Take the law with you. Anywhere.

LexisNexis® Electronic Books for Law Enforcement

Check criminal and traffic laws, research critical case notes, and study for promotion exams anywhere and in any way you want.

TABLET   SMARTPHONE   COMPUTER   BOOKS

After you download your new LexisNexis eBook you can access its content wherever, without the need to find Wi-Fi.

Covering over 40 states, LexisNexis print and eBook publications bring you:

- State Traffic and Criminal Laws
- Supreme Court Decisions
- Legal Guidelines
- Spanish Language Guides
- Case Notes
- Exam Prep Guides

SHOP
www.lexisnexis.com/lawenforcement

CALL
877.861.3389

FREE SAMPLE
lexisnexis.com/ebooks/le

WATCH VIDEO

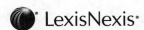

NEW HAMPSHIRE CRIMINAL CODE ANNOTATED

2013-2014 EDITION

Reprinted from LEXIS New Hampshire Revised Statutes Annotated
and 2013 Cumulative Supplement

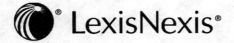 LexisNexis®

QUESTIONS ABOUT THIS PUBLICATION?

For CUSTOMER SERVICE ASSISTANCE concerning replacement pages, shipments, billing, reprint permission, or other matters,

    please call Customer Service Department at 800-833-9844
    email *customer.support@lexisnexis.com*
    or visit our interactive customer service website at *www.lexisnexis.com/printcdsc*

For EDITORIAL **content questions** concerning this publication,

    please email: *LEpublications@lexisnexis.com*

For **information on other LEXISNEXIS MATTHEW BENDER publications**,

    please call us at 877-461-8801
    or visit our online bookstore at *www.lexisnexis.com/bookstore*

ISBN: 978-0-7698-9191-0

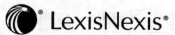

Matthew Bender & Company, Inc.
Editorial Offices
701 E. Water Street
Charlottesville, VA 22902
800-446-3410
www.lexisnexis.com

Product Number 2881729

(Pub. 28817)

Foreword

As publishers of the LEXIS *New Hampshire Statutes Annotated,* we are pleased to offer to the legal and criminal practice communities this 2013-2014 edition of **New Hampshire Criminal Code**. The statutes included in this publication include new legislation and amendments enacted through Chapter 279 of the 2013 Session of the General Court.

This book features the provisions of Title LXII, the Criminal Code of New Hampshire, as well as miscellaneous related laws. Additionally, we have included a convenient listing of sections affected by recent legislation, as well as a comprehensive index.

This publication contains annotations taken from decisions of the New Hampshire Supreme Court and from decisions of the appropriate federal courts posted on *lexis.com* with decisions dates up through October 9, 2013. These cases will be printed in the following reports:

New Hampshire Reports
Atlantic Reporter, 3rd Series
Federal Supplement, 2nd Series
Bankruptcy Reporter
Federal Rules Decisions
Federal Reporter, 3rd Series
United States Supreme Court Reports, Lawyers' Edition, 2nd Series

As practice aids, references to the following publications have been included: New Hampshire Practice; Criminal Practice and Procedure; and New Hampshire Criminal Jury Instructions.

For rules of court governing practice in the New Hampshire courts, and annotations pertaining thereto, see New Hampshire Court Rules Annotated.

In planning this publication, suggestions as to format and content were solicited from many sources, and we are indebted to all those professionals who provided us with direction.

We are committed to providing attorneys and criminal law professionals with the most comprehensive, current and useful manuals possible. Accordingly, regular revisions of this book are planned, and we also publish a host of other publications covering various topics of New Hampshire law.

We actively solicit your comments and suggestions. If you believe that there are statutes which should be included (or excluded), or if you have suggestions regarding index improvements, please write to us or call us toll-free at 1-800-833-9844; fax us toll-free at 1-800-643-1280; or visit our website at http://lexisnexis.com/lawenforcement; or E-mail us at LEpublications@lexisnexis.com. By providing us with your informed comments, you will be assured of having available a working tool which increases in value with each edition.

December 2013

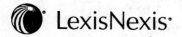

Table of Contents

	PAGE
Sections Affected by 2013 Legislation	ix

Constitution of the State of New Hampshire

Part I. Bill of Rights

ARTICLE

15. Right of Accused	1
16. Former Jeopardy; Jury Trial in Capital Cases	40
17. Venue of Criminal Prosecutions	46
18. Penalties to be Proportioned to Offenses; True Design of Punishment	47
19. Searches and Seizures Regulated	49
21. Jurors; Compensation	67
33. Excessive Bail, Fines, and Punishments Prohibited	67

Part II. Form of Government

91. Habeas Corpus	67

Title V

Taxation

CHAPTER

78 Tobacco Tax, 78:1 to 78:34	69

Title VII

Sheriffs, Constables, and Police Officers

106-J Missing Adults, Persons with Developmental Disabilities, and Senior Citizens, 106-J:1 to 106-J:5	83
106-K Criminal Justice Information System, 106-K:1 to 106-K:7	84

Title X

Public Health

126-K Youth Access to and Use of Tobacco Products, 126-K:1 to 126-K:19	89
135 New Hampshire Hospital and Insane Persons, 135:17, 135:17-a to 135:17-c	94

Title XII

Public Safety and Welfare

158 Explosives and Explosive Substances, 158:1 to 158:40	98
159 Pistols and Revolvers, 159:1 to 159:26	108
159-A Purchase of Shotguns and Rifles [Repealed]	122
159-C Sale of Handguns; Criminal Record Check [Repealed]	122
159-D Criminal Background Checks, 159-D:1 to 159-D:3	123
167 Public Assistance to Blind, Aged, or Disabled Persons, and to Dependent Children, 167:17-b, 167:17-c	123
172 Study, Treatment and Care of Inebriates, 172:1, 172:13, 172:15	125
172-B Alcoholism and Alcohol Abuse, 172-B:1, 172-B:2, 172-B:3	128
173-B Protection of Persons from Domestic Violence, 173-B:1 to 173-B:25	131

CHAPTER   PAGE

173-C   Confidential Communications Between Victims and Counselors, 173-C:1 to 173-C:10 146

Title XIII

Alcoholic Beverages

179   Enforcement, Requirements and Penalties, 179:1 to 179:62 150

Title XVIII

Fish and Game

215-C   Snowmobiles, 215-C:31 173

Title XXX

Occupations and Professions

318-B   Controlled Drug Act, 318-B:1 to 318-B:38 174
318-C   Model Drug Dealer Liability Act, 318-C:1 to 318-C:18 210
318-D   Methamphetamine-Related Offenses, 318-D:1 to 318-D:5 215

Title LI

Courts

502-A   District Courts, 502-A:12 218

Title LIII

Proceedings in Court

516   Witnesses, 516:1 to 516:38 219
517   Depositions, 517:13 231

Title LV

Proceedings in Special Cases

539   Wilful Trespass, 539:7, 539:9 234

Title LVIII

Public Justice

570-A   Wiretapping and Eavesdropping, 570-A:1 to 570-A:11 236

Title LIX

Proceedings in Criminal Cases

594   Arrests In Criminal Cases, 594:1 to 594:25 249
595-A   Search Warrants, 595-A:1 to 595-A:9 258
597   Bail and Recognizances, 597:1 to 597:42 263
599   Appeals from Convictions in Municipal or District Court, 599:1 to 599:4 281
600   Grand Juries, 600:1 to 600:5 ....
600-A   Multicounty Grand Juries, 600-A:1 to 600-A:8 285
601   Indictments, Informations, and Complaints, 601:1 to 601:9 286
602   Venue, 602:1, 602:2 290
603   Limitation of Prosecutions [Repealed] 291
604   Rights of Accused, 604:1 to 604:3 291

CHAPTER		PAGE
604-A	Adequate Representation for Indigent Defendants in Criminal Cases, 604-A:1 to 604-A:10	292
604-B	Public Defender Program, 604-B:1 to 604-B:8	302
605	Pleas and Refusal to Plead, 605:1 to 605:6	303
606	Trial, 606:1 to 606:10	304
606-A	Agreement on Detainers, 606-A:1 to 606-A:6	308
607	Sentence and Execution; Parole [Repealed]	314
607-A	Uniform Act on Status of Convicted Persons, 607-A:1 to 607-A:8	315
608	Surety of the Peace, 608:1 to 608:10	317
609	Suppression of Riots [Repealed]	319
609-A	Mob Action [Repealed]	319
610	Rewards and Compensations to Prosecutors, 610:1, 610:2	319
611	Medical Examiners [Repealed]	320
611-A	Office of Chief Medical Examiner [Repealed]	320
611-B	Office of the Chief Medical Examiner, 611-B:1 to 611-B:31	320
612	Uniform Criminal Extradition Law, 612:1 to 612:30	327
613	Summoning Witnesses from Without a State, 613:1 to 613:6	335
613-A	Uniform Rendition of Prisoners as Witnesses in Criminal Proceedings Act, 613-A:1 to 613-A:11	337
614	Fresh Pursuit, 614:1 to 614:10	338

Title LX

Correction and Punishment

616	Pecuniary Penalties and Forfeitures, 616:1 to 616:9	342
617	Forfeitures of Personal Property, 617:1 to 617:10	343
618	Fines, Costs, and Discharges, 618:1 to 618:15	346
619	Common Jails and Prisoners Therein [Repealed]	349
620	Houses of Correction [Repealed]	351
621	Youth Development Center, 621:1 to 621:35	351
621-A	Youth Services Center, 621-A:1 to 621-A:11	361
622	The State Prisons, 622:1 to 622:58	364
622-A	New England Interstate Corrections Compact, 622-A:1 to 622-A:3	381
622-B	Interstate Corrections Compact, 622-B:1 to 622-B:3	384
622-C	International Prisoner Transfers, 622-C:1	387
623	Temporary Removal of Prisoners, 623:1 to 623:4	387
623-A	Approved Absences from New Hampshire State Prisons, 623-A:1 to 623-A:9	389

Title LXII

Criminal Code

625	Preliminary, 625:1 to 625:11	392
626	General Principles, 626:1 to 626:8	402
627	Justification, 627:1 to 627:9	413
628	Responsibility, 628:1, 628:2	421
629	Inchoate Crimes, 629:1 to 629:3	423
630	Homicide, 630:1 to 630:6	427
631	Assault and Related Offenses, 631:1 to 631:8	444
632	Rape [Repealed]	455
632-A	Sexual Assault and Related Offenses, 632-A:1 to 632-A:24	455
633	Interference with Freedom, 633:1 to 633:10	478
634	Destruction of Property, 634:1 to 634:3	489
635	Unauthorized Entries, 635:1 to 635:8	493
636	Robbery, 636:1	498
637	Theft, 637:1 to 637:11	500

Chapter		Page
638	Fraud, 638:1 to 638:29	512
639	Offenses Against the Family, 639:1 to 639:5	528
639-A	Methamphetamine-Related Crimes, 639-A:1 to 639-A:4	531
640	Corrupt Practices, 640:1 to 640:7	532
641	Falsification in Official Matters, 641:1 to 641:8	533
642	Obstructing Governmental Operations, 642:1 to 642:10	539
643	Abuse of Office, 643:1, 643:2	546
644	Breaches of the Peace and Related Offenses, 644:1 to 644:20	547
645	Public Indecency, 645:1 to 645:3	562
646	Offenses Against the Flag [Repealed]	564
646-A	Desecration of the Flag, 646-A:1 to 646-A:4	564
647	Gambling Offenses, 647:1, 647:2	565
648	Subversive Activities [Repealed]	568
649	Sabotage Prevention, 649:1 to 649:12	568
649-A	Child Pornography, 649-A:1 to 649-A:7	571
649-B	Computer Pornography and Child Exploitation Prevention, 649-B:1 to 649-B:6	575
650	Obscene Matter, 650:1 to 650:6	576
650-A	Felonious Use of Firearms, 650-A:1	579
650-B	Felonious Use of Body Armor, 650-B:1, 650-B:2	580
650-C	Negligent Storage of Firearms, 650-C:1	580
651	Sentences, 651:1 to 651:70	581
651-A	Parole of Prisoners, 651-A:1 to 651-A:38	622
651-B	Registration of Criminal Offenders, 651-B:1 to 651-B:12	641
651-C	DNA Testing of Criminal Offenders, 651-C:1 to 651-C:7	654
651-D	Post-Conviction DNA Testing, 651-D:1 to 651-D:5	656
651-E	Interbranch Criminal and Juvenile Justice Council, 651-E:1 to 651-E:5	658
651-F	Information and Analysis Center, 651-F:1 to 651-F:8	659

User's Guide to the Index		665
Index		I-1

Sections Affected by 2013 Legislation

NOTE: In addition to the sections listed below, users of this edition should be aware that additional section and case note annotations have also been appropriately incorporated throughout this publication. The sections with new and/or revised annotations do *not* appear in this listing.

RSA	Effect	Bill No.	Act Chap.	Act Sec.
78:1*XVII	Amended	HB488	35	1
78-A:26*I	Amended	HB2	144	70
172-B:2*IV	Amended	HB2	144	107
173-B:2	Amended	SB69	62	I.
173-B:2*I	Amended	SB69	62	1
173-B:3	Amended	SB69	62	II.
173-B:3*IV	Amended	SB69	62	2
173-B:3*VI	Amended	SB69	62	3
173-B:4*Intro. Par. I	Amended	SB69	62	4
173-B:5*IV	Amended	SB69	62	5
173-B:11*I	Amended	SB69	62	6
173-B:13*IV	Amended	SB69	62	7
173-B:14*II	Amended	SB69	62	8
179:17*II(b)	Amended	HB575	213	1
179:21	Amended	HB599	258	8
179:22*II	Amended	HB599	258	9
179:33*II	Amended	HB639	72	1
179:56*I	Amended	HB599	258	10
318-B:2*I-b	Amended	HB573	242	3
318-B:13*IV	Amended	HB313	121	7
318-B:17*I-a, I-b	Amended	SB44	222	1
318-B:26*IX-a	Amended	HB573	242	4
318-B:31	Repealed	SB83	79	3(II)
318-B:32	Repealed	SB83	79	3(II)
318-B:33	Repealed	SB83	79	3(II)
318-B:34	Repealed	SB83	79	3(II)
318-B:35	Repealed	SB83	79	3(II)
318-B:36	Repealed	SB83	79	3(II)
318-B:37	Repealed	SB83	79	3(II)
318-B:38	Repealed	SB83	79	3(II)
318-B:38*I(m)	Amended	SB83	79	1
516:29-b*II(b)	Amended	SB105	65	1
604-A:1-a	Amended	HB2	144	58
621:1*III	Amended	HB260	249	19
621:19*I-a	Amended	HB260	249	20
651:2*V(i)	Amended	HB644	156	8
651:5*X(c), (d)	Amended	HB450	123	1
651:19	Amended	HB224	277	1
651-A:6*I(b)	Amended	HB644	156	10
651-A:11*I	Amended	HB644	156	1
651-A:11*II-a	Amended	HB644	156	2
651-A:16*I(e)	Amended	HB644	156	3
651-A:16-a	Amended	HB644	156	4

RSA	Effect	Bill No.	Act Chap.	Act Sec.
651-A:19*I	Amended	HB644	156	5
651-A:19*III(a)	Amended	HB644	156	6
651-A:19*VII(a)	Amended	HB644	156	7

New Hampshire Criminal Code Annotated

Constitution
Of The
State Of New Hampshire

PART FIRST—Bill Of Rights

Article
15. [Right of Accused.]
16. [Former Jeopardy; Jury Trial in Capital Cases.]
17. [Venue of Criminal Prosecutions.]
18. [Penalties to be Proportioned to Offenses; True Design of Punishment.]
19. [Searches and Seizures Regulated.]
21. [Jurors; Compensation.]
33. [Excessive Bail, Fines, and Punishments Prohibited.]

PART SECOND—Form Of Government

OATHS AND SUBSCRIPTIONS—EXCLUSION FROM OFFICES—COMMISSIONS—WRITS— CONFIRMATION OF LAWS—HABEAS CORPUS—THE ENACTING STYLE— CONTINUANCE OF OFFICERS—PROVISIONS FOR A FUTURE REVISION OF THE CONSTITUTION—ETC.

91. [Habeas Corpus.]

PART FIRST

Bill Of Rights

Art. 15.   [Right of Accused.]

No subject shall be held to answer for any crime, or offense, until the same is fully and plainly, substantially and formally, described to him; or be compelled to accuse or furnish evidence against himself. Every subject shall have a right to produce all proofs that may be favorable to himself; to meet the witnesses against him face to face, and to be fully heard in his defense, by himself, and counsel. No subject shall be arrested, imprisoned, despoiled, or deprived of his property, immunities, or privileges, put out of the protection of the law, exiled or deprived of his life, liberty, or estate, but by the judgment of his peers, or the law of the land; provided that, in any proceeding to commit a person acquitted of a criminal charge by reason of insanity, due process shall require that clear and convincing evidence that the person is potentially dangerous to himself or to others and that the person suffers from a mental disorder must be established. Every person held to answer in any crime or offense punishable by deprivation of liberty shall have the right to counsel at the expense of the state if need is shown; this right he is at liberty to waive, but only after the matter has been thoroughly explained by the court.

Amendments
—**1984.** Deleted "and" preceding "every" at the beginning of the second sentence and preceding "no" at the beginning of the third sentence and added "provided that, in any proceeding to commit a person acquitted of a criminal charge by reason of insanity, due process shall require that clear and convincing evidence that the person is potentially dangerous to himself or to others and that the person suffers from a mental disorder must be established" following "land" at the end of that sentence.
—**1966.** Added the fourth sentence.

Cross References.
Committal of persons found not guilty by reason of insanity, see RSA 651:8-b–11-a.
Double jeopardy, see New Hampshire Constitution, Part 1, Article 16.
Granting of immunity to witness compelled to waive constitutional protection against self-incrimination in criminal proceedings, see RSA 516:34.
Indictments, informations and complaints generally, see RSA 601.
Representation of indigent defendants, see RSA 604-A, 604-B.
Rights under federal constitution of person accused of crime, see United States Constitution, Amendments V, VI.
Right to speedy trial, see New Hampshire Constitution, Part 1, Article 14.
Securing attendance of witnesses, see RSA 516:1 et seq. 613.
Trial of criminal cases generally, see RSA 606.

NOTES TO DECISIONS

I. GENERALLY

1. Purpose
2. Conflict of rights
3. Classification of crimes
4. Burden of proof
5. Statutory vagueness
6. Statutory overbreadth
7. Guilty plea
8. Right to be tried as juvenile

II. INDICTMENTS, INFORMATIONS AND COMPLAINTS

51. Sufficiency generally
52. Elements of offense
53. Statutory language
54. Time of offense
55. Bill of particulars
56. Former convictions
57. Grand jury
58. Corporations
59. Conduct of trial
60. Accomplice liability
61. Duplicitous indictments
62. Attempt
63. Misdemeanors
64. Sexual assault
65. Amendment of indictment

III. SELF-INCRIMINATION

101. Construction with federal constitution
102. Scope of right
103. Application of right
104. Exclusion of evidence
105. Civil proceedings
106. Legislative investigations
107. Miranda warning
108. Assertion of right—Questioning after
109. —Procedure
110. —Who may assert right

1

111. Waiver of right—Generally
112. —Voluntariness of confessions
113. —Juveniles
114. Immunity from prosecution
115. Implied consent law
116. Admissibility of evidence of silence
117. Publicity concerning silence
118. Reference to defendant's silence
119. Voluntary admissions
120. Psychiatric evaluations
121. Accident reports
122. Records
123. Corporations and other entities
124. Predicating parole on participation in sexual offender program
125. Custody
126. Incarcerated suspects

IV. Evidence

127. Sentencing
150. Right to present witnesses
151. Relevancy
152. Discovery
153. Rights of witnesses
154. Rape shield law
155. Hearsay
156. Privileged information
157. Identification procedure
158. Child abuse records
159. All favorable proofs
160. Extrinsic evidence
161. Excluding or limiting evidence
162. Blood alcohol tests
163. Failure to preserve evidence

V. Confrontation of Witnesses

201. Cross-examination
202. Videotaped testimony
203. Hearsay
204. Chemical analysis of controlled substance
205. Juvenile certification hearing
206. Termination of parental rights
207. Nontestimonial statements
208. Laboratory tests
209. Trustworthiness
210. Availability of witness
211. Bias of witness
212. Disguised witness

VI. Right to Represent Oneself

251. Generally
252. Construction with right to counsel
253. Acting as co-counsel
254. Waiver of right to counsel
255. Duty of court
256. Practice and procedure

VII. Right to Counsel

257. Appointment of standby counsel
301. Construction with federal constitution
302. When right attaches
303. Privileged communications
304. Waiver
305. Effective assistance—Generally
306. —Standards
307. —Burden of proof
308. —Guilty pleas
309. —Actual prejudice
310. —Conflict of interest
311. —Contingent fee
312. —Tactics and strategy
313. —Argument of counsel
314. —Appeals
315. —Objection to instructions

316. Habitual offender proceedings
317. Contempt proceedings
318. Indigents
319. Fees
320. Uncounselled convictions
321. Right to counsel for misdemeanor appeal
322. Right to counsel in appeals of denial of postconviction relief
323. Child in need of services proceedings
324. Sentencing

VIII. Jury Trial

325. Abuse or neglect proceedings
351. Generally
352. When required
353. Public trial
354. Right to be present at trial—Generally
355. Waiver of right
356. Number of jurors
357. Selection by jury
358. Alternate jurors
359. Issues determined by jury
360. Impartial jury
361. Instructions
362. Suspension of license
363. Referees
364. Court fees
365. Sequestration of jury
366. Jury misconduct
367. Right to fair trial
368. Unanimous jury
369. Juveniles
370. Disqualification of juror
371. Jury orientation
372. Misdemeanors

IX. Law of the Land; Due Process

401. Generally
402. Statutes
403. Arrest
404. Property interest
405. Liberty interests
406. Implied consent law
407. Arraignment
408. Plea agreements
409. Competency to stand trial
410. Public trial
411. Admissibility of evidence
412. Sentencing
413. Appeals
414. Vicarious liability
415. Notice and hearing
416. Administrative procedures
417. Immunity of witnesses
418. Eminent domain
419. Prosecutorial misconduct
420. Comments by trial court
421. Indictments and informations
422. Informants
423. Jury instructions
424. Identifications
425. Pretrial publicity

I. Generally

1. Purpose

The clause of this article which states that no subject shall be arrested, imprisoned, despoiled, or deprived of his property, immunities, or privileges, put out of the protection of the law, exiled, or deprived of his life, liberty, or estate, but by the judgment of his peers or the law of the land, has for its object the protection of private rights from all interference of single branches of the government and of individual magistrates, not warranted by law. Trustees of Dartmouth College v. Woodward, 1 N.H. 111, 1817 N.H. LEXIS 33 (1817).

2. Conflict of rights

Trial court did not violate due process under the Fifth Amendment or the New Hampshire Constitution by failing to continue a hearing to impose a suspended sentence until after a collateral criminal prosecution; the decision whether to testify or to present evidence and witnesses at a hearing to impose was left to a defendant and did not force the defendant to make an impermissible election between the constitutional right to testify and the constitutional right to remain silent. For constitutional purposes, all that mattered was whether defendant had the option to testify at her imposition hearing. State v. Flood, 159 N.H. 353, 986 A.2d 626, 2009 N.H. LEXIS 119 (2009).

A defendant's right to cross-examine prosecution witnesses may be restricted when it conflicts with a witness's right against self-incrimination, and when presented with these competing constitutional protections, trial court must engage in a delicate balancing by weighing conflicting interests of parties involved. State v. Donnelly, 145 N.H. 562, 765 A.2d 680, 2000 N.H. LEXIS 109 (2000).

Trial court did not violate forgery defendant's right of confrontation by permitting complaining witnesses to testify but limiting defendant's cross-examination of them in response to their invocation of their rights against self-incrimination; areas precluded from cross-examination were essentially collateral to charged crimes, and defendant had ample opportunity to impeach witnesses' credibility generally and to advance her theory that they had a motive to fabricate charges against her. State v. Donnelly, 145 N.H. 562, 765 A.2d 680, 2000 N.H. LEXIS 109 (2000).

Constitutional right to produce all proofs that may be favorable to a defendant is not absolute when it conflicts with a witness' privilege against self-incrimination. State v. Lavallee, 119 N.H. 207, 400 A.2d 480, 1979 N.H. LEXIS 278 (1979), superseded by statute as stated in, State v. Newell, 141 N.H. 199, 679 A.2d 1142, 1996 N.H. LEXIS 72 (1996).

When a witness' right to remain silent conflicts with a defendant's right to produce all proofs favorable to himself, the court must delicately balance these conflicting interests. State v. Lavallee, 119 N.H. 207, 400 A.2d 480, 1979 N.H. LEXIS 278 (1979), superseded by statute as stated in, State v. Newell, 141 N.H. 199, 679 A.2d 1142, 1996 N.H. LEXIS 72 (1996).

3. Classification of crimes

A violation subject to a penalty less than the amount constitutionally entitling civil litigants to a jury determination is a petty offense. Opinion of Justices, 135 N.H. 538, 608 A.2d 202, 1992 N.H. LEXIS 213 (1992).

4. Burden of proof

New Hampshire Supreme Court concluded that the vehicular assault statute, RSA 265:79-a, is valid as enacted and requires proof of a mental state of criminal negligence to sustain a conviction, RSA 626:2, II(d); the final sentence of RSA 265:79-a must be stricken, however, because it removes the evidence weighing function from the jury and shifts the burdens of proof and production to the defendant in violation of N.H. Const. pt. I, art. 15. State v. Rollins-Ercolino, 149 N.H. 336, 821 A.2d 953, 2003 N.H. LEXIS 48 (2003).

New Hampshire Legislature cannot directly enact a statute requiring a defendant to furnish evidence at a criminal prosecution, N.H. Const. pt. I, art. 15. State v. Rollins-Ercolino, 149 N.H. 336, 821 A.2d 953, 2003 N.H. LEXIS 48 (2003).

This article poses no obstacle to placing the burden on a defendant to prove his insanity. State v. Bertrand, 123 N.H. 719, 465 A.2d 912, 1983 N.H. LEXIS 340 (1983).

There is no prohibition against a criminal defendant waiving his right to produce all proofs that may be favorable to himself, to meet the witnesses against him face to face, and to be fully heard in his defense, by himself, and counsel, as the result of a defendant's voluntary absence from certain proceeding; therefore, there is no prohibition against the trial court proceedings to try the defendant in absentia. State v. Lister, 119 N.H. 713, 406 A.2d 967, 1979 N.H. LEXIS 438 (1979).

Whether the defendant has voluntarily absented himself from criminal proceedings and thereby voluntarily waived his right to be present at trial is a question of fact for the trial court to be established by the state by a preponderance of the evidence. State v. Lister, 119 N.H. 713, 406 A.2d 967, 1979 N.H. LEXIS 438 (1979).

Where a trial has commenced, proceeding in absentia of defendant who has voluntarily absented himself from trial does not violate this article. State v. Lister, 119 N.H. 713, 406 A.2d 967, 1979 N.H. LEXIS 438 (1979).

Where defendant voluntarily had absented himself from criminal court proceedings for first degree murder after completion of suppression hearings and selection, but not swearing, of five jurors, defendant had thereby voluntarily waived his right to be present at trial and he could be tried in absentia. State v. Lister, 119 N.H. 713, 406 A.2d 967, 1979 N.H. LEXIS 438 (1979).

5. Statutory vagueness

When a vagueness claim does not involve a fundamental right, a facial attack on the challenged statutory scheme is unwarranted. Accordingly, because respondent did not argue that the privilege to operate a boat was a fundamental right, the court rejected her argument that RSA 270-E:17. was unconstitutionally vague on its face in violation of N.H. Const. pt. I, art. 15. Appeal of Blizzard, 163 N.H. 326, 42 A.3d 791, 2012 N.H. LEXIS 27 (2012).

RSA 625:11, V should be construed to include only death or serious bodily injury to a human, not that of an animal. To hold otherwise renders the statute impermissibly vague, as such an expansive interpretation would not provide the ordinary person with adequate notice of those substances or things which would constitute a deadly weapon. State v. Pratte, 158 N.H. 45, 959 A.2d 200, 2008 N.H. LEXIS 135 (2008).

Imposition of consecutive sentences for convictions on multiple counts of aggravated felonious sexual assault did not violate due process under N.H. Const. pt. I, art. 15 because of vagueness in that the language of RSA 632-A:10-a, RSA chapter 651 and judicial construction of that language puts a person of ordinary intelligence on notice that a person guilty of aggravated felonious sexual assault may receive the maximum statutory sentence for each aggravated felonious sexual assault conviction. Duquette v. Warden, N.H. State Prison, 154 N.H. 737, 919 A.2d 767, 2007 N.H. LEXIS 10 (2007).

RSA 318-B:1, X-a was not impermissibly vague under the State or Federal Constitution as: (1) the statute provided ample notice of the objects it proscribed as objects were considered drug paraphernalia if they were used, intended for use, or customarily intended for use, to introduce controlled substances into the human body, (2) the use of the word "customarily" in the statute was comprehensible, and presented an evidentiary question, rather than a constitutional validity question, (3) RSA 318-B:1, X-a(a)–(k) contained a nonexhaustive list of items that could be considered drug paraphernalia, (4) the person who had to use an item, design it for use, or intend it for use with drugs in order for it to be drug paraphernalia, was the person charged with one of the statute's substantive violations, and (5) the statute did not authorize or encourage arbitrary and discriminatory enforcement because the statutory scheme provided comprehensive guidelines under RSA 318-B:2, IV to govern law enforcement. State v. Smoke Signals Pipe & Tobacco Shop, LLC, 155 N.H. 234, 922 A.2d 634, 2007 N.H. LEXIS 53 (2007).

RSA 633:3-a, the stalking statute, is not vague in violation of the Due Process Clause or N.H. Const. pt. I, art. 15. The phrase "legitimate purpose" read in the context of the entire statute, coupled with an objective standard, does not give too much discretion to a trial court and does not require a person of common intelligence to guess at its meaning. Miller v. Blackden, 154 N.H. 448, 913 A.2d 742, 2006 N.H. LEXIS 184 (2006), rehearing denied, 2007 N.H. LEXIS 16 (N.H. Jan. 12, 2007).

References in the child endangerment definition to knowing endangerment by purposely ignoring a duty to a child did not make the prohibition unconstitutionally vague, because many conceivable purposeful failures to perform less critical duties to a child could occur without knowingly exposing the child to danger. State v. Bortner, 150 N.H. 504, 841 A.2d 80, 2004 N.H. LEXIS 11 (2004).

Provisions of the New Hampshire stalking statute, subsections I(d)(5)(A) and II(b) of RSA 633:3-a, were not unconstitutionally vague either on their face or as applied to the defendant who was convicted of stalking his wife during their divorce proceedings by following her car in his car after the wife obtained a domestic violence restraining order against him because in reading the statute in a common sense manner, together with the protective order, it was clear what these portions of the stalking statute prohibited and it gave adequate warning that defendant's actions were prohibited. State v. Porelle, 149 N.H. 420, 822 A.2d 562, 2003 N.H. LEXIS 58 (2003).

A criminal statute is void for vagueness under this article when it forbids or requires the doing of an act in terms so vague that men of common intelligence must necessarily guess at its meaning and differ as to its application. State v. Wong, 125 N.H. 610, 486 A.2d 262, 1984 N.H. LEXIS 413 (1984).

6. Statutory overbreadth

Even if it were assumed that a savings clause in RSA 644:4, I(f) was an affirmative defense to harassment and the burdens of proof were not shifted, the statute is unconstitutionally overbroad and violates N.H. Const., pt. I, art. 15, and U.S. Const. amends. I, V, XIV. State v. Pierce, 152 N.H. 790, 887 A.2d 132, 2005 N.H. LEXIS 172 (2005).

A statute is overbroad in violation of this article when it sweeps unnecessarily broadly and thereby invades the area of a protected freedom. State v. Wong, 125 N.H. 610, 486 A.2d 262, 1984 N.H. LEXIS 413 (1984).

7. Guilty plea

Defendant, who was 19 and had a general equivalency diploma and some technical college experience, had not shown that his guilty plea to simple assault was not knowing, intelligent, and voluntary under the Fourteenth Amendment or N.H. Const. pt. I, art. 15. The trial court did not assume that defendant understood the charge, which it read to him and which he stated that he understood; defendant signed an acknowledgment and waiver form and did not ask questions when given the opportunity; the trial court affirmatively inquired into his knowledge and volition; and defendant's age and limited experience with the criminal justice system were insufficient to compel a finding that his plea was unknowingly entered. State v. Davies, 164 N.H. 71, 53 A.3d 517, 2012 N.H. LEXIS 107 (2012).

A guilty plea followed the administration of a proper plea colloquy to determine whether the petitioner understood his constitutional rights. The petitioner argued that the trial judge was obligated to explicitly name each constitutional right that he was waiving and failed to do so. However, the trial judge asked the petitioner if he understood that he was waiving certain constitutional rights, the petitioner answered in the affirmative, and the trial judge also adverted to an acknowledgment of rights form that the petitioner completed and signed that contained all of his Boykin/Richard rights. Millette v. Warden, N.H. State Prison, 141 N.H. 653, 692 A.2d 963, 1997 N.H. LEXIS 16 (1997).

A guilty plea was valid, notwithstanding the petitioner's assertion that he was unable to understand the constitutional rights that he was waiving because of a learning disability. The petitioner's attorney explained to the trial judge that he went over the entire acknowledgment of rights form with the petitioner in detail, and the petitioner admitted that he signed the acknowledgment of rights form, that he went over the form with his attorney, that he understood his constitutional rights, and that he signed the form willingly and freely. Millette v. Warden, N.H. State Prison, 141 N.H. 653, 692 A.2d 963, 1997 N.H. LEXIS 16 (1997).

In order for a plea to be knowing, voluntary, and intelligent, the defendant must understand the essential elements of the crime to which he is pleading guilty. During the plea colloquy, however, the court need not inquire whether the defendant understands each element of the crime; the court may assume that defense counsel routinely explained the nature of the offense in sufficient detail to give the accused notice of what he is being asked to admit. State v. Thornton, 140 N.H. 532, 669 A.2d 791, 1995 N.H. LEXIS 186 (1995).

A subjective belief in one's innocence does not render a guilty plea involuntary as long as there are grounds for doubting the reliability of that belief and for believing that one's defense at trial would be unsuccessful. State v. Thornton, 140 N.H. 532, 669 A.2d 791, 1995 N.H. LEXIS 186 (1995).

Given the state's offer of proof and the defendant's admission that he committed the substance of the charged offense described by the state, the defendant's denial of certain aspects of the crime was insufficient to reverse the trial court's finding that the defendant understood the elements of the crime to which he pleaded guilty. State v. Thornton, 140 N.H. 532, 669 A.2d 791, 1995 N.H. LEXIS 186 (1995).

It was reasonable for the trial court to rely on the assertions of the defendant's trial counsel, as well as the defendant's presence at the hearing on a motion to dismiss where the mens rea of the accomplice charge was discussed, in concluding that the defendant understood the elements of the crime to which he pleaded guilty. State v. Thornton, 140 N.H. 532, 669 A.2d 791, 1995 N.H. LEXIS 186 (1995).

The defendant's guilty plea was not rendered involuntary and unknowing by the fact that the state's plea offer letter stated that it could be withdrawn by the state upon the filing of motions or taking of depositions by defense counsel. The condition imposed by the plea offer was not a mandatory one, the defendant was free to pursue discovery if he chose to do so, either with or without the agreement of the state, and he had no right to the benefit of the plea agreement. State v. Laforest, 140 N.H. 286, 665 A.2d 1083, 1995 N.H. LEXIS 142 (1995).

Defendant's confessions to police were involuntary under the totality of the circumstances where the police did more than merely exhort the defendant to be truthful; they made specific promises of leniency. The message was clear: if the defendant confessed, he would not be charged with any offense other than those he allegedly committed on the night of his arrest, if he did not confess, he faced harsher treatment. State v. Rezk, 150 N.H. 483, 840 A.2d 758, 2004 N.H. LEXIS 10 (2004).

Officer's comments that he would try to get defendant back to her kids after defendant had calmed down in the police cruiser was a response to defendant's conduct and it was unlikely that she would have interpreted the statement as being a promise for a future Miranda waiver and confession. State v. Spencer, 149 N.H. 622, 826 A.2d 546, 2003 N.H. LEXIS 92 (2003).

When defendant confessed to a murder before she was warned of her Miranda rights, and confessed again after being advised of those rights, whether the second confession was admissible involved a traditional due process voluntariness inquiry, considering the totality of the circumstances, into whether the second confession was the product of an essentially free and unconstrained choice. State v. Fleetwood, 149 N.H. 396, 824 A.2d 1061, 2003 N.H. LEXIS 57 (2003), rehearing denied, 2003 N.H. LEXIS 102 (N.H. June 25, 2003).

Inquiry into whether defendant's warned confession, following an unwarned custodial confession, was admissible encompassed an evaluation of several factors, including (1) the time lapse between the initial confession and the subsequent statements; (2) the defendant's contacts, if any, with friends or family members during that period of time; (3) the degree of police influence exerted over the defendant; (4) whether the defendant was advised that her prior admission could not be used against her; and (5) whether the defendant was told that her previous statement could be used against her, and no one factor in isolation was determinative. State v. Fleetwood, 149 N.H. 396, 824 A.2d 1061, 2003 N.H. LEXIS 57 (2003), rehearing denied, 2003 N.H. LEXIS 102 (N.H. June 25, 2003).

Defendant's properly warned second confession was not rendered inadmissible as a result of a first unwarned and uncoerced confession where the second confession occurred more than 17 hours after the first interview and the defendant was not in custody during that period and defendant was advised of his Miranda rights and waived them. State v. Aubuchont, 141 N.H. 206, 679 A.2d 1147, 1996 N.H. LEXIS 75 (1996).

8. Right to be tried as juvenile

There is no constitutional right to a juvenile certification hearing. State v. Rayes, 142 N.H. 496, 703 A.2d 1381, 1997 N.H. LEXIS 127 (1997).

II. Indictments, Informations and Complaints

51. Sufficiency generally

Informations charging vehicular assault did not violate N.H. Const. pt. I, art. 15. They alleged that defendant acted negligently and provided the date of the offense, the names of the victims, and some of the acts that were alleged to have been negligent. State v. Demond-surace, 162 N.H. 17, 27 A.3d 793, 2011 N.H. LEXIS 67 (2011).

Indictments that charged defendant with violations of the statute were sufficient because they alleged the essential elements of the alleged crimes and the place and approximate date of the crimes and further, defendant was sufficiently apprised of the crimes that he was accused of. State v. Davis, 149 N.H. 698, 828 A.2d 293, 2003 N.H. LEXIS 103 (2003).

New Hampshire constitution protects a defendant from being convicted of a crime not charged in an indictment. State v. Glanville, 145 N.H. 631, 765 A.2d 173, 2000 N.H. LEXIS 114 (2000).

In order to satisfy Part I, Article 15 of New Hampshire Constitution, indictment must describe offense with sufficient specificity to ensure that defendant can prepare for trial and avoid double jeopardy. State v. Johnson, 144 N.H. 175, 738 A.2d 1284, 1999 N.H. LEXIS 95 (1999).

Indictment charging Medicaid fraud was sufficient as the indictment tracked the language of RSA 167:17-b and adequately described the offense; furthermore, the indictment included a two page listing of all the transactions on which the charge was based. State v. Hermsdorf, 135 N.H. 360, 605 A.2d 1045, 1992 N.H. LEXIS 42, (1992).

An indictment is adequate, under the New Hampshire Constitution, when it informs the defendant of the offense charged with enough specificity to enable him or her to prepare adequately for trial and to guard against double jeopardy. State v. DeMatteo, 134 N.H. 296, 591 A.2d 1323, 1991 N.H. LEXIS 56 (1991).

An indictment must inform the defendant of the offense for which he is charged with sufficient specificity so that he knows what he must be prepared to meet and so that he is protected from being put in jeopardy again for the same offense. State v. Smith, 127 N.H. 836, 508 A.2d 1082, 1986 N.H. LEXIS 229 (1986).

This article requires that a complaint or indictment inform the defendant of the offense for which he is charged with sufficient specificity so that he knows what he must be prepared to meet and so that he is protected from being put in jeopardy once again for the same offense. State v. Cote, 126 N.H. 514, 493 A.2d 1170, 1985 N.H. LEXIS 336 (1985).

A sufficient indictment informs the defendant of each element charged with sufficient specificity to enable the defendant to prepare his defense. State v. Portigue, 125 N.H. 352, 481 A.2d 534, 1984 N.H. LEXIS 266 (1984).

For an indictment to be sufficient under this article, it must give the defendant enough information to allow him to prepare for trial and it must include all of the elements which constitute the offense charged. State v. Shannon, 125 N.H. 653, 484 A.2d 1164, 1984 N.H. LEXIS 380 (1984).

Although reference to a particular paragraph of a statute or to a specific felony is not the touchstone of the sufficiency of an indictment, it is essential that the indictment inform the defendant of the charges against him with adequate definiteness. State v. Shannon, 125 N.H. 653, 484 A.2d 1164, 1984 N.H. LEXIS 380 (1984).

An indictment or information must inform defendant of offense for which he is charged with sufficient specificity so that he knows what he must be prepared to meet and so that he is protected from being twice put in jeopardy. State v. Manchester News Co., 118 N.H. 255, 387 A.2d 324, 1978 N.H. LEXIS 392 (1978), appeal dismissed, Manchester News Co. v. New Hampshire, 439 U.S. 949, 99 S. Ct. 343, 58 L. Ed. 2d 340, 1978 U.S. LEXIS 3691 (1978).

An information need contain only elements of offense and enough facts to warn accused of specific charges against him. State v. Manchester News Co., 118 N.H. 255, 387 A.2d 324, 1978 N.H. LEXIS 392 (1978), appeal dismissed, Manchester News Co. v. New Hampshire, 439 U.S. 949, 99 S. Ct. 343, 58 L. Ed. 2d 340, 1978 U.S. LEXIS 3691 (1978).

An indictment must inform defendant of the offense charged with sufficient specificity so that he knows what he must be prepared to meet and is protected from being twice put in jeopardy. State v. Bean, 117 N.H. 185, 371 A.2d 1152, 1977 N.H. LEXIS 298 (1977).

A complaint must inform the defendant of the offense for which he is charged with sufficient specificity so that he knows what he must be prepared to meet and is protected from being put in jeopardy once again for the same offense. State v. Inselburg, 114 N.H. 824, 330 A.2d 457, 1974 N.H. LEXIS 384 (1974).

It is not essential to the validity of a complaint or indictment that it could possibly be made more comprehensive and certain; it is necessary only that it allege every element of the offense charged in language sufficiently definite to apprise respondents of what they must be prepared to meet for trial. State v. Farwell, 102 N.H. 3, 148 A.2d 653, 1959 N.H. LEXIS 2 (1959).

The true test of a sufficient indictment is not whether it could possibly be more definite and certain but rather whether it alleges every element of the offense charged in language sufficiently definite to apprise the accused of what he must be prepared to meet for trial. State v. Story, 97 N.H. 141, 83 A.2d 142, 1951 N.H. LEXIS 39 (1951).

The state is not required to set forth in the indictment the evidence in detail on which it expects to rely to sustain the charges. State v. Story, 97 N.H. 141, 83 A.2d 142, 1951 N.H. LEXIS 39 (1951).

Any complaint or indictment should be considered adequate if it informs the defendant of the nature and the cause of the accusation with sufficient definiteness to enable him to prepare for trial. State v. Rousten, 84 N.H. 140, 146 A. 870, 1929 N.H. LEXIS 66 (1929); State v. Langelier, 95 N.H. 97, 58 A.2d 315, 1948 N.H. LEXIS 190 (1948); State v. Donovan, 97 N.H. 190, 84 A.2d 405, 1951 N.H. LEXIS 49 (1951); State v. Ball, 101 N.H. 62, 132 A.2d 144, 1957 N.H. LEXIS 17 (1957); State v. Webster, 105 N.H. 415, 200 A.2d 856, 1964 N.H. LEXIS 90 (1964); State v. Strescino, 106 N.H. 554, 215 A.2d 706, 1965 N.H. LEXIS 213 (1965); State v. Mower, 107 N.H. 481, 225 A.2d 627, 1967 N.H. LEXIS 203 (1967).

It must appear to the court from the indictment that if the facts alleged are proved as stated, without any additional fact or circumstances, there can be no doubt of the illegality of the conduct charged, nor of its criminality. State v. Piper, 73 N.H. 226, 60 A. 742, 1905 N.H. LEXIS 21 (1905).

52. Elements of offense

Indictment for dispensing a controlled drug with death resulting under RSA 318-B:26, IX, satisfied N.H. Const. pt. I, art. 15, as it communicated to defendant that he was charged with dispensing a proscribed controlled drug and that a death resulted from injecting, inhaling, or ingesting that controlled drug. The use of the phrase "resulting in" apprised defendant that causation was an element; furthermore, assuming that the state constitution required any fact, other than a prior conviction, to be alleged, this rule was not violated, as the factor that the heroin dispensed by defendant caused the decedent's death was charged in the indictment, submitted to the jury, and found to exist by proof beyond a reasonable doubt. State v. Marshall, 162 N.H. 657, 34 A.3d 540, 2011 N.H. LEXIS 152 (2011).

Where the mens rea of purposely or knowingly was not included in a juvenile delinquency petition under RSA 169-B:6, II and RSA 169-B:2, IV that charged a juvenile with the offense of misdemeanor simple assault, in violation of RSA 631:2-a, I(a), the petition was constitutionally deficient under N.H. Const. pt. I, art. 15. In re Alex C., 158 N.H. 525, 969 A.2d 399, 2009 N.H. LEXIS 39 (2009).

Indictment for attempted burglary was not inadequate under N.H. Const. pt. I, art. 15 because it did not allege what crime defendant would have committed in furtherance of the burglary. Charging defendant with attempted burglary did not require the State to specify the offense defendant would have committed in furtherance of the burglary; furthermore, juror unanimity was required only for the elements of attempted burglary, not as to the crime or offense defendant would have committed in furtherance of the burglary. State v. Munoz, 157 N.H. 143, 949 A.2d 155, 2008 N.H. LEXIS 47 (2008).

Defendant was entitled to have vacated his conviction for failure to register with police under RSA 651-B:4, I because his guilty plea to the charge was not knowing and voluntary as he was not informed by either the trial court or the complaint that the statute afforded him 30 days in which to register after he moved to New Hampshire, and thus, his due process rights under N.H. Const. pt. 1, art. 15, were violated; further, the 30-day time period was an element of the offense pursuant to RSA 625:11, III(a) as it was included in the definition of the offense. State v. Offen, 156 N.H. 435, 938 A.2d 879, 2007 N.H. LEXIS 203 (2007).

"Three strikes" provision for sex offenders did not require three separate proceedings, but, rather, three separate adjudications of guilt, so that multiple separate incidents adjudicated in a single trial counted as multiple prior felonies; the possibility of enhanced sentencing was not an element of the offense for purposes of due process, so the State's desire to seek an enhanced sentence did not have to be included in the indictment. State v. Melvin, 150 N.H. 134, 834 A.2d 247, 2003 N.H. LEXIS 152 (2003).

Indictment which failed to make any reference to intended victim was legally insufficient to charge defendant with attempted armed robbery, and trial court's instruction supplying that reference was an improper amendment of the indictment in violation of New Hampshire constitution. State v. Glanville, 145 N.H. 631, 765 A.2d 173, 2000 N.H. LEXIS 114 (2000).

An indictment was sufficient as it alleged all of the elements of second degree murder, as well as the date of the offense, the name of the victim, and how the defendant committed the offense, i.e., by shooting her in the head; other specific acts of the defendant or circumstances that would demonstrate his extreme indifference did not have to be alleged. State v. Burley, 137 N.H. 286, 627 A.2d 98, 1993 N.H. LEXIS 73 (1993).

In determining the sufficiency of an indictment, the question is not whether the indictment could be more certain and comprehensive, but whether it contains the elements of the offense and enough facts to warn the accused of the specific charges against him. State v. Hermsdorf, 135 N.H. 360, 605 A.2d 1045, 1992 N.H. LEXIS 42, (1992).

Fact that indictment for fraud failed to allege a specific object of the fraud would not expose a defendant to additional, separate charges in violation of constitutional protection against double jeopardy, where indictment required only an intent to defraud anyone in the community and indictment contained an adequate description of such mens rea. State v. DeMatteo, 134 N.H. 296, 591 A.2d 1323, 1991 N.H. LEXIS 56 (1991).

In order for an indictment to be deemed constitutionally sufficient, for purposes of double jeopardy it must allege all the elements of an offense that is identified by the pleaded facts. State v. DeMatteo, 134 N.H. 296, 591 A.2d 1323, 1991 N.H. LEXIS 56 (1991).

As a threshold for meeting the standards of this article, an indictment must set forth all of the necessary elements constituting the offense. State v. Cote, 126 N.H. 514, 493 A.2d 1170, 1985 N.H. LEXIS 336 (1985).

An indictment is sufficient only if it clearly sets out all of the necessary elements constituting the offense. State v. Bussiere, 118 N.H. 659, 392 A.2d 151, 1978 N.H. LEXIS 263 (1978).

An indictment is not sufficient merely because the state deems a crime charged to be generally understood; the necessary elements of the crime must be included in it. State v. Bussiere, 118 N.H. 659, 392 A.2d 151, 1978 N.H. LEXIS 263 (1978).

As a threshold for meeting constitutional standards, an indictment must state all of the necessary elements constituting the offense. State v. Smith, 127 N.H. 836, 508 A.2d 1082, 1986 N.H. LEXIS 229 (1986).

53. Statutory language

An indictment is generally sufficient if it uses the language of the applicable statute, but it need not state the specific means by which the crime was carried out. State v. Hermsdorf, 135 N.H. 360, 605 A.2d 1045, 1992 N.H. LEXIS 42, (1992).

Indictment for arson alleged the nature of the offense with sufficient definiteness to withstand a motion to dismiss where indictment tracked wording of arson statute providing: "A person is guilty of arson if he knowingly starts a fire ... which unlawfully damages the property of another." State v. Champagne, 119 N.H. 118, 399 A.2d 287, 1979 N.H. LEXIS 253 (1979).

An indictment or information will generally give sufficient notice to defendant of a statutory offense when charge follows language of statute and alleges all necessary elements of offense with sufficient specificity. State v. Manchester News Co., 118 N.H. 255, 387 A.2d 324, 1978 N.H. LEXIS 392 (1978), appeal dismissed, Manchester News Co. v. New Hampshire, 439 U.S. 949, 99 S. Ct. 343, 58 L. Ed. 2d 340, 1978 U.S. LEXIS 3691 (1978).

When a statutory offense is alleged, it is not sufficient to merely quote the statute unless it clearly sets out all the elements of the offense. State v. Inselburg, 114 N.H. 824, 330 A.2d 457, 1974 N.H. LEXIS 384 (1974).

Generally, in offenses created by statute it is sufficient to describe the offense in the words of the statute, but a complaint so drawn does not always meet the constitutional requirements that a full description of the offense must be alleged. State v. Mower, 107 N.H. 481, 225 A.2d 627, 1967 N.H. LEXIS 203 (1967).

In indictments or complaints created by statute it is generally sufficient to describe the offense in the words of the statute but a complaint so drawn does not always meet the constitutional re-

quirements that a fair and full description of the offense must be alleged. State v. Webster, 105 N.H. 415, 200 A.2d 856, 1964 N.H. LEXIS 90 (1964).

54. Time of offense

Indictment alleging a number of acts each month for 23 months against defendant's stepdaughter 10 years before adequately informed defendant of the charges against him pursuant to N.H. Const. pt. I, art. 15; particular time of the offenses was not an element of the crime. State v. Dupont, 149 N.H. 70, 816 A.2d 954, 2003 N.H. LEXIS 8 (2003).

An indictment charging one with being an accessory before the fact to a crime committed on a certain day, without setting forth the means and specific facts by which the alleged accessory procured, aided and abetted the commission of the crime sufficiently meets the requirement of this provision, though it would have been better practice to have alleged a day or dates when the offense of the accessory was committed and that it occurred prior to the commission of the principal crime. State v. Ball, 101 N.H. 62, 132 A.2d 144, 1957 N.H. LEXIS 17 (1957).

The date stated in an indictment is usually immaterial, and a respondent may be convicted upon proof of the offense on any other date prior to the time when the indictment was returned. Hurd v. Varney, 83 N.H. 467, 144 A. 266, 1929 N.H. LEXIS 87 (1929).

55. Bill of particulars

Decision concerning issuance of a bill of particulars is within the discretion of the trial court and will not be disturbed unless defendant can demonstrate that the ruling was clearly untenable or unreasonable to the prejudice of defendant's case. State v. Woodard, 146 N.H. 221, 769 A.2d 379, 2001 N.H. LEXIS 64 (2001).

Defendant charged with felonious sexual assault was not entitled to a bill of particulars specifying whether the victim was age twelve or thirteen at the time of the alleged offenses because the intent of the legislature in creating two classes of felony offenses for any act of sexual penetration committed against a child under sixteen years of age was to protect all young victims against sexual assault but to establish an enhanced penalty for assaults against younger victims. State v. Woodard, 146 N.H. 221, 769 A.2d 379, 2001 N.H. LEXIS 64 (2001).

Where indictment did not inform defendant of the nature and cause of the accusation against him with sufficient definiteness so that he could prepare for trial, the defect could not be cured by permitting the state to file a bill of particulars. State v. Gilbert, 89 N.H. 134, 194 A. 728, 1937 N.H. LEXIS 28 (1937).

56. Former convictions

In imposing sentence enhancement based on prior convictions, trial court could properly sentence defendant to prison terms exceeding one year for crimes charged by information; portion of extended terms that exceeded maximum generally applicable sentence did not transform charged misdemeanor offenses into crimes required to be charged by indictment. State v. Smith, 144 N.H. 1, 736 A.2d 1236, 1999 N.H. LEXIS 66 (1999).

An indictment charging a second offense is sufficient where it sets forth the court, time, offense, and fact of former conviction; no allegation is necessary as to the facts surrounding the former conviction or upon which it was based. State v. Adams, 64 N.H. 440, 13 A. 785, 1887 N.H. LEXIS 48 (1888), overruled in part, State v. LeBaron, 148 N.H. 226, 808 A.2d 541, 2002 N.H. LEXIS 112 (2002).

57. Grand jury

On appeal from conviction of manslaughter, claim that trial court impermissibly amended grand jury's indictment would be examined by supreme court under state constitution despite normally preclusive effect of defendant's failure to raise state constitutional issue below; claim alleged violation of state statute guaranteeing individual's right to an indictment by grand jury for crimes punishable by greater than one year of imprisonment which must be considered in conjunction with constitutional provision guaranteeing that individual may only be convicted of crime charged in grand jury's indictment. State v. Elliott, 133 N.H. 759, 585 A.2d 304, 1990 N.H. LEXIS 135 (1990).

Citizens of New Hampshire have the right to indictment by a grand jury before they may be tried for any offense punishable by imprisonment for more than one year. State v. Erickson, 129 N.H. 515, 533 A.2d 23, 1987 N.H. LEXIS 253 (1987).

The guaranty of this article that no subject shall be arrested, imprisoned, or deprived of his life, liberty, or estate, but by the judgment of his peers, or the law of the land, guaranties to an accused the common law right to be placed upon trial for a crime upon a lawful accusation by a grand jury. State v. Canatella, 96 N.H. 202, 72 A.2d 507, 1950 N.H. LEXIS 144 (1950).

58. Corporations
An information charging corporation with an offense need not indicate for whose acts corporation is being charged. State v. Manchester News Co., 118 N.H. 255, 387 A.2d 324, 1978 N.H. LEXIS 392 (1978), appeal dismissed, Manchester News Co. v. New Hampshire, 439 U.S. 949, 99 S. Ct. 343, 58 L. Ed. 2d 340, 1978 U.S. LEXIS 3691 (1978).

59. Conduct of trial
The requirement that a defendant be tried only for crimes for which he or she has been indicted is not necessarily violated when a trial judge provides a jury instruction that does not mirror the indictment. State v. Hutchinson, 137 N.H. 591, 631 A.2d 523, 1993 N.H. LEXIS 131 (1993).

60. Accomplice liability
When a defendant is sufficiently charged by an indictment as a principal, the indictment is sufficient to allow the defendant to prepare a defense to the substantive offense for principal or accomplice liability. Therefore, an instruction with regard to accomplice liability does not impermissibly amend the indictment in violation of part I, article 15 of the New Hampshire Constitution. State v. Barton, 142 N.H. 391, 702 A.2d 336, 1997 N.H. LEXIS 109 (1997).

61. Duplicitous indictments
Indictments on nine counts of felonious sexual assault did not violate defendant's constitutional guarantees against double jeopardy where each indictment accused the defendant of engaging in the act of sexual penetration with the victim when the victim was "either twelve or thirteen years old" and charged the defendant with a class B felony, and, because the victim's age was in question, the court limited the state to prosecuting the defendant only on class B felonies. State v. Woodard, 146 N.H. 221, 769 A.2d 379, 2001 N.H. LEXIS 64 (2001).

Second count of two-count sexual assault indictment could not reasonably be read to charge a violation of both RSA 632-A:2, X-a and RSA 632-A:2, III, and thus indictment was not unconstitutionally duplicitous. State v. Marti, 143 N.H. 608, 732 A.2d 414, 1999 N.H. LEXIS 50 (1999).

62. Attempt
Statute governing attempts to commit crime did not require State to plead and prove elements of intended offense, and therefore indictment which alleged attempted aggravated felonious sexual assault, and factually identified offense in describing overt steps defendant took to accomplish it, was sufficient to enable defendant to prepare his defense and to protect him from double jeopardy. State v. Johnson, 144 N.H. 175, 738 A.2d 1284, 1999 N.H. LEXIS 95 (1999).

63. Misdemeanors
Indictment is required for a misdemeanor charge that results in extended imprisonment greater than one year, when a sentencing enhancement factor is related to offense itself. State v. Ouellette, 145 N.H. 489, 764 A.2d 914, 2000 N.H. LEXIS 96 (2000).

Trial court erred in sentencing misdemeanor defendant to prison for more than one year for offenses that were charged by information and not by indictment, since his extended terms were based on punishment related to offenses themselves and not upon his recidivism. State v. Ouellette, 145 N.H. 489, 764 A.2d 914, 2000 N.H. LEXIS 96 (2000).

Misdemeanor assault defendant did not waive his right to indictment by stipulating that he knew victim was a law enforcement officer acting in the line of duty at time of assault. State v. Ouellette, 145 N.H. 489, 764 A.2d 914, 2000 N.H. LEXIS 96 (2000).

64. Sexual assault
Indictment alleged the pattern variant of aggravated felonious sexual assault under RSA 632-A:2 with the requisite specificity to satisfy N.H. Const. pt. I, art. 15 when it specified a location for the alleged conduct, the time period in which it was alleged to have occurred, the identity and age of the victim, and the conduct against which defendant had to defend. Defendant's ability to prepare a defense was not impaired by the indictment's failure to allege more specifically the predicate acts comprising the pattern, because the essential culpable act was the pattern itself. State v. Ericson, 159 N.H. 379, 986 A.2d 488, 2009 N.H. LEXIS 125 (2009).

65. Amendment of indictment
Trial court did not amend the indictments by changing the offense charged or adding an offense not charged by the grand jury. Moreover, defendant received notice that the State could attempt to prove that he was reckless because he was voluntarily intoxicated. State v. Dilboy, 160 N.H. 135, 999 A.2d 1092, 2010 N.H. LEXIS 36 (2010).

It was not error to grant the State's motions to amend the indictments. Defendant never asserted an alibi defense or lack of access to the victim, and had never established any prejudice to his defense due to the change in the time frame of the indictments; furthermore, defendant had sufficient time to understand the charges and prepare any additional defenses before trial. State v. Oakes, 161 N.H. 270, 13 A.3d 293, 2010 N.H. LEXIS 149 (Dec. 7, 2010).

III. Self-Incrimination

101. Construction with federal constitution
Since State Constitution afforded greater protection to criminal defendant than Federal Constitution, in requiring State to prove voluntariness of defendant's statements beyond reasonable doubt rather than by preponderance of evidence, court was not required to undertake a separate federal analysis on appeal. State v. Ford, 144 N.H. 57, 738 A.2d 937, 1999 N.H. LEXIS 71 (1999).

Under this article, state must prove voluntariness of defendant's statements beyond a reasonable doubt, a more stringent standard than the preponderance of evidence standard required under the Federal Constitution. State v. Beland, 138 N.H. 735, 645 A.2d 79, 1994 N.H. LEXIS 96 (1994).

Because state's burden of proving voluntariness of defendant's confession beyond a reasonable doubt, grounded in the state constitution, is more stringent than the preponderance of the evidence standard required under the federal constitution, trial court's decision need only be reviewed under the more demanding state constitutional standard. State v. Laurie, 135 N.H. 438, 606 A.2d 1077, 1992 N.H. LEXIS 59 (1992), cert. denied, Laurie v. New Hampshire, 506 U.S. 886, 113 S. Ct. 245, 121 L. Ed. 2d 178, 1992 U.S. LEXIS 6039 (1992).

This article's privilege against self-incrimination is comparable in scope to the fifth amendment. State v. Cormier, 127 N.H. 253, 499 A.2d 986, 1985 N.H. LEXIS 424 (1985).

102. Scope of right
There was no plain error under N.H. Sup. Ct. R. 16-A by the trial court's consideration of defendant's lack of remorse as a factor in determining what sentence to impose, based on defendant's request to return to the house of corrections in time to shower after the second day of trial, as defendant had admitted that his actions led to death and injury although he maintained it was an accident; there was no violation of defendant's privilege against self-incrimination because defendant did not maintain his innocence throughout the trial. State v. Lamy, 158 N.H. 511, 969 A.2d 451, 2009 N.H. LEXIS 45 (2009).

Sentencing court may not draw a negative inference of lack of remorse from defendant's silence at sentencing, but that holding does not preclude a sentencing court from considering other evidence besides defendant's silence that indicates his lack of remorse, nor does it prevent a sentencing court from considering defendant's false trial testimony as a sentencing factor. The holding was limited to situations where a defendant maintains his innocence throughout the criminal process and risks incriminating himself if he expresses remorse at sentencing. N.H. v. Burgess, 156 N.H. 746, 943 A.2d 727, 2008 N.H. LEXIS 18 (2008).

Sentencing court did not abuse its discretion by imposing the maximum sentence of 10 to 30 years in prison on each of defendant's two counts involving escape because the trial court did not violate his privilege against self-incrimination by using his silence at the sentencing hearing and failure to participate in the presentence investigation as sentencing factors as, although the sentencing court could not draw a negative inference of lack of remorse from his silence at sentencing, it was permitted to consider other evidence as indications of a lack of remorse, such as his denial that he ever intended to escape. The sentencing court only considered defendant's lack of involvement with the pre-sentence investigation, not his silence, as a sentencing factor. N.H. v. Burgess, 156 N.H. 746, 943 A.2d 727, 2008 N.H. LEXIS 18 (2008).

A reciprocal discovery order, which required that the defendant disclose the identity and statements of witnesses he intended to call at trial, did not violate his constitutional privileges against compelled self-incrimination. The order did not require the defendant to say or testify to anything he would not otherwise say or testify to; it merely determined the time of his disclosures. Moreover, such disclosure would not lighten the state's burden of proof. State v. Drewry, 139 N.H. 678, 661 A.2d 1181, 1995 N.H. LEXIS 71 (1995).

The decision to admit guilt of a lesser-included offense of a crime with which he is charged should remain inviolably personal to the defendant. State v. Anaya, 134 N.H. 346, 592 A.2d 1142, 1991 N.H. LEXIS 68 (1991).

Statute applicable to crime of capital murder that explicitly allowed consideration of an imposition of the death penalty only where a jury had rendered a verdict of guilty and not where defendants had pled guilty was violative of defendants' rights to assert innocence and to a jury trial and thus was unconstitutional on its face. State v. Johnson, 134 N.H. 570, 595 A.2d 498, 1991 N.H. LEXIS 101 (1991).

State constitutional provision forbidding the government from compelling an accused to furnish evidence against himself guarantees a defendant procedural protections, such as warning and the requirement of a waiver, which safeguard the underlying state right of freedom from self-incrimination. State v. Gravel, 135 N.H. 172, 601 A.2d 678, 1991 N.H. LEXIS 171 (1991).

The privilege against self-incrimination guaranteed by this article is an option for the witness to refuse to answer each particular question as it is propounded, and not a prohibition of all further inquiry by the examiner. State v. Bell, 112 N.H. 444, 298 A.2d 753, 1972 N.H. LEXIS 240 (1972).

The self-incrimination provision of this article is intended to preserve the common law privilege afforded a witness to refuse to give testimony which may possibly expose him to a criminal prosecution, but does not protect him from disgrace, infamy or other consequences which might follow from his disclosures. Wyman v. De Gregory, 101 N.H. 171, 137 A.2d 512, 1957 N.H. LEXIS 47 (1957), appeal dismissed, 360 U.S. 717, 79 S. Ct. 1454, 3 L. Ed. 2d 1540, 1959 U.S. LEXIS 667 (1959).

The privilege against self-incrimination accorded by this article prevents a witness from being compelled to speak about an offense for which he could be criminally punished. Wyman v. De Gregory, 100 N.H. 163, 121 A.2d 805, 1956 N.H. LEXIS 21 (1956).

The constitutional guaranty against self-incrimination means not only that a person shall not be compelled to disclose his guilt upon the trial of a criminal proceeding against himself, but also that he shall not be required to disclose, on the trial of issues between others, facts that can be used against him as admissions tending to prove his guilt of any crime or offense of which he may then or afterwards be charged, or the source from which, or the means by which, evidence of its commission or his connection with it may be obtained. State v. Nowell, 58 N.H. 314, 1878 N.H. LEXIS 46 (1878).

103. Application of right

DNA samples are non-testimonial in nature. Compelling an accused to provide a DNA sample does not violate N.H. Const. pt. I, art. 15. State v. Hearns, 151 N.H. 226, 855 A.2d 549, 2004 N.H. LEXIS 129 (2004).

Blood test evidence, although an incriminating product of compulsion, is neither testimony nor evidence relating to some communicative act and does not violate N.H. Const. pt. I, art. 15. State v. Hearns, 151 N.H. 226, 855 A.2d 549, 2004 N.H. LEXIS 129 (2004).

Privilege against self-incrimination applies only to evidence provided by a defendant that is of testimonial character. The privilege does not protect an accused from compulsion which makes him the source of real or physical evidence. State v. Hearns, 151 N.H. 226, 855 A.2d 549, 2004 N.H. LEXIS 129 (2004).

Requiring a defendant to furnish a handwriting exemplar does not violate the defendant's rights under part I, article 15 of the New Hampshire constitution because the action is non-testimonial in nature. Therefore, if a defendant refuses to comply with a court's order to furnish an exemplar, such a refusal is not compelled by the state and the court may instruct the jury regarding the defendant's refusal. State v. Robidoux, 139 N.H. 657, 662 A.2d 268, 1995 N.H. LEXIS 66 (1995).

Privilege against self-incrimination applies only to evidence provided by a defendant that is of testimonial character. State v. Cormier, 127 N.H. 253, 499 A.2d 986, 1985 N.H. LEXIS 424 (1985).

The procedural protections against involuntary self-incrimination provided under this article attach only after an individual has been taken into custody. State v. Damiano, 124 N.H. 742, 474 A.2d 1045, 1984 N.H. LEXIS 337 (1984).

The constitutional privilege against self-incrimination ceases to apply where the danger of criminal prosecution is removed by a statute so designed. Wyman v. De Gregory, 101 N.H. 171, 137 A.2d 512, 1957 N.H. LEXIS 47 (1957), appeal dismissed, 360 U.S. 717, 79 S. Ct. 1454, 3 L. Ed. 2d 1540, 1959 U.S. LEXIS 667 (1959).

If at the time of the claim of the privilege against self-incrimination the liability of the witness to be convicted of the offense inquired about has been terminated because of an acquittal, prior conviction, pardon, or otherwise, the privilege does not exist for such conduct. Wyman v. De Gregory, 100 N.H. 163, 121 A.2d 805, 1956 N.H. LEXIS 21 (1956).

104. Exclusion of evidence

To determine whether statements made by a criminal defendant should be suppressed as fruit of an unlawful arrest, the Supreme Court of New Hampshire must determine whether the act of giving the statement was sufficiently a product of the defendant's free will so as to break the causal connection between the illegality and the confession. In making this determination, the court considers the following four factors: (1) whether Miranda warnings were given; (2) the temporal proximity of the arrest and the confession; (3) the presence of intervening circumstances; and (4) the purpose and flagrancy of the official misconduct. State v. Belton, 150 N.H. 741, 846 A.2d 526, 2004 N.H. LEXIS 67 (2004), cert. denied, Belton v. New Hampshire, 543 U.S. 1028, 125 S. Ct. 674, 160 L. Ed. 2d 509, 2004 U.S. LEXIS 8093 (2004).

Failure of police who were interrogating defendant to inform him of his attorney's efforts to contact him vitiated defendant's waiver of his Miranda rights, and all statements he made after his attorney called the police were properly suppressed. State v. Roache, 148 N.H. 45, 803 A.2d 572, 2002 N.H. LEXIS 89 (2002).

Although proof of a deranged or deficient mental state may be highly significant in determining whether any given police conduct was overbearing in its effect, mere proof that a defendant's confession or admission was the product of his own mental condition is not a sufficient basis to exclude the confession or admission from evidence at trial. State v. Chapman, 135 N.H. 390, 605 A.2d 1055, 1992 N.H. LEXIS 48 (1992).

The "fruit of the poisonous tree" doctrine requires the exclusion from trial of evidence derivatively obtained through a violation of constitutional guarantee against compelled self-incrimination. State v. Gravel, 135 N.H. 172, 601 A.2d 678, 1991 N.H. LEXIS 171 (1991).

Because warrant application to search defendant's bedroom for drugs failed to establish probable cause when stripped of information obtained in violation of defendant's *Miranda* rights, drug evidence seized from defendant's bedroom should have been suppressed. State v. Gravel, 135 N.H. 172, 601 A.2d 678, 1991 N.H. LEXIS 171 (1991).

105. Civil proceedings

Trial court erred in ruling that divorce defendant improperly asserted his privilege against self-incrimination, where nearly all questions related to defendant's financial or business dealings and could possibly serve as a link in the chain of evidence, or could tend to incriminate him. Defendant's answers to questions to which he erroneously asserted his privilege would not have provided plaintiff with any additional information material to determining size of marital estate. DeMauro v. DeMauro, 142 N.H. 879, 712 A.2d 623, 1998 N.H. LEXIS 53 (1998).

In a case involving the efforts of the plaintiff bank to collect a judgment of nearly $3 million from the defendant, the defendant was entitled to rely on his privilege against self-incrimination in refusing to answer certain questions pertaining to his finances as answers to such questions could constitute links in the chain of evidence needed to prosecute the defendant for overstating his wealth on a financial statement; the defendant was thus entitled to refuse to answer questions pertaining to his finances near the time that the financial statement was filed, but was not entitled to refuse to answer questions pertaining to his finances over one year later. Key Bank v. Latshaw, 137 N.H. 665, 633 A.2d 952, 1993 N.H. LEXIS 141 (1993).

In a case involving the efforts of the plaintiff bank to collect a judgment of nearly $3 million from the defendant, the defendant's wife was not entitled to rely on her privilege against self-incrimination in refusing to answer some questions pertaining to the defendant's finances as answers to such questions could not have subjected her to criminal liability in connection with a financial statement filed by the defendant. Key Bank v. Latshaw, 137 N.H. 665, 633 A.2d 952, 1993 N.H. LEXIS 141 (1993).

The fact that proceedings in which questions are asked are civil rather than criminal does not deprive a person of the privilege against self-incrimination. Sevigny v. Burns, 108 N.H. 95, 227 A.2d 775, 1967 N.H. LEXIS 129 (1967).

The privilege against self-incrimination is not to be used as the means of preventing an orderly investigation of civil matters. State v. Cote, 95 N.H. 108, 58 A.2d 749, 1948 N.H. LEXIS 195 (1948).

The guaranty of this article that no subject shall be compelled to furnish evidence against himself relates to criminal proceedings only and not to civil actions; that disclosure may result in pecuniary loss to the witness provides no privilege.Boston & M. R.R. v. State, 75 N.H. 513, 77 A. 996, 1910 N.H. LEXIS 36, 31 L.R.A. (n.s.) 539 (1910).

106. Legislative investigations

This privilege against self-incrimination applies to an investigation by a legislative committee. Wyman v. De Gregory, 100 N.H. 163, 121 A.2d 805, 1956 N.H. LEXIS 21 (1956).

107. Miranda warning

Defendant's Miranda rights under N.H. Const. pt. I, art. 15 and the Fifth Amendment had not been violated because a trooper did not engage in the functional equivalent of interrogation. The trooper's statements were made in direct response to defendant's questions about whether his job was hard and could not be characterized as interrogatory. State v. Gribble, — N.H. —, 66 A.3d 1194, 2013 N.H. LEXIS 47 (May 7, 2013).

In determining whether defendant's Miranda rights under the New Hampshire and United States constitutions were violated, the trial court did not err in finding that defendant was not subject to custodial interrogation before receiving and waiving his Miranda rights; determining whether defendant was interrogated prior to his Miranda warnings required the trial court to weigh the credibility of the witnesses, in which it had broad discretion. Similarly, the interview transcript established that a detective terminated his first interview with defendant upon defendant's request for a lawyer and that during the second interview, he offered defendant an opportunity to use the telephone to contact an attorney, which defendant declined; the detective did not have an obligation to independently contact a public defender on behalf of defendant. State v. Kousounadis, 159 N.H. 413, 986 A.2d 603, 2009 N.H. LEXIS 136 (2009).

Trial court did not err in denying defendant's motion to suppress evidence that defendant made while in the custody of police that were incriminating regarding the subsequent drug charges brought against him, as the State proved that defendant was warned of his constitutional rights, that he waived those rights, and that any subsequent statements he made were made knowingly, voluntarily, and intelligently. State v. Zwicker, 151 N.H. 179, 855 A.2d 415, 2004 N.H. LEXIS 112 (2004).

Barnett rule requiring that post-Miranda confessions be tape-recorded and complete before being admitted in evidence was not extended to require tape recording of pre-Miranda statements; giving of warnings was adopted as the dividing line for due process purposes because at that point a defendant would clearly be aware that a statement could be used in court. State v. Velez, 150 N.H. 589, 842 A.2d 97, 2004 N.H. LEXIS 35 (2004).

Officer's action of showing a surveillance photograph of defendant in response to her repeated questions about the basis for her arrest and claims of innocence were not interrogatory as the photographs did not require an affirmative response; thus defendant's pre-Miranda response to viewing the photographs was properly admitted. State v. Spencer, 149 N.H. 622, 826 A.2d 546, 2003 N.H. LEXIS 92 (2003).

Evidence before the trial court was sufficient, despite possibly conflicting times written on the Miranda waiver form and the consent to search form, to support the trial court's factual finding that the defendant was given Miranda warnings at the police station by the police officers after the questioning of the defendant began but before the substantive questioning began and that the defendant voluntarily waived the Miranda rights. Therefore, the defendant's statements were admissible. State v. Higgins, 149 N.H. 290, 821 A.2d 964, 2003 N.H. LEXIS 41 (2003).

Defendant's motion to exclude evidence regarding his identity on the basis that the information was derivative evidence and "fruit of the poisonous tree" following an alleged Miranda violation was properly denied because the evidence compelled a finding that his identity would inevitably have been discovered through motor vehicle records, court records "or other means." State v. Hill, 146 N.H. 568, 781 A.2d 979, 2001 N.H. LEXIS 114 (2001).

Tape recording of only the inculpatory part of defendant's statement to police was not excluded from evidence on due process grounds; instead, the court established a rule in the exercise of its supervisory authority requiring that once Miranda warnings had been issued, in order for a tape recording to be subsequently admissible, it had to include the whole interrogation, not just the inculpatory portions. State v. Barnett, 147 N.H. 334, 789 A.2d 629, 2001 N.H. LEXIS 216 (2001).

School principal was not a law enforcement officer, nor was she acting as an agent of police when she searched defendant for drugs, and therefore Miranda warnings were not required to be given to defendant. State v. Tinkham, 143 N.H. 73, 719 A.2d 580, 1998 N.H. LEXIS 69 (1998).

Where a defendant asserts Miranda rights while in custody, but before interrogation has begun, the state's ability to go forward with interrogation depends on the nature of the request for counsel. Pre-interrogation, there is no irrebuttable presumption that a defendant's request for counsel was for the purpose of having counsel present during the imminent interrogation. State v. Grant-Chase, 140 N.H. 264, 665 A.2d 380, 1995 N.H. LEXIS 139 (1995), cert. denied, Grant-Chase v. New Hampshire, 517 U.S. 1140, 116 S. Ct. 1431, 134 L. Ed. 2d 553, 1996 U.S. LEXIS 2503 (1996).

If a defendant's pre-interrogation assertion of the right to counsel is ambiguous as to the purpose for which counsel is sought, the police have a right to clarify the ambiguity by asking the defendant if he or she wishes to go forward with interrogation. If, upon clarification, the defendant states that the purpose of the request for counsel was unrelated to the subject matter of the imminent questioning or that the purpose of the call was merely to seek advice of counsel on how to proceed with imminent questioning, the police may proceed with questioning if they first secure a knowing, intelligent, and voluntary Miranda waiver. However, if, upon clarification, after talking with counsel, the defendant states that she does not wish to proceed with questioning until counsel is present, that right must be scrupulously honored and no police questioning may follow. State v. Grant-Chase, 140 N.H. 264, 665 A.2d 380, 1995 N.H. LEXIS 139 (1995), cert. denied, Grant-Chase v. New Hampshire, 517 U.S. 1140, 116 S. Ct. 1431, 134 L. Ed. 2d 553, 1996 U.S. LEXIS 2503 (1996).

State historically has mandated more protection for a suspect's rights where *Miranda* is concerned than has the United States Supreme Court. State v. Gravel, 135 N.H. 172, 601 A.2d 678, 1991 N.H. LEXIS 171 (1991).

The police must advise a suspect that he has a right to remain silent and the right to counsel before engaging in custodial interrogation. State v. Munson, 126 N.H. 191, 489 A.2d 646, 1985 N.H. LEXIS 245 (1985).

108. Assertion of right—Questioning after

Privilege against self-incrimination is a personal one, and if a witness desires the protection of the privilege, the witness must claim it him or herself; thus, it is error for a trial court to bar a witness from testifying based upon its own concerns regarding that witness's privilege before the witness has claimed that right. State v. King, 146 N.H. 717, 781 A.2d 1002, 2001 N.H. LEXIS 145 (2001).

Trial court erred when it sua sponte asserted the privilege against self-incrimination on witness's behalf. State v. King, 146 N.H. 717, 781 A.2d 1002, 2001 N.H. LEXIS 145 (2001).

Standard set forth in Michigan v. Mosley, 423 U.S. 96, 96 S. Ct. 321, 46 L. Ed. 2d 313, 1975 U.S. LEXIS 100 (1975), adequately protects a defendant's privilege against self-incrimination under the state constitution; accordingly, whenever a suspect in police custody exercises his option to cut off questioning, the police must scrupulously honor the suspect's desire to remain silent. State v. Laurie, 135 N.H. 438, 606 A.2d 1077, 1992 N.H. LEXIS 59 (1992), cert. denied, Laurie v. New Hampshire, 506 U.S. 886, 113 S. Ct. 245, 121 L. Ed. 2d 178, 1992 U.S. LEXIS 6039 (1992).

Fact that third interview resulting in defendant's murder confession involved same crime as first and second interviews, and that therefore one factor identified in Michigan v. Mosley, 423 U.S. 96, 96 S. Ct. 321, 46 L. Ed. 2d 313, 1975 U.S. LEXIS 100 (1975), was not met, did not automatically prohibit finding that police scrupulously honored defendant's desire to remain silent. State v. Laurie, 135 N.H. 438, 606 A.2d 1077, 1992 N.H. LEXIS 59 (1992), cert. denied, Laurie v. New Hampshire, 506 U.S. 886, 113 S. Ct. 245, 121 L. Ed. 2d 178, 1992 U.S. LEXIS 6039 (1992).

If a suspect asserts his right to remain silent or his right to counsel, all questioning by the police must cease. State v. Munson, 126 N.H. 191, 489 A.2d 646, 1985 N.H. LEXIS 245 (1985).

109. —Procedure

In order to legitimately exclude testimony based upon witness's Fifth Amendment right, trial court must conduct a hearing to determine if the privilege is being properly invoked. State v. King, 146 N.H. 717, 781 A.2d 1002, 2001 N.H. LEXIS 145 (2001).

In giving Miranda warnings, police are not constitutionally required to inform defendant of every possible charge that may be brought against him, or the elements thereof, nor must defendant understand every possible charge that may be brought against him so long as he understands that anything he says may be used against him. State v. LaFountain, 138 N.H. 225, 636 A.2d 1028, 1994 N.H. LEXIS 5 (1994).

In order to determine whether, after initially waiving his *Miranda* rights, defendant subsequently invoked his right to remain silent, defendant's statements would be examined by considering the totality of the circumstances. State v. Chapman, 135 N.H. 390, 605 A.2d 1055, 1992 N.H. LEXIS 48 (1992).

The privilege against self-incrimination may be effectively invoked by any language that a court should reasonably understand to be a claim of the privilege. State v. Bell, 112 N.H. 444, 298 A.2d 753, 1972 N.H. LEXIS 240 (1972).

In order for a court to dispense with the usual procedure of requiring a witness to claim his privilege against self-incrimination as each question is propounded and instead allow a blanket assertion of the privilege, the court should carefully question the witness as to questions proffered by counsel calling the witness, and if it then clearly appears that there is no relevant nonprivileged testimony which the witness can offer, the witness may be excused from further testifying upon his claim of the privilege. State v. Bell, 112 N.H. 444, 298 A.2d 753, 1972 N.H. LEXIS 240 (1972).

110. —Who may assert right

This article does not provide a defendant with a privilege of silence that may be asserted against another individual acting in his private capacity. State v. Brown, 128 N.H. 606, 517 A.2d 831, 1986 N.H. LEXIS 328 (1986).

Ordinarily, a witness must personally claim the privilege against self-incrimination, although there may be occasions when an attorney may properly invoke the privilege. State v. Bell, 112 N.H. 444, 298 A.2d 753, 1972 N.H. LEXIS 240 (1972).

The objection that the testimony of a witness in a criminal case is self-incriminating is not available to the accused. State v. Geddes, 101 N.H. 164, 136 A.2d 818, 1957 N.H. LEXIS 45 (1957).

111. Waiver of right—Generally

The burden lies with the State to demonstrate beyond a reasonable doubt that a defendant has knowingly and voluntarily waived his Miranda rights. State v. Duffy, 146 N.H. 648, 778 A.2d 415, 2001 N.H. LEXIS 125 (2001).

Where there was no express waiver, defendant's course of conduct and the surrounding circumstances were looked to in order to determine if defendant impliedly waived his rights. State v. Duffy, 146 N.H. 648, 778 A.2d 415, 2001 N.H. LEXIS 125 (2001).

Where defendant first orally indicates that he understands his right to remain silent and then initiates a dialogue with the police, courts generally conclude that a knowing and voluntary waiver has occurred. State v. Duffy, 146 N.H. 648, 778 A.2d 415, 2001 N.H. LEXIS 125 (2001).

To overcome presumption that a defendant would not normally forfeit constitutional right against self-incrimination, State must prove beyond a reasonable doubt that defendant knowingly, intelligently, and voluntarily waived that right. State v. Farrell, 145 N.H. 733, 766 A.2d 1057, 2001 N.H. LEXIS 14 (2001).

Record supported trial court's finding that, despite defendant's borderline intelligence, he was capable of understanding meaning and effect of his waiver of Miranda rights. State v. Dumas, 145 N.H. 301, 761 A.2d 1063, 2000 N.H. LEXIS 61 (2000).

Officers' pre-polygraph Miranda warning provided defendant with sufficient safeguards to protect his right against self-incrimination during post-polygraph interview. State v. Monroe, 142 N.H. 857, 711 A.2d 878, 1998 N.H. LEXIS 51 (1998), cert. denied, Monroe v. New Hampshire, 525 U.S. 1073, 119 S. Ct. 807, 142 L. Ed. 2d 667, 1999 U.S. LEXIS 190 (1999).

Where defendant was obviously intoxicated at time he was interrogated and never gave any indication, verbal or otherwise, that he understood his rights and chose to waive them, totality of circumstances did not support trial court's finding beyond a reasonable doubt that defendant validly waived his rights. State v. Gagnon, 139 N.H. 175, 651 A.2d 5, 1994 N.H. LEXIS 126 (1994).

A waiver of the privilege against self-incrimination is limited to the particular proceeding in which the witness appears; thus, the waiver of the privilege at a pretrial deposition does not prevent the assertion of the privilege at trial. State v. Roberts, 136 N.H. 731, 622 A.2d 1225, 1993 N.H. LEXIS 24 (1993).

State must establish beyond a reasonable doubt that it did not violate defendant's *Miranda* rights before defendant's confession may be admitted as evidence. State v. Chapman, 135 N.H. 390, 605 A.2d 1055, 1992 N.H. LEXIS 48 (1992).

Before statements made by a defendant during custodial interrogation may be considered as evidence, the state must prove beyond a reasonable doubt that the defendant was warned of his constitutional rights, that the defendant waived those rights, and that the statements were made voluntarily, knowingly and intelligently. State v. Benoit, 126 N.H. 6, 490 A.2d 295, 1985 N.H. LEXIS 240 (1985).

State constitutional protections that support the right to freedom from self-incrimination include the requirement that a voluntary oral or written express waiver, not induced by further interrogation, be obtained once the right to counsel is asserted. State v. Nash, 119 N.H. 728, 407 A.2d 365, 1979 N.H. LEXIS 377 (1979).

The right to refuse to give incriminating evidence is one that can be waived, and, when it has been waived, the party may be compelled to furnish the evidence as any other party might. State v. Ober, 52 N.H. 459, 1873 N.H. LEXIS 72 (1873); State v. Sterrin, 78 N.H. 220, 98 A. 482, 1916 N.H. LEXIS 41 (1916); State v. Fogg, 80 N.H. 533, 119 A. 799, 1923 N.H. LEXIS 56 (1923).

112. —Voluntariness of confessions

Defendant's statements could be found to be voluntary under the Fifth Amendment and N.H. Const. pt. I, art. 15. Defendant was not under arrest and specifically stated at each interview that he was participating freely and voluntarily; he was advised he could end the interviews but continued with them; there was no evidence of threats, violence, or coercion on the videotapes of the interviews; the first interview was less than three hours and the second less than an hour; although defendant lacked experience with police and was possibly dyslexic, he had made very good grades and graduated from high school; the fact that police used minimization techniques and were friendly to defendant did not alter the voluntariness of his statements; based upon the conflicting evidence as to whether defendant was threatened with being charged with resisting arrest if he left the first interview, the jury was not required to find that a threat was made; and the failure of police to give Miranda warnings before the first interview did not make the statements involuntary. State v. Wilmot, 163 N.H. 148, 37 A.3d 422, 2012 N.H. LEXIS 8 (2012).

Defendant's statements were not involuntary in violation of due process under the Fourteenth Amendment or N.H. Const. pt. I, art. 15. Defendant was not in custody; the detectives did not take advantage of her distressed emotional state; the detectives did not deny her food or access to a telephone; the detectives offered her beverages, the detectives accurately informed defendant of her daughter's medical condition; defendant confirmed that she was at the interview voluntarily; defendant was read her Miranda rights and signed a Miranda waiver; the eight-by-ten-feet room in which defendant was questioned was not inordinately small; and the six-and-a-half hour duration of the interview did not in itself make the statements involuntary. State v. Belonga, 163 N.H. 343, 42 A.3d 764, 2012 N.H. LEXIS 32 (Mar. 16, 2012).

Six and one-half hours is a lengthy period of time to be faced with the stress and pressure inherent in police questioning. Nevertheless, an interview of this length, in and of itself, does not render a statement involuntary, for although the length of an interview is a relevant factor in determining voluntariness, what is of paramount importance is what occurred during the interview. State v. Belonga, 163 N.H. 343, 42 A.3d 764, 2012 N.H. LEXIS 32 (Mar. 16, 2012).

Officer had not made an impermissible promise of confidentiality that would render defendant's statements involuntary under the Fourteenth Amendment and N.H. Const. pt. I, art. 15. He used the phrase "between you and me" only once, and he made it clear that defendant's statements could be used to prosecute her. State v. Hernandez, 162 N.H. 698, 34 A.3d 669, 2011 N.H. LEXIS 168 (2011).

Circumstances surrounding defendant's interview did not render her statements involuntary. Although defendant apparently did not have any prior experience with police, she was of at least average intelligence; although she had been drinking the evening before, there was no evidence that she was drunk or significantly impaired at the time of the interview; the interview lasted less than two hours; an officer read and carefully explained defendant's Miranda rights; the officers never promised defendant leniency; and although the detectives admittedly used minimization techniques and were "friendly" to defendant, this did not render the statements involuntary. State v. Hernandez, 162 N.H. 698, 34 A.3d 669, 2011 N.H. LEXIS 168 (2011).

Confession was not involuntary under N.H. Const. pt. I, art. 15 despite the fact that defendant was in a psychiatric unit and was taking psychiatric medications at the time. In January 2007, two months before the confession, he invoked his Miranda rights and inquired about getting outside counsel; he confessed in March only after he requested to speak to detectives, who complied with Miranda; the interview only lasted 15 minutes; defendant confessed immediately; and although the response he received in January to his inquiries about the status of the investigation might have been "minimal," it did not force him to speak with the officers to get the information he desired. State v. Bilodeau, 159 N.H. 759, 992 A.2d 557, 2010 N.H. LEXIS 20 (2010).

In a case in which defendant was convicted of aggravated and felonious sexual assault on two minors under the age of 13, defendant's confessions were involuntary under N.H. Const. pt. I, art. 15, where the interviewing detective made a promise of confidentiality that defendant relied upon. State v. Parker, 160 N.H. 203, 999 A.2d 314, 2010 N.H. LEXIS 38 (2010).

Defendant's confessions to police were involuntary under the totality of the circumstances where the police did more than merely exhort the defendant to be truthful; they made specific promises of leniency. The message was clear: if the defendant confessed, he would not be charged with any offense other than those he allegedly committed on the night of his arrest, and if he did not confess, he faced harsher treatment. State v. Rezk, 150 N.H. 483, 840 A.2d 758, 2004 N.H. LEXIS 10 (2004).

A promise not to charge the defendant with the very crime for which he was arrested is a promise that is "so attractive" as to "render a resulting confession involuntary"; while an officer can ordinarily tell a suspect that it is better to tell the truth, the officer crosses the line if he tells the suspect what advantage is to be gained or is likely from making a confession. State v. Rezk, 150 N.H. 483, 840 A.2d 758, 2004 N.H. LEXIS 10 (2004).

Viewing the totality of the circumstances, it was against the manifest weight of the evidence to find that the State met its heavy burden of proving beyond a reasonable doubt that defendant voluntarily and intelligently waived defendant's Miranda rights

because (1) defendant's questions about defendant's antique car involved in the accident did not amount to waiver of the right to remain silent and (2) the officer's question regarding how many drinks defendant had that night exceeded the scope of a routine booking question and was improperly designed to elicit incriminatory admissions. State v. Chrisicos, 148 N.H. 546, 813 A.2d 513, 2002 N.H. LEXIS 167 (2002).

Detectives' attempts to interview defendant, despite his repeating that he would contact them, did not indicate that they would persist until they obtained a confession, and thus did not make his confession involuntary. State v. Aubuchont, 147 N.H. 142, 784 A.2d 1170, 2001 N.H. LEXIS 186 (2001).

Police adequately accommodated suspect with borderline intelligence by reading his Miranda rights to him slowly prior to questioning, and no other special accommodations were necessary. State v. Dumas, 145 N.H. 301, 761 A.2d 1063, 2000 N.H. LEXIS 61 (2000).

Under New Hampshire Constitution, State must prove beyond a reasonable doubt that an accused's statements were voluntary. In re Wesley B., 145 N.H. 428, 764 A.2d 888, 2000 N.H. LEXIS 82 (2000).

If a person suffers from a mental or developmental condition that impairs that person's ability to comprehend his or her choices, that impairment must be factored into court's determination as to voluntariness of person's confession. In re Wesley B., 145 N.H. 428, 764 A.2d 888, 2000 N.H. LEXIS 82 (2000).

Part I, Article 15 of New Hampshire Constitution requires State to prove that defendant's incriminating statements were voluntary beyond a reasonable doubt. State v. Hammond, 144 N.H. 401, 742 A.2d 532, 1999 N.H. LEXIS 129 (1999).

Defendant's confession to shaking seven-month-old victim, who subsequently died, was voluntarily made and was therefore admissible; fact that police knew defendant was undergoing counseling and taking anti-depressant medication did not change result, where totality of circumstances demonstrated that defendant's depression was not so debilitating as to prevent him from making a conscious choice to confess, and mere selection of officer with whom defendant was friendly to serve subpoena did not by itself amount to improper police influence. State v. Hammond, 144 N.H. 401, 742 A.2d 532, 1999 N.H. LEXIS 129 (1999).

Officers questioning defendant regarding armed robbery made no promise that he and his family would be protected from harm or that he would serve a reduced sentence, and there were no allegations that interviews were excessively long or that defendant was deprived of food, sleep, or medical attention, and therefore by agreeing to inform authorities of defendant's willingness to bargain, police did not exert such an influence on defendant that his will was overborne. State v. Ford, 144 N.H. 57, 738 A.2d 937, 1999 N.H. LEXIS 71 (1999).

Defendant's confessions to murder were voluntary, since undercover officer's earlier portrayal of witness did not trick or coerce defendant into subsequently confessing, and "witness" posed no threat of violence or extortion to defendant at time of his confession. Moreover, neither use of polygraph results nor statements and presence of defendant's wife contributed to involuntariness of his confessions. State v. Monroe, 142 N.H. 857, 711 A.2d 878, 1998 N.H. LEXIS 51 (1998), cert. denied, Monroe v. New Hampshire, 525 U.S. 1073, 119 S. Ct. 807, 142 L. Ed. 2d 667, 1999 U.S. LEXIS 190 (1999).

Evidence supported the determination that the defendant's confession to the murder of a fellow inmate was voluntary. The defendant asserted that a prison doctor had prescribed sleeping pills for him and that the prescription was later revoked because the state was attempting to induce a confession. However, the doctor testified that he revoked the prescription primarily because he had not examined the defendant, the defendant was scheduled for an exam by the prison psychiatrist on the next day, the defendant was not suffering from a serious medical problem, and prison policy favored having the prison psychiatrist write prescriptions for psychotropic drugs, such as sleeping pills. State v. Robidoux, 139 N.H. 657, 662 A.2d 268, 1995 N.H. LEXIS 66 (1995).

Trial court did not err in ruling that Ethiopian defendant made a knowing, voluntary, and intelligent waiver of his rights, where he had studied English since third grade and his ability to speak and understand English was very good; although defendant questioned what advantage might exist in having a lawyer present, police officers were not obligated to explain what possible legal advantage might accrue from such presence, and officers' responses were not misleading, evasive, or distracting. State v. Girmay, 139 N.H. 292, 652 A.2d 150, 1994 N.H. LEXIS 148 (1994).

Trial court did not err in ruling that defendant's confession was voluntary, where police officer made no direct promises but merely told defendant that his cooperation would in some manner be taken into consideration by authorities, and that he should ask others what form that consideration might take. State v. Beland, 138 N.H. 735, 645 A.2d 79, 1994 N.H. LEXIS 96 (1994).

Inmate's waiver of counsel and confession to prison murder were not induced by stress and anxiety of three months' special confinement, or by an implied promise of improved living conditions; his waiver of rights was thus voluntary and his confession was not required to be suppressed. State v. Decker, 138 N.H. 432, 641 A.2d 226, 1994 N.H. LEXIS 44 (1994).

Police officer's statement that defendant would be spending time in jail did not improperly induce defendant to waive his rights against self-incrimination. State v. LaFountain, 138 N.H. 225, 636 A.2d 1028, 1994 N.H. LEXIS 5 (1994).

Determination of the voluntariness of a confession is a question of fact for trial court to decide and such a finding is entitled to stand unless it is contrary to the manifest weight of evidence, as viewed in the light most favorable to the state. State v. Chapman, 135 N.H. 390, 605 A.2d 1055, 1992 N.H. LEXIS 48 (1992).

In determining the voluntariness of a confession, question is whether the confession was the product of an essentially free and unconstrained choice and was not extracted by any sort of threats or violence, or obtained by any direct or implied promises, however slight, or by the exertion of any improper influences. State v. Chapman, 135 N.H. 390, 605 A.2d 1055, 1992 N.H. LEXIS 48 (1992).

Police officer's comment during questioning that defendant "could go to jail for a long, long time" was an effort to convince defendant of the seriousness of the charges against him, was not inherently coercive and did not render defendant's confession involuntary. State v. Chapman, 135 N.H. 390, 605 A.2d 1055, 1992 N.H. LEXIS 48 (1992).

Videotape of police questioning showed that the police did not take advantage of defendant's intoxication and did not obtain his confession by making direct or implied promises or by exerting influence. State v. Chapman, 135 N.H. 390, 605 A.2d 1055, 1992 N.H. LEXIS 48 (1992).

Trial court's finding that state established beyond a reasonable doubt that defendant's murder confession was voluntary was upheld, where on appeal defendant failed to present any arguments not adequately considered by trial court, and review of record uncovered no evidence suggesting trial court's analysis was contrary to the manifest weight of the evidence. State v. Laurie, 135 N.H. 438, 606 A.2d 1077, 1992 N.H. LEXIS 59 (1992), cert. denied, Laurie v. New Hampshire, 506 U.S. 886, 113 S. Ct. 245, 121 L. Ed. 2d 178, 1992 U.S. LEXIS 6039 (1992).

113. —Juveniles

Juvenile defendant's waiver of his right against self-incrimination was valid under N.H. Const. pt. I, art. 15 and the Fifth and Fourteenth Amendments. The trial court made findings on each of the 15 factors prescribed for use when evaluating a juvenile's purported waiver, and atleast 12 indicated that the waiver was knowing, intelligent, and voluntary; defendant was never prevented from speaking with a lawyer, his mother, or any other interested adult; defendant's mother was never denied the opportunity to speak with him; and given the other findings, the fact that he was not told he could consult with his mother or another adult did not render the waiver invalid. State v. Garcia, 162 N.H. 426, 33 A.3d 1087, 2011 N.H. LEXIS 126 (2011).

If statute governing notice of arrest is not followed when a juvenile is arrested, absence of opportunity to consult with an adult is to be given greater weight when assessing totality of circumstances surrounding juvenile's waiver of right against self-incrimination. State v. Farrell, 145 N.H. 733, 766 A.2d 1057, 2001 N.H. LEXIS 14 (2001).

When a parent or guardian arrives at a police station or other site of custodial detention and requests to see a juvenile in custody, police must: (1) immediately cease interrogating juvenile; (2) notify him that his parent or guardian is present at station; and (3) immediately allow parent or guardian into interrogation room. State v. Farrell, 145 N.H. 733, 766 A.2d 1057, 2001 N.H. LEXIS 14 (2001).

Because police failed to notify parents or other interested adult with whom juvenile suspect may have wished to consult, and juvenile was interrogated while his father waited to consult with him, juvenile's Miranda waiver was rendered invalid and his statements to police were required to be suppressed on remand for retrial. State v. Farrell, 145 N.H. 733, 766 A.2d 1057, 2001 N.H. LEXIS 14 (2001).

State failed to establish beyond a reasonable doubt that juvenile's confession to arson was voluntary, where he was eleven years old, developmentally impaired, and unaccompanied by his mother or any other person responsible for his welfare; police officer's repeated and prolonged questioning of juvenile under these conditions, despite his continued denial of any involvement in fire, led to conclusion that juvenile's will was overborne. In re Wesley B., 145 N.H. 428, 764 A.2d 888, 2000 N.H. LEXIS 82 (2000).

Before a juvenile can be deemed to have waived the constitutional privilege against self-incrimination, he or she must be informed, in language understandable to a child, of his or her rights, the trial court must review and make findings on the circumstances which surround the giving of any incriminating statement, the judge and jury, if the confession is admitted, must be persuaded by an adequate number of favorable findings that the waiver was made voluntarily, intelligently and with full knowledge of the consequences, and if facing possible adult felony charges, the juvenile must be informed of the consequences of a certification to stand trial as an adult criminal defendant. State v. Benoit, 126 N.H. 6, 490 A.2d 295, 1985 N.H. LEXIS 240 (1985).

When a confession is to be admitted against a child charged with a felony in adult criminal court, for a judge to conclude that the child's statements were made knowingly and intelligently, the child, when facing a charge that would be a felony if committed by an adult, must have been advised of the possibility of his being tried as an adult and of his being subject to adult criminal sanctions. State v. Benoit, 126 N.H. 6, 490 A.2d 295, 1985 N.H. LEXIS 240 (1985).

Any juvenile who is not given Miranda warnings in a simplified juvenile form will be presumed to have been given an inadequate explanation of his or her rights in the supreme court's evaluation of the circumstances surrounding any incriminating statements subsequently made. State v. Benoit, 126 N.H. 6, 490 A.2d 295, 1985 N.H. LEXIS 240 (1985).

The confession of a fifteen-year-old child, who was tried and convicted as an adult of armed robbery and theft, should have been suppressed where, before the confession, the interrogating officer read the defendant his rights from the standard adult Miranda form, did not explain any of the rights, and did not discuss the possibility of the youth's being tried as an adult. State v. Benoit, 126 N.H. 6, 490 A.2d 295, 1985 N.H. LEXIS 240 (1985).

114. Immunity from prosecution

An immunity statute which protects a witness against criminal prosecution in New Hampshire courts from disclosures he may be compelled to make satisfies the constitutional requirements, although it cannot be invoked in other states or in the federal courts. Wyman v. De Gregory, 101 N.H. 171, 137 A.2d 512, 1957 N.H. LEXIS 47 (1957), appeal dismissed, 360 U.S. 717, 79 S. Ct. 1454, 3 L. Ed. 2d 1540, 1959 U.S. LEXIS 667 (1959).

A statute which provides that a clerk, servant, or agent shall not be excused from testifying against his principal, but that his testimony so given shall not in any prosecution be used as evidence against himself, and that he shall not be thereafter prosecuted for any offense so disclosed by him, does not deprive the witness of his constitutional guaranty against self-incrimination. State v. Nowell, 58 N.H. 314, 1878 N.H. LEXIS 46 (1878).

115. Implied consent law

Under the New Hampshire Constitution, Miranda warnings need not precede implied consent law questioning, and voluntary admissions, comments, or explanations spoken in response to implied consent law questioning are admissible as evidence in criminal trials. State v. Goding, 128 N.H. 267, 513 A.2d 325, 1986 N.H. LEXIS 285 (1986).

At trial for driving while intoxicated, defendant's post-arrest admissions, uttered in response to implied consent law questioning, were properly admitted, where record did not indicate that arresting officer exceeded the bounds of the questioning necessary under the implied consent law, nor was there any indication of the use of subtle coercion to obtain an incriminating response. State v. Goding, 128 N.H. 267, 513 A.2d 325, 1986 N.H. LEXIS 285 (1986).

Defendant's unsolicited comments, or explanations, spoken in response to implied consent law questioning by a police officer, after defendant's arrest but prior to the time he was advised of his Miranda rights, were properly admissible as evidence at his negligent homicide trial. State v. Lescard, 128 N.H. 495, 517 A.2d 1158, 1986 N.H. LEXIS 338 (1986).

Since there is no good reason in general constitutional principle, in the particular facts of the testing procedures or in constitutional history to classify a defendant's refusal as compelled, guarantee of this article against compelled self-incrimination does not preclude the evidentiary use of a driving-while-intoxicated defendant's refusal to provide a sample of breath or bodily substance for chemical testing. State v. Cormier, 127 N.H. 253, 499 A.2d 986, 1985 N.H. LEXIS 424 (1985).

Field sobriety tests performed by a driver suspected of intoxication, such as walking, balancing, turning, touching the nose and picking up a coin do not infringe upon privilege against self-incrimination. State v. Arsenault, 115 N.H. 109, 336 A.2d 244, 1975 N.H. LEXIS 236 (1975).

116. Admissibility of evidence of silence

Defendant was entitled to a new trial on charges of sexually assaulting a 12-year-old where the prosecutor impermissibly commented in closing argument on defendant's failure to testify, the trial court allowed the prosecutor to "explain" the argument to jurors instead of issuing a prompt curative instruction, and the comment was likely to have prejudiced defendant's outcome, since the only evidence was the alleged victim's accusation and, by attacking defendant for not testifying, the prosecution went to the heart of the defense of insufficient evidence. State v. Ellsworth, 151 N.H. 152, 855 A.2d 474, 2004 N.H. LEXIS 110 (2004).

Where defense counsel moved for a mistrial arguing that the State intended to elicit testimony that defendant had exercised his right to remain silent during interrogation, a mistrial was unwarranted under N.H. Const. pt. I, § 15, because no reference was ever made to defendant's refusal to answer certain questions during interrogation. State v. Spaulding, 147 N.H. 583, 794 A.2d 800, 2002 N.H. LEXIS 34 (2002).

State's comment on defendant's post-arrest, pre-Miranda silence did not violate his due process rights under this article. State v. Hill, 146 N.H. 568, 781 A.2d 979, 2001 N.H. LEXIS 114 (2001).

By offering testimony at trial that differed from his post-Miranda statements, defendant placed his credibility in issue, thus permitting prosecution to probe all post-arrest statements and the circumstances under which they were made, including defendant's failure to provide critical details. State v. McLellan, 139 N.H. 132, 649 A.2d 843, 1994 N.H. LEXIS 121 (1994).

A defendant's decision not to testify or present evidence in his own defense can provide no basis for an adverse comment by the prosecutor, and comments which can be construed as unfavorable references to a defendant's failure to testify are contrary to this section and violations of defendant's constitutional rights against self-incrimination (decision under former RSA 516:32). State v. Fowler, 132 N.H. 540, 567 A.2d 557, 1989 N.H. LEXIS 142 (1989).

Once a defendant has chosen to take the witness stand, this article does not require the exclusion of evidence that a defendant maintained silence toward a private third person. State v. Brown, 128 N.H. 606, 517 A.2d 831, 1986 N.H. LEXIS 328 (1986).

A suspect's silence in the face of accusation may not be used against him at trial. State v. Munson, 126 N.H. 191, 489 A.2d 646, 1985 N.H. LEXIS 245 (1985).

Admission of testimony by police officer that defendant, after being arrested and advised of his rights, stated that he did not want to say anything, but wanted to call his attorney, violated the rule that a suspect's silence in the face of accusation may not be used against him at trial. State v. Munson, 126 N.H. 191, 489 A.2d 646, 1985 N.H. LEXIS 245 (1985).

Comment either by a prosecutor or the court which may be construed as an unfavorable reference to the failure of a defendant to testify is contrary to this section and a violation of defendant's constitutional rights against self-incrimination (decision under former RSA 516:32). State v. Fowler, 110 N.H. 110, 261 A.2d 429, 1970 N.H. LEXIS 112 (1970).

Although prosecutor's argument to jury in prosecution for rape, that defendants had offered nothing in rebuttal to evidence against them, and although his questioning jurors as to how they would have gone about establishing their innocence if they were in defendants' position, was of the sort that should be avoided, any error was corrected by court's immediate instruction that jury should not draw improper inferences from defendants' failure to testify in their defense (decision under former RSA 516:32). State v. Fowler, 110 N.H. 110, 261 A.2d 429, 1970 N.H. LEXIS 112 (1970).

When a respondent does not elect to make himself a witness in his own cause, the fact that he does not choose to testify cannot be commented upon by the state's counsel, nor can the jury draw any inference detrimental to him from his silence (decision under former RSA 516:32). State v. Ober, 52 N.H. 459, 1873 N.H. LEXIS 72 (1873).

117. Publicity concerning silence

The freedom of a witness to exercise his constitutional privilege against self-incrimination may not be hampered by the prior restraint or deterrence of notice that publicity will be given to its exercise but not to its waiver. Nelson v. Wyman, 99 N.H. 33, 105 A.2d 756, 1954 N.H. LEXIS 10 (1954).

118. Reference to defendant's silence

Trial court did not err in denying a mistrial after the State introduced evidence of defendant's silence in violation of the Sixth Amendment and N.H. Const. pt. I, art. 15. The line of questioning was cut off immediately after the witness confirmed an attempt to interview defendant, who then declined the offer of a cautionary instruction; furthermore, the question did not constitute prosecutorial misconduct, as the officer referred to his attempt to interview defendant without being asked by the prosecutor, and the prosecutor later asked him to confirm his statement in an attempt to diffuse any claim of inadequate police work. State v. Reid, 161 N.H. 569, 20 A.3d 298, 2011 N.H. LEXIS 31 (2011).

Prosecutor did not elicit testimony about defendant's post-arrest, post-Miranda silence in violation of N.H. Const. pt. I, art. 15 and U.S. Const. amends. V and XIV when an officer's statement that defendant invoked his right to counsel was not responsive to the prosecutor's question. Furthermore, any prejudice was alleviated by a curative instruction and the jurors' response that they could comply with it. State v. Neeper, 160 N.H. 11, 999 A.2d 251, 2010 N.H. LEXIS 22 (2010).

Taken in context, the prosecutor's comment in closing argument that defendant "never told anyone" referred to his statements immediately following the assault and not his post-Miranda silence. State v. Neeper, 160 N.H. 11, 999 A.2d 251, 2010 N.H. LEXIS 22 (2010).

119. Voluntary admissions

In a complaint for grossly careless and grossly negligent operation of a motor vehicle the admission by the respondent a few hours after the accident, when questioned by the police, that she was the operator of the vehicle was not rendered inadmissible for the reason that she was not previously warned of her constitutional rights under this article where there was no evidence that the admission was anything but voluntary. State v. Hamson, 104 N.H. 526, 191 A.2d 89, 1963 N.H. LEXIS 86 (1963).

120. Psychiatric evaluations

Right against self-incrimination does not prevent the State from compelling a defendant to undergo a psychological or psychiatric examination when he raises an insanity defense; however, the results of the examination may be used only to rebut the defendant's insanity claim. Only the expert's ultimate conclusion should be provided to the prosecution and defense prior to trial; any other information derived from or related to the examination may be shared with the prosecution only at the point in the trial when such information is necessary for the prosecution to prepare for its rebuttal to the defendant's insanity claim. State v. Marchand, 164 N.H. 26, 48 A.3d 856, 2012 N.H. LEXIS 100 (2012).

This article protects statements a defendant may make to a court-appointed psychiatrist. State v. Briand, 130 N.H. 650, 547 A.2d 235, 1988 N.H. LEXIS 77 (1988).

A post-trial psychiatric evaluation order issued by a superior court was not a per se violation of the privilege against self-incrimination; since the purpose of the order was not to elicit statements for the purposes of convicting or punishing the defendant, there was, therefore, no incriminating objective or consequence inherent in the order. State v. Mercier, 128 N.H. 57, 509 A.2d 1246, 1986 N.H. LEXIS 255 (1986).

121. Accident reports

A statute requiring information to be furnished by the operator of a motor vehicle in case of accident is merely a condition attached to the privilege of using the public highways and is not in violation of the constitutional guaranty against self-incrimination. State v. Sterrin, 78 N.H. 220, 98 A. 482, 1916 N.H. LEXIS 41 (1916).

122. Records

The privilege against self-incrimination is strictly a personal one applicable to records held by an individual in a purely personal capacity. State v. Cote, 95 N.H. 108, 58 A.2d 749, 1948 N.H. LEXIS 195 (1948).

123. Corporations and other entities

The privilege against self-incrimination does not apply to organizations or companies, incorporated or unincorporated, whose character is essentially impersonal rather than purely private and personal, and is no bar to a judicial examination of corporate books and records. State v. Cote, 95 N.H. 108, 58 A.2d 749, 1948 N.H. LEXIS 195 (1948).

124. Predicating parole on participation in sexual offender program

An inmate's right against compelled self-incrimination was not violated by a parole board requirement that he complete a sexual offender program before becoming eligible for parole. The inmate could choose not to participate in the program and, therefore, the compulsion element of a violation of his privilege against compelled self-incrimination was missing. Knowles v. Warden, 140 N.H. 387, 666 A.2d 972, 1995 N.H. LEXIS 158 (1995).

125. Custody

Trial court erred in concluding that a defendant was in custody during his conversation with the police officer at the hospital where the officer had asked permission to speak with the defendant, he had informed the defendant that he did not have to speak, there was only one officer present, the conversation lasted only 20 to 30 minutes, and the defendant was never physically restrained; even assuming the defendant was unable to leave the hospital during the interrogation, it was because hospital staff required him to undergo certain tests, and the officer's confrontation of the defendant with his suspicions occurred near the end of an otherwise casual conversation. State v. Steimel, 155 N.H. 141, 921 A.2d 378, 2007 N.H. LEXIS 38 (2007).

Where defendant was informed that an interview at the police station was voluntary, the officer insisted that defendant ride in the police cruiser and defendant made incriminating statements during a two-hour interview behind closed doors, defendant was restrained from early on in the encounter, although no handcuffs were used. The duration and character of the encounter and interview suggested that defendant was in custody and, therefore, N.H. Const. pt. I, art. 15 was violated when the police exerted control over defendant in a manner that limited defendant's freedom and subjected defendant to a custodial interrogation without being informed of his Miranda rights. Thus, his statements were properly suppressed. State v. Jennings, 155 N.H. 768, 929 A.2d 982, 2007 N.H. LEXIS 131 (2007).

Statements made in defendant's grandmother's home where defendant was not physically restrained were not custodial and thus, Miranda warnings were not required. State v. Goupil, 154 N.H. 208, 908 A.2d 1256, 2006 N.H. LEXIS 146 (2006).

When an individual is incarcerated for an offense unrelated to subject of his interrogation, custody for Miranda purposes occurs when there is some act or circumstance that places additional limitations on prisoner. State v. Dorval, 144 N.H. 455, 743 A.2d 836, 1999 N.H. LEXIS 140 (1999).

Defendant was not in custody for Miranda purposes when he met with two plain-clothes police officers in jail library; interview was short and conducted in an amicable way by officers, defendant was not restrained or in handcuffs, and he was told that he could leave

at any time and did not have to talk to officers. State v. Dorval, 144 N.H. 455, 743 A.2d 836, 1999 N.H. LEXIS 140 (1999).

The trial court's conclusion that the defendant was not "in custody" for Miranda purposes until after he pointed out the location of drugs in his apartment was supported by the record. The initial questioning of the defendant occurred in a trooper's vehicle, the trooper informed the defendant that he was free to leave after a search of his person, and a reasonable person would have felt free to walk away accordingly. State v. Johnson, 140 N.H. 573, 669 A.2d 222, 1995 N.H. LEXIS 194 (1995).

The location of questioning is not, by itself, determinative of whether a defendant is entitled to Miranda warnings. A defendant may be "in custody" in his own home, but not "in custody" at a police station; a defendant is not "in custody" for Miranda purposes merely because his freedom of movement has been curtailed so that he has been "seized" in a fourth amendment sense. State v. Johnson, 140 N.H. 573, 669 A.2d 222, 1995 N.H. LEXIS 194 (1995).

126. Incarcerated suspects

Where there was no act or circumstance that placed additional limitations upon incarcerated defendant, he was not in custody when he made his confession; in light of this conclusion, and because the right to counsel had not attached, the fact that defendant's attorney indicated by letter that defendant did not wish to speak with the police was irrelevant. State v. Pehowic, 147 N.H. 52, 780 A.2d 1289, 2001 N.H. LEXIS 168 (2001), cert. denied, Pehowic v. New Hampshire, 535 U.S. 956, 122 S. Ct. 1362, 152 L. Ed. 2d 357, 2002 U.S. LEXIS 1980 (2002).

When an individual is incarcerated for an offense unrelated to subject of his interrogation, custody for *Miranda* purposes occurs when there is some act or circumstance that places additional limitations on prisoner; there must be some further restriction on prisoner's freedom of movement in anticipation of or associated with interrogation itself. State v. Ford, 144 N.H. 57, 738 A.2d 937, 1999 N.H. LEXIS 71 (1999).

IV. Evidence

127. Sentencing

When a defendant has maintained his innocence throughout the criminal process, a trial court's consideration at sentencing of a defendant's failure to affirmatively express remorse at trial offends his constitutional privilege against self-incrimination. This holding —that a sentencing court may not consider a defendant's failure to express remorse at trial—does not preclude a court from considering other evidence that indicates a defendant's lack of remorse. State v. Willey, 163 N.H. 532, 44 A.3d 431, 2012 N.H. LEXIS 57 (2012).

Resentencing was required under N.H. Const. pt. I, art. 15 and 18. The trial court's comments implied that the trial court might have penalized defendant for his attorney's trial strategy; furthermore, it might have considered his failure to affirmatively express remorse, which violated his right against self-incrimination. State v. Willey, 163 N.H. 532, 44 A.3d 431, 2012 N.H. LEXIS 57 (2012).

150. Right to present witnesses

Defendant's fundamental due process right to seek out and present witnesses on his behalf is dependent entirely on his affirmative exercise of that right, and, as such, either through action or inaction, defendant may waive his right to present witness testimony. State v. Cromlish, 146 N.H. 277, 780 A.2d 486, 2001 N.H. LEXIS 72 (2001).

151. Relevancy

Defendant had no constitutional right to present irrelevant evidence and no right under N.H. Const. pt. I, art. 15, to introduce evidence of the victim's prior sexual abuse and the proceedings that followed since that evidence would have little effect other than to confuse the issues or confound the jury, for such evidence was not competent, favorable proof. State v. Mitchell, 148 N.H. 293, 808 A.2d 62, 2002 N.H. LEXIS 128 (2002).

At rape trial, denial of defendant's motion for transportation costs to bring defendant's wife to trial did not deny defendant constitutional right to produce all proofs that might be favorable to himself, where defense counsel stated she did not know whether wife would be called as witness and made no offer of proof as to what she would say if called. State v. Fecteau, 133 N.H. 860, 587 A.2d 591, 1991 N.H. LEXIS 11 (1991).

Criminal defendant does not have an absolute right to introduce testimony which is not relevant. State v. Brooks, 126 N.H. 618, 495 A.2d 1258, 1985 N.H. LEXIS 366 (1985).

152. Discovery

Defendant in a sexual assault case was entitled to a new trial under the due process provision of N.H. Const. pt. I, art. 15 based on the State's failure to disclose evidence about the victim's mental health that was redacted from a physician's report. Evidence about the victim's mental stability could be useful as impeachment evidence, and the case hinged on the victim's credibility and whether she accurately described her level of consciousness. State v. Shepherd, 159 N.H. 163, 977 A.2d 1029, 2009 N.H. LEXIS 105 (2009).

In a case in which defendant was issued a citation for failure to yield after being involved in a motor vehicle accident with a vehicle driven by an off-duty police officer, to the extent the officer's confidential personnel file contained exculpatory information, defendant was entitled to that information under N.H. Const. pt. I, art. 15. In re State (Theodosopoulos), 153 N.H. 318, 893 A.2d 712, 2006 N.H. LEXIS 29 (2006).

Defendant was not denied due process by the State's destruction of her blood samples where multiple notices were sent to defendant stating that she had 30 days to pick up the samples or they would be destroyed; the destruction of the blood samples may have constituted negligence but, without more, did not amount to culpable negligence. State v. Lavoie, 152 N.H. 542, 880 A.2d 432, 2005 N.H. LEXIS 136 (2005).

In a prosecution for aggravated felonious sexual assault, felonious sexual assault, kidnapping, and violation of child pornography laws, it was a violation of the defendant's due process rights for the trial court to refuse to order the disclosure of the full investigatory file of a charge that the state's principal witness committed sexual misconduct of a three-year-old child. Such evidence was exculpatory, as the credibility of the witness was crucial to the state's case. State v. Lucius, 140 N.H. 60, 663 A.2d 605, 1995 N.H. LEXIS 97 (1995).

In trial for attempted felonious sexual assault, trial court's denial of defendant's motion for video tape deposition of victim did not deprive defendant of state or federal constitutional rights to due process and effective assistance of counsel where defendant had access to a statement by victim that would enable him to anticipate the victim's testimony and defendant failed to otherwise show he was unable to prepare adequately for trial without video tape deposition discovery. State v. Adams, 133 N.H. 818, 585 A.2d 853, 1991 N.H. LEXIS 3 (1991).

A criminal defendant does not have a constitutional right to unlimited discovery. State v. Booton, 114 N.H. 750, 329 A.2d 376, 1974 N.H. LEXIS 366 (1974), cert. denied, Booton v. New Hampshire, 421 U.S. 919, 95 S. Ct. 1584, 43 L. Ed. 2d 787, 1975 U.S. LEXIS 1352 (1975).

Criminal defendant had no right under this article to discovery of any and all state's evidence which might be potentially useful for impeachment purposes. State v. Booton, 114 N.H. 750, 329 A.2d 376, 1974 N.H. LEXIS 366 (1974), cert. denied, Booton v. New Hampshire, 421 U.S. 919, 95 S. Ct. 1584, 43 L. Ed. 2d 787, 1975 U.S. LEXIS 1352 (1975).

153. Rights of witnesses

A defense witness' use of the fifth amendment privilege against self-incrimination does not violate the right of the accused under this article to produce all proofs that may be favorable. State v. Taylor, 118 N.H. 859, 395 A.2d 1239, 1978 N.H. LEXIS 306 (1978).

154. Rape shield law

Defendant's claim that the trial court denied his right to confrontation under N.H. Const. pt. I, § 15, because the trial court refused to allow defendant to cross-examine the victims about sexual relations between the victims, failed where defendant failed to demonstrate that trial court's ruling was clearly untenable or unreasonable to the prejudice of the defendant's case. State v. Spaulding, 147 N.H. 583, 794 A.2d 800, 2002 N.H. LEXIS 34 (2002).

Part I, Article 15 of the New Hampshire Constitution did not prohibit the enactment of a bill to prohibit the introduction of evidence of the victim's manner of dress at the time of a sexual assault in order to infer consent. The statute in question would not preempt an accused's right to produce all proofs that may be favorable to the accused and to cross-examine witnesses. Opinion of the Justices (Certain Evidence in Sexual Assault Cases), 140 N.H. 22, 662 A.2d 294, 1995 N.H. LEXIS 87 (1995).

Since automatic and total exclusion of evidence of rape victim's prior consensual sexual activity is improper because it might preempt the accused's right to confront witnesses against him, admission of such evidence may be proper upon showing of particular relevance by the defendant in cases in which reputation of the rape victim and in which specific prior sexual activity of the victim may become relevant and its probative value may outweigh the detrimental impact of its introduction. State v. Howard, 121 N.H. 53, 426 A.2d 457, 1981 N.H. LEXIS 248 (1981).

The effect of State v. Howard, 121 N.H. 53, 426 A.2d 457, 1981 N.H. LEXIS 248 (1981), is to make evidence of a prosecutrix's prior sexual activity with persons other than the defendant admissible when trial court, in the exercise of its discretion, determines that due process so requires. State v. La Clair, 121 N.H. 743, 433 A.2d 1326, 1981 N.H. LEXIS 391 (1981).

155. Hearsay

Defendant's argument that the trial court had violated N.H. Const. pt. I, art. 15 by admitting certain evidence failed because the New Hampshire Supreme Court had not adopted the United States Supreme Court's Crawford v. Washington, 541 U.S. 36, 124 S. Ct. 1354, 158 L. Ed. 2d 177 (2004) analysis, the standard argued by defendant, with regard to the state constitution. State v. Munoz, 157 N.H. 143, 949 A.2d 155, 2008 N.H. LEXIS 47 (2008).

In a prosecution for witness tampering, hearsay statements made by the witness tampered with were properly admitted into evidence based on the trial court's determination of particularized guarantees of trustworthiness where (1) the witness made the statements in confidence to persons providing psychological treatment rather than to the police; (2) the witness had an "open and honest, professional relationship" with the counselors to whom he made the statements; (3) the witness cried spontaneously for 20 minutes when he first admitted to having had a sexual relationship with the defendant; and (4) the statements revealing the defendant's identity and his sexual relationship with the witness placed the witness "in a light where others may look unfavorably upon him." State v. Roberts, 136 N.H. 731, 622 A.2d 1225, 1993 N.H. LEXIS 24 (1993).

The admission in evidence of statements made by an alleged accomplice if implicating the accused in the commission of the crime is a violation of due process where the accomplice is not present and testifying and the accused has no opportunity to face him or cross-examine him. State v. Clapp, 94 N.H. 62, 46 A.2d 119, 1946 N.H. LEXIS 144 (1946).

156. Privileged information

Sexual assault defendant's right to produce all favorable proofs was not violated by preclusion of evidence of his good character, or of privileged information regarding victim's history. State v. Graf, 143 N.H. 294, 726 A.2d 1270, 1999 N.H. LEXIS 1 (1999).

A criminal defendant's constitutional right to produce all proofs that may be favorable to himself and to confront witnesses may overcome an evidentiary privilege, such as attorney-client privilege, if the defendant meets his burden to show the privileged information is reasonably necessary to his defense. State v. Eason, 133 N.H. 335, 577 A.2d 1203, 1990 N.H. LEXIS 66 (1990).

A trial court may not summarily reject a criminal defendant's claim of his right to cross-examine a witness who has correctly invoked the attorney-client privilege. State v. Eason, 133 N.H. 335, 577 A.2d 1203, 1990 N.H. LEXIS 66 (1990).

157. Identification procedure

In a robbery case, a photo array was not unnecessarily suggestive for due process purposes under U.S. Const. amend. XIV and N.H. Const. pt. I, art. 15 because defendant was the only person wearing a white tank top. Nothing indicated that the identifications were affected by clothing; the witnesses' trial testimony and written statements indicated that they had focused on defendant's facial features rather than his clothing; because the robber had been wearing a sweatshirt or a sweater, defendant's clothing in the array did not connect him to the crime; and three others in the array wore either tank tops or white shirts. State v. Bell-Rogers, 159 N.H. 178, 977 A.2d 1017, 2009 N.H. LEXIS 103 (2009).

Supreme Court of New Hampshire joins the apparent majority of courts in concluding that *Neil v. Biggers* does not apply to in-court identifications and that the remedy for any alleged suggestiveness of an in-court identification is cross-examination and argument; the manner in which in-court identifications are conducted is not of constitutional magnitude but rests within the sound discretion of the trial court. Thus, a victim's in-court identification of defendant as the man who exposed himself to the victim did not violate defendant's due process rights under U.S. Const. amend. XIV and N.H. Const. pt. I, art. 15 because the *Biggers* test was inapplicable, and the pretrial photo array was not impermissibly suggestive, and because the in-court identification was not improper, the district court identification did not taint the subsequent identification in superior court. State v. King, 156 N.H. 371, 934 A.2d 556, 2007 N.H. LEXIS 191 (2007).

In a state constitutional challenge to an identification procedure, defendant has the initial burden of establishing that the out-of-court conduct of which he complains was unnecessarily suggestive. State v. Allen, 133 N.H. 306, 577 A.2d 801, 1990 N.H. LEXIS 68 (1990).

In state constitutional challenge to identification procedure used at sexual assault trial, defendant failed to establish that pre-trial comments made by victim-witness advocate to the victim, about the defendant's appearance, were unnecessarily suggestive. State v. Allen, 133 N.H. 306, 577 A.2d 801, 1990 N.H. LEXIS 68 (1990).

Record did not support a finding of state due process violation in a criminal case where apparently relevant evidence, a photographic array from which victim was unable to identify defendant, was not preserved by the state, since defendant did not show bad faith on part of police. State v. Smagula, 133 N.H. 600, 578 A.2d 1215, 1990 N.H. LEXIS 107 (1990).

158. Child abuse records

Due process considerations require trial courts to balance the state's interest in protecting the confidentiality of child abuse records against the defendant's right to obtain evidence helpful to his defense. State v. Gagne, 136 N.H. 101, 612 A.2d 899, 1992 N.H. LEXIS 135 (1992).

159. All favorable proofs

While as a general matter, cross-examination helps to preserve a defendant's right to all favorable proofs, this right is not vitiated when a defendant is unable to conduct his desired cross-examination of an available declarant. The right to produce all favorable proofs under N.H. Const. pt. I, art. 15 gives a defendant only the right to produce witnesses, not to produce their testimony; while a declarant's lack of memory may thwart the cross-examination the defendant wishes to attempt, the fact remains that the declarant is present to be examined. State v. Ata, 158 N.H. 406, 969 A.2d 419, 2009 N.H. LEXIS 25 (2009).

Where defendant, who was convicted of four counts of being a felon in possession of a firearm in violation of former RSA 159:3, I, argued that the trial court deprived defendant of the right to produce all favorable proofs under N.H. Const. pt. I, art. 15 when it denied defendant's motions for discovery of records regarding the ownership of the four firearms, the argument failed; ownership of the weapons was not relevant to defendant's prosecution, given that only possession or control of the weapons was necessary for a conviction under former RSA 159:3, I(a). State v. Fox, 150 N.H. 623, 843 A.2d 309, 2004 N.H. LEXIS 39 (2004).

In order to establish a violation of his constitutional right to present all proofs in his favor, defendant must show that testimony he was precluded from introducing would have been material and favorable to his defense in ways not merely cumulative of other evidence. State v. King, 146 N.H. 717, 781 A.2d 1002, 2001 N.H. LEXIS 145 (2001).

Trial court did not violate defendant's constitutional right to present all proofs in his favor by barring testimony of his co-venturer because it would have been cumulative of other testimony. State v. King, 146 N.H. 717, 781 A.2d 1002, 2001 N.H. LEXIS 145 (2001).

Where trial court misconstrued State's constitutional duty to disclose favorable evidence, and police report that had been withheld was favorable to defendant, case was remanded for further proceedings on whether report was knowingly withheld, and whether defendant was entitled to a new trial. State v. Dewitt, 143 N.H. 24, 719 A.2d 570, 1998 N.H. LEXIS 65 (1998).

The constitutional right to produce all proofs that may be favorable does not require that a juvenile be given a right of allocution in a transfer proceeding. In re Farrell, 142 N.H. 424, 702 A.2d 809, 1997 N.H. LEXIS 111 (1997).

The right to produce favorable proofs does not entitle a defendant to introduce evidence in violation of the rules of evidence. State v. Seymour, 140 N.H. 736, 673 A.2d 786, 1996 N.H. LEXIS 24 (1996), cert. denied, Seymour v. New Hampshire, 519 U.S. 853, 117 S. Ct. 146, 136 L. Ed. 2d 93, 1996 U.S. LEXIS 5265 (1996).

Record supported trial court's determination that no probative evidence favorable to defendant would derive from witnesses' assertion, before jury, of their privilege against self-incrimination. State v. Seymour, 140 N.H. 736, 673 A.2d 786, 1996 N.H. LEXIS 24 (1996), cert. denied, Seymour v. New Hampshire, 519 U.S. 853, 117 S. Ct. 146, 136 L. Ed. 2d 93, 1996 U.S. LEXIS 5265 (1996).

Under narrow circumstances, where the defendant shows that the testimony sought would be directly exculpatory or would present a highly material variance from the tenor of the state's evidence, failure to immunize a witness may have due process implications. State v. Roy, 140 N.H. 478, 668 A.2d 41, 1995 N.H. LEXIS 179 (1995).

The trial court's decision to allow the introduction of an unsworn prior inconsistent statement of a witness only for impeachment purposes, and not to allow full substantive admissibility, did not deprive the defendant of the right to present all favorable proof. The statement did not possess sufficient indicia of trustworthiness to fall within any hearsay exception and thus to be allowed full substantive admissibility. State v. Newcomb, 140 N.H. 72, 663 A.2d 613, 1995 N.H. LEXIS 101 (1995).

In a prosecution for simple assault arising from an altercation with a police officer, the trial court's exclusion of proffered expert testimony regarding the defendant's bipolar manic depressive disorder was not error. Such evidence was essentially a classic insanity defense claim, and the defendant failed to comply with the notice requirements for such a claim. State v. James, 140 N.H. 50, 663 A.2d 83, 1995 N.H. LEXIS 99 (1995).

The New Hampshire constitutional right to present all favorable proofs affords greater protection to a criminal defendant than does the federal constitution. Upon a showing by the defendant that favorable, exculpatory evidence has been knowingly withheld by the prosecution, the burden shifts to the state to prove beyond a reasonable doubt that the undisclosed evidence would not have affected the verdict. State v. Laurie, 139 N.H. 325, 653 A.2d 549, 1995 N.H. LEXIS 8 (1995).

Trial court did not deny defendant his right to present all proofs favorable to his case, since excluded expert testimony would have been merely cumulative, and thus defendant was unable to establish that evidence he was precluded from introducing would have been material and favorable to his defense. State v. Girmay, 139 N.H. 292, 652 A.2d 150, 1994 N.H. LEXIS 148 (1994).

Because there is little, if any, probative value in the rejection of a plea offer, while there is invariably a high risk that its admission would infuse extraneous, confusing issues into a trial, evidence of a defendant's rejection of a plea offer is not admissible in the ensuing criminal trial under the defendant's right to produce all favorable proofs. State v. Woodsum, 137 N.H. 198, 624 A.2d 1342, 1993 N.H. LEXIS 64 (1993).

The right to produce favorable proofs does not grant the right to present cumulative testimony; thus, the court properly refused to allow the defendant to recall two coperpetrators to impeach their credibility on the basis of letters written by the coperpetrators while imprisoned where defense counsel had already cross-examined the coperpetrators with regard to their credibility and admitted that the letters did not raise new issues. State v. Smart, 136 N.H. 639, 622 A.2d 1197, 1993 N.H. LEXIS 11 (1993), cert. denied, Smart v. New Hampshire, 510 U.S. 917, 114 S. Ct. 309, 126 L. Ed. 2d 256, 1993 U.S. LEXIS 6384 (1993).

Where witnesses expressly denied any involvement in murders and their invocations of the privilege against self-incrimination related to theft of stolen property belonging to victim and to drug use, the record amply supported the trial court's determination that no probative evidence favorable to defendant would derive from the witnesses' assertion of the privilege before the jury. State v. Seymour, 140 N.H. 736, 673 A.2d 786, 1996 N.H. LEXIS 24 (1996), cert. denied, Seymour v. New Hampshire, 519 U.S. 853, 117 S. Ct. 146, 136 L. Ed. 2d 93, 1996 U.S. LEXIS 5265 (1996).

160. Extrinsic evidence

Sexual assault defendant's right to present all favorable proofs under New Hampshire Constitution was not violated by his inability to impeach victims' credibility by using their prior allegations of sexual assaults, since right to produce all favorable proofs gave defendant only the right to produce witnesses, not to produce their testimony, and he did not argue that he was prevented from producing victims as witnesses. State v. White, 145 N.H. 544, 765 A.2d 156, 2000 N.H. LEXIS 107 (2000), cert. denied, White v. New Hampshire, 533 U.S. 932, 121 S. Ct. 2557, 150 L. Ed. 2d 722, 2001 U.S. LEXIS 4763 (2001).

Duty to disclose evidence favorable to an accused applies to any investigating officer or law enforcement official in possession of favorable evidence. State v. Lavallee, 145 N.H. 424, 765 A.2d 671, 2000 N.H. LEXIS 83 (2000).

Prosecutor's duty to produce exculpatory evidence did not extend to evidence in possession of division for children, youth and families, but only to evidence in prosecutor's possession or in possession of law enforcement agency charged with investigation and presentation of case; sexual assault defendant was therefore not entitled to dismissal due to State's alleged failure to produce exculpatory evidence. State v. Lavallee, 145 N.H. 424, 765 A.2d 671, 2000 N.H. LEXIS 83 (2000).

Due process did not require admission of extrinsic evidence that sexual assault victim had made false allegations of sexual voyeurism and theft against other children at treatment facility. Defendant failed to make a threshold showing of probity and similarity of allegations necessary to justify admission of such evidence. State v. Ellsworth, 142 N.H. 710, 709 A.2d 768, 1998 N.H. LEXIS 25 (1998).

161. Excluding or limiting evidence

When considering excluding or limiting evidence offered under this article, as a discovery sanction, trial court should consider such factors as the probative value and reliability of the proposed evidence, the effectiveness of less severe sanctions, the integrity of the adversary process, the interest in the fair and efficient administration of justice, and the potential prejudice to the truth-determining function of the trial process. State v. Cromlish, 146 N.H. 277, 780 A.2d 486, 2001 N.H. LEXIS 72 (2001).

Trial court's order precluding testimony from defendant's proposed firearms training expert did not violate defendant's rights under this article because the low probative value of the proposed testimony indicated that its absence at trial did not deny defendant the ability to present an issue at trial; in addition, defendant's unexplained delay in requesting the testimony would have resulted in either prejudicing the prosecution or interfering with the efficient administration of justice. State v. Cromlish, 146 N.H. 277, 780 A.2d 486, 2001 N.H. LEXIS 72 (2001).

162. Blood alcohol tests

Since defendant voluntarily consented to the breath test after being advised of her right to refuse, the "fruit of the poisonous tree" doctrine did not apply. The fact that the trooper did not provide a mandated advisory to an initial test did not preclude the administration of the second test. State v. Barkus, 152 N.H. 701, 888 A.2d 398, 2005 N.H. LEXIS 160 (2005), rehearing denied, 2005 N.H. LEXIS 193 (N.H. Dec. 28, 2005).

163. Failure to preserve evidence

Dismissal of charges of possession of alcohol by a minor, transportation of alcohol by a minor, and violation of a local open container ordinance based on officer's act of pouring out contents of beer can, and thus discarding evidence, was error as the amount of beer in the can was immaterial. Neither reference to "liquor" nor to "beverage" under RSA 175:1 references a minimum amount needed to compose the regulated liquid; even a de minimis amount of alcohol is sufficient to trigger a violation. State v. Flagg, 154 N.H. 690, 918 A.2d 1286, 2007 N.H. LEXIS 4 (2007).

The unexplained loss of 12 photographs taken at the scene of the burglary at issue showed some negligence on the part of the police

department, but did not reach the level of culpable negligence, and, therefore, did not constitute a violation of the defendant's right to due process. State v. Giordano, 138 N.H. 90, 635 A.2d 482, 1993 N.H. LEXIS 172 (1993).

V. Confrontation of Witnesses

201. Cross-examination

Trial court did not err in prohibiting defendant from cross-examining the victim regarding certain drugs found in the apartment where the attack on her occurred. Balanced against the minimal probative value of the drug evidence, the trial court could readily have found that its potential to confuse the issues and mislead the jury was sufficient to require its exclusion under N.H. R. Evid. 403; furthermore, defendant's confrontation rights under N.H. Const. pt. I, art. 15 and the Sixth Amendment had not been violated, as defendant was given ample opportunity to challenge the victim's credibility and expose her bias. State v. Alwardt, 164 N.H. 52, 53 A.3d 545, 2012 N.H. LEXIS 111 (2012).

Defendant failed to establish that the trial court's decision precluding him from questioning a witness regarding his statements to the investigating officer was clearly untenable or unreasonable to the prejudice of his case under N.H. R. Evid. 608(b) or in violation of the Sixth Amendment and N.H. Const. pt. I, art. 15. The trial court could have found that the purported discrepancy between the witness's initial statement to the police and his later testimony at the court proceedings was ambiguous, thereby making the probative value marginal; moreover, the record demonstrated that defendant was permitted to cross-examine the witness on numerous alleged inconsistencies between his testimony at trial and statements he made under oath at a prior court proceeding and to the police. State v. Stowe, 162 N.H. 464, 34 A.3d 678, 2011 N.H. LEXIS 128 (2011).

In defendant's prosecution for aggravated felonious sexual assault and felonious sexual assault, in which he was denied the ability to cross-examine the victim about her prior, allegedly false, allegations of physical and emotional abuse against her father, defendant's right to confrontation under N.H. Const. pt. I, art. 15 was not denied because he was not barred from making a threshold inquiry into the victim's character for truthfulness or untruthfulness, so his ability to effectively impeach her was not impermissibly limited. State v. Miller, 155 N.H. 246, 921 A.2d 942, 2007 N.H. LEXIS 51 (2007).

Confrontation clauses of the federal and state constitutions do not mandate that a defendant be allowed to cross-examine a victim about prior allegations of sexual assault, under N.H. R. Evid. 608(b), unless a defendant meets the standard of showing the victim's prior allegations were "demonstrably false." State v. Miller, 155 N.H. 246, 921 A.2d 942, 2007 N.H. LEXIS 51 (2007).

Defendant's right to cross-examine the victim was not violated when the trial court limited defendant's cross-examination of the victim as to two differing reports regarding a prior sexual assault incident because defendant was permitted to ask the victim about all but one of the discrepancies between the reports and, therefore, was permitted a threshold level of inquiry about the subject and defendant failed to demonstrate that the trial court's ruling was untenable or unreasonable to the prejudice of defendant's case. State v. Brum, 155 N.H. 408, 923 A.2d 1068, 2007 N.H. LEXIS 71 (2007).

Trial court did not err in granting State's motion in limine that prohibited the cross-examination of sexual abuse victims and admission of extrinsic evidence concerning allegations made by the victims that defendant had also sexually abused their two younger brothers in a case where defendant had been charged with multiple offenses arising out of defendant's sexual abuse of the victims over a two-year period; although defendant sought to establish that the victims had made prior false allegations of abuse, defendant's Confrontation Clause and due process rights were not violated because the prior allegations of abuse were not demonstrably false and admission of such evidence would have produced significant confusion of the issues. State v. Abram, 153 N.H. 619, 903 A.2d 1042, 2006 N.H. LEXIS 81 (2006).

Trial court did not err in granting State's motion in limine that prohibited the cross-examination of sexual abuse victims and admission of extrinsic evidence concerning allegations made by the victims that defendant had also sexually abused their two younger brothers in a case where defendant had been charged with multiple offenses arising out of defendant's sexual abuse of the victims over a two-year period; although defendant sought to establish that the victims had made prior false allegations of abuse, defendant's confrontation clause and due process rights were not violated because the prior allegations of abuse were not demonstrably false and admission of such evidence would have produced significant confusion of the issues. State v. Abram, 153 N.H. 619, 903 A.2d 1042, 2006 N.H. LEXIS 81 (2006).

Trial court did not violate juvenile defendant's right to due process by refusing to allow his expert to disassemble handgun at trial, since this demonstrative evidence was merely duplicative of other evidence from expert already presented to jury in form of testimony, photographs and illustrations. State v. Farrell, 145 N.H. 733, 766 A.2d 1057, 2001 N.H. LEXIS 14 (2001).

Defendant's offer of proof was insufficient to allow defendant to impeach the credibility of a witness through cross-examination into mental instability and delusional thinking where the offer of proof did not allege that the witness's unusual beliefs were symptoms of a mental illness that caused the witness to lie or hallucinate or dramatically impaired the witness's ability to perceive and tell the truth. Thus, the trial court did not violate defendant's right to confrontation by barring defendant from cross-examining the witness. State v. Fichera, 153 N.H. 588, 903 A.2d 1030, 2006 N.H. LEXIS 76 (2006).

It was not an unsustainable abuse of discretion for trial court to decide not to allow defendant to cross-examine the victim regarding prior drug use, since defendant had ample opportunity to impeach the victim on other grounds and had failed to show how allegations of drug use related to the charges in question. State v. Flynn, 151 N.H. 378, 855 A.2d 1254, 2004 N.H. LEXIS 158 (2004).

Trial court did not violate U.S. Const. amends. VI, XIV and N.H. Const. pt. I, art. 15 Confrontation Clauses and did violate N.H. R. Evid. 403, 608(b) by not allowing a defendant who was accused of sex crimes under RSA 629:1, 632-A:2, 632-A:3 to cross-examine the victim with evidence that she stole money from her employer since that evidence was prejudicial and was not probative of her credibility regarding the sex crimes. State v. Hokenstrom, 2003 N.H. LEXIS 214 (N.H. Feb. 14, 2003). (Unpublished opinion.)

Trial court did not violate defendant's rights under the Confrontation Clause, N.H. Const. pt.1, art. 15, by denying him the right to introduce portions of his accomplice's statement to a police witness to impeach the witness's credibility, as defendant could have explored this area by recalling the witness after the accomplice testified. State v. Locke, 149 N.H. 1, 813 A.2d 1182, 2002 N.H. LEXIS 210 (2002), cert. denied, Locke v. New Hampshire, 538 U.S. 1043, 123 S. Ct. 2096, 155 L. Ed. 2d 1079, 2003 U.S. LEXIS 3860 (2003).

In a sexual assault trial, the trial court did not violate N.H. Const. pt. I, art. 15, where it barred defendant from cross-examining the eight-year-old victim about the impact the victim's friend's sexual assault allegation against a babysitter may have had on the victim's allegation, where defendant claimed that the testimony was relevant to defendant's fabrication theory, in which defendant claimed that the victim knew that the allegation could result in defendant's removal from the victim's home; although the trial court did not permit questions about the friend's allegations, defendant was permitted to ask the victim whether the victim knew that the victim's complaint could have resulted in defendant being removed from the home. State v. Newman, 148 N.H. 287, 808 A.2d 7, 2002 N.H. LEXIS 124 (2002).

Defendant's claim that the trial court denied his right to confrontation under N.H. Const. pt. I, § 15, because the trial court refused to allow defendant to cross-examine the victims about sexual relations between the victims, failed where defendant failed to demonstrate that trial court's ruling was clearly untenable or unreasonable to the prejudice of defendant's case. State v. Spaulding, 147 N.H. 583, 794 A.2d 800, 2002 N.H. LEXIS 34 (2002).

While a trial court may not completely deny defendant the opportunity to cross-examine a witness on a proper matter of inquiry, it may limit cross-examination after allowing a threshold level of inquiry that satisfies the Sixth Amendment. State v. Munson, 146 N.H. 712, 781 A.2d 1, 2001 N.H. LEXIS 147 (2001).

Trial court did not err by precluding cross-examination of witness regarding a court order finding her incompetent to stand trial, because inquiry into the incompetency ruling had only minimal

probative value, and the risk that it would confuse the jury was substantial. State v. Munson, 146 N.H. 712, 781 A.2d 1, 2001 N.H. LEXIS 147 (2001).

Where the only evidence of a prior false allegation by the victim in a sexual assault case was defendant's uncorroborated assertion to that effect, even if the trial judge required him to satisfy a more stringent standard of proof than clear and convincing evidence, its restriction on his right to cross-examine the victim on this issue was correct and did not constitute a violation of defendant's constitutional rights to due process and confrontation. State v. Gordon, 146 N.H. 258, 770 A.2d 702, 2001 N.H. LEXIS 70 (2001), overruled in part, State v. Miller, 155 N.H. 246, 921 A.2d 942, 2007 N.H. LEXIS 51 (2007).

Defendant's right to cross-examine prosecution witnesses is not unfettered, and supreme court will uphold trial court's decision limiting scope of cross-examination absent an abuse of discretion. State v. Michaud, 146 N.H. 29, 777 A.2d 840, 2001 N.H. LEXIS 22 (2001).

Court at trials for assault and criminal trespass did not err by limiting defendant's cross-examination of his ex-wife, since defendant had all the ammunition he needed to argue that his ex-wife had a motive to lie and had lied in the past, and whatever evidence prohibited inquiries might have yielded would have been cumulative at best. State v. Michaud, 146 N.H. 29, 777 A.2d 840, 2001 N.H. LEXIS 22 (2001).

Although trial court has discretion to limit cross-examination, defendant may not be denied opportunity to make at least a threshold level of inquiry. State v. Etienne, 146 N.H. 115, 767 A.2d 455, 2001 N.H. LEXIS 34 (2001).

A criminal defendant's right to confront adverse witnesses necessarily includes right to cross-examine regarding motive and bias arising from contemporaneous civil actions in which witness has a financial interest. State v. Etienne, 146 N.H. 115, 767 A.2d 455, 2001 N.H. LEXIS 34 (2001).

Trial court did not violate defendant's due process or confrontation rights by not permitting him to cross-examine victims regarding their prior sexual assault allegations against other individuals; prior allegations were not probative of victims' motives because defendant failed to demonstrate clearly and convincingly that prior allegations were false. State v. White, 145 N.H. 544, 765 A.2d 156, 2000 N.H. LEXIS 107 (2000), cert. denied, White v. New Hampshire, 533 U.S. 932, 121 S. Ct. 2557, 150 L. Ed. 2d 722, 2001 U.S. LEXIS 4763 (2001).

Denial of sexual assault defendant's motion for bill of particulars did not violate his right of confrontation under New Hampshire Constitution, since he was not precluded from questioning victim about his access to her or dates of assaults, and he also had opportunity to cross-examine State's witnesses. State v. Dixon, 144 N.H. 273, 741 A.2d 580, 1999 N.H. LEXIS 109 (1999).

The trial court's decision to allow a witness' privilege against self-incrimination to curtail cross-examination on his use of cocaine did not violate the defendant's right to confront the witness or to impeach his credibility at trial by eliciting testimony that cocaine had impaired his memory; the jury required no further information to conclude that drugs had impaired the witness' ability to remember relevant events where the jury actually heard the witness read from his earlier deposition transcript that his use of drugs and alcohol during the relevant time period had rendered his memory very unclear and manifested other memory defects in response to questions posed by counsel. State v. Roberts, 136 N.H. 731, 622 A.2d 1225, 1993 N.H. LEXIS 24 (1993).

Criminal defendant's sixth amendment confrontation right triggers correlative right to impeach witness' credibility; since cross-examination is principal means by which defendant can test witness' credibility, this right is fundamental. State v. Rodriguez, 136 N.H. 505, 618 A.2d 810, 1992 N.H. LEXIS 193 (1992).

In determining limits of cross-examination, trial court must balance prejudice, confusion, and delay of proffered testimony against its probative value; consequently, while they may not completely deny defendant opportunity to cross-examine witness on proper mattter of inquiry, trial courts may limit cross-examination after allowing threshhold level of inquiry that satisfies sixth amendment. State v. Rodriguez, 136 N.H. 505, 618 A.2d 810, 1992 N.H. LEXIS 193 (1992).

Murder defendant's inquiry into prior inconsistent statement made by state's witness was properly restricted, where defendant had no admissible evidence with which to contradict witness's response, only two affidavits from unavailable witness which arguably made good faith basis for believing statement was made, since defendant's several opportunities to question witness about perpetrator and statement at issue satisfied sixth amendment confrontation requirements and inquiry would have improperly inferred that defendant had evidence witness was lying and that another person committed crime. State v. Rodriguez, 136 N.H. 505, 618 A.2d 810, 1992 N.H. LEXIS 193 (1992).

Under the New Hampshire Constitution, the guarantee that criminal defendants may face witnesses against them face to face must occasionally give way to considerations of public policy and the necessities of the case; necessity may not be established by legislative presumption that certain classes of witnesses, such as child victims of sexual abuse, are unable to testify at trial. State v. Peters, 133 N.H. 791, 587 A.2d 587, 1991 N.H. LEXIS 2 (1991).

In trial for attempted felonious assault prosecuted following entry of nolle prosequi on charge of felonious sexual assault, trial court properly quashed defendant's subpoena of government attorney whose testimony as to why nolle prosequi was entered on higher charge, lack of physical evidence of penetration, would have been merely cumulative. State v. Adams, 133 N.H. 818, 585 A.2d 853, 1991 N.H. LEXIS 3 (1991).

In order to sustain an exception to a defendant's constitutional right to confront witnesses face to face at trial, there must be an individualized finding that the witness in a particular case is unavailable to testify at trial. State v. Peters, 133 N.H. 791, 587 A.2d 587, 1991 N.H. LEXIS 2 (1991).

Rights of accused under New Hampshire Constitution include the fundamental right to cross-examine witnesses to impeach their credibility. State v. Benoit, 126 N.H. 6, 490 A.2d 295, 1985 N.H. LEXIS 240 (1985).

Cross-examination is necessary to ensure that the defendant shall have a right to produce all proofs that may be favorable to himself, to meet the witnesses against him face to face, and be fully heard in his defense. State v. Ramos, 121 N.H. 863, 435 A.2d 1122, 1981 N.H. LEXIS 430 (1981).

Criminal defendant has right under this article to meet the proof against him and to cross-examine witnesses to impeach their testimony. State v. La Clair, 121 N.H. 743, 433 A.2d 1326, 1981 N.H. LEXIS 391 (1981).

202. Videotaped testimony

The proponent of videotape evidence offered in lieu of live testimony has the burden of proving by a preponderance of the evidence that the witness is unavailable, in the constitutional sense of the word, as used in confrontation clause jurisprudence, to testify at trial. State v. Peters, 133 N.H. 791, 587 A.2d 587, 1991 N.H. LEXIS 2 (1991).

Statute which authorizes taking of videotaped trial depositions of certain child victims and witnesses of crimes which, properly interpreted, requires trial judge to make specific finding at time of trial that witness is still unavailable in a constitutional sense, is not unconstitutional on its face. State v. Peters, 133 N.H. 791, 587 A.2d 587, 1991 N.H. LEXIS 2 (1991).

In trial for attempted felonious sexual assault, trial court's denial of defendant's motion for videotape deposition of victim did not deprive defendant of state or federal constitutional rights to due process and effective assistance of counsel where defendant had access to a statement by victim that would enable him to anticipate the victim's testimony and defendant failed to otherwise show he was unable to prepare adequately for trial without videotape deposition discovery. State v. Adams, 133 N.H. 818, 585 A.2d 853, 1991 N.H. LEXIS 3 (1991).

Videotaped trial deposition of eight-year-old alleged victim of sexual abuse was not properly admitted as evidence at trial in absence of showing by state that victim, at the same time of trial, continued to be "unavailable" to testify in the constitutional sense of the word. State v. Peters, 133 N.H. 791, 587 A.2d 587, 1991 N.H. LEXIS 2 (1991).

203. Hearsay

Because experts had each applied their independent judgment to a decedent's hearsay statements and were not acting as mere "transmitters" of testimonial hearsay, the Confrontation Clause did not prohibit them from testifying regarding their opinions, so long as they did not testify as to the decedent's statements on direct

examination. Because there was no Sixth Amendment violation, there was also no violation of N.H. Const. pt. I, art. 15. State v. McLeod, — N.H. —, 66 A.3d 1221, 2013 N.H. LEXIS 53 (May 14, 2013).

Admission of an identification by a witness who claimed to have no current memory of her interactions with police did not violate defendant's right to confrontation under the New Hampshire Constitution. Her earlier statement of identification fell within N.H. R. Evid. 801(d)(1)(C), a firmly rooted hearsay exception, as she had been produced for cross-examination at trial. State v. Legere, 157 N.H. 746, 958 A.2d 969, 2008 N.H. LEXIS 118 (2008), cert. denied, Legere v. New Hampshire, 556 U.S. 1133, 129 S. Ct. 1623, 173 L. Ed. 2d 1005, 2009 U.S. LEXIS 2085 (2009).

Where the defendant had a full and fair chance to confront witnesses, the hearsay did not violate the Confrontation Clause. State v. Gabusi, 149 N.H. 327, 821 A.2d 1064, 2003 N.H. LEXIS 47 (2003).

Findings of trial court with respect to reliability of hearsay statements admitted under exception for declarations against penal interest, and whether introduction of this evidence infringed on defendant's constitutional right of confrontation, will not be overturned unless clearly erroneous. State v. McLaughlin, 135 N.H. 669, 610 A.2d 809, 1992 N.H. LEXIS 100 (1992).

Spontaneity and temporal proximity to the event are factors supporting a finding of reliability of hearsay statements admitted under exception for declarations against penal interest, for purposes of determining whether introduction of this evidence infringed on defendant's constitutional right of confrontation. State v. McLaughlin, 135 N.H. 669, 610 A.2d 809, 1992 N.H. LEXIS 100 (1992).

In determining whether hearsay statements admitted under exception for declarations against penal interest violated defendant's constitutional right of confrontation, issue of reliability looks to circumstances surrounding declarant's making of statement; whether or not witness was a reliable reporter of the statements goes to witness's credibility, a matter for exploration by the defendant before the jury. State v. McLaughlin, 135 N.H. 669, 610 A.2d 809, 1992 N.H. LEXIS 100 (1992).

In determining whether hearsay statements admitted under exception for declarations against penal interest violated defendant's constitutional right of confrontation, fact that admissions were made in benign setting of declarant's own home, in front of her husband, to his son, at a time when she was neither under arrest nor suspicion, negated presumption of unreliability usually attaching to statements by a declarant implicating another. State v. McLaughlin, 135 N.H. 669, 610 A.2d 809, 1992 N.H. LEXIS 100 (1992).

At trial for first degree murder and conspiracy to commit murder, introduction of defendant's wife's inculpatory statements to the defendant's son under hearsay exception did not violate defendant's constitutional right of confrontation; statements were shown to be reliable and trustworthy, based on six separate indicia of reliability. State v. McLaughlin, 135 N.H. 669, 610 A.2d 809, 1992 N.H. LEXIS 100 (1992).

Under New Hampshire Constitution, hearsay testimony implicating a person other than the declarant, which may otherwise be admissible against the declarant under an exception to the hearsay rule, must possess particularized guarantees of trustworthiness to be admissible; state must present trial court with evidence that testimony was so trustworthy that adversarial testing would add little to reliability. State v. Cook, 135 N.H. 655, 610 A.2d 800, 1992 N.H. LEXIS 99 (1992).

204. Chemical analysis of controlled substance

Because former RSA 265:90 (see now RSA 265-A:12) allows for the testimony of a certifying scientist in place of the analyst who conducted the test, the admission of a blood test report does not violate a defendant's rights under the Confrontation Clause of the United States Constitution or N.H. Const. pt. I, art. 15. State v. Coombs, 149 N.H. 319, 821 A.2d 1030, 2003 N.H. LEXIS 45 (2003).

Where, pursuant to former RSA 265:90 (see now RSA 265-A:12), defendant was permitted to cross-examine the scientist who certified defendant's blood alcohol test results but not the analyst who conducted the test, defendant's ability to subpoena the analyst during the presentation of defendant's case did not ameliorate the State's duty to confront a defendant with a witness pursuant to

N.H. Const. pt. I, § 15. State v. Coombs, 149 N.H. 319, 821 A.2d 1030, 2003 N.H. LEXIS 45 (2003).

Cross-examination of the scientist that certified the blood-alcohol test results was not useless under former RSA 265:90 (see now RSA 265-A:12) and in violation of N.H. Const. pt. I, § 15, despite the fact that the scientist did not conduct the specific blood test at issue; an analyst who conducted 40 blood tests per day would not remember the performance of a specific test months later either. State v. Coombs, 149 N.H. 319, 821 A.2d 1030, 2003 N.H. LEXIS 45 (2003).

RSA 318-B:26-a, II, requiring defendant charged with selling marijuana to demonstrate "specific grounds" for objection to admission of certificate of chemical analysis in order to question the analyst who prepared it violated defendant's right to confront witnesses against him, since without confronting the analyst, defendant could not practicably identify "specific grounds" under the statute, yet without identifying "specific grounds," he could not confront the analyst. State v. Christensen, 135 N.H. 583, 607 A.2d 952, 1992 N.H. LEXIS 84 (1992).

205. Juvenile certification hearing

Due process does not require a right to confront witnesses in a hearing to certify the transfer of a juvenile to Superior Court. In re Eduardo L., 136 N.H. 678, 621 A.2d 923, 1993 N.H. LEXIS 14 (1993).

206. Termination of parental rights

Relying in part on an interpretation by the highest court in Massachusetts of that state's very similar confrontation clause, the court interpreted New Hampshire's constitution as not providing a right of confrontation in proceedings to terminate parental rights. In re Juvenile 2003-195, 150 N.H. 644, 843 A.2d 318, 2004 N.H. LEXIS 44 (2004).

207. Nontestimonial statements

Admission of business records and their certifications under N.H. R. Evid. 902(11) did not violate the Confrontation Clause of the Sixth Amendment or N.H. Const. pt. I, art. 15. The records were not created for the purpose of litigation and thus were not testimonial, and the certifications served only as the foundation for the admission of the substantive evidence. State v. Brooks, 164 N.H. 272, 56 A.3d 1245, 2012 N.H. LEXIS 141 (2012).

Admission of statements by defendant's wife, who did not testify at trial, that defendant had said that he was going to shoot the victim and had been waiting for him in his truck did not violate the Confrontation Clause or N.H. Const. pt. I, art. 15. The statements, made shortly after the shooting and at the scene, were not testimonial as the purpose of an officer's interrogation of the wife was to meet an ongoing emergency. State v. Ayer, 154 N.H. 500, 917 A.2d 214, 2006 N.H. LEXIS 191 (2006), rehearing denied, 2007 N.H. LEXIS 35 (N.H. Jan. 30, 2007), cert. denied, Ayer v. New Hampshire, 552 U.S. 834, 128 S. Ct. 63, 169 L. Ed. 2d 52, 2007 U.S. LEXIS 9174 (2007).

208. Laboratory tests

In a prosecution for dispensing a controlled drug with death resulting, testimony by a certifying toxicologist who did not himself perform tests was admissible under N.H. Const. pt. I, art. 15. At least a dozen separate analysts performed tests in the case and were unlikely to remember how specific procedures were performed or even which specific testing was done; the certifying toxicologist's testimony about lab procedures and lab protocol and his steps in certifying the results of the tests was a sufficient substitute for that of the actual analysts and established the laboratory report's reliability. State v. Silva, 158 N.H. 96, 960 A.2d 715, 2008 N.H. LEXIS 145 (2008).

209. Trustworthiness

There was no merit to defendant's argument that the trial court failed to make a particularized determination of guarantees of trustworthiness as there was ample evidence from which the trial court could have concluded that a certifying toxicologist's testimony was trustworthy; the trial court permitted him to testify, and the court would assume that in doing so, it made all necessary findings to support its decision. State v. Silva, 158 N.H. 96, 960 A.2d 715, 2008 N.H. LEXIS 145 (2008).

210. Availability of witness

Because a codefendant was on the stand to answer questions, he was "available," despite his lack of memory. Thus, it was not error under N.H. Const. pt. I, art. 15 to allow the introduction of his prior statements that inculpated defendant, regardless of whether they bore adequate indicia of reliability. State v. Ata, 158 N.H. 406, 969 A.2d 419, 2009 N.H. LEXIS 25 (2009).

211. Bias of witness

Trial court did not impermissibly limit defendant's ability to effectively impeach the principal witness against him in violation of defendant's right to confrontation. That the trial court restricted defendant on cross-examination from inquiring about the specific underlying events giving rise to the hostilities between him and the witness did not equate to precluding him from engaging in a threshold inquiry on the matters of bias and motive. State v. Stowe, 162 N.H. 464, 34 A.3d 678, 2011 N.H. LEXIS 128 (2011).

Any error under N.H. Const. pt. I, art. 15 in the trial court's refusal to allow the defense to question a witness about her potential bias stemming from her arrest and night in jail was harmless. The State presented overwhelming alternative evidence to support defendant's conviction beyond a reasonable doubt. State v. Rogers, 159 N.H. 50, 977 A.2d 493, 2009 N.H. LEXIS 85 (2009).

212. Disguised witness

Trial court did not violate the Confrontation Clauses of the federal and state constitutions by allowing the investigating officer to testify while wearing a mask. It found that the mask allowed the jury to see most of his face and that the jury could evaluate the witness's credibility, hear his tone of voice, and see his movements. State v. Walker, — N.H. —, — A.3d —, 2011 N.H. LEXIS 40 (Mar. 21, 2011).

Assuming without deciding that allowing a detective to testify while wearing a ski mask violated N.H. Const. pt. I, art. 15 and the Sixth and Fourteenth Amendments, the error was harmless. The evidence that defendant had sexual intercourse with the victim, who was less than 13 at the time, was overwhelming; the masked detective's testimony was merely cumulative. State v. Hernandez, 159 N.H. 394, 986 A.2d 480, 2009 N.H. LEXIS 127 (2009).

In the future, when a trial court is considering whether to allow a prosecution witness to testify while wearing a disguise, such as a mask, the court must make specific findings that the disguise is necessary to further an important state interest and that the reliability of the evidence is otherwise assured. Determining whether the reliability of the testimony is otherwise assured turns upon the extent to which the proceedings respect the four elements of confrontation: physical presence, oath, cross-examination, and observation of demeanor by the trier of fact; additionally, as with decisions to close the courtroom, the trial court's findings supporting allowing the witness to testify while wearing a disguise must be specific enough that a reviewing court can determine whether the order was properly entered. State v. Hernandez, 159 N.H. 394, 986 A.2d 480, 2009 N.H. LEXIS 127 (2009).

VI. Right to Represent Oneself

251. Generally

Conditional request for self-representation is not equivocal. State v. Towle, 162 N.H. 799, 35 A.3d 490, 2011 N.H. LEXIS 180 (2011).

When defendant essentially said that if the trial court would not dismiss his lawyer or grant a continuance, then he wanted to represent himself, this request for self-representation, though conditional, was not equivocal. Thus, the trial court's failure to inquire further was structural error under N.H. Const. pt. I, art. 15, requiring a new trial. State v. Towle, 162 N.H. 799, 35 A.3d 490, 2011 N.H. LEXIS 180 (2011).

Trial court did not violate N.H. Const. pt. I, art. 15 or the Sixth Amendment in appointing counsel for defendant where he had not clearly invoked his right to self-representation; defendant had only declined to decide whether he would accept appointed counsel or proceed pro se. State v. Ayer, 154 N.H. 500, 917 A.2d 214, 2006 N.H. LEXIS 191 (2006), rehearing denied, 2007 N.H. LEXIS 35 (N.H. Jan. 30, 2007), cert. denied, Ayer v. New Hampshire, 552 U.S. 834, 128 S. Ct. 63, 169 L. Ed. 2d 52, 2007 U.S. LEXIS 9174 (2007).

Defendant had no due process right to proceed pro se on appeal. State v. Thomas, 150 N.H. 327, 840 A.2d 803, 2003 N.H. LEXIS 192 (2003), rehearing denied, 2004 N.H. LEXIS 23 (N.H. Jan. 27, 2004).

Where defendant was not granted the right to proceed in his criminal trial by self-representation, and he was instead represented by counsel for two days and thereafter, was completely on his own, such constituted a structural defect and was a clear violation of defendant's Farretta rights, as well as a violation of his constitutional rights under U.S. Const. amend. VI and N.H. Const. pt. I, art. 15, requiring that his conviction be reversed and vacated, and a new trial be granted; there was no double jeopardy attachment, pursuant to N.H. Const. pt. I, art. 16, as defendant was successful in appealing his conviction on constitutional grounds. State v. Ayer, 150 N.H. 14, 834 A.2d 277, 2003 N.H. LEXIS 133 (2003), cert. denied, Ayer v. New Hampshire, 124 S. Ct. 1668, 158 L. Ed. 2d 366, 2004 U.S. LEXIS 2130 (2004).

A defendant has a right under this article to represent himself in a criminal trial. State v. Barham, 126 N.H. 631, 495 A.2d 1269, 1985 N.H. LEXIS 363 (1985).

252. Construction with right to counsel

The right to self-representation does not coexist with that of a defendant to be represented by counsel; rather, its exercise extinguishes the constitutional right to counsel. Lewis v. Powell, 135 N.H. 490, 607 A.2d 603, 1992 N.H. LEXIS 67 (1992), cert. denied, Lewis v. New Hampshire, 506 U.S. 891, 113 S. Ct. 259, 121 L. Ed. 2d 190, 1992 U.S. LEXIS 6115 (1992).

The constitutional right to represent oneself in a criminal trial does not coexist with the right to be represented by counsel; rather, its exercise extinguishes the right to counsel. State v. Barham, 126 N.H. 631, 495 A.2d 1269, 1985 N.H. LEXIS 363 (1985).

253. Acting as co-counsel

Provision of this article guaranteeing every defendant the right "to be fully heard in his defense, by himself, and counsel" does not guarantee a defendant the right to act as co-counsel. State v. Settle, 123 N.H. 34, 455 A.2d 1031, 1983 N.H. LEXIS 218 (1983).

254. Waiver of right to counsel

In order to represent himself, an accused must knowingly and intelligently relinquish the traditional benefits associated with the right to counsel. Lewis v. Powell, 135 N.H. 490, 607 A.2d 603, 1992 N.H. LEXIS 67 (1992), cert. denied, Lewis v. New Hampshire, 506 U.S. 891, 113 S. Ct. 259, 121 L. Ed. 2d 190, 1992 U.S. LEXIS 6115 (1992).

Waiver of the right to counsel is required when a criminal defendant represents himself, even though counsel will act in a standby capacity. Lewis v. Powell, 135 N.H. 490, 607 A.2d 603, 1992 N.H. LEXIS 67 (1992), cert. denied, Lewis v. New Hampshire, 506 U.S. 891, 113 S. Ct. 259, 121 L. Ed. 2d 190, 1992 U.S. LEXIS 6115 (1992).

A criminal defendant must plainly and unequivocally state his intention to represent himself and such an election is tantamount to waiver of the right to counsel. Lewis v. Powell, 135 N.H. 490, 607 A.2d 603, 1992 N.H. LEXIS 67 (1992), cert. denied, Lewis v. New Hampshire, 506 U.S. 891, 113 S. Ct. 259, 121 L. Ed. 2d 190, 1992 U.S. LEXIS 6115 (1992).

Express waiver of the right to counsel is not required whenever a criminal defendant chooses to proceed pro se. Lewis v. Powell, 135 N.H. 490, 607 A.2d 603, 1992 N.H. LEXIS 67 (1992), cert. denied, Lewis v. New Hampshire, 506 U.S. 891, 113 S. Ct. 259, 121 L. Ed. 2d 190, 1992 U.S. LEXIS 6115 (1992).

Where petitioner plainly and unequivocally stated his intention to proceed pro se with the assistance of standby counsel, both prior to trial and at hearing on his motions to suppress and to dismiss, an express waiver of counsel was not required. Lewis v. Powell, 135 N.H. 490, 607 A.2d 603, 1992 N.H. LEXIS 67 (1992), cert. denied, Lewis v. New Hampshire, 506 U.S. 891, 113 S. Ct. 259, 121 L. Ed. 2d 190, 1992 U.S. LEXIS 6115 (1992).

255. Duty of court

Where defendant was repeatedly made aware of the dangers and disadvantages of self-representation, while his decision to proceed pro se might have been to his detriment, defendant's decision to proceed pro se at trial was knowing, intelligent, and voluntary; however, defendant had no due process right to proceed pro se on appeal. State v. Thomas, 150 N.H. 327, 840 A.2d 803, 2003 N.H. LEXIS 192 (2003), rehearing denied, 2004 N.H. LEXIS 23 (N.H. Jan. 27, 2004).

When a criminal defendant states his intention to represent himself, the court must make the defendant aware of the dangers and disadvantages of self-representation. Lewis v. Powell, 135 N.H. 490, 607 A.2d 603, 1992 N.H. LEXIS 67 (1992), cert. denied, Lewis v. New Hampshire, 506 U.S. 891, 113 S. Ct. 259, 121 L. Ed. 2d 190, 1992 U.S. LEXIS 6115 (1992).

256. Practice and procedure

Although, due to defendant's voluntary absence, trial court could not engage defendant in a colloquy on the subject of his waiver of right to counsel at the time his motion to proceed pro se was granted, court had previously discussed consequences of proceeding pro se with defendant, and court was able to reasonably conclude at a subsequent hearing that defendant intended to waive his right to counsel and that his waiver had been knowingly and intelligently made. State v. Davis, 139 N.H. 185, 650 A.2d 1386, 1994 N.H. LEXIS 132 (1994).

VII. Right to Counsel

257. Appointment of standby counsel

Use of standby counsel did not violate defendant's right of self-representation under N.H. Const. pt. I, art. 15 and the Sixth Amendment. Standby counsel did not request a limiting instruction, but merely stated his opinion that certain language in the instruction was a good idea; furthermore, his participation in two sidebar conferences and the trial court's comment to the jury that it had "discussed the issue with the attorneys" did not destroy the jury's perception that defendant was representing himself. State v. Russo, 164 N.H. 585, 62 A.3d 798, 2013 N.H. LEXIS 16 (2013).

301. Construction with federal constitution

The provision of this article providing the right to counsel covers a broader range of criminal defendants than are granted a right to counsel by the sixth and fourteenth amendments to the United States Constitution. State v. Scarborough, 124 N.H. 363, 470 A.2d 909, 1983 N.H. LEXIS 417 (1983).

The supreme court's discussion of the defendant's right to counsel under this article by reference to decisions in the federal context only represented the minimum extent of the protections afforded by this article, which covers a broader range of defendants than are granted a right to counsel by the sixth and fourteenth amendments to the United States Constitution, and the supreme court would depart from that context when it was persuaded that such a departure was mandated by the state constitution's clear intent to "stay in the van" of protecting its citizens' rights against governmental interference. State v. Scarborough, 124 N.H. 363, 470 A.2d 909, 1983 N.H. LEXIS 417 (1983).

302. When right attaches

Because judicial proceedings had not yet commenced against defendant with respect to a shooting, his right to counsel had not attached as to those charges. Thus, an informant's questioning him about the shooting after defendant was arrested on drug charges did not violate his right to counsel under Sixth Amendment and N.H. Const. pt. I, art. 15, despite the fact that the informant also asked defendant about the drug charges after being told not to do so. State v. White, 163 N.H. 303, 42 A.3d 783, 2012 N.H. LEXIS 28 (2012).

While the New Hampshire Supreme Court has implicitly held that the right to counsel under N.H. Const. pt. I, art. 15 is also offense specific, the court now explicitly adopts, under the New Hampshire Constitution, the "offense specific" nature of the right to counsel. This means that the right to counsel attaches only to offenses for which prosecution has commenced and cannot be invoked once for all future prosecutions; thus, a defendant's statements regarding offenses for which he has not been charged are admissible notwithstanding the attachment of his right to counsel on other charged offenses. State v. White, 163 N.H. 303, 42 A.3d 783, 2012 N.H. LEXIS 28 (2012).

New Hampshire Supreme Court has never construed the state constitutional right to counsel as arising earlier than the Sixth Amendment right to counsel; nor has it found that the use of an informant, in and of itself, violates the state constitution. State v. White, 163 N.H. 303, 42 A.3d 783, 2012 N.H. LEXIS 28 (2012).

Trial court committed plain error pursuant to N.H. Sup. Ct. R. 16-A when it failed to appoint counsel for defendant prior to imposing a deferred sentence, as that constituted a critical stage of the proceeding, entitling defendant to counsel pursuant to N.H. Const. pt. I, art. 15. State v. Almodovar, 158 N.H. 548, 969 A.2d 479, 2009 N.H. LEXIS 46 (2009).

Because the particular language of a 1990 sentencing order provided that sentencing would not be completed until 2005 when the trial court considered whether to impose a deferred seven-year term, it was a critical state of the proceeding to which defendant was entitled to counsel under N.H. Const. pt. I, art 15. State v. Parker, 155 N.H. 89, 921 A.2d 366, 2007 N.H. LEXIS 31 (2007).

When, after probation revocation proceedings had been initiated against defendant, he admitted probation violations other than those alleged to his probation officer, outside the presence of his counsel, it did not violate his right to counsel to admit those admissions against him in the revocation proceedings because the right to counsel was offense-specific, and the alleged probation violations as to which the right to counsel had attached, upon the initiation of revocation proceedings, were distinct from the violations defendant admitted to his probation officer, even though they were violations of the same rule of probation as had been alleged in the complaint filed. State v. Matey, 153 N.H. 263, 891 A.2d 592, 2006 N.H. LEXIS 11 (2006).

When an attorney calls or arrives at the police station and identifies himself or herself as counsel retained for the suspect, the interrogating officers have a duty to stop questioning the suspect and inform the suspect that the attorney is attempting to contact him or her. State v. Roache, 148 N.H. 45, 803 A.2d 572, 2002 N.H. LEXIS 89 (2002).

The defendant had no right to confer with counsel prior to the taking of a blood sample pursuant to a search warrant since the execution of a warrant to seize blood is not a critical stage of a criminal proceeding. State v. Delisle, 137 N.H. 549, 630 A.2d 767, 1993 N.H. LEXIS 119 (1993).

The defendant's right to counsel was not violated when a conversation she had with a third party was intercepted with the consent of the third party where, at the time of the intercepted conversations, the defendant had not been arrested and had no charges pending, notwithstanding that she and her attorney had notified the attorney general's office of her desire to deal with the state only through an attorney. State v. Smart, 136 N.H. 639, 622 A.2d 1197, 1993 N.H. LEXIS 11 (1993), cert. denied, Smart v. New Hampshire, 510 U.S. 917, 114 S. Ct. 309, 126 L. Ed. 2d 256, 1993 U.S. LEXIS 6384 (1993).

Once judicial proceedings have commenced against a defendant, this article entitles the defendant to the benefit of counsel during interrogation; absent a valid waiver of that right, any government interrogation of the defendant would be improper. State v. Roberts, 131 N.H. 512, 556 A.2d 302, 1989 N.H. LEXIS 20 (1989).

The advice of counsel is not constitutionally required when a person has to make a choice whether to take a blood alcohol test under the implied consent law. State v. Greene, 128 N.H. 317, 512 A.2d 429, 1986 N.H. LEXIS 276 (1986).

In a nonfatal DWI case, the point at which a defendant had to decide whether to take or to refuse to take a breath test was not a "critical stage" so as to entitle defendant constitutionally to consult with counsel, even though defendant's refusal to take the test could be admitted into evidence. State v. Greene, 128 N.H. 317, 512 A.2d 429, 1986 N.H. LEXIS 276 (1986).

In prosecution for robbery, the defendant's right to assistance of counsel attached no later than the time of his indictment. State v. Scarborough, 124 N.H. 363, 470 A.2d 909, 1983 N.H. LEXIS 417 (1983).

Defendant's statement that "he thought he had better talk to an attorney" was sufficient to assert his rights under Miranda; therefore, his subsequent confession would be admissible only if state could establish that defendant later waived his right to counsel. State v. Nash, 119 N.H. 728, 407 A.2d 365, 1979 N.H. LEXIS 377 (1979).

303. Privileged communications

The defendant's right to counsel serves to protect communications between a defendant and the defendant's attorney, not the defendant's conversations with third parties where defense counsel happens to be in the same room. State v. Jaroma, 137 N.H. 143, 625 A.2d 1049, 1993 N.H. LEXIS 54 (1993).

304. Waiver

Where, when given a clear choice between accepting a continuance or proceeding pro se, defendant explicitly elected the latter, and the choice presented to defendant did not rise to the level of a due process violation, and where pretrial delay of less than six months— had defendant agreed to a six-week continuance— was not presumptively prejudicial, the manifest certainty with which defendant made his decision rendered his waiver of right to counsel voluntary. State v. Panzera, 139 N.H. 235, 652 A.2d 136, 1994 N.H. LEXIS 138 (1994).

Evidence was sufficient to establish that the defendant waived his right to counsel during a conversation with a police officer where (1) the defendant asserted his right to counsel at his arraignment, (2) about two weeks later, in response to the officer's direct inquiry about whether he wanted to continue speaking with him without counsel present, he indicated that he understood his right to have counsel present, and (3) the defendant then knowingly and voluntarily chose to continue his discussion with the officer. State v. Jaroma, 137 N.H. 143, 625 A.2d 1049, 1993 N.H. LEXIS 54 (1993).

The defendant's statements made to a police officer before he was advised of his Miranda rights were properly admitted since there was no interrogation or its functional equivalent for the first 70 minutes of the meeting between the defendant and the officer where the officer testified that, during this period, he did not interview the defendant and did not recall interrupting the defendant's recitation to clarify any of his statements. State v. Jaroma, 137 N.H. 143, 625 A.2d 1049, 1993 N.H. LEXIS 54 (1993).

The court would not extend the requirement that police obtain a waiver of a previously-asserted right to counsel before questioning a defendant about a situation in which the defendant, who has been released from custody and is awaiting trial, voluntarily approaches the police and makes a statement; law enforcement personnel are required to honor the invocation of an individual's right to counsel, but they are not required to prevent that individual from voluntarily approaching a police officer and making injudicious statements. State v. Jaroma, 137 N.H. 143, 625 A.2d 1049, 1993 N.H. LEXIS 54 (1993).

A valid waiver of the right to the presence of counsel does not require the presence of counsel. State v. Lamb, 125 N.H. 495, 484 A.2d 1074, 1984 N.H. LEXIS 408 (1984).

Trial court properly ruled in prosecution for robbery that this article requires an explanation from the trial court before a defendant can validly waive his right to have counsel appointed, but that this article did not require an explanation from the trial court before he could validly waive his right to have counsel present during any questioning. State v. Scarborough, 124 N.H. 363, 470 A.2d 909, 1983 N.H. LEXIS 417 (1983).

To prove a constitutionally effective waiver of counsel, state must first show that suspect's right to terminate questioning by requesting counsel was scrupulously honored, and second, that suspect intentionally waived right once it was asserted. State v. Nash, 119 N.H. 728, 407 A.2d 365, 1979 N.H. LEXIS 377 (1979).

If individual states that he wants an attorney, the interrogation must cease until an attorney is present; however, an individual may waive his right to counsel after he has asserted it. State v. Nash, 119 N.H. 728, 407 A.2d 365, 1979 N.H. LEXIS 377 (1979).

A first offense conviction is invalid absent a knowing and intelligent waiver of right to counsel and cannot be the basis for conviction for committing the same type of offense a second time, where statute provides for more severe sanctions upon a subsequent offense. State v. Maxwell, 115 N.H. 363, 341 A.2d 766, 1975 N.H. LEXIS 306 (1975).

305. Effective assistance—Generally

While the New Hampshire Supreme Court has indicated a preference for collaterally reviewing ineffective assistance claims, it is now persuaded, in agreement with numerous other state appellate courts, that direct review of such a claim may be permitted in certain, limited circumstances where all of the facts necessary to adjudicate the claim appear in the trial record. Under no circumstance, however, shall the failure to bring an ineffectiveness claim on direct appeal result in the procedural default of that claim. State v. Thompson, 161 N.H. 507, 20 A.3d 242, 2011 N.H. LEXIS 23 (2011).

Counsel was ineffective under N.H. Const. pt. I, art. 15, as his failure to object to hearsay defied all rational explanation and was not protected as trial strategy. The prejudice was manifest, as the State was able to prove its case only because of defense counsel's failure. State v. Thompson, 161 N.H. 507, 20 A.3d 242, 2011 N.H. LEXIS 23 (2011).

Counsel was not ineffective for failing to highlight certain inconsistencies between out-of-court statements and trial testimony. Defense counsel developed testimony addressing the inconsistencies highlighted in his opening statement and closing argument; his decisions as to whether to further highlight inconsistencies necessarily included consideration of whether the additional testimony would allow the State to offer otherwise inadmissible evidence and whether the jury might perceive him as being overly technical and aggressive. State v. Kidd, — N.H. —, — A.3d —, 2010 N.H. LEXIS 211 (Aug. 31, 2010).

Broad language of Avery v. Cunningham, 131 N.H. 138, 551 A.2d 952, 1988 N.H. LEXIS 107 (1988), has been significantly undermined so that claims of ineffective assistance of counsel based upon alleged trial errors are not procedurally barred by the failure to raise those errors on direct appeal. Accordingly, the trial court should have heard the merits of defendant's ineffective assistance of counsel claims concerning due process and double jeopardy. State v. Pepin, 159 N.H. 310, 982 A.2d 364, 2009 N.H. LEXIS 116 (2009).

Trial counsel was ineffective under U.S. Const. amend. VI and N.H. Const. pt. I, art. 15 by failing to consult with an expert. Had he done so, he might have been able to present a case that defendant's impairment did not cause the victim's death; and the testimony of an expert might have been admissible, even if it was based upon assumptions. State v. Whittaker, — N.H. —, 973 A.2d 299, 2009 N.H. LEXIS 75 (June 3, 2009).

Counsel was not ineffective for failing to file a motion to suppress, as such a motion would have been meritless. The language of RSA 641:6 did not make admissibility of the evidence at trial an element of the offense of falsifying physical evidence; furthermore, any taint of violation of N.H. Const. pt. I, art. 19 and the U.S. Constitution was purged when defendant ingested marijuana, which supported a new criminal charge distinct from the prior illegal seizure. State v. McGurk, 157 N.H. 765, 958 A.2d 1005, 2008 N.H. LEXIS 119 (2008).

Defendant failed to show prejudice from his attorney's asserted failure to adequately inform him of his absolute right to testify at trial, because no reasonable probability existed that result of trial would have been different had defendant testified at trial and denied the allegations. State v. Paulsen, 143 N.H. 447, 726 A.2d 902, 1999 N.H. LEXIS 23 (1999).

Sexual assault defendant failed to demonstrate that his counsel's representation was constitutionally deficient. Counsel lacked sufficient information to justify further investigation, made reasonably competent strategic and tactical decisions not to submit certain evidence at trial, and otherwise competently investigated and presented defendant's case. State v. Dewitt, 143 N.H. 24, 719 A.2d 570, 1998 N.H. LEXIS 65 (1998).

The defendant's right to effective assistance of counsel was violated when the defendant's trial counsel inadvertently submitted a jury instruction to the trial court that expanded the grand jury indictment in such a way as to negate the defense presented by the defendant at trial. State v. Henderson, 141 N.H. 615, 689 A.2d 1336, 1997 N.H. LEXIS 13 (1997).

Where the trial court's finding that trial counsel's performance with respect to alleged error was based on its implicit finding that defendant's version of events was not credible, trial court's finding would not be overturned. State v. Seymour, 140 N.H. 736, 673 A.2d 786, 1996 N.H. LEXIS 24 (1996), cert. denied, Seymour v. New Hampshire, 519 U.S. 853, 117 S. Ct. 146, 136 L. Ed. 2d 93, 1996 U.S. LEXIS 5265 (1996).

Evidence was insufficient to establish ineffective assistance of counsel where trial counsel's decision to take full advantage of the court's pretrial rulings by portraying the defendant in a most favorable light was a calculated risk falling within the limits of reasonable practice notwithstanding fact that it opened the door to prosecution's introduction of evidence relating to defendant's arrest on similar charges; furthermore, trial counsel was not ineffective in failing to take adequate steps to ensure the presence and testimony of defendant's then-wife because fact that wife's testimony would have been speculative and cumulative was amply supported by the record and any advantage of her testimony would have been overshadowed by the damaging revelations of her troubled history with defendant. State v. Fecteau, 140 N.H. 498, 667 A.2d 1384, 1995 N.H. LEXIS 178 (1995).

A reciprocal discovery order, which required that the defendant disclose the identity and statements of witnesses he intended to call at trial, did not violate the defendant's right to effective assistance of counsel, notwithstanding the argument that defense counsel, in fear of unwittingly helping prepare the state's case, would not dig as zealously as the law requires, possibly missing the basis for a defense. State v. Drewry, 139 N.H. 678, 661 A.2d 1181, 1995 N.H. LEXIS 71 (1995).

Evidence did not establish ineffective assistance of counsel where defendant was unable to establish actual prejudice resulting from his trial counsel's failure to object to substitution of an ill juror; the defendant was properly tried by twelve jurors and his allegation that the dismissed juror might have been a lone dissenter in favor of acquittal was purely speculative. State v. Colbert, 139 N.H. 367, 654 A.2d 963, 1995 N.H. LEXIS 6 (1995).

Evidence was insufficient to establish ineffective assistance of counsel where the defendant failed to show that his counsel's performance failed to meet the objective standard of reasonable competence. State v. Wisowaty, 137 N.H. 298, 627 A.2d 572, 1993 N.H. LEXIS 74 (1993).

A criminal defendant is entitled to reasonably competent assistance of counsel under the New Hampshire and United States Constitutions. State v. Matiyosus, 134 N.H. 686, 597 A.2d 1068, 1991 N.H. LEXIS 122 (1991).

In guaranteeing a right to the effective assistance of counsel, this article does not guarantee either perfection in trial tactics by defense counsel, or success by the defendant. State v. Labonville, 126 N.H. 451, 492 A.2d 1376, 1985 N.H. LEXIS 302 (1985).

Success in criminal trials and perfection in trial tactics are not guaranteed by this article. State v. Glidden, 127 N.H. 359, 499 A.2d 1349, 1985 N.H. LEXIS 438 (1985).

This article guarantees, as a fundamental right, the effective assistance of counsel. Abbott v. Potter, 125 N.H. 257, 480 A.2d 118, 1984 N.H. LEXIS 282 (1984); State v. Labonville, 126 N.H. 451, 492 A.2d 1376, 1985 N.H. LEXIS 302 (1985).

This article guarantees a criminal defendant the right to effective assistance of counsel. State v. Perron, 122 N.H. 941, 454 A.2d 422, 1982 N.H. LEXIS 496 (1982); Breest v. Perrin, 125 N.H. 703, 484 A.2d 1192, 1984 N.H. LEXIS 383 (1984); State v. Glidden, 127 N.H. 359, 499 A.2d 1349, 1985 N.H. LEXIS 438 (1985); State v. Guaraldi, 127 N.H. 303, 500 A.2d 360, 1985 N.H. LEXIS 444 (1985); State v. Dennehy, 127 N.H. 425, 503 A.2d 769, 1985 N.H. LEXIS 462 (1985).

Effective assistance of counsel is a right fundamental to criminal defendants and is required by this article. State v. Staples, 121 N.H. 959, 437 A.2d 266, 1981 N.H. LEXIS 441 (1981).

Effective assistance of counsel is a fundamental right to criminal defendants, a principle deeply ingrained in the criminal justice system, and is required by this article. Smith v. State, 118 N.H. 764, 394 A.2d 834, 1978 N.H. LEXIS 289, 3 A.L.R.4th 568 (1978).

306. —Standards

To successfully assert a claim for ineffective assistance of counsel, defendant must show that counsel's representation was constitutionally deficient and actually prejudiced outcome of case. State v. Croft, 145 N.H. 90, 749 A.2d 1284, 2000 N.H. LEXIS 24 (2000).

To prevail on an ineffective assistance claim, the defendant must demonstrate that his counsel's conduct so undermined the proper functioning of the adversarial process that the trial could not be relied on as having produced a just result. This test contains two prongs; the defendant must show that: (1) his attorney's performance was deficient, or not reasonably competent, and (2) the deficient performance resulted in actual prejudice to the outcome of the defendant's trial. State v. Sanchez, 140 N.H. 162, 663 A.2d 629, 1995 N.H. LEXIS 117 (1995).

To prevail on a claim of ineffective assistance of counsel, the defendant must show first that counsel's performance was deficient and second that counsel's deficient performance resulted in actual prejudice by affecting the outcome of the trial. Reid v. Warden, New Hampshire State Prison, 139 N.H. 530, 659 A.2d 429, 1995 N.H. LEXIS 45 (1995).

Standard for attorney performance under both state and federal constitutions is that of reasonably effective assistance. State v. Morse, 135 N.H. 565, 607 A.2d 619, 1992 N.H. LEXIS 79 (1992).

In determining whether reasonably effective assistance of counsel was rendered, supreme court starts with the strong presumption that counsel's conduct falls within the limits of reasonable practice, bearing in mind the limitless variety of strategic and tactical decisions that counsel must make. State v. Morse, 135 N.H. 565, 607 A.2d 619, 1992 N.H. LEXIS 79 (1992).

To overcome presumption that counsel's conduct fell within the limits of reasonable practice, defendant must prove that counsel made such egregious errors that counsel was not functioning as the "counsel" guaranteed by state and federal constitutions and that counsel's conduct actually prejudiced defendant such that there is a reasonable probability that the result of the proceeding would have been different had counsel been competent. State v. Morse, 135 N.H. 565, 607 A.2d 619, 1992 N.H. LEXIS 79 (1992).

Analysis of the right to effective counsel is the same under both the federal and state constitutions, and the benchmark for judging any claim of ineffectiveness must be whether counsel's conduct so undermined the proper functioning of the adversarial process that the trial cannot be relied on as having produced a just result. State v. Anaya, 134 N.H. 346, 592 A.2d 1142, 1991 N.H. LEXIS 68 (1991).

To make successful claim of ineffective assistance of counsel, the defendant must show counsel's performance was deficient, and that this allegedly deficient performance actually prejudiced him or her by affecting the outcome of the proceeding. State v. Anaya, 134 N.H. 346, 592 A.2d 1142, 1991 N.H. LEXIS 68 (1991).

Ineffective assistance of counsel will only be found if the defendant can prove that (1) counsel's errors were so egregious that he was not acting as the "counsel" guaranteed under the state and federal constitutions and (2) a reasonable probability exists that counsel's errors prejudiced the outcome of the proceedings. State v. Matiyosus, 134 N.H. 686, 597 A.2d 1068, 1991 N.H. LEXIS 122 (1991).

The standard for measuring attorney performance, under the right to counsel provisions of both the federal and state constitutions, is one of reasonably effective assistance. State v. Chase, 135 N.H. 209, 600 A.2d 931, 1991 N.H. LEXIS 169 (1991).

For purposes of ineffectiveness of counsel analysis, a claim of deficient performance must overcome the strong presumption that counsel's conduct falls within the limits of reasonable practice. State v. Anaya, 134 N.H. 346, 592 A.2d 1142, 1991 N.H. LEXIS 68 (1991).

The prejudice necessary to make out successful claim of ineffective assistance of counsel was presumed without requirement of proof where in contravention of defendant's express wishes, counsel argued strenuously for conviction on lesser-included offense of crime charged; severity of counsel's error prevented meaningful testing of prosecution's case against defendant on the lesser charge, rendered meaningless defendant's right to proclaim his innocence on the stand, and eliminated state's burden to prove guilt beyond reasonable doubt. State v. Anaya, 134 N.H. 346, 592 A.2d 1142, 1991 N.H. LEXIS 68 (1991).

The standard for attorney performance under both state and federal constitutions is reasonably effective assistance. State v. Fennell, 133 N.H. 402, 578 A.2d 329, 1990 N.H. LEXIS 79 (1990).

The totality of the circumstances test is the appropriate standard in determining a claim of ineffective assistance of counsel under the New Hampshire Constitution. State v. Settle, 127 N.H. 756, 512 A.2d 1083, 1986 N.H. LEXIS 266 (1986).

This article measures the defendant's right to assistance of counsel under an objective standard of reasonable competence. State v. Faragi, 127 N.H. 1, 498 A.2d 723, 1985 N.H. LEXIS 401 (1985).

New Hampshire and federal constitutional standards are identical as to the right to effective assistance of counsel. State v. Glidden, 127 N.H. 359, 499 A.2d 1349, 1985 N.H. LEXIS 438 (1985).

The analysis and result of a claim of ineffective assistance of counsel is the same under the United States Constitution and the New Hampshire Constitution, and the state and federal standards are identical. State v. Dennehy, 127 N.H. 425, 503 A.2d 769, 1985 N.H. LEXIS 462 (1985).

The standard by which the performance of a lawyer representing his client in a criminal case is measured is reasonable competence. Breest v. Perrin, 125 N.H. 703, 484 A.2d 1192, 1984 N.H. LEXIS 383 (1984); State v. Labonville, 126 N.H. 451, 492 A.2d 1376, 1985 N.H. LEXIS 302 (1985); State v. Glidden, 127 N.H. 359, 499 A.2d 1349, 1985 N.H. LEXIS 438 (1985).

307. —Burden of proof

In order to show a denial of the right to effective assistance of counsel and obtain a new trial, defendant must overcome the strong presumption that counsel's conduct falls within the limits of reasonable practice, and then must also show that he was actually prejudiced. State v. Glidden, 127 N.H. 359, 499 A.2d 1349, 1985 N.H. LEXIS 438 (1985).

308. —Guilty pleas

Counsel was not ineffective for not persuading defendant to accept a capped plea agreement. Because counsel secured a promise from the prosecutor that he would not increase his sentencing recommendation for the non-negotiated plea, there was little risk that the sentence would be greater than with the capped plea arrangement; furthermore, the non-negotiated plea preserved defendant's right to sentence review, whereas a capped plea would likely have required him to waive his right to review. State v. Hall, 160 N.H. 581, 8 A.3d 12, 2010 N.H. LEXIS 89 (2010).

Trial court erred in denying defendant's motion to withdraw his guilty plea to driving under the influence of alcohol based upon ineffective assistance of counsel where defendant's counsel incorrectly informed defendant that the collateral consequence of his guilty plea in New Hampshire would be a suspension in Massachusetts for the same time period as in New Hampshire and, instead, Massachusetts revoked defendant's driver's license indefinitely pursuant to a mandatory statute and defendant relied on counsel's gross misinformation and probably would not have pled guilty to the New Hampshire charge had he known that it would result in the permanent revocation of his Massachusetts driver's license. State v. Sharkey, 155 N.H. 638, 927 A.2d 519, 2007 N.H. LEXIS 114 (2007).

Defense counsel fails to supply the effective assistance of counsel guaranteed by N.H. Const. pt. I, art. 15 if counsel grossly misinforms a criminal defendant about the collateral consequences of pleading guilty, the defendant relies upon that advice in deciding to plead guilty, and there is a reasonable probability that the defendant would not have pled guilty but for that erroneous advice; "gross misinformation" is defined as information that creates an objectively significant discrepancy between what a defendant was told defendant's collateral consequences would be and what they actually became, which is in line with the requirement that an attorney must make an "egregious error" to satisfy the first prong of the test for ineffective assistance of counsel. State v. Sharkey, 155 N.H. 638, 927 A.2d 519, 2007 N.H. LEXIS 114 (2007).

309. —Actual prejudice

Defendant's attorneys' failure to object to a police witness's testimony was improper, but as it was not prejudicial, the representation was not constitutionally deficient under N.H. Const. pt. I, art. 15; the police witness only indirectly revealed that he regarded the victim as credible, and the most reasonable interpretation of the testimony was that the police had sufficient grounds to arrest and question defendant. State v. Eschenbrenner, 164 N.H. 532, 62 A.3d 820, 2013 N.H. LEXIS 8 (2013).

Trial counsel's failure to ask for a redaction of defendant's statement could not have caused actual prejudice, given the other evidence in the case. State v. Brown, 160 N.H. 408, 999 A.2d 295, 2010 N.H. LEXIS 70 (June 30, 2010).

Even if it was error to fail to object when the trial court and the prosecutor used the term "victim," prejudice was not established on that basis alone. The court could not conclude that there was a reasonable probability that had counsel objected and had the trial court sustained the objection, the result would have been different. State v. Kidd, — N.H. —, — A.3d —, 2010 N.H. LEXIS 211 (Aug. 31, 2010).

Defendant, who claimed ineffective assistance of counsel under the Sixth Amendment and N.H. Const. part. I, art. 15, had not shown prejudice from his trial counsel's failure to object to statements in the prosecution's opening and closing arguments. Trial counsel's opening and closing arguments were not evidence, and, to the extent that they were improper, they were only marginally so. State v. Breed, 159 N.H. 61, 977 A.2d 463, 2009 N.H. LEXIS 88 (2009).

Defendant's representation was not constitutionally deficient under N.H. Const. art. I, § 15 or the Sixth Amendment because trial counsel failed to argue that the State actually disproved the concealment or surprise element of RSA 632-A:2, I(i) as: (1) a victim was legally surprised as the victim became aware of what defendant was doing to her during the assault, the victim was startled enough by the victim's realization to flee the scene, and defendant provided the victim with alcohol, the consumption of which placed the victim in a mental state that allowed the victim to be assaulted without fully realizing what was happening to the victim, (2) the victim was factually surprised in light of the victim's initial detachment, contrasted with the victim's subsequent realization of the situation and the victim's flight from it, and (3) during closing, trial counsel argued that the victim was not sufficiently impaired to have been surprised by defendant's actions by calling into question the State's proof as to the degree of the victim's impairment. State v. Kepple, 155 N.H. 267, 922 A.2d 661, 2007 N.H. LEXIS 52 (2007).

Defense counsel's failure to depose or interview prosecution witness prior to sexual assault trial did not result in actual prejudice and thus could not have been constitutionally deficient, where defendant's opportunity to have made admissions to witness the morning after assault would not have been negated, and even if counsel had interviewed witness and he failed to disclose defendant's rape admission or provided a statement inconsistent with his ultimate testimony, defendant's ability to impeach witness at trial would not have been significantly enhanced. State v. Croft, 145 N.H. 90, 749 A.2d 1284, 2000 N.H. LEXIS 24 (2000).

The defendant established actual prejudice where the indictment required the state to prove that he actually caused serious injury to the victim and defense counsel inadvertently submitted a jury instruction to the trial court that allowed the jury to convict the defendant for an attempt to cause serious injury to the victim. Defense counsel's error expanded the indictment and gave legal significance to the defendant's otherwise insignificant admission that he swung at the victim. State v. Henderson, 141 N.H. 615, 689 A.2d 1336, 1997 N.H. LEXIS 13 (1997).

The defendant failed to show that he was sufficiently prejudiced by the introduction of disputed testimony to meet his burden under the Strickland/Fennell test where the sum of the evidence against him was overwhelming. State v. Killam, 137 N.H. 155, 626 A.2d 401, 1993 N.H. LEXIS 55 (1993).

310. —Conflict of interest

Because conflict of interest rules of N.H. R. Prof. Conduct 1.10 and 1.7 applied to public defenders and appellate defenders, which functioned as a single firm, defendant's appeal of an incompetency ruling under RSA 135:17-a was stayed until a lower court ruled on the merits of defendant's ineffective assistance of counsel claim against the public defender and any actual conflict of interest. State v. Veale, 154 N.H. 730, 919 A.2d 794, 2007 N.H. LEXIS 18 (2007).

In claims of ineffective assistance of counsel based on an alleged conflict of interest unrelated to multiple representation, standard of Cuyler v. Sullivan, 446 U.S. 335, 100 S. Ct. 1708, 64 L. Ed. 2d 333, 1980 U.S. LEXIS 96 (1980), is applicable; defendant must demonstrate that an actual conflict of interest adversely affected his lawyer's performance. State v. Cyrs, 129 N.H. 497, 529 A.2d 947, 1987 N.H. LEXIS 209 (1987).

Reversal of conviction was required based on ineffective assistance of counsel, where the state had actual knowledge that defendant's attorney was a subject of the same criminal investigation which resulted in the indictment of his client. State v. Cyrs, 129 N.H. 497, 529 A.2d 947, 1987 N.H. LEXIS 209 (1987).

When a defendant has not objected at trial to his lawyer's simultaneous representation of more than one of the defendants, in order to demonstrate a denial of effective assistance of counsel, a defendant must establish that an actual conflict of interest adversely affected his lawyer's performance. Hopps v. State Bd. of Parole, 127 N.H. 133, 500 A.2d 355, 1985 N.H. LEXIS 443 (1985).

311. —Contingent fee

Test for determining whether an attorney's representation of a criminal defendant under a contingent fee agreement is constitutionally defective is whether there was an actual conflict of interest which adversely affected the attorney's performance. State v. Labonville, 126 N.H. 451, 492 A.2d 1376, 1985 N.H. LEXIS 302 (1985).

312. —Tactics and strategy

Defendant's attorneys' failure to object to a police witness's redirect examination testimony was not constitutionally deficient under N.H. Const. pt. I, art. 15, as any objection to the failure by the State to disclose her as an expert witness would not have been

successful; further, counsel's decision to cross-examine the witness and expose defendant to the potentially detrimental redirect examination testimony was a calculated risk within the limits of reasonable practice. State v. Eschenbrenner, 164 N.H. 532, 62 A.3d 820, 2013 N.H. LEXIS 8 (2013).

Counsel was not ineffective under the Sixth and Fourteenth Amendments and N.H. Const. pt. I, art. 15 for failing to request an instruction on voluntary renunciation. Counsel made a strategic decision to challenge the attempted murder charge by arguing that defendant did not possess the requisite mens rea, and this decision to pursue one viable defense over another was a tactical decision that fell within the wide range of reasonable professional assistance. State v. Brown, 160 N.H. 408, 999 A.2d 295, 2010 N.H. LEXIS 70 (June 30, 2010).

Counsel was not ineffective for failing to request jury instructions on various lesser-included offenses of attempted first-degree murder. Trial counsel and defendant chose to pursue an all-or-nothing strategy, eliminating the possibility of a compromise verdict; under this strategy, which was not unreasonable, trial counsel could concede that defendant was guilty of a lesser-included offense, but could argue that he was not guilty of the charged offense. State v. Brown, 160 N.H. 408, 999 A.2d 295, 2010 N.H. LEXIS 70 (June 30, 2010).

Defendant's representation was not constitutionally deficient under N.H. Const. art. I, § 15 or the Sixth Amendment because trial counsel failed to object to the admission of a tape recording of the victim's side of a phone conversation with defendant as victim impact evidence under N.H. R. Evid. 403 since: (1) the victim's side of the conversation came from a script prepared by the investigating officers, and (2) the tape recording had no capacity to inflame the passions of a reasonable juror. State v. Kepple, 155 N.H. 267, 922 A.2d 661, 2007 N.H. LEXIS 52 (2007).

Defendant's representation was not constitutionally deficient under N.H. Const. art. I, § 15 or the Sixth Amendment because trial counsel failed to object to the prosecutor's comparison of defendant to a "jungle animal" as: (1) the prosecutor used the term "predator," which was a term of art in the realm of sexual offenses as RSA ch. 135-E bore the title "Involuntary Civil Commitment of Sexually Violent Predators," and (2) if the prosecutor's use of the predator analogy was improper, it was only marginally so; defendant failed to show a reasonable probability that the result of defendant's trial would have been different if trial counsel had objected to the prosecutor's predator analogy. State v. Kepple, 155 N.H. 267, 922 A.2d 661, 2007 N.H. LEXIS 52 (2007).

Defense counsel's decision not to call inmate as witness was a classic tactical choice that did not amount to ineffective assistance of counsel, where trial court had indicated it would probably allow a county attorney to rebut inmate by vouching for truthfulness of prosecution witness whose testimony inmate would have impeached. State v. Croft, 145 N.H. 90, 749 A.2d 1284, 2000 N.H. LEXIS 24 (2000).

Defendant failed to demonstrate deficient performance in his attorneys' tactical decision not to investigate statements made by two putative witnesses. State v. Seymour, 140 N.H. 736, 673 A.2d 786, 1996 N.H. LEXIS 24 (1996), cert. denied, Seymour v. New Hampshire, 519 U.S. 853, 117 S. Ct. 146, 136 L. Ed. 2d 93, 1996 U.S. LEXIS 5265 (1996).

Where defense counsel stated he was not aware of whether there were so-called experts on "blood drying times," defendant did not suggest that such experts existed or were available or would have provided evidence favorable to him, and defense counsel developed a time-of-death theory through other witnesses, defendant did not show that his counsel's performance was not adequate in this area. State v. Seymour, 140 N.H. 736, 673 A.2d 786, 1996 N.H. LEXIS 24 (1996), cert. denied, Seymour v. New Hampshire, 519 U.S. 853, 117 S. Ct. 146, 136 L. Ed. 2d 93, 1996 U.S. LEXIS 5265 (1996).

Reviewing court affords a high degree of deference to strategic decisions of trial counsel, bearing in mind the limitless variety of strategic and tactical decisions that counsel must make. State v. Seymour, 140 N.H. 736, 673 A.2d 786, 1996 N.H. LEXIS 24 (1996), cert. denied, Seymour v. New Hampshire, 519 U.S. 853, 117 S. Ct. 146, 136 L. Ed. 2d 93, 1996 U.S. LEXIS 5265 (1996).

The defendant was not denied effective assistance of counsel when his counsel opened the door to evidence of a prior arrest. Counsel's conduct was a calculated risk falling within the limits of reasonable practice and the court gave a limiting instruction to the jury. State v. Fecteau, 140 N.H. 498, 667 A.2d 1384, 1995 N.H. LEXIS 178 (1995).

The defendant was not denied effective assistance of counsel when defendant and his counsel made a tactical decision not to pursue depositions prior to entering a plea after receiving a plea offer letter which stated that it could be withdrawn by the state upon the filing of motions or taking of depositions by defense counsel. State v. Laforest, 140 N.H. 286, 665 A.2d 1083, 1995 N.H. LEXIS 142 (1995).

The defendant was not deprived of effective assistance of counsel where, during opening statements, his trial counsel urged the jury to find him guilty of a lesser-included, uncharged offense and charges for resisting arrest, but to acquit him of two felony charges where the trial court found that the plaintiff authorized the concession of guilt. Reid v. Warden, New Hampshire State Prison, 139 N.H. 530, 659 A.2d 429, 1995 N.H. LEXIS 45 (1995).

Defense counsel's presentation of the insanity defense at trial, even though it ultimately proved unsuccessful, was not clearly indicative of deficient representation, especially as, in light of the obvious strength of the state's case, the insanity defense might well have been one of the few options available to the defendant's attorney at trial. State v. Wisowaty, 137 N.H. 298, 627 A.2d 572, 1993 N.H. LEXIS 74 (1993).

At trial for aggravated felonious sexual assault on two eight-year-old girls, defense counsel's decision to question defendant about his prior arrest for indecent exposure did not deprive defendant of his right to effective assistance of counsel where counsel's strategy was to show that a lifeguard had upset one girl's mother by telling her of the prior arrest and that the lifeguard and the mother coerced the children into fabricating the charges against defendant. State v. Morse, 135 N.H. 565, 607 A.2d 619, 1992 N.H. LEXIS 79 (1992).

At trial for being accomplice to first degree murder in which defense counsel argued in favor of jury's conviction of defendant on lesser-included offense of being accomplice to second degree murder, defendant adequately objected to his counsel's strategy, for purposes of asserting ineffective assistance of counsel on appeal, where he refused to accept proposed plea agreement to admit guilt to the lesser offense, testified at trial as to his innocence to both charges, and urged counsel, at close of the evidence, to argue his total innocence in closing argument. State v. Anaya, 134 N.H. 346, 592 A.2d 1142, 1991 N.H. LEXIS 68 (1991).

Defendant was deprived of effective assistance of counsel, requiring reversal of conviction for being accomplice to second degree murder and remand for new trial, where defense counsel presumptively prejudiced defendant's constitutional rights by urging jury to convict on lesser-included offense, despite defendants' express desire that counsel argue defendant's total innocence. State v. Anaya, 134 N.H. 346, 592 A.2d 1142, 1991 N.H. LEXIS 68 (1991).

For purposes of ineffective assistance of counsel analysis, under both state and federal constitutions, the test of the propriety of defense counsel's strategy to argue in favor of jury's conviction of defendant on lesser-included offense of crime charged was whether defendant authorized counsel to make this argument, particularly where defendant expressly rejected counsel's proposed argument during client consultation at the close of the evidence. State v. Anaya, 134 N.H. 346, 592 A.2d 1142, 1991 N.H. LEXIS 68 (1991).

Tactical decision of counsel not to call witnesses at the sentencing hearing did not violate defendant's right to effective assistance of counsel. State v. Glidden, 127 N.H. 359, 499 A.2d 1349, 1985 N.H. LEXIS 438 (1985).

Right to effective assistance of counsel was not denied on the grounds that counsel should have used as a defense to the criminal charges defendant's alleged chronic alcoholism, where counsel reasonably determined that pursuit of this defense would be ineffectual. State v. Glidden, 127 N.H. 359, 499 A.2d 1349, 1985 N.H. LEXIS 438 (1985).

313. —Argument of counsel

Defendant's representation was not constitutionally deficient under N.H. Const. art. I, § 15 or the Sixth Amendment because trial counsel failed to argue that the evidence did not support a finding that defendant owed the victim a duty of care as: (1) defendant's precise affinal relationship to the victim was not an element of an offense under RSA 639:3, I, and (2) defendant owed the victim a duty of care as defendant's contact with the victim came about through familial channels, and the arrangements for the victim's contact with defendant on the day of the assault were made between two adult family members. State v. Kepple, 155 N.H. 267, 922 A.2d 661, 2007 N.H. LEXIS 52 (2007).

Right to effective assistance of counsel was not denied, under the circumstances, due to counsel's use of inappropriate language during closing argument, where counsel had consistently maintained his theory of defense throughout the trial. State v. Glidden, 127 N.H. 359, 499 A.2d 1349, 1985 N.H. LEXIS 438 (1985).

It was clear that purportedly inculpatory statements made by trial counsel during opening argument were reasonable tactics designed to weaken, in advance, any testimony that might be given by the victim's spouse; further, there was no showing that defendant's outcome had been prejudiced. State v. Flynn, 151 N.H. 378, 855 A.2d 1254, 2004 N.H. LEXIS 158 (2004).

314. —Appeals

The defendant failed to establish ineffective assistance of counsel because he failed to demonstrate a reasonable probability that, but for his counsel's failure to preserve the record, his conviction would have been reversed on appeal, and that the verdict on a subsequent retrial would be different. State v. Sanchez, 140 N.H. 162, 663 A.2d 629, 1995 N.H. LEXIS 117 (1995).

If counsel has not fulfilled his duty to see to it that an adequate record is before the appellate court, he has not provided that advocacy which permits full consideration and resolution of his appeal as required by this article. State v. Staples, 121 N.H. 959, 437 A.2d 266, 1981 N.H. LEXIS 441 (1981).

315. —Objection to instructions

The defendant's right to effective assistance of counsel was violated when the defendant's trial counsel inadvertently submitted a jury instruction to the trial court that expanded the grand jury indictment in such a way as to negate the defense presented by the defendant at trial. State v. Henderson, 141 N.H. 615, 689 A.2d 1336, 1997 N.H. LEXIS 13 (1997).

316. Habitual offender proceedings

Since the results of hearings held pursuant to RSA 262:21 to determine habitual offender status under the motor vehicle laws are civil rather than criminal in nature, they do not give rise to any right to counsel under this article, which applies only to criminal cases when deprivation of liberty is possible. State v. Cook, 125 N.H. 452, 481 A.2d 823, 1984 N.H. LEXIS 300 (1984).

Imprisonment pursuant to RSA 262:23, governing penalty for violation of an habitual offender order issued pursuant to RSA 262:22, does not violate the right to counsel provided by this article when the order rests upon uncounselled convictions for motor vehicle violations, since the risk of unreliable motor vehicle convictions in the absence of counsel is small and the burden on the public from requiring counsel in all motor vehicle violation cases would be very heavy. State v. Cook, 125 N.H. 452, 481 A.2d 823, 1984 N.H. LEXIS 300 (1984).

317. Contempt proceedings

A possible loss of liberty for civil contempt will not automatically give rise to a right to counsel under the due process standards of this article. State v. Cook, 125 N.H. 452, 481 A.2d 823, 1984 N.H. LEXIS 300 (1984).

This article does not guarantee assistance of counsel in a civil contempt action, as the term "offense" refers to public, not private, wrongs. Duval v. Duval, 114 N.H. 422, 322 A.2d 1, 1974 N.H. LEXIS 292 (1974).

318. Indigents

Defendant was not automatically entitled to appointed counsel under N.H. Const. pt. I, art. 15 relating to a postconviction motion for new trial; however, the trial court had discretion to appoint counsel for the motion for new trial, and since defendant's motion was denied without explanation, remand was required. State v. Hall, 154 N.H. 180, 908 A.2d 766, 2006 N.H. LEXIS 141 (2006).

Because a defendant facing no loss of liberty does not have a right to appointed counsel at trial, he does not have such a right at the appellate level, where the constitutional concerns are lessened. State v. Westover, 140 N.H. 375, 666 A.2d 1344, 1995 N.H. LEXIS 159 (1995).

An indigent criminal defendant is entitled at public expense to the services that provide the working tools essential to the establishment of a tenable defense, without which the right to counsel would be meaningless. In re Allen R., 127 N.H. 718, 506 A.2d 329, 1986 N.H. LEXIS 210 (1986).

The right to counsel, as guaranteed by this article, would be meaningless if counsel for an indigent defendant is denied the use of the working tools essential to the establishment of a tenable defense because there are no funds to pay for these items; therefore, the state must provide the defense with these tools. State v. Robinson, 123 N.H. 665, 465 A.2d 1214, 1983 N.H. LEXIS 331 (1983).

While all indigent defendants have constitutional right to court-appointed counsel, it is not required that they remain forever immune from any obligation to shoulder expenses of legal defense. Opinion of Justices, 121 N.H. 531, 431 A.2d 144, 1981 N.H. LEXIS 342 (1981).

This article requires that the cost of services rendered by attorneys on behalf of indigent defendants be borne by the state. Smith v. State, 118 N.H. 764, 394 A.2d 834, 1978 N.H. LEXIS 289, 3 A.L.R.4th 568 (1978).

Where this article requires that the state provide legal representation for indigent defendants and the state transferred a major part of its own burden onto the shoulders of the New Hampshire bar by means of a statutory compensation scheme for court-appointed attorneys, such statutes are unconstitutional insofar as they shift much of the state's obligation to the legal profession and intrude impermissibly upon an exclusive judicial function to determine the reasonableness of compensation for court-appointed counsel. Smith v. State, 118 N.H. 764, 394 A.2d 834, 1978 N.H. LEXIS 289, 3 A.L.R.4th 568 (1978).

Footnote in appropriation bill making indigent defendants personally responsible for certain percentage of legal fees of court-appointed counsel which applied to defendant who had no funds and no probability of acquiring any either because of imprisonment or destitution was invalid as being in conflict with this article. Opinion of Justices, 109 N.H. 508, 256 A.2d 500, 1969 N.H. LEXIS 193 (1969).

319. Fees

Requiring an acquitted defendant to reimburse the State under RSA 604-A:9, I for the costs of his appointed counsel was constitutional under N.H. Const. pt. I, art. 15 and U.S. Const. amend. 14 where the statute's purpose was to require that those who were financially able to do so, pay for a service that they received from the State, there was nothing illegitimate in the governmental interest in recouping costs expended for public defense whether or not a defendant was convicted, and the statutory scheme was rationally related to that purpose in that it inquired into a defendant's ability to pay and outlined procedures for recoupment order, collection, and appeal of such orders. State v. Haas, 155 N.H. 612, 927 A.2d 1209, 2007 N.H. LEXIS 102 (2007), rehearing denied, 2007 N.H. LEXIS 134 (N.H. July 26, 2007).

Court-appointed attorneys should be paid a reasonable fee, but one somewhat less than that which an ordinary fee-paying client would pay. Smith v. State, 118 N.H. 764, 394 A.2d 834, 1978 N.H. LEXIS 289, 3 A.L.R.4th 568 (1978).

320. Uncounselled convictions

Defendant's right to counsel was not violated by trial court's revocation of her suspended sentence, based on her prior, uncounseled class B misdemeanor conviction. State v. Weeks, 141 N.H. 248, 681 A.2d 86, 1996 N.H. LEXIS 85 (1996).

Use of an uncounselled conviction for driving while intoxicated to convert the sentence for a subsequent offense for driving while intoxicated into a term of imprisonment does not violate the right to counsel guaranteed by this article. State v. Jacobson, 125 N.H. 838, 485 A.2d 1048 (1984).

321. Right to counsel for misdemeanor appeal

The defendant was not entitled to appointed counsel for his class B misdemeanor appeal where the maximum fine for the offense at issue set by the legislature was $1,200. State v. Westover, 140 N.H. 375, 666 A.2d 1344, 1995 N.H. LEXIS 159 (1995).

322. Right to counsel in appeals of denial of postconviction relief

Under N.H. Const. pt. I, art. 15, a defendant has no right to counsel in a collateral challenge to a conviction based on a guilty plea; thus, he has no such right on appeal of the denial of the collateral challenge. But if the defendant can show that "complicating factors" such as those identified in State v. Hall, 154 N.H. 180, 908 A.2d 766, 2006 N.H. LEXIS 141 (2006), are present— the defendant's capability to speak for himself, the character of the proceeding, the complexity of the issues, or other circumstances showing the defendant would be treated unfairly if not represented —appellate counsel may be appointed. State v. Lopez, 156 N.H. 193, 931 A.2d 1186, 2007 N.H. LEXIS 166 (2007).

Inmate had no right to counsel under N.H. Const. pt. I, Art. 15 in an appeal of a collateral challenge to a conviction based on a guilty plea; as the record did not contain any evidence that the inmate would have directly appealed his plea had he been correctly advised, counsel's alleged incorrect advice, standing alone, did not complicate the inmate's challenge to his plea-conviction to the extent that appellate counsel was required under the guidelines established by State v. Hall, 154 N.H. 180, 908 A.2d 766, 2006 N.H. LEXIS 141 (2006). State v. Lopez, 156 N.H. 193, 931 A.2d 1186, 2007 N.H. LEXIS 166 (2007).

323. Child in need of services proceedings

Because the Supreme Court of New Hampshire has not yet held that a juvenile in a child-in-need-of-services (CHINS) proceeding has a due process right to counsel and because it has not been established that such a right exists, the court necessarily rejects the assertion that, to be able to exercise this right, the Due Process Clause of the State Constitution requires that a juvenile be adjudged competent to stand trial before being adjudicated a CHINS. As the United States Supreme Court has also not yet established a due process right to counsel in a CHINS case, the court rejects this assertion under the Federal Constitution for the same reason. In re Kotey M., 158 N.H. 358, 965 A.2d 1146, 2009 N.H. LEXIS 15 (2009).

324. Sentencing

Counsel was not ineffective for failing to strongly advise defendant not to pursue sentence review. There were a letter asking for leniency from the victim's mother, a presentence investigation report recommending a lighter sentence, and several mitigating factors; furthermore, it was defendant who decided to pursue sentence review because he was focused upon reducing his minimum sentence. State v. Hall, 160 N.H. 581, 8 A.3d 12, 2010 N.H. LEXIS 89 (2010).

VIII. Jury Trial

325. Abuse or neglect proceedings

On balance, due process under N.H. Const. pt. I, arts. 2 and 15 or the Fourteenth Amendment does not require that indigent parents have a per se right to appointed counsel in abuse or neglect proceedings under RSA ch. 169-C. While due process does not require that counsel be appointed for indigent parents in every proceeding brought under RSA ch. 169-C, a determination of whether appointed counsel is necessary to adequately reduce the risk of erroneous deprivation should be made on a case-by-case basis in the first instance by the trial court. In re C.M., 163 N.H. 768, 48 A.3d 942, 2012 N.H. LEXIS 85 (2012).

351. Generally

Penalty provisions of drug enterprise leader statute did not impermissibly burden defendant's right to jury trial, by encouraging defendant to enter a negotiated plea or post-conviction agreement in order to avoid a twenty-five-year mandatory minimum sentence. State v. Marcano, 138 N.H. 643, 645 A.2d 661, 1994 N.H. LEXIS 82 (1994).

It is a fundamental precept of our system of justice that a defendant has the right to be tried by a fair and impartial jury. State v. VandeBogart, 136 N.H. 107, 612 A.2d 906, 1992 N.H. LEXIS 145 (1992).

Right to jury trial does not include the option to specify where and when the right will be executed. Opinion of Justices, 135 N.H. 549, 608 A.2d 874, 1992 N.H. LEXIS 214 (1992).

On interlocutory appeal at trial for capital murder, the trial court properly ruled that statute in effect at time of trial could not be retrospectively applied and capital punishment procedures under statute in effect at time of crime, which permitted jury to consider imposition of death penalty only where jury had rendered guilty verdict and not where defendant had pled guilty, could not be enforced as statute was unconstitutional on its face. State v. Johnson, 134 N.H. 570, 595 A.2d 498, 1991 N.H. LEXIS 101 (1991).

Provisions of United States Constitution, as well as this article guarantee every criminal defendant the right to a jury trial. State v. Williams, 133 N.H. 631, 581 A.2d 78, 1990 N.H. LEXIS 111 (1990).

The right to a jury trial is a fundamental one under the New Hampshire Constitution in both the civil and the criminal contexts. State v. Morrill, 123 N.H. 707, 465 A.2d 882, 1983 N.H. LEXIS 338 (1983).

Right to a jury trial for a criminal defendant is fundamental to our system of criminal justice. State v. Cushing, 119 N.H. 147, 399 A.2d 297, 1979 N.H. LEXIS 256 (1979).

352. When required

Patient who was under a psychiatrist's care was not entitled to a trial by jury in an action which was filed by a state hospital, seeking the patient's involuntary commitment, and the state supreme court found that the record was sufficient to sustain the probate court's judgment ordering that the patient be involuntarily committed for up to two years. In re Sandra H., 150 N.H. 634, 846 A.2d 513, 2004 N.H. LEXIS 43 (2004), rehearing denied, 2004 N.H. LEXIS 84 (N.H. Apr. 23, 2004).

This article guarantees criminal defendants right to trial by jury either in the first instance or on appeal to superior court. Opinion of Justices, 135 N.H. 538, 608 A.2d 202, 1992 N.H. LEXIS 213 (1992).

Legislative enactment entirely eliminating right to jury trial and providing maximum sentence of six months imprisonment would violate this article. Opinion of Justices, 135 N.H. 538, 608 A.2d 202, 1992 N.H. LEXIS 213 (1992).

The right to a jury trial under the New Hampshire Constitution is not without limitation; it extends only to those cases for which the jury trial right existed when the constitution was adopted in 1784, and New Hampshire does not require as a matter of constitutional right that a jury trial be available even for petty criminal offenses. State v. Morrill, 123 N.H. 707, 465 A.2d 882, 1983 N.H. LEXIS 338 (1983).

A fine exceeding $500, the amount presently established as constitutionally entitling civil litigants to a jury trial, cannot be levied against individuals charged with offenses under the penal code, without granting them a jury trial on appeal. State v. Morrill, 123 N.H. 707, 465 A.2d 882, 1983 N.H. LEXIS 338 (1983).

This article guarantees the right of trial by jury in all cases where the right existed at common law in this state at the time of the adoption of the constitution. State ex rel. Cunningham v. Ray, 63 N.H. 406, 1885 N.H. LEXIS 55 (1885).

353. Public trial

In a prosecution for aggravated felonious sexual assault and felonious sexual assault, the trial court violated the defendant's constitutional right to a public trial by requiring him to show good cause why the courtroom should not be closed during the victim's testimony. State v. Weber, 137 N.H. 193, 624 A.2d 967, 1993 N.H. LEXIS 60 (1993).

354. Right to be present at trial—Generally

The defendant's right to be present at trial derives from the specific rights to produce all favorable proofs, confront witnesses, and be fully heard in one's defense, as well as the right to due process. State v. Castle, 128 N.H. 649, 517 A.2d 848, 1986 N.H. LEXIS 341 (1986).

Trial court's determination that defendant's waiver was voluntary was not against the manifest weight of the evidence where the judge reviewed videotapes of defendant's interview which showed defendant as articulate and comprehending. State v. Plch, 149 N.H. 608, 826 A.2d 534, 2003 N.H. LEXIS 93 (2003), cert. denied, Vaclav Plch v. New Hampshire, 540 U.S. 1009, 124 S. Ct. 546, 157 L. Ed. 2d 419, 2003 U.S. LEXIS 8294 (2003).

355. Waiver of right

While a detective's statements regarding defendant's disclosure of the location of the victim's body parts were reasonably likely to evoke an incriminating response from defendant who had invoked his right to counsel, the incriminating statements were admissible given the significant time lapse of one hour before defendant's self-initiated statements. State v. Plch, 149 N.H. 608, 826 A.2d 534,

2003 N.H. LEXIS 93 (2003), cert. denied, Vaclav Plch v. New Hampshire, 540 U.S. 1009, 124 S. Ct. 546, 157 L. Ed. 2d 419, 2003 U.S. LEXIS 8294 (2003).

Although it would have been advisable for the court to have secured an express waiver of jury trial directly from a defendant, it was not constitutionally mandated nor statutorily required and, where the waiver was knowing, intelligent and voluntary, it was proper. State v. Foote, 149 N.H. 323, 821 A.2d 1072, 2003 N.H. LEXIS 46 (2003).

Defendant's constitutional right to jury trial was not violated by superior court's denial of motion to reinstate, in that forum, defendant's appeal from district court requesting a trial de novo by jury, where defendant failed to appear in superior court and prosecute his appeal; contention was rejected that defendant could only waive his jury trial right with an express personal waiver indicating his understanding of that right. State v. Bousquet, 133 N.H. 485, 578 A.2d 853, 1990 N.H. LEXIS 84 (1990), cert. denied, Bousquet v. New Hampshire, 498 U.S. 1035, 111 S. Ct. 700, 112 L. Ed. 2d 690, 1991 U.S. LEXIS 241 (1991), US Supreme Crt. cert. denied, Adamu v. United States, 498 U.S. 1036, 111 S. Ct. 700, 112 L. Ed. 2d 690, 1991 U.S. LEXIS 223 (1991).

356. Number of jurors

Regardless of the procedural mechanisms employed, late substitution does not in itself violate a defendant's right to a 12 person jury. State v. Colbert, 139 N.H. 367, 654 A.2d 963, 1995 N.H. LEXIS 6 (1995).

State constitution mandates that jury of twelve must unanimously reach verdict of guilty before defendant's liberty may be compromised. State v. Dushame, 136 N.H. 309, 616 A.2d 469, 1992 N.H. LEXIS 173 (1992).

An accused felon's right to trial by jury as guaranteed by the state constitution is a right to a jury of twelve. State v. Hewitt, 128 N.H. 557, 517 A.2d 820, 1986 N.H. LEXIS 336 (1986).

Where a juror was excused in the course of defendant's trial for forgery, leaving an eleven-person jury panel, which rendered a guilty verdict, the defendant's silence and his counsel's acceptance of the depleted panel were not sufficient to waive the right to trial by a full jury; in these circumstances, a personal waiver by the defendant, indicating his understanding of the right to a full jury, was required to effectuate the constitutional guarantee. State v. Hewitt, 128 N.H. 557, 517 A.2d 820, 1986 N.H. LEXIS 336 (1986).

357. Selection by jury

This article requires that any discussion by the court with a venire panelist during the process of jury selection be recorded. State v. Bailey, 127 N.H. 416, 503 A.2d 762, 1985 N.H. LEXIS 461 (1985).

The constitutional guaranty of right of trial by jury does not guarantee to the accused any particular mode or manner of selecting such jury so long as the jury finally selected and sworn to try the case is impartial. State v. Wilson, 48 N.H. 398, 1869 N.H. LEXIS 46 (1869).

358. Alternate jurors

When the trial court replaced a juror with an alternate under RSA 500-A:13, it should have asked each remaining juror whether he or she could and would start the deliberations anew. Each juror should be certain of his or her ability to set aside all opinions and conclusions formed during prior deliberations; only in cases where this is possible is a defendant's constitutional right to have a jury of 12 arrive at a common verdict sufficiently protected in the event that it becomes necessary to seat an alternate juror after the commencement of deliberations. State v. Sullivan, 157 N.H. 124, 949 A.2d 140, 2008 N.H. LEXIS 48 (2008).

The late substitution of an alternate juror does not violate a defendant's right to a trial by jury under part I, article 15 of the New Hampshire Constitution, so long as procedural mechanisms are utilized to protect the parties' rights, including establishing a valid reason for juror discharge, polling the substitute for bias, and instructing the jury to begin deliberating anew. State v. Colbert, 139 N.H. 367, 654 A.2d 963, 1995 N.H. LEXIS 6 (1995).

Substitution of alternate jurors after deliberations have begun is constitutionally permissible when procedural mechanisms are utilized to protect the parties' rights. Opinion of Justices, 137 N.H. 100, 623 A.2d 1334, 1993 N.H. LEXIS 48 (1993).

Alternate jurors may be substituted after deliberations have begun only where the discharge of a particular juror is for a meritorious reason; it is to be done only in special circumstances and with special precautions, and great care must be taken to ensure that a lone dissenting juror is not permitted to evade his responsibilities. Opinion of Justices, 137 N.H. 100, 623 A.2d 1334, 1993 N.H. LEXIS 48 (1993).

When substituting alternate jurors after deliberations have begun, the trial court must instruct the jury to set aside and disregard all past deliberations and begin deliberating anew, the trial court must make a finding on the record that the alternate juror has not been tainted subsequent to the original panel retiring to deliberate, the remaining jurors must affirmatively state that they can and will start the deliberations anew, and the trial court must find on the record that, taking into consideration the circumstances of the particular case, recommencing deliberations is practically feasible. Opinion of Justices, 137 N.H. 100, 623 A.2d 1334, 1993 N.H. LEXIS 48 (1993).

359. Issues determined by jury

Although there was an expectation in New Hampshire that evidence would be taken into the jury room, it was not a right of constitutional proportions; therefore, when an item of evidence was inadvertently left out, the high court engaged in harmless error analysis, and, finding no prejudice, let the verdict stand. State v. MacDonald, 150 N.H. 237, 836 A.2d 764, 2003 N.H. LEXIS 170 (2003).

Defendant's due process rights were not violated under N.H. Const. pt. I, art. 15 where the trial court did not allow him to argue self-defense or receive a jury instruction on the issue but did allow defendant to cross-examine the victim in regard to self-defense where defendant did not file a self-defense claim prior to trial pursuant to N.H. Super. Ct. R. 101 and there was no evidence supporting self-defense other than defendant's assertion that one week prior to defendant throwing hot oil on the victim three different times, there was an incident which led defendant to believe that the victim would assault defendant. State v. Ke Tong Chen, 148 N.H. 565, 813 A.2d 424, 2002 N.H. LEXIS 169 (2002).

In a prosecution for manslaughter, the court committed reversible error when it refused to allow the defendant to introduce evidence that medical negligence actually caused the victim's death. Since the issue of whether the defendant caused the death of the victim was a factual element of the crime, the proper role of the trial court was to determine the proper supervening cause test, admit the appropriate medical evidence relevant to whether that test was met, and instruct the jury as to that test. State v. Soucy, 139 N.H. 349, 653 A.2d 561, 1995 N.H. LEXIS 4 (1995).

The provision of this article establishing the right to a jury trial in criminal cases entitles a defendant to a jury determination on all factual elements of a crime, but this right does not extend to consideration of questions of law; these issues obviously fall within the domain of the trial court. State v. Sands, 123 N.H. 570, 467 A.2d 202, 1983 N.H. LEXIS 362, 37 A.L.R.4th 904 (1983).

One who pleads guilty to an indictment for murder, upon which conviction either in the first or in the second degree is warranted, has no constitutional right to a trial by jury to determine the degree of his guilt. State v. Almy, 67 N.H. 274, 28 A. 372, 1892 N.H. LEXIS 44, 22 L.R.A. 744 (1892).

360. Impartial jury

Trial court properly denied defendant's motion to set aside the verdict after finding that the jury had not reached a compromise verdict, as jurors' use of the word "compromise" could appropriately describe the give and take which customarily occurred in jury deliberations. State v. Fandozzi, 159 N.H. 773, 992 A.2d 685, 2010 N.H. LEXIS 19 (2010).

Instructing the jury that defendant had been indicted for the unrelated shooting of a police officer did not violate defendant's rights to a fair trial before an impartial jury under N.H. Const. pt. I, arts. 15, 17, and 35 and U.S. Const. amends. V, VI, and XIV. The charge was given to determine whether each juror could lay aside impressions or opinions and render a verdict based upon the evidence presented in court; furthermore, the trial judge called all potential jurors to the bench individually to question them about possible bias and was able to observe each juror's demeanor and make her own determination regarding his or her credibility. State v. Addison, 160 N.H. 493, 8 A.3d 53, 2010 N.H. LEXIS 78 (2010).

Defendant's right to an impartial jury was not violated where a juror posted derogatory and biased opinions regarding criminal defendants and judicial process in a blog, which was available to public and other jurors, because defendant did not allege any other jurors even knew of the blog, and the statement, on its face, did not reference anything specifically related to defendant's case. State v. Goupil, 154 N.H. 208, 908 A.2d 1256, 2006 N.H. LEXIS 146 (2006).

Defendant failed to establish that a "distinctive group" or "cognizable class" was excluded from his jury venire in violation of N.H. Const. pt. I, art. 15, as the trial court excluded those who indicated that they would suffer economic difficulty of having to serve on a jury for multiple weeks; accordingly, there was no violation of his right to a jury comprised of a fair cross-section of the community. State v. Ayer, 150 N.H. 14, 834 A.2d 277, 2003 N.H. LEXIS 133 (2003), cert. denied, Ayer v. New Hampshire, 124 S. Ct. 1668, 158 L. Ed. 2d 366, 2004 U.S. LEXIS 2130 (2004).

Where the court's inquiry into alleged jury misconduct, including the decision not to conduct individual juror voir dire, was not error, there was no violation of a defendant's right to be tried by a fair and impartial jury under the New Hampshire Constitution or the United States Constitution. State v. Bader, 148 N.H. 265, 808 A.2d 12, 2002 N.H. LEXIS 123 (2002), cert. denied, Bader v. New Hampshire, 538 U.S. 1014, 123 S. Ct. 1945, 155 L. Ed. 2d 850, 2003 U.S. LEXIS 3498 (2003).

Where State was permitted to obtain criminal records of potential jurors for use during jury selection, and any information as to discrepancies between selected jurors' questionnaires and their criminal record history was made equally available to parties for use in challenging selected jurors, either peremptorily or for cause, assault defendant's equal knowledge of criminal records of unselected members of jury venire was not constitutionally required to ensure ultimate impartiality of defendant's jury. State v. Goodale, 144 N.H. 224, 740 A.2d 1026, 1999 N.H. LEXIS 102 (1999).

A juror found to be disqualified at any time before or during trial should be removed from further service. State v. Rideout, 143 N.H. 363, 725 A.2d 8, 1999 N.H. LEXIS 10 (1999).

Although requests for excusals due to medical reasons and for inconvenience were improperly granted by the clerk, rather than by the court, and although the clerk failed to institute proceedings to pursue prospective jurors who failed to return their jury questionnaires, the defendant nonetheless was afforded a randomly selected pool of prospective jurors from a fair cross-section of the community. Therefore, he was not denied an impartial jury. State v. Martel, 141 N.H. 599, 689 A.2d 1327, 1997 N.H. LEXIS 10 (1997).

The trial court's finding that the jury was impartial did not constitute manifest error where no member of the defendant's jury expressed an opinion on voir dire that she was guilty and, importantly, none sat on her jury over her objection. State v. Smart, 136 N.H. 639, 622 A.2d 1197, 1993 N.H. LEXIS 11 (1993), cert. denied, Smart v. New Hampshire, 510 U.S. 917, 114 S. Ct. 309, 126 L. Ed. 2d 256, 1993 U.S. LEXIS 6384 (1993).

An "avalanche of media attention" to the murder for which the defendant was prosecuted did not give rise to a presumption of prejudice where the bulk of the publicity was merely factual reporting and an analysis of the material submitted by the defendant for review indicated that most of the items appeared after the jury had been selected and had been continually instructed by the trial court not to read or watch anything connected to the case. State v. Smart, 136 N.H. 639, 622 A.2d 1197, 1993 N.H. LEXIS 11 (1993), cert. denied, Smart v. New Hampshire, 510 U.S. 917, 114 S. Ct. 309, 126 L. Ed. 2d 256, 1993 U.S. LEXIS 6384 (1993).

The defendant was denied his right to an impartial jury when the court only asked one of three requested voir dire questions as all of the questions involved the credibility of police officers as witnesses and the single question asked provided the defendant with insufficient information to intelligently challenge potential jurors. State v. Jaroma, 137 N.H. 562, 630 A.2d 1173, 1993 N.H. LEXIS 121 (1993).

Ex parte discussions between the judge and venire panelists which occur without a record being made violate constitutional policy involving the defendant's right to an impartial jury, and also thwart effective appellate review. State v. Brodowski, 135 N.H. 197, 600 A.2d 925, 1991 N.H. LEXIS 166 (1991).

Due process requires that an accused receive a trial by a fair and impartial jury. State v. Laaman, 114 N.H. 794, 331 A.2d 354, 1974

N.H. LEXIS 377 (1974), cert. denied, Laaman v. New Hampshire, 423 U.S. 854, 96 S. Ct. 101, 46 L. Ed. 2d 79, 1975 U.S. LEXIS 2632 (1975).

Mere existence of a preconceived opinion as to guilt or innocence of accused is insufficient to rebut presumption of impartiality; it must be shown that juror cannot lay aside his impression or opinion and render a verdict on the evidence presented in court. State v. Laaman, 114 N.H. 794, 331 A.2d 354, 1974 N.H. LEXIS 377 (1974), cert. denied, Laaman v. New Hampshire, 423 U.S. 854, 96 S. Ct. 101, 46 L. Ed. 2d 79, 1975 U.S. LEXIS 2632 (1975).

Publicity can result either in inherent prejudice, which exists when, by its nature, the publicity has so tainted the trial atmosphere as to necessarily result in a lack of due process, in which case actual identifiable prejudice need not be shown, or in actual prejudice, which exists when publicity has infected the jurors to such an extent that the defendant cannot receive a fair trial, in which case it must be shown that the publicity induced the jurors to form opinions such that the jurors cannot set them aside and render a verdict based on the evidence presented in court. State v. Laaman, 114 N.H. 794, 331 A.2d 354, 1974 N.H. LEXIS 377 (1974), cert. denied, Laaman v. New Hampshire, 423 U.S. 854, 96 S. Ct. 101, 46 L. Ed. 2d 79, 1975 U.S. LEXIS 2632 (1975).

The constitutional guaranty of right of trial by jury guarantees to the accused a right of trial by an impartial jury, and not a jury partial to him or his cause. State v. Wilson, 48 N.H. 398, 1869 N.H. LEXIS 46 (1869).

361. Instructions

Informing jurors that defendant also faced a murder charge did not violate defendant's rights to due process, a fair trial, and a trial before a fair and impartial jury under N.H. Const. pt. I, arts. 15, 17, and 35 and U.S. Const. amends. V, VI, and XIV. In VandeBogart, the court had held that given the difficulty of selecting impartial jurors otherwise, the trial court was within its discretion in informing the venire that the defendant also faced a first-degree murder charge, and the same reasoning justified the use of the instruction here. State v. Addison, 161 N.H. 300, 13 A.3d 214, 2010 N.H. LEXIS 186 (2010), cert. denied, Addison v. New Hampshire, 131 S. Ct. 2107, 179 L. Ed. 2d 903, 2011 U.S. LEXIS 3106 (U.S. 2011).

Firearm was a deadly weapon under RSA 625:11, V, if, in the manner it was used, intended to be used, or threatened to be used, it was known to be capable of producing death or serious bodily injury. Thus, as to felony criminal threatening under RSA 631:4, it was error to instruct the jury that a shotgun was a deadly weapon per se; the error was not subject to harmless error analysis because under the state constitution, a jury instruction that omitted an element of the offense charged was an error that partially or completely denied a defendant the right to the basic trial process. State v. Kousounadis, 159 N.H. 413, 986 A.2d 603, 2009 N.H. LEXIS 136 (2009).

Under the New Hampshire Constitution, a jury instruction that omits an element of the offense charged is an error that partially or completely denies a defendant the right to the basic trial process, and thus is not subject to harmless error analysis. State v. Kousounadis, 159 N.H. 413, 986 A.2d 603, 2009 N.H. LEXIS 136 (2009).

Where a defendant took the stand and admitted an element of the charge against him, and maintained that admission throughout the trial, his right to jury trial under this article was not violated when the trial judge instructed the jury that the defendant had made that admission and that they need not consider that element of the offense. State v. O'Leary, 128 N.H. 661, 517 A.2d 1174, 1986 N.H. LEXIS 326 (1986).

362. Suspension of license

Statute requiring suspension of motor vehicle license after conviction in district or municipal court on charge of operating a motor vehicle while under the influence of intoxicating liquor and pending appeal to superior court for trial by jury is not an unconstitutional impairment of the right to trial by jury. State v. Despres, 107 N.H. 297, 220 A.2d 758, 1966 N.H. LEXIS 178 (1966).

A statute requiring the suspension of an automobile driver's license upon a conviction, in a municipal court, of drunken driving, and pending an appeal, is not unconstitutional because this may be done without a jury trial. State v. Wood, 98 N.H. 418, 101 A.2d 774, 1953 N.H. LEXIS 93 (1953).

363. Referees

A statute which provides for committing certain causes to referees for trial, and further provides an unfettered and absolute right of appeal to a court where the issues may be tried in their entirety before a jury, is not unconstitutional. Copp v. Henniker, 55 N.H. 179, 1875 N.H. LEXIS 59 (1875).

364. Court fees

Superior court rule requiring payment of an eight dollar fee to superior court before a misdemeanor appeal from a district or municipal court may be tried by jury is void only insofar as it relates to jury trials for criminal cases. State v. Cushing, 119 N.H. 147, 399 A.2d 297, 1979 N.H. LEXIS 256 (1979).

365. Sequestration of jury

A defendant challenging a trial court's denial of a motion to sequester the jury during trial must show that the court's ruling was unreasonable and prejudicial. State v. Smart, 136 N.H. 639, 622 A.2d 1197, 1993 N.H. LEXIS 11 (1993), cert. denied, Smart v. New Hampshire, 510 U.S. 917, 114 S. Ct. 309, 126 L. Ed. 2d 256, 1993 U.S. LEXIS 6384 (1993).

366. Jury misconduct

Although a juror told other jurors that the juror enjoyed watching people involved in defendant's trial from the juror's car during the lunch hour, and made comments regarding people she observed with the defendant leaving the courthouse, the remaining jurors stated that they could remain impartial; therefore, defendant's N.H. Const. pt. I, art. 15 and U.S. Const. amends VI, XIV rights to an impartial jury were not violated. State v. Brown, 154 N.H. 345, 910 A.2d 1203, 2006 N.H. LEXIS 168 (2006).

In a case where plaintiff received a jury verdict on claims that defendant violated the fiduciary duties of good faith and due diligence in conducting a foreclosure sale, the trial court did not err in denying defendant's motion to set aside the verdict based on juror misconduct because a disqualified juror's brief presence in the jury room did not affect the fairness or impartiality of the trial where deliberations had not begun. Anderson v. Smith, 150 N.H. 788, 846 A.2d 1165, 2004 N.H. LEXIS 69 (2004), rehearing denied, 2004 N.H. LEXIS 88 (N.H. May 12, 2004).

The trial court did not abuse its discretion in refusing to poll the jury based on the defendant's sheer conjecture that the jurors were deliberating in their separate motel rooms on the night they were sequestered or that they drank alcoholic beverages that evening. State v. Smart, 136 N.H. 639, 622 A.2d 1197, 1993 N.H. LEXIS 11 (1993), cert. denied, Smart v. New Hampshire, 510 U.S. 917, 114 S. Ct. 309, 126 L. Ed. 2d 256, 1993 U.S. LEXIS 6384 (1993).

The existence of tape-recorded recollections of a juror was not evidence of juror misconduct which required a new trial where the juror stated on the tapes that she made them for her personal use only and there was no evidence that she formed an intent to sell the tapes at any time during her service as a juror. State v. Smart, 136 N.H. 639, 622 A.2d 1197, 1993 N.H. LEXIS 11 (1993), cert. denied, Smart v. New Hampshire, 510 U.S. 917, 114 S. Ct. 309, 126 L. Ed. 2d 256, 1993 U.S. LEXIS 6384 (1993).

367. Right to fair trial

Jury charge on accident did not violate defendant's rights to due process and a fair trial under N.H. Const. pt. I, art. 15 and the Fourteenth Amendment. A reasonable juror would have understood from the instructions in their entirety that the State had the burden of proving beyond a reasonable doubt that defendant's conduct was not an accident. State v. Leveille, 160 N.H. 630, 7 A.3d 1175, 2010 N.H. LEXIS 95 (2010).

Although a prosecutor's comment regarding the credibility of police officers' testimony was improper because it was a personal assurance of credibility, the error was harmless; defendant confessed to injuring the victim, and defendant's confession was strongly corroborated by the medical evidence and testimony of the treating doctors, who testified that the victim's injuries could have been caused by the actions to which the defendant confessed. Therefore, defendant's right to a fair trial was not violated by the prosecutor's misconduct. State v. Mussey, 153 N.H. 272, 893 A.2d 701, 2006 N.H. LEXIS 20 (2006).

Defendant was not denied due process by trial court's refusal to order State to either grant immunity to her fiance, who she alleged would provide exculpatory evidence, or dismiss indictment, since fiance's proffered testimony fell short of being directly exculpatory and did not present a highly material variance from tenor of State's evidence. State v. Kivlin, 145 N.H. 718, 766 A.2d 274, 2001 N.H. LEXIS 12 (2001).

State failed to rebut presumption of prejudice arising from assistance provided to juror by prosecution witness during medical emergency. Therefore, reversal and remand for new trial was therefore required. State v. Rideout, 143 N.H. 363, 725 A.2d 8, 1999 N.H. LEXIS 10 (1999).

Prosecutor's inquiry into identity of witnesses and their availability for trial did not create impermissible inference of a missing witness, and there was no violation of due process where jury was clearly instructed that defendant did not have to produce any evidence; moreover, at close of case, court instructed jury on presumption of innocence and burden of proof in criminal cases. State v. Laurent, 144 N.H. 517, 744 A.2d 598, 1999 N.H. LEXIS 149 (1999).

Comments by defense counsel regarding State's missing witnesses opened the door to State's remarks concerning defendant's missing witnesses, and any harm caused by prosecutor was cured by trial court's curative and final jury instructions, in which it reiterated burden of proof in criminal cases and stated that defendant had no obligation to call any witnesses at all. State v. Laurent, 144 N.H. 517, 744 A.2d 598, 1999 N.H. LEXIS 149 (1999).

Child pornography defendant's right to due process and fair trial was not violated by introduction of evidence that police had received report of a man matching defendant's description approaching two children in same town as charged crimes. Report was not offered for its truth, but rather as relevant background information to explain conduct of police on day of charged crimes. State v. Cobb, 143 N.H. 638, 732 A.2d 425, 1999 N.H. LEXIS 53 (1999).

Consolidation of child pornography charges with attempted sexual assault charge did not deprive defendant of his rights to a fair trial or to testify in his own defense. Much of the evidence underlying the charges was the same, the court gave adequate instructions and typewritten verdict forms to jury, and defendant failed to make a convincing showing that he had important testimony to offer on pornography charges and a need to refrain from testifying on attempted sexual assault charge. State v. Cobb, 143 N.H. 638, 732 A.2d 425, 1999 N.H. LEXIS 53 (1999).

A defendant in custody may waive his right to attend court proceedings. State v. Davis, 139 N.H. 185, 650 A.2d 1386, 1994 N.H. LEXIS 132 (1994).

Defendant was not denied his right to due process by trial court's permitting State to amend bill of particulars four days before trial. State v. Crooker, 139 N.H. 226, 651 A.2d 470, 1994 N.H. LEXIS 128 (1994).

368. Unanimous jury

Jury instructions at assault trial did not violate defendant's right to jury unanimity under New Hampshire Constitution; although instructions did not require that all jurors agree on which object was used to inflict injury, instructions did require jury to be unanimous on essential elements of first degree assault. State v. Francoeur, 146 N.H. 83, 767 A.2d 429, 2001 N.H. LEXIS 31 (2001).

Right to jury unanimity as to each element of a criminal offense may ordinarily be satisfied through a general unanimity instruction. State v. Sinbandith, 143 N.H. 579, 729 A.2d 994, 1999 N.H. LEXIS 47 (1999).

369. Juveniles

To the extent that paragraphs III and III-a of RSA 169-B:19 authorize incarceration of juveniles in adult correctional facilities without first affording the juvenile the right to a jury trial, they are unconstitutional. In re Jeffery C., 146 N.H. 722, 781 A.2d 4, 2001 N.H. LEXIS 152 (2001).

Even though a juvenile is not entitled to a jury trial in a juvenile delinquency proceeding because it is not a criminal proceeding, when commitment to an adult criminal facility is permitted, the juvenile is constitutionally entitled to a trial by jury. In re Jeffery C., 146 N.H. 722, 781 A.2d 4, 2001 N.H. LEXIS 152 (2001).

Failure of juvenile to seek certification to be tried as an adult does not constitutes a waiver of his constitutional right to a jury trial. In re Jeffery C., 146 N.H. 722, 781 A.2d 4, 2001 N.H. LEXIS 152 (2001).

370. Disqualification of juror

Defendant's right to a fair and impartial jury under N.H. Const. pt. I, art. 15 was violated when the trial court dismissed a deliberating juror without a meritorious reason. The record did not support the finding that the juror had engaged in a pattern of disobedience, as the trial court had dismissed the juror's sleeping as insignificant, found his submission of questions to show attentiveness, and found no concrete evidence of an inability to deliberate; furthermore, the final act leading to the juror's dismissal, his failed attempt to use a legal dictionary, had no demonstrable impact on the deliberative process. State v. Sullivan, 157 N.H. 124, 949 A.2d 140, 2008 N.H. LEXIS 48 (2008).

371. Jury orientation

Where defendant alleged that the trial court had a practice of verbally instructing prospective jurors on legal concepts and responding to questions of individual prospective jurors during jury orientation, defendant's constitutional rights were not violated, because defendant had no right to be present since orientation of prospective jurors was not a critical stage of criminal proceedings instituted against a defendant, and did not bear the hallmarks of a proceeding in which defendant's presence was necessary to preserve defendant's ability to defend against pending criminal charges; also, the failure to record the orientation proceeding caused no constitutional infringement. State v. Cosme, 157 N.H. 40, 943 A.2d 810, 2008 N.H. LEXIS 31 (2008).

Orientation of prospective jurors is not a critical stage of criminal proceedings instituted against defendant, and does not bear the hallmarks of a proceeding in which defendant's presence is necessary to preserve the defendant's ability to defend against pending criminal charges. State v. Cosme, 157 N.H. 40, 943 A.2d 810, 2008 N.H. LEXIS 31 (2008).

372. Misdemeanors

When defendant was convicted in district court of two class A misdemeanors and was punished only with a fine of $350 plus a $70 penalty on each charge, converting the convictions to class B misdemeanors under RSA 625:9, VIII operated to deny defendant his right to a jury trial under N.H. Const. part. I, art. 15. Because defendant faced possible incarceration, he was entitled to a de novo jury trial in the superior court under RSA 599:1. State v. Bilc, 158 N.H. 651, 972 A.2d 1029, 2009 N.H. LEXIS 56 (2009).

IX. Law of the Land; Due Process

401. Generally

Defendant's due process and effective assistance of counsel rights under U.S. Const. amend. V, VI, and XIV and N.H. Const. pt. I, art 15 were not violated by interpreting RSA ch. 173-B as prohibiting contact with a victim protected under a temporary protective order as a defendant's constitutional rights do not confer upon him unfettered access to witnesses, especially when the witness is a victim of domestic violence and holds a protective order against the defendant; if a defendant has a legitimate reason to contact a victim, he can petition the court for an exception to or modification of the protective order. State v. Kidder, 150 N.H. 600, 843 A.2d 312, 2004 N.H. LEXIS 37 (2004).

Because the Fourteenth Amendment provides no greater protection to a defendant than N.H. Const. art I, § 15, courts need not conduct a separate due process analysis under the Federal Constitution. State v. Gourlay, 148 N.H. 75, 802 A.2d 1203, 2002 N.H. LEXIS 96 (2002).

The New Hampshire Constitution does not guarantee a right to appeal. State v. Landry, 146 N.H. 635, 776 A.2d 1289, 2001 N.H. LEXIS 123 (2001).

Because defendant based his due process argument only on Part I, Article 15 of New Hampshire Constitution, no separate analysis was necessary under United States Constitution, and court would consider cases from federal courts only as an analytical aid. State v. Dumont, 145 N.H. 240, 761 A.2d 454, 2000 N.H. LEXIS 48 (2000).

State agency could not invoke protection of this article, because State due process clause protects only "subjects," not governments. Appeal of New Hampshire Dep't of Empl. Sec., 140 N.H. 703, 672 A.2d 697, 1996 N.H. LEXIS 23 (1996).

A bill which would prohibit a defendant charged with sexual assault from commencing a civil action against a victim of the alleged crime if the civil action is "based upon statements or reports made by the victim that pertain to an incident from which the criminal action is derived" would not deprive the defendant of due process of law as an individual subject to the provisions of the bill would not be irretrievably foreclosed from access to the courts. Opinion of Justices, 137 N.H. 260, 628 A.2d 1069, 1993 N.H. LEXIS 99 (1993).

The phrase "the law of the land" is synonymous with "due process of law." Riblet Tramway Co. v. Stickney, 129 N.H. 140, 523 A.2d 107, 1987 N.H. LEXIS 153 (1987).

This article guarantees due process. State v. Cooper, 127 N.H. 119, 498 A.2d 1209, 1985 N.H. LEXIS 375 (1985).

Due process has, as a primary consideration, the notion that no matter how rich or how poor, all citizens are entitled to fundamental fairness when the government seeks to take action which will deprive them of their property or liberty interests. Claremont v. Truell, 126 N.H. 30, 489 A.2d 581, 1985 N.H. LEXIS 280 (1985).

This article guarantees every citizen due process of the law. State v. Damiano, 124 N.H. 742, 474 A.2d 1045, 1984 N.H. LEXIS 337 (1984); State v. Denney, 130 N.H. 217, 536 A.2d 1242, 1987 N.H. LEXIS 299 (1987).

This article guarantees due process to individuals facing a potential deprivation of liberty. In re Gamble, 118 N.H. 771, 394 A.2d 308, 1978 N.H. LEXIS 290 (1978).

"Law of the land" in this article means due process of law. In re Harvey, 108 N.H. 196, 230 A.2d 757, 1967 N.H. LEXIS 152 (1967); State v. Denney, 130 N.H. 217, 536 A.2d 1242, 1987 N.H. LEXIS 299 (1987).

The phrase "law of the land" as used in this article means due course and process of law. In re Opinion of Justices, 66 N.H. 629, 33 A. 1076, 1891 N.H. LEXIS 105 (1891).

The phrase "the law of the land" means that process warranted by law. Hutchins v. Edson, 1 N.H. 139, 1817 N.H. LEXIS 35 (1817).

402. Statutes

Apportioning fault to an immune employer pursuant to RSA 507:7-e does not violate due process under N.H. Const. pt. I, art. 15. Thus, the trial court did not err in apportioning liability between plaintiff, defendant, and plaintiff's employer, a nonparty which was immune from suit because of plaintiff's recovery of federal workers' compensation benefits from it. Ocasio v. Fed. Express Corp., 162 N.H. 436, 33 A.3d 1139, 2011 N.H. LEXIS 124 (2011).

Assuming arguendo that the due process protections provided by N.H. Const. pt. I, art. 15 applied to the passage of legislation, an inmate's due process rights were not violated by the enactment of RSA 651:2, II-e, as the session during which this occurred was open to the public, as required by RSA 91-A:1-a, I(a) and 91-A:2, II. Starr v. Governor, 154 N.H. 174, 910 A.2d 1247, 2006 N.H. LEXIS 140 (2006), rehearing denied, 2006 N.H. LEXIS 193 (N.H. Nov. 27, 2006).

Defendant, who received a parking ticket for parking for more than 30 minutes on a downtown city street, failed to prove a due process violation as the city did not have to post a parking ordinance where defendant parked. State v. Hofland, 151 N.H. 322, 857 A.2d 1271, 2004 N.H. LEXIS 146 (2004), rehearing denied, 2004 N.H. LEXIS 173 (N.H. Sept. 24, 2004).

Defendant did not argue, nor did the record contain evidence, that the purported selective enforcement of the parking ordinance against defendant was a conscious intentional discrimination, nor did he assert that the city impermissibly established classifications and, therefore, treated similarly situated individuals in a different manner. Accordingly, defendant failed to meet the burden of establishing that the city's parking citation for parking longer than 30 minutes violated defendant's right to equal protection of the law. State v. Hofland, 151 N.H. 322, 857 A.2d 1271, 2004 N.H. LEXIS 146 (2004), rehearing denied, 2004 N.H. LEXIS 173 (N.H. Sept. 24, 2004).

A bill which would prohibit a defendant charged with sexual assault from commencing a civil action against a victim of the alleged crime if the civil action is "based upon statements or reports made by the victim that pertain to an incident from which the criminal action is derived" would not deprive the defendant of due process of law as an individual subject to the provisions of the bill would not be irretrievably foreclosed from access to the courts. Opinion of Justices, 137 N.H. 260, 628 A.2d 1069, 1993 N.H. LEXIS 99 (1993).

The preponderance of the evidence standard in RSA 169-C:13 meets the due process requirements of this article. In re Tracy M., 137 N.H. 119, 624 A.2d 963, 1993 N.H. LEXIS 51 (1993).

All statutes not repugnant to any other clauses in the constitution have always been considered as the "law of the land" within the meaning of this clause. Trustees of Dartmouth College v. Woodward, 1 N.H. 111, 1817 N.H. LEXIS 33 (1817).

403. Arrest

The constitutional guaranty that no subject shall be arrested but by the judgment by his peers or the law of the land means that no subject shall be arrested but by due process of law, which is awarded by the constitution, by the common law adopted by the constitution and not altered, or by statute made in pursuance of the constitution. Mayo v. Wilson, 1 N.H. 53, 1817 N.H. LEXIS 13 (1817).

404. Property interest

State employee had not shown a property interest in his employment for purposes of due process. He failed to cite a specific provision of the relevant statutes or of the collective bargaining agreement that created such an interest; moreover, notwithstanding that the employee might have been entitled to certain procedural protections and rights of appeal by statute and administrative rule, a substantive property right could not exist exclusively by virtue of a procedural right. Appeal of Alexander, 163 N.H. 397, 42 A.3d 804, 2012 N.H. LEXIS 41 (2012).

Purchasers of real property obtained a protected property interest when they received a deed from the seller. Berube v. Belhumeur, 139 N.H. 562, 663 A.2d 598, 1995 N.H. LEXIS 55 (1995).

A petitioner who was licensed to practice medicine in New Hampshire for nearly 10 years until, as a result of the terms of a consent order, his license became suspended pursuant to RSA 329:16-e, still possessed a property right entitled to due process protection in a relicensing proceeding. Appeal of Dell, 140 N.H. 484, 668 A.2d 1024, 1995 N.H. LEXIS 176 (1995).

Since the right to inherit has no immediate value, children whose right to inherit from a natural parent was substituted for the right to inherit from an adoptive parent through the operation of the adoption statute, had no property taken from them at the time of their adoption and suffered no unconstitutional "taking" in violation of the state constitution. In re Estate of McQuesten, 133 N.H. 420, 578 A.2d 335, 1990 N.H. LEXIS 80 (1990).

Claim of entitlement to unemployment compensation benefits is a claim to a property interest that is subject to protection under the due process guarantees of this article. Appeal of Eno, 126 N.H. 650, 495 A.2d 1277, 1985 N.H. LEXIS 361 (1985).

A proceeding for reimbursement of expenses incurred in care of children in need of services pursuant to RSA 169-D:29 is one in which an individual may be deprived of significant property rights and, therefore, implicates due process considerations. Claremont v. Truell, 126 N.H. 30, 489 A.2d 581, 1985 N.H. LEXIS 280 (1985).

405. Liberty interests

Imposition of a suspended sentence is not part of a criminal prosecution and thus the full panoply of rights due a defendant in such a proceeding does not apply. Nevertheless, the liberty interest involved is valuable and its termination calls for some orderly process, however informal. State v. Laplaca, 162 N.H. 174, 27 A.3d 719, 2011 N.H. LEXIS 86 (2011).

The admittee did not show that his substantive due process were rights violated in extending the conditional discharge of the admittee's involuntary commitment, as the relevant statute was narrowly drawn to protect both the admittee and society, and promoted the compelling interest of protecting both from the admittee's dangerousness. Due process under the State Constitution is not violated by the renewal of a conditional discharge based upon a finding of dangerousness in the past and a finding that the person, because of mental illness, poses a potentially serious likelihood of danger in the future. In re Christopher K., 155 N.H. 219, 923 A.2d 187, 2007 N.H. LEXIS 49 (2007), rehearing denied, 2007 N.H. LEXIS 107 (N.H. May 30, 2007).

Procedures employed in "3JX docket," which uses a three-justice panel, rather than the full five justice court, provides for five minutes of uninterrupted oral argument, followed by an unlimited period of questioning by the justices, and decides cases by order, rather than by full opinion, do not create a risk of erroneous deprivation of defendant's liberty interest. State v. Landry, 146 N.H. 635, 776 A.2d 1289, 2001 N.H. LEXIS 123 (2001).

Defendant's right to due process was violated by superior court denying him opportunity to testify and to present witnesses and evidence on issue of whether he violated good conduct provision of his probation. State v. Dumont, 145 N.H. 240, 761 A.2d 454, 2000 N.H. LEXIS 48 (2000).

Probation may be revoked, consistent with requirements of due process, upon proof by a preponderance of evidence that defendant violated terms of his freedom. State v. Dumont, 145 N.H. 240, 761 A.2d 454, 2000 N.H. LEXIS 48 (2000).

Due process requires that preponderance of evidence standard apply in any hearing to determine whether an individual's name should be added to central registry of sexual offenders, where the individual would be excluded from working in his or her profession due to that listing. In re Preisendorfer, 143 N.H. 50, 719 A.2d 590, 1998 N.H. LEXIS 71 (1998).

Special education aide's interest in his profession was a protected liberty interest, since decision to enter his name into sexual offender registry essentially barred him from working with children, and caused him to become unemployed and unemployable in his profession. In re Preisendorfer, 143 N.H. 50, 719 A.2d 590, 1998 N.H. LEXIS 71 (1998).

Due process protects a probationer against unreasonable deprivations of his or her conditional liberty interest, including unreasonable delay between probationer's arrest and final revocation hearing. State v. Leavitt, 136 N.H. 475, 617 A.2d 652, 1992 N.H. LEXIS 188 (1992).

State's termination of contract with corporation did not deny the corporation's liberty interests under this article, since, even assuming that the termination of the contract incidentally damaged the corporation's reputation and indirectly made it more difficult to find work, this "injury" would not be cognizable under this article. Riblet Tramway Co. v. Stickney, 129 N.H. 140, 523 A.2d 107, 1987 N.H. LEXIS 153 (1987).

In determining that a report of child neglect against parents was "founded," and in entering and maintaining a record of this determination in the central registry, the division for children and youth services engaged in an official adjudication of status of potentially injurious consequences and thus deprived petitioners of their "liberty" within the meaning of this article. In re Bagley, 128 N.H. 275, 513 A.2d 331, 1986 N.H. LEXIS 283 (1986).

The due process clause of this article provides mentally ill persons, like all other individuals, with certain fundamental liberty interests, and accordingly, mentally ill persons have a right to be free from unjustified intrusion upon their personal security. Opinion of Justices, 123 N.H. 554, 465 A.2d 484, 1983 N.H. LEXIS 321 (1983).

406. Implied consent law

Under circumstances of DUI case, implied consent procedure which permitted the destruction of a second breath sample when defendant did not retrieve it within thirty days did not violate due process clause of this article. State v. Symonds, 131 N.H. 532, 556 A.2d 1175, 1989 N.H. LEXIS 24 (1989).

Due process guarantee contained in this article requires that those arrested for driving while intoxicated be informed that the fact of their refusal to submit to a blood alcohol test can be admitted against them at the trial arising out of their arrest. State v. Denney, 130 N.H. 217, 536 A.2d 1242, 1987 N.H. LEXIS 299 (1987).

The due process clause of the state constitution does not require that individuals arrested for driving while intoxicated under RSA 265:82 be apprised, before submitting to a chemical test for intoxication, that the results of the test may result in their being charged under RSA 265:82-a for the more serious offense of aggravated driving while intoxicated. State v. Jenkins, 128 N.H. 672, 517 A.2d 1182, 1986 N.H. LEXIS 348 (1986).

407. Arraignment

Arraignments and bail hearings conducted by video teleconference did not violate due process. Such a procedure does not pose a greater risk of erroneous deprivation of liberty, saves the state thousands of dollars in transportation and security fees, and decreases the likelihood of violence during such proceedings. Larose v. Superintendent, Hillsborough County Correction Admin., 142 N.H. 364, 702 A.2d 326, 1997 N.H. LEXIS 104 (1997).

408. Plea agreements

New Hampshire Supreme Court joins the other jurisdictions that have concluded that immigration consequences are collateral consequences of a plea, and holds that New Hampshire's constitutional due process protections do not require trial courts to advise defendants of such potential consequences during plea colloquies. State v. Ortiz, 163 N.H. 506, 44 A.3d 425, 2012 N.H. LEXIS 48 (2012).

Trial court did not violate due process under the Fourteenth Amendment or the New Hampshire Constitution in failing to advise defendant of the immigration consequences of her nolo contendere plea. Immigration consequences were collateral consequences of a plea, and due process did not require that defendant be advised of such consequences. State v. Ortiz, 163 N.H. 506, 44 A.3d 425, 2012 N.H. LEXIS 48 (2012).

Although the prosecution did violate a drunk driving defendant's due process guarantees by sending a letter suggesting that an early guilty plea was the only way to avoid maximum penalties (failure to fully explain the collateral consequences of administrative license suspension, however, was not a rights violation), dismissal of the criminal charges was not an appropriate remedy, because it provided defendant windfall relief from punishment and potentially endangered the public; therefore, on remand, the trial court was to consider what other sanction might be more appropriate under the circumstances. State v. Chace, 151 N.H. 310, 856 A.2d 1, 2004 N.H. LEXIS 144 (2004).

A defendant who is a party to a wholly executory plea agreement has no claim to its enforcement on due process grounds because neither the agreement nor its repudiation is sufficient to affect his liberty interest; however, a defendant who has performed his part of a plea agreement has a claim to relief, if not specific enforcement, because a prosecutor's failure to honor his side of the agreement invalidates the defendant's waiver of substantive constitutional rights. State v. O'Leary, 128 N.H. 661, 517 A.2d 1174, 1986 N.H. LEXIS 326 (1986).

409. Competency to stand trial

Defendant, who was found incompetent to stand trial, had not shown that due process under N.H. Const. pt. I, art. 15 and U.S. Const. amend. XIV required the appointment of additional counsel and/or guardians to protect his reputational interest. The procedure used sufficiently protected that interest by ensuring a reliable competency determination; furthermore, fully litigating the competency issue in an adversrial proceeding with two sets of appointed counsel also counseled against the additional process defendant sought. State v. Veale, 158 N.H. 632, 972 A.2d 1009, 2009 N.H. LEXIS 58 (2009), cert. denied, Veale v. New Hampshire, 558 U.S. 1053, 130 S. Ct. 748, 175 L. Ed. 2d 524, 2009 U.S. LEXIS 8587 (2009).

Competency determinations sufficiently implicate reputational interests to warrant the protection afforded by the New Hampshire Due Process Clause. State v. Veale, 158 N.H. 632, 972 A.2d 1009, 2009 N.H. LEXIS 58 (2009), cert. denied, Veale v. New Hampshire, 558 U.S. 1053, 130 S. Ct. 748, 175 L. Ed. 2d 524, 2009 U.S. LEXIS 8587 (2009).

Declining to appoint counsel solely to vindicate a defendant's reputational interest does not offend fundamental fairness. Where a criminal defendant is at odds with counsel because counsel believes that the defendant is not competent, while the defendant believes that he or she is competent, due process does not require the appointment of additional counsel. State v. Veale, 158 N.H. 632, 972 A.2d 1009, 2009 N.H. LEXIS 58 (2009), cert. denied, Veale v. New Hampshire, 558 U.S. 1053, 130 S. Ct. 748, 175 L. Ed. 2d 524, 2009 U.S. LEXIS 8587 (2009).

Had defendant, who sought based on his due process reputational interest to vacate a finding that he was incompetent to stand trial, requested to testify or call other witnesses at the competency hearing, due process might well have afforded him that right. On the record, however, it appeared that defendant never requested as much; had he wished to testify, he should have informed his counsel and/or the trial court instead of raising the issue for the first time in his pro se notice of appeal. State v. Veale, 158 N.H. 632, 972 A.2d 1009, 2009 N.H. LEXIS 58 (2009), cert. denied, Veale v. New Hampshire, 558 U.S. 1053, 130 S. Ct. 748, 175 L. Ed. 2d 524, 2009 U.S. LEXIS 8587 (2009).

Defendant's claim that he had no memory of the accident underlying the charges against him did not automatically raise a bona fide or a legitimate doubt triggering a due process right to a competency hearing under N.H. Const. pt. I, art. 15 and the Fourteenth Amendment, as a defendant could assist and consult with counsel without necessarily remembering an event. As the record essentially contained only a representation that defendant suffered amnesia, the trial court could have reasonably concluded that no bona fide or legitimate doubt arose as to his competency. State v. Kincaid, 158 N.H. 90, 960 A.2d 711, 2008 N.H. LEXIS 144 (2008).

Claim of loss of memory alone does not automatically raise a bona fide or legitimate doubt triggering a due process right to a competency hearing. There are many ways a defendant can consult with and assist his trial counsel with a reasonable degree of rational understanding without necessarily remembering the details or circumstances of an event that led to his arrest. State v. Kincaid, 158 N.H. 90, 960 A.2d 711, 2008 N.H. LEXIS 144 (2008).

Defendant, who threw hot oil onto the victim three times, was not denied due process under N.H. Const. pt. I, art. 15 where the trial court determined he was competent to stand trial as there was evidence supporting the trial court's finding that defendant had a rational and factual understanding of the proceedings against him. State v. Ke Tong Chen, 148 N.H. 565, 813 A.2d 424, 2002 N.H. LEXIS 169 (2002).

State bears burden of proving, by a preponderance of evidence, that a criminal defendant has both a factual and a rational understanding of proceedings against him. State v. Haycock, 146 N.H. 5, 766 A.2d 720, 2001 N.H. LEXIS 17 (2001).

Trial court erred in finding defendant competent to stand trial, where court failed to make specific findings to support its conclusion that defendant had a rational understanding of proceedings against him, and court's conclusion was directly contrary to the only expert opinion offered at defendant's competency hearing. State v. Haycock, 146 N.H. 5, 766 A.2d 720, 2001 N.H. LEXIS 17 (2001).

There was not sufficient evidence to raise a bona fide doubt as to the defendant's competency to stand trial and, therefore, the superior court did not err when it failed to order an evidentiary hearing to evaluate the defendant's competency to stand trial where, although the defendant exhibited disruptive and often annoying behavior, he appeared to have a factual as well as rational understanding of the proceedings against him; the superior court's observation that the defendant may have had "problems with [his] noggin" could be regarded as an attempt to chide the defendant for his obstinate refusal to comply with court decorum. State v. Zorzy, 136 N.H. 710, 622 A.2d 1217, 1993 N.H. LEXIS 19 (1993).

Due process requires that a defendant not be subject to criminal prosecution if he is not competent. State v. Bertrand, 123 N.H. 719, 465 A.2d 912, 1983 N.H. LEXIS 340 (1983).

A defendant's due process rights prohibit him or her from being placed on trial if legally incompetent, meaning that he or she is not capable of understanding the proceedings against him or her or assisting his or her lawyer in the preparation of his or her defense. State v. Gagne, 129 N.H. 93, 523 A.2d 76, 1986 N.H. LEXIS 380 (1986).

In the exercise of its inherent authority to protect a defendant's constitutional rights, a district court is empowered to order a pre-trial evaluation to determine the competency of a defendant charged with a felony prior to the probable cause hearing. State v. Gagne, 129 N.H. 93, 523 A.2d 76, 1986 N.H. LEXIS 380 (1986).

410. Public trial

A defendant's public trial right is not violated upon closure of a proceeding as long as: (1) party seeking to close courtroom advances an overriding interest that is likely to be prejudiced; (2) closure is no broader than necessary to protect that interest; (3) trial court considers reasonable alternatives to closing proceeding; and (4) trial court makes adequate findings supporting closure. State v. Cote, 143 N.H. 368, 725 A.2d 652, 1999 N.H. LEXIS 12 (1999).

Remand was required where trial court exclusively focused on justifying closure of post-conviction hearing to defendant, and failed to make specific findings justifying closure to public, which would enable reviewing court to determine whether such closure was proper. State v. Cote, 143 N.H. 368, 725 A.2d 652, 1999 N.H. LEXIS 12 (1999).

The right to a public trial is protected by the due process requirement of the article. Martineau v. Helgemoe, 117 N.H. 841, 379 A.2d 1040, 1977 N.H. LEXIS 445 (1977).

411. Admissibility of evidence

Any error in excluding certain testimony was harmless and thus did not violate due process under N.H. Const. pt. I, art. 15 and the Fifth and Fourteenth Amendments. The alternative evidence of defendant's guilt of second-degree murder under RSA 630:1-b, I(b), and of riot under RSA 644:1, I, including eyewitness testimony, was of an overwhelming nature, and the testimony was cumulative. State v. Garcia, 162 N.H. 426, 33 A.3d 1087, 2011 N.H. LEXIS 126 (2011).

Trial court did not violate sexual assault defendant's due process rights by refusing to conduct an in camera review of counseling records and presentence investigation report (PSI) related to victim's conviction for a driving offense since, no matter how little time elapsed between victim's driving offense and her first report of assaults to police, it was mere speculation that either PSI or counseling records would concern themselves with her past sexual assaults. State v. Pandolfi, 145 N.H. 508, 765 A.2d 1037, 2000 N.H. LEXIS 101 (2000).

Because sexual assault victim relied on medication to explain her memory difficulties, defendant was entitled to an in camera review to discover the type of medication she took, if any, but victim's reliance on medication to explain her inaccurate recall did not justify disclosure of her underlying clinical diagnosis. State v. Pandolfi, 145 N.H. 508, 765 A.2d 1037, 2000 N.H. LEXIS 101 (2000).

The enactment of a bill to prohibit the introduction of evidence of the victim's manner of dress at the time of a sexual assault in order to infer consent would not impinge upon an accused's right to due process in violation of Part I, Article 15 of the New Hampshire Constitution. Opinion of the Justices (Certain Evidence in Sexual Assult Cases), 140 N.H. 22, 662 A.2d 294, 1995 N.H. LEXIS 87 (1995).

Admission of prior convictions solely for impeachment purposes does not constitute a denial of a defendant's right to due process of law. State v. Kelley, 120 N.H. 14, 413 A.2d 300, 1980 N.H. LEXIS 220 (1980).

412. Sentencing

As the conditions of probation that defendant was found to have violated under N.H. Super. Ct. R. 107(a) and (b) were implicitly imposed in the original sentencing order pursuant to RSA 504-A:1, VII, there was no due process violation of U.S. Const. amends. V and XIV or N.H. Const. pt. I, art. 15. State v. Kay, 162 N.H. 237, 27 A.3d 749, 2011 N.H. LEXIS 100 (July 21, 2011).

Trial court misread the sentencing sheets, imposing a concurrent instead of a consecutive sentence. Thus, even though the original sentence was clear and unambiguous on its face, the trial court had inherent authority to amend it nine minutes later because it was the result of a clerical error, and there was no due process violation under N.H. Const. pt. I, art. 15. State v. Ortiz, 162 N.H. 585, 34 A.3d 599, 2011 N.H. LEXIS 146 (2011).

Under the language of the original 1996 sentencing order, the sentencing court retained only the authority to impose or terminate defendant's deferred sentence. Thus, it lacked the authority to suspend sua sponte the deferred sentence, and there was a violation of due process under N.H. Const. pt. I, art. 15. State v. French, 163 N.H. 1, 35 A.3d 625, 2011 N.H. LEXIS 181 (2011).

When the trial court intended to sentence defendant to a minimum of 15 years but failed to consider his entitlement to good time credit, the sentence was not the result of scrivener's error. Thus, the trial court lacked the authority to change one of his sentences from concurrent to consecutive, and doing so violated his state due process rights. State v. Fletcher, 158 N.H. 207, 965 A.2d 1000, 2009 N.H. LEXIS 2 (2009).

Defendant's due process rights were violated after he obtained reversal of 9 out of 21 child sexual abuse charges but received a restructuring of the same 150-year aggregate prison term on remand, which amounted to a harsher sentence that was not within the bounds of the trial court's sentencing authority. State v. Abram, 156 N.H. 646, 941 A.2d 576, 2008 N.H. LEXIS 3 (2008).

Trial court committed plain error by sentencing defendant to 12 months in jail, a $2,000 fine and two years probation for misdemeanor simple assault constituting a violation of his probation because under RSA 651:2, VII, the trial court, in order to impose probation, was required to retain a portion of its sentencing power as an enforcement mechanism and could not impose probation where the maximum fine and imprisonment terms had been given;

due process requires a sentencing court to make clear at the time of sentencing in plain and certain terms what punishment it is exacting as well as the extent to which the court retains discretion to impose punishment at a later date and under what conditions the sentence may be modified. No further penalty was ascertainable at the time of sentencing, and in fact, there was uncertainty as to whether defendant could have been punished at all. State v. Hancock, 156 N.H. 301, 934 A.2d 551, 2007 N.H. LEXIS 183 (2007).

As RSA 651:58, I and II provide that a defendant must be given both statutory and actual notice of the State's right to seek a review of his sentence within 30 days of the imposition of that sentence, and the extent to which jurisdiction is retained to either increase or decrease the sentence after a hearing conducted by a sentencing review board, RSA 651:58, I does not violate the Due Process Clause of the New Hampshire Constitution. In re Guardarramos-Cepeda, 154 N.H. 7, 904 A.2d 609, 2006 N.H. LEXIS 112 (2006).

Trial court's reinterpretation of its authority to suspend defendant's sentence in light of the time limitations in RSA 651:20, I(a), which resulted in the trial court denying defendant's motion seeking the suspension that the trial court indicated he could seek after his successful completion of a sexual offender treatment program, was not unconstitutional and did not violate the doctrine against judicial ex post facto decisions under either the U.S. Constitution or the New Hampshire State Constitution. State v. Horner, 153 N.H. 306, 893 A.2d 683, 2006 N.H. LEXIS 28 (2006), rehearing denied, 2006 N.H. LEXIS 74 (N.H. Apr. 26, 2006).

While a trial court's denial of defendant's request to suspend his sentence due to defendant's failure to complete a treatment program did not violate defendant's due process rights under either the New Hampshire Constitution or the Federal Constitution, the order was vacated as imposing impossible conditions upon the motion, as the department of corrections was not offering a treatment program in which the defendant could enroll. State v. LeCouffe, 152 N.H. 148, 872 A.2d 773, 2005 N.H. LEXIS 56 (2005).

Trial court did not violate defendant's N.H. Const. pt. I, art. 15 due process rights by amending a clerical error in defendant's sentence which led to a longer sentence of incarceration; the parties understood the court's intention as to the sentence, the court notified the parties of its error and original sentencing intent approximately two hours after sentencing, and held a hearing on the amendment the same day, and defendant was not prejudiced by the lapse of time between the first and second sentencing hearing because after the first hearing, the court stayed the sentence pending appeal and defendant was free on bail. State v. Stern, 150 N.H. 705, 846 A.2d 64, 2004 N.H. LEXIS 59 (2004).

Constitutional mandate of unanimity in the jury verdict to enhance the defendant's sentences was met because, in light of the jury instructions as a whole and the evidence presented at trial, a reasonable jury would understand that the deadly weapon element of both the criminal threatening charges against the defendant exclusively referred to the use of a firearm. Therefore, the guilty verdicts reflected a unanimous conclusion that the defendant used a firearm, and no other object, as a deadly weapon to commit the crimes. State v. Higgins, 149 N.H. 290, 821 A.2d 964, 2003 N.H. LEXIS 41 (2003).

In accordance with due process, the sentencing order must clearly communicate to defendant the exact nature of the sentence. State v. Budgett, 146 N.H. 135, 769 A.2d 351, 2001 N.H. LEXIS 43 (2001).

Termination of freedom by revocation of a suspended sentence involves constitutional liberty interests protected by the due process clause. State v. Budgett, 146 N.H. 135, 769 A.2d 351, 2001 N.H. LEXIS 43 (2001).

There is an implied condition of good behavior in suspended sentences and this condition does not offend due process. State v. Budgett, 146 N.H. 135, 769 A.2d 351, 2001 N.H. LEXIS 43 (2001).

There is an implied condition of good behavior in deferred sentences and that condition does not offend due process; therefore, defendant's right to due process was not violated by the court's imposition of his deferred sentence because of his criminal conduct. State v. Graham, 146 N.H. 142, 769 A.2d 355, 2001 N.H. LEXIS 44 (2001).

Due process required proof beyond a reasonable doubt of prior sexual assault convictions used to enhance defendant's sentence to life in prison without parole under provisions of statute. State v. McLellan, 146 N.H. 108, 767 A.2d 953, 2001 N.H. LEXIS 36 (2001).

Revocation of defendant's suspended sentence based on her prior, uncounseled misdemeanor stalking conviction did not violate her right to due process. State v. Weeks, 141 N.H. 248, 681 A.2d 86, 1996 N.H. LEXIS 85 (1996).

New Hampshire Constitution requires that a defendant be informed at the time of sentencing in plain and certain terms what punishment has been exacted by the court as well as the extent to which the court retained discretion to impose punishment at a later date and under what conditions the sentence may be modified. State v. Huot, 136 N.H. 96, 612 A.2d 362, 1992 N.H. LEXIS 131 (1992).

Due process was denied to defendant who pleaded no contest to two misdemeanor charges and was sentenced on the first charge to sixty days in the house of correction, suspended on condition of the defendant's "good behavior," and the second charge was marked "continued for sentence," because the length of time in which either sentence could be called forward was uncertain. State v. Ingerson, 130 N.H. 112, 536 A.2d 161, 1987 N.H. LEXIS 292 (1987).

413. Appeals

Although N.H. Const. pt. I, arts. 15, 18, and 33 entitle a defendant to a fair appellate procedure, free from arbitrary and discriminatory enforcement, the constitution does not require that the procedure be adopted through the formal rulemaking process. State v. Addison, 159 N.H. 87, 977 A.2d 520, 2009 N.H. LEXIS 86 (2009).

As a church did not cite or discuss the three-factor analysis for purposes of a claim that due process was violated under N.H. Const. pt. I, art. 15 by a trial court's failure to hold an evidentiary hearing on its preliminary objections to the State's condemnation proceeding against church property, and the church also failed to point to controlling precedent that showed it had a right to such a hearing, an argument on appeal was deemed not developed and accordingly, not reviewable. State v. Korean Methodist Church of N.H., 157 N.H. 254, 949 A.2d 738, 2008 N.H. LEXIS 59 (2008).

Because the transcripts that defendant sought could only be for the purpose of pursuing a successive collateral proceeding that had not yet been filed, defendant was not entitled to preparation of hearing transcripts at the State's expense; therefore, defendant's due process and equal protection rights under N.H. Const. pt. I, arts. 8, 14, 15 were not violated when the request was denied. State v. Dupont, 155 N.H. 644, 931 A.2d 583, 2007 N.H. LEXIS 111 (2007), rehearing denied, 2007 N.H. LEXIS 155 (N.H. Aug. 20, 2007).

Considering that "3JX docket" procedures as applied in criminal appeals pose little or no risk of erroneous deprivation of defendant's liberty and that the government's interest in providing a timely, fair and effective forum for the resolution of matters of all parties before the supreme court is substantial, the procedures conform with due process. State v. Landry, 146 N.H. 635, 776 A.2d 1289, 2001 N.H. LEXIS 123 (2001).

Because Fourteenth Amendment to United States Constitution provided no greater due process protection than Part I, Article 15 of New Hampshire Constitution, supreme court was not required to engage in a separate federal analysis of defendant's constitutional claims. State v. Haycock, 146 N.H. 5, 766 A.2d 720, 2001 N.H. LEXIS 17 (2001).

Where defendant appealed violation of probation finding based on theory that twenty-two month wait between arrest and final revocation hearing violated state and federal due process rights, defendant's claim was first considered under state constitution, using federal case law only as an aid to analysis. State v. Leavitt, 136 N.H. 475, 617 A.2d 652, 1992 N.H. LEXIS 188 (1992).

Guarantee of due process requires that each and every criminal defendant be offered a fair and equal opportunity to have his case accepted on appeal by the supreme court and thereby to obtain an adjudication on the merits of his appeal. State v. Cooper, 127 N.H. 119, 498 A.2d 1209, 1985 N.H. LEXIS 375 (1985).

Declination of appeal procedure of the supreme court does not violate due process guarantee of this article, since it is neither arbitrary nor capricious, and is rationally related to discharging its responsibilities equitably and effectively. State v. Cooper, 127 N.H. 119, 498 A.2d 1209, 1985 N.H. LEXIS 375 (1985).

Due process is violated where a prosecutor makes threats of stiffer penalties on appeal than in the trial below if a defendant exercises his right to a de novo appeal following a conviction and defendant could reasonably fear the prosecutor had the power to carry out the threats; it is not necessary to find the prosecutor actually had the power to implement the threats. Koski v. Samaha, 491 F. Supp. 432, 1980 U.S. Dist. LEXIS 9157 (D.N.H. 1980).

Where anti-nuclear power plant demonstrator received 15-day sentence in district court for criminal trespass and prosecutor made it clear that if she sought de novo appeal in superior court he would "slap her" with a six-month sentence, there was a due process violation in the chilling of the exercise of the right to a de novo appeal and writ of habeas corpus would be granted; and whether prosecutor had the power to pass sentence or implement his threat was not relevant as the issue was whether demonstrator reasonably believed the threat. Koski v. Samaha, 491 F. Supp. 432, 1980 U.S. Dist. LEXIS 9157 (D.N.H. 1980).

414. Vicarious liability

Off highway recreational vehicle operation and licensing statute, which seeks to impose vicarious criminal liability on parents for minors' violations, solely because of parental status, and which does not base liability on any voluntary act or omission on part of parents, offends the due process clause. State v. Akers, 119 N.H. 161, 400 A.2d 38, 1979 N.H. LEXIS 265, 12 A.L.R.4th 667 (1979).

415. Notice and hearing

Teacher's New Hampshire and federal due process rights were not violated when the New Hampshire Public Employee Labor Relations Board (PELRB) held that because the collective bargaining agreement provided for a three-step grievance process, with the third step being a final and binding hearing before the school board, it lacked jurisdiction over his unfair labor practices complaint. A union could waive its members' customary procedural rights, such as de novo judicial review, by way of the ordinary bargaining process; furthermore, the teacher had not cited any holding that a public school teacher had a constitutionally based due process right to a termination hearing before a third party, such as an arbitrator or the PELRB, rather than before the school board. Appeal of Silverstein, 163 N.H. 192, 37 A.3d 382, 2012 N.H. LEXIS 7 (2012), cert. denied, Silverstein v. Andover Sch. Bd., 133 S. Ct. 167, 184 L. Ed. 2d 35, 2012 U.S. LEXIS 7003 (U.S. 2012).

Notice of hearing respondent received regarding the suspension of her boating privileges was not inadequate under N.H. Const. pt. I, art. 15 when the notice informed respondent of the specific date, location and nature of the conduct that the hearing would address and of the legal authority, RSA 270-E:17, for revoking her operating privilege; the notice enabled respondent to present objections both before and during the hearing; and the hearing addressed only that conduct to which the notice specifically referred. Furthermore, although the notice failed to cite the negligent boating statute upon which the Department of Safety ultimately relied to suspend the respondent's operating privilege, the notice adequately informed her of the facts and legal standards involved. Appeal of Blizzard, 163 N.H. 326, 42 A.3d 791, 2012 N.H. LEXIS 27 (2012).

Once defendant was convicted of robbery, a final parole revocation hearing was not necessary to protect his due process rights associated with the parole violation charge stemming from the robbery. Thus, the calculation of his pretrial confinement credit did not violate due process under N.H. Const. pt. I, art. 15 and the Fifth and Fourteenth Amendments. State v. Mwangi, 161 N.H. 699, 20 A.3d 940, 2011 N.H. LEXIS 49 (2011).

Trial court violated due process under N.H. Const. pt. I, art. 15 in denying defendant's motion for a hearing on the issue of whether his suspended sentence should be imposed. Defendant's advance waiver of the right to any hearings was akin to pleading guilty to any future allegations brought against him because the effect of such a waiver eliminated the obligation of the State to prove the allegations against him, and deprived him of the opportunity to contest them. State v. Laplaca, 162 N.H. 174, 27 A.3d 719, 2011 N.H. LEXIS 86 (2011).

Because it was clear that the deliberate violation of a court order could be punished as a criminal contempt, defendant had sufficient notice that an attempt to violate a no-contact order could trigger imposition of his suspended felony sentences. Thus, there was no due process violation under N.H. Const. pt. I, art. 15 or U.S. Const. amend. XIV. State v. Smith, 163 N.H. 13, 35 A.3d 646, 2011 N.H. LEXIS 184 (2011).

Trial court did not violate due process by not holding a hearing on defendant's motion to amend the conditions of his suspended sentence. The facts were not in dispute, and because the condition

in question was reasonably related to defendant's rehabilitation and supervision, defendant would not have been entitled to relief regardless of additional evidence he might have presented. State v. Perfetto, 160 N.H. 675, 7 A.3d 1179, 2010 N.H. LEXIS 102 (2010).

Board of Tax and Land Appeals erred in finding that due process under N.H. Const. pt. I, art. 15 required a taxpayer to receive actual notice of the land-use-change-tax bills it was mailed. The city placed the bills in the mail, and nothing in the record indicated that the mail was returned unclaimed or undeliverable; the city's reliance on the United States Postal Service was reasonably calculated, under all the circumstances, to apprise interested parties of the pendency of the action and afford them an opportunity to present their objections. City of Concord, 161 N.H. 169, 13 A.3d 287, 2010 N.H. LEXIS 135 (2010).

Residential utility customers did not have a statutory or due process right to a hearing when the public utilities commission approved an amendment to a previously approved special contract. Appeal of Office of the Consumer Advocate, 148 N.H. 134, 803 A.2d 1054, 2002 N.H. LEXIS 103 (2002).

Notice to intervenors did not violate due process and was sufficient because, by definition intervenors have a direct and apparent interest in the subject matter of the litigation, and by virtue of their status, they were parties to the case. Town of Nottingham v. Bonser, 146 N.H. 418, 777 A.2d 851, 2001 N.H. LEXIS 90 (2001).

An actual hearing is not required to satisfy due process; rather, a party must be given an adequate opportunity to present objections and make its case. Town of Nottingham v. Bonser, 146 N.H. 418, 777 A.2d 851, 2001 N.H. LEXIS 90 (2001).

Trial court did not violate intervenors' due process rights by failing to conduct a hearing on plaintiff's fraudulent conveyance motion where it provided them sixty days to present evidence to counter its prima facie finding of fraud and instructed the parties that no hearing would be scheduled unless the intervenors offered contrary evidence establishing such a need. Town of Nottingham v. Bonser, 146 N.H. 418, 777 A.2d 851, 2001 N.H. LEXIS 90 (2001).

State due process clause requires that, prior to any proceeding involving the deprivation of significant property rights, State must provide notice reasonably calculated, under all the circumstances, to apprise interested parties of the pendency of the action and afford them an opportunity to present objections. Town of Nottingham v. Bonser, 146 N.H. 418, 777 A.2d 851, 2001 N.H. LEXIS 90 (2001).

Divorce defendant was adequately apprised of fact that she was, as a party, required to be available for trial in person, and that she could not simply send counsel in her absence. Douglas v. Douglas, 143 N.H. 419, 728 A.2d 215, 1999 N.H. LEXIS 20 (1999).

A town failed to give adequate notice of tax deedings to a bank that held mortgages on the properties at issue. The notices did not contain a warning that the mortgages would be eradicated if the properties were not redeemed. Dime Sav. Bank of N.Y., FSB v. Town of Pembroke, 142 N.H. 235, 698 A.2d 539, 1997 N.H. LEXIS 83 (1997).

The failure of board members to be present at an evidentiary hearing did not violate the petitioner's right to due process in a license reinstatement proceeding. Appeal of Dell, 140 N.H. 484, 668 A.2d 1024, 1995 N.H. LEXIS 176 (1995).

The board's decision to reject the hearing officer's recommendation did not violate the petitioner's right to due process in a license reinstatement proceeding. Appeal of Dell, 140 N.H. 484, 668 A.2d 1024, 1995 N.H. LEXIS 176 (1995).

Even assuming, arguendo, that the notice received by the plaintiff prior to a trial court hearing did not adequately apprise him of the court's intention to hear testimony and decide issues of fact, he could not prevail on his due process claim absent a showing of actual prejudice. McIntire v. Woodall, 140 N.H. 228, 666 A.2d 934, 1995 N.H. LEXIS 130 (1995).

A tax sale notice for a condominium unit gave adequate notice of the property interests that might be affected. Although the notice identified the condominium unit only by reference to its parcel number on the town's tax map and the parcel number comprised more than one condominium unit, the description was sufficient to alert anyone reading the notice that any or all of the units at the parcel might be auctioned. Berube v. Belhumeur, 139 N.H. 562, 663 A.2d 598, 1995 N.H. LEXIS 55 (1995).

Town selectmen did not violate the plaintiffs' rights to due process by denying them a hearing before posting a weight limit on the only road that allowed access to the plaintiffs' property. Before and after the imposition of the weight limit, the selectmen sought to confer personally with the plaintiffs, to no avail, and, after the limit was enacted, the selectmen invited the plaintiffs to participate in a selectmen's meeting to discuss the matter, but the plaintiffs failed to reply and did not attend. Kerouac v. Town of Hollis, 139 N.H. 554, 660 A.2d 1080, 1995 N.H. LEXIS 51 (1995).

Fundamental fairness requires notice to mortgagee of issue date of tax lien deeds and expiration date of right of redemption, and warning that mortgage will be eradicated by tax lien deed if property is not redeemed. First NH Bank v. Town of Windham, 138 N.H. 319, 639 A.2d 1089, 1994 N.H. LEXIS 28 (1994).

By dismissing an equitable proceeding initiated by executors of an estate to ascertain ownership of certain personal property without notice and an opportunity for a hearing, the trial court violated the plaintiff's due process rights under the New Hampshire Constitution. King v. Mosher, 137 N.H. 453, 629 A.2d 788, 1993 N.H. LEXIS 103 (1993).

To establish due process violation under federal and state constitutions, defendant must show that delay between arrest and trial resulted in actual prejudice to conduct of his or her defense; once defendant has shown that, trial court must balance prejudice against reasonableness of delay. State v. Leavitt, 136 N.H. 475, 617 A.2d 652, 1992 N.H. LEXIS 188 (1992).

Defendant appealing revocation of probation on theory that twenty-two month period between arrest and final revocation hearing constituted violation of state and federal due process did not so prove, where he did not satisfy burden to prove actual prejudice to conduct of his defense. State v. Leavitt, 136 N.H. 475, 617 A.2d 652, 1992 N.H. LEXIS 188 (1992).

Where governmental action would affect a legally protected interest, the due process clause of the New Hampshire Constitution guarantees to the holder of the interest the right to be heard at a meaningful time and in a meaningful manner. Appeal of Concord Steam Corp., 130 N.H. 422, 543 A.2d 905, 1988 N.H. LEXIS 41 (1988).

A fundamental requirement of the constitutional right to be heard is notice of the impending action that affords the party an opportunity to protect the interest through the presentation of objections and evidence. Appeal of Concord Steam Corp., 130 N.H. 422, 543 A.2d 905, 1988 N.H. LEXIS 41 (1988).

When the government seeks to take action which will deprive someone of property or liberty interests, notice must be given at a time when the deprivation can still be prevented. Claremont v. Truell, 126 N.H. 30, 489 A.2d 581, 1985 N.H. LEXIS 280 (1985).

The type of notice required to satisfy due process in a given case depends on the nature of the governmental interest and the private interests affected. Claremont v. Truell, 126 N.H. 30, 489 A.2d 581, 1985 N.H. LEXIS 280 (1985).

An elementary and fundamental requirement of due process is notice reasonably calculated, under all the circumstances, to apprise interested parties of the pendency of an action and afford them an opportunity to present their objections. Claremont v. Truell, 126 N.H. 30, 489 A.2d 581, 1985 N.H. LEXIS 280 (1985).

When the government seeks to take action which will deprive someone of property or liberty interests, due process requires meaningful notice of the government's action. Claremont v. Truell, 126 N.H. 30, 489 A.2d 581, 1985 N.H. LEXIS 280 (1985).

To satisfy the notice requirements of due process, notice to parents that they may be held liable for expenses incurred in the care of a child in need of services (CHINS) must be included in the summons issued by the court to the parents under RSA 169-D:6 informing them of the impending CHINS petition. Claremont v. Truell, 126 N.H. 30, 489 A.2d 581, 1985 N.H. LEXIS 280 (1985).

RSA 169-D:29, when read to require that the notice be given to the persons in custody and control and the parents of a child, in the summons informing them of the pending CHINS petition, that they may be held liable for expenses incurred, does not violate the due process protections of the New Hampshire or United States Constitutions. Claremont v. Truell, 126 N.H. 30, 489 A.2d 581, 1985 N.H. LEXIS 280 (1985).

The use of an ex parte capias writ to initiate collection or civil contempt proceedings before the debtor has been given an opportunity to appear voluntarily for a hearing concerning his reasons for nonpayment and his present ability to pay violates the debtor's procedural due process rights under both the United States and

New Hampshire Constitutions. Vermont Nat'l Bank v. Taylor, 122 N.H. 442, 445 A.2d 1122, 1982 N.H. LEXIS 366 (1982).

Where the district court used the ex parte capias procedure to initiate civil contempt proceedings against debtors who had defaulted in payment on an agreement for judgment, and the procedure resulted in the arrest of one of the debtors before she had notice or any opportunity to be heard on her present ability to pay the judgment, use of the writ was unconstitutional. Vermont Nat'l Bank v. Taylor, 122 N.H. 442, 445 A.2d 1122, 1982 N.H. LEXIS 366 (1982).

Fundamental requisite of due process is the right to be heard at a meaningful time and in a meaningful manner; furthermore, the right to be heard is grounded in the need for confrontation when adjudicative rights are in dispute. Hampton Nat'l Bank v. State, 114 N.H. 38, 314 A.2d 668, 1974 N.H. LEXIS 203 (1974).

The due process provision of this article requires notice and hearing before deprivation of a property interest. Royer v. State Dep't of Employment Sec., 118 N.H. 673, 394 A.2d 828, 1978 N.H. LEXIS 269 (1978).

416. Administrative procedures

Since the police officer informed the driver that the preliminary breath test (PBT) would be used to prove or disprove the sobriety test results, it was not fundamentally unfair or a violation of due process to admit the PBT result at the administrative license suspension hearing as the driver was informed what the test would be used for. Even if the admission of the PBT result was error, it was harmless as there was other evidence, such as the officers' observations, which showed the driver was impaired. Saviano v. Dir., N.H. DMV, 151 N.H. 315, 855 A.2d 1278, 2004 N.H. LEXIS 142 (2004).

There was no denial of due process to fireworks retailer that faced license suspension for violation of various provisions of RSA 160-B where the retailer received a summary of charges with a list of statutes allegedly violated and also received, well before the hearing, copies of detailed police reports. Appeal of N.H. Fireworks, Inc. (N.H. Dep't of Safety), 151 N.H. 335, 856 A.2d 725, 2004 N.H. LEXIS 152 (2004).

Where defendant's trial record was destroyed 10 years after it was recorded as provided for in N.H. Super. Ct. Admin. R. 3-9(b) but before defendant's sentence because defendant fled the jurisdiction before sentencing, defendant's due process rights under N.H. Const. pt. I, art. 15 were not denied; the rule allowing the destruction only disadvantaged defendant due to defendant's flight, and because the destruction of the record was defendant's own making, defendant could not complain of a due process violation. State v. Brenes, 151 N.H. 11, 846 A.2d 1211, 2004 N.H. LEXIS 80 (2004).

Property owner failed to meet his burden of establishing that agricultural lands preservation committee had a conflict of interest, entertained ill-will towards him, or unalterably prejudged facts of his case, and thus there was no violation of property owner's constitutional right to fair hearing. State v. Rattee (Petition of Rattee), 145 N.H. 341, 761 A.2d 1076, 2000 N.H. LEXIS 65 (2000).

Absent an adjudicative component, alleged combination of investigative and accusative functions in same individual was insufficient to render psychologist's disciplinary proceeding unconstitutional. Appeal of Trotzer, 143 N.H. 64, 719 A.2d 584, 1998 N.H. LEXIS 68 (1998).

The plaintiff's due process rights were not violated where: (1) he refused to take a chemical test after his arrest for driving while intoxicated on March 25, 1995, and his driver's license was suspended for 180 days pursuant to former RSA 265:91-a (see now RSA 265-A:30); (2) on April 27, 1995, the Division of Motor Vehicles (DMV) held an administrative hearing to review the license suspension pursuant to RSA 265:91-b; (3) on May 12, 1995, the suspension was upheld until October 21, 1995; (4) the plaintiff appealed this decision to the superior court on May 25, 1995, and (5) on July 17, 1995, the plaintiff learned that the superior court's record review of the DMV decision would begin after November 4, 1995, approximately two weeks after his license was scheduled to be restored. Bragg v. Director, N.H. DMV, 141 N.H. 677, 690 A.2d 571, 1997 N.H. LEXIS 20 (1997).

The application of the preponderance of the evidence burden of proof to psychologist disciplinary proceedings satisfies due process. In re Grimm, 138 N.H. 42, 635 A.2d 456, 1993 N.H. LEXIS 169 (1993).

The court would vacate a decision of the New Hampshire Board of Examiners of Psychologists revoking the petitioner's psychologist certificate as the failure of every member of the hearing panel, acting in a fact-finding capacity, to attend all of his and the complainant's testimony violated his right to due process. In re Grimm, 138 N.H. 42, 635 A.2d 456, 1993 N.H. LEXIS 169 (1993).

In determining whether challenged administrative procedures satisfy the due process requirement of this article, the touchstone of the analysis of whether the interest at stake is a protected liberty or property interest is not whether the government benefit conferred is characterized as a right or a privilege, but whether it is a protected property interest under this article. Appeal of Plantier, 126 N.H. 500, 494 A.2d 270, 1985 N.H. LEXIS 341, 51 A.L.R.4th 1129 (1985).

The following factors are considered in determining whether challenged procedures afford appropriate procedural safeguards for state due process purposes: first, the private interest that will be affected by the official action; second, the risk of an erroneous deprivation of such interest through the procedures used, and the probable value, if any, of additional or substitute procedural safeguards; and finally, the government's interest, including the function involved and the fiscal and administrative burdens that the additional or substitute procedural requirement would entail. Appeal of Plantier, 126 N.H. 500, 494 A.2d 270, 1985 N.H. LEXIS 341, 51 A.L.R.4th 1129 (1985).

417. Immunity of witnesses

Trial court did not violate due process under the Fifth and Fourteenth Amendments and N.H. Const. pt. I, art. 15 by failing to grant immunity to a witness for the purpose of investigating his alleged perjury. Even a complete recantation by the witness could not place defendant elsewhere or preclude the possibility that he committed the crime of which he was convicted. State v. Etienne, 163 N.H. 57, 35 A.3d 523, 2011 N.H. LEXIS 189 (Dec. 21, 2011).

State's refusal to immunize two defense witnesses under RSA 516:34 did not violate defendant's due process rights under the state constitution because the testimony was not the sort of exculpatory evidence that would have prevented conviction: their testimony could not place defendant elsewhere or preclude the possibility that he had an agreement with a second person to kidnap and terrorize the victim. Furthermore, the testimony was cumulative, and there was no suggestion of prosecutorial misconduct. State v. Rogers, 159 N.H. 50, 977 A.2d 493, 2009 N.H. LEXIS 85 (2009).

418. Eminent domain

Fact that the Public Utilities Commission imposed conditions upon a city's acquisition of a utility through eminent domain, as RSA 38:11 expressly allowed it to do, did not mean that it was not fair and impartial under U.S. Const. amends. V and XIV and N.H. Const. pt. I, art. 15. Furthermore, the utilities had ample opportunity to be heard about the concerns that prompted the conditions. Appeal of Pennichuck Water Works, Inc., 160 N.H. 18, 992 A.2d 740, 2010 N.H. LEXIS 23 (2010).

419. Prosecutorial misconduct

Trial court did not violate defendant's rights to due process and a fair trial by failing to re-instruct the jury. The State's closing remarks, viewed in context, did not communicate to the jury that the charging instruments had evidentiary value or shift the burden of proof to defendant. State v. Stowe, 162 N.H. 464, 34 A.3d 678, 2011 N.H. LEXIS 128 (2011).

In determining whether evidence withheld by the State was material under the New Hampshire Constitution, the Court would treat the trial court's determination as a mixed question of law and fact and review it de novo, as the State did not argue otherwise. State v. Etienne, 163 N.H. 57, 35 A.3d 523, 2011 N.H. LEXIS 189 (Dec. 21, 2011).

Trial court properly denied defendant's motion for a new trial under RSA 526:1 based on the prosecution's failure to disclose exculpatory information in violation of due process under the Fourteenth Amendment and N.H. Const. pt. I, art. 15. Disclosure of a witness's immunity agreement and plea deal in other cases would not have affected defense counsel's strategy or the ultimate verdict. State v. Etienne, 163 N.H. 57, 35 A.3d 523, 2011 N.H. LEXIS 189 (Dec. 21, 2011).

Double jeopardy and due process did not prohibit a retrial based on intentional prosecutorial misconduct. The State had immediately informed the trial court and defendant about an eyewitness's untruthful grand jury testimony, had sought a continuance to reindict defendant, and had provided defendant with all of the witness's prior statements; there was no evidence that the State intentionally sought the witness's false testimony; and the trial court credited the State's assertion that it did not know that defendant had applied for a concealed handgun permit until the day before trial and that it did not know the contents of that application until after the trial. State v. Glenn, 160 N.H. 480, 9 A.3d 161, 2010 N.H. LEXIS 81 (July 20, 2010).

420. Comments by trial court

Comments by the trial court were not plain error that had violated due process under the Fifth Amendment and N.H. Const. pt. I, art. 15. The first comment could not reasonably be construed to imply that the trial court believed defendant to be "a bad person who had committed a crime," the second reflected the evidence offered by officers in their testimony regarding their investigation, and the third was not a specific comment on defendant's guilt or credibility; moreover, defendant had not shown that the comments affected the outcome of the proceeding, and the trial judge had instructed the jurors to disregard any opinions they believed he had expressed. State v. Euliano, 161 N.H. 601, 20 A.3d 223, 2011 N.H. LEXIS 29 (2011).

421. Indictments and informations

Indictments for perjury under RSA 641:1, I(a) were not insufficient under N.H. Const. pt. I, art. 15 and the Fourteenth Amendment because they did not allege specific statements. An indictment that attributes a false statement to a defendant does not fail for insufficiency even though the statement represents a summary of the defendant's testimony. State v. Bisbee, — N.H. —, 69 A.3d 95, 2013 N.H. LEXIS 51 (May 14, 2013).

In evaluating the sufficiency of a perjury indictment, the trial court need not compare the allegedly perjurious statement with the defendant's prior testimony. Whether the defendant made the statements alleged in the indictments raises an issue of proof that is distinct from the indictment's sufficiency. State v. Bisbee, — N.H. —, 69 A.3d 95, 2013 N.H. LEXIS 51 (May 14, 2013).

It is a faulty premise that the sufficiency of an indictment depends in part on its ability to assure jury unanimity. The sufficiency of an indictment is measured against the defendant's ability to prepare for trial and avoid double jeopardy. State v. Bisbee, — N.H. —, 69 A.3d 95, 2013 N.H. LEXIS 51 (May 14, 2013).

Trial court did not violate due process under N.H. Const. pt. I, art. 15 by refusing to give an instruction under Williams without also permitting the State to amend the indictments to include the time period evidenced by a photograph proffered by defendant the day before trial. Had defendant provided the photograph to the State 30 days prior to trial, as required by N.H. Super. Ct. R. 98(B)(3), the State could have amended the indictments sufficiently in advance of trial to avoid any undue prejudice to the defense. State v. Quintero, 162 N.H. 526, 34 A.3d 612, 2011 N.H. LEXIS 142 (2011).

Clear and convincing standard of proof in RSA ch. 135-E does not violate the state constitutional due process guarantee. State v. Ploof, 162 N.H. 609, 34 A.3d 563, 2011 N.H. LEXIS 148 (2011).

RSA ch. 135-E, governing involuntary civil commitment of sexually violent predators, did not violate due process under the Fifth and Fourteenth Amendments or N.H. Const. pt. I, art. 15. Neither the procedures nor the burden of proof set forth in the statute carried undue risk of an erroneous deprivation of a defendant's private interests, and the State had a strong interest in protecting the public from, and providing care and treatment for, sexually violent predators. State v. Ploof, 162 N.H. 609, 34 A.3d 563, 2011 N.H. LEXIS 148 (2011).

Defendant was not denied due process under N.H. Const. pt. I, art. 15 and the Fifth and Fourteenth Amendments based on the incompleteness of the record. He had not shown specific prejudice to his appeal from the fact that part of an expert witness's cross-examination testimony was missing. State v. Marshall, 162 N.H. 657, 34 A.3d 540, 2011 N.H. LEXIS 152 (2011).

422. Informants

When an informant assigned to discuss shooting charges with defendant after defendant's arrest on drug charges also questioned him about the drug charges, this violated defendant's right to counsel with respect to the drug charges; however, these facts did not demonstrate the kind of misbehavior that so shocked the sensibilities of civilized society as to constitute a due process violation under N.H. Const. pt. I, art. 15. State v. White, 163 N.H. 303, 42 A.3d 783, 2012 N.H. LEXIS 28 (2012).

423. Jury instructions

In a criminal case that included direct evidence, it was error for the trial court to include in its instructions language indicating that the evidence need not exclude all rational conclusions other than guilt. There was no due process violation, however, as the jury heard the correct instruction on burden of proof about 20 times and could not have understood the challenged instruction as allowing it to convict defendant based on proof less than beyond a reasonable doubt. State v. Saunders, 164 N.H. 342, 55 A.3d 1014, 2012 N.H. LEXIS 149 (2012).

424. Identifications

That the police did not follow every recommendation of the New Hampshire Attorney General guidelines did not, in and of itself, satisfy defendant's burden to show that the manner of presenting the photographs in an array was unnecessarily suggestive. Furthermore, there was no evidence that police told the victim that defendant's photograph depicted a person of interest or that the officers rushed the victim or implied that she should select a particular photograph, and the array did not highlight defendant's photograph. State v. Perri, 164 N.H. 400, 58 A.3d 627, 2012 N.H. LEXIS 162 (2012).

Victim's out-of-court identification of defendant was sufficiently reliable to be admitted when the victim had two opportunities to view defendant on the day of the assault, including in a well-lit area, her degree of attention was high, and she previously accurately described defendant. Because her out-of-court identification was admissible, her in-court identification was as well. State v. Perri, 164 N.H. 400, 58 A.3d 627, 2012 N.H. LEXIS 162 (2012).

425. Pretrial publicity

Pretrial publicity did not result in presumptive prejudice requiring a change of venue under N.H. Const. pt. I, arts. 15 and 17 and the Sixth Amendment. The jury was drawn from a county with a population over 400,000; the overwhelming amount of the material submitted by defendant consisted of straightforward, factual accounts of the crime; defendant's trial occurred nearly a year and a half after the crimes; and given that defendant admitted his participation in the crimes and pleaded not guilty by reason of insanity, his codefendant's trial had little relevance to defendant's state of mind at the time of the crime. State v. Gribble, — N.H. —, 66 A.3d 1194, 2013 N.H. LEXIS 47 (May 7, 2013).

Statements of potential jurors on voir dire did not show that a change of venue under N.H. Const. pt. I, arts. 15 and 17 and the Sixth Amendment was required due to pretrial publicity. The trial court conducted a thorough jury selection process over a period of eight days and went to great lengths to ensure that the empaneled jury was fair and impartial; there was ample support for the trial court's conclusion that defendant was unable to demonstrate any actual bias or prejudice in the seated jury panel. State v. Gribble, — N.H. —, 66 A.3d 1194, 2013 N.H. LEXIS 47 (May 7, 2013).

Cited:

Cited in State v. Flynn, 36 N.H. 64, 1858 N.H. LEXIS 40 (1858); East Kingston v. Towle, 48 N.H. 57, 1868 N.H. LEXIS 13 (1868); State v. Gerry, 68 N.H. 495, 38 A. 272, 1896 N.H. LEXIS 41, 38 L.R.A. 228 (1896); State v. Jackson, 69 N.H. 511, 43 A. 749, 1898 N.H. LEXIS 72 (1899); State v. Silverman, 76 N.H. 309, 82 A. 536, 1912 N.H. LEXIS 42 (1912); In re Opinion of Justices, 88 N.H. 500, 190 A. 801, 1937 N.H. LEXIS 90 (1936); State v. Liptzer, 90 N.H. 395, 10 A.2d 232, 1939 N.H. LEXIS 83 (1939); Perley v. Roberts, 138 F.2d 518, 1943 U.S. App. LEXIS 2569 (1st Cir. N.H. 1943) certiorari denied, 321 U.S. 788, 64 S. Ct. 786, 88 L. Ed. 2d 1078 (1944); State v. Fogg, 92 N.H. 308, 30 A.2d 491, 1943 N.H. LEXIS 81 (1943); State v. Moore, 93 N.H. 169, 37 A.2d 15, 1944 N.H. LEXIS 116 (1944); State v. Sturtevant, 96 N.H. 99, 70 A.2d 909, 1950 N.H. LEXIS 5 (1950); In re Moulton, 96 N.H. 370, 77 A.2d 26, 1950 N.H. LEXIS

210 (1950); In re Mundy, 97 N.H. 239, 85 A.2d 371, 1952 N.H. LEXIS 2 (1952); State v. Morris, 98 N.H. 517, 103 A.2d 913, 1954 N.H. LEXIS 101 (1954); Wyman v. De Gregory, 101 N.H. 82, 133 A.2d 787, 1957 N.H. LEXIS 23 (1957); State ex rel. Regan v. Superior Court, 102 N.H. 224, 153 A.2d 403, 1959 N.H. LEXIS 51 (1959); Manchester Hous. Auth. v. Fisk, 102 N.H. 280, 155 A.2d 186, 1959 N.H. LEXIS 65 (1959); Corning Glass Works v. Max Dichter Co., 102 N.H. 505, 161 A.2d 569, 1960 N.H. LEXIS 67 (1960); Massachusetts Bonding & Ins. Co. v. Nudd, 103 N.H. 1, 164 A.2d 242, 1960 N.H. LEXIS 1 (1960); State v. Davis, 103 N.H. 79, 165 A.2d 42, 1960 N.H. LEXIS 18 (1960); State v. La Palme, 104 N.H. 97, 179 A.2d 284, 1962 N.H. LEXIS 26 (1962); State v. Ring, 106 N.H. 509, 214 A.2d 748, 1965 N.H. LEXIS 202 (1965); State v. Charest, 109 N.H. 201, 247 A.2d 515, 1968 N.H. LEXIS 156 (1968); State v. Thomson, 109 N.H. 205, 247 A.2d 179, 1968 N.H. LEXIS 157 (1968); State v. Desjardins, 110 N.H. 511, 272 A.2d 599, 1970 N.H. LEXIS 214 (1970); State v. Hudson, 111 N.H. 25, 274 A.2d 878, 1971 N.H. LEXIS 114 (1971); State v. Larochelle, 112 N.H. 392, 297 A.2d 223, 1972 N.H. LEXIS 227 (1972); Hartford Accident & Indem. Co. v. Duvall, 113 N.H. 28, 300 A.2d 732, 1973 N.H. LEXIS 191 (1973); State v. Nickerson, 114 N.H. 47, 314 A.2d 648, 1974 N.H. LEXIS 205 (1974); State v. Russell, 114 N.H. 222, 317 A.2d 781, 1974 N.H. LEXIS 243 (1974); State v. Fleury, 114 N.H. 325, 321 A.2d 108, 1974 N.H. LEXIS 270 (1974); State v. Clough, 115 N.H. 7, 332 A.2d 386, 1975 N.H. LEXIS 209 (1975); New Hampshire Ins. Co. v. Duvall, 115 N.H. 215, 337 A.2d 533, 1975 N.H. LEXIS 263 (1975); Wheeler v. State, 115 N.H. 347, 341 A.2d 777, 1975 N.H. LEXIS 302 (1975) certiorari denied, 423 U.S. 1075, 96 S. Ct. 860, 47 L. Ed. 2d 86 (1976); State v. Williams, 115 N.H. 437, 343 A.2d 29, 1975 N.H. LEXIS 331 (1975); State v. New Hampshire Retail Grocers Ass'n, 115 N.H. 623, 348 A.2d 360, 1975 N.H. LEXIS 380 (1975); State v. Allard, 116 N.H. 240, 356 A.2d 671, 1976 N.H. LEXIS 319 (1976); State v. Harlan, 116 N.H. 598, 364 A.2d 1254, 1976 N.H. LEXIS 423 (1976); Jenkins v. Canaan Mun. Court, 116 N.H. 616, 366 A.2d 208, 1976 N.H. LEXIS 428 (1976); State v. Lantaigne, 117 N.H. 266, 371 A.2d 1170, 1977 N.H. LEXIS 313 (1977); State v. Smagula, 117 N.H. 663, 377 A.2d 608, 1977 N.H. LEXIS 405 (1977); State v. Whiting, 117 N.H. 701, 378 A.2d 736, 1977 N.H. LEXIS 413 (1977); Proctor v. Butler, 117 N.H. 927, 380 A.2d 673, 1977 N.H. LEXIS 463 (1977); Novosel v. Helgemoe, 118 N.H. 115, 384 A.2d 124, 1978 N.H. LEXIS 356 (1978); State v. Gregoire, 118 N.H. 140, 384 A.2d 132, 1978 N.H. LEXIS 360 (1978); Nizza v. Adams, 118 N.H. 383, 387 A.2d 336, 1978 N.H. LEXIS 423 (1978); State v. Breest, 118 N.H. 416, 387 A.2d 643, 1978 N.H. LEXIS 428 (1978) certiorari denied, 442 U.S. 931, 99 S. Ct. 2864, 61 L. Ed. 2d 300, 99 S. Ct. 2864 (1979); Hudson v. Miller, 119 N.H. 141, 399 A.2d 612, 1979 N.H. LEXIS 257 (1979); State v. Boisvert, 119 N.H. 174, 400 A.2d 48, 1979 N.H. LEXIS 268 (1979); State v. Osborne, 119 N.H. 427, 402 A.2d 493, 1979 N.H. LEXIS 346 (1979); State v. Heinz, 119 N.H. 717, 407 A.2d 814, 1979 N.H. LEXIS 382 (1979); State v. Gullick, 120 N.H. 99, 411 A.2d 1113, 1980 N.H. LEXIS 237 (1980) certiorari denied, 449 U.S. 879, 101 S. Ct. 226, 66 L. Ed. 2d 101, 1980 U.S. LEXIS 3313 (1980); In re G., 120 N.H. 153, 412 A.2d 1012, 1980 N.H. LEXIS 250 (1980); State v. Morehouse, 120 N.H. 738, 424 A.2d 798, 1980 N.H. LEXIS 406 (1980); State v. Degrenier, 120 N.H. 919, 424 A.2d 412, 1980 N.H. LEXIS 421 (1980); Fournier v. State, 121 N.H. 283, 428 A.2d 1238, 1981 N.H. LEXIS 302 (1981); State v. Gilbert, 121 N.H. 305, 429 A.2d 323, 1981 N.H. LEXIS 308 (1981); In re D., 121 N.H. 547, 431 A.2d 789, 1981 N.H. LEXIS 364 (1981); State v. Merski, 121 N.H. 901, 437 A.2d 710, 1981 N.H. LEXIS 435 (1981) certiorari denied, 455 U.S. 943, 102 S. Ct. 1439, 71 L. Ed. 2d 655 (1982); State v. Hunt, 122 N.H. 59, 440 A.2d 1126, 1982 N.H. LEXIS 284 (1982); Opinion of Justices, 122 N.H. 199, 442 A.2d 594, 1982 N.H. LEXIS 309 (1982); In re Clark, 122 N.H. 888, 451 A.2d 1303, 1982 N.H. LEXIS 486 (1982); State v. Comtois, 122 N.H. 1173, 453 A.2d 1324, 1982 N.H. LEXIS 535 (1982); Kozerski v. Smith, 555 F. Supp. 212, 1983 U.S. Dist. LEXIS 20099 (D.N.H. 1983); State v. Chaisson, 123 N.H. 17, 458 A.2d 95, 1983 N.H. LEXIS 236 (1983); Seabrook Citizens for Defense of Home Rule v. Yankee Greyhound Racing, 123 N.H. 103, 456 A.2d 973, 1983 N.H. LEXIS 234 (1983); Chasan v. Village Dist. of Eastman, 572 F. Supp. 578, 1983 U.S. Dist. LEXIS 13323 (D.N.H. 1983); Armstrong v. Armstrong, 123 N.H. 291, 461 A.2d 103, 1983 N.H. LEXIS 278 (1983); State v. LaFrance, 124 N.H. 171, 471 A.2d 340, 1983 N.H. LEXIS 377 (1983); In re Scott L., 124 N.H. 327, 469 A.2d 1336, 1983 N.H. LEXIS 398 (1983); State v. Baillargeon, 124

N.H. 355, 470 A.2d 915, 1983 N.H. LEXIS 422 (1983); State v. Laliberte, 124 N.H. 621, 474 A.2d 1025, 1984 N.H. LEXIS 354 (1984); State v. Lovely, 124 N.H. 690, 480 A.2d 847, 1984 N.H. LEXIS 295 (1984); State v. Elbert, 125 N.H. 1, 480 A.2d 854, 1984 N.H. LEXIS 371 (1984); State v. Etzweiler, 125 N.H. 57, 480 A.2d 870, 1984 N.H. LEXIS 369 (1984); State v. Ballou, 125 N.H. 304, 481 A.2d 260, 1984 N.H. LEXIS 270 (1984); State v. Brown, 125 N.H. 346, 480 A.2d 901, 1984 N.H. LEXIS 265 (1984); State v. Merrill, 125 N.H. 479, 484 A.2d 1065, 1984 N.H. LEXIS 412 (1984); State v. Jones, 125 N.H. 490, 484 A.2d 1070, 1984 N.H. LEXIS 409 (1984); State v. Robb, 125 N.H. 581, 484 A.2d 1130, 1984 N.H. LEXIS 310 (1984); State v. Alcorn, 125 N.H. 672, 484 A.2d 1176, 1984 N.H. LEXIS 379 (1984); State v. Kilgus, 125 N.H. 739, 484 A.2d 1208, 1984 N.H. LEXIS 375 (1984); Kilgus v. Cunningham, 602 F. Supp. 735, 1985 U.S. Dist. LEXIS 22685 (D.N.H. 1985) (D.N.H.), State v. Chaisson, 126 N.H. 323, 493 A.2d 1114, 1985 N.H. LEXIS 325 (1985); State v. Corey, 127 N.H. 56, 497 A.2d 1196, 1985 N.H. LEXIS 400 (1985); State v. Abbott, 127 N.H. 444, 503 A.2d 791, 1985 N.H. LEXIS 465 (1985); State v. Perra, 127 N.H. 533, 503 A.2d 814, 1985 N.H. LEXIS 456 (1985); State v. Dukette, 127 N.H. 540, 506 A.2d 699, 1986 N.H. LEXIS 227 (1986); In re Melissa M., 127 N.H. 710, 506 A.2d 324, 1986 N.H. LEXIS 226 (1986); State v. Allison, 127 N.H. 829, 508 A.2d 1084, 1986 N.H. LEXIS 228 (1986); Opinion of Justices, 128 N.H. 1, 509 A.2d 734, 1986 N.H. LEXIS 246 (1986); State v. Saucier, 128 N.H. 291, 512 A.2d 1120, 1986 N.H. LEXIS 292 (1986); Appeal of Catholic Medical Ctr., 128 N.H. 410, 515 A.2d 1205, 1986 N.H. LEXIS 320 (1986); State v. Grimshaw, 128 N.H. 431, 515 A.2d 1201, 1986 N.H. LEXIS 323 (1986); Ladd v. Coleman, 128 N.H. 543, 517 A.2d 811, 1986 N.H. LEXIS 340 (1986); State v. Dellorfano, 128 N.H. 628, 517 A.2d 1163, 1986 N.H. LEXIS 343 (1986); State v. Lakin, 128 N.H. 639, 517 A.2d 846, 1986 N.H. LEXIS 344 (1986); State v. Cross, 128 N.H. 732, 519 A.2d 272, 1986 N.H. LEXIS 351 (1986); State v. Wheeler, 128 N.H. 767, 519 A.2d 289, 1986 N.H. LEXIS 367 (1986); In re Champagne, 128 N.H. 791, 519 A.2d 310, 1986 N.H. LEXIS 357 (1986); State v. Heath, 129 N.H. 102, 523 A.2d 82, 1986 N.H. LEXIS 395 (1986); Opinion of the Justices, 129 N.H. 290, 525 A.2d 1095, 1987 N.H. LEXIS 177 (1987); State v. Cote, 129 N.H. 358, 530 A.2d 775, 1987 N.H. LEXIS 217 (1987); State v. Day, 129 N.H. 378, 529 A.2d 887, 1987 N.H. LEXIS 204 (1987); State v. Erickson, 129 N.H. 515, 533 A.2d 23, 1987 N.H. LEXIS 253 (1987); State v. Murray, 129 N.H. 645, 531 A.2d 323, 1987 N.H. LEXIS 233 (1987); State v. Richards, 129 N.H. 669, 531 A.2d 338, 1987 N.H. LEXIS 241 (1987); State v. Allegra, 129 N.H. 720, 533 A.2d 338, 1987 N.H. LEXIS 247 (1987); State v. Therrien, 129 N.H. 765, 533 A.2d 346, 1987 N.H. LEXIS 261 (1987); State v. Lewis, 129 N.H. 787, 533 A.2d 358, 1987 N.H. LEXIS 246 (1987); State v. MacManus, 130 N.H. 256, 536 A.2d 203, 1987 N.H. LEXIS 283 (1987); State v. Colbath, 130 N.H. 316, 540 A.2d 1212, 1988 N.H. LEXIS 13 (1988); State v. Riccio, 130 N.H. 376, 540 A.2d 1239, 1988 N.H. LEXIS 8 (1988); In re Sanborn, 130 N.H. 430, 545 A.2d 726, 1988 N.H. LEXIS 40 (1988); State v. Stearns, 130 N.H. 475, 547 A.2d 672, 1988 N.H. LEXIS 72 (1988); Bedford Residents Group v. Bedford, 130 N.H. 632, 547 A.2d 225, 1988 N.H. LEXIS 65 (1988); Stewart v. Cunningham, 131 N.H. 68, 550 A.2d 96, 1988 N.H. LEXIS 84 (1988); State v. O'Connell, 131 N.H. 92, 550 A.2d 747, 1988 N.H. LEXIS 92 (1988); State v. Bruneau, 131 N.H. 104, 552 A.2d 585, 1988 N.H. LEXIS 106 (1988); Avery v. Cunningham, 131 N.H. 138, 551 A.2d 952, 1988 N.H. LEXIS 107 (1988); State v. Sundstrom, 131 N.H. 203, 552 A.2d 81, 1988 N.H. LEXIS 116 (1988); Richardson v. Chevrefils, 131 N.H. 227, 552 A.2d 89, 1988 N.H. LEXIS 117 (1988); State v. Gosselin, 131 N.H. 243, 552 A.2d 974, 1988 N.H. LEXIS 114 (1988); State v. Ramos, 131 N.H. 276, 553 A.2d 275, 1988 N.H. LEXIS 133 (1988); State v. Reynolds, 131 N.H. 291, 556 A.2d 298, 1988 N.H. LEXIS 128 (1988); State v. Moulton, 131 N.H. 467, 554 A.2d 1292, 1989 N.H. LEXIS 10 (1989); Opinion of Justices, 131 N.H. 504, 555 A.2d 1095, 1989 N.H. LEXIS 13 (1989); Opinion of Justices, 131 N.H. 583, 557 A.2d 1355, 1989 N.H. LEXIS 37 (1989); Vachon v. New Durham Zoning Bd. of Adjustment, 131 N.H. 623, 557 A.2d 649, 1989 N.H. LEXIS 29 (1989); State v. Pelky, 131 N.H. 715, 559 A.2d 1345, 1989 N.H. LEXIS 52 (1989); State v. Derby, 131 N.H. 760, 561 A.2d 504, 1989 N.H. LEXIS 57 (1989); Grote v. Powell, 132 N.H. 96, 562 A.2d 152, 1989 N.H. LEXIS 70 (1989); State v. Carpentier, 132 N.H. 123, 562 A.2d 181, 1989 N.H. LEXIS 80 (1989); State v. Wood, 132 N.H. 162, 562 A.2d 1312, 1989 N.H. LEXIS 85 (1989); State v. Grondin, 132 N.H. 194, 563 A.2d 435, 1989 N.H. LEXIS 90 (1989); State v.

Kulikowski, 132 N.H. 281, 564 A.2d 439, 1989 N.H. LEXIS 99 (1989); State v. Frederick, 132 N.H. 349, 566 A.2d 180, 1989 N.H. LEXIS 105 (1989); State v. Pond, 132 N.H. 472, 567 A.2d 992, 1989 N.H. LEXIS 129 (1989); State v. Vanderheyden, 132 N.H. 536, 567 A.2d 553, 1989 N.H. LEXIS 135 (1989); State v. Settle, 132 N.H. 626, 570 A.2d 895, 1990 N.H. LEXIS 3 (1990); State v. Smith, 132 N.H. 756, 571 A.2d 279, 1990 N.H. LEXIS 14 (1990); State v. Lachapelle, 133 N.H. 1, 572 A.2d 584, 1990 N.H. LEXIS 27 (1990); State v. Cox, 133 N.H. 261, 575 A.2d 1320, 1990 N.H. LEXIS 46 (1990); State v. Monsalve, 133 N.H. 268, 574 A.2d 1384, 1990 N.H. LEXIS 60 (1990); Appeal of Sullivan County Nursing Home, 133 N.H. 389, 578 A.2d 325, 1990 N.H. LEXIS 77 (1990); Appeal of Office of Consumer Advocate, 134 N.H. 651, 597 A.2d 528, 1991 N.H. LEXIS 115 (1991); State v. Hurlburt, 135 N.H. 143, 603 A.2d 493, 1991 N.H. LEXIS 157 (1991); Appeal of Atlantic Connections, 135 N.H. 510, 608 A.2d 861, 1992 N.H. LEXIS 69 (1992); State v. Ryan, 135 N.H. 587, 607 A.2d 954, 1992 N.H. LEXIS 82 (1992); State v. Mills, 136 N.H. 46, 611 A.2d 1104, 1992 N.H. LEXIS 128 (1992); State v. Huffman, 136 N.H. 149, 613 A.2d 476, 1992 N.H. LEXIS 149 (1992); Avery v. Powell, 806 F. Supp. 7, 1992 U.S. Dist. LEXIS 17074 (D.N.H. 1992); State v. Delisle, 137 N.H. 549, 630 A.2d 767, 1993 N.H. LEXIS 119 (1993); In re Grimm, 138 N.H. 42, 635 A.2d 456, 1993 N.H. LEXIS 169 (1993); State v. Martin, 138 N.H. 508, 643 A.2d 946, 1994 N.H. LEXIS 57 (1994); State v. Colbert, 139 N.H. 367, 654 A.2d 963, 1995 N.H. LEXIS 6 (1995); Asselin v. Conway, 135 N.H. 576, 607 A.2d 132, 1992 N.H. LEXIS 83 (1992); Opinion of the Justices (Certain Evidence in Sexual Assult Cases), 140 N.H. 22, 662 A.2d 294, 1995 N.H. LEXIS 87 (1995); Wellington v. Commissioner, State Dep't of Corrections, 140 N.H. 399, 666 A.2d 969, 1995 N.H. LEXIS 155 (1995); State v. Doucette, 146 N.H. 583, 776 A.2d 744, 2001 N.H. LEXIS 112 (2001).

RESEARCH REFERENCES

New Hampshire Bar Journal.

For article, "Lex Loci: A Survey of New Hampshire Supreme Court Decisions," see 49 N.H.B.J. 40 (Spring 2008).

For article, "Lex Loci: A Survey of New Hampshire Supreme Court Decisions," see 47 N.H.B.J. 78 (Autumn 2006).

For article, "Lex Loci: A Survey of New Hampshire Supreme Court Decisions," see 45 N.H.B.J. 64 (July 2004).

For article, "I'm Guilty — I Think? In re Wesley B.: An Anlysis of the Voluntariness of Juvenile Confessions," see 42 N.H.B.J. 24 (Sept. 2001).

Art. 16. [Former Jeopardy; Jury Trial in Capital Cases.]

No subject shall be liable to be tried, after an acquittal, for the same crime or offense. Nor shall the legislature make any law that shall subject any person to a capital punishment, (excepting for the government of the army and navy, and the militia in actual service) without trial by jury.

Cross References.

Appointment of counsel for indigent charged with capital offense, see RSA 604-A:2.

Double jeopardy prohibited by federal constitution, see United States Constitution, Amendment V.

Procedure in capital murder, see RSA 630:5.

Rights of accused generally, see New Hampshire Constitution, Part 1, Article 15.

Rights of persons indicted in capital cases, see RSA 604:1.

NOTES TO DECISIONS

1. Double jeopardy—Generally
2. —Attachment
3. —Construction with federal constitution
4. —Purpose
5. —Identity of offenses
6. —Tests

7. —Burden of proof
8. —Nolle prosequi
9. —Separate trials
10. —Retrial following mistrial
11. —Sentencing
12. —Retrial following reversal on appeal
13. —Civil proceedings
14. —Res judicata
15. —Collateral estoppel
16. —Federal and state prosecutions
17. —Administrative punishment
18. —Prosecution for greater charge after conviction of lesser
19. Jury trial
20. Criminal contempt
21. Prosecutorial misconduct

1. Double jeopardy—Generally

There was no merit to defendant's argument that the jury, by acquitting him of first-degree felony murder, necessarily found that he did not shoot and kill the victim, thereby barring his reprosecution under the Double Jeopardy Clause; the jury could have based its acquittal for the first-degree felony murder on other grounds, such as finding that defendant did not attempt to rob the victim at the time of the shooting. Therefore, the United States Supreme Court's decision in *Yeager* did not bar defendant's retrial for second degree knowing or reckless murder, neither of which required proof of robbery for conviction. State v. Glenn, 160 N.H. 480, 9 A.3d 161, 2010 N.H. LEXIS 81 (July 20, 2010).

No double jeopardy violation since proof of the elements of either of the crimes charged could not sustain a conviction on the elements of the other crime. State v. Hull, 149 N.H. 706, 827 A.2d 1001, 2003 N.H. LEXIS 106 (2003).

Double jeopardy clause of New Hampshire Constitution prohibits State from placing a criminal defendant in jeopardy more than once for the same offense, thereby preserving defendant's valued right to have his trial completed by a particular tribunal. In re Mello, 145 N.H. 358, 761 A.2d 506, 2000 N.H. LEXIS 68 (2000).

Double jeopardy generally precludes State from pursuing a second prosecution stemming from same conduct or events charged in a previous prosecution, provided charges constitute the same offense. State v. Nickles, 144 N.H. 673, 749 A.2d 290, 2000 N.H. LEXIS 9 (2000).

Absence of bill of particulars specifying exact dates did not place sexual assault defendant in jeopardy of being prosecuted for same crime twice, since State was barred from prosecuting defendant for same type of act during any part of entire period alleged in earlier indictments. State v. Dixon, 144 N.H. 273, 741 A.2d 580, 1999 N.H. LEXIS 109 (1999).

This article protects an accused from prosecution for the same crime not only after acquittal, but also after conviction. State v. Constant, 135 N.H. 254, 605 A.2d 206, 1992 N.H. LEXIS 17 (1992).

Double jeopardy is to be distinguished from the protection the state constitution offers against the mere duplication of trials in two jurisdictions for the same offense. State v. McNally, 122 N.H. 892, 451 A.2d 1305, 1982 N.H. LEXIS 487 (1982).

Protection afforded by double jeopardy does not prevent the threat of twice being punished for the same act, but rather, forbids twice being tried and convicted for the same offense. State v. Goodwin, 116 N.H. 37, 351 A.2d 59, 1976 N.H. LEXIS 257 (1976).

2. —Attachment

Trial court did not err in denying defendant's motion for mistrial, as defendant's double jeopardy rights were not violated due to two earlier trials of his case which were both dismissed when police officers inadvertently gave improper testimony that defendant previously had been involved in crimes, as the record did not show that the officers intentionally tried to introduce prejudicial evidence or that there was prosecutorial misconduct sufficient to bar reprosecution, and, thus there was no showing that jeopardy had attached as a result of either of the earlier trials. State v. Zwicker, 151 N.H. 179, 855 A.2d 415, 2004 N.H. LEXIS 112 (2004).

Where defendant was not granted the right to proceed in his criminal trial by self-representation, and he was instead represented by counsel for two days and thereafter, was completely on his own, such constituted a structural defect and was a clear violation of defendant's Farretta rights, as well as a violation of his constitutional rights under U.S. Const. amend. VI and N.H. Const. pt. I, art. 15, requiring that his conviction be reversed and vacated, and a new trial be granted; there was no double jeopardy attachment, pursuant to N.H. Const. pt. I, art. 16, as defendant was successful in appealing his conviction on constitutional grounds. State v. Ayer, 150 N.H. 14, 834 A.2d 277, 2003 N.H. LEXIS 133 (2003), cert. denied, Ayer v. New Hampshire, 124 S. Ct. 1668, 158 L. Ed. 2d 366, 2004 U.S. LEXIS 2130 (2004).

Because federal standard for collateral estoppel afforded criminal defendant no greater double jeopardy protection than that provided by New Hampshire Constitution, court was not required to undertake a separate federal analysis. State v. Hutchins, 144 N.H. 669, 746 A.2d 447, 2000 N.H. LEXIS 8 (2000).

A defendant is put in jeopardy at the moment a jury is empaneled and sworn. State v. Paquin, 140 N.H. 525, 668 A.2d 47, 1995 N.H. LEXIS 180 (1995).

3. —Construction with federal constitution

Federal and state sovereignty concept under which United States Supreme Court has held that federal constitution does not protect citizens from dual prosecutions permits the states independently to construe their own constitutions as affording such protection. State v. Hogg, 118 N.H. 262, 385 A.2d 844, 1978 N.H. LEXIS 393 (1978).

United States Supreme Court decision which held on basis of dual sovereignty that double jeopardy clause of federal constitution did not prohibit trial of defendant in state court after trial and acquittal in federal courts even though both offenses result from same transaction was not binding on New Hampshire Supreme Court in construing this article or in applying state's due process protection in the area. State v. Hogg, 118 N.H. 262, 385 A.2d 844, 1978 N.H. LEXIS 393 (1978).

4. —Purpose

Underlying basis for double jeopardy provisions in both federal and state constitutions is protection of the individual against repeated prosecutions for the same crime, it being fundamentally and morally wrong to try a man for a crime of which he has already been tried and found not guilty. State v. Hogg, 118 N.H. 262, 385 A.2d 844, 1978 N.H. LEXIS 393 (1978).

5. —Identity of offenses

One of two counts of criminal restraint had to be vacated based on double jeopardy grounds under N.H. Const. pt. I, art. 16, as both the confinement and the risk of serious bodily injury were continuous during the period in question. The victim's confinement began from the time he was tied to a column in a basement, continued when he was brought upstairs and tied to a chair, and ended only when he was able to free himself; the victim was exposed to the risk of bodily injury throughout this period. State v. Gibbs, 164 N.H. 439, 58 A.3d 656, 2012 N.H. LEXIS 169 (2012).

Defendant's criminal threatening and reckless conduct convictions under RSA 631:3 and RSA 631:4, I(a), which arose out of the same transaction, did not violate double jeopardy under N.H. Const. pt. I, art. 16 and the federal Constitution because the indictments each required the State to prove a separate element. Whereas the criminal threatening statute required proof that defendant placed or attempted to place the victim in fear of imminent bodily injury, it did not require proof that the victim was actually placed in danger; by contrast, the reckless conduct statute did require that defendant placed or might have placed the victim in actual danger of serious bodily injury regardless of whether he feared such injury. State v. Gingras, 162 N.H. 633, 34 A.3d 659, 2011 N.H. LEXIS 149 (2011).

Possession of a controlled substance required proof that defendant knowingly possessed a controlled drug, and falsifying physical evidence required the State to prove that defendant, believing that there was a proceeding pending, knowingly altered, destroyed, concealed or removed anything, and did so with a purpose to impair its availability; thus, although each offense arose out of the same act of ingesting marijuana, they were separate offenses and there was no violation of the Double Jeopardy Clauses of the United States and New Hampshire Constitutions. State v. McGurk, 157 N.H. 765, 958 A.2d 1005, 2008 N.H. LEXIS 119 (2008).

The charging of three discrete patterns of sexual assault under RSA 632-A:2, III inflicted on a single victim did not run afoul of double jeopardy as the pattern statute allows the State to charge more than one pattern of a given sexual assault variant within a five-year time frame, each as an individual unit of prosecution, when the evidence of discrete patterns so warrants. Because the indictments charged three discrete patterns of sexual assault, as permitted by the statute, and because the prosecution at trial would have to prove that the acts occurred within each of the alleged, discrete periods of time, the defendant was not subject to multiple punishments for the same offense and his federal double jeopardy right was not infringed. Furthermore, the requirement when seeking convictions on multiple pattern indictments that charge numerous assaults within a common time frame inflicted on a single victim that the indictments could not rely on the same underlying act or acts to comprise the charged pattern was met because the pattern indictments alleged three separate sets of acts during three discrete time periods at three different locations.State v. Jennings, 155 N.H. 768, 929 A.2d 982, 2007 N.H. LEXIS 131 (2007).

Defendant's double jeopardy rights under N.H. Const. pt. I, art. 16, and U.S. Const. amend. V, were not violated because, as charged, each indictment required the State to prove a fact not necessary to the other; specifically, the State did not have to prove the existence of an agreement, required for the conspiracy conviction, to prove the first degree murder charge, and the conspiracy indictment did not require the State to prove the enhanced mental state of deliberation and premeditation, required for a first degree murder conviction. State v. Sanchez, 152 N.H. 625, 883 A.2d 292, 2005 N.H. LEXIS 149 (2005).

Charging defendant with both assault by sexual intercourse and assault by digital penetration was not impermissible multiplicity because it was clear that jurors were not confused, acquitting defendant on the sexual intercourse charges and convicting defendant of digital penetration. State v. Flynn, 151 N.H. 378, 855 A.2d 1254, 2004 N.H. LEXIS 158 (2004).

Prosecution of defendant for sexual assaults using both indictments alleging a broad time frame and indictments alleging a narrow time frame for the same crimes was a violation of double jeopardy. State v. Currier, 148 N.H. 203, 808 A.2d 527, 2002 N.H. LEXIS 110 (2002).

Separate indictments of defendant for aggravated felonious sexual assault could be sustained where each image of defendant's actions depicted on videotape presented additional evidence of how he repeatedly renewed his intention to coax child into the act of penetration, and evidence to sustain each of the carefully worded indictments was different from evidence required to sustain any of the other indictments. State v. Krueger, 146 N.H. 541, 776 A.2d 720, 2001 N.H. LEXIS 108 (2001).

Even though the time frame alleged in pattern indictments overlapped several felonious sexual assault indictments alleging specific incidents of sexual assault, defendant suffered no infringement upon his right to be free from double jeopardy because he was not sentenced on any felonious sexual assault indictment alleging that he committed a sexual assault within the same time period as alleged in the pattern indictments. State v. Fortier, 146 N.H. 784, 780 A.2d 1243, 2001 N.H. LEXIS 163 (2001).

Indictments charging that defendant digitally penetrated the victim and engaged in sexual intercourse with the victim were not duplicative because each indictment alleged that defendant committed a separate offense against the victim, sexual intercourse and digital penetration, and, thus, conviction on both indictments did not result in defendant receiving multiple punishments for the same offense. State v. DeCosta, 146 N.H. 405, 772 A.2d 340, 2001 N.H. LEXIS 89 (2001).

State may simultaneously prosecute multiple charges which constitute the same offense, based on a single act or transaction, provided it seeks a single conviction and each charge alleges a distinct, alternative method of committing the offense. State v. Nickles, 144 N.H. 673, 749 A.2d 290, 2000 N.H. LEXIS 9 (2000).

Defendant's armed robbery of jewelry store clerk and theft from store constituted two distinct acts involving different property and separated in time and space, and therefore evidence was sufficient to support two separate convictions without violating double jeopardy. State v. Ford, 144 N.H. 57, 738 A.2d 937, 1999 N.H. LEXIS 71 (1999).

Because elemental evidence for each child pornography charge was different, multiple prosecutions did not violate defendant's rights under this article. State v. Cobb, 143 N.H. 638, 732 A.2d 425, 1999 N.H. LEXIS 53 (1999).

An offense is lesser-included if the elements of the lesser offense form a subset of the elements of the greater offense. State v. Liakos, 142 N.H. 726, 709 A.2d 187, 1998 N.H. LEXIS 27 (1998).

Evidence of defendant's intoxication was necessary to aggravated driving while intoxicated charge but not to second degree assault charge, and proof of defendant's excessive rate of speed was essential to second degree assault indictment but not to aggravated driving while intoxicated indictment. Therefore, defendant's convictions for both offenses did not violate the "same evidence" or "difference in evidence" double jeopardy test under the State Constitution. State v. MacLeod, 141 N.H. 427, 685 A.2d 473, 1996 N.H. LEXIS 120 (1996).

Multiple convictions for both solicitation of aggravated felonious sexual assault and solicitation of kidnapping violated double jeopardy. Under the indictments in the case, the defendant could have been convicted for solicitation of aggravated felonious sexual assault for asking a third party to engage in sexual penetration of another female while the victim submitted under circumstances involving false imprisonment or kidnapping. State v. Lucius, 140 N.H. 60, 663 A.2d 605, 1995 N.H. LEXIS 97 (1995).

Multiple convictions for both solicitation of kidnapping and solicitation of violation of the child pornography laws violated double jeopardy. Under the indictments, the defendant could have been convicted for solicitation of kidnapping for asking a third party to knowingly confine a female with a purpose that he commit the offense of violation of the child pornography laws. State v. Lucius, 140 N.H. 60, 663 A.2d 605, 1995 N.H. LEXIS 97 (1995).

Dual convictions and sentences violated the double jeopardy clause of this article where the indictment for first degree assault charged that the defendant purposely caused the victim serious bodily injury "in the form of [brain] damage" by "pressing his hands tightly around her neck, thereby depriving her brain of oxygen," and the indictment for attempted murder alleged the same conduct, that is, the defendant's strangulation of the victim. State v. Hutchinson, 137 N.H. 591, 631 A.2d 523, 1993 N.H. LEXIS 131 (1993).

The defendant's conviction for driving while intoxicated and his subsequent conviction for driving after certification as an habitual offender did not violate the prohibition against double jeopardy as the facts charged in the habitual offender indictment could not have sustained a conviction for driving while intoxicated. State v. Brooks, 137 N.H. 541, 629 A.2d 1347, 1993 N.H. LEXIS 118 (1993).

The defendant's conviction for felony criminal mischief and felonious use of a firearm did not subject him to multiple punishments for the same offense in violation of the guarantees against double jeopardy in the New Hampshire Constitution as only the penalty enhancement for felonious use of a firearm turned on the defendant's use of a firearm and the enhancement provision in the underlying criminal mischief statute was triggered not by use of a firearm, but by purposely causing pecuniary loss exceeding $1,000. State v. Paris, 137 N.H. 322, 627 A.2d 582, 1993 N.H. LEXIS 78 (1993).

Double jeopardy would not bar prosecution of DWI charge after the state obtained a conviction for violating the habitual offender statute where the DWI charge required proof of elements not contained in the habitual offender statute, specifically, for the DWI charge the state had to prove that the defendant was under the influence of intoxicating liquor. State v. Brooks, 137 N.H. 541, 629 A.2d 1347, 1993 N.H. LEXIS 118 (1993).

As a general rule, it is a violation of double jeopardy protection to prosecute for a greater offense after a conviction or acquittal for the lesser-included one. State v. Constant, 135 N.H. 254, 605 A.2d 206, 1992 N.H. LEXIS 17 (1992).

When considering the issue of double jeopardy, a subsequent prosecution is permissible only if proof of the elements of the crimes as charged will in actuality require a difference in evidence. State v. Constant, 135 N.H. 254, 605 A.2d 206, 1992 N.H. LEXIS 17 (1992).

Where defendant was charged with misdemeanor transportation of a controlled drug and felony possession of a controlled drug, conviction on the felony possession charge was barred by double jeopardy since the possession charge lacked any element not common to the transportation charge, and, therefore, was a lesser-included offense of the transportation charge. State v. Constant, 135 N.H. 254, 605 A.2d 206, 1992 N.H. LEXIS 17 (1992).

For purposes of double jeopardy protection under this article, two offenses are the same unless each requires proof of a fact the other does not. State v. Moses, 128 N.H. 617, 517 A.2d 839, 1986 N.H. LEXIS 347 (1986).

A conviction on two counts of negligent homicide from two deaths arising out of one accident did not violate the double jeopardy clause of this article since each count required proof of a fact not necessary to the other. State v. Bailey, 127 N.H. 811, 508 A.2d 1066, 1986 N.H. LEXIS 243 (1986).

Where plaintiff was convicted of robbery while armed with a deadly weapon and of the felonious use of a firearm, the conviction and sentence for the felonious use of a firearm were vacated since, as the offenses were charged and proven, not a single difference in evidence was required, which violated this article. Heald v. Perrin, 123 N.H. 468, 464 A.2d 275, 1983 N.H. LEXIS 310 (1983), superseded by statute as stated in, State v. Nickles, 144 N.H. 673, 749 A.2d 290, 2000 N.H. LEXIS 9 (2000). (But see State v. Nickles, 144 N.H. 673, 749 A.2d 290, 2000 N.H. LEXIS 9 (2000)).

Double jeopardy only prohibits reprosecution where the second offense charged is the same as the first, both in law and in fact. State v. Heinz, 119 N.H. 717, 407 A.2d 814, 1979 N.H. LEXIS 382 (1979).

Proof of theft by misapplication over a three-year period under a state indictment will necessarily involve evidence different from or in addition to that which would have been presented at trial of a federal charge of embezzlement over a four-month period, and the fact that both charges relate to and grow out of one transaction does not make them a single offense. State v. Heinz, 119 N.H. 717, 407 A.2d 814, 1979 N.H. LEXIS 382 (1979).

Plea of former jeopardy will not be sustained unless it appears that offense previously charged was same in law and in fact as that presently charged. State v. Harlan, 103 N.H. 31, 164 A.2d 562, 1960 N.H. LEXIS 7 (1960).

6. —Tests

Dismissal of an indictment that charged defendant with a criminal offense, based on the trial court's grant of defendant's directed verdict motion at the close of the evidence due to improper venue, did not bar a retrial under the double jeopardy clause of N.H. Const. pt. I, § 16, as none of the material elements of the charged offense were determined; the dismissal was not the same as an "acquittal," and the determination of improper venue was not a material element under RSA 625:11, III(e) and IV. State v. Johanson (In re State), 156 N.H. 148, 932 A.2d 848, 2007 N.H. LEXIS 152 (2007).

New Hampshire Supreme Court would not adopt "same transaction" test of double jeopardy, which treats consequences of same transaction, episode, or conduct as constituting one offense, although such consequences may be in violation of more than one criminal statute. State v. Gosselin, 117 N.H. 115, 370 A.2d 264, 1977 N.H. LEXIS 281 (1977).

Protection afforded by this article does not prevent threat of twice being punished for same act, but rather, forbids twice being tried and convicted for same offense; and this doctrine is effectuated by means of the "same evidence" test of identity of offenses. State v. Gosselin, 117 N.H. 115, 370 A.2d 264, 1977 N.H. LEXIS 281 (1977).

7. —Burden of proof

Where defendant moved to dismiss eight indictments for theft by misapplication on the ground of former jeopardy from a federal conviction for embezzlement, defendant had the burden of showing by a preponderance of the evidence that the offense for which he was previously acquitted or convicted was the same as the one subsequently charged. State v. Heinz, 119 N.H. 717, 407 A.2d 814, 1979 N.H. LEXIS 382 (1979).

8. —Nolle prosequi

Where State at trial de novo filed a substituted criminal complaint which charged same offense, and then nol prossed the original complaint, substituted complaint did not constitute an impermissible second prosecution for double jeopardy purposes, so as to preclude prosecution of new charges. State v. Anderson, 142 N.H. 918, 714 A.2d 227, 1998 N.H. LEXIS 58 (1998).

A criminal complaint for a misdemeanor may properly be nol prossed in the reasonable discretion of the prosecution and an information filed in substitution thereof charging a different offense and such substitution does not result in double jeopardy. State v. Green, 105 N.H. 260, 197 A.2d 204, 1964 N.H. LEXIS 58 (1964).

9. —Separate trials

Simultaneous prosecution of alternative charges of same statutory offense is proper as long as charges are neither identical in fact and law nor prejudicial; in such a case, when mistrial is granted on one charge due to jury deadlock, an acquittal on other does not, in itself, bar retrial for deadlocked charge because jury deadlock prevents original jeopardy from terminating on that charge. State v. Nickles, 144 N.H. 673, 749 A.2d 290, 2000 N.H. LEXIS 9 (2000).

As charged, sexual assault by false imprisonment indictment was sufficiently distinct in fact and law from sexual assault by physical force indictment, such that dual indictments were properly presented to jury for its deliberation, and since jury deadlock prevented original jeopardy from terminating on physical force indictment, State could permissibly retry defendant on that charge following mistrial, notwithstanding jury's acquittal of defendant on false imprisonment indictment. State v. Nickles, 144 N.H. 673, 749 A.2d 290, 2000 N.H. LEXIS 9 (2000).

Embezzlement or misapplication of multiple sums of money on various occasions constitute separate and distinct offenses for which multiple punishments may be imposed, and while it may be appropriate to require that all charges be joined in one trial if possible, where neither court can obtain jurisdiction over both sets of offenses separate trials do not constitute double jeopardy. State v. Heinz, 119 N.H. 717, 407 A.2d 814, 1979 N.H. LEXIS 382 (1979).

10. —Retrial following mistrial

Double jeopardy under U.S. Const. amend. V and N.H. Const. pt. I, art. 16 did not prohibit defendant's trial for reckless second-degree murder and knowing second-degree murder after his acquittal of first-degree felony murder and a declaration of mistrial on a second-degree murder charge. The charges of first-degree felony murder and the charge of reckless second-degree murder did not require proof of the same mens rea; the charge of reckless second-degree murder did not include the element that defendant killed the victim while engaged in robbery; and while the trial court had instructed the jury on knowing second-degree murder as a lesser included offense of first-degree felony murder, the jury made no finding on that offense. State v. Glenn, 160 N.H. 480, 9 A.3d 161, 2010 N.H. LEXIS 81 (July 20, 2010).

Double jeopardy under U.S. Const. amend. V and N.H. Const. pt. I, art. 16 did not bar reprosecution after indictments had been dismissed and a mistrial declared. The State's actions were not the type of misconduct preventing a finding of manifest necessity for a mistrial, as it did not make its tactical decision to amend the original indictments with the knowledge that they violated the Ex Post Facto Clause; furthermore, the trial court considered alternatives before declaring a mistrial. State v. Howell, 158 N.H. 717, 973 A.2d 926, 2009 N.H. LEXIS 65 (2009).

Retrial was not barred following a mistrial under circumstances in which the jury had deadlocked and, when given the opportunity by the trial court, defendant declined an invitation to object to a mistrial; the fact that a juror may have been prejudiced against defendant based upon her undisclosed history did not change this result. State v. Kornbrekke, 156 N.H. 821, 943 A.2d 797, 2008 N.H. LEXIS 25 (2008).

Because the State failed in its burden of showing that any consideration was given to the possible effect on defendant's constitutional rights, or that any measures were taken to ensure those rights were protected after the initial justice, a member of the New Hampshire National Guard, volunteered to be deployed, a successor judge's order granting a mistrial based on a manifest necessity, over defendant's objection, was reversed. State v. Solomon, 157 N.H. 47, 943 A.2d 819, 2008 N.H. LEXIS 32 (2008).

Defendant's second trial did not violate double jeopardy because the trial court properly found that the prosecutor had not intentionally provoked a mistrial by eliciting testimony from an officer about an inadmissible statement as to whether defendant was the driver of a vehicle. The record did not demonstrate that the State had any tactical reason to provoke a mistrial; the officer's testimony that defendant had been the driver had been unequivocal. State v. Murray, 153 N.H. 674, 917 A.2d 203, 2006 N.H. LEXIS 92 (2006).

To bar retrial after a mistrial, an additional showing beyond prosecutorial gross negligence is required: the prosecutorial over-reaching must also be intended either to provoke the defendant into requesting a mistrial or to prejudice his prospects for an acquittal. This New Hampshire standard is consistent with the federal standard; thus, there was no merit to defendant's argument that the New Hampshire Constitution provided more protection than the federal one. State v. Murray, 153 N.H. 674, 917 A.2d 203, 2006 N.H. LEXIS 92 (2006).

Trial court properly allowed defendant to be retried after his first trial ended in a mistrial; the retrial did not violate defendant's double jeopardy rights under N.H. Const. pt. I, art. 16, because defendant's argument that the jury in the first trial was not genuinely deadlocked but had effectively found him not guilty failed, as the jury foreman's post-mistrial letter was not admissible evidence to impeach the mistrial, because the affidavit or testimony of a single juror was inadmissible where it was offered as a basis for setting the verdict aside, and this applied where the mistrial directly resulted from the jurors' inability to reach a verdict because the conduct of the jury during deliberations was at issue. State v. Cook, 148 N.H. 735, 813 A.2d 480, 2002 N.H. LEXIS 183 (2002).

Trial court's mistrial order was not unreasonable where defendant created his predicament by interjecting into his testimony evidence that he had been told was inadmissible and the trial court reasonably concluded that no fully curative, non-prejudicial instruction could be fashioned and that defendant's disclosure created actual, incurable prejudice. In re Brosseau, 146 N.H. 339, 771 A.2d 579, 2001 N.H. LEXIS 80 (2001).

Jury voir dire is not required as a prerequisite to declaring a mistrial in all cases; thus, where the trial court determined that a curative instruction would not remove the prejudicial impact of the defendant's testimony, questioning the jurors about the prejudicial testimony could have exacerbated the prejudice and compounded the futility of a curative instruction. In re Brosseau, 146 N.H. 339, 771 A.2d 579, 2001 N.H. LEXIS 80 (2001).

Defendant's reprosecution following mistrial was barred by double jeopardy, because trial court had an independent obligation to voir dire jurors individually once court became aware that one juror may have failed to reveal information on questionnaire that could have been grounds for her disqualification and, if court determined that juror should have been disqualified, it could have excused that juror and proceeded with an eleven-person panel by stipulation. In re Mello, 145 N.H. 358, 761 A.2d 506, 2000 N.H. LEXIS 68 (2000).

Because defendant is put in jeopardy at moment a jury is empanelled and sworn, constitution recognizes defendant's valued right to have his trial completed by a particular tribunal, and when this right is frustrated by declaration of mistrial without defendant's consent, prosecution must demonstrate that mistrial was justified by manifest necessity; absent such proof, a retrial is barred. State v. Gould, 144 N.H. 415, 743 A.2d 300, 1999 N.H. LEXIS 130 (1999).

Even though two negligent homicide indictments arose out of the same incident, evidence required to prove negligence in first indictment was different than evidence required to prove that defendant was under influence of Valium while operating vehicle, as alleged in second indictment. Similarity of evidence used to prove some elements did not mean that same evidence was required for all elements, and since each offense required a difference in evidence, double jeopardy did not attach to bar retrial on first indictment. State v. Liakos, 142 N.H. 726, 709 A.2d 187, 1998 N.H. LEXIS 27 (1998).

Since each set of sexual assault indictments, as charged, obliged State to prove a particular fact not necessary to the other—physical force in one and surprise in the other—double jeopardy did not prohibit State from retrying defendant on "force" and oral penetration charges following mistrial on those indictments. State v. Crate, 141 N.H. 489, 686 A.2d 318, 1996 N.H. LEXIS 129 (1996).

The double jeopardy clause barred further prosecution of the defendant on the original indictments against her because a mistrial was not necessarily required. The jury foreperson took notes in violation of the court's directive during closing arguments and the judge's instructions and shared those notes with other members of the jury. Before declaring a mistrial, the trial court should have considered whether and to what extent the deliberative process was affected by the foreperson's conduct and whether alternatives to a mistrial could have neutralized any prejudicial effect the notes

might have had on jury members. State v. Paquin, 140 N.H. 525, 668 A.2d 47, 1995 N.H. LEXIS 180 (1995).

Constitutional protections against double jeopardy are of no avail when a prosecution has resulted in a mistrial, unless defendant, by conduct and design of state, has been painted into a corner so as to require a successful motion for mistrial as the only reasonable means of extrication to avoid becoming a victim of unlawful trial tactics or inadmissible evidence. State v. Montella, 135 N.H. 698, 610 A.2d 351, 1992 N.H. LEXIS 108 (1992).

At attempted murder trial in which mistrial was found because state's witness made specific reference in direct testimony to previously suppressed evidence, court properly held that defendant had not been "painted into a corner" by state so as to require a successful motion for mistrial as the only means of extrication to avoid becoming a victim of unlawful tactics or inadmissible evidence, where defendant did not show that state intended to provoke or goad defendant into asking for a mistrial. State v. Montella, 135 N.H. 698, 610 A.2d 351, 1992 N.H. LEXIS 108 (1992).

Generally, when a first trial is terminated as a result of the court's granting the defendant's motion for a mistrial, the guarantee against double jeopardy does not bar a second trial, but an exception to this rule applies when the conduct giving rise to the defendant's successful motion for a mistrial was intended to provoke the motion, or to prejudice the defendant's prospects for an acquittal. State v. Berry, 124 N.H. 203, 470 A.2d 881, 1983 N.H. LEXIS 423 (1983), overruled, State v. Duhamel, 128 N.H. 199, 512 A.2d 420, 1986 N.H. LEXIS 267 (1986).

To preserve fundamental constitutional rights under double jeopardy clause for a defendant to have trial completed by a particular tribunal, judge may declare mistrial without defendant's consent only if there is a manifest necessity for the act, or the ends of public justice would otherwise be defeated. State v. Pugliese, 120 N.H. 728, 422 A.2d 1319, 1980 N.H. LEXIS 384 (1980).

In trial for homicide involving greater offense of manslaughter and a lesser-included offense of negligent homicide, declaration of mistrial on manslaughter charge where all possible alternatives to a mistrial were not considered, employed, or found wanting, violated defendant's double jeopardy rights and barred a retrial on the greater offense. State v. Pugliese, 120 N.H. 728, 422 A.2d 1319, 1980 N.H. LEXIS 384 (1980).

Trial court's determination in criminal trespass proceeding that jury's impartiality was impaired indicated not only that there was a manifest necessity to declare a mistrial but also that the ends of public justice would otherwise be defeated if it were not declared; thus, there was no double jeopardy bar to retrial of defendants. State v. Brady, 120 N.H. 899, 424 A.2d 407, 1980 N.H. LEXIS 417 (1980).

11. —Sentencing

As RSA 651:58, I provides for notice to the defendant that the imposed sentence may be increased after a review hearing before the sentencing review board, he or she has no expectation of finality until the 30-day period to request a sentence review has passed. Because this limited appeal does not involve a retrial or approximate the ordeal of a trial on the basic issue of guilt or innocence, RSA 651:58, I does not violate the Double Jeopardy Clause of the New Hampshire Constitution. In re Guardarramos-Cepeda, 154 N.H. 7, 904 A.2d 609, 2006 N.H. LEXIS 112 (2006).

Even though, at defendant's initial sentencing hearing, the State had failed to prove beyond a reasonable doubt that he had two prior aggravated felonious sexual assault convictions, double jeopardy did not bar the State from attempting to prove on remand that the defendant had been twice previously convicted of aggravated felonious sexual assault. State v. McLellan, 149 N.H. 237, 817 A.2d 309, 2003 N.H. LEXIS 32 (2003).

There was no violation of the protection against double jeopardy when an extended sentence of 10 to 30 years was imposed on the defendant for aggravated felonious sexual assault based on the age of the victim. The defendant argued that the sentence was improper because the victim's age had already been used to elevate the offense from a class B felony to a class A felony. However, the defendant was only convicted once and sentenced once, and there was no violation. State v. Hennessey, 142 N.H. 149, 697 A.2d 930, 1997 N.H. LEXIS 68 (1997).

Double jeopardy was not violated when the defendant was sentenced to 12 months' imprisonment for stalking and sentenced to an additional 12 months' imprisonment for committing the offense while released on bail with a condition that he not bother the victim or go within 300 yards of her. The court rejected the contention that the defendant was subjected to multiple punishments for the same offense because the sentencing enhancement factor constituted an element of the substantive offense of stalking. Rather, the defendant was convicted of one offense for which the defendant received a constitutionally permissible single sentencing enhancement. State v. Ringuette, 142 N.H. 163, 142 N.H. 168, 697 A.2d 507, 1997 N.H. LEXIS 67 (1997).

When cumulative punishments are sought for offenses arising out of a single transaction, the focus of the inquiry under the double jeopardy prohibition of this article is whether proof of the elements of the crimes as charged will in actuality require a difference in evidence. State v. Gooden, 133 N.H. 674, 582 A.2d 607, 1990 N.H. LEXIS 120 (1990).

Imposition of consecutive sentences for first degree assault and the felonious use of a firearm violated constitutional guarantee against double jeopardy, because the underlying crime of knowing assault was itself enhanced by the use of a deadly weapon, and the perpetrator could therefore not be properly sentenced a second time for the felonious use of the firearm. State v. Houtenbrink, 130 N.H. 385, 539 A.2d 714, 1988 N.H. LEXIS 17 (1988).

The guarantee against double jeopardy contained in this article does not forbid the imposition of a single enhanced penalty for an underlying offense, even though the underlying offense and the allegations justifying the penalty enhancement are contained in separate indictments containing identical allegations. State v. Elbert, 128 N.H. 210, 512 A.2d 1114, 1986 N.H. LEXIS 280 (1986).

A motion to vacate a conviction for felonious use of a firearm filed by a defendant who had been convicted and sentenced for attempted murder, involving the use of a firearm, also was properly denied since the defendant was not subjected to multiple punishments for the same offense. State v. Elbert, 128 N.H. 210, 512 A.2d 1114, 1986 N.H. LEXIS 280 (1986).

Defendant convicted of first degree murder who had started sentence of life imprisonment at time trial judge certified, at next term of court, that the murder was psychosexual in nature, which resulted in extending time in which defendant would be eligible for parole from 18 years to 40 years, was not subjected to double jeopardy by subjecting him to multiple punishments for same offense contrary to this article, as defendant was subjected to only one valid and complete judgment. State v. Breest, 116 N.H. 734, 367 A.2d 1320, 1976 N.H. LEXIS 463 (1976).

12. —Retrial following reversal on appeal

Where defendant's conviction for first degree assault was reversed on appeal, double jeopardy barred his retrial on charges of attempted first degree murder and the felonious use of a firearm, of which he had already been acquitted, but the defendant could be retried for the offense of first degree assault, or any other lesser-included offense. State v. Lessard, 123 N.H. 788, 465 A.2d 516, 1983 N.H. LEXIS 329 (1983).

13. —Civil proceedings

Double jeopardy did not bar the State's forfeiture petition following defendant's guilty plea in federal court, since RSA 318-B:17-b was a civil, non-punitive statute. In re Toyota Avalon, 155 N.H. 720, 927 A.2d 1239, 2007 N.H. LEXIS 124 (2007).

An administrative license suspension, pursuant to RSA 263:56, I(g), is not so punitive as to be considered punishment for double jeopardy purposes. State v. Liakos, 142 N.H. 726, 709 A.2d 187, 1998 N.H. LEXIS 27 (1998).

New Hampshire's in rem forfeiture statute was a civil, nonpunitive measure, and thus forfeiture of defendant's vehicle did not constitute a second punishment for double jeopardy purposes. In re 1994 Chevrolet Cavalier, 142 N.H. 705, 708 A.2d 397, 1998 N.H. LEXIS 22 (1998).

Administrative license suspension pursuant to RSA 263:56 was not punishment for purposes of double jeopardy, and did not bar defendant's subsequent prosecution on negligent homicide indictments. State v. Drewry, 141 N.H. 514, 687 A.2d 991, 1996 N.H. LEXIS 133 (1996).

By failing to contest forfeiture, defendant never became a party to proceeding and effectively renounced any interest in property forfeited. As a result, there was no judicial determination that the property belonged to defendant, and he could not claim that forfeiture of property punished him. Without punishment, there was no former jeopardy, and thus double jeopardy did not bar defendant's prosecution on indictment for conspiracy to sell cocaine. State v. Natalcolon, 140 N.H. 689, 671 A.2d 556, 1996 N.H. LEXIS 16 (1996).

Civil forfeiture did not implicate double jeopardy because defendant's forfeiture of property was purely voluntary and not the result of any State-initiated forfeiture proceeding. Therefore, no civil sanction was imposed by State. State v. Guenzel, 140 N.H. 685, 671 A.2d 545, 1996 N.H. LEXIS 14 (1996).

In a prosecution for driving under the influence of liquor, the doctrine of collateral estoppel as guaranteed by part 1, article 16 of the New Hampshire Constitution and the fifth and fourteenth Amendments to the United States Constitution did not prevent the state from relitigating issues of fact previously decided in the defendant's favor in a prior administrative license suspension hearing held in accordance with RSA 265:91-b. State v. Cassady, 140 N.H. 46, 662 A.2d 955, 1995 N.H. LEXIS 92 (1995).

Traffic violations adjudicable under the mail-in procedure provided for in RSA 262:44 are civil in nature, and the penalties imposed for these traffic violations are not criminal sanctions or punishment; thus, a conviction for such a traffic violation does not trigger the prohibition against double jeopardy. State v. Fitzgerald, 137 N.H. 23, 622 A.2d 1245, 1993 N.H. LEXIS 29 (1993).

Express and sole purpose of defendant's involuntary commitment proceedings was to determine whether defendant's mental condition was such that he was dangerous to himself or others, and fact that evidence used to establish defendant's dangerousness related to an incident for which he had already been tried and convicted did not convert the civil proceedings into a criminal trial; thus, involuntary commitment proceeding did not violate provision of this article against double jeopardy. State v. Hudson, 121 N.H. 6, 425 A.2d 255, 1981 N.H. LEXIS 237 (1981).

A civil proceeding raises no double jeopardy question. State v. Bowles, 113 N.H. 571, 311 A.2d 300, 1973 N.H. LEXIS 322 (1973).

14. —Res judicata

In the criminal context, collateral estoppel mandates that an issue of ultimate fact that has been fully tried and determined cannot again be litigated between parties in a future prosecution; however, a second prosecution will be barred only if an essential element of second prosecution was necessarily determined in defendant's favor at first trial, and burden is on defendant to establish that such an issue was decided in his favor. State v. Hutchins, 144 N.H. 669, 746 A.2d 447, 2000 N.H. LEXIS 8 (2000).

Where defendant at sexual assault trial denied that anything of a sexual nature ever occurred between himself and victim, defendant's later prosecution for perjury was not barred by double jeopardy, since sexual assault jury's general verdict of acquittal only reflected that State failed to prove beyond a reasonable doubt that defendant committed the crimes charged in the indictment. State v. Hutchins, 144 N.H. 669, 746 A.2d 447, 2000 N.H. LEXIS 8 (2000).

The constitutional provision against being placed twice in jeopardy for the same offense does not operate to prevent the application of the doctrine of res judicata if its constituent elements are present. State v. Hentschel, 98 N.H. 382, 101 A.2d 456, 1953 N.H. LEXIS 86 (1953).

15. —Collateral estoppel

Collateral estoppel did not bar evidence that a murder defendant was attempting to rob the victim. Neither the knowing nor reckless second-degree murder indictments as charged required the State to prove beyond a reasonable doubt that defendant was attempting to rob the victim at the time of the murder; therefore, under these indictments, the alleged attempted robbery was merely an evidentiary fact, not an ultimate fact that had to be proved beyond a reasonable doubt. State v. Glenn, 160 N.H. 480, 9 A.3d 161, 2010 N.H. LEXIS 81 (July 20, 2010).

This article's protections against double jeopardy incorporate the doctrine of collateral estoppel. State v. Crate, 141 N.H. 489, 686 A.2d 318, 1996 N.H. LEXIS 129 (1996).

Under the rule of collateral estoppel mandated by this article as a corollary to the right to be free of double jeopardy, in criminal cases, when an issue of ultimate fact has once been determined by a valid and final judgment, that issue cannot again be litigated between the same parties in any future lawsuit. State v. Sefton, 125 N.H. 533, 485 A.2d 284, 1984 N.H. LEXIS 400 (1984).

The rule of collateral estoppel mandated by this article as a corollary to the right to be free of double jeopardy does not forbid relitigation of an issue as one of evidentiary fact, even though the state had lost on the same issue as one of ultimate fact to be proven beyond a reasonable doubt in a prior trial. State v. Sefton, 125 N.H. 533, 485 A.2d 284, 1984 N.H. LEXIS 400 (1984).

The doctrine of collateral estoppel is embodied within the double jeopardy clause of this article. State v. Fielders, 124 N.H. 310, 470 A.2d 897, 1983 N.H. LEXIS 415 (1983).

Collateral estoppel, embodied within the double jeopardy clause of this article, means that when an issue of ultimate fact has once been determined by a valid and final judgment, that issue cannot again be litigated between the same parties in any future lawsuit. State v. Fielders, 124 N.H. 310, 470 A.2d 897, 1983 N.H. LEXIS 415 (1983).

16. —Federal and state prosecutions

Action of a federal sentencing judge in taking into account circumstances surrounding the offense charged, including indications of criminal conduct for which the defendant had not been tried or convicted, was not a bar to subsequent prosecution for that conduct in state court. State v. Heinz, 119 N.H. 717, 407 A.2d 814, 1979 N.H. LEXIS 382 (1979).

In overruling State v. Whittemore, 50 NH 245, 1870 N.H. LEXIS 90 (1870), to extent that it was inconsistent with its present decision, supreme court would hold that defendants' acquittals in federal court on charges of robbery and of being an accessory before the fact barred prosecution by the state on charges arising out of same criminal transaction. State v. Hogg, 118 N.H. 262, 385 A.2d 844, 1978 N.H. LEXIS 393 (1978).

This article does not prohibit a prosecution for the transportation of intoxicating liquors in violation of a state statute against one who has previously been convicted in the federal court for illegally transporting the same liquor in violation of a federal statute. State v. Gendron, 80 N.H. 394, 118 A. 814, 1922 N.H. LEXIS 37 (1922).

17. —Administrative punishment

An administrative review hearing in accordance with RSA 265:91-b is not a criminal proceeding, and the sanction of license revocation is not criminal punishment for purposes of double jeopardy. State v. Cassady, 140 N.H. 46, 662 A.2d 955, 1995 N.H. LEXIS 92 (1995).

A conviction for the crime of escape does not constitute double jeopardy merely because the prisoner has been subjected to administrative discipline by the incarcerating authorities. State v. Gonyer, 102 N.H. 527, 162 A.2d 172, 1960 N.H. LEXIS 72 (1960).

18. —Prosecution for greater charge after conviction of lesser

When after defendant was convicted of attempted murder, the victim died, double jeopardy did not bar his murder indictment as double jeopardy did not bar a subsequent prosecution for a greater offense where all of the necessary elements of that offense did not exist at the time of the first trial. The societal interest in prosecuting defendant for an alleged homicide completed after his initial trial outweighed defendant's interest in finality and did not offend the New Hampshire Double Jeopardy Clause; the court was not persuaded that it should interpret the state constitution differently from the federal one in this context. State v. Hutchinson, 156 N.H. 790, 942 A.2d 1289, 2008 N.H. LEXIS 20 (2008).

19. Jury trial

Trial by jury as used in this article means trial by twelve men, who returned their unanimous verdict upon the issue submitted to them, and the accused may avail himself of it or waive it at his election, but when he enters a plea of guilty to the charge of a capital offense he has waived all right to a jury trial in relation to that offense, as the guaranty does not extend to the point of affording him a jury to determine the degree of his guilt or the punishment therefor. State v. Almy, 67 N.H. 274, 28 A. 372, 1892 N.H. LEXIS 44, 22 L.R.A. 744 (1892).

20. Criminal contempt

Although not found in the Criminal Code, criminal contempt is an offense and the sentence is punitive. State v. Goodnow, 140 N.H. 38, 662 A.2d 950, 1995 N.H. LEXIS 93 (1995).

When a defendant has been convicted of direct criminal contempt for physically attacking police officers in open court, a subsequent prosecution for assault on the basis of the same conduct is prohibited by Part 1, article 16 of the New Hampshire State Constitution. This result does not undermine a court's authority to deal effectively with disruptive conduct in the courtroom. State v. Goodnow, 140 N.H. 38, 662 A.2d 950, 1995 N.H. LEXIS 93 (1995).

21. Prosecutorial misconduct

Double jeopardy and due process did not prohibit a retrial based on intentional prosecutorial misconduct. The State had immediately informed the trial court and defendant about an eyewitness's untruthful grand jury testimony, had sought a continuance to reindict defendant, and had provided defendant with all of the witness's prior statements; there was no evidence that the State intentionally sought the witness's false testimony; and the trial court credited the State's assertion that it did not know that defendant had applied for a concealed handgun permit until the day before trial and that it did not know the contents of that application until after the trial. State v. Glenn, 160 N.H. 480, 9 A.3d 161, 2010 N.H. LEXIS 81 (July 20, 2010).

Double jeopardy did not bar a retrial on the basis of prosecutorial misconduct where prosecutor's intent was not to deny the defendant a fair trial but to punish defendant for appealing; for retrial to be barred, the prosecutor's aim needed the be to subvert the protections of double jeopardy. State v. Marti, 147 N.H. 168, 784 A.2d 1193, 2001 N.H. LEXIS 189 (2001).

Cited:

Cited in State v. Janvrin, 121 N.H. 370, 430 A.2d 152, 1981 N.H. LEXIS 321 (1981); State v. Pugliese, 122 N.H. 1141, 455 A.2d 1018, 1982 N.H. LEXIS 541 (1982); State v. Beaudette, 124 N.H. 579, 474 A.2d 1012, 1984 N.H. LEXIS 355 (1984); State v. Cote, 126 N.H. 514, 493 A.2d 1170, 1985 N.H. LEXIS 336 (1985); Bunnell v. Lucas, 126 N.H. 663, 495 A.2d 1282, 1985 N.H. LEXIS 360 (1985); State v. Smith, 127 N.H. 836, 508 A.2d 1082, 1986 N.H. LEXIS 229 (1986); State v. Duhamel, 128 N.H. 199, 512 A.2d 420, 1986 N.H. LEXIS 267 (1986); State v. Wonyetye, 129 N.H. 452, 529 A.2d 927, 1987 N.H. LEXIS 212 (1987); State v. Beaupre, 129 N.H. 486, 529 A.2d 944, 1987 N.H. LEXIS 218 (1987); State v. King, 131 N.H. 173, 551 A.2d 973, 1988 N.H. LEXIS 102 (1988); State v. Stratton, 132 N.H. 451, 567 A.2d 986, 1989 N.H. LEXIS 124 (1989); State v. Hartford, 132 N.H. 580, 567 A.2d 577, 1989 N.H. LEXIS 137 (1989); State v. Pond, 133 N.H. 738, 584 A.2d 770, 1990 N.H. LEXIS 133 (1990); State v. Bertrand, 133 N.H. 843, 587 A.2d 1219, 1991 N.H. LEXIS 8 (1991); State v. Lucius, 140 N.H. 60, 663 A.2d 605, 1995 N.H. LEXIS 97 (1995).

RESEARCH REFERENCES

New Hampshire Bar Journal.

For article, "Lex Loci: A Survey of New Hampshire Supreme Court Decisions," see 49 N.H.B.J. 40 (Spring 2008).

For article, "The Role of the Primacy Doctrine in New Hampshire Criminal Procedure: An Expansion of Individual Constitutional Rights," see 28 N.H.B.J. 357 (1987).

For article, "State v. Gould: Setting the Standard for when Broad Judicial Discretion Encounters Double Jeopardy," see 42 N.H.B.J. 31 (Sept. 2001).

Art. 17. [Venue of Criminal Prosecutions.]

In criminal prosecutions, the trial of facts, in the vicinity where they happened, is so essential to the security of the life, liberty and estate of the citizen, that no crime or offense ought to be tried in any other county or judicial district than that in which it is committed; except in any case in any particular county or judicial district, upon motion by the defendant, and after a finding by the court that a fair and impartial trial cannot be had where the offense may be committed, the court shall direct the trial to a county or judicial district in which a fair and impartial trial can be obtained.

Amendments

—**1978.** Rewritten to the extent that a detailed comparison would be impracticable.

—**1793.** Substituted "legislature" for "assembly".

Cross References.

Venue of offenses committed in more than one county, see RSA 602:1.

NOTES TO DECISIONS

1. Judicial districts
2. Preliminary hearings
3. Jury
4. Place where crime is committed
5. Juvenile proceedings
6. Pretrial publicity

1. Judicial districts

Proposed legislation which would create a judicial district comprised of contiguous municipalities located in different counties did not violate this article since this article had been amended with the intent of broadening venue in a criminal case, and the possibility of creating judicial districts comprised of contiguous municipalities in different counties was therefore intended. Opinion of Justices, 126 N.H. 486, 494 A.2d 259, 1985 N.H. LEXIS 339 (1985).

2. Preliminary hearings

A justice of the peace having statewide jurisdiction may conduct a preliminary examination of a charge against an accused and order the accused to recognize for his appearance before the proper court of a county in which the crime was committed, even though the county in which the preliminary hearing is held and the county in which the crime was committed are different, since a preliminary hearing is not a trial within the meaning of the term as used in this article. State v. Thompson, 20 N.H. 250, 1850 N.H. LEXIS 2 (1850).

3. Jury

Instructing the jury that defendant had been indicted for the unrelated shooting of a police officer did not violate defendant's rights to a fair trial before an impartial jury under N.H. Const. pt. I, arts. 15, 17, and 35 and U.S. Const. amends. V, VI, and XIV. The charge was given to determine whether each juror could lay aside impressions or opinions and render a verdict based upon the evidence presented in court; furthermore, the trial judge called all potential jurors to the bench individually to question them about possible bias and was able to observe each juror's demeanor and make her own determination regarding his or her credibility. State v. Addison, 160 N.H. 493, 8 A.3d 53, 2010 N.H. LEXIS 78 (2010).

Informing jurors that defendant also faced a murder charge did not violate defendant's rights to due process, a fair trial, and a trial before a fair and impartial jury under N.H. Const. pt. I, arts. 15, 17, and 35 and U.S. Const. amends. V, VI, and XIV. In VandeBogart, the court had held that given the difficulty of selecting impartial jurors otherwise, the trial court was within its discretion in informing the venire that the defendant also faced a first-degree murder charge, and the same reasoning justified the use of the instruction here. State v. Addison, 161 N.H. 300, 13 A.3d 214, 2010 N.H. LEXIS 186 (2010), cert. denied, Addison v. New Hampshire, 131 S. Ct. 2107, 179 L. Ed. 2d 903, 2011 U.S. LEXIS 3106 (U.S. 2011).

The right to trial of a criminal case in the county in which the act was committed does not mean that the jurors trying the case must come from all the towns in the county, or from towns scattered over all the county, but rather the right secured to the accused is to be tried by an impartial jury of the county and such jury may be selected from such towns in the county as the court directs. State v. Jackson, 77 N.H. 287, 90 A. 791, 1914 N.H. LEXIS 145 (1914).

4. Place where crime is committed

Where defendant's criminal matter was transferred to a county other than where his criminal act was allegedly committed due to the recusal of all of the judges in the county where the crime occurred, and defendant was thereafter tried in a bench trial, his motion for a directed verdict at the end of the case based on improper venue under N.H. Const. pt. I, art. 17 and RSA 602:1 was untimely; the objection to venue was accordingly deemed waived,

and the trial court's grant of the directed verdict was erroneous in the circumstances. State v. Johanson (In re State), 156 N.H. 148, 932 A.2d 848, 2007 N.H. LEXIS 152 (2007).

The county that a particular city or town lies within is a matter of law, thus, when the state proved the crime occurred in Rye, this constituted proof that the crime occurred in Rockingham County and the venue of the trial was properly in Rockingham County. State v. Huffman, 136 N.H. 149, 613 A.2d 476, 1992 N.H. LEXIS 149 (1992).

Fact that body was found in Hillsborough County and absence of evidence that homicide was committed elsewhere warranted inference crime was committed in that county. State v. Coolidge, 109 N.H. 403, 260 A.2d 547, 1969 N.H. LEXIS 170 (1969).

5. Juvenile proceedings

This article is not implicated and does not apply to juvenile delinquency hearings. In re Kevin E., 143 N.H. 417, 725 A.2d 669, 1999 N.H. LEXIS 21 (1999).

6. Pretrial publicity

Pretrial publicity did not result in presumptive prejudice requiring a change of venue under N.H. Const. pt. I, arts. 15 and 17 and the Sixth Amendment. The jury was drawn from a county with a population over 400,000; the overwhelming amount of the material submitted by defendant consisted of straightforward, factual accounts of the crime; defendant's trial occurred nearly a year and a half after the crimes; and given that defendant admitted his participation in the crimes and pleaded not guilty by reason of insanity, his codefendant's trial had little relevance to defendant's state of mind at the time of the crime. State v. Gribble, — N.H. —, 66 A.3d 1194, 2013 N.H. LEXIS 47 (May 7, 2013).

Statements of potential jurors on voir dire did not show that a change of venue under N.H. Const. pt. I, arts. 15 and 17 and the Sixth Amendment was required due to pretrial publicity. The trial court conducted a thorough jury selection process over a period of eight days and went to great lengths to ensure that the empaneled jury was fair and impartial; there was ample support for the trial court's conclusion that defendant was unable to demonstrate any actual bias or prejudice in the seated jury panel. State v. Gribble, — N.H. —, 66 A.3d 1194, 2013 N.H. LEXIS 47 (May 7, 2013).

Cited:

Cited in State v. Albee, 61 N.H. 423, 1881 N.H. LEXIS 95 (1881); State v. Sawtelle, 66 N.H. 488, 32 A. 831, 1891 N.H. LEXIS 62 (1891) petition for new trial dismissed, 67 NH 590, 35 A 1130, 36 A. 605, 1891 N.H. LEXIS 41 (1892); State v. Thomson, 109 N.H. 205, 247 A.2d 179, 1968 N.H. LEXIS 157 (1968); State v. Fleury, 114 N.H. 325, 321 A.2d 108, 1974 N.H. LEXIS 270 (1974); State v. Sullivan, 121 N.H. 301, 428 A.2d 1247, 1981 N.H. LEXIS 307 (1981); State v. Lister, 122 N.H. 603, 448 A.2d 395, 1982 N.H. LEXIS 410 (1982); State v. Wentzell, 131 N.H. 151, 551 A.2d 960, 1988 N.H. LEXIS 100 (1988).

RESEARCH REFERENCES

New Hampshire Bar Journal.

For article, "Lex Loci: A Survey of New Hampshire Supreme Court Decisions," see 48 N.H.B.J. 84 (Autumn 2007).

Art. 18. [Penalties to be Proportioned to Offenses; True Design of Punishment.]

All penalties ought to be proportioned to the nature of the offense. No wise legislature will affix the same punishment to the crimes of theft, forgery, and the like, which they do to those of murder and treason. Where the same undistinguishing severity is exerted against all offenses, the people are led to forget the real distinction in the crimes themselves, and to commit the most flagrant with as little compunction as they do the lightest offenses. For the same reason a multitude of sanguinary laws is both impolitic and unjust. The true design of all punishments being to reform, not to exterminate mankind.

Amendments

—1793. Deleted "those of" preceding "the lightest" and substituted "offenses" for "dye" thereafter at the end of the third sentence.

Cross References.

Excessive fines and punishments prohibited, see New Hampshire Constitution, Part 1, Article 33.

Sentences, see RSA 651.

NOTES TO DECISIONS

1. Construction
2. Discretion of sentencing court
3. Standards of review
4. Harsher penalty for lesser offense
5. Disparity in sentencing
6. Penalty not intended as punishment
7. Juveniles
8. Rehabilitation
9. Deterrence
10. Parole
11. Administrative sanctions
12. Appeals
13. Factors considered

1. Construction

This article forbids only gross disproportionality between offense and penalty. State v. Elbert, 125 N.H. 1, 480 A.2d 854, 1984 N.H. LEXIS 371 (1984).

2. Discretion of sentencing court

Sentencing court may not draw a negative inference of lack of remorse from defendant's silence at sentencing, but that holding does not preclude a sentencing court from considering other evidence besides defendant's silence that indicates his lack of remorse, nor does it prevent a sentencing court from considering defendant's false trial testimony as a sentencing factor. The holding was limited to situations where a defendant maintains his innocence throughout the criminal process and risks incriminating himself if he expresses remorse at sentencing. N.H. v. Burgess, 156 N.H. 746, 943 A.2d 727, 2008 N.H. LEXIS 18 (2008).

Sentencing court did not abuse its discretion by imposing the maximum sentence of 10 to 30 years in prison on each of defendant's two counts involving escape because the trial court did not violate his privilege against self-incrimination by using his silence at the sentencing hearing and failure to participate in the presentence investigation as sentencing factors as, although the sentencing court could not draw a negative inference of lack of remorse from his silence at sentencing, it was permitted to consider other evidence as indications of a lack of remorse, such as his denial that he ever intended to escape. The sentencing court only considered defendant's lack of involvement with the pre-sentence investigation, not his silence, as a sentencing factor. N.H. v. Burgess, 156 N.H. 746, 943 A.2d 727, 2008 N.H. LEXIS 18 (2008).

Consecutive sentences imposed for multiple convictions of aggravated felonious sexual assault under RSA 632-A:2 did not violate N.H. Const. pt. I, art. 18 because the provision required only that a trial court consider all of the relevant factors necessary to exercise its discretion, which include whether the sentence imposed will meet the traditional goals of sentencing—punishment, deterrence and rehabilitation. In light of the commands of Part I, Article 18, and as the petitioner had failed to cite any relevant authority for his assertion that for a sentencing scheme to be constitutional, objective factors must be set forth by statute to guide judicial discretion in sentencing, the sentencing scheme does not violate the State Constitution for the reasons he posited. Duquette v. Warden, N.H. State Prison, 154 N.H. 737, 919 A.2d 767, 2007 N.H. LEXIS 10 (2007).

To violate this article, a sentence must be grossly disproportionate to the crime, and such an abuse of sentencing discretion will also occur if the trial court fails to consider all the relevant factors necessary to the exercise of its discretion. State v. Stearns, 130 N.H. 475, 547 A.2d 672, 1988 N.H. LEXIS 72 (1988).

3. Standards of review

In assessing whether a criminal punishment is cruel and unusual, or unreasonably disproportionate to the offense charged, a statute is presumed valid and the legislature may not be required to select the least severe penalty possible so long as the penalty selected is not cruelly inhumane or disproportionate to the crime involved. State v. Deflorio, 128 N.H. 309, 512 A.2d 1133, 1986 N.H. LEXIS 286 (1986).

In determining whether a second degree murder sentence was an abuse of discretion and constitutionally disporportionate, it was important and useful to compare not only the minimum sentence imposed with earlier minimum sentences, but also the times of eligibility for parole in the two cases. State v. Pliskaner, 128 N.H. 486, 517 A.2d 795, 1986 N.H. LEXIS 329 (1986).

4. Harsher penalty for lesser offense

Sentence of life imprisonment with a minimum of thirty-five years was disproportionate to the offense of second degree murder, where the sentence was harsher than the maximum provided for first degree murder. State v. Dayutis, 127 N.H. 101, 498 A.2d 325, 1985 N.H. LEXIS 379 (1985).

5. Disparity in sentencing

Not all persons convicted of a particular crime must receive the same sentence; for even if crimes were identical, defendants may not be. State v. Fraser, 120 N.H. 117, 411 A.2d 1125, 1980 N.H. LEXIS 241 (1980).

6. Penalty not intended as punishment

Penalty assessment, under proposed legislation, of $2.00 or 10 percent, whichever is greater, on each fine, penalty or forfeiture imposed by court for a criminal offense, to provide funding for police training programs established by police standards and training council, was not an excessive fine or penalty disproportional to the offense within meaning of this article, since assessments were not intended for purpose of punishment, but rather, were to be levied to raise revenue for the training of police officers by imposing a special charge upon those who occasion the need for law enforcement. Opinion of Justices, 117 N.H. 382, 373 A.2d 640, 1977 N.H. LEXIS 342 (1977).

7. Juveniles

Incarceration of a sixteen or seventeen-year-old minor with adult prisoners on a misdemeanor offense is not cruel and unusual punishment, nor is it unreasonably disproportionate to the offense charged, and there is, therefore, no constitutional bar to the application of a statute subjecting such minors to adult process for motor vehicle violations. State v. Deflorio, 128 N.H. 309, 512 A.2d 1133, 1986 N.H. LEXIS 286 (1986).

8. Rehabilitation

Language of this article that "the true design of all punishments [is] to reform" is best read as a general statement of principle rather than as a mandatory standard which creates affirmative rights. State v. Evans, 127 N.H. 501, 506 A.2d 695, 1985 N.H. LEXIS 478 (1985).

While this article creates no substantive right to rehabilitation for prison inmates, it does place a constitutional imprimatur on this goal. State v. Evans, 127 N.H. 501, 506 A.2d 695, 1985 N.H. LEXIS 478 (1985).

Lack of rehabilitative programs in prison does not violate this article. State v. Evans, 127 N.H. 501, 506 A.2d 695, 1985 N.H. LEXIS 478 (1985).

Rehabilitation, which in the modern sense of the word includes counseling and training, is not required by this article for a prison inmate. State v. Evans, 127 N.H. 501, 506 A.2d 695, 1985 N.H. LEXIS 478 (1985).

A convicted defendant has no claim under this article that a particular sentence is not meaningful and rehabilitative. State v. Evans, 127 N.H. 501, 506 A.2d 695, 1985 N.H. LEXIS 478 (1985).

While this article's provision that the design of all punishments is to reform, not exterminate, mankind, is a statement of general purpose and intent, and may not create substantive rights, it is clear that the state espouses reform as a primary goal of its correctional system, and where the state places its constitutional imprimatur upon the goal of reform and rehabilitation, it cannot slough it off in the name of security, and a balance must be reached which accommodates all the state's penal objectives, not the least of which is the reform of the criminal. Laaman v. Helgemoe, 437 F. Supp. 269, 1977 U.S. Dist. LEXIS 15128 (D.N.H. 1977).

9. Deterrence

Emphasis on deterrence is not inconsistent with this article. State v. Wentworth, 118 N.H. 832, 395 A.2d 858, 1978 N.H. LEXIS 302 (1978).

10. Parole

Whether language of this article, "true design of all punishments being to reform, not to exterminate mankind," is directory or mandatory, such language does not create right to parole. State v. Farrow, 118 N.H. 296, 386 A.2d 808, 1978 N.H. LEXIS 402 (1978).

11. Administrative sanctions

Ample documentary evidence, as well as pharmacist's own admissions, supported board of pharmacy's sanctions against pharmacist for violations of recordkeeping and data entry requirements; moreover, second penalty imposed following rehearing was not more severe than first, and was not an abuse of discretion or violative of constitution. Appeal of Morgan (New Hampshire Bd. of Pharm.), 144 N.H. 44, 742 A.2d 101, 1999 N.H. LEXIS 75 (1999).

12. Appeals

Although N.H. Const. pt. I, arts. 15, 18, and 33 entitle a defendant to a fair appellate procedure, free from arbitrary and discriminatory enforcement, the constitution does not require that the procedure be adopted through the formal rulemaking process. State v. Addison, 159 N.H. 87, 977 A.2d 520, 2009 N.H. LEXIS 86 (2009).

13. Factors considered

Resentencing was required under N.H. Const. pt. I, art. 15 and 18. The trial court's comments implied that the trial court might have penalized defendant for his attorney's trial strategy; furthermore, it might have considered his failure to affirmatively express remorse, which violated his right against self-incrimination. State v. Willey, 163 N.H. 532, 44 A.3d 431, 2012 N.H. LEXIS 57 (2012).

Cited:

Cited in State v. Foster, 80 N.H. 1, 113 A. 211, 1921 N.H. LEXIS 1 (1921); State v. Burroughs, 113 N.H. 21, 300 A.2d 315, 1973 N.H. LEXIS 189 (1973); State v. Streeter, 113 N.H. 402, 308 A.2d 535, 1973 N.H. LEXIS 284 (1973); State v. Belanger, 114 N.H. 616, 325 A.2d 789, 1974 N.H. LEXIS 333 (1974); State v. Dean, 115 N.H. 520, 345 A.2d 408, 1975 N.H. LEXIS 352 (1975); State v. Goodwin, 118 N.H. 862, 395 A.2d 1234, 1978 N.H. LEXIS 307 (1978); State v. Wheeler, 120 N.H. 496, 416 A.2d 1384, 1980 N.H. LEXIS 331 (1980); State v. Darcy, 121 N.H. 220, 427 A.2d 516, 1981 N.H. LEXIS 283 (1981); State v. Peabody, 121 N.H. 1075, 438 A.2d 305, 1981 N.H. LEXIS 469 (1981); State v. Etzweiler, 125 N.H. 57, 480 A.2d 870, 1984 N.H. LEXIS 369 (1984); State v. McLaughlin, 126 N.H. 98, 489 A.2d 114, 1985 N.H. LEXIS 270 (1985); Gangi v. Cunningham, 127 N.H. 780, 508 A.2d 1050, 1986 N.H. LEXIS 235 (1986).

Art. 19.   [Searches and Seizures Regulated.]

Every subject hath a right to be secure from all unreasonable searches and seizures of his person, his houses, his papers, and all his possessions. Therefore, all warrants to search suspected places, or arrest a person for examination or trial in prosecutions for criminal matters, are contrary to this right, if the cause or foundation of them be not previously supported by oath or affirmation; and if the order, in a warrant to a civil officer, to make search in suspected places, or to arrest one or more suspected persons or to seize their property, be not accompanied with a special designation of the persons or objects of search, arrest, or seizure; and no warrant ought to be issued; but in cases, and with the formalities, prescribed by law.

Amendments

—1793.   This article was substituted for original Article 19.

Cross References.

Administrative inspection warrants, see RSA 595-B.
Arrests in criminal cases, see RSA 594.
Searches and seizures regulated by federal constitution, see United States Constitution, Amendment IV.
Search warrants, see RSA 595-A.

NOTES TO DECISIONS

1. Applicability
2. Construction with federal constitution
3. Definitions
4. Reasonableness
5. Search by private party
6. Probable cause—Generally
7. —Required
8. —Determination by magistrate
9. —Information from informant
10. Dispelled
11. Waiver of rights
12. Arrest
13. Custody
14. Seizure—Generally
15. —Plain view exception
16. —Community caretaking exception
17. Investigative detention
18. Motor vehicles
19. Sobriety checkpoints
·20. Use of dogs
21. Warrants—Issuance
22. —Supporting affidavit
23. —Contents
24. —Execution
25. Warrantless search—Generally
26. —Probationer
27. —Burden of proof
28. —Consent
29. —Abandonment of property
30. —Exigent circumstances
31. —Incident to arrest
32. —Administrative search exception
33. —Schools
34. —Community caretaking exception
35. —Detention
36. Warrantless arrest
37. Knock and announce rule
38. Open fields
39. Electronic interception and recording of private conversations
40. Administrative searches
41. Standing to challenge search or seizure
42. Admissibility of evidence
43. Forfeiture of property seized
44. Complaints
45. Medical records
46. Search valid
47. Anticipatory searches
48. Exclusionary rule
49. Warrantless entry
50. Apparent authority to consent to search
51. Attenuation test
52. Curtilage
53. Aerial observation
54. Expectation of privacy
55. Observations by conservation officer
55. Stop and frisk

1. Applicability

RSA 318-B:16 is not facially overbroad in violation of a defendant's rights under the Fourth Amendment or N.H. Const. pt. I, art. 19, as neither constitutional provision authorizes knowingly keeping a place where drug-dependent persons can use drugs. Furthermore, the operation of RSA 318-B:16 does not require a physical intrusion into the home so does not implicate search and seizure protections and the defendant in this case did not allege a search and seizure of her home. State v. MacElman, 154 N.H. 304, 910 A.2d 1267, 2006 N.H. LEXIS 160 (2006).

2. Construction with federal constitution

Because State Constitution provided at least as much protection as Federal Constitution with respect to probable cause to search, court was not required to conduct a separate federal analysis. State v. Roach, 141 N.H. 64, 677 A.2d 157, 1996 N.H. LEXIS 50 (1996).

Since supreme court found search illegal under state constitution, court was not required to reach defendant's fourth amendment argument in appeal from conviction for marijuana possession. State v. Silvestri, 136 N.H. 522, 618 A.2d 821, 1992 N.H. LEXIS 203 (1992).

For purposes of determining what constitutes an invasion of protected interests under this article, New Hampshire has neither adopted nor rejected the reasonable expectation of privacy analysis adhered to by the United States Supreme Court in interpreting the fourth amendment to the federal constitution. State v. Pellicci, 133 N.H. 523, 580 A.2d 710, 1990 N.H. LEXIS 104 (1990).

This article provides greater protection for individual rights than does the fourth amendment. State v. Koppel, 127 N.H. 286, 499 A.2d 977, 1985 N.H. LEXIS 425 (1985).

In its determination whether the seizure of a person was reasonable under this article, this article may be interpreted as more protective of individual rights than the minimal federal constitutional standards. State v. Brodeur, 126 N.H. 411, 493 A.2d 1134, 1985 N.H. LEXIS 317 (1985).

Where the search and seizure of a motor vehicle is involved, this article provides significantly greater protection than the fourth amendment against intrusion by the state. State v. Koppel, 127 N.H. 286, 499 A.2d 977, 1985 N.H. LEXIS 425 (1985).

The supreme court may impose a heavier burden on the state to prove a valid consent to search under this article than the federal constitution requires. State v. Osborne, 119 N.H. 427, 402 A.2d 493, 1979 N.H. LEXIS 346 (1979).

3. Definitions

A police officer's random computer check of a passing vehicle registration is not a search subject to protections of Fourth Amendment or Part I, Article 19 of New Hampshire constitution. State v. Richter, 145 N.H. 640, 765 A.2d 687, 2000 N.H. LEXIS 111 (2000).

For purposes of this article, a search ordinarily implies a quest by an officer of the law, a prying into hidden places for that which is concealed. State v. Pellicci, 133 N.H. 523, 580 A.2d 710, 1990 N.H. LEXIS 104 (1990).

In criminal law enforcement, a search ordinarily implies a quest by an officer of the law, a prying into hidden places for that which is concealed; a seizure contemplates forcible dispossession of the owner. State v. Coolidge, 106 N.H. 186, 208 A.2d 322, 1965 N.H. LEXIS 126 (1965).

4. Reasonableness

Absent some indication that an informant may not be telling the truth, such as the clear presence of bias, the police are not obligated to inquire into or to demonstrate the informant's credibility when relying on the informant for reasonable suspicion, and if the informant is identified, the tip must contain sufficient indicia of reliability to justify an investigatory stop; an informant who has personally observed incriminating behavior has a stronger basis of knowledge than does an informant who relates not what she knows personally, but what she has heard another say. State v. Gowen, 150 N.H. 286, 837 A.2d 297, 2003 N.H. LEXIS 182 (2003).

There is a twofold requirement for a reasonable expectation of privacy analysis: first, that a person have exhibited an actual (subjective) expectation of privacy and, second, that the expectation be one that society is prepared to recognize as "reasonable." State v. Goss, 150 N.H. 46, 834 A.2d 316, 2003 N.H. LEXIS 137 (2003).

Under the New Hampshire Constitution, warrantless entries are per se unreasonable searches and seizures and are thus illegal unless entry is made pursuant to one of a few recognized exceptions. State v. Santana, 133 N.H. 798, 586 A.2d 77, 1991 N.H. LEXIS 4 (1991).

New Hampshire citizens are entitled to protection from unreasonable searches and seizures; all searches and seizures must be reasonable. State v. Cote, 129 N.H. 358, 530 A.2d 775, 1987 N.H. LEXIS 217 (1987).

This article prohibits all unreasonable searches of all a citizen's possessions. State v. Pinder, 128 N.H. 66, 514 A.2d 1241, 1986 N.H. LEXIS 313 (1986); State v. Kilgus, 128 N.H. 577, 519 A.2d 231, 1986 N.H. LEXIS 372 (1986).

Unless a warrantless search or seizure falls within one of the few specifically established and well-delineated exceptions to the warrant requirement, it is per se unreasonable. State v. Pinder, 128 N.H. 66, 514 A.2d 1241, 1986 N.H. LEXIS 313 (1986).

The reasonableness of a search and seizure may not be determined solely by reference to general rules or to concepts of authority, agency or privity. State v. Coolidge, 106 N.H. 186, 208 A.2d 322, 1965 N.H. LEXIS 126 (1965).

The validity of a search and seizure is to be determined by reference to whether the particular search and seizure was reasonable or unreasonable and that determination is to be made on a case-to-case basis in the light of the surrounding circumstances. State v. Coolidge, 106 N.H. 186, 208 A.2d 322, 1965 N.H. LEXIS 126 (1965).

5. Search by private party

Where a college acted for its own reasons enforcing it's drug policy, the college's officers acted unilaterally, unaided by police in the college's interests and the trial court erred finding an agency relationship between college officers and police. State v. Nemser, 148 N.H. 453, 807 A.2d 1289, 2002 N.H. LEXIS 152 (2002).

Once a woman began producing contraband as she gathered her belongings from an apartment after being served with a restraining order which required her to vacate the apartment, the officer to whom she gave the contraband had no duty to prevent the woman from further gathering evidence and to obtain a warrant. State v. Patch, 142 N.H. 453, 702 A.2d 1278, 1997 N.H. LEXIS 118 (1997).

Drugs and drug paraphernalia were properly seized where (1) the defendant was granted a restraining order against the woman with whom he had been living which required her to leave their apartment, (2) an officer served the restraining order on the woman, and permitted her to gather her personal belongings before leaving the apartment, and (3) as she gathered her belongings, the woman proceeded to retrieve drugs and drug paraphernalia from cabinets and other areas of the apartment and handed them to the officer and then detailed to the officer her knowledge of the defendant's involvement in illegal marijuana trafficking. State v. Patch, 142 N.H. 453, 702 A.2d 1278, 1997 N.H. LEXIS 118 (1997).

6. Probable cause—Generally

Because the police did not violate the state constitution in entering the woods behind defendant's home, where they observed a smell of fresh marijuana each time a vent turned on, the information from their observations contained in their affidavits established probable cause to issue a warrant to search defendant's home. State v. Smith, 163 N.H. 169, 37 A.3d 409, 2012 N.H. LEXIS 1 (2012).

Under the totality of the circumstances, there was probable cause under the Fourth and Fourteenth Amendments and N.H. Const. pt. I, art. 19 to search defendant's home and computer pursuant to a search warrant, in light of a neighbor's statements that child pornography he saw in defendant's garage appeared to be computer printouts and that he had seen defendant use a laptop in his home. State v. Ward, 163 N.H. 156, 37 A.3d 353, 2012 N.H. LEXIS 2 (2012).

Police officers have a duty to reassess probable cause based upon information acquired after the warrant issues but before or during a search. The police must, of course, have some latitude to conduct searches pursuant to warrants; what the police cannot do, however, is treat the search warrant as an authorization for a full-scale search irrespective of developments subsequent to the warrant's issuance. State v. Schulz, 164 N.H. 217, 55 A.3d 933, 2012 N.H. LEXIS 129 (2012).

In many situations involving risky and high-intensity searches, police officers will not have an opportunity to reconsider with sober reflection the basis of probable cause each time a new piece of information comes to light. Thus, a reviewing court must consider not only whether such new information undermines the initial probable cause determination, but also the circumstances under which the police discovered the mistake, including the degree to which the police had secured the area and no longer faced an ongoing threat. State v. Schulz, 164 N.H. 217, 55 A.3d 933, 2012 N.H. LEXIS 129 (2012).

Because marijuana plants and defendant's statements were illegally obtained, they could not be used to establish probable cause for a search warrant; assuming that an officer was able to lawfully view a garden hose, this alone could not establish probable cause that evidence of illegal drug manufacturing was occurring on the property. Accordingly, any evidence obtained through the search warrant had to be suppressed. State v. Orde, 161 N.H. 260, 13 A.3d 338, 2010 N.H. LEXIS 145 (Nov. 30, 2010).

Trial court did not err in issuing search warrant that was used to obtain incriminating drug offense evidence against defendant at a specific location, as probable cause based on the totality of the circumstances supported issuance of the search warrant; the police officer's application for the warranted recounted information from at least five cooperating individuals who had dealt with defendant in recent weeks such that the officer presented the magistrate with sufficient facts to demonstrate a substantial likelihood that drug-related activities were occurring at defendant's residence. State v. Zwicker, 151 N.H. 179, 855 A.2d 415, 2004 N.H. LEXIS 112 (2004).

An affidavit is not rendered insufficient to establish probable cause by the fact that it does not establish the veracity and reliability of the informants; such a showing is not required where the affidavit otherwise establishes probable cause. State v. Daniel, 142 N.H. 54, 694 A.2d 989, 1997 N.H. LEXIS 54 (1997).

An affidavit was sufficient to establish probable cause, notwithstanding the assertion that it failed to indicate the veracity and reliability of the affiant's informants, where other information contained in the affidavit sufficiently corroborated their statements. State v. Daniel, 142 N.H. 54, 694 A.2d 989, 1997 N.H. LEXIS 54 (1997).

Probable cause supported a warrant to search the defendant's residence and person for drugs where (1) the supporting affidavit described an informant as having been "very reliable" in the past, his information having recently led to the arrest of a suspect on drug possession charges and the seizure of a quantity of cocaine, (2) the basis of the informant's knowledge was personal observation, as the informant described purchasing drugs directly from the defendant, such constituting a declaration against his penal interest, and (3) the supporting affidavit described two controlled buys involving the defendant, which independently corroborated the informant's statements. State v. Johnson, 140 N.H. 573, 669 A.2d 222, 1995 N.H. LEXIS 194 (1995).

Where the passage of time between the suspected criminal activity and the application for the warrant is at issue, circumstances such as the nature of the activity and the items sought must be considered in determining whether probable cause exists. State v. Kirsch, 139 N.H. 647, 662 A.2d 937, 1995 N.H. LEXIS 67 (1995).

In a prosecution for aggravated felonious sexual assault, probable cause supported the issuance of a search warrant for "pornographic or erotic materials to include but not limited to books, magazines, articles, photographs, slides, movies, albums, letters, diaries, sexual aids or toys or other items relating to sexual acts or sexual acts with children," where one victim told the police that she had been shown pornographic movies by the defendant or his wife during some of the assaults upon her and that she and other young girls were photographed in the nude by the defendant. State v. Kirsch, 139 N.H. 647, 662 A.2d 937, 1995 N.H. LEXIS 67 (1995).

Probable cause existed to search the remains of an entire home which was destroyed by fire where (1) the supporting affidavit identified a propane tank and water heater as a possible source of the fire, but in no way suggested that this was the only evidence of arson to be found in a search of the defendant's residence, and (2) the affidavit expressly stated that the speed with which the fire consumed the entire structure was consistent with the use of accelerants; thus, a reasonable interpretation of the evidence in the affidavit was that the defendant manipulated a propane tank and hot water heater to cause an explosion and fire, and then used accelerants to ensure the rapid and complete destruction of the entire residence, and a search to prove or disprove this theory necessarily encompassed not only the section of the home where the propane tank and water heater were located, but also the surround-

ing structure where accelerants might have been used. State v. Decoteau, 137 N.H. 106, 623 A.2d 1338, 1993 N.H. LEXIS 49 (1993).

Trial court's decision that police had probable cause to arrest defendant would not be reversed unless the decision when viewed in the light most favorable to the state was contrary to the manifest weight of the evidence. State v. Reid, 135 N.H. 376, 605 A.2d 1050, 1992 N.H. LEXIS 47 (1992).

Probable cause, which must support the issuance of a search warrant, exists if a person of ordinary caution would justifiably believe that what is sought will be found through the search and will aid in a particular apprehension or conviction. State v. Grimshaw, 128 N.H. 431, 515 A.2d 1201, 1986 N.H. LEXIS 323 (1986).

Probable cause exists where the facts and circumstances within the officer's knowledge and of which he had reasonably trustworthy information are in themselves sufficient to warrant a man of reasonable caution in the belief that an offense has been or is being committed. State v. Coolidge, 106 N.H. 186, 208 A.2d 322, 1965 N.H. LEXIS 126 (1965).

7. —Required

Application for search warrant need only contain sufficient facts and circumstances to establish a substantial likelihood that items sought will be found in place to be searched. State v. McMinn, 144 N.H. 34, 737 A.2d 1093, 1999 N.H. LEXIS 69 (1999).

Search warrant application established probable cause that a search of defendant's knapsack could provide evidence of crime to which search warrant related, and it was not required that facts and circumstances be sufficient to prove guilt beyond a reasonable doubt, to make out a prima facie case, or even to establish that guilt was more probable than not. State v. Cobb, 143 N.H. 638, 732 A.2d 425, 1999 N.H. LEXIS 53 (1999).

This article requires that search warrants be issued only upon a determination of probable cause. State v. Carroll, 131 N.H. 179, 552 A.2d 69, 1988 N.H. LEXIS 103 (1988).

This article requires that probable cause exist to support the issuance of a search. State v. Corey, 127 N.H. 56, 497 A.2d 1196, 1985 N.H. LEXIS 400 (1985); State v. Kellenbeck, 124 N.H. 760, 474 A.2d 1388, 1984 N.H. LEXIS 339 (1984).

To allow a law enforcement officer to act on less than probable cause and to conduct a search in an attempt to find something incriminating violates the defendant's protection against unreasonable search and seizure provided in this article. State v. Berthiaume, 124 N.H. 264, 470 A.2d 893, 1983 N.H. LEXIS 421 (1983).

To allow a police officer to seize an object on less than probable cause in order to further investigate whether it is contraband violates the defendant's protection against unreasonable search and seizure provided in this article. State v. Ball, 124 N.H. 226, 471 A.2d 347, 1983 N.H. LEXIS 426 (1983).

A warrantless seizure based on mere suspicion rather than probable cause is not valid, since to allow a police officer to act upon less than probable cause would violate the protection against unreasonable search and seizure afforded in this article and would allow an officer to seize anything in plain view on mere suspicion, thus permitting the unreasonable seizure of a person's property while a further investigation was made in an effort to find something incriminating. State v. Ball, 124 N.H. 226, 471 A.2d 347, 1983 N.H. LEXIS 426 (1983).

Probable cause must precede a warrantless search and mere suspicion is not enough, since allowing a police officer to seize an object on less than probable cause in order to further investigate whether it is contraband violates the defendant's protection against unreasonable search and seizure provided in this article. State v. Berthiaume, 124 N.H. 264, 470 A.2d 893, 1983 N.H. LEXIS 421 (1983).

It is a constitutional requirement that search warrants be issued only upon probable cause supported by oath or affirmation. State v. Coolidge, 106 N.H. 186, 208 A.2d 322, 1965 N.H. LEXIS 126 (1965).

8. —Determination by magistrate

This article protects the right to be secure from all unreasonable searches and seizures by requiring an objective determination of probable cause by a neutral and detached magistrate. State v. Kellenbeck, 124 N.H. 760, 474 A.2d 1388, 1984 N.H. LEXIS 339 (1984).

A grand jury indictment alone cannot substitute for the objective determination of probable cause to search by a neutral and detached magistrate when that magistrate isunaware of the evidence before the grand jury, and when the information before the magistrate, aside from the allegation of an indictment, is insufficient to support probable cause. State v. Kellenbeck, 124 N.H. 760, 474 A.2d 1388, 1984 N.H. LEXIS 339 (1984).

9. —Information from informant

Search warrant for storage unit was supported by probable cause, where information provided by three confidential informants was corroborated by each others' statements and by independent police searches of two of defendant's drug suppliers' residences, and a reasonable and prudent person would have been justified in believing that it was more probable than not that items listed in warrant application would be found in storage unit in question. State v. McMinn, 144 N.H. 34, 737 A.2d 1093, 1999 N.H. LEXIS 69 (1999).

The police established probable cause both to believe that the defendant was involved in drug trafficking and that there was a nexus between his drug activity and his residence as the self-incriminating nature of information given by a confidential informant and corroboration of such information was sufficient to establish reliability. State v. Fish, 142 N.H. 524, 703 A.2d 1377, 1997 N.H. LEXIS 124 (1997).

Informant's tip was reliable and, when combined with other information available to police, provided reasonable suspicion to stop pickup truck in which defendant and another individual were riding. State v. Hood, 141 N.H. 196, 679 A.2d 594, 1996 N.H. LEXIS 70 (1996).

An informant's basis of knowledge can reasonably be inferred where the tip includes such a wealth of intimate detail that it reasonably implies firsthand knowledge. State v. Christy, 138 N.H. 352, 639 A.2d 261, 1994 N.H. LEXIS 32 (1994).

Although anonymous telephone informant neither had an established track record with police nor had offered to demonstrate her reliability, her veracity could also be established where police were able to independently corroborate details provided by her. State v. Christy, 138 N.H. 352, 639 A.2d 261, 1994 N.H. LEXIS 32 (1994).

There was probable cause to support defendant's arrest based on tip from an anonymous informant where, by the time of arrest, police could reasonably have ascertained informant's identity and that she shared a close relationship with defendant, and that even the incompletely corroborated statements in her anonymous tip were true. State v. Christy, 138 N.H. 352, 639 A.2d 261, 1994 N.H. LEXIS 32 (1994).

10. Dispelled

When an officer obtained a search warrant on the belief that the guns he saw in defendant's house were firearms, and learned after the search began that the guns were BB guns and therefore not firearms, the continued search of the home was unreasonable under N.H. Const. pt. I, art. 19. Learning that the guns were BB guns dispelled probable cause. State v. Schulz, 164 N.H. 217, 55 A.3d 933, 2012 N.H. LEXIS 129 (2012).

Police officers must discontinue a search under the authority of a warrant when an unambiguous and material change has occurred in the facts, eliminating probable cause. To the extent that the police have encountered new information that casts doubt upon the ongoing justification for the search, they would be well-advised to refrain from continuing the search until a neutral magistrate determines that probable cause continues to exist: should they fail to do so, the remedy of suppression will be warranted if a reviewing court finds that the magistrate would not have issued the warrant had the magistrate known about the new information. State v. Schulz, 164 N.H. 217, 55 A.3d 933, 2012 N.H. LEXIS 129 (2012).

11. Waiver of rights

Since defendant voluntarily consented to the breath test after being advised of her right to refuse, the "fruit of the poisonous tree" doctrine did not apply. The fact that the trooper did not provide a mandated advisory to an initial test did not preclude the administration of the second test. State v. Barkus, 152 N.H. 701, 888 A.2d 398, 2005 N.H. LEXIS 160 (2005), rehearing denied, 2005 N.H. LEXIS 193 (N.H. Dec. 28, 2005).

The right to be secure against unreasonable search and seizure is one that may be yielded; but the right is not to be diminished or diluted for reasons of convenience or expediency or violated on the basis of assumptions or presumptions. State v. Laro, 106 N.H. 500, 213 A.2d 909, 1965 N.H. LEXIS 200 (1965).

Public policy does not forbid the waiver of the constitutional right to be secure against unreasonable search and seizure. Manchester Press Club v. State Liquor Comm'n, 89 N.H. 442, 200 A. 407, 1938 N.H. LEXIS 51, 116 A.L.R. 1093 (1938).

12. Arrest

Passenger's unlawful arrest claim failed because probable cause justified the arrest based on the heroin found in the car and an outstanding warrant. Machado v. Weare Police Dep't, — F.3d —, 2012 U.S. App. LEXIS 20538 (Oct. 2, 2012).

Where defendant assaulted defendant's girlfriend in one jurisdiction, the police in that jurisdiction notified other jurisdictions of the offense, and the police department in the jurisdiction in which defendant resided sent officers without a warrant to defendant's home to arrest defendant, the trial court erroneously dismissed the charges against defendant, as the arresting officers had territorial jurisdiction to arrest defendant; RSA 105:4 did not address where the underlying conduct had to occur for the arresting jurisdiction to legally make the arrest, the probable cause pursuant to N.H. Const. pt. I, art. 19 to arrest was transferred by the department where the conduct occurred to the arresting officers, and the arresting officers had authority under RSA 594:10, I(b) to make the warrantless arrest, because they had probable cause to believe that defendant had, within the previous six hours, committed abuse as defined in RSA 173-B:1 against a person eligible for protection from domestic violence as defined in RSA 173-B:1. State v. Merriam, 150 N.H. 548, 842 A.2d 102, 2004 N.H. LEXIS 19 (2004), rehearing denied, 2004 N.H. LEXIS 46 (N.H. Mar. 12, 2004).

Officer's investigatory stop of defendant was based on specific, articulable facts where his testimony was that he was investigating recent burglaries in the area, that he went to the location of the burglary two days previously because he knew that burglars who take cash often return to the same place to take more, and that he saw the defendant coming right from a previously burglarized house wearing dark clothing and a hooded sweatshirt. State v. Graham, 146 N.H. 142, 769 A.2d 355, 2001 N.H. LEXIS 44 (2001).

The defendant's assumed detention did not rise to the level of an arrest until after he made certain statements at issue since the detention was not unreasonably intrusive, he was not confined or physically restrained during questioning by a police officer, and the detention lasted no longer than necessary to effectuate the purpose of the stop, which was to ascertain whether the defendant knew that an outboard motor was stolen. State v. Wong, 138 N.H. 56, 635 A.2d 470, 1993 N.H. LEXIS 157 (1993).

A police officer had probable cause to arrest the defendant for loitering and prowling where (1) the officer observed the defendant quickly depart from the parking lot of a commercial building at 4:30 a.m., a time at which all the businesses were closed, (2) the officer knew that there had been several burglaries in the area during the past several months, and upon stopping the vehicle, learned that the defendant was not an owner or employee of any of the businesses, and (3) shortly after stopping the defendant, the officer became aware that the defendant had a reputation as a burglar. State v. Jaroma, 137 N.H. 562, 630 A.2d 1173, 1993 N.H. LEXIS 121 (1993).

The defendant was not arrested when, after the pickup truck in which he was a passenger was stopped on a reasonable suspicion that the furniture in the truck was stolen, he and the driver were given a choice between taking the furniture to the police station or being arrested; if the police had not received notice that a burglary was discovered near the location where the pickup truck was first spotted prior to arriving at the police station, the defendant and his partner would have been free to leave as soon as they deposited the furniture, and if the defendant had deposited the furniture according to plan, the continued detention of the furniture would have been permissible as a limited investigatory seizure. State v. Noel, 137 N.H. 384, 628 A.2d 692, 1993 N.H. LEXIS 88 (1993).

Determination of when an arrest occurs depends upon the facts and circumstances of a particular case. State v. Reid, 135 N.H. 376, 605 A.2d 1050, 1992 N.H. LEXIS 47 (1992).

An arrest, to be valid, must meet the requirement for reasonable searches and seizures of this article. State v. Jones, 127 N.H. 515, 503 A.2d 802, 1985 N.H. LEXIS 454 (1985).

Absent exigent circumstances or consent, the police must obtain an arrest warrant to enter a suspect's home to arrest him in order for the arrest to pass state constitutional muster. State v. Jones, 127 N.H. 515, 503 A.2d 802, 1985 N.H. LEXIS 454 (1985).

13. Custody

In the absence of formal arrest, trial court deciding whether custody exists for purposes of this article must determine whether a suspect's freedom of movement was sufficiently curtailed by considering how a reasonable man in the suspect's position would have understood his situation. State v. Green, 133 N.H. 249, 575 A.2d 1308, 1990 N.H. LEXIS 55 (1990).

14. Seizure—Generally

Seizure of a plastic bag containing ecstasy pills was proper under the plain view doctrine. Before he seized the bag, an officer observed that the pills were abnormally shaped and partially crumbled; he knew from his training and experience that ecstasy pills were manufactured to have different shapes and patterns; he recognized the bag as being tied in a way associated with storing illicit drugs; and defendant's behavior was suggestive of recent drug use. State v. Bell, 164 N.H. 452, 58 A.3d 665, 2012 N.H. LEXIS 171 (2012).

Defendant had been seized under N.H. Const. pt. I, art. 19 when he overheard one officer call another to come to the scene with a narcotics-sniffing dog. At that point, defendant reasonably could have concluded that he would not be allowed to leave the scene until the officer and the dog arrived and completed their investigation. State v. Joyce, 159 N.H. 440, 986 A.2d 642, 2009 N.H. LEXIS 135 (2009).

When an officer asked defendant to open the locked door of an inn, then asked him what he was "up to" and for an identification, defendant had not been seized under U.S. Const. amend. IV and N.H. Const. pt. I, art. 19. Nothing suggested that defendant felt bound to open the door, and the record was devoid of evidence that once defendant opened the door, the officer touched him or used authoritative language or tone; furthermore, a reasonable person would not have taken the officer's question about what the men were "up to" as a show of authority, and the officer's request to see defendant's identification did not constitute a seizure. State v. Daoud, 158 N.H. 779, 973 A.2d 294, 2009 N.H. LEXIS 72 (2009).

Defendant had not been "seized" under N.H. Const. pt. I, art. 19 when he went to the victim's home to find out what was going on with the investigation, thus voluntarily placing himself in a situation where it could only be expected that police would request further communication. He readily agreed to hold such communication at the police department and to be transported there, and he experienced neither physical force nor coercive commands. State v. Sullivan, 157 N.H. 124, 949 A.2d 140, 2008 N.H. LEXIS 48 (2008).

Where the officer drove the officer's boat within 50 feet of defendant's kayak and asked defendant if defendant had a life jacket, this was a stop without an articulable suspicion as required by New Hampshire Department of Safety Standard Operating Procedures, which contained the same requirement as New Hampshire case law under N.H. Const. pt. I, art. 19, and defendant's motion to suppress should have been granted; the actions of the officer coupled with the officer's stated practice of waiting to determine from a boater's response as to whether the boater had a personal flotation device indicated that defendant's compliance with the officer's questioning was mandatory and that a reasonable person would not have felt free to leave, and the State conceded that the officer lacked an articulable suspicion. State v. McKeown, 151 N.H. 95, 849 A.2d 127, 2004 N.H. LEXIS 96 (2004).

Encounters between police officers and individuals that are purely voluntary or very brief generally do not constitute seizures. State v. Brunelle, 145 N.H. 656, 766 A.2d 272, 2000 N.H. LEXIS 124 (2000).

Officer's encounter with defendant transcended a mere request to communicate where it fairly indicated that compliance was mandatory, and no reasonable person would have believed he was free to ignore the officer and simply walk away; defendant was therefore seized within meaning of this article. State v. Quezada, 141 N.H. 258, 681 A.2d 79, 1996 N.H. LEXIS 86 (1996).

A person is considered seized for purposes of state constitution if, in view of all the circumstances surrounding the incident, a reasonable person would have believed that he was not free to leave. State v. Reid, 135 N.H. 376, 605 A.2d 1050, 1992 N.H. LEXIS 47 (1992).

Defendant was seized but not under arrest when he was handcuffed and placed in a police cruiser, as he could not have reasonably believed that he was free to leave at that time. State v. Reid, 135 N.H. 376, 605 A.2d 1050, 1992 N.H. LEXIS 47 (1992).

The test for determining whether a "seizure" has occurred is whether, in view of all the circumstances surrounding the incident, a reasonable person would have believed that he was not free to leave. State v. Cote, 129 N.H. 358, 530 A.2d 775, 1987 N.H. LEXIS 217 (1987).

It is not enough to establish a "seizure" that the person asking questions was a law enforcement official. State v. Cote, 129 N.H. 358, 530 A.2d 775, 1987 N.H. LEXIS 217 (1987).

An individual is seized, for purposes of this article, if under all of the circumstances a reasonable person would have believed that he was not free to leave. State v. Brodeur, 126 N.H. 411, 493 A.2d 1134, 1985 N.H. LEXIS 317 (1985).

15. —Plain view exception

Plain view exception did not apply to marijuana seized on defendant's deck because an officer's initial intrusion onto the deck was not lawful. State v. Orde, 161 N.H. 260, 13 A.3d 338, 2010 N.H. LEXIS 145 (Nov. 30, 2010).

With respect to the plain view exception to the warrant requirement, the inadvertency requirement under the New Hampshire Constitution is abolished for drugs, weapons, and other items dangerous in themselves. State v. Nieves, 160 N.H. 245, 999 A.2d 389, 2010 N.H. LEXIS 42 (2010).

Although the inadvertency requirement under the New Hampshire Constitution is abolished for drugs, weapons, and other items dangerous in themselves, the initial intrusion under the plain view exception must still be justified by a warrant or an exception to the warrant requirement. State v. Nieves, 160 N.H. 245, 999 A.2d 389, 2010 N.H. LEXIS 42 (2010).

Trial court properly denied defendant's motion to suppress illegal weapons that were seized without a warrant by police during a plain-clothes sweep of a flea market because the plain view exception applied where the police were lawfully on the premises; discovery of the weapons was inadvertent because although the police had a justifiable suspicion that they would find contraband, they did not have probable cause to obtain a warrant for defendant's booths; and the weapons' incriminating nature was immediately apparent given the police officers' observations of the contraband. State v. Davis, 149 N.H. 698, 828 A.2d 293, 2003 N.H. LEXIS 103 (2003).

Knives and stockpile of guns were admissible since they were inadvertently discovered and their incriminating nature was apparent; defendant controlled them due to his proximity to them and the ammunition in his pocket; mere access to the guns hanging in the hallway did not constitute control. State v. Hammell, 147 N.H. 313, 787 A.2d 850, 2001 N.H. LEXIS 218 (2001).

State bears burden of establishing that a warrantless seizure falls within a judicially crafted exception to the warrant requirement. State v. Brunelle, 145 N.H. 656, 766 A.2d 272, 2000 N.H. LEXIS 124 (2000).

Police had a legitimate concern for their safety when they entered defendant's trailer, and this concern justified a protective sweep of bedroom, and where evidence in bedroom was found in plain view, there was no violation of this article. State v. Smith, 141 N.H. 271, 681 A.2d 1215, 1996 N.H. LEXIS 90 (1996).

Under the New Hampshire Constitution, in order to justify a warrantless seizure under the "plain view" exception, the state must prove by a preponderance of the evidence that: (1) the initial intrusion which afforded the view was lawful; (2) the discovery of the evidence was inadvertent; and (3) the incriminating nature of the evidence was immediately apparent. State v. Murray, 134 N.H. 613, 598 A.2d 206, 1991 N.H. LEXIS 107 (1991).

16. —Community caretaking exception

Officers investigating a noise complaint were justified under the state and federal constitutions in effecting a limited seizure of defendant based upon a reasonable suspicion that he was disturbing the peace. The reasonable suspicion was not eliminated when the loud music was turned off, as reasonable suspicion could relate to past criminal activity; there was no indication that the police extended the encounter beyond what was minimally necessary to identify defendant; and to the extent the encounter was prolonged, it was by defendant's refusal to identify himself. State v. Bell, 164 N.H. 452, 58 A.3d 665, 2012 N.H. LEXIS 171 (2012).

Although New Hampshire's highest court recognized that community caretaking and investigative functions could be performed at the same time and in the same place, it further held that the State had not met its burden of showing that the seizure of defendant's backpack was a community caretaking activity where the police officer who found it testified to having been sent to the crime scene to check for further property damage; although a claim of inventory search could not be sustained as to a search before defendant's ownership of the backpack could be established, the State could try, on remand, if the community caretaking exception were established upon further taking of evidence, that a second search did qualify as an inventory search. State v. D'Amour, 150 N.H. 122, 834 A.2d 214, 2003 N.H. LEXIS 151 (2003).

Emergency aid provision of the community caretaking exception to the warrant requirement applied to a situation where police arrived at defendant's premises to investigate a report of a car in danger of sliding over an embankment onto an interstate highway and discovered, simultaneously with their realization that the car was not in danger, that its occupants were all smoking marijuana. State v. MacElman, 149 N.H. 795, 834 A.2d 322, 2003 N.H. LEXIS 128 (2003).

It was error to deny defendant's motion to suppress a wallet left in a car that was to be towed because although the community care-taking exception to the warrant requirement applied to the wallet's seizure, it did not apply to the wallet's search and the court declined the invitation to extend it to do so. State v. Denoncourt, 149 N.H. 308, 821 A.2d 997, 2003 N.H. LEXIS 42 (2003).

Absent any indication that defendant needed aid, a police officer was not justified in seizing defendant under the community care-taking exception where defendant claimed defendant was stopped in a travel lane on a residential street after dropping off a drunk female and the officer thought the answer was "unusual." State v. Boyle, 148 N.H. 306, 807 A.2d 1234, 2002 N.H. LEXIS 126 (2002).

Investigative stop of defendant's vehicle was not justified as a valid exercise of community caretaking function, where police had no evidence of any ongoing threat to public safety and only an anonymous tip about a possible motor vehicle violation which had already been completed. State v. Blake, 146 N.H. 1, 766 A.2d 725, 2001 N.H. LEXIS 16 (2001).

State trooper's limited request for license and registration of motorist whom she was assisting with disabled vehicle fell within community caretaking exception to warrant requirement, and therefore motorist's motion to suppress was properly denied. State v. Brunelle, 145 N.H. 656, 766 A.2d 272, 2000 N.H. LEXIS 124 (2000).

The seizure of property by the police is justified by the community caretaking exception when it constitutes no more than a routine and good faith attempt, in the exercise of reasonable caution, to safeguard the defendant's own property. State v. Psomiades, 139 N.H. 480, 658 A.2d 1190, 1995 N.H. LEXIS 33 (1995).

The community caretaking exception justified a police officer's seizure of the defendant's purse where the defendant was arrested for driving while intoxicated and the officer removed the purse, which was located on the front seat, turned on the hazard lights, and locked the car doors before transporting the defendant to the police station pursuant to departmental policy to remove any valuables located in plain view when securing an automobile. State v. Psomiades, 139 N.H. 480, 658 A.2d 1190, 1995 N.H. LEXIS 33 (1995).

17. Investigative detention

Based upon defendant's behavior, including a lack of eye contact and unclear response when asked whether defendant had any other weapons in his car, a police officer doubted defendant's truthfulness in answering questions regarding a fight. The officer had a reasonable suspicion that defendant was armed and dangerous, and the officer was justified in assuring himself that defendant did not possess a weapon by conducting a protective frisk. State v. Michelson, 160 N.H. 270, 999 A.2d 372, 2010 N.H. LEXIS 45 (2010).

Because defendant was seized when an officer called for another officer and a narcotics-sniffing dog, any information that the police acquired after the seizure could not support a reasonable suspicion that the defendant was engaged in criminal activity. Therefore, even though a detective testified that he smelled marijuana on the defendant after he called for the narcotics-sniffing dog, this fact could not justify the seizure of defendant. State v. Joyce, 159 N.H. 440, 986 A.2d 642, 2009 N.H. LEXIS 135 (2009).

When defendant was seized, officers lacked reasonable suspicion under N.H. Const. pt. I, art. 19 that he was engaged in criminal activity. A tip that a woman was smoking marijuana outside a building contained no reference to defendant or his car and thus could not have provided reasonable suspicion that he was engaged in criminal activity; the record did not support a reasonable suspicion that the woman was linked to defendant other than the fact that they were together in defendant's car; an officer smelled the odor of fresh marijuana coming from the woman only after she left the car; and no officer smelled marijuana in the car, or the odor of burnt marijuana, before defendant was seized. State v. Joyce, 159 N.H. 440, 986 A.2d 642, 2009 N.H. LEXIS 135 (2009).

Seizure was lawful as an officer possessed more than a general sense that defendant, who was driving a vehicle, had possibly committed some kind of crime, and had reasonable suspicion that defendant had been involved in the reported sexual assaults since: (1) the car was the make and color reported to have been driven by the assailant, (2) a license plate check revealed that the car belonged to defendant, whom the officer knew was familiar with wooded areas where the assaults took place, and (3) an object shaped like a sneaker hung from the car's rearview mirror that was similar to the air freshener reportedly hanging in the assailant's car. State v. Giddens, 155 N.H. 175, 922 A.2d 650, 2007 N.H. LEXIS 46 (2007), rehearing denied, 2007 N.H. LEXIS 106 (N.H. June 7, 2007).

Investigatory stop of defendant's vehicle violated N.H. Const. pt. I, art. 19 because the only support for it was that an officer heard defendant squeal his tires, and, absent some evidence of the car's acceleration or speed, this was insufficient, alone, to create a reasonable suspicion that defendant had been, was, or was about to be violating the road racing statute, RSA 265:75, I, nor did it create a reasonable suspicion of driving under the influence, under RSA 265:82, I, because there was no evidence of any erratic driving or traffic violation, and the fact that it was "club night" in the town was insufficient. State v. Pepin, 155 N.H. 364, 920 A.2d 1209, 2007 N.H. LEXIS 59 (2007).

Officer's encounter with defendant when officer approached defendant's parked vehicle was consensual where restrictions on defendant's movement were not the result of the officer's actions, and, inter alia, the officer did not draw his weapon, did not order defendant out of car, and did not ask defendant to roll down his window, but rather asked if defendant was "all set". State v. Licks, 154 N.H. 491, 914 A.2d 1246, 2006 N.H. LEXIS 189 (2006).

Seizure did not violate the Fourth Amendment or N.H. Const. pt. I, art. 19, because the police officer conducted a valid investigatory stop after the officer observed defendant drive through a stop sign and weave all over the road, nearly causing a head-on collision. State v. Smith, 154 N.H. 113, 908 A.2d 786, 2006 N.H. LEXIS 125 (2006).

In affirming RSA 265:82, I(a) (Repealed, see now RSA 265A:2) driving under the influence of intoxicating liquor conviction on sufficient evidence, a defendant's failure of five field sobriety tests was properly not suppressed; an officer watching a building after its alarm rang had reasonable, articulable suspicion to seize defendant after he parked in its lot by approaching him, questioning him, and noticing indicia of intoxication before administering the tests. State v. Wiggin, 151 N.H. 305, 855 A.2d 1250, 2004 N.H. LEXIS 143 (2004).

Officer's questions did not exceed the scope of a Terry stop, and defendant's motion to suppress was therefore properly denied, where a reasonable, articulable suspicion of wrongdoing was aroused by defendant's conduct after an ordinary traffic stop: in approaching the police car, in having stopped near a restricted area where drug transfers often occurred, and in claiming to have been on the way to a destination that did not accord with the route taken. State v. McKinnon-Andrews, 151 N.H. 19, 846 A.2d 1198, 2004 N.H. LEXIS 82 (2004).

Police officer had reasonable suspicion of wrongdoing that justified stopping defendant's car once officer heard from dispatcher that the driver's license of the registered owner of the car—as to which the dispatcher and the officer had already received a report of possible drunk driving—had been suspended. State v. Reno, 150 N.H. 466, 840 A.2d 786, 2004 N.H. LEXIS 4 (2004).

Even though officer's stop of defendant for speeding and a broken taillight was a lawful investigatory stop, the scope of the stop must have been carefully tailored to its underlying justification, must have been temporary and have lasted no longer than was necessary to effectuate its purpose. State v. Hight, 146 N.H. 746, 781 A.2d 11, 2001 N.H. LEXIS 155 (2001).

Investigative stop of defendant's vehicle violated New Hampshire Constitution, where stop was based on uncorroborated telephone report from an anonymous informant, and report lacked information necessary to establish that caller's tip was self-verifying. State v. Blake, 146 N.H. 1, 766 A.2d 725, 2001 N.H. LEXIS 16 (2001).

Police officer's random computer check of passing vehicle registration, which indicated that registered owner of vehicle had a suspended driver's license, provided reasonable suspicion for officer to stop vehicle since it was reasonable for officer to infer that driver was owner of vehicle, which gave rise to reasonable suspicion that driver was driving with a suspended license. State v. Richter, 145 N.H. 640, 765 A.2d 687, 2000 N.H. LEXIS 111 (2000).

Premises-wide warrant included authority to search knapsack owned by defendant, a visitor, since defendant was neither wearing nor in possession of knapsack at time warrant was executed, and knapsack was a container that could hold either the marijuana or hallucinogenic mushrooms identified in warrant. State v. Leiper, 145 N.H. 233, 761 A.2d 458, 2000 N.H. LEXIS 51 (2000).

A police officer may make an investigative stop of a vehicle provided that stop is based on a reasonable suspicion that person detained had committed, was committing, or was about to commit a crime, and officer is able to point to specific and articulable facts which, taken together with rational inferences from those facts, reasonably warrant the intrusion. State v. Galgay, 145 N.H. 100, 750 A.2d 52, 2000 N.H. LEXIS 23 (2000).

Officer had reasonable suspicion, based on specific and articulable facts, to justify his investigative stop of suspected drunk driver; despite passage of approximately fifty minutes, officer could reasonably infer that defendant was same person who had earlier been reported as driving erratically, and fact that defendant was able to walk to his car and drive away from restaurant without apparent difficulty did not negate officer's reasonable suspicion. State v. Galgay, 145 N.H. 100, 750 A.2d 52, 2000 N.H. LEXIS 23 (2000).

The ultimate test of the propriety of an investigatory stop is whether, viewing the circumstances objectively, an officer had a specific and articulable basis for concluding that an individual had committed, was committing, or was about to commit a crime; if such a justification is found, the stop will be deemed constitutional, and this is so regardless of whether a hypothetical "reasonable" officer, absent any allegedly illegitimate motivation, would have elected not to investigate. State v. McBreairty, 142 N.H. 12, 697 A.2d 495, 1997 N.H. LEXIS 48 (1997).

An officer properly stopped the defendant's vehicle where, after receiving a report that another police department was looking for a similar vehicle, he followed the vehicle and determined that it was being operated at 10 to 15 miles per hour over the speed limit; a contrary result was not required by the fact that the officer acknowledged that he had previously been told by local residents of a vehicle with the defendant's license plate number, often driven by a male under suspension and while intoxicated. State v. McBreairty, 142 N.H. 12, 697 A.2d 495, 1997 N.H. LEXIS 48 (1997).

The court refused to validate an officer's search of the defendant's wallet for identification papers as a "narrow extension" of the permissible scope of an investigatory stop. State v. Webber, 141 N.H. 817, 694 A.2d 970, 1997 N.H. LEXIS 44 (1997).

Police officer had reasonable, articulable suspicion to justify a seizure at the time he ordered defendant to remove his hands from his pockets, where defendant's behavior was suspicious and took place in an alley in city's "combat zone" at 3:55 a.m., and during his encounter with officer, defendant acted evasive, nervous, confused, and uncooperative. State v. Roach, 141 N.H. 64, 677 A.2d 157, 1996 N.H. LEXIS 50 (1996).

Investigatory stop was justified by officers' observation of defendant emerging, at 1:15 a.m., from a building known as a center for drug sales, and by defendant's suspicious actions both before and after officers stopped automobile which defendant had entered. State v. Vadnais, 141 N.H. 68, 677 A.2d 155, 1996 N.H. LEXIS 49 (1996).

A police officer had reasonable suspicion sufficient to justify the stop of the defendant's vehicle to investigate the possibility of driving while intoxicated where (1) an anonymous caller provided information including the specific description of the car, knowledge of its exact location at a moment in time, and specific information regarding the car's movements, (2) while the police had no information on the caller, they were able to corroborate certain details provided by the caller within a few minutes of the call, and (3) the officer faced the potential of a dangerous public safety hazard. State v. Melanson, 140 N.H. 199, 665 A.2d 338, 1995 N.H. LEXIS 127 (1995).

An officer possessed a reasonable suspicion, based on specific, articulable facts, that the defendant was committing the offense of driving after having been certified an habitual offender and, therefore, his stop of the defendant's vehicle was proper where (1) the police department received a telephone call from a local resident who was concerned that her child was riding in a vehicle driven by the defendant who, according to the caller's belief, was driving while his license was under suspension, and (2) a police officer subsequently spotted the defendant, whom he recognized, driving the defendant's vehicle, which he also recognized. State v. Mortrud, 139 N.H. 423, 654 A.2d 464, 1995 N.H. LEXIS 19 (1995).

An investigative stop was justified since the police had an articulable suspicion that the defendant had received stolen property where (1) a police officer knew that an outboard motor had been reported stolen and that when delivered by the defendant it was packaged in half of its original crate and was missing several parts, and (2) the officer also knew that the defendant lived in Massachusetts and might reasonably have suspected that the defendant brought the motor, as well as a boat and another motor, to the area so as to avoid Massachusetts marine dealers more likely to discover that the property was stolen. State v. Wong, 138 N.H. 56, 635 A.2d 470, 1993 N.H. LEXIS 157 (1993).

A police officer had a sufficient basis to make an investigatory stop of the defendant where the officer knew the area, knew that several burglaries had occurred at local businesses within the past year, observed the defendant's vehicle emerge from behind a commercial building at 4:30 a.m. and enter onto a main street at approximately 30 miles per hour without yielding, knew that the businesses would not have been open for several hours, and knew that the vehicle did not belong to an owner of any of the businesses. State v. Jaroma, 137 N.H. 562, 630 A.2d 1173, 1993 N.H. LEXIS 121 (1993).

Police may temporarily detain a suspect for investigatory purposes on grounds that do not amount to probable cause to arrest him for commission of a crime. State v. Reid, 135 N.H. 376, 605 A.2d 1050, 1992 N.H. LEXIS 47 (1992).

For an investigatory detention to be lawful under state constitution, police must have articulable suspicion that the individual detained has committed or is about to commit a crime. State v. Reid, 135 N.H. 376, 605 A.2d 1050, 1992 N.H. LEXIS 47 (1992).

Scope of an investigatory detention must be carefully tailored to its underlying justification and the detention must be temporary and last no longer than is necessary to effectuate the purpose of the stop. State v. Reid, 135 N.H. 376, 605 A.2d 1050, 1992 N.H. LEXIS 47 (1992).

For purposes of determining whether reasonable suspicion exists, under state constitutional standards, to justify an investigative stop based on information received by an informant, the supreme court will examine the reliability and credibility of the informant, and his basis of knowledge, and will render final judgment on the totality of the circumstances. State v. Kennison, 134 N.H. 243, 590 A.2d 1099, 1991 N.H. LEXIS 52 (1991).

An investigative stop passes constitutional muster under the New Hampshire Constitution where it is substantially less intrusive than an arrest, where the investigating officer had a reasonable suspicion that the person detained had committed, was committing, or was about to commit a crime, and where the officer can point to specific and articulable facts which, taken together with rational inferences from those facts, reasonably warrant the intrusion. State v. Kennison, 134 N.H. 243, 590 A.2d 1099, 1991 N.H. LEXIS 52 (1991).

At the heart of every state constitutional analysis involving an investigative stop is a balancing of the governmental interest that allegedly justified the stop against the extent of the intrusion of protected interests. State v. Kennison, 134 N.H. 243, 590 A.2d 1099, 1991 N.H. LEXIS 52 (1991).

Fact that officer had seen defendant, at least four years prior to investigatory stop, associating with drug users and sellers, and that one year prior to the stop reliable informant informed officer that defendant sold marijuana could not justify stop under state constitutional standard of reasonable suspicion; information and tips were stale, vague and conclusory. State v. Kennison, 134 N.H. 243, 590 A.2d 1099, 1991 N.H. LEXIS 52 (1991).

The factors used to evaluate an informant's reliability, credibility, and the basis of knowledge for purposes determining whether reasonable suspicion exists to warrant an investigatory stop, under state constitutional standards, are the same as those used in analysis of probable cause; the quality of information is, however, less than that required for probable cause. State v. Kennison, 134 N.H. 243, 590 A.2d 1099, 1991 N.H. LEXIS 52 (1991).

Investigative stop based upon an anonymous, uncorroborated tip from an informant that defendant had four pounds of marijuana in trunk of automobile and would drive home from work and later make deliveries of the marijuana was an unjustifiable intrusion upon defendant state constitutional privacy rights; officers lacked the requisite level of reasonable suspicion under the totality of the circumstances where general predictions about defendant's behavior failed to demonstrate a special familiarity with defendant's itinerary. State v. Kennison, 134 N.H. 243, 590 A.2d 1099, 1991 N.H. LEXIS 52 (1991).

Under carefully defined circumstances, certain investigative stops on the basis of less than probable cause to arrest are permissible under this article, because stops are substantially less intrusive than an arrest. State v. Pellicci, 133 N.H. 523, 580 A.2d 710, 1990 N.H. LEXIS 104 (1990).

A temporary detention of a suspect by police, on grounds that do not amount to probable cause to arrest is lawful under this article only where the investigating officer undertook to stop on the basis of a reasonable suspicion that the person detained had committed, was committing, or was about to commit a crime, the officer can point to specific and articulable facts which, taken together with rational inferences from those facts, reasonably warrants the intrusion, and the scope of the detention was carefully tailored to its underlying justification, is temporary, and lasts no longer than is necessary to effectuate the purpose of the stop. State v. Pellicci, 133 N.H. 523, 580 A.2d 710, 1990 N.H. LEXIS 104 (1990).

In determining whether an investigatory stop is lawful under this article, governmental interests justifying the stop are balanced against the extent of intrusion on protected interests. State v. Pellicci, 133 N.H. 523, 580 A.2d 710, 1990 N.H. LEXIS 104 (1990).

An investigatory stop by police, a limited seizure based on articulable suspicion, is permissible under this article. State v. Brodeur, 126 N.H. 411, 493 A.2d 1134, 1985 N.H. LEXIS 317 (1985).

A temporary detention of a suspect by police, on grounds that do not amount to probable cause to arrest, is lawful under this article only if the police have an articulable suspicion that the person detained has committed or is about to commit a crime. State v. Maya, 126 N.H. 590, 493 A.2d 1139, 1985 N.H. LEXIS 347 (1985).

The scope of a temporary detention must be carefully tailored to its underlying justification, must be temporary and must last no longer than is necessary to effectuate the purpose of the stop. State v. Maya, 126 N.H. 590, 493 A.2d 1139, 1985 N.H. LEXIS 347 (1985).

Temporary detention of suspect was lawful under this article, where officer had articulable basis for his suspicion that suspect had committed a burglary, the scope of his questioning of the detained suspect did not exceed legitimate limits, and the duration of the detention was not unreasonably long. State v. Maya, 126 N.H. 590, 493 A.2d 1139, 1985 N.H. LEXIS 347 (1985).

RSA 594:2 is unconstitutional to the extent that it permits temporary detention for questioning on grounds less than probable cause. State v. White, 119 N.H. 567, 406 A.2d 291, 1979 N.H. LEXIS 356 (1979).

18. Motor vehicles

Officer who stopped a car for not having an inspection sticker did not violate the New Hampshire Constitution or the Fourth Amendment by continuing the stop after realizing that it had a transparent sticker, as he could not determine whether the sticker was still valid and was permitted to ask for defendant's registration, license, and inspection paperwork. State v. Dalton, — N.H. —, — A.3d —, 2013 N.H. LEXIS 95 (Aug. 21, 2013).

Officer was protected by qualified immunity as to the initial stop of a car because the officer's suspicion was based on the fact that the driver abruptly turned into the parking lot of a closed business late at night, and the location had recently been investigated for incidents of burglary and vandalism. Machado v. Weare Police Dep't, — F.3d —, 2012 U.S. App. LEXIS 20538 (Oct. 2, 2012).

Because vehicles must be registered and display license plates, who owns a car is not private information. Rather, the private information protected by N.H. Const. I, art. 19 is what lies behind the door. State v. Robinson, — N.H. —, 973 A.2d 277, 2009 N.H. LEXIS 78 (June 12, 2009).

By inserting a key found at the crime scene into a car door, an officer did not violate N.H. Const. pt. I, art. 19 or U.S. Const. amend. IV. The officer inserted the key into the lock and turned it, but did not open the door or conduct any search of the car; thus, he had not intruded upon defendant's reasonable expectation of privacy. State v. Robinson, — N.H. —, 973 A.2d 277, 2009 N.H. LEXIS 78 (June 12, 2009).

Because an officer had not yet seized the defendant when he stopped behind defendant's motorcycle and first spoke with him, and because defendant's appearance and conduct created a reasonable suspicion that he was driving under the influence of alcohol, the officer lawfully administered additional field sobriety tests, and there was no violation of U.S. Const. amend. IV and N.H. Const. pt. I, art. 19. A single officer approached a parked vehicle from behind, parked his cruiser so as not to block or restrict defendant's movement, kept his weapon holstered, and refrained from issuing orders to defendant; requesting defendant's license and registration did not constitute a seizure; activating the spotlight and two takedown lights in order to illuminate what would otherwise be plainly in daylight was not an act of seizure because such lighting was necessary to view and evaluate the situation; and the officer's activating his rear blue lights was not a seizure, as there was a strong need to warn passing traffic because the road lacked a breakdown lane. State v. Steeves, 158 N.H. 672, 972 A.2d 1033, 2009 N.H. LEXIS 63 (2009).

Trial court did not err in denying defendant's motion to suppress because the police had reasonable suspicion to stop his pickup truck where: (1) another driver, who told police that they believed defendant was driving while intoxicated was not an anonymous informant, but rather an identifiable witness; thus, the police were not obligated to inquire into or to demonstrate her credibility; (2) the driver's statement to the police concerned conduct that was publicly observed and although the information itself was conclusory, it was partially corroborated by the driver simultaneously pointing out the pickup truck as it drove by; and, (3) although the police officer did not observe impaired driving while he pursued defendant, defendant's apparent ability to competently drive the truck for approximately one mile did not negate the officer's reasonable suspicion. State v. Gowen, 150 N.H. 286, 837 A.2d 297, 2003 N.H. LEXIS 182 (2003).

Inventory search of closed container in back seat of motor vehicle violated defendant's rights under State Constitution, requiring suppression of evidence found in container, since police department's inventory policy did not include any procedure for searching a closed container. State v. Finn, 146 N.H. 59, 767 A.2d 413, 2001 N.H. LEXIS 27 (2001).

The court declined to adopt an automobile exception under part I, article 19 of the New Hampshire Constitution. State v. Sterndale, 139 N.H. 445, 656 A.2d 409, 1995 N.H. LEXIS 26 (1995).

To justify a warrantless search of an automobile conducted at a location other than where the automobile is first stopped, state must prove by a preponderance of the evidence the presence of public safety or law enforcement factors requiring removal from the location where probable cause and exigency would have allowed a warrantless search; furthermore, the state must show that the search took place as soon as the public safety concerns or the law enforcement considerations no longer existed. State v. Gallant, 133 N.H. 138, 574 A.2d 385, 1990 N.H. LEXIS 44 (1990).

Trial court properly denied defendant's motion to suppress evidence uncovered in warrantless search of automobile conducted at police station and public works garage, rather than location where automobile was first stopped and defendant arrested; search was conducted within twenty minutes of defendant's arrest, and removal of the automobile from the location before the search was justified by public safety and law enforcement considerations. State v. Gallant, 133 N.H. 138, 574 A.2d 385, 1990 N.H. LEXIS 44 (1990).

This article gives persons a right to be secure from unreasonable searches of their vehicles. State v. Pellicci, 133 N.H. 523, 580 A.2d 710, 1990 N.H. LEXIS 104 (1990).

An officer who stops a motor vehicle "seizes" both vehicle and occupants for purposes of this article. State v. Pellicci, 133 N.H. 523, 580 A.2d 710, 1990 N.H. LEXIS 104 (1990).

Sobriety checkpoint stops authorized in accordance with proposed legislation under which law enforcement agencies could obtain prior judicial authorization to implement such checkpoints as a means of detecting and apprehending impaired drivers, and of deterring those who might otherwise drive, while under the influence of intoxicating liquor or controlled drugs, would not violate this article. Opinion of Justices, 128 N.H. 14, 509 A.2d 744, 1986 N.H. LEXIS 249 (1986).

Stopping and detaining an automobile and its occupants, whether by roving patrol or roving roadblock, constitutes a seizure within the meaning of this article. State v. Koppel, 127 N.H. 286, 499 A.2d 977, 1985 N.H. LEXIS 425 (1985).

Stop of defendant's vehicle by police officer constituted a seizure under this article. State v. Parker, 127 N.H. 525, 503 A.2d 809, 1985 N.H. LEXIS 455 (1985).

To justify the search or seizure of a motor vehicle, absent probable cause or even a reasonable suspicion that a criminal offense is being committed, the state must prove that its conduct significantly advances the public interest in a manner that outweighs the accompanying intrusion on individual rights, and must further prove that no less intrusive means are available to accomplish the state's goal. State v. Koppel, 127 N.H. 286, 499 A.2d 977, 1985 N.H. LEXIS 425 (1985).

The use of police roadblocks specifically established for the purpose of determining whether the driver of a motor vehicle is driving under the influence of intoxicating liquor violates a defendant's guarantees against unreasonable searches and seizures as provided by this article. State v. Koppel, 127 N.H. 286, 499 A.2d 977, 1985 N.H. LEXIS 425 (1985).

Police officer's observation of defendant's erratic driving, including a traffic violation committed by defendant, formed a reasonable basis for officer's suspicion that defendant was driving while intoxicated, and therefore officer's subsequent stop of the defendant did not violate defendant's right to be free from unreasonable seizures under this article. State v. Brodeur, 126 N.H. 411, 493 A.2d 1134, 1985 N.H. LEXIS 317 (1985).

19. Sobriety checkpoints

Sobriety checkpoints did not violate N.H. Const. pt. I, art. 19, because, inter alia, the police department's distribution of a press release to many press agencies in the state, despite being made only one day before checkpoints and despite the fact that only one media outlet printed the release, was sufficient to provide the public with advance notice of the checkpoints. State v. Hunt, 155 N.H. 465, 924 A.2d 424, 2007 N.H. LEXIS 85 (2007).

20. Use of dogs

Employing a trained canine to sniff a person's private vehicle in order to determine whether controlled substances are concealed is a search subject to the strictures of this article. State v. Pellicci, 133 N.H. 523, 580 A.2d 710, 1990 N.H. LEXIS 104 (1990).

Where a canine sniff: (1) is part of an investigative stop based on a reasonable and articulable suspicion of imminent criminal activity involving controlled substances; (2) is employed to search a vehicle; (3) in no way increases the time necessary for moderate questioning; and (4) is itself based on a reasonable and articulable suspicion that the property searched contains a controlled substances, it satisfies requirements of this article. State v. Pellicci, 133 N.H. 523, 580 A.2d 710, 1990 N.H. LEXIS 104 (1990).

A canine sniff of a suspect's vehicle, made during the course of an otherwise constitutionally permissible investigative stop, based on reasonable and articulable suspicion that the vehicle contained controlled substances and which lasted no longer than the questioning, was sufficiently limited, and the legitimate state interest sufficiently great, to justify the search on the basis of less than probable cause. State v. Pellicci, 133 N.H. 523, 580 A.2d 710, 1990 N.H. LEXIS 104 (1990).

21. Warrants—Issuance

In reviewing magistrate's determination of probable cause, court will not invalidate a warrant by interpreting evidence submitted in a hypertechnical sense. State v. Silvestri, 136 N.H. 522, 618 A.2d 821, 1992 N.H. LEXIS 203 (1992).

In appeal from conviction for marijuana possession, supreme court refused to adopt per se rule that if magistrate determines person is a drug dealer, finding of probable cause to search that person's residence automatically follows, and fact that defendant sold marijuana twice in one week did not provide probable cause to search his residence. State v. Silvestri, 136 N.H. 522, 618 A.2d 821, 1992 N.H. LEXIS 203 (1992).

Fact that police officer at suppression hearing informed court there had been a "controlled buy" of marijuana between informant and defendant did not supply corroboration sufficient to establish probable cause to search, because supporting affidavit did not indicate there was a controlled buy and court was not allowed to consider information not presented to magistrate who issued search warrant. State v. Silvestri, 136 N.H. 522, 618 A.2d 821, 1992 N.H. LEXIS 203 (1992).

Totality-of-the-circumstances test, similar to the one adopted by the United States Supreme Court in Illinois v. Gates, 462 U.S. 213, 103 S. Ct. 2317, 76 L. Ed. 2d 527, 1983 U.S. LEXIS 54 (1983), is the appropriate standard to be applied under this article when determining the validity of a search warrant based upon information obtained from an informant. State v. Hazen, 131 N.H. 196, 552 A.2d 77, 1988 N.H. LEXIS 104 (1988).

Totality-of-the-circumstances test akin to that set out by the United States Supreme Court in Illinois v. Gates, 462 U.S. 213, 103 S. Ct. 2317, 76 L. Ed. 2d 527, 1983 U.S. LEXIS 54 (1983), is adopted to determine whether probable cause exists for purposes of this article in cases involving the issuance of search warrants based on informants' tips. State v. Bradberry, 129 N.H. 68, 522 A.2d 1380, 1986 N.H. LEXIS 397 (1986).

Evidence relied upon by a complaining officer or the magistrate to justify issuance of a search warrant is not required to be fully contained in the complaint upon which the warrant is issued but may be presented with the complaint; and in such case, the issue of probable cause may be determined on the basis of all the evidence before the magistrate. State v. Titus, 106 N.H. 219, 212 A.2d 458, 1965 N.H. LEXIS 131 (1965).

In criminal proceedings, hearsay information may properly furnish probable cause for the issuance of a search warrant when the underlying circumstances surrounding the information received by the complaining officer can be found to reasonably justify evidence of belief in its credibility. State v. Titus, 106 N.H. 219, 212 A.2d 458, 1965 N.H. LEXIS 131 (1965).

22. —Supporting affidavit

Under the totality of the circumstances, the affidavit supporting an application for a search warrant afforded a substantial basis under the Fourth Amendment and the New Hampshire Constitution to believe that defendant's computer contained child pornography. Although there was no child pornography observed on defendant's computer, the affidavit alleged that the cell phone belonging to the victim's stepfather contained sexually explicit images of children and that he used it to transmit such images to others; that the stepfather and defendant exchanged messages; that defendant touched the minor victim sexually and watched her and the stepfather engage in sexual activity; and that the officer knew from his training and experience that those who had demonstrated an interest or preference in sexual activity with children were likely to keep secreted, but readily at hand, sexually explicit visual images depicting children, which they often carried upon their person in the form of USB drives or other media storage devices, and that persons receiving such images would copy them onto their computers' hard drives. State v. Ball, 164 N.H. 204, 53 A.3d 603, 2012 N.H. LEXIS 127 (2012), cert. denied, Ball v. New Hampshire, 133 S. Ct. 1467, 185 L. Ed. 2d 364, 2013 U.S. LEXIS 1762 (U.S. 2013).

Under N.H. Const. pt. I, art. 19, an affidavit in support of a search warrant supported a finding of probable cause. The affidavit recounted recent firsthand observations by defendant's girlfriend of his use of crack and his method of manufacturing it, and the officer explained how his experience corroborated the girlfriend's observations. State v. Dalling, 159 N.H. 183, 978 A.2d 261, 2009 N.H. LEXIS 102 (2009).

Under N.H. Const. pt. I, art. 19, a magistrate could still have found probable cause even if the affidavit in support of a search warrant for a search of the house of defendant's girlfriend had not omitted the information that the girlfriend, who said that defendant had manufactured crack cocaine at the house, believed that defendant had removed all of the illegal items from the house. He could have done so by finding that her belief was speculation or that there was a substantial likelihood that even if defendant did remove some incriminating objects from the house, others remained. State v. Dalling, 159 N.H. 183, 978 A.2d 261, 2009 N.H. LEXIS 102 (2009).

Under N.H. Const. pt. I, art. 19, an officer's handwritten annotation on a typed affidavit in support of a search warrant, referencing the suspicion of defendant's girlfriend that defendant had removed cocaine from her residence, did not defeat a finding of probable cause. The note did not posit that defendant also removed the utensils to cook crack cocaine; because such utensils often contained cocaine residue, as the affidavit noted, there still remained a substantial likelihood that the police would discover evidence of the commission of a crime upon a search. State v. Dalling, 159 N.H. 183, 978 A.2d 261, 2009 N.H. LEXIS 102 (2009).

Affidavit seeking a search warrant for child pornography adequately established probable cause for such a warrant, without providing copies of the images defendant was alleged to possess, or detailed factual descriptions of them, because it alleged that defendant admitted that about 25 percent of the image files on his computer and disks contained child pornography, and this admission provided a sufficient "other indicia of probable cause" to issue a search warrant. State v. Dowman, 151 N.H. 162, 855 A.2d 524, 2004 N.H. LEXIS 109 (2004).

An affidavit may establish probable cause to search without observance of contraband at location to be searched. State v. Silvestri, 136 N.H. 522, 618 A.2d 821, 1992 N.H. LEXIS 203 (1992).

Standard for determining if affidavit in support of search warrant establishes probable cause is whether, given all circumstances set forth in affidavit, including veracity and basis for knowledge of persons supplying hearsay information, there is a fair probability that contraband or evidence of crime will be found in particular place described in warrant. State v. Silvestri, 136 N.H. 522, 618 A.2d 821, 1992 N.H. LEXIS 203 (1992).

At trial for marijuana possession, defendant's motion to suppress evidence seized from home should have been granted, where affidavit in support of search warrant contained nothing to indicate that evidence of the crime was kept at or picked up from defendant's residence, other than mere fact that defendant was suspected of being a criminal. State v. Silvestri, 136 N.H. 522, 618 A.2d 821, 1992 N.H. LEXIS 203 (1992).

Common sense reading of search warrant affidavit supported defendant's argument that affidavit did not establish probable cause to search his residence, where affidavit provided no indication of informants' veracity, and informant who had purchased marijuana lacked personal knowledge of presence of drugs in defendant's residence. State v. Silvestri, 136 N.H. 522, 618 A.2d 821, 1992 N.H. LEXIS 203 (1992).

If an affidavit supporting an application for a search warrant contains a material misrepresentation that is recklessly made, the search warrant is invalid, and all evidence obtained as a result of the search should be suppressed. State v. Chaisson, 125 N.H. 810, 486 A.2d 297, 1984 N.H. LEXIS 320 (1984).

A facially sufficient but misrepresentative affidavit cannot be the basis for a search warrant. State v. Spero, 117 N.H. 199, 371 A.2d 1155, 1977 N.H. LEXIS 301 (1977).

The affidavit on which an application for a search warrant is based must set forth the underlying circumstances from which an informant reached his or her conclusions as well as facts from which the magistrate can conclude that the informant is reliable. State v. Spero, 117 N.H. 199, 371 A.2d 1155, 1977 N.H. LEXIS 301 (1977).

A defendant is entitled to a hearing for the purpose of attacking a facially sufficient affidavit once a preliminary showing has been made that the affidavit contains material misrepresentations by a police officer or other government agent. State v. Spero, 117 N.H. 199, 371 A.2d 1155, 1977 N.H. LEXIS 301 (1977).

23. —Contents

Although affidavit in support of search warrant contained information collected over a period of time, totality of information was not stale because it included recent information of defendant's suspicious activity at storage facility on day before warrant was issued and executed for search of storage unit. State v. McMinn, 144 N.H. 34, 737 A.2d 1093, 1999 N.H. LEXIS 69 (1999).

Business records were of an enduring quality and district court could reasonably have inferred that defendant moved records to safeguard them, and thus a person of ordinary caution could justifiably believe that records would be present at residence eleven months later; superior court therefore erred in suppressing evidence obtained pursuant to search warrant. State v. Cannuli, 143 N.H. 149, 722 A.2d 450, 1998 N.H. LEXIS 82 (1998).

A search warrant which sought "pornographic or erotic materials to include but not limited to books, magazines, articles, photographs, slides, movies, albums, letters, diaries, sexual aids or toys or other items relating to sexual acts or sexual acts with children," was sufficiently particularized. State v. Kirsch, 139 N.H. 647, 662 A.2d 937, 1995 N.H. LEXIS 67 (1995).

Lack of facts attesting to veracity of informant does not preclude finding of probable cause to search, because other indicia of reliability, such as corroboration by police officers, may be used to supply missing factors relative to informant and informant's information in determining existence of probable cause. State v. Silvestri, 136 N.H. 522, 618 A.2d 821, 1992 N.H. LEXIS 203 (1992).

Warrant authorizing search of secondhand merchandise store for "fireworks, smokebombs, records, ledgers, U.S. currency, and slot machines" met particularity standards of this article. State v. Fitanides, 131 N.H. 298, 552 A.2d 1379, 1988 N.H. LEXIS 139 (1988), cert. denied, Fitanides v. New Hampshire, 490 U.S. 1080, 109 S. Ct. 2100, 104 L. Ed. 2d 662, 1989 U.S. LEXIS 2555 (1989).

Search warrants must describe with particularity the area to be searched and things to be seized. State v. Moreau, 113 N.H. 303, 306 A.2d 764, 1973 N.H. LEXIS 260 (1973).

A description in a search warrant which identifies with reasonable certainty the place or places to be searched is sufficient. Metcalf v. Weed, 66 N.H. 176, 19 A. 1091, 1889 N.H. LEXIS 27 (1890).

24. —Execution

The plain language of the article does not require that police have a warrant physically in hand upon commencing a search authorized by that warrant. State v. Cavanaugh, 138 N.H. 193, 635 A.2d 1382, 1993 N.H. LEXIS 183 (1993).

The police, in executing a search warrant for a dwelling, may remain on the premises only so long as it is reasonably necessary to conduct the search. State v. Chaisson, 125 N.H. 810, 486 A.2d 297, 1984 N.H. LEXIS 320 (1984).

25. Warrantless search—Generally

Under Part I, Article 19 of New Hampshire Constitution, all warrantless police entries are *per se* unreasonable and thus illegal unless made pursuant to a judicially created exception, and State bears burden of proving existence of exigent circumstances, such as hot pursuit, to justify a warrantless home intrusion. State v. Ricci, 144 N.H. 241, 739 A.2d 404, 1999 N.H. LEXIS 104 (1999).

The court refused to validate an officer's search of the defendant's wallet for identification papers under a novel "identification search" exception to the warrant requirement. State v. Webber, 141 N.H. 817, 694 A.2d 970, 1997 N.H. LEXIS 44 (1997).

The warrantless search of the defendant's purse, which occurred when the defendant asked to use the bathroom during the execution of a warrant for the search of a residence in which she was found, was unreasonable and, therefore, contraband found in the search was improperly admitted into evidence where the officer made no effort to pat down the purse in order to determine whether there was a weapon in it, but proceeded to empty it of its entire contents. State v. Coons, 137 N.H. 365, 627 A.2d 1064, 1993 N.H. LEXIS 91 (1993).

In the absence of a lawful warrant, all searches are per se unreasonable unless conducted within the narrow confines of a judicially crafted exception. State v. Murray, 135 N.H. 369, 605 A.2d 676, 1992 N.H. LEXIS 41 (1992).

A warrantless search is per se unreasonable and invalid unless it comes within one of a few recognized exceptions to the requirement of a warrant. State v. Plante, 134 N.H. 585, 594 A.2d 165, 1991 N.H.

LEXIS 106 (1991), cert. denied, Plante v. New Hampshire, 502 U.S. 984, 112 S. Ct. 590, 116 L. Ed. 2d 614, 1991 U.S. LEXIS 6966 (1991).

A warrantless search is per se unreasonable, and evidence derived from such a search is inadmissible unless the state proves that the search comes within one of the recognized exceptions to the warrant requirement. State v. Turmelle, 132 N.H. 148, 562 A.2d 196, 1989 N.H. LEXIS 78 (1989).

A warrantless search may be justified under this article when both probable cause and exigent circumstances exist. State v. Camargo, 126 N.H. 766, 498 A.2d 292, 1985 N.H. LEXIS 418 (1985).

Unless a warrantless search falls within one of the few specifically established and well-delineated exceptions to the warrant requirement, it is per se unreasonable. State v. Farnsworth, 126 N.H. 656, 497 A.2d 835, 1985 N.H. LEXIS 421 (1985).

This article reflects the intent of the framers that all searches and seizures must be reasonable, and unless a warrantless search falls within one of the few specifically established and well-delineated exceptions, it is per se unreasonable. State v. Ball, 124 N.H. 226, 471 A.2d 347, 1983 N.H. LEXIS 426 (1983).

A warrantless search is per se unreasonable and invalid, unless it comes within one of the few recognized exceptions. State v. Theodosopoulos, 119 N.H. 573, 409 A.2d 1134, 1979 N.H. LEXIS 435 (1979), cert. denied, Theodosopoulos v. New Hampshire, 446 U.S. 983, 100 S. Ct. 2964, 64 L. Ed. 2d 839, 1980 U.S. LEXIS 1903 (1980).

26. —Probationer

Where a fraternity was sentenced to two years probation for the felony conviction of illegal sale of alcohol on the condition that the fraternity not allow the consumption on its premises of alcoholic beverages, the fraternity's premises were properly made subject to unannounced searches by the Department of Corrections to determine compliance with the condition. State v. Zeta Chi Fraternity, 142 N.H. 16, 696 A.2d 530, 1997 N.H. LEXIS 50 (1997), cert. denied, Zeta Chi Fraternity v. New Hampshire, 522 U.S. 995, 118 S. Ct. 558, 139 L. Ed. 2d 400, 1997, 1997 U.S. LEXIS 7080 (1997).

Probation authorities do not need a particularized suspicion that a probationer is violating the conditions of its probation in order to conduct a search based on a reasonably imposed probation condition and do not need to announce their intention to search in advance; however, this does not give probation officers carte blanche to execute a search in an unreasonable manner. State v. Zeta Chi Fraternity, 142 N.H. 16, 696 A.2d 530, 1997 N.H. LEXIS 50 (1997), cert. denied, Zeta Chi Fraternity v. New Hampshire, 522 U.S. 995, 118 S. Ct. 558, 139 L. Ed. 2d 400, 1997, 1997 U.S. LEXIS 7080 (1997).

In order for a warrantless probation search condition to be constitutional, it must be related to the rehabilitation or supervision of the defendant, and the search itself must be conducted in a manner that is reasonable in time, scope, and frequency. State v. Zeta Chi Fraternity, 142 N.H. 16, 696 A.2d 530, 1997 N.H. LEXIS 50 (1997), cert. denied, Zeta Chi Fraternity v. New Hampshire, 522 U.S. 995, 118 S. Ct. 558, 139 L. Ed. 2d 400, 1997, 1997 U.S. LEXIS 7080 (1997).

Because the police do not have the same special statutory responsibilities toward a probationer as does a probation officer, a condition of probation authorizing the police to conduct warrantless searches is unreasonable under part I, article 19 of the New Hampshire Constitution; however, a proper visitation by a probation officer does not cease to be so because he is accompanied by a law enforcement official. State v. Zeta Chi Fraternity, 142 N.H. 16, 696 A.2d 530, 1997 N.H. LEXIS 50 (1997), cert. denied, Zeta Chi Fraternity v. New Hampshire, 522 U.S. 995, 118 S. Ct. 558, 139 L. Ed. 2d 400, 1997, 1997 U.S. LEXIS 7080 (1997).

When a condition of probation authorizes random warrantless searches and the condition is reasonably related to the supervision and rehabilitation of the probationer, a warrantless probation search is constitutionally permissible. State v. Zeta Chi Fraternity, 142 N.H. 16, 696 A.2d 530, 1997 N.H. LEXIS 50 (1997), cert. denied, Zeta Chi Fraternity v. New Hampshire, 522 U.S. 995, 118 S. Ct. 558, 139 L. Ed. 2d 400, 1997, 1997 U.S. LEXIS 7080 (1997).

Decision to conduct warrantless search of probationer's apartment was properly made on basis of a reasonable suspicion that he had violated terms of his probation. State v. Berrocales, 141 N.H. 262, 681 A.2d 95, 1996 N.H. LEXIS 89 (1996).

27. —Burden of proof

In the absence of a warrant, burden is on state to show that the conduct of a search falls within claimed exception to warrant requirement. State v. Murray, 135 N.H. 369, 605 A.2d 676, 1992 N.H. LEXIS 41 (1992).

The burden is on the state to prove, by a preponderance of the evidence, that a warrantless search was permissible under this article. State v. Farnsworth, 126 N.H. 656, 497 A.2d 835, 1985 N.H. LEXIS 421 (1985).

The state has the burden of proving, by a preponderance of the evidence, that a warrantless search was constitutionally permissible. State v. Ball, 124 N.H. 226, 471 A.2d 347, 1983 N.H. LEXIS 426 (1983).

28. —Consent

Trial court properly found that defendant consented to a search of her home for purposes of N.H. Const. pt. I, art. 19 and the Fourth Amendment. Even assuming that defendant's initial verbal consent could be construed as limited, the evidence demonstrated that she subsequently gave written consent for a general search of the house and the vehicles on the premises; insofar as the trial court relied on a detective's testimony in finding that defendant consented to a general search of her home and vehicles, the court deferred to the trial court's determination of credibility. State v. Saunders, 164 N.H. 342, 55 A.3d 1014, 2012 N.H. LEXIS 149 (2012).

Evidence supported the finding that defendant was not coerced into giving consent to a search of her home. Although one officer held a gun, it was pointed at the ground in an "administrative carry," and defendant described that officer as "quiet"; defendant said that she "let in" the officers; defendant admitted officers into her home without hesitation when they asked her if they could check whether the victim was there; defendant was familiar with the police; and officers testified that she had been assertive with them in the past. State v. Labarre, 160 N.H. 1, 992 A.2d 733, 2010 N.H. LEXIS 21 (2010).

Warrantless search of the hotel room defendant lived in with his girlfriend did not violate the Fourth Amendment and N.H. Const. pt. I, art. 19. The girlfriend, a probationer, had consented to the search as part of the conditions of her probation, and defendant had not expressly refused to consent to the search, even if his body language implied that he did not consent. State v. Tarasuik, 160 N.H. 323, 999 A.2d 409, 2010 N.H. LEXIS 50 (2010).

Because the New Hampshire Supreme Court finds persuasive the United States Supreme Court's decision in Randolph, which limits the general rule that consent provided by a co-tenant is valid against another co-tenant in cases in which a present co-tenant expressly refuses consent, the court adopts it for purposes of state constitutional analysis under N.H. Const. pt. I, art. 19. State v. Tarasuik, 160 N.H. 323, 999 A.2d 409, 2010 N.H. LEXIS 50 (2010).

Because the actual leaseholder no longer lived in the apartment and did not have the requisite actual authority to consent to its search, the police lacked authority to search the bedroom where defendant's possessions were found under U.S. Const. amend. IV, and N.H. Const. pt. I, art. 19 without defendant's consent. State v. Sodoyer, 156 N.H. 84, 931 A.2d 548, 2007 N.H. LEXIS 145 (2007).

Trial court properly held that defendant had consented to a search of his truck where two police officers testified that defendant consented and that he freely signed a consent form, and the trial court had reviewed a videotaped interview with defendant during which he signed a consent form without objection. State v. Ayer, 154 N.H. 500, 917 A.2d 214, 2006 N.H. LEXIS 191 (2006), rehearing denied, 2007 N.H. LEXIS 35 (N.H. Jan. 30, 2007), cert. denied, Ayer v. New Hampshire, 552 U.S. 834, 128 S. Ct. 63, 169 L. Ed. 2d 52, 2007 U.S. LEXIS 9174 (2007).

Photograph of defendant's tattoo was admissible because defendant verbally consented to an officer's request to take the photograph and defendant was aware that defendant was not required to consent because, during the same interview, defendant refused to allow police to take a DNA swab of defendant's mouth. State v. Goupil, 154 N.H. 208, 908 A.2d 1256, 2006 N.H. LEXIS 146 (2006).

Defendant's consent to search of his vehicle was voluntary when, in response to defendant's initial refusal, an officer told him that a refusal would result in a canine sniff search of the vehicle that, if positive, would lead to the officer applying for a search warrant; this response was explanatory rather than coercive. Furthermore, neither defendant's exit from the vehicle before he reviewed and signed the written consent nor his prior refusal invalidated the consent as involuntary. State v. Livingston, 153 N.H. 399, 897 A.2d 977, 2006 N.H. LEXIS 42 (2006).

When a trial court, based on a determination of credibility, found that defendant had not limited the scope of an officer's search of his vehicle, the court held that a reasonable person would determine that the officer did not exceed the scope of defendant's consent. State v. Livingston, 153 N.H. 399, 897 A.2d 977, 2006 N.H. LEXIS 42 (2006).

Defendant consented to the search as (1) at all times, the officers acted in a non-coercive manner, (2) even after the officers explained that they were looking for child pornography, the defendant directed them to the two computers in his home and the alleged child pornography that he stored under his bed, and (3) importantly, the defendant also signed a consent to search form, which permitted the officers to search his computers. State v. Johnston, 150 N.H. 448, 839 A.2d 830, 2004 N.H. LEXIS 2 (2004).

Trial court properly denied defendant's motion to suppress; while N.H. Const. pt. I, art. 19 protected all people, their papers, their possessions and their homes from unreasonable searches and seizures, consensual entries were reasonable under the New Hampshire constitution, whether the consent to enter was granted expressly through words or impliedly through conduct, and in the instant case defendant's grandparents gave implied consent to a police entry into the home to investigate criminal conduct when they requested that the police watch their home while the grandparents were on an extended vacation. State v. Grey, 148 N.H. 666, 813 A.2d 465, 2002 N.H. LEXIS 186 (2002).

Although a search of defendant was not a permissible extension of an initial investigatory stop, defendant's subsequent consent to a search of defendant's person was not based on "flagrant" conduct by the police and extended to a search of defendant's knapsack where evidence of illegal drugs was found. State v. Szczerbiak, 148 N.H. 352, 807 A.2d 1219, 2002 N.H. LEXIS 136 (2002).

When deciding the validity of consent that is the product of an unlawful detention during a motor vehicle stop, proper disposition follows as an application of the well-settled law that, when consent to search is the product of an unlawful detention, such consent is "tainted" by the illegality of the detention. State v. Hight, 146 N.H. 746, 781 A.2d 11, 2001 N.H. LEXIS 155 (2001).

In considering the suppression of evidence obtained during a consent search that stems from an unlawful detention, the question is whether, granting establishment of the primary illegality, the evidence to which instant objection is made has been come at by exploitation of that illegality or instead by means sufficiently distinguishable to be purged of the primary taint. State v. Hight, 146 N.H. 746, 781 A.2d 11, 2001 N.H. LEXIS 155 (2001).

When determining whether the State has purged the taint of an unlawful detention followed by a consent to search, consideration of the following factors is instructive: (1) temporal proximity between the police illegality and the consent to search; (2) presence of intervening circumstances; and (3) purpose and flagrancy of the official misconduct. State v. Hight, 146 N.H. 746, 781 A.2d 11, 2001 N.H. LEXIS 155 (2001).

Factors considered when determining whether the State has purged the taint of an unlawful detention followed by a consent to search, should not be confused with factors considered to determine whether consent is voluntary. State v. Hight, 146 N.H. 746, 781 A.2d 11, 2001 N.H. LEXIS 155 (2001).

There was absolute temporal proximity between unlawful detention and defendant's consent since defendant gave consent while he was unlawfully detained. State v. Hight, 146 N.H. 746, 781 A.2d 11, 2001 N.H. LEXIS 155 (2001).

There were no intervening circumstances between unlawful detention and defendant's consent, such as the officer informing defendant of his right to refuse consent, that would purge the taint of the unlawful detention and support a conclusion that the consent was an "act of free will." State v. Hight, 146 N.H. 746, 781 A.2d 11, 2001 N.H. LEXIS 155 (2001).

Purpose and flagrancy of official misconduct was troubling where officer sought consent to search not only defendant's car, but his person, based upon such innocuous facts as he had driven to Boston with a purpose to "hang out," had attended a "frat party" there and was returning to college in Vermont. State v. Hight, 146 N.H. 746, 781 A.2d 11, 2001 N.H. LEXIS 155 (2001).

A tenant's signal to come in and throwing his arms in the air after being asked for permission to search constituted consent to the search. State v. Hammell, 147 N.H. 313, 787 A.2d 850, 2001 N.H. LEXIS 218 (2001).

The operator of a motor vehicle gave the police voluntary and uncoerced consent to search her car, notwithstanding that she initially refused to sign the consent form and requested an attorney, where she subsequently did not hesitate in signing the consent form after an officer explained that he planned to tow her car and seek a search warrant. State v. Prevost, 141 N.H. 647, 690 A.2d 1029, 1997 N.H. LEXIS 15 (1997).

A third party bailee properly gave consent to a search of an outboard motor where (1) the defendant delivered the motor to a business with which he had no prior dealing, (2) the motor was not enclosed in a container, locked or otherwise, (3) it was implicit in the defendant's instructions to switch the motors on a boat that the bailee would necessarily become thoroughly acquainted with the motor and would perhaps refer to the serial number for such purposes as ordering parts, and (4) nothing in the record suggested that the defendant ever instructed the bailee not to show the motor to anyone else. State v. Wong, 138 N.H. 56, 635 A.2d 470, 1993 N.H. LEXIS 157 (1993).

The superior court properly employed an objective standard in determining the scope of a consent to a search, basing its findings on the totality of the circumstances as reasonably construed by the police officers, rather than on a determination of the defendant's actual state of mind at the time of the search. State v. Baroudi, 137 N.H. 62, 623 A.2d 750, 1993 N.H. LEXIS 39 (1993).

State carries the burden of establishing by a preponderance of the evidence, based upon the totality of the surrounding circumstances, that consent to a warrantless search was free, knowing and voluntary. State v. Diaz, 134 N.H. 662, 596 A.2d 725, 1991 N.H. LEXIS 116 (1991).

A trial court's finding of voluntary consent to a warrantless search will not be overturned on appeal unless it is without support in the record. State v. Green, 133 N.H. 249, 575 A.2d 1308, 1990 N.H. LEXIS 55 (1990).

Submission to a search does not constitute consent. State v. Pinder, 126 N.H. 220, 489 A.2d 653, 1985 N.H. LEXIS 252 (1985).

Voluntary consent to a warrantless search is a question of fact that trial court must determine from the totality of the circumstances. State v. Pinder, 126 N.H. 220, 489 A.2d 653, 1985 N.H. LEXIS 252 (1985).

A trial court's finding of voluntary consent to a warrantless search will not be over-turned on appeal unless it is without support in the record. State v. Pinder, 126 N.H. 220, 489 A.2d 653, 1985 N.H. LEXIS 252 (1985).

When the police are relying upon consent as a basis for their warrantless search, they have no more authority than they have been given by the consent. State v. Pinder, 126 N.H. 220, 489 A.2d 653, 1985 N.H. LEXIS 252 (1985).

To justify a warrantless search on a theory of consent, the state must demonstrate that the consent was free, knowing and voluntary. State v. Pinder, 126 N.H. 220, 489 A.2d 653, 1985 N.H. LEXIS 252 (1985).

The state must meet its burden of proof on the issue of the existence of voluntary consent to a warrantless search by a preponderance of the evidence. State v. Pinder, 126 N.H. 220, 489 A.2d 653, 1985 N.H. LEXIS 252 (1985).

Where defendant signed a consent form which authorized a search of his house, the meaning of the form was explained to him by the police, and after speaking with his attorney, he reaffirmed his consent to the police, there was ample evidence to support a finding that the defendant voluntarily consented to a search of his house. State v. Pinder, 126 N.H. 220, 489 A.2d 653, 1985 N.H. LEXIS 252 (1985).

A trial court erred in failing to grant a defendant's motion to suppress items taken in a search of his barn where the defendant never explicitly authorized or consented to such a search, and had signed a consent form which only referred to a search of the "premises" or "residence." State v. Pinder, 126 N.H. 220, 489 A.2d 653, 1985 N.H. LEXIS 252 (1985).

29. —Abandonment of property

Compact disc left behind when defendant moved had been abandoned; thus, he had no reasonable expectation of privacy in it under N.H. Const. pt. I, art. 19 and the Fourth Amendment.

Defendant went twice to retrieve items during the week he had been given to be out and did not say he would return again; he had no further contact with the couple with whom he had been staying; 12 days elapsed from the time the couple told him to leave to the day on which the wife searched the room; and the wife told him that she intended to throw away any items remaining after seven days, which reasonably would entail going through the drawers and any property he left behind. State v. Howe, 159 N.H. 366, 986 A.2d 631, 2009 N.H. LEXIS 124 (2009).

While the possibility of a generalized intent to return to the property at some time does not per se preclude a finding of abandonment, there must be a significant dissociation of the property from the defendant for a finding of abandonment; "temporary abandonment," therefore, is not a valid general exception to the warrant requirement. State v. Westover, 140 N.H. 375, 666 A.2d 1344, 1995 N.H. LEXIS 159 (1995).

The defendant did not abandon his sweatshirt when he tossed it aside before entering a store and, therefore, a warrantless search of the sweatshirt was invalid. State v. Westover, 140 N.H. 375, 666 A.2d 1344, 1995 N.H. LEXIS 159 (1995).

30. —Exigent circumstances

Although exigent circumstances existed under N.H. Const. pt. I, art. 19 once another occupant of an apartment told officers that defendant had a knife to his own chest, police had no knowledge of this until after they entered the home. Thus, the State could not rely upon the ensuing emergency to justify the initial entry. State v. Robinson, — N.H. —, 973 A.2d 277, 2009 N.H. LEXIS 78 (June 12, 2009).

Exigent circumstances did not exist to justify entry into an apartment under N.H. Const. pt. I, art. 19. There was no evidence that defendant continued to pose a danger to himself or to others; the police had blocked any routes of escape; and officers had no reason to believe evidence was being or would be destroyed. State v. Robinson, — N.H. —, 973 A.2d 277, 2009 N.H. LEXIS 78 (June 12, 2009).

Evidence that: (1) police officers smelled burning marijuana while they were at a hotel conducting an unrelated investigation; (2) they could track the smell to a particular room; and (3) they heard several people conducting what sounded like a small party in the room provided exigent circumstances that justified their warrantless entry into the hotel room. Defendant's right to be free from unreasonable searches pursuant to N.H. Const. pt. 1, art. 19 and the Fourth Amendment to the United States Constitution was not violated since the smell of burning marijuana indicated an offense was being committed and that evidence of that offense was being destroyed, which under the totality of the circumstances justified the officers' warrantless entry into the hotel room. State v. Rodriguez, 157 N.H. 100, 945 A.2d 676, 2008 N.H. LEXIS 42 (2008).

Trial court erred in suppressing a defendant's blood test results where the potential for drugs to metabolize in the body and the timing of the traffic accident late at night on a holiday weekend constituted exigent circumstances for conducting a warrantless search. State v. Steimel, 155 N.H. 141, 921 A.2d 378, 2007 N.H. LEXIS 38 (2007).

Evidence presented, including that defendant was in custody, was insufficient to support a reasonable belief that evidence would be destroyed or that there was a threat of imminent danger to life or public safety; thus the warrantless search of defendant's locked bedroom and the seizure of a rifle violated the Fourth and Fourteenth Amendments and N.H. Const. pt. I, art. 19. The error was harmless in light of the overwhelming evidence against defendant, including the fact that defendant threatened to commit a crime, murder, against a person defendant knew was a police officer with the purpose to terrorize that person. State v. Pseudae, 154 N.H. 196, 908 A.2d 809, 2006 N.H. LEXIS 142 (2006).

Trial court properly denied defendant's motion to suppress three blood alcohol tests in a trial for negligent homicide, RSA 630:3, and aggravated driving while intoxicated, RSA 265:82-a; one test was justified by exigent circumstances, as officers had observed defendant display signs of intoxication and the evidence of alcohol would have diminished over time, and two tests were taken pursuant to a valid search warrant, so defendant's rights pursuant to N.H. Const. pt. I, art. 19 were not violated. State v. Stern, 150 N.H. 705, 846 A.2d 64, 2004 N.H. LEXIS 59 (2004).

Because defendant had walked away from an automobile accident and was later not alone in an apartment, she was not in dire, life-threatening distress or in need of immediate assistance; therefore, the entry into the apartment was impermissible because it fell within no recognized exception to the warrant requirement. State v. Seavey, 147 N.H. 304, 789 A.2d 621, 2001 N.H. LEXIS 215 (2001).

Totality of circumstances demonstrated that police were in hot pursuit of defendant when he continued to elude them by disobeying order and entering his house; exigent circumstances thus justified officer's warrantless entry into defendant's home to arrest him for driving under influence of alcohol, and district court did not err in denying defendant's motion to suppress results of blood test taken subsequent to arrest. State v. Ricci, 144 N.H. 241, 739 A.2d 404, 1999 N.H. LEXIS 104 (1999).

Officer's search of automobile trunk was justified by exigent circumstances, where officer had just been informed of one suspect's recent arrest for armed robbery, and had just been surprised by an unexpected person in back seat of car and thought that yet another suspect might be in trunk, which was ajar. State v. Graca, 142 N.H. 670, 708 A.2d 393, 1998 N.H. LEXIS 18 (1998).

Where police officers had as much information to justify the issuance of a warrant one day after a person was reported missing as they did on the following day and yet made no effort to obtain a warrant and then, after deciding to enter a defendant's apartment, delayed several more hours before entering, no exigent circumstances existed which would excuse a search without a warrant. State v. Beede, 119 N.H. 620, 406 A.2d 125, 1979 N.H. LEXIS 364 (1979), cert. denied, Beede v. New Hampshire, 445 U.S. 967, 100 S. Ct. 1659, 64 L. Ed..2d 244, 1980 U.S. LEXIS 1480 (1980).

31. —Incident to arrest

The search of a paper bag found in the defendant's automobile could not be justified as a proper search incident to arrest as the bag was not within the defendant's immediate control where she was secured, in handcuffs, in the rear of a police cruiser. State v. Sterndale, 139 N.H. 445, 656 A.2d 409, 1995 N.H. LEXIS 26 (1995).

In order for search incident to arrest exception to warrant requirement to be applicable, search and seizure must be made contemporaneously with arrest and only with respect to those items within defendant's immediate control. State v. Murray, 135 N.H. 369, 605 A.2d 676, 1992 N.H. LEXIS 41 (1992).

Search of defendant's purse after defendant had been placed under arrest and was in an ambulance about to be transported to a hospital was not incident to arrest. State v. Murray, 135 N.H. 369, 605 A.2d 676, 1992 N.H. LEXIS 41 (1992).

This article does not require that the police show independent probable cause to retain and examine evidence seized during a search incident to a lawful arrest. State v. Wheeler, 128 N.H. 767, 519 A.2d 289, 1986 N.H. LEXIS 367 (1986).

At burglary trial, court properly allowed introduction of evidence of the testing of the defendant's boots which were seized when he was arrested on an unrelated charge, since retention and examination of the boots was constitutionally permissible without further demonstration of probable cause or the issuance of further legal process. State v. Wheeler, 128 N.H. 767, 519 A.2d 289, 1986 N.H. LEXIS 367 (1986).

Superior court properly denied defendant's motion to suppress folded paper packets containing cocaine, found by police in defendant's wallet while he was being searched at the police station after being arrested, since the search was permissible as a search incident to a lawful arrest and did not violate warrant requirement of this article. State v. Farnsworth, 126 N.H. 656, 497 A.2d 835, 1985 N.H. LEXIS 421 (1985).

A warrantless search incident to a valid arrest and substantially contemporaneous therewith is a reasonable intrusion and does not violate this article. State v. Schofield, 114 N.H. 454, 322 A.2d 603, 1974 N.H. LEXIS 300 (1974).

32. —Administrative search exception

Routine stop of vehicle under RSA 266:72-a, I, and 49 C.F.R. § 390 was valid under the administrative search exception to the warrant requirement when an officer reasonably believed it was a commercial motor vehicle for purposes of federal motor safety regulations. Once the officer realized that defendant's vehicle was not a commercial one, he did not exceed his authority in continuing to question defendant, as the strong odor of marijuana, defendant's bloodshot eyes, and defendant's nervousness gave the officer a reasonable suspicion that defendant had engaged or was about to engage in criminal activity. State v. Livingston, 153 N.H. 399, 897 A.2d 977, 2006 N.H. LEXIS 42 (2006).

Three criteria must be satisfied before administrative search exception applies to justify warrantless search by a government body: (1) there must be a substantial government interest that informs regulatory scheme pursuant to which inspection is made; (2) warrantless inspections must be necessary to further the regulatory scheme; and (3) implementation of statutory inspection program must provide a constitutionally adequate substitute for a warrant. Appeal of Morgan (New Hampshire Bd. of Pharm.), 144 N.H. 44, 742 A.2d 101, 1999 N.H. LEXIS 75 (1999).

Audit by board of pharmacy investigators came within administrative search exception to search warrant requirement, where State had a substantial, long-recognized interest in regulating sale and distribution of drugs, warrantless access to records was necessary to quickly investigate wrongdoing and encourage compliance with law, and statutory scheme was sufficiently limited in time, place, and scope so as to constitute an adequate substitute for a warrant. Appeal of Morgan (New Hampshire Bd. of Pharm.), 144 N.H. 44, 742 A.2d 101, 1999 N.H. LEXIS 75 (1999).

New Hampshire recognizes the administrative search exception to the warrant requirement. State v. Plante, 134 N.H. 585, 594 A.2d 165, 1991 N.H. LEXIS 106 (1991), cert. denied, Plante v. New Hampshire, 502 U.S. 984, 112 S. Ct. 590, 116 L. Ed. 2d 614, 1991 U.S. LEXIS 6966 (1991).

At trial for possession of a controlled drug, sufficient evidence supported the trial court's conclusion that bailiff's search of small metal container in defendant's purse during the course of administrative search for weapons conducted at entrance of county courthouse was reasonable, in light of fact bailiff had on previous occasions found deadly weapons concealed in containers of that size and in light of notice to defendant that administrative searches, once commenced, would be completed, which rendered nugatory defendant's attempt to withdraw consent prior to opening of the specific container. State v. Plante, 134 N.H. 585, 594 A.2d 165, 1991 N.H. LEXIS 106 (1991), cert. denied, Plante v. New Hampshire, 502 U.S. 984, 112 S. Ct. 590, 116 L. Ed. 2d 614, 1991 U.S. LEXIS 6966 (1991).

33. —Schools

Search of defendant, a juvenile, was not justified at its inception and thus was unreasonable under N.H. Const. pt. I, art. 19. Although it was school policy to search all students who returned to school after leaving an assigned area, defendant was leaving, not returning; furthermore, nothing linked defendant to the infraction for which he was searched, namely, possession of drugs, weapons, or alcohol. In re Anthony F., 163 N.H. 163, 37 A.3d 429, 2012 N.H. LEXIS 4 (2012).

There had been a search of defendant, a juvenile, when two assistant principals twice informed him that he was going to be searched and then immediately inquired into what he had on his person, after which defendant handed over marijuana. Their conduct was akin to a command. In re Anthony F., 163 N.H. 163, 37 A.3d 429, 2012 N.H. LEXIS 4 (2012).

Search of defendant, a juvenile, could not be upheld under the United States Supreme Court's suspicionless school search jurisprudence. That line of cases was readily distinguishable from the present case in that the consequences to the student resulting from the search in those cases did not include turning over the results to law enforcement or lead to academic discipline. In re Anthony F., 163 N.H. 163, 37 A.3d 429, 2012 N.H. LEXIS 4 (2012).

In a delinquency petition, the trial court properly denied a juvenile's motion to suppress evidence, because a search of the student's locker by school officials which uncovered a pot pipe and marijuana did not violate N.H. Const. pt. I, art. 19, as a tip from student informants provided reasonable grounds for the search. In re Juvenile 2006-406, 156 N.H. 233, 931 A.2d 1229, 2007 N.H. LEXIS 170 (2007).

Student's statement that she had purchased drugs from defendant the previous day justified school principal's search of defendant in order to preempt future drug sales and confiscate any drugs in his possession, and principal's search of defendant's book bag, and request for him to remove his shoes and socks and empty his pockets, were logical and not excessively intrusive given that these were obvious places where contraband could be hidden. State v. Tinkham, 143 N.H. 73, 719 A.2d 580, 1998 N.H. LEXIS 69 (1998).

A search of a student by a school principal was reasonable where an anonymous telephone call informed the administrative assistant to the principal that the student "would be carrying a substantial amount of drugs including LSD with him in school that day," and teachers had previously expressed concern to the principal that the student was likely using, and possibly distributing, drugs. State v. Drake, 139 N.H. 662, 662 A.2d 265, 1995 N.H. LEXIS 69 (1995).

Public school officials are not exempt from constitutional prohibitions against unreasonable searches and seizures. State v. Drake, 139 N.H. 662, 662 A.2d 265, 1995 N.H. LEXIS 69 (1995).

Public school students have legitimate privacy interests in a variety of personal items they bring to school, and these privacy interests are not waived when the student merely passes through the schoolhouse door; however, while students bring certain rights with them when they enter a public school, additional rights attach upon that entry, including the right to a safe and healthy educational environment. State v. Drake, 139 N.H. 662, 662 A.2d 265, 1995 N.H. LEXIS 69 (1995).

A warrantless search of a student by a public school official is constitutional if it is reasonable under all of the circumstances; it must be justified at its inception and reasonably related in scope to the circumstances giving rise to the search; prior to beginning a search, the school official must have reasonable grounds to believe that the search will turn up evidence that the student has violated or is violating either the law or the rules of the school; and the action taken must be reasonably related to the objectives of the search and not excessively intrusive in light of the age and sex of the student and the nature of the infraction. State v. Drake, 139 N.H. 662, 662 A.2d 265, 1995 N.H. LEXIS 69 (1995).

34. —Community caretaking exception

Seizure was not valid under the community caretaking exception to the warrant requirement of N.H. Const. pt. I, art. 19 and the Fourth Amendment. Defendant's car was parked legally in a pull-off area and the officer did not observe any obvious signs of an accident, that the car was disabled, or that the passengers were in any type of distress. State v. Boutin, 161 N.H. 139, 13 A.3d 334, 2010 N.H. LEXIS 133 (2010).

New Hampshire Supreme Court is cognizant that police officers perform a broad range of community caretaking functions such as helping stranded motorists, returning lost children to their parents, and generally assisting and protecting citizens in need. The court recognizes the importance of these functions and encourages police officers to perform them, but to do so in a nonintrusive manner and without seizing the occupants of a vehicle. State v. Boutin, 161 N.H. 139, 13 A.3d 334, 2010 N.H. LEXIS 133 (2010).

Warrantless search of defendant's property was justified by the community caretaking exception to the warrant requirement of N.H. Const. pt. I, art. 19 and the Fourth Amendment, as the facts were enough to cause a person of reasonable caution to believe that the victim might have been injured and at defendant's residence; furthermore, the officers' concerns for the victim's well-being, and the likelihood that he was still at defendant's home, outweighed the intrusion onto defendant's property. The victim's family made numerous calls to police indicating concern for the victim's safety; when officers saw the victim a second time, he was visibly injured; the victim's mother stated that he had not contacted his family, which was unusual for him; defendant played a tape for police where the victim could be heard vomiting; defendant had previously lied to police about the victim's whereabouts; and police knew that defendant had a history of arguing with partners who left her home but returned later. State v. Labarre, 160 N.H. 1, 992 A.2d 733, 2010 N.H. LEXIS 21 (2010).

Motor vehicle stop was not justified under the community caretaking exception to the warrant requirement where, although defendant drove through flood waters, the police chief made no effort to warn drivers or stop defendant until the chief recognized defendant, who the chief knew had previously been convicted of driving under suspension, as the driver. State v. Craveiro, 155 N.H. 423, 924 A.2d 361, 2007 N.H. LEXIS 67 (2007).

35. —Detention

Passenger's unlawful frisk and unlawful detention claims failed because it could not be said that an officer was unreasonable in suspecting that the bulge near the passenger's waistband was a weapon and that a frisk was necessary to ensure the officer's own safety, and the officer was entitled to qualified immunity as to the decision to handcuff the passenger and detain the passenger in the cruiser while conducting a background check. Machado v. Weare Police Dep't, — F.3d —, 2012 U.S. App. LEXIS 20538 (Oct. 2, 2012).

36. Warrantless arrest

Police officer was constitutionally justified in stopping defendant's automobile, where officer had personally observed defendant yelling and gesturing in a parking lot, was told by an eyewitness that defendant had kicked over a parking sign and saw that sign was in fact on the ground, and officer thus had reasonable grounds to suspect defendant of having committed offense of disorderly conduct. State v. Hayes, 138 N.H. 410, 640 A.2d 288, 1994 N.H. LEXIS 40 (1994).

A warrantless arrest in a public place is reasonable if it is supported by probable cause. State v. Chaisson, 125 N.H. 810, 486 A.2d 297, 1984 N.H. LEXIS 320 (1984).

If the police, while lawfully on the premises, discover probable cause and arrest a suspect, then that seizure is lawful under this article. State v. Chaisson, 125 N.H. 810, 486 A.2d 297, 1984 N.H. LEXIS 320 (1984).

Where following a search of defendant's apartment pursuant to a search warrant a police officer remained in the apartment for the purpose of arresting defendant when he came home, the officer's conduct, although physically passive, constituted a search for defendant within his home and the warrant requirement of this article was applicable. State v. Chaisson, 125 N.H. 810, 486 A.2d 297, 1984 N.H. LEXIS 320 (1984).

Where following a search of defendant's apartment pursuant to a search warrant a police officer remained in the apartment and arrested defendant upon his return, since the officer was on the premises merely to await defendant's return and was not conducting or waiting to resume the search, the officer was not lawfully on the premises when the arrest occurred and the state should have obtained a warrant before arresting defendant. State v. Chaisson, 125 N.H. 810, 486 A.2d 297, 1984 N.H. LEXIS 320 (1984).

37. Knock and announce rule

Entry of police into a hotel room did not trigger the knock-and-announcement rule of N.H. Const. pt. I, art. 19 or the Fourth Amendment because the entry was not forcible. Fully uniformed police executing an arrest warrant followed a woman into the room after she opened the door in response to their knock and turned to walk toward defendant, leaving the door open. State v. Sconsa, 161 N.H. 113, 13 A.3d 164, 2010 N.H. LEXIS 128 (2010).

Knock and announce rule has its basis in the common law rather than this article; therefore, a violation of the knock and announce rule is not per se unconstitutional. State v. Pinder, 128 N.H. 66, 514 A.2d 1241, 1986 N.H. LEXIS 313 (1986).

38. Open fields

This article, which protects "possessions," was not designed to protect "open fields," which are unoccupied and undeveloped lands somewhat removed from dwellings and other protected structures, from warrantless searches; accordingly, the word "possessions" does not include "open fields." State v. Pinder, 128 N.H. 66, 514 A.2d 1241, 1986 N.H. LEXIS 313 (1986).

39. Electronic interception and recording of private conversations

Under this article, each participant in a telephone conversation is free to waive the interest in keeping the conversation private and to make the discussion public, and where one participant consents to share the discussion with the police, the rights of other participants are no longer protected. State v. Kilgus, 128 N.H. 577, 519 A.2d 231, 1986 N.H. LEXIS 372 (1986).

Where a police informant consented to wear a hidden tape recorder during a private conversation between him and the defendant, since the informant agreed to provide the police with the tape, no warrant was required in order to make the interception and recording of the discussion lawful. State v. Kilgus, 128 N.H. 577, 519 A.2d 231, 1986 N.H. LEXIS 372 (1986).

This article does not preclude the use in a criminal prosecution of evidence obtained by wire tapping. State v. Tracey, 100 N.H. 267, 125 A.2d 774, 1956 N.H. LEXIS 48 (1956).

40. Administrative searches

A regulation of the state liquor commission requiring a club licensed to sell liquors to members and guests to furnish the commission's law enforcement department a key or entry to the premises at any time does not violate constitutional provisions against unreasonable search. Manchester Press Club v. State Liquor Comm'n, 89 N.H. 442, 200 A. 407, 1938 N.H. LEXIS 51, 116 A.L.R. 1093 (1938).

A statute authorizing the tax commissioner in the process of collecting a sales tax to search a retail dealer's place of business and to demand from him information of unlimited scope authorizes no unreasonable searches. In re Opinion of Justices, 88 N.H. 500, 190 A. 801, 1937 N.H. LEXIS 90 (1936).

41. Standing to challenge search or seizure

Defendant had no reasonable expectation of privacy in his telephone records as they were never in his possession, and they only contained information that he voluntarily conveyed to the cell phone company in order to make use of its telephone service. State v. Gubitosi, 152 N.H. 673, 886 A.2d 1029, 2005 N.H. LEXIS 159 (2005).

When a defendant communicates information to the telephone company in order to make the telephone system work for him, there is no violation of a protected privacy interest when the record of that information is later disclosed. Likewise, the defendant does not have a reasonable expectation of privacy in information concerning his cellular telephone calls that was recorded for billing purposes and retained by a company in the ordinary course of its business. State v. Gubitosi, 152 N.H. 673, 886 A.2d 1029, 2005 N.H. LEXIS 159 (2005).

Defendant did not have a reasonable expectation of privacy in the records obtained from a cell phone company; thus, he did not have standing to claim that the subpoena was overbroad. State v. Gubitosi, 152 N.H. 673, 886 A.2d 1029, 2005 N.H. LEXIS 159 (2005).

School custodian on trial for theft from classroom did not have automatic standing to challenge video surveillance as an unlawful search under New Hampshire Constitution, where he had no possessory interest in classroom, desk, or money in desk prior to time of his offending act. State v. McLellan, 144 N.H. 602, 744 A.2d 611, 1999 N.H. LEXIS 162 (1999).

Defendant lacked automatic standing to challenge canine sniff of suspicious parcel found to contain marijuana, where defendant failed to demonstrate that he had requisite possessory interest in parcel prior to, or at time of, canine sniff. State v. Gonzalez, 143 N.H. 693, 738 A.2d 1247, 1999 N.H. LEXIS 59 (1999).

In a prosecution for conspiracy to possess marijuana with the intent to distribute and being an accomplice to the possession of marijuana with the intent to distribute, the defendant was not entitled to automatic standing to challenge the seizure of marijuana by a Federal Express official as possession by the defendant was not an element of either of the charges against him. State v. Alosa, 137 N.H. 33, 623 A.2d 218, 1993 N.H. LEXIS 37 (1993).

Where police entered and searched third party's apartment based on invalid search warrant at 9:50 p.m. and found cocaine, and while search was being executed defendant called and told detective he wanted to buy cocaine, and at 11:30 p.m. detective gave defendant the seized cocaine for $100, defendant had no standing to challenge validity of search warrant; defendant had no possessory interest in the cocaine prior to, or at the time of, its seizure. State v. Paige, 136 N.H. 208, 612 A.2d 1331, 1992 N.H. LEXIS 154 (1992).

This article requires that automatic standing be afforded to all persons within the state who are charged with crimes in which possession of an article or thing is an element. State v. Sidebotham, 124 N.H. 682, 474 A.2d 1377, 1984 N.H. LEXIS 344 (1984).

This article prohibits all unreasonable searches and seizures of all a citizen's possessions and, in order to assert this constitutional right, a citizen must be given standing to challenge any search or seizure of his possessions. State v. Sidebotham, 124 N.H. 682, 474 A.2d 1377, 1984 N.H. LEXIS 344 (1984).

Since the right to be secure from all unreasonable searches and seizures of all one's possessions without a concurrent right to challenge the legality of any search or seizure is meaningless, a defendant who has been charged with an offense arising out of his possession of a motor vehicle must be afforded "automatic standing" under the provisions of this article to challenge the legality of any search of that motor vehicle, even if the alleged search was conducted by a title investigator while the vehicle was located at a repair shop. State v. Sidebotham, 124 N.H. 682, 474 A.2d 1377, 1984 N.H. LEXIS 344 (1984).

This article requires that automatic standing to challenge an unlawful search or seizure be afforded to all persons within the State of New Hampshire who are charged with crimes in which possession of any article or thing is an element. State v. Settle, 122 N.H. 214, 447 A.2d 1284, 1982 N.H. LEXIS 373 (1982).

Defendants, charged with receiving stolen property and conspiracy to receive stolen property, were improperly denied standing by the trial court to contest an illegal warrantless search conducted by law enforcement personnel of the premises of a third party, since this article requires that automatic standing to challenge an unlawful search or seizure be afforded to all persons within the State of New Hampshire who are charged with crimes in which possession of any article or thing is an element. State v. Settle, 122 N.H. 214, 447 A.2d 1284, 1982 N.H. LEXIS 373 (1982).

42. Admissibility of evidence

Taint of a violation of the New Hampshire Constitution was not purged before defendant made incriminating statements to the police; thus, the statements had to be suppressed as fruit of the illegal seizure. Defendant made the statements immediately after being confronted with the illegally seized evidence; furthermore, the officer induced defendant to speak about the illegally seized evidence by stating that the defendant would have "to answer to the plants on the porch." State v. Orde, 161 N.H. 260, 13 A.3d 338, 2010 N.H. LEXIS 145 (Nov. 30, 2010).

Defendant's confession following his illegal arrest was inadmissible under N.H. Const. pt. I, art. 19. The factors of temporal proximity and intervening circumstances outweighed those favoring admission, as the circumstances suggested that defendant found it futile to refuse to speak to the officer to whom he confessed or to say anything different from what he had previously told other officers. State v. Miller, 159 N.H. 125, 977 A.2d 561, 2009 N.H. LEXIS 98 (2009).

Any taint of violation of N.H. Const. pt. I, art. 19 and the U.S. Constitution was purged when defendant ingested marijuana, which supported a new criminal charge distinct from the prior illegal seizure. State v. McGurk, 157 N.H. 765, 958 A.2d 1005, 2008 N.H. LEXIS 119 (2008).

Denial of defendant's motion to suppress evidence was reversed as the search of his garbage violated his state constitutional right to privacy; because the warrantless search of defendant's garbage violated N.H. Const. pt. I, art. 19, the information obtained from that search had to be excised from the affidavit in support of the warrant and the remainder of the affidavit examined to determine whether it established probable cause. State v. Goss, 150 N.H. 46, 834 A.2d 316, 2003 N.H. LEXIS 137 (2003).

Out-of-court identification of child pornography defendant through use of his arrest picture in newspaper was not required to be suppressed as the fruit of his illegal arrest, where intervening events with little or no connection to illegal police action broke causal link between illegal arrest and out-of-court identification. State v. Cobb, 143 N.H. 638, 732 A.2d 425, 1999 N.H. LEXIS 53 (1999).

Defendant's confession to murder was sufficiently the product of free will so as to break causal connection with his earlier illegal arrest, and therefore confession was not required to be suppressed as the fruit of an unlawful arrest. State v. Gotsch, 143 N.H. 88, 719 A.2d 606, 1998 N.H. LEXIS 74 (1998), cert. denied, Gotsch v. New Hampshire, 525 U.S. 1164, 119 S. Ct. 1080, 143 L. Ed. 2d 82, 1999 U.S. LEXIS 1398 (1999).

A good faith exception to the exclusionary rule is incompatible with the guarantees contained in part I, article 19 of the constitution. State v. Canelo, 139 N.H. 376, 653 A.2d 1097, 1995 N.H. LEXIS 3 (1995).

Because security officer was employed by store, not the state, and the state did not instigate or participate in the search and seizure, there was no constitutional reason under this article to exclude evidence of property seized, at defendant's subsequent trial for attempted theft by deception. State v. Keyser, 117 N.H. 45, 369 A.2d 224, 1977 N.H. LEXIS 263 (1977).

At a preliminary hearing to suppress evidence obtained on search warrants the respondent as the moving party has the burden of proving that the evidence was illegally obtained. State v. Coolidge, 106 N.H. 186, 208 A.2d 322, 1965 N.H. LEXIS 126 (1965).

Upon the offer at trial of evidence allegedly obtained illegally, on objection that the evidence was illegally obtained, the state has the burden of presenting evidence to the trial court of facts in existence when the warrants were issued which established to the magistrate the probable cause upon which their issuance was based. State v. Coolidge, 106 N.H. 186, 208 A.2d 322, 1965 N.H. LEXIS 126 (1965).

43. Forfeiture of property seized

There can be no decree for a forfeiture of property taken under a search warrant unless all the formalities of the law are complied with regarding search, seizure, and forfeiture proceedings. State v. Teletypewriter Mach., 97 N.H. 282, 86 A.2d 333, 1952 N.H. LEXIS 11 (1952).

44. Complaints

Federal constitution and this article neither require nor suggest by analogy that a post-arrest misdemeanor complaint used only to begin criminal proceedings and not to secure arrest or search warrants must meet the constitutional requirements of affidavits in support of warrants. State v. Fields, 119 N.H. 249, 400 A.2d 1175, 1979 N.H. LEXIS 282 (1979).

Constitutional guarantee afforded by this article securing the right of the people to be secure from all unreasonable searches and seizures concerns only searches and seizures, and its express requirement of probable cause can be read to encompass only situations involving searches and seizures; such provision does not purport to govern the issuance of post-arrest traffic complaints. State v. Fields, 119 N.H. 249, 400 A.2d 1175, 1979 N.H. LEXIS 282 (1979).

This article precludes the bringing one into court upon a criminal complaint not sworn to by complainant. State v. Thibodeau, 101 N.H. 136, 135 A.2d 715, 1957 N.H. LEXIS 40 (1957).

45. Medical records

Physician-patient privilege is no less valid, and its rationale is no less important, because a magistrate has found probable cause to believe that the privileged records contain evidence of a crime. The immediacy and intrusiveness of searches, combined with the potential for irreparable injury to privilege-holders, lead the New Hampshire Supreme Court to conclude that when privileged medical records are sought by search warrant, at least a minimal level of procedural protection is required. In re Search Warrant for Med. Records of C.T., 160 N.H. 214, 999 A.2d 210, 2010 N.H. LEXIS 39 (2010).

Henceforth, any search warrant for privileged medical records shall order the hospital or medical provider to comply within a reasonable time by producing the records under seal for in camera review by the trial court; the trial court shall then determine the manner by which the patient shall be provided notice that such records were produced and shall give the patient and hospital or medical provider an opportunity to object to their disclosure. Upon objection, the State must demonstrate "essential need" for the information contained in the record, i.e., the State must prove both that the information is unavailable from another source and that there is a compelling justification for its disclosure. In re Search Warrant for Med. Records of C.T., 160 N.H. 214, 999 A.2d 210, 2010 N.H. LEXIS 39 (2010).

Trial court did not err in requiring a hospital to turn over, pursuant to a search warrant, the medical records of a patient it treated following an automobile accident. Given the legislature's silence as to the treatment due privileged records sought by search warrant, the trial court's order was in accordance with the law governing search warrants. In re Search Warrant for Med. Records of C.T., 160 N.H. 214, 999 A.2d 210, 2010 N.H. LEXIS 39 (2010).

Because any agency relationship created between a police officer and ambulance personnel, where the officer requested the ambulance personnel take defendant to a particular hospital, did not extend to hospital staff who subsequently drew defendant's blood without a request from the police, there was no violation of N.H. Const. pt. I, art. 19 or the Fourth Amendment. State v. Wall, 154 N.H. 237, 910 A.2d 1253, 2006 N.H. LEXIS 151 (2006).

A trooper's asking doctors to voluntarily disclose information previously conveyed to them by the defendant did not constitute a search within the meaning of the New Hampshire Constitution. State v. Summers, 142 N.H. 429, 702 A.2d 819, 1997 N.H. LEXIS 115 (1997).

46. Search valid

Although defendant's car was only ten to fifteen feet from his house, his driveway was only semi-private in nature and thus police were not required to obtain a warrant before entering driveway and investigating defendant, still in his car, for drunk driving. State v. Pinkham, 141 N.H. 188, 679 A.2d 589, 1996 N.H. LEXIS 71 (1996).

Fact that consent form was silent with respect to search of defendant's sneakers in particular was of no moment where, prior to signing consent form, defendant was advised by detective that requested search of his person included a search of his sneakers. State v. Seymour, 140 N.H. 736, 673 A.2d 786, 1996 N.H. LEXIS 24 (1996), cert. denied, Seymour v. New Hampshire, 519 U.S. 853, 117 S. Ct. 146, 136 L. Ed. 2d 93, 1996 U.S. LEXIS 5265 (1996).

47. Anticipatory searches

An anticipatory search warrant involving the controlled delivery of contraband must recite the following specific conditions: (1) triggering event must be ascertainable and preordained, restricting police discretion in detecting occurrence of event to almost ministerial proportions; and (2) contraband must be on a sure and irreversible course to its destination, and a future search of destination must be made expressly contingent upon contraband's arrival there. State v. Gonzalez, 143 N.H. 693, 738 A.2d 1247, 1999 N.H. LEXIS 59 (1999).

Requirements for an anticipatory search warrant were satisfied, where it was clear from context of warrant application, supporting affidavit, and resulting warrant that the necessary triggering event was delivery of package and acceptance into apartment. State v. Gonzalez, 143 N.H. 693, 738 A.2d 1247, 1999 N.H. LEXIS 59 (1999).

An anticipatory search warrant was invalid where the warrant was made contingent on a confidential informant observing cocaine in the defendant's apartment, but the affidavit in support of the warrant application offered no facts to support a determination that event was both ascertainable and preordained and on a sure and irreversible course to transpiring. State v. Canelo, 139 N.H. 376, 653 A.2d 1097, 1995 N.H. LEXIS 3 (1995).

Anticipatory search warrants do not categorically violate part I, article 19 of the constitution; however, in order for such a warrant to be valid, the magistrate must ensure that the triggering event is both ascertainable and preordained, the warrant must restrict the officers' discretion in detecting the occurrence of the event to almost ministerial proportions, the contraband must be on a sure and irreversible course to its destination, and a future search of the destination must be made expressly contingent upon the contraband's arrival there. State v. Canelo, 139 N.H. 376, 653 A.2d 1097, 1995 N.H. LEXIS 3 (1995).

48. Exclusionary rule

United States Supreme Court's statement that the identity of a defendant was never suppressible as the fruit of an illegal arrest was limited solely to jurisdiction. Accordingly, because the trial court had determined that defendant was illegally arrested under N.H. Const. pt. I, art. 19, it should have excluded his driver's license, which was obtained after the illegal arrest, along with any testimony about the license. State v. Moscone, 161 N.H. 355, 13 A.3d 137, 2011 N.H. LEXIS 1 (2011).

Denial of defendant's suppression motion was proper, as a police officer's investigatory stop of defendant's vehicle was based on a reasonable suspicion that the radio in the vehicle was being played at an unnecessarily loud volume in violation of a local ordinance; the officer's objectively reasonable reliance on the ordinance, even if it was unconstitutional, was within an exception to the exclusionary rule under N.H. Const. pt. I, art. 19. State v. De La Cruz, 158 N.H. 564, 969 A.2d 413, 2009 N.H. LEXIS 41 (2009).

An officer's objectively reasonable reliance upon an ordinance or statute in forming reasonable suspicion is an exception to the exclusionary rule in N.H. Const. pt. I, art. 19. State v. De La Cruz, 158 N.H. 564, 969 A.2d 413, 2009 N.H. LEXIS 41 (2009).

The New Hampshire Supreme Court adopts the "new crime" exception to the exclusionary rule; under this exception, where the response to an unlawful entry, search or seizure has been a physical attack (or threat of same) upon an officer, the evidence of this new crime is admissible. State v. Panarello, 157 N.H. 204, 949 A.2d 732, 2008 N.H. LEXIS 53 (2008).

Under the "new crime" exception to the exclusionary rule, the trial court erred in suppressing evidence that defendant allegedly pointed a gun at an officer who unlawfully entered his home. State v. Panarello, 157 N.H. 204, 949 A.2d 732, 2008 N.H. LEXIS 53 (2008).

A good faith exception to exclusionary rule is incompatible with and detrimental to citizens' strong right of privacy inherent in New Hampshire Constitution. State v. Martin, 145 N.H. 362, 761 A.2d 516, 2000 N.H. LEXIS 69 (2000).

State's failure to prove that bench warrant was valid at time of defendant's arrest removed mantle of judicial authorization for that arrest and grounds for police to be at defendant's residence, and thus trial court erred in denying defendant's motion to suppress evidence of firearms seized during arrest. State v. Martin, 145 N.H. 362, 761 A.2d 516, 2000 N.H. LEXIS 69 (2000).

49. Warrantless entry

Defendant had no reasonable expectation of privacy in the curtilage of his home because (1) defendant's mobile home and garage were approximately 100 feet from the road, and no large shrubs or fences hid the front curtilage of the home, (2) as such, the house, garage and driveway were visible from the road, and (3) moreover, the driveway was not blocked by a gate or posted with "No Trespassing" signs. State v. Johnston, 150 N.H. 448, 839 A.2d 830, 2004 N.H. LEXIS 2 (2004).

Although the New Hampshire Supreme Court does not adopt the Ferrier rule announced by the Washington State Supreme Court, trial courts in New Hampshire should scrutinize the facts of each knock and talk case with special care to determine whether the procedures rise to a level of coercion that is constitutionally impermissible. State v. Johnston, 150 N.H. 448, 839 A.2d 830, 2004 N.H. LEXIS 2 (2004).

Trial court erred in concluding that officer's conduct did not trigger defendant's constitutional protections, since Part I, Article 19 of New Hampshire Constitution protected individuals from warrantless police entries as well as warrantless searches. State v. Sawyer, 145 N.H. 704, 764 A.2d 936, 2001 N.H. LEXIS 4 (2001).

Defendant did not manifest unambiguous consent for officer to enter her apartment, where she entered apartment while engaged in conversation with officer and failed to instruct him not to enter; officer's presence in defendant's apartment was thus in violation of New Hampshire Constitution, and trial court erred in refusing to suppress fruits of searches which followed officer's warrantless entry. State v. Sawyer, 145 N.H. 704, 764 A.2d 936, 2001 N.H. LEXIS 4 (2001).

50. Apparent authority to consent to search

Supreme Court of New Hampshire adopted the doctrine of apparent authority regarding consensual searches; apparent authority existed when, under totality of circumstances, it was objectively reasonable to believe that third party had authority to consent to search. State v. Sawyer, 147 N.H. 191, 784 A.2d 1208, 2001 N.H. LEXIS 194 (2001), cert. denied, Sawyer v. New Hampshire, 537 U.S. 822, 123 S. Ct. 107, 154 L. Ed. 2d 31, 2002 U.S. LEXIS 6017 (2002).

51. Attenuation test

Where the issue on appeal was whether defendant's confession was tainted by the prior unlawful arrest at his home after he had eluded the pursing officer, the appellate court, applying the attenuation test set forth in State v. Gotsch, 143 N.H. 88, 719 A.2d 606, 1998 N.H. LEXIS 74 (1998), held: (1) that because Miranda warnings were given, same favored the admissibility of defendant's confession; (2) the temporal proximity between the illegal arrest and the confession (estimated at 45 minutes), was essentially a neutral factor; (3) there were no intervening circumstances to consider; (4) the police misconduct was not flagrant as the officer was in hot pursuit of defendant while he was committing a felony (operating after having been certified a habitual offender), and the officer did have probable cause for an arrest; and finally; (5) the taint of the unlawful arrest was purged. State v. Cowles, 152 N.H. 369, 877 A.2d 219, 2005 N.H. LEXIS 103 (2005).

52. Curtilage

Police did not violate N.H. Const. pt. I, art. 19 by entering a wooded area behind defendant's home, as it fell outside defendant's curtilage. No general enclosure surrounded it; there was no indication that it was used as an adjunct to the home or for domestic purposes; and defendant did not limit outsiders' access to it. State v. Smith, 163 N.H. 169, 37 A.3d 409, 2012 N.H. LEXIS 1 (2012).

Under the Fourth Amendment and N.H. Const. pt. I, art. 19, police did not need a warrant to search an overgrown field behind defendant's house where marijuana was found, as the area was not within the curtilage of defendant's home. It was not necessary, convenient and habitually used for family purposes or for carrying on domestic employment, and defendant had no reasonable expectation of privacy in it. State v. Johnson, 159 N.H. 109, 977 A.2d 548, 2009 N.H. LEXIS 91 (2009).

53. Aerial observation

Because no warrant was required to search a field where marijuana was found, even if the court assumed, without deciding, that a previous aerial observation constituted a search, no constitutional violation occurred. State v. Johnson, 159 N.H. 109, 977 A.2d 548, 2009 N.H. LEXIS 91 (2009).

54. Expectation of privacy

Defendant has no reasonable expectation of privacy in subscriber information voluntarily provided to an Internet service provider. Thus, although a search warrant requesting such records from an out-of-state corporation was defective, there was no violation of the Fourth Amendment or N.H. Const. pt. I, art. 19. State v. Mello, 162 N.H. 115, 27 A.3d 771, 2011 N.H. LEXIS 77 (2011).

Defendant had a reasonable expectation of privacy in his deck under N.H. Const. pt. I, art. 19, requiring the suppression of evidence seized from the deck. The placement of the deck and lilac bushes prevented the public from viewing the activities on the deck from the driveway; the deck was attached to the home and used for family activities; and an officer's departure from obvious paths and his entrance onto the deck exceeded his implied invitation onto the property. State v. Orde, 161 N.H. 260, 13 A.3d 338, 2010 N.H. LEXIS 145 (Nov. 30, 2010).

To the extent that a defendant may have a reasonable expectation of privacy in his medical records generally, society does not recognize a reasonable expectation of privacy in blood alcohol test results obtained and recorded by a hospital as part of its consensual treatment of a patient, where those results are requested by law enforcement for law enforcement purposes in connection with an incident giving rise to an investigation for driving while under the influence of intoxicating liquors or controlled drugs. State v. Davis, 161 N.H. 292, 12 A.3d 1271, 2010 N.H. LEXIS 182 (Dec. 17, 2010).

When a hospital tested defendant's blood alcohol content as part of its treatment of him, the State's warrantless request for and acquisition of the blood test results did not implicate N.H. Const. pt. I, art. 19 or the Fourth Amendment. Society did not recognize a reasonable expectation of privacy in blood alcohol test results obtained and recorded by a hospital as part of its consensual treatment of a patient, when those results were requested by law enforcement for law enforcement purposes in connection with an incident giving rise to an investigation for driving while under the influence of intoxicating liquors or controlled drugs. State v. Davis, 161 N.H. 292, 12 A.3d 1271, 2010 N.H. LEXIS 182 (Dec. 17, 2010).

Defendant had no reasonable expectation of privacy in his girlfriend's vehicle when the vehicle was parked in a multi-space lot in defendant's apartment building, there were no gates blocking the entrance to the lot and no signs restricting access to it, and the lot was clearly visible to officers from the street. The fact that the police made their observations at night and that the windows of the vehicle were tinted did not affect this conclusion. State v. Collanzo, — N.H. —, — A.2d —, 2009 N.H. LEXIS 152 (Feb. 23, 2009).

55. Observations by conservation officer

Conservation officer's presence on defendant's porch was not a violation of N.H. Const. pt. I, art. 19 or the Fourth Amendment. When conservation officers entered private property to conduct an investigation and restricted their movements to places visitors could be expected to go, observations made from these places were not protected, and defendant's porch was a place visitors could be expected to go in order to knock on the front door. State v. Beauchemin, 161 N.H. 654, 20 A.3d 936, 2011 N.H. LEXIS 36 (2011).

Because an inventory search was not conducted according to the standardized procedures of the local police department, it violated N.H. Const. pt. I, art. 19. The department's policy prohibited the search of any locked area or container that was not a trunk or glove compartment, and the back compartment of defendant's rental truck was not a trunk. State v. Newcomb, 161 N.H. 666, 20 A.3d 881, 2011 N.H. LEXIS 46 (2011).

55. Stop and frisk

Police were justified in conducting a protective frisk of defendant, given that defendant's appearance closely corresponded to that of the person described in the report of a violent rape occurring in the same area. State v. Perri, 164 N.H. 400, 58 A.3d 627, 2012 N.H. LEXIS 162 (2012).

Cited:

Cited in Opinion of the Justices, 25 N.H. 537 (1852); State v. Spirituous Liquors, 68 N.H. 47, 40 A. 398, 1894 N.H. LEXIS 22 (1894); Fletcher v. Merrimack County, 71 N.H. 96, 51 A. 271, 1901 N.H. LEXIS 24 (1901); State v. Cohen, 73 N.H. 543, 63 A. 928, 1906 N.H. LEXIS 28 (1906); State v. Drew, 89 N.H. 54, 192 A. 629, 1937 N.H. LEXIS 11 (1937); State v. Mara, 96 N.H. 463, 78 A.2d 922, 1951 N.H. LEXIS 190 (1951); State v. Morris, 98 N.H. 517, 103 A.2d 913, 1954 N.H. LEXIS 101 (1954); State v. Comeau, 114 N.H. 431, 321 A.2d 590, 1974 N.H. LEXIS 294 (1974); State v. Levesque, 123 N.H. 52, 455 A.2d 1045, 1983 N.H. LEXIS 221 (1983); State v. Miskolczi, 123 N.H. 626, 465 A.2d 919, 1983 N.H. LEXIS 325 (1983); State v. Tapply, 124 N.H. 318, 470 A.2d 900, 1983 N.H. LEXIS 399 (1983); State v. Sheedy, 124 N.H. 738, 474 A.2d 1042, 1984 N.H. LEXIS 336 (1984); State v. Doyle, 126 N.H. 153, 489 A.2d 639, 1985 N.H. LEXIS 262 (1985); State v. Cote, 126 N.H. 514, 493 A.2d 1170, 1985 N.H. LEXIS 336 (1985); State v. Cimino, 126 N.H. 570, 493 A.2d 1197, 1985 N.H. LEXIS 346 (1985); State v. Westover, 127 N.H. 130, 497 A.2d 1218, 1985 N.H. LEXIS 374 (1985); State v. Oxley, 127 N.H. 407, 503 A.2d 756, 1985 N.H. LEXIS 460 (1985); State v. Jaroma, 128 N.H. 423, 514 A.2d 1274, 1986 N.H. LEXIS 304 (1986); State v. Steer, 128 N.H. 490, 517 A.2d 797, 1986 N.H. LEXIS 334 (1986); State v. Dellorfano, 128 N.H. 628, 517 A.2d 1163, 1986 N.H. LEXIS 343 (1986); State v. MacDonald, 129 N.H. 13, 523 A.2d 35, 1986 N.H. LEXIS 375 (1986); State v. Maguire, 129 N.H. 165, 523 A.2d 120, 1987 N.H. LEXIS 161 (1987); State v. Allegra, 129 N.H. 720, 533 A.2d 338, 1987 N.H. LEXIS 247 (1987); State v. Lewis, 129 N.H. 787, 533 A.2d 358, 1987 N.H. LEXIS 246 (1987); State v. Valenzuela, 130 N.H. 175, 536 A.2d 1252, 1987 N.H. LEXIS 302 (1987); State v. Houtenbrink, 130 N.H. 385, 539 A.2d 714, 1988 N.H. LEXIS 17 (1988); State v. Chaloux, 130 N.H. 809, 546 A.2d 1081, 1988 N.H. LEXIS 75 (1988); State v. Coyman, 130 N.H. 815, 547 A.2d 307, 1988 N.H. LEXIS 68 (1988); State v. Glaude, 131 N.H. 218, 552 A.2d 85, 1988 N.H. LEXIS 119 (1988); State v. Gosselin, 131 N.H. 243, 552 A.2d 974, 1988 N.H. LEXIS 114 (1988); State v. Thompson, 132 N.H. 730, 571 A.2d 266, 1990 N.H. LEXIS 24 (1990); State v. Field, 132 N.H. 760, 571 A.2d 1276, 1990 N.H. LEXIS 17 (1990); State v. Tucker, 133 N.H. 204, 575 A.2d 810, 1990 N.H. LEXIS 61 (1990); State v. Davis, 133 N.H. 211, 575 A.2d 4, 1990 N.H. LEXIS 49 (1990); State v. Caicedo, 135 N.H. 122, 599 A.2d 895, 1991 N.H. LEXIS 149 (1991); State v. Dodier, 135 N.H. 134, 600 A.2d 913, 1991 N.H. LEXIS 152 (1991); State v. Wilkinson, 136 N.H. 170, 612 A.2d 926, 1992 N.H. LEXIS 141 (1992); State v. Smart, 136 N.H. 639, 622 A.2d 1197, 1993 N.H. LEXIS 11 (1993); State v. Barron, 137 N.H. 29, 623 A.2d 216, 1993 N.H. LEXIS 36 (1993); State v. Jaroma, 137 N.H. 143, 625 A.2d 1049, 1993 N.H. LEXIS 54 (1993); State v. Mortrud, 139 N.H. 423, 654 A.2d 464, 1995 N.H. LEXIS 19 (1995); State v. Psomiades, 139 N.H. 480, 658 A.2d 1190, 1995 N.H. LEXIS 33 (1995); State v. Fish, 142 N.H. 524, 703 A.2d 1377, 1997 N.H. LEXIS 124 (1997).

RESEARCH REFERENCES

New Hampshire Bar Journal.

For article, "Lex Loci: A Survey of New Hampshire Supreme Court Decisions," see N.H.B.J. 64 (Spring 2005).

For article, "The *Lopez* Decision: Drivers Beware," see 42 N.H. Bar Journal 38 (March 2001).

For article, "The Role of the Primacy Doctrine in New Hampshire Criminal Procedure: An Expansion of Individual Constitutional Rights," see 28 N.H.B.J. 357 (1987).

"For article, *"State v. Pellicci:* Making Scents About the Use of Drug Detection Dogs," see 32 N.H.B.J. 186 (1991).

For note, "The State of New Hampshire v. Zeta Chi Fraternity: The Creation of a New Standard Regarding Warrantless Searches of Probationers," see 39 N.H. Bar Journal 30 (September 1998).

For note, "School Personnel as Third Party Agents of the Police," see 40 N.H. Bar Journal 8 (September 1999).

For note, "Reaching Deep: The N.H. Supreme Court Delves into Constitutionality of Warrantless Searches into Wallets and Pockets," see 39 N.H. Bar Journal 70 (September 1998).

Art. 21. [Jurors; Compensation.]

In order to reap the fullest advantage of the inestimable privilege of the trial by jury, great care ought to be taken, that none but qualified persons should be appointed to serve; and such ought to be fully compensated for their travel, time, and attendance.

Cross References.
Jurors generally, see RSA 500-A.

NOTES TO DECISIONS

1. Impartiality
2. Compensation

1. Impartiality
It cannot be said as a matter of law that a juror who entertains an opinion of the merits of a case which can be overcome only by very strong evidence is as impartial as the lot of humanity will admit. State v. Rheaume, 80 N.H. 319, 116 A. 758, 1922 N.H. LEXIS 17 (1922).

2. Compensation
Where defendant gave a laundry list of citations in support of his argument that the juror compensation scheme was in violation of the U.S. and N.H. Constitutions, but he did not argue that the actual juror compensation statute, RSA 500-A:15, violated constitutional requirement of jurors being fully compensated, pursuant to N.H. Const. pt. I, art. 21, the court found that the argument, which had no developed legal claims in support of it, was not subject to appellate review. State v. Ayer, 150 N.H. 14, 834 A.2d 277, 2003 N.H. LEXIS 133 (2003), cert. denied, Ayer v. New Hampshire, 124 S. Ct. 1668, 158 L. Ed. 2d 366, 2004 U.S. LEXIS 2130 (2004).

Cited:
Cited in State v. Thomson, 109 N.H. 205, 247 A.2d 179, 1968 N.H. LEXIS 157 (1968); State v. Fleury, 114 N.H. 325, 321 A.2d 108, 1974 N.H. LEXIS 270 (1974).

Art. 33. [Excessive Bail, Fines, and Punishments Prohibited.]

No magistrate, or court of law, shall demand excessive bail or sureties impose excessive fines, or inflict cruel or unusual punishments.

Cross References.
Bail and recognizances generally, see RSA 597.
Excessive bail, fines and punishments prohibited by federal constitution, see United States Constitution, Amendment VIII.
Penalties to be proportioned to offenses; true design of punishment, see New Hampshire Constitution, Part 1, Article 18.
Sentences, see RSA 651.

NOTES TO DECISIONS

1. Bail
2. Cruel or unusual punishment
3. Remedies
4. Fines
5. Appeals

1. Bail
Penalty assessment, under proposed legislation, of $2.00 or 10 percent, whichever is greater, computed on basis of offender's "bail," to provide funding for police training programs established by police standards and training council, would violate provision of this article prohibiting imposition of excessive bail or sureties, as well as a similar prohibition of eighth amendment to the United States Constitution. Opinion of Justices, 117 N.H. 382, 373 A.2d 640, 1977 N.H. LEXIS 342 (1977).

An act for the suppression of drinking houses and tippling shops which provides in part that no person shall be surety for an accused, directly or indirectly, under the provisions of this act, in more than one case, is inconsistent with the constitutional prohibition against excessive bail in that it regards exclusively the person who becomes bail, without considering his sufficiency, and tends to render it as difficult as possible for the accused to procure bail. Opinion of the Justices, 25 N.H. 537 (1852).

2. Cruel or unusual punishment
A commitment for contempt in refusing to answer a question until such time as the witness shall purge himself is not within the constitutional prohibition of cruel and unusual punishments. Wyman v. Uphaus, 100 N.H. 436, 130 A.2d 278, 1957 N.H. LEXIS 73 (1957), vacated, 355 U.S. 16, 78 S. Ct. 57, 2 L. Ed. 2d 22, 1957 U.S. LEXIS 332 (1957), aff'd, 101 N.H. 139, 136 A.2d 221, 1957 N.H. LEXIS 41 (1957).

In granting to the attorney general the power to publish testimony of witnesses in a legislative investigation concerned with matters violative of the subversive activities act, the legislature does not permit the infliction of cruel or unusual punishment. Nelson v. Wyman, 99 N.H. 33, 105 A.2d 756, 1954 N.H. LEXIS 10 (1954).

3. Remedies
A civil action will not lie against a judicial officer for his requirement of excessive bail, since such action is a crime punishable by means of indictment. Evans v. Foster, 1 N.H. 374, 1819 N.H. LEXIS 42 (1819).

4. Fines
Trial court's judgment imposing a fine of $160,000 on defendant who was convicted of 80 counts of gambling, in violation of RSA 647:2 (1996), was not excessive or disproportionate to the offenses. State v. Enderson, 148 N.H. 252, 804 A.2d 448, 2002 N.H. LEXIS 116 (2002).

5. Appeals
Although N.H. Const. pt. I, arts. 15, 18, and 33 entitle a defendant to a fair appellate procedure, free from arbitrary and discriminatory enforcement, the constitution does not require that the procedure be adopted through the formal rulemaking process. State v. Addison, 159 N.H. 87, 977 A.2d 520, 2009 N.H. LEXIS 86 (2009).

Cited:
Cited in Doe v. O'Brien, 107 N.H. 79, 217 A.2d 189, 1966 N.H. LEXIS 125 (1966); State v. Hutton, 107 N.H. 426, 223 A.2d 416, 1966 N.H. LEXIS 205 (1966); Peters v. University of New Hampshire, 112 N.H. 120, 289 A.2d 396, 1972 N.H. LEXIS 156 (1972); State v. Wheeler, 120 N.H. 496, 416 A.2d 1384, 1980 N.H. LEXIS 331 (1980).

PART SECOND

Form Of Government

OATHS AND SUBSCRIPTIONS—EXCLUSION FROM OFFICES—COMMISSIONS—WRITS—CONFIRMATION OF LAWS—HABEAS CORPUS—THE ENACTING STYLE—CONTINUANCE OF OFFICERS—PROVISIONS FOR A FUTURE REVISION OF THE CONSTITUTION—ETC.

Art. 91. [Habeas Corpus.]

The privilege and benefit of the habeas corpus, shall be enjoyed in this state, in the most free, easy, cheap, expeditious, and ample manner, and shall not be suspended by the legislature, except upon the most urgent and pressing occasions, and for a time not exceeding three months.

Cross References.

Habeas Corpus generally, see RSA 534.

NOTES TO DECISIONS

Federal jurisdiction

A prisoner in custody under the authority of the state should not, except in a case of peculiar urgency, be discharged by a court or judge of the United States on a writ of habeas corpus, in advance of any proceedings in the courts of the state to test validity of his detention. Lyon v. Harkness, 151 F.2d 731, 1945 U.S. App. LEXIS 3030 (1st Cir. N.H. 1945), cert. denied, 327 U.S. 782, 66 S. Ct. 682, 90 L. Ed. 1009, 1946 U.S. LEXIS 2754 (1946).

TITLE V

TAXATION

CHAPTER 78

TOBACCO TAX

SECTION
78:1.   Definitions.
78:2.   Licenses.
78:3.   Tampering with Seal. [Repealed.]
78:4.   Term of License; Renewals.
78:5.   Unclassified Importers. [Repealed.]
78:6.   Suspension and Revocation of License by Commissioner.
78:6-a.   Denial of License Application.
78:7.   Tax Imposed.
78:7-a.   Nature of Tax.
78:7-b.   Exemption.
78:7-c.   Tax Imposed on Tobacco Products Other Than Cigarettes.
78:8.   Stock-in-Trade Tax. [Repealed.]
78:9.   Stamps.
78:9-a.   Compensation for Collecting and Remitting Tax. [Repealed.]
78:10.   Resale of Stamps; Redemption.
78:11.   Metering Machines.
78:12.   Affixing Stamps.
78:12-a. Unauthorized Sales.
78:12-b. Sale and Distribution of Tobacco Products to Persons Under 18 Years of Age Prohibited. [Repealed.]
78:12-c. Possession of Tobacco by Persons Under 18 Years of Age and Misrepresentation of Age for the Purpose of Procuring Tobacco Products. [Repealed.]
78:12-d. Vending Machines. [Repealed.]
78:12-e. Access and Dissemination of Information Required.
78:13.   Authorization to Affix Stamps or Use Metering Machine.
78:14.   Unstamped Tobacco Products.
78:14-a. Possession of Tobacco Products of Foreign States.
78:15.   Sales Between Licensees. [Repealed.]
78:16.   Seizure, Forfeiture, and Destruction of Illegal Tobacco Products.
78:17.   Fraudulent Stamps. [Repealed.]
78:18.   Required Taxpayer Records.
78:18-a. Additions to Tax.
78:19.   Newspaper Advertisements. [Repealed.]
78:20.   State Tax. [Repealed.]

Administration

78:21.   Division of Tobacco Products. [Repealed.]
78:22.   Administration by Director of Division of Tobacco Products. [Repealed.]
78:23.   Jurisdiction of Director. [Repealed.]

Protection of Revenue of the State

78:24.   Report of Importation. [Repealed.]
78:25.   Required Records. [Repealed.]
78:26.   Inspection Authorized.
78:27.   Transportation. [Repealed.]
78:28.   Exception. [Repealed.]
78:29.   Enforcement of Provisions. [Repealed.]
78:30.   Penalty. [Repealed.]
78:31.   Appeal. [Repealed.]
78:31-a. Appeals of License Revocation or Suspension Orders and Seizure, Forfeiture, or Destruction of Illegal Tobacco Products Orders.
78:32.   Distribution of Funds.

Importation of Certain Tobacco Products Prohibited

SECTION
78:33.   Preservation of Revenues.
78:34.   Federal Requirements; Cigarettes and Other Tobacco Products; Placement of Labels; Penalty.

NOTES TO DECISIONS

1. Constitutionality
2. Effect on dealer

1. Constitutionality

Tobacco so distinctively stands in a class of its own that the imposition of a tax upon its sale is neither arbitrary nor unreasonable. Havens v. Attorney Gen., 91 N.H. 115, 14 A.2d 636, 1940 N.H. LEXIS 32 (1940).

The tax upon "tobacco products sold at retail" is not invalid because of the exemption of other property by failure to enumerate it as taxable. Havens v. Attorney Gen., 91 N.H. 115, 14 A.2d 636, 1940 N.H. LEXIS 32 (1940).

2. Effect on dealer

The fact that a retail dealer suffers some loss of profit through diminished business because some customers buy cheaper tobacco products is immaterial. Havens v. Attorney Gen., 91 N.H. 115, 14 A.2d 636, 1940 N.H. LEXIS 32 (1940).

The absence of a provision in this chapter for the deduction of a federal excise tax paid by manufacturers is immaterial, since the retailer does not pay that tax except as included in the price charged by the wholesaler. Havens v. Attorney Gen., 91 N.H. 115, 14 A.2d 636, 1940 N.H. LEXIS 32 (1940).

Cited:

Cited in Opinion of Justices, 94 N.H. 506, 52 A.2d 294, 1947 N.H. LEXIS 219 (1947).

RESEARCH REFERENCES

New Hampshire Code of Administrative Rules.

Rules of the Department of Revenue Administration, Rev. 207.04, 1001.01 et seq., New Hampshire Code of Administrative Rules Annotated.

78:1. Definitions.

Whenever used in this chapter the following words shall have the meanings set opposite them below:

I. "Commissioner", the commissioner of revenue administration.

II. "Person," any individual, firm, fiduciary, partnership, corporation, trust, or association, however formed.

III. "Manufacturer" means any person engaged in the business of importing, exporting, producing, or manufacturing tobacco products who sells his product only to licensed wholesalers.

III-a. "Wholesale sales price" means the established price for which a manufacturer sells tobacco products other than cigarettes to a wholesaler, exclusive of any discount or other reduction.

IV. "Licensed manufacturer," a manufacturer licensed hereunder.

V. "Wholesaler" means any person doing business in this state who shall purchase all of his unstamped tobacco products directly from a licensed manufacturer, and who shall sell all of his products to licensed wholesalers, sub-jobbers, vending machine operators, retailers, and those persons exempted from the tobacco tax under RSA 78:7-b.

VI. "Licensed wholesaler," a wholesaler licensed hereunder.

VII. "Sub-jobber" means any person doing business in this state who buys stamped tobacco products from a licensed wholesaler and who sells all of his tobacco products to other licensed sub-jobbers, vending machine operators and retailers.

VIII. "Licensed sub-jobber," a sub-jobber licensed hereunder.

IX. "Vending machine operator" means any person operating one or more tobacco product vending machines on property or premises other than his own.

X. "Licensed vending machine operator," a vending machine operator licensed hereunder.

XI. "Retailer" means any person who sells tobacco products to consumers, and any vending machine in which tobacco products are sold.

XII. "Licensed retailer," a retailer licensed hereunder.

XIII. "Sale" or "sell," any transfer, whether by bargain, gift, exchange, barter or otherwise.

XIV. "Tobacco products" means cigarettes, loose tobacco, smokeless tobacco, snuff, and cigars, but shall not include premium cigars.

XIV-a–XVI. [Repealed.]

XVII. (a) In conformity with RSA 541-C:2, IV, "cigarette" means any product that contains nicotine, is intended to be burned or heated under ordinary conditions of use, and consists of or contains:

(1) Any roll of tobacco wrapped in paper or in any substance not containing tobacco; or

(2) Tobacco, in any form, that is functional in the product, which, because of its appearance, the type of tobacco used in the filler, or its packaging and labeling, is likely to be offered to, or purchased by, consumers as a cigarette; or

(3) Any roll of tobacco wrapped in any substance containing tobacco which, because of its appearance, the type of tobacco used in the filler, or its packaging and labeling, is likely to be offered to, or purchased by, consumers as a cigarette described in subparagraph (a)(1).

(b) The term "cigarette" includes "roll-your-own" (i.e., any tobacco which, because of its appearance, type, packaging, or labeling is suitable for use and likely to be offered to, or purchased by, consumers as tobacco for making cigarettes). For purposes of this definition of "cigarette," 0.09 ounces of "roll-your-own" tobacco shall constitute one individual "cigarette."

XVIII. "Licensee" means the person in whose name the license is issued.

XIX. "Sampler" means any person who distributes free tobacco products to consumers for promotional purposes.

XX. "Vending machine" means any self-service device which, upon insertion of money, tokens, or any other form of payment, dispenses tobacco, cigarettes, or any other tobacco product.

XXI. "Premium cigars" means cigars which are made entirely by hand of all natural tobacco leaf, hand constructed and hand wrapped, wholesaling for $2 or more, and weighing more than 3 pounds per 1000 cigars. These cigars shall be kept in a humidor at the proper humidity.

Source.
1939, 167:1; 180:1. RL 79:1. 1947, 133:1; 238:1. 1949, 187:1, 2. RSA 78:1. 1970, 5:12. 1973, 544:11, XII. 1975, 466:2, 6. 1977, 200:1. 1981, 210:1–6, 24. 1991, 292:1, 2, eff. July 1, 1991. 1997, 338:1, eff. Jan. 1, 1998. 2003, 152:5, eff. Jan. 1, 2004; 152:8, eff. July 1, 2003. 2005, 177:140, July 1, 2005. 2008, 236:1, eff. July 1, 2008. 2009, 144:177, 178, eff. July 1, 2009. 2013, 35:1, eff. May 31, 2013.

Amendments
—2013. The 2013 amendment rewrote XVII to the extent that a detailed comparison would be impracticable.

—2009. The 2009 amendment added "snuff, and cigars, but shall not include premium cigars" in XIV; added XXI; and made a related change.

—2008. The 2008 amendment rewrote XVII to the extent that a detailed comparison would be impracticable.

—2005. Paragraph XIV: Inserted "loose tobacco" following "cigarettes".

—2003. Paragraph III-a: Added.
Paragraph XIV-a: Repealed.

—1997. Paragraphs XVIII–XX: Added.

—1991. Paragraph XIV: Added "and smokeless tobacco" following "cigarettes".
Paragraph XIV-a: Added.

—1981. Paragraph III: Inserted "means" following "manufacturer", "importing, exporting, producing, or" preceding "manufacturing" and "who sells his product only to licensed wholesalers" following "products".
Paragraphs V, VII and IX: Rewritten to the extent that a detailed comparison would be impracticable.
Paragraph XI: Deleted "thereof" following "consumers" and added "and any vending machine in which tobacco products are sold".
Paragraph XVI: Repealed.
Paragraph XVII: Added.

—1977. Paragraph III: Deleted "in this state" preceding "engaged".

—1975. Rewrote par. XIV and repealed par. XV.

—1973. Paragraph I: Rewritten to the extent that a detailed comparison would be impracticable.

—1970. Paragraph XV: Inserted "but which shall exclude any federal tax thereon excepting the federal tax thereon on the effective date of this paragraph as last amended" following "commission" in the first sentence.

Severability of enactment.
1947, 133 was subject to a severability clause. See 1947, 133:15.

Severability of 2003 amendments.
2003, 152:4, eff. Jan. 1, 2004, provided: "If a court of competent jurisdiction finds that the provisions of this act [which enacted RSA 541-D, and amended this section, RSA 21-J:14, RSA 78:7, and 78:7-c], and of RSA 541-C conflict and cannot be harmonized, then such provisions of RSA 541-C shall control. If any provision of this act causes RSA 541-C to no longer constitute a qualifying or model

statute, as those terms are defined in the Master Settlement Agreement, then that portion of this act shall not be valid. If any provision of this act is for any reason held to be invalid, unlawful, or unconstitutional, such decision shall not affect the validity of the remaining provisions of this act."

NOTES TO DECISIONS

1. Chain organizations
2. Tobacco products

1. Chain organizations

The separate stores or vending machines of a chain organization are properly classed as retail outlets each of which requires a dealer's license. Havens v. Attorney Gen., 91 N.H. 115, 14 A.2d 636, 1940 N.H. LEXIS 32 (1940).

2. Tobacco products

Whether the legislature in imposing a tax upon the sale of tobacco products may exempt therefrom any tax upon the sale of cigars, doubted. Opinion of Justices, 97 N.H. 543, 81 A.2d 851, 1951 N.H. LEXIS 63 (1951).

A statutory exemption of tobacco used for insecticides and other agricultural purposes is not unreasonable. Havens v. Attorney Gen., 91 N.H. 115, 14 A.2d 636, 1940 N.H. LEXIS 32 (1940).

Cited:

Cited in State v. 483 Cases, 98 N.H. 180, 96 A.2d 568, 1953 N.H. LEXIS 44 (1953).

78:2. Licenses.

I. Each manufacturer, wholesaler, and sub-jobber shall secure a license from the commissioner before engaging in the business of selling or distributing tobacco products in this state or continuing to engage in such business. Each wholesale and sub-job outlet shall have a separate license regardless of the fact that one or more outlets may be owned or controlled by a single person. The commissioner shall issue a license upon application stating such information necessary to identify the outlet and the character of business transacted. The fees for licenses shall be: $100 for a manufacturer's license; $250 for a wholesaler's license; and $150 for a sub-jobber's license, for the purpose of helping to pay the cost of administering this chapter. Each license shall be prominently displayed on the premises described in it. Any person who shall sell, offer for sale or possess with intent to sell any tobacco products without such license as provided in this section or under RSA 178 shall be subject to the penalty provisions of RSA 21-J:39.

II. Notwithstanding RSA 21-J:14, information regarding licenses issued pursuant to this section and information regarding enforcement actions taken pursuant to this chapter and RSA 126-K shall be public records.

Source.

1939, 167:2. RL 79:2. 1947, 133:2. RSA 78:2. 1973, 531:156; 544:9. 1975, 439:33. 1977, 563:53. 1981, 210:7. 1991, 163:23. 1993, 114:1, eff. Jan. 1, 1994. 1995, 259:1, eff. Aug. 18, 1995. 1997, 338:2, 3, eff. Jan. 1, 1998. 2008, 341:1, eff. January 1, 2009.

Amendments

—2008. The 2008 amendment rewrote the section to the extent that a detailed comparison would be impracticable.

—1997. Paragraph I: Substituted "operator, retailer, and sampler" for "operator and retailer" following "vending machine" and inserted "or distributing" preceding "tobacco products" in the first sentence, and "$10 for a sampler's license; and $10 for each vending machine location" following "retailer's license"and made a minor stylistic change in the sixth sentence.

Paragraph I-a: Inserted "and information regarding enforcement actions taken pursuant to this chapter and RSA 126-I" following "section" and substituted "records" for "record" following "public".

Paragraph I-b: Added.

—1995. Paragraph I-a: Added.

—1993. Paragraph I: In the sixth sentence, substituted "$100" for "$50", "$250" for "$125", "$150" for "$75", "$70" for "$35" and "$10" for "$5".

—1991. Paragraph I: Substituted "subject to the penalty provisions of RSA 21-J:39" for "guilty of a violation for the first offense" following "section shall be" in the eighth sentence and deleted the ninth sentence.

—1981. Rewritten to the extent that a detailed comparison would be impracticable.

—1977. Increased fees in fifth sentence.

—1975. Substituted "two dollars" for "one dollar" preceding "for a retailer's" in the fifth sentence.

—1973. Chapter 544 substituted "commissioner" for "commission" preceding "before engaging" in the first sentence, and in two places in the third sentence and in two places in the fourth sentence.

Chapter 531 substituted "guilty of a violation for the first offense" for "fined not more than twenty-five dollars for the first offense and not less than twenty-five dollars and not more than two hundred dollars for each subsequent offense" following "provided shall be" in the seventh sentence and added the eighth sentence.

Severability of enactment.

1977, 563:53 was subject to a severability clause. See 1977, 563:100.

Cross References.

Classification of crimes, see RSA 625:9.
Revocation of license, see RSA 78:6.
Sentences, see RSA 651.
Term and renewal of license, see RSA 78:4.

NOTES TO DECISIONS

Fee

The registration of dealers is properly required as essential to the proper administration of the law, and the fee therefor, which covers hardly more than expense involved, is not a tax. Havens v. Attorney Gen., 91 N.H. 115, 14 A.2d 636, 1940 N.H. LEXIS 32 (1940).

Cited:

Cited in State v. 483 Cases, 98 N.H. 180, 96 A.2d 568, 1953 N.H. LEXIS 44 (1953).

78:3. Tampering with Seal.

[Repealed 2008, 341:19, I, eff. January 1, 2009.]

Former section(s).

Former RSA 78:3, which was derived from 1947, 238:2; RSA 78:3; 1973, 531:157, 544:9; 1977, 563:54; and 1981, 210:8, related to tampering with vending machine seal.

78:4. Term of License; Renewals.

Licenses issued under RSA 78:2 shall expire on June 30 in each even-numbered year, unless sooner revoked or unless the business in respect to which the license was issued should change ownership. Licenses may be renewed upon signed application as provided in RSA 78:2 and upon paying the prescribed fee, provided that a license shall not be renewed if there are unpaid fees, fines, or penalties resulting from violations of this chapter or RSA 126-K attributable to the license or the licensee.

Source.
1939, 167:3; 180:1. RL 79:3. 1947, 133:3. RSA 78:4. 1973, 544:9. 1981, 210:9. 1993, 114:2, eff. Jan. 1, 1994. 1997, 338:4, eff. Jan. 1, 1998. 2008, 341:2, eff. January 1, 2009.

Amendments
—2008. The 2008 amendment substituted "RSA 126-K" for "RSA 126-I" in the second sentence.

—1997. Added the proviso in the second sentence.

—1993. Substituted "in each even-numbered year" for "following the date of issuance" following "June 30" in the first sentence.

—1981. Substituted "under RSA 78:2" for "hereunder" and "June 30 following" for "June thirtieth next succeeding" in the first sentence and "RSA 78:2 and upon paying the prescribed fee" for "section 2 and paying fee therein prescribed" in the second sentence and deleted the former third sentence.

—1973. Substituted "commissioner" for "commission" in two places in the third sentence.

78:5. Unclassified Importers.

[Repealed 1981, 210:25, eff. July 1, 1981.]

Former section(s).
Former RSA 78:5, relating to expiration and renewal of unclassified importers' licenses, was derived from 1947, 238:3; RSA 78:5; and 1973, 544:9.

78:6. Suspension and Revocation of License by Commissioner.

The commissioner may adopt rules pursuant to RSA 541-A relative to establishing procedures and criteria for tobacco license applications, tobacco enforcement penalties, and tobacco hearings for new licenses and renewals of licenses. The commissioner may suspend or revoke any license issued under RSA 78:2 for failure to comply with the provisions of this chapter and with any rules which the commissioner may adopt. The commissioner shall suspend or revoke any license issued under RSA 78:2 if ordered to do so pursuant to RSA 126-K.

Source.
1939, 167:4. RL 79:4. 1947, 133:4. RSA 78:6. 1973, 544:9. 1981, 210:10, eff. July 1, 1981. 1997, 338:5, eff. Jan. 1, 1998. 2008, 341:3, eff. January 1, 2009.

Amendments
—2008. The 2008 amendment in the first sentence, substituted "establishing procedures and criteria for tobacco license applications, tobacco enforcement penalties, and tobacco hearings for new licenses and renewals of licenses" for "accomplishing the purpose of RSA 78" and in the third sentence, substituted "RSA 126-K" for "RSA 126-I" at the end.

—1997. Added "suspension and" preceding "revocation" in the section catchline, inserted "suspend or" preceding "revoke" in the second sentence, and added the third sentence.

—1981. Inserted "by Commissioner" following "License" in the section catchline, added the first sentence and substituted "under RSA 78:2" for "hereunder" and "this chapter and with any rules which the commissioner may adopt" for "sections 1 through 18 and lawful rules and regulations established thereunder" following "provisions of" in the second sentence.

—1973. Substituted "commissioner" for "commission" preceding "may revoke".

RESEARCH REFERENCES

New Hampshire Code of Administrative Rules.
Rules of the Department of Revenue Administration, Rev. 207.05, New Hampshire Code of Administrative Rules Annotated.
Rules of the Department of Revenue Administration, Rev 207.05, New Hampshire Code of Administrative Rules Annotated.

78:6-a. Denial of License Application.

I. The commissioner shall deny a license application for tobacco manufacturer, wholesaler, sub-jobber, vending machine operator, retailer, or sampler for any one of the following reasons:

(a) The license of the applicant has been previously revoked by the commissioner under RSA 78:6.

(b) The commissioner has reason to believe that the application is filed by a person as a subterfuge for the real person in interest whose license has been previously revoked by the commissioner under RSA 78:6.

(c) The applicant fails to provide security, as required under RSA 78:9, for stamps purchased on credit.

(d) Any tax payable under this chapter has been finally determined to be due from the applicant and has not been paid in full.

(e) The applicant has been convicted of a crime provided for in this chapter, or in any other state for a crime related to tobacco tax, within one year from the date on which such application is filed.

II. The commissioner shall notify the applicant of a denied application, in writing.

III. A license applicant aggrieved by the denial of a license may petition for redetermination or reconsideration within 60 days after issuance of the notice of denial pursuant to the procedures provided under RSA 21-J:28-b.

Source.
2008, 80:1, eff. July 20, 2008.

78:7. Tax Imposed.

A tax upon the retail consumer is hereby imposed at the rate of $1.78 for each package containing 20 cigarettes or at a rate proportional to such rate for packages containing more or less than 20 cigarettes, on all cigarettes sold at retail in this state. The payment of the tax shall be evidenced by affixing stamps to the smallest packages containing the cigarettes in which such products usually are sold at retail. The word "package" as used in this section shall not include individual cigarettes. No tax is imposed on any transactions, the taxation of which by this state is prohibited by the Constitution of the United States.

Source.

1939, 167:5; 180:1. RL 79:5. 1947, 238:4. RSA 78:7. 1955, 256:1. 1965, 132:1. 1967, 159:1. 1970, 5:10. 1971, 475:1. 1973, 530:3; 544:9. 1975, 466:3. 1981, 210:11. 1983, 469:103. 1985, 396:1. 1986, 75:1. 1989, 336:1. 1990, 5:1, eff. Feb. 20, 1990. 1997, 351:57, eff. July 1, 1997. 1999, 183:1, eff. July 6, 1999. 2003, 152:6, eff. July 1, 2003. 2005, 177:56, eff. July 1, 2005. 2007, 263:6, eff. July 1, 2007. 2008, 296:15, eff. October 15, 2008. 2009, 144:2, eff. July 1, 2009. 2011, 224:377, eff. July 1, 2011; 224:379, eff. July 15, 2013.

Amendments

—2011. The 2011 amendment by 224:377, substituted "$1.68" for "$1.78" in the first sentence.

The 2011 amendment by 224:379, substituted "$1.78" for "$1.68" in the first sentence.

—2009. The 2009 amendment substituted "$1.78" for "$1.33" in the first sentence.

—2008. The 2008 amendment substituted "rate of $1.33" for "rate of $1.08" in the first sentence.

—2007. Substituted "$1.08" for "$.80" preceding "for each" in the first sentence.

—2005. Substituted "$.80" for "52 cents" in the first sentence.

—2003. Substituted "cigarettes" for "tobacco products" in the first and second sentences.

—1999. Substituted "52 cents" for "37 cents" in the first sentence.

—1997. Substituted "37 cents" for "25 cents" following "rate of" in the first sentence.

—1990. Substituted "25" for "21" preceding "cents" in the first sentence.

—1989. Substituted "21" for "17" preceding "cents" in the first sentence.

—1986. Rewritten to the extent that a detailed comparison would be impracticable.

—1985. Designated the existing provisions of the section as par. I and added par. II.

—1983. Added the proviso at the end of the first sentence.

—1981. Rewritten to the extent that a detailed comparison would be impracticable.

—1975. Rewritten to the extent that a detailed comparison would be impracticable.

—1973. Chapter 544 substituted "commissioner" for "tax commission" following "notify the" in the third sentence, preceding "thereupon" in the fourth sentence and preceding "shall be" in the sixth sentence.

Chapter 530 substituted "guilty of a misdemeanor if a natural person, or guilty of a felony if any other person" for "subject to a fine of not less than twenty-five dollars or more than one hundred dollars" following "shall be" in the sixth sentence.

—1971. Substituted "forty-two" for "thirty-four" preceding "per cent" in the first and fourth sentences.

—1970. Substituted "thirty-four" for "thirty" preceding "per cent" in the first and fourth sentences.

—1967. Substituted "thirty" for "twenty-one" preceding "per cent" in the first and fourth sentences.

—1965. Substituted "twenty-one" for "fifteen" preceding "per cent" in the first and fourth sentences.

—1955. Inserted "upon the retail consumer" following "tax" in the first sentence and made a minor stylistic change in the second sentence.

Contingent 2011 amendment; Reporting of Tobacco Revenue.

2011, 224:381, eff. July 1, 2011, provided: "On or before July 15, 2013, the department of revenue administration shall report to the speaker of the house of representatives, the senate president, the fiscal committee of the general court, the secretary of state, and the director of the office of legislative services, the amount of tobacco tax revenue received, as reported in the department's daily cash basis revenue report, for the period of July 1, 2011 through June 30, 2013. If the department reports that the amount of tobacco tax revenue received for the period was below the amounts received for the period of July 1, 2009 through June 30, 2011, then sections 379 and 380 of this act shall take effect on August 1, 2013. If the department reports that the amount of tobacco tax revenue received for the period was equal to or above the amount received for the period of July 1, 2009 through June 30, 2011, then sections 379 and 380 of this act shall not take effect."

Severability of 2003 amendments.

2003, 152:4, eff. Jan. 1, 2004, provided: "If a court of competent jurisdiction finds that the provisions of this act [which enacted RSA 541-D, and amended this section, RSA 21-J:14, RSA 78:1, and 78:7-c], and of RSA 541-C conflict and cannot be harmonized, then such provisions of RSA 541-C shall control. If any provision of this act causes RSA 541-C to no longer constitute a qualifying or model statute, as those terms are defined in the Master Settlement Agreement, then that portion of this act shall not be valid. If any provision of this act is for any reason held to be invalid, unlawful, or unconstitutional, such decision shall not affect the validity of the remaining provisions of this act."

Tobacco Tax; Applicability of 2009 amendment.

2009, 144:3, eff. July 1, 2009, provided: "Section 2 [which amended this section] of this act shall apply to all persons licensed under RSA 78:2. Such persons shall inventory all taxable tobacco products in their possession and file a report of such inventory with the department of revenue administration on a form prescribed by the commissioner within 20 days after the effective date of this act. The tax rate effective July 1, 2009 shall apply to such inventory. The inventory form shall be treated as a tax return for the purpose of computing penalties under RSA 21-J."

Applicability of 2005 amendment.

2005, 177:57, eff. July 1, 2005, provided: "Section 56 of this act [which amended this section], shall apply to all persons licensed under RSA 78:2. Such persons shall inventory all taxable tobacco products in their possession and file a report of such inventory with the department of revenue administration on a form prescribed by the commissioner within 20 days after the effective date of this act. The tax rate effective July 1, 2005 shall apply to such inventory and the difference, if any, in the amount paid previously on such inventory and the current effective rate of tax shall be paid with the inventory form. The inventory form shall be treated as a tax return for the purpose of computing penalties under RSA 21-J."

Applicability of 1999 amendment.

1999, 183:2, effective July 6, 1999, provided that section 1 of this act, which amended this section, shall apply to all persons licensed under RSA 78:2. Such persons shall inventory all taxable tobacco products in their possession and file a report of such inventory with the department of revenue administration on a form prescribed by the commissioner within 20 days after the effective date of this act. The tax rate effective July 6, 1999, shall apply to such inventory and the difference, if any, in the amount paid previously on such inventory and the current effective rate of tax shall be paid with the inventory form. The inventory form shall be treated as a tax return for the purpose of computing penalties under RSA 21-J.

Applicability of 1997 amendment.

1997, 351:58, eff. July 1, 1997, provided: "Section 57 of this act [which amended this section], shall apply to all persons licensed under RSA 78:2. Such persons shall inventory all taxable tobacco products in their possession and file a report of such inventory with the department of revenue administration on a form prescribed by the commissioner within 20 days after July 1, 1997. The tax rate effective July 1, 1997, shall apply to such inventory and the difference, if any, in the amount paid previously on such inventory and the current effective rate of tax shall be paid with the inventory form. The inventory form shall be treated as a tax return for the purpose of computing penalties under RSA 21-J."

Applicability of cigarette tax.

1999, 17:56, effective April 29, 1999, provided: "Any increase in the cigarette tax rate in RSA 78:7 over 37 cents adopted and enacted by any act of the 1999 general court shall apply to all persons licensed under RSA 78:2. Such persons shall inventory all taxable tobacco products in their possession and file a report of such inventory with the department of revenue administration on a form prescribed by the commissioner within 20 days after the effective date of the tax rate increase. The tax rate increase shall apply to such inventory and the difference, if any, in the amount paid previously on such inventory and the current effective rate of tax shall be paid with the inventory form. The inventory form shall be treated as a tax return for the purpose of computing penalties under RSA 21-J."

Tobacco Tax; Applicability of 2008 amendment.

2008, 296:16, eff. June 27, 2008, provided: "Section 15 of this act [which amended RSA 78:7] shall apply to all persons licensed under RSA 78:2. Such persons shall inventory all taxable tobacco products in their possession and file a report of such inventory with the department of revenue administration on a form prescribed by the commissioner within 20 days after the effective date of this section. The tax rate effective on the date of certification from the commissioner of the department of revenue administration that the amount of tobacco tax revenue for the period of July 1, 2008 through September 30, 2008 was below $50,000,000, shall apply to such inventory. The inventory form shall be treated as a tax return for the purpose of computing penalties under RSA 21-J. Payment of the additional tax on said inventory shall be due 60 days from the effective date of this section, accompanied by a form prescribed by the department of revenue administration."

Contingent 2008 amendment; Reporting of Tobacco Revenue.

2008, 296:17, eff. June 27, 2008, provided: "On or before October 15, 2008, the commissioner of the department of revenue administration shall certify to the speaker of the house of representatives, the senate president, and the fiscal committee of the general court, the amount of tobacco tax revenue received for the period of July 1, 2008 through September 30, 2008, without any material change in cigarette tax stamp inventory. If the commissioner certifies that the amount of tobacco tax revenue received for the period was below $50,000,000, then sections 15 and 16 of this act shall take effect on the date of certification. If the commissioner certifies that the amount of tobacco tax revenue received for the period was equal to or above $50,000,000, then sections 15 and 16 of this act shall not take effect."

On October 15, 2008, the commissioner of the department of revenue administration certified that the amount of tobacco tax revenue for the period of July 1, 2008 through September 30, 2008 was below $50,000,000 and therefore, 2008, 296:15 and 16 took effect October 15, 2008.

Tobacco Tax; Applicability of 2007 amendment.

2007, 263:7, eff. July 1, 2007, provided: "Section 6 of this act [which amended this section] shall apply to all persons licensed under RSA 78:2. Such persons shall inventory all taxable tobacco products in their possession and file a report of such inventory with the department of revenue administration on a form prescribed by the commissioner within 20 days after the effective date of this act. The tax rate effective July 1, 2007 shall apply to such inventory. The inventory form shall be treated as a tax return for the purpose of computing penalties under RSA 21-J."

NOTES TO DECISIONS

Cited:
Cited in Havens v. Attorney Gen., 91 N.H. 115, 14 A.2d 636, 1940 N.H. LEXIS 32 (1940); State v. 483 Cases, 98 N.H. 180, 96 A.2d 568,

1953 N.H. LEXIS 44 (1953); Opinion of Justices, 99 N.H. 517, 113 A.2d 119, 1955 N.H. LEXIS 65 (1955).

RESEARCH REFERENCES

New Hampshire Practice.
16-6 N.H.P. Municipal Law & Taxation § 6.13.

78:7-a. Nature of Tax.

All taxes upon tobacco products under this chapter are declared to be a direct tax upon the consumer at retail and shall conclusively be presumed to be pre-collected for the purpose of convenience and facility only. Accordingly, the commissioner may collect the tax directly from consumers who purchase unstamped tobacco products.

Source.
1955, 256:2, eff. July 14, 1955. 2008, 341:20, eff. September 5, 2008.

Amendments
—**2008.** The 2008 amendment added the second sentence.

78:7-b. Exemption.

Notwithstanding the provisions of RSA 78, no state tax shall be imposed on tobacco products sold at the New Hampshire veterans' home to residents of said home; provided, that no such resident shall be permitted to purchase more than 2 such tax exempt cartons of cigarettes in any one week.

Source.
1971, 376:1. 1975, 466:5, eff. July 1, 1975.

Amendments
—**1975.** Substituted "New Hampshire veterans' home" for "New Hampshire soldiers' home" and deleted "or equivalent products" following "cigarettes".

78:7-c. Tax Imposed on Tobacco Products Other Than Cigarettes.

A tax upon the retail consumer is hereby imposed on tobacco products other than cigarettes at a rate of 65.03 percent of the wholesale sales price. The tax under this section may be rounded to the nearest cent if the commissioner determines that the amount of tax would not thereby be made materially disproportionate. No such tax is imposed on any transactions, the taxation of which by this state is prohibited by the Constitution of the United States. No such tax shall be imposed on premium cigars.

Source.
1991, 292:3, eff. July 1, 1991. 2003, 152:7, eff. July 1, 2003. 2009, 144:179, eff. July 1, 2009. 2010S, 1:45, eff. June 10, 2010. 2011, 224:378, eff. July 1, 2011; 224:380, eff. July 15, 2013.

Amendments
—**2011.** The 2011 amendment by Chapter 224:378, substituted "48 percent" for "65.03 percent" in the first sentence.
The 2011 amendment by Chapter 224:380, substituted "65.03 percent" for "48 percent" in the first sentence.

—**2010.** The 2010 amendment substituted "65.03 percent" for "48.59 percent" in the first sentence.

—2009. The 2009 amendment substituted "rate of 48.59 percent" for "rate of 19 percent" in the first sentence and added the last sentence.

—2003. Substituted "of 19 percent of the wholesale sales price" for "proportional to the cigarette tax, having such ratio to the usual wholesale price of the tobacco product other than cigarettes as the cigarette tax bears to the usual wholesale price of the cigarettes" in the first sentence.

Contingent 2011 amendment; Reporting of Tobacco Revenue.
2011, 224:381, eff. July 1, 2011, provided: "On or before July 15, 2013, the department of revenue administration shall report to the speaker of the house of representatives, the senate president, the fiscal committee of the general court, the secretary of state, and the director of the office of legislative services, the amount of tobacco tax revenue received, as reported in the department's daily cash basis revenue report, for the period of July 1, 2011 through June 30, 2013. If the department reports that the amount of tobacco tax revenue received for the period was below the amounts received for the period of July 1, 2009 through June 30, 2011, then sections 379 and 380 of this act shall take effect on August 1, 2013. If the department reports that the amount of tobacco tax revenue received for the period was equal to or above the amount received for the period of July 1, 2009 through June 30, 2011, then sections 379 and 380 of this act shall not take effect."

Severability of 2003 amendments.
2003, 152:4, eff. Jan. 1, 2004, provided: "If a court of competent jurisdiction finds that the provisions of this act [which enacted RSA 541-D, and amended this section, RSA 21-J:14, RSA 78:1, and 78:7], and of RSA 541-C conflict and cannot be harmonized, then such provisions of RSA 541-C shall control. If any provision of this act causes RSA 541-C to no longer constitute a qualifying or model statute, as those terms are defined in the Master Settlement Agreement, then that portion of this act shall not be valid. If any provision of this act is for any reason held to be invalid, unlawful, or unconstitutional, such decision shall not affect the validity of the remaining provisions of this act."

78:8. Stock-in-Trade Tax.

[Repealed 1971, 363:12, eff. June 28, 1971.]

Former section(s).
Former RSA 78:8, relating to tax on stock-in-trade, was derived from 1939, 167:6; RL 79:6; and 1947, 133:5.

78:9. Stamps.

I. The commissioner shall adopt rules pursuant to RSA 541-A relative to the design and denomination of stamps to be secured by the commissioner for affixing to packages of tobacco products as evidence of the payment of the tax imposed by this chapter. The commissioner shall sell such stamps to each licensed wholesaler. The commissioner may permit a licensed wholesaler to pay for such stamps within 30 days after the date of purchase, provided a bond satisfactory to the commissioner in an amount not less than the sale price of such stamps shall have been filed with the commissioner, conditioned upon the payment of such stamps. The commissioner shall keep accurate records of all stamps sold to each wholesaler and shall pay over all receipts from the sale of such stamps to the state treasurer daily.

II. Any wholesaler who fails to pay any amount owing to the purchase of stamps or meter-registered settings within the time required shall pay, in addition to the amount, interest as prescribed in RSA 21-J:28.

III. At the sole discretion of the commissioner, the commissioner may place a lien on property of the licensed wholesaler in lieu of the bond requirement under paragraph I, provided that:

(a) The licensed wholesaler submits a written request for the lien and detailed proposal acceptable to the commissioner; and

(b) The property on which the proposed lien shall be placed is of adequate value, marketability, and liquidity to protect the state's interests to the same degree or greater than a bond.

Source.
1939, 167:7; 180:1. RL 79:7. 1947, 133:6. RSA 78:9. 1965, 132:2. 1967, 159:2. 1970, 5:11; 57:1. 1973, 544:9. 1975, 505:26. 1976, 49:1. 1977, 200:2. 1981, 128:20; 210:12; 465:6. 1982, 42:100. 1983, 441:6. 1985, 204:13. 2003, 319:43, eff. July 1, 2003. 2007, 263:43, eff. July 1, 2007.

Amendments
—2007. Paragraph III: Added.

—2003. Paragraph I: Substituted "the commissioner" for "him" in the first sentence, deleted "on a cash basis" following "sell such stamps" and "at a discount of 2 ¾ percent up to the first $500,000, 2 ⅜ percent from $500,001 to $1,000,000 and 2 percent for all sales in excess of $1,000,000 of their face value on an annual basis from July 1 to June 30 to encourage each wholesaler to affix such stamps and compensate them for so doing" following "wholesaler" in the second sentence and "in his discretion" preceding "permit a licensed" in the third sentence.

—1985. Paragraph II: Substituted "as prescribed in RSA 21-J:28" for "at the rate of 1-¼ percent per month from the date on which the amount becomes due and payable until the date of payment" following "interest".

—1983. Paragraph II: Substituted "of 1-¼ percent per month" for "determined by the commissioner under RSA 71-A:11, XIII" following "rate".

—1982. Paragraph II: Substituted "determined by the commissioner under RSA 71-A:11, XIII" for "of 1-½ percent per month" following "rate".

—1981. Paragraph I: Chapter 128 rewrote the first sentence.
Chapter 210 inserted "on a cash basis" following "stamps" and deleted "manufacturer" preceding "wholesaler" and "or sub-jobber" thereafter in two places in the second sentence and "and to licensed vending machine operators and retailers at their face value" following "doing" in that sentence, and deleted "manufacturer" preceding "wholesaler" and "sub-jobber, vending machine operator or retailer" thereafter in the third and fourth sentences.
Paragraph II: Chapter 210 deleted "manufacturer" preceding "wholesaler" and "sub-jobber, vending machine operator or retailer" thereafter.
Chapter 465 substituted "1-½ percent" for "1 percent".

—1977. Designated the existing provisions of the section as par. I and added par. II.

—1976. Substituted "wholesaler or sub-jobber at a discount of 2-¾ per cent up to the first $500,000, 2-¾ per cent from $500,001 to $1,000,000 and 2 per cent for all sales in excess of $1,000,000 of their face value on an annual basis from July 1 to June 30" for "wholesalers and sub-jobbers at a discount of two percent of their face value" preceding "to encourage" in the second sentence.

—1975. Substituted "two" for "three and one-half" preceding "percent" in the second sentence.

—1973. Substituted "commissioner" for "tax commission" preceding "shall secure" in the first sentence, preceding "may in its" in the third sentence and preceding "shall keep" in the fourth sentence and substituted "commissioner" for "commission" preceding "conditioned" in the third sentence and made minor changes in phraseology throughout the section.

—1970. Chapter 5 substituted "three" for "three and one-half" preceding "percent" in the second sentence.

Chapter 57 substituted "three and one-half" for "three" preceding "percent" in the second sentence.

—1967. Substituted "three and one-half" for "four" preceding "per cent" in the second sentence.

—1965. Substituted "four" for "five" preceding "per cent" in the second sentence.

Effective date of 1985 amendment

1985, 204:24, provided that 1985, 204:13, would take effect when the reorganized department of revenue administration became operational on the date set according to 1983, 372:5, II. Pursuant to 1983, 372:5, II, the joint committee on implementation of reorganization and the governor determined the effective date upon which the department became operational to be Jan. 1, 1986.

NOTES TO DECISIONS

Discount

The provision of this section allowing the distributor a discount on the purchase of stamps is not discriminatory, but sustainable as a means of preventing tax evasions. Havens v. Attorney Gen., 91 N.H. 115, 14 A.2d 636, 1940 N.H. LEXIS 32 (1940).

Cited:

Cited in State v. 483 Cases, 98 N.H. 180, 96 A.2d 568, 1953 N.H. LEXIS 44 (1953).

78:9-a. Compensation for Collecting and Remitting Tax.

[Repealed 2003, 319:44, eff. July 1, 2003.]

Former section(s).

Former RSA 78:9-a, which was derived from 1991, 292:4, related to compensation for collecting and remitting tax.

78:10. Resale of Stamps; Redemption.

No wholesaler shall sell or transfer any stamps issued under RSA 78:9. The commissioner shall redeem any unused, uncancelled stamps presented by any licensed wholesaler at a price equal to the amount paid by such licensee. In case such stamps are destroyed before they are affixed, the commissioner shall refund the purchase price upon presentation of evidence of such destruction satisfactory to the commissioner. The commissioner shall refund the purchase price for stamps and metered impressions which are destroyed after affixing to outdated, damaged, or unsaleable tobacco products. The commissioner also shall refund or provide a credit for future tax payments on outdated, damaged, or unsaleable tobacco products exempted from bearing stamps by the commissioner under rules adopted under RSA 541-A. The state treasurer shall provide, out of money collected under this chapter, the funds necessary for redemption or refund.

Source.

1939, 167:9; 180:1. RL 79:9. 1947, 6:1; 133:8. RSA 78:10. 1981, 210:13. 1987, 106:1. 1992, 13:8, eff. May 19, 1992.

Amendments
—1992. Added the fifth sentence.

—1987. Rewrote the fourth sentence.

—1981. Deleted "manufacturer" preceding "wholesaler" and "sub-jobber, vending machine operator or retailer" thereafter in the first and second sentences, substituted "RSA 78:9" for "the provisions hereof" in the first sentence, deleted "therefor" following "paid" in the second sentence, rewrote the third sentence as the new third and fourth sentences and substituted "under this chapter" for "hereunder" following "collected" in the fifth sentence.

OPINIONS OF THE ATTORNEY GENERAL

Refunds

Practice of department of revenue administration to give tobacco refunds to wholesalers for the tax value of stamped products returned to manufacturers for destruction was unauthorized by statute. 1986 Op. Att'y Gen. 146.

78:11. Metering Machines.

The commissioner shall adopt rules pursuant to RSA 541-A relative to the authorization of any licensee to use a metering machine in lieu of stamps and the insuring of the payment of all taxes properly due under RSA 78. The commissioner shall not permit the use of any such machine until prepayment covering the cost of the tax less discount, for which the meter is set, shall have been made or unless a bond satisfactory to the commissioner shall have been filed, conditioned upon the payment of said amount. Cash may be used as security in place of surety bond.

Source.

1939, 167:8; 180:1. RL 79:8. 1947, 133:7. RSA 78:11. 1973, 544:9. 1981, 128:21, eff. May 11, 1981; 210:14, eff. July 1, 1981.

Amendments
—1981. Chapter 128 rewrote the first sentence and made a minor change in punctuation in the fourth sentence.

Chapter 210 deleted "if any" following "discount" in the second sentence and deleted the former fourth sentence.

—1973. Substituted "commissioner" for "commission" preceding "may authorize" in the first sentence and in two places in the second sentence.

78:12. Affixing Stamps.

I. The commissioner shall adopt rules pursuant to RSA 541-A relative to the affixing of stamps to each package or tobacco products sold or distributed by a licensed wholesaler. At any time before tobacco products are transferred out of the possession of a licensed wholesaler, stamps shall be affixed, at the location for which the license is issued, to each package of tobacco products sold or distributed.

II. The commissioner is authorized to exempt such tobacco products other than cigarettes from the requirement of affixing stamps to their packages under paragraph I, as to which he finds that the affixing of stamps is physically impractical due to the size or nature of the package or that the cost of affixing the stamps is unreasonably disproportionate to the tax revenue to be collected. In lieu of stamps, the commissioner may, by rules adopted under RSA 541-A, require the submission of periodic returns to the commissioner by wholesalers thereof exempted under this paragraph, setting forth the total amount of such unstamped tobacco products distributed and transmitting payment of the tax due under this chapter.

III. Any person who violates the provisions of this section by failing to file the returns and to pay the taxes due shall be guilty of a felony.

Source.
1939, 167:11, 12. RL 79:11, 12. 1947, 133:10. RSA 78:12. 1973, 544:9. 1981, 128:22; 210:15. 1991, 292:5, eff. July 1, 1991. 2011, 27:1, eff. June 27, 2011.

Amendments
—2011. The 2011 amendment substituted "returns" for "reports" in the second sentence of II and in III and substituted "file" for "make" in III.

—1991. Designated the existing provisions of the section as par. I, deleted the third sentence of that paragraph and added pars. II and III.

—1981. Rewritten by chs. 128 and 210 to the extent that a detailed comparison would be impracticable.

Cross References.
Classification of crimes, see RSA 625:9.
Sentences, see RSA 651.

NOTES TO DECISIONS

Cited:
Cited in State v. 483 Cases, 98 N.H. 180, 96 A.2d 568, 1953 N.H. LEXIS 44 (1953).

78:12-a. Unauthorized Sales.

Manufacturers, wholesalers, and sub-jobbers shall not sell tobacco products to any licensee who does not possess a valid or current license issued by the commissioner or issued by the liquor commission under RSA 178. Any person who violates the provisions of this section shall be subject to the penalty provisions of RSA 21-J:39.

Source.
1981, 210:16. 1991, 163:24, eff. May 27, 1991. 2008, 341:4, eff. January 1, 2009.

Amendments
—2008. The 2008 amendment added "or issued by the liquor commission under RSA 178" at the end of the first sentence.

—1991. Substituted "subject to the penalty provisions of RSA 21-J:39" for "guilty of a misdemeanor" at the end of the second sentence.

Cross References.
Classification of crimes, see RSA 625:9.
Sentences, see RSA 651.

78:12-b. Sale and Distribution of Tobacco Products to Persons Under 18 Years of Age Prohibited.

[Repealed 1997, 338:9, I, eff. Jan. 1, 1998.]

Former section(s).
Former RSA 78:12-b, relating to prohibition of the sale and

distribution of tobacco products to persons under 18 years of age, was derived from 1986, 162:2; 1991, 292:9; and 1995, 259:2, 3.

78:12-c. Possession of Tobacco by Persons Under 18 Years of Age and Misrepresentation of Age for the Purpose of Procuring Tobacco Products.

[Repealed 1997, 338:9, II, eff. Jan. 1, 1998.]

Former section(s).
Former RSA 78:12-c, relating to possession of tobacco by persons under 18 years of age and misrepresentation of age for the purpose of procuring tobacco products, was derived from 1986, 162:2 and 1995, 259:4.

78:12-d. Vending Machines.

[Repealed 341:19, II, eff. January 1, 2009.]

Former section(s).
Former RSA 78:12-d, which was derived from 1995, 259:5; 1997, 338:7; 2000, 303:4; and 2001, 280:4, related to tobacco vending machines.

78:12-e. Access and Dissemination of Information Required.

I. For the purpose of protecting the public health, the commissioner of the department of health and human services shall obtain annually from the Commonwealth of Massachusetts Department of Public Health, or other sources if they become available, a public report containing the list of additives for each brand of tobacco products sold.

II. The department shall make available to the public any information received under paragraph I above.

Source.
1998, 165:1, eff. Aug. 14, 1998.

78:13. Authorization to Affix Stamps or Use Metering Machine.

The commissioner may adopt rules, pursuant to RSA 541-A, relative to authorizing any person resident or located outside this state and engaged in a business which would make such person if he carried it on in this state a wholesaler as defined in this chapter, to affix the stamps required by this chapter on behalf of the purchasers of such tobacco products. The commissioner may sell stamps to such person or the commissioner may authorize the use of a metering machine as provided in this chapter. No stamps shall be sold or no such authorization shall issue, however, until such nonresident person shall have appointed the secretary of state his attorney for the service of process in this state in the same manner as provided in RSA 300. Service shall be made on the secretary of state as agent of such person in the same manner as is provided in RSA 300. The commissioner may adopt rules pursuant to RSA 541-A relative to the conditions which must be met upon a grant of authorization to a nonresident to affix stamps. Such conditions shall include the right to inspect the books of the nonresident and the posting of a bond by the nonresident conditioned upon the payment of all taxes imposed under this chapter.

Source.
1939, 167:10; 180:1. RL 79:10. 1947, 133:9. RSA 78:13. 1973, 544:9. 1981, 128:23, eff. May 11, 1981; 210:17, eff. July 1, 1981.

References in text.
RSA 300, referred to in this section, was repealed by 1981, 557:2, eff. Feb. 1, 1982. The current New Hampshire Business Corporation Act provisions governing appointment of a registered agent for service on a nonresident corporation, RSA 293-A:15.07–15.10 do not provide for appointment of the secretary of state as agent.

Amendments
—1981. Chapter 128 rewrote the first sentence, deleted "chapter" preceding "300" in the third sentence, rewrote the fifth sentence and added the sixth sentence.
Chapter 210 substituted "RSA 300" for "said chapter" in the fourth sentence.

—1973. Substituted "commissioner" for "commission" preceding "shall find" in the first sentence, in two places in the second sentence and preceding "may establish" in the fifth sentence.

78:14. Unstamped Tobacco Products.

No sub-jobber, vending machine operator, or retailer, and no other person who is not licensed under the provisions of this chapter or licensed under the provisions of RSA 178, shall sell, offer for sale, display for sale, ship, store, import, transport, carry, or possess with or without intent to sell, any tobacco products not properly stamped under RSA 78:12 or 78:13, except as provided in RSA 78:12, II. This section shall not prevent any unlicensed person able to purchase unstamped tobacco products by statute from possessing such products for his or her own use or consumption, if the tax otherwise due under this chapter is paid by the unlicensed person to the department directly. The provisions of this section shall not apply to common carriers transporting unstamped tobacco products. Any person who violates the provisions of this section shall be guilty of a felony.

Source.
1939, 167:13. RL 79:13. 1947, 133:10. RSA 78:14. 1973, 528:24. 1981, 210:18. 1991, 292:6, eff. July 1, 1991. 2008, 341:5, eff. September 5, 2008.

Amendments
—2008. The 2008 amendment in the first sentence, added "or licensed under the provisions of RSA 178", in the second sentence, added "if the tax otherwise due under this chapter is paid by the unlicensed person to the department directly" at the end and made a stylistic change.

—1991. Added "except as provided in RSA 78:12, II" following "78:13" in the first sentence.

—1981. Rewritten to the extent that a detailed comparison would be impracticable.

—1973. Rewrote the third sentence.

Cross References.
Classification of crimes, see RSA 625:9.
Sentences, see RSA 651.

Cited:
Cited in 1986 Op. Att'y Gen. 225.

78:14-a. Possession of Tobacco Products of Foreign States.

Licensed wholesalers, sub-jobbers and vending machine operators may possess tobacco products bearing a foreign state's tax stamp or indicia with an intent to sell such products only if the licensee is currently and legitimately doing business in that state.

Source.
1981, 210:19, eff. July 1, 1981.

78:15. Sales Between Licensees.

[Repealed 1981, 210:26, eff. July 1, 1981.]

Former section(s).
Former RSA 78:15, relating to sale of unstamped tobacco products between licensees, was derived from 1939, 167:14; RL 79:14; and 1947, 133:11.

78:16. Seizure, Forfeiture, and Destruction of Illegal Tobacco Products.

I. Unless the tobacco products are subject to the exemption under RSA 78:12, II, tobacco products found at any place in this state without the necessary stamps affixed to them, unless they shall be in the possession of a licensed manufacturer or wholesaler, or unless they shall be in the course of transit by common carrier from a bonded warehouse and consigned to a licensed manufacturer, wholesaler or anyone exempted by statute, shall be declared to be contraband goods and subject to forfeiture to the state.
II. The commissioner, the commissioner's authorized agents, sheriffs, deputy sheriffs, and police officers shall have the power to seize such tobacco products in the manner provided under RSA 617 or by immediately seizing the contraband tobacco products and providing the owner with the opportunity to appeal the seizure through an administrative proceeding before the department. The commissioner shall adopt rules, pursuant to RSA 541-A, relative to the seizure and destruction of contraband tobacco products and the hearings procedure.

Source.
1939, 167:15. RL 79:15. 1947, 133:12; 238:5. RSA 78:16. 1973, 544:9. 1981, 210:20. 1991, 292:7, eff. July 1, 1991. 2007, 152:2, eff. August 17, 2007. 2008, 341:21, eff. September 5, 2008.

Amendments
—2008. The 2008 amendment added designation I to existing first sentence and II to existing second and third sentences; and in II, substituted "hearings" for "appeals" near the end of the second sentence.

—2007. Added "seizure" preceding "forfeiture" and added "and destruction of illegal tobacco products" thereafter in the section heading, substituted "the commissioner's" for "his" preceding "authorized" and added "or by immediately seizing the contraband tobacco products and providing the owner with the opportunity to appeal the seizure through an administrative proceeding before the department" in the second sentence, and added the third sentence.

—**1991.** Substituted "unless the tobacco products are subject to the exemption under RSA 78:2, II" for "any" preceding "tobacco products found" in the first sentence.

—**1981.** Rewritten to the extent that a detailed comparison would be impracticable.

—**1973.** Substituted "commissioner" for "tax commission" preceding "as provided".

NOTES TO DECISIONS

Application

Cigarettes imported into the state by one not shown to have had an established regular place of business in the state within the statutory definition of a wholesaler or sub-jobber and not shown to have been engaged in selling at retail or to have acquired the cigarettes for use or consumption within the state or for sale therein, are not subject to forfeiture immediately upon their arrival because unstamped. State v. 483 Cases, 98 N.H. 180, 96 A.2d 568, 1953 N.H. LEXIS 44 (1953).

OPINIONS OF THE ATTORNEY GENERAL

Cited:

Cited in 1986 Op. Att'y Gen. 225.

78:17. Fraudulent Stamps.

[Repealed 1991, 163:43, XVII, eff. May 27, 1991.]

Former section(s).

Former RSA 78:17, relating to penalty for making or using fraudulent stamps, was derived from 1939, 167:16; RL 79:16; RSA 78:17; 1973, 528:25; and 544:9. See now RSA 21-J:39.

78:18. Required Taxpayer Records.

The commissioner shall adopt rules, pursuant to RSA 541-A, relative to the form for records of all tobacco products manufactured, produced, purchased, and sold. Each manufacturer, wholesaler, sub-jobber, vending machine operator and retailer shall keep complete and accurate records of all such tobacco products. Such records shall be safely preserved for 3 years in such manner as to insure permanency and accessibility for inspection by the commissioner and the commissioner's authorized agents. The commissioner and the authorized agents may examine the books, papers and records of any manufacturer, wholesaler, sub-jobber, vending machine operator or retailer doing business in this state, for the purpose of determining whether the tax imposed by this chapter has been fully paid, and they may investigate and examine the stock of tobacco products in or upon any premises where such tobacco products are possessed, stored or sold, for the purpose of determining whether the provisions of this chapter are being obeyed. Each sampler shall keep complete and accurate records of tobacco products distributed free to consumers in New Hampshire for promotional purposes. The commis-

sioner and the commissioner's authorized agents may examine such records.

Source.

1939, 167:17. RL 79:17. 1947, 133:13. RSA 78:18. 1973, 544:9. 1981, 210:21, eff. July 1, 1981. 1997, 338:6, eff. Jan. 1, 1998.

Amendments

—**1997.** Made two minor gender neutral changes and added the fifth and sixth sentences.

—**1981.** Rewrote the section catchline, added the first sentence, inserted "such" preceding "tobacco products" and deleted "manufactured, produced, purchased and sold" thereafter in the second sentence, deleted "shall be of such kind and in such form as the commissioner may prescribe" following "records" in the third sentence, and substituted "his" for "its" preceding "authorized" in that sentence and in the fourth sentence.

—**1973.** Substituted "commissioner" for "tax commission" preceding "may prescribe" and "commissioner" for "commission" following "inspection by the" in the second sentence and preceding "and its authorized" in the third sentence and made other minor changes in phraseology.

Cross References.

Inspection of premises, see RSA 78:26.

78:18-a. Additions to Tax.

If after any examination as provided in RSA 78:18, the commissioner or his agent determines that there is a deficiency with respect to the purchase of tax indicia, the commissioner shall assess the tax and all applicable additions due the state. At the time such additional assessment is made, the commissioner shall give notice of the assessment to the person liable and make demand upon him for immediate payment.

Source.

1981, 210:22, eff. July 1, 1981.

78:19. Newspaper Advertisements.

[Repealed 1981, 210:27, eff. July 1, 1981.]

Former section(s).

Former RSA 78:19, relating to newspaper advertisements by out-of-state tobacco dealers, was derived from 1947, 238:6; RSA 78:19; 1973, 544:8; and 1975, 466:4.

78:20. State Tax.

[Repealed 1999, 17:58, I, eff. April 29, 1999.]

Former section(s).

Former RSA 78:20, relating to state tax, was derived from 1939, 18:1 and RL 79:19.

Administration

78:21. Division of Tobacco Products.

[Repealed 1975, 439:34, XII, eff. July 1, 1975.]

Former section(s).

Former RSA 78:21, relating to the division of tobacco products of the department of revenue administration, was derived from 1950, 5, part 8:4; RSA 78:21; and 1973, 544:11, XIII.

78:22. Administration by Director of Division of Tobacco Products.

[Repealed 1975, 439:34, XII, eff. July 1, 1975.]

Former section(s).

Former RSA 78:22, relating to administration of the tobacco tax by the director of the division of tobacco products, was derived from 1939, 167:18; RL 19:18; 1950, 5, part 8:5; RSA 78:22; and 1973, 544:9, 11, XIV.

78:23. Jurisdiction of Director.

[Repealed 1975, 439:5, eff. July 1, 1975.]

Former section(s).

Former RSA 78:23, relating to jurisdiction of the director of the division of tobacco products, was derived from 1947, 133:14; RSA 78:23; 1961, 172:1; 1973, 544:10; and also repealed by 1975, 466:7.

Protection of Revenue of the State

78:24. Report of Importation.

[Repealed 1981, 210:28, eff. July 1, 1981.]

Former section(s).

Former RSA 78:24, relating to reports of importation of tobacco products, was derived from 1953, 244:1, par. 1; 1973, 544:11, XV; and 1977, 200:3.

78:25. Required Records.

[Repealed 1981, 210:29, eff. July 1, 1981.]

Former section(s).

Former RSA 78:25, relating to records of imported tobacco products, was derived from 1953, 244:1; RSA 78:25; and 1973, 544:9.

78:26. Inspection Authorized.

The commissioner or any agent or employee of the department of revenue administration, and any policeman, constable, sheriff or deputy sheriff, or agent of the liquor commission may enter in and upon any place or premises where tobacco products are held, kept, located, or stored for the purpose of inspecting such products and ascertaining that the tobacco products at such premises, or any portion thereof, shall not be sold, used, or consumed in this state without the tobacco products tax first having been paid.

Source.

1953, 244:1, par. 3. RSA 78:26. 1973, 544:11, XVI. 1981, 210:23, eff. July 1, 1981. 2008, 341:6, eff. January 1, 2009.

Amendments

—2008. The 2008 amendment added "or agent of the liquor commission".

—1981. Deleted "such" following "where", substituted "such products" for "the same" preceding "and ascertaining" and "tobacco products at such premises" for "same" preceding "or any portion".

—1973. Substituted "commissioner" for "members of the state tax commission" preceding "or any agent" and "department of revenue administration" for "state tax commission".

78:27. Transportation.

[Repealed 1981, 210:30, eff. July 1, 1981.]

Former section(s).

Former RSA 78:27, relating to permits to transport tobacco products, was derived from 1953, 244:1, par. 4; RSA 78:27; and 1973, 544:10.

78:28. Exception.

[Repealed 1981, 210:31, eff. July 1, 1981.]

Former section(s).

Former RSA 78:28, relating to transportation of unstamped tobacco products by common carriers, was derived from 1953, 244;1, par. 5.

78:29. Enforcement of Provisions.

[Repealed 1981, 210:32, eff. July 1, 1981.]

Former section(s).

Former RSA 78:29, relating to enforcement of RSA 78:24–78:30, was derived from 1953, 244:1, par. 6.

78:30. Penalty.

[Repealed 1981, 210:33, eff. July 1, 1981.]

Former section(s).

Former RSA 78:30, relating to penalties for violating RSA 78:24–78:29, was derived from 1953, 244:1 and amended by 1973, 528:26.

78:31. Appeal.

[Repealed 1991, 163:43, XVIII, eff. May 27, 1991.]

Former section(s).

Former RSA 78:31, relating to appeals, was derived from 1983, 394:7. See now RSA 21-J:28-b.

78:31-a. Appeals of License Revocation or Suspension Orders and Seizure, Forfeiture, or Destruction of Illegal Tobacco Products Orders.

I. This section shall apply only to appeals of final orders regarding license revocation or suspension under RSA 78:6 and final orders regarding seizure, forfeiture, and destruction of illegal tobacco products under RSA 78:16. Proceedings regarding assessments of tax, penalties, and interest and requests for refund of tax, penalties, and interest shall be taken under RSA 21-J:28-b.

II. Within 30 days of the notice of a final order by the commissioner, the owner or licensee, as applicable, may appeal such order by written application to the board of tax and land appeals. The board of tax and land appeals shall hear the appeal de novo.

Source.

2008, 341:22, eff. September 5, 2008.

78:32. Distribution of Funds.

I. The commissioner shall determine the additional amount of revenue produced by any additional tax in excess of $1.00 for each package containing 20 cigarettes or at a rate proportional to such rate for packages containing more or less than 20 cigarettes, on all tobacco products sold at retail in this state imposed by RSA 78:7 and shall certify such amount to the state treasurer by October 1 of each year for deposit in the education trust fund established by RSA 198:39.

II. The commissioner shall make quarterly estimates of the amount of additional revenues that will be produced by such increase in tax rate for the next fiscal year and shall certify such amount to the state treasurer for deposit in the education trust fund established by RSA 198:39. Such estimates shall be certified on June 1, September 1, December 1, and March 1 of each year.

Source.
1999, 17:23, eff. April 29, 1999. 2009, 144:257, eff. July 1, 2009.

Amendments
—2009. The 2009 amendment substituted "$1.00" for "37 cents" in I.

Contingency; constitutional amendment; reenactment of laws.
1999, 17:57, eff. April 29, 1999, provided: "If voters of the state adopt an amendment to the New Hampshire Constitution which substantially relates to the role of the general court in determining the nature and means for funding public education, then the provisions of this act not relative to the education property tax shall be without effect as of July 1 following such adoption.

"If such constitutional amendment is adopted, the provisions of this act relative to the education property tax shall be without effect as of April 1 following such adoption.

"If such constitutional amendment is adopted, the rate of the real estate transfer tax in RSA 78-B:1, I shall revert to the rate imposed by section 32 of this act, unless specifically amended or repealed by an act of the legislature.

"Upon the proclamation of the adoption of such constitutional amendment, the director of legislative services is authorized to make changes to the Revised Statutes Annotated mentioned above."

Importation of Certain Tobacco Products Prohibited

78:33. Preservation of Revenues.

The general court hereby finds, determines, and declares that this subdivision is necessary for the protection of revenues to which the state is entitled under the Master Settlement Agreement between the state and the tobacco industry. The general court also finds, determines, and declares that this subdivision is necessary for the preservation of the public health and safety.

Source.
2000, 323:1, eff. Jan. 1, 2001.

78:34. Federal Requirements; Cigarettes and Other Tobacco Products; Placement of Labels; Penalty.

I. No person shall import into this state any package of tobacco products that does not comply with all federal requirements for the placement of labels, warnings, and other information on a package of tobacco products manufactured, packaged, or imported for sale, distribution or use in the United States, including but not limited to the precise warning labels specified in the Federal Cigarette Labeling and Advertising Act, 15 United States Code, section 1333.

II. No person shall knowingly sell or offer to sell a package of tobacco products or affix the stamp or imprint required by this title on a package of tobacco products unless that package of tobacco products complies with all federal tax laws, federal trademark and copyright laws, and federal laws regarding the placement of labels, warnings, or any other information upon a package of tobacco products.

III. No person shall knowingly sell or offer to sell a package of tobacco products or affix the stamp or imprint required by this title on a package of cigarettes if the package bears any mark indicating that the manufacturer did not intend the tobacco products to be sold, distributed, or used in the United States, including but not limited to labels stating "For Export Only," "U.S. Tax-Exempt," "For Use Outside U.S.," or similar wording, or if any label or language has been altered from the manufacturer's original packaging and labeling to conceal the fact that the product or package was manufactured for use outside of the United States.

IV. No person shall knowingly sell or offer to sell a package of tobacco products or affix the stamp or imprint required by this title on a package of cigarettes if the tobacco products were imported into the United States in violation of 26 United States Code, section 5754 or any other federal law, or implementing federal regulations, or if the person knows or has reason to know that the manufacturer did not intend the tobacco product to be sold, distributed, or used in the United States.

V. No person shall knowingly sell or offer to sell a package of cigarettes or affix the stamp or imprint required by this title on a package of cigarettes if there has not been submitted to the Secretary of the U.S. Department of Health and Human Services the list or lists of ingredients added to tobacco in the manufacture of such cigarettes required by the Federal Cigarette Labeling and Advertising Act, 15 United States Code, section 1335a.

VI. (a) No person shall alter the package of any tobacco product prior to sale to the ultimate consumer, so as to remove, conceal, or obscure the fact that the package was manufactured for use outside of the United States.

(b) No person shall knowingly sell or offer to sell a package of tobacco products that has been altered in violation of subparagraph (a).

VII. The penalty for violation of any provision of this section is loss of license for a period of 90 days for a first offense, loss of license for a period of one year for subsequent offenses, and a fine to be determined by the commissioner which shall not exceed $10,000.

VIII. (a) Any tobacco product or package of tobacco products found for sale at retail or wholesale at any place in this state in violation of this section shall be subject to forfeiture pursuant to RSA 78:16. Nothing in this section shall be construed to require the commissioner to confiscate packages of tobacco products in quantities of one carton or less when the commissioner has reason to believe that the owner possesses the tobacco products for personal use.

(b) Any tobacco products seized by virtue of the provisions of subparagraph (a) shall be confiscated, and the department shall cause such confiscated goods to be destroyed.

IX. This subdivision shall not apply to:

(a) Tobacco products allowed to be imported or brought into the United States for personal use; and

(b) Tobacco products sold or intended to be sold as duty-free merchandise by a duty-free sales enterprise in accordance with the provisions of 19 United States Code, section 1555(b) and any implementing regulations, provided, however, that this act shall apply to any such tobacco products that are brought back into the customs territory for resale within the customs territory.

Source.
  2000, 323:1, eff. Jan. 1, 2001.

TITLE VII

SHERIFFS, CONSTABLES, AND POLICE OFFICERS

CHAPTER 106-J

MISSING ADULTS, PERSONS WITH DEVELOPMENTAL DISABILITIES, AND SENIOR CITIZENS

SECTION
106-J:1.   Definitions.
106-J:2.   Procedures.

Missing Persons With a Developmental Disability and Missing Senior Citizen Alert Program

106-J:3.   Definitions.
106-J:4.   Program Established.
106-J:5.   Rulemaking.

Amendments
—**2009.** The 2009 amendment by 2009, 279:2, eff. July 1, 2010, added "Persons With Developmental Disabilities, and Senior Citizens" in the chapter heading.

106-J:1. Definitions.

In this chapter, "missing adult" means any person:

I. Who is 18 years of age or older;

II. Whose residence is in New Hampshire or is believed to be in New Hampshire;

III. Who has been reported to a law enforcement agency as missing; and

IV. Who falls within one of the following categories:

(a) The person is under proven physical or mental disability or is senile, thereby subjecting himself or herself or others to personal and immediate danger;

(b) The circumstances indicate that the person's physical safety may be in danger;

(c) The circumstances indicate that the person's disappearance may not have been voluntary; or

(d) The person is missing after a catastrophe.

Source.
2005, 247:3, eff. September 12, 2005.

106-J:2. Procedures.

I. Upon receiving notice of a missing adult, a law enforcement agency shall complete a missing person report by providing identifying and descriptive information about the missing adult within 72 hours to the National Crime Information Center (NCIC) for inclusion in the missing person file of its computerized database.

II. It shall be the duty of the initial investigating law enforcement agency to immediately notify the NCIC when the missing adult is located or returned.

III. The provisions of this chapter are not intended to remove the discretion of a law enforcement agency to notify the NCIC when an adult is missing under circumstances other than those specified in RSA 106-J:1, IV, when the law enforcement agency has reasonable concern for such adult's safety.

Source.
2005, 247:3, eff. September 12, 2005.

Missing Persons With a Developmental Disability and Missing Senior Citizen Alert Program

106-J:3. Definitions.

In this subdivision:

I. "Department" means the department of safety.

II. "Missing person with developmental disabilities" means a person:

(a) Whose whereabouts are unknown;

(b) Whose domicile at the time he or she is reported missing is in New Hampshire;

(c) Who has a verified developmental disability; and

(d) Whose disappearance poses a credible threat to the safety and health of himself or herself, as determined by a local law enforcement agency.

III. "Missing senior citizen" means a person:

(a) Whose whereabouts are unknown;

(b) Whose domicile at the time he or she is reported missing is in New Hampshire;

(c) Whose age at the time he or she is first reported missing is 55 years of age or older and who has a verified impaired mental condition; and

(d) Whose disappearance poses a credible threat to the safety and health of the person, as determined by a local law enforcement agency.

Source.
2009, 279:3, eff. July 1, 2010.

106-J:4. Program Established.

I. The department shall establish an alert program for missing persons with a developmental disability and missing senior citizens.

II. (a) When a local law enforcement agency receives notice that a senior citizen is missing, the agency shall require the senior citizen's family or legal guardian to provide information relative to the senior citizen's impaired mental condition. The local law enforcement agency shall follow a procedure to verify that the senior citizen is missing and has an impaired mental condition. Once the local law enforcement agency verifies that the senior citizen is missing and has a verified impaired mental condition, the local law enforcement agency shall notify the department.

(b) When a local law enforcement agency receives notice that a person with developmental disabilities is missing, the agency shall require the family, legal guardian, or service provider of the missing person with developmental disabilities to provide information relative to the person's developmental disability. The local law enforcement agency shall follow a procedure to verify the person is missing and has a developmental disability. Once the local law enforcement agency verifies the person with developmental disabilities is missing, the local law enforcement agency shall notify the department.

III. When notified by a local law enforcement agency that a senior citizen is missing and has a verified impaired mental condition or a person with developmental disabilities is missing, the department shall confirm the accuracy of the information and then issue an alert. The alert shall be sent to designated media outlets in New Hampshire. Participating radio stations, television stations, and other media outlets may issue the alert at designated intervals. The alert shall include all appropriate information from the local law enforcement agency that may assist in the safe recovery of the missing senior citizen or missing person with developmental disabilities and a statement instructing anyone with information related to the missing senior citizen or missing person with developmental disabilities to contact his or her local law enforcement agency.

IV. The alert shall be cancelled upon notification to the department that the missing senior citizen or missing person with developmental disabilities has been found or at the end of the notification period, whichever occurs first. A local law enforcement agency that locates a missing senior citizen or missing person with developmental disabilities who is the subject of an alert shall notify the department as soon as possible that the missing senior citizen or missing person with developmental disabilities has been located.

Source.
2009, 279:3, eff. July 1, 2010.

Statement of Intent.
2009, 279:1, eff. July 1, 2010, provided: "The general court finds that in the case of a missing person with developmental disabilities or a missing senior citizen the first few hours are critical in finding such person. Therefore, the general court hereby establishes an alert program to aid in the identification and location of missing persons with developmental disabilities and missing senior citizens."

106-J:5. Rulemaking.

The commissioner of the department shall adopt rules, pursuant to RSA 541-A, relative to:

I. Procedures for a local law enforcement agency to use to verify whether a senior citizen or person with developmental disabilities is missing and to verify whether a senior citizen has an impaired mental condition or a person has a developmental disability and the circumstances under which the agency shall report the missing senior citizen or missing person with developmental disabilities to the department.

II. The process to be followed by the department in confirming the local law enforcement agency's information.

III. The process for reporting the information to designated media outlets in New Hampshire.

Source.
2009, 279:3, eff. July 1, 2010.

CHAPTER 106-K

CRIMINAL JUSTICE INFORMATION SYSTEM

SECTION
106-K:1.   Definitions.
106-K:2.   Criminal Justice Information System (J-One).
106-K:3.   Requirements for J-One.
106-K:4.   Design, Implementation, and Operation.
106-K:5.   Board Established.
106-K:6.   Confidentiality.
106-K:7.   Criminal Penalties.

Redesignation of chapter; revision of internal references.
RSA 106-K was originally enacted as RSA 106-J by 2005, 244:2, but was redesignated, pursuant to 2005, 244:5, in light of the enactment of RSA 106-J by 2005, 247:3. All internal references to RSA 106-J appearing in this chapter have been revised to refer to RSA 106-K pursuant to 2005, 244:5.

106-K:1. Definitions.

In this chapter:

I. "Administration of criminal justice" means the performance of detection, apprehension, detention, pre-trial release, prosecution, post-trial release, adjudication, correctional supervision, rehabilitation of accused persons or criminal offenders, criminal identification activities, and the collection, storage, and dissemination of criminal history record information.

II. "Board" means the New Hampshire criminal justice information system board, established in RSA 106-K:5.

III. "Criminal justice agency" means any court other than a probate court or any government agency, or subunit thereof, which performs the administration of criminal justice pursuant to the New Hampshire constitution, a statute, or an executive order and which allocates a substantial part of its annual budget to the administration of criminal justice.

IV. "Criminal justice information" means information pertaining to natural persons collected by criminal justice agencies that provide individual identification of record subjects together with notations relating to such persons' involvement in the criminal justice system as alleged or convicted offenders. The term includes information relating to arrests; pre-trial detention or release; formal documents setting out criminal charges; dispositions; post-trial release; sentences; correctional pre-sentence investigations; probation and parole status and conditions; parole or probation violations; warrants; and court scheduling orders, such as transport orders and hearing notices. The term also includes juvenile protective orders issued pursuant to RSA 169-C:16, I(d)(1) or RSA 169-C:19, II(a)(1), domestic violence protective orders issued pursuant to RSA 173-B, restraining orders issued pursuant to RSA 458:16, I(a), (b), (c), or (d), and stalking orders issued pursuant to RSA 633:3-a. The term "criminal justice information" does not include:

(a) Information relating to juveniles other than those who are charged as adults.

(b) Information contained in intelligence files, investigation records, law enforcement work product record files, or law enforcement work product records used solely for law enforcement investigation purposes.

(c) Fingerprints or other biometric data taken for non-criminal purposes.

V. "Disposition" means information disclosing that criminal proceedings have concluded, and the nature of the termination. The term includes, but is not limited to, the following types of terminations: dismissal, nolle prosequi, acquittal, guilty plea, mistrial, not guilty by reason of insanity, a finding of incompetency to stand trial, pardon, commutation, probation, parole, as well as information that a law enforcement agency has elected not to refer a matter for prosecution, that a prosecutor has elected not to pursue criminal charges, or that the proceedings have been indefinitely postponed and the reason therefor.

VI. "Driver's license information" means information in motor vehicle records that identifies a person, including a person's photograph or computerized image, social security number, driver identification number, name, address, and telephone number.

VII. "Member" refers to any criminal justice agency that contributes data to J-One.

VIII. "Member user" means any individual employed by a member agency who is authorized by the head of that agency to access J-One.

IX. "Motor vehicle records" has the same meaning as in RSA 260:14, I(a).

X. "Personal information" means information that identifies a person, including a person's photograph or computerized image, social security number, driver identification number, name, address, telephone number, fingerprints, and physical description.

Source.
2005, 244:2, eff. January 1, 2006.

106-K:2. Criminal Justice Information System (J-One).

There is established an integrated criminal justice information system, hereafter known as J-One, the purpose of which is to improve the effectiveness and efficiency of the criminal justice agencies through the capture of data at its source; to facilitate the distribution of criminal justice data electronically to authorized members; and to provide individual case and statistical queries electronically. J-One shall consist of a network of computers, including hardware, software, and telecommunications lines, which shall be accessible only by criminal justice agencies and used only for the administration of criminal justice.

Source.
2005, 244:2, eff. January 1, 2006.

106-K:3. Requirements for J-One.

I. J-One shall be designed to capture from member agencies criminal justice information relating to the following, and consisting solely of the data elements identified in the February 15, 2002 NH - CJIS Data Dictionary Version 1.0:

(a) Arrests and criminal incidents: including statistical data on criminal incidents, which is currently submitted to the National Incident Based Reporting System; and information relating to felony, misdemeanor and violation-level arrests such as the arrestee's name, date of birth, address, physical description, tracking number, motor vehicle registration information, driver's license information, aliases, social security number, photograph, fingerprint data, bail status, custody status, arraignment date, name of arresting officer, arresting agency, type of offense, charge or charges, date of offense, and date of arrest.

(b) Disposition and sentencing: including, but not limited to, the defendant's personal information and tracking number, court identifier, type of offense and statutory reference, manner of disposition, type and terms of sentence.

(c) Bail orders, bench warrants, and restraining orders: including, but not limited to, bail conditions, active arrest warrants and capiases, juvenile protective orders issued pursuant to RSA 169-C:16 or RSA 169-C:19, domestic violence protective orders issued pursuant to RSA 173-B, restraining orders issued pursuant to RSA 458:16, I(a), (b), (c), or (d), and stalking orders issued pursuant to RSA 633:3-a. Member agencies shall be able to access information through a query/response function.

II. (a) All criminal justice information entered into J-One related to a criminal charge, including arrest and bail information, shall be expunged from J-One upon the occurrence of any of the following events:

(1) The charge is nolle prossed.

(2) The defendant is acquitted of the charge.

(3) The charge is dismissed.

(4) A court has ordered expungement of the records pursuant to RSA 651:5.

(b) If an arrest resulted in multiple charges against a person, and less than all of the charges were disposed of in a manner listed above, only the information specifically relating to charge or charges that were dismissed, nolle prossed, or resulted in an acquittal shall be expunged.

(c) J-One shall, on a monthly basis, identify all criminal charges in the criminal justice information database that were entered 3 years earlier for which no dispositional data has been entered. J-One shall notify the court of record for each charge. If the charge has been disposed of, the court shall, within 90 days, enter the disposition into J-One. If the charge is still pending, the court shall so indicate in J-One. If, after 90 days, the court has not entered either a disposition or status update in J-One, J-One shall notify the charging agency. That agency shall, within 90 days, take the necessary steps to have the charge disposed of and the disposition entered into J-One. If the charging agency is pursuing the charge, it shall, within 90 days, submit a report to J-One indicating that the case remains active. If the agency does not respond, all criminal justice information relating to that specific charge shall be expunged. If the agency indicates that the charge is still active, J-One shall, every year thereafter, require a status update from the agency, provided no disposition has been entered in the interim.

III. J-One shall provide a communication link to the court case management system, for the purpose of exchanging case management information such as arraignment and hearing dates and transport orders.

IV. Until such time as the department of corrections is a fully-functional member of J-One, and as the department upgrades its computer system, J-One shall provide a query/response communications link to the department's offender management and field services case management computer system.

V. J-One shall include a notification function, which will alert a member agency that data matching a set of criteria, established by the agency with the approval of the board, has become available in the central repository. A notification may include, for example, notice to a parole/probation officer that a particular parolee has been detained or arrested by the police; or notice to a police officer that a person on whom the officer has submitted a query has outstanding warrants, bail conditions, or protective orders

VI. (a) The J-One system shall maintain a master name index, which shall only be populated by, and accessible to, authorized individuals within the state police, member police and sheriff's departments, and authorized investigators within the department of justice and the county attorneys' offices.

Authorized member users may access the index only for purposes of obtaining information related to an on-going criminal investigation. For each query, the member user shall provide his or her name, the name of the person initiating the request, the name of the specific individual being queried and the agency case number to which the query is related.

(b) The master name index shall serve as a pointer system, enabling authorized users to determine which, if any, member agencies have information relating to a specific individual that the agency is willing to share. The data contained in the index shall be provided by law enforcement agencies on a voluntary basis, and shall consist of the following only: the individual's name, date of birth if known, known aliases, the contributing law enforcement agency, the agency case number, and the associated crime.

(c) The master name index shall not include the names of individuals who were witnesses to, or victims of the identified crime, nor shall it include non-criminal complainants.

(d) The master name index shall be maintained separately from the database for criminal justice information. It shall be accessible through a query function, by authorized member users only. A query in the master name index shall not enable the user to access the criminal justice information database. There shall be an audit trail for each query and for each entry of a name into the index.

(e) J-One shall, on a monthly basis, expunge from the master name index any name that has had no activity for 5 years. For purposes of this subparagraph, "activity" means any submission of additional information or query on the name with a new agency case number.

Source.

2005, 244:2, eff. January 1, 2006.

Cross References.

Classification of crimes, see RSA 625:9.

Sentences, see RSA 651.

106-K:4. Design, Implementation, and Operation.

J-One shall be designed, implemented, and operated to:

I. Ensure that all criminal justice data is validated as complete, accurate and meeting the business rules established by the board prior to its inclusion in J-One;

II. Provide for varying levels of access to criminal justice information, in order to ensure that member agencies will have access only to that information that is relevant for an articulated purpose consistent with their statutory or constitutional responsibilities;

III. Prevent access to anyone other than a criminal justice agency; provided, however that access in print and over the internet to statistical and aggregate criminal justice information from which personal information has been removed, shall be provided to the general public;

IV. Prevent the unauthorized addition, destruction, or modification of criminal justice information; and

V. Provide an audit function that will track each transaction, including but not limited to access, data input, and data modification.

Source.
2005, 244:2, eff. January 1, 2006.

106-K:5. Board Established.

I. There is hereby established the New Hampshire criminal justice information system board, which shall oversee the development and implementation of J-One. The board shall consist of the following members:

(a) The commissioner of the department of safety, or designee.

(b) The attorney general, or designee.

(c) The commissioner of the department of corrections, or designee.

(d) The director of the administrative office of the courts, or designee.

(e) The chief information officer of the department of information technology, or designee.

(f) The president of the New Hampshire Association of Chiefs of Police, or designee.

(g) The president of the New Hampshire Sheriffs' Association, or designee.

(h) The director of the New Hampshire police standards and training council, or designee.

(i) The director of Justiceworks, or designee.

(j) The director of the American Civil Liberties Union of New Hampshire, or designee.

(k) The president of the New Hampshire Association of Counties, Corrections Affiliate, or designee.

II. The board shall:

(a) Oversee the planning, implementation, operation, and management of J-One.

(b) Pursue, develop, and coordinate grants and other funding opportunities for the continued development, operation, and maintenance of the J-One system.

(c) Adopt strategic and tactical planning goals and objectives that implement, maintain, and enhance the sharing and integrated delivery of criminal justice information within the parameters set forth in RSA 106-K:3 and RSA 106-K:4.

(d) Adopt bylaws and rules to govern the functions and decision-making processes of the board.

(e) Recommend to the governor, the speaker of the house of representatives, and the president of the senate those legislative changes and appropriations needed to implement, maintain, and enhance J-One, to ensure the timely, accurate, and complete exchange of criminal justice information.

(f) Establish and staff advisory committees, the purpose of which will be to advise the board and to draft rules and standard operating procedures with respect to the following areas, at a minimum: operations, technology, finances, privacy, security, and the master name index.

(g) Establish a procedure by which an individual, upon written request and submission of a fee established by the board, may obtain a copy of any criminal justice information contained in J-One relating to the individual, and have corrections made to any of the data proven to be incorrect.

(h) Create a database of criminal justice information from which all personal information has been deleted, which shall be accessible by the public. The board shall establish a fee schedule for access to the database by individuals, researchers, government entities, public officials, and not-for-profit and for-profit enterprises, which shall cover the costs of maintaining the database. In establishing the fee schedule, the board shall ensure, to the extent possible, that individuals will not be prevented from gaining access to the database due to an inability to pay.

Source.
2005, 244:2, eff. January 1, 2006. 2008, 335:5, eff. September 5, 2008.

Amendments
—2008. The 2008 amendment substituted "department of information technology" for "office of information technology" in I(e).

106-K:6. Confidentiality.

All data stored in J-One shall be confidential and shall be exempt from disclosure under RSA 91-A; provided, however, that nothing in this chapter shall affect the continued application of RSA 91-A to such information, to the extent that it is collected and maintained separately by a member agency.

Source.
2005, 244:2, eff. January 1, 2006.

106-K:7. Criminal Penalties.

I. It shall be a class B misdemeanor for any person to access J-One, or cause another to access J-One, knowing that the person gaining access is unauthorized to do so.

II. It shall be a class B misdemeanor for any authorized user of J-One to access J-One for a purpose unrelated to that person's official duties in connection with the administration of justice; provided, however, that if the authorized user accepts money or other consideration from another in exchange for the unauthorized access, it shall be a class A misdemeanor for a first offense or a class B felony for a second or subsequent offense.

III. Any person who pays, or provides any other consideration to, an authorized user of J-One in exchange for that user gaining access to J-One for an unauthorized purpose shall be guilty of a class A misdemeanor for a first offense or a class B felony for a second or subsequent offense.

IV. For purposes of this section, the term "access" has the same meaning as in RSA 638:16, I.

V. Each act in violation of this statute shall constitute a separate offense.

Source.
2005, 244:2, eff. January 1, 2006.

Cross References.
Classification of crimes, see RSA 625:9.
Sentences, see RSA 651.

TITLE X
PUBLIC HEALTH

CHAPTER 126-K

YOUTH ACCESS TO AND USE OF TOBACCO PRODUCTS

SECTION
126-K:1.   Purpose.
126-K:2.   Definitions.
126-K:3.   Proof of Age of Purchaser.
126-K:4.   Sale and Distribution of Tobacco Products, E-ciga-
             rettes, or Liquid Nicotine to Minors Prohibited.
126-K:4-a.   Rolling Papers.
126-K:5.   Distribution of Free Samples.
126-K:6.   Possession and Use of Tobacco Products, E-cigarettes,
             or Liquid Nicotine by Minors.
126-K:7.   Use of Tobacco Products, E-cigarettes, or Liquid Nico-
             tine on Public Educational Facility Grounds
             Prohibited.
126-K:8.   Special Provisions.
126-K:9.   Enforcement Authority.
126-K:10.   Rulemaking.
126-K:11.   Fines.
126-K:12.   Penalties.
126-K:13.   Severability.
126-K:14.   Preemption.

Tobacco Use Prevention and Cessation Program

126-K:15.   Tobacco Use Prevention and Cessation Program.
126-K:16.   Definitions.
126-K:17.   Purpose of Grants; Grants Process.
126-K:18.   Rulemaking.
126-K:19.   Advisory Committee. [Repealed.]

Codification.
  This chapter, which was originally enacted as RSA 126-I, comprising RSA 126-I:1–126-I:14, was redesignated as RSA 126-K, comprising RSA 126-K:1–126-K:14, pursuant to 1997, 338:10, eff. Jan. 1, 1998, and internal references were revised to conform to the redesignation.

126-K:1. Purpose.

The purpose of this chapter is to protect the children of New Hampshire from the possibility of addiction, disability, and death resulting from the use of tobacco products by ensuring that tobacco products will not be supplied to minors.

Source.
  1997, 338:8, eff. Jan. 1, 1998.

126-K:2. Definitions.

In this chapter:

I. "Cigarette" means any roll for smoking made wholly or in part of tobacco, and wrapped in any material except tobacco.

II. "Commission" means the liquor commission.

II-a. "E-cigarette" means any electronic smoking device composed of a mouthpiece, a heating element, a battery, and electronic circuits that provides a vapor of pure nicotine mixed with propylene glycol to the user as the user simulates smoking. This term shall include such devices whether they are manufactured as e-cigarettes, e-cigars, or e-pipes, or under any other product name.

III. "Licensee" means the person in whose name a license issued pursuant to RSA 78:2 was granted.

III-a. "Liquid nicotine" means any liquid product composed either in whole or in part of pure nicotine and propylene glycol and manufactured for use with e-cigarettes.

IV. "Manufacturer" means any person engaged in the business of importing, exporting, producing, or manufacturing tobacco products who sells the product only to licensed wholesalers.

V. "Minor" means a person under the age of 18.

VI. "Person" means any individual, firm, fiduciary partnership, corporation, trust, or association, however formed.

VII. "Public educational facility" means any enclosed place or portion of such place, which is supported by public funds and which is used for the instruction of students enrolled in preschool programs and in grades kindergarten through 12. This definition shall include all administrative buildings and offices and areas within facilities supportive of instruction and subject to educational administration including, but not limited to, lounge areas, passageways, rest rooms, laboratories, study areas, cafeterias, gymnasiums, libraries, maintenance rooms, and storage areas.

VIII. "Retailer" means any person who sells tobacco products to consumers.

VIII-a. "Rolling paper" means any paper product that is designed to encase or wrap tobacco or similar products and marketed for the purpose of smoking or manufacturing hand-rolled cigarettes.

IX. "Sampler" means any person who distributes free tobacco products to consumers for promotional purposes.

X. "Sub-jobber" means any person doing business in this state who buys stamped tobacco products from a licensed wholesaler and who sells all the sub-jobber's tobacco products to other licensed sub-jobbers, vending machine operators, and retailers.

XI. "Tobacco product" means any product containing tobacco including, but not limited to, cigarettes, smoking tobacco, cigars, chewing tobacco, snuff, pipe tobacco, smokeless tobacco, and smokeless cigarettes.

XII. "Vending machine" means any self-service device which, upon insertion of money, tokens, or any other form of payment, dispenses tobacco, cigarettes, or any other tobacco product.

XIII. "Vending machine operator" means any person operating one or more tobacco product vending machines on property or premises other than the operator's own.

XIV. "Wholesaler" means any person doing business in this state who shall purchase all the wholesaler's unstamped tobacco products directly from a licensed manufacturer and who shall sell all of the wholesaler's products to licensed wholesalers, sub-jobbers, vending machine operators, retailers, samplers, and those persons exempted from the tobacco tax under RSA 78:7-b.

Source.
1997, 338:8, eff. Jan. 1, 1998. 2001, 171:1, eff. Jan. 1, 2002. 2010, 113:1, 2, eff. July 31, 2010.

Amendments
—**2010.** The 2010 amendment added II-a and III-a.

—**2001.** Paragraph VIII-a: Added.

126-K:3. Proof of Age of Purchaser.

I. For the purposes of this chapter, any person responsible for monitoring sales from a tobacco vending machine or any person making the sale of tobacco products, e-cigarettes, or liquid nicotine which vending machine or other sale is to be made to any person who does not appear to be at least 18 years of age, shall require the purchaser to furnish any of the following documentation that such person is 18 years of age or over:

(a) A motor vehicle driver's license issued by the state of New Hampshire, or a valid driver's license issued by another state, or province of Canada, which bears the date of birth, name, address, and picture of the individual.

(b) An identification card issued by the director of motor vehicles under the provisions of RSA 260:21, or any picture identification card issued by another state which bears the date of birth, name, and address of the individual.

(c) An armed services identification card.

(d) A valid passport from a country with whom the United States maintains diplomatic relations.

II. Photographic identification presented under this section shall be consistent with the appearance of the person, and shall be correct and free of alteration, erasure, blemish, or other impairment.

III. The establishment of all of the following facts by a person responsible for monitoring sales from a vending machine or a person or sampler making a sale or distribution of tobacco products, e-cigarettes, or liquid nicotine to a person under 18 years of age shall constitute prima facie evidence of innocence and a defense to any prosecution for such sale:

(a) That the person falsely represented in writing and supported by some official documents that the person was 18 years of age or older;

(b) That the appearance of the person was such that an ordinary and prudent person would believe such person to be at least 18 years of age or older; and

(c) That the sale was made in good faith relying on such written representation and appearance in the reasonable belief that the person was actually 18 years of age or over.

Source.
1997, 338:8, eff. Jan. 1, 1998. 2010, 113:3, 4, eff. July 31, 2010.

Amendments
—**2010.** The 2010 amendment added "e-cigarettes, or liquid nicotine" in the introductory language of I and III.

126-K:4. Sale and Distribution of Tobacco Products, E-cigarettes, or Liquid Nicotine to Minors Prohibited.

I. No person shall sell, give, or furnish or cause or allow or procure to be sold, given, or furnished tobacco products, e-cigarettes, or liquid nicotine to a minor. The prohibition established by this paragraph shall not be deemed to prohibit minors employed by any manufacturer, wholesaler, sub-jobber, vending machine operator, sampler, or retailer from performing the necessary handling of tobacco products, e-cigarettes, or liquid nicotine during the duration of their employment.

II. Violations of this section shall be civil infractions punishable by administrative action of the commission against the licensee. The fines for violations of this section shall not exceed $250 for the first offense and $500 for the second offense. For the third offense, the commission shall issue a letter of warning detailing necessary corrective actions and an administrative fine ranging from $500 to $1500. In addition, the license to sell tobacco products of the manufacturer, wholesaler, sub-jobber, vending machine operator, or retailer where the offense occurred shall be suspended for a period of 10 consecutive days and not exceeding 30 consecutive days. For the fourth offense, the commission shall issue either an administrative fine and a suspension of a minimum of 10 consecutive days not to exceed 40 consecutive days, or a suspension. The administrative fine shall range from $750 to $3,000 while any suspension without a fine shall be 40 consecutive days. For any violation beyond the fourth, the commission shall revoke any license for the business or business entity at the location where the infraction occurred or any principal thereof for a period of one year from the date of revocation. The commission shall determine the level of the violation by reviewing the licensee's record and counting violations that have occurred within 3 years of the date of the violation being considered.

III. In addition to the civil penalty described in paragraph II, a person who violates this section shall be guilty of a violation for a first offense and a misdemeanor for each subsequent offense.

Source.
1997, 338:8, eff. Jan. 1, 1998. 2000, 303:1, eff. Jan. 1, 2001. 2001, 280:1, eff. Jan. 1, 2002. 2010, 113:5, eff. July 31, 2010.

Amendments
—**2010.** The 2010 amendment added "e-cigarettes, or liquid nicotine" in the section heading and the first and second sentences of I.

—**2001.** Paragraph II: Added "for the business or business entity at the location where the infraction occurred or any principal thereof for a period of one year from the date of revocation" in the penultimate sentence and added the last sentence.

—2000. Paragraph II: Rewritten to the extent that a detailed comparison would be impracticable.

Cross References.
Classification of crimes, see RSA 625:9.

126-K:4-a. Rolling Papers.

I. No person shall sell, give, or furnish rolling papers to a minor. Violations of this paragraph shall be civil infractions punishable by administrative action of the commission against the licensee. The fines for violations of this paragraph shall not exceed $250 for the first offense, $500 for the second offense, and $750 for the third and subsequent offenses.

II. No person under 18 years of age shall purchase, attempt to purchase, possess, or use any rolling paper. Any minor who violates this section shall be guilty of a violation and shall be punished by a fine not to exceed $100 for each offense.

Source.
2001, 171:2, eff. Jan. 1, 2002.

126-K:5. Distribution of Free Samples.

I. No person may distribute or offer to distribute samples of tobacco products, e-cigarettes, or liquid nicotine in a public place. This prohibition shall not apply to sampling:

(a) In an area to which minors are denied access.

(b) In a store to which a retailer's license has been issued.

(c) At factory sites, construction sites, conventions, trade shows, fairs, or motorsport facilities in areas to which minors are denied access.

II. The commission shall adopt rules, pursuant to RSA 541-A, concerning the distribution of free samples of tobacco products, e-cigarettes, or liquid nicotine to prevent their distribution to minors.

III. Violations of this section shall be civil infractions punishable by administrative action of the commission against the licensee. The fines for violations of this section shall not exceed $250 for the first offense and $500 for the second offense. For the third offense, the commission shall issue a letter of warning detailing necessary corrective actions and an administrative fine ranging from $500 to $1,500. In addition, the sampler's license shall be suspended for a period of 10 consecutive days and not exceeding 30 consecutive days. For the fourth offense, the commission shall issue either an administrative fine and a suspension of a minimum of 10 consecutive days not to exceed 40 consecutive days, or a suspension. The administrative fine shall range from $750 to $3,000 while any suspension without a fine shall be 40 consecutive days. For any violation beyond the fourth, the commission shall revoke any license for the business or business entity at the location where the infraction occurred or any principal thereof for a period of one year from the date of revocation. The commission shall determine the level of the violation by reviewing the licensee's record and counting violations that have occurred within 3 years of the date of the violation being considered.

Source.
1997, 338:8, eff. Jan. 1, 1998. 2000, 303:2, eff. Jan. 1, 2001. 2001, 280:2, eff. Jan. 1, 2002. 2010, 113:6, eff. July 31, 2010.

Amendments
—2010. The 2010 amendment added "e-cigarettes, or liquid nicotine" in the first sentence of the introductory language of I and in II.

—2001. Paragraph III: Added "for the business or business entity at the location where the infraction occurred or any principal thereof for a period of one year from the date of revocation" in the penultimate sentence and added the last sentence.

—2000. Paragraph III: Rewritten to the extent that a detailed comparison would be impracticable.

126-K:6. Possession and Use of Tobacco Products, E-cigarettes, or Liquid Nicotine by Minors.

I. No person under 18 years of age shall purchase, attempt to purchase, possess, or use any tobacco product, e-cigarette, or liquid nicotine.

II. The prohibition on possession of tobacco products, e-cigarettes, or liquid nicotine shall not be deemed to prohibit minors employed by any manufacturer, wholesaler, sub-jobber, vending machine operator, sampler, or retailer from performing the necessary handling of tobacco products, e-cigarettes, or liquid nicotine during the duration of their employment.

III. A minor shall not misrepresent his or her age for the purpose of purchasing tobacco products.

IV. Notwithstanding RSA 169-B and RSA 169-D, a person 12 years of age and older who violates this section shall not be considered a delinquent or a child in need of services.

V. Any minor who violates this section shall be guilty of a violation and shall be punished by a fine not to exceed $100 for each offense or shall be required to complete up to 20 hours of community service for each offense, or both. Where available, punishment may also include participation in an education program.

Source.
1997, 338:8, eff. Jan. 1, 1998. 2010, 113:7, eff. July 31, 2010.

Amendments
—2010. The 2010 amendment added "e-cigarettes, or liquid nicotine" or variants wherever it appears in the section heading and in I and II.

126-K:7. Use of Tobacco Products, E-cigarettes, or Liquid Nicotine on Public Educational Facility Grounds Prohibited.

I. No person shall use any tobacco product, e-cigarette, or liquid nicotine in any public educational facility or on the grounds of any public educational facility.

II. Any person who violates this section shall be guilty of a violation and, notwithstanding RSA 651:2, shall be punished by a fine not to exceed $100 for each offense.

Source.
1997, 338:8, eff. Jan. 1, 1998. 2010, 113:8, eff. July 31, 2010.

Amendments
—**2010.** The 2010 amendment added "e-cigarettes, or liquid nicotine" or variants in the section heading and in I.

126-K:8. Special Provisions.

I. No person shall sell, give, or furnish tobacco products, e-cigarettes, or liquid nicotine to a minor who has a note from an adult requesting such sale, gift, or delivery.

II. All tobacco products shall be sold in their original packaging bearing the Surgeon General's warning.

III. The sale of single cigarettes is prohibited.

IV. Violations of this section shall be civil infractions punishable by administrative action of the commission against the licensee. The fines for violations of this section shall not exceed $250 for the first offense and $500 for the second offense. For the third offense, the commission shall issue a letter of warning detailing necessary corrective actions and an administrative fine ranging from $500 to $1,500. In addition, the license to sell tobacco products of the manufacturer, wholesaler, sub-jobber, vending machine operator, or retailer where the offense occurred shall be suspended for a period of 10 consecutive days and not exceeding 30 consecutive days. For the fourth offense, the commission shall issue either an administrative fine and a suspension of a minimum of 10 consecutive days not to exceed 40 consecutive days, or a suspension. The administrative fine shall range from $750 to $3,000 while any suspension without a fine shall be 40 consecutive days. For any violation beyond the fourth, the commission shall revoke any license for the business or business entity at the location where the infraction occurred or any principal thereof for a period of one year from the date of revocation. The commission shall determine the level of the violation by reviewing the licensee's record and counting violations that have occurred within 3 years of the date of the violation being considered.

V. In addition to the civil penalty described in paragraph IV, a person who violates this section shall be guilty of a violation for the first offense and a misdemeanor for each subsequent offense.

Source.
1997, 338:8, eff. Jan. 1, 1998. 2000, 303:3, eff. Jan. 1, 2001. 2001, 280:3, eff. Jan. 1, 2002. 2010, 113:9, eff. July 31, 2010.

Amendments
—**2010.** The 2010 amendment added "e-cigarettes, or liquid nicotine" in I.

—**2001.** Paragraph IV: Inserted "at the location where the infraction occurred" in the second to last sentence and added the last sentence.

—**2000.** Paragraph IV: Rewritten to the extent that a detailed comparison would be impracticable.

Cross References.
Classification of crimes, see RSA 625:9.

126-K:9. Enforcement Authority.

The commission shall have the primary responsibility for enforcing this chapter. Local, county, and state law enforcement officers shall also have jurisdiction to enforce this chapter. Such authority may be delegated to agents working under their authority.

Source.
1997, 338:8, eff. Jan. 1, 1998.

126-K:10. Rulemaking.

The commission shall adopt rules, pursuant to RSA 541-A, relative to the hearings and appeals process and relative to the proper administration of this chapter.

Source.
1997, 338:8, eff. Jan. 1, 1998.

126-K:11. Fines.

I. All fines imposed by any court and collected for the violation of the provisions of this chapter shall be paid to the state, county, or town, the officials of which instituted the prosecution.

II. All fines imposed by the commission shall be deposited into the general fund.

Source.
1997, 338:8, eff. Jan. 1, 1998.

126-K:12. Penalties.

I. Violations of this chapter may be prosecuted by local, county, or state law enforcement officials.

II. The commission may issue administrative warnings and assess fines and may order the commissioner of revenue administration to suspend or revoke a license issued pursuant to RSA 78 for a specified period of time for violations of this chapter.

III. The commission may issue administrative warnings, assess fines, and suspend or revoke a license issued pursuant to RSA 178 for a specified period of time for violations of this chapter.

Source.
1997, 338:8, eff. Jan. 1, 1998. 2008, 341:18, eff. January 1, 2009.

Amendments

—**2008.** The 2008 amendment rewrote III to the extent that a detailed comparison would be impracticable.

Cross References.

Department of revenue administration, see RSA 21-J.

126-K:13. Severability.

If any provision of this chapter or the application thereof to any person or circumstance is held invalid, the invalidity does not affect other provisions or applications of the chapter which can be given effect without the invalid provisions or applications, and to this end the provisions of this chapter are severable.

Source.

1997, 338:8, eff. Jan. 1, 1998.

126-K:14. Preemption.

Nothing in this chapter shall be construed to restrict the power of any county, city, town, village, or other subdivision of the state to adopt local laws, ordinances, and regulations that are more stringent than this chapter and RSA 78.

Source.

1997, 338:8, eff. Jan. 1, 1998.

Tobacco Use Prevention and Cessation Program

Amendments

—**2007.** 2007, 263:112, eff. June 30, 2007, deleted "Fund" following "Prevention" and substituted "and Cessation Program" for "and Tobacco Control Program" at the end of the subdivision heading.

—**2000.** 2000, 62:1, eff. June 16, 2000, added "and Tobacco Control Program" following "Fund" in the subdivision heading.

126-K:15. Tobacco Use Prevention and Cessation Program.

There is hereby established in the department of health and human services the tobacco use prevention and cessation program, which shall be administered with funds appropriated to the department for such purpose, and which shall include but not be limited to:

I. Tobacco use prevention community programs and grants.

II. Tobacco use prevention school programs and grants.

III. Tobacco use prevention state-wide programs and grants.

IV. Tobacco use cessation programs.

V. Tobacco use prevention and cessation counter marketing.

VI. Evaluation of tobacco control initiatives.

VII. Administration and enforcement.

Source.

1999, 183:3, eff. July 6, 1999. 2000, 62:2, eff. June 16, 2000. 2007, 263:113, eff. June 30, 2007.

Amendments

—**2007.** Rewritten to the extent that a detailed comparison would be impracticable.

—**2000.** Paragraph VI: Rewritten to the extent that a detailed comparison would be impracticable.

126-K:16. Definitions.

In this subdivision:

I. "Commissioner" means the commissioner of the department of health and human services.

II. "Department" means the department of health and human services.

III. [Repealed.]

Source.

2000, 62:3, eff. June 16, 2000. 2007, 263:116, II, eff. June 30, 2007.

Amendments

—**2007.** Paragraph III: Repealed.

126-K:17. Purpose of Grants; Grants Process.

Grants shall be available in accordance with the following procedures:

I. Requests for funding consideration in any given year shall be forwarded to the commissioner by January 1 to be reviewed for a grant beginning in the following fiscal year.

II. The commissioner shall review all requests and recommend awards, including amounts and duration. The commissioner shall submit recommendations to the governor and executive council for approval.

III. Additional requests may be considered throughout the year if funds are available. The commissioner shall forward recommendations to the governor and council for approval.

Source.

2000, 62:3, eff. June 16, 2000.

126-K:18. Rulemaking.

The commissioner shall adopt rules, pursuant to RSA 541-A, necessary for the administration of this subdivision.

Source.

2000, 62:3, eff. June 16, 2000.

126-K:19. Advisory Committee.

[Repealed 2008, 144:1, II, eff. August 5, 2008.]

Former section(s).

Former RSA 126-K:19, which was derived from 2000, 62:3 and 2007, 263:114, related to the tobacco use advisory committee.

CHAPTER 135

NEW HAMPSHIRE HOSPITAL AND INSANE PERSONS

Commitment to Hospitals

SECTION
135:17.   Competency; Commitment for Evaluation.
135:17-a.   Competency Hearing; Commitment for Treatment.
135:17-b.   Notification Authorized.
135:17-c.   Information Related to Competency Determinations.

Commitment to Hospitals

135:17. Competency; Commitment for Evaluation.

I. (a) When a person is charged or indicted for any offense, or is bound over by any district or superior court to await the action of the grand jury, the district or superior court before which he or she is to be tried, if a plea of insanity is made in court, or said court is notified by either party that there is a question as to the competency or sanity of the person, may make such order for a pre-trial examination of such person by a qualified psychiatrist or psychologist on the staff of any public institution or by a private qualified psychiatrist or psychologist as the circumstances of the case may require, which order may include, though without limitation, examination at the secure psychiatric unit on an out-patient basis, the utilization of local mental health clinics on an in- or out-patient basis, or the examination of such person, should he or she be incarcerated for any reason, at his or her place of detention by qualified psychiatrists or psychologists assigned to a state or local mental health facility. Such pre-trial examination shall be completed within 45 days in the case of a person being held at a county correctional facility, otherwise 90 days after the date of the order for such examination, unless either party requests an extension of this period. For the purposes of this paragraph and RSA 135:17-a, III, "qualified" means board-eligible or board-certified in forensic psychiatry or psychology, or demonstrated competence and experience in completing court-ordered forensic criminal evaluations. A licensed out-of-state psychiatrist or psychologist who meets the definition of qualified may also conduct evaluations under this paragraph and RSA 135:17-a, III.

(b) In cases where the person is being held at a county correctional facility, the facility may request a pre-trial examination of such person for the purpose of determining if the person is competent to stand trial. Such request shall be reviewed, and a decision rendered by the district or superior court before which he or she is to be tried.

(c) In cases where the person is incarcerated and a pre-trial examination has not been performed within 45 days of the court's order, the court shall, upon request of the person, order an evaluation by a qualified psychiatrist or psychologist. The court shall favorably consider a request that the psychiatrist or psychologist be treated as a defense expert who shall be compensated pursuant to RSA 604-A:6.

(d) In cases where the person is incarcerated and an examination has not been performed, the court before which he or she is to be tried shall review the person's bail status on a monthly basis.

II. The district or superior court may allow the parties to obtain separate competency evaluations if such request is made and the circumstances require it. The competency evaluations shall address:

(a) Whether the defendant suffers from a mental disease or defect; and

(b) Whether the defendant has a rational and factual understanding of the proceedings against him or her, and sufficient present ability to consult with and assist his or her lawyer on the case with a reasonable degree of rational understanding.

III. If the examiner concludes that the defendant is not competent to stand trial under the definition set forth in II(b), the evaluation shall include the examiner's findings as to whether there is a course of treatment which is reasonably likely to restore the defendant to competency.

Source.
1901, 21:1. 1911, 13:1. PL 11:13. RL 17:13. RSA 135:17. 1967, 132:4. 1969, 184:1. 1973, 532:28. 1975, 83:1. 1985, 337:12, eff. July 1, 1985. 2000, 229:1, eff. Jan. 1, 2001. 2009, 263:1, eff. July 16, 2009. 2010, 250:1, eff. September 4, 2010.

Revision note.
"State hospital" changed to "New Hampshire Hospital" pursuant to 1963, 39:2.
"Its trustees" changed to "the director of the division of mental health" and "them" changed to "him" pursuant to 1961, 222:1.

Amendments
—2010. The 2010 amendment added the I(a) designation; in I(a), substituted "superior" for "municipal" following "any district or" in the first sentence and "45 days in the case of a person being held at a county correctional facility, otherwise 90 days" for "60 days"; and added I(b) through I(d).

—2009. The 2009 amendment, in I, in the first sentence, substituted "pre-trial examination" for "pre-trial psychiatric examination" and substituted "qualified psychiatrist or psychologist" for "psychiatrist" each time it appears and added the third and fourth sentences; substituted "competency" for "psychiatric" in the second sentence of the introductory paragraph of II; and in III, deleted "psychiatric" preceding "examiner concludes" and preceding "evaluation shall."

—2000. Rewritten to the extent that a detailed comparison would be impracticable.

—1985. Substituted "secure psychiatric unit" for "New Hampshire Hospital" in the first sentence.

—1975. Added the second sentence.

—1973. Rewritten to the extent that a detailed comparison would be impracticable.

—1969. Substituted "bound over by any district or municipal court" for "committed to jail on any criminal charge" preceding "to await".

—1967. Substituted "the superior" for "any justice of the" following "grand jury", "court" for "justice" preceding "is notified" and deleted "in term time or vacation" following "respondent, may".

Cross References.
Expenses for commitment for observation, see RSA 126-A:45.
Insanity defense, see RSA 628:2.
Secure psychiatric unit at state prison, see RSA 622:40 et seq.

NOTES TO DECISIONS

1. Constitutionality
2. Jurisdiction
3. Procedure
4. Second examination
5. Firearms

1. Constitutionality

Defendant, who was found incompetent to stand trial, had not shown that due process under N.H. Const. pt. I, art. 15 and U.S. Const. amend. XIV required the appointment of additional counsel and/or guardians to protect his reputational interest. The procedure used sufficiently protected that interest by ensuring a reliable competency determination; furthermore, fully litigating the competency issue in an adversarial proceeding with two sets of appointed counsel also counseled against the additional process defendant sought. State v. Veale, 158 N.H. 632, 972 A.2d 1009, 2009 N.H. LEXIS 58 (2009), cert. denied, Veale v. New Hampshire, 558 U.S. 1053, 130 S. Ct. 748, 175 L. Ed. 2d 524, 2009 U.S. LEXIS 8587 (2009).

Declining to appoint counsel solely to vindicate a defendant's reputational interest does not offend fundamental fairness. Where a criminal defendant is at odds with counsel because counsel believes that the defendant is not competent, while the defendant believes that he or she is competent, due process does not require the appointment of additional counsel. State v. Veale, 158 N.H. 632, 972 A.2d 1009, 2009 N.H. LEXIS 58 (2009), cert. denied, Veale v. New Hampshire, 558 U.S. 1053, 130 S. Ct. 748, 175 L. Ed. 2d 524, 2009 U.S. LEXIS 8587 (2009).

Had defendant, who sought based on his due process reputational interest to vacate a finding that he was incompetent to stand trial, requested to testify or call other witnesses at the competency hearing, due process might well have afforded him that right. On the record, however, it appeared that defendant never requested as much; had he wished to testify, he should have informed his counsel and/or the trial court instead of raising the issue for the first time in his pro se notice of appeal. State v. Veale, 158 N.H. 632, 972 A.2d 1009, 2009 N.H. LEXIS 58 (2009), cert. denied, Veale v. New Hampshire, 558 U.S. 1053, 130 S. Ct. 748, 175 L. Ed. 2d 524, 2009 U.S. LEXIS 8587 (2009).

2. Jurisdiction

If the grand jury indicts a defendant, or the defendant waives his right to a preliminary hearing prior to the issue of competency having been raised, the district court loses jurisdiction and the issue of competency must be resolved before the superior court. State v. Gagne, 129 N.H. 93, 523 A.2d 76, 1986 N.H. LEXIS 380 (1986).

3. Procedure

In the exercise of its inherent authority to protect a defendant's constitutional rights, a district court may order competency evaluations on a defendant charged with a misdemeanor, adhering to this section insofar as it prescribes the manner in which an individual may be evaluated. State v. Gagne, 129 N.H. 93, 523 A.2d 76, 1986 N.H. LEXIS 380 (1986).

Motions under this section must be in writing, specifying in detail behavior observed by counsel that forms basis for questioning accused's sanity or competency to stand trial, and order must specify whether examining psychiatrists are to determine accused's competency to stand trial and to assist counsel in defense of case or to determine insanity at time of commission of alleged crime, or to do both. Novosel v. Helgemoe, 118 N.H. 115, 384 A.2d 124, 1978 N.H. LEXIS 356 (1978), superseded by statute as stated in, State v. Blair, 143 N.H. 669, 732 A.2d 448, 1999 N.H. LEXIS 57 (1999).

4. Second examination

State prisoner was not entitled to habeas corpus relief because RSA 135:17, which provided for a neutral, third-party psychiatric evaluation of a defendant's competency to stand trial upon notice that the defendant's competency was at issue, adequately protected a criminal defendant's Fourteenth Amendment right not to be tried while legally incompetent, both on its face and as applied to the prisoner. The Fourteenth Amendment did not guarantee the prisoner the right to a second evaluation. Fox v. Cattell, 2005 U.S. Dist. LEXIS 8491 (D.N.H. 2005).

A defendant does not have an absolute right to a second pretrial psychiatric examination. State v. Osborne, 119 N.H. 427, 402 A.2d 493, 1979 N.H. LEXIS 346 (1979).

5. Firearms

Denial of defendant's motion for return of firearms seized pursuant to his bail order was error because, contrary to the trial court's finding, "adjudicated as a mental defective" pursuant to 18 U.S.C.S. § 922(g)(4) of the Federal Gun Control Act did not mean the same thing as incompetent to stand trial; the trial court's prior incompetency finding under RSA 135:17 did not bar defendant's possession of firearms. Competency for purposes of RSA 135:17 was not directly related to dangerousness or the ability to contract or manage one's own affairs-requirements of the federal definition of "adjudicated as a mental defective." State v. Buchanan, 155 N.H. 505, 924 A.2d 422, 2007 N.H. LEXIS 86 (2007).

Cited:

Cited in State v. Mercier, 128 N.H. 57, 509 A.2d 1246, 1986 N.H. LEXIS 255 (1986); In re Petition of Demers, 130 N.H. 31, 533 A.2d 380, 1987 N.H. LEXIS 267 (1987); State v. Briand, 130 N.H. 650, 547 A.2d 235, 1988 N.H. LEXIS 77 (1988).

RESEARCH REFERENCES

New Hampshire Bar Journal.

For article, "Competency to Stand Trial Evaluations in New Hampshire: Who Is Evaluated? What Are the Findings?," see 46 N.H.B.J. 48 (Winter 2006).

135:17-a. Competency Hearing; Commitment for Treatment.

I. If, after hearing, the district court or superior court determines that the defendant is not competent to stand trial, the court shall order treatment for the restoration of competency unless it determines, by clear and convincing evidence, that there is no reasonable likelihood that the defendant can be restored to competency through appropriate treatment within 12 months. If the court finds, by clear and convincing evidence, that the defendant cannot be restored to competency within 12 months, the case against the defendant shall be dismissed without prejudice and the court shall proceed as provided in paragraph V.

II. If the defendant is to undergo treatment to restore competency, he or she may be treated in the state mental health system or at the secure psychiatric unit only under an order for involuntary admission or involuntary emergency admission ordered by the district court or probate court having jurisdiction pursuant to RSA 135-C. In all other cases, the accused shall, if otherwise qualified, be admitted to bail. The court may order bail supervision by the division of field services and impose such conditions, in addition to the appropriate course of treatment to restore competency, as the court deems necessary to ensure the appearance of the defendant for further proceedings in the case, and the safety of the defendant and the community.

III. Except for good cause shown, a further hearing to determine the defendant's competency shall be held no later than 12 months after the order committing the defendant for treatment. The hearing may be held earlier if the court is notified that the defendant has been restored to competency, or that there is no longer a reasonable likelihood of such restoration. Prior to the scheduled hearing, the qualified psychiatrist or psychologist who conducted the initial competency evaluation shall conduct a further evaluation pursuant to RSA 135:17, and furnish a copy of the report of such evaluation to the court and the parties. If that qualified psychiatrist or psychologist is unavailable or unable to conduct such further evaluation, the court may order that the evaluation be conducted by another qualified psychiatrist or psychologist other than the treating qualified psychiatrist or psychologist.

IV. If following the hearing, the court determines that the defendant has regained competency, the court shall docket the matter for trial. If the court finds that the defendant has not regained competency, the case against the defendant shall be dismissed without prejudice.

V. If the court has determined that the defendant has not regained competency, and the court determines that he or she is dangerous to himself or herself or others, the court shall order the person to remain in custody for a reasonable period of time, not to exceed 90 days, to be evaluated for the appropriateness of involuntary treatment pursuant to RSA 135-C:34 or RSA 171-B:2. The court may order the person to submit to examinations by a physician, psychiatrist, or psychologist designated by the state for the purpose of evaluating appropriateness and completing the certificate for involuntary admission into the state mental health services system, the state developmental services delivery system, or the secure psychiatric unit, as the case may be. If a defendant who was charged with a sexually violent offense, as defined in RSA 135-E:2, XI, has not regained competency, the court shall proceed pursuant to RSA 135-E.

VI. If the person is ordered to be involuntarily committed following proceedings pursuant to RSA 135-C or RSA 171-B, the court may, upon motion of the attorney general or county attorney at any time during the period of the involuntary commitment and before expiration of the limitations period applicable to the underlying criminal offense, order a further competency evaluation, to be conducted as prescribed in paragraph III. Such further competency evaluations may be ordered if the court finds that there is a reasonable basis to believe that the person's condition has changed such that competency to stand trial may have been affected. During proceedings authorized by this paragraph, the person is entitled to the assistance of counsel, including appointed counsel under RSA 135-C:22.

VII. Upon a finding that the defendant is not competent to stand trial, the court, at the competency hearing, shall determine if the competency report shall be available to the receiving facility, as defined in RSA 135-C:26, or the secure psychiatric unit. Before the court determines whether to provide the competency report to the receiving facility or the secure psychiatric unit, the court shall provide the defendant with an opportunity to object. The court shall consider the defendant's privacy interest in the content of the competency report and the receiving facility's, or the secure psychiatric unit's, need to review the competency report for purposes of treatment.

Source.
1990, 266:1. 1994, 55:1, eff. Jan. 1, 1995; 408:2, eff. at 12:01 a.m., Jan. 1, 1995. 1999, 195:1–3, eff. Jan. 1, 2000. 2000, 229:2, eff. Jan. 1, 2001. 2001, 243:3, eff. Sept. 11, 2001. 2005, 201:1, 2, eff. Jan. 1, 2006. 2006, 327:22, eff. January 1, 2007. 2009, 263:2, eff. July 16, 2009. 2010, 46:1, eff. May 18, 2010.

Amendments
—**2010.** The 2010 amendment added VII.

—**2009.** The 2009 amendment, in III, substituted "qualified psychiatrist or psychologist" for "psychiatrist" in the third sentence and twice in the last sentence and added "or psychologist" preceding "other than" in the last sentence.

—**2006.** Paragraph V: Added the third sentence.

—**2005.** Paragraphs III and VI: Rewritten to the extent that a detailed comparison would be impracticable.

—**2001.** Paragraph II: Substituted "only under an order for involuntary admission or involuntary emergency admission ordered by the district court or probate court having jurisdiction pursuant to RSA 135-C" for "if the criteria set forth in RSA 135-C:27 are met" in the first sentence.

—**2000.** Rewritten to the extent that a detailed comparison would be impracticable.

—**1999.** Paragraph I: Substituted "60 days" for "90 days" in the first sentence.
Paragraph II: Substituted "60 days" for "90 days" following "not to exceed" in the first sentence of subpar. (c).
Paragraph III: Added.

—**1994.** Chapter 55:1 inserted "following a hearing and a determination that such person is dangerous to self or others" preceding "order" in par. I and Ch. 408 amended the section generally.

Applicability of 1994 amendment.
1994, 408:13, eff. Jan. 1, 1995, provided that the amendment to this section by 1994, 408:2 shall apply to acts leading to a felony charge which occur on or after January 1, 1995.

NOTES TO DECISIONS

1. Burden of proof
2. "Dangerous"
3. Restoration of competency
4. Reassessment of capacity

1. Burden of proof
Clear and convincing standard of proof did not have to be applied to a dangerousness determination regarding a 90-day involuntary commitment under RSA 135:17-a, V because, using a three-factor due process analysis under the New Hampshire constitution, defendant's and the State's interests were substantially equivalent so that the preponderance of the evidence burden of proof was appropriate. State v. Lavoie, 155 N.H. 477, 924 A.2d 370, 2007 N.H. LEXIS 84 (2007).

2. "Dangerous"

Superior court utilized the proper criteria in ordering defendant's involuntary commitment for 90 days under RSA 135:17-a, V although it did not specifically apply or refer to the definition of the term "dangerous" as found in RSA 135-C:27, II, the involuntary emergency admission (IEA) statute. State v. Lavoie, 155 N.H. 477, 924 A.2d 370, 2007 N.H. LEXIS 84 (2007).

3. Restoration of competency

Appellate court will not infer from silence in the record that the trial court found by clear and convincing evidence that a defendant cannot be restored to competency. Such a finding must be explicit. State v. Demesmin, 159 N.H. 595, 992 A.2d 569, 2010 N.H. LEXIS 7 (2010).

RSA 135:17-a plainly contemplated that whatever course of treatment a trial court ordered for the restoration of competency be under the supervision of a psychiatrist; the trial court erred, therefore, when it ordered "tutelage in the law" by defendant's attorneys. In addition, RSA 135:17-a dictated that any further competency evaluation be undertaken by defendant's "treating psychiatrist." State v. Leonard, 151 N.H. 201, 855 A.2d 531, 2004 N.H. LEXIS 114 (2004).

4. Reassessment of capacity

Trial court did not lack jurisdiction to order a re-assessment of defendant's capacity to stand trial because it had impliedly dismissed without prejudice the original indictment by operation of law. For a case to be dismissed without prejudice, the trial court had to find that a defendant could not be restored to competency, and the trial court had made no such finding; thus, the trial court had never dismissed the original indictment against defendant, and the State was not required to re-indict him to continue prosecuting him. State v. Demesmin, 159 N.H. 595, 992 A.2d 569, 2010 N.H. LEXIS 7 (2010).

Trial courts possess the inherent authority to order a second evaluation and competency hearing when there is evidence of malingering, and the common law governing malingering is consistent with a plain and ordinary reading of RSA 135:17-a. RSA 135:17-a does not preclude a trial court from conducting necessary proceedings to determine whether a defendant is malingering; the statute provides no safe harbor for the artful malingerer. State v. Demesmin, 159 N.H. 595, 992 A.2d 569, 2010 N.H. LEXIS 7 (2010).

When the State alleged that defendant was malingering, the trial court did not err in permitting a re-evaluation of his competency to stand trial. Under the common law, trial courts possessed the inherent authority to order a second evaluation and competency hearing when there was evidence of malingering, and RSA 135:17-a did not preclude this. State v. Demesmin, 159 N.H. 595, 992 A.2d 569, 2010 N.H. LEXIS 7 (2010).

135:17-b. Notification Authorized.

I. Notwithstanding any provision of law to the contrary, in the event that a person who has been charged with a violent crime, found incompetent to stand trial pursuant to RSA 135:17-a, and civilly committed pursuant to RSA 135-C or RSA 171-B, or committed pursuant to RSA 651:9-a, is transferred to another facility or discharged to the community, either conditionally or absolutely, the department of health and human services shall immediately notify the attorney general, who shall notify the victim as defined in RSA 21-M:8-k, I(a) and, in the event of a discharge, the law enforcement agency in the community to which the person is being discharged. For purposes of this section, discharge shall include the initial authorization by the administrative review committee of New Hampshire hospital to allow a person to leave the grounds of the hospital unaccompanied by a hospital staff member.

II. For purposes of this section, the term "violent crime" includes those crimes listed in RSA 651:5, XIII and the following:

(a) RSA 173-B:9, violation of protective order.

(b) RSA 631:2, second degree assault.

(c) RSA 631:3, felony reckless conduct.

(d) RSA 631:4, criminal threatening involving the use of a deadly weapon.

(e) RSA 633:3-a, stalking.

(f) RSA 635:1, burglary.

(g) RSA 641:5, tampering with witnesses and informants.

(h) RSA 650-A:1, felonious use of firearms.

Source.

2010, 293:4, eff. September 11, 2010. 2011, 251:1, eff. September 11, 2011. 2012, 151:1, eff. August 6, 2012.

Amendments

—**2012.** The 2012 amendment added the I designation; in the first sentence of I, substituted "a violent crime" for "murder, pursuant to RSA 630:1, I-a, or I-b, manslaughter, or aggravated felonious sexual assault," "or RSA 171-B, or committed pursuant to RSA 651:9-a, is transferred to another facility or discharged" for "is discharged," and "victim as defined in RSA 21-M:8-k, I(a) and, in the event of a discharge" for "family of the victim, or the victim of aggravated felonious sexual assault if an adult, and"; and added II.

—**2011.** The 2011 amendment, in the first sentence, substituted "absolutely" for "otherwise" and "victim, or the victim of aggravated felonious sexual assault if an adult" for "homicide victim" and added the second sentence.

Applicability of 2011 amendment.

2011, 251:2, eff. September 11, 2011, provided: "RSA 135:17-b as amended by section 1 of this act shall be applicable to the discharge of any qualified individual who is under an order of civil commitment on or after September 11, 2010."

135:17-c. Information Related to Competency Determinations.

All evaluation reports, recommendations, medical records, or other documents related to the court's determinations under RSA 135:17-a, I, II, and III shall be kept separately from the public court file and shall not be disclosed except as follows:

I. The court may order release with the written consent of the parties.

II. The competency report may be provided to the receiving facility or the secure psychiatric unit pursuant to RSA 135:17-a, VII.

III. In any case in which the court finds that the defendant is not competent to stand trial pursuant to RSA 135:17-a, I, or has not been restored to competency pursuant to RSA 135:17-a, IV, the court shall make written findings which describe the evidence which was relied upon to make its determination. Such written findings shall be part of the public court file. The prosecutor shall provide a copy of the written findings to the victim, as defined in RSA 21-M:8-k.

Source.

2012, 151:2, eff. August 6, 2012.

TITLE XII
PUBLIC SAFETY AND WELFARE

CHAPTER 158

EXPLOSIVES AND EXPLOSIVE SUBSTANCES

Keeping

SECTION
158:9.   Possession of Explosives.

License to Purchase, Store and Transport

158:9-a.   Acts Unlawful.
158:9-b.   Application.
158:9-c.   Fees and Disposition.
158:9-d.   License Forms.
158:9-e.   Penalties.
158:9-f.   Rules; Enforcement.
158:9-g.   Availability of Information.
158:9-h.   Certificates of Competency for Explosives.
158:10.   Recovery of Penalties, etc. [Repealed.]

Transportation

158:11.   With Passengers.
158:12.   Rulemaking. [Repealed.]
158:15.   Picture Films, etc. [Repealed.]
158:16.   Marking.
158:17.   Penalty.
158:18.   Personal Injury.

Control of Storage, Sale, and Use

158:19.   Control of Explosives.

Sale, etc., of Inflammable Polishes

158:20.   Test, Domestic Use. [Repealed.]
158:21.   Other Cases. [Repealed.]
158:22.   Penalty. [Repealed.]

Electrical Material, Devices, Appliances and Equipment

158:23.   Prohibition.
158:24.   Authority.
158:25.   Penalty.

Electric Fence Controllers

158:26.   Sale and Use.
158:27.   Penalty.

Space Heaters and Stoves

158:28.   Sale or Installation of Heaters.

Unlawful Use of Explosives

158:29.   Definitions.
158:30.   Classes of Explosives.
158:31.   Duties of Certain Officials.
158:32.   Possession of Bomb or Explosive; Penalty.
158:33.   Notice of Seizure.
158:34.   Malicious Explosion; Penalty.
158:35.   Possession of Infernal Machine; Penalty.
158:36.   Throwing or Placing of Explosives; Penalty.
158:37.   Use of Molotov Cocktail; Penalty.
158:38.   False Reports as to Explosives.
158:38-a.   Placement of Simulated Explosives.
158:39.   Exceptions.

Enforcement

SECTION
158:40.   Exceptions and Exemptions Not Required to be Negated.

Cross References.
Arson, see RSA 634:1.
Fireworks, see RSA 160-B.
Fishing with explosive substances, see RSA 211:7.
Permissible fireworks, see RSA 160-C.

RESEARCH REFERENCES

New Hampshire Practice.
11-55 N.H.P. Probate Law & Procedure § 55-1.
11-56 N.H.P. Probate Law & Procedure § 56-1.
11-62 N.H.P. Probate Law & Procedure § 62-1.

Keeping

158:1–158:8.

[Repealed 1955, 190:1, eff. June 3, 1955.]

Former section(s).
Former RSA 158:1, which was derived from RS 112:1; CS 118:1; GS 98:2; GL 108:2; PS 117:2; PL 148:1; and RS 177:1, related to searching buildings and vessels suspected of containing more than twenty-five pounds of gunpowder.

Former RSA 158:2, which was derived from RS 112:2; CS 118:2; GS 98:3; 1878, 31:1; GL 108:3; PS 117:3; PL 148:2; and RL 177:2, related to storing more than twenty-five pounds of gunpowder.

Former RSA 158:3, which was derived from RS 112:3; CS 118:3; GS 98:4; GL 108:4; PS 117:4; PL 148:3; and RL 177:3, related to keeping gunpowder for retail sale.

Former RSA 158:4, which was derived from RS 112:5; CS 118:5; GS 98:7; GL 108:7; PS 117:7; PL 148:4; and RL 177:4, related to peddling and night sales of gunpowder.

Former RSA 158:5, which was derived from RS 112:7; CS 118:7; GS 98:6; GL 108:6; PS 117:6; PL 148:5; and RL 177:5, related to gunpowder on carriages.

Former RSA 158:6, which was derived from RS 112:9; CS 118:9; GS 98:9; GL 108:9; PS 117:9; PL 148:6; and RL 177:6, related to depositing cargos of gunpowder in the public magazine.

Former RSA 158:7, which was derived from 1854, 1543:1; GS 98:1; GL 108:1; PS 117:1; PL 148:7; and RL 177:7, related to municipal regulations relative to gunpowder.

Former RSA 158:8, which was derived from RS 112:1, 6; CS 118:1, 6; GS 98:8; GL 108:8; PS 117:8; PL 148:8; and RL 177:8, related to seizure and forfeiture of gunpowder.

158:9. Possession of Explosives.

No person shall leave, deposit or have in his custody or possession in any building used in whole or in part as a dwelling house, tenement house, apartment building, office building, shop or store, or in or within 500 feet of any building used in whole or in part as a school, theater, church, public building or other place of public assembly, any high explosive, such as and including dynamite, any explosive compound of which nitroglycerin forms a part, fulminate in bulk or dry condition, blasting caps, detonating fuses, black powder or other similar explosive, except as may be permitted by regulations issued pursuant to RSA 158. Whoever violates the provisions of this section shall be guilty of a misdemeanor if a natural person, or guilty of a felony if any other person.

Source.
1885, 96:1. PS 117:11. PL 148:9. RL 177:9. RSA 158:9. 1955, 190:2. 1973, 529:29. 1977, 361:12, eff. July 1, 1977.

Amendments
—**1977.** Substituted "RSA 158" for "RSA 153" at the end of the first sentence.

—**1973.** Made minor stylistic changes in the first sentence and rewrote the second sentence.

—**1955.** Rewritten to the extent that a detailed comparison would be impracticable.

Cross References.
Classification of crimes, see RSA 625:9.
Sentences, see RSA 651.

License to Purchase, Store and Transport

158:9-a. Acts Unlawful.

I. No person shall purchase, store, or transport or attempt to purchase, store or transport any high explosive without first obtaining a license therefor as provided in RSA 158:9-b.

II. No person shall sell any high explosive to another unless the purchaser exhibits a license to purchase obtained as provided in RSA 158:9-b. In such case, the seller shall record the name and address of the purchaser, the license number, the date of the sale, the type and quantity of explosive sold, the serial number of said explosive, if any, and the purpose for which it is to be used. Said record shall be kept by the seller for a period of 2 years.

III. No person shall store or keep any high explosive unless such explosive is stored or kept in accordance with regulations pursuant to RSA 158:9-f.

IV. Notwithstanding the provisions of paragraph I, any employee of any person, firm, corporation or association whose usual business requires the use of any high explosive may transport the same in the course of his employment if the employer has obtained a license in its name as provided in RSA 158:9-b.

V. Notwithstanding the provisions of paragraph II, any employee of any person, firm, corporation or association whose usual business requires the use of any high explosive may purchase the same in the name of his employer if said employer has obtained a license in its name as provided in RSA 158:9-b. In such case, the seller shall record the name, address and license number of the employer, the name and address of the employee, the date of the sale, the type and quantity of explosive, the serial number of the explosive sold, if any, and the purpose for which it is to be used. Said record shall be kept by the seller for a period of 2 years.

VI. For the purposes of this section, the term "high explosive" shall mean and include dynamite, any explosive compound of which nitroglycerin forms a part, fulminate in bulk or dry condition, blasting caps, detonating fuses, blasting powder, blasting agents or other similar explosive but shall not include black powder used in sporting rifles purchased or sold in quantities of 50 pounds or less or stored in quantities of 5 pounds or less.

Source.
1970, 45:1. 1977, 361:6, eff. July 1, 1977.

Amendments
—**1977.** Paragraph III: Substituted "in accordance with regulations pursuant to RSA 158:9-f" for "under lock and key or in a safe, secure place".
Paragraph VI: Inserted "blasting agents" following "powder" and added "purchased or sold in quantities of 50 pounds or less or stored in quantities of 5 pounds or less" following "sporting rifles".

Cross References.
Penalties, see RSA 158:9-e.
Proof of exceptions or exemptions generally, see RSA 158:40.

158:9-b. Application.

I. Upon application of any resident or non-resident, the director of state police, or some person designated by the director, shall issue a license to such applicant authorizing the applicant to use, purchase and transport explosives in this state for not more than 2 years from the date of issue, if the applicant has a certificate of competency pursuant to RSA 158:9-h, has any proper purposes, and the applicant is a suitable person to be licensed. The license shall be in duplicate and shall bear the name, address, description and signature of the licensee. The original thereof shall be delivered to the licensee and the duplicate shall be preserved by the director. The license shall be issued within a reasonable time after application therefor, and, if such application is denied, the reasons for such denial shall be stated in writing, in duplicate, the original of which shall be delivered to the applicant, and the copy thereof kept in the office of the department of safety, division of state police.

I-a. Upon application of any corporation, partnership, or similar entity, the director of state police, or designee, shall issue a license to a corporation, partnership, or similar entity authorizing the use, purchase, and transport of explosives in this state for not more than 2 years from the date of issue, if an employee of such corporation, partnership, or similar entity has a certificate of competency pursuant to RSA 158:9-h. The license shall be in duplicate and shall bear the name, address, description, and signature of the licensee. The original thereof shall be delivered to the licensee and the duplicate shall be preserved by the director. The license shall be issued within a reasonable time after application therefor, and if such application is denied, the reasons for such denial shall be stated in writing, in duplicate, the original of which shall be delivered to the applicant, and the copy thereof kept in the office of the department of safety, division of state police.

II. Upon application of any person, the director of state police, or some person designated by the director, shall issue a license to such applicant authorizing the applicant to store explosives in this state for not more than one year from the date of issue. The license shall be in duplicate and shall bear the name, address, description and signature of the licensee. The original thereof shall be delivered to the licensee and the duplicate shall be preserved by the director. The license shall be issued within a reasonable time after application therefor, and, if such application is denied, the reasons for such denial shall be stated in writing, in duplicate, the original of which shall be delivered to the applicant, and the copy thereof kept in the office of the department of safety, division of state police.

III. Upon application of any person, the director of state police, or some person designated by the director, shall issue a license to such applicant authorizing the applicant to sell or market explosives in this state for not more than one year from the date of issue. The license shall be in duplicate and shall bear the name, address, description and signature of the licensee. The original thereof shall be delivered to the licensee and the duplicate shall be preserved by the director. The license shall be issued within a reasonable time after application therefor, and, if such application is denied, the reasons for such denial shall be stated in writing, in duplicate, the original of which shall be delivered to the applicant, and the copy thereof kept in the office of the department of safety, division of state police.

IV. Upon application of any person, the director of state police, or designee, shall issue a license to such applicant authorizing the use, purchase, and transport of black powder and other flash powders, in excess of 50 pounds, for the use of fireworks manufacturing, if the applicant has a certificate of competency pursuant to RSA 158:9-f, has any proper purpose, and the applicant is a suitable person to be licensed. For the purposes of any corporation, partnership, or other similar entity, the applicant must be an employee who fulfills all other criteria under this section. The use, purchase, and transport license for black powder or flash powders shall not be issued for more than 2 years from the date of issuance. The license shall be in duplicate and shall bear the name, address, description, and signature of the licensee. The original thereof shall be delivered to the licensee and the duplicate shall be preserved by the director. The license shall be issued within a reasonable time after application therefor, and if such application is denied, the reasons for such denial shall be stated in writing, in duplicate, the original of which shall be delivered to the applicant, and the copy thereof kept in the office of the department of safety, division of state police.

Source.
1970, 45:1. 1977, 361:7, eff. July 1, 1977. 2002, 280:2, eff. July 17, 2002.

Amendments
—**2002.** Paragraph I: Substituted "the director" for "him" preceding "shall issue" and "the applicant" for "him" following "authorizing", deleted "it appears that" preceding "the applicant" and inserted "has a certificate of competency pursuant to RSA 158:9-h" thereafter and deleted "that" following "proper purposes, and" in the first sentence.
Paragraphs I-a and IV: Added.
Paragraphs II and III: Substituted "the director" for "him" following "designated by" and "the applicant" for "him" following "authorizing" in the first sentence.

—**1977.** Rewritten to the extent that a detailed comparison would be impracticable.

158:9-c. Fees and Disposition.

I. The fee for licenses issued under RSA 158:9-b, I shall be $100.

II. The fee for licenses for explosives storage facilities as defined by federal regulation in 27 CFR 181 shall be as follows:

(a) For a type I storage facility, a fee of $50;

(b) For a type II outdoor storage facility, a fee of $50, and for a type II indoor storage facility, a fee of $10;

(c) For a type IV outdoor storage facility, a fee of $50, and for a type IV indoor storage facility, a fee of $10;

(d) For a type V outdoor storage facility, a fee of $50, and for a type V indoor storage facility, a fee of $10;

(e) There shall be no license required for a type III storage facility.

III. The fee for licenses issued under RSA 158:9-b, III shall be $100.

III-a. There shall be a storage facility fee for a storage permit issued by the director of state police for the storage of display fireworks as defined in 27 C.F.R. section 555.11, packaged or unpackaged. This fee shall be the same as that provided under paragraph II(a) through (e).

IV. All fees received under this section shall be used for administration and enforcement, any excess to be deposited as unrestricted general fund revenue.

V. The state, county, or municipal governments or units thereof shall be exempt from the payment of license fees under this chapter.

VI. There shall be a fee of $100 for any competency examination or renewal certificate given by the director of state police for any examination or certificate given under this subdivision.

Source.
1970, 45:1. 1977, 361:8. 1987, 323:1, 2. 1988, 292:1, 2, eff. at 12:01 a.m., May 3, 1988. 1999, 348:1, eff. Jan. 21, 2000. 2002, 280:3, eff. July 17, 2002. 2008, 192:8, 9, eff. June 11, 2008. 2011, 160:1, eff. June 14, 2011.

Amendments
—**2011.** The 2011 amendment substituted "27 C.F.R. section 555.11" for "27 C.F.R. section 55.11" in the first sentence of III-a.

—**2008.** The 2008 amendment in I and VI, substituted "$100" for "$40".

—**2002.** Paragraphs I and VI: Substituted "$40" for "$4".

Paragraph II: Increased the fees throughout subpars. (a)–(d) and substituted "type IV" for "type V" preceding "indoor storage" in subpar.(c)

Paragraph III: Substituted "$100" for "$10".

—1999. Paragraph III-a: Substituted "display fireworks" for "class B special fireworks" and "27 C.F.R. section 55.11" for "49 CFR 173.88(d)" in the first sentence.

—1988. Paragraph III-a: Deleted the former first sentence, "in addition" preceding "there shall be" at the beginning of the present first sentence and inserted "for a storage permit issued by the director of state police" preceding "for the storage" in that sentence, and substituted "(e)" for "(c)" following "II(a) through" at the end of the second sentence.

Paragraph VI: Substituted "examination or certificate given" for "license issued" preceding "under this subdivision".

—1987. Paragraphs III-a and VI: Added.

—1977. Rewritten to the extent that a detailed comparison would be impracticable.

158:9-d. License Forms.

The director of state police is hereby authorized and directed to prepare forms for the licenses required by RSA 158:9-a.

Source.
1970, 45:1. 1977, 361:9, eff. July 1, 1977.

Amendments
—1977. Deleted "and to supply the same to the officials of the cities and towns authorized to issue said licenses" at the end of the first sentence and deleted the second sentence.

158:9-e. Penalties.

I. Any person convicted of violating the provisions of RSA 158:9-a, I and II shall be guilty of a misdemeanor for first and second offense and of a felony for any subsequent offense.

II. Any person convicted of violating the provisions of RSA 158:9-a, III or regulations promulgated pursuant thereto shall be guilty of a misdemeanor for first and second offense and of a felony for any subsequent offense.

III. Any person convicted of larceny of any high explosive as defined in RSA 158:9-a, IV, shall be guilty of a class B felony.

IV. The director, or his designee, shall have the authority to, at the owner's expense, require the immediate removal to a safe and secure location, any explosive found to be kept in violation of any rule or regulation covered under RSA 158 provided that said violation constitutes an immediate threat to public safety. The director shall also have the authority to suspend or revoke any license issued under RSA 158:9-b when it has been determined by a hearing board, the members of which shall be designated by the commissioner of safety, that a violation of any of the requirements of RSA 158 has occurred.

Source.
1970, 45:1. 1973, 528:77. 1977, 361:10, eff. July 1, 1977.

Revision note.
In par. II, substituted "provisions" for "provision" preceding "of RSA 158:9-a, III" to correct an apparent typographical error in 1977, 361:10.

Amendments
—1977. Paragraph I: Substituted "misdemeanor for first and second offense and of a felony for any subsequent offense" for "class B felony if a natural person, or guilty of a felony if any other person."

Paragraph II: Substituted "provision" for "provisions" preceding "of RSA 158:9-a, III", inserted "or regulations promulgated pursuant thereto" thereafter and substituted "misdemeanor for first and second offense and of a felony for any subsequent offense" for "misdemeanor if a natural person, or guilty of a felony if any other person."

Paragraph III: Substituted "RSA 158:9-a, IV" for "RSA 158:9-a, VI".

Paragraph IV: Added.

—1973. Paragraph I: Substituted "guilty of a class B felony if a natural person, or guilty of a felony if any other person" for "fined not more than one thousand dollars or imprisoned not more than five years, or both" following "shall be".

Paragraph II: Substituted "guilty of a misdemeanor if a natural person, or guilty of a felony if any other person" for "fined not more than five hundred dollars or imprisoned not more than one year, or both" following "shall be".

Paragraph III: Substituted "guilty of a class B felony" for "fined not more than one thousand dollars or imprisoned not more than five years or both" following "shall be".

Cross References.
Classification of crimes, see RSA 625:9.
Sentences, see RSA 651.

158:9-f. Rules; Enforcement.

I. The director of the division of state police may adopt rules pursuant to RSA 541-A relative to:

(a) The sale, storage, handling, transportation, inspection, administration, and use of explosives, including provisions relative to the purchase of insurance by commercial entities.

(b) The procedures for the sale, storage, handling, transportation, inspection, administration, permit fees, and use of display fireworks to be followed by the licensing board of any city or town, or if a duly constituted licensing board does not exist, the chief of police of a city or town, if any, or the governing board of a town, city, or village district, when issuing permits for the sale or display of display fireworks pursuant to RSA 160-B. Rules adopted pursuant to this subparagraph shall include a requirement that no person may be issued a display permit for display fireworks unless the person has previously demonstrated his or her competence to handle such displays and has been issued a certificate of competency by the division of state police.

(c) The purchase of insurance by commercial entities, relative to the sale, storage, handling, transportation, inspection, administration and display of display fireworks.

II. The director shall enforce all laws of the state relative to the sale, storage, handling, transportation, inspection, administration, and use of explosives and display fireworks and rules adopted under this section. The director shall assist the several counties, cities, towns, village districts, and precincts in supervising and enforcing local laws, by-laws, and ordinances where existent, relative to the storage, transportation, sale, and use of explosives and display fireworks. The powers and duties authorized by this section shall not be restricted by the provisions of RSA 106-B:15.

III. As used in this section "display fireworks" shall mean the same as display fireworks defined in 27 C.F.R. section 555.11, packaged or unpackaged.

Source.
  1977, 361:11. 1987, 323:3. 1988, 292:3, 4. 1991, 286:3, eff. March 1, 1992. 1999, 348:2, eff. Jan. 21, 2000. 2011, 160:1, eff. June 14, 2011.

Amendments
  —2011. The 2011 amendment substituted "27 C.F.R. section 555.11" for "27 C.F.R. section 55.11" in III.

  —1999. Substituted "display fireworks" for "class B special fireworks" wherever it appeared throughout the section, "27 C.F.R. section 55.11" for "49 CFR 173.88(d)" in par. III and made minor stylistic changes throughout the section.

  —1991. Paragraph I(b): Substituted "RSA 160-B" for "RSA 160-A" at the end of the first sentence.

  —1988. Paragraph I(b): Rewritten to the extent that a detailed comparison would be impracticable.
  Paragraph I(c): Added.

  —1987. Rewritten to the extent that a detailed comparison would be impracticable.

Cross References.
  Transportation of permissible fireworks from point of purchase, see RSA 160-C:14.

158:9-g. Availability of Information.

Except as provided in this section, all records and papers pertaining to licenses issued pursuant to RSA 158:9-b and any hearing conducted pursuant to RSA 158:9-e, IV, shall be open to the inspection of any person. Notwithstanding any other law to the contrary, the commissioner of safety may refuse to release any information or may exclude the public from any portion of a hearing if he determines that the information or hearing concerns the storage of explosives or other matters which, if made available to the public, would jeopardize public safety.

Source.
  1979, 106:2. 1987, 20:1, eff. June 6, 1987.

Amendments
  —1987. Rewritten to the extent that a detailed comparison would be impracticable.

158:9-h. Certificates of Competency for Explosives.

I. No person shall use explosives unless at least one natural person with a current and valid certificate of competency is physically present to conduct the blasting operation. A certificate of competency shall not constitute a license under RSA 158:9-b but shall be in addition to any other license required under that section.

II. No natural person shall conduct blasting operations without a current certificate of competency issued by the director of the division of state police and valid for the category of use involved. Such certificate shall be valid for 4 years from the date of issue unless suspended or revoked by the director.

III. The commissioner of the department of safety shall adopt rules, pursuant to RSA 541-A, establishing the categories of certificates of competency based on the use of the explosives and the procedure and criteria for issuing, renewing, suspending, and revoking such certificates.

IV. Any person convicted of violating the provisions of RSA 158:9-h, I, and any natural person convicted of violating RSA 158:9-h, II, shall be guilty of a misdemeanor for the first and second offense and of a felony for any subsequent offense.

V. The fee for a certificate of competency or its renewal shall be as stated in RSA 158:9-c, VI.

Source.
  1995, 226:13, eff. Aug. 13, 1995.

Cross References.
  Classification of crimes, see RSA 625:9.
  Sentences, see RSA 651.

158:10. Recovery of Penalties, etc.

[Repealed 1955, 190:1, eff. June 3, 1955.]

Former section(s).
  Former RSA 158:10, which was derived from RS 112:10; CS 118:10; GS 98:10; GL 108:10; PS 117:10; PL 148:10; and RL 177:10, related to recovery and use of penalties.

Transportation

Cross References.
  Transporting hazardous materials and explosives, see RSA 265:115 et seq.

158:11. With Passengers.

It shall be unlawful to transport, carry or convey, from one place to another in this state, any dynamite, gunpowder or other explosive on any vessel or vehicle of any description operated by a common carrier, which vessel or vehicle is carrying passengers for hire by railroad or on the public waters of the state; provided, that it shall be lawful to transport on any such vessel or vehicles small arms ammunition in any quantity, and such fuses, torpedoes, rockets or other signal devices as may be essential to promote safety in operation, and properly packed and marked samples of explosives for laboratory examination, not exceeding a net weight of ½ pound each, and not exceeding 20 samples at one time in a single vessel or vehicle, but such samples shall not be carried in that part of a vessel or vehicle which is intended for transportation of passengers for hire. Nothing in this section shall prevent the transportation of military or naval forces with their accompanying munitions of war on passenger equipment vessels or vehicles.

Source.
1913, 128:1. PL 148:11. RL 177:11. RSA 158:11. 1955, 190:3, eff. June 9, 1955.

Amendments
—**1955.** Inserted "by railroad or on the public waters of the state" preceding "provided" and made other minor stylistic changes in the first sentence.

Cross References.
Proof of exceptions or exemptions generally, see RSA 158:40.

158:12. Rulemaking.

[Repealed 1996, 227:4, XI, eff. June 10, 1996.]

Former section(s).
Former RSA 158:12, which was derived from 1913, 128:2; PL 148:12; RL 177:12; 1951, 203:1; RSA 158:12; 1955, 190:4; 1981, 435:3; and 1985, 402:6, I(e)(1), related to rulemaking authority realtive to the transportation of explosives through the compact part of a town or village.

158:13, 158:14.

[Repealed 1955, 190:1, eff. June 3, 1955.]

Former section(s).
Former RSA 158:13, which was derived from RS 112:4; CS 118:4; GS 98:5; GL 108:5; PS 117:5; PL 148:13; and RL 177:13, related to transportation of gunpowder through the compact part of a town or village.
Former RSA 158:14, which was derived from 1913, 128:3; PL 148:14; and RL 177:14, related to transportation of nitroglycerine.

158:15. Picture Films, etc.

[Repealed 2007, 168:2, eff. June 18, 2007.]

Former section(s).
Former RSA 158:15, which was derived from 1919, 127:1; PL 148:15; and RL 177:15, related to transportation of picture films in the passenger cabin of trains.

158:16. Marking.

Every package containing explosives or other dangerous articles, when presented to a common carrier for shipment, shall have the contents plainly marked on the outside thereof; and it shall be unlawful for any person to deliver, or cause to be delivered, to any common carrier any explosive or other dangerous article under any false or deceptive marking, description, invoice, shipping order or other declaration, or without informing the agent of such carrier of the true character thereof, at or before the time such delivery or carriage is made.

Source.
1913, 128:4. PL 148:16. RL 177:16.

158:17. Penalty.

Any person who shall knowingly violate, or cause to be violated, any provision of this subdivision, or any regulation made by the commissioner of transportation in pursuance thereof, shall, except as otherwise provided, be guilty of a class B felony if a natural person, or guilty of a felony if any other person.

Source.
1913, 128:4. PL 148:17. RL 177:17. RSA 158:17. 1973, 528:78, eff. at 11:59 p.m., Oct. 31, 1973.

Revision note.
Substituted "public utilities commission" for "public service commission" pursuant to 1951, 203:10, par. 1.
Substituted "commissioner of transportation" for "public utilities commission" in light of 1985 amendment of RSA 158:12.

Amendments
—**1973.** Substituted "any person who" for "whoever" preceding "shall knowingly" and "guilty of a class B felony if a natural person, or guilty of a felony if any other person" for "fined not more than two thousand dollars, or imprisoned not more than eighteen months, or both" following "provided, be".

Cross References.
Classification of crimes, see RSA 625:9.
Sentences, see RSA 651.

158:18. Personal Injury.

When the death or bodily injury of any person is caused by the explosion of any article named in this subdivision, while the same is being placed upon any vessel or vehicle to be transported in violation hereof, or while the same is being so transported, or while the same is being removed from such vessel or vehicle, the person knowingly placing, or aiding or permitting the placing, of such articles upon any such vessel or vehicle, to be so transported, shall be guilty of a class A felony.

Source.
1913, 128:5. PL 148:18. RL 177:18. RSA 158:18. 1973, 528:79, eff. at 11:59 p.m., Oct. 31, 1973.

Amendments
—**1973.** Substituted "guilty of a class A felony" for "imprisoned not more than ten years" at the end of the section.

Cross References.
Classification of crimes, see RSA 625:9.
Sentences, see RSA 651.

Control of Storage, Sale, and Use

158:19. Control of Explosives.

Whenever in his judgment the common defense of public safety of the state requires such action, the governor is hereby authorized to direct the adjutant general of this state to control the storage, sale, and use of explosives, except small arms ammunition, for the purpose of preventing such explosives from endangering the public safety by coming into the possession of unfriendly forces, domestic or foreign, and for the purpose of advising the military, naval, and civil defense authorities of this state of the quantities and location of such explosives for use in the common defense of this state. Upon the governor so directing, the adjutant general is hereby authorized to promulgate regulations requiring dealers to register their stocks and sales of such explosives, and requiring boards of firewards, police officers, or selectmen, as the case may be, to assist in such control measures as he shall institute in the exercise of this authority. No records of the location and amounts of explosives compiled by the adjutant general hereunder shall be deemed public records, but shall be subject to such security classification and restricted to such military, naval, and civil defense uses as the adjutant general, with the approval of the governor and council, may prescribe.

Source.
1951, 204:1, eff. Aug. 7, 1951.

Sale, etc., of Inflammable Polishes

158:20. Test, Domestic Use.

[Repealed 2011, 67:1, I, eff. January 1, 2012.]

Former section(s).
Former RSA 158:20, which was derived from 1923, 118:1; PL 148:19; and RL 177:19, related to the sale of stove polish.

158:21. Other Cases.

[Repealed 2011, 67:1, II, eff. January 1, 2012.]

Former section(s).
Former RSA 158:21, which was derived from 1921, 101:1; PL 148:20; and RL 177:20, related to the sale of certain inflammable polishes.

158:22. Penalty.

[Repealed 2011, 67:1, III, eff. January 1, 2012.]

Former section(s).
Former RSA 158:22, which was derived from 1921, 101:2; 1923, 119:2; PL 148:21; RL 177:21; RSA 158:22; and 1973, 528:80, related to penalties for the sale of certain polishes.

Electrical Material, Devices, Appliances and Equipment

158:23. Prohibition.

It shall be unlawful for any person, firm or corporation to offer for sale, manufacture for sale, expose for sale at retail, or rent to the general public or dispose of by gift as premiums or in any similar manner, any material, devices, appliances or equipment requiring electrical energy to function and designed for household or other domestic uses which are not in conformity with standard approved methods of construction for safety to life and property.

Source.
1957, 192:1, eff. Aug. 20, 1957.

158:24. Authority.

To carry out the provisions of this chapter, the state fire marshal is authorized to take such actions as he may deem necessary to inform the public of the intent and purposes of this chapter and to adopt such rules, under RSA 541-A, as may be required for its effective enforcement.

Source.
1957, 192:1. 1987, 124:8, eff. July 1, 1987.

Amendments
—**1987.** Rewritten to the extent that a detailed comparison would be impracticable.

158:25. Penalty.

Any person who violates any of the provisions set forth in this subdivision shall be guilty of a misdemeanor.

Source.
1957, 192:1. 1973, 528:81, eff. at 11:59 p.m., Oct. 31, 1973.

Amendments
—**1973.** Rewritten to the extent that a detailed comparison would be impracticable.

Cross References.
Classification of crimes, see RSA 625:9.
Sentences, see RSA 651.

Electric Fence Controllers

158:26. Sale and Use.

No person or individual shall sell, utilize, install or have installed within this state equipment, devices or methods whereby fence wires may be energized with electricity unless a standard type of controller is used which has the approval of the Underwriters Laboratories or the state fire marshal's office, or both. All existing fence controllers shall conform to the requirements of this section not later than one year from January 1, 1968. Enforcement of this section shall be the responsibility of the fire control board.

Source.
1967, 135:1, eff. Jan. 1, 1968.

Revision note.
Substituted "January 1, 1968" for "the effective date of this act" at the end of the second sentence.
Substituted "section" for "act" following "enforcement of this" in the third sentence to conform reference to style employed in LEXIS New Hampshire Revised Statutes Annotated.

158:27. Penalty.

Any person who violates the provisions of RSA 158:26 shall be guilty of a violation if a natural person, or guilty of a misdemeanor if any other person.

Source.
1967, 135:1. 1973, 530:14, eff. at 11:59 p.m., Oct. 31, 1973.

Amendments
—1973. Rewritten to the extent that a detailed comparison would be impracticable.

Cross References.
Classification of crimes, see RSA 625:9.
Sentences, see RSA 651.

Space Heaters and Stoves

158:28. Sale or Installation of Heaters.

I. For the purposes of this section, "unvented space heater" means any heating appliance, either wick, wickless, or pot burner type, which uses oil, gas, or kerosene for fuel, is either stationary or portable, and the products of combustion of which are not directly conducted to the outside of the building via a chimney connector pipe.

II. No person shall sell, offer for sale, install, or operate an unvented space heater that does not comply with the standards established pursuant to this section. Nothing in this section shall prevent the sale, installation, or use of:

(a) Flameless catalyst type heaters; or

(b) Unvented space heaters used as antiques or curios, provided they are rendered inoperative.

III. The commissioner of safety shall adopt rules, pursuant to RSA 541-A, relative to:

(a) Approval, installation, and operation of unvented space heaters.

(b) Safekeeping, safe storage, and safe handling of any fuel recommended by the manufacturer of any approved unvented space heater for use in such space heater.

IV. The state fire marshal may test or cause to be tested, at the expense of the manufacturer, any type or brand of unvented space heater proposed for sale or distribution in this state to ensure that such heater meets the standards established pursuant to this section.

V. Any person who violates this section or any rule adopted pursuant to this section shall be guilty of a violation if a natural person, or guilty of a misdemeanor if any other person.

Source.
1971, 400:1. 1973, 530:15. 1979, 398:4. 1982, 40:1, eff. May 24, 1982. 1998, 104:1, eff. Jan. 1, 1999.

Amendments
—1998. Rewritten to the extent that a detailed comparison would be impracticable.

—1982. Rewritten to the extent that a detailed comparison would be impracticable.

—1979. Rewritten to the extent that a detailed comparison would be impracticable.

—1973. Substituted "guilty of a violation if a natural person, or guilty of a misdemeanor if any other person" for "punished by a fine of not more than one hundred dollars" at the end of the third sentence.

Cross References.
Classification of crimes, see RSA 625:9.
Sentences, see RSA 651.

Purpose
A majority of the language of the legislative history of this section indicates that it was enacted to prohibit the sale of unvented space heaters for use in occupied buildings. Linlee Enters. v. State, 122 N.H. 455, 445 A.2d 1130, 1982 N.H. LEXIS 369 (1982).

The purpose of this section, as set forth in the legislative subcommittee report, was to prevent accidental asphyxiation resulting from the use of unvented space heaters in occupied buildings. Linlee Enters. v. State, 122 N.H. 455, 445 A.2d 1130, 1982 N.H. LEXIS 369 (1982).

The purpose of this section was to promote safety by discouraging the use of unvented space heaters in occupied structures by forbidding the sale of these items for that use and by prohibiting their installation in occupied structures. Linlee Enters. v. State, 122 N.H. 455, 445 A.2d 1130, 1982 N.H. LEXIS 369 (1982).

Unlawful Use of Explosives

158:29. Definitions.

For the purpose of this subdivision:

I. "Detonators" shall mean any devices for the purpose of exploding an explosive charge and shall include blasting caps, blasting caps with safety fuse, electric blasting caps, detonating fuses, primers, boosters and igniters.

II. "Primers, percussion fuses, combination fuses and time fuses" shall mean devices used to ignite powder charges of ammunition or the black powder bursting charges of projectiles.

III. "Explosive bombs" shall mean containers filled with explosives and provided with a detonating device.

IV. "Detonating fuse" shall mean a fuse containing high explosives of sufficient strength to detonate other high explosives lying alongside and explode the entire charge almost instantaneously through its whole length.

V. "Boosters" shall mean casings containing several ounces of a high explosive used to increase the intensity of explosion of the detonator of a detonating fuse.

VI. "Delay electric igniters" shall mean small metal tubes containing a wire bridge in contact with a small quantity of ignition compound.

VII. "Fuse lighters" shall mean small cylindrical hollow pasteboard or metal tubes containing an igniting composition in one end, the other being open.

VIII. "Blasting caps" shall mean thin metal shells containing dry fulminate of mercury or other similar substance either alone or in combination with fulminate of mercury and fired by a slow-burning safety fuse, or arranged to be fired by an electric current.

IX. "Tracer fuses" shall mean devices attached to projectiles and containing a slow-burning composition.

X. "Electric squibs" shall mean small tubes or blocks containing a small quantity of ignition compound in contact with a wire bridge.

XI. "Explosives", "high explosive or explosive substance" shall mean any material or container containing a chemical compound or mixture that is commonly used or intended for the purpose of producing an explosion and that contains any oxidizing or combustible materials or other ingredients in such proportions, quantities, or packing that an ignition by fire, friction, concussion, or detonation of any part of the compound or mixture may cause such a sudden generation of highly heated gases that the resultant gaseous pressure is capable of producing destructive effects on contiguous objects. This definition shall not include the components for hand loading rifle, pistol, and shotgun ammunition and or rifle, pistol, and shotgun ammunition.

XII. "Infernal machine" shall mean any device which would endanger life or do damage to property, or both, by fire or explosion, whether or not contrived to ignite or explode automatically and whether or not disguised so as to appear harmless.

Source.
1973, 419:1, eff. Aug. 29, 1973. 2002, 280:4, eff. July 17, 2002.

Amendments
—**2002.** Paragraph XI: Rewritten to the extent that a detailed comparison would be impracticable.

158:30. Classes of Explosives.

I. Class A explosives or so-called dangerous explosives shall include: ammunition for cannon with explosive projectile; explosive projectiles; explosive grenades; explosive bombs; explosive mines; explosive torpedoes; rocket ammunition; chemical ammunition; explosive boosters; jet thrust units (JATO), class A; detonating primers; detonating fuses, boosters, or other detonating fuse parts containing an explosive; cartridge bags empty, with black powder igniters; percussion, tracer, combination time fuses and tracers; nitroglycerine blasting caps and electric blasting caps in quantity exceeding 1,000 caps in the aggregate; dynamite; T.N.T. (trinitrotoluene); fulminate of mercury; ammonia nitrate, when stored with, transported with, or used with explosives, or with any substance which, when mixed with ammonium nitrate, creates an explosive; or any substance highly susceptible to detonation or otherwise of a maximum hazard.

II. Class B explosives or so-called flammable hazards shall include: ammunition for cannon with empty projectiles, inert loaded projectiles, solid projectiles, or without projectiles or shell; rocket ammunition; jet thrust units (JATO), Class B; or any other substance highly susceptible to detonation.

III. Class C explosives or so-called minimum hazards shall include: explosives cable cutters; empty grenades, primed; explosive rivets; blasting caps and electric blasting caps, not exceeding 1,000 caps; smokeless powder; small arms ammunition; igniters; delay igniters or fuse lighters; ammunition for

cannon; ammunition for small arms with explosive bullets or explosive projectiles; black powder; primers.

Source.
1973, 419:1, eff. Aug. 29, 1973.

158:31. Duties of Certain Officials.

I. Heads of police and fire departments in cities and towns shall investigate the cause and circumstances of every explosion in their respective jurisdictions by which property has been destroyed or damaged, especially to ascertain whether it was caused by carelessness or design. They shall begin such investigation forthwith after such explosion, and if it appears to the official making such investigation that the explosion is of suspicious origin or is the result of a violation of law, or if the department head is unable to determine the cause, he or she shall immediately notify the director of the division of state police.

II. For the purposes of statistical reporting and intelligence information gathering, criminal threats which are conveyed by any means of communication and which involve the potential use of any explosive device, radiological or nuclear material, or any chemical or biological agent, military or otherwise, or any combination of such agents or materials, shall be reported to the director of the division of state police.

Source.
1973, 419:1, eff. Aug. 29, 1973. 2002, 280:5, eff. July 17, 2002.

Amendments
—**2002.** Designated the existing provisions of the section as par. I and in that paragraph substituted "the department head" for "he" preceding "is unable" and inserted "the division of" preceding "state police" in the second sentence and added par. II.

158:32. Possession of Bomb or Explosive; Penalty.

No person shall have in his possession or under his control any high explosive Class A as defined in RSA 158:30, I, or any bomb manufactured from any substance or device as defined in RSA 158:30, I–III, contrary to the provisions of this chapter or any rule or regulation made thereunder. Whoever violates the provisions of this section shall be subject to the following penalty:

I. If the offense occurs prior to November 1, 1973, he shall be fined not more than $1,000 or imprisoned for not more than 2-½ years, or both.

II. If the offense occurs on or after November 1, 1973, he shall, if a natural person, be guilty of a Class B felony, and any other person shall be guilty of a felony.

III. Any bomb or explosive found in possession or under the control of a person violating the provisions hereof shall be forfeited to the state.

Source.
1973, 419:1, eff. Aug. 29, 1973.

Cross References.
  Classification of crimes, see RSA 625:9.
  Sentences, see RSA 651.

158:33. Notice of Seizure.

Notice of the seizure of any bomb or explosive found in the possession or under the control of any person in violation of RSA 158:32 shall immediately be sent to the director of state police by the officer making the seizure, and upon final conviction of such person, such bomb or explosive shall be adjudged forfeited to the state and safely delivered to the director of state police or his authorized representative and disposed of at his discretion.

Source.
  1973, 419:1, eff. Aug. 29, 1973.

158:34. Malicious Explosion; Penalty.

Whoever wilfully, intentionally and without right, by the explosion of gunpowder or of any other explosive, unlawfully damages or destroys property or injures a person, shall be subject to the following penalty:

I. If the offense occurs prior to November 1, 1973, he shall be fined not more than $1,000 or imprisoned in the state prison for not more than 20 years, or both.

II. If the offense occurs on or after November 1, 1973, he shall, if a natural person, be guilty of a Class A felony, and any other person shall be guilty of a felony.

Source.
  1973, 419:1, eff. Aug. 29, 1973.

Cross References.
  Classification of crimes, see RSA 625:9.
  Sentences, see RSA 651.

158:35. Possession of Infernal Machine; Penalty.

Whoever, other than a police or other law enforcement officer acting in the discharge of his official duties, or fire or military personnel while in performance of their duties, has in his possession or under his control an infernal machine or a similar instrument, contrivance, or device shall be subject to the following penalty:

I. If the offense occurs prior to November 1, 1973, he shall be fined not more than $1,000 or imprisoned in the state prison for not more than 10 years, or both.

II. If the offense occurs on or after November 1, 1973, he shall, if a natural person, be guilty of a Class A felony, and any other person shall be guilty of a felony.

III. The said machine, instrument, contrivance, or device shall be forfeited to the state. Notice of the seizure of any such machine, instrument, contriv-ance or device shall be sent forthwith to the director of state police and the article seized shall be subject to his order.

Source.
  1973, 419:1, eff. Aug. 29, 1973.

Cross References.
  Classification of crimes, see RSA 625:9.
  Sentences, see RSA 651.

158:36. Throwing or Placing of Explosives; Penalty.

Whoever wilfully and intentionally throws at or near any person and whoever wilfully, intentionally and without right throws into, against or upon, any property real or personal, or puts, places or explodes or causes to be exploded in, upon or near such property, or near any person, the following: gunpowder or other explosive, or a bombshell, torpedo or other instrument filled or loaded with an explosive; with an intent unlawfully to destroy or damage property or to injure any person, or whoever has in his possession or under his control such an article or instrument with such intent, shall be subject to the following penalty:

I. If the offense occurs prior to November 1, 1973, he shall be fined not more than $5,000 or imprisoned in the state prison for not more than 20 years, or both.

II. If the offense occurs on or after November 1, 1973, he shall, if a natural person, be guilty of a Class A felony, and any other person shall be guilty of a felony.

Source.
  1973, 419:1, eff. Aug. 29, 1973.

Cross References.
  Classification of crimes, see RSA 625:9.
  Sentences, see RSA 651.

158:37. Use of Molotov Cocktail; Penalty.

Whoever makes, sells, uses or has in his possession or under his control a bottle or other breakable container containing a flammable liquid into which has been fixed or placed a wick or similar device, and which bottle or container when ignited and thrown will cause a fire or explosion, shall be subject to the following penalty:

I. If the offense occurs prior to November 1, 1973, he shall be fined not more than $1,000 or imprisoned for not more than 2-½ years, or both.

II. If the offense occurs on or after November 1, 1973, he shall, if a natural person, be guilty of a Class B felony, and any other person shall be guilty of a felony.

The provisions of this section shall not apply to flares, lanterns, fireworks or other such devices used for signal or illumination purposes, or items used for any other lawful purpose.

Source.
1973, 419:1, eff. Aug. 29, 1973.

Cross References.
Classification of crimes, see RSA 625:9.
Sentences, see RSA 651.

158:38. False Reports as to Explosives.

Any person who knowingly communicates a report known by him to be false regarding the location of an explosive or other similar dangerous substance or contrivance, thereby causing anxiety, unrest, fear, or personal discomfort to any person, shall be guilty of a class B felony.

Source.
1973, 419:1. 1981, 553:1, eff. Aug. 29, 1981.

Amendments
—**1981.** Rewritten to the extent that a detailed comparison would be impracticable.

Cross References.
Classification of crimes, see RSA 625:9.
False public alarm regarding explosion, see RSA 644:3.
False report to law enforcement officer concerning explosive, see RSA 641:4.
Sentences, see RSA 651.

NOTES TO DECISIONS

Cited:
Cited in State v. Sorrell, 120 N.H. 472, 416 A.2d 1375, 1980 N.H. LEXIS 326 (1980).

158:38-a. Placement of Simulated Explosives.

Any person who places or causes the placement of any device simulating an explosive or other similar dangerous substance or contrivance in any location, thereby causing anxiety, unrest, fear, or personal discomfort to any person, shall be guilty of a class A felony.

Source.
1981, 553:2, eff. Aug. 29, 1981.

Cross References.
Classification of crimes, see RSA 625:9.
Sentences, see RSA 651.

158:39. Exceptions.

I. Nothing contained in this subdivision shall apply to the regular military or naval forces or coast guard of the United States, or any federal agency, or the duly authorized militia of this state, nor to the police or fire departments of this state, provided they are acting within their official capacity and in the proper performance of their duties.

II. Nothing contained in this subdivision shall apply to explosives while being transported by certified carriers in motor vehicles, railroad cars, or vessels in conformity with the regulations adopted by the federal government.

III. Nothing contained in this subdivision shall apply to black powder used by an association or nonprofit entity organized to conduct historical re-enactments, portrayals, or demonstrations, or to the storage of up to 50 pounds of black powder by such an association or entity, provided that no more than 50 pounds of black powder is contained in a type 4 magazine as defined in 27 C.F.R. 55.203 and 27 C.F.R. 55.210(b) located at least 50 feet from an occupied dwelling in such a way as to be secure from unauthorized persons. The location of such magazine shall be registered with the local fire department and such information shall be for local fire department or local law enforcement use only.

Source.
1973, 419:1, eff. Aug. 29, 1973. 2007, 70:1, eff. June 11, 2007; 183:2, eff. at 12:01 a.m., June 11, 2007.

Amendments
—**2007.** Chapter 70 designated existing provisions of the section as par. I and par. II; substituted "the federal government" for "the interstate commerce commission or the United States Coast Guard" at the end of par. II.
Paragraph III: Added by Chapter 70.
Paragraph III: Rewritten by Chapter 183.

Contingent 2007 amendment.
2007, 183:3, eff. June 18, 2007, provided in part: "If HB 117 [ch. 70] of the 2007 legislative session becomes law, section 2 of this act shall take effect at 12:01 a.m. on the effective date of HB 117." Pursuant to the terms of this provisions par. III is set out above as amended by Ch. 198:2, eff. June 11, 2007 at 12:01 a.m.

Cross References.
Proof of exceptions or exemptions generally, see RSA 158:40.

Enforcement

158:40. Exceptions and Exemptions Not Required to be Negated.

In any complaint, information, or indictment, and in any action or proceeding brought for the enforcement of any provision of this chapter, it shall not be necessary to negate any exception, excuse, proviso, or exemption contained herein, and the burden of proof of any such exception, excuse, proviso or exemption shall be upon the defendant.

Source.
1987, 181:1, eff. May 12, 1987.

CHAPTER 159

PISTOLS AND REVOLVERS

SECTION
159:1. Definition.
159:2. Carrying by Offenders. [Repealed.]
159:3. Convicted Felons.
159:3-a. Armed Career Criminals.
159:4. Carrying Without License.
159:5. Exceptions.
159:5-a. Exceptions and Exemptions Not Required to be Negated.
159:6. License to Carry.
159:6-a. Confidentiality of Licenses.
159:6-b. Suspension or Revocation of License.
159:6-c. Appeal From Denial, Suspension, or Revocation.
159:6-d. Full Faith and Credit for Licenses From Other States; Reciprocity.
159:6-e. Violation.

SECTION
159:6-f.   Remedies.
159:7.   Sales to Felons.
159:8.   License to Sell.
159:8-a.   Sales to Nonresidents; Attorney General.
159:8-b.   Penalties.
159:9.   Record of Sale. [Repealed.]
159:10.   Sale Without License.
159:11.   False Information.
159:12.   Sale to Minors.
159:13.   Changing Marks.
159:14.   Exemption.
159:15.   Possession of Dangerous Weapon While Committing a
             Violent Crime.
159:16.   Carrying or Selling Weapons.
159:17.   Exceptions.
159:18.   Felonious Use of Teflon-coated, Armor-piercing and
             Exploding Bullets and Cartridges.
159:19.   Courthouse Security.
159:19-a.   Criminal Use of Pistol Cane or Sword Cane.

Self-Defense Weapons

159:20.   Self-Defense Weapons Defined.
159:21.   Possession by Felons Prohibited.
159:22.   Restricted Sale.
159:23.   Criminal Use of Electronic Defense or Aerosol Self-
             Defense Spray Weapons.

Martial Arts Weapons

159:24.   Sale of Martial Arts Weapons.

Voluntarily Surrendered Firearms

159:25.   Voluntarily Surrendered Firearms.

State Jurisdiction

159:26.   Firearms, Ammunition, and Knives; Authority of the
             State.

Cross References.
Criminal record check for sale of handguns, see RSA 159-D.
Felonious use of firearms, see RSA 650-A:1.
Noise pollution from shooting ranges, see RSA 159-B.
Unauthorized use of firearms, see RSA 644:13.

NOTES TO DECISIONS

Appeals
RSA ch. 159 does not provide a choice of appellate forum. Garand v. Town of Exeter, 159 N.H. 136, 977 A.2d 540, 2009 N.H. LEXIS 95 (2009).

Cited:
Cited in United States v. Kozerski, 518 F. Supp. 1082, 1981 U.S. Dist. LEXIS 13519 (D.N.H. 1981).

159:1. Definition.

Pistol or revolver, as used herein, means any firearm with barrel less than 16 inches in length. It does not include antique pistols, gun canes, or revolvers. An antique pistol, gun cane, or revolver, for the purposes of this chapter means any pistol, gun cane, or revolver utilizing an early type of ignition, including, but not limited to, flintlocks, wheel locks, matchlocks, percussions and pin-fire, but no pistol, gun cane, or revolver which utilizes readily available center fire or rim-fire cartridges which are in common, current use shall be deemed to be an antique pistol, gun cane, or revolver. Noth-

ing in this section shall prevent antique pistols, gun canes, or revolvers from being owned or transferred by museums, antique or arms collectors, or licensed gun dealers at auctions, gun shows, or private premises provided such ownership or transfer does not conflict with federal statutes.

Source.
1923 118:1. PL 149:1. RL 179:1. RSA 159:1. 1967, 220:1. 1992, 273:1, eff. July 17, 1992.

Amendments
—1992. In the second sentence inserted "gun canes" following "pistols" in the third sentence inserted "gun cane" following "pistol" in four places readily available preceding "center fire"and "which are in common current use" following "cartridges" and added the fourth sentence.

—1967. Substituted "sixteen" for "twelve" preceding "inches" in the first sentence pistols or revolvers for "weapons incapable of use" following "antique" in the second sentence and added the third sentence.

Cross References.
Proof of exceptions or exemptions generally, see RSA 159:5-a.

NOTES TO DECISIONS

Tear gas weapon
A loaded tear gas pencil which could not be used except with alteration or adaptation for any purpose other than the discharge of tear gas was not a loaded pistol or firearm within the meaning of this section and RSA 159:4 prohibiting the carrying of concealed loaded pistols or revolvers without license. State v. Umbrello, 106 N.H. 336, 211 A.2d 400, 1965 N.H. LEXIS 160 (1965).

159:2. Carrying by Offenders.

[Repealed 1977, 403:3, eff. Sept. 3, 1977.]

Former section(s).
Former RSA 159:2, which was derived from 1923, 118:2; PL 149:20; RL 179:2; RSA 159:2; 1967, 220:2; and 1973, 528:82, related to additional punishment for commission of a crime when armed with a pistol or revolver.

159:3. Convicted Felons.

I. A person is guilty of a class B felony if he:

(a) Owns or has in his possession or under his control, a pistol, revolver, or other firearm, or slung-shot, metallic knuckles, billies, stiletto, switchblade knife, sword cane, pistol cane, blackjack, dagger, dirk-knife, or other deadly weapon as defined in RSA 625:11, V; and

(b) Has been convicted in either a state or federal court in this or any other state, the District of Columbia, the Commonwealth of Puerto Rico, or any territory or possession of the United States of:

(1) A felony against the person or property of another; or

(2) A felony under RSA 318-B; or

(3) A felony violation of the laws of any other state, the District of Columbia, the United States, the Commonwealth of Puerto Rico or any territory or possession of the United States relating to controlled drugs as defined in RSA 318-B.

I-a. A person is guilty of a class B felony if such person completes and signs an application for purchase of a firearm and the person is a convicted felon under the provisions of paragraph I.

II. The state shall confiscate to the use of the state the weapon or weapons of persons convicted under this section.

III. It is an affirmative defense to a charge under this section that a felony of which a defendant has been convicted in another jurisdiction would not have constituted a felony in the state of New Hampshire at the time such felony was committed.

Source.
1923, 118:3. PL 149:3. RL 179:3. RSA 159:3. 1973, 405:1; 528:83. 1981, 553:4. 1993, 157:1, eff. Jan. 1, 1994. 2001, 189:1, eff. Jan. 1, 2002; 214:1, eff. Jan. 1, 2002.

Amendments
—2001. Paragraph I(a): Chapter 214 substituted "or other deadly weapon as defined in RSA 625:11, V" for "or any other dangerous weapon".
Paragraph I-a: Added by ch. 189.

—1993. Rewritten to the extent that a detailed comparison would be impracticable.

—1981. Rewritten to the extent that a detailed comparison would be impracticable.

—1973. Rewritten by chs. 405 and 528 to the extent that a detailed comparison would be impracticable.

Cross References.
Classification of crimes, see RSA 625:9.
Exceptions, see RSA 159:5.
Possession of electronic defense weapons by felons, see RSA 159:21.
Selling firearms to convicted felons, see RSA 159:7.
Sentences, see RSA 651.

NOTES TO DECISIONS

1. Constitutionality
2. Purpose
3. Elements
4. Felony conviction
5. Control of weapon
6. Dangerous weapon
7. Deadly weapon
8. Indictments
9. Hearing
10. Ignorance
11. Sentencing
12. Evidence

1. Constitutionality
Where defendant, who was convicted of four counts of being a felon in possession of a firearm in violation of former RSA 159:3, I, argued that the trial court deprived defendant of the right to produce all favorable proofs under N.H. Const. pt. I, art. 15 when it denied defendant's motions for discovery of records regarding the ownership of the four firearms, the argument failed; ownership of the weapons was not relevant to defendant's prosecution, given that only possession or control of the weapons was necessary for a conviction under former RSA 159:3, I(a). State v. Fox, 150 N.H. 623, 843 A.2d 309, 2004 N.H. LEXIS 39 (2004).

Use of term "dangerous weapon" in felon in possession statute was not unconstitutionally vague, where a fair reading of statute informed by its purpose placed defendant on notice that possession of a six-inch hunting knife under circumstances alleged could constitute a "dangerous weapon." State v. Beckert, 144 N.H. 315,

741 A.2d 63, 1999 N.H. LEXIS 114 (1999).

This section, prohibiting felons from possessing firearms, does not violate state constitutional right to bear arms. State v. Smith, 132 N.H. 756, 571 A.2d 279, 1990 N.H. LEXIS 14 (1990).

This section, prohibiting convicted felons from having control or possession of firearms, is not unconstitutionally vague. State v. Pike, 128 N.H. 447, 514 A.2d 1279, 1986 N.H. LEXIS 305, 66 A.L.R.4th 1233 (1986).

This section, prohibiting convicted felons from having control or possession of firearms, is not unconstitutionally over broad. State v. Pike, 128 N.H. 447, 514 A.2d 1279, 1986 N.H. LEXIS 305, 66 A.L.R.4th 1233 (1986).

2. Purpose
The plain purpose of this section prohibiting convicted felons from having control or possession of firearms is to impose upon convicted felons the prescribed sanctions when they deal with the weapons described by this section. State v. Pike, 128 N.H. 447, 514 A.2d 1279, 1986 N.H. LEXIS 305, 66 A.L.R.4th 1233 (1986).

3. Elements
With respect to the crime of being a felon in possession of a firearm, prosecution is required to prove that the defendant knowingly owned possessed or controlled the firearms and that he was a convicted felon. State v. Stratton, 132 N.H. 451, 567 A.2d 986, 1989 N.H. LEXIS 124 (1989).

Failure of this section to state a specific culpable mental state did not prevent valid prosecution. State v. Stratton, 132 N.H. 451, 567 A.2d 986, 1989 N.H. LEXIS 124 (1989).

Charge that defendant possessed a pistol concealed on his person when he had previously been convicted of a felony stated an offense under this section, and did not also state one under RSA 159:4, and thus was not duplicitous and bad for uncertainty. State v. Hoyt, 114 N.H. 256, 319 A.2d 286, 1974 N.H. LEXIS 251 (1974).

4. Felony conviction
With regard to defendant's charge of being a felon in possession of a firearm, the trial court was not obligated to accept defendant's stipulation to felon status without reading it to the jury. Defendant's status as a convicted felon was what rendered his gun possession illegal; thus, his stipulation pertained to an essential element of the crime. State v. Young, 159 N.H. 332, 986 A.2d 497, 2009 N.H. LEXIS 122 (2009).

There was sufficient evidence to support a conviction for being a felon in possession of a firearm. The State submitted evidence of defendant's felony convictions, and several witnesses testified that they saw him holding a gun or saw him extend his arm as if he were holding a gun and witnessed muzzle flashes coming from where a gun would be located in his hand. State v. Young, 159 N.H. 332, 986 A.2d 497, 2009 N.H. LEXIS 122 (2009).

A conviction of the offense of being an accessory after the fact to the crime of breaking, entering and larceny constitutes a conviction "of a felony against the person or property of another" within the meaning of this section prohibiting the possession of certain firearms by felons. State v. Colcord, 106 N.H. 90, 205 A.2d 32, 1964 N.H. LEXIS 45 (1964).

5. Control of weapon
There was sufficient evidence that defendant possessed weapons in violation of RSA 159:3 where there was testimony that he had rifles inside a gun locker in his home, that he and his wife jointly owned and exercised control over them, and that he could access the locker if needed; the fact that the key was in the wife's jewelry box did not prevent defendant from gaining access to the weapons. State v. Crie, 154 N.H. 403, 913 A.2d 767, 2006 N.H. LEXIS 179 (2006).

Where defendant was convicted of four counts of being a felon in possession of a firearm in violation of former RSA159:3, I, there was overwhelming evidence that defendant controlled the four firearms at issue; although defendant's trailer was owned by the father and was on the father's property, defendant exclusively used the trailer, witnesses had seen defendant either display or use three of the guns, and defendant exercised sufficient control over the fourth gun such that he made the previously inoperable gun operable. State v. Fox, 150 N.H. 623, 843 A.2d 309, 2004 N.H. LEXIS 39 (2004).

Whether a defendant has "control" over weapons for purposes of this section is not based upon their location at any particular place, or upon his relationship with any individual; rather, it is based upon his ability to determine use and disposition of the guns. State v. Haycock, 136 N.H. 361, 616 A.2d 481, 1992 N.H. LEXIS 180 (1992).

State did not present sufficient evidence for rational trier of fact to conclude beyond reasonable doubt that felon defendant exercised control over a firearm, where state showed at best only that defendant had access to certain rifles and rational conclusions inconsistent with defendant exercising control over rifles could be drawn from evidence, which was circumstantial. State v. Haycock, 136 N.H. 361, 616 A.2d 481, 1992 N.H. LEXIS 180 (1992).

A defendant charged with being a convicted felon having control of firearms did not have to be in the proximity of the firearms when arrested; the defendant need only have had the ability to exercise "control" over the firearms in the sense that he could determine who could use the firearms. State v. Pike, 128 N.H. 447, 514 A.2d 1279, 1986 N.H. LEXIS 305, 66 A.L.R.4th 1233 (1986).

An argument by a defendant charged with being a convicted felon having control of firearms, that the statutory language did not adequately forewarn him that his presence in his girlfriend's house or his relationship with her constituted control over firearms located in her house, was rejected, since control over the firearms was not based upon these factors, but only upon the defendant's ability to determine the use and disposition of the firearms. State v. Pike, 128 N.H. 447, 514 A.2d 1279, 1986 N.H. LEXIS 305, 66 A.L.R.4th 1233 (1986).

6. Dangerous weapon

Where a felon is charged with possession of a "dangerous weapon" not specifically enumerated in statute, test of whether instrument is included in statute's reach is whether it has the capacity to cause serious injury or death as allegedly used or intended to be used; factors relevant to this determination include nature of instrument itself, circumstances and manner of its possession, its actual or intended use, and possible peaceful purposes justifying its possession and use. State v. Beckert, 144 N.H. 315, 741 A.2d 63, 1999 N.H. LEXIS 114 (1999).

Defendant's concealed, six-inch hunting knife constituted a "dangerous weapon" within meaning of felon in possession statute; under circumstances in which defendant was apprehended, a reasonable jury could find knife constituted a "dangerous weapon" because of serious and immediate danger it posed to police and members of public. State v. Beckert, 144 N.H. 315, 741 A.2d 63, 1999 N.H. LEXIS 114 (1999).

Evidence was sufficient to show that a "zip gun" was a dangerous weapon, where an expert witness testified as to the construction of zip guns and testified that the device possessed by the defendant was a zip gun, and where the jurors themselves were allowed to examine the zip gun. State v. Surette, 137 N.H. 20, 622 A.2d 1254, 1993 N.H. LEXIS 31 (1993).

7. Deadly weapon

Shank possessed by defendant, a prison inmate, was a deadly weapon under RSA 625:11, V, for purposes of RSA 159:3, I. The circumstances surrounding defendant's possession of a shank in a prison indicated only one potential use—to cause death or serious bodily injury to another human. State v. Duran, 162 N.H. 369, 33 A.3d 1183, 2011 N.H. LEXIS 122 (2011).

When defendant used a bow and arrow to kill a porcupine on his property, the evidence was insufficient to support his conviction of being a felon in possession of a deadly weapon under RSA 159:3, I. "Deadly weapon" as defined in RSA 625:11, V, was to be construed to include only death or serious bodily injury to a human, not an animal. State v. Pratte, 158 N.H. 45, 959 A.2d 200, 2008 N.H. LEXIS 135 (2008).

8. Indictments

In a prosecution of defendant for possession of a firearm by a felon, in violation of RSA 159:3, the trial court erred in applying the mandatory minimum sentencing provision of RSA 651:2, II-g, where the indictments to which defendant pled guilty did not allege that defendant possessed, used, or attempted to use a firearm. State v. Taylor, 152 N.H. 719, 886 A.2d 1012, 2005 N.H. LEXIS 164 (2005).

Indictments that charged defendant with violations of the stat-

ute were sufficient because they alleged the essential elements of the alleged crimes and the place and approximate date of the crime and further, defendant was sufficiently apprised of the crimes of which he was accused. State v. Davis, 149 N.H. 698, 828 A.2d 293, 2003 N.H. LEXIS 103 (2003).

Where police search of defendant's residence resulted in seizure of seven firearms, and defendant was charged on seven counts of being a felon in possession of a firearm, each firearm possessed or controlled by defendant was the legitimate subject of a separate indictment, and the multiple indictments did not violate defendant's double jeopardy rights under either the New Hampshire or the Federal Constitution. State v. Stratton, 132 N.H. 451, 567 A.2d 986, 1989 N.H. LEXIS 124 (1989).

9. Hearing

Defendant charged with being a felon in possession of a firearm is not entitled to a hearing to determine whether he is too dangerous to possess a firearm. State v. Smith, 132 N.H. 756, 571 A.2d 279, 1990 N.H. LEXIS 14 (1990).

10. Ignorance

Defendant's assertion that he was ignorant of the law was not a valid defense to crime of being a felon in possession of a firearm, and, in any event, was contrary to the findings of the jury. State v. Stratton, 132 N.H. 451, 567 A.2d 986, 1989 N.H. LEXIS 124 (1989).

11. Sentencing

When defendant was convicted of being a felon in possession of a firearm under RSA 159:3, I, it was plain error to sentence him to the minimum mandatory sentence pursuant to RSA 651:2, II-g. The elements of the crime did not include a showing that the firearm was a deadly weapon, and a firearm was not a deadly weapon per se. State v. Charest, 164 N.H. 252, 55 A.3d 960, 2012 N.H. LEXIS 135 (2012).

Where an indictment specifically alleges that a defendant had firearms in his possession, the offense as alleged under RSA 159:3 is within the scope of RSA 651:2, II-g. State v. Crie, 154 N.H. 403, 913 A.2d 767, 2006 N.H. LEXIS 179 (2006).

12. Evidence

There was sufficient evidence for the jury to find that defendant, an inmate, possessed a shank. A corrections officer found the shank in a sock, which was in defendant's bag and in the bathroom where defendant was showering; defendant's name was on the sock; the laundry bag, which defendant admitted belonged to him, contained other items belonging to defendant; and defendant declined to pick up his belongings, including sneakers and a radio, when ordered to by the corrections officer, who testified that it was unusual for an inmate to leave expensive property unattended. State v. Duran, 162 N.H. 369, 33 A.3d 1183, 2011 N.H. LEXIS 122 (2011).

Cited:

Cited in State v. Kelley, 120 N.H. 12, 413 A.2d 308, 1980 N.H. LEXIS 219 (1980); State v. Gorham, 120 N.H. 162, 412 A.2d 1017, 1980 N.H. LEXIS 253 (1980); Kozerski v. Steere, 121 N.H. 469, 433 A.2d 1244, 1981 N.H. LEXIS 387 (1981); State v. Marcotte, 123 N.H. 245, 459 A.2d 278, 1983 N.H. LEXIS 260 (1983); State v. Berube, 123 N.H. 771, 465 A.2d 509, 1983 N.H. LEXIS 348 (1983); State v. Nocella, 124 N.H. 163, 467 A.2d 575, 1983 N.H. LEXIS 375 (1983); State v. Kellenbeck, 124 N.H. 760, 474 A.2d 1388, 1984 N.H. LEXIS 339 (1984); State v. Holt, 126 N.H. 394, 493 A.2d 483, 1985 N.H. LEXIS 314 (1985); State v. St. John, 129 N.H. 1, 523 A.2d 26, 1986 N.H. LEXIS 383 (1986); State v. Hurlburt, 132 N.H. 674, 569 A.2d 1306, 1990 N.H. LEXIS 8 (1990); State v. Field, 132 N.H. 760, 571 A.2d 1276, 1990 N.H. LEXIS 17 (1990); State v. Hurlburt, 135 N.H. 143, 603 A.2d 493, 1991 N.H. LEXIS 157 (1991); State v. Taylor, 136 N.H. 131, 612 A.2d 917, 1992 N.H. LEXIS 147 (1992); State v. Prevost, 141 N.H. 647, 690 A.2d 1029, 1997 N.H. LEXIS 15 (1997); In re T.J.S., 141 N.H. 697, 692 A.2d 498, 1997 N.H. LEXIS 24 (1997); State v. Hammell, 147 N.H. 313, 787 A.2d 850, 2001 N.H. LEXIS 218 (2001); Hammell v. Cattell, 2004 U.S. Dist. LEXIS 17415 (D.N.H. 2004); State v. Henderson, 154 N.H. 95, 907 A.2d 968, 2006 N.H. LEXIS 128 (2006); Bleiler v. Chief, Dover Police Dep't, 155 N.H. 693, 927 A.2d 1216, 2007 N.H. LEXIS 118 (2007).

159:3-a. Armed Career Criminals.

I. No person who has been convicted of any combination of 3 or more felonies in this state or any other state under homicide, assault, sexual assault, arson, burglary, robbery, extortion, child pornography, or controlled drug laws, shall own or have in his possession or under his control, a pistol, revolver, rifle, shotgun, or any other firearm.

II. Any person who violates paragraph I shall be guilty of a felony and, notwithstanding RSA 651:2, II, shall be sentenced to a minimum mandatory term of 10 years imprisonment and a maximum term of imprisonment of not more than 40 years and shall be fined not more than $25,000.

III. Notwithstanding any other provision of law, neither the whole, nor any part of the minimum mandatory sentence provided under paragraph II shall be served concurrently with any other term, nor shall the whole or any part of such additional term of imprisonment be suspended or deferred. No action brought to enforce sentencing under this section shall be continued for sentencing, nor shall the provisions of RSA 651:20 relative to suspensions or RSA 651-A relative to parole apply to any sentence of imprisonment imposed.

Source.
1989, 295:1, eff. Jan. 1, 1990.

Cross References.
Classification of crimes, see RSA 625:9.
Selling firearms to convicted felons, see RSA 159:7.

NOTES TO DECISIONS

1. Sufficiency of evidence
There was sufficient evidence that defendant possessed a handgun to support his conviction of being an armed career criminal. Defendant told a witness that he and his accomplice "had guns" at the time of the home invasion; the victim testified that one man had a gun; and a holster was found in the vehicle in which defendant was riding. State v. Gibbs, 164 N.H. 439, 58 A.3d 656, 2012 N.H. LEXIS 169 (2012).

Cited:
Cited in Phelan v. Thompson, 889 F. Supp. 517, 1994 U.S. Dist. LEXIS 17726 (D.N.H. 1994); In re T.J.S., 141 N.H. 697, 692 A.2d 498, 1997 N.H. LEXIS 24 (1997); State v. Rothe, 142 N.H. 483, 703 A.2d 884, 1997 N.H. LEXIS 122 (1997); Bleiler v. Chief, Dover Police Dep't, 155 N.H. 693, 927 A.2d 1216, 2007 N.H. LEXIS 118 (2007).

159:4. Carrying Without License.

No person shall carry a loaded pistol or revolver in any vehicle or concealed upon his person, except in his dwelling, house or place of business, without a valid license therefor as hereinafter provided. A loaded pistol or revolver shall include any pistol or revolver with a magazine, cylinder, chamber or clip in which there are loaded cartridges. Whoever violates the provisions of this section shall, for the first such offense, be guilty of a misdemeanor. For the second and for each subsequent violation of the provisions of this section, such person shall be guilty

of a class B felony, provided such second or subsequent violation has occurred within 7 years of the previous conviction.

Source.
1923, 118:4. PL 149:4. RL 179:4. 1951, 151:1. RSA 159:4. 1967, 220:3. 1973, 528:84. 1994, 48:1, eff. Jan. 1, 1995.

Amendments
—1994. Inserted "valid" preceding "license" in the first sentence and added "provided such second or subsequent violation has occurred within 7 years of the previous conviction" following "felony" in the fourth sentence.

—1973. Made a minor stylistic change in the first sentence and substituted "guilty of a misdemeanor" for "fined not more than one hundred dollars, or imprisoned not more than one year" at the end of the third sentence and "guilty of a class B felony" for "imprisoned not less than two years nor more than five years" at the end of the fourth sentence.

—1967. Inserted "for the first such offense" preceding "be fined" and deleted "or both" following "one year" in the third sentence and added the fourth sentence.

Cross References.
Classification of crimes, see RSA 625:9.
Exceptions, see RSA 159:5.
Proof of exceptions or exemptions generally, see RSA 159:5-a.
Sentences see RSA 651.

NOTES TO DECISIONS

1. Constitutionality
2. Construction with other law
3. Elements
4. Tear gas weapon
5. Construction

1. Constitutionality
State statute reasonably regulating right to bear arms does not violate Second Amendment to United States Constitution. State v. Sanne, 116 N.H. 583, 364 A.2d 630, 1976 N.H. LEXIS 418 (1976).

2. Construction with other law
This section and RSA 159:5 and RSA 159:6 limit the right to keep and bear arms granted by Part I Article 2-a of the New Hampshire Constitution by requiring individuals who want to carry a concealed weapon to receive a license from the town. Conway v. King, 718 F. Supp. 1059, 1989 U.S. Dist. LEXIS 10591 (D.N.H. 1989).

3. Elements
In order for a pistol or revolver to be considered "loaded" within the meaning of the carrying-without-a-license statute, the pistol or revolver must contain a cartridge in the chamber or must contain a magazine, cylinder, or clip inserted in or otherwise adjoined to the firearm such that the firearm can be discharged through normal operation. State v. Dor, — N.H. —, — A.3d —, 2013 N.H. LEXIS 87 (Aug. 7, 2013).

Offenses charged under this section and under RSA 159:3 are not identical; proof that individual is a convicted felon is necessary for conviction under section RSA 159:3 but not under this section, while proof that gun is loaded and concealed is necessary for conviction under this section but not under RSA 159:3. State v. Gosselin, 117 N.H. 115, 370 A.2d 264, 1977 N.H. LEXIS 281 (1977).

4. Tear gas weapon
A loaded tear gas pencil which could not be used except with alteration or adaptation for any purpose other than the discharge of tear gas was held not to be a loaded pistol or firearm within the meaning of this section and RSA 159:1 prohibiting the carrying of concealed loaded pistols or revolvers without license. State v. Umbrello, 106 N.H. 336, 211 A.2d 400, 1965 N.H. LEXIS 160 (1965).

5. Construction

Carrying-without-a-license statute is interpreted narrowly so as to set forth a clear demarcation between that conduct which is allowed and that which is prohibited. State v. Dor, — N.H. —, — A.3d —, 2013 N.H. LEXIS 87 (Aug. 7, 2013).

Cited:

Cited in State v. Fielders, 124 N.H. 310, 470 A.2d 897, 1983 N.H. LEXIS 415 (1983); Bleiler v. Chief, Dover Police Dep't, 155 N.H. 693, 927 A.2d 1216, 2007 N.H. LEXIS 118 (2007).

159:5. Exceptions.

The provisions of RSA 159:3 and 4 shall not apply to marshals, sheriffs, policemen or other duly appointed peace and other law enforcement officers, or bailiffs and court officers responsible for court security; nor to the regular and ordinary transportation of pistols or revolvers as merchandise, nor to members of the armed services of the United States when on duty; nor to the national guard when on duty; nor to organizations by law authorized to purchase or receive such weapons; nor to duly authorized military or civil organizations when parading, or the members thereof when at, or going to or from, their customary places of assembly.

Source.

1923, 118:5. PL 149:5. RL 179:5. 1951, 151:2. RSA 159:5. 1985, 258:1, eff. Jan. 1, 1986.

Amendments

—1985. Substituted "RSA 159:3 and 4" for "the preceding sections" following "provisions of" and inserted "or bailiffs and court officers responsible for court security" following "officers".

Cross References.

Proof of exceptions or exemptions generally, see RSA 159:5-a.

NOTES TO DECISIONS

Construction with other law

RSA 159:4, RSA 159:6 and this section limit the right to keep and bear arms granted by Part I, Article 2-a of the New Hampshire Constitution by requiring individuals who want to carry a concealed weapon to receive a license from the town. Conway v. King, 718 F. Supp. 1059, 1989 U.S. Dist. LEXIS 10591 (D.N.H. 1989).

Cited:

Cited in Kozerski v. Steere, 121 N.H. 469, 433 A.2d 1244, 1981 N.H. LEXIS 387 (1981).

159:5-a. Exceptions and Exemptions Not Required to be Negated.

In any complaint, information, or indictment, and in any action or proceeding brought for the enforcement of any provision of this chapter, it shall not be necessary to negate any exception, excuse, proviso, or exemption contained herein, and the burden of proof of any such exception, excuse, proviso or exemption shall be upon the defendant.

Source.

1987, 181:2, eff. May 12, 1987.

159:6. License to Carry.

I. (a) The selectmen of a town, the mayor or chief of police of a city or a full-time police officer designated by them respectively, the county sheriff for a resident of an unincorporated place, or the county sheriff if designated by the selectmen of a town that has no police chief, upon application of any resident of such town, city, or unincorporated place, or the director of state police, or some person designated by such director, upon application of a nonresident, shall issue a license to such applicant authorizing the applicant to carry a loaded pistol or revolver in this state for not less than 4 years from the date of issue, if it appears that the applicant has good reason to fear injury to the applicant's person or property or has any proper purpose, and that the applicant is a suitable person to be licensed. Hunting, target shooting, or self-defense shall be considered a proper purpose. The license shall be valid for all allowable purposes regardless of the purpose for which it was originally issued.

(b) The license shall be in duplicate and shall bear the name, address, description, and signature of the licensee. The original shall be delivered to the licensee and the duplicate shall be preserved by the people issuing the same for 4 years. When required, license renewal shall take place within the month of the fourth anniversary of the license holder's date of birth following the date of issuance. The license shall be issued within 14 days after application, and, if such application is denied, the reason for such denial shall be stated in writing, the original of which such writing shall be delivered to the applicant, and a copy kept in the office of the person to whom the application was made. The fee for licenses issued to residents of the state shall be $10, which fee shall be for the use of the law enforcement department of the town or city granting said licenses; the fee for licenses granted to out-of-state residents shall be $100, which fee shall be for the use of the state. The director of state police is hereby authorized and directed to prepare forms for the licenses required under this chapter and forms for the application for such licenses and to supply the same to officials of the cities and towns authorized to issue the licenses. No other forms shall be used by officials of cities and towns. The cost of the forms shall be paid out of the fees received from nonresident licenses.

II. No photograph or fingerprint shall be required or used as a basis to grant, deny, or renew a license to carry for a resident or nonresident, unless requested by the applicant.

Source.

1923, 118:6. PL 149:6. 1941, 172:1. RL 179:6. 1951, 151:3. RSA 159:6. 1959, 100:1. 1967, 220:4. 1977, 563:76. 1979, 355:1. 1993, 27:1, eff. Jan. 1, 1994; 203:1, eff. at 12:01 a.m., Jan. 1, 1994. 1994,

115:1, eff. Jan. 1, 1995; 257:1, eff. Aug. 1, 1994; 257:2, eff. Jan. 1, 1995. 1996, 167:2, eff. Aug. 2, 1996. 2003, 90:1, eff. July 29, 2003. 2009, 144:194, eff. July 1, 2009. 2012, 255:1, eff. August 17, 2012.

Revision note.

In the first sentence, substituted "director of state police" for "superintendent of the state police" pursuant to 1961, 166:3, which established a division of state police in department of safety, under a director of state police, and provided that the term of office of superintendent of state police expired upon appointment and qualification of director of state police.

Amendments

—2012. The 2012 amendment added the I(a) and I(b) designations; in the first sentence of I(a), substituted "a full-time" for "some full-time," added "the county sheriff for a resident of an unincorporated place, or the county sheriff if designated by the selectmen of a town that has no police chief," and added "unincorporated place, or"; and made related changes.

—2009. The 2009 amendment, in the eighth sentence of I, added "or city" following "of the town" and substituted "$100" for "$20."

—2003. Designated the existing provisions of the section as par. I and added par. II.

—1996. Substituted "less" for "more" preceding "than 4 years" in the first sentence, "the" for "said" following "issue" in the seventh sentence and "the" for "said" preceding "forms" in the ninth sentence.

—1994. Chapter 257:1 substituted "such" for "said" following "resident of", "such director" for "him" following "designated by", "the applicant" for "him" following "authorizing", "the applicant's" for "his" following "injury to" and "the applicant" for "he" preceding "is a suitable" in the first sentence, deleted "or" following "hunting" and inserted "or self-defense" following "shooting" in the second sentence, and added the third sentence.

Chapter 257:2 deleted "thereof" following "original" in the fifth sentence, added the sixth sentence, and deleted "therefor" following "after application" and "thereof" following "copy" in the seventh sentence.

—1993. Chapter 27 inserted "and forms for the application for such licenses" following "chapter" in the seventh sentence and added the eighth sentence.

Chapter 203 substituted "4" for "2" preceding "years" in the first and fourth sentences, "$10" for "$4" following "residents of the state shall be" and "$20" for "$10" following "out-of-state residents shall be" in the sixth sentence.

—1979. Substituted "people" for "person" preceding "issuing" in the fourth sentence, "14" for "7" preceding "days" in the fifth sentence and "$4" for "$2" following "state shall be" in the sixth sentence and added the seventh and eighth sentences.

—1977. Substituted "$10" for "four dollars" in the sixth sentence and made other minor stylistic changes throughout the section.

—1967. Added the fifth sentence.

—1959. Substituted "two years" for "one year" following "more than" in the first sentence, and at the end of the fourth sentence, and "two dollars" for "fifty cents" and "four dollars" for "one dollar" in the fifth sentence.

Severability of enactment.

1977, 563:76 was subject to a severability clause. See 1977, 563:100.

Nullification of 1994 amendment.

1994, 115:1, eff. Jan. 1, 1995, provided for the amendment of this section; however, under the terms of 1994, 257:3, the amendment of this section did not take effect.

Cross References.

Reciprocity with other states for non-residents carrying a loaded pistol or revolver, see RSA 159:6-d.

NOTES TO DECISIONS

1. Constitutionality
2. Construction
3. Construction with other law
4. Nonrenewal
5. Denial of application
6. Evidence

1. Constitutionality

A state statute reasonably regulating right to bear arms does not violate Second Amendment to the United States Constitution. State v. Sanne, 116 N.H. 583, 364 A.2d 630, 1976 N.H. LEXIS 418 (1976).

2. Construction

Town police chief plainly acts as a municipal policymaker when he decides on criteria to be considered in granting or denying a request for a gun permit. Penney v. Town of Middleton, 888 F. Supp. 332, 1994 U.S. Dist. LEXIS 16698 (D.N.H. 1994).

3. Construction with other law

RSA 159:6-e, read as a whole and construed in light of RSA 159:6 and RSA 159:6-c, applies only to alleged derelictions of a licensing authority's ministerial duties and does not provide a means to appeal a determination that the applicant does not meet the suitability or proper purpose requirements for licensure. Rather, it offers a means of enforcing those procedural provisions of RSA ch. 159 that require strict compliance by the licensing authority rather than the exercise of deliberation. Garand v. Town of Exeter, 159 N.H. 136, 977 A.2d 540, 2009 N.H. LEXIS 95 (2009).

RSA 159:4, RSA 159:5 and this section limit the right to keep and bear arms granted by Part I, Article 2-a of the New Hampshire Constitution by requiring individuals who want to carry a concealed weapon to receive a license from the town. Conway v. King, 718 F. Supp. 1059, 1989 U.S. Dist. LEXIS 10591 (D.N.H. 1989).

4. Nonrenewal

Nonrenewal of a license to carry a concealed weapon did not deprive plaintiff of a constitutionally protected liberty interest. Conway v. King, 718 F. Supp. 1059, 1989 U.S. Dist. LEXIS 10591 (D.N.H. 1989).

5. Denial of application

Although the record was incomplete, there was evidence that a licensee did not provide a town's police chief with requested information and that he had a significant and unexplained arrest history, which allowed the trial court to make a finding of unsuitability under RSA 159:6-c without shifting the ultimate burden of proof; therefore, the state supreme court had to assume that there was sufficient evidence to support a town's denial of a licensee's RSA 159:6, I application to carry a concealed weapon. Silverstein v. Town of Alexandria, 150 N.H. 679, 843 A.2d 963, 2004 N.H. LEXIS 52 (2004), overruled in part, Garand v. Town of Exeter, 159 N.H. 136, 977 A.2d 540, 2009 N.H. LEXIS 95 (2009).

6. Evidence

Pursuant to RSA 159:6-c, the trial court could make a finding of unsuitability without shifting the ultimate burden of proof; therefore, the issue of the licensee's residency did not have to be reached. In the absence of a sufficient record (required by N.H. Sup. Ct. R. 13(3)), it was assumed that the evidence supported the trial court's decision to deny licensee's RSA 159:6, I application for a license to carry a concealed weapon. Silverstein v. Town of Alexandria, 150 N.H. 679, 843 A.2d 963, 2004 N.H. LEXIS 52 (2004), overruled in part, Garand v. Town of Exeter, 159 N.H. 136, 977 A.2d 540, 2009 N.H. LEXIS 95 (2009).

Cited:

Cited in Kozerski v. Steere, 121 N.H. 469, 433 A.2d 1244, 1981

N.H. LEXIS 387 (1981); Bleiler v. Chief, Dover Police Dep't, 155 N.H. 693, 927 A.2d 1216, 2007 N.H. LEXIS 118 (2007).

RESEARCH REFERENCES

New Hampshire Bar Journal.
For article, "Lex Loci: A Survey of New Hampshire Supreme Court Decisions," see 45 N.H.B.J. 64 (July 2004).

159:6-a. Confidentiality of Licenses.

Notwithstanding the provisions of RSA 91-A:4 or any other provision of law to the contrary, all papers and records, including applications, pertaining to the issuance of licenses pursuant to RSA 159:6 and all licenses issued pursuant to said section are subject to inspection only by law enforcement officials of the state or any political subdivision thereof or of the federal government while in the performance of official duties or upon written consent, for good cause shown, of the superior court in the county where said license was issued.

Source.
1979, 106:1, eff. July 10, 1979.

159:6-b. Suspension or Revocation of License.

I. The issuing authority may order a license to carry a loaded pistol or revolver issued to any person pursuant to RSA 159:6 to be suspended or revoked for just cause, provided written notice of the suspension or revocation and the reason therefore is given to the licensee. A licensee whose license has been suspended or revoked shall be permitted a hearing on such suspension or revocation if a hearing is requested by the licensee to the issuing authority within 7 days of the suspension or revocation.

II. When the licensee hereunder ceases to be a resident of the community in which the license was issued he shall notify in writing the issuing authority at his new place of residence that he has a current license. Such license shall remain in effect until it expires pursuant to RSA 159:6.

Source.
1979, 355:2, eff. Aug. 22, 1979.

NOTES TO DECISIONS

1. Constitutionality
2. Revocation upheld

1. Constitutionality
RSA 159:6-b is a reasonable limitation upon the state constitutional right to bear arms. Bleiler v. Chief, Dover Police Dep't, 155 N.H. 693, 927 A.2d 1216, 2007 N.H. LEXIS 118 (2007).
Given the compelling state interest in public safety, RSA 159:6-b is a reasonable regulation of the time, place, and manner in which the state constitutional right to bear arms may be exercised. Bleiler v. Chief, Dover Police Dep't, 155 N.H. 693, 927 A.2d 1216, 2007 N.H. LEXIS 118 (2007).
RSA 159:6-b is not unconstitutionally vague on its face. Bleiler v. Chief, Dover Police Dep't, 155 N.H. 693, 927 A.2d 1216, 2007 N.H. LEXIS 118 (2007).
Plain language of RSA 159:6-b, read in conjunction with other provisions in the same statutory scheme, as well as prior New Hampshire court decisions, gives notice to a person of ordinary intelligence of the conduct that may result in the revocation of his or her license to carry loaded weapons concealed. Bleiler v. Chief, Dover Police Dep't, 155 N.H. 693, 927 A.2d 1216, 2007 N.H. LEXIS 118 (2007).
RSA 159:6-b does not subvert unduly the self-defense aspect of the state constitutional right to bear arms. Bleiler v. Chief, Dover Police Dep't, 155 N.H. 693, 927 A.2d 1216, 2007 N.H. LEXIS 118 (2007).

2. Revocation upheld
Petitioner's permit to carry a concealed weapon was properly revoked pursuant to RSA 159:6-b, where petitioner went to the city attorney's office and removed a loaded firearm from his pocket and placed it on a desk to tell a story about organized crime threats that allegedly had been made against him. The statute was not impermissibly vague as applied to petitioner, who knew the proper procedure for handling a loaded weapon but failed to follow it. Bleiler v. Chief, Dover Police Dep't, 155 N.H. 693, 927 A.2d 1216, 2007 N.H. LEXIS 118 (2007).

RESEARCH REFERENCES

New Hampshire Bar Journal.
For article, "Lex Loci: A Survey of New Hampshire Supreme Court Decisions," see 48 N.H.B.J. 84 (Autumn 2007).

159:6-c. Appeal From Denial, Suspension, or Revocation.

Any person whose application for a license to carry a loaded pistol or revolver has been denied pursuant to RSA 159:6 or whose license to carry a loaded pistol or revolver has been suspended or revoked pursuant to RSA 159:6-b may within 30 days thereafter, petition the district or municipal court in the jurisdiction in which such person resides to determine whether the petitioner is entitled to a license. The court shall conduct a hearing within 14 days after receipt of the petition. During this hearing the burden shall be upon the issuing authority to demonstrate by clear and convincing proof why any denial, suspension, or revocation was justified, failing which the court shall enter an order directing the issuing authority to grant or reinstate the petitioner's license. The court shall issue its decision not later than 14 days after the hearing on whether the petitioner is entitled to a license.

Source.
1979, 355:2, eff. Aug. 22, 1979. 1998, 380:2, eff. Jan. 1, 1999.

Amendments
—1998. Rewritten to the extent that a detailed comparison would be impracticable.

NOTES TO DECISIONS

1. Construction
2. Construction with other law
3. Review
4. Findings

1. Construction
Although the statutory standard of review is far from deferential, RSA 159:6-c still clearly provides an appeal from a decision of the issuing authority. Garand v. Town of Exeter, 159 N.H. 136, 977 A.2d 540, 2009 N.H. LEXIS 95 (2009).

2. Construction with other law

RSA 159:6-e, read as a whole and construed in light of RSA 159:6 and RSA 159:6-c, applies only to alleged derelictions of a licensing authority's ministerial duties and does not provide a means to appeal a determination that the applicant does not meet the suitability or proper purpose requirements for licensure. Rather, it offers a means of enforcing those procedural provisions of RSA ch. 159 that require strict compliance by the licensing authority rather than the exercise of deliberation. Garand v. Town of Exeter, 159 N.H. 136, 977 A.2d 540, 2009 N.H. LEXIS 95 (2009).

3. Review

Superior court does not have subject matter jurisdiction over RSA 159:6-c proceedings. Garand v. Town of Exeter, 159 N.H. 136, 977 A.2d 540, 2009 N.H. LEXIS 95 (2009).

RSA 159:6-e applied only to alleged derelictions of a licensing authority's ministerial duties and did not provide a means to appeal a determination that an applicant did not meet the suitability or proper purpose requirements for pistol licensure. Thus, an appeal could be brought only under RSA 159:6-c and had to be brought in district court. Garand v. Town of Exeter, 159 N.H. 136, 977 A.2d 540, 2009 N.H. LEXIS 95 (2009).

Pursuant to RSA 159:6-c, the trial court could make a finding of unsuitability without shifting the ultimate burden of proof; therefore, the issue of the licensee's residency did not have to be reached. In the absence of a sufficient record (required by N.H. Sup. Ct. R. 13(3)), it was assumed that the evidence supported the trial court's decision to deny licensee's RSA 159:6, I application for a license to carry a concealed weapon. Silverstein v. Town of Alexandria, 150 N.H. 679, 843 A.2d 963, 2004 N.H. LEXIS 52 (2004), overruled in part, Garand v. Town of Exeter, 159 N.H. 136, 977 A.2d 540, 2009 N.H. LEXIS 95 (2009).

RSA 159:6 which permits selectmen to issue licenses authorizing persons to carry a loaded pistol or revolver appears to contemplate that the district court would hear evidence and make its own determination whether the petitioner is entitled to a license. Kozerski v. Steere, 121 N.H. 469, 433 A.2d 1244, 1981 N.H. LEXIS 387 (1981).

The standard of review in appeals under RSA 159:6 which permits selectmen to issue licenses authorizing persons to carry a loaded pistol or revolver allows the court to substitute its judgment for that of the selectmen. Kozerski v. Steere, 121 N.H. 469, 433 A.2d 1244, 1981 N.H. LEXIS 387 (1981).

4. Findings

Although the record was incomplete, there was evidence that a licensee did not provide a town's police chief with requested information and that he had a significant and unexplained arrest history, which allowed the trial court to make a finding of unsuitability under RSA 159:6-c without shifting the ultimate burden of proof; therefore, the state supreme court had to assume that there was sufficient evidence to support a town's denial of a licensee's RSA 159:6, I application to carry a concealed weapon. Silverstein v. Town of Alexandria, 150 N.H. 679, 843 A.2d 963, 2004 N.H. LEXIS 52 (2004), overruled in part, Garand v. Town of Exeter, 159 N.H. 136, 977 A.2d 540, 2009 N.H. LEXIS 95 (2009).

Cited:

Cited in Allard v. Power, 122 N.H. 27, 440 A.2d 450, 1982 N.H. LEXIS 279 (1982); Conway v. King, 718 F. Supp. 1059, 1989 U.S. Dist. LEXIS 10591 (D.N.H. 1989); Bleiler v. Chief, Dover Police Dep't, 155 N.H. 693, 927 A.2d 1216, 2007 N.H. LEXIS 118 (2007).

159:6-d. Full Faith and Credit for Licenses From Other States; Reciprocity.

Notwithstanding the provisions of RSA 159:6, no nonresident holding a current and valid license to carry a loaded pistol or revolver in the state in which he resides or who is a peace officer in the state in which he resides, shall be required to obtain a license to carry a loaded pistol or revolver within this state if:

I. Such nonresident carries upon his person the license held from the state in which he resides; and

II. The state in which such person is a resident provides a reciprocal privilege for residents of this state.

Source.
1993, 130:1, eff. Jan. 1, 1994.

159:6-e. Violation.

Any person aggrieved by a violation of the licensing sections of this chapter by a licensing entity may petition the superior court of the county in which the alleged violation occurred for injunctive relief. The court shall give proceedings under this chapter priority on the court calendar. Such a petitioner may appear with or without counsel. The petition shall be deemed sufficient if it states facts constituting a violation of the licensing sections of this chapter by the licensing entity, and may be filed by the petitioner or the petitioner's counsel with the clerk of court or the justice. The clerk of court or any justice shall order service by copy of the petition on the licensing entity or a person employed by the entity. If the justice finds that time is of the essence, the justice may order notice by any reasonable means, and shall have authority to issue an order ex parte when the justice reasonably deems such an order necessary to insure compliance with the provisions of this chapter.

Source.
1996, 122:1, eff. Jan. 1, 1997.

NOTES TO DECISIONS

1. Construction
2. Applicability

1. Construction

RSA 159:6-e, read as a whole and construed in light of RSA 159:6 and RSA 159:6-c, applies only to alleged derelictions of a licensing authority's ministerial duties and does not provide a means to appeal a determination that the applicant does not meet the suitability or proper purpose requirements for licensure. Rather, it offers a means of enforcing those procedural provisions of RSA ch. 159 that require strict compliance by the licensing authority rather than the exercise of deliberation. Garand v. Town of Exeter, 159 N.H. 136, 977 A.2d 540, 2009 N.H. LEXIS 95 (2009).

In Silverstein v. Town of Alexandria, 150 N.H. 679, 843 A.2d 963, 2004 N.H. LEXIS 52 (2004), after stating that "an appeal under RSA 159:6-c is limited to the issue of whether the petitioner is entitled to a license," the court stated in dicta that "a separate appeal avenue to superior court is provided for alleged violations of the licensing sections of RSA ch. 159 by a licensing authority. See RSA 159:6-e (2002)." The court now clarifies that its reference to RSA 159:6-e as an avenue of appeal was mistaken; a petition under that section is addressed to the original jurisdiction of the superior court. Garand v. Town of Exeter, 159 N.H. 136, 977 A.2d 540, 2009 N.H. LEXIS 95 (2009).

2. Applicability

RSA 159:6-e applied only to alleged derelictions of a licensing authority's ministerial duties and did not provide a means to appeal a determination that an applicant did not meet the suitability or proper purpose requirements for pistol licensure. Thus, an appeal could be brought only under RSA 159:6-c and had to be brought in district court. Garand v. Town of Exeter, 159 N.H. 136, 977 A.2d 540, 2009 N.H. LEXIS 95 (2009).

Cited:

Cited in Bleiler v. Chief, Dover Police Dep't, 155 N.H. 693, 927 A.2d 1216, 2007 N.H. LEXIS 118 (2007).

159:6-f. Remedies.

I. If any licensing entity or employee or member of the city council or board of selectmen, in violation of the provisions of this chapter, refuses to comply with this chapter, such entity or person shall be liable for reasonable attorney's fees and costs incurred in a lawsuit under this chapter to enforce the terms of this chapter, provided that the court finds that such lawsuit was necessary in order to obtain compliance with this chapter by the licensing authority. Fees shall not be awarded unless the court finds that the entity or person knew or should have known that the conduct engaged in was a violation of this chapter or when the parties, by agreement, provide that no such fees shall be paid. In any case in which fees are awarded under this chapter, upon a finding that an employee, or other official of a licensing entity has acted in bad faith in refusing to comply with this chapter, the court may award such fees personally against such employee or other official.

II. The court may invalidate an action of a licensing entity taken in violation of the provisions of this chapter, if the circumstances justify such invalidation, and may require the licensing entity to issue a license or otherwise comply with the provisions of this chapter.

III. In addition to any other relief awarded pursuant to this chapter, the court may issue an order to enjoin future violations of this chapter.

Source.

1996, 122:1, eff. Jan. 1, 1997.

159:7. Sales to Felons.

No person shall sell, deliver, or otherwise transfer a pistol, revolver or any other firearm, to a person who has been convicted, in any jurisdiction, of a felony. Whoever violates the provisions of this section shall be guilty of a class B felony.

Source.

1923, 118:8. PL 149:7. RL 179:7. RSA 159:7. 1973, 405:2; 528:85. 1981, 553:5, eff. Aug. 29, 1981.

Amendments

—1981. Rewritten to the extent that a detailed comparison would be impracticable.

—1973. Chapter 405 deleted "is an unnaturalized foreign-born person, or" preceding "has been convicted" in the first sentence.

Chapter 528 substituted "guilty of a misdemeanor" for "fined not more than one hundred dollars, or imprisoned not more than one year, or both" at the end of the sixth sentence.

Cross References.

Classification of crimes, see RSA 625:9.

Sentences, see RSA 651.

NOTES TO DECISIONS

Cited:

Cited in State v. Kelley, 120 N.H. 12, 413 A.2d 308, 1980 N.H. LEXIS 219 (1980); Kozerski v. Steere, 121 N.H. 469, 433 A.2d 1244, 1981 N.H. LEXIS 387 (1981); State v. Smith, 132 N.H. 756, 571 A.2d 279, 1990 N.H. LEXIS 14 (1990).

159:8. License to Sell.

The selectmen of a town and the chief of police of a city may grant licenses, the form of which shall be prescribed by the director of the division of state police, effective for not more than 3 years from date of issue, permitting the licensee to sell at retail pistols and revolvers subject to the following conditions, for breach of any of which the licensee shall be subject to forfeiture:

I. The business shall be carried on only in the building designated in the license or at any organized sporting show or arms collectors' meeting sponsored by a chartered club or organization.

II. The license or a copy thereof, certified by the issuing authority, shall be displayed on the premises where it can easily be read.

III. No pistol, revolver, or other firearm shall be delivered to a purchaser not personally known to the seller or who does not present clear evidence of his identity; nor to a person who has been convicted of a felony.

Source.

1923, 118:10. PL 149:8. RL 179:8. RSA 159:8. 1967, 220:5. 1979, 44:1. 1981, 553:6. 1991, 254:2, eff. Aug. 9, 1991. 1996, 167:1, eff. Aug. 2, 1996.

Amendments

—1996. Substituted "3 years" for "one year" preceding "from date of issue" in the introductory paragraph.

—1991. Substituted "director of the division of state police" for "secretary of state" preceding "effective" in the introductory paragraph.

—1981. Paragraph III: Substituted "revolver, or other firearm" for "or revolver" following "pistol" and deleted "unless he has a permit as required by RSA 159:7" following "felony".

—1979. Paragraph III: Deleted "an unnaturalized foreign-born person or" preceding "a person".

—1967. Paragraph I: Added "or at any organized sporting show or arms collectors'" meeting sponsored by a chartered club or organization" following "license".

Cross References.

Sales to nonresidents, see RSA 159:8-a, 8-b.

Sale without license, see RSA 159:10.

OPINIONS OF THE ATTORNEY GENERAL

1. Criteria
2. License required

1. Criteria

Under this section the selectmen of a town and chiefs of police of cities may grant licenses after determining whether a dealer or a person seeking a license is a fit subject to be permitted to sell pistols and revolvers. 1 N.H.Op.A.G. 224.

2. License required

If selectmen of town or chief of police of a city do not issue license under this section dealers or other persons may not engage in business of selling pistols and revolvers. 1 N.H.Op.A.G. 224.

159:8-a. Sales to Nonresidents; Attorney General.

No person holding a license issued under the provisions of RSA 159:8 shall sell a pistol or revolver to a nonresident unless such nonresident has authority under the laws of the state of his residence, to purchase a pistol or revolver in the state of his residence, or unless the director of the division of state police, for good cause shown, has issued to such nonresident a permit for the purchase of a pistol or revolver. The attorney general shall, at least once annually, file with the secretary of state a summary of the laws of each state of the United States relative to the purchase of pistols and revolvers in such states; and a licensee may rely upon such summary in determining if a nonresident offering to purchase a pistol or revolver has authority to make such purchase under the laws of the state of his residence.

Source.
1967, 220:6, eff. Aug. 21, 1967.

159:8-b. Penalties.

If a licensee shall in any court be found guilty of a violation of any of the provisions of RSA 159:8-a, such court shall, for each such violation, order the suspension of his license for a period of 3 months, and may, in addition, impose a fine not in excess of $100.

Source.
1967, 220:6, eff. Aug. 21, 1967.

159:9. Record of Sale.

[Repealed 1996, 116:1, I, eff. July 14, 1996.]

Former section(s).
Former RSA 159:9, which was derived from 1923, 118:10; PL 149:9; RL 179:9; RSA 159:9; and 1991, 254:3, related to the making and keeping of records of sale for pistols and revolvers.

159:10. Sale Without License.

Any person who, without being licensed as herein provided, sells, advertises or exposes for sale, or has in his possession with intent to sell, pistols or revolvers shall be guilty of a class B felony if a natural person, or guilty of a felony if any other person.

Source.
1923, 118:9. PL 149:10. RL 179:10. RSA 159:10. 1967, 220:7. 1973, 528:86, eff. at 11:59 p.m., Oct. 31, 1973.

Amendments
—1973. Rewritten to the extent that a detailed comparison would be impracticable.

—1967. Rewritten to the extent that a detailed comparison would be impracticable.

Cross References.
Classification of crimes, see RSA 625:9.
Sentences, see RSA 651.

159:11. False Information.

Any person who, in purchasing or otherwise securing delivery of a pistol, revolver, or other firearm, gives false information or offers false evidence of his identity, shall be guilty of a misdemeanor for the first offense, and be guilty of a class B felony for any subsequent offense.

Source.
1923, 118:11. PL 149:11. RL 179:11. RSA 159:11. 1967, 220:8. 1981, 553:7, eff. Aug. 29, 1981.

Amendments
—1981. Rewritten to the extent that a detailed comparison would be impracticable.

—1967. Rewritten to the extent that a detailed comparison would be impracticable.

Cross References.
Classification of crimes, see RSA 625:9.
Sentences, see RSA 651.

NOTES TO DECISIONS

Construction

Plain language of RSA 159:11 criminalizes conveying false information, including information upon a federal form that is false based upon federal definitions of the form's terms; the statute is not limited to the conveying of false information pertinent to the acquisition of a firearm under New Hampshire gun acquisition laws. State v. Brown, 155 N.H. 590, 927 A.2d 493, 2007 N.H. LEXIS 98 (2007).

Dismissal of the State's complaint against defendant for providing false information to secure a firearm in violation of RSA 159:11 was reversed and remanded because, contrary to the trial court's reading, RSA 159:11 did not limit the type of false information that it criminalized when conveyed in the acquisition of a firearm, and the plain language of RSA 159:11 criminalized conveying false information, including information upon a federal form that was false based upon federal definitions of the form's terms. State v. Brown, 155 N.H. 590, 927 A.2d 493, 2007 N.H. LEXIS 98 (2007).

159:12. Sale to Minors.

I. Any person who shall sell, barter, hire, lend or give to any minor any pistol or revolver shall be guilty of a misdemeanor.

II. This section shall not apply to:

(a) Fathers, mothers, grandparents, guardians, administrators or executors who give a revolver to their children or wards or to heirs to an estate.

(b) Individuals instructing minors in the safe use of firearms during a supervised firearms training program, provided the minor's parent or legal guardian has granted the minor permission to participate in such program.

(c) Licensed hunters accompanying a minor while lawfully taking wildlife.

(d) Individuals supervising minors using firearms during a lawful shooting event or activity.

Source.

1923, 118:7. PL 149:12. RL 179:12. RSA 159:12. 1973, 528:87, eff. at 11:59 p.m., Oct. 31, 1973. 2006, 73:2, eff. April 28, 2006.

Amendments

—**2006.** Rewritten to the extent that detailed comparison would be impracticable.

—**1973.** Substituted "guilty of a misdemeanor" for "fined not more than one hundred dollars, or imprisoned not more than three months, or both" at the end of the first sentence.

Cross References.

Classification of crimes, see RSA 625:9.
Furnishing arms to persons under age 16, see RSA 644:15.
Proof of exceptions or exemptions generally, see RSA 159:5-a.
Selling air rifles to minors, see RSA 644:14.
Selling electronic defense weapons to minors, see RSA 159:22.
Sentences, see RSA 651.

159:13. Changing Marks.

No person shall change, alter, remove or obliterate the name of the maker, model, manufacturer's number or other mark of identification on any pistol or revolver. Possession of any such firearms upon which the same shall have been changed, altered, removed or obliterated shall be presumptive evidence that such possessor has changed, altered, removed or obliterated the same. Any person who violates the provisions of this section shall be guilty of a misdemeanor.

Source.

1923, 118:12. PL 149:13. RL 179:13. RSA 159:13. 1973, 528:88, eff. at 11:59 p.m., Oct. 31, 1973.

Amendments

—**1973.** Substituted "any person who" for "whoever" preceding "violates" and "guilty of a misdemeanor" for "fined not more than two hundred dollars, or imprisoned not more than one year, or both" following "shall be" in the third sentence.

Cross References.

Classification of crimes, see RSA 625:9.
Sentences, see RSA 651.

RESEARCH REFERENCES

New Hampshire Trial Bar News.

For article, "Presumptions in New Hampshire Law—A Guide Through the Impenetrable Jungle (Part II)," see 11 N.H. Trial Bar News 31, 44 n.116 (Fall 1991).

159:14. Exemption.

None of the provisions of this chapter shall prohibit an individual not licensed under the provisions thereof who is not engaged in the business of selling pistols or revolvers from selling a pistol or revolver to a person licensed under this chapter or to a person personally known to him.

Source.

1967, 220:9, eff. Aug. 21, 1967.

Cross References.

Proof of exceptions or exemptions generally, see RSA 159:5-a.

159:15. Possession of Dangerous Weapon While Committing a Violent Crime.

I. A person shall be guilty of a class A misdemeanor if that person uses or employs slung shot, metallic knuckles, billies, or other deadly weapon as defined in RSA 625:11, V during the commission or attempted commission of a violent crime.

II. "Violent crime," for purposes of this section, means "violent crime" as defined in RSA 651:5, XIII.

Source.

1973, 370:15, eff. Nov. 1, 1973. 1998, 373:1, eff. Jan. 1, 1999. 2001, 214:2, eff. Jan. 1, 2002.

Amendments

—**2001.** Paragraph I: Substituted "deadly weapon as defined in RSA 625:11, V" for "dangerous weapons".

—**1998.** Rewritten to the extent that a detailed comparison would be impracticable.

Cross References.

Classification of crimes, see RSA 625:9.
Sentences, see RSA 651.

NOTES TO DECISIONS

1. Constitutionality
2. Construction

1. Constitutionality

Statute gave juvenile adequate warning that coin rolls reinforced with duct tape constituted a dangerous weapon, and thus statute was not unconstitutionally vague as applied, where the phrase "other dangerous weapons" was construed to include items of a similar character to "slung shot, metallic knuckles, [or] billies," and juvenile carried reinforced coin rolls with him to prearranged fist fight, admitted that he kept them for protection, and pointed to no evidence of any use for coin rolls other than as a weapon. In re Justin D., 144 N.H. 450, 743 A.2d 829, 1999 N.H. LEXIS 132 (1999) (Decided under prior law.)

This section and RSA 159:16 do not threaten a fundamental right such as freedom of speech so as to require special judicial scrutiny. State v. Piper, 117 N.H. 64, 369 A.2d 199, 1977 N.H. LEXIS 268 (1977).

This section gave defendant adequate warning that a blade, four or five inches long, attached to belt buckle, which when worn was concealed by belt, was a dangerous weapon and therefore was not unconstitutionally vague as applied to these facts. State v. Piper, 117 N.H. 64, 369 A.2d 199, 1977 N.H. LEXIS 268 (1977).

That this section applies only to those who have the prohibited weapons upon their person when arrested does not violate the Equal Protection Clause, since RSA 159:16 prohibits the weapons from being carried upon one's person at any time and the same penalty is applicable; and in any event, there is a rational basis to treat arrested persons differently than those who are not arrested, due to the danger to the arresting officer and the need to guard against the use of a weapon to effect escape. State v. Piper, 117 N.H. 64, 369 A.2d 199, 1977 N.H. LEXIS 268 (1977).

2. Construction

Even though statute governing possession of dangerous weapons was not part of Criminal Code, it would be construed as would a criminal code provision, according to fair import of its terms and to promote justice. In re Justin D., 144 N.H. 450, 743 A.2d 829, 1999 N.H. LEXIS 132 (1999) (Decided under prior law.)

159:16. Carrying or Selling Weapons.

Whoever, except as provided by the laws of this state, sells, has in his possession with intent to sell, or carries on his person any blackjack, slung shot, or metallic knuckles shall be guilty of a misdemeanor; and such weapon or articles so carried by him shall be confiscated to the use of the state.

Source.
1973, 370:16. 1992, 273:2, eff. July 17, 1992. 2010, 67:1, eff. May 18, 2010.

Amendments
—2010. The 2010 amendment substituted "blackjack" for "stiletto, switch knife, blackjack, dagger, dirk-knife" and made a stylistic change.

—1992. Deleted "sword cane, pistol cane" preceding "blackjack".

Cross References.
Classification of crimes, see RSA 625:9.
Criminal use of pistol cane or sword cane, see RSA 159:19-a.
Exceptions, see RSA 159:17.
Sentences, see RSA 651.

NOTES TO DECISIONS

Constitutionality
This section and RSA 159:15 do not threaten a fundamental right such as freedom of speech so as to require special judicial scrutiny. State v. Piper, 117 N.H. 64, 369 A.2d 199, 1977 N.H. LEXIS 268 (1977).

Cited:
Cited in State v. Beckert, 144 N.H. 315, 741 A.2d 63, 1999 N.H. LEXIS 114 (1999); State v. Davis, 149 N.H. 698, 828 A.2d 293, 2003 N.H. LEXIS 103 (2003).

159:17. Exceptions.

The provisions of the preceding section shall not apply to officers of the law, to persons holding hunting or fishing licenses when lawfully engaged in hunting or fishing, to employees of express companies while on duty, to watchmen while on duty, to emergency medical technicians, firefighters, or military personnel while in the course of their duties, or to duly authorized military or civic organizations when parading, or to the members thereof when at, or going to or from, their customary places of assembly.

Source.
1973, 370:17, eff. Nov. 1, 1973. 2006, 227:1, eff. July 31, 2006.

Amendments
—2006. Substituted "hunting or fishing licenses" for "hunters' licenses", inserted "or fishing" following "in hunting", and deleted "or" preceding "to watchmen while on duty" and added the end of the sentence thereafter.

Cross References.
Proof of exceptions or exemptions or exemptions generally, see RSA 159:5-a.

159:18. Felonious Use of Teflon-coated, Armor-piercing and Exploding Bullets and Cartridges.

I. A person is guilty of a class B felony if he uses or attempts to use any teflon-coated or armor-piercing bullet or cartridge, or any bullet or cartridge which contains any explosive substance in the projectile and is designed to explode upon impact, in the course of committing any misdemeanor or felony.

II. Neither the whole nor any part of a sentence of imprisonment imposed for a violation of this section shall be served concurrently with any other term of imprisonment.

Source.
1983, 311:1, eff. Aug. 17, 1983.

Cross References.
Classification of crimes, see RSA 625:9.
Felonious use of body armor, see RSA 650-B.
Sentences, see RSA 651.

159:19. Courthouse Security.

I. No person shall knowingly carry a loaded or unloaded pistol, revolver, or firearm or any other deadly weapon as defined in RSA 625:11, V, whether open or concealed or whether licensed or unlicensed, upon the person or within any of the person's possessions owned or within the person's control in a courtroom or area used by a court. Whoever violates the provisions of this paragraph shall be guilty of a class B felony.

II. Firearms may be secured at the entrance to a courthouse by courthouse security personnel.

III. For purposes of paragraph I, "area used by a court" means:

(a) In a building dedicated exclusively to court use, the entire building exclusive of the area between the entrance and the courthouse security.

(b) In any other building which includes a court facility, courtrooms, jury assembly rooms, deliberation rooms, conference and interview rooms, the judge's chambers, other court staff facilities, holding facilities, and corridors, stairways, waiting areas, and elevators directly connecting these rooms and facilities.

IV. The provisions of this section shall not apply to marshals, sheriffs, deputy sheriffs, police or other duly appointed or elected law enforcement officers, bailiffs and court security officers, or persons with prior authorization of the court for the purpose of introducing weapons into evidence and as otherwise provided for in RSA 159:5.

V. It shall be an affirmative defense to any prosecution under paragraph I that there was no notice of the provisions of paragraph I posted in a conspicuous place at each public entrance to the court building.

Source.
1985, 258:2, eff. Jan. 1, 1986. 2000, 175:1, eff. Jan. 1, 2001.

Amendments
—2000. Rewritten to the extent that a detailed comparison would be impracticable.

159:19-a. Criminal Use of Pistol Cane or Sword Cane.

I. Any person who uses a pistol cane or sword cane on another person with intent to commit a crime punishable as a misdemeanor shall be guilty of a misdemeanor.

II. Any person who uses a pistol cane or sword cane on another person with intent to commit a crime punishable as a felony shall be guilty of a class B felony.

III. Neither the whole nor any part of a sentence of imprisonment imposed for a violation of this section shall be served concurrently with any other term of imprisonment.

Source.
1992, 273:3, eff. July 17, 1992.

Cross References.
Classification of crimes, see RSA 625:9.
Sentences, see RSA 651.

Self-Defense Weapons

Amendments
—1994. 1994, 139:1, eff. July 1, 1995, substituted "self-defense" for "electronic defense" in the subdivision heading.

159:20. Self-Defense Weapons Defined.

In this subdivision:

I. "Electronic defense weapon" means an electronically activated non-lethal device which is designed for or capable of producing an electrical charge of sufficient magnitude to immobilize or incapacitate a person temporarily.

II. "Aerosol self-defense spray weapon" means any aerosol self-defense spray weapon which is designed to immobilize or incapacitate a person temporarily.

Source.
1986, 46:1. 1994, 139:2, eff. July 1, 1995.

Amendments
—1994. Rewritten to the extent that a detailed comparison would be impracticable.

NOTES TO DECISIONS

1. Electronic defense weapon
There was insufficient evidence to support a conviction for being a felon in possession of an electronic defense weapon. Testimony that a device was a "taser" from which an officer observed sparks and could hear the crackling of electricity was insufficient to establish that it was designed for or capable of an electrical charge. State v. Tabaldi, — N.H. —, — A.3d —, 2013 N.H. LEXIS 102 (Oct. 1, 2013).

159:21. Possession by Felons Prohibited.

Any person who has been convicted of a felony in this or any other state who possesses an electronic defense weapon away from the premises where he resides shall be guilty of a class B felony. Neither the whole nor any part of a sentence of imprisonment imposed for a violation of this section shall be served concurrently with any other term of imprisonment.

Source.
1986, 46:1, eff. May 5, 1986.

Cross References.
Classification of crimes, see RSA 625:9.
Criminal use of electronic defense weapons, see RSA 159:23.
Sentences, see RSA 651.

NOTES TO DECISIONS

1. Evidence
There was insufficient evidence to support a conviction for being a felon in possession of an electronic defense weapon. Testimony that a device was a "taser" from which an officer observed sparks and could hear the crackling of electricity was insufficient to establish that it was designed for or capable of an electrical charge. State v. Tabaldi, — N.H. —, — A.3d —, 2013 N.H. LEXIS 102 (Oct. 1, 2013).

159:22. Restricted Sale.

Any person who knowingly sells an electronic defense weapon to a person under 18 years of age shall be guilty of a violation.

Source.
1986, 46:1, eff. May 5, 1986.

Cross References.
Classification of crimes, see RSA 625:9.
Furnishing arms to persons under age 16, see RSA 644:15.
Selling air rifles to minors, see RSA 644:14.
Selling pistols or revolvers to minors, see RSA 159:12.
Sentences, see RSA 651.

159:23. Criminal Use of Electronic Defense or Aerosol Self-Defense Spray Weapons.

I. Any person who uses an electronic defense or aerosol self-defense spray weapon on a law enforcement officer or another person with intent to commit a crime punishable as a misdemeanor shall be guilty of a misdemeanor.

II. Any person who uses an electronic defense or aerosol self-defense spray weapon on a law enforcement officer or another person with intent to commit a crime punishable as a felony shall be guilty of a class B felony.

III. Neither the whole nor any part of a sentence of imprisonment imposed for a violation of this section shall be served concurrently with any other term of imprisonment.

Source.
1986, 46:1. 1994, 139:3, eff. July 1, 1995.

Amendments
—1994. Inserted "or aerosol self-defense spray" preceding "weapons" in the section catchline and preceding "weapon on" in pars. I and II and inserted "a law enforcement officer or" preceding "another" in those paragraphs.

Cross References.
Classification of crimes, see RSA 625:9.
Felonious use of firearms generally, see RSA 650-A.
Possession of electronic defense weapons by felons, see RSA 159:21.
Sentences, see RSA 651.

Martial Arts Weapons

159:24. Sale of Martial Arts Weapons.

I. "Martial arts weapon" means any kind of sword, knife, spear, throwing star, throwing dart, or nunchaku or any other object designed for use in the martial arts which is capable of being used as a lethal or dangerous weapon.

II. Any person who shall sell, deliver, or otherwise transfer any martial arts weapon to a person under the age of 18 without first obtaining the written consent of such person's parent or guardian shall be guilty of a misdemeanor.

III. Paragraph II shall not apply to fathers, mothers, guardians, administrators or executors who give a martial arts weapon to their children or wards or to heirs to an estate.

Source.
1986, 222:3, eff. Jan. 1, 1987.

Cross References.
Classification of crimes, see RSA 625:9.
Proof of exceptions or exemptions generally, see RSA 159:5-a.
Sentences, see RSA 651.

Voluntarily Surrendered Firearms

159:25. Voluntarily Surrendered Firearms.

No state agency shall operate a firearms "voluntary surrender and destroy" program. Firearms which are voluntarily surrendered to a state agency shall be sold at public auction or kept by the state agency for its own use. Proceeds from firearms sold at public auction by the state shall be deposited in the general fund.

Source.
1998, 380:1, eff. Aug. 25, 1998.

State Jurisdiction

159:26. Firearms, Ammunition, and Knives; Authority of the State.

I. To the extent consistent with federal law, the state of New Hampshire shall have authority and jurisdiction over the sale, purchase, ownership, use, possession, transportation, licensing, permitting, taxation, or other matter pertaining to firearms, firearms components, ammunition, firearms supplies, or knives in the state. Except as otherwise specifically provided by statute, no ordinance or regulation of a political subdivision may regulate the sale, purchase, ownership, use, possession, transportation, licensing, permitting, taxation, or other matter pertaining to firearms, firearms components, ammunition, or firearms supplies in the state. Nothing in this section shall be construed as affecting a political subdivision's right to adopt zoning ordinances for the purpose of regulating firearms or knives businesses in the same manner as other businesses or to take any action allowed under RSA 207:59.

II. Upon the effective date of this section, all municipal ordinances and regulations not authorized under paragraph I relative to the sale, purchase, ownership, use, possession, transportation, licensing, permitting, taxation, or other matter pertaining to firearms, firearm components, ammunition, firearms supplies, or knives shall be null and void.

Source.
2003, 283:2, eff. July 18, 2003. 2011, 139:1, eff. August 6, 2011.

Amendments
—2011. The 2011 amendment added "and Knives" in the section heading; added "or knives" wherever it appears in I and II; and made related changes.

CHAPTER 159-A

PURCHASE OF SHOTGUNS AND RIFLES

159-A:1, 159-A:2.

[Repealed 1996, 116:1, II, eff. July 14, 1996.]

Former section(s).
Former RSA 159-A, consisting of RSA 159-A:1 and 159-A:2, which was derived from 1969, 309:1, related to the purchase of rifles and shotguns in contiguous states.

CHAPTER 159-C

SALE OF HANDGUNS; CRIMINAL RECORD CHECK

[Repealed 1994, 391:2, eff. November 30, 1998.]

Former section(s).
Former RSA 159-C, comprising RSA 159-C:1–159-C:11, which was derived from 1994, 391:1, related to the sale of handguns and criminal record checks. RSA 159-C:2 was amended by 1999, 240:2 prior to repeal. See now RSA 159-D.

Contingent repeal.
1994, 391:2, provided for the repeal of Chapter 159-C "on the date that any federal law is effective that requires federally licensed firearms dealers to contact a federal or state government agency or official to determine whether receipt of a firearm by a prospective purchaser would violate federal or state law. If such federal law becomes effective, the commissioner of safety shall certify to the secretary of state the date that such federal law took effect."
The commissioner of safety certified to the secretary of state that

18 U.S.C.S. section 923, commonly referred to as the Brady Act, became effective on November 30, 1998. Therefore, this chapter was effectively repealed on that date.

CHAPTER 159-D

CRIMINAL BACKGROUND CHECKS

SECTION
159-D:1.   Sale of Firearms; Criminal History Record and Protective Order Check.
159-D:2.   Confidentiality.
159-D:3.   Penalties for Attempts to Purchase Firearms Illegally.

159-D:1. Sale of Firearms; Criminal History Record and Protective Order Check.

The department of safety may become the point of contact for the federal government for the purposes of the National Instant Criminal Background Check System (NICS).

Source.
1999, 336:1, eff. Nov. 3, 1999.

159-D:2. Confidentiality.

I. If the department of safety conducts criminal background checks under RSA 159-D:1, any records containing information pertaining to a potential buyer or transferee who is not found to be prohibited from receipt or transfer of a firearm by reason of state or federal law, which are created by the department of safety to conduct the criminal background check, shall be confidential and may not be disclosed by the department or any officers or employees to any person or to another agency. The department shall destroy any such records after it communicates the corresponding approval number to the licensee and, in any event, such records shall be destroyed within one day after the day of the receipt of the licensee's request.

II. The department shall retain records containing any information pertaining to a potential buyer or transferee who is prohibited from receipt or transfer of a firearm for 3 years.

III. Notwithstanding the provisions of this section, the department may maintain only a log of dates of requests for criminal background checks and unique approval numbers corresponding to such dates for an indefinite period.

IV. Nothing in this section shall be construed to allow the department to maintain records containing the names of licensees who receive unique approval numbers or to maintain records of firearm transactions, including the names or other identification of licensees and potential buyers or transferees, including persons not otherwise prohibited by law from the receipt or possession of firearms.

Source.
1999, 336:1, eff. Nov. 3, 1999.

159-D:3. Penalties for Attempts to Purchase Firearms Illegally.

A person who completes and signs an application for purchase of a firearm and who knows that such purchase is illegal because he or she is subject to a protective order shall be guilty of a class A misdemeanor for a first offense and a class B felony for a second or subsequent offense.

Source.
2000, 152:1, eff. Jan. 1, 2001.

CHAPTER 167

PUBLIC ASSISTANCE TO BLIND, AGED, OR DISABLED PERSONS, AND TO DEPENDENT CHILDREN

SECTION
167:17-b.   Prohibited Acts.
167:17-c.   Penalties.

167:17-b. Prohibited Acts.

I. No person shall:

(a) By means of an intentionally false statement or misrepresentation or by impersonation or other fraudulent act or device, obtain or attempt to obtain, or aid or abet any person in obtaining any assistance or benefit or payment under RSA 161 or RSA 167 to which he is not entitled;

(b) With intent to defraud the department of health and human services, buy or aid or abet in the purchase or the disposal of the property of a person receiving assistance or food stamps under RSA 161 or RSA 167, so as to affect the recipient's eligibility for assistance, without the consent of the commissioner of the department of health and human services;

(c) [Repealed.]

(d) Intentionally fail to disclose the receipt of property, wages, income or resources or any change in circumstances which would affect his eligibility for assistance or his initial or continued right to any benefit or payment for the purpose of receiving any assistance, benefit or payment under RSA 167 or RSA 161 to which he is not entitled;

(e) Knowingly use, transfer, acquire, alter, sell or possess food stamps or authorization to issue food stamps in any manner not authorized by the Federal Food Stamp Act, as amended, or by the federal regulations or state rules adopted pursuant to the act;

(f) Present or cause to be presented food stamps for payment or redemption, knowing the stamps were received, transferred or used in any manner not authorized by the Federal Food Stamp Act, as amended, or by the federal regulations or state rules adopted pursuant to the act;

(g), (h) [Repealed.]

II. When a person receiving assistance is convicted of an offense under this section, the commissioner of the department of health and human services shall discontinue his assistance, if such action has not already been taken.

Source.
1973, 364:2. 1975, 399:5, 6; 406:2. 1981, 189:3. 1983, 291:1, II. 1987, 207:2. 1990, 260:4. 1995, 310:180, 182, eff. Nov. 1, 1995.

References in text.
The Federal Food Stamp Act, referred to in pars. I(e) and (f), are classified to 7 U.S.C.S. §§ 2011 et seq.

Revision note.
Substituted "director of human services" for "director of welfare" in view of 1983, 291:1, II, which changed the name of the division of welfare to the division of human services.

Amendments
—1995. Substituted "department of health and human services" for "division of health and human services" in par. I(b) and "commissioner of the department of health and human services" for "director of the division of human services" in par. II.

—1990. Paragraph I: Repealed subpars. (c), (g) and (h).

—1987. Paragraph I: Added subpars. (g) and (h).

—1983. Paragraph I: Substituted "division of human services" for "division of welfare" preceding "buy or aid" in subpar. (b) and "for merchandise not sold" in subpar. (c).
Paragraph II: Substituted "division of human services" for "division of welfare" preceding "shall discontinue".

—1981. Rewritten to the extent that a detailed comparison would be impracticable.

—1975. Paragraph II: Rewritten by ch. 399:6 to the extent that a detailed comparison would be impracticable.
Paragraph III: Chapter 399:5 rewrote the first sentence.
Rewritten by ch. 406:2 to the extent that a detailed comparison would be impracticable.
Paragraphs IV, V: Added.

Cross References.
Fraud on the women, infants, and children (WIC) program, see RSA 638:15.

NOTES TO DECISIONS

1. Constitutionality
2. Indictments

1. Constitutionality
Provision of this section that no person shall fail to disclose changed circumstances that would affect his eligibility to welfare benefits under aid to families with dependent children (AFDC) program was not unconstitutionally vague in failing to notify parents of eligible parties, who were the needy children themselves, that the parent's failure to disclose changed circumstances was a crime; statute read in a commonsense manner and in conjunction with other provisions gave parents constitutionally sufficient notice. State v. Winslow, 134 N.H. 398, 593 A.2d 238, 1991 N.H. LEXIS 70 (1991).

2. Indictments
Indictment charging medicaid fraud was sufficient. State v. Hermsdorf, 135 N.H. 360, 605 A.2d 1045, 1992 N.H. LEXIS 42, (1992).
This section does not make specification of the date of the false representation an essential element. Settle v. New Hampshire, 769 F. Supp. 428, 1990 U.S. Dist. LEXIS 19062 (D.N.H. 1990).
Indictments for welfare fraud alleging that defendant falsely stated that he had no income sufficiently apprised defendant of the subject matter of the false representations even though they failed to identify precisely the false statements at issue. Settle v. New Hampshire, 769 F. Supp. 428, 1990 U.S. Dist. LEXIS 19062 (D.N.H. 1990).
Precise language of the allegedly false statement need not be set forth in indictment for receiving public benefits based upon a false statement or representation. State v. Settle, 132 N.H. 626, 570 A.2d 895, 1990 N.H. LEXIS 3 (1990).

Cited:
Cited in State v. Adams, 123 N.H. 64, 455 A.2d 1030, 1983 N.H. LEXIS 223 (1983); State v. Williams, 127 N.H. 79, 497 A.2d 858, 1985 N.H. LEXIS 405 (1985); State v. McPherson, 127 N.H. 826, 508 A.2d 1076, 1986 N.H. LEXIS 231 (1986).

167:17-c. Penalties.

I. Any natural person who violates RSA 167:17-b shall, unless otherwise specified, be guilty of:
(a) A class A felony if the value of the monetary award or goods or services in question is $1,000 or more;
(b) A class B felony if the value of the monetary award or goods or services in question exceeds $100 but does not exceed $1,000; or
(c) A misdemeanor if the value of the monetary award or goods or services in question is $100 or less.

II. Any other person who violates RSA 167:17-b shall, unless otherwise specified, be guilty of:
(a) A felony if the value of the monetary award or goods or services in question exceeds $100; or
(b) A misdemeanor if the value of the monetary award or goods or services in question is $100 or less.

III. In the case of any natural person convicted of fraudulently using, presenting, transferring, acquiring, receiving, possessing or altering food stamps, the court may permit such person to perform work approved by the court for the purpose of providing restitution for losses incurred by the United States and the department of health and human services as a result of the offense for which such person was convicted. If the court permits such person to perform such work and such person agrees thereto, the court shall withhold the imposition of the sentence on the condition that such person perform the assigned work. Upon the successful completion of the assigned work the court may suspend such sentence.

Source.
1981, 189:4. 1983, 387:2; 291:1. 1995, 310:181, eff. Nov. 1, 1995.

Amendments
—1995. Paragraph III: Deleted "division of human services" preceding "department of health and human services" in the first sentence.

—1983. Paragraph III: Added by ch. 387.
Chapter 291 substituted "division of human services, department of health and human services" for "division of welfare, department of health and welfare" in the first sentence.

Cross References.
Classification of crimes, see RSA 625:9.
Penalties for violation of RSA 167:31, see RSA 167:32.
Sentences, see RSA 651.

Suspension or termination of medicaid provider, see RSA 167:60.

Aggregation of amounts

This section allows aggregation of small sums in order to create a felony count. State v. Hermsdorf, 135 N.H. 360, 605 A.2d 1045, 1992 N.H. LEXIS 42, (1992).

Where nineteen separate transactions resulted in fraudulent medicaid billings that ranged from $0.27 to $30.48 and the total amount fraudulently obtained was $154.21, the offenses could be aggregated and defendants were properly charged with felonies. State v. Hermsdorf, 135 N.H. 360, 605 A.2d 1045, 1992 N.H. LEXIS 42, (1992).

CHAPTER 172

STUDY, TREATMENT AND CARE OF INEBRIATES

SECTION
172:1.   Definitions.
172:13.   Acceptance and Admissions.
172:15.   Treatment and Services.

172:1. Definitions.

Certain terms used in this chapter shall be construed as follows unless a different meaning is clearly apparent from the language or context.

I, II. [Repealed.]

III. "Commissioner" means the commissioner of health and human services.

IV–IX. [Repealed.]

IX-a. "Client" means a person who voluntarily seeks substance abuse treatment as provided by the office of alcohol and drug abuse prevention through its agents or substance abuse treatment contractors.

X. "Abuse of drugs" means the use of controlled drugs solely for their stimulant, depressant or hallucinogenic effect upon the higher functions of the central nervous system and not as a therapeutic agent recommended by a practitioner in the course of medical treatment or in a program of research operated under the direction of a physician, or pharmacologist, physiologist, or chemist.

XI. [Repealed.]

XII. "Amphetamine-type drugs" means amphetamine, optical isomers thereof, salts of amphetamine and its isomers, and chemical compounds which are similar thereto in physiological effect, and which show a like potential for abuse.

XIII. "Barbiturate-type drugs" means barbituric acid and its salts, derivatives thereof and chemical compounds which are similar thereto in physiological effect, and which show a like potential for abuse.

XIV. "Cannabis-type drug" means all parts of any plant of the Cannabis genus of plants, whether growing or not; the seeds thereof; the resin extracted from any part of such plant; and every compound, manufacture, salt, derivative, mixture or preparation of such plant, its seeds or resin. Such term does not include the mature stalks of such plant, fiber produced from such stalks, oil or cake made from the seeds of such plants, any other compound, manufac-

ture, salt, derivative, mixture, or preparation of such mature stalks (except the resin extracted therefrom), fiber, oil or cake, or the sterilized seeds of such plants which are incapable of germination.

XV. "Cocaine-type drugs" means coca leaves, cocaine, ecgouine, and chemical compounds which are similar thereto in physiological effect, and which show a like potential for abuse.

XVI. "Controlled drugs" has the same meaning as in RSA 318-B:1, VI.

XVII. "Drug abuser" means any person who uses controlled drugs solely for their stimulant, depressant, or hallucinogenic effect upon the higher functions of the central nervous system and not as a therapeutic agent recommended by a practitioner in the course of medical treatment or in a program of research operated under the direction of a physician or pharmacologist.

XVIII. "Drug dependence" means a state of physical addiction or psychic dependence, or both, upon a drug following use of that drug upon a repeated periodic or continuous basis except:

(a) Upon a morphine-type drug as an incident to current medical treatment of a demonstrable physical disorder, other than produced by the use of the drug itself, or

(b) Upon amphetamine-type, ataractic, barbiturate-type, hallucinogenic or other stimulant or depressant drugs as an incident to current medical treatment of a demonstrable physical or psychological disorder, or both, other than produced by the drug itself.

XIX. "Drug dependent person" means any person who has developed a state of psychic or physical dependence, or both, upon a controlled drug following administration of that drug upon a repeated periodic or continuous basis. No person shall be classified as drug dependent who is dependent:

(a) Upon a morphine-type drug as an incident to current medical treatment of a demonstrable physical disorder other than drug dependence, or

(b) Upon amphetamine-type, ataractic, barbiturate-type, hallucinogenic or other stimulant and depressant drugs as an incident to current medical treatment of a demonstrable physical or psychological disorder, or both, other than drug dependence.

XX. "Hallucinogenic drugs" are psychodysleptic drugs which assert a confusional or disorganizing effect upon mental processes or behavior and mimic acute psychotic disturbances. Exemplary of such drugs are mescaline, peyote, psilocybin and d-lysergic acid diethylamide.

XXI. "Morphine-type drugs" means morphine and chemical compounds which are similar thereto in chemical structure or which are similar thereto in physiological effect, and which show a like potential for abuse.

XXII. "Other stimulant and depressant drugs" means controlled drugs other than amphetamine-type, barbiturate-type, cannabis-type, cocaine-type, hallucinogenics and morphine-type which are found to exert a stimulant and depressant effect upon the higher functions of a central nervous system and which are found to have a potential for abuse.

XXIII. [Repealed.]

XXIV. "Certified substance abuse treatment facility" means a facility funded in part or in whole by the office of alcohol and drug abuse prevention, and certified under rules adopted pursuant to RSA 541-A.

XXV. "Certified alcohol and drug abuse counselor" means a person who is certified by the director of the office of alcohol and drug abuse prevention as qualified to provide alcohol abuse counseling, drug abuse counseling, combined alcohol and drug abuse counseling, counseling to families with one or more substance abusing members, and counseling to children of alcoholics.

XXVI. "Incapacitated" means that a person as a result of his or her use of drugs is in a state of intoxication, or mental confusion resulting from withdrawal, such that:

(a) He or she appears to need medical care or supervision by approved drug treatment personnel to assure his or her safety; or

(b) He or she appears to present a direct active or passive threat to the safety of others.

XXVII. "Intoxicated" means a condition in which the mental or physical functioning of an individual is substantially impaired as a result of the presence of drugs in his or her system.

XXVIII. "Protective custody" means a civil status in which an incapacitated person is detained by a peace officer for the purposes of:

(a) Assuring the safety of the individual or the public or both; and

(b) Assisting the individual to return to a functional condition.

XXIX. "Designated drug counselor" means a person approved by the commissioner to evaluate and treat drug users and drug abusers. A "designated drug counselor" may be, but is not required to be, a certified alcohol and drug abuse counselor.

Source.
1947, 254:1. 1949, 313:1, par. 1. RSA 172:1. 1961, 222:8. 1969, 501:1. 1975, 255:1. 1979, 378:3, II; 378:7–10; 378:27–29. 1988, 242:1, 2, 10, I, II, eff. June 29, 1988. 2003, 96:2, eff. Jan. 1, 2004.

Revision note.
In par. III, substituted "commissioner of health and human services" for "commissioner of health and welfare" in light of 1983, 291:1, I, eff. July 1, 1985, which renamed the department of health and welfare as the department of health and human services.

Amendments
—**2003.** Paragraphs XXVI–XXIX: Added.

—**1988.** Paragraphs IX and XXIII: Repealed.
Paragraphs IX-a, XXIV, and XXV: Added.

—**1979.** Paragraphs I, II, IV–VIII, XI: Repealed by ch. 378:3, II.
Paragraph III: Rewritten by ch. 378:7 to the extent that a detailed comparison would be impracticable.
Rewritten by ch. 378:27 to the extent that a detailed comparison would be impracticable.
Paragraph IX: Chapter 378:8 substituted "office" for "commission".

Chapter 378:28 substituted "commissioner" for "commission".
Paragraph XVI: Rewritten by ch. 378:9 to the extent that a detailed comparison would be impracticable.
Paragraph XXIII: Added by ch. 378:10.
Chapter 378:29 substituted "commissioner" for "office director".

—**1975.** Paragraph XIV: Rewritten to the extent that a detailed comparison would be impracticable.

—**1969.** Added pars. X–XXII.

—**1961.** Paragraph III: Substituted "department of health and welfare, division of public health services" for "commission on alcoholism".

172:13. Acceptance and Admissions.

I. Any resident of the state, or the parent, person in loco parentis, or the legal guardian of a resident under 18 years of age or mentally incompetent, may apply to the commissioner for voluntary admission of such resident for care, treatment and guidance. The commissioner may adopt such rules regarding the admission, care and treatment of voluntary patients as he deems best. The rules of the commissioner in regard to voluntary clients shall be printed and made available to the public. No voluntary client shall, by asking the help or care of the commissioner, abridge any of his civil rights nor shall evidence of his voluntary submission to the commissioner's care and control be admissible against him in any court. All records pertaining to voluntary clients shall be kept confidential and not divulged, except that the commissioner may release such records to hospitals, institutions and physicians whenever in his discretion such information may assist in further treatment of the voluntary client.

II. When a person is indicted for any felony, is bound over by any district or municipal court to await the action of the grand jury on any felony, or is charged with a misdemeanor, and question as to the drug or alcohol dependency of the person is raised by either party, any justice of the superior, district or municipal court may, after hearing, order such person to be examined in accordance with the instructions of the commissioner to determine whether said person is drug or alcohol dependent. The commissioner shall report the results of the examination and his findings to the court in writing.

III. If a person examined pursuant to the provisions of paragraph II is found to be drug or alcohol dependent, the superior court having jurisdiction over the criminal action may, after hearing, without regard to the result of the criminal action, issue an order requiring the person to accept treatment at a certified substance abuse treatment facility when an opening becomes available. During treatment no further action shall be taken in respect to the original charges made against such a person unless otherwise ordered by the court. The court may release the person conditionally for treatment at any alcohol-drug abuse clinic, certified facility, mental health clinic or center or other appropriate sources of care.

IV. Nothing in this section shall prevent the court from placing a person convicted of a violation of RSA 318-B on probation conditioned upon the requirement that the person receive treatment at a treatment facility such as a certified substance abuse facility or other alcohol-drug abuse clinic, mental health clinic or center, or other appropriate sources of care.

V–VIII. [Repealed.]

Source.

1947, 254:10. 1949, 313:1, par. 12. 1950, 5, part 19:9. 1953, 207:1. RSA 172:13. 1967, 229:1. 1969, 501:6. 1973, 72:11. 1979, 378:23, 41. 1985, 337:13. 1988, 89:19, eff. June 17, 1988; 242:6, 7, 10, V, eff. June 29, 1988.

Amendments

—1988. Chapter 242 rewrote the section catchline.

Paragraphs I, III, and IV: Rewritten by ch. 242 to the extent that a detailed comparison would be impracticable.

Paragraph II: Chapter 89 substituted "a county correctional facility" for "the county jail" preceding "until further order of the court" at the end of the second sentence.

Rewritten by ch. 242 to the extent that a detailed comparison would be impracticable.

Paragraphs V–VIII: Repealed by ch. 242.

—1985. Paragraph II: Inserted "secure psychiatric unit" following "New Hampshire Hospital" in the second sentence.

—1979. Rewritten by chs. 378:23 and 41 to the extent that a detailed comparison would be impracticable.

—1973. Paragraph I: Substituted "eighteen" for "twenty-one" preceding "years" in the first sentence.

—1971. Paragraph II-a: Rewritten to the extent that a detailed comparison would be impracticable.

—1969. Paragraphs II-a–II-c: Added.

—1967. Paragraph II: Rewritten to the extent that a detailed comparison would be impracticable.

Cross References.

Admissibility of evidence of intoxication to negate element of criminal offense, see RSA 626:4.

Classification of crimes, see RSA 625:9.

Sentences, see RSA 651.

NOTES TO DECISIONS

1. Examination of accused—Discretion
2. —Sufficiency of evidence

1. Examination of accused—Discretion

This section does not require trial judge to order a defendant into the care and custody of the Executive Director upon the mere raising of the question of drug dependency, nor does it require a finding that a defendant is in fact drug dependent before the order may be made; it is the judge's discretion whether to make the order, depending upon whether the evidence at the hearing raises a sufficient question as to defendant's drug dependency to warrant examination by the Executive Director. State v. Garland, 111 N.H. 250, 279 A.2d 593, 1971 N.H. LEXIS 169 (1971).

2. —Sufficiency of evidence

Evidence by defendant and his friend that he used drugs extensively, by defendant that he had used heroin a couple of times, and by his wife and that she had seen him take marijuana two to three dozen times in the past two years, would have supported an examination order, but did not require one, and refusal of defendant's motion for commitment was not an abuse of discretion. State v. Garland, 111 N.H. 250, 279 A.2d 593, 1971 N.H. LEXIS 169 (1971).

172:15. Treatment and Services.

I. When a peace officer encounters a person who, in the judgment of the officer, is intoxicated as defined in RSA 172:1, XXVII, the officer may take such person into protective custody and shall take whichever of the following actions is, in the judgment of the officer, the most appropriate to ensure the safety and welfare of the public, the individual, or both:

(a) Assist the person, if the person consents, to his or her home, an approved drug treatment program, or some other appropriate location; or

(b) Release the person to some other person assuming responsibility for the intoxicated person; or

(c) Lodge the person in a local jail or county correctional facility for said person's protection, for up to 24 hours or until the keeper of said jail or facility judges the person to be no longer intoxicated.

II. When a peace officer encounters a person who, in the judgment of the officer, is incapacitated as defined in RSA 172:1, XXVI, the officer may take such person into protective custody and shall take whichever of the following actions is, in the judgment of the officer, the most appropriate to ensure the safety and welfare of the public, the individual, or both:

(a) Transport the person to an approved drug treatment program with detoxification capabilities or to the emergency room of a licensed general hospital for treatment, except that if a designated drug counselor exists in the vicinity and is available, the person may be released to the counselor at any location mutually agreeable between the officer and the counselor. The period of protective custody shall end when the person is released to a designated drug counselor, a clinical staff person of an approved drug treatment program with detoxification capabilities, or a professional medical staff person at a licensed general hospital emergency room. The person may be released to his or her own devices if at any time the officer judges the person to be no longer incapacitated. Protective custody shall in no event exceed 24 hours.

(b) Lodge the person in protective custody in a local jail or county correctional facility for up to 24 hours, or until judged by the keeper of the facility to be no longer incapacitated, or until a designated drug counselor has arranged transportation for the person to an approved drug treatment program with detoxification capabilities or to the emergency room of a licensed general hospital.

III. No person shall be lodged in a local jail or county correctional facility under paragraph II unless the person in charge of the facility, immediately upon lodging said person in protective custody, contacts a designated drug counselor, a clinical staff person of an approved drug treatment program with detoxification capabilities or a professional medical staff person at a licensed general hospital emergency room to determine whether said person is indeed incapacitated. If, and only if none of the foregoing is available, such a medical or clinical determination shall be made by a registered nurse or registered emergency medical technician on the staff of the detention facility.

IV. No local jail or county correctional facility shall refuse to admit an intoxicated or incapacitated person in protective custody whose admission is requested by a peace officer, in compliance with the conditions of this section.

V. Notwithstanding any other provisions of law, whenever a person under 18 years of age who is judged by a peace officer to be intoxicated or incapacitated and who has not been charged with a crime is taken into protective custody, the person's parent or guardian shall be immediately notified and such person may be held at a police station or a local jail or a county correctional facility in a room or ward separate from any adult or any person charged with juvenile delinquency until the arrival of his or her parent or guardian. If such person has no parent or guardian in the area, arrangements shall be made to house him or her according to the provisions of RSA 169-D:17.

VI. If an incapacitated person in protective custody is lodged in a local jail or county correctional facility his or her family or next of kin shall be notified as promptly as possible. If the person requests that there be no notification, the person's request shall be respected.

VII. A taking into protective custody under this section is not an arrest, however nothing in this section shall be construed so as to prevent an officer or jailer from obtaining proper identification from a person taken into protective custody or from conducting a search of such person to reduce the likelihood of injury to the officer or jailer, the person taken into protective custody, or others. No unnecessary or unreasonable force or means of restraint may be used in detaining any person taken into protective custody.

VIII. Peace officers or persons responsible for supervision in a local jail or designated drug counselors who act under the authority of this section are acting in the course of their official duty and are not criminally or civilly liable therefor, unless for gross negligence or willful or wanton injury.

Source.
2003, 96:3, eff. Jan. 1, 2004.

CHAPTER 172-B

ALCOHOLISM AND ALCOHOL ABUSE

SECTION
172-B:1.   Definitions.
172-B:2.   Provision of Services; Acceptance into Treatment.
172-B:3.   Treatment and Services.

172-B:1. Definitions.

In this chapter:

I. "Alcohol abuser" means anyone who drinks to an extent or with a frequency which impairs or endangers his health, or his social and economic functioning, or the health and welfare of others. The class of alcohol abusers includes the smaller class of alcoholics.

II. "Alcoholic" means a person suffering from the condition of alcoholism.

III. "Alcoholism" means addiction to alcoholic beverages. It is characterized by:

(a) Chronic absence of control by the drinker over the frequency or the volume of his alcohol intake; and

(b) Inability of the drinker to consistently moderate his drinking practices in spite of the onset of a variety of consequences deleterious to his health or his socio-economic functions.

IV. "Approved alcohol treatment program" means an alcohol treatment program which is approved by the commissioner as qualified to provide treatment for alcoholism and alcohol abuse.

V. "Client" means a person who is provided services by programs funded by the department of health and human services.

V-a. "Commissioner" means the commissioner of the department of health and human services.

V-b. "Department" means the department of health and human services.

VI. "Designated alcohol counselor" means a person approved by the commissioner to evaluate and treat alcoholics and alcohol abusers, pursuant to the provisions of this chapter.

VII. "Detoxification" means the planned withdrawal of an individual from a state of acute or chronic alcohol intoxication, under qualified supervision and with or without the use of medication. Detoxification is monitoring and management of the physical and psychological effects of withdrawal, for the purpose of assuring safe and rapid return of the individual to normal bodily and mental functioning.

VIII. "Director" means the director of the office of alcohol and drug abuse prevention.

IX. "Incapacitated" means that a person as a result of his use of alcohol is in a state of intoxication, or mental confusion resulting from withdrawal, such that:

(a) He appears to need medical care or supervision by approved alcohol treatment personnel, as defined in this section, to assure his safety; or

(b) He appears to present a direct active or passive threat to the safety of others.

X. "Intoxicated" means a condition in which the mental or physical functioning of an individual is substantially impaired as a result of the presence of alcohol in his system.

XI. "Licensed hospital" means a hospital licensed under RSA 151.

XII. "Peace officer" shall have the same meaning as set out in RSA 594:1, III.

XIII. "Protective custody" means a civil status in which an incapacitated person is detained by a peace officer for the purposes of:

(a) Assuring the safety of the individual or the public or both; and

(b) Assisting the individual to return to a functional condition.

XIV. "Treatment" means the broad range of medical, detoxification, residential, outpatient, aftercare and follow-up services which are needed by alcoholics and alcohol abusers, and may include a variety of other medical, social, vocational and educational services relevant to the rehabilitation of these persons.

Source.
1979, 378:2. 1995, 310:147, 177, 183, eff. Nov. 1, 1995.

Amendments
—1995. Paragraphs IV, VI: Substituted "commissioner" for "director".
Paragraph V: Substituted "department of health and human services" for "office of alcohol and drug abuse prevention".
Paragraphs V-a, V-b: Added.
Paragraph VIII: Rewritten to the extent that a detailed comparison would be impracticable.

NOTES TO DECISIONS

Protective custody
Trial court did not err in ruling that defendant was properly placed in protective custody by police, where officers observed defendant with characteristic signs of intoxication, officer observed a can of beer by defendant's truck and a small fire on the front seat, and where defendant misunderstood the officers' directions to move his truck and smashed into a police cruiser. State v. Green, 133 N.H. 249, 575 A.2d 1308, 1990 N.H. LEXIS 55 (1990).

Cited:
Cited in State v. Harlow, 123 N.H. 547, 465 A.2d 1210, 1983 N.H. LEXIS 320 (1983); State v. Toto, 123 N.H. 619, 465 A.2d 894, 1983 N.H. LEXIS 344 (1983); State v. Leary, 133 N.H. 46, 573 A.2d 135, 1990 N.H. LEXIS 25 (1990); Kidd v. Gowen, 829 F. Supp. 16, 1993 U.S. Dist. LEXIS 11794 (D.N.H. 1993).

172-B:2. Provision of Services; Acceptance into Treatment.

I. The commissioner shall have the authority and accountability for providing or arranging for the provision of a comprehensive system of alcoholism prevention and treatment services.

II. All state funds appropriated specifically for the prevention and treatment of alcoholism, and any federal or private funds which are received by the state for these purposes shall be in the budget of, and be administered by, the department of health and human services.

III. The commissioner shall have the authority to adopt rules, pursuant to RSA 541-A, relative to admission to alcohol treatment programs. In establishing such rules, the commissioner shall adhere to the following guidelines:

(a) A client shall be initially assigned or transferred to outpatient treatment, unless he is found to require medical treatment, detoxification or residential treatment;

(b) A person shall not be denied treatment solely because he has withdrawn from treatment against medical advice on a prior occasion or because he has relapsed after earlier treatment;

(c) An individualized treatment plan shall be prepared and maintained on a current basis for each client; and

(d) Provision shall be made for a continuum of coordinated treatment services, so that a person who leaves a program or a form of treatment shall have available and utilize other appropriate treatment.

IV. The commissioner shall establish, by rules adopted under RSA 541-A, a uniform, sliding-fee scale, based on the client's income, for voluntary services provided by approved alcohol treatment programs.

Source.
1979, 378:2. 1995, 310:177, 183, eff. Nov. 1, 1995. 2013, 144:107, eff. July 1, 2013.

Amendments
—2013. The 2013 amendment added IV.

—1995. Substituted "commissioner" for "director" preceding "shall have" in par. I and in two places in the introductory paragraph of in par. III and "department of health and human services" for "office of alcohol and drug abuse prevention" following "administered by, the" in par. II.

NOTES TO DECISIONS

Cited:
Cited in State v. Donovan, 128 N.H. 702, 519 A.2d 252, 1986 N.H. LEXIS 365 (1986).

172-B:3. Treatment and Services.

I. When a peace officer encounters a person who, in the judgment of the officer, is intoxicated as defined in RSA 172-B:1, X, the officer may take such person into protective custody and shall take whichever of the following actions is, in the judgment of the officer, the most appropriate to ensure the safety and welfare of the public, the individual, or both:

(a) Assist the person, if he consents, to his home, an approved alcohol treatment program, or some other appropriate location; or

(b) Release the person to some other person assuming responsibility for the intoxicated person; or

(c) Lodge the person in a local jail or county correctional facility for said person's protection, for up to 24 hours or until the keeper of said jail or facility judges the person to be no longer intoxicated.

II. When a peace officer encounters a person who, in the judgment of the officer, is incapacitated as defined in RSA 172-B:1, IX, the officer may take such person into protective custody and shall take whichever of the following actions is, in the judgment of the officer, the most appropriate to ensure the safety and welfare of the public, the individual, or both:

(a) Transport the person to an approved alcohol treatment program with detoxification capabilities or to the emergency room of a licensed general hospital for treatment, except that if a designated alcohol counselor exists in the vicinity and is available, the person may be released to the counselor at any location mutually agreeable between the officer and the counselor. The period of protective custody shall end when the person is released to a designated alcohol counselor, a clinical staff person of an approved alcohol treatment program with detoxification capabilities, or a professional medical staff person at a licensed general hospital emergency room. The person may be released to his own devices if at any time the officer judges him to be no longer incapacitated. Protective custody shall in no event exceed 24 hours.

(b) Lodge the person in protective custody in a local jail or county correctional facility for up to 24 hours, or until judged by the keeper of the facility to be no longer incapacitated, or until a designated alcohol counselor has arranged transportation for the person to an approved alcohol treatment program with detoxification capabilities or to the emergency room of a licensed general hospital.

III. No person shall be lodged in a local jail or county correctional facility under paragraph II unless the person in charge of the facility, immediately upon lodging said person in protective custody, contacts a designated alcohol counselor, a clinical staff person of an approved alcohol treatment program with detoxification capabilities or a professional medical staff person at a licensed general hospital emergency room to determine whether said person is indeed incapacitated. If, and only if none of the foregoing are available, such a medical or clinical determination shall be made by a registered nurse or registered emergency medical technician on the staff of the detention facility.

IV. No local jail or county correctional facility shall refuse to admit an intoxicated or incapacitated person in protective custody whose admission is requested by a peace officer, in compliance with the conditions of this section.

V. Notwithstanding any other provisions of law, whenever a person under 18 years of age who is judged by a peace officer to be intoxicated or incapacitated and who has not been charged with a crime is taken into protective custody, if no needed treatment is available, his parent or guardian shall be immediately notified and such person may be held at a police station or a local jail or a county correctional facility in a room or ward separate from any adult or any person charged with juvenile delinquency until the arrival of his parent or guardian. If such person has no parent or guardian in the area, arrangements shall be made to house him according to the provisions of RSA 169-D:17.

VI. If an incapacitated person in protective custody is lodged in a local jail or county correctional facility his family or next of kin shall be notified as promptly as possible. If the person requests that there be no notification, his request shall be respected.

VII. A taking into protective custody under this section is not an arrest, however nothing in this section shall be construed so as to prevent an officer or jailer from obtaining proper identification from a person taken into protective custody or from conducting a search of such person to reduce the likelihood of injury to the officer or jailer, the person taken into protective custody, or others. No unnecessary or unreasonable force or means of restraint may be used in detaining any person taken into protective custody.

VIII. Peace officers or persons responsible for supervision in a local jail or designated alcohol counselors who act under the authority of this section are acting in the course of their official duty and are not criminally or civilly liable therefor, unless for gross negligence or willful or wanton injury.

Source.
1979, 378:2. 1988, 89:20. 1989, 285:10, eff. July 28, 1989.

Amendments
—1989. Paragraph V: Substituted "18" for "16" preceding "years of age" in the first sentence.

—1988. Paragraph I(c): Inserted "jail" preceding "or county", substituted "correctional facility" for "jail" thereafter and inserted "or facility" preceding "judges the person".
Paragraph II(b): Inserted "jail" following "local" and substituted "correctional facility" for "jail" preceding "for up to 24 hours".
Paragraph III: Inserted "jail" following "local" and substituted "correctional facility" for "jail" preceding "under paragraph II" in the first sentence.
Paragraph IV: Inserted "jail" preceding "or county" and substituted "correctional facility" for "jail" thereafter.
Paragraph V: Deleted "or county" preceding "jail" and inserted "or a county correctional facility" thereafter in the first sentence.
Paragraph VI: Inserted "jail" preceding "or county" and substituted "correctional facility" for "jail" thereafter in the first sentence.

Cross References.
Forfeiture of liquor or beverage by person taken into protective custody, see RSA 179:4.

NOTES TO DECISIONS

1. Intoxication
2. Protective custody
3. Preemption by federal statute
4. Search—Generally
5. —Pockets
6. —Bag
7. —Wallet
8. Resisting arrest
9. Immunity

1. Intoxication
RSA 172-B:3, I does not authorize the police to take individuals into protective custody if, in the police officer's judgment, the individual is under the influence of drugs. State v. Novak, 147 N.H. 580, 801 A.2d 202, 2002 N.H. LEXIS 27 (2002).

In order to take a person into protective custody under this section, a police officer is not required to eliminate completely the possibility that the intoxication was, in fact due to drugs, and not to alcohol. State v. Toto, 123 N.H. 619, 465 A.2d 894, 1983 N.H. LEXIS 344 (1983).

Even assuming that this section requires a police officer to have probable cause to believe that a person is intoxicated due to alcohol, rather than to drugs, in order to take that person into protective custody, that standard was satisfied in the case of defendant who was charged with unauthorized possession of a narcotic drug, where the evidence indicated that there was an odor of alcohol on the defendant's breath, that his eyes were glassy, that his speech was slurred and that he was staggering in a drunkenlike state. State v. Toto, 123 N.H. 619, 465 A.2d 894, 1983 N.H. LEXIS 344

(1983).

In prosecution for unauthorized possession of a narcotic drug, where the police officer, who took the defendant into protective custody pursuant to this section, testified that he believed the defendant was "intoxicated" when he took him into custody, the officer was not required to have probable cause to believe that the defendant was "incapacitated" prior to lodging the defendant in jail. State v. Toto, 123 N.H. 619, 465 A.2d 894, 1983 N.H. LEXIS 344 (1983).

2. Protective custody

In his civil rights action, plaintiff could not establish that officers used excessive force in taking him into protective custody, RSA 172-B:3, I(c), because plaintiff's own deposition provided no evidence to indicate that the force exerted (however considerable) to handcuff him was unnecessary, or that a reasonable police officer would have thought otherwise. Statchen v. Palmer, 623 F.3d 15, 2010 U.S. App. LEXIS 21345 (2010).

The provisions of this section do not require the police to exhaust all other options before placing an "intoxicated" or "incapacitated" person in jail, but this section does require the officer to consider all of the options listed in the section, and to decide which, in his judgment, is most appropriate to ensure the safety of the public, the individual, or both. State v. Harlow, 123 N.H. 547, 465 A.2d 1210, 1983 N.H. LEXIS 320 (1983).

3. Preemption by federal statute

There was an actual conflict between RSA 172-B:3 and the Federal Emergency Medical Treatment and Active Labor Act, 42 U.S.C.S. § 1395dd, preempting the doctor's argument that his conduct, in placing the patient in the protective custody of the police, was justified by RSA 172-B:3. Carlisle v. Frisbie Mem'l Hosp., 152 N.H. 762, 888 A.2d 405, 2005 N.H. LEXIS 168 (2005).

4. Search—Generally

To construe the language of this section as limiting the scope of searches of individuals in protective custody to what is necessary to obtain identification and to protect the officer, jailer, or others, is consistent with the legislature's intent to treat such persons as sick and socially disabled persons, not as criminals. State v. Harlow, 123 N.H. 547, 465 A.2d 1210, 1983 N.H. LEXIS 320 (1983).

Through this section, the legislature has expressed its concern that police be permitted to conduct a search in order to reduce the likelihood of injury to themselves and others; such danger of injury arises not only from the person taken into protective custody but also from objects in his possession which may pose a threat of injury to persons even if the object is taken into police custody. State v. Toto, 123 N.H. 619, 465 A.2d 894, 1983 N.H. LEXIS 344 (1983).

Under fourth amendment analysis, the inventory search of the person and the property of one lodged in jail pursuant to this section is permissible for the limited purposes identified in State v. Harlow, 123 N.H. 547, 465 A.2d 1210, 1983 N.H. LEXIS 320 (1983), even though the person has not been arrested. State v. Toto, 123 N.H. 619, 465 A.2d 894, 1983 N.H. LEXIS 344 (1983).

5. —Pockets

A motion to suppress evidence obtained in a search conducted pursuant to this section after placing the defendant in protective custody was properly denied since the search was not a violation of paragraph VII of this section because the police searched the defendant's pockets without reason to believe that they contained a weapon; the police acted legitimately in searching the defendant's pockets because they could have contained a small object or substance dangerous to the officers or to the defendant himself. State v. Donovan, 128 N.H. 702, 519 A.2d 252, 1986 N.H. LEXIS 365 (1986).

6. —Bag

Where defendant had been taken into protective custody pursuant to this section, a police search at the police station of a large garbage bag that the defendant had been carrying did not violate the permissible scope of searches under this section, although the search was apparently not necessary to obtain identification in the defendant's case, since a search was necessary to reduce the likelihood of injury to persons because a large garbage bag could contain a number of objects which would pose a threat of injury to

persons, as for instance, a gun. State v. Toto, 123 N.H. 619, 465 A.2d 894, 1983 N.H. LEXIS 344 (1983).

7. —Wallet

Where defendant had been taken into protective custody pursuant to this section, a search by police of the defendant's wallet, while the defendant was being placed in a jail cell, which revealed what was later determined to be three LSD capsules, violated the provisions of this section, where the facts indicated that the police officer who initially detained the defendant had determined the defendant's identity at the scene and therefore that the search was not necessary for that purpose, and where the search of the wallet was not necessary to protect the police, the jailer, the defendant, or others because, once it was taken from the defendant, the wallet posed no danger of injury to the defendant or to others since it could have been placed in an envelope and sealed. State v. Harlow, 123 N.H. 547, 465 A.2d 1210, 1983 N.H. LEXIS 320 (1983).

8. Resisting arrest

Because the word "detain" did not have to be applied in a criminal context to the exclusion of other applications, defendant could be convicted for resisting arrest or detention under RSA 642:2 where defendant knowingly or purposely physically interfered with being taken into protective custody under RSA 172-B:3. State v. Kelley, 153 N.H. 481, 899 A.2d 236, 2006 N.H. LEXIS 62 (2006).

9. Immunity

Decision of police officers not to detain the driver of a vehicle under their authority as peace officers to take a person into protective custody under RSA 135-C:28 and RSA 172-B:3, after giving the driver field sobriety tests, was not the type of discretionary function protected under the discretionary function immunity exception and the officers' discretion in this case did not involve legislative or executive policy-making or government planning. However, the court found for the first time that municipal police officers are immune from personal liability for decisions, acts or omissions that are: (1) made within the scope of their official duties while in the course of their employment; (2) discretionary, rather than ministerial; and (3) not made in a wanton or reckless manner and, thus, the trial court was to determine on remand whether the officers were entitled to official immunity, and whether the town was thereby entitled to vicarious immunity. Everitt v. GE, 156 N.H. 202, 932 A.2d 831, 2007 N.H. LEXIS 164 (2007).

Cited:

Cited in State v. Shannon, 125 N.H. 653, 484 A.2d 1164, 1984 N.H. LEXIS 380 (1984); State v. Leary, 133 N.H. 46, 573 A.2d 135, 1990 N.H. LEXIS 25 (1990); State v. Green, 133 N.H. 249, 575 A.2d 1308, 1990 N.H. LEXIS 55 (1990); Kidd v. Gowen, 829 F. Supp. 16, 1993 U.S. Dist. LEXIS 11794 (D.N.H. 1993); State v. Greene, 137 N.H. 126, 623 A.2d 1342, 1993 N.H. LEXIS 52 (1993).

RESEARCH REFERENCES

New Hampshire Practice.
8-4 N.H.P. Personal Injury-Tort & Insurance Practice § 4.03.
8-4 N.H.P. Personal Injury-Tort & Insurance Practice § 4.05.
8-9 N.H.P. Personal Injury-Tort & Insurance Practice § 9.40.

CHAPTER 173-B

PROTECTION OF PERSONS FROM DOMESTIC VIOLENCE

SECTION
173-B:1.   Definitions.
173-B:2.   Jurisdiction and Venue.
173-B:3.   Commencement of Proceedings; Hearing.
173-B:4.   Temporary Relief.
173-B:5.   Relief.
173-B:5-a. Permissible Contact.
173-B:6.   Guardian Ad Litem.
173-B:7.   Minority not a Preclusion for Services.
173-B:8.   Notification.

SECTION
173-B:9.   Violation of Protective Order; Penalty.
173-B:10. Protection by Peace Officers.
173-B:11. Notice to the Victim.
173-B:12. Emergency Care; Limitation and Liability.
173-B:13. Orders Enforceable.
173-B:14. Orders of Support.
173-B:15. Fund for Domestic Violence Grant Program.
173-B:16. Grant Program Established.
173-B:17. Duties of the Commissioner.
173-B:18. Selection of Coordinator.
173-B:19. Compensation for Coordinating Domestic Violence Grant Program.
173-B:20. Duties of Coordinator.
173-B:21. Criteria for Selection of Direct Service Grantees.
173-B:22. Confidentiality.
173-B:23. Referral.
173-B:24. Rights Reserved.
173-B:25. Severability.

Repeal and reenactment of chapter.

1999, 240:3, eff. Jan. 1, 2000, provided for the repeal and reenactment of RSA 173-B. Original RSA 173-B, consisting of RSA 173-B:1–173-B:24, was derived from 1979, 377:2, 10; 1981, 223:2, 522:1–13; 1982, 25:1; 1983, 291:1; 1989, 297:1–18; 1990, 241:1–6, 10, 250:6, 7; 1993, 173:5, 6; 1994, 255:1, 259:1–9; 1995, 310:175, 181–183; 1996, 272:1; and 1997, 263:25.

Cross References.

Confidential communications between domestic violence victims and counselors, see RSA 173-C.

Protection of children from abuse and neglect, see RSA 169-C.

Protective services to adults, see RSA 161-F:42 et seq.

Standardized domestic violence protocol, see RSA 21-M:8-d.

NOTES TO DECISIONS

Constitutionality

Defendant's due process and effective assistance of counsel rights under U.S. Const. amend. V, VI, and XIV and N.H. Const. pt. I, art 15 were not violated by interpreting RSA ch. 173-B as prohibiting contact with a victim protected under a temporary protective order as a defendant's constitutional rights did not confer upon him unfettered access to witnesses, especially when the witness was a victim of domestic violence and held a protective order against the defendant; if a defendant has a legitimate reason to contact a victim, he can petition the court for an exception to or modification of the protective order. State v. Kidder, 150 N.H. 600, 843 A.2d 312, 2004 N.H. LEXIS 37 (2004).

RESEARCH REFERENCES

New Hampshire Practice.

3-5 N.H.P. Family Law § 5.16.

New Hampshire Bar Journal.

For article, "New Hampshire Revises Its Domestic Violence Law," see 40 N.H.B.J. 6 (December 1999).

For article, "Identifying the Assaultive Husband in Court: You Be the Judge," see 40 N.H.B.J. 54 (December 1999).

173-B:1. Definitions.

In this chapter:

I. "Abuse" means the commission or attempted commission of one or more of the acts described in subparagraphs (a) through (g) by a family or household member or by a current or former sexual or intimate partner, where such conduct is determined to constitute a credible present threat to the petitioner's safety. The court may consider evidence of such acts, regardless of their proximity in time to the filing of the petition, which, in combination with recent conduct, reflects an ongoing pattern of behavior which reasonably causes or has caused the petitioner to fear for his or her safety or well-being:

(a) Assault or reckless conduct as defined in RSA 631:1 through RSA 631:3.

(b) Criminal threatening as defined in RSA 631:4.

(c) Sexual assault as defined in RSA 632-A:2 through RSA 632-A:5.

(d) Interference with freedom as defined in RSA 633:1 through RSA 633:3-a.

(e) Destruction of property as defined in RSA 634:1 and RSA 634:2.

(f) Unauthorized entry as defined in RSA 635:1 and RSA 635:2.

(g) Harassment as defined in RSA 644:4.

II. "Applicant" means any private, town, city, or regional agency or organization applying for funds under RSA 173-B:16.

III. "Commissioner" means the commissioner of the department of health and human services.

IV. "Contact" means any action to communicate with another either directly or indirectly, including, but not limited to, using any form of electronic communication, leaving items, or causing another to communicate in such fashion.

V. "Coordinator" means the agency or organization appointed by the commissioner to administer the domestic violence grant program.

VI. "Cross orders for relief" means separate orders granted to parties in a domestic violence situation where each of the parties has filed a petition pursuant to this chapter on allegations arising from the same incident or incidents of domestic violence.

VII. "Deadly weapon" means "deadly weapon" as defined in RSA 625:11, V.

VIII. "Department" means the department of health and human services.

IX. "Domestic violence" means abuse as defined in RSA 173-B:1, I.

X. "Family or household member" means:

(a) Spouses, ex-spouses, persons cohabiting with each other, and persons who cohabited with each other but who no longer share the same residence.

(b) Parents and other persons related by consanguinity or affinity, other than minor children who reside with the defendant.

XI. "Firearm" means any weapon, including a starter gun, which will or is designed to or may readily be converted to expel a projectile by force of gunpowder.

XII. "Foreign protective order" means an order enforceable under RSA 173-B:13.

XIII. "Fund" means the special fund for domestic violence programs established by RSA 173-B:15.

XIV. "Grantee" means any private, town, city, or regional agency or organization receiving funds under RSA 173-B:16.

XV. "Intimate partners" means persons currently or formerly involved in a romantic relationship, whether or not such relationship was ever sexually consummated.

XVI. "Mutual order for relief" means an order restraining both parties from abusing the other originating from a petition filed by one of the parties and arising from the same incident or incidents of domestic violence.

XVII. "Program" means services or facilities provided to domestic violence victims.

Source.
1999, 240:3, eff. Jan. 1, 2000. 2010, 289:1, eff. January 1, 2011.

Amendments
—2010. The 2010 amendment rewrote the introductory paragraph of I, which formerly read: "'Abuse' means the commission or attempted commission of one or more of the following acts by a family or household member or current or former sexual or intimate partner and where such conduct constitutes a credible threat to the plaintiff's safety."

NOTES TO DECISIONS

1. "Abuse"
2. Relationship to RSA 173-B:5
3. Credible threat
4. "Contact"
5. Jury instructions

1. "Abuse"
In issuing a protective order, the trial court properly found defendant husband to be a threat to plaintiff wife. The definition of "abuse" in RSA 173-B:1 did not require defendant to have committed a violent act; defendant's history of angry, destructive behavior supported the conclusion that plaintiff was in fear of physical contact from defendant when he followed her from room to room, repeatedly demanding certain papers, while holding a propane torch; and the trial court found, and defendant did not dispute on appeal, that he committed the offense of criminal threatening. In re McArdle & McArdle, 162 N.H. 482, 34 A.3d 700, 2011 N.H. LEXIS 127 (2011).

Family court was not required to award a former wife sole decision-making power because of a prior court's finding that her former husband had assaulted her. The family court properly awarded the husband sole decision-making power because it found no abuse had occurred; RSA 461-A:5, III was not triggered by finding of another court that abuse occurred. In re Mannion, 155 N.H. 52, 917 A.2d 1272, 2007 N.H. LEXIS 28 (2007).

In a proceeding on a domestic violence petition, based on testimony of plaintiff's father that defendant stated to him "if I catch [plaintiff] after dark, you won't recognize her the next time you see her," district court could reasonably conclude that the statement constituted criminal threatening as defined in RSA 631:3, and that it constituted a credible threat to plaintiff's safety. Fichtner v. Pittsley, 146 N.H. 512, 774 A.2d 1239, 2001 N.H. LEXIS 104 (2001).

2. Relationship to RSA 173-B:5
Because RSA 173-B:1 contains an enumerated list of prohibited conduct, RSA 173-B:5 requires that a trial court must make a specific finding of criminal conduct in order to issue a final restraining order against a defendant. Fillmore v. Fillmore, 147 N.H. 283, 786 A.2d 849, 2001 N.H. LEXIS 206 (2001).

3. Credible threat
In a case where plaintiff sought a domestic violence protective order, the evidence supported a finding of a present credible threat to her safety under RSA 173-B:1, I. The trial court specifically relied upon an attempted assault that occurred within six months of the filing of the petition, defendant's threatening statement regarding a loaded shotgun made within three months of the filing, and a further message including the words "die bitch" sent just days prior to the filing. Thompson v. D'errico, 163 N.H. 20, 35 A.3d 584, 2011 N.H. LEXIS 185 (2011).

The trial court erred in entering a final domestic violence protective order against an ex-husband, because the evidence submitted by the ex-wife was insufficient to support a finding that the ex-husband's harassment constituted a credible threat to the ex-wife's safety pursuant to RSA 173-B:1, I (Supp. 2001). In re Alexander, 147 N.H. 441, 790 A.2d 142, 2002 N.H. LEXIS 7 (2002).

4. "Contact"
RSA 173-B:1, IV contains no exceptions to the definition of "contact," and defendant's claim that interpreting RSA 173-B:1, IV without a legitimate purpose exception rendered RSA ch. 173-B overbroad was rejected as any contact with a victim of domestic violence, whether legitimate or not, may be perceived by the victim as harassment, intimidation, or abuse; because RSA 173-B:1, IV does not attempt to control activities by means which invade areas of protected freedom, the statute is not overbroad. State v. Kidder, 150 N.H. 600, 843 A.2d 312, 2004 N.H. LEXIS 37 (2004).

5. Jury instructions
Trial court did not err when it denied defendant's request to instruct the jury to use the definition of "household members" contained in RSA 173-B:1 in his sexual assault trial with regard to his alleged assaults upon the minor daughter of an ex-girlfriend, who had commenced living with defendant, as RSA 632-A:2, I(j)(1), which he was charged as having violated, specifically excluded minor children. State v. Hearns, 151 N.H. 226, 855 A.2d 549, 2004 N.H. LEXIS 129 (2004).

Cited:
Cited in State v. Small, 150 N.H. 457, 843 A.2d 932, 2004 N.H. LEXIS 3 (2004); State v. Merriam, 150 N.H. 548, 842 A.2d 102, 2004 N.H. LEXIS 19 (2004).

RESEARCH REFERENCES

New Hampshire Practice.
3-5 N.H.P. Family Law § 5.04.

New Hampshire Trial Bar News.
For article, "New Hampshire Health Care Providers' Duty to Warn Third Parties: How Far Does It Extend?," see 15 N.H. Trial Bar News 37, 39 n.16 (Summer 1993).

New Hampshire Bar Journal.
For article, "Understanding and Representing Adult Clients Who Are Victims of Domestic Abuse," see 35 N.H.B.J. 8 (1994).
For article, "Interspousal Torts," see 35 N.H.B.J. 45 (1994).

173-B:2. Jurisdiction and Venue.

I. The district division and the judicial branch family division of the circuit courts shall have concurrent jurisdiction over all proceedings under this chapter.

II. If the plaintiff has left the household or premises to avoid further abuse, the plaintiff shall have the option to commence proceedings pursuant to RSA 173-B:3 in the county or district where the plaintiff temporarily resides.

III. Proceedings under this chapter may be transferred to another court upon the motion of any party or of the court as the interests of justice or the convenience of the parties may require.

[Effective until January 1, 2014; see prospective repeal note below.]

IV. In any county where the family division is located, the family division shall have jurisdiction over domestic violence cases consistent with 1995, 152.

Source.
1999, 240:3, eff. Jan. 1, 2000. 2013, 62:1, 10, January 1, 2014.

References in text.
1995, 152, referred to in par. IV of this section, provided for the establishment of the family division court pilot program in Rockingham and Grafton counties no later than July 1, 1996. For provisions relating to jurisdiction, location, and operation, see 1995, ch. 152.

Amendments
—2013. The 2013 amendment, in I, substituted "The district division and the judicial branch family division of the circuit" for "All district" and deleted "with the superior court" following "jurisdiction" and deleted IV.

Prospective repeal of Paragraph IV.
2013, 62:10, provides for the repeal of paragraph IV on January 1, 2014.

NOTES TO DECISIONS

Cited:
Cited in Fichtner v. Pittsley, 146 N.H. 512, 774 A.2d 1239, 2001 N.H. LEXIS 104 (2001).

RESEARCH REFERENCES

New Hampshire Bar Journal.
For article, "Understanding and Representing Adult Clients Who Are Victims of Domestic Abuse," see 35 N.H.B.J. 8 (1994).

173-B:3. Commencement of Proceedings; Hearing.

I. Any person may seek relief pursuant to RSA 173-B:5 by filing a petition, in the county or district where the plaintiff or defendant resides, alleging abuse by the defendant. Any person filing a petition containing false allegations of abuse shall be subject to criminal penalties. Notice of the pendency of the action and of the facts alleged against the defendant shall be given to the defendant, either personally or as provided in paragraph III. The plaintiff shall be permitted to supplement or amend the petition only if the defendant is provided an opportunity prior to the hearing to respond to the supplemental or amended petition. All petitions filed under this section shall include the home and work telephone numbers of the defendant, if known. Notice of the whereabouts of the plaintiff shall not be revealed except by order of the court for good cause shown. Any answer by the defendant shall be filed with the court and a copy shall be provided to the plaintiff by the court.

II. (a) The minority of the plaintiff shall not preclude the court from issuing protective orders against a present or former intimate partner, spouse, or ex-spouse under this chapter.

(b) A minor plaintiff need not be accompanied by a parent or guardian to receive relief or services under this chapter.

III. No filing fee or fee for service of process shall be charged for a petition or response under this section, and the plaintiff or defendant may proceed without legal counsel. Either a peace officer or the sheriff's department shall serve process under this section. Any proceeding under this chapter shall not preclude any other available civil or criminal remedy.

IV. The clerks of the circuit courts shall supply forms for petitions and for relief under this chapter designed to facilitate pro se proceedings. All such petitions shall contain the following words: I swear that the foregoing information is true and correct to the best of my knowledge. I understand that making a false statement on this petition will subject me to criminal penalties.

[Effective until January 1, 2014; see prospective repeal note below.]

V. Upon entry of any action in a district court, where the court determines that there is pending in the superior court a cause of action involving the same parties arising out of the same situation on which the district court action is based, the case shall be transferred to the superior court to be heard as if originally entered in the superior court, unless the district court determines that the interests of justice or expediency require the district court to exercise jurisdiction. Any transfer to the superior court under this paragraph shall be made as soon as practicable following entry of the action.

VI. The findings of facts shall be final, but questions of law may be transferred from the circuit court to the supreme court.

VII. (a) The court shall hold a hearing within 30 days of the filing of a petition under this section or within 10 days of service of process upon the defendant, whichever occurs later.

(b) The time frame established in this paragraph may be extended for an additional 10 days upon motion by either party for good cause shown. A recusal by the judge or any act of God or closing of the court that interferes with the originally scheduled hearing shall not be cause for the dismissal of the petition. The court shall reschedule any hearing under this section in an expeditious manner.

VIII. In any proceeding under this chapter, the court shall not be bound by the technical rules of evidence and may admit evidence which it considers relevant and material.

Source.
1999, 240:3, eff. Jan. 1, 2000. 2007, 284:1, eff. Jan. 1, 2008. 2013, 62:2, 3, 10, January 1, 2014.

Amendments
—2013. The 2013 amendment substituted "circuit" for "district and superior" in the first sentence of IV; deleted V; and in VI,

substituted "circuit" for "district" and deleted "in the same manner as from the superior court" at the end.

—2007. Paragraph VII: Designated existing provisions as subpar. (a) and added subpar. (b).

Prospective repeal of Paragraph V.
2013, 62:10, provides for the repeal of paragraph V on January 1, 2014.

NOTES TO DECISIONS

1. Protective orders
2. Timeliness of hearing
3. Evidence
4. Amendment of petition
5. Attestation

1. Protective orders

Because the trial court failed to make specific factual findings to support its final stalking order, entered pursuant to RSA 633:3-a, and evidence pertaining to unnoticed allegations should not have been admitted, insufficient evidence supported the order, warranting vacation of the same and remand. Moreover, petitioner's assertion that her specific allegations were part of respondent's "ongoing pattern of behavior" did not satisfy the notice provision under RSA 173-B:3, I. South v. McCabe, 156 N.H. 797, 943 A.2d 779, 2008 N.H. LEXIS 23 (2008).

Although the trial court had broad discretion to admit evidence it deemed relevant and material to facts alleged in a mother's RSA 173-B:3, I petition for a domestic violence restraining order, it erred in admitting evidence on unnoticed charges. In re Aldrich, 156 N.H. 33, 930 A.2d 393, 2007 N.H. LEXIS 140 (2007).

Defendant was not allowed to collaterally attack the validity of a temporary restraining order that was issued pursuant to RSA 173-B:3 in defending charges that he violated RSA 633:3-a and RSA 173-B:9, by stalking his wife, and the trial court did not err by denying his motion to dismiss the charges on grounds that the order had expired. State v. Small, 150 N.H. 457, 843 A.2d 932, 2004 N.H. LEXIS 3 (2004), rehearing denied, 2004 N.H. LEXIS 56 (N.H. Mar. 25, 2004).

2. Timeliness of hearing

Where a trial court failed to conduct a timely hearing on a domestic violence temporary restraining order (TRO) pursuant to RSA 173-B:4, I and RSA 173-B:3, VII, dismissal of both the TRO and the petition was required. McCarthy v. Wheeler, 152 N.H. 643, 886 A.2d 972, 2005 N.H. LEXIS 153 (2005).

3. Evidence

Husband's due process rights were not violated in case where husband was not permitted to call 15 and 16-year-old children as witnesses in domestic violence action filed by wife, under RSA ch. 173-B, as husband was able to present children's handwritten statements and was otherwise given the opportunity to be heard in a meaningful way and to adequately present his case. In re Morrill, 147 N.H. 116, 784 A.2d 690, 2001 N.H. LEXIS 180 (2001).

4. Amendment of petition

Court rejected defendant husband's argument that because the allegations contained in plaintiff wife's motion to amend were unverified, defendant did not have proper notice of them. First, defendant received a copy of the motion to amend the day before the hearing and, therefore, received notice of the subject allegations; second, plaintiff attested to the factual allegations in the motion to amend at the start of the hearing; third, the Family Division was empowered under N.H. Fam. Div. R. 1.2 to waive its rules when good cause and the interests of justice might require. In re McArdle & McArdle, 162 N.H. 482, 34 A.3d 700, 2011 N.H. LEXIS 127 (2011).

Trial court did not lack authority under RSA 173-B:3, I to insert an explanatory sentence into a wife's domestic violence petition; the wife herself amended the petition by clarifying her allegation that defendant threatened to take the parties' children "at whatever cost." Furthermore, the trial court had not violated N.H. Const. pt. II, art. 79; it did not advocate for the wife, provide her with legal advice, or undertake any prosecutorial function, but clarified an ambiguous allegation. Walker v. Walker, 158 N.H. 602, 972 A.2d 1083, 2009 N.H. LEXIS 49 (2009).

5. Attestation

New Hampshire Supreme Court cannot conclude, based on the language of RSA 173-B:3, IV, that it was the intent of the legislature to prohibit the court from waiving the attestation requirement for the petition form under circumstances where the plaintiff later attests to the facts at the hearing on the petition. In re McArdle & McArdle, 162 N.H. 482, 34 A.3d 700, 2011 N.H. LEXIS 127 (2011).

Cited:
Cited in Fichtner v. Pittsley, 146 N.H. 512, 774 A.2d 1239, 2001 N.H. LEXIS 104 (2001).

RESEARCH REFERENCES

New Hampshire Bar Journal.
For article, "McCarthy v. Wheeler: Double Jeopardy for Domestic Violence Victims?," see 47 N.H.B.J. 30 (Summer 2006).

173-B:4. Temporary Relief.

I. Upon a showing of an immediate and present danger of abuse, the court may enter temporary orders to protect the plaintiff with or without actual notice to defendant. The court may issue such temporary orders by telephone or facsimile. Such telephonically issued orders shall be made by a circuit court judge to a law enforcement officer, shall be valid in any jurisdiction in the state, and shall be effective until the close of the next regular court business day. Such orders shall be returnable to the circuit court where the plaintiff resides or to which the plaintiff has fled, unless otherwise ordered by the issuing judge. If non-telephonic temporary orders are made ex parte, the party against whom such relief is issued may file a written request with the clerk of the court and request a hearing on such orders. Such hearing shall be held no less than 3 business days and no more than 5 business days after the request is received by the clerk. Such hearings may constitute the final hearing described in RSA 173-B:3, VII. Such temporary relief may direct the defendant to relinquish to a peace officer any and all firearms and ammunition in the control, ownership, or possession of the defendant, or any other person on behalf of the defendant for the duration of the protective order. Other temporary relief may include:

(a) Protective orders:

(1) Restraining the defendant from abusing the plaintiff.

(2) Restraining the defendant from entering the premises and curtilage where the plaintiff resides, except when the defendant is accompanied by a peace officer and, upon reasonable notice to the plaintiff, is allowed entry by the plaintiff for the sole purpose of retrieving toiletries, medication, clothing, business equipment, and any other items as determined by the court.

(3) Restraining the defendant from withholding items of the plaintiff's personal property which are specified in the order. A peace officer shall accompany the plaintiff in retrieving such

property to protect the plaintiff.

(4) Awarding custody of minor children to either party or, upon actual notice, to the department when it is in the best interest of a child.

(5) Denying the defendant visitation, ordering that visitation shall be supervised, or ordering a specific visitation schedule. Visitation shall only be ordered on an ex parte basis where such order can be entered consistent with the following requirements. In determining whether visitation can be safely ordered, the court shall consider the following factors:

(A) The degree to which visitation exposes the plaintiff or the children to physical or psychological harm.

(B) Whether the risk of physical or psychological harm can be removed by ordering supervised visitation.

(C) Whether visitation can be ordered without requiring the plaintiff and defendant to have contact regarding the exchange of children.

(6) Restraining the defendant from contacting the plaintiff or entering the plaintiff's place of employment, school, or any specified place frequented regularly by the plaintiff or by any family or household member.

(7) Restraining the defendant from abusing the plaintiff, plaintiff's relatives, regardless of their place of residence, or plaintiff's household members in any way.

(8) Restraining the defendant from taking, converting, or damaging property in which the plaintiff may have a legal or equitable interest.

(9) Directing the defendant to relinquish to the peace officer, in addition to the relief specified in RSA 173-B:4, I, any and all deadly weapons specified in the protective order that are in the control, ownership, or possession of the defendant, or any other person on behalf of the defendant, for the duration of the protective order.

(b) Other relief, including but not limited to:

(1) Awarding to the plaintiff the exclusive use and possession of an automobile, home, and household furniture, if the defendant has the legal duty to support the plaintiff or the plaintiff's minor children, or the plaintiff has contributed to the household expenses. The court shall consider the type and amount of contribution to be a factor.

(2) Restraining the defendant from taking any action which would lead to the disconnection of any and all utilities and services to the parties' household, or the discontinuance of existing business or service contracts, including, but not limited to, mortgage or rental agreements.

II. The defendant may be prohibited from purchasing, receiving, or possessing any deadly weapons and any and all firearms and ammunition for the duration of the order. The court may subsequently issue a search warrant authorizing the peace officer to seize any deadly weapons specified in the protective order and any and all firearms and ammunition, if there is probable cause to believe such firearms and ammunition and specified deadly weapons are kept on the premises or curtilage of the defendant and if the court has reason to believe that all such firearms and ammunition and specified deadly weapons have not been relinquished by the defendant.

Source.
1999, 240:3, eff. Jan. 1, 2000. 2013, 62:4, eff. January 1, 2014.

Amendments
—2013. The 2013 amendment, in the introductory paragraph of I, substituted "circuit" for "district or superior" in the third sentence and in the fourth sentence, substituted "circuit" for "district" and "judge" for "justice."

Cross References.
Notification of local law enforcement agency, see RSA 173-B:8.
Violation of protective orders, see RSA 173-B:9.

NOTES TO DECISIONS

1. Custody matters
2. Allegations insufficient to support order
3. No exception for "legitimate" contact
4. Prosecutorial discretion
5. Timeliness of hearing
6. Allegations sufficient to justify order
7. Pleading requirements
8. Constitutional concerns

1. Custody matters
Where in a proceeding on a domestic violence petition, district court was concerned with the general welfare of the parties' child under an existing custodial order, it could have immediately transferred the proceedings to the superior court to be heard as if originally entered in the superior court. Fichtner v. Pittsley, 146 N.H. 512, 774 A.2d 1239, 2001 N.H. LEXIS 104 (2001).

2. Allegations insufficient to support order
Plaintiff wife's petition for domestic violence protective order against defendant husband contained insufficient allegations to justify the trial court's issuance of an ex parte domestic violence protective order under RSA 173-B:4, I. Fillmore v. Fillmore, 147 N.H. 283, 786 A.2d 849, 2001 N.H. LEXIS 206 (2001).

3. No exception for "legitimate" contact
Nothing in the plain language of RSA 173-B:4 or the legislative history indicates a legislative intent to except legitimate contact by certain third parties, and a trier of fact can find that a defendant violated a protective order if the trier of fact finds that the defendant knowingly contacted the unrepresented protected person through his attorney; this interpretation effectuates the legislative intent in enacting RSA ch. 173-B of preventing and deterring domestic violence through equal enforcement of the criminal laws and the provision of judicial relief for domestic violence victims. State v. Kidder, 150 N.H. 600, 843 A.2d 312, 2004 N.H. LEXIS 37 (2004).

4. Prosecutorial discretion
While a defendant may properly be found guilty of violating a protective order when he knowingly contacts the victim through an attorney, teacher, doctor, or other party, prosecutorial discretion should be exercised to distinguish between cases when a third party makes innocent contact with the protected party and those where the defendant uses a third party as a conduit. State v. Kidder, 150 N.H. 600, 843 A.2d 312, 2004 N.H. LEXIS 37 (2004).

5. Timeliness of hearing
Where a trial court failed to conduct a timely hearing on a domestic violence temporary restraining order (TRO) pursuant to RSA 173-B:4, I and RSA 173-B:3, VII, dismissal of both the TRO

and the petition was required. McCarthy v. Wheeler, 152 N.H. 643, 886 A.2d 972, 2005 N.H. LEXIS 153 (2005).

6. Allegations sufficient to justify order

Wife's allegations justified a temporary domestic violence protective order under RSA 173-B:4, I. She alleged that the husband had hit and choked her on many occasions and had threatened her life on three occasions; she was not obliged to set forth the specific dates on which she allegedly was abused. In re Sawyer, 161 N.H. 11, 8 A.3d 80, 2010 N.H. LEXIS 117 (2010).

7. Pleading requirements

While Tosta and Fillmore mandate that the misconduct prompting a domestic violence petition not be too distant in time, neither obliges a plaintiff seeking a temporary protective order to set forth the specific dates upon which he or she allegedly suffered abuse; indeed, such a requirement would conflict with the intent of RSA ch. 173-B, which is to entitle such victims to immediate and effective police protection and judicial relief. The New Hampshire Supreme Court declines to read such a requirement into the relevant statutory scheme. In re Sawyer, 161 N.H. 11, 8 A.3d 80, 2010 N.H. LEXIS 117 (2010).

8. Constitutional concerns

Trial court's issuance of a temporary domestic violence protective order and its failure to dismiss the wife's petition because it did not contain dates did not violate due process under N.H. Const. pt. I, art. 15 and U.S. Const. amend. XIV. The allegations were sufficiently specific to allow the husband to prepare for the hearing; furthermore, he did not present any evidence that he in fact had a time-based defense which he would have presented had he known the alleged dates. In re Sawyer, 161 N.H. 11, 8 A.3d 80, 2010 N.H. LEXIS 117 (2010).

Cited:

Cited in Walker v. Walker, 158 N.H. 602, 972 A.2d 1083, 2009 N.H. LEXIS 49 (2009).

RESEARCH REFERENCES

New Hampshire Practice.
3-5 N.H.P. Family Law § 5.25.

New Hampshire Bar Journal.
For article, "Lex Loci: A Survey of New Hampshire Supreme Court Decisions," see 47 N.H.B.J. 78 (Autumn 2006).
For article, "McCarthy v. Wheeler: Double Jeopardy for Domestic Violence Victims?," see 47 N.H.B.J. 30 (Summer 2006).
For article, "Understanding and Representing Adult Clients Who Are Victims of Domestic Abuse," see 35 N.H.B.J. 8 (1994).
For article, "Role of Judges' Response to Domestic Violence," see 35 N.H.B.J 37 (1994).

173-B:5. Relief.

I. A finding of abuse shall mean the defendant represents a credible threat to the safety of the plaintiff. Upon a showing of abuse of the plaintiff by a preponderance of the evidence, the court shall grant such relief as is necessary to bring about a cessation of abuse. Such relief shall direct the defendant to relinquish to the peace officer any and all firearms and ammunition in the control, ownership, or possession of the defendant, or any other person on behalf of the defendant for the duration of the protective order. Other relief may include:

(a) Protective orders:

(1) Restraining the defendant from abusing the plaintiff.

(2) Restraining the defendant from entering the premises and curtilage where the plaintiff resides, except when the defendant is accompanied by a peace officer and is allowed entry by the plaintiff for the sole purpose of retrieving personal property specified by the court.

(3) Restraining the defendant from contacting the plaintiff or entering the plaintiff's place of employment, school, or any specified place frequented regularly by the plaintiff or by any family or household member.

(4) Restraining the defendant from abusing the plaintiff, plaintiff's relatives, regardless of their place of residence, or plaintiff's household members in any way.

(5) Restraining the defendant from taking, converting, or damaging property in which the plaintiff may have a legal or equitable interest.

(6) Directing the defendant to relinquish to the peace officer, in addition to the relief specified in RSA 173-B:5, I, any and all deadly weapons specified in the protective order that are in the control, ownership, or possession of the defendant, or any other person on behalf of the defendant.

(b) Other relief including, but not limited to:

(1) Granting the plaintiff the exclusive use and possession of the premises and curtilage of the plaintiff's place of residence, unless the defendant exclusively owns or leases and pays for the premises and the defendant has no legal duty to support the plaintiff or minor children on the premises.

(2) Restraining the defendant from withholding items of the plaintiff's personal property specified by the court. A peace officer shall accompany the plaintiff in retrieving such property to protect the plaintiff.

(3) Granting to the plaintiff the exclusive right of use and possession of the household furniture, furnishings, or a specific automobile, unless the defendant exclusively owns such personal property and the defendant has no legal duty to support the plaintiff or minor children.

(4) Ordering the defendant to make automobile, insurance, health care, utilities, rent, or mortgage payments.

(5) Awarding temporary custody of the parties' minor children to either party or, where appropriate, to the department, provided that:

(A) Where custody of the parties' minor children with the department may be appropriate, the department shall receive actual notice of the hearing 10 days prior to such hearing provided that, if necessary, such hearing may be continued 10 days to provide the department adequate notice.

(B) The department may move at any time to rescind its custody of the parties' minor children.

(6) Establishing visitation rights with regard to the parties' minor children. The court shall consider, and may impose on a custody

award, conditions necessary to assure the safety of the plaintiff and minor children. This may include orders denying visitation or requiring supervised visitation, where such order can be entered consistent with the following requirements. In determining whether visitation shall be granted, the court shall consider whether visitation can be exercised by the non-custodial parent without risk to the plaintiff's or children's safety. In making such determination, the court shall consider, in addition to any other relevant factors, the following:

(A) The degree to which visitation exposes the plaintiff or the children to physical or psychological harm.

(B) Whether the risk of physical or psychological harm can be removed by ordering supervised visitation.

(C) Whether visitation can be ordered without requiring the plaintiff and defendant to have contact regarding the exchange of children.

(7) Directing the defendant to pay financial support to the plaintiff or minor children, unless the defendant has no legal duty to support the plaintiff or minor children.

(8) Directing the abuser to engage in a batterer's intervention program or personal counseling. If available, such intervention and counseling program shall focus on alternatives to aggression. The court shall not direct the plaintiff to engage in joint counseling services with the defendant. Court-ordered and court-referred mediation of cases involving domestic violence shall be prohibited.

(9) Ordering the defendant to pay the plaintiff monetary compensation for losses suffered as a direct result of the abuse which may include, but not be limited to, loss of earnings or support, medical and dental expenses, damage to property, out-of-pocket losses for injuries sustained, and moving and shelter expenses.

(10) Ordering the defendant to pay reasonable attorney's fees.

II. The defendant shall be prohibited from purchasing, receiving, or possessing any deadly weapons and any and all firearms and ammunition for the duration of the order. The court may subsequently issue a search warrant authorizing a peace officer to seize any deadly weapons specified in the protective order and any and all firearms and ammunition, if there is probable cause to believe such firearms and ammunition and specified deadly weapons are kept on the premises or curtilage of the defendant.

III. Reconciliation after a previous order, prior to filing the current action, shall not be grounds for denying or terminating a new or existing protective order. Furthermore, the court shall not deny the plaintiff protective orders based solely on a lapse of time between an act of domestic violence and the filing of a petition, provided that the underlying act presents a credible threat to the plaintiff's current safety.

IV. No order made under this section shall supersede or affect any court order pertaining to the possession of a residence; household furniture; custody of children pursuant to RSA 169-B, 169-C, or 169-D; support or custody made under RSA 458; or custody of children of unwed parents as determined by a circuit court, or title to real or personal property.

V. (a) Mutual orders for relief shall not be granted. A foreign mutual order for relief shall only be granted full faith and credit in New Hampshire if it meets the requirements set out in RSA 173-B:13, VII.

(b) Cross orders for relief may be granted only if:

(1) The court has made specific findings that each party has committed abuse against the other; and

(2) The court cannot determine who is the primary physical aggressor.

VI. Any order under this section shall be for a fixed period of time not to exceed one year, but may be extended by order of the court upon a motion by the plaintiff, showing good cause, with notice to the defendant, for one year after the expiration of the first order and thereafter each extension may be for up to 5 years, upon the request of the plaintiff and at the discretion of the court. The court shall review the order, and each renewal thereof and shall grant such relief as may be necessary to provide for the safety and well-being of the plaintiff. A defendant shall have the right to a hearing on the extension of any order under this paragraph to be held within 30 days of the extension. The court shall state in writing, at the respondent's request, its reason or reasons for granting the extension. The court shall retain jurisdiction to enforce and collect the financial support obligation which accrued prior to the expiration of the protective order.

VII. Both parties shall be issued written copies of any orders issued by the court, and all orders shall bear the following language: "A willful violation of this order is a crime, as well as contempt of court. Violations of the protective provisions shall result in arrest and may result in imprisonment." Orders shall clearly state how any party can request a further hearing and how the plaintiff may bring a criminal complaint or a petition for contempt if there is a violation of any court order.

VIII. (a) No order issued under this chapter shall be modified other than by the court. Temporary reconciliations shall not revoke an order.

(b) If either party wishes the defendant to be excused from any provisions of an order of protection, the remedy is to petition the court for modification of such order.

(c) A defendant who is restrained from contacting the plaintiff or entering the premises of the plaintiff is prohibited from doing so even if invited by the plaintiff unless the restraining order has been modified by the court.

(d) This paragraph shall give unequivocal direction to peace officers that orders for protection are to be enforced as written and that no action by a party relieves them of the duty to enforce the order.

VIII-a. Upon issuing an order against a defendant, in which a defendant is restrained from having any contact with the plaintiff, the court shall advise the plaintiff that it would be unwise and possibly unsafe for the plaintiff to contact the defendant. If the plaintiff wishes to contact the defendant for any reason, the court shall advise the plaintiff that such contact be made only after petitioning the court for a modification of the order. In an emergency situation, the plaintiff or plaintiff's family may request that the local police department notify the defendant and the local police may accompany the defendant to a designated location, such as a hospital, if appropriate.

IX. (a) A copy of each protective order issued under this chapter shall be transmitted to the administrative office of the courts by facsimile or computer. An emergency protective order issued telephonically shall be transmitted by telephone or facsimile to the department of safety.

(b) The administrative office of the courts shall enter information regarding the protective orders into the state database which shall be made available to police and sheriff departments statewide. The department of safety shall make available information regarding emergency protective orders issued telephonically to police and sheriff departments statewide.

(c) The administrative office of the courts shall update the database upon expiration or termination of a protective order.

(d) Notwithstanding any other provision of law, the administrative office of the courts or the department of safety, its employees and agents, and law enforcement officials shall not be held criminally or civilly liable for action taken under this chapter or RSA 458:16, provided they are acting in good faith and without gross negligence, and within the scope of their duties and authority.

IX-a. If a criminal records check conducted by the department of safety indicates that a potential buyer or transferee is prohibited from receipt or possession of a firearm pursuant to a protective order issued under this chapter, the department of safety shall notify the administrative office of the courts of the denial. The administrative office of the courts shall immediately notify the plaintiff that the defendant has attempted to purchase or obtain a firearm in violation of the protective order.

X. (a) Within 15 days prior to the expiration of the protective orders, the defendant may request, by motion to the court, the return of any and all firearms and ammunition and specified deadly weapons held by the law enforcement agency while the protective order was in effect. Upon receipt of such a motion, the court shall schedule a hearing no later than 15 days after the expiration of the order. The court shall provide written notice to the plaintiff who shall have the right to appear and be heard, and to the law enforcement agency which has control of the firearms, ammunition, and specified deadly weapons. The scope of the hearing shall be limited to:

(1) Establishing whether the defendant is subject to any state or federal law or court order that precludes the defendant from owning or possessing a firearm; and

(2) Under circumstances where the plaintiff has requested an extension of the protective order, whether the plaintiff has established by a preponderance of the evidence that the defendant continues to represent a credible threat to the safety of the plaintiff.

(b) If the court finds that the defendant is not subject to any state or federal law or court order precluding the ownership or possession of firearms, or if the court denies the plaintiff's request to extend the protective order, the court shall issue a written order directing the law enforcement agency to return the requested firearms, ammunition, or deadly weapon to the defendant.

(c) Law enforcement agencies shall not release firearms and ammunition and specified deadly weapons without a court order granting such release. The law enforcement agency may charge the defendant a reasonable fee for the storage of any firearms and ammunition and specified deadly weapons taken pursuant to a protective order. The fee shall not exceed the actual cost incurred by the law enforcement agency for the storage of the firearms and ammunition and specified deadly weapons. The defendant may make alternative arrangements with a federally licensed firearms dealer for the storage of firearms, at the defendant's own expense, upon approval of the court. Such firearms shall be turned over to the appropriate law enforcement agency for transfer to the storage facility. Retrieval of such firearms shall be through the law enforcement agency responsible for their transfer to the storage facility pursuant to a court order as prescribed in this paragraph.

(d) No law enforcement agency shall be held liable for alleged damage or deterioration due to storage or transportation to any firearms and ammunition and specified deadly weapons held by a law enforcement agency, so long as due care is used.

Source.

1999, 240:3, eff. Jan. 1, 2000. 2000, 230:1, eff. July 1, 2000. 2001, 189:2, eff. Jan. 1, 2002. 2004, 206:1, eff. Jan. 1, 2005. 2005, 284:1, eff. August 21, 2005. 2006, 214:4, eff. July 31, 2006. 2013, 62:5, eff. January 1, 2014.

Amendments

—2013. The 2013 amendment substituted "circuit" for "superior court, probate court, or family division" in IV.

—2006. Paragraph VII: Inserted "or a petition for contempt" following "criminal complaint" in the third sentence.

—2005. Paragraph VI: Inserted "for one year after the expiration of the first order and thereafter each extension may be for up to 5 years, upon the request of the plaintiff and at the discretion of the court" at the end of the first sentence, and added the second sentence.

—2004. Paragraph VI: Added the third sentence.

—2001. Paragraph IX-a: Added.

—2000. Paragraph VIII-a: Added.

Applicability of 2005 amendment.
2005, 284:3, eff. Aug. 21, 2005, provided: "This act shall apply to any order in effect under RSA 173-B:5, VI and RSA 633:3-a, III-c on the effective date [Aug. 21, 2005] of this act as well as any order entered thereafter."

Cross References.
Notification of local law enforcement agency, see RSA 173-B:8.
Temporary relief, see RSA 173-B:4.
Violation of protective orders, see RSA 173-B:9.

NOTES TO DECISIONS

1. Custody matters
2. Allegations insufficient to support finding of abuse
3. Finding of criminal conduct required
4. Firearms, ammunition, and deadly weapons
5. Sufficient evidence to issue protective order
6. Attorney's fees
7. Reconsideration
8. Property
9. Relevance of evidence

1. Custody matters
Under paragraph IV of this section, district court is prohibited from modifying custody orders that have previously been judicially determined in any of the proceedings enumerated therein. Fichtner v. Pittsley, 146 N.H. 512, 774 A.2d 1239, 2001 N.H. LEXIS 104 (2001).

Since district court had no authority to issue an order that affected a prior custody award made in the superior court under RSA 458:17, part of its protective order that included awarding plaintiff custody of parties' minor child, while permitting defendant unsupervised visitation with the child, was vacated. Fichtner v. Pittsley, 146 N.H. 512, 774 A.2d 1239, 2001 N.H. LEXIS 104 (2001).

2. Allegations insufficient to support finding of abuse
Assault that occurred nine months before a wife filed for a protection order did not qualify as a threshold element of misconduct that was a prerequisite to a finding of abuse; the parties had since lived together without physical violence, despite the commencement of divorce proceedings, and the husband's sudden and unexplained decision to leave home had prompted the wife to seek a protective order. Tosta v. Bullis, 156 N.H. 763, 943 A.2d 824, 2008 N.H. LEXIS 16 (2008).

After plaintiff wife's petition for an ex parte domestic violence protective order against defendant husband was granted, the trial court's finding of abuse as defined in RSA 173-B:1 was unsupported by the evidence presented at the final hearing, since the incidents described by the wife were too distant in time or too non-specific to be abuse in the form of criminal threatening or harassment as defined in RSA 631:4 (Supp. 2000) and RSA 644:4 (Supp. 2000), respectively. Fillmore v. Fillmore, 147 N.H. 283, 786 A.2d 849, 2001 N.H. LEXIS 206 (2001).

3. Finding of criminal conduct required
Because RSA 173-B:1 contains an enumerated list of prohibited conduct, RSA 173-B:5 requires that a trial court must make a specific finding of criminal conduct in order to issue a final restrain-

ing order against a defendant. Fillmore v. Fillmore, 147 N.H. 283, 786 A.2d 849, 2001 N.H. LEXIS 206 (2001).

4. Firearms, ammunition, and deadly weapons
Court order which prohibited a husband from interfering with ex-wife's person or liberty or from harassing, intimidating, or threatening her did not trigger 18 U.S.C.S. § 922(d)(8)(B)(ii) (2000), and the state supreme court held that the trial court erred as a matter of law when it ruled that § 922(d)(8)(B)(ii) prohibited a sheriff's office from returning firearms it seized under court order after the husband's wife filed a stalking petition, once that petition was dismissed. Magoon v. Thoroughgood, 148 N.H. 139, 803 A.2d 1070, 2002 N.H. LEXIS 105 (2002).

5. Sufficient evidence to issue protective order
It was error to grant a former husband a domestic violence protective order against his former wife under RSA 173-B:5, I(a), as there was insufficient evidence that she posed a threat to his physical safety. The former husband's concern was based upon his speculation that as a result of the former wife's statements about him, unknown persons might take it upon themselves to harm him. Knight v. Maher, 161 N.H. 742, 20 A.3d 901, 2011 N.H. LEXIS 51 (2011).

In issuing a protective order, the trial court properly found defendant husband to be a threat to plaintiff wife. The definition of "abuse" in RSA 173-B:1 did not require defendant to have committed a violent act; defendant's history of angry, destructive behavior supported the conclusion that plaintiff was in fear of physical contact from defendant when he followed her from room to room, repeatedly demanding certain papers, while holding a propane torch; and the trial court found, and defendant did not dispute on appeal, that he committed the offense of criminal threatening. In re McArdle & McArdle, 162 N.H. 482, 34 A.3d 700, 2011 N.H. LEXIS 127 (2011).

There was sufficient evidence to support the decision in favor of a wife who sought a domestic protective order when the husband threatened the wife's life multiple times within several weeks of her petition. Although the wife testified that things were "okay" during the weekend preceding her petition, she stated that the parties were at a campground with other people nearby and that she did not do anything to make the husband believe she intended to leave and that she intended to proceed following the weekend. Walker v. Walker, 158 N.H. 602, 972 A.2d 1083, 2009 N.H. LEXIS 49 (2009).

Although a wife's allegations could have been read to support a conclusion that the husband's conduct posed a credible and continuing threat to her safety, there was insufficient evidence to support a finding that he was engaged in abuse that warranted a protective order; there was no evidence that a husband had in any way threatened his wife's safety in the weeks or months leading up to her filing within the meaning of RSA 173-B:5. The link between the wife's request for protection and a prior assault was attenuated at best. Tosta v. Bullis, 156 N.H. 763, 943 A.2d 824, 2008 N.H. LEXIS 16 (2008).

Because a daughter threatened the administrator of an assisted living center and other staff members, the acts constituted a course of conduct, as defined in RSA 633:3-a, II; therefore, the district court properly issued a stalking protective order under RSA ch. 173-B against the daughter and in favor of the administrator. Fisher v. Minichiello, 155 N.H. 188, 921 A.2d 385, 2007 N.H. LEXIS 45 (2007), rehearing denied, 2007 N.H. LEXIS 105 (N.H. May 23, 2007).

6. Attorney's fees
Trial court did not engage in an unsustainable exercise of discretion in denying the wife's requests for attorney's fees because the parties were engaged in a contentious divorce, which was adversarial by nature, and the wife's assertions of the husband's bad faith amounted to disagreements and accusations in which both parties engaged. In re Martel, 157 N.H. 53, 944 A.2d 575, 2008 N.H. LEXIS 35 (2008), rehearing denied, 2008 N.H. LEXIS 54 (N.H. Apr. 16, 2008).

7. Reconsideration
In a domestic protective order case, the trial court did not err in denying the husband's motion for reconsideration based on a note written by the wife after the hearing. Even if the note was

inconsistent with the wife's testimony that the husband had deprived her of her debit card and checkbook, the husband conceded that the allegation was not essential to a finding of abuse. Walker v. Walker, 158 N.H. 602, 972 A.2d 1083, 2009 N.H. LEXIS 49 (2009).

8. Property

For a court to make an order regarding the right to use or possess household property under RSA 173-B:5, I(b)(3), it must make a determination regarding ownership of that property. The family court made such a determination when it allowed a former boyfriend to "retrieve his belongings." Gray v. Kelly, 161 N.H. 160, 13 A.3d 848, 2010 N.H. LEXIS 134 (2010).

Relief available concerning property in a replevin action is available in a domestic violence action. Thus, when a family court had given a boyfriend 30 days to retrieve his property from his girlfriend, res judicata barred his action for replevin against the girlfriend. Gray v. Kelly, 161 N.H. 160, 13 A.3d 848, 2010 N.H. LEXIS 134 (2010).

9. Relevance of evidence

In considering a domestic violence petition filed by plaintiff wife against defendant husband, the trial court did not err in considering events detailed in plaintiff's motion to amend because they were too stale. The trial court's ruling was based on the incident which occurred the day before plaintiff filed the domestic violence petition; furthermore, the prior incidents were relevant to the trial court's finding that defendant had committed criminal threatening and posed a credible threat to plaintiff's safety. In re McArdle & McArdle, 162 N.H. 482, 34 A.3d 700, 2011 N.H. LEXIS 127 (2011).

Cited:

Cited in State v. Small, 150 N.H. 457, 843 A.2d 932, 2004 N.H. LEXIS 3 (2004).

RESEARCH REFERENCES

New Hampshire Practice.
3-5 N.H.P. Family Law § 5.25.

New Hampshire Bar Journal.
For article, "Understanding and Representing Adult Clients Who Are Victims of Domestic Abuse," see 35 N.H.B.J. 8 (1994).

173-B:5-a. Permissible Contact.

I. A protective order issued pursuant to RSA 173-B:4 or RSA 173-B:5 shall not be construed to prohibit an attorney, or any person acting on the attorney's behalf, who is representing the defendant in an action brought under this chapter, or in any criminal proceeding concerning the abuse alleged under this chapter, from contacting the plaintiff for a legitimate purpose within the scope of the civil or criminal proceeding; provided, that the attorney or person acting on behalf of the attorney: identifies himself or herself as a representative of the defendant; acknowledges the existence of the protective order and informs the plaintiff that he or she has no obligation to speak; terminates contact with the plaintiff if the plaintiff expresses an unwillingness to talk; and ensures that any personal contact with the plaintiff occurs outside of the defendant's presence, unless the court has modified the protective order to permit such contact.

II. A no-contact provision in a protective order issued pursuant to RSA 173-B:4 or RSA 173-B:5 shall not be construed to:

(a) Prevent contact between counsel for represented parties; or

(b) Prevent a party from appearing at a scheduled court or administrative hearing; or

(c) Prevent a defendant or defendant's counsel from sending the plaintiff copies of any legal pleadings filed in court relating to the domestic violence petition or related civil or criminal matters.

III. A violation of this section may result in a finding of contempt of court.

Source.
2006, 214:1, eff. July 31, 2006.

173-B:6. Guardian Ad Litem.

In all proceedings under this chapter, the court may appoint a guardian ad litem to represent the interests of the children of either or both parties. The guardian ad litem may continue to serve after the final disposition of the case.

Source.
1999, 240:3, eff. Jan. 1, 2000.

173-B:7. Minority not a Preclusion for Services.

The minority of any individual seeking assistance from any domestic violence program, as defined by RSA 173-B:1, shall not preclude provision of such requested services.

Source.
1999, 240:3, eff. Jan. 1, 2000.

173-B:8. Notification.

I. A copy of any order made under this chapter which prohibits any person from abusing another shall be promptly transmitted to the local law enforcement agency having jurisdiction to enforce such order.

II. Temporary orders shall be promptly served on the defendant by a peace officer. Subsequent orders shall be sent to the defendant's last address of record. The defendant shall be responsible for informing the court of any changes of address. Law enforcement agencies shall establish procedures whereby a peace officer at the scene of an alleged violation of such an order may be informed of the existence and terms of such order.

III. Any court-ordered changes or modifications of the order shall be effective upon issuance of such changes or modifications, and shall be mailed or otherwise provided to the appropriate local law enforcement agency and transmitted to the department of safety within 24 hours of the entry of such changes or modifications.

Source.
1999, 240:3, eff. Jan. 1, 2000.

173-B:9. Violation of Protective Order; Penalty.

I. (a) When the defendant violates either a temporary or permanent protective order issued or enforced under this chapter, peace officers shall arrest the defendant and ensure that the defendant is detained until arraignment, provided that in extreme circumstances, such as when the health of the defendant would be jeopardized by the temporary detention, a judge in response to a request by the arresting law enforcement officer or agency, may order an alternative to detention pending arraignment. Such arrests may be made within 12 hours without a warrant upon probable cause, whether or not the violation is committed in the presence of a peace officer.

(b) Subsequent to an arrest, the peace officer shall seize any firearms and ammunition in the control, ownership, or possession of the defendant and any deadly weapons which may have been used, or were threatened to be used, during the violation of the protective order. The law enforcement agency shall maintain possession of the firearms, ammunition, or deadly weapons until the court issues an order directing that the firearms, ammunition, or deadly weapons be relinquished and specifying the person to whom the firearms and ammunition or deadly weapons will be relinquished.

II. The prosecution and sentencing for criminal contempt for a violation of a protective order shall not preclude the prosecution of or sentencing for other criminal charges underlying the contempt.

III. A person shall be guilty of a class A misdemeanor if such person knowingly violates a protective order issued under this chapter, or RSA 458:16, III, or any foreign protective order enforceable under the laws of this state. Charges made under this chapter shall not be reduced to a lesser charge, as permitted in other instances under RSA 625:9.

IV. Any person convicted under RSA 173-B:9, III, or who has been convicted in another jurisdiction of violating a protective order enforceable under the laws of this state, who, within 6 years of such conviction or the completion of the sentence imposed for such conviction, whichever is later, subsequently commits and is convicted of one or more offenses involving abuse may be charged with an enhanced penalty for each subsequent offense as follows:

(a) There shall be no enhanced charge under this section if the subsequent offense is a class A felony or an unclassified felony;

(b) If the subsequent offense would otherwise constitute a class B felony, it may be charged as a class A felony;

(c) If the subsequent offense would otherwise constitute a class A misdemeanor, it may be charged as a class B felony;

(d) If the subsequent offense would otherwise constitute a class B misdemeanor, it may be charged as a class A misdemeanor;

(e) If the subsequent offense would otherwise constitute a violation, it may be charged as a class B misdemeanor.

V. A victim of domestic violence shall be entitled to all rights granted to victims of crime under RSA 21-M:8-k.

Source.

1999, 240:3, eff. Jan. 1, 2000. 2002, 79:1, eff. Jan. 1, 2003. 2003, 219:1, eff. Jan. 1, 2004.

Amendments

—2003.   Paragraph I(a): Added the proviso in the first sentence.

—2002.   Paragraph I(a): Substituted "12 hours" for "6 hours" in the second sentence.

Cross References.
Sentences, see RSA 651.

NOTES TO DECISIONS

1.   Validity of order
2.   Foreign order
3.   Construction with other laws

1. Validity of order

Defendant was not allowed to collaterally attack the validity of a temporary restraining order that was issued pursuant to RSA 173-B:3 in defending charges that he violated RSA 633:3-a and RSA 173-B:9, by stalking his wife, and the trial court did not err by denying his motion to dismiss the charges on grounds that the order had expired. State v. Small, 150 N.H. 457, 843 A.2d 932, 2004 N.H. LEXIS 3 (2004), rehearing denied, 2004 N.H. LEXIS 56 (N.H. Mar. 25, 2004).

2. Foreign order

Trial court properly denied defendant's motion to dismiss a charge of violating a Massachusetts protective order under RSA 173-B:9, III. Defendant did not argue that the Massachusetts order was invalid for lack of jurisdiction or due process, nor did he offer any other reason why it should not be enforced. State v. Kousounadis, 159 N.H. 413, 986 A.2d 603, 2009 N.H. LEXIS 136 (2009).

3. Construction with other laws

To the extent RSA 173-B:9, IV, and RSA 633:3-a, VI, conflict, RSA 173-B:9, IV, as the more specific statute, controls. Accordingly, when defendant was convicted of stalking, the trial court did not err in imposing felony sentences. State v. Moussa, 164 N.H. 108, 53 A.3d 630, 2012 N.H. LEXIS 117 (2012).

Cited:

Cited in State v. Kidder, 150 N.H. 600, 843 A.2d 312, 2004 N.H. LEXIS 37 (2004).

RESEARCH REFERENCES

New Hampshire Practice.
3-5 N.H.P. Family Law § 5.17.

New Hampshire Bar Journal.
For article, "Understanding and Representing Adult Clients Who Are Victims of Domestic Abuse," see 35 N.H.B.J. 8 (1994).

173-B:10. Protection by Peace Officers.

I. Whenever any peace officer has probable cause to believe that a person has been abused, as defined in RSA 173-B:1, that officer shall use all means within reason to prevent further abuse including, but not limited to:

(a) Confiscating any deadly weapons involved in the alleged domestic abuse and any firearms and ammunition in the defendant's control, ownership, or possession.

(b) Transporting or obtaining transportation for the victim and any child, to a designated place to meet with a domestic violence counselor, local family member, or friend.

(c) Assisting the victim in removing toiletries, medication, clothing, business equipment, and any other items determined by the court.

(d) Giving the victim immediate and written notice of the rights of victims and of the remedies and services available to victims of domestic violence. The written notice shall include a statement substantially as follows:

"If you are the victim of domestic violence and you believe that law enforcement protection is needed for your physical safety, you have the right to request that the officer assist in providing for your safety, including asking for an emergency telephonic order for protection. You may also request that the officer assist you in obtaining from your premises and curtilage, toiletries, medication, clothing, business equipment, and any other items as determined by the court, and in locating and taking you to a local safe place including, but not limited to, a designated meeting place to be used as a crisis center, a family member's or friend's residence, or a similar place of safety. If you are in need of medical treatment, you have the right to request that the officer assist you in obtaining an ambulance. You may request a copy of the report filed by the peace officer, at no cost, from the law enforcement department."

II. Pursuant to RSA 594:10, an arrest for abuse may be made without a warrant upon probable cause, whether or not the abuse is committed in the presence of the peace officer. When the peace officer has probable cause to believe that the persons are committing or have committed abuse against each other, the officer need not arrest both persons, but should arrest the person the officer believes to be the primary physical aggressor. In determining who is the primary physical aggressor, an officer shall consider the intent of this chapter to protect the victims of domestic violence, the relative degree of injury or fear inflicted on the persons involved, and any history of domestic abuse between these persons if that history can reasonably be obtained by the officer.

Source.
1999, 240:3, eff. Jan. 1, 2000.

NOTES TO DECISIONS

Probable cause standard
RSA 173-B:10, II, was irrelevant to the Fourth Amendment analysis regarding probable cause to arrest plaintiff husband for simple assault because the choice of a more restrictive probable cause standard did not render less restrictive ones unreasonable, and hence unconstitutional. Holder v. Town of Sandown, 585 F.3d 500, 2009 U.S. App. LEXIS 23853 (2009).

RESEARCH REFERENCES

New Hampshire Bar Journal.
For article, "Who's to Blame," see 35 N.H.B.J. 34 (1994).

173-B:11. Notice to the Victim.

I. Notwithstanding the peace officer's obligations in RSA 173-B:9 and RSA 173-B:10, all peace officers shall give victims of abuse immediate and adequate notice of their right to go to the circuit court of their county to file a petition asking for protective orders against the abusive person and to seek a private criminal complaint.

II. The clerk of the court shall be responsible for advising victims of their right to request that the judge issue an order which may include removing any and all firearms and ammunition in the control, ownership, or possession of the defendant and may include:

(a) Restraining the defendant from abusing the victim.

(b) Directing the defendant to leave and stay away from the victim's premises and curtilage.

(c) Giving the victim custody of any minor children, denying the defendant visitation, or requiring that visitation be supervised to ensure safety for the victim and minor children.

(d) Directing the defendant to support the victim and any minor children if the defendant has the legal responsibility to support either or both.

(e) Restraining the defendant from contacting the victim, or entering the victim's place of employment, school, or any specified place frequented regularly by the victim or by any family or household member.

(f) Restraining the defendant from abusing, in any way, the victim, household members, or victim's relatives, regardless of their place of residence.

(g) Restraining the defendant from taking, converting, or damaging property in which the victim may have a legal or equitable interest.

(h) Directing the defendant to temporarily relinquish to the peace officer specific deadly weapons in the control, ownership, or possession of the defendant which may have been used, or were threatened to be used, in an incident of abuse against the victim or any member of the victim's household.

(i) Ordering the defendant to pay the victim monetary compensation for losses suffered as a direct result of the abuse which may include, but not be limited to, loss of earnings or support, medical and dental expenses, damage to property, out-of-pocket losses for injuries sustained, and moving and shelter expenses.

(j) Ordering the defendant to pay reasonable attorney's fees.

Source.
1999, 240:3, eff. Jan. 1, 2000. 2013, 62:6, eff. January 1, 2014.

Amendments
—**2013.** The 2013 amendment substituted "circuit" for "district or superior" in I.

173-B:12. Emergency Care; Limitation and Liability.

Any act or omission of any peace officer rendering emergency care or assistance to a victim of domestic violence including, but not limited to transportation, shall not impose civil liability upon the peace officer or the peace officer's supervisors or employer if the care or assistance is rendered in good faith, unless the act or omission is a result of gross negligence or willful misconduct.

Source.
1999, 240:3, eff. Jan. 1, 2000.

173-B:13. Orders Enforceable.

I. Any protective order issued under this chapter shall be effective throughout the state.

II. Any protective order issued by any other state, tribal, or territorial court related to domestic or family violence, including an ex parte order, shall be deemed valid if the issuing court had jurisdiction over the parties and matter under the law of the state, tribe, or territory, and the person against whom the order was made was given reasonable notice and opportunity to be heard. There shall be a presumption of validity where an order appears facially valid.

III. Any valid protective order, as defined in paragraph II, shall be accorded full faith and credit throughout the state.

IV. A person entitled to protection under a foreign protective order, as defined in paragraph II, may file such order in any circuit court by filing with the court a certified copy of the order. Such person shall swear under oath in an affidavit to the best of such person's knowledge that the order is presently in effect as written. Such filing shall be without fee or cost. The clerk of the circuit court shall forward such order to the administrative office of the courts which shall enter such order in the state database. Such filing shall not be a precondition to arrest or enforcement of a foreign order.

V. A peace officer may rely upon a copy of any protective order issued under this chapter, or under RSA 458, or upon a copy of a foreign protective order, as defined in this section, which has been provided to the peace officer by any source.

VI. Law enforcement personnel may rely on the statement of the person protected by the order that the order remains in effect as written.

VII. A mutual protective order issued by any other state, tribal, or territorial court against one who has petitioned, filed a complaint, or otherwise filed a written pleading for protection relating to domestic or family violence shall be accorded full faith and credit only if:

(a) A cross or counter petition, complaint, or other written pleading was filed seeking such protection order; and

(b) The court made specific findings of domestic or family violence by both parties and that each party was entitled to such order.

Source.
1999, 240:3, eff. Jan. 1, 2000. 2001, 189:3, eff. Jan. 1, 2002. 2013, 62:7, eff. January 1, 2014.

Amendments
—2013. The 2013 amendment substituted "circuit" for "district or superior" in the first and fourth sentences of IV.

—2001. Paragraph IV: Substituted "administrative office of the courts which" for "state police who" in the fourth sentence.

173-B:14. Orders of Support.

I. In any action determining the obligation of the obligor to support the obligee or the parties' minor children including, but not limited to, actions for divorce pursuant to RSA 458; determination of parental rights and responsibilities pursuant to RSA 461-A; paternity pursuant to RSA 168-A; child support pursuant to RSA 161-B, RSA 161-C, and RSA 458; reimbursement of public assistance pursuant to RSA 161-C; and the uniform interstate family support act pursuant to RSA 546-B; the court shall take judicial notice of any support obligation established pursuant to this chapter upon the filing of a certified copy of the order by:

(a) Either party to the domestic violence proceeding.

(b) The department.

(c) Any other agency or person legally entitled to enforce the obligation of support for the minor children.

II. Any circuit court order for financial support shall include enforcement of any duly filed circuit court order from the date of filing forward, and shall include enforcement of any arrears which have been:

(a) Reduced to judgment by the circuit court;

(b) Documented by the department pursuant to an order to make payable through the department; or

(c) Documented by the obligee in a notarized statement, provided that the obligor shall have 30 days to object and request a hearing on the issue of arrears.

Source.
1999, 240:3, eff. Jan. 1, 2000. 2005, 273:13, eff. October 1, 2005. 2013, 62:8, eff. January 1, 2014.

Amendments
—2013. The 2013 amendment, in the introductory language of II, substituted "Any circuit" for "Any superior" and "filed circuit" for "filed district" and substituted "circuit" for "district" in II(a).

—2005. Paragraph I: Rewritten to the extent that a detailed comparison would be impracticable.

173-B:15. Fund for Domestic Violence Grant Program.

A special fund for domestic violence programs is established. The sole purpose of the fund shall be to provide revenues for the domestic violence program established in RSA 173-B:16, and shall not be available for any other purpose. The state treasurer shall deposit all fees received by the department under RSA 457:29 in the fund. All moneys deposited in the fund shall be continually appropriated for the purposes of the domestic violence grant program and shall not lapse.

Source.
1999, 240:3, eff. Jan. 1, 2000.

173-B:16. Grant Program Established.

A grant program is established within the department for the allocation of grant money to New Hampshire programs which provide aid and assistance to victims of domestic violence. The grant program shall be funded by the fund established under RSA 173-B:15.

Source.
1999, 240:3, eff. Jan. 1, 2000.

173-B:17. Duties of the Commissioner.

The commissioner shall:
I. Administer the grant program established in RSA 173-B:16 through a coordinator. The costs of administration shall be covered by the fund, and shall not exceed 2 percent.
II. Adopt rules, under RSA 541-A, relative to procedures under which interested New Hampshire programs may apply for funding.
III. Appoint the coordinator.
IV. Enter into a contract with the coordinator, subject to the approval of the governor and council.

Source.
1999, 240:3, eff. Jan. 1, 2000.

173-B:18. Selection of Coordinator.

The commissioner shall be satisfied that the organization or agency chosen as the coordinator shall be qualified to provide at least those services listed in RSA 173-B:20.

Source.
1999, 240:3, eff. Jan. 1, 2000.

173-B:19. Compensation for Coordinating Domestic Violence Grant Program.

Compensation for the functions and duties of coordinating the program shall not exceed 30 percent of the total revenues of the fund.

Source.
1999, 240:3, eff. Jan. 1, 2000.

173-B:20. Duties of Coordinator.

The coordinator shall be a statewide organization or agency which has demonstrated its ability, at a minimum, to:

I. Serve as a clearinghouse for information relating to domestic violence.
II. Conduct educational programs on domestic violence, both for the general public and for specialized interest groups, such as law enforcement and medical personnel.
III. Provide technical assistance to local domestic violence programs in the areas of budget, management, and other such skills.
IV. Enlist the assistance of public and voluntary health, education, welfare, legal, and rehabilitation agencies in a concerted effort to prevent domestic violence.
V. Provide coordination and supervision of programs.
VI. Assist the commissioner in the administration of the fund.
VII. Publicize the availability of the fund and the date by which applications must be received, and act on all applications within 45 days of the application deadline.
VIII. Notify each appropriate agency or organization in writing whether or not it is eligible for funds, and specify the amount available.
IX. Publicize the availability of domestic violence programs to the public.
X. Provide training for court advocates and social services agency advocates to accompany domestic violence victims.
XI. Apply for and receive any federal funds for which this program may be eligible.
XII. Ensure, as far as possible, that grants are awarded on a reasonable geographical basis throughout the state.
XIII. Obtain and evaluate reports from each grantee, at least annually, on its operations under this chapter.

Source.
1999, 240:3, eff. Jan. 1, 2000.

173-B:21. Criteria for Selection of Direct Service Grantees.

The coordinator shall use all of the following criteria for selecting grantees:
I. A grantee's ability to provide direct services to victims of domestic violence as follows:
(a) Shelter or safe homes on a 24-hours-a-day, 7-days-a-week basis.
(b) A 24-hours-a-day, 7-days-a-week switchboard for crisis calls.
(c) Temporary housing and food facilities.
(d) Psychological support and peer counseling.
(e) Referrals to existing services in the community and follow-up on the outcome of the referrals.
(f) A drop-in center to assist victims of domestic violence who have not yet made the decision to leave their homes, or who have found other shelter but who have a need for support services.

(g) Arrangements for school-aged children to continue their education during their stay at the center.

(h) Emergency transportation to a shelter and, when appropriate, arrangements with local law enforcement for assistance in providing such transportation.

(i) Trained court advocates and social service agency advocates to accompany domestic violence victims.

II. A grantee shall be a private or private nonprofit organization, or a public agency.

III. A grantee shall demonstrate the need for the services proposed by the program.

IV. A grantee shall establish its ability to secure community support and its efficiency of administration.

V. A grantee shall receive at least 50 percent of its funding from sources other than the fund, including town, city, county, federal, or private sources. Contributions in kind, whether material, commodities, transportation, office space, or personal services, may be evaluated and counted as part of the required non-state funding.

Source.
1999, 240:3, eff. Jan. 1, 2000.

173-B:22. Confidentiality.

All persons who are employed, appointed, or who volunteer under this chapter shall maintain confidentiality with regard to persons served by the coordinator and grantees and files kept by the coordinator and grantees, except for reasons of safety for other shelter residents or staff.

Source.
1999, 240:3, eff. Jan. 1, 2000.

173-B:23. Referral.

Where centers are available, any law enforcement officer who investigates an alleged incident of domestic violence shall advise the person subject to such violence of the availability of programs from which that person may receive services.

Source.
1999, 240:3, eff. Jan. 1, 2000.

173-B:24. Rights Reserved.

A person shall not be prejudiced by the court having jurisdiction under RSA 173-B for having left the residence or household with or without the children to avoid further domestic violence.

Source.
1999, 240:3, eff. Jan. 1, 2000.

173-B:25. Severability.

If any provision of this chapter or the application of such provision to any person or circumstance is held invalid, the invalidity does not affect other provisions or applications of the chapter which can be given effect without the invalid provisions or applications, and to this end the provisions of this chapter are severable.

Source.
1999, 240:3, eff. Jan. 1, 2000.

CHAPTER 173-C

CONFIDENTIAL COMMUNICATIONS BETWEEN VICTIMS AND COUNSELORS

SECTION
173-C:1. Definitions.
173-C:2. Privilege.
173-C:3. Assertion or Waiver of Privilege.
173-C:4. Partial Waiver.
173-C:5. Limitation on the Privilege; Criminal Proceedings.
173-C:6. Locations of Centers Privileged.
173-C:7. Involuntary Waiver.
173-C:8. Failure to Testify.
173-C:9. Appeal.
173-C:10. Counselor's Duty to Report Child Abuse.

RESEARCH REFERENCES

New Hampshire Bar Journal.
For article, "The Advocate's Role in Working With Battered Victims," see 35 N.H.B.J. 30 (1994).

173-C:1. Definitions.

In this chapter:

I. "Confidential communication" means information transmitted between a victim, as defined in paragraph VI, of an alleged sexual assault, alleged domestic abuse, alleged sexual harassment, or alleged stalking, and a sexual assault or domestic violence counselor in the course of that relationship and in confidence by means which, so far as the victim is aware, does not disclose the information to a third person. The presence of an interpreter for the hearing impaired, a foreign language interpreter, or any other interpreter necessary for that communication to take place shall not affect the confidentiality of the communication nor shall it be deemed a waiver of the privilege. The term includes all information received by the sexual assault or domestic violence counselor in the course of that relationship.

II. "Domestic violence center" means any organization or agency which would qualify as a direct service grantee under RSA 173-B:21.

III. "Domestic violence counselor" means any person who is employed or appointed or who volunteers in a domestic violence center who renders support, counseling, or assistance to victims of domestic abuse or attempted domestic abuse, who has satisfactorily completed 30 hours of training in a bona fide program which has been developed by a center as defined in RSA 173-C:1, II.

IV. "Rape crisis center" means any public or private agency, office, or center that primarily offers assistance to victims of sexual assault and their families and provides all the following services:

(a) Crisis intervention to victims of sexual assault 24 hours per day.

(b) Support services to victims of sexual assault by trained volunteers during the hospital examination, police investigation, and court proceedings.

(c) Referral of victims of sexual assault to public and private agencies offering needed services.

(d) The establishment of peer counseling services for the victims of sexual assault.

(e) The development of training programs and the standardization of procedures for law enforcement, hospital, legal and social service personnel to enable them to respond appropriately to the needs of victims.

(f) The coordination of services which are being provided by existing agencies.

(g) Education of the public about the nature and scope of sexual assault and the services which are available.

(h) Development of services to meet the needs of special populations, for example, children, the elderly, and minorities.

(i) Court advocacy through the criminal justice system.

V. "Sexual assault counselor" means any person who is employed or appointed or who volunteers in a rape crisis center who renders support, counseling, or assistance to victims of sexual assault or attempted sexual assault, who has satisfactorily completed 30 hours of training in a bona fide program which has been developed by a rape crisis center as defined in RSA 173-C:1, IV.

VI. "Victim" means any person alleging sexual assault under RSA 632-A, domestic abuse as defined in RSA 173-B:1, stalking under RSA 633:3-a, or sexual harassment as defined under state or federal law, who consults a sexual assault counselor or a domestic violence counselor for the purpose of securing support, counseling or assistance concerning a mental, physical, emotional, legal, housing, medical, or financial problem caused by an alleged act of sexual assault or domestic abuse, stalking, or sexual harassment, or an alleged attempted sexual assault or domestic abuse.

Source.
1985, 98:1. 1990, 241:7, eff. May 27, 1990. 1998, 345:1, 2, eff. Aug. 25, 1998.

Amendments
—**1999.** Paragraph II: Substituted "RSA 173-B:21" for "RSA 173-B:19".

—**1998.** Paragraph I: Deleted "or" preceding "alleged domestic abuse" and inserted "alleged sexual harassment, or alleged stalking" thereafter in the first sentence.
Paragraph VI: Deleted "or" preceding "domestic abuse as defined in RSA 173-B:1" and inserted "stalking under RSA 633:3-a, or sexual harassment as defined under state or federal law" thereafter and inserted "stalking, or sexual harassment" following "domestic abuse".

—**1990.** Paragraph I: Added the second sentence.

173-C:2. Privilege.

I. A victim has the privilege to refuse to disclose and to prevent any other person from disclosing a confidential communication made by the victim to a sexual assault counselor or a domestic violence counselor, including any record made in the course of support, counseling, or assistance of the victim. Any confidential communication or record may be disclosed only with the prior written consent of the victim. This privilege terminates upon the death of the victim.

I-a. The privilege and confidentiality under paragraph I shall extend to:

(a) A third person present to assist communication with the victim.

(b) A third person present to assist a victim who is physically challenged.

(c) Co-participants in support group counseling of the victim.

II. Persons prevented from disclosing a confidential communication or record pursuant to paragraph I shall be exempt from the provisions of RSA 631:6.

Source.
1985, 98:1. 1990, 241:8. 1994, 259:10, eff. June 2, 1994.

Amendments
—**1994.** Paragraph I-a: Added.

—**1990.** Designated the existing provisions of the section as par. I and added par. II.

Cross References.
Disclosure of privileged information in criminal proceedings, see RSA 173-C:5.
Involuntary waiver of privilege, see RSA 173-C:7.
Location of rape crisis center and domestic violence center privileged, see RSA 173-C:6.

RESEARCH REFERENCES

New Hampshire Trial Bar News.
For article, "New Hampshire Health Care Providers' Duty to Warn Third Parties: How Far Does It Extend?" See 15 N.H. Trial Bar News 37 (Fall 1993).

173-C:3. Assertion or Waiver of Privilege.

The privilege may be claimed or waived in all civil, administrative, and criminal legal proceedings, including discovery proceedings, by the following persons:

(a) The victim or an attorney on the victim's behalf.

(b) The guardian of the victim, if the victim has been found incompetent by a court of competent jurisdiction.

(c) A minor victim who is emancipated, married, or over the age of 15, unless, in the opinion of the court, the minor is incapable of knowingly waiving the privilege. A guardian ad litem shall be appointed in all cases in which there is a potential conflict of interest between a victim under the age of 18 and his parent or guardian.

Source.
1985, 98:1, eff. May 10, 1985.

Cross References.
Disclosure of privileged information in criminal proceedings, see RSA 173-C:5.

173-C:4. Partial Waiver.

Waiver as to a specific portion of communication between the victim and the counselor shall not constitute a waiver of the privilege as to other portions of the confidential communication between victim and counselor, relating to the alleged crime.

Source.
1985, 98:1, eff. May 10, 1985.

173-C:5. Limitation on the Privilege; Criminal Proceedings.

In criminal proceedings when a defendant seeks information privileged under this chapter in discovery or at trial, the procedure below shall be followed:

I. A written pretrial motion shall be made by the defendant to the court stating that the defendant seeks discovery of records of a rape crisis center or domestic violence center or testimony of a sexual assault counselor or domestic violence counselor. The written motion shall be accompanied by an affidavit setting forth specific grounds as to why discovery is requested and showing that there is a substantial likelihood that favorable and admissible information would be obtained through discovery or testimony. No discovery or hearing shall occur pursuant to the information sought to be disclosed for at least 3 business days after the filing of a motion for disclosure.

II. The only information subject to discovery from the records of a rape crisis center or a domestic violence center or which may be elicited during the testimony of a sexual assault or domestic violence counselor are those statements of the victim which relate to the alleged crime being prosecuted in the instant trial.

III. Prior to admission of information at deposition, trial, or other legal proceeding, when a claim of privilege has been asserted and whether or not the information was obtained through discovery, the burden of proof shall be upon the defendant to establish by a preponderance of the evidence that:

(a) The probative value of the information, in the context of the particular case, outweighs its prejudicial effect on the victim's emotional or physical recovery, privacy, or relationship with the counselor or the rape crisis or domestic violence center.

(b) That the information sought is unavailable from any other source.

(c) That there is a substantial probability that the failure to disclose that information will interfere with the defendant's right to confront the witnesses against him and his right to a fair trial.

IV. The trial court shall review each motion for disclosure of information on a case by case basis and determine on the totality of the circumstances that the information sought is or is not subject to the privilege established in RSA 173-C:2. In finding that the privilege shall not apply in a particular case, the trial court shall make written findings as to its reasons therefor.

V. The records and testimony of a rape crisis center or domestic violence center shall be disclosed solely to the trial judge to determine, as a matter of law, whether the information contained in the records or testimony is admissible under this chapter.

VI. That portion of any record and testimony of a rape crisis center or domestic violence center which is not disclosed to the defendant shall be preserved by the court under seal for appeal. For the purpose of preservation, a copy of the record shall be retained with the original released to the center. Costs of duplication shall be borne by the defendant.

VII. If, after disclosure of privileged information, the court upholds the privilege claim, the court shall impose a protective order against revealing any of the information without the consent of the person authorized to permit disclosure.

Source.
1985, 98:1, eff. May 10, 1985.

Cross References.
Interlocutory appeal of decision to require disclosure of privileged information, see RSA 173-C:9.

173-C:6. Locations of Centers Privileged.

Notwithstanding any other provisions of this chapter, the location and the street address of a rape crisis center or domestic violence center are absolutely privileged.

Source.
1985, 98:1, eff. May 10, 1985.

173-C:7. Involuntary Waiver.

The privilege established by this chapter shall not apply when the sexual assault counselor or the domestic violence counselor has knowledge that the victim has given perjured testimony and when the defendant has made an offer of proof that there is probable cause to believe that perjury has been committed.

Source.
1985, 98:1, eff. May 10, 1985.

173-C:8. Failure to Testify.

Failure of any person to testify as a witness pursuant to the provisions of this chapter shall not give rise to an inference unfavorable to the prosecution or the defense.

Source.
1985, 98:1, eff. May 10, 1985.

173-C:9. Appeal.

The victim shall have a right to interlocutory appeal to the supreme court from any decision by a court to require the disclosure of records or testimony of a rape crisis or domestic violence center or sexual assault or domestic violence counselor.

Source.
1985, 98:1, eff. May 10, 1985.

173-C:10. Counselor's Duty to Report Child Abuse.

The domestic violence or sexual assault counselor shall have the same reporting duties under RSA 169-C:29 as other professionals, providing that this duty shall not apply where a minor is seeking relief pursuant to RSA 173-B:3 for abuse by a spouse or former spouse of the minor, or by an intimate partner who is not related to the minor by consanguinity or affinity. As used in this section, "abuse" and "intimate partners" shall be as defined in RSA 173-B:1.

Source.
1985, 98:1. 1994, 259:11, eff. June 2, 1994.

Amendments
—1994. Rewritten to the extent that a detailed comparison would be impracticable.

TITLE XIII
ALCOHOLIC BEVERAGES

CHAPTER 179

ENFORCEMENT, REQUIREMENTS AND PENALTIES

SECTION
179:1.   Possession.
179:2.   Seizure.
179:3.   Forfeiture.
179:4.   Forfeiture of Liquor and Beverage.
179:5.   Prohibited Sales.
179:5-a.   Sale of Kegs of Malt Beverages; Penalty.
179:5-b.   Enforcement Activity Verifying Noncompliance.
179:6.   Sale of Cider to Persons Under 21.
179:7.   Sales to Persons Under 21.
179:8.   Statement From Purchaser as to Age.
179:9.   Person Misrepresenting Age.
179:10.   Unlawful Possession and Intoxication.
179:10-a. Attempt to Purchase Alcohol.
179:11.   Holders of Beverage Manufacturer, Wholesale Distributor, Beverage Vendor, and Other Licenses; Prohibited Interests.
179:12.   Wine Manufacturer's, Liquor and Wine Representative's, Liquor and Wine Salesperson's, and Table Wine Vendor's Interests Prohibited. [Repealed.]
179:13.   Limited Credits.
179:14.   Reports.
179:15.   Transportation of Beverages and Wine.
179:16.   Adulteration.
179:17.   Hours of Sales.
179:18.   Posting of Age Requirements.
179:19.   Entertainment and Entertainers.
179:20.   Employee Restrictions.
179:21.   Employment Prohibited.
179:22.   Employment Intervention; Penalty.
179:23.   Employment; Employment of Minors; Felon Exception.
179:24.   Change of Manager.
179:25.   Sign Restrictions.
179:26.   Compliance With Other Agencies.
179:27.   Restrictions on Serving and Congregating of Patrons.
179:27-a. Removal of Opened Table Wine Bottle.

Advertising

179:28.   Product Advertisement.
179:29.   Retailer Advertising Specialties.
179:30.   Consumer Advertising Specialties and Coupons.
179:31.   Advertising Restrictions.

Purchase and Supply Restrictions

179:32.   Purchase of Supplies.
179:33.   Sizes of Beer Containers; Promotions; Notification.
179:34.   Sizes of Wine Containers.
179:35.   Retention of Invoices and Sale and Delivery Slips.
179:36.   Registration of Wine Brand Sizes. [Repealed.]
179:37.   Services From Wine Vendors. [Repealed.]
179:38.   Liquor and Wine Payment Procedures.

Sales Restrictions

179:39.   Serving Containers and Sizes. [Repealed.]
179:40.   Substitution of Brand; Refilling Bottles.
179:40-a. Specialty Beer Label Requirements.
179:41.   Gifts of Coupons for Beverage or Liquor.
179:42.   Package Deals.
179:43.   Sale on Credit.
179:44.   Free Drinks.

SECTION
179:45.   Mini-Bars. [Repealed.]
179:46.   Sales of Holders of Wine Vendor Licenses; Fees; Sales Figures. [Repealed.]
179:47.   Off-Premises Special License Restriction.

Premises Restrictions

179:48.   Leasing or Renting Concessions or Part of Business.
179:49.   Storage of Surplus Liquor and Beverage.
179:50.   Loitering; Unlawful Purpose.
179:51.   Lighting and Conduct Requirements for On-Premises Licensees.
179:52.   Posting of Licenses.
179:53.   Alteration of Premises.
179:54.   Beverage Taps in View of Public; Names Displayed on Beer Dispensers.
179:55.   Notification of Change in Corporate Officers.

Enforcement Proceedings and Penalties

179:56.   Hearings; Investigations; False Statement; Enforcement Policy.
179:57.   Suspension or Revocation; Administrative Fines.
179:58.   Penalties.
179:59.   Prosecutions.
179:60.   Interference With Liquor Investigators.
179:61.   Fines.
179:62.   Manufacture, Sale, and Possession of False Identification.

Cross References.

Liability for damages of alcoholic beverage licenses serving beverages to minors or intoxicated persons, see RSA 507-F.

NOTES TO DECISIONS

Regulation generally

Strict regulations are necessary to control the liquor industry. Dugan v. Bridges, 16 F. Supp. 694, 1936 U.S. Dist. LEXIS 1852 (D.N.H. 1936), appeal dismissed, 300 U.S. 684, 57 S. Ct. 668, 81 L. Ed. 887, 1937 U.S. LEXIS 264 (1937), dismissed, North German Lloyd v. Elting, 300 U.S. 675, 57 S. Ct. 668, 81 L. Ed. 881, 1937 U.S. LEXIS 229 (1937). (Decided under prior law.)

Cited:

Cited in Casico, Inc. v. City of Manchester, 142 N.H. 312, 702 A.2d 302, 1997 N.H. LEXIS 95 (1997).

179:1. Possession.

No person shall possess, transport, procure, furnish, or give away any beverage or liquor except such as has been sold under the provisions of this title or legally purchased outside the state and except as otherwise provided in this title.

Source.

1990, 255:1, eff. July 1, 1990.

NOTES TO DECISIONS

1. Construction with other laws
2. Federal law

1. Construction with other laws

This section does not modify the provisions of former RSA 175:14 [see now RSA 175:6], but the two are to be read in light of each other, under principle of contextual consideration. State v. Muscarello, 92 N.H. 214, 29 A.2d 115, 1942 N.H. LEXIS 60 (1942).

2. Federal law

Conviction in a state court of illegally transporting liquor within the state does not bar a prosecution based on same transaction for transporting liquor without obtaining permit required by federal law. United States v. Regan, 273 F. 727, 1921 U.S. Dist. LEXIS 1299 (D.N.H. 1921).

179:2. Seizure.

Any beverage or liquor possessed, kept for sale, or transported in violation of the provisions of this title or any law of the state, together with the casks, bottles, or other paraphernalia used in such illegal possession, keeping, or transportation, shall be subject to seizure either upon a warrant issued upon a complaint against the person charged with violating the law, and containing a command for such seizure, or upon a libel directed against the property, filed in accordance with the provisions of RSA 617, and upon due proceedings may be adjudged forfeited. When any sheriff or deputy sheriff, duly appointed police officer or constable of any city or town, or other duly appointed law enforcement officer, shall discover any person in the act of transporting beverages or liquor in violation of this chapter or any other law of this state, in any wagon, buggy, automobile, watercraft, aircraft, or other vehicle, or any other conveyance, it shall be his duty to seize all beverage and liquor found therein being transported contrary to law. No officer shall, without a warrant, cause any automobile or other vehicle traveling upon a public highway in this state to be stopped for the purpose of searching the same for beverages or liquor unless he has reasonable cause to believe that such automobile or other vehicle is, at the time of said stopping or search, being used for the illegal transportation of beverage or liquor. Whenever beverage or liquor being illegally transported shall be seized by an officer he shall take possession of any vehicle, team, automobile, boat, aircraft, watercraft, or any other conveyance engaged in such illegal transportation, and shall arrest any person or persons in charge of such transportation. Such officer shall at once proceed against the person or persons arrested under the provisions of this chapter in any court having competent jurisdiction, and the vehicle or conveyance, on due proceedings in accordance with the provisions of RSA 617, may be adjudged forfeited, unless by intervention or otherwise at hearing, or in some other proceeding brought for the purpose, a lien or liens shall be established to have been created without notice that such vehicle was being used or was to be used for the illegal transportation of beverage or liquor. The vehicle may be ordered sold by the court, and the proceeds of the sale, after deducting the expenses of keeping and sale, used for the purpose of paying such liens in the order of their priority, and the balance disposed of as provided in RSA 179:3. If a lien or liens shall be established in excess of the value of such vehicle, the court shall order its surrender to the first lienholder upon payment of costs of seizure, but subsequent lienholders shall have the right of redemption in the order of

their liens upon satisfaction of prior liens and charges, provided such right is asserted within such time as the court shall fix in its order of surrender.

Source.

1990, 255:1, eff. July 1, 1990.

NOTES TO DECISIONS

Negligence

A violation of this section constitutes negligence only if the violation causes an injury by creating a danger that the section was intended to prevent. Weldy v. Kingston, 128 N.H. 325, 514 A.2d 1257, 1986 N.H. LEXIS 315 (1986). (Decided under prior law.)

OPINIONS OF THE ATTORNEY GENERAL

1. Duty to arrest
2. Duty to seize

1. Duty to arrest

An officer cannot utilize discretion to release on a summons when confronted with a situation involving underage transportation of alcohol without incurring liability therefor. 1994 Op. Att'y Gen. 4.

Failure to arrest when confronted with a situation involving underage transportation of alcohol is a breach of statutory duty of care for which the Liquor Commission and its investigators can be held liable. 1994 Op. Att'y Gen. 4.

2. Duty to seize

The language of RSA 265:81-a, together with the language of RSA 179:2, leaves no room for discretion and obligates the arresting officer to seize the vehicle when confronted with a situation involving underage transportation of alcohol. 1994 Op. Att'y Gen. 4.

While there is no authority to seize liquor that is lawfully possessed by a person age 21 or older, once a person under age 21 is "engaged in" illegal transportation, the liquor and the vehicle must be seized. 1994 Op. Att'y Gen. 4.

179:3. Forfeiture.

Upon a decree of forfeiture, the beverage and liquor, with the casks, bottles, cases, or containers, may be adjudged to be destroyed, or they, and any other property which may be seized or forfeited under the provisions of this chapter, may be sold in accordance with the decree of the court. The proceeds of any sale of such property duly forfeited, after deducting the expense of the seizure and proceedings, shall be paid into the treasury of the county in which the proceedings were determined, for its use.

Source.

1990, 255:1, eff. July 1, 1990.

179:4. Forfeiture of Liquor and Beverage.

Any person who is taken into protective custody for intoxication or convicted of driving a motor vehicle under the influence of beverage or liquor shall forfeit any liquor or beverage upon his person or in the vehicle, if any, at the time of the commission of the offense. This section shall not apply to liquor or beverage legally in his possession for the purpose of sale. Any liquor or beverage so forfeited shall be disposed of as the court may determine and the proceeds, if any, shall be paid into the treasury of the county in which the proceedings were determined for its use.

Source.

1990, 255:1, eff. July 1, 1990.

179:5. Prohibited Sales.

I. No licensee, salesperson, direct shipper, common carrier, delivery agent, nor any other person, shall sell or give away or cause or allow or procure to be sold, delivered, or given away any liquor or beverage to a person under the age of 21 or serve an individual who is visibly intoxicated or who a reasonable and prudent person would know is intoxicated. For all deliveries of packages by common carrier or delivery agent marked "alcoholic beverages" or "alcoholic products," the carrier shall obtain an adult signature. A licensed carrier shall not transport any liquor, wine, or beverage that has been identified by the commission as originating from a person who does not hold a valid New Hampshire direct shipper permit, provided that such identification has first been provided to and received by the licensed carrier in writing. The commission shall notify carriers by mail on a monthly basis of the identity of unauthorized shippers, which notification shall be effective 15 days after such mailing.

II. No licensee, manager or person in charge of a licensed premises shall allow or permit any individual, who is under the age of 21, to possess or consume any liquor or beverage on the licensed premises.

Source.

1990, 255:1, eff. July 1, 1990. 1996, 275:16, eff. June 10, 1996. 1998, 167:6, eff. July 1, 1998; 331:13, eff. July 1, 1998. 2009, 95:1, eff. January 1, 2010. 2010, 300:6, eff. January 1, 2011.

Amendments

—2010. The 2010 amendment, in I, substituted "carrier shall obtain an adult signature" for "addressee shall sign a delivery receipt" in the second sentence, deleted the former last sentence, which read: "In no case shall any section of this title be so construed as to permit sale of liquor or beverages in any so-called saloon or speakeasy", and added the last two sentences.

—2009. The 2009 amendment substituted "serve an individual who is visibly intoxicated or who a reasonable and prudent person would know is intoxicated" for "to an intoxicated individual" at the end of the first sentence of I and made a stylistic change.

—1998. Paragraph I: Chapter 167 substituted "an intoxicated individual" for "a person under the influence of liquor or beverage" following "age of 21 or to" in the first sentence.

Chapter 331 inserted "direct shipper, common carrier, delivery agent" following "salesperson" in the first sentence and added the second sentence.

—1996. Designated the existing text of the section as par. I and added par. II.

Contingent 1996, 331 amendment.

1998, 331:10, provided for amendment of this section. However, under the terms of 1998, 331:14, eff. July 1, 1998, the amendment did not become effective.

Cross References.

Liability for damages of alcoholic beverage licensees serving beverages to minors or intoxicated persons, see RSA 507-F.

NOTES TO DECISIONS

1. Construction
2. Minors
3. Torts—Generally
4. —Evidence of negligence
5. Corporate liability

1. Construction

RSA 179:5, I is a strict liability statute; thus, a bar owner was properly found to be in violation of the statute for serving alcohol to an intoxicated person because it was irrelevant whether a bartender knew that a patron was intoxicated before being served three mixed drinks. Appeal of Baldoumas Enters., (N.H. State Liquor Comm'n), 149 N.H. 736, 829 A.2d 1056, 2003 N.H. LEXIS 114 (2003).

Words "nor any other person" are not restricted by "No licensee, sales agent" which precede them. State v. Small, 99 N.H. 349, 111 A.2d 201, 1955 N.H. LEXIS 22 (1955). (Decided under prior law.)

2. Minors

Where defendant, charged with giving alcohol to a minor, raised a defense of lack of opportunity, trial court did not err in failing to dismiss informations on the basis that the State failed to prove when the acts occurred because time is not an element of the offense and evidence demonstrated that the victim spent considerable time at defendant's home within the time frame alleged. State v. DeCosta, 146 N.H. 405, 772 A.2d 340, 2001 N.H. LEXIS 89 (2001).

This chapter makes it a crime for individuals generally, who are not licensees or sales agents, to sell or give away intoxicating liquor and beverages to minors. State v. Small, 99 N.H. 349, 111 A.2d 201, 1955 N.H. LEXIS 22 (1955). (Decided under prior law.)

3. Torts—Generally

The statute grants no civil right of action based on its violation. Hickingbotham v. Burke, 140 N.H. 28, 662 A.2d 297, 1995 N.H. LEXIS 94 (1995); MacLeod v. Ball, 140 N.H. 159, 663 A.2d 632, 1995 N.H. LEXIS 114 (1995).

Common-law action may be maintained for injuries received as a result of being served additional liquor, while intoxicated, by liquor licensee. Ramsey v. Anctil, 106 N.H. 375, 211 A.2d 900, 1965 N.H. LEXIS 172 (1965). (Decided under prior law.)

Repeal of dramshop law or civil damage law did not abrogate the common-law principles of negligence. Ramsey v. Anctil, 106 N.H. 375, 211 A.2d 900, 1965 N.H. LEXIS 172 (1965). (Decided under prior law.)

4. —Evidence of negligence

The sale of liquor to intoxicated persons in violation of this section is evidence of negligence. Brown v. Cathay Island, 125 N.H. 112, 480 A.2d 43, 1984 N.H. LEXIS 286 (1984). (Decided under prior law.)

Selling liquor to an intoxicated person is prohibited by this section and a violation thereof is evidence of negligence. Burns v. Bradley, 120 N.H. 542, 419 A.2d 1069, 1980 N.H. LEXIS 345 (1980). (Decided under prior law.)

Violation of this section prohibiting sale of liquor to specified persons is evidence of negligence. Ramsey v. Anctil, 106 N.H. 375, 211 A.2d 900, 1965 N.H. LEXIS 172 (1965). (Decided under prior law.)

5. Corporate liability

Evidence was insufficient to convict a fraternity of selling alcohol to a person under the age of 21 at a party, notwithstanding the assertion that the fraternity voted not to allow alcohol at the party and moved a soda machine with beer in it from the main area in the fraternity house to a separate apartment at the back of the house, where: (1) the fraternity had control over the apartment in which the soda machine was located, (2) the fraternity had control over the soda machine, (3) only the fraternity had an interest in the proceeds from the machine, (4) only fraternity members had keys to the apartment in which the soda machine was located, (5) someone made change for the soda machine, and (6) no one would have an interest in making change except a member of the fraternity. State v. Zeta Chi Fraternity, 142 N.H. 16, 696 A.2d 530, 1997 N.H. LEXIS 50 (1997), cert. denied, Zeta Chi Fraternity v. New Hampshire, 522 U.S. 995, 118 S. Ct. 558, 139 L. Ed. 2d 400, 1997, 1997 U.S. LEXIS 7080 (1997).

Cited:
Cited in State v. Hall, 148 N.H. 671, 813 A.2d 501, 2002 N.H. LEXIS 208 (2002).

179:5-a. Sale of Kegs of Malt Beverages; Penalty.

I. The commission by rule shall require the identification of kegs of malt beverages sold directly to consumers who are not licensees of the commission and the signing of a receipt therefor by the purchaser in order to allow the kegs to be traced if the contents are consumed in violation of the Title XIII. The keg identification shall be in a form prescribed by the commission which identifies the seller and which is removable or obliterated when the keg is processed for refilling. The receipt shall be on a form prescribed and supplied by the commission and shall include the purchaser's name, address, and motor vehicle operator's license number, if any. The receipt shall contain a statement that shall be signed by the purchaser that, under penalty of unsworn falsification, the purchaser shall not allow consumption of any malt beverage in the keg in violation of the provisions of RSA 179:5. A copy of the receipt shall be given to the purchaser and the seller shall retain the original receipt for such period as the commission by rule may require.

II. Possession of a keg containing malt beverage, which is not identified as required by paragraph I of this section, shall be a violation.

III. Any person, other than a beverage manufacturer or wholesaler, who removes the identification prescribed by paragraph I shall be guilty of a violation.

IV. A person who signs a receipt described in paragraph I in order to obtain a keg, knowing the receipt to be false, or who falsifies any information required on the receipt, is guilty of unsworn falsification as prescribed by RSA 641:3.

V. As used in this section, "keg" means any brewery-sealed, individual container of malt beverage having a liquid capacity of more than 7 gallons.

Source.
2000, 259:1, eff. Jan. 1, 2001.

References in text.
Title XIII, referred to in the first sentence of par. I, is classified to Title 13 of LEXIS New Hampshire Revised Statutes Annotated, which is comprised of chapters 175–180.

179:5-b. Enforcement Activity Verifying Noncompliance.

It shall be a violation to sell any liquor or beverage to a minor during enforcement activity initiated solely for the purpose of verifying noncompliance with RSA 179:5. It shall be a misdemeanor to knowingly sell liquor or beverage to a minor at the time of any such enforcement activity. The commission shall retain the right to require the licensee in such a circumstance to initiate additional training of its staff or individual employee. This section shall not apply to law enforcement initiatives involving surveillance, investigations, or criminal complaints of prohibited sales.

Source.
2010, 283:1, eff. January 1, 2011.

179:6. Sale of Cider to Persons Under 21.

Notwithstanding any other provisions of this chapter, it shall be unlawful for any person to sell or cause or allow or procure to be sold to any person under 21 years of age, cider containing not less than ½ of one percent of alcohol by volume at 60 degrees Fahrenheit.

Source.
1990, 255:1. 1995, 34:12, eff. June 23, 1995.

Amendments
—1995. Deleted "provided that the provisions of this section shall not apply to sales of cider made within 15 days of its manufacture" following "Fahrenheit".

179:7. Sales to Persons Under 21.

The establishment of all the following facts by a person making a sale of liquor or beverage to a person under the age of 21 shall constitute prima facie evidence of innocence and a defense to any prosecution for such sale:

I. That the person falsely represented in writing and supported by some official document that he was 21 years of age or over;

II. That the appearance of the person was such that an ordinary and prudent person would believe him to be 21 years of age or over; and

III. That the sale was made in good faith relying upon such written representation and appearance in the reasonable belief that the person was actually 21 years of age or over.

Source.
1990, 255:1, eff. July 1, 1990.

NOTES TO DECISIONS

Cited:

Cited in Appeal of Baldoumas Enters., (N.H. State Liquor Comm'n), 149 N.H. 736, 829 A.2d 1056, 2003 N.H. LEXIS 114 (2003).

RESEARCH REFERENCES

New Hampshire Trial Bar News.

For article, "Presumptions in New Hampshire Law—A Guide Through the Impenetrable Jungle (Part 1)," see 10 N.H. Trial Bar News 55, 60 n.82 (Winter 1990).

179:8. Statement From Purchaser as to Age.

I. For the purposes of RSA 179:7, any person making the sale of beverages or liquor to any person whose age is in question shall require the purchaser to furnish any of the following documentation that such person is 21 years of age or over:

(a) A motor vehicle driver's license issued by the state of New Hampshire, or a valid driver's license issued by another state, or province of Canada, which bears the date of birth, name, address and picture of the licensee.

(b) An identification card issued by the director of motor vehicles under the provisions of RSA 260:21, or any picture identification card issued by another state which bears the date of birth, name and address of the individual.

(c) An armed services identification card.

(d) A valid passport from a country with whom the United States maintains diplomatic relations.

II. Photographic identification presented under this section shall be consistent with the appearance of the person, shall not be expired, and shall be correct and free of alteration, erasure, blemish, or other impairment.

Source.

1990, 255:1, eff. July 1, 1990. 1998, 167:7, eff. July 1, 1998.

Amendments

—**1998.** Paragraph II: Inserted "shall not be expired" following "person".

179:9. Person Misrepresenting Age.

I. A person who falsely represents his age for the purpose of procuring liquor or beverage and who procures such liquor or beverage shall be guilty of a misdemeanor. Any person who violates any of the provisions of this section shall be fined for his first offense a minimum of $500. No portion of this mandatory minimum fine shall be waived, continued for sentencing, or suspended by the court. A second or subsequent offense shall carry a $1,000 minimum fine.

II. Notwithstanding paragraph I or any other law to the contrary, any person who possesses or uses or displays in any manner a false identification card, document, license, or any other document which represents such person's age for the purpose of purchasing liquor, beverages, or beer as defined in RSA 175:1 by the bottle, can, glass, container, or drink in any manner shall be fined a minimum of $500. No portion of this mandatory minimum fine shall be waived, continued for sentencing, or suspended by the court. The provisions of this paragraph do not reduce the maximum penalty which could be imposed for such an offense pursuant to paragraph I. A second or subsequent offense shall carry a $1,000 minimum fine.

III. An identification card issued under the provisions of RSA 260:21 shall be withdrawn for violation of this section for 90 days. In addition, the director of the division of motor vehicles shall withdraw, for 90 days, the identification card of any person who allows his card to be used or displayed by another person for the purpose of purchasing liquor or beverages as defined in RSA 175:1.

Source.

1990, 255:1, eff. July 1, 1990. 1996, 275:17, eff. June 10, 1996. 2002, 107:1, eff. Jan. 1, 2003.

Amendments

—**2002.** Paragraph I: Substituted "$500" for "$250" in the second sentence, and "$1,000" for "$500" in the fourth sentence.

Paragraph II: Substituted "$500" for "$250" in the first sentence, and "$1,000" for "$500" in the fourth sentence.

—**1996.** Paragraph II: Substituted "possesses or" for "has in his possession and" preceding "uses", substituted "any other document" for "other form" preceding "which represents" and "such person's" for "his" thereafter, deleted "or" preceding "beverages" and inserted "or beer" thereafter in the first sentence.

Cross References.

Classification of crimes, see RSA 625:9.

Sentences, see RSA 651.

179:10. Unlawful Possession and Intoxication.

I. Except as provided in RSA 179:23, any person under the age of 21 years who has in his or her possession any liquor or alcoholic beverage, or who is intoxicated by consumption of an alcoholic beverage, shall be guilty of a violation and shall be fined a minimum of $300. Any second and subsequent offense shall be fined at least $600. For purposes of this section, alcohol concentration as defined in RSA 259:3-b of .02 or more shall be prima facie evidence of intoxication. No portion of this mandatory minimum fine shall be waived, continued for sentencing, or suspended by the court. In addition to the penalties provided in this section, the court may, in its discretion, impose further penalties authorized by RSA 263:56-b.

II. Except for persons convicted on the basis of intoxication, any person under the age of 21 years convicted of unlawful possession of liquor or beverage shall forfeit the same, and it shall be disposed of as the court directs. The proceeds, if any, shall be paid into the treasury of the county in which the proceedings were determined.

Source.

1990, 255:1, eff. July 1, 1990. 1998, 167:8, eff. July 1, 1998. 2002, 256:1, eff. Jan. 1, 2003. 2005, 177:47, eff. July 1, 2005.

Amendments

—2005. Paragraph I: Substituted "$300" for "$250" in the first sentence, and "$600" for "$500" in the second sentence.

—2002. Added "and intoxication" in the section catchline, designated the former first through third sentences of the section as par. I, and in that paragraph inserted "or her" preceding "possession", "or who is intoxicated by consumption of an alcoholic beverage" preceding "shall be guilty" in the first sentence, and added the second and fourth sentences, and designated the former fourth and fifth sentences as par. II and in that paragraph added "Except for persons convicted on the basis of intoxication" preceding "any person".

—1998. Substituted "$250" for "$50" at the end of the first sentence and substituted "$500" for "$250" at the end of the second sentence.

Effective date of 2006 amendment.

2006, 259:34, III, provided: "The remainder of this act [including 259:1, which amends this section] shall take effect one day after the passage of the state operating budget for the biennium ending June 30, 2009." (See below regarding repeal of 2006 amendments)

Purpose of 2005 amendment.

2005, 177:23, eff. July 1, 2005, provided: "Sections 24–52 of this act [which amended this section and RSA 261:176, 261:40, 261:61, 261:176, 263:30, 263:64, 263:92, 265:107-a, 265:120, 265:15, 265:17, 265:22, 265:23, 265:25, 265:26, 265:3, 265:31, 265:57, 265:60, 265:79, 265:81, 265:82-b, 265:94, 265:95, 265:99, 266:5, 318-B:26 and enacted RSA 265:50-a], are increases to current motor vehicle fines contained in the uniform fine schedule which, pursuant to RSA 502-A:19-b, V, may be changed only by statute."

Repeal of 2006, ch. 259 amendment.

2007, 263:66, eff. June 29, 2007, provided for the repeal of 2006, 259:1, which was to amend this section by reducing fines set forth in par. I eff. on day after the passage of the state operating budget for the biennium ending June 30, 2009.

Cross References.

Classification of crimes, see RSA 625:9.

Sentences, see RSA 651.

NOTES TO DECISIONS

Evidence

Dismissal of charges of possession of alcohol by a minor, transportation of alcohol by a minor, and violation of a local open container ordinance based on officer's act of pouring out contents of beer can, and thus discarding evidence, was error as the amount of beer in the can was immaterial. Neither reference to "liquor" nor to "beverage" under RSA 175:1 references a minimum amount needed to compose the regulated liquid; even a de minimis amount of alcohol is sufficient to trigger a violation. State v. Flagg, 154 N.H. 690, 918 A.2d 1286, 2007 N.H. LEXIS 4 (2007).

179:10-a. Attempt to Purchase Alcohol.

Notwithstanding any other law to the contrary, any person under the age of 21 years, who possesses beverage or liquor with the intent to purchase said beverage or liquor, and who does or omits to do anything which, under the circumstances as such person believes them to be, is an act or omission constituting a substantial step towards the purchase of an alcoholic beverage shall be guilty of a violation.

Source.

1996, 275:18, eff. June 10, 1996.

179:11. Holders of Beverage Manufacturer, Wholesale Distributor, Beverage Vendor, and Other Licenses; Prohibited Interests.

I. No holder of a beverage manufacturer license, brew pub license, wholesale distributor license, or beverage vendor license shall sell, cause to be sold, rent, lend or cause to be loaned, or give to any on-premises or off-premises licensee or to the owner of the premises on which the business of any on-premises or off-premises licensee is to be conducted any money, equipment, furniture, fixtures, or property with which the business of any on-premises or off-premises licensee is to be conducted, nor shall any on-premises or off-premises licensee purchase, cause to be purchased, rent, borrow, solicit, or accept from any holder of a beverage manufacturer license, brew pub license, wholesale distributor license, or beverage vendor license any money, equipment, furniture, fixtures, or property with which the business of the on-premises or off-premises licensee is to be conducted, nor shall any holder of a beverage manufacturer license, brew pub license, wholesale distributor license, or beverage vendor license install or service equipment, furniture, fixtures, or property of any on-premises or off-premises licensee, except as may be designated by the commission.

II. There shall be no restriction on the number of off-premises licenses held by any person. No holder of a beverage manufacturer license, brew pub license, wholesale distributor license, or beverage vendor license shall in any way contribute or pay any money or anything in lieu thereof to any on-premises or off-premises licensee, or the licensee's agent or employees, or to any group, association, or organization thereof, including, but not limited to, payment for the placement, display, or sale of any beverage. Nothing in this section shall prohibit any licensee from being a member of a club holding a permit or license under this title, nor prohibit the sale or purchase, for resale, of merchandise or beverages for the conduct of the business of any on-premises or off-premises licensee. Nothing in this section shall prohibit a holder of a beverage manufacturer license, brew pub license, wholesale distributor license, or beverage vendor license from bringing such holder's own product from the storeroom of an on-premises or off-premises licensee to a warm shelf, display, refrigerated retail space, or refrigerated storage. Nothing in this section shall prohibit the holder of a beverage manufacturers license, wholesale distributors license, brew pub license, or beverage vendors license from rotating, reorganizing, cleaning, and resetting such holder's own product once the product is on an on-premises or off-premises licensee's warm shelf, or in an on-premises or off-premises licensee's refrigerated retail space, or refrigerated storage.

III. No holder of an on-premises or off-premises license shall knowingly employ in any capacity any person who is the holder of any license provided under this title, except that the holder of an on-premises license may employ the holder of an off-premises license in an entertainment capacity.

IV. Except as provided in paragraphs IV-a and IV-b, no holder of a beverage manufacturer license, brew pub license, or beverage vendor license and no member of a limited liability company, officer, director, employee, or agent of a beverage manufacturer licensee, brew pub licensee, or beverage vendor licensee shall have an interest, either direct or indirect, in the business of the holder of a wholesale distributor on-premises or off-premises license.

IV-a. Notwithstanding RSA 179:11, IV or any other provision of this chapter, a beverage manufacturer or beverage vendor may participate in a limited partnership as defined in RSA 304-B with a wholesale distributor in which the beverage manufacturer or beverage vendor is a limited partner and the wholesale distributor is a general partner. The duration of any such limited partnership arrangement shall not exceed 10 years.

IV-b. This section shall not prohibit a beverage manufacturer or beverage vendor from extending financing to a wholesale distributor. In the event of a default by the wholesale distributor, the beverage manufacturer or beverage vendor shall not control or operate the wholesale distributor for more than 180 days.

IV-c. Any financial agreement allowed under paragraph IV-a or IV-b shall be submitted to the commission for approval and shall comply with all applicable statutes and administrative rules of the commission.

IV-d. No holder of a beverage manufacturer license or beverage vendor license, who enters into a limited partnership or lender/debtor relationship with a wholesale distributor shall have any managerial control over the day-to-day operations of such wholesale distributorship.

V. Except as provided under RSA 178:12, II or RSA 178:16, III, no holder of a wholesale distributor license and no officer, director, stockholder, member of a limited liability company, employee, or agent of the holder of a wholesale distributor license shall through interlocking stock ownership, interlocking directors, or otherwise, have an interest, either direct or indirect, in the business of the holder of an on-premises license. Nothing in this paragraph shall be construed to apply to normal credit relations between licensees.

VI. The provisions of paragraphs IV through V shall also apply to liquor and wine manufacturers, liquor and wine vendors, and liquor and wine representatives.

Source.
1990, 255:1. 1992, 226:4. 1994, 6:1, eff. April 5, 1994; 236:5, eff. July 26, 1994. 1995, 139:13, eff. July 1, 1995. 1996, 275:37, eff. at 12:01 a.m., June 10, 1996; 289:6, 7, eff. June 10, 1996. 1997, 63:1, 2, eff. Jan. 1, 1998. 1998, 42:1, eff. July 1, 1998. 2002, 54:1, eff. July 1, 2002. 2003, 231:14, eff. July 1, 2003.

Amendments
—2003. Deleted "beverage vendor importer" and "beverage representative" in the section catchline; substituted "on-premises or off-premises" for "on-sale or off-sale", "off-premises" for "off-sale" and "on-premises" for "on-sale" wherever they appeared throughout the section; deleted "beverage vendor importer license, or beverage representative license" following "vendor license" throughout the section; substituted "RSA 178:12, II or RSA 178:16, III" for "RSA 178:10, II or RSA 178:13, IV" in par. V, and deleted "and liquor and wine salespersons" following "representatives" in par. VI.

—2002. Paragraph VI: Substituted "paragraphs IV through V" for "this section".

—1998. Paragraph II: Deleted the last sentence.

—1997. Paragraph IV: Added "except as provided in paragraphs IV-a and IV-b" preceding "no holder".
Paragraphs IV-a–IV-d: Added.

—1996. Chapter 289 inserted "brew pub" following "manufacturer" in the section catchline.
Paragraph I: Chapter 289 inserted "brew pub license" preceding "wholesale" in three places.
Paragraph II: Chapter 289 substituted "the licensee's" for "his" preceding "agent" and substituted "or" for "his" thereafter in the second sentence and inserted "brew pub license" following "manufacturer license" in the second and fourth sentences and following "wholesale distributors license" in the fifth sentence.
Chapter 275 added the sixth sentence.
Paragraph IV: Rewritten by ch. 289 to the extent that a detailed comparison would be impracticable.

—1995. Paragraph V: Inserted "member of a limited liability company" following "stockholder" in the first sentence.

—1994. Paragraph II: Chapter 6 added the fourth and fifth sentences.
Chapter 236 added "including, but not limited to, payment for the placement, display or sale of any beverage" following "thereof" in the second sentence.

—1992. Paragraph VI: Added.

Contingent 1996 amendment.
1996, 275:19, provided for amendment of this section. However, under the terms of 1996, 275:38, eff. June 10, 1996, the amendment did not become effective.

Severability of 2003 amendment.
2003, 231, which amended this section, was subject to a severability clause. See 2003, 231:53.

NOTES TO DECISIONS

1. Constitutionality
2. Purpose
3. Prohibited interests

1. Constitutionality
The restrictive provisions of this section have a rational basis, and do not discriminate against domestic wholesalers. Nashua Wholesale Grocers v. State Liquor Comm'n, 95 N.H. 224, 60 A.2d 124, 1948 N.H. LEXIS 222 (1948). (Decided under prior law.)

2. Purpose
The legislative purpose to prevent control of retailers by either wholesalers or any manufacturer is clear. Nashua Wholesale Grocers v. State Liquor Comm'n, 95 N.H. 224, 60 A.2d 124, 1948 N.H. LEXIS 222 (1948). (Decided under prior law.)

3. Prohibited interests
Business corporation with wholesale beverage permit which sells only to stockholders and refunds profits to stockholders is sufficient

control over retailers by wholesalers to violate this section. Nashua Wholesale Grocers v. State Liquor Comm'n, 95 N.H. 224, 60 A.2d 124, 1948 N.H. LEXIS 222 (1948). (Decided under prior law.)

179:12. Wine Manufacturer's, Liquor and Wine Representative's, Liquor and Wine Salesperson's, and Table Wine Vendor's Interests Prohibited.

[Repealed 1996, 275:35, I, eff. June 10, 1996.]

Former section(s).
Former RSA 179:12, which was derived from 1990, 255:1; 1992, 144:7; and 1995, 139:14, related to prohibition against wine manufacturer's, liquor and wine representative's and salesperson's and table wine vendor's interests.

179:13. Limited Credits.

I. Each holder of a wholesale distributor, brew pub, nano brewery, or beverage manufacturer license shall report to the commission the name and license number of any on-premises or off-premises licensee who is delinquent in making payment of accounts over a total of $100 within 10 days, including Sundays and holidays, from the date of delivery of beverages on the premises of such on-premises or off-premises licensee or on the premises of a liquor/wine/beverage warehouser storing the beverages for an on-premises or off-premises licensee. Each holder of a wholesale distributor license, brew pub license, nano brewery license, beverage manufacturer license, or beverage vendor license shall report to the commission the name and license number of any holder of a wholesale distributor license who is delinquent in making payments of accounts within 30 days from the date of delivery of beverages on the premises of such holder of a wholesale distributor license. Such report to the commission shall include the amounts purchased and the dates when payments were due and shall be forwarded to the commission within 5 days after said accounts become delinquent, unless the fifth day of such period is a Sunday or holiday in which case the report shall be forwarded the day following such Sunday or holiday.

II. Each holder of a beverage manufacturer license, beverage vendor license, brew pub license, nano brewery license, or wholesale distributor license shall immediately notify the commission of the receipt of the payment of any account which has been reported to the commission as delinquent. Post-dated checks beyond the 5-day reporting period shall not constitute payments of accounts for the purchases of beverages. Checks given in payment for beverages which are returned for nonpayment after the 5-day reporting period shall immediately constitute a delinquency and shall, upon return, be reported to the commission. Payments collected by agents shall be reported as delinquent unless actually received at the place of business of the holder of the beverage manufacturer license, beverage vendor license, brew pub license, nano brewery license, or

wholesale distributor license on or before the fifth day of the reporting period. When collections are made by an agent, the sales slips or invoices shall be clearly marked with the name of the person making the collection and the date of such collection.

III. The commission shall inform holders of beverage manufacturer licenses, beverage vendor licenses, brew pub licenses, nano brewery licenses, and wholesale distributor licenses of the names of licensees who are delinquent in making payments of a total amount of $100 or more under the provisions of this section and no holder of a beverage manufacturer license, beverage vendor license, brew pub license, nano brewery license, or wholesale distributor license shall knowingly make any delivery of beverages to any licensee whose payments for purchases of beverages are reported as delinquent under this section. The commission may withhold names of delinquent licensees under circumstances in which there is a dispute over payments, an agreement to liquidate which has been approved by the commission, or other reason which the commission may deem proper.

IV. The commission may impose a fine of not less than $100 nor more than $500 for a violation of this section. Determinations of a failure to comply with this section shall be made by the commission.

V. Each wholesale distributor, brew pub licensee, nano brewery, or beverage manufacturer shall notify any retailer reported to the commission pursuant to RSA 179:13, I who is delinquent in making payment of accounts. Notification shall be delivered in writing to the licensee by a representative of the wholesaler, brew pub licensee, nano brewery, or beverage manufacturer. Proof of notification shall be forwarded to the commission, whose enforcement division shall issue an administrative notice for a violation of the provisions of RSA 179:13, I and shall forward a report of violation for administrative action. Any license issued to any business violating the provisions of RSA 179:13, I may be suspended by the commission for nonpayment of accounts which are delinquent more than 15 days from the date of the wholesale distributor's, brew pub licensee's, nano brewery's, or beverage manufacturer's notification, providing the requirements of this section have been met.

Source.
1990, 255:1. 1992, 115:2, 3, eff. June 30, 1992. 1996, 275:20, eff. June 10, 1996. 1998, 42:2, eff. July 1, 1998; 78:1, 2, eff. July 18, 1998. 1999, 169:5, 6, eff. Aug. 30, 1999. 2003, 231:15, eff. July 1, 2003. 2009, 144:169, eff. July 1, 2011 (see effective date note below). 2011, 128:2, eff. at 12:01 a.m., July 1, 2011.

Amendments
—2011. The 2011 amendment added "nano brewery" or variants in the first sentence of I and throughout V; added "nano brewery license" or variants wherever it appears in I through III; and made a stylistic change.

—2009. The 2009 amendment, in the third sentence of V, substituted "who shall issue" for "whose enforcement division shall issue" and deleted "and shall forward a report of violation for administrative action" at the end.

—2003. Paragraph I: Substituted "on-premises or off-premises" for "on-sale or off-sale" in three places in the first sentence, and deleted "or beverage vendor importer license" preceding "shall report" in the second sentence.

Paragraph II: Deleted "beverage vendor importer license" following "brew pub license" in the first and fourth sentences, "beverage representatives or" following "collected by" in the fourth sentence, deleted the former fifth sentence, substituted "an" for "a beverage representative or" preceding "agent" in the present fifth sentence, and made minor stylistic changes throughout the paragraph.

Paragraph III: Deleted "beverage vendor importer licenses" following "brew pub licenses" and following "beverage vendor license", deleted "or" preceding "wholesale" and deleted "or beverage representative license" preceding "shall knowingly" in the first sentence.

—1999. Paragraph I: Inserted "brew pub" following "distributor" near the beginning of the first sentence.

Paragraph V: Inserted "brew pub licensee" following "wholesaler" in the second sentence.

—1998. Paragraph I: Chapter 78 inserted "over a total of $100" in the first sentence and "brew pub license" following "distributor license" in the second sentence.

Paragraph II: Chapter 78 inserted "brew pub license" preceding "beverage vendor" in the first and fourth sentences.

Paragraph III: Chapter 42 inserted "brew pub licenses" following "beverage vendor licenses", "who are" preceding "delinquent" and "in making payments of a total amount of $100 or more" thereafter, and "brew pub license" preceding "wholesale distributor license or" in the first sentence.

Paragraph IV: Chapter 42 rewrote the first sentence.

Paragraph V: Chapter 78 inserted "brew pub licensee" following "wholesale distributor" in the first sentence and "brew pub licensee's" following "wholesale distributor's" in the last sentence.

—1997. Paragraph I: Inserted "beverage manufacturer license" preceding "beverage vendor license" in the second sentence.

—1996. Paragraph I: Added "or on the premises of a liquor/wine/beverage warehouser storing the beverages for an on-sale or off-sale licensee" at the end of the first sentence and inserted "wholesale distributor license" following "each holder of a" at the beginning of the second sentence.

—1992. Paragraph I: Inserted "or beverage manufacturer" following "distributor" in the first sentence.

Paragraph III: Inserted "beverage manufacturer licenses" following "inform holders of" and "beverage manufacturer license" following "no holder of a" in the first sentence.

Paragraph IV: Inserted "beverage manufacturer license" following "holder of a" in the first sentence.

Paragraph V: Added.

Effective date of amendment by 2009, 144:169.
2010, 248:1, eff. July 2, 2010, amended 2009, 144:301, VIII to change the effective date of 2009, 144:169 from July 1, 2010 to July 1, 2011.

Severability of 2003 amendment.
2003, 231, which amended this section, was subject to a severability clause. See 2003, 231:53.

Repeal of 2009, 144:169 amendment.
2011, 38:1, I, eff. May 9, 2011, provided for the repeal of the amendment to par. V by 2009, 144:169 (see note regarding effective date of amendments).

179:14. Reports.

Each beverage manufacturer licensee, beverage vendor licensee, brew pub licensee, and wholesale distributor of beverages within the state shall, on or before the tenth day of each month, furnish to the commission, on a form prescribed, a statement under penalty of perjury showing the quantity of beverages sold for resale and the quantity of beverages sold under an off-premises license during the preceding calendar month, within the state.

Source.
1990, 255:1. 1992, 115:4, eff. June 30, 1992. 1999, 169:7, eff. Aug. 30, 1999. 2003, 231:16, eff. July 1, 2003.

Amendments
—2003. Deleted "beverage vendor importer licensee" preceding "brew pub" and substituted "off-premises" for "off-sale".

—1999. Inserted "brew pub licensee" following "importer licensee".

—1992. Inserted "beverage manufacturer licensee" preceding "beverage vendor licensee".

Severability of 2003 amendment.
2003, 231, which amended this section, was subject to a severability clause. See 2003, 231:53.

Cross References.
Perjury generally, see RSA 641:1.
Reporting delinquent accounts, see RSA 179:13.

179:15. Transportation of Beverages and Wine.

A person may transport or deliver beverages and wines in this state without a license, provided such beverages and wines were obtained as authorized by this title and provided such beverages and wines are for consumption only and not for resale purposes. Licensees may transport and deliver to their place of business beverages and wines purchased as authorized under this title, and, except on-premises licensees, may transport and deliver anywhere in the state such beverages and wines ordered from and sold by them in vehicles operated under the control of themselves or of their employees or agents, provided that the owner of such vehicles shall carry a copy of the license issued by the commission in the vehicle driven on behalf of the licensee for whom they are transporting such beverages and wines. Every person operating such a vehicle, when engaged in such transportation or delivery, shall carry a copy of the license in the vehicle so operated, and shall carry such evidence as the commission by rule may prescribe showing the origin and destination of the beverages and wines being transported or delivered. Upon demand of any law enforcement officer, investigator, or employee of the commission, the person operating such vehicle shall produce for inspection a copy of the license and the evidence required by this section. Failure to produce such license or evidence shall constitute prima facie evidence of unlawful transportation. Except as otherwise provided, beverages and wines may be transported within the state only by a railroad or steamboat corporation or by a person regularly and lawfully conducting a general express or trucking business, and in each case holding a valid carrier's license issued by the commission. Nothing in this section shall prohibit individual retail licensees from arranging for the delivery of wine products to a location central for the parties involved.

Source.
1990, 255:1, eff. July 1, 1990. 1997, 207:17, eff. July 1, 1997. 2003, 231:17, eff. July 1, 2003. 2009, 144:170, eff. July 1, 2011 (see effective date note below).

Amendments
—2009. The 2009 amendment substituted "department of safety" for "commission" in the fourth sentence.

—2003. Substituted "on-premises" for "on-sale" in the second sentence.

—1997. Deleted "table" preceding "wine" in the section catch-line and "table" preceding "wine" or "wines" wherever it appeared throughout the section, and inserted "such" preceding "beverages" in two places in the second sentence.

Effective date of amendment by 2009, 144:170.
2010, 248:1, eff. July 2, 2010, amended 2009, 144:301, VIII to change the effective date of 2009, 144:170 from July 1, 2010 to July 1, 2011.

Severability of 2003 amendment.
2003, 231, which amended this section, was subject to a severability clause. See 2003, 231:53.

Repeal of 2009, 144:170 amendment.
2011, 38:1, I, eff. May 9, 2011, provided for the repeal of the amendment to the section by 2009, 144:170 (see note regarding effective date of amendments).

Cross References.
Transportation of liquor, see RSA 175:6.
Transportation of liquor or beverages by persons under age 21, see RSA 265-A:45.
Transportation of partially consumed bottle of table wine, see RSA 179:27-a.

RESEARCH REFERENCES

New Hampshire Trial Bar News.
For article, "Presumptions in New Hampshire Law—A Guide Through the Impenetrable Jungle (Part 1)," see 10 N.H. Trial Bar News 55, 60 n.82 (Winter 1990).

179:16. Adulteration.

Any licensee allowed to sell beverages and wines to be consumed on the premises as provided in this title who shall allow any adulteration of said beverages or wines so as to increase their alcoholic content shall be guilty of a misdemeanor if a natural person, or guilty of a felony if any other person, and shall lose his license to sell for a period of not less than 6 months. Any person adulterating or causing to be adulterated beverages which are consumed on the premises under such a license shall be guilty of a misdemeanor if a natural person, or guilty of a felony if any other person.

Source.
1990, 255:1, eff. July 1, 1990.

Cross References.
Classification of crimes, see RSA 625:9.
Sentences, see RSA 651.

179:17. Hours of Sales.

I. The commission may from time to time fix either generally or specially for each license the hours between which licensees may sell beverages or liquor and may adopt such rules as to the conduct of persons holding sellers' licenses as it deems proper.

II. The following restrictions on hours of sale reflect the times during which a licensee may sell beverages or liquor, unless further extended by the commission:

(a) Off-premises licensees may sell from 6:00 a.m. to 11:45 p.m., 7 days a week.

(b) On-premises licensees may sell from 6:00 a.m. to 1:00 a.m., 7 days a week. The licensee may sell until 2:00 a.m. under conditions authorized by the legislative body of the city or town in which the premises are located if the legislative body adopts an ordinance authorizing such sales.

(c) Wine manufacturer licensees may sell from 6:00 a.m. to midnight, 7 days a week.

(d) Wholesale distributor licensees may sell from 6:00 a.m. to midnight, 7 days a week.

(e) Beverage manufacturer licensees may sell from 6:00 a.m. to midnight, 7 days a week.

(f) Brew pub licensees may sell off-sale from 8:00 a.m. to 10:00 p.m., 7 days a week.

III. There shall be no additional restrictions on sales by any licensees on election days.

IV. All beverages and liquor served on the premises of on-premises licensees shall be consumed no later than 30 minutes after expiration of the serving hour. No beverages shall be moved from any off-premises licensee's establishment at any time except during those periods indicated as hours of sale.

V. No bottle club shall be operated or maintained after the hours fixed for the sale of beverages by on-premises licensees.

VI. Any person who violates any provision of paragraph V shall be guilty of a misdemeanor.

Source.
1990, 235:7; 255:1. 1994, 236:6, eff. July 26, 1994. 1995, 129:3, eff. July 1, 1995. 2003, 231:18, 19, eff. July 1, 2003. 2013, 213:1, eff. January 1, 2014.

Amendments
—2013. The 2013 amendment added the second sentence of II(b).

—2003. Paragraph II: Substituted "off-premises" for "off-sale" in subpar. (a), and "on-premises" for "on-sale" in subpar. (b).
Paragraph IV: Substituted "on-premises" for "on-sale" in the first sentence and "off-premises" for "off-sale" in the second sentence.
Paragraph V: Substituted "on-premises" for "on-sale" preceding "licensees".

—1995. Paragraph II(f): Added.

—1994. Paragraph II: Substituted "7 days a week" for "Monday–Saturday and 9:00 a.m. to 11:45 p.m. on Sunday" in sub pars. (a) and (c), "Monday–Saturday and 9:00 a.m. to 1:00 a.m. on Sunday" in subpar. (b) and "Monday–Saturday and shall not sell on Sunday" in subpars. (d) and (e).

—1990. Paragraph II(c): Substituted "9:00 a.m. to 11:45 p.m." for "shall not sell" preceding "on Sunday".

Severability of 2003 amendment.
2003, 231, which amended this section, was subject to a severability clause. See 2003, 231:53.

Cross References.
Classification of crimes, see RSA 625:9.
Sentences, see RSA 651.

179:18. Posting of Age Requirements.

The commission shall prepare and distribute to business establishments which sell, serve or otherwise dispense liquor or beverage to the general public, posters to be displayed on the premises in a conspicuous place. The posters shall contain a summary and explanation of the laws relative to drinking age restrictions.

Source.
1990, 255:1, eff. July 1, 1990.

179:19. Entertainment and Entertainers.

I. In this section:

(a) "Dancer" means a person or a group of people who, with or without compensation, move their feet, or body, or both, to the accompaniment of music in a premises approved to sell alcoholic beverages. "Dancer" shall not be construed to mean a person or group of individuals who perform dances based upon ethnic, cultural, or historical customs.

(b) "Entertainer" means a person who, with or without compensation, performs in a premises licensed to sell alcoholic beverages. "Entertainer" shall not include a "dancer" as defined under subparagraph I(a).

II. On-premises licensees may provide entertainment and dancing, in clearly defined areas on their licensed premises, provided they have received written authorization by the town or city and they have provided the commission with a copy of that authorization. A cover charge may be assessed to cover the cost of live entertainment. Notwithstanding any other provision of law, paragraph III shall not be construed to permit a person under the age of majority to perform, paid or unpaid, as a dancer in any licensed premise.

III. No person licensed to sell liquor or beverage under RSA 178 may employ as an entertainer any person who is under 17 years of age in a cocktail lounge where liquor or beverages are sold.

IV. [Repealed.]

V. On-premises or off-premises licensees may install amusement machines on their premises. Nothing in this paragraph shall be construed in any way to limit the powers of municipalities under RSA 31:41-d to adopt bylaws relative to licensing amusement machines and to determining the number, location, and types of machines allowed in the municipality.

VI. Licensees shall not allow gambling or wagering on their premises.

VII. The use of darts shall be allowed in clearly defined areas.

Source.
1990, 255:1. 1992, 153:4; 227:2. 1995, 37:1, eff. April 24, 1995. 1996, 275:21, eff. June 10, 1996. 1998, 374:1, eff. Jan. 1, 1999. 2003, 231:20, 21, 52, VI, eff. July 1, 2003.

Amendments
—**2003.** Paragraph II: Substituted "on-premises" for "on-sale"

preceding "licensees" in the first sentence, and "paragraph III" for "paragraphs III and IV" in the third sentence.
Paragraph IV: Repealed.
Paragraph V: Substituted "on-premises or off-premises" for "on-sale or off-sale" in the first sentence.

—**1998.** Rewritten to the extent that a detailed comparison would be impracticable.

—**1996.** Rewritten to the extent that a detailed comparison would be impracticable.

—**1995.** Paragraph I: Inserted "and dancing, in clearly defined areas" following "entertainment" in the first sentence and added the second sentence.
Paragraph II: Inserted "in clearly defined areas" following "dancing" in the first sentence and added the second sentence.

—**1992.** Paragraph VI: Rewritten by ch. 227 to the extent that a detailed comparison would be impracticable.
Paragraph VII: Chapter 153 substituted "gambling or wagering" for "card games" preceding "on their premises" and deleted "except that golf clubs, veterans' clubs, social clubs, and military clubs may allow card games, provided that no gambling or wagering shall be allowed" thereafter.

Contingent 1999 amendment.
1999, 278:16, eff. July 14, 1999, provided: "If a constitutional amendment to the New Hampshire constitution providing that municipalities shall have home rule authority to exercise any powers not specifically prohibited by the state or federal constitutions is adopted by the voters in the 2000 general election, then sections 1–15 of this act [which amended this section and RSA 31:39; 41:11; 47:17; 143-A:5, I, III; 149-M:17, II(b); 231:132-a, Intro. par.; 266:24, I; 466:30-b, V; 502:14, and 502-A:8, enacted RSA 31:39-b and 47:17-a, and repealed RSA 31:39-a; 31:40–43], shall take effect January 1, 2001. If such a constitutional amendment is not adopted, then sections 1–15 of this act shall not take effect."

Contingent 1999 amendment; outcome of 2000 general election.
In the 2000 general election, the voters of New Hampshire rejected the constitutional amendment referred to above, which would have provided that municipalities would have home rule authority to exercise any powers not specifically prohibited by the state or federal constitutions. Consequently, sections 1–15 of 1999, 278:16 [which amended this section and RSA 31:39; 41:11; 47:17; 143-A:5, I, III; 149-M:17, II(b); 231:132-a, Intro. par.; 266:24, I; 466:30-b, V; 502:14, and 502-A:8, enacted RSA 31:39-b and 47:17-a, and repealed RSA 31:39-a; 31:40–43] did not take effect.

Severability of 2003 amendment.
2003, 231, which amended this section, was subject to a severability clause. See 2003, 231:53.

179:20. Employee Restrictions.

I. No person, except a citizen of the United States or legal resident alien, shall be employed to sell or deliver any liquor or beverage.

II. No on-premises or off-premises licensee shall consume beverage or liquor while working. No employee, as defined in RSA 275:4, II, shall consume beverage or liquor while working.

Source.
1990, 255:1, eff. July 1, 1990. 2003, 231:22, eff. July 1, 2003. 2008, 327:1, eff. January 1, 2009.

Amendments
—**2008.** The 2008 amendment substituted "as defined in RSA 275:4, II" for "with or without compensation" in II.

—**2003.** Paragraph II: Substituted "on-premises or off-premises" for "on-sale or off-sale".

Severability of 2003 amendment.

2003, 231, which amended this section, was subject to a severability clause. See 2003, 231:53.

179:21. Employment Prohibited.

No elected state official, liquor commissioner, or employee of the liquor commission responsible for making recommendations to the commission relative to the purchase of liquor, wine, or beer shall hold a liquor or wine representative license for a period of one year from the date that such person leaves office or terminates such employment.

Source.

1990, 255:1, eff. July 1, 1990. 1996, 275:22, eff. June 10, 1996. 2004, 76:1, eff. July 6, 2004. 2013, 258:8, eff. September 22, 2013.

Amendments

—2013. The 2013 amendment substituted "liquor commissioner" for "member of the liquor commission" and made a stylistic change.

—2004. Inserted "responsible for making recommendations to the commission relative to the purchase of liquor, wine, or beer" and deleted "or salesperson's liquor or wine license" following "representative license" and substituted "1 year" for "one year".

—1996. Substituted "one year" for "2 years" following "period of".

179:22. Employment Intervention; Penalty.

I. It shall be unlawful for any elected state official knowingly to:

(a) Intervene in the selection, employment or dismissal of any liquor or wine representative, or other agent or employee of any distiller, importer, rectifier, or other holder of a liquor or wine manufacturer license or liquor or wine vendor license.

(b) Intervene in the stocking, displaying, listing, delisting, or marketing policies, practices, or decisions of the commission regarding products authorized by the commission to be sold in this state.

II. It shall be unlawful for the liquor commissioner or any employee of the commission knowingly to intervene in the selection, employment, or dismissal of any liquor or wine representative, or other agent or employee of any distiller, importer, rectifier, or other holder of a liquor or wine manufacturer license or liquor or wine vendor license.

III. It shall be unlawful, except as authorized by procedural rules adopted by the commission under RSA 541-A, for any liquor or wine representative or liquor or wine vendor, to knowingly intervene in the stocking, displaying, listing, delisting or marketing policies, practices, or decisions of the commission regarding products authorized by the commission to be sold in this state.

IV. Any person who shall be convicted of violating any provision of this section shall be guilty of a class B felony.

Source.

1990, 255:1, eff. July 1, 1990. 2013, 258:9, eff. September 22, 2013.

Amendments

—2013. The 2013 amendment substituted "the liquor commissioner or any" for "any member or" in II.

Cross References.

Classification of crimes, see RSA 625:9.

Sentences, see RSA 651.

179:23. Employment; Employment of Minors; Felon Exception.

I. No licensee shall employ any minor, with or without compensation, to serve or otherwise handle liquor or beverages, except that off-premises licensees may employ minors of not less than 15 years of age when beverages or wine is sold in the original container and delivered in the place of business of the seller, or at the vehicle of the buyer parked on or adjacent to the premises of the seller. To act as a cashier in a selling capacity a minor shall be at least 16 years of age, providing a person at least 18 years of age is in attendance and is designated in charge of the employees and business.

II. An on-premises licensee may employ any person not less than 18 years of age to serve or otherwise handle liquor and beverages while employed as a waiter, waitress, bartender, or hostess in a licensed premises. Minors not less than 15 years of age may be employed in dining areas and minors not less than 16 years of age may be employed in lounge areas to clean tables, remove empty containers and glasses, and assist in stocking. A person at least 18 years of age shall be in attendance and be designated in charge of the employees and business.

III. The provisions of this section shall in no way prohibit an on-premises or off-premises licensee from employing persons 18 years of age or older to sell, serve, or otherwise handle or be left in charge of the employees and the business.

IV. Each licensee shall designate one or more persons to be in charge of the premises. Each designated person in charge shall file an affidavit with the commission attesting to the fact such person is 18 years of age or older and has not been convicted of a felony. For the purposes of this section, any corporate officer or member of a limited liability company shall be deemed to be a person in charge of the licensed premises. For the purposes of this section, any person designated as a person in charge by a licensee shall be considered so designated for all licenses held by the licensee. The commission shall maintain records of all affidavits filed by licensees.

V. Notwithstanding paragraph IV, the commission may in its discretion approve the designation of any person who has been convicted of a felony as a person to be in charge of the premises, provided that not less than 6 months shall have passed since such person was placed on parole or probation and that during this interim period such person shall have led an exemplary life and not have been convicted of any further crime excluding minor traffic violations. The commission shall periodically review the status of such person in respect to the continuance of his or her good behavior and may revoke, in its discretion, the approval for designation as a person to be in charge of the premises granted under this section.

VI. Notwithstanding paragraph V, a licensee may employ a person convicted of a felony to sell, serve, or otherwise handle alcoholic beverages in a non-managerial capacity for a period of 60 days without meeting the provisions of paragraph V. A convicted felon employed under this section shall not be allowed to work longer than 60 days without the licensee complying with the provisions of paragraph V. Any licensee knowingly employing a person convicted of a felony to serve alcoholic beverages longer than 60 days without obtaining a waiver under paragraph V shall be fined not more than $50 per day for each day of employment beyond 60 days.

Source.
1990, 255:1. 1992, 227:3. 1993, 88:1, eff. April 29, 1993. 1998, 167:9, eff. July 1, 1998. 2000, 253:1, eff. July 12, 2000. 2003, 231:23, eff. July 1, 2003.

Amendments
—**2003.** Paragraph I: Substituted "off-premises" for "off-sale" in the first sentence.
Paragraph II: Substituted "on-premises" for "on-sale" in the first sentence.
Paragraph III: Substituted "on-premises or off-premises" for "on-sale or off-sale".

—**2000.** Rewrote par. V and added par. VI.

—**1998.** Paragraph IV: Rewritten to the extent that a detailed comparison would be impracticable.

—**1993.** Paragraph II: Substituted "15 years" for "16 years" preceding "of age may be employed in dining" and inserted "minors not less than 16 years of age may be employed in" preceding "lounge" in the second sentence.

—**1992.** Paragraph II: Rewritten to the extent that a detailed comparison would be impracticable.

Severability of 2003 amendment.
2003, 231, which amended this section, was subject to a severability clause. See 2003, 231:53.

Cross References.
Employment of persons under age seventeen as entertainers, see RSA 179:19.
Prohibition against employment of felons in licensed establishments, see RSA 179:57.
Transportation of alcoholic beverages by persons under age twenty one generally, see RSA 265-A:44.
Youth Employment Law, see RSA 276-A.

179:24. Change of Manager.

In the event a licensee has designated a person approved by the commission to manage the business for him and the employment of such manager shall terminate, such licensee shall notify the commission of such termination and shall within 30 days after termination designate a new manager. If no manager acceptable to the commission is designated within the 30-day period, the license may, in the discretion of the commission, be revoked.

Source.
1990, 255:1, eff. July 1, 1990.

179:25. Sign Restrictions.

I. No brand advertising of liquor or beverages sold in this state shall be allowed through the use of internally illuminated signs outside the licensed premises. Brand advertising of liquor or beverages sold in this state shall be allowed through the use of internally illuminated signs inside the licensed premises. Notwithstanding the above, beverage manufacturers and wholesale distributors may advertise on the site of their licensed premises through the use of internally illuminated signs.

II. For the purposes of this section, internally illuminated signs shall include back lighted, or similar signs, but shall not include neon signs.

III. All exterior signs shall be in conformance with city or town requirements.

IV. For purposes of this section only, "brand advertising" means advertising that includes a name, trademark, symbol, logo, slogan, or other distinguishing mark or device that identifies any product or manufacturer.

Source.
1990, 255:1. 1992, 115:5, eff. June 30, 1992; 195:1, eff. July 11, 1992. 1996, 275:23, eff. June 10, 1996. 2002, 54:2, eff. July 1, 2002.

Amendments
—**2002.** Paragraph I: Inserted "brand" preceding "advertising" and deleted "inside or" following "signs" in the first sentence and added the present second sentence.
Paragraph II: Deleted "neon" preceding "back lighted" and "flashing" thereafter and added "but shall not include neon signs" at the end of the sentence.
Paragraph IV: Added.

—**1996.** Rewritten to the extent that a detailed comparison would be impracticable.

—**1992.** Paragraph I: Chapter 195 added the second sentence.
Paragraph VI: Chapter 115 substituted "internally" for "either electric or directly or indirectly" preceding "illuminated" and inserted "or outside" following "inside" in the first sentence and substituted "internally" for "electric or directly or indirectly" preceding "illuminated" in the second sentence.

179:26. Compliance With Other Agencies.

I. All on-premises licensees shall have a valid license or certificate issued by state or local public health officials before the commission shall issue a license.

II. All on-premises licensees shall have a valid permit of assembly or certificate issued by state or local fire authorities before the commission shall issue a license.

Source.
1990, 255:1, eff. July 1, 1990. 2003, 231:24, eff. July 1, 2003.

Amendments
—**2003.** Substituted "on-premises" for "on-sale" in pars. I and II.

Severability of 2003 amendment.

2003, 231, which amended this section, was subject to a severability clause. See 2003, 231:53.

179:27. Restrictions on Serving and Congregating of Patrons.

I. Liquor and beverages may be served to patrons in on-premises establishments while seated at tables or booths, at the bar, seated at drink rails, or while standing at the bar or drink rails.

II. No beverages or liquor shall be served or consumed in foyers, hallways, kitchens, restrooms, or other areas not approved for service by the commission.

Source.

1990, 255:1. 1991, 2:2, eff. May 27, 1991. 1996, 275:24, eff. June 10, 1996. 2003, 231:25, eff. July 1, 2003.

Amendments

—2003. Paragraph I: Substituted "on-premises" for "on-sale".

—1996. Rewritten to the extent that a detailed comparison would be impracticable.

—1991. Paragraph I: Inserted "or drink rails" preceding "provided" and substituted "or seated at the bar or" for "at the bar or seated at" following "person standing".

Severability of 2003 amendment.

2003, 231, which amended this section, was subject to a severability clause. See 2003, 231:53.

NOTES TO DECISIONS

Golf courses

RSA 179:27 does not prohibit consumption of alcohol on a golf course. Werne v. Exec. Women's Golf Ass'n, 158 N.H. 373, 969 A.2d 346, 2009 N.H. LEXIS 17 (2009).

179:27-a. Removal of Opened Table Wine Bottle.

I. Notwithstanding any other provision of law, any food service business holding an on-premises license may allow any person who has purchased a full course meal and purchased and partially consumed a bottle of table wine with said meal, to remove such partially consumed bottle from the premises upon departure, provided that the person is not in a state of intoxication as defined in RSA 507-F:1, IV and such bottle of table wine is removed and transported in a manner consistent with paragraph II.

II. Any partially consumed bottle of table wine which is to be removed from the premises under paragraph I shall be securely sealed and bagged, by the licensee, either to be in conformance with any applicable local open container law for those patrons on foot, or transported as required by RSA 265-A:44, in the trunk of a motor vehicle. If the vehicle is not equipped with a trunk, the securely sealed opened table wine bottles may be stored and transported in that compartment or area of the vehicle which is the least accessible to the driver.

Source.

1994, 125:4, eff. July 22, 1994. 2003, 231:26, eff. July 1, 2003. 2006, 260:7, eff. January 1, 2007.

Amendments

—2006. Paragraph II: Substituted "RSA 265-A:44" for "RSA 265:81" in the first sentence.

—2003. Paragraph I: Substituted "food service business holding an on-premises" for "on-sale licensee, which maintains a license for a restaurant, as defined by RSA 175:1, XXXIII or LIX, where full course meals are regularly served in conjunction with such" and made a minor change in punctuation.

Severability of 2003 amendment.

2003, 231, which amended this section, was subject to a severability clause. See 2003, 231:53.

Advertising

Cross References.

Advertising generally, see RSA 175:4.
Sign restrictions, see RSA 179:25.

179:28. Product Advertisement.

An industry member may furnish, give, rent, loan, or sell product displays or other things of value to a retailer, subject to the following conditions and limitations:

I. Equipment, inside signs, supplies, services, or other things of value furnished by an industry member to a retailer shall not be conditioned on the purchase of liquor, wine or beverages.

II. Product displays shall bear conspicuous and substantial advertising material.

III. The total value of all product displays furnished by an industry member may not exceed the dollar amount established annually for product displays by the Bureau of Alcohol, Tobacco and Firearms per brand in use at any one time in any one retail establishment. The value of a product display shall be the actual cost to the industry member who initially purchased it. Transportation and installation costs shall be excluded.

IV. Industry members shall not pool or combine, as of July 1, 1989, their dollar limitations to provide a retailer a product display valued in excess of the dollar amount established annually for product displays by the Bureau of Alcohol, Tobacco and Firearms.

V. [Repealed.]

Source.

1990, 255:1, eff. July 1, 1990. 1996, 275:25, 35, II, eff. June 10, 1996. 2002, 54:3, eff. July 1, 2002.

Amendments

—2002. Inserted "or other things of value" following "displays" in the introductory paragraph.

—1996. Paragraphs III, IV: Rewritten to the extent that a detailed comparison would be impracticable.

Paragraph V: Repealed.

179:29. Retailer Advertising Specialties.

I. An industry member may furnish, give, rent, loan, or sell retailer advertising specialties to a retailer if such items bear advertising material and are primarily valuable to the retailer as a means of advertising. These items may include, but are not limited to: coasters, mats, menu cards, wine lists, meal checks, paper napkins, foam scrapers, back bar mats, thermometers, clocks and calendars. The name or name and address of the retailer may be added to the advertising specialty.

II. An industry member may sell glassware to a retailer if the glassware is sold at a price not less than it cost the industry member who initially purchased it, and if the price is collected within 30 days of the date of the sale.

III. The total value of all retail advertising specialties furnished by an industry member to a retailer may not exceed the dollar amount established annually for retailer advertising specialties by the Bureau of Alcohol, Tobacco and Firearms per brand in any calendar year per retail establishment. The value of a retailer advertising specialty shall be the actual cost of that item to the industry member who initially purchased it. Transportation and installation costs shall be excluded.

IV. Industry members shall not pool or combine their dollar limitations to provide a retailer with advertising specialties valued in excess of the dollar amount established annually for retailer advertising specialities by the Bureau of Alcohol, Tobacco and Firearms.

Source.
1990, 255:1. 1992, 115:6, eff. June 30, 1992. 1996, 275:26, eff. June 10, 1996.

Amendments
—1996. Paragraphs III, IV: Rewritten to the extent that a detailed comparison would be impracticable.

—1992. Paragraph I: Deleted the former third sentence.

179:30. Consumer Advertising Specialties and Coupons.

I. Consumer advertising specialties, such as ash trays, bottle or can openers, corkscrews, shopping bags, matches, printed recipes, pamphlets, cards, leaflets, blotters, postcards, and pencils, which bear advertising material may be furnished, given, or sold to a retailer for unconditional distribution by the retailer to the general public. The retailer shall not be paid or credited in any manner directly or indirectly for the distribution of such items.

II. Contest prizes, premium offers, refunds, and similar items may be offered by industry members directly to consumers. Officers, members of a limited liability company, employees, and representatives of wholesale distributors or retailers shall be excluded from participation.

Source.
1990, 255:1. 1995, 139:15, eff. July 1, 1995.

Amendments
—1995. Paragraph II: Inserted "members of a limited liability company" following "officers" in the second sentence.

179:31. Advertising Restrictions.

I. Advertising or promotion of liquor or beverages by the use of billboards, sound trucks, or outdoor internally illuminated screen displays is prohibited.

II. Manufacturers, wholesale distributors, or wine and liquor vendors or their salespersons may distribute samples of their products to licensees for purposes of tasting. The following restrictions shall apply:

(a) Beer samples shall not exceed one 6-pack.

(b) Wine samples shall not exceed 2 750 ml. bottles.

(c) Liquor samples shall not exceed one 750 ml. bottle.

(d) Wine coolers samples shall not exceed one 4-pack, or the product's normal marketing unit.

(e) All liquor or wine for this purpose shall be purchased from the commission.

(f) All beverage, wine, or liquor samples may be added to the retailer's inventory for sale.

(g) All beverage furnished as samples shall be considered sales for the requirements of RSA 178:26.

III. Liquor and wine representatives or salespersons shall not enter state operated stores or warehouses operated by the commission for the purpose of sales promotion or to secure information regarding inventory sales movement without specific permission from the commission.

IV. The listing of retail prices on behalf of retail licensees, by a holder of a wholesale distributor license, is prohibited in all newspaper, magazine, periodical, radio or television advertising.

V. All liquor and beverage advertising, or any claims for liquor or beverage advertising shall conform with the standards set forth in regulations under the provisions of the federal Alcoholic Administration Act.

VI. Liquor and beverage advertising shall not be inconsistent with the description of the contents on labels of any such liquor or beverage.

VII. Advertising of liquor or beverages shall not contain:

(a) Any reference to minors, pictorial or otherwise.

(b) Any subject matter or illustrations inducing persons under the legal drinking age to drink. All coupon offers requiring consumer participation shall contain reference that the coupon offer is available only to persons of legal drinking age.

(c) Any statement that is false or misleading.

VIII. Coupon offers shall be redeemed by the vendor or the vendor's agent as specified in the offer. No redemptions shall be made by state stores.

IX. Advertising of liquor or beverages shall be consistent with the spirit of public health or safety. The commission may suspend any single advertising or promotion of liquor or beverage, at its discretion, that is inconsistent with the spirit of public health or safety.

X. It shall be the responsibility of the advertiser to insure that all advertising copy is in complete conformity with the New Hampshire laws and rules.

XI. Licensees may advertise liquor and beverage prices separately from any other advertisement or promotion.

XI-a. Notwithstanding paragraph XI, if the legislative body of a city or town adopts a provision prohibiting exterior signs or signs in view of any public way promoting the sale of liquor or beverages at reduced prices by an on-premises licensee, such signs shall not be permitted in that city or town.

XII. No holder of a beverage manufacturer license, wholesale distributor license, or beverage vendor license, and no on-premises licensee or off-premises licensee, or group thereof, shall advertise, either directly or indirectly, promoting the consumption of alcohol in any yearbook or other publication distributed predominantly to persons under 21 years of age.

XIII. On-premises licensees shall make food readily available to guests any time alcoholic beverages are being advertised or promoted at a reduced price.

Source.
1990, 255:1. 1991, 355:59. 1992, 195:2, eff. July 11, 1992. 1996, 275:27, eff. June 10, 1996. 2003, 231:27, 28, eff. July 1, 2003. 2011, 238:1–4, eff. July 5, 2011. 2012, 54:1, eff. May 14, 2012.

References in text.
The federal Alcoholic Administration Act, referred to in par. V, is classified to 27 U.S.C.S. §§ 201 et seq.

Amendments
—2012. The 2012 amendment rewrote XII, which formerly read: "No holder of a beverage manufacturer license, wholesale distributor license, or beverage vendor license shall advertise, either directly or indirectly, in any booklet, program, program book, yearbook, magazine, newspaper, periodical, brochure, circular, or other similar publication published by, for, or in behalf of any religious, fraternal, educational, patriotic, social, or civic group. No on-premises licensee or off-premises licensee, any group thereof, or any holder of a beverage manufacturer license, wholesale distributor license, or vendor license, through any control, ownership, interlocking ownership, interlocking directors, or otherwise shall advertise or cause any manner or form of advertising to be inserted in such publications."

—2011. The 2011 amendment, in I, added "or promotion" and "billboards"; in IX, substituted "public health or safety" for "safety or safe driving" in the first sentence and added the second sentence; rewrote XI, which formerly read: "No advertising or promotion shall be done by the use of a billboard. Advertising shall not contain any reference to a 'happy hour' except that a 'happy hour schedule' may be posted within the licensed premises, not in view of any public way and an on-premises licensee may advertise or promote the holding of a 'champagne brunch' or similar package"; added XI-a and XIII; and made a stylistic change.

—2003. Paragraph II(g): Substituted "RSA 178:26" for "RSA 178:28, I and RSA 178:30, I".
Paragraph XI: Substituted "on-premises" for "on-sale" in the second sentence.
Paragraph XII: Substituted "or" for "beverage representative license" preceding "beverage vendor license" and deleted "or a beverage vendor importer license" thereafter in the first sentence, and substituted "on-premises" for "on-sale" and "off-premises" for "off-sale" and "or" for "beverage representative license" preceding "vendor license" and deleted "vendor importer license" thereafter in the second sentence.

—1996. Rewritten to the extent that a detailed comparison would be impracticable.

—1992. Paragraph XIII: Deleted "or off-sale" preceding "license" and added "or wine list" following "menu".
Paragraph XIV: Deleted "or off-sale" following "on-sale".

—1991. Paragraph V: Substituted "on" for "by, for or in" following "prices" and "by a holder of a wholesale distributor or license" for "except for wine by off-premise licensees" preceding "is prohibited" in the first sentence and added the second sentence.

Severability of 2003 amendment.
2003, 231, which amended this section, was subject to a severability clause. See 2003, 231:53.

Label Approval Not Required.
2012, 54:2, eff. May 14, 2012, provided: "The liquor commission shall not, by rule or otherwise, require a beverage vendor, beverage manufacturer, nano brewery, or brew pub to obtain federal label approval for beer, as defined in RSA 175:1, VII, sold exclusively in the state of New Hampshire."

Temporary Local Advertising Restrictions.
2011, 238:6, eff. July 5, 2011, provided: "The governing body of a city or town may adopt a temporary provision prohibiting exterior signs or signs in view of any public way promoting the sale of liquor or beverages at reduced prices by an on-premises licensee. The temporary prohibition shall be enforceable in the same manner as a prohibition adopted under RSA 179:31, XI-a. The temporary prohibition shall expire on the earliest of the following dates:
"I. The date on which the legislative body of the city or town votes on whether to adopt a permanent prohibition under RSA 179:31, XI-a.
"II. The date specified by the governing body when adopting the temporary prohibition.
"III. July 1, 2012."

Purchase and Supply Restrictions

179:32. Purchase of Supplies.

I. All licensees shall purchase their supplies of liquor and wine from the commission or as provided by law.

II. An on-premises licensee, with the approval of the commission, may purchase its supplies of liquor and wine from an agency store.

III. All on-premises or off-premises licensees shall purchase their supplies of beverages from licensed wholesale distributors, manufacturers, brew pubs, or as otherwise specifically provided by law.

IV. The commission may, upon request, grant licensees permission to purchase product not otherwise available in New Hampshire from direct shipper permit holders.

Source.
1990, 255:1, eff. July 1, 1990. 2003, 231:29, eff. July 1, 2003. 2010, 300:7, eff. January 1, 2011; 310:1, eff. September 11, 2010.

Editor's note.
Paragraph III, as added by 2010, 300:7, was redesignated as par. IV in light of the amendments to this section by 2010, 310:1.

Amendments
—2010. The 2010 amendment by Chapter 300 added IV (see editor's note).
The 2010 amendment by Chapter 310 added II and redesignated former II as III.

—2003. Designated the existing provisions of the section as par. I and added par. II.

Severability of 2003 amendment.
2003, 231, which amended this section, was subject to a severability clause. See 2003, 231:53.

179:33. Sizes of Beer Containers; Promotions; Notification.

I. Holders of beverage vendor, nano brewery, or beverage manufacturer licenses shall use bottles or cans, and cases or containers for the sale of beer in the state which shall be specifically authorized by the commission.

II. Holders of beverage vendor, nano brewery, or beverage manufacturer licenses shall have their packaging or containers specifically approved by the commission and shall be fined $250 for each packaging or container violation. Container and packaging approval shall not require delivery of physical sample of beer under 6 percent alcohol by volume at 60 degrees Fahrenheit unless the commission determines a physical sample is necessary for approval.

III. All details of transactions between retailers and wholesale distributors, beverage manufacturers, nano breweries, or brew pubs shall be reflected on pertinent invoices. Promotions shall be clearly identified by both brands and sizes and cash discounts shall be shown as credit and itemized as such. All items noted on delivery slips shall also be noted on wholesale distributor's account receivable ledger records.

IV. All wholesale distributors, beverage manufacturers, nano breweries, and brew pubs shall make their current prices for wholesale sales available to the commission in writing by brand package. Prices shall remain in effect until such time as they are changed in writing by the wholesale distributor, beverage manufacturer, nano brewery, or brew pub to the commission. Price changes shall be in the commission offices no later than 5 working days prior to any change of prices.

Source.
1990, 255:1, eff. July 1, 1990. 1996, 275:28, eff. June 10, 1996. 1999, 169:8, eff. Aug. 30, 1999. 2003, 231:30, eff. July 1, 2003. 2011, 128:3, eff. at 12:01 a.m., July 1, 2011. 2013, 72:1, eff. August 5, 2013.

Amendments
—**2013.** The 2013 amendment added the second sentence of II.

—**2011.** The 2011 amendment added "nano brewery" in I and II and in the second sentence of IV and added "nano breweries" in the first sentence of III and IV.

—**2003.** Deleted "beverage vendor importer or" preceding "beverage manufacturer" in pars. I and II.

—**1999.** Paragraph III: Inserted "retailers and" preceding "wholesale distributors" and substituted "beverage manufacturers, or brew pubs" for "and retailers" thereafter in the first sentence.
Paragraph IV: Inserted "beverage manufacturers, and brew pubs" following "distributors" and "for wholesale sales" following "current prices" in the first sentence, and "beverage manufacturer, or brew pub" following "distributor" in the second sentence.

—**1996.** Paragraph I: Deleted "in the usual and customary industry sizes" following "containers".
Paragraph III: Deleted the former third sentence.
Paragraph IV: Rewritten to the extent that a detailed comparison would be impracticable.

Severability of 2003 amendment.
2003, 231, which amended this section, was subject to a severability clause. See 2003, 231:53.

179:34. Sizes of Wine Containers.

A holder of a wine manufacturer license shall use bottles and containers for the sale of wine in the state which shall be specifically authorized by the commission.

Source.
1990, 255:1, eff. July 1, 1990. 2003, 231:31, eff. July 1, 2003.

Amendments
—**2003.** Deleted "wine vendor license or" preceding "wine manufacturer".

Severability of 2003 amendment.
2003, 231, which amended this section, was subject to a severability clause. See 2003, 231:53.

179:35. Retention of Invoices and Sale and Delivery Slips.

All invoices, sales slips and delivery slips, current and covering a period of 60 days prior to the current date pertaining to purchases of beverages and liquor shall be retained by the licensee on the premises or be readily available for examination by the commission or its liquor investigators.

Source.
1990, 255:1, eff. July 1, 1990. 2009, 144:171, eff. July 1, 2011 (see effective date note below).

Amendments
—**2009.** The 2009 amendment substituted "department of safety" for "commission or its liquor investigators" at the end and made a stylistic change.

Effective date of amendment by 2009, 144:171.
2010, 248:1, eff. July 2, 2010, amended 2009, 144:301, VIII to change the effective date of 2009, 144:171 from July 1, 2010 to July 1, 2011.

Repeal of 2009, 144:171 amendment.
2011, 38:1, I, eff. May 9, 2011, provided for the repeal of the amendment to the section by 2009, 144:171 (see note regarding effective date of amendments).

179:36. Registration of Wine Brand Sizes.

[Repealed 2000, 259:5, eff. January 1, 2001.]

Former section(s)
Former RSA 179:36, which was derived from 1990, 255:1, related to the registration of wine brand sizes.

179:37. Services From Wine Vendors.

[Repealed 1996, 275:35, III, eff. June 10, 1996.]

Former section(s).
Former RSA 179:37, which was derived from 1990, 255:1, related to services from wine vendors.

179:38. Liquor and Wine Payment Procedures.

All invoices submitted to the commission for payment of liquor or wine purchases shall be submitted in duplicate and shall contain the state of New

Hampshire liquor commission purchase order number, the state of New Hampshire brand code numbers, brand names, brand size, quantity in cases, unit and extension prices and discounts allowed. A single invoice with a duplicate copy shall be submitted for each purchase order. Payment for merchandise received shall be made as stated on the purchase order.

Source.
1990, 255:1, eff. July 1, 1990.

Sales Restrictions

179:39. Serving Containers and Sizes.

[Repealed 1996, 275:35, IV, eff. June 10, 1996.]

Former section(s).
Former RSA 179:39, which was derived from 1990, 255:1 and 147:4, 5, related to serving containers and sizes of alcoholic beverages.

179:40. Substitution of Brand; Refilling Bottles.

I. No licensee shall substitute any other brand of beer, ale, liquor or wine in place of the brand specified by a patron unless the licensee has advised the patron that his desired brand is not available and has received his approval of a substitution.

II. No licensee shall refill any bottle of legally purchased beverage or liquor.

Source.
1990, 255:1, eff. July 1, 1990.

179:40-a. Specialty Beer Label Requirements.

No person shall sell any specialty beer having an alcohol content greater than 12 percent unless the label on the container and any packaging for the consumer clearly states the percent of alcohol by volume of the specialty beer.

Source.
2007, 380:5, eff. January 1, 2008.

179:41. Gifts of Coupons for Beverage or Liquor.

A licensee may exchange a coupon, ticket or check for beverages or liquor in connection with an admission price or fee if the licensee has obtained prior approval of the commission.

Source.
1990, 255:1. 1992, 115:7, eff. June 30, 1992. 1996, 275:29, eff. June 10, 1996.

Amendments
—**1996.** Rewritten to the extent that a detailed comparison would be impracticable.

—**1992.** Paragraph I: Substituted "liquor, or" for "and" preceding "wine".

Paragraph II: Substituted "exchange" for "change" preceding "any coupon".

179:42. Package Deals.

Licensees may promote the sale of so-called package deals in which a single price is charged for lodging and beverages and liquor, food and beverages and liquor, or any combination thereof. A package deal shall state the amount of beverages and liquor included. It shall be incumbent upon the licensee to insure that patrons contracting for such package deals meet all requirements of law for the purchase of beverages and liquor.

Source.
1990, 255:1. 1993, 90:1, eff. April 29, 1993.

Amendments
—**1993.** Inserted "food and beverages and liquor" preceding "or any combination" and added "thereof" thereafter in the first sentence.

179:43. Sale on Credit.

I. No licensee shall sell beverages or liquor on credit.

II. Notwithstanding the provisions of paragraph I, on-premises and off-premises licensees may extend credit through the medium of credit cards or to commercial accounts, for which payment is received within 30 days of the date of the transaction.

Source.
1990, 255:1, eff. July 1, 1990. 1996, 275:30, eff. June 10, 1996. 2003, 231:32, eff. July 1, 2003.

Amendments
—**2003.** Paragraph II: Substituted "on-premises and off-premises" for "on-sale and off-sale".

—**1996.** Rewritten to the extent that a detailed comparison would be impracticable.

Severability of 2003 amendment.
2003, 231, which amended this section, was subject to a severability clause. See 2003, 231:53.

179:44. Free Drinks.

I. No licensee shall give away free drinks to customers, patrons, members or guests, in any manner.

II. Notwithstanding the above, beverage manufacturers, beverage vendors, brew pubs, wholesale distributors and their liquor or wine vendors, their liquor and wine representatives, domestic wine manufacturers, and on-premises and off-premises licensees may conduct beverage, liquor, or wine tasting, as applicable, on licensed premises. Liquor, beverage, or wine tasting shall be conducted only during such hours as are authorized by the commission for the sale of the product on the premises.

III. Liquor, beverage, or wine samples shall be consumed on the premises, and, except for wine samples provided by wine manufacturers, liquor or wine for this purpose shall be purchased from the commission under conditions prescribed by this title. Beverage samples for a tasting shall only be obtained as prescribed by this title.

IV. The commission may adopt rules, pursuant to RSA 541-A, establishing the criteria and procedures for liquor, beverage, and wine tasting within the state.

V. All samples furnished for tasting shall be considered sales for the requirements of RSA 178:26.

Source.
1990, 255:1. 1995, 122:1, eff. July 16, 1995. 1996, 44:1, eff. June 23, 1996; 275:31, eff. June 10, 1996; 275:36, eff. June 23, 1996. 2003, 231:33, 34, eff. July 1, 2003. 2011, 165:4, eff. August 13, 2011.

Amendments
—**2011.** The 2011 amendment added "except for wine samples provided by wine manufacturers" in the first sentence of III.

—**2003.** Paragraph II: Deleted "beverage vendor importers" preceding "brew pubs", "beverage representatives or" preceding "liquor or" and substituted "on-premises and off-premises" for "on-sale and off-sale" in the first sentence.
Paragraph V: Substituted "RSA 178:26" for "RSA 178:28, I and RSA 178:30, I".

—**1996.** Chapter 275:31 added the fifth sentence.
Chapters 44 and 275:36 rewrote section to the extent that a detailed comparison would be impractical.

—**1995.** Inserted "liquor or" preceding "wine" wherever it appeared in the second through fourth sentences and added the fifth sentence.

Severability of 2003 amendment.
2003, 231, which amended this section, was subject to a severability clause. See 2003, 231:53.

179:45. Mini-Bars.

[Repealed 1996, 275:35, V, eff. June 10, 1996.]

Former section(s).
Former RSA 179:45, which was derived from 1990, 255:1, related to mini-bars in hotels.

179:46. Sales of Holders of Wine Vendor Licenses; Fees; Sales Figures.

[Repealed 2003, 231:52, VII, eff. July 1, 2003.]

Former section(s).
Former RSA 179:46, which was derived from 1990, 255:1 and 1996, 275:32, related to sales of holders of wine vendor licenses.

Severability of 2003 repeal.
2003, 231, which repealed this section, was subject to a severability clause. See 2003, 231:53.

179:47. Off-Premises Special License Restriction.

I. Holders of a license for an auction or sheriff's sale shall advise all buyers that no liquor or beverage purchased shall be resold.

II. Any holder of a special license for an auction or sheriff's sale shall supply to the commission within 10 days of the sale the following information:

(a) Name and address of all buyers.

(b) The brands, quantity and purchase price of all items purchased by each buyer.

Source.
1990, 255:1, eff. July 1, 1990. 2003, 231:35, eff. July 1, 2003.

Amendments
—**2003.** Substituted "off-premises" for "off-sale" in the section catchline.

Severability of 2003 amendment.
2003, 231, which amended this section, was subject to a severability clause. See 2003, 231:53.

Premises Restrictions

179:48. Leasing or Renting Concessions or Part of Business.

I. No licensee shall lease or rent concession of selling liquor or beverage to any person, firm, limited liability company, or corporation.

II. No persons shall be employed by any on-premises or off-premises licensee to serve or sell beverages or liquor whose compensation is based on a percentage of the sale price of such liquor or beverage.

III. No licensee shall rent or lease any part of his business without prior permission of the commission.

IV. No licensee shall have a direct entrance to such licensee's business from that of another person, without prior permission of the commission.

V. [Repealed.]

Source.
1990, 255:1. 1995, 139:16, eff. July 1, 1995. 1996, 275:33, 35, VI, eff. June 10, 1996. 2003, 231:36, eff. July 1, 2003.

Amendments
—**2003.** Paragraph II: Substituted "on-premises or off-premises" for "on-sale or off-sale".

—**1996.** Paragraph IV: Rewritten to the extent that a detailed comparison would be impractical.
Paragraph V: Repealed.

—**1995.** Paragraph I: Inserted "limited liability company" following "firm".

Severability of 2003 amendment.
2003, 231, which amended this section, was subject to a severability clause. See 2003, 231:53.

179:49. Storage of Surplus Liquor and Beverage.

No licensee shall store beverages or liquor in any other building or buildings other than that designated in his license, except by written permission from the commission.

Source.
1990, 255:1, eff. July 1, 1990.

179:50. Loitering; Unlawful Purpose.

I. No licensee shall allow any person to loiter on his or her premises who is disorderly or who loiters for any illegal purpose.

II. No licensee shall use, or allow to be used, such premises for any purpose contrary to law.

Source.
1990, 255:1, eff. July 1, 1990. 2010, 185:1, eff. January 1, 2011.

Amendments
—2010. The 2010 amendment deleted "Intoxication" following "Loitering" in the section heading; deleted "intoxicated or" preceding "disorderly" in I; and made a stylistic change.

179:51. Lighting and Conduct Requirements for On-Premises Licensees.

Holders of on-premises licenses shall conduct their premises in an orderly manner at all times, and the premises shall be well lighted.

Source.
1990, 255:1, eff. July 1, 1990. 2003, 231:37, eff. July 1, 2003.

Revision note.
Substituted "on-premises" for "on-sale" in the section catchline in light of the changes made by 2003, 231:37.

Amendments
—2003. Substituted "on-premises" for "on-sale".

Severability of 2003 amendment.
2003, 231, which amended this section, was subject to a severability clause. See 2003, 231:53.

179:52. Posting of Licenses.

Every on-premises or off-premises license shall be posted in a conspicuous place on the premises named in the license.

Source.
1990, 255:1, eff. July 1, 1990. 2003, 231:37, eff. July 1, 2003.

Amendments
—2003. Substituted "on-premises or off-premises" for "off-sale or on-sale".

Severability of 2003 amendment.
2003, 231, which amended this section, was subject to a severability clause. See 2003, 231:53.

179:53. Alteration of Premises.

I. An on-premises or off-premises licensee shall notify the commission of any alteration to the licensed premises.

II. No licensee shall alter the premises so as to provide for both on-sale and off-sale on the same premises.

III. No licensee shall sell liquor or beverage from a drive-in window.

Source.
1990, 255:1, eff. July 1, 1990. 1996, 275:34, eff. June 10, 1996. 2003, 231:37, eff. July 1, 2003.

Amendments
—2003. Paragraph I: Substituted "on-premises or off-premises" for "off-sale or on-sale".
Paragraph II: Deleted "except as provided in RSA 178:17, I" following "same premises".

—1996. Rewritten to the extent that a detailed comparison would be impracticable.

Severability of 2003 amendment.
2003, 231, which amended this section, was subject to a severability clause. See 2003, 231:53.

179:54. Beverage Taps in View of Public; Names Displayed on Beer Dispensers.

I. All new beverage installations on on-premises licensees' premises, except in food service businesses holding on-premises licenses, shall have their taps in view of the public.

II. On-premises licensees shall display on dispensers of draught beer a knob or sign, illuminated or otherwise, clearly visible to patrons describing the brand or beverage dispensed from such outlets.

Source.
1990, 255:1, eff. July 1, 1990. 2003, 231:37, eff. July 1, 2003.

Amendments
—2003. Paragraph I: Substituted "on-premises" for "on-sale" and "food service businesses holding on-premises licenses" for "the part of premises of licensees operating as a full service restaurant".
Paragraph II: Substituted "on-premises" for "on-sale".

Severability of 2003 amendment.
2003, 231, which amended this section, was subject to a severability clause. See 2003, 231:53.

179:55. Notification of Change in Corporate Officers.

Sole proprietorships, partnerships, limited liability companies, or corporations shall notify the commission in writing of any change in the sole proprietorship, partnership, memberships of a limited liability company, or corporation or of its officers. Notification shall be made within 30 days of such change.

Source.
1990, 255:1. 1995, 139:17, eff. July 1, 1995.

Amendments
—1995. Substituted "business organization" for "corporate officers" in the section catchline, and inserted "limited liability companies" following "partnerships" and "memberships of a limited liability company" following "partnership" in the first sentence.

Enforcement Proceedings and Penalties

179:56. Hearings; Investigations; False Statement; Enforcement Policy.

I. The commission shall adopt and publish rules pursuant to RSA 541-A, to govern its proceedings and to regulate the mode and manner of all investigations and hearings before it. All hearings before the commission shall be in accordance with RSA 541-A:31-36. In any such investigation or hearing the commission shall not be bound by the technical rules of evidence. The commission may subpoena witnesses and administer oaths in any proceeding or examination instituted before or conducted by it, and may compel, by subpoena, the production of any accounts, books, contracts, records, documents, memoranda, and papers of any kind whatever. Witnesses summoned before the commission shall be paid the same fees as witnesses summoned to appear before the superior court, and such summons issued by any justice of the peace shall have the same effect as though issued for appearance before such court.

II. If any false statement is knowingly made in any statement under oath which may be required by the provisions of this title or by the commission, the person making the same shall be deemed guilty of perjury. The making of any such false statement in any such application or in any such accompanying statements, whether made with or without the knowledge or consent of the applicant, shall, in the discretion of the commission, constitute sufficient cause for the revocation of the license.

III. (a) The commission shall adopt by rule under RSA 541-A a formal enforcement policy for licensees under its jurisdiction. This policy shall specify the disciplinary action which the commission shall take for violations of various laws under its jurisdiction. The enforcement policy shall also specify mitigating and aggravating factors which the commission shall consider in determining penalties for specific actions. Except as provided in subparagraph (c), the commission shall not suspend or revoke a license until the licensee has been provided a hearing under RSA 541-A.

(b) In applying its enforcement policy, the liquor commission shall establish and enforce specific determinate penalties for specific offenses. The commission shall not apply penalties such as license suspensions for indefinite periods of time.

(c) The commission may suspend, for a period of not more than 24 hours, any license issued under the provisions of this title, if a risk to public health, safety, or welfare constitutes an emergency requiring such suspension. Any such suspension shall be approved directly by at least one member of the commission before taking effect.

Source.
1990, 255:1. 1991, 204:4, 5. 1994, 412:23, eff. Aug. 9, 1994. 2004, 142:2, eff. May 24, 2004. 2009, 144:172, eff. July 1, 2011 (see effective date note below). 2013, 258:10, eff. September 22, 2013.

Amendments
—2013. The 2013 amendment deleted "or any member" following "The commission" in the fourth sentence of I.

—2009. The 2009 amendment deleted "Investigations" following "Hearings" in the section heading; in I, deleted "investigations and" following "manner of all" in the first sentence and deleted "investigation or" preceding "hearing the commission" in the third sentence; and made a stylistic change.

—2004. Paragraph III: Added "Except as provided in subparagraph (c)" in the fourth sentence of subpar. (a) and added subpar. (c).

—1994. Paragraph I: Substituted "RSA 541-A:31–36" for "RSA 541-A:16–22" following "accordance with" in the second sentence.

—1991. Paragraph I: Added the second sentence.
Paragraph III(a): Added the fourth sentence.

Effective date of amendment by 2009, 144:172.
2010, 248:1, eff. July 2, 2010, amended 2009, 144:301, VIII to change the effective date of 2009, 144:172 from July 1, 2010 to July 1, 2011.

Repeal of 2009, 144:172 amendment.
2011, 38:1, I, eff. May 9, 2011, provided for the repeal of the amendment to the section heading and par. I by 2009, 144:172 (see note regarding effective date of amendments).

Cross References.
Fees of witnesses, see RSA 516:16 et seq.
Perjury generally, see RSA 641:1.

179:57. Suspension or Revocation; Administrative Fines.

I. The commission shall cause frequent inspections to be made of all the premises with respect to which any license has been issued under the provisions of this title. If any licensee violates any of the provisions of law or any of the rules of the commission adopted under this title or fails to superintend in person or through a manager approved by the commission the business for which the license was issued or allows the premises with respect to which the license was issued to be used for any unlawful purposes or knowingly designates to be in charge of the premises any person who has been convicted of a felony, unless the person has been approved by the commission pursuant to RSA 179:23, V, or otherwise fails to carry out in good faith the purposes of this title or if the premises are regularly the site of violence the license of such licensee may be suspended or revoked after notice and hearing, in accordance with RSA 541-A:31–36. Notwithstanding any other provisions of this chapter, the commission after the appropriate hearing may impose a fine of a specific sum, which shall not be less than $100 nor more than $5,000 for any one offense. Such a fine may be imposed instead of, or in addition to, any suspension or revocation of a license by the commission.

I-a. Notwithstanding any other provision of law, the commission may accept at any time, a petition from the governing body of a city or town who has voted to accept the provisions of RSA 663:5, I(b), (c) and (d), to revoke a license to sell alcoholic beverages held by a licensee who is located within that community. Any petition filed under this paragraph shall state with particularity all relevant facts and circumstances that sustain the opinion of the petitioner to revoke a license. A licensee against whom a petition is filed shall be entitled to a public hearing before any decision by the commission. All proceedings conducted in conjunction with this paragraph shall conform to the requirements of RSA 541-A.

II. Appeals from a decision of the commission shall be in accordance with RSA 541.

III. The commission shall, upon notification by the commissioner of the department of revenue administration of a tobacco tax violation, suspend or revoke any tobacco license issued under RSA 178. Any challenge to such suspension or revocation shall be made to the commissioner of the department of revenue administration.

Source.

1990, 255:1. 1991, 204:6. 1994, 412:24, eff. Aug. 9, 1994. 1997, 207:18, eff. July 1, 1997. 1998, 48:1, eff. Jan. 1, 1999. 2000, 253:2, eff. July 12, 2000. 2008, 341:17, eff. January 1, 2009. 2012, 49:2, eff. July 13, 2012.

Amendments

—2012. The 2012 amendment added "or if the premises are regularly the site of violence" in the second sentence of I.

—2008. The 2008 amendment added III.

—2000. Paragraph I: Substituted "designates to be in charge of the premises" for "employs in the sale or distribution of liquor or beverages" following "knowingly" in the second sentence.

—1998. Paragraph I-a: Added.

—1997. Paragraph I: Inserted "unless the person has been approved by the commission pursuant to RSA 179:23, V" following "felony" in the second sentence.

—1994. Paragraph I: Substituted "RSA 541-A:31–36" for "RSA 541-A:16–22" following "accordance with" in the second sentence.

—1991. Designated the existing provisions of the section as par. I, deleted "disorderly or immoral" following "unlawful", substituted "or" for "by the commission without hearing, and may be" following "suspended" and added "in accordance with RSA 541-A:16–22" following "and hearing" in the second sentence and substituted "after the appropriate hearing" for "in its discretion" following "commission" in the third sentence of that paragraph and added par. II.

NOTES TO DECISIONS

Access to licensed premises

Liquor commission may issue a regulation requiring a licensed club to furnish to commission's law enforcement department a key for entrance into premises at any time. Manchester Press Club v. State Liquor Comm'n, 89 N.H. 442, 200 A. 407, 1938 N.H. LEXIS 51, 116 A.L.R. 1093 (1938). (Decided under prior law.)

Cited:

Cited in Hickingbotham v. Burke, 140 N.H. 28, 662 A.2d 297, 1995 N.H. LEXIS 94 (1995).

179:58. Penalties.

I. Any person who violates any of the provisions of this title or any of the rules adopted pursuant to this title shall be guilty of a misdemeanor if a natural person, or guilty of a felony if any other person. In case of appeal by a licensee, the license of such licensee may be suspended at the discretion of the commission during the pendency of such appeal.

II. Any person who holds any license pursuant to this title who offers for sale any beverage or liquor without paying all fees due shall, if a natural person, be guilty of a class B felony and, if any other person, be guilty of a felony and upon conviction shall have his license permanently revoked.

Source.

1990, 255:1, eff. July 1, 1990.

Cross References.

Classification of crimes, see RSA 625:9.
Sentences, see RSA 651.

NOTES TO DECISIONS

Cited:

Cited in Hickingbotham v. Burke, 140 N.H. 28, 662 A.2d 297, 1995 N.H. LEXIS 94 (1995).

179:59. Prosecutions.

The commission shall appoint liquor investigators whose primary function shall be the proper prosecution of this title. The liquor investigators shall have all the powers of the sheriff in any county, with reference to enforcement of all laws either in cooperation with, or independently of, the officers of any county or town. The commission shall have the primary responsibility for the enforcement of all liquor and beverage laws upon premises where liquor and beverages are lawfully sold, stored, distributed, or manufactured. Any person violating the provisions of any law may be prosecuted by the commission or any of its investigators as provided in this section, or by county or city attorneys, or by sheriffs or their deputies, or by police officials of towns.

Source.

1990, 255:1. 1995, 34:13, eff. June 23, 1995. 2009, 144:173, eff. July 1, 2011 (see effective date note below).

Amendments

—2009. The 2009 amendment deleted the former first and second sentences, which read: "The commission shall appoint liquor investigators whose primary function shall be the proper prosecution of this title. The liquor investigators shall have all the powers of the sheriff in any county, with reference to enforcement of all laws either in cooperation with, or independently of, the officers of any county or town"; substituted "department of safety" for "commission" in the first sentence; and substituted "department of safety" for "commission or any of its investigators as provided in this section" in the second sentence.

—1995. Deleted the former third sentence and deleted "herein" preceding "provided" and inserted "in this section" thereafter in the present fourth sentence.

Effective date of amendment by 2009, 144:173.

2010, 248:1, eff. July 2, 2010, amended 2009, 144:301, VIII to change the effective date of 2009, 144:173 from July 1, 2010 to July 1, 2011.

Repeal of 2009, 144:173 amendment.

2011, 38:1, I, eff. May 9, 2011, provided for the repeal of the amendment to the section by 2009, 144:173 (see note regarding effective date of amendments).

Cross References.

Enforcement policy, see RSA 179:56.

179:60. Interference With Liquor Investigators.

It shall be unlawful to resist or attempt to resist arrest by a liquor investigator, or to obstruct, or to intimidate or interfere with a liquor investigator in the performance of his duty. Any person who violates any of the provisions of this section shall be guilty of a misdemeanor.

Source.
1990, 255:1, eff. July 1, 1990.

Repeal of prospective repeal of section.
2009, 144:174, II, as amended by 2010, 248:1, eff. July 2, 2010, provided for the repeal of this section effective July 1, 2011, was repealed by 2011, 38:1, I, eff. May 9, 2011.

Cross References.
Classification of crimes, see RSA 625:9.
Sentences, see RSA 651.

179:61. Fines.

I. All fines imposed by any court and collected for the violation of the provisions of this title shall be paid to the state, county, or town, the officials of which instituted the prosecution.

II. All fines imposed by the commission shall be deposited into the general fund.

Source.
1990, 255:1, eff. July 1, 1990.

179:62. Manufacture, Sale, and Possession of False Identification.

I. No person shall knowingly manufacture, sell, advertise for sale, solicit orders for, deliver or cause to be delivered, or produce in any manner any photographic identification card that purports to be an official document issued by a local, state, or federal government, or any political subdivision thereof, which contains false or inaccurate information regarding the name, address, date of birth, or height and weight characteristics of the cardholder. A person who violates this paragraph shall be guilty of:

(a) A misdemeanor.

(b) A class B felony if such person has had 2 or more prior convictions in this state or another state for the conduct described in this paragraph.

(c) A class B felony if such person is engaged in the business of manufacturing, selling, advertising for sale, soliciting orders for, delivering, or causing to be delivered photographic identification cards in violation of this paragraph.

II. In this section, "engaged in the business" means manufacturing, selling, advertising for sale, soliciting orders for, delivering, or causing to be delivered 5 or more photographic identification cards in violation of paragraph I.

III. No person shall possess a photographic identification card that purports to be an official document issued by a local, state, or federal government, or any political subdivision thereof, which contains false or inaccurate information regarding the name, address, date of birth, or height and weight characteristics of the card holder. Any person who violates this paragraph shall be guilty of a misdemeanor.

IV. Interests in any tools, instruments, computer or computerized records, products, and equipment of any kind, or other paraphernalia used in the manufacture, sale, advertising for sale, delivery, or solicitation of any order for sale, of a false identification card, shall, upon petition of the attorney general, be subject to forfeiture to the state and shall be vested in the state.

Source.
1998, 374:2, eff. Jan. 1, 1999.

TITLE XVIII
FISH AND GAME

CHAPTER 215-C
SNOWMOBILES

SECTION
215-C:31.   Regulations of Political Subdivisions.

215-C:31. Regulations of Political Subdivisions.

I. With bylaws or ordinances city or town councils and boards of selectmen may regulate the operation of snowmobiles within city or town limits, providing they do not conflict with provisions of this chapter.

II. Speed limits for snowmobiles traveling on the frozen surface of Turtle Pond, also known as Turtle Town Pond, in the city of Concord shall not exceed 55 miles per hour.

III. Enforcement of paragraph II shall be the joint responsibility of the city of Concord and the state of New Hampshire.

IV. The local legislative body of a municipality shall not by ordinance or resolution authorize the planning board to review and approve or disapprove site plans for the development, siting, maintenance, or use of trails on private property for snowmobiles, as defined in RSA 215-C:1.

Source.
2005, 210:1, eff. July 1, 2006.

TITLE XXX
OCCUPATIONS AND PROFESSIONS
CHAPTER 318-B
CONTROLLED DRUG ACT

SECTION
318-B:1. Definitions.
318-B:1-a. Scheduling by the Commissioner.
318-B:1-b. Schedule Tests.
318-B:1-c. Flunitrazepam.
318-B:2. Acts Prohibited.
318-B:2-a. Exception. [Repealed.]
318-B:2-b. Counterfeit Drugs; Affirmative Defense.
318-B:3. Licensing of Manufacturers and Wholesalers Required.
318-B:4. Licenses. [Repealed.]
318-B:5. Sale by Manufacturer or Wholesaler.
318-B:6. Possession Lawful.
318-B:7. Written Orders.
318-B:8. Limitation on Use.
318-B:9. Sale by Pharmacists.
318-B:10. Professional Use of Narcotic Drugs.
318-B:11. Preparations Exempted.
318-B:12. Records to be Kept; Confidentiality.
318-B:12-a. Treatment for Drug Abuse.
318-B:13. Labels.
318-B:14. Authorized Possession of Controlled Drugs by Individuals. [Repealed.]
318-B:15. Persons and Corporations Exempted.
318-B:16. Common Nuisances.
318-B:17. Disposal of Controlled Drugs in Possession of Law Enforcement Officer.
318-B:17-a. Disposal of Controlled Drugs in Possession of Practitioner.
318-B:17-b. Forfeiture of Items Used in Connection with Drug Offense.
318-B:17-c. Drug Forfeiture Fund.
318-B:17-d. Administrative Forfeiture of Items Used in Connection With Drug Offenses.
318-B:17-e. Drug Asset Forfeiture Guidelines Required.
318-B:17-f. Forfeiture Reports.
318-B:18. Notice of Conviction to be Sent to Licensing Board.
318-B:19. Records, Confidential. [Repealed.]
318-B:20. Prohibited Acts. [Repealed.]
318-B:21. Certain Communications Not Privileged.
318-B:22. Exceptions and Exemptions Not Required to be Negatived.
318-B:23. Enforcement and Cooperation.
318-B:24. Rulemaking.
318-B:25. Authority for Inspection.
318-B:26. Penalties.
318-B:26-a. Chemical Analyses.
318-B:27. Prior Offenses.
318-B:28. Recording of Sentences as Misdemeanors or Felonies. [Repealed.]
318-B:28-a. Annulments of Criminal Records.
318-B:29. Effect of Acquittal or Conviction Under the Comprehensive Drug Abuse Prevention and Control Act of 1970.
318-B:30. Severability.

Controlled Drug Prescription Health and Safety Program. [Repealed.]

318-B:31. Definitions. [Repealed.]
318-B:32. Controlled Drug Prescription Health and Safety Program Established. [Repealed.]

SECTION
318-B:33. Controlled Drug Prescription Health and Safety Program Operation. [Repealed.]
318-B:34. Confidentiality. [Repealed.]
318-B:35. Providing Controlled Drug Prescription Health and Safety Information. [Repealed.]
318-B:36. Unlawful Act and Penalties. [Repealed.]
318-B:37. Rulemaking. [Repealed.]
318-B:38. Advisory Council Established. [Repealed.]

Cross References.

Arrest without warrant of persons suspected of driving while under the influence of controlled drugs, see RSA 265-A:2 et seq.

Establishment of drug-free school zones, see RSA 193-B.

Establishment of public housing property as drug-free zone, see RSA 31:41-e, 47:17.

Regulation of dentists generally, see RSA 317-A.

Regulation of food and drugs generally, see RSA 146.

Regulation of optometrists generally, see RSA 327.

Regulation of pharmacists and pharmacies generally, see RSA 318.

Regulation of physicians and surgeons generally, see RSA 329.

Regulation of veterinarians generally, see RSA 332-B.

NOTES TO DECISIONS

Cited:

Cited in Opinion of Justices, 121 N.H. 542, 431 A.2d 152, 1981 N.H. LEXIS 343 (1981); State v. Andrews, 125 N.H. 158, 480 A.2d 889, 1984 N.H. LEXIS 361 (1984); State v. Doyle, 126 N.H. 153, 489 A.2d 639, 1985 N.H. LEXIS 262 (1985); State v. Valenzuela, 130 N.H. 175, 536 A.2d 1252, 1987 N.H. LEXIS 302 (1987); State v. Hazen, 131 N.H. 196, 552 A.2d 77, 1988 N.H. LEXIS 104 (1988); State v. Smith, 132 N.H. 756, 571 A.2d 279, 1990 N.H. LEXIS 14 (1990); State v. Hughes, 135 N.H. 413, 605 A.2d 1062, 1992 N.H. LEXIS 51 (1992); State v. Conant, 139 N.H. 728, 662 A.2d 283, 1995 N.H. LEXIS 79 (1995); State v. Sanchez, 140 N.H. 162, 663 A.2d 629, 1995 N.H. LEXIS 117 (1995).

RESEARCH REFERENCES

Criminal Jury Instructions.

New Hampshire Criminal Jury Instructions, Instruction # 2.21.

318-B:1. Definitions.

The following words and phrases, as used in this chapter, shall have the following meanings, unless the context otherwise requires:

I. "Abuse of drugs" means the use of controlled drugs solely for their stimulant, depressant or hallucinogenic effect upon the higher functions of the central nervous system and not as a therapeutic agent recommended by a practitioner in the course of medical treatment or in a program of research operated under the direction of a physician, pharmacologist, physiologist, chemist, or advanced practice registered nurse;

I-a. "Administer" means an act whereby a single dose of a drug is instilled into the body of or given to a person or animal for immediate consumption or use.

I-aa. "Advanced emergency medical care provider" means a person licensed to provide advanced emergency medical care under RSA 151-B.

I-b. "Advanced practice registered nurse" means a person licensed to practice as an advanced practice registered nurse in this state pursuant to RSA 326-B:18.

II. "Amphetamine-type drugs" means amphetamine, optical isomers thereof, salts of amphetamine and its isomers, and chemical compounds which are similar thereto in physiological effect, and which show a like potential for abuse;

II-a. "Anabolic steroid" includes any of the following or any isomer, ester, salt, or derivative of the following that acts in the same manner on the human body:

(a) Clostebol;

(b) Dehydrochlormethyltestosterone;

(c) Ethylestrenol;

(d) Fluoxymesterone;

(e) Mesterolone;

(f) Methandienone;

(g) Methandrostenolone;

(h) Methenolone;

(i) Methyltestosterone;

(j) Nandrolone;

(k) Norethandrolone;

(l) Oxandrolone;

(m) Oxymesterone;

(n) Oxymetholone;

(o) Stanozolol; and

(p) Testosterone;

III. "Barbiturate-type drugs" means barbituric acid and its salts, derivatives thereof and chemical compounds which are similar thereto in physiological effect, and which show a like potential for abuse;

IV. "Cannabis-type drug" means all parts of any plant of the Cannabis genus of plants, whether growing or not; the seeds thereof; the resin extracted from any part of such plant; and every compound, manufacture, salt, derivative, mixture or preparation of such plant, its seeds or resin. Such term does not include the mature stalks of such plants, fiber produced from such stalks, oil or cake made from the seeds of such plants, any other compound, manufacture, salt, derivative, mixture, or preparation of such mature stalks (except the resin extracted therefrom), fiber, oil or cake, or the sterilized seeds of such plants which are incapable of germination;

V. "Cocaine-type drugs" means coca leaves, cocaine, ecgonine, and chemical compounds which are similar thereto in chemical structure or which are similar thereto in physiological effect and which show a like potential for abuse;

V-a. "Commissioner" means the commissioner of the department of health and human services.

VI. "Controlled drugs" means any drug or substance, or immediate precursor, which is scheduled pursuant to RSA 318-B:1-a.

VI-a. "Controlled drug analog" means a substance that has a chemical structure substantially similar to that of a controlled drug and that was specifically designed to produce an effect substantially similar to that of a controlled drug. The term shall not include a drug manufactured or distributed in conformance with the provisions of an approved new drug application or an exemption for investigational use within the meaning of section 505 of the Federal Food, Drug and Cosmetic Act, 52 Stat. 1052 (21 U.S.C. 355);

VI-b. "Crack cocaine", also known as cocaine base or rock cocaine, means the free base form of cocaine in which the molecule is not chemically combined as an acid salt.

VII. "Dentist" means a person authorized by law to practice dentistry in this state;

VII-a. "Department" means the department of health and human services.

VIII. "Dispense" means to distribute, leave with, give away, dispose of, deliver, or sell one or more doses of and shall include the transfer of more than a single dose of a medication from one container to another and the labelling or otherwise identifying a container holding more than a single dose of a drug;

IX. "Drug dependence" means a state of physical addiction or psychic dependence, or both, upon a drug following use of that drug upon a repeated periodic or continuous basis except:

(a) Upon a morphine-type drug as an incident to current medical treatment of a demonstrable physical disorder, other than produced by the use of the drug itself, or

(b) Upon amphetamine-type, ataractic, barbiturate-type, hallucinogenic or other stimulant and depressant drugs as an incident to current medical treatment of a demonstrable physical or psychological disorder, or both, other than produced by the drug itself;

X. "Drug-dependent person" means any person who has developed a state of psychic or physical dependence, or both, upon a controlled drug following administration of that drug upon a repeated periodic or continuous basis. No person shall be classified as drug dependent who is dependent:

(a) Upon a morphine-type drug as an incident to current medical treatment of a demonstrable physical disorder other than drug dependence, or

(b) Upon amphetamine-type, ataractic, barbiturate-type, hallucinogenic or other stimulant and depressant drugs as an incident to current medical treatment of a demonstrable physical or psychological disorder, or both, other than drug dependence;

X-a. "Drug paraphernalia" means all equipment, products and materials of any kind which are used or intended for use or customarily intended for use in planting, propagating, cultivating, growing, harvesting, manufacturing, compounding, converting, producing, processing, preparing, testing, analyzing, packaging, repackaging, storing, containing, concealing, ingesting, inhaling, or otherwise introducing into the human body a controlled substance in violation of this chapter. It includes, but is not limited to:

(a) Kits used or intended for use or customarily intended for use in planting, propagating, cultivating, growing or harvesting of any species of plant which is a controlled substance or from which a controlled substance can be derived;

(b) Kits including but not limited to cocaine kits, used or intended for use or customarily intended for use in manufacturing, compounding, converting, producing, processing, or preparing controlled substances;

(c) Isomerization devices used or intended for use or customarily intended for use in increasing the potency of any species of plant which is a controlled substance;

(d) Testing equipment used or intended for use or customarily intended for use in identifying, or analyzing the strength, effectiveness or purity of controlled substances;

(e) Scales and balances used or intended for use or customarily intended for use in weighing or measuring controlled substances;

(f) Diluents and adulterants, such as quinine hydrochloride, mannitol, mannite, dextrose and lactose, used or intended for use or customarily intended for use in cutting controlled substances;

(g) Separation gins and sifters used or intended for use or customarily intended for use in removing twigs and seeds from, or in otherwise cleaning or refining, marijuana;

(h) Blenders, bowls, containers, spoons and mixing devices used or intended for use or customarily intended for use in compounding controlled substances;

(i) Capsules, balloons, envelopes and other containers used or intended for use or customarily intended for use in packaging small quantities of controlled substances;

(j) Containers and other objects used or intended for use or customarily intended for use in storing or concealing controlled substances;

(k) Objects used or intended for use or customarily intended for use in ingesting, inhaling, or otherwise introducing marijuana, cocaine, hashish, or hashish oil into the human body, such as:

(1) Metal, wooden, acrylic, glass, stone, plastic, or ceramic pipes with or without screens, permanent screens, hashish heads, or punctured metal bowls;

(2) Water pipes;

(3) Carburetion tubes and devices;

(4) Smoking and carburetion masks;

(5) Chamber pipes;

(6) Carburetor pipes;

(7) Electric pipes;

(8) Air-driven pipes;

(9) Chillums;

(10) Bongs;

(11) Ice pipes or chillers;

XI. "Federal food and drug laws" means the Federal Food, Drug and Cosmetic Act, as amended (Title 21 U.S.C. § 301 et seq.);

XII. "Comprehensive Drug Abuse Prevention and Control Act of 1970" means the applicable law of the United States relating to opium, coca leaves and other narcotic drugs;

XIII. "Hallucinogenic drugs" are psychodysleptic drugs which assert a confusional or disorganizing effect upon mental processes or behavior and mimic acute psychotic disturbances. Exemplary of such drugs are mescaline, peyote, psilocybin and d-lysergic acid diethylamide;

XIV. "Laboratory" means a scientific or medical establishment entrusted with the custody of controlled drugs and the use of controlled drugs for scientific and medical purposes and for purposes of instruction, research or analysis;

XIV-a. "Law enforcement officer" means any officer of the state or political subdivision of the state who is empowered by law to conduct investigations of or to make arrests for offenses enumerated in this chapter.

XV. "Manufacturer" means a person who, by compounding, mixing, cultivating, growing or other process, produces or prepares controlled drugs, but shall not mean a pharmacist who compounds controlled drugs to be sold or dispensed on prescription;

XVI. "Morphine-type drugs" means morphine and chemical compounds which are similar thereto in physiological effect and which show a like potential for abuse;

XVII. "Narcotic drugs" means cocaine-type and morphine-type drugs, and drugs other than cannabis-type regulated under the Comprehensive Drug Abuse Prevention and Control Act of 1970;

XVIII. "Nurse" means a person licensed to perform nursing as defined in RSA 326-B;

XIX. "Official written order" means an order written on a form provided for that purpose by the United States Attorney General under the laws of the United States making provision therefor, if such order forms are authorized and required by federal law, or conforming to the requirements of such a form and provided by the department of health and human services, or, if no such order form is provided, on an official form provided for that purpose by the department of health and human services;

XIX-a. "Optometrist" means a person authorized by law to practice optometry in this state pursuant to RSA 327;

XX. "Other stimulant and depressant drugs" means controlled drugs other than amphetamine-type, barbiturate-type, cannabis-type, cocaine-type, hallucinogenics and morphine-type which are found to exert a stimulant and depressant effect upon the higher functions of the central nervous system and which are found to have a potential for abuse;

XXI. "Person" means any corporation, association or partnership, or one or more individuals;

XXII. "Pharmacist" means a person authorized by law to practice pharmacy pursuant to RSA 318;

XXIII. "Pharmacy" means an establishment licensed pursuant to RSA 318;

XXIV. "Physician" means a person authorized by law to practice medicine in this state pursuant to RSA 329;

XXIV-a. "Podiatrist" means a person authorized by law to practice podiatry in this state pursuant to RSA 315.

XXV. "Potential for abuse" means that there is a likelihood that a drug will be used solely for its stimulant, depressant or hallucinogenic effect upon the higher functions of the central nervous system as distinguished from use recommended by a practitioner as a therapeutic agent in a course of medical treatment or in a program of research operated under the direction of a physician, pharmacologist, or advanced practice registered nurse;

XXVI. "Practitioner" means any person who is lawfully entitled to prescribe, administer, dispense or distribute controlled drugs to patients;

XXVI-a. "Practitioner-patient relationship" means a medical connection between a licensed practitioner and a patient that includes an in-person exam, a history, a diagnosis, a treatment plan appropriate for the licensee's scope of practice, and documentation of all prescription drugs including name and dosage. A licensee may prescribe for a patient whom the licensee does not have a practitioner-patient relationship under the following circumstances: for a patient of another licensee for whom the prescriber is taking call; for a patient examined by another New Hampshire licensed practitioner; or for medication on a short-term basis for a new patient prior to the patient's first appointment. The definition of a practitioner-patient relationship shall not apply to a practitioner licensed in another state who is consulting to a New Hampshire licensed practitioner with whom the patient has a relationship.

XXVII. "Prescribe" means order or designate a remedy or any preparation containing controlled drugs;

XXVIII. "Prescription" means an oral, written, or facsimile or electronically transmitted order for any controlled drug or preparation issued by a licensed practitioner to be compounded and dispensed by a pharmacist and delivered to a patient for a medicinal or therapeutic purpose arising from a practitioner-patient relationship.

XXIX. "Registry number" means the number assigned to each person registered under the federal narcotic laws;

XXX. "Sale" means barter, exchange or gift, or offer therefor, and each such transaction made by any person whether as principal, proprietor, agent, servant, or employee;

XXXI. "State food, drug and cosmetic laws" means RSA 146;

XXXII. "Veterinarian" means a person authorized by law to practice veterinary medicine in this state pursuant to RSA 332-B;

XXXIII. "Wholesaler" means a person who supplies or distributes controlled drugs that he himself has not produced or prepared to hospitals, practitioners, pharmacies, other wholesalers, manufacturers or federal, state and municipal agencies.

Source.
1969, 421:1. 1975, 255:2. 1977, 547:1–4. 1981, 513:1. 1985, 190:98; 293:1, 2; 324:17, 18. 1988, 6:1. 1989, 195:1; 361:1. 1993, 333:3, eff. Jan. 1, 1994. 1994, 186:1, eff. Jan. 1, 1995; 333:16–18, eff. Jan. 1, 1995. 1995, 310:155, 156, 181, eff. Nov. 1, 1995. 1996, 267:22, eff. Aug. 9, 1996. 2000, 176:4, eff. Jan. 1, 2001. 2001, 15:3, eff. Jan. 1, 2002; 282:8, eff. July 1, 2001. 2005, 293:8, eff. at 12:02 a.m., July 1, 2005. 2008, 217:3, 4, eff. January 1, 2009. 2009, 54:5, eff. July 21, 2009. 2011, 63:4, eff. July 1, 2011.

References in text.
RSA 151-B, referred to in par. I-aa, was repealed by 1999, 345:11, eff. July 1, 1999. See now RSA 153-A.

The Comprehensive Drug Abuse Prevention and Control Act of 1970, referred to in pars. XII and XVII, is classified principally to 42 U.S.C.S. §§ 218, 246, 4541.

In par. XVIII, substituted "RSA 326-B" for "RSA 326-A" as RSA 326-A was repealed and the substance of that chapter incorporated in RSA 326-B.

In par. XIX, substituted "Attorney General" for "commissioner of narcotics". The office of United States commissioner of narcotics was abolished by Reorg. Plan No. 1 of 1968, effective April 8, 1968, 33 F.R. 5611, 82 Stat. 1367 and the functions thereof were transferred to the Department of Justice. Written order forms are now prescribed and issued by the Attorney General of the United States pursuant to 21 U.S.C.S. § 828.

In par. XXXII, substituted "RSA 332-B" for "RSA 332" as RSA 332 was repealed and the substance of that chapter incorporated in RSA 332-B.

—**2011.** The 2011 amendment added XIV-a.

—**2009.** The 2009 amendment substituted "advanced practice registered nurse" for "advanced registered nurse practitioner" in I and XXV, and twice in I-b.

—**2008.** The 2008 amendment added XXVI-a and rewrote XXVIII to the extent that a detailed comparison would be impracticable.

—**2005.** Paragraph I-b: Substituted "RSA 326-B:18" for "RSA 326-B:10".

—**2001.** Paragraph XXIV-a: Added by ch. 15.
Paragraph XXVIII: Chapter 282 inserted "verbal" preceding "written, or" and substituted "facsimile or electronically transmitted" for "oral" thereafter.

—**2000.** Paragraph X-a: Substituted "concealing" for "injecting" preceding "ingesting" in the first sentence of the introductory paragraph.

—**1996.** Paragraph I-aa: Added.

—**1995.** Paragraph V-a: Added.
Paragraph VII-a: Rewritten to the extent that a detailed comparison would be impracticable.
Paragraph XIX: Substituted "department of health and human services" for "division of public health services" in two places.

—**1994.** Paragraph I: Chapter 333 deleted "or" preceding "chemist" and added "or advanced registered nurse practitioner" thereafter.
Paragraph I-b: Added by ch. 333.
Paragraph VI-b: Added by ch. 186.
Paragraph XXV: Chapter 333 deleted "or" preceding "pharmacologist" and added "or advanced registered nurse practitioner" thereafter.

—**1993.** Paragraph XIX-a: Added.

—**1989.** Paragraph II-a: Added by ch. 195.
Paragraph X-a: Chapter 361 inserted "or customarily intended

for use" following "used or intended for use" throughout the paragraph and inserted "including but not limited to cocaine kits" at the beginning of subpar. (b).

—**1988.** Paragraph VI-a: Added.

—**1985.** Paragraph VI: Chapter 190 substituted "rule" for "regulation" preceding "after investigation" in the first sentence.
Rewritten by ch. 293 to the extent that a detailed comparison would be impracticable.
Paragraph VII-a: Added by ch. 293.
Paragraphs VIII, XXXIII: Rewritten by ch. 324 to the extent that a detailed comparison would be impracticable.

—**1981.** Paragraph X-a: Added.

—**1977.** Paragraph I-a: Added.
Paragraphs VI, XVII: Substituted "Comprehensive Drug Abuse Prevention and Control Act of 1970" for "federal narcotic laws".
Paragraph XII: Defined "Comprehensive Drug Abuse Prevention and Control Act of 1970".

—**1975.** Paragraph IV: Redefined cannabis-type drug.

Severability of 1995 amendment.
1995, 310, which amended this section, was subject to a severability clause. See 1995, 310:186.

Severability of 1989 amendment.
1989, 361 was subject to a severability clause. See 1989, 361:4.

Severability of 1981 amendment.
1981, 513:1 was subject to a severability clause. See 1981, 513:5.

Construction of 1995 amendment.
1995, 310:187, eff. Nov. 1, 1995, provided:
"Nothing in this act is intended to, nor shall it be construed as, mandating or assigning any new, expanded, or modified program or responsibility for any political subdivision in violation of part I, article 28-a of the constitution of the state of New Hampshire."

NOTES TO DECISIONS

1. Controlled drugs
2. Drug-dependent person
3. Drug paraphernalia

1. Controlled drugs
The definition of "controlled drugs" in paragraph VI of this section is not limited by federal designations under the Comprehensive Drug Abuse Prevention and Control Act or under other food and drug laws. State v. Stiles, 128 N.H. 81, 512 A.2d 1084, 1986 N.H. LEXIS 289 (1986). (Decided under section prior to 1985 amendment.)
The definition of "controlled drugs" includes "narcotic drugs;" "narcotic drugs" include "cocaine type drugs;" and "cocaine type drugs" include cocaine of any isomer. State v. Stiles, 128 N.H. 81, 512 A.2d 1084, 1986 N.H. LEXIS 289 (1986). (Decided under section prior to 1985 amendment.)

2. Drug-dependent person
RSA 318-B:16's phrase, "drug-dependent person," is not unconstitutionally vague on its face. RSA 318-B:16, read in conjunction with RSA 318-B:1, X (defining "drug-dependent person"), gives clear notice to a person of ordinary intelligence of the precise conduct, involving drug-dependent persons, that constitutes the nuisance. State v. MacElman, 154 N.H. 304, 910 A.2d 1267, 2006 N.H. LEXIS 160 (2006).

3. Drug paraphernalia
RSA 318-B:1, X-a is not impermissibly vague under the State or Federal Constitutions as: (1) the statute provides ample notice of the objects it proscribes as objects are considered drug paraphernalia if they are used, intended for use, or customarily intended for use, to introduce controlled substances into the human body, (2) the use of the word "customarily" in the statute is comprehensible, and presents an evidentiary question, rather than a constitutional

validity question, (3) RSA 318-B:1, X-a(a)–(k) contains a nonexhaustive list of items that can be considered drug paraphernalia, (4) the person who must use an item, design it for use, or intend it for use with drugs in order for it to be drug paraphernalia, is the person charged with one of the statute's substantive violations, and (5) the statute does not authorize or encourage arbitrary and discriminatory enforcement because the statutory scheme provides comprehensive guidelines under RSA 318-B:2, IV to govern law enforcement. State v. Smoke Signals Pipe & Tobacco Shop, LLC, 155 N.H. 234, 922 A.2d 634, 2007 N.H. LEXIS 53 (2007).

Cited:
Cited in State v. Stone, 114 N.H. 114, 316 A.2d 196, 1974 N.H. LEXIS 220 (1974); State v. Pelillo, 117 N.H. 674, 377 A.2d 615, 1977 N.H. LEXIS 407 (1977); Opinion of Justices, 121 N.H. 542, 431 A.2d 152, 1981 N.H. LEXIS 343 (1981); State v. Cimino, 126 N.H. 570, 493 A.2d 1197, 1985 N.H. LEXIS 346 (1985); State v. Cartier, 133 N.H. 217, 575 A.2d 347, 1990 N.H. LEXIS 54 (1990); State v. Pike, 134 N.H. 690, 597 A.2d 1071, 1991 N.H. LEXIS 120 (1991); State v. Coons, 137 N.H. 365, 627 A.2d 1064, 1993 N.H. LEXIS 91 (1993).

RESEARCH REFERENCES

Workers Compensation Manual.
Misconduct of Employee as Defense see §§ 6.01 et seq.

318-B:1-a. Scheduling by the Commissioner.

I. The commissioner may add, delete, or reschedule all substances, by rule, pursuant to RSA 541-A, after hearing and after consulting with the pharmacy board. In making a determination regarding a substance, the commissioner shall consider the following:
(a) Actual or relative potential for abuse;
(b) Scientific evidence of its pharmacological effect, if known;
(c) State of current scientific knowledge regarding the substance;
(d) History and current pattern of abuse;
(e) Scope, duration, and significance of abuse;
(f) Risk to the public health;
(g) Potential of the substance to produce psychic or physical dependence liability; and
(h) Whether the substance is an immediate precursor of a substance already controlled under this chapter.
II. After considering the factors in paragraph I, the commissioner shall make findings relative to the substance and adopt a rule controlling the substance if he finds the substance has a potential for abuse.
III. In addition to the provisions of RSA 541-A, the commissioner shall give due notice of the time, place and purpose of all hearings required under this chapter to podiatrists, osteopaths, hospitals, pharmacists, physicians, dentists, veterinarians, advanced registered nurse practitioners, optometrists, laboratories, registered manufacturers, suppliers and to the general public by such means as he shall deem adequate. From and after the hearing date, the sale or dispensation (except by prescription) of a drug or chemical containing any quantity of such substance as is the subject matter of the hearing shall be suspended pending a determination as to whether such substance is to be designated as a controlled drug. Designation as a controlled drug

shall result in the continued suspension of the sale or dispensation (except by prescription) of any drug or chemical containing any quantity of such substance until the effective date of the designation. The substance shall thereafter be a controlled drug subject to this chapter. If any substance is so designated, the commissioner shall publish the designation in a newspaper of general circulation in the state once each week for 3 successive weeks.

IV. Substances which are precursors of the controlled precursor shall not be subject to control solely because they are precursors of the controlled precursor.

V. If any substance is designated, rescheduled, or deleted as a controlled substance under federal law and notice thereof is given to the commissioner, the commissioner shall similarly control the substance under this chapter after the expiration of 30 days from publication in the Federal Register of a final order designating a substance as a controlled substance or rescheduling or deleting a substance, unless, within that 30 day period, the commissioner objects to inclusion, rescheduling, or deletion. In that case, the commissioner shall publish the reasons for objection and afford all interested persons an opportunity to be heard. At the conclusion of the hearing, the commissioner shall publish his decision, which shall be final unless altered by law. Upon publication of objection to inclusion, rescheduling, or deletion under this chapter by the commissioner, control under this chapter shall be stayed until the commissioner publishes his decision.

VI. Authority to control under this section shall not extend to distilled spirits, wine, malt beverages, or tobacco.

VII. Controlled drugs shall be scheduled by whatever official, common, usual, chemical or trade name designated.

VIII. The commissioner shall revise and republish the schedules in RSA 318-B:1-b semi-annually for 2 years from the effective date of this section, and thereafter annually.

Source.
1985, 293:3. 1993, 333:4, eff. Jan. 1, 1994. 1994, 333:19, eff. Jan. 1, 1995. 1995, 310:183, eff. Nov. 1, 1995.

Amendments
—1995. Substituted "commissioner" for "director" wherever it appeared in pars. I–III, V, and VIII.

—1994. Paragraph III: Inserted "advanced registered nurse practitioners" following "veterinarians" in the first sentence.

—1993. Paragraph III: Inserted "optometrists" following "veterinarians" in the first sentence.

Severability of 1995 amendment.
1995, 310, which amended this section, was subject to a severability clause. See 1995, 310:186.

Construction of 1995 amendment.
1995, 310:187, eff. Nov. 1, 1995, provided:
"Nothing in this act is intended to, nor shall it be construed as, mandating or assigning any new, expanded, or modified program or responsibility for any political subdivision in violation of part I, article 28-a of the constitution of the state of New Hampshire."

Establishment of initial schedules of controlled drugs.
1985, 293:8, eff. Aug. 13, 1985, provided: "There are hereby established 5 schedules of controlled drugs to be known as schedules I, II, III, IV and V. Such schedules shall initially consist of substances listed in this section [of the act]. The schedules established by this section [of the act] shall be updated and republished pursuant to RSA 318-B:1-a.

"I. Schedule I shall include the controlled substances listed in schedule I of the current chapter 21, Code of Federal Regulations.

"II. Schedule II shall include the controlled substances listed in schedule II of the current chapter 21, Code of Federal Regulations.

"III. Schedule III shall include the controlled substances listed in schedule III of the current chapter 21, Code of Federal Regulations.

"IV. Schedule IV shall include the controlled substances listed in schedule IV of the current chapter 21, Code of Federal Regulations.

"V. Schedule V shall include the controlled substances listed in schedule V of the current chapter 21, Code of Federal Regulations."

NOTES TO DECISIONS

Republication
Argument was rejected that director of division of public health services was obliged under this section to "republish" schedules of controlled drugs semi-annually for 2 years and thereafter annually, and that failure to republish rendered drug possession laws a nullity; republication was not required where director took no action to revise schedules as initially provided by session law. State v. Cartier, 133 N.H. 217, 575 A.2d 347, 1990 N.H. LEXIS 54 (1990).

318-B:1-b. Schedule Tests.

I. SCHEDULE I TESTS. The commissioner shall place a substance in schedule I if he finds that the substance:

(a) Has high potential for abuse; and

(b) Has no accepted medical use in treatment in the United States or lacks accepted safety for use in treatment under medical supervision.

II. SCHEDULE II TESTS. The commissioner shall place a substance in schedule II if he finds that:

(a) The substance has high potential for abuse;

(b) The substance has currently accepted medical use in treatment in the United States, or currently accepted medical use with severe restrictions; and

(c) The abuse of the substance may lead to severe psychic or physical dependence.

III. SCHEDULE III TESTS. The commissioner shall place a substance in schedule III if he finds that:

(a) The substance has a potential for abuse less than the substances listed in schedules I and II of the current chapter 21, Code of Federal Regulations;

(b) The substance has currently accepted medical use in treatment in the United States; and

(c) Abuse of the substance may lead to moderate or low physical dependence or high psychological dependence.

IV. SCHEDULE IV TESTS. The commissioner shall place a substance in schedule IV if he finds that:

(a) The substance has a low potential for abuse relative to substances listed in schedule III of the current chapter 21, Code of Federal Regulations;

(b) The substance has currently accepted medical use in treatment in the United States; and

(c) Abuse of the substance may lead to limited physical dependence or psychological dependence relative to the substances in schedule III of the current chapter 21, Code of Federal Regulations.

V. SCHEDULE V TESTS. The commissioner shall place a substance in schedule V if he finds that:

(a) The substance has a low potential for abuse relative to substances listed in schedule IV of the current chapter 21, Code of Federal Regulations;

(b) The substance has currently accepted medical use in treatment in the United States; and

(c) The substance has limited physical dependence liability or psychological dependence liability relative to the substances in schedule IV of the current chapter 21, Code of Federal Regulations.

Source.
1985, 293:3. 1995, 310:183, eff. Nov. 1, 1995.

Amendments
—**1995.** Substituted "commissioner" for "director" in the introductory paragraph of pars. I–V.

Severability of 1995 amendment.
1995, 310, which amended this section, was subject to a severability clause. See 1995, 310:186.

Construction of 1995 amendment.
1995, 310:187, eff. Nov. 1, 1995, provided:
"Nothing in this act is intended to, nor shall it be construed as, mandating or assigning any new, expanded, or modified program or responsibility for any political subdivision in violation of part I, article 28-a of the constitution of the state of New Hampshire."

[RSA 318-B:1-c contingently repealed by 1998, 359:2; see contingent repeal note set out below.]

318-B:1-c. Flunitrazepam.

I. The legislature intends that the provisions of paragraph III of this section shall remain in effect until such time as flunitrazepam is scheduled by the commissioner of the department of human services in accordance with and pursuant to RSA 318-B.

II. The legislature finds that flunitrazepam, marketed under the trade name rohypnol, which has a sedative, hypnotic, and amnesiac effect, has no acceptable medical uses in the United States and carries a high potential for abuse. Therefore, flunitrazepam meets the criteria for placement on schedule I of controlled drugs.

III. Notwithstanding the provisions of RSA 318-B:1-a, relative to scheduling by rulemaking of the commissioner of the department of health and human services, flunitrazepam shall be scheduled as a schedule I controlled drug.

Source.
1998, 359:1, eff. June 26, 1998. 2005, 177:138, eff. July 1, 2005.

Amendments
—**2005.** Rewritten to the extent that a detailed comparison would be impracticable.

Contingent repeal of RSA 318-B:1-c.
1998, 359:2, eff. June 26, 1998, provided: "If the commissioner of health and human services chooses to schedule flunitrazepam, gamma-hydroxy-butyrate, or ketamine hydrochloride pursuant to an administrative rule adopted by the commissioner and pursuant to RSA 318-B, then the affected part of RSA 318-B:1-c as inserted by section 1 of this act, as it pertains to each individual substance so scheduled, shall be repealed at 12:01 a.m. the day after such substance is scheduled. The commissioner of the department of health and human services shall certify to the secretary of state the date on which flunitrazepam, gamma-hydroxy-butyrate, or ketamine hydrochloride is scheduled by rule."

318-B:2. Acts Prohibited.

I. It shall be unlawful for any person to manufacture, possess, have under his control, sell, purchase, prescribe, administer, or transport or possess with intent to sell, dispense, or compound any controlled drug, or controlled drug analog, or any preparation containing a controlled drug, except as authorized in this chapter.

I-a. It shall be unlawful for any person to manufacture, sell, purchase, transport or possess with intent to sell, dispense, compound, package or repackage (1) any substance which he represents to be a controlled drug or controlled drug analog, or (2) any preparation containing a substance which he represents to be a controlled drug or controlled drug analog, except as authorized in this chapter.

I-b. It shall be unlawful for a qualifying patient or designated caregiver as defined under RSA 126-W:1 to sell cannabis to another person who is not a qualifying patient or designated caregiver. A conviction for the sale of cannabis to a person who is not a qualifying patient or designated caregiver shall not preclude or limit a prosecution or conviction of any person for sale of cannabis or any other offense defined in this chapter.

II. It shall be unlawful for any person to deliver, possess with intent to deliver, or manufacture with intent to deliver, drug paraphernalia, knowing that it will be used or is customarily intended to be used to plant, propagate, cultivate, grow, harvest, manufacture, compound, convert, produce, process, prepare, test, analyze, pack, repack, store, contain, conceal, ingest, inhale, or otherwise introduce into the human body a controlled substance.

II-a. It shall be unlawful for any person, at retail, to sell or offer for sale any drug paraphernalia listed in RSA 318-B:1, X-a.

III. It shall be unlawful for any person to place in any newspaper, magazine, handbill, or other publication any advertisement, knowing that the purpose of the advertisement, when viewed as a whole, is to promote the sale of objects intended for use or customarily intended for use as drug paraphernalia.

IV. In determining whether an object is drug paraphernalia under this chapter, a court or other authority should consider, in addition to all other logically relevant factors, the following:

(a) Statements by an owner or by anyone in control of the object concerning its use;

(b) Prior convictions, if any, of an owner, or of anyone in control of the object, under any state or federal law relating to any controlled substance;

(c) The proximity of the object, in time and space, to a direct violation of this chapter;

(d) The proximity of any residue of controlled substances;

(e) The existence of any residue of controlled substances on the object;

(f) Direct or circumstantial evidence of the intent of an owner, or of anyone in control of the object, to deliver it to persons whom he knows intend to use the object to facilitate a violation of this chapter; the innocence of an owner, or of anyone in control of the object, as to a direct violation of this chapter shall not prevent a finding that the object is intended for use as drug paraphernalia;

(g) Instructions, oral or written, provided with the object concerning its use;

(h) Descriptive materials accompanying the object which explain or depict its use;

(i) National and local advertising concerning its use;

(j) The manner in which the object is displayed for sale;

(k) Direct or circumstantial evidence of the ratio of sales of the objects to the total sales of the business enterprise;

(l) Whether the object is customarily intended for use as drug paraphernalia and the existence and scope of other legitimate uses for the object in the community; and

(m) Expert testimony concerning its use.

V. No person shall obtain or attempt to obtain a controlled drug:

(a) By fraud, deceit, misrepresentation, or subterfuge;

(b) By the forgery or alteration of a prescription or of any written order;

(c) By the concealment of a material fact;

(d) By the use of a false name or the giving of a false address; or

(e) By submission of an electronic or on-line medical history form that fails to establish a valid practitioner-patient relationship.

VI. No person shall willfully make a false statement in any prescription, order, report, or record required hereby.

VII. No person shall, for the purpose of obtaining a controlled drug, falsely assume the title of, or represent himself to be, a manufacturer, wholesaler, pharmacist, practitioner, or other authorized person.

VIII. No person shall make or utter any false or forged prescription or false or forged written order.

IX. No person shall affix any false or forged label to a package or receptacle containing controlled drugs.

X. Possession of a false or forged prescription for a controlled drug by any person, other than a pharmacist in the pursuance of his profession, shall be prima facie evidence of his intent to use the same for the purpose of illegally obtaining a controlled drug.

XI. It shall be unlawful for any person 18 years of age or older to knowingly use, solicit, direct, hire or employ a person 17 years of age or younger to manufacture, sell, prescribe, administer, transport or possess with intent to sell, dispense or compound any controlled drug or any preparation containing a controlled drug, except as authorized in this chapter, or to manufacture, sell, transport or possess with intent to sell, dispense, compound, package or repackage (1) any substance which he represents to be a controlled drug or controlled drug analog, or (2) any preparation containing a substance which he represents to be a controlled drug or controlled drug analog, except as authorized in this chapter. It shall be no defense to a prosecution under this section that the actor mistakenly believed that the person who the actor used, solicited, directed, hired or employed was 18 years of age or older, even if such mistaken belief was reasonable. Nothing in this section shall be construed to preclude or limit a prosecution or conviction for a violation of any other offense defined in this chapter or any other provision of law governing an actor's liability for the conduct of another.

XII. A person is a drug enterprise leader if he conspires with one or more persons as an organizer, supervisor, financier, or manager to engage for profit in a scheme or course of conduct to unlawfully manufacture, sell, prescribe, administer, dispense, bring with or transport in this state methamphetamine, lysergic acid diethylamide, phencyclidine (PCP) or any controlled drug classified in schedule I or II, or any controlled drug analog thereof. A conviction as a drug enterprise leader shall not merge with the conviction for any offense which is the object of the conspiracy. Nothing in this section shall be construed to preclude or limit a prosecution or conviction of any person for conspiracy or any other offense defined in this chapter.

XII-a. It shall be unlawful for any person to knowingly acquire, obtain possession of or attempt to acquire or obtain possession of a controlled drug by misrepresentation, fraud, forgery, deception or subterfuge. This prohibition includes the situation in which a person independently consults 2 or more practitioners for treatment solely to obtain additional controlled drugs or prescriptions for controlled drugs.

XII-b. It shall be unlawful for any person to knowingly obtain, or attempt to obtain, or to assist a person in obtaining or attempting to obtain a prescription for a controlled substance without having formed a valid practitioner-patient relationship.

XII-c. It shall be unlawful for any person to, by written or electronic means, solicit, facilitate or enter into any agreement or contract to solicit or facilitate the dispensing of controlled substances pursuant to prescription orders that do not meet the federal and state requirements for a controlled drug prescription, and without an established valid practitioner-patient relationship.

XII-d. It shall be unlawful for any pharmacy to ship finished prescription products, containing controlled substances, to patients residing in the state of New Hampshire, pursuant to any oral, written or online prescription order that was generated based upon the patient's submission of an electronic or online medical history form. Such electronic or online medical questionnaires, even if followed by telephonic communication between practitioner and patient, shall not be deemed to form the basis of a valid practitioner-patient relationship.

XII-e. It shall be unlawful for any pharmacist to knowingly dispense a controlled substance pursuant to any oral, written, or electronic prescription order, which he or she knows or should have known, was generated based upon the patient's submission of an electronic or online medical history form. Such electronic or online medical questionnaires, even if followed by telephonic communication between practitioner and patient, shall not be deemed to form the basis of a valid practitioner-patient relationship.

XIII. Nothing in this section shall be deemed to preclude or limit a prosecution for theft as defined in RSA 637.

XIV. It shall be an affirmative defense to prosecution for a possession offense under this chapter that the person charged had a lawful prescription for the controlled drug in question or was, at the time charged, acting as an authorized agent for a person holding a lawful prescription. An authorized agent shall mean any person, including but not limited to a family member or caregiver, who has the intent to deliver the controlled drug to the person for whom the drug was lawfully prescribed.

XV. Persons who have lawfully obtained a controlled substance in accordance with this chapter or a person acting as an authorized agent for a person holding a lawful prescription for a controlled substance may deliver any unwanted or unused controlled substances to law enforcement officers acting within the scope of their employment and official duties for the purpose of collection, storage, and disposal of such controlled drugs in conjunction with a pharmaceutical drug take-back program established pursuant to RSA 318-E.

Source.
   1969, 421:1. 1977, 547:5. 1981, 513:2. 1983, 36:1; 292:1, 2. 1988, 6:2, 3. 1989, 207:1; 361:2, 3. 1990, 207:1; 361:2, 3. 1990, June 18, 1990. 2000, 176:5, eff. Jan. 1, 2001. 2008, 145:1, eff. January 1, 2009; 217:5, 6, eff. January 1, 2009. 2011, 63:5, eff. July 1, 2011. 2013, 242:3, eff. July 23, 2013.

Amendments
   —2013. The 2013 amendment added I-b.

   —2011. The 2011 amendment added XV.

   —2008. The 2008 amendment by Chapter 145 added XIV.
   The 2008 amendment by Chapter 217, added V(e) and made related changes; and added XII-b through XII-e.

   —2000. Paragraph II: Substituted "conceal" for "inject" preceding "ingest".

   —1990. Paragraph XII-a: Added.

   —1989. Paragraph II: Chapter 361 inserted "or is customarily intended to be used" preceding "to plant".
   Paragraph II-a: Added by ch. 361.
   Paragraph III: Chapter 361 inserted "or customarily intended for use" preceding "as drug paraphernalia".
   Paragraph IV(*l*): Chapter 361 added "whether the object is customarily intended for use as drug paraphernalia and" preceding "the existence" and inserted "other" preceding "legitimate".
   Paragraph XIII: Chapter 207 deleted the former first sentence.

   —1988. Paragraph I: Inserted "or controlled drug analog" preceding "or any preparation".
   Paragraph I-a: Inserted "or controlled drug analog" following "a controlled drug" in two places.
   Paragraphs XI–XIII: Added.

   —1983. Paragraph I-a: Added by ch. 36.
   Paragraph IV(d): Ch. 292:1 substituted "any residue of" for "the object to" preceding "controlled".
   Paragraphs V–X: Added by ch. 292:2.

   —1981. Designated the existing provision of the section as par. I and added pars. II–IV.

   —1977. Inserted "or transport or possess with intent to sell" following "administer".

Severability of 1989 amendment.
   1989, 361 was subject to a severability clause. See 1989, 361:4.

Severability of 1981 amendment.
   1981, 513:2 was subject to a severability clause. See 1981, 513:5.

Cross References.
   Affirmative defense to prosecution, see RSA 318-B:2-b.
   Exceptions generally, see RSA 318-B:15.
   Forgery generally, see RSA 638:1.
   Lawful possession of controlled drugs by individuals, see RSA 318-B:14.
   Lawful possession or control of controlled drugs generally, see RSA 318-B:6.
   Lawful sale and dispensation of controlled drugs by manufacturers or wholesalers, see RSA 318-B:5.
   Lawful sale and dispensation of controlled drugs by pharmacists, see RSA 318-B:9.
   Obtaining a drug that is to be sold or dispensed only by prescription through fraud or deceit, see RSA 318:52-a.
   Possession of a controlled drug while operating boat on public waters, see RSA 270:12-d.
   Possession, sale, etc., of hypodermic syringes, needles or other instruments adapted for administration of drugs, see RSA 318:52-c et seq.

NOTES TO DECISIONS

1.   Constitutionality
2.   Construction
3.   Elements
4.   Drug paraphernalia
5.   Controlled drugs
6.   Evidence
7.   Lesser-included offenses
8.   Obtaining of drugs by fraud, deceit, misrepresentation or subterfuge—Generally
9.   —Use of false drug enforcement administration number
10. Sentencing

1. Constitutionality

The language in paragraph II of this section is not void for vagueness under the due process clause of the fourteenth amendment in permitting prosecution of one person on the basis of the unknown intent of another; a fair reading of the section as a whole indicates that the intent referred to is that of the person alleged to have violated the section. New England Accessories Trade Asso. v. Nashua, 679 F.2d 1, 1982 U.S. App. LEXIS 18983 (1st Cir. N.H. 1982).

Paragraph II of this section is not void for vagueness under the due process clause for failure to provide proper standards for law enforcement officials to determine whether a merchant has intentionally sold drug paraphernalia to a customer knowing that it was going to be used with a controlled substance; the thirteen factors listed in paragraph IV of the section are not vague and confusing and consideration of the factors is not mandatory, but even assuming that the factors are considered and that some of them are part of the basis for a person's arrest and prosecution, that does not reduce in any way the state's burden of proving beyond a reasonable doubt that the accused intended to sell drug paraphernalia knowing that it was to be used by the customer with a controlled substance. New England Accessories Trade Asso. v. Nashua, 679 F.2d 1, 1982 U.S. App. LEXIS 18983 (1st Cir. N.H. 1982).

Paragraph III of this section does restrict the right to advertise; it is a limitation on commercial speech, to which the constitution accords a lesser protection than to other constitutionally guaranteed expression, the protection available turning on the nature both of the expression and of the governmental interests served by its regulation. New England Accessories Trade Asso. v. Nashua, 679 F.2d 1, 1982 U.S. App. LEXIS 18983 (1st Cir. N.H. 1982).

For commercial speech to come within the first amendment, it at least must concern lawful activity and not be misleading; paragraph III of this section forbids only advertisements which promote the sale of objects designed or intended for use as drug paraphernalia and does not reach speech which merely glorifies the drug culture without direct invitation to purchase specific items and, consequently, does not unconstitutionally impinge on first amendment rights. New England Accessories Trade Asso. v. Nashua, 679 F.2d 1, 1982 U.S. App. LEXIS 18983 (1st Cir. N.H. 1982).

Paragraph III of this section, making it illegal to place an advertisement promoting the sale of drug paraphernalia outside the state, even if the sale of drug paraphernalia is legal in jurisdictions outside the state, does not violate the first amendment of the federal constitution; the section, read as a whole, is aimed at conduct that is criminal in all jurisdictions—the ingestion of illegal drugs into the human body—and the advertisement proscribed promotes activity which has been determined to be criminal in all jurisdictions. New England Accessories Trade Asso. v. Nashua, 679 F.2d 1, 1982 U.S. App. LEXIS 18983 (1st Cir. N.H. 1982).

2. Construction

Since this section used plain and unambiguous language, it was not subject to judicial modification. State v. Pike, 134 N.H. 690, 597 A.2d 1071, 1991 N.H. LEXIS 120 (1991).

Where this section displayed no contrary intent to exclude "unusable" or "immeasurable" amounts from definition of "controlled drug," imposition of such qualifiers would be an impermissible judicial construction; possession of any quantity of a controlled substance, sufficient to permit proper identification, is prohibited. State v. Pike, 134 N.H. 690, 597 A.2d 1071, 1991 N.H. LEXIS 120 (1991).

3. Elements

The precise time of defendant's knowledge of the possession is not a necessary element of the offense of possession of a controlled substance. State v. Donovan, 128 N.H. 702, 519 A.2d 252, 1986 N.H. LEXIS 365 (1986).

The identity of the purchaser is not a material element of the offense of selling of a controlled drug. State v. Bell, 125 N.H. 425, 480 A.2d 906, 1984 N.H. LEXIS 253 (1984).

4. Drug paraphernalia

Items used in defendant's trial for sale of drug paraphernalia had to be returned to defendant under RSA 595-A:6 as they were not contraband under RSA 318-B:2, II, II-a where: (1) none of the items seized were alleged to be "designed for use" with controlled substances, (2) the items were not contraband under federal law from the time they were manufactured, (3) defendant was acquitted of all pending charges, (4) the State made clear to defendant after a prior prosecution that there were six specific categories of items that it could not sell, and returned to defendant certain glass pipes and

other items, and (5) the State then reversed course and prosecuted defendant for items virtually indistinguishable from many of the items returned to defendant after the first prosecution. State v. Smoke Signals Pipe & Tobacco Shop, LLC, 155 N.H. 234, 922 A.2d 634, 2007 N.H. LEXIS 53 (2007).

The mere possession of an item of drug paraphernalia, without an intent to deliver, is not a crime. State v. Berthiaume, 124 N.H. 264, 470 A.2d 893, 1983 N.H. LEXIS 421 (1983).

5. Controlled drugs

The reference in paragraph I of this section to a controlled drug refers to the same narcotic controlled drugs that fall within the scope of RSA 318-B:26, I. State v. Stiles, 128 N.H. 81, 512 A.2d 1084, 1986 N.H. LEXIS 289 (1986).

Possession, or possession with intent to sell, of cocaine of any isomer is a felony under this chapter. State v. Stiles, 128 N.H. 81, 512 A.2d 1084, 1986 N.H. LEXIS 289 (1986).

6. Evidence

Trial court properly denied defendant's motion to dismiss a charge of possession of a controlled drug commonly known as "ecstasy," in violation of RSA 318-B:2, I, as the evidence was sufficient to prove both that defendant possessed the ecstasy and that he knew of its presence. State v. Trebian, 164 N.H. 629, 63 A.3d 1205, 2013 N.H. LEXIS 18 (2013).

There was sufficient evidence that defendant had constructive possession of crack cocaine. The cocaine was in a cigarette box found between the driver's seat and the center console of the car which defendant was driving; additionally, several of his possessions were located near the crack cocaine, including his black bag containing drug paraphernalia State v. Tabaldi, — N.H. —, — A.3d —, 2013 N.H. LEXIS 102 (Oct. 1, 2013).

Evidence that a prescription bottle contained the named prescription and 113 tablets of oxycodone and that defendant first stated he did not know where the drugs had come from, but later claimed that the prescription belonged to his wife and he would been in trouble for having it supported defendant's conviction for possession of a controlled drug. State v. Drake, 155 N.H. 169, 921 A.2d 403, 2007 N.H. LEXIS 44 (2007).

Where the process of randomly selecting packets of contraband for testing was accepted in the scientific community, the chemical testing methods were consistent with those used in the scientific community, and the tested and untested samples were similar in both appearance and packaging, there was sufficient reliability to permit the admission of the untested packets; a reasonable inference could be drawn about both the contents and weight of the untested packets. State v. Tucker, 149 N.H. 792, 837 A.2d 1078, 2003 N.H. LEXIS 127 (2003).

Although a search of defendant was not a permissible extension of an initial investigatory stop, defendant's subsequent consent to a search of defendant's person was not based on "flagrant" conduct by the police and extended to a search of defendant's knapsack where evidence of illegal drugs was found. State v. Szczerbiak, 148 N.H. 352, 807 A.2d 1219, 2002 N.H. LEXIS 136 (2002).

Trial court did not err in concluding that evidence of drug defendant's unexplained wealth was relevant, where this evidence was linked with other evidence showing existence of conspiracies to sell drugs, and it thus tended to increase probability that charged conspiracies existed. State v. Sonthikoummane, 145 N.H. 316, 769 A.2d 330, 2000 N.H. LEXIS 64 (2000).

Trial court did not err in refusing to admit, as irrelevant, expert testimony regarding medicinal use of marijuana, where testimony had been offered to support defendant's attempt to obtain jury nullification. State v. Hokanson, 140 N.H. 719, 672 A.2d 714, 1996 N.H. LEXIS 18 (1996).

Drug evidence is generally fungible, especially where State offers no proof that marked bags are sealed such that tampering would be evident; however, precision in developing "chain of custody" is not an iron-clad requirement, and fact of a missing link does not prevent admission of real evidence, particularly where defendant produces no evidence of alteration or other foul play. State v. Moscillo, 139 N.H. 79, 649 A.2d 57, 1994 N.H. LEXIS 110 (1994).

Out-of-court statements by co-conspirators are admissible as exceptions to hearsay rule when made during pendency of the criminal enterprise and in furtherance of the criminal object, as long as existence of conspiracy is sufficiently proved by independent evidence. State v. Gonzalez, 136 N.H. 354, 615 A.2d 640, 1992 N.H. LEXIS 177 (1992).

State made prima facie case that defendant was conspiracy member, ensuring that statements by co-conspirator were allowable as hearsay exceptions, where trooper testified that defendant was recognized by person in conspiracy and defendant committed overt acts in furtherance of conspiracy. State v. Gonzalez, 136 N.H. 354, 615 A.2d 640, 1992 N.H. LEXIS 177 (1992).

At trial for sale or possession of a controlled substance, state produced sufficient evidence to support admission into evidence of infrared spectrophotometer test results showing the presence and identity of a controlled substance, notwithstanding laboratory's failure to keep calibration logs, where evidence as to standard laboratory procedures and machine's internal checking mechanism supported inference of its accuracy, and where the logic of the test indicated any error of miscalibration would only benefit the defendant. State v. Lee, 134 N.H. 392, 593 A.2d 235, 1991 N.H. LEXIS 73 (1991).

Proof of intent to distribute a controlled substance does not require possession of some minimum quantity as a matter of law. State v. Cartier, 133 N.H. 217, 575 A.2d 347, 1990 N.H. LEXIS 54 (1990).

At trial for possession of controlled drugs and possession with intent to distribute, status of marijuana or cocaine as a controlled drug was an issue of law for the court, and there was therefore no occasion to present evidence on these points to the jury. State v. Cartier, 133 N.H. 217, 575 A.2d 347, 1990 N.H. LEXIS 54 (1990).

Where defendant was one of two occupants of premises where controlled drugs were found, proof of joint possession of the drugs was sufficient for a possession conviction. State v. Cartier, 133 N.H. 217, 575 A.2d 347, 1990 N.H. LEXIS 54 (1990).

7. Lesser-included offenses

Where defendant was charged with misdemeanor transportation of a controlled drug and felony possession of a controlled drug, conviction on the felony possession charge was barred by double jeopardy since the possession charge lacked any element not common to the transportation charge, and, therefore, was a lesser-included offense of the transportation charge. State v. Constant, 135 N.H. 254, 605 A.2d 206, 1992 N.H. LEXIS 17 (1992).

8. Obtaining of drugs by fraud, deceit, misrepresentation or subterfuge—Generally

The clear purpose of paragraph V of this section, which prohibits any person from obtaining or attempting to obtain controlled drugs by "fraud, deceit, misrepresentation or subterfuge", is to proscribe the obtaining of controlled substances through untruthfulness or nondisclosure, regardless of whether the means employed constitutes "fraud", "deceit", "misrepresentation" or "subterfuge" in the technical sense. (Decided under former RSA 318-B:20.)

In a prosecution for obtaining a controlled drug through fraud, deceit, misrepresentation or other subterfuge, the state need not prove all the technical elements of fraud, deceit or misrepresentation in order to establish the guilt of the defendant; rather, it is sufficient to establish that the defendant obtained or attempted to obtain controlled drugs through trickery, nondisclosure or any other subterfuge. (Decided under former RSA 318-B:20.)

In a prosecution for obtaining or attempting to obtain a controlled drug by fraud, where the defendant, whether or not he knew that the drug purchased was a controlled drug, did have knowledge that he could not obtain it without a prescription and that he could not have the prescription refilled without returning to a physician, and employed a scheme designed solely to circumvent this procedure, the evidence clearly demonstrated the defendant's fraudulent intent in obtaining the drug. (Decided under former RSA 318-B:20.)

Where the evidence indicated that the defendant, who photocopied a prescription for a controlled substance, did so because he knew that if he presented the original to a pharmacist, it would be retained by the pharmacist and because he wished to obtain more of the substance without returning to see the prescribing physician, the evidence demonstrated the defendant's intent to obtain unauthorized amounts of a controlled substance through trickery and nondisclosure. State v. Basinow, 121 N.H. 815, 435 A.2d 829, 1981 N.H. LEXIS 414 (1981)(Decided under former RSA 318-B:20.)

9. —Use of false drug enforcement administration number

Obtaining controlled drugs by knowing use of a false Drug Enforcement Administration number violates this section, even if the accused is a doctor or practitioner in another state.

Evidence that the defendant gave a false Drug Enforcement Administration number to a pharmacist, and that no number had been issued to him, was sufficient to support a finding that he was not a practitioner authorized to prescribe drugs in this or any other state.

10. Sentencing

After defendant was placed on probation for possession of a controlled drug, under RSA 318-B:2, a class B felony, and his violation of probation was found, to the extent the term of his probation was extended beyond five years, the trial court's judgment was plain error, under N.H. Sup. Ct. R. 16-A, because a term of probation exceeding the five-year maximum allowable under RSA 651:2, V(a) was illegal.

Cited:

Cited in State v. Harlow, 123 N.H. 547, 465 A.2d 1210, 1983 N.H. LEXIS 320 (1983); State v. Toto, 123 N.H. 619, 465 A.2d 894, 1983 N.H. LEXIS 344 (1983); State v. Miskolczi, 123 N.H. 626, 465 A.2d 919, 1983 N.H. LEXIS 325 (1983); State v. Berger, 125 N.H. 83, 480 A.2d 27, 1984 N.H. LEXIS 366 (1984); State v. Mayo, 125 N.H. 200, 480 A.2d 85, 1984 N.H. LEXIS 255 (1984); State v. Desmond, 125 N.H. 448, 480 A.2d 208, 1984 N.H. LEXIS 248 (1984); State v. Kelly, 125 N.H. 484, 484 A.2d 1066, 1984 N.H. LEXIS 410 (1984); State v. Smith, 125 N.H. 522, 484 A.2d 1091, 1984 N.H. LEXIS 402 (1984); State v. Pinder, 126 N.H. 220, 489 A.2d 653, 1985 N.H. LEXIS 252 (1985); State v. Farnsworth, 126 N.H. 656, 497 A.2d 835, 1985 N.H. LEXIS 421 (1985); State v. Ruffing, 127 N.H. 370, 499 A.2d 1351, 1985 N.H. LEXIS 431 (1985); State v. Grote, 127 N.H. 748, 506 A.2d 346, 1986 N.H. LEXIS 218 (1986); State v. Pinder, 128 N.H. 66, 514 A.2d 1241, 1986 N.H. LEXIS 313 (1986); State v. Varagianis, 128 N.H. 226, 512 A.2d 1117, 1986 N.H. LEXIS 265 (1986); State v. De Grenier, 128 N.H. 547, 517 A.2d 814, 1986 N.H. LEXIS 349 (1986); State v. Cyrs, 129 N.H. 497, 529 A.2d 947, 1987 N.H. LEXIS 209 (1987); State v. Richards, 129 N.H. 669, 531 A.2d 338, 1987 N.H. LEXIS 241 (1987); State v. Torres, 130 N.H. 340, 540 A.2d 1217, 1988 N.H. LEXIS 11 (1988); State v. Svoleantopoulos, 130 N.H. 471, 543 A.2d 410, 1988 N.H. LEXIS 24 (1988); State v. Cannata, 130 N.H. 545, 543 A.2d 421, 1988 N.H. LEXIS 21 (1988); State v. Ramos, 131 N.H. 276, 553 A.2d 275, 1988 N.H. LEXIS 133 (1988); State v. Gigas, 131 N.H. 389, 553 A.2d 321, 1988 N.H. LEXIS 123 (1988); Grote v. Powell, 132 N.H. 96, 562 A.2d 152, 1989 N.H. LEXIS 70 (1989); State v. Turmelle, 132 N.H. 148, 562 A.2d 196, 1989 N.H. LEXIS 78 (1989); State v. Stratton, 132 N.H. 451, 567 A.2d 986, 1989 N.H. LEXIS 124 (1989); State v. Hartford, 132 N.H. 580, 567 A.2d 577, 1989 N.H. LEXIS 137 (1989); State v. Gallant, 133 N.H. 138, 574 A.2d 385, 1990 N.H. LEXIS 44 (1990); State v. Davis, 133 N.H. 211, 575 A.2d 4, 1990 N.H. LEXIS 49 (1990); State v. Monsalve, 133 N.H. 268, 574 A.2d 1384, 1990 N.H. LEXIS 60 (1990); State v. Gooden, 133 N.H. 674, 582 A.2d 607, 1990 N.H. LEXIS 120 (1990); State v. Kennison, 134 N.H. 243, 590 A.2d 1099, 1991 N.H. LEXIS 52 (1991); State v. Favreau, 134 N.H. 336, 592 A.2d 1136, 1991 N.H. LEXIS 63 (1991); State v. Plante, 134 N.H. 585, 594 A.2d 165, 1991 N.H. LEXIS 106 (1991); State v. Diaz, 134 N.H. 662, 596 A.2d 725, 1991 N.H. LEXIS 116 (1991); State v. Caicedo, 135 N.H. 122, 599 A.2d 895, 1991 N.H. LEXIS 149 (1991); State v. Dodier, 135 N.H. 134, 600 A.2d 913, 1991 N.H. LEXIS 152 (1991); State v. Murray, 135 N.H. 369, 605 A.2d 676, 1992 N.H. LEXIS 41 (1992); State v. Christensen, 135 N.H. 583, 607 A.2d 952, 1992 N.H. LEXIS 84 (1992); State v. Silvestri, 136 N.H. 522, 618 A.2d 821, 1992 N.H. LEXIS 203 (1992); State v. Lamontagne, 136 N.H. 575, 618 A.2d 849, 1992 N.H. LEXIS 200 (1992); State v. Coons, 137 N.H. 365, 627 A.2d 1064, 1993 N.H. LEXIS 91 (1993); State v. Marcano, 138 N.H. 643, 645 A.2d 661, 1994 N.H. LEXIS 82 (1994); State v. Moscillo, 139 N.H. 79, 649 A.2d 57, 1994 N.H. LEXIS 110 (1994); State v. Canelo, 139 N.H. 376, 653 A.2d 1097, 1995 N.H. LEXIS 3 (1995); State v. Puzzanghera, 140 N.H. 105, 663 A.2d 94, 1995 N.H. LEXIS 104 (1995); Diamontopoulas v. State, 140 N.H. 182, 664 A.2d 81, 1995 N.H. LEXIS 122 (1995); State v. Westover, 140 N.H. 375, 666 A.2d 1344, 1995 N.H. LEXIS 159 (1995); State v. Johnson, 140 N.H. 573, 669 A.2d 222, 1995 N.H. LEXIS 194 (1995); State v. Guenzel, 140 N.H. 685, 671 A.2d 545,

1996 N.H. LEXIS 14 (1996); State v. Taylor, 142 N.H. 6, 694 A.2d 977, 1997 N.H. LEXIS 49 (1997); State v. Daniel, 142 N.H. 54, 694 A.2d 989, 1997 N.H. LEXIS 54 (1997); State v. Fish, 142 N.H. 524, 703 A.2d 1377, 1997 N.H. LEXIS 124 (1997); State v. Tinkham, 143 N.H. 73, 719 A.2d 580, 1998 N.H. LEXIS 69 (1998); State v. Gonzalez, 143 N.H. 693, 738 A.2d 1247, 1999 N.H. LEXIS 59 (1999); Vasquez v. Warden, 2002 U.S. Dist. LEXIS 20982 (D.N.H. 2002); State v. MacElman, 149 N.H. 795, 834 A.2d 322, 2003 N.H. LEXIS 128 (2003); State v. McKinnon-Andrews, 151 N.H. 19, 846 A.2d 1198, 2004 N.H. LEXIS 82 (2004).

RESEARCH REFERENCES

Criminal Jury Instructions.
New Hampshire Criminal Jury Instructions, Instruction ## 2.33, 2.38.

New Hampshire Trial Bar News.
For article, "Presumptions in New Hampshire Law—A Guide Through the Impenetrable Jungle (Part 1)," see 10 N.H. Trial Bar News 55, 60 n.82 (Winter 1990).

318-B:2-a. Exception.

[Repealed 1994, 333:34, eff. Jan. 1, 1995.]

Former section(s).
Former RSA 318-B:2-a, which was derived from 1977, 547:6 and 1983, 292:3, related to conditions for possession of controlled drugs by advanced registered nurse practitioners.

318-B:2-b. Counterfeit Drugs; Affirmative Defense.

It is an affirmative defense to prosecution under RSA 318-B:2, I-a that the actor is:

I. A physician or advanced practice registered nurse who sells, dispenses, or prescribes a substance which he represents to be or contain a controlled drug, but which in fact neither is nor contains a controlled drug, to a patient under his care for a bona fide therapeutic purpose; or

II. A pharmacist who sells or dispenses a substance which he represents to be or contain a controlled drug, but which in fact neither is nor contains a controlled drug, to a person at the direction of and upon the written prescription of an attending physician or advanced practice registered nurse, provided any written prescription is properly executed, dated, and signed by the person prescribing on the day when issued and bears the full name and address of the patient for whom the drug is dispensed; or

III. A nurse or intern who, at the explicit direction of and under the supervision of an attending physician, administers a substance which he represents to be or contain a controlled drug, but which in fact neither is nor contains a controlled drug, to a patient for a bona fide therapeutic purpose; or

IV. An advanced emergency medical care provider who, upon receipt directly or by phone or by radio or by other communication medium of directions to do so from the supervising physician or an emergency/trauma advanced practice registered nurse, administers a substance which he represents to be or to contain a controlled drug, but which in fact neither

is nor contains a controlled drug, to a patient for a bona fide therapeutic purpose.

Source.
1983, 36:2. 1992, 48:7. 1994, 333:20, eff. Jan. 1, 1995. 2009, 54:5, eff. July 21, 2009.

Amendments
—2009. The 2009 amendment substituted "advanced practice registered nurse" for "advanced registered nurse practitioner" in I, II, and IV.

—1994. Inserted "or advanced registered nurse practitioner" following "physician" in pars. I and II and "or an emergency/trauma advanced registered nurse practitioner" following "physician" in par. IV.

—1992. Paragraph IV: Inserted "advanced" preceding "emergency" and substituted "care provider" for "technician-paramedic" following "medical".

Cross References.
Necessity not necessary for negation of exceptions, exemptions or provisos in prosecutions under chapter, see RSA 318-B:22.

318-B:3. Licensing of Manufacturers and Wholesalers Required.

No person shall manufacture controlled drugs, and no person as a wholesaler shall supply the same, without first having obtained a license to do so as provided in RSA 318:51-a.

Source.
1969, 421:1. 1973, 198:1. 1985, 324:19. 1990, 129:3, eff. June 18, 1990.

Amendments
—1990. Inserted "and" following "manufacture controlled drugs" and deleted "and no professional association or corporation engaged in the practice of medicine or pharmacy or both shall possess or dispense controlled drugs" preceding "without".

—1985. Deleted "group" preceding "practice of medicine" and inserted "or pharmacy or both" thereafter and substituted "first having" for "having first" and "as provided in RSA 318:51-a" for "from the division of public health services of the department of health and welfare" following "license to do so".

—1973. Rewritten to the extent that a detailed comparison would be impracticable.

Cross References.
Offenses generally, see RSA 318-B:2.
Sales by licensees generally, see RSA 318-B:5.

318-B:4. Licenses.

[Repealed 1985, 324:25, eff. Jan. 1, 1986.]

Former section(s).
Former RSA 318-B:4, which was derived from 1969, 421:1; 1977, 563:56; and 1982, 42:6, related to the issuing of licenses and applicable requirements.

318-B:5. Sale by Manufacturer or Wholesaler.

A duly licensed manufacturer or wholesaler may sell and dispense controlled drugs only to any of the following persons, and only on official written orders:

I. To a manufacturer, wholesaler, or pharmacist.

II. To a practitioner.

III. To that person in each hospital designated as in charge of controlled drugs, but only for use by that hospital, pursuant to the restrictions of the board of pharmacy license.

IV. To that person in each laboratory designated as in charge of controlled drugs, but only for use in that laboratory for scientific and medical purposes.

V. To a person in the employ of the United States government or of any state, territorial, district, county, municipal, or insular government purchasing, receiving, possessing, or dispensing controlled drugs by reason of his official duties, upon an exempt official order form as required by the Comprehensive Drug Abuse Prevention and Control Act of 1970, as amended.

VI. To a master of a ship or a person in charge of any aircraft upon which no physician is regularly employed, or to a physician or surgeon, duly licensed in some state, territory, or the District of Columbia to practice his profession, or to a retired commissioned medical officer of the United States Army, Navy, or Public Health Service employed upon such ship or aircraft for the medical needs of persons on board such ship or aircraft, or to a physician, surgeon, or retired commissioned medical officer of the United States Army, Navy, or Public Health Service employed upon such ship or aircraft only in pursuance of a special order form approved by the Attorney General of the United States.

VII. To a person in a foreign country if the provisions of the Comprehensive Drug Abuse Prevention and Control Act of 1970, as amended, are complied with.

Source.
1969, 421:1. 1977, 547:7, 8. 1983, 292:4, eff. Aug. 17, 1983.

References in text.
The Comprehensive Drug Abuse Prevention and Control Act of 1970, referred to in pars. V and VII, is classified principally to 42 U.S.C.S. §§ 218, 246, 4541.

Revision note.
At the end of par. VI, substituted "the Attorney General of the United States" for "a commissioned medical officer or acting assistant surgeon of the United States Public Health Service". Written order forms for distribution of controlled substances are prescribed and issued by the Attorney General of the United States pursuant to 21 U.S.C.S. § 828.

Amendments
—1983. Rewritten to the extent that a detailed comparison would be impracticable.

—1977. Paragraph V: Substituted "the Comprehensive Drug Abuse Prevention and Control Act of 1970" for "federal narcotics laws".

Paragraph VII: Substituted "Comprehensive Drug Abuse Prevention and Control Act of 1970" for "federal narcotic laws".

Cross References.
License requirements generally, see RSA 318-B:3.
Restrictions on use of controlled drugs by authorized possessors, see RSA 318-B:6, 8.

NOTES TO DECISIONS

Cited:
Cited in State v. Nickerson, 114 N.H. 47, 314 A.2d 648, 1974 N.H. LEXIS 205 (1974).

318-B:6. Possession Lawful.

Possession of or control of controlled drugs obtained as authorized shall be lawful if in the regular course of business, occupation, profession, employment, or duty of the possessor. A person who obtains controlled drugs under the provisions of RSA 318-B:5 or otherwise shall not administer, dispense, or otherwise use such drugs within the state, except within the scope of his employment or official duty, and then only for scientific or medical purposes and subject to the provisions of this chapter.

Source.
1969, 421:1. 1983, 292:5, eff. Aug. 17, 1983.

Amendments
—1983. Deleted "by section 5" following "authorized" in the first sentence and added the second sentence.

Cross References.
Offenses generally, see RSA 318-B:2.
Restrictions generally, see RSA 318-B:8.

NOTES TO DECISIONS

Cited:
Cited in State v. Nickerson, 114 N.H. 47, 314 A.2d 648, 1974 N.H. LEXIS 205 (1974).

318-B:7. Written Orders.

An official written order for any controlled drug in schedule II shall be signed in triplicate by the person giving said order or by his duly authorized agent. The original shall be presented to the person who sells or dispenses the controlled drug or drugs named therein. In the event of the acceptance of such order by said person, each party to the transaction shall preserve his copy of such order for a period of 2 years in such a way as to be readily accessible for inspection by any public officer or employee engaged in the enforcement of this chapter. It shall be deemed compliance with this section if the parties to the transaction have complied with the Comprehensive Drug Abuse Prevention and Control Act of 1970, as amended, or the federal food and drug laws, respecting the requirements governing the use of order forms.

Source.
1969, 421:1. 1977, 547:9. 1983, 292:6. 1985, 293:4, eff. Aug. 13, 1985.

References in text.
The Comprehensive Drug Abuse Prevention and Control Act of 1970, referred to in this section, is classified principally to 42 U.S.C.S. §§ 218, 246, 4541.

The federal food and drug laws, referred to in this section, are classified principally to 21 U.S.C.S. §§ 301 et seq.

Amendments

—1985. Deleted "of the current chapter 21, Code of Federal Regulations" following "schedule II" in the first sentence.

—1983. Deleted "narcotic" preceding "drug" and inserted "in schedule II of the current chapter 21, Code of Federal Regulations" thereafter in the first sentence and inserted "the" preceding "event" in the third sentence and "as amended" following "1970" in the fourth sentence.

—1977. Substituted "Comprehensive Drug Abuse Prevention and Control Act of 1970" for "federal narcotic laws" in the fourth sentence.

Cross References.

Forms for written orders for controlled substances generally, see 21 U.S.C.S. § 828.

Schedules of controlled substances generally, see 21 U.S.C.S. § 812.

318-B:8. Limitation on Use.

A person in charge of controlled drugs in a hospital or of a laboratory, or in the employ of this state or of any other state or of any political subdivision thereof, or a master of a ship or a person in charge of any aircraft upon which no physician is regularly employed, or a physician or surgeon duly licensed in some state, territory, or the District of Columbia to practice his profession, or a retired commissioned medical officer of the United States Army, Navy, or Public Health Service employed upon such ship or aircraft who obtains controlled drugs under the provisions of RSA 318-B:5, or otherwise, shall not administer, nor dispense, nor otherwise use such drugs within the state, except within the scope of his employment or official duty, and then only for scientific or medical purposes and subject to the provisions of this chapter.

Source.

1969, 421:1, eff. Aug. 31, 1969.

Cross References.

Restrictions generally, see RSA 318-B:6.

NOTES TO DECISIONS

Cited:

Cited in State v. Nickerson, 114 N.H. 47, 314 A.2d 648, 1974 N.H. LEXIS 205 (1974).

318-B:9. Sale by Pharmacists.

I. A pharmacist, in good faith and in the course of his or her professional practice, may sell and dispense controlled drugs exempt under the Comprehensive Drug Abuse Prevention and Control Act of 1970, as amended, and federal food and drug laws from prescription requirements. A pharmacist, in good faith, may sell and dispense controlled drugs requiring prescriptions to any person upon the written or electronically transmitted prescription of a practitioner, provided it is properly executed, dated and when required by law, manually or electronically signed by the person prescribing on the day when issued and bears the full name and address of the patient for whom, or of the owner of the animal for which, the drug is dispensed, or upon oral prescription, in pursuance of regulations promulgated by the Department of Justice of the United States, under the provisions of the Comprehensive Drug Abuse Prevention and Control Act of 1970, as amended where applicable, provided said oral prescription is promptly reduced to writing by the pharmacist or authorized technician, stating the name of the practitioner so prescribing, the date, the full name and address of the patient for whom, or the owner of the animal for which, the drug is dispensed, and, in all instances, the full name, address and registry number under the Comprehensive Drug Abuse Prevention and Control Act of 1970, as amended, or federal food and drug laws of the person so prescribing. If the prescription is for an animal, it shall state the species of animal for which the drug is prescribed. The person filling the prescription shall indicate the date of filling and his or her name on the face or record of the prescription. The prescription shall be retained on file by the proprietor of the pharmacy in which it is filled for a period of 4 years so as to be readily accessible for the inspection of any officers engaged in the enforcement of this chapter. The prescription as to a controlled drug may be refilled pursuant to the Comprehensive Drug Abuse Prevention and Control Act of 1970, as amended. The person refilling a prescription for a controlled drug shall record on the prescription record the date of refill, the quantity dispensed, and his or her initials.

II. The legal owner of any stock of controlled drugs in a pharmacy, upon discontinuance of dealing in said drugs, may sell said stock to a manufacturer, wholesaler, or registered pharmacy but only upon an official written order, and in accordance with the Comprehensive Drug Abuse Prevention and Control Act of 1970, as amended, and regulations where applicable. A licensed pharmacy only upon an official written order may sell controlled drugs in schedule II to a practitioner to be used for medical purposes.

III. Prescriptions issued by practitioners for controlled drugs shall be executed in clear, concise, readable form. Each prescription shall contain the following information and comply with the following requirements:

(a) The full name and complete address of the patient or of the owner of the animal for which the drug is prescribed.

(b) The day, month, and year the prescription is issued.

(c) The name of the controlled drug prescribed. Only one controlled drug shall appear on a prescription blank.

(d) The strength of the controlled drug prescribed.

(e) The specific directions for use of the controlled drug by the patient.

(f) No refills shall be authorized for controlled drugs in schedule II of the current chapter 21, Code of Federal Regulations.

(g) The federal Drug Enforcement Administration registration number of the practitioner.

(h) The practitioner shall manually or electronically sign the prescription on the date of issuance.

(i) The practitioner's full name shall be printed, rubber stamped, or typewritten above or below the manual or electronic signature.

(j) A practitioner shall not issue a prescription in order to obtain controlled substances for the purpose of general dispensing to his or her patients.

(k) A practitioner shall not issue a prescription to himself or herself or his or her immediate family which includes a spouse, children or parents.

(*l*) A prescription shall be deemed invalid if it is not filled within 6 months from the date prescribed.

IV. No prescription shall be filled for more than a 34-day supply upon any single filling for controlled drugs of schedules II or III; provided, however, that for controlled drugs, in schedules II or III, that are commercially packaged for dispensing directly to the patient, such as metered sprays and inhalers, liquids packaged in bottles with calibrated droppers, and certain topical preparations packaged with metered dispensing pumps may be filled for greater than a 34-day supply, but not more than 60 days, utilizing the smallest available product size, in order to maintain the dosing integrity of the commercially packaged containers; and, provided that with regard to amphetamines and methylphenidate hydrochloride, a prescription may be filled for up to a 60-day supply if either such prescription specifies it is being used for the treatment of attention deficit disorder, attention deficit disorder with hyperactivity, or narcolepsy.

V. Notwithstanding the provisions of RSA 318-B:26, it shall be a misdemeanor for a practitioner to issue or a pharmacist to fill a prescription that does not meet the requirements of this section.

VI. A pharmacist employed by a pharmacy located in a hospital may dispense cannabis-type drugs prescribed under RSA 318-B:10, VI, to any person upon the written prescription of an attending physician, provided it is properly executed, dated, and signed by the person prescribing on the day when issued and bears the full name and address of the patient for whom the drug is dispensed. The pharmacist filling the prescription shall write the date of filling and his own signature on the face of the prescription.

Source.
1969, 421:1. 1977, 547:10. 1979, 398:5. 1981, 107:2; 226:1–3. 1983, 292:7. 1985, 293:5, 6, eff. Aug. 13, 1985. 1997, 30:1, eff. June 24, 1997. 2005, 177:136, 137, eff. July 1, 2005. 2008, 222:1, eff. January 1, 2009.

References in text.
The Comprehensive Drug Abuse Prevention and Control Act of 1970, referred to in pars. I and II, is classified principally to 21 U.S.C.S. §§ 801 et seq.
The federal food and drug laws, referred to in par. I, are classified principally to 21 U.S.C.S. §§ 301 et seq.
—**2008.** The 2008 amendment in IV, deleted "or 100 dosage units, whichever is less" following "34-day supply" and added "for controlled drugs...and, provided that".

—**2005.** Paragraph I: Inserted "or her" following "his" in the first sentence, "or electronically transmitted" following "written", "when required by law, manually or electronically" preceding "signed" and "or authorized technician" following "pharmacist" in the second sentence, substituted "indicate" for "write" following "shall" and "or her name" for "own signature" and inserted "or record" following "face" in the third sentence, and inserted "record" following "prescription" and "or her" following "his" in the last sentence.
Paragraph III: Substituted "issued" for "written" and deleted "and may be typewritten" following "readable form" in the first sentence of the introductory paragraph, inserted "manually or electronically" and deleted "in ink" following "prescription" in subpar. (h), substituted "manual or electronic" for "hand-written" in subpar. (i), inserted "or her" following "his" in subpar. (j), and "or herself" and "or her" in subpar. (k).

—**1997.** Paragraph IV: Substituted "amphetamines and methylphenidate hydrochloride" for "dextro amphetamine sulphate and methyl phenidate hydrochloride" and "attention deficit disorder, attention deficit disorder with hyperactivity" for "minimum brain dysfunction".

—**1985.** Paragraph II: Substituted "licensed" for "registered" preceding "pharmacy" in the second sentence and deleted "of the current chapter 21, Code of Federal Regulations" following "schedule II" in that sentence.
Paragraph IV: Deleted "of the current chapter 21, Code of Federal Regulations" preceding "provided".

—**1983.** Rewritten to the extent that a detailed comparison would be impracticable.

—**1981.** Paragraph III: Repealed by ch. 226:3.
Paragraph IV(f): Rewritten by ch. 226:1 to the extent that a detailed comparison would be impracticable.
Paragraph V: Rewritten by ch. 226:2 to the extent that a detailed comparison would be impracticable.
Paragraph VII: Added by ch. 107.

—**1979.** Paragraphs III–VI: Added.

—**1977.** Rewritten to the extent that a detailed comparison would be impracticable.

Cross References.
Affirmative defense to prosecution under RSA 318-B:2, I-a, see RSA 318-B:2-b.
Classification of crimes, see RSA 625:9.
Labeling of controlled drugs and packages generally, see RSA 318-B:13.
Offenses generally, see RSA 318-B:2.
Regulation of pharmacists and pharmacies generally, see RSA 318.
Scheduling of controlled drugs generally, see RSA 318-B:1-a.
Sentences, see RSA 651.

NOTES TO DECISIONS

Cited:
Cited in State v. Nickerson, 114 N.H. 47, 314 A.2d 648, 1974 N.H. LEXIS 205 (1974); State v. Basinow, 121 N.H. 815, 435 A.2d 829, 1981 N.H. LEXIS 414 (1981); State v. Bell, 125 N.H. 425, 480 A.2d

906, 1984 N.H. LEXIS 253 (1984); State v. Summers, 142 N.H. 429, 702 A.2d 819, 1997 N.H. LEXIS 115 (1997).

318-B:10. Professional Use of Narcotic Drugs.

I. A practitioner other than a veterinarian, in good faith, in the course of his professional practice, and for a legitimate medical purpose, may administer and prescribe controlled drugs, or the practitioner may cause the same to be administered by a nurse or intern under his direction and supervision. In a bona fide emergency situation, the practitioner may dispense a controlled drug to a patient under his care but only in a quantity not to exceed a 48-hour supply for all schedule II substances or a 7-day supply of schedule III, IV, or V substances.

II. A veterinarian, in good faith, in the course of his professional practice only, and not for use by a human being, may administer and prescribe controlled drugs, and the veterinarian may cause them to be administered to an animal under his care, but only in a quantity not to exceed a 48-hour supply of a schedule II substance or a 7-day supply of schedule III, IV, or V substances.

III, IV. [Repealed.]

V. An advanced emergency medical care provider licensed under RSA 153-A may possess, for emergency use only, such controlled prescription drugs as are specified by the state emergency medical services medical control board, with the concurrence of the pharmacy board, provided that there has been prior establishment of medical control for the possession of such drugs. The advanced emergency medical care provider may only administer such controlled prescription drugs upon receipt of orders to do so from a supervising physician or an emergency trauma advanced practice registered nurse, practicing within such nurse practitioner's specialty. Such orders may be transmitted either directly or by telephone or by radio or by other communication medium, or by standing order of local medical control delineated in a protocol as defined in RSA 153-A.

VI. Notwithstanding any other law to the contrary, an attending physician, in good faith and in the course of the attending physician's professional practice only, may prescribe and administer federal Food and Drug Administration approved and classified cannabis-type drugs, or the attending physician may cause such drugs to be administered by a nurse or intern under such physician's direction and supervision.

VII. (a) The department of health and human services is hereby declared to be the state methadone authority.

(b) The commissioner of the department of health and human services shall adopt and have in effect rules, pursuant to RSA 541-A, relative to methadone detoxification and maintenance programs as follows:

(1) Application procedure and standards for approval for certification and re-certification of providers to operate methadone detoxification

and maintenance programs, including certification period, for each type of certification. The department shall utilize accreditation reports obtained from national accreditation bodies that are approved by the United States Department of Health and Human Services Substance Abuse and Mental Health Services Administration in certifying methadone detoxification and maintenance programs in New Hampshire.

(2) Eligibility of individuals for admission to such programs.

(3) Qualifications of program personnel.

(4) Program content, including, but not limited to, services to be offered by the program.

(5) Mandatory records and reports to the department.

(6) Security measures to prevent diversion of methadone to illegal use.

(7) Confidentiality and disclosure of identifying information, records and reports.

(8) Financial responsibility.

(9) Any other provisions necessary to implement the purposes of this paragraph.

(c) Providers may operate a methadone detoxification or methadone maintenance program, or both, in the state of New Hampshire only if the providers are certified to operate pursuant to rules adopted under subparagraph VII(b). In implementing subparagraph VII(b), the commissioner shall not use the interim rulemaking process in RSA 541-A:19.

(d) For the purposes of this paragraph:

(1) "Heroin" means an illegal semi-synthetic drug produced from the morphine contained in sap of the opium poppy, and known to have the potential for devastating addictive properties in vulnerable individuals.

(2) "Methadone" means a legal drug, methadone hydrochloride, which is a synthetic opiod that has been demonstrated to be an effective treatment agent for heroin abuse and dependence.

(3) "Methadone detoxification treatment" means the dispensing of methadone or similar substance in decreasing doses to an individual in order to reduce or eliminate adverse physiological or psychological effects incident to the withdrawal from the sustained use of heroin.

(4) "Methadone maintenance program" means a substance abuse treatment program substituting methadone or any of its derivatives, over time, to relieve withdrawal symptoms of heroin dependence, to reduce craving, and to permit normal functioning and engagement in rehabilitative services.

(e) Nothing in this paragraph shall prohibit a licensed health care practitioner from administering, prescribing, or dispensing a controlled drug under paragraph I.

(f) The department shall assess a fee to be paid by providers of methadone detoxification and maintenance programs for certification and administration by the department. The fee shall be $8 per client based on the annual client census of the previous calendar year. If the provider had no clients in the previous calendar year, then the fee shall be $1,000. All moneys collected by the department from fees authorized under this subparagraph shall be deposited into the general fund.

(g) The commissioner of the department of health and human services shall report by July 31, 2010, and each July 31 thereafter, to the chairpersons of the house and senate ways and means committees, the house and senate committees having jurisdiction over health and human services, and the oversight committee on health and human services under RSA 126-A:13, on the number of methadone detoxification and maintenance program clinics certified under RSA 318-B:10, VII, the number of clients, the average annual census data, the amount of fees assessed providers, and any recommendations for changes to the fee structure.

VIII. (a) Notwithstanding paragraph VII or any other law to the contrary, methadone may be administered, prescribed, and dispensed to pregnant and postpartum heroin addicts and administered as part of an alcohol and drug abuse treatment program, which may include extended detoxification and which is approved by the commissioner of health and human services.

(b) The commissioner of health and human services shall adopt rules pursuant to RSA 541-A, relative to:

(1) Eligibility for the program.

(2) Length of time in the program.

(3) Requirements for participation in prenatal and postnatal care.

(4) Security measures to prevent diversion of methadone to illegal use.

(5) Any other provisions necessary to implement the purposes of this paragraph.

IX. If, in the judgment of a physician licensed under RSA 329, appropriate pain management warrants a high dosage of controlled drugs and the benefit of the relief expected outweighs the risk of the high dosage, the licensed physician may administer or cause to be administered such a dosage, even if its use may increase the risk of death, so long as it is not furnished for the purpose of causing, or the purpose of assisting in causing, death for any reason and so long as it falls within rules of the board of medicine.

Source.
1969, 421:1. 1973, 392:3. 1977, 106:2; 547:11, 12. 1981, 107:1. 1983, 292:8, 9, 21. 1985, 293:7; 324:20. 1992, 48:8. 1994, 186:2, eff. May 24, 1994; 333:21, eff. Jan. 1, 1995. 1995, 286:25, eff. Jan. 1, 1996. 1996, 252:1, 2, eff. June 10, 1996; 267:23, eff. Aug. 9, 1996. 1998, 149:1, eff. Jan. 1, 1999. 1999, 345:8, eff. July 1, 1999. 2000, 268:2, eff. Aug. 11, 2000; 271:1, eff. June 12, 2000. 2009, 54:5, eff. July 21, 2009; 205:1, 2, July 15, 2009.

References in text.
The federal Food and Drug Administration, referred to in par. VI, is classified principally to 21 U.S.C.S. §§ 321, 351, 360, 371.

Amendments
—2009. The 2009 amendment by Chapter 54 substituted "advanced practice registered nurse" for "advanced registered nurse practitioner" in the second sentence of V.

The 2009 amendment by Chapter 205, deleted "on or before June 30, 2001" following "services shall" in the introductory language of VII(b); substituted "methadone detoxification and" for "detoxification and methadone" in the introductory language of VII(b) and in the first sentence of VII(b)(1); added the second sentence of VII(b)(1); and added VII(f) and VII(g).

—2000. Paragraph IX: Added by chapter 268.
Paragraph VII: Rewritten by ch. 271 to the extent that a detailed comparison would be impracticable.

—1999. Paragraph V: Chapter 345:8 substituted "RSA 153-A" for "RSA 151-B" wherever it appeared.

—1998. Paragraph VI: Substituted "the attending physician's" for "his" preceding "professional", inserted "federal Food and Drug Administration approved and classified" following "administer", substituted "such physician's" for "his" preceding "direction", and deleted "to a patient who is receiving radiation or chemotherapy treatment for cancer" following "supervision".

—1996. Paragraph V: Rewritten by ch. 267 to the extent that a detailed comparison would be impracticable.
Paragraph VII: Chapter 252 added "Except as provided in paragraph VIII" preceding "no person" in the first sentence.
Paragraph VIII: Added by ch. 252.

—1995. Paragraph V: Deleted "and certified by the board of registration in medicine" following "approved" and "registration in" following "state board of" in the first sentence.

—1994. Paragraph V: Chapter 333 added "or advanced registered nurse practitioner, practicing within such nurse practitioner's specialty" following "physician" in the second sentence.
Paragraph VII: Added by ch. 186.

—1992. Paragraph V: Inserted "advanced" preceding "emergency medical" and substituted "care provider" for "technician-paramedic" thereafter in the first sentence.

—1985. Paragraph I: Chapter 293 deleted "of the current chapter 21, Code of Federal Regulations" following "IV, or V substances" at the end of the second sentence.
Paragraph II: Chapter 293 deleted "of the current chapter 21, Code of Federal Regulations" following "IV, or V substances".
Paragraph V: Chapter 324 substituted "administer" for "dispense" in the second sentence.

—1983. Paragraphs I, II, and V: Rewritten to the extent that a detailed comparison would be impracticable.
Paragraphs III and IV: Repealed.

—1981. Paragraph VI: Added.

—1977. Paragraphs I and II: Rewritten by ch. 547 to the extent that a detailed comparison would be impracticable.
Paragraph V: Added by ch. 106.

—1973. Paragraph IV: Added.

Applicability of 2000, 271 amendment.
2000, 271:2, eff. June 12, 2000, provided: "Notwithstanding RSA 318-B:10, VII(c) as inserted by section 1 of this act, methadone detoxification programs licensed pursuant to federal statute and regulations may operate without certification under paragraph VII for up to 90 days after the effective date of rules adopted under RSA 318-B:10, VII(b) as inserted by section 1 of this act."

2000, 271:3, eff. June 12, 2000, further provided:
"I. Notwithstanding the above, nothing in this act [which amended this section and RSA 318:1 and 318:42 and enacted RSA 3318:51-b] shall be construed as prohibiting or limiting the provision of methadone detoxification treatment or from prohibiting or limiting treatment for those persons in treatment under RSA 318-B:10, VIII. Any other methadone detoxification treatment shall cease to operate on June 30, 2001 if the rules required under section 1 of this act have not been adopted.

"II.   Any provider under this section may provide treatment as long as the provider meets Commission on Accreditation of Rehabilitation Facilities (CARF) accreditation standards and is licensed by the federal Food and Drug Administration and the federal Drug Enforcement Administration, and otherwise meets all applicable state and federal laws and regulations."

Cross References.
Regulation of veterinarians generally, see RSA 332-B.
Scheduling of controlled drugs generally, see RSA 318-B:1-a.

NOTES TO DECISIONS

Cited:
Cited in Cited in State v. Nickerson, 114 N.H. 47, 314 A.2d 648, 1974 N.H. LEXIS 205 (1974).

318-B:11. Preparations Exempted.

I. NOT DEPENDENCE FORMING OR OF SUSTAINING CHARACTER.   The department of health and human services may by rule exempt from the application of this chapter, to such extent as it determines to be consistent with the public welfare, pharmaceutical preparations found by the department of health and human services after due notice and hearing:

(a) Either to possess no physiological or psychological dependence forming or sustaining character, or to possess physiological or psychological dependence forming or sustaining character not sufficient to warrant imposition of all the requirements of this chapter, and,

(b) Not to permit recovery of the minute quantity of a controlled drug from the pharmaceutical preparation having such a physiological or psychological dependence forming or sustaining character, with such relative technical chemical separation simplicity and degree of quantitative yield as to create a risk of improper use.

II. EXEMPT UNDER FEDERAL LAW.   In exercising the authority granted in paragraph I, the commissioner of the department of health and human services by rule and without special findings, may grant exempt status to such pharmaceutical preparations as are or may be determined to be exempt under the Comprehensive Drug Abuse Prevention and Control Act of 1970 and regulations and permit the administering, dispensing, or selling of such preparations under the same conditions as permitted by the Comprehensive Drug Abuse Prevention and Control Act of 1970 and regulations and the federal food and drug laws and regulations.

III. REVOCATION.   If the department of health and human services shall find after due notice and a hearing, as required by RSA 318-B:1, VI, that any exempt pharmaceutical preparation does possess a degree of physiological or psychological dependence character that results in material abusive use, it shall by designation publish, once each week for 3 successive weeks, the findings in a newspaper of general circulation in the state. The findings shall be effective, and the exempt status shall cease to apply to such pharmaceutical preparation, 7 days after the date of the publication of the findings. The suspen-

sion procedure specified in RSA 318-B:1, VI, shall also apply to such exempt preparation after the hearing date.

Source.
1969, 421:1. 1977, 547:13. 1985, 190:99, 100. 1995, 310:181, 182, eff. Nov. 1, 1995.

References in text.
The Comprehensive Drug Abuse Prevention and Control Act of 1970, referred to in par. II, is classified principally to 42 U.S.C.S. §§ 218, 246, 4541.
The federal food and drug laws, referred to in par. II, are classified principally to 21 U.S.C.S. §§ 301 et seq.
The provisions of RSA 318-B:1, VI, referred to in two places in par. III, are now classified to RSA 318-B:1-a, III.

Amendments
—1995. Substituted "department of health and human services" for "division of public health services" in two places in the introductory paragraph of par. I and in par. III and "commissioner of the department of health and human services" for "director of the division of public health services" in par. II.

—1985. Paragraph I: Substituted "rule" for "regulation" preceding "exempt".
Paragraph II: Inserted "director of the" preceding "division of public health services, by" and substituted "rule" for "regulation" thereafter.

—1977. Paragraph II: Substituted "Comprehensive Drug Abuse Prevention and Control Act of 1970" for "federal narcotic laws" in two places.

Severability of 1995 amendment.
1995, 310, which amended this, was subject to a severability clause. See 1995, 310:186.

Construction of 1995 amendments
1995, 310:187, eff. Nov. 1, 1995, provided:
"Nothing in this act is intended to, nor shall it be construed as, mandating or assigning any new, expanded, or modified program or responsibility for any political subdivision in violation of part I, article 28-a of the constitution of the state of New Hampshire."

Cross References.
Administrative Procedure Act, see RSA 541-A.
Adoption of rules and regulations generally, see RSA 318-B:24.

318-B:12. Records to be Kept; Confidentiality.

I. Practitioners, including physicians, podiatrists, dentists, veterinarians, optometrists, advanced registered nurse practitioners, manufacturers, wholesalers, pharmacists, clinics, hospitals, and laboratories, shall keep separate records, so as not to breach the confidentiality of patient records, to show the receipt and disposition of all controlled drugs. Such records shall meet the requirements of the department of health and human services and federal laws and regulations relative to the receipt, manufacture, inventory, distributions, sale, dispensing, loss, theft, and any other disposition of controlled drugs. The records shall indicate at least the name, dosage form, strength, and quantity of the controlled drug; the name and address of any person to whom the drug was administered, dispensed, sold or transferred and the date of any and all transactions involved with the controlled drug.

II. Prescription orders and records required by this chapter and stocks of controlled drugs shall be open for inspection only to federal, state, county and municipal law enforcement officers; all officers, agents, inspectors, and representatives of the board of pharmacy who are charged with the responsibility to enforce this chapter; all peace officers within the state; the attorney general; and all county attorneys whose duty it is to enforce the laws of this state or of the United States relating to controlled drugs. No officer having knowledge by virtue of his office of any such prescription, order, or record shall divulge such knowledge, except in connection with a prosecution or proceeding in court or before a licensing or registration board or officer, to which prosecution or proceeding the person to whom such prescriptions, orders or records relate is a party.

III. Practitioners including physicians, podiatrists, dentists, veterinarians, optometrists, advanced registered nurse practitioners, manufacturers, wholesalers, pharmacies, clinics, hospitals, laboratories, and any other person required by federal law to conduct biennial controlled substance inventories, shall do so beginning May 1, 1991, and thereafter on May 1 of every odd-numbered year.

IV. Records relative to prescription information containing patient-identifiable and prescriber-identifiable data shall not be licensed, transferred, used, or sold by any pharmacy benefits manager, insurance company, electronic transmission intermediary, retail, mail order, or Internet pharmacy or other similar entity, for any commercial purpose, except for the limited purposes of pharmacy reimbursement; formulary compliance; care management; utilization review by a health care provider, the patient's insurance provider or the agent of either; health care research; or as otherwise required by law. Commercial purpose includes, but is not limited to, advertising, marketing, promotion, or any activity that could be used to influence sales or market share of a pharmaceutical product, influence or evaluate the prescribing behavior of an individual health care professional, or evaluate the effectiveness of a professional pharmaceutical detailing sales force. Nothing in this paragraph shall prohibit the dispensing of prescription medications to a patient or to the patient's authorized representative; the transmission of prescription information between an authorized prescriber and a licensed pharmacy; the transfer of prescription information between licensed pharmacies; the transfer of prescription records that may occur in the event a pharmacy ownership is changed or transferred; care management educational communications provided to a patient about the patient's health condition, adherence to a prescribed course of therapy or other information about the drug being dispensed, treatment options, or clinical trials. Nothing in this section shall prohibit the collection, use, transfer, or sale of patient and prescriber de-identified data by zip code, geographic region, or medical specialty for commercial purposes. In addition to other appropriate remedies under this chapter, a violation of this paragraph is an unfair or deceptive act or practice within the meaning of RSA 358-A:2. Any right or remedy set forth in RSA 358-A may be used to enforce the provisions of this paragraph.

Source.
1969, 421:1. 1977, 547:14. 1983, 292:10. 1985, 324:21. 1990, 129:4. 1993, 333:5, 6, eff. Jan. 1, 1994. 1994, 333:22, 23, eff. Jan. 1, 1995. 1995, 310:181, eff. Nov. 1, 1995. 2006, 328:2, eff. June 30, 2006.

Amendments
—**2006.** Paragraph IV: Added.

—**1995.** Paragraph I: Substituted "department of health and human services" for "division of public health services" in the second sentence.

—**1994.** Inserted "advanced registered nurse practitioners" following "optometrists" in the first sentence of par. I and in par. III.

—**1993.** Inserted "optometrists" following "veterinarians" in the first sentence of paragraphs I and III.

—**1990.** Paragraph III: Added.

—**1985.** Paragraph II: Inserted "law enforcement" following "county and municipal" in the first sentence and made minor stylistic changes.

—**1983.** Designated the existing provisions of the section as par. I, inserted "podiatrists" following "physicians" in the first sentence, deleted "the name and address of the person or firm supplying the controlled drug" following "quantity of the controlled drug" in the third sentence, and made other minor changes in style in that paragraph, and added par. II.

—**1977.** Rewritten to the extent that a detailed comparison would be impracticable.

Severability of 1995 amendment.
1995, 310, which amended this section, was subject to a severability clause. See 1995, 310:186.

Construction of 1995 amendment.
1995, 310:187, eff. Nov. 1, 1995, provided:
"Nothing in this act is intended to, nor shall it be construed as, mandating or assigning any new, expanded, or modified program or responsibility for any political subdivision in violation of part I, article 28-a of the constitution of the state of New Hampshire."

Cross References.
Non-privileged communications, see RSA 318-B:21.

NOTES TO DECISIONS

Construction
Statute governing confidentiality of prescription orders and records allowed disclosure of otherwise confidential records during agency proceedings, when relevant to conduct of a licensee subject to a board of pharmacy action or proceeding. Appeal of Morgan (New Hampshire Bd. of Pharm.), 144 N.H. 44, 742 A.2d 101, 1999 N.H. LEXIS 75 (1999).

318-B:12-a. Treatment for Drug Abuse.

Any minor 12 years of age or older may voluntarily submit himself to treatment for drug dependency as defined in RSA 318-B:1, IX, or any problem related to the use of drugs at any municipal health department, state institution or facility, public or private hospital or clinic, any licensed physician or advanced practice registered nurse practicing within such nurse practitioner's specialty, or other accredited state or local social welfare agency, without the consent of a parent, guardian, or any other person charged with the care or custody of said minor. Such parent or legal guardian shall not be liable for the payment for any treatment rendered pursuant to this section. The treating facility, agency or individual shall keep records on the treatment given to minors as provided under this section in the usual and customary manner, but no reports or records or information contained therein shall be discoverable by the state in any criminal prosecution. No such reports or records shall be used for other than rehabilitation, research, or statistical and medical purposes, except upon the written consent of the person examined or treated. Nothing contained herein shall be construed to mean that any minor of sound mind is legally incapable of consenting to medical treatment provided that such minor is of sufficient maturity to understand the nature of such treatment and the consequences thereof.

Source.
1971, 136:1. 1994, 333:24, eff. Jan. 1, 1995. 2009, 54:5, eff. July 21, 2009.

Amendments
—2009. The 2009 amendment substituted "advanced practice registered nurse" for "advanced registered nurse practitioner" in the first sentence.

—1994. Inserted "or advanced registered nurse practitioner practicing within such nurse practitioner's specialty" following "physician" in the first sentence.

Cross References.
Confidentiality of records generally, see RSA 318-B:12.
Non-privileged communications, see RSA 318-B:21.

318-B:13. Labels.

I. Whenever a manufacturer sells or dispenses a controlled drug, and whenever a wholesaler sells or dispenses a controlled drug in a package prepared by him, he shall securely affix to each package in which the drug is contained a label showing in legible English the name and address of the vendor and the quantity, kind, and form of controlled drug contained therein. If any controlled drug is determined by rule of the department of health and human services to be habit forming, the container label shall show clearly the statement "Warning—May be Habit Forming". No person, except a pharmacist for the purpose of filling a prescription under this chapter, shall alter, deface, or remove any label so affixed.

II. Whenever a pharmacist dispenses any controlled drug on prescription issued by a practitioner, he or she shall affix to the container in which such drug is dispensed a label showing the name, address, and registry number of the pharmacy and name or the initials of the pharmacist; the name of the prescribing practitioner; the prescription identification number; the name of the patient; the date dispensed; any directions as may be stated on the prescription; and the name and strength and quantity of the drug dispensed. All drugs dispensed to a patient that have been filled using a centralized prescription processing system shall bear a label containing an identifiable code that provides a complete audit trail of the dispensing of the drug and pharmaceutical care activities. No person shall alter, deface, or remove any label so affixed.

III. Whenever a practitioner other than a pharmacist, but including a physician, dentist, podiatrist, optometrist, veterinarian, or advanced practice registered nurse dispenses a controlled drug, he shall indicate on the container in which such drug is dispensed at least the name of the practitioner; the name and address of the patient, or, in the case of an animal, the name and address of the owner and the species of animal; the date dispensed; the name, strength, and quantity of drug dispensed; and the directions for administering the medication.

IV. A compounded drug product shall also be labeled as provided in RSA 318:14-a.

Source.
1969, 421:1. 1977, 547:15, 16. 1983, 292:11. 1985, 324:22. 1993, 333:7, eff. Jan. 1, 1994. 1994, 333:25, eff. Jan. 1, 1995. 1995, 310:181, eff. Nov. 1, 1995. 2002, 281:6, eff. July 22, 2002. 2009, 54:5, eff. July 21, 2009. 2013, 121:7, eff. January 1, 2014.

Amendments
—2013. The 2013 amendment added IV.

—2009. The 2009 amendment substituted "advanced practice registered nurse" for "advanced registered nurse practitioner" in III.

—2002. Paragraph II: Inserted "or she" following "he" in the first sentence, and inserted the second sentence.

—1995. Substituted "department of health and human services" for "division of public health services" following "rule of the" in the second sentence.

—1994. Paragraph III: Deleted "or" preceding "veterinarian" and inserted "or advanced registered nurse practitioner" thereafter.

—1993. Paragraph III: Inserted "optometrist" following "podiatrist".

—1985. Paragraph II: Inserted "and quantity" following "name and strength" in the first sentence.

—1983. Paragraph I: Deleted "Manufacturer or Wholesaler" following "I" and substituted "English" for "english" preceding "the name and address" in the first sentence.
Paragraphs II, III: Rewritten to the extent that a detailed comparison would be impracticable.

—1977. Paragraph II: Rewritten to the extent that a detailed comparison would be impracticable.
Paragraph III: Added.

Severability of 1995 amendment.
1995, 310, which amended this section, was subject to a severability clause. See 1995, 310:186.

Construction of 1995 amendment.
1995, 310:187, eff. Nov. 1, 1995, provided:
"Nothing in this act is intended to, nor shall it be construed as, mandating or assigning any new, expanded, or modified program or responsibility for any political subdivision in violation of part I, article 28-a of the constitution of the state of New Hampshire."

Cross References.
Offenses generally, see RSA 318-B:2.
Requirements as to sales by pharmacists and prescriptions generally, see RSA 318-B:9.

318-B:14. Authorized Possession of Controlled Drugs by Individuals.

[Repealed 2010, 173:2, eff. January 1, 2011.]

Former section(s).

Former RSA 318-B:14, which was derived from 1969, 421:1; 1979, 244:1; 1983, 292:12; and 2002, 281:8, related to authorized possession of controlled drugs by individuals.

318-B:15. Persons and Corporations Exempted.

The provisions of this chapter restricting the possession and having control of controlled drugs shall not apply to:

I. Common carriers or to warehousemen while engaged in lawfully transporting or storing such drugs, or to an employee of the same acting within the scope of his employment; or to public officers or their employees in the performance of their official duties requiring possession or control of controlled drugs; or to temporary incidental possession by employees or agents or persons lawfully entitled to possession, or by persons whose possession is for the purpose of aiding public officers in performing their official duties.

II. Persons possessing prescription drugs dispensed to them pursuant to a lawful prescription or who are acting as an authorized agent for a person holding a lawful prescription. For purposes of this section, an authorized agent shall mean any person, including but not limited to a family member or caregiver, who has the intent to deliver the prescription drug to the person to whom the prescription drugs are lawfully prescribed. This exemption does not extend to persons possessing drugs with an intent to sell.

III. Law enforcement officers engaged in the collection, storage, and disposal of controlled drugs in conjunction with a pharmaceutical drug take-back program established under RSA 318-E.

Source.

1969, 421:1, eff. Aug. 31, 1969. 2010, 173:1, eff. January 1, 2011. 2011, 63:6, eff. July 1, 2011.

Amendments

—**2011.** The 2011 amendment added III.

—**2010.** The 2010 amendment added the I designation and added II.

318-B:16. Common Nuisances.

Any store, shop, warehouse, dwelling-house, building, vehicle, boat, aircraft, or any place whatever which is resorted to by drug-dependent persons for the purpose of using controlled drugs or which is used for the illegal keeping or selling of the same shall be deemed a common nuisance. No person shall knowingly keep or maintain such a common nuisance.

Source.

1969, 421:1, eff. Aug. 31, 1969.

Cross References.

Forfeiture and disposition of contraband generally, see RSA 318-B:17 et seq.

NOTES TO DECISIONS

1. Constitutionality
2. Indictments

1. Constitutionality

RSA 318-B:16's phrase, "drug-dependent person," is not unconstitutionally vague on its face. RSA 318-B:16, read in conjunction with RSA 318-B:1, X (defining "drug-dependent person"), gives clear notice to a person of ordinary intelligence of the precise conduct, involving drug-dependent persons, that constitutes the nuisance. State v. MacElman, 154 N.H. 304, 910 A.2d 1267, 2006 N.H. LEXIS 160 (2006).

RSA 318-B:16 is not facially overbroad in violation of a defendant's rights under the Fourth Amendment or N.H. Const. pt. I, art. 19, as neither constitutional provision authorizes knowingly keeping a place where drug-dependent persons can use drugs. Furthermore, the operation of RSA 318-B:16 does not require a physical intrusion into the home so does not implicate search and seizure protections and the defendant in this case did not allege a search and seizure of her home. State v. MacElman, 154 N.H. 304, 910 A.2d 1267, 2006 N.H. LEXIS 160 (2006).

RSA 318-B:16 does not prohibit a substantial amount of protected associational activities in the federal constitutional sense, as it does not punish anyone for associating with anyone else in contravention of the First Amendment. Rather, RSA 318-B:16 proscribes keeping a place to which drug-dependent persons resort for the purpose of using controlled drugs. State v. MacElman, 154 N.H. 304, 910 A.2d 1267, 2006 N.H. LEXIS 160 (2006).

2. Indictments

Where an indictment alleged the defendant maintained a common nuisance in violation of RSA 318-B:16, inserting names of particular drug-dependent persons into the indictment was neither required by RSA 318-B:16 nor necessary to the defendant's preparation for trial. State v. MacElman, 154 N.H. 304, 910 A.2d 1267, 2006 N.H. LEXIS 160 (2006).

318-B:17. Disposal of Controlled Drugs in Possession of Law Enforcement Officer.

All controlled drugs, the lawful possession of which is not established or the title to which cannot be ascertained, which have come into the custody of a law enforcement officer shall be forfeited and disposed of as follows:

I. The superior court shall order such controlled drugs forfeited and destroyed. A record of the place where the drugs were seized, of the kinds and quantities of drugs so destroyed, and of the time, place and manner of destruction shall be kept, and return under oath, reporting said destruction, shall be made to the superior court and to the Drug Enforcement Administration, if controlled drugs are involved, by the officer who destroys them.

I-a. The circuit court having jurisdiction over a misdemeanor or violation controlled drug offense may order such controlled drugs forfeited and destroyed upon written motion. Such order shall not be entered until after the period for appeal of the offense has expired.

I-b. The circuit court shall require the same record and reporting of the officer who is destroying the controlled drugs as is required under paragraph

I for the superior court, with the exception of notification to the Drug Enforcement Administration.

I-c. All unwanted or unused controlled drugs which have come into the custody of a law enforcement officer, pursuant to a pharmaceutical drug take-back program, shall be disposed of in accordance with the disposal requirements for controlled drugs set forth under RSA 318-E.

II, III. [Repealed.]

Source.
1969, 421:1. 1983, 292:13. 1995, 310:181, eff. Nov. 1, 1995. 1998, 362:1, 2, eff. Jan. 1, 1999. 2003, 80:1, eff. Jan. 1, 2004. 2011, 63:7, 8, eff. July 1, 2011. 2013, 222:1, eff. January 1, 2014.

References in text.
The Drug Enforcement Administration, referred to in par. I, is classified to 21 U.S.C.S. §§ 871 et seq.

Amendments
—2013. The 2013 amendment substituted "circuit" for "district" in the first sentence of I-a and in I-b and added "or violation" in the first sentence of I-a.

—2011. The 2011 amendment substituted "law enforcement officer" for "peace officer" in the section heading and the introductory paragraph and added I-c.

—2003. Paragraphs I-a and I-b: Added.

—1998. Paragraph I: Deleted "Except as otherwise provided in this section" preceding "the superior court" at the beginning of the first sentence.
Paragraphs II and III: Repealed.

—1995. Substituted "department of health and human services" for "division of public health services" wherever it appeared in pars. II and III.

—1983. Paragraph I: Deleted "Forfeited or Destroyed" following "I", rewrote the first sentence, and substituted "Drug Enforcement Administration, if" for "United States commissioner of narcotics, if narcotic" preceding "controlled drugs" at the end of the second sentence.
Paragraph II: Rewritten to the extent that a detailed comparison would be impracticable.
Paragraph III: Deleted "Records Required" following "III" and "state" preceding "division".

Severability of 1995 amendment.
1995, 310, which amended this section, was subject to a severability clause. See 1995, 310:186.

Construction of 1995 amendment.
1995, 310:187, eff. Nov. 1, 1995, provided:
"Nothing in this act is intended to, nor shall it be construed as, mandating or assigning any new, expanded, or modified program or responsibility for any political subdivision in violation of part I, article 28-a of the constitution of the state of New Hampshire."

Cross References.
Forfeiture of items used in connection with drugs, see RSA 318-B:17-b.

318-B:17-a. Disposal of Controlled Drugs in Possession of Practitioner.

No person other than the pharmacy board, its officers, agents, and inspectors is authorized to destroy any out-dated, deteriorated, excessive or otherwise unwanted or confiscated controlled drugs which are in the possession of a practitioner, veterinarian, pharmacy, peace officer, nursing home, manufacturer, wholesaler, clinic, or laboratory or hospital. No payment shall be made to any person or institution for any drug surrendered for destruction. A record shall be maintained which indicates the name, strength, and quantity of all drugs destroyed; the place and manner of destruction; the date and time destroyed; the name of the practitioner or institution surrendering the drugs; and the signature and title of the person witnessing destruction. Such records shall conform to any federal requirements and shall be open to inspection by all federal or state officers charged with the enforcement of federal or state controlled drug laws.

Source.
1977, 547:17. 1983, 292:14, eff. Aug. 17, 1983.

Amendments
—1983. Substituted "no person other than the pharmacy board" for "the pharmacy commission" preceding "its" and "is" for "are solely" preceding "authorized" at the beginning of the first sentence, deleted "the name of the practitioner or institution surrendering the drugs, the signature and title of the person requesting destruction" preceding "the signature" in the third sentence, and made other minor changes in style.

Cross References.
Forfeiture of items used in connection with drugs, see RSA 318-B:17-b.

318-B:17-b. Forfeiture of Items Used in Connection with Drug Offense.

I. Interests in the following property, upon petition of the attorney general, shall be subject to forfeiture to the state and said property interest shall be vested in the state:

(a) All materials, products and equipment of any kind, including, but not limited to, firearms, scales, packaging equipment, surveillance equipment and grow lights, which are used or intended for use in procurement, manufacture, compounding, processing, concealing, trafficking, delivery or distribution of a controlled drug in felonious violation of this chapter.

(b) Property interest in any conveyance, including but not limited to aircraft, vehicles, or vessels, which is used or intended for use in the procurement, manufacture, compounding, processing, concealing, trafficking, delivery or distribution of a controlled drug in felonious violation of this chapter.

(c) Any moneys, coin, currency, negotiable instruments, securities or other investments knowingly used or intended for use in the procurement, manufacture, compounding, processing, concealing, trafficking, delivery or distribution of a controlled drug in felonious violation of this chapter and all proceeds, including moneys, coin, currency, negotiable instruments, securities or other investments, and any real or personal property, traceable thereto. All moneys, coin, currency, negotiable instruments, securities and other investments found in proximity to controlled substances are presumed to be forfeitable under this paragraph. The claimant of the property shall bear the burden of rebutting this presumption.

(d) Any books, records, ledgers and research material, including formulae, microfilm, tapes and any other data which are used or intended for use in felonious violation of this chapter.

(e) Any real property, including any right, title, leasehold interest, and other interest in the whole of any lot or tract of land and any appurtenances or improvements, which real property is knowingly used or intended for use, in any manner or part, in the procurement, manufacture, compounding, processing, concealing, trafficking, delivery or distribution of a controlled drug in felonious violation of this chapter.

I-a. The state shall have a lien on any property subject to forfeiture under this section upon seizure thereof. Upon forfeiture, the state's title to the property relates back to the date of seizure.

I-b. Property may be seized for forfeiture by any law enforcement agency designated by the department of justice, as follows:

(a) Upon process issued by any justice, associate justice or special justice of the municipal, district or superior court. The court may issue a seizure warrant on an affidavit under oath demonstrating that probable cause exists for its forfeiture or that the property has been the subject of a previous final judgment of forfeiture in the courts of any state or of the United States. The application for process and the issuance, execution and return of process shall be subject to applicable state law. The court may order that the property be seized and secured on such terms and conditions as are reasonable in the discretion of the court. Such order may include an order to a financial institution or to any fiduciary or bailee to require the entity to impound any property in its possession or control and not to release it except upon further order of the court. The order may be made on or in connection with a search warrant;

(b) Physically, without process on probable cause to believe that the property is subject to forfeiture under this chapter; or

(c) Constructively, without process on probable cause to believe that the property is subject to forfeiture under this chapter, by recording a notice of pending forfeiture in the registry of deeds in the county where the real property is located or at the town clerk's office where the personal property is located stating that the state intends to seek forfeiture of the identified property pursuant to this chapter.

(d) A seizure for forfeiture without process under subparagraph (b) or (c) is reasonable if made under circumstances in which a warrantless seizure or arrest would be valid in accordance with state law.

I-c. Upon seizure of any items or property interests the property shall not be subject to alienation, sequestration or attachment but is deemed to be in the custody of the department of justice subject only to the order of the court.

II. (a) Upon the seizure of any personal property under paragraph I, the person making or directing such seizure shall inventory the items or property interests and issue a copy of the resulting report to any person or persons having a recorded interest, or claiming an equitable interest in the item within 7 days of said seizure.

(b) Upon seizure of any real property under paragraph I, the person making or directing such seizure shall notify any person having a recorded interest or claiming an equitable interest in the property within 7 days of said seizure.

(c) The seizing agency shall cause an appraisal to be made of the property as soon as possible and shall promptly send to the department of justice a written request for forfeiture. This request shall include a statement of all facts and circumstances supporting forfeiture of the property, including the names of all witnesses then known, and the appraised value of the property.

(d) The department of justice shall examine the facts and applicable law of the cases referred pursuant to subparagraph (c), and if it is probable that the property is subject to forfeiture, shall cause the initiation of administrative or judicial proceedings against the property. If upon inquiry and examination, the department of justice determines that such proceedings probably cannot be sustained or that the ends of justice do not require the institution of such proceedings, the department shall make a written report of such findings and send a copy to the seizing agency, and, if appropriate, shall also authorize and direct the release of the property.

(e) The department of justice shall, within 60 days of the seizure, either file a petition in the superior court having jurisdiction under this section or seek administrative forfeiture pursuant to RSA 318-B:17-d. If no such petition is filed or administrative procedure initiated within 60 days, the items or property interest seized shall be released or returned to the owners.

II-a. Pending forfeiture and final disposition, the law enforcement agency making the seizure shall:

(a) Place the property under seal; or

(b) Remove the property to a storage area for safekeeping; or

(c) Remove the property to a place designated by the court; or

(d) Request another agency to take custody of the property and remove it to an appropriate location within the state; or

(e) In the case of moneys, file a motion for transfer of evidence under RSA 595-A:6. Upon the court's granting of the motion the moneys shall be immediately forwarded to an interest-bearing seized asset escrow account to be administered by the attorney general. Upon resolution of the forfeiture proceeding the moneys deposited shall be transferred to the drug forfeiture fund or returned to the owners thereof as directed by the court. Unless otherwise ordered by a court in a specific case, interest on all moneys deposited in the seized asset escrow account shall be deposited annually into the drug forfeiture fund established under RSA 318-B:17-c.

III. The court may order forfeiture of all items or property interests subject to the provisions of paragraph I, except as follows:

(a) No item or property interest shall be subject to forfeiture unless the owner or owners thereof were consenting parties to a felonious violation of this chapter and had knowledge thereof.

(b) No items or property interests shall be subject to forfeiture unless involved in an offense which may be charged as a felony.

IV. (a) The department of justice may petition the superior court in the name of the state in the nature of a proceeding in rem to order forfeiture of items or property interests subject to forfeiture under the provisions of this section. Such petition shall be filed in the court having jurisdiction over any related criminal proceedings which could be brought under this chapter.

(b) Such proceeding shall be deemed a civil suit in equity in which the state shall have the burden of proving all material facts by a preponderance of the evidence and in which the owners or other persons claiming an exception pursuant to paragraph III shall have the burden of proving such exception.

(c) The court shall issue orders of notice to all persons who have a recorded interest or claim an equitable interest in said items or property interests seized under this chapter and shall schedule a hearing on the petition to be held within 90 days of the return date on said petition.

(d) At the request of any party to the forfeiture proceeding, the court may grant a continuance until the final resolution of any criminal proceedings which were brought against a party under this chapter and which arose from the transaction which gave rise to the forfeiture proceeding. No asset forfeiture may be maintained against a person's interest in property if that person has been found not guilty of the underlying felonious charge.

(e) At the hearing, the court shall hear evidence and make findings of fact and rulings of law as to whether the property is subject to forfeiture under this chapter. Except in the case of proceeds, upon a finding that the property is subject to forfeiture the court shall determine whether the forfeiture of the property is not excessive in relation to the underlying criminal offense. In making this determination the court shall consider whether in addition to any other pertinent considerations:

(1) There is a substantial connection between the property to be forfeited and the underlying drug offense;

(2) Criminal activities conducted by or through the use of the property were extensive; and

(3) The value of the property to be forfeited greatly outweighs the value of the drugs that were

or would have been likely to be distributed, the costs of the investigation and prosecution, and the harm caused by the criminal conduct.

The court shall, thereupon, make a final order, from which all parties shall have a right of appeal.

V. Final orders for forfeiture of property under this section or under RSA 318-B:17-d shall be implemented by the department of justice and shall provide for disposition of the items or property interests by the state in any manner not prohibited by law, including retention for official use by law enforcement or other public agencies or sale at public auction. The department of justice shall pay the reasonable expenses of the forfeiture proceeding, seizure, storage, maintenance of custody, advertising, court costs and notice of sale from any money forfeited and from the proceeds of any sale or public auction of forfeited items. All outstanding recorded liens on said items or property interests seized shall be paid in full upon conclusion of the court proceedings from the proceeds of any sale or public auction of forfeited items. The balance remaining shall be distributed by the department of justice as follows:

(a) Of the first $500,000:

(1) Forty-five percent shall be returned to the fiscal officer or officers of the municipal, county, state, or federal government which provided the law enforcement agency or agencies responsible for the seizure. Moneys returned to each fiscal officer shall be deposited in a special account and shall be used primarily for meeting expenses incurred by law enforcement agencies in connection with drug-related investigations. Except as provided in RSA 31:95-b, such funds shall be available for expenditure without further appropriation by the legislative body of the municipal, county, state or federal government, and shall not be transferred or expended for any other purpose. Moneys returned to a state law enforcement agency shall be deposited in a special nonlapsing account established within the office of the state treasurer and shall be in addition to all other state appropriations to such agency;

(2) Ten percent shall be deposited into a special nonlapsing account established within the office of the state treasurer for the department of health and human services; and

(3) Forty-five percent shall be deposited in a revolving drug forfeiture fund, administered by the department of justice pursuant to RSA 318-B:17-c; and

(b) Of any balance remaining:

(1) Ten percent shall be deposited in the manner prescribed in subparagraph V(a)(2) of this section; and

(2) Ninety percent shall be deposited in the manner prescribed in subparagraph V(a)(3) of this section.

The total amount of payments made to the special account for the department of health and human services pursuant to subparagraphs V(a)(2) and V(b)(1) of this section shall not exceed $400,000 in any fiscal year and any excess over $400,000 which would otherwise be paid to such special account under this section shall be deposited in the general fund. The revolving drug forfeiture fund shall at no time exceed $1,000,000. All sums in the revolving drug forfeiture fund in excess of $1,000,000 shall be credited to the general fund.

Source.
1981, 166:2. 1983, 292:15. 1985, 327:1–4. 1986, 232:1. 1988, 94:1. 1989, 380:1, 2. 1992, 182:1. 1994, 343:1–3, eff. Aug. 7, 1994. 1995, 310:177, eff. Nov. 1, 1995.

Amendments
—1995. Paragraph V: Substituted "department of health and human services" for "office of alcohol and drug abuse prevention" in subpar. (a)(2) and in the first sentence of the concluding paragraph.

—1994. Paragraph III(a): Deleted "it shall appear that" following "unless".
Paragraph IV(d): Added the second sentence.
Paragraph IV(e): Rewritten to the extent that a detailed comparison would be impracticable.

—1992. Rewritten to the extent that a detailed comparison would be impracticable.

—1989. Paragraph IV: Substituted "$200,000" for "$50,000" in the introductory clause of subpar. (a), added "except as provided in RSA 31:95-b" following "investigations" in the second sentence of subpar. (a)(1), and substituted "$400,000" for "$200,000" in the first and second sentences and "$1,000,000" for "$300,000" in the third and fourth sentences of the unnumbered concluding paragraph.

—1988. Paragraph IV: Rewritten to the extent that a detailed comparison would be impracticable.

—1986. Paragraph I: Substituted "interest" for "interests" in the introductory clause and rewrote subpar. (b).
Paragraph II: Substituted "interest" for "interests" following "items or property" in the third sentence.
Paragraph III: Substituted "interest" for "interests" following "property" in subpar. (a) and "may be charged as" for "constitutes" preceding "a felony" in subpar. (b) and deleted subpar. (c).
Paragraph IV: Rewritten to the extent that a detailed comparison would be impracticable.

—1985. Paragraph I: Rewrote subpar. (c), added subpars. (e) and (f), and made other minor stylistic changes.
Paragraph III(c): Added.
Paragraph IV: Inserted "which could be" preceding "brought" in the second sentence, rewrote the fourth and tenth sentences, and added the fifth and eleventh sentences.

—1983. Paragraph III(b): Deleted "at the time of seizure" following "felony" at the end of the paragraph.
Paragraph IV: Deleted "any provision of" preceding "this chapter" at the end of the second sentence, substituted "the" for "said" preceding "hearing" at the beginning of the fifth sentence, "the" for "said" preceding "items" in the sixth sentence, and "the" for "said" preceding "seized" in the last sentence and made other minor changes in style.

Purpose.
1981, 166:1, eff. Aug. 1, 1981, provided: "The purpose of this bill is to allow the attorney general to seize any money, books, records, ledgers and research material, any materials, products and equipment, and any vehicle, aircraft or vessel used in connection with a felonious drug offense and to provide an equitable proceeding to determine the disposition of the goods seized by the attorney general. This act is intended also to provide that all persons holding liens on seized property be compensated in full for the amount of their liens and to protect all innocent owners from having any items forfeited to the state."

Severability of 1995 amendment.
1995, 310, which amended this section, was subject to a severability clause. See 1995, 310:186.

Construction of 1995 amendment.
1995, 310:187, eff. Nov. 1, 1995, provided:
"Nothing in this act is intended to, nor shall it be construed as, mandating or assigning any new, expanded, or modified program or responsibility for any political subdivision in violation of part I, article 28-a of the constitution of the state of New Hampshire."

Applicability of 1988 amendment.
1988, 94:3, eff. July 1, 1988, provided that the amendment to this section shall apply only to items or property interests related to drug offenses seized on or after July 1, 1988.

Cross References.
Classification of crimes, see RSA 625:9.
Forfeiture of controlled drugs, see RSA 318-B:17-a.
Properties and places deemed common nuisances generally, see RSA 318-B:16.
Sentences, see RSA 651.

NOTES TO DECISIONS

1. Jurisdiction
2. Burden of proof
3. Sufficiency of evidence
4. Double jeopardy
5. Nonpunitive nature of statute

1. Jurisdiction
Proceedings under this section with respect to motorcycle seized in connection with drug offenses were in the nature of in personam, and therefore were not of such type or character as to prevent federal court, by medium of the doctrine of "adoptive forfeiture" from claiming prior jurisdiction over motorcycle and issuing warrant in rem under federal forfeiture statute. United States v. Certain Real Property Known As Lot B Governor's Rd., 755 F. Supp. 487, 1990 U.S. Dist. LEXIS 18665 (D.N.H. 1990).

2. Burden of proof
In forfeiture proceeding, state has burden to prove by a preponderance of the evidence that property owner knowingly used or intended to use his real property for activities proscribed by this chapter. In re Parcel of Land Located in Effingham, 132 N.H. 1, 561 A.2d 1061, 1989 N.H. LEXIS 55 (1989).

3. Sufficiency of evidence
Order granting the State's petition for forfeiture of defendant's vehicle was proper because, inter alia, the record supported the trial court's findings that the vehicle was used in the trafficking and distribution of drugs valued at about $4,000, the investigation cost $3,000 to $6,000, and the vehicle was worth $10,000 to $11,000; the trial court had jurisdiction despite the fact that the underlying criminal case was referred for federal prosecution. Double jeopardy did not bar the State's forfeiture petition following defendant's guilty plea in federal court, and, because a forfeiture action was a civil suit, it was explicitly exempt from the terms of defendant's plea agreement. In re Toyota Avalon, 155 N.H. 720, 927 A.2d 1239, 2007 N.H. LEXIS 124 (2007).
Paragraph I(c) of this section, providing for forfeiture of moneys used or intended for use in felonious violation of this chapter, does not require proof connecting the money to be forfeited with a particular narcotics transaction. In re Two Hundred Seven Thousand Five Hundred Twenty-Three Dollars & Forty-Six Cents in United States Currency, 130 N.H. 202, 536 A.2d 1270, 1987 N.H. LEXIS 300 (1987).
In order to justify a forfeiture under paragraph I(c) of this section, the state is not required to demonstrate that the moneys were associated with drug transactions occurring after the 1981 effective date of the section statute. In re Two Hundred Seven Thousand Five Hundred Twenty-Three Dollars & Forty-Six Cents in United States Currency, 130 N.H. 202, 536 A.2d 1270, 1987 N.H. LEXIS 300 (1987).

4. Double jeopardy

By failing to contest forfeiture, defendant never became a party to proceeding and effectively renounced any interest in property forfeited, and as a result, there was no judicial determination that the property was his; defendant therefore could not claim that forfeiture of property punished him, and without punishment there was no former jeopardy, and thus double jeopardy did not bar defendant's prosecution on indictment for conspiracy to sell cocaine. State v. Natalcolon, 140 N.H. 689, 671 A.2d 556, 1996 N.H. LEXIS 16 (1996).

Civil forfeiture did not implicate double jeopardy, where defendant's forfeiture of property was purely voluntary and not the result of any State-initiated forfeiture proceeding, and thus no civil sanction was imposed by State. State v. Guenzel, 140 N.H. 685, 671 A.2d 545, 1996 N.H. LEXIS 14 (1996).

5. Nonpunitive nature of statute

New Hampshire's in rem forfeiture statute was a civil, nonpunitive measure, and thus forfeiture of defendant's vehicle did not constitute a second punishment for double jeopardy purposes. In re 1994 Chevrolet Cavalier, 142 N.H. 705, 708 A.2d 397, 1998 N.H. LEXIS 22 (1998).

318-B:17-c. Drug Forfeiture Fund.

I. There is hereby established within the office of the state treasurer a special revolving fund to be designated as the drug forfeiture fund. This fund shall be administered by the attorney general and may be used to pay the costs of local, county and state drug related investigations, as well as drug control law enforcement programs within New Hampshire. The fund may also be used to pay extraordinary costs of local, county and state drug prosecutions and trial expenses.

II. Law enforcement agencies may apply to the department of justice for grants from the forfeiture fund. Such grants shall be utilized exclusively for meeting expenses associated with drug related investigations. The attorney general shall report 60 days after the close of each fiscal year to the governor and council and to the fiscal committee of the general court a summary of the grants provided to law enforcement agencies under this paragraph for the preceding fiscal year.

III. The attorney general shall adopt rules, pursuant to RSA 541-A, relative to:

(a) The administration of the drug forfeiture fund.

(b) The grant application procedures and forms to be used by law enforcement agencies.

Source.
1985, 327:5. 1986, 232:2. 1989, 380:3, eff. June 5, 1989. 2012, 247:29, eff. August 17, 2012.

Amendments
—**2012.** The 2012 amendment, in the last sentence of II, substituted "60 days after the close of each fiscal year" for "on or before December 31 of each calendar year" and added "of the general court."

—**1989.** Paragraph I: Added the third sentence.

—**1986.** Rewritten to the extent that a detailed comparison would be impracticable.

Cross References.
Department of justice, see RSA 21-M.

318-B:17-d. Administrative Forfeiture of Items Used in Connection With Drug Offenses.

I. Interests in property subject to forfeiture under the provisions of RSA 318-B:17-b, subparagraphs I(a), I(b), I(c) excepting proceeds and I(d), but not real property, shall be subject to administrative forfeiture by the department of justice provided that the total amount or value of such property does not exceed $75,000. The provisions of RSA 318-B:17-b shall apply in any case of administrative forfeiture except as otherwise provided in this section.

II. The department of justice may administratively forfeit property seized under paragraph I of this section as follows:

(a) The department of justice shall provide a notice of intent to forfeit property administratively by publication for 3 consecutive weeks in a local newspaper of general circulation where the property was seized.

(b) In addition, to the extent practicable, the department of justice shall provide notice by certified mail return receipt addressee only requested, of intent to forfeit the property administratively to all persons having a recorded interest or claiming an equitable interest in the property seized.

(c) Notice by publication and by mail shall include:

(1) A description of the property;

(2) Its appraised value;

(3) The date and place of seizure;

(4) The violation of law alleged against the subject property;

(5) Instructions for filing a claim and posting bond or filing a petition for remission or mitigation; and

(6) Notice that the property will be forfeited to the state if a petition for remission or mitigation has not been filed in a timely manner or a claim has not been filed and bond has not been posted in a timely manner.

(d) Persons claiming an interest in the property may file petitions for remission or mitigation of forfeiture or file a claim and post bond with the department of justice within 30 days of the first notice by publication or 30 days from the receipt of written notice, whichever is later.

(e) It shall be the duty of the department of justice to inquire into the facts and circumstances surrounding petitions for remission or mitigation of forfeiture.

(f) The department of justice shall provide the seizing agency and the petitioner a written decision on each petition for remission or mitigation within 60 days of receipt of such petition unless the circumstances of the case require additional time in which case the department of justice shall notify the petitioner in writing and with specificity within the 60-day period that the circumstances of the case require additional time, and further notify the petitioner of the expected decision date.

(g) Any person claiming an interest in seized property may institute judicial review of the seizure and proposed forfeiture by timely filing with the department of justice a claim and bond to the state in the amount of 10 percent of the appraised value or in the penal sum of $2,500, whichever is less, with sureties to be approved by the department of justice, upon condition that in the case of forfeiture the claimant shall pay all costs and expenses of the proceedings at the discretion of the court. A sworn affidavit of indigency may be filed in lieu of a cost bond. Upon receipt of the claim and bond, or, if the department of justice otherwise so elects, the department shall file with the court a petition in rem to order forfeiture of items or property interests subject to forfeiture under the provisions of this section. All judicial proceedings thereafter shall be conducted in accordance with the provisions of RSA 318-B:17-b, IV. Any bonds received by the department of justice shall be held by the department pending final disposition of the case.

(h) If no petitions or claims with bonds are timely filed, the department of justice shall prepare a written declaration of forfeiture of the subject property to the state and dispose of the property in accordance with this section and the department of justice rules, if any, relative to this section.

(i) If the petition is denied, the department of justice shall prepare a written declaration of forfeiture to the state and dispose of the property in accordance with this section and the department of justice rules, if any, relative to this section.

(j) A written declaration of forfeiture signed by the attorney general or designee pursuant to this chapter shall be deemed good and sufficient title to the forfeited property.

Source.
1988, 94:2. 1989, 207:6. 1992, 182:2, eff. June 11, 1992.

Amendments
—**1992.** Rewritten to the extent that a detailed comparison would be impracticable.

—**1989.** Paragraph VI(g): Substituted "less" for "greater" following "whichever is" in the first sentence and added the second sentence.

Applicability of enactment.
1988, 94:3, eff. July 1, 1988, provided that this section shall apply only to items or property interests related to drug offenses seized on or after July 1, 1988.

NOTES TO DECISIONS

Voluntary forfeiture
Civil forfeiture did not implicate double jeopardy, where defendant's forfeiture of property was purely voluntary and not the result of any State-initiated forfeiture proceeding, and thus no civil sanction was imposed by State. State v. Guenzel, 140 N.H. 685, 671 A.2d 545, 1996 N.H. LEXIS 14 (1996).

318-B:17-e. Drug Asset Forfeiture Guidelines Required.

The department of justice shall adopt and maintain drug asset forfeiture guidelines. The attorney general shall submit the guidelines and any proposed amendments to such guidelines to the house judiciary and family law committee and to the senate judiciary committee for review and comment at least as often as annually. The attorney general shall submit any proposed amendments to the guidelines for legislative review and comment prior to their becoming effective.

Source.
1994, 343:4, eff. Aug. 7, 1994. 1995, 9:39, eff. June 11, 1995.

Amendments
—**1995.** In the second sentence, deleted "and senate" preceding "judiciary" and substituted "and family law committee and to the senate judiciary committee" for "committee" thereafter.

318-B:17-f. Forfeiture Reports.

The attorney general shall submit a biennial report to the governor, senate president, and speaker of the house relative to the seizure of any items or property interests under RSA 318-B:17-b. Such report shall include:

I. A full and complete description of any items or property interests seized including the property's location and value.

II. The name and address of all known persons having a legal or equitable interest in the property.

III. Any findings of fact relative to the justice of the forfeiture as determined under RSA 318-B:17-b, IV(e).

The attorney general has the authority to exclude any information which would reveal the identity of an informant or compromise an ongoing investigation.

Source.
1994, 343:5, eff. Aug. 7, 1994.

318-B:18. Notice of Conviction to be Sent to Licensing Board.

On the conviction of any person for violation of any provision of this chapter, a copy of the judgment and sentence, and of the opinion of the superior court if any opinion is filed, shall be sent by the clerk of the court to the board by whom the convicted defendant has been licensed or registered to practice his profession or to carry on his business. The board may summarily suspend, limit or revoke the license or registration of the convicted defendant to practice his profession or to carry on his business.

Source.
1969, 421:1. 1983, 292:17, eff. Aug. 17, 1983.

Amendments
—**1983.** Substituted "for" for "of the" preceding "violation" and deleted "or officer, if any" following "board" in the first sentence, rewrote the second sentence, deleted the former third sentence, and made other minor changes in style.

318-B:19. Records, Confidential.

[Repealed 1983, 292:21, eff. Aug. 17, 1983.]

Former section(s).

Former RSA 318-B:19, which was derived from 1969, 421:1, related to inspection and confidentiality of prescriptions, orders, records, etc. See now RSA 318-B:12.

318-B:20. Prohibited Acts.

[Repealed 1983, 292:21, eff. Aug. 17, 1983.]

Former section(s).

Former RSA 318-B:20, which was derived from 1969, 421:1, related to prohibited acts. See now RSA 318-B:2.

318-B:21. Certain Communications Not Privileged.

Information communicated to a practitioner in an effort unlawfully to procure a controlled drug, or unlawfully to procure the administration of any such drug, shall not be deemed a privileged communication.

Source.

1969, 421:1. 1983, 292:18, eff. Aug. 17, 1983.

Amendments

—1983. Substituted "practitioner" for "physician" following "communicated to a".

Cross References.

Confidentiality of records relating to treatment of minors for drug abuse, see RSA 318-B:12-a.

NOTES TO DECISIONS

Cited:

Cited in State v. Summers, 142 N.H. 429, 702 A.2d 819, 1997 N.H. LEXIS 115 (1997).

318-B:22. Exceptions and Exemptions Not Required to be Negatived.

In any complaint, information, or indictment, and in any action or proceeding brought for the enforcement of any provision of this chapter, it shall not be necessary to negate any exception, excuse, proviso, or exemption contained herein, and the burden of proof of any such exception, excuse, proviso or exemption shall be upon the defendant.

Source.

1969, 421:1, eff. Aug. 31, 1969.

NOTES TO DECISIONS

Construction with other law

RSA 625:7 generally makes the Criminal Code applicable to offenses outside the Code, and under RSA 625:10 (burden of proof) and RSA 625:11 (elements of an offense under the Code) the non-applicability of exemptions to an offense must be established during the state's case-in-chief in order for the state's case to survive a motion for acquittal; however, the general rule found within the Criminal Code does not displace the clear and specific intent of this section, and the defendant has the burden to prove the application of any exemption. State v. Bell, 125 N.H. 425, 480 A.2d 906, 1984 N.H. LEXIS 253 (1984).

Cited:

Cited in State v. Nickerson, 114 N.H. 47, 314 A.2d 648, 1974 N.H. LEXIS 205 (1974).

318-B:23. Enforcement and Cooperation.

It is hereby made the duty of the department of health and human services, its officers, agents, inspectors, and representatives; the pharmacy board, its officers, agents, inspectors and representatives; and of all peace officers within the state, and of all county attorneys, to enforce all provisions of this chapter, except those specifically delegated, and to cooperate with all agencies charged with the enforcement of the laws of the United States, of this state, and of all other states relating to controlled drugs.

Source.

1969, 421:1. 1977, 547:18. 1995, 310:181, eff. Nov. 1, 1995.

Revision note.

Substituted "pharmacy board" for "pharmacy commission" for purposes of conformity with RSA 318, as amended by 1981, 484.

Amendments

—1995. Substituted "department of health and human services" for "division of public health services".

—1977. Inserted "the pharmacy commission, its officers, agents, inspectors and representatives" preceding "and of all peace officers".

Severability of 1995 amendment.

1995, 310, which amended this section, was subject to a severability clause. See 1995, 310:186.

Construction of 1995 amendment.

1995, 310:187, eff. Nov. 1, 1995, provided:

"Nothing in this act is intended to, nor shall it be construed as, mandating or assigning any new, expanded, or modified program or responsibility for any political subdivision in violation of part I, article 28-a of the constitution of the state of New Hampshire."

318-B:24. Rulemaking.

I. The commissioner of the department of health and human services, in conjunction with the pharmacy board, shall adopt rules, pursuant to RSA 541-A, relative to:

(a) Investigations and hearings on controlled drugs under RSA 318-B:1, VI.

(b) Official forms required by RSA 318-B:1, XIX.

(c) Licenses under RSA 318-B:4.

(d) Revocation procedures under RSA 318-B:11.

(e) Labels under RSA 318-B:13.

(f) [Repealed.]

II. The commissioner of the department of health and human services and the pharmacy board are hereby required to adopt rules under this chapter to conform with regulations promulgated by the Secretary of the Treasury of the United States, his delegate, the Secretary of Health and Human Services of the United States, or the United States Attorney General under the Comprehensive Drug Abuse Prevention and Control Act of 1970 and the federal food and drug laws.

Source.

1969, 421:1. 1977, 547:19. 1985, 190:101; 324:23. 1995, 310:182, eff. Nov. 1, 1995. 2012, 171:26, XIII, eff. August 10, 2012.

References in text.

The reference to RSA 318-B:4 in par. I(c) is obsolete. RSA 318-B:4 was repealed by 1985, 324:25. Provisions relating to licensing of drug manufacturers and wholesalers generally appear in RSA 318:51-a.

The Comprehensive Drug Abuse Prevention and Control Act of 1970, referred to in par. II, is classified principally to 42 U.S.C.S. §§ 218, 246, 4541.

The federal food and drug laws, referred to in par. II, are classified principally to 21 U.S.C.S. §§ 301 et seq.

Revision note.

Near the end of the section, substituted "Secretary of Health and Human Services of the United States" and "Attorney General" for "commissioner of narcotics". The functions of the Secretary of Health, Education and Welfare were divided among the Secretary of Health and Human Services and the Secretary of Education pursuant to Section 509(b) of Pub. L. 96-88. See generally 42 U.S.C.S. § 202 and notes thereunder.

Rules and regulations under the Comprehensive Drug Abuse Prevention and Control Act of 1970 are promulgated by the Attorney General of the United States. See 21 U.S.C.S. § 821.

Amendments

—2012. The 2012 amendment deleted I(f).

—1995. Substituted "commissioner of the department of health and human services" for "director, division of public health services" in the introductory paragraph of par. I and preceding "and the pharmacy" in par. II.

—1985. Rewritten by ch. 190 to the extent that a detailed comparison would be impracticable.

Chapter 324 inserted "in conjunction with the pharmacy board" preceding "shall" in the introductory paragraph of par. I and substituted "and the pharmacy board are" for "is" preceding "hereby" in par. II.

—1977. Substituted "Comprehensive Drug Abuse Prevention and Control Act of 1970" for "federal narcotic laws".

Severability of 1995 amendment.

1995, 310, which amended this section, was subject to a severability clause. See 1995, 310:186.

Construction of 1995 amendment.

1995, 310:187, eff. Nov. 1, 1995, provided:

"Nothing in this act is intended to, nor shall it be construed as, mandating or assigning any new, expanded, or modified program or responsibility for any political subdivision in violation of part I, article 28-a of the constitution of the state of New Hampshire."

318-B:25. Authority for Inspection.

All officers, agents, inspectors and representatives of the department of health and human services who are charged with the responsibility to enforce this chapter; all officers, agents, inspectors, and representatives of the pharmacy board who are charged with the responsibility to enforce this chapter; all peace officers within the state; the attorney general and all county attorneys; and federal, state, county and municipal law enforcement officers are authorized to enter during normal business hours upon the premises used by a practitioner for the purpose of his practice and to inspect such original records or prescriptions or both for controlled drugs as defined herein. Every practitioner, his clerk, agent, or servant shall exhibit to such person on demand every such original record or prescription or both so kept on file.

Source.

1969, 421:1. 1977, 547:20. 1983, 292:19. 1985, 324:24. 1995, 310:181, eff. Nov. 1, 1995.

Amendments

—1995. Substituted "department of health and human services" for "division of public health services" in the first sentence.

—1985. Rewritten to the extent that a detailed comparison would be impracticable.

—1983. Substituted "board" for "commission" following "pharmacy", inserted "federal, state, county and municipal officers" following "county attorneys", and deleted "or her" following "his" wherever it appeared.

—1977. Rewritten to the extent that a detailed comparison would be impracticable.

Severability of 1995 amendment.

1995, 310, which amended this section, was subject to a severability clause. See 1995, 310:186.

Construction of 1995 amendment.

1995, 310:187, eff. Nov. 1, 1995, provided:

"Nothing in this act is intended to, nor shall it be construed as, mandating or assigning any new, expanded, or modified program or responsibility for any political subdivision in violation of part I, article 28-a of the constitution of the state of New Hampshire."

Cross References.

Administrative inspection warrants generally, see RSA 595-B.

Enforcement generally, see RSA 318-B:23.

NOTES TO DECISIONS

Constitutionality

Statutes governing authority of board of pharmacy and procedure to inspect pharmacies were not impermissibly vague, where they clearly notified licensees that they had a duty to comply with all federal, State, and local pharmacy and drug laws, and authorized board inspections to enforce that duty; fact that perfect compliance with law was rarely possible did not mean that express standards were required, but that decisions to investigate and prosecute were committed to sound discretion of agency. Appeal of Morgan (New Hampshire Bd. of Pharm.), 144 N.H. 44, 742 A.2d 101, 1999 N.H. LEXIS 75 (1999).

Cited:

Cited in State v. Summers, 142 N.H. 429, 702 A.2d 819, 1997 N.H. LEXIS 115 (1997).

318-B:26. Penalties.

I. Any person who manufactures, sells, prescribes, administers, or transports or possesses with intent to sell, dispense, or compound any controlled drug, controlled drug analog or any preparation containing a controlled drug, except as authorized in this chapter; or manufactures, sells, or transports or possesses with intent to sell, dispense, compound, package or repackage (1) any substance which he represents to be a controlled drug, or controlled drug analog, or (2) any preparation containing a substance which he represents to be a controlled drug, or controlled drug analog, shall be sentenced as follows, except as otherwise provided in this section:

(a) In the case of a violation involving any of the following, a person shall be sentenced to a maximum term of imprisonment of not more than 30 years, a fine of not more than $500,000, or both. If any person commits such a violation after one or more prior offenses as defined in RSA 318-B:27, such person may be sentenced to a maximum term of life imprisonment, a fine of not more than $500,000, or both:

 (1) Five ounces or more of a mixture or substance containing any of the following, including any adulterants or dilutants:

  (A) Coca leaves, except coca leaves and extracts of coca leaves from which cocaine, ecgonine, and derivatives of ecgonine or their salts have been removed; or

  (B) Cocaine other than crack cocaine, its salts, optical and geometric isomers, and salts of isomers; or

  (C) Ecgonine, its derivatives, their salts, isomers, and salts of isomers.

 (2) Lysergic acid diethylamide, or its analog, in a quantity of 100 milligrams or more including any adulterants or dilutants, or phencyclidine (PCP), or its analog, in a quantity of 10 grams or more including any adulterants or dilutants.

 (3) Heroin or its analog or crack cocaine in a quantity of 5 grams or more, including any adulterants or dilutants.

 (4) Methamphetamine or its analog, in a quantity of 5 ounces or more, including adulterants or dilutants.

 (b) In the case of a violation involving any of the following, a person may be sentenced to a maximum term of imprisonment of not more than 20 years, a fine of not more than $300,000, or both. If any person commits such a violation after one or more prior offenses as defined in RSA 318-B:27, such person may be sentenced to a term of imprisonment of not more than 40 years, a fine of not more than $500,000, or both:

 (1) A substance or mixture referred to in subparagraph I(a)(1) of this section, other than crack cocaine, in a quantity of ½ ounce or more, including any adulterants or dilutants;

 (2) A substance classified in schedule I or II other than those specifically covered in this section, or the analog of any such substance, in a quantity of one ounce or more including any adulterants or dilutants;

 (3) Lysergic acid diethylamide, or its analog, in a quantity of less than 100 milligrams including any adulterants or dilutants, or where the amount is undetermined, or phencyclidine (PCP) or its analog, in a quantity of less than 10 grams, including any adulterants or dilutants, or where the amount is undetermined;

 (4) Heroin or its analog or crack cocaine in a quantity of one gram or more, including any adulterants or dilutants;

 (5) Methamphetamine or its analog, in a quantity of one ounce or more including any adulterants or dilutants;

 (6) Marijuana in a quantity of 5 pounds or more including any adulterants or dilutants, or hashish in a quantity of one pound or more

including any adulterants and dilutants;

 (7) Flunitrazepam in a quantity of 500 milligrams or more.

 (c) In the case of a violation involving any of the following, a person may be sentenced to a maximum term of imprisonment of not more than 7 years, a fine of not more than $100,000, or both. If any person commits such a violation after one or more prior offenses as defined in RSA 318-B:27, such person may be sentenced to a maximum term of imprisonment of not more than 15 years, a fine of not more than $200,000, or both:

 (1) A substance or mixture referred to in subparagraph I(a)(1) of this section, other than crack cocaine, in a quantity less than ½ ounce including any adulterants or dilutants;

 (2) A substance or mixture classified as a narcotic drug in schedule I or II other than those specifically covered in this section, or the analog of any such substance, in a quantity of less than one ounce including any adulterants or dilutants;

 (3) Methamphetamine, or its analog in a quantity of less than one ounce including any adulterants or dilutants;

 (4) Heroin or its analog or crack cocaine in a quantity of less than one gram, including any adulterants or dilutants;

 (5) Marijuana in a quantity of one ounce or more including any adulterants or dilutants, or hashish in a quantity of 5 grams or more including any adulterants or dilutants;

 (6) Flunitrazepam in a quantity of less than 500 milligrams;

 (7) Any other controlled drug or its analog, other than those specifically covered in this section, classified in schedules I, II, III or IV.

 (d) In the case of a violation involving any of the following, a person may be sentenced to a maximum term of imprisonment of not more than 3 years, a fine of not more than $25,000, or both. If any person commits such a violation after one or more prior offenses as defined in RSA 318-B:27, such person may be sentenced to a maximum term of imprisonment of not more than 6 years, a fine of not more than $50,000, or both:

 (1) Marijuana in a quantity of less than one ounce including any adulterants or dilutants, or hashish in a quantity of less than 5 grams including any adulterants or dilutants;

 (2) Any schedule V substance or its analog.

II. Any person who knowingly or purposely obtains, purchases, transports, or possesses actually or constructively, or has under his control, any controlled drug or controlled drug analog, or any preparation containing a controlled drug or controlled drug analog, except as authorized in this chapter, shall be sentenced as follows, except as otherwise provided in this section:

 (a) In the case of a controlled drug or its analog, classified in schedules I, II, III or IV, other than those specifically covered in this section, the person shall be guilty of a class B felony, except that notwithstanding the provisions of RSA 651:2, IV(a), a fine of not more than $25,000 may be imposed. If any person commits such a violation after one or more prior offenses as defined in RSA 318-B:27, such person shall be guilty of a class A felony, except that notwithstanding the provisions of RSA 651:2, IV(a), a fine of up to $50,000 may be imposed;

(b) In the case of a controlled drug or its analog classified in schedule V, the person shall be sentenced to a maximum term of imprisonment of not more than 3 years, a fine of not more than $15,000, or both. If a person commits any such violation after one or more prior offenses as defined in RSA 318-B:27, such person shall be guilty of a class B felony, except that notwithstanding the provisions of RSA 651:2, IV(a), a fine of not more than $25,000 may be imposed;

(c) In the case of more than 5 grams of hashish, the person shall be guilty of a misdemeanor, except that notwithstanding the provisions of RSA 651:2, IV(a), a fine of not more than $5,000 may be imposed.

(d) In the case of marijuana, including any adulterants or dilutants, or 5 grams or less of hashish, the person shall be guilty of a class A misdemeanor.

III. A person shall be guilty of a misdemeanor who:

(a) Controls any premises or vehicle where he knows a controlled drug or its analog is illegally kept or deposited;

(b) Aids, assists or abets a person in his presence in the perpetration of a crime punishable under paragraph II of this section, knowing that such person is illegally in possession of a controlled drug or its analog.

(c) Manufactures with the intent to deliver, delivers or possesses with the intent to deliver any drug paraphernalia when such paraphernalia is knowingly manufactured, delivered or possessed for one or more of the uses set forth in RSA 318-B:2, II.

(d) Places an advertisement in violation of RSA 318-B:2, III.

III-a. [Repealed.]

IV. Any person who attempts or conspires to commit any offense defined in this chapter is punishable by imprisonment or a fine or both, which may not exceed the maximum punishment prescribed for the offense, the commission of which was the object of the attempt or conspiracy.

V. Any person who violates this chapter by manufacturing, selling, prescribing, administering, dispensing, or possessing with intent to sell, dispense, or compound any controlled drug or its analog, in or on or within 1,000 feet of the real property comprising a public or private elementary, secondary, or secondary vocational-technical school, may be sentenced to a term of imprisonment or fine, or both, up to twice that otherwise authorized by this section. Except to the extent a greater minimum sentence is

otherwise provided by this chapter, a sentence imposed under this paragraph shall include a mandatory minimum term of imprisonment of not less than one year. Neither the whole nor any part of the mandatory minimum sentence imposed under this paragraph shall be suspended or reduced.

VI. Except as otherwise provided in this paragraph, a person convicted under RSA 318-B:2, XII as a drug enterprise leader shall be sentenced to a mandatory minimum term of not less than 25 years and may be sentenced to a maximum term of not more than life imprisonment. The court may also impose a fine not to exceed $500,000 or 5 times the street value of the controlled drug or controlled drug analog involved, whichever is greater. Upon conviction, the court shall impose the mandatory sentence unless the defendant has pleaded guilty pursuant to a negotiated agreement or, in cases resulting in trial, the defendant and the state have entered into a post-conviction agreement which provides for a lesser sentence. The negotiated plea or post-conviction agreement may provide for a specified term of imprisonment within the range of ordinary or extended sentences authorized by law, a specified fine, or other disposition. In that event, the court at sentencing shall not impose a lesser term of imprisonment or fine than that expressly provided for under the terms of the plea or post-conviction agreement.

VII. Any person who violates RSA 318-B:2, XI may be sentenced to a maximum term of imprisonment of not more than 20 years, a fine of not more than $300,000, or both. If any person commits such a violation after one or more prior offenses, as defined in RSA 318-B:27, such person may be sentenced to a term of imprisonment of not more than 40 years, a fine of not more than $500,000, or both.

VIII. Any person who knowingly or purposely obtains or purchases (1) any substance which he represents to be a controlled drug or controlled drug analog, or (2) any preparation containing a substance which he represents to be a controlled drug or controlled drug analog, except as authorized in this chapter, shall be guilty of a misdemeanor. If any person commits such a violation after one or more prior offenses as defined in RSA 318-B:27, such person shall be guilty of a class B felony.

IX. Any person who manufactures, sells, or dispenses methamphetamine, lysergic acid, diethylamide phencyclidine (PCP) or any other controlled drug classified in schedules I or II, or any controlled drug analog thereof, in violation of RSA 318-B:2, I or I-a, is strictly liable for a death which results from the injection, inhalation or ingestion of that substance, and may be sentenced to imprisonment for life or for such term as the court may order. For purposes of this section, the person's act of manufacturing, dispensing, or selling a substance is the cause of a death when:

(a) the injection, inhalation or ingestion of the substance is an antecedent but for which the death would not have occurred; and

(b) the death was not:

(1) too remote in its occurrence as to have just bearing on the person's liability; or

(2) too dependent upon conduct of another person which was unrelated to the injection, inhalation or ingestion of the substance or its effect, as to have a just bearing on the person's liability. It shall not be a defense to a prosecution under this section that the decedent contributed to his own death by his purposeful, knowing, reckless or negligent injection, inhalation or ingestion of the substance or by his consenting to the administration of the substance by another. Nothing in this section shall be construed to preclude or limit any prosecution for homicide. A conviction arising under this section shall not merge with a conviction of one as a drug enterprise leader or for any other offense defined in this chapter.

IX-a. A qualifying patient or designated caregiver as defined in RSA 126-W:1 who sells cannabis to a person who is not a qualifying patient or a designated caregiver shall be guilty of a class B felony and shall be sentenced to a maximum term of imprisonment of not more than 7 years, a fine of not more than $300,000, or both.

X. Any penalty imposed for violation of this chapter shall be in addition to, and not in lieu of, any civil or administrative penalty or sanction authorized by law.

XI. Any person who violates any provision of this chapter for which a penalty is not provided by paragraphs I through IX shall be guilty of a class B felony if a natural person, or guilty of a felony if any other person.

XII. The penalty categories set forth in this section based upon the weight of the drug involved are material elements of the offense; however, the culpability requirement shall not apply to that element of the offense.

XIII. Any person who violates any provision of this chapter shall be fined a minimum of $350 for a first offense and $500 for a second or subsequent offense.

Source.
1969, 421:1. 1970, 48:3. 1973, 528:204. 1977, 547:21. 1981, 114:2; 513:3, 4. 1988, 6:4. 1989, 195:2; 207:2–5. 1991, 364:2. 1993, 291:1, eff. June 23, 1993. 1994, 186:3–11, eff. Jan. 1, 1995. 1998, 359:3, 4, eff. June 26, 1998. 2005, 177:52, eff. July 1, 2005. 2006, 241:2, eff. January 1, 2007. 2013, 242:4, eff. July 23, 2013.

Amendments
—**2013.** The 2013 amendment added IX-a.

—**2006.** Paragraph I(a)(4): Added.

—**2005.** Paragraph XIII: Added.

—**1998.** Paragraph I(b): Made a minor change in punctuation in subpar. (6) and added subpar. (7).
Paragraph I(c): Added new subpar. (6) and redesignated former subpar. (6) as subpar. (7).

—**1994.** Paragraph I(a): Inserted "other than crack cocaine" preceding "its salts" in subpar. (1)(B) and "or crack cocaine" following "analog" in subpar. (3).
Paragraph I(b): Inserted "other than crack cocaine" following "section" and deleted "but less than 5 ounces" preceding "including" in subpar. (1) and inserted "or crack cocaine" following "analog" and "one gram or" preceding "more" and deleted "than one gram but less than 5 grams" thereafter in subpar. (4).
Paragraph I(c): Inserted "other than crack cocaine" following "section" in subpar. (1) and "or crack cocaine" following "analog" in subpar. (4) and deleted "but less than 5 pounds" following "ounce or more" and "but less than one pound" following "grams or more" in subpar. (5).
Paragraph II: Deleted "of possession" following "case" in subpars. (c) and (d) and inserted "class A" preceding "misdemeanor" in subpar. (d).
Paragraph XII: Added.

—**1993.** Paragraph III-a: Repealed.

—**1991.** Paragraph V: Substituted "violates this chapter by manufacturing, selling, prescribing, administering, dispensing, or possessing" for "manufactures, sells, prescribes, administers, dispenses, or possesses" preceding "with intent" and "secondary, or secondary vocational-technical" for "vocational, or secondary" preceding "school" and made other minor stylistic changes in the first sentence and added the second and third sentences.

—**1989.** Paragraphs I and VII: Rewritten by ch. 207 to the extent that a detailed comparison would be impracticable.
Paragraph III-a: Added by ch. 195.
Paragraph VIII: Chapter 207 rewrote the first sentence.
Paragraph XI: Added by ch. 207.

—**1988.** Rewritten to the extent that a detailed comparison would be impracticable.

—**1981.** Paragraphs II(a), II(b): Rewritten by ch. 114 to the extent that a detailed comparison would be impracticable.
Paragraphs II(c), II(d): Added by ch. 513.
Paragraph III: Chapter 513 inserted "except those of RSA 318-B:2, II or III" following "this chapter" in the first sentence and added the second sentence.

—**1977.** Paragraph I(a): Inserted "or possesses" following "transports" in the introductory clause.

—**1973.** Rewritten to the extent that a detailed comparison would be impracticable.

—**1970.** Paragraph I(c): Added.

Purpose of 2005 amendments.
2005, 177:23, eff. July 1, 2005, provided: "Sections 24–52 of this act [which amended this section and RSA 179:10, 261:40, 261:61, 261:176, 263:30, 263:64, 263:92, 265:3, 265:15, 265:17, 265:22, 265:23, 265:25, 265:26, 265:31, 265:57, 265:60, 265:79, 265:81, 265:82-b, 265:94, 265:95, 265:99, 265:107-a, 265:120, 266:5, and enacted RSA 265:50-a], are increases to current motor vehicle fines contained in the uniform fine schedule which, pursuant to RSA 502-A:19-b, V, may be changed only by statute."

Purpose of 1981 amendment of paragraph II.
1981, 114:1, eff. July 3, 1981, provided: "It is the intent of this act [which amended par. II of this section] to prevent the prosecution of persons under the controlled drug laws who do not act to aid, assist, or abet the perpetration of a crime. Mere presence at and knowledge of the commission of a crime do not justify criminal prosecution; rather, it is the element of participation or abetting by lending approbation to a wrong through one's presence which is at the heart of the wrong prohibited."

Severability of 1981 amendments.
1981, 513:3 and 513:4 were subject to a severability clause. See 1981, 513:5.

Cross References.
Classification of crimes, see RSA 625:9.
Offenses generally, see RSA 318-B:2.

Sentences, see RSA 651.

NOTES TO DECISIONS

1. Constitutionality
2. Construction with other law
3. Admissibility of evidence
4. Possession
5. Possession with intent to sell
6. Dispensing with death resulting

1. Constitutionality

Penalty provisions of drug enterprise leader statute did not impermissibly burden defendant's right to jury trial, by encouraging defendant to enter a negotiated plea or post-conviction agreement in order to avoid a twenty-five-year mandatory minimum sentence. State v. Marcano, 138 N.H. 643, 645 A.2d 661, 1994 N.H. LEXIS 82 (1994).

2. Construction with other law

Where defendant was charged with misdemeanor transportation of a controlled drug and felony possession of a controlled drug, conviction on the felony possession charge was barred by double jeopardy since the possession charge lacked any element not common to the transportation charge, and, therefore, was a lesser-included offense of the transportation charge. State v. Constant, 135 N.H. 254, 605 A.2d 206, 1992 N.H. LEXIS 17 (1992).

The reference in RSA 318-B:2, I, to a controlled drug refers to the same narcotic controlled drugs that fall within the scope of paragraph I of this section. State v. Stiles, 128 N.H. 81, 512 A.2d 1084, 1986 N.H. LEXIS 289 (1986).

Possession of cocaine of any isomer is a felony under subparagraph I(b)(1) of this section and like possession with intent to sell is a felony under subparagraph I(a)(1) of this section. State v. Stiles, 128 N.H. 81, 512 A.2d 1084, 1986 N.H. LEXIS 289 (1986).

Defendant charged with felony of transporting a controlled drug with intent to dispense it was not entitled to a jury instruction on former RSA 265:80 [see now RSA 265-A:43] the misdemeanor of driving while possessing a controlled drug, as a lesser-included offense, since the misdemeanor offense was not a lesser-included offense under the felony offense and since, even if it were, defendant conceded by his own testimony the existence of the claimed uncommon element distinguishing the two offenses, intent to dispense the drugs. State v. Cimino, 126 N.H. 570, 493 A.2d 1197, 1985 N.H. LEXIS 346 (1985).

3. Admissibility of evidence

Where the process of randomly selecting packets of contraband for testing was accepted in the scientific community, the chemical testing methods were consistent with those used in the scientific community, and the tested and untested samples were similar in both appearance and packaging, there was sufficient reliability to permit the admission of the untested packets; a reasonable inference could be drawn about both the contents and weight of the untested packets. State v. Tucker, 149 N.H. 792, 837 A.2d 1078, 2003 N.H. LEXIS 127 (2003).

Out-of-court statements by co-conspirators are admissible as exceptions to hearsay rule when made during pendency of the criminal enterprise and in furtherance of the criminal object, as long as existence of conspiracy is sufficiently proved by independent evidence. State v. Gonzalez, 136 N.H. 354, 615 A.2d 640, 1992 N.H. LEXIS 177 (1992).

State made prima facie case that defendant was conspiracy member, ensuring that statements by co-conspirator were allowable as hearsay exceptions, where trooper testified that defendant was recognized by person in conspiracy and defendant committed overt acts in furtherance of conspiracy. State v. Gonzalez, 136 N.H. 354, 615 A.2d 640, 1992 N.H. LEXIS 177 (1992).

In prosecution for possession of marijuana with intent to sell, where only a representative sample of seized contraband was chemically analyzed, trial judge did not abuse his discretion in admitting into evidence baggies containing unanalyzed material, since this evidence had considerable probative value, and was a representative sample of the seized material. State v. Rodrigue, 127 N.H. 496, 506 A.2d 299, 1985 N.H. LEXIS 477 (1985).

4. Possession

Warrantless entry of police officers into defendant's hotel room was justified by a totality of circumstances that indicated exigent circumstances existed because the officers smelled burning marijuana, which was an indication that evidence was being destroyed. The officers could conclude that a serious crime was being committed because possession of marijuana was a class A misdemeanor pursuant to RSA 318-B:26, II(d) and a class A misdemeanor was punishable by a prison term not to exceed one year pursuant to RSA 651:2, II(c). State v. Rodriguez, 157 N.H. 100, 945 A.2d 676, 2008 N.H. LEXIS 42 (2008).

To obtain a conviction under paragraph I(b) of this section for possession of a narcotic drug, the state must prove beyond a reasonable doubt: (1) that the defendant had knowledge of the nature of the drug, (2) that he had knowledge of its presence in his vicinity, and (3) that he had custody of the drug and exercised dominion and control over it. State v. Sweeney, 124 N.H. 396, 469 A.2d 1362, 1983 N.H. LEXIS 419 (1983).

In order to sustain a conviction under this section for the offense of possession, the state must prove beyond a reasonable doubt: (1) that defendant had knowledge of the nature of the drug, (2) that he had knowledge of its presence in his vicinity, and (3) that he had custody of the drug and exercised dominion and control over it. State v. Fossett, 119 N.H. 155, 399 A.2d 966, 1979 N.H. LEXIS 259 (1979).

5. Possession with intent to sell

Evidence was sufficient for the jury to find that the defendant took a substantial step towards commission of the crime of attempted possession of marijuana with intent to dispense where: (1) the defendant agreed to meet with an undercover officer and his source to purchase one pound of marijuana, (2) she inspected the marijuana, smelled it, voiced her displeasure that it was brown, and decided not to purchase it, and (3) she evidenced familiarity with other dealers and the market price for green marijuana, stated her ability and intent to resell marijuana, and asked the undercover officer to contact her if he obtained green marijuana; the fact that the defendant did not go through with the purchase of marijuana did not require a contrary result. State v. Allcock, 137 N.H. 458, 629 A.2d 99, 1993 N.H. LEXIS 102 (1993).

In prosecution for possession of marijuana with intent to sell, the state had the burden of proving that the defendant possessed drugs with an intent to sell or give them to another person. State v. Rodrigue, 127 N.H. 496, 506 A.2d 299, 1985 N.H. LEXIS 477 (1985).

In order to sustain a conviction under this section for the offense of possession of a controlled drug with intent to sell, the state must prove beyond a reasonable doubt: (1) that the defendant knew the nature of the drug, (2) that he knew the drug was in his vicinity, and (3) that he possessed the drugs with intent to sell or give them to another person. State v. Renfrew, 122 N.H. 308, 444 A.2d 527, 1982 N.H. LEXIS 334 (1982).

6. Dispensing with death resulting

Indictment for dispensing a controlled drug with death resulting under RSA 318-B:26, IX, satisfied N.H. Const. pt. I, art. 15, as it communicated to defendant that he was charged with dispensing a proscribed controlled drug and that a death resulted from injecting, inhaling, or ingesting that controlled drug. The use of the phrase "resulting in" apprised defendant that causation was an element; furthermore, assuming that the state constitution required any fact, other than a prior conviction, to be alleged, this rule was not violated, as the factor that the heroin dispensed by defendant caused the decedent's death was charged in the indictment, submitted to the jury, and found to exist by proof beyond a reasonable doubt. State v. Marshall, 162 N.H. 657, 34 A.3d 540, 2011 N.H. LEXIS 152 (2011).

RSA 318-B:26, IX(a) and (b) are not additional "elements" to be proved, but rather explain further the kind of causation required before criminal liability may attach under this statute. RSA 318-B:26, IX(a) and (b) constitute the law to be applied when determining whether the element of causation, that is, "death resulting," has been met. State v. Marshall, 162 N.H. 657, 34 A.3d 540, 2011 N.H. LEXIS 152 (2011).

Indictment under RSA 318-B:26, IX, is sufficient if it states that the victim's death resulted from the victim's ingestion of the controlled drug that the defendant dispensed. In the indictment here, the use of the phrase "resulting in" apprised defendant that causation was an element of the offense. State v. Marshall, 162 N.H. 657, 34 A.3d 540, 2011 N.H. LEXIS 152 (2011).

Rational juror could have found that defendant's act of dispensing heroin to the decedent caused his death. Defendant conceded that the State introduced sufficient evidence to satisfy RSA 318-B:26, IX(a), and made no argument concerning RSA 318-B:26, IX(b)(1); the jury could have found that the "too dependent" exception of the statute did not apply here because the decedent's consumption of alcohol was related to the effect of the heroin, in that the alcohol and the heroin worked together to cause his inadequate breathing that precipitated his death. State v. Marshall, 162 N.H. 657, 34 A.3d 540, 2011 N.H. LEXIS 152 (2011).

In a trial for dispensing a controlled drug with death resulting, the jury could have found that defendant and the victim did not jointly acquire heroin because defendant called his drug dealer to purchase heroin; only defendant and the dealer orchestrated the meetings in order to facilitate the sales; during both sales, the dealer interacted only with defendant; and the dealer was unaware that the victim intended to use the heroin. Even though the victim was present during both drug sales, withdrew money to buy the heroin, and wanted to purchase it, the jury could have reasonably concluded that defendant dispensed the heroin to her only after acquiring it from the dealer. State v. Silva, 158 N.H. 96, 960 A.2d 715, 2008 N.H. LEXIS 145 (2008).

Cited:
Cited in State v. Streeter, 113 N.H. 402, 308 A.2d 535, 1973 N.H. LEXIS 284 (1973); State v. Nickerson, 114 N.H. 47, 314 A.2d 648, 1974 N.H. LEXIS 205 (1974); State v. Comeau, 114 N.H. 431, 321 A.2d 590, 1974 N.H. LEXIS 294 (1974); State v. Dearborn, 114 N.H. 457, 322 A.2d 924, 1974 N.H. LEXIS 301 (1974); State v. Dunphy, 114 N.H. 740, 328 A.2d 787, 1974 N.H. LEXIS 363 (1974); State v. Horan, 115 N.H. 35, 332 A.2d 175, 1975 N.H. LEXIS 216 (1975); State v. Greely, 115 N.H. 461, 344 A.2d 12, 1975 N.H. LEXIS 335 (1975); State v. Gilbert, 115 N.H. 665, 348 A.2d 713, 1975 N.H. LEXIS 391 (1975); State v. Goodwin, 116 N.H. 37, 351 A.2d 59, 1976 N.H. LEXIS 257 (1976); State v. Wolfson, 116 N.H. 227, 356 A.2d 692, 1976 N.H. LEXIS 315 (1976); State v. Gilson, 116 N.H. 230, 356 A.2d 689, 1976 N.H. LEXIS 316 (1976); State v. Thorp, 116 N.H. 303, 358 A.2d 655, 1976 N.H. LEXIS 338 (1976); State v. Jarret, 116 N.H. 590, 364 A.2d 624, 1976 N.H. LEXIS 420 (1976); Shea v. Helgemoe, 116 N.H. 640, 365 A.2d 1043, 1976 N.H. LEXIS 434 (1976); State v. Desbiens, 117 N.H. 433, 374 A.2d 651, 1977 N.H. LEXIS 352 (1977); State v. Maxfield, 121 N.H. 103, 427 A.2d 12, 1981 N.H. LEXIS 261 (1981); State v. Francoeur, 122 N.H. 386, 445 A.2d 1095, 1982 N.H. LEXIS 356 (1982); State v. Levesque, 123 N.H. 52, 455 A.2d 1045, 1983 N.H. LEXIS 221 (1983); State v. Philibotte, 123 N.H. 240, 459 A.2d 275, 1983 N.H. LEXIS 259 (1983); State v. Toto, 123 N.H. 619, 465 A.2d 894, 1983 N.H. LEXIS 344 (1983); State v. Miskolczi, 123 N.H. 626, 465 A.2d 919, 1983 N.H. LEXIS 325 (1983); State v. Ball, 124 N.H. 226, 471 A.2d 347, 1983 N.H. LEXIS 426 (1983); State v. Baldwin, 124 N.H. 770, 475 A.2d 522, 1984 N.H. LEXIS 341 (1984); State v. Berger, 125 N.H. 83, 480 A.2d 27, 1984 N.H. LEXIS 366 (1984); State v. Mayo, 125 N.H. 200, 480 A.2d 85, 1984 N.H. LEXIS 255 (1984); State v. Meister, 125 N.H. 435, 480 A.2d 200, 1984 N.H. LEXIS 245 (1984); State v. Cote, 126 N.H. 514, 493 A.2d 1170, 1985 N.H. LEXIS 336 (1985); State v. Farnsworth, 126 N.H. 656, 497 A.2d 835, 1985 N.H. LEXIS 421 (1985); State v. Whiting, 127 N.H. 110, 497 A.2d 1217, 1985 N.H. LEXIS 378 (1985); State v. Ruffing, 127 N.H. 370, 499 A.2d 1351, 1985 N.H. LEXIS 431 (1985); State v. Dellorfano, 128 N.H. 628, 517 A.2d 1163, 1986 N.H. LEXIS 343 (1986); State v. Bradberry, 129 N.H. 68, 522 A.2d 1380, 1986 N.H. LEXIS 397 (1986); State v. Maguire, 129 N.H. 165, 523 A.2d 120, 1987 N.H. LEXIS 161 (1987); State v. Isaacson, 129 N.H. 438, 529 A.2d 923, 1987 N.H. LEXIS 222 (1987); State v. Otero, 129 N.H. 444, 529 A.2d 381, 1987 N.H. LEXIS 220 (1987); State v. Torres, 130 N.H. 340, 540 A.2d 1217, 1988 N.H. LEXIS 11 (1988); State v. Carroll, 131 N.H. 179, 552 A.2d 69, 1988 N.H. LEXIS 103 (1988); State v. Gigas, 131 N.H. 389, 553 A.2d 321, 1988 N.H. LEXIS 123 (1988); State v. Stratton, 132 N.H. 451, 567 A.2d 986, 1989 N.H. LEXIS 124 (1989); State v. Thompson, 132 N.H. 730, 571 A.2d 266, 1990 N.H. LEXIS 24 (1990); State v. Davis, 133 N.H. 211, 575 A.2d 4, 1990 N.H. LEXIS 49 (1990); State v. Cartier, 133 N.H. 217, 575 A.2d 347, 1990 N.H. LEXIS 54 (1990); State v. Gooden, 133 N.H. 674, 582 A.2d 607, 1990 N.H. LEXIS 120 (1990); United States v. Isabel, 945 F.2d 1193, 1991 U.S. App. LEXIS 21208 (1st Cir. N.H. 1991); State v. Murray, 134 N.H. 613, 598 A.2d 206, 1991 N.H. LEXIS 107 (1991); State v. Dodier, 135 N.H. 134, 600 A.2d 913, 1991 N.H. LEXIS 152 (1991); State v. Paige, 136 N.H. 208, 612 A.2d 1331, 1992 N.H. LEXIS 154 (1992); State v. Alosa, 137 N.H. 33, 623 A.2d 218, 1993 N.H. LEXIS 37 (1993); State v. Drake, 139 N.H. 662, 662 A.2d 265, 1995 N.H. LEXIS 69 (1995); State v. Conant, 139 N.H. 728, 662 A.2d 283, 1995 N.H. LEXIS 79 (1995); State v. Johnson, 140 N.H. 573, 669 A.2d 222, 1995 N.H. LEXIS 194 (1995); State v. Gonzalez, 143 N.H. 693, 738 A.2d 1247, 1999 N.H. LEXIS 59 (1999); In re Toyota Avalon, 155 N.H. 720, 927 A.2d 1239, 2007 N.H. LEXIS 124 (2007).

RESEARCH REFERENCES

Criminal jury instructions.
New Hampshire Criminal Jury Instructions, Instruction # 2.34.

318-B:26-a. Chemical Analyses.

I. Upon the request of the attorney general, a county attorney or any law enforcement agency, the laboratory employee performing the chemical analysis shall prepare a certificate. The employee shall sign the certificate under oath and shall include in the certificate an attestation as to the result of the analysis. The presentation of this certificate to a court by any party to a proceeding shall be evidence that all of the requirements and provisions of this section have been complied with. This certificate shall be sworn to before a notary public or other person empowered by law to take oaths and shall contain a statement establishing the following: the type of analysis performed; the result achieved; any conclusions reached based upon that result; that the subscriber is the person who performed the analysis and made the conclusions; the subscriber's training or experience to perform the analysis; and the nature and condition of the equipment used. When properly executed, the certificate shall, subject to paragraph II of this section and notwithstanding any other provision of law, be admissible evidence of the composition, quality, and quantity of the substance submitted to the laboratory for analysis, and the court shall take judicial notice of the signature of the person performing the analysis and of the fact that he is that person.

II. Whenever a party intends to proffer in a criminal proceeding a certificate executed pursuant to this section, notice of an intent to proffer that certificate and all reports relating to the analysis in question, including a copy of the certificate, shall be conveyed to the opposing party or parties at least 25 days before the proceeding begins. An opposing party who intends to object to the admission into evidence of a certificate shall give notice of objection and the specific grounds for the objection within 10 days upon receiving the adversary's notice of intent to proffer the certificate. Whenever a notice of objection is filed, admissibility of the certificate shall be determined not later than 10 days before the beginning of the trial. A proffered certificate shall be admitted in evidence unless it appears from the notice of objection and specific grounds for that objection that the composition, quality, or quantity of the substance submitted to the laboratory for analysis will be contested at trial. A failure to comply with the time limitations regarding the notice of objection required by this section shall constitute a waiver of any objection to the admission of the certificate. The time limitations set forth in this section shall not be relaxed except upon a showing of good cause.

Source.
1981, 207:1. 1983, 19:2. 1988, 6:5, eff. July 1, 1988.

Amendments
—**1988.** Rewritten to the extent that a detailed comparison would be impracticable.

—**1983.** Paragraph I: Substituted "certified mail" for "registered mail" in the second sentence.

Construction of 1981 amendment.
1981, 207:2, eff. Aug. 7, 1981, provided: "Nothing in this act [this section] shall be construed to limit a defendant's right to compel the presence at trial of the person having performed a chemical analysis under RSA 318-B:26-a, I, by subpoena."

Cross References.
Admissibility in evidence of results of test for determination of controlled drug content of blood of motor vehicle operators, see RSA 265-A:9 et seq.
Furnishing of copy of report of chemical analysis of blood of operator of motor vehicle, see RSA 265-A:4.
Preliminary tests of controlled drug content of blood of motor vehicle operators, see RSA 265:92-a.
Testing for purposes of determination of controlled drug content of blood of motor vehicle operators, see RSA 265-A:4 et seq.

NOTES TO DECISIONS

Constitutionality
Paragraph II of this section, requiring defendant charged with selling marijuana to demonstrate "specific grounds" for objection to admission of certificate of chemical analysis in order to question the analyst who prepared it, violated defendant's right to confront witnesses against him, since without confronting the analyst, defendant could not practicably identify "specific grounds", yet without identifying "specific grounds", he could not confront the analyst. State v. Christensen, 135 N.H. 583, 607 A.2d 952, 1992 N.H. LEXIS 84 (1992).

RESEARCH REFERENCES

New Hampshire Court Rules Annotated.
Motions to suppress evidence, see Rule 94, Rules of the Superior Court, New Hampshire Court Rules Annotated.

318-B:27. Prior Offenses.

In the case of any person charged with a violation of any provision of this chapter or RSA 318-D, who has previously been convicted of a violation of the laws of the United States or any state, territory or the District of Columbia relating to controlled drugs as defined in this chapter, such previous conviction shall be deemed a prior offense.

Source.
1969, 421:1, eff. Aug. 31, 1969. 2006, 241:3, eff. January 1, 2007.

Amendments
—**2006.** Inserted "or RSA 318-D" following "this chapter".

Cross References.
Offenses and penalties generally, see RSA 318-B:26.

318-B:28. Recording of Sentences as Misdemeanors or Felonies.

[Repealed 1988, 6:6, eff. July 1, 1988.]

Former section(s).
Former RSA 318-B:28, which was derived from 1969, 421:1 and 1973, 370:21, related to the recording of sentences as misdemeanors or felonies as a function of the fines imposed and disposition of time imposed and served.

318-B:28-a. Annulments of Criminal Records.

No court shall order an annulment, pursuant to RSA 651:5 or any other provision of law, of any record of conviction for a felony under RSA 318-B until 7 years after the date of conviction.

Source.
1985, 205:1. 1988, 238:5, eff. Jan. 1, 1989.

Amendments
—**1988.** Rewritten to the extent that a detailed comparison would be impracticable.

Cross References.
Classification of crimes, see RSA 625:9.
Sentences, see RSA 651.

NOTES TO DECISIONS

Construction with other law
Where RSA 651:5, III(d) would permit a petition for annulment of a conviction to be filed sooner than seven years following a Controlled Drug Act (CDA) conviction, then CDA's seven-year minimum period, set forth in RSA 318-B:28-a, controls; however, for any CDA conviction involving a sentence longer than two years, the five and ten-year provisions of RSA 651:5, III(d) and III(e) control, and the CDA's seven-year minimum is not violated. State v. Patterson, 145 N.H. 462, 764 A.2d 901, 2000 N.H. LEXIS 91 (2000).

318-B:29. Effect of Acquittal or Conviction Under the Comprehensive Drug Abuse Prevention and Control Act of 1970.

No person shall be prosecuted for a violation of any provision of this chapter if such person has been acquitted or convicted under the Comprehensive Drug Abuse Prevention and Control Act of 1970, as amended, or under the federal food and drug laws of the same act or omission which it is alleged constitutes a violation of this chapter.

Source.
1969, 421:1. 1977, 547:22. 1983, 292:20, eff. Aug. 17, 1983.

References in text.
The Comprehensive Drug Abuse Prevention and Control Act of 1970, referred to in this section, is classified principally to 42 U.S.C.S. §§ 218, 246, 4541.
The federal food and drug laws, as referred to in this section, are classified principally to 21 U.S.C.S. §§ 301 et seq.

Amendments
—**1983.** Inserted "as amended" following "Act of 1970" and made other minor changes in style.

—1977. Substituted "the Comprehensive Drug Abuse Prevention and Control Act of 1970" for "federal narcotic laws".

Cross References.
Offenses generally, see RSA 318-B:2.
Prohibition against multiple prosecutions for same crime or offense generally, see New Hampshire Constitution, Part 1, Article 16.

318-B:30. Severability.

If any provision of this chapter or the application thereof to any person or circumstances is held invalid, such invalidity shall not affect other provisions or applications of the chapter which can be given effect without the invalid provision or application, and to this end the provisions of this chapter are declared to be severable.

Source.
1969, 421:1, eff. Aug. 31, 1969.

Controlled Drug Prescription Health and Safety Program

Statement of Intent.
2012, 196:1, eff. June 12, 2012, provided:
"I.   The general court recognizes that there is a significant problem with the abuse, misuse, and diversion of controlled prescription drugs, resulting in over 100 deaths annually in New Hampshire and thousands of unnecessary visits to health care practitioners and our hospital emergency rooms.
"II.   The controlled prescription drugs most misused are found in schedules II, III, and IV, such as the stimulants Ritalin and Adderall and pain reliever oxycodone (Oxycontin and others), all in schedule II; the pain medication Vicodin, the number one abused drug in the nation, in schedule III; and tranquilizers (benzodiazepines) such as Valium, Xanax, and Ativan, in schedule IV.
"III.   The general court understands that health practitioners are challenged everyday with the difficult task of discerning between patients in need of legitimate pain treatment and the 'doctor shoppers' who seek a controlled drug prescription for their own addiction or for diversion on the street. Access to a controlled drug prescription health and safety program can help physicians and other health practitioners provide better care to patients truly in need of such medications. A controlled drug prescription health and safety program will also help identify health practitioners who are fraudulently prescribing controlled drugs and adding to prescription drug abuse in New Hampshire.
"IV.   The general court believes that a controlled drug prescription health and safety program that fully complies with all state and federal Health Insurance Portability and Accountability Act (HIPPA) privacy and security laws and regulations should be established as a tool to improve medical treatment.
"V.   The general court intends that a controlled drug prescription health and safety program will reduce patient morbidity and mortality associated with controlled drugs by providing a secure program through which the prescriber and the dispenser may access information on a patient's controlled drug prescription history. The program established by this act is designed to create a greater sense of safety, security, and comfort in the health practitioner-patient relationship when controlled drugs are prescribed.
"VI.   The general court believes, to achieve these goals, New Hampshire should join 48 other states to enact a controlled drug prescription health and safety program that physicians and other legal practitioners can access when prescribing or dispensing controlled drugs."

Applicability; Reports Required.
2012, 196:3, eff. June 12, 2012, as amended by 2013, 79:2, 3, I, eff. June 7, 2013, provides:
"I.   In the event that there is not adequate funding for the controlled drug prescription health and safety program established in section 2 of this act, the pharmacy board may curtail, temporarily suspend, or cancel the program.
"II.   The office of the legislative budget assistant shall conduct a performance audit of the program on or before December 31, 2017 for the use of the speaker of the house of representatives, the president of the senate, and the governor, in evaluating the effectiveness of the program established in section 2 of this act, including bu't not limited to changes in the number and type of drug-related deaths, the number of instances of drug abuse, and the number of instances of overprescribing.
"III.   The pharmacy board shall report annually to the oversight committee on health and human services relative to the effectiveness of the program established in section 2 of this act.
"IV.   [Repealed.]

318-B:31. Definitions.

[Repealed 2013, 79:3, II, eff. June 7, 2013.]

Effective date of 2013 amendment.
2013, 79:3, III, eff. June 7, 2013, amended 2012, 196:5, to change the effective date from September 1, 2015 to June 7, 2013.

Former section(s).
Former RSA 318-B:31, which was derived from 2012, 196:2, related to definitions.

318-B:32. Controlled Drug Prescription Health and Safety Program Established.

[Repealed 2013, 79:3, II, eff. June 7, 2013.]

Effective date of 2013 amendment.
2013, 79:3, III, eff. June 7, 2013, amended 2012, 196:5, to change the effective date from September 1, 2015 to June 7, 2013.

Former section(s).
Former RSA 318-B:31, which was derived from 2012, 196:2, related to controlled drug prescription health and safety program Established.

318-B:33. Controlled Drug Prescription Health and Safety Program Operation.

[Repealed 2013, 79:3, II, eff. June 7, 2013.]

Effective date of 2013 amendment.
2013, 79:3, III, eff. June 7, 2013, amended 2012, 196:5, to change the effective date from September 1, 2015 to June 7, 2013.

Former section(s).
Former RSA 318-B:31, which was derived from 2012, 196:2, related to controlled drug prescription health and safety operation.

318-B:34. Confidentiality.

[Repealed 2013, 79:3, II, eff. June 7, 2013.]

Effective date of 2013 amendment.
2013, 79:3, III, eff. June 7, 2013, amended 2012, 196:5, to change the effective date from September 1, 2015 to June 7, 2013.

Former section(s).

Former RSA 318-B:31, which was derived from 2012, 196:2, related to confidentiality.

318-B:35. Providing Controlled Drug Prescription Health and Safety Information.

[Repealed 2013, 79:3, II, eff. June 7, 2013.]

Effective date of 2013 amendment.

2013, 79:3, III, eff. June 7, 2013, amended 2012, 196:5, to change the effective date from September 1, 2015 to June 7, 2013.

Former section(s).

Former RSA 318-B:31, which was derived from 2012, 196:2, related to providing controlled drug prescription health and safety information.

318-B:36. Unlawful Act and Penalties.

[Repealed 2013, 79:3, II, eff. June 7, 2013.]

Effective date of 2013 amendment.

2013, 79:3, III, eff. June 7, 2013, amended 2012, 196:5, to change the effective date from September 1, 2015 to June 7, 2013.

Former section(s).

Former RSA 318-B:31, which was derived from 2012, 196:2, related to unlawful act and penalties.

318-B:37. Rulemaking.

[Repealed 2013, 79:3, II, eff. June 7, 2013.]

Effective date of 2013 amendment.

2013, 79:3, III, eff. June 7, 2013, amended 2012, 196:5, to change the effective date from September 1, 2015 to June 7, 2013.

Former section(s).

Former RSA 318-B:31, which was derived from 2012, 196:2, related to rulemaking.

318-B:38. Advisory Council Established.

[Repealed 2013, 79:3, II, eff. June 7, 2013.]

Effective date of 2013 amendment.

2013, 79:3, III, eff. June 7, 2013, amended 2012, 196:5, to change the effective date from September 1, 2015 to June 7, 2013.

Former section(s).

Former RSA 318-B:31, which was derived from 2012, 196:2, related to advisory council established.

CHAPTER 318-C

MODEL DRUG DEALER LIABILITY ACT

SECTION
318-C:1.   Title.
318-C:2.   Purpose.
318-C:3.   Findings.
318-C:4.   Definitions.
318-C:5.   Liability for Participation in the Illegal Drug Market.
318-C:6.   Recovery of Damages.
318-C:7.   Limited Recovery of Damages.
318-C:8.   Third Party Cases.
318-C:9.   Illegal Drug Market Target Community.
318-C:10. Joinder of Parties.
318-C:11. Comparative Responsibility.
318-C:12. Contribution Among and Recovery from Multiple Defendants.
318-C:13. Standard of Proof; Effect of Criminal Drug Conviction.
SECTION
318-C:14. Prejudgment Attachment and Execution on Judgments.
318-C:15. Statute of Limitations.
318-C:16. Representation of Governmental Entities: Stay of Action.
318-C:17. Effect on Existing Laws.
318-C:18. Severability.

318-C:1. Title.

This chapter may be cited as the Drug Dealer Liability Act.

Source.

2004, 252:1, eff. Jan. 1, 2005.

318-C:2. Purpose.

The purpose of this chapter is to:

I. Provide a civil remedy for damages to persons in a community injured as a result of illegal drug use. These persons include parents, employers, insurers, governmental entities, and others who pay for drug treatment or employee assistance programs, as well as infants injured as a result of exposure to drugs in utero ("drug babies"). The chapter will enable them to recover damages from those persons in the community who have joined the illegal drug market.

II. Shift, to the extent possible, the cost of the damage caused by the existence of the illegal drug market in a community to those who illegally profit from that market.

III. Establish the prospect of substantial monetary loss as a deterrent to those who have not yet entered into the illegal drug distribution market.

IV. Establish an incentive for drug users to identify and seek payment for their own drug treatment from those dealers who have sold drugs to the user in the past.

Source.

2004, 252:1, eff. Jan. 1, 2005.

318-C:3. Findings.

The legislature finds and declares all of the following:

I. Every community in the country is affected by the marketing and distribution of illegal drugs. A vast amount of state and local resources are expended in coping with the financial, physical, and emotional toll that results from the existence of the illegal drug market. Families, employers, insurers, and society in general bear the substantial costs of coping with the marketing of illegal drugs. Drug babies and parents, particularly those of adolescent illegal drug users, suffer significant non-economic injury as well.

II. Although the criminal justice system is an important weapon against the illegal drug market, the civil justice system can and must also be used. The civil justice system can provide an avenue of compensation for those who have suffered harm as a result of the marketing and distribution of illegal drugs. The persons who have joined the illegal drug market should bear the cost of the harm caused by that market in the community.

III. The threat of liability under this chapter serves as an additional deterrent to a recognizable segment of the illegal drug network. A person who has non-drug related assets, who markets illegal drugs at the workplace, who encourages friends to become users, among others, is likely to decide that the added cost of entering the market is not worth the benefit. This is particularly true for a first-time casual dealer who has not yet made substantial profits. This act provides a mechanism for the cost of the injury caused by illegal drug use to be borne by those who benefit from illegal drug dealing.

IV. This chapter imposes liability against all participants in the illegal drug market, including small dealers, particularly those in the workplace, who are not usually the focus of criminal investigations. The small dealers increase the number of users and are the people who become large dealers. These small dealers are most likely to be deterred by the threat of liability.

V. A parent of an adolescent illegal drug user often expends considerable financial resources, typically in the tens of thousands of dollars, for the child's drug treatment. Local and state governments provide drug treatment and related medical services made necessary by the distribution of illegal drugs. The treatment of drug babies is a considerable cost to local and state governments. Insurers pay large sums for medical treatment relating to drug addiction and use. Employers suffer losses as a result of illegal drug use by employees due to lost productivity, employee drug-related workplace accidents, employer contributions to medical plans, and the need to establish and maintain employee assistance programs. Large employers, insurers, and local and state governments have existing legal staffs that can bring civil suits against those involved in the illegal drug market, in appropriate cases, if a clear legal mechanism for liability and recovery is established.

VI. Drug babies, who are clearly the most innocent and vulnerable of those affected by illegal drug use, are often the most physically and mentally damaged due to the existence of an illegal drug market in a community. For many of these babies, the only hope is extensive medical and psychological treatment, physical therapy, and special education. All of these potential remedies are expensive. These babies, through their legal guardians and through court appointed guardians ad litem, should be able to recover damages from those in the community who have entered and participated in the marketing of the types of illegal drugs that have caused their injuries.

VII. (a) In theory, civil actions for damages for distribution of illegal drugs can be brought under existing law. They are not. Several barriers account for this. Under existing tort law, only those dealers in the actual chain of distribution to a particular user could be sued. Drug babies, parents of adolescent illegal drug users, and insurers are not likely to be able to identify the chain of distribution to a particular user. Furthermore, drug treatment experts largely agree that users are unlikely to identify and bring suit against their own dealers, even after they have recovered, given the present requirements for a civil action.

(b) Recovered users are similarly unlikely to bring suit against others in the chain of distribution, even if they know the user. A user is unlikely to know other dealers in the chain of distribution. Unlike the chain of distribution for legal products, in which records identifying the parties to each transaction in the chain are made and shared among the parties, the distribution of illegal drugs is clandestine. Its participants expend considerable effort to keep the chain of distribution secret.

VIII. Those involved in the illegal drug market in a community are necessarily interrelated and interdependent, even if their identities are unknown to one another. Each new dealer obtains the benefit of the existing illegal drug distribution system to make illegal drugs available to him or her. In addition, the existing market aids a new entrant by the prior development of people as users. Many experts on the illegal drug market agree that all participants are ultimately likely to be indirectly related. That is, beginning with any one dealer, given the theoretical ability to identify every person known by that dealer to be involved in illegal drug trafficking, and in turn each of such others know to them, and so on, the illegal drug market in a community would ultimately be fully revealed.

IX. Market liability has been created with respect to legitimate products by judicial decision in some states. It provides for civil recovery by plaintiffs who are unable to identify the particular manufacturer of the product that is claimed to have caused them harm, allowing recovery from all manufacturers of the product who participated in that particular market. The market liability theory has been shown to be destructive of market initiative and product development when applied to legitimate markets. Because of its potential for undermining markets, this chapter expressly adopts a legislatively crafted form of liability for those who intentionally join the illegal drug market. The liability established by this chapter grows out of, but is distinct from, existing judicially crafted market liability.

X. The prospect of a future suit for the costs of drug treatment may drive a wedge between prospective dealers and their customers by encouraging users to turn on their dealers. Therefore, liability for those costs, even to the user, is imposed under this chapter as long as the user identifies and brings suit against his or her own dealers.

XI. Allowing dealers who face a civil judgment for their illegal drug marketing to bring suit against their own sources for contribution may also drive a wedge into the relationships among some participants in the illegal drug distribution network.

XII. While not all persons who have suffered losses as a result of the marketing of illegal drugs will pursue an action for damages, at least some individuals, guardians of drug babies, government agencies that provide treatment, insurance companies, and employers will find such an action worthwhile. These persons deserve the opportunity to recover their losses. Some new entrants to retail illegal drug dealing are likely to be deterred even if only a few of these suits are actually brought.

Source.
2004, 252:1, eff. Jan. 1, 2005.

318-C:4. Definitions.

As used in this chapter:

I. "Illegal drug" means any drug which is a schedule I-IV drug under RSA 318-B.

II. "Illegal drug market" means the support system of illegal drug related operations, from production to retail sales, through which an illegal drug reaches the user.

III. "Illegal drug market target community" is the area described under RSA 318-C:9.

IV. "Individual drug user" means the individual whose illegal drug use is the basis of an action brought under this chapter.

V. "Level 1 offense" means possession of ¼ ounce or more, but less than 4 ounces, or distribution of less than one ounce of an illegal drug other than marijuana, or possession of one pound or more or 25 plants or more, but less than 4 pounds or 50 plants, or distribution of more than ½ pound but less than one pound of marijuana.

VI. "Level 2 offense" means possession of 4 ounces or more, but less than 8 ounces, or distribution of one ounce or more, but less than 2 ounces, of an illegal drug other than marijuana, or possession of 4 pounds or more or 50 plants or more but less than 8 pounds or 75 plants or distribution of one pound or more but less than 5 pounds of marijuana.

VII. "Level 3 offense" means possession of 8 ounces or more, but less than 16 ounces, or distribution of 2 ounces or more, but less than 4 ounces, of an illegal drug other than marijuana, or possession of 8 pounds or more or 75 plants or more, but less than 16 pounds or 100 plants, or distribution of 5 pounds or more but less than 10 pounds of marijuana.

VIII. "Level 4 offense" means possession of 16 ounces or more or distribution of 4 ounces or more of an illegal drug other than marijuana, or possession of 16 pounds or more or 100 plants or more or distribution of 10 pounds or more of marijuana.

IX. "Participate in the illegal drug market" means to distribute, possess with an intent to distribute, commit an act intended to facilitate the marketing or distribution of, or agree to distribute, possess with an intent to distribute, or commit an act intended to facilitate the marketing and distribution of an illegal drug. "Participate in the illegal drug market" does not include the purchase or receipt of an illegal drug for personal use only.

X. "Person" means an individual, governmental entity, corporation, firm, trust, partnership, or incorporated or unincorporated association, existing under or authorized by the laws of this state, another state, or foreign country.

XI. "Period of illegal drug use" means, in relation to the individual drug user, the time of the individual's first use of an illegal drug to the accrual of the cause of action. The period of illegal drug use is presumed to commence 2 years before the cause of action accrues unless the defendant proves otherwise by clear and convincing evidence.

XII. "Place of illegal drug activity" means, in relation to the individual drug user, each house of representatives' legislative district in which the individual possesses or uses an illegal drug or in which the individual resides, attends school, or is employed during the period of the individual's illegal drug use, unless the defendant proves otherwise by clear and convincing evidence.

XIII. "Place of participation" means, in relation to a defendant in an action brought under this chapter, each house of representatives' legislative district in which the person participates in the illegal drug market or in which the person resides, attends school, or is employed during the period of the person's participation in the illegal drug market.

Source.
2004, 252:1, eff. Jan. 1, 2005.

318-C:5. Liability for Participation in the Illegal Drug Market.

I. A person who knowingly participates in the illegal drug market within this state is liable for civil damages as provided in this chapter. A person may recover damages under this chapter for injury resulting from an individual's use of an illegal drug.

II. A law enforcement officer or agency, the state, or a person acting at the direction of a law enforcement officer or agency or the state is not liable for participating in the illegal drug market, if the participation is in furtherance of an official investigation.

Source.
2004, 252:1, eff. Jan. 1, 2005.

318-C:6. Recovery of Damages.

I. One or more of the following persons may bring an action for damages caused by an individual's use of an illegal drug:

(a) A parent, legal guardian, child, spouse, or sibling of the individual drug user.

(b) An individual who was exposed to an illegal drug in utero.

(c) An employer of the individual drug user.

(d) A medical facility, insurer, governmental entity, employer, or other entity that funds a drug treatment program or employee assistance program for the individual drug user or that otherwise expended money on behalf of the individual drug user.

(e) A person injured as a result of the willful, reckless, or negligent actions of an individual drug user.

II. A person entitled to bring an action under this section may seek damages from a person convicted of a drug offense or a person who knowingly distributed, or knowingly participated in the chain of distribution of, the illegal drug that was actually used by the individual drug user and that was the proximate cause of the recoverable losses.

II-a. No governmental entity may bring an action against a person until after that person has been convicted of a criminal act related to the possession, manufacture, or distribution of drugs.

III. A person entitled to bring an action under this section may recover all of the following damages:

(a) Economic damages, including, but not limited to, the cost of treatment and rehabilitation, medical expenses, loss of economic or educational potential, loss of productivity, absenteeism, support expenses, accidents or injury, and any other pecuniary loss proximately caused by the illegal drug use.

(b) Non-economic damages, including, but not limited to, physical and emotional pain, suffering, physical impairment, emotional distress, mental anguish, disfigurement, loss of enjoyment, loss of companionship, services and consortium, and other non-pecuniary losses proximately caused by an individual's use of an illegal drug.

(c) Reasonable attorney fees.

(d) Costs of suit, including, but not limited to, reasonable expenses for expert testimony.

Source.
2004, 252:1, eff. Jan. 1, 2005.

318-C:7. Limited Recovery of Damages.

I. An individual drug user shall not bring an action for damages caused by the use of an illegal drug, except as otherwise provided in this paragraph. An individual drug user may bring an action for damages caused by the use of an illegal drug only if all of the following conditions are met:

(a) The individual personally discloses to narcotics enforcement authorities, more than 6 months before filing the action, all of the information known to the individual regarding all that individual's sources of illegal drugs;

(b) The individual has not used an illegal drug within the 6 months before filing the action; and

(c) The individual continues to remain free of the use of an illegal drug throughout the pendency of the action.

II. A person entitled to bring an action under this section may seek damages only from a person who distributed, or is in the chain of distribution of, an illegal drug that was actually used by the individual drug user.

III. A person entitled to bring an action under this section may recover only the following damages:

(a) Economic damages, including, but not limited to, the cost of treatment, rehabilitation, and medical expenses, loss of economic or educational potential, loss of productivity, absenteeism, accidents or injury, and any other pecuniary loss proximately caused by the person's illegal drug use.

(b) Reasonable attorney fees.

(c) Costs of suit, including, but not limited to, reasonable expenses for expert testimony.

Source.
2004, 252:1, eff. Jan. 1, 2005.

318-C:8. Third Party Cases.

A third party shall not pay damages awarded under this chapter, or provide a defense or money for a defense, on behalf of an insured under a contract of insurance or indemnification.

Source.
2004, 252:1, eff. Jan. 1, 2005.

318-C:9. Illegal Drug Market Target Community.

A person whose participation in the illegal drug market constitutes the following level offense shall be considered to have the following illegal drug market target community:

I. For a level 1 offense, the New Hampshire house of representatives' legislative district in which the defendant's place of participation is situated.

II. For a level 2 offense, the target community described in paragraph I plus all New Hampshire house of representatives' legislative districts with a border contiguous to that target community.

III. For a level 3 offense, the target community described in paragraph II plus all New Hampshire house of representatives' legislative districts with a border contiguous to that target community.

IV. For a level 4 offense, the state.

Source.
2004, 252:1, eff. Jan. 1, 2005.

Revision note.
Substituted "representatives'" for "representative's" in par. II to correct a typographical error.

318-C:10. Joinder of Parties.

I. Two or more persons may join in one action under this chapter as plaintiffs if their respective actions have at least one place of illegal drug activity in common and if any portion of the period of illegal drug use overlaps with the period of illegal drug use for every other plaintiff.

II. Two or more persons may be joined in one action under this chapter as defendants if those persons are liable to at least one plaintiff.

III. A plaintiff need not be interested in obtaining and a defendant need not be interested in defending against all the relief demanded. Judgment may be given for one or more plaintiffs according to their respective rights to relief and against one or more defendants according to their respective liabilities.

Source.
2004, 252:1, eff. Jan. 1, 2005.

318-C:11. Comparative Responsibility.

I. An action by an individual drug user is governed by the principles of comparative responsibility. Comparative responsibility attributed to the plaintiff does not bar recovery but diminishes the award of compensatory damages proportionally, according to the measure of responsibility attributed to the plaintiff.

II. The burden of proving the comparative responsibility of the plaintiff is on the defendant, which shall be shown by clear and convincing evidence.

III. Comparative responsibility shall not be attributed to a plaintiff who is not an individual drug user.

Source.
2004, 252:1, eff. Jan. 1, 2005.

318-C:12. Contribution Among and Recovery from Multiple Defendants.

A person subject to liability under this chapter has a right of action for contribution against another person subject to liability under this chapter. Contribution may be enforced either in the original action or by a separate action brought for that purpose. A plaintiff may seek recovery in accordance with this chapter and existing law against a person against whom a defendant has asserted a right of contribution.

Source.
2004, 252:1, eff. Jan. 1, 2005..

318-C:13. Standard of Proof; Effect of Criminal Drug Conviction.

I. Proof of participation in the illegal drug market in an action brought under this chapter shall be shown by clear and convincing evidence. Except as otherwise provided in this chapter, other elements of the cause of action shall be shown by a preponderance of the evidence.

II. A person against whom recovery is sought who has a criminal conviction pursuant to RSA 318-B or other state drug laws or the Comprehensive Drug Abuse Prevention and Control Act of 1970, Public Law 91-513, 84 Stat. 1236, codified at 21 U.S.C. 801 et seq., is estopped from denying participation in the illegal drug market. Such a conviction is also prima facie evidence of the person's participation in the illegal drug market during the 2 years preceding the date of an act giving rise to a conviction.

III. The absence of a criminal drug conviction of a person against whom recovery is sought does not bar an action against that person.

Source.
2004, 252:1, eff. Jan. 1, 2005.

318-C:14. Prejudgment Attachment and Execution on Judgments.

I. A plaintiff under this chapter, subject to paragraph II, may request an ex parte prejudgment attachment order from the court against all assets of a defendant sufficient to satisfy a potential award. If attachment is instituted, a defendant is entitled to an immediate hearing. Attachment may be lifted if the defendant demonstrates that the assets will be available for a potential award or if the defendant posts a bond sufficient to cover a potential award.

II. Any assets sought to satisfy a judgment under this chapter that are named in a forfeiture action or have been seized for forfeiture by any state or federal agency may not be used to satisfy a judgment unless and until the assets have been released following the conclusion of the forfeiture action or released by the agency that seized the assets.

Source.
2004, 252:1, eff. Jan. 1, 2005.

318-C:15. Statute of Limitations.

I. Except as otherwise provided in this section, a claim under this chapter shall not be brought more than 2 years after the cause of action accrues. A cause of action accrues under this chapter when a person who may recover has reason to know of the harm from illegal drug use that is the basis for the cause of action and has reason to know that the illegal drug use is the cause of the harm.

II. For a plaintiff, the statute of limitations under this section is tolled while the individual potential plaintiff is incapacitated by the use of an illegal drug to the extent that the individual cannot reasonably be expected to seek recovery under this chapter or as otherwise provided by law. For a defendant, the statute of limitations under this section is tolled until 6 months after the individual potential defendant is convicted of a criminal drug offense or as otherwise provided by law.

III. The statute of limitations under this chapter for a claim based on participation in the illegal drug market that occurred prior to the effective date of this chapter does not begin to run until the effective date of this chapter.

Source.
2004, 252:1, eff. Jan. 1, 2005.

318-C:16. Representation of Governmental Entities: Stay of Action.

I. A prosecuting attorney may represent the state or a political subdivision of the state in an action brought under this chapter.

II. Upon the filing of an action under this chapter, the plaintiff shall give immediate notice in writing and provide a copy of the writ to the attorney general. The attorney general shall notify the United States Department of Justice or other appropriate federal agency of such action.

III. On motion by a governmental agency involved in a drug investigation or prosecution, an action brought under this chapter shall be stayed until the completion of the criminal investigation or prosecution that gave rise to the motion for a stay of the action.

Source.
2004, 252:1, eff. Jan. 1, 2005.

318-C:17. Effect on Existing Laws.

The provisions of this chapter are not intended to alter the law regarding intra-family tort immunity.

Source.
2004, 252:1, eff. Jan. 1, 2005.

318-C:18. Severability.

If any provision of this chapter or the application of any provision to any person or circumstance is held invalid, the remainder of this chapter and the application of such provision to any other person or circumstance shall not be affected by that invalidation.

Source.
2004, 252:1, eff. Jan. 1, 2005.

CHAPTER 318-D

METHAMPHETAMINE-RELATED OFFENSES

SECTION
318-D:1.   Definitions.
318-D:2.   Manufacture of Methamphetamine.
318-D:3.   Injury Resulting From the Manufacture of Methamphetamine.
318-D:4.   Sale, Transfer, Lease, or Rental of Real Property on Which Methamphetamine has Been Produced.
318-D:5.   Anhydrous Ammonia; Prohibited Conduct.

318-D:1. Definitions.

In this chapter:

I. "Anhydrous ammonia" means ammonia that has been cooled, pressurized, or both so that it exists in liquid form. Water may be present in varying degrees, if at all. This definition shall not include commercially available water solutions of ammonia such as glass cleaners.

II. "Clandestine lab site" means any structure or conveyance or location occupied or affected by conditions or chemicals typically associated with the manufacturing of methamphetamine.

III. "Emergency response" includes, but is not limited to, removing and collecting evidence, securing the site, removal, remediation, and hazardous chemical assessment or inspection of the site where the relevant offense or offenses took place, regardless of whether these actions are performed by a public entity, a private contractor paid by a public entity, or the property owner.

IV. "Remediation" means proper cleanup, treatment, or containment of hazardous substances or methamphetamine at or in a clandestine lab site, and may include demolition or disposal of structures or other property.

V. "Removal" means the removal from the clandestine lab site of precursor or waste chemicals, chemical containers, or equipment associated with the manufacture, packaging, or storage of illegal drugs.

Source.
2006, 241:1, eff. January 1, 2007.

318-D:2. Manufacture of Methamphetamine.

I. It shall be unlawful for any person to knowingly manufacture or attempt to manufacture methamphetamine. A person is guilty of an attempt to manufacture methamphetamine if the person:

(a) With the purpose that the crime of manufacturing methamphetamine be committed, the person engages in any conduct that, under the circumstances as the person believes them to be, is an act constituting a substantial step toward the commission of the crime; or

(b) Possesses one or more of the following substances or their salts or isomers, with the intent to manufacture methamphetamine:

   (1) Acetic acid.
   (2) Acetic anhydride.
   (3) Aluminum.
   (4) Ammonium nitrate.
   (5) Anhydrous ammonia.
   (6) Benzaldehyde.
   (7) Benzyl chloride.
   (8) Benzyl cyanide.
   (9) Chloroephedrine.
   (10) Chloropseudoephedrine.
   (11) Elemental phosphorous.
   (12) Ephedrine.
   (13) Ethylamine.
   (14) Formic acid.
   (15) Hydriodic acid.
   (16) Hydrochloric acid.
   (17) Hydrogen.
   (18) Hydrogen peroxide.
   (19) Hypophosphorus acid.
   (20) Iodine.
   (21) Lithium metal.

(22) Mercuric chloride.

(23) Methylamine.

(24) N-methyl formamide.

(25) Nitroethane.

(26) Palladium.

(27) Perchloric acid.

(28) Phenylacetic acid.

(29) Phosphorous pentachloride.

(30) Platinum.

(31) Raney nickel.

(32) Sodium acetate.

(33) Sodium hydroxide.

(34) Sodium hypochlorite.

(35) Sodium hypophosphite.

(36) Sodium metal.

(37) Sodium/potassium cyanide.

(38) Sulfuric acid.

(39) Thionyl chloride.

(40) Tincture of iodine.

(c) Possesses one or more of the following organic solvents with the intent to manufacture methamphetamine:

(1) Acetone.

(2) Chloroform.

(3) Cyclohexane.

(4) Ethanol.

(5) Ether.

(6) Light petroleum distillates.

(7) Methanol.

(8) Methyl isobutyl ketone.

(9) Phenyl-2 porpanone.

(10) Tetrachloroethylene.

(11) Toluene.

II. Notwithstanding the provisions of RSA 318-B:26, I, a person convicted under this section may be sentenced to imprisonment for not more than 30 years, a fine of not more than $500,000, or both. A person convicted under this section who has one or more prior offenses as defined in RSA 318-B:27, shall be sentenced to imprisonment for not less than 5 years and not more than life imprisonment, a fine of not more than $500,000, or both.

III. A court may require a person convicted of manufacturing or attempting to manufacture methamphetamine, where the response to the crime involved an emergency response or a hazardous substance cleanup operation, to pay restitution to all public entities, or private entities under contract to a public entity, that participated in the response or the cleanup. The restitution ordered shall cover the reasonable costs of the entities' participation in the response and the reasonable costs of the site cleanup.

IV. In addition to the restitution authorized in paragraph III, a court may require a person convicted of manufacturing or attempting to manufacture methamphetamine to pay restitution to a property owner who incurred removal or remediation costs as a result of the crime.

Source.
2006, 241:1, eff. January 1, 2007.

318-D:3. Injury Resulting From the Manufacture of Methamphetamine.

I. A person shall be guilty of an offense if that person recklessly causes serious bodily injury to a law enforcement officer, firefighter, emergency medical technician, ambulance operator, ambulance attendant, or social worker, civilian government employee, or hazardous material contractor acting in his or her official duties, as a result of the hazards posed by the person's conduct in manufacturing or attempting to manufacture methamphetamine. For purposes of this section, a person who takes any substantial step towards the manufacture of methamphetamine acts recklessly.

II. A person convicted of an offense under this section may be sentenced to imprisonment for not more than 20 years, or a fine of not more than $300,000 or both.

Source.
2006, 241:1, eff. January 1, 2007.

318-D:4. Sale, Transfer, Lease, or Rental of Real Property on Which Methamphetamine has Been Produced.

Any sale, transfer, lease, or rental of real property on which methamphetamine has been produced shall be subject to the provisions of RSA 477:4-g.

Source.
2006, 241:1, eff. January 1, 2007.

318-D:5. Anhydrous Ammonia; Prohibited Conduct.

I. In this section, "tamper" means action taken by a person not authorized to take that action by law, or by the owner or authorized custodian of an anhydrous ammonia container, or of equipment where anhydrous ammonia is used, stored, distributed, or transported.

II. No person shall:

(a) Steal or unlawfully take or carry away any amount of anhydrous ammonia.

(b) Purchase, possess, transfer, or distribute any amount of anhydrous ammonia, knowing, or having reason to know, that it will be used to unlawfully manufacture a controlled substance or explosive device.

(c) Place, have placed, or possess anhydrous ammonia in a container that is not designed, constructed, maintained, and authorized to contain or transport anhydrous ammonia.

(d) Transport anhydrous ammonia in a container that is not designed, constructed, maintained, and authorized to transport anhydrous ammonia.

(e) Use, deliver, receive, sell, or transport a container designed and constructed to contain anhydrous ammonia without the express consent of the owner or authorized custodian of the container.

(f) Tamper with any equipment or facility used to contain, store, or transport anhydrous ammonia.

III. The department of safety shall adopt rules, pursuant to RSA 541-A, in order to implement and enforce the provisions of this section.

IV. Except as provided in paragraph V, a person who tampers with anhydrous ammonia containers or equipment under this section shall have no cause of action for damages arising out of the tampering against:

(a) The owner or lawful custodian of the container or equipment;

(b) A person responsible for the installation or maintenance of the container or equipment; or

(c) A person lawfully selling or offering for sale the anhydrous ammonia.

V. Paragraph IV shall not apply to a cause of action against a person who unlawfully obtained the anhydrous ammonia or anhydrous ammonia container or who possesses the anhydrous ammonia or anhydrous ammonia container for any unlawful purpose.

VI. A person who knowingly violates paragraph II may be sentenced to imprisonment for not more than 5 years or a fine of not more than $50,000, or both.

Source.
2006, 241:1, eff. January 1, 2007.

TITLE LI

COURTS

CHAPTER 502-A

DISTRICT COURTS

Jurisdiction

SECTION
502-A:12.   Appeals from Sentence.

Jurisdiction

502-A:12. Appeals from Sentence.

I. A person sentenced by a district court for a class A misdemeanor after trial or after proceedings pursuant to District Court Rule 2.14 may appeal therefrom to the superior court for a jury trial as provided in RSA 599, except in cases in district courts served by regional jury trial courts as provided in RSA 502-A:12-a.

II. A person sentenced by a district court for a class A misdemeanor may, if no appeal for a jury trial in superior court is taken, appeal therefrom to the supreme court at the time the sentence is declared or within 30 days after the sentence is declared. The supreme court's review shall be limited to questions of law.

Source.
1963, 331:1. 1983, 382:5. 1993, 190:16, eff. Jan. 1, 1994. 1995, 277:16, eff. Aug. 19, 1995. 2006, 64:1, eff. January 1, 2007.

Amendments
—2006. Rewritten to the extent that a detailed comparison would be impracticable.

—1995. Substituted "in cases in district courts served by regional jury trial courts as provided in RSA 502-A:12-a" for "as modified in accordance with the pilot program in 1992, 223" following "except".

—1993. Inserted "class A" preceding "misdemeanor", deleted "or for any offense which provides the basis for enhanced penalties if the offender is subsequently convicted of the same offense" thereafter and added "except as modified in accordance with the pilot program in 1992, 223" following "RSA 599".

—1983. Rewritten to the extent that a detailed comparison would be impracticable.

Cross References.
Classification of crimes, see RSA 625:9.

NOTES TO DECISIONS

1. Right to appeal
2. Effect of appeal

1. Right to appeal
Where defendant was found guilty of violations in the district court, denial of his motion to appeal to the superior court, based upon the 1983 amendment to this section, which took effect after the defendant was charged with the violations, violated part 1, article 23 of the State Constitution, limiting the retrospective application of the law. State v. McKenney, 126 N.H. 184, 489 A.2d 644, 1985 N.H. LEXIS 243 (1985), overruled in part, State v. Matthews, 157 N.H. 415, 951 A.2d 155, 2008 N.H. LEXIS 79 (2008).

2. Effect of appeal
Appeal to the superior court vacates the sentence of the district court and entitles the defendant to a trial de novo. State v. Flynn, 110 N.H. 451, 272 A.2d 591, 1970 N.H. LEXIS 197 (1970). See also State v. Hennessey, 110 N.H. 447, 270 A.2d 613, 1970 N.H. LEXIS 195 (1970).

Cited:
Cited in State v. Lambert, 125 N.H. 442, 480 A.2d 205, 1984 N.H. LEXIS 246 (1984); State v. Langone, 127 N.H. 49, 498 A.2d 731, 1985 N.H. LEXIS 399 (1985); State v. Homo, 132 N.H. 514, 567 A.2d 540, 1989 N.H. LEXIS 150 (1989); Hammell v. Warden, 146 N.H. 557, 776 A.2d 740, 2001 N.H. LEXIS 130 (2001).

RESEARCH REFERENCES

New Hampshire Court Rules Annotated.
Appeal to the superior court after waiver of trial, see Rule 2.14, Rules of the District Courts, New Hampshire Court Rules Annotated.
Appeal to the superior court generally, see Rule 2.13, Rules of the District Courts, New Hampshire Court Rules Annotated.
Withdrawal of appeal, see Rule 2.15, Rules of the District Courts, New Hampshire Court Rules Annotated.

CHAPTER 516

WITNESSES

Attendance of Witnesses

SECTION
516:1.   Summons.
516:2.   Issue of Summons by Clerks.
516:3.   Issue of Summons by Justices or Judges.
516:4.   Issue, for Depositions.
516:5.   Service of Summons.
516:6.   Neglect to Attend.
516:7.   Penalty.
516:7-a.   Victim/Witness Advocates as Witnesses.

Nonresident Officers, etc., of Corporations

516:8.   Inclusions.
516:9.   Duty to Testify.
516:10.   Order; Summons.
516:11.   Service of Summons.
516:12.   Commissioner, Issuance of Summons by.
516:13.   Fees.
516:14.   Double Fees.
516:15.   Neglect to Attend.

Fees of Witnesses

516:16.   Attendance; Travel.
516:16-a.   Defaults; Witness Fees for Law Enforcement Officers.
516:17.   Ferry, etc. [Repealed.]
516:18.   Limitation.

Competency of Witnesses, etc.

516:19.   Swearing.
516:20.   Affirmation.
516:21.   Religious Opinions.
516:22.   Interest.
516:23.   Party Deponent.
516:24.   Adverse Party. [Repealed.]
516:25.   Declarations of Deceased Persons. [Repealed.]
516:25-a.   Statements of Minors in Certain Civil Cases.
516:26.   Negotiated Paper.
516:27.   Husband and Wife. [Repealed.]
516:28.   Wills, etc.
516:29.   Opinions. [Repealed.]
516:29-a.   Testimony of Expert Witnesses.
516:29-b.   Disclosure of Expert Testimony in Civil Cases.
516:30.   Public Records. [Repealed.]
516:31.   Respondents in Criminal Cases. [Repealed.]
516:32.   Limitation. [Repealed.]
516:33.   Felons. [Repealed.]
516:33-a.   Confidential Settlement Agreements.

Grant of Immunity in Criminal Cases

516:34.   Compelling Evidence in Criminal Proceedings; Immunity.

Privileged Communications

516:35.   Religious Leaders.

Law Enforcement Agency Documents and Records

516:36.   Written Policy Directives to Police Officers and Investigators.

Testimony by Video Teleconference in Criminal and Motor Vehicle Cases

SECTION
516:37.   Testimony by Video Teleconference in Criminal Cases.
516:38.   Testimony by Video Teleconference for Motor Vehicle Violations.

Cross References.
Perjury as criminal offense, see RSA 641:1.
Recognizances of, in criminal cases, see RSA 597:22-26.
Summons for, in criminal proceedings, see RSA 592-A:11.

RESEARCH REFERENCES

New Hampshire Court Rules Annotated.
Witnesses, see Rule 601 et seq., New Hampshire Rules of Evidence.

New Hampshire Trial Bar News.
For article, "Trial Practice," see 14 N.H. Trial Bar News 19, 20 n.9 (Summer 1993).

New Hampshire Evidence Manual.
Douglas, New Hampshire Rules of Evidence Manual.

Attendance of Witnesses

Cross References.
Arbitration proceedings, see RSA 542:5.
Criminal proceedings, summoning from without the state, see RSA 613.

516:1. Summons.

A summons or subpoena not executed under seal shall be as effectual as though sealed. Writs of summons to witnesses shall be substantially in the form following:

THE STATE OF NEW HAMPSHIRE

_____ ss. To_____ :
You are required to appear at _____, in the county of _____, on the _____ day of _____, to testify what you know relating to _____, then and there to be heard, in which _____ is _____ and _____ is _____.
Hereof fail not, as you will answer your default under the penalties prescribed by law.
Dated at ____ , the ____ day of ____ , ____ .
(Signed)

Source.
RS 188:2. CS 200:2. GS 209:1. GL 228:1. PS 224:1. PL 336:1. RL 392:1. RSA 516:1. 1977, 366:1, eff. date, see note set out below.

Amendments
—1977. Amended generally by eliminating the need for legal seals on summonses.

Effective Date.
1977, 366:11, provided: "This act [which amended this section and RSA 477:1, 3, 7-a, 9, 16, 27 and 29–31] shall take effect 60 days

after its passage but shall not apply to summonses or subpoenas or deeds or conveyances executed prior to said effective date but such summonses, subpoenas, deeds, and conveyances shall remain subject to the provisions of the laws in force prior to the effective date of this act [Aug. 30, 1977.]"

NOTES TO DECISIONS

1. Nonresidents
2. Depositions

1. Nonresidents

Nonresident witnesses cannot be compelled, as resident witnesses may be, to attend a trial, at least in civil actions; their consent must be secured. Ela v. Ela, 68 N.H. 312, 36 A. 15, 1895 N.H. LEXIS 25 (1895).

2. Depositions

The form of summons of witnesses, as set forth in this section, is a suitable form to use in summoning witnesses for the purpose of taking their depositions. Burnham v. Stevens, 33 N.H. 247, 1856 N.H. LEXIS 75 (1856).

RESEARCH REFERENCES

New Hampshire Code of Administrative Rules.

Rules of the Department of Revenue Administration, Rev 204.07, New Hampshire Code of Administrative Rules Annotated.

516:2. Issue of Summons by Clerks.

Such writ may be issued by the clerk of any court for witnesses in any case pending therein.

Source.

RS 188:3, 4. CS 200:3, 4. GS 209:2. GL 228:2. PS 224:2. PL 336:2. RL 392:2.

NOTES TO DECISIONS

Cited:

Cited in Ela v. Ela, 68 N.H. 312, 36 A. 15, 1895 N.H. LEXIS 25 (1895).

516:3. Issue of Summons by Justices or Judges.

Any justice or judge may issue such writs for witnesses, in cases pending before himself or herself or any other justice or judge, in any case in any court, in all matters before the general court, or before auditors, referees, arbitrators or commissioners.

Source.

RS 188:4. CS 200:4. GS 209:3. GL 228:3. PS 224:3. PL 336:3. RL 392:3. 2007, 117:3, eff. June 11, 2007.

Amendments

—2007. Inserted "or judges" following "justices" in the section heading; "or judge" following "justice" in two places and "or herself" following "before himself".

NOTES TO DECISIONS

Conflict of interests

The action of plaintiff's counsel in issuing subpoenas as a justice of the peace was authorized by this section. R. C. Hazelton Co. v. Southwick Constr. Co., 105 N.H. 25, 192 A.2d 610, 1963 N.H. LEXIS 7 (1963).

Cited:

Cited in Robertson v. Hale, 68 N.H. 538, 44 A. 695, 1896 N.H. LEXIS 46 (1896); Ela v. Ela, 68 N.H. 312, 36 A. 15, 1895 N.H. LEXIS 25 (1895); Opinion of Justices, 131 N.H. 443, 554 A.2d 466, 1989 N.H. LEXIS 3 (1989).

516:4. Issue, for Depositions.

Any justice or notary may issue such writs for witnesses to appear before himself or any other justice or notary, to give depositions in any matter or cause in which the same may be lawfully taken.

Source.

RS 188:5. CS 200:5. GS 209:4. GL 228:4. PS 224:4. PL 336:4. RL 392:4.

NOTES TO DECISIONS

Cited:

Cited in Robertson v. Hale, 68 N.H. 538, 44 A. 695, 1896 N.H. LEXIS 46 (1896); Ela v. Ela, 68 N.H. 312, 36 A. 15, 1895 N.H. LEXIS 25 (1895); Burnham v. Stevens, 33 N.H. 247, 1856 N.H. LEXIS 75 (1856); Opinion of Justices, 131 N.H. 443, 554 A.2d 466, 1989 N.H. LEXIS 3 (1989).

516:5. Service of Summons.

Any person may be summoned to attend and testify or give his deposition, by reading to him, or by giving to him in hand an attested copy, of the writ of summons, and by paying or tendering to him the fees established for his travel to and from the place where his attendance is required, and for one day's attendance.

Source.

RS 188:6. CS 200:6. GS 209:5. GL 228:5. PS 224:5. 1895, 9:1. PL 336:5. RL 392:5.

NOTES TO DECISIONS

1. Generally
2. Change of residence
3. Attendance without payment
4. Action for fees

1. Generally

When a witness is summoned to attend a court and to testify in any specific case, or to testify before the grand jury at any term of the court, by having a proper subpoena read to him and his legal fees for travel and attendance paid or tendered to him by a proper officer or by a private individual, it is the duty of the witness to attend such court and testify according to the command of the summons. State v. Tebbetts, 54 N.H. 240, 1874 N.H. LEXIS 34 (1874).

2. Change of residence

A witness who is summoned and paid his fee while residing in this state, but who afterwards removes to another state, is bound to attend court in pursuance of the summons unless, before removing, he shall give notice of his intention to leave and be relieved from his obligation, or is subsequently released therefrom, and if he does attend in good faith he is entitled to his fees for such attendance and for the additional travel from the other state. Gunnison v. Gunnison, 41 N.H. 121, 1860 N.H. LEXIS 50 (1860).

3. Attendance without payment

When a subpoena is sent out under the endorsement of the attorney general or the county solicitor and is properly served upon the witness, it is his duty to attend the court and testify according to the command of the summons without having any fees paid or tendered to him, since such endorsement of the subpoena by the prosecuting officer of the state is a sufficient guarantee that his fees will be paid by the county. State v. Tebbetts, 54 N.H. 240, 1874 N.H. LEXIS 34 (1874).

4. Action for fees

A witness who was subpoenaed, and in good faith attends court as a witness, without being paid, may maintain an action against the party summoning him for his legal fees for travel and attendance, and he is equally entitled to recover such fees if he attends and is examined without being summoned or if he is summoned and attends without being examined. Gunnison v. Gunnison, 41 N.H. 121, 1860 N.H. LEXIS 50 (1860).

A witness who is summoned to attend court and paid for his travel and one day's attendance, or who is summoned and attends without being paid, if he remains in attendance in good faith until the cause is tried or otherwise disposed of, without notice that his attendance is no longer required, is entitled to his fees for such attendance from the party summoning him, and if they are not paid may maintain an action to recover them. Gunnison v. Gunnison, 41 N.H. 121, 1860 N.H. LEXIS 50 (1860).

Cited:

Cited in Robertson v. Hale, 68 N.H. 538, 44 A. 695, 1896 N.H. LEXIS 46 (1896) (in relation to the power of a justice to summon witnesses before him to be heard in the cause pending in his court, and to punish for contempt those witnesses who refuse to appear and testify); Ela v. Ela, 68 N.H. 312, 36 A. 15, 1895 N.H. LEXIS 25 (1895) (as one of the statutes compelling attendance of resident witnesses at a trial of a civil action); Burnham v. Stevens, 33 N.H. 247, 1856 N.H. LEXIS 75 (1856); Fenlon v. Thayer, 127 N.H. 702, 506 A.2d 319, 1986 N.H. LEXIS 224, 66 A.L.R.4th 203 (1986).

516:6. Neglect to Attend.

If a person so summoned neglects to attend or to give his attendance so long as may be necessary for the purpose for which he was summoned, or refuses to testify or to give his deposition if required, having no reasonable excuse therefor, he shall be liable to the party aggrieved for all damages sustained thereby.

Source.

RS 188:7. CS 200:7. GS 209:6. GL 228:6. PS 224:6. PL 336:6. RL 392:6.

NOTES TO DECISIONS

Nature of relief

Where a person has been summoned to attend court as a witness and his fees have been paid him, but neglects to attend, assumpsit for money had and received will not lie to recover the money thus paid, but rather the witness, under this section, will be liable to the party aggrieved for all damages sustained by the failure of the witness to testify, since process requiring the attendance of a witness is wholly compulsory and does not partake of the nature of a contract. Leighton v. Twombly, 9 N.H. 483, 1838 N.H. LEXIS 69 (1838).

Cited:

Cited in Ela v. Ela, 68 N.H. 312, 36 A. 15, 1895 N.H. LEXIS 25 (1895); Robertson v. Hale, 68 N.H. 538, 44 A. 695, 1896 N.H. LEXIS 46 (1896) (as applying to resident witnesses only); Burnham v. Stevens, 33 N.H. 247, 1856 N.H. LEXIS 75 (1856); Baker v. Cestari, 569 F. Supp. 842, 1983 U.S. Dist. LEXIS 13983 (D.N.H. 1983).

516:7. Penalty.

Every court, justice, and notary, before whom a person has been summoned to appear and testify or to give a deposition, may bring the person neglecting or refusing to appear or to testify or to give a deposition, by attachment, before them, and if, on examination, such person has no reasonable excuse, such person shall be guilty of a violation, and may be ordered to pay costs.

Source.

RS 188:8. CS 200:8. GS 209:7. GL 228:7. PS 224:7. PL 336:7. RL 392:7. RSA 516:7. 1973, 531:150, eff. at 11:59 p.m., Oct. 31, 1973. 2003, 128:1, eff. Jan. 1, 2004.

Amendments

—2003. Substituted "give a deposition" for "give his deposition", "such person" for "he" following "examination", "such person shall be" for "may find him", and "be ordered" for "order him" preceding "to pay costs".

—1973. Amended generally to conform provisions to new criminal code.

NOTES TO DECISIONS

1. Justice of the peace
2. Contempt
3. Due process

1. Justice of the peace

Justice of the peace acted within the limits of his jurisdiction in causing the arrest of a witness who neglected to appear before him conformably to a summons and order of adjournment, and was not liable therefor in an action for damages. Robertson v. Hale, 68 N.H. 538, 44 A. 695, 1896 N.H. LEXIS 46 (1896).

Justice of the peace had jurisdiction to take a deposition to be used in another state and to impose a fine for neglect to appear and give a deposition upon a witness duly summoned and neglecting to attend. Burnham v. Stevens, 33 N.H. 247, 1856 N.H. LEXIS 75 (1856).

2. Contempt

Where a witness, duly summoned to appear and testify before a magistrate, appears but refuses to testify on the ground that his answers to questions propounded would disclose his case and the manner in which he proposes to prove it, and his reasons for refusing to answer are thereupon considered and adjudged to be insufficient, the magistrate has power to punish such witness for contempt. State v. Towle, 42 N.H. 540, 1861 N.H. LEXIS 137 (1861).

3. Due process

Debtor, who is arrested to secure his attendance in court after he fails to appear under subpoena at hearing to discover his assets, is entitled to due process of law including right to be brought before court without unreasonable delay, right to bail, and right to move for hearing on grounds for his arrest. Mason Furniture Corp. v. George, 116 N.H. 451, 362 A.2d 188, 1976 N.H. LEXIS 380 (1976).

Cited:

Cited in Ela v. Ela, 68 N.H. 312, 36 A. 15, 1895 N.H. LEXIS 25 (1895).

516:7-a. Victim/Witness Advocates as Witnesses.

If a victim/witness advocate is called as a witness, a party opposing such action may move for an order requiring the party desiring to use such testimony to show cause why such victim/witness advocate's testimony is necessary. In no case shall a victim/witness advocate be sequestered unless the court finds and orders, based on the facts of the case, that failure to sequester would violate a defendant's rights.

Source.
1994, 393:4, eff. June 10, 1994.

Applicability of enactment.
1994, 394:5, eff. June 10, 1994, provided that section 4 of the act, which enacted this section, shall apply to all offenses committed on or before June 10, 1994.

Nonresident Officers, etc., of Corporations

516:8. Inclusions.

The words director, officer and agent as used in this subdivision shall include all persons who may be directors, officers and agents of such corporation at the commencement of the proceeding or who may become such during the pendency thereof, and all persons who may have the custody or possession of the books, records or papers of the corporation.

Source.
1903, 37:6. PL 336:15. RL 392:15.

516:9. Duty to Testify.

Whenever any domestic corporation is a party to any legal proceeding in this state before any court or other lawful tribunal, every nonresident director, officer or agent of such corporation may be required to appear and testify in such proceeding within the state, or to give his deposition for use in such proceeding before a special commissioner or commissioners within or without the state, and to produce all books, records and papers of such corporation or relating to its affairs in his possession or control so far as the same may be material upon the question involved in such proceedings.

Source.
1903, 37:1. PL 336:8. RL 392:8.

NOTES TO DECISIONS

Discovery
This section does not deprive the court of its equitable power to order discovery. Ingram v. Boston & M. R.R., 89 N.H. 277, 197 A. 822, 1938 N.H. LEXIS 17 (1938).

Cited:
Cited in New Castle v. Rand, 101 N.H. 201, 136 A.2d 914, 1957 N.H. LEXIS 51, 70 A.L.R.2d 669 (1957).

516:10. Order; Summons.

Upon the petition of a party to such proceeding, a justice of the superior court may issue such order as shall seem to the court to be reasonable and just, requiring such director, officer or agent to appear and testify in such proceeding, and upon such order the clerk of the superior court for any county may issue a summons requiring compliance with the order.

Source.
1903, 37:2. PL 336:9. RL 392:9.

516:11. Service of Summons.

Such summons may be served either within or without the state, and may require the person summoned to produce books, records and papers in connection with his testimony.

Source.
1903, 37:2. PL 336:10. RL 392:10.

516:12. Commissioner, Issuance of Summons by.

Upon like petition, the court may issue a commission to any special commissioner, authorizing him to summon or cause to be summoned such director, officer or agent to appear before him and give his deposition for use in such proceeding, and such summons may require the person so summoned to produce books, records and papers in connection with his deposition.

Source.
1903, 37:3. PL 336:11. RL 392:11.

516:13. Fees.

Any witness so summoned to testify or give his deposition shall be paid such fees for attendance and travel as witnesses are entitled to under the laws of the state in which the testimony or deposition is to be given.

Source.
1903, 37:4. PL 336:12. RL 392:12.

NOTES TO DECISIONS

Parties
A party who testifies or gives his deposition to be used in his own favor upon trial is not entitled to fees as a witness, but when such party compels his adversary to testify or give a deposition to be used on such trial, he shall pay him the same as any other witness. George v. Starrett, 40 N.H. 135, 1860 N.H. LEXIS 129 (1860).

516:14. Double Fees.

If the witness shall be summoned to come from another state into this state he shall be paid double fees for his travel and attendance.

Source.
1903, 37:4. PL 336:13. RL 392:13.

516:15. Neglect to Attend.

If any such director, officer or agent shall wilfully neglect or refuse to appear, produce books, records or papers, or to testify or give his deposition as required by such order or summons, the superior court, upon notice and hearing, may thereupon appoint a receiver to manage and control such corporation until the reasonable and just orders of the court shall be complied with, and when such orders shall have been complied with, such receiver shall be discharged.

Source.
1903, 37:5. PL 366:14. RL 392:14.

Fees of Witnesses

Cross References.
Payment of witnesses in criminal cases, see RSA 592-A:12.

516:16. Attendance; Travel.

The fees of law enforcement officers shall be $30 for each day's attendance and for all other witnesses shall be $12 for each half day's attendance before a municipal, district, superior, or probate court or legally constituted auditors, referees, magistrates or officials having the power to summon witnesses, except as otherwise specially provided; for each mile's travel to and from the place of testifying, mileage shall be paid at the rate of $.17 per mile; mileage to be allowed for each day's attendance where the witness is required to leave the town or city in which he resides to testify.

Source.
RS 229:12. 1850, 963:1. CS 245:12. GS 272:12. GL 290:12. 1883, 91:1. PS 287:13. 1905, 52:3. 1917, 14:1. 1925, 54:1. PL 336:18. RL 392:16. RSA 516:16. 1957, 11:1; 244:33. 1974, 29:3. 1979, 259:2. 1991, 355:99. 1992, 158:1, eff. July 1, 1992.

Amendments
—1992. Inserted "law enforcement officers shall be $30 for each day's attendance and for all other" following "fees of".

—1991. Substituted "$12" for "$30" and inserted "half" preceding "day's attendance before".

—1979. Fee raised to $30 and mileage shall be paid at the rate of $.17 per mile.

—1974. Added reference to district court and changed fees.

—1957. Omitted reference to justices of the peace and increased fees to $5 a day.

NOTES TO DECISIONS

  1. Administrative proceedings
  2. Number of cases

1. Administrative proceedings
The fees of witnesses attending before road commissioners were the same as if they were attending before a justice of the peace. Hanson v. Effingham, 20 N.H. 460, 1846 N.H. LEXIS 95 (1846).

2. Number of cases
A witness who testifies before a grand jury in several cases on the same day is entitled to fees for mileage and for one day's attendance only. Healy v. Hillsboro County, 70 N.H. 588, 49 A. 89, 1900 N.H. LEXIS 72 (1901).

Cited:
Cited in Edgerly v. Hale, 71 N.H. 138, 51 A. 679, 1901 N.H. LEXIS 31 (1901).

RESEARCH REFERENCES

New Hampshire Bar Journal.
For a commentary on this section, see Taxation of Costs in New Hampshire, 5 N.H.B.J. 114 (April 1963).

516:16-a. Defaults; Witness Fees for Law Enforcement Officers.

Any person who defaults on a scheduled court appearance on a motor vehicle offense shall be responsible for paying the current witness fee for any law enforcement officer required to attend such appearance, unless the court determines that such person is indigent.

Source.
1992, 39:1, eff. Jan. 1, 1993.

516:17. Ferry, etc.

[Repealed 1994, 273:4, eff. June 6, 1994.]

Former section(s).
Former 516:17, which was derived from RS 229:13; CS 245:13; GS 272:13; GL 290:13; PS 287:14; PL 336:19 and RL 329:17, related to travel allowance for ferry or toll bridge.

516:18. Limitation.

In civil causes the party prevailing shall be entitled to tax for the travel of witnesses residing out of the state to the line of the state only, unless the court specially orders otherwise.

Source.
1883, 66:1. PS 287:15. PL 336:20. RL 392:18.

Competency of Witnesses, etc.

516:19. Swearing.

No other ceremony shall be necessary in swearing than holding up the right hand, but any other form or ceremony may be used which the person to whom the oath is administered professes to believe more binding upon the conscience.

Source.
RS 188:10. CS 200:10. 1860, 2364. GS 209:10. GL 228:10. PS 224:10. PL 336:21. RL 392:19.

NOTES TO DECISIONS

  1. Construction
  2. Purpose of oath
  3. Wording of oath
  4. Signature

1. Construction
Hearings examiner erred in dismissing State's petition for driver's license suspension on grounds that police officer's report was not properly sworn; where officer raised his right hand and swore to contents of his report, and signed it in presence of oathtaker, this was sufficient to satisfy prerequisites for a sworn statement, and no affirmative act by oathtaker was required. Appeal of State (New Hampshire Dep't of Safety), 144 N.H. 85, 736 A.2d 1242, 1999 N.H. LEXIS 74 (1999).

2. Purpose of oath
The purpose of an oath is to ensure that the affiant consciously

recognizes his legal obligation to tell the truth. State v. Sands, 123 N.H. 570, 467 A.2d 202, 1983 N.H. LEXIS 362, 37 A.L.R.4th 904 (1983).

3. Wording of oath

Neither this section nor RSA 516:20, governing affirmation, expressly requires that the oath be made to God. State v. Sands, 123 N.H. 570, 467 A.2d 202, 1983 N.H. LEXIS 362, 37 A.L.R.4th 904 (1983).

Where the oath administered by the magistrate required the affiant of an affidavit for a search warrant, a deputy sheriff, simply to raise his hand and answer whether his words were true, to which the affiant answered in the affirmative, the oath constituted "swearing" within the meaning of this section and RSA 516:20, governing affirmation, despite the magistrate's failure to use the words "So help you God," since it sufficiently impressed upon the deputy sheriff his obligation to tell the truth. State v. Sands, 123 N.H. 570, 467 A.2d 202, 1983 N.H. LEXIS 362, 37 A.L.R.4th 904 (1983).

4. Signature

The Department of Safety did not lack jurisdiction over a license suspension appeal because the arresting officer failed to sign the section of the administrative license suspension form entitled "Officer's Report." The plain language of RSA 265-A:30 does not require a report to be signed in order to be a "sworn report"; RSA 516:19 also does not require that such a statement be signed; and assuming that RSA 456-B:2, II applied, the form here satisfied its requirements because the officer signed another section of the form, from which a justice of the peace was able to verify that he was the person whose true signature appeared on the form. Kerouac v. Dir., N.H. Division of Motor Vehicles, 158 N.H. 353, 965 A.2d 1111, 2009 N.H. LEXIS 18 (2009).

516:20. Affirmation.

Persons scrupulous of swearing may affirm; the word "affirm" being used in administering the oath, instead of the word "swear," and the words *this you do under the pains and penalties of perjury,* instead of the words *"So help you God."*

Source.

RS 188:11. CS 200:11. GS 209:11. GL 228:11. PS 224:11. PL 336:22. RL 392:20.

NOTES TO DECISIONS

1. Purpose of oath
2. Wording of oath

1. Purpose of oath

The purpose of an oath is to ensure that the affiant consciously recognizes his legal obligation to tell the truth. State v. Sands, 123 N.H. 570, 467 A.2d 202, 1983 N.H. LEXIS 362, 37 A.L.R.4th 904 (1983).

2. Wording of oath

Neither RSA 516:19, governing swearing, nor this section expressly requires that the oath be made to God. State v. Sands, 123 N.H. 570, 467 A.2d 202, 1983 N.H. LEXIS 362, 37 A.L.R.4th 904 (1983).

Where the oath administered by the magistrate required the affiant of an affidavit for a search warrant, a deputy sheriff, simply to raise his hand and answer whether his words were true, to which the affiant answered in the affirmative, the oath constituted "swearing" within the meaning of RSA 516:19, governing swearing, and this section despite the magistrate's failure to use the words "So help you God," since it sufficiently impressed upon the deputy sheriff his obligation to tell the truth. State v. Sands, 123 N.H. 570, 467 A.2d 202, 1983 N.H. LEXIS 362, 37 A.L.R.4th 904 (1983).

516:21. Religious Opinions.

No person who believes in the existence of a supreme being shall be excluded from testifying on account of his opinions on matters of religion.

Source.

RS 188:9. CS 200:9. GS 209:12. GL 228:12. PS 224:12. PL 336:23. RL 392:21.

516:22. Interest.

No person shall be excused or excluded from testifying or giving his deposition in any civil cause by reason of his interest therein, as a party or otherwise.

Source.

1857, 1952:1. 1858, 2090:1. GS 209:13. GL 228:13. 1885, 27:1. PS 224:13. PL 336:24. RL 392:22.

NOTES TO DECISIONS

1. Constitutionality
2. Purpose
3. Applicability
4. Adultery
5. Paternity proceedings
6. Executors and administrators
7. Interest in land
8. Principal and surety
9. Partnership

1. Constitutionality

This section in removing the disqualification of interest in witnesses and thereby enabling parties in actions to testify, is one affecting the remedy and therefore not violative of the constitutional provision against the passing of retrospective laws. Rich v. Flanders, 39 N.H. 304, 1859 N.H. LEXIS 47 (1859), overruled in part, Caswell v. Maplewood Garage, 84 N.H. 241, 149 A. 746, 1930 N.H. LEXIS 72, 73 A.L.R. 433 (1930) (overruled in Caswell v. Maplewood Garage (1929) Caswell v. Maplewood Garage, 84 N.H. 241, 149 A. 746, 1930 N.H. LEXIS 72, 73 A.L.R. 433 (1930).

2. Purpose

This section was designed to enlarge and not contract the field of testimony. Stevens v. Moulton, 68 N.H. 254, 38 A. 732, 1894 N.H. LEXIS 87 (1895).

3. Applicability

This section, by its terms, is applicable to civil causes only and not to criminal actions. State v. Connell, 38 N.H. 81, 1859 N.H. LEXIS 93 (1859); State v. Flanders, 38 N.H. 324, 1859 N.H. LEXIS 129 (1859).

4. Adultery

In an action for alienation of affections, a defendant against whom adultery is alleged is a competent witness, and cannot refuse to testify. Whitcher v. Davis, 70 N.H. 237, 46 A. 458, 1899 N.H. LEXIS 107 (1900).

5. Paternity proceedings

Before the disability of parties to an action to testify was removed, the mother was a competent witness as to the paternity of the child in a bastardy proceeding, provided she declared when in travail that the defendant was the father and continued constant in that accusation, but under this section no such declaration is necessary to make her a competent witness. Heath v. Heath, 58 N.H. 292, 1878 N.H. LEXIS 34 (1878).

6. Executors and administrators

Where one of the parties to an action is an executor, he is not excused or excluded from testifying to all facts which occurred after the death of his testator. Parsons v. Wentworth & Drew, 73 N.H. 122, 59 A. 623, 1904 N.H. LEXIS 26 (1904).

7. Interest in land

A plaintiff who seeks to establish an equitable ownership in realty, by an action against the residuary legatee of the person in whom the legal title is vested, is not excluded as a witness in his own behalf. Crowley v. Crowley, 72 N.H. 241, 56 A. 190, 1903 N.H. LEXIS 56 (1903).

8. Principal and surety

A principal upon a joint and several promissory note who became defaulted in an action against him and the surety, is a competent witness for the surety if released from liability to him, and without such release if the surety's defense is a personal one, although the witness has an interest in the event of the suit and the plaintiff is an administrator who does not elect to testify. Chase v. Pitman, 69 N.H. 423, 43 A. 617, 1898 N.H. LEXIS 37 (1899).

9. Partnership

One partner may be a witness to prove the existence of the partnership whether he is a party to the suit in which he testifies or not. Rich v. Flanders, 39 N.H. 304, 1859 N.H. LEXIS 47 (1859), overruled in part, Caswell v. Maplewood Garage, 84 N.H. 241, 149 A. 746, 1930 N.H. LEXIS 72, 73 A.L.R. 433 (1930) (overruled in Caswell v. Maplewood Garage (1929) Caswell v. Maplewood Garage, 84 N.H. 241, 149 A. 746, 1930 N.H. LEXIS 72, 73 A.L.R. 433 (1930).

Cited:

Cited in Reynolds v. Burgess Sulphite Fibre Co., 71 N.H. 332, 51 A. 1075, 1902 N.H. LEXIS 34, 57 L.R.A. 949 (1902); Smyth v. Balch, 40 N.H. 363, 1860 N.H. LEXIS 160 (1860) (as applicable to actions pending at the time of passage of the original statute).

516:23. Party Deponent.

No party shall be compelled, in testifying or giving a deposition, to disclose the names of the witnesses by whom nor the manner in which he proposes to prove his case, nor, in giving a deposition, to produce any writing which is material to his case or defense, unless the deposition is taken in his own behalf.

Source.

1858, 2090:1. GS 209:14. GL 228:14. PS 224:14. PL 336:25. RL 392:23.

NOTES TO DECISIONS

1. Construction and application
2. Construction with other law
3. Generally
4. Parties as witnesses
5. Incidental or common evidence
6. Personal knowledge
7. Privilege
8. Notes of testimony
9. Agents and employees
10. Experts
11. Attorneys
12. Discovery

1. Construction and application

The limited exemption from discovery on deposition granted by this section does not extend to third persons. Therrien v. Public Serv. Co., 99 N.H. 197, 108 A.2d 48, 1954 N.H. LEXIS 45 (1954).

2. Construction with other law

Secrecy permitted by this section is inconsistent with the policies underlying new superior court rule which allows very broad discovery. Barry v. Horne, 117 N.H. 693, 377 A.2d 623, 1977 N.H. LEXIS 411 (1977).

3. Generally

This section does not require plaintiff to answer a question on the taking of her deposition as to name of a certain witness, nor was she required to confirm a name furnished by party taking the deposition. Huntress v. Tucker, 104 N.H. 270, 184 A.2d 562, 1962 N.H. LEXIS 65 (1962).

A party to an action stands in exactly the same position as any other witness except that he cannot be compelled to disclose the names of the witnesses by whom nor the manner in which he proposes to prove his case. La Coss v. Lebanon, 78 N.H. 413, 101 A. 364, 1917 N.H. LEXIS 28 (1917).

4. Parties as witnesses

A party to an action who is called as a witness is on the same footing as every other witness insofar as the production of documents is concerned, and while a party cannot be compelled to produce material writings when he is giving a deposition, he may be compelled to produce them when he is called as witness, whenever the court finds that that will promote the discovery of truth. La Coss v. Lebanon, 78 N.H. 413, 101 A. 364, 1917 N.H. LEXIS 28 (1917).

5. Incidental or common evidence

This section did not prevent incidental disclosure of defendant's evidence necessary to plaintiff's case nor discovery of evidence common to both parties' cases; Trial Court could permit discovery if evidence sought would aid the party either in his own case or in defending against the case of the other party. Humphreys Corp. v. Margo Lyn, Inc., 109 N.H. 498, 256 A.2d 149, 1969 N.H. LEXIS 189 (1969).

An order, in a personal injury action by a passenger against a bus company, to the effect that the defendant shall produce for the use of the plaintiff names and addresses of witnesses who were passengers in the bus at the time of the accident and whose names and addresses were taken by the driver at that time, in no way violates the letter or the spirit of this section or the equitable safeguards which surround the remedy of discovery, since these passengers as witnesses to this accident are not the exclusive property of either party and in the interest of justice both parties are entitled to have their testimony introduced in the action for whatever help it may furnish in arriving at a just determination. Reynolds v. Boston & Me. Transp. Co., 98 N.H. 251, 98 A.2d 157, 1953 N.H. LEXIS 55, 37 A.L.R.2d 1149 (1953).

The court may order the production of certain writings in advance of trial although they were prepared by the defendant to preserve evidence on which he intends to rely in the trial of the case, if they are also material to the plaintiff's case and justice requires their production. La Coss v. Lebanon, 78 N.H. 413, 101 A. 364, 1917 N.H. LEXIS 28 (1917).

6. Personal knowledge

When necessary to prevent injustice the provisions of this section do not preclude a court of equity, on a motion for discovery, from ordering the defendant to disclose the identity of a witness at whose house the defendant visited prior to the accident. Gibbs v. Prior, 107 N.H. 218, 220 A.2d 151, 1966 N.H. LEXIS 160 (1966).

The provisions of this section to the effect that no party shall be compelled to disclose the names of his witnesses nor the manner of proving his case, does not excuse him from testifying to all matters within his personal knowledge and capable of being proved by his own testimony which relate directly to the matter in issue. Penniman v. Jones, 59 N.H. 119, 1879 N.H. LEXIS 162 (1879).

This section does not excuse a defendant from stating what may bear upon or support his defense unless it will disclose his witnesses or the manner of proving his case, and in a suit against a railroad conductor charging him with receiving money for the fare of passengers which he has not accounted for, he may be required to state the condition of his property at the commencement and close of his service, to be weighed with other evidence in the case, even if it be alleged that this is part of his defense. State ex rel. Eaton v. Farmer, 46 N.H. 200, 1865 N.H. LEXIS 56 (1865).

7. Privilege

The rules of evidence governing privileged matters at trial govern such matters when they arise in discovery proceedings. Riddle Spring Realty Co. v. State, 107 N.H. 271, 220 A.2d 751, 1966 N.H. LEXIS 172 (1966).

8. Notes of testimony

Where an attorney for the contestants of a will takes minutes of the testimony of the witnesses to the instrument upon a proceeding for its probate, his possession of the writing is that of his clients, and neither the attorney nor his clients may be compelled, upon giving depositions, to produce the writings, although either the client or his attorney might be compelled to disclose the names and testimony of the witnesses to the probate of the will. Ex parte Snow, 75 N.H. 7, 70 A. 120, 1908 N.H. LEXIS 23 (1908).

9. Agents and employees

The exemption given by this section does not extend to a corporation's agents or employees. Humphreys Corp. v. Margo Lyn, Inc., 109 N.H. 498, 256 A.2d 149, 1969 N.H. LEXIS 189 (1969).

Where the servant of a corporation, whose duty it is to procure and report in writing the names of witnesses to an accident, is summoned to give a deposition in an action against his employer, he cannot refuse to disclose the information so obtained, since this section applies only to parties to an action and this witness, not being a party to the action, is not within the exemption provided by this section. In re Bradley, 71 N.H. 54, 51 A. 264, 1901 N.H. LEXIS 12 (1901).

10. Experts

Where full answers to interrogatories may require party to disclose names of experts which party does not propose to call as witnesses, order of discovery should be so limited as to exclude those answers. Humphreys Corp. v. Margo Lyn, Inc., 109 N.H. 498, 256 A.2d 149, 1969 N.H. LEXIS 189 (1969).

11. Attorneys

An attorney who gives a deposition cannot be compelled to produce papers of his client, which are in his possession, if the client would be excused from producing them by virtue of the provisions of this section. Ex parte Snow, 75 N.H. 7, 70 A. 120, 1908 N.H. LEXIS 23 (1908).

12. Discovery

Discovery will be best accomplished by direct exchange between counsel with only occasional resort to trial court, and counsel should exercise discrimination as to the limitations sought in opposing discovery. Humphreys Corp. v. Margo Lyn, Inc., 109 N.H. 498, 256 A.2d 149, 1969 N.H. LEXIS 189 (1969).

Party deponent's determination that a question on deposition calls for name of witness by whom he proposes to prove his case is binding upon his opponent. Huntress v. Tucker, 104 N.H. 270, 184 A.2d 562, 1962 N.H. LEXIS 65 (1962).

A party may be required in a deposition to testify to all matters in issue, except that he shall not be required to disclose the names of his witnesses and the manner of proving his case, and if the party declines to answer, because it will disclose his witnesses or the manner of proving his case, and it reasonably appears to the court that it may do so, he will not be required to state how it will have that effect lest in doing that he be compelled to disclose the very facts which the law excuses him from stating. State ex rel. Eaton v. Farmer, 46 N.H. 200, 1865 N.H. LEXIS 56 (1865).

Where defendant, in deposition, properly declined to answer several questions upon the ground that the answering of them would disclose the manner in which she proposed to prove her case, upon the trial of the case, the plaintiff will not be allowed to read those questions and replies to the jury or to inquire of the defendant, who testified at the trial, how the answering of such questions would disclose the manner in which she proposed to prove her case. Carter v. Beals, 44 N.H. 408, 1862 N.H. LEXIS 77 (1862).

Cited:

Cited in State ex rel. Regan v. Superior Court, 102 N.H. 224, 153 A.2d 403, 1959 N.H. LEXIS 51 (1959) (determining the scope of disclosure requirable in taking depositions of police officers.); Whitcher v. Davis, 70 N.H. 237, 46 A. 458, 1899 N.H. LEXIS 107 (1900).

516:24. Adverse Party.

[Repealed 1986, 210:1, I, eff. Jan. 1, 1987.]

Former section(s).

Former RSA 516:24, which was derived from 1857, 1952:2; GS 209:15; GL 228:15; PS 224:15; PL 336:26; RL 392:24, related to adverse parties.

For provisions relating to impeachment and cross-examination of witnesses generally, see Rules 607–611, Rules of Evidence, New Hampshire Court Rules Annotated.

516:25. Declarations of Deceased Persons.

[Repealed 1994, 57:1, II, eff. Jan. 1, 1995.]

Former section(s).

Former RSA 516:25, which was derived from 1857, 1952:3; 1858, 2090:2; 1861, 2496; 1865, 4074:1; GS 209:16, 17, 18; GL 228:16, 17, 18; 1889, 74:1; PS 224:16, 17, 18; PL 336:27, 28, 29; 1941, 132:1, 2; RL 392:25, 26, 27; 1953, 182:1, eff. May 26, 1953, related to declarations of deceased persons.

For provisions relating to the admissibility of statement of a deceased person, see Rule 804(b)(5), Rules of Evidence, New Hampshire Court Rules Annotated.

516:25-a. Statements of Minors in Certain Civil Cases.

In all civil actions, suits or proceedings to recover damages on behalf of a minor child for abuse or assault, including sexual abuse or sexual assault, any statement of the minor child alleged to have been the victim of such abuse or assault shall not be excluded as hearsay, provided that the trial judge, prior to the admission of such testimony, shall make findings of fact that the statement sought to be admitted is apparently trustworthy and that the witness seeking to testify to such statement is competent.

Source.

1989, 30:1, eff. Jan. 1, 1990.

RESEARCH REFERENCES

New Hampshire Bar Journal.

For article, "Child Testimony in Civil Sexual Abuse Cases," see 34 N.H.B.J. 49 (Sept. 1993).

516:26. Negotiated Paper.

In an action brought by an indorsee or assignee of a bill of exchange, promissory note or mortgage against an original party thereto, the defendant shall not testify in his own behalf if either of the original parties to the bill, note or mortgage is dead or insane, unless the plaintiff elects to testify himself or to offer the testimony of an original party thereto.

Source.
1862, 2601:1, 2. GS 209:19. GL 228:19. PS 224:19. PL 336:30. RL 392:28.

516:27. Husband and Wife.

[Repealed 1994, 57:1, III, eff. Jan. 1, 1995.]

Former section(s).
Former RSA 516:27, which was derived from GS 209:20, 21, 22. 1866, 4268:2. 1868, 1:52. 1869, 29:1. 1870, 20:1. 1871, 38:2. GL 228:20, 21. PS 224:20. 1899, 41:1. PL 336:31. RL 392:29 related to husband and wife testimony.
For provisions relating to spousal privilege, see Rule 504, Rules of Evidence, New Hampshire Court Rules Annotated.

516:28. Wills, etc.

The provisions of this chapter shall not affect the law relative to the attestation of wills or other instruments required to be attested by subscribing witnesses.

Source.
1858, 2090:2. GS 209:23. GL 228:22. PS 224:21. PL 336:32. RL 392:30.

NOTES TO DECISIONS

Purpose
The purpose and effect of this section is to measure the competency of subscribing witnesses to wills or other instruments by the rules of common law regardless of the provisions of other sections relating to the general competency of witnesses. Cochran v. Brown, 76 N.H. 9, 78 A. 1072, 1911 N.H. LEXIS 138 (1911); Lord v. Lord, 58 N.H. 7, 1876 N.H. LEXIS 7 (1876).

516:29. Opinions.

[Repealed 1994, 57:1, IV, eff. Jan. 1, 1995.]

Former section(s).
Former RSA 516:29, which was derived from GS 209:24. GL 228:23. PS 224:22. PL 336:33. RL 392:31, related to the opinions of witnesses.
For provisions relating to opinions and expert testimony generally, see Rules 701–705, Rules of Evidence, New Hampshire Court Rules Annotated.

516:29-a. Testimony of Expert Witnesses.

I. A witness shall not be allowed to offer expert testimony unless the court finds:

(a) Such testimony is based upon sufficient facts or data;

(b) Such testimony is the product of reliable principles and methods; and

(c) The witness has applied the principles and methods reliably to the facts of the case.

II. (a) In evaluating the basis for proffered expert testimony, the court shall consider, if appropriate to the circumstances, whether the expert's opinions were supported by theories or techniques that:

(1) Have been or can be tested;

(2) Have been subjected to peer review and publication;

(3) Have a known or potential rate of error; and

(4) Are generally accepted in the appropriate scientific literature.

(b) In making its findings, the court may consider other factors specific to the proffered testimony.

Source.
2004, 118:1, eff. July 16, 2004.

NOTES TO DECISIONS

1. Qualifications of expert
2. Basis for testimony
3. Waiver of objection to admissibility
4. Abuse of discretion
5. Reliability

1. Qualifications of expert
Where plaintiffs in medical malpractice action involving injury to their baby during birth challenged a doctor's qualifications to offer an opinion regarding timing of the baby's injury as required by Rule 702 and RSA 516:29-a, because: (1) her specialty was maternal fetal medicine; (2) she had never seen the particular condition at issue in a premature infant; and (3) she admitted that she would defer to a pediatric neurologist or radiologist on the timing of injuries, the trial court did not err in admitting the doctor's expert testimony on the cause and timing of the injuries as court reasonably could have found that the doctor was qualified to give her opinion regarding the injury given the doctor's years of experience in the field of obstetrics and gynecology, the numerous reasons she gave as to her opinion on the injuries and her experience with many births. The lack of specialization in a particular medical field did not automatically disqualify a doctor from testifying as an expert in that field. Milliken v. Dartmouth-Hitchcock Clinic, 154 N.H. 662, 914 A.2d 1226, 2006 N.H. LEXIS 209 (2006).

2. Basis for testimony
Boston Process Approach as a flexible battery approach was deemed a sufficiently reliable methodology to assist a fact finder in understanding a minor's neuropsychological status in an action based on the minor's exposure to lead paint and the minor's poisoning therefrom, such that a neuropsychologist's use thereof was proper under RSA 516:29-a. Baxter v. Temple, 157 N.H. 280, 949 A.2d 167, 2008 N.H. LEXIS 65 (2008).
Trial court's exclusion of a neuropsychologist's testimony as unreliable under N.H. R. Evid. 702 and RSA 516:29-a in an action by a minor, through her mother, arising from lead paint poisoning in a rented apartment, was error, as the methodology used by the neuropsychologist was reliable and it was properly and reliably applied to the facts of the case. Baxter v. Temple, 157 N.H. 280, 949 A.2d 167, 2008 N.H. LEXIS 65 (2008).

3. Waiver of objection to admissibility
Where plaintiffs in malpractice action arising out of a birth injury to their child challenged the admission of an expert's testimony as to the timing of the child's injuries arguing that the testimony was the product of unreliable principles and methods, plaintiff's counsel's statement during a bench conference stating that the expert was capable of testifying as to timing of the injury based upon edema conceded the very issue that the plaintiffs were trying to appeal and counsel's admission was binding upon the plaintiffs and the issue was waived on appeal. Milliken v. Dartmouth-Hitchcock Clinic, 154 N.H. 662, 914 A.2d 1226, 2006 N.H. LEXIS 209 (2006).

4. Abuse of discretion
Trial court unsustainably exercised its discretion in excluding a criminalist's expert testimony concerning the identification of a latent fingerprint of defendant found at a crime scene because the trial court exceeded its gatekeeping function by finding the criminalist's testimony unreliable because the criminalist failed to take

bench notes. Moreover, while blind verification of the fingerprint may have ensured with a higher level of certainty that an identification was correct, the record contained no indication that non-blind verification was unreliable. State v. Langill, 157 N.H. 77, 945 A.2d 1, 2008 N.H. LEXIS 39 (2008).

5. Reliability

In a title insurance case, the insurer's expert had not conducted a market analysis of the lot as a buildable one. Thus, when the insured sought to have him testify on the value of the lot as a buildable one, the trial court properly concluded that the testimony did not meet the standard for reliability under RSA 516:29-a. Gray v. Commonwealth Land Title Ins. Co., 162 N.H. 71, 27 A.3d 852, 2011 N.H. LEXIS 72 (2011).

516:29-b. Disclosure of Expert Testimony in Civil Cases.

I. A party in a civil case shall disclose to other parties the identity of any person who may be used at trial to present evidence under Rules 702, 703, or 705 of the New Hampshire rules of evidence.

II. Except as otherwise stipulated or directed by the court, this disclosure shall, with respect to a witness who is retained or specially employed to provide expert testimony in the case or whose duties as an employee of the party regularly involve giving expert testimony, be accompanied by a written report signed by the witness. The report shall contain a complete statement of:

(a) All opinions to be expressed and the basis and reasons therefor;

(b) The facts or data considered by the witness in forming the opinions;

(c) Any exhibits to be used as a summary of or support for the opinions;

(d) The qualifications of the witness, including a list of all publications authored by the witness within the preceding 10 years;

(e) The compensation to be paid for the study and testimony; and

(f) A listing of any other cases in which the witness has testified as an expert at trial or by deposition within the preceding 4 years.

III. These disclosures shall be made at the times and in the sequence directed by the court. In the absence of other directions from the court or stipulation by the parties, the disclosures shall be made at least 90 days before the trial date or the date the case is to be ready for trial or, if the evidence is intended solely to contradict or rebut evidence on the same subject matter identified by another party, within 30 days after the disclosure made by the other party. The parties shall supplement these disclosures when required in accordance with the court's rules.

IV. The deposition of any person who has been identified as an expert whose opinions may be presented at trial, and whose testimony has been the subject of a report under this section, shall not be conducted until after such report has been provided.

V. The provisions of this section shall not apply in criminal cases.

Source.

2004, 118:1, eff. July 16, 2004. 2005, 279:1, eff. July 22, 2005. 2013, 65:1, eff. January 1, 2014.

Amendments

—**2013.** The 2013 amendment substituted "facts or data" for "data or other information" in II(b).

—**2005.** Inserted "in civil cases" in the section catchline and following "a party" in paragraph I, and added paragraph V.

NOTES TO DECISIONS

1. Applicability
2. Exhibits
3. Preservation of objection on appeal
4. Prejudice

1. Applicability

RSA 516:29-b, requiring a party to disclose a retained expert witness, did not apply in a nonemergency involuntary civil commitment proceeding where a psychiatrist was not retained by either party, but was independent of the parties and was appointed by the trial court under RSA 135-C:40 to evaluate respondent. In re Nicholas L., 158 N.H. 700, 973 A.2d 924, 2009 N.H. LEXIS 64 (2009).

2. Exhibits

Where plaintiffs in medical malpractice action objected to doctor's exhibits presented during his expert testimony at trial, on the ground that they were not part of the expert disclosure under RSA 516:29-b, II(c), the trial court engaged in a sustainable exercise of discretion in overruling the plaintiffs' objection and permitting admission of the doctor's exhibits as the exhibits were part of the exhibit list submitted one month prior to trial, the exhibits themselves were disclosed two weeks before the expert's testimony and, although RSA 516:29-b, II may contain additional requirements regarding exhibit disclosure, the trial court was permitted to exercise its discretion and impose different requirements. Milliken v. Dartmouth-Hitchcock Clinic, 154 N.H. 662, 914 A.2d 1226, 2006 N.H. LEXIS 209 (2006).

3. Preservation of objection on appeal

Where plaintiffs in medical malpractice action filed a pretrial motion in limine to preclude a doctor from testifying about the timing of their baby's injury, claiming that it lacked the requisite indicia of reliability required by New Hampshire Rule of Evidence 702, the motion in limine preserved for appeal the issue of the doctor's qualifications to testify on the timing of the injury although the plaintiffs made no objection on this issue at trial; however, issues regarding the doctor's report and her qualifications to testify on the cause of the injury were not preserved by the plaintiffs' motion in limine. The motion did not argue that the testimony was inadmissible because the defendants failed to comply with the disclosure requirements of RSA 516:29-b or Superior Court Rule 35(f), the trial court's order denying the plaintiffs' motion specifically focused upon the issue of reliability and did not discuss disclosure issues and neither the plaintiffs' motion nor the court's order addressed the doctor's testimony about the cause of the injury. Milliken v. Dartmouth-Hitchcock Clinic, 154 N.H. 662, 914 A.2d 1226, 2006 N.H. LEXIS 209 (2006).

Where plaintiffs in medical malpractice action filed a pretrial motion in limine seeking to preclude "exclude any opinion testimony from physicians testifying for the defense for whom no expert opinions have been disclosed" but the trial court did not directly rule on this motion finding that the issue was not ripe, the motion in limine was insufficient to preserve the issue on appeal with respect to a particular expert witness's disclosure; the court made no definitive ruling on the motion and the particular doctor was not even specifically mentioned in the motion. Since the motion in limine was insufficient to preserve this issue, a timely objection at trial was required; the plaintiffs' first objection to the doctor's testimony came during the defendant's cross-examination and was too late to preserve the issue on appeal. Furthermore, issues regarding the doctor's qualifications to offer an opinion on causation and timing were not preserved for the same reasons. Milliken v. Dartmouth-Hitchcock Clinic, 154 N.H. 662, 914 A.2d 1226, 2006 N.H. LEXIS 209 (2006).

4. Prejudice

Defendant had not shown that it was prejudiced by plaintiff's failure to disclose the qualifications of its expert witness, the compensation to be paid to the witness, and a list of prior cases in which the witness testified. Defendant still had ample tools at its disposal, including the expert's report, his name, and the organization for which he worked; it had the ability to challenge the expert's damage theory on its merits through the testimony of its own expert; and it did not appear that either of the experts' qualifications were significant factors in the trial court's conclusion. Barking Dog v. Citizens Ins. Co. of Am., 164 N.H. 80, 53 A.3d 554, 2012 N.H. LEXIS 109 (2012).

Business owner had failed to demonstrate that an expert witness disclosure's lack of specifics caused him any prejudice, and thus had failed to show that the trial court's decision to allow the expert to testify about the corporate financial records that he reviewed was clearly untenable or unreasonable to the prejudice of his case. J & M Lumber & Constr. Co. v. Smyjunas, 161 N.H. 714, 20 A.3d 947, 2011 N.H. LEXIS 52 (2011).

516:30. Public Records.

[Repealed 1994, 57:1, V, eff. Jan. 1, 1995.]

Former section(s).
Former RSA 516:30, which was derived from 1846, 322:3. CS 147:10. GS 209:25. 1870, 11:1. GL 228:24. 1881, 19:1; 47:1. 1885, 59:1. PS 224:23. PL 336:34. RL 392:32 related to public records as evidence.
For provisions relating to admissibility of public records, see Rules 803, 901, 902, Rules of Evidence, New Hampshire Court Rules Annotated. For provisions relating to access to public records generally, see RSA 91-A.

516:31. Respondents in Criminal Cases.

[Repealed 1994, 57:1, VI, eff. Jan. 1, 1995.]

Former section(s).
Former RSA 516:31, which was derived from 1869, 23:1. GL 228:25. PS 224:24. PL 336:35. RL 392:33 related to respondents as witnesses in criminal cases.
For provisions relating to rights of accused, see New Hampshire Constitution, Part I, Article 15.

516:32. Limitation.

[Repealed 1994, 57:1, VII, eff. Jan. 1, 1995.]

Former section(s).
Former RSA 516:32, which was derived from 1869, 23:2; GL 228:26; PS 224:25; PL 336:36; and RL 392:34, related to limitations on respondents as witnesses in criminal cases.
For provisions relating to rights of accused, see New Hampshire Constitution, Part I, Article 15.

516:33. Felons.

[Repealed 1994, 57:1, VIII, eff. Jan. 1, 1995.]

Former section(s).
Former RSA 516:33, which was derived from 1871, 38:1; GL 228:27; PS 224:26; PL 336:37; and RL 392:35, related to the competency of felons to testify.
For provisions relating to lack of privilege to refuse to be a witness, see Rule 501(a)(1), Rules of Evidence, New Hampshire Court Rules Annotated.

516:33-a. Confidential Settlement Agreements.

For purposes of testimony, confidential settlement agreements in prior court actions shall not prevent a person from disclosing information other than the amount of the settlement, if the court finds the information is relevant to the pending action.

Source.
2004, 125:1, eff. Jan. 1, 2005.

Grant of Immunity in Criminal Cases

516:34. Compelling Evidence in Criminal Proceedings; Immunity.

I. Whenever:

(a) A witness refuses, on the basis of his privilege against self-incrimination, to testify or provide information in a proceeding before, or ancillary to a district or superior court or a grand jury; and

(b) The person presiding over the proceeding communicates on the record to the witness an order issued under paragraph II,
the witness may not refuse to comply with the order on the basis of the privilege against self-incrimination. No testimony or other information compelled under the order, or any information directly or indirectly derived from such testimony or other information, may be used against the witness in any criminal case or forfeiture. However, the witness may be prosecuted or subject to penalty or forfeiture for any perjury, false swearing, or contempt committed in answering or failing to answer, or in producing or failing to produce evidence in accordance with the order.

II. A prosecutor may, with the prior written approval of the attorney general or county attorney for the jurisdiction where offenses are alleged to have occurred, request an order requiring such individual to give testimony or provide other information which he refuses to give or provide on the basis of his privilege against self-incrimination, when in the judgment of the attorney general or county attorney:

(a) The testimony or other information from such individual may be necessary to the public interest.

(b) Such individual has refused or is likely to refuse to testify or provide other information on the basis of his privilege against self-incrimination.

Source.
1967, 427:1. 1993, 115:1, eff. July 1, 1993.

Amendments
—1993. Rewritten to the extent that a detailed comparison would be impracticable.

NOTES TO DECISIONS

1. Generally
2. Review

3. Use immunity—Relation to transactional immunity
4. —As a right
5. Denial of immunity

1. Generally

Since trial court does not have power to grant immunity to defense witnesses on its own, or to require government to seek immunity for defense witnesses, defendants could not have been denied right to call witnesses in their behalf because trial court refused to grant immunity to, or seal testimony of, defense witnesses who invoked fifth amendment. State v. Linsky, 117 N.H. 866, 379 A.2d 813, 1977 N.H. LEXIS 450 (1977).

2. Review

Where possibility of immunity for defense witness was not argued or considered below, supreme court would not consider whether present case involved situation in which to deny a defense witness immunization from prosecution would deprive defendant of due process. State v. Lavallee, 119 N.H. 207, 400 A.2d 480, 1979 N.H. LEXIS 278 (1979), superseded by statute as stated in, State v. Newell, 141 N.H. 199, 679 A.2d 1142, 1996 N.H. LEXIS 72 (1996).

3. Use immunity—Relation to transactional immunity

The power to request an order compelling testimony is vested solely with the state. State v. Roy, 140 N.H. 478, 668 A.2d 41, 1995 N.H. LEXIS 179 (1995).

4. —As a right

Defendant was not denied due process by trial court's refusal to order State to either grant immunity to her fiance, who she alleged would provide exculpatory evidence, or dismiss indictment, since fiance's proffered testimony fell short of being directly exculpatory and did not present a highly material variance from tenor of State's evidence. State v. Kivlin, 145 N.H. 718, 766 A.2d 274, 2001 N.H. LEXIS 12 (2001).

A defendant has no per se right to have a defense witness immunized. State v. Roy, 140 N.H. 478, 668 A.2d 41, 1995 N.H. LEXIS 179 (1995).

Under narrow circumstances where the defendant shows that the testimony sought would be directly exculpatory or would present a highly material variance from the tenor of the State's evidence, failure to immunize a witness may have due process implications. State v. Roy, 140 N.H. 478, 668 A.2d 41, 1995 N.H. LEXIS 179 (1995).

5. Denial of immunity

State's refusal to immunize two defense witnesses under RSA 516:34 did not violate defendant's due process rights under the state constitution because the testimony was not the sort of exculpatory evidence that would have prevented conviction: their testimony could not place defendant elsewhere or preclude the possibility that he had an agreement with a second person to kidnap and terrorize the victim. Furthermore, the testimony was cumulative, and there was no suggestion of prosecutorial misconduct. State v. Rogers, 159 N.H. 50, 977 A.2d 493, 2009 N.H. LEXIS 85 (2009).

In a prosecution for conspiracy to possess marijuana with the intent to sell which arose from the interception of a package containing marijuana sent by private courier service to the defendant, it was not error for the court to refuse to compel the grant of immunity to a coconspirator, notwithstanding the assertion that the coconspirator was expected to testify that the defendant was not involved in the conspiracy, as the defendant made an insufficient showing that the testimony would be directly exculpatory or at a highly material variance to the state's evidence where the anticipated testimony was that the defendant was aware of, and interfered with, the coconspirator's activities. State v. Winn, 141 N.H. 812, 694 A.2d 537, 1997 N.H. LEXIS 45 (1997).

Cited:

Cited in State v. MacManus, 130 N.H. 256, 536 A.2d 203, 1987 N.H. LEXIS 283 (1987); Avery v. Cunningham, 131 N.H. 138, 551 A.2d 952, 1988 N.H. LEXIS 107 (1988); State v. Monsalve, 133 N.H. 268, 574 A.2d 1384, 1990 N.H. LEXIS 60 (1990).

RESEARCH REFERENCES

New Hampshire Bar Journal.

For article, "State v. Bortner: NH Begins to Develop Law on Immunity and Cooperation Agreements in Criminal Cases," see 45 N.H.B.J. 16 (Sept. 2004).

Privileged Communications

516:35. Religious Leaders.

A priest, rabbi or ordained or licensed minister of any church or a duly accredited Christian Science practitioner shall not be required to disclose a confession or confidence made to him in his professional character as spiritual adviser, unless the person confessing or confiding waives the privilege.

Source.

1979, 197:1, eff. Aug. 10, 1979.

NOTES TO DECISIONS

1. Presence of third party
2. Child abuse

1. Presence of third party

Religious privilege did not apply to a statement that defendant made to his pastor in the presence of the pastor's wife, as there was no evidence that her presence was necessary for the communication or essential to and in furtherance of the communication. State v. Willis, — N.H. —, — A.3d —, 2013 N.H. LEXIS 91 (Aug. 21, 2013).

2. Child abuse

Trial court properly admitted defendant's statement to his pastor that he had been sexually involved with the victim twice, as any statement to a clergyperson that might be helpful in establishing child abuse was not protected by the religious privilege State v. Willis, — N.H. —, — A.3d —, 2013 N.H. LEXIS 91 (Aug. 21, 2013).

Law Enforcement Agency Documents and Records

516:36. Written Policy Directives to Police Officers and Investigators.

I. In any civil action against any individual, agency or governmental entity, including the state of New Hampshire, arising out of the conduct of a law enforcement officer having the powers of a peace officer, standards of conduct embodied in policies, procedures, rules, regulations, codes of conduct, orders or other directives of a state, county or local law enforcement agency shall not be admissible to establish negligence when such standards of conduct are higher than the standard of care which would otherwise have been applicable in such action under state law.

II. All records, reports, letters, memoranda, and other documents relating to any internal investigation into the conduct of any officer, employee, or agent of any state, county, or municipal law enforcement agency having the powers of a peace officer shall not be admissible in any civil action other than in a disciplinary action between the agency and its officers, agents, or employees. Nothing in this paragraph shall preclude the admissibility of otherwise relevant records of the law enforcement agency which relate to the incident under investigation that are not generated by or part of the internal investigation. For the purposes of this paragraph, "internal investigation" shall include any inquiry conducted by the chief law enforcement officer within a law enforcement agency or authorized by him.

Source.
  1986, 111:1, eff. July 19, 1986.

Cross References.
  Confidentiality of police personnel files in criminal proceedings, see RSA 105:13-b.

NOTES TO DECISIONS

Cited:
  Cited in Union Leader Corp. v. Fenniman, 136 N.H. 624, 620 A.2d 1039, 1993 N.H. LEXIS 4 (1993).

Testimony by Video Teleconference in Criminal and Motor Vehicle Cases

Amendments
  —**2011.** The 2011 amendment by 2011, 220:2, eff. August 7, 2011, added "and Motor Vehicle" in the subdivision heading.

516:37. Testimony by Video Teleconference in Criminal Cases.

I. In any criminal case at which a certifying scientist, criminalist, laboratory scientist, or technical specialist from the forensic laboratory of the department of safety, division of state police is summoned to testify, the state may move to take the testimony of the scientist, criminalist, or specialist by video teleconference, provided that the testimony is limited to expert testimony or to the results of and matters relating to tests conducted at the forensic laboratory. Notice shall be provided to the defendant, and the defendant shall have an opportunity to object to the introduction of testimony by video teleconference. No video teleconference testimony shall be permitted during a felony prosecution, except with the affirmative assent of the defendant. Examination and cross-examination of the scientist, criminalist, or specialist shall proceed in the same manner as permitted at trial.

II. In any criminal case at which the defendant summons a toxicologist, criminalist, laboratory scientist, or other person of similar expertise to testify as an expert witness, the defendant may move to take the testimony of that witness by video teleconference, provided that the testimony is limited to expert testimony or to the results of and matters relating to tests conducted at the forensic laboratory of the department of safety, division of state police. Notice shall be provided to the state, and the state shall have an opportunity to object to the introduction of testimony by video teleconference. No video teleconference testimony shall be permitted during

a felony prosecution, except with the affirmative assent of the state. Examination and cross-examination of the expert witness shall proceed in the same manner as permitted at trial.

Source.
  2003, 247:1, eff. Jan. 1, 2004.

516:38. Testimony by Video Teleconference for Motor Vehicle Violations.

In any contested case for an alleged motor vehicle violation in district court at which a keeper of the records or technical specialist from the department of safety, bureau of hearings or division of motor vehicles is summoned to testify, the state may move to take the testimony of the keeper of the records or technical specialist by video teleconference, provided that the testimony is limited to expert testimony or to the results of and matters relating to records of the department of safety. Notice shall be provided to the defendant, and the defendant shall have an opportunity to object to the introduction of testimony by video teleconference. Similarly, in any contested case for an alleged motor vehicle violation in district court, the defendant may move to take the testimony of his or her own expert witness by video teleconference, provided that the testimony is limited to expert testimony or to the results of and matters relating to records of the department of safety. Notice shall be provided to the state, and the state shall have an opportunity to object to the introduction of testimony by video teleconference. Examination and cross-examination of the expert witness shall proceed in the same manner as permitted at a contested case for an alleged motor vehicle violation in district court. For purposes of this section, "video teleconference" includes the use of any technology that provides live, interactive aural and visual communication.

Source.
  2011, 220:3, eff. August 27, 2011.

CHAPTER 517

DEPOSITIONS

In Criminal Cases

SECTION
517:13.   Discovery Depositions in Criminal Cases.

In Criminal Cases

517:13. Discovery Depositions in Criminal Cases.

I. Except as otherwise provided in this section or by order of the court, depositions shall be taken in the manner provided in civil actions.

II. The court in its discretion may permit either party to take the deposition of any witness, except the defendant, in any criminal case, upon a finding by a preponderance of the evidence that such deposition is necessary:

(a) To preserve the testimony of any witness who is unlikely to be available for trial due to illness, absence from the jurisdiction or reluctance to cooperate; or

(b) To ensure a fair trial, avoid surprise or for other good cause shown. In determining the necessity, the court shall consider the complexity of the issues involved, other opportunities or information available to discover the information sought by the deposition, and any other special or exceptional circumstances which may exist.

III. In any felony case either party may take a discovery deposition of any expert witness who may be called by the other party to testify at trial.

IV. Nothing in this section shall be construed as limiting discovery depositions by agreement between the parties.

V. Notwithstanding this section, no party in a criminal case shall take the discovery deposition of a victim or witness who has not achieved the age of 16 years at the time of the deposition.

Source.

1869, 24:1. GL 229:12. PS 225:13. PL 337:13. RL 339:13. RSA 517:13. 1959, 12:1. 1985, 228:1. 1988, 195:1. 1990, 206:1, eff. Jan. 1, 1991. 2003, 141:1, eff. Jan. 1, 2004.

Amendments

—2003. Paragraph V: Substituted "or witness who has not achieved the age of 16 years at the time of the deposition" for "who was 16 years of age or under at the time of the alleged offense or of any witness who was 16 years of age or under at the time of the alleged offense".

—2003. Paragraph V: Rewritten to the extent that a detailed comparison would be impracticable.

—1990. Rewritten to the extent that a detailed comparison would be impracticable.

—1988. Substituted "16 years of age or under" for "under 16 years of age" preceding "shall take the discovery" and following "witness who was" in the third sentence.

—1985. Added "of depositions" in the section catchline, substituted "prosecutor" for "county attorney" preceding "that is required" in the first sentence, inserted "discovery" preceding "deposition" in the second sentence, and added the third sentence.

Cross References.

Taking of video tape depositions of witnesses under 16 years of age, see RSA 517:13-a.

NOTES TO DECISIONS

1. Constitutionality
2. Grounds for deposition
3. Time
4. Production of documents
5. Scope of questioning
6. Court's discretion
7. Necessity
8. Experts
9. Motion to compel depositions

1. Constitutionality

This section, barring discovery depositions of crime victims who were sixteen years of age or under at time of offense regardless of age of victim when discovery deposition was requested, violated equal protection guarantees of state and federal constitutions in that once victim passed age of sixteen protection of this section was no longer deemed necessary; in light of legislative history, this section would be construed to bar discovery depositions where crime victim was sixteen years or under at time of deposition. State v. LaPorte, 134 N.H. 73, 587 A.2d 1237, 1991 N.H. LEXIS 25 (1991).

At trial for aggravated felonious sexual assault, this section applied to bar discovery deposition of victim who was under sixteen years of age at time of alleged offense but who had attained age of sixteen at time of discovery request violated equal protection guarantees of state and federal constitutions in that defendant was subject to classification not rationally related to purported goal of protecting children under age sixteen from repetitive subjection to interrogation without judicial supervision, since once victim reached age sixteen protection of this section was deemed no longer necessary. State v. LaPorte, 134 N.H. 73, 587 A.2d 1237, 1991 N.H. LEXIS 25 (1991).

Where this section, which barred discovery depositions of crime victims who were sixteen at time alleged offense occurred, violated state and federal equal protection guarantees and legislative history indicated legislature would have enacted this section had it been worded to bar discovery depositions of crime victims under sixteen years of age at time of deposition, the supreme court would so construe statute. State v. LaPorte, 134 N.H. 73, 587 A.2d 1237, 1991 N.H. LEXIS 25 (1991).

2. Grounds for deposition

Although the victim was in good health, he was 83 years old and had exceeded the life expectancy for males, also, several delays had occurred in scheduling the case for trial; thus, the court properly exercised its discretion in allowing a deposition to be taken as good cause existed to ensure that the jury could hear the victim's testimony. State v. Schonarth, 152 N.H. 560, 883 A.2d 305, 2005 N.H. LEXIS 138 (2005), rehearing denied, 2005 N.H. LEXIS 156 (N.H. Oct. 25, 2005).

Trial court did not abuse its discretion by denying defendant's motion to take depositions and funds to take them. Defendant had access to detailed police reports about witnesses in question and had received extensive discovery throughout case, and chance for surprise at trial was slight. State v. Haines, 142 N.H. 692, 709 A.2d 762, 1998 N.H. LEXIS 23 (1998).

A deposition for discovery purposes is authorized where respondent in criminal case contends there was insufficient evidence to support issuance of search warrant by justice of peace. State ex rel. Childs v. Hayward, 109 N.H. 228, 248 A.2d 88, 1968 N.H. LEXIS 165 (1968).

Respondent charged with misdemeanor has no right to take depositions prior to arraignment and plea. State v. Karafotis, 104 N.H. 191, 182 A.2d 609, 1962 N.H. LEXIS 45 (1962); State v. Sargent, 104 N.H. 211, 182 A.2d 607, 1962 N.H. LEXIS 51 (1962).

Fair, prompt and orderly disposition of criminal cases requires that plea be entered and issue joined before motions to take depositions or for discovery may be entertained. State v. Sargent, 104 N.H. 211, 182 A.2d 607, 1962 N.H. LEXIS 51 (1962).

A person who has been arraigned upon a criminal charge and is awaiting the action of the grand jury has no right to take depositions under this section, since no case is then pending against him. State v. Naud, 73 N.H. 531, 63 A. 673, 1906 N.H. LEXIS 23 (1906).

3. Time

This section is no longer applicable at the conclusion of a criminal trial unfavorable to the respondent. State v. Bruneau, 131 N.H. 104, 552 A.2d 585, 1988 N.H. LEXIS 106 (1988).

Accused charged with misdemeanor may not take depositions in advance of arraignment and plea and an accused charged with felony may not do so before indictment. State ex rel. McLetchie v. Laconia Dist. Court, 106 N.H. 48, 205 A.2d 534, 1964 N.H. LEXIS 35 (1964).

4. Production of documents

The right to take depositions does not extend to requiring the production by police officers of reports made and of photographs and statements of witnesses taken by them, or procured by direction of the prosecuting officer. Whether such production should be required is in the reasonable discretion of the court. State ex rel. Regan v. Superior Court, 102 N.H. 224, 153 A.2d 403, 1959 N.H. LEXIS 51 (1959).

5. Scope of questioning

While this section, as amended, limits the use of discovery depositions in criminal cases when the victim is under sixteen at the time of the offense alleged, RSA 517:13-a authorizes a trial court to order videotaped depositions of such victims or witnesses, and such depositions may include questions posed for discovery purposes, calling for answers that might not be admissible at the trial. State v. Heath, 129 N.H. 102, 523 A.2d 82, 1986 N.H. LEXIS 395 (1986).

6. Court's discretion

A defendant has no unqualified due process right under either State or Federal Constitution to compel depositions in criminal cases, although trial court may allow a witness deposition upon a finding that it is necessary to ensure a fair trial, avoid surprise, or for other good cause shown. State v. Hilton, 144 N.H. 470, 744 A.2d 96, 1999 N.H. LEXIS 139 (1999).

The trial court did not abuse its discretion by denying the defendant's motion to depose the victim, notwithstanding inconsistencies in her testimony, since the case was not complex, the defendant was provided open file discovery, which included the police report and a two-page, handwritten statement by the victim thoroughly detailing her allegations, and the defendant was aware that the victim had given an inconsistent statement to a Division of Children and Youth Services worker. State v. Rhoades, 139 N.H. 432, 655 A.2d 414, 1995 N.H. LEXIS 20 (1995).

In prosecution for burglary, ruling denying defendant permission to impeach a witness by the use of a deposition of another witness, who was available as a witness and could have been called by defendant, was within trial court's discretion. State v. Seeley, 116 N.H. 831, 368 A.2d 1171, 1976 N.H. LEXIS 480 (1976).

7. Necessity

Under statute governing depositions in criminal cases, burden is on defendant requesting deposition to establish necessity. State v. Howe, 145 N.H. 41, 750 A.2d 48, 2000 N.H. LEXIS 18 (2000).

Defendant failed to establish necessity for depositions in connection with probation revocation proceeding, where facts of underlying incident and any animosity between defendant and witnesses were known to defendant, issues involved were not complex, and prosecution provided written statements of witnesses and police reports to defendant well in advance of hearing. State v. Howe, 145 N.H. 41, 750 A.2d 48, 2000 N.H. LEXIS 18 (2000).

Kidnapping and sexual assault defendant failed to establish necessity for deposition of victim and police officers who interviewed her, where defendant had ample information to prepare his defense, and there was no merit to his allegation of surprise with respect to victim's testimony at trial. State v. Hilton, 144 N.H. 470, 744 A.2d 96, 1999 N.H. LEXIS 139 (1999).

Bare assertions of defense counsel were insufficient to demonstrate necessity for deposition of sexual assault victim's counselor. State v. Ellsworth, 142 N.H. 710, 709 A.2d 768, 1998 N.H. LEXIS 25 (1998).

Trial court did not err in ruling that sexual assault defendant had not made a sufficient showing that deposition of victim was necessary to investigate her delay in reporting assaults. State v.

Chick, 141 N.H. 503, 688 A.2d 553, 1996 N.H. LEXIS 131 (1996).

The defendant must make some showing of necessity before the trial court can grant a motion to depose, which showing must be made with reference to the facts and circumstances of the particular case. State v. Rhoades, 139 N.H. 432, 655 A.2d 414, 1995 N.H. LEXIS 20 (1995).

8. Experts

Assault defendant at pretrial hearing did not argue that State's witnesses were experts he was entitled as a matter of law to depose, but rather that witnesses were non-experts as to whom he had shown requisite necessity for deposing, and therefore "invited error" doctrine precluded defendant from claiming, on appeal, that trial court erred in denying his motion to depose witnesses by using the very standard he asked the court to apply. State v. Goodale, 144 N.H. 224, 740 A.2d 1026, 1999 N.H. LEXIS 102 (1999).

While the statute requires the court to make a finding of necessity before ordering the deposition of a lay witness, no such finding is required before an expert witness may be deposed. State v. Martin, 142 N.H. 63, 694 A.2d 999, 1997 N.H. LEXIS 55 (1997).

If a victim's treating physician is an expert witness, the plain language of the statute expressly allows the defendant to take her deposition. State v. Martin, 142 N.H. 63, 694 A.2d 999, 1997 N.H. LEXIS 55 (1997).

The defendant in a prosecution for felonious aggravated sexual assault was entitled to a new trial since the trial court committed reversible error when it refused to treat the victim's treating physician as an expert witness and denied the defendant his right to depose the physician; although the physician did not offer opinions to the jury, her observations and findings, some based on an internal gynecological examination, required special skills and knowledge not possessed by the average layperson and, therefore, she was an expert for purposes of the statute. State v. Martin, 142 N.H. 63, 694 A.2d 999, 1997 N.H. LEXIS 55 (1997).

9. Motion to compel depositions

Trial court properly denied defendant's motion to compel depositions of police officers and of a polygraph examiner under RSA 517:13, II. Defendant could have challenged the voluntariness of his confession and moved to suppress it; at the hearing, he would have had an opportunity to cross-examine both of the officers and the polygraph examiner. State v. Oakes, 161 N.H. 270, 13 A.3d 293, 2010 N.H. LEXIS 149 (Dec. 7, 2010).

Cited:

Cited in State v. Preston, 121 N.H. 147, 427 A.2d 32, 1981 N.H. LEXIS 269 (1981).

RESEARCH REFERENCES

New Hampshire Court Rules Annotated.

Taking of depositions generally, see Rules 37–44, Rules of the Superior Court, New Hampshire Court Rules Annotated.

Taking of video tape depositions generally, see Rules 45 and 45-A, Rules of the Superior Court, New Hampshire Court Rules Annotated.

TITLE LV

PROCEEDINGS IN SPECIAL CASES

CHAPTER 539

WILFUL TRESPASS

SECTION
539:7.   Theft of Utility Services.
539:9.   Agricultural Vandalism; Penalties.

539:7. Theft of Utility Services.

I. A person shall be guilty of a misdemeanor, if a natural person, or a felony, if any other person, who:

(a) Knowingly injures, destroys, or causes to be injured or destroyed any meter, pipe, conduit, wire, line, post, lamp or other device or attachment belonging to a person or corporation engaged in the manufacture or sale of electricity, gas, water, or telephone communications services;

(b) Knowingly interferes with the proper action or just registration of any meter or other recording device belonging to a person or corporation described in subparagraph (a);

(c) Knowingly participates in causing the prohibited result in either subparagraph (a) or (b); or

(d) Without the consent of the person or corporation described in subparagraph (a), knowingly diverts, causes to be diverted, or allows to be diverted for his use any utility service from such person or corporation.

II. The existence of any of the results prohibited in paragraph I with reference to meters, recording devices or attachments shall be evidence that the person to whom such utility service is at the time being furnished by or through such meters, recording devices, or attachments, has knowingly created or caused to be created the conditions so existing; provided that the evidence referred to in this paragraph shall not apply to any person who has been furnished with electric, gas, water or telephone service for less than 31 days, or until the first meter reading has been made; and, provided further that the evidence referred to in this paragraph shall not apply to any person whose electric meter, recording devices and attachments are on the property of another person or under the control of another person.

III. Nothing in this section shall limit any civil right of action lying in favor of any utility as a result of damage occurring from any act prohibited under paragraph I. Damages shall include the cost of the utility service wrongfully used, the cost of the equipment repair or replacement as necessary, attorney's fees, and all costs to the utility, including labor in undertaking and completing the investigation resulting in a determination of liability under this section.

IV. Nothing in this section shall limit or restrict the prosecution of a person under RSA 637:8.

Source.
1901, 41:1. PL 355:7. RL 411:7. RSA 539:7. 1973, 529:124. 1981, 448:1. 1985, 134:1, eff. Jan. 1, 1986.

Amendments
—**1985.** Paragraph IV: Added.

—**1981.** Expanded provisions relating to theft of utilities services and increased penalties.

—**1973.** Amended generally to conform provisions to new criminal code.

Cross References.
Classification of crimes, see RSA 625:9.
Sentences, see RSA 651.

NOTES TO DECISIONS

1. Scope
2. Circumstantial evidence
3. Proof

1. Scope
To constitute the offense described in this section, it is not necessary that the electricity diverted from a meter should be supplied to the person who commits the offense. State v. Rousten, 84 N.H. 140, 146 A. 870, 1929 N.H. LEXIS 66 (1929).

2. Circumstantial evidence
Circumstantial evidence was held to warrant submission of the case to the jury in State v. Rousten, 84 N.H. 140, 146 A. 870, 1929 N.H. LEXIS 66 (1929).

3. Proof
In the trial of an indictment under this section, a charge that the electricity was "supplied to" defendant, and evidence that the electricity was supplied to a corporation of which there was evidence that the defendant was the sole proprietor, does not constitute a variance, since defendant was not thereby misled. State v. Rousten, 84 N.H. 140, 146 A. 870, 1929 N.H. LEXIS 66 (1929).

539:9. Agricultural Vandalism; Penalties.

I. Whoever shall knowingly cut, fell, destroy, injure, damage, cause to be damaged, carry away, tamper with, worry, or vandalize any legal crop or legal crop bearing tree or plant, cropland, pasture or pasture land, livestock or other farm raised animals, as defined in RSA 21:34-a, and all farm buildings, enclosures, structures, or equipment used in the care and production of crops, livestock or other farm raised animals, or aid in such action without permission of the owner, shall forfeit to the person injured up to 10 times the market value or repair cost.

II. A person who violates the provisions of paragraph I shall also be guilty of a class B felony if the actual loss or cost of repair is $10,000 or more, or a misdemeanor if the actual loss or cost of repair is less than $10,000.

Source.
  2003, 181:1, eff. Jan. 1, 2004.

Cross References.
  Classification of crimes, see RSA 625:9.
  Sentences, see RSA 651.

TITLE LVIII
PUBLIC JUSTICE

CHAPTER 570-A

WIRETAPPING AND EAVESDROPPING

SECTION
570-A:1.   Definitions.
570-A:2.   Interception and Disclosure of Telecommunication or Oral Communications Prohibited.
570-A:3.   Manufacture, Distribution, Possession, and Advertising of Telecommunication or Oral Communication Intercepting Devices Prohibited.
570-A:4.   Confiscation of Telecommunication or Oral Communication Intercepting Devices.
570-A:5.   Immunity of Witnesses.
570-A:6.   Prohibition of Use as Evidence of Intercepted Telecommunications or Oral Communications.
570-A:7.   Authorization for Interception of Telecommunications or Oral Communications.
570-A:8.   Authorization for Disclosure and Use of Intercepted Telecommunications or Oral Communications.
570-A:9.   Procedure for Interception of Telecommunication or Oral Communications.
570-A:9-a. Authorization for Installation and Use of Pen Register Devices. [Repealed.]
570-A:9-b. Use of Interpreters.
570-A:10.   Reports Concerning Intercepted Telecommunications or Oral Communications.
570-A:11.   Recovery of Civil Damages Authorized.

Cross References.

Involuntary admission for persons found not competent to stand trial, see RSA 171-B.

Regulation of searches and seizures, see New Hampshire Constitution, Part 1, Article 19.

Search warrants generally, see RSA 595-A.

Unlawful use of devices for hearing, recording, amplifying or broadcasting sounds in private places, see RSA 644:9.

NOTES TO DECISIONS

1. Purpose
2. Construction

1. Purpose

In enacting and later amending this chapter, legislature balanced state's duty to protect public and enforce laws with individual's right to privacy by carefully regulating use of wiretapping and eavesdropping devices for law enforcement purposes. State v. Lamontagne, 136 N.H. 575, 618 A.2d 849, 1992 N.H. LEXIS 200 (1992).

This chapter is not intended to prevent a telephone user from misrepresenting his or her identity on the telephone. State v. Lamontagne, 136 N.H. 575, 618 A.2d 849, 1992 N.H. LEXIS 200 (1992).

The legislature enacted this chapter to carefully regulate the use of wiretapping and eavesdropping devices for law enforcement purposes and to maintain a proper balance between the state's duty to protect the public and the individual's right to privacy and free expression. State v. Lee, 113 N.H. 313, 307 A.2d 827, 1973 N.H. LEXIS 262 (1973), superseded by statute as stated in, State v. Lamontagne, 136 N.H. 575, 618 A.2d 849, 1992 N.H. LEXIS 200 (1992).

2. Construction

This chapter is a stricter wiretapping and eavesdropping law, and protects the individual's right to privacy to a greater degree, than the United States Constitution or the federal statute, 18 U.S.C.S. § 2510 et seq. State v. Ayres, 118 N.H. 90, 383 A.2d 87, 1978 N.H. LEXIS 350 (1978), superseded by statute as stated in, State v. Kilgus, 128 N.H. 577, 519 A.2d 231, 1986 N.H. LEXIS 372 (1986).

Cited:

Cited in State v. Andrews, 125 N.H. 158, 480 A.2d 889, 1984 N.H. LEXIS 361 (1984) (Set out to correct an error in the citation carried in the bound volume.); State v. Allcock, 137 N.H. 458, 629 A.2d 99, 1993 N.H. LEXIS 102 (1993); State v. Telles, 139 N.H. 344, 653 A.2d 554, 1995 N.H. LEXIS 11 (1995); Desilets v. Wal-Mart Stores, Inc., 171 F.3d 711, 1999 U.S. App. LEXIS 5629 (1st Cir. N.H. 1999)

570-A:1. Definitions.

As used in this chapter:

I. "Telecommunication" means the transfer of any form of information in whole or in part through the facilities of a communications common carrier. "Telecommunication" does not include any communication made through a tone-only paging system or from a tracking device.

II. "Oral communication" means any verbal communication uttered by a person who has a reasonable expectation that the communication is not subject to interception, under circumstances justifying such expectation.

III. "Intercept" means the aural or other acquisition of, or the recording of, the contents of any telecommunication or oral communication through the use of any electronic, mechanical, or other device.

IV. "Electronic, mechanical, or other device" means any device or apparatus which can be used to intercept a telecommunication or oral communication other than:

(a) Any telephone or telegraph instrument, equipment, facility or any component thereof:

(1) Furnished to the subscriber or user by a communication carrier in the ordinary course of its business and being used by the subscriber or user in the ordinary course of its business or furnished by such subscriber or user for connection to the facilities of such service and used in the ordinary course of its business in accordance with applicable provisions of telephone and telegraph company rules and regulations, as approved by the public utilities commission;

(2) Being used by a communication common carrier in the ordinary course of its business, or by an investigative or law enforcement officer in the ordinary course of his duties pursuant to this chapter;

(b) A hearing aid or similar device being used to correct subnormal hearing to not better than normal.

V. "Person" means any employee or agent of the state or political subdivision thereof, and any individual, partnership, association, joint stock company, trust, or corporation.

VI. "Investigative or law enforcement officer" means any officer of the state or political subdivision thereof who is empowered by law to conduct investigations of or to make arrests for offenses enumerated in this chapter, and any attorney authorized by law to prosecute or participate in the prosecution of such offenses.

VII. "Contents", when used with respect to any telecommunication or oral communication, includes any information concerning the identity of the parties to such communication or the existence, substance, purport, or meaning of that communication.

VIII. "Judge of competent jurisdiction" means a judge of the superior court.

IX. "Communications common carrier" means a person engaged in providing communications services to the general public through transmission of any form of information between subscribers by means of wire, cable, radio or electromagnetic transmission, optical or fiber-optic transmission, or other means which transfers information without physical transfer of medium, whether by switched or dedicated facilities. A person engaged in radio or television broadcasting or any other general distribution of any form of communications shall not thereby be deemed a communications common carrier.

X. "Aggrieved person" means a person who was a party to any intercepted telecommunication or oral communication or a person against whom the interception was directed.

XI. "Organized crime" means the unlawful activities of the members of a highly organized, disciplined association engaged in supplying illegal goods and services, including but not limited to homicide, gambling, prostitution, narcotics, marijuana or other dangerous drugs, bribery, extortion, blackmail and other unlawful activities of members of such organizations.

XII. [Repealed.]

Source.
1969, 403:1. 1975, 385:1. 1985, 263:1. 1986, 53:1. 1988, 25:1, 2, 7, I. 1992, 174:1. 1995, 280:1, 2, 10, I, eff. Aug. 20, 1995. 2012, 65:1, eff. July 14, 2012.

Amendments
—2012. The 2012 amendment, in II, substituted "verbal communication" for "oral communication" and "who has a reasonable expectation that the" for "exhibiting an expectation that such" and made a stylistic change.

—1995. Rewrote pars. I and IX and substituted "telecommunication" for "wire" preceding "or oral communication" in par. III, in the introductory paragraph of par. IV and in pars. VII and X.

—1992. Paragraph IV(a): Deleted former subpar. (2), renumbered former subpar. (3) as subpar. (2) and added "pursuant to this chapter" following "duties" in that subparagraph.

—1988. Paragraph III: Inserted "or other" preceding "acquisition of" and "or the recording of" preceding "the contents of any wire".

Paragraph IV(a)(1): Substituted "user" for "used" preceding "by a

communication" and added "or furnished by such subscriber or user for connection to the facilities of such service and used in the ordinary course of its business in accordance with applicable provisions of telephone and telegraph company rules and regulations, as approved by the public utilities commission" following "ordinary course of its business" at the end of the paragraph.

Paragraph XII: Repealed.

—1986. Paragraph XII: Added.

—1985. Paragraph IV(a): Rewritten to the extent that a detailed comparison would be impracticable.

—1975. Paragraph IV(a): Inserted "and in accordance with applicable provisions of telephone and telegraph company rules and regulations, as approved by the public utilities commission" following "subscriber or user in the ordinary course of its business" and "pertaining to the conducting of investigations of or making of arrests for offenses enumerated in this chapter and when authorization for interception of wire or oral communications has been approved pursuant to this chapter" following "enforcement officer in the ordinary course of his duties".

Former paragraph XII.
Former paragraph XII, which was derived from 1986, 53:1, defined pen register devices.

NOTES TO DECISIONS

1. Construction
2. Oral communication
3.. Computer communications

1. Construction
No violation of this chapter occurs if telephone caller consents to speak over telephone with person who answers call and no unauthorized monitoring or recording takes place. State v. Lamontagne, 136 N.H. 575, 618 A.2d 849, 1992 N.H. LEXIS 200 (1992).

Police officers did not violate this chapter where officers were in separate residences on other matters, answered telephone calls, and spoke directly with defendants without any unauthorized monitoring or recording, since chapter did not prohibit conversations in which all parties consented to the aural acquisition of information and defendants so consented, having continued to speak with officers after hearing officers answer. State v. Lamontagne, 136 N.H. 575, 618 A.2d 849, 1992 N.H. LEXIS 200 (1992).

2. Oral communication
Trial court properly denied defendant's own motion for directed verdict on invasion of privacy claim brought by his former wife. Although they could have expected the content of her conversations with her daughter to be repeated by the defendant to his therapist, a reasonable jury could conclude that the plaintiff did not expect her actual words to be tape recorded. Fischer v. Hooper, 143 N.H. 585, 732 A.2d 396, 1999 N.H. LEXIS 160 (1999).

3. Computer communications
Detective's recording of defendant's telecommunication with his computer and/or instant messaging program was an interception under RSA 570-A:2, however, there was no violation where defendant knew his messages were recorded and implicitly consented to the recording; even if the detective illegally intercepted the communication by enabling the message archiving feature, admission of that evidence was harmless as the evidence, identical in form and content to the lawfully-obtained recording, was merely cumulative. State v. Lott, 152 N.H. 436, 879 A.2d 1167, 2005 N.H. LEXIS 111 (2005).

Cited:
Cited in State v. Lee, 113 N.H. 313, 307 A.2d 827, 1973 N.H. LEXIS 262 (1973); State v. Kilgus, 128 N.H. 577, 519 A.2d 231, 1986 N.H. LEXIS 372 (1986); State v. Valenzuela, 130 N.H. 175, 536 A.2d 1252, 1987 N.H. LEXIS 302 (1987); State v. Telles, 139 N.H. 344, 653 A.2d 554, 1995 N.H. LEXIS 11 (1995).

570-A:2. Interception and Disclosure of Telecommunication or Oral Communications Prohibited.

I. A person is guilty of a class B felony if, except as otherwise specifically provided in this chapter or without the consent of all parties to the communication, the person:

(a) Wilfully intercepts, endeavors to intercept, or procures any other person to intercept or endeavor to intercept, any telecommunication or oral communication;

(b) Wilfully uses, endeavors to use, or procures any other person to use or endeavor to use any electronic, mechanical, or other device to intercept any oral communication when:

(1) Such device is affixed to, or otherwise transmits a signal through, a wire, cable, or other like connection used in telecommunication, or

(2) Such device transmits communications by radio, or interferes with the transmission of such communication, or

(3) Such use or endeavor to use (A) takes place on premises of any business or other commercial establishment, or (B) obtains or is for the purpose of obtaining information relating to the operations of any business or other commercial establishment; or

(c) Wilfully discloses, or endeavors to disclose, to any other person the contents of any telecommunication or oral communication, knowing or having reason to know that the information was obtained through the interception of a telecommunication or oral communication in violation of this paragraph; or

(d) Willfully uses, or endeavors to use, the contents of any telecommunication or oral communication, knowing or having reason to know that the information was obtained through the interception of a telecommunication or oral communication in violation of this paragraph.

I-a. A person is guilty of a misdemeanor if, except as otherwise specifically provided in this chapter or without consent of all parties to the communication, the person knowingly intercepts a telecommunication or oral communication when the person is a party to the communication or with the prior consent of one of the parties to the communication, but without the approval required by RSA 570-A:2, II(d).

II. It shall not be unlawful under this chapter for:

(a) Any operator of a switchboard, or an officer, employee, or agent of any communication common carrier whose facilities are used in the transmission of a telecommunication, to intercept, disclose, or use that communication in the normal course of employment while engaged in any activity which is a necessary incident to the rendition of service or to the protection of the rights or property of the carrier of such communication; provided, however, that said communication common carriers shall not utilize service observing or random monitoring except for mechanical or service quality control checks.

(b) An officer, employee, or agent of any communication common carrier to provide information, facilities, or technical assistance to an investigative or law enforcement officer who, pursuant to this chapter, is authorized to intercept a telecommunication or oral communication.

(c) Any law enforcement officer, when conducting investigations of or making arrests for offenses enumerated in this chapter, to carry on the person an electronic, mechanical or other device which intercepts oral communications and transmits such communications by radio.

(d) An investigative or law enforcement officer in the ordinary course of the officer's duties pertaining to the conducting of investigations of organized crime, offenses enumerated in this chapter, solid waste violations under RSA 149-M:9, I and II, or harassing or obscene telephone calls to intercept a telecommunication or oral communication, when such person is a party to the communication or one of the parties to the communication has given prior consent to such interception; provided, however, that no such interception shall be made unless the attorney general, the deputy attorney general, or an assistant attorney general designated by the attorney general determines that there exists a reasonable suspicion that evidence of criminal conduct will be derived from such interception. Oral authorization for the interception may be given and a written memorandum of said determination and its basis shall be made within 72 hours thereafter. The memorandum shall be kept on file in the office of the attorney general.

(e) Where the offense under investigation is defined in RSA 318-B, the attorney general may delegate authority under RSA 570-A:2, II(d) to a county attorney. The county attorney may exercise this authority only in the county where the county attorney serves. The attorney general shall, prior to the effective date of this subparagraph, adopt specific guidelines under which the county attorney may give authorization for such interceptions. Any county attorney may further delegate authority under this section to any assistant county attorney in the county attorney's office.

(f) An officer, employee, or agent of the Federal Communications Commission, in the normal course of employment and in discharge of the monitoring responsibilities exercised by the commission in the enforcement of chapter 5 of title 47 of the United States Code, to intercept a telecommunication, or oral communication transmitted by radio, or to disclose or use the information thereby obtained.

(g) Any law enforcement officer, when conducting investigations of or making arrests for offenses enumerated in this chapter, to carry on the person an electronic, mechanical or other device which intercepts oral communications and transmits such communications by radio.

(h) Any municipal, county, or state fire or police department, the division of emergency services and communications as created by RSA 21-P:48-a, including the bureau of emergency communications as defined by RSA 106-H, or any independently owned emergency service, and their employees in the course of their employment, when receiving or responding to emergency calls, to intercept, record, disclose or use a telecommunication, while engaged in any activity which is a necessary incident to the rendition of service or the protection of life or property.

(i) Any public utility regulated by the public utilities commission, and its employees in the course of employment, when receiving central dispatch calls or calls for emergency service, or when responding to central dispatch calls or calls for emergency service, to intercept, record, disclose or use a telecommunication, while engaged in any activity which is a necessary incident to the rendition of service, or the protection of life and property. Any public utility recording calls pursuant to this subparagraph shall provide an automatic tone warning device which automatically produces a distinct signal that is repeated at regular intervals during the conversation. The public utilities commission may adopt rules relative to the recording of emergency calls under RSA 541-A.

(j) A uniformed law enforcement officer to make an audio recording in conjunction with a video recording of a routine stop performed in the ordinary course of patrol duties on any way as defined by RSA 259:125, provided that the officer shall first give notification of such recording to the party to the communication.

(k) (1) The owner or operator of a school bus, as defined in RSA 259:96, to make an audio recording in conjunction with a video recording of the interior of the school bus while students are being transported to and from school or school activities, provided that the school board authorizes audio recording, the school district provides notification of such recording to the parents and students as part of the district's pupil safety and violence prevention policy required under RSA 193-F, and there is a sign informing the occupants of such recording prominently displayed on the school bus.

(2) Prior to any audio recording, the school board shall hold a public hearing to determine whether audio recording should be authorized in school buses, and if authorized, the school board shall establish an administrative procedure to address the length of time which the recording is retained, ownership of the recording, limitations on who may listen to the recording, and provisions for erasing or destroying the recording. Such administrative procedure shall permit the parents or legal guardian of any student against whom a recording is being used as part of a disciplinary proceeding to listen to the recording. In no event, however, shall the recording be retained for longer than 10 school days unless the school district determines that the recording is relevant to a disciplinary proceeding, or a court orders that it be retained for a longer period of time. An audio recording shall only be reviewed if there has been a report of an incident or a complaint relative to conduct on the school bus, and only that portion of the audio recording which is relevant to the incident or complaint shall be reviewed.

(*l*) A law enforcement officer in the ordinary course of the officer's duties using any device capable of making an audio or video recording, or both, and which is attached to and used in conjunction with a TASER or other similar electroshock device. Any person who is the subject of such recording shall be informed of the existence of the audio or video recording, or both, and shall be provided with a copy of such recording at his or her request.

Source.
1969, 403:1. 1975, 385:2. 1977, 588:16. 1979, 282:1. 1985, 263:2. 1988, 25:3. 1990, 96:1; 191:2. 1992, 174:2. 1995, 195:1, eff. Aug. 11, 1995; 280:10, I–III, eff. Aug. 20, 1995. 1996, 251:24, eff. Aug. 9, 1996; 274:1–5, eff. Jan. 1, 1997. 2002, 257:11, eff. July 1, 2002. 2003, 319:129, eff. Sept. 4, 2003. 2004, 171:21, eff. July 24, 2004. 2006, 69:1, eff. June 24, 2006. 2008, 139:1, eff. August 5, 2008; 361:11, eff. July 11, 2008. 2010, 155:4, eff. July 1, 2010.

Amendments
—2010. The 2010 amendment substituted "RSA 193-F" for "RSA 193-F:3, I(b)" in II(k)(1).

—2008. The 2008 amendment by Chapter 139, added II(*l*).

The 2008 amendment by Chapter 361, in II(h), deleted "and management" and made a related change and substituted "RSA 21-P:48-a" for "RSA 21-P:36".

—2006. Paragraph II(k): Added.

—2004. Paragraph II(h): Substituted "the division of emergency services, communications, and management as created by RSA 21-P:36, including" for "the bureau of emergency management as created by RSA 21-P:36".

—2003. Paragraph II(h): Substituted "the bureau of emergency management" for "the office of emergency management".

—2002. Paragraph II(h): Substituted "RSA 21-P:36" for "RSA 107-C:3".

—1996. Paragraph I: Chapter 274 substituted "the person" for "he" following "communication" in the introductory paragraph.

Paragraph I-a: Chapter 274 substituted "the person" for "he" preceding "knowingly intercepts" and preceding "is a party".

Paragraph II(a): Chapter 274 deleted "his" preceding "employment" and preceding "service or".

Paragraph II(c): Chapter 274 substituted "carry on the" for "carry with him on his" preceding "person".

Paragraph II(d): Chapter 274 substituted "the officer's" for "his" preceding "duties pertaining" in the first sentence.

Chapter 251 substituted "RSA 149-M:9, I and II" for "RSA 149-M:10, I and I-a" in the first sentence.

Paragraph II(e): Chapter 274 substituted "may delegate" for "to delegate" and deleted "his" preceding "authority" in the first sentence, substituted "the" for "said" preceding "county attorney" and "the county attorney" for "he" preceding "serves" in the second sentence, deleted "his" preceding "authority" in the third sentence, and substituted "the county attorney's" for "his" preceding "office" in the fourth sentence.

Paragraph II(f): Chapter 274 deleted "his" preceding "employment".

Paragraph II(g): Chapter 274 substituted "carry on the" for "carry with him on his" preceding "person".

Paragraph II(h): Chapter 274 inserted "county or state" preceding "fire" and "the office of emergency management as created by

RSA 107-C:3, the bureau of emergency communications as defined by RSA 106-H" following "department".

—1995. Chapter 195 added subpar. II(j).

Chapter 280 substituted "telecommunications" for "wire" preceding "or oral communications" in the section catchline, in par. I(a), in two places in par. I(c) and (d) and in pars. I-a, II(b) and (d) and "telecommunication" for "wire communication" in pars. I(b)(1) and II(a), (e), (f), (h) and (i).

—1992. Paragraph II: Added subpars. (h) and (i).

—1990. Paragraph II: Chapter 96 added a new subpar. (e) and redesignated former subpars. (e) and (f) as subpars. (f) and (g), respectively.

Chapter 191 inserted "solid waste violations under RSA 149-M:10, I and I-a" preceding "or harassing" in the first sentence of subpar. (d).

—1988. Paragraph I-a: Added.

—1985. Paragraph II: Rewritten to the extent that a detailed comparison would be impracticable.

—1979. Paragraph II: Rewritten to the extent that a detailed comparison would be impracticable.

—1977. Paragraph I: Rewritten to the extent that a detailed comparison would be impracticable.

—1975. Added the last paragraph.

Cross References.

Annoying or alarming telephone calls, see RSA 644:4.

Authorization for disclosure and use of intercepted wire or oral communications, see RSA 570-A:8.

Authorization for interception of wire or oral communications, see RSA 570-A:7.

Classification of crimes, see RSA 625:9.

Criminal solicitation generally, see RSA 629:2.

Procedure for interception of communications, see RSA 570-A:9.

Recovery of damages for unlawful interceptions or disclosures, see RSA 570-A:11.

Reports concerning interceptions, see RSA 570-A:10.

Sentences, see RSA 651.

NOTES TO DECISIONS

1. Legislative intent
2. Applicability of section
3. Existence of reasonable suspicion
4. Use of body bug
5. Interception of communications involving police officers or consented to by parties thereto
6. Use of recorded conversations as evidence
7. Consent
8. Written memorandum requirement

1. Legislative intent

Legislature did not intend to impose a mens rea of "knowingly" in subdivision I of this section. Because this subdivision closely tracks language of former federal wiretapping statute, use of term "willfully" means that defendant must act with an intentional or reckless disregard for the lawfulness of his conduct. A defendant has not violated this subdivision if he has a good faith belief that his conduct was lawful. Fischer v. Hooper, 143 N.H. 585, 732 A.2d 396, 1999 N.H. LEXIS 160 (1999).

In enacting the last paragraph of this section, the legislature intended to provide a narrow exception to the eavesdropping prohibition in order to protect undercover police officers; it did not intend to allow a recording of the eavesdropping to be used as evidence. State v. Ayres, 118 N.H. 90, 383 A.2d 87, 1978 N.H. LEXIS 350 (1978), superseded by statute as stated in, State v. Kilgus, 128 N.H. 577, 519 A.2d 231, 1986 N.H. LEXIS 372 (1986).

2. Applicability of section

Mens rea necessary to give rise to a violation of RSA 570-A, prohibiting unlawful wiretapping and eavesdropping, requires that

a defendant must act with an intentional or reckless disregard for the lawfulness of his conduct, and the defendant has not violated the statute if he has a good faith belief that his conduct was lawful. Karch v. BayBank FSB, 147 N.H. 525, 794 A.2d 763, 2002 N.H. LEXIS 21 (2002).

In case involving only federal officers engaged in the investigation of an alleged federal crime, with the trial of the offense to be held in federal court before a federal jury, the admissibility of intercepted communications was not governed by the provisions of this section or interpretations thereof by the Supreme Court of New Hampshire. United States v. Upton, 502 F. Supp. 1193, 1980 U.S. Dist. LEXIS 15000 (D.N.H. 1980).

3. Existence of reasonable suspicion

In an analysis of this section, the court would interpret the phrase "reasonable suspicion" in the same manner as constitutional cases involving investigative stops; thus, reasonable suspicion exists when specific and articulable facts which, taken together with rational inferences from those facts, lead the authorizing official to believe that evidence of criminal conduct will be derived from an interception. State v. Conant, 139 N.H. 728, 662 A.2d 283, 1995 N.H. LEXIS 79 (1995).

Absence of information concerning an informant's reliability, in and of itself, does not require a finding of no reasonable suspicion if the basis of knowledge is otherwise sufficient; an informant who has personally observed incriminating behavior has a stronger basis of knowledge than does an informant who relates not what he knows personally, but what he has heard others say, and an explicit and detailed description of alleged wrongdoing is entitled to greater weight than a general assertion of criminal activity. State v. Conant, 139 N.H. 728, 662 A.2d 283, 1995 N.H. LEXIS 79 (1995).

An informant's tip exhibited sufficient indicia of reliability to justify use of electronic interception devices and, therefore, suppression of the evidence thus obtained was not warranted; notwithstanding the argument that the informant lacked reliability because (1) he had no track record with the police, having initially lied to them by supplying false names, and (2) he was from the "criminal milieu," the informant's offer to demonstrate his reliability by wearing a body wire and personally arranging a drug purchase gave reason to believe that the informant was telling the truth regarding the defendant. State v. Conant, 139 N.H. 728, 662 A.2d 283, 1995 N.H. LEXIS 79 (1995).

4. Use of body bug

Interception of oral communication through a body bug concealed on a police officer was authorized by the last paragraph of this section, which provides that a law enforcement officer conducting an investigation or making an arrest may carry on his person a listening device to intercept and transmit oral communications. State v. Ayres, 118 N.H. 90, 383 A.2d 87, 1978 N.H. LEXIS 350 (1978), superseded by statute as stated in, State v. Kilgus, 128 N.H. 577, 519 A.2d 231, 1986 N.H. LEXIS 372 (1986).

5. Interception of communications involving police officers or consented to by parties thereto

Detective's recording of defendant's telecommunication with his computer and/or instant messaging program was an interception under RSA 570-A:2, but there was no violation since defendant knew his messages were recorded and implicitly consented to the recording; even if the detective illegally intercepted the communication by enabling the message archiving feature, admission of that evidence was harmless as the evidence, identical in form and content to the lawfully-obtained recording, was merely cumulative. State v. Lott, 152 N.H. 436, 879 A.2d 1167, 2005 N.H. LEXIS 111 (2005).

When investigating the offenses enumerated in RSA 570-A:7, the police may intercept communications pursuant to subparagraph II(d) of this section without judicial authorization when a police officer is a party to the communication or a party to the communication consents to the interception; otherwise, the police must obtain judicial authorization. State v. Kilgus, 128 N.H. 577, 519 A.2d 231, 1986 N.H. LEXIS 372 (1986).

6. Use of recorded conversations as evidence

Because RSA 570-A:2, II(d) did not require that defendant's identity be known prior to the recording of a confidential informant's purchase of marijuana from defendant, the trial court did not err in denying defendant's motion to suppress. State v. Corrado, 154 N.H. 43, 904 A.2d 642, 2006 N.H. LEXIS 114 (2006).

The interceptions permitted by subparagraph II:(d) of this section are exempt from the prohibition in RSA 570-A:6 against using recorded conversations as evidence. State v. Kilgus, 128 N.H. 577, 519 A.2d 231, 1986 N.H. LEXIS 372 (1986).

7. Consent

Publishing the transcript of defendant's Internet chat with an undercover detective posing as a teenage girl did not violate RSA 570-A:2 because defendant engaged in online instant messaging and knew that the messages were capable of being recorded. The fact that the defendant told the "girl" to "delete her archives" after their online conversation did not vitiate his consent because his consent was implicit in his use of instant messaging technology. State v. Moscone, 161 N.H. 355, 13 A.3d 137, 2011 N.H. LEXIS 1 (2011).

Consent to interception of communication is valid under wiretap statute when surrounding circumstances demonstrate that consenting party knew that law enforcement personnel were intercepting conversation with an "electronic, mechanical or other device," even if the precise method of interception is not disclosed. State v. Locke, 144 N.H. 348, 761 A.2d 376, 1999 N.H. LEXIS 123 (1999), superseded by statute as stated in, State v. Anthony, 151 N.H. 492, 861 A.2d 773, 2004 N.H. LEXIS 184 (2004), superseded by statute as stated in, State v. Rivera, 162 N.H. 182, 27 A.3d 676, 2011 N.H. LEXIS 84 (2011).

A minor's consent to tape record conversations with the defendant was voluntary where the minor's mother was present at the times the minor gave her consent and discussed with the minor the advisability of participating in the conversations prior to each one. Futhermore, the police explained to the minor, before she signed the consent forms for each intercept, that she had the right to refuse and that she "wasn't in any trouble at all." In addition, the minor stated that she did not consent to the intercepts out of fear of being arrested. State v. Smart, 136 N.H. 639, 622 A.2d 1197, 1993 N.H. LEXIS 11 (1993), cert. denied, Smart v. New Hampshire, 510 U.S. 917, 114 S. Ct. 309, 126 L. Ed. 2d 256, 1993 U.S. LEXIS 6384 (1993).

Trial court erred in ruling that, in order to obtain valid consent under wiretap statute, law enforcement personnel were required to expressly inform co-defendant of the manner in which they intended to intercept targeted communication between co-defendant and defendant; although certain facts were undisputed, record was insufficient to allow court to determine whether co-defendant's consent was valid under statute, and therefore remand was required. State v. Locke, 144 N.H. 348, 761 A.2d 376, 1999 N.H. LEXIS 123 (1999), superseded by statute as stated in, State v. Anthony, 151 N.H. 492, 861 A.2d 773, 2004 N.H. LEXIS 184 (2004), superseded by statute as stated in, State v. Rivera, 162 N.H. 182, 27 A.3d 676, 2011 N.H. LEXIS 84 (2011).

8. Written memorandum requirement

Trial court erred in excluding an audio recording of a one-party consensual telephonic interception under RSA 570-A:6. The State obtained the intercepted information lawfully, and its three-day delay in meeting the post-intercept written memorandum requirement of RSA 570-A:2, II(d) did not vitiate the lawfulness of the intercept. State v. McLeod, — N.H. —, 66 A.3d 1221, 2013 N.H. LEXIS 53 (May 14, 2013).

Cited:

Cited in Baker v. Cestari, 569 F. Supp. 842, 1983 U.S. Dist. LEXIS 13983 (D.N.H. 1983); State v. Sheedy, 125 N.H. 108, 480 A.2d 887, 1984 N.H. LEXIS 285 (1984); State v. Stiles, 128 N.H. 81, 512 A.2d 1084, 1986 N.H. LEXIS 289 (1986); State v. Lewis, 129 N.H. 787, 533 A.2d 358, 1987 N.H. LEXIS 246 (1987); State v. Davis, 133 N.H. 211, 575 A.2d 4, 1990 N.H. LEXIS 49 (1990); State v. Lamontagne, 136 N.H. 575, 618 A.2d 849, 1992 N.H. LEXIS 200 (1992).

RESEARCH REFERENCES

New Hampshire Bar Journal.

For article, "Lex Loci: A Survey of New Hampshire Supreme Court Decisions," see 46 N.H.B.J. 76 (Summer 2005).

570-A:3. Manufacture, Distribution, Possession, and Advertising of Telecommunication or Oral Communication Intercepting Devices Prohibited.

I. A person is guilty of a class B felony if, except as otherwise specifically provided in this chapter, he:

(a) Manufactures, assembles, possesses, or sells any electronic, mechanical, or other device, knowing or having reason to know that the design of such device renders it primarily useful for the purpose of the surreptitious interception of telecommunications or oral communications; or

(b) Places in any newspaper, magazine, handbill, or other publication any advertisement of:

(1) Any electronic, mechanical, or other device knowing or having reason to know that the design of such device renders it primarily useful for the purpose of the surreptitious interception of telecommunications or oral communications, or

(2) Any other electronic, mechanical, or other device, where such advertisement promotes the use of such device for the purpose of the surreptitious interception of telecommunications or oral communications.

II. It shall not be unlawful under this section for:

(a) A communications common carrier or an officer, agent, or employee of, or a person under contract with, a communications common carrier, in the normal course of the communications common carrier's business, or

(b) An officer, agent, or employee of, or a person under contract with, the state, or a political subdivision thereof, in the normal course of the activities of the state, or a political subdivision thereof, to manufacture, assemble, possess, or sell any electronic, mechanical, or other device knowing or having reason to know that the design of such device renders it primarily useful for the purpose of the surreptitious interception of telecommunications or oral communications.

Source.

1969, 403:1. 1977, 588:17. 1995, 280:10, I, III, eff. Aug. 20, 1995.

Amendments

—1995. Substituted "telecommunication" for "wire" preceding "or oral communication" in the section catchline and "telecommunications" for "wire" preceding "or oral communications" wherever it appeared in par. I and in par. II(b).

—1977. Paragraph I: Rewritten to the extent that a detailed comparison would be impracticable.

570-A:4. Confiscation of Telecommunication or Oral Communication Intercepting Devices.

Any electronic, mechanical, or other device used, sent, carried, manufactured, assembled, possessed, sold, or advertised in violation of RSA 570-A:2 or 570-A:3 may be seized and forfeited to the state according to the procedure set forth in RSA 617.

Source.
1969, 403:1. 1995, 280:10, I, eff. Aug. 20, 1995.

Amendments
—1995. Substituted "telecommunication" for "wire" preceding "or oral" in the section catchline.

570-A:5. Immunity of Witnesses.

Whenever, in the judgment of the attorney general, the testimony of any witness, or the production of books, papers, or other evidence by any witness, in any case or proceeding before any grand jury or superior court involving any violation of this chapter or any of the offenses enumerated in RSA 570-A:7, or any conspiracy to violate this chapter or any of the offenses enumerated in RSA 570-A:7, is necessary to the public interest, the attorney general, or a county attorney upon the written approval of the attorney general, shall make application to the superior court that the witness shall be instructed to testify or produce evidence subject to the provisions of this section, and upon order of the court such witness shall not be excused from testifying or from producing books, papers, or other evidence on the ground that the testimony or evidence required of him may tend to incriminate him or subject him to a penalty or forfeiture. No such witness shall be prosecuted or subjected to any penalty or forfeiture for or on account of any transaction, matter or thing concerning which he is compelled, after having claimed his privilege against self-incrimination, to testify or produce evidence, nor shall testimony so compelled be used as evidence in any criminal proceeding (except in the proceeding described in the next sentence) against him in any court. No witness shall be exempt under this section from prosecution for perjury or contempt committed while giving testimony or producing evidence under compulsion as provided in this section.

Source.
1969, 403:1, eff. Aug. 31, 1969.

Cross References.
Grant of immunity in criminal cases, see RSA 516:34.
Perjury generally, see RSA 641:1.
Privilege against self-incrimination, see New Hampshire Constitution, Part 1, Article 15.

570-A:6. Prohibition of Use as Evidence of Intercepted Telecommunications or Oral Communications.

Whenever any telecommunication or oral communication has been intercepted, no part of the contents of such communication and no evidence derived therefrom may be received in evidence in any trial, hearing, or other proceeding in or before any court, grand jury, department, officer, agency, regulatory body, legislative committee, or other authority of the state, or a political subdivision thereof, if the disclosure of that information would be in violation of this chapter.

Source.
1969, 403:1. 1995, 280:10, I, III, eff. Aug. 20, 1995.

Amendments
—1995. Substituted "telecommunications" for "wire" preceding "or oral communications" in the section catchline and "telecommunication" for "wire" preceding "or oral communication" in the text of the section.

Cross References.
Prohibition of interception of wire or oral communications, see RSA 570-A:2.
Recovery of damages for unlawful interceptions or disclosures, see RSA 570-A:11.

NOTES TO DECISIONS

1. Construction
2. Recordings of police officers or parties consenting to interception
3. Domestic eavesdropping
4. Particular cases

1. Construction
Based on the plain language of RSA 570-A:6, evidence is excluded from trial only if its disclosure would violate New Hampshire's wiretap statute. State v. Ruggiero, 163 N.H. 129, 35 A.3d 616, 2011 N.H. LEXIS 190 (Dec. 28, 2011).

2. Recordings of police officers or parties consenting to interception
The interceptions permitted by RSA 570-A:2, II(d), are exempt from the prohibition in this section against using recorded conversations as evidence. State v. Kilgus, 128 N.H. 577, 519 A.2d 231, 1986 N.H. LEXIS 372 (1986).

3. Domestic eavesdropping
There was no violation of this section where the court allowed the introduction of evidence regarding a telephone conversation between the defendant and the victim which was overheard by the witness on an extension telephone, since domestic eavesdropping is not prohibited by the chapter. State v. Telles, 139 N.H. 344, 653 A.2d 554, 1995 N.H. LEXIS 11 (1995).

4. Particular cases
Trial court erred in excluding an audio recording of a one-party consensual telephonic interception under RSA 570-A:6. The State obtained the intercepted information lawfully, and its three-day delay in meeting the post-intercept written memorandum requirement of RSA 570-A:2, II(d) did not vitiate the lawfulness of the intercept. State v. McLeod, — N.H. —, 66 A.3d 1221, 2013 N.H. LEXIS 53 (May 14, 2013).
Trial court did not err in admitting recordings of certain telephone calls. Under the plain language of RSA 570-A:6, evidence was excluded from trial only if its disclosure would violate the New Hampshire wiretap statute, and the calls here, which were legally

intercepted in South Carolina, did not violate RSA ch. 570-A. State v. Ruggiero, 163 N.H. 129, 35 A.3d 616, 2011 N.H. LEXIS 190 (Dec. 28, 2011).

Cited:

Cited in State v. Stiles, 128 N.H. 81, 512 A.2d 1084, 1986 N.H. LEXIS 289 (1986); State v. Conant, 139 N.H. 728, 662 A.2d 283, 1995 N.H. LEXIS 79 (1995); State v. Locke, 144 N.H. 348, 761 A.2d 376, 1999 N.H. LEXIS 123 (1999).

RESEARCH REFERENCES

New Hampshire Bar Journal.

For article, "Lex Loci: A Survey of New Hampshire Supreme Court Decisions," see 46 N.H.B.J. 76 (Summer 2005).

570-A:7. Authorization for Interception of Telecommunications or Oral Communications.

The attorney general, deputy attorney general, or a county attorney, upon the written approval of the attorney general or deputy attorney general, may apply to a judge of competent jurisdiction for an order authorizing or approving the interception of telecommunications or oral communications, and such judge may grant, in conformity with RSA 570-A:9, an order authorizing or approving the interception of telecommunications or oral communications by investigative or law enforcement officers having responsibility for the investigation of the offenses as to which the application is made, when such interception may provide, or has provided, evidence of the commission of organized crime, as defined in RSA 570-A:1, XI, or evidence of the commission of the offenses of homicide, kidnapping, gambling, theft as defined in RSA 637, corrupt practices as defined in RSA 640, child pornography under RSA 649-A, computer pornography and child exploitation under RSA 649-B, criminal conduct in violation of the securities law, as defined in RSA 421-B:3, 421-B:4, 421-B:5, 421-B:19, and 421-B:24, criminal conduct in violation of the security take-over disclosure laws, as defined in RSA 421-A:3, 421-A:7, 421-A:8, 421-A:11, and 421-A:13, robbery as defined in RSA 636:1, arson as defined in RSA 634:1, hindering apprehension or prosecution as defined in RSA 642:3, tampering with witnesses and informants as defined in RSA 641:5, aggravated felonious sexual assault as defined in RSA 632-A:2, felonious sexual assault as defined in RSA 632-A:3, escape as defined in RSA 642:6, bail jumping as defined in RSA 642:8, insurance fraud as defined in RSA 638:20, dealing in narcotic drugs, marijuana, or other dangerous drugs, hazardous waste violations under RSA 147-A:4, I, or any conspiracy to commit any of the foregoing offenses.

Source.

1969, 403:1. 1985, 263:3. 1988, 25:4. 1990, 191:1. 1995, 280:10, III, eff. Aug. 20, 1995. 1998, 361:4, eff. Jan. 1, 1999. 2001, 224:10, eff. Sept. 9, 2001.

Revision note.

Following "an order authorizing or approving the interception of wire or oral communications," deleted "may apply to such judge for" as being redundant with "may apply to a judge of competent jurisdiction for".

Amendments

—2001. Inserted "insurance fraud as defined in RSA 638:20" following "RSA 642:8".

—1998. Inserted "child pornography under RSA 649-A, computer pornography and child exploitation under RSA 649-B" following "RSA 640".

—1995. Substituted "telecommunications" for "wire" preceding "or oral" in the section catchline and in two places in the text of the section.

—1990. Inserted "investigative or" preceding "law enforcement", "criminal conduct in violation of the securities law, as defined in RSA 421-B:3, 421-B:4, 421-B:5, 421-B:19, and 421-B:24, criminal conduct in violation of the security takeover disclosure laws, as defined in RSA 421-A:3, 421-A:7, 421-A:8, 421-A:11, and 421-A:13" following "RSA 640", deleted "or" following "RSA 642:8" and inserted "hazardous waste violations under RSA 147-A:4, I" following "dangerous drugs".

—1988. Substituted "RSA 636:1" for "RSA 636" following "robbery as defined in" and inserted "tampering with witnesses and informants as defined in RSA 641:5, aggravated felonious sexual assault as defined in RSA 632-A:2, felonious sexual assault as defined in RSA 632-A:3" preceding "escape as defined".

—1985. Rewritten to the extent that a detailed comparison would be impracticable.

Cross References.

Procedure for interception of communications, see RSA 570-A:9. Reports of interceptions of communications, see RSA 570-A:10.

NOTES TO DECISIONS

Construction with other laws

When investigating the offenses enumerated in this section, the police may intercept communications pursuant to RSA 570-A:2, II(d), without judicial authorization when a police officer is a party to the communication or the party to the communication consents to the interception; otherwise, the police must obtain judicial authorization. State v. Kilgus, 128 N.H. 577, 519 A.2d 231, 1986 N.H. LEXIS 372 (1986).

Cited:

Cited in State v. Doyle, 126 N.H. 153, 489 A.2d 639, 1985 N.H. LEXIS 262 (1985); State v. Stiles, 128 N.H. 81, 512 A.2d 1084, 1986 N.H. LEXIS 289 (1986).

570-A:8. Authorization for Disclosure and Use of Intercepted Telecommunications or Oral Communications.

I. Any law enforcement officer who, by any means authorized by this chapter, has obtained knowledge of the contents of any telecommunication or oral communication, or evidence derived therefrom, may disclose such contents to another law enforcement officer to the extent that such disclosure is appropriate to the proper performance of the official duties of the officer making or receiving the disclosure.

II. Any law enforcement officer who, by any means authorized by this chapter, has obtained knowledge of the contents of any telecommunication or oral communication or evidence derived therefrom may use such contents to the extent such use is appropriate to the proper performance of the officer's official duties.

III. Any person who has received, by any means authorized by this chapter, any information concerning a telecommunication or oral communication or evidence derived therefrom intercepted in accordance with the provisions of this chapter may disclose the contents of that communication or such derivative evidence while giving testimony under oath or affirmation in any criminal proceeding in any court of the United States or of any state or in any federal or state grand jury proceeding.

IV. No otherwise privileged telecommunication or oral communication intercepted in accordance with, or in violation of, the provisions of this chapter shall lose its privileged character.

V. When a law enforcement officer, while engaged in intercepting telecommunications or oral communications in the manner authorized herein, intercepts telecommunications or oral communications relating to offenses other than those specified in the order of authorization or approval, the contents thereof, and evidence derived therefrom, may be disclosed or used as provided in paragraphs I and II. Such contents and any evidence derived therefrom may be used under paragraph III, when authorized or approved by a judge of competent jurisdiction where such judge finds on subsequent application that the contents were otherwise intercepted in accordance with the provisions of this chapter. Such application shall be made as soon as practicable.

Source.
1969, 403:1. 1995, 280:3, 10, I, III, eff. Aug. 20, 1995.

Amendments
—1995. Substituted "telecommunications" for "wire" preceding "or oral communications" in the section catchline and in two places in par. V, substituted "telecommunication" for "wire" preceding "or oral communication" wherever it appeared in pars. I–IV and substituted "the officer's" for "his" preceding "official" in par. II.

Cross References.
Procedure for interception of communications, see RSA 570-A:9.
Prohibition of disclosure of wire or oral communications generally, see RSA 570-A:2.

NOTES TO DECISIONS

Cited:
Cited in State v. Lee, 113 N.H. 313, 307 A.2d 827, 1973 N.H. LEXIS 262 (1973).

570-A:9. Procedure for Interception of Telecommunication or Oral Communications.

I. Each application for an order authorizing or approving the interception of a telecommunication or oral communication shall be made in writing upon oath or affirmation to a judge of competent jurisdiction and shall state the applicant's authority to make such application. Each application shall include the following information:

(a) The identity of the law enforcement officer making the application, and the officer authorizing the application;

(b) A full and complete statement of the facts and circumstances relied upon by the applicant to justify the applicant's belief that an order should be issued, including: (1) Details as to the particular offense that has been, is being, or is about to be committed, (2) A particular description of the nature and location of the facilities from which or the place where the communication is to be intercepted, (3) A particular description of the type of communications sought to be intercepted, (4) The identity of the person, if known, committing the offense and whose communications are to be intercepted;

(c) A full and complete statement as to whether or not other investigative procedures have been tried and failed or why they reasonably appear to be unlikely to succeed if tried or to be too dangerous;

(d) A statement of the period of time for which the interception is required to be maintained. If the nature of the investigation is such that the authorization for interception should not automatically terminate when the described type of communication has been first obtained, the application shall include a particular description of facts establishing probable cause to believe that additional communications of the same type will occur thereafter;

(e) A full and complete statement of the facts concerning all previous applications known to the individual authorizing and making the application, made to any judge for authorization to intercept, or for approval of interceptions of, telecommunications or oral communications involving any of the same persons, facilities or places specified in the application, and the action taken by the judge on each such application; and

(f) Where the application is for the extension of an order, a statement setting forth the results thus far obtained from the interception, or a reasonable explanation of the failure to obtain such results.

II. The judge may require the applicant to furnish additional testimony or documentary evidence in support of the application.

III. Upon such application, the judge may enter an ex parte order, as requested or as modified, authorizing or approving interception of telecommunication or oral communications, if the judge determines on the basis of the facts submitted by the applicant that:

(a) There is probable cause for belief that an individual is committing, has committed, or is about to commit a particular offense enumerated in RSA 570-A:7;

(b) There is probable cause for belief that particular communications concerning that offense will be obtained through such interception;

(c) Normal investigative procedures have been tried and have failed or reasonably appear to be unlikely to succeed if tried or to be too dangerous;

(d) There is probable cause for belief that the facilities from which, or the place where, the telecommunications or oral communications are to be intercepted are being used, or are about to be used, in connection with the commission of such offense, or are leased to, listed in the name of, or commonly used by such person.

IV. Each order authorizing or approving the interception of any telecommunication or oral communication shall specify:

(a) The identity of the person, if known, whose communications are to be intercepted;

(b) The nature and location of the communications facilities as to which, or the place where, authority to intercept is granted;

(c) A particular description of the type of communication sought to be intercepted, and a statement of the particular offense to which it relates;

(d) The identity of the agency authorized to intercept the communications, and of the person authorizing the application; and

(e) The period of time during which such interception is authorized, including a statement as to whether or not the interception shall automatically terminate when the described communication has been first obtained.

V. No order entered under this section may authorize or approve the interception of any telecommunication or oral communication for any period longer than is necessary to achieve the objective of the authorization, nor in any event longer than 10 days. Extensions of an order may be granted, but only upon application for an extension made in accordance with paragraph I, and the court making the findings required by paragraph III. The period of extension shall be no longer than the authorizing judge deems necessary to achieve the purposes for which it was granted and in no event for longer than 10 days. Every order and extension thereof shall contain a provision that the authorization to intercept shall be executed as soon as practicable, shall be conducted in such a way as to minimize the interception of communications not otherwise subject to interception under this chapter, and must terminate upon attainment of the authorized objective, or in any event in 10 days.

VI. Whenever an order authorizing interception is entered pursuant to this chapter, the order may require reports to be made to the judge who issued the order showing what progress has been made toward achievement of the authorized objective and the need for continued interception. Such reports shall be made at such intervals as the judge may require.

VII. (a) The contents of any telecommunication or oral communication intercepted by any means authorized by this chapter shall, if possible, be recorded on tape or wire or other comparable device. The recording of the contents of any telecommunication or oral communication under this paragraph shall be done in such way as will protect the recording from editing or other alterations. Immediately upon the expiration of the period of the order or extensions thereof, such recordings shall be made available to the judge issuing such order and sealed under the judge's directions. Custody of the recordings shall be wherever the judge orders. They shall not be destroyed except upon an order of the issuing or denying judge and in any event shall be kept for 10 years. Duplicate recordings may be made for use or disclosure pursuant to the provisions of RSA 570-A:8, I and II, for investigations. The presence of the seal provided for by this paragraph, or a satisfactory explanation for the absence thereof, shall be a prerequisite for the use or disclosure of the contents of any telecommunication or oral communication or evidence derived therefrom under RSA 570-A:8, III.

(b) Applications made and orders granted under this chapter shall be sealed by the judge. Custody of the applications and orders shall be wherever the judge directs. Such applications and orders shall be disclosed only upon a showing of good cause before a judge of competent jurisdiction and shall not be destroyed except on order of the issuing or denying judge, and in any event shall be kept for 10 years.

(c) Any violation of the provisions of this paragraph may be punished as contempt of the issuing or denying judge.

VIII. The contents of any intercepted telecommunication or oral communication or evidence derived therefrom shall not be received in evidence or otherwise disclosed in any trial, hearing, or other proceeding in a state court unless each party, not less than 10 days before the trial, hearing, or proceeding, has been furnished with a copy of the court order, and accompanying application, under which the interception was authorized or approved. This 10-day period may be waived by the judge if the judge finds that it was not possible to furnish the party with the above information 10 days before the trial, hearing, or proceeding and that the party will not be prejudiced by the delay in receiving such information.

IX. (a) Any aggrieved person in any trial, hearing, or proceeding in or before any court, department, officer, agency, regulatory body, or other authority of the state, or a political subdivision thereof, may move to suppress the contents of any intercepted telecommunication or oral communication, or evidence derived therefrom, on the grounds that:

(1) The communication was unlawfully intercepted;

(2) The order of authorization or approval under which it was intercepted is insufficient on its face; or

(3) The interception was not made in conformity with the order of authorization or approval.

Such motion shall be made before the trial, hearing, or proceeding unless there was no opportunity to make such motion or the person was not aware of the grounds of the motion. If the motion is granted, the contents of the intercepted telecommunication or oral communication, or evidence derived therefrom, shall be treated as having been obtained in violation of this chapter. The judge, upon the filing of such motion by the aggrieved person, may, in the judge's discretion, make available to the aggrieved person or such person's counsel for inspection such portions of the intercepted communication or evidence derived therefrom as the judge determines to be in the interests of justice.

(b) In addition to any other right to appeal, the state shall have the right to appeal from an order granting a motion to suppress made under subparagraph IX(a), or the denial of an application for an order of approval, if the attorney shall certify to the judge or other official granting such motion or denying such application that the appeal is not taken for purposes of delay. Such appeal shall be taken within 30 days after the date the order was entered and shall be diligently prosecuted.

X. If an order authorizing interception is entered pursuant to this chapter, the order, upon request of the attorney general or deputy attorney general, shall direct that a communication common carrier shall furnish to the law enforcement agency designated by the attorney general all information, facilities or technical assistance necessary to accomplish the interception unobtrusively and with a minimum of interference with the services that such communication common carrier is according the person whose communications are to be intercepted. The communication common carrier shall furnish such facilities or technical assistance at its prevailing rate or tariff.

Source.
1969, 403:1. 1975, 385:3. 1995, 280:4-7, 10, I, III, eff. Aug. 20, 1995.

Revision note.
In the second sentence of subpar. I(d), inserted "the application shall include" preceding "a particular description of facts" for purposes of clarity.

Amendments
—**1995.** Substituted "telecommunications" for "wire" preceding "or oral communications" and "telecommunication" for "wire" preceding "or oral communication" wherever it appeared and substituted "the applicant's" for "his" preceding "belief" in par. I(b), "the judge's" for "his" preceding "directions" in the third sentence of par. VII(a), "the judge" for "he" preceding "finds" in the second sentence of par. VIII and "the judges" for "his" preceding "discretion" and "such person's" for "his" preceding "counsel" in the third sentence of the concluding paragraph of par. IX(a).

—**1975.** Paragraph X: Added.

Cross References.
Authorization for interception of communications generally, see RSA 570-A:7.
Reports of interceptions of communications generally, see RSA 570-A:10.

NOTES TO DECISIONS

1. Constitutionality
2. Contents of application—Statement as to inadequacy of traditional investigative techniques
3. —Statement as to previous applications involving persons named in application
4. Contents of authorization order
5. Minimization of intrusions upon communications not subject to interception

1. Constitutionality
The fact that this section does not provide for post-surveillance notice of a wiretap to persons whose communications have been intercepted does not make the section unconstitutional. State v. Rowman, 116 N.H. 41, 352 A.2d 737, 1976 N.H. LEXIS 259 (1976).

2. Contents of application—Statement as to inadequacy of traditional investigative techniques
In prosecution for possession with intent to distribute and conspiracy to distribute controlled drugs, state's application for wiretap order complied with subparagraph III(c) of this section where the affidavit in support of application described a four-month police investigation which, although establishing probable cause for issuance of a wiretap order, could not establish the amount of evidence necessary to conclusively demonstrate the criminal culpability of the members of the drug conspiracy, asserted that continued surveillance of the defendant's home was likely to be detected by the defendant's neighbors and could more than likely be compromised, and that the successful introduction of a state police undercover agent to the drug conspiracy was unlikely because of the absence of a legitimate contact with the conspirators. State v. Andrews, 125 N.H. 158, 480 A.2d 889, 1984 N.H. LEXIS 361 (1984).

A court must find from the application the existence of one of the circumstances enumerated in subparagraph I(c) as a prerequisite for entering an interception order under subparagraph III(c). State v. Rowman, 116 N.H. 41, 352 A.2d 737, 1976 N.H. LEXIS 259 (1976).

A judge reviewing a wiretap application is handicapped without a showing why traditional investigative techniques are not sufficient in a particular case, and, if he considers it necessary, he should not hesitate to require the applicant to furnish additional testimony or documentary evidence in support of the application. State v. Rowman, 116 N.H. 41, 352 A.2d 737, 1976 N.H. LEXIS 259 (1976).

A boilerplate recitation of the difficulties of gathering usable evidence in bookmaking operations prosecutions is not a sufficient basis for granting a wiretap order under paragraph III of this section. State v. Rowman, 116 N.H. 41, 352 A.2d 737, 1976 N.H. LEXIS 259 (1976).

Where affidavits presented with wiretap application in an effort to establish probable cause showed in detail the methods used by the police to uncover the crimes charged in the complaints, and from such details the judge could draw inferences as to the limits of the traditional investigative techniques, the judge reasonably concluded that normal investigative procedures had been tried and failed, or reasonably appeared unlikely to succeed if tried, as required by paragraph III of this section. State v. Rowman, 116 N.H. 41, 352 A.2d 737, 1976 N.H. LEXIS 259 (1976).

3. —Statement as to previous applications involving persons named in application
Under subparagraph I(e), requiring that an applicant for an interception order report all previous applications involving any of the persons mentioned in the application, the test of whether a previous application involved a person involved in the current application is whether the applicant had a duty under this section to name that person in the previous application. State v. Rowman, 116 N.H. 41, 352 A.2d 737, 1976 N.H. LEXIS 259 (1976).

Where an affidavit supporting a wiretap application did not report previous applications involving a person involved in the current application, but it did contain conversations intercepted under the previous applications and regarding the person, or in which that person participated, and all the applications were presented to the same judge, the requirement of subparagraph I(e) that all previous applications involving any of the same persons as those involved in the current application be reported was satisfied, although ordinarily reports of conversations regarding a person, or in which he participated, intercepted under prior orders would not be sufficient to inform the judge that the person was a target of the prior applications. State v. Rowman, 116 N.H. 41, 352 A.2d 737, 1976 N.H. LEXIS 259 (1976).

4. Contents of authorization order

In prosecution for possession with intent to distribute and conspiracy to distribute controlled drugs, the issuing magistrate was not required by paragraph V of this section to restrict interception in his wiretap order to incoming and outgoing calls of specific numbers already obtained through the use of pen register since the application for the wiretap order supported the conclusion that the police investigation had not established the boundaries of the illicit drug distribution network of which the defendant was a part and had not established within any boundary all of the network's members, and since the goal of the wiretap, as stated in the affidavit, was to delineate the contours of the conspiracy between the defendant and others known and yet unknown. State v. Andrews, 125 N.H. 158, 480 A.2d 889, 1984 N.H. LEXIS 361 (1984).

Paragraph V of this section requires the inclusion of all of its provisions in the authorization order. State v. Moccia, 119 N.H. 169, 400 A.2d 44, 1979 N.H. LEXIS 267 (1979).

Authorization order which included statement that the authorization should be executed in any event for no longer than ten days, but did not include a statement that the authorization must terminate upon attainment of the authorized objective, was defective. State v. Moccia, 119 N.H. 169, 400 A.2d 44, 1979 N.H. LEXIS 267 (1979).

The failure to specify in a wiretap authorization order that the interception must terminate when the objective had been achieved did not prejudice defendants and was harmless beyond a reasonable doubt since the interception did terminate upon attainment of the authorized objective, even though the ten-day period of authorization had not been exhausted. State v. Moccia, 119 N.H. 169, 400 A.2d 44, 1979 N.H. LEXIS 267 (1979).

5. Minimization of intrusions upon communications not subject to interception

The proper test for the minimization required by paragraph V of this section is the reasonableness under the facts and circumstances of each case. State v. Andrews, 125 N.H. 158, 480 A.2d 889, 1984 N.H. LEXIS 361 (1984).

In prosecution for possession with intent to distribute and conspiracy to distribute controlled drugs, where the police officers, in executing a wiretap order, intercepted 207 calls over a period of nine days, and where 3 of those calls were minimized, 58 calls were incriminating and 145 calls were non-pertinent, the minimization, required by paragraph V of this section, was reasonable, since the police were investigating an apparently large-scale drug conspiracy whose members used code language, the terms of which made it difficult to identify immediately those calls that were inquiries into the defendant's legitimate business interests as a lobster dealer, thus making it difficult for the officers to develop a pattern of innocent calls that would clearly require minimization, and since the wiretap was of a relatively short duration—nine days—and was far too brief a period for such a pattern to develop. State v. Andrews, 125 N.H. 158, 480 A.2d 889, 1984 N.H. LEXIS 361 (1984).

In determining whether the requirement of paragraph V that interception be conducted in such a way as to minimize the interception of communications not otherwise subject to interception has been satisfied, the test is the reasonableness of the intrusions under the facts and circumstances of each case. State v. Moccia, 119 N.H. 169, 400 A.2d 44, 1979 N.H. LEXIS 267 (1979).

Among the factors to be considered in determining whether the police minimized unnecessary intrusions upon communications not subject to interception are (1) the percentage of nonpertinent calls intercepted, (2) the nature and scope of the criminal activity under investigation, and (3) the state's reasonable expectation of the contents of particular calls. State v. Moccia, 119 N.H. 169, 400 A.2d 44, 1979 N.H. LEXIS 267 (1979).

Where the purpose of a wiretap was to investigate a large scale drug conspiracy, and the police had difficulty identifying the relevant conversations because of the large number of people involved, and the uncertainty of their identity, compounded by the use of guarded language and code words, the interception of virtually every call during the period of the tap did not violate the minimization requirement of paragraph V of this section. State v. Moccia, 119 N.H. 169, 400 A.2d 44, 1979 N.H. LEXIS 267 (1979).

Cited:

Cited in State v. Lee, 113 N.H. 313, 307 A.2d 827, 1973 N.H. LEXIS 262 (1973); State v. Doyle, 126 N.H. 153, 489 A.2d 639, 1985 N.H. LEXIS 262 (1985); State v. Valenzuela, 130 N.H. 175, 536 A.2d 1252, 1987 N.H. LEXIS 302 (1987); State v. Horne, 136 N.H. 348, 615 A.2d 1251, 1992 N.H. LEXIS 175 (1992).

RESEARCH REFERENCES

New Hampshire Court Rules Annotated.
Motions to suppress evidence generally, see Rule 94, Rules of the Superior Court, New Hampshire Court Rules Annotated.

570-A:9-a. Authorization for Installation and Use of Pen Register Devices.

[Repealed 1988, 25:7, II, eff. July 1, 1988.]

Former section(s).
Former RSA 570-A:9-a, which was derived from 1986, 53:2, related to authorization for installation and use of pen register devices.

570-A:9-b. Use of Interpreters.

Notwithstanding any other provision of this chapter, an investigative or law enforcement officer supervising an interception under this chapter in which the intercepted communication is in a code or foreign language may utilize the assistance and participation of a qualified interpreter to translate the language being used into English. Such interpreter, before entering upon his or her duties, shall take an oath that he or she will make a true interpretation in an understandable manner to the best of his or her skill and judgment.

Source.
2008, 361:13, eff. July 11, 2008.

570-A:10. Reports Concerning Intercepted Telecommunications or Oral Communications.

I. Within 30 days after the expiration of an order, or each extension thereof, entered under RSA 570-A:9, or the denial of an order approving an interception, the issuing or denying judge shall report to the administrative office of the United States Courts:

(a) The fact that an order or extension was applied for;

(b) The kind of order or extension applied for;

(c) The fact that the order or extension was granted as applied for, was modified, or was denied;

(d) The period of interceptions authorized by the order, and the number and duration of any extensions of the order;

(e) The offense specified in the order or application, or extension of an order;

(f) The identity of the applying investigative or law enforcement officer and agency making the application and the person authorizing the application; and

(g) The nature of the facilities from which or the place where communications were to be intercepted.

II. In January of each year, each county attorney shall report to the attorney general who shall report, in turn, to the administrative office of the United States Courts:

(a) The information required by subparagraphs I(a) through (g) with respect to each application for an order or extension made during the preceding calendar year;

(b) A general description of the interceptions made under such order or extension, including: (1) The approximate nature and frequency of incriminating communications intercepted, (2) The approximate nature and frequency of other communications intercepted, (3) The approximate number of persons whose communications were intercepted, and (4) The approximate nature, amount, and cost of the manpower and other resources used in the interceptions;

(c) The number of arrests resulting from interceptions made under such order or extension, and the offenses for which arrests were made;

(d) The number of trials resulting from such interceptions;

(e) The number of motions to suppress made with respect to such interceptions, and the number granted or denied;

(f) The number of convictions resulting from such interceptions and the offenses for which the convictions were obtained and a general assessment of the importance of the interceptions; and

(g) The information required by subparagraphs (b) through (f) of this paragraph with respect to orders or extensions obtained in a preceding calendar year.

III. On or before December 1 of each odd numbered year, the attorney general shall include in the report required by RSA 7:37, a report concerning the number of applications for orders authorizing or approving the interception of telecommunications or oral communications and the number of orders and extensions granted or denied during the preceding 2 years.

Source.
1969, 403:1. 1995, 280:8, 10, III, eff. Aug. 20, 1995.

Revision note.
In par. III, substituted "of each odd numbered year" for "preceding each biennial session of the general court" for purposes of conformity with RSA 7:37, as amended by 1985, 300:11.

Amendments
—**1995.** Substituted "telecommunications" for "wire" preceding "or oral communications" in the section catchline and in par. III and deleted "of him" preceding "by RSA 7:37" in that paragraph.

570-A:11. Recovery of Civil Damages Authorized.

Any person whose telecommunication or oral communication is intercepted, disclosed, or used in violation of this chapter shall have a civil cause of action against any person who intercepts, discloses, or uses, or procures any other person to intercept, disclose or use such communications, and be entitled to recover from any such person: (a) actual damages but not less than liquidated damages computed at the rate of $100 a day for each day of violation or $1,000, whichever is higher; (b) punitive damages; and (c) a reasonable attorney's fee and other litigation costs reasonably incurred. Good faith reliance on a court order or on a representation made by the attorney general, deputy attorney general or a county attorney shall constitute a complete defense to any civil or criminal action brought under this chapter.

Source.
1969, 403:1. 1995, 280:10I, eff. Aug. 20, 1995.

Amendments
—**1995.** Substituted "telecommunication" for "wire" preceding "or oral".

Cross References.
Prohibition of interception and disclosure of communications generally, see RSA 570-A:2.

NOTES TO DECISIONS

1. Construction
2. Attorneys' fees and costs
3. Applicability

1. Construction
Recovery under this section requires a reasonable expectation by plaintiff that her communications will not be intercepted. Fischer v. Hooper, 143 N.H. 585, 732 A.2d 396, 1999 N.H. LEXIS 160 (1999).

2. Attorneys' fees and costs
Trial court did not err in declining to reduce plaintiffs' award of attorneys' fees and costs to account for their lack of success in recovering punitive damages, since plaintiffs' failure to recover punitive damages was not a "failed claim," but a category of relief denied by the jury. Desilets v. Wal-Mart Stores, Inc., 171 F.3d 711, 1999 U.S. App. LEXIS 5629 (1st Cir. N.H. 1999).

3. Applicability
Nothing in RSA 570-A:11 or RSA 570-A:2, I (defining violations under RSA ch. 570-A, prohibiting illegal wiretapping or eavesdropping) limits the prohibited use of an intercepted communication to any particular circumstances; cordless telephone communication fell within the definition of wire communication. Karch v. BayBank FSB, 147 N.H. 525, 794 A.2d 763, 2002 N.H. LEXIS 21 (2002).

CHAPTER 594

ARRESTS IN CRIMINAL CASES

General Provisions

SECTION
594:1.   Definitions.

Arrest

594:1-a.   Bailiffs and Court Security Officers.
594:2.   Questioning and Detaining Suspects.
594:3.   Searching for Weapons.
594:4.   Permissible Force.
594:5.   Resisting Arrest.
594:6.   Aid to Officers.
594:7.   Arrest on Warrant.
594:8.   Conveying Prisoner.
594:9.   Arrest by Virtue of a Warrant Not in Officer's Possession.
594:10.   Arrest Without a Warrant.
594:10-a. Notice of Arrest.
594:11.   Judge's Order to Arrest.
594:12.   Duty to Obey.
594:13.   Arrest on Improper Grounds.
594:14.   Summons Instead of Arrest.
594:14-a. Arrest Records.

Notice of Arrest; Right to Advice of Counsel, etc.

594:15.   Notice of Arrest.
594:16.   Conference with Friends or Counsel.
594:17.   Penalty.

Release or Detention

594:18.   Release of Persons Arrested Without Warrant. [Repealed.]
594:18-a. Release of Persons Arrested Without Warrant.
594:19.   Detention of Person Arrested on Warrant. [Repealed.]
594:19-a. Detention of Person Arrested; With Warrant; Without Warrant.
594:20.   Detention, Night Arrest. [Repealed.]
594:20-a. Place and Time of Detention.
594:21.   Authority of Jailer. [Repealed.]
594:21-a. Authority of Superintendent.
594:22, 594:23. [Repealed.]

Armed Guards

594:24, 594:25. [Repealed.]

Severability of enactment.
1941, 163:1-9 were subject to a severability clause. See 1941, 163:12.

Cross References.
Annulment of arrest records, see RSA 651:5.
Arrest in extradition proceedings, see RSA 612.
Fresh pursuit, see RSA 614.
Powers of fire investigators generally, see RSA 21-P:4.
Powers of police officers generally, see RSA 105:3.
Powers of sheriffs and deputies generally, see RSA 106-B:12.
Powers of state police generally, see RSA 106-B:12.

Powers of watchmen, see RSA 105:12.

NOTES TO DECISIONS

Cited:
Cited in United States v. Kozerski, 518 F. Supp. 1082, 1981 U.S. Dist. LEXIS 13519 (D.N.H. 1981).

General Provisions

594:1. Definitions.

As used in this chapter:

I. "Arrest" is the taking of a person into custody in order that he may be forthcoming to answer for the commission of a crime.

II. "Felony" is any crime that may be punished by death or imprisonment in the state prison. Other crimes are "misdemeanors."

III. "Officer" or "peace officer" is any sheriff or deputy sheriff, mayor or city marshal, constable, police officer or watchman, member of the national guard acting under orders while in active state service ordered by the governor under RSA 110-B:6, or other person authorized to make arrests in a criminal case.

Source.
GS 236:1. GL 254:1. PS 250:1. 1941, 163:1. PL 364:1. RL 423:1; 423:20. RSA 594:1. 1965, 98:1, eff. July 17, 1965.

Amendments
—**1965.** Paragraph III: Inserted "member of the national guard acting under orders while in active state service ordered by the governor under RSA 110-A:6" following "watchman".

Revision note.
In par. III, substituted "RSA 110-B:6" for "RSA 110-A:6". 1981, 434:2, eff. Aug. 22, 1981, provided for the repeal of RSA 110-A and the enactment of RSA 110-B.

Cross References.
Classification of crimes, see RSA 625:9.
Use of summons, see RSA 594:14.

NOTES TO DECISIONS

I. Generally

1. Construction of section with other laws

II. Arrests

11. Requisites generally
12. Manner of effecting arrest
13. Apprehension of escaped prisoner

III. Crimes

21. Generally
22. Offenses classified as violations
23. Particular offenses

IV. Peace Officers

31. Generally
32. Police officers generally
33. Particular officers

I. Generally

1. Construction of section with other laws

In determining whether there was a violation of the privilege from arrest granted to a member of the national guard by RSA 110-A:77, III (now RSA 110-B:71, II) by the act of a police officer in stopping the motor vehicle of a guard member and issuing a summons to him, the definition of "arrest" is governed by arrests in criminal cases as in this section and not that pertaining to military offenses as in RSA 110-A:58 (now RSA 110-B:44, I). State v. Murray, 106 N.H. 71, 205 A.2d 29, 1964 N.H. LEXIS 41 (1964).

II. Arrests

11. Requisites generally

To constitute an arrest, there must exist an intent on the part of the arresting officer to take the person into custody and corresponding understanding by the person arrested that he is in custody. State v. Hutton, 108 N.H. 279, 235 A.2d 117, 1967 N.H. LEXIS 172 (1967), overruled in part, State v. Riley, 126 N.H. 257, 490 A.2d 1362, 1985 N.H. LEXIS 292 (1985); State v. Brodhead, 116 N.H. 39, 351 A.2d 57, 1976 N.H. LEXIS 258 (1976); State v. Wolfson, 116 N.H. 227, 356 A.2d 692, 1976 N.H. LEXIS 315 (1976). But see State v. Riley, 126 N.H. 257, 490 A.2d 1362, 1985 N.H. LEXIS 292 (1985).

To constitute an arrest, there must be an intent on the part of the arresting officer to take the person into custody and the corresponding understanding by the person arrested that he is in custody; it is not necessary that the defendant subsequently remain in custody or that a criminal complaint be instituted. State v. Rocheleau, 117 N.H. 792, 378 A.2d 1381, 1977 N.H. LEXIS 434 (1977). But see State v. Riley, 126 N.H. 257, 490 A.2d 1362, 1985 N.H. LEXIS 292 (1985).

Although possibly relevant to the issue of when an arrest occurs, any subjective beliefs of the arresting officer and the arrestee are not determinative of that issue. State v. Riley, 126 N.H. 257, 490 A.2d 1362, 1985 N.H. LEXIS 292 (1985).

An individual is "seized" for purposes of the Fourth Amendment of the United States Constitution and this section, if, in view of all the circumstances surrounding the incident, a reasonable person would have believed that he was not free to leave. State v. Riley, 126 N.H. 257, 490 A.2d 1362, 1985 N.H. LEXIS 292 (1985).

In order for a "seizure" of a person to have occurred, there must have been a "show of authority" such that the liberty of the individual has been restrained; circumstances indicating a "show of authority" include the threatening presence of several officers, the display of a weapon by an officer, some physical touching of the person of the citizen, or the use of language or tone of voice indicating that compliance with the officer's request might be compelled. State v. Riley, 126 N.H. 257, 490 A.2d 1362, 1985 N.H. LEXIS 292 (1985).

A person was not seized when he was approached by a police officer and asked to come to a police cruiser for questioning, or when he was questioned at the cruiser. State v. Riley, 126 N.H. 257, 490 A.2d 1362, 1985 N.H. LEXIS 292 (1985).

A person was seized when, after being asked to come to a police cruiser for questioning, he was told by the police officer administering the questions to remain in the cruiser. State v. Riley, 126 N.H. 257, 490 A.2d 1362, 1985 N.H. LEXIS 292 (1985).

12. Manner of effecting arrest

Under this section, an arrest may be effected by an actual or constructive seizure or detention of the accused or by his voluntary submission to custody, both of which subject him to the actual control and will of the person making the arrest. State v. Hutton, 108 N.H. 279, 235 A.2d 117, 1967 N.H. LEXIS 172 (1967), overruled in part, State v. Riley, 126 N.H. 257, 490 A.2d 1362, 1985 N.H. LEXIS 292 (1985).

13. Apprehension of escaped prisoner

Apprehension of an escaped prisoner was not an arrest as defined by paragraph I of this section since the prisoner was not "taken into custody" when recaptured because he was never lawfully out of state custody, and was not apprehended to answer for the commission of a crime, but to be returned to prison to serve a previously imposed sentence. State v. Sampson, 125 N.H. 544, 484 A.2d 1104, 1984 N.H. LEXIS 397 (1984).

III. Crimes

21. Generally

The use of the word "crime" in paragraph I of this section was not intended as a word of limitation, but rather to encompass broadly all offenses prohibited by statute or ordinance. State v. Miller, 115 N.H. 662, 348 A.2d 345, 1975 N.H. LEXIS 390 (1975).

The definition of a crime contained in paragraph I of this section is determined by reference to other statutes concerned with arrest and criminal procedure rather than the criminal code definition, restricted as it is to sentencing. State v. Miller, 115 N.H. 662, 348 A.2d 345, 1975 N.H. LEXIS 390 (1975).

22. Offenses classified as violations

Where a professor unleashed a tirade against a colleague, the false arrest claim based on a disorderly conduct charge failed because there was probable cause for the professor's arrest on the disorderly conduct charge, and the professor's argument regarding an alleged distinction between crimes and violations under New Hampshire law was rejected. Collins v. Univ. of N.H., 664 F.3d 8, 2011 U.S. App. LEXIS 25146 (2011).

Until the enactment of the criminal code all "offenses" were either misdemeanors or felonies and the terms "crimes" and "offenses" were synonymous; in the statutes outside of the criminal code, "crimes" are "offenses" and "offenses" are "crimes" and, while for the purpose of the criminal code a "violation" is an "offense" but not a "crime", no such distinction exists outside the code. State v. Miller, 115 N.H. 662, 348 A.2d 345, 1975 N.H. LEXIS 390 (1975).

The language in RSA 625:9, II(b), providing that a violation does not constitute a crime, does not by implication repeal the right to arrest for such an offense conferred by this section. State v. Miller, 115 N.H. 662, 348 A.2d 345, 1975 N.H. LEXIS 390 (1975).

23. Particular offenses

Arrest on warrant for operating an uninspected motor vehicle in violation of RSA 260:16 (now RSA 266:5), which offense was classified as a violation, was not improper. State v. Miller, 115 N.H. 662, 348 A.2d 345, 1975 N.H. LEXIS 390 (1975).

IV. Peace Officers

31. Generally

This section and RSA 594:10 grant the power of arrest to an extensive list of persons, indicating a legislative intent to provide maximum protection to the community. State v. Swan, 116 N.H. 132, 352 A.2d 700, 1976 N.H. LEXIS 285 (1976).

32. Police officers generally

The words "police officer" in paragraph III of this section are to be construed according to their common and approved usage and must be taken to mean all police officers, whether regular, special or auxiliary. State v. Swan, 116 N.H. 132, 352 A.2d 700, 1976 N.H. LEXIS 285 (1976).

33. Particular officers

An auxiliary policeman has the power to make an arrest without a warrant for a misdemeanor committed in his presence. State v. Swan, 116 N.H. 132, 352 A.2d 700, 1976 N.H. LEXIS 285 (1976).

Cited:

Cited in Park v. United States, 294 F. 776, 1924 U.S. App. LEXIS 2959 (1st Cir. N.H. 1924); Nelson v. Hancock, 239 F. Supp. 857, 1965 U.S. Dist. LEXIS 7108 (D.N.H. 1965); Hancock v. Nelson, 363 F.2d 249, 1966 U.S. App. LEXIS 5544 (1st Cir. N.H. 1966); State v. Preston, 124 N.H. 118, 467 A.2d 243, 1983 N.H. LEXIS 370 (1983); State v. Oxley, 127 N.H. 407, 503 A.2d 756, 1985 N.H. LEXIS 460 (1985); In re Justin D., 144 N.H. 450, 743 A.2d 829, 1999 N.H. LEXIS 132 (1999); State v. Diamond, 146 N.H. 691, 785 A.2d 887, 2001 N.H. LEXIS 144 (2001).

Arrest

Cross References.
Notice of arrest, see RSA 594:15.
Release or detention, see RSA 594:18-a et seq.

Right to conference with attorney, relatives, etc., see RSA 594:16.

594:1-a. Bailiffs and Court Security Officers.

I. Bailiffs and supreme court security officers responsible for court security shall have the powers of arrest provided in this chapter when performing their duties relating to court security.

II. The sheriff, through the sheriff's deputies and bailiffs, shall be responsible for court security and shall be responsible for the conduct and control of detained defendants and prisoners during the time period that such defendants and prisoners are in all state courts, except for the supreme court.

Source.
1985, 258:3, eff. Jan. 1, 1986. 1998, 297:5, eff. Jan. 1, 1999.

Amendments
—**1998.** Inserted "Security" following "Court" in the section catchline, designated the existing provisions of the section as par. I and substituted "supreme court security officers" for "court officers" in that paragraph, and added par. II.

Cross References.
Courtroom security generally, see RSA 159:19.

594:2. Questioning and Detaining Suspects.

A peace officer may stop any person abroad whom he has reason to suspect is committing, has committed or is about to commit a crime, and may demand of him his name, address, business abroad and where he is going.

Source.
1941, 163:2. RL 423:21. RSA 594:2. 1985, 255:2, eff. Jan. 1, 1986.

Amendments
—**1985.** Rewritten to the extent that a detailed comparison would be impracticable.

Cross References.
Searches of persons detained, see RSA 594:3.
Warrantless arrests, see RSA 594:10.

NOTES TO DECISIONS

1. Constitutionality
2. Consensual encounter
3. Detention

1. Constitutionality
This section is unconstitutional to the extent that it permits temporary detention for questioning on grounds less than probable cause to arrest. State v. White, 119 N.H. 567, 406 A.2d 291, 1979 N.H. LEXIS 356 (1979).

2. Consensual encounter
Officer's encounter with defendant when officer approached defendant's parked vehicle was consensual where restrictions on defendant's movement were not the result of the officer's actions, and, inter alia, the officer did not draw his weapon, did not order defendant out of car, and did not ask defendant to roll down his window, but rather asked if defendant was "all set." State v. Licks, 154 N.H. 491, 914 A.2d 1246, 2006 N.H. LEXIS 189 (2006).

3. Detention
Passenger's unlawful frisk and unlawful detention claims failed because, inter alia, the officer saw the passenger toss something into the back of the car, New Hampshire law authorized the officer

to demand the passenger's full name pursuant to a lawful stop, and the passenger enhanced suspicion when the passenger refused to give it. Machado v. Weare Police Dep't, — F.3d —, 2012 U.S. App. LEXIS 20538 (Oct. 2, 2012).

Cited:
Cited in Nelson v. Hancock, 239 F. Supp. 857, 1965 U.S. Dist. LEXIS 7108 (D.N.H. 1965); Hancock v. Nelson, 363 F.2d 249, 1966 U.S. App. LEXIS 5544 (1st Cir. N.H. 1966); State v. Gilson, 116 N.H. 230, 356 A.2d 689, 1976 N.H. LEXIS 316 (1976).

594:3. Searching for Weapons.

A peace officer may search for a dangerous weapon any person whom he is questioning or about to question as provided in RSA 594:2 whenever he reasonably believes that he might be in danger if such person possessed a dangerous weapon. If the officer finds a weapon, he may take and keep it until the completion of the questioning, when he shall either return it or arrest the person.

Source.
1941, 163:3. RL 423:22.

594:4. Permissible Force.

I. No unnecessary or unreasonable force or means of restraint may be used in detaining or arresting any person.

II. A peace officer is justified in using deadly force to effect an arrest as provided in RSA 627:5, II.

Source.
1941, 163:4. RL 423:23. RSA 594:4. 1981, 373:4, eff. Aug. 22, 1981.

Amendments
—**1981.** Paragraph II: Rewritten to the extent that a detailed comparison would be impracticable.

594:5. Resisting Arrest.

If a person has reasonable ground to believe that he is being arrested and that the arrest is being made by a peace officer, it is his duty to submit to arrest and refrain from using force or any weapon in resisting it, regardless of whether there is a legal basis for the arrest.

Source.
1941, 163:5. RL 423:24.

Cross References.
Hindering apprehension or prosecution, see RSA 642:3.
Resisting arrest or detention, see RSA 642:2.

NOTES TO DECISIONS

Construction
At trial for simple assault and resisting arrest, regardless of whether chief of police properly or improperly ordered arresting officer to tow defendant's vehicle, defendant enjoyed no privilege to use self-help to prevent removal of his property or to effect its return nor was he entitled to resist arrest; any such privileges that may have existed at common law have been statutorily superceded. State v. Haas, 134 N.H. 480, 596 A.2d 127, 1991 N.H. LEXIS 88 (1991).

Cited:

Cited in State v. Reid, 134 N.H. 418, 594 A.2d 160, 1991 N.H. LEXIS 81 (1991); State v. Cavanaugh, 138 N.H. 193, 635 A.2d 1382, 1993 N.H. LEXIS 183 (1993).

594:6. Aid to Officers.

Every law enforcement officer who encounters a need for assistance in the execution of his office in a criminal case or emergency situation may require any person to render suitable aid. Any person who, when so required, neglects or refuses to give such aid shall be guilty of a violation.

Source.

RS 178:12. CS 189:12. GS 236:2. GL 254:2. PS 250:2. PL 364:2. RL 423:2. RSA 594:6. 1994, 286:1, eff. Jan. 1, 1995.

Amendments

—1994. Rewritten to the extent that a detailed comparison would be impracticable.

Cross References.

Classification of crimes, see RSA 625:9.

Sentences, see RSA 651.

NOTES TO DECISIONS

Cited:

Cited in La Chance v. Berlin S. Ry., 79 N.H. 291, 109 A. 720, 1919 N.H. LEXIS 56 (1919).

594:7. Arrest on Warrant.

An officer to whom a warrant for the arrest of an offender may be addressed has power to make the arrest at any time and in any place, and shall have, in any county, the same powers in relation to the process as an officer of that county.

Source.

RS 222:16. CS 237:16. GS 236:9. GL 254:9. PS 250:9. PL 364:12. RL 423:12.

Cross References.

Warrantless arrest, see RSA 594:10.

NOTES TO DECISIONS

Cited:

Cited in State v. Jones, 127 N.H. 515, 503 A.2d 802, 1985 N.H. LEXIS 454 (1985); State v. Martin, 145 N.H. 362, 761 A.2d 516, 2000 N.H. LEXIS 69 (2000).

594:8. Conveying Prisoner.

An officer, having made an arrest under a warrant to him directed, may, if convenient, convey the prisoner through any town or county, and, in respect to such prisoner, shall have the powers of an officer of such town or county.

Source.

RS 222:19. CS 237:19. GS 236:11. GL 254:11. PS 250:11. PL 364:14. RL 423:14.

594:9. Arrest by Virtue of a Warrant Not in Officer's Possession.

An arrest by a peace officer acting under a warrant is lawful even though the officer does not have the warrant in his possession at the time of the arrest, but, if the person arrested so requests, the warrant shall be shown to him as soon as practicable.

Source.

1941, 163:8. RL 423:27.

Cross References.

Arrest on warrant generally, see RSA 594:7.

NOTES TO DECISIONS

Cited:

Cited in State v. Dumais, 126 N.H. 532, 493 A.2d 501, 1985 N.H. LEXIS 337 (1985).

594:10. Arrest Without a Warrant.

I. An arrest by a peace officer without a warrant on a charge of a misdemeanor or a violation is lawful whenever:

(a) He has probable cause to believe that the person to be arrested has committed a misdemeanor or violation in his presence; or

(b) He has probable cause to believe that the person to be arrested has within the past 12 hours committed abuse as defined in RSA 173-B:1, I against a person eligible for protection from domestic violence as defined in RSA 173-B:1, has within the past 12 hours violated a temporary or permanent protective order issued under RSA 173-B or RSA 458:16 by committing assault, criminal trespass, criminal mischief or another criminal act, or has within the last 12 hours violated stalking provisions under RSA 633:3-a.

(c) He has probable cause to believe that the person to be arrested has committed a misdemeanor or violation, and, if not immediately arrested, such person will not be apprehended, will destroy or conceal evidence of the offense, or will cause further personal injury or damage to property.

II. An arrest by a peace officer without a warrant on a charge of felony is lawful whenever:

(a) A felony has actually been committed by the person arrested, regardless of the reasons which led the officer to make the arrest.

(b) The officer has reasonable ground to believe that the person arrested has committed a felony.

Source.

1941, 163:6. RL 423:25. RSA 594:10. 1979, 377:4. 1981, 344:3. 1989, 297:19. 1990, 241:9. 1993, 173:3, eff. July 26, 1993. 2002, 79:4, eff. Jan. 1, 2003.

Amendments

—2002. Paragraph I(b): Substituted "12 hours" for "6 hours" in three places.

—1993. Paragraph I(b): Deleted "or" following "violence as defined in RSA 173-B:1" and inserted "or RSA 458:16" preceding "by committing" and "or has within the last 6 hours violated stalking provisions under RSA 633:3-a" following "criminal act".

—1990. Paragraph 1(b): Rewritten to the extent that a detailed comparison would be impracticable.

—1989. Paragraph I(b): Substituted "person eligible for protection from domestic violence" for "family or household member" following "assaulted a" and "RSA 173-B:1" for "RSA 173-B:1, II".

—1981. Paragraph I: Rewritten to the extent that a detailed comparison would be impracticable.

—1979. Paragraph I: Inserted "or whenever he has probable cause to believe that the person to be arrested has assaulted a family or household member as defined in RSA 173-B:1, II within the past 6 hours" following "presence".

Cross References.

Arrest on warrant generally, see RSA 594:7, 9.

Classification of crimes, see RSA 625:9.

Validity of defective arrest for which lawful cause exists, see RSA 594:13.

NOTES TO DECISIONS

1. Persons authorized to make arrests
2. Basis for arrest—Generally
3. —Loss of evidence from reduction of blood alcohol level
4. —Reasonable grounds
5. —Exigent circumstances
6. —Offense committed in officer's presence
7. Driving under the influence

1. Persons authorized to make arrests

Officers of university police department had the authority to arrest where they were found to have been appointed as police officers for town, and to be ultimately accountable to and under the control of the town police chief. State v. Diamond, 146 N.H. 691, 785 A.2d 887, 2001 N.H. LEXIS 144 (2001).

An auxiliary policeman is a "police officer" as that term is employed in RSA 594:1, III, and is thus empowered to arrest without a warrant for a misdemeanor committed in his presence as provided in paragraph I of this section. State v. Swan, 116 N.H. 132, 352 A.2d 700, 1976 N.H. LEXIS 285 (1976).

2. Basis for arrest—Generally

Where defendant assaulted defendant's girlfriend in one jurisdiction, the police in that jurisdiction notified other jurisdictions of the offense, and the police department in the jurisdiction in which defendant resided sent officers without a warrant to defendant's home to arrest defendant, the trial court erroneously dismissed the charges against defendant, as the arresting officers had territorial jurisdiction to arrest defendant; RSA 105:4 did not address where the underlying conduct had to occur for the arresting jurisdiction to legally make the arrest, the probable cause pursuant to N.H. Const. pt. I, art. 19 to arrest was transferred by the department where the conduct occurred to the arresting officers, and the arresting officers had authority under RSA 594:10, I(b) to make the warrantless arrest, because they had probable cause to believe that defendant had, within the previous six hours, committed abuse as defined in RSA 173-B:1 against a person eligible for protection from domestic violence as defined in RSA 173-B:1. State v. Merriam, 150 N.H. 548, 842 A.2d 102, 2004 N.H. LEXIS 19 (2004), rehearing denied, 2004 N.H. LEXIS 46 (N.H. Mar. 12, 2004).

A police officer is authorized to conduct a warrantless arrest whenever he has probable cause to believe that the person to be arrested has committed a misdemeanor or violation in his presence. State v. Crotty, 134 N.H. 706, 597 A.2d 1078, 1991 N.H. LEXIS 126 (1991).

An officer may take into consideration what he sees or learns through his senses at the time and also other sources of information, and if such sources of information furnish reasonable ground

to believe an arrest ought to be made, and he acts in good faith, he is justified in making the arrest. Park v. United States, 294 F. 776, 1924 U.S. App. LEXIS 2959 (1st Cir. N.H. 1924).

3. —Loss of evidence from reduction of blood alcohol level

Since the effectiveness and reliability of a breathalyzer diminishes with the passage of time because alcohol is metabolized by the blood so as to be undetectable with a breathalyzer, any significant delay in taking a breathalyzer test may serve to deprive the state of an accurate indication of the driver's condition; such delay could result in the loss of evidence within the meaning of subparagraph I(c) of this section authorizing a warrantless arrest. State v. Schneider, 124 N.H. 242, 470 A.2d 887, 1983 N.H. LEXIS 418 (1983).

Where an individual was initially stopped around midnight by two police officers after he had been observed driving his truck erratically, a state trooper arrived on the scene some four minutes after the initial stop, and, after being told what the police officers had observed and conducting a field sobriety test, as well as noting the smell of alcohol in the truck's cab and the individual's glassy eyes and slurred speech, arrested the individual, the trooper had probable cause to believe that an arrest under subparagraph I(c) of this section was warranted, given the fact that the incident occurred at midnight, combined with the established fact of the metabolization of alcohol by the blood. State v. Schneider, 124 N.H. 242, 470 A.2d 887, 1983 N.H. LEXIS 418 (1983).

4. —Reasonable grounds

Where police officer asked defendant whether he had drugs in his pocket, defendant's affirmative response gave officer probable cause to arrest him, and to conduct a search incident to arrest. State v. Roach, 141 N.H. 64, 677 A.2d 157, 1996 N.H. LEXIS 50 (1996).

A warrantless arrest by a police officer is generally lawful if the officer has "reasonable ground" to believe that the person arrested has committed a felony; "reasonable ground" in this context means substantially the same thing as "probable cause." State v. Vachon, 130 N.H. 37, 533 A.2d 384, 1987 N.H. LEXIS 266 (1987).

In the context of subparagraph II(b) of this section, "reasonable ground" means substantially the same thing as "probable cause". State v. Rodrigue, 127 N.H. 496, 506 A.2d 299, 1985 N.H. LEXIS 477 (1985).

"Probable cause" and "reasonable ground" are synonymous, and determination of the existence of probable cause requires only a showing of reasonable probabilities; proof beyond a reasonable doubt is not required. Kay v. Bruno, 605 F. Supp. 767, 1985 U.S. Dist. LEXIS 22282 (D.N.H. 1985).

As used in this section, "reasonable ground" means substantially the same thing as "probable cause". State v. Hutton, 108 N.H. 279, 235 A.2d 117, 1967 N.H. LEXIS 172 (1967), overruled in part, State v. Riley, 126 N.H. 257, 490 A.2d 1362, 1985 N.H. LEXIS 292 (1985); State v. Schofield, 114 N.H. 454, 322 A.2d 603, 1974 N.H. LEXIS 300 (1974).

5. —Exigent circumstances

When a police officer has probable cause to believe that an intoxicated person has been driving, and unless detained, may continue to drive, risking injury to himself and others, exigent circumstances exist which permit a seizure of the person without warrant; therefore, active or passive threat posed to public safety by an intoxicated driver could justify warrantless arrest to protect against further personal injury or damage to property; officer is not automatically required to place driver into protective custody until arrest warrant can be obtained. State v. Leary, 133 N.H. 46, 573 A.2d 135, 1990 N.H. LEXIS 25 (1990).

Warrantless arrest for driving while intoxicated was authorized by exigent circumstances, to prevent risk to defendant's life as well as the safety of others, where police officers had probable cause to believe that the defendant was driving the vehicle minutes before they arrived at the scene, there was adequate support for the officers' reasonable belief that defendant was intoxicated while operating the vehicle, where the defendant, although not in the driver's seat, was found in the vehicle, where there was no evidence that the vehicle was incapable of further operation, and where the officers had probable cause to believe that defendant might resume driving. State v. Leary, 133 N.H. 46, 573 A.2d 135, 1990 N.H. LEXIS 25 (1990).

6. —Offense committed in officer's presence

Where a store customer was arrested after store security showed a police officer a partial videotape of the customer allegedly shoplifting, the jury was properly instructed that the arrest was unlawful as a matter of law because the officer did not have probable cause to believe that the customer committed a misdemeanor in his presence as required under RSA 594:10, I(a); the videotape alone did not provide a sufficient basis to satisfy the "presence" requirement for warrantless arrests under RSA 594:10, I(a). Forgie-Buccioni v. Hannaford Bros., Inc., 413 F.3d 175, 2005 U.S. App. LEXIS 13137 (1st Cir. N.H. 2005).

Where there was no evidence that police officers observed the defendant operate or even attempt to operate the vehicle, and the officers in fact were unaware that defendant had been driving until so informed by a witness to the events preceding their arrival, warrantless arrest for driving while intoxicated on basis that offense was committed in officer's presence, was not justified. State v. Leary, 133 N.H. 46, 573 A.2d 135, 1990 N.H. LEXIS 25 (1990).

7. Driving under the influence

Because an officer had not yet seized the defendant when he stopped behind defendant's motorcycle and first spoke with him, and because defendant's appearance and conduct created a reasonable suspicion that he was driving under the influence of alcohol, the officer lawfully administered additional field sobriety tests, and there was no violation of U.S. Const. amend. IV and N.H. Const. pt. I, art. 19. A single officer approached a parked vehicle from behind, parked his cruiser so as not to block or restrict defendant's movement, kept his weapon holstered, and refrained from issuing orders to defendant; requesting defendant's license and registration did not constitute a seizure; activating the spotlight and two takedown lights in order to illuminate what would otherwise be plainly in daylight was not an act of seizure because such lighting was necessary to view and evaluate the situation; and the officer's activating his rear blue lights was not a seizure, as there was a strong need to warn passing traffic because the road lacked a breakdown lane. State v. Steeves, 158 N.H. 672, 972 A.2d 1033, 2009 N.H. LEXIS 63 (2009).

Cited:

Cited in La Chance v. Berlin S. Ry., 79 N.H. 291, 109 A. 720, 1919 N.H. LEXIS 56 (1919); State v. Davis, 108 N.H. 45, 226 A.2d 873, 1967 N.H. LEXIS 117 (1967); State v. Scanlon, 110 N.H. 179, 263 A.2d 669, 1970 N.H. LEXIS 124 (1970); State v. McComb, 111 N.H. 312, 282 A.2d 673, 1971 N.H. LEXIS 186 (1971); State v. Brodhead, 116 N.H. 39, 351 A.2d 57, 1976 N.H. LEXIS 258 (1976); State v. Wolfson, 116 N.H. 227, 356 A.2d 692, 1976 N.H. LEXIS 315 (1976); State v. Standish, 116 N.H. 483, 363 A.2d 404, 1976 N.H. LEXIS 388 (1976); State v. Lemire, 121 N.H. 1, 424 A.2d 1135, 1981 N.H. LEXIS 238 (1981); State v. Conway, 463 A.2d 1319, 1983 R.I. LEXIS 1039 (R.I. 1983); State v. Sweeney, 124 N.H. 396, 469 A.2d 1362, 1983 N.H. LEXIS 419 (1983); State v. Christy, 138 N.H. 352, 639 A.2d 261, 1994 N.H. LEXIS 32 (1994).

RESEARCH REFERENCES

New Hampshire Practice.
3-5 N.H.P. Family Law § 5.23.

594:10-a. Notice of Arrest.

A peace officer making an arrest on complaints for felony, misdemeanor, or violation charges arising from the same facts or circumstances shall within 24 hours, excluding weekends and holidays or before a plea is accepted or entered in court, give notice in writing of all charges pending to the county attorney. Failure to provide such notice shall not affect the validity of the arrest or the prosecution of any charges arising from the arrests.

Source.
1992, 75:1, eff. Jan. 1, 1993.

Cross References.
Notice of arrest generally, see RSA 594:15.

594:11. Judge's Order to Arrest.

Any justice of any court, upon view of a breach of the peace or other transgression of the law proper for his cognizance, or if necessary for the preservation of the peace, may command any officer or other person to arrest, bring before him, and detain the offender, until complaint can be made against him.

Source.
RS 222:8. CS 237:8. GS 236:7. GL 254:7. PS 250:7. PL 364:10. RL 423:10. RSA 594:11. 1985, 258:4, eff. Jan. 1, 1986.

Amendments
—1985. Substituted "judge's" for "justice's" in the section catchline, inserted "of any court" following "justice" in the text of the section, and made other minor stylistic changes.

NOTES TO DECISIONS

1. Arrests authorized by section
2. Effect of knowledge and beliefs of arresting officer

1. Arrests authorized by section

This section gives justices of the peace authority to require any person, when no proper officer is present, to apprehend and bring before them any offenders who have violated the law in the presence of the justice, but the authority does not extend to violations not in the presence of the justice. Bissell v. Bissell, 3 N.H. 520, 1826 N.H. LEXIS 44 (1826).

2. Effect of knowledge and beliefs of arresting officer

Where a justice of the peace, assuming to act under the authority of this section, by verbal warrant orders an officer to arrest an alleged offender against the law, it is the province and duty of the justice alone to decide as to what constitutes an offense, and it makes no difference whether the arresting officer observes the commission of the offense or not. Forrist v. Leavitt, 52 N.H. 481, 1872 N.H. LEXIS 63 (1872).

Cited:

Cited in State v. Lemire, 121 N.H. 1, 424 A.2d 1135, 1981 N.H. LEXIS 238 (1981).

594:12. Duty to Obey.

Every officer or person, upon receipt of a command pursuant to RSA 594:11, may arrest and detain the offender. If the officer or person shall not obey such command, he shall be subject to the same penalty as for disobeying an officer.

Source.
RS 222:8. CS 237:8. GS 236:8. GL 254:8. PS 250:8. PL 364:11. RL 423:11.

Revision note.

At the beginning of the section, substituted "upon receipt of a command pursuant to RSA 594:11" for "upon such command" for purposes of clarity.

NOTES TO DECISIONS

Cited:

Cited in Forrist v. Leavitt, 52 N.H. 481, 1872 N.H. LEXIS 63 (1872).

594:13. Arrest on Improper Grounds.

If a lawful cause of arrest exists, the arrest will be lawful even though the officer charged the wrong offense or gave a reason that did not justify the arrest.

Source.

1941, 163:7. RL 423:26.

Cross References.

Warrantless arrests generally, see RSA 594:10.

NOTES TO DECISIONS

Cited:

Cited in State v. McBreairty, 142 N.H. 12, 697 A.2d 495, 1997 N.H. LEXIS 48 (1997).

594:14. Summons Instead of Arrest.

I. In any case in which it is lawful for a peace officer to arrest without a warrant a person for a misdemeanor or violation, he may instead issue to him in hand a written summons in substantially the following form:

THE STATE OF NEW HAMPSHIRE

To ....

You are hereby notified to appear before the .... district (municipal) court of the State of New Hampshire, to be holden on the .... day of .... 19 .... at .... o'clock in the forenoon (afternoon) to answer to a complaint (to be filed in said court) charging you with .... in violation of the laws of the State of New Hampshire.

Hereof fail not, as you will answer your default under the penalty of the law in that behalf made and provided.

Dated at ....

                 Name

the .... day of .... 19 ....

                 Title

Upon failure to appear, a warrant of arrest may issue. Any person who fails to appear in answer to such summons shall be guilty of a misdemeanor.

II. A summons may be issued after an arrest for a misdemeanor or violation in lieu of bail.

Source.

1941, 163:9. RL 423:28. RSA 594:14. 1965, 38:1. 1977, 588:11. 1983, 347:1, eff. Aug. 17, 1983.

Amendments

—1983. Rewritten to the extent that a detailed comparison would be impractical.

—1977. Rewrote the last sentence.

—1965. Inserted "in hand" following "him" and "written" preceding "summons" in the introductory clause and substituted "district (municipal) court" for "municipal court" in the body of the form.

Cross References.

Classification of crimes, see RSA 625:9.

Warrantless arrests generally, see RSA 594:10.

594:14-a. Arrest Records.

I. For the purposes of this section, an "arrest record" means a record created by law enforcement personnel to document the arrest of an individual 17 years of age or older. Arrest records are "governmental records" as defined in RSA 91-A and subject to disclosure in accordance with that chapter, with the exception noted in RSA 106-B:14.

II. Arrest records shall contain, at a minimum:

(a) The identity of the individual arrested;

(b) The identity of the arresting officer or officers unless the officer's supervisor has good cause to believe that identifying the officer would not serve the public interest;

(c) A statement as to reasons why and how the arrest was made;

(d) The alleged crime; and

(e) Whether the arrest was made pursuant to a warrant.

Source.

2012, 263:1, eff. January 1, 2013.

Notice of Arrest; Right to Advice of Counsel, etc.

594:15. Notice of Arrest.

The officer in charge of a police station to which an arrested person is brought shall immediately secure from the prisoner, if possible, the name of the parent, nearest relative, friend or attorney with whom the prisoner may desire to consult, and shall immediately notify such relative, friend or attorney of the detention of the prisoner, when possible. Notice shall be given by telephone or messenger when practicable.

Source.

1917, 92:1. PL 364:7. RL 423:7.

Cross References.
Notice of arrest to county attorney, see RSA 594:10-a.
Representation of indigent defendants in criminal cases, see RSA 604-A.

NOTES TO DECISIONS

Construction with other law
If statute governing notice of arrest is not followed when a juvenile is arrested, absence of opportunity to consult with an adult is to be given greater weight when assessing totality of circumstances surrounding juvenile's waiver of right against self-incrimination. State v. Farrell, 145 N.H. 733, 766 A.2d 1057, 2001 N.H. LEXIS 14 (2001).

Because police failed to notify parents or other interested adult with whom juvenile suspect may have wished to consult, and juvenile was interrogated while his father waited to consult with him, juvenile's Miranda waiver was rendered invalid and his statements to police were required to be suppressed on remand for retrial. State v. Farrell, 145 N.H. 733, 766 A.2d 1057, 2001 N.H. LEXIS 14 (2001).

Cited:
Cited in State v. George, 93 N.H. 408, 43 A.2d 256, 1945 N.H. LEXIS 148 (1945); Nelson v. Hancock, 239 F. Supp. 857, 1965 U.S. Dist. LEXIS 7108 (D.N.H. 1965); Hancock v. Nelson, 363 F.2d 249, 1966 U.S. App. LEXIS 5544 (1st Cir. N.H. 1966); State v. Benoit, 126 N.H. 6, 490 A.2d 295, 1985 N.H. LEXIS 240 (1985).

594:16. Conference with Friends or Counsel.

I. The officer in charge of a police station shall permit the prisoner to confer with his attorney at all reasonable times.

II. Such officer shall establish regular visiting hours during which the prisoner shall be allowed to confer with relatives and friends.

Source.
1917, 92:1. PL 364:8. RL 423:8. RSA 594:16. 1981, 563:1, eff. Aug. 29, 1981.

Amendments
—**1981.** Rewritten to the extent that a detailed comparison would be impracticable.

NOTES TO DECISIONS

Construction with other laws
The right to consult with counsel provided for by paragraph I of this section was not violated by the denial of an opportunity for a defendant, arrested for driving while intoxicated, to contact her attorney prior to deciding whether to take or refuse to take an alcohol breath test under RSA 265:84 since this section does not confer such a specific right and the delay which would result from permitting a defendant to contact an attorney before the observation period and performance of the test could frustrate the purpose of the test and reduce its reliability and effectiveness. State v. Greene, 128 N.H. 317, 512 A.2d 429, 1986 N.H. LEXIS 276 (1986).

Cited:
Cited in State v. George, 93 N.H. 408, 43 A.2d 256, 1945 N.H. LEXIS 148 (1945); Nelson v. Hancock, 239 F. Supp. 857, 1965 U.S. Dist. LEXIS 7108 (D.N.H. 1965); Hancock v. Nelson, 363 F.2d 249, 1966 U.S. App. LEXIS 5544 (1st Cir. N.H. 1966); State v. Beaupre, 123 N.H. 155, 459 A.2d 233, 1983 N.H. LEXIS 243 (1983).

594:17. Penalty.

A person who violates the requirements of this subdivision is guilty of a misdemeanor.

Source.
1917, 92:2. PL 364:9. RL 423:9. RSA 594:17. 1977, 588:18, eff. Sept. 16, 1977.

Amendments
—**1977.** Rewritten to the extent that a detailed comparison would be impracticable.

Cross References.
Classification of crimes, see RSA 625:9.
Sentences, see RSA 651.

NOTES TO DECISIONS

Cited:
Cited in State v. Beaupre, 123 N.H. 155, 459 A.2d 233, 1983 N.H. LEXIS 243 (1983).

Release or Detention

Cross References.
Arrests generally, see RSA 594:1-a et seq.
Bail and recognizances generally, see RSA 597.
Preliminary examinations generally, see RSA 596-A.

594:18. Release of Persons Arrested Without Warrant.

[Repealed 1965, 158:2, eff. Aug. 15, 1965.]

Former section(s).
Former RSA 594:18, which was derived from 1941, 163:10 and RL 423:29, related to release of persons arrested without warrants. See now RSA 594:18-a.

594:18-a. Release of Persons Arrested Without Warrant.

When a peace officer makes an arrest without a warrant, either he or his superior officer may release the person arrested instead of taking him before a district or municipal court if satisfied either that there is no ground for making a criminal complaint against such person or that such person has been arrested for drunkenness and no further proceedings are necessary. A person released as above provided shall have no right to sue any peace officer on the ground that he was released without being brought before a court.

Source.
1965, 158:1, eff. Aug. 15, 1965.

Cross References.
Detention of persons arrested, see RSA 594:19-a, 20-a.

NOTES TO DECISIONS

Purpose
The purpose of this section is to permit the arresting officer to determine whether to charge the arrested person with a crime or to release him. State v. Hutton, 108 N.H. 279, 235 A.2d 117, 1967 N.H. LEXIS 172 (1967), overruled in part, State v. Riley, 126 N.H. 257, 490 A.2d 1362, 1985 N.H. LEXIS 292 (1985).

594:19. Detention of Person Arrested on Warrant.

[Repealed 1965, 158:2, eff. Aug. 15, 1965.]

Former section(s).
Former RSA 594:19, which was derived from CS 185:11; GS 236:10; GL 254:10; PS 250:10; PL 364:13; and RL 423:13, related to detention of persons arrested. See now RSA 594:19-a.

594:19-a. Detention of Person Arrested; With Warrant; Without Warrant.

I. Every officer making an arrest or holding a person in custody under a warrant shall take the accused to the court as directed in the warrant without unreasonable delay.

II. An officer arresting a person without a warrant shall without unreasonable delay take such person to the court to answer a complaint for the offense.

Source.
1965, 158:1, eff. Aug. 15, 1965. 1998, 297:6, eff. Jan. 1, 1999.

Amendments
—**1998.** Rewritten to the extent that a detailed comparison would be impracticable.

Cross References.
Arrest without warrant of person violating restraining order, see RSA 458:16.
Release without court appearance of persons arrested without warrant, see RSA 594:18-a.

594:20. Detention, Night Arrest.

[Repealed 1965, 158:2, eff. Aug. 15, 1965.]

Former section(s).
Former RSA 594:20, which was derived from RS 114:5; CS 120:7; GS 236:4; GL 254:4; PS 250:4; PL 364:4; and RL 423:4, related to detention of persons arrested at night. See now RSA 594:20-a.

594:20-a. Place and Time of Detention.

I. When a person is arrested with or without a warrant he or she may be committed to a county correctional facility, to a police station or other place provided for the detention of offenders, or otherwise detained in custody; provided, however, that he or she shall be taken before a district court without unreasonable delay, but not exceeding 24 hours, Saturdays, Sundays, and holidays excepted, to answer for the offense.

II. Notwithstanding the provisions of paragraph I, defendants detained under RSA 173-B shall have timely access to a bail hearing by telephonic means or otherwise as determined by the district court.

Source.
1965, 158:1. 1988, 89:22, eff. June 17, 1988. 2004, 119:1, eff. May 17, 2004.

Amendments
—**2004.** Designated the existing provisions of the section as par. I, inserted "or she" following "he" in two places, deleted "or municipal" following "a district" and inserted "Saturdays" preceding "Sundays" in that paragraph and added par. II.

—**1988.** Substituted "a county correctional facility" for "jail, to a house of correction" preceding "to a police station or other place".

Cross References.
Detention of person arrested generally, see RSA 594:19-a.

NOTES TO DECISIONS

Cited:
Cited in State v. Hughes, 135 N.H. 413, 605 A.2d 1062, 1992 N.H. LEXIS 51 (1992).

ANNOTATIONS UNDER FORMER RSA 594:20, 594:23

1. Application of section
2. Video teleconference

1. Application of section
The provisions of this section, requiring arraignment of an accused within 24 hours after his arrest, did not apply where the accused was seriously wounded and in a hospital. State v. George, 93 N.H. 408, 43 A.2d 256, 1945 N.H. LEXIS 148 (1945). (Decided under former RSA 594:20.)

2. Video teleconference
The statute permits arraignments and bail hearings conducted by video teleconference. Larose v. Superintendent, Hillsborough County Correction Admin., 142 N.H. 364, 702 A.2d 326, 1997 N.H. LEXIS 104 (1997).
Arraignments and bail hearings conducted by video teleconference did not violate due process since such a procedure does not pose a greater risk of erroneous deprivation of liberty, saves the state thousands of dollars in transportation and security fees, and decreases the likelihood of violence during such proceedings. Larose v. Superintendent, Hillsborough County Correction Admin., 142 N.H. 364, 702 A.2d 326, 1997 N.H. LEXIS 104 (1997).

594:21. Authority of Jailer.

[Repealed 1965, 158:2, eff. Aug. 15, 1965.]

Former section(s).
Former RSA 594:21, which was derived from RS 114:6; CS 120:8; GS 236:5; GL 254:5; PS 250:5; PL 364:5; and RL 423:5, related to the authority of the jailer to detain a prisoner. See now RSA 594:21-a.

594:21-a. Authority of Superintendent.

The request of the officer making the arrest shall be sufficient authority if accompanied by an arrest report, uniform report of crime form, or other substantiating documentation, for the superintendent of the county department of corrections, for the police station, or for any other officer or person, for keeping the person arrested in custody pursuant to RSA 594:20-a.

Source.
1965, 158:1. 1988, 89:23, eff. June 17, 1988.

Amendments
—**1988.** Rewritten to the extent that a detailed comparison would be impracticable.

594:22, 594:23.

[Repealed 1965, 158:2, eff. Aug. 15, 1965.]

Former section(s).
Former RSA 594:22 and 594:23, which were derived from 1852, 1282:11; CS 185:11; GS 236:6; GL 254:6; PS 250:6; PL 364:6; 1941,

163:11; and RL 423:6, 30, related to bringing persons arrested before the court. See now RSA 594:19-a and 594:20-a.

Armed Guards

594:24, 594:25.

[Repealed 1977, 588:32, eff. Sept. 16, 1977.]

Former section(s).

Former RSA 594:24 and 594:25, which were derived from 1917, 166:1; PL 364:18, 19; and RL 423:18, 19, related to the authority and duties of public officers detailed as armed guards of property.

CHAPTER 595-A

SEARCH WARRANTS

SECTION
595-A:1.   Issuance of Search Warrants; Purposes.
595-A:2.   Requisites of Warrant.
595-A:3.   Form of Warrant.
595-A:4.   Affidavit in Support of Application for Warrant; Contents and Form.
595-A:4-a.   Electronic Communication and Signature.
595-A:5.   Receipt, Inventory, and Return.
595-A:6.   Seizure, Custody and Disposition of Articles; Exceptions.
595-A:7.   Time for Return of Warrant.
595-A:8.   Assistants.
595-A:9.   Scope and Definition.

Cross References.

Administrative inspection warrants, see RSA 595-B.

Right to be free from unreasonable searches and seizures, see New Hampshire Constitution, Part 1, Article 19.

NOTES TO DECISIONS

Effect of violations of chapter

Technical violations of this chapter do not require suppression of the items seized. State v. Brown, 125 N.H. 346, 480 A.2d 901, 1984 N.H. LEXIS 265 (1984).

Cited:

Cited in State v. Cavanaugh, 138 N.H. 193, 635 A.2d 1382, 1993 N.H. LEXIS 183 (1993).

RESEARCH REFERENCES

New Hampshire Court Rules Annotated.

Motions to suppress evidence, see Rule 94, Rules of the Superior Court, New Hampshire Court Rules Annotated.

595-A:1. Issuance of Search Warrants; Purposes.

A search warrant authorized by this chapter may be issued by any justice, associate justice or special justice of the municipal, district or superior courts to search for and seize any property which is:

I. Stolen, embezzled or fraudulently obtained;

II. Designed or intended for use or which is or has been used as the means of committing a criminal offense;

III. Contraband; or

IV. Evidence of the crime to which the probable cause upon which the search warrant is issued relates.

Source.

1969, 317:1, eff. Aug. 29, 1969.

Cross References.

Affidavit supporting application for warrant, see RSA 595-A:4.

Applicability of chapter, see RSA 595-A:9.

NOTES TO DECISIONS

1.   Medical records
2.   Search warrants

1. Medical records

Trial court did not err in requiring a hospital to turn over pursuant to a search warrant the medical records of a patient it treated following an automobile accident. Given the legislature's silence as to the treatment due privileged records sought by search warrant, the trial court's order was in accordance with the law governing search warrants. In re Search Warrant for Med. Records of C.T., 160 N.H. 214, 999 A.2d 210, 2010 N.H. LEXIS 39 (2010).

2. Search warrants

Physician-patient privilege is no less valid, and its rationale is no less important, because a magistrate has found probable cause to believe that the privileged records contain evidence of a crime. The immediacy and intrusiveness of searches, combined with the potential for irreparable injury to privilege-holders, lead the New Hampshire Supreme Court to conclude that when privileged medical records are sought by search warrant, at least a minimal level of procedural protection is required. In re Search Warrant for Med. Records of C.T., 160 N.H. 214, 999 A.2d 210, 2010 N.H. LEXIS 39 (2010).

Henceforth, any search warrant for privileged medical records shall order the hospital or medical provider to comply within a reasonable time by producing the records under seal for in camera review by the trial court; the trial court shall then determine the manner by which the patient shall be provided notice that such records were produced and shall give the patient and hospital or medical provider an opportunity to object to their disclosure. Upon objection, the State must demonstrate "essential need" for the information contained in the record, i.e., the State must prove both that the information is unavailable from another source and that there is a compelling justification for its disclosure. In re Search Warrant for Med. Records of C.T., 160 N.H. 214, 999 A.2d 210, 2010 N.H. LEXIS 39 (2010).

Cited:

Cited in State v. Sands, 123 N.H. 570, 467 A.2d 202, 1983 N.H. LEXIS 362, 37 A.L.R.4th 904 (1983).

ANNOTATIONS UNDER FORMER RSA 595:1

1.   Articles subject to seizure—Intoxicating liquors and related items
2.   —Gambling implements

1. Articles subject to seizure—Intoxicating liquors and related items

Where an officer, by virtue of a warrant which directed him to search in a certain dwelling house for liquors kept for sale and concealed there and, if found, to seize them, on the day the warrant was issued took from a wagon, in which they were being carried to another place of concealment, liquors which, when the warrant was issued, were kept for sale and concealed in the dwelling house, the seizure was lawful. State v. Whiskey, 54 N.H. 164, 1873 N.H. LEXIS 24 (1873).

A beer faucet, adapted for the illegal keeping and sale of intoxicating liquors in the place searched, was liable to seizure under this section. Collins v. Noyes, 66 N.H. 619, 27 A. 225, 1891 N.H. LEXIS 97 (1891).

2. —Gambling implements

A teletypewriter machine designed for receiving purposes only, which had no facilities for sending messages or for receiving or transmitting money or wagers, was not a gambling implement per se. State v. Teletypewriter Mach., 97 N.H. 282, 86 A.2d 333, 1952 N.H. LEXIS 11 (1952).

595-A:2. Requisites of Warrant.

Search warrants shall designate or describe the person, building, vessel, or vehicle to be searched and shall particularly describe the property or articles to be searched for. They shall be substantially in the form prescribed in RSA 595-A:3 and shall be directed to a sheriff or his deputy or to a constable or police officer, commanding him to search in the daytime, or if the warrant so directs, in the nighttime, the person, building, vessel, or vehicle where the property or articles for which he is required to search are believed to be concealed, and to bring such property or articles when found, and the persons in whose possession they are found, before any district or municipal court named therein.

Source.

1969, 317:1. 1971, 255:1, eff. Aug. 22, 1971.

Amendments

—1971. Substituted "any district or municipal court named therein" for "a court having jurisdiction" following "before" at the end of the section.

Cross References.

Execution and return of warrant, see RSA 595-A:5, 7.

NOTES TO DECISIONS

Nighttime search

The statute sets forth no specific requirement for a specific request for a nighttime search or a sufficient factual basis to justify a nighttime search. State v. Barron, 137 N.H. 29, 623 A.2d 216, 1993 N.H. LEXIS 36 (1993).

The magistrate is not required to cross out the words "the daytime," which precede the parenthetical "(or at any time of the day or night)," or to circle the parenthetical provision in order to authorize a nighttime search. Instead, the form allows for both contingencies, "daytime" and "any time of the day or night," thus requiring the issuing magistrate to strike out the nighttime language if a nighttime search is not authorized. State v. Barron, 137 N.H. 29, 623 A.2d 216, 1993 N.H. LEXIS 36 (1993).

There were sufficient facts to demonstrate the need for an immediate nighttime search where the supporting affidavit detailed the evidence that led the police to believe that the items listed in the warrant application would be in the defendant's apartment. The affidavit established that the police were searching for the body of a missing person, without knowing whether the person was dead or injured, that a neighbor reported hearing a loud confrontation in the defendant's apartment, and that an inventory search of a stolen truck driven by the defendant revealed bloodstained items and a knife. The affidavit also established that the defendant's clothing at the time of his arrest was bloodstained, that at the time of the booking procedure, the defendant had discarded two identification cards belonging to the missing person, and that the victim's vehicle had been seen in the parking lot where the defendant lived on the day the victim was reported as missing. State v. Barron, 137 N.H. 29, 623 A.2d 216, 1993 N.H. LEXIS 36 (1993).

Cited:

Cited in State v. Valenzuela, 130 N.H. 175, 536 A.2d 1252, 1987 N.H. LEXIS 302 (1987).

ANNOTATIONS UNDER FORMER RSA 595:1

Seizure of property not described in warrant

A search warrant issued upon a complaint for keeping gambling implements and authorizing a search for such implements did not authorize the seizure or forfeiture of property found upon the premises not falling within the class of gambling implements and not described in the search warrant. State v. Teletypewriter Mach., 97 N.H. 282, 86 A.2d 333, 1952 N.H. LEXIS 11 (1952).

595-A:3. Form of Warrant.

The warrant shall be in substantially the following form:

The State of New Hampshire

(County), ss. (Name) Court.

To the Sheriffs of our several counties, or their deputies, any State Police Officer, or any Constable or Police Officer of any city or town, within our said State.

Proof by affidavit (supplemented by oral statements under oath) having been made this day before (name of person authorized to issue warrant) by (names of person or persons whose affidavits have been taken) that there is probable cause for believing that (certain property has been stolen, embezzled, or fraudulently obtained; certain property is intended for use or has been used as the means of committing a crime; contraband; evidence of the crime to which the probable cause upon which the search warrant is issued relates.)

We therefore command you in the daytime (or at any time of the day or night) to make an immediate search of (identify premises) (occupied by A.B.) and (of the person of A.B.) and of any person present who may be found to have such property in his possession or under his control or to whom such property may have been delivered, for the following property:

(description of property)

and if you find any such property or any part thereof to bring it and the persons in whose possession it is found before (name of court and location).

Dated at (city or town) this .... day of ...., 19 .

Source.

1969, 317:1. 1971, 255:2, eff. Aug. 22, 1971.

Amendments

—1971. Deleted "(court having jurisdiction) at" following "found before" near the end of the form.

NOTES TO DECISIONS

Nighttime search

The magistrate is not required to either cross out the words "the daytime," which precede the parenthetical "(or at any time of the day or night)," or to circle the parenthetical provision in order to authorize a nighttime search. Instead, the form allows for both contingencies, "daytime" and "any time of the day or night," thus requiring the issuing magistrate to strike out the nighttime language if a nighttime search is not authorized. State v. Barron, 137 N.H. 29, 623 A.2d 216, 1993 N.H. LEXIS 36 (1993).

ANNOTATIONS UNDER FORMER RSA 595:1

1. Description of property to be seized
2. Description of premises to be searched

1. Description of property to be seized

In a warrant to search for liquors concealed, it was sufficient to describe them as "certain spirituous and intoxicating liquors to wit, rum, gin, brandy, whiskey, wine, alcohol, and ale." State v. Whiskey, 54 N.H. 164, 1873 N.H. LEXIS 24 (1873).

2. Description of premises to be searched

A description in a search warrant which identified with reasonable certainty the place or places to be searched was sufficient, and where the place to be searched was described as "the premises now occupied by P.M. situated in Haverhill" it was sufficient upon its face. Metcalf v. Weed, 66 N.H. 176, 19 A. 1091, 1889 N.H. LEXIS 27 (1890).

595-A:4. Affidavit in Support of Application for Warrant; Contents and Form.

A person seeking a search warrant shall appear personally before a court or justice authorized to issue search warrants in criminal cases and shall give an affidavit in substantially the form hereinafter prescribed. Such affidavit shall contain facts, information, and circumstances upon which such person relies to establish probable cause for the issuance of the warrant and such affidavit may be supplemented by oral statements under oath for the establishment of probable cause. The person issuing the warrant shall retain the affidavit and shall make notes, personally, of the substance, or arrange for a transcript, of any oral statements under oath supplementing the affidavit. The person issuing the search warrant shall deliver the affidavit and the notes or transcript within 3 days after the issuance of the warrant to the court to which the warrant is returnable. Upon the return of said warrant, the affidavit and the notes or transcript shall be attached to it and shall be filed therewith, and they shall be a public document when the warrant is returned, unless otherwise ordered by a court of record.

The affidavit in support of the application for a search warrant shall be in substantially the following form:

The State of New Hampshire
(County), ss. (Name) Court.
................................., 19 .

I, (name of applicant) being duly sworn, depose and say:

1. I am (describe position, assignment, office, etc.).
2. I have information, based upon (describe source, facts indicating reliability of source and nature of information; if based on personal knowledge, so state).

3. Based upon the foregoing reliable information (and upon my personal knowledge) there is probable cause to believe that the property hereinafter described (has been stolen, etc.) and may be found (in the possession of A.B. or any other person) at premises (identify).

4. The property for which I seek the issuance of a search warrant is the following: (here describe the property as particularly as possible).

Wherefore, I request that the court issue a warrant and order of seizure, authorizing the search of (identify premises and the persons to be searched) and directing that if such property or evidence or any part thereof be found that it be seized and brought before the court; together with such other and further relief that the court may deem proper.

....
Name.

Then personally appeared the above named .... and made oath that the foregoing affidavit by him subscribed is true.

Before me this .... day of ...., 19 .

....
Justice of the Court

Source.
1969, 317:1, eff. Aug. 29, 1969.

Cross References.
Execution and return of warrant, see RSA 595-A:5, 7.
Form of warrant, see RSA 595-A:3.
Issuance of warrants generally, see RSA 595-A:1.

NOTES TO DECISIONS

Access to court records

The public right of access to court records is not absolute, and may be overcome when a sufficiently compelling interest for nondisclosure is identified. In re State (Bowman Search Warrants), 146 N.H. 621, 781 A.2d 988, 2001 N.H. LEXIS 121 (2001).

The existence of an investigation itself will provide the overriding consideration or special circumstance, that is, a sufficiently compelling interest, that would justify preventing public access to search warrants and associated documents in an on-going, preindictment criminal investigation. In re State (Bowman Search Warrants), 146 N.H. 621, 781 A.2d 988, 2001 N.H. LEXIS 121 (2001).

In a case arising out of a complex on-going criminal investigation in which no indictments had been returned, no arrests made, and which involved a search for two individuals who disappeared, seemingly without a trace, the State satisfied its burden of proof by making a strong showing that disclosure of search warrants, applications, affidavits and returns would impede its investigation into a matter which might involve serious wrongdoing. In re State (Bowman Search Warrants), 146 N.H. 621, 781 A.2d 988, 2001 N.H. LEXIS 121 (2001).

Cited:
Cited in State v. Decoteau, 137 N.H. 106, 623 A.2d 1338, 1993 N.H. LEXIS 49 (1993).

RESEARCH REFERENCES

New Hampshire Bar Journal.
For article, "Role of Judges Response to Domestic Violence," see 35 N.H.B.J. 37 (1994).

For article, "Lex Loci: A Survey of New Hampshire Supreme Court Decisions," see 42 N.H.B.J. 67 (Sept. 2001).

595-A:4-a. Electronic Communication and Signature.

The personal appearance and authorization for a search warrant under RSA 595-A:4 may be by means of telecommunication or electronic communication, and electronic signature pursuant to RSA 294-E.

Source.
2005, 76:3, eff. January 1, 2006.

595-A:5. Receipt, Inventory, and Return.

The officer taking property under the warrant shall give to the person from whom, or from whose premises, the property was taken a copy of the warrant and a receipt for the property taken, or shall leave the copy and receipt at the place from which the property was taken. The return shall be made promptly and shall be accompanied by a written inventory of any property taken. The inventory shall be made in the presence of the applicant for the warrant and the person from whose possession or premises the property was taken, if they are present, or in the presence of at least one creditable person other than the applicant for the warrant or the person from whose possession or premises the property was taken, and shall be verified by the officer. The justice of a court of record shall upon request deliver a copy of the inventory to the person from whom or from whose premises the property was taken and to the applicant for the warrant. The justice of a court of record shall attach to the warrant a copy of the return, inventory and all other papers in connection therewith and shall file them with the clerk of the court to which the warrant is returnable. The return shall be in substantially the following form:

Return

I received the attached search warrant on ...., 19 , and have executed it as follows:

On ...., 19 , at .... o'clock .... M, I searched (the person) (the premises) described in the warrant and I left a copy of the warrant with (name of person searched or owner) at (the place of search) together with a receipt for the items seized.

The following is an inventory of property taken pursuant to the warrant:

....
....
....
....

This inventory was made in the presence of .... and ....

I swear that this inventory is a true and detailed account of all the property taken by me on the warrant

....

Subscribed and sworn to and returned before me this .... day of ...., 19 .

....
Justice of the Court

Source.
1969, 317:1. 1971, 255:3, eff. Aug. 22, 1971.

Amendments
—1971. Substituted "court to which the warrant is returnable" for "court of record having jurisdiction" in the fifth sentence.

Cross References.
Time for return of warrant, see RSA 595-A:7.

NOTES TO DECISIONS

1. Issuance of receipt for property seized
2. Verification of inventory of property seized
3. Possession of warrant

1. Issuance of receipt for property seized
The failure of police officers to give a receipt for seized items at the scene of the search does not require that the evidence seized be suppressed. State v. Saide, 114 N.H. 735, 329 A.2d 148, 1974 N.H. LEXIS 362 (1974).

2. Verification of inventory of property seized
This section does not mandate that the person verifying the inventory be an individual different from the applicant. State v. Sands, 123 N.H. 570, 467 A.2d 202, 1983 N.H. LEXIS 362, 37 A.L.R.4th 904 (1983).

The fact that the same person had both applied for a search warrant and verified the inventory did not require suppression of the documents seized since this section does not mandate that the person verifying the inventory be an individual different from the applicant. State v. Sands, 123 N.H. 570, 467 A.2d 202, 1983 N.H. LEXIS 362, 37 A.L.R.4th 904 (1983).

3. Possession of warrant
Police need not have a warrant physically in hand upon commencing a search authorized by that warrant. State v. Cavanaugh, 138 N.H. 193, 635 A.2d 1382, 1993 N.H. LEXIS 183 (1993).

Cited:
Cited in State v. Tucker, 133 N.H. 204, 575 A.2d 810, 1990 N.H. LEXIS 61 (1990).

ANNOTATIONS UNDER FORMER RSA 595:3

1. Requirement of inventory
2. Amendment of return

1. Requirement of inventory
A search warrant was to require the officer to make return of his proceeding thereon with an inventory. Hussey v. Davis, 58 N.H. 317, 1878 N.H. LEXIS 48 (1878).

2. Amendment of return
Where justice required it, a defective return of an officer's proceedings under a search warrant could be amended to show a legal search and seizure. State v. Spirituous Liquors, 75 N.H. 273, 73 A. 168, 73 A. 169, 1909 N.H. LEXIS 30 (1909).

595-A:6. Seizure, Custody and Disposition of Articles; Exceptions.

If an officer in the execution of a search warrant,

or by some other authorized method, finds property or articles he is empowered to take, he shall seize and safely keep them under the direction of the court or justice so long as necessary to permit them to be produced or used as evidence in any trial. Upon application by a prosecutor, defendant, or civil claimants, the court, prior to trial or upon an appeal after trial, shall, upon notice to a defendant and hearing, and except for good cause shown, order returned to the rightful owners any stolen, embezzled or fraudulently obtained property, or any other property of evidential value, not constituting contraband. This section shall apply regardless of how possession of the property was obtained by the state. Photographs or other identification or analysis made of the returned property shall be admissible at trial as secondary evidence, in lieu of the originals, for all relevant purposes, including ownership. In the case of unknown, unapprehended defendants, or defendants wilfully absent from the jurisdiction, the court shall have discretion to appoint a guardian ad litem to represent the interest of such unknown or absent defendants. The judicial findings on such matters as ownership, identification, chain of possession or value made at such an evidentiary hearing for the restoration of property to the rightful owners shall thereafter be admissible at trial, to be considered with other evidence on the same issues, if any, as may be admitted before the finder of fact. All other property seized in execution of a search warrant or otherwise coming into the hands of the police shall be returned to the owner of the property, or shall be disposed of as the court or justice orders, which may include forfeiture and either sale or destruction as the public interest requires, in the discretion of the court or justice, and in accordance with due process of law. Any property, the forfeiture and disposition of which is specified in any general or special law, shall be disposed of in accordance therewith.

Source.

1969, 317:1. 1977, 320:1. 1981, 553:9. 1988, 88:3, eff. Jan. 1, 1989.

Amendments

—1988. Substituted "shall" for "may" following "or upon an appeal after trial" and inserted "and except for good cause shown" following "upon notice to a defendant and hearing" in the second sentence.

—1981. Rewritten to the extent that a detailed comparison would be impracticable.

—1977. Rewritten to the extent that a detailed comparison would be impracticable.

Chapter nullified

1988, 88:2, eff. April 18, 1988, provided that Chapter 43 of the 1988 regular legislative session, which amended RSA 595-A:6, relating to return of recovered property, shall be null and void and shall be deemed to never have taken effect.

Cross References.

Execution and return of warrant generally, see RSA 595-A:5.

NOTES TO DECISIONS

1. Standard of review of ruling on motion for return of property
2. Remedies for violations of section
3. Return of goods
4.. Required findings not made
5. Burden of proof

1. Standard of review of ruling on motion for return of property

The standard of review of trial court's order issued pursuant to this section was whether the court abused its discretion in denying the defendant's motion for the return of property seized by the state at the time of his arrest. State v. Gullick, 120 N.H. 99, 411 A.2d 1113, 1980 N.H. LEXIS 237 (1980), cert. denied, Gullick v. New Hampshire, 449 U.S. 879, 66 L. Ed. 2d 101, 101 S. Ct. 226, 1980 U.S. LEXIS 3313 (1980); State v. Hebert, 122 N.H. 1089, 453 A.2d 1310, 1982 N.H. LEXIS 526 (1982).

2. Remedies for violations of section

A violation of this section does not require the dismissal of the indictment. State v. Brown, 125 N.H. 346, 480 A.2d 901, 1984 N.H. LEXIS 265 (1984).

Since this section focuses on the owner of the items seized and provides procedures by which the owner may recover possession of the items, a violation of this section may give rise to civil liability but not criminal sanctions. State v. Brown, 125 N.H. 346, 480 A.2d 901, 1984 N.H. LEXIS 265 (1984).

3. Return of goods

RSA 595-A:6 does not require the submission of the NHJB-2055-DFS motion and affidavit by an individual seeking the return of seized evidence once ownership of the property in question has been established. State v. Pessetto, 160 N.H. 813, 8 A.3d 75, 2010 N.H. LEXIS 115 (2010).

Neither the State nor the trial court can impose requirements beyond those contained in RSA 595-A:6, and then consider the defendant's refusal to comply with them to be good cause to withhold the seized item. State v. Pessetto, 160 N.H. 813, 8 A.3d 75, 2010 N.H. LEXIS 115 (2010).

It was error when the trial court found good cause to withhold a seized firearm based upon defendant's failure to submit to a background check, without any showing beyond mere speculation by the State that he was legally disqualified from possessing the firearm. Remand was required, however, as the trial court did not have the benefit of the ruling that the State bore the burden of proof as to whether an item was contraband under RSA 595-A:6. State v. Pessetto, 160 N.H. 813, 8 A.3d 75, 2010 N.H. LEXIS 115 (2010).

Items used in defendant's trial for sale of drug paraphernalia had to be returned to defendant under RSA 595-A:6 as they were not contraband under RSA 318-B:2, II, II-a where: (1) none of the items seized were alleged to be "designed for use" with controlled substances, (2) the items were not contraband under federal law from the time they were manufactured, (3) defendant was acquitted of all pending charges, (4) the State made clear to defendant after a prior prosecution that there were six specific categories of items that it could not sell, and returned to defendant certain glass pipes and other items, and (5) the State then reversed course and prosecuted defendant for items virtually indistinguishable from many of the items returned to defendant after the first prosecution. State v. Smoke Signals Pipe & Tobacco Shop, LLC, 155 N.H. 234, 922 A.2d 634, 2007 N.H. LEXIS 53 (2007).

Trial court properly denied defendant's motion for return of property as, although possession of the compact discs did not violate RSA 352-A:2, the compact discs were either contraband per se or derivative contraband under RSA 595-A:6, and were subject to a court's disposal since defendant conceded that the compact discs were counterfeit. State v. Cohen, 154 N.H. 89, 907 A.2d 983, 2006 N.H. LEXIS 122 (2006).

Even though trial court erroneously ruled that, in order for the state to return seized goods to their rightful owner, the court must determine the goods are stolen, since this section also permits return when the goods have evidential value, trial court's order to return the good would not be disturbed, since the correct result was reached. In re Trailer & Plumbing Supplies, 133 N.H. 432, 578 A.2d 343, 1990 N.H. LEXIS 82 (1990).

4. Required findings not made

Order that remaining items seized from defendant be destroyed was vacated because the trial court failed to find that the property directly related to the acts underlying the crime in that they either influenced defendant's behavior, or were relevant to an understanding of the psychological or physical circumstances under which the crime was committed, or that returning the property to defendant would be so offensive to basic concepts of decency, or would justifiably spark outrage, disgust, and incredulity on the part of the general public that it would undermine public confidence in the criminal justice system. State v. Gero, 152 N.H. 379, 877 A.2d 201, 2005 N.H. LEXIS 104 (2005).

5. Burden of proof

State bears the burden of proof as to whether an item is contraband under RSA 595-A:6. State v. Pessetto, 160 N.H. 813, 8 A.3d 75, 2010 N.H. LEXIS 115 (2010).

Cited:

Cited in Soucy v. State, 127 N.H. 451, 506 A.2d 288, 1985 N.H. LEXIS 474 (1985); Decker v. Hillsborough County Attorney's Office, 845 F.2d 17, 1988 U.S. App. LEXIS 5395 (1st Cir. N.H. 1988); State v. Reynolds, 131 N.H. 291, 556 A.2d 298, 1988 N.H. LEXIS 128 (1988).

RESEARCH REFERENCES

New Hampshire Court Rules Annotated.

Proof of contents of writings, recordings and photographs, see Rule 1001 et seq., Rules of Evidence, New Hampshire Court Rules Annotated.

595-A:7. Time for Return of Warrant.

Every officer to whom a warrant to search is issued shall return the same to the court to which it was made returnable as soon as it has been served, and in any event not later than 7 days from the date of issuance thereof, with a return of his actions thereon.

Source.

1969, 317:1. 1971, 255:4, eff. Aug. 22, 1971.

Revision note.

At the end of the section, substituted "actions" for "doings" following "with a return of his" for purposes of clarity.

Amendments

—1971. Rewritten to the extent that a detailed comparison would be impracticable.

Cross References.

Execution and return of warrant generally, see RSA 595-A:5.

NOTES TO DECISIONS

Cited:

Cited in State v. Marcotte, 123 N.H. 245, 459 A.2d 278, 1983 N.H. LEXIS 260 (1983).

595-A:8. Assistants.

An officer executing a search warrant may take with him suitable assistants and suffer no others to be with him.

Source.

1969, 317:1, eff. Aug. 29, 1969.

595-A:9. Scope and Definition.

This chapter does not modify any act inconsistent with it regulating search, seizure and the issuance and execution of search warrants in circumstances for which special provision is made. The term "property" is used in this chapter to denote everything which is the subject of ownership.

Source.

1969, 317:1, eff. Aug. 29, 1969.

CHAPTER 597

BAIL AND RECOGNIZANCES

General Provisions

SECTION

597:1.	Release and Detention Authority Generally.
597:1-a.	Release or Detention of a Defendant Pending Sentence or Appeal.
597:1-b.	Probationers and Parolees Excepted. [Repealed.]
597:1-c.	Offenses Punishable by Life Imprisonment.
597:1-d.	Probationees and Parolees.
597:2.	Release of a Defendant Pending Trial.
597:2-a.	Ten Percent Bail Authorized. [Repealed.]
597:3.	Money Deposited.
597:4.	In Superior Court.
597:5.	When Requirable.
597:5-a.	When Requirable; Bail and Recognizances for Person Detained for Probation Violation.
597:6.	Appearance at Superior Court.
597:6-a.	Release or Detention of a Defendant Pending Trial. [Repealed.]
597:6-b.	Hearing Before a Justice. [Repealed.]
597:6-c.	Petition to Superior Court to Review Bail. [Repealed.]
597:6-d.	Release or Detention of Material Witness.
597:6-e.	Review and Appeal of Release or Detention Order.
597:7.	Commitment in Default of Recognizance.
597:7-a.	Detention and Sanctions for Default or Breach of Conditions.
597:7-b.	Bail Agents and Recovery Agents; Certification and Registration; Notification to Local Law Enforcement Required.
597:8.	Subsequent Bail.
597:9.	Copies, Subsequent Bail.
597:10.	Copies, on Appeal.
597:11.	Copies, Binding Over.
597:12.	Penalty.
597:13.	Accepting Insufficient Bail, etc.
597:14.	Minors.
597:14-a.	Failure to Appear; Punishment. [Repealed.]
597:14-b.	Penalty for Offense Committed While on Release.

Bail Commissioners

597:15.	Superior Court.
597:15-a.	Circuit Court.
597:15-b.	Judicial Branch Family Division. [Repealed.]
597:16.	Municipal Courts. [Repealed.]
597:17.	Term.
597:18.	Powers.
597:18-a.	Educational Requirements for Bail Commissioners.
597:19.	Returns.
597:20.	Fees.
597:21.	Bail on Sunday.

Recognizances of Witnesses

| 597:22. | Recognizances After Arrest. |
| 597:23. | Commitment in Default of Recognizance. |

Form of Recognizance

SECTION
597:24.   To the State; Sureties.
597:25.   Condition.
597:26.   Variations.

Discharge of Bail

597:27.   Surrender, in Court.
597:28.   Surrender, to Jailer.
597:29.   Jailer's Authority; New Bail.
597:30.   Excusing Surrender.

Forfeitures of Recognizances and Actions Thereon

597:31.   Declaration of Forfeiture.
597:32.   Striking Off Default.
597:33.   Judgment.
597:34.   Venue.
597:35.   Defective Records, etc.
597:36.   Declaration.
597:37.   Bench Warrants.
597:38.   Forfeit of Recognizance.
597:38-a. Default Fees.
597:38-b. Collection of Forfeitures; Motor Vehicles.

Discharge of Prisoner Unable to Procure Bail

597:39.   Procedure.

Recognizances Upon Arrest for Offense Committed in Another County

597:40.   Recognizance for Appearance in Superior Court.
597:41.   Recognizance for Appearance Before Court or Justice Named in Warrant.
597:42.   Return of Recognizance, etc.

Cross References.
Bail jumping, see RSA 642:8.
Excessive bail as grounds for writ of habeas corpus, see RSA 534:6.
Extradition proceedings, see RSA 612.
Fixing of bail in habeas corpus proceedings, see RSA 534:23.
Peace bonds, see RSA 608.
Preliminary examinations, see RSA 596-A.
Professional bondsmen, see RSA 598-A.
Prohibition against excessive bail, see New Hampshire Constitution, Part 1, Article 33.
Release or detention upon arrest generally, see RSA 594:18-a et seq.

NOTES TO DECISIONS

Liability for bail decisions
RSA 597:1 et seq. placed the power to set bail with the courts and individuals appointed as bail commissioners by the courts, and while a police officer's lack of statutory authority to set bail was insufficient to shield the officer from liability under 42 U.S.C.S. § 1983 if he helped to shape, and exercised significant influence over, the bail decision, where the record showed that defendant police chief did not actively participate in plaintiff arrestee's bail proceedings, did not initiate bail activity, and did not control or limit sources of information about the arrestee, the arrestee's § 1983 claim, which alleged a violation of the right to be free from excessive bail under the Eighth Amendment and the right to due process under the Fourteenth Amendment, failed. Briand v. Strout, 2003 U.S. Dist. LEXIS 8966 (D.N.H. 2003).

Cited:
Cited in State v. Gagne, 129 N.H. 93, 523 A.2d 76, 1986 N.H. LEXIS 380 (1986); State v. Hall, 131 N.H. 634, 557 A.2d 997, 1989 N.H. LEXIS 30 (1989); Briand v. Morin, 2003 U.S. Dist. LEXIS 2710 (D.N.H. 2003).

RESEARCH REFERENCES

New Hampshire Court Rules Annotated.
Bail in civil contempt proceedings, see Rule 1.21, Rules of the District and Municipal Courts and Rules 142, 143, Rules of the Superior Court, New Hampshire Court Rules Annotated.
Bail in criminal contempt proceedings, see Rule 95, Rules of the Superior Court, New Hampshire Court Rules Annotated.
Procedure for taking and forfeiture of bail, see Rule 2.2, Rules of the District and Municipal Courts, New Hampshire Court Rules Annotated.

General Provisions

Cross References.
Discharge of prisoner unable to procure bail, see RSA 597:39.
Release upon recognizance of persons arrested for offenses committed outside county in which accused arrested, see RSA 597:40 et seq.

597:1. Release and Detention Authority Generally.

Except as provided in RSA 597:1-a, 597:1-c, or 597:1-d, all persons arrested for an offense shall be eligible to be released pending judicial proceedings upon compliance with the provisions of this chapter.

Source.
GS 240:18. GL 258:18. PS 252:12. PL 366:13. RL 425:13. RSA 597:1. 1969, 78:1. 1974, 34:4. 1988, 110:1. 1989; 386:1. 1993, 258:1, eff. Aug. 14, 1993.

Amendments
—1993. Rewritten to the extent that a detailed comparison would be impracticable.

—1989. Inserted "eligible to be" preceding "released", deleted "or detained" thereafter, and substituted "upon compliance with" for "pursuant to" following "proceedings" in the second sentence.

—1988. Rewritten to the extent that a detailed comparison would be impracticable.

—1974. Substituted "offenses punishable by death or for murder in the first degree" for "capital offenses".

—1969. Rewritten to the extent that a detailed comparison would be impracticable.

Cross References.
Arrest and detention of parolees generally, see RSA 651-A:15-a.
Arrest and detention of probationers and parolees, see RSA 504-A:4, 5.
Classification of crimes generally, see RSA 625:9.
Determination of bail in cases involving murder, see RSA 597:4.
Homicide generally, see RSA 630.
Release of persons appealing convictions, see RSA 597:1-a.
Rights of persons charged with capital offenses and first degree murder generally, see RSA 604:1.
Taking of recognizance generally, see RSA 597:5.

NOTES TO DECISIONS

Cited:
Cited in Ex parte Thaw, 209 F. 954, 1913 U.S. Dist. LEXIS 1170 (D.N.H. 1913); State v. Ricciardi, 81 N.H. 223, 123 A. 606, 1924 N.H. LEXIS 10, 34 A.L.R. 609 (1924); State v. Small, 99 N.H. 349, 111 A.2d 201, 1955 N.H. LEXIS 22 (1955); State v. Williams, 115 N.H. 437, 343 A.2d 29, 1975 N.H. LEXIS 331 (1975); Thompson v. Sanborn, 568 F. Supp. 385, 1983 U.S. Dist. LEXIS 15256 (D.N.H. 1983).

597:1-a. Release or Detention of a Defendant Pending Sentence or Appeal.

I. After conviction for an offense punishable by death or, by a term of life imprisonment without possibility of parole, or for aggravated felonious sexual assault or felonious sexual assault, a defendant shall not be allowed bail.

II. Except as provided in paragraph I, the court shall order that a person who has been found guilty of a felony and who is awaiting imposition or execution of sentence be detained, unless the court finds by clear and convincing evidence that the person is not likely to flee or pose a danger to the safety of the person or to any other person or the community. If the court makes such a finding, it shall order the release of the person in accordance with the provisions of RSA 597:2.

III. (a) The court shall order that a person found guilty of a felony and sentenced to a term of imprisonment and who has made a good faith representation that he or she shall file a timely appeal be detained, unless the person establishes and the court finds:

(1) By clear and convincing evidence, taking into consideration the nature of the crime and the length of the sentence imposed, that the person is not likely to fail to appear to answer the judgment following the conclusion of the appellate proceeding, or to pose a danger to himself or herself or to any other person or the community, or to intimidate witnesses, or otherwise to interfere with the administration of justice; and

(2) By a preponderance of the evidence that the appeal will not likely be frivolous or taken merely for delay.

(b) Upon making the findings specified in subparagraph (a), the court shall order the release of the person in accordance with the provisions of RSA 597:2.

IV. Any person who has been found guilty of a misdemeanor and who is awaiting imposition or execution of sentence, or who has been sentenced to a term of imprisonment and who has filed an appeal shall, before the conclusion of the appellate proceeding, be released upon compliance with the provisions of RSA 597:2.

V. In any case where release is denied pending appeal, the court shall provide for the record the reasons for such denial.

VI. The court shall treat a defendant in a case in which an appeal has been taken by the state pursuant to the provisions of RSA 606:10, in accordance with the provisions of RSA 597:2, unless the defendant is otherwise subject to a release or a detention order.

Source.

1975, 275:1. 1985, 26:1. 1988, 110:2. 1989, 386:2. 1992, 254:12, eff. Jan. 1, 1993. 2008, 200:1, eff. June 11, 2008.

Amendments
—2008. The 2008 amendment rewrote III to the extent that a detailed comparison would be impracticable.

—1992. Paragraph I: Inserted "or for aggravated felonious sexual assault or felonious sexual assault" following "parole".

—1989. Paragraph II: Deleted "in accordance with the provisions of RSA 597:6-a, II or III" following "community" in the first sentence and substituted "RSA 597:2" for "RSA 597:6-a, II or III" following "provisions of" in the second sentence.
Paragraph III: Substituted "RSA 597:2" for "RSA 597:6-a, II or III" following "pursuant to" in the first sentence of subpar. (a) and following "provisions of" in the last sentence of the paragraph.
Paragraph IV: Added "released upon compliance with the provisions of RSA 597:2" following "proceeding, be" and deleted subpars. (a) and (b).
Paragraph VI: Substituted "RSA 597:2" for "RSA 597:6-a" preceding "unless".

—1988. Rewritten to the extent that a detailed comparison would be impracticable.

—1985. Rewritten to the extent that a detailed comparison would be impracticable.

Cross References.
Arrest and detention of parolees generally, see RSA 651-A:15-a.
Arrest and detention of probationers and parolees, see RSA 504-A:4, 5.
Classification of crimes generally, see RSA 625:9.
Detention and sanctions for default or breach of conditions, see RSA 597:7-a.
Determination of bail in cases involving murder, see RSA 597:4.
Filing of copies of complaint, etc., see RSA 597:10.
Homicide generally, see RSA 630.
Penalties for offenses committed while on release, see RSA 597:14-b.
Release of persons prior to conviction, see RSA 597:1.
Review and appeal of release or detention order, see RSA 597:6-e.
Taking of recognizance generally, see RSA 597:5.

NOTES TO DECISIONS

1. Constitutionality
2. Purpose of section
3. Granting of bail
   —Generally
4. —Burden of proof
5. —Factors considered
6. —Propriety of particular determinations

1. Constitutionality
The legislature's inclusion of felonious sexual assault among nonbailable offenses in paragraph I, while excluding other class B felonies, is not a violation of equal protection under the State Constitution. The legislature could rationally have determined that individuals convicted of felonious sexual assault constitute a special danger to the community, as distinguished from other class B felons. In re Hamel, 137 N.H. 488, 629 A.2d 802, 1993 N.H. LEXIS 111 (1993).
The application of the 1992 amendment to a defendant who committed felonious sexual assault prior to the effective date of the statute was not a violation of the state constitutional prohibition against ex post facto laws. Convicted felons have no fundamental right to post-conviction bail; therefore, the amendment did not alter

any substantial right the petitioner had prior to the amendment. In re Hamel, 137 N.H. 488, 629 A.2d 802, 1993 N.H. LEXIS 111 (1993).

2. Purpose of section

The purpose of this section is to encourage the release on bail of defendants pending appeal. State v. Seeley, 116 N.H. 57, 357 A.2d 870, 1976 N.H. LEXIS 264 (1976).

3. Granting of bail

—Generally

The granting of bail pending appeal is within the discretion of the trial court judge, though that discretion must be exercised in accordance with the legislature's intention, as expressed in this section, to strongly endorse granting bail pending appeal. State v. Marini, 117 N.H. 71, 369 A.2d 202, 1977 N.H. LEXIS 271 (1977).

The question of bail is a discretionary matter. State v. Seeley, 116 N.H. 57, 357 A.2d 870, 1976 N.H. LEXIS 264 (1976).

4. —Burden of proof

A trial court denial of bail because the defendant failed to demonstrate that granting of bail was proper and right was not improper as a matter of law. State v. Marini, 117 N.H. 71, 369 A.2d 202, 1977 N.H. LEXIS 271 (1977).

5. —Factors considered

Under paragraph III of this section, controlling bail pending appeal, length of sentence alone is not justification for denying bail; all the criteria listed must be weighed in making the determination. State v. Blum, 132 N.H. 396, 566 A.2d 1131, 1989 N.H. LEXIS 113 (1989).

For purposes of paragraph III of this section, an appeal is not "frivolous" where there exist reasonable grounds to argue that the record contains assignable error, the type of which may result in reversal; modifying rule in State v. Marini, 117 NH 71, 369 A.2d 202, 1977 N.H. LEXIS 271 (1977), by requiring the trial court, in deciding whether an appeal is frivolous, to consider the outcome of the defendant's appeal only to the extent necessary to determine whether the appeal may result in reversal. State v. Blum, 132 N.H. 396, 566 A.2d 1131, 1989 N.H. LEXIS 113 (1989).

A trial court did not err in considering, as one factor bearing on the question of bail, its opinion as to the probable outcome of the defendant's appeal and the reasons for which the appeal was taken. State v. Marini, 117 N.H. 71, 369 A.2d 202, 1977 N.H. LEXIS 271 (1977).

One factor to be considered in deciding on bail is the risk that the defendant will not appear to answer the judgment following the conclusion of the appellate proceedings. State v. Gross, 116 N.H. 527, 363 A.2d 408, 1976 N.H. LEXIS 402 (1976).

A factor to be considered in deciding upon bail is that the denial of bail pending appeal may make any appeal meaningless because the defendant may have served his sentence before his appeal can be concluded. State v. Gross, 116 N.H. 527, 363 A.2d 408, 1976 N.H. LEXIS 402 (1976).

6. —Propriety of particular determinations

When defendant received a deferred sentence, his sentence included the implied condition of good behavior, with which he was to immediately comply, the sentence began to run on the date it was imposed, so he was not awaiting the execution of his sentence, for purposes of RSA 597:1-a, IV, nor was he awaiting trial or an appeal, under RSA 597:2 and RSA 597:1-a, respectively, so his bail should have been released when he was sentenced. State v. Clark, 151 N.H. 56, 849 A.2d 143, 2004 N.H. LEXIS 86 (2004).

Since there is no reason for other than personal recognizance in a routine DWI case appealed to the supreme court by a New Hampshire resident, a requirement of $200 bail pending appeal, set by a trial court without hearing, was excessive. State v. Wheeler, 120 N.H. 496, 416 A.2d 1384, 1980 N.H. LEXIS 331 (1980), overruled in part, State v. Landry, 131 N.H. 65, 550 A.2d 94, 1988 N.H. LEXIS 83 (1988).

A trial court's finding that, in view of the crime charged, the conviction, and the sentence imposed, a defendant was much more likely to attempt escape or not to appear if liberated on bail than he was before sentencing, did not substantiate this section's requirement, as a basis for denying bail, that there be substantial risk that

the defendant will not appear to answer the judgment following the conclusion of the appellate proceedings. State v. Marini, 117 N.H. 71, 369 A.2d 202, 1977 N.H. LEXIS 271 (1977).

Where nearly all of the defendants whose appeals were pending following conviction for criminal contempt were residents of New Hampshire and the others had close affiliations with the state, most of the defendants owned property or worked or attended school in the state, and all of the defendants except one had no criminal record, denial of bail pending their appeals was improper. State v. Adams, 116 N.H. 529, 363 A.2d 410, 1976 N.H. LEXIS 403 (1976).

Denial of bail pending appeal by defendant, who had been convicted for criminal contempt and sentenced to six months imprisonment, three months suspended; who was a married resident of the state; who was a member of the New Hampshire bar, employed by New Hampshire Legal Assistance on a regular basis; and who had no criminal record, was improper, particularly since denial of bail pending appeal could make any appeal meaningless because the defendant might serve his sentence before the appeal could be concluded. State v. Gross, 116 N.H. 527, 363 A.2d 408, 1976 N.H. LEXIS 402 (1976).

A finding that there was substantial risk that if a defendant was released on bail he would, once again, interfere with the administration of justice, as he had done previously by attempting to break and enter a county administration building and carry away evidence, was sufficient to deny bail pending appeal. State v. Seeley, 116 N.H. 57, 357 A.2d 870, 1976 N.H. LEXIS 264 (1976).

Cited:

Cited in State v. Moccia, 120 N.H. 298, 414 A.2d 1275, 1980 N.H. LEXIS 283 (1980); State v. Aikens, 135 N.H. 569, 607 A.2d 948, 1992 N.H. LEXIS 78 (1992); State v. Cook, 135 N.H. 702, 609 A.2d 742, 1992 N.H. LEXIS 107 (1992); State v. Taylor, 139 N.H. 96, 649 A.2d 375, 1994 N.H. LEXIS 116 (1994).

597:1-b. Probationers and Parolees Excepted.

[Repealed 1988, 110:12, I, eff. June 17, 1988.]

Former section(s).
Former RSA 597:1-b, which was derived from 1986, 156:2, provided for special bail procedures for probationers and parolees.

597:1-c. Offenses Punishable by Life Imprisonment.

Any person arrested for an offense punishable by up to life in prison, where the proof is evident or the presumption great, shall not be allowed bail.

Source.
1993, 258:2, eff. Aug. 14, 1993. 2006, 327:14, eff. January 1, 2007.

Amendments
—2006. Substituted "Offenses Punishable By Life Imprisonment" for "Capital Offenses and Murder in the First Degree" in the title and substituted "up to life in prison" for "death or murder in the first degree" in the sentence.

NOTES TO DECISIONS

1. Constitutionality
2. Construction
3. Burden of proof
4. Right to counsel

1. Constitutionality

RSA 597:1-c did not violate due process under the federal or state constitutions. It was not necessary for there to be an individualized inquiry into a defendant's dangerousness or risk of flight for a statute to pass constitutional muster; moreover, both risk of flight and dangerousness were inherent in the statute's "proof is evident" analysis. State v. Furgal, 161 N.H. 206, 13 A.3d 272, 2010 N.H. LEXIS 142 (2010).

2. Construction

Plain language of RSA 597:1-c does not permit the trial court to consider factors such as flight risk or dangerousness. The "proof is evident" analysis focuses solely upon the strength of the evidence against a defendant charged with a crime punishable by life in prison. State v. Furgal, 161 N.H. 206, 13 A.3d 272, 2010 N.H. LEXIS 142 (2010).

Plain language of RSA 597:1-c does not shift the burden of proof to the defendant once the State establishes that the proof is evident or the presumption great. The plain language of the statute provides that once the State meets its burden, the defendant "shall not be allowed bail." State v. Furgal, 161 N.H. 206, 13 A.3d 272, 2010 N.H. LEXIS 142 (2010).

3. Burden of proof

Clear and convincing evidence standard is the standard for determining whether or not the State has shown that the proof is evident or the presumption great under RSA 597:1-c State v. Furgal, 161 N.H. 206, 13 A.3d 272, 2010 N.H. LEXIS 142 (2010).

4. Right to counsel

At a minimum a defendant has a right to counsel at a hearing under RSA 597:1-c. A criminal defendant's initial appearance before a judicial officer, where he learns the charge against him and his liberty is subject to restriction, marks the start of adversary judicial proceedings that trigger attachment of the Sixth Amendment right to counsel. State v. Furgal, 161 N.H. 206, 13 A.3d 272, 2010 N.H. LEXIS 142 (2010).

597:1-d. Probationees and Parolees.

I. If there is a judicial finding of probable cause to believe that a person has committed a violation of RSA 630, RSA 631, RSA 632-A:2-4 or RSA 633:1-3 from an arrest warrant affidavit or an affidavit issued pursuant to district court administrative order number 91-03 or any other district court administrative order which supercedes it and the person is on probation or parole for a conviction of a violent crime listed in RSA 651:4-a or a substantially similar crime in any state or federal court in this or any other state, the District of Columbia, the Commonwealth of Puerto Rico, or any territory or possession of the United States, it is presumed that release on bail and imposition of any condition or set of conditions listed in RSA 597:2 will not reasonably assure the appearance of the person as required and will endanger the safety of the person or of any other person or the community.

II. The court shall not release such person on bail unless the court finds by a preponderance of the evidence that some condition or set of conditions found in RSA 597:2 will assure the person's appearance and assure that release will not pose a danger to the safety of the person or of any person or the community.

III. Such person shall be detained without bail pending a bail hearing before the court to be held as soon after arraignment as possible but in no event later than 72 hours after arraignment. At such hearing, the arresting agency shall present, and the court shall consider, all relevant records or other documentation concerning the arrested person's parole or probation, as well as the offense for which the person is on parole or probation.

Source.
1993, 258:2, eff. Aug. 14, 1993.

597:2. Release of a Defendant Pending Trial.

I. Upon the appearance before the court or justice of a person charged with an offense, the court or justice shall issue an order that, pending arraignment or trial, the person be:

(a) Released on his personal recognizance or upon execution of an unsecured appearance bond, pursuant to the provisions of paragraph II;

(b) Released on a condition or combination of conditions pursuant to the provisions of paragraph III; or

(c) Temporarily detained to permit revocation of conditional release pursuant to the provisions of paragraph V.

I-a. Except as provided in RSA 597:1-d, a person charged with a probation violation shall be entitled to a bail hearing. The court shall issue an order that, pending a probation violation hearing, the person be:

(a) Released on his or her personal recognizance or upon execution of an unsecured appearance bond, pursuant to the provisions of paragraph II;

(b) Released on a condition or combination of conditions pursuant to the provisions of paragraph III; or

(c) Detained.

II. The court or justice shall order the prearraignment or pretrial release of the person on his or her personal recognizance, or upon execution of an unsecured appearance bond in an amount specified by the court, subject to the condition that the person not commit a crime during the period of his or her release, and subject to such further condition or combination of conditions that the court may require, unless the court determines that such release will not reasonably assure the appearance of the person as required or will endanger the safety of the person or of any other person or the community. The court may also consider as a factor in its determination under this paragraph or paragraph III that a person who is detained as a result of his or her inability to meet the required conditions or post the required bond is the parent and sole caretaker of a child and whether, as a result, such child would become the responsibility of the division of children, youth, and families.

III. If the court or justice determines that the release described in paragraph II will not reasonably assure the appearance of the person as required or, as described in paragraph II or VI, will endanger the safety of the person or of any other person or the community, he shall issue an order that includes the following conditions:

(a) The condition that the person not commit a crime during the period of release; and

(b) Such further condition or combination of conditions that he determines will reasonably assure the appearance of the person as required and the safety of the person or of any other person or the community, which may include the condition that the person:

(1) Execute an agreement to forfeit, upon failing to appear within 45 days of the date required, such designated property, including money, as is reasonably necessary to assure the appearance of the person as required, and post with the court such indicia of ownership of the property or such percentage of the money as the court or justice may specify;

(2) Furnish bail for his appearance by recognizance with sufficient sureties or by deposit of moneys equal to the amount of the bail required as the court or justice may direct; and

(3) Satisfy any other condition that is reasonably necessary to assure the appearance of the person as required and to assure the safety of the person or of any other person or the community. In considering the conditions of release described in subparagraph III(b)(1) or III(b)(2), the court may upon its own motion, or shall upon the motion of the state, conduct an inquiry into the source of the property to be designated for potential forfeiture or offered as collateral to secure a bond, and shall decline to accept the designation, or the use as collateral, of property that because of its source will not reasonably assure the appearance of the person as required.

III-a. If a person is charged with any of the offenses listed in RSA 173-B:1, I or with violation of a protective order issued under RSA 458:16, III or RSA 173-B, the court or justice may order preventive detention without bail, or, in the alternative, restrictive conditions including but not limited to electronic monitoring and supervision, if there is clear and convincing evidence that the person poses a danger to another. The court or justice may consider, but shall not be limited to considering, any of the following conduct as evidence of posing a danger:

(a) Threats of suicide.

(b) Acute depression.

(c) History of violating protective orders.

(d) Possessing or attempting to possess a deadly weapon in violation of an order.

(e) Death threats or threats of possessiveness toward another.

(f) Stalking, as defined in RSA 633:3-a.

(g) Cruelty to or violence directed toward pets.

III-b. A no-contact provision contained in any bail order shall not be construed to:

(a) Prevent counsel for the defendant to have contact with counsel for any of the individuals protected by such provision; or

(b) Prevent the parties, if the defendant and one of the protected individuals are parties in a domestic violence or marital matter, from attending court hearings scheduled in such matters or exchanging copies of legal pleadings filed in court in such matters.

IV. In a release order issued pursuant to the provisions of this section, the court or justice shall include a written statement that sets forth:

(a) All of the conditions to which the release is subject, in a manner sufficiently clear and specific to serve as a guide for the person's conduct; and

(b) The provisions of RSA 641:5, relative to intimidation of witnesses and informants.

V. A person charged with an offense who is, and was at the time the offense was committed, on

(a) Release pending trial for a felony or misdemeanor under federal or state law;

(b) Release pending imposition or execution of sentence, appeal of sentence or conviction, or completion of sentence, for any offense under federal or state law; or

(c) Probation or parole for any offense under federal or state law, except as provided in RSA 597:1-d, III may be detained for a period of not more than 72 hours from the time of his arrest, excluding Saturdays, Sundays and holidays. The law enforcement agency making the arrest shall notify the appropriate court, probation or parole official, or federal, state or local law enforcement official. Upon such notice the court shall also direct the clerk to notify by telephone the division of field services, department of corrections, of the pending bail hearing. If the official fails or declines to take the person into custody during that period, the person shall be treated in accordance with the provisions of law governing release pending trial. Probationers and parolees who are arrested and fail to advise their supervisory probation officer or parole officer in accordance with the conditions of probations and parole may be subject to arrest and detention as probation and parole violators.

VI. Notwithstanding any law to the contrary, upon the appearance of a person charged with a class B misdemeanor, the court or justice shall issue an order that, pending arraignment, the person be released on his personal recognizance, unless the court determines that such release will endanger the safety of the person or of any other person or the community. The court shall appoint an attorney to represent any indigent person charged with a class B misdemeanor denied release for the purpose of representing such person at any detention hearing.

Source.

1903, 28:1. 1919, 49:1. PL 366:14. RL 425:14. RSA 597:2. 1969, 78:2. 1989, 386:3. 1992, 269:3, 4. 1993, 258:3, eff. Aug. 14, 1993. 1999, 229:1, eff. Jan. 1, 2000. 2005, 230:1, eff. Jan. 1, 2006. 2006, 214:3, eff. July 31, 2006. 2009, 91:1, eff. August 11, 2009. 2011, 236:2, eff. September 3, 2011.

Amendments

—**2011.** The 2011 amendment added "within 45 days of the date" in III(b)(1) and made a stylistic change.

—**2009.** The 2009 amendment added the second sentence of II and made stylistic changes.

—**2006.** Paragraph III-b: Added.

—**2005.** Paragraph I-a: Added.

—1999. Paragraph III-a: Added.

—1993. Paragraph V(c): Rewrote the former first sentence as the first and second sentences and added the third sentence.

—1992. Paragraph III: Inserted "as described in paragraph II or VI" preceding "will endanger" in the introductory paragraph. Paragraph VI: Added.

—1989. Rewritten to the extent that a detailed comparison would be impracticable.

—1969. Inserted "personal recognizance" preceding "recognizance with sufficient sureties" and added "as the court or justice may direct" following "amount of bail required" in the first sentence.

Applicability of 1992 amendment.
1992, 269:21, eff. July 1, 1992, provided that the act, which amended this section and RSA 502-A:27-d, 599:1, 625:9, 634:2, 635:5, 637:11, 638:1, 638:6, 642:8, 644:11, 644:12, 645:3, 651:2, and 651:5, shall apply to offenses committed on or after July 1, 1992.

Cross References.
Arrest and detention of parolees generally, see RSA 651-A:15-a.
Detention and sanctions for default or breach of conditions, see RSA 597:7-a.
Form of recognizances generally, see RSA 597:24 et seq.
Penalties for offenses committed while on release, see RSA 597:14-b.
Probationers and parolees generally, see RSA 504-A.
Release or detention of defendant pending sentence or appeal, see RSA 597:1-a.
Release or detention of material witnesses, see RSA 597:6-d.
Review and appeal of release or detention order, see RSA 597:6-e.

NOTES TO DECISIONS
1. Notification of parole officer
2. Discharge of bail

1. Notification of parole officer
Subsection V requires a law enforcement agency to notify a parole official of the arrest of a parolee only if the court decides to detain the parolee. Goss v. City of Manchester, 140 N.H. 449, 669 A.2d 785, 1995 N.H. LEXIS 169 (1995).

Where a parolee was released on personal recognizance after his arrest, subsection V did not apply, and the police were not obligated to inform the parolee's parole officer of his arrest. Goss v. City of Manchester, 140 N.H. 449, 669 A.2d 785, 1995 N.H. LEXIS 169 (1995).

Where a parolee was released on personal recognizance after his arrest, the decision whether to notify his parole officer remained a discretionary one and was entitled to discretionary immunity. Goss v. City of Manchester, 140 N.H. 449, 669 A.2d 785, 1995 N.H. LEXIS 169 (1995).

2. Discharge of bail
When defendant received a deferred sentence, his sentence included the implied condition of good behavior, with which he was to immediately comply, the sentence began to run on the date it was imposed, so he was not awaiting the execution of his sentence, for purposes of RSA 597:1-a, IV, nor was he awaiting trial or an appeal, under RSA 597:2 and RSA 597:1-a, respectively, so his bail should have been released when he was sentenced. State v. Clark, 151 N.H. 56, 849 A.2d 143, 2004 N.H. LEXIS 86 (2004).

597:2-a. Ten Percent Bail Authorized.

[Repealed 1988, 110:12, II, eff. June 17, 1988.]

Former section(s).
Former RSA 597:2-a which was derived from 1983, 382:12, related to acceptance of deposit in escrow of ten percent of bail.

597:3. Money Deposited.

All money deposited for bail shall be held for the use of the state until the clerk of the superior court where the bail is deposited shall certify that no liability exists against the bail.

Source.
1903, 28:2. PL 366:15. RL 425:15. RSA 597:3. 1983, 383:60, eff. Jan. 1, 1984.

Amendments
—1983. Substituted "state" for "county" following "use of the" and inserted "where the bail is deposited" following "superior court".

597:4. In Superior Court.

If any person is charged with murder, the superior court or any justice thereof, upon application and notice to the attorney general or county attorney, and examination of such evidence as may be laid before them, may determine the amount of the bail, and take the recognizance required or authorize the clerk or any suitable justice to take it.

Source.
GS 240:19. GL 258:19. PS 252:13. PL 366:16. RL 425:16. RSA 597:4. 1969, 78:3. 1973, 370:20, eff. Nov. 1, 1973.

Amendments
—1973. Substituted "murder" for "an offense punishable by death, or imprisonment for life or for twenty years or upward" and deleted "may release said person on personal recognizance or" preceding "may determine the amount of bail".

—1969. Inserted "may release said person on personal recognizance or" preceding "may determine the amount of bail".

Cross References.
Bail in cases involving murder generally, see RSA 597:1, 1-a.
Homicide generally, see RSA 630.

NOTES TO DECISIONS
Construction
The post-arraignment detention of a minor charged with felony-murder was not illegal because the district court refused to set bail; a district court has no jurisdiction to set bail in a murder case. In re E., 121 N.H. 836, 435 A.2d 833, 1981 N.H. LEXIS 421 (1981).

The fact that this section does not contain the further limitation of "and no other court or justice" does not abrogate the limitation of the power to determine bail in cases involving murder, which is exclusively in the superior court and may not be exercised by a municipal court or justice. State v. Ricciardi, 81 N.H. 223, 123 A. 606, 1924 N.H. LEXIS 10, 34 A.L.R. 609 (1924); State v. Ricciardi, 81 N.H. 223, 123 A. 606, 1924 N.H. LEXIS 10, 34 A.L.R. 609 (1924).

597:5. When Requirable.

Every court and justice may, when a person is accused of an offense in which said court or justice is authorized to receive bail, release said person on personal recognizance or require him to recognize, with sureties, to appear at a future time before himself or any other competent tribunal.

Source.
RS 222:3. CS 237:3. GS 241:1. GL 259:1. PS 252:14. PL 366:17. RL 425:17. RSA 597:5. 1969, 78:4, eff. June 3, 1969.

Amendments
—**1969.** Rewritten to the extent that a detailed comparison would be impracticable.

Cross References.
Allowances of bail generally, see RSA 597:1, 1-a.
Conditions for release on personal recognizance, see RSA 597:2.
Form of recognizances generally, see RSA 597:24 et seq.
Requirement of appearance before superior court, see RSA 597:6.

NOTES TO DECISIONS

Authority of municipal court
A municipal court had jurisdiction under this section to set bail for appearance before a municipal court in another municipality of a defendant charged with violation of the provisions of the unemployment compensation law. MacNeil v. Lathe, 102 N.H. 439, 158 A.2d 292 (1960).

Cited:
Cited in State v. Small, 99 N.H. 349, 111 A.2d 201, 1955 N.H. LEXIS 22 (1955).

597:5-a. When Requirable; Bail and Recognizances for Person Detained for Probation Violation.

Upon motion duly made, a court shall schedule a bail hearing. Every court may, when a person is accused of an offense or a probation violation in which said court is authorized to receive bail, release said person on personal recognizance or require him or her to recognize, with sureties, to appear at a future time before the court or any other competent tribunal.

Source.
2005, 230:2, eff. January 1, 2006.

597:6. Appearance at Superior Court.

If the offense is bailable by the municipal or district court, the accused shall be ordered to recognize, in accordance with the provisions of RSA 597:2, for the accused's appearance at the superior court, at the next term thereof for the county or judicial district thereof at which a grand jury is required to attend, and to stand committed until the order is complied with.

Source.
RS 222:3. CS 237:3. 1859, 2211:8. GS 240:6. 1873, 34:1. GL 258:6. PS 252:15. PL 366:18. RL 425:18. RSA 597:6. 1965, 86:2. 1988, 110:3. 1989, 386:4. 1992, 284:73, eff. July 1, 1992.

Amendments
—**1992.** Substituted "the accused's" for "his" preceding "appearance" and inserted "or judicial district thereof" following "county".

—**1989.** Substituted "RSA 597:2" for "RSA 597:6-a" following "provisions of".

—**1988.** Substituted "in accordance with the provisions of RSA 597:6-a" for "with sufficient sureties in a reasonable amount, or personal recognizance" following "shall be ordered to recognize" and made other minor stylistic changes.

—**1965.** Substituted "or district court" for "court or justice" following "municipal" and inserted "or personal recognizance" following "reasonable amount".

Cross References.
Filing of copies of complaint, etc., see RSA 597:11.

NOTES TO DECISIONS

Cited:
Cited in State v. Ricciardi, 81 N.H. 223, 123 A. 606, 1924 N.H. LEXIS 10, 34 A.L.R. 609 (1924); State v. Ricciardi, 81 N.H. 223, 123 A. 606, 1924 N.H. LEXIS 10, 34 A.L.R. 609 (1924).

597:6-a. Release or Detention of a Defendant Pending Trial.

[Repealed 1989, 386:11, eff. June 5, 1989.]

Former section(s).
Former RSA 597:6-a, which was derived from 1969, 78:5 and 1988, 110:4, related to release or detention of defendant pending trial.

NOTES TO DECISIONS

ANNOTATIONS UNDER FORMER RSA 597:6-a

Detention hearing
Under this section, no matter when the district court established conditions for a defendant's release, the state had to move for a detention hearing in the superior court within 72 hours of the defendant's arrest, if it believed that whatever conditions would be set would not reasonably assure the appearance of the person as required or the safety of the person or of any other person or the community; the state could not move for a detention hearing once the 72-hour deadline passed unless it learned of a change of circumstances or new information, in which case the state could move for a hearing at any time. State v. Hall, 131 N.H. 634, 557 A.2d 997, 1989 N.H. LEXIS 30 (1989).

During pretrial detention hearing under this section, the court should use its discretion to make meaningful defendants' statutory rights to present their own witnesses and to cross-examine state witnesses, without transforming the hearing into a full-fledged trial. State v. Hall, 131 N.H. 634, 557 A.2d 997, 1989 N.H. LEXIS 30 (1989).

Under this section, the trial court at a pretrial detention hearing generally could require a defendant to proceed by offer of proof; if unpersuaded by the defendant's proffer, however, the court had to permit the defendant to present witnesses. State v. Hall, 131 N.H. 634, 557 A.2d 997, 1989 N.H. LEXIS 30 (1989).

Where state anticipated that court might substantially reduce bail amount, and state believed that only the risk of forfeiting a significant bail amount would reasonably assure the defendant's appearance, the likelihood that bail would be reduced constituted a change in the defendant's circumstances authorizing the state to initiate pretrial detention proceedings even though post-arrest 72-hour deadline had passed. State v. Hall, 131 N.H. 634, 557 A.2d 997, 1989 N.H. LEXIS 30 (1989).

Order of pretrial detainment by superior court under this section was reversed and remanded, where superior court policy at pretrial detainment hearing limiting evidence to offers of proof was error. State v. Hall, 131 N.H. 634, 557 A.2d 997, 1989 N.H. LEXIS 30 (1989).

At pretrial detention hearing, if defendant is unsatisfied with the opportunity for cross-examination, and if the accuracy of the state's proffer is in question, a defendant can call as adverse witnesses other sources of the state's information. State v. Poulicakos, 131 N.H. 709, 559 A.2d 1341, 1989 N.H. LEXIS 44 (1989).

Witnesses may present hearsay testimony at pretrial detention hearing, since this section suspends the rules of evidence for detention hearings. State v. Poulicakos, 131 N.H. 709, 559 A.2d 1341, 1989 N.H. LEXIS 44 (1989).

At pretrial detention hearing, state need not make available all the sources of the information underlying its offer of proof. State v. Poulicakos, 131 N.H. 709, 559 A.2d 1341, 1989 N.H. LEXIS 44 (1989).

At pretrial detention hearing, if defendant raises question about the accuracy of the state's proffer, the state must supply a witness or witnesses capable of being effectively cross-examined; witness must be more than a mere reporter of information gathered by others. State v. Poulicakos, 131 N.H. 709, 559 A.2d 1341, 1989 N.H. LEXIS 44 (1989).

At pretrial detention hearing, the government may proceed by offer of proof; if the defendant raises questions about the accuracy of the state's proffer, the court can require the prosecution to present witnesses to buttress its offer of proof. State v. Poulicakos, 131 N.H. 709, 559 A.2d 1341, 1989 N.H. LEXIS 44 (1989).

At pretrial detention hearing, the state is not required to put on live witnesses when arguing for a defendant's pretrial detention; the defendant's right to cross-examination guaranteed by this section and the due process clause is satisfied by state's supplying a knowledgeable witness who can be cross-examined effectively. State v. Poulicakos, 131 N.H. 709, 559 A.2d 1341, 1989 N.H. LEXIS 44 (1989).

597:6-b. Hearing Before a Justice.

[Repealed 1988, 110:12, III, eff. June 17, 1988.]

Former section(s).
Former RSA 597:6-b, which was derived from 1975, 334:1; and 1979, 377:5, related to hearings on conditions for release.

597:6-c. Petition to Superior Court to Review Bail.

[Repealed 1988, 110:12, IV, eff. June 17, 1988.]

Former section(s).
Former RSA 597:6-c, which was derived from 1979, 377:5, related to petition for reduction of bail or release on personal recognizance.
For present provisions relating to review and appeal of release or detention order, see RSA 597:6-e.

Cross References.
Fixing of bail generally, see RSA 597:1, 1-a.

597:6-d. Release or Detention of Material Witness.

If it appears from an affidavit filed by a party that the testimony of a person is material in a criminal proceeding, and if it is shown that it may become impracticable to secure the presence of the person by subpoena, a justice of the court in which the defendant will be tried may order the arrest of the person and treat the person in accordance with the provisions of RSA 597:2. No material witness may be detained because of inability to comply with any condition of release if the trial testimony of such witness can adequately be secured by deposition, and if further detention is not necessary to prevent a failure of justice. Release of a material witness may be delayed for a reasonable period of time until the trial deposition of the witness may be taken.

Source.
1988, 110:5. 1989, 386:5, eff. June 5, 1989.

Amendments
—1989. Substituted "RSA 597:2" for "597:6-a" at the end of the first sentence.

597:6-e. Review and Appeal of Release or Detention Order.

I. If a person is ordered released by a bail commissioner, the person, or the state, shall be entitled to a hearing, if requested, on the conditions of bail before a justice within 48 hours, Sundays and holidays excepted.

II. The person or the state may file with the superior court a motion for revocation of the order or amendment of the conditions of release set by a municipal or district court, by a justice or by a bail commissioner. The motion shall be determined promptly. However, no action shall be taken on any such motion until the moving party has provided to the superior court certified copies of the complaint, affidavit, warrant, bail slip, and any other court orders relative to each charge for which a release or detention order was issued by a justice or a bail commissioner. In cases where a district court justice has made a finding, pursuant to RSA 597:2, III-a that the person poses a danger to another, the superior court shall, after notification to both parties, the police department that brought the charges in district court, and the victim, conduct a hearing and make written findings supporting any modifications and reasons for new conditions or changes from the district court order. The reviewing court shall take into consideration the district court's written findings, orders, pleadings, or transcript when making a modification.

III. The person, or the state pursuant to RSA 606:10, V, may appeal to the supreme court from a court's release or detention order, or from a decision denying revocation or amendment of such an order. The appeal shall be determined promptly.

Source.
1988, 110:5. 1989, 386:6, eff. June 5, 1989. 1999, 229:2, eff. Jan. 1, 2000. 2000, 51:1, eff. Jan. 1, 2001.

Amendments
—2000. Paragraph II: Added the third sentence.

—1999. Paragraph II: Added the third and fourth sentences.

—1989. Paragraph I: Rewritten to the extent that a detailed comparison would be impracticable.
Paragraph II: Rewritten to the extent that a detailed comparison would be impracticable.
Paragraph III: Deleted "the provisions of" preceding "RSA 606:10, V".

NOTES TO DECISIONS

Cited:
Cited in State v. Hall, 131 N.H. 634, 557 A.2d 997, 1989 N.H. LEXIS 30 (1989); State v. Poulicakos, 131 N.H. 709, 559 A.2d 1341, 1989 N.H. LEXIS 44 (1989).

597:7. Commitment in Default of Recognizance.

If the order to recognize for his appearance is not complied with in a reasonable time, the court or justice, by warrant, shall cause the accused to be committed to jail until he complies therewith.

Source.
RS 222:6. CS 237:6. GS 240:7. GL 258:7. PS 252:16. PL 366:19. RL 425:19.

Revision note.
At the beginning of the section, substituted "the order to recognize for his appearance" for "such order" for purposes of clarity.

597:7-a. Detention and Sanctions for Default or Breach of Conditions.

I. A peace officer may detain an accused until he can be brought before a justice if he has a warrant issued by a justice for default of recognizance or for breach of conditions of release or if he witnesses a breach of conditions of release. The accused shall be brought before a justice for a bail revocation hearing within 48 hours, Saturdays, Sundays and holidays excepted.

I-a. If a person violates a restraining order issued under RSA 458:16, III, or a protective order issued under RSA 633:3-a, or a temporary or permanent protective order issued under RSA 173-B by committing assault, criminal trespass, criminal mischief, or another criminal act, a peace officer shall arrest the accused, detain the accused pursuant to RSA 594:19-a, bring the accused before a justice pursuant to RSA 594:20-a, and refer the accused for prosecution. Such arrest may be made within 12 hours after a violation without a warrant upon probable cause whether or not the violation is committed in the presence of the peace officer.

II. A person who has been released pursuant to the provisions of this chapter and who has violated a condition of his release is subject to a revocation of release, an order of detention, and a prosecution for contempt of court.

III. The state may initiate a proceeding for revocation of an order of release by filing a motion with the court which ordered the release and the order of which is alleged to have been violated. The court may issue a warrant for the arrest of a person charged with violating a condition of release, and the person shall be brought before the court for a proceeding in accordance with this section. The court shall enter an order of revocation and detention if, after a hearing, the court:

(a) Finds that there is:

(1) Probable cause to believe that the person has committed a federal, state, or local crime while on release; or

(2) Clear and convincing evidence that the person has violated any other condition of release or has violated a temporary or permanent protective order by conduct indicating a potential danger to another; and

(b) Finds that:

(1) There is no condition or combination of conditions of release that will assure that the person will not flee or that the person will not pose a danger to the safety of himself or any other person or the community; or

(2) The person is unlikely to abide by any condition or combination of conditions of release.

If there is probable cause to believe that, while on release, the person committed a federal or state felony, a rebuttable presumption arises that no condition or combination of conditions will assure that the person shall not pose a danger to the safety of any other person or the community. If the court finds that there are conditions of release that shall assure that the person will not flee or pose a danger to the safety of himself or any other person or the community, and that the person will abide by such conditions, he shall treat that person in accordance with the provisions of RSA 597:2 and may amend the conditions of release accordingly.

IV. The state may commence a prosecution for contempt if the person has violated a condition of his release.

Source.
1979, 377:6. 1988, 110:6. 1989, 386:7. 1993, 303:1, eff. Jan. 1, 1994. 1999, 229:3, eff. Jan. 1, 2000. 2002, 79:3, eff. Jan. 1, 2003.

Amendments
—**2002.** Paragraph I-a: Inserted "or a protective order issued under RSA 633:3-a" following "RSA 458:16, III" in the first sentence and substituted "12 hours" for "6 hours" in the second sentence.

—**1999.** Paragraph III(a)(2): Deleted "his" preceding "release" and inserted "or has violated a temporary or permanent protective order by conduct indicating a potential danger to another" thereafter.

—**1993.** Paragraph I-a: Added.

—**1989.** Paragraph I: Substituted "48 hours" for "24 hours" and inserted "Saturdays" thereafter.
Paragraph II: Substituted "this chapter" for "RSA 597:6-a" following "provisions of".
Paragraph III: Substituted "state" for "attorney general or county attorney" preceding "may initiate" and "court which" for "justice who" preceding "ordered the release and", deleted "whose" thereafter and inserted "of which" preceding "is alleged" in the first sentence, deleted "based on the factors set forth in RSA 597:6-a, VIII" preceding "there is no condition" in the third sentence, inserted "or" preceding "state" and deleted "or local" thereafter in the fourth sentence, and inserted "himself or" following "safety of" and substituted "RSA 597:2" for "RSA 597:6-a" following "provisions of" in the fifth sentence.
Paragraph IV: Substituted "state" for "court" preceding "may commence".

—**1988.** Rewritten to the extent that a detailed comparison would be impracticable.

NOTES TO DECISIONS

1. Contempt proceedings
2. Revocation of bail pending appeal

1. Contempt proceedings
Contempt proceedings were an appropriate mechanism for punishing defendant's violation of the conditions of bail release given the purpose of criminal contempt and New Hampshire law. State v. Nott, 149 N.H. 280, 821 A.2d 976, 2003 N.H. LEXIS 38 (2003).

2. Revocation of bail pending appeal

Where defendant had not violated a condition of his release, a superior court did not have authority to revoke his bail pursuant to RSA 597:7-a; instead, defendant's bail pending appeal was properly revoked after defendant's conviction was affirmed, the effective date of which was when a mandate was issued under Sup. Ct. R. 24. State v. Gubitosi, 153 N.H. 79, 888 A.2d 1262, 2005 N.H. LEXIS 192 (2005).

597:7-b. Bail Agents and Recovery Agents; Certification and Registration; Notification to Local Law Enforcement Required.

I. In this section:

(a) "Bail agent" means any person appointed by an insurer by power of attorney to execute or countersign bail bonds for the insurer in connection with judicial proceedings and who receives a premium.

(b) "Recovery agent" means a person who meets the requirements of paragraph II of this section and who is offered or given any compensation by a bail agent or surety in exchange for assisting the bail agent or surety in apprehending or surrendering any defendant, or keeping the defendant under necessary surveillance.

II. Any person who operates as a recovery agent in this state, excluding licensed private detectives, shall be trained and certified through a program approved by the Professional Bail Agents of the United States and shall register annually with the secretary of state. The secretary of state shall issue to each registered recovery agent proof of such registration. Effective July 1, 2000, each bail agency operating in this state shall annually provide to the secretary of state proof of liability insurance coverage in the amount of $300,000 for bail recovery activities of the agency's bail agents and bail recovery agents. This proof of insurance coverage shall be provided before the agency's bail agents are licensed or relicensed, and before the agency's bail recovery agents are registered or reregistered. Bail recovery agents acting as independent contractors shall provide proof of liability insurance coverage in the amount of $300,000 to the secretary of state before registration or reregistration. Any person who operates as a recovery agent in this state without meeting such certification, insurance, and registration requirements shall be guilty of a class A misdemeanor.

III. A bail agent or recovery agent searching for a person who has violated conditions of release shall notify a municipality's chief law enforcement officer if the search is to be conducted in the municipality's jurisdiction. A bail agent or recovery agent who violates the provisions of this paragraph shall be guilty of a class A misdemeanor.

Source.
1995, 287:1, eff. Jan. 1, 1996. 1999, 299:1, eff. Jan. 1, 2000.

Amendments
—1999. Rewritten to the extent that a detailed comparison would be impracticable.

Cross References.
Classification of crimes, see RSA 625:9.
Sentences, see RSA 651.

597:8. Subsequent Bail.

A prisoner committed to jail pursuant to RSA 597:7 may at any time recognize agreeably to the order to recognize for his appearance, before a justice, and thereupon the justice shall issue his warrant for the discharge of the prisoner, and he shall be discharged from custody.

Source.
GS 240:8. GL 258:8. PS 252:17. PL 366:20. RL 425:20.

Revision note.
At the beginning of the section, substituted "a prisoner committed to jail pursuant to RSA 597:7" for "such prisoner" and "the order to recognize for his appearance" for "such order" for purposes of clarity.

Cross References.
Filing of copies of discharge, see RSA 597:9, 10.

597:9. Copies, Subsequent Bail.

The justice issuing an order for the discharge of a prisoner shall file, in the office of the clerk of the superior court for the county or judicial district thereof in which the offense is alleged to have been committed, true and attested copies of the application to the justice to take such recognizance, of the order made by the justice on the application, of the recognizance taken, and a note of the warrant of discharge issued by the justice.

Source.
GS 240:10. GL 258:10. PS 252:19. PL 366:21. RL 425:21. RSA 597:9. 1992, 284:74, eff. July 1, 1992.

Amendments
—1992. Inserted "or judicial district thereof" following "county", substituted "the justice" for "him" following "application to" and "made by the justice on the application" for "by him made thereon" following "the order", deleted "by him" preceding "issued" and added "by the justice" thereafter.

Cross References.
Discharge of prisoner generally, see RSA 597:8.

597:10. Copies, on Appeal.

In case of appeal, the municipal and district courts shall cause true and attested copies of the complaint, other process, records and recognizances, together with any cash bail in the case, to be filed with the clerk of the superior court within 10 days after the date of such order for recognizance.

Source.
RS 222:4. CS 237:4. GS 240:9. GL 258:9. PS 252:18. 1911, 113:1. PL 366:22. 1937, 49:3. RL 425:22. RSA 597:10. 1957, 71:2. 1959, 19:1. 1965, 86:3, eff. July 10, 1965.

Amendments
—1965. Rewritten to the extent that a detailed comparison would be impracticable.

—1959. Deleted "or justice" following "municipal court".

—1957. Inserted "including cash bail" following "records and recognizances".

Cross References.
Release on bail or personal recognizance pending appeal generally, see RSA 597:1-a.

NOTES TO DECISIONS

Effect of failure of complaint to show attestation
The failure of a municipal court justice to attest to a complaint did not entitle the defendant to dismissal of the charges in superior court; the requirement of attestation could be met by amendment of the complaint in superior court. State v. Pomeroy, 113 N.H. 610, 312 A.2d 697, 1973 N.H. LEXIS 332 (1973).

597:11. Copies, Binding Over.

In the case of an order to recognize for appearance before the superior court, the district or municipal court shall cause true and attested copies of the complaint, other process, records and recognizances, together with any cash bail in the case, to be mailed or delivered to the clerk of the superior court of the county or judicial district thereof within 10 days after the date of such order for recognizance. A true and attested copy of the complaint or other process shall also be mailed or delivered to the county attorney and the state probation office for the county within said 10 days.

Source.
RS 222:4. CS 237:4. GS 240:9. GL 258:9. PS 252:18. 1911, 113:1. PL 366:23. RL 425:23. RSA 597:11. 1965, 86:4. 1992, 284:75, eff. July 1, 1992.

Amendments
—1992. Inserted "or judicial district thereof" following "county" in the first sentence.

—1965. Rewritten to the extent that a detailed comparison would be impracticable.

NOTES TO DECISIONS

Effect of failure to transfer documents to superior court
When a magistrate, in binding over an accused in a criminal case, fails to transfer to the superior court attested copies of the process, records, and recognizance within the statutory time limit, he subjects himself to a personal liability, but the accused will not be discharged because of a failure to transfer such copies within the time limit. State v. Davis, 43 N.H. 600, 1862 N.H. LEXIS 117 (1862).

597:12. Penalty.

Whoever violates any provision of RSA 597:10 and 11 shall be guilty of a violation.

Source.
RS 222:4. CS 237:4. GS 240:9. GL 258:9. PS 252:18. 1911, 113:1. PL 366:24. RL 425:24. RSA 597:12. 1973, 531:151, eff. at 11:59 p.m., Oct. 31, 1973.

Amendments
—1973. Rewritten to the extent that a detailed comparison would be impracticable.

Cross References.
Classification of crimes, see RSA 625:9.
Sentences, see RSA 651.

597:13. Accepting Insufficient Bail, etc.

If a justice knowingly accepts insufficient bail or fails to make return of his proceedings as required by law, he shall be liable to the same punishment as for aiding an escape in a like case; provided, that this section shall not apply to release on personal recognizance upon a finding by the justice that such release is proper under the circumstances of the case.

Source.
GS 240:11. GL 258:11. PS 252:20. PL 366:25. RL 425:25. RSA 597:13. 1969, 78:6, eff. June 3, 1969.

Amendments
—1969. Added "provided, that this section shall not apply to release on personal recognizance upon a finding by the justice that such release is proper under the circumstances of the case" following "like case".

Cross References.
Hindering apprehension or prosecution, see RSA 642:3.

597:14. Minors.

Minors and their sureties shall be bound by their recognizance in the same manner as if their principals were of full age.

Source.
GS 241:5. GL 259:5. PS 252:21. PL 366:26. RL 425:26. RSA 597:14. 1988, 110:7, eff. June 17, 1988.

Amendments
—1988. Deleted "etc." in the catchline, "and married women" preceding "and their sureties", and "and unmarried" following "were of full age"; substituted "recognizance" for "recognizances" following "bound by their" and "their" for "the" following "same manner as if".

Cross References.
Age of majority, see RSA 21:44.

597:14-a. Failure to Appear; Punishment.

[Repealed 1988, 110:12, V, eff. June 17, 1988.]

Former section(s).
Former RSA 597:14-a, which was derived from 1965, 88:1, related to punishment for failure to appear before the court.

597:14-b. Penalty for Offense Committed While on Release.

I. A person convicted of an offense while released pursuant to this chapter shall be sentenced, in addition to the sentence prescribed for the offense to:

(a) A maximum term of imprisonment of not more than 7 years if the offense is a felony; or

(b) A maximum term of imprisonment of not more than one year if the offense is a misdemeanor.

II. A term of imprisonment imposed pursuant to this section shall be consecutive to any other sentence of imprisonment. Neither the penalty provided by this section or any prosecution under this section shall interfere with or prevent the forfeiture of any bail or the exercise by the court of its power to punish for contempt.

Source.
1988, 110:8. 1989, 386:8, eff. June 5, 1989.

Amendments
—1989. Paragraph I(a): Inserted "maximum" preceding "term". Paragraph II: Deleted "but this section shall be construed to provide an additional penalty for failure to appear" following "contempt" in the second sentence.

NOTES TO DECISIONS

Sentence enhancement
Defendant was properly subjected to an enhanced penalty for selling cocaine while on bail based on a reading of the legislative history and RSA 597:14-b as a whole; for purposes of future sentence enhancement, however, defendant's record would reflect only one conviction. State v. Rosario, 148 N.H. 488, 809 A.2d 1283, 2002 N.H. LEXIS 159 (2002).

Cited:
Cited in Duquette v. Warden, N.H. State Prison, 154 N.H. 737, 919 A.2d 767, 2007 N.H. LEXIS 10 (2007).

Bail Commissioners

Cross References.
General provisions relating to bail, see RSA 597:1 et seq.

597:15. Superior Court.

The superior court may appoint justices of the peace and quorum as commissioners authorized to fix and receive bail in criminal or civil cases as hereinafter provided. The superior court shall not appoint as a bail commissioner anyone whose appointment would present a conflict of interest or an appearance of bias in the carrying out of his or her duties as a bail commissioner.

Source.
1895, 37:1. PL 366:27. RL 425:27. RSA 597:15. 1967, 302:1, eff. Aug. 29, 1967. 2007, 189:1, eff. June 18, 2007. 2013, 59:1, eff. June 6, 2013.

Amendments
—2013. The 2013 amendment rewrote the section heading, which formerly read: "Appointment" and added the second sentence.

—2007. Inserted "or civil" following "bail in criminal".

—1967. Rewritten to the extent that a detailed comparison would be impracticable.

Applicability of 2013 amendment.
2013, 59:3, eff. June 6, 2013, provided: "Nothing in this act shall require the removal from office of any currently commissioned bail commissioner."

NOTES TO DECISIONS

Contempt
Defendant was properly subject to criminal contempt as a sanction for violation of an order issued by a bail commissioner, as opposed to an order issued by a court, because contempt against a subordinate officer appointed by a court, such as a bail commissioner, was contempt of the authority of the appointing court. State v. Nott, 149 N.H. 280, 821 A.2d 976, 2003 N.H. LEXIS 38 (2003).

Cited:
Cited in Thompson v. Sanborn, 568 F. Supp. 385, 1983 U.S. Dist. LEXIS 15256 (D.N.H. 1983); Opinion of Justices, 131 N.H. 443, 554 A.2d 466, 1989 N.H. LEXIS 3 (1989).

597:15-a. Circuit Court.

The circuit court may appoint justices of the peace and quorum as commissioners authorized to fix and receive bail and other fines and fees as authorized by law in criminal or civil cases as hereinafter provided. The circuit court shall not appoint as a bail commissioner anyone whose appointment would present a conflict of interest or an appearance of bias in the carrying out of his or her duties as a bail commissioner.

Source.
1963, 331:9. 1985, 341:9, eff. Jan. 1, 1986. 1998, 288:5, eff. Jan. 1, 1999. 2008, 105:1, eff. May 28, 2008. 2013, 59:2, eff. June 6, 2013.

Amendments
—2013. The 2013 amendment rewrote the section heading, which formerly read: "District Courts"; in the first sentence, substituted "The circuit court may appoint" for "District courts may appoint 3 or more" and "as hereinafter provided" for "to be brought before the appointing court or any other district court"; and added the second sentence.

—2008. The 2008 amendment substituted "the appointing court or any other district court" for "said courts as hereafter provided" at the end.

—1998. Inserted "and other fines and fees as authorized by law" preceding "in criminal" and inserted "or civil" thereafter.

—1985. Rewritten to the extent that a detailed comparison would be impracticable.

NOTES TO DECISIONS

Contempt
Defendant was properly subject to criminal contempt as a sanction for violation of an order issued by a bail commissioner, as opposed to an order issued by a court, because contempt against a subordinate officer appointed by a court, such as a bail commissioner, was contempt of the authority of the appointing court. State v. Nott, 149 N.H. 280, 821 A.2d 976, 2003 N.H. LEXIS 38 (2003).

597:15-b. Judicial Branch Family Division.

[Repealed 2013, 59:4, I, eff. June 6, 2013.]

Former section(s).
Former RSA 597:15-b, which was derived from 2007, 189:2, related to appointment of bail commissioners in the judicial branch family division.

597:16. Municipal Courts.

[Repealed 2013, 59:4, II, eff. June 6, 2013.]

Former section(s).
Former RSA 597:16, which was derived from 1951, 224:5 and 1998, 288:6, related to appointment of bail commissioners in the municipal courts.

597:17. Term.

Bail commissioners shall be commissioned for 5 years and continue in office until their successors shall have qualified.

Source.
1895, 37:2. PL 366:28. RL 425:28.

Revision note.

At the beginning of the section, substituted "bail commissioners" for "they" for purposes of clarity.

NOTES TO DECISIONS

Contempt

Defendant was properly subject to criminal contempt as a sanction for violation of an order issued by a bail commissioner, as opposed to an order issued by a court, because contempt against a subordinate officer appointed by a court, such as a bail commissioner, was contempt of the authority of the appointing court. State v. Nott, 149 N.H. 280, 821 A.2d 976, 2003 N.H. LEXIS 38 (2003).

597:18. Powers.

On application of a person who is arrested for a bailable offense, at any time before his arraignment therefor, any commissioner may fix the amount of and receive bail in the same manner as the court might do, except in cases provided for by RSA 597:4.

Source.

1895, 37:3. PL 366:29. RL 425:29.

NOTES TO DECISIONS

Cited:

Cited in Thompson v. Sanborn, 568 F. Supp. 385, 1983 U.S. Dist. LEXIS 15256 (D.N.H. 1983); State v. Nott, 149 N.H. 280, 821 A.2d 976, 2003 N.H. LEXIS 38 (2003).

597:18-a. Educational Requirements for Bail Commissioners.

I. During September or October of each year beginning in 1995, a justice of each district or municipal court, under the direction of the administrative judge of the district and municipal courts, shall hold a meeting with all bail commissioners under the jurisdiction of such court. This meeting shall be for the purpose of educating bail commissioners on the laws concerning their powers and duties.

II. A copy of all laws concerning bail commissioners and a copy of the latest edition of the Bail Commissioner's Handbook shall be provided to each bail commissioner at this annual meeting.

Source.

1995, 61:2, eff. July 8, 1995.

597:19. Returns.

Every recognizance taken by a commissioner shall be certified and returned to the clerk of the court before which the party is bound to appear, on or before the day of the sitting thereof.

Source.

1895, 37:4. PL 366:30. RL 425:30.

597:20. Fees.

The bail commissioners in such cases shall be entitled to a fee of $40. However, clerks of court or members of their staffs who are bail commissioners shall be entitled to collect such fee only when called while not on active duty. In jurisdictions where the bail commissioner is a full-time salaried police officer, constable, sheriff, deputy sheriff, state police employee, or anyone else authorized to execute police powers, such person shall not receive the fee established in this section, but instead such amount shall be remitted to the town or city in which the district court is situated.

Source.

1895, 37:5. 1905, 9:1. 1921, 83:1. PL 366:31. RL 425:31. 1949, 135:1. RSA 597:20. 1965, 195:1. 1969, 215:1. 1971, 112:1. 1981, 139:1. 1989, 150:1. 1995, 61:1, eff. July 1, 1995. 2001, 154:1, eff. Aug. 28, 2001. 2008, 117:1, eff. August 2, 2008.

Amendments

—2008. The 2008 amendment in the first sentence, substituted "$40" for "$30" at the end; and in the third sentence, deleted "municipal or" following "which the" near the end.

—2001. Substituted "$30" for "$20" in the first sentence.

—1995. Substituted "$20" for "$15" in the first sentence.

—1989. Substituted "$15" for "$7 when called between the hours of 9 o'clock in the morning and 5 o'clock at night, Monday through Friday; and a fee of $12 when called at any other time" following "fee of" in the first sentence.

—1981. Rewritten to the extent that a detailed comparison would be impracticable.

—1971. Substituted "four dollars" for "two dollars" and "six dollars" for "four dollars" in the first sentence.

—1969. Added the second sentence.

—1965. Substituted "nine o'clock" for "seven o'clock", "five o'clock" for "ten o'clock" and added "Monday through Friday" following "at night".

NOTES TO DECISIONS

Constitutionality

Imposition of $30 fee on arrestee's who sought an immediate bail proceeding at times when court was not in session bore a rational relationship to the need to offer convenient service to arrestees and did not violate arrestees' rights to equal access to the courts so long as arrestees were informed of how long they would have to wait for a hearing if they did not incur the fee and that they could choose to have a bail hearing and simply pay the fee later or, if they qualified as indigent, have it waived. Follansbee v. Plymouth Dist. Court, 151 N.H. 365, 856 A.2d 740, 2004 N.H. LEXIS 155 (2004).

597:21. Bail on Sunday.

Persons arrested on Sunday, or on the evening or afternoon preceding, may be admitted to bail on that day when in the opinion of the commissioner an application for that purpose appears to be proper.

Source.

1895, 37:6. PL 366:32. RL 425:32.

Recognizances of Witnesses

Cross References.

General provisions relating to bail and recognizances, see RSA 597:1 et seq.

Issuance of summons to witnesses in criminal cases, see RSA 592-A:11.

597:22. Recognizances After Arrest.

Any police officer may detain any person who he deems to be a necessary witness to a crime; provided, however, within 24 hours, including Sundays and holidays, he shall be brought before a justice of the superior court who may, upon the showing that the testimony of said person is necessary in any court, release the person on personal recognizance or take the recognizance of the witness in such sum as the justice may deem reasonable for his appearance before the court.

Source.
RS 222:5. CS 237:5. GS 240:16. GL 258:16. PS 252:22. PL 366:33. RL 425:33. RSA 597:22. 1959, 159:1. 1965, 86:5. 1969, 78:7. 1975, 407:1, eff. Aug. 15, 1975.

Amendments
—**1975.** Rewritten to the extent that a detailed comparison would be impracticable.

—**1969.** Rewritten to the extent that a detailed comparison would be impracticable.

—**1965.** Inserted "or district" following "municipal" in the first sentence.

—**1959.** Deleted "justice or" preceding "municipal court" in the first sentence and added the second sentence.

NOTES TO DECISIONS

Cited:
Cited in State v. Bruneau, 131 N.H. 104, 552 A.2d 585, 1988 N.H. LEXIS 106 (1988).

597:23. Commitment in Default of Recognizance.

Whenever a witness, upon being ordered by a superior court justice to recognize, neglects or refuses to do so, the justice may issue a warrant and cause such witness to be committed to jail until he complies with the order.

Source.
RS 222:6. CS 237:6. GS 240:17. GL 258:17. PS 252:23. PL 366:34. RL 425:34. RSA 597:23. 1959, 159:2. 1965, 86:6. 1975, 407:2, eff. Aug. 15, 1975.

Amendments
—**1975.** Rewritten to the extent that a detailed comparison would be impracticable.

—**1965.** Inserted "district" following "superior" in two places.

—**1959.** Rewritten to the extent that a detailed comparison would be impracticable.

Form of Recognizance

Cross References.
General provisions relating to bail and recognizances, see RSA 597:1.

597:24. To the State; Sureties.

Recognizance shall be taken in the name of the state, and with sufficient sureties, unless, in proper cases, the recognizance of the party shall be deemed by the superior court to be sufficient.

Source.
RS 211:17. CS 224:17. GS 241:2. GL 259:2. PS 252:24. PL 366:35. RL 425:35.

597:25. Condition.

Recognizances may be taken with condition to attend the court or before the justice at the next term, from term to term, at a fixed day to which the case may be continued, or from day to day, there to wait and abide the order of the court, and not to depart without leave until discharged by order of court.

Source.
GS 241:3. GL 259:3. PS 252:25. PL 366:36. RL 425:36.

597:26. Variations.

Recognizances may be taken in any other form which the court, considering the circumstances of the case, may direct or allow.

Source.
GS 241:4. GL 259:4. PS 252:26. PL 366:37. RL 425:37. RSA 597:26. 1967, 132:38, eff. July 18, 1967.

Amendments
—**1967.** Deleted "or justice" following "court".

Discharge of Bail

Cross References.
Forfeitures of and actions on recognizances, see RSA 597:31 et seq.
General provisions relating to bail and recognizances, see RSA 597:1 et seq.

597:27. Surrender, in Court.

A surety for the appearance of a party or witness may be discharged by order of the superior court from further liability upon surrendering the party in open court, during the pendency of the original cause and before trial, on payment of the costs of any proceeding against them, and the principal shall be committed unless again recognized.

Source.
RS 201:6. CS 214:6. GS 241:6. GL 259:6. PS 252:27. PL 366:38. RL 425:38. RSA 597:27. 1969, 78:8, eff. June 3, 1969.

Amendments
—**1969.** Substituted "a surety" for "bail" preceding "for the appearance of a party".

Cross References.
Discharge of sureties unable to surrender principals, see RSA 597:30.

NOTES TO DECISIONS

Prerequisites to effective surrender
A bail cannot make an effectual surrender of the principal in court unless there is an action pending against the principal or the bail. Sloan v. Bryant, 28 N.H. 67, 1853 N.H. LEXIS 39 (1853).

597:28. Surrender, to Jailer.

Sureties may be discharged before forfeiture of the recognizance by committing the principal to the jail of the county, by leaving with the jailer a certified copy of the order to recognize and of the names of the bail, and a certificate of the bail thereon that they have committed the principal in discharge of their liability as bail, and by giving written notice thereof to the attorney general or county attorney.

Source.

RS 201:4. CS 214:4. GS 241:7. GL 259:7. PS 252:28. PL 366:39. RL 425:39. RSA 597:28. 1967, 132:39, eff. July 18, 1967.

Amendments

—**1967.** Deleted "in vacation" following "discharged" and substituted "attorney" for "solicitor" following "county".

Cross References.

Discharge of sureties unable to surrender principals, see RSA 597:30.

597:29. Jailer's Authority; New Bail.

The copies and certificates provided for in RSA 597:28 shall be sufficient authority for the keeper of the jail to detain the party committed until he shall be discharged by due order of law; and the accused may be again recognized with sureties, agreeably to the original order of the court requiring such recognizance.

Source.

GS 241:8. GL 259:8. PS 252:29. PL 366:40. RL 425:40. RSA 597:29. 1967, 132:40, eff. July 18, 1967.

Amendments

—**1967.** Deleted "or justice" following "court".

Revision note.

At the beginning of the section, substituted "provided for in RSA 597:28" for "aforesaid" following "copies and certificates" for purposes of clarity.

597:30. Excusing Surrender.

When the sureties in a recognizance, without their fault, are prevented from surrendering their principal by an act of God or of the government of the state or of the United States, or by sentence of law, the superior court, on petition and notice thereof to the county commissioners and state's counsel, may discharge them on such terms as may be deemed just.

Source.

GS 241:12. GL 259:12. PS 252:30. PL 366:41. RL 425:41.

NOTES TO DECISIONS

1. Construction generally
2. Particular cases

1. Construction generally

Sureties upon a recognizance will not be discharged under this section if the surrender of the principal was prevented by any fault of the sureties in connection with an act of God or of the government or the sentence of the law. State v. McAllister, 54 N.H. 156 (1873).

Because RSA 597:30 applies only in the enumerated situations, it cannot be construed to excuse the surety when another state's

government prevents the defendant's appearance. Accordingly, a bond surety was not entitled to discharge under RSA 597:30 when defendant failed to appear because he was being held on charges in Vermont. State v. McGurk, 163 N.H. 584, 44 A.3d 568, 2012 N.H. LEXIS 62 (May 11, 2012).

2. Particular cases

With regard to a bond forfeiture, the surety failed to establish prejudice from the lack of an evidentiary hearing. Whatever a hearing might have revealed, defendant's incarceration in Vermont would nonetheless fall outside the circumstances under which RSA 597:30 permitted discharging a surety. State v. McGurk, 163 N.H. 584, 44 A.3d 568, 2012 N.H. LEXIS 62 (May 11, 2012).

The fact that sureties in a recognizance were prevented from surrendering the principal by reason of his voluntary enlistment in the United States Navy without their knowledge did not furnish sufficient ground for their discharge since the absence of the principal was purely voluntary and was the very thing that the recognizance was designed to prevent. Lamphire v. State, 73 N.H. 463, 62 A. 786, 1906 N.H. LEXIS 4 (1906).

Where sureties failed to produce their principal in court at the time called for in the recognizance due to the voluntary absence of the principal, but were successful in making an arrangement with the state whereby, if they produced their principal at a later date the recognizance would not be forfeited, and, at this later date, the principal was incarcerated as a violator of a federal law, that fact did not bring the sureties within this section since it did not excuse their failure to produce their principal as originally contemplated in the recognizance in the first instance. State v. McAllister, 54 N.H. 156 (1873).

Forfeitures of Recognizances and Actions Thereon

Cross References.

Discharge of sureties generally, see RSA 597:27 et seq.

General provisions relating to bail and recognizances, see RSA 597:1 et seq.

597:31. Declaration of Forfeiture.

If any party recognized to appear makes default, the recognizance shall be declared forfeited, and the state may cause proceedings to be had immediately for the recovery of such forfeiture.

Source.

1865, 4077:3, 4. GS 241:9. GL 259:9. 1889, 27:1. PS 252:31. PL 366:42. RL 425:42. RSA 597:31. 1959, 12:1. 1988, 110:9. 1989, 386:9, eff. June 5, 1989.

Amendments

—**1989.** Rewritten to the extent that a detailed comparison would be impracticable.

—**1988.** Rewritten to the extent that a detailed comparison would be impracticable.

Cross References.

Contents of declaration, see RSA 597:36.

Venue of action, see RSA 597:34.

NOTES TO DECISIONS

1. Particular cases

In ordering forfeiture after defendant failed to appear because he was being held on charges in Vermont, the trial court did not treat the bonds as performance rather than appearance bonds. Although the trial court noted that defendant's failure to appear resulted from his decision to travel to Vermont and commit crimes, its order made clear that it forfeited the bonds because defendant failed to appear, not because of his criminal activity. State v. McGurk, 163 N.H. 584, 44 A.3d 568, 2012 N.H. LEXIS 62 (May 11, 2012).

With regard to a bond forfeiture, the surety failed to establish prejudice from the lack of an evidentiary hearing. Whatever a hearing might have revealed, defendant's incarceration in Vermont would nonetheless fall outside the circumstances under which RSA 597:30 permitted discharging a surety. State v. McGurk, 163 N.H. 584, 44 A.3d 568, 2012 N.H. LEXIS 62 (May 11, 2012).

Cited:
Cited in State v. Walker, 56 N.H. 176, 1875 N.H. LEXIS 27 (1875); Belknap County v. Laconia, 80 N.H. 251, 116 A. 434, 1922 N.H. LEXIS 1 (1922).

597:32. Striking Off Default.

Any court, for good cause, may strike off a default upon a recognizance or order it to be struck off at a future day, upon a substantial compliance with the condition.

Source.
GS 241:10. GL 259:10. 1889, 27:2. PS 252:32. PL 366:43. RL 425:43.

NOTES TO DECISIONS

Cited:
Cited in State v. Moccia, 120 N.H. 298, 414 A.2d 1275, 1980 N.H. LEXIS 283 (1980).

597:33. Judgment.

The superior court may render judgment for the whole amount of any forfeited recognizance and interest and costs, or for such part thereof as, after hearing counsel, the court may think proper, according to any special circumstances in evidence affecting the case or the party liable.

Source.
1865, 4075:2. GS 241:11. GL 259:11. PS 252:33. PL 366:44. RL 425:44. RSA 597:33. 1983, 383:61, eff. July 1, 1984.

Amendments
—**1983.** Deleted "the county commissioners and state's" preceding "counsel".

NOTES TO DECISIONS

Common law
In the absence of a statute such as this, which confers upon the court the authority to consider in equity the forfeiture of a recognizance and render judgment for the amount due thereon in good conscience, when any condition of a recognizance is breached, the whole amount of the forfeiture is due. Philbrick v. Buxton, 40 N.H. 384, 1860 N.H. LEXIS 164 (1860).

Cited:
Cited in State v. Moccia, 120 N.H. 298, 414 A.2d 1275, 1980 N.H. LEXIS 283 (1980).

597:34. Venue.

Actions upon recognizances may be brought and tried in the county or judicial district thereof in which they were taken, unless the court shall order the venue to be changed.

Source.
RS 211:17. CS 224:17. GS 241:14. GL 259:14. PS 252:34. PL 366:45. RL 425:45. RSA 597:34. 1992, 284:76, eff. July 1, 1992.

Amendments
—**1992.** Inserted "or judicial district thereof" following "county".

597:35. Defective Records, etc.

No action on a recognizance shall be defeated, nor judgment thereon be arrested, for any omission to record a default at the proper term, nor for any defect in the form of recognizance or of the *scire facias*, but the court may order the record of process to be amended to conform to the facts, without costs.

Source.
GS 241:15. GL 259:15. PS 252:35. PL 366:46. RL 425:46.

Revision note.
At the end of the section, substituted "to conform" for "agreeably" for purposes of clarity.

597:36. Declaration.

In actions brought upon recognizances taken in criminal prosecutions, it shall be sufficient to set forth in the writ the substance of the recognizance and the time and place at which the same was declared forfeited, without setting forth the complaint or indictment or any subsequent proceedings thereon.

Source.
1865, 4075:1. GS 241:17. GL 259:17. PS 252:36. PL 366:47. RL 425:47.

NOTES TO DECISIONS

Sufficiency of declaration
In an action upon a recognizance where the condition contained therein was that the accused would appear at a future time and not depart without leave of the court, but abide by the order of the court in the premises, and there was no averment in the declaration that the accused, being called to appear according to the tenor of the recognizance, made default, the declaration was insufficient and judgment would be entered for the defendant. State v. Chesley, 4 N.H. 366, 1828 N.H. LEXIS 18 (1828).

597:37. Bench Warrants.

Any court may issue a warrant for the arrest of a person under recognizance to appear before the court who fails to appear according to the condition thereof or of any person who, being party to a criminal proceeding, is, by escape or otherwise, improperly at large.

Source.
GS 241:16. GL 259:16. PS 252:37. PL 366:48. RL 425:48. RSA 597:37. 1967, 132:41, eff. July 18, 1967.

Amendments
—**1967.** Deleted "or justice" following "any court".

Cross References.
Arrests generally, see RSA 594.

NOTES TO DECISIONS

Cited:
Cited in State v. Jones, 127 N.H. 515, 503 A.2d 802, 1985 N.H. LEXIS 454 (1985).

597:38. Forfeit of Recognizance.

If a recognizance is forfeited and paid in any case in which, if the recognizor had been convicted, any sum might have been due and payable to the complainant or to any other person, the superior court may ascertain the amount and may order it to be paid from the state treasury.

Source.
RS 211:16. CS 224:16. GS 245:3. GL 263:3. PS 261:3. PL 375:3. RL 435:3. RSA 597:38. 1983, 383:62, eff. July 1, 1984.

Amendments
—**1983.** Deleted "on notice to the county commissioners" following "superior court" and substituted "state" for "county" preceding "treasury".

NOTES TO DECISIONS

Restitution
The legislative history of this section reveals that it was not intended to provide authority for judicial awards of restitution from forfeited bail. State v. Schachter, 133 N.H. 439, 577 A.2d 1222, 1990 N.H. LEXIS 81 (1990).

597:38-a. Default Fees.

I. Whenever a party recognized to appear for any offense defaults, the court may impose an administrative processing fee in the amount of $50 in addition to any other fine or penalty assessment.

II. The administrative processing fee provided for in paragraph I shall be retained by the court.

Source.
1991, 347:7, eff. July 1, 1991.

597:38-b. Collection of Forfeitures; Motor Vehicles.

I. Whenever a party recognized to appear for any offense involving driving makes default and the recognizance is declared forfeited, the court shall send a notice of default to the division of motor vehicles. The division shall send a notice to the person owing the recognizance, demanding payment within 30 days and stating that failure to make payment within the 30-day period shall result in suspension of such person's driver's license or driving privilege until such time as the person provides proof to the department of safety that he has paid the amount of the forfeited recognizance to the court.

II. Payments of the forfeited recognizance under paragraph I shall be sent to the department of safety and deposited into a special fund, known as the default bench warrant fund, established in RSA 263:56-d to pay the costs of state, county and local law enforcement officials who make arrests pursuant to bench warrants issued for persons improperly at large for driving-related offenses and to pay the cost of breath analyzer machines.

Source.
1991, 366:1, eff. Jan. 1, 1992. 1998, 288:10, eff. Jan. 1, 1999.

Amendments
—**1998.** Paragraph II: Substituted "default bench warrant fund" for "DWI bench warrant fund" and "driving-related offenses and to pay the cost of breath analyzer machines" for "driving while intoxicated offenses".

Revision note.
This section, which was originally enacted as RSA 597:38-a, was redesignated pursuant to 1991, 366:4, eff. Jan. 1, 1992.

Discharge of Prisoner Unable to Procure Bail

597:39. Procedure.

The court, upon petition and notice to the county attorney, prosecutor or party interested, may order the discharge of any person imprisoned for inability to find sureties in a recognizance, upon such terms as may be deemed just.

Source.
1858, 2118:1. GS 241:13. GL 259:13. PS 252:38. PL 366:49. RL 425:49. RSA 597:39. 1967, 132:42, eff. July 18, 1967.

Amendments
—**1967.** Deleted "or any justice thereof" following "court" and substituted "county attorney" for "solicitor".

Cross References.
Right to release on bail or recognizance generally, see RSA 597:1, 1-a.

Recognizances Upon Arrest for Offense Committed in Another County

Cross References.
General provisions relating to bail and recognizance, see RSA 597:1 et seq.

597:40. Recognizance for Appearance in Superior Court.

If a person is arrested in one county on a warrant for an offense alleged to have been committed in another county exceeding the jurisdiction of a justice to determine, the officer, on the arrestee's request, shall take the arrestee before a justice for the county or judicial district thereof in which the arrest was made, and, upon the arrestee's waiving examination, such justice may take the arrestee's personal recognizance or recognizance with sufficient sureties upon the terms and conditions prescribed by this chapter for the arrestee's appearance at the next term of the superior court for the county or judicial district thereof in which the offense is alleged to have been committed, and the arrestee shall return to said court certified copies of the warrant and recognizance.

Source.
RS 222:16. CS 237:16. GS 236:12. GL 254:12. PS 250:12. PL 364:15. RL 423:15. RSA 597:40. 1969, 78:9. 1992, 284:77, eff. July 1, 1992.

Amendments
—**1992.** Rewritten to the extent that a detailed comparison would be impracticable.

—1969. Substituted "personal recognizance or recognizance with sufficient sureties upon the terms and conditions prescribed by this chapter" for "recognizance, with sufficient sureties".

597:41. Recognizance for Appearance Before Court or Justice Named in Warrant.

A justice before whom a party is taken pursuant to RSA 597:40 may, upon good cause shown, take the recognizance of the party to appear before the court or justice as directed in the warrant on a day and hour named, within 10 days following. He shall certify the fact upon the warrant and deliver it, with the recognizance, to the officer.

Source.
GS 236:13. GL 254:13. PS 250:13. PL 364:16. RL 423:16.

Revision note.
At the beginning of the section, substituted "a justice before whom a party is taken pursuant to RSA 597:40" for "such justice" for purposes of clarity.

597:42. Return of Recognizance, etc.

The officer shall forthwith deliver the warrant and recognizance to the justice or court before whom the warrant is returnable, who may thereupon summon before him and order to recognize any witness that he may deem necessary to appear at the same time and place.

Source.
GS 236:14. GL 254:14. PS 250:14. PL 364:17. RL 423:17.

CHAPTER 599

APPEALS FROM CONVICTIONS IN MUNICIPAL OR DISTRICT COURT

SECTION
599:1.   Appeals.
599:1-a.   Petition; Late Appeal.
599:1-b.   Petition for Appeal.
599:1-c.   Records Required.
599:2.   Recognizance of Appellant.
599:3.   Failure to Prosecute Appeal.
599:4.   Enforcing Original Sentence.

Cross References.
District courts generally, see RSA 502-A.
Municipal courts generally, see RSA 502.

NOTES TO DECISIONS

Cited:
Cited in State v. Bardsley, 125 N.H. 696, 484 A.2d 1187, 1984 N.H. LEXIS 385 (1984).

RESEARCH REFERENCES

New Hampshire Court Rules Annotated.
Notice of appeal to superior court, see Rule 2.13, Rules of the District and Municipal Courts, New Hampshire Court Rules Annotated.

Proceedings before superior court in criminal appeals, see Rules 92 and 93, Rules of the Superior Court, New Hampshire Court Rules Annotated.

Withdrawal of appeal to superior court, see Rule 2.15, Rules of the District and Municipal Courts, New Hampshire Court Rules Annotated.

599:1. Appeals.

A person convicted by a district court of a class A misdemeanor, at the time the sentence is declared, may appeal therefrom to obtain a de novo jury trial in the superior court, which shall hear the appeal. The appeal shall be entered by the defendant at the next return day unless for good cause shown the time is extended by the superior court. If, after a jury trial in the superior court, the defendant is found guilty, the superior court shall sentence the defendant, and the defendant may appeal questions of law arising therefrom to the supreme court. In the event the defendant waives the right to jury trial after the case has been appealed, the superior court shall forthwith remand the case to the district court for imposition of the sentence originally imposed by the district court, and the defendant may appeal questions of law arising therefrom to the supreme court. In all misdemeanor cases which are appealed to superior court or in which defendants are bound over, it shall be the duty of the superior court to transmit to the justice of the district court, within 10 days after the case is finally disposed of, a certificate showing the final disposition of the case.

Source.
RS 222:2. CS 237:2. 1860, 239:3. GS 240:2. GL 258:2. PS 252:2. PL 366:2. 1927, 10:1. 1937, 49:1. RL 425:2. 1947, 121:14. 1951, 163:13. RSA 599:1. 1957, 244:38. 1965, 86:1. 1983, 382:6. 1988, 19:3. 1992, 269:6. 2006, 64:2, eff. January 1, 2007. 2011, 88:28, eff. July 1, 2011.

Amendments
—2011. The 2011 amendment rewrote the section to the extent that a detailed comparison would be impracticable.

—2006. Rewritten to the extent that a detailed comparison would be impracticable.

—1995. Added "except in cases in district courts served by regional jury trial courts as provided in RSA 502-A:12-a" following "the appeal" in the first sentence and deleted "so" preceding "appealed" and added "to the superior court" thereafter in the third sentence.

—1992. Rewrote the first sentence.

—1988. Inserted "or who has been sentenced by the imposition of a civil penalty bringing the total fines and penalties for a violation to an amount in excess of $500" following "convicted of the same offense" in the first sentence; deleted "the clerk of" following "shall be the duty of" in the third sentence.

—1983. Rewrote the former first sentence as the present first and second sentences, substituted "misdemeanor" for "criminal" preceding "cases which are so appealed" in the present third sentence, and made other minor stylistic changes.

—1965. Inserted "district or" preceding "municipal court" in the first sentence and deleted the second sentence.

—1957. Deleted "or justice of the peace" following "municipal court" in the first sentence.

Applicability of 1992 amendment.

1992, 269:21, eff. July 1, 1992, provided that the act, which amended this section and RSA 502-A:27-d, 597:2, 625:9, 634:2. 635:5, 637:11, 638:1, 638:6, 642:8, 644:11, 644:12, 645:3, 651:2, and 651:5, shall apply to offenses committed on or after July 1, 1992.

Cross References.

Appeals from convictions for violations not providing basis for enhanced penalties for subsequent convictions, see RSA 599:1-c.

Classification of crimes, see RSA 625:9.

Late appeals, see RSA 599:1-a, 1-b.

Sentences, see RSA 651.

NOTES TO DECISIONS

1. Construction
2. Right to appeal—Generally
3. —Probation revocation
4. —License revocation
5. Effect of appeal
6. Right to jury trial

1. Construction

An assessment on a penalty is in and of itself a penalty to be taken into account when determining whether total fines and penalties exceed amount entitling a defendant to appeal a sentence to the superior court. State v. Corson, 134 N.H. 430, 593 A.2d 248, 1991 N.H. LEXIS 77 (1991).

2. Right to appeal—Generally

Levy of penalty assessment upon defendant fined $500 for violation of statute prohibiting reckless operation of a motor vehicle clearly brought total fines and penalties to an amount in excess of $500, and therefore the trial court properly denied the state's motion to vacate defendant's appeal. State v. Corson, 134 N.H. 430, 593 A.2d 248, 1991 N.H. LEXIS 77 (1991).

A defendant has an absolute right of appeal to the superior court from a criminal conviction of a misdemeanor in the municipal court under this section and RSA 592-A:2, and the effect of such an appeal to the superior court is to vacate the judgment and transfer the whole proceedings for trial de novo on the original complaint, unless amended, or on an information substituted for the original complaint. State v. Green, 105 N.H. 260, 197 A.2d 204, 1964 N.H. LEXIS 58 (1964).

3. —Probation revocation

A probation violation hearing held pursuant to RSA 504:4, which governs violation and termination of probation, is not part of a criminal prosecution and, therefore, the superior court has no jurisdiction to hear an appeal from a probation hearing, either under RSA 592-A:2, governing appeals to the superior court, which applies only to criminal cases, or under this section, which allows a person sentenced for an offense to appeal to the superior court and which does not apply to probation revocation since that is not being "sentenced for an offense". State v. Brackett, 122 N.H. 716, 449 A.2d 1210, 1982 N.H. LEXIS 436 (1982).

4. —License revocation

A defendant convicted of reckless driving was not entitled to a trial de novo in superior court since a driver's license revocation resulting from the conviction was not a penalty within the meaning of this section. State v. Penn, 127 N.H. 351, 499 A.2d 1014, 1985 N.H. LEXIS 428 (1985).

5. Effect of appeal

The effect of an appeal under this section is to vacate the judgment and transfer the whole proceeding to the superior court, there to be tried de novo on the original complaint, unless amended. State v. Lambert, 125 N.H. 442, 480 A.2d 205, 1984 N.H. LEXIS 246 (1984).

The effect of an appeal to the superior court from a conviction in a municipal court is to vacate that judgment and transfer the whole proceeding to the higher court, there to be tried de novo on the original complaint, unless amended, or on an information substituted for the original complaint. State v. Cook, 96 N.H. 212, 72 A.2d 778, 1950 N.H. LEXIS 147 (1950).

Where a defendant was found guilty in the municipal court upon a complaint for operating a motor vehicle while under the influence of intoxicating liquor and, after his appeal to the superior court was perfected, a nolle prosequi was entered there by the solicitor (now county attorney), the substitution of an information for the complaint did not give the defendant the right to plead former jeopardy thereto since, by his appeal, he gave up that right. State v. Cook, 96 N.H. 212, 72 A.2d 778, 1950 N.H. LEXIS 147 (1950).

6. Right to jury trial

When defendant was convicted in district court of two class A misdemeanors and was punished only with a fine of $350 plus a $70 penalty on each charge, converting the convictions to class B misdemeanors under RSA 625:9, VIII operated to deny defendant his right to a jury trial under N.H. Const. part. I, art. 15. Because defendant faced possible incarceration, he was entitled to a de novo jury trial in the superior court under RSA 599:1. State v. Bilc, 158 N.H. 651, 972 A.2d 1029, 2009 N.H. LEXIS 56 (2009).

Cited:

Cited in State v. Griffin, 66 N.H. 326, 29 A. 414, 1890 N.H. LEXIS 32 (1890); State v. Gerry, 68 N.H. 495, 38 A. 272, 1896 N.H. LEXIS 41, 38 L.R.A. 228 (1896); State v. Jackson, 69 N.H. 511, 43 A. 749, 1898 N.H. LEXIS 72 (1899); State v. Charpentier, 117 N.H. 647, 377 A.2d 131, 1977 N.H. LEXIS 400 (1977); Kozerski v. Smith, 555 F. Supp. 212, 1983 U.S. Dist. LEXIS 20099 (D.N.H. 1983); State v. Bardsley, 125 N.H. 696, 484 A.2d 1187, 1984 N.H. LEXIS 385 (1984); State v. Langone, 127 N.H. 49, 498 A.2d 731, 1985 N.H. LEXIS 399 (1985); State v. Goding, 128 N.H. 267, 513 A.2d 325, 1986 N.H. LEXIS 285 (1986); State v. Landry, 131 N.H. 65, 550 A.2d 94, 1988 N.H. LEXIS 83 (1988); State v. Hodgkiss, 132 N.H. 376, 565 A.2d 1059, 1989 N.H. LEXIS 114 (1989); State v. Homo, 132 N.H. 514, 567 A.2d 540, 1989 N.H. LEXIS 150 (1989); State v. Bousquet, 133 N.H. 485, 578 A.2d 853, 1990 N.H. LEXIS 84 (1990); Appeal of Nolan, 134 N.H. 723, 599 A.2d 112, 1991 N.H. LEXIS 144 (1991); State v. Gagnon, 135 N.H. 217, 600 A.2d 937, 1991 N.H. LEXIS 168 (1991); Opinion of Justices, 135 N.H. 549, 608 A.2d 874, 1992 N.H. LEXIS 214 (1992); State v. Steed, 140 N.H. 153, 665 A.2d 1072, 1995 N.H. LEXIS 115 (1995); State v. Hoyt, 141 N.H. 371, 684 A.2d 1349, 1996 N.H. LEXIS 105 (1996); Hammell v. Warden, 146 N.H. 557, 776 A.2d 740, 2001 N.H. LEXIS 130 (2001).

599:1-a. Petition; Late Appeal.

A person sentenced for an offense by a district or municipal court who fails to appeal as provided in RSA 599:1 may petition said court to enter a late appeal. The petition shall be in writing and shall be made within 3 days from the date sentence is declared. The court shall grant such petition, provided that the person appealing shall appear in person or by his attorney at the next regular session of the court, or at such time and place as the justice of the court shall designate, to perfect his appeal by providing such bail as is determined proper by the court. All other requirements provided for in RSA 599:1 shall be in force.

Source.

1961, 131:1, eff. July 17, 1961.

Revision note.

In the first sentence, inserted "district or" preceding "municipal court" in light of the enactment of RSA 502-A and of the amendment of RSA 599:1 by 1965, 86:1. See RSA 502-A:11 for criminal jurisdiction of district courts generally. See also RSA 502-A:34.

Cross References.

Time for entry of appeal generally, see RSA 599:1.

1. Generally
2. Effect of three-day limit

1. Generally

This section, extending the time for appeal by three days, was not intended to otherwise change the long established practice of requiring prompt appeal if finality of the conviction is to be prevented. State v. Flynn, 110 N.H. 451, 272 A.2d 591, 1970 N.H. LEXIS 197 (1970).

2. Effect of three-day limit

The three-day period for late appeal established by this section marks the outside limit of the jurisdiction of a municipal or district court to modify or vacate a verdict in a criminal case; therefore, a district court order vacating a finding of guilty and a sentence entered thereon and dismissing the complaint was void as beyond the jurisdiction of the court to enter it where it was entered more than three days after the sentence was declared. State v. Flynn, 110 N.H. 451, 272 A.2d 591, 1970 N.H. LEXIS 197 (1970).

Cited:

Cited in State v. Bousquet, 133 N.H. 485, 578 A.2d 853, 1990 N.H. LEXIS 84 (1990).

599:1-b. Petition for Appeal.

Any person aggrieved by a decision of a district or municipal court who was prevented from appealing therefrom, as provided in RSA 599:1 or RSA 599:1-a, through mistake, accident or misfortune, and not from his own neglect, may petition the superior court at any time within 30 days from the time the sentence is declared, to be allowed an appeal, setting forth his interest, his reason for appealing and the cause of his delay. The court may make such order thereon as justice may require.

Source.

1961, 131:2, eff. July 17, 1961.

Revision note.

At the beginning of the section, inserted "district or" preceding "municipal court" in light of the enactment of RSA 502-A and of the amendment of RSA 599:1 by 1965, 86:1. See RSA 502-A:11 for criminal jurisdiction of district courts generally. See also RSA 502-A:34.

Burden of proof

Under this section, the burden of showing that the statutory requirements were met is on defendant. State v. Hess, 118 N.H. 491, 387 A.2d 1183, 1978 N.H. LEXIS 446 (1978).

Cited:

Cited in State v. Bousquet, 133 N.H. 485, 578 A.2d 853, 1990 N.H. LEXIS 84 (1990).

599:1-c. Records Required.

I. Any person charged with any violation or class B misdemeanor may, at least 5 days prior to trial, request the district or municipal court that a sound recording be kept of all proceedings in his trial. If such a request is made, the district or municipal court shall make the sound recording at no cost to the person requesting it.

II. A person sentenced by a district or municipal court for a violation or class B misdemeanor may, at the time the sentence is declared or within 30 days thereafter, appeal therefrom to the supreme court. On any such appeal, the district or municipal court shall, at no cost to the person, provide to the supreme court the sound recording requested under paragraph I.

Source.

1983, 382:18. 1985, 341:8. 1993, 190:18, eff. Jan. 1, 1994.

Amendments

—1993. Substituted "or class B misdemeanor" for "which does not provide a basis for enhanced penalties for subsequent convictions for the same offense or who is charged with any other offense which might result in a conviction for a violation which does not provide a basis for enhanced penalties for subsequent convictions for the same offense" following "any violation" in the first sentence or par. I and for "which does not provide a basis for enhanced penalties for subsequent convictions for the same offense" preceding "may, at the time" in the first sentence of par. II.

—1985. Paragraph I: Substituted "sound recording" for "record" in the second sentence.

Paragraph II: Substituted "sound recording" for "record" in the second sentence.

Cross References.

Appeals from convictions in district or municipal courts generally, see RSA 599:1-1-b.

Classification of crimes, see RSA 625:9.

Recording of proceeding in district courts generally, see RSA 502-A:27-d.

Sentences, see RSA 651.

Cited:

Cited in State v. Penn, 127 N.H. 351, 499 A.2d 1014, 1985 N.H. LEXIS 428 (1985); State v. Hodgkiss, 132 N.H. 376, 565 A.2d 1059, 1989 N.H. LEXIS 114 (1989); State v. Homo, 132 N.H. 514, 567 A.2d 540, 1989 N.H. LEXIS 150 (1989); Lillios v. Justices of New Hampshire Dist. Court, 735 F. Supp. 43, 1990 U.S. Dist. LEXIS 4130 (D.N.H. 1990); State v. Hofland, 151 N.H. 322, 857 A.2d 1271, 2004 N.H. LEXIS 146 (2004).

599:2. Recognizance of Appellant.

Before the appeal is allowed, the appellant shall enter into recognizance, with sufficient sureties, in such sum as the court shall order, not exceeding $2,000, to appear at the court of appeal, to prosecute his appeal with effect, to abide the order of the court thereon and, if so required, to be of good behavior in the meantime, or shall surrender himself to the proper authority for the purpose of commitment to the county jail or house of correction pending such appeal.

Source.

RS 222:2. CS 237:2. GS 240:3. GL 258:3. PS 252:3. 1913, 68:1. 1915, 38:1. PL 366:3. 1931, 161:1. RL 425:3.

Cross References.

Allowance of bail or recognizance pending appeal, see RSA 597:1-a.

Forfeiture of recognizance, see RSA 599:3.

NOTES TO DECISIONS

Cited:

Cited in State v. Griffin, 66 N.H. 326, 29 A. 414, 1890 N.H. LEXIS 32 (1890); State v. Gerry, 68 N.H. 495, 38 A. 272, 1896 N.H. LEXIS 41, 38 L.R.A. 228 (1896); State v. Bousquet, 133 N.H. 485, 578 A.2d 853, 1990 N.H. LEXIS 84 (1990).

599:3. Failure to Prosecute Appeal.

If the appellant fails to enter his appeal within the time limited and prosecute his appeal, a record thereof shall be made, his recognizance shall be declared forfeited, and, within 10 days, the clerk of court shall transmit to the district or municipal court appealed from a certificate of such forfeiture.

Source.

1862, 2606. GS 240:4. GL 258:4. PS 252:4. PL 366:4. 1927, 10:2. 1937, 49:2. RL 425:4. RSA 599:3. 1957, 244:39, eff. Sept. 23, 1957.

Amendments

—1957. Deleted "justice or" preceding "clerk of court".

Revision note.

At the end of the section, inserted "district or" preceding "municipal court" in light of the enactment of RSA 502-A and of the amendment of RSA 599:1 by 1965, 86:1. See RSA 502-A:11 for criminal jurisdiction of district courts generally. See also RSA 502-A:34.

NOTES TO DECISIONS

1. Constitutionality
2. Absence from hearing

1. Constitutionality

Defendant's constitutional right to jury trial was not violated by superior court's denial of motion to reinstate, in that forum, defendant's appeal from district court requesting a trial de novo by jury, where defendant failed to appear in superior court and prosecute his appeal; contention was rejected that defendant could only waive his jury trial right with an express personal waiver indicating his understanding of that right. State v. Bousquet, 133 N.H. 485, 578 A.2d 853, 1990 N.H. LEXIS 84 (1990), cert. denied, Bousquet v. New Hampshire, 498 U.S. 1035, 111 S. Ct. 700, 112 L. Ed. 2d 690, 1991 U.S. LEXIS 241 (1991), US Supreme Crt. cert. denied, Adamu v. United States, 498 U.S. 1036, 111 S. Ct. 700, 112 L. Ed. 2d 690, 1991 U.S. LEXIS 223 (1991).

2. Absence from hearing

Defendant's failure to appear personally at motion hearing did not constitute a failure to prosecute for purposes of this section, and thus he could not reasonably be deemed to have waived his right to trial by jury. State v. Hoyt, 141 N.H. 371, 684 A.2d 1349, 1996 N.H. LEXIS 105 (1996).

Cited:

Cited in State v. Gerry, 68 N.H. 495, 38 A. 272, 1896 N.H. LEXIS 41, 38 L.R.A. 228 (1896); State v. Reenstierna, 101 N.H. 286, 140 A.2d 572, 1958 N.H. LEXIS 18 (1958); Appeal of Nolan, 134 N.H. 723, 599 A.2d 112, 1991 N.H. LEXIS 144 (1991).

599:4. Enforcing Original Sentence.

The justice shall record the certificate of forfeiture, and he shall issue a mittimus or other process to carry into effect the original sentence.

Source.

1862, 2606. GS 240:4. GL 258:4. PS 252:4. PL 366:5. RL 425:5. RSA 599:4. 1955, 322:4, eff. Aug. 5, 1955.

Amendments

—1955. Rewritten to the extent that a detailed comparison would be impracticable.

Revision note.

For purposes of clarity, substituted "the certificate of forfeiture" for "such certificate" following "justice shall record".

NOTES TO DECISIONS

Cited:

Cited in State v. Gerry, 68 N.H. 495, 38 A. 272, 1896 N.H. LEXIS 41, 38 L.R.A. 228 (1896); State v. Reenstierna, 101 N.H. 286, 140 A.2d 572, 1958 N.H. LEXIS 18 (1958); State v. Bousquet, 133 N.H. 485, 578 A.2d 853, 1990 N.H. LEXIS 84 (1990); Appeal of Nolan, 134 N.H. 723, 599 A.2d 112, 1991 N.H. LEXIS 144 (1991).

CHAPTER 600

GRAND JURIES

SECTION
600:1.   Drawing Jurors.
600:2.   Issuance of Venires in Emergencies.
600:3.   Oath.
600:4.   Oath to Witnesses.
600:5.   Clerk; Minutes.

Cross References.

Indictments, informations and complaints, see RSA 601.
Multi county grand juries, see RSA 600-A.
Payment of jurors' fees, see RSA 500-A:15.

NOTES TO DECISIONS

Generally

In this state, a grand jury is an investigatory body as well as an accusatory body; its investigation may result in an indictment, or it may not; and its investigations are not subject to legislative control and its common law powers are not restricted. Powell v. Pappagianis, 108 N.H. 523, 238 A.2d 733, 1968 N.H. LEXIS 204 (1968).

600:1. Drawing Jurors.

Grand jurors shall be drawn, summoned and returned in the same manner as jurors for trials, and talesmen, not exceeding 5, under the direction of the court may be returned by the sheriff or other officer.

Source.

RS 176:20. CS 186:21. GS 242:2. GL 260:2. PS 253:2. PL 367:2. RL 427:2.

Cross References.

Drawing, summoning and selection of jurors generally, see RSA 500-A.

600:2. Issuance of Venires in Emergencies.

In case of emergency, venires may be issued for grand jurors to be drawn and notified and to attend forthwith as in the case of petit jurors.

Source.
RS 176:15. CS 186:16. GS 242:3. GL 260:3. PS 253:3. PL 367:3. RL 427:3.

Cross References.
Drawing, summoning and selection of jurors generally, see RSA 500-A.

600:3. Oath.

Grand jurors before entering upon their duties shall take the following oath: You, as grand jurors, do solemnly swear that you will diligently inquire, and a true presentment make, of all such matters and things as shall be given you in charge; the state's counsel, your fellows' and your own you shall keep secret; and shall present no person for envy, hatred or malice; neither shall you leave any unpresented for love, fear, favor, affection or hope of reward; but you shall present things truly as they come to your knowledge, according to the best of your understanding. So help you God.

Source.
RS 176:22. CS 186:23. GS 242:5. GL 260:5. PS 253:5. PL 367:4. RL 427:4. RSA 600:3. 1992, 284:78, eff. Jan. 1, 1993.

Amendments
—**1992.** Deleted "for the body of this county" preceding "do solemnly" and substituted "person" for "man" preceding "for envy" in the first sentence of the oath.

NOTES TO DECISIONS

Legislative investigation of grand jurors
The investigatory power of the legislature does not extend to interrogation of grand jurors concerning their votes, deliberations, or opinions, as to which they are sworn to secrecy; legislative investigation of alleged irregularities in grand jury proceedings by interrogation of the grand jurors is limited to inquiries concerning occurrences during the jury's investigations, and is permissible only when their testimony is necessary to promote or protect public or private rights of sufficient importance to warrant releasing them from their oath. Opinion of Justices, 96 N.H. 530, 73 A.2d 433, 1950 N.H. LEXIS 202 (1950).

Cited:
Cited in Powell v. Pappagianis, 108 N.H. 523, 238 A.2d 733, 1968 N.H. LEXIS 204 (1968); State v. Cobb, 143 N.H. 638, 732 A.2d 425, 1999 N.H. LEXIS 53 (1999).

600:4. Oath to Witnesses.

The foreman of the grand jury, the prosecuting officer or any justice upon the jury may administer oaths to witnesses to be examined before them.

Source.
GS 242:6. GL 260:6. PS 253:6. PL 367:5. RL 427:5.

Cross References.
Oath of witnesses generally, see RSA 516:19, 20.

NOTES TO DECISIONS

Cited:
Cited in State v. Canatella, 96 N.H. 202, 72 A.2d 507, 1950 N.H. LEXIS 144 (1950).

600:5. Clerk; Minutes.

The grand jury may appoint one of their number to be clerk to preserve minutes of the proceedings before them, which shall be delivered to the attorney general or county attorney.

Source.
GS 242:7. GL 260:7. PS 253:7. PL 367:7 RL 427:6.

NOTES TO DECISIONS

Transcription of proceedings
This section does not mention a stenographer, nor does it contain any provision for the superior court to approve a transcript of the grand jury proceeding. State v. Purrington, 122 N.H. 458, 446 A.2d 451, 1982 N.H. LEXIS 377 (1982).
Since there is neither legislation nor court rule in New Hampshire authorizing a court to order the transcription of testimony given before a grand jury, the supreme court will not sanction any transcription of grand jury testimony. State v. Purrington, 122 N.H. 458, 446 A.2d 451, 1982 N.H. LEXIS 377 (1982).

Cited:
Cited in State v. Vanderheyden, 132 N.H. 536, 567 A.2d 553, 1989 N.H. LEXIS 135 (1989).

CHAPTER 600-A

MULTICOUNTY GRAND JURIES

SECTION
600-A:1.   Application for Multicounty Grand Jury.
600-A:2.   Contents of Order Convening Multicounty Grand Jury.
600-A:3.   Term.
600-A:4.   Applicable Law.
600-A:5.   Presentation of Evidence to Multicounty Grand Jury.
600-A:6.   Indictment; Designation of Venue; Consolidation.
600-A:7.   Prosecution of Indictments.
600-A:8.   Costs and Expenses.

Cross References.
Grand juries generally, see RSA 600.
Indictments, informations and complaints, see RSA 601.
Payment of juror's fees, see RSA 500-A:15.

600-A:1. Application for Multicounty Grand Jury.

Application for a multicounty grand jury may be made by the attorney general to the supreme court. In such application the attorney general shall state that, in his or her judgment, the convening of a multicounty grand jury is necessary because of an alleged crime or crimes involving more than one county or judicial district thereof of the state and that, in his or her judgment, the grand jury functions cannot be effectively performed by a county grand jury. The application shall specify for which counties or judicial districts thereof the multicounty grand jury is to be convened.

Source.
1985, 133:1. 1992, 284:79, eff. July 1, 1992.

Amendments
—**1992.** Inserted "or her" following "his" in two places in the second sentence, "or judicial district thereof" following "county" in that sentence and "or judicial districts thereof" following "counties" in the third sentence.

600-A:2. Contents of Order Convening Multicounty Grand Jury.

I. An order issued upon an application made pursuant to RSA 600-A:1 shall:

(a) Convene a multicounty grand jury having statewide jurisdiction, or jurisdiction over all counties and judicial districts thereof requested in the application by the attorney general;

(b) Designate a judge of a superior court to be supervising judge over such multicounty grand jury and provide that such judge shall, with respect to all proper activities of said multicounty grand jury, have jurisdiction over all counties or judicial districts thereof in the jurisdiction of said multicounty grand jury;

(c) Designate the counties or judicial districts thereof which shall supply jurors and in what ratios;

(d) Designate a location or locations for the multicounty grand jury proceeding; and

(e) Provide for such other incidental arrangements as may be necessary.

II. All matters to be included in such order shall be determined by the justice issuing the order in any manner which he deems appropriate, except that the supreme court may adopt general rules, consistent with the provisions of this chapter, establishing standard procedures for the convening of multicounty grand juries.

Source.
1985, 133:1. 1992, 284:80, eff. July 1, 1992.

Amendments
—**1992.** Paragraph I: Inserted "and judicial districts thereof" following "counties" in subpar. (a) and "or judicial districts thereof" following "counties" in subpars. (b) and (c).

600-A:3. Term.

The regular term of the multicounty grand jury shall be 6 months. The terms may be shortened by the supervising judge at the request of the attorney general. The term may be extended by the supervising judge for a specified time period upon a written petition by the attorney general stating that an extension is needed to conclude a multicounty grand jury begun prior to the expiration of its term.

Source.
1985, 133:1, eff. Jan. 1, 1986.

600-A:4. Applicable Law.

The law applicable to county grand juries, including their powers, duties and functions, shall apply to multicounty grand juries except insofar as it is in conflict with this chapter.

Source.
1985, 133:1, eff. Jan. 1, 1986.

Cross References.
Grand juries generally, see RSA 600.

600-A:5. Presentation of Evidence to Multicounty Grand Jury.

Evidence shall be presented a multicounty grand jury by the attorney general or his designee.

Source.
1985, 133:1, eff. Jan. 1, 1986.

600-A:6. Indictment; Designation of Venue; Consolidation.

Any indictment by any multicounty grand jury shall be returned to the supervising judge and shall include a finding as to the county, judicial district thereof, or counties in which the alleged offense was committed. Thereupon, the supervising judge shall, by order, designate the county of venue for the purpose of trial. The supervising judge may, by order, direct the consolidation of an indictment returned by a county grand jury with an indictment returned by a multicounty grand jury and fix venue for trial.

Source.
1985, 133:1. 1992, 284:81, eff. July 1, 1992.

Amendments
—**1992.** Inserted "judicial district thereof" following "county" in the first sentence.

Cross References.
Indictments, informations and complaints generally, see RSA 601.
Trial generally, see RSA 606.
Venue generally, see RSA 602.

600-A:7. Prosecution of Indictments.

The attorney general or his designee shall prosecute all indictments returned by a multicounty grand jury.

Source.
1985, 133:1, eff. Jan. 1, 1986.

600-A:8. Costs and Expenses.

The costs and expenses incurred by impaneling a multicounty grand jury and in the performance of its functions and duties shall be paid by the state.

Source.
1985, 133:1, eff. Jan. 1, 1986.

CHAPTER 601

INDICTMENTS, INFORMATIONS, AND COMPLAINTS

SECTION
601:1.   Indictments, Necessity.
601:2.   Waiving Indictment.

SECTION
601:3.   Additional Charges.
601:3-a.   Waiving Indictment in Other Cases.
601:4.   Sufficiency.
601:5.   Charging Intent to Defraud.
601:6.   Charging Manner of Death.
601:6-a.   Joining Charges.
601:7.   Charging Assaults.
601:8.   Formal Errors, etc.
601:9.   Lotteries.

Cross References.

Form of indictments, etc., see New Hampshire Constitution, Part 2, Article 88.

Grand juries generally, see RSA 600.

Limitation periods for criminal prosecutions, see RSA 625:8.

Multi county grand juries, see RSA 600-A.

Pleas generally, see RSA 605.

Right of persons accused of capital offenses and first degree murder to copy of indictment, see RSA 604:1.

601:1. Indictments, Necessity.

No person shall be tried for any offense, the punishment of which may be death or imprisonment for more than one year, unless upon an indictment found against such person by the grand jury of the county or judicial district thereof in which the offense is committed or is triable.

Source.

RS 225:1. CS 240:1. GS 242:1. GL 260:1. PS 253:1. PL 367:1. RL 427:1. RSA 601:1. 1992, 284:82, eff. July 1, 1992.

Amendments

—1992. Deleted "for" following "Necessity" in the section catchline, substituted "such person" for "him" following "against" and inserted "or judicial district thereof" following "county".

Cross References.

Classification of crimes, see RSA 625:9.

Right of accused to copy of indictment, see RSA 604:1.

Sentences, see RSA 651.

Sufficiency of indictments generally, see RSA 601:4 et seq.

NOTES TO DECISIONS

1. Amendment of indictment
2. Amendment of indictment

1. Amendment of indictment

Indictment is required for a misdemeanor charge that results in extended imprisonment greater than one year, when a sentencing enhancement factor is related to offense itself. State v. Ouellette, 145 N.H. 489, 764 A.2d 914, 2000 N.H. LEXIS 96 (2000).

Trial court erred in sentencing misdemeanor defendant to prison for more than one year for offenses that were charged by information and not by indictment, since his extended terms were based on punishment related to offenses themselves and not upon his recidivism. State v. Ouellette, 145 N.H. 489, 764 A.2d 914, 2000 N.H. LEXIS 96 (2000).

Misdemeanor assault defendant did not waive his right to indictment by stipulating that he knew victim was a law enforcement officer acting in the line of duty at time of assault. State v. Ouellette, 145 N.H. 489, 764 A.2d 914, 2000 N.H. LEXIS 96 (2000).

In imposing sentence enhancement based on prior convictions, trial court could properly sentence defendant to prison terms exceeding one year for crimes charged by information; portion of extended terms that exceeded maximum generally applicable sentence did not transform charged misdemeanor offenses into crimes required to be charged by indictment. State v. Smith, 144 N.H. 1, 736 A.2d 1236, 1999 N.H. LEXIS 66 (1999).

This section should be considered in conjunction with the requirement of part 1, article 15 of the state constitution that no subject shall be held to answer for any crime or offense until the same is fully and plainly, substantially and formally, described to him; the allegations of indictment must inform the defendant of the offense charged with sufficient specificity so that he knows what he must be prepared to meet and so that he is protected from being twice put in jeopardy. State v. Bean, 117 N.H. 185, 371 A.2d 1152, 1977 N.H. LEXIS 298 (1977).

2. Amendment of indictment

On appeal from conviction of manslaughter, claim that trial court impermissibly amended grand jury's indictment would be examined by supreme court under state constitution despite normally preclusive effect of defendant's failure to raise state constitutional issue below; claim alleged violation of this section guaranteeing individual's right to an indictment by grant jury for crimes punishable by greater than one year of imprisonment which must be considered in conjunction with constitutional provision guaranteeing that individual may only be convicted of crime charged in grand jury's indictment. State v. Elliott, 133 N.H. 759, 585 A.2d 304, 1990 N.H. LEXIS 135 (1990).

Cited:

Cited in State v. Webster, 105 N.H. 415, 200 A.2d 856, 1964 N.H. LEXIS 90 (1964); State v. Erickson, 129 N.H. 515, 533 A.2d 23, 1987 N.H. LEXIS 253 (1987); State v. Allegra, 130 N.H. 720, 533 A.2d 338, 1987 N.H. LEXIS 247 (1987); State v. Johnson, 130 N.H. 578, 547 A.2d 213, 1988 N.H. LEXIS 64 (1988); State v. Pelky, 131 N.H. 715, 559 A.2d 1345, 1989 N.H. LEXIS 52 (1989); State v. Pond, 132 N.H. 472, 567 A.2d 992, 1989 N.H. LEXIS 129 (1989).

601:2. Waiving Indictment.

Any person who has been bound over or committed by a justice or district or municipal court under the provisions of RSA 592-A:4 or 6 for trial in the superior court upon a complaint charging a crime not punishable by death, and who desires to waive indictment, may apply in writing to the superior court for prompt arraignment upon such complaint. Upon the filing of such an application, the county attorney may, with the approval of the court, proceed against the defendant by complaint, and in such case he shall be held to answer and the court shall have as full jurisdiction of the complaint as if an indictment had been found. The arraignment of the defendant shall be at such time as the court may designate. Every person when so committed or bound over upon such a complaint shall be notified by the court of his right to apply for waiver of indictment and prompt arraignment as aforesaid.

Source.

1945, 38:1, eff. March 6, 1945.

Revision note.

In the first sentence, inserted "district or" preceding "municipal court" in light of the enactment of RSA 502-A. See RSA 502-A:11 for criminal jurisdiction of district courts generally. See also RSA 502-A:34.

Cross References.

Classification of crimes, see RSA 625:9.

Sentences, see RSA 651.

Waiver of indictment upon other charges, see RSA 601:3, 3-a.

RESEARCH REFERENCES

New Hampshire Court Rules Annotated.

Waiver of arraignment, see Rule 97, Rules of the Superior Court, New Hampshire Court Rules Annotated.

601:3. Additional Charges.

If the county attorney desires to charge a defendant making application under RSA 601:2 with a crime or crimes not punishable by death other than a crime charged in the complaint upon which the defendant has been committed or bound over, the county attorney may, before consenting to such application, prepare a complaint or complaints charging such other crime or crimes and serve the same upon the defendant in order that he may have an opportunity to waive indictment upon such other charges. If an application for waiver of indictment as to any such other charge is subsequently filed, the court shall, before approving such application, require an affidavit of service upon the defendant as part of the record of the case. The superior court shall by rule establish forms for application to waive indictment under this chapter and may by rule make such other regulations of procedure under this chapter as justice may require.

Source.
1945, 38:1, eff. March 6, 1945.

Revision note.
For purposes of clarity, substituted "under RSA 601:2" for "hereunder" and "the defendant" for "he" in the first sentence and "under this chapter" for "hereunder" in the third sentence.

Cross References.
Classification of crimes, see RSA 625:9.
Sentences, see RSA 651.
Waiver of indictment generally, see RSA 601:2.
Waiver of indictment upon felonies generally, see RSA 601:3-a.

601:3-a. Waiving Indictment in Other Cases.

If there is no provision in RSA 601:2 or 3, any county attorney may charge a person with a felony not punishable by death by preparing a complaint charging such felony and serving the same on the defendant in order that the defendant may have an opportunity to waive indictment on such felony, and if the defendant does so waive indictment, and the superior court approves the waiver, after an affidavit of service on the defendant has been filed, the defendant shall be held to answer and the superior court shall have as full jurisdiction of the complaint as if an indictment had been found.

Source.
1965, 302:1, eff. Sept. 5, 1965.

Cross References.
Classification of crimes, see RSA 625:9.
Sentences, see RSA 651.
Waiver of indictment generally, see RSA 601:2.
Waiver of indictment upon offenses charged after original complaint, see RSA 601:3.

601:4. Sufficiency.

An indictment, information or complaint is sufficient if it sets forth the offense fully, plainly, substantially and formally, and it is not necessary to set forth therein the special statute, bylaw or ordinance on which it is founded.

Source.
1855, 1699:17. GS 242:10. GL 260:10. PS 253:9. PL 367:8. RL 427:8.

Cross References.
Effect of formal errors, etc., see RSA 601:8.
Necessity for indictment, see RSA 601:1.

NOTES TO DECISIONS

1. Generally
2. Particular offenses
3. Errors of form

1. Generally
An indictment is sufficient if it sets forth the offense fully, plainly, substantially, and formally. State v. Brewer, 127 N.H. 799, 508 A.2d 1058, 1986 N.H. LEXIS 232 (1986).

An indictment is not sufficient merely because the state deems a crime charged in an indictment to be generally understood; the necessary elements of the crime must be included in it. State v. Bussiere, 118 N.H. 659, 392 A.2d 151, 1978 N.H. LEXIS 263 (1978).

2. Particular offenses
An indictment alleging that a victim submitted to sexual penetration under circumstances involving kidnapping (a violation of RSA 632-A:2) must enumerate the facts establishing the necessary elements of the offense of kidnapping. State v. Bussiere, 118 N.H. 659, 392 A.2d 151, 1978 N.H. LEXIS 263 (1978).

3. Errors of form
Where indictment stated clearly that defendant was charged with second degree assault, incorrect statutory reference therein was merely error of form not requiring abatement of the indictment. State v. Mansfield, 134 N.H. 287, 592 A.2d 512, 1991 N.H. LEXIS 54 (1991).

Cited:
Cited in State v. Thresher, 122 N.H. 63, 442 A.2d 578, 1982 N.H. LEXIS 288 (1982); State v. Pelky, 131 N.H. 715, 559 A.2d 1345, 1989 N.H. LEXIS 52 (1989); State v. Homo, 132 N.H. 514, 567 A.2d 540, 1989 N.H. LEXIS 150 (1989); State v. Lachapelle, 133 N.H. 1, 572 A.2d 584, 1990 N.H. LEXIS 27 (1990); State v. Bird, 161 N.H. 31, 8 A.3d 146, 2010 N.H. LEXIS 125 (2010).

601:5. Charging Intent to Defraud.

When an intent to defraud is necessary to constitute any offense, it is sufficient to allege in the indictment or information such intent generally, and proof of an intent to defraud some person or body corporate is competent to support such indictment or information.

Source.
RS 225:18. CS 240:21. GS 242:11. GL 260:11. PS 253:10. PL 367:9. RL 427:9.

Cross References.
Offenses involving fraud generally, see RSA 638.
Sufficiency of indictments generally, see RSA 601:4.

NOTES TO DECISIONS

Law governing

Enactment of comprehensive criminal code did not render pre-existing forgery statute inapplicable. State v. DeMatteo, 134 N.H. 296, 591 A.2d 1323, 1991 N.H. LEXIS 56 (1991).

601:6. Charging Manner of Death.

In indictments charging any degree of murder, including capital murder, it is not necessary to set forth the manner in which or the means by which the death of the deceased was caused, but it is sufficient in an indictment for murder to charge the culpable mental state applicable and, where appropriate, the particular circumstances set forth in RSA 630:1, I, RSA 630:1-a, I, or RSA 630:1-b, I, constituting an element of the offense charged, and in an indictment for manslaughter to charge the culpable mental state applicable and, where appropriate, the particular circumstances set forth in RSA 630:2 constituting an element of the offense charged.

Source.

GS 242:14. GL 260:14. PS 253:11. PL 367:10. RL 427:10. RSA 601:6. 1977, 315:1, eff. Aug. 26, 1977.

Amendments

—1977. Rewritten to the extent that a detailed comparison would be impracticable.

Cross References.

Culpable mental states generally, see RSA 626:2.
Sufficiency of indictments generally, see RSA 601:4.

NOTES TO DECISIONS

1. Allegation of cause of death
2. Allegation of mental state

1. Allegation of cause of death

An indictment for second-degree murder need not state the exact cause of death of the victim provided that all elements of the crime charged are alleged with sufficient specificity for the defendant to prepare his defense. State v. Thresher, 122 N.H. 63, 442 A.2d 578, 1982 N.H. LEXIS 288 (1982).

Where an indictment for second-degree murder stated that death was caused by beating "with hands, feet and a bottle," the indictment stated the necessary information. State v. Thresher, 122 N.H. 63, 442 A.2d 578, 1982 N.H. LEXIS 288 (1982).

An indictment for murder which charged that the accused "in some way and manner, and by some means, instrument, and weapon to the jurors unknown" killed and murdered the deceased was sufficient. State v. Burke, 54 N.H. 92, 1873 N.H. LEXIS 10 (1873).

2. Allegation of mental state

An indictment for being an accomplice to first-degree murder, which did not allege malice aforethought or premeditation and deliberation, but did allege that the defendant did certain acts "with the purpose of facilitating the first degree murder" of the victim and that he performed the specified acts "with the purpose of causing the death" of the victim, was sufficient since murder had been redefined, eliminating the requirement that premeditation and deliberation be specifically alleged; the word "purposely," as defined in RSA 630:1-a governing first-degree murder, satisfies the common-law "malice aforethought" requirement in a first-degree murder indictment; and the indictment satisfied even the more rigid requirements of this section before it was amended in 1977 to require only that "the culpable mental state applicable" be charged. State v. Glidden, 123 N.H. 126, 459 A.2d 1136, 1983 N.H. LEXIS 240 (1983).

The words "deliberately and with premeditation" in a first-degree murder indictment satisfied the requirement of this section that an allegation of malice aforethought appear in the indictment. State v. Conklin, 115 N.H. 331, 341 A.2d 770, 1975 N.H. LEXIS 299 (1975), overruled, State v. Dayutis, 127 N.H. 101, 498 A.2d 325, 1985 N.H. LEXIS 379 (1985).

601:6-a. Joining Charges.

The crime of murder shall not be charged in the same indictment with the offense of concealing the death of a newborn child.

Source.

1859, 2221:3. GS 264:6. GL 282:6. PS 278:6. PL 392:7. RL 455:7. RSA 585:7. 1973, 370:5, eff. Nov. 1, 1973.

Cross References.

Concealing death of newborn child, see RSA 639:5.
Murder, see RSA 630:1-a, 1-b.

601:7. Charging Assaults.

It is not necessary, in an indictment for assault and battery, to allege that any preliminary proceedings have been had in the case before a justice or district or municipal court.

Source.

1860, 2360. GS 242:12. GL 260:12. PS 253:12. PL 367:11. RL 427:11.

Revision note.

At the end of the section, inserted "district or" preceding "municipal court" in light of the enactment of RSA 502-A.

Cross References.

Offenses involving assault, see RSA 631.

601:8. Formal Errors, etc.

No indictment, complaint, return, process, judgment or other proceeding in any criminal case in the courts or course of justice shall be abated, quashed or reversed for any error or mistake where the person or case may be rightly understood by the court, nor through any defect or want of form or addition, and courts and justices may, on motion, order amendments in any such case.

Source.

1863, 2724:1. GS 242:13. GL 260:13. PS 253:13. PL 367:12. RL 427:12.

Cross References.

Sufficiency of indictments generally, see RSA 601:4.

NOTES TO DECISIONS

1. In general
2. Purpose
3. Documents subject to amendment—Indictment
4. —Information
5. —Return on search warrant
6. Defects subject to correction—Date in caption of indictment
7. —Date or time of commission of alleged offense
8. —Value and description of objects alleged to have been stolen
9. —Ownership of goods alleged to have been stolen
10. —Residence of victim of offense

1. In general

Courts are allowed to amend indictments in form, but not substance, and, therefore, instructing the jury on an element not charged by the grand jury substantively changes the offense and is grounds for automatic reversal. State v. Prevost, 141 N.H. 559, 689 A.2d 121, 1997 N.H. LEXIS 1 (1997).

2. Purpose

This section is meant only to prevent technical defects or imperfections in matters of form from frustrating the orderly administration of justice; the section does not allow the court to disregard a defect in respect of a matter of substance. State v. Bean, 117 N.H. 185, 371 A.2d 1152, 1977 N.H. LEXIS 298 (1977).

3. Documents subject to amendment—Indictment

This section does not authorize amendments of indictments in matters of substance, but rather in form only, and where there is a variance between the description of a place stated in an indictment as a matter of local description and the evidence at trial, the variance is fatal since it involves a matter of substance. State v. Kelley, 66 N.H. 577, 29 A. 843, 1891 N.H. LEXIS 85 (1891).

4. —Information

A criminal information which is defective may seasonably be amended under this section in the same manner as a criminal complaint. State v. Green, 105 N.H. 260, 197 A.2d 204, 1964 N.H. LEXIS 58 (1964).

An information is subject to amendment under this section. State v. Lothrops-Farnham Co., 84 N.H. 322, 150 A. 551, 1930 N.H. LEXIS 87 (1930).

5. —Return on search warrant

Under the provisions of this section, a court may permit a return on a search warrant to be signed by the officer making the search, even after a motion to quash the complaint has been made. State v. Agalos, 79 N.H. 241, 107 A. 314, 1919 N.H. LEXIS 40 (1919).

6. Defects subject to correction—Date in caption of indictment

An erroneous statement in the caption of an indictment of the year in which it was found does not furnish a ground for a motion to quash since the defect may be cured by amendment as provided by this section. State v. Jenkins, 64 N.H. 375, 10 A. 699, 1887 N.H. LEXIS 19 (1887).

7. —Date or time of commission of alleged offense

If time is not of the essence of an offense charged, an erroneous or defective allegation as to the time of the commission of the crime is a matter of form which may be corrected under this section; however, amendment is not allowed when the circumstances of the case are such that a change must be regarded as a matter of substance, as affecting a change in the offense charged, or as adding an offense. State v. Spade, 118 N.H. 186, 385 A.2d 115, 1978 N.H. LEXIS 373 (1978).

An indictment which improperly charged the date of the commission of a burglary could be amended so as to state the true date of the commission of the alleged offense. State v. Blaisdell, 49 N.H. 81, 1869 N.H. LEXIS 11 (1869).

8. —Value and description of objects alleged to have been stolen

An indictment for robbery charging the accused with taking "eighteen dollars of the lawful currency and money of the United States of America of the value of eighteen dollars of the goods and chattels" of the complaining witness sufficiently described the money alleged to have been taken, even though there was no particular description of the bills and coins and no recital that a more particular description was, to the grand jurors, unknown. State v. Canatella, 96 N.H. 202, 72 A.2d 507, 1950 N.H. LEXIS 144 (1950).

In an indictment for receiving stolen goods knowing the same to have been stolen, an allegation as to the value of the goods was a matter of substance rather than form where it was determinative of the question of what court had original jurisdiction in the matter, and the indictment could not be amended to give a justice or municipal court jurisdiction, which, under the terms of the original indictment, was vested in the superior court. State v. Dolby, 49 N.H. 483, 1870 N.H. LEXIS 37 (1870).

An indictment for larceny must state the value of the goods alleged to have been stolen, and if it does not, it is bad in substance and cannot be amended. State v. Goodrich, 46 N.H. 186, 1865 N.H. LEXIS 53 (1865).

9. —Ownership of goods alleged to have been stolen

In an indictment for larceny, the name of the owner of the goods alleged to have been stolen is a matter of substance, and cannot be supplied by amendment. State v. Lyon, 47 N.H. 416, 1867 N.H. LEXIS 33 (1867), overruled in part, State v. Fennelly, 123 N.H. 378, 461 A.2d 1090, 1983 N.H. LEXIS 288 (1983).

10. —Residence of victim of offense

The failure of an indictment for embezzlement to describe the place of residence of the person defrauded does not render it invalid if the identity of such person is understood. State v. Goodwin, 101 N.H. 252, 139 A.2d 630, 1958 N.H. LEXIS 10 (1958).

Cited:

Cited in State v. Clark, 54 N.H. 456, 1874 N.H. LEXIS 64 (1874); State v. George, 93 N.H. 408, 43 A.2d 256, 1945 N.H. LEXIS 148 (1945); State v. Crockett, 116 N.H. 324, 358 A.2d 414, 1976 N.H. LEXIS 343 (1976); State v. Erickson, 129 N.H. 515, 533 A.2d 23, 1987 N.H. LEXIS 253 (1987); State v. Johnson, 130 N.H. 578, 547 A.2d 213, 1988 N.H. LEXIS 64 (1988); State v. Comley, 130 N.H. 688, 546 A.2d 1066, 1988 N.H. LEXIS 50 (1988); State v. Pond, 132 N.H. 472, 567 A.2d 992, 1989 N.H. LEXIS 129 (1989); State v. Settle, 132 N.H. 626, 570 A.2d 895, 1990 N.H. LEXIS 3 (1990).

601:9. Lotteries.

In a complaint or indictment in any case arising under RSA 647:1, a lottery may be described as a pretended lottery, which shall be sufficient, whatever the proof may be, and it shall not be necessary to allege or prove, upon trial, who is the owner of the property, nor who manages, conducts, or draws the lottery, or participates therein.

Source.

1855, 1697. GS 254:4. GL 272:4. PS 270:4. PL 384:4. RL 447:4. RSA 577:4. 1973, 532:17, eff. Nov. 1, 1973.

CHAPTER 602

VENUE

SECTION
602:1.   Parts of Offense in More Than One County, etc.
602:2.   Arraignment and Bail of Defaulters.

Cross References.

Jurisdiction of criminal offenses generally, see RSA 625:4.
Trial generally, see RSA 606.
Venue of criminal prosecutions generally, see New Hampshire Constitution, Part 1, Article 17.

NOTES TO DECISIONS

Cited:

Cited in State v. Wentzell, 131 N.H. 151, 551 A.2d 960, 1988 N.H. LEXIS 100 (1988); State v. Enderson, 148 N.H. 252, 804 A.2d 448, 2002 N.H. LEXIS 116 (2002).

602:1. Parts of Offense in More Than One County, etc.

Offenders shall be prosecuted and tried in the county or judicial district thereof in which the offense was committed. But if any person is feloniously stricken, wounded or poisoned in one county or judicial district thereof and dies thereof in another, or if parts of an offense are committed in more than one county or judicial district thereof, the offense shall be deemed to have been committed, the offender may be prosecuted, and the trial may be had in either county or judicial district thereof.

Source.

RS 225:2. CS 240:2. 1863, 2722. GS 242:9. GL 260:9. PS 253:8. PL 367:7. RL 427:7. RSA 602:1. 1992, 284:83, eff. July 1, 1992.

Amendments

—1992. Inserted "or judicial district thereof" following "county" in the first sentence and in three places in the second sentence.

NOTES TO DECISIONS

1. Procurement of commission of a crime
2. Waiver of venue

1. Procurement of commission of a crime

Where a felony is incited and procured in another state, but designed to be committed in this state, the accessory before the fact cannot be tried in the county in this state within which the principal offense is committed for the offense of procuring the commission of the crime since the crime alleged to have been committed by the accessory was committed and completed in another state. State v. Moore, 26 N.H. 448, 1853 N.H. LEXIS 82 (1853).

2. Waiver of venue

Where defendant's criminal matter was transferred to a county other than where his criminal act was allegedly committed due to the recusal of all of the judges in the county where the crime occurred, and defendant was thereafter tried in a bench trial, his motion for a directed verdict at the end of the case based on improper venue under N.H. Const. pt. I, art. 17 and RSA 602:1 was untimely; the objection to venue was accordingly deemed waived, and the trial court's grant of the directed verdict was erroneous in the circumstances. State v. Johanson (In re State), 156 N.H. 148, 932 A.2d 848, 2007 N.H. LEXIS 152 (2007).

602:2. Arraignment and Bail of Defaulters.

A justice of any district, municipal, or superior court in this state shall hold an arraignment and bail hearing on any person who has been arrested on a warrant for default of a court appearance or nonpayment of a fine, regardless of the county or judicial district in which the warrant was issued. The court, with the agreement of the state and the defendant, may accept a plea of guilty or no contest.

Source.

1996, 182:1, eff. June 3, 1996.

CHAPTER 603

LIMITATION OF PROSECUTIONS

[Repealed 1977, 588:19, eff. Sept. 16, 1977.]

Former section(s).

Former RSA 603:1, which was derived from RS 211:8, 9; CS 224:8, 9; GS 242:8; GL 260:8; PS 253:14; PL 367:13; RL 427:13; RSA 603:1; and 1967, 240:1, related to periods of limitation of prosecutions, on information and indictments. See now RSA 625:8.

CHAPTER 604

RIGHTS OF ACCUSED

SECTION
604:1.　　　Capital Cases and First Degree Murder.
604:1-a.　　Discovery in Criminal Matters.
604:2, 604:3. [Repealed.].

Cross References.

Constitutional rights of accused generally, see New Hampshire Constitution, Part 1, Article 15.

604:1. Capital Cases and First Degree Murder.

Every person indicted for an offense punishable by death or for murder in the first degree shall be entitled to a copy of the indictment before he is arraigned thereon; to a list of the witnesses to be used and of the jurors returned to serve on the trial, with the place of abode of each, to be delivered to him 24 hours before the trial; and to process from court to compel witnesses to appear and testify at the trial; provided, however, the justice presiding at the trial may admit the testimony of any witness whose name and place of abode is not on the list hereinbefore provided for upon such notice to the respondent as he, the presiding justice, shall direct, whenever, in his discretion, he deems such action will promote justice.

Source.

RS 225:3. CS 240:3. GS 243:1. GL 261:1, 13. PS 254:1. PL 368:1. 1939, 178:1. RL 428:1. RSA 604:1. 1965, 296:3. 1974, 34:11, eff. April 15, 1974.

Amendments

—1974. Substituted "an offense punishable by death or for murder in the first degree" for "a felony the punishment of which may be death" preceding "shall be entitled" in the first sentence.

—1965. Substituted "felony" for "offense" preceding "the punishment of which" and deleted "to counsel learned in the law, not exceeding two, to be assigned him by the court, at his request, who shall leave access to him at all reasonable hours" preceding "and to process" in the first sentence.

Cross References.

Classification of crimes, see RSA 625:9.
Depositions generally, see RSA 517.

Homicide generally, see RSA 630.
Provision of legal counsel, see RSA 604-A--604-B.
Trial generally, see RSA 606.
Witnesses generally, see RSA 516.

NOTES TO DECISIONS

1. Applicability of section
2. Furnishing of copy of indictment
3. Furnishing of list of witnesses

1. Applicability of section

A person indicted for the crime of murder in the second degree is not entitled to be furnished with a list of the state's witnesses under this section since murder in the second degree is not a capital offense. State v. Wood, 53 N.H. 484, 1873 N.H. LEXIS 41 (1873).

2. Furnishing of copy of indictment

An accused cannot, after proceeding to trial, object that no copy of the indictment was furnished to him before his arraignment; he must be held to have waived his right to insist that a copy of the indictment be furnished. Lord v. State, 18 N.H. 173, 1846 N.H. LEXIS 18 (1846).

3. Furnishing of list of witnesses

The purpose of the requirement of this section that a defendant be furnished with a list of witnesses is to inform a defendant what witnesses are to be called to testify against him; where no surprise results, the omission of a witness' name from the list does not preclude calling the witness. State v. Coolidge, 109 N.H. 403, 260 A.2d 547, 1969 N.H. LEXIS 170 (1969).

No prejudice was caused to an accused by the failure to state in the list of witnesses the street address of a witness identified on the list as living in Boston where the witness was not called to testify. State v. Thorp, 86 N.H. 511, 171 A. 633, 172 A. 879 (1934).

A witness was properly not excluded where the list of witnesses furnished to the accused did not contain the true name of a witness where the name contained in the list was the name by which the witness was commonly known. State v. Burke, 54 N.H. 92, 1873 N.H. LEXIS 10 (1873).

If, following the names of the witnesses in the list furnished the accused, there is a designation of a town and state, this is a sufficient designation of the place of abode of the witnesses. Lord v. State, 18 N.H. 173, 1846 N.H. LEXIS 18 (1846).

If the list of witnesses which this section requires has not been furnished to a defendant before trial, he may object, when the case is called, to proceeding with the trial until the section is complied with; if he does not object at that time and for that purpose, but proceeds with the trial without objection, he must be regarded as waiving it, unless the court, in its discretion, should afterwards receive the objection for the purpose of postponing the trial in order that a proper list be furnished. Lord v. State, 18 N.H. 173, 1846 N.H. LEXIS 18 (1846).

Cited:

Cited in State v. Arlin, 39 N.H. 179, 1859 N.H. LEXIS 26 (1859); State v. Archer, 54 N.H. 465, 1874 N.H. LEXIS 66 (1874); Logan v. United States, 144 U.S. 263, 12 S. Ct. 617, 36 L. Ed. 429, 1892 U.S. LEXIS 2080 (1892); Betts v. Brady, 316 U.S. 455, 62 S. Ct. 1252, 86 L. Ed. 1595, 1942 U.S. LEXIS 489 (1942); State ex rel. Regan v. Superior Court, 102 N.H. 224, 153 A.2d 403, 1959 N.H. LEXIS 51 (1959).

RESEARCH REFERENCES

New Hampshire Court Rules Annotated.
Discovery procedure, see Rules 98-102, Rules of the Superior Court, New Hampshire Court Rules Annotated.

604:1-a. Discovery in Criminal Matters.

After an accused person has been bound over to the superior court and prior to indictment, he shall have the same rights to discovery and deposition as he has subsequent to indictment, provided that all judicial proceedings with respect thereto shall be within the jurisdiction of the superior court, and notice of petition therefor and hearing thereon shall be given to the county attorney, or the attorney general if he shall have entered the case.

Source.
1971, 506:1, eff. Sept. 4, 1971.

RESEARCH REFERENCES

New Hampshire Court Rules Annotated.
Discovery procedure, see Rules 98-102, Rules of the Superior Court, New Hampshire Court Rules Annotated.

604:2, 604:3.

[Repealed 1965, 296:4, eff. July 1, 1965.]

Former section(s).
Former RSA 604:2, which was derived from 1901, 104:1; 1907, 136:1; PL 368:2; 1937, 22:1; RSA 604:2; and 1963, 221:1, related to rights of persons charged with offenses punishable by imprisonment for three years.

Former RSA 604:3, which was derived from 1901, 104:6; PL 368:3; RL 428:3; RSA 604:3; and 1955, 215:1, related to compensation of counsel appointed for defendants. See now RSA 604-A-604-B.

CHAPTER 604-A

ADEQUATE REPRESENTATION FOR INDIGENT DEFENDANTS IN CRIMINAL CASES

SECTION
604-A:1.   Representation of Defendants.
604-A:1-a. Neglected or Abused Children.
604-A:1-b. Additional Funding.
604-A:2.   Appointment of Counsel.
604-A:2-a. Additional Inquiry.
604-A:2-b. Contract Attorneys.
604-A:2-c. Determination of Financial Ability.
604-A:2-d. Partial Liability.
604-A:3.   Duration and Substitution of Appointments.
604-A:4.   Compensation of Counsel.
604-A:5.   Compensation Limited.
604-A:6.   Services Other Than Counsel.
604-A:6-a. Contract Services.
604-A:7.   Rules and Regulations.
604-A:8.   Payment of Expenses.
604-A:9.   Repayment.
604-A:10.   Rulemaking; Records Required; Judicial Council; Commissioner of Administrative Services.

Cross References.
Constitutional right to counsel, see New Hampshire Constitution, Part 1, Article 15.
Domestic violence proceedings, see RSA 173-B.
Parole of delinquents, see RSA 170-H.
Proceedings relating to abused or neglected children generally, see RSA 169-C.
Proceedings relating to children in need of services generally, see RSA 169-D.
Proceedings relating to delinquent children generally, see RSA 169-B.
Public defender program, see RSA 604-B.
Right of arrested persons to confer with attorney, see RSA 594:16.
Waiver of court costs and fees, see RSA 499:18-b.

NOTES TO DECISIONS

Applicability

This chapter clearly and unambiguously guarantees legal representation only to indigent defendants in criminal cases and to any juveniles charged with being delinquent, and imposes such obligation to provide legal counsel on the state. In re D., 121 N.H. 547, 431 A.2d 789, 1981 N.H. LEXIS 364 (1981).

Cited:

Cited in State v. Howard, 109 N.H. 518, 257 A.2d 17, 1969 N.H. LEXIS 196 (1969).

604-A:1. Representation of Defendants.

The purpose of this chapter is to provide adequate representation for indigent defendants in criminal cases, as a precondition of imprisonment, and indigent juveniles charged with being delinquent in any court of this state. Representation of juveniles shall include all court ordered representation and shall be paid from funds appropriated for indigent defense pursuant to this chapter. Representation shall include counsel and investigative, expert and other services and expenses, including process to compel the attendance of witnesses, as may be necessary for an adequate defense before the courts of this state.

Source.

1965, 296:1. 1967, 422:1. 1973, 370:22. 1981, 568:20, I, eff. July 1, 1981. 2009, 144:182, eff. July 1, 2009.

Amendments
—2009. The 2009 amendment added the second sentence.

—1981. Substituted "as a precondition of imprisonment, and indigent juveniles" for "charged with felonies or misdemeanors, or any juvenile" in the first sentence.

—1973. Deleted "other than petty offenses" following "misdemeanors" in the first sentence and deleted the second sentence.

—1967. Inserted "or any juvenile charged with being delinquent" following "petty offenses" and substituted "provide for imprisonment or a fine exceeding five hundred dollars" for "exceed imprisonment for six months or a fine of five hundred dollars, or both" following "penalty for which does not" in the second sentence.

Severability of enactment.
1981, 568:20 was subject to a severability clause. See 1981, 568:21.

Cross References.
Proceedings involving delinquent children generally, see RSA 169-B.
Securing attendance of witnesses generally, see RSA 516:1 et seq.

NOTES TO DECISIONS

Cited:

Cited in Opinion of Justices, 121 N.H. 531, 431 A.2d 144, 1981 N.H. LEXIS 342 (1981); State v. Cooper, 127 N.H. 119, 498 A.2d 1209, 1985 N.H. LEXIS 375 (1985); In re Allen R., 127 N.H. 718, 506 A.2d 329, 1986 N.H. LEXIS 210 (1986).

604-A:1-a. Neglected or Abused Children.

In cases involving a neglected or abused child, when a guardian ad litem is appointed for the child as provided in RSA 169-C:10, the cost of such appointment shall be paid from funds appropriated for indigent defense pursuant to this chapter. In cases involving a neglected or abused child, when an attorney is appointed to represent a parent determined to be indigent pursuant to RSA 169-C:10, II, at the preliminary hearing or a hearing pursuant to RSA 169-C:6-a, III, whichever occurs earlier, the cost of such appointment shall be paid from funds appropriated for indigent defense pursuant to this chapter.

Source.

1973, 522:1, eff. July 1, 1973. 1996, 248:9, eff. July 1, 1996. 2008, 296:24, eff. June 27, 2008. 2009, 144:183, eff. July 1, 2009. 2011, 224:74, eff. July 1, 2011. 2013, 144:58, eff. July 1, 2013.

Amendments
—2013. The 2013 amendment added the second sentence.

—2011. The 2011 amendment deleted the former second sentence, which read: "In cases involving a neglected or abused child, when an attorney is appointed to represent a parent determined to be indigent pursuant to RSA 169-C:10, II, the cost of such appointment shall be paid from funds appropriated for indigent defense pursuant to this chapter."

—2009. The 2009 amendment added the second sentence.

—2008. The 2008 amendment substituted "from funds appropriated for indigent defense pursuant to this chapter" for "by the indigent defense fund".

—1996. Rewritten to the extent that a detailed comparison would be impracticable.

Cross References.
Proceedings relating to abused or neglected children generally, see RSA 169-C.
Securing attendance of witnesses generally, see RSA 516:1 et seq.

604-A:1-b. Additional Funding.

In the event that expenditures for indigent defense by the judicial council are greater than amounts appropriated in the operating budget, the judicial council may request, with prior approval of the fiscal committee of the general court, that the governor and council authorize additional funding. For funds requested and approved, the governor is authorized to draw a warrant from any money in the treasury not otherwise appropriated.

Source.

2008, 296:25, eff. June 27, 2008.

604-A:2. Appointment of Counsel.

I. In every criminal case in which the defendant is charged with a felony or a class A misdemeanor and appears without counsel, the court before which he appears shall advise the defendant that he has a right to be represented by counsel and that counsel will be appointed to represent him if he is financially unable to obtain counsel. Unless the defendant waives the appointment of counsel, if the defendant indicates to the court that he is financially unable to obtain counsel, the court shall instruct the defendant to complete a financial affidavit in such form as designated by the unit of cost containment. If after review of the financial affidavit and application of the rules established pursuant to RSA 604-A:10, IV the commissioner of administrative services, is satisfied that the defendant is financially unable to obtain counsel, the court shall appoint counsel to represent him; provided, however, that in any case in which the defendant is charged with a capital offense, the court may appoint 2 counsel to represent him. Whenever defendants have such conflicting interests that they cannot be properly represented by the same counsel, or when other good cause is shown, the court shall appoint separate counsel for each of them.

II. Whenever the court makes an appointment under paragraph I, the appointment shall be made as follows: first, appointment of the public defender program under RSA 604-B if that office is available; second, in the event the public defender program is not available, appointment of a contract attorney under RSA 604-A:2-b if such an attorney is available; and third, in the event that neither the public defender program nor a contract attorney is available, the appointment of any qualified attorney under paragraph I.

III. In the event that the defendant disagrees with the commissioner's decision on eligibility, the defendant shall have the right to appeal to the court having jurisdiction over the case within 7 days of notification of the commissioner's findings. An appeals hearing shall be held before the court in which the defendant will be tried and the burden of persuasion shall be upon the defendant to demonstrate why the determination procedures specified in the rules pursuant to RSA 604-A:10, IV, should not be controlling in the case. In any such hearing the court shall receive such evidence and argument as justice may require and shall enter an order setting forth its decision within 7 days of the filing of the appeal. In the event the court alters the commissioner's eligibility decision on appeal, its order shall contain specific findings outlining why the commissioner's decision was not sustained.

IV. (a) The court shall review any information available to it regarding the defendant's mental condition and shall require the state to disclose any information as to the defendant's mental condition. If the court has information indicating the defendant has a mental illness, the court shall act on any application for appointed counsel on the same day as the defendant's first court appearance. If the application is approved, the court shall, by phone, notify the attorney appointed to represent the defendant and immediately transmit all relevant court documents to the attorney by facsimile or other electronic transmission.

(b) The court shall appoint counsel without formal application if the defendant is without counsel and mental illness appears to be interfering with the defendant's ability to communicate, understand court proceedings, or to complete a formal application on a timely basis.

(c) If a public defender is appointed, the public defender, upon receiving notification that the defendant may have a mental illness, shall, on the day notice of the appointment is received, designate a specific attorney to represent the defendant.

Source.
1965, 296:1. 1973, 370:23. 1981, 568:20, II. 1985, 342:1. 1989, 345:3, 4. 1993, 190:19, eff. Jan. 1, 1994. 2010, 250:3, eff. January 2, 2011.

Amendments
—2010. The 2010 amendment added IV.

—1993. Paragraph I: Inserted "class A" preceding "misdemeanor" in the first sentence.

—1989. Paragraph I: Substituted "instruct the defendant to complete a financial affidavit in such form as designated by the unit of cost containment" for "conduct an appropriate inquiry of the defendant as to his financial ability to obtain counsel" following "court shall" in the second sentence and "review of the financial affidavit and application of the rules established pursuant to RSA 604-A:10, IV the commissioner of administrative services" for "such inquiry, the court" preceding "is satisfied" in the third sentence.
Paragraph III: Added.

—1985. Designated the existing provisions of the section as par. I and added par. II.

—1981. Rewrote the former second sentence as the present second and third sentences.

—1973. Deleted "other than a petty offense" following "misdemeanor" in the first sentence.

Severability of enactment.
1981, 568:20 was subject to a severability clause. See 1981, 568:21.

Cross References.
Classification of crimes, see RSA 625:9.
Duration of appointment, see RSA 604-A:3.
Maintenance of records by commissioner of administrative services, see RSA 604-A:10.
Payment of expenses by defendants financially able to pay portion of expenses of obtaining private counsel, see RSA 604-A:2-d.
Reimbursement of state by persons other than defendants, see RSA 604-A:2-a.
Repayment of fees and expenses, see RSA 604-A:9.
Standards for determination of financial ability to obtain counsel, see RSA 604-A:2-c.

NOTES TO DECISIONS

1. Number of counsel
2. Assets of spouse

1. Number of counsel
A defendant not charged with a capital offense is not entitled to more than one counsel. State v. Cameron, 121 N.H. 348, 430 A.2d 138, 1981 N.H. LEXIS 317 (1981).

2. Assets of spouse
In determining eligibility for court-appointed counsel, court may consider a spouse's income and assets insofar as they may reduce a defendant's other expenses and free more of his income to pay for counsel. State v. Atkins, 143 N.H. 242, 723 A.2d 939, 1998 N.H. LEXIS 98 (1998).

Cited:
Cited in Opinion of Justices, 121 N.H. 531, 431 A.2d 144, 1981 N.H. LEXIS 342 (1981); In re D., 121 N.H. 547, 431 A.2d 789, 1981

N.H. LEXIS 364 (1981); State v. Gagnon, 135 N.H. 217, 600 A.2d 937, 1991 N.H. LEXIS 168 (1991).

RESEARCH REFERENCES

New Hampshire Court Rules Annotated.

Filing of petitions for appointment of counsel, see Rule 90, Rules of the Superior Court, New Hampshire Court Rules Annotated.

604-A:2-a. Additional Inquiry.

Whenever a court appoints counsel pursuant to the provisions of RSA 604-A:2, the court shall conduct an appropriate inquiry as to whether any person who, pursuant to RSA 546-A:2, is liable for the support of the defendant is financially able to pay for such defendant's counsel. If the court determines that the person liable for support is financially able to pay for said counsel, in whole or in part, the court shall enter an appropriate order requiring said person to reimburse the state for the representation provided; provided, however, that a child shall not be required to reimburse the state for representation provided to his mother or father, a parent shall not be required to reimburse the state for representation provided to a child 18 years of age or older, and any person who was a victim of the crime with which the defendant has been charged shall not be required to reimburse the state for the representation provided. For the purposes of this section, the inquiry conducted by the court shall include notice and hearing to the person liable for support.

Source.

1981, 568:20, III. 1982, 42:41, eff. June 29, 1982.

Amendments

—1982. Added "a parent shall not be required to reimburse the state for representation provided to a child 18 years of age or older, and any person who was a victim of the crime with which the defendant has been charged shall not be required to reimburse the state for the representation provided" following "mother or father" at the end of the second sentence.

Severability of enactment.

1981, 568:20 was subject to a severability clause. See 1981, 568:21.

Cross References.

Determination of financial ability of defendant to obtain private counsel, see RSA 604-A:2-c.

Payment of expenses by defendants financially able to pay portion of expenses of obtaining private counsel, see RSA 604-A:2-d.

Repayment of fees and expenses by defendant, see RSA 604-A:9.

NOTES TO DECISIONS

1. Construction
2. Application

1. Construction

This section clearly requires court to inquire into finances of defendant's spouse. State v. Atkins, 143 N.H. 242, 723 A.2d 939, 1998 N.H. LEXIS 98 (1998).

2. Application

This section requires court to take any additional steps to secure reimbursement for State for cost of providing court-appointed counsel. State v. Atkins, 143 N.H. 242, 723 A.2d 939, 1998 N.H. LEXIS 98 (1998).

604-A:2-b. Contract Attorneys.

The state of New Hampshire, by the judicial council and with the approval of governor and council, may, within the limits of available appropriations, contract with any qualified attorney in the state to provide for the representation of indigents in circumstances where, pursuant to RSA 604-B, the public defender program is unavailable to provide such representation. The executive director of the judicial council shall authorize payments to contract attorneys provided for under this section.

Source.

1985, 342:2. 1987, 406:17. 1991, 46:1, eff. June 25, 1991. 1997, 351:8, eff. July 1, 1997.

Amendments

—1997. Substituted "executive director of the judicial council" for "commissioner of administrative services" at the beginning of the second sentence.

—1991. Deleted the former second sentence.

—1987. Added the second sentence.

Cross References.

Department of administrative services, see RSA 21-I.

Repayment of fees and expenses, see RSA 604-A:9.

604-A:2-c. Determination of Financial Ability.

The determination of a defendant's financial ability to obtain counsel shall be made by comparing the defendant's assets and incomes with the minimum cost of obtaining qualified private counsel. The defendant's assets shall include all real and personal property owned in any manner by the defendant, excluding only those assets which are exempt from attachment and execution under RSA 511:2. The defendant's income shall include all income, whether earned or not, from any source, unless exempt from attachment under any state or federal law, and shall be reduced only by the amount of expenses which are reasonably necessary for the maintenance of the defendant and his dependents. In determining a defendant's financial ability to obtain counsel, the rules adopted by the commissioner under RSA 604-A:10, IV, shall contain a method for considering the defendant's ability to borrow some or all of the necessary funds. The rules shall also consider the possibility of the defendant paying his counsel fees in periodic installments.

Source.

1985, 342:2. 1989, 345:5, eff. July 1, 1989.

Amendments
—**1989.** Inserted "unless exempt from attachment under any state or federal law" following "source" in the third sentence, substituted "the rules adopted by the commissioner under RSA 604-A:10, IV, shall contain a method for considering" for "the court shall consider" following "counsel" in the fourth sentence, and substituted "rules" for "court" preceding "shall also" in the fifth sentence.

Cross References.
Payment of expenses by defendants financially able to pay portion of expenses of obtaining private counsel, see RSA 604-A:2-d.
Procedure for appointment of counsel generally, see RSA 604-A:2, 2-b.
Repayment of fees and expenses, see RSA 604-A:9.

604-A:2-d. Partial Liability.

If the commissioner of administrative services determines, in accordance with the standards set forth in RSA 604-A:2-c, that a defendant is able to pay some, but not all of the expenses of obtaining private counsel, the court shall appoint counsel and shall require the defendant to pay a fixed contribution in accordance with rules adopted pursuant to RSA 604-A:10, IV. The defendant's full payment shall be made to the court prior to the conclusion of the proceedings, unless otherwise ordered by the court. The clerk of court shall remit such payments to the department of administrative services with the documentation required by the commissioner.

Source.
1985, 342:2. 1989, 345:6, eff. July 1, 1989.

Amendments
—**1989.** Substituted "Liability" for "Eligibility" in the section catchline, "commissioner of administrative services" for "court" preceding "determines" and "a fixed contribution in accordance with rules adopted pursuant to RSA 604-A:10, IV" for "so much of the costs as he is able" following "require the defendant to pay" in the first sentence, "department" for "office" preceding "of administrative services" in the third sentence and "with the documentation required by the commissioner" for "following receipt of the attorney's statement" thereafter.

Cross References.
Appeal from decision on eligibility, see RSA 604-A:2.
Procedure for appointment of counsel generally, see RSA 604-A:2, 2-b.
Repayment of fees and expenses generally, see RSA 604-A:9.

604-A:3. Duration and Substitution of Appointments.

A defendant for whom counsel is appointed shall be represented by counsel from his initial appearance before the court at every stage of the proceedings until the entry of final judgment. If at any time after the appointment of counsel the defendant is financially able to obtain counsel or to make partial payment for representation, the court having jurisdiction of the case may terminate the appointment of counsel or direct the application of the funds available to the defendant to meet the expense of representation, as justice may require. If at any stage of the proceedings, the court having jurisdiction of the case finds that the defendant is financially unable to pay counsel whom he had retained, the court may appoint counsel to represent him, as justice may require. The court having jurisdiction of the case may, in the interest of justice, at any stage of the proceedings, substitute one appointed counsel for another.

Source.
1965, 296:1, eff. July 1, 1965.

Cross References.
Payment of expenses by defendant financially able to pay portion of expenses of obtaining private counsel generally, see RSA 604-A:2-d.
Procedure for appointment of counsel generally, see RSA 604-A:2, 2-b.
Repayment of fees and expenses, see RSA 604-A:9.

NOTES TO DECISIONS

Cited:
Cited in Opinion of Justices, 109 N.H. 508, 256 A.2d 500, 1969 N.H. LEXIS 193 (1969).

604-A:4. Compensation of Counsel.

Subject to the provisions of RSA 604-A:6, counsel appointed pursuant to this chapter to represent the defendant, at the conclusion of the representation or any segment thereof, shall be reasonably compensated therefor and shall be reimbursed for expenses reasonably incurred. A separate claim for compensation and reimbursement shall be made to each court before which the counsel represented the defendant. Each claim shall be supported by a written statement specifying the time expended, services rendered and expenses incurred while the case was pending before the court. Each court before which the counsel represented the defendant shall fix the compensation and reimbursement to be paid the counsel for services rendered and expenses incurred while representing the defendant in proceedings before the court; however, no justice shall approve any unreasonable or unnecessary charge.

Source.
1965, 296:1. 1969, 364:1, eff. July 1, 1969.

Amendments
—**1969.** Added "however, no justice shall approve any unreasonable or unnecessary charge" following "before the court" at the end of the fourth sentence.

Cross References.
Limitation on compensation of counsel generally, see RSA 604-A:5.
Limitation on payment of expenses generally, see RSA 604-A:6.

NOTES TO DECISIONS

Cited:
Cited in Opinion of Justices, 109 N.H. 508, 256 A.2d 500, 1969 N.H. LEXIS 193 (1969).

RESEARCH REFERENCES

New Hampshire Court Rules Annotated.
Maximum fees for appeals to supreme court, see Rule 32, Rules of the Supreme Court, New Hampshire Court Rules Annotated.

Maximum fees for representation of indigents generally, see Rules 47 and 48, Rules of the Supreme Court, New Hampshire Court Rules Annotated.

604-A:5. Compensation Limited.

For representation of a defendant in any criminal case in which one or more felonies are charged, the total compensation paid counsel shall not exceed $500; provided that in cases alleging a capital offense in which 2 counsel are appointed to represent a defendant, each may be paid not exceeding $500. For representation of a defendant in any criminal case in which only misdemeanors are charged, the total compensation to be paid counsel shall not exceed $200. For representation of any juvenile charged with being delinquent or for representation of a neglected or abused child, the total compensation to be paid counsel shall not exceed $100. Provided, that of the above specified amounts, the proportion allowed by a justice of a district or municipal court for services rendered by counsel while representing the defendant in proceedings before said court shall not be in excess of $175 for a preliminary examination in the case of a felony; $100 for the trial of a misdemeanor or $50 for a juvenile case or a case involving a neglected or abused child. Each clerk of a district or municipal court shall certify to the clerk of the superior court the amount approved by the district or municipal court. In cases where homicides are charged or the penalty exceeds 25 years and there are extraordinary circumstances, payment in excess of these limits may be made if the court finds that the nature of the case is such as to require intensive and protracted representation.

Source.
1965, 296:1. 1967, 422:2. 1969, 364:2. 1973, 522:2, eff. July 1, 1973.

Amendments
—1973. Inserted "or for representation of a neglected or abused child" following "delinquent" in the third sentence and "or a case involving a neglected or abused child" following "juvenile case" in the fourth sentence.

—1969. Rewritten to the extent that a detailed comparison would be impracticable.

—1967. Added the third sentence.

Cross References.
Classification of crimes, see RSA 625:9.
Compensation of counsel generally, see RSA 604-A:4.

NOTES TO DECISIONS

Constitutionality
The courts of the state have the exclusive authority to determine the reasonableness of compensation for court-appointed counsel; this section, by attempting to impose a fee schedule for court-appointed counsel, intrudes upon this judicial function in violation of the constitutional separation of powers mandate in part 1, article 37 of the state constitution. Smith v. State, 118 N.H. 764, 394 A.2d 834, 1978 N.H. LEXIS 289, 3 A.L.R.4th 568 (1978).
This section is unconstitutional as the maximum fees it establishes shift much of the state's obligation to furnish counsel to the legal profession and intrude impermissibly upon the exclusive judicial authority to determine the reasonableness of compensation for court-appointed counsel. Smith v. State, 118 N.H. 764, 394 A.2d 834, 1978 N.H. LEXIS 289, 3 A.L.R.4th 568 (1978).

Cited:
Cited in Opinion of Justices, 109 N.H. 508, 256 A.2d 500, 1969 N.H. LEXIS 193 (1969).

RESEARCH REFERENCES

New Hampshire Court Rules Annotated.
Approval of counsel fees, see Rule 90, Rules of the Superior Court, New Hampshire Court Rules Annotated.
Maximum fees for appeals to supreme court, see Rule 32, Rules of the Supreme Court, New Hampshire Court Rules Annotated.
Maximum fees for representation of indigents generally, see Rules 47 and 48, Rules of the Supreme Court, New Hampshire Court Rules Annotated.

604-A:6. Services Other Than Counsel.

In any criminal case in which counsel has been appointed to represent a defendant who is financially unable to obtain investigative, expert or other services necessary to an adequate defense in his case, counsel may apply therefor to the court, and, upon finding that such services are necessary and that the defendant is financially unable to obtain them, the court shall authorize counsel to obtain the necessary services on behalf of the defendant. The court may, in the interests of justice and upon finding that timely procurement of necessary services could not await prior authorization, ratify and approve such services after they have been obtained. The court shall determine reasonable compensation for the services and direct payment upon the filing of a claim for compensation supported by an affidavit specifying the time expended, the nature of the services rendered, the expenses incurred on behalf of the defendant, and the compensation, if any, received in the same case for the same services from any other source. The compensation to be paid to any person or association for such services shall not exceed $300 unless the court determines that the nature or quantity of such services reasonably merits greater compensation. The $300 limit for compensation shall not include or apply to reimbursement for expenses reasonably incurred. In any case in which appointed counsel seeks funds for services other than counsel under this section, the application for such funds may be filed with the court on an ex parte basis and may, upon the request of appointed counsel, be sealed until the conclusion of the representation.

Source.
1965, 296:1. 1983, 321:1. 1989, 188:1, eff. Jan. 1, 1990. 2005, 135:1, eff. January 1, 2006.

Amendments
—2005. Added the last sentence.

—1989. Deleted "superior" following "therefor to the" in the first sentence and preceding "court" in the second, third and fourth sentences.

—**1983.** Deleted "and" following "services rendered" and "or" following "same case" in the third sentence, rewrote the former fourth sentence as the present fourth and fifth sentences, and made other minor stylistic changes.

Cross References.

Compensation of counsel and reimbursement of expenses generally, see RSA 604-A:4, 5.

Repayment of fees and expenses generally, see RSA 604-A:9.

NOTES TO DECISIONS

1. Generally
2. Compensation of expert witnesses
3. Preparation of record of proceedings
4. Necessity for prior authorization to obtain services
5. Approval of orders for pre-trial psychiatric competency evaluations
6. Particular cases

1. Generally

Where defendant did not show how allegedly improper interview techniques required an expert to ensure effective preparation of defendant's case, as required by RSA 604-A:6, and where the fact that the victim might have masturbated on prior occasions was not probative of the victim's independent knowledge of the sexual activity with which defendant was charged, the trial court did not abuse its discretion or violate N.H. Cons. pt. I, art. 15, U.S. Const. amends. V, VI, and XIV by refusing defendant's requests for funds to hire an expert and to introduce evidence of the victim's sexual knowledge. State v. Wellington, 150 N.H. 782, 846 A.2d 1171, 2004 N.H. LEXIS 71 (2004).

The fact that funds for services other than counsel are in limited supply is not an appropriate reason for denying an indigent defendant access to experts. A denial of access based solely on this reason constitutes an abuse of discretion. State v. Stow, 136 N.H. 598, 620 A.2d 1023, 1993 N.H. LEXIS 8 (1993).

There was no need for a psychologist's impeachment testimony with regard to the reliability of the victim's identification of the defendant as the man who kidnapped and sexually assaulted her. Therefore, the court did not abuse its discretion in denying compensation to this witness. State v. Stow, 136 N.H. 598, 620 A.2d 1023, 1993 N.H. LEXIS 8 (1993).

It was unreasonable for a trial court to deny any reimbursement to the counsel for an indigent criminal defendant for the fee of a psychologist where there was no question that such services were needed and the court's prior denial of a motion to retain a psychologist was made on the basis that such services could be obtained for less expense at a mental health agency; counsel should have been reimbursed for the amount the mental health agency would have charged. In re Allen R., 127 N.H. 718, 506 A.2d 329, 1986 N.H. LEXIS 210 (1986).

2. Compensation of expert witnesses

The proper defense of some criminal cases may require the retention of experts, without whose services a conviction may be held to have been improperly obtained—a fact which must be kept in mind by trial judges in interpreting the phrase "extraordinary circumstances". State v. Shute, 122 N.H. 498, 446 A.2d 1162, 1982 N.H. LEXIS 392 (1982).

Where the trial court, in the first trial of a defendant, which ended in a mistrial, approved the $600 bill of an expert medical witness who appeared for the defense, due to the extraordinary circumstances resulting from the fact that the witness had been hired hurriedly the evening before the trial began and had been inconvenienced by a late-night conference and other last-minute preparations, and, after the retrial, refused to allow the witness more than the $300 maximum allowed by this section, since the court felt that the witness did not prepare anything new for the second trial and wanted to be compensated for travel time, which the court had never approved, the court's order would be upheld as there were no extraordinary circumstances with regard to the expert's role for the second trial. State v. Shute, 122 N.H. 498, 446 A.2d 1162, 1982 N.H. LEXIS 392 (1982).

3. Preparation of record of proceedings

A trial court did not abuse its discretion in denying a post-trial request by counsel for an indigent criminal defendant for reimbursement of expenses incurred in hiring a court reporter where, in denying a motion for approval to hire a court reporter prior to the proceedings, the court had indicated it would provide a tape recording of the proceedings in lieu of a court reporter's record, counsel had nonetheless hired the court reporter, and nothing in the record indicated that the tape recording would be unintelligible as a basis for a later transcript. In re Allen R., 127 N.H. 718, 506 A.2d 329, 1986 N.H. LEXIS 210 (1986).

4. Necessity for prior authorization to obtain services

This section requires that counsel request the trial court's prior authorization to obtain services necessary for the adequate defense of an indigent criminal defendant where there is sufficient time to do so. In re Allen R., 127 N.H. 718, 506 A.2d 329, 1986 N.H. LEXIS 210 (1986).

5. Approval of orders for pre-trial psychiatric competency evaluations

If a district court orders a pre-trial psychiatric evaluation for a defendant charged with a misdemeanor for the purpose of determining competency to stand trial, utilizing the services of a private psychiatrist or a private mental health clinic, superior court approval must be obtained since only the superior court has authority to approve of payment for such services. State v. Gagne, 129 N.H. 93, 523 A.2d 76, 1986 N.H. LEXIS 380 (1986).

6. Particular cases

Defendant, who was convicted of reckless manslaughter under RSA 630:2 after his gun discharged while he was sitting in a car, was not substantially prejudiced by the denial of additional funds under RSA 604-A:6. Even without an expert, his misfire theory was substantially explored at trial; his statements were not consistent with how the gun could have misfired; and even if he had proven that the gun misfired, it did not necessarily follow that he would have prevailed on his defense, as there was ample evidence that he had handled the gun unsafely. State v. Mentus, 162 N.H. 792, 35 A.3d 572, 2011 N.H. LEXIS 182 (Dec. 14, 2011).

In allowing defendant only $1,200 of the $3,000 he requested to hire a firearms expert under RSA 604-A:6, the trial court did not rely solely on the limited supply of state funds in reaching its decision, but was open to approving more funds if needed. State v. Mentus, 162 N.H. 792, 35 A.3d 572, 2011 N.H. LEXIS 182 (Dec. 14, 2011).

Cited:

Cited in State v. Robinson, 123 N.H. 665, 465 A.2d 1214, 1983 N.H. LEXIS 331 (1983); State v. Campbell, 127 N.H. 112, 498 A.2d 330, 1985 N.H. LEXIS 376 (1985); State v. Lewis, 129 N.H. 787, 533 A.2d 358, 1987 N.H. LEXIS 246 (1987); State v. Bruneau, 131 N.H. 104, 552 A.2d 585, 1988 N.H. LEXIS 106 (1988); State v. Monroe, 142 N.H. 857, 711 A.2d 878, 1998 N.H. LEXIS 51 (1998); State v. Monroe, 142 N.H. 857, 711 A.2d 878, 1998 N.H. LEXIS 51 (1998).

RESEARCH REFERENCES

New Hampshire Court Rules Annotated.

Maximum fees for representation of indigents generally, see Rules 47 and 48, Rules of the Supreme Court, New Hampshire Court Rules Annotated.

604-A:6-a. Contract Services.

The state of New Hampshire, by the judicial council and with the approval of governor and council, may, within the limits of appropriations, contract with qualified firms or individuals in the state to provide stenographic and clerical services where, pursuant to RSA 604-A:6, the defendant has been found to be eligible for such services. The executive director of the judicial council shall authorize payments to such individuals and firms as provided for under this section.

Source.
1991, 46:2, eff. June 25, 1991. 1997, 351:9, eff. July 1, 1997.

Amendments
—**1997.** Substituted "executive director of the judicial council" for "commissioner of administrative services" at the beginning of the second sentence.

Cross References.
Department of administrative services, see RSA 21-I.
Maintenance of records by commissioner of administrative services, see RSA 604-A:10.

604-A:7. Rules and Regulations.

The supreme court, superior court, district court, and judicial branch family division shall each have the authority to establish such rules and regulations and prescribe such forms as may be deemed necessary or advisable for the performance of their respective duties hereunder.

Source.
1965, 296:1, eff. July 1, 1965. 2006, 267:2, eff. June 9, 2006.

Amendments
—**2006.** Deleted "and the" preceding "superior court" and inserted "district court, and judicial branch family division" thereafter and deleted the end of the sentence following "duties hereunder".

RESEARCH REFERENCES

New Hampshire Court Rules Annotated.
Maximum fees for representation of indigents generally, see Rules 47 and 48, Rules of the Supreme Court, New Hampshire Court Rules Annotated.

604-A:8. Payment of Expenses.

I. Each claim and written statement in support thereof when approved by the court shall be forwarded to the judicial council for payment. The commissioner of administrative services may adopt rules, under RSA 541-A, in addition to the requirements of paragraph II, to carry out the provisions of this section.

II. Statements submitted by counsel for payments of fees shall in each case be examined by the trial and appellate judges and certified by them as to the reasonableness of the fee requested and whether the defendant continued to be eligible for assignment of counsel during the duration of the trial. Such certificates shall be attached to the request for payment of counsel fees. Counsel must submit bills to the appropriate court for payment within 60 days of the disposition of a case unless the trial judge finds that there are extenuating circumstances. Courts shall, within 30 days of receipt, certify statements as outlined above and forward the certified statements to the judicial council for payment.

Source.
1965, 296:1. 1977, 600:23. 1981, 568:66. 1985, 399:3, eff. July 1, 1985. 2002, 250:4, eff. May 17, 2002.

Amendments
—**2002.** Paragraphs I and II: Substituted "judicial council" for "commissioner of administrative services".

—**1985.** Substituted "commissioner of administrative services" for "comptroller" throughout the section.

—**1981.** Designated the existing provisions of the section as par. I, substituted "comptroller" for "judicial council" in the first sentence and rewrote the second sentence of that paragraph, and added par. II.

—**1977.** Substituted "judicial council" for "comptroller" throughout the section.

Cross References.
Department of administrative services generally, see RSA 21-I.
Maintenance of records by commissioner of administrative services, see RSA 604-A:10.

604-A:9. Repayment.

I. Any adult defendant who has had counsel or a public defender assigned to the defendant at the expense of the state shall be ordered by the court under paragraph I-b to repay the state through the unit of cost containment, the fees and expenses paid by the state on the defendant's behalf according to a schedule established by the administrator of the cost containment unit with the approval of the administrative justices of the courts on such terms as the court may order consistent with the defendant's present or future ability to pay, such ability to be determined by the unit of cost containment. The state may collect from the defendant a service charge of up to 10 percent of the total amount of fees and expenses owed by such defendant. At no time shall the defendant be required to repay, for legal services, an amount greater than the state's flat rate for a contract attorney as established contractually pursuant to RSA 604-B. If the defendant is placed on probation or sentenced to a period of conditional discharge, the defendant shall repay the state, through the department of corrections, all fees and expenses paid on his behalf on such terms as the court may order consistent with the defendant's present or future ability to pay.

I-a. Notwithstanding the provisions of paragraph I, any juvenile charged with being delinquent who has had counsel or a public defender assigned to him at the expense of the state, or any person liable for the support of the juvenile pursuant to RSA 604-A:2-a, shall be ordered by the court to repay the state through the unit of cost containment, the fees and expenses paid by the state on the defendant's behalf according to a schedule established by the administrator of the cost containment unit with the approval of the administrative justices of the courts on such terms as the court may order consistent with the defendant's present or future ability to pay. The office of cost containment may collect from the defendant or the person liable for his support a service charge of up to 10 percent of the total amount of fees and expenses owed by such defendant. At no time shall the defendant be required to repay, for legal services, an amount greater than the state's flat rate for a contract attorney as established contractually pursuant to RSA 604-B. Liability for repayment under this paragraph shall end when the juvenile reaches the age of majority, except in a case where the juvenile was certified and tried as an adult.

I-b. The court shall enter a separate order, pursuant to the rules adopted by the commissioner of administrative services under RSA 604-A:10, IV, setting forth the terms of repayment of fees and expenses to the state, or if the court finds that the defendant is financially unable to make such payment or payments setting forth the reasons therefor. A copy of each order shall be forwarded to the commissioner of administrative services. Any defendant subject to an order under this section may petition the court for relief from the obligation imposed by this section, which may be granted only upon a finding that the defendant is unable to comply with the terms of the court's order or any modification of the order by the court. If the court does not order full payment for representation under RSA 604-A, the commissioner of administrative services or his designee shall perform an investigation to determine the defendant's present financial condition and his ability to make repayment and may petition the court for a new repayment order at any time within 6 years from the date of the original order.

I-c. In a case where counsel has been appointed, the defendant shall be required to notify the clerk of the court and the office of cost containment of each change of mail address and actual street address. Whenever notice to the defendant is required, notice to the last mail address on file shall be deemed notice to and binding on the defendant.

II. All petitions for court appointed counsel shall bear the following words in capital letters:

I UNDERSTAND THAT I MAY BE REQUIRED TO REPAY THE SERVICES PROVIDED TO ME BY COURT APPOINTED COUNSEL UNLESS THE COURT FINDS THAT I AM OR WILL BE FINANCIALLY UNABLE TO PAY.

III. If any repayment ordered pursuant to paragraph I becomes overdue, the court having originally appointed counsel may order any employer of a former defendant to deduct from that person's wages or salary the appropriate amount due and to pay such amount to the appropriate department as determined under paragraph I, which shall refund such amount to the state, provided that no money, rights, or credits listed in RSA 512:21 shall be subject to deduction.

IV. Notwithstanding any other provision of law, any defendant whose sentence does not include actual incarceration in the state prison and who has had counsel or a public defender assigned to him at the expense of the state and who, as part of his sentence, is placed on probation or sentenced to a period of conditional discharge shall be required as a condition of such probation or conditional discharge to reimburse the state for all fees and expenses paid on his behalf in accordance with the terms of any order entered pursuant to paragraph I.

V. If the defendant is incarcerated in the state prison, orders for repayment, pursuant to paragraph I may be suspended until the time of the defendant's release. The adult parole board may make repayment of any order for repayment a condition of parole or early release. If the defendant has not been ordered to repay the state for expenses incurred on the defendant's behalf, at any time within 6 years of the time the defendant is released from the state prison the state may petition the superior court for repayment, and upon such petition the superior court shall order repayment unless the court finds the defendant is unable to comply with the terms of any order for repayment.

VI. At any time within 6 years of the disposition of an action in which the court finds at the time of disposition or thereafter that the defendant is not able to make payments to the state as provided in paragraph I, the state may petition the court for an order of repayment. The court shall order such repayment in whole or in partial payments, unless the court finds the defendant is unable to pay, in whole or in partial payments, the amounts paid on his behalf for fees and expenses pursuant to this chapter. Notice of each such order shall be forwarded to the commissioner of administrative services.

VII. The commissioner of administrative services, with the approval of governor and council, is authorized to enter into contracts to secure the repayment of fees and expenses paid by the state as provided for in this section. Any person or entity with whom the commissioner so contracts may bring any legal or equitable action authorized by law, including any petition authorized by this section, to secure an order for repayment, or repayment pursuant to any order, of fees and expenses paid by the state which are recoverable by the state under this section. The contract or contracts authorized by this paragraph may include provisions by which the contractor may, as consideration in whole or in part for services, receive a percentage of the amounts recovered on behalf of the state.

Source.
1969, 475:1. 1973, 370:24. 1981, 568:20, VI. 1983, 201:1. 1985, 342:3. 1987, 406:14-16. 1989, 345:7-10. 1991, 135:1, 2. 1992, 284:84. 1994, 288:1, eff. Jan. 1, 1995. 1995, 156:1-3, eff. July 1, 1995.

Amendments
—1995. Paragraph I: Substituted "the defendant" for "him" following "assigned to", deleted "provided that the defendant's sentence does not include actual incarceration in the state prison, if the defendant is not placed on probation or sentenced to a period of conditional discharge" preceding "be ordered" and substituted "the defendant's" for "his" preceding "behalf" in the first sentence, substituted "state" for "office of containment" preceding "may

collect" in the second sentence, and deleted "be ordered by the court to" preceding "repay" in the fourth sentence.

Paragraph I-c: Added.

Paragraph V: Rewritten to the extent that a detailed comparison would be impracticable.

—1994. Paragraph I: Substituted "the fees and expenses paid by the state on his behalf according to a schedule established by the administrator of the cost containment unit with the approval of the administrative justices of the courts" for "all fees and expenses paid on his behalf" preceding "on such terms" in the first sentence and added the third sentence.

Paragraph I-a: Substituted "the fees and expenses paid by the state on the defendant's behalf according to a schedule established by the administrator of the cost containment unit with the approval of the administrative justices of the courts" for "all fees and expenses paid on the defendant's behalf" preceding "on such terms" in the first sentence and added the third and fourth sentences.

—1992. Deleted "at the time of disposition" preceding "provided" in the first sentence of par. I and preceding "be ordered" in the first sentence of par. I-a.

—1991. Paragraph I-a: Deleted "where the defendant was not convicted or through the defendant's juvenile services officer where the defendant is convicted" following "containment" in the first sentence.

Paragraph II: Deleted "if I am convicted" preceding "I may be" in the form for the petition for court appointed counsel.

—1989. Paragraph I: Rewritten to the extent that a detailed comparison would be impracticable.

Paragraphs I-a, I-b: Added.

Paragraph III: Inserted "appropriate" preceding "department" and substituted "as determined under paragraph I" for "of corrections" thereafter.

Paragraph VI: Substituted "disposition" for "sentence" preceding "or thereafter" in the first sentence.

—1987. Paragraph I: Added the second and third sentences.

Paragraph V: Substituted "6" for "3" preceding "years".

Paragraphs VI, VII: Added.

—1985. Rewritten to the extent that a detailed comparison would be impracticable.

—1983. Paragraph I: Substituted "may" for "shall" following "expense of the state".

Paragraph II: Substituted "may" for "will" preceding "be required to repay" in the first sentence and deleted the second sentence of the form for the petition for court appointed counsel.

Paragraph IV: Substituted "may" for "shall" following "expense of the state" in the first sentence and deleted the second, third, and fourth sentences.

Paragraph V: Deleted "and the work performed" following "amount repaid".

—1981. Rewritten to the extent that a detailed comparison would be impracticable.

—1973. Rewritten to the extent that a detailed comparison would be impracticable.

Severability of enactment.

1981, 568:20 was subject to a severability clause. See 1981, 568:21.

Contingent 1989 amendment.

1989, 285:11, provided for amendment of this section. However, under the terms of 1989, 345:15, eff. July 1, 1989, the amendment did not become effective.

Cross References.

Classification of crimes, see RSA 625:9.

Department of administrative services, see RSA 21-I.

Department of corrections, see RSA 21-H.

Payment of expenses by persons other than defendants, see RSA 604-A:2-a.

Sentences, see RSA 651.

Standards for determination of financial ability to obtain counsel, see RSA 604-A:2-c.

NOTES TO DECISIONS

Constitutionality

Requiring an acquitted defendant to reimburse the State under RSA 604-A:9, I for the costs of his appointed counsel was constitutional under N.H. Const. pt. I, art. 15 and U.S. Const. amend. 14 where the statute's purpose was to require that those who were financially able to do so, pay for a service that they received from the State, there was nothing illegitimate in the governmental interest in recouping costs expended for public defense whether or not a defendant was convicted, and the statutory scheme was rationally related to that purpose in that it inquired into a defendant's ability to pay and outlined procedures for recoupment order, collection, and appeal of such orders. State v. Haas, 155 N.H. 612, 927 A.2d 1209, 2007 N.H. LEXIS 102 (2007), rehearing denied, 2007 N.H. LEXIS 134 (N.H. July 26, 2007).

Cited:

Cited in Opinion of Justices, 109 N.H. 508, 256 A.2d 500, 1969 N.H. LEXIS 193 (1969); Opinion of Justices, 121 N.H. 531, 431 A.2d 144, 1981 N.H. LEXIS 342 (1981).

RESEARCH REFERENCES

New Hampshire Court Rules Annotated.

Filing of petitions for appointment of counsel generally, see Rule 90, Rules of the Superior Court, New Hampshire Court Rules Annotated.

604-A:10. Rulemaking; Records Required; Judicial Council; Commissioner of Administrative Services.

I. The judicial council shall keep records of the notification of eligibility and assignment of counsel as submitted by the courts of the state pursuant to supreme court order 81-5A and subsequent related orders. In addition to any other use the judicial council shall make of these records, the judicial council shall keep records including the following information and compile such information on a monthly basis:

(a) The name of the courts, including the location and the type of the court.

(b) The type of the case as defined by the most serious offense charged in the case, according to the following categories:

(1) Homicide

(2) Other felony

(3) Misdemeanor

(4) Juvenile

(5) Other

(c) Whether the case was assigned to a private attorney or a public defender.

II. When a final bill has been approved for payment to a private attorney, the judicial council shall record the following information:

(a) The type of case as defined in RSA 604-A:10, I(b).

(b) The amount of the attorney's fee.

III. The judicial council shall also compile the gross monthly cost for bills approved for payment for expenses other than counsel, including those pursuant to RSA 604-A:6.

IV. The commissioner of administrative services shall, with the approval of the attorney general, adopt rules pursuant to RSA 541-A, governing determinations of eligibility for payment of indigent defense expenditures, determinations of repayment schedules, financial and credit investigations, and any other matters the commissioner deems necessary or advisable for the performance of duties under this chapter.

Source.
1983, 120:4. 1985, 399:3. 1989, 345:11, 12, eff. July 1, 1989. 2002, 250:5, eff. May 17, 2002.

Amendments
—**2002.** Inserted "judicial council" in the section catchline, substituted "judicial council" for "commissioner of administrative services" in three places in the introductory paragraph of par. I, in the introductory paragraph of par. II, and in par. III and substituted "the commissioner" for "he" preceding "deems necessary", and deleted "his" following "performance of" in par. IV.

—**1989.** Added "Rulemaking" preceding "Records" in the section catchline and added par. IV.

—**1985.** Substituted "commissioner of administrative services" for "comptroller" in the catchline and throughout the section.

Cross References.
Assignment of counsel generally, see RSA 604-A:2, 2-b.
Procedure for submission and approval of claims for compensation and expenses, see RSA 604-A:8.

CHAPTER 604-B

PUBLIC DEFENDER PROGRAM

SECTION
604-B:1. Declaration of Purpose.
604-B:2. Representation of Indigent Defendants.
604-B:3. Limitation of Representation.
604-B:4. Contract.
604-B:5. Supervision.
604-B:6. Allocation of Cases.
604-B:7. Public Defenders.
604-B:8. Alternate Public Defender Program.

Severability of enactment.
1981, 568:19 was subject to a severability clause. See 1981, 568:21.

Recodification of chapter.
1981, 568:19, provided for the recodification of RSA 604-B. former RSA 604-B, comprising RSA 604-B: 1-604-B:8 was derived from 1977, 296:1.

Cross References.
Constitutional right to counsel, see New Hampshire Constitution, Part 1 Article 15.
Proceedings relating to abused or neglected children generally, see RSA 169-C.
Proceeding relating to children in need of services generally, see RSA 169-D.
Proceedings relating to delinquent children generally, see RSA 169-B.
Provision of counsel and other services for defendants in criminal cases generally, see RSA 604-A.

604-B:1. Declaration of Purpose.

It is hereby declared to be the policy of the state to continue a public defender program for representa-

tion of indigent criminal defendants in Belknap, Merrimack, Hillsborough and Rockingham counties and to extend that program to the remaining 6 counties in the state.

Source.
1977, 296:1. 1981, 568:19, eff. July 1, 1981.

604-B:2. Representation of Indigent Defendants.

Notwithstanding any other provisions of law to the contrary, when the appointment of counsel is required:

I. For indigent defendants in criminal cases, or

II. For juveniles charged as delinquents under RSA 169-B, the district, municipal, superior and supreme courts shall appoint the public defender program or a qualified attorney assigned by the court. The public defender program shall also provide such other representation of indigents as is necessary and consistent with normal criminal defense as required by the New Hampshire and United States Constitutions.

Source.
1977, 296:1. 1981, 568:19, eff. July 1, 1981.

604-B:3. Limitation of Representation.

The public defender program shall not represent more than one person where a conflict of interest exists under the code of professional responsibility.

Source.
1977, 296:1. 1981, 568:19, eff. July 1, 1981.

604-B:4. Contract.

The state of New Hampshire, by the judicial council and with the approval of governor and council, shall contract with any organization or groups of lawyers approved by the board of governors of the New Hampshire Bar Association to operate the public defender program and provide public defender representation as provided in RSA 604-B:2 and 3. The contract shall fix the number of defender attorneys providing representation in each county and shall permit the public defender program to subcontract for attorney services, including appellate services, as may be necessary to provide such representation. No such contract shall be effective for longer than 2 years. The compensation for operation of the public defender program shall be such sums as may be fixed by the contract, subject to the appropriations made therefor.

Source.
1977, 296:1. 1981, 568:19, eff. July 1, 1981.

Cross References.
Assignment of cases to public defenders, see RSA 604-B:6.
Duties of public defenders, see RSA 604-B:7.

604-B:5. Supervision.

The public defender program shall be under the general supervision of the judicial council for such matters pertaining to, but not limited to, allocation of cases between the public defender program and assigned counsel, performance, professional competence, and fiscal and budgetary matters. The supreme court shall recommend a fee schedule for assigned counsel which shall be graduated to reflect years of legal experience of such counsel.

Source.
1977, 296:1. 1981, 568:19, eff. July 1, 1981.

RESEARCH REFERENCES

New Hampshire Court Rules Annotated.
Maximum fees for representation of indigents in criminal cases, see Rules 47 and 48, Rules of the Supreme Court, New Hampshire Court Rules Annotated.

604-B:6. Allocation of Cases.

The allocation of cases between the public defender program and assigned counsel shall be in accordance with a plan adopted by the public defender program and approved by the judicial council. The plan shall establish caseload limits for defender attorneys in accordance with professional standards under the code of professional responsibility and shall provide for appointment of assigned counsel only where maximum caseloads have been reached or public defender attorneys are otherwise unavailable.

Source.
1977, 296:1. 1981, 568:19, eff. July 1, 1981.

Revision note.
At the end of the second sentence, inserted "public" preceding "defender attorneys" for purposes of clarity.

604-B:7. Public Defenders.

Public defenders shall serve in accordance with the terms of a contract entered into pursuant to RSA 604-B:4. Public defender responsibilities shall be exclusively concerned with rights of indigent criminal defendants.

Source.
1977, 269:1. 1978, 52:4. 1981, 568:19, eff. July 1, 1981.

Severability of enactment.
This section is subject to a severability clause.

604-B:8. Alternate Public Defender Program.

The state of New Hampshire by the judicial council and with the approval of the governor and council may, in addition to the contract for the public defender program referred to in RSA 604-B:4, contract for an alternate public defender program to represent indigent defendants in circumstances where, because of conflict of interest or otherwise, the public defender program is unable to provide representation to a defendant. The alternate public defender program and the contract between it and the state shall be governed by the provisions of this chapter.

Source.
1988, 225:1, eff. April 30, 1988.

CHAPTER 605

PLEAS AND REFUSAL TO PLEAD

SECTION
605:1.   Minors, etc.
605:2.   Counsel Fees.
605:3.   Plea of Lesser Offense.
605:4.   Nonacceptance of Plea.
605:5.   Refusal to Plead.
605:6.   Plea of Nolo Contendere.

Cross References.
Bail and recognizances generally, see RSA 597.
Indictments, informations and complaints generally, see RSA 601.
Preliminary examinations generally, see RSA 596-A.

RESEARCH REFERENCES

New Hampshire Court Rules Annotated.
Admissibility in evidence of pleas, plea discussions and related statements, see Rule 410, Rules of Evidence, New Hampshire Court Rules Annotated.
Entry and acceptance of pleas in district and municipal courts generally, see Rule 2.4, Rules of the District and Municipal Courts, New Hampshire Court Rules Annotated.
Entry of not guilty plea and waiver of formal arraignment in superior court, see Rule 97, Rules of the Superior Court, New Hampshire Court Rules Annotated.
Entry of pleas by mail in district and municipal courts, see Rule 2.5, Rules of the District and Municipal Courts, New Hampshire Court Rules Annotated.

605:1. Minors, etc.

No minor under the age of 17 years, except with the consent of his parent, nor any person supposed to be of unsound mind shall be permitted to plead guilty or shall be put upon trial until counsel has been appointed to advise him and conduct his defense. If such person is poor, witnesses may, on motion of his counsel, be summoned in his behalf at the expense of the county.

Source.
GS 243:4. GL 261:4. PS 254:4. 1913, 31:1. PL 368:5. RL 428:5.

Cross References.
Civil commitment of mentally ill persons generally, see RSA 135-C.
Commitment for observation of persons charged with criminal offenses, see RSA 135:17, 172:13.
Commitment of mentally ill persons charged with or acquitted of criminal offenses generally, see RSA 651:8 et seq.
Constitutional right to counsel, see New Hampshire Constitution, Part 1, Article 15.

Representation of indigent defendants generally, see RSA 604-A, 604-B.

Cited:
Cited in Fitzgibbons v. Hancock, 97 N.H. 162, 82 A.2d 769, 1951 N.H. LEXIS 40 (1951).

605:2. Counsel Fees.

Whenever counsel is appointed to advise with a minor or a person of unsound mind and to conduct his defense as provided by RSA 605:1, the counsel shall be entitled to receive, from the town or county in whose behalf the action is prosecuted, reasonable compensation for his services.

Source.
1873, 47:1. GL 261:5. PS 254:5. PL 368:6. RL 428:6.

Revision note.
For purposes of clarity, substituted "is" for "shall be" preceding "appointed".

605:3. Plea of Lesser Offense.

A person indicted may plead guilty of any minor offense which is included in the indictment, and if such plea is accepted by the state's counsel, judgment shall be rendered thereon.

Source.
1850, 962:5. CS 240:6. GS 243:5. GL 261:6. PS 254:6. PL 368:7. RL 428:7.

Cross References.
Indictments, information and complaints generally, see RSA 601.

605:4. Nonacceptance of Plea.

If a plea of guilty to a minor offense tendered under RSA 605:3 is not accepted, it may be withdrawn and a plea of not guilty may be entered, and in such case the former plea shall not operate against the accused at his trial.

Source.
1850, 962:5. CS 240:6. GS 243:5. GL 261:6. PS 254:6. PL 368:8. RL 428:8.

Revision note.
For purposes of clarity, substituted "a plea of guilty to a minor offense tendered under RSA 605:3" for "the plea" preceding "is not accepted" and "the accused at" for "him on" preceding "his trial".

RESEARCH REFERENCES

New Hampshire Court Rules Annotated.
Admissibility in evidence of pleas, plea discussions and related statements, see Rule 410, Rules of Evidence, New Hampshire Court Rules Annotated.

605:5. Refusal to Plead.

Whenever a person indicted stands mute or refuses to plead, the court shall order the plea of not guilty to be entered, and it shall have the same effect as if the accused had pleaded not guilty.

Source.
RS 225:4. CS 240:5. GS 243:3. GL 261:3. PS 254:3. PL 368:4. RL 428:4.

Revision note.
At the end of the sentence, substituted "the accused" for "he" preceding "had pleaded not guilty" for purposes of clarity.

605:6. Plea of Nolo Contendere.

A plea of nolo contendere may be accepted in any criminal case, and when such a plea is accepted, the court or justice may enter a finding of guilty upon such plea. Evidence of a plea of nolo contendere or of the finding entered thereon shall not be admissible in any civil action against the defendant.

Source.
1967, 197:1, eff. Aug. 13, 1967.

RESEARCH REFERENCES

New Hampshire Court Rules Annotated.
Admissibility in evidence of pleas, plea discussions and related statements, see Rule 410, Rules of Evidence, New Hampshire Court Rules Annotated.

CHAPTER 606

TRIAL

SECTION
606:1.   Impanelling Jury.
606:2.   Oath of Jurors.
606:3.   Challenges; Defendant.
606:4.   Challenges; State.
606:5.   Custody of Jury.
606:6.   Rebutting Evidence.
606:7.   Waiver of Jury Trial in Certain Cases.
606:8.   Offenses Punishable by Imprisonment not Exceeding One Year.
606:9.   Procedure; Challenges.
606:10.   Appeals by the State.

Cross References.
Compensation of jurors, see New Hampshire Constitution, Part 1, Article 21.
Criminal jurisdiction of district courts, see RSA 502-A:11.
Criminal jurisdiction of municipal courts, see RSA 502:18.
Criminal jurisdiction of superior court, see RSA 491:7.
Depositions generally, see RSA 517:13 et seq.
Juries generally, see RSA 500-A.
Rights of accused generally, see New Hampshire Constitution, Part 1, Article 15, and RSA 604.
Right to jury trial generally, see New Hampshire Constitution, Part 1, Article 16.
Venue generally, see New Hampshire Constitution, Part 1, Article 17, and RSA 602.
Witnesses generally, see RSA 516.

RESEARCH REFERENCES

New Hampshire Court Rules Annotated.
Appeals from convictions in municipal or district courts, see RSA 599 and Rules 2.13 and 2.14, Rules of the District and Municipal Courts, New Hampshire Court Rules Annotated.
Evidence generally, see Rules of Evidence, New Hampshire Court Rules Annotated.
Rules governing criminal proceedings in the superior court generally, see Rules 94-105, Rules of the Superior Court, New Hampshire Court Rules Annotated.

Criminal Jury Instructions.
New Hampshire Criminal Jury Instructions, Instruction ##
1.01–1.11.

606:1. Impanelling Jury.

Petit jurors attending the court may be impanelled for the trial of any criminal case and may be examined as in civil cases and otherwise, as to their fitness and capacity to perform the duty of jurors on the trial.

Source.
RS 176:21. CS 186:22. GS 243:6. GL 261:7. PS 254:7. PL 368:9. RL 428:9.

Cross References.
Challenges to jurors generally, see RSA 606:3, 4, and 9.
Examination of jurors generally, see RSA 500-A:12.
Selection of jurors generally, see New Hampshire Constitution, Part 1, Article 21.

NOTES TO DECISIONS

1. Propounding of questions to jurors
2. Ruling on disqualification of juror
3. Dismissal of juror
4. Questioning by attorneys

1. Propounding of questions to jurors
It is the duty of the court to impanel for the trial of a case a competent and impartial jury, and in the execution of this duty, the court may propound to the jurors returned other interrogatories than those which are required to be put by the law. Pierce v. State, 13 N.H. 536, 1843 N.H. LEXIS 117 (1843), aff'd, Peirce v. New Hampshire, 46 U.S. 554, 5 How. 554, 12 L. Ed. 279 (1847), aff'd, Thurlow v. Massachusetts, 46 U.S. 504, 12 L. Ed. 256, 1847 U.S. LEXIS 322 (1847).

2. Ruling on disqualification of juror
Whether a juror is disqualified to sit in a cause on account of his interest therein is a question of fact for the court, and if he is interested, it does not follow as a conclusion of law that he is not indifferent; he may nevertheless be found to be unbiased and impartial. In re Opinion of Justices, 75 N.H. 613, 72 A. 754, 1909 N.H. LEXIS 83 (1909).
Whether a juror is indifferent is a question of fact to be decided at the trial. Rowell v. Boston & M. R.R., 58 N.H. 514, 1879 N.H. LEXIS 229 (1879).

3. Dismissal of juror
On motion of either party, a juror may be set aside if it appears he is not indifferent. Rowell v. Boston & M. R.R., 58 N.H. 514, 1879 N.H. LEXIS 229 (1879).

4. Questioning by attorneys
By its express terms, RSA 606:1 does not require that jurors in criminal trials be subject to the same voir dire process as jurors in civil trials. Accordingly, RSA 606:1 does not mandate that the attorney voir dire process outlined in RSA 500-A:12-a, III and IV apply to criminal trials. State v. Wamala, 158 N.H. 583, 972 A.2d 1071, 2009 N.H. LEXIS 50 (2009).

Cited:
Cited in State v. Webster, 13 N.H. 491, 1843 N.H. LEXIS 109 (1843); Hutchinson v. Manchester S. Ry., 73 N.H. 271, 60 A. 1011, 1905 N.H. LEXIS 36 (1905); State v. Isabelle, 80 N.H. 191, 115 A. 806, 1921 N.H. LEXIS 61 (1921); Shulinsky v. Boston & M. R.R., 83 N.H. 86, 139 A. 189, 1927 N.H. LEXIS 41 (1927).

606:2. Oath of Jurors.

The following oath shall be administered to petit jurors in criminal cases: You solemnly swear or affirm that you will carefully consider the evidence and the law presented to you in this case and that you will deliver a fair and true verdict as to the charge or charges against the defendant. So help you God.

Source.
RS 176:22. CS 186:23. GS 243:7. GL 261:8. PS 254:8. PL 368:10. RL 428:10. RSA 606:2. 1989, 5:1, eff. Jan. 1, 1990.

Amendments
—1989.   Rewrote the first sentence of the oath.

Cross References.
Oath of jurors in civil cases, see RSA 500-A:18.

NOTES TO DECISIONS

1. Generally
2. Administration of incorrect oath

1. Generally
This section prescribes the form of oath to be administered to petit jurors in criminal trials and imperatively requires its administration; any other form of oath is insufficient. State v. Rollins, 22 N.H. 528, 1851 N.H. LEXIS 109 (1851).

2. Administration of incorrect oath
If, in a criminal case, an oath in the form prescribed for civil trials is administered to the jurors, the verdict returned will be set aside upon exception by the accused, and a new trial will be granted. State v. Rollins, 22 N.H. 528, 1851 N.H. LEXIS 109 (1851).

Cited:
Cited in State v. Sawtelle, 66 N.H. 488, 32 A. 831, 1891 N.H. LEXIS 62 (1891).

606:3. Challenges; Defendant.

Every person arraigned and put on trial for an offense may, in addition to challenges for cause or unless he stands wilfully mute, peremptorily challenge:
I. 20 jurors for capital murder.
II. 15 jurors for murder in the first degree.
III. 3 jurors in any other case.

Source.
RS 225:5. CS 240:7. 1859, 2213:1. GS 243:8. GL 261:9. PS 254:9. 1919, 40:1. PL 368:11. RL 428:11. RSA 606:3. 1974, 34:5. 1993, 143:1, eff. Jan. 1, 1994.

Amendments
—1993.   Rewritten to the extent that a detailed comparison would be impracticable.

—1974.   Substituted "punishable by death or for murder in the first degree" for "which may be punishable by death".

Revision note.
For purposes of clarity, substituted "peremptorily" for "so" preceding "challenge 3" and deleted "of the" thereafter.

Cross References.
Capital murder, see RSA 630:1.
Classification of crimes, see RSA 625:9.

First degree murder, see RSA 630:1-a.

Number of peremptory challenges in cases tried by juries of six persons, see RSA 606:9.

NOTES TO DECISIONS

1. Construction with other law
2. Crimes deemed capital offenses
3. Number of challenges available to joint defendants
4. Exercise of challenge after acceptance of juror

1. Construction with other law

Under the United States Constitution, peremptory challenges may be made based on age, but not on gender. State v. Taylor, 142 N.H. 6, 694 A.2d 977, 1997 N.H. LEXIS 49 (1997).

2. Crimes deemed capital offenses

Upon the trial of an indictment charging second degree murder, the accused is not entitled to peremptorily challenge twenty jurors since second degree murder is not a capital offense. State v. Wood, 53 N.H. 484, 1873 N.H. LEXIS 41 (1873).

3. Number of challenges available to joint defendants

Where two or more defendants are jointly indicted for a capital offense and tried together, each is entitled to the full number of challenges allowed by this section. State v. Doolittle, 58 N.H. 92, 1877 N.H. LEXIS 23 (1877).

4. Exercise of challenge after acceptance of juror

The trial court in a criminal case has discretionary authority before the jury panel is sworn to allow the state or the respondent to exercise a peremptory challenge of a juror that has been accepted by both parties. State v. Prevost, 105 N.H. 90, 193 A.2d 22, 1963 N.H. LEXIS 23 (1963).

Cited:

Cited in Shulinsky v. Boston & M. R.R., 83 N.H. 86, 139 A. 189, 1927 N.H. LEXIS 41 (1927); State v. Farrow, 118 N.H. 296, 386 A.2d 808, 1978 N.H. LEXIS 402 (1978); State v. Anaya, 131 N.H. 330, 553 A.2d 297, 1988 N.H. LEXIS 121 (1988).

606:4. Challenges; State.

The state shall be entitled to the following number of peremptory challenges, in addition to challenges for cause, in the following cases:

I. Upon the trial for capital murder, 10 challenges.

II. Upon the trial for murder in the first degree, 15 challenges.

III. Upon the trial for any other case, 3 challenges.

Source.

GS 243:9. 1877, 6:1. GL 261:10. 1879, 57:31. PS 254:10. 1919, 40:1. PL 368:12. RL 428:12. RSA 606:4. 1974, 34:6. 1979, 283:1. 1993, 143:2, eff. Jan. 1, 1994.

Amendments

—**1993.** Paragraph I: Substituted "for capital murder" for "of any offense punishable by death" following "trial".

Paragraph II: Substituted "for" for "of" preceding "murder" and "15" for "20".

Paragraph III: Substituted "upon the trial for" for "in" preceding "any other".

—**1979.** Rewritten to the extent that a detailed comparison would be impracticable.

—**1974.** Substituted "punishable by death or of murder in the first degree" for "which may be punishable by death".

Cross References.

Capital murder, see RSA 630:1.

Classification of crimes, see RSA 625:9.

First degree murder, see RSA 630:1-a.

Number of peremptory challenges available to defendants generally, see RSA 606:3.

Number of peremptory challenges in cases tried by juries of six persons, see RSA 606:9.

NOTES TO DECISIONS

1. Constitutionality
2. Exercise of challenge after acceptance of juror
3. Gender discrimination

1. Constitutionality

This section is constitutional. State v. Wilson, 48 N.H. 398, 1869 N.H. LEXIS 46 (1869).

Under the United States Constitution, peremptory challenges may be made based on age, but not on gender. State v. Taylor, 142 N.H. 6, 694 A.2d 977, 1997 N.H. LEXIS 49 (1997).

2. Exercise of challenge after acceptance of juror

The trial court in a criminal case has discretionary authority before the jury panel is sworn to allow the state or the respondent to exercise a peremptory challenge of a juror who has been accepted by both parties. State v. Prevost, 105 N.H. 90, 193 A.2d 22, 1963 N.H. LEXIS 23 (1963).

3. Gender discrimination

The defendant failed to make out a prima facie case of gender discrimination where the state exercised two peremptory challenges to male prospective jurors, but three men were empaneled as jurors despite the availability to the state of another unexercised peremptory challenge. State v. Taylor, 142 N.H. 6, 694 A.2d 977, 1997 N.H. LEXIS 49 (1997).

Cited:

Cited in Shulinsky v. Boston & M. R.R., 83 N.H. 86, 139 A. 189, 1927 N.H. LEXIS 41 (1927); State v. Farrow, 118 N.H. 296, 386 A.2d 808, 1978 N.H. LEXIS 402 (1978); State v. Anaya, 131 N.H. 330, 553 A.2d 297, 1988 N.H. LEXIS 121 (1988).

606:5. Custody of Jury.

The jury impanelled to try any criminal case may be kept separate from all other persons during the trial, if, upon cause shown, the court shall so order, and not otherwise.

Source.

GS 243:12. GL 261:12. PS 254:11. 1919, 48:1. PL 368:13. RL 428:13.

NOTES TO DECISIONS

Effect of improper sequestration

The mere separation of jurors who have been impanelled to try a capital offense from their fellow jurors, without the attendance of an officer, although an irregularity, is not a sufficient cause for setting aside the verdict if the court is satisfied that the accused has not sustained any injury by reason of such separation. State v. Prescott, 7 N.H. 287, 1834 N.H. LEXIS 35 (1834).

Where there has been an improper separation of jurors during the trial, if the verdict is against the accused he is entitled to the benefit of the presumption that the irregularity has been prejudicial to him, and the burden of proof is upon the state to show beyond a reasonable doubt that the accused has suffered no injury by reason of the separation; if the state fails in this proof, the verdict will be set aside. State v. Prescott, 7 N.H. 287, 1834 N.H. LEXIS 35 (1834).

606:6. Rebutting Evidence.

In capital cases witnesses may be called in behalf

of the state to rebut or explain any evidence of new matter offered by the defendant, or to discredit his witnesses, though the names of such witnesses have not been furnished to the defendant, but time may be allowed the defendant to answer such evidence, if, in the opinion of the court, justice shall require it.

Source.
1843, 34:17. CS 240:4. GS 243:11. GL 261:11. PS 254:12. PL 368:14. RL 428:14.

RESEARCH REFERENCES

New Hampshire Court Rules Annotated.
Control of mode and order of interrogation of witnesses and presentation of evidence, see Rule 611, Rules of Evidence, New Hampshire Court Rules Annotated.

606:7. Waiver of Jury Trial in Certain Cases.

Any defendant in the superior court in a criminal case other than a capital case may, if he shall so elect, when called upon to plead, or later and before a jury has been impanelled to try him, waive his right to trial by jury by signing a written waiver thereof and filing the same with the clerk of the court, whereupon he shall be tried by the court instead of by a jury, but not, however, unless all the defendants, if there are 2 or more to be tried together for the same offense, shall have exercised such election before a jury has been impanelled to try any of the defendants. In every such case the court shall have jurisdiction to hear and try the case and render judgment and sentence thereon.

Source.
1933, 96:1. RL 428:15.

Revision note.
For purposes of clarity, substituted "whereupon" for "thereupon" following "filing the same with the clerk of court" and "the case" for "such case" following "hear and try".

Cross References.
Right to jury trial in capital cases, see New Hampshire Constitution, Part 1, Article 16.

NOTES TO DECISIONS

Cited:
Cited in State v. Geddes, 101 N.H. 164, 136 A.2d 818, 1957 N.H. LEXIS 45 (1957).

606:8. Offenses Punishable by Imprisonment not Exceeding One Year.

Six persons shall constitute a jury for the trial in the superior court of any offense punishable by imprisonment for any period not exceeding one year.

Source.
1973, 485:1, eff. Aug. 29, 1973.

Cross References.
Classification of crimes, see RSA 625:9.
Procedure for trial by juries of six persons, see RSA 606:9.
Sentences, see RSA 651.

NOTES TO DECISIONS

Cited:
Cited in Opinion of Justices, 121 N.H. 480, 431 A.2d 135, 1981 N.H. LEXIS 345 (1981).

606:9. Procedure; Challenges.

Trials by juries of 6 shall proceed in accordance with provisions of law applicable to trials of criminal cases in the superior court, except that the number of peremptory challenges shall be limited to 2 for each defendant. The state shall be entitled to as many challenges as equal the whole number to which all the defendants in the case are entitled.

Source.
1973, 485:1, eff. Aug. 29, 1973.

Cross References.
Number of peremptory challenges in criminal cases generally, see RSA 606:3, 4.
Offenses subject to trial by juries of six persons, see RSA 606:8.

NOTES TO DECISIONS

Cited:
Cited in Opinion of Justices, 121 N.H. 480, 431 A.2d 135, 1981 N.H. LEXIS 345 (1981).

606:10. Appeals by the State.

I. As used in this section, "order" shall mean any decision by a court on a question of law including, but not limited to, any order, ruling, decision or judgment.

II. An appeal may be taken by the state in criminal cases on questions of law from the district or municipal courts or from the superior court to the supreme court from:

(a) An order of the court prior to trial which suppresses any evidence including, but not limited to, physical or identification evidence or evidence of a confession or admission;

(b) An order prior to trial which prevents the state from obtaining evidence;

(c) A pretrial dismissal of an indictment, information or complaint; or

(d) Any other order of the court prior to trial if, either because of the nature of the order in question or because of the particular circumstances of the case, there is a reasonable likelihood that such order will cause either serious impairment to or termination of the prosecution of any case.

III. An appeal may be taken by the state from the superior court or the district or municipal courts to the supreme court, after trial and after a finding of guilty by a jury or the court, from:

(a) The granting of a motion for a new trial;

(b) Dismissal; or

(c) Any other order requiring a new trial or resulting in termination of the prosecution in favor of the accused if an appeal of such order would be permitted by the double jeopardy provisions of the constitutions of the United States and New Hampshire.

IV. An appeal taken pursuant to paragraph II shall be taken before the defendant has been placed in jeopardy.

V. No appeal may be taken pursuant to this section unless the attorney general approves such appeal. Written approval of the attorney general shall be filed:

(a) At the time the notice of the appeal is filed; or

(b) Within 5 business days, if the attorney for the state filing the notice of appeal states in such notice that the attorney general has orally given his approval.

VI. The provisions of this section shall be liberally construed to effectuate its purpose of insuring that the state is able to proceed to trial with all of the evidence which it is legally entitled to introduce, in view of the limited ability of the state to have error reviewed after trial.

VII. The supreme court may adopt rules implementing the provisions of this section.

Source.
1985, 32:1, eff. Jan. 1, 1986.

NOTES TO DECISIONS

1. Timeliness
2. Certiorari review

1. Timeliness

Appeals filed by State in criminal matters, pursuant to RSA 606:10, are subject to same timeliness requirements that govern all supreme court appeals under Supreme Court Rules 7 through 9. State v. Dukette, 145 N.H. 226, 761 A.2d 442, 2000 N.H. LEXIS 46 (2000).

State's interlocutory appeal from denial of its motion in limine was untimely, since State neither filed an appeal within thirty days of clerk's written notice of decision nor stayed running of appeal period by filing a timely motion for reconsideration. State v. Dukette, 145 N.H. 226, 761 A.2d 442, 2000 N.H. LEXIS 46 (2000).

2. Certiorari review

State's petition for a writ of certiorari was granted pursuant to N.H. Sup. Ct. R. 11 and RSA 490:4 with respect to its request for review of a dismissal of an indictment against defendant after the State had presented its case, as jeopardy had already attached and accordingly, there was no other available avenue for review of the dismissal. State v. Laporte (in re State), 157 N.H. 229, 950 A.2d 147, 2008 N.H. LEXIS 55 (2008).

As jeopardy already attached to a criminal matter where a trial court granted defendant's dismissal motion of the grand jury indictment against him after trial but before the verdict was rendered, certiorari pursuant to RSA 606:10 was within the court's discretion under N.H. Sup. Ct. R. 11 and it was the only avenue that the State had to seek relief from the dismissal order. State v. Johanson (In re State), 156 N.H. 148, 932 A.2d 848, 2007 N.H. LEXIS 152 (2007).

State's petition for certiorari review of defendant's sentence was granted as defendant was not sentenced to an enhanced sentence for driving while intoxicated and certiorari was the only avenue by which the State could appeal the sentencing order. State v. Marcoux (In re State), 154 N.H. 118, 908 A.2d 155, 2006 N.H. LEXIS 126 (2006).

Cited:
Cited in State v. Fischer, 152 N.H. 205, 876 A.2d 232, 2005 N.H.

LEXIS 77 (2005); State v. Wonyetye, 129 N.H. 452, 529 A.2d 927, 1987 N.H. LEXIS 212 (1987); State v. Briand, 130 N.H. 650, 547 A.2d 235, 1988 N.H. LEXIS 77 (1988); State v. McDermott, 131 N.H. 495, 554 A.2d 1302, 1989 N.H. LEXIS 14 (1989); State v. Symonds, 131 N.H. 532, 556 A.2d 1175, 1989 N.H. LEXIS 24 (1989); State v. Pelky, 131 N.H. 715, 559 A.2d 1345, 1989 N.H. LEXIS 52 (1989); State v. O'Neill, 134 N.H. 182, 589 A.2d 999, 1991 N.H. LEXIS 51 (1991); State v. DeMatteo, 134 N.H. 296, 591 A.2d 1323, 1991 N.H. LEXIS 56 (1991); State v. Caplin, 134 N.H. 302, 592 A.2d 188, 1991 N.H. LEXIS 62 (1991); State v. Caicedo, 135 N.H. 122, 599 A.2d 895, 1991 N.H. LEXIS 149 (1991); State v. Lamontagne, 136 N.H. 575, 618 A.2d 849, 1992 N.H. LEXIS 200 (1992); State v. Decoteau, 137 N.H. 106, 623 A.2d 1338, 1993 N.H. LEXIS 49 (1993); State v. Hayes, 138 N.H. 410, 640 A.2d 288, 1994 N.H. LEXIS 40 (1994); State v. Dolbeare, 140 N.H. 84, 663 A.2d 85, 1995 N.H. LEXIS 96 (1995); State v. Hungerford, 142 N.H. 110, 697 A.2d 916, 1997 N.H. LEXIS 64 (1997); State v. Hayes, 138 N.H. 410, 640 A.2d 288, 1994 N.H. LEXIS 40 (1994); State v. Spinale, 156 N.H. 456, 937 A.2d 938, 2007 N.H. LEXIS 209 (2007); State v. Langill, 157 N.H. 77, 945 A.2d 1, 2008 N.H. LEXIS 39 (2008).

RESEARCH REFERENCES

New Hampshire Court Rules Annotated.

Appeals from convictions in municipal or district courts, see RSA 599 and Rules 2.13 and 2.14, Rules of the District and Municipal Courts, New Hampshire Court Rules Annotated.

Appeals to supreme court generally, see Rules 7-9, Rules of the Supreme Court, New Hampshire Court Rules Annotated.

CHAPTER 606-A

AGREEMENT ON DETAINERS

SECTION
606-A:1.   Agreement Enacted.
606-A:2.   Definition.
606-A:3.   Enforcement of Agreement.
606-A:4.   Application.
606-A:5.   Duty of Warden.
606-A:6.   Compact Administrator.

Cross References.

Department of corrections, see RSA 21-H.
Department of justice, see RSA 21-M.
Extradition, see RSA 612.
Interstate corrections compact, see RSA 622-B.
New England Interstate Corrections Compact, see RSA 622-A.
Rendition of prisoners as witnesses in criminal proceedings, see RSA 613-A.
Securing attendance of witnesses in criminal proceedings generally, see RSA 613.

NOTES TO DECISIONS

Purpose of chapter

The purpose of this chapter is to give formal recognition to the practice of honoring detainers filed by other states against prisoners confined in this state and to provide for trial here of persons serving sentences in other states prior to the expiration of their sentences there. Allen v. Hancock, 109 N.H. 254, 248 A.2d 632, 1968 N.H. LEXIS 173 (1968).

The purpose of this chapter is to secure the speedy trial of persons incarcerated in jurisdictions that have enacted similar statutes. In re Lemieux, 109 N.H. 258, 248 A.2d 634, 1968 N.H. LEXIS 174 (1968).

Cited:

Cited in Cross v. Warden, N.H. State Prison, 138 N.H. 591, 644 A.2d 542, 1994 N.H. LEXIS 69 (1994).

606-A:1. Agreement Enacted.

The agreement on detainers is hereby enacted into law and entered into by this state with all other jurisdictions legally joining therein in the form substantially as follows:

The contracting states solemnly agree that:

Article I

The party states find that charges outstanding against a prisoner, detainers based on untried indictments, informations or complaints, and difficulties in securing speedy trial of persons already incarcerated in other jurisdictions, produce uncertainties which obstruct programs of prisoner treatment and rehabilitation. Accordingly, it is the policy of the party states and the purpose of this agreement to encourage the expeditious and orderly disposition of such charges and determination of the proper status of any and all detainers based on untried indictments, informations or complaints. The party states also find that proceedings with reference to such charges and detainers, when emanating from another jurisdiction, cannot properly be had in the absence of cooperative procedures. It is the further purpose of this agreement to provide such cooperative procedures.

Article II

As used in this agreement:

(a) "State" shall mean a state of the United States; the United States of America; a territory or possession of the United States; the District of Columbia; the Commonwealth of Puerto Rico.

(b) "Sending state" shall mean a state in which a prisoner is incarcerated at the time that he initiates a request for final disposition pursuant to Article III hereof or at the time that a request for custody or availability is initiated pursuant to Article IV hereof.

(c) "Receiving state" shall mean the state in which trial is to be had on an indictment, information or complaint pursuant to Article III or Article IV hereof.

Article III

(a) Whenever a person has entered upon a term of imprisonment in a penal or correctional institution of a party state, and whenever during the continuance of the term of imprisonment there is pending in any other party state any untried indictment, information or complaint on the basis of which a detainer has been lodged against the prisoner, he shall be brought to trial within 180 days after he shall have caused to be delivered to the prosecuting officer and the appropriate court of the prosecuting officer's jurisdiction written notice of the place of his imprisonment and his request for a final disposition

to be made of the indictment, information or complaint; provided that for good cause shown in open court, the prisoner or his counsel being present, the court having jurisdiction of the matter may grant any necessary or reasonable continuance. The request of the prisoner shall be accompanied by a certificate of the appropriate official having custody of the prisoner, stating the term of commitment under which the prisoner is being held, the time already served, the time remaining to be served on the sentence, the amount of good time earned, the time of parole eligibility of the prisoner, and any decisions of the state parole agency relating to the prisoner.

(b) The written notice and request for final disposition referred to in paragraph (a) hereof shall be given or sent by the prisoner to the warden, commissioner of corrections or other official having custody of him, who shall promptly forward it together with the certificate to the appropriate prosecuting official and court by registered or certified mail, return receipt requested.

(c) The warden, commissioner of corrections or other official having custody of the prisoner shall promptly inform him of the source and contents of any detainer lodged against him and shall also inform him of his right to make a request for final disposition of the indictment, information or complaint on which the detainer is based.

(d) Any request for final disposition made by a prisoner pursuant to paragraph (a) hereof shall operate as a request for final disposition of all untried indictments, informations or complaints on the basis of which detainers have been lodged against the prisoner from the state to whose prosecuting official the request for final disposition is specifically directed. The warden, commissioner of corrections or other official having custody of the prisoner shall forthwith notify all appropriate prosecuting officers and courts in the several jurisdictions within the state to which the prisoner's request for final disposition is being sent of the proceeding being initiated by the prisoner. Any notification sent pursuant to the paragraph shall be accompanied by copies of the prisoner's written notice, request, and the certificate. If trial is not had on any indictment, information or complaint contemplated hereby prior to the return of the prisoner to the original place of imprisonment, such indictment, information or complaint shall not be of any further force or effect, and the court shall enter an order dismissing the same with prejudice.

(e) Any request for final disposition made by a prisoner pursuant to paragraph (a) hereof shall also be deemed to be a waiver of extradition with respect to any charge or proceeding contemplated thereby or included therein by reason of paragraph (d) hereof, and a waiver of extradition to the receiving state to serve any sentence there imposed upon him, after completion of his term of imprisonment in the sending state. The request for final disposition shall also constitute a consent by the prisoner to the production of his body in any court where his presence may be required in order to effectuate the purposes of this agreement and a further consent voluntarily to be returned to the original place of imprisonment in accordance with the provisions of this agreement. Nothing in this paragraph shall prevent the imposition of a concurrent sentence if otherwise permitted by law.

(f) Escape from custody by the prisoner subsequent to his execution of the request for final disposition referred to in paragraph (a) hereof shall void the request.

Article IV

(a) The appropriate officer of the jurisdiction in which an untried indictment, information or complaint is pending shall be entitled to have a prisoner against whom he has lodged a detainer and who is serving a term of imprisonment in any party state made available in accordance with Article V(a) hereof upon presentation of a written request for temporary custody or availability to the appropriate authorities of the state in which the prisoner is incarcerated; provided that the court having jurisdiction of such indictment, information or complaint shall have duly approved, recorded and transmitted the request; and provided further that there shall be a period of 30 days after receipt by the appropriate authorities before the request be honored, within which period the governor of the sending state may disapprove the request for temporary custody or availability, either upon his own motion or upon motion of the prisoner.

(b) Upon receipt of the officer's written request as provided in paragraph (a) hereof, the appropriate authorities having the prisoner in custody shall furnish the officer with a certificate stating the term of commitment under which the prisoner is being held, the time already served, the time remaining to be served on the sentence, the amount of good time earned, the time of parole eligibility of the prisoner, and any decisions of the state parole agency relating to the prisoner. Said authorities simultaneously shall furnish all other officers and appropriate courts in the receiving state who have lodged detainers against the prisoner with similar certificates and with notices informing them of the request for custody or availability and of the reasons therefor.

(c) In respect to any proceeding made possible by this Article, trial shall be commenced within 120 days of the arrival of the prisoner in the receiving state, but for good cause shown in open court, the prisoner or his counsel being present, the court having jurisdiction of the matter may grant any necessary or reasonable continuance.

(d) Nothing contained in this Article shall be construed to deprive any prisoner of any right which he may have to contest the legality of his delivery as provided in paragraph (a) hereof, but such delivery may not be opposed or denied on the ground that the executive authority of the sending state has not affirmatively consented to or ordered such delivery.

(e) If trial is not had on any indictment, information or complaint contemplated hereby prior to the prisoner being returned to the original place of imprisonment pursuant to Article V(e) hereof, such indictment, information or complaint shall not be of any further force or effect, and the court shall enter an order dismissing the same with prejudice.

Article V

(a) In response to a request made under Article III or Article IV hereof, the appropriate authority in a sending state shall offer to deliver temporary custody of such prisoner to the appropriate authority in the state where such indictment, information or complaint is pending against such person in order that speedy and efficient prosecution may be had. If the request for final disposition is made by the prisoner, the offer of temporary custody shall accompany the written notice provided for in Article III of this agreement. In the case of a federal prisoner, the appropriate authority in the receiving state shall be entitled to temporary custody as provided by this agreement or to the prisoner's presence in federal custody at the place for trial, whichever custodial arrangement may be approved by the custodian.

(b) The officer or other representative of a state accepting an offer of temporary custody shall present the following upon demand:

(1) Proper identification and evidence of his authority to act for the state into whose temporary custody the prisoner is to be given.

(2) A duly certified copy of the indictment, information or complaint on the basis of which the detainer has been lodged and on the basis of which the request for temporary custody of the prisoner has been made.

(c) If the appropriate authority shall refuse or fail to accept temporary custody of said person, or in the event that an action of the indictment, information or complaint on the basis of which the detainer has been lodged is not brought to trial within the period provided in Article III or Article IV hereof, the appropriate court of the jurisdiction where the indictment, information or complaint has been pending shall enter an order dismissing the same with prejudice, and any detainer based thereon shall cease to be of any force or effect.

(d) The temporary custody referred to in this agreement shall be only for the purpose of permitting prosecution on the charge or charges contained in one or more untried indictments, informations or complaints which form the basis of the detainer or detainers or for prosecution on any other charge or charges arising out of the same transaction. Except for his attendance at court and while being transported to or from any place at which his presence may be required, the prisoner shall be held in a suitable jail or other facility regularly used for persons awaiting prosecution.

(e) At the earliest practicable time consonant with the purposes of this agreement, the prisoner shall be returned to the sending state.

(f) During the continuance of temporary custody or while the prisoner is otherwise being made available for trial as required by this agreement, time being served on the sentence shall continue to run but good time shall be earned by the prisoner only if, and to the extent that, the law and practice of the jurisdiction which imposed the sentence may allow.

(g) For all purposes other than that for which temporary custody as provided in this agreement is exercised, the prisoner shall be deemed to remain in the custody of and subject to the jurisdiction of the sending state and any escape from temporary custody may be dealt with in the same manner as an escape from the original place of imprisonment or in any other manner permitted by law.

(h) From the time that a party state receives custody of a prisoner pursuant to this agreement until such prisoner is returned to the territory and custody of the sending state, the state in which the one or more untried indictments, informations or complaints are pending or in which trial is being had shall be responsible for the prisoner and shall also pay all costs of transporting, caring for, keeping and returning the prisoner. The provisions of this paragraph shall govern unless the states concerned shall have entered into a supplementary agreement providing for a different allocation of costs and responsibilities as between or among themselves. Nothing herein contained shall be construed to alter or affect any internal relationship among the departments, agencies and officers of and in the government of a party state, or between a party state and its subdivisions, as to the payment of costs, or responsibilities therefor.

Article VI

(a) In determining the duration and expiration dates of the time periods provided in Articles III and IV of this agreement, the running of said time periods shall be tolled whenever and for as long as the prisoner is unable to stand trial, as determined by the court having jurisdiction of the matter.

(b) No provision of this agreement, and no remedy made available by this agreement, shall apply to any person who is adjudged to be mentally ill.

Article VII

Each state party to this agreement shall designate an officer who, acting jointly with like officers of other party states, shall promulgate rules and regulations to carry out more effectively the terms and provisions of this agreement, and who shall provide, within and without the state, information necessary to the effective operation of this agreement.

Article VIII

This agreement shall enter into full force and effect as to a party state when such state has enacted the same into law. A state party to this agreement may withdraw herefrom by enacting a statute repealing the same. However, the withdrawal of any state shall not affect the status of any proceedings already initiated by inmates or by state officers at the time such withdrawal takes effect, nor shall it affect their rights in respect thereof.

Article IX

This agreement shall be liberally construed so as to effectuate its purposes. The provisions of this agreement shall be severable and if any phrase, clause, sentence or provision of this agreement is declared to be contrary to the constitution of any party state or of the United States or the applicability thereof to any government, agency, person or circumstance is held invalid, the validity of the remainder of this agreement and the applicability thereof to any government, agency, person or circumstances shall not be affected thereby. If this agreement shall be held contrary to the constitution of any state party hereto, the agreement shall remain in full force and effect as to the remaining states and in full force and effect as to the state affected as to all severable matters.

Source.
1959, 107:1, eff. July 17, 1959.

Cross References.
Department of corrections, see RSA 21-H.
Department of justice, see RSA 21-M.
Parole of delinquents, see RSA 170-H.
Parole of prisoners generally, see RSA 651-A.
Probation generally, see RSA 504-A.
State prison, see RSA 622.

NOTES TO DECISIONS

1. Application of agreement—Generally
2. —Application to multiple indictments
3. —Right to speedy trial
4. —Appeals
5. Continuances
6. Tolling of time period
7. Waiver of time period
8. Computation of time period

1. Application of agreement—Generally
Where defendant was indicted on armed robbery charges in New Hampshire, and subsequently indicted and convicted of robbery in Rhode Island, his right to a speedy trial on New Hampshire charge attached on the date he pled guilty to the Rhode Island charge. Humphrey v. Cunningham, 133 N.H. 727, 584 A.2d 763, 1990 N.H. LEXIS 138 (1990).

The language of Article III(a), governing when the interstate agreement on detainers may be invoked by a defendant, is sufficiently broad to include those indictments arising before incarceration in the sending state, and those for which the defendant has been released on bail in the receiving state. State v. McGann, 126

N.H. 316, 493 A.2d 452, 1985 N.H. LEXIS 323 (1985).

Applying the interstate agreement on detainers where a defendant has been indicted, arraigned, and released on bail prior to his out-of-state confinement is consistent with the agreement's stated purpose. State v. McGann, 126 N.H. 316, 493 A.2d 452, 1985 N.H. LEXIS 323 (1985).

2. —Application to multiple indictments

Nothing in the interstate agreement on detainers requires that the defendant be brought to trial on each and every indictment within the 180-day limitation period provided in the agreement if trial of the other indictments is continued, if the limitation period is tolled as to these indictments, or if trial is commenced within 180 days on one indictment and subsequent trials are commenced within a reasonable time after resolution of the first trial. State v. McGann, 126 N.H. 316, 493 A.2d 452, 1985 N.H. LEXIS 323 (1985).

3. —Right to speedy trial

The words "brought to trial" contained in Article III mean only that a proceeding must be initiated, not that the case must be finally disposed of. State v. Sprague, 146 N.H. 334, 771 A.2d 583, 2001 N.H. LEXIS 82 (2001).

The state is required to provide a trial within 180 days after a prisoner has requested a final disposition of his indictment, and the burden of providing such a trial, after excluding delays that are caused by the defendant's conduct, plus a reasonable period for court response, is squarely on the shoulders of the state. State v. Dolbeare, 140 N.H. 84, 663 A.2d 85, 1995 N.H. LEXIS 96 (1995).

4. —Appeals

Failure of state authorities to return defendant to Massachusetts custody during pendency of his direct appeal of bank robbery convictions to New Hampshire Supreme Court did not violate article V(e). Absent defendant's specific waiver agreeing to be returned to New Hampshire if his appeal resulted in a new trial, State was justified in delaying his return to Massachusetts. Therefore, the defendant was returned to Massachusetts at the earliest possible time consistent with expeditious and orderly disposition of bank robbery charges against him. Cross v. Warden, N.H. State Prison, 138 N.H. 591, 644 A.2d 542, 1994 N.H. LEXIS 69 (1994), cert. denied, Cross v. Cunningham, 513 U.S. 1111, 115 S. Ct. 901, 130 L. Ed. 2d 785, 1995 U.S. LEXIS 541 (1995).

5. Continuances

Continuance was granted for good cause on the basis that the jury pool had seen defendant in prison clothes, the defense wished to interview one of the State's witnesses who had recently been granted immunity, and the State wished to correct a pleading defect in one of three indictments. State v. Sprague, 146 N.H. 334, 771 A.2d 583, 2001 N.H. LEXIS 82 (2001).

Under the circumstances of the case, a continuance of sixty-one days was not unreasonable; therefore, delay occasioned by the continuance should not be included in the 180-day period in bringing defendant to trial. State v. Sprague, 146 N.H. 334, 771 A.2d 583, 2001 N.H. LEXIS 82 (2001).

The fact that a delay is not called a "continuance" is not controlling as to its character as a continuance for purposes of the 180-day limitation period of Article III. State v. McGann, 126 N.H. 316, 493 A.2d 452, 1985 N.H. LEXIS 323 (1985).

Decision of the superior court on a pending indictment against defendant, to take under advisement state's motion for production of information and deposition, and continue the trial itself, was a reasonable continuance which tolled the 180-day limitation period for bringing defendant to trial provided in Article III. State v. McGann, 126 N.H. 316, 493 A.2d 452, 1985 N.H. LEXIS 323 (1985).

Article III of this section expressly allows for reasonable and necessary continuances in order to prevent the state or the defendant from sacrificing adequate trial preparation. State v. Brown, 125 N.H. 346, 480 A.2d 901, 1984 N.H. LEXIS 265 (1984).

Where in the time between defendant's request for final disposition of indictment and trial three continuances were granted to the defendant, all of which were necessary to allow the defendant time for adequate trial preparation, since the continuances were, therefore, for good cause, the delay occasioned by them was not to be included in completing the 180-day period between defendant's request for final disposition of the indictment and trial prescribed by Article III(a) of this section. State v. Brown, 125 N.H. 346, 480 A.2d 901, 1984 N.H. LEXIS 265 (1984).

Where in time between defendant's request for final disposition of indictment and trial defendant requested and was granted three continuances, all of which were necessary to allow the defendant time for adequate trial preparation and were, therefore, for good cause, fact that circumstances necessitating the requests resulted in part from failure to transfer defendant to New Hampshire until six months after his request for final disposition of indictment did not mean that the delay should be attributed to the state and, therefore, not excluded from the 180-day period between request for final disposition of indictment and trial prescribed by Article III(a) of this section. State v. Brown, 125 N.H. 346, 480 A.2d 901, 1984 N.H. LEXIS 265 (1984).

6. Tolling of time period

When defendant sought court-appointed counsel, the trial court had good cause under the Interstate Agreement on Detainers (IAD) to grant a continuance to allow counsel time for prepare to trial; furthermore, for this adequate preparation, defendant had waived the IAD time limits from the time of his arraignment until the time of a status conference. Accordingly, defendant was brought to trial within the 180-day limit required by the IAD. State v. Nelson, 161 N.H. 58, 8 A.3d 40, 2010 N.H. LEXIS 120 (2010).

When a defendant has not waived his right to counsel, the 180-day statutory limit in the Interstate Agreement on Detainers Act (IAD) is tolled starting from the time that he is not represented by counsel until new counsel is either appointed or retained, because during this period, a defendant is unable to stand trial in accordance with the IAD. State v. Brown, 157 N.H. 555, 953 A.2d 1174, 2008 N.H. LEXIS 96 (2008).

Period of time between the filing of counsel's motions to withdraw and the appointment of new counsel was excluded from the 180-day limitation period of the Interstate Agreement on Detainers Act. During this time period, defendant was without counsel and thus, no action of consequence to defendant could have occurred in the case until the motion was resolved. State v. Brown, 157 N.H. 555, 953 A.2d 1174, 2008 N.H. LEXIS 96 (2008).

Period of time before defense counsel filed motions to withdraw because of a conflict of interest was not excluded from the 180-day limitation period of the Interstate Agreement on Detainers Act. Nothing in the record suggested that during this period, each of defendant's former attorneys was not representing the defendant. State v. Brown, 157 N.H. 555, 953 A.2d 1174, 2008 N.H. LEXIS 96 (2008).

Even assuming that a continuance of defendant's trial was for good cause, because it was not granted in open court or in the presence of defendant or his counsel, the 180-day limitation period was not tolled for the length of this continuance. State v. Brown, 157 N.H. 555, 953 A.2d 1174, 2008 N.H. LEXIS 96 (2008).

Because there is substantially less reason to view the filing of defense motions as open-ended waivers of the 180-day deadline, where a defendant timely advises the court that he or she is claiming protections under the Interstate Agreement on Detainers Act and the court takes more time than is necessary to resolve the defendant's pretrial motions, the delay may not be fully excluded from the 180-day clock. Thus, the exception applies only in those instances where a defendant's motion occasions the relevant period of delay. State v. Brown, 157 N.H. 555, 953 A.2d 1174, 2008 N.H. LEXIS 96 (2008).

Where a period of delay in trial was occasioned not by defendant's motion to dismiss, but instead by the trial court's sua sponte continuance of trial, it was unnecessary to determine whether defendant timely advised the trial court that he was claiming the protections of the Interstate Agreement on Detainers Act (IAD) or whether the trial court took more time than necessary to resolve defendant's motion. Thus, because the day the parties resolved defendant's charges was the 181st day after the State received defendant's request for final disposition of his charges, his IAD speedy trial rights were violated, and he was entitled to dismissal of the charges with prejudice. State v. Brown, 157 N.H. 555, 953 A.2d 1174, 2008 N.H. LEXIS 96 (2008).

Delays in bringing defendant to trial caused by defendant's

request or a delay to accommodate the defendant are not counted toward the 180-day limitation period provided in Article III. State v. McGann, 126 N.H. 316, 493 A.2d 452, 1985 N.H. LEXIS 323 (1985).

Where delay between indictments and trial was caused by defendant's filing of a motion to suppress, and a subsequent motion to dismiss, trial on the pending indictments was not barred by the 180-day limitation period of Article III. State v. McGann, 126 N.H. 316, 493 A.2d 452, 1985 N.H. LEXIS 323 (1985).

Where there are multiple charges, if the state cannot conduct the trials simultaneously, the 180-day limitation period provided in Article III is not tolled as to a second trial unless the state obtains a continuance until resolution of the first trial. State v. McGann, 126 N.H. 316, 493 A.2d 452, 1985 N.H. LEXIS 323 (1985).

A defendant indicted on more than one charge, who asserts his right to be present at one trial, and is therefore unable to stand trial at the same time on other charges, causes the 180-day limitation period provided in Article III to toll as to a second trial on the other charges. State v. McGann, 126 N.H. 316, 493 A.2d 452, 1985 N.H. LEXIS 323 (1985).

7. Waiver of time period
A defendant may waive his right to trial within the 180-day limitation period provided in Article III. State v. McGann, 126 N.H. 316, 493 A.2d 452, 1985 N.H. LEXIS 323 (1985).

The defendant did not waive his statutory right under the Interstate Agreement on Detainers (IAD) to a speedy disposition of charges pending against him in New Hampshire by filing and subsequently withdrawing a notice of intent to plead guilty and a speedy trial waiver; the defendant waived his statutory speedy trial right only with respect to 39 days between the filing and withdrawal of his notice of intent to plead guilty and, even when those 39 days were subtracted from the calculated time period, the period exceeded the 180 day limit mandated by the IAD. State v. Dolbeare, 140 N.H. 84, 663 A.2d 85, 1995 N.H. LEXIS 96 (1995).

8. Computation of time period
Where the last day of the 180-day limitation period for bringing defendant to trial fell on Sunday, and defendant was scheduled for trial on the following Monday, the State complied with Article III. State v. Sprague, 146 N.H. 334, 771 A.2d 583, 2001 N.H. LEXIS 82 (2001).

Cited:
Cited in State v. Bugely, 103 N.H. 376, 172 A.2d 370, 1961 N.H. LEXIS 54 (1961); Herbert v. New Hampshire State Parole Bd., 106 N.H. 401, 211 A.2d 907, 1965 N.H. LEXIS 178 (1965); Allen v. Hancock, 109 N.H. 254, 248 A.2d 632, 1968 N.H. LEXIS 173 (1968); State v. Monahan, 125 N.H. 17, 480 A.2d 863, 1984 N.H. LEXIS 372 (1984); Stow v. Horan, 829 F. Supp. 504, 1993 U.S. Dist. LEXIS 12283 (D.N.H. 1993); Cross v. Cunningham, 87 F.3d 586, 1996 U.S. App. LEXIS 15419 (1st Cir. N.H. 1996).

606-A:2. Definition.

The phrase "appropriate court" as used in the agreement on detainers shall, with reference to the courts of this state, mean the municipal court, the district court or the superior court.

Source.
1959, 107:2. 1977, 588:20, eff. Sept. 16, 1977.

Amendments
—**1977.** Inserted "the district court" following "municipal court".

Cross References.
District courts generally, see RSA 502-A.
Municipal courts generally, see RSA 502.
Superior court generally, see RSA 490.

606-A:3. Enforcement of Agreement.

All courts, departments, agencies, officers and employees of this state and its political subdivisions are hereby directed to enforce the agreement on detainers and to cooperate with one another and with other party states in enforcing the agreement and effectuating its purpose.

Source.
1959, 107:3, eff. July 17, 1959.

NOTES TO DECISIONS

Generally
Prosecuting authorities have no duty to respond to a request for a speedy trial filed in accordance with this chapter unless the state of incarceration is a jurisdiction which has enacted similar legislation. Quinlan v. Bussiere, 106 N.H. 527, 214 A.2d 877, 1965 N.H. LEXIS 207 (1965); In re Lemieux, 109 N.H. 258, 248 A.2d 634, 1968 N.H. LEXIS 174 (1968).

Cited:
Cited in Guglielmo v. Cunningham, 811 F. Supp. 31, 1993 U.S. Dist. LEXIS 924 (D.N.H. 1993).

606-A:4. Application.

Nothing in this chapter or in the agreement on detainers shall be construed to require the application of the habitual offenders law to any person on account of any conviction had in a proceeding brought to final disposition by reason of the use of said agreement.

Source.
1959, 107:4, eff. July 17, 1959.

Cross References.
Imposition of extended terms of imprisonment generally, see RSA 651:6.

606-A:5. Duty of Warden.

It shall be lawful and mandatory upon the warden or other official in charge of a penal or correctional institution in this state to give over the person of any inmate thereof whenever so required by the operation of the agreement on detainers.

Source.
1959, 107:5, eff. July 17, 1959.

Cross References.
Department of corrections, see RSA 21-H.
State prison generally, see RSA 622.

606-A:6. Compact Administrator.

The governor may designate an officer of the state to act as compact administrator of and information agent for the agreement.

Source.
1959, 107:6, eff. July 17, 1959.

Cross References.
Department of corrections, see RSA 21-H.

CHAPTER 607

SENTENCE AND EXECUTION; PAROLE

[Repealed 1973, 370:44, eff. Nov. 1, 1973.]

Former section(s).
Former RSA 607:1, which was derived from RSA 225:21; CS 240:24; GS 244:1; GL 262:1; PS 255:1; PL 369:1; and RL 429:1, related to the grand jury's finding and certification of insanity. See now RSA 651:8.

Former RSA 607:2, which was derived from 1850, 962: 1; CS 240:28; GS 244:2; GL 262:2; PS 255:2; PL 369:2; and RL 429:2, related to entering a plea of not guilty by reason of insanity generally. See now RSA 651:8-a.

Former RSA 607:3, which was derived from 1850, 962:2; CS 240:29; GS 244:3; GL 262:3; PS 255:3; PL 369:3; RL 429:3; and 1955, 177:1, related to committal of a person to the state prison or state hospital upon a finding or plea of insanity. See now RSA 651:9-a.

Former RSA 607:4, which was derived from RS 225:24; 1850, 962:4; CS 9:19, 240:26, 31; GS 10:20, 244:4; GL 10:27, 262:4; PS 255:4; 1917, 56:1; PL 369:4; and RL 429:4, related to the procedure for discharge of insane persons from the state prison and transfer of insane prisoners to the state hospital. See now RSA 651:10.

Former RSA 607:5, which was derived from RS 9:12; CS 9:12; GS 10:13; GL 10:13; PS 255:5; PL 369:5; and RL 429:5, related to the transfer of insane persons confined in jail to the state hospital. See now RSA 651:11.

Former RSA 607:6, which was derived from 1849, 855; CS 240:9, 10; GS 244:5; GL 262:5; PS 255:6; PL 369:6; and RL 429:6, related to the manner of execution of a defendant under the penalty of death generally. See now RSA 630:5.

Former RSA 607:7, which was derived from RS 225:7; CS 240:10; GS 244:6; GL 262:6; PS 255:7; PL 369:7; and RL 429:7, related to the location of and witnesses to an execution. See now RSA 630:6.

Former RSA 607:8, which was derived from RS 225:14; CS 240:17; GS 244:7; GL 262:7; PS 255:8; PL 369:8; and RL 429:8, and was previously repealed by 1967, 289:2, related to the civil effects of a sentence of death. See now RSA 607-A:3.

Former RSA 607:9, which was derived from GS 244:8; GL 262:8; PS 255:9; PL 369:9; and RL 429:9, related to the sentencing of persons to the state prison for conviction of offenses punishable by imprisonment for more than one year. See now RSA 651:17 and 651:18.

Former RSA 607:10, which was derived from RS 225:8; CS 240:11; GS 244:11; GL 262:11; PS 255:10; PL 369:10; and RL 429:10, related to the sentencing of convicts to solitary confinement in the state prison.

Former RSA 607:11, which was derived from GS 244:10; GL 262:10; PS 255:12; PL 369:11; and RL 429:11, related to confinement of persons to house of correction or jail for conviction of offenses punishable by imprisonment for one year or less. See now RSA 651:17.

Former RSA 607:12, which was derived from 1929, 98:1; 1935, 36:1; and RL 429:12, related to suspension of a sentence to the house of correction in case of a misdemeanor. See now RSA 651:17 and 651:18.

Former RSA 607:13, which was derived from 1899, 7:3; PL 369:12; RL 429:13; 1949, 208:1; RSA 607:13; and 1971, 337:1, related to the discretion of the court in the place of confinement to jail or a house of corrections and the reduction in sentence for meritorious conduct. See now RSA 651:18.

Former RSA 607:14, which was derived from GS 244:12; GL 262:12; PS 255:13; PL 369:13; and RL 429:14, related to sentencing of persons convicted of common law offenses.

Former RSA 607:14-a, which was derived from 1967, 291:1, related to the release of persons committed to penal institutions other than the state prison for obtaining or working at gainful employment or for other purposes conducive to rehabilitation. See now RSA 651:19.

Former RSA 607:14-b, which was derived from 1967, 291:1, related to incarceration of a person given a suspended sentence. See now RSA 651:20.

Former RSA 607:14-c, which was derived from 1967, 291:1, related to the terms and conditions imposed by the court upon revocation of a suspended sentence. See now RSA 651:21.

Former RSA 607:14-d, which was derived from 1967, 291:1, related to jurisdiction of the court over and disposition of wages earned by a defendant released from a penal institution other than the state prison for employment purposes. See now RSA 651:22.

Former RSA 607:14-e, which was derived from 1967, 291:1, related to changing the place of confinement of a prisoner before the expiration of the original sentence. See now RSA 651:23.

Former RSA 607:14-f, which was derived from 1967, 291:1, related to failure of person to report for confinement as an attempt to escape. See now RSA 651:25.

Former RSA 607:14-g, which was derived from 1967, 291:1, related to release of a person from the state prison for the purpose of obtaining and working at gainful employment, disposition of the person's wages, and conditions for recall of a person from release status. See now RSA 651:25.

Former RSA 607:15, which was derived from GS 244:14; GL 262:14; PS 255:15; PL 369:14; and RL 429:15, related to award of a conditional sentence to a person convicted of an offense punishable by a fine or imprisonment, or both. See now RSA 651:2.

Former RSA 607:16, which was derived from GS 244:15; GL 262:15; PS 255:16; PL 369:15; and RL 429:16, related to the term of imprisonment for a person awarded a conditional sentence. See now RSA 651:2.

Former RSA 607:17, which was derived from GS 244:16; GL 262:16; PS 255:17; PL 369:16, and RL 429:17, and was previously repealed by 1967, 295:4, related to the committal of a person to the custody of an officer until the terms of the conditional sentence have been met. See now RSA 651:2.

Former RSA 607:18, which was derived from GS 244:17; GL 262:17; PS 255:18; PL 369:17; and RL 429:18, related to rendition of judgment upon the failure of an indicted corporation to appear. See now RSA 651:28.

Former RSA 607:19, which was derived from GS 244:17; GL 262:18; PS 255:19; PL 369:18; and RL 429:19, related to issuance of a writ of execution upon a judgment against a corporation. See now RSA 651:2.

Former RSA 607:20, which was derived from 1909, 120:1; PL 369:19; and RL 429:20, related to the establishment of a maximum and minimum term of imprisonment for a person sentenced to the state prison generally. See now RSA 651:2.

Former RSA 607:21, which was derived from 1909, 120:1; PL 369:20; and RL 429:21, related to the length of the minimum and maximum terms generally. See now RSA 651:2.

Former RSA 607:22, which was derived from 1917, 119:1; PL 369:41; and RL 429:41, related to the power of the commissioner of public works and highways to employ convicts from the state prison to work on state highways.

Former RSA 607:23, which was derived from 1917, 119:2; PL 369:42; and RL 429:42, related to delivery of requisitioned convicts to the commissioner of public works and highways.

Former RSA 607:24, which was derived from 1917, 119:3; PL 369:43; and RL 429:43, related to supervision of the employed convicts by the commissioner of public works and highways.

Former RSA, 607:25, which was derived from 1917, 119:4; PL 369:44; and RL 429:44, related to jurisdiction of the state prison warden in matters of discipline and control of convicts employed by the commissioner of public works and highways.

Former RSA 607:26, which was derived from 1917, 119:5; PL 369:45; and RL 429:45, related to the expense of transporting, paying wages to and guarding convicts while employed on state highways.

Former RSA 607:27, which was derived from 1917, 119:6; PL 369:46; and RL 429:46, related to deductions from the sentence of a prisoner whose record of employment with the commissioner of public works and highways showed he had observed the rules of the state prison regarding his employment.

Former RSA 607:28, which was derived from 1917, 119:7; PL 369:47; and RL 429:47, related to employment of prisoners from the county jail or the house of correction on state highways.

Former RSA 607:29, which was derived from 1917, 119:7, PL 369:48; and RL 429:48, related to custody of prisoners from the county jail or the house of corrections employed in work on state highways.

Former RSA 607:30, which was derived from 1917, 119:8; PL 369:49; and RL 429:49, related to the penalty for interfering or interrupting the work of prisoner employed on state highways.

Former RSA 607:31, which was derived from 1921, 136:1; PL 369:27; 1939, 148:6; RL 429:28; 1949, 171:1; RSA 607:31; 1969, 140:1; and 1971, 419:1, related to the composition, general duties, compensation of members and reports of the state board of parole. See now RSA 651-A:3—651-A:5.

Former RSA 607:32, which was derived from 1919, 116:1; 1921, 136:1; PL 369:28, 29: 1927, 67:1; 1939, 148:6; and RL 429:29, related to the appointment of the state parole officer.

Former RSA 607:33, which was derived from 1953, 265:1, related to the salary of the state parole officer.

Former RSA 607:34, which was derived from 1939, 148:6 and RL 429:30, related to employment of clerical assistance by the state parole officer.

Former RSA 607:35, which was derived from 1921, 136:1; PL 369:30; 1939, 148:6; and RL 429:31, related to general duties of the state parole officer.

Former RSA 607:36, which was derived from 1939, 148:6 and RL 429:32, related to appointment of assistant parole officers.

Former RSA 607:37, which was derived from 1939, 148:6 and RL 429:33, related to compensation for expenses incurred by the state parole officers and assistant parole officers.

Former RSA 607:38, which was derived from 1909, 120:7; PL 369:38; 1935, 66:1; and RL 429:38, related to provision of information and assistance to parole officers relative to the conduct and investigations of paroled convicts.

Former RSA 607:39, which was derived from 1909, 120:2; PL 369:21; RL 429:22; RSA 607:39; 1969, 62:1; and 1971, 419:2, related to release of convicts upon expiration of the minimum terms of their sentences. See now RSA 651-A:6.

Former RSA 607:40, which was derived from 1909, 120:2; PL 369:22; 1939, 148:1; and RL 429:23, related to the terms and conditions of release of convicts upon expiration of the minimum terms of their sentence. See now RSA 651-A:6.

Former RSA 607:41, which was derived from 1909, 120:2; PL 369:23; 1939, 148:2; and RL 429:24, related to release of convicts who had violated prison rules after the expiration of the minimum terms of their sentences. See now RSA 651-A:6.

Former RSA 607:41-a, which was derived from 1971, 419:3 and 1972, 22:1, related to eligibility for release of prisoners serving sentences of life imprisonment. See now RSA 651-A:7.

Former RSA 607:41-b, which was derived from 1972, 22:2, related to eligibility for parole of prisoners serving sentences of life imprisonment for convictions of psycho-sexual murder. See now RSA 651-A:8.

Former RSA 607:41-c, which was derived from 1972, 22:2, related to certification, upon first degree murder conviction, of psycho-sexual nature of offense. See now RSA 651-A:9.

Former RSA 607:41-d, which was derived from 1972, 22:2, related to the definition of psycho-sexual murder. See now RSA 651-A:10.

Former RSA 607:42, which was derived from 1917, 52:1; PL 369:24; 1939, 148:3; and RL 429:25, and was previously repealed by 1969, 141:1, related to release of prisoners prior to expiration of minimum terms for exceptionally meritorious conduct. See now RSA 651-A:14.

Former RSA 607:43, which was derived from 1923, 64:1; PL 369:25; 1939, 148:4; RL 429:26; 1943, 84:1; RSA 607:43; and 1969, 141:2, and was previously repealed by 1969, 141:2 and 1971, 419:9, related to release of prisoners having served two thirds of their sentence whose conduct had been meritorious. See now RSA 651-A:6.

Former RSA 607:44, which was derived from 1909, 120:2; 1923, 64:1; PL 369:26; 1939, 148:5; RL 429:27; and 1943, 45:1, related to the release of prisoners to the custody of the state parole board and the requirement that they report at specified intervals to a parole officer.

Former RSA 607:44-a, which was derived from 1969, 142:1, related to reduction of the maximum sentences of prisoners in parole. See now RSA 651-A:12.

Former RSA 607:45, which was derived from 1943, 43:1, related to suspension of parole supervision of paroled prisoners having entered the armed services. See now RSA 651-A:13.

Former RSA 607:45-a, which was derived from 1969, 238:1, related to issuance of certificates of discharge to paroles no longer in need of supervision due to good conduct. See now RSA 651-A:14.

Former RSA 607:46, which was derived from 1909, 120:4; 1921, 136:2; PL 369:32; 1939, 148:7; and RL 429:34, related to arrest of parolees violating the conditions of their parole. See now RSA 504-A:4.

Former RSA 607:47, which was derived from 1909, 120:5; PL 369:35; 1939, 148:8; and RL 429:35, related to recommittal of parole violators to state prison. See now RSA 651-A:17.

Former RSA 607:48, which was derived from 1909, 120:6; PL 369:36; 1939, 148:9; RL 429:36; 1951, 136:1; RSA 607:48; 1969, 143:1; and 1971, 419:4, related to the general requirements of parole for a recommitted parolee. See now RSA 651-A:19.

Former RSA 607:49, which was derived from 1921, 136:3; PL 369:37; and RL 429:37, related to deductions from the maximum term for good behavior of persons recommitted for parole violations. See now RSA 651-A:22.

Former RSA 607:50, which was derived from 1909, 120:8; PL 369:39; RL 429:39; and 1953, 236:1, related to issuance of permits for release of convicts serving two or more sentences in the state prison. See now RSA 651-A:6.

Former RSA 607:51, which was derived from 1909, 120:9; PL: 369:40; and RL 429:40, related to final discharge of paroled prisoner upon expiration of the terms of their maximum sentences. See now RSA 651-A:21.

Former RSA 607:51-a, which was derived from 1969, 95:1, 333:1 and 1971, 419:6, related to reduction of minimum terms of sentences for donations of blood by prisoners. See now RSA 651-A:22.

Former RSA 607:51-b, which was derived from 1971, 419:6, related to credit against minimum and maximum terms for obedience to rules of state prison and good conduct. See now RSA 651-A:22.

Former RSA 607:51-c, which was derived from 1971, 419:6, related to credit against maximum and minimum terms for confinement in jail prior to sentencing. See now RSA 651-A:23.

Former RSA 607:52, which was derived from 1937, 64:1; RSA 607:52; and 1957, 63:1, related to the compact for out-of-state parolee supervision. See now RSA 651-A:25.

Former RSA 607:53, which was derived from 1937, 64:4, related to citation of the compact for out-of-state parolee supervision.

CHAPTER 607-A

UNIFORM ACT ON STATUS OF CONVICTED PERSONS

SECTION
607-A:1.   Definition.
607-A:2.   Rights Lost.
607-A:3.   Rights Retained by Convicted Person.
607-A:4.   Savings Provisions.
607-A:5.   Certificate of Discharge.
607-A:6.   Uniformity of Interpretation.
607-A:7.   Short Title.
607-A:8.   Severability.

607-A:1. Definition.

In this chapter, "felony" means:

I. A crime committed against the laws of this state or of the federal government for which a sentence of death or imprisonment in the state prison or a federal prison or penitentiary; or

II. A crime committed against the laws of another state for which a sentence of death or imprisonment in a prison or penitentiary is imposed, if the act would permit a sentence of death or imprisonment in the state prison in this state had it been committed in this state.

Source.

1967, 289:1, eff. Aug. 26, 1967.

Cross References.

Classification of crimes generally, see RSA 625:9.

Imposition of civil penalties, see RSA 651:1.

NOTES TO DECISIONS

Construction with other laws

This section, read in pari materia with RSA 625:9, III, defining a felony as an offense "where the maximum penalty provided is imprisonment in excess of one year," leads to the conclusion that the legislature intended the potential sentence, rather than the actual sentence imposed, to be the determining factor as to the application of this chapter. Paey v. Rodrigue, 119 N.H. 186, 400 A.2d 51, 1979 N.H. LEXIS 269 (1979).

Where a town selectman found guilty in federal court of the felony of interstate transportation of stolen merchandise and conspiracy under 18 U.S.C.S. §§ 371, 2314 was sentenced to a "jail type institution" for the first forty days of his three-year sentence, the remainder of his sentence being suspended and he being placed on probation, the selectman forfeited his office under this chapter because he could have been sentenced to a state or federal prison for more than one year. Paey v. Rodrigue, 119 N.H. 186, 400 A.2d 51, 1979 N.H. LEXIS 269 (1979).

607-A:2. Rights Lost.

I. A person sentenced for a felony, from the time of his sentence until his final discharge, may not:

(a) Vote in an election, but if execution of sentence is suspended with or without the defendant being placed on probation or he is paroled after commitment to imprisonment, he may vote during the period of the suspension or parole; or

(b) Become a candidate for or hold public office.

II. A public office held at the time of sentence is forfeited as of the date of the sentence if the sentence is in this state or, if the sentence is in another state or in a federal court, as of the date a certification of the sentence from the sentencing court is filed in the office of secretary of state, who shall receive and file it as a public document. An appeal or other proceeding taken to set aside or otherwise nullify the conviction or sentence does not affect the application of this section, but if the conviction is reversed the defendant shall be restored to any public office forfeited under this chapter from the time of the reversal and shall be entitled to the emoluments thereof from the time of the forfeiture.

Source.

1967, 289:1, eff. Aug. 26, 1967.

Cross References.

Restoration of rights, see RSA 607-A:5.

NOTES TO DECISIONS

1. Constitutionality
2. Application

1. Constitutionality

This section does not violate the provisions of part 1, article 11 of the state constitution; the right to hold office is subject to reasonable qualifications established by the legislature. Paey v. Rodrigue, 119 N.H. 186, 400 A.2d 51, 1979 N.H. LEXIS 269 (1979).

Felon disenfranchisement statutes did not violate Part I, Article 11 of New Hampshire Constitution, since legislature retained authority under Article 11 to determine voter qualifications and such statutes were a reasonable exercise of legislative authority; incarcerated felons were therefore not "qualified" absentee voters under absentee ballot provision of Article 11. Fischer v. Governor, 145 N.H. 28, 749 A.2d 321, 2000 N.H. LEXIS 16 (2000).

The qualifications for public office contained in this section promote honesty and integrity in candidates for and holders of public office and are, therefore, reasonable and not violative of part 1, article 11 of the state constitution. Paey v. Rodrigue, 119 N.H. 186, 400 A.2d 51, 1979 N.H. LEXIS 269 (1979).

This section did not violate the right to equal protection of the laws under the fourteenth amendment to the United States Constitution of a town selectman whose office was declared forfeited under this section after conviction of interstate transportation of stolen merchandise and conspiracy; the state has a legitimate interest in excluding from office those who would impair efficiency and honesty in government operations. Paey v. Rodrigue, 119 N.H. 186, 400 A.2d 51, 1979 N.H. LEXIS 269 (1979).

2. Application

Where a town selectman found guilty in federal court of the felony of interstate transportation of stolen merchandise and conspiracy under 18 U.S.C.S. §§ 371, 2314 was sentenced to a "jail type institution" for the first forty days of his three-year sentence, the remainder of his sentence being suspended and he being placed on probation, the selectman forfeited his office under this section because he could have been sentenced to a state or federal prison for more than one year, he was sentenced for a "felony" within the meaning of this section. Paey v. Rodrigue, 119 N.H. 186, 400 A.2d 51, 1979 N.H. LEXIS 269 (1979).

RESEARCH REFERENCES

New Hampshire Practice.

14-30 N.H.P. Local Government Law § 1191.

New Hampshire Bar Journal.

For article, "Commentary: The Disenfranchisement of New Hampshire's Incarcerated Felons," see 42 N.H.B.J. 38 (Sept. 2001).

607-A:3. Rights Retained by Convicted Person.

Except as otherwise provided by this chapter or by the constitution of this state, a person convicted of a crime does not suffer civil death or corruption of blood or sustain loss of civil rights or forfeiture of estate or property, but retains all of his rights, political, personal, civil, and otherwise, including the right to hold public office or employment, to vote, to hold, receive, and transfer property, to enter into contracts, to sue and be sued, and to hold offices of private trust in accordance with law.

Source.

1967, 289:1, eff. Aug. 26, 1967.

Cross References.

Forfeiture of electoral rights and right to hold public office, see RSA 607-A:2.

Forfeiture of personal property, see RSA 617.

Pecuniary penalties and forfeitures, see RSA 616.

607-A:4. Savings Provisions.

I. This chapter does not affect the power of a court, otherwise given by law, to impose sentence, to suspend imposition or execution of sentence on any conditions, or to impose conditions of probation, or the power of the adult parole board to impose conditions of parole.

II. This chapter does not deprive or restrict the authority and powers of officials of a penal institution or other penal facility, otherwise provided by law, for the administration of the institution or facility or for the control of the conduct and conditions of confinement of a convicted person in their custody.

III. This chapter does not affect the qualifications or disqualifications otherwise required or imposed by law for a designated office, public or private, for service as a juror, for voting, or for any designated profession, trust, or position or any designated license or privilege conferred by public authority.

IV. This chapter does not affect the rights of others arising out of the conviction or out of the conduct on which the conviction is based and not dependent upon the doctrines of civil death, the loss of civil rights, the forfeiture of estate, or corruption of blood.

V. This chapter does not affect laws governing rights of inheritance of a murderer from his victim.

Source.
1967, 289:1, eff. Aug. 26, 1967.

Revision note.
In par. I, substituted "adult parole board" for "state board of parole" for purposes of conformity with RSA 651-A:3.

In par. III, substituted "for service" for "or to serve" and "for voting" for "or to vote" in order to correct grammatical errors.

Cross References.
County correctional facilities, see RSA 30-B.
Department of corrections, see RSA 21-H.
Parole of delinquents, see RSA 170-H.
Parole of prisoners generally, see RSA 651-A.
Probation generally, see RSA 504-A.
Sentences, see RSA 651.
State prison generally, see RSA 622.
Youth development center, see RSA 621.

607-A:5. Certificate of Discharge.

I. If the sentence was imposed in this state, the order, certificate, or other instrument of discharge given to a person sentenced for a felony upon his discharge after completion of service of his sentence or after service under probation or parole shall state that the defendant's rights to vote and to hold any future public office, of which he was deprived by this chapter, are thereby restored and that he suffers no other disability by virtue of his conviction and sentence except as otherwise provided by this chapter. A copy of the order or other instrument of discharge shall be filed with the clerk of the court of conviction.

II. If the sentence was imposed in another state or in a federal court and the convicted person has similarly been discharged by the appropriate authorities, the governor of this state, upon application and proof of the discharge in such form as the governor may require, shall issue a certificate stating that the rights enumerated in paragraph I have been restored to the defendant under the laws of this state.

III. If another state having a similar act issues its certificate of discharge to a convicted person stating that the defendant's rights have been restored, the rights of which he was deprived in this state under this chapter are restored to him in this state.

Source.
1967, 289:1, eff. Aug. 26, 1967.

Revision note.
For purposes of clarity, inserted "imposed" following "the sentence was" in pars. I and II and substituted "the rights enumerated in paragraph I" for "such rights" preceding "have been restored to" and "the defendant" for "him" thereafter in par. II.

Cross References.
Parole generally, see RSA 651-A.
Sentences generally, see RSA 651.

NOTES TO DECISIONS

Cited:
Cited in United States v. Kozerski, 518 F. Supp. 1082, 1981 U.S. Dist. LEXIS 13519 (D.N.H. 1981).

607-A:6. Uniformity of Interpretation.

This chapter shall be so construed as to effectuate its general purpose to make uniform the law of those states which enact it.

Source.
1967, 289:1, eff. Aug. 26, 1967.

607-A:7. Short Title.

This chapter may be cited as the Uniform Act on Status of Convicted Persons.

Source.
1967, 289:1, eff. Aug. 26, 1967.

607-A:8. Severability.

If any provision of this chapter or the application thereof to any person or circumstance is held invalid, the invalidity does not affect other provisions or applications of the chapter which can be given effect without the invalid provision or application and to this end the provisions of the chapter are severable.

Source.
1967, 289:1, eff. Aug. 26, 1967.

CHAPTER 608

SURETY OF THE PEACE

SECTION
608:1.   Complaint.
608:2.   Order.
608:3.   Appeal.
608:4.   Order.
608:5.   Failure to Prosecute Appeal.
608:6.   Recognizing after Committal.
608:7.   Certifying to Court.
608:8.   Order on Conviction, etc.
608:9.   Order on View.
608:10.   Committal by Surety.

Cross References.
Arrests generally, see RSA 594.
Bail and recognizances generally, see RSA 597.
Pecuniary penalties and forfeitures generally, see RSA 616.

608:1. Complaint.

Anyone fearing that another person may do injury to himself, his family or property may make complaint thereof, under oath, before a justice, who shall, by warrant, cause the person accused to be brought before him or some other justice for examination.

Source.
RS 222:9. CS 237:9. GS 238:1. 1868, 1:53. GL 256:1. PS 259:1. PL 373:1. RL 433:1.

Cross References.
Hearing and order, see RSA 608:2.

NOTES TO DECISIONS

Purpose
The purpose of this section and RSA 608:2 is to protect the complainant and public from injury by another person. State ex rel. Fortin v. Harris, 109 N.H. 394, 253 A.2d 830, 1969 N.H. LEXIS 168 (1969).

608:2. Order.

If, upon hearing the parties and their evidence, it appears to the justice that there is just cause to fear that the offense described in the complaint filed under RSA 608:1 may be committed, he may order the party named in the complaint to recognize, with sufficient sureties, in a reasonable sum, to keep the peace toward all the people of the state, and especially toward the complainant, for a term not exceeding one year, to pay costs of prosecution, and to stand committed until the order is complied with.

Source.
RS 222:9. CS 237:9. GS 238:2. GL 256:2. PS 259:2. PL 373:2. RL 433:2.

Revision note.
For purposes of clarity, substituted "the offense described in the complaint filed under RSA 608:1" for "such offense" preceding "may be committed" and "the party named in the complaint" for "such party" preceding "to recognize".

Cross References.
Fines and costs generally, see RSA 618.
Issuance of order requiring recognizance for appearance or to keep peace subsequent to conviction, see RSA 608:8.
Issuance of order requiring recognizance upon commission of offense in the presence of a court or justice, see RSA 608:9.
Proceedings upon appeal, see RSA 608:4.
Proceedings upon failure to recognize, see RSA 608:6.

NOTES TO DECISIONS

Purpose
The purpose of RSA 608:1 and this section is to protect the complainant and public from injury by another person. State ex rel. Fortin v. Harris, 109 N.H. 394, 253 A.2d 830, 1969 N.H. LEXIS 168 (1969).

608:3. Appeal.

The party ordered to recognize may appeal to the superior court at the next term to be held for the county on giving the security required by the order and security to pay such costs as may be awarded against him on the appeal.

Source.
GS 238:3. GL 256:3. PS 259:3. PL 373:3. RL 433:3.

Revision note.
For purposes of clarity, substituted "next term to be held" for "term next to be holden".

Cross References.
Terms of superior court, see RSA 496.

608:4. Order.

The superior court may affirm the order issued under RSA 608:2, discharge the appellant, or require him to enter into a new recognizance, with sufficient sureties, in such sum and for such time as it may think proper, and may make such order in relation to the costs of prosecution as may be deemed just.

Source.
GS 238:4. GL 256:4. PS 259:4. PL 373:4. RL 433:4.

Revision note.
For purposes of clarity, substituted "the order issued under RSA 608:2" for "such order, or" following "affirm".

Cross References.
Fines and costs generally, see RSA 618.

608:5. Failure to Prosecute Appeal.

If the appellant fails to prosecute his appeal, his recognizance shall remain in force, and the court may award such costs to the complainant as it deems just.

Source.
GS 238:5. GL 256:5. PS 259:5. PL 373:5. RL 433:5.

Cross References.
Appeals generally, see RSA 608:3, 4.
Fines and costs generally, see RSA 618.

608:6. Recognizing after Committal.

A person committed for not finding sureties or refusing to recognize as required by the court or magistrate may recognize agreeably to the order before any justice, and, on payment of the costs of his application, he shall be discharged.

Source.
GS 238:6. GL 256:6. PS 259:6. PL 373:6. RL 433:6.

Cross References.
Issuance of order requiring recognizance, see RSA 608:2.

608:7. Certifying to Court.

Every recognizance taken in pursuance of the

foregoing provisions shall be transmitted by the justice to the superior court for the county on or before the first day of the next term, and shall be filed by the clerk.

Source.
GS 238:7. GL 256:7. PS 259:7. PL 373:7. RL 433:7.

608:8. Order on Conviction, etc.

A person sentenced by a justice or court for a criminal offense, or ordered to recognize for his appearance before the same or another court, may be required to recognize to keep the peace and to be of good behavior for such time as the court or justice may direct.

Source.
RS 116:4; 118:7, 8; 218:1. CS 122:4; 124:7; 232:1. 1855, 1658:5. GS 238:8. GL 256:8. PS 259:8. PL 373:8. RL 433:8.

Cross References.
Bail and recognizances generally, see RSA 597.
Issuance of orders requiring recognizances pursuant to complaints, see RSA 608:2.

608:9. Order on View.

A person who, in the presence of a court or justice, makes an affray, threatens to kill or beat another or to commit any violence or outrage to person or property, or who contends with hot and angry words to the disturbance of the peace, may be ordered, without process or any other proof, to recognize for keeping the peace and being of good behavior for a term not exceeding 3 months, and to stand committed until the order is complied with.

Source.
RS 222:8. GS 238:9. GL 256:9. PS 259:9. PL 373:9. RL 433:9.

Cross References.
Breaches of the peace and related offenses generally, see RSA 644.
Issuance of orders requiring recognizances for appearances or to keep peace subsequent to convictions, see RSA 608:8.
Issuance of orders requiring recognizances pursuant to complaints, see RSA 608:2.

608:10. Committal by Surety.

A surety in a recognizance to keep the peace may commit the principal to the common jail, and shall be discharged in the same manner as sureties in other recognizances in criminal cases.

Source.
GS 238:10. GL 256:10. PS 259:10. PL 373:10. RL 433:10.

Cross References.
Bail and recognizances generally, see RSA 597.

CHAPTER 609

SUPPRESSION OF RIOTS

[Repealed 1965, 167:2, eff. June 17, 1965.]

Former section(s).
Former RSA 609:1, which was derived from RS 218:3; CS 232:3; GS 239:1; GL 257:1; PS 260:1; PL 374:1; and RL 434:1, related to the duty of officials to command persons unlawfully or riotously assembled to depart to their homes.
Former RSA 609:2, which was derived from GS 239:2; GL 257:2; PS 260:2; PL 374:2; and RL 434:2, related to the duty and authority of officials to command persons to assist in arresting and securing rioters.
Former RSA 609:3, which was derived from GS 239:3; GL 257:3; PS 260:3; PL 374:3; and RL 434:3, related to military aid in suppression of riots.
Former RSA 609:4, which was derived from GS 239:4; GL 257:4; PS 260:4; PL 374:4; and RL 434:4, related to the immunity of officials from guilt liability for death or injury to persons or property during suppression of riots.
Former RSA 609:5, which was derived from GS 239:5; GL 257:5; PS 260:5; PL 374:5; and RL 434:5, related to the liability of rioters for death or injury to persons suppressing riots.
Former RSA 609:6, which was derived from GS 239:6; GL 257:6; PS 260:6; PL 374:6, related to the penalty for failure of officials with knowledge of unlawful assemblies to act to suppress the assemblies.
Former RSA 609:7, which was derived from GS 239:7; GL 257:7; PS 260:7; PL 374:7; and RL 434:7, related to the penalty for refusal to assist in suppression of riots.
Former RSA 609:8, which was derived from GS 239:8; GL 257:8; PS 260:8; PL 374:8; and RL 434:8, related to the criminal liability of principals for any crimes or offense committed by mobs.
Former RSA 609:9, which was derived from RS 218:4; CS 232:4; GS 239:9; GL 257:9; PS 260:9; PL 374:9; and RL 434:9, related to the penalty for refusal to disperse.
Former RSA 609:10, which was derived from GS 239:10; GL 257:10; PS 260:10; PL 374:10; and RS 434:10, related to the immunity from prosecution of participants in riots acting as witnesses.
For present provisions relating to riots generally, see RSA 644:1.

CHAPTER 609-A

MOB ACTION

[Repealed 1973, 370:31, eff. Nov. 1, 1973.]

Former section(s).
Former RSA ch. 609-A, comprising RSA 609-A:1–609-A:6, which was derived from 1965, 167:2, related to mob action. See now RSA 644:1.

CHAPTER 610

REWARDS AND COMPENSATIONS TO PROSECUTORS

SECTION
610:1.   Offer of Reward.
610:2.   Compensation for Service.

610:1. Offer of Reward.

The county commissioners of any county, the city council of a city and the selectmen of a town are authorized, whenever in their opinion the public good requires it, to offer and pay from the treasury of such county, city or town a suitable reward, not exceeding $300 in any one case, to any person who shall, in consequence of such offer, apprehend and secure any person or persons charged with having committed a capital or other high crime.

Source.
1848, 735. CS 236:1. GS 245:1. GL 263:1. PS 261:1. 1911, 143:1. PL 375:1. RL 435:1.

Cross References.
Classification of crimes, see RSA 625:9.

NOTES TO DECISIONS

Recovery of reward
Where the selectmen of a city or town acting under this section offer a reward for the apprehension of an alleged criminal, the city or town is bound by the offer, and any person who apprehends the alleged criminal in reliance upon the offer may recover from the city or town in a civil action. Janvrin v. Exeter, 48 N.H. 83, 1868 N.H. LEXIS 17 (1868).

Cited:
Cited in State v. Schachter, 133 N.H. 439, 577 A.2d 1222, 1990 N.H. LEXIS 81 (1990).

610:2. Compensation for Service.

If any service is performed by a person by direction of a court or justice, of the attorney general, or of the county attorney in bringing to justice an offender charged with a crime or misdemeanor, the superior court shall allow a reasonable sum therefor to be paid from the county treasury.

Source.
RS 211:15. CS 224:15. GS 245:2. GL 263:2. PS 261:2. PL 375:2. RL 435:2. RSA 610:2. 1959, 12:1.

Cross References.
Classification of crimes, see RSA 625:9.

NOTES TO DECISIONS

Cited:
Cited in In re Ricker, 66 N.H. 207, 29 A. 559 (1890); Wyman v. De Gregory, 101 N.H. 171, 137 A.2d 512, 1957 N.H. LEXIS 47 (1957); State v. Schachter, 133 N.H. 439, 577 A.2d 1222, 1990 N.H. LEXIS 81 (1990).

CHAPTER 611

MEDICAL EXAMINERS

[Repealed 2007, 324:18, I, eff. July 16, 2007.]

Former section(s).
Former RSA ch. 611, comprising RSA 611:1–611:22, which was derived from 1995, 278:1, 310:181, 200; 1997, 325:21; 2003, 319:17, 95; and 2007, 263:12, related to medical examiners.
The responsibilities of the Office of the Chief Medical Examiner and the procedure for medico-legal death investigations have been recodified into one new chapter. See now RSA 611-B.

CHAPTER 611-A

OFFICE OF CHIEF MEDICAL EXAMINER

[Repealed 2007, 324:18, II, eff. July 16, 2007.]

Former section(s).
Former RSA Ch. 611-A, comprising RSA 611-A:1–611-A:12, which was derived from 1979, 471:1; 1985, 300:5; 1987, 406:12, 13; 1990, 238:1, 2, 5, 6; 1991, 355:100; 1994, 181:4, 5; 1995, 278:2–11, 310:39; and 2005, 50:1, related to office of the chief medical examiner.
The responsibilities of the Office of the Chief Medical Examiner and the procedure for medico-legal death investigations have been recodified into one new chapter. See now RSA 611-B.

CHAPTER 611-B

OFFICE OF THE CHIEF MEDICAL EXAMINER

SECTION
611-B:1.   Definitions.
611-B:2.   Chief Medical Examiner; Authority; Rulemaking.
611-B:3.   Deputy Chief Medical Examiner.
611-B:4.   Acting Chief Medical Examiner.
611-B:5.   Assistant Deputy Medical Examiners.
611-B:6.   Indemnification of Medical Examiner.
611-B:7.   Supervision.
611-B:8.   Affiliation and Training.
611-B:9.   Temporary Expert Assistance.
611-B:10.   Administrative and Technical Assistance.
611-B:11.   Oath; Duty to Investigate in Medico-Legal Case.
611-B:12.   Mandatory Reporting of Medico-Legal Deaths.
611-B:13.   Charge of Body.
611-B:14.   Survey of Location.
611-B:14-a. Medical Records.
611-B:15.   Postmortem Examination.
611-B:16.   Property of Deceased.
611-B:17.   Performance of Autopsies.
611-B:18.   Retention and Disposal of Organs, Unidentified Remains, Body Fragments, and Body Fluids.
611-B:19.   Duty of the State Forensic Science Laboratory.
611-B:20.   Report to County Attorney.
611-B:21.   Autopsy and Investigative Reports.
611-B:22.   Report to Bureau of Maternal and Child Health.
611-B:23.   Dental Examinations.
611-B:24.   Release of Body.
611-B:25.   Unclaimed Body.
611-B:26.   Death Record.
611-B:27.   Assistant Deputy Medical Examiner Accounts.
611-B:27-a. Autopsy Expenses.
611-B:28.   Medico-Legal Investigation Fund.

Missing Persons

611-B:29.   Dental Records.
611-B:30.   Identification by Scoring Probabilities.
611-B:31.   Destruction of Records.

611-B:1. Definitions.

In this chapter:

I. "Acting chief medical examiner" means the physician designated pursuant to RSA 611-B:4.

II. "Assistant deputy medical examiner" means a person appointed by the chief medical examiner pursuant to RSA 611-B:5.

III. "Chief medical examiner" means the licensed physician certified by the American Board of Pathology as a qualified pathologist and appointed pursuant to RSA 611-B:2.

IV. "Death investigation" means an investigation conducted by a medical examiner pursuant to this chapter, which may involve one or more of the following: a telephone consultation, investigation of the scene of death, or post-mortem examination.

V. "Deputy chief medical examiner" means the licensed physician certified by the American Board of Pathology as a qualified pathologist and appointed pursuant to RSA 611-B:3.

VI. "Designee" means the medical examiner designated by the chief medical examiner to act on behalf of the chief medical examiner, who shall be either the deputy chief medical examiner or the acting chief medical examiner.

VII. "Medical examiner" means any person authorized pursuant to RSA 611-B to investigate medico-legal cases.

VIII. "Post-mortem examination" means any external or internal examination of a decedent's body.

IX. "Supervising medical examiner" means the chief medical examiner, deputy chief medical examiner, or acting chief medical examiner.

X. "Telephone consultation" means a type of death investigation that does not involve a visual examination of the deceased by the medical examiner.

Source.
2007, 324:1, eff. September 14, 2007.

611-B:2. Chief Medical Examiner; Authority; Rulemaking.

I. There is hereby established within the department of justice the office of chief medical examiner. The office shall be under the immediate supervision of a person who shall be known as the "chief medical examiner," and who shall be a duly licensed physician and certified by the American Board of Pathology to possess special competence in forensic pathology and who has had experience in forensic medicine. The chief medical examiner shall be nominated by the attorney general and appointed by the governor and council and shall serve for a term of 5 years and until a successor is appointed, unless sooner removed by the governor and council for cause in accordance with the provisions of RSA 4:1. The chief medical examiner shall be subject to direction and control by the attorney general in all matters relating to the enforcement of the criminal law. The chief medical examiner shall enforce the provisions of this chapter. The chief medical examiner or designee shall be continually available for emergency consultation as necessary for carrying out the functions of this office.

II. The chief medical examiner shall have the authority to adopt rules, pursuant to RSA 541-A, relative to:

(a) The methods and procedures for medico-legal death investigations.

(b) The examination of substances taken from dead bodies or human remains in order to determine the manner of death, provided that such examinations shall be conducted, whenever possible, at existing qualified state facilities.

(c) Training and certification of medical examiners under RSA 611-B.

(d) The fee schedule for medical examiners under RSA 611-B.

(e) Forms, blank returns, and other documents necessary for medical examiners to carry out the provisions of this chapter.

Source.
2007, 324:1, eff. September 14, 2007.

611-B:3. Deputy Chief Medical Examiner.

There is hereby established within the office of chief medical examiner the position of deputy chief medical examiner. The deputy chief medical examiner shall be appointed in the same manner as the chief medical examiner as provided in RSA 611-B:2, and shall be a licensed physician, certified by the American Board of Pathology as a qualified pathologist, with training and experience in forensic medicine. The deputy chief medical examiner shall serve under the professional direction and supervision of the chief medical examiner and shall act as the chief medical examiner whenever the latter is absent, or unable to act for any cause.

Source.
2007, 324:1, eff. September 14, 2007.

611-B:4. Acting Chief Medical Examiner.

The chief medical examiner may designate in writing an acting chief medical examiner who shall be a licensed physician, certified by the American Board of Pathology as a qualified pathologist with training and experience in forensic medicine. The acting chief medical examiner shall act as the chief medical examiner whenever the chief medical examiner and the deputy chief medical examiner are absent, or unable to act from any cause.

Source.
2007, 324:1, eff. September 14, 2007.

611-B:5. Assistant Deputy Medical Examiners.

The chief medical examiner shall appoint assistant deputy medical examiners to perform the duties of medical examiner under this chapter. Assistant deputy medical examiners shall serve without geographic restriction. An assistant deputy medical examiner shall be a person educated in the science of medicine and shall serve under the direction and supervision of the chief medical examiner. An assistant deputy medical examiner shall possess all the powers granted to medical examiners under this chapter and be sworn in the same manner. Assistant deputy medical examiners shall serve at the pleasure of the chief medical examiner.

Source.
2007, 324:1, eff. September 14, 2007.

611-B:6. Indemnification of Medical Examiner.

The provisions of RSA 99-D shall apply to the chief medical examiner and any other medical examiner or investigator employed in the office of the chief medical examiner for claims arising from the scope of their official duties, including, but not limited to, the practice of forensic pathology and the practice of clinical forensic medicine.

Source.
2007, 324:1, eff. September 14, 2007.

611-B:7. Supervision.

The chief medical examiner shall have general supervision over the administration of and shall enforce the provisions of this chapter. Medical examiners shall serve under the professional direction and supervision of the chief medical examiner.

Source.
2007, 324:1, eff. September 14, 2007.

611-B:8. Affiliation and Training.

I. The chief medical examiner shall have the authority to enter into agreements, subject to approval of the attorney general and governor and council, with state departments and with any public or private college or university, school of medicine, or hospital for the use of certain laboratories, morgues, and other technical facilities, and, pursuant to such agreements, shall have authority to make medical examiners available to such educational institutions for the teaching of legal medicine and other subjects closely related to their duties.

II. The chief medical examiner and, at the chief medical examiner's direction, other medical examiners shall assist in the training of police officers in police training programs authorized by the police standards and training council under RSA 188-F:22 through RSA 188-F:32.

Source.
2007, 324:1, eff. September 14, 2007.

611-B:9. Temporary Expert Assistance.

The supervising medical examiner shall have authority to call upon and employ such persons, skilled in science, pathology, or otherwise, as are necessary for the performance of duties, as occasion may necessitate.

Source.
2007, 324:1, eff. September 14, 2007.

611-B:10. Administrative and Technical Assistance.

The chief medical examiner may employ adequate administrative, clerical, and technical assistants to carry out the purposes of this chapter, all of whom shall be in the classified service of the state.

Source.
2007, 324:1, eff. September 14, 2007.

611-B:11. Oath; Duty to Investigate in Medico-Legal Case.

I. Each medical examiner shall, before entering upon the duties of the office, take an oath of office.

II. A medical examiner shall make investigations in medico-legal cases. A medico-legal case exists when death is pronounced or remains are found indicating that a human has died and that death is known or suspected to have resulted from:

(a) Any death known or suspected to have occurred during or as a result of any criminal act regardless of the time interval between incident and death and regardless of whether criminal violence appears to have been the immediate cause of death or a contributory factor thereto.

(b) Any death by suicide regardless of the time interval between the incident and death.

(c) Any death due to accidental or unintentional injury regardless of the time interval between the incident and death and regardless of whether such injury appears to have been the immediate cause of death or a contributory factor thereto.

(d) Deaths associated with fire or explosion.

(e) Deaths associated with firearms or other mortal weapons.

(f) Any death which occurs in or associated with any public or private conveyance, including but not limited to any motor vehicle, recreational vehicle, bicycle, aircraft, watercraft, motorcycle, bus, train, or the like.

(g) Abortion or the complications thereof if the abortion was known or suspected to have been performed by an unlicensed practitioner.

(h) Poison, illicit drug use, or an overdose of any drug or medication.

(i) Disease, injury, or exposure to a toxic agent resulting from or occurring during the course of employment.

(j) Disease or agent which constitutes a public health hazard or environmental hazard.

(k) Sudden unexpected death when in apparent good health of a person under the age of 60 years.

(*l*) Death of a person whose medical care has not been regularly followed by a physician.

(m) Death occurring in legal custody, including any death that occurs in any prison or penal institution.

(n) Death associated with diagnostic or therapeutic procedures, including intraoperative and perioperative deaths.

(*o*) Death in which a body is to be cremated in the state of New Hampshire or buried at sea regardless of the jurisdiction in which the death occurred.

(p) Death occurring less than 24 hours after admission to a health care facility or hospital, except when the decedent was known to have been terminally ill from natural disease and the death is imminent and expected.

(q) Death of a child under the age of 18 years unless the child is known to be terminally ill from natural disease or congenital anomaly and the death is expected.

(r) The death of any child from any cause when such death occurs at a day care facility, or when the child is in foster care, or when the child is in the custody of or being investigated by the department of health and human services.

(s) Fetal deaths that result from intrauterine trauma when the fetus has attained 20 weeks gestation or 350 grams weight.

(t) Death known to have been improperly certified, including but not limited to any remains brought into the state of New Hampshire without proper certification.

(u) Death of any unidentified person regardless of cause and manner.

(v) Discovery of buried remains which are known or thought to be human and which are uncovered other than by an exhumation order.

(w) The discovery of decomposed remains, including partially or completely skeletonized remains.

(x) Suspicious or unusual circumstances surrounding a presumed natural death.

Source.
2007, 324:1, eff. September 14, 2007.

611-B:12. Mandatory Reporting of Medico-Legal Deaths.

It shall be the duty of anyone who finds the body of any person whose death is suspected to have been caused or to have occurred in any manner described in RSA 611-B:11, or who finds remains which are thought to be human to immediately notify the medical examiner and the county attorney for the county where the body or remains are found.

Source.
2007, 324:1, eff. September 14, 2007.

611-B:13. Charge of Body.

Whenever the medical examiner has notice of the body of a person whose death is supposed to have been caused in a manner described in RSA 611-B:11, the medical examiner shall take charge of the body and may go to the place where such body lies. The medical examiner may authorize the moving of the body.

Source.
2007, 324:1, eff. September 14, 2007.

611-B:14. Survey of Location.

I. Before a body is removed or disturbed, the medical examiner shall make or cause to be made a careful survey of the body and its surroundings, and reduce or cause to be reduced to writing an accurate and detailed description of the location, position, and condition of the body and any other facts concerning the body or its surroundings that will aid in determining the cause and manner of death.

II. A body shall not be altered or disturbed, personal effects shall not be removed or altered, and physical or biological evidence, including samples of blood and other body fluids for analysis, shall not be obtained or collected from the body, without the permission of the medical examiner.

Source.
2007, 324:1, eff. September 14, 2007.

611-B:14-a. Medical Records.

For the purpose of any medical examination into the cause and manner of death, and where medical treatment has been provided to the decedent who is the subject of the examination, upon written request of the supervising medical examiner any individual, partnership, association, corporation, institution, or governmental entity which has rendered such treatment shall provide the supervising medical examiner with all medical records pertaining to the decedent and the treatment rendered. This section shall not preclude the supervising medical examiner from directly inspecting or obtaining any medical records pertaining to a case under the jurisdiction of the chief medical examiner. The records shall be promptly provided to the supervising medical examiner. When the records are incorporated into the files of the medical examiner or the office of the chief medical examiner, they shall be confidential and shall not be available for public inspection.

Source.
2008, 197:2, eff. June 11, 2008.

611-B:15. Postmortem Examination.

I. If the medical examiner determines that an external examination of the body is necessary to determine the manner and cause of death, the medical examiner may arrange for the body to be transported to a funeral home or other facility where an examination can be conducted. In the event that the decedent's family or next of kin does not employ the services of the funeral home or other facility used to transport the body, the cost of that transport shall be billed to the state.

II. In the event an autopsy is ordered, the medical examiner shall arrange for the body to be transported to the morgue. The cost of that transport shall be billed to the state.

III. The medical examiner performing the postmortem examination shall take and preserve, under proper seal, such portions of the body and its contents, together with such other articles that may require subsequent examination in order to determine the manner and cause of death.

Source.
2007, 324:1, eff. September 14, 2007.

611-B:16. Property of Deceased.

In all cases arising under the provisions of this chapter, the medical examiner shall take charge of any money and other personal property of the deceased found upon or near the body. Unless held as evidence, all money and other personal property shall be released with the body to the legal next of kin. If any personal property is retained, the medical examiner shall inventory the property on a form prescribed by the chief medical examiner. The inventory shall list the total of any cash received and a complete description of any other items, including quantity and any identifying information. The original inventory form shall be retained on file for a period of at least 5 years by the office of the chief medical examiner, together with the case file. A copy of the inventory form shall be forwarded to the next of kin of the decedent, if that person's identity is known, either directly or through the funeral home to which the decedent's body is released.

Source.
2007, 324:1, eff. September 14, 2007.

611-B:17. Performance of Autopsies.

I. If the supervising medical examiner, attorney general, or county attorney deems that an autopsy is necessary, he or she shall direct that one be made. The commissioner of the department of health and human services may, pursuant to RSA 126-A:5, V, request an autopsy of any individual who dies while admitted to, a resident of, or receiving care from New Hampshire hospital, Glencliff home, or any other residential facility operated by the department or a contract service provider.

II. The supervising medical examiner shall have the authority to conduct an autopsy and shall comply with any request by the attorney general, a county attorney, or the commissioner of health and human services to perform an autopsy.

Source.
2007, 324:1, eff. September 14, 2007.

611-B:18. Retention and Disposal of Organs, Unidentified Remains, Body Fragments, and Body Fluids.

I. Except as provided in RSA 227-C:8-a through RSA 227-C:8-g, whenever unidentified human skeletal remains are recovered, the chief medical examiner may store the remains, release them to an educational institution, direct that they be interred in an appropriate resting place, or have them cremated in accordance with RSA 325-A. Ashes of remains cremated shall be disposed of in an appropriate manner. Human skeletal remains recovered in a cared-for cemetery shall not be subject to the provisions of this paragraph.

II. The chief medical examiner or a designated pathologist may retain body tissues or body fluids for evidence, further study, documentation, or research. Subject to RSA 651-D:3, body tissue or body fluids retained for such purposes, or those which have been recovered after the body has been released from the custody of the medical examiner, may, unless claimed in writing by the person responsible for burial, be disposed of:

(a) According to the practices of the laboratory responsible for analysis;

(b) By the office of the chief medical examiner; or

(c) By the medical examiner or pathologist retaining those tissues or fluids.

III. Subject to RSA 651-D:3, the chief medical examiner may dispose of substantial body tissues that have been retained for evidence, further study, or documentation or that have been recovered after the rest of the body has been finally released, in accordance with paragraph I, unless claimed by the person responsible for burial.

Source.
2007, 324:1, eff. September 14, 2007.

611-B:19. Duty of the State Forensic Science Laboratory.

Whenever the supervising medical examiner requires expert investigation, either chemical or pathological, of any substance or article preserved from an autopsy, such investigation may be made at the forensic science laboratory of the department of safety established in RSA 106-B:2-a, without charge or expense to the state or county, and the expert making such investigation shall submit a report of the results of the work to the person requesting it.

Source.
2007, 324:1, eff. September 14, 2007.

611-B:20. Report to County Attorney.

If, upon completion of a death investigation, the medical examiner is of the opinion that the death of the person was caused or occurred in any manner described in RSA 611-B:11, the medical examiner shall file a record of the case with the county attorney or the attorney general, in accordance with rules adopted by the chief medical examiner under RSA 541-A.

Source.
2007, 324:1, eff. September 14, 2007.

611-B:21. Autopsy and Investigative Reports.

I. The medical examiner shall charge a reasonable fee for each autopsy report made available upon request. Such fee shall be credited to the medicolegal investigation fund established under RSA 611-B:28.

II. Homicide autopsy reports shall be made available only to the department of justice unless a written release is provided by the department of justice.

III. Except as provided otherwise by law and in rules adopted by the chief medical examiner pursuant to RSA 541-A, autopsy reports, investigative reports, and supporting documentation are confidential medical records and, as such, are exempt from the provisions of RSA 91-A. Copies of such documents may be made available to the next of kin, a law enforcement, prosecutorial, or other governmental agency involved in the investigation of the death, the decedent's treating physician, and a medical or scientific body or university or similar organization for educational or research purposes. Autopsy reports, investigative reports, and supporting documents shall not otherwise be released without the authorization of next of kin.

IV. For any autopsy conducted pursuant to RSA 126-A:5, V, a report of any autopsy requested by the commissioner of health and human services shall be provided to the commissioner's quality assurance program and any autopsy findings, test results, reports, or any other information pertaining to the autopsy shall be treated by the department of health and human services in accordance with the quality assurance program under RSA 126-A:4, IV. The copy of the report provided to the department under this section shall be privileged and confidential as provided in RSA 126-A:4, IV(b), except that the medical examiner may forward a copy of the report to the department of justice if the medical examiner finds that the cause of death may be attributable to criminal conduct, or may otherwise disclose the report in accordance with this statute.

Source.
2007, 324:1, eff. September 14, 2007.

611-B:22. Report to Bureau of Maternal and Child Health.

In any case in which the deceased whose death is being investigated is a child whose death is determined to have been the result of sudden unexplained infant death, the supervising medical examiner shall file a record of the case with the bureau of maternal and child health, department of health and human services. The bureau shall not release this report to any person without the written permission of the supervising medical examiner. The bureau may inform the parents of the child of the disposition of the case in a letter, but shall not include any portion of the autopsy report.

Source.
2007, 324:1, eff. September 14, 2007.

611-B:23. Dental Examinations.

In deaths investigated by a medical examiner, when the identity of a dead body cannot be established by visual means, fingerprints, or other identifying data, the medical examiner shall have a qualified dentist, as determined by the supervising medical examiner, carry out a dental examination of the dead body. If the medical examiner with the aid of the dental examination and other sources of identification is still not able to establish the identity of the dead body, he or she shall prepare and forward the dental examination records to the division of state police on a form supplied by the division for that purpose.

Source.
2007, 324:1, eff. September 14, 2007.

611-B:24. Release of Body.

The medical examiner, upon the completion of the investigation, shall release the dead body, upon their claim therefor, to one of the following persons:

I. The husband or wife, as the case may be.

II. The next of kin.

III. Any friend of the deceased.

Source.
2007, 324:1, eff. September 14, 2007.

611-B:25. Unclaimed Body.

If a dead body is unidentified or unclaimed for a period of not less than 48 hours following completion of the death investigation, the medical examiner shall release the body to the overseer of public welfare in the town or, in the case of an unincorporated place, to a county commissioner, who shall decently bury or cremate the body, or, with the consent of the commissioners or the overseer, it may be sent to the medical department of a medical school or university, to be used for the advancement of the science of anatomy and surgery, as provided for by law.

Source.
2007, 324:1, eff. September 14, 2007.

611-B:26. Death Record.

When the body is released pursuant to RSA 611-B:24 or RSA 611-B:25, the medical examiner shall provide to the person taking custody of the body a state of New Hampshire death certificate form with the pronouncing and certifying sections completed.

Source.
2007, 324:1, eff. September 14, 2007.

611-B:27. Assistant Deputy Medical Examiner Accounts.

I. Assistant deputy medical examiners shall be paid at the following rates: telephone consultations - $25; death investigations involving an external examination of the body - $140, plus mileage at the state rate; pre-cremation examinations conducted pursuant to RSA 325-A:18 - $50.

II. Assistant deputy medical examiners shall submit all claims for telephone consultation fees, death investigation fees and expenses, and pre-cremation examination fees to the office of the chief medical examiner, which shall authorize such claims and submit them for payment to the state treasurer, chargeable to the medico-legal investigation fund established pursuant to RSA 611-B:28. On a monthly basis, the office of the chief medical examiner shall bill each of the counties for the services provided to that county by the assistant deputy medical examiners during the previous month, and any body transportation costs associated with the billed services, as provided under RSA 611-B:15, I. Services shall be billed at the following rates: telephone consultation - $25; death investigation - $140; travel expenses – the state mileage rate. The county treasurer shall submit payment to the state treasurer, for deposit in the medico-legal investigation fund.

Source.
2007, 324:1, eff. September 14, 2007. 2008, 197:3, eff. June 11, 2008.

Amendments
—2008. The 2008 amendment substituted "$140" for "$125" preceding "plus mileage" in I.

611-B:27-a. Autopsy Expenses.

I. All autopsy-related bills shall be submitted to the office of the chief medical examiner, which shall authorize them and submit them for payment to the state treasurer, chargeable to the medico-legal investigative fund established pursuant to RSA 611-B:28.

II. For purposes of this section, autopsy expenses shall include morgue costs, microscopic processes, toxicology, body transportation, x-ray costs, and other ancillary testing costs.

Source.
2007, 324:1, eff. September 14, 2007.

611-B:28. Medico-Legal Investigation Fund.

I. There is established in the office of the state treasurer a nonlapsing fund to be known as the medico-legal investigation fund, which shall be kept distinct and separate from all other funds. The medico-legal investigation fund is established to receive all fees paid to the state related to medico-legal investigations and reports, to receive autopsy expenses paid to the state, to pay autopsy expenses authorized by the office of the chief medical examiner, fees due to assistant deputy medical examiners for investigations conducted, related administrative salaries, and the costs of recruitment, training, administration, and supervision of assistant deputy medical examiners.

II. The treasurer shall deposit in the medico-legal investigation fund all fees collected by the department of justice, office of the chief medical examiner pursuant to RSA 611-B. The treasurer shall also deposit in the medico-legal investigation fund such other funds received under state or federal law, or donated to the state by private parties, for the purposes related to medico-legal investigations, the recruitment, training, administration, and supervision of assistant deputy medical examiners, and related technology projects and improvements, and the treasurer shall credit any interest or income earned on moneys on deposit to the fund.

III. The attorney general is authorized to accept, budget, and expend moneys in the medico-legal investigation fund received from any party without the approval of the governor and council for the purposes of paying fees due by law to assistant deputy medical examiners, and for recruitment, training, administration, and supervision of assistant deputy medical examiners, administrative support costs, and related information technology.

IV. All moneys in the medico-legal investigation fund shall be continually appropriated to the department of justice and shall not lapse.

V. The treasurer, upon approval of the attorney general, shall pay assistant deputy medical examiners fees to which they are entitled by law, the expenses of recruiting, training, administering, and supervising assistant deputy medical examiners, administrative support costs, and the expenses of related information technology.

VI. The attorney general shall include the medico-legal investigation fund in the department budget submitted pursuant to RSA 9:4.

Source.
2007, 324:1, eff. September 14, 2007.

Missing Persons

611-B:29. Dental Records.

If a person reported missing has not been found within 30 days, the county sheriff, chief of police of a city or town, medical examiner, or other law enforcement authority initiating or conducting the investigation for the missing person shall request the family or next of kin of the missing person to give them written consent to contact and request from the dentist of the missing person the person's dental records. The dental records of the missing person shall be forwarded to the division of state police on a form supplied by the division for that purpose.

Source.
2007, 324:1, eff. September 14, 2007.

611-B:30. Identification by Scoring Probabilities.

The division of state police shall act as a repository or computer center, or both, for the dental examination records and dental records filed with it under this chapter. The division shall compare the dental examination records filed pursuant to RSA 611-B:29 with the dental records filed pursuant to RSA 611-B:23 and shall determine which scoring probabilities are the highest for purposes of identification, and shall submit the information to the agency that prepared and forwarded the dental examination records. The division files shall be made available to any law enforcement agency attempting to locate a missing person.

Source.
2007, 324:1, eff. September 14, 2007.

611-B:31. Destruction of Records.

If a person reported missing has been found, the county sheriff, chief of police of a city or town, medical examiner, or other law enforcement authority shall report the fact to the division of state police. After receiving the report, the division shall erase or destroy the dental records with respect to the person, which are maintained pursuant to this subdivision.

Source.
2007, 324:1, eff. September 14, 2007.

CHAPTER 612

UNIFORM CRIMINAL EXTRADITION LAW

SECTION
612:1.   Definitions.
612:2.   Fugitives from Justice; Duty of Governor.
612:3.   Form of Demand.
612:4.   Governor May Investigate Case.
612:5.   Extradition of Persons Imprisoned or Awaiting Trial in Another State or Who Have Left the Demanding State Under Compulsion.
612:5-a.   Violation of Terms of Release; Presigned Waiver of Extradition.
612:6.   Extradition of Persons not Present in Demanding State at Time of Commission of Crime.
612:7.   Issue of Governor's Warrant of Arrest; Its Recitals.
612:8.   Manner and Place of Execution.
612:9.   Authority of Arresting Officer.
612:10.   Rights of Accused Person; Application for Writ of Habeas Corpus.
612:11.   Penalty for Noncompliance with Preceding Section.
612:12.   Confinement in Jail When Necessary.
612:13.   Arrest Prior to Requisition.
612:14.   Arrest Without a Warrant.
612:15.   Commitment to Await Requisition; Bail.
612:16.   Bail; In What Cases; Conditions of Bond.
612:17.   Extension of Time of Commitment, Adjournment.
612:18.   Forfeiture of Bail.

SECTION
612:19.   Persons Under Criminal Prosecution in This State at Time of Requisition.
612:20.   Guilt or Innocence of Accused, When Inquired Into.
612:21.   Governor may Recall Warrant or Issue Alias.
612:22.   Fugitives from This State; Duty of Governors.
612:23.   Application for Issuance of Requisition; By Whom Made; Contents.
612:24.   Expenses.
612:25.   Immunity from Service of Process in Certain Civil Actions.
612:26.   Written Waiver of Extradition Proceedings.
612:27.   Nonwaiver by This State.
612:28.   No Right of Asylum; No Immunity from Other Criminal Prosecutions While in This State.
612:29.   Interpretation.
612:30.   Constitutionality.

Cross References.
Agreement on detainers, see RSA 606-A.
Rendition of prisoners as witnesses in criminal proceedings, see RSA 613-A.
Rendition of juveniles charged as delinquents, see RSA 169-A:11.
Securing attendance of witnesses in criminal proceedings generally, see RSA 613.

NOTES TO DECISIONS

Cited:
Cited in Robichaud v. Macaskill, 123 N.H. 110, 456 A.2d 389, 1983 N.H. LEXIS 233 (1983).

612:1. Definitions.

Where appearing in this chapter, the term "governor" includes any person performing the functions of governor by authority of the law of this state. The term "executive authority" includes the governor, and any person performing the functions of governor in a state other than this state. The term "state," referring to a state other than this state, includes any other state or territory, organized or unorganized, of the United States of America.

Source.
1937, 70:1. RL 437:1.

612:2. Fugitives from Justice; Duty of Governor.

Subject to the provisions of this chapter, the provisions of the Constitution of the United States controlling, and any and all acts of Congress enacted in pursuance thereof, it is the duty of the governor of this state to have arrested and delivered up to the executive authority of any other state of the United States any person charged in that state with treason, felony, or other crime, who has fled from justice and is found in this state.

Source.
1937, 70:1. RL 437:2.

Cross References.
Classification of crimes, see RSA 625:9.
Procedure for extradition of persons by governor of this state, see RSA 612:22 et seq.

NOTES TO DECISIONS

1. Construction
2. Procedure generally
3. Sufficiency of requisition papers
4. Sufficiency of proof of fugitive status

1. Construction

The word "crime," as used in this section, embraces every offense known to the law of the demanding state, including misdemeanors. Bracco v. Wooster, 91 N.H. 413, 20 A.2d 640, 1941 N.H. LEXIS 43 (1941).

2. Procedure generally

In an extradition proceeding, the governor of the asylum state must consider whether the requisition papers are in order, whether the person demanded is substantially charged with a crime, and whether the person is a fugitive from justice; it is the governor's duty to issue a warrant for the person's arrest once these findings have been made. Reeves v. Cox, 118 N.H. 271, 385 A.2d 847, 1978 N.H. LEXIS 396 (1978).

3. Sufficiency of requisition papers

The requisition papers are valid and sufficiently describe the person sought to be extradited if they contain the name of the person and the date and place of the offense. Reeves v. Cox, 118 N.H. 271, 385 A.2d 847, 1978 N.H. LEXIS 396 (1978).

4. Sufficiency of proof of fugitive status

In criminal extradition proceedings, evidence that the accused was in the foreign state when the crime was committed and is now in this state supports a finding that he is fugitive from justice irrespective of his purpose in leaving the state in which the alleged crime was committed, since the mission, motive, or purpose inducing a person accused of being a fugitive from justice to leave the demanding state is immaterial. Pearson v. Campbell, 97 N.H. 444, 91 A.2d 453, 1952 N.H. LEXIS 50 (1952).

Evidence that the accused left the demanding state after the commission of the alleged offense and was found in this state supported a finding that he was a fugitive from justice. Bracco v. Wooster, 91 N.H. 413, 20 A.2d 640, 1941 N.H. LEXIS 43 (1941); Thomas v. O'Brien, 98 N.H. 111, 95 A.2d 120, 1953 N.H. LEXIS 28 (1953).

Cited:

Cited in Koch v. O'Brien, 101 N.H. 11, 131 A.2d 63, 1957 N.H. LEXIS 4 (1957).

612:3. Form of Demand.

No demand for the extradition of a person charged with a crime in another state shall be recognized by the governor, unless in writing alleging, except in cases arising under RSA 612:6, that the accused was present in the demanding state at the time of the commission of the alleged crime and that thereafter he fled from the state, and accompanied by a copy of an indictment found, by information supported by affidavit in the state having jurisdiction of the crime, by a copy of an affidavit made before a magistrate there, together with a copy of any warrant which was issued thereupon, or by a copy of a judgment of conviction or of a sentence imposed in execution thereof, together with a statement by the executive authority of the demanding state that the person claimed has escaped from confinement or has broken the terms of his bail, probation, or parole. The indictment, information, or affidavit made before the magistrate must substantially charge the person demanded with having committed a crime under the law of that state, and the copy of indictment, infor-

mation, affidavit, judgment of conviction, or sentence must be authenticated by the executive authority making the demand.

Source.

1937, 70:1. RL 437:3.

Revision note.

In the first sentence, deleted "or" following "indictment found" and following "state having jurisdiction of the crime" and substituted a comma for a semicolon following "warrant which was issued thereupon" for purposes of clarity.

Cross References.

Arrest of persons prior to demand for extradition, see RSA 612:13.

Extradition of persons subject to pending criminal prosecutions at time of demand, see RSA 612:19.

Extradition without Governor's warrant, see RSA 612:5-a.

Right to challenge extradition by writ of habeas corpus, see RSA 612:10.

NOTES TO DECISIONS

1. Procedure generally
2. Sufficiency of requisition papers—Description of accused
3. —Presence of accused in state at time of offense
4. —Fugitive status of accused
5. Sufficiency of charging documents

1. Procedure generally

In an extradition proceeding, the governor of the asylum state must consider whether the requisition papers are in order, whether the person demanded is substantially charged with a crime, and whether the person is a fugitive from justice; it is the governor's duty to issue a warrant for the person's arrest once these findings have been made. Reeves v. Cox, 118 N.H. 271, 385 A.2d 847, 1978 N.H. LEXIS 396 (1978).

2. Sufficiency of requisition papers—Description of accused

Requisition papers are valid and sufficiently describe the person sought to be extradited if they contain the name of the person and the date and place of the offense. Reeves v. Cox, 118 N.H. 271, 385 A.2d 847, 1978 N.H. LEXIS 396 (1978).

The fact that requisition papers do not contain a personal description of an alleged fugitive from justice or any identification other than his name and the date and place of the alleged crime does not make the rendition invalid. Thomas v. O'Brien, 98 N.H. 111, 95 A.2d 120, 1953 N.H. LEXIS 28 (1953).

3. —Presence of accused in state at time of offense

An express allegation in the demand that the accused was present in the demanding state at the time of the commission of the alleged crime is not essential. Fortier v. Frink, 92 N.H. 50, 24 A.2d 604, 1942 N.H. LEXIS 15 (1942).

A demand for extradition is not invalid merely because it fails to allege that the accused was present in the demanding state at the time of the commission of the alleged crime, since this is necessarily implied from the allegations of the indictment, which is referred to in the demand and annexed thereto. Fortier v. Frink, 92 N.H. 50, 24 A.2d 604, 1942 N.H. LEXIS 15 (1942).

4. —Fugitive status of accused

In criminal extradition proceedings, evidence that the accused was in the foreign state when the crime was committed and is now in this state supports a finding that he is fugitive from justice irrespective of his purpose in leaving the state in which the alleged crime was committed, since the mission, motive, or purpose inducing a person accused of being a fugitive from justice to leave the demanding state is immaterial. Pearson v. Campbell, 97 N.H. 444, 91 A.2d 453, 1952 N.H. LEXIS 50 (1952).

The fact that an accused was in the demanding state only temporarily and for an innocent purpose does not preclude the finding that he is a fugitive from justice under this section. Hinz v. Perkins, 97 N.H. 114, 82 A.2d 423, 1951 N.H. LEXIS 31 (1951).

Evidence that the accused left the demanding state after the commission of the alleged offense and was found in this state supported a finding that he was a fugitive from justice. Bracco v. Wooster, 91 N.H. 413, 20 A.2d 640, 1941 N.H. LEXIS 43 (1941); Thomas v. O'Brien, 98 N.H. 111, 95 A.2d 120, 1953 N.H. LEXIS 28 (1953).

5. Sufficiency of charging documents

Extradition on the basis of a sworn complaint is authorized under this chapter. Smith v. Helgemoe, 117 N.H. 91, 369 A.2d 218, 1977 N.H. LEXIS 277 (1977).

A governor's authentication covered all documents included in the extradition requisition request, including a police officer's affidavit on the basis of which arrest warrants were issued, and met requirements of this section. Smith v. Helgemoe, 117 N.H. 91, 369 A.2d 218, 1977 N.H. LEXIS 277 (1977).

A copy of a complaint duly authenticated before a municipal judge of the demanding state indicating that the complaint was signed and sworn to before the judge, who certified the copy under oath before a notary public, and a warrant charging commission of a crime in the demanding state, met the requirements of this section that the demand for extradition must be accompanied by the copy of an affidavit made before a magistrate in the demanding state together with any warrant which had been issued thereupon. Loulakis v. Walker, 103 N.H. 526, 176 A.2d 314, 1961 N.H. LEXIS 80 (1961).

612:4. Governor May Investigate Case.

When a demand shall be made upon the governor of this state by the executive authority of another state for the surrender of a person so charged with a crime, the governor may call upon the attorney general or any prosecuting officer in this state to investigate or assist in investigating the demand, and to report to him the situation and circumstances of the person so demanded and whether he ought to be surrendered.

Source.
1937, 70:1. RL 437:4.

612:5. Extradition of Persons Imprisoned or Awaiting Trial in Another State or Who Have Left the Demanding State Under Compulsion.

When it is desired to have returned to this state a person charged in this state with a crime, and such person is imprisoned or is held under criminal proceedings then pending against him in another state, the governor of this state may agree with the executive authority of such other state for the extradition of such person before the conclusion of such proceedings or of his term of sentence in such other state, upon condition that such person be returned to such other state at the expense of this state as soon as the prosecution in this state is terminated. The governor of this state may also surrender, on demand of the executive authority of any other state, any person in this state who is charged in the manner provided in RSA 612:23 with having violated the laws of the state whose executive authority is making the demand, even though such person left the demanding state involuntarily.

Source.
1937, 70:1. RL 437:5.

Cross References.
Extradition of persons not present in demanding state at time of commission of crime, see RSA 612:6.
Extradition of persons subject to pending criminal prosecutions at time of demand, see RSA 612:19.
Persons subject to extradition generally, see RSA 612:2.

612:5-a. Violation of Terms of Release; Pre-signed Waiver of Extradition.

Notwithstanding any other law to the contrary, a law enforcement agency shall deliver a person in custody to the accredited agent or agents of a demanding state without the governor's warrant provided that:

I. Such person is alleged to have broken the terms of his probation, parole, bail or any other release of the demanding state; and

II. The law enforcement agency has received from the demanding state an authenticated copy of a prior waiver of extradition signed by such person as a term of his probation, parole, bail or any other release of the demanding state. The copy shall contain photographs, fingerprints or other evidence properly identifying such person as the person who signed the waiver.

Source.
1993, 121:1, eff. Jan. 1, 1994.

Cross References.
Bail agents and recovery agents; notification required, see RSA 597:7-b.
Waiver of extradition procedures, see RSA 612:26.

612:6. Extradition of Persons not Present in Demanding State at Time of Commission of Crime.

The governor of this state may also surrender, on demand of the executive authority of any other state, any person in this state charged in such other state in the manner provided in RSA 612:3 with committing an act in this state or in a third state, intentionally resulting in a crime in the state whose executive authority is making the demand, and the provisions of this chapter not otherwise inconsistent shall apply to such cases, even though the accused was not in that state at the time of the commission of the crime and has not fled therefrom.

Source.
1937, 70:1. RL 437:6.

NOTES TO DECISIONS

Cited:
Cited in Hinz v. Perkins, 97 N.H. 114, 82 A.2d 423, 1951 N.H. LEXIS 31 (1951); Hardy v. Betz, 105 N.H. 169, 195 A.2d 582, 1963 N.H. LEXIS 42 (1963).

612:7. Issue of Governor's Warrant of Arrest; Its Recitals.

If the governor decides that the demand should be complied with, he shall sign a warrant of arrest, which shall be sealed with the state seal and shall be directed to any peace officer or other person whom he may think fit to entrust with the execution thereof. The warrant must substantially recite the facts necessary to the validity of its issuance.

Source.
1937, 70:1. RL 437:7.

Revision note.
In the first sentence, inserted "shall" preceding "be directed to any peace officer" for purposes of clarity.

Cross References.
Arrest prior to demand for extradition, see RSA 612:13.
Arrests generally, see RSA 594.
Execution of warrant, see RSA 612:8, 9.
Extradition without Governor's warrant, see RSA 612:5-a.
Recall of or issuance of new warrant by governor, see RSA 612:21.
Right to challenge extradition by writ of habeas corpus, see RSA 612:10.
Waiver of extradition procedures, see RSA 612:26.
Warrantless arrests, see RSA 612:14.

612:8. Manner and Place of Execution.

The warrant issued pursuant to RSA 612:7 shall authorize the peace officer or other person to whom it is directed to arrest the accused at any time and any place where he may be found within the state, to command the aid of all peace officers or other persons in the execution of the warrant, and to deliver the accused, subject to the provisions hereof, to the duly authorized agent of the demanding state.

Source.
1937, 70:1. RL 437:8.

Revision note.
For purposes of clarity, substituted "the warrant issued pursuant to RSA 612:7" for "such warrant" preceding "shall authorize", inserted "it is" preceding "directed to arrest" and deleted "and" preceding "to command the aid".

Cross References.
Waiver of extradition procedures, see RSA 612:26.

612:9. Authority of Arresting Officer.

Every peace officer or other person empowered to make an arrest pursuant to RSA 612:8 shall have the same authority to command assistance in arresting the accused as peace officers have by law in the execution of any criminal process directed to them, with like penalties against those who refuse their assistance.

Source.
1937, 70:1. RL 437:9.

Revision note.
For purposes of clarity, deleted "such" preceding "peace officer or other person", substituted "an arrest pursuant to RSA 612:8" for "the arrest", and inserted "to command assistance" preceding "in arresting the accused" and deleted "to command assistance therein" thereafter.

612:10. Rights of Accused Person; Application for Writ of Habeas Corpus.

No person arrested upon a warrant issued pursu-

ant to RSA 612:7 shall be delivered over to the agent whom the executive authority demanding him shall have appointed to receive him unless he shall first be taken forthwith before a judge of a court of record in this state, who shall inform him of the demand made for his surrender and of the crime with which he is charged, and that he has the right to demand and procure legal counsel. If the prisoner or his counsel shall state that he or they desire to test the legality of his arrest, the judge of such court of record shall fix a reasonable time to be allowed him within which to apply for a writ of habeas corpus. When such writ is applied for, notice thereof, and of the time and place of hearing thereon, shall be given to the prosecuting officer of the county in which the arrest is made and in which the accused is in custody, and to the agent of the demanding state. Pending the outcome of such hearing, the accused shall be held in custody without bail, and, following such hearing, if the court denies the application for writ of habeas corpus, he shall continue to be so held until delivery to the agent of the demanding state. If after a reasonable time the agents of the demanding state have not taken custody of the accused, the accused shall be allowed to apply to the superior court for review of his custody status.

Source.
1937, 70:1. RL 437:10. RSA 612:10. 1993, 121:2, eff. Jan. 1, 1994.

Amendments
—1993. Rewrote the former first sentence as the first and second sentences and added the fourth and fifth sentences.

Revision note.
In the first sentence, substituted "a warrant issued pursuant to RSA 612:7" for "such warrant" following "person arrested upon" for purposes of clarity.

Cross References.
Habeas corpus proceedings generally, see RSA 534.
Waiver of extradition procedures, see RSA 612:26.

NOTES TO DECISIONS

1. Generally
2. Issues in habeas corpus proceedings—Generally
3. —Identity of accused

1. Generally
Any decision made in extradiction proceedings is subject to a defendant's right to file a writ of habeas corpus. State v. Murray, 104 N.H. 38, 178 A.2d 507, 1962 N.H. LEXIS 12 (1962).

2. Issues in habeas corpus proceedings—Generally
The office of habeas corpus in interstate rendition is generally confined to: (1) the correctness of the requisition papers; (2) the relator's identity; (3) whether the relator is a fugitive; and (4) whether a crime is substantially charged. Hinz v. Perkins, 97 N.H. 114, 82 A.2d 423, 1951 N.H. LEXIS 31 (1951).

3. —Identity of accused
In an extradition proceeding, the person who is arrested has the right, through a petition for a writ of habeas corpus, to question whether he is the person named in the requisition papers, and at this stage of the proceedings, the parties can present evidence to prove or disprove that the accused is that person. Reeves v. Cox, 118 N.H. 271, 385 A.2d 847, 1978 N.H. LEXIS 396 (1978).
If the evidence which the state produces at the hearing on a petition for habeas corpus contesting a proposed extradition con-

sists of only rendition papers, and the papers contain only the accused's name and date of birth, there would not be sufficient evidence to support a finding that the accused is the person requested. Reeves v. Cox, 118 N.H. 271, 385 A.2d 847, 1978 N.H. LEXIS 396 (1978).

Cited:
Cited in Ex parte Lyon, 58 F. Supp. 746, 1945 U.S. Dist. LEXIS 2605 (D.N.H. 1945); Robichaud v. Macaskill, 123 N.H. 110, 456 A.2d 389, 1983 N.H. LEXIS 233 (1983).

612:11. Penalty for Noncompliance with Preceding Section.

Any officer who shall deliver to the agent for extradition of the demanding state a person in his custody under the governor's warrant in wilful disobedience to RSA 612:10 shall be guilty of a misdemeanor.

Source.
1973, 70:1. RL 437:11. RSA 612:11. 1973, 528:318, eff. at 11:59 p.m., Oct. 31, 1973.

Amendments
—1973. Rewritten to the extent that a detailed comparison would be impracticable.

Cross References.
Classification of crimes, see RSA 625:9.
Sentences, see RSA 651.

612:12. Confinement in Jail When Necessary.

The officer or person executing the governor's warrant of arrest, or the agent of the demanding state to whom the prisoner has been delivered, may, when necessary, confine the prisoner in the jail of any county or city through which he may pass, and the keeper of such jail must receive and safely keep the prisoner until the officer or person having charge of him is ready to proceed on his route, such officer or person being chargeable with the expense of keeping. The officer or agent of a demanding state to whom a prisoner has been delivered following extradition proceedings in another state, or to whom a prisoner has been delivered after waiving extradition in such other state, and who is passing through this state with the prisoner for the purpose of immediately returning such prisoner to the demanding state may, when necessary, confine the prisoner in the jail of any county or city through which he may pass, and the keeper of such jail must receive and safely keep the prisoner until the officer or agent having charge of him is ready to proceed on his route, such officer or agent, however, being chargeable with the expense of keeping; provided, however, that such officer or agent shall produce and show to the keeper of such jail satisfactory written evidence of the fact that he is actually transporting such prisoner to the demanding state after a requisition by the executive authority of such demanding state. Such prisoner shall not be entitled to demand a new requisition while in this state.

Source.
1937, 70:1. RL 437:12.

Revision note.
For purposes of clarity, substituted "has" for "may have" preceding "been delivered" in three places in the first and second sentences and "the" for "such a" preceding "prisoner for the purpose" in the second sentence.

612:13. Arrest Prior to Requisition.

Whenever any person within this state shall be charged on the oath of any credible person before any judge or magistrate of this state with the commission of any crime in any other state and, except in cases arising under RSA 612:6, with having fled from justice, or with having been convicted of a crime in that state and having escaped from confinement or having broken the terms of his bail, probation, or parole, or whenever complaint shall have been made before any judge or magistrate in this state setting forth on the affidavit of any credible person in another state that a crime has been committed in such other state and that the accused has been charged in such state with the commission of the crime, and, except in cases arising under RSA 612:6, has fled from justice, or has been convicted of a crime in that state and has escaped from confinement, or has broken the terms of his bail, probation, or parole, and is believed to be in this state, the judge or magistrate shall issue a warrant directed to any peace officer commanding him to apprehend the person named therein, wherever he may be found in this state, and to bring him before the same or any other judge, magistrate, or court who or which may be available in or convenient of access to the place where the arrest is made, to answer the charge or complaint and affidavit, and a certified copy of the sworn charge or complaint and affidavit upon which the warrant is issued shall be attached to the warrant.

Source.
1937, 70:1. RL 437:13.

Revision note.
For purposes of clarity, substituted "has" for "with having" preceding "been convicted of a crime in that state", for "having" preceding "escaped from confinement" and for "having" preceding "broken the terms of his bail" and substituted "is" for "may be" following "where the arrest".

Cross References.
Arrest upon governor's warrant, see RSA 612:7-9.
Commitment of accused pending issuance of demand for extradition, see RSA 612:15.
Demand for extradition generally, see RSA 612:3.

612:14. Arrest Without a Warrant.

The arrest of a person may be lawfully made also by any peace officer or a private person without a warrant upon reasonable information that the accused stands charged in the courts of a state with a crime punishable by death or imprisonment for a term exceeding one year, but when so arrested the accused must be taken before a judge or magistrate with all practicable speed, and complaint must be made against him, under oath, setting forth the ground for the arrest as in RSA 612:13, and, thereafter, his answer shall be heard as if he had been arrested on a warrant.

Source.
1937, 70:1. RL 437:14.

Revision note.
For purposes of clarity, substituted "RSA 612:13" for "the preceding section".

Cross References.
Classification of crimes, see RSA 625:9.
Commitment of accused pending issuance of demand for extradition, see RSA 612:15.
Right to challenge extradition by writ of habeas corpus, see RSA 612:10.
Sentences, see RSA 651.

612:15. Commitment to Await Requisition; Bail.

If from the examination before the judge or magistrate it appears that the person held is the person charged with having committed the crime alleged and, except in cases arising under RSA 612:6, that he has fled from justice, the judge or magistrate must, by a warrant reciting the accusation, commit him to the county jail for such a time, not exceeding 30 days and specified in the warrant, as will enable the arrest of the accused to be made under a warrant of the governor on a requisition of the executive authority of the state having jurisdiction of the offense, unless the accused gives bail as provided in RSA 612:16, or until he shall be legally discharged.

Source.
1937, 70:1. RL 437:15.

Revision note.
For purposes of clarity, substituted "RSA 612:16" for "the next section".

Cross References.
Arrests on governor's warrant generally, see RSA 612:7.
Bail and recognizances generally, see RSA 597.
Demand for extradition generally, see RSA 612:3.
Extension of commitment, see RSA 612:17.
Extradition without Governor's warrant, see RSA 612:5-a.
Forfeiture of bail, see RSA 612:18.

612:16. Bail; In What Cases; Conditions of Bond.

Unless the offense with which the prisoner is charged is shown to be an offense punishable by death or life imprisonment under the laws of the state in which it was committed, a judge or magistrate in this state may admit the person arrested to bail by bond, with sufficient sureties in such sum as he deems proper, conditioned for his appearance before the judge or magistrate at a time specified in such bond, and for his surrender, to be arrested upon the warrant of the governor of this state.

Source.
1937, 70:1. RL 437:16.

Revision note.
For purposes of clarity, substituted "the judge or magistrate" for "him" preceding "at a time specified in such bond".

Cross References.
Arrests on governor's warrant generally, see RSA 612:7.
Bail and recognizances generally, see RSA 597.
Forfeiture of bail, see RSA 612:18.

NOTES TO DECISIONS

Right to bail of persons charged with misdemeanors
Where a prisoner is charged with the commission of a misdemeanor in the demanding state which is requesting his extradition, he has an absolute right to bail unless his liberty would be a menace to the community. Ex parte Thaw, 209 F. 954, 1913 U.S. Dist. LEXIS 1170 (D.N.H. 1913).

612:17. Extension of Time of Commitment, Adjournment.

If the accused is not arrested under warrant of the governor by the expiration of the time specified in the warrant or bond, a judge or magistrate may discharge him or may recommit him for a further period, not to exceed 60 days, or a judge or magistrate may again take bail for his appearance and surrender, as provided in RSA 612:16, but within a period not to exceed 60 days after the date of such new bond.

Source.
1937, 70:1. RL 437:17.

612:18. Forfeiture of Bail.

If a prisoner is admitted to bail and fails to appear and surrender himself according to the conditions of his bond, the judge or magistrate, by proper order, shall declare the bond forfeited and order his immediate arrest without warrant if he is within this state. Recovery may be had on such bond in the name of the state as in the case of other bonds given by the accused in criminal proceedings within this state.

Source.
1937, 70:1. RL 437:18.

Cross References.
Bail and recognizances generally, see RSA 597.
Bail of accused generally, see RSA 612:15, 16.
Extension of commitment and bail, see RSA 612:17.

612:19. Persons Under Criminal Prosecution in This State at Time of Requisition.

If a criminal prosecution has been instituted against such person under the laws of this state and is still pending, when a demand for extradition is received, the governor, in his discretion, may surrender the person on demand of the executive authority of another state or hold him until he has been tried and discharged or convicted and punished in this state.

Source.
1937, 70:1. RL 437:19.

Revision note.
For purposes of clarity, inserted "when a demand for extradition is received" following "still pending" and substituted "the person" for "him" following "may surrender".

Cross References.
Demand for extradition and proceedings thereon generally, see RSA 612:3 et seq.
Extradition without Governor's warrant, see RSA 612:5-a.

NOTES TO DECISIONS

Generally
Whether one undergoing imprisonment in the state should be extradited to another state before completion of service of his sentence is within the discretion of the governor, and the exercise of such discretion does not violate the separation of powers provision of part 1, article 37 of the state constitution. Koch v. O'Brien, 101 N.H. 11, 131 A.2d 63, 1957 N.H. LEXIS 4 (1957).

612:20. Guilt or Innocence of Accused, When Inquired Into.

The guilt or innocence of the accused as to the crime of which he is charged may not be inquired into by the governor or in any proceeding after the demand for extradition accompanied by a charge of crime in legal form as provided in RSA 612:3 has been presented to the governor, except as it may be involved in identifying the person held as the person charged with the crime.

Source.
1937, 70:1. RL 437:20.

Revision note.
For purposes of clarity, substituted "provided in RSA 612:3 has" for "above provided shall have" following "legal form as".

Cross References.
Demand for extradition and proceedings thereon generally, see RSA 612:3 et seq.
Habeas corpus proceedings, see RSA 612:10.

NOTES TO DECISIONS

Identification of accused
A person who is arrested has the right, through a petition for habeas corpus, to question whether he is the person named in the requisition papers. Reeves v. Cox, 118 N.H. 271, 385 A.2d 847, 1978 N.H. LEXIS 396 (1978).

612:21. Governor may Recall Warrant or Issue Alias.

The governor may recall his warrant of arrest or may issue another warrant whenever he deems proper.

Source.
1937, 70:1. RL 437:21.

Cross References.
Issuance of warrant by governor generally, see RSA 612:7.

612:22. Fugitives from This State; Duty of Governors.

Whenever the governor of this state shall demand a person charged with a crime or with escaping from confinement or breaking the terms of his bail, probation, or parole in this state from the executive authority of any other state, or from the chief justice or an associate justice of the supreme court of the District of Columbia authorized to receive such demand under the laws of the United States, he shall issue a warrant under the seal of this state to some agent, commanding him to receive the person so charged if delivered to him and convey him to the proper officer of the county in this state in which the offense was committed.

Source.
1937, 70:1. RL 437:22.

Cross References.
Classification of crimes, see RSA 625:9.
Procedure for extradition of persons by governors of other states, see RSA 612:2 et seq.

612:23. Application for Issuance of Requisition; By Whom Made; Contents.

I. When the return to this state of a person charged with a crime in this state is required, the prosecuting attorney shall present to the governor his written application for a requisition for the return of the person charged, in which application shall be stated the name of the person so charged, the crime charged against him, the approximate time, place, and circumstances of its commission, the state in which he is believed to be, including the location of the accused therein, at the time the application is made and a certification that, in the opinion of the prosecuting attorney, the ends of justice require the arrest and return of the accused to this state for trial and that the proceeding is not instituted to enforce a private claim.

II. When the return to this state is required of a person who has been convicted of a crime in this state and has escaped from confinement or broken the terms of his bail, probation, or parole, the prosecuting attorney of the county in which the offense was committed, the parole board, or the warden of the institution or sheriff of the county from which escape was made shall present to the governor a written application for a requisition for the return of such person, in which application shall be stated the name of the person, the crime of which he was convicted, the circumstances of his escape from confinement or of the breach of the terms of his bail, probation, or parole, and the state in which he is believed to be, including the location of the person therein at the time application is made.

III. The application shall be verified by affidavit, shall be executed in duplicate and shall be accompanied by 2 certified copies of the indictment returned, or information and affidavit filed, or of the complaint made to the judge or magistrate, stating the offense with which the accused is charged, or of the judgment of conviction or of the sentence. The prosecuting officer, parole board, warden, or sheriff may also attach such further affidavits and other documents in duplicate as he shall deem proper to be submitted with such application. One copy of the application, with the action of the governor indicated by endorsement thereon, and one of the certified copies of the indictment, complaint, information, and affidavits, or of the judgment of conviction or of the sentence, shall be filed in the office of the secretary of state to remain of record in that office. The other copies of all papers shall be forwarded with the governor's requisition.

Source.
1937, 70:1. RL 437:23.

Revision note.
In par. I, substituted "a certification" for "certifying" following "at the time the application is made and" for purposes of clarity.

Cross References.
Trial of persons extradited for offenses not named in requisition papers, see RSA 612:28.

612:24. Expenses.

All expenses of officers of this state in connection with extradition proceedings under the provision of this chapter shall be paid out of the county treasury in the county wherein the crime is alleged to have been committed, except as provided in the case of recommitment of certain paroled convicts as provided by RSA 651:44.

Source.
1937, 70:1. RL 437:24.

References in text.
RSA 651:44, referred to in this section, was repealed by 1983, 461:33, eff. July 1, 1983. For present provisions relating to parole of prisoners, see RSA 651-A.

612:25. Immunity from Service of Process in Certain Civil Actions.

A person brought into this state by, or after waiver of, extradition based on a criminal charge shall not be subject to service of personal process in civil actions arising out of the same facts as the criminal proceedings to answer which he is being or has been returned, until he has been convicted in the criminal proceeding, or if acquitted, until he has had reasonable opportunity to return to the state from which he was extradited.

Source.
1937, 70:1. RL 437:25.

612:26. Written Waiver of Extradition Proceedings.

Any person arrested in this state charged with having committed any crime in another state or alleged to have escaped from confinement or broken the terms of his bail, probation, or parole may waive the issuance and service of the warrant provided for in RSA 612:7 and 612:8 and all other procedures incidental to extradition proceedings by executing or

subscribing in the presence of a judge of any court of record within this state a writing which states that he consents to return to the demanding state; provided, however, that before such waiver shall be executed or subscribed by such person, it shall be the duty of such judge to inform such person of his right to the issuance and service of a warrant of extradition and to obtain a writ of habeas corpus as provided for in RSA 612:10. Following the execution of a waiver of extradition by such person, he shall be placed in custody without bail to await delivery to the agent of the demanding state. If after a reasonable time the agents of the demanding state have not taken custody of the accused, the accused shall be allowed to apply to the superior court for review of his custody status. If and when such consent has been duly executed, it shall forthwith be forwarded to the office of the governor of this state and filed therein. The judge shall direct the officer having such person in custody to deliver forthwith such person to the duly accredited agent or agents of the demanding state, and shall deliver or cause to be delivered to such agent or agents a copy of such consent; provided, however, that nothing in this section shall be deemed to limit the right of the accused person to return voluntarily and without formality to the demanding state, nor shall this waiver procedure be deemed to be an exclusive procedure or to limit the powers, rights, or duties of the officers of the demanding state or of this state.

Source.
1937, 70:1. RL 437:26. RSA 612:26. 1993, 121:3, eff. Jan. 1, 1994.

Amendments
—**1993.** Added the second and third sentences.

Cross References.
Extradition under authority of prior waiver signed in demanding state, see RSA 612:5-a.

612:27. Nonwaiver by This State.

Nothing contained in this chapter shall be deemed to constitute a waiver by this state of its right, power, or privilege to try a demanded person for a crime committed within this state, or of its right, power, or privilege to regain custody of such person by extradition proceedings or otherwise for the purpose of trial, sentence, or punishment for any crime committed within this state, nor shall any proceedings had under this chapter which result in, or fail to result in, extradition be deemed a waiver by this state of any of its rights, privileges, or jurisdiction in any way whatsoever.

Source.
1937, 70:1. RL 437:27.

Revision note.
At the beginning of the section, substituted "nothing contained in this chapter" for "nothing in this chapter contained" for purposes of clarity.

Cross References.
Territorial jurisdiction of criminal offenses, see RSA 625:4.

NOTES TO DECISIONS

Cited:

Cited in Koch v. O'Brien, 101 N.H. 11, 131 A.2d 63, 1957 N.H. LEXIS 4 (1957).

612:28. No Right of Asylum; No Immunity from Other Criminal Prosecutions While in This State.

After a person has been brought back to this state by, or after waiver of, extradition proceedings, he may be tried in this state for other crimes which he may be charged with having committed here as well as that specified in the requisition for his extradition.

Source.

1937, 70:1. RL 437:28.

Cross References.

Application for requisition for extradition, see RSA 612:23.

612:29. Interpretation.

The provisions of this chapter shall be so interpreted and construed as to effectuate its general purposes to make uniform the law of those states which enact it.

Source.

1937, 70:1. RL 437:29.

612:30. Constitutionality.

If any provision of this chapter or the application thereof to any person or circumstances is held invalid, such invalidity shall not affect other provisions or applications of the chapter which can be given effect without the invalid provision or application, and to this end the provisions hereof are declared to be severable.

Source.

1937, 70:1. RL 437:30.

CHAPTER 613

SUMMONING WITNESSES FROM WITHOUT A STATE

SECTION
613:1.   Definitions.
613:2.   Summoning Witness in This State to Testify in Another State.
613:3.   Witness from Another State Summoned to Testify in This State.
613:4.   Exemption from Arrest and Service of Process.
613:5.   Uniformity of Interpretation.
613:6.   Constitutionality.

Cross References.

Rendition of prisoners as witnesses in criminal proceedings, see RSA 613-A.

Securing attendance of witnesses generally, see RSA 516:1 et seq.

NOTES TO DECISIONS

Cited:

Cited in Isaac v. Perrin, 659 F.2d 279, 1981 U.S. App. LEXIS 17363 (1st Cir. N.H. 1981).

613:1. Definitions.

I. "Witness" as used in this chapter shall include a person whose testimony is desired in any proceeding or investigation by a grand jury or in a criminal action, prosecution, or proceeding.

II. The word "state" shall include any territory of the United States and District of Columbia.

III. The word "summons" shall include a subpoena, order, or other notice requiring the appearance of a witness.

Source.

1937, 65:1. RL 438:1.

613:2. Summoning Witness in This State to Testify in Another State.

I. If a judge of a court of record in any state which by its laws has made provision for commanding persons within that state to attend and testify in this state certifies under the seal of such court that there is a criminal prosecution pending in such court or that a grand jury investigation has commenced or is about to commence, that a person being within this state is a material witness in such prosecution or grand jury investigation, and that his presence will be required for a specified number of days, upon presentation of such certificate to any judge of a court of record in the county in which such person is found, such judge shall fix a time and place for a hearing, and shall make an order directing the witness to appear at a time and place certain for the hearing.

II. If at a hearing the judge determines that the witness is material and necessary, that it will not cause undue hardship to the witness to be compelled to attend and testify in the prosecution or grand jury investigation in the other state, and that the laws of the state in which the prosecution is pending or grand jury investigation has commenced or is about to commence and of any other state through which the witness may be required to pass by ordinary course of travel, will give to him protection from arrest and the service of civil and criminal process, he shall issue a summons, with a copy of the certificate attached, directing the witness to attend and testify in the court where the prosecution is pending or where the grand jury investigation has commenced or is about to commence at a time and place specified in the summons. In any such hearing, the certificate shall be prima facie evidence of all the facts stated therein.

III. If said certificate recommends that the witness be taken into immediate custody and delivered to an officer of the requesting state to assure his attendance in the requesting state, such judge may, in lieu of notification of the hearing, direct that such witness be forthwith brought before him for said hearing; and the judge at the hearing being satisfied of the desirability of such custody and delivery, for which determination the certificate shall be prima facie proof of such desirability, may, in lieu of issuing subpoena or summons, order that said witness be forthwith taken into custody and delivered to an officer of the requesting state.

IV. If the witness who is summoned as above provided, after being paid or tendered by some properly authorized person the sum of $.10 a mile for each mile by the ordinary traveled route to and from the court where the prosecution is pending and $5 for each day that he is required to travel and attend as a witness, fails without good cause to attend and testify as directed in the summons, he shall be punished in the manner provided for the punishment of any witness who disobeys a summons issued from a court of record in this state.

Source.
1937, 65:2. RL 438:2.

Revision note.
Near the end of par. I, inserted "found" following "county in which such person is" for purposes of clarity.

Cross References.
Exemption from arrest and service of process of persons summoned to testify in this state, see RSA 613:4.
Securing attendance of witnesses generally, see RSA 516:1 et seq.
Witnesses fees generally, see RSA 516:16 et seq.

RESEARCH REFERENCES

New Hampshire Trial Bar News.
For article, "Presumptions in New Hampshire Law—A Guide Through the Impenetrable Jungle (Part 1)," see 10 N.H. Trial Bar News 55, 60 n.82 (Winter 1990).

613:3. Witness from Another State Summoned to Testify in This State.

I. If a person in any state which by its laws has made provision for commanding persons within its borders to attend and testify in criminal prosecutions or grand jury investigations commenced or about to commence in this state is a material witness in a prosecution pending in a court of record in this state or in a grand jury investigation which has commenced or is about to commence, a judge of such court may issue a certificate under the seal of the court stating these facts and specifying the number of days the witness will be required. Said certificate may include a recommendation that the witness be taken into immediate custody and delivered to an officer of this state to assure his attendance in this state. This certificate shall be presented to a judge of a court of record in the county in which the witness is found.

II. If the witness is summoned to attend and testify in this state he shall be tendered the sum of $.10 a mile for each mile by the ordinary traveled route to and from the court where the prosecution is

pending and $5 for each day that he is required to travel and attend as a witness. A witness who has appeared in accordance with the provisions of the summons shall not be required to remain within this state a longer period of time than the period mentioned in the certificate, unless otherwise ordered by the court. If such witness, after coming into this state, fails without good cause to attend and testify as directed in the summons, he shall be punished in the manner provided for the punishment of any witness who disobeys a summons issued from a court of record in this state.

Source.
1937, 65:3. RL 438:3.

Cross References.
Exemption from arrest and service of process, see RSA 613:4.
Securing attendance of witnesses generally, see RSA 516:1 et seq.
Witnesses fees generally, see RSA 516:16 et seq.

613:4. Exemption from Arrest and Service of Process.

I. If a person comes into this state in obedience to a summons directing him to attend and testify in this state he shall not while in this state pursuant to such summons be subject to arrest or the service of process, civil or criminal, in connection with matters which arose before his entrance into this state under the summons.

II. If a person passes through this state while going to another state in obedience to a summons to attend and testify in that state or while returning therefrom, he shall not while so passing through this state be subject to arrest or the service of process, civil or criminal, in connection with matters which arose before his entrance into this state under the summons.

Source.
1937, 65:4. RL 438:4.

NOTES TO DECISIONS

1. Purpose of exemption
2. Application of exemption

1. Purpose of exemption
The exemption under this section is not established for the benefit of the witnesses but to protect the administration of justice. Pitman v. Cunningham, 100 N.H. 49, 118 A.2d 884, 1955 N.H. LEXIS 12 (1955).

2. Application of exemption
The exemption under this section does not extend to a nonresident attorney coming into the state to represent a client. Pitman v. Cunningham, 100 N.H. 49, 118 A.2d 884, 1955 N.H. LEXIS 12 (1955).

613:5. Uniformity of Interpretation.

This chapter shall be so interpreted and construed as to effectuate its general purpose to make uniform the law of the states which enact it.

Source.
1937, 65:5. RL 438:5.

613:6. Constitutionality.

If any provision of this chapter or the application thereof to any person or circumstances is held invalid, such invalidity shall not affect other provisions or applications of the chapter which can be given effect without the invalid provision or application, and to this end the provisions hereof are declared to be severable.

Source.
1937, 65:6. RL 438:6.

CHAPTER 613-A

UNIFORM RENDITION OF PRISONERS AS WITNESSES IN CRIMINAL PROCEEDINGS ACT

SECTION
613-A:1.   Definitions.
613-A:2.   Summoning Witness in This State to Testify in Another State.
613-A:3.   Court Order.
613-A:4.   Terms and Conditions.
613-A:5.   Exceptions.
613-A:6.   Prisoner from Another State Summoned to Testify in This State.
613-A:7.   Compliance.
613-A:8.   Exemption from Arrest and Service of Process.
613-A:9.   Uniformity of Interpretation.
613-A:10.   Short Title.
613-A:11.   Severability Clause.

Cross References.
Securing attendance of witnesses generally, see RSA 613.
Summoning witnesses from without state in criminal proceedings generally, see RSA 613.

613-A:1. Definitions.

As used in this chapter:

I. "Witness" means a person who is confined in a penal institution in any state and whose testimony is desired in another state in any criminal proceeding or investigation by a grand jury or in any criminal action before a court.

II. "Penal institutions" includes a jail, prison, penitentiary, house of correction, or other place of penal detention.

III. "State" includes any state of the United States, the District of Columbia, the Commonwealth of Puerto Rico, and any territory of the United States.

Source.
1959, 83:1, eff. July 5, 1959.

613-A:2. Summoning Witness in This State to Testify in Another State.

A judge of a state court of record in another state which by its laws has made provision for commanding persons confined in penal institutions within that state to attend and testify in this state may certify (1) that there is a criminal proceeding or investigation by a grand jury or a criminal action pending in the court, (2) that a person who is confined in a penal institution in this state may be a material witness in the proceeding, investigation, or action, and (3) that his presence will be required during a specified time. Upon presentation of the certificate to any judge having jurisdiction over the person confined, and upon notice to the attorney general, the judge in this state shall fix a time and place for a hearing and shall make an order directed to the person having custody of the prisoner requiring that the prisoner be produced before him at the hearing.

Source.
1959, 83:1, eff. July 5, 1959.

Cross References.
Application of chapter, see RSA 613-A:5.
Orders requiring attendance of witnesses in out-of-state proceedings, see RSA 613-A:3, 4.
Procedure for securing attendance of witnesses from other states in proceedings in this state, see RSA 613-A:6-8.

613-A:3. Court Order.

If at the hearing provided for in RSA 613-A:2 the judge determines (1) that the witness may be material and necessary, (2) that his attending and testifying are not adverse to the interests of this state or to the health or legal rights of the witness, (3) that the laws of the state in which he is requested to testify will give him protection from arrest and the service of civil and criminal process because of any act committed prior to his arrival in the state under the order, and (4) that as a practical matter the possibility is negligible that the witness may be subject to arrest or to the service of civil or criminal process in any state through which he will be required to pass, the judge shall issue an order, with a copy of the certificate attached, (a) directing the witness to attend and testify, (b) directing the person having custody of the witness to produce him in the court where the criminal action is pending or where the grand jury investigation is pending, at a time and place specified in the order, and (c) prescribing such conditions as the judge shall determine.

Source.
1959, 83:1, eff. July 5, 1959.

Revision note.
Near the beginning of the section, inserted "provided for in RSA 613-A:2" following "at the hearing" for purposes of clarity.

613-A:4. Terms and Conditions.

The order to the witness and to the person having custody of the witness issued pursuant to RSA 613-A:3 shall provide for the return of the witness at the conclusion of his testimony, proper safeguards on his custody, and proper financial reimbursement or prepayment by the requesting jurisdiction for all expenses incurred in the production and return of the witness, and may prescribe such other conditions as the judge thinks proper or necessary. The order shall not become effective until the judge of the state requesting the witness enters an order directing compliance with the conditions prescribed.

Source.
    1959, 83:1, eff. July 5, 1959.

Revision note.
    In the first sentence, inserted "issued pursuant to RSA 613-A:3" following "person having custody of the witness" for purposes of clarity.

613-A:5. Exceptions.

This chapter does not apply to any person in this state confined as insane or mentally ill or as a defective delinquent or under sentence of death.

Source.
    1959, 83:1, eff. July 5, 1959.

613-A:6. Prisoner from Another State Summoned to Testify in This State.

If a person confined in a penal institution in any other state may be a material witness in a criminal action pending in a court of record or in a grand jury investigation in this state, a judge of the court may certify (1) that there is a criminal proceeding or investigation by a grand jury or a criminal action pending in the court, (2) that a person who is confined in a penal institution in the other state may be a material witness in the proceeding, investigation, or action, and (3) that his presence will be required during a specified time. The certificate shall be presented to a judge of a court of record in the other state having jurisdiction over the prisoner confined, and a notice shall be given to the attorney general of the state in which the prisoner is confined.

Source.
    1959, 83:1, eff. July 5, 1959.

Cross References.
    Application of chapter, see RSA 613-A:5.
    Exemption from arrest and service of process, see RSA 613-A:8.
    Orders requiring attendance of witnesses in proceedings in this state, see RSA 613-A:7.
    Procedure for securing attendance of witnesses from this state in proceedings in other states, see RSA 613-A:2-4.

613-A:7. Compliance.

The judge of the court in this state may enter an order directing compliance with the terms and conditions prescribed by the judge of the state in which the witness is confined.

Source.
    1959, 83:1, eff. July 5, 1959.

613-A:8. Exemption from Arrest and Service of Process.

If a witness from another state comes into or passes through this state under an order directing him to attend and testify in this or another state, he shall not while in this state pursuant to the order be subject to arrest or the service of process, civil or criminal, because of any act committed prior to his arrival in this state under the order.

Source.
    1959, 83:1, eff. July 5, 1959.

613-A:9. Uniformity of Interpretation.

This chapter shall be so construed as to effectuate its general purpose to make uniform the law of those states which enact it.

Source.
    1959, 83:1, eff. July 5, 1959.

613-A:10. Short Title.

This act may be cited as the Uniform Rendition of Prisoners as Witnesses in Criminal Proceedings Act.

Source.
    1959, 83:1, eff. July 5, 1959.

613-A:11. Severability Clause.

If any provision of this chapter or the application thereof to any person or circumstance is held invalid, the invalidity shall not affect other provisions or applications of the chapter which can be given effect without the invalid provision or application, and to this end the provisions of this chapter are severable.

Source.
    1959, 83:1, eff. July 5, 1959.

CHAPTER 614

FRESH PURSUIT

Uniform Law on Interstate Fresh Pursuit

SECTION
614:1.   Authority Granted to Make Arrest.
614:1-a.   Reciprocity Requirement.
614:2.   Court Hearing.
614:3.   Limitation.
614:4.   Definition.
614:5.   What Constitutes Fresh Pursuit.
614:6.   Separability Clause.

Uniform Law on Intrastate Fresh Pursuit

614:7.   Authority Granted to Make Arrest.
614:8.   Court Hearing.
614:9.   What Constitutes Fresh Pursuit.
614:10.   Limitation.

Cross References.
    Arrests generally, see RSA 594.

Territorial jurisdiction over criminal offenses, see RSA 625:4.

Uniform Law on Interstate Fresh Pursuit

Adoption of agreement.
This law has been adopted by the following states and is codified as indicated:
(1)   Maine ...... 15 M.R.S.A. §§ 151–155.
(2)   Massachusetts ...... M.G.L.A. c. 276 §§ 10–10D.
(3)   Vermont ...... 13 V.S.A. §§ 5041–5045.

Cross References.
Intrastate fresh pursuit, see RSA 614:7 et seq.

NOTES TO DECISIONS

Generally
The territorial jurisdiction of New Hampshire police generally extends only to the borders of the state; the one exception to this principle is contained in this chapter which allows a border crossing if in fresh or "hot" pursuit for a felony. State v. Goff, 118 N.H. 724, 393 A.2d 562, 1978 N.H. LEXIS 279 (1978).

614:1. Authority Granted to Make Arrest.

Except as provided in RSA 614:1-a, any member of a duly organized state, county, or municipal peace unit of another state of the United States who enters this state in fresh pursuit, and continues within this state in such fresh pursuit, of a person in order to arrest him or her on the ground that he or she is believed to have committed a felony or to have driven a motor vehicle or operated a boat while under the influence of intoxicating liquor or a controlled drug in such other state, shall have the same authority to arrest and hold such person in custody as has any member of any duly organized state, county, or municipal peace unit of this state to arrest and hold in custody a person on the ground that he or she is believed to have committed a felony or to have driven a motor vehicle or operated a boat in this state while under the influence of intoxicating liquor or a controlled drug.

Source.
1937, 54:1. RL 439:1. RSA 614:1. 1986, 193:5, eff. Aug. 2, 1986. 2003, 252:4, eff. July 14, 2003.

Amendments
—2003.   Inserted "or operated a boat" following "motor vehicle" in two places and "or a controlled drug" following "intoxicating liquor" in two places, and made gender neutral changes throughout the section.

—1986.   Added "except as provided in RSA 614:1-a" at the beginning of the section, inserted "or to have driven a motor vehicle while under the influence of intoxicating liquor" following "arrest him on the ground that he is believed to have committed a felony" and substituted "or to have driven a motor vehicle in this state while under the influence of intoxicating liquor" for "in this state" following "hold in custody a person on the ground that he is believed to have committed a felony".

Cross References.
Fresh pursuit defined, see RSA 614:5.

614:1-a. Reciprocity Requirement.

The provisions of RSA 614 shall not authorize members of state, county or local peace units from other states to pursue persons driving or suspected of driving a motor vehicle or operating or suspected of operating a boat under the influence of intoxicating liquor or a controlled drug into New Hampshire unless the state of origin of such peace unit accords reciprocal authority to pursue such persons to members of duly authorized New Hampshire state, county or local peace units.

Source.
1986, 193:5, eff. Aug. 2, 1986. 2003, 252:5, eff. July 14, 2003.

Amendments
—2003.   Inserted "a motor vehicle or operating or suspected of operating a boat" following "driving" and "or a controlled drug" following "intoxicating liquor".

614:2. Court Hearing.

If an arrest is made in this state by an officer of another state in accordance with the provisions of RSA 614:1, he shall without unnecessary delay take the person arrested before any justice of the superior court or of the district court or the municipal court of any city who shall conduct a hearing for the purpose of determining the lawfulness of the arrest. If said justice determines that the arrest was lawful, he shall commit the person arrested to await for a reasonable time the issuance of an extradition warrant by the governor of this state, or admit such person to bail pending the issuance of such warrant. If the said justice determines that the arrest was unlawful, he shall discharge the person arrested.

Source.
1937, 54:2. RL 439:2.

Revision note.
In the first sentence, inserted "district court or the" preceding "municipal court" in light of the enactment of RSA 502-A. See RSA 502-A:34 and 502-A:35.

Cross References.
Arrests generally, see RSA 594.
Bail and recognizances generally, see RSA 597.

614:3. Limitation.

RSA 614:1 shall not be construed so as to make unlawful any arrest in this state which would otherwise be lawful.

Source.
1937, 54:3. RL 439:3.

614:4. Definition.

For the purpose hereof the word "state" shall include the District of Columbia.

Source.
1937, 54:4. RL 439:4.

614:5. What Constitutes Fresh Pursuit.

The term "fresh pursuit" as used in this subdivision shall include fresh pursuit as defined by the common law, and also the pursuit of a person who has committed a felony or who is reasonably suspected of having committed a felony or who is reasonably suspected of driving a motor vehicle or operating a boat while under the influence of intoxicating liquor or a controlled drug. It shall also include the pursuit of a person suspected of having committed a supposed felony, though no felony has actually been committed, if there is reasonable ground for believing that a felony has been committed. Fresh pursuit as used herein shall not necessarily imply instant pursuit, but pursuit without unreasonable delay.

Source.
1937, 54:5. RL 439:5. RSA 614:5. 1986, 193:6, eff. Aug. 2, 1986. 2003, 252:6, eff. July 14, 2003.

Amendments
—**2003.** Inserted "or operating a boat" following "motor vehicle" and added "or a controlled drug" following "intoxicating liquor" in the first sentence.

—**1986.** Added "or who is reasonably suspected of driving a motor vehicle while under the influence of intoxicating liquor" following "suspected of having committed a felony" at the end of the first sentence.

Cross References.
Classification of crimes, see RSA 625:9.

614:6. Separability Clause.

If any part of this subdivision is for any reason declared void, it is declared to be the intent hereof that such invalidity shall not affect the validity of the remaining portions.

Source.
1937, 54:6. RL 439:6.

Uniform Law on Intrastate Fresh Pursuit

Cross References.
Interstate fresh pursuit, see RSA 614:1 et seq.

614:7. Authority Granted to Make Arrest.

I. Any peace officer of this state or other person authorized to make arrests in a criminal case in this state in fresh pursuit of a person who is reasonably believed by such officer to have committed a felony in this state or who has committed or attempted to commit any criminal offense in this state in the presence of such officer, or for whom such officer holds a warrant of arrest for any offense, shall have the authority to arrest and hold in custody such person anywhere in this state.

II. Any peace officer of this state in fresh pursuit of a person who is reasonably believed by such officer to be driving under the influence of intoxicating liquor or controlled drugs, or has violated any motor vehicle statute in the presence of such officer, or for whom such officer holds a warrant of arrest for any

offense, shall have the authority to arrest and hold in custody such person anywhere in this state.

Source.
1941, 34:1. RL 439:7. RSA 614:7. 1995, 193:1, eff. Jan. 1, 1996.

Amendments
—**1995.** Designated the existing provisions of the section as par. I and substituted "such officer" for "him" following "believed by" and "any" for "a criminal" preceding "offense" in that paragraph and added par. II.

Cross References.
Classification of crimes, see RSA 625:9.
Fresh pursuit defined, see RSA 614:9.

614:8. Court Hearing.

If an arrest pursuant to RSA 614:7 is made in obedience to a warrant, the disposition of the prisoner shall be as in other cases of arrest under a warrant; if the arrest is without a warrant, the prisoner shall without unnecessary delay be admitted to bail, if the offense is bailable, by a magistrate or bail commissioner of either the jurisdiction where the offense was committed or where the prisoner was apprehended, by taking security by way of recognizance of the appearance of such prisoner before the court having jurisdiction of such criminal offense.

Source.
1941, 34:2. RL 439:8. 2002, 53:1, eff. Jan. 1, 2003.

Revision note.
At the beginning of the section, substituted "an arrest pursuant to RSA 614:7" for "such an arrest" for purposes of clarity.
In light of the enactment of RSA 502-A, inserted "district court or" preceding "municipal court". See RSA 502-A:34 and 502-A:35.

Amendments
—**2002.** Substituted "admitted" for "taken before a district court or municipal court or a justice of the peace or other magistrate of the county wherein such an arrest was made, and such court shall admit such person" preceding "to bail" and inserted "by a magistrate or bail commissioner of either the jurisdiction where the offense was committed or where the prisoner was apprehended".

Cross References.
Bail and recognizances generally, see RSA 597.

614:9. What Constitutes Fresh Pursuit.

The term "fresh pursuit" as used in this subdivision shall include fresh pursuit as defined by the common law and also the pursuit of a person who has committed a felony or is reasonably suspected of having committed a felony in this state, or under RSA 614:7, II a person who is reasonably suspected of driving under the influence of intoxicating liquor or controlled drugs, or who has violated any motor vehicle statute, ordinance, or any other law in this state in the presence of the arresting officer referred to in RSA 614:7, or for whom such officer holds a warrant of arrest for any offense. It shall also include the pursuit of a person suspected of having committed a supposed felony in this state, though no felony has actually been committed, if there is reasonable ground for so believing. Fresh pursuit as used herein shall not necessarily imply instant pursuit, but pursuit without unreasonable delay.

Source.
  1941, 34:3. RL 439:9. RSA 614:9. 1995, 193:2, eff. Jan. 1, 1996.

Amendments
  —1995. Substituted "or under RSA 614:7, II a person who is reasonably suspected of driving under the influence of intoxicating liquor or controlled drugs, or who has violated any motor vehicle statute, ordinance, or any other law" for "or who has committed or attempted to commit any criminal offense" preceding "in this state" and "any" for "a criminal" following "arrest for" in the first sentence.

Cross References.
  Classification of crimes, see RSA 625:9.

614:10. Limitation.

  RSA 614:7 shall not make unlawful an arrest which would otherwise be lawful.

Source.
  1941, 34:4. RL 439:10.

TITLE LX

CORRECTION AND PUNISHMENT

CHAPTER 616

PECUNIARY PENALTIES AND FORFEITURES

SECTION
616:1.   Jurisdiction.
616:2.   For Whose Use.
616:3.   Execution.
616:4.   Right of Town, etc.
616:5.   Powers of Selectmen.
616:6.   Computation of Time, etc.
616:7.   Disqualification of Justice.
616:8.   General Issue.
616:9.   Limitation of Action.

Cross References.
Fines generally, see RSA 618.
Forfeitures of personal property, see RSA 617.
Restitution, see RSA 651:61-a et seq.

616:1. Jurisdiction.

Any penalty or forfeiture of money may be recovered by action of debt before a justice if it does not exceed $13.33, before a municipal court if it does not exceed $100, and before the superior court in other cases.

Source.
RS 211:1. CS 224:1. GS 248:1. GL 266:1. PS 257:1. PL 371:1. RL 431:1.

Cross References.
Civil jurisdiction of district court, see RSA 502-A:14.
Criminal jurisdiction generally, see RSA 592-A.
Criminal jurisdiction of district court, see RSA 502-A:11.
Criminal jurisdiction of municipal court, see RSA 502:18.
Criminal jurisdiction of superior court, see RSA 491:7.
Limitation period, see RSA 616:9.

NOTES TO DECISIONS

Cited:
Cited in State v. McConnell, 70 N.H. 158, 46 A. 458, 1899 N.H. LEXIS 79 (1900); Noyes v. Edgerly, 71 N.H. 500, 53 A. 311, 1902 N.H. LEXIS 71 (1902).

616:2. For Whose Use.

Every such penalty and forfeiture shall be for the use of the county in which the offense is committed, unless otherwise limited.

Source.
RS 211:2. CS 224:2. GS 248:2. GL 266:2. PS 257:2. PL 371:2. RL 431:2.

Editor's note.
The disposition of penalties and forfeitures provided for in this section appears to be inconsistent with the scheme established in Laws of 1983, Chapter 383, which established a state funded, unified court system. See, in particular, 1983, 383:63–65.

616:3. Execution.

Whenever judgment is rendered for any such penalty or forfeiture, a writ of execution may issue in favor of the county for the penalty and costs.

Source.
GS 248:3. GL 266:3. PS 257:3. PL 371:3. RL 431:3.

Cross References.
Costs generally, see RSA 618.

616:4. Right of Town, etc.

If part of a penalty or forfeiture is payable to a town, corporation or board of public officers, they shall have the same rights in relation to such action and penalty as the county has in the cases aforesaid.

Source.
GS 248:6. GL 266:6. PS 257:6. PL 371:4. RL 431:4.

616:5. Powers of Selectmen.

Whenever a penalty or forfeiture or any part thereof is given to a town, the selectmen may sue therefor in the name of the town, shall defray the expenses of the action and may remit the penalty or forfeiture.

Source.
RS 211:11. CS 224:11. GS 248:12. GL 266:12. PS 257:12. PL 371:5. RL 431:5.

Cross References.
Limitation period, see RSA 616:9.
Rights of towns generally, see RSA 616:4.

616:6. Computation of Time, etc.

Whenever a fine or penalty is imposed for neglect for any period of time, the neglect may be alleged to have begun at any specified time and shall be reckoned from the time so alleged; but no suit or prosecution in such case shall be begun against a town or town officers until 20 days after notice in writing of the intention to begin it, nor then, if, within that time, the duty is performed.

Source.
RS 211:3. CS 224:3. GS 248:7. GL 266:7. PS 257:7. PL 371:6. RL 431:6.

Cross References.
Limitation period, see RSA 616:9.

NOTES TO DECISIONS

Construction and application
This section is distinctively a penal statute; its provisions are to be construed strictly against the plaintiff. Stanyan v. Peterboro, 69

N.H. 372, 46 A. 191, 1898 N.H. LEXIS 23 (1898).

The phrase "neglect for any period of any time" may mean neglect for a definite or an indefinite period. Stanyan v. Peterboro, 69 N.H. 372, 46 A. 191, 1898 N.H. LEXIS 23 (1898).

The phrase "neglect for any period of time" does not mean only such neglects as must continue for a specified period of time in order to expose those guilty of them to a penalty. Stanyan v. Peterboro, 69 N.H. 372, 46 A. 191, 1898 N.H. LEXIS 23 (1898).

616:7. Disqualification of Justice.

In actions for the recovery of a penalty before a justice, it shall be no cause of exception that the justice resides or has property within the town in which the offense was committed, nor that the penalty or any part thereof may belong to the town.

Source.
RS 211:6. CS 224:6. GS 248:8. GL 266:8. PS 257:8. PL 371:7. RL 431:7.

NOTES TO DECISIONS

Cited:
Cited in State v. Sawtelle, 66 N.H. 488, 32 A. 831, 1891 N.H. LEXIS 62 (1891).

616:8. General Issue.

In any such action the defendant may plead the general issue, and under it give any special matter in evidence.

Source.
RS 211:7. CS 224:7. GS 248:9. GL 266:9. PS 257:9. PL 371:8. RL 431:8.

NOTES TO DECISIONS

Statute of limitations
In a prosecution under a penal statute, the limitation period as to the time within which suit must be brought need not be pleaded in defense, but may be given in evidence under the general issue. Pike v. Jenkins, 12 N.H. 255, 1841 N.H. LEXIS 34 (1841).

616:9. Limitation of Action.

All suits or prosecutions founded upon any penal statute for penalties or forfeitures shall be brought within 2 years after the commission of the offense, unless otherwise specially provided. This section shall apply only to suits or prosecutions brought under this chapter.

Source.
RS 211:9, 10. CS 224:9. GS 248:10. GL 266:10. PS 257:10. PL 371:9. RL 431:9. RSA 616:9. 1990, 191:3, eff. Jan. 1, 1991.

Amendments
—1990. Added the second sentence.

NOTES TO DECISIONS

1. Application of section—Claims for unliquidated damages generally
2. —Federal antitrust actions
3. Effect of section upon public prosecutions
4. Drug forfeitures

1. Application of section—Claims for unliquidated damages generally
This section does not apply to claims of unliquidated damages, even though the statute upon which the claim is founded may be in some respects penal. Whitaker v. Warren, 60 N.H. 20, 1880 N.H. LEXIS 57 (1880).

2. —Federal antitrust actions
The limitation period prescribed in RSA 508:4, rather than the limitation period prescribed by this section, applies to actions under the federal anti-trust laws for treble damages. Le Witt v. Warner Bros. Pictures Distributing Corp., 158 F. Supp. 307, 1957 U.S. Dist. LEXIS 2667 (D.N.H. 1957).

3. Effect of section upon public prosecutions
This section does not postpone an indictment upon a penal statute for the period prescribed in the section; a public prosecution by indictment or information may be brought at any time within the limitation period if no private prosecution has been commenced. State v. McConnell, 70 N.H. 158, 46 A. 458, 1899 N.H. LEXIS 79 (1900).

4. Drug forfeitures
This section has no application to a forfeiture proceeding under RSA 318-B:17-b based on a demonstration of intended activity. In re Two Hundred Seven Thousand Five Hundred Twenty-Three Dollars & Forty-Six Cents in United States Currency, 130 N.H. 202, 536 A.2d 1270, 1987 N.H. LEXIS 300 (1987).

CHAPTER 617

FORFEITURES OF PERSONAL PROPERTY

SECTION
617:1.   Seizure.
617:2.   Libel.
617:3.   Warrant.
617:4.   Notice.
617:5.   Sale.
617:6.   Delivery to Claimant.
617:7.   Trial.
617:8.   Costs.
617:9.   Appeal.
617:10.   Order for Destruction.

Cross References.
Forfeiture of gambling equipment, see RSA 647:2.
Pecuniary penalties and forfeitures, see RSA 616.

NOTES TO DECISIONS

1. Nature and purpose of proceedings
2. Forfeiture of property subject to bona fide liens

1. Nature and purpose of proceedings
A forfeiture of personal property under this chapter is not a further penalty upon the owner of the property; it is a penalty upon the property itself as a means of confiscating property employed in furthering a particular offense. State v. Ford Victoria Auto., 98 N.H. 114, 95 A.2d 126, 1953 N.H. LEXIS 29 (1953).

The proceedings under this chapter, though criminal in form, are civil in essential elements and must be governed by the rules applicable to civil causes. State v. Tufts, 56 N.H. 137, 1875 N.H. LEXIS 18 (1875).

Proceedings for the forfeiture of property are to be considered and tried as civil causes; the question involved is only as to the title of property. State v. Barrels of Liquor, 47 N.H. 369, 1867 N.H. LEXIS 21 (1867).

2. Forfeiture of property subject to bona fide liens
A forfeiture of personal property under this chapter does not exempt property upon which bona fide liens are held; RSA 617:7

clearly expresses the intention of the legislature that there is to be no exemption in favor of innocent lienholders, and that there shall be put upon the lienholder the burden of chance as to what one in lawful possession of the property may do with it. State v. Ford Victoria Auto., 98 N.H. 114, 95 A.2d 126, 1953 N.H. LEXIS 29 (1953).

617:1. Seizure.

Whenever personal property is forfeited for violation of law, any officer or person by law authorized to seize the same may take and retain it until he shall deliver it to a proper officer having a warrant to detain it.

Source.
RS 212:1. CS 225:1. GS 249:1. GL 267:1. PS 258:1. PL 372:1. RL 432:1.

Cross References.
Administrative inspection warrants, see RSA 595-B.
Search warrants, see RSA 595-A.

NOTES TO DECISIONS

Authorization of searches
This section and RSA 617:2 authorize the seizure of property kept in violation of law but do not authorize a search for such property. State v. Spirituous Liquors, 68 N.H. 47, 40 A. 398, 1894 N.H. LEXIS 22 (1894).
An officer who makes a search under an invalid search warrant cannot justify his actions by invoking the provisions of this section and RSA 617:2. State v. Spirituous Liquors, 68 N.H. 47, 40 A. 398, 1894 N.H. LEXIS 22 (1894).

Cited:
Cited in Park v. United States, 294 F. 776, 1924 U.S. App. LEXIS 2959 (1st Cir. N.H. 1924); Sinkevich v. Nashua Police Comm'n, 97 N.H. 262, 86 A.2d 562, 1952 N.H. LEXIS 7 (1952); State v. Ford Victoria Auto., 98 N.H. 114, 95 A.2d 126, 1953 N.H. LEXIS 29 (1953); 1986 Op. Att'y Gen. 225.

617:2. Libel.

The person making or directing a seizure pursuant to RSA 617:1 shall, without unnecessary delay, file a libel before a district court or a municipal court in towns and cities in which there is such court if the property does not exceed in value $500, and in other cases in the office of the clerk of the superior court, stating the cause and praying for a decree of forfeiture.

Source.
RS 212:2. CS 225:2. GS 249:2. GL 267:2. PS 258:2. PL 372:2. RL 432:2. 1951, 224:1, eff. Aug. 29, 1951.

Revision note.
For purposes of clarity, substituted "a seizure pursuant to RSA 617:1" for "such seizure" following "making or directing".
In view of the abolition of the civil and criminal jurisdiction of justices of the peace by 1957, 244, deleted "before a justice if the property does not exceed in value thirteen dollars and thirty-three cents" following "file a libel".
In light of the enactment of RSA 502-A, inserted "a district court or" preceding "a municipal court". See RSA 502-A:34 and 502-A:35.

Cross References.
Criminal jurisdiction generally, see RSA 592-A.
Jurisdiction of district courts generally, see RSA 502-A:11, 14.
Jurisdiction of municipal courts generally, see RSA 502:18.
Jurisdiction of superior court generally, see RSA 491:7.

NOTES TO DECISIONS

1. Construction with other laws
2. Timeliness of filing of libel
3. Prosecution of action

1. Construction with other laws
RSA 617:1 and this section authorize the seizure of property kept in violation of law, but do not authorize a search therefor, and an officer who makes a search and seizure under and by virtue of an invalid search warrant is not proceeding under these sections and cannot justify his actions under them. State v. Spirituous Liquors, 68 N.H. 47, 40 A. 398, 1894 N.H. LEXIS 22 (1894).

2. Timeliness of filing of libel
Whether a libel for the forfeiture of liquor seized upon a search warrant is filed without unnecessary delay is ordinarily a question determinable by the trial court. State v. Spirituous Liquors, 75 N.H. 273, 73 A. 168, 73 A. 169, 1909 N.H. LEXIS 30 (1909).

3. Prosecution of action
The provision that the person making or directing a seizure shall, without unnecessary delay, file a libel does not limit the right to file a libel to the person making or directing the seizure. State v. Spirituous Liquors, 75 N.H. 273, 73 A. 168, 73 A. 169, 1909 N.H. LEXIS 30 (1909).
Where a justice of the peace had issued a search warrant directing seizure of spirituous liquors, a county solicitor, who was specially charged with the enforcement of the liquor law, was a proper party to file the libel and institute forfeiture proceedings. State v. Spirituous Liquors, 75 N.H. 273, 73 A. 168, 73 A. 169, 1909 N.H. LEXIS 30 (1909).
A complainant who files a libel under this section to procure the forfeiture of personal property for violation of the law and prosecutes the same wholly at his own expense is entitled to do so without interference from the county or state's attorney. State v. Tufts, 56 N.H. 137, 1875 N.H. LEXIS 18 (1875).

Cited:
Cited in Park v. United States, 294 F. 776, 1924 U.S. App. LEXIS 2959 (1st Cir. N.H. 1924); State v. Ford Victoria Auto., 98 N.H. 114, 95 A.2d 126, 1953 N.H. LEXIS 29 (1953); 1986 Op. Att'y Gen. 225.

617:3. Warrant.

Upon the filing, before or after seizure, of a libel for a forfeiture, a warrant shall be issued to the proper officer, requiring him to take such property into his custody and to detain it until it is legally disposed of.

Source.
RS 212:3. CS 225:3. GS 249:3. GL 267:3. PS 258:3. PL 372:3. RL 432:3.

Cross References.
Sale, see RSA 617:5.
Trial and decree, see RSA 617:7, 8.

NOTES TO DECISIONS

Cited:
Cited in State v. Barrels of Liquor, 47 N.H. 369, 1867 N.H. LEXIS 21 (1867); Park v. United States, 294 F. 776, 1924 U.S. App. LEXIS 2959 (1st Cir. N.H. 1924); 1986 Op. Att'y Gen. 225.

617:4. Notice.

Notice of the libel shall be given to the owner, if known; otherwise, a notice shall be published to all persons interested, to appear at the time and place appointed for trial, and to show cause why a decree of forfeiture should not be passed.

Source.
RS 212:4. CS 225:4. GS 249:4. GL 267:4. PS 258:4. PL 372:4. RL 432:4.

Cross References.
Trial, see RSA 617:7.

NOTES TO DECISIONS

Cited:
Cited in State v. Ford Victoria Auto., 98 N.H. 114, 95 A.2d 126, 1953 N.H. LEXIS 29 (1953); 1986 Op. Att'y Gen. 225.

617:5. Sale.

If a person interested shall appear and claim the property, it may be sold by consent of the parties or upon examination and certificate of its perishable nature or of its being expensive to keep, as in case of sale of like property attached, unless it is provided by law that it shall be destroyed, or unless the court shall otherwise order.

Source.
RS 212:5. CS 225:5. GS 249:5. GL 267:5. PS 258:5. PL 372:5. RL 432:5.

Cross References.
Sale of attached perishable goods, see RSA 511:31 et seq.

NOTES TO DECISIONS

Cited:
Cited in 1986 Op. Att'y Gen. 225.

617:6. Delivery to Claimant.

If the claimant requests it, the property may be appraised and delivered to him in the same manner as property attached, upon his giving bond to pay to the persons entitled thereto the appraised value thereof, and costs, in case a decree of forfeiture is made.

Source.
RS 212:6. CS 225:6. GS 249:6. GL 267:6. PS 258:6. PL 372:6. RL 432:6.

Cross References.
Awarding of costs, see RSA 617:8.
Restoration of attached property generally, see RSA 511:35 et seq.

NOTES TO DECISIONS

Cited:
Cited in State v. Barrels of Liquor, 47 N.H. 369, 1867 N.H. LEXIS 21 (1867); 1986 Op. Att'y Gen. 225.

617:7. Trial.

The case may be tried by a jury, if in the superior court, upon the request of either party, otherwise by the court; and, the cause of forfeiture alleged being

proved, the court or justice shall make a decree for the forfeiture and disposition of the property and a distribution of its proceeds according to law.

Source.
RS 212:7. CS 225:7. GS 249:7. GL 267:7. PS 258:7. PL 372:7. RL 432:7.

Cross References.
Appeal, see RSA 617:9.

NOTES TO DECISIONS

Cited:
Cited in State v. Whippet Coach, 85 N.H. 561, 160 A. 443, 1932 N.H. LEXIS 130 (1932); State v. 483 Cases, 98 N.H. 180, 96 A.2d 568, 1953 N.H. LEXIS 44 (1953); State v. Ford Victoria Auto., 98 N.H. 114, 95 A.2d 126, 1953 N.H. LEXIS 29 (1953); 1986 Op. Att'y Gen. 225.

617:8. Costs.

Costs may be awarded to the libelant if a reasonable cause for seizure appears, in which shall be included the necessary expenses of the seizure, detention and sale of the property; otherwise, reasonable costs and damages shall be awarded to the claimant.

Source.
RS 212:8. CS 225:8. GS 249:8. GL 267:8. PS 258:8. PL 372:8. RL 432:8.

Revision note.
In order to correct a grammatical error, substituted "appears" for "appear" following "cause for seizure".

NOTES TO DECISIONS

Cited:
Cited in 1986 Op. Att'y Gen. 225.

617:9. Appeal.

An appeal may be claimed by either party from a decree made by a justice of a district court or municipal court in the same manner as in other civil actions, and like proceedings may be had therein as in the case of libels originally filed in the superior court.

Source.
RS 212:9. CS 225:9. GS 249:9. GL 267:9. PS 258:9. PL 372:9. RL 432:9.

Revision note.
In light of the repeal of the civil and criminal jurisdiction of justices of the peace, deleted "the peace" following "justice of".
In light of the enactment of RSA 502-A, inserted "a district court" preceding "or municipal court". See RSA 502-A:34 and 502-A:35.
For purposes of clarity, inserted "other" preceding "civil actions".

NOTES TO DECISIONS

Cited:
Cited in State v. Whippet Coach, 85 N.H. 561, 160 A. 443, 1932 N.H. LEXIS 130 (1932); 1986 Op. Att'y Gen. 225.

RESEARCH REFERENCES

New Hampshire Court Rules Annotated.
Appeals to the superior court generally, see Rule 2.13, Rules of the District and Municipal Courts, New Hampshire Court Rules Annotated.

617:10. Order for Destruction.

The court, unless otherwise specially provided, may order that any property which has been forfeited shall be destroyed, whenever the public good requires it, and it may direct how and by whom it shall be done.

Source.
PS 258:10. PL 372:10. RL 432:10.

Cross References.
Trial and disposition generally, see RSA 617:7.

CHAPTER 618

FINES, COSTS, AND DISCHARGES

Imposition and Payment of Fines

SECTION
618:1.   Imposition; Definition of Fine.
618:2.   For Whose Use.
618:3.   Fines, to Whom Paid.
618:3-a.   Payment of Fines.
618:4.   Paying Over to County.
618:5.   Paying Over by County.

Enforcement of Fines

618:6.   Place of Committal.
618:7.   Execution.

Discharge of One Committed in Default of Payment of Fine

618:8.   At End of Term, or on Payment of Balance.
618:9.   Committal for Nonpayment; Term.
618:10.   Petition for Discharge.
618:11.   Procedure for Discharge.
618:12.   Discharge by Selectmen.
618:13.   Effect.

Costs

618:14.   Costs.
618:15.   Liability for Costs.

Cross References.
Application of earnings of prisoners, see RSA 30-B:19.
Pecuniary penalties and forfeitures generally, see RSA 616.
Sentences generally, see RSA 651.

NOTES TO DECISIONS

Confinement for nonpayment of fine
The confinement authorized by this chapter for failure to pay a fine is neither sentence nor punishment, but rather simply a means to compel financially able but recalcitrant individuals to pay fines they owe. State v. Morrill, 123 N.H. 707, 465 A.2d 882, 1983 N.H. LEXIS 338 (1983).

Imposition and Payment of Fines

618:1. Imposition; Definition of Fine.

I. Fines are imposed by the sentence of a court of criminal jurisdiction in a prosecution begun by indictment or information, or upon complaint before a justice of a municipal court.

II. In this chapter, "fine" means a fine, a penalty assessment, or an administrative fee imposed for a default on a court appearance or a default of payment of a fine.

Source.
GS 250:1. GL 268:1. PS 256:1. PL 370:1. RL 430:1. RSA 618:1. 1957, 244:40, eff. Sept. 23, 1957. 1998, 353:1, eff. Jan. 1, 1999.

Amendments
—**1998.** Added "Definition of Fine" in the section catchline, designated the existing provisions of the section as par. I, and added par. II.

—**1957.** Added "of a municipal court" following "justice".

Cross References.
Criminal jurisdiction generally, see RSA 592-A.
District courts generally, see RSA 502-A.
Municipal courts generally, see RSA 502.

NOTES TO DECISIONS

Cited:
Cited in State v. Marshall, 64 N.H. 549, 15 A. 210, 1888 N.H. LEXIS 56, 1 L.R.A. 51 (1888); State v. McConnell, 70 N.H. 158, 46 A. 458, 1899 N.H. LEXIS 79 (1900).

618:2. For Whose Use.

Unless otherwise specially provided, all fines and forfeitures imposed by a municipal court shall be for the use of the town in which the court is established, and all other fines and forfeitures shall be for the use of the county within which the offense was committed.

Source.
RS 211:13. CS 224:13. GS 250:7. 1868, 17:1. 1874, 48:1. GL 268:7. PS 256:2. PL 370:2. RL 430:2. RSA 618:2. 1957, 244:41, eff. Sept. 23, 1957.

Amendments
—**1957.** Rewritten to the extent that a detailed comparison would be impracticable.

Cross References.
Disposition of fines by counties, see RSA 618:5.
Disposition of fines collected by district courts, see RSA 502-A:8.
Disposition of fines collected by municipal courts, see RSA 502:14.
Forfeitures generally, see RSA 616.
Payment of fines to counties, see RSA 618:4.

NOTES TO DECISIONS

Cited:
Cited in Hillsborough County v. Manchester, 49 N.H. 57, 1869

N.H. LEXIS 6 (1869); Batchelder v. Rockingham County, 66 N.H. 374, 23 A. 429, 1890 N.H. LEXIS 44 (1890); State v. Sawtelle, 66 N.H. 488, 32 A. 831, 1891 N.H. LEXIS 62 (1891); Rockingham County v. Chase, 75 N.H. 127, 71 A. 634, 1908 N.H. LEXIS 53 (1908); State by Tucker v. Gratta, 101 N.H. 87, 133 A.2d 482, 1957 N.H. LEXIS 25 (1957).

618:3. Fines, to Whom Paid.

No fines or other money belonging to a county shall be paid to the county attorney; but when imposed or recovered in the superior court they shall be paid to the clerk of court or to the sheriff having a precept therefor.

Source.
1861, 2486:2. GS 271:11. GL 289:11. PS 256:16. PL 370:16. RL 430:16. 1951, 163:11, eff. July 1, 1951.

Cross References.
Disposition of fines by judges, see RSA 618:4.
Payment of fines to clerk of court, see RSA 618:3-a.

618:3-a. Payment of Fines.

All fines, except parking fines or except as otherwise specifically provided by law, shall be paid to the clerk of the court imposing the fine.

Source.
1957, 166:2, eff. Aug. 5, 1957.

Cross References.
Payment of fines generally, see RSA 618:3.

618:4. Paying Over to County.

Every justice of a municipal court shall pay over to the town or county to which any fine or forfeiture accrues every such fine or forfeiture received by him within 6 months after the receipt of the same. Upon default thereof, he shall forfeit double the amount of such fine or forfeiture.

Source.
RS 222:11. 1859, 2237:1, 2. GS 24:11. GL 25:11. PS 256:3. PL 370:3. RL 430:3. RSA 618:4. 1957, 244:42, eff. Sept. 23, 1957.

Amendments
—**1957.** Substituted "a" for "the peace and" following "justice of" in the first sentence.

Cross References.
Entitlement to fines and forfeitures imposed by municipal courts, see RSA 618:2.
Forfeitures generally, see RSA 616.

618:5. Paying Over by County.

If any fine appropriated to the use of any town or person or for any particular use is paid into the county treasury, the county commissioners, upon application, shall draw their order upon the county treasurer for the same, in favor of the party so entitled.

Source.
GS 250:8. GL 25:12; 268:8. PS 256:4. PL 370:4. RL 430:4.

Enforcement of Fines

Cross References.
Sentences generally, see RSA 651.

618:6. Place of Committal.

Any person sentenced to pay a fine shall be ordered to be imprisoned until sentence is performed, or he or she is otherwise legally discharged, in the county correctional facility in which the crime was committed. This section shall not be construed as authorizing the confinement of any juvenile under the age of 17 years in a county correctional facility for the nonpayment of a fine.

Source.
1861, 2510. GS 250:4. GL 268:4. PS 256:7. PL 370:7. RL 430:7. 1951, 163:4. RSA 618:6. 1963, 213:2. 1965, 256:10. 1979, 150:2. 1988, 89:33, eff. June 17, 1988. 2003, 237:6, eff. Jan. 1, 2004.

Amendments
—**2003.** Inserted "or she" following "or he", and substituted "the county" for "any county" and "in which the crime was committed" for "at the discretion of the court" in the first sentence.

—**1988.** Substituted "county correctional facility" for "house of correction or jail" preceding "at the discretion of the court" in the first sentence and preceding "for the nonpayment of a fine" in the second sentence.

—**1979.** Substituted "in any house of correction or jail in the discretion of the court" for "in the house of correction or jail of the county" following "discharged" in the first sentence.

—**1965.** Substituted "17" for "eighteen" in the second sentence.

—**1963.** Added the second sentence.

Cross References.
Discharge of fines, see RSA 618:10–12.
Duration of commitment for nonpayment of fine, see RSA 618:9.
Release of persons committed for nonpayment of fines, see RSA 618:8.

NOTES TO DECISIONS

Constitutional law
A defendant may not be imprisoned if his indigency renders him unable to pay the fine imposed. State v. Morrill, 123 N.H. 707, 465 A.2d 882, 1983 N.H. LEXIS 338 (1983).
Incarceration of defendant convicted of speeding in violation of RSA 265:60 when he was unable to pay a fine due to his indigency violated his right to equal protection of the laws under the United States Constitution. Kozerski v. Smith, 555 F. Supp. 212, 1983 U.S. Dist. LEXIS 20099 (D.N.H. 1983).

618:7. Execution.

A writ of execution may be issued for any fine in a criminal case, notwithstanding the respondent may be committed or detained in a county correctional facility for nonpayment thereof, and if the fine is collected upon the execution, the convict shall not be further detained on account thereof.

Source.
GS 250:5. GL 268:5. PS 256:8. PL 370:8. RL 430:8. 1951, 163:5. RSA 618:7. 1988, 89:34, eff. June 17, 1988.

Amendments
—**1988.** Substituted "a county correctional facility" for "jail" following "may be committed or detained in".

Discharge of One Committed in Default of Payment of Fine

Cross References.
Enforcement of fines, see RSA 618:6, 7.
Imposition and payment of fines generally, see RSA 618:1 et seq.

618:8. At End of Term, or on Payment of Balance.

Any person sentenced conditionally to pay a fine or to be imprisoned for a term shall be discharged at the expiration of the term, and may be discharged at any time on payment of the balance of the fine, after deducting $50 for each day such person has been imprisoned under the sentence.

Source.
GS 250:6. GL 268:6. PS 256:10. PL 370:10. RL 430:10. 1951, 163:6. RSA 618:8. 1967, 295:2. 1987, 81:1, eff. Jan. 1, 1988. 2003, 237:7, eff. Jan. 1, 2004.

Amendments
—**2003.** Substituted "$50" for "$20" and "such person" for "he".

—**1987.** Substituted "$20" for "$5" following "after deducting".

—**1967.** Substituted "$5" for "one dollar".

Cross References.
Sentences generally, see RSA 651:2.

NOTES TO DECISIONS

Cited:
Cited in Kozerski v. Smith, 555 F. Supp. 212, 1983 U.S. Dist. LEXIS 20099 (D.N.H. 1983); State v. Morrill, 123 N.H. 707, 465 A.2d 882, 1983 N.H. LEXIS 338 (1983).

618:9. Committal for Nonpayment; Term.

Whenever a person is committed to a county correctional facility in default of payment of a fine imposed by a justice of a municipal court or a district court, he or she shall be discharged from custody by the superintendent thereof at the expiration of a number of days after the date of his or her commitment equal to one day for each $50 of the fine so imposed. The superintendent shall keep a record of all discharges made under the provisions of this section.

Source.
1883, 96:1. PS 256:11. PL 370:11. RL 430:11. 1951, 163:7. 1953, 80:1. RSA 618:9. 1957, 244:43. 1967, 295:3. 1987, 81:2. 1988, 89:35, eff. June 17, 1988. 2003, 237:7, eff. Jan. 1, 2004.

Revision note.
In the first sentence, inserted "or a district court" following "municipal court" in light of the enactment of RSA 502-A. See RSA 502-A:34 and 502-A:35.

Amendments
—**2003.** Inserted "or she" following "he" and "or her" following "his" and substituted "$50" for "$20" in the first sentence.

—**1988.** Substituted "a county correctional facility" for "jail or to a house of correction" preceding "in default of payment" and "superintendent" for "keeper" following "from custody by the" in the first sentence and preceding "shall keep a record" in the second sentence.

—**1987.** Made minor stylistic changes in the section catchline and substituted "$20" for "$5" preceding "of the fine" in the first sentence.

—**1967.** Substituted "one day for each $5" for "the number of dollars and the fraction of a dollar" following "equal to" in the first sentence.

—**1957.** Deleted "the peace or" following "justice of" in the first sentence.

NOTES TO DECISIONS

Construction with other laws
This section, which requires that certain persons committed to jail be discharged by the jailor at the expiration of a specified time, does not restrict the power of discharging such persons given by RSA 618:10. Siskin's Petition, 63 N.H. 389, 1885 N.H. LEXIS 43 (1885).

Cited:
Cited in Kozerski v. Smith, 555 F. Supp. 212, 1983 U.S. Dist. LEXIS 20099 (D.N.H. 1983); State v. Morrill, 123 N.H. 707, 465 A.2d 882, 1983 N.H. LEXIS 338 (1983).

618:10. Petition for Discharge.

Whenever a person under conviction for a criminal offense and confined in a county correctional facility is unable to pay the fine, the superior court, upon petition of the prisoner or the superintendent and satisfactory proof of such inability, may order the prisoner to be discharged upon such terms as they may think proper.

Source.
RS 226:12. 1846, 351. CS 241:12. GS 250:9. 1872, 80:1. GL 268:9. PS 256:12. PL 370:12. RL 430:12. 1951, 163:8. RSA 618:10. 1957, 244:44. 1988, 89:36, eff. June 17, 1988. 2003, 237:7, eff. Jan. 1, 2004.

Amendments
—**2003.** Substituted "superintendent" for "county commissioners" preceding "and satisfactory".

—**1988.** Substituted "a county correctional facility" for "jail" preceding "is unable to pay the fine".

—**1957.** Deleted "or any justice thereof in vacation" following "superior court".

Cross References.
Discharge by selectmen, see RSA 618:12.
Effect of discharge, see RSA 618:13.

NOTES TO DECISIONS

1. Construction with other laws
2. Conditions of discharge

1. Construction with other laws
RSA 618:9, which requires that certain persons committed to jail be discharged by the jailor at the expiration of a specified time, does not restrict the power of discharging such persons given by this section. Siskin's Petition, 63 N.H. 389, 1885 N.H. LEXIS 43 (1885).

2. Conditions of discharge
The superior court or a justice thereof may annex terms and conditions to the remission of a fine and costs, and a condition that the prisoner give his own note for the amount of the fine and costs for the payment of which he was committed is not illegal. County of Strafford v. Jackson, 14 N.H. 16, 1843 N.H. LEXIS 2 (1843).

Cited:

Cited in Kozerski v. Smith, 555 F. Supp. 212, 1983 U.S. Dist. LEXIS 20099 (D.N.H. 1983); State v. Morrill, 123 N.H. 707, 465 A.2d 882, 1983 N.H. LEXIS 338 (1983).

618:11. Procedure for Discharge.

No discharge shall be granted pursuant to RSA 618:10 unless the petition shall be approved by the county attorney, or it shall appear to the court that the county attorney has been served with a copy of the petition, and that notice has been given to him of the time and place when and where the petition is to be presented to the court at least 10 days before the hearing upon the petition, and the petition, evidence and order of the court shall be filed in the office of the clerk of court.

Source.

1863, 2723. GS 250:10. 1872, 30:2. GL 268:10. PS 256:13. PL 370:13. RL 430:13. RSA 618:11. 1957, 244:45, eff. Sept. 23, 1957.

Amendments

—1957. Deleted "or justice" following "court" throughout the section.

NOTES TO DECISIONS

Cited:

Cited in Kozerski v. Smith, 555 F. Supp. 212, 1983 U.S. Dist. LEXIS 20099 (D.N.H. 1983).

618:12. Discharge by Selectmen.

Any person convicted of an offense against the police of towns or against a bylaw of a town may, upon petition and proof of inability to pay the fine, be discharged by the selectmen, and the town shall be liable for prison charges if the prisoner is unable to pay them.

Source.

RS 114:9. CS 120:11. GS 250:11. GL 268:11. PS 256:14. PL 370:14. RL 430:14. 1951, 163:9, eff. July 1, 1951.

Cross References.

Discharge by superior court, see RSA 618:10, 11.
Effect of discharge, see RSA 618:13.

618:13. Effect.

In neither of the cases specified in RSA 618:10 and 12 shall a fine be released by the discharge of the prisoner, but a writ of execution therefor against the goods or estate of the prisoner may be at any time issued, upon request of the county commissioners or selectmen, without a writ of scire facias.

Source.

GS 250:12. GL 268:12. PS 256:15. PL 370:15. RL 430:15. 1951, 163:10, eff. July 1, 1951.

Costs

618:14. Costs.

Except as otherwise provided by statute, the as-

sessment of any costs against respondents in criminal cases is hereby forbidden; provided, however, that costs involving transportation of prisoners up to the time of court arraignment may be assessed against respondents, in the discretion of the superior court.

Source.

1951, 163:1. RSA 618:14. 1992, 39:2, eff. Jan. 1, 1993.

Amendments

—1992. Added "except as otherwise provided by statute" at the beginning of the section and deleted "and all laws whether or not specifically designated hereinafter are hereby repealed insofar as they assess costs against respondents in criminal cases" following "forbidden".

Cross References.

Exception, see RSA 516:16-a.

NOTES TO DECISIONS

Penalty assessment

The addition of a ten percent penalty assessment to a twenty-dollar fine imposed upon a defendant convicted of speeding pursuant to RSA 105-A:8 did not violate this section. State v. Holland, 119 N.H. 200, 399 A.2d 976, 1979 N.H. LEXIS 275 (1979).

618:15. Liability for Costs.

All legal costs attending the arrest, examination or conveyance of an offender, except when directed or approved in writing by the counsel of the state or county commissioners, shall be paid by the complainant.

Source.

RS 222:21. CS 237:21. GS 250:13. 1876, 10:1. GL 268:13. PS 256:9. PL 370:9. RL 430:9.

NOTES TO DECISIONS

Construction

This section relates solely to expenses incurred in prosecutions for alleged crimes; it has nothing to do with the regulation of allowances to or on behalf of defendants. State v. Weeks, 78 N.H. 408, 101 A. 35, 1917 N.H. LEXIS 26 (1917).

Cited:

Cited in Upton v. Manchester, 56 N.H. 54, 1875 N.H. LEXIS 12 (1875); Rockingham County v. Chase, 75 N.H. 127, 71 A. 634, 1908 N.H. LEXIS 53 (1908); Kirke v. Strafford County, 76 N.H. 181, 80 A. 1046, 1911 N.H. LEXIS 180 (1911).

CHAPTER 619

COMMON JAILS AND PRISONERS THEREIN

[Repealed 1988, 89:37, I, eff. June 17, 1988.]

Former section(s).

Former RSA 619:1, which was derived from RS 226:1; CS 241:1; GS 267:1; GL 285:1; PS 282:1; PL 397:1; RL 461:1, related to the maintaining of county jails.

Former RSA 619:1-a, which was derived from 1905, 105:2; PL 378:17; RL 440:17; RSA 570:17; 1957, 244:10. 1973, 532:2, related to the expense of detention.

Former RSA 619:2, which was derived from 1921, 135:1; PL 397:2; and RL 461:2, related to the requirement for location and maintenance of two jails in the state and was previously repealed by 1981, 288:1.

Former RSA 619:3, which was derived from 1921, 135:1; PL 397:4; RL 461:4; RSA 619:3; 1967, 132:43, related to the removal of prisoners upon the closing of a jail.

Former RSA 619:4, which was derived from 1921, 135:2; PL 397:5; RL 461:5, related to commitments of persons held for trial.

Former RSA 619:5, which was derived from 1923, 114:1; PL 397:7; 1927, 91:1; 1931, 100:1; RL 461:7; 1950, 16:9; RSA 619:5; 1961, 14:1, related to imprisonment in Rockingham, Strafford, Cheshire, Merrimack and Sullivan Counties.

Former RSA 619:6, which was derived from RS 226:2; CS 241:2; GS 267:2; GL 285:2; PS 282:2; PL 397:8; RL 461:8; 1945, 130:1, related to inspection and reports of county jail conditions.

Former RSA 619:7, which was derived from RS 226:3, 4; CS 241:3, 4; GS 267:3; GL 285:3; PS 282:3; PL 397:9; 1931, 112:1; RL 461:9; RSA 619:7; 1965, 316:1; 1973, 150:2; 1979, 22:1; 1985, 69:1, related to the custodian of the jail in each county.

Former RSA 619:8, which was derived from RS 226:3, 4; CS 241:3, 4; GS 267:3; GL 285:3; PS 282:3; PL 397:10; RL 461:10, related to the deputy jailer.

Former RSA 619:9, which was derived from RS 226:5; CS 241:5; GS 267:4; GL 285:4; PS 282:4; 1917, 77:1; PL 397:11; RL 461:11, related to sustenance and other support for prisoners.

Former RSA 619:10, which was derived from RS 226:6; CS 241:6; GS 267:5; GL 285:5; PS 282:5; PL 397:12; RL 461:12; RSA 619:10; 1973, 531:152, related to the jailer's fraud or neglect.

Former RSA 619:11, which was derived from RS 226:7; CS 241:7; GS 267:6; GL 285:6; PS 282:6; PL 397:13; RL 461:13; RSA 619:11; 1973, 531:153, related to certified lists of prisoners to be maintained by jailers.

Former RSA 619:12, which was derived from RS 226:8; CS 241:8; GS 267:7; GL 285:7; PS 282:7; PL 397:14; RL 461:14, related to jailer liability for the escape of prisoners committed for debt or nonpayment of a forfeiture.

Former RSA 619:13, which was derived from RS 226:9; CS 241:9; GS 267:8; GL 285:8; PS 282:8; PL 397:15; RL 461:15, related to the sheriff's recovery of amounts paid under RSA 619:12.

Former RSA 619:14, which was derived from RS 226:10; CS 241:10; GS 267:9; GL 285:9; PS 282:9; PL 397:16; RL 461:16, related to the commitment of United States prisoners.

Former RSA 619:15, which was derived from RS 226:13; CS 241:13; GS 267:10; GL 285:10; PS 282:10; PL 397:17; RL 461:17, related to the removal of prisoners because of an epidemic or repairs to the jail.

Former RSA 619:16, which was derived from RS 226:14; CS 241:14; GS 267:11; GL 285:11; PS 282:11; PL 397:18; RL 461:18, related to the expenses of removing and maintaining prisoners.

Former RSA 619:17, which was derived from 1866, 4248:2; GS 267:13; GL 285:12; PS 282:12; PL 397:19; RL 461:19, related to fuel expenses for jails.

Former RSA 619:18, which was derived from 1862, 2591:2, 3; GS 267:14; GL 285:13; PS 282:13; PL 397:20; RL 461:20, related to the accounting and payment of sheriff's bills.

Former RSA 619:19, which was derived from 1852, 1289:1; 1866, 4248:2; GS 272:17; GL 290:17; PS 287:20; 1917, 72:1; PL 397:21; RL 461:21, related to jailer's fees.

Former RSA 619:20, which was derived from 1877, 48:1; GL 285:14; PS 282:14; PL 397:22; 1927, 112:1; RL 461:22, related to authorization for setting prisoners to labor.

Former RSA 619:20-a, which was derived from 1977, 141:1, related to voluntary labor by prisoners awaiting trial.

Former RSA 619:21, which was derived from 1877, 48:2; GL 285:15; PS 282:15; PL 397:23; RL 461:23, related to the application of prisoner earnings to payment of fines and costs in certain circumstances.

Former RSA 619:22, which was derived from 1921, 135:3; PL 397:6; RL 461:6, related to employment of prisoners.

Former RSA 619:23, which was derived from 1877, 48:3; GL 285:16; PS 282:16; PL 397:24; RL 461:24, related to earnings of persons not indicted or of witnesses held for want of bail.

Former RSA 619:24, which was derived from 1877, 48:4; GL 285:17; PS 282:17; PL 397:25; RL 461:25, related to the payment of earnings to prisoners upon discharge.

Former RSA 619:25, which was derived from 1877, 48:5; GL 285:18, 19; PS 282:18; PL 397:26; RL 461:26, related to prisoner

accounts.

Former RSA 619:26, which was derived from 1877, 48:6; GL 285:20; PS 282:19; PL 397:27; RL 461:27, related to the auditing and reconciling of accounts maintained by the jailer.

Former RSA 619:27, which was derived from 1877, 48:7; GL 285:20; PS 282:20; PL 397:28; RL 461:28, related to penalties for jailers failing to comply with the provisions of RSA 619:25 and 619:26.

Former RSA 619:28, which was derived from 1877, 48:8; GL 285:21; PS 282:21; PL 397:29; RL 461:29, related to the compensation of jailers for extra services rendered in connection with the employment of prisoners.

Former RSA 619:29, which was derived from 1963, 197:1, related to the prohibited delivery of certain articles to prisoners.

Former RSA 619:30, which was derived from 1963, 197:1; 1973, 528:319, related to the penalty for violating the provisions of RSA 619:29.

For present provisions relating to county correctional facilities, see RSA 30-B.

NOTES TO DECISIONS

Annotations Under Former RSA 619:6

Liability for expenses of precautionary measures

It is the duty of county commissioners under this section to take all necessary precautions against sickness and infection in the common jails of the county, and that implies that the necessary expenses of such precautions shall be paid, in the first instance at least, by the county. Slotts v. Rockingham County, 53 N.H. 598, 1873 N.H. LEXIS 60 (1873).

Where the county commissioners failed to have the body of an inmate of the jail, who died of smallpox, immediately removed and buried, and the jailer, after the lapse of thirty-two hours, employed persons to remove and bury the body, the charge for such service was to be paid by the county, whether the deceased was a pauper when committed to jail or not. Slotts v. Rockingham County, 53 N.H. 598, 1873 N.H. LEXIS 60 (1873).

Annotations Under Former RSA 619:8

Right to fees

Where the duties of receiving and discharging prisoners had been performed by a deputy jailer, with the assent and under the express authority of the sheriff, the deputy jailer was entitled to receive the fees provided for in RSA 619:19, and the sheriff could not recover such fees from the county. Locke v. Belknap County, 71 N.H. 208, 51 A. 914, 1902 N.H. LEXIS 3 (1902).

Annotations Under Former RSA 619:9

Construction and application generally

Since under this section the jailer is entitled to a reasonable compensation for the support of all prisoners confined on criminal process, his compensation will naturally vary with the amount and quality of the service rendered; a sheriff who has not furnished support to prisoners confined in the jail of his county on criminal process, nor incurred any expense on that account, is not entitled to any compensation therefor. Locke v. Belknap County, 71 N.H. 208, 51 A. 914, 1902 N.H. LEXIS 3 (1902).

This section applies only to prisoners confined in jail on criminal process. Locke v. Belknap County, 71 N.H. 208, 51 A. 914, 1902 N.H. LEXIS 3 (1902).

This section has no application to prisoner confined in jail on civil process. Spinney v. Seabrook, 79 N.H. 34, 104 A. 248, 1918 N.H. LEXIS 11 (1918).

Annotations Under Former RSA 619:12

Sufficiency of pleadings

In an action against a jailer under this section for negligently permitting the escape of a prisoner confined on civil process for debt, a declaration alleging generally an arrest and commitment of the prisoner without averring that a copy of the writ was left with the jailer, or giving the name of the jailer except that the sheriff was keeper of the prison, was sufficient. Atherton v. Gilmore, 9 N.H. 185, 1838 N.H. LEXIS 9 (1838).

ANNOTATIONS UNDER FORMER RSA 619:19

Cited:
Cited in Locke v. Belknap County, 71 N.H. 208, 51 A. 914, 1902 N.H. LEXIS 3 (1902).

ANNOTATIONS UNDER FORMER RSA 619:23

Purpose
The purpose of this section in relation to witnesses held in jail is to give to the witnesses some slight recompense for the inconvenience and loss which their detention occasions, and to place them, as nearly as possible, on the same footing as the ordinary witness who is entitled to use, for his own advantage, such portion of his time as is not required for the service of the public; the section is not intended to deny any witness his right to a regular witness fee. Kirke v. Strafford County, 76 N.H. 181, 80 A. 1046, 1911 N.H. LEXIS 180 (1911).

CHAPTER 620

HOUSES OF CORRECTION

[Repealed 1988, 89:37, II, eff. June 17, 1988.]

Former section(s).
Former RSA 620:1, which was derived from 1921, 135:4; PL 398:1; RL 462:1, related to the maintaining by counties of houses of correction.

Former RSA 620:1-a, which was derived from 1913, 50:1; PL 378:28; RL 440:27; RSA 570:30; 1971, 11:1; 1973, 532:6; 1979, 150:1, related to places of imprisonment.

Former RSA 620:2, which was derived from 1899, 7:2; PL 398:2; RL 462:2; RSA 620:2; 1973, 150:3, related to superintendency of houses of correction.

Former RSA 620:3, which was derived from 1862, 2590:1; GS 268:2; GL 286:2; PS 283:3; PL 398:3; RL 462:3, related to the labor of inmates.

Former RSA 620:4, which was derived from 1862, 2590:1; GS 268:3; GL 286:3; PS 283:4; PL 398:4; RL 462:4, related to county commissioners' visiting houses of correction.

Former RSA 620:5, which was derived from 1862, 2590:1; GS 268:3; GL 286:3; PS 283:4; PL 398:5; RL 462:5, related to the removal of officers of a house of corrections.

Former RSA 620:6, which was derived from 1862, 2590:2; GS 268:4; GL 286:4; PS 283:5; PL 398:6; RL 462:6, related to the superintendent's duties.

Former RSA 620:7, which was derived from 1862, 2590:2; GS 268:4; GL 286:4; PS 283:5; PL 398:7; RL 462:7; RSA 620:7; 1981, 227:5, related to prisoner discipline.

Former RSA 620:8, which was derived from 1862, 2590:3; GS 268:5; GL 286:5; PS 283:6; PL 398:8; RL 462:8, related to action taken upon the escape of a prisoner.

Former RSA 620:9, which was derived from 1953, 55:2; RSA 620:9; and 1963, 122:1, related to the penalty for escape from a house of correction, and was previously repealed by 1985, 90:1.

Former RSA 620:10, which was derived from 1862, 2590:4; GS 268:7; GL 286:7; PS 283:8; PL 398:10; RL 462:10, related to accounting of the expenses of a house of corrections.

Former RSA 620:11, which was derived from 1862, 2590:4; GS 268:8; GL 286:8; PS 283:9; PL 398:11; RL 462:11, related to inmates unable to work.

Former RSA 620:12, which was derived from 1955, 29:1, related to the transfer of prisoners.

Former RSA 620:13, which was derived from 1979, 150:3, related to the transfer of female prisoners.

For present provisions relating to county correctional facilities, see RSA 30-B.

CHAPTER 621

YOUTH DEVELOPMENT CENTER

SECTION
621:1.   Youth Development Center.
621:2.   Philosophy of the New Hampshire Youth Development Center.
621:3.   Definitions.
621:4.   Duties Relative to Property.
621:5.   Supervisory Control Over the Board of Trustees. [Repealed.]
621:6.   Books and Records of Account.
621:7.   Bylaws.
621:8.   Fire Code Compliance.
621:9.   Care of Children.
621:9-a.   Extended Commitment at the Center.
621:10.   Limits to Population at the Youth Development Center.
621:11.   Superintendent. [Repealed.]
621:12.   Department's Duties.
621:13.   Deputy Superintendent. [Repealed.]
621:14.   Compensation of Superintendent and Deputy. [Repealed.]
621:15.   Records of Children Committed or Detained.
621:16.   Erroneous Committal Elsewhere.
621:17.   Committal by the United States.
621:18.   Detention.
621:19.   Releases and Discharges.
621:20.   Contract for Board.
621:21.   Payment of Board.
621:22.   Children in Residential Care.
621:23.   Religious Preference.
621:24.   Effect of Release.
621:25.   Remands and Changes in Conditions of Release.
621:26.   Discharge by Superior Court.
621:27.   Incorrigibles.
621:28.   Modification of Transfer.
621:29.   Orders.
621:30.   Children's Funds.
621:31.   Parents or Estate of Child to Contribute to Costs.
621:32.   Contraband.
621:33.   Authority to Apprehend.
621:34.   Reimbursement for Transportation Costs.
621:35.   Rulemaking Authority. [Repealed.]

Transfer of functions, powers, duties, etc., from the department of youth development services to the department of health and human services.
2001, 286:1, eff. Sept. 14, 2001, provided that the functions, powers, duties, personnel, records, property and funds of department of youth development services are transferred to the department of health and human services.

Transfer of functions, powers, duties, etc., from the youth development center to the department of youth development services.
1995, 181:24, eff. July 1, 1995, provided that the functions, powers, duties, personnel, records, property and funds of the youth development center are transferred to the department of youth development services.

Salary enhancement for youth services educational administrators; severability.
1993, 358:52, eff. July 8, 1993, provided: "Beginning July 1, 1993, educational management personnel at the youth development center and the youth services center on the academic pay scale shall receive a 25 percent salary enhancement. This salary enhancement is deemed necessary based on the enhancement previously granted to teachers at such centers as a result of the U.S. District Court decree in the case of James O. v. Martin, rendered on August 23, 1991."
1993, 358 was subject to a severability clause. See 1993, 358:106.

Cross References.
Children in need of services, see RSA 169-D.

Delinquent children, see RSA 169-B.

Department of corrections, see RSA 21-H.

Department of justice, see RSA 21-M.

Division for children, youth, and families generally, see RSA 170-G.

Neglected or abused children, see RSA 169-C.

Organization of executive branch of government generally, see RSA 21-G.

Parole of delinquents, see RSA 170-H.

Procedure after exposure of public safety workers to infectious disease, see RSA 141-G.

NOTES TO DECISIONS

Cited:

Cited in In re Bryan L., 123 N.H. 420, 462 A.2d 108, 1983 N.H. LEXIS 296 (1983).

621:1. Youth Development Center.

I. The New Hampshire youth development center, a juvenile correctional facility formerly known as the industrial school, may also be referred to as the YDC or the center. References to the industrial school or the YDC in statutes or other documents shall mean the youth development center.

II. The programs and policies of the New Hampshire youth development center shall be administered by the department of health and human services.

III. To ensure that juveniles are placed in the least restrictive environment consistent with their treatment needs, their safety, and the safety of the community, the department shall not establish treatment services at the youth development center or other architecturally secure facility which are not also available to children living in the community or in settings other than architecturally secure settings.

Source.

1913, 101:3. PL 399:1. RL 463:1. 1953, 205:1, par. 1. RSA 621:1. 1973, 17:2. 1981, 539:3. 1983, 416:10. 1994, 81:3, eff. July 1, 1994; 212:2, eff. May 24, 1994. 1995, 181:12, eff. July 1, 1995. 2001, 286:19, eff. Sept. 14, 2001. 2013, 249:19, eff. September 22, 2013.

Amendments

—2013. The 2013 amendment added III.

—2001. Paragraph II: Substituted "department of health and human services" for "department of youth development services".

—1995. Paragraph II: Substituted "by the department of youth development services" for "through the bureau of residential services, division for children, youth, and families" following "administered".

—1994. Paragraph II: Chapter 81 substituted "residential services" for "secure care" following "bureau of".

Chapter 212 substituted "youth, and families" for "and youth services" following "children".

—1983. Designated the existing provisions of the section as par. I and added par. II.

Restructuring of Department of Youth Development Services.

2001, 286:22, eff. September 14, 2001, provided: "The restructuring of the department of youth development services as a unit of the department of health and human services shall occur within 60 days of the effective date of this act [September 14, 2001]."

Cross References.

Division for children and youth services generally, see RSA 170-G.

Youth services center, see RSA 621-A:1 et seq.

621:2. Philosophy of the New Hampshire Youth Development Center.

The New Hampshire youth development center shall be administered to effect the following purposes and policies:

I. To provide a wholesome physical and emotional setting for each child detained at or committed to the center;

II. To provide protection, care, counseling, supervision, and rehabilitative services as required by the individual child;

III. To assure that the child has not been deprived of those rights to which he or she is entitled by law;

IV. To teach the child to accept responsibility for his or her actions;

V. To recognize that the child's interests are of major importance while also acknowledging the interests of public safety;

VI. To cooperate with the courts, law enforcement agencies, and other agencies in juvenile matters to ensure that the needs of each child who is involved with these agencies are met with minimum adverse impact upon the child; and

VII. To return each child committed to the center to a community setting with an improved attitude toward society.

Source.

1981, 539:3, eff. June 30, 1981.

Cross References.

Commission on juvenile justice, see RSA 169-H:1.

Review of dispositional orders in juvenile cases, see RSA 169-G:1.

621:3. Definitions.

In this chapter:

I. "Administrative release to parole" means an administrative procedure to provide a period of community adjustment before parole status is granted.

I-a. "Board" means the juvenile parole board established in RSA 170-H:3.

II. "Child," "minor," or "juvenile" means a person under the age of 17 years.

II-a. "Commissioner" means the commissioner of the department of health and human services.

III. "Commitment" or "committed" refers to children who are in the custody of the center as a result of being adjudicated delinquent by a district or superior court and who are placed in the custody and care of the center for their minority.

IV. "Court" means the district court, unless otherwise indicated.

V. "Delinquent" or "delinquent child" means a minor who has committed an offense before reaching the age of 17 years which would be a felony or misdemeanor under the criminal code of this state if committed by an adult.

V-a. "Department" means the department of health and human services.

VI. "Detention" means the care of a minor in a physically restricted facility while awaiting further action by a court.

VI-a. [Repealed.]

VI-b. [Repealed.]

VII. "Minority" means the period of time before the age of 17 years and terminates on the seventeenth birthday.

VIII. "Parole" means a conditional release from the center which allows the child to serve the remainder of his or her commitment outside the center, supervised by a juvenile probation and parole officer, contingent upon satisfactory compliance with the terms and conditions set forth in the parole agreement.

Source.
   1981, 539:3. 1983, 291:1, 416:11, 12, 20. 1994, 212:2, eff. May 24, 1994. 1995, 181:13, 14, 20, 23, X, eff. July 1, 1995; 308:114–116, eff. Jan. 1, 1996. 1999, 219:12, eff. July 6, 1999. 2000, 294:8, eff. July 1, 2000. 2001, 286:19, eff. Sept. 14, 2001.

Amendments
   —2001. In pars. II-a and V-a, substituted "department of health and human services" for "department of youth development services".

   —2000. Paragraph VIII: Inserted "probation and" following "juvenile".

   —1999. Paragraph I: Deleted "subject to approval by the department at its next regular meeting" following "granted".

   —1995. Paragraph I: Chapter 181 substituted "department" for "division" following "approval by the".
   Paragraph II: Chapter 308 substituted "17" for "18".
   Paragraph II-a: Added by ch. 181.
   Paragraph V: Chapter 308 substituted "17" for "18".
   Paragraph V-a: Added by ch. 181.
   Paragraphs VI-a, VI-b: Repealed by ch. 181.
   Paragraph VII: Chapter 308 substituted "17" for "18" and "seventeenth" for "eighteenth".

   —1994. Substituted "youth, and families" for "and youth services" following "children" in pars. VI-a and VI-b.

   —1983. Paragraph I: Chapter 416:20 substituted "division" for "board of trustees".
   Paragraph I-a: Added by ch. 416:11.
   Paragraph VI-a: Added by ch. 416:12.
   Chapter 291 substituted "department of health and human services" for "department of health and welfare".
   Paragraph VI-b: Added by ch. 416:12.
   Chapter 291 substituted "department of health and human services" for "department of health and welfare".

Cross References.
   Delinquent generally, see RSA 169-B:2.

621:4. Duties Relative to Property.

   With the approval of the fiscal committee, the department shall be authorized to take, hold, and manage, in trust for the state, lands, money, or other property granted, devised, or bequeathed for the use of the center, and to sell and convey the lands, money, or other property and to invest the proceeds

therefrom in such investments as are legal for New Hampshire savings banks or in the physical plant of the center.

Source.
   1981, 539:3. 1983, 416:13. 1995, 181:20, eff. July 1, 1995.

Amendments
   —1995. Substituted "department" for "division" preceding "shall be authorized".

   —1983. Rewritten to the extent that a detailed comparison would be impracticable.

Cross References.
   Duties of division generally, see RSA 621:12.
   Investments of savings banks generally, see RSA 387.

621:5. Supervisory Control Over the Board of Trustees.

   [Repealed 1983, 416:37, IV, eff. July 1, 1983.]

Former section(s).
   Former RSA 621:5, which was derived from 1981, 539:3, related to supervision of the board of trustees of the center.

621:6. Books and Records of Account.

   All books of account and documents relating to the center shall be open to examination by the bank commissioner, the governor and council, or either legislative branch.

Source.
   1913, 101:4. PL 399:4. RL 463:4. 1953, 205:1, par. 3. RSA 621:3. 1981, 539:3, eff. June 30, 1981.

Cross References.
   Administration of special funds, see RSA 621:30.

621:7. Bylaws.

   The commissioner shall adopt and may amend bylaws for the governance of the center and for the management of its concerns, and shall prescribe in the bylaws the powers and duties of the persons connected with the center, in conformity with the rules of the department of personnel.

Source.
   1913, 101:5. PL 399:5. RL 463:5. 1953, 205:1, par. 4. RSA 621:4. 1981, 539:3, 416:20. 1994, 81:3, eff. July 1, 1994. 1995, 181:15, eff. July 1, 1995.

Amendments
   —1995. Substituted "commissioner" for "division" preceding "shall adopt" and deleted "administrator of the bureau of residential services and other" preceding "persons connected".

   —1994. Substituted "residential services" for "secure care" following "bureau of".

   —1983. Substituted "division" for "board of trustees".

621:8. Fire Code Compliance.

   The state fire marshal, with the assistance of the department of health and human services and the commissioner of the department of youth center development services, shall inspect all youth development facilities once every 6 months. In order to insure compliance with the fire safety rules which he is authorized to promulgate under RSA 153:5, the fire marshal shall assist the center administration in developing a plan to bring all center buildings into compliance with such rules.

Source.

1981, 539:3. 1983, 416:21. 1994, 81:3, eff. July 1, 1994. 1995, 181:21, eff. July 1, 1995; 310:181, eff. Nov. 1, 1995.

Revision note.

Inserted "of the department of youth development services" preceding "shall inspect" for purposes of clarity.

Amendments

—1995. Chapter 181 substituted "commissioner" for "administrator of the bureau of residential services" preceding "shall inspect" in the first sentence.

Chapter 310 substituted "department of health and human services" for "division of public health services".

—1994. Substituted "residential services" for "secure care" following "bureau of" in the first sentence.

—1983. Substituted "administrator of the bureau of secure care" for "superintendent of the center" in the first sentence.

Severability

—1995, 310 amendment. 1995, 310, which amended this section, was subject to a severability clause. See 1995, 310:186.

Construction of amendments

—1995, 310. 1995, 310:187, eff. Nov. 1, 1995, provided:

"Nothing in this act is intended to, nor shall it be construed as, mandating or assigning any new, expanded, or modified program or responsibility for any political subdivision in violation of part I, article 28-a of the constitution of the state of New Hampshire."

621:9. Care of Children.

The department shall ensure that children sent to the center are properly accounted for and are provided with those services to which they are entitled by statute, the bylaws of the center, and other directives.

Source.

1913, 101:6. PL 399:6. RL 463:6. 1953, 205:1, par. 6. RSA 621:5. 1981, 539:3. 1983, 416:20. 1995, 181:20, eff. July 1, 1995.

Amendments

—1995. Substituted "department" for "division" preceding "shall ensure".

—1983. Substituted "division" for "board of trustees".

Cross References.

Duties regarding children on release or in residential care, see RSA 621:20–22.

621:9-a. Extended Commitment at the Center.

Notwithstanding any provision of law to the contrary, a minor over whom the court has exercised jurisdiction pursuant to RSA 169-B:4, I or retained jurisdiction pursuant to RSA 169-B:4, V(c), may be committed or continue to be committed at the center pursuant to RSA 169-B:19, I(j) until the minor's eighteenth birthday.

Source.

2002, 170:5, eff. July 14, 2002.

621:10. Limits to Population at the Youth Development Center.

I. No residential facility at or under the control of the youth development center shall exceed, for a period of more than 24 hours, Sundays and holidays excluded, the maximum capacity for the facility as fixed by a population oversight panel composed of the fire marshal, the commissioner of the department of health and human services, and the assistant commissioner of transportation.

II. The panel shall meet annually during the month of October to review or modify population limits for each residential facility controlled by the center. Minutes of annual meetings shall be kept for at least 7 years and shall be maintained by the commissioner. If new facilities are made available or existing facilities are modified, the panel shall convene to fix the population limit before any residential use is made of the new or modified facility. Population limits shall be supplied to the commissioner in letter form at the conclusion of each meeting.

III. Population limits fixed by the panel for each facility shall be prominently displayed in the administrative area of the center.

IV. When youth development center facilities used for detention approach maximum population capability as fixed by the panel, the district courts shall be notified by the commissioner or his agent so that the courts may determine alternatives to detention at the center. Courts shall be notified to consider other facilities when all space in the detention houses is assigned. Expenses arising from alternative detention shall be borne by the city or town in which the minor resides at the time the petition is filed or, if such place of residence cannot be determined, by the city or town in which the alleged offense occurred. Either city or town shall have a right of action for these expenses against the person chargeable by law for the minor's support and necessities. A court may make such order as to reimbursement as may be reasonable and just, based on the person's ability to pay.

Source.

1981, 539:3. 1983, 416:21. 1994, 81:3, eff. July 1, 1994. 1995, 181:21, eff. July 1, 1995; 310:182, eff. Nov. 1, 1995.

Revision note.

In par. I, substituted "assistant commissioner of transportation" for "chief engineer of public works and highways" pursuant to 1985, 402:6. 1985, 402:2, I, provided for the abolition of the department of public works and highways and the transfer of the functions, powers, duties and officials of that department to the department of transportation as established by 1985, 402:1. The qualifications and general duties of the assistant commissioner of transportation, who is also known as the chief engineer of the department of transportation, are provided for in RSA 21-L:5.

In the fourth sentence of par. IV, inserted "city or" preceding "town" for purposes of conformity with the provisions of the third sentence of the paragraph.

Amendments

—1995. Paragraph I: Chapter 310 substituted "commissioner of the department of health and human services" for "director of the division of public health services".

Paragraph II: Chapter 181 substituted "commissioner" for "administrator of the bureau of residential services" following "maintained by the" in the second sentence and preceding "in letter" in the fourth sentence.

Paragraph IV: Chapter 181 substituted "commissioner" for "administrator of the bureau of residential services" following "notified by the" in the first sentence.

—**1994.** Substituted "residential services" for "secure care" following "bureau of" in the second and fourth sentences of par. II and in the first sentence of par. IV.

—**1983.** Paragraph II: Substituted "administrator of the bureau of secure care" for "superintendent" in the second and fourth sentences.

Paragraph IV: Substituted "administrator of the bureau of secure care" for "superintendent" in the first sentence.

Severability
—**1995, 310 amendment.** 1995, 310, which amended this section, was subject to a severability clause. See 1995, 310:186.

Construction of amendments
—**1995, 310.** 1995, 310:187, eff. Nov. 1, 1995, provided:
"Nothing in this act is intended to, nor shall it be construed as, mandating or assigning any new, expanded, or modified program or responsibility for any political subdivision in violation of part I, article 28-a of the constitution of the state of New Hampshire."

Cross References.
Liability of parents of children committed to center for support of child, see RSA 621:31.

NOTES TO DECISIONS

Maximum population
Superior court order providing that the population at the youth development center was not to exceed 107 juveniles under any circumstances at any time was ordered to be amended to allow the population to exceed that number to the extent permitted by paragraph I of this section, which permits the limit to be exceeded for periods not to exceed twenty-four hours and on Sundays and holidays. Harry P. v. Sheridan, 129 N.H. 391, 529 A.2d 894, 1987 N.H. LEXIS 191 (1987).

621:11. Superintendent.

[Repealed 1983, 416:37, V, eff. July 1, 1983.]

Former section(s).
Former RSA 621:11, which was derived from 1981, 539:3, related to the appointment of the superintendent of the center.

621:12. Department's Duties.

I. The department shall have charge of the lands, buildings, furniture, tools, implements, stock, provisions, and other property of the center. The department shall keep, in suitable books, regular and complete accounts of all receipts and expenditures, and of the debts, credits, contracts and property of the center, showing its income and expenses. Such accounts shall be specific and contain the dates and amounts of all receipts, and the date, quantity, and price of every article purchased or procured. There is specifically excepted from the foregoing such accounts and accountability as the department of administrative services otherwise requires. The de-

partment shall be responsible for the organization of the center to effect the maximum in economy and efficiency, and shall be the appointing authority for employees of the center. The department shall have custody and charge of the children committed to their care and shall provide maintenance to those children detained at the center awaiting further court action.

II. The commissioner shall develop and periodically revise a juvenile section of the comprehensive plan for the state's correctional system required by RSA 21-H:8, X which shall contain the elements required by law to be addressed in that plan. The juvenile section shall be fully integrated into the overall plan provided for by RSA 21-H:8, X.

Source.
1913, 101:12. PL 399:13. RL 463:13. 1953, 205:1, par. 7. RSA 621:7. 1981, 539:3. 1983, 416:54. 1995, 181:16, 20, eff. July 1, 1995.

Revision note.
Substituted "department's" for "division's" preceding "duties" in the section catchline for purposes of conformity with 1995, 181:20.

In par. II, substituted "RSA 21-H:8, X" for "RSA 21-G:8, X" in the first and third sentences in order to conform reference to current designation of provisions relating to department of corrections, which were originally enacted as RSA 21-G, but were redesignated as RSA 21-H pursuant to 1983, 461:34.

Amendments
—**1995.** Paragraph I: Substituted "department" for "division" preceding "shall" in the first, second, fifth and sixth sentences.

Paragraph II: Substituted "commissioner" for "director" preceding "shall develop" in the first sentence, deleted the former second sentence and deleted "but the director shall be solely responsible for its contents" following "RSA 21-H:8, X" in the present second sentence.

—**1983.** Chapter 416:54, III, rewrote section to the extent that a detailed comparison would be impracticable.

Contingent 1983 amendments
1983, 416:14, eff. July 1, 1983, and 461:32, eff. July 1, 1983, provided for amendment of this section. However, under the terms of 1983, 416:54, III, eff. July 1, 1983, the amendments did not become effective.

Cross References.
Department of administrative services, see RSA 21-I.
Department of corrections, see RSA 21-H.
Detention of children generally, see RSA 621:18.
Duties of division relating to property generally, see RSA 621:4.
Examination of accounts, see RSA 621:6.

621:13. Deputy Superintendent.

[Repealed 1983, 416:37, VI, eff. July 1, 1983.]

Former section(s).
Former RSA 621:13, which was derived from 1981, 539:3, related to the appointment and duties of the deputy superintendent of the center.

621:14. Compensation of Superintendent and Deputy.

[Repealed 1983, 416:37, VII, eff. July 1, 1983.]

Former section(s).
Former RSA 621:14, which was derived from 1981, 539:3, related to the salaries of the superintendent and deputy superintendent of the center.

621:15. Records of Children Committed or Detained.

The commissioner shall cause accurate records to be kept which shall contain, as a minimum, the child's name, address, age, parents' or guardians' names and addresses, commitment documents, and such other data as may be appropriate. The commissioner shall issue directives to ensure compliance with state and federal privacy laws and regulations.

Source.
1913, 101:13. PL 399:14. RL 463:14. 1953, 205:1, par. 9. RSA 621:10. 1981, 539:3. 1983, 416:21. 1994, 81:3, eff. July 1, 1994. 1995, 181:21, eff. July 1, 1995.

Amendments
—**1995.** Substituted "commissioner" for "administrator of the bureau of residential services" preceding "shall cause" in the first sentence and preceding "shall issue" in the second sentence.

—**1994.** Substituted "residential services" for "secure care" following "bureau of" in the first and second sentences.

—**1983.** Substituted "administrator of the bureau of secure care" for "superintendent" in the first and second sentences.

621:16. Erroneous Committal Elsewhere.

If a child shall be committed by error of any court to a correctional institution other than the center, the commissioner, the county attorney, the minor, or any person interested in the minor may apply to a justice of the superior court for an order for the commitment of the minor to the center for the term of minority, and the justice shall issue a new mittimus accordingly.

Source.
1913, 101:17. PL 399:18. RL 463:18. 1953, 205:1, par. 12. RSA 621:13. 1965, 256:8. 1973, 72:46. 1981, 539:3. 1983, 416:15. 1995, 181:19, eff. July 1, 1995.

Amendments
—**1995.** Substituted "commissioner" for "director" preceding "the county attorney".

—**1983.** Deleted "the trustees" following "other than the center" and "of the division of welfare" following "the director" and made other minor stylistic changes.

Cross References.
Discharge of minors erroneously committed to center, see RSA 621:26.
Receipt of juveniles committed by United States, see RSA 621:17.
Transfer from center of minors deemed dangerous or incorrigible, see RSA 621:27–29.

NOTES TO DECISIONS

Cited:
Cited in In re H., 121 N.H. 759, 433 A.2d 1336, 1981 N.H. LEXIS 372 (1981).

621:17. Committal by the United States.

The department may receive and maintain juvenile offenders sent to the center by virtue of any act of the Congress of the United States for such reasonable compensation as may be agreed upon with the United States authorities. The commissioner shall receive, detain, and treat these offenders as if they had been detained or committed by a juvenile proceeding in a New Hampshire court, except that no such juvenile shall be released to parole or furlough without approval of the United States authorities.

Source.
1913, 101:19. PL 399:20. RL 463:20. 1953, 205:1, par. 14. RSA 621:15. 1981, 539:3. 1983, 416:20, 21. 1994, 81:3, eff. July 1, 1994. 1995, 181:20, 21, eff. July 1, 1995.

Amendments
—**1995.** Substituted "department" for "division" preceding "may receive" in the first sentence and "commissioner" for "administrator of the bureau of residential services" preceding "shall receive" in the second sentence.

—**1994.** Substituted "residential services" for "secure care" following "bureau of" in the second sentence.

—**1983.** Chapter 416:20 substituted "division" for "trustees" in the first sentence.
Chapter 416:21 substituted "administrator of the bureau of secure care" for "superintendent" in the second sentence.

Cross References.
Releases and discharges generally, see RSA 621:19–25.

NOTES TO DECISIONS

Cited:
Cited in In re H., 121 N.H. 759, 433 A.2d 1336, 1981 N.H. LEXIS 372 (1981).

621:18. Detention.

Children detained at the center under RSA 169-B shall not be subject to the provisions of this chapter relative to release, administrative release to parole, parole, and discharge, but shall be subject to the transfer provided for incorrigibles until the court disposes of their cases.

Source.
1913, 101:20. PL 399:21. RL 463:21. 1953, 205:1, par. 15. RSA 621:16. 1981, 539:3, eff. June 30, 1981.

Cross References.
Releases and discharges generally, see RSA 621:19–25.
Transfer from center of minors deemed dangerous or incorrigible, see RSA 621:27–29.

NOTES TO DECISIONS

Cited:
Cited in In re H., 121 N.H. 759, 433 A.2d 1336, 1981 N.H. LEXIS 372 (1981).

621:19. Releases and Discharges.

I. The board may release any child committed to its care on administrative release to parole or parole, not to exceed the minority of the child, but no release shall be effective until provisions have been made for the proper care of the released child.

I-a. The board shall release, pursuant to paragraph I, any child committed to its care for a delinquency adjudication based on an offense other than a violent crime as defined in RSA 169-B:35-a no later than 6 months following the child's commitment pursuant to RSA 169-B:19, I(j). Release is not required under this paragraph during the period that a child is the subject of a delinquency petition which is awaiting adjudication or disposition. The department may seek a waiver of this provision from the court which ordered the commitment of the child, which may be granted by the court following written findings of fact supported by clear and convincing evidence that continued commitment is necessary to protect the safety of the minor or of the community. Such a waiver may be granted for up to 90 days. The number of waivers which may be granted in a particular case is not limited.

II. Any child may be discharged by the board whenever it finds the discharge to be in the best interest of the child and of the state. Every discharge shall be in writing and shall be a full release from all the penalties and disabilities created by the commitment and may be in such terms of commendation as the child deserves.

Source.
1913, 101:21. PL 399:22, 23. RL 463:22, 23. 1953, 205:1, par. 16. RSA 621:17. 1981, 539:3. 1983, 416:16, eff. July 1, 1983. 2013, 249:20, eff. September 22, 2013.

Amendments
—**2013.** The 2013 amendment added I-a.

—**1983.** Paragraph I: Substituted "board" for "trustees" and "its care" for "their care".
Paragraph II: Substituted "board" for "trustees" and "it finds" for "they find" in the first sentence.

Cross References.
Discharge of minors erroneously committed to center, see RSA 621:26.
Parole of delinquents generally, see RSA 170-H.
Payment of costs of support of children released from center, see RSA 621:20–22.
Procedure for releases, see RSA 621:23–25.
Release of children committed by United States, see RSA 621:17.
Release of children detained at center under RSA 169-B, see RSA 621:18.
Transfer from center of minors deemed dangerous or incorrigible, see RSA 621:27–29.

NOTES TO DECISIONS

Cited:
Cited in In re C., 120 N.H. 221, 412 A.2d 1037, 1980 N.H. LEXIS 263 (1980).

621:20. Contract for Board.

The department may contract to pay the board of a released child when the child, because of age or other conditions, is unable to earn board and no proper place may be found for him or her without payment of board.

Source.
1913, 101:22. PL 399:24. RL 463:24. 1953, 205:1, par. 17. RSA 621:18. 1981, 539:3. 1983, 416:20. 1995, 181:20, eff. July 1, 1995.

Amendments
—**1995.** Substituted "department" for "division" preceding "may contract".

—**1983.** Substituted "division" for "trustees".

Cross References.
Payments for board of children released to residential care facilities, see RSA 621:22.
Payments for board of released children generally, see RSA 621:21.

621:21. Payment of Board.

Payments of board shall be charged to the expenses of the center as if they were payments for boarding, instructing, and disciplining the child at the center, with a right of recovery against the legally liable unit in accordance with RSA 169-B:40 and RSA 621:31.

Source.
1913, 101:22. PL 399:25. RL 463:25. 1953, 205:1, par. 18. RSA 621:19. 1981, 539:3, eff. June 30, 1981.

Cross References.
Releases generally, see RSA 621:19.

621:22. Children in Residential Care.

Notwithstanding the provisions of any other statute, whenever the department releases a child and contracts for the child's residential care in a facility which has been approved by the department of health and human services, payment for the care shall be charged in accordance with RSA 169-B:40 and RSA 621:31.

Source.
1967, 174:1. 1981, 539:3. 1983, 291:1; 416:20. 1995, 181:20, eff. July 1, 1995.

Revision note.
Near the beginning of the section, substituted "releases" for "release" and "contracts" for "contract" for purposes of agreement with "division".

Amendments
—**1995.** Substituted "department" for "division" preceding "releases".

—**1983.** Chapter 416 substituted "division" for "trustees".
Chapter 291 substituted "department of health and human services" for "department of health and welfare".

Cross References.
Payments for support of released children generally, see RSA 621:20, 21.
Releases generally, see RSA 621:19.

Cited:
Cited in In re John M., 122 N.H. 1120, 454 A.2d 887, 1982 N.H. LEXIS 529 (1982).

621:23. Religious Preference.

In all questions of release, the department shall investigate the religious and moral character of those into whose custody a released child is placed.

Source.
1913, 101:24. PL 399:27. RL 463:27. 1953, 205:1, par. 19. RSA 621:20. 1981, 539:3. 1983, 416:20. 1995, 181:20, eff. July 1, 1995.

Amendments
—**1995.** Substituted "department" for "division" preceding "shall investigate".

—**1983.** Substituted "division" for "trustees".

Cross References.
Releases generally, see RSA 621:19.

621:24. Effect of Release.

No administrative release or parole of a child shall operate as a discharge of the child from the center. The department shall continue to have control of children on administrative release to parole or parole until they reach the age of 17 years or until age 18 if the child's commitment is extended pursuant to RSA 169-B:19, III-b, and the control conferred by the department upon others shall be conferred upon them as agents of the department, except where a child is discharged under RSA 621:19.

Source.
1913, 101:25. PL 399:28. RL 463:28. 1953, 205:1, par. 20. RSA 621:21. 1973, 72:42. 1981, 539:3. 1983, 416:20. 1995, 181:20, eff. July 1, 1995; 308:117, eff. Jan. 1, 1996. 2002, 170:6, eff. July 14, 2002.

Amendments
—**2002.** Inserted "or until age 18 if the child's commitment is extended pursuant to RSA 169-B:19, III-b" following "age of 17 years" in the second sentence.

—**1995.** Chapter 181 substituted "department" for "division" in three places in the second sentence.
Chapter 308 substituted "17 years" for "18 years" in the second sentence.

—**1983.** Substituted "division" for "trustees" in three places in the second sentence.

Applicability of 1995 amendment.
1995, 308:118, eff. Jan. 1, 1996, provided that the amendment to this section by 1995, 308:117, shall apply to offenses committed on or after Jan. 1, 1996.

Cross References.
Changes in conditions of release, see RSA 621:25.
Parole of delinquents generally, see RSA 170-H.
Releases generally, see RSA 621:19.

621:25. Remands and Changes in Conditions of Release.

The board or the commissioner, subject to the approval of the board, may modify or cancel any arrangements or conditions relative to release, other than discharge of a child, or may order a child remanded to the center, until the child reaches the age of 17 years, or until age 18 if the child's commitment is extended pursuant to RSA 169-B:19, III-b, or until the child is discharged under RSA 621:19. Under the direction of the board and subject to rules adopted by the commissioner the department shall:

I. Seek out proper places for children who are qualified for administrative release to parole or parole and keep in contact with these children after they are so released;

II. Make reports of its activities to the board when so required. When the department deems it to be in the best interest of a child on administrative release to parole or parole to be placed under different conditions, it shall report the case fully to the board, together with its recommendations, and the board shall act on the case in whatever manner seems to them to be in the best interests of the child; and

III. Remand children to the center with the same power and authority as provided to the board or under such terms and conditions as the board may prescribe.

Source.
1913, 101:25. PL 399:29. RL 463:29. 1953, 205:1, par. 21. RSA 621:22. 1973, 72:43. 1981, 539:3. 1983, 416:17. 1995, 181:19, 20, eff. July 1, 1995; 308:117, eff. Jan. 1, 1996. 2002, 170:6, eff. July 14, 2002.

Amendments
—**2002.** Inserted "until age 18 if the child's commitment is extended pursuant to RSA 169-B:19, III-b, or until the child" following "17 years, or" in the first sentence of the introductory paragraph.

—**1995.** Chapter 181 substituted "commissioner" for "director" preceding "subject" in the first sentence and "department" for "division" preceding "shall" in the second sentence of the introductory paragraph and substituted "department" for "division" preceding "deems" in par. II.
Chapter 308 substituted "17 years" for "18 years" in the first sentence of the introductory paragraph.

—**1983.** Rewritten to the extent that a detailed comparison would be impracticable.

Applicability of 1995 amendment.
1995, 308:118, eff. Jan. 1, 1996, provided that the amendment to this section by 1995, 308:117, shall apply to offenses committed on or after Jan. 1, 1996.

Cross References.
Effect of release generally, see RSA 621:24.

621:26. Discharge by Superior Court.

A minor erroneously committed to the center may be discharged by a justice of the superior court, upon petition of the county attorney or a selectman of the town or mayor of the city in which the minor resides, when continued commitment is unnecessary. Upon petition to the superior court by the division or the board, the court may review the case of a child, modify or amend the order of commitment, or order the release of the child.

Source.
1913, 183:1. PL 399:31. RL 463:31. 1953, 205:1, par. 22. RSA
621:23. 1981, 539:3. 1983, 416:18, eff. July 1, 1983.

Amendments
—**1983.** Substituted "the division or the board" for "the superintendent or by an agent of the board of trustees" in the second
sentence.

Cross References.
Commitment of minors erroneously committed to other correc-
tional institutions, see RSA 621:16.
Discharges generally, see RSA 621:19.

621:27. Incorrigibles.

I. If a minor committed or detained at the center
shall be found by the department to be incorrigible
and dangerous to the discipline of the center, the
department may order the minor to be transferred
and committed to another institution with facilities
for minors for a time not exceeding the time when
the commitment to the center expires.

II. The department shall cause an attested copy
of its order to be served on the minor and his or her
father or mother or guardian, or other person standing in loco parentis, either personally or by certified
mail. No defect or insufficiency in the service of the
copy shall invalidate the order of transfer and
commitment. The minor, or any interested person in
the minor's behalf, may, within 30 days from the
entry of the order, petition the superior court or any
justice of the superior court for a review of the
findings and order of transfer and commitment to
determine whether the order was justified. The
court or justice shall immediately fix a time and
place for hearing and make such orders relative to
the giving of notice of the hearing as may be proper
and, upon hearing all relevant evidence, an order
shall be entered as justice may require.

III. The minor may be transferred to any institution upon payment by the center of a reasonable sum
for the minor's care and maintenance, and for such
time, not exceeding the minority, as the department
may determine. The center shall have the right of
recovery in accordance with RSA 169-B:40 and RSA
621:31.

Source.
1913, 101:30. PL 399:37. RL 463:37. 1953, 205:1, pars. 23, 24.
RSA 621:24, 25. 1963, 172:1. 1981, 539:3. 1983, 416:20. 1995,
181:20, eff. July 1, 1995.

Revision note.
In par. II, substituted "its" for "their" preceding "order" in the
first sentence for purposes of agreement with "division".

Amendments
—**1995.** Paragraph I: Substituted "department" for "division"
preceding "to be incorrigible" and "may order".
Paragraph II: Substituted "department" for "division" preceding
"shall cause" in the first sentence.
Paragraph III: Substituted "department" for "division" preceding
"may determine" in the first sentence.

—**1983.** Paragraph I: Substituted "division" for "trustees" in
two places.
Paragraph II: Substituted "division" for "trustees" in the first
sentence.

Paragraph III: Substituted "division" for "trustees" in the first
sentence.

Cross References.
Terms and conditions of transfers generally, see RSA 621:28.
Transfer orders, see RSA 621:29.
Transfers of children detained under RSA 169-B, see RSA 621:18.

621:28. Modification of Transfer.

The terms and condition of transfer and commitment of a child pursuant to RSA 621:27 may be
modified at the discretion of the department, as with
released children.

Source.
1913, 101:30. PL 399:39. RL 463:39. 1953, 205:1, par. 25. RSA
621:26. 1981, 539:3. 1983, 416:20. 1995, 181:20, eff. July 1, 1995.

Revision note.
For purposes of clarity, inserted "pursuant to RSA 621:27" following"commitment of a child".

Amendments
—**1995.** Substituted "department" for "division" following "discretion of the".

—**1983.** Substituted "division" for "trustees".

Cross References.
Changes in conditions of release generally, see RSA 621:25.
Transfers generally, see RSA 621:27.

621:29. Orders.

A written order of the commissioner shall authorize the keeper of any state, county, city, or town
facility to receive and keep, or to discharge into the
keeping of an employee of the center, any child
transferred pursuant to RSA 621:27.

Source.
1913, 101:30. PL 399:40. RL 463:40. 1953, 205:1, par. 26. RSA
621:27. 1981, 539:3. 1983, 416:21. 1994, 81:3, eff. July 1, 1994.
1995, 181:21, eff. July 1, 1995.

Revision note.
For purposes of clarity, added "transferred pursuant to RSA
621:27" following "any child".

Amendments
—**1995.** Substituted "commissioner" for "administrator of the
bureau of residential services" preceding "shall authorize".

—**1994.** Substituted "residential services" for "secure care"
following "bureau of".

—**1983.** Substituted "administrator of the bureau of secure
care" for "superintendent".

Cross References.
Terms and conditions of transfers, see RSA 621:28.
Transfers generally, see RSA 621:27.

621:30. Children's Funds.

Accounts shall be established to administer the
following funds:

I. The children's benefit fund, a budgetary line
item, shall be used for allowances to residents,
payment to residents for their services, funding for
resident projects, and other expenditures directly
benefiting the residents as determined by the

commissioner.

II. (a) Except as provided in subparagraph II(b), the personal funds of residents in their possession while at the center shall be transferred to and held in trust by the commissioner in a pooled account kept in approved facilities in accordance with the manual of procedures of the department of administrative services. Notwithstanding RSA 6:11 or any other provision of law, any interest on such pooled account:

(1) Accrued prior to July 1, 1994, shall be appropriated to the department and shall be expended only for the direct benefit of the residents.

(2) Accruing after July 1, 1994, shall be the property of the individual residents as determined by the commissioner.

(b) Residents who receive social security benefits or veterans administration benefits, who are receiving regular income from sources other than the resident's own labor, or whose personal funds in their possession while at the center total more than $200, shall have individual bank accounts established, to be administered for the residents by the commissioner. Notwithstanding RSA 6:11 or any other provision of law, the interest accrued or accruing on such individual accounts shall be the property of the individual resident.

III. The special projects fund shall consist of moneys from gifts, bequests, and miscellaneous contributions and shall be administered by the commissioner for the direct benefit of residents or in accordance with donor instructions. Notwithstanding RSA 6:11 or any other provision of law and unless otherwise prohibited by donor instructions, any interest accrued or accruing on the special project fund shall be continually appropriated to the department and shall be expended only for the direct benefit of the residents.

IV. Trust funds shall be administered separately and held in the state treasury, with the state treasurer designated as custodian.

V. In addition to the accounts described in paragraphs II and III of this section, the commissioner may establish such other accounts for the deposit of residents' personal funds, proceeds of program activities, donations, and other miscellaneous contributions or moneys as are necessary to meet the needs of the center. Such accounts shall be kept in approved facilities in accordance with the manual of procedures of the department of administrative services. Notwithstanding RSA 6:11 or any other provision of law, any interest accrued or accruing on such accounts shall be continually appropriated to the department and shall be expended only for the direct benefit of the residents, except that the interest accrued or accruing on such accounts established with the personal funds of residents shall be the property of the individual residents as determined by the commissioner.

Source.
1929, 19:1. RL 463:42, 43. 1953, 205:1, pars. 27, 28. RSA 621:28, 29. 1981, 539:3. 1983, 416:21. 1985, 399:3, II. 1994, 81:1–3, eff. July 1, 1994. 1995, 181:20, 21, eff. July 1, 1995.

Amendments
—1995. Substituted "commissioner" for "administrator of the bureau of residential services" wherever it appeared and "department" for "division" in par. II(a)(1), in the second sentence of par. II and in the third sentence of par. V.

—1994. Paragraph I: Substituted "residential services" for "secure care" following "bureau of".
Paragraph II: Rewritten to the extent that a detailed comparison would be impracticable.
Paragraph III: Substituted "residential services" for "secure care" following "bureau of" in the first sentence and added the second sentence.
Paragraph V: Added.

—1985. Paragraph II: Substituted "department of administrative services" for "department of administration and control" at the end of the first sentence.

—1983. Paragraph I: Substituted "administrator of the bureau of secure care" for "superintendent".
Paragraph II: Substituted "administrator of the bureau of secure care" for "superintendent" in the first and second sentences.
Paragraph III: Substituted "administrator of the bureau of secure care" for "superintendent".

Cross References.
Examination of books and accounts, see RSA 621:6.
Powers and duties of division as to lands, money or property generally, see RSA 621:4, 12.

621:31. Parents or Estate of Child to Contribute to Costs.

I. If it appears that the parent or estate of a child who is subject to the provisions of this chapter is able to contribute to the support of the child, the court may enter an order requiring the parent, guardian, or executor of the child's estate to pay a reasonable sum toward the support, education, or maintenance of the child.

II. The order of the court shall direct the money to be paid to the probation department serving that court for disbursement to the state of New Hampshire general fund, from which it shall be further disbursed to the New Hampshire youth development center, upon its request.

III. On application and on such notice as the court may direct, the court may make modifications in the requirement for contribution as justice may require. The court may require security for payment of sums due and shall have the power of a court of equity to enforce its orders. Failure of the parent, guardian, or executor to comply with the orders of the court shall constitute prima facie evidence of contempt of court and shall be admissible as evidence in contempt proceedings.

Source.
1981, 539:3, eff. June 30, 1981.

Revision note.
In par. II, substituted "from which" for "where" preceding "it shall be further disbursed" for purposes of clarity.

Cross References.

Recovery of costs of return to center of children absent without authority from center, see RSA 621:34.

Right of recovery for payments for board of children released from center generally, see RSA 621:21.

Right of recovery for payments for children released to residential care facilities, see RSA 621:22.

Right of recovery for payments for minors transferred to other institutions, see RSA 621:27.

Right of towns and cities to recover expenses of support of children from persons legally chargeable for support, see RSA 621:10.

RESEARCH REFERENCES

New Hampshire Trial Bar News.

For article, "Presumptions in New Hampshire Law—A Guide Through the Impenetrable Jungle (Part 1)," see 10 N.H. Trial Bar News 55, 60 n.82 (Winter 1990).

621:32. Contraband.

No person shall have in his or her possession, with the intent to deliver or otherwise convey to any child committed to or detained at the center, any article contrary to the rules of the center. No person shall deposit or conceal any such item in or about the center, in any building or vehicle, or on any land adjacent to the center, with the intent that a resident of the center shall receive it. No person shall convey out of the center any article contrary to the rules of the center. A person who violates this section shall be guilty of a class B felony.

Source.

1981, 539:3, eff. June 30, 1981.

Cross References.

Classification of crimes, see RSA 625:9.

Sentences, see RSA 651.

621:33. Authority to Apprehend.

Certain employees of the department who satisfactorily complete a prescribed course of instruction and are certified by the commissioner shall be designated as ex officio constables to possess general police powers, including the power of arrest, but limited as follows:

I. These powers shall extend to employees only during the period of duty with the department.

II. These powers shall extend only to property controlled by the department with 3 exceptions:

(a) When an employee is in hot pursuit of a person who has committed a crime while on grounds, in buildings, or in vehicles controlled by the department;

(b) When an on duty employee observes a child whom the employee knows has escaped from the department or failed to return from furlough, or who is in violation of the terms of parole; or

(c) When an employee is transporting a detained or committed child to another location.

Source.

1981, 539:3. 1983, 416:21. 1994, 81:3, eff. July 1, 1994. 1999, 219:13, eff. July 6, 1999.

Amendments

—1999. Substituted "commissioner" for "administrator of the bureau of residential services" preceding "shall be" in the introductory paragraph and "department" for "center" wherever it appeared throughout the section.

—1994. Substituted "residential services" for "secure care" following "bureau of" in the introductory paragraph.

—1983. Substituted "administrator of the bureau of secure care" for "superintendent" in the introductory paragraph.

Cross References.

Arrests generally, see RSA 594.

Fresh pursuit, see RSA 614.

Parole of delinquents generally, see RSA 170-H.

Recovery of transportation costs, see RSA 621:34.

621:34. Reimbursement for Transportation Costs.

When a child who is committed to the center escapes or is in violation of the parole agreement by being absent from placement, and is apprehended at a distance from the center requiring expenditure of funds for transportation to the center, the commissioner may petition a court having jurisdiction to conduct a hearing under RSA 621:31 to assess reimbursement for travel expenses.

Source.

1981, 539:3. 1983, 416:21. 1994, 81:3, eff. July 1, 1994. 1995, 181:21, eff. July 1, 1995.

Amendments

—1995. Substituted "commissioner" for "administrator of the bureau of residential services" preceding "may petition".

—1994. Substituted "residential services" for "secure care" following "bureau of".

—1983. Substituted "administrator of the bureau of secure care" for "superintendent".

Cross References.

Apprehension of children by employees of center generally, see RSA 621:33.

Parole of delinquents generally, see RSA 170-H.

621:35. Rulemaking Authority.

[Repealed 1999, 219:17, II, eff. July 6, 1999.]

Former section(s).

Former RSA 621:35, which was derived from 1981, 539:3; and 1983, 416:19, related to the rulemaking authority of the commissioner of health and human services over the youth development center.

CHAPTER 621-A

YOUTH SERVICES CENTER

SECTION
621-A:1. Definitions.
621-A:2. Establishment. [Repealed.]
621-A:3. Commissioner; Appointment; Qualification; Compensation. [Repealed.]
621-A:4. Powers and Duties of Commissioner.
621-A:5. Purposes.
621-A:6. Admission.
621-A:7. Records.
621-A:8. Rulemaking. [Repealed.]

Advisory Board

SECTION
621-A:9.   Juvenile Justice Advisory Board Established.
621-A:10.   Terms of Office; Organization.
621-A:11.   Duties of the Advisory Board.

Amendments
—2001. 2001, 286:11, eff. Sept. 14, 2001, substituted "Youth Services Center" for "Youth Development Services" in the chapter heading.

Restructuring of Department of Youth Development Services.
2001, 286:22, eff. September 14, 2001, provided: "The restructuring of the department of youth development services as a unit of the department of health and human services shall occur within 60 days of the effective date of this act [September 14, 2001]."

Transfer of functions, powers, duties, etc., from the department of youth development services to the department of health and human services.
2001, 286:1, eff. Sept. 14, 2001, provided that the functions, powers, duties, personnel, records, property and funds of department of youth development services are transferred to the department of health and human services.

Transfer of functions, powers, duties, etc., from the youth services center to the department of youth development services.
1995, 181:24, eff. July 1, 1995, provided that the functions, powers, duties, personnel, records, property and funds of the youth services center are transferred to the department of youth development services.

Repeal of former subdivision heading.
2001, 286:21, V, eff. September 14, 2001, provided for the repeal of the subdivision heading "Youth Services Center" which had preceded RSA 621-A:5.

621-A:1. Definitions.

In this chapter:

I. "Commissioner" means the commissioner of the department of health and human services.

II. "Department" means the department of health and human services.

III. "Detention" means the care of a child in a physically restricted facility while awaiting further action by a court.

Source.
1995, 181:17, eff. July 1, 1995. 2001, 286:12, eff. Sept. 14, 2001.

Amendments
—2001. Substituted "health and human services" for "youth development services" in pars. I and II and added par. III.

621-A:2. Establishment.

[Repealed 2001, 286:21, III, eff. September 14, 2001.]

Former section(s).
Former RSA 621-A:2, which was derived from 1995, 181:17, related to the establishment of the department of youth development services.

621-A:3. Commissioner; Appointment; Qualification; Compensation.

[Repealed 2001, 286:21, IV, eff. September 14, 2001.]

Former section(s).
Former RSA 621-A:3, which was derived from 1995, 181:17, related to the appointment, qualifications, and compensation of the commissioner of youth development services.

621-A:4. Powers and Duties of Commissioner.

I. The commissioner shall maintain the youth services center for such purposes as the commissioner shall determine, which may include, but are not limited to, the purposes described in RSA 621-A:5.

II. The commissioner shall adopt rules under RSA 541-A relative to:

(a) The discharge of any child admitted to the center when further detention is either unnecessary or undesirable.

(b) The return of the child to such custody as may be determined appropriate or as ordered by the court.

Source.
1995, 181:17, eff. July 1, 1995. 1998, 184:3, eff. Aug. 14, 1998. 1999, 219:14, eff. July 6, 1999. 2001, 286:13, eff. Sept. 14, 2001.

Editor's note.
In the introductory paragraph of par. II, substituted "RSA 541-A" for "RSA 541-a" to correct a typographical error.

Amendments
—2001. Rewrote this section to the extent that a detailed comparison would be impracticable.

—1999. Paragraph IV: Rewritten to the extent that a detailed comparison would be impracticable.

—1998. Paragraph V: Added.

621-A:5. Purposes.

The youth services center may be used for the following purposes:

I. Receiving facility for the temporary detention of children who are awaiting disposition of the court pursuant to RSA 169-B:14.

II. Receiving facility for children determined educationally disabled pursuant to RSA 186-C.

Source.
1995, 181:17, eff. July 1, 1995.

621-A:6. Admission.

Children, subject to proceedings in juvenile court, may be admitted to the youth services center for temporary detention while awaiting disposition of the court pursuant to RSA 169-B:14, for educational services pursuant to RSA 186-C, RSA 169-B, RSA 169-C, or RSA 169-D, only upon prior approval of the commissioner.

Source.
1995, 181:17, eff. July 1, 1995. 2001, 286:14, eff. Sept. 14, 2001.

Amendments
—2001. Deleted the par. I designation and made stylistic changes in that paragraph and deleted former par. II concerning discharge from the youth services center.

621-A:7. Records.

I. Full and complete records shall be kept by the commissioner of the care and study of each child admitted to the youth services center. The records shall not be open to the inspection of any persons not on the staff of the commissioner except that such records shall be available, by court order, to any court having competent jurisdiction of the child in any matter pending in this state or to such person or persons as may be authorized by the court. Notwithstanding any other provision of law, exchange of medical or psychiatric records between the Philbrook center and the department shall be permitted.

II. Nothing in this section shall be construed to prohibit the disclosure by the commissioner to the legislature or the public of the generalized facts relating to the children admitted to the youth services center, together with conclusions as to the proper means for the control and child guidance for such children, provided that the names and identities of particular children shall not be disclosed.

Source.
1995, 181:17, eff. July 1, 1995.

621-A:8. Rulemaking.

[Repealed 2001, 286:21, VI, eff. September 14, 2001.]

Former section(s).
RSA 621-A:8, which was derived from 1995, 181:17; and 1999, 219:15, related to the rulemaking authority of the department of youth development services.

Advisory Board

621-A:9. Juvenile Justice Advisory Board Established.

I. There is hereby established a juvenile justice advisory board. The board shall act in an advisory capacity and make recommendations to the commissioner relative to programs and services provided to children at the youth development center and the youth services center.

II. The board shall be composed of the following members:

(a) Four members from the house of representatives, one of whom shall be a member of the house finance committee, 2 of whom shall be members of the children and family law committee, and one of whom shall be a member of the criminal justice and public safety committee, appointed by the speaker of the house of representatives.

(b) One member from the senate, appointed by the president of the senate.

(c) The director of the unit of juvenile justice services within the department.

(d) A representative of the department of health and human services who is responsible for mental health services, designated by the commissioner of health and human services.

(e) The commissioner of the department of education or designee.

(f) One district or family court judge, appointed by the administrative justice of the district courts.

(g) Two human services administrators, one from an urban county and one from a rural county, appointed by the executive director or other appropriate appointing authority of the New Hampshire Association of Counties.

(h) Seven members, appointed by the governor with the advice and consent of the council, which shall include 2 members representing the interests of business and industry, 2 parents of children who are receiving or have received services from the department, one member of state or local law enforcement, and 2 members from the general public.

(i) One juvenile probation and parole officer, appointed by the commissioner of the department of health and human services.

(j) [Repealed.]

III. Members of the advisory board shall serve without compensation provided that legislative members shall receive mileage at the legislative rate while attending to the duties of the board.

Source.
2000, 294:6, eff. July 1, 2000. 2001, 30:1–3, eff. June 8, 2001; 286:15–17, eff. Sept. 14, 2001. 2009, 272:1, eff. July 29, 2009. 2010, 368:28, IX, eff. December 31, 2010.

Amendments
—2010. The 2010 amendment deleted II(j).

—2009. The 2009 amendment, in II(a), substituted "Four members" for "Three members" at the beginning and added "2 of whom shall be members of the children and family law committee, and one of whom shall be a member of the criminal justice and public safety committee"; deleted "who shall serve as an ex officio member" at the end of II(c) and II(e); rewrote II(d), which formerly read: "The commissioner of the department of health and human services or designee, who shall serve as an ex officio member"; in II(h), substituted "Seven members" for "Six members" at the beginning and "2 members" for "one member"; and rewrote II(j), which formerly read: "One member of the house children and family law committee, appointed by the speaker of the house."

—2001. Section catchline: Chapter 286 substituted "Juvenile Justice" for "Department of Youth Development Services".
Paragraph I: Chapter 286 substituted "juvenile justice" for "department of youth development services" in the first sentence and "at the youth development center and the youth services center" for "referred to the department pursuant to RSA 169-B" in the second sentence.
Paragraph II(a): Chapter 30 substituted "three members" for "two members".
Paragraph II(c): Chapter 30 deleted "or designee" following "services".

Chapter 286 substituted "director of the unit of juvenile justice services within the department" for "commissioner of the department of youth development".

Paragraph II(i): Added by ch. 30.

Paragraph II(j): Added by ch. 286.

621-A:10. Terms of Office; Organization.

I. The legislative members and the members listed in RSA 621-A:9, II(c)–(e) shall serve terms which are coterminous with their terms in office. The remaining members shall serve 3-year terms.

II. Each appointed member of the advisory board shall hold office until a successor is appointed and qualified. The appointment of successors for the filling of vacancies for unexpired terms shall be by appointment in the same manner as the original appointment. Non-legislative appointed members shall not serve more than 2 consecutive terms.

III. The advisory board shall elect its own chairperson and officers annually. The board shall meet as deemed necessary, provided that the board shall meet at least 4 times per year.

Source.
2000, 294:6, eff. July 1, 2000. 2009, 272:1, eff. July 29, 2009.

Amendments
—**2009.** The 2009 amendment, in I, substituted "RSA 621-A:9, II(c)–(e)" for "RSA 621-A:9, II(c)–(f)" in the first sentence, deleted the former second sentence, which read: "The members listed in RSA 621-A:12, II(g) shall serve for 3 years," and in the second sentence, substituted "The remaining" for "Three of the members listed in RSA 621-A:9, II(h) shall serve for 4 years, and 3" and "3-year terms" for "for 3 years"; added the last sentence of II; and in the second sentence of III, deleted "monthly, or" preceding "as deemed" and substituted "4 times per year" for "once every 3 months."

621-A:11. Duties of the Advisory Board.

I. The advisory board shall act in an advisory capacity to assist the commissioner of the department of health and human services relative to juvenile justice programs and services provided to children at the youth development center [and] and other juvenile justice facilities. The board may also provide advice and input on fiscal and budgetary matters related to such facilities, the availability of state and federal grants, business partnerships, and other funding sources available to the department for such facilities.

I-a. The board shall seek information from the director of the division of juvenile justice services in the department of health and human services concerning the successes and challenges relative to the state's juvenile justice programs and services.

I-b. The board shall be available to address emergent issues identified by the commissioner of health and human services, the director of the division of juvenile justice services, the chair of the advisory board, or any board member. In furtherance of this paragraph, the board may solicit comments from the public or any other entities as it deems appropriate.

II. Beginning in December 2010, and biennially thereafter, the board shall submit a written report to the speaker of the house, the president of the senate, the governor, and the following legislative committees: the house children and family law committee, the house criminal justice and safety committee, and the senate judiciary committee. The report shall detail the activities of the board and any recommendations made by the board to the department relative to juvenile justice services.

Source.
2000, 294:6, eff. July 1, 2000. 2001, 286:18, eff. Sept. 14, 2001. 2009, 272:1, eff. July 29, 2009.

Amendments
—**2009.** The 2009 amendment substituted "and other juvenile justice facilities" for "the youth services center" in the first sentence of I; added I-a and I-b; in II, in the first sentence, substituted "December 2010, and biennially" for "December 2000, and annually" and "and the following legislative committees: the house children and family law committee, the house criminal justice and safety committee, and the senate judiciary committee" for "detailing" and added "The report shall detail" at the beginning of the second sentence; and made a related change.

—**2001.** Paragraph I: Rewritten to the extent that a detailed comparison would be impracticable.

Paragraph II: Added "relative to juvenile justice services" following "department".

CHAPTER 622

THE STATE PRISONS

General Provisions

SECTION

622:1.   General Penitentiary. [Repealed.]

622:2.   Superintendence.

622:2-a.   Wardens.

622:2-b.   Superintendent, Lakes Region Facility. [Repealed.]

622:3..   Deputy Warden. [Omitted.]

622:4..   Compensation. [Omitted.]

622:5.   Powers of Commissioner of Corrections.

622:6.   Visitation.

622:7.   Duties of Commissioner of Corrections.

622:7-a.   Prisoner's Fund.

622:7-b.   Victims' Fund.

622:8.   Committals.

622:9.   Mittimus; Return.

622:10.   United States Prisoners.

622:11.   Illegal Privileges.

622:12.   Assaults by Life Prisoners. [Repealed.]

622:13.   Assaults by Other Prisoners. [Repealed.]

622:14.   Discipline.

622:15.   Communication by Inmates with Commissioner of Corrections, etc.

622:16.   Supplies for Discharged Prisoners.

622:17.   Committal of One Held on Civil Process.

622:18.   Detention of One Held on Civil Process.

622:19.   Execution on Judgment against Commissioner of Corrections.

622:20.   Failure of Commissioner of Corrections to Pay Judgment.

622:21.   Appraisers. [Repealed.]

622:22.   Religious Ministrations.

622:23.   Religious Preferences.

Delivery of Articles to Prisoners

622:24.   Regulations.

622:25.   Penalty.

Prison Labor and Its Products

622:26.   Sales of Prison Products.

SECTION
622:27.   Sale of Prison-Made Goods.
622:28.   Provision of Products for State Agencies.
622:28-a. Industries Inventory Account.
622:28-b. Correctional Industries Advisory Board. [Repealed.]
622:29.   Prisoner's Earnings, etc.
622:30.   Source of Payment.
622:31.   Application of Earnings.
622:31-a. Medical Care; Inmate Copayment Required.
622:32.   Effect of Misconduct.

Care and Custody of Female Convicts

622:33.   Contracts Authorized. [Repealed.]
622:33-a. Care and Custody of Female Prisoners.
622:34.   Transfer of Prisoners. [Repealed.]
622:34-a. Expenses of Confinement.
622:35.   Good Behavior.
622:36.   Return or Transfer of Convicts.
622:37.   Cost.

State Prison Security Force

622:38.   Prison Security Force.
622:39.   Authority.

Secure Psychiatric Unit

622:40.   Definitions.
622:41.   Unit Established.
622:42.   Coordination of Responsibility. [Repealed.]
622:43.   Staffing.
622:44.   Rulemaking.
622:45.   Commitment.
622:46.   Treatment Standards.
622:47.   Medical Records.
622:48.   Discharge.
622:49.   Notification of Granting of Off-Grounds Privileges by
           Director.
622:50.   Parole.
622:51.   Investigation of Detention.
622:52.   Conduct of Hearings for Commitment, Detention, or
           Parole.

Reimbursement of Cost of Care by Inmates

622:53.   Definitions.
622:54.   Financial Resources Form.
622:55.   Cost of Care Reimbursement by Inmate.
622:56.   Post-Imprisonment Action for Reimbursement of Cost
           of Care.
622:57.   Legal Costs.
622:58.   Deposit of Recovered Moneys.

Amendments

—1998. 1998, 386:16, eff. Aug. 26, 1998, substituted "prisons" for "prison" in the chapter heading.

Transfer of functions, powers and duties of state prison to department of corrections.

1983, 461:6, eff. July 1, 1983, provided: "All functions, powers and duties of the probation department, the parole department, and the state prison are hereby transferred to the department of corrections, except as specified elsewhere in this act [1983, ch. 461]."

Transfer of state prison and satellite facilities to department of corrections; assignment and operation of other similar institutions and agencies.

1983, 461:5, eff. July 1, 1983, provided: "The facilities of the state prison and its satellite facilities are hereby transferred to the control of the department of corrections. Any state facilities established or acquired for any purpose similar to the above institutions and agencies shall be assigned to, maintained and operated by the department of corrections."

Validity of previously adopted orders or rules.

1983, 461:8, eff. July 1, 1983, provided: "This act shall not affect the orders and rules previously made or adopted by any division, bureau, board, or other agency, the functions, powers, and duties of which have been reassigned or transferred to the department of corrections or to any agency designated, continued, or constituted under this act."

Compliance with requirements of federal law.

1983, 461:11, eff. July 1, 1983, provided: "This act shall not be construed or applied in any way which will prevent full compliance by the department of corrections or any agency designated, continued or established under this act with the requirements of any act of the Congress of the United States or any regulation made thereunder by which federal aid or other federal assistance has been or is hereafter made available."

Sunset provisions.

For provisions relating to review and renewal or termination of state agencies and programs, see RSA 17-G:5 and notes thereunder.

Cross References.

Approved absences from state prison, see RSA 623-A.
County correctional facilities, see RSA 30-B.
Department of corrections, see RSA 21-H.
Department of justice, see RSA 21-M.
Interstate Corrections Compact, see RSA 622-B.
New England Interstate Corrections Compact, see RSA 622-A.
Procedure after exposure of public safety workers to infectious disease, see RSA 141-G.
Sentences generally, see RSA 651.
Temporary removal of prisoners from prison, see RSA 623.
Youth development center, see RSA 621.

NOTES TO DECISIONS

Cited:

Cited in State v. Johnson, 96 N.H. 4, 69 A.2d 515, 1949 N.H. LEXIS 3 (1949).

General Provisions

622:1. General Penitentiary.

[Repealed 1999, 296:11, eff. Sept. 14, 1999.]

Former section(s).

Former RSA 622:1, which was derived from RS 227:1; CS 242:1; GS 270:1; GL 288:1; PS 285:1; PL 400:1; RL 464:1; RSA 622:1; and 1998, 386:3, related to the general penitentiary.

622:2. Superintendence.

The state prisons shall be under the superintendence and general management of the commissioner of corrections.

Source.

RS 227:2, 4. CS 242:2, 4. GS 270:2, 4. 1870, 22:1, 3. GL 288:2, 4. PS 285:2. PL 400:2. 1927, 101:1. RL 464:2. 1998, 386:16, eff. Aug. 26, 1998.

Revision note.

At the beginning of the section, substituted "the state prison" for "it" for purposes of clarity.

At the end of the section, substituted "the commissioner of corrections" for "a warden" pursuant to 1983, 461:3, which provided for the abolition of the position of warden of the state prison and the transfer of all powers, duties, and functions of that position to the commissioner of corrections. See RSA 21-H.

Amendments

—1998. Substituted "prisons" for "prison".

Cross References.
Powers and duties of commissioner of corrections generally, see RSA 21-H:8.

622:2-a. Wardens.

The wardens of the New Hampshire state prisons shall serve at the pleasure of the commissioner and shall be unclassified employees qualified by education and experience.

Source.
1996, 159:5, eff. July 1, 1996. 1999, 296:8, eff. Sept. 14, 1999.

Amendments
—1999. Substituted "wardens" for "warden" in two places and "prisons" for "prison for men" preceding "shall serve" and deleted "an" preceding "unclassified" and substituted "employees" for "employee" thereafter.

Terms of office for incumbent warden and superintendent.
1996, 159:7, eff. July 1, 1996, provided that the warden and superintendent of the state prison for women shall serve out their current terms of office and shall thereafter serve as provided for in this section, RSA 622:2-b and 622:33-a, II.

622:2-b. Superintendent, Lakes Region Facility.

[Repealed 1999, 296:12, eff. Sept. 14, 1999.]

Former section(s).
RSA 622:2-b, which was derived from 1996, 159:5, related to the superintendent of the lakes region facility.

622:3. Deputy Warden.

[Omitted.]

RSA 622:3, which was derived from RS 227:9; CS 242:9; GS 270:9; GL 288:9; PS 285:4; PL 400:5; RL 464:5; and 1953, 265:14, related to the appointment, powers and duties of the deputy warden, and was omitted as obsolete in view of 1983, 461:3, which provided for the abolition of the position of deputy warden of the state prison and the transfer of the powers, duties and functions of that position to the commissioner of corrections. See RSA 21-H.

622:4. Compensation.

[Omitted.]

RSA 622:4, which was derived from 1953, 265:1, related to the compensation of the warden and deputy warden of the state prison, and was omitted as obsolete in view of 1983, 461:3, which provided for the abolition of the positions of warden and deputy warden of the state prison and the transfer of the powers, duties and functions of those positions to the commissioner of corrections. See RSA 21-H.

622:5. Powers of Commissioner of Corrections.

The commissioner of corrections, subject to the supervision and direction of the governor and council, shall have power:

I. To appoint all officers and servants necessary for the management of the prisons, and to remove them, subject to the regulations of the state personnel commission.

II. To define the powers, duties, and compensation of such officers and agents, subject to the regulations of the state personnel commission.

III. To establish bylaws for the government of the prisons.

IV. To provide for the purchase of articles necessary for the use of the prisons and for the health and comfort of the officers and prisoners.

V. To provide for the sale of articles manufactured in the prisons or not necessary for the use thereof.

VI. To make contracts, if expedient, for the support and employment of the prisoners or any portion of them, or to provide such other employment for the prisoners as they may deem desirable; to organize, conduct, and manage such industries as in his judgment may be best adapted to the needs of the prisons and the prisoners; and to provide machinery, tools, materials, supplies, and other instrumentalities useful therein. As far as may be practicable, the commissioner shall dispose of the products of every prison industry under his control and management to public institutions within the state.

VII. To make necessary additions, alterations, and repairs within the prisons or their enclosures.

VIII. To provide a military guard for the security of the prisons.

IX. To provide such books and other instruction as shall be deemed necessary for the convicts.

Source.
RS 227:5. CS 242:5. GS 270:5. GL 288:5. PS 285:5. 1917, 45:1. PL 400:6. RL 464:6. 1998, 386:4, 16, eff. Aug. 26, 1998.

Revision note.
In the catchline of the section and in the introductory clause of the text, substituted "commissioner of corrections" for "trustees" pursuant to 1983, 461:2, which provided for the abolition of the state prison board of trustees and the transfer of all the powers, functions and duties of the board to the commissioner of corrections. See RSA 21-H. Appropriate changes in pronouns were made throughout the section for purposes of conformity with the substitutes described above.

Amendments
—1998. Paragraphs I, III–V: Substituted "prisons" for "prison".
Paragraph VI: Substituted "prisons" for "prison" following "adapted to the needs of the" in the first sentence.
Paragraph VII: Substituted "prisons or their enclosures" for "prison or its inclosure".
Paragraph VIII: Substituted "prisons" for "prison".

Cross References.
Adoption of rules by police standards and training council regarding certification of state corrections officers, see RSA 188-F:26.
Powers and duties of commissioner generally, see RSA 21-H:8.
Sale or lease of goods and products produced at prison, see RSA 622:26–28-a.
State prison security force, see RSA 622:38, 39.

NOTES TO DECISIONS

Cited:
Cited in Piccoli v. Board of Trustees & Warden, 87 F. Supp. 672, 1949 U.S. Dist. LEXIS 2100 (D.N.H. 1949); Opinion of Justices, 116 N.H. 531, 363 A.2d 1005, 1976 N.H. LEXIS 405 (1976); Laaman v. Helgemoe, 437 F. Supp. 269, 1977 U.S. Dist. LEXIS 15128 (D.N.H. 1977).

622:6. Visitation.

The governor and council shall be visitors of the state prisons and shall annually, and as much oftener as may be proper, visit the prisons and see that all regulations made for the government thereof are proper and properly executed.

Source.
RS 227:10. CS 242:10. GS 270:10. GL 288:10. 1883, 28:1. PS 285:6. PL 400:7. RL 464:7. 1998, 386:16, eff. Aug. 26, 1998.

Amendments
—**1998.** Substituted "prisons" for "prison".

Cross References.
Site visits by commissioner, see RSA 21-H:9.

622:7. Duties of Commissioner of Corrections.

It shall be the duty of the commissioner of corrections:

I. To receive, safely keep, and employ in the prisons all convicts pursuant to their sentence and until discharged according to law. The commissioner may employ convicts outside of the prison walls, upon terms to be prescribed by the commissioner. A prisoner, while so employed, or while going to or from the prisons in connection with such employment, shall be deemed to be in prison as far as all laws relating to escape, attempts to escape, and aiding escape are concerned.

II. To have the custody and superintendence of all persons confined in the prisons, and of all property belonging thereto.

III. To obey and enforce all orders, bylaws, and regulations which the commissioner may make for the management of the prisons.

IV. To command the military guard for the prisons.

V. To be the fiscal officer of the prisons.

VI. To keep a regular and true account upon the books of the prisons of all money received and expended on account of the prisons and of all their concerns.

VII. Not to be a contractor for the prisons and not to be interested in any contract therewith.

VIII. [Repealed.]

IX. To conduct and manage the industries at the prisons.

X. To conduct and manage the educational program of the prisons.

Source.
RS 227:6. CS 242:6. GS 270:6. GL 288:6. PS 285:7. 1917, 45:2. PL 400:8. 1927, 101:2. 1941, 15:1. RL 464:8. RSA 622:7. 1977, 600:36. 1988, 170:4, I, eff. June 25, 1988. 1998, 386:5, eff. Aug. 26, 1998.

Revision note.
In the catchline and in the introductory clause substituted "commissioner of corrections" for "warden" pursuant to 1983, 461:3, which provided for the abolition of the position of warden of the state prison and the transfer of all powers, duties, and functions of that position to the commissioner of corrections. See RSA 21-H.

In the second sentence of par. I, substituted "commissioner" for "board of trustees" pursuant to 1983, 461:2, which provided for the abolition of the state prison board of trustees and the transfer of all the powers, functions, and duties of the board to the commissioner of corrections. See RSA 21-H.

In par. III, substituted "he may make" for "may be made by the trustees" pursuant to 1983, 461:2, which is described above.

In par. VIII, substituted "the governor and council and to the general court" for "trustees" pursuant to the transfers of functions provided for in 1983, 461:2 and 461:3, which are described above, and for purposes of conformity with RSA 21-H:8, IX.

In par. IX, deleted "it shall be the duty of the warden" preceding "to conduct and manage" and "under the direct supervision of the trustees of the prison" thereafter pursuant to 1983, 461:2 and 461:3, which are described above.

In par. X, deleted "it shall be the duty of the warden" preceding "to conduct and manage" pursuant to the transfer of functions in 1983, 461:3, which is described above, and for purposes of conformity with the style of the remainder of the section.

Amendments
—**1998.** Substituted "prisons" for "prison" and "the commissioner" for "he" wherever they appeared throughout the section and "their" for "its" preceding "concerns" in par. VI.

—**1988.** Paragraph VIII: Repealed.

—**1977.** Paragraph X: Added.

Cross References.
Escape and related offenses, see RSA 642:6, 7.
Powers and duties of commissioner generally, see RSA 21-H:8.
State prison security force, see RSA 622:38, 39.

NOTES TO DECISIONS

Cited:
Cited in Piccoli v. Board of Trustees & Warden, 87 F. Supp. 672, 1949 U.S. Dist. LEXIS 2100 (D.N.H. 1949); In re Mason, 101 N.H. 335, 143 A.2d 117, 1958 N.H. LEXIS 33 (1958); Hoitt v. Vitek, 361 F. Supp. 1238, 1973 U.S. Dist. LEXIS 12455 (D.N.H. 1973); Laaman v. Helgemoe, 437 F. Supp. 269, 1977 U.S. Dist. LEXIS 15128 (D.N.H. 1977); In re Caulk, 125 N.H. 226, 480 A.2d 93, 1984 N.H. LEXIS 364 (1984); State v. Evans, 127 N.H. 501, 506 A.2d 695, 1985 N.H. LEXIS 478 (1985).

622:7-a. Prisoner's Fund.

Notwithstanding RSA 6:11, any interest accruing on moneys in any account established by the commissioner of corrections for the benefit of prisoners and their families or dependent relatives is hereby continually appropriated to the state prisons and may be expended by the commissioner of corrections for the benefit of all prisoners.

Source.
1975, 304:1, eff. Aug. 6, 1975. 1998, 386:16, eff. Aug. 26, 1998.

Revision note.
At the beginning and end of the section, substituted "commissioner of corrections" for "warden" pursuant to 1983, 461:3, which provided for the abolition of the position of warden of the state prison and the transfer of all powers, duties and functions of that position to the commissioner of corrections. See RSA 21-H.

At the end of the section, deleted "with the consent of the trustees" pursuant to 1983, 461:2, which provided for the abolition of the state prison board of trustees and transfer of all powers, functions and duties of the board to the commissioner of corrections. See RSA 21-H.

Amendments
—**1998.** Substituted "state prisons" for "state prison".

622:7-b. Victims' Fund.

Every commissary in a state prison operated for the sale of commodities shall collect a surcharge of 5 percent of the sales price of every item sold. All funds collected pursuant to this section shall be deposited in and continually appropriated to the victims' assistance fund.

Source.
1999, 261:5, eff. July 1, 1999.

NOTES TO DECISIONS

Constitutionality
Surcharge on purchases made at the state prisons' commissaries was an unconstitutionally disproportionate tax, contrary to N.H. Const. pt. II, art. 5, because there was no legitimate reason to impose a surcharge on these retail purchases. Starr v. Governor, 148 N.H. 72, 802 A.2d 1227, 2002 N.H. LEXIS 93 (2002).

Surcharge on purchases made at the state prisons' commissaries was not a special cost assessment because inmates neither made use of nor benefitted from the victims' assistance fund for which the surcharge raised revenue. Starr v. Governor, 148 N.H. 72, 802 A.2d 1227, 2002 N.H. LEXIS 93 (2002).

622:8. Committals.

Whenever any convict shall be sentenced to confinement at hard labor the court shall order the sheriff of the county to remove him to the state prisons and deliver him to the commissioner of corrections.

Source.
RS 227:7. CS 242:7. GS 270:7. GL 288:7. PS 285:8. PL 400:9. RL 464:9. 1998, 386:16, eff. Aug. 26, 1998.

Revision note.
At the end of the sentence, substituted "commissioner of corrections" for "warden" pursuant to 1983, 461:3, which provided for the abolition of the position of warden of the state prison and the transfer of all powers, duties and functions of that position to the commissioner of corrections. See RSA 21-H.

Amendments
—**1998.** Substituted "prisons" for "prison".

Cross References.
Commitment of adult offenders generally, see RSA 21-H:10.
Sentences generally, see RSA 651:2.
Sentences to state prison generally, see RSA 651:15.

622:9. Mittimus; Return.

The clerk of the court shall deliver a copy of the conviction, judgment and order issued pursuant to RSA 622:8 to the sheriff, who shall deliver the same, with a copy of his return indorsed thereon, to the commissioner of corrections, and shall make due return to the court of the service of the order, upon an attested copy thereof.

Source.
RS 227:8. CS 242:8. GS 270:8. GL 288:8. PS 285:9. PL 400:10. RL 464:10.

Revision note.
Following "judgment and order", substituted "issued pursuant to RSA 622:8" for "thereon" for purposes of clarity.

Preceding "and shall make due return", substituted "commissioner of corrections" for "warden" pursuant to 1983, 461:3, which provided for the abolition of the position of warden of the state prison and the transfer of all powers, duties and functions of that position to the commissioner of corrections. See RSA 21-H.

622:10. United States Prisoners.

The commissioner of corrections shall receive all convicts sentenced to confinement to hard labor by any court of the United States within this state who may be delivered to him by the marshal of the district or his deputy, and shall safely keep such convicts until discharged by due course of the laws of the United States.

Source.
RS 227:14. CS 242:14. GS 270:14. GL 288:14. PS 285:10. PL 400:11. RL 464:11.

Revision note.
At the beginning of the section, substituted "commissioner of corrections" for "warden" pursuant to 1983, 461:3, which provided for the abolition of the position of warden of the state prison and the transfer of all powers, functions and duties of that position to the commissioner of corrections. See RSA 21-H.

622:11. Illegal Privileges.

A person employed in the prisons is guilty of a misdemeanor if he negligently suffers a prisoner to be at large, or to be visited, comforted, or relieved contrary to the regulations of the prisons or the terms of the sentence of the prisoner, and is guilty of a class B felony if he knowingly allows a controlled substance to be passed to a prisoner.

Source.
RS 227:11. CS 242:11. GS 270:11. GL 288:11. PS 285:11. PL 400:12. RL 464:12. RSA 622:11. 1977, 588:21, eff. Sept. 16, 1977. 1998, 386:6, eff. Jan. 1, 1999.

Amendments
—**1998.** Substituted "prisons" for "prison" in two places and added "and is guilty of a class B felony if he knowingly allows a controlled substance to be passed to a prisoner" following "sentence of the prisoner" at the end of the section.

—**1977.** Rewritten to the extent that a detailed comparison would be impracticable.

Cross References.
Classification of crimes, see RSA 625:9.
Escape and related offenses, see RSA 642:6, 7.
Sentences, see RSA 651.

622:12. Assaults by Life Prisoners.

[Repealed 1985, 80:2, I, eff. Jan. 1, 1986.]

Former section(s).
Former RSA 622:12, which was derived from RS 227:12; CS 242:12; GS 270:12; GL 288:12; PS 285:12; PL 400:13; RL 464:13; RSA 622;12; and 1975, 458:1, related to the penalties for assaults or escapes by persons serving sentences of life imprisonment. See now RSA 642:6 and 642:9.

622:13. Assaults by Other Prisoners.

[Repealed 1985, 80:2, II, eff. Jan. 1, 1986.]

Former section(s).
Former RSA 622:13, which was derived from RS 227:13; CS 242:13; GS 270:13; GL 288:13; PS 285:13; PL 400:14; RL 464:14; RSA 622:13; and 1975, 458:2, related to the penalties for assaults or escapes by prisoners. See now RSA 642:6 and 642:9.

622:14. Discipline.

The commissioner of corrections may offer suitable encouragement and indulgences to those convicts who distinguish themselves by obedience, industry, and faithfulness, and may punish any convict guilty of insolence or ill language to any officer of the prisons or guilty of obstinate and refractory behavior by solitary imprisonment not more than 30 days at one time or by such other reasonable and effective modes of punishment and discipline as the commissioner of corrections may from time to time prescribe.

Source.

RS 227:15. CS 242:15. GS 270:16. GL 288:16. 1885, 72:1. PS 285:15. PL 400:16. RL 464:15. 1998, 386:16, eff. Aug. 26, 1998.

Revision note.

At the beginning of the sentence, substituted "commissioner of corrections" for "warden, with the consent of the trustees" pursuant to 1983, 461:2 and 461:3, which, respectively, provided for the abolition of the state prison board of trustees and the abolition of the position of warden of the state prison and for the transfer of all powers, duties and functions of the board and of the warden to the commissioner of corrections. See RSA 21-H.

At the end of the section, substituted "commissioner of corrections" for "trustees" pursuant to 1983, 461:2, which is described above.

Amendments

—**1998.** Substituted "prisons" for "prison".

Cross References.

Adoption by commissioner of standards relating to behavior of inmates, see RSA 21-H:14.

Adoption of rules by commissioner generally, see RSA 21-H:8.

622:15. Communication by Inmates with Commissioner of Corrections, etc.

Whenever a prisoner desires to communicate with the governor and council, the commissioner of corrections, or the attorney general, he shall be permitted to do so in a direct manner, without any supervision being exercised over his letters by the prison officials or other persons.

Source.

1879, 97:1. PS 285:16. PL 400:17. RL 464:16. 1949, 25:1, eff. Feb. 23, 1949.

Revision note.

In the catchline of the section and in the text, substituted "commissioner of corrections" for "trustees" pursuant to 1983, 461:2, which provided for abolition of the state prison board of trustees and the transfer of all powers, functions and duties of the board to the commissioner of corrections. See RSA 21-H.

622:16. Supplies for Discharged Prisoners.

The commissioner of corrections may furnish, at the expense of the state, to each convict discharged from the prisons a suit of clothes, decent and suitable for the season in which he is discharged, and a sum of money, not more than $100.

Source.

RS 227:16. CS 270:17. GS 242:16. GL 288:17. PS 285:17. 1903, 84:1. PL 400:18. RL 464:17. 1951, 138:1. RSA 622:16. 1965, 25:1. 1971, 299:1. 1975, 210:1, eff. Aug. 1, 1975. 1998, 386:16, eff. Aug. 26, 1998.

Revision note.

At the beginning of the section, substituted "commissioner of corrections" for "warden" pursuant to 1983, 461:3, which provided for the abolition of the position of warden of the state prison and the transfer of all the powers, duties and functions of that position to the commissioner of corrections. See RSA 21-H.

Amendments

—**1998.** Substituted "prisons" for "prison".

—**1975.** Substituted "$100" for "sixty dollars".

—**1971.** Substituted "sixty dollars" for "thirty dollars".

—**1965.** Substituted "thirty dollars" for "twenty dollars".

622:17. Committal of One Held on Civil Process.

If any convict sentenced to confinement to hard labor or solitary imprisonment shall, at the time of his sentence, be in custody of the sheriff on civil process, mesne or final, the sheriff shall, on the delivery of such convict to the commissioner of corrections, leave with the commissioner of corrections an attested copy of such process.

Source.

RS 227:17. CS 242:17. GS 270:18. GL 288:18. PS 285:18. PL 400:19. RL 464:18.

Revision note.

At the end of the section, substituted "commissioner of corrections" for "warden" in two places pursuant to 1983, 461:3, which provided for the abolition of the position of warden of the state prison and the transfer of all powers, duties and functions of the position to the commissioner of corrections. See RSA 21-H.

Editor's note.

The language relating to a sentence of solitary imprisonment appears to be no longer relevant in light of the repeal of RSA 651:16, relating to sentences to solitary confinement, by 1981, 228:2.

622:18. Detention of One Held on Civil Process.

The commissioner of corrections shall detain a convict committed under the circumstances provided for in RSA 622:17 by virtue of the civil process as well as of his sentence, and, if, at the expiration of the sentence, the civil process is not withdrawn, discharged, satisfied, or annulled, shall still detain the convict thereon until he is discharged or remanded by due course of law.

Source.

RS 227:18. CS 242:18. GS 270:19. GL 288:19. PS 285:19. PL 400:20. RL 464:19.

Revision note.

At the beginning of the section, substituted "commissioner of corrections" for "warden" pursuant to 1983, 461:3, which provided for the abolition of the position of warden of the state prison and the transfer of all powers, duties and functions of the position to the commissioner of corrections. See RSA 21-H.

For purposes of clarity, substituted "a convict committed under the circumstances provided for in RSA 622:17" for "the convict, as well", "the civil" for "such" preceding "process" in two places, "is not" for "shall not be" preceding "withdrawn" and "the convict" for "him" preceding "thereon", inserted "as well" preceding "as of his sentence", and deleted "whence he came" following "remanded".

622:19. Execution on Judgment against Commissioner of Corrections.

If judgment shall be rendered against a person holding the office of commissioner of corrections, for a sum of money, the execution thereon shall be against his goods, chattels, and lands, but not against his body; and, if the execution is returned unsatisfied, the creditor may file a certified copy of it, and of the return thereon, with the secretary of state.

Source.

RS 227:19. CS 242:19. GS 270:20. GL 288:20. PS 285:20. PL 400:21. RL 464:20.

Revision note.

In the catchline and at the beginning of the section, substituted "commissioner of corrections" for "warden" pursuant to 1983, 461:3, which provided for the abolition of the position of warden of the state prison and the transfer of all powers, duties, and functions of that position to the commissioner of corrections. See RSA 21-H.

Editor's note.

The provisions of this section, originally relating to execution of judgments against the warden of the state prison, may be obsolete in view of the abolition of the position of warden of the state prison and the transfer of the powers, duties, and functions thereof to the commissioner of corrections by 1983, 461:3, and the enactment of the provisions of RSA 21-H:8, II(g), requiring the commissioner to furnish a bond pursuant to RSA 93-B.

622:20. Failure of Commissioner of Corrections to Pay Judgment.

The secretary shall immediately notify the commissioner of corrections thereof, in writing, with the day on which the copy was filed. If the execution shall remain unsatisfied for the space of 90 days after such notification, the commissioner of corrections shall be removed from his office, and execution may then issue against him in common form.

Source.

RS 227:20. CS 242:20. GS 270:21. GL 288:21. PS 285:21. PL 400:22. RL 464:21.

Revision note.

In the catchline and in the first sentence, substituted "commissioner of corrections" for "warden" pursuant to 1983, 461:3, which provided for the abolition of the position of warden of the state prison and the transfer of all powers, duties and functions of that position to the commissioner of corrections. See RSA 21-H.

In the second sentence, substituted "commissioner of corrections shall be removed" for "trustees shall remove the warden" pursuant to 1983, 461:2, which provided for the abolition of the state prison board of trustees and the transfer of all the powers, duties, and functions of the board to the commissioner of corrections. See RSA 21-H.

Editor's note.

The provisions of this section, originally relating to proceedings upon unsatisfied judgments against the warden, may be obsolete in

view of the abolition of the position of warden of the state prison and the powers, duties and functions thereof to the commissioner of corrections by 1983, 461:3, and the enactment of the provisions of RSA 21-H:8, II(g), requiring the commissioner to furnish a bond pursuant to RSA 93-B.

622:21. Appraisers.

[Repealed 1988, 170:4, II, eff. June 25, 1988.]

Former section(s).

Former RSA 622:21, which was derived from 1850, 984; CS 242:21; GS 270:22; GL 288:22; PS 285:22; PL 400:23; and RL 464:22, related to the appointment of appraisers by the commissioner of corrections.

622:22. Religious Ministrations.

The rules and regulations established for the government of any prison, county correctional facility, or public charitable or reformatory institution shall provide for suitable religious instruction and ministration to the inmates.

Source.

1881, 39:1. PS 285:24. PL 400:25. RL 464:23. RSA 622:22. 1988, 89:24, eff. June 17, 1988.

Amendments

—1988. Substituted "county correctional facility" for "house of correction" following "the government of any prison".

Cross References.

Adoption of rules by commissioner of corrections, see RSA 21-H:13.

622:23. Religious Preferences.

The inmates shall have freedom of religious belief and freedom to worship God according to the dictates of their consciences, but this shall not permit anything inconsistent with proper discipline and management or any expense beyond that made under RSA 622:22.

Source.

1881, 39:1. PS 285:25. PL 400:26. RL 464:24.

Delivery of Articles to Prisoners

622:24. Regulations.

No person shall deliver or procure to be delivered or have in his possession with intent to deliver to a prisoner confined in the state prisons, or deposit or conceal in or about the prisons, or in any building or upon any land appurtenant thereto, or in any vehicle entering the premises belonging to the prisons, any article with intent that a prisoner shall receive or obtain it, or receive from a prisoner any article with intent to convey it out of the prisons, or bring into or attempt to take from the prisons any article contrary to the rules and regulations established by the commissioner of corrections and without the knowledge and permission of the commissioner of corrections.

Source.
1925, 57:1. PL 400:31. RL 464:29. 1998, 386:16, eff. Aug. 26, 1998.

Revision note.
At the end of the section, substituted "commissioner of corrections" for "prison trustees" and "warden" pursuant to 1983, 461:2 and 461:3, which, respectively, provided for the abolition of the state prison board of trustees and the abolition of the position of warden of the state prison and for the transfer of all powers, duties and functions of the board and of the warden to the commissioner of corrections. See RSA 21-H.

Amendments
—1998. Substituted "prisons" for "prison" wherever it appeared throughout the section.

Cross References.
Adoption of rules by commissioner of corrections, see RSA 21-H:13.
Provision of implements of escape or contraband to prisoners, see RSA 642:7.

622:25. Penalty.

Any person who violates any provision of RSA 622:24 shall be guilty of a class B felony.

Source.
1925, 57:1. PL 400:32. RL 464:30. RSA 622:25. 1973, 528:320, eff. at 11:59 p.m., Oct. 31, 1973.

Amendments
—1973. Rewritten to the extent that a detailed comparison would be impracticable.

Cross References.
Classification of crimes, see RSA 625:9.
Sentences, see RSA 651.

Prison Labor and Its Products

622:26. Sales of Prison Products.

I. The commissioner of corrections may contract for the sale or lease of goods and products which are produced at the state prisons on the open market at competitive prices, when, in his opinion, such sale or lease is in the best interests of the inmates and of the prisons and does not conflict unduly with the availability of prison manufactured goods to state and public institutions as provided for in RSA 622:5, VI and RSA 622:28, and results in the best utilization of the prison production capacity.

II. The commissioner of corrections shall not, nor shall any other authority, make any contract by which the labor or time of any prisoner in the state prisons or in any reformatory, penitentiary, or jail in the state shall be farmed out, given or sold to any person.

Source.
1933, 42:1. RL 464:31. RSA 622:26. 1979, 113:1. 1982, 6:1, eff. Feb. 19, 1982. 1998, 386:7, eff. Aug. 26, 1998.

Revision note.
In pars. I and II, substituted "commissioner of corrections" for "warden" pursuant to 1983, 461:3, which provided for the abolition of the position of warden of the state prison and the transfer of all powers, duties and functions of the position to the commissioner of corrections. See RSA 21-H.

Amendments
—1998. Substituted "prisons" for "prison" following "state" and preceding "and does not conflict" in par. I and preceding "or in any reformatory" in par. II.

—1982. Paragraph I: Rewritten to the extent that a detailed comparison would be impracticable.

—1979. Rewritten to the extent that a detailed comparison would be impracticable.

Cross References.
Powers and duties of commissioner generally, see RSA 21-H:8, 622:5 and 622:7.
Release of prisoners for purposes of engaging in gainful employment, see RSA 651:19, 25.

622:27. Sale of Prison-Made Goods.

No goods, wares, or merchandise, manufactured, or mined wholly or in part by convicts or prisoners of other states, except convicts or prisoners on parole or probation, shall be sold on the open market, or be sold to, or exchanged with, an institution of this state or with any of its political subdivisions, except under arrangements which have been entered into between the commissioner of corrections and another state's correctional institution engaged in industrial activities.

Source.
1933, 42:1. RL 464:32. RSA 622:27. 1981, 495:3, eff. July 1, 1981.

Revision note.
At the end of the section, substituted "commissioner of corrections" for "warden of the New Hampshire state prison" pursuant to 1983, 461:3, which provided for the abolition of the position of warden of the state prison and the transfer of all powers, duties and functions of the position to the commissioner of corrections. See RSA 21-H.

Amendments
—1981. Rewritten to the extent that a detailed comparison would be impracticable.

Cross References.
Sale of prison products, see RSA 622:26.

622:28. Provision of Products for State Agencies.

No articles or supplies, except printing, such as are manufactured at the state prisons or for the state prisons in accordance with arrangements with other prison systems shall be purchased from any other source for the state or its departments or institutions if the director of plant and property management determines that such purchases may be made at fair market value. The commissioner of corrections will advise the director of plant and property management as to what articles or supplies are available for purchase and their current prices.

Source.
1933, 42:1. RL 464:33. RSA 622:28. 1977, 485:2. 1981, 495:4, eff. July 1, 1981. 1998, 386:8, eff. Aug. 26, 1998.

Revision note.
In the first and second sentences, substituted "director of plant and property management" for "director of purchase and property". 1983, 416:53, II, repealed RSA 8:14 et seq., relating to the division of purchase and property. 1983, 416:40, enacted RSA 21-I:11,

relating to the division of plant and property management.

In the second sentence, substituted "commissioner of corrections" for "superintendent of prison industries" pursuant to 1983, 461:6, which provided for the transfer of all powers, duties and functions of the state prison to the commissioner of corrections. See RSA 21-H.

Amendments

—1998. Substituted "prisons" for "prison" in two places in the first sentence.

—1981. Rewritten to the extent that a detailed comparison would be impracticable.

—1977. Inserted "except printing" following "no articles or supplies" and substituted "inmates" for "convicts" following "labor of".

Cross References.

Sale of prison products, see RSA 622:26.

622:28-a. Industries Inventory Account.

I. An industries inventory account shall be maintained to enable the state prisons to implement RSA 622:26–28. Except for permanent personnel, all operating expenses, materials, supplies, overtime and purchase and repair of equipment determined to be necessary for the growing or manufacture of products for resale shall be a proper charge against this account. Charges for the sale of goods and services produced by the industries program shall be sufficient to defray the expenditures charged against this account and any sums obtained therefrom shall be a credit to the account.

II. The state treasurer, upon presentation of manifests prepared by the commissioner of corrections and certified by the commissioner of administrative services, is authorized to pay for materials, supplies and equipment from any money in the treasury not otherwise appropriated.

III. The commissioner of corrections shall prepare a monthly profit and loss statement and at the end of each fiscal year shall file a report with the commissioner of administrative services in such format and containing such information as the commissioner of administrative services shall require. The commissioner of administrative services at the end of each fiscal year shall cause any profit which accrued during that year to lapse to the general fund.

IV. [Omitted.]

V. All purchases of materials, supplies, and equipment into the inventory account shall be made in accordance with the provisions of RSA 21-I:11 and any equipment purchase in excess of $5,000 made under the provisions of this section shall require the prior approval of both the fiscal committee of the general court and the governor and council.

Source.

1979, 268:1. 1985, 399:3, I, eff. July 1, 1985. 1998, 386:9, 16, eff. Aug. 26, 1998.

Revision note.

In pars. II and III, substituted "commissioner of corrections" for "state prison warden" pursuant to 1983, 461:3, which provided for the abolition of the position of warden of the state prison and the transfer of all powers, duties and functions of the position to the

commissioner of corrections. See RSA 21-H.

Paragraph IV which provided for the inventory of materials, supplies and manufactured products on hand on July 1, 1980, and for purchase of those items into the inventory account, has been omitted as no longer having any purpose.

In par. V, substituted "RSA 21-I:11" for "RSA 8:19". RSA 8:19 was repealed by 1983, 416:53, II.

Amendments

—1998. Paragraph I: Substituted "state prisons" for "state prison" in the first sentence.

Paragraph V: Substituted "$5,000" for "$1,000".

—1985. Paragraph II: Substituted "commissioner of administrative services" for "comptroller".

Paragraph III: Substituted "commissioner of administrative services" for "comptroller" in the first and second sentences.

Cross References.

Department of administrative services, see RSA 21-I.

622:28-b. Correctional Industries Advisory Board.

[Repealed 1997, 25:1, eff. June 24, 1997.]

Former section(s).

Former RSA 622:28-b, which was derived from 1993, 221:1 and 1995, 182:29, related to the correctional industries advisory board.

622:29. Prisoner's Earnings, etc.

The commissioner of corrections may provide for the payment to prisoners confined in the state prisons of such pecuniary earnings, and render to their families such pecuniary assistance, as the commissioner of corrections may deem proper, under such rules as he may prescribe.

Source.

1913, 178:1. PL 400:27. RL 464:25. RSA 622:29. 1998, 386:16, eff. Aug. 26, 1998.

Revision note.

In two places, substituted "commissioner of corrections" for "trustees" pursuant to 1983, 461:2, which provided for abolition of the state prison board of trustees and the transfer of all powers, functions and duties of the board to the commissioner of corrections. See RSA 21-H. Appropriate changes in pronouns were made throughout the section for purposes of conformity with the substitution described above.

Amendments

—1998. Substituted "prisons" for "prison".

Cross References.

Adoption of rules by commissioner generally, see RSA 21-H:13.

Disposition of wages or other income of prisoners on work release or released on suspended sentences, see RSA 651:22.

Prisoner's fund, see RSA 622:7-a.

622:30. Source of Payment.

When allowed, the earnings and assistance provided for in RSA 622:29 shall be paid out of such money as may be available for current running expenses of the state prisons.

Source.

1913, 178:1. PL 400:28. RL 464:26. RSA 622:30. 1998, 386:16, eff. Aug. 26, 1998.

Revision note.

At the beginning of the section, substituted "when allowed, the earnings and assistance provided for in RSA 622:29" for "such earnings and such assistance, when allowed" for purposes of clarity.

Amendments
—1998. Substituted "prisons" for "prison".

622:31. Application of Earnings.

Any money accruing under RSA 622:29 shall be and remain under the control of the commissioner of corrections, to be used for the benefit of the prisoner, his family or dependent relatives under such regulation as to time, manner, and amount of disbursement as the commissioner of corrections may prescribe.

Source.
   1913, 178:2. PL 400:29. RL 464:27.

Revision note.
   In two places, substituted "commissioner of corrections" for "trustees" pursuant to 1983, 461:2, which provided for abolition of the state prison board of trustees and the transfer of all powers, functions and duties of the board to the commissioner of corrections. See RSA 21-H.

Cross References.
   Adoption of rules by commissioner generally, see RSA 21-H:13.

622:31-a. Medical Care; Inmate Copayment Required.

I. The commissioner of the department of corrections shall adopt policies and procedures establishing reasonable medical and health service fees for the medical services that are provided to inmates at any state facility.

II. Except as provided in paragraph III, the commissioner may charge each inmate a reasonable fee for medical and mental health services, including prescriptions, medication, or prosthetic devices. The fee shall be deducted from the inmate's account.

III. The commissioner shall exempt the following inmates or medical visits by inmates from payment of medical and health services fees:

   (a) Medical visits initiated by the medical or mental health staff, consultants, or contract personnel of the department.

   (b) Inmates at reception centers.

   (c) Juvenile inmates.

   (d) Pregnant inmates.

   (e) Seriously mentally ill inmates.

   (f) Developmentally disabled inmates, as determined by authorized staff.

   (g) Inmates who are housed in the secure psychiatric unit.

   (h) Inmates who are undergoing follow-up medical treatment for chronic diseases.

IV. An inmate shall not be refused medical treatment for financial reasons.

V. The commissioner shall establish criteria for reasonable deductions from moneys credited to the inmate's account to repay the cost of medical treatment for injuries that were self-inflicted or inflicted by the inmate on others.

VI. All moneys received by the department for medical and health service fees shall be deposited in the general fund.

VII. The commissioner shall establish criteria for reasonable deductions from moneys credited to the inmate's account to repay the cost of:

   (a) Property that the inmate willfully damages or destroys during the inmate's incarceration.

   (b) Searching for and apprehending an inmate who escapes or attempts to escape.

   (c) Quelling a riot or other disturbance in which the inmate is unlawfully involved.

No inmate shall be subject to deductions from moneys credited to the inmate's account under paragraphs V and VII until the inmate has been afforded a due process hearing and has been found guilty.

VIII. For purposes of this section, "reasonable fee" and "reasonable deduction" mean an amount to be determined by the commissioner of corrections, and which shall be based upon the actual or approximate costs of the property or service for which reimbursement is required.

IX. For purposes of this section, "inmate's account" means the moneys belonging to an inmate which are held in the department of corrections trust fund.

Source.
   1995, 296:1, eff. Jan. 1, 1996.

Applicability of enactment.
   1995, 296:4, eff. Jan. 1, 1995, provided that 1995, 296:1, which added this section, shall apply to all inmates incarcerated before, on or after Jan. 1, 1996, but the provisions of 1995, 296:1 shall not apply retroactively to costs incurred prior to Jan. 1, 1996.

622:32. Effect of Misconduct.

If any prisoner shall willfully escape from a state prison or commit a breach of discipline while confined in said prison, or when at liberty on parole shall violate any of the terms and conditions governing prisoners on parole, the commissioner of corrections may, in his or her discretion, cause the forfeiture of all earnings remaining to the prisoner's credit, and the same shall be credited to the account from which it was taken. Any restitution ordered by a court or through the inmate disciplinary system shall, upon payment, be used to defray the operating expenses of the prisons.

Source.
   1913, 178:2. PL 400:30. RL 464:28. 1998, 386:10, eff. Aug. 26, 1998. 2007, 239:1, eff. June 25, 2007.

Revision note.
   At the beginning of the section, substituted "any prisoner" for "any such prisoners" preceding "shall wilfully escape" for purposes of clarity.
   Following "prisoners on parole", substituted "the commissioner of corrections" for "the trustees" pursuant to 1983, 461:2, which provided for abolition of the state prison board of trustees and the transfer of all powers, functions and duties of the board to the commissioner of corrections. See RSA 21-H.

Amendments

—2007. Inserted "or her" preceding "discretion" in the first sentence and added the second sentence.

—1998. Substituted "a state prison" for "the state prison" following "wilfully escape from".

Cross References.

Disposition of wages or other income of prisoners on work release or released on suspended sentences generally, see RSA 651:22.

Parole of prisoners generally, see RSA 651-A.

Care and Custody of Female Convicts

Cross References.

Agreements between counties for custody of female prisoners, see RSA 30-B:24.

Housing of females committed to custody of commissioner of corrections generally, see RSA 21-H:11.

Interstate compacts, see RSA 622-A, 622-B.

Temporary transfers of inmates from state prison, see RSA 623.

Transfer of inmates by commissioner, see RSA 21-H:12.

622:33. Contracts Authorized.

[Repealed 1990, 211:4, I, eff. June 26, 1990.]

Former section(s).

Former RSA 622:33, which was derived from 1941, 123:1; RL 464:34; and 1955, 38:1; 61:1, related to contracts with counties or other states for care and custody of female prisoners.

622:33-a. Care and Custody of Female Prisoners.

I. There is established a state confinement facility for female prisoners which shall be called the New Hampshire state prison for women.

II. The New Hampshire state prison for women shall be under the superintendence of a warden. The warden shall serve at the pleasure of the commissioner of corrections and shall be an unclassified employee qualified by education and experience.

III. The operation of the New Hampshire state prison for women and the inmates confined to the New Hampshire state prison for women shall be governed by the same laws, rules and regulations which govern the state prisons for men and inmates of the state prisons for men, except as otherwise specified by law.

Source.

1990, 211:1, eff. June 26, 1990. 1996, 159:6, eff. July 1, 1996. 1998, 386:11, eff. Aug. 26, 1998. 1999, 296:7, eff. Sept. 14, 1999.

Amendments

—1999. Paragraph II: Substituted "warden" for "superintendent" in the first and second sentences.

—1998. Paragraph III: Substituted "prisons for men" for "prison" in two places.

—1996. Paragraph II: Substituted "at the pleasure of the commissioner of corrections" for "for a term of 4 years" following "shall serve" in the second sentence.

Terms of office for incumbent warden and superintendent.

1996, 159:7, eff. July 1, 1996, provided that the warden and superintendent of the state prison for women shall serve out their current terms of office and shall thereafter serve as provided for in this section, RSA 622:2-a and 622:2-b.

622:34. Transfer of Prisoners.

[Repealed 1990, 211:4, II, eff. June 26, 1990.]

Former section(s).

Former RSA 622:34, which was derived from 1941, 123:1; RL 464:35; and 1955, 61:2, related to transfer of female prisoners.

622:34-a. Expenses of Confinement.

The expenses of confinement of any female transferred to the custody of the state prisons shall be paid by the institution making the transfer.

Source.

1955, 61:3, eff. April 1, 1955. 1998, 386:16, eff. Aug. 26, 1998.

Amendments

—1998. Substituted "prisons" for "prison".

622:35. Good Behavior.

The law of this state with respect to diminution of the length of a sentence for good behavior or other cause shall apply to all sentences served in whole or in part in county prison facilities or out-of-state institutions.

Source.

1941, 123:1. RL 464:36. 1955, 38:2, eff. March 12, 1955.

Cross References.

Reduction in sentences of persons on release from state prison generally, see RSA 651:25.

622:36. Return or Transfer of Convicts.

Upon the termination of any contract entered into in accordance with the provisions of this subdivision, or when the terms of any such contract shall so provide, convicts confined in county prison facilities or out-of-state institutions shall be returned by the commissioner of corrections or his assistant to the state prisons or shall be delivered to such other county prison facility or out-of-state penal institution as the commissioner of corrections shall have contracted with under the provisions of this subdivision. The commissioner of corrections shall provide for the return to this state of all such convicts as shall desire to return upon the expiration of their sentences or other discharge by law.

Source.

1941, 123:1. RL 464:37. 1955, 38:3, eff. March 12, 1955. 1998, 386:12, eff. Aug. 26, 1998.

Revision note.

In the first and second sentences, substituted "commissioner of corrections" for "trustees" pursuant to 1983, 461:2, which provided for abolition of the state prison board of trustees and the transfer of all powers, functions and duties of the board to the commissioner of corrections. See RSA 21-H.

In the first sentence, substituted "commissioner of corrections" for "warden" pursuant to 1983, 461:3, which provided for the abolition of the position of warden of the state prison and the transfer of all powers, functions and duties of the position to the commissioner of corrections. See RSA 21-H.

In the first sentence, substituted "of this subdivision" for "hereof" following "provisions" for purposes of clarity.

Amendments
—**1998.** Substituted "prisons" for "prison" following "assistant to the state" in the first sentence.

622:37. Cost.

The cost of maintenance of convicts transferred pursuant to this subdivision and the expenses incident to their transfer shall be payable out of the funds provided for the maintenance of the state prisons.

Source.
1941, 123:1. RL 464:38. 1998, 386:16, eff. Aug. 26, 1998.

Revision note.
For purposes of clarity, substituted "convicts transferred pursuant to this subdivision" for "such convicts".

Amendments
—**1998.** Substituted "prisons" for "prison".

State Prison Security Force

Cross References.
Secure psychiatric unit of state prison, see RSA 622:40 et seq.

622:38. Prison Security Force.

The commissioner of corrections is authorized to organize a prison security force, consisting of members of the prisons' correctional line personnel, for the purpose of patrolling prison buildings, roads, and grounds and providing for general security at the prisons. The prison security force shall be under the immediate control of and responsible to the commissioner of corrections.

Source.
1977, 599:2, eff. July 30, 1977. 1998, 386:13, eff. Aug. 26, 1998.

Revision note.
In the first sentence, substituted "commissioner of corrections" for "warden of the New Hampshire state prison" pursuant to 1983, 461:3, which provided for the abolition of the position of warden of the state prison and the transfer of all powers, duties and functions of the position to the commissioner of corrections. See RSA 21-H.
In the second sentence, substituted "commissioner of corrections" for "warden of the prison" pursuant to 1983, 461:3, which is described above.

Amendments
—**1998.** Deleted "State" preceding "Prison" in the section catchline and substituted "prisons'" for "prison's" preceding "correctional line" and "prisons" for "prison" in two places in the first sentence.

Cross References.
Certification of state corrections officers by police standards and training council, see RSA 188-F:22 et seq.
Powers and duties of commissioner of corrections generally, see RSA 21-H:8.

622:39. Authority.

All security officers of the prison security force shall be ex officio constables and shall possess general police powers including the power of arrest, but such powers shall extend only to the confines of the grounds of the prisons and only to the period during which such officers are on official active duty. The only 2 instances where the authority of members of the prison security force shall extend beyond the prisons' grounds are:

I. Where a member of the security force is in hot pursuit of a person or persons who have committed a crime or violation while on prison grounds or who have committed the crime of escape from the prisons; and

II. Where a member of the prison security force is transporting a court committed inmate.

Source.
1977, 599:2, eff. July 30, 1977. 1998, 386:14, eff. Aug. 26, 1998.

Revision note.
In the first sentence, substituted "officers" for "members" preceding "are on official active duty" for purposes of clarity.
Deleted "of the" preceding "prison grounds" in the second sentence of the introductory paragraph to correct a typographical error.
Substituted "prisons'" for "prisons" in the second sentence of the introductory paragraph to correct a typographical error.

Amendments
—**1998.** Substituted "the grounds of the prisons" for "the prison grounds" in the first sentence and "of the prisons" for "prison" preceding "grounds" in the second sentence of the introductory paragraph and substituted "prisons" for "prison" at the end of par. I.

Cross References.
Arrests generally, see RSA 594.
Escape and related offenses generally, see RSA 642:6, 7.
Fresh pursuit, see RSA 614.

Secure Psychiatric Unit

Cross References.
Civil commitment of mentally-ill persons generally, see RSA 135-C.
Commitment for observation of persons charged with criminal offenses, see RSA 135:17, 172:13.
Commitment of mentally-ill persons charged with or acquitted of criminal offenses generally, see RSA 651:8 et seq.

622:40. Definitions.

In this subdivision:

I. "Commissioner" means the commissioner of the department of corrections under RSA 21-H:2.

II. "Department" means the department of health and human services.

III. [Repealed.]

IV. "Unit" means the secure psychiatric unit.

Source.
1985, 337:1. 1995, 310:170, XI, eff. Nov. 1, 1995.

Amendments
—**1995.** Paragraph III: Repealed.

Severability
—**1995 amendment.** 1995, 310, which amended this section, was subject to a severability clause. See 1995, 310:186.

Construction of amendments
—**1995.** 1995, 310:187, eff. Nov. 1, 1995, provided:
"Nothing in this act is intended to, nor shall it be construed as, mandating or assigning any new, expanded, or modified program or responsibility for any political subdivision in violation of part I, article 28-a of the constitution of the state of New Hampshire."

622:41. Unit Established.

There is hereby established a secure psychiatric unit to receive and provide appropriate treatment for persons transferred under RSA 622:45 to a secure environment.

Source.
1985, 337:1, eff. July 1, 1985.

NOTES TO DECISIONS

Cited:
Cited in 1986 Op. Att'y Gen. 69.

622:42. Coordination of Responsibility.

[Repealed 1995, 310:166, eff. Nov. 1, 1995.]

Former section(s).
Former RSA 622:42, which was derived from 1985, 337:1, related to cooperative agreements between the commissioner of corrections and the department of health and human services for the operation of the secure psychiatric unit.

Construction of repeal
1995, 310:187, eff. Nov. 1, 1995, provided "Nothing in this act is intended to, nor shall it be construed as, mandating or assigning any new, expanded, or modified program or responsibility for any political subdivision in violation of part I, article 28-a of the constitution of the state of New Hampshire."

Severability of repeal
1995, 310, which amended this section, was subject to a severability clause. See 1995, 310:186.

622:43. Staffing.

I. There are hereby established the following unclassified positions:

(a) A medical director, who shall be a board certified psychiatrist and shall be under the administrative supervision of the commissioner. The medical director shall be responsible for the provision, supervision, and administration of the medical and psychiatric services of the department of corrections and the unit.

(b) A psychiatrist, who shall be board eligible and who shall provide psychiatric and medical services under the supervision of the medical director.

(c) A non-medical director, who shall administer programs and services of the division of medical and psychiatric services and the unit.

II. The positions established by paragraph I shall carry with them an annual salary as set forth in RSA 94:1-a.

III. The commissioner shall appoint qualified personnel, who shall serve at the pleasure of the commissioner, to the positions established by paragraph I of this section.

Source.
1985, 337:1. 1993, 321:4, 5, eff. July 1, 1993.

Amendments
—1993. Paragraph I(a): Deleted "unit" preceding "director" in the first sentence.

Paragraph I(c): Deleted "unit" preceding "director" and substituted "of the division of medical and psychiatric services and" for "at" preceding "the unit".

NOTES TO DECISIONS

Cited:
Cited in Disabilities Rights Ctr., Inc. v. Commissioner, N.H. Dep't of Corrections, 143 N.H. 674, 732 A.2d 1021, 1999 N.H. LEXIS 56 (1999).

622:44. Rulemaking.

I. The commissioner shall adopt rules, pursuant to RSA 541-A, which provide for effective treatment for persons found to be dangerous to themselves or others and committed or transferred pursuant to RSA 622:45 to an environment which provides for safety and security for the public, the staff, and those committed.

II. The rules shall reflect the general policy that persons committed or transferred to the unit, who may be convicted offenders, persons found not guilty because of insanity, pre-trial detainees, or persons civilly committed, shall retain all their individual rights, except where safety or security mandates restriction.

Source.
1985, 337:1, eff. July 1, 1985.

Cross References.
Powers of commissioner generally, see RSA 21-H:8.
Rulemaking powers of commissioner generally, see RSA 21-H:13.
Standards for discharge, see RSA 622:48.
Standards for treatment, see RSA 622:46.

622:45. Commitment.

Commitment may occur as follows:

I. Any person subject to an involuntary admission to the state mental health services system pursuant to RSA 135-C or any person subject to involuntary admission pursuant to RSA 171-B may at any time be transferred to the unit upon a determination that the person would present a serious likelihood of danger to himself or to others if admitted to or retained in a receiving facility in the state mental health services system. The admission to the unit may be ordered by:

(a) A probate court pursuant to RSA 135-C:34–54; or

(b) An administrator of a designated receiving facility to which a person has been involuntarily admitted pursuant to an involuntary emergency admission or an involuntary admission; or

(c) A probate court pursuant to RSA 171-B or an administrator of a receiving facility to which a person has been involuntarily admitted pursuant to RSA 171-B.

II. Except upon an order of court under subparagraph I(a) or in an emergency, no admission or transfer to the unit shall occur without the prior approval of the commissioner and the commissioner of the department of health and human services, or their designees. In such instances, if the person to be admitted or transferred objects to the transfer, the person may request a hearing or review of the decision by the commissioner of the department of health and human services or designee in accordance with rules adopted pursuant to RSA 541-A. The review or hearing may occur following the admission or transfer where immediate admission or transfer has been determined necessary to protect the person or others. If the commissioner of the department of health and human services upholds the objection of a person to be transferred, the transfer shall not be made. If the commissioner of the department of health and human services upholds the objection of a person already transferred, the person shall promptly be delivered to a receiving facility named by the commissioner of the department of health and human services.

III. Except where ordered by a court of competent jurisdiction, if the commissioner objects to a proposed admission or transfer approved by the commissioner of the department of health and human services, the commissioners may agree to have the disagreement resolved by a mutually acceptable third party.

IV. Any person admitted or transferred to the unit shall be under the care and custody of the commissioner and the medical unit director and shall be subject to the rules of the commissioner until the person is transferred to a receiving facility in the state mental health services system. No person may be retained within the unit longer than the period of the order of involuntary admission to the state mental health services system.

V. A person in the custody of the commissioner who needs treatment for a mental illness may be transferred to the unit following a due process hearing. If the person requires immediate transfer, the due process review shall occur within a reasonable time following the transfer.

Source.

1985, 337:1. 1994, 248:9, eff. June 2, 1994; 408:10, 14, eff. Jan. 1, 1995. 1995, 310:167, eff. Nov. 1, 1995.

Amendments

—1995. Paragraph II: Substituted "commissioner of the department of health and human services" for "director" wherever it appeared, deleted "admission or" preceding "transfer" and substituted "the person" for "he" thereafter and deleted "or his" preceding "designee" in the second sentence and deleted "admitted or" preceding "transferred" in the fifth sentence.

Paragraph III: Deleted "director" following "approved by the" and substituted "commissioner of the department of health and human services, the commissioners" for "and director" preceding "may agree".

—1994. Paragraph I: Chapter 248 substituted "RSA 135-C" for "RSA 135-B" in the first sentence of the introductory paragraph and "RSA 135-C:34–54" for "RSA 135-B:26–41" in subpar. (a).

Chapter 408 inserted "or any person subject to involuntary admission pursuant to RSA 171-B" following "RSA 135-C" in the first sentence of the introductory paragraph, substituted "admission" for "hospitalization" following "emergency" and made a minor change in punctuation in subpar. (b) and added subpar. (c).

Severability

—1995 amendment. 1995, 310, which amended this section, was subject to a severability clause. See 1995, 310:186.

Construction of amendments

—1995. 1995, 310:187, eff. Nov. 1, 1995, provided:

"Nothing in this act is intended to, nor shall it be construed as, mandating or assigning any new, expanded, or modified program or responsibility for any political subdivision in violation of part I, article 28-a of the constitution of the state of New Hampshire."

Applicability of 1994, 408 amendment.

1994, 408:13, eff. Jan. 1, 1995, provided that the amendment to this section by section 14 of the act shall apply to acts leading to a felony charge which occur on or after Jan. 1, 1995.

Contingent 1994 amendment.

1994, 408:10, provided for amendment of this section. However, under the terms of 1994, 408:15, I, eff. Jan. 1, 1995, the amendment did not take effect.

Cross References.

Adoption of rules by commissioner generally, see RSA 622:44. Discharge, see RSA 622:48.

NOTES TO DECISIONS

Burden of proof for transfer to unit

In order to effect a transfer from within the state mental health services system to the secure psychiatric unit (SPU), a probate court need determine only by a preponderance of the evidence, and not beyond a reasonable doubt, that the individual would be a danger to himself or others if admitted or retained in a receiving facility in the state mental health services system. In re Champagne, 128 N.H. 791, 519 A.2d 310, 1986 N.H. LEXIS 357 (1986).

622:46. Treatment Standards.

I. The commissioner shall establish clinical and treatment standards for the operation of the unit in consultation with the commissioner of the department of health and human services. The commissioners shall review, at least annually, any interagency agreements and the mental health program at the unit to determine which provisions, standards, or practices should be revised to improve treatment.

II. The governor shall appoint the director ex officio to the advisory committee of the New Hampshire department of corrections pursuant to RSA 21-G:11.

Source.

1985, 337:1. 1995, 310:168, eff. Nov. 1, 1995.

Amendments

—1995. Paragraph I: Substituted "commissioner of the department of health and human services" for "director" following "consultation with" in the first sentence and "commissioners" for "commissioner and the director" preceding "shall review" in the second sentence.

Severability

—1995 amendment. 1995, 310, which amended this section, was subject to a severability clause. See 1995, 310:186.

Construction of amendments

—1995. 1995, 310:187, eff. Nov. 1, 1995, provided:

"Nothing in this act is intended to, nor shall it be construed as, mandating or assigning any new, expanded, or modified program or responsibility for any political subdivision in violation of part I, article 28-a of the constitution of the state of New Hampshire."

Adoption of rules by commissioner generally, see RSA 622:44.
Discharge, see RSA 622:48.
Rights regarding treatment of civilly committed persons generally, see RSA 135-C:55 et seq.

NOTES TO DECISIONS

Requirement of treatment plans

Treatment plans must be implemented for individuals in the secure psychiatric unit (SPU) in order to meet the requirements of this section. In re Champagne, 128 N.H. 791, 519 A.2d 310, 1986 N.H. LEXIS 357 (1986).

Since treatment plans must be implemented for individuals transferred to the secure psychiatric unit (SPU) pursuant to this section, and RSA 135-B:44 requires that persons confined within the mental health services system be provided with a treatment plan and follow-up treatment after that plan is established, the statutory scheme does not violate the equal protection provisions of the state and federal constitutions by treating similar classes of persons differently, depending upon their admittance to a facility controlled by the mental health services system or to a facility controlled by the department of corrections. In re Champagne, 128 N.H. 791, 519 A.2d 310, 1986 N.H. LEXIS 357 (1986).

622:47. Medical Records.

Notwithstanding the provisions of RSA 329:26 and RSA 330-A:32, medical and mental health records concerning current patients shall be exchanged between other state medical and mental health facilities and the unit to facilitate treatment.

Source.
1985, 337:1, eff. July 1, 1985. 1998, 234:16, eff. Oct. 31, 1998.

Amendments
—**1998.** Substituted "RSA 330-A:32" for "RSA 330-A:19".

622:48. Discharge.

I. When a person committed or transferred to the unit no longer requires the security provided by the unit, the commissioner shall initiate his discharge as follows:

(a) A person who was in pre-trial or post-trial confinement when admitted to the unit shall be returned to the sending facility or other appropriate facility;

(b) The commissioner or designee may transfer to the state mental health services system, or the state developmental services system only if the person was admitted or transferred to the unit pursuant to RSA 171-B, any person admitted or transferred to the unit, pursuant to RSA 622:45, I, upon a determination that the person no longer presents a serious likelihood of danger to self or others if such person were to be confined within a receiving facility in the state mental health services system or the state developmental services delivery system. If the commissioner of health and human services objects to a proposed transfer, the commissioners may agree to have the disagreement resolved by a mutually acceptable third party, or if none is acceptable, by the attorney general.

(c) The commissioner or designee may transfer to the state mental health services system any person committed to the unit under RSA 651:9-a upon a determination by a physician that the person presents a potentially serious likelihood of danger to self or others as a result of mental illness, but the person no longer requires the degree of safety and security provided by the unit. No transfer may occur under this subparagraph without the prior approval of the commissioner of the department of health and human services and administrative due process pursuant to rules adopted by the commissioner under RSA 541-A. If the commissioner of health and human services objects to a proposed transfer, the commissioners may agree to have the disagreement resolved by a mutually acceptable third party. No transfer may occur under this subparagraph without the prior approval of the superior court. Any person transferred under this subparagraph shall, for purposes of treatment, be under the care and custody of the commissioner of health and human services but shall for all other purposes, including, but not limited to, discharge, granting of privileges, parole, and recommittal, remain under the jurisdiction of the commissioner of the department of corrections and the superior court.

(d) When a person is transferred to another facility pursuant to subparagraphs (b) or (c), the commissioner or designee shall provide notice to the attorney general in accordance with RSA 135:17-b.

II. Any person who was committed or transferred to the unit may participate in prison pre-release programs if the commissioner deems it appropriate. However, persons who object and who do not have a state prison sentence shall not be placed in state prison programs.

III. Any person committed to the unit by criminal proceedings may be discharged by a justice of the superior court under RSA 622:51 whenever further detention at the unit is unnecessary, but any person so discharged who was under sentence of imprisonment at the time of his commitment, the period of which has not expired, shall be remanded to prison.

Source.
1985, 337:1. 1986, 220:1, 2. 1994, 408:11, eff. Jan. 1, 1995. 1995, 310:169, eff. Nov. 1, 1995. 2012, 151:4, eff. August 6, 2012.

Amendments
—**2012.** The 2012 amendment added I(d).

—**1995.** Paragraph I: Rewrote subpars. (b) and (c).

—**1994.** Paragraph I(b): Rewrote the first sentence and added "or if none is acceptable, by the attorney general" following "party" in the second sentence.

—**1986.** Paragraph I(c): Deleted "the" preceding "administrative due process" in the second sentence, added the fourth sentence and rewrote the fifth sentence.
Paragraph III: Added.

Severability
—**1995 amendment.** 1995, 310, which amended this section, was subject to a severability clause. See 1995, 310:186.

Construction of amendments
—**1995.** 1995, 310:187, eff. Nov. 1, 1995, provided:
"Nothing in this act is intended to, nor shall it be construed as, mandating or assigning any new, expanded, or modified program or

responsibility for any political subdivision in violation of part I, article 28-a of the constitution of the state of New Hampshire."

Applicability of 1994 amendment.

1994, 408:13, eff. Jan. 1, 1995, provided that the amendment to this section by section 11 of the act shall apply to acts leading to a felony charge which occur on or after Jan. 1, 1995.

Cross References.

Action for discharge by person admitted, see RSA 135-C:53.

Adoption of rules by commissioner generally, see RSA 622:44.

Granting of off-grounds privileges, see RSA 622:49.

Parole generally, see RSA 622:50.

Procedure for conduct of hearings relating to commitment, detention or parole, see RSA 622:52.

Releases from state prison generally, see RSA 651:25.

622:49. Notification of Granting of Off-Grounds Privileges by Director.

Not less than 30 days before the intended date of the granting of off-grounds privileges by the director to any person committed to the unit by criminal proceedings and subsequently transferred to the state mental health services system, the director shall give notice of such intention to the commissioner. The commissioner shall give notice of the director's intention to the superior court for the county in which said person was committed, to the attorney general, and to the county attorney, if any, who prosecuted the case. The superior court justice, the attorney general, or the county attorney, if any, who prosecuted the case may request a hearing before the superior court, in which case the director shall not grant off-grounds privileges to such person prior to the hearing. Following such hearing, the court may approve such off-grounds privileges or may order that no off-grounds privileges be granted at the time. In the event that the order of commitment by the superior court shall expressly provide restrictions upon the manner of commitment, such restrictions shall be observed until such restrictions are modified by further order of the court.

Source.

1986, 220:3, eff. June 6, 1986.

Cross References.

Parole of persons committed to unit by criminal proceedings, see RSA 622:50.

Procedure for conduct of hearings, see RSA 622:52.

622:50. Parole.

The superior court may, with notice to the attorney general and to the county attorney, if any, who prosecuted the case and after a hearing, for due cause shown, parole any person committed to the unit by criminal proceedings upon such terms and conditions as justice may require; and said court may at any time thereafter, for due cause shown, revoke said parole and order said person returned to the unit under the original commitment.

Source.

1986, 220:3, eff. June 6, 1986.

Cross References.

Granting of off-grounds privileges to persons committed to unit by criminal proceedings, see RSA 622:49.

Probation and parole generally, see RSA 504-A.

Procedure for conduct of hearing, see RSA 622:52.

622:51. Investigation of Detention.

The superior court may at any time, with notice to the attorney general and to the county attorney, if any, who prosecuted the case, upon application and after a hearing, for due cause shown, investigate the question whether there is sufficient reason for the detention in the unit of any person who has been committed thereto by criminal proceedings, and may order his discharge, when such order ought to be made, without the formality of a writ.

Source.

1986, 220:3, eff. June 6, 1986.

Cross References.

Discharge of persons committed to unit by criminal proceedings generally, see RSA 622:48.

Procedure for conduct of hearings, see RSA 622:52.

622:52. Conduct of Hearings for Commitment, Detention, or Parole.

Whenever provisions of this chapter relative to the commitment, detention, or parole of the mentally ill by criminal proceedings require that a hearing be conducted by the superior court, such hearing shall be ordered in accordance with the following requirements:

I. Such person shall have the right to be represented by counsel and shall have the right to present independent testimony. The court shall appoint counsel for such person whom it finds to be indigent and who is not represented by counsel, unless such person refuses the appointment of counsel.

II. The court may provide an independent medical examination for such indigent person upon the request of his counsel or upon his own request if he is not represented by counsel.

III. The person shall be allowed not less than 2 days after the appearance of his counsel in which to prepare his case and a hearing shall be conducted forthwith after such period unless counsel requests a delay.

IV. Notice of the time and place of hearing shall be furnished by the court to the commissioner, the person, his counsel, and his nearest relative or guardian.

V. The person or the commissioner may request either an open or a closed hearing and the court in its discretion may grant such a request.

Source.

1986, 220:3, eff. June 6, 1986.

Cross References.

Probation and parole generally, see RSA 504-A.

Reimbursement of Cost of Care by Inmates

Applicability of enactment.

1995, 296:4, eff. Jan. 1, 1995, provided that 1995, 296:3, which added RSA 622:53–58, shall apply to all inmates incarcerated before, on, or after Jan. 1, 1996, but the provisions of 1995, 296:3 shall not apply retroactively to costs incurred prior to Jan. 1, 1996.

622:53. Definitions.

In this subdivision:

I. "Commissioner" means the commissioner of the department of corrections.

II. "Cost of care" means the cost to the department for providing room, board, clothing, medical care, and other living expenses excluding capital costs for an inmate confined to a correctional facility, or any costs associated with maintaining an inmate in a home detention program incurred by the department of corrections.

III. "Department" means the department of corrections.

IV. "Estate" means any tangible or intangible properties, real or personal, belonging to or due an inmate, including income or payments to such inmate from previously earned salary or wages, bonuses, annuities, pensions, or retirement benefits, or any source whatsoever.

V. "Inmate" means a person confined to a correctional facility as the result of conviction of a crime or violation of parole or probation, or an offender sentenced to a home detention program.

VI. "Inmate's account" means the moneys belonging to an inmate which are held in the department of corrections trust fund.

Source.

1995, 296:3, eff. Jan. 1, 1996.

622:54. Financial Resources Form.

I. Each inmate shall complete the form provided to the department by the department of justice pursuant to RSA 622:55. Each completed form shall be forwarded to the department.

II. The commissioner or the sentencing court shall immediately notify the department of any information regarded as a significant change in the financial circumstances of any inmate.

Source.

1995, 296:3, eff. Jan. 1, 1996.

622:55. Cost of Care Reimbursement by Inmate.

I. The attorney general shall prepare a form which shall be designed to elicit information from an inmate regarding such person's estate and other pertinent financial information, for the purpose of determining whether such person has sufficient assets to pay all or part of the inmate's cost of care.

Such forms shall be provided by the department of justice to the department and to the chief justice of the superior court.

II. Each inmate shall complete the form under oath when required to do so by the department or the department of justice. Any failure by an inmate to complete such form truthfully shall be considered by the state board of parole in determining whether such inmate should be paroled.

III. The department shall adopt policies and procedures for determining the cost of care of inmates. The cost of care for any inmate shall not be in excess of the per capita cost of maintaining the inmate in the facility or facilities in which the inmate is or was incarcerated.

IV. The department shall review each completed form and determine whether the estate of the inmate is sufficient to reimburse the state for all or part of the cost of care of the inmate. The department shall adopt policies and procedures by which such a determination shall be made. The attorney general or the department may also conduct independent investigations as appropriate to determine whether an inmate has sufficient estate to pay for all or part of the cost of care of such inmate.

V. If the attorney general determines that an inmate possesses a sufficient estate to reimburse the state for all or part of the cost of care of such inmate, the attorney general shall file a petition in superior court. The petition shall state that the person is an inmate, that the department has or shall incur cost of care for the inmate, and that the inmate has a sufficient estate to reimburse the state for all or part of the cost of care of such inmate.

VI. The petition shall be served upon the inmate. When the court determines that the inmate has been properly notified, the court shall issue an order to show cause why the request of the petitioner should not be granted.

VII. If the inmate files an objection, the court shall determine at a hearing whether the department has or will incur the cost of care for the inmate. If the court determines that the inmate has a sufficient estate to pay all or part of the cost of care, the court shall determine the amount which shall be paid by the inmate for the cost of care. The amount shall not be in excess of the per capita cost of maintaining inmates in the institution or facility in which the inmate is residing. The court shall order the inmate to pay such payments toward the cost of care as are appropriate under the circumstances. In setting the amount of such payments, the court shall take into consideration and make allowances for any restitution ordered to the victim or victims of a crime which shall take priority over any payments ordered pursuant to this section, and for the maintenance and support of an inmate's spouse, dependent children, or any other persons having a legal right to support and maintenance out of the estate of the inmate. The court shall also consider the financial needs of the inmate for the 6-month period immediately following the inmate's release for the purpose of allowing the inmate to seek employment.

VIII. If the inmate fails to make any payments as ordered by the court, the attorney general may bring appropriate actions pursuant to RSA 512, for execution and levy of assets of the inmate consistent with the provisions of RSA 480 in the amount necessary to satisfy the unpaid portions of the court's order.

Source.
1995, 296:3, eff. Jan. 1, 1996.

622:56. Post-Imprisonment Action for Reimbursement of Cost of Care.

After release, the department may seek reimbursement of cost of care against any inmate within 6 years of release from imprisonment of such inmate. The department may recover the expenses incurred by an inmate during the entire period such inmate was confined in a correctional facility.

Source.
1995, 296:3, eff. Jan. 1, 1996.

622:57. Legal Costs.

The attorney general shall provide to the department a report on the number of petitions brought under this section and the amount of money recovered. Such report shall be included in the biennial report of the department.

Source.
1995, 296:3, eff. Jan. 1, 1996.

622:58. Deposit of Recovered Moneys.

All moneys recovered under this subdivision shall be deposited in the general fund.

Source.
1995, 296:3, eff. Jan. 1, 1996.

CHAPTER 622-A

NEW ENGLAND INTERSTATE CORRECTIONS COMPACT

SECTION
622-A:1.   Name.
622-A:2.   Compact.
622-A:3.   Authority of Commissioner of Corrections.

Adoption of compact.
This law has been adopted by the following states and is codified as indicated:
  (1)   Connecticut .... C.G.S.A. §§ 18-102–18-104.
  (2)   Massachusetts .... M.G.L.A. c. 125 App., §§ 1-1–1-3.
  (3)   Rhode Island .... Gen. Laws § 13-11-1 et seq.
  (4)   Vermont .... 28 V.S.A. §§ 1401–1410.

Cross References.
Agreements, for care and custody of female convicts, see RSA 622:33 et seq.
  Agreement on detainers, see RSA 606-A.
  Department of corrections, see RSA 21-H.
  Extradition, see RSA 612.
  Interstate corrections compact, see RSA 622-B.
  Sentences generally, see RSA 651.
  State prison, see RSA 622.

NOTES TO DECISIONS

Cited:
  Cited in Hoitt v. Vitek, 361 F. Supp. 1238, 1973 U.S. Dist. LEXIS 12455 (D.N.H. 1973); State v. Harnum, 142 N.H. 195, 697 A.2d 1380, 1997 N.H. LEXIS 75 (1997).

622-A:1. Name.

This chapter may be cited as the New England interstate corrections compact.

Source.
1961, 101:1, eff. May 4, 1961.

622-A:2. Compact.

The New England interstate corrections compact is hereby enacted into law and entered into by this state with any other of the hereinafter mentioned states legally joining therein in the form substantially as follows:

New England Interstate Corrections Compact

Article I

Purpose and Policy

The party states, desiring by common action to fully utilize and improve their institutional facilities and provide adequate programs for the confinement, treatment and rehabilitation of various types of offenders, declare that it is the policy of each of the party states to provide such facilities and programs on a basis of cooperation with one another, thereby serving the best interests of such offenders and of society and effecting economies in capital expenditures and operational costs. The purpose of this compact is to provide for the mutual development and execution of such programs of cooperation for the confinement, treatment and rehabilitation of offenders with the most economical use of human and material resources.

Article II

Definitions

As used in this compact, unless the context clearly requires otherwise:

(a) "State" means a state of the United States, located in New England, to wit, Maine, New Hampshire, Vermont, Massachusetts, Connecticut, Rhode

Island.

(b) "Sending state" means a state party to this compact in which conviction or court commitment was had.

(c) "Receiving state" means a state party to this compact to which an inmate is sent for confinement other than a state in which conviction or court commitment was had.

(d) "Inmate" means a male or female offender who is committed, under sentence to or confined in a penal or correctional institution.

(e) "Institution" means any penal or correctional facility (including but not limited to a facility for the mentally ill or mentally defective) in which inmates as defined in (d) above may lawfully be confined.

Article III

Contracts

(a) Each party state may make one or more contracts with any one or more of the other party states for the confinement of inmates on behalf of a sending state in institutions situated within receiving states. Any such contract shall provide for:

1. Its duration.

2. Payments to be made to the receiving state by the sending state for inmate maintenance, extraordinary medical and dental expenses, and any participation in or receipt by inmates of rehabilitative or correctional services, facilities, programs or treatment not reasonably included as part of normal maintenance.

3. Participation in programs of inmate employment, if any; the disposition or crediting of any payments received by inmates on account thereof; and the crediting of proceeds from or disposal of any products resulting therefrom.

4. Delivery and retaking of inmates.

5. Such other matters as may be necessary and appropriate to fix the obligations, responsibilities and rights of the sending and receiving states.

(b) Subject to legislative approval by the states concerned and prior to the construction or completion of construction of any institution or addition thereto by a party state, any other party state or states may contract therewith for the enlargement of the planned capacity of the institution or addition thereto, or for the inclusion therein of particular equipment or structures, and for the reservation of a specific percentum of the capacity of the institution to be kept available for use by inmates of the sending state or states so contracting. Any sending state so contracting may, to the extent that monies are legally available therefor, pay to the receiving state a reasonable sum as consideration for such enlargement of capacity, or provision of equipment or structures, and reservation of capacity.

(c) The terms and provisions of this compact shall be a part of any contract entered into by the author-ity of or pursuant thereto, and nothing in any such contract shall be inconsistent therewith.

Article IV

Procedures and Rights

(a) Whenever the duly constituted authorities in a state party to this compact, and which has entered into a contract pursuant to Article III, shall decide that confinement in, or transfer of an inmate to, an institution within the territory of another party state is necessary or desirable in order to provide adequate quarters and care or an appropriate program of rehabilitation or treatment, said officials may direct that the confinement be within an institution within the territory of said other party state, the receiving state to act in that regard solely as agent for the sending state.

(b) The appropriate officials of any state party to this compact shall have access, at all reasonable times, to any institution in which it has a contractual right to confine inmates for the purpose of inspecting the facilities thereof and visiting such of its inmates as may be confined in the institution.

(c) Inmates confined in an institution pursuant to the terms of this compact shall at all times be subject to the jurisdiction of the sending state and may at any time be removed therefrom for transfer to a prison or other institution within the sending state, for transfer to another institution in which the sending state may have a contractual or other right to confine inmates, for release on probation or parole, for discharge, or for any other purpose permitted by the laws of the sending state; provided that the sending state shall continue to be obligated to such payments as may be required pursuant to the terms of any contract entered into under the terms of Article III.

(d) Each receiving state shall provide regular reports to each sending state on the inmates of that sending state in institutions pursuant to this compact, including a conduct record of each inmate, and certify said record to the official designated by the sending state, in order that each inmate may have official review of his or her record in determining and altering the disposition of said inmate in accordance with the law which may obtain in the sending state and in order that the same may be a source of information for the sending state.

(e) All inmates who may be confined in an institution pursuant to the provisions of this compact shall be treated in a reasonable and humane manner and shall be treated equally with such similar inmates of the receiving state as may be confined in the same institution. The fact of confinement in a receiving state shall not deprive any inmate so confined of any legal rights which said inmate would have had if confined in an appropriate institution of the sending state.

(f) Any hearing or hearings to which an inmate confined pursuant to this compact may be entitled by the laws of the sending state may be had before the appropriate authorities of the sending state, or of the receiving state if authorized by the sending state. The receiving state shall provide adequate facilities for such hearings as may be conducted by the appropriate officials of a sending state. In the event such hearing or hearings are had before officials of the receiving state, the governing law shall be that of the sending state and a record of the hearing or hearings as prescribed by the sending state shall be made. Said record together with any recommendations of the hearing officials shall be transmitted forthwith to the official or officials before whom the hearing would have been had if it had taken place in the sending state. In any and all proceedings had pursuant to the provisions of this subdivision, the officials of the receiving state shall act solely as agents of the sending state and no final determination shall be made in any matter except by the appropriate officials of the sending state.

(g) Any inmate confined pursuant to this compact shall be released within the territory of the sending state unless the inmate, and the sending and receiving states, shall agree upon release in some other place. The sending state shall bear the cost of such return to its territory.

(h) Any inmate confined pursuant to the terms of this compact shall have any and all rights to participate in and derive any benefits or incur or be relieved of any obligations or have such obligations modified or his status changed on account of any action or proceeding in which he could have participated if confined in any appropriate institution of the sending state located within such state.

(i) The parent, guardian, trustee, or other person or persons entitled under the laws of the sending state to act for, advise, or otherwise function with respect to any inmate shall not be deprived of or restricted in his exercise of any power in respect of any inmate confined pursuant to the terms of this compact.

Article V

Acts Not Reviewable in Receiving State: Extradition

(a) Any decision of the sending state in respect of any matter over which it retains jurisdiction pursuant to this compact shall be conclusive upon and not reviewable within the receiving state, but if at the time the sending state seeks to remove an inmate from an institution in the receiving state there is pending against the inmate within such state any criminal charge or if the inmate is formally accused of having committed within such state a criminal offense, the inmate shall not be returned without the consent of the receiving state until discharged from prosecution or other form of proceeding, imprison-

ment or detention for such offense. The duly accredited officers of the sending state shall be permitted to transport inmates pursuant to this compact through any and all states party to this compact without interference.

(b) An inmate who escapes from an institution in which he is confined pursuant to this compact shall be deemed a fugitive from the sending state and from the state in which the institution is situated. In the case of an escape to a jurisdiction other than the sending or receiving state, the responsibility for institution of extradition or rendition proceedings shall be that of the sending state, but nothing contained herein shall be construed to prevent or affect the activities of officers and agencies of any jurisdiction directed toward the apprehension and return of an escapee.

Article VI

Federal Aid

Any state party to this compact may accept federal aid for use in connection with any institution or program, the use of which is or may be affected by this compact or any contract pursuant hereto, and any inmate in the receiving state pursuant to this compact may participate in any such federally aided program or activity for which the sending and receiving states have made contractual provision; provided that if such program or activity is not part of the customary correctional regimen, the express consent of the appropriate official of the sending state shall be required therefor.

Article VII

Entry into Force

This compact shall enter into force and become effective and binding upon the states so acting when it has been enacted into law by any 2 states from among the states in New England. Thereafter, this compact shall enter into force and become effective and binding as to any other of said states upon similar action by such state.

Article VIII

Withdrawal and Termination

This compact shall continue in force and remain binding upon a party state until it shall have enacted a statute repealing the same and providing for the sending of formal written notice of withdrawal from the compact to the appropriate officials of all other party states. An actual withdrawal shall not take effect until one year after the notices provided in said statute have been sent. Such withdrawal shall not relieve the withdrawing state from its obligations assumed hereunder prior to the effective date of withdrawal. Before the effective date of withdrawal, a withdrawing state shall remove to its territory, at its own expense, such inmates as it may have confined pursuant to the provisions of this compact.

Article IX

Other Arrangements Unaffected

Nothing contained in this compact shall be construed to abrogate or impair any agreement or other arrangement which a party state may have with a nonparty state for the confinement, rehabilitation or treatment of inmates nor to repeal any other laws of a party state authorizing the making of cooperative institutional arrangements.

Article X

Construction and Severability

The provisions of this compact shall be liberally construed and shall be severable. If any phrase, clause, sentence or provision of this compact is declared to be contrary to the constitution of any particular state or of the United States, or the applicability thereof to any government, agency, person or circumstance is held invalid, the validity of the remainder of the compact and the applicability thereof to any government, agency, person or circumstance shall not be affected thereby. If this compact shall be held contrary to the constitution of any state participating therein, the compact shall remain in full force and effect as to the remaining states and in full force and effect as to the state affected as to all severable matters.

Source.
1961, 101:1, eff. May 4, 1961.

622-A:3. Authority of Commissioner of Corrections.

The commissioner of corrections is hereby authorized and directed to do all things necessary or incidental to the carrying out of the compact in every particular.

Source.
1961, 101:1, eff. May 4, 1961.

Revision note.
In the catchline of the section, substituted "commissioner of corrections" for "warden" pursuant to 1983, 461:3, which provided for the abolition of the position of warden of the state prison and the transfer of all powers, duties and functions of the position to the commissioner of corrections. See RSA 21-H.
In the text of the section, substituted "commissioner of corrections" for "warden of the state prison" pursuant to 1983, 461:3, which is described above.

CHAPTER 622-B

INTERSTATE CORRECTIONS COMPACT

SECTION
622-B:1.   Name.
622-B:2.   Compact.
622-B:3.   Duty of the Commissioner of Corrections.

Cross References.
Agreement on detainers, see RSA 606-A.
Agreements for care and custody of female convicts, see RSA 622:33 et seq.
Department of corrections, see RSA 21-H.
Extradition, see RSA 612.
New England interstate corrections compact, see RSA 622-A.
Sentences generally, see RSA 651.
State prison, see RSA 622.

NOTES TO DECISIONS

Cited:
Cited in State v. Harnum, 142 N.H. 195, 697 A.2d 1380, 1997 N.H. LEXIS 75 (1997).

622-B:1. Name.

This chapter may be cited as the national interstate corrections compact.

Source.
1979, 111:1, eff. July 20, 1979.

622-B:2. Compact.

The national interstate corrections compact is hereby enacted into law and entered into by this state with any other states legally joining therein in the form substantially as follows:

Interstate Corrections Compact

Article I

Purpose and Policy

The party states, desiring by common action to fully utilize and improve their institutional facilities and provide adequate programs for the confinement, treatment and rehabilitation of various types of offenders, declare that it is the policy of each of the party states to provide such facilities and programs on a basis of cooperation with one another, thereby serving the best interest of such offenders and of society and effecting economies in capital expenditures and operational costs. The purpose of this compact is to provide for the mutual development and execution of such programs of cooperation for the confinement, treatment and rehabilitation of offenders with the most economical use of human and material resources.

Article II

Definitions

As used in this compact, unless the context clearly requires otherwise:

(a) "State" means a state of the United States; the United States of America; a territory or possession of the United States; the District of Columbia; the commonwealth of Puerto Rico.

(b) "Sending state" means a state party to this compact in which conviction or court commitment was had.

(c) "Receiving state" means a state party to this compact to which an inmate is sent for confinement other than a state in which conviction or court commitment was had.

(d) "Inmate" means a male or female offender who is committed, under sentence to or confined in a penal or correctional institution.

(e) "Institution" means any penal or correctional facility, including but not limited to a facility for the mentally ill or mentally defective, in which inmates as defined in (d) may lawfully be confined.

Article III

Contracts

(a) Each party state may make one or more contracts with any one or more of the other party states for the confinement of inmates on behalf of a sending state in institutions situated within receiving states. Any such contract shall provide for:

(i) Its duration.

(ii) Payments to be made to the receiving state by the sending state for inmate maintenance, extraordinary medical and dental expenses, and any participation in or receipt by inmates of rehabilitative or correctional services, facilities, programs or treatment not reasonably included as part of normal maintenance.

(iii) Participation in programs of inmate employment, if any; the disposition or crediting of any payments received by inmates on account thereof; and the crediting of proceeds from or disposal of any product resulting therefrom.

(iv) Delivery and retaking of inmates.

(v) Such other matters as may be necessary and appropriate to fix the obligations, responsibilities and rights of the sending and receiving states.

(b) The terms and provisions of this compact shall be a part of any contract entered into by the authority of or pursuant thereto, and nothing in any such contract shall be inconsistent therewith.

Article IV

Procedures and Rights

(a) Whenever the duly constituted authorities in a state party to this compact, and which has entered into a contract pursuant to Article III, shall decide that confinement in, or transfer of an inmate to, an institution within the territory of another party state is necessary or desirable in order to provide adequate quarters and care or an appropriate program of rehabilitation or treatment, said officials may direct that the confinement be within an institution within the territory of said other party state, the receiving state to act in that regard solely as agent for the sending state.

(b) The appropriate officials of any state party to this compact shall have access, at all reasonable times, to any institution in which it has a contractual right to confine inmates for the purpose of inspecting the facilities thereof and visiting such of its inmates as may be confined in the institution.

(c) Inmates confined in an institution pursuant to the terms of this compact shall at all times be subject to the jurisdiction of the sending state and may at any time be removed therefrom for transfer to a prison or other institution within the sending state, for transfer to another institution in which the sending state may have a contractual or other right to confine inmates, for release on probation or parole, for discharge or for any other purpose permitted by the laws of the sending state; provided that the sending state shall continue to be obligated to such payments as may be required pursuant to the terms of any contract entered into under the terms of Article III.

(d) Each receiving state shall provide regular reports to each sending state on the inmates of that sending state in institutions pursuant to this compact, including a conduct record of each inmate, and certify said record to the official designated by the sending state, in order that each inmate may have official review of his or her record in determining and altering the disposition of said inmate in accordance with the law which may obtain in the sending state and in order that the same may be a source of information for the sending state.

(e) All inmates who may be confined in an institution pursuant to the provisions of this compact shall be treated in a reasonable and humane manner and shall be treated equally with such similar inmates of the receiving state as may be confined in the same institution. The fact of confinement in a receiving state shall not deprive any inmate so confined of any legal rights which said inmate would have had if confined in an appropriate institution of the sending state.

(f) Any hearing or hearings to which an inmate confined pursuant to this compact may be entitled by the laws of the sending state may be had before the appropriate authorities of the sending state, or of the receiving state if authorized by the sending state. The receiving state shall provide adequate facilities for such hearings as may be conducted by the appropriate officials of a sending state. In the event such hearing or hearings are had before officials of the receiving state, the governing law shall be that of the sending state and a record of the hearing or hearings as prescribed by the sending state shall be made. Said record, together with any recommendations of the hearing officials, shall be transmitted forthwith to the official or officials before whom the hearing would have been had if it had taken place in the sending state. In any and all proceedings had pursuant to the provisions of this subdivision, the officials of the receiving state shall act solely as agents of the sending state and no final determination shall be made in any matter except by the appropriate officials of the sending state.

(g) Any inmate confined pursuant to this compact shall be released within the territory of the sending state unless the inmate, and the sending and receiving states, shall agree upon release in some other place. The sending state shall bear the cost of such return to its territory.

(h) Any inmate confined pursuant to the terms of this compact shall have any and all rights to participate in and derive any benefits or incur or be relieved of any obligations or have such obligations modified or his status changed on account of any action or proceeding in which he could have participated if confined in any appropriate institution of the sending state located within such state.

(i) The parent, guardian, trustee, or other person or persons entitled under the laws of the sending state to act for, advise, or otherwise function with respect to any inmate shall not be deprived of or restricted in his exercise of any power in respect of any inmate confined pursuant to the terms of this compact.

Article V

Acts Not Reviewable in Receiving State; Extradition

(a) Any decision of the sending state in respect of any matter over which it retains jurisdiction pursuant to this compact shall be conclusive upon and not reviewable within the receiving state, but if at the time the sending state seeks to remove an inmate from an institution in the receiving state there is pending against the inmate within such state any criminal charge or if the inmate is formally accused of having committed within such state a criminal offense, the inmate shall not be returned without the consent of the receiving state until discharged from prosecution or other form of proceeding, imprisonment, or detention for such offense. The duly accredited officers of the sending state shall be permitted to transport inmates pursuant to this compact through any and all states party to this compact without interference.

(b) An inmate who escapes from an institution in which he is confined pursuant to this compact shall be deemed a fugitive from the sending state and from the state in which the institution is situated. In the case of an escape to a jurisdiction other than the sending or receiving state, the responsibility for institution of extradition or rendition proceedings shall be that of the sending state, but nothing contained herein shall be construed to prevent or affect the activities of officers and agencies of any jurisdiction directed toward the apprehension and return of an escapee.

Article VI

Federal Aid

Any state party to this compact may accept federal aid for use in connection with any institution or program, the use of which is or may be affected by this compact or any contract pursuant hereto, and any inmate in a receiving state pursuant to this compact may participate in any such federally aided program or activity for which the sending and receiving states have made contractual provisions; provided that if such program or activity is not part of the customary correctional regimen, the express consent of the appropriate official of the sending state shall be required therefor.

Article VII

Entry into Force

This compact shall enter into force and become effective and binding upon the state so acting when it has been enacted into law by any 2 states. Thereafter, this compact shall enter into force and become effective and binding as to any other of said states upon similar action by such state.

Article VIII

Withdrawal and Termination

This compact shall continue in force and remain binding upon a party state until it shall have enacted a statute repealing the same and providing for the sending of formal written notice of withdrawal from the compact to the appropriate officials of all other party states. An actual withdrawal shall not take effect until one year after the notices provided in said statute have been sent. Such withdrawal shall not relieve the withdrawing state from its obligations assumed hereunder prior to the effective date of withdrawal. Before the effective date of withdrawal, a withdrawing state shall remove to its territory, at its own expense, such inmates as it may have confined pursuant to the provisions of this compact.

Article IX

Other Agreements Unaffected

Nothing contained in this compact shall be construed to abrogate or impair any agreement or other arrangement which a party state may have with a nonparty state for the confinement, rehabilitation or treatment of inmates nor to repeal any other laws of a party authorizing the making of cooperative institutional arrangements.

Article X

Construction and Severability

The provisions of this compact shall be liberally construed and shall be severable. If any phrase, clause, sentence or provision of this compact is declared to be contrary to the constitution of any participating state or of the United States, or the applicability thereof to any government, agency, person or circumstance is held invalid, the validity of the remainder of this compact and the applicability thereof to any government, agency, person or circumstance shall not be affected thereby. If this compact shall be held contrary to the constitution of any state participating therein, the compact shall remain in full force and effect as to the remaining states and in full force and effect as to the state affected as to all severable matters.

Source.
1979, 111:1, eff. July 20, 1979.

622-B:3. Duty of the Commissioner of Corrections.

The commissioner of corrections is authorized and directed to do all things necessary or incidental to implement this compact and he may, in his discretion, delegate this authority to other persons.

Source.
1979, 111:1, eff. July 20, 1979.

Revision note.
In the catchline of the section and in the text, substituted "commissioner of corrections" for "warden of the state prison" pursuant to 1983, 461:3, which provided for the abolition of the position of warden of the state prison and the transfer of all powers, duties, and functions of the position to the commissioner of corrections. See RSA 21-H.

CHAPTER 622-C

INTERNATIONAL PRISONER TRANSFERS

SECTION
622-C:1.   International Prisoner Transfer.

622-C:1. International Prisoner Transfer.

Whenever a treaty is in force between the United States and a foreign country providing for the transfer or exchange of convicted offenders to the country of which they are citizens or nationals, the governor may, on behalf of the state and subject to the terms of the treaty, authorize the commissioner of corrections to consent to the transfer or exchange of offenders and to take any other action necessary to implement the participation of this state in the treaty.

Source.
1986, 156:3, eff. May 28, 1986.

CHAPTER 623

TEMPORARY REMOVAL OF PRISONERS

SECTION
623:1.   Illness or Emergency.
623:1-a.   Court Appearances.
623:2.   Transfer From State Prisons.
623:3.   Transfer to State Prison. [Repealed.]
623:4.   Transfer Procedure.

Cross References.
County correctional facilities generally, see RSA 30-B.
Department of corrections, see RSA 21-H.
Procedure after exposure of public safety workers to infectious disease, see RSA 141-G.
Sentences generally, see RSA 651.
State prison generally, see RSA 622.
Youth development center generally, see RSA 621.

623:1. Illness or Emergency.

I. Any person confined in a county department of corrections facility, state prison or other place of detention may, under necessary precautions, be taken by some regular or specially authorized officer from such place of detention to a medical facility for the purpose of receiving medical examination or treatment upon recommendation of a physician, a physician's assistant, or an advanced practice registered nurse (APRN) and upon approval of the superintendent of the institution in which the person is confined. In the case of a transfer of a pretrial prisoner for medical purposes for a period in excess of 10 days, the justice of the court who originally ordered the prisoner's commitment shall be given written notice of the transfer within 15 days of said transfer, and shall be given notice upon the return of the prisoner within 15 days of the prisoner's return, provided the prisoner is not in the custody of correctional personnel while at the medical facility. The provisions of RSA 402:79 shall apply to payments for medical care provided pursuant to this section.

II. Any person confined in a county department of corrections facility, state prison or other place of detention may be temporarily taken from his place of confinement because of the imminently approaching death or funeral of a member of his immediate family or for other imperative and extraordinary purpose, including treatment, counseling or rehabilitation programs, for a period not exceeding 72 hours without approval by a justice of the superior court.

III, IV. [Repealed.]

Source.

1917, 18:1. 1919, 58:1. PL 397:30. RL 461:30. RSA 623:1. 1975, 388:7. 1977, 306:1. 1979, 290:1. 1987, 250:2. 1988, 89:25, eff. June 17, 1988. 2000, 225:2, eff. July 31, 2000. 2002, 255:1, eff. Jan. 1, 2003. 2003, 32:1, eff. Jan. 1, 2004; 237:8, eff. at 12:01 a.m., Jan. 1, 2004. 2004, 218:2, eff. June 11, 2004. 2009, 54:4, 5, eff. July 21, 2009.

Amendments

—2009. The 2009 amendment substituted "advanced practice registered nurse (APRN)" for "advanced registered nurse practitioner (ARNP)" in the first sentence of I.

—2004. Paragraphs III, IV: Repealed.

—2003. Paragraph I: Chapter 32 added the proviso in the second sentence.

Chapter 237 inserted "a physician's assistant" following "physician" and substituted "superintendent" for "administrator" in the first sentence, and inserted "of a pretrial prisoner" preceding "for medical" and substituted "10 days" for "24 hours" and "15 days" for "5 days" in two places in the second sentence.

Paragraph II: Chapter 237 substituted "72 hours" for "48 hours".

—2002. Paragraphs III and IV: Added.

—2000. Paragraph I: Inserted "or an advanced registered nurse practitioner (ARNP)" following "physician" in the first sentence.

—1988. Paragraph I: Substituted "department of corrections facility" for "jail, house of correction" preceding "state prison or other place of detention" in the first sentence.

Paragraph II: Substituted "department of corrections facility" for "jail, house of correction" preceding "state prison or other place of detention".

—1987. Paragraph I: Deleted "within the state of New Hampshire" following "medical facility" in the first sentence and added the third sentence.

—1979. Rewritten to the extent that a detailed comparison would be impracticable.

—1977. Rewritten to the extent that a detailed comparison would be impracticable.

—1975. Added the second and third sentences.

NOTES TO DECISIONS

1. Involuntary interstate transfers—Generally

2. —Emergency transfers

1. Involuntary interstate transfers—Generally

An involuntary out-of-state transfer of a prisoner does not in and of itself constitute cruel and unusual punishment. Hoitt v. Vitek, 361 F. Supp. 1238, 1973 U.S. Dist. LEXIS 12455 (D.N.H. 1973), aff'd, 495 F.2d 219, 1974 U.S. App. LEXIS 9244 (1st Cir. N.H. 1974), aff'd, 497 F.2d 598, 1974 U.S. App. LEXIS 8588 (1st Cir. 1974), aff'd without op., Laaman v. Vitek, 502 F.2d 1158 (1st Cir. N.H. 1973).

Whatever the state's interest, procedural due process must be met in involuntary interstate transfers of prisoners because of the adverse effects such transfers impose on those transferred; due process requires, prior to the transfer, (1) written notice, of at least three days, of the basis for the recommendation to transfer; (2) assistance of a lay advocate of inmate's choice; (3) a hearing before three or more impartial persons, at least one of whom is not a prison official; (4) the right to present evidence and cross-examine; (5) a record of the hearing; (6) written findings with a copy to the inmate; (7) a determination based on reliable evidence adduced at the hearing; and (8) an opportunity for administrative review before at least a three member panel none of whom sat at the original hearing. Hoitt v. Vitek, 361 F. Supp. 1238, 1973 U.S. Dist. LEXIS 12455 (D.N.H. 1973), aff'd, 495 F.2d 219, 1974 U.S. App. LEXIS 9244 (1st Cir. N.H. 1974), aff'd, 497 F.2d 598, 1974 U.S. App. LEXIS 8588 (1st Cir. 1974), aff'd without op., Laaman v. Vitek, 502 F.2d 1158 (1st Cir. N.H. 1973).

2. —Emergency transfers

In an emergency prison situation, all inmates transferred to out-of-state prisons must be returned immediately after the emergency has subsided, given a due process hearing with notice and opportunity for review if permanent transfer is contemplated, and given a hearing if the transfers have a detrimental effect on parole or "good time." Hoitt v. Vitek, 361 F. Supp. 1238, 1973 U.S. Dist. LEXIS 12455 (D.N.H. 1973), aff'd, 495 F.2d 219, 1974 U.S. App. LEXIS 9244 (1st Cir. N.H. 1974), aff'd, 497 F.2d 598, 1974 U.S. App. LEXIS 8588 (1st Cir. 1974), aff'd without op., Laaman v. Vitek, 502 F.2d 1158 (1st Cir. N.H. 1973).

Cited:

Cited in Laaman v. Helgemoe, 437 F. Supp. 269, 1977 U.S. Dist. LEXIS 15128 (D.N.H. 1977).

RESEARCH REFERENCES

New Hampshire Trial Bar News.

For article, "Competency to Stand Trial (Part 1)," see 6 N.H. Trial Bar News 22, 24 (Summer 1986).

623:1-a. Court Appearances.

Any person confined in a county department of corrections facility, state prison, or other place of detention may, under necessary precautions and upon approval of the administrator of the institution in which said person is confined, be taken by some regular or specially authorized officer from such place of detention to a state or federal court within the state of New Hampshire to appear in a proceeding before that court. During the time period such person is in a state courthouse, the sheriff, through the sheriff's deputies and bailiffs, shall be responsible for such person's custody and control.

Source.

1977, 306:2. 1979, 290:2. 1988, 89:26, eff. June 17, 1988. 1998, 297:7, eff. Jan. 1, 1999. 2003, 32:2, eff. Jan. 1, 2004.

Amendments

—2003. Deleted the proviso in the first sentence.

—1998. Added the last sentence.

—**1988.** Substituted "department of corrections facility" for "jail, house of correction" preceding "state prison, or other place".

—**1979.** Deleted "the governor or" following "12 hours without approval of".

623:2. Transfer From State Prisons.

Any person confined in a state prison may, upon recommendation of the commissioner of corrections, be transferred to a county correctional facility if such transfer is approved by the county commissioners of the county in which the receiving facility is located.

Source.
1971, 312:1. 1988, 89:27, eff. June 17, 1988. 1998, 386:15, eff. Aug. 26, 1998.

Revision note.
At the beginning of the section, substituted "commissioner of corrections" for "warden" pursuant to 1983, 461:3, which provided for the abolition of the position of warden of the state prison and the transfer of all powers, functions and duties of the position to the commissioner of corrections. See RSA 21-H.

Amendments
—**1998.** Substituted "Prisons" for "Prison" in the section catchline, and substituted "a state prison" for "the state prison".

—**1988.** Deleted "and with the approval of the governor or a justice of the superior court" following "recommendation of the commissioner of corrections" and substituted "correctional facility if such transfer is approved by the county commissioners of the county in which the receiving facility is located" for "jail or house of correction" following "transferred to a county".

Cross References.
County correctional facilities, see RSA 30-B.

NOTES TO DECISIONS

Cited:
Cited in Hoitt v. Vitek, 361 F. Supp. 1238, 1973 U.S. Dist. LEXIS 12455 (D.N.H. 1973); State v. Schulte, 120 N.H. 344, 415 A.2d 670, 1980 N.H. LEXIS 286 (1980).

623:3. Transfer to State Prison.

[Repealed 1992, 143:3, eff. July 5, 1992.]

Former section(s).
Former RSA 623:3, which was derived from 1971, 312:1 and 1988, 89:28, related to transfer of persons awaiting trial on felony charges to state prison. See now RSA 21-H:8.

623:4. Transfer Procedure.

No person shall be transferred pursuant to the provisions of RSA 623:2 and RSA 21-H:8, VI, unless both the commissioner of corrections and the respective superintendent of the county department of corrections sign an authorization to permit such a transfer.

Source.
1971, 312:1. 1988, 89:29. 1992, 143:2, eff. July 5, 1992.

Revision note.
At the beginning of the section, substituted "commissioner of

corrections" for "warden of the state prison" pursuant to 1983, 461:3, which provided for the abolition of the position of warden of the state prison and the transfer of all powers, functions and duties of the position to the commissioner of corrections. See RSA 21-H.

Amendments
—**1992.** Substituted "RSA 623:2 and RSA 21-H:8, VI" for "RSA 623:2 and 3" following "provisions of".

—**1988.** Substituted "superintendent of the county department of corrections" for "county sheriff" preceding "sign an authorization".

CHAPTER 623-A

APPROVED ABSENCES FROM NEW HAMPSHIRE STATE PRISONS

SECTION
623-A:1.   Authority to Establish Regulations.
623-A:2.   Eligibility for Approved Absence.
623-A:3.   Purposes of Approved Absence.
623-A:4.   Duration of Approved Absence.
623-A:5.   Expenses.
623-A:6.   Waiver of Extradition.
623-A:7.   Status During Absence.
623-A:8.   Violation of Terms of Approved Absence.
623-A:9.   Interpretation of Chapter.

Amendments
—**1998.** 1998, 386:16, eff. Aug. 26, 1998, substituted "prisons" for "prison" in the chapter heading.

Cross References.
Department of corrections, see RSA 21-H.
Extradition, see RSA 612.
Sentences generally, see RSA 651.
State prison generally, see RSA 622.
Temporary removal of prisoners from prison, see RSA 623.

623-A:1. Authority to Establish Regulations.

The commissioner of corrections is hereby authorized to establish rules permitting approved absences of eligible inmates who are in his official custody. The rules shall be subject to the limitations, restrictions and conditions of this chapter and may impose additional limitations, restrictions or conditions. The rules may be amended from time to time or rescinded.

Source.
1975, 241:1, eff. Aug. 3, 1975.

Revision note.
In the first sentence, substituted "commissioner of corrections" for "warden of the state prison" pursuant to 1983, 461:3, which provided for the abolition of the position of warden of the state prison and the transfer of all powers, duties and functions of the position to the commissioner of corrections. See RSA 21-H.
In the first sentence preceding "is hereby authorized" and in the third sentence following "rescinded", deleted "with the approval of the board of prison trustees" pursuant to 1983, 461:2, which provided for the abolition of the state prison board of trustees and the transfer of all powers, functions and duties of the board to the commissioner of corrections. See RSA 21-H.

Cross References.
Administrative Procedure Act, see RSA 541-A.

623-A:2. Eligibility for Approved Absence.

I. Upon the application of an inmate, the commissioner of corrections may grant an approved absence if he determines that the inmate:

(a) Is serving the last 90 days of his sentence;

(b) Pursuant to RSA 651:25, is on work or study release or is a resident of a community correctional center or halfway house;

(c) Is physically and mentally capable of conducting himself during an approved absence without escort; and

(d) Has demonstrated a level of responsibility which provides reasonable assurance that he will comply fully with the requirements of approved absence and will not jeopardize the safety of persons or property in the community.

II. If otherwise eligible under subparagraphs I(a), (b), (c) and (d), inmates confined at the state prison or other institution under the control of the commissioner of corrections under RSA 622-A may be eligible for approved absence only if, upon the request of the commissioner of corrections, the sending state authorizes such approved absence.

Source.
1975, 241:1, eff. Aug. 3, 1975.

Revision note.
In pars. I and II, substituted "commissioner of corrections" for "warden" pursuant to 1983, 461:3, which provided for the abolition of the position of warden of the state prison and the transfer of all powers, duties and functions of the position to the commissioner of corrections. See RSA 21-H.

In par. II, substituted "subparagraphs" for "paragraphs" preceding "I(a), (b), (c) and (d)" in order to conform terminology to that employed generally in New Hampshire Revised Statutes Annotated.

623-A:3. Purposes of Approved Absence.

I. An eligible inmate may be considered for approved absence only for the following purposes:

(a) Visits with the inmate's family.

(b) Attendance at the funeral of a close relative.

(c) Obtaining medical treatment.

(d) Seeking or securing employment.

(e) Seeking or securing admission to an educational or vocational program.

(f) Attendance at specific community religious, educational, vocational, social, civic or recreational activities.

II. In unusual circumstances, an approved absence may be granted for purposes not specified in this section.

Source.
1975, 241:1, eff. Aug. 3, 1975.

Revision note.
In par. II following "specified in this section", deleted "only with the concurrence of the board of prison trustees" pursuant to 1983, 461:2, which provided for the abolition of the state prison board of trustees and the transfer of all powers, functions and duties of the board to the commissioner of corrections. RSA 623-A:2 provides for granting of absences by the commissioner of corrections under specified conditions.

Cross References.
Temporary removal of inmates from correctional facilities for medical treatment or emergencies generally, see RSA 623:1.

623-A:4. Duration of Approved Absence.

Every approved absence shall be for a specified period of time which shall be no longer than necessary to accomplish the purpose of the approved absence. An approved absence shall not exceed 7 days except where necessary for extended medical treatment. An approved absence once begun may be extended by the commissioner of corrections only where necessary to permit accomplishment of the purpose for which the approved absence was originally granted. The commissioner of corrections may shorten or terminate an approved absence in his discretion.

Source.
1975, 241:1, eff. Aug. 3, 1975.

Revision note.
In the third and fourth sentences, substituted "commissioner of corrections" for "warden" pursuant to 1983, 461:3, which provided for the abolition of the position of warden of the state prison and the transfer of all powers, duties and functions of the position to the commissioner of corrections. See RSA 21-H.

Cross References.
Authorized purposes for absences generally, see RSA 623-A:3.

623-A:5. Expenses.

All expenses of an approved absence for transport, food, lodging and incidentals shall be borne by the inmate or his family or from other sources approved by the commissioner of corrections.

Source.
1975, 241:1, eff. Aug. 3, 1975.

Revision note.
At the end of the section, substituted "commissioner of corrections" for "warden" pursuant to 1983, 461:3, which provided for the abolition of the position of warden of the state prison and the transfer of all powers, duties and functions of the position to the commissioner of corrections. See RSA 21-H.

623-A:6. Waiver of Extradition.

Prior to commencement of an approved absence, the inmate shall be required to execute a waiver of extradition.

Source.
1975, 241:1, eff. Aug. 3, 1975.

Cross References.
Extradition generally, see RSA 612.

623-A:7. Status During Absence.

While on approved absence, an inmate continues in the official custody of the commissioner of corrections.

Source.
1975, 241:1, eff. Aug. 3, 1975.

Revision note.

At the end of the section, substituted "commissioner of corrections" for "warden" pursuant to 1983, 461:3, which provided for the abolition of the position of warden of the state prison and the transfer of all powers, duties and functions of the position to the commissioner of corrections. See RSA 21-H.

623-A:8. Violation of Terms of Approved Absence.

I. If the commissioner of corrections has reason to believe that an inmate has violated the terms of an approved absence, he may certify that the inmate has escaped and thereafter shall take all necessary steps to secure the return of the inmate as promptly as possible. Escape from approved absence is escape from official custody within the meaning and subject to the provisions of RSA 642:6.

II. A person is guilty of a misdemeanor if he willfully obstructs, intimidates or abets an inmate on approved absence and thereby causes or contributes to cause the inmate to violate the terms of approved absence.

Source.

1975, 241:1, eff. Aug. 3, 1975.

Revision note.

In the first sentence of par. I, substituted "commissioner of corrections" for "warden" pursuant to 1983, 461:3, which provided for the abolition of the position of warden of the state prison and the transfer of all powers, duties and functions of the position to the commissioner of corrections. See RSA 21-H.

Cross References.

Classification of crimes, see RSA 625:9.

Sentences, see RSA 651.

623-A:9. Interpretation of Chapter.

This chapter shall not be interpreted as establishing any rights to approved absence, but only as authorizing establishment of provisions for approved absence as part of a program for rehabilitation and reintegration of inmates into the community. This chapter does not affect nor is it affected by the provisions of RSA 651:19 and 25, relating to work release, and RSA 623, relating to temporary removal of prisoners.

Source.

1975, 241:1, eff. Aug. 3, 1975.

TITLE LXII
CRIMINAL CODE

CHAPTER

625   Preliminary.
626   General Principles.
627   Justification.
628   Responsibility.
629   Inchoate Crimes.
630   Homicide.
631   Assault and Related Offenses.
632   Rape. [Repealed.].
632-A   Sexual Assault and Related Offenses.
633   Interference with Freedom.
634   Destruction of Property.
635   Unauthorized Entries.
636   Robbery.
637   Theft.
638   Fraud.
639   Offenses Against the Family.
639-A   Methamphetamine-Related Crimes.
640   Corrupt Practices.
641   Falsification in Official Matters.
642   Obstructing Governmental Operations.
643   Abuse of Office.
644   Breaches of the Peace and Related Offenses.
645   Public Indecency.
646   Offenses Against the Flag. [Repealed.].
646-A   Desecration of the Flag.
647   Gambling Offenses.
648   Subversive Activities. [Repealed.].
649   Sabotage Prevention.
649-A   Child Pornography.
649-B   Computer Pornography and Child Exploitation Prevention.
650   Obscene Matter.
650-A   Felonious Use of Firearms.
650-B   Felonious Use of Body Armor.
650-C   Negligent Storage of Firearms.
651   Sentences.
651-A   Parole of Prisoners.
651-B   Registration of Criminal Offenders.
651-C   DNA Testing of Criminal Offenders.
651-D   Post-Conviction DNA Testing.
651-E   Interbranch Criminal and Juvenile Justice Council.
651-F   Information and Analysis Center.

Cross References.

Appeals from convictions in municipal or district court, see RSA 599.

Arrests in criminal cases, see RSA 594.

Bail and recognizances, see RSA 597.

Depositions in criminal cases, see RSA 517:13 et seq.

Discovery in criminal cases, see RSA 604:1-a.

Extradition, see RSA 612.

Fingerprinting and measuring of defendants, see RSA 593.

Fresh pursuit, see RSA 614.

Immunity in criminal cases, see RSA 516:34.

Indictments, information, and complaints, see RSA 601.

Jurisdiction and procedure generally, see RSA 592-A.

Pleas and refusal to plead, see RSA 605.

Preliminary examination of accused, see RSA 596-A.

Proceedings in cases of willful trespass, see RSA 539.

Representation of indigent defendants, see RSA 604-A.

Rights of accused, see New Hampshire Constitution, Part 1, Article 15.

Trial of criminal cases, see RSA 606.

Venue in criminal cases, see RSA 602:1.

CHAPTER 625
PRELIMINARY

SECTION

625:1.   Name.
625:2.   Effective Date.
625:3.   Construction of the Code.
625:4.   Territorial Jurisdiction.
625:5.   Civil Actions.
625:6.   All Offenses Defined by Statute.
625:7.   Application to Offenses Outside the Code.
625:8.   Limitations.
625:9.   Classification of Crimes.
625:10.   Burden of Proof.
625:11.   General Definitions.

625:1. Name.

This title shall be known as the Criminal Code.

Source.

1971, 518:1, eff. Nov. 1, 1973.

625:2. Effective Date.

I. This code shall take effect on November 1, 1973.

II. Prosecution for offenses committed prior to the effective date of this code shall be governed by the prior law, which is continued in effect for that purpose as if this code were not in force; provided, however, that in any such prosecution the court may, with the consent of the defendant, impose sentence under the provisions of this code.

III. For purposes of this section, an offense was committed prior to the effective date if any of the elements of the offense occurred prior thereto.

Source.

1971, 518:1, eff. Nov. 1, 1973.

NOTES TO DECISIONS

Sentencing

Defendant convicted of first-degree manslaughter committed prior to effective date of new criminal code was not entitled to be sentenced solely upon his election under the more lenient code provisions, as sentencing under this code is also in the discretion of the court. Nichols v. Helgemoe, 117 N.H. 57, 369 A.2d 614, 1977 N.H. LEXIS 266 (1977).

If defendant consents, the trial court may, in its discretion, sentence under this code, but the consent of defendant does not require the court to sentence under this code. State v. McMillan, 115 N.H. 268, 339 A.2d 21, 1975 N.H. LEXIS 283 (1975).

Where state conceded it did not appear trial court considered paragraph II of this section, whereby court may impose sentence under this code with the consent of defendant, the case would be remanded in order that the court could exercise its discretion under paragraph II to sentence under this code if defendant should consent to it. State v. McMillan, 115 N.H. 268, 339 A.2d 21, 1975 N.H. LEXIS 283 (1975).

Cited:

Cited in Doe v. State, 114 N.H. 714, 328 A.2d 784, 1974 N.H. LEXIS 359 (1974); State v. Dean, 115 N.H. 520, 345 A.2d 408, 1975 N.H. LEXIS 352 (1975); State v. McMillan, 116 N.H. 126, 352 A.2d

702, 1976 N.H. LEXIS 283 (1976); State v. Musumeci, 116 N.H. 136, 355 A.2d 434, 1976 N.H. LEXIS 287 (1976).

625:3. Construction of the Code.

The rule that penal statutes are to be strictly construed does not apply to this code. All provisions of this code shall be construed according to the fair import of their terms and to promote justice.

Source.
1971, 518:1, eff. Nov. 1, 1973.

Cross References.
Statutory construction generally, see RSA 21.

NOTES TO DECISIONS

1. Common law
2. Liberal construction

1. Common law
New Hampshire did not follow the common law rule of strict construction of criminal statutes, and because the theft statute broadly defined "theft," the crime of burglary with the purpose to commit theft was considered to be a theft crime for the purpose of sentencing enhancement. Derosia v. Warden, N.H. State Prison, 149 N.H. 579, 826 A.2d 575, 2003 N.H. LEXIS 78 (2003), rehearing denied, 2003 N.H. LEXIS 111 (N.H. July 18, 2003).
New Hampshire does not follow the common law rule that criminal statutes are to be strictly construed. State v. Harper, 126 N.H. 815, 498 A.2d 310, 1985 N.H. LEXIS 409 (1985).

2. Liberal construction
Criminal code must be construed liberally to promote justice. State v. Roger A., 121 N.H. 19, 424 A.2d 1139, 1981 N.H. LEXIS 243 (1981).

Cited:
Cited in State v. Littlefield, 152 N.H. 331, 876 A.2d 712, 2005 N.H. LEXIS 100 (2005); Doe v. State, 114 N.H. 714, 328 A.2d 784, 1974 N.H. LEXIS 359 (1974); State v. Lemire, 116 N.H. 395, 359 A.2d 644, 1976 N.H. LEXIS 363 (1976); State v. McPhail, 116 N.H. 440, 362 A.2d 199, 1976 N.H. LEXIS 377 (1976); State v. Partlow, 117 N.H. 78, 369 A.2d 221, 1977 N.H. LEXIS 274 (1977); State v. Berry, 117 N.H. 352, 373 A.2d 355, 1977 N.H. LEXIS 337 (1977); State v. French, 117 N.H. 785, 378 A.2d 1377, 1977 N.H. LEXIS 432 (1977); State v. Scott, 117 N.H. 996, 380 A.2d 1092, 1977 N.H. LEXIS 479 (1977); State v. Goodwin, 118 N.H. 862, 395 A.2d 1234, 1978 N.H. LEXIS 307 (1978); State v. Aldrich, 124 N.H. 43, 466 A.2d 938, 1983 N.H. LEXIS 356 (1983); State v. Bailey, 127 N.H. 811, 508 A.2d 1066, 1986 N.H. LEXIS 243 (1986); State v. Hamel, 138 N.H. 392, 643 A.2d 953, 1994 N.H. LEXIS 35 (1994); Appeal of Soucy, 139 N.H. 110, 649 A.2d 60, 1994 N.H. LEXIS 115 (1994); State v. Goodwin, 140 N.H. 672, 671 A.2d 554, 1996 N.H. LEXIS 13 (1996); State v. Bernard, 141 N.H. 230, 680 A.2d 609, 1996 N.H. LEXIS 77 (1996); State v. Williams, 143 N.H. 559, 729 A.2d 416, 1999 N.H. LEXIS 44 (1999); State v. Williams, 143 N.H. 559, 729 A.2d 416, 1999 N.H. LEXIS 44 (1999); State v. Hatt, 144 N.H. 246, 740 A.2d 1037, 1999 N.H. LEXIS 107 (1999); In re Justin D., 144 N.H. 450, 743 A.2d 829, 1999 N.H. LEXIS 132 (1999); State v. Woodard, 146 N.H. 221, 769 A.2d 379, 2001 N.H. LEXIS 64 (2001); State v. Grant-Chase, 150 N.H. 248, 837 A.2d 322, 2003 N.H. LEXIS 171 (2003); In re Juvenile 2003-187, 151 N.H. 14, 846 A.2d 1207, 2004 N.H. LEXIS 81 (2004).

625:4. Territorial Jurisdiction.

I. Except as otherwise provided in this section, a person may be convicted under the laws of this state for any offense committed by his own conduct or by the conduct of another for which he is legally accountable if:

(a) Either conduct which is an element of the offense or the result which is such an element occurs within this state; or
(b) Conduct occurring outside this state constitutes an attempt to commit an offense under the laws of this state and the purpose is that the offense take place within this state; or
(c) Conduct occurring outside this state would constitute a criminal conspiracy under the laws of this state, and an overt act in furtherance of the conspiracy occurs within this state, and the object of the conspiracy is that an offense take place within this state; or
(d) Conduct occurring within this state would constitute complicity in the commission of, or an attempt, solicitation or conspiracy to commit an offense in another jurisdiction which is also an offense under the law of this state; or
(e) The offense consists of the omission to perform a duty imposed on a person by the law of this state regardless of where that person is when the omission occurs; or
(f) Jurisdiction is otherwise provided by law.
II. Subparagraph I(a) does not apply if:
(a) Causing a particular result or danger of causing that result is an element and the result occurs or is designed or likely to occur only in another jurisdiction where the conduct charged would not constitute an offense; or
(b) Causing a particular result is an element of an offense and the result is caused by conduct occurring outside the state which would not constitute an offense if the result had occurred there.
III. When the offense is homicide, either the death of the victim or the bodily impact causing death constitutes a "result" within the meaning of subparagraph I(a) and if the body of a homicide victim is found within this state, it is presumed that such result occurred within the state.
IV. This state includes the land and water and the air space above such land and water with respect to which the state has legislative jurisdiction.

Source.
1971, 518:1, eff. Nov. 1, 1973.

Cross References.
Attempt, see RSA 629:1.
Conspiracy, see RSA 629:3.
Criminal liability for conduct of another, see RSA 626:8.
Criminal solicitation, see RSA 629:2.

NOTES TO DECISIONS

1. Construction
2. Results of conduct
3. Knowledge
4. State's burden of proof
5. Evidence
6. Jurisdiction

1. Construction
Subparagraph II(b) of this section is designed to give limited effect to foreign law by withholding jurisdiction when the conduct is legal by the law of the place where it takes place, and such intent dictates that it be read to apply not only to legally operative

conduct, but also to conduct of defendant that allegedly gives rise to its legal accountability. State v. Luv Pharmacy, 118 N.H. 398, 388 A.2d 190, 1978 N.H. LEXIS 426, 16 A.L.R.4th 1304 (1978).

2. Results of conduct

New Hampshire courts can properly exercise territorial jurisdiction where illegal act occurred outside State, if result of that act is felt in New Hampshire and constitutes an element of an offense under New Hampshire law. State v. Stewart, 142 N.H. 610, 706 A.2d 171, 1998 N.H. LEXIS 6 (1998).

Although Delaware corporation had its principal place of business in New York, maintained no office in New Hampshire, and was not registered to do business in New Hampshire, trial court had territorial jurisdiction under this section, where corporation's conduct of publishing obscene material resulted in sale of such material within state of New Hampshire. State v. Luv Pharmacy, 118 N.H. 398, 388 A.2d 190, 1978 N.H. LEXIS 426, 16 A.L.R.4th 1304 (1978).

3. Knowledge

Where national distributor of magazines with offices in New Jersey and Pennsylvania, who was not registered to do business in New Hampshire and who had not appointed an agent to receive service of process in New Hampshire, knew that the New Hampshire wholesaler whose orders it solicited or received would distribute allegedly obscene magazine to New Hampshire retailers, distributor could be found to have intended and attempted to facilitate and promote the retail sale of such allegedly obscene magazine, and therefore, was subject to state's territorial jurisdiction in regard to its New Hampshire activities. State v. Luv Pharmacy, 118 N.H. 398, 388 A.2d 190, 1978 N.H. LEXIS 426, 16 A.L.R.4th 1304 (1978).

4. State's burden of proof

In action seeking abatement of proceedings on claim that court lacked criminal jurisdiction, where national distributor of magazines with offices in New Jersey and Pennsylvania, who was not registered to do business in New Hampshire and had not appointed an agent to receive service of process in New Hampshire, was charged with purposely selling obscene material by conduct of another for whom it was accountable, in that distributor's conduct of distributing said obscene material resulted in sale within state of New Hampshire, the state, to the extent it wished to rely on distributor's out-of-state activities, was required to prove that there existed statutes in the states in which distributor's alleged activities occurred that proscribed distribution of obscene materials. State v. Luv Pharmacy, 118 N.H. 398, 388 A.2d 190, 1978 N.H. LEXIS 426, 16 A.L.R.4th 1304 (1978).

Where Delaware corporation's conduct that allegedly made it legally accountable for pharmacy's alleged conduct in selling obscene material in New Hampshire occurred in New York, corporation would be subject to criminal jurisdiction in New Hampshire only if the state could prove that a New York statute existed that would proscribe publication and distribution of obscene materials; state could meet its burden by showing that there was a New York statute directly so providing, or by showing that there was a New York statute criminalizing the sale of obscene materials and that the corporation by its activities would be subject to criminal penalties as an aider or abettor of, or as legally accountable for, such sale. State v. Luv Pharmacy, 118 N.H. 398, 388 A.2d 190, 1978 N.H. LEXIS 426, 16 A.L.R.4th 1304 (1978).

5. Evidence

Where national distributor of magazines with offices in New Jersey and Pennsylvania, who was not registered to do business in New Hampshire and who had not appointed an agent to receive service of process in New Hampshire, was charged with purposely selling obscene material by conduct of another for whom it was accountable, in that distributor's conduct of distributing said obscene material resulted in sale within state of New Hampshire, testimony that under New Jersey law distributor would have been subject to criminal prosecution if ultimate sale had taken place in New Jersey supported trial court's implied finding that subparagraph II(b) of this section did not insulate distributor from prosecution for its New Jersey activities. State v. Luv Pharmacy, 118 N.H. 398, 388 A.2d 190, 1978 N.H. LEXIS 426, 16 A.L.R.4th 1304 (1978).

6. Jurisdiction

Under RSA 625:4, I(a), New Hampshire had jurisdiction over charges of theft by deception because defendant, a medical examiner, took money from the Commonwealth of Massachusetts by submitting medical examiner fee forms to a New Hampshire entity in New Hampshire that gave the false impression that he had examined bodies in New Hampshire. State v. Breed, 159 N.H. 61, 977 A.2d 463, 2009 N.H. LEXIS 88 (2009).

New Hampshire trial court had jurisdiction over defendant's conviction, even though defendant intended to commit the crime that was the object of the conspiracy in Massachusetts, since the crime that was the object of the conspiracy was the possession of marijuana with the intent to sell, which was a crime in New Hampshire. State v. Blackmer, 149 N.H. 47, 816 A.2d 1014, 2003 N.H. LEXIS 3 (2003).

The trial court had territorial jurisdiction over an indictment charging the defendant with witness tampering where the defendant offered to take a potential witness against him to Canada and offered to rent an apartment for the witness in Canada. Whether the defendant's attempt to induce or otherwise cause the witness to elude legal process took place in New Hampshire, in Canada, or both, was of no consequence, because the defendant was attempting to pervert New Hampshire's system of justice by distorting the fact finding function of the courts. State v. Roberts, 136 N.H. 731, 622 A.2d 1225, 1993 N.H. LEXIS 24 (1993).

Cited:

Cited in State v. Gilbert, 115 N.H. 665, 348 A.2d 713, 1975 N.H. LEXIS 391 (1975); State v. Harlan, 116 N.H. 598, 364 A.2d 1254, 1976 N.H. LEXIS 423 (1976); State v. Goff, 118 N.H. 724, 393 A.2d 562, 1978 N.H. LEXIS 279 (1978).

625:5. Civil Actions.

This code does not bar, suspend, or otherwise affect any right or liability for damages, penalty, forfeiture or other remedy authorized by law to be recovered or enforced in a civil action, regardless of whether the conduct involved in such civil action constitutes an offense defined in this code.

Source.
1971, 518:1, eff. Nov. 1, 1973.

625:6. All Offenses Defined by Statute.

No conduct or omission constitutes an offense unless it is a crime or violation under this code or under another statute.

Source.
1971, 518:1, eff. Nov. 1, 1973.

NOTES TO DECISIONS

1. Parking violations
2. Nonstatutory offense
3. Miscellaneous

1. Parking violations

The authority of a city to prosecute a violator of its parking ordinance is limited to the institution of an action for the commission of an offense under the criminal code. Portsmouth v. Karosis, 126 N.H. 717, 498 A.2d 291, 1985 N.H. LEXIS 395 (1985).

2. Nonstatutory offense

This section does not abrogate offense of criminal contempt which is a nonstatutory offense, which is not founded upon, nor does it rely upon legislative authority. State v. Martina, 135 N.H. 111, 600 A.2d 132, 1991 N.H. LEXIS 145 (1991).

3. Miscellaneous

Where a professor unleashed a tirade against a colleague, the false arrest claim based on a disorderly conduct charge failed because there was probable cause for the professor's arrest on the disorderly conduct charge, and the professor's argument regarding an alleged distinction between crimes and violations under New Hampshire law was rejected. Collins v. Univ. of N.H., 664 F.3d 8, 2011 U.S. App. LEXIS 25146 (2011).

625:7. Application to Offenses Outside the Code.

The provisions of RSA 625 through 629 are applicable to offenses defined outside this code unless the code otherwise provides.

Source.
1971, 518:1, eff. Nov. 1, 1973.

NOTES TO DECISIONS

1. Parking violations
2. Possession of dangerous weapons

1. Parking violations

The authority of a city to prosecute a violator of its parking ordinance is limited to the institution of an action for the commission of an offense under the criminal code. Portsmouth v. Karosis, 126 N.H. 717, 498 A.2d 291, 1985 N.H. LEXIS 395 (1985).

2. Possession of dangerous weapons

Even though statute governing possession of dangerous weapons was not part of Criminal Code, it would be construed as would a criminal code provision, according to fair import of its terms and to promote justice. In re Justin D., 144 N.H. 450, 743 A.2d 829, 1999 N.H. LEXIS 132 (1999).

Cited:

Cited in State v. French, 117 N.H. 785, 378 A.2d 1377, 1977 N.H. LEXIS 432 (1977); State v. Goff, 118 N.H. 724, 393 A.2d 562, 1978 N.H. LEXIS 279 (1978); State v. Etzweiler, 125 N.H. 57, 480 A.2d 870, 1984 N.H. LEXIS 369 (1984); State v. Bell, 125 N.H. 425, 480 A.2d 906, 1984 N.H. LEXIS 253 (1984).

625:8. Limitations.

I. Except as otherwise provided in this section, prosecutions are subject to the following periods of limitations:

(a) For a class A felony, 6 years;

(b) For a class B felony, 6 years;

(c) For a misdemeanor, one year;

(d) For a violation, 3 months;

(e) For an offense defined by RSA 282-A, 6 years.

II. Murder may be prosecuted at any time.

II-a. [Repealed.]

III. If the period prescribed in paragraph I has expired, a prosecution may nevertheless be commenced:

(a) Within one year after its discovery by an aggrieved party or by a person who has a duty to represent such person and who is himself not a party to the offense for a theft where possession of the property was lawfully obtained and subsequently misappropriated or for any offense, a material element of which is either fraud or a breach of fiduciary duty.

(b) For any offense based upon misconduct in office by a public servant, at any time when the defendant is in public office or within 2 years thereafter.

(c) For any offense under RSA 208, RSA 210, or RSA 215, within 3 years thereafter.

(d) For any offense under RSA 632-A or for an offense under RSA 639:2, where the victim was under 18 years of age when the alleged offense occurred, within 22 years of the victim's eighteenth birthday.

(e) For any offense where destruction or falsification of evidence, witness tampering, or other unlawful conduct delayed discovery of the offense, within one year of the discovery of the offense.

(f) For any offense under RSA 153:24 and RSA 153:5, the state fire code, within one year of its discovery.

(g) For any offense under RSA 641:1 through 641:7, if committed with the purpose to assist in a murder, to conceal a murder, or to conceal or hinder the investigation or apprehension of an individual responsible for murder, at any time.

(h) For any violation-level offense involving a motor vehicle accident resulting in death or serious bodily injury, within 6 months of the accident.

IV. Time begins to run on the day after all elements of an offense have occurred or, in the case of an offense comprised of a continuous course of conduct, on the day after that conduct or the defendant's complicity therein terminates.

V. A prosecution is commenced on the day when a warrant or other process is issued, an indictment returned, or an information is filed, whichever is the earliest.

VI. The period of limitations does not run:

(a) During any time when the accused is continuously absent from the state or has no reasonably ascertained place of abode or work within this state; or

(b) During any time when a prosecution is pending against the accused in this state based on the same conduct.

Source.
1971, 518:1. 1973, 370:45. 1989, 97:1. 1990, 153:2; 213:2. 1993, 215:3, eff. Jan. 1, 1994. 2000, 173:1, eff. May 24, 2000. 2003, 265:3, eff. Jan. 1, 2004. 2007, 183:1, eff. January 1, 2008. 2009, 100:1, eff. January 1, 2010. 2012, 208:1, eff. January 1, 2013.

Revision note.
At the end of par. III(b), added "or" following "thereafter" for purposes of conformity with the remainder of the paragraph. In subpar. I(e), substituted "RSA 282-A" for "RSA 282" pursuant to 1981, 408:9.

Amendments

—**2012.** The 2012 amendment added III(h).

—**2009.** The 2009 amendment added III(g).

—**2007.** Paragraph III: Added subpar. (f) and made minor stylistic changes.

—**2003.** Paragraph III(e): Added.

—2000. Paragraph III(d): Inserted "or for an offense under RSA 639:2" following "RSA 632-A".

—1993. Paragraph II-a. Repealed.

—1990. Paragraph II-a: Added by ch. 153.
Paragraph III(c): Chapter 213 added "or" following "thereafter".
Paragraph III(d): Added by ch. 213.

—1989. Paragraph III(c): Added.

—1973. Paragraph I(e): Added.

Purpose of 1990 amendment.
1990, 213:1, eff. April 27, 1990, provided: "The general court finds that juvenile victims of sexual assault often suffer profound psychological harm resulting in repression of memory of the assault. Such victims are frequently financially dependent upon their assailants, and are often the sole witnesses to the assault. As a result, charges for sexual assault against youthful victims are frequently not brought because the criminal conduct is not brought to light within the current statute of limitations. The general court finds that an extension of the period of limitations is warranted in this situation so that justice is not lost because of the psychological harm to the victim."

Severability
—1990 amendment. 1990, 213:5, eff. April 27, 1990, provided: "If any provision of this act [which amended this section] or the application thereof to any person or circumstance is held invalid, the invalidity does not affect other provisions of the act which can be given effect without the invalid provisions or applications, and to this end the provisions of this act are severable."

Applicability of 1990 amendment.
1990, 213:4, eff. April 27, 1990, provided that the amendment to this section by section 2 of the act shall apply to victims injured under RSA 632-A before, on, or after April 27, 1990.

Cross References.
Classification of crimes, see RSA 625:9.

NOTES TO DECISIONS

1. Constitutionality
2. Construction
3. Purpose
4. Computation of time
5. Discovery of offense
6. Concealment of crime
7. Continuing offenses
8. Fraud or breach of fiduciary duty

1. Constitutionality
Retrospective application of statutory amendments, which extended statute of limitations in sexual assault cases where victim was under age of 18, was not prohibited by ex post facto clause of New Hampshire Constitution. State v. Martin, 138 N.H. 508, 643 A.2d 946, 1994 N.H. LEXIS 57 (1994).

Until statute runs, a defendant has no "defense under the statute of limitations" and, within constitutional limitations, the legislature can extend the limitations period without affecting a defendant's substantive rights, thereby precluding any possibility that retrospective application of law violates constitutional ex post facto prohibitions. State v. Hamel, 138 N.H. 392, 643 A.2d 953, 1994 N.H. LEXIS 35 (1994).

2. Construction
This section limits only the period during which state may commence a prosecution. State v. Roe, 118 N.H. 690, 393 A.2d 553, 1978 N.H. LEXIS 271 (1978).

Although criminal statutes of limitations are to be accorded a rational meaning in harmony with the obvious intent and purpose of the law, they are to be construed liberally in favor of the accused. State v. Morey, 103 N.H. 529, 176 A.2d 328, 1961 N.H. LEXIS 81 (1961). (Decided under prior law.)

3. Purpose
Applicable statute of limitations for an offense provides the primary guarantee against bringing overly stale criminal charges. State v. Ramos, 131 N.H. 276, 553 A.2d 275, 1988 N.H. LEXIS 133 (1988).

4. Computation of time
State was not barred by former RSA 603:1 (see now RSA 625:8) from prosecuting defendant who allegedly committed unnatural and lascivious acts in 1967, while he was a college student in New Hampshire, because the six-year statute of limitations contained in former RSA 603:1 was tolled when defendant left the State and had not expired at the time defendant was indicted, and there was no evidence that the State was responsible for the pre-indictment delay. State v. Nadler, 151 N.H. 244, 855 A.2d 490, 2004 N.H. LEXIS 128 (2004).

Argument was rejected that indictments alleging aggravated felonious sexual assault were barred by this section because the state relied on threats that had occurred more than six years prior to the date of the arrest warrant; defendant was not prosecuted for merely threatening the victim more than six years prior to the date of the warrant, but for committing aggravated felonious sexual assault within the limitations period. State v. Kulikowski, 132 N.H. 281, 564 A.2d 439, 1989 N.H. LEXIS 99 (1989).

5. Discovery of offense
The one-year discovery provision applied to a prosecution for theft by unauthorized taking and brought the indictments within the statute of limitations where the offenses occurred more than six years before the indictment but were not discovered until a date witin one year of the indictment. State v. Weeks, 137 N.H. 687, 635 A.2d 439, 1993 N.H. LEXIS 145 (1993).

6. Concealment of crime
The fraudulent concealment by the accused of his crime did not extend the statutory period of limitation within which an indictment must be brought. State v. Nute, 63 N.H. 79, 1884 N.H. LEXIS 26 (1884) (Decided under prior law); State v. Parady, 95 N.H. 417, 64 A.2d 319, 1949 N.H. LEXIS 185 (1949). (Decided under prior law.)

Under this statute an indictment for grand larceny had to be filed or found within six years after the offense was committed, and fraudulent concealment by the accused of his crime did not operate to extend the statutory time, nor was the statute tolled by the filing of a complaint and warrant within the statutory six year period as the result of which the accused was bound over to the superior court since the statute required that the indictment itself be filed within the six year period. State v. Parady, 95 N.H. 417, 64 A.2d 319, 1949 N.H. LEXIS 185 (1949). (Decided under prior law.)

7. Continuing offenses
Because the applicable statute of limitations in a criminal case provides the primary guarantee against bringing stale criminal charges, the doctrine of continuing offenses is applied in limited circumstances. State v. AmeriGas Propane LP, Inc., 146 N.H. 267, 769 A.2d 401, 2001 N.H. LEXIS 68 (2001).

Offense is not continuous unless explicit language of the substantive criminal statute compels such a conclusion, or the nature of the crime is such that the legislature must have intended that it be treated as a continuing one. State v. AmeriGas Propane LP, Inc., 146 N.H. 267, 769 A.2d 401, 2001 N.H. LEXIS 68 (2001).

For purposes of application of the statute of limitations, the plain language of RSA 153:24, prescribing the penalty for violation of any rule or regulation of the state fire marshal, does not evince legislative intent to create a continuing offense. State v. AmeriGas Propane LP, Inc., 146 N.H. 267, 769 A.2d 401, 2001 N.H. LEXIS 68 (2001).

Defendant company's offense in failing to vent a propane furnace in accordance with the state fire code was not a continuing one and the state's charges were untimely because they were brought over one year after defendant's work on the venting system. State v. AmeriGas Propane LP, Inc., 146 N.H. 267, 769 A.2d 401, 2001 N.H. LEXIS 68 (2001).

8. Fraud or breach of fiduciary duty

When an attorney revealed information about his former representation of a client because he believed it was reasonably necessary to prevent the client from committing criminal activity to the substantial detriment of the client's mother, under RSA 638:11, I, the applicable statute of limitations in RSA 625:8, III(a) did not bar the client's prosecution because, even if the time period had run, a prosecution was allowed where a material element of the crime was fraud or a breach of a fiduciary duty, as was the case here. Lane's Case, 153 N.H. 10, 889 A.2d 3, 2005 N.H. LEXIS 178 (2005).

Cited:

Cited in State v. Sampson, 120 N.H. 251, 413 A.2d 590, 1980 N.H. LEXIS 268 (1980); Appeal of Rochester, 125 N.H. 399, 480 A.2d 181, 1984 N.H. LEXIS 258 (1984); Appeal of Plantier, 126 N.H. 500, 494 A.2d 270, 1985 N.H. LEXIS 341, 51 A.L.R.4th 1129 (1985); State v. O'Flynn, 126 N.H. 706, 496 A.2d 348, 1985 N.H. LEXIS 349 (1985); Portsmouth v. Karosis, 126 N.H. 717, 498 A.2d 291, 1985 N.H. LEXIS 395 (1985); State v. Varagianis, 128 N.H. 226, 512 A.2d 1117, 1986 N.H. LEXIS 265 (1986).

RESEARCH REFERENCES

New Hampshire Practice.
15-7 N.H.P. Land Use Planning & Zoning § 7.14.
15-7 N.H.P. Land Use Planning & Zoning § 7.19.

625:9. Classification of Crimes.

I. The provisions of this section govern the classification of every offense, whether defined within this code or by any other statute.

II. Every offense is either a felony, misdemeanor or violation.

(a) Felonies and misdemeanors are crimes.

(b) A violation does not constitute a crime and conviction of a violation shall not give rise to any disability or legal disadvantage based on conviction of a criminal offense.

III. A felony is murder or a crime so designated by statute within or outside this code or a crime defined by statute outside of this code where the maximum penalty provided is imprisonment in excess of one year; provided, however, that a crime defined by statute outside of this code is a felony when committed by a corporation or an unincorporated association if the maximum fine therein provided is more than $200.

(a) Felonies other than murder are either class A felonies or class B felonies when committed by an individual. Felonies committed by a corporation or an unincorporated association are unclassified.

(1) Class A felonies are crimes so designated by statute within or outside this code and any crime defined by statute outside of this code for which the maximum penalty, exclusive of fine, is imprisonment in excess of 7 years.

(2) Class B felonies are crimes so designated by statute within or outside this code and any crime defined outside of this code for which the maximum penalty, exclusive of fine, is imprisonment in excess of one year but not in excess of 7 years.

IV. Misdemeanors are either class A misdemeanors or class B misdemeanors when committed by an individual. Misdemeanors committed by a corporation or an unincorporated association are unclassified.

(a) A class A misdemeanor is any crime so designated by statute within or outside this code and any crime defined outside of this code for which the maximum penalty, exclusive of fine, is imprisonment not in excess of one year.

(b) A class B misdemeanor is any crime so designated by statute within or outside this code and any crime defined outside of this code for which the maximum penalty does not include any term of imprisonment or any fine in excess of the maximum provided for a class B misdemeanor in RSA 651:2, IV(a).

(c) Any crime designated within or outside this code as a misdemeanor without specification of the classification shall be presumed to be a class B misdemeanor unless:

(1) An element of the offense involves an "act of violence" or "threat of violence" as defined in paragraph VII; or

(2) The state files a notice of intent to seek class A misdemeanor penalties on or before the date of arraignment. Such notice shall be on a form approved in accordance with RSA 490:26-d.

(d) Nothing in this paragraph shall prohibit the state from reducing any offense originally charged as a class A misdemeanor to a class B misdemeanor at any time with the agreement of the person charged.

V. A violation is an offense so designated by statute within or outside this code and, except as provided in this paragraph, any offense defined outside of this code for which there is no other penalty provided other than a fine or fine and forfeiture or other civil penalty. In the case of a corporation or an unincorporated association, offenses defined outside of this code are violations if the amount of any such fine provided does not exceed $50.

V-a. The violation of any requirement created by statute or by municipal regulation enacted pursuant to an enabling statute, where the statute neither specifies the penalty or offense classification, shall be deemed a violation, and the penalties to be imposed by the court shall be those provided for a violation under RSA 651:2.

VI. Prior to or at the time of arraignment, the state may, in its discretion, charge any offense designated a misdemeanor, as defined by paragraph IV, as a violation. At such time, the prosecutor shall make an affirmative statement to the court as to whether he intends to proceed under this paragraph. In such cases the penalties to be imposed by the court shall be those provided for a violation under RSA 651:2. This paragraph shall not apply to any offense for which a statute prescribes an enhanced penalty for a subsequent conviction of the same offense.

VII. The state may change any offense designated or defined as a class A misdemeanor as defined by paragraph IV to a class B misdemeanor, so long as no element of the offense involves an act of violence or threat of violence. The term "act of violence" means attempting to cause or purposely or recklessly causing bodily injury or serious bodily injury with or without a deadly weapon; and the term "threat of violence" means placing or attempting to place another in fear of imminent bodily injury either by physical menace or by threats to commit a crime against the person of the other. The state may change an offense pursuant to this paragraph if such change is in the interest of public safety and welfare and is not inconsistent with the societal goals of deterrence and prevention of recidivism, as follows:

(a) In its own discretion prior to or at the time of arraignment in the district court;

(b) In its own discretion following an entry of appeal in the superior court or within 20 days thereafter;

(c) With the agreement of the person charged at any other time; or

(d) In its own discretion, following entry of a complaint at a regional jury trial court or within 21 days thereafter.

VIII. If a person convicted of a class A misdemeanor has been sentenced and such sentence does not include any period of actual incarceration or a suspended or deferred jail sentence or any fine in excess of the maximum provided for a class B misdemeanor in RSA 651:2, IV(a), the court shall record such conviction and sentence as a class B misdemeanor.

Source.
1971, 518:1. 1973, 370:26–28. 1983, 382:7. 1988, 225:2. 1992, 269:1, 2. 1995, 277:21, eff. Aug. 19, 1995. 1996, 93:1, eff. Jan. 1, 1997. 2001, 274:5, eff. Jan. 1, 2002. 2006, 64:3, eff. January 1, 2007. 2009, 142:1, 2, eff. October 1, 2009.

Amendments
—2009. The 2009 amendment deleted the IV(a)(1) designation; deleted former IV(a)(2), which read: "Any crime designated within or outside this code as a misdemeanor, without specification of the classification"; added IV(c) and IV(d); deleted "For purposes of this paragraph" at the beginning of the second sentence of the introductory paragraph of VII; and made related changes.

—2006. Paragraph VIII: Deleted the second sentence.

—2001. Paragraph V-a: Added.

—1996. Paragraph VII: Rewritten to the extent that a detailed comparison would be impractical.

—1995. Paragraph VII(d): Added.

—1992. Rewrote par. VI and added pars. VII and VIII.

—1988. Paragraph VI: Added the second sentence.

—1983. Paragraph VI: Added.

—1973. Paragraphs III–V: Substituted "by statute within or outside" for "in" following "designated" whenever it appeared.

Applicability of 2009 amendment.
2009, 142:3, eff. October 1, 2009, provided: "This act shall apply to offenses committed on or after October 1, 2009."

Applicability of 1992 amendment.
1992, 269:21, eff. July 1, 1992, provided that the amendments to this section by 1992, 269:1, 2, shall apply to all offenses committed on or after July 1, 1992.

NOTES TO DECISIONS

1. Constitutionality
2. Construction
3. Reduction of charges
4. Parking violations
5. Criminal mischief
6. Violation-level offenses
7. Misdemeanors

1. Constitutionality
When defendant was convicted in district court of two class A misdemeanors and was punished only with a fine of $350 plus a $70 penalty on each charge, converting the convictions to class B misdemeanors under RSA 625:9, VIII operated to deny defendant his right to a jury trial under N.H. Const. part. I, art. 15. Because defendant faced possible incarceration, he was entitled to a de novo jury trial in the superior court under RSA 599:1. State v. Bilc, 158 N.H. 651, 972 A.2d 1029, 2009 N.H. LEXIS 56 (2009).

Superior court properly relied upon the amendment to RSA 625:9, VIII when it remanded defendant's case to district court to be entered as a conviction for a class B misdemeanor. The amendment, involving appellate rights, was procedural in nature and did not affect substantive rights; thus, its retrospective application was not ex post facto under N.H. Const. pt. I, art. 23. State v. Matthews, 157 N.H. 415, 951 A.2d 155, 2008 N.H. LEXIS 79 (2008).

2007 amendment to RSA 625:9, VIII affecting defendant's appellate rights, was procedural in nature; it neither made criminal a theretofore innocent act, nor aggravated a crime previously committed, nor provided greater punishment, nor changed the proof necessary to convict. Since the amendment did not affect defendant's substantive rights, the retrospective application of the revised statute was not ex post facto and did not violate N.H. Const. pt. I, art. 23. State v. Matthews, 157 N.H. 415, 951 A.2d 155, 2008 N.H. LEXIS 79 (2008).

2. Construction
Plain language of RSA 637:11, II(b), together with RSA 625:9, III and IV(a), expressed the legislature's intent to include out-of-state theft convictions as predicate sentence enhancement offenses. Thus, defendant, who had two theft convictions in another state, could be charged with class B felony theft as a third offense under RSA 637:11, II(b). State v. Lukas, 164 N.H. 693, 62 A.3d 883, 2013 N.H. LEXIS 25 (2013).

Provision of this section allowing prosecutor to reduce a misdemeanor charge to a violation only prior to or at the time of "arraignment" refers to either a district court arraignment or a superior court arraignment. State v. Gagnon, 135 N.H. 217, 600 A.2d 937, 1991 N.H. LEXIS 168 (1991).

Under the criminal code, a violation of driving while intoxicated is not a crime. State v. Dery, 134 N.H. 370, 594 A.2d 149, 1991 N.H. LEXIS 72 (1991).

"Violation", as used in this section, does not refer to any and all offenses, but rather only to those which are neither felonies nor misdemeanors. State v. Doe, 116 N.H. 646, 365 A.2d 1044, 1976 N.H. LEXIS 437 (1976).

3. Reduction of charges
The state's post-appeal election to change a matter from a class A misdemeanor to a class B misdemeanor did not remove from the defendant his right to appeal for a trial de novo; if the state's argument to the contrary were valid, both the statutory guarantee of a defendant's right to a trial de novo in superior court for a conviction of a class A misdemeanor and the statutory provision deeming all persons convicted of class A misdemeanors so convicted for purposes of appeal would be meaningless and, moreover, such an interpretation of the statute would give the state the power to

rescind retroactively a statutory right that has already been exercised. State v. Guy, 140 N.H. 453, 667 A.2d 1026, 1995 N.H. LEXIS 170 (1995). (Referring to provision of statute deleted by 2006 amendment to subpara. VIII effective January 1, 2007.)

When the state changes an offense from a class A misdemeanor to a class B misdemeanor after a defendant has exercised his or her right to appeal, the matter goes forward, de novo, as a class B misdemeanor and the defendant has no right to a jury trial. State v. Guy, 140 N.H. 453, 667 A.2d 1026, 1995 N.H. LEXIS 170 (1995). (Referring to provision of statute deleted by 2006 amendment to subpara. VIII effective January 1, 2007.)

Where a defendant was charged with a class A misdemeanor and on this basis was tried, convicted, and sentenced, but the sentence imposed on the defendant amounted to less than the statutory maximum for a class B misdemeanor, the conviction and sentence necessarily were recorded as for a class B misdemeanor; nevertheless, the defendant was deemed to have been convicted of a class A misdemeanor for the purposes of appeal. State v. Guy, 140 N.H. 453, 667 A.2d 1026, 1995 N.H. LEXIS 170 (1995). (Referring to provision of statute deleted by 2006 amendment to subpara. VIII effective January 1, 2007.)

Reduction of defendant's misdemeanor charge to a violation prior to arraignment in superior court after defendant appealed her district court conviction on the charge was within the prosecutor's discretion, cost-effective, and not contrary to the supposed purpose of the statute of reducing costs of providing indigent defendants with court-appointed counsel. State v. Gagnon, 135 N.H. 217, 600 A.2d 937, 1991 N.H. LEXIS 168 (1991).

Superior court properly allowed the prosecutor to reduce defendant's misdemeanor charge to a violation, but erred in remanding case to district court for sentencing only; case should have been remanded for trial de novo. State v. Gagnon, 135 N.H. 217, 600 A.2d 937, 1991 N.H. LEXIS 168 (1991).

4. Parking violations

The authority of a city to prosecute a violator of its parking ordinance is limited to the institution of an action for the commission of an offense under the criminal code. Portsmouth v. Karosis, 126 N.H. 717, 498 A.2d 291, 1985 N.H. LEXIS 395 (1985).

5. Criminal mischief

Because provision of criminal mischief statute that "[a]ll other criminal mischief is a misdemeanor" does not specify a classification, pursuant to subparagraph IV(a)(2) of this section it must be categorized as a class A misdemeanor. State v. Bruce, 147 N.H. 37, 780 A.2d 1270, 2001 N.H. LEXIS 165 (2001).

6. Violation-level offenses

A former RSA 265:81-a (repealed effective January 1, 2007, see now RSA 265-A:45) violation was a "violation-level offense," and, since a former RSA 265:81-a violation did not constitute a "crime," the supreme court answered the district court's interlocutory question, stating that the district court could not impose the defendant's suspended sentences upon proof that he committed a former RSA 265:81-a violation, citing RSA 625:9, II(b) (Supp. 2001). State v. Auger, 147 N.H. 752, 802 A.2d 1209, 2002 N.H. LEXIS 77 (2002).

7. Misdemeanors

Because the notice of intent to seek enhanced sentence purported to authorize a sentence beyond that which the district division had the power to impose under RSA 502-A:11, the State's filing of that notice in the circuit court was wholly ineffective. Furthermore, there was no merit to the State's position that the RSA 651:6 notice could nonetheless be treated as a "proxy" for the notice required by RSA 625:9, IV(c)(2), as not only was the RSA 651:6 notice devoid of any indication that its purpose was to authorize the imposition of class A misdemeanor penalties, but the notice was not filed at or before the defendant's arraignment. State v. Blunt, 164 N.H. 679, 62 A.3d 1285, 2013 N.H. LEXIS 27 (2013).

Complaints for simple assault under RSA 631:2-a and for resisting arrest under RSA 642:2 did not allege a crime that involved as an element an act of violence or a threat of violence for purposes of class A misdemeanor classification under RSA 625:9, IV(c)(1). The variant of simple assault alleged here involved causing unprivileged physical contact, not bodily injury, and the resisting arrest statute could be violated by conduct that fell short of causing or attempting to cause bodily injury. State v. Blunt, 164 N.H. 679, 62 A.3d 1285, 2013 N.H. LEXIS 27 (2013).

Important consideration under RSA 625:9, IV(c)(1) is not whether a particular offense was actually committed in a violent manner, but whether an act of violence must be involved as an element of the offense. State v. Blunt, 164 N.H. 679, 62 A.3d 1285, 2013 N.H. LEXIS 27 (2013).

Merely checking the "class A misdemeanor" box on the standard complaint form does not constitute compliance with RSA 625:9, IV(c)(2). State v. Blunt, 164 N.H. 679, 62 A.3d 1285, 2013 N.H. LEXIS 27 (2013).

Pursuant to RSA 625:9, when it is necessary to classify a crime designated only as "a misdemeanor," such crime will be classified as a class A misdemeanor; however, the phrase "any misdemeanor" in RSA 262:23, III is not used to classify the crime of driving after certification as a habitual offender, but is used to define a sentencing factor. The crimes that form the basis of driving after certification as a habitual offender have already been classified. State v. Hayden, 158 N.H. 597, 972 A.2d 1043, 2009 N.H. LEXIS 48 (2009).

Cited:

Cited in State v. Dean, 115 N.H. 520, 345 A.2d 408, 1975 N.H. LEXIS 352 (1975); State v. Payne, 115 N.H. 595, 347 A.2d 157, 1975 N.H. LEXIS 370 (1975); State v. Miller, 115 N.H. 662, 348 A.2d 345, 1975 N.H. LEXIS 390 (1975); State v. Martin, 116 N.H. 47, 351 A.2d 52, 1976 N.H. LEXIS 260 (1976); State v. Komisarek, 116 N.H. 427, 362 A.2d 190, 1976 N.H. LEXIS 373 (1976); State v. Bennett, 116 N.H. 433, 362 A.2d 184, 1976 N.H. LEXIS 375 (1976); State v. Cushing, 119 N.H. 147, 399 A.2d 297, 1979 N.H. LEXIS 256 (1979); Paey v. Rodrigue, 119 N.H. 186, 400 A.2d 51, 1979 N.H. LEXIS 269 (1979); State v. Brady, 122 N.H. 110, 441 A.2d 1165, 1982 N.H. LEXIS 296 (1982); State v. Morrill, 123 N.H. 707, 465 A.2d 882, 1983 N.H. LEXIS 338 (1983); State v. Sweeney, 124 N.H. 396, 469 A.2d 1362, 1983 N.H. LEXIS 419 (1983); State v. Cook, 125 N.H. 452, 481 A.2d 823, 1984 N.H. LEXIS 300 (1984); State v. McKenney, 126 N.H. 184, 489 A.2d 644, 1985 N.H. LEXIS 243 (1985); State v. Dery, 126 N.H. 747, 496 A.2d 357, 1985 N.H. LEXIS 355 (1985); State v. Perra, 127 N.H. 533, 503 A.2d 814, 1985 N.H. LEXIS 456 (1985); State v. Deflorio, 128 N.H. 309, 512 A.2d 1133, 1986 N.H. LEXIS 286 (1986); Kiluk v. Potter, 133 N.H. 67, 572 A.2d 1157, 1990 N.H. LEXIS 26 (1990); State v. Murray, 135 N.H. 369, 605 A.2d 676, 1992 N.H. LEXIS 41 (1992); Opinion of Justices, 135 N.H. 538, 608 A.2d 202, 1992 N.H. LEXIS 213 (1992); Opinion of Justices, 135 N.H. 549, 608 A.2d 874, 1992 N.H. LEXIS 214 (1992); State v. Woods, 139 N.H. 399, 654 A.2d 960, 1995 N.H. LEXIS 12 (1995); State v. Rothe, 142 N.H. 483, 703 A.2d 884, 1997 N.H. LEXIS 122 (1997); State v. Polk, 155 N.H. 585, 927 A.2d 514, 2007 N.H. LEXIS 100 (2007).

RESEARCH REFERENCES

New Hampshire Practice.
1-1 N.H.P. Criminal Practice & Procedure § 1.03.
2-30 N.H.P. Criminal Practice & Procedure § 30.16.
16-50 N.H.P. Municipal Law & Taxation § 50.02.

625:10. Burden of Proof.

No person may be convicted of an offense unless each element of such offense is proved beyond a reasonable doubt. In the absence of such proof, the innocence of the defendant is assumed.

Source.
1971, 518:1, eff. Nov. 1, 1973.

NOTES TO DECISIONS

1.   Elements
2.   Jury instructions

1. Elements

As committing penetration or touching for sexual gratification were statutory variants of attempted aggravated felonious sexual assault, in violation of RSA 629:1 and 632-A:2, it was sufficient that the jury determined that defendant intended to commit either variant for purposes of supporting his conviction; they did not have to agree which act he intended to commit pursuant to RSA 625:10. State v. Casanova, 164 N.H. 563, 63 A.3d 169, 2013 N.H. LEXIS 11 (2013).

Where discrete factual predicates can provide alternative bases for finding an element of the offense to have been established, a defendant is entitled to jury unanimity as to the factual predicate supporting a finding of guilt. State v. Greene, 137 N.H. 126, 623 A.2d 1342, 1993 N.H. LEXIS 52 (1993).

By properly categorizing the element of materiality in RSA 641:1, governing perjury, as a question of law for the trial court, the legislature has clearly recognized that this element is not subject to the requirement of this section that each element of an offense be proved beyond a reasonable doubt. State v. Sands, 123 N.H. 570, 467 A.2d 202, 1983 N.H. LEXIS 362, 37 A.L.R.4th 904 (1983).

2. Jury instructions

Because the jury needed to be unanimous only as to the elements of the crime of accomplice to second degree murder, and because a question asked by the jury regarding the offense did not reflect confusion about the need for unanimity on the elements, no supplemental unanimity instruction was required. State v. Doucette, 146 N.H. 583, 776 A.2d 744, 2001 N.H. LEXIS 112 (2001).

Trial court's failure to incorporate into its jury instructions the verbatim language of this section was not error where the instructions correctly and adequately conveyed the concepts of reasonable doubt and presumption of innocence and several times referred to reasonable doubt, stating the substance, if not the exact wording, of this section. State v. Theodore, 118 N.H. 548, 392 A.2d 122, 1978 N.H. LEXIS 238 (1978).

In prosecution for criminal trespass, trial court did not err in instructing jury that a reasonable doubt exists "where our belief in a fact is so uncertain that we would hesitate to act upon the strength of it to undertake something of importance and seriousness equal to this case." State v. Wentworth, 118 N.H. 832, 395 A.2d 858, 1978 N.H. LEXIS 302 (1978).

In prosecution for criminal trespass, even assuming that it was error to instruct the jury that reasonable doubt was "a strong and abiding conviction that still remains after a careful consideration of all the evidence," any possible prejudicial effect of the phrase was harmlessly lost in the totality of the instructions that also stated that the defendant had no burden of proving anything and that the entire burden rested with the state; taken in context, the phrase "a strong and abiding conviction" did not shift the burden of proof to the defendant. State v. Wentworth, 118 N.H. 832, 395 A.2d 858, 1978 N.H. LEXIS 302 (1978).

Cited:

Cited in State v. Boone, 119 N.H. 594, 406 A.2d 113, 1979 N.H. LEXIS 360 (1979); State v. Preston, 121 N.H. 147, 427 A.2d 32, 1981 N.H. LEXIS 269 (1981); State v. Qualters, 121 N.H. 484, 431 A.2d 780, 1981 N.H. LEXIS 355 (1981); State v. Condict, 122 N.H. 1133, 455 A.2d 1013, 1982 N.H. LEXIS 544 (1982); State v. Nocella, 124 N.H. 163, 467 A.2d 575, 1983 N.H. LEXIS 375 (1983); State v. King, 124 N.H. 643, 474 A.2d 575, 1984 N.H. LEXIS 227 (1984); State v. Bell, 125 N.H. 425, 480 A.2d 906, 1984 N.H. LEXIS 253 (1984); State v. O'Leary, 128 N.H. 661, 517 A.2d 1174, 1986 N.H. LEXIS 326 (1986); State v. Johnson, 130 N.H. 578, 547 A.2d 213, 1988 N.H. LEXIS 64 (1988); State v. Wentzell, 131 N.H. 151, 551 A.2d 960, 1988 N.H. LEXIS 100 (1988); State v. Pinardville Athletic Club, 134 N.H. 462, 594 A.2d 1284, 1991 N.H. LEXIS 96 (1991); State v. Fitzgerald, 137 N.H. 23, 622 A.2d 1245, 1993 N.H. LEXIS 29 (1993); In re Gina D., 138 N.H. 697, 645 A.2d 61, 1994 N.H. LEXIS 91 (1994); State v. McMinn, 141 N.H. 636, 690 A.2d 1017, 1997 N.H. LEXIS 11 (1997); State v. Sinbandith, 143 N.H. 579, 729 A.2d 994, 1999 N.H. LEXIS 47 (1999); State v. Goodman, 145 N.H. 526, 764 A.2d 925, 2000 N.H. LEXIS 104 (2000); State v. French, 146 N.H. 97, 776 A.2d 1253, 2001 N.H. LEXIS 35 (2001); In re Nathan L., 146 N.H. 614, 776 A.2d 1277, 2001 N.H. LEXIS 119 (2001).

625:11. General Definitions.

The following definitions apply to this code.

I. "Conduct" means an action or omission, and its accompanying state of mind, or, a series of acts or omissions.

II. "Person", "he", and "actor" include any natural person and, a corporation or an unincorporated association.

III. "Element of an offense" means such conduct, or such attendant circumstances, or such a result of conduct as:

(a) Is included in the definition of the offense; or

(b) Establishes the required kind of culpability; or

(c) Negatives an excuse or justification for such conduct; or

(d) Negatives a defense under the statute of limitations; or

(e) Establishes jurisdiction or venue.

IV. "Material element of an offense" means an element that does not relate exclusively to the statute of limitations, jurisdiction, venue or to any other matter similarly unrelated to (1) the harm sought to be prevented by the definition of the offense, or (2) any justification or excuse for the prescribed conduct.

V. "Deadly weapon" means any firearm, knife or other substance or thing which, in the manner it is used, intended to be used, or threatened to be used, is known to be capable of producing death or serious bodily injury.

VI. "Serious bodily injury" means any harm to the body which causes severe, permanent or protracted loss of or impairment to the health or of the function of any part of the body.

Source.

1971, 518:1, eff. Nov. 1, 1973.

NOTES TO DECISIONS

1. Conduct
2. Elements of offense
3. Material element
4. Deadly weapon
5. Serious bodily injury
6. "Person"

1. Conduct

Several acts may constitute one crime if impelled by one intent. State v. Sampson, 120 N.H. 251, 413 A.2d 590, 1980 N.H. LEXIS 268 (1980).

2. Elements of offense

Defendant did not file a statute of limitations claim prior to trial, as required by N.H. Super. Ct. R. 101; instead, he first raised the issue at the close of the State's case. Thus, the statute of limitations did not become an element of the offense under RSA 625:11, III(d), and the trial court properly denied defendant's motion to dismiss a misdemeanor charge based on the statute of limitations. State v. Cook, 158 N.H. 708, 972 A.2d 1059, 2009 N.H. LEXIS 66 (2009).

Defendant was entitled to have vacated his conviction for failure to register with police under RSA 651-B:4, I because his guilty plea to the charge was not knowing and voluntary as he was not informed by either the trial court or the complaint that the statute afforded him 30 days in which to register after he moved to New Hampshire, and, thus, his due process rights under N.H. Const. pt. 1, art. 15, were violated; further, the 30-day time period was an element of the offense pursuant to RSA 625:11, III(a) as it was included in the definition of the offense. State v. Offen, 156 N.H. 435, 938 A.2d 879, 2007 N.H. LEXIS 203 (2007).

Where evidence pertaining to the statute of limitations was not admitted at trial and the issue was presented for the first time in the defendant's proposed jury instruction, the state was not required to disprove a statute of limitations defense. State v. Weeks, 137 N.H. 687, 635 A.2d 439, 1993 N.H. LEXIS 145 (1993).

Statutory definition of "element of an offense" cannot be read to include the defense of consent. State v. Cooper, 135 N.H. 258, 603 A.2d 499, 1992 N.H. LEXIS 16 (1992).

Because consent is not a justification, lack of consent is not an element of the offense of sexual assault. State v. Cooper, 135 N.H. 258, 603 A.2d 499, 1992 N.H. LEXIS 16 (1992).

Consent is not an excuse or justification. State v. Cooper, 135 N.H. 258, 603 A.2d 499, 1992 N.H. LEXIS 16 (1992).

To plead a justification, defendant must admit the substance of the allegation but point to facts that excuse, exonerate or justify his actions. State v. Cooper, 135 N.H. 258, 603 A.2d 499, 1992 N.H. LEXIS 16 (1992).

Since RSA 318:52-e, prohibiting the control or possession of hypodermic needles, is specifically made inapplicable to certain designated individuals so that those persons falling within any of the enumerated exceptions and possessing those instruments are "excused" from what would otherwise be criminal conduct, the non-applicability of these exceptions is an element of the offense, pursuant to subparagraph III(c) of this section, which element must be proved by the state. State v. King, 124 N.H. 643, 474 A.2d 575, 1984 N.H. LEXIS 227 (1984).

Where provisions of former RSA 249:51 (now RSA 266:72), which made it a violation to carry a load of sand, gravel or other particulate substance on public highways without a close-fitting tarpaulin covering the load, were inapplicable to certain persons and classes of vehicles, the non-applicability of these exceptions were elements of the offense pursuant to subparagraph III(c) of this section. State v. Qualters, 121 N.H. 484, 431 A.2d 780, 1981 N.H. LEXIS 355 (1981).

3. Material element

Dismissal of an indictment that charged defendant with a criminal offense, based on the trial court's grant of defendant's directed verdict motion at the close of the evidence due to improper venue, did not bar a retrial under the double jeopardy clause of N.H. Const. pt. I, § 16, as none of the material elements of the charged offense were determined; the dismissal was not the same as an "acquittal," and the determination of improper venue was not a material element under RSA 625:11, III(e) and IV. State v. Johanson (In re State), 156 N.H. 148, 932 A.2d 848, 2007 N.H. LEXIS 152 (2007).

Although use of deadly weapon was an element of crime of felony criminal threatening, it was not a material element, and therefore State was not obligated to prove a specific mens rea with respect to that element. State v. McCabe, 145 N.H. 686, 765 A.2d 176, 2001 N.H. LEXIS 7 (2001).

4. Deadly weapon

"Protracted" impairment is one that is "delayed or prolonged in time"; thus, whether an impairment is protracted for purposes of determining whether there was serious bodily injury is a question of degree, State v. Dorrance, — N.H. —, 70 A.3d 451, 2013 N.H. LEXIS 81 (July 16, 2013).

Shank possessed by defendant, a prison inmate, was a deadly weapon under RSA 625:11, V, for purposes of RSA 159:3, I. The circumstances surrounding defendant's possession of a shank in a prison indicated only one potential use—to cause death or serious bodily injury to another human. State v. Duran, 162 N.H. 369, 33 A.3d 1183, 2011 N.H. LEXIS 122 (2011).

Possessed by a prison inmate, a shank has no recreational uses; simply stated, the only reason an individual would have a shank in prison is to cause death or serious bodily injury. Unlike the felon who may arguably have a legitimate nonviolent reason for possessing a weapon outside of prison, there is simply no acceptable use for a weapon by an inmate in a prison. State v. Duran, 162 N.H. 369, 33

A.3d 1183, 2011 N.H. LEXIS 122 (2011).

Definitions of "deadly weapon" and "deadly force" in RSA 625:11, V, and RSA 627:9, II, are not synonymous, and a finding of the use of deadly force does not necessarily follow from a finding that a person brandished or threatened to use a deadly weapon. State v. Gingras, 162 N.H. 633, 34 A.3d 659, 2011 N.H. LEXIS 149 (2011).

Firearm was a deadly weapon under RSA 625:11, V, if, in the manner it was used, intended to be used, or threatened to be used, it was known to be capable of producing death or serious bodily injury. Thus, as to felony criminal threatening under RSA 631:4, it was error to instruct the jury that a shotgun was a deadly weapon per se; the error was not subject to harmless error analysis because under the state constitution, a jury instruction that omitted an element of the offense charged was an error that partially or completely denied a defendant the right to the basic trial process. State v. Kousounadis, 159 N.H. 413, 986 A.2d 603, 2009 N.H. LEXIS 136 (2009).

Legislature, in adopting the Commission to Recommend Codification of Criminal Laws' Report, intended for the qualifying phrase comprising the latter portion of the deadly weapon statute to modify each item listed, including "firearm." Accordingly, a firearm is a deadly weapon under RSA 625:11, V, if, in the manner it is used, intended to be used, or threatened to be used, it is known to be capable of producing death or serious bodily injury. State v. Kousounadis, 159 N.H. 413, 986 A.2d 603, 2009 N.H. LEXIS 136 (2009).

RSA 625:11, V should be construed to include only death or serious bodily injury to a human, not that of an animal. To hold otherwise renders the statute impermissibly vague, as such an expansive interpretation would not provide the ordinary person with adequate notice of those substances or things which would constitute a deadly weapon. State v. Pratte, 158 N.H. 45, 959 A.2d 200, 2008 N.H. LEXIS 135 (2008).

When defendant used a bow and arrow to kill a porcupine on his property, the evidence was insufficient to support his conviction of being a felon in possession of a deadly weapon under RSA 159:3, I. "Deadly weapon" as defined in RSA 625:11, V, was to be construed to include only death or serious bodily injury to a human, not an animal. State v. Pratte, 158 N.H. 45, 959 A.2d 200, 2008 N.H. LEXIS 135 (2008).

Where evidence showed defendant drove his vehicle while intoxicated, defendant drove his vehicle so close to a police officer engaged in a traffic stop that he hit the officer, and defendant testified that he drove into oncoming traffic to go around the officer, a reasonably jury could have found that defendant's truck, in the manner in which it was used, was known to be capable of causing death or serious bodily injury and, thus, was a deadly weapon. State v. Hull, 149 N.H. 706, 827 A.2d 1001, 2003 N.H. LEXIS 106 (2003).

Although unloaded, firearm which defendant threatened to fire at victim was objectively understood to be capable of causing death or serious bodily injury, and thus trial court did not err in concluding that unloaded handgun was a "deadly weapon" for purposes of defendant's conviction and sentence for armed robbery. State v. Hatt, 144 N.H. 246, 740 A.2d 1037, 1999 N.H. LEXIS 107 (1999).

5. Serious bodily injury

Evidence was sufficient to show that a law enforcement officer suffered a protracted impairment to the function of his eye and thus suffered a serious bodily injury for purposes of the second-degree assault statute. The jury could have believed that he had consistently impaired vision for up to 19 days and, for at least some time thereafter, intermittently impaired vision requiring medical attention. State v. Dorrance, — N.H. —, 70 A.3d 451, 2013 N.H. LEXIS 81 (July 16, 2013).

Contrary to defendant's claim, the evidence was sufficient to support a finding that he caused serious injury to his assault victim, his wife; the jury heard evidence that the victim suffered a broken nose, a broken tooth, a lacerated lip, a bruised neck, a swollen chin, and, for about a week after the incident, she was unable to drink, except through a straw, and unable to eat anything other than soft foods. The jury also heard testimony that, because of the beating, the victim had to have a root canal and, eventually braces, and that, at the time of trial, nearly a year later, her lip was still tender, numb and tingling. State v. Pepin, 156 N.H. 269, 940 A.2d 221, 2007 N.H. LEXIS 182 (2007).

Decisions allowing the State access to defendants' privileged medical records to prove the "serious bodily injury" element of the crime of felony aggravated driving while intoxicated were vacated to determine whether the State had appropriately tried to discover other sources of competent evidence before invading the doctor-patient privilege. In re Grand Jury Subpoena for Med. Records of Payne v. Barka, 150 N.H. 436, 839 A.2d 837, 2004 N.H. LEXIS 1 (2004).

Evidence was sufficient to support finding that defendant's violent acts toward the victim caused serious bodily injury where a medical expert testified that a life-threatening infection could have resulted from the smashing of the victim's nose in the absence of medical intervention and where the victim testified to still feeling the effects of the incident a year later. State v. Scognamiglio, 150 N.H. 534, 842 A.2d 109, 2004 N.H. LEXIS 17 (2004).

"Serious bodily injury" element does not require permanent injury, and in order to establish this element, State need not have victim or a medical expert parrot words of statute. State v. MacArthur, 138 N.H. 597, 644 A.2d 68, 1994 N.H. LEXIS 70 (1994).

Evidence that victim required sutures and also sustained a scratched eyeball resulting in blurred vision was sufficient to sustain a finding of serious bodily injury. State v. Kiluk, 120 N.H. 1, 410 A.2d 648, 1980 N.H. LEXIS 218 (1980).

Since health means the state of being sound in both body and mind, the definition of serious bodily injury in paragraph VI of this section includes psychological injury. State v. Goodwin, 118 N.H. 862, 395 A.2d 1234, 1978 N.H. LEXIS 307 (1978).

6. "Person"

Town and defendant's employer, a corporation, were "persons" within the meaning of RSA 625:11, II. State v. Seymour, 161 N.H. 450, 20 A.3d 347, 2011 N.H. LEXIS 17 (2011).

Cited:

Cited in State v. Champagne, 119 N.H. 118, 399 A.2d 287, 1979 N.H. LEXIS 253 (1979); State v. Boone, 119 N.H. 594, 406 A.2d 113, 1979 N.H. LEXIS 360 (1979); State v. Arillo, 122 N.H. 107, 441 A.2d 1163, 1982 N.H. LEXIS 295 (1982); State v. Bell, 125 N.H. 425, 480 A.2d 906, 1984 N.H. LEXIS 253 (1984); State v. Shannon, 125 N.H. 653, 484 A.2d 1164, 1984 N.H. LEXIS 380 (1984); State v. Holt, 126 N.H. 394, 493 A.2d 483, 1985 N.H. LEXIS 314 (1985); State v. Bailey, 127 N.H. 416, 503 A.2d 762, 1985 N.H. LEXIS 461 (1985); State v. Smith, 127 N.H. 836, 508 A.2d 1082, 1986 N.H. LEXIS 229 (1986); State v. Elbert, 128 N.H. 210, 512 A.2d 1114, 1986 N.H. LEXIS 280 (1986); State v. Allen, 128 N.H. 390, 514 A.2d 1263, 1986 N.H. LEXIS 309 (1986); State v. Hotchkiss, 129 N.H. 260, 525 A.2d 270, 1987 N.H. LEXIS 167 (1987); State v. Day, 129 N.H. 378, 529 A.2d 887, 1987 N.H. LEXIS 204 (1987); State v. Allegra, 129 N.H. 720, 533 A.2d 338, 1987 N.H. LEXIS 247 (1987); State v. Dean, 129 N.H. 744, 533 A.2d 333, 1987 N.H. LEXIS 263 (1987); State v. Wentzell, 131 N.H. 151, 551 A.2d 960, 1988 N.H. LEXIS 100 (1988); Opinion of Justices, 131 N.H. 583, 557 A.2d 1355, 1989 N.H. LEXIS 37 (1989); State v. Wheeler, 132 N.H. 552, 567 A.2d 996, 1989 N.H. LEXIS 148 (1989); State v. Pinardville Athletic Club, 134 N.H. 462, 594 A.2d 1284, 1991 N.H. LEXIS 96 (1991); State v. Hamel, 138 N.H. 392, 643 A.2d 953, 1994 N.H. LEXIS 35 (1994); State v. Hamel, 138 N.H. 392, 643 A.2d 953, 1994 N.H. LEXIS 35 (1994); State v. MacLeod, 141 N.H. 427, 685 A.2d 473, 1996 N.H. LEXIS 120 (1996); State v. McMinn, 141 N.H. 636, 690 A.2d 1017, 1997 N.H. LEXIS 11 (1997); State v. Beckert, 144 N.H. 315, 741 A.2d 63, 1999 N.H. LEXIS 114 (1999); State v. Francoeur, 146 N.H. 83, 767 A.2d 429, 2001 N.H. LEXIS 31 (2001); In re Nathan L., 146 N.H. 614, 776 A.2d 1277, 2001 N.H. LEXIS 119 (2001); State v. Higgins, 149 N.H. 290, 821 A.2d 964, 2003 N.H. LEXIS 41 (2003).

RESEARCH REFERENCES

New Hampshire Trial Bar News.

For article, "Presumptions in New Hampshire Law—A Guide Through the Impenetrable Jungle (Part II)," see 11 N.H. Trial Bar News 31, 43 (Fall 1991).

CHAPTER 626

GENERAL PRINCIPLES

SECTION
626:1.   Requirement of a Voluntary Act.
626:2.   General Requirements of Culpability.
626:3.   Effect of Ignorance or Mistake.
626:4.   Intoxication.
626:5.   Entrapment.
626:6.   Consent.
626:7.   Defenses; Affirmative Defenses and Presumptions.
626:8.   Criminal Liability for Conduct of Another.

626:1. Requirement of a Voluntary Act.

I. A person is not guilty of an offense unless his criminal liability is based on conduct that includes a voluntary act or the voluntary omission to perform an act of which he is physically capable.

II. Possession is a voluntary act if the possessor knowingly procured or received the thing possessed or was aware of his control thereof for a sufficient period to have been able to terminate his possession.

Source.

1971, 518:1, eff. Nov. 1, 1973.

NOTES TO DECISIONS

1. Defenses
2. Duress

1. Defenses

When evidence of alcoholism is offered as a defense to the commission of a criminal act because it is involuntary, it must be on the basis of a mental disease. State v. Plummer, 117 N.H. 320, 374 A.2d 431, 1977 N.H. LEXIS 330 (1977).

2. Duress

Duress cannot, as a matter of law, make criminal conduct involuntary within meaning of subdivision I of this section. State v. Daoud, 141 N.H. 142, 679 A.2d 577, 1996 N.H. LEXIS 65 (1996).

Cited:

Cited in State v. Adelson, 118 N.H. 484, 389 A.2d 1382, 1978 N.H. LEXIS 444 (1978); State v. Akers, 119 N.H. 161, 400 A.2d 38, 1979 N.H. LEXIS 265, 12 A.L.R.4th 667 (1979); State v. Thresher, 122 N.H. 63, 442 A.2d 578, 1982 N.H. LEXIS 288 (1982); State v. Donovan, 128 N.H. 702, 519 A.2d 252, 1986 N.H. LEXIS 365 (1986); State v. Stratton, 132 N.H. 451, 567 A.2d 986, 1989 N.H. LEXIS 124 (1989); State v. DeMatteo, 134 N.H. 296, 591 A.2d 1323, 1991 N.H. LEXIS 56 (1991); State v. Burrell, 135 N.H. 715, 609 A.2d 751, 1992 N.H. LEXIS 112 (1992).

626:2. General Requirements of Culpability.

I. A person is guilty of murder, a felony, or a misdemeanor only if he acts purposely, knowingly, recklessly or negligently, as the law may require, with respect to each material element of the offense. He may be guilty of a violation without regard to such culpability. When the law defining an offense prescribes the kind of culpability that is sufficient for its commission, without distinguishing among the material elements thereof, such culpability shall apply to all the material elements, unless a contrary purpose plainly appears.

II. The following are culpable mental states:

(a) "Purposely." A person acts purposely with respect to a material element of an offense when his conscious object is to cause the result or engage in the conduct that comprises the element.

(b) "Knowingly." A person acts knowingly with respect to conduct or to a circumstance that is a material element of an offense when he is aware that his conduct is of such nature or that such circumstances exist.

(c) "Recklessly." A person acts recklessly with respect to a material element of an offense when he is aware of and consciously disregards a substantial and unjustifiable risk that the material element exists or will result from his conduct. The risk must be of such a nature and degree that, considering the circumstances known to him, its disregard constitutes a gross deviation from the conduct that a law-abiding person would observe in the situation. A person who creates such a risk but is unaware thereof solely by reason of having voluntarily engaged in intoxication or hypnosis also acts recklessly with respect thereto.

(d) "Negligently." A person acts negligently with respect to a material element of an offense when he fails to become aware of a substantial and unjustifiable risk that the material element exists or will result from his conduct. The risk must be of such a nature and degree that his failure to become aware of it constitutes a gross deviation from the conduct that a reasonable person would observe in the situation.

III. When the law provides that negligence suffices to establish an element of an offense, such element is also established if the person acts purposely, knowingly or recklessly. When recklessness suffices, the element is also established if the person acts purposely or knowingly. When acting knowingly suffices, the element is also established if a person acts purposely.

IV. A requirement that an offense be committed wilfully is satisfied if the person acts knowingly with respect to the material elements of the offense, unless a purpose to impose further requirements appears.

V. Neither knowledge nor recklessness nor negligence as to whether conduct constitutes an offense or as to the existence or meaning of the law defining the offense is an element of such offense, unless the law so provides.

Source.

1971, 518:1. 1973, 370:29, 30, eff. Nov. 1, 1973.

Amendments

—1973. Paragraphs I, II (d): Substituted "negligently" for "gross negligence" and "with gross negligence".

Cross References.

Classification of crimes, see RSA 625:9.

NOTES TO DECISIONS

1. Construction
2. Construction with other laws
3. Negligence
4. Mens rea
5. Knowingly
6. Recklessness
7. Indictment
8. Insanity
9. Sexual assault

1. Construction

This section does not permit a criminal defendant to be charged with whichever one of the four culpable mental states defined herein a prosecutor may choose, wherever a criminal statute fails to provide a specific mental state for the offense; rather the section must be read as requiring proof of a culpable mental state which is appropriate in light of the nature of the offense and the policy considerations for punishing the conduct in question. State v. Aldrich, 124 N.H. 43, 466 A.2d 938, 1983 N.H. LEXIS 356 (1983).

This section does not vest prosecutors with unfettered discretion to charge any one of the four culpable mental states, depending upon the circumstances of a particular case, wherever a criminal statute fails to prescribe a specific mental state; such an interpretation would, for instance, leave prosecutors free to charge escape defendants criminally for acting "negligently", a mental state not even requiring awareness, and would be broader than even the standard set forth in the Model Penal Code, which provides that whenever a statute fails to prescribe a specific mental state such element is established if a person acts purposely, knowingly or recklessly. State v. Aldrich, 124 N.H. 43, 466 A.2d 938, 1983 N.H. LEXIS 356 (1983).

The difference between recklessness and negligence is that a person is reckless if he is aware of and consciously disregards a substantial risk that a material element of the crime exists or will result from his conduct, whereas one is negligent when he fails to become aware of the substantial risk that an essential element of the crime exists or will result from his conduct, and both must constitute a gross deviation from the conduct of a reasonable person. State v. Cameron, 121 N.H. 348, 430 A.2d 138, 1981 N.H. LEXIS 317 (1981).

2. Construction with other laws

One cannot conspire to commit a crime where the culpability is based upon the result of reckless conduct; thus, defendant's motion to dismiss the portion of an indictment that charged conspiracy to commit reckless second-degree assault should have been granted because the indictment failed to allege facts that, if proven, would have constituted a cognizable crime. State v. Donohue, 150 N.H. 180, 834 A.2d 253, 2003 N.H. LEXIS 158 (2003).

In reversing a defendant's conviction for false report to law enforcement under RSA 641:4, I for insufficient evidence, the supreme court stated that since freedom of speech under N.H. Const. pt. I, art. 22 was implicated and its protection was broader than the First Amendment's, special scrutiny was necessary in evaluating the purpose requirement of RSA 641:4 when a defendant alleged police misconduct, and that, in such a case, the State was to offer evidence that the defendant's purpose in issuing a false report was to instigate a criminal investigation of a police officer's conduct, and that the State was to prove that it was the defendant's "conscious object" to cause such an investigation, pursuant to RSA 626:2, II(a); this interpretation effectively balanced the right of the individual to criticize police conduct with the State's interest in preventing the misdirection of police resources for the investigation of crime. State v. Allard, 148 N.H. 702, 813 A.2d 506, 2002 N.H. LEXIS 181 (2002).

In prosecution for criminal mischief, defendant was expected to know that this section defines elements requiring proof that he acted recklessly as constituting a subset of the elements requiring proof that he acted purposely, and, thus, RSA 634:2 on its face gave him notice that recklessly causing damage to property is a lesser-included offense of purposely causing damage to property. State v. Bruce, 147 N.H. 37, 780 A.2d 1270, 2001 N.H. LEXIS 165 (2001).

To convict defendant of driving after being certified an habitual offender, jury must find beyond a reasonable doubt that defendant knowingly drove a motor vehicle in the state while an order prohibiting such driving was in effect, and to prove defendant acted knowingly state must prove knowledge as to all material elements. State v. Baker, 135 N.H. 447, 606 A.2d 309, 1992 N.H. LEXIS 58 (1992).

A conviction on the charge of operation of a motor vehicle after certification as an habitual offender requires proof of three elements: (1) that an habitual offender order barring the defendant from driving a motor vehicle was in force; (2) that the defendant drove a motor vehicle on the ways of this state while that order remained in effect; and (3) that the defendant did so with knowledge of his status as an habitual offender. State v. Crotty, 134 N.H. 706, 597 A.2d 1078, 1991 N.H. LEXIS 126 (1991).

Under statute defining crime of resisting arrest, the requisite mental state, "knowingly," applies to each material element of the offense, and therefore in order to convict, a finding that defendant subjectively knew that the individual effecting the arrest was a law enforcement official is required. State v. Reid, 134 N.H. 418, 594 A.2d 160, 1991 N.H. LEXIS 81 (1991).

Requirement of forgery statute that defendant act "with purpose to defraud anyone" did not require allegation in indictment as to specific person defendant intended to defraud by uttering a forged check, and therefore trial court erred in quashing indictment for insufficiency. State v. DeMatteo, 134 N.H. 296, 591 A.2d 1323, 1991 N.H. LEXIS 56 (1991).

An indictment for witness tampering under RSA 641:5, I(a), which stated that the defendant "intentionally" attempted to induce one to testify falsely, rather than using the statutory term "purposely," sufficiently alleged the requisite culpable mental state, since the two terms are synonymous. State v. Brewer, 127 N.H. 799, 508 A.2d 1058, 1986 N.H. LEXIS 232 (1986).

This section and RSA 626:4 provided a defendant charged with manslaughter and second-degree assault with fair notice that a person may act recklessly while voluntarily intoxicated, since this section states that a person acts recklessly when he creates the requisite risk and is unaware of the risk solely by reason of having voluntarily engaged in intoxication, and RSA 626:4, which states that a person may introduce evidence of intoxication whenever it is relevant to negate an element of the offense charged, did not apply since intoxication is not relevant to negate the element of recklessness. State v. Glidden, 122 N.H. 41, 441 A.2d 728, 1982 N.H. LEXIS 285 (1982).

3. Negligence

Defendant's conviction for negligent homicide, in violation of RSA 630:3, I, was supported by sufficient evidence, as her use of a cellular telephone while driving, although not prohibited by RSA 265:105-a, constituted the requisite wrongful or blameworthy conduct to establish the culpable mental state of criminal negligence pursuant to RSA 626:2, II(d); further, she had a duty to yield to the victim, who was a pedestrian within a crosswalk pursuant to RSA 265:35. State v. Dion, 164 N.H. 544, 62 A.3d 792, 2013 N.H. LEXIS 7 (2013).

Criminal negligence does not depend upon the consequences of the defendant's act, no matter how tragic. Rather, it is the circumstances of the defendant's conduct that control the outcome. State v. Shepard, — N.H. —, 973 A.2d 318, 2009 N.H. LEXIS 73 (May 29, 2009).

Evidence did not support convictions of negligent homicide and vehicular assault under RSA 630:3, I and RSA 265:79-a when there was no evidence that defendant had consumed alcohol or drugs before driving and no evidence that he was speeding; at most, the evidence showed that his car inexplicably drifted over the double yellow line and into oncoming traffic for no more than two seconds. This did not constitute criminal negligence under RSA 626:2, II as a matter of law. State v. Shepard, — N.H. —, 973 A.2d 318, 2009 N.H. LEXIS 73 (May 29, 2009).

Without more, a defendant's violation of a traffic law due to momentary inattention is insufficient to impose criminal liability. State v. Shepard, — N.H. —, 973 A.2d 318, 2009 N.H. LEXIS 73 (May 29, 2009).

Sufficient evidence existed to support defendant's conviction for negligent homicide with regard to a collision between defendant's 36-foot Baja performance boat and the stern of a 20-foot motorboat where the evidence showed that the night of the collision was clear, moonless, there was smooth water and good visibility, that defen-

dant consumed alcohol before operating his boat and that he failed to keep a proper lookout. State v. Littlefield, 152 N.H. 331, 876 A.2d 712, 2005 N.H. LEXIS 100 (2005).

New Hampshire Supreme Court concluded that the vehicular assault statute, RSA 265:79-a, is valid as enacted and requires proof of a mental state of criminal negligence to sustain a conviction, RSA 626:2, II(d); the final sentence of RSA 265:79-a must be stricken, however, because it removes the evidence weighing function from the jury and shifts the burdens of proof and production to the defendant in violation of N.H. Const. pt. I, art. 15. State v. Rollins-Ercolino, 149 N.H. 336, 821 A.2d 953, 2003 N.H. LEXIS 48 (2003).

Jury could reasonably have found that defendant boat operator failed to become aware of a substantial and unjustifiable risk that death would result from his conduct where the evidence showed that victim was swimming with a group of five other people near a known swimming area, that victim's mother was visible from the waist up and members of group were using assorted visible flotation devices, and that defendant turned away from his direction of travel, pointing to property on shore, prior to accident. State v. Pittera, 139 N.H. 257, 651 A.2d 931, 1994 N.H. LEXIS 141 (1994).

4. Mens rea

Where a specific mental state is not provided for a statutory offense, subdivision I of this section requires proof of a culpable mental state which is appropriate in light of the nature of the offense and the policy considerations for punishing the conduct in question. State v. Bergen, 141 N.H. 61, 677 A.2d 145, 1996 N.H. LEXIS 47 (1996).

While RSA 263:64, IV, does not contain an explicit mens rea requirement, this section makes it clear that the defendant's knowledge of the suspension constitutes an element of the crime. State v. Curran, 140 N.H. 530, 669 A.2d 798, 1995 N.H. LEXIS 188 (1995).

There is no indication in the language of RSA 263:64 that the legislature intended the misdemeanor of driving after suspension or revocation to be merely a penalty enhancement not subject to the mens rea requirement of this section. State v. Curran, 140 N.H. 530, 669 A.2d 798, 1995 N.H. LEXIS 188 (1995).

5. Knowingly

Word "attempt" in RSA 649-B:4, I(a) does not incorporate the attempt statute, RSA 629:1, I, or the mental state of "purposely." Accordingly, under RSA 626:2, I, the mental state of "knowingly" applies to all of the material elements of RSA 649-B:4, I(a), and the trial court did not err in its jury instruction as to the mental state required for conviction. State v. Moscone, 161 N.H. 355, 13 A.3d 137, 2011 N.H. LEXIS 1 (2011).

In a trial for aggravated felonious sexual assault under RSA 632-A:2, I(l), there was sufficient evidence that defendant acted knowingly. The victim testified that she awoke when she felt defendant's fingers inside her vagina, that her shorts and underwear were pushed to one side, that defendant was standing over her, and that when she moved, defendant ran back to the cot where he was sleeping. State v. Tayag, 159 N.H. 21, 977 A.2d 510, 2009 N.H. LEXIS 80 (2009).

Trial court's instruction that New Hampshire law presumed all persons were aware of their actions and that defendant could not rebut this presumption because he had not raised insanity as a defense during his trial relieved the State of its burden of proving that defendant acted knowingly, and the state supreme court reversed defendant's conviction for second-degree murder. State v. Hall, 148 N.H. 394, 808 A.2d 55, 2002 N.H. LEXIS 146 (2002).

6. Recklessness

Determination that N.H. Rev. Stat. Ann. § 626:2, and § 631.3 reckless conduct was necessarily reprehensible because its definition included "serious bodily injury" and satisfied the scienter element because it required a classic formulation of recklessness was reasonable, and perfectly reflected moral turpitude as contemplated in 8 U.S.C.S. § 1182. Idy v. Holder, 674 F.3d 111, 2012 U.S. App. LEXIS 6098 (2012).

The evidence was sufficient to support the convictions of first-degree assault for recklessly causing serious bodily injury to a person under 13 in violation of RSA 631:1, I(d). On the two occasions when the infant victim exhibited symptoms of abuse, he was with defendant immediately beforehand; there was no evidence that his other caregivers mistreated him; defendant's admissions were consistent with medical evidence about the baby's injuries; from defendant's statements and the medical testimony, a rational juror could have found beyond a reasonable doubt that defendant was aware of and consciously disregarded the risk that violently handling the infant could cause serious bodily injury. State v. Wilmot, 163 N.H. 148, 37 A.3d 422, 2012 N.H. LEXIS 8 (2012).

Evidence was sufficient to establish that defendant was criminally reckless when, while intoxicated, he fired a handgun into a couch inside an occupied residence. State v. McCabe, 145 N.H. 686, 765 A.2d 176, 2001 N.H. LEXIS 7 (2001).

Trial court did not abuse its discretion in allowing State to present evidence of degree of force used by manslaughter defendant, in order to prove that defendant acted recklessly. State v. Bennett, 144 N.H. 13, 737 A.2d 640, 1999 N.H. LEXIS 64 (1999).

The act of kicking an unconscious person repeatedly in the head comes well within the definition of recklessly in subparagraph II(c) of this section. State v. Benson, 124 N.H. 767, 474 A.2d 576, 1984 N.H. LEXIS 340 (1984).

The last sentence of subparagraph II(c) of this section establishes two distinct requirements for recklessness: first, a person must create the specified risk, and second, the individual must be unaware of this risk solely because of voluntary intoxication. State v. Glidden, 122 N.H. 41, 441 A.2d 728, 1982 N.H. LEXIS 285 (1982).

The last sentence of subparagraph II(c) of this section implicitly provides for consideration of conditions, other than intoxication, which might cause a lack of awareness, because it permits a finding of recklessness only when an individual's lack of awareness results solely from voluntary intoxication. State v. Glidden, 122 N.H. 41, 441 A.2d 728, 1982 N.H. LEXIS 285 (1982).

Requested instruction, "that if the defendant was sufficiently intoxicated or had been struck in the head with a kick or a combination of both, then he would be … incapable of conduct of recklessness," stated the law incorrectly, because, under the terms of subparagraph II(c) of this section, a person suffering from a physical ailment or from intoxication might still possess the requisite mental state for recklessness. State v. Glidden, 122 N.H. 41, 441 A.2d 728, 1982 N.H. LEXIS 285 (1982).

7. Indictment

Where defendant was indicted for second degree assault and charged with recklessly causing bodily injury, the trial court did not substantively amend the indictment by instructing the jury, based on paragraph III of this section, that if they found that defendant acted purposely or knowingly, such a finding would satisfy the State's burden of proving recklessness as charged in the indictment. State v. Bathalon, 146 N.H. 485, 778 A.2d 1109, 2001 N.H. LEXIS 99 (2001).

Indictment sufficiently alleged all of the elements of negligent homicide, and it was not required to allege other specific acts of defendant or circumstances that would constitute a failure to become aware of a substantial and unjustifiable risk. State v. Pittera, 139 N.H. 257, 651 A.2d 931, 1994 N.H. LEXIS 141 (1994).

Where defendant was indicted for burglary and conspiracy to receive stolen property, the state was not required to allege that each action specified in the indictments was done with the purpose to commit the crimes charged, since this section did not require an indictment to charge redundantly. State v. Chaisson, 123 N.H. 17, 458 A.2d 95, 1983 N.H. LEXIS 236 (1983).

This section does not require an indictment to charge redundantly that a person charged as an accomplice of another purposely acted with purpose of promoting or facilitating the commission of an offense. State v. Bussiere, 118 N.H. 659, 392 A.2d 151, 1978 N.H. LEXIS 263 (1978).

8. Insanity

If not guilty plea is coupled with insanity defense, accused shall, upon request, receive bifurcated hearing before same judge and jury; evidence relating to accused's mental state is admissible in guilt determination phase only to show whether accused had requisite intent (e.g., purposely or knowingly) for commission of crime; evidence tending to show legal sanity or legal insanity, such

as expert psychiatric testimony, would not be admissible in first stage. Novosel v. Helgemoe, 118 N.H. 115, 384 A.2d 124, 1978 N.H. LEXIS 356 (1978), superseded by statute as stated in, State v. Blair, 143 N.H. 669, 732 A.2d 448, 1999 N.H. LEXIS 57 (1999).

9. Sexual assault

Defendant's motive of acting as his cousin's accomplice to avoid shame did not mean that he did not act with the purpose of making the crime of aggravated felonious sexual assault succeed. Defendant took off his clothes, got onto the bed with the victim, and penetrated her twice; regardless of why he acted, he had the conscious object of penetrating the victim. State v. Jenot, 158 N.H. 181, 965 A.2d 1086, 2008 N.H. LEXIS 142 (2008).

State did not have to prove defendant knew that a victim was under age of legal consent for statutory rape conviction under RSA 632-A:3, II because legislature had amended statute many times and did not insert a mens rea pursuant to RSA 626:2, I and did not provide a reasonable mistake of age defense. Thus, the offense remained a strict liability crime. State v. Holmes, 154 N.H. 723, 920 A.2d 632, 2007 N.H. LEXIS 9 (2007).

"Knowingly" is the appropriate mens rea for felonious sexual assault involving sexual penetration. State v. Goodwin, 140 N.H. 672, 671 A.2d 554, 1996 N.H. LEXIS 13 (1996).

While the underlying act common to each variant of the offense of aggravated sexual assault is sexual penetration, no mens rea is expressed in RSA 632-A:2; notwithstanding this omission, one cannot be convicted of this felony without proof that the act was accompanied by a culpable mental state. State v. Ayer, 136 N.H. 191, 612 A.2d 923, 1992 N.H. LEXIS 139 (1992).

Paragraph I of this section does not apply to a sexual assault victim's lack of consent and, thus, for conviction of crime of aggravated felonious sexual assault, there is no requirement that the defendant actually know that the victim did not consent. State v. Ayer, 136 N.H. 191, 612 A.2d 923, 1992 N.H. LEXIS 139 (1992).

Cited:

Cited in State v. Lantaigne, 117 N.H. 266, 371 A.2d 1170, 1977 N.H. LEXIS 313 (1977); State v. Plummer, 117 N.H. 320, 374 A.2d 431, 1977 N.H. LEXIS 330 (1977); State v. Howland, 119 N.H. 413, 402 A.2d 188, 1979 N.H. LEXIS 313 (1979); State v. Rullo, 120 N.H. 149, 412 A.2d 1009, 1980 N.H. LEXIS 248 (1980); Appeal of Metropolitan Property & Liab. Ins. Co., 120 N.H. 733, 422 A.2d 1037, 1980 N.H. LEXIS 385 (1980); State v. Weitzman, 121 N.H. 83, 427 A.2d 3, 1981 N.H. LEXIS 265 (1981); Opinion of Justices, 121 N.H. 542, 431 A.2d 152, 1981 N.H. LEXIS 343 (1981); State v. Pugliese, 122 N.H. 1141, 455 A.2d 1018, 1982 N.H. LEXIS 541 (1982); Pugliese v. Perrin, 567 F. Supp. 1337, 1983 U.S. Dist. LEXIS 15416 (D.N.H. 1983); State v. Fennelly, 123 N.H. 378, 461 A.2d 1090, 1983 N.H. LEXIS 288 (1983); Pugliese v. Perrin, 731 F.2d 85, 1984 U.S. App. LEXIS 23974 (1st Cir. N.H. 1984); State v. Monahan, 125 N.H. 17, 480 A.2d 863, 1984 N.H. LEXIS 372 (1984); State v. Etzweiler, 125 N.H. 57, 480 A.2d 870, 1984 N.H. LEXIS 369 (1984); State v. Fleming, 125 N.H. 238, 480 A.2d 107, 1984 N.H. LEXIS 365 (1984); State v. Wong, 125 N.H. 610, 486 A.2d 262, 1984 N.H. LEXIS 413 (1984); State v. Goding, 126 N.H. 50, 489 A.2d 579, 1985 N.H. LEXIS 241 (1985); State v. Dow, 126 N.H. 205, 489 A.2d 650, 1985 N.H. LEXIS 248 (1985); In re Dubuque, 46 B.R. 156, 1985 Bankr. LEXIS 6762 (Bankr. D.N.H. 1985); State v. Cote, 126 N.H. 514, 493 A.2d 1170, 1985 N.H. LEXIS 336 (1985); State v. Stone, 127 N.H. 747, 506 A.2d 345, 1986 N.H. LEXIS 214 (1986); State v. Allison, 127 N.H. 829, 508 A.2d 1084, 1986 N.H. LEXIS 228 (1986); State v. Pinder, 128 N.H. 66, 514 A.2d 1241, 1986 N.H. LEXIS 313 (1986); State v. Dominguez, 128 N.H. 288, 512 A.2d 1112, 1986 N.H. LEXIS 270 (1986); State v. Allen, 128 N.H. 390, 514 A.2d 1263, 1986 N.H. LEXIS 309 (1986); State v. Brown, 128 N.H. 606, 517 A.2d 831, 1986 N.H. LEXIS 328 (1986); State v. Guglielmo, 130 N.H. 240, 544 A.2d 25, 1987 N.H. LEXIS 303 (1987); King v. Prudential Property & Casualty Ins. Co., 684 F. Supp. 347, 1988 U.S. Dist. LEXIS 4173 (D.N.H. 1988); State v. Comley, 130 N.H. 688, 546 A.2d 1066, 1988 N.H. LEXIS 50 (1988); State v. Dufield, 131 N.H. 35, 549 A.2d 1205, 1988 N.H. LEXIS 88 (1988); State v. Pelky, 131 N.H. 715, 559 A.2d 1345, 1989 N.H. LEXIS 52 (1989); State v. Stratton, 132 N.H. 451, 567 A.2d 986, 1989 N.H. LEXIS 124 (1989); State v. Evans, 134 N.H. 378, 594 A.2d 154, 1991 N.H. LEXIS 71 (1991); State v. Ebinger, 135 N.H. 264, 603 A.2d 924, 1992 N.H. LEXIS 19 (1992); State v. Dushame, 136 N.H. 309, 616 A.2d 469, 1992 N.H. LEXIS

173 (1992); State v. Hutchinson, 137 N.H. 591, 631 A.2d 523, 1993 N.H. LEXIS 131 (1993); State v. Low, 138 N.H. 86, 635 A.2d 478, 1993 N.H. LEXIS 165 (1993); State v. Bassett, 139 N.H. 493, 659 A.2d 891, 1995 N.H. LEXIS 40 (1995); Fischer v. Hooper, 143 N.H. 585, 732 A.2d 396, 1999 N.H. LEXIS 160 (1999); Fischer v. Hooper, 143 N.H. 585, 732 A.2d 396, 1999 N.H. LEXIS 160 (1999); State v. Kidder, 150 N.H. 600, 843 A.2d 312, 2004 N.H. LEXIS 37 (2004).

RESEARCH REFERENCES

New Hampshire Practice.
8-7 N.H.P. Personal Injury-Tort & Insurance Practice § 7.10[1].

New Hampshire Bar Journal.
For article, "Lex Loci: A Survey of New Hampshire Supreme Court Decisions," see 44 N.H.B.J. 38 (Sept. 2003).

626:3. Effect of Ignorance or Mistake.

I. A person is not relieved of criminal liability because he acts under a mistaken belief of fact unless:

(a) The mistake negatives the culpable mental state required for commission of the offense; or

(b) The statute defining the offense expressly provides that such mistake is a defense; or

(c) Such mistake supports a defense of justification as defined in RSA 627.

II. A person is not relieved of criminal liability because he acts under a mistaken belief that his conduct does not, as a matter of law, constitute an offense unless his belief is founded upon a statement of the law contained in a statute or other enactment, or an administrative order or grant of permission, or a judicial decision of a state or federal court, or a written interpretation of the law relating to the offense officially made by a public servant, agency or body legally empowered with authority to administer, enforce or interpret such law. The defendant must prove a defense arising under this subsection by a preponderance of evidence.

Source.
1971, 518:1, eff. Nov. 1, 1973.

NOTES TO DECISIONS

1. Mistake as to law
2. Mistake of fact

1. Mistake as to law
Mistake as to law is a defense only when the mistaken belief is founded in such reliable sources as legal enactments, administrative orders, judicial decisions or official written interpretations of the law. State v. Stratton, 132 N.H. 451, 567 A.2d 986, 1989 N.H. LEXIS 124 (1989).

The affirmative defense provided in paragraph II of this section is in essence a question of fact: whether the defendant believed that the law in question did not apply to him because of his knowledge of a statute or administrative or judicial decision. State v. Sheedy, 125 N.H. 108, 480 A.2d 887, 1984 N.H. LEXIS 285 (1984).

2. Mistake of fact
Defendant provided a rational basis under RSA 626:3, I for finding defendant not guilty of driving while certified as a habitual offender under RSA 262:23 where defendant's testimony included (1) his memory problems, (2) his limited memory of his certification hearing, (3) his lack of understanding that habitual offender status continues until removed in writing, (4) the significance of his prior

conviction for operating after certification as a habitual offender and the ensuing jail sentence, and (5) his meeting with the department of motor vehicles employee which reinforced his belief that although his license was suspended, he was no longer certified as a habitual offender; thus, the trial court abused its discretion in denying defendant's request for a jury instruction on a lesser-included offense. State v. Gauntt, 154 N.H. 204, 908 A.2d 771, 2006 N.H. LEXIS 147 (2006).

Indictment's allegation that the defendant shot at an object "which he believed to be a deer," did not make it impossible for the state to disprove the defendant's mistake of fact defense. The indictment alleged that the defendant negligently caused the victim's death, and mistake of fact is an affirmative defense only if the mistake negatives the culpable mental state required for the commission of the offense. State v. Low, 138 N.H. 86, 635 A.2d 478, 1993 N.H. LEXIS 165 (1993).

Cited:
Cited in State v. Guaraldi, 124 N.H. 93, 467 A.2d 233, 1983 N.H. LEXIS 365 (1983); State v. W.J.T. Enters., 136 N.H. 490, 618 A.2d 806, 1992 N.H. LEXIS 211 (1992).

626:4. Intoxication.

Intoxication is not, as such, a defense. The defendant may, however, introduce evidence of intoxication whenever it is relevant to negate an element of the offense charged, and it shall be taken into consideration in determining whether such element has been proved beyond a reasonable doubt.

Source.
1971, 518:1, eff. Nov. 1, 1973.

NOTES TO DECISIONS

1. Construction with other laws
2. Intent—Specific intent
3. —Questions for jury
4. Voir dire

1. Construction with other laws
Imposing a culpable mental state requirement would have, in many cases, defeated the purpose of former RSA 265:82-a (repealed 2006, see now RSA 265-A:3 for similar provisions) entirely because to prove the core offense of driving while intoxicated, the State had to prove that defendant was impaired by alcohol, and that proof would simultaneously provide defendant a basis under RSA 626:4 to claim that his level of intoxication prevented defendant from acting purposely with respect to the aggravating factor of eluding the police. The legislature did not intend such a result when it enacted former RSA 265:82-a (repealed 2006, see now RSA 265-A:3 for similar provisions). State v. Polk, 155 N.H. 585, 927 A.2d 514, 2007 N.H. LEXIS 100 (2007).

This section and RSA 626:2 provided a defendant charged with manslaughter and second-degree assault with fair notice that a person may act recklessly while voluntarily intoxicated, since RSA 626:2 states that a person acts recklessly when he creates the requisite risk and is unaware of the risk solely by reason of having voluntarily engaged in intoxication, and this section, which states that a person may introduce evidence of intoxication whenever it is relevant to negate an element of the offense charged, did not apply since intoxication is not relevant to negate the element of recklessness. State v. Glidden, 122 N.H. 41, 441 A.2d 728, 1982 N.H. LEXIS 285 (1982).

2. Intent—Specific intent
Court at trial of attorney for theft of client funds did not err in ruling that evidence of acute alcohol dependence was limited to insanity defense and could not be used to prove lack of specific intent to commit theft; case law distinguishes between intoxication and alcoholism, and expert testimony offered by defendant as to his acute alcoholism had no bearing on whether he was so intoxicated as to be unable to form specific intent to commit theft. State v.

Sylvia, 136 N.H. 428, 616 A.2d 507, 1992 N.H. LEXIS 185 (1992).

Intoxication, whether by drugs or alcohol, may negate the existence of specific intent. State v. Noel, 119 N.H. 522, 404 A.2d 290, 1979 N.H. LEXIS 347 (1979).

Jury charge that burglary and arson required a finding of specific intent and that the effect of defendant's consumption of alcohol was a factor to be considered in resolving the issues in the case properly informed the jury that intoxication could prevent the formation of specific intent. State v. Warren, 114 N.H. 196, 317 A.2d 566, 1974 N.H. LEXIS 235 (1974).

3. —Questions for jury

Testimony of expert psychologist as to defendant's intoxication was properly excluded, since expert testimony on ultimate issue of whether defendant in fact formed or was capable of forming requisite intent for crimes charged would not aid jury in its search for truth. State v. St. Laurent, 138 N.H. 492, 642 A.2d 335, 1994 N.H. LEXIS 55 (1994).

In prosecution for first degree murder, where the defendant argued that he was unable to deliberate and premeditate the murder because he was highly intoxicated, and the jury chose to reject that argument, having been instructed on the relevance of intoxication to deliberation and premeditation, the jury's finding would not be disturbed on appeal since it was the province of the jury to determine whether intoxication negated deliberation and premeditation. State v. Hamel, 123 N.H. 670, 466 A.2d 555, 1983 N.H. LEXIS 332 (1983), overruled in part, State v. Riley, 126 N.H. 257, 490 A.2d 1362, 1985 N.H. LEXIS 292 (1985).

It is for the jury to resolve whether intoxication negates the element of intent. State v. Goodwin, 118 N.H. 862, 395 A.2d 1234, 1978 N.H. LEXIS 307 (1978).

Where there was substantial evidence that defendant was intoxicated when he allegedly broke into and entered dwelling in the nighttime with intent to commit rape, and the crime charged was one of specific intent and intent was a separate element of the crime, the jury could consider whether intoxication could prevent the formation of the requisite intent and the trial court erred in not so charging the jury. State v. Caldrain, 115 N.H. 390, 342 A.2d 628, 1975 N.H. LEXIS 318 (1975).

4. Voir dire

Trial court did not abuse its discretion by denying defendant's request for voir dire questions directed specifically to defendant's alleged intoxication as defense to robbery charge. State v. Dunbar, 117 N.H. 904, 379 A.2d 831, 1977 N.H. LEXIS 455 (1977) (per curiam decision).

Cited:

Cited in State v. Aldrich, 124 N.H. 43, 466 A.2d 938, 1983 N.H. LEXIS 356 (1983); MacKinnon v. Hanover Ins. Co., 124 N.H. 456, 471 A.2d 1166, 1984 N.H. LEXIS 215 (1984); State v. Guglielmo, 130 N.H. 240, 544 A.2d 25, 1987 N.H. LEXIS 303 (1987); McLaughlin v. Moore, 152 F. Supp. 2d 123, 2001 U.S. Dist. LEXIS 6908 (D.N.H. 2001).

626:5. Entrapment.

It is an affirmative defense that the actor committed the offense because he was induced or encouraged to do so by a law enforcement official or by a person acting in cooperation with a law enforcement official, for the purpose of obtaining evidence against him and when the methods used to obtain such evidence were such as to create a substantial risk that the offense would be committed by a person not otherwise disposed to commit it. However, conduct merely affording a person an opportunity to commit an offense does not constitute entrapment.

Source.
1971, 518:1, eff. Nov. 1, 1973.

NOTES TO DECISIONS

1. Purpose
2. Questions for jury
3. Evidence of predisposition
4. Continuing entrapment
5. Particular cases

1. Purpose

General purpose of entrapment defense is to prevent conviction of a crime manufactured by law enforcement officers. State v. Bacon, 114 N.H. 306, 319 A.2d 636, 1974 N.H. LEXIS 265 (1974).

2. Questions for jury

Entrapment is a question of fact for the jury, if there is evidence presenting the issue and allowing entrapment to be found. State v. Bacon, 114 N.H. 306, 319 A.2d 636, 1974 N.H. LEXIS 265 (1974).

3. Evidence of predisposition

In cases where the defense of entrapment is raised, evidence of the defendant's predisposition to commit the crime is relevant and admissible. State v. Little, 121 N.H. 765, 435 A.2d 517, 1981 N.H. LEXIS 410 (1981).

When the defense of entrapment is raised but the evidence supports a finding that the defendant was ready to commit the crime, the conviction will be upheld. State v. Little, 121 N.H. 765, 435 A.2d 517, 1981 N.H. LEXIS 410 (1981).

This section, by its terms, does not mandate that the inquiry as to existence of the defense focus solely on the conduct of the police, because in order for the defense to succeed the conduct must be "such as to create a substantial risk that the offense would be committed by a person not otherwise disposed to commit it"; therefore, disposition to commit the offense is relevant to the determination of the existence of the defense. State v. Little, 121 N.H. 765, 435 A.2d 517, 1981 N.H. LEXIS 410 (1981).

In case where defense of entrapment was raised, trial court did not err in allowing state to introduce rebuttal predisposition evidence, where defendant first raised issue of predisposition and testified to the effect that he was not so predisposed. State v. Little, 121 N.H. 765, 435 A.2d 517, 1981 N.H. LEXIS 410 (1981).

4. Continuing entrapment

A jury instruction on either the theory of continuing entrapment or the presumption of continuing entrapment is not required by RSA 626:5. Nothing in the entrapment statute indicated that a finding of entrapment as to a first charge precluded a finding of guilt as to subsequent crimes also charged, nor did the statute create a presumption of such an outcome. Interpreting the statute to include theory of continuing entrapment would grant defendant entrapped into committing an offense license to commit subsequent offenses regardless of whether defendant's disposition to commit changed over timeState v. Gelinas, 147 N.H. 437, 790 A.2d 138, 2002 N.H. LEXIS 9 (2002).

5. Particular cases

In a trial for criminal solicitation to commit murder, the trial court did not err in refusing to instruct on entrapment when there was no evidence that a trooper who posed as a hit man did anything other than offer his services to defendant. Although defendant argued that her roommate threatened her, his acts could only constitute inducement if they occurred during the brief time in which he acted as a government agent, and the only evidence that he threatened defendant during this time came from her own self-serving account. State v. Mendola, 160 N.H. 550, 8 A.3d 127, 2010 N.H. LEXIS 86 (2010).

Defendant's claim that he sold cocaine to an undercover officer because of police entrapment, under RSA 626:5, failed because defendant failed to produce "some evidence" that he was induced to commit the charged offenses of selling cocaine to an undercover police officer, because: (1) there was no evidence that the undercover officer engaged in any improper inducement; (2) the officer merely asked defendant for drugs; (3) while defendant implied that he would never have sold cocaine to the officer had a police informant not induced him to return to his drug addiction by repeatedly doing drugs with him, his own testimony established that even before the informant contacted him, he had been party-

ing; (4) that the informant asked defendant twice was not inducement; and (5) it was not inducement that defendant was lured by
the promise of a good cocaine customer and the ability to keep some
of the cocaine for himself. State v. Larose, 157 N.H. 28, 944 A.2d
566, 2008 N.H. LEXIS 33 (2008).

There was no entrapment where defendant's friend telephoned
and asked if he could send two men over to buy marijuana,
defendant told his friend, and the two men when they arrived, that
he maybe had some of his own, the men had asked if defendant had
any, and stated they had been talking to defendant's friend after
defendant said he was not sure he had any, and defendant then sold
the men some of his own. State v. Bacon, 114 N.H. 306, 319 A.2d
636, 1974 N.H. LEXIS 265 (1974).

Cited:
Cited in State v. Linsky, 117 N.H. 866, 379 A.2d 813, 1977 N.H.
LEXIS 450 (1977); State v. Guaraldi, 124 N.H. 93, 467 A.2d 233,
1983 N.H. LEXIS 365 (1983); State v. Saulnier, 132 N.H. 412, 566
A.2d 1135, 1989 N.H. LEXIS 118 (1989).

626:6. Consent.

I. The consent of the victim to conduct constituting an offense is a defense if such consent negatives
an element of the offense or precludes the harm
sought to be prevented by the law defining the
offense.

II. When conduct constitutes an offense because
it causes or threatens bodily harm, consent to the
conduct is a defense if the bodily harm is not serious;
or the harm is a reasonably foreseeable hazard of
lawful activity.

III. Consent is no defense if it is given by a person
legally incompetent to authorize the conduct or by
one who, by reason of immaturity, insanity, intoxication or use of drugs is unable and known by the
actor to be unable to exercise a reasonable judgment
as to the harm involved.

Source.
1971, 518:1, eff. Nov. 1, 1973.

NOTES TO DECISIONS

1. Construction with other laws
2. Instructions

1. Construction with other laws
Statutory definition of "element of an offense" cannot be read to
include the defense of consent. State v. Cooper, 135 N.H. 258, 603
A.2d 499, 1992 N.H. LEXIS 16 (1992).

Because consent is not a justification, lack of consent is not an
element of the offense of sexual assault. State v. Cooper, 135 N.H.
258, 603 A.2d 499, 1992 N.H. LEXIS 16 (1992).

2. Instructions
Assuming without deciding that the defendant was entitled to a
jury instruction on consent, trial court's decision not to give the
defendant's requested instruction on that theory was sustainable
where the trial court charged the jury on the elements of aggravated felonious sexual assault by concealment or surprise and
where defendant's requested consent instruction did not correctly
state the law. State v. Ramos, 149 N.H. 272, 821 A.2d 979, 2003
N.H. LEXIS 37 (2003).

Trial court's inclusion of "physically helpless to resist" language,
in instruction on consent at sexual assault trial, improperly
amended subdivision III of this section and was erroneous as a
matter of law. State v. Jackson, 141 N.H. 152, 679 A.2d 572, 1996
N.H. LEXIS 67 (1996).

Cited:
Cited in State v. Guaraldi, 124 N.H. 93, 467 A.2d 233, 1983 N.H.
LEXIS 365 (1983); State v. Ayer, 136 N.H. 191, 612 A.2d 923, 1992
N.H. LEXIS 139 (1992).

626:7. Defenses; Affirmative Defenses and Presumptions.

I. When evidence is admitted on a matter declared by this code to be:

(a) A defense, the state must disprove such
defense beyond a reasonable doubt; or

(b) An affirmative defense, the defendant has
the burden of establishing such defense by a preponderance of the evidence.

II. When this code establishes a presumption
with respect to any fact which is an element of an
offense, it has the following consequences:

(a) When there is evidence of the facts which
give rise to the presumption, the issue of the existence of the presumed fact must be submitted to the
jury, unless the court is satisfied that the evidence as
a whole clearly negatives the presumed fact; and

(b) When the issue of the existence of the presumed fact is submitted to the jury, the court shall
charge that while the presumed fact must, on all the
evidence, be proved beyond a reasonable doubt, the
law declares that the jury may regard the facts
giving rise to the presumption as sufficient evidence
of the presumed fact.

Source.
1971, 518:1, eff. Nov. 1, 1973.

NOTES TO DECISIONS

1. Constitutionality
2. Affirmative defenses
3. Presumption of sanity
4. Defense of consent
5. Statute of limitations defense

1. Constitutionality
This section, placing the burden of proving the affirmative
defense of entrapment upon the defendant, does not violate due
process, because the burden of proving all the elements of the crime
charged beyond a reasonable doubt remains with the state. State v.
Little, 121 N.H. 765, 435 A.2d 517, 1981 N.H. LEXIS 410 (1981).

2. Affirmative defenses
Defendant's claim that he sold cocaine to an undercover officer
because of police entrapment, under RSA 626:5, failed because
defendant failed to produce "some evidence" that he was induced to
commit the charged offenses of selling cocaine to an undercover
police officer, because: (1) there was no evidence that the undercover officer engaged in any improper inducement; (2) the officer
merely asked defendant for drugs; (3) while defendant implied that
he would never have sold cocaine to the officer had a police
informant not induced him to return to his drug addiction by
repeatedly doing drugs with him, his own testimony established
that even before the informant contacted him, he had been party-
ing; (4) that the informant asked defendant twice was not inducement; and (5) it was not inducement that defendant was lured by
the promise of a good cocaine customer and the ability to keep some
of the cocaine for himself. State v. Larose, 157 N.H. 28, 944 A.2d
566, 2008 N.H. LEXIS 33 (2008).

The affirmative defense of insanity must be proven by clear and
convincing evidence. State v. Rullo, 120 N.H. 149, 412 A.2d 1009,

1980 N.H. LEXIS 248 (1980), superseded by statute as stated in, State v. Blair, 143 N.H. 669, 732 A.2d 448, 1999 N.H. LEXIS 57 (1999).

3. Presumption of sanity

Sanity is properly in nature of a policy presumption because it is inherent in human nature and is natural and normal condition of mankind, and is not properly an element of the crime. Novosel v. Helgemoe, 118 N.H. 115, 384 A.2d 124, 1978 N.H. LEXIS 356 (1978), superseded by statute as stated in, State v. Blair, 143 N.H. 669, 732 A.2d 448, 1999 N.H. LEXIS 57 (1999).

4. Defense of consent

Once defendant charged with sexual assault raises the defense of consent, the burden of proving lack of consent shifts to the state. State v. Cooper, 135 N.H. 258, 603 A.2d 499, 1992 N.H. LEXIS 16 (1992).

5. Statute of limitations defense

Where evidence pertaining to the statute of limitations was not admitted at trial and the issue was presented for the first time in the defendant's proposed jury instruction, the state was not required to disprove a statute of limitations defense as the state's burden is only triggered when evidence pertaining to the statute of limitations is admitted at trial. State v. Weeks, 137 N.H. 687, 635 A.2d 439, 1993 N.H. LEXIS 145 (1993).

Cited:

Cited in State v. Millette, 112 N.H. 458, 299 A.2d 150, 1972 N.H. LEXIS 243 (1972); State v. Arillo, 122 N.H. 107, 441 A.2d 1163, 1982 N.H. LEXIS 295 (1982); Pugliese v. Perrin, 567 F. Supp. 1337, 1983 U.S. Dist. LEXIS 15416 (D.N.H. 1983); State v. Guaraldi, 124 N.H. 93, 467 A.2d 233, 1983 N.H. LEXIS 365 (1983); State v. Patten, 126 N.H. 227, 489 A.2d 657, 1985 N.H. LEXIS 253 (1985); State v. Smith, 127 N.H. 433, 503 A.2d 774, 1985 N.H. LEXIS 463 (1985); State v. Abbott, 127 N.H. 444, 503 A.2d 791, 1985 N.H. LEXIS 465 (1985); State v. Jernigan, 133 N.H. 396, 577 A.2d 1214, 1990 N.H. LEXIS 78 (1990); State v. Wallace, 136 N.H. 267, 615 A.2d 1243, 1992 N.H. LEXIS 165 (1992); State v. McMinn, 141 N.H. 636, 690 A.2d 1017, 1997 N.H. LEXIS 11 (1997); State v. Dukette, 145 N.H. 226, 761 A.2d 442, 2000 N.H. LEXIS 46 (2000).

RESEARCH REFERENCES

New Hampshire Trial Bar News.

For article, "Presumptions in New Hampshire Law—A Guide Through the Impenetrable Jungle (Part II)," see 11 N.H. Trial Bar News 31, 35, nn.82, 90, 96, 36, 43 (Fall 1991).

626:8. Criminal Liability for Conduct of Another.

I. A person is guilty of an offense if it is committed by his own conduct or by the conduct of another person for which he is legally accountable, or both.

II. A person is legally accountable for the conduct of another person when:

(a) Acting with the kind of culpability that is sufficient for the commission of the offense, he causes an innocent or irresponsible person to engage in such conduct; or

(b) He is made accountable for the conduct of such other person by the law defining the offense; or

(c) He is an accomplice of such other person in the commission of the offense.

III. A person is an accomplice of another person in the commission of an offense if:

(a) With the purpose of promoting or facilitating the commission of the offense, he solicits such other person in committing it, or aids or agrees or attempts to aid such other person in planning or committing it; or

(b) His conduct is expressly declared by law to establish his complicity.

IV. Notwithstanding the requirement of a purpose as set forth in paragraph III(a), when causing a particular result is an element of an offense, an accomplice in the conduct causing such result is an accomplice in the commission of that offense, if he acts with the kind of culpability, if any, with respect to that result that is sufficient for the commission of the offense. In other words, to establish accomplice liability under this section, it shall not be necessary that the accomplice act with a purpose to promote or facilitate the offense. An accomplice in conduct can be found criminally liable for causing a prohibited result, provided the result was a reasonably foreseeable consequence of the conduct and the accomplice acted purposely, knowingly, recklessly, or negligently with respect to that result, as required for the commission of the offense.

V. A person who is legally incapable of committing a particular offense himself may be guilty thereof if it is committed by the conduct of another person for which he is legally accountable, unless such liability is inconsistent with the purpose of the provision establishing his incapacity.

VI. Unless otherwise provided, a person is not an accomplice in an offense committed by another person if:

(a) He is the victim of that offense; or

(b) The offense is so defined that his conduct is inevitably incident to its commission; or

(c) He terminates his complicity prior to the commission of the offense and wholly deprives it of effectiveness in the commission of the offense or gives timely warning to the law enforcement authorities or otherwise makes proper effort to prevent the commission of the offense.

VII. An accomplice may be convicted on proof of the commission of the offense and of his complicity therein, though the person claimed to have committed the offense has not been prosecuted or convicted or has been convicted of a different offense or degree of offense or has an immunity to prosecution or conviction or has been acquitted.

Source.

1971, 518:1, eff. Nov. 1, 1973. 2001, 216:1, eff. Jan. 1, 2002.

Amendments

—2001. Paragraph IV: Added "notwithstanding the requirement of a purpose as set forth in paragraph III(a)" in the first sentence and added the second and third sentences.

NOTES TO DECISIONS

1. Construction
2. Construction with other laws
3. Extent of liability
4. Presence during crime
5. Affirmative act
6. Intent

7. Purpose of accomplice
8. Facilitation
9. Aid
10. Guilt of principal
11. Indictment and information
12. Instructions
13. Particular cases

1. Construction

RSA 626:8, IV, plainly states that accomplice liability can flow from conduct provided the result was a reasonably foreseeable consequence of the conduct. To require the State to prove that the defendant had a purpose to promote or facilitate the actus reus of a prohibited results crime would limit accomplice liability to only the direct, not the "reasonably foreseeable," consequences of the defendant's conduct. State v. Rivera, 162 N.H. 182, 27 A.3d 676, 2011 N.H. LEXIS 84 (2011).

It has been stated that "the standard interpretation of the phrase 'intent to promote or facilitate the commission of the offense' is that it requires proof of the accomplice's intent to promote or facilitate another person's conduct that constitutes the actus reus of the offense," but this passage addresses RSA 626:8, III, alone. When causing a prohibited result is an element of an offense, RSA 626:8, IV, modifies the formulation stated in RSA 626:8, III; it specifically provides that in such a case, it shall not be necessary that the accomplice act with a purpose to promote or facilitate the offense. State v. Rivera, 162 N.H. 182, 27 A.3d 676, 2011 N.H. LEXIS 84 (2011).

Classic formulation of the felony-murder doctrine declares that one is guilty of murder if a death results from conduct during the commission or attempted commission of any felony; as thus conceived, the rule operated without separate proof of any culpability with regard to the death. New Hampshire's statutory scheme does not allow imposition of guilt regardless of the actor's mental state, but requires that the State prove that the defendant possessed the mental state required by the underlying offense—in the case of second-degree murder, recklessness. State v. Rivera, 162 N.H. 182, 27 A.3d 676, 2011 N.H. LEXIS 84 (2011).

The 2001 amendment to paragraph IV of this section constitutes a legislative rejection of the interpretation of the statute stated by the plurality in State v. Etzweiler, 125 N.H. 57 (1984) and reiterated by the court in State v. Locke, 144 N.H. 348 (1999) and was intended to clarify RSA 626:8, IV in response to Etzweiler. Accordingly, consistent with the majority of courts interpreting accomplice liability statutes derived from the Model Penal Code, accomplice liability under RSA 626:8, III and IV requires proof (1) that the accomplice intended to promote or facilitate another's unlawful or dangerous conduct, and (2) that the accomplice acted with the culpable mental state specified in the underlying statute with respect to the result. State v. Anthony, 151 N.H. 492, 861 A.2d 773 (2004).

Paragraph IV of this section, governing liability when causing a particular result is an element of an offense, is not independent of paragraph III of this section, which defines when a person is an accomplice, and therefore the elements set forth in paragraph III must be alleged and proven by the state to establish accomplice liability. State v. Horne, 125 N.H. 254, 480 A.2d 121, 1984 N.H. LEXIS 283 (1984). (Decided under prior law.)

This section eradicated the distinctions between principal and accomplice. State v. Thresher, 122 N.H. 63, 442 A.2d 578, 1982 N.H. LEXIS 288 (1982).

2. Construction with other laws

An individual may not be an accomplice to negligent homicide, since to satisfy the requirements of paragraph III of this section, the state must establish that the accomplice's acts were designed to aid the primary actor in committing the substantive offense, yet under RSA 626:2, II(d) setting forth the necessary accompanying mental state of negligence, the primary actor must be unaware of the risk that his conduct created, and an accomplice could not intentionally aid the primary actor in a crime that the primary actor was unaware that he was committing. State v. Etzweiler, 125 N.H. 57, 480 A.2d 870, 1984 N.H. LEXIS 369 (1984), superseded by statute as stated in, State v. Anthony, 151 N.H. 492, 861 A.2d 773,

2004 N.H. LEXIS 184 (2004), superseded by statute as stated in, State v. Rivera, 162 N.H. 182, 27 A.3d 676, 2011 N.H. LEXIS 84 (2011). (Decided under prior law; see para. IV as subsequently amended.)

The legislature, in enacting RSA 630:3, I, governing negligent homicide, and this section, did not intend to impose criminal liability upon a person who lends his automobile to an intoxicated driver but does not accompany the driver, when the driver's operation of the borrowed automobile causes death. State v. Etzweiler, 125 N.H. 57, 480 A.2d 870, 1984 N.H. LEXIS 369 (1984), superseded by statute as stated in, State v. Anthony, 151 N.H. 492, 861 A.2d 773, 2004 N.H. LEXIS 184 (2004), superseded by statute as stated in, State v. Rivera, 162 N.H. 182, 27 A.3d 676, 2011 N.H. LEXIS 84 (2011). (Decided under prior law.)

3. Extent of liability

An accomplice's liability ought not to extend beyond the criminal purposes that he or she shares. State v. Etzweiler, 125 N.H. 57, 480 A.2d 870, 1984 N.H. LEXIS 369 (1984), superseded by statute as stated in, State v. Anthony, 151 N.H. 492, 861 A.2d 773, 2004 N.H. LEXIS 184 (2004), superseded by statute as stated in, State v. Rivera, 162 N.H. 182, 27 A.3d 676, 2011 N.H. LEXIS 84 (2011).

4. Presence during crime

In a trial for attempted burglary under RSA 635:1, RSA 626:8, and RSA 629:1, the evidence revealed more than defendant's mere presence at the scene. A witness saw three men fleeing from his home and later identified them; he found a bent window screen in the grass and testified that he was sure that one of the men removed the screen; another witness heard three men having a "panicked" conversation and then saw them fleeing together; the three men, including defendant, were found hiding near the scene; and when police questioned defendant regarding the whereabouts of any accomplices, he was uncooperative, physically aggressive and used vulgar language. State v. Winward, 161 N.H. 533, 20 A.3d 338, 2011 N.H. LEXIS 21 (2011).

Crime of accomplice liability requires some active participation by accomplice, and mere presence at scene of crime is insufficient; defendant's presence may constitute aiding and abetting, however, when it is shown to encourage perpetrator or facilitate perpetrator's unlawful deed. State v. Merritt, 143 N.H. 714, 738 A.2d 343, 1999 N.H. LEXIS 63 (1999).

Evidence was insufficient to sustain defendant's conviction under first count of acting in concert with another in fraudulent use of credit cards, where no rational jury could have found him guilty as an accomplice for first jewelry purchase, since there was no evidence that defendant did anything other than accompany his girlfriend to jewelry store. State v. Merritt, 143 N.H. 714, 738 A.2d 343, 1999 N.H. LEXIS 63 (1999).

The circumstances under which a defendant is present at the scene of a crime may be such as to warrant the jury's inferring beyond a reasonable doubt that he sought thereby to make the crime succeed. State v. Goodwin, 118 N.H. 862, 395 A.2d 1234, 1978 N.H. LEXIS 307 (1978).

Mere presence at the scene of a crime is insufficient to make a person criminally responsible. State v. Goodwin, 118 N.H. 862, 395 A.2d 1234, 1978 N.H. LEXIS 307 (1978).

5. Affirmative act

Jury could have found that defendant aided his girlfriend in all fraudulent credit card transactions after their first one, where defendant selected or assisted his girlfriend in selecting merchandise that was ultimately purchased, and distracted sales clerks from closely examining credit cards while merchandise was being purchased. State v. Merritt, 143 N.H. 714, 738 A.2d 343, 1999 N.H. LEXIS 63 (1999).

The crime of accomplice liability under subparagraph III(a) of this section requires some active participation by the accomplice. State v. Arillo, 131 N.H. 295, 553 A.2d 281, 1988 N.H. LEXIS 124 (1988).

The crime of accomplice liability under subparagraph III(a) of this section necessitates some active participation by the accomplice. State v. Vaillancourt, 122 N.H. 1153, 453 A.2d 1327, 1982 N.H. LEXIS 530 (1982).

Knowledge and mere presence at the scene of a crime cannot support a conviction for accomplice liability because they do not constitute sufficient affirmative acts to satisfy the actus reus requirement of subparagraph III(a) of this section. State v. Vaillancourt, 122 N.H. 1153, 453 A.2d 1327, 1982 N.H. LEXIS 530 (1982).

6. Intent

Jury could have reasonably excluded all rational conclusions other than guilt with respect to defendant's intent, at trial for acting in concert with another in fraudulent use of credit cards, where defendant and his girlfriend had a relationship and were living together, credit cards were used six times in six stores over a period of about five hours, for merchandise totaling over $2,600, jewelry and clothes purchased either fit defendant or were items defendant expressed an intent to give to his girlfriend, and defendant gave a false name on diamond certificate that accompanied purchase of a men's diamond ring. State v. Merritt, 143 N.H. 714, 738 A.2d 343, 1999 N.H. LEXIS 63 (1999).

7. Purpose of accomplice

Under accomplice liability statute, State must establish that accomplice acted with purpose of promoting or facilitating commission of the substantive offense; this requires State to prove that accomplice's acts were designed to aid primary actor in committing offense, and that accomplice had purpose to make crime succeed. State v. Locke, 144 N.H. 348, 761 A.2d 376, 1999 N.H. LEXIS 123 (1999), superseded by statute as stated in, State v. Anthony, 151 N.H. 492, 861 A.2d 773, 2004 N.H. LEXIS 184 (2004), superseded by statute as stated in, State v. Rivera, 162 N.H. 182, 27 A.3d 676, 2011 N.H. LEXIS 84 (2011).

Under paragraph III of this section, the state has the burden of establishing that the accomplice acted with the purpose of promoting or facilitating the commission of the substantive offense, and this encompasses the requirement that the accomplice's acts were designed to aid the primary actor in committing the offense and that the accomplice had the purpose to make the crime succeed. State v. Etzweiler, 125 N.H. 57, 480 A.2d 870, 1984 N.H. LEXIS 369 (1984), superseded by statute as stated in, State v. Anthony, 151 N.H. 492, 861 A.2d 773, 2004 N.H. LEXIS 184 (2004), superseded by statute as stated in, State v. Rivera, 162 N.H. 182, 27 A.3d 676, 2011 N.H. LEXIS 84 (2011).

To prosecute one as an accomplice, paragraph III of this section requires that the state must prove that the defendant acted with the purpose of promoting or facilitating the offense. State v. Horne, 125 N.H. 254, 480 A.2d 121, 1984 N.H. LEXIS 283 (1984).

8. Facilitation

Jury could have reasonably concluded that defendant's presence facilitated and encouraged principal's actions where there was evidence that defendant owned the car in which victim was abducted and owned the apartment where rape occurred, and was present during the kidnapping and rape of the victim. State v. Goodwin, 118 N.H. 862, 395 A.2d 1234, 1978 N.H. LEXIS 307 (1978).

9. Aid

Trial court erred in upholding defendant's indictment for accomplice liability where the state alleged the requisite mens rea but further alleged only that the defendant aided another "by accompanying him to the location of the crime and watching ...", since accompaniment and observation are not sufficient acts to constitute "aid" under subparagraph III(a) of this section. State v. Vaillancourt, 122 N.H. 1153, 453 A.2d 1327, 1982 N.H. LEXIS 530 (1982).

10. Guilt of principal

Paragraph VII of this section excludes the guilt of the named principal as an element necessary for the conviction of an accomplice. State v. Kaplan, 124 N.H. 382, 469 A.2d 1354, 1983 N.H. LEXIS 388 (1983).

Language of paragraph VII of this section that "an accomplice may be convicted on proof of the commission of the offense and of his complicity therein ..." excludes the guilt of the named principal as an element necessary for the conviction of the accomplice. State v. Jansen, 120 N.H. 616, 419 A.2d 1108, 1980 N.H. LEXIS 354 (1980).

11. Indictment and information

Trial court did not constructively amend the indictment for attempted burglary under RSA 635:1, RSA 626:8, and RSA 629:1 by refusing to instruct the jury that the State had to prove that defendant himself removed a window screen. Because the indictment clearly alleged both principal and accomplice liability, it provided sufficient notice that defendant was charged with either removing the window screen himself or soliciting, aiding or attempting to aid another in removing it; the indictment was more than sufficient for defendant to prepare his defense because it put him on notice that the State would have to prove that he in some way solicited, aided, agreed or attempted to aid in the attempted burglary State v. Winward, 161 N.H. 533, 20 A.3d 338, 2011 N.H. LEXIS 21 (2011).

Defendant's double jeopardy rights under N.H. Const. pt. I, art. 16, and U.S. Const. amend. V, were not violated because, as charged, each indictment required the State to prove a fact not necessary to the other; specifically, the State did not have to prove the existence of an agreement, required for the conspiracy conviction, to prove the first degree murder charge under RSA 630:1-a and RSA 626:8, and the conspiracy indictment did not require the State to prove the enhanced mental state of deliberation and premeditation, required for a first degree murder conviction. State v. Sanchez, 152 N.H. 625, 883 A.2d 292, 2005 N.H. LEXIS 149 (2005).

Trial court erred in ruling that defendant could not be charged as an accomplice to a crime requiring proof of recklessness as the culpable mental state; as a matter of law, a person could act with purpose of promoting or facilitating commission of a reckless homicide, and thus defendant could properly be charged as an accomplice to reckless second degree murder. State v. Locke, 144 N.H. 348, 761 A.2d 376, 1999 N.H. LEXIS 123 (1999), superseded by statute as stated in, State v. Anthony, 151 N.H. 492, 861 A.2d 773, 2004 N.H. LEXIS 184 (2004), superseded by statute as stated in, State v. Rivera, 162 N.H. 182, 27 A.3d 676, 2011 N.H. LEXIS 84 (2011).

Indictments alleging that defendant acted "in concert with" another were sufficient to charge defendant both as a principal and an accomplice. Therefore, defendant had sufficient notice that he was being charged as a principal, and accomplice indictments were not defective in alleging that defendant acted "knowingly", as opposed to "purposely." State v. Sinbandith, 143 N.H. 579, 729 A.2d 994, 1999 N.H. LEXIS 47 (1999).

An indictment sufficiently alleges accomplice liability to an attempted felony if it alleges an attempted felony on the part of the principal and the acts and intent of the accomplice to aid the principal in that activity. State v. Abbis, 125 N.H. 646, 484 A.2d 1156, 1984 N.H. LEXIS 387 (1984).

Because accomplice liability holds an individual criminally liable for actions done by another, it is important that the prosecution fall squarely within this section. State v. Etzweiler, 125 N.H. 57, 480 A.2d 870, 1984 N.H. LEXIS 369 (1984), superseded by statute as stated in, State v. Anthony, 151 N.H. 492, 861 A.2d 773, 2004 N.H. LEXIS 184 (2004), superseded by statute as stated in, State v. Rivera, 162 N.H. 182, 27 A.3d 676, 2011 N.H. LEXIS 84 (2011).

An information charging the defendant with being an accomplice to receiving stolen property had to set forth the acts that constituted the offense and not merely the language of this section. State v. Lurvey, 122 N.H. 190, 442 A.2d 592, 1982 N.H. LEXIS 316 (1982).

Language of indictment stating that defendant was indicted for "acting in concert with" another defendant adequately informed defendant that he was charged as an accomplice and could be held criminally liable under this section. State v. Burke, 122 N.H. 565, 448 A.2d 962, 1982 N.H. LEXIS 401 (1982).

Trial court's interpretation of language in an indictment for robbery and second-degree murder, which alleged that the defendant committed the crimes "in concert with" a codefendant, as charging the defendant as a principal and/or accomplice rather than only as a principal was proper since the "in concert with" language has been interpreted as charging the defendants as accomplices and this section has been interpreted as eradicating the distinctions between principal and accomplice and, therefore, the defendant could have been found guilty of second-degree murder whether he was the principal or accomplice. State v. Thresher, 122 N.H. 63, 442 A.2d 578, 1982 N.H. LEXIS 288 (1982).

12. Instructions

In a trial for attempted burglary, the trial court did not err in not giving a "mere presence" instruction. Its instruction made clear that to find defendant guilty, the jury had to conclude that he in some way actively aided or participated in the attempted burglary. State v. Winward, 161 N.H. 533, 20 A.3d 338, 2011 N.H. LEXIS 21 (2011).

In a manslaughter case, the State presented sufficient evidence to support a jury instruction on accomplice liability under RSA 626:8, III. There was evidence that defendant had the purpose to make the crime succeed in that a witness testified that he was present when defendant kicked the victim, and evidence that defendant jumped up and down on the victim's head showed that he had aided in the commission of the crime and that he possessed the requisite mens rea for manslaughter, recklessness. State v. Duran, 158 N.H. 146, 960 A.2d 697, 2008 N.H. LEXIS 139 (2008).

When a defendant is sufficiently charged by an indictment as a principal, the indictment is sufficient to allow the defendant to prepare a defense to the substantive offense for principal or accomplice liability and an instruction with regard to accomplice liability does not impermissibly amend the indictment in violation of part I, article 15 of the New Hampshire Constitution. State v. Barton, 142 N.H. 391, 702 A.2d 336, 1997 N.H. LEXIS 109 (1997).

Where the trial court instructed the jury that if it found that the defendant had committed all of the acts necessary for murder or if he had committed the acts in conjunction with his accomplice, provided he was accountable for his accomplice's acts, then it could find him guilty of murder, because this charge was consistent with this section which eradicated the distinctions between principals and accessories, and because the trial court's interpretation of the indictment as charging the defendant as either a principal or accomplice, rather than only as a principal, was valid, the jury instructions were proper. State v. Thresher, 122 N.H. 63, 442 A.2d 578, 1982 N.H. LEXIS 288 (1982).

13. Particular cases

Error in admitting post-arrest statements of co-conspirators under N.H. R. Evid. 801(d)(2)(E) was not harmless as to accomplice and conspiracy first-degree assault charges under RSA 626:8, RSA 629:3, and RSA 631:1, as the evidence did not overwhelmingly establish that defendant had at least a tacit understanding that deadly weapons would be used in the commission of the assault. State v. Rodriguez, 164 N.H. 800, 64 A.3d 962, 2013 N.H. LEXIS 45 (2013).

There was sufficient evidence to support defendant's conviction for being an accomplice to armed robbery where a witness testified that defendant told her and a decedent that he wanted to commit robbery, traveled with them to the house in question, directed her to park behind the house, and wore a ski mask and armed himself. Furthermore, defendant admitted that he was inside the house during the robbery and used force against the victim; a ski mask and a rubber glove recovered from the scene contained defendant's DNA; and the decedent was found wearing rubber gloves with a baseball bat nearby. State v. Noucas, — N.H. —, 70 A.3d 476, 2013 N.H. LEXIS 83 (July 16, 2013).

Fact that defendant might not have been an active participant in the crime from the outset did not shelter him from accomplice liability for second-degree assault under RSA 631:2, I(c) and 626:8. The jury could find that when defendant aided and assisted the assailants, the assault was a work in progress; furthermore, there was sufficient evidence that defendant could have reasonably foreseen that the victim would sustain further bodily injury as a consequence of his acts and that he acted recklessly with extreme indifference to the value of human life State v. Alwardt, 164 N.H. 52, 53 A.3d 545, 2012 N.H. LEXIS 111 (2012).

In a prosecution for being an accomplice to reckless second-degree murder under RSA 626:8, and RSA 630:1-b, I(b), the victim's death was a reasonably foreseeable consequence of defendant's actions in planning an armed burglary of a house occupied by a person he knew to have a gun; driving his companions, one of whom he knew was armed with a gun, to the victim's home; entering the home with his companions; confronting and scuffling with the victim; and searching the victim's property while a companion, armed with a gun, remained with the victim. State v. Rivera, 162 N.H. 182, 27 A.3d 676, 2011 N.H. LEXIS 84 (2011).

Evidence that defendant acted as his cousin's accomplice because he feared that the cousin would reveal having sexually assaulted him was properly excluded under N.H. R. Evid. 403. It was of limited probative value under N.H. R. Evid 401 because potential embarrassment did not excuse unlawful actions, and its probative value was outweighed by its prejudicial potential to create jury sympathy for defendant. State v. Jenot, 158 N.H. 181, 965 A.2d 1086, 2008 N.H. LEXIS 142 (2008).

Defendant's motive of acting as his cousin's accomplice to avoid shame did not mean that he did not act with the purpose of making the crime of aggravated felonious sexual assault succeed. Defendant took off his clothes, got onto the bed with the victim, and penetrated her twice; regardless of why he acted, he had the conscious object of penetrating the victim. State v. Jenot, 158 N.H. 181, 965 A.2d 1086, 2008 N.H. LEXIS 142 (2008).

Evidence was sufficient to support convictions for attempted murder as an "accomplice/principal" based on the shooting of the victims where shoe print evidence and the defendant's own statement placed him at the scene of the shooting and additional evidence supported the jury's conclusion that the defendant's involvement exceeded mere presence. State v. Duguay, 142 N.H. 221, 698 A.2d 5, 1997 N.H. LEXIS 79 (1997).

Evidence was sufficient to establish that the defendant, as an accomplice, committed two counts of attempted murder, one count of attempted arson, and one count of attempted falsification of evidence, where a witness testified that, mere hours after the incident, the defendant admitted that he had accompanied his coperpetrator to the scene of the crime, that they planned to rob whomever they discovered there, by violent means if necessary, that the defendant and the coperpetrator hid behind a bush while the latter twice shot at a car, that after the victims abandoned the car they searched it for valuables and money, and that there was an attempt to destroy the car following the search for valuables. State v. Laudarowicz, 142 N.H. 1, 694 A.2d 980, 1997 N.H. LEXIS 47 (1997).

Cited:

Cited in State v. Acton, 115 N.H. 254, 339 A.2d 4, 1975 N.H. LEXIS 279 (1975); State v. Gilbert, 115 N.H. 665, 348 A.2d 713, 1975 N.H. LEXIS 391 (1975); State v. Shippee, 115 N.H. 694, 349 A.2d 587, 1975 N.H. LEXIS 401 (1975); State v. Luv Pharmacy, 118 N.H. 398, 388 A.2d 190, 1978 N.H. LEXIS 426, 16 A.L.R.4th 1304 (1978); State v. Bussiere, 118 N.H. 659, 392 A.2d 151, 1978 N.H. LEXIS 263 (1978); State v. Akers, 119 N.H. 161, 400 A.2d 38, 1979 N.H. LEXIS 265, 12 A.L.R.4th 667 (1979); State v. Glidden, 123 N.H. 126, 459 A.2d 1136, 1983 N.H. LEXIS 240 (1983); State v. McDuffee, 123 N.H. 184, 459 A.2d 251, 1983 N.H. LEXIS 249 (1983); State v. Mitchell, 124 N.H. 247, 469 A.2d 1310, 1983 N.H. LEXIS 411 (1983); State v. Palamia, 124 N.H. 333, 470 A.2d 906, 1983 N.H. LEXIS 392 (1983); State v. Beaudette, 124 N.H. 579, 474 A.2d 1012, 1984 N.H. LEXIS 355 (1984); State v. Damiano, 124 N.H. 742, 474 A.2d 1045, 1984 N.H. LEXIS 337 (1984); State v. Champagne, 125 N.H. 648, 484 A.2d 1161, 1984 N.H. LEXIS 381 (1984); State v. Pierce, 126 N.H. 84, 489 A.2d 109, 1985 N.H. LEXIS 278 (1985); State v. Wellman, 128 N.H. 340, 513 A.2d 944, 1986 N.H. LEXIS 294 (1986); State v. Kaplan, 128 N.H. 562, 517 A.2d 1162, 1986 N.H. LEXIS 325 (1986); State v. Dellorfano, 128 N.H. 628, 517 A.2d 1163, 1986 N.H. LEXIS 343 (1986); State v. Therrien, 129 N.H. 765, 533 A.2d 346, 1987 N.H. LEXIS 261 (1987); State v. Riccio, 130 N.H. 376, 540 A.2d 1239, 1988 N.H. LEXIS 8 (1988); State v. Hamel, 130 N.H. 615, 547 A.2d 223, 1988 N.H. LEXIS 76 (1988); State v. Prisby, 131 N.H. 57, 550 A.2d 89, 1988 N.H. LEXIS 85 (1988); State v. Anaya, 134 N.H. 346, 592 A.2d 1142, 1991 N.H. LEXIS 68 (1991); State v. Alosa, 137 N.H. 33, 623 A.2d 218, 1993 N.H. LEXIS 37 (1993); State v. Huard, 138 N.H. 256, 638 A.2d 787, 1994 N.H. LEXIS 11 (1994); State v. Puzzanghera, 140 N.H. 105, 663 A.2d 94, 1995 N.H. LEXIS 104 (1995); State v. Koehler, 140 N.H. 469, 669 A.2d 788, 1995 N.H. LEXIS 173 (1995); State v. Thornton, 140 N.H. 532, 669 A.2d 791, 1995 N.H. LEXIS 186 (1995); State v. Duguay, 142 N.H. 221, 698 A.2d 5, 1997 N.H. LEXIS 79 (1997); State v. Doucette, 146 N.H. 583, 776 A.2d 744, 2001 N.H. LEXIS 112 (2001); State v. Donohue, 150 N.H. 180, 834 A.2d 253, 2003 N.H. LEXIS 158 (2003).

RESEARCH REFERENCES

New Hampshire Bar Journal.

For article, "Purposely Negligent: Revisiting New Hampshire's Accomplice Liability Precedent after State v. Anthony," see 46 N.H.B.J. 14 (Fall 2005).

For article, "Lex Loci: A Survey of New Hampshire Supreme Court Decisions," see 45 N.H.B.J. 52 (Winter 2005).

For article, "Accomplice Liability for Unintentional Crime: Etzweiler and Horne Revisited," see 30 N.H.B.J. 95 (1989).

For note, "New Hampshire's Accomplice Liability Statute: All Dressed Up and No Place to Go," see 39 N.H. Bar Journal 20 (September 1998).

For article, "Purposely Negligent: Revisiting New Hampshire's Accomplice Liability Precedent after State v. Anthony, 46 N.H.B.J. 14 (2005).

CHAPTER 627

JUSTIFICATION

SECTION
627:1.   General Rule.
627:1-a.   Civil Immunity.
627:2.   Public Duty.
627:3.   Competing Harms.
627:4.   Physical Force in Defense of a Person.
627:5.   Physical Force in Law Enforcement.
627:6.   Physical Force by Persons with Special Responsibilities.
627:7.   Use of Force in Defense of Premises.
627:8.   Use of Force in Property Offenses.
627:8-a.   Use of Force by Merchants.
627:8-b.   Detention Powers of County Fair Security Guards.
627:9.   Definitions.

627:1. General Rule.

Conduct which is justifiable under this chapter constitutes a defense to any offense. The fact that such conduct is justifiable shall constitute a complete defense to any civil action based on such conduct.

Source.

1971, 518:1. 1979, 429:2, eff. Aug. 22, 1979.

Amendments

—1979. Substituted "shall constitute a complete defense to any civil action based on such conduct" for "however, does not abolish or impair any remedy for such conduct which is available in any civil action" following "justifiable" at the end of the second sentence.

Cross References.

Civil liability for action which would constitute justification, see RSA 507:8-d.

NOTES TO DECISIONS

1. Generally
2. Commitment proceedings
3. Riot

1. Generally

This section establishes a defense akin to the common-law defense of necessity. State v. O'Brien, 132 N.H. 587, 567 A.2d 582, 1989 N.H. LEXIS 138 (1989).

2. Commitment proceedings

Statutory defense of justification does not apply in civil commitment proceedings, and any specific acts alleged in petition may be appropriately considered as prognostic evidence of dangerousness, whether or not the acts are justified under statutory criteria; however, petitionee in rebuttal may show that the acts alleged in a petition were in fact justified. In re Fasi, 132 N.H. 478, 567 A.2d 178, 1989 N.H. LEXIS 130 (1989).

3. Riot

Self-defense is an available defense to riot. State v. McMinn, 141 N.H. 636, 690 A.2d 1017, 1997 N.H. LEXIS 11 (1997).

Cited:

Cited in Pugliese v. Perrin, 567 F. Supp. 1337, 1983 U.S. Dist. LEXIS 15416 (D.N.H. 1983); State v. Guaraldi, 124 N.H. 93, 467 A.2d 233, 1983 N.H. LEXIS 365 (1983); Panas v. Harakis, 129 N.H. 591, 529 A.2d 976, 1987 N.H. LEXIS 224 (1987); State v. Bruce, 132 N.H. 465, 566 A.2d 1144, 1989 N.H. LEXIS 122 (1989); State v. O'Brien, 132 N.H. 587, 567 A.2d 582, 1989 N.H. LEXIS 138 (1989); State v. McMinn, 141 N.H. 636, 690 A.2d 1017, 1997 N.H. LEXIS 11 (1997); State v. Bernard, 141 N.H. 230, 680 A.2d 609, 1996 N.H. LEXIS 77 (1996).

RESEARCH REFERENCES

New Hampshire Practice.

8-9 N.H.P. Personal Injury-Tort & Insurance Practice § 9.09.

New Hampshire Trial Bar News.

For article, "Presumptions in New Hampshire Law—A Guide Through the Impenetrable Jungle (Part II)," see 11 N.H. Trial Bar News 31, 34, 35 nn.82, 112 (Fall 1991).

627:1-a. Civil Immunity.

A person who uses force in self-protection or in the protection of other persons pursuant to RSA 627:4, in the protection of premises and property pursuant to RSA 627:7 and 627:8, in law enforcement pursuant to RSA 627:5, or in the care or welfare of a minor pursuant to RSA 627:6, is justified in using such force and shall be immune from civil liability for personal injuries sustained by a perpetrator which were caused by the acts or omissions of the person as a result of the use of force. In a civil action initiated by or on behalf of a perpetrator against the person, the court shall award the person reasonable attorney's fees, and costs, including but not limited to, expert witness fees, court costs, and compensation for loss of income.

Source.

2011, 268:3, eff. November 13, 2011.

627:2. Public Duty.

I. Any conduct, other than the use of physical force under circumstances specifically dealt with in other sections of this chapter, is justifiable when it is authorized by law, including laws defining functions of public servants or the assistance to be rendered public servants in the performance of their duties; laws governing the execution of legal process or of military duty; and judgments or orders of courts or other tribunals.

II. The justification afforded by this section to public servants is not precluded by the fact that the law, order or process was defective provided it appeared valid on its face or, as to persons assisting public servants, by the fact that the public servant to whom assistance was rendered exceeded his legal authority or that there was a defect of jurisdiction in the legal process or decree of the court or tribunal, provided the actor believed the public servant to be engaged in the performance of his duties or that the legal process or court decree was competent.

Source.
1971, 518:1, eff. Nov. 1, 1973.

627:3. Competing Harms.

I. Conduct which the actor believes to be necessary to avoid harm to himself or another is justifiable if the desirability and urgency of avoiding such harm outweigh, according to ordinary standards of reasonableness, the harm sought to be prevented by the statute defining the offense charged. The desirability and urgency of such conduct may not rest upon considerations pertaining to the morality and advisability of such statute, either in its general or particular application.

II. When the actor was reckless or negligent in bringing about the circumstances requiring a choice of harms or in appraising the necessity of his conduct, the justification provided in paragraph I does not apply in a prosecution for any offense for which recklessness or negligence, as the case may be, suffices to establish criminal liability.

Source.
1971, 518:1, eff. Nov. 1, 1973.

NOTES TO DECISIONS

1. Construction
2. Application
3. Requirements
4. Particular offenses

1. Construction

This section establishes a defense akin to the common-law defense of necessity. State v. O'Brien, 132 N.H. 587, 567 A.2d 582, 1989 N.H. LEXIS 138 (1989).

This section is not meant to excuse illegal actions carried out with good intentions. State v. O'Brien, 132 N.H. 587, 567 A.2d 582, 1989 N.H. LEXIS 138 (1989).

An individual is protected from prosecution for a criminal act under this section if he commits a criminal act that was urgently necessary to avoid a clear and imminent danger. State v. Fee, 126 N.H. 78, 489 A.2d 606, 1985 N.H. LEXIS 276 (1985).

This section establishes statutory defense akin to common-law defense of necessity. State v. Dorsey, 118 N.H. 844, 395 A.2d 855, 1978 N.H. LEXIS 303 (1978).

This section is intended to deal only with harms that are readily apparent and recognizable to the average juror. State v. Dorsey, 118 N.H. 844, 395 A.2d 855, 1978 N.H. LEXIS 303 (1978).

2. Application

Evidence that a neighbor early on the morning of the incident heard a dog barking, sounds of people arguing, a series of bangs, and then a woman screaming hysterically, and testimony that the victim proposed three-way sex and that defendant was turned off by the suggestion was insufficient to support a competing harms defense to defendant's charges of manslaughter arising from the victim's death, based on defendant's theory that she was subject to unwanted sexual advances by the victim. State v. Lavoie, 152 N.H. 542, 880 A.2d 432, 2005 N.H. LEXIS 136 (2005).

Where defendant, who was intoxicated, left a friend's home because he was fearful of a neighbor who was brandishing a rifle, there was no one else to drive him, and he could not get a taxi, the trial court erred in determining that the defense of competing

harms pursuant to RSA 627:3 was not available to him in his trial for operating a motor vehicle with an alcohol concentration of .08 or more, in violation of RSA 265:82, I(b). The trial court found that there were other available legal alternatives; however, the court indicated that the standard employed by the trial court was in error, as the true test for whether that defense was available was whether there were "available" legal alternatives, and "available" was interpreted to mean reasonable. State v. L'Heureux, 150 N.H. 822, 846 A.2d 1193, 2004 N.H. LEXIS 77 (2004).

Trial court erred in ruling that defense of competing harms was not available in prosecution under habitual offender statute. State v. Bernard, 141 N.H. 230, 680 A.2d 609, 1996 N.H. LEXIS 77 (1996).

This section cannot lightly be allowed to justify acts taken to foreclose speculative and uncertain dangers, but must be limited to acts directed to the prevention of harm that is reasonably certain to occur. State v. Fee, 126 N.H. 78, 489 A.2d 606, 1985 N.H. LEXIS 276 (1985).

3. Requirements

In order for the competing harms defense to be available, a number of requirements must be satisfied; the otherwise illegal conduct must be urgently necessary, there must be no lawful alternative, and the harm sought to be avoided must outweigh, according to ordinary standards of reasonableness, the harm sought to be prevented by the violated statute. State v. O'Brien, 132 N.H. 587, 567 A.2d 582, 1989 N.H. LEXIS 138 (1989).

This section sets up a balancing test; in order for the competing harms defense to be available, the desire or need to avoid the present harm must outweigh the harm sought to be prevented by the violated statute. State v. O'Brien, 132 N.H. 587, 567 A.2d 582, 1989 N.H. LEXIS 138 (1989).

4. Particular offenses

Trial court correctly ruled that, as a matter of law, competing harms defense was not available to defendant charged with driving a motor vehicle while an habitual offender, where defendant drove a co-employee to the hospital for treatment of a twisted ankle; the relatively minor injury did not demand immediate action necessary to avoid a clear and imminent danger required by this section, and even if the defendant reasonably believed an imminent danger existed, alternative courses of conduct were available. State v. O'Brien, 132 N.H. 587, 567 A.2d 582, 1989 N.H. LEXIS 138 (1989).

Danger alleged by defendant pharmacist to have been created by possibility of distribution of stolen prescription drugs did not justify conduct of defendant in driving, while under the influence of intoxicating liquor, to pharmacy of which he was in charge, where an alarm had been tripped, since he was not told of any burglary or that any drugs had been taken, and since he had experience with false alarms in the past, facts which precluded any reasonable certainty of the danger alleged. State v. Fee, 126 N.H. 78, 489 A.2d 606, 1985 N.H. LEXIS 276 (1985).

Trial court did not err in ruling that defense of competing harms was not available to one charged with criminal trespass for occupying the construction site of a nuclear power plant, where both state legislature and Congress of the United States had made deliberate choices in support of nuclear power. State v. Dorsey, 118 N.H. 844, 395 A.2d 855, 1978 N.H. LEXIS 303 (1978).

Cited:
Cited in State v. Dupuy, 118 N.H. 848, 395 A.2d 851, 1978 N.H. LEXIS 304 (1978); State v. Koski, 120 N.H. 112, 411 A.2d 1122, 1980 N.H. LEXIS 240 (1980); State v. Gorham, 120 N.H. 162, 412 A.2d 1017, 1980 N.H. LEXIS 253 (1980); State v. Brady, 120 N.H. 899, 424 A.2d 407, 1980 N.H. LEXIS 417 (1980); Brady v. Samaha, 667 F.2d 224, 1981 U.S. App. LEXIS 15036 (1st Cir. N.H. 1981); State v. Weitzman, 121 N.H. 83, 427 A.2d 3, 1981 N.H. LEXIS 265 (1981); State v. Williams, 127 N.H. 79, 497 A.2d 858, 1985 N.H. LEXIS 405 (1985).

RESEARCH REFERENCES

New Hampshire Practice.
8-3 N.H.P. Personal Injury-Tort & Insurance Practice § 3.14.

627:4. Physical Force in Defense of a Person.

I. A person is justified in using non-deadly force upon another person in order to defend himself or a third person from what he reasonably believes to be the imminent use of unlawful, non-deadly force by such other person, and he may use a degree of such force which he reasonably believes to be necessary for such purpose. However, such force is not justifiable if:

(a) With a purpose to cause physical harm to another person, he provoked the use of unlawful, non-deadly force by such other person; or

(b) He was the initial aggressor, unless after such aggression he withdraws from the encounter and effectively communicates to such other person his intent to do so, but the latter notwithstanding continues the use or threat of unlawful, non-deadly force; or

(c) The force involved was the product of a combat by agreement not authorized by law.

II. A person is justified in using deadly force upon another person when he reasonably believes that such other person:

(a) Is about to use unlawful, deadly force against the actor or a third person;

(b) Is likely to use any unlawful force against a person present while committing or attempting to commit a burglary;

(c) Is committing or about to commit kidnapping or a forcible sex offense; or

(d) Is likely to use any unlawful force in the commission of a felony against the actor within such actor's dwelling or its curtilage.

II-a. A person who responds to a threat which would be considered by a reasonable person as likely to cause serious bodily injury or death to the person or to another by displaying a firearm or other means of self-defense with the intent to warn away the person making the threat shall not have committed a criminal act.

III. A person is not justified in using deadly force on another to defend himself or herself or a third person from deadly force by the other if he or she knows that he or she and the third person can, with complete safety:

(a) Retreat from the encounter, except that he or she is not required to retreat if he or she is within his or her dwelling, its curtilage, or anywhere he or she has a right to be, and was not the initial aggressor; or

(b) Surrender property to a person asserting a claim of right thereto; or

(c) Comply with a demand that he or she abstain from performing an act which he or she is not obliged to perform; nor is the use of deadly force justifiable when, with the purpose of causing death or serious bodily harm, the person has provoked the use of force against himself or herself in the same encounter; or

(d) If he or she is a law enforcement officer or a private person assisting the officer at the officer's direction and was acting pursuant to RSA 627:5, the person need not retreat.

Source.
1971, 518:1. 1981, 347:1, 2, eff. Aug. 16, 1981. 2010, 361:1, eff. January 1, 2011. 2011, 268:1, eff. November 13, 2011.

Amendments
—2011. The 2011 amendment made gender neutral changes in III.

—2010. The 2010 amendment added II-a.

—1981. Paragraph II(d): Added.
Paragraph III(a): Added "or its curtilage" following "dwelling".

NOTES TO DECISIONS

1. Provocation
2. Unreasonable belief
3. Elements
4. Sufficiency of evidence
5. Instructions
6. Reasonable necessity

1. Provocation
The term "provoke" connotes speech as well as action and a jury may correctly conclude that a defendant's use of words alone to bring about a fight in which he intended at the outset to kill his opponent was sufficient to destroy his legal defense of self-defense. State v. Gorham, 120 N.H. 162, 412 A.2d 1017, 1980 N.H. LEXIS 253 (1980).

2. Unreasonable belief
A defendant's unreasonable belief that another is likely to use an unlawful force in the commission of a felony against him, even if the belief is honest, will not support a defense of justification for the use of deadly force. State v. Holt, 126 N.H. 394, 493 A.2d 483, 1985 N.H. LEXIS 314 (1985).

3. Elements
RSA 627:4, II(d) does not justify the use of deadly force against an assailant when the assailant is a cohabitant of the home. State v. Warren, 147 N.H. 567, 794 A.2d 790, 2002 N.H. LEXIS 30 (2002).

A victim's aggressive character is not among the elements set forth in this section for a defense of self-defense. State v. Newell, 141 N.H. 199, 679 A.2d 1142, 1996 N.H. LEXIS 72 (1996).

4. Sufficiency of evidence
Evidence was sufficient to support a finding that assault defendant did not act in self-defense, where jury could have found that defendant initially provoked victim verbally, that victim's response constituted non-deadly force, and that defendant was not justified in using deadly force because there was no reason for him to believe victim was about to use unlawful, deadly force against him. State v. Santamaria, 145 N.H. 138, 756 A.2d 589, 2000 N.H. LEXIS 29 (2000).

5. Instructions
In a prosecution for armed robbery, the trial court did not err in not instructing on defense of another, as defendant did not admit to any of the facts alleged in the indictment, but testified to a different factual scenario. Furthermore, had the trial court given the model jury instructions on self-defense and defense of another, the jury would have been improperly told to acquit defendant even if it found evidence sufficient to convict him independent of his admitted use of force. State v. Noucas, — N.H. —, 70 A.3d 476, 2013 N.H. LEXIS 83 (July 16, 2013).

RSA 627:4, II(a), when read in conjunction with RSA 627:9, II, allows a person to use deadly force against another if he reasonably believes that person is about to confine or restrain him so as to allow others to employ deadly force against him. In the future, where supported by some evidence in the record, a trial court should instruct the jury that a defendant was entitled to use deadly force in self-defense against a person that the defendant reasonably believed, acting alone or in concert with others, was about to confine him with the purpose of causing or with knowledge of a substantial risk of causing death or serious bodily injury. State v. Furgal, 164 N.H. 430, 58 A.3d 648, 2012 N.H. LEXIS 167 (2012).

Trial court's failure to include the "in-concert" language requested by defendant in its self-defense instruction under RSA 627:4 did not entitle him to a new trial. A reasonable juror would have understood that he had to consider whether the victim, acting alone or in concert with others, was about to use unlawful deadly force against defendant. State v. Furgal, 164 N.H. 430, 58 A.3d 648, 2012 N.H. LEXIS 167 (2012).

In instructing the jury on the issue of self-defense under RSA 627:4, I, the trial court erred in failing to give the portion of the "deadly force" definition of RSA 627:9, II, relating to the discharge of a firearm. If the jury had been given the full definition, then it could have concluded that defendant's merely pointing his gun at the victim without discharging it constituted the use of non-deadly force. State v. Gingras, 162 N.H. 633, 34 A.3d 659, 2011 N.H. LEXIS 149 (2011).

Given New Hampshire's common law and the canons of statutory interpretation, the New Hampshire Supreme Court does not find that the legislature has expressed an intent to abrogate the deeply entrenched principle that in order for a killing to be justified, it must be reasonably necessary under the circumstances. Accordingly, the trial court's instructions requiring reasonable necessity for the defensive use of deadly force were not erroneous. State v. Etienne, 163 N.H. 57, 35 A.3d 523, 2011 N.H. LEXIS 189 (Dec. 21, 2011).

Jury instructions properly assigned to the State the burden of proof as to all elements of the offense. To the extent the instructions erroneously advised the jury that the State could disprove self-defense or defense of others by establishing a third party's provocation of the encounter, the record established beyond a reasonable doubt that such instruction did not contribute to the defendant's conviction. State v. Etienne, 163 N.H. 57, 35 A.3d 523, 2011 N.H. LEXIS 189 (Dec. 21, 2011).

In instructing the jury on self-defense under RSA 627:4, II(c), the trial court properly explained the law of self-defense and used the exact language of the statute. It was not required to further define the term "forcible sex offense" because the phrase had a commonly understood ordinary meaning. State v. McDonald, 163 N.H. 115, 35 A.3d 605, 2011 N.H. LEXIS 192 (Dec. 28, 2011).

Although the trial court committed plain error in not instructing the jury on self-defense under RSA 627:4, the error did not require reversal because it did not seriously affect the fairness, integrity or public reputation of judicial proceedings. The evidence that defendant did not act in self-defense was overwhelming, and the trial court instructed the jury that the State had to prove guilt. State v. Richard, 160 N.H. 780, 7 A.3d 1195, 2010 N.H. LEXIS 109 (2010).

In a murder trial where defendant had shot a caseworker, the trial court did not err in refusing to give an instruction on defense of a person. Although defendant had presented evidence of his alleged mistreatment by the New Hampshire Division for Children, Youth and Families and other agencies, nothing supported his claim that the caseworker, the division, or any other entity intended to kidnap his son or that defendant reasonably believed that they had such intent. State v. Ayer, 154 N.H. 500, 917 A.2d 214, 2006 N.H. LEXIS 191 (2006), rehearing denied, 2007 N.H. LEXIS 35 (N.H. Jan. 30, 2007), cert. denied, Ayer v. New Hampshire, 552 U.S. 834, 128 S. Ct. 63, 169 L. Ed. 2d 52, 2007 U.S. LEXIS 9174 (2007).

Because there was some evidence that defendant reasonably believed that his brother was about to use deadly force where the brother had threatened to kill defendant and his mother prior to leaving for his garage room where a gun was located, the trial court should have given a self defense instruction. State v. Vassar, 154 N.H. 370, 910 A.2d 1193, 2006 N.H. LEXIS 171 (2006).

Defendant was not entitled to a jury instruction on self-defense, even if the defendant had timely filed his claim, where there was no evidence to support that claim other than defendant's assertion that one week prior to defendant throwing hot oil on the victim three different times, there was an incident which led defendant to believe that the victim would assault defendant. State v. Ke Tong Chen, 148 N.H. 565, 813 A.2d 424, 2002 N.H. LEXIS 169 (2002).

Convictions for first degree assault were reversed where the jury

was improperly instructed regarding the circumstances under which a defendant could not use deadly force in self-defense, under RSA 627:4, III(c); the jury, as instructed, could have concluded that use of deadly force was not justified merely because defendant started an argument. State v. Bashaw, 147 N.H. 238, 785 A.2d 897, 2001 N.H. LEXIS 203 (2001).

Because defendant's testimony provided at least some evidence that his assault on victim was in defense of his son, trial court erred in denying defendant's request to instruct jury on use of force in defense of another. State v. Haycock, 146 N.H. 5, 766 A.2d 720, 2001 N.H. LEXIS 17 (2001).

It was error for the court to refuse to instruct the jury with regard to self-defense in a prosecution for riot where there was evidence that a three-on-one beating of the victim never occurred and that the defendant acted, throughout the altercation, under a reasonable belief that his conduct was necessary to defend himself from two others. State v. McMinn, 141 N.H. 636, 690 A.2d 1017, 1997 N.H. LEXIS 11 (1997).

Trial court did not err in using phrase "the one who started the encounter" rather than statutory term "the initial aggressor" since, in context of entire jury instruction as well as evidence introduced at trial, there was no meaningful distinction between the two. State v. Newell, 141 N.H. 199, 679 A.2d 1142, 1996 N.H. LEXIS 72 (1996).

In appeal from conviction for simple assault in which superior court declined to give requested jury instructions concerning justifications of self-defense, defense of another, and defense of property, all three claims of error were preserved for review where the record showed timely objection made to failure to charge justifications of self-defense and defense of property; format of this section combined self-defense and defense of another in same paragraph and parties and court understood objection included instruction on defense of others. State v. Hast, 133 N.H. 747, 584 A.2d 175, 1990 N.H. LEXIS 127 (1990).

In trial for simple assault, defendant was entitled to jury instruction on defense of others where some evidence was presented that defendant had assaulted victim in response to unlawful unprivileged physical contact by another on defendant's wife. State v. Hast, 133 N.H. 747, 584 A.2d 175, 1990 N.H. LEXIS 127 (1990).

6. Reasonable necessity

New Hampshire Supreme Court declines to infer from the legislature's silence regarding the reasonable necessity requirement in the deadly force provision of the justification statute that New Hampshire citizens have the right to kill when it is not necessary under the circumstances. State v. Etienne, 163 N.H. 57, 35 A.3d 523, 2011 N.H. LEXIS 189 (Dec. 21, 2011).

To construe the term "forcible sex offense" in RSA 627:4, II(c) to mean any aggravated felonious sexual assault would render the word "forcible" as used in the self-defense statute meaningless, and would require the court to insert language the legislature did not see fit to include. It would also lead to the illogical result that a person could use deadly force to defend against any non-consensual sex act, but in all other circumstances, could only use deadly force to the extent necessary, and proportionate with, the harm threatened. State v. McDonald, 163 N.H. 115, 35 A.3d 605, 2011 N.H. LEXIS 192 (Dec. 28, 2011).

In light of the plain language of RSA 627:4, II(c) and the overall statutory scheme, the New Hampshire Supreme Court need not set forth a technical meaning for the term "forcible." Despite the multiple definitions of the word "forcible," the ordinary meaning of the word is unambiguous because each definition has in common the use of some amount of "strength" or "power." State v. McDonald, 163 N.H. 115, 35 A.3d 605, 2011 N.H. LEXIS 192 (Dec. 28, 2011).

As construing "forcible sex offense" in RSA 627:4, II(c) to include any aggravated felonious assault would render the word "forcible" meaningless, the trial court did not err by prohibiting the defense from referring to the aggravated felonious sexual assault statute, RSA 632-A:2, I(i), in its closing argument. State v. McDonald, 163 N.H. 115, 35 A.3d 605, 2011 N.H. LEXIS 192 (Dec. 28, 2011).

Cited:

Cited in State v. Kawa, 113 N.H. 310, 306 A.2d 791, 1973 N.H. LEXIS 261 (1973); State v. Pugliese, 120 N.H. 728, 422 A.2d 1319, 1980 N.H. LEXIS 384 (1980); State v. Arillo, 122 N.H. 107, 441 A.2d 1163, 1982 N.H. LEXIS 295 (1982); State v. McAvenia, 122 N.H. 580, 448 A.2d 967, 1982 N.H. LEXIS 404 (1982); State v. Pugliese,

122 N.H. 1141, 455 A.2d 1018, 1982 N.H. LEXIS 541 (1982); Pugliese v. Perrin, 567 F. Supp. 1337, 1983 U.S. Dist. LEXIS 15416 (D.N.H. 1983); State v. Lesnick, 141 N.H. 121, 677 A.2d 686, 1996 N.H. LEXIS 59 (1996); State v. McMinn, 141 N.H. 636, 690 A.2d 1017, 1997 N.H. LEXIS 11 (1997); State v. Warren, 143 N.H. 633, 732 A.2d 1017, 1999 N.H. LEXIS 52 (1999); State v. Dukette, 145 N.H. 226, 761 A.2d 442, 2000 N.H. LEXIS 46 (2000); State v. Smalley, 151 N.H. 193, 855 A.2d 401, 2004 N.H. LEXIS 113 (2004).

RESEARCH REFERENCES

New Hampshire Practice.
8-3 N.H.P. Personal Injury-Tort & Insurance Practice § 3.14.

New Hampshire Trial Bar News.
For article, "Presumptions in New Hampshire Law—A Guide Through the Impenetrable Jungle (Part II)," see 11 N.H. Trial Bar News 31, 34, 35 nn.82, 112 (Fall 1991).

627:5. Physical Force in Law Enforcement.

I. A law enforcement officer is justified in using non-deadly force upon another person when and to the extent that he reasonably believes it necessary to effect an arrest or detention or to prevent the escape from custody of an arrested or detained person, unless he knows that the arrest or detention is illegal, or to defend himself or a third person from what he reasonably believes to be the imminent use of non-deadly force encountered while attempting to effect such an arrest or detention or while seeking to prevent such an escape.

II. A law enforcement officer is justified in using deadly force only when he reasonably believes such force is necessary:

(a) To defend himself or a third person from what he reasonably believes is the imminent use of deadly force; or

(b) To effect an arrest or prevent the escape from custody of a person whom he reasonably believes:

(1) Has committed or is committing a felony involving the use of force or violence, is using a deadly weapon in attempting to escape, or otherwise indicates that he is likely to seriously endanger human life or inflict serious bodily injury unless apprehended without delay; and

(2) He had made reasonable efforts to advise the person that he is a law enforcement officer attempting to effect an arrest and has reasonable grounds to believe that the person is aware of these facts.

(c) Nothing in this paragraph constitutes justification for conduct by a law enforcement officer amounting to an offense against innocent persons whom he is not seeking to arrest or retain in custody.

III. A private person who has been directed by a law enforcement officer to assist him in effecting an arrest or preventing an escape from custody is justified in using:

(a) Non-deadly force when and to the extent that he reasonably believes such to be necessary to carry out the officer's direction, unless he believes the arrest is illegal; or

(b) Deadly force only when he reasonably believes such to be necessary to defend himself or a third person from what he reasonably believes to be the imminent use of deadly force, or when the law enforcement officer directs him to use deadly force and he believes such officer himself is authorized to use deadly force under the circumstances.

IV. A private person acting on his own is justified in using non-deadly force upon another when and to the extent that he reasonably believes it necessary to arrest or prevent the escape from custody of such other whom he reasonably believes to have committed a felony and who in fact has committed that felony: but he is justified in using deadly force for such purpose only when he reasonably believes it necessary to defend himself or a third person from what he reasonably believes to be the imminent use of deadly force.

V. A guard or law enforcement officer in a facility where persons are confined pursuant to an order of the court or as a result of an arrest is justified in using deadly force when he reasonably believes such force is necessary to prevent the escape of any person who is charged with, or convicted of, a felony, or who is committing the felony of escape from official custody as defined in RSA 642:6. The use of non-deadly force by such guards and officers is justified when and to the extent the person effecting the arrest believes it reasonably necessary to prevent any other escape from the facility.

VI. A reasonable belief that another has committed an offense means such belief in facts or circumstances which, if true, would in law constitute an offense by such person. If the facts and circumstances reasonably believed would not constitute an offense, an erroneous though reasonable belief that the law is otherwise does not make justifiable the use of force to make an arrest or prevent an escape.

VII. Use of force that is not justifiable under this section in effecting an arrest does not render illegal an arrest that is otherwise legal and the use of such unjustifiable force does not render inadmissible anything seized incident to a legal arrest.

VIII. Deadly force shall be deemed reasonably necessary under this section whenever the arresting law enforcement officer reasonably believes that the arrest is lawful and there is apparently no other possible means of effecting the arrest.

Source.
1971, 518:1. 1981, 373:1–3, eff. Aug. 22, 1981.

Amendments
—1981. Paragraph II(b)(1): Inserted "or is committing" preceding "a felony" and substituted "involving the use of force or violence"

for "or" thereafter.

Paragraph V: Rewritten to the extent that a detailed comparison would be impracticable.

Paragraph VIII: Added.

NOTES TO DECISIONS

Justification not found

(Unpublished) Special operations unit officers who allegedly pointed rifles at the heads of occupants, who were detained in their residence during the execution of a search warrant, for several minutes after the occupants had been handcuffed were not entitled to summary judgment on assault and battery claims asserted by the occupants because the officers did not show that they had a reasonable belief that it was necessary to handcuff the occupants, who had not resisted arrest or taken any action to threaten the safety of the officers, and hold the occupants at gunpoint for as long as they allegedly did in order to effect the detention of the occupants during the execution of the search warrant. Mlodzinski v. Lewis, 731 F. Supp. 2d 157, 2010 U.S. Dist. LEXIS 72030 (July 16, 2010), aff'd in part, rev'd in part, 648 F.3d 24, 2011 U.S. App. LEXIS 11117 (1st Cir. N.H. 2011).

Sufficient evidence supported the convictions of defendant, a correctional officer, for simple assault under RSA 631:2-a when defendant shoved the small of the victim's back and swept one of the victim's legs out from under him after the victim was brought to defendant's facility. A rational juror could have found that defendant's physical contact with the victim was unprivileged and unjustified under RSA 627:5, as there was evidence that the victim did not pose a threat to defendant at the time of the incidents. State v. Cunningham, 159 N.H. 103, 977 A.2d 506, 2009 N.H. LEXIS 89 (2009).

Cited:

Cited in Blais v. Goffstown, 119 N.H. 613, 406 A.2d 295, 1979 N.H. LEXIS 440 (1979).

RESEARCH REFERENCES

New Hampshire Practice.
8-3 N.H.P. Personal Injury-Tort & Insurance Practice § 3.14.
8-9 N.H.P. Personal Injury-Tort & Insurance Practice § 9.49.

627:6. Physical Force by Persons with Special Responsibilities.

I. A parent, guardian or other person responsible for the general care and welfare of a minor is justified in using force against such minor when and to the extent that he reasonably believes it necessary to prevent or punish such minor's misconduct.

II. (a) A teacher or person otherwise entrusted with the care or supervision of a minor for special purposes is justified on the premises in using necessary force against any such minor, when the minor creates a disturbance, or refuses to leave the premises or when it is necessary for the maintenance of discipline.

(b) In a child care program licensed or exempt from licensure under RSA 170-E, necessary force shall be limited to the minimum physical contact necessary to protect the child, other children present, the staff, or the general public from harm.

III. A person responsible for the general care and supervision of an incompetent person is justified in using force for the purpose of safeguarding his welfare, or, when such incompetent person is in an institution for his care and custody, for the mainte-

nance of reasonable discipline in such institution.

IV. The justification extended in paragraphs I, II, and III does not apply to the malicious or reckless use of force that creates a risk of death, serious bodily injury, or substantial pain.

V. A person authorized by law to maintain decorum or safety in a vessel, aircraft, vehicle, train or other carrier, or in a place where others are assembled may use non-deadly force when and to the extent that he reasonably believes it necessary for such purposes, but he may use deadly force only when he reasonably believes it necessary to prevent death or serious bodily injury.

VI. A person acting under a reasonable belief that another person is about to commit suicide or to inflict serious bodily injury upon himself may use a degree of force on such person as he reasonably believes to be necessary to thwart such a result.

VII. A licensed physician, or a person acting under his or her direction, or an advanced practice registered nurse (APRN) working for the department of corrections may use force for the purpose of administering a recognized form of treatment which he or she reasonably believes will tend to promote the physical or mental health of the patient, provided such treatment is administered:

(a) With consent of the patient or, if the patient is a minor or incompetent person, with the consent of the person entrusted with his care and supervision; or

(b) In an emergency when the physician or the advanced practice registered nurse (APRN) reasonably believes that no one competent to consent can be consulted and that a reasonable person concerned for the welfare of the patient would consent.

Source.
1971, 518:1, eff. Nov. 1, 1973. 2000, 225:1, eff. July 31, 2000. 2002, 112:1, eff. July 2, 2002. 2009, 54:4, 5, eff. July 21, 2009.

Amendments
—2009. The 2009 amendment substituted "advanced practice registered nurse (APRN)" for "advanced registered nurse practitioner (ARNP)" in the introductory language of VII and in VII(b).

—2002. Paragraph II: Designated the existing provisions of the paragraph as subpar. (a), and added subpar. (b).

—2000. Paragraph VII: In the introductory paragraph inserted "or her" preceding "direction" and "or an advanced registered nurse practitioner (ARNP) working for the department of corrections" thereafter, and "or she" following "which he", and in subpar. (b) inserted "or the advanced registered nurse practitioner (ARNP)" following "physician".

NOTES TO DECISIONS

1. Construction
2. Justification

1. Construction

Paragraph I of this section, justifying use of force by parent or one standing in loco parentis against minor when necessary to prevent or punish misconduct, merely codifies well-recognized precept of Anglo-American jurisprudence. In re Ethan H., 135 N.H. 681, 609 A.2d 1222, 1992 N.H. LEXIS 102 (1992).

2. Justification

Where the evidence showed that there were less harmful ways that the doctor could have treated the patient and kept her safe from harm, there was nothing to justify the doctor's decision to have the patient placed in protective custody and the trial court's finding of professional negligence was sustained. Carlisle v. Frisbie Mem'l Hosp., 152 N.H. 762, 888 A.2d 405, 2005 N.H. LEXIS 168 (2005).

Use of force to prevent or punish misconduct by a child is justified only if it is "reasonable". Reasonableness is determined by an objective standard, and a belief which is unreasonable, even though honest, will not support the defense. State v. Leaf, 137 N.H. 97, 623 A.2d 1329, 1993 N.H. LEXIS 47 (1993).

Cited:

Cited in In re Caulk, 125 N.H. 226, 480 A.2d 93, 1984 N.H. LEXIS 364 (1984); In re Doe, 126 N.H. 719, 495 A.2d 1293, 1985 N.H. LEXIS 358 (1985); In re Doe, 132 N.H. 270, 564 A.2d 433, 1989 N.H. LEXIS 101 (1989); State v. Bruce, 132 N.H. 465, 566 A.2d 1144, 1989 N.H. LEXIS 122 (1989).

RESEARCH REFERENCES

New Hampshire Practice.

8-3 N.H.P. Personal Injury-Tort & Insurance Practice § 3.14.
8-9 N.H.P. Personal Injury-Tort & Insurance Practice § 9.09.

627:7. Use of Force in Defense of Premises.

A person in possession or control of premises or a person who is licensed or privileged to be thereon is justified in using non-deadly force upon another when and to the extent that he reasonably believes it necessary to prevent or terminate the commission of a criminal trespass by such other in or upon such premises, but he may use deadly force under such circumstances only in defense of a person as prescribed in RSA 627:4 or when he reasonably believes it necessary to prevent an attempt by the trespasser to commit arson.

Source.

1971, 518:1, eff. Nov. 1, 1973.

NOTES TO DECISIONS

1. Jury instructions
2. Reasonableness of belief

1. Jury instructions

In a murder and arson case, the trial court properly denied a requested charge under RSA 627:7. By his own admission, defendant stabbed the victim with the sole intention of fleeing the premises; there was no evidence in the record suggesting that defendant stabbed the victim and fled in order to prevent further arson or extinguish existing fires. State v. Balliro, 158 N.H. 1, 959 A.2d 212, 2008 N.H. LEXIS 126 (2008).

In a murder and arson case, the trial court properly denied a requested charge under RSA 627:7. Defendant's testimony that he had made arrangements to keep his troubled restaurant operating by borrowing money from his parents and having family members help him operate it was a mere scintilla of evidence; a jury could not reasonably infer from this that in stabbing the victim, defendant acted justifiably under RSA 627:7. State v. Balliro, 158 N.H. 1, 959 A.2d 212, 2008 N.H. LEXIS 126 (2008).

2. Reasonableness of belief

With regard to defendant's claim of defense of premises, a rational juror could have found that defendant's belief that it was necessary to wave his pistol to terminate the victim's trespass was not objectively reasonable. While the victim drove past "no tres-

passing" signs onto defendant's property, she had been given directions to follow the roads with these signs by defendant's niece, who had then telephoned defendant to tell him that the victim was going to look at certain property that was for sale and might stop at his property; furthermore, the victim testified that she asked defendant if he was the boyfriend of the woman selling the property, and he responded by yelling "get the F off my property!" and pointing a gun at her. State v. Bird, 161 N.H. 31, 8 A.3d 146, 2010 N.H. LEXIS 125 (2010).

Cited:

Cited in State v. Arillo, 122 N.H. 107, 441 A.2d 1163, 1982 N.H. LEXIS 295 (1982); State v. Smith, 123 N.H. 46, 455 A.2d 1041, 1983 N.H. LEXIS 220 (1983).

RESEARCH REFERENCES

New Hampshire Practice.

8-3 N.H.P. Personal Injury-Tort & Insurance Practice § 3.14.

627:8. Use of Force in Property Offenses.

A person is justified in using force upon another when and to the extent that he reasonably believes it necessary to prevent what is or reasonably appears to be an unlawful taking of his property, or criminal mischief, or to retake his property immediately following its taking; but he may use deadly force under such circumstances only in defense of a person as prescribed in RSA 627:4.

Source.

1971, 518:1, eff. Nov. 1, 1973.

NOTES TO DECISIONS

1. Construction
2. Jury instructions

1. Construction

Plain language of RSA 627:8 does not limit the use of force in defense of property to instances of "theft." RSA 627:8 does not require that the taker act with any particular intent in order for the actor's use of force to be justified. State v. Davidson, 163 N.H. 462, 44 A.3d 454, 2012 N.H. LEXIS 46 (2012).

Legislative intent behind RSA 627:8 is that the justified use of force in defense of property is not limited to instances of theft, but applies to any instance of what would reasonably appear to be an unlawful taking, regardless of the taker's intent. State v. Davidson, 163 N.H. 462, 44 A.3d 454, 2012 N.H. LEXIS 46 (2012).

At trial for simple assault and resisting arrest, regardless of whether chief of police properly or improperly ordered arresting officer to tow defendant's vehicle, defendant enjoyed no privilege to use self-help to prevent removal of his property or to effect its return nor was he entitled to resist arrest; any such privileges that may have existed at common law have been statutorily superseded. State v. Haas, 134 N.H. 480, 596 A.2d 127, 1991 N.H. LEXIS 88 (1991).

2. Jury instructions

Because RSA 627:8 did not limit the use of force in defense of property to instances of "theft," the trial court erred in refusing to give defendant's requested jury instruction on defense of property on the basis of insufficient evidence that the complainant had committed a theft. State v. Davidson, 163 N.H. 462, 44 A.3d 454, 2012 N.H. LEXIS 46 (2012).

Cited:

Cited in State v. Cavanaugh, 138 N.H. 193, 635 A.2d 1382, 1993 N.H. LEXIS 183 (1993).

RESEARCH REFERENCES

New Hampshire Practice.
8-3 N.H.P. Personal Injury-Tort & Insurance Practice § 3.14.

627:8-a. Use of Force by Merchants.

I. A merchant, or his or her agent, is justified in detaining any person who he or she has reasonable grounds to believe has committed the offense of willful concealment, as defined by RSA 637:3-a, on his or her premises as long as necessary to surrender the person to a peace officer, provided such detention is conducted in a reasonable manner.

II. A motion picture theater owner, or his or her agent, is justified in detaining any person who he or she has reasonable grounds to believe has committed the offense of unauthorized recording in a motion picture theater on his or her premises, as defined by RSA 644:19, as long as necessary to surrender the person to a peace officer, provided such detention is conducted in a reasonable manner.

III. Notwithstanding RSA 594:10, a peace officer may arrest a person who has been detained pursuant to this section, without a warrant, if the peace officer has probable cause to believe that the person has committed the offense of willful concealment and if the merchant or his or her agent witnessed the offense or if the unlawfully obtained goods or merchandise of the store were recovered from the person.

Source.
1981, 344:2, eff. Aug. 16, 1981. 2005, 70:1, eff. January 1, 2006. 2009, 209:8, eff. January 1, 2010. 2012, 205:1, eff. January 1, 2013.

Amendments
—**2012.** The 2012 amendment added III.

—**2009.** The 2009 amendment substituted "as defined by RSA 637:3-a" for "or shoplifting, as defined by RSA 644:17" in I.

—**2005.** Designated the existing provisions of the section as par. I and made gender-neutral changes in that paragraph, and added par. II.

NOTES TO DECISIONS

Jury instructions
In a false arrest action, the court's instruction that "the good faith of the instigator or participator, or his/her reasonable belief is not a defense," did not conflict with and negate the merchant's privilege because the instruction only referenced the "reasonable belief" and "good faith" of the instigator if the arrest was unlawful, and the court also instructed the jury that the arrest was unlawful as a matter of law. Forgie-Buccioni v. Hannaford Bros., Inc., 413 F.3d 175, 2005 U.S. App. LEXIS 13137 (1st Cir. N.H. 2005).

In action based on allegedly improper arrest and detention of plaintiff for shoplifting, trial court's failure to instruct the jury that this section was a complete defense was harmless error, if error at all, since a reasonable jury could only have found that this section was inapplicable because the defendant did not have reasonable grounds to detain plaintiff. Panas v. Harakis, 129 N.H. 591, 529 A.2d 976, 1987 N.H. LEXIS 224 (1987).

RESEARCH REFERENCES

New Hampshire Practice.
8-3 N.H.P. Personal Injury-Tort & Insurance Practice §§ 3.07, 3.14.

8-9 N.H.P. Personal Injury-Tort & Insurance Practice § 9.09.

627:8-b. Detention Powers of County Fair Security Guards.

I. Any county fair security guard who meets the requirements of paragraph II shall have the power to detain any person who he has reasonable grounds to believe has committed any offense under the laws of the state, on the premises of the county fair association as long as necessary to surrender the person to a peace officer, provided such detention is accomplished in a reasonable manner.

II. Only security guards who have completed a program of police training for part-time police officers, meeting standards established by the New Hampshire police standards and training council pursuant to RSA 188-F:26 and appropriate to a security guard's exercise of limited police powers, shall have the powers of detention granted in paragraph I.

Source.
1987, 85:1, eff. May 6, 1987.

627:9. Definitions.

As used in this chapter:

I. "Curtilage" means those outbuildings which are proximately, directly and intimately connected with a dwelling, together with all the land or grounds surrounding the dwelling such as are necessary, convenient, and habitually used for domestic purposes.

II. "Deadly force" means any assault or confinement which the actor commits with the purpose of causing or which he knows to create a substantial risk of causing death or serious bodily injury. Purposely firing a firearm capable of causing serious bodily injury or death in the direction of another person or at a vehicle in which another is believed to be constitutes deadly force.

III. "Dwelling" means any building, structure, vehicle, boat or other place adapted for overnight accommodation of persons, or sections of any place similarly adapted. It is immaterial whether a person is actually present.

IV. "Non-deadly force" means any assault or confinement which does not constitute deadly force. The act of producing or displaying a weapon shall constitute non-deadly force.

Source.
1971, 518:1. 1981, 347:3, eff. Aug. 16, 1981. 2011, 268:4, eff. November 13, 2011.

Amendments
—**2011.** The 2011 amendment added the second sentence of IV.

—**1981.** Paragraph I: Former par. I redesignated as par. II and new par. I added.
Paragraph II: Former par. II redesignated as par. IV and former par. I redesignated as par. II.
Paragraph III: Added.
Paragraph IV: Redesignated from former par. II.

NOTES TO DECISIONS

1. Instructions
2. "Deadly force"

1. Instructions

RSA 627:4, II(a), when read in conjunction with RSA 627:9, II, allows a person to use deadly force against another if he reasonably believes that person is about to confine or restrain him so as to allow others to employ deadly force against him. In the future, where supported by some evidence in the record, a trial court should instruct the jury that a defendant was entitled to use deadly force in self-defense against a person that the defendant reasonably believed, acting alone or in concert with others, was about to confine him with the purpose of causing or with knowledge of a substantial risk of causing death or serious bodily injury. State v. Furgal, 164 N.H. 430, 58 A.3d 648, 2012 N.H. LEXIS 167 (2012).

In instructing the jury on the issue of self-defense under RSA 627:4, I, the trial court erred in failing to give the portion of the "deadly force" definition of RSA 627:9, II, relating to the discharge of a firearm. If the jury had been given the full definition, then it could have concluded that defendant's merely pointing his gun at the victim without discharging it constituted the use of non-deadly force. State v. Gingras, 162 N.H. 633, 34 A.3d 659, 2011 N.H. LEXIS 149 (2011).

2. "Deadly force"

Definitions of "deadly weapon" and "deadly force" in RSA 625:11, V, and RSA 627:9, II, are not synonymous, and a finding of the use of deadly force does not necessarily follow from a finding that a person brandished or threatened to use a deadly weapon. State v. Gingras, 162 N.H. 633, 34 A.3d 659, 2011 N.H. LEXIS 149 (2011).

That the legislature found it necessary to include the second sentence in RSA 627:9, II, is a strong indication that, in the absence of this provision, such discharge of a firearm would not, without more, constitute the use of deadly force—otherwise there would have been no need for the legislature to include it. State v. Gingras, 162 N.H. 633, 34 A.3d 659, 2011 N.H. LEXIS 149 (2011).

CHAPTER 628

RESPONSIBILITY

SECTION
628:1.   Immaturity.
628:2.   Insanity.

628:1. Immaturity.

I. Except as provided in paragraph II, a person less than 15 years old is not criminally responsible for his conduct, but may be adjudged to be a juvenile delinquent.

II. Except as provided in paragraph III, a person 13 years of age or older may be held criminally responsible for the following offenses if the person's case is transferred to the superior court under the provisions of RSA 169-B:24:

(a) (1) First degree murder as defined in RSA 630:1-a.

(2) Second degree murder as defined in RSA 630:1-b.

(3) Manslaughter as defined in RSA 630:2.

(b) First degree assault as defined in RSA 631:1.

(c) Second degree assault as defined in RSA 631:2.

(d) Kidnapping as defined in RSA 633:1.

(e) Aggravated felonious sexual assault as defined in RSA 632-A:2.

(f) Criminal restraint as defined in RSA 633:2.

(g) Class A felony robbery as defined in RSA 636:1.

(h) Attempted murder.

(i) Negligent homicide as defined in RSA 630:3, II.

III. If a person is charged after his or her 17th birthday for an offense set forth in paragraph II which is alleged to have been committed when such person was 13 years of age but less than 15 years of age, and the statute of limitations has not expired, and no juvenile petition based on the acts constituting the offense has been filed, the provisions of RSA 169-B:24 shall not apply. In such cases, the superior court shall hold a hearing prior to trial to determine, based on a preponderance of the evidence, whether the defendant may be held criminally responsible. In making such determination, the court shall consider, but shall not be limited to, the following criteria:

(a) The seriousness of the alleged offense to the community;

(b) The aggressive, violent, premeditated, or willful nature of the alleged offense;

(c) Whether the alleged offense was committed against persons or property;

(d) The prosecutorial merit of the charge;

(e) The sophistication and maturity of the defendant at the time of the alleged offense; and

(f) The defendant's prior record and prior contacts with law enforcement as of the date of the hearing.

Source.

1971, 518:1. 1988, 204:6. 1995, 308:113, eff. Jan. 1, 1996. 1998, 381:3, eff. Jan. 1, 1999. 2003, 265:2, eff. Jan. 1, 2004. 2004, 158:1, 2, eff. May 24, 2004.

Amendments

—**2004.** Paragraph II: Added "except as provided in paragraph III" to the beginning of the introductory par.

Paragraph III: Rewritten to the extent that a detailed comparison would be impractical.

—**2003.** Paragraph III: Added.

—**1998.** Paragraph II(i): Added.

—**1995.** Paragraph II: Rewritten to the extent that a detailed comparison would be impractical.

—**1988.** Designated the existing provisions of the section as par. I, added "except as provided in paragraph II" preceding "a person" at the beginning of that paragraph and added par. II.

Applicability of 1995 amendment.

1995, 308:118, eff. Jan. 1, 1996, provided that the amendment to par. II of this section by 1995, 308:113 shall apply to offenses committed on or after Jan. 1, 1996.

Cross References.

Delinquent children, see RSA 169-B.

Parole of delinquents, see RSA 170-H.

NOTES TO DECISIONS

1. Jurisdiction
2. Juveniles who are 17

1. Jurisdiction

Jurisdiction over the issue of the criminal responsibility of 22-year-old defendant for acts committed when he was 13 years old, was controlled by RSA 628:1, II, as opposed to RSA 169-B:4, VII, as RSA 628:1, II, was intended to protect defendant at time of the alleged act; thus, defendant could not be held responsible unless the State could persuade the district court that defendant was responsible and that the case should have been transferred to the superior court. State v. Gifford, 148 N.H. 215, 808 A.2d 1, 2002 N.H. LEXIS 113 (2002).

2. Juveniles who are 17

Since the juvenile, who was 17, was afforded all the protections that attend juvenile proceedings, including confidentiality of the proceedings and the closing of his case once he became 21, and the adjudication of "true" was not equivalent to a finding of guilt in a criminal proceeding, there was no violation of RSA 628:1 where he was sentenced to a suspended term in an adult correctional facility. In re Juvenile 2004-822, 153 N.H. 115, 888 A.2d 1258, 2005 N.H. LEXIS 189 (2005).

Cited:

Cited in State v. Guaraldi, 124 N.H. 93, 467 A.2d 233, 1983 N.H. LEXIS 365 (1983); State v. Benoit, 126 N.H. 6, 490 A.2d 295, 1985 N.H. LEXIS 240 (1985); In re T.J.S., 141 N.H. 697, 692 A.2d 498, 1997 N.H. LEXIS 24 (1997).

RESEARCH REFERENCES

New Hampshire Bar Journal.
For article: "Lex Loci: A Survey of New Hampshire Supreme Court Decisions," see 43 N.H.B.J. 57 (Dec. 2002).

628:2. Insanity.

I. A person who is insane at the time he acts is not criminally responsible for his conduct. Any distinction between a statutory and common law defense of insanity is hereby abolished and invocation of such defense waives no right an accused person would otherwise have.

II. The defendant shall have the burden of proving the defense of insanity by clear and convincing evidence.

III. Evidence of insanity is not admissible unless:

(a) The defendant, within 10 days after entering his plea of not guilty or at such later time as the court may for good cause permit, notifies the court and the state of his purpose to rely on such defense; and

(b) Such notice is given at least 30 days before the scheduled commencement of trial.

Source.
1971, 518:1. 1982, 34:1. 1987, 13:1, eff. June 2, 1987.

Amendments
—1987. Paragraph II: Rewritten to the extent that a detailed comparison would be impracticable.

—1982. Paragraph II: Former par. II redesignated as subpar. III(a) and new par. II added.
Paragraph III: Former par. II redesignated as introductory clause and subpar. (a), made minor changes in phraseology in that subparagraph and added subpar. (b).

Cross References.
Committal of accused acquitted by reason of insanity, see RSA 651:9-a.
Committal of accused for pre-trial psychiatric examination, see RSA 135:17.

Duration of order committing accused acquitted by reason of insanity, see RSA 651:11-a.
Evidence required to commit accused acquitted by reason of insanity, see New Hampshire Constitution, Part 1, Article 15.
Plea of insanity, see RSA 651:8-a.

NOTES TO DECISIONS

1. Constitutionality
2. Presumption of sanity
3. Test
4. Trial procedure
5. Alcoholism
6. Notice
7. Expert testimony

1. Constitutionality

Requiring a defendant to prove insanity by clear and convincing evidence does not violate Part I, Article 15 of New Hampshire Constitution. State v. Blair, 143 N.H. 669, 732 A.2d 448, 1999 N.H. LEXIS 57 (1999).

Failure of legislature to delineate a legal standard concerning the factual question of criminal insanity is not an unconstitutional delegation of legislative authority. State v. Shackford, 127 N.H. 695, 506 A.2d 315, 1986 N.H. LEXIS 223 (1986).

2. Presumption of sanity

Sanity is properly in nature of a policy presumption because it is inherent in human nature and is natural and normal condition of mankind, and is not properly an element of the crime. Novosel v. Helgemoe, 118 N.H. 115, 384 A.2d 124, 1978 N.H. LEXIS 356 (1978), superseded by statute as stated in, State v. Blair, 143 N.H. 669, 732 A.2d 448, 1999 N.H. LEXIS 57 (1999).

3. Test

The test for criminal insanity is whether insanity negated criminal intent. State v. Shackford, 127 N.H. 695, 506 A.2d 315, 1986 N.H. LEXIS 223 (1986).

4. Trial procedure

If accused does not desire a bifurcated hearing, but instead wishes to plead not guilty and raise insanity issue as affirmative defense, he may go forward with his affirmative insanity defense after state has rested upon evidence probative of requisite intent or culpability, and other elements of crime charged, and in such case, jury should be instructed about consequences of finding of not guilty by reason of insanity, and if jury certifies to court that they have acquitted defendant by reason of insanity, court will then proceed to determination of present dangerousness. Novosel v. Helgemoe, 118 N.H. 115, 384 A.2d 124, 1978 N.H. LEXIS 356 (1978), superseded by statute as stated in, State v. Blair, 143 N.H. 669, 732 A.2d 448, 1999 N.H. LEXIS 57 (1999).

5. Alcoholism

Though intoxication has been recognized as a defense to a crime on grounds of insanity in the form of dipsomania, it is only when defendant claims that his condition of chronic alcoholism constitutes a mental disease or insanity which renders him incapable of exercising his volition and thus constitutes a complete defense to an alleged criminal act that he will be allowed to present evidence of this condition, and in order to do so, notice provisions of this section must first be complied with. State v. Plummer, 117 N.H. 320, 374 A.2d 431, 1977 N.H. LEXIS 330 (1977).

6. Notice

Trial court erred in granting the State's motion to strike defendant's insanity defense where defendant's offer of proof was sufficient to give notice of defendant's intent to raise an insanity defense and the grounds upon which the defense was based. State v. Fichera, 153 N.H. 588, 903 A.2d 1030, 2006 N.H. LEXIS 76 (2006).

In a prosecution for simple assault arising from an altercation with a police officer, the trial court's exclusion of proffered expert testimony regarding the defendant's bipolar manic depressive disorder was not error since such evidence was essentially a classic insanity defense claim and the defendant failed to comply with the notice requirements for such a claim. State v. James, 140 N.H. 50, 663 A.2d 83, 1995 N.H. LEXIS 99 (1995).

7. Expert testimony

Trial court properly denied defendant's motion to exclude the testimony of the State's expert psychiatrist on the issue of whether defendant's murder of his mother was the product of mental illness or defect, and it did not engage in an unsustainable exercise of its discretion in admitting the testimony of the expert, as the expert had a medical background and experience in treating mental illness and his opinion likely aided the jury to understand the complexities of mental illness and the multitude of behaviors likely to stem from mental illness. The trial court also gave the jury a clear instruction that, as the fact finder, it was not bound by the expert's opinion, and was free to reject it. State v. Labranche, 156 N.H. 740, 942 A.2d 1284, 2008 N.H. LEXIS 17 (2008).

Cited:

Cited in State v. Warren, 114 N.H. 196, 317 A.2d 566, 1974 N.H. LEXIS 235 (1974); State v. Holler, 123 N.H. 195, 459 A.2d 1143, 1983 N.H. LEXIS 251 (1983); State v. Sadvari, 123 N.H. 410, 462 A.2d 102, 1983 N.H. LEXIS 294 (1983); State v. Guaraldi, 124 N.H. 93, 467 A.2d 233, 1983 N.H. LEXIS 365 (1983); State v. Faragi, 127 N.H. 1, 498 A.2d 723, 1985 N.H. LEXIS 401 (1985); State v. Abbott, 127 N.H. 444, 503 A.2d 791, 1985 N.H. LEXIS 465 (1985); State v. Plante, 134 N.H. 585, 594 A.2d 165, 1991 N.H. LEXIS 106 (1991).

RESEARCH REFERENCES

New Hampshire Practice.
2-32 N.H.P. Criminal Practice & Procedure § 32.34.

CHAPTER 629

INCHOATE CRIMES

SECTION
629:1.   Attempt.
629:2.   Criminal Solicitation.
629:3.   Conspiracy.

629:1. Attempt.

I. A person is guilty of an attempt to commit a crime if, with a purpose that a crime be committed, he does or omits to do anything which, under the circumstances as he believes them to be, is an act or omission constituting a substantial step toward the commission of the crime.

II. As used in this section, "substantial step" means conduct that is strongly corroborative of the actor's criminal purpose.

III. (a) It is an affirmative defense to prosecution under this section that the actor voluntarily renounces his criminal purpose by abandoning his effort to commit the crime or otherwise preventing its commission under circumstances manifesting a complete withdrawal of his criminal purpose.

(b) A renunciation is not "voluntary" if it is substantially motivated by circumstances the defendant was not aware of at the inception of his conduct which increase the probability of his detection or which make more difficult the commission of the crime. Renunciation is not complete if the purpose is to postpone the criminal conduct until a more advantageous time or to transfer the criminal effort to another but similar objective or victim.

IV. The penalty for attempt is the same as that authorized for the crime that was attempted, except that in the case of attempt to commit murder the punishment shall be imprisonment for life or such other term as the court shall order.

Source.

1971, 518:1. 1979, 126:5, eff. Aug. 4, 1979. 1999, 158:1, eff. June 28, 1999.

Revision note.

Undesignated subparagraphs of par. III designated as subpars. (a) and (b) to conform to the paragraph style of LEXIS New Hampshire Revised Statutes Annotated.

Amendments

—1999. Paragraph IV: Substituted "punishment shall be imprisonment for life or such other term as the court shall order" for "penalty shall be as provided in RSA 651:2, II-c" at the end of the paragraph.

—1979. Paragraph IV: Substituted "the penalty shall be as provided in RSA 651:2, II-c" for "it is a class A felony" following "murder".

Cross References.

Attempted sabotage, see RSA 649:4.
Victims permitted to speak before sentencing for attempted murder, see RSA 651:4-a.

NOTES TO DECISIONS

1.   Generally
2.   Construction
3.   Renunciation of criminal purpose
4.   Substantial step
5.   Murder
6.   Driving while intoxicated
7.   Assault
8.   Indictments
9.   Evidence
10. Lesser included offenses
11. Merger with other offenses
12. Crime of dishonesty or false statement
13. Appeal

1. Generally

Word "attempt" in RSA 649-B:4, I(a) does not incorporate the attempt statute, RSA 629:1, I, or the mental state of "purposely." Accordingly, under RSA 626:2, I, the mental state of "knowingly" applies to all of the material elements of RSA 649-B:4, I(a), and the trial court did not err in its jury instruction as to the mental state required for conviction. State v. Moscone, 161 N.H. 355, 13 A.3d 137, 2011 N.H. LEXIS 1 (2011).

An attempt is a substantive crime in and of itself. State v. Harper, 126 N.H. 815, 498 A.2d 310, 1985 N.H. LEXIS 409 (1985).

If the essence of a certain crime is the attempt to do a certain act, there cannot be an attempt to commit the crime because it is committed whether or not the certain act is performed. State v. Davis, 108 N.H. 158, 229 A.2d 842, 1967 N.H. LEXIS 142 (1967), overruled in part, State v. Ayer, 136 N.H. 191, 612 A.2d 923, 1992 N.H. LEXIS 139 (1992). (Decided under prior law.)

2. Construction

Any act or omission constituting a substantial step toward the commission of the crime is enough to trigger this section. State v. Harper, 126 N.H. 815, 498 A.2d 310, 1985 N.H. LEXIS 409 (1985).

3. Renunciation of criminal purpose

A defendant who raises renunciation as an affirmative defense bears the burden of showing by a preponderance of the evidence both that he completely abandoned his criminal purpose and that the abandonment was voluntary. State v. Jernigan, 133 N.H. 396, 577 A.2d 1214, 1990 N.H. LEXIS 78 (1990).

The "transferred effort" exception of RSA 629:1, III(b) applies only when defendant continues to engage in a similar course of criminal conduct after the purported renunciation; where defendant did not resume any criminal conduct after his renunciation, the exception did not apply.State v. Jernigan, 133 N.H. 396, 577 A.2d 1214, 1990 N.H. LEXIS 78 (1990).

Unless the undisputed testimony and required inferences compel a finding that defendant renounced his criminal purpose, courts are precluded from so finding as a matter of law. State v. Jernigan, 133 N.H. 396, 577 A.2d 1214, 1990 N.H. LEXIS 78 (1990).

Defendant claiming an affirmative defense of renunciation of criminal purpose in a case of aggravated felonious sexual assault failed to prove that he abandoned his effort because the victim "invoked God" where victim also invoked God earlier in the assault without deterring him, and abandonment could have been caused by extraneous physical causes, such as struggle. State v. Jernigan, 133 N.H. 396, 577 A.2d 1214, 1990 N.H. LEXIS 78 (1990).

In a trial for attempted aggravated felonious sexual assault, where victim struggled with defendant, told defendant she was menstruating, and where defendant held his penis against her vagina for at least thirty seconds before abandoning his assault, a jury could reasonably find that defendant's renunciation was not voluntary because extraneous circumstances may have made more difficult the commission of his crime. State v. Jernigan, 133 N.H. 396, 577 A.2d 1214, 1990 N.H. LEXIS 78 (1990).

Voluntary renunciation of criminal purpose, which constitutes an affirmative defense to prosecution for attempt, will be found as a matter of law only where the undisputed testimony and required inferences compel a finding that the defendant renounced his criminal purpose. State v. Patten, 126 N.H. 227, 489 A.2d 657, 1985 N.H. LEXIS 253 (1985).

4. Substantial step

Fact that the prison phone system blocked defendant's telephone call to the victim did not mean that there was insufficient evidence of attempted criminal contempt. Defendant's conduct in dialing the victim's telephone number from the prison was sufficient to establish that with the purpose of contacting the victim in violation of a no-contact order, he took a substantial step toward accomplishing that end under RSA 629:1, I. State v. Smith, 163 N.H. 13, 35 A.3d 646, 2011 N.H. LEXIS 184 (2011).

Trial court properly denied defendant's motion to set aside conviction of attempted felonious sexual assault where viewed in light most favorable to the state, the evidence supported finding that defendant's act(s) or failure to act constituted a substantial step toward commission of the crime of felonious sexual assault despite fact that physical evidence was lacking to support victim's claim of penetration. State v. Adams, 133 N.H. 818, 585 A.2d 853, 1991 N.H. LEXIS 3 (1991).

5. Murder

Evidence was sufficient to support convictions for attempted murder as an "accomplice/principal" based on the shooting of the victims where shoe print evidence and the defendant's own statement placed him at the scene of the shooting and additional evidence supported the jury's conclusion that the defendant's involvement exceeded mere presence. State v. Duguay, 142 N.H. 221, 698 A.2d 5, 1997 N.H. LEXIS 79 (1997).

Attempted murder is a single, generic crime comprising an act committed with the purpose to cause the death of another, when that act is a substantial step toward the causation of death; there are no varieties of attempted murder corresponding to varieties of murder as a completed crime. State v. Allen, 128 N.H. 390, 514 A.2d 1263, 1986 N.H. LEXIS 309 (1986).

Solicitation of another to commit murder may constitute an attempt to commit murder when the defendant has completed all the necessary preliminary steps for the hired murder to take place. State v. Kilgus, 128 N.H. 577, 519 A.2d 231, 1986 N.H. LEXIS 372 (1986).

There was sufficient evidence which could reasonably support a finding of guilt beyond a reasonable doubt of attempted first degree murder where it could reasonably be inferred from the defendant's actions of repeatedly striking the victim on the head with a metal hammer that he believed that he had succeeded in killing her, and even if the accused voluntarily ceased striking the victim before he believed he caused her death, the jury was not precluded from reasonably inferring that the accused intended to kill the victim

when he began the assault. State v. Morehouse, 120 N.H. 738, 424 A.2d 798, 1980 N.H. LEXIS 406 (1980).

6. Driving while intoxicated

Where motor vehicle was pulled over to the side of the road with the motor running and the lights out, driver was in the driver's seat asleep, and state trooper awoke driver and noted a moderate odor of alcoholic beverage on driver's breath, there was probable cause to believe driver was engaged in an attempt to operate the vehicle which, though temporarily suspended, would probably be resumed, quite likely at a time when driver's impaired judgment might satisfy him that his competence to operate the vehicle had been restored. State v. Martin, 116 N.H. 47, 351 A.2d 52, 1976 N.H. LEXIS 260 (1976).

7. Assault

Defendant's conviction for attempted first degree assault was affirmed, where based on victim's testimony, jury could rationally have concluded beyond a reasonable doubt that the defendant had intended to cause bodily injury to the victim when he came at her with a knife and that this act was a substantial step towards the commission of first degree assault. State v. Meaney, 129 N.H. 448, 529 A.2d 384, 1987 N.H. LEXIS 193 (1987).

8. Indictments

Trial court did not constructively amend the indictment for attempted burglary under RSA 635:1, RSA 626:8, and RSA 629:1 by refusing to instruct the jury that the State had to prove that defendant himself removed a window screen. Because the indictment clearly alleged both principal and accomplice liability, it provided sufficient notice that defendant was charged with either removing the window screen himself or soliciting, aiding or attempting to aid another in removing it; the indictment was more than sufficient for defendant to prepare his defense because it put him on notice that the State would have to prove that he in some way solicited, aided, agreed or attempted to aid in the attempted burglary State v. Winward, 161 N.H. 533, 20 A.3d 338, 2011 N.H. LEXIS 21 (2011).

Indictment for attempted burglary was not inadequate under N.H. Const. pt. I, art. 15 because it did not allege what crime defendant would have committed in furtherance of the burglary. Charging a defendant with attempted burglary did not require the State to specify the offense the defendant would have committed in furtherance of the burglary; furthermore, juror unanimity was required only for the elements of attempted burglary, not as to the crime or offense defendant would have committed in furtherance of the burglary. State v. Munoz, 157 N.H. 143, 949 A.2d 155, 2008 N.H. LEXIS 47 (2008).

Statute governing attempts to commit crime did not require State to plead and prove elements of intended offense, and therefore indictment which alleged attempted aggravated felonious sexual assault, and factually identified offense in describing overt steps defendant took to accomplish it, was sufficient to enable defendant to prepare his defense and to protect him from double jeopardy. State v. Johnson, 144 N.H. 175, 738 A.2d 1284, 1999 N.H. LEXIS 95 (1999).

A trial court properly denied a defendant's motion to quash an attempted murder indictment because of its failure to specify the degree of murder attempted. State v. Allen, 128 N.H. 390, 514 A.2d 1263, 1986 N.H. LEXIS 309 (1986).

The word "capital" in indictment for attempted capital murder may be considered surplusage under paragraph IV of this section because the state is not required to prove attempted capital murder to sustain a charge of attempted murder; all classifications of murder are included in the charge. State v. McPhail, 116 N.H. 440, 362 A.2d 199, 1976 N.H. LEXIS 377 (1976).

9. Evidence

As committing penetration or touching for sexual gratification were statutory variants of attempted aggravated felonious sexual assault, in violation of RSA 629:1 and 632-A:2, it was sufficient that the jury determined that defendant intended to commit either variant for purposes of supporting his conviction; they did not have to agree which act he intended to commit pursuant to RSA 625:10. State v. Casanova, 164 N.H. 563, 63 A.3d 169, 2013 N.H. LEXIS 11

(2013).

Evidence was sufficient to convict defendant of attempted burglary under RSA 629:1 and RSA 635:1. A rational trier of fact could have found that defendant took a substantial step towards committing the crime of burglary when, without the victim's permission, he pulled on the door of her screened-in porch; a rational trier of fact could also have found that he acted with the specific intent of committing a crime inside the victim's home. State v. Gordon, 161 N.H. 410, 13 A.3d 201, 2011 N.H. LEXIS 6 (2011).

In a trial for attempted burglary under RSA 635:1, RSA 626:8, and RSA 629:1, the evidence revealed more than defendant's mere presence at the scene. A witness saw three men fleeing from his home and later identified them; he found a bent window screen in the grass and testified that he was sure that one of the men removed the screen; another witness heard three men having a "panicked" conversation and then saw them fleeing together; the three men, including defendant, were found hiding near the scene; and when police questioned defendant regarding the whereabouts of any accomplices, he was uncooperative, physically aggressive and used vulgar language. State v. Winward, 161 N.H. 533, 20 A.3d 338, 2011 N.H. LEXIS 21 (2011).

Evidence was sufficient to support an attempted murder conviction under RSA 630:1-a and RSA 629:1, either as a principal or as an accomplice. Witness testimony supported the facts that defendant and a second man possessed guns, tracked the car occupied by the victim, took aim at multiple targets on the car where people would be expected to be located, and together discharged numerous gunshots with the intention of killing the victim, against whom defendant bore a longtime grudge; even if the evidence failed to establish that any bullet fired by the defendant actually struck the victim, actual injury was not an element of the crime. State v. Young, 159 N.H. 332, 986 A.2d 497, 2009 N.H. LEXIS 122 (2009).

Sufficient evidence supported defendant's attempted kidnapping conviction where the record revealed ample evidence from which a jury could conclude that defendant had the purpose to commit the crime of kidnapping, and the jury also heard testimony about statements made by defendant that pointed to his own consciousness of guilt. State v. Bean, 153 N.H. 380, 897 A.2d 946, 2006 N.H. LEXIS 45 (2006).

Evidence was sufficient to establish that the defendant, as an accomplice, committed two counts of attempted murder, one count of attempted arson, and one count of attempted falsification of evidence, where a witness testified that, mere hours after the incident, the defendant admitted that he had accompanied his coperpetrator to the scene of the crime, that they planned to rob whomever they discovered there, by violent means if necessary, that the defendant and the coperpetrator hid behind a bush while the latter twice shot at a car, that after the victims abandoned the car they searched it for valuables and money, and that there was an attempt to destroy the car following the search for valuables. State v. Laudarowicz, 142 N.H. 1, 694 A.2d 980, 1997 N.H. LEXIS 47 (1997).

10. Lesser included offenses

Conviction for attempted murder was reversed because the jury should have been instructed on the lesser-included offenses of attempted first degree assault and reckless conduct; the issue of intent was sufficiently disputed to provide a rational basis for the jury to conclude defendant acted only recklessly or with a purpose to cause only serious bodily injury where he was reacting to his wife's infidelity and stabbed her as she came towards him and where court could not say that there was no rational basis for the jury to find that severe intoxication may have negated any purpose to kill the victim. State v. Thomas, 154 N.H. 189, 908 A.2d 774, 2006 N.H. LEXIS 144 (2006).

11. Merger with other offenses

Merger doctrine rendered it unlikely that the Legislature intended to criminalize restraint that was integral to other crimes, such that it was irrelevant whether the charges against defendant of attempted kidnapping and attempted aggravated felonious sexual assault, in violation of RSA 629:1, 633:1, and 632-A:2, were intended to prohibit different types of criminal activity; accordingly, the merger doctrine should have been employed. State v. Casanova, 164 N.H. 563, 63 A.3d 169, 2013 N.H. LEXIS 11 (2013).

Merger doctrine applied to the crime of attempted kidnapping, in violation of RSA 629:1 and 633:1, as the purpose of the doctrine was arguably even more germane in such a case, where actual confinement did not need to be proven. State v. Casanova, 164 N.H. 563, 63 A.3d 169, 2013 N.H. LEXIS 11 (2013).

Intentionally trying to kill a person and knowingly inflicting bodily injury on that same person do not constitute two distinct criminal activities when the identical criminal conduct is the basis of both charges; the legislature did not intend for identical criminal conduct to give rise to distinct charges for first degree assault and attempted murder. Thus, because the same shooting was the basis of both the attempted murder and assault indictments, under the common law doctrine of merger, the trial court erred by imposing consecutive sentences for the convictions regarding the same victim. State v. Young, 159 N.H. 332, 986 A.2d 497, 2009 N.H. LEXIS 122 (2009).

12. Crime of dishonesty or false statement

In establishing the elements of RSA 638:5, I(a), the State must prove that a defendant knowingly used a stolen credit card to obtain goods or services; thus, because this act necessarily involves falsely claiming to be someone else, conviction under this statute clearly falls within N.H. R. Evid. 609(a)(2). Furthermore, even if the act constituting the attempt, e.g., entering a store, is not itself an act of dishonesty or false statement, the act is done with the purpose of ultimately posing as someone else and using that person's stolen credit card to obtain goods and services; thus, because the ultimate purpose is to commit an act of dishonesty, an attempt to commit credit card fraud comes within Rule 609(a)(2). State v. Long, 161 N.H. 364, 12 A.3d 1289, 2011 N.H. LEXIS 3 (2011).

Defendant was properly impeached under N.H. R. Evid. 609(a)(2) with attempted credit card fraud under RSA 638:5, I(a) and RSA 629:1, I. The act constituting the attempt was done with the purpose of ultimately posing as someone else and using that person's stolen credit card to obtain goods and services, an act of dishonesty. State v. Long, 161 N.H. 364, 12 A.3d 1289, 2011 N.H. LEXIS 3 (2011).

In a trial for attempted burglary, the trial court did not err in not giving a "mere presence" instruction. Its instruction made clear that to find defendant guilty, the jury had to conclude that he in some way actively aided or participated in the attempted burglary. State v. Winward, 161 N.H. 533, 20 A.3d 338, 2011 N.H. LEXIS 21 (2011).

13. Appeal

As defendant had sought dismissal in the trial court of a charge of attempted kidnapping, in violation of RSA 629:1 and 633:1, arguing that it was not independent of an attempted aggravated felonious sexual assault charge, even though his motion was denied the issue was properly preserved for review. State v. Casanova, 164 N.H. 563, 63 A.3d 169, 2013 N.H. LEXIS 11 (2013).

Cited:

Cited in Welch v. Bergeron, 115 N.H. 179, 337 A.2d 341, 1975 N.H. LEXIS 253 (1975); State v. Hanley, 116 N.H. 235, 356 A.2d 687, 1976 N.H. LEXIS 317 (1976); State v. Lordan, 116 N.H. 479, 363 A.2d 201, 1976 N.H. LEXIS 387 (1976); State v. Stewart, 116 N.H. 585, 364 A.2d 621, 1976 N.H. LEXIS 419 (1976); State v. La Roche, 117 N.H. 127, 370 A.2d 631, 1977 N.H. LEXIS 283 (1977); State v. Laplante, 117 N.H. 417, 374 A.2d 643, 1977 N.H. LEXIS 349 (1977); State v. Theodosopoulos, 119 N.H. 573, 409 A.2d 1134, 1979 N.H. LEXIS 435 (1979); State v. Fraser, 120 N.H. 117, 411 A.2d 1125, 1980 N.H. LEXIS 241 (1980); State v. Aubert, 120 N.H. 634, 421 A.2d 124, 1980 N.H. LEXIS 367 (1980); State v. Baker, 120 N.H. 773, 424 A.2d 171, 1980 N.H. LEXIS 401 (1980); State v. Stiles, 123 N.H. 680, 465 A.2d 908, 1983 N.H. LEXIS 333 (1983); State v. Lessard, 123 N.H. 788, 465 A.2d 516, 1983 N.H. LEXIS 329 (1983); State v. Fielders, 124 N.H. 310, 470 A.2d 897, 1983 N.H. LEXIS 415 (1983); State v. Leuthner, 124 N.H. 638, 474 A.2d 1029, 1984 N.H. LEXIS 226 (1984); State v. Elbert, 125 N.H. 1, 480 A.2d 854, 1984 N.H. LEXIS 371 (1984); State v. Woodman, 125 N.H. 381, 480 A.2d 169, 1984 N.H. LEXIS 250 (1984); State v. Abbis, 125 N.H. 646, 484 A.2d 1156, 1984 N.H. LEXIS 387 (1984); Elbert v. Cunningham, 616 F. Supp. 433, 1985 U.S. Dist. LEXIS 16980 (D.N.H. 1985); State v. Batchelder, 126 N.H. 700, 496 A.2d 346, 1985 N.H. LEXIS 351 (1985); State v. Parker, 127 N.H. 525, 503 A.2d 809,

1985 N.H. LEXIS 455 (1985); State v. Elbert, 128 N.H. 210, 512 A.2d 1114, 1986 N.H. LEXIS 280 (1986); State v. Brown, 128 N.H. 606, 517 A.2d 831, 1986 N.H. LEXIS 328 (1986); State v. Allegra, 129 N.H. 720, 533 A.2d 338, 1987 N.H. LEXIS 247 (1987); State v. Guglielmo, 130 N.H. 240, 544 A.2d 25, 1987 N.H. LEXIS 303 (1987); State v. Trainor, 130 N.H. 371, 540 A.2d 1236, 1988 N.H. LEXIS 9 (1988); Bussiere v. Cunningham, 132 N.H. 747, 571 A.2d 908, 1990 N.H. LEXIS 19 (1990); State v. Allen, 133 N.H. 306, 577 A.2d 801, 1990 N.H. LEXIS 68 (1990); State v. Plante, 133 N.H. 384, 577 A.2d 95, 1990 N.H. LEXIS 75 (1990); State v. Jones, 133 N.H. 562, 578 A.2d 864, 1990 N.H. LEXIS 101 (1990); State v. Whittey, 134 N.H. 310, 591 A.2d 1326, 1991 N.H. LEXIS 58 (1991); State v. Smith, 135 N.H. 524, 607 A.2d 611, 1992 N.H. LEXIS 71 (1992); State v. Eldredge, 135 N.H. 562, 607 A.2d 617, 1992 N.H. LEXIS 80 (1992); State v. Ayer, 136 N.H. 191, 612 A.2d 923, 1992 N.H. LEXIS 139 (1992); State v. Stow, 136 N.H. 598, 620 A.2d 1023, 1993 N.H. LEXIS 8 (1993); State v. Decoteau, 137 N.H. 106, 623 A.2d 1338, 1993 N.H. LEXIS 49 (1993); State v. Patten, 137 N.H. 627, 631 A.2d 921, 1993 N.H. LEXIS 134 (1993); State v. Panzera, 139 N.H. 235, 652 A.2d 136, 1994 N.H. LEXIS 138 (1994); State v. Lopez, 139 N.H. 309, 652 A.2d 696, 1994 N.H. LEXIS 144 (1994); State v. Rhoades, 139 N.H. 432, 655 A.2d 414, 1995 N.H. LEXIS 20 (1995); State v. McGlew, 139 N.H. 505, 658 A.2d 1191, 1995 N.H. LEXIS 42 (1995); Reid v. Warden, New Hampshire State Prison, 139 N.H. 530, 659 A.2d 429, 1995 N.H. LEXIS 45 (1995); State v. Fecteau, 140 N.H. 498, 667 A.2d 1384, 1995 N.H. LEXIS 178 (1995); State v. Glanville, 145 N.H. 631, 765 A.2d 173, 2000 N.H. LEXIS 114 (2000); N.H. v. Burgess, 156 N.H. 746, 943 A.2d 727, 2008 N.H. LEXIS 18 (2008).

629:2. Criminal Solicitation.

I. A person is guilty of criminal solicitation if, with a purpose that another engage in conduct constituting a crime, he commands, solicits or requests such other person to engage in such conduct.

II. It is an affirmative defense to prosecution under this section that the actor renounced his criminal purpose by persuading the other not to engage in the criminal conduct or by otherwise preventing commission of the crime under circumstances manifesting a purpose that it not occur.

III. It is no defense to prosecution under this section that the person solicited would be immune from liability for engaging in the criminal conduct by virtue of irresponsibility, incapacity or exemption.

IV. The penalty for criminal solicitation is the same as that authorized for the crime that was solicited, except that in the case of solicitation of murder the punishment shall be imprisonment for a term of not more than 30 years.

Source.
1971, 518:1, eff. Nov. 1, 1973. 1999, 158:2, eff. June 28, 1999.

Amendments
—**1999.** Paragraph IV: Substituted "the punishment shall be imprisonment for a term of not more than 30 years" for "it is a class A felony" at the end of the paragraph.

Cross References.
Causing or aiding suicide, see RSA 630:4.
Classification of crimes, see RSA 625:9.
Solicitation of sabotage, see RSA 649:4.

NOTES TO DECISIONS

1. Construction with other laws
2. Murder

1. Construction with other laws
Defendant is guilty of solicitation pursuant to RSA 639:3, III if the defendant entices or strongly urges a child under the age of 16 to engage in sexual penetration, as the plain language of RSA 639:3, III does not incorporate the definition of criminal solicitation in RSA 629:2, I; the use of the term "solicits" in RSA 639:3, III is not synonymous with the use of the term "criminal solicitation" in RSA 629:2, I. State v. Laporte (in re State), 157 N.H. 229, 950 A.2d 147, 2008 N.H. LEXIS 55 (2008).

Under this section, if one solicits another to commit murder and the one solicited does not kill, then the one who solicited is guilty of criminal solicitation. State v. Kilgus, 128 N.H. 577, 519 A.2d 231, 1986 N.H. LEXIS 372 (1986).

If one solicits another to commit murder and the one solicited does kill, the one solicited is guilty of capital murder under RSA 630:1. State v. Kilgus, 128 N.H. 577, 519 A.2d 231, 1986 N.H. LEXIS 372 (1986).

Solicitation of another to commit murder may constitute an attempt to commit murder within RSA 629:1 when the defendant has completed all the necessary preliminary steps for the hired murder to take place. State v. Kilgus, 128 N.H. 577, 519 A.2d 231, 1986 N.H. LEXIS 372 (1986).

2. Murder
Criminal solicitation of solicitation to murder is a crime under RSA 629:2. State v. Grant-Chase, 150 N.H. 248, 837 A.2d 322, 2003 N.H. LEXIS 171 (2003).

Cited:
Cited in State v. Martineau, 116 N.H. 797, 368 A.2d 592, 1976 N.H. LEXIS 472 (1976); State v. Ayres, 118 N.H. 90, 383 A.2d 87, 1978 N.H. LEXIS 350 (1978); State v. Feole, 121 N.H. 164, 427 A.2d 43, 1981 N.H. LEXIS 272 (1981); State v. Kaplan, 124 N.H. 382, 469 A.2d 1354, 1983 N.H. LEXIS 388 (1983); State v. Chandonnet, 124 N.H. 778, 474 A.2d 578, 1984 N.H. LEXIS 331 (1984); In re Tinkham, 59 B.R. 209, 1986 Bankr. LEXIS 6367 (Bankr. D.N.H. 1986); State v. Kaplan, 128 N.H. 562, 517 A.2d 1162, 1986 N.H. LEXIS 325 (1986); State v. Hermsdorf, 135 N.H. 360, 605 A.2d 1045, 1992 N.H. LEXIS 42, (1992); State v. Conant, 139 N.H. 728, 662 A.2d 283, 1995 N.H. LEXIS 79 (1995); State v. Lucius, 140 N.H. 60, 663 A.2d 605, 1995 N.H. LEXIS 97 (1995).

629:3. Conspiracy.

I. A person is guilty of conspiracy if, with a purpose that a crime defined by statute be committed, he agrees with one or more persons to commit or cause the commission of such crime, and an overt act is committed by one of the conspirators in furtherance of the conspiracy.

II. For purposes of paragraph I, "one or more persons" includes, but is not limited to, persons who are immune from criminal liability by virtue of irresponsibility, incapacity or exemption.

III. It is an affirmative defense to prosecution under this statute that the actor renounces his criminal purpose by giving timely notice to a law enforcement official of the conspiracy and of the actor's part in it, or by conduct designed to prevent commission of the crime agreed upon.

IV. The penalty for conspiracy is the same as that authorized for the crime that was the object of the conspiracy, except that in the case of a conspiracy to commit murder the punishment shall be imprisonment for a term of not more than 30 years.

Source.
1971, 518:1, eff. Nov. 1, 1973. 1999, 158:3, eff. June 28, 1999.

Amendments

—1999. Paragraph IV: Substituted "the punishment shall be imprisonment for a term of not more than 30 years" for "it is a class A felony" at the end of the paragraph.

Cross References.

Classification of crimes, see RSA 625:9.
Conspiracy to commit sabotage, see RSA 649:5.

NOTES TO DECISIONS

1. Construction
2. Construction with other laws
3. Particular offenses

1. Construction

The crime of conspiracy does not necessarily require that both parties to the conspiracy possess criminal intent, and the phrase "one or more persons" in RSA 629:3, II, expressly includes those who are immune from criminal liability; therefore, fact that defendant's co-conspirator was a police officer who did not intend to actually commit the crime for which they were conspiring, did not affect defendant's conviction for conspiracy. State v. Blackmer, 149 N.H. 47, 816 A.2d 1014, 2003 N.H. LEXIS 3 (2003).

2. Construction with other laws

Defendant's double jeopardy rights under N.H. Const. pt. I, art. 16, and U.S. Const. amend. V, were not violated because, as charged, each indictment required the State to prove a fact not necessary to the other; specifically, the State did not have to prove the existence of an agreement, required for the conspiracy conviction, to prove the first degree murder charge, and the conspiracy indictment did not require the State to prove the enhanced mental state of deliberation and premeditation, required for a first degree murder conviction. State v. Sanchez, 152 N.H. 625, 883 A.2d 292, 2005 N.H. LEXIS 149 (2005).

Conspiracy to receive stolen property is a separate and distinct crime of receiving stolen property set forth in RSA 637:7. State v. Chaisson, 123 N.H. 17, 458 A.2d 95, 1983 N.H. LEXIS 236 (1983).

3. Particular offenses

Error in admitting post-arrest statements of co-conspirators under N.H. R. Evid. 801(d)(2)(E) was not harmless as to accomplice and conspiracy first-degree assault charges under RSA 626:8, RSA 629:3, and RSA 631:1, as the evidence did not overwhelmingly establish that defendant had at least a tacit understanding that deadly weapons would be used in the commission of the assault. State v. Rodriguez, 164 N.H. 800, 64 A.3d 962, 2013 N.H. LEXIS 45 (2013).

Error in admitting post-arrest statements of co-conspirators under N.H. R. Evid. 801(d)(2)(E) was harmless as to defendant's conviction for conspiracy to commit burglary under RSA 629:3 and RSA 635:1. Given defendant's admission that he intended to go to the victim's residence to assault the victim as well as evidence that he enlisted the help of others to do so, the alternative evidence of his guilt was overwhelming. State v. Rodriguez, 164 N.H. 800, 64 A.3d 962, 2013 N.H. LEXIS 45 (2013).

One cannot conspire to commit a crime where the culpability is based upon the result of reckless conduct; thus, defendant's motion to dismiss the portion of an indictment that charged conspiracy to commit reckless second-degree assault should have been granted because the indictment failed to allege facts that, if proven, would have constituted a cognizable crime. State v. Donohue, 150 N.H. 180, 834 A.2d 253, 2003 N.H. LEXIS 158 (2003).

A conviction for conspiracy to commit murder was proper where the evidence, when read in the light most favorable to the state, was sufficient for a rational trier of fact to conclude beyond a reasonable doubt that the defendant and another entered into a conspiracy to kill, and that three overt acts were carried out in furtherance of the conspiracy. State v. Kilgus, 128 N.H. 577, 519 A.2d 231, 1986 N.H. LEXIS 372 (1986).

At the trial of defendant for conspiring to transport controlled drug into this state with intent to sell, essence of crime was secrecy and concealment and state was entitled to rely on inferences drawn from course of conduct of alleged conspirators. State v. Gilbert, 115 N.H. 665, 348 A.2d 713, 1975 N.H. LEXIS 391 (1975).

Where trip was mutually planned together, taken together and expenses were shared, and there was uncontroverted evidence that defendant was present when marijuana was purchased in California, there was ample evidence to sustain conviction for conspiring to transport controlled drug into this state with intent to sell. State v. Gilbert, 115 N.H. 665, 348 A.2d 713, 1975 N.H. LEXIS 391 (1975).

Cited:

Cited in State v. Rowman, 116 N.H. 41, 352 A.2d 737, 1976 N.H. LEXIS 259 (1976); State v. Colby, 116 N.H. 790, 368 A.2d 587, 1976 N.H. LEXIS 471 (1976); State v. Martineau, 116 N.H. 797, 368 A.2d 592, 1976 N.H. LEXIS 472 (1976); State v. Gilbert, 121 N.H. 305, 429 A.2d 323, 1981 N.H. LEXIS 308 (1981); State v. Settle, 123 N.H. 34, 455 A.2d 1031, 1983 N.H. LEXIS 218 (1983); State v. Holt, 124 N.H. 645, 474 A.2d 1031, 1984 N.H. LEXIS 228 (1984); State v. Damiano, 124 N.H. 742, 474 A.2d 1045, 1984 N.H. LEXIS 337 (1984); State v. Chaisson, 125 N.H. 810, 486 A.2d 297, 1984 N.H. LEXIS 320 (1984); State v. Labonville, 126 N.H. 451, 492 A.2d 1376, 1985 N.H. LEXIS 302 (1985); State v. Mayo, 127 N.H. 67, 497 A.2d 853, 1985 N.H. LEXIS 391 (1985); State v. Dennehy, 127 N.H. 425, 503 A.2d 769, 1985 N.H. LEXIS 462 (1985); In re Tinkham, 59 B.R. 209, 1986 Bankr. LEXIS 6367 (Bankr. D.N.H. 1986); State v. Riccio, 130 N.H. 376, 540 A.2d 1239, 1988 N.H. LEXIS 8 (1988); State v. Prisby, 131 N.H. 57, 550 A.2d 89, 1988 N.H. LEXIS 85 (1988); State v. Gallant, 133 N.H. 138, 574 A.2d 385, 1990 N.H. LEXIS 44 (1990); State v. Gibney, 133 N.H. 890, 587 A.2d 607, 1991 N.H. LEXIS 7 (1991); State v. Perez, 134 N.H. 667, 597 A.2d 73, 1991 N.H. LEXIS 113 (1991); State v. Matiyosus, 134 N.H. 686, 597 A.2d 1068, 1991 N.H. LEXIS 122 (1991); State v. Gonzalez, 136 N.H. 354, 615 A.2d 640, 1992 N.H. LEXIS 177 (1992); State v. Alosa, 137 N.H. 33, 623 A.2d 218, 1993 N.H. LEXIS 37 (1993); State v. Beland, 138 N.H. 735, 645 A.2d 79, 1994 N.H. LEXIS 96 (1994); State v. Gonzalez, 143 N.H. 693, 738 A.2d 1247, 1999 N.H. LEXIS 59 (1999); State v. Gonzalez, 143 N.H. 693, 738 A.2d 1247, 1999 N.H. LEXIS 59 (1999); McLaughlin v. Moore, 152 F. Supp. 2d 123, 2001 U.S. Dist. LEXIS 6908 (D.N.H. 2001); State v. Doucette, 146 N.H. 583, 776 A.2d 744, 2001 N.H. LEXIS 112 (2001).

CHAPTER 630

HOMICIDE

SECTION
630:1.　　Capital Murder.
630:1-a.　First Degree Murder.
630:1-b.　Second Degree Murder.
630:2.　　Manslaughter.
630:3.　　Negligent Homicide.
630:4.　　Causing or Aiding Suicide.
630:5.　　Procedure in Capital Murder.
630:6.　　Place; Witnesses.

Cross References.

Limitation of prosecutions, see RSA 625:8.
Shooting human beings while hunting, see RSA 207:37-b.

RESEARCH REFERENCES

New Hampshire Bar Journal.

For Attorney General article, "The New Hampshire Office of Chief Medical Examiner: Medicolegal Death Investigation in the Granite State, see 45 N.H.B.J. 14 (2004).

For article, "Purposely Negligent: Revisiting New Hampshire's Accomplice Liability Precedent After State v. Anthony, see 46 N.H.B.J. 14 (2005).

630:1. Capital Murder.

I. A person is guilty of capital murder if he knowingly causes the death of:

(a) A law enforcement officer or a judicial officer acting in the line of duty or when the death is caused as a consequence of or in retaliation for such person's actions in the line of duty;

(b) Another before, after, while engaged in the commission of, or while attempting to commit kidnapping as that offense is defined in RSA 633:1;

(c) Another by criminally soliciting a person to cause said death or after having been criminally solicited by another for his personal pecuniary gain;

(d) Another after being sentenced to life imprisonment without parole pursuant to RSA 630:1-a, III;

(e) Another before, after, while engaged in the commission of, or while attempting to commit aggravated felonious sexual assault as defined in RSA 632-A:2;

(f) Another before, after, while engaged in the commission of, or while attempting to commit an offense punishable under RSA 318-B:26, I(a) or (b); or

(g) Another, who is licensed or privileged to be within an occupied structure, or separately secured or occupied section thereof, before, after, or while in the commission of, or while attempting to commit, burglary as defined in RSA 635:1.

II. As used in this section, a "law enforcement officer" is a sheriff or deputy sheriff of any county, a state police officer, a constable or police officer of any city or town, an official or employee of any prison, jail or corrections institution, a probation-parole officer, or a conservation officer.

II-a. As used in this section, a "judicial officer" is a judge of a district, probate, superior or supreme court; an attorney employed by the department of justice or a municipal prosecutor's office; or a county attorney; or attorney employed by the county attorney.

III. A person convicted of a capital murder may be punished by death.

IV. As used in this section and RSA 630:1-a, 1-b, 2, 3 and 4, the meaning of "another" does not include a foetus.

V. In no event shall any person under the age of 18 years at the time the offense was committed be culpable of a capital murder.

Source.
1971, 518:1. 1974, 34:1. 1977, 440:1; 588:41. 1988, 69:1, 2. 1990, 199:1. 1994, 128:1, 2, eff. Jan. 1, 1995. 2005, 35:1, eff. January 1, 2006. 2011, 222:2, eff. July 1, 2011.

Amendments
—2011. The 2011 amendment added I(g) and made a related change.

—2005. Paragraph V: Substituted "of 18 years at the time the offense was committed be culpable" for "of 17 years be culpable".

—1994. Paragraph I(a): Inserted "or a judicial officer" preceding "acting in the line of duty" and added "or when the death is caused as a consequence of or in retaliation for such person's actions in the line of duty" thereafter.
Paragraph II-a: Added.

—1990. Paragraph I: Added subpars. (e) and (f).

—1988. Paragraph I: Made a minor stylistic change at the end of subpar. (c) and added subpar. (d).
Paragraph II: Inserted "a probation-parole officer" preceding "or a conservation officer" at the end of the paragraph.

—1977. Paragraph III: Chapter 440 substituted "may" for "shall" following "murder".
Paragraph IV: Chapter 588 inserted "and" preceding "4" and deleted "and 5" thereafter.

—1974. Rewritten to the extent that a detailed comparison would be impracticable.

Findings and Purpose.
2011, 222:1, eff. July 1, 2011, provided: "The legislature finds and declares that:
"I. The purposes of the criminal justice system include providing an organized means for achieving justice so that individuals do not need or feel compelled to seek justice on their own; and
"II. It is in the interest of the community to ensure that all know justice for personal wrongs committed against them may be achieved through the criminal justice system and that the state has criminal sanctions that properly and proportionately respond to the acts being sanctioned; and
"III. Protection of law-abiding residents in their homes may be promoted in part by the state imposing sanctions that are commensurate with the wrongs committed by criminals who would invade the homes of others; and
"IV. An additional purpose of the criminal justice system is to protect law-abiding residents of the state from the violence of others, particularly in their homes whether they are alone or with family, and deserving of a place of respite and safety; and
"V. In order to realize these purposes and address community interest, the legislature has determined that there is a need to increase the sanction for such home invasions which are perpetrated with the intent to commit murder. In doing so, the legislature intends to enhance, and has determined and found that it will enhance, the potential for prevention of such acts by others who may contemplate such acts, while at the same time vindicating the community's belief in justice and the legitimacy of the criminal justice system when adjudicating the worst of crimes; and
"VI. In response to recent incidents involving home invasions in which the intent of those committing such invasions is to murder the occupants and in which deaths of occupants have resulted, and in response to the October 4, 2009 murder of Kimberly L. Cates of Mont Vernon, the legislature declares this act to be known as The Kimberly L. Cates Law."

Cross References.
Appointment of counsel for indigent charged with capital offense, see RSA 604-A:2.
Charging manner of death, see RSA 601:6.
Disallowance of bail, see RSA 597:1-c.
Jury trial in capital cases, see New Hampshire Constitution, Part 1, Article 16.
Procedure in capital murder, see RSA 630:5.
Rights of persons indicted in capital cases, see RSA 604:1.
Victims permitted to speak before sentencing, see RSA 651:4-a.

NOTES TO DECISIONS

1. Constitutionality
2. Construction
3. Elements
4. Kidnapping
5. Jury instructions

1. Constitutionality
This section is not unconstitutional as a bill of attainder, since it does not provide for a legislative, rather than a judicial, determination of guilt. State v. McPhail, 116 N.H. 440, 362 A.2d 199, 1976 N.H. LEXIS 377 (1976).

2. Construction
Plain language of RSA 630:1, I(c) creates two categories: those who solicit and those who are solicited. The "last antecedent rule" supports applying the qualifying phrase "for his own pecuniary

gain" to only the second category, those who are solicited to kill; accordingly, the statute did not require that defendant must have acted for his own pecuniary gain. State v. Brooks, 164 N.H. 272, 56 A.3d 1245, 2012 N.H. LEXIS 141 (2012).

Based on the definition of live birth in RSA 5-C:1, XIX and the legislative intent, the Supreme Court of New Hampshire holds that, at the very least, an expelled or extracted fetus must show some spontaneous sign of life before it is considered "another" and its death can result in criminal prosecution under the codified continuation of the born alive rule in RSA 630:1, IV. State v. Lamy, 158 N.H. 511, 969 A.2d 451, 2009 N.H. LEXIS 45 (2009).

If one solicits another to commit murder and the one solicited does kill, then the one who solicited is guilty of capital murder under this section. State v. Kilgus, 128 N.H. 577, 519 A.2d 231, 1986 N.H. LEXIS 372 (1986).

If one solicits another to commit murder and the one solicited does not kill, then the one who solicited is guilty of criminal solicitation under RSA 629:2. State v. Kilgus, 128 N.H. 577, 519 A.2d 231, 1986 N.H. LEXIS 372 (1986).

Solicitation of another to commit murder may constitute an attempt to commit murder under RSA 629:1 when the defendant has completed all the necessary preliminary steps for the hired murder to take place. State v. Kilgus, 128 N.H. 577, 519 A.2d 231, 1986 N.H. LEXIS 372 (1986).

3. Elements

As a fetus that was born early following injuries to its mother as a result of a vehicle collision caused by defendant never displayed any spontaneous sign of life prior to its death, it was error to convict defendant of involuntary manslaughter and negligent homicide, in violation of RSA 630:2, I and RSA 630:3; the fetus was not "another" for purposes of a homicide prosecution under the "born alive" rule under RSA 630:1, IV. State v. Lamy, 158 N.H. 511, 969 A.2d 451, 2009 N.H. LEXIS 45 (2009).

In order to support a conviction under paragraph I of this section, it must be shown that the accused acted purposely to cause the death of another: there must be not only an intention to kill, but also a deliberate and premeditated design to kill. Elbert v. Cunningham, 616 F. Supp. 433, 1985 U.S. Dist. LEXIS 16980 (D.N.H. 1985).

Where the evidence in a prosecution for attempted first degree murder indicated that the victim, after perceiving her attacker and being threatened, ran several steps before she was shot in the head from behind, there was sufficient evidence that the defendant had time for reflection and consideration and deliberately attempted to inflict a lethal wound on the victim to warrant submission of the charge to a jury for consideration. Elbert v. Cunningham, 616 F. Supp. 433, 1985 U.S. Dist. LEXIS 16980 (D.N.H. 1985).

4. Kidnapping

New Hampshire Supreme Court considers the merger doctrine to apply to a capital murder charge based upon kidnapping, since the kidnapping is an element of the offense that the State must prove beyond a reasonable doubt. The court agrees with the view taken by the majority of jurisdictions, and hold that a kidnapping conviction cannot rest on unlawful confinements or movements incidental to the commission of other felonies. State v. Brooks, 164 N.H. 272, 56 A.3d 1245, 2012 N.H. LEXIS 141 (2012).

5. Jury instructions

With regard to capital murder based on kidnapping, the trial court's instructions to the jury required a unanimous decision as to whether defendant confined the victim for the purpose of terrorizing him, or, if the purpose of the confinement was to kill the victim, whether "the confinement was contemplated or expected to last for some appreciable period of time beyond that necessary to accomplish the killing." There was no error in this instruction. State v. Brooks, 164 N.H. 272, 56 A.3d 1245, 2012 N.H. LEXIS 141 (2012).

Cited:

Cited in State v. Lordan, 116 N.H. 479, 363 A.2d 201, 1976 N.H. LEXIS 387 (1976); State v. Stewart, 116 N.H. 585, 364 A.2d 621, 1976 N.H. LEXIS 419 (1976); State v. Darcy, 121 N.H. 220, 427 A.2d 516, 1981 N.H. LEXIS 283 (1981); Pugliese v. Perrin, 567 F. Supp. 1337, 1983 U.S. Dist. LEXIS 15416 (D.N.H. 1983); State v. Plante,

133 N.H. 384, 577 A.2d 95, 1990 N.H. LEXIS 75 (1990); State v. Tallard, 143 N.H. 228, 723 A.2d 574, 1998 N.H. LEXIS 95 (1998).

630:1-a. First Degree Murder.

I. A person is guilty of murder in the first degree if he:

(a) Purposely causes the death of another; or

(b) Knowingly causes the death of:

(1) Another before, after, while engaged in the commission of, or while attempting to commit felonious sexual assault as defined in RSA 632-A:3;

(2) Another before, after, while engaged in the commission of, or while attempting to commit robbery or burglary while armed with a deadly weapon, the death being caused by the use of such weapon;

(3) Another in perpetrating or attempting to perpetrate arson as defined in RSA 634:1, I, II, or III;

(4) The president or president-elect or vice-president or vice-president-elect of the United States, the governor or governor-elect of New Hampshire or any state or any member or member-elect of the congress of the United States, or any candidate for such office after such candidate has been nominated at his party's primary, when such killing is motivated by knowledge of the foregoing capacity of the victim.

II. For the purpose of RSA 630:1-a, I(a), "purposely" shall mean that the actor's conscious object is the death of another, and that his act or acts in furtherance of that object were deliberate and premeditated.

III. A person convicted of a murder in the first degree shall be sentenced to life imprisonment and shall not be eligible for parole at any time.

Source.
1974, 34:2. 1986, 132:3. 1990, 199:2, eff. Jan. 1, 1991.

Amendments
—1990. Paragraph I(b)(1): Deleted "aggravated felonious sexual assault as defined in RSA 632-A:2 or" following "commit".

—1986. Paragraph I(b)(1): Rewritten to the extent that a detailed comparison would be impracticable.

Cross References.
Charging manner of death, see RSA 601:6.
Disallowance of bail, see RSA 597:1-c.
Rights of persons indicted for first degree murder, see RSA 604:1.
Victims permitted to speak before sentencing, see RSA 651:4-a.

NOTES TO DECISIONS

1. Constitutionality
2. Elements
3. Lesser included offenses
4. Indictment
5. State's burden of proof
6. Classification of offense
7. Felony-murder
8. Evidence
9. Instructions
10. Right of allocution
11. Sentence

12. Parole
13. Subsequent wrongful death suit
14. Merger with other offenses
15. Double jeopardy
16. Provocation

1. Constitutionality

Paragraph III of this section does not constitute cruel and unusual punishment, either on grounds that the sentence is disproportional or on grounds that the sentence does not comport with basic notions of human dignity. State v. Farrow, 118 N.H. 296, 386 A.2d 808, 1978 N.H. LEXIS 402 (1978).

2. Elements

Defendant's double jeopardy rights under N.H. Const. pt. I, art. 16, and U.S. Const. amend. V, were not violated because, as charged, each indictment required the State to prove a fact not necessary to the other; specifically, the State did not have to prove the existence of an agreement, required for the conspiracy conviction, to prove the first degree murder charge, and the conspiracy indictment did not require the State to prove the enhanced mental state of deliberation and premeditation, required for a first degree murder conviction. State v. Sanchez, 152 N.H. 625, 883 A.2d 292, 2005 N.H. LEXIS 149 (2005).

Defendant's conviction for first-degree murder in the course of rape, in violation of RSA 630:1-a, was proper even though New Hampshire's rape statute had been repealed at the time of the offense; the legislature's failure to remove the word "rape" from RSA 630:1-a, I(b)(1) when it repealed RSA 632 was an oversight and did not nullify that provision of the first-degree murder statute. State v. Whittey, 149 N.H. 463, 821 A.2d 1086, 2003 N.H. LEXIS 64 (2003).

The elements of premeditation and deliberation necessary to prove first degree murder require that there be not only intention to kill, but also a deliberate and premeditated design to kill; such design must precede the killing by some appreciable space of time, but the time need not be long. State v. Place, 126 N.H. 613, 495 A.2d 1253, 1985 N.H. LEXIS 369 (1985); State v. Shackford, 127 N.H. 695, 506 A.2d 315, 1986 N.H. LEXIS 223 (1986).

While the object of the requirement of premeditation and deliberation, in a first degree murder charge, is to rule out action on sudden impulse, no particular period of premeditation and deliberation is required. State v. Shackford, 127 N.H. 695, 506 A.2d 315, 1986 N.H. LEXIS 223 (1986).

Whether the deliberate and premeditated design to kill necessary for a charge of first degree murder was formed must be determined from all the circumstances of the case. State v. Place, 126 N.H. 613, 495 A.2d 1253, 1985 N.H. LEXIS 369 (1985); State v. Shackford, 127 N.H. 695, 506 A.2d 315, 1986 N.H. LEXIS 223 (1986).

As elements of first-degree murder under paragraph II of this section, premeditation and deliberation require proof beyond a reasonable doubt of some reflection and consideration upon the choice to kill or not to kill, and the formation of a definite purpose to kill, and while the object of the requirement is to rule out action on sudden impulse, no particular period of premeditation and deliberation is required. State v. Elbert, 125 N.H. 1, 480 A.2d 854, 1984 N.H. LEXIS 371 (1984).

Malice, as an essential element of the crime of murder, is not an inference of law from the mere act of killing, but like any other fact in issue it must be found by the jury upon competent evidence. State v. Greenleaf, 71 N.H. 606, 54 A. 38, 1902 N.H. LEXIS 91 (1902). (Decided under prior law.)

3. Lesser included offenses

Manslaughter is a lesser included offense of murder and indictment for murder contains all allegations essential to charge manslaughter, so that one indicted for murder may be convicted of manslaughter. Nichols v. Vitek, 114 N.H. 453, 321 A.2d 570, 1974 N.H. LEXIS 299 (1974).

4. Indictment

The word "purposely" as defined in paragraph II of this section satisfies the common law malice aforethought requirement in a first-degree murder indictment. State v. Glidden, 123 N.H. 126, 459

A.2d 1136, 1983 N.H. LEXIS 240 (1983).

Supreme court would quash attempted murder indictment where, by reading the indictment, defendant could not know whether he was indicted for attempting to purposely cause the death of another or for attempting to knowingly cause the death of another after having been engaged in the commission of rape. State v. Bussiere, 118 N.H. 659, 392 A.2d 151, 1978 N.H. LEXIS 263 (1978).

5. State's burden of proof

To warrant a conviction of murder in the first degree, the state had to prove beyond a reasonable doubt not only that the killing was done with malice, but also that it was deliberate and premeditated or done in perpetrating or attempting to perpetrate a collateral felony. State v. Nelson, 103 N.H. 478, 175 A.2d 814, 1961 N.H. LEXIS 71 (1961), cert. denied, Nelson v. New Hampshire, 369 U.S. 879, 82 S. Ct. 1153, 8 L. Ed. 2d 282, 1962 U.S. LEXIS 1339 (1962), cert. denied, Martineau v. New Hampshire, 369 U.S. 881, 82 S. Ct. 1155, 8 L. Ed. 2d 283, 1962 U.S. LEXIS 1351 (1962). (Decided under prior law.)

To warrant a conviction of murder in the first degree, it was incumbent on the state to prove beyond a reasonable doubt that the homicide was malicious, and also that the crime was deliberate and premeditated, in the natural or ordinary sense of those words, or else committed in perpetrating or attempting to perpetrate one of the collateral felonies specified in this section. State v. Greenleaf, 71 N.H. 606, 54 A. 38, 1902 N.H. LEXIS 91 (1902). (Decided under prior law.)

6. Classification of offense

A husband who can supply his wife with the necessities of life, and neglects to do so while she is living with him and is incapable of taking care of herself by reason of sickness or other cause, is guilty of the crime of murder or manslaughter, according to the nature and degree of the negligence in respect to premeditation, wilfulness, recklessness, and culpability, if her death is caused or hastened by such neglect. Gendron v. St. Pierre, 73 N.H. 419, 62 A. 966, 1905 N.H. LEXIS 74 (1905). (Decided under prior law.)

Under an indictment alleging that the accused feloniously, wilfully and of his malice aforethought, did kill and murder the named victim, the jury may return a verdict of guilty of murder in the first degree upon proof of murder by deliberate and premeditated killing, or under such indictment the jury may return the same verdict upon proof of murder committed in perpetrating robbery. State v. Pike, 49 N.H. 399, 1870 N.H. LEXIS 33 (1870), overruled in part, Hardy v. Merrill, 56 N.H. 227, 1875 N.H. LEXIS 38 (1875). (Decided under prior law.)

7. Felony-murder

Where death results to the victim as a result of the commission of the crime of robbery, it is not error for the court to refuse to give an instruction on any other degree of homicide other than first degree murder. State v. Thorp, 86 N.H. 501, 171 A. 633, 1934 N.H. LEXIS 91 (1934). (Decided under prior law.)

Homicide in furtherance of a design to commit rape was murder in the first degree, although the rape intended was neither consummated nor begun. State v. Greenleaf, 71 N.H. 606, 54 A. 38, 1902 N.H. LEXIS 91 (1902). (Decided under prior law.)

Murder committed in perpetrating a robbery is murder of the first degree, although not committed with a deliberate and premeditated design to kill. State v. Pike, 49 N.H. 399, 1870 N.H. LEXIS 33 (1870), overruled in part, Hardy v. Merrill, 56 N.H. 227, 1875 N.H. LEXIS 38 (1875). (Decided under prior law.)

8. Evidence

In a first-degree murder case under RSA 630:1-a, there was sufficient evidence that defendant's assault on the victim caused the victim's death 14 years later. The victim had no preexisting medical condition; six experts testified to her brain damage, its cause, and its risks; and a medical examiner testified that her death was caused by defendant's 1991 assault on her. State v. Hutchinson, 161 N.H. 765, 20 A.3d 972, 2011 N.H. LEXIS 57 (2011).

In a first-degree murder trial, any error in admitting cell phone records and in excluding evidence of alternative perpetrators was harmless. Even without the phone evidence, there was ample evidence that defendant was at or near the crime scene, and compared to evidence of his motive and opportunity, the alternative perpetrator evidence was inconsequential. State v. Peters, 162 N.H. 30, 27 A.3d 765, 2011 N.H. LEXIS 65 (2011).

When an officer testifying under N.H. R. Evid. 701 characterized defendant's emotions as "feigned," and described his body language as overexaggerated and overly dramatic, this was tantamount to a improper comment on his credibility. The error was harmless, however, given the overwhelming evidence of guilt of first-degree murder and the cumulative nature of the inadmissible evidence. State v. McDonald, 163 N.H. 115, 35 A.3d 605, 2011 N.H. LEXIS 192 (Dec. 28, 2011).

Evidence was sufficient to support an attempted murder conviction under RSA 630:1-a and RSA 629:1, either as a principal or as an accomplice. Witness testimony supported the facts that defendant and a second man possessed guns, tracked the car occupied by the victim, took aim at multiple targets on the car where people would be expected to be located, and together discharged numerous gunshots with the intention of killing the victim, against whom defendant bore a longtime grudge; even if the evidence failed to establish that any bullet fired by the defendant actually struck the victim, actual injury was not an element of the crime. State v. Young, 159 N.H. 332, 986 A.2d 497, 2009 N.H. LEXIS 122 (2009).

Trial court properly denied defendant's motion to exclude the testimony of the State's expert psychiatrist on the issue of whether defendant's murder of his mother was the product of mental illness or defect, and it did not engage in an unsustainable exercise of its discretion in admitting the testimony of the expert, as the expert had a medical background and experience in treating mental illness and his opinion likely aided the jury to understand the complexities of mental illness and the multitude of behaviors likely to stem from mental illness. The trial court also gave the jury a clear instruction that, as the fact finder, it was not bound by the expert's opinion, and was free to reject it. State v. Labranche, 156 N.H. 740, 942 A.2d 1284, 2008 N.H. LEXIS 17 (2008).

Where defendant who was on trial for first-degree murder in violation of RSA 630:1-a asserted self-defense and placed his state of mind at issue, the State had the burden to prove that defendant acted purposely when he shot the victim and did so with premeditation and deliberation. Evidence of his drug dealings was properly admitted to show that his motivation for going to the motel where he killed the victim was to preserve his drug business and not to protect his friend. State v. Smalley, 151 N.H. 193, 855 A.2d 401, 2004 N.H. LEXIS 113 (2004).

Assuming that a trial court erred in denying an evidentiary hearing on the admission of certain deoxyribonucleic acid (DNA) evidence, the other evidence at trial was so overwhelming that the murder verdict was not affected by the error: defendant admitted that the bloodstained clothing found at the scene was his, defendant and the victim had recently argued, the wounds on the victim's body and skull matched a hatchet that defendant had recently purchased, and defendant fled after the murder, changed his appearance, and assumed a new identity. State v. Thompson, 149 N.H. 565, 825 A.2d 490, 2003 N.H. LEXIS 81 (2003).

Evidence was sufficient to convince a rational juror that defendant acted with premeditation and deliberation in killing his mother and stepfather where defendant used a heavy wooden mallet, a weapon capable of producing death, to carry out the attack, and inflicted several severe wounds on each victim. State v. Patten, 148 N.H. 659, 813 A.2d 497, 2002 N.H. LEXIS 198 (2002).

Evidence was sufficient to support convictions for attempted murder as an "accomplice/principal" based on the shooting of the victims where shoe print evidence and the defendant's own statement placed him at the scene of the shooting and additional evidence supported the jury's conclusion that the defendant's involvement exceeded mere presence. State v. Duguay, 142 N.H. 221, 698 A.2d 5, 1997 N.H. LEXIS 79 (1997).

Evidence was sufficient to establish that the defendant, as an accomplice, committed two counts of attempted murder, one count of attempted arson, and one count of attempted falsification of evidence, where a witness testified that, mere hours after the incident, the defendant admitted that he had accompanied his coperpetrator to the scene of the crime, that they planned to rob whomever they discovered there, by violent means if necessary, that the defendant and the coperpetrator hid behind a bush while the latter twice shot at a car, that after the victims abandoned the car they searched it for valuables and money, and that there was an attempt to destroy the car following the search for valuables. State v. Laudarowicz, 142 N.H. 1, 694 A.2d 980, 1997 N.H. LEXIS 47 (1997).

Graphic color photographs and videotape of the bloodied and strangled victims were clearly relevant to prove defendant possessed the mental state that he so vigorously denied possessing; the condition of the bodies supported an inference concerning the amount of force used by the perpetrator, and evidence of degree of force was relevant because it tended to prove that defendant acted with the requisite mental state. State v. Seymour, 140 N.H. 736, 673 A.2d 786, 1996 N.H. LEXIS 24 (1996), cert. denied, Seymour v. New Hampshire, 519 U.S. 853, 117 S. Ct. 146, 136 L. Ed. 2d 93, 1996 U.S. LEXIS 5265 (1996).

Defendant failed to establish that the trial court's decision to permit the introduction of photograph of victims together while alive was clearly untenable or unreasonable to the prejudice of his case where the State maintained that it was admissible to allow the jury to identify the people who were the subjects of the murder prosecution. State v. Seymour, 140 N.H. 736, 673 A.2d 786, 1996 N.H. LEXIS 24 (1996), cert. denied, Seymour v. New Hampshire, 519 U.S. 853, 117 S. Ct. 146, 136 L. Ed. 2d 93, 1996 U.S. LEXIS 5265 (1996).

There was sufficient evidence of premeditation and deliberation to sustain a verdict of first degree murder, where defendant abandoned his plans and instead followed the victim, loaded his .357 magnum revolver, pulled out the gun, cocked it, aimed it at victim's head, then forced the gun into victim's back and pulled the trigger. State v. Herrick, 133 N.H. 694, 582 A.2d 613, 1990 N.H. LEXIS 123 (1990).

Circumstantial evidence which may be weighed by the jury, in its determination whether there was sufficient premeditation and deliberation to support a charge of first degree murder, includes the character of the weapon employed, the force and number of blows inflicted, the location and severity of the wounds, the place of the crime, previous remarks and conduct indicating preparation, subsequent acts and statements, and every circumstance having a legitimate bearing upon the subject. State v. Place, 126 N.H. 613, 495 A.2d 1253, 1985 N.H. LEXIS 369 (1985).

Upon the trial of a charge of murder in the first degree, each subsidiary fact based on the issue of premeditation did not have to be established beyond a reasonable doubt, provided the evidence as a whole was sufficient to warrant the verdict returned. State v. George, 93 N.H. 408, 43 A.2d 256, 1945 N.H. LEXIS 148 (1945). (Decided under prior law.)

Upon the trial of the charge of murder in the first degree, uncontradicted evidence of the jealousy and anger of the accused could justify conclusions by the jury that he brought the murder weapon to the house of the deceased with the purpose of using it as he did, and this fact would clearly establish premeditation beyond a reasonable doubt. State v. George, 93 N.H. 408, 43 A.2d 256, 1945 N.H. LEXIS 148 (1945). (Decided under prior law.)

Upon trial of an indictment for murder, evidence as to the character of the weapon employed, the force and number of the blows inflicted, the location and severity of the wounds, the place of the crime, previous conduct and remarks of the accused indicating preparation, and his subsequent acts and statements inconsistent with innocence, was properly submitted to the jury as bearing upon the questions of malice and deliberation. State v. Greenleaf, 71 N.H. 606, 54 A. 38, 1902 N.H. LEXIS 91 (1902). (Decided under prior law.)

9. Instructions

In a first-degree murder prosecution under RSA 630:1-a, I(a), where a defendant presents evidence to support a rational finding of provocation manslaughter, juries should be instructed that to find the defendant guilty of first-degree murder the State must prove beyond a reasonable doubt: (1) that the defendant caused the death of the victim; (2) that he acted "purposely" under the special definition of that term in RSA 630:1-a, II; and (3) that he did not act under the influence of extreme mental or emotional disturbance caused by extreme provocation. The jury should also be given an acquittal first instruction indicating that, if the jury finds the defendant not guilty of first-degree murder pursuant to the foregoing instructions, it should next consider whether the State has proved, again beyond a reasonable doubt, the elements of second-degree murder under RSA 630:1-b, I(a): (1) that the defendant caused the death of the victim; (2) that he acted knowingly; and (3) that he did not act under the influence of extreme mental or emotional disturbance caused by extreme provocation. State v. Soto, 162 N.H. 708, 34 A.3d 738, 2011 N.H. LEXIS 169 (2011).

In a first-degree murder prosecution under RSA 630:1-a, I(a) (2007), where a defendant presents evidence to support a rational finding of provocation manslaughter, the jury should be given the acquittal first instruction and told that if it finds the defendant not guilty of second-degree murder, it should then go on to consider whether he is guilty of provocation manslaughter, the elements of this offense being: (1) that the defendant caused the death of the victim; and (2) that the defendant acted either purposely or knowingly. The jury should also be instructed that, if it reaches the crime of provocation manslaughter in its deliberations, the defendant may be found guilty of this crime if the State proves the foregoing two elements beyond a reasonable doubt even if the jury concludes that the defendant acted under the influence of extreme mental or emotional disturbance caused by extreme provocation. State v. Soto, 162 N.H. 708, 34 A.3d 738, 2011 N.H. LEXIS 169 (2011).

In a murder case, the evidence, taken in a light most favorable to defendant, supported the conclusion that no reasonable jury could have found defendant guilty of provocation manslaughter, even if the trial court had instructed the jury as defendant requested regarding provocation manslaughter as a lesser-included offense of first degree murder. Given the overwhelming evidence of defendant's guilt of first degree murder, the trial court's error did not affect the verdict. State v. O'Leary, 153 N.H. 710, 903 A.2d 997, 2006 N.H. LEXIS 95 (2006), rehearing denied, 2006 N.H. LEXIS 137 (N.H. Aug. 24, 2006).

Trial court did not abuse its discretion in refusing the "mere presence" instruction because to the extent there was any question about defendant's mere presence at the scene, instructions to the jury that the State must prove, first, that the defendant caused the death of another person and, second, that the defendant did so purposely were adequate to convey to the jurors their obligation to acquit if mere presence were all that had been proved. State v. Seymour, 140 N.H. 736, 673 A.2d 786, 1996 N.H. LEXIS 24 (1996), cert. denied, Seymour v. New Hampshire, 519 U.S. 853, 117 S. Ct. 146, 136 L. Ed. 2d 93, 1996 U.S. LEXIS 5265 (1996).

10. Right of allocution

Trial court did not abuse its discretion in refusing to allow defendant to speak to court before it imposed the only possible sentence, which was a mandatory life sentence without possibility of parole. State v. Vandebogart, 139 N.H. 145, 652 A.2d 671, 1994 N.H. LEXIS 125 (1994).

11. Sentence

When this section, RSA 651:1, I, and RSA 651:20, I(a), are read together, RSA 651:20, I(a), cannot be construed to allow persons convicted of first degree murder to petition for sentence suspension; such a construction, if adopted, would defeat the underlying legislative intent of these statutes by providing new opportunities for first degree murderers to return to society. State v. Farrow, 140 N.H. 473, 667 A.2d 1029, 1995 N.H. LEXIS 174 (1995).

Although RSA 651:20, I(a), confers general discretion upon a sentencing court to suspend a sentence, this section and RSA 651:1, I, clearly and specifically limit the court's authority in sentencing first degree murderers and, because this section and RSA 651:1, I, provide specific exceptions to the more general rule found in RSA 651:20, I(a), they control. State v. Farrow, 140 N.H. 473, 667 A.2d 1029, 1995 N.H. LEXIS 174 (1995).

Permanent isolation from the community of persons convicted of first-degree murder, prescribed by paragraph III of this section, bears a rational relationship to the need to protect society against murderers. State v. Farrow, 118 N.H. 296, 386 A.2d 808, 1978 N.H. LEXIS 402 (1978).

12. Parole

Seeking to avert any miscarriage of justice that occurs when parole authorities release dangerous felons by restricting power to release persons convicted of first-degree murder to governor through his pardoning power furthers state's goal of protecting society against murderers. State v. Farrow, 118 N.H. 296, 386 A.2d 808, 1978 N.H. LEXIS 402 (1978).

13. Subsequent wrongful death suit

Conduct underlying a conviction of first-degree murder, as a matter of law, was wanton, malicious, and oppressive and therefore justified an award of liberal compensatory damages in a civil wrongful death case. Stewart v. Bader, 154 N.H. 75, 907 A.2d 931, 2006 N.H. LEXIS 121 (2006).

14. Merger with other offenses

Intentionally trying to kill a person and knowingly inflicting bodily injury on that same person do not constitute two distinct criminal activities when the identical criminal conduct is the basis of both charges; the legislature did not intend for identical criminal conduct to give rise to distinct charges for first degree assault and attempted murder. Thus, because the same shooting was the basis of both the attempted murder and assault indictments, under the common law doctrine of merger, the trial court erred by imposing consecutive sentences for the convictions regarding the same victim. State v. Young, 159 N.H. 332, 986 A.2d 497, 2009 N.H. LEXIS 122 (2009).

15. Double jeopardy

Double jeopardy under U.S. Const. amend. V and N.H. Const. pt. I, art. 16 did not prohibit defendant's trial for reckless second-degree murder and knowing second-degree murder after his acquittal of first-degree felony murder and a declaration of mistrial on a second-degree murder charge. The charges of first-degree felony murder and the charge of reckless second-degree murder did not require proof of the same mens rea; the charge of reckless second-degree murder did not include the element that defendant killed the victim while engaged in robbery; and while the trial court had instructed the jury on knowing second-degree murder as a lesser included offense of first-degree felony murder, the jury made no finding on that offense. State v. Glenn, 160 N.H. 480, 9 A.3d 161, 2010 N.H. LEXIS 81 (July 20, 2010).

There was no merit to defendant's argument that the jury, by acquitting him of first-degree felony murder, necessarily found that he did not shoot and kill the victim, thereby barring his reprosecution under the Double Jeopardy Clause; the jury could have based its acquittal for the first-degree felony murder on other grounds, such as finding that defendant did not attempt to rob the victim at the time of the shooting. Therefore, the United States Supreme Court's decision in *Yeager* did not bar defendant's retrial for second degree knowing or reckless murder, neither of which required proof of robbery for conviction. State v. Glenn, 160 N.H. 480, 9 A.3d 161, 2010 N.H. LEXIS 81 (July 20, 2010).

16. Provocation

Although provocation is only a partial rather than a full defense, because it can operate both to reduce the mens rea required for murder and to provide a basis for the jury's invocation of the community's sense of compassion, provocation, when properly raised, should be treated similarly to self-defense. Accordingly, in a murder prosecution, the State must prove the absence of provocation beyond a reasonable doubt when the defendant presents some evidence to support a rational finding that he caused the death at issue under the influence of extreme mental or emotional disturbance caused by extreme provocation. State v. Soto, 162 N.H. 708, 34 A.3d 738, 2011 N.H. LEXIS 169 (2011).

Cited:

Cited in State v. Williams, 115 N.H. 437, 343 A.2d 29, 1975 N.H. LEXIS 331 (1975); State v. Lordan, 116 N.H. 479, 363 A.2d 201, 1976 N.H. LEXIS 387 (1976); State v. Breest, 116 N.H. 734, 367 A.2d 1320, 1976 N.H. LEXIS 463 (1976); State v. La Roche, 117 N.H. 127, 370 A.2d 631, 1977 N.H. LEXIS 283 (1977); State v. Smith, 119 N.H. 674, 406 A.2d 135, 1979 N.H. LEXIS 353 (1979); State v. Baker, 120 N.H. 773, 424 A.2d 171, 1980 N.H. LEXIS 401 (1980); State v. Darcy, 121 N.H. 220, 427 A.2d 516, 1981 N.H. LEXIS 283 (1981); In re E., 121 N.H. 836, 435 A.2d 833, 1981 N.H. LEXIS 421 (1981); Roy v. Perrin, 122 N.H. 88, 441 A.2d 1151, 1982 N.H. LEXIS 292 (1982); State v. Lister, 122 N.H. 603, 448 A.2d 395, 1982 N.H. LEXIS 410 (1982); State v. Comtois, 122 N.H. 1173, 453

A.2d 1324, 1982 N.H. LEXIS 535 (1982); State v. Sadvari, 123 N.H. 410, 462 A.2d 102, 1983 N.H. LEXIS 294 (1983); State v. Hamel, 123 N.H. 670, 466 A.2d 555, 1983 N.H. LEXIS 332 (1983); State v. Lessard, 123 N.H. 788, 465 A.2d 516, 1983 N.H. LEXIS 329 (1983); State v. Labonville, 126 N.H. 451, 492 A.2d 1376, 1985 N.H. LEXIS 302 (1985); State v. Dayutis, 127 N.H. 101, 498 A.2d 325, 1985 N.H. LEXIS 379 (1985); State v. Elbert, 128 N.H. 210, 512 A.2d 1114, 1986 N.H. LEXIS 280 (1986); State v. Allen, 128 N.H. 390, 514 A.2d 1263, 1986 N.H. LEXIS 309 (1986); State v. Pliskaner, 128 N.H. 486, 517 A.2d 795, 1986 N.H. LEXIS 329 (1986); State v. Therrien, 129 N.H. 765, 533 A.2d 346, 1987 N.H. LEXIS 261 (1987); State v. Riccio, 130 N.H. 376, 540 A.2d 1239, 1988 N.H. LEXIS 8 (1988); State v. Briand, 130 N.H. 650, 547 A.2d 235, 1988 N.H. LEXIS 77 (1988); State v. Bruneau, 131 N.H. 104, 552 A.2d 585, 1988 N.H. LEXIS 106 (1988); State v. Moulton, 131 N.H. 467, 554 A.2d 1292, 1989 N.H. LEXIS 10 (1989); State v. McDermott, 131 N.H. 495, 554 A.2d 1302, 1989 N.H. LEXIS 14 (1989); State v. Nicholas H., 131 N.H. 569, 560 A.2d 1156, 1989 N.H. LEXIS 21 (1989); State v. Brown, 132 N.H. 520, 567 A.2d 544, 1989 N.H. LEXIS 140 (1989); State v. Fowler, 132 N.H. 540, 567 A.2d 557, 1989 N.H. LEXIS 142 (1989); Bussiere v. Cunningham, 132 N.H. 747, 571 A.2d 908, 1990 N.H. LEXIS 19 (1990); State v. Eason, 133 N.H. 335, 577 A.2d 1203, 1990 N.H. LEXIS 66 (1990); State v. Gibney, 133 N.H. 890, 587 A.2d 607, 1991 N.H. LEXIS 7 (1991); State v. Whittey, 134 N.H. 310, 591 A.2d 1326, 1991 N.H. LEXIS 58 (1991); State v. VandeBogart, 136 N.H. 365, 616 A.2d 483, 1992 N.H. LEXIS 181 (1992); Brown v. Powell, 975 F.2d 1, 1992 U.S. App. LEXIS 16048 (1st Cir. N.H. 1992); State v. Hutchinson, 137 N.H. 591, 631 A.2d 523, 1993 N.H. LEXIS 131 (1993); State v. Girmay, 139 N.H. 292, 652 A.2d 150, 1994 N.H. LEXIS 148 (1994); State v. Vandebogart, 139 N.H. 145, 652 A.2d 671, 1994 N.H. LEXIS 125 (1994); State v. Lopez, 139 N.H. 309, 652 A.2d 696, 1994 N.H. LEXIS 144 (1994); State v. Taylor, 141 N.H. 89, 677 A.2d 1093, 1996 N.H. LEXIS 56 (1996); McLaughlin v. Moore, 152 F. Supp. 2d 123, 2001 U.S. Dist. LEXIS 6908 (D.N.H. 2001).

630:1-b. Second Degree Murder.

I. A person is guilty of murder in the second degree if:

(a) He knowingly causes the death of another; or

(b) He causes such death recklessly under circumstances manifesting an extreme indifference to the value of human life. Such recklessness and indifference are presumed if the actor causes the death by the use of a deadly weapon in the commission of, or in an attempt to commit, or in immediate flight after committing or attempting to commit any class A felony.

II. Murder in the second degree shall be punishable by imprisonment for life or for such term as the court may order.

Source.
1974, 34:2, eff. April 15, 1974.

Cross References.
Charging manner of death, see RSA 601:6.
Extended term of imprisonment, see RSA 651:6.
Maximum sentence for second degree murder, see RSA 651:2, II(d).
Parole of prisoner convicted of psycho-sexual murder, see RSA 651-A:8.
Parole of prisoner serving sentence of life imprisonment, see RSA 651-A:7.
Victims permitted to speak before sentencing, see RSA 651:4-a.

NOTES TO DECISIONS

1. Constitutionality
2. Construction
3. Elements
4. Voluntary intoxication
5. Lesser included offenses
6. Indictment
7. Accomplice liability
8. Evidence
9. Questions for jury
10. Jury instructions
11. Sentence
12. Double jeopardy
13. —Collateral estoppel
14. Provocation

1. Constitutionality

The phrase "extreme indifference to the value of human life" in subparagraph I(b) of this section is easily understood and not unconstitutionally vague. State v. Dow, 126 N.H. 205, 489 A.2d 650, 1985 N.H. LEXIS 248 (1985).

2. Construction

The phrase "circumstances manifesting an extreme indifference to the value of human life" in subparagraph I(b) of this section means something more than merely being aware of and consciously disregarding a substantial and unjustifiable risk. State v. Howland, 119 N.H. 413, 402 A.2d 188, 1979 N.H. LEXIS 313 (1979); State v. Dow, 126 N.H. 205, 489 A.2d 650, 1985 N.H. LEXIS 248 (1985).

3. Elements

Extreme indifference does not require proof of particularly vicious conduct; rather, critical factor is the degree to which defendant disregards the risk of death to another. State v. Schultz, 141 N.H. 101, 677 A.2d 675, 1996 N.H. LEXIS 54 (1996).

Where the accused's behavior "constitutes a gross deviation" from law-abiding conduct, but does not manifest "an extreme indifference to the value of human life," the jury may properly find only manslaughter; where, however, the evidence supports the additional element of "extreme indifference," the jury may find murder in the second degree. State v. Howland, 119 N.H. 413, 402 A.2d 188, 1979 N.H. LEXIS 313 (1979); State v. Dow, 126 N.H. 205, 489 A.2d 650, 1985 N.H. LEXIS 248 (1985).

4. Voluntary intoxication

At trial for second degree murder, evidence, that defendant, who was experienced in the safe use of operation of firearms, cocked a loaded revolver and held it point-blank against victim, after consuming alcoholic beverages, supported finding beyond a reasonable doubt that defendant acted recklessly under circumstances manifesting extreme indifference to the value of human life. State v. Eldridge, 134 N.H. 118, 588 A.2d 1222, 1991 N.H. LEXIS 28 (1991).

At trial for reckless second degree murder, court properly refused to recognize a defense of voluntary intoxication rendering the defendant unable to experience a mental state of "extreme indifference to the value of human life." State v. Dufield, 131 N.H. 35, 549 A.2d 1205, 1988 N.H. LEXIS 88 (1988).

5. Lesser included offenses

Conviction for the lesser-included offense of manslaughter constituted an acquittal on the charge of second-degree murder which bars a retrial on that charge. State v. Cameron, 121 N.H. 348, 430 A.2d 138, 1981 N.H. LEXIS 317 (1981).

Manslaughter is a lesser included offense to murder in the second degree. State v. Howland, 119 N.H. 413, 402 A.2d 188, 1979 N.H. LEXIS 313 (1979).

6. Indictment

In prosecution for murder, trial court did not err in denying pretrial motion to require state to elect to try only one of two indictments, one charging that the defendant knowingly caused the death of the victim, the other charging that he caused the death under circumstances manifesting extreme indifference to the value of human life. State v. Allison, 126 N.H. 111, 489 A.2d 620, 1985 N.H. LEXIS 255 (1985).

An amendment, prior to trial, of the date of death of the victim specified in an indictment for robbery and second-degree murder is permissible since the exact date of death is not an element of either offense. State v. Thresher, 122 N.H. 63, 442 A.2d 578, 1982 N.H.

LEXIS 288 (1982).

A husband who can supply his wife with the necessities of life, and neglects to do so while she is living with him and is incapable of taking care of herself by reason of sickness or other cause, is guilty of the crime of murder or manslaughter, according to the nature and degree of the negligence in respect to premeditation, wilfulness, recklessness, and culpability, if her death is caused or hastened by such neglect. Gendron v. St. Pierre, 73 N.H. 419, 62 A. 966, 1905 N.H. LEXIS 74 (1905). (Decided under prior law.)

7. Accomplice liability

In a prosecution for being an accomplice to reckless second-degree murder under RSA 626:8, and RSA 630:1-b, I(b), the victim's death was a reasonably foreseeable consequence of defendant's actions in planning an armed burglary of a house occupied by a person he knew to have a gun; driving his companions, one of whom he knew was armed with a gun, to the victim's home; entering the home with his companions; confronting and scuffling with the victim; and searching the victim's property while a companion, armed with a gun, remained with the victim. State v. Rivera, 162 N.H. 182, 27 A.3d 676, 2011 N.H. LEXIS 84 (2011).

Classic formulation of the felony-murder doctrine declares that one is guilty of murder if a death results from conduct during the commission or attempted commission of any felony; as thus conceived, the rule operated without separate proof of any culpability with regard to the death. New Hampshire's statutory scheme does not allow imposition of guilt regardless of the actor's mental state, but requires that the State prove that the defendant possessed the mental state required by the underlying offense--in the case of second-degree murder, recklessness. State v. Rivera, 162 N.H. 182, 27 A.3d 676, 2011 N.H. LEXIS 84 (2011).

Trial court erred in ruling that defendant could not be charged as an accomplice to a crime requiring proof of recklessness as the culpable mental state; as a matter of law, a person could act with purpose of promoting or facilitating commission of a reckless homicide, and thus defendant could properly be charged as an accomplice to reckless second degree murder. State v. Locke, 144 N.H. 348, 761 A.2d 376, 1999 N.H. LEXIS 123 (1999), superseded by statute as stated in, State v. Anthony, 151 N.H. 492, 861 A.2d 773, 2004 N.H. LEXIS 184 (2004), superseded by statute as stated in, State v. Rivera, 162 N.H. 182, 27 A.3d 676, 2011 N.H. LEXIS 84 (2011). (Superseded by statute as stated in State v. Anthony, 151 N.H. 492 (2004); see RSA 626:8, IV as amended in 2001.)

8. Evidence

Under the second-degree murder statute, there was a presumption that participation in an armed burglary was proof that the defendant acted recklessly with extreme difference to the value of human life, and the instruction made clear that the presumption applied to the mens rea, not the actus reus, of the crime of murder. Further, the evidence was sufficient for a jury to find beyond a reasonable doubt, even without the operation of the presumption, that defendant acted recklessly with extreme indifference to human life; defendant entered the victim's home at night with two other men, one of whom he knew carried a loaded gun, with the intention of stealing money and drugs; the men had agreed that the second man would hold the victim at gun point while defendant and the third man searched the house; defendant was also aware that the victim might be armed and had discussed the possibility that the second man would shoot the victim if there was a stand-off. RSA 630:1-b, I(b). State v. Rivera, 162 N.H. 182, 27 A.3d 676, 2011 N.H. LEXIS 84 (2011).

Any error in excluding certain testimony was harmless and thus did not violate due process under N.H. Const. pt. I, art. 15 and the Fifth and Fourteenth Amendments. The alternative evidence of defendant's guilt of second-degree murder under RSA 630:1-b, I(b), and of riot under RSA 644:1, I, including eyewitness testimony, was of an overwhelming nature, and the testimony was cumulative. State v. Garcia, 162 N.H. 426, 33 A.3d 1087, 2011 N.H. LEXIS 126 (2011).

Evidence was sufficient to show extreme indifference where: (1) the defendant was familiar with the operation of a semi-automatic handgun, knew he had loaded the .22 with which his ex-wife was shot, and knew his ex-wife was in the next room, (2) the defendant had been drinking beer all afternoon and his blood alcohol content nearly five hours after the shooting was .15, (3) at the time of the

shooting, he was sitting with his elbows resting on raised knees with the barrel of a gun he knew to be loaded pointing into the kitchen where his ex-wife was located, the gun was cocked and ready to fire, and the defendant's finger was in the trigger housing, (4) a firearms expert testified that due to its safety features the gun could not have fired without simultaneously gripping the safety on the back of the handle and squeezing the trigger, and (5) the defendant, who had told the police he knew not to point a gun at anyone, finally admitted that he had been "fooling around" with it after consistently lying by saying he had been cleaning it. State v. Burley, 137 N.H. 286, 627 A.2d 98, 1993 N.H. LEXIS 73 (1993).

Evidence presented at defendant's trial for second degree murder which showed a killing accomplished by a brutal beating and asphyxiation conclusively supported allegation that defendant manifested an extreme indifference to the value of human life. State v. Dow, 126 N.H. 205, 489 A.2d 650, 1985 N.H. LEXIS 248 (1985).

9. Questions for jury

In determining whether to convict accused of second degree murder or of manslaughter, the existence and extent of disregard manifested is a factual determination to be made by the jury. State v. Howland, 119 N.H. 413, 402 A.2d 188, 1979 N.H. LEXIS 313 (1979); State v. Dow, 126 N.H. 205, 489 A.2d 650, 1985 N.H. LEXIS 248 (1985).

10. Jury instructions

In a first-degree murder prosecution under RSA 630:1-a, I(a), where a defendant presents evidence to support a rational finding of provocation manslaughter, juries should be instructed that to find the defendant guilty of first-degree murder the State must prove beyond a reasonable doubt: (1) that the defendant caused the death of the victim; (2) that he acted "purposely" under the special definition of that term in RSA 630:1-a, II; and (3) that he did not act under the influence of extreme mental or emotional disturbance caused by extreme provocation. The jury should also be given an acquittal first instruction indicating that, if the jury finds the defendant not guilty of first-degree murder pursuant to the foregoing instructions, it should next consider whether the State has proved, again beyond a reasonable doubt, the elements of second-degree murder under RSA 630:1-b, I(a): (1) that the defendant caused the death of the victim; (2) that he acted knowingly; and (3) that he did not act under the influence of extreme mental or emotional disturbance caused by extreme provocation. State v. Soto, 162 N.H. 708, 34 A.3d 738, 2011 N.H. LEXIS 169 (2011).

Any error in refusing to instruct the jury on reckless manslaughter under RSA 630:2, I(b) as a lesser-included offense of reckless second-degree murder under RSA 630:1-b, I(b) was harmless. Because the jury had convicted defendant of purposeful first-degree murder despite having the option to convict him of the less serious offense of reckless second-degree murder, it followed that it would not have convicted him of the still less serious offense of reckless manslaughter. State v. Soto, 162 N.H. 708, 34 A.3d 738, 2011 N.H. LEXIS 169 (2011).

Trial court's instruction that New Hampshire law presumed all persons were aware of their actions and that defendant could not rebut this presumption because he had not raised insanity as a defense during his trial relieved the State of its burden of proving that defendant acted knowingly, and the state supreme court reversed defendant's conviction for second-degree murder. State v. Hall, 148 N.H. 394, 808 A.2d 55, 2002 N.H. LEXIS 146 (2002).

11. Sentence

Sentence of thirty-six years to life imposed on defendant convicted of second degree murder, which was reviewed and upheld by the sentence review board, although greater than that recommended by the state, was well within the limits permitted by this section and was not excessive, in view of the violent nature of the defendant's crime and all of the circumstances presented by the record. State v. Little, 123 N.H. 433, 462 A.2d 117, 1983 N.H. LEXIS 300 (1983).

12. Double jeopardy

Double jeopardy under U.S. Const. amend. V and N.H. Const. pt. I, art. 16 did not prohibit defendant's trial for reckless second-degree murder and knowing second-degree murder after his acquittal of first-degree felony murder and a declaration of mistrial on a second-degree murder charge. The charges of first-degree felony murder and the charge of reckless second-degree murder did not require proof of the same mens rea; the charge of reckless second-degree murder did not include the element that defendant killed the victim while engaged in robbery; and while the trial court had instructed the jury on knowing second-degree murder as a lesser included offense of first-degree felony murder, the jury made no finding on that offense. State v. Glenn, 160 N.H. 480, 9 A.3d 161, 2010 N.H. LEXIS 81 (July 20, 2010).

There was no merit to defendant's argument that the jury, by acquitting him of first-degree felony murder, necessarily found that he did not shoot and kill the victim, thereby barring his reprosecution under the Double Jeopardy Clause; the jury could have based its acquittal for the first-degree felony murder on other grounds, such as finding that defendant did not attempt to rob the victim at the time of the shooting. Therefore, the United States Supreme Court's decision in *Yeager* did not bar defendant's retrial for second degree knowing or reckless murder, neither of which required proof of robbery for conviction. State v. Glenn, 160 N.H. 480, 9 A.3d 161, 2010 N.H. LEXIS 81 (July 20, 2010).

13. —Collateral estoppel

Collateral estoppel did not bar evidence that a murder defendant was attempting to rob the victim. Neither the knowing nor reckless second-degree murder indictments as charged required the State to prove beyond a reasonable doubt that defendant was attempting to rob the victim at the time of the murder; therefore, under these indictments, the alleged attempted robbery was merely an evidentiary fact, not an ultimate fact that had to be proved beyond a reasonable doubt. State v. Glenn, 160 N.H. 480, 9 A.3d 161, 2010 N.H. LEXIS 81 (July 20, 2010).

14. Provocation

Although provocation is only a partial rather than a full defense, because it can operate both to reduce the mens rea required for murder and to provide a basis for the jury's invocation of the community's sense of compassion, provocation, when properly raised, should be treated similarly to self-defense. Accordingly, in a murder prosecution, the State must prove the absence of provocation beyond a reasonable doubt when the defendant presents some evidence to support a rational finding that he caused the death at issue under the influence of extreme mental or emotional disturbance caused by extreme provocation. State v. Soto, 162 N.H. 708, 34 A.3d 738, 2011 N.H. LEXIS 169 (2011).

Cited:

Cited in State v. Conklin, 115 N.H. 331, 341 A.2d 770, 1975 N.H. LEXIS 299 (1975); State v. Roy, 118 N.H. 2, 381 A.2d 1198, 1978 N.H. LEXIS 329 (1978); State v. French, 119 N.H. 500, 403 A.2d 424, 1979 N.H. LEXIS 328 (1979); State v. Beede, 119 N.H. 620, 406 A.2d 125, 1979 N.H. LEXIS 364 (1979); State v. Rullo, 120 N.H. 149, 412 A.2d 1009, 1980 N.H. LEXIS 248 (1980); State v. Gorham, 120 N.H. 162, 412 A.2d 1017, 1980 N.H. LEXIS 253 (1980); State v. Darcy, 121 N.H. 220, 427 A.2d 516, 1981 N.H. LEXIS 283 (1981); State v. Cameron, 121 N.H. 348, 430 A.2d 138, 1981 N.H. LEXIS 317 (1981); State v. Torres, 121 N.H. 828, 435 A.2d 527, 1981 N.H. LEXIS 423 (1981); Roy v. Perrin, 122 N.H. 88, 441 A.2d 1151, 1982 N.H. LEXIS 292 (1982); State v. Purrington, 122 N.H. 458, 446 A.2d 451, 1982 N.H. LEXIS 377 (1982); State v. Tapply, 124 N.H. 318, 470 A.2d 900, 1983 N.H. LEXIS 399 (1983); State v. Baillargeon, 124 N.H. 355, 470 A.2d 915, 1983 N.H. LEXIS 422 (1983); State v. Kaplan, 124 N.H. 382, 469 A.2d 1354, 1983 N.H. LEXIS 388 (1983); State v. Elbert, 125 N.H. 1, 480 A.2d 854, 1984 N.H. LEXIS 371 (1984); State v. Fleming, 125 N.H. 238, 480 A.2d 107, 1984 N.H. LEXIS 365 (1984); State v. Portigue, 125 N.H. 338, 480 A.2d 896, 1984 N.H. LEXIS 264 (1984); State v. Allison, 126 N.H. 111, 489 A.2d 620, 1985 N.H. LEXIS 255 (1985); State v. Cote, 126 N.H. 514, 493 A.2d 1170, 1985 N.H. LEXIS 336 (1985); State v. Glidden, 127 N.H. 359, 499 A.2d 1349, 1985 N.H. LEXIS 438 (1985); State v. Baillargeon, 127 N.H. 782, 508 A.2d 1051, 1986 N.H. LEXIS 238 (1986); State v. Allison, 127 N.H. 829, 508 A.2d 1084, 1986 N.H. LEXIS 228 (1986); State v. Duhamel, 128 N.H. 199, 512 A.2d 420, 1986 N.H. LEXIS 267 (1986); State v. Dominguez, 128 N.H. 288, 512 A.2d 1112, 1986 N.H. LEXIS 270 (1986); State v. Saucier, 128

N.H. 291, 512 A.2d 1120, 1986 N.H. LEXIS 292 (1986); State v. Allen, 128 N.H. 390, 514 A.2d 1263, 1986 N.H. LEXIS 309 (1986); State v. Pliskaner, 128 N.H. 486, 517 A.2d 795, 1986 N.H. LEXIS 329 (1986); State v. Kaplan, 128 N.H. 562, 517 A.2d 1162, 1986 N.H. LEXIS 325 (1986); State v. Sundstrom, 131 N.H. 203, 552 A.2d 81, 1988 N.H. LEXIS 116 (1988); State v. Gosselin, 131 N.H. 243, 552 A.2d 974, 1988 N.H. LEXIS 114 (1988); State v. Anaya, 134 N.H. 346, 592 A.2d 1142, 1991 N.H. LEXIS 68 (1991); State v. Thornton, 140 N.H. 532, 669 A.2d 791, 1995 N.H. LEXIS 186 (1995); State v. Taylor, 141 N.H. 89, 677 A.2d 1093, 1996 N.H. LEXIS 56 (1996); State v. Monroe, 142 N.H. 857, 711 A.2d 878, 1998 N.H. LEXIS 51 (1998); State v. Gotsch, 143 N.H. 88, 719 A.2d 606, 1998 N.H. LEXIS 74 (1998); State v. Doucette, 146 N.H. 583, 776 A.2d 744, 2001 N.H. LEXIS 112 (2001); State v. Smalley, 151 N.H. 193, 855 A.2d 401, 2004 N.H. LEXIS 113 (2004).

RESEARCH REFERENCES

New Hampshire Practice.
2 N.H.P. Criminal Practice & Procedure § 33.10.

New Hampshire Trial Bar News.
For article, "Presumptions in New Hampshire Law—A Guide Through the Impenetrable Jungle (Part II)," see 11 N.H. Trial Bar News 31, 36 n.112 (Fall 1991).

630:2. Manslaughter.

I. A person is guilty of manslaughter when he causes the death of another:

(a) Under the influence of extreme mental or emotional disturbance caused by extreme provocation but which would otherwise constitute murder; or

(b) Recklessly.

II. Manslaughter shall be punishable by imprisonment for a term of not more than 30 years.

III. In addition to any other penalty imposed, if the death of another person resulted from the driving of a motor vehicle, the court may revoke the license or driving privilege of the convicted person indefinitely.

Source.
1971, 518:1. 1974, 34:3. 1979, 126:4, eff. Aug. 4, 1979. 2000, 318:1, eff. June 21, 2000.

Amendments
—2000. Paragraph III: Added.

—1979. Paragraph I: Substituted "manslaughter" for "a class A felony" preceding "when" in the introductory clause.
Paragraph II: Added.

—1974. Rewritten to the extent that a detailed comparison would be impracticable.

Cross References.
Charging manner of death, see RSA 601:6.
Penalty for manslaughter committed while boating under the influence of intoxicating liquor or controlled drugs, see RSA 265-A:19.

NOTES TO DECISIONS

1. Constitutionality
2. Construction
3. Classification of offense
4. Lesser included offense
5. Indictment
6. Provocation
7. Recklessness

8. Fetus
9. Voluntary act
10. Defenses
11. Questions for jury
12. Jury instructions
13. Sentence
14. Harmless error

1. Constitutionality

Use of the phrase "but which would otherwise constitute murder" in subparagraph I(a) of this section does not render this section unconstitutionally vague, since one need only turn to the preceding sections of this chapter to find the definition of the various degrees of murder. State v. Darcy, 121 N.H. 220, 427 A.2d 516, 1981 N.H. LEXIS 283 (1981).

2. Construction

The word "cause" in paragraph I of this section is not a technical term requiring an elaborate definition by the court. State v. Bird, 122 N.H. 10, 440 A.2d 441, 1982 N.H. LEXIS 275 (1982).

3. Classification of offense

A husband who can supply his wife with the necessities of life, and neglects to do so while she is living with him and is incapable of taking care of herself by reason of sickness or other cause, is guilty of the crime of murder or manslaughter, according to the nature and degree of the negligence in respect to premeditation, wilfulness, recklessness, and culpability, if her death is caused or hastened by such neglect. Gendron v. St. Pierre, 73 N.H. 419, 62 A. 966, 1905 N.H. LEXIS 74 (1905). (Decided under prior law.)

4. Lesser included offense

Manslaughter is a lesser included offense to murder in the second degree. State v. Howland, 119 N.H. 413, 402 A.2d 188, 1979 N.H. LEXIS 313 (1979).

Where the accused's behavior "constitutes a gross deviation" from law-abiding conduct but does not manifest "an extreme indifference to the value of human life," the jury may properly find only manslaughter; where, however, the evidence supports the additional element of "extreme indifference," the jury may find murder in the second degree. State v. Howland, 119 N.H. 413, 402 A.2d 188, 1979 N.H. LEXIS 313 (1979); State v. Dow, 126 N.H. 205, 489 A.2d 650, 1985 N.H. LEXIS 248 (1985).

5. Indictment

Indictment alleging defendant did knowingly cause death of victim by shooting her once in the chest with a rifle while he was under the influence of extreme mental or emotional disturbance, caused by extreme provocation, gave defendant ample information to enable him to prepare for trial and was therefore constitutionally sufficient. State v. Darcy, 121 N.H. 220, 427 A.2d 516, 1981 N.H. LEXIS 283 (1981).

6. Provocation

New Hampshire Supreme Court has never treated provocation manslaughter under RSA 630:2, I(a), as a true "defense" under the Criminal Code triggering the notice requirements of N.H. Super. Ct. R. 98(B) and 101, and it declines to do so. Rather, provocation is best understood as a "partial defense" because, unlike traditional defenses that serve to discharge a defendant's liability for conduct that otherwise constitutes a crime, provocation manslaughter comprises a set of mitigating circumstances that can negate the mens rea required for intentional murder and, even where they do not have this negation effect, can warrant a jury in finding the defendant guilty of a separate, less culpable offense than murder under the Code. State v. Soto, 162 N.H. 708, 34 A.3d 738, 2011 N.H. LEXIS 169 (2011).

Although provocation is only a partial rather than a full defense, because it can operate both to reduce the mens rea required for murder and to provide a basis for the jury's invocation of the community's sense of compassion, provocation, when properly raised, should be treated similarly to self-defense. Accordingly, in a murder prosecution, the State must prove the absence of provocation beyond a reasonable doubt when the defendant presents some evidence to support a rational finding that he caused the death at

issue under the influence of extreme mental or emotional disturbance caused by extreme provocation. State v. Soto, 162 N.H. 708, 34 A.3d 738, 2011 N.H. LEXIS 169 (2011).

In a murder case where defendant shot a caseworker from the New Hampshire Division for Children, Youth and Families, the trial court properly denied defendant's request for an instruction on provocation manslaughter. In coming to defendant's home pursuant to his assignment to his case, the caseworker was engaged in a lawful act, and his refusal to leave did not provide sufficient provocation to support a finding of manslaughter. State v. Ayer, 154 N.H. 500, 917 A.2d 214, 2006 N.H. LEXIS 191 (2006), rehearing denied, 2007 N.H. LEXIS 35 (N.H. Jan. 30, 2007), cert. denied, Ayer v. New Hampshire, 552 U.S. 834, 128 S. Ct. 63, 169 L. Ed. 2d 52, 2007 U.S. LEXIS 9174 (2007).

According to common-law rule which measures provocation under a reasonable-person standard to determine whether it is legally sufficient to reduce murder to manslaughter, provocation is adequate only if it is so severe or extreme as to provoke a reasonable man to commit the act. State v. Little, 123 N.H. 433, 462 A.2d 117, 1983 N.H. LEXIS 300 (1983).

A lawful act cannot provide sufficient provocation to support a finding of manslaughter, since subparagraph I(a) of this section requires that the provocation be "extreme." State v. Smith, 123 N.H. 46, 455 A.2d 1041, 1983 N.H. LEXIS 220 (1983).

Trial court's instruction to the jury on manslaughter, that "a lawful act, even if it involves physical violence, is not recognized by the law as a sufficient provocation," was proper. State v. Smith, 123 N.H. 46, 455 A.2d 1041, 1983 N.H. LEXIS 220 (1983).

7. Recklessness

Defendant, who was convicted of reckless manslaughter under RSA 630:2 after his gun discharged while he was sitting in a car, was not substantially prejudiced by the denial of additional funds under RSA 604-A:6. Even without an expert, his misfire theory was substantially explored at trial; his statements were not consistent with how the gun could have misfired; and even if he had proven that the gun misfired, it did not necessarily follow that he would have prevailed on his defense, as there was ample evidence that he had handled the gun unsafely. State v. Mentus, 162 N.H. 792, 35 A.3d 572, 2011 N.H. LEXIS 182 (Dec. 14, 2011).

Complaints, records of conviction, and notices of revocation from past DWI convictions were properly admitted in manslaughter prosecution, where evidence was relevant for purpose of determining whether defendant acted recklessly by driving his vehicle in an intoxicated condition, and prejudice to defendant did not outweigh probativeness. State v. Dushame, 136 N.H. 309, 616 A.2d 469, 1992 N.H. LEXIS 173 (1992).

Subparagraph I(b) of this section proscribes an undesirable result and requires that a defendant have a mental state of recklessness with respect to the result of death; thus, to obtain a conviction, the state must prove that a defendant was aware that his or her conduct created a substantial and unjustifiable risk, but consciously disregarded that risk, pursuant to RSA 626:2, II(c), defining recklessness as a culpable mental state. State v. Etzweiler, 125 N.H. 57, 480 A.2d 870, 1984 N.H. LEXIS 369 (1984), superseded by statute as stated in, State v. Anthony, 151 N.H. 492, 861 A.2d 773, 2004 N.H. LEXIS 184 (2004), superseded by statute as stated in, State v. Rivera, 162 N.H. 182, 27 A.3d 676, 2011 N.H. LEXIS 84 (2011). (Superseded by statute as stated in State v. Anthony, 151 N.H. 492, 861 A.2d 773 (2004); since 2001 amendment to 626:8, IV, accomplice liability under RSA 626:8, III and IV requires proof (1) that the accomplice intended to promote or facilitate another's unlawful or dangerous conduct, and (2) that the accomplice acted with the culpable mental state specified in the underlying statute with respect to the result.)

8. Fetus

As a fetus that was born early following injuries to its mother as a result of a vehicle collision caused by defendant never displayed any spontaneous sign of life prior to its death, it was error to convict defendant of involuntary manslaughter and negligent homicide, in violation of RSA 630:2, I and RSA 630:3; the fetus was not "another" for purposes of a homicide prosecution under the "born alive" rule under RSA 630:1, IV. State v. Lamy, 158 N.H. 511, 969 A.2d 451, 2009 N.H. LEXIS 45 (2009).

9. Voluntary act

Court at manslaughter trial properly refused to employ defendant's requested jury instruction that defendant's fatal last act of pulling trigger of revolver needed to be voluntary, where no requirement existed that criminal conduct's last act be voluntary, simply that conduct include a voluntary act. State v. Burrell, 135 N.H. 715, 609 A.2d 751, 1992 N.H. LEXIS 112 (1992).

10. Defenses

Because there was some evidence that defendant reasonably believed that his brother was about to use deadly force where the brother had threatened to kill defendant and his mother prior to leaving for his garage room where a gun was located, the trial court should have given a self defense instruction. State v. Vassar, 154 N.H. 370, 910 A.2d 1193, 2006 N.H. LEXIS 171 (2006).

Self-defense may still be asserted as a defense and proved under this section when the facts support such a claim. State v. Darcy, 121 N.H. 220, 427 A.2d 516, 1981 N.H. LEXIS 283 (1981).

11. Questions for jury

In determining whether to convict accused of second degree murder or of manslaughter, the existence and extent of disregard manifested is a factual determination to be made by the jury. State v. Howland, 119 N.H. 413, 402 A.2d 188, 1979 N.H. LEXIS 313 (1979); State v. Dow, 126 N.H. 205, 489 A.2d 650, 1985 N.H. LEXIS 248 (1985).

12. Jury instructions

In a first-degree murder prosecution under RSA 630:1-a, I(a), where a defendant presents evidence to support a rational finding of provocation manslaughter, juries should be instructed that to find the defendant guilty of first-degree murder the State must prove beyond a reasonable doubt: (1) that the defendant caused the death of the victim; (2) that he acted "purposely" under the special definition of that term in RSA 630:1-a, II; and (3) that he did not act under the influence of extreme mental or emotional disturbance caused by extreme provocation. The jury should also be given an acquittal first instruction indicating that, if the jury finds the defendant not guilty of first-degree murder pursuant to the foregoing instructions, it should next consider whether the State has proved, again beyond a reasonable doubt, the elements of second-degree murder under RSA 630:1-b, I(a): (1) that the defendant caused the death of the victim; (2) that he acted knowingly; and (3) that he did not act under the influence of extreme mental or emotional disturbance caused by extreme provocation. State v. Soto, 162 N.H. 708, 34 A.3d 738, 2011 N.H. LEXIS 169 (2011).

In a first-degree murder prosecution under RSA 630:1-a, I(a) (2007), where a defendant presents evidence to support a rational finding of provocation manslaughter, the jury should be given the acquittal first instruction and told that if it finds the defendant not guilty of second-degree murder, it should then go on to consider whether he is guilty of provocation manslaughter, the elements of this offense being: (1) that the defendant caused the death of the victim; and (2) that the defendant acted either purposely or knowingly. The jury should also be instructed that, if it reaches the crime of provocation manslaughter in its deliberations, the defendant may be found guilty of this crime if the State proves the foregoing two elements beyond a reasonable doubt even if the jury concludes that the defendant acted under the influence of extreme mental or emotional disturbance caused by extreme provocation. State v. Soto, 162 N.H. 708, 34 A.3d 738, 2011 N.H. LEXIS 169 (2011).

In a murder trial, the trial court did not err in not instructing on provocation manslaughter under RSA 630:2, I. A reasonable person would not remain in an extreme emotional state after driving to a different city, meeting with friends to discuss how to retaliate, taking the time to smoke marijuana, and again driving to search for the provokers; defendant's actions leading up to the killing revealed a calm and calculating state of mind, guided not by a sudden, uncontrollable passion but by a desire to avenge the beating of his friend. State v. Soto, 162 N.H. 708, 34 A.3d 738, 2011 N.H. LEXIS 169 (2011).

Any error in refusing to instruct the jury on reckless manslaughter under RSA 630:2, I(b) as a lesser-included offense of reckless second-degree murder under RSA 630:1-b, I(b) was harmless. Because the jury had convicted defendant of purposeful first-degree murder despite having the option to convict him of the less serious offense of reckless second-degree murder, it followed that it would not have convicted him of the still less serious offense of reckless manslaughter. State v. Soto, 162 N.H. 708, 34 A.3d 738, 2011 N.H. LEXIS 169 (2011).

In a manslaughter case, the State presented sufficient evidence to support a jury instruction on accomplice liability under RSA 626:8, III. There was evidence that defendant had the purpose to make the crime succeed in that a witness testified that he was present when defendant kicked the victim, and evidence that defendant jumped up and down on the victim's head showed that he had aided in the commission of the crime and that he possessed the requisite mens rea for manslaughter, recklessness. State v. Duran, 158 N.H. 146, 960 A.2d 697, 2008 N.H. LEXIS 139 (2008).

In a prosecution on charges of manslaughter, misdemeanor reckless conduct, and first-degree assault, the trial court properly instructed the jury that to find defendant guilty of manslaughter and first-degree assault, it had to find that the State had proven beyond a reasonable doubt that defendant's conduct was a substantial factor in causing the death of a child who died when defendant lost control of a pickup truck and the truck hit a tree, or the serious bodily injuries sustained by the five other children who were riding in the bed of the pickup truck. State v. Lamprey, 149 N.H. 364, 821 A.2d 1080, 2003 N.H. LEXIS 54 (2003).

Where a defendant in a manslaughter case can proffer some evidence of medical malpractice in the causal link between the criminal act and the death of the victim, the issue of causation must be submitted to the jury with appropriate instructions on the supervening cause; such instructions must be based on the principle that when such alternate causes are asserted and are supported by some evidence, the medical malpractice will break the causal link and defeat the element of causation only when such malpractice is the sole substantial cause of the death. State v. Soucy, 139 N.H. 349, 653 A.2d 561, 1995 N.H. LEXIS 4 (1995).

13. Sentence

Trial court did not abuse its discretion in imposing a twenty-to-forty year sentence for defendant's convictions of manslaughter and first degree assault in connection with death of seven-month-old child; there was no requirement that all sentences for a particular crime be identical, and court considered all relevant factors, including misrepresentations defendant made regarding cause of victim's injuries, fact that shaking incident was not the only instance of abuse, and defendant's lack of remorse. State v. Hammond, 144 N.H. 401, 742 A.2d 532, 1999 N.H. LEXIS 129 (1999).

The character of the fault of the accused can be considered in imposing sentence under a charge of manslaughter, and the sentence may be merely nominal. State v. Karvelos, 80 N.H. 528, 120 A. 263, 1923 N.H. LEXIS 54 (1923). (Decided under prior law.)

14. Harmless error

Although defendant's statement that she had struck her daughter months before the incident in question and evidence that she had attended anger management classes should have been excluded under N.H. R. Evid. 404(b), the errors were harmless, as there was overwhelming evidence of defendant's guilt of manslaughter under RSA 630:2, I(b). Defendant's description of the incidents in which she used physical force against her infant daughter closely corresponded with the doctors' testimony; defendant's testimony, together with the doctors' testimony, strongly supported the conclusion that defendant was caring for the daughter when the daughter's injuries occurred; defendant made several statements suggesting she had used too much physical force against her daughter and that she did something wrong; and defendant's general description of the events painted a picture of a person using unwarranted and dangerous physical force against a very young child. State v. Belonga, 163 N.H. 343, 42 A.3d 764, 2012 N.H. LEXIS 32 (Mar. 16, 2012).

Cited:

Cited in State v. Conklin, 115 N.H. 331, 341 A.2d 770, 1975 N.H. LEXIS 299 (1975); State v. Plummer, 117 N.H. 320, 374 A.2d 431, 1977 N.H. LEXIS 330 (1977); State v. Laplante, 117 N.H. 417, 374 A.2d 643, 1977 N.H. LEXIS 349 (1977); State v. Theodosopoulos, 119 N.H. 573, 409 A.2d 1134, 1979 N.H. LEXIS 435 (1979); State v. Gorham, 120 N.H. 162, 412 A.2d 1017, 1980 N.H. LEXIS 253

(1980); Mitchell v. Aetna Life & Casualty Ins. Co., 121 N.H. 458, 431 A.2d 120, 1981 N.H. LEXIS 351 (1981); State v. Glidden, 122 N.H. 41, 441 A.2d 728, 1982 N.H. LEXIS 285 (1982); State v. Pugliese, 122 N.H. 1141, 455 A.2d 1018, 1982 N.H. LEXIS 541 (1982); Pugliese v. Perrin, 567 F. Supp. 1337, 1983 U.S. Dist. LEXIS 15416 (D.N.H. 1983); State v. Baillargeon, 124 N.H. 355, 470 A.2d 915, 1983 N.H. LEXIS 422 (1983); Pugliese v. Perrin, 731 F.2d 85, 1984 U.S. App. LEXIS 23974 (1st Cir. N.H. 1984); State v. Fleming, 125 N.H. 238, 480 A.2d 107, 1984 N.H. LEXIS 365 (1984); State v. Cote, 126 N.H. 514, 493 A.2d 1170, 1985 N.H. LEXIS 336 (1985); State v. Glidden, 127 N.H. 359, 499 A.2d 1349, 1985 N.H. LEXIS 438 (1985); State v. Bailey, 127 N.H. 811, 508 A.2d 1066, 1986 N.H. LEXIS 243 (1986); State v. Allison, 127 N.H. 829, 508 A.2d 1084, 1986 N.H. LEXIS 228 (1986); State v. Dominguez, 128 N.H. 288, 512 A.2d 1112, 1986 N.H. LEXIS 270 (1986); State v. Dufield, 131 N.H. 35, 549 A.2d 1205, 1988 N.H. LEXIS 88 (1988); State v. Hartford, 132 N.H. 580, 567 A.2d 577, 1989 N.H. LEXIS 137 (1989); State v. Stetson, 135 N.H. 267, 603 A.2d 498, 1992 N.H. LEXIS 15 (1992); State v. Pittera, 139 N.H. 257, 651 A.2d 931, 1994 N.H. LEXIS 141 (1994); State v. Taylor, 141 N.H. 89, 677 A.2d 1093, 1996 N.H. LEXIS 56 (1996); State v. Demeritt, 148 N.H. 435, 813 A.2d 393, 2002 N.H. LEXIS 149 (2002); State v. O'Leary, 153 N.H. 710, 903 A.2d 997, 2006 N.H. LEXIS 95 (2006).

RESEARCH REFERENCES

New Hampshire Bar Journal.
For article, "Purposely Negligent: Revisiting New Hampshire's Accomplice Liability Precedent After State v. Anthony," see 46 N.H.B.J. 14 (2005).

630:3. Negligent Homicide.

I. A person is guilty of a class B felony when he causes the death of another negligently.

II. A person is guilty of a class A felony when in consequence of being under the influence of intoxicating liquor or a controlled drug or any combination of intoxicating liquor and controlled drug while operating a propelled vehicle, as defined in RSA 637:9, III or a boat as defined in RSA 265-A:1, II, he or she causes the death of another.

III. In addition to any other penalty imposed, if the death of another person resulted from the negligent driving of a motor vehicle, the court may revoke the license or driving privilege of the convicted person for up to 7 years. In cases where the person is convicted under paragraph II, the court shall revoke the license or driving privilege of the convicted person indefinitely and the person shall not petition for eligibility to reapply for a driver's license for at least 7 years. In a case in which alcohol was involved, the court may also require that the convicted person shall not have a license to drive reinstated until after the division of motor vehicles receives certification of installation of an ignition interlock device as described in RSA 265-A:36, which shall remain in place for a period not to exceed 5 years.

Source.
1971, 518:1. 1977, 588:40. 1985, 290:2. 1989, 415:2. 1992, 257:10. 1993, 272:2, eff. July 15, 1993. 2000, 287:4, eff. Jan. 1, 2002; 318:2, eff. June 21, 2000. 2006, 260:32, eff. January 1, 2007.

Amendments
—2006. Paragraph II: Substituted "RSA 265-A:1" for "RSA 270:48" and made a gender neutral change.
Paragraph III: Substituted "RSA 265-A:36" for "RSA 265:82-e."

—2000. Paragraph III: Chapter 318:2, eff. June 21, 2000, added the second and third sentences.
Chapter 287:4, eff. Jan. 1, 2002, inserted "as described in RSA 265:82-e" following "interlock device" in the third sentence.

—1993. Paragraph II: Deleted "his" following "consequence of" and inserted "or any combination of intoxicating liquor and controlled drug" preceding "while operating".

—1992. Paragraph II: Substituted "RSA 270:48, II" for "RSA 631:5, II" preceding "he causes".

—1989. Rewrote par. I, added a new par. II and redesignated former par. II as par. III.

—1985. Designated existing provisions of the introductory paragraph as par. I, redesignated former pars. I and II as present subpars. (a) and (b), and added present par. II.

—1977. Paragraph II: Substituted "III" for "II" following "RSA 637:9".

Severability
—1989 amendment. 1989, 415:2, was subject to a severability clause. See 1989, 415:4.

The Brooke Blanchard Act.
1998, 381:1, eff. Jan. 1, 1999, provided: "The creation of the presumption that a juvenile is certifiable as an adult where a juvenile is charged with negligent homicide driving while intoxicated under RSA 630:3, II shall be known as the 'Brooke Blanchard Act.' Brooke Blanchard was the victim in a motor vehicle fatality where the driver was a 16-year-old alleged to have consumed alcohol."

Cross References.
Classification of crimes, see RSA 625:9.
Conditions for restoration of license or driving privilege, see RSA 265-A:22
Penalty for negligent homicide committed while boating under the influence of intoxicating liquor or controlled drug, see RSA 265-A:19.
Sentences, see RSA 651.
Simultaneous revocation of motor vehicle registration for conviction of negligent homicide by motor vehicle, see RSA 261:180.
Victims permitted to speak before sentencing, see RSA 651:4-a.

NOTES TO DECISIONS

1. Constitutionality
2. Construction
3. Construction with other laws
4. Accomplice liability
5. Culpable mental state
6. Causal connection
7. Defenses
8. Lesser included offenses
9. Evidence

1. Constitutionality
Subparagraph I(b) (now, as amended, paragraph II) of this section is not unconstitutionally vague, since it gives clear notice to a person of ordinary intelligence that the act of driving an automobile while under the influence of intoxicating liquor, with death resulting as a consequence of that act, is proscribed. State v. Wong, 125 N.H. 610, 486 A.2d 262, 1984 N.H. LEXIS 413 (1984).

Subparagraph I(b) (now, as amended, paragraph II) of this section is not unconstitutionally over broad, since prohibiting a person from causing death as a consequence of driving an automobile while under the influence of intoxicating liquor does not infringe a protected freedom. State v. Wong, 125 N.H. 610, 486 A.2d 262, 1984 N.H. LEXIS 413 (1984).

This section does not create a constitutionally impermissible classification which treats defendants indicted under subparagraph I(b) (now, as amended, paragraph II) differently from those indicted under subparagraph I(a) (now paragraph I). State v. Wong, 125 N.H. 610, 486 A.2d 262, 1984 N.H. LEXIS 413 (1984).

The legislature's determination that proof of the elements of subparagraph I(b) (now, as amended, paragraph II) of this section constitutes proof of criminal negligence per se is consistent with its authority under part II, article 5 of the New Hampshire Constitution to define criminal acts and to prescribe punishments which conform to constitutional limits. State v. Wong, 125 N.H. 610, 486 A.2d 262, 1984 N.H. LEXIS 413 (1984).

2. Construction

Element of being "under the influence" of a controlled drug under RSA 630:3, II may be proved by evidence that the defendant was suffering symptoms of withdrawal from drug usage. To prove a driver was "under the influence," the State need prove only that the driver was impaired "to any degree"; nothing in the statute limits such impairment to the time immediately following the ingestion of the drugs. State v. Dilboy, 160 N.H. 135, 999 A.2d 1092, 2010 N.H. LEXIS 36 (2010).

Nothing in the plain language of RSA 630:3, II indicates that the legislature intended to require a person to have controlled drugs present in their blood, resulting in an impaired driving ability. Rather, the language merely requires that one be under the influence of drugs. State v. Dilboy, 160 N.H. 135, 999 A.2d 1092, 2010 N.H. LEXIS 36 (2010).

Subdivision III of this section allows sentencing courts to effectuate administrative license suspension statute's remedial purpose once a jury has determined, beyond a reasonable doubt, that defendant has caused death of another person by negligent driving of a motor vehicle. State v. Drewry, 141 N.H. 514, 687 A.2d 991, 1996 N.H. LEXIS 133 (1996).

Allowance of multiple charges under subparagraph I(b) (now, as amended, paragraph II) of this section where there are multiple victims resulting from one episode of drunken driving does not violate principles of statutory construction since the meaning of the provision is clear and since the legislative intent is to punish drunken drivers who kill and to protect individuals from them. State v. Bailey, 127 N.H. 811, 508 A.2d 1066, 1986 N.H. LEXIS 243 (1986).

That this section mistakenly referred to "a propelled vehicle, as defined in RSA 637:9, II", in that the proper citation was RSA 637:9, III, at time appellant was charged with negligent homicide, did not mean that complaint failed to allege a criminal offense and that the complaint should have been quashed on motion; for to grant the motion when the legislative intent was clear would be to defeat or interfere with the legislative direction, and the mistaken reference would be disregarded and the section read so as to refer to the proper statutory provision. State v. Murgatroy, 115 N.H. 717, 349 A.2d 600, 1975 N.H. LEXIS 408 (1975).

3. Construction with other laws

Former RSA 265:84 (now RSA 265-A:4), governing implied consent to chemical testing to determine blood alcohol content, applied to all offenses arising from driving while intoxicated, including negligent homicide. State v. Dery, 126 N.H. 747, 496 A.2d 357, 1985 N.H. LEXIS 355 (1985).

4. Accomplice liability

The 2001 amendment to RSA 626:8, IV was a legislative rejection of the interpretation of that statute stated by the plurality in State v. Etzweiler and the amendment was enacted to clarify the intent of the statute in response to Etzweiler. Accordingly, consistent with the majority of courts interpreting accomplice liability statutes derived from the Model Penal Code, accomplice liability under RSA 626:8, III and IV requires proof (1) that the accomplice intended to promote or facilitate another's unlawful or dangerous conduct, and (2) that the accomplice acted with the culpable mental state specified in the underlying statute with respect to the result. If the offense's mental state with respect to the result is something less than purposeful, the State need only establish that lesser mens rea on the part of the accomplice to prove him or her guilty of the offense. State v. Anthony, 151 N.H. 492, 861 A.2d 773 (2004).

An individual may not be an accomplice to negligent homicide, since to satisfy the requirements of RSA 626:8, III, setting forth the conduct element of accomplice liability, the state must establish that the accomplice's acts were designed to aid the primary actor in committing the substantive offense, yet under RSA 626:2, II(d), setting forth the necessary accompanying mental state of negligence, the primary actor must be unaware of the risk that his

conduct created, and an accomplice could not intentionally aid the primary actor in a crime that the primary actor was unaware that he was committing. State v. Etzweiler, 125 N.H. 57, 480 A.2d 870, 1984 N.H. LEXIS 369 (1984), superseded by statute as stated in, State v. Anthony, 151 N.H. 492, 861 A.2d 773, 2004 N.H. LEXIS 184 (2004), superseded by statute as stated in, State v. Rivera, 162 N.H. 182, 27 A.3d 676, 2011 N.H. LEXIS 84 (2011). (Decided under prior law; see RSA 626:8, IV as amended in 2001.)

The legislature, in enacting paragraph I of this section and RSA 626:8, governing accomplice liability, did not intend to impose criminal liability upon a person who lends his automobile to an intoxicated driver but does not accompany the driver, when the driver's operation of the borrowed automobile causes death. State v. Etzweiler, 125 N.H. 57, 480 A.2d 870, 1984 N.H. LEXIS 369 (1984), superseded by statute as stated in, State v. Anthony, 151 N.H. 492, 861 A.2d 773, 2004 N.H. LEXIS 184 (2004), superseded by statute as stated in, State v. Rivera, 162 N.H. 182, 27 A.3d 676, 2011 N.H. LEXIS 84 (2011). (Decided under prior law.)

5. Culpable mental state

Defendant's conviction for negligent homicide, in violation of RSA 630:3, I, was supported by sufficient evidence, as her use of a cellular telephone while driving, although not prohibited by RSA 265:105-a, constituted the requisite wrongful or blameworthy conduct to establish the culpable mental state of criminal negligence pursuant to RSA 626:2, II(d); further, she had a duty to yield to the victim, who was a pedestrian within a crosswalk pursuant to RSA 265:35. State v. Dion, 164 N.H. 544, 62 A.3d 792, 2013 N.H. LEXIS 7 (2013).

Defendant was properly convicted of negligent homicide where jury could have found that defendant's behavior constituted a gross deviation from the conduct that a reasonable person would have exhibited in the same situation. State v. Ebinger, 135 N.H. 264, 603 A.2d 924, 1992 N.H. LEXIS 19 (1992).

In order to prove that a defendant negligently caused death under paragraph I of this section, the state must, under RSA 262:2, II(d), defining negligence as a culpable mental state, establish that defendant failed to become aware of a substantial and unjustifiable risk that his or her conduct might cause the death of another human being, and that risk must be of such a nature and degree that his or her failure to become aware of it constituted a gross deviation from the conduct that a reasonable person would observe in the situation. State v. Etzweiler, 125 N.H. 57, 480 A.2d 870, 1984 N.H. LEXIS 369 (1984), superseded by statute as stated in, State v. Anthony, 151 N.H. 492, 861 A.2d 773, 2004 N.H. LEXIS 184 (2004), superseded by statute as stated in, State v. Rivera, 162 N.H. 182, 27 A.3d 676, 2011 N.H. LEXIS 84 (2011). (Decided under prior law.)

Proof of subparagraph I(b) (now, as amended, paragraph II) of this section constitutes proof of negligence per se and, as such, satisfies the mens rea requirement of RSA 626:2, I. State v. Wong, 125 N.H. 610, 486 A.2d 262, 1984 N.H. LEXIS 413 (1984).

In those circumstances in which the state proceeds on two different indictments separately charging negligent homicide based, respectively, on subparagraphs (a) (now paragraph I) or (b) (now, as amended, paragraph II) of paragraph I of this section, and the trial court instructs on both charges, proof of either charge would satisfy the culpability requirement of this section. State v. Wong, 125 N.H. 610, 486 A.2d 262, 1984 N.H. LEXIS 413 (1984).

6. Causal connection

To sustain a conviction under subparagraph I(b) (now, as amended, paragraph II) of this section, the state must establish a causal connection between the person's driving under the influence, the subsequent collision and the resulting death. State v. Wong, 125 N.H. 610, 486 A.2d 262, 1984 N.H. LEXIS 413 (1984).

7. Defenses

Because a person who is proven to have driven an automobile while intoxicated is criminally negligent per se under subparagraph I(b) (now, as amended, paragraph II) of this section, that person may not in turn defend the negligent homicide charge by demonstrating due care or the state's failure to prove an element of criminal negligence under RSA 626:2, II(d). State v. Wong, 125 N.H. 610, 486 A.2d 262, 1984 N.H. LEXIS 413 (1984).

8. Lesser included offenses

Charge of negligent homicide for crossing yellow line, pursuant to subdivision I of this section, was not a lesser-included offense of negligent homicide for operating vehicle under influence of Valium, pursuant to subdivision II of this section. State v. Liakos, 142 N.H. 726, 709 A.2d 187, 1998 N.H. LEXIS 27 (1998).

The offense of simple assault under RSA 631:2-a, I(b), based on recklessly causing bodily injury to another, is not a lesser included offense of negligent homicide, because simple assault requires a more culpable mental state than negligent homicide. State v. Mallar, 127 N.H. 816, 508 A.2d 1070, 1986 N.H. LEXIS 251 (1986).

The offense of simple assault under RSA 631:2-a, I(c), based on negligently causing bodily injury to another by means of a deadly weapon, is not a lesser included offense of negligent homicide, since use of a deadly weapon is not an essential element of negligent homicide. State v. Mallar, 127 N.H. 816, 508 A.2d 1070, 1986 N.H. LEXIS 251 (1986).

9. Evidence

Where defendant was allegedly on her cell phone while driving at the time when she caused her car to hit a pedestrian in a crosswalk, such cell phone records were properly admitted in her criminal proceeding for negligent homicide under RSA 630:3, I, as the probative value thereof substantially outweighed any prejudicial impact under N.H. R. Evid. 403. State v. Dion, 164 N.H. 544, 62 A.3d 792, 2013 N.H. LEXIS 7 (2013).

As a fetus that was born early following injuries to its mother as a result of a vehicle collision caused by defendant never displayed any spontaneous sign of life prior to its death, it was error to convict defendant of involuntary manslaughter and negligent homicide, in violation of RSA 630:2, I and RSA 630:3; the fetus was not "another" for purposes of a homicide prosecution under the "born alive" rule under RSA 630:1, IV. State v. Lamy, 158 N.H. 511, 969 A.2d 451, 2009 N.H. LEXIS 45 (2009).

Evidence did not support convictions of negligent homicide and vehicular assault under RSA 630:3, I and RSA 265:79-a when there was no evidence that defendant had consumed alcohol or drugs before driving and no evidence that he was speeding; at most, the evidence showed that his car inexplicably drifted over the double yellow line and into oncoming traffic for no more than two seconds. This did not constitute criminal negligence under RSA 626:2, II as a matter of law. State v. Shepard, — N.H. —, 973 A.2d 318, 2009 N.H. LEXIS 73 (May 29, 2009).

Trial court did not err in failing to instruct the jury that certain deposition testimony of a forensic laboratory analyst with regard to the boat defendant was operating colliding with another boat and killing the operator of the smaller boat could be considered as substantive evidence because, contrary to defendant's contention, the instructions did not prevent substantive use of any inconsistent sworn deposition testimony of the analyst in that all of the analyst's testimony concerning his earlier deposition was elicited either during direct or cross-examination, and the jury was specifically instructed that it should consider both. Further, the trial court's instructions, viewed in their entirety, explained in clear and intelligible language the issues of law applicable to the case. State v. Littlefield, 152 N.H. 331, 876 A.2d 712, 2005 N.H. LEXIS 100 (2005).

Sufficient evidence existed to support defendant's conviction for negligent homicide with regard to a collision between defendant's 36-foot Baja performance boat and the stern of a 20-foot motorboat where the evidence showed that the night of the collision was clear, moonless, there was smooth water and good visibility, that defendant consumed alcohol before operating his boat and that he failed to keep a proper lookout. State v. Littlefield, 152 N.H. 331, 876 A.2d 712, 2005 N.H. LEXIS 100 (2005).

Trial court properly denied defendant's motion to suppress three blood alcohol tests in a trial for negligent homicide, RSA 630:3, and aggravated driving while intoxicated, former RSA 265:82-a (see now RSA 265-A:3); one test was justified by exigent circumstances, as officers had observed defendant display signs of intoxication and the evidence of alcohol would have diminished over time, and two tests were taken pursuant to a valid search warrant, so defendant's rights pursuant to N.H. Const. pt. I, art. 19 were not violated. State v. Stern, 150 N.H. 705, 846 A.2d 64, 2004 N.H. LEXIS 59 (2004).

Where defendant was charged in a two-count indictment for negligent homicide, the first count alleging that defendant was driving while under the influence of alcohol and caused the death of another, and the second count alleging that defendant negligently crossed over into the breakdown lane, thereby causing the death of another, the jury's failure to reach a verdict on the first count did not preclude it from factoring evidence of alcoholic consumption into its conclusion that defendant was criminally negligent. State v. Ebinger, 135 N.H. 264, 603 A.2d 924, 1992 N.H. LEXIS 19 (1992).

Former RSA 265:87 (see now RSA 265-A:8), listing prerequisites necessary to admit blood alcohol content tests into evidence, applied to an individual arrested for negligent homicide. State v. Dery, 126 N.H. 747, 496 A.2d 357, 1985 N.H. LEXIS 355 (1985).

The results of a breathalyzer test may be used in the prosecution of offenses other than driving under the influence violations of former RSA 262-A:62 (see now RSA 265-A:2), and defendant charged under this section with negligent homicide with a motor vehicle while intoxicated could not successfully challenge admission of breathalyzer test results. State v. Murgatroy, 115 N.H. 717, 349 A.2d 600, 1975 N.H. LEXIS 408 (1975).

Cited:

Cited in State v. Plummer, 117 N.H. 320, 374 A.2d 431, 1977 N.H. LEXIS 330 (1977); State v. Driscoll, 120 N.H. 907, 424 A.2d 410, 1980 N.H. LEXIS 419 (1980); State v. Berry, 121 N.H. 324, 428 A.2d 1250, 1981 N.H. LEXIS 310 (1981); State v. Buckingham, 121 N.H. 339, 430 A.2d 135, 1981 N.H. LEXIS 315 (1981); State v. Pugliese, 122 N.H. 1141, 455 A.2d 1018, 1982 N.H. LEXIS 541 (1982); Pugliese v. Perrin, 567 F. Supp. 1337, 1983 U.S. Dist. LEXIS 15416 (D.N.H. 1983); Pugliese v. Perrin, 731 F.2d 85, 1984 U.S. App. LEXIS 23974 (1st Cir. N.H. 1984); State v. Sefton, 125 N.H. 533, 485 A.2d 284, 1984 N.H. LEXIS 400 (1984); State v. Goding, 126 N.H. 50, 489 A.2d 579, 1985 N.H. LEXIS 241 (1985); State v. Riley, 126 N.H. 257, 490 A.2d 1362, 1985 N.H. LEXIS 292 (1985); State v. Place, 128 N.H. 75, 513 A.2d 321, 1986 N.H. LEXIS 288 (1986); State v. Dominguez, 128 N.H. 288, 512 A.2d 1112, 1986 N.H. LEXIS 270 (1986); State v. Lescard, 128 N.H. 495, 517 A.2d 1158, 1986 N.H. LEXIS 338 (1986); State v. Elwell, 132 N.H. 599, 567 A.2d 1002, 1989 N.H. LEXIS 139 (1989); State v. Dery, 134 N.H. 370, 594 A.2d 149, 1991 N.H. LEXIS 72 (1991); State v. Allison, 134 N.H. 550, 595 A.2d 1089, 1991 N.H. LEXIS 99 (1991); State v. Dushame, 136 N.H. 309, 616 A.2d 469, 1992 N.H. LEXIS 173 (1992); State v. Fitzgerald, 137 N.H. 23, 622 A.2d 1245, 1993 N.H. LEXIS 29 (1993).

RESEARCH REFERENCES

New Hampshire Bar Journal.

For article, "Purposely Negligent: Revisiting New Hampshire's Accomplice Liability Precedent After State v. Anthony," see 46 N.H.B.J. 14 (2005).

630:4. Causing or Aiding Suicide.

I. A person is guilty of causing or aiding suicide if he purposely aids or solicits another to commit suicide.

II. Causing or aiding suicide is a class B felony if the actor's conduct causes such suicide or an attempted suicide. Otherwise it is a misdemeanor.

Source.
1971, 518:1, eff. Nov. 1, 1973.

Cross References.
Classification of crimes, see RSA 625:9.
Sentences, see RSA 651.

NOTES TO DECISIONS

Cited:
Cited in In re Caulk, 125 N.H. 226, 480 A.2d 93, 1984 N.H. LEXIS 364 (1984).

630:5. Procedure in Capital Murder.

I. Whenever the state intends to seek the sentence of death for the offense of capital murder, the attorney for the state, before trial or acceptance by the court of a plea of guilty, shall file with the court and serve upon the defendant, a notice:

(a) That the state in the event of conviction will seek the sentence of death; and

(b) Setting forth the aggravating factors enumerated in paragraph VII of this section and any other aggravating factors which the state will seek to prove as the basis for the death penalty.

The court may permit the attorney for the state to amend this notice for good cause shown. Any such amended notice shall be served upon the defendant as provided in this section.

II. When the attorney for the state has filed a notice as required under paragraph I and the defendant is found guilty of or pleads guilty to the offense of capital murder, the judge who presided at the trial or before whom the guilty plea was entered, or any other judge if the judge who presided at the trial or before whom the guilty plea was entered is unavailable, shall conduct a separate sentencing hearing to determine the punishment to be imposed. The hearing shall be conducted:

(a) Before the jury which determined the defendant's guilt;

(b) Before a jury impaneled for the purpose of the hearing if:

(1) the defendant was convicted upon a plea of guilty; or

(2) the jury which determined the defendant's guilt has been discharged for good cause; or

(3) after initial imposition of a sentence under this section, redetermination of the sentence under this section is necessary.

A jury impaneled under subparagraph (b) shall consist of 12 members, unless at any time before the conclusion of the hearing, the parties stipulate with the approval of the court that it shall consist of any number less than 12.

III. When a defendant is found guilty of or pleads guilty to the offense of capital murder, no presentence report shall be prepared. In the sentencing hearing, information may be presented as to matters relating to any of the aggravating or mitigating factors set forth in paragraphs VI and VII, or any other mitigating factor or any other aggravating factor for which notice has been provided under subparagraph I(b). Where information is presented relating to any of the aggravating factors set forth in paragraph VII, information may be presented relating to any other aggravating factor for which notice has been provided under subparagraph I(b). Information presented may include the trial transcript and exhibits if the hearing is held before a jury or judge not present during the trial, or at the trial judge's discretion. Any other information relevant to such mitigating or aggravating factors may be presented by either the state or the defendant, regard-

less of its admissibility under the rules governing admission of evidence at criminal trials, except that information may be excluded if its probative value is substantially outweighed by the danger of unfair prejudice, confusion of the issues, or misleading the jury. The state and the defendant shall be permitted to rebut any information received at the hearing and shall be given fair opportunity to present argument as to the adequacy of the information to establish the existence of any of the aggravating or mitigating factors and as to appropriateness in that case of imposing a sentence of death. The state shall open and the defendant shall conclude the argument to the jury. The burden of establishing the existence of any aggravating factor is on the state, and is not satisfied unless established beyond a reasonable doubt. The burden of establishing the existence of any mitigating factor is on the defendant, and is not satisfied unless established by a preponderance of the evidence.

IV. The jury shall consider all the information received during the hearing. It shall return special findings identifying any aggravating factors set forth in paragraph VII, which are found to exist. If one of the aggravating factors set forth in subparagraph VII(a) and another of the aggravating factors set forth in subparagraphs VII(b)–(j) is found to exist, a special finding identifying any other aggravating factor for which notice has been provided under subparagraph I(b) may be returned. A finding with respect to a mitigating factor may be made by one or more of the members of the jury, and any member of the jury who finds the existence of a mitigating factor may consider such a factor established for purposes of this section, regardless of the number of jurors who concur that the factor has been established. A finding with respect to any aggravating factor must be unanimous. If an aggravating factor set forth in subparagraph VII(a) is not found to exist or an aggravating factor set forth in subparagraph VII(a) is found to exist but no other aggravating factor set forth in paragraph VII is found to exist, the court shall impose a sentence of life imprisonment without possibility of parole. If an aggravating factor set forth in subparagraph VII(a) and one or more of the aggravating factors set forth in subparagraph VII (b)–(j) are found to exist, the jury shall then consider whether the aggravating factors found to exist sufficiently outweigh any mitigating factor or factors found to exist, or in the absence of mitigating factors, whether the aggravating factors are themselves sufficient to justify a sentence of death. Based upon this consideration, if the jury concludes that the aggravating factors outweigh the mitigating factors or that the aggravating factors, in the absence of any mitigating factors, are themselves sufficient to justify a death sentence, the jury, by unanimous vote only, may recommend that a sentence of death be imposed rather than a sentence of life imprisonment without possibility of parole. The jury, regardless of its findings with respect to aggravating and mitigating factors, is never required to impose a death sentence and the jury shall be so instructed.

V. Upon the recommendation that the sentence of death be imposed, the court shall sentence the defendant to death. Otherwise the court shall impose a sentence of life imprisonment without possibility of parole.

VI. In determining whether a sentence of death is to be imposed upon a defendant, the jury shall consider mitigating factors, including the following:

(a) The defendant's capacity to appreciate the wrongfulness of his conduct or to conform his conduct to the requirements of law was significantly impaired, regardless of whether the capacity was so impaired as to constitute a defense to the charge.

(b) The defendant was under unusual and substantial duress, regardless of whether the duress was of such a degree as to constitute a defense to the charge.

(c) The defendant is punishable as an accomplice (as defined in RSA 626:8) in the offense, which was committed by another, but the defendant's participation was relatively minor, regardless of whether the participation was so minor as to constitute a defense to the charge.

(d) The defendant was youthful, although not under the age of 18.

(e) The defendant did not have a significant prior criminal record.

(f) The defendant committed the offense under severe mental or emotional disturbance.

(g) Another defendant or defendants, equally culpable in the crime, will not be punished by death.

(h) The victim consented to the criminal conduct that resulted in the victim's death.

(i) Other factors in the defendant's background or character mitigate against imposition of the death sentence.

VII. If the defendant is found guilty of or pleads guilty to the offense of capital murder, the following aggravating factors are the only aggravating factors that shall be considered, unless notice of additional aggravating factors is provided under subparagraph I(b):

(a) The defendant:

(1) purposely killed the victim;

(2) purposely inflicted serious bodily injury which resulted in the death of the victim;

(3) purposely engaged in conduct which:

(A) the defendant knew would create a grave risk of death to a person, other than one of the participants in the offense; and

(B) resulted in the death of the victim.

(b) The defendant has been convicted of another state or federal offense resulting in the death of a person, for which a sentence of life imprisonment or a sentence of death was authorized by law.

(c) The defendant has previously been convicted of 2 or more state or federal offenses punishable by a term of imprisonment of more than one

year, committed on different occasions, involving the infliction of, or attempted infliction of, serious bodily injury upon another person.

(d) The defendant has previously been convicted of 2 or more state or federal offenses punishable by a term of imprisonment of more than one year, committed on different occasions, involving the distribution of a controlled substance.

(e) In the commission of the offense of capital murder, the defendant knowingly created a grave risk of death to one or more persons in addition to the victims of the offense.

(f) The defendant committed the offense after substantial planning and premeditation.

(g) The victim was particularly vulnerable due to old age, youth, or infirmity.

(h) The defendant committed the offense in an especially heinous, cruel or depraved manner in that it involved torture or serious physical abuse to the victim.

(i) The murder was committed for pecuniary gain.

(j) The murder was committed for the purpose of avoiding or preventing a lawful arrest or effecting an escape from lawful custody.

VIII. If a person is convicted of the offense of capital murder and the court does not impose the penalty of death, the court shall impose a sentence of life imprisonment without possibility of parole.

IX. If the jury cannot agree on the punishment within a reasonable time, the judge shall impose the sentence of life imprisonment without possibility of parole. If the case is reversed on appeal because of error only in the presentence hearing, the new trial which may be ordered shall apply only to the issue of punishment.

X. In all cases of capital murder where the death penalty is imposed, the judgment of conviction and the sentence of death shall be subject to automatic review by the supreme court within 60 days after certification by the sentencing court of the entire record unless time is extended for an additional period not to exceed 30 days by the supreme court for good cause shown. Such review by the supreme court shall have priority over all other cases and shall be heard in accordance with rules adopted by said court.

XI. With regard to the sentence the supreme court shall determine:

(a) Whether the sentence of death was imposed under the influence of passion, prejudice or any other arbitrary factor; and

(b) Whether the evidence supports the jury's finding of an aggravating circumstance, as authorized by law; and

(c) Whether the sentence of death is excessive or disproportionate to the penalty imposed in similar cases, considering both the crime and the defendant.

XII. In addition to its authority regarding correction of errors, the court, with regard to review of death sentences, shall be authorized to:

(a) Affirm the sentence of death; or

(b) Set the sentence aside and remand the case for resentencing.

XIII. When the penalty of death is imposed, the sentence shall be that the defendant be imprisoned in the state prison at Concord until the day appointed for his execution, which shall not be within one year from the day sentence is passed. The punishment of death shall be inflicted by continuous, intravenous administration of a lethal quantity of an ultrashort-acting barbiturate in combination with a chemical paralytic agent until death is pronounced by a licensed physician according to accepted standards of medical practice.

XIV. The commissioner of corrections or his designee shall determine the substance or substances to be used and the procedures to be used in any execution, provided, however, that if for any reason the commissioner finds it to be impractical to carry out the punishment of death by administration of the required lethal substance or substances, the sentence of death may be carried out by hanging under the provisions of law for the death penalty by hanging in effect on December 31, 1986.

XV. An execution carried out by lethal injection shall be performed by a person selected by the commissioner of the department of corrections and trained to administer the injection. The person administering the injection need not be a physician, registered nurse, or licensed practical nurse, licensed or registered under the laws of this or any other state.

XVI. The infliction of the punishment of death by administration of the required lethal substance or substances in the manner required by this section shall not be construed to be the practice of medicine, and any pharmacist or pharmaceutical supplier is authorized to dispense drugs to the commissioner of corrections or his designee, without prescription, for carrying out the provisions of this section, notwithstanding any other provision of law.

XVII. The governor and council or their designee shall determine the time of performing such execution and shall be responsible for providing facilities for the implementation thereof. In no event shall a sentence of death be carried out upon a pregnant woman or a person for an offense committed while a minor.

Source.

1974, 34:10. 1977, 440:2. 1986, 82:1. 1990, 199:3, eff. Jan. 1, 1991.

Amendments

—1990. Rewritten to the extent that a detailed comparison would be impracticable.

—1986. Paragraph IX: Deleted "and he shall then be hanged by the neck until he is dead" following "sentence is passed" at the end of the first sentence, rewrote the second sentence and deleted the third sentence.

Paragraphs X–XIII: Added.

—1977. Rewritten to the extent that a detailed comparison would be impracticable.

Applicability of 1986 amendment.

1986, 82:2, eff. Jan. 1, 1987, provided: "This act shall apply to all executions carried out on or after January 1, 1987, irrespective of the date sentence was imposed."

Manner of imposition of death sentence in event of decision holding 1986 amendment unconstitutional

1986, 82:3, eff. Jan. 1, 1987, provided: "If the execution of the death sentence as provided in RSA 630:5, IX as amended by this act is held unconstitutional, then the sentence of death shall be carried out by hanging, under the provisions of law for the death penalty by hanging in effect on December 31, 1986."

Cross References.

Commutation of death sentence, see RSA 4:23.

Respite from execution of death sentence, see RSA 4:24.

True design of punishment, see New Hampshire Constitution, Part 1, Article 18.

NOTES TO DECISIONS

1. Construction
2. Prior law
3. Retroactive effect
4. Law governing
5. Reprieve
6. Time of execution
7. Rules governing appeals
8. Proportionality review

1. Construction

In enacting the current death penalty statutory scheme, the legislature intended to incorporate the then-existing jurisprudential background of the United States Supreme Court, and the New Hampshire Supreme Court will interpret the statutory scheme accordingly. State v. Addison, 160 N.H. 732, 7 A.3d 1225, 2010 N.H. LEXIS 110 (2010).

2. Prior law

This section explicitly allowed consideration of an imposition of the death penalty only where a jury had rendered a verdict of guilty and not where defendants had pled guilty and, thus, was violative of defendants' rights to assert innocence and to a jury trial and thus was unconstitutional on its face. State v. Johnson, 134 N.H. 570, 595 A.2d 498, 1991 N.H. LEXIS 101 (1991). (Decided under former RSA 630:5.)

3. Retroactive effect

Questions of whether New Hampshire and federal constitutions barred retrospective application of this section was moot, where the supreme court determined that the legislature had not intended retrospective application of this section. State v. Johnson, 134 N.H. 570, 595 A.2d 498, 1991 N.H. LEXIS 101 (1991).

Where statute that was in effect at time of defendants' trial but not at time of commission of the crime provided new statutory grounds upon which the state could seek the death penalty, thus substantially and adversely affecting defendants' rights, and the new statute contained no expression of the legislature's intent to apply the statute retroactively, the statute would not be retroactively applied against defendants. State v. Johnson, 134 N.H. 570, 595 A.2d 498, 1991 N.H. LEXIS 101 (1991).

4. Law governing

On interlocutory appeal at trial for capital murder, the trial court properly ruled that statute in effect at time of trial could not be retrospectively applied and capital punishment procedures under statute in effect at time of crime, which permitted jury to consider imposition of death penalty only where jury had rendered guilty verdict and not where defendant had pled guilty, could not be enforced as statute was unconstitutional on its face. State v. Johnson, 134 N.H. 570, 595 A.2d 498, 1991 N.H. LEXIS 101 (1991).

5. Reprieve

A postponement of the time of execution, by reprieve, does not affect the sentence; it remains to be enforced at the end of the period of respite, or by a new order, if no other disposition has been made of the case. Ex parte Howard, 17 N.H. 545, 1845 N.H. LEXIS 41 (1845). (Decided under prior law.)

6. Time of execution

The time designated for executing a sentence of death is not a part of the sentence but simply an order prescribing the time when the sentence shall take effect. Ex parte Howard, 17 N.H. 545, 1845 N.H. LEXIS 41 (1845). (Decided under prior law.)

7. Rules governing appeals

Portion of RSA 630:5 requiring that cases "shall be heard in accordance with rules adopted by said court" does not require special rules; instead, based upon its plain language, the statute requires simply that the court have appellate rules and that such rules are followed. Thus, review of death sentences may be completed consistent with preexisting appellate rules. State v. Addison, 159 N.H. 87, 977 A.2d 520, 2009 N.H. LEXIS 86 (2009).

RSA 630:5 and the Supreme Court Rules govern the appellate procedure in capital sentence review. Neither the state nor the federal constitution mandates formal rulemaking. State v. Addison, 159 N.H. 87, 977 A.2d 520, 2009 N.H. LEXIS 86 (2009).

8. Proportionality review

Under RSA 630:5, XI(c), a death penalty is excessive or disproportionate if it is aberrant from, or substantially out of line with, a pattern of jury verdicts which demonstrate that juries generally do not impose death in similar cases. This appellate monitoring function serves to ensure that defendants will not incur a death sentence that is arbitrary and capricious, or wanton and freakish, in relation to penalties imposed by juries in similar cases, considering both the crime and the defendant. State v. Addison, 160 N.H. 732, 7 A.3d 1225, 2010 N.H. LEXIS 110 (2010).

In keeping with the plain language of RSA 630:5 and the fair import of its terms, the universe of "similar cases" is limited to those with the following procedural characteristics: the defendant committed the offense of capital murder; a separate sentencing hearing occurred; the jury found predicate aggravating factors; and the penalty imposed was either death or life imprisonment without possibility of parole. New Hampshire therefore aligns with jurisdictions that rely upon a death-and-life-imprisonment universe. State v. Addison, 160 N.H. 732, 7 A.3d 1225, 2010 N.H. LEXIS 110 (2010).

Based upon the plain language of RSA 630:5, XI(c), and the fair import of its terms, the legislature did not intend that the universe of similar cases be confined to a death-only universe. State v. Addison, 160 N.H. 732, 7 A.3d 1225, 2010 N.H. LEXIS 110 (2010).

Considering both the procedural and substantive boundaries for "similar cases," the comparison case inventory is restricted to cases in which a defendant committed the same kind of capital murder as the defendant whose death sentence is under review, a separate sentencing hearing occurred, the jury unanimously found predicate aggravating factors, and the penalty imposed was either death or life imprisonment without possibility of parole. State v. Addison, 160 N.H. 732, 7 A.3d 1225, 2010 N.H. LEXIS 110 (2010).

Plain language of RSA 630:5, XI(c) anticipates that the New Hampshire Supreme Court conduct comparative proportionality review in a fact-specific manner by considering both the crime and the defendant. The precedent-seeking method fulfills this statutory prescription and accords with the individualized sentencing considerations that juries are required to engage in when deciding whether to impose the death penalty; the approach is consistent with the plain language and fair import of RSA 630:5, XI(c). State v. Addison, 160 N.H. 732, 7 A.3d 1225, 2010 N.H. LEXIS 110 (2010).

Ultimately, the New Hampshire Supreme Court will not vacate a death sentence as excessive or disproportionate unless it is aberrant from, or substantially out of line with, a pattern of jury verdicts which demonstrate that juries generally do not impose death in similar cases. State v. Addison, 160 N.H. 732, 7 A.3d 1225, 2010 N.H. LEXIS 110 (2010).

Neither party bears the burden of proof on comparative proportionality review. RSA 630:5, XI(c) requires the Supreme Court of New Hampshire to conduct an independent review; this inquiry is a question of law that the court must definitively decide de novo, and it is not amenable to traditional burdens of proof. State v. Addison, 160 N.H. 732, 7 A.3d 1225, 2010 N.H. LEXIS 110 (2010).

When defendant's sentence of death was the first sentence subject to comparative proportionality review under RSA 630:5, XI(c), this did not by itself signify that his death sentence was excessive or disproportionate or render the comparative proportionality provision ineffective or inoperative. In this case, the court would consider published opinions of out-of-state cases to the extent such comparison would be meaningful for performing comparative proportionality review under the framework set forth by the court. State v. Addison, 160 N.H. 732, 7 A.3d 1225, 2010 N.H. LEXIS 110 (2010).

Cited:

Cited in State v. Polk, 154 N.H. 59, 907 A.2d 966, 2006 N.H. LEXIS 115 (2006).

630:6. Place; Witnesses.

The punishment of death shall be inflicted within the walls or yard of the state prison. The sheriff of the county in which the person was convicted, and 2 of his deputies, shall be present, unless prevented by unavoidable casualty. He shall request the presence of the attorney general or county attorney, clerk of the court and a surgeon, and may admit other reputable citizens not exceeding 12, the relations of the convict, his counsel and such priest or clergyman as he may desire, and no others.

Source.

1974, 34:10, eff. April 15, 1974.

CHAPTER 631

ASSAULT AND RELATED OFFENSES

SECTION

631:1.   First Degree Assault.
631:2.   Second Degree Assault.
631:2-a.   Simple Assault.
631:3.   Reckless Conduct.
631:3-a.   Conduct Involving Laser Pointing Devices.
631:4.   Criminal Threatening.
631:4-a.   Harm or Threats to Certain Government Officials.
631:5.   Operating Boats Under Influence of Liquor or Drugs. [Repealed.]
631:6.   Failure to Report Injuries.
631:7.   Student Hazing.
631:8.   Criminal Neglect of Elderly, Disabled, or Impaired Adults.

Cross References.

Assault of election official, see RSA 659:41.

Sexual assault and related offenses, see RSA 632-A.

631:1. First Degree Assault.

I. A person is guilty of a class A felony if he:

(a) Purposely causes serious bodily injury to another; or

(b) Purposely or knowingly causes bodily injury to another by means of a deadly weapon, except that if the deadly weapon is a firearm, he shall be sentenced in accordance with RSA 651:2, II-g; or

(c) Purposely or knowingly causes injury to another resulting in miscarriage or stillbirth; or

(d) Knowingly or recklessly causes serious bodily injury to a person under 13 years of age.

II. In this section:

(a) "Miscarriage" means the interruption of the normal development of the fetus other than by a live birth and not an induced abortion, resulting in the complete expulsion or extraction of a fetus; and

(b) "Stillbirth" means the death of a fetus prior to complete expulsion or extraction and not an induced abortion.

Source.

1971, 518:1. 1979, 126:1. 1990, 95:2. 1991, 75:1. 1992, 71:1, eff. Jan. 1, 1993.

Amendments

—1992. Paragraph I: Added "or" at the end of subpar. (c) and added subpar. (d).

—1991. Rewritten to the extent that a detailed comparison would be impracticable.

—1990. Paragraph II: Added "except that if the deadly weapon is a firearm, he shall be sentenced in accordance with RSA 651:2, II-g" at the end of the paragraph.

—1979. Rewritten to the extent that a detailed comparison would be impracticable.

Cross References.

Assaults by prisoners, see RSA 642:9.

Charging assaults, see RSA 601:7.

Classification of crimes, see RSA 625:9.

Involuntary admission for persons charged with felonious assault found not competent to stand trial, see RSA 171-B.

Limitation of prosecutions, see RSA 625:8.

Sentences, see RSA 651.

Victims permitted to speak before sentencing, see RSA 651:4-a.

Violating temporary restraining order by committing assault, see RSA 458:16.

NOTES TO DECISIONS

1. Double jeopardy
2. Loaded weapon
3. Expert testimony
4. Jury instructions
5. Sufficiency of the evidence
6. Merger with other offenses
7. Serious bodily injury
8. Particular cases

1. Double jeopardy

Imposition of consecutive sentences for first degree assault and the felonious use of a firearm violated constitutional guarantee against double jeopardy, because the underlying crime of knowing assault was itself enhanced by the use of a deadly weapon, and the perpetrator could therefore not be properly sentenced a second time for the felonious use of the firearm. State v. Houtenbrink, 130 N.H. 385, 539 A.2d 714, 1988 N.H. LEXIS 17 (1988).

2. Loaded weapon

In prosecution for attempted first degree assault, the fact whether the defendant's gun was loaded was not an essential element of the state's case, but rather only an evidentiary fact. State v. Fielders, 124 N.H. 310, 470 A.2d 897, 1983 N.H. LEXIS 415 (1983).

3. Expert testimony

In a prosecution for first degree assault of a two-year-old child by placing the child in a bathtub containing scalding water, it was error to permit expert testimony regarding evidence of prior intentional injuries to the child in the form of battered child syndrome since, without any connection to the defendant, such evidence did not tend to prove that the defendant purposely scalded her child. State v. Guyette, 139 N.H. 526, 658 A.2d 1204, 1995 N.H. LEXIS 39 (1995).

The fact that the defendant in a prosecution for first degree assault never suggested that the injuries sustained by the victim were not caused by him or that the injuries were the product of insignificant force did not affect the relevance of expert testimony concerning the nature and severity of the victim's injury as the state was required to prove beyond a reasonable doubt all the elements of the crime charged. State v. Walsh, 139 N.H. 435, 655 A.2d 912, 1995 N.H. LEXIS 21 (1995).

4. Jury instructions

Conviction for attempted murder was reversed because the jury should have been instructed on the lesser-included offenses of attempted first degree assault and reckless conduct; the issue of intent was sufficiently disputed to provide a rational basis for the jury to conclude defendant acted only recklessly or with a purpose to cause only serious bodily injury where he was reacting to his wife's infidelity and stabbed her as she came towards him and where court could not say that there was no rational basis for the jury to find that severe intoxication may have negated any purpose to kill the victim. State v. Thomas, 154 N.H. 189, 908 A.2d 774, 2006 N.H. LEXIS 144 (2006).

In a prosecution on charges of involuntary manslaughter, misdemeanor reckless conduct, and first-degree assault, the trial court properly instructed the jury that to find defendant guilty of involuntary manslaughter and first-degree assault, it had to find that the State had proven beyond a reasonable doubt that defendant's conduct was a substantial factor in causing the death of a child who died when defendant lost control of a pickup truck and the truck hit a tree, or the serious bodily injuries sustained by the five other children who were riding in the bed of the pickup truck. State v. Lamprey, 149 N.H. 364, 821 A.2d 1080, 2003 N.H. LEXIS 54 (2003).

5. Sufficiency of the evidence

The evidence was sufficient to support the convictions of first-degree assault for recklessly causing serious bodily injury to a person under 13 in violation of RSA 631:1, I(d). On the two occasions when the infant victim exhibited symptoms of abuse, he was with defendant immediately beforehand; there was no evidence that his other caregivers mistreated him; defendant's admissions were consistent with medical evidence about the baby's injuries; from defendant's statements and the medical testimony, a rational juror could have found beyond a reasonable doubt that defendant was aware of and consciously disregarded the risk that violently handling the infant could cause serious bodily injury. State v. Wilmot, 163 N.H. 148, 37 A.3d 422, 2012 N.H. LEXIS 8 (2012).

In a first-degree assault case involving defendant's infant child, there was sufficient evidence that the child's injury occurred in New Hampshire. The uncontroverted evidence at trial was that the only time the child was out of New Hampshire was when he was brought to Connecticut by defendant's wife to visit her friends and family, and the jury could have believed the testimony of all of the individuals who cared for him while he was in Connecticut, who appeared at trial and testified that nothing improper occurred and that he was not injured while in their care. State v. Fandozzi, 159 N.H. 773, 992 A.2d 685, 2010 N.H. LEXIS 19 (2010).

There was sufficient evidence to convict defendant of the first-degree assault of his infant child, who had broken ribs. By defendant's own admission, he was "with the kids ninety-nine point nine percent of the time"; given expert testimony about the age of the fractures, the jury could have rejected defendant's argument that he accidentally fell while holding the child four months prior to the child's hospitalization; the State's medical expert opined that the fractures were not caused by a genetic or metabolic condition and that all the fractures were the result of abuse; and there was evidence that after learning of the child's injuries, defendant's demeanor was uncharacteristic of a parent whose child was injured by unknown causes. State v. Fandozzi, 159 N.H. 773, 992 A.2d 685, 2010 N.H. LEXIS 19 (2010).

Evidence supported a conviction of first-degree assault. Even if none of defendant's bullets actually hit either victim, the evidence was sufficient that his purposeful acts were intended to, and actually did, aid the other shooter in accomplishing the assaults. State v. Young, 159 N.H. 332, 986 A.2d 497, 2009 N.H. LEXIS 122 (2009).

Contrary to defendant's claim, the evidence was sufficient to support a finding that he caused serious injury to his assault victim, his wife; the jury heard evidence that the victim suffered a broken nose, a broken tooth, a lacerated lip, a bruised neck, a swollen chin, and, for about a week after the incident, she was unable to drink, except through a straw, and unable to eat anything other than soft foods. The jury also heard testimony that, because of the beating, the victim had to have a root canal and, eventually braces, and that, at the time of trial, nearly a year later, her lip was still tender, numb and tingling. State v. Pepin, 156 N.H. 269, 940 A.2d 221, 2007 N.H. LEXIS 182 (2007).

6. Merger with other offenses

Intentionally trying to kill a person and knowingly inflicting bodily injury on that same person do not constitute two distinct criminal activities when the identical criminal conduct is the basis of both charges; the legislature did not intend for identical criminal conduct to give rise to distinct charges for first degree assault and attempted murder. Thus, because the same shooting was the basis of both the attempted murder and assault indictments, under the common law doctrine of merger, the trial court erred by imposing consecutive sentences for the convictions regarding the same victim. State v. Young, 159 N.H. 332, 986 A.2d 497, 2009 N.H. LEXIS 122 (2009).

7. Serious bodily injury

In an assault case, any error in allowing the victim to testify about corrective options for his teeth was harmless. Evidence of the injury to the victim's mouth was overwhelming, and the evidence of treatment options for the victim's teeth was cumulative and inconsequential in relation to the State's evidence of serious bodily injury. State v. Richard, 160 N.H. 780, 7 A.3d 1195, 2010 N.H. LEXIS 109 (2010).

8. Particular cases

Error in admitting post-arrest statements of co-conspirators under N.H. R. Evid. 801(d)(2)(E) was not harmless as to accomplice and conspiracy first-degree assault charges under RSA 626:8, RSA 629:3, and RSA 631:1, as the evidence did not overwhelmingly establish that defendant had at least a tacit understanding that deadly weapons would be used in the commission of the assault. State v. Rodriguez, 164 N.H. 800, 64 A.3d 962, 2013 N.H. LEXIS 45 (2013).

Cited:

Cited in State v. Boone, 119 N.H. 594, 406 A.2d 113, 1979 N.H. LEXIS 360 (1979); State v. Kelley, 120 N.H. 12, 413 A.2d 308, 1980 N.H. LEXIS 219 (1980); State v. Kelley, 120 N.H. 14, 413 A.2d 300, 1980 N.H. LEXIS 220 (1980); State v. McAvenia, 122 N.H. 580, 448 A.2d 967, 1982 N.H. LEXIS 404 (1982); State v. Niquette, 122 N.H. 870, 451 A.2d 1292, 1982 N.H. LEXIS 482 (1982); State v. Stone, 122 N.H. 987, 453 A.2d 1272, 1982 N.H. LEXIS 505 (1982); State v. Beaupre, 123 N.H. 155, 459 A.2d 233, 1983 N.H. LEXIS 243 (1983); State v. Allard, 123 N.H. 209, 459 A.2d 259, 1983 N.H. LEXIS 253 (1983); State v. Lessard, 123 N.H. 788, 465 A.2d 516, 1983 N.H. LEXIS 329 (1983); State v. Leuthner, 124 N.H. 638, 474 A.2d 1029, 1984 N.H. LEXIS 226 (1984); State v. Morse, 125 N.H. 403, 480 A.2d 183, 1984 N.H. LEXIS 259 (1984); State v. Bell, 125 N.H. 425, 480 A.2d 906, 1984 N.H. LEXIS 253 (1984); State v. Shackford, 127 N.H. 695, 506 A.2d 315, 1986 N.H. LEXIS 223 (1986); State v. Wood, 128 N.H. 739, 519 A.2d 277, 1986 N.H. LEXIS 360 (1986); State v. Meaney, 129 N.H. 448, 529 A.2d 384, 1987 N.H. LEXIS 193 (1987); State v. Beaupre, 129 N.H. 486, 529 A.2d 944, 1987 N.H. LEXIS 218 (1987); State v. Dellner, 130 N.H. 89, 534 A.2d 396, 1987 N.H. LEXIS 277 (1987); State v. Guglielmo, 130 N.H. 240, 544 A.2d 25, 1987 N.H. LEXIS 303 (1987); State v. Thomas, 133 N.H. 360, 577 A.2d 89, 1990 N.H. LEXIS 74 (1990); State v. Plante, 133 N.H. 384, 577 A.2d 95, 1990 N.H. LEXIS 75 (1990); State v. Brown, 134 N.H. 334, 591 A.2d 1331, 1991 N.H. LEXIS 60 (1991); State v. King, 136 N.H. 674, 621 A.2d 921, 1993 N.H. LEXIS 13 (1993); State v. Delgado, 137 N.H. 380, 628 A.2d 263, 1993 N.H. LEXIS 94 (1993); State v. Wright, 137 N.H. 558, 630 A.2d 772, 1993 N.H. LEXIS 125 (1993); State v. St. Laurent, 138 N.H. 492, 642 A.2d 335, 1994 N.H. LEXIS 55 (1994); State v. Lopez, 139 N.H. 309, 652 A.2d 696, 1994 N.H. LEXIS 144 (1994); State v. Soucy, 139 N.H. 349, 653 A.2d 561, 1995 N.H. LEXIS 4 (1995); State v. Walsh, 139 N.H. 435, 655 A.2d 912, 1995 N.H. LEXIS 21 (1995); Reid v. Warden, New Hampshire State Prison, 139 N.H. 530, 659 A.2d 429, 1995 N.H. LEXIS 45

(1995); State v. Grant-Chase, 140 N.H. 264, 665 A.2d 380, 1995 N.H. LEXIS 139 (1995); State v. Aubuchont, 141 N.H. 206, 679 A.2d 1147, 1996 N.H. LEXIS 75 (1996); State v. Croft, 142 N.H. 76, 696 A.2d 1117, 1997 N.H. LEXIS 58 (1997); State v. Santamaria, 145 N.H. 138, 756 A.2d 589, 2000 N.H. LEXIS 29 (2000); State v. Looney, 148 N.H. 656, 813 A.2d 495, 2002 N.H. LEXIS 212 (2002).

RESEARCH REFERENCES

New Hampshire Practice.
8-3 N.H.P. Personal Injury-Tort & Insurance Practice § 3.10.

New Hampshire Bar Journal.
For article, "Understanding and Representing Adult Clients Who Are Victims of Domestic Abuse," see 35 N.H.B.J. 8 (1994).

631:2. Second Degree Assault.

I. A person is guilty of a class B felony if he or she:

(a) Knowingly or recklessly causes serious bodily injury to another; or

(b) Recklessly causes bodily injury to another by means of a deadly weapon, except that if the deadly weapon is a firearm, he or she shall be sentenced in accordance with RSA 651:2, II-g; or

(c) Recklessly causes bodily injury to another under circumstances manifesting extreme indifference to the value of human life; or

(d) Purposely or knowingly causes bodily injury to a child under 13 years of age; or

(e) Recklessly or negligently causes injury to another resulting in miscarriage or stillbirth; or

(f) Purposely or knowingly engages in the strangulation of another.

II. In this section:

(a) "Miscarriage" means the interruption of the normal development of the fetus other than by a live birth and not an induced abortion, resulting in the complete expulsion or extraction of a fetus.

(b) "Stillbirth" means the death of a fetus prior to complete expulsion or extraction and not an induced abortion.

(c) "Strangulation" means the application of pressure to another person's throat or neck, or the blocking of the person's nose or mouth, that causes the person to experience impeded breathing or blood circulation or a change in voice.

Source.
1971, 518:1. 1979, 126:2. 1985, 181:1. 1990, 95:3. 1991, 75:2, eff. Jan. 1, 1992. 2010, 8:1, eff. January 1, 2011.

Amendments
—2010. The 2010 amendment added I(f) and II(c) and made related and stylistic changes.

—1991. Rewritten to the extent that a detailed comparison would be impracticable.

—1990. Paragraph II: Inserted "except that if the deadly weapon is a firearm, he shall be sentenced in accordance with RSA 651:2, II-g" following "means of a deadly weapon".

—1985. Paragraph III: Added "or" following "life".
Paragraph IV: Added.

—1979. Rewritten to the extent that a detailed comparison would be impracticable.

Cross References.

Assaults by prisoners, see RSA 642:9.
Charging assaults, see RSA 601:7.
Child Protection Act, see RSA 169-C.
Classification of crimes, see RSA 625:9.
Limitation of prosecutions, see RSA 625:8.
Sentences, see RSA 651.

NOTES TO DECISIONS

1. Constitutionality
2. Construction with other laws
3. Indictment
4. Serious bodily injury
5. Circumstances manifesting extreme indifference
6. Deadly weapon
7. Recklessness
8. Evidence
9. Lesser included offense
10. Instructions
11. Defenses
12. Double jeopardy

1. Constitutionality

In the context of this section, the phrase "under circumstances manifesting an extreme indifference to the value of human life" is not unconstitutionally vague. State v. Saucier, 128 N.H. 291, 512 A.2d 1120, 1986 N.H. LEXIS 292 (1986).

2. Construction with other laws

One cannot conspire to commit a crime where the culpability is based upon the result of reckless conduct; thus, defendant's motion to dismiss the portion of an indictment that charged conspiracy to commit reckless second-degree assault should have been granted because the indictment failed to allege facts that, if proven, would have constituted a cognizable crime. State v. Donohue, 150 N.H. 180, 834 A.2d 253, 2003 N.H. LEXIS 158 (2003).

3. Indictment

Where defendant was indicted for second degree assault and charged with recklessly causing bodily injury, the trial court did not substantively amend the indictment by instructing the jury, based on RSA 626:2, III, that if they found that defendant acted purposely or knowingly, such a finding would satisfy the State's burden of proving recklessness as charged in the indictment. State v. Bathalon, 146 N.H. 485, 778 A.2d 1109, 2001 N.H. LEXIS 99 (2001).

At trial for second degree assault in which defendant had fired pistol injuring thirteen-year-old victim, allegation of victim's age in indictment was surplusage; therefore, trial court properly denied motion for judgment notwithstanding the verdict based on state's failure to prove victim's date of birth at trial. State v. Mansfield, 134 N.H. 287, 592 A.2d 512, 1991 N.H. LEXIS 54 (1991).

4. Serious bodily injury

Evidence was sufficient to show that a law enforcement officer suffered a protracted impairment to the function of his eye and thus suffered a serious bodily injury for purposes of the second-degree assault statute. The jury could have believed that he had consistently impaired vision for up to 19 days and, for at least some time thereafter, intermittently impaired vision requiring medical attention. State v. Dorrance, — N.H. —, 70 A.3d 451, 2013 N.H. LEXIS 81 (July 16, 2013).

Evidence was sufficient to support finding that defendant's violent acts toward the victim caused serious bodily injury where a medical expert testified that a life-threatening infection could have resulted from the smashing of the victim's nose in the absence of medical intervention and where the victim testified to still feeling the effects of the incident a year later. State v. Scognamiglio, 150 N.H. 534, 842 A.2d 109, 2004 N.H. LEXIS 17 (2004).

In prosecution for second-degree assault, whether the victim's injuries constituted "serious bodily injury" was a question of fact for the jury to decide. State v. Plaut, 124 N.H. 813, 474 A.2d 587, 1984 N.H. LEXIS 335 (1984).

In the case of defendant convicted of second-degree assault, where the jury heard the testimony of the victim, who described slipping in and out of consciousness immediately after the assault,

his inability to move at the time of the assault, the presence of blood in his urine, dizziness and inability to walk steadily during his two-day stay at the hospital, and the pain and reduced mobility he experienced after his release from the hospital, the supreme court held that that testimony, viewed in the light most favorable to the prosecution, supported the verdict, and that a rational jury could have found beyond a reasonable doubt that the victim had suffered "serious bodily injury." State v. Plaut, 124 N.H. 813, 474 A.2d 587, 1984 N.H. LEXIS 335 (1984).

5. Circumstances manifesting extreme indifference

Defendant's conviction for second-degree assault, RSA 631:2, I(c), was affirmed as there was sufficient evidence to prove that defendant caused bodily injury to the victim under circumstances manifesting an extreme indifference to the value of human life where defendant repeatedly hit and kicked the officer. State v. Edson, 153 N.H. 45, 889 A.2d 420, 2005 N.H. LEXIS 179 (2005).

For purposes of paragraph III (now paragraph I(c)) of this section, an attacker acts with "extreme indifference" when he inflicts any degree of bodily injury on a victim and when the circumstances of the attack demonstrate a blatant disregard for the risk of the victim's life. State v. Saucier, 128 N.H. 291, 512 A.2d 1120, 1986 N.H. LEXIS 292 (1986); State v. Fletcher, 129 N.H. 641, 531 A.2d 321, 1987 N.H. LEXIS 231 (1987).

In order to support a finding that the defendant acted with extreme indifference to the value of human life, as provided in paragraph III (now paragraph I(c)) of this section, it is not necessary that the particular assaults or injuries charged themselves be life threatening, but instead that the circumstances of the crime manifest extreme indifference. State v. Saucier, 128 N.H. 291, 512 A.2d 1120, 1986 N.H. LEXIS 292 (1986).

Second degree assault committed in violation of paragraph III (now paragraph I(c)) of this section requires proof that the circumstances of the crime manifest extreme indifference; neither paragraph III (now paragraph I(c)) nor common sense limits the relevant circumstances to the injuries themselves. State v. Bailey, 127 N.H. 416, 503 A.2d 762, 1985 N.H. LEXIS 461 (1985).

To prove second degree assault committed in violation of paragraph III (now paragraph I(c)) of this section, the injury or series of injuries need not themselves threaten life. State v. Bailey, 127 N.H. 416, 503 A.2d 762, 1985 N.H. LEXIS 461 (1985).

6. Deadly weapon

The use of a deadly weapon is not an essential element of second degree assault. State v. Fletcher, 129 N.H. 641, 531 A.2d 321, 1987 N.H. LEXIS 231 (1987).

7. Recklessness

At trial for second degree assault on an infant in which infant's injuries reflected "shaken baby syndrome," under culpability standard of recklessness, jury was not required to find that defendant anticipated the severe brain damage that resulted from his conduct, but only to find that (1) the shaking of a newborn baby in the manner discernible from the evidence involved the substantial and unjustifiable risk to that baby of any serious bodily injury; (2) the defendant was aware of that risk yet consciously disregarded it; and (3) that defendant was aware of the existence of circumstances permitting the characterization of the disregard as a gross deviation from law-abiding conduct. State v. Evans, 134 N.H. 378, 594 A.2d 154, 1991 N.H. LEXIS 71 (1991).

8. Evidence

Fact that defendant might not have been an active participant in the crime from the outset did not shelter him from accomplice liability for second-degree assault under RSA 631:2, I(c) and 626:8. The jury could find that when defendant aided and assisted the assailants, the assault was a work in progress; furthermore, there was sufficient evidence that defendant could have reasonably foreseen that the victim would sustain further bodily injury as a consequence of his acts and that he acted recklessly with extreme indifference to the value of human life State v. Alwardt, 164 N.H. 52, 53 A.3d 545, 2012 N.H. LEXIS 111 (2012).

A rational trier of fact could find beyond a reasonable doubt that the defendant was guilty of second-degree assault by hitting the victim in the mouth where victim's guidance counselor reported that, the day after the assault, the victim had an injury to her lip, and that the victim said that the defendant had punched her, and a doctor also testified that the victim reported having been hit by defendant. State v. Mason, 150 N.H. 53, 834 A.2d 339, 2003 N.H. LEXIS 138 (2003).

Conviction of defendant of second degree assault was vacated because the State presented no direct evidence that the defendant broke the victim's nose, but rather relied solely upon circumstantial evidence to prove culpability. State v. Haycock, 146 N.H. 302, 771 A.2d 570, 2001 N.H. LEXIS 74 (2001).

Evidence was sufficient to allow a rational jury to find, beyond a reasonable doubt, that the defendant knowingly injured the four-year-old victim where testimony showed that, acting out of anger or frustration, the defendant handled the victim in such a way that he was aware would cause injury. State v. Lowe, 140 N.H. 271, 665 A.2d 740, 1995 N.H. LEXIS 140 (1995).

At trial for second degree assault on infant whose injuries reflected "shaken baby syndrome," evidence was sufficient to find beyond a reasonable doubt that defendant was subjectively aware of the risk shaking posed of severe bodily injury and consciously disregarded such risk, and that defendant was aware of circumstances permitting characterization of such conduct as a gross deviation from law-abiding conduct, and jury was entitled to weigh defendant's numerous subsequent explanations for the baby's injuries other than shaking in determining his earlier subjective knowledge. State v. Evans, 134 N.H. 378, 594 A.2d 154, 1991 N.H. LEXIS 71 (1991).

Evidence was sufficient to uphold defendant's conviction for second degree assault on his infant son, where evidence indicated that the baby had been in the defendant's care at the approximate time he suffered a broken femur, and expert testimony stressed the likelihood that the injury was not accidental. State v. Amell, 131 N.H. 309, 553 A.2d 286, 1988 N.H. LEXIS 125 (1988).

At a trial for second degree assault, the court properly admitted a photograph of the victim, a five-week-old baby, pursuant to a finding of relevancy, where the photograph was offered to prove the contested element of serious bodily injury. State v. Hotchkiss, 129 N.H. 260, 525 A.2d 270, 1987 N.H. LEXIS 167 (1987).

There was sufficient evidence for a jury to find beyond a reasonable doubt that defendant committed second degree assault where he repeatedly held the victim by the throat, choked her, dragged her across a parking lot while holding her throat, and repeatedly threw her against parked cars. State v. Saucier, 128 N.H. 291, 512 A.2d 1120, 1986 N.H. LEXIS 292 (1986).

At a trial for second degree assault committed in violation of paragraph III (now paragraph I(c)) of this section, doctor's testimony concerning the life-threatening tendency of the acts committed by defendant was clearly admissible, since from this evidence of the fatal tendency of the defendant's course of conduct the jury could infer an indifference to that tendency. State v. Bailey, 127 N.H. 416, 503 A.2d 762, 1985 N.H. LEXIS 461 (1985).

Evidence that defendant, who was being detained at police station, refused to enter a cell in which he was being placed in order to avoid further fighting between his girlfriend and another female cellmate, and took hold of an officer's revolver and fired shot which superficially wounded another officer, clearly supported conviction for aggravated assault on the ground the defendant recklessly caused bodily injury to another by means of a deadly weapon. State v. Jones, 120 N.H. 652, 421 A.2d 1004, 1980 N.H. LEXIS 368 (1980).

9. Lesser included offense

Where juvenile was charged as a delinquent with second-degree assault, the trial court erred in concluding that simple assault by unprivileged physical contact is a lesser-included offense of second-degree assault. In re Nathan L., 146 N.H. 614, 776 A.2d 1277, 2001 N.H. LEXIS 119 (2001).

10. Instructions

Robbery and assault defendant was not entitled to jury instruction on defense of accident in connection with injury to police officer inflicted during defendant's escape from scene of shoplifting, where testimony of officer, his partner, and two loss prevention officers was that defendant held officer's arm inside car as he drove away; although some evidence of accident was presented, it was not legally sufficient to support a rational finding that injuries to officer were caused by accident. State v. Rosciti, 144 N.H. 198, 740 A.2d 623, 1999 N.H. LEXIS 99 (1999).

In charging the jury in a prosecution under this section, a trial court did not commit error in declining to read verbatim the comments to the 1969 Report of the Commission to Recommend Codification of the Criminal Laws which related to this section. State v. Bailey, 127 N.H. 416, 503 A.2d 762, 1985 N.H. LEXIS 461 (1985); State v. Saucier, 128 N.H. 291, 512 A.2d 1120, 1986 N.H. LEXIS 292 (1986).

11. Defenses

Use of force to prevent or punish misconduct by a child constitutes a defense in a prosecution for second degree assault only if it is "reasonable." Reasonableness is determined by an objective standard, and a belief which is unreasonable, even though honest, will not support the defense. State v. Leaf, 137 N.H. 97, 623 A.2d 1329, 1993 N.H. LEXIS 47 (1993).

12. Double jeopardy

Evidence of defendant's intoxication was necessary to aggravated driving while intoxicated charge but not to second degree assault charge, and proof of defendant's excessive rate of speed was essential to second degree assault indictment but not to aggravated driving while intoxicated indictment; defendant's convictions for both offenses therefore did not violate the "same evidence" or "difference in evidence" double jeopardy test under the State Constitution. State v. MacLeod, 141 N.H. 427, 685 A.2d 473, 1996 N.H. LEXIS 120 (1996).

Defendant's convictions for armed robbery under RSA 636:1 and assault under this section did not violate the double jeopardy clause of the federal constitution, since proof that defendant used physical force while in the course of committing theft is essential to a conviction for armed robbery, but it is not necessary that defendant be in the course of committing theft for a conviction under this section, and the state must establish that defendant caused bodily injury to obtain a conviction under this section, while bodily injury is not essential to a conviction for armed robbery. State v. Shannon, 125 N.H. 653, 484 A.2d 1164, 1984 N.H. LEXIS 380 (1984).

Cited:

Cited in State v. Varney, 114 N.H. 642, 325 A.2d 784, 1974 N.H. LEXIS 339 (1974); State v. McMillan, 116 N.H. 126, 352 A.2d 702, 1976 N.H. LEXIS 283 (1976); State v. Ober, 116 N.H. 381, 359 A.2d 624, 1976 N.H. LEXIS 359 (1976); State v. Slade, 116 N.H. 436, 362 A.2d 194, 1976 N.H. LEXIS 376 (1976); State v. Martin, 118 N.H. 102, 382 A.2d 1107, 1978 N.H. LEXIS 352 (1978); State v. Perron, 118 N.H. 245, 385 A.2d 225, 1978 N.H. LEXIS 389 (1978); State v. Lavallee, 119 N.H. 207, 400 A.2d 480, 1979 N.H. LEXIS 278 (1979); State v. Osborne, 119 N.H. 427, 402 A.2d 493, 1979 N.H. LEXIS 346 (1979); State v. Kiluk, 120 N.H. 1, 410 A.2d 648, 1980 N.H. LEXIS 218 (1980); State v. Kelley, 120 N.H. 14, 413 A.2d 300, 1980 N.H. LEXIS 220 (1980); State v. Glidden, 122 N.H. 41, 441 A.2d 728, 1982 N.H. LEXIS 285 (1982); State v. Arillo, 122 N.H. 107, 441 A.2d 1163, 1982 N.H. LEXIS 295 (1982); State v. Perron, 122 N.H. 941, 454 A.2d 422, 1982 N.H. LEXIS 496 (1982); State v. Paradis, 123 N.H. 68, 455 A.2d 1070, 1983 N.H. LEXIS 225 (1983); La Vallee v. Perrin, 124 N.H. 33, 466 A.2d 932, 1983 N.H. LEXIS 354 (1983); In re Eric C., 124 N.H. 222, 469 A.2d 1305, 1983 N.H. LEXIS 382 (1983); State v. Benson, 124 N.H. 767, 474 A.2d 576, 1984 N.H. LEXIS 340 (1984); State v. Horne, 125 N.H. 254, 480 A.2d 121, 1984 N.H. LEXIS 283 (1984); Abbott v. Potter, 125 N.H. 257, 480 A.2d 118, 1984 N.H. LEXIS 282 (1984); State v. Ballou, 125 N.H. 304, 481 A.2d 260, 1984 N.H. LEXIS 270 (1984); State v. Glidden, 127 N.H. 359, 499 A.2d 1349, 1985 N.H. LEXIS 438 (1985); State v. Smith, 127 N.H. 836, 508 A.2d 1082, 1986 N.H. LEXIS 229 (1986); State v. MacManus, 130 N.H. 256, 536 A.2d 203, 1987 N.H. LEXIS 283 (1987); State v. Pelky, 131 N.H. 715, 559 A.2d 1345, 1989 N.H. LEXIS 52 (1989); State v. Allen, 133 N.H. 306, 577 A.2d 801, 1990 N.H. LEXIS 68 (1990); State v. Michaud, 135 N.H. 723, 610 A.2d 354, 1992 N.H. LEXIS 110 (1992); State v. Mills, 136 N.H. 46, 611 A.2d 1104, 1992 N.H. LEXIS 128 (1992); State v. Bernaby, 139 N.H. 420, 653 A.2d 1124, 1995 N.H. LEXIS 18 (1995); Reid v. Warden, New Hampshire State Prison, 139 N.H. 530, 659 A.2d 429, 1995 N.H. LEXIS 45 (1995); State v. Horne, 140 N.H. 90, 663 A.2d 92, 1995 N.H. LEXIS 110 (1995); State v. James, 140 N.H. 50, 663 A.2d 83, 1995 N.H. LEXIS 99 (1995); Tsiatsios v. Tsiatsios, 140 N.H. 173, 663 A.2d 1335, 1995 N.H. LEXIS 120 (1995); State v. Lowe, 140

N.H. 271, 665 A.2d 740, 1995 N.H. LEXIS 140 (1995); State v. Russo, 140 N.H. 751, 674 A.2d 156, 1996 N.H. LEXIS 29 (1996).

RESEARCH REFERENCES

New Hampshire Practice.
8-3 N.H.P. Personal Injury-Tort & Insurance Practice § 3.10.

New Hampshire Bar Journal.
For article, "Understanding and Representing Adult Clients Who Are Victims of Domestic Abuse," see 35 N.H.B.J. 8 (1994).

631:2-a. Simple Assault.

I. A person is guilty of simple assault if he:

(a) Purposely or knowingly causes bodily injury or unprivileged physical contact to another; or

(b) Recklessly causes bodily injury to another; or

(c) Negligently causes bodily injury to another by means of a deadly weapon.

II. Simple assault is a misdemeanor unless committed in a fight entered into by mutual consent, in which case it is a violation.

Source.
1979, 126:3, eff. Aug. 4, 1979.

Cross References.
Assaults by prisoners, see RSA 642:9.
Charging assaults, see RSA 601:7.
Classification of crimes, see RSA 625:9.
Sentences, see RSA 651.

NOTES TO DECISIONS

1. Constitutionality
2. Elements
3. Juvenile delinquency petition
4. Provocation
5. Lesser included offense
6. Defense
7. Sufficient evidence to convict
8. Juvenile delinquency petition
9. Classification

1. Constitutionality

RSA 631:2-a, I(a), which criminalizes "unprivileged physical contact," is not unconstitutionally vague under the Due Process Clause, because the plain meaning of that phrase includes all physical contact not justified by law or consent, and this construction of RSA 631:2-a, I(a) limits police discretion so as to make it unlikely that the law will be applied in an ad hoc and subjective manner. State v. Burke, 153 N.H. 361, 897 A.2d 996, 2006 N.H. LEXIS 38 (2006).

2. Elements

The means used by the accused in making a simple assault is not an essential element of the offense and need not be specifically alleged in the complaint. State v. Twarog, 97 N.H. 101, 81 A.2d 855, 1951 N.H. LEXIS 27 (1951)(decided under prior law).

3. Juvenile delinquency petition

Where the mens rea of purposely or knowingly was not included in a juvenile delinquency petition under RSA 169-B:6, II and RSA 169-B:2, IV that charged a juvenile with the offense of misdemeanor simple assault, in violation of RSA 631:2-a, I(a), the petition was constitutionally deficient under N.H. Const. pt. I, art. 15. In re Alex C., 158 N.H. 525, 969 A.2d 399, 2009 N.H. LEXIS 39 (2009).

4. Provocation

In a complaint for committing a simple assault upon a sheriff while he was serving process, it was proper on direct examination to inquire of the sheriff whether he did anything on that day in any way to provoke the assault. State v. Cornwell, 97 N.H. 446, 91 A.2d 456, 1952 N.H. LEXIS 51 (1952). (Decided under prior law.)

5. Lesser included offense

Simple assault under RSA 631:2-a, I(a), although perhaps a lesser-included offense of aggravated felonious sexual assault by means of application of physical force, is not a lesser-included offense of felonious sexual assault under RSA 632-A:3, III. "Unprivileged physical contact" is not an element of felonious sexual assault by means of sexual contact with a victim under the age of thirteen. State v. Michaud, 161 N.H. 785, 20 A.3d 1012, 2011 N.H. LEXIS 60 (2011).

Defendant, who was charged with violating RSA 632-A:3, III, by engaging in sexual contact with a person other than his legal spouse who was under 13, was not entitled to a lesser-included-offense instruction on simple assault under RSA 631:2-a, I(a). "Unprivileged physical contact" was not an element of felonious sexual assault under RSA 632-A:3, III. State v. Michaud, 161 N.H. 785, 20 A.3d 1012, 2011 N.H. LEXIS 60 (2011).

Where juvenile was charged as a delinquent with second-degree assault, the trial court erred in concluding that simple assault by unprivileged physical contact is a lesser-included offense of second-degree assault. In re Nathan L., 146 N.H. 614, 776 A.2d 1277, 2001 N.H. LEXIS 119 (2001).

In relation to a conviction on the charge of disobeying an officer with personal injury to another, where the elements of the crime of a purported lesser-included offense of simple assault contained a reckless mental state, and the elements of the charged crime did not contain any culpable mental state, defendant was properly denied a lesser-included offense instruction. State v. Hall, 133 N.H. 446, 577 A.2d 1225, 1990 N.H. LEXIS 89 (1990).

The offense of simple assault under subparagraph I(b) of this section, based on recklessly causing bodily injury to another, is not a lesser included offense of negligent homicide as defined in RSA 630:3, because simple assault requires a more culpable mental state than negligent homicide. State v. Mallar, 127 N.H. 816, 508 A.2d 1070, 1986 N.H. LEXIS 251 (1986).

The offense of simple assault under subparagraph I(c) of this section, based on negligently causing bodily injury to another by means of a deadly weapon, is not a lesser included offense of negligent homicide, as defined in RSA 630:3, since use of a deadly weapon is not an essential element of negligent homicide. State v. Mallar, 127 N.H. 816, 508 A.2d 1070, 1986 N.H. LEXIS 251 (1986).

In prosecution for aggravated felonious sexual assault, where there was no physical evidence of rape, the prosecutrix stated that she was raped and the defendant claimed that he hit or pushed the prosecutrix in an attempt to secure the return of his property, but did not rape her, there was sufficient evidence to permit a jury rationally to convict the defendant of the lesser offense of simple assault and acquit him of the greater offense of aggravated felonious sexual assault, and the failure of the trial court to give a requested instruction on the lesser included offense seriously undermined the integrity of the fact finding process and denied the defendant of due process of law. Dukette v. Perrin, 564 F. Supp. 1530, 1983 U.S. Dist. LEXIS 16363 (D.N.H. 1983).

6. Defense

Reversal and remand were required where the court's response to a jury question on the date of the crime constructively amended the complaint to defendant's prejudice because the defendant's alibi defense was based upon the particular date charged in the complaint by the state and the court instructed the jury that it need not find that the offense occurred on the date alleged. State v. Poole, 150 N.H. 299, 837 A.2d 307, 2003 N.H. LEXIS 186 (2003).

In trial for simple assault, defendant was entitled to jury instruction on defense of others where some evidence was presented that defendant had assaulted victim in response to unlawful unprivileged physical contact by another on defendant's wife. State v. Hast, 133 N.H. 747, 584 A.2d 175, 1990 N.H. LEXIS 127 (1990).

7. Sufficient evidence to convict

Although there was no direct evidence of physical contact between defendant and the victim, the trial court properly denied the motion to dismiss a simple assault charge. If the jury accepted the circumstantial evidence, including defendant's statements that were recounted by a witness and the victim's injuries, if credibility issues were resolved in favor of the State, and if the evidence was taken in a light favorable to the State, a jury could find that the State proved all the elements of the charge beyond a reasonable doubt. State v. Schwartz, 160 N.H. 68, 993 A.2d 220, 2010 N.H. LEXIS 29 (2010).

Sufficient evidence supported the convictions of defendant, a correctional officer, for simple assault under RSA 631:2-a when defendant shoved the small of the victim's back and swept one of the victim's legs out from under him after the victim was brought to defendant's facility. A rational juror could have found that defendant's physical contact with the victim was unprivileged and unjustified under RSA 627:5, as there was evidence that the victim did not pose a threat to defendant at the time of the incidents. State v. Cunningham, 159 N.H. 103, 977 A.2d 506, 2009 N.H. LEXIS 89 (2009).

As defendant conceded engaging in physical contact with the victim, and the record contained testimony that she acted knowingly and that her conduct was not justified by law or consent, the trial court reasonably could have concluded that defendant committed simple assault under RSA 631:2-a, I(a) by knowingly causing unprivileged physical contact to the victim by knowingly pushing her. State v. Burke, 153 N.H. 361, 897 A.2d 996, 2006 N.H. LEXIS 38 (2006).

There was sufficient evidence to convict defendant of simple assault under RSA 631:2-a, I(a), where a contemporaneous 911 call from a witness stated that defendant struck the victim, and the 911 call was corroborated by another witness in a written statement to police. State v. Jordan, 148 N.H. 115, 803 A.2d 604, 2002 N.H. LEXIS 101 (2002).

8. Juvenile delinquency petition

As the mens rea of purposely or knowingly is an element of the offense of misdemeanor simple assault pursuant to RSA 631:2-a, I(a) which is required in a charging document against an adult, a juvenile delinquency petition requires that the requisite mental state be alleged pursuant to RSA 169-B:2, IV. In re Alex C., 158 N.H. 525, 969 A.2d 399, 2009 N.H. LEXIS 39 (2009).

9. Classification

Complaints for simple assault under RSA 631:2-a and for resisting arrest under RSA 642:2 did not allege a crime that involved as an element an act of violence or a threat of violence for purposes of class A misdemeanor classification under RSA 625:9, IV(c)(1). The variant of simple assault alleged here involved causing unprivileged physical contact, not bodily injury, and the resisting arrest statute could be violated by conduct that fell short of causing or attempting to cause bodily injury. State v. Blunt, 164 N.H. 679, 62 A.3d 1285, 2013 N.H. LEXIS 27 (2013).

Cited:

Cited in State v. Sullivan, 121 N.H. 301, 428 A.2d 1247, 1981 N.H. LEXIS 307 (1981); State v. Randall, 122 N.H. 19, 440 A.2d 11, 1982 N.H. LEXIS 276 (1982); State v. Miner, 122 N.H. 86, 441 A.2d 1150, 1982 N.H. LEXIS 291 (1982); State v. Thaxton, 122 N.H. 1148, 455 A.2d 1016, 1982 N.H. LEXIS 542 (1982); State v. Smith, 123 N.H. 46, 455 A.2d 1041, 1983 N.H. LEXIS 220 (1983); State v. Lessard, 123 N.H. 788, 465 A.2d 516, 1983 N.H. LEXIS 329 (1983); State v. Baldwin, 124 N.H. 770, 475 A.2d 522, 1984 N.H. LEXIS 341 (1984); State v. Wright, 126 N.H. 643, 496 A.2d 702, 1985 N.H. LEXIS 362 (1985); State v. Bailey, 127 N.H. 416, 503 A.2d 762, 1985 N.H. LEXIS 461 (1985); State v. Smith, 127 N.H. 836, 508 A.2d 1082, 1986 N.H. LEXIS 229 (1986); State v. Fletcher, 129 N.H. 641, 531 A.2d 321, 1987 N.H. LEXIS 231 (1987); State v. Pierce, 130 N.H. 7, 533 A.2d 34, 1987 N.H. LEXIS 252 (1987); State v. Houtenbrink, 130 N.H. 385, 539 A.2d 714, 1988 N.H. LEXIS 17 (1988); State v. Leary, 133 N.H. 46, 573 A.2d 135, 1990 N.H. LEXIS 25 (1990); State v. Bousquet, 133 N.H. 485, 578 A.2d 853, 1990 N.H. LEXIS 84 (1990); State v. Sammataro, 135 N.H. 579, 607 A.2d 135, 1992 N.H. LEXIS 85 (1992); State v. VandeBogart, 136 N.H. 107, 612 A.2d 906, 1992 N.H. LEXIS 145 (1992); State v. Vaillancourt, 136 N.H. 206, 612 A.2d 1329, 1992 N.H. LEXIS 152 (1992); State v. Dushame, 136 N.H. 309, 616 A.2d 469, 1992 N.H. LEXIS 173 (1992); State v. Richardson, 138 N.H. 162, 635 A.2d 1361, 1993 N.H. LEXIS 187 (1993); State v. Woods, 139 N.H. 399, 654 A.2d 960, 1995 N.H. LEXIS 12 (1995).

RESEARCH REFERENCES

New Hampshire Practice.

8-3 N.H.P. Personal Injury-Tort & Insurance Practice §§ 3.10, 3.14.

New Hampshire Bar Journal.

For article, "Understanding and Representing Adult Clients Who Are Victims of Domestic Abuse," see 35 N.H.B.J. 8 (1994).

631:3. Reckless Conduct.

I. A person is guilty of reckless conduct if he recklessly engages in conduct which places or may place another in danger of serious bodily injury.

II. Reckless conduct is a class B felony if the person uses a deadly weapon as defined in RSA 625:11, V. All other reckless conduct is a misdemeanor.

III. A person convicted of a class B felony offense under this section shall not be subject to the provisions of RSA 651:2, II-g.

Source.

1971, 518:1. 1994, 187:1, eff. Jan. 1, 1995. 2006, 163:2, eff. January 1, 2007.

Amendments
—**2006.** Paragraph III: Added.

—**1994.** Designated the existing provisions of the section as par. I, substituted "reckless conduct" for "a misdemeanor" following "guilty of" in that paragraph, and added par. II.

Cross References.
Classification of crimes, see RSA 625:9.
Sentences, see RSA 651.

NOTES TO DECISIONS

1. Construction with other law
2. Double jeopardy
3. Sufficiency of evidence
4. Jury instructions
5. Sufficiency of indictment/information

1. Construction with other law

Determination that N.H. Rev. Stat. Ann. § 626:2, and § 631:3 reckless conduct was necessarily reprehensible because its definition included "serious bodily injury" and satisfied the scienter element because it required a classic formulation of recklessness was reasonable, and perfectly reflected moral turpitude as contemplated in 8 U.S.C.S. § 1182. Idy v. Holder, 674 F.3d 111, 2012 U.S. App. LEXIS 6098 (2012).

Minimum mandatory sentence provision of RSA 651:2, II-g, applied to defendant's felony conviction of reckless conduct with a deadly weapon under subdivision II of this section. State v. Haines, 142 N.H. 692, 709 A.2d 762, 1998 N.H. LEXIS 23 (1998). (Decided under prior law.)

2. Double jeopardy

Defendant's criminal threatening and reckless conduct convictions under RSA 631:3 and RSA 631:4, I(a), which arose out of the same transaction, did not violate double jeopardy under N.H. Const. pt. I, art. 16 and the federal Constitution because the indictments each required the State to prove a separate element. Whereas the criminal threatening statute required proof that defendant placed or attempted to place the victim in fear of imminent bodily injury, it did not require proof that the victim was actually placed in danger; by contrast, the reckless conduct statute did require that defendant placed or might have placed the victim in actual danger of serious bodily injury regardless of whether he feared such injury. State v. Gingras, 162 N.H. 633, 34 A.3d 659,

2011 N.H. LEXIS 149 (2011).

Double jeopardy provision of State Constitution was not violated by sentence enhancement under statute requiring minimum mandatory sentence for firearms, in combination with enhancement of reckless conduct from misdemeanor to Class B felony for use of deadly weapon. State v. Haines, 142 N.H. 692, 709 A.2d 762, 1998 N.H. LEXIS 23 (1998). (Decided under prior law.)

3. Sufficiency of evidence

Evidence was sufficient to establish that defendant was criminally reckless when, while intoxicated, he fired a handgun into a couch inside an occupied residence. State v. McCabe, 145 N.H. 686, 765 A.2d 176, 2001 N.H. LEXIS 7 (2001).

A rational trier of fact could find that brandishing a loaded rifle at another individual in middle of town constituted reckless behavior placing another in danger of serious bodily injury. Therefore, the evidence was sufficient to support defendant's conviction under this section. State v. Haines, 142 N.H. 692, 709 A.2d 762, 1998 N.H. LEXIS 23 (1998).

4. Jury instructions

Conviction for attempted murder was reversed because the jury should have been instructed on the lesser-included offenses of attempted first degree assault and reckless conduct; the issue of intent was sufficiently disputed to provide a rational basis for the jury to conclude defendant acted only recklessly or with a purpose to cause only serious bodily injury where he was reacting to his wife's infidelity and stabbed her as she came towards him and where court could not say that there was no rational basis for the jury to find that severe intoxication may have negated any purpose to kill the victim. State v. Thomas, 154 N.H. 189, 908 A.2d 774, 2006 N.H. LEXIS 144 (2006).

5. Sufficiency of indictment/information

Reckless conduct indictments did not violate the Fifth and Sixth Amendments. They tracked RSA 631:3 in alleging misdemeanor reckless conduct, and any insufficiency in alleging felony reckless conduct was harmless because any rational grand jury presented with proper indictments would have charged defendant with felony-level reckless conduct. State v. Euliano, 161 N.H. 601, 20 A.3d 223, 2011 N.H. LEXIS 29 (2011).

Cited.

Cited in State v. Dowdle, 148 N.H. 345, 807 A.2d 1237, 2002 N.H. LEXIS 133 (2002); State v. Demeritt, 148 N.H. 435, 813 A.2d 393, 2002 N.H. LEXIS 149 (2002); State v. Lamprey, 149 N.H. 364, 821 A.2d 1080, 2003 N.H. LEXIS 54 (2003).

RESEARCH REFERENCES

New Hampshire Practice.

8-3 N.H.P. Personal Injury-Tort & Insurance Practice § 3.10.

631:3-a. Conduct Involving Laser Pointing Devices.

I. Any person who knowingly shines the beam of a laser pointing device at an occupied motor vehicle, window, or person shall be guilty of a violation and the laser pointing device shall be forfeited upon conviction.

II. Notwithstanding the provisions of paragraph I, any person who knowingly shines the beam of a laser pointing device at a law enforcement officer or law enforcement vehicle shall be guilty of a class A misdemeanor and the laser pointing device shall be forfeited upon conviction.

III. It shall be an affirmative defense under this section if the laser pointing device was used in an organized meeting or training class by the instructor or speaker. Nothing in this section shall be con-

strued so as to limit the use of medical lasers by qualified medical personnel, or construction lasers used by construction personnel, or laser devices utilized by law enforcement personnel in the performance of their official duties.

Source.

1999, 230:1, eff. Jan. 1, 2000.

Cross References.

Classification of crimes, see RSA 625:9.
Sentences, see RSA 651.

RESEARCH REFERENCES

New Hampshire Practice.

8-3 N.H.P. Personal Injury-Tort & Insurance Practice § 3.10.

631:4. Criminal Threatening.

I. A person is guilty of criminal threatening when:

(a) By physical conduct, the person purposely places or attempts to place another in fear of imminent bodily injury or physical contact; or

(b) The person places any object or graffiti on the property of another with a purpose to coerce or terrorize any person; or

(c) The person threatens to commit any crime against the property of another with a purpose to coerce or terrorize any person; or

(d) The person threatens to commit any crime against the person of another with a purpose to terrorize any person; or

(e) The person threatens to commit any crime of violence, or threatens the delivery or use of a biological or chemical substance, with a purpose to cause evacuation of a building, place of assembly, facility of public transportation or otherwise to cause serious public inconvenience, or in reckless disregard of causing such fear, terror or inconvenience; or

(f) The person delivers, threatens to deliver, or causes the delivery of any substance the actor knows could be perceived as a biological or chemical substance, to another person with the purpose of causing fear or terror, or in reckless disregard of causing such fear or terror.

II. (a) Criminal threatening is a class B felony if the person:

(1) Violates the provisions of subparagraph I(e); or

(2) Uses a deadly weapon as defined in RSA 625:11, V in the violation of the provisions of subparagraph I(a), I(b), I(c), or I(d).

(b) All other criminal threatening is a misdemeanor.

III. (a) As used in this section, "property" has the same meaning as in RSA 637:2, I; "property of another" has the same meaning as in RSA 637:2, IV.

(b) As used in this section, "terrorize" means to cause alarm, fright, or dread; the state of mind induced by the apprehension of hurt from some hostile or threatening event or manifestation.

IV. A person who responds to a threat which would be considered by a reasonable person as likely to cause serious bodily injury or death to the person or to another by displaying a firearm or other means of self-defense with the intent to warn away the person making the threat shall not have committed a criminal act under this section.

Source.

1971, 518:1. 1983, 338:1. 1994, 187:2, eff. Jan. 1, 1995. 1996, 92:1, eff. Jan. 1, 1997. 2002, 222:7, eff. Jan. 1, 2003. 2003, 69:1, eff. Jan. 1, 2004. 2010, 361:2, eff. January 1, 2011.

Amendments

—2010. The 2010 amendment added IV.

—2003. Paragraph III: Designated the existing provisions as subpar. (a) and added subpar. (b).

—2002. Paragraph I(e): Inserted "or threatens the delivery or use of a biological or chemical substance" following "violence", and added "or" following "inconvenience".

Paragraph I(f): Added.

—1996. Paragraph I: Rewritten to the extent that a detailed comparison would be impracticable.

Paragraph II(a)(1): Substituted "subparagraph I(e)" for "subparagraph I(c)".

Paragraph II(a)(2): Inserted "I(c)" preceding "or I(d)".

—1994. Paragraph II: Rewritten to the extent that a detailed comparison would be impracticable.

—1983. Redesignated former pars. I-III as present subpars. (a)-(c) of par. I and added subpar. (d) of that paragraph, redesignated former par. IV as present par. II and substituted "subparagraph I(c)" for "paragraph III" in that paragraph, and added par. III.

Cross References.

Classification of crimes, see RSA 625:9.

Sentences, see RSA 651.

NOTES TO DECISIONS

1. Construction
2. Evidence
3. Double jeopardy
4. Jury instructions
5. Deadly weapon
6. Indictment
7. Sentence

1. Construction

Since the trial court committed reversible error by interpreting RSA 631:4, I to include a mens rea of "knowingly," which was a lesser mental state than "purposely," defendant's conviction for criminal threatening had to be reversed. State v. Morabito, 153 N.H. 302, 893 A.2d 691, 2006 N.H. LEXIS 26 (2006).

In order for a jury to conclude that defendant intended to terrorize his employee, in violation of RSA 631:4, I(d), it had to conclude that his purpose was to cause extreme fear, and trial court's instruction which defined "a purpose to terrorize another" as seeking "to cause alarm, fright, dread, or the state of mind which is induced by the apprehension of hurt from some hostile or threatening event" was legally insufficient. State v. Fuller, 147 N.H. 210, 785 A.2d 408, 2001 N.H. LEXIS 196 (2001).

Although use of deadly weapon was an element of crime of felony criminal threatening, it was not a material element, and therefore State was not obligated to prove a specific mens rea with respect to that element. State v. McCabe, 145 N.H. 686, 765 A.2d 176, 2001 N.H. LEXIS 7 (2001).

Criminal threatening statute did not require defendant to have acted with purpose of placing victim in fear of imminent bodily injury or physical contact when he used deadly weapon, but only that he had such a purposeful mental state when he made threat,

and therefore trial court did not err in its answer to jury's question concerning intent required for criminal threatening. State v. McCabe, 145 N.H. 686, 765 A.2d 176, 2001 N.H. LEXIS 7 (2001).

2. Evidence

Evidence was sufficient to support a conviction of criminal threatening under RSA 631:4. A rational juror could have found that defendant's actions of waving and pointing a gun toward the victim, while yelling "get the F off my property," constituted felony criminal threatening. State v. Bird, 161 N.H. 31, 8 A.3d 146, 2010 N.H. LEXIS 125 (2010).

Trial court did not err in denying defendant's motion to set aside the verdict of guilty on a charge of felony criminal threatening. By defendant's own admission, he pulled out a gun with the purpose of frightening the victim; whether he purposely placed or attempted to place her in fear of imminent bodily injury was a question of fact for the jury, and the jury was so instructed. State v. Kousounadis, 159 N.H. 413, 986 A.2d 603, 2009 N.H. LEXIS 136 (2009).

Where wife asserted that (1) 11 years before she filed her request, the husband struck her in anger; (2) 8 years prior to the request, the husband pushed her into a slide during an argument; and (3) the husband threatened during an argument some months prior to the request to make her life a living hell if she did not comply with his wishes, trial court's finding of abuse in issuing protective order was not supported by sufficient evidence that husband committed abuse in the form of criminal threatening as the incidents the wife described were either too distant in time or were too non-specific to constitute criminal threatening. Fillmore v. Fillmore, 147 N.H. 283, 786 A.2d 849, 2001 N.H. LEXIS 206 (2001).

3. Double jeopardy

Defendant's criminal threatening and reckless conduct convictions under RSA 631:3 and RSA 631:4, I(a), which arose out of the same transaction, did not violate double jeopardy under N.H. Const. pt. I, art. 16 and the federal Constitution because the indictments each required the State to prove a separate element. Whereas the criminal threatening statute required proof that defendant placed or attempted to place the victim in fear of imminent bodily injury, it did not require proof that the victim was actually placed in danger; by contrast, the reckless conduct statute did require that defendant placed or might have placed the victim in actual danger of serious bodily injury regardless of whether he feared such injury. State v. Gingras, 162 N.H. 633, 34 A.3d 659, 2011 N.H. LEXIS 149 (2011).

Defendant was properly convicted and sentenced for separate kidnapping and criminal threatening charges, as each element of two offenses differed and each charge required different evidence, and therefore there was no double jeopardy violation; the kidnapping elements were set forth in RSA 633:1, I(c), and the criminal threatening elements were set forth in RSA 631:4, I(a), II(a)(2). State v. McKean, 147 N.H. 198, 785 A.2d 404, 2001 N.H. LEXIS 195 (2001).

4. Jury instructions

Court could not conclude, as a matter of law, that charging the jury to determine whether shooting a firearm "in the vicinity" of a person necessarily required the jury to render an essential factual finding on an element of a felony criminal threatening charge—namely, that defendant used, intended to use, or threatened to use a firearm in a manner that was known to be capable of producing death or serious bodily injury. Whether the specific manner in which defendant used a shotgun and the circumstances surrounding that use rendered the shotgun a deadly weapon was a factual issue within the exclusive province of the jury. State v. Kousounadis, 159 N.H. 413, 986 A.2d 603, 2009 N.H. LEXIS 136 (2009).

Firearm was a deadly weapon under RSA 625:11, V, if, in the manner it was used, intended to be used, or threatened to be used, it was known to be capable of producing death or serious bodily injury. Thus, as to felony criminal threatening under RSA 631:4, it was error to instruct the jury that a shotgun was a deadly weapon per se; the error was not subject to harmless error analysis because under the state constitution, a jury instruction that omitted an element of the offense charged was an error that partially or completely denied a defendant the right to the basic trial process. State v. Kousounadis, 159 N.H. 413, 986 A.2d 603, 2009 N.H. LEXIS 136 (2009).

5. Deadly weapon

State bears the burden in a criminal threatening case to prove beyond a reasonable doubt that the defendant used a firearm in such a manner that it constituted a deadly weapon. State v. Kousounadis, 159 N.H. 413, 986 A.2d 603, 2009 N.H. LEXIS 136 (2009).

6. Indictment

Indictment sufficiently alleged felony criminal threatening when it stated that defendant waved a 45 caliber handgun, a firearm and deadly weapon pursuant to RSA 625:11, at the victim while telling her to get off of his property. Implicit in these allegations was a threat to use the gun. State v. Bird, 161 N.H. 31, 8 A.3d 146, 2010 N.H. LEXIS 125 (2010).

7. Sentence

Imposition of a mandatory sentence of three to six years in state prison under RSA 651:2, II-g for conviction of criminal threatening under RSA 631:4 did not violate N.H. Const. pt. I, art. 18 or U.S. Const. amends. VIII and XIV. Defendant failed to persuade the court that the sentencing scheme was unconstitutional because it necessarily resulted in sentences that were disproportionate. State v. Bird, 161 N.H. 31, 8 A.3d 146, 2010 N.H. LEXIS 125 (2010).

Cited:

Cited in State v. Miner, 122 N.H. 86, 441 A.2d 1150, 1982 N.H. LEXIS 291 (1982); State v. Cantara, 123 N.H. 737, 465 A.2d 887, 1983 N.H. LEXIS 341 (1983); State v. Gagne, 129 N.H. 93, 523 A.2d 76, 1986 N.H. LEXIS 380 (1986); State v. Bousquet, 133 N.H. 485, 578 A.2d 853, 1990 N.H. LEXIS 84 (1990); State v. DeLong, 136 N.H. 707, 621 A.2d 442, 1993 N.H. LEXIS 18 (1993); State v. Richardson, 138 N.H. 162, 635 A.2d 1361, 1993 N.H. LEXIS 187 (1993); State v. Horne, 140 N.H. 90, 663 A.2d 92, 1995 N.H. LEXIS 110 (1995); State v. Higgins, 149 N.H. 290, 821 A.2d 964, 2003 N.H. LEXIS 41 (2003); In re McArdle & McArdle, 162 N.H. 482, 34 A.3d 700, 2011 N.H. LEXIS 127 (2011).

RESEARCH REFERENCES

New Hampshire Practice.
8-3 N.H.P. Personal Injury-Tort & Insurance Practice § 3.10.

New Hampshire Bar Journal.
For article, "Understanding and Representing Adult Clients Who Are Victims of Domestic Abuse," see 35 N.H.B.J. 8 (1994).

631:4-a. Harm or Threats to Certain Government Officials.

I. A person is guilty of a class A felony if he or she causes bodily injury to, or commits any other crime against, a sitting member of the general court, an executive councilor, a past or present governor, member of the judiciary, marital master, or member of their immediate family, for the purpose of influencing such official's action or in retaliation for action taken as a part of an official's government duties.

II. A person is guilty of a class B felony if he or she threatens bodily injury or threatens to commit any other crime against a sitting member of the general court, an executive councilor, a past or present governor, member of the judiciary, marital master, or member of their immediate family, for the purpose of influencing such official's action or in retaliation for action taken as a part of an official's government duties.

III. Violations of this statute shall be prosecuted by the office of the attorney general.

Source.

2006, 47:1, eff. January 1, 2007. 2012, 66:6, eff. April 5, 2016. 2013, 89:2, II, eff. June 20, 2013.

Editor's note.

2013, 89:2 (II), eff. June 20, 2013, repealed the prospective repeal of Paragraphs I and II, which provided postponed repeal by 2012, 66:6, effective April 5, 2016.

Amendments

—2012. The 2012 amendment deleted "marital master" following "of the judiciary" in I and II.

631:5. Operating Boats Under Influence of Liquor or Drugs.

[Repealed 1992, 257:22, II, eff. Jan. 1, 1993.]

Former section(s).

Former RSA 631:5, which was derived from 1971, 518:1; 1985, 28:2; and 1989, 353:28, related to penalties for operating boats under the influence of liquor or drugs. See now RSA 270:48-a.

631:6. Failure to Report Injuries.

I. Except as provided in paragraph II, a person is guilty of a misdemeanor if, having knowingly treated or assisted another for a gunshot wound or for any other injury he believes to have been caused by a criminal act, he fails immediately to notify a law enforcement official of all the information he possesses concerning the injury.

II. A person who has rendered treatment or assistance is excepted from the reporting provisions of paragraph I if the person seeking or receiving treatment or other assistance: (a) is 18 years of age or older, (b) has been a victim of a sexual assault offense or abuse as defined in RSA 173-B:1, and (c) objects to the release of any information to law enforcement officials. This exception shall not apply if the sexual assault or abuse victim is also being treated for a gunshot wound or other serious bodily injury.

III. [Repealed.]

Source.

1971, 518:1. 1991, 59:1. 1993, 95:1, 3, eff. Jan. 1, 1994.

Amendments

—1993. Paragraph II: Inserted "or abuse as defined in RSA 173-B:1" following "offense" in the first sentence and "or abuse" preceding "victim" in the second sentence and substituted "serious bodily" for "life threatening" preceding "injury" at the end of that sentence.

Paragraph III: Repealed.

—1991. Designated the existing provisions of the section as par. I, added "except as provided in paragraph II" preceding "a person" in that paragraph, and added pars. II and III.

Cross References.

Classification of crimes, see RSA 625:9.

Privilege of victim to bar disclosure of confidential communication or records by counselor, see RSA 173-C:2.

Sentences, see RSA 651.

NOTES TO DECISIONS

Medical records

Physician reporting statute did not provide unilateral authority to the State to subpoena records protected by the doctor-patient privilege. In re Grand Jury Subpoena for Med. Records of Payne v. Barka, 150 N.H. 436, 839 A.2d 837, 2004 N.H. LEXIS 1 (2004).

RESEARCH REFERENCES

New Hampshire Trial Bar News.
For article, "New Hampshire Health Care Providers' Duty to Warn Third Parties: How Far Does It Extend?," see 15 N.H. Trial Bar News 37 (Fall 1993).

631:7. Student Hazing.

I. For the purposes of this section:

(a) "Educational institution" means any public or private high school, college, university, or other secondary or postsecondary educational establishment.

(b) "Organization" means a fraternity, sorority, association, corporation, order, society, corps, athletic group, cooperative, club, or service, social or similar group, whose members are or include students, operating at or in conjunction with an educational institution.

(c) "Student" means any person regularly enrolled on a full-time or part-time basis as a student in an educational institution.

(d) "Student hazing" means any act directed toward a student, or any coercion or intimidation of a student to act or to participate in or submit to any act, when:

(1) Such act is likely or would be perceived by a reasonable person as likely to cause physical or psychological injury to any person; and

(2) Such act is a condition of initiation into, admission into, continued membership in or association with any organization.

II. (a) A natural person is guilty of a class B misdemeanor if such person:

(1) Knowingly participates as actor in any student hazing; or

(2) Being a student, knowingly submits to hazing and fails to report such hazing to law enforcement or educational institution authorities; or

(3) Is present at or otherwise has direct knowledge of any student hazing and fails to report such hazing to law enforcement or educational institution authorities.

(b) An educational institution or an organization operating at or in conjunction with an educational institution is guilty of a misdemeanor if it:

(1) Knowingly permits or condones student hazing; or

(2) Knowingly or negligently fails to take reasonable measures within the scope of its authority to prevent student hazing; or

(3) Fails to report to law enforcement authorities any hazing reported to it by others or of which it otherwise has knowledge.

III. The implied or express consent of any person toward whom an act of hazing is directed shall not be a defense in any action brought under this section.

Source.
1993, 155:1, eff. July 1, 1993.

Cross References.
Classification of crimes, see RSA 625:9.
Sentences, see RSA 651.

631:8. Criminal Neglect of Elderly, Disabled, or Impaired Adults.

I. In this section:

(a) "Adult" means any person who is 18 years of age or older.

(b) "Caregiver" means any person who has been entrusted with, or has assumed the responsibility voluntarily, by contract, or by order of the court, for frequent and regular care of or services to an elderly, disabled, or impaired adult, including subsistence, medical, custodial, personal or other care, on a temporary or permanent basis. A caregiver shall not include an uncompensated volunteer, unless such person has agreed to provide care and is aware that the person receiving the care is dependent upon the care provided.

(c) "Disabled adult" means an adult who has a diagnosed physical or mental impairment.

(d) "Elderly adult" means an individual who is 60 years of age or older.

(e) "Impaired adult" means any adult who suffers from an impairment by reason of mental illness, developmental disability, organic brain disorder, physical illness or disability, chronic use of drugs, chronic intoxication, memory loss, or other cause, that causes an adult to lack sufficient understanding or capacity to make or communicate reasonable decisions concerning the adult's person or property or to be substantially impaired in the adult's ability to provide adequately for his or her own care and custody.

(f) "Neglect" means the failure or omission on the part of the caregiver to provide the care, supervision, and services which he or she has voluntarily, or by contract, or by order of the court agreed to provide and which are necessary to maintain the health of an elderly, disabled, or impaired adult, including, but not limited to, food, clothing, medicine, shelter, supervision, and medical services, that a prudent person would consider necessary for the well-being of an elderly, disabled, or impaired adult. "Neglect" may be repeated conduct or a single incident.

(g) "Person" means any natural person, corporation, trust, partnership, unincorporated association, or any other legal entity.

(h) "Serious bodily injury" means serious bodily injury as defined in RSA 625:11, VI.

II. Any caregiver who purposely causes serious bodily injury to an elderly, disabled, or impaired adult by neglect shall be guilty of a class A felony.

III. Any caregiver who knowingly or recklessly causes serious bodily injury to an elderly, disabled, or impaired adult by neglect shall be guilty of a class B felony.

IV. Nothing in this section shall be construed to alter or impair a person's right to self-determination or right to refuse medical treatment as described in RSA 151:21 and RSA 151:21-b.

V. Nothing in this section shall be construed to mean a person is abused, neglected, exploited, or in need of protective services for the sole reason that such person relies on or is being furnished treatment by spiritual means alone through prayer, in accordance with the tenets and practices of a church or religious denomination of which such person is a member or an adherent.

VI. Nothing in this section shall be construed to impose criminal liability on a person who has made a good faith effort to provide for the care of an elderly, disabled, or impaired adult, but through no fault of his or her own, has been unable to provide such care, or on a person who is carrying out the lawful request of an elderly or disabled adult who is competent to make his or her own decisions.

Source.
2002, 226:1, eff. July 16, 2002.

Cross References.
Classification of crimes, see RSA 625:9.
Sentences, see RSA 651.

RESEARCH REFERENCES

New Hampshire Bar Journal.
For Attorney General article, "Combating Health Care Fraud and Patient Abuse: The Role of the Medicaid Fraud Unit," see 45 N.H.B.J. 71 (2004).

CHAPTER 632

RAPE

[Repealed 1975, 302:2, eff. Aug. 6, 1975.]

Former section(s).
Former RSA 632, comprising RSA 632:1–632:5, which was derived from 1971, 518:1, related to sexual offenses. See now RSA 632-A.

CHAPTER 632-A

SEXUAL ASSAULT AND RELATED OFFENSES

SECTION
632-A:1. Definitions.
632-A:2. Aggravated Felonious Sexual Assault.
632-A:3. Felonious Sexual Assault.
632-A:4. Sexual Assault.
632-A:5. Spouse as Victim; Evidence of Husband and Wife.
632-A:6. Testimony and Evidence.
632-A:7. Limitations of Prosecutions. [Repealed.]
632-A:8. In Camera Testimony.
632-A:9. Speedy Trial.
632-A:10. Prohibition from Child Care Service of Persons Convicted of Certain Offenses.
632-A:10-a. Penalties.
632-A:10-b. HIV Testing.
632-A:10-c. Limitations on Civil Actions.

Registration of Sexual Offenders
SECTION
632-A:11–632-A:19. [Repealed.]

DNA Testing of Sexual Offenders 632-A:20–632-A:24. [Repealed.]

Cross References.
Annulment of record of conviction for offense under this chapter, see RSA 651:5.
Confidential communications between victims of sexual assault and counselors, see RSA 173-C.
DNA testing of criminal offenders, see RSA 651-C.
Involuntary admission for persons charged with felonious sexual assault found not competent to stand trial, see RSA 171-B.
Parole of prisoner convicted of psycho-sexual murder, see RSA 651-A:8.
Physical force in defense of a person, see RSA 627:4.
Registration of Criminal Offenders, see RSA 651-B.
Testimony of minor in civil proceedings to recover damages on behalf of minor for abuse or assault, see RSA 516:25-a.

NOTES TO DECISIONS

Cited:
Cited in State v. Cressey, 137 N.H. 402, 628 A.2d 696, 1993 N.H. LEXIS 83 (1993).

RESEARCH REFERENCES

New Hampshire Bar Journal.
For article, "Repressed Memory or False Memory: New Hampshire Courts Consider the Dispute," 35 N.H.B.J. 51 (1994).
For Attorney General article, "State Office of Victim/Witness Assistance," see 45 N.H.B.J. 87 (2004).

632-A:1. Definitions.

In this chapter:

I. "Actor" means a person accused of a crime of sexual assault.

I-a. "Affinity" means a relation which one spouse because of marriage has to blood relatives of the other spouse.

I-b. "Genital openings" means the internal or external genitalia including, but not limited to, the vagina, labia majora, labia minora, vulva, urethra or perineum.

I-c. "Pattern of sexual assault" means committing more than one act under RSA 632-A:2 or RSA 632-A:3, or both, upon the same victim over a period of 2 months or more and within a period of 5 years.

II. "Retaliate" means to undertake action against the interests of the victim, including, but not limited to:

(a) Physical or mental torment or abuse.

(b) Kidnapping, false imprisonment or extortion.

(c) Public humiliation or disgrace.

III. "Serious personal injury" means extensive bodily injury or disfigurement, extreme mental anguish or trauma, disease or loss or impairment of a sexual or reproductive organ.

IV. "Sexual contact" means the intentional touching whether directly, through clothing, or otherwise, of the victim's or actor's sexual or intimate parts, including emissions, tongue, anus, breasts, and buttocks. Sexual contact includes only that aforementioned conduct which can be reasonably construed as being for the purpose of sexual arousal or gratification.

V. (a) "Sexual penetration" means:

    (1) Sexual intercourse; or

    (2) Cunnilingus; or

    (3) Fellatio; or

    (4) Anal intercourse; or

    (5) Any intrusion, however slight, of any part of the actor's body, including emissions, or any object manipulated by the actor into genital or anal openings of the victim's body; or

    (6) Any intrusion, however slight, of any part of the victim's body, including emissions, or any object manipulated by the victim into the oral, genital, or anal openings of the actor's body; or

    (7) Any act which forces, coerces, or intimidates the victim to perform any sexual penetration as defined in subparagraphs (1)–(6) on the actor, on another person, or on himself.

(b) Emissions include semen, urine, and feces. Emission is not required as an element of any form of sexual penetration.

(c) "Objects" include animals as defined in RSA 644:8, II.

VI. "Therapy" means the treatment of bodily, mental, or behavioral disorders by remedial agents or methods.

Source.

1975, 302:1. 1979, 127:1. 1981, 553:10. 1986, 132:2. 1992, 254:3–5. 1994, 185:1, eff. Jan. 1, 1995. 1998, 240:1, eff. Jan. 1, 1999. 1999, 177:1, eff. Aug. 30, 1999. 2008, 334:8, eff. January 1, 2009.

Amendments

—2008. The 2008 amendment in IV, in the first sentence, added "emissions, tongue, anus"; added designation V(a); redesignated former V(a) through V(g) as V(a)(1) through V(a)(7); in V(a)(5), added "including emissions"; in V(a)(6), added "including emissions, or any object manipulated by the victim" and "the oral" preceding "genital"; in V(a)(7), substituted "subparagraphs (1)–(6)" for "subparagraphs (a)–(f)"; redesignated former V(h) as V(b); in V(b), added the first sentence; added V(c); and made stylistic changes.

—1999. Paragraph IV: Inserted "whether directly, through clothing, or otherwise" following "touching" and deleted "and the intentional touching of the victim's or actor's clothing covering the immediate area of the victim's or actor's sexual or intimate parts" following "buttocks" in the first sentence.

—1998. Paragraph VI: Added.

—1994. Paragraph I-c: Added.

—1992. Paragraph I-b: Added.

Paragraph II: Rewritten to the extent that a detailed comparison would be impracticable.

Paragraph V: Added a new subpar. (g) and redesignated former subpar. (g) as subpar. (h).

—1986. Paragraph I-a: Added.

—1981. Paragraph V: Rewritten to the extent that a detailed comparison would be impracticable.

—1979. Paragraph IV: Inserted "or actor's" following "victim's" wherever it appeared.

NOTES TO DECISIONS

1. Sexual penetration
2. Sexual contact
3. Pattern of sexual assault
4. Therapy
5. "Intimate part"

1. Sexual penetration

Although "vagina" is defined by RSA 632-A:1 as a "genital opening," that definition does not establish that touching the vagina constitutes penetration; on the contrary, the statute defines penetration as "intrusion . . . into genital or anal openings of the victim's body." Thus, in a prosecution for aggravated felonious sexual assault under 632-A:2, I(l), the State was required to prove digital intrusion into the victim's vagina. State v. Guay, 162 N.H. 375, 33 A.3d 1166, 2011 N.H. LEXIS 121 (2011).

Gross sexual assault under Me. Rev. Stat. Ann. tit. 17-A, § 253(2)(D) was reasonably equivalent to aggravated felonious sexual assault under RSA 632-A:2, as New Hampshire's definition of "sexual penetration" in RSA 632-A:1, V is substantially similar to Maine's definition of "sexual act" in Me. Rev. Stat. Ann. tit. 17-A, § 251(C). Accordingly, petitioner, who had pleaded guilty to violating the Maine statute, was required under RSA 651-B:1 to register for life as a sex offender. Doe v. N.H. Dep't of Safety, 160 N.H. 474, 999 A.2d 362, 2010 N.H. LEXIS 63 (2010).

An indictment that alleges that a defendant "knowingly" solicited a child under the age of 16 to engage in sexual penetration as defined by RSA 632-A:1, V satisfies the requirements of RSA 639:3, III, as the "knowingly" mental state in RSA 639:3, I applies to the conduct defined in RSA 639:3, III. State v. Laporte (in re State), 157 N.H. 229, 950 A.2d 147, 2008 N.H. LEXIS 55 (2008).

Circumstantial evidence of semen and saliva found on the victim's body and other circumstances were ample to support defendant's conviction of aggravated felonious sexual assault by surprise, and there was plenty of direct evidence indicating assault by digital penetration, particularly the victim's own account. State v. Flynn, 151 N.H. 378, 855 A.2d 1254, 2004 N.H. LEXIS 158 (2004).

If the victim is forced to commit fellatio upon the defendant or the defendant performs the act upon the victim, the act falls within the definition of sexual penetration in paragraph V of this section. State v. Vonklock, 121 N.H. 697, 433 A.2d 1299, 1981 N.H. LEXIS 399 (1981), overruled in part, State v. Smith, 127 N.H. 433, 503 A.2d 774, 1985 N.H. LEXIS 463 (1985).

Subparagraph V(e) of this section relates to acts not otherwise covered in paragraph IV and does limit sexual penetration to the genital or anal openings of the victim. State v. Scott, 117 N.H. 996, 380 A.2d 1092, 1977 N.H. LEXIS 479 (1977).

The act of cunnilingus as sexual penetration does not require actual penetration. State v. Zeta Chi Fraternity, 142 N.H. 16, 696 A.2d 530, 1997 N.H. LEXIS 50 (1997), cert. denied, Zeta Chi Fraternity v. New Hampshire, 522 U.S. 995, 118 S. Ct. 558, 139 L. Ed. 2d 400, 1997, 1997 U.S. LEXIS 7080 (1997).

2. Sexual contact

RSA 645:2, I(f) was overbroad under N.H. Const. pt. I, art. 22 when applied to the specific facts of the case, where defendant offered to pay a couple for engaging in sexual intercourse while he videotaped them. The only evidence in the record as to defendant's intent was that he intended to make pornography, which as a general rule could be banned only if obscene; the State had not charged defendant with offering to pay the couple to engage in sexual contact, which under RSA 632-A:1, IV would have required the State to prove that he acted for the purpose of sexual arousal or gratification and thus engaged in conduct that was not constitutionally protected. State v. Theriault, 158 N.H. 123, 960 A.2d 687, 2008 N.H. LEXIS 138 (2008).

Even before the statute was clarified by amendment in 1999, touching through clothing included touching through blankets. State v. Barnett, 147 N.H. 334, 789 A.2d 629, 2001 N.H. LEXIS 216 (2001).

Victim's testimony and illustrations, together with testimony of victim's brother and investigating officer, were sufficient to support jury's verdict on counts alleging sexual contact, fellatio and cunnilingus. State v. Hodgdon, 143 N.H. 399, 725 A.2d 660, 1999 N.H. LEXIS 17 (1999).

3. Pattern of sexual assault

With regard to an indictment for pattern aggravated felonious sexual assault, there was no plain error arising from the indictment's failure to include the statutory definition of the word "pattern" because the court had not previously decided whether the definition had to be included. State v. Ortiz, 162 N.H. 585, 34 A.3d 599, 2011 N.H. LEXIS 146 (2011).

Victim's testimony that defendant digitally penetrated her at least three times in a four-month period satisfied the requirements of a pattern of sexual assault. State v. DeCosta, 146 N.H. 405, 772 A.2d 340, 2001 N.H. LEXIS 89 (2001).

4. Therapy

Legislature intended the term "therapy" in RSA 632-A:1, VI to encompass activity whereby an actor implements a planned action for another person's "bodily, mental, or behavioral" disorder by affording him or her some systematic cause or measure, procedure, or technique or particular approach in order to cure, remove, counteract, relieve, or abate that disorder. State v. Flodin, 159 N.H. 358, 986 A.2d 470, 2009 N.H. LEXIS 126 (2009).

Defendant's aggravated felonious sexual assault and sexual assault convictions under RSA 632-A:2, I(g)(1) and RSA 632-A:4, I were reversed because he had not provided "therapy" under RSA 632-A:1, VI to the victim, an inmate whom defendant met while serving as a "spiritual services coordinator" at a correctional institution. Having regular meetings centered on different topics which ultimately generated encouraging and helpful discussions did not give rise to a rational conclusion that defendant engaged in a planned action or a systematic cause or measure, procedure, technique or any particular approach in order to relieve the alleged victim's bodily, mental, or behavioral disorders; defendant's own characterization of his work as therapeutic in nature did not satisfy the statutorily defined dimensions of therapy. State v. Flodin, 159 N.H. 358, 986 A.2d 470, 2009 N.H. LEXIS 126 (2009).

5. "Intimate part"

In RSA 632-A:1, IV, an "intimate part" means any part of the body the touching of which, for sexual arousal or gratification, is offensive to an objectively reasonable sense of personal dignity, privacy, and modesty. State v. Bakunczyk, 164 N.H. 77, 53 A.3d 569, 2012 N.H. LEXIS 110 (2012).

Six-year-old victim's inner thigh adjacent to her genitals was an "intimate part" of her body as defined by RSA 632-A:1, IV. Accordingly, there was sufficient evidence to support defendant's conviction of felonious sexual assault under RSA 632-A:3, III. State v. Bakunczyk, 164 N.H. 77, 53 A.3d 569, 2012 N.H. LEXIS 110 (2012).

Cited:

Cited in State v. Goodwin, 118 N.H. 862, 395 A.2d 1234, 1978 N.H. LEXIS 307 (1978); State v. St. John, 120 N.H. 61, 410 A.2d 1126, 1980 N.H. LEXIS 224 (1980); State v. Mitchell, 124 N.H. 247, 469 A.2d 1310, 1983 N.H. LEXIS 411 (1983); State v. Lovely, 124 N.H. 690, 480 A.2d 847, 1984 N.H. LEXIS 295 (1984); State v. Smith, 127 N.H. 433, 503 A.2d 774, 1985 N.H. LEXIS 463 (1985); Lovely v. Cunningham, 796 F.2d 1, 1986 U.S. App. LEXIS 26377 (1st Cir. N.H. 1986); State v. Smith, 127 N.H. 836, 508 A.2d 1082, 1986 N.H. LEXIS 229 (1986); Opinion of Justices, 129 N.H. 180, 522 A.2d 989, 1987 N.H. LEXIS 176 (1987); State v. Hood, 131 N.H. 606, 557 A.2d 995, 1989 N.H. LEXIS 36 (1989); State v. Wood, 132 N.H. 162, 562 A.2d 1312, 1989 N.H. LEXIS 85 (1989); State v. Pond, 132 N.H. 472, 567 A.2d 992, 1989 N.H. LEXIS 129 (1989); State v. Fennell, 133 N.H. 402, 578 A.2d 329, 1990 N.H. LEXIS 79 (1990); State v. Letourneau, 133 N.H. 565, 578 A.2d 865, 1990 N.H. LEXIS 99 (1990); State v. O'Neill, 134 N.H. 182, 589 A.2d 999, 1991 N.H. LEXIS 51 (1991); State v. Vaillancourt, 136 N.H. 206, 612 A.2d 1329, 1992 N.H. LEXIS 152 (1992); State v. Demmons, 137 N.H. 716, 634 A.2d 998, 1993 N.H. LEXIS 149 (1993); State v. Arris, 139 N.H. 469, 656 A.2d 828, 1995 N.H. LEXIS 31 (1995); State v. Cole, 142 N.H. 519, 703 A.2d 658, 1997 N.H. LEXIS 125 (1997); State v. Krueger, 146 N.H. 541, 776 A.2d 720, 2001 N.H. LEXIS 108 (2001); State v. Richard, 147 N.H. 340, 786 A.2d 876, 2001 N.H. LEXIS 221 (2001).

632-A:2. Aggravated Felonious Sexual Assault.

I. A person is guilty of the felony of aggravated felonious sexual assault if such person engages in sexual penetration with another person under any of the following circumstances:

(a) When the actor overcomes the victim through the actual application of physical force, physical violence or superior physical strength.

(b) When the victim is physically helpless to resist.

(c) When the actor coerces the victim to submit by threatening to use physical violence or superior physical strength on the victim, and the victim believes that the actor has the present ability to execute these threats.

(d) When the actor coerces the victim to submit by threatening to retaliate against the victim, or any other person, and the victim believes that the actor has the ability to execute these threats in the future.

(e) When the victim submits under circumstances involving false imprisonment, kidnapping or extortion.

(f) When the actor, without the prior knowledge or consent of the victim, administers or has knowledge of another person administering to the victim any intoxicating substance which mentally incapacitates the victim.

(g) When the actor provides therapy, medical treatment or examination of the victim and in the course of that therapeutic or treating relationship or within one year of termination of that therapeutic or treating relationship:

(1) Acts in a manner or for purposes which are not professionally recognized as ethical or acceptable; or

(2) Uses this position as such provider to coerce the victim to submit.

(h) When, except as between legally married spouses, the victim has a disability that renders him or her incapable of freely arriving at an independent choice as to whether or not to engage in sexual conduct, and the actor knows or has reason to know that the victim has such a disability.

(i) When the actor through concealment or by the element of surprise is able to cause sexual penetration with the victim before the victim has an adequate chance to flee or resist.

(j) When, except as between legally married spouses, the victim is 13 years of age or older and under 16 years of age and:

(1) the actor is a member of the same household as the victim; or

(2) the actor is related by blood or affinity to the victim.

(k) When, except as between legally married spouses, the victim is 13 years of age or older and under 18 years of age and the actor is in a position of authority over the victim and uses this authority to coerce the victim to submit.

(*l*) When the victim is less than 13 years of age.

(m) When at the time of the sexual assault, the victim indicates by speech or conduct that there is not freely given consent to performance of the sexual act.

(n) When the actor is in a position of authority over the victim and uses this authority to coerce the victim to submit under any of the following circumstances:

(1) When the actor has direct supervisory or disciplinary authority over the victim by virtue of the victim being incarcerated in a correctional institution, the secure psychiatric unit, or juvenile detention facility where the actor is employed; or

(2) When the actor is a probation or parole officer or a juvenile probation and parole officer who has direct supervisory or disciplinary authority over the victim while the victim is on parole or probation or under juvenile probation.

Consent of the victim under any of the circumstances set forth in subparagraph (n) shall not be considered a defense.

II. A person is guilty of aggravated felonious sexual assault without penetration when he intentionally touches whether directly, through clothing, or otherwise, the genitalia of a person under the age of 13 under circumstances that can be reasonably construed as being for the purpose of sexual arousal or gratification.

III. A person is guilty of aggravated felonious sexual assault when such person engages in a pattern of sexual assault against another person, not the actor's legal spouse, who is less than 16 years of age. The mental state applicable to the underlying acts of sexual assault need not be shown with respect to the element of engaging in a pattern of sexual assault.

IV. A person is guilty of aggravated felonious sexual assault when such person engages in sexual penetration as defined in RSA 632-A:1, V with another person under 18 years of age whom such person knows to be his or her ancestor, descendant, brother or sister of the whole or half blood, uncle, aunt, nephew, or niece. The relationships referred to herein include blood relationships without regard to legitimacy, stepchildren, and relationships of parent and child by adoption.

Source.
1975, 302:1. 1981, 415:2, 3. 1986, 132:1. 1992, 254:6. 1994, 185:2, eff. Jan. 1, 1995. 1995, 66:1, eff. Jan. 1, 1996. 1997, 220:2, eff. Jan. 1, 1998. 1998, 240:2, eff. Jan. 1, 1999. 1999, 177:2, eff. Aug. 30, 1999. 2003, 226:1, 2, eff. Jan. 1, 2004. 2008, 334:13, eff. January 1, 2009. 2012, 105:1, eff. July 28, 2012.

Amendments
—2012. The 2012 amendment, in I(h), substituted "has a disability that renders him or her incapable of freely arriving at an independent choice as to whether or not to engage in sexual conduct" for "is mentally defective" and "has such a disability" for "is mentally defective."

—2008. The 2008 amendment added IV.

—2003. Paragraph I: Substituted "such person" for "he" in the introductory paragraph.

Paragraph I(n): Substituted "has direct supervisory or disciplinary authority" for "has supervisory authority", inserted "the secure psychiatric unit" and "where the actor is employed" in subpar. (1), inserted "the actor is" preceding "a probation" and substituted "officer or a juvenile probation and parole officer who has direct supervisory or disciplinary authority" for "officer has supervisory authority" in subpar (2), and deleted "above" preceding "circumstances" and inserted "set forth" in the concluding paragraph.

—1999. Paragraph II: Inserted "whether directly, through clothing, or otherwise" following "intentionally touches".

—1998. Paragraph I(g): Rewritten to the extent that a detailed comparison would be impracticable.

—1997. Paragraph I(n): Added.

—1995. Paragraph I(m): Added.

—1994. Paragraph III: Added.

—1992. Designated the existing introductory paragraph as par. I and substituted "the felony of aggravated felonious sexual assault" for "a class A felony" following "guilty of" in that paragraph, redesignated former pars. I–VI as subpars. (a)–(f), respectively, redesignated former par. VII as subpar. (g) and substituted "provides therapy" for "engages in the" following "actor" and "professionally" for "medically" preceding "recognized" in that subparagraph, and redesignated former pars. VIII–XI as subpars. (h)–(*l*), respectively, and added par. II.

—1986. Paragraph X: Rewritten to the extent that a detailed comparison would be impracticable.

Paragraph X-a: Added.

—1981. Paragraph VIII: Inserted "except as between legally married spouses" following "when".

Paragraph X: Inserted "except as between legally married spouses" following "when" and "when the actor" preceding "is related" and substituted "13" for "thirteen" and "16" for "sixteen".

Cross References.
Bail prohibited, see RSA 597:1-a.
Classification of crimes, see RSA 625:9.
Limitations on civil actions brought by defendant against victim, see RSA 632-A:10-c.
Penalties, see RSA 632-A:10-a.
Registration of criminal offenders, see RSA 651-B.
Sentences, see RSA 651.
Victims permitted to speak before sentencing, see RSA 651:4-a.

NOTES TO DECISIONS

1. Constitutionality
2. Construction
3. Construction with other laws
4. Burden of proof
5. Elements
6. Mens rea
7. Threats of retaliation
8. Mentally defective victim
9. Coercion
10. Proof of authority
11. Pattern of sexual assault
12. Indictment
13. Lesser included offenses
14. Severance of charges
15. Double jeopardy
16. Defenses
17. Consent
18. Evidence
19. Expert testimony
20. Instructions
21. Consecutive sentencing
22. Proof of victim's age
23. Therapeutic relationship

24.   Registration as sex offender
25.   Member of household

1. Constitutionality

RSA 632-A:2, I(g)(1), which criminalizes a therapist engaging in sex with a client within one year of the termination of the therapeutic or treating relationship between them, is not facially unconstitutional as violative of substantive due process under the Fourteenth Amendment or the state constitution. It is rationally related to the governmental interests in protecting those who are vulnerable to exploitation and in maintaining the integrity of the mental health profession. State v. Hollenbeck, 164 N.H. 154, 53 A.3d 591, 2012 N.H. LEXIS 120 (2012).

Where the statute of limitations had not run when it was extended by the legislature, application of the extended statute of limitations for aggravated felonious sexual assault under RSA 632-A:2, II, to defendant did not violate N.H. Const. pt. 1, art. 23 or U.S. Const. art. I, § 10. State v. Martin, 151 N.H. 107, 849 A.2d 138, 2004 N.H. LEXIS 98 (2004).

A construction of paragraph IV (now paragraph I(d)) of this section, which includes as one of the prescribed means of coercing sex through threats to retaliate, a threat to extort, to embrace the definition of extortion in RSA 637:5, II, which includes threats of economic reprisal, without the objective of acquiring the victim's property, did not constitute an interpretation so novel and unforeseeable as to render retroactive application of the interpretation a violation of the Due Process Clause of the United States Constitution. Lovely v. Cunningham, 796 F.2d 1, 1986 U.S. App. LEXIS 26377 (1st Cir. N.H. 1986).

In prosecution under paragraph IV (now paragraph I(d)) of this section, predicated on the use or threats of economic reprisal to coerce the victim to engage in sexual acts with the defendant in which the state presented evidence of a plethora of threats by the defendant to cause trouble for the victim with the police and to cause the victim to lose his job unless he continued to provide sexual favors, resulting in apprehension by the victim of being deprived of financial resources, the facts supported the conclusion of the jury that the situation was one involving coercion of the victim by the defendant, rather than a bargain by the victim, in response to pressure by the defendant, to continue sexual favors and, thus, application of the statute to the defendant did not involve an unconstitutional application of the statute to criminalize a lover's quarrel. Lovely v. Cunningham, 796 F.2d 1, 1986 U.S. App. LEXIS 26377 (1st Cir. N.H. 1986).

Since routine and ordinary penetrations of a child which occur in the course of caring for him or her do not fall within the prohibitions of this section, this section is thus not over broad because it does not prohibit any protected conduct. State v. Smith, 127 N.H. 433, 503 A.2d 774, 1985 N.H. LEXIS 463 (1985).

Use of the word "involving" in paragraph V (now paragraph I(e)) of this section does not render that paragraph unconstitutionally vague. State v. Taylor, 121 N.H. 489, 431 A.2d 775, 1981 N.H. LEXIS 356 (1981).

Paragraph V (now paragraph I(e)) of this section gave fair warning to defendant that the conduct with which he was charged, sexual penetration of a victim whom he had kidnapped or falsely imprisoned, was forbidden. State v. Taylor, 121 N.H. 489, 431 A.2d 775, 1981 N.H. LEXIS 356 (1981).

Paragraph VII (now paragraph I(h)) of this section is not void for vagueness or overbreadth because of undefined use of the term "mentally defective" since the term is no more vague than many other statutory terms describing criminal offenses, any reasonable person would know that the language was meant to describe people who are of marked subnormal intelligence and the fact that paragraph VII (now paragraph I(h)) imposes criminal liability only on one who either knows or should have known that the victim was mentally defective bears heavily on the issue of fair warning of the conduct proscribed. State v. Degrenier, 120 N.H. 919, 424 A.2d 412, 1980 N.H. LEXIS 421 (1980).

2. Construction

Legislature's use of the phrase "overcomes the victim through the actual application of physical force" in RSA 632-A:2, I(a), means that the State must prove the use of actual physical force, and not simply lack of consent. The State is not required, however, to prove that the victim resisted. In re D.B., 164 N.H. 46, 53 A.3d 646, 2012

N.H. LEXIS 116 (2012).

Statute governing sexual assault without penetration was not limited to skin-to-skin touching, but encompassed touching of genitalia through clothing, and therefore defendant was not entitled to a jury instruction that only type of touching prohibited under statute was direct skin-to-skin touching. State v. Dixon, 144 N.H. 273, 741 A.2d 580, 1999 N.H. LEXIS 109 (1999).

Where victim lived in defendant's home at time of incidents and was subject to parental-like control while there, jury could reasonably find that victim and defendant were members of the same household for purposes of subdivision I(j)(1) of this section. State v. Paglierani, 139 N.H. 37, 648 A.2d 209, 1994 N.H. LEXIS 105 (1994).

Under this section, although the threat and sexual penetration must be close in time, the threat need not be explicit. State v. Kulikowski, 132 N.H. 281, 564 A.2d 439, 1989 N.H. LEXIS 99 (1989).

The exact date of the assault is not an element of the aggravated felonious sexual assault crime. State v. Tynan, 132 N.H. 461, 566 A.2d 1142, 1989 N.H. LEXIS 119 (1989).

Normally, the exact date of the sexual assault is not required for a conviction. State v. Lacasse, 129 N.H. 651, 531 A.2d 327, 1987 N.H. LEXIS 236 (1987).

This section does not require proof of the exact date of the assault as an element, and therefore a defendant need only be informed that he must meet proof that he committed the assaultive acts at some time during a specified period. State v. Lakin, 128 N.H. 639, 517 A.2d 846, 1986 N.H. LEXIS 344 (1986).

Sexual contact is not a necessary element of aggravated felonious assault. State v. Smith, 127 N.H. 433, 503 A.2d 774, 1985 N.H. LEXIS 463 (1985).

This section was not intended to include penetration of a child for benign purposes such as washing, administering an enema, or taking a child's temperature. State v. Smith, 127 N.H. 433, 503 A.2d 774, 1985 N.H. LEXIS 463 (1985).

This section does not define the offense so as to make proof of exact date essential. State v. Boire, 124 N.H. 622, 474 A.2d 568, 1984 N.H. LEXIS 230 (1984), overruled in part, State v. French, 146 N.H. 97, 776 A.2d 1253, 2001 N.H. LEXIS 35 (2001).

A defendant may be separately indicted for and convicted of proscribed intercourse and fellatio, two separate offenses against the person. State v. Bussiere, 118 N.H. 659, 392 A.2d 151, 1978 N.H. LEXIS 263 (1978).

A male commits an aggravated felonious sexual assault if he forces a female to commit act of fellatio upon him. State v. Scott, 117 N.H. 996, 380 A.2d 1092, 1977 N.H. LEXIS 479 (1977).

3. Construction with other laws

As construing "forcible sex offense" in RSA 627:4, II(c) to include any aggravated felonious sexual assault would render the word "forcible" meaningless, the trial court did not err by prohibiting the defense from referring to the aggravated felonious sexual assault statute, RSA 632-A:2, I(i), in its closing argument. State v. McDonald, 163 N.H. 115, 35 A.3d 605, 2011 N.H. LEXIS 192 (Dec. 28, 2011).

Argument was rejected that indictments alleging aggravated felonious sexual assault were barred by RSA 625:8, the statute of limitations, because the state relied on threats that had occurred more than six years prior to the date of the arrest warrant; defendant was not prosecuted for merely threatening the victim more than six years prior to the date of the warrant, but for committing aggravated felonious sexual assault within the limitations period. State v. Kulikowski, 132 N.H. 281, 564 A.2d 439, 1989 N.H. LEXIS 99 (1989).

The distinguishing feature between the crimes of sexual assault and aggravated sexual assault is that a person must commit sexual penetration to be guilty of aggravated felonious sexual assault under this section, but to be guilty of sexual assault under RSA 632-A:4, he need only commit sexual contact under circumstances set forth in this section. State v. Vonklock, 121 N.H. 697, 433 A.2d 1299, 1981 N.H. LEXIS 399 (1981), overruled in part, State v. Smith, 127 N.H. 433, 503 A.2d 774, 1985 N.H. LEXIS 463 (1985).

4. Burden of proof

In a prosecution for aggravated felonious sexual assault, the state must prove beyond a reasonable doubt that the defendant engaged in sexual penetration with another person when the defendant overcame the victim through the application of physical force, physical violence or superior physical strength. State v. Simpson, 133 N.H. 704, 582 A.2d 619, 1990 N.H. LEXIS 124 (1990). (Decided under prior law.)

5. Elements

Although "vagina" is defined by RSA 632-A:1 as a "genital opening," that definition does not establish that touching the vagina constitutes penetration; on the contrary, the statute defines penetration as "intrusion . . . into genital or anal openings of the victim's body." Thus, in a prosecution for aggravated felonious sexual assault under 632-A:2, I(*l*), the State was required to prove digital intrusion into the victim's vagina. State v. Guay, 162 N.H. 375, 33 A.3d 1166, 2011 N.H. LEXIS 121 (2011).

Defendant's representation was not constitutionally deficient under N.H. Const. art. I, § 15 or the Sixth Amendment because trial counsel failed to argue that the State actually disproved the concealment or surprise element of RSA 632-A:2, I(i) as: (1) a victim was legally surprised as the victim became aware of what defendant was doing to her during the assault, the victim was startled enough by the victim's realization to flee the scene, and defendant provided the victim with alcohol, the consumption of which placed the victim in a mental state that allowed the victim to be assaulted without fully realizing what was happening to the victim; (2) the victim was factually surprised in light of the victim's initial detachment, contrasted with the victim's subsequent realization of the situation and the victim's flight from it; and (3) during closing, trial counsel argued that the victim was not sufficiently impaired to have been surprised by defendant's actions by calling into question the State's proof as to the degree of the victim's impairment. State v. Kepple, 155 N.H. 267, 922 A.2d 661, 2007 N.H. LEXIS 52 (2007).

There need not be an overt, express verbal threat prior to each separate act in order to satisfy the requirements of RSA 632-A:2, I(c) or the language of the indictments. State v. Goupil, 154 N.H. 208, 908 A.2d 1256, 2006 N.H. LEXIS 146 (2006).

Because "fellatio" is one of the definitions of "sexual penetration" in this section, fellatio is "sexual penetration" for purposes of statute, whether or not it involves actual penetration in the sense of "passing through or into." State v. Melcher, 140 N.H. 823, 678 A.2d 146, 1996 N.H. LEXIS 37 (1996).

Where the state alleges a time frame for the occurrence of the crime, rather than a specific time and date, the state has the obligation to prove that the offense occurred within that time frame when the defendant asserts a defense based on lack of opportunity within that time frame. State v. Williams, 137 N.H. 343, 629 A.2d 83, 1993 N.H. LEXIS 79 (1993), overruled, State v. Quintero, 162 N.H. 526, 34 A.3d 612, 2011 N.H. LEXIS 142 (2011).

6. Mens rea

In a trial for aggravated felonious sexual assault under RSA 632-A:2, I(*l*), there was sufficient evidence that defendant acted knowingly. The victim testified that she awoke when she felt defendant's fingers inside her vagina, that her shorts and underwear were pushed to one side, that defendant was standing over her, and that when she moved, defendant ran back to the cot where he was sleeping. State v. Tayag, 159 N.H. 21, 977 A.2d 510, 2009 N.H. LEXIS 80 (2009).

Defendant's motive of acting as his cousin's accomplice to avoid shame did not mean that he did not act with the purpose of making the crime of aggravated felonious sexual assault succeed. Defendant took off his clothes, got onto the bed with the victim, and penetrated her twice; regardless of why he acted, he had the conscious object of penetrating the victim. State v. Jenot, 158 N.H. 181, 965 A.2d 1086, 2008 N.H. LEXIS 142 (2008).

While the underlying act common to each variant of the offense of aggravated sexual assault is sexual penetration, no mens rea is expressed in this section; notwithstanding this omission, one cannot be convicted of this felony without proof that the act was accompanied by a culpable mental state. State v. Ayer, 136 N.H. 191, 612 A.2d 923, 1992 N.H. LEXIS 139 (1992). (Decided under prior law.)

For conviction of crime of aggravated felonious sexual assault, there is no requirement that the defendant actually know that the victim did not consent. State v. Ayer, 136 N.H. 191, 612 A.2d 923,

1992 N.H. LEXIS 139 (1992).

Indictment for aggravated felonious assault could properly charge defendant for acting "knowingly," rather than "intentionally" or "purposely," since common-law crime of rape was general-intent, rather than a specific intent, crime; holding in State v. Davis, 108 N.H. 158, 229 A.2d 842, 1967 N.H. LEXIS 142 (1967), that same intent was required for rape and attempted rape, is overruled insofar as it is inconsistent. State v. Ayer, 136 N.H. 191, 612 A.2d 923, 1992 N.H. LEXIS 139 (1992).

Aggravated felonious sexual assault indictment alleging that defendant acted "knowingly", rather than "purposely", was sufficient, since state only needed to prove defendant acted knowingly. State v. Reynolds, 136 N.H. 325, 615 A.2d 637, 1992 N.H. LEXIS 170 (1992).

Requisite mental state for conviction of aggravated felonious sexual assault is "knowingly", not "purposely". State v. Lemieux, 136 N.H. 329, 615 A.2d 635, 1992 N.H. LEXIS 171 (1992).

7. Threats of retaliation

Retaliatory threats, within the meaning of paragraph IV (now I(d)) of this section, are not required to be express. State v. Johnson, 130 N.H. 578, 547 A.2d 213, 1988 N.H. LEXIS 64 (1988).

In the case of defendant convicted of aggravated felonious sexual assault where the victim testified that the defendant had threatened him with loss of employment and housing, institution of criminal charges, and proceedings in court to collect money owed the defendant, the threats directed to the victim amounted to threats of retaliation within the meaning of paragraph IV (now I(d)) of this section. State v. Lovely, 124 N.H. 690, 480 A.2d 847, 1984 N.H. LEXIS 295 (1984).

8. Mentally defective victim

Testimony that the 22-year-old complainant had been born with disabilities and could not read, testimony that she required assistance with daily activities such as dressing and maintaining hygiene, the fact that she attended a center that provided services for people with acquired brain disorders and developmental disabilities, and her own testimony that failed to establish her competency as a witness all supported a finding that she had a mental disorder or defect under RSA 632-A:2, I(h). Her testimony also showed confusion about the sexual act taking place. State v. Horak, 159 N.H. 576, 986 A.2d 596, 2010 N.H. LEXIS 2 (2010).

Defendant had dated the 22-year-old complainant's mother for nine years, was living with her and the complainant at the time of the incident, and would help to put the complainant to bed; thus, it could not be said that no rational trier of fact could find defendant knew that the complainant was mentally defective. Furthermore, although defendant contended that the State did not prove that he knew that the complainant was incapable of choosing whether or not to engage in sexual conduct, the complainant testified about her confusion at the time of the assault. State v. Horak, 159 N.H. 576, 986 A.2d 596, 2010 N.H. LEXIS 2 (2010).

A person is "mentally defective" within meaning of subdivision I(h) of this section only if he or she (1) suffers from a "mental disease or defect" and (2) is incapable of freely arriving at an independent choice whether or not to engage in sexual conduct. State v. Frost, 141 N.H. 493, 686 A.2d 1172, 1996 N.H. LEXIS 132 (1996).

Evidence was insufficient to prove beyond a reasonable doubt that victim was incapable of legally consenting to sexual act and was thus "mentally defective" within meaning of subdivision I(h) where the State introduced evidence that the victim had been living in a group home for several years and that she took some form of medication, witnesses testified that the victim was "handicapped", that she "looked mentally retarded" and that she was once a resident of a hospital and that there was something mentally wrong with her, but offered no expert or medical testimony to explain the victim's mental condition. State v. Call, 139 N.H. 102, 650 A.2d 331, 1994 N.H. LEXIS 117 (1994).

Paragraph VIII (now I(h)) of this section prohibits intercourse only with those persons whose mental deficiency is such as to make them incapable of legally consenting to the act. State v. Degrenier, 120 N.H. 919, 424 A.2d 412, 1980 N.H. LEXIS 421 (1980).

Although the degree of mental defectiveness intended to be covered by paragraph VIII (now paragraph I(h)) of this section may not be entirely clear, the term "mentally defective" is sufficient to give defendant fair warning that, by engaging in sexual intercourse with one who he knows or has reason to know is mentally defective in any recognizable and appreciable degree, he is violating paragraph VIII (now paragraph I(h)). State v. Degrenier, 120 N.H. 919, 424 A.2d 412, 1980 N.H. LEXIS 421 (1980).

9. Coercion

Nothing in this statute eliminated coercion as an element of the offense; the conviction of a correctional officer was reversed where an inmate willingly engaged in sexual conduct with the officer and there was no proof the officer's sexual contact with an inmate came about due to the officer's coercion. State v. Foss, 148 N.H. 209, 804 A.2d 462, 2002 N.H. LEXIS 115 (2002).

"Coercion" as used in this section need not be overt, but may consist of the subtle persuasion arising from the position of authority. State v. Fortier, 146 N.H. 784, 780 A.2d 1243, 2001 N.H. LEXIS 163 (2001).

A person in a position of authority who uses such authority in any way to coerce a child's submission to sexual activity is subject to prosecution under this section, whether the coercion involves undue influence, physical force, threats, or any combination thereof. State v. Collins, 129 N.H. 488, 529 A.2d 945, 1987 N.H. LEXIS 219 (1987).

10. Proof of authority

There was ample evidence to support defendant's conviction of aggravated felonious sexual assault by coercion using a position of authority; even though defendant did not hire and fire at the sandwich shop where defendant was assistant manager and the victim was a 15-year-old employee, it was clear that defendant was regarded as the boss and that the victim felt that there was no choice about acceding to defendant's demands for oral sex. State v. Cossette, 151 N.H. 355, 856 A.2d 732, 2004 N.H. LEXIS 156 (2004).

Trial court did not err in allowing aggravated felonious sexual assault coercion indictments to go to the jury because defendant's role as the victims' personal religious leader, and their subservient role as his altar servers, sufficiently established defendant's right to expect obedience and power to receive submission from the victims; accordingly, a rational jury could have found beyond a reasonable doubt that defendant maintained a position of authority over the victims at the time of charged assaults. State v. Fortier, 146 N.H. 784, 780 A.2d 1243, 2001 N.H. LEXIS 163 (2001).

Evidence supported finding that defendant, a Roman Catholic priest, used his respected position of authority to employ a tactic of manipulation and exertion of subtle pressure to succeed in sexually assaulting young boys who were alter servers; accordingly, a rational jury could have found beyond a reasonable doubt that defendant used his position of authority to coerce the victims to submit to his sexual assaults. State v. Fortier, 146 N.H. 784, 780 A.2d 1243, 2001 N.H. LEXIS 163 (2001).

In the prosecution of an eighth grade teacher for aggravated felonious sexual assault upon a former student, evidence was sufficient to show that the defendant was in a position of authority over the victim at the time of the sexual acts, since his authority over the victim continued even after her departure from the junior high school where he taught as the proximity of the high school and the involvement of its students in activities at the junior high school supported the inference that the defendant had the right to expect obedience from the victim. State v. Carter, 140 N.H. 114, 663 A.2d 101, 1995 N.H. LEXIS 108 (1995).

Evidence was sufficient to establish that an eighth grade teacher used his position of authority to coerce a former student through undue psychological influence into submitting to sexual acts where there was evidence that the teacher knew of the victim's vulnerability and the potentially great influence over her his position as a teacher afforded him and that he used this knowledge to manipulate her and pursue a plan of seduction. State v. Carter, 140 N.H. 114, 663 A.2d 101, 1995 N.H. LEXIS 108 (1995).

The power to grade is not the only weapon in a teacher's arsenal, nor the only proof of authority. State v. Carter, 140 N.H. 114, 663 A.2d 101, 1995 N.H. LEXIS 108 (1995).

11. Pattern of sexual assault

With regard to an indictment for pattern aggravated felonious sexual assault, there was no plain error arising from the indictment's failure to include the statutory definition of the word "pattern" because the court had not previously decided whether the definition had to be included. State v. Ortiz, 162 N.H. 585, 34 A.3d 599, 2011 N.H. LEXIS 146 (2011).

Because under RSA 632-A:2, III, the State did not need to prove an additional mental state to prove the pattern element of sexual assault, it was error to admit evidence of past acts under N.H. R. Evid. 404(b) to show intent to commit a pattern of sexual assault; furthermore, because the victim's delay in reporting the acts against her was never questioned at trial, evidence of the past acts was not relevant to show any delay in disclosure. The error was not harmless, given the fact that the inadmissible and admissible evidence was intertwined and the nature of the evidence; because of the prejudicial impact of the inadmissible evidence, the additional burden that a limiting jury instruction created did not render the error harmless. State v. Cook, 158 N.H. 708, 972 A.2d 1059, 2009 N.H. LEXIS 66 (2009).

Federal continuing criminal enterprise statute, 21 U.S.C.S. § 848(a)–(c), unlike the aggravated felonious sexual assault statute, RSA 632-A:2, III, does not define the sole actus reus as the pattern, but criminalizes the individual violations underlying the pattern as well. Therefore, although jury unanimity is required for a conviction under 21 U.S.C.S. § 848(a)–(c), it does not follow that unanimity is therefore also necessary for a conviction of a pattern of sexual assault under RSA 632-A:2. State v. Sleeper, 150 N.H. 725, 846 A.2d 545, 2004 N.H. LEXIS 64 (2004).

Dispensing with unanimity on the predicate acts that comprise the pattern element of charges of pattern sexual assault under RSA 632-A:2 is consistent with federal due process because the underlying acts involve the sexual abuse of a child under the age of 16, crimes of the same or similar nature and level of culpability, and any variation that may exist is not of such a degree or nature as to call into question the basic moral and conceptual equivalence of the underlying acts. Therefore, it is not unfair or irrational to lift the requirement of jury unanimity as to the specific underlying acts as long as unanimity is required regarding the existence of the pattern, defined by the temporal requirements set forth in the statute. State v. Sleeper, 150 N.H. 725, 846 A.2d 545, 2004 N.H. LEXIS 64 (2004).

"Pattern of sexual assault" is the commission of at least two acts of sexual assault as described under the crimes of aggravated felonious sexual assault or felonious sexual assault within a defined time frame. State v. Fortier, 146 N.H. 784, 780 A.2d 1243, 2001 N.H. LEXIS 163 (2001).

That individual acts of sexual assault are required for a "pattern" to occur, and that such acts would be unlawful under other sections of the Criminal Code, does not remove the pattern statute from the course of conduct category of offenses. State v. Fortier, 146 N.H. 784, 780 A.2d 1243, 2001 N.H. LEXIS 163 (2001).

To secure a conviction under the pattern statute in a manner that preserves defendant's right to a unanimous jury verdict, the jury must be unanimous on the statutory element that a defendant engaged in behavior constituting a pattern of sexual assault; the jury must unanimously agree that defendant engaged in more than one act of sexual assault as described in aggravated felonious sexual assault and felonious sexual assault statutes, but need not agree on the particular acts, provided that they find the requisite number of acts occurred during the statutory time period. State v. Fortier, 146 N.H. 784, 780 A.2d 1243, 2001 N.H. LEXIS 163 (2001).

Where defendant stood charged under statute proscribing a "pattern of sexual assault," not single acts of sexual contact or assault, his right to a unanimous jury verdict was not compromised by the State's failure to specify the particular predicate acts underlying the charged pattern indictments, or the trial court's failure to require unanimity on the particular acts underlying the pattern charges. State v. Fortier, 146 N.H. 784, 780 A.2d 1243, 2001 N.H. LEXIS 163 (2001).

Even though the time frame alleged in pattern indictments overlapped several felonious sexual assault indictments alleging specific incidents of sexual assault, defendant suffered no infringement upon his right to be free from double jeopardy because he was not sentenced on any felonious sexual assault indictment alleging that he committed a sexual assault within the same time period as alleged in the pattern indictments. State v. Fortier, 146 N.H. 784, 780 A.2d 1243, 2001 N.H. LEXIS 163 (2001).

12. Indictment

Indictment alleged the pattern variant of aggravated felonious sexual assault under RSA 632-A:2 with the requisite specificity to satisfy N.H. Const. pt. I, art. 15 when it specified a location for the alleged conduct, the time period in which it was alleged to have occurred, the identity and age of the victim, and the conduct against which defendant had to defend. Defendant's ability to prepare a defense was not impaired by the indictment's failure to allege more specifically the predicate acts comprising the pattern, because the essential culpable act was the pattern itself. State v. Ericson, 159 N.H. 379, 986 A.2d 488, 2009 N.H. LEXIS 125 (2009).

Indictments charging that defendant digitally penetrated the victim and engaged in sexual intercourse with the victim were not duplicative because each indictment alleged that defendant committed a separate offense against the victim, sexual intercourse and digital penetration, and, thus, conviction on both indictments did not result in defendant receiving multiple punishments for the same offense. State v. DeCosta, 146 N.H. 405, 772 A.2d 340, 2001 N.H. LEXIS 89 (2001).

Statute governing attempts to commit crime did not require State to plead and prove elements of intended offense, and therefore indictment which alleged attempted aggravated felonious sexual assault, and factually identified offense in describing overt steps defendant took to accomplish it, was sufficient to enable defendant to prepare his defense and to protect him from double jeopardy. State v. Johnson, 144 N.H. 175, 738 A.2d 1284, 1999 N.H. LEXIS 95 (1999).

Second count of two-count sexual assault indictment could not reasonably be read to charge a violation of both RSA 632-A:2, X-a (now I(k)), and RSA 632-A:2, III (now I(c)) as the state alleged facts in the second count sufficient to meet the requirements of RSA 632-A:2, X-a (now I(k)), but not RSA 632-A:2, III (now I(c)), namely, the second count failed to allege threats to the victim. Therefore, indictment was not unconstitutionally duplicitous. State v. Marti, 143 N.H. 608, 732 A.2d 414, 1999 N.H. LEXIS 50 (1999).

An indictment which alleged that an act of aggravated felonious sexual assault occurred sometime within a two-year time period was adequate. State v. Williams, 137 N.H. 343, 629 A.2d 83, 1993 N.H. LEXIS 79 (1993), overruled, State v. Quintero, 162 N.H. 526, 34 A.3d 612, 2011 N.H. LEXIS 142 (2011).

Three indictments for aggravated felonious sexual assault properly alleged the element of coercion by threatening, where they clearly alleged present coercion occasioned by repeated prior threats. State v. Kulikowski, 132 N.H. 281, 564 A.2d 439, 1989 N.H. LEXIS 99 (1989).

The omission from the indictment of the name of an under-thirteen victim of an aggravated felonious sexual assault did not, per se, render the indictment constitutionally insufficient, where the omission did not hobble the defendant's preparation of his defense. State v. Day, 129 N.H. 378, 529 A.2d 887, 1987 N.H. LEXIS 204 (1987).

Although indictment charging defendant with violating paragraph III (now I(c)) of this section did not allege that the victim believed that the actor had the present ability to execute his threats, since it informed defendant of the factual basis of the charge by stating that he forced the prosecutrix to submit to sexual penetration by threatening her with a knife, and she would not have been forced to submit if she had not believed that the defendant had the present ability to carry out his threat, the indictment was constitutionally sufficient. State v. Shute, 122 N.H. 498, 446 A.2d 1162, 1982 N.H. LEXIS 392 (1982).

13. Lesser included offenses

Simple assault under RSA 631:2-a, I(a), although perhaps a lesser-included offense of aggravated felonious sexual assault by means of application of physical force, is not a lesser-included offense of felonious sexual assault under RSA 632-A:3, III. "Unprivileged physical contact" is not an element of felonious sexual assault by means of sexual contact with a victim under the age of thirteen. State v. Michaud, 161 N.H. 785, 20 A.3d 1012, 2011 N.H. LEXIS 60 (2011).

Sexual assault cannot be a lesser-included offense of aggravated felonious sexual assault because sexual assault requires element of "sexual contact" for purpose of sexual arousal or gratification, an element not required for a conviction of aggravated felonious sexual assault. State v. Smith, 127 N.H. 433, 503 A.2d 774, 1985 N.H.

LEXIS 463 (1985).

State v. Vonklock, 121 N.H. 697, 433 A.2d 1299, 1981 N.H. LEXIS 399 (1981), is overruled to the extent it held that sexual assault is a lesser-included offense of aggravated felonious sexual assault. State v. Smith, 127 N.H. 433, 503 A.2d 774, 1985 N.H. LEXIS 463 (1985).

A person must necessarily commit the crime of sexual assault before he can commit aggravated felonious sexual assault inasmuch as there is no means by which a person could commit sexual penetration without engaging in sexual contact; therefore, sexual assault is a lesser-included offense of aggravated felonious sexual assault. State v. Vonklock, 121 N.H. 697, 433 A.2d 1299, 1981 N.H. LEXIS 399 (1981), overruled in part, State v. Smith, 127 N.H. 433, 503 A.2d 774, 1985 N.H. LEXIS 463 (1985).

In prosecution for aggravated felonious sexual assault, where there was no physical evidence of rape, the prosecutrix stated that she was raped and the defendant claimed that he hit or pushed the prosecutrix in an attempt to secure the return of his property, but did not rape her, there was sufficient evidence to permit a jury rationally to convict the defendant of the lesser offense of simple assault and acquit him of the greater offense of aggravated felonious sexual assault, and the failure of the trial court to give a requested instruction on the lesser included offense seriously undermined the integrity of the fact finding process and denied the defendant of due process of law. Dukette v. Perrin, 564 F. Supp. 1530, 1983 U.S. Dist. LEXIS 16363 (D.N.H. 1983).

14. Severance of charges

Defendant's convictions of aggravated felonious sexual assault, RSA 632-A:2, and felonious sexual assault, RSA 632-A:3, III, were reversed, because under newly-adopted rules concerning severance which applied retroactively, the trial court erred in denying defendant's motion to sever the charges concerning the two child victims. State v. Tierney, 150 N.H. 339, 839 A.2d 38, 2003 N.H. LEXIS 196 (2003).

15. Double jeopardy

The charging of three discrete patterns of sexual assault under RSA 632-A:2, III, inflicted on a single victim did not run afoul of double jeopardy as the pattern statute allows the State to charge more than one pattern of a given sexual assault variant within a five-year time frame, each as an individual unit of prosecution, when the evidence of discrete patterns so warrants. Because the indictments charged three discrete patterns of sexual assault, as permitted by the statute, and because the prosecution at trial would have to prove that the acts occurred within each of the alleged, discrete periods of time, the defendant was not subject to multiple punishments for the same offense and his federal double jeopardy right was not infringed. Furthermore, the requirement when seeking convictions on multiple pattern indictments that charge numerous assaults within a common time frame inflicted on a single victim that the indictments could not rely on the same underlying act or acts to comprise the charged pattern was met because the pattern indictments alleged three separate sets of acts during three discrete time periods at three different locations. State v. Jennings, 155 N.H. 768, 929 A.2d 982, 2007 N.H. LEXIS 131 (2007).

Separate indictments of defendant for aggravated felonious sexual assault could be sustained where each image of defendant's actions depicted on videotape presented additional evidence of how he repeatedly renewed his intention to coax child into the act of penetration, and evidence to sustain each of the carefully worded indictments was different from evidence required to sustain any of the other indictments. State v. Krueger, 146 N.H. 541, 776 A.2d 720, 2001 N.H. LEXIS 108 (2001).

Defendant's double jeopardy right was not infringed upon since the pattern indictments against him did not rely upon any act charged in another pattern indictment; thus, the same pattern was never charged twice. State v. Richard, 147 N.H. 340, 786 A.2d 876, 2001 N.H. LEXIS 221 (2001).

Physical force and false imprisonment variants of aggravated felonious sexual assault each required proof of an element or elements the other did not, and thus these statutory variants could, for double jeopardy purposes, be charged as distinct alternative methods of committing aggravated felonious sexual assault. State

v. Nickles, 144 N.H. 673, 749 A.2d 290, 2000 N.H. LEXIS 9 (2000).

As charged, sexual assault by false imprisonment indictment was sufficiently distinct in fact and law from sexual assault by physical force indictment, such that dual indictments were properly presented to jury for its deliberation, and since jury deadlock prevented original jeopardy from terminating on physical force indictment, State could permissibly retry defendant on that charge following mistrial, notwithstanding jury's acquittal of defendant on false imprisonment indictment. State v. Nickles, 144 N.H. 673, 749 A.2d 290, 2000 N.H. LEXIS 9 (2000).

There was no violation of the protection against double jeopardy found in part I, article 16 of the New Hampshire Constitution when an extended sentence of 10 to 30 years was imposed on the defendant for aggravated felonious sexual assault based on the age of the victim, notwithstanding the contention that the sentence was improper because the victim's age had already been used to elevate the offense from a class B felony to a class A felony; the defendant was only convicted once and sentenced once, and there was no violation. State v. Hennessey, 142 N.H. 149, 697 A.2d 930, 1997 N.H. LEXIS 68 (1997).

Since each set of sexual assault indictments, as charged, obliged State to prove a particular fact not necessary to the other—physical force in one and surprise in the other—double jeopardy did not prohibit State from retrying defendant on "force" and oral penetration charges following mistrial on those indictments. State v. Crate, 141 N.H. 489, 686 A.2d 318, 1996 N.H. LEXIS 129 (1996).

For purposes of double jeopardy, each of the statutory variants of aggravated felonious sexual assault listed under subdivision I of this section plainly requires proof of an element or elements the others do not. State v. Crate, 141 N.H. 489, 686 A.2d 318, 1996 N.H. LEXIS 129 (1996).

16. Defenses

Where a defendant is charged with the variant of aggravated felonious sexual assault through concealment or the element of surprise, a consensual sex defense instruction is inappropriate since, for the jury to find that penetration occurred only through defendant's concealment or by surprise, it necessarily would have had to find the victim did not consent to such penetration; therefore, lack of consent is an element of the crime rather than a defense requiring a consent instruction.State v. Ramos, 149 N.H. 272, 821 A.2d 979, 2003 N.H. LEXIS 37 (2003).

Once defendant in an aggravated felonious sexual assault case raises defense of consent, State must prove beyond a reasonable doubt that victim did not consent. State v. Jackson, 141 N.H. 152, 679 A.2d 572, 1996 N.H. LEXIS 67 (1996).

This section implicitly creates a defense in any prosecution, for penetration necessary for the health, hygiene, or safety of a child. State v. Smith, 127 N.H. 433, 503 A.2d 774, 1985 N.H. LEXIS 463 (1985).

Penetration for a legitimate purpose is a defense to aggravated felonious sexual assault. State v. Smith, 127 N.H. 433, 503 A.2d 774, 1985 N.H. LEXIS 463 (1985).

17. Consent

Under RSA 632-A:2, I(g)(1), lack of consent is irrelevant. The legislature has determined that all patients are legally incapable, for an admittedly arbitrary period of one year after the termination of therapy, of consenting to sex with a former therapist. State v. Hollenbeck, 164 N.H. 154, 53 A.3d 591, 2012 N.H. LEXIS 120 (2012).

Lack of consent, a necessary element to make a prima facie case of rape, could be proved in a variety of ways, including but not limited to an attempt to escape, outcry or offer of resistance, except where the complaining witness was restrained by fear of violence. State v. Lemire, 115 N.H. 526, 345 A.2d 906, 1975 N.H. LEXIS 353 (1975). (Decided under prior law.)

Since a necessary element to make a prima facie case of rape was lack of consent, a showing of consent would constitute a complete defense to the crime. State v. Lemire, 115 N.H. 526, 345 A.2d 906, 1975 N.H. LEXIS 353 (1975). (Decided under prior law.)

18. Evidence

Merger doctrine rendered it unlikely that the Legislature intended to criminalize restraint that was integral to other crimes, such that it was irrelevant whether the charges against defendant

of attempted kidnapping and attempted aggravated felonious sexual assault, in violation of RSA 629:1, 633:1, and 632-A:2, were intended to prohibit different types of criminal activity; accordingly, the merger doctrine should have been employed. State v. Casanova, 164 N.H. 563, 63 A.3d 169, 2013 N.H. LEXIS 11 (2013).

As committing penetration or touching for sexual gratification were statutory variants of attempted aggravated felonious sexual assault, in violation of RSA 629:1 and 632-A:2, it was sufficient that the jury determined that defendant intended to commit either variant for purposes of supporting his conviction; they did not have to agree which act he intended to commit pursuant to RSA 625:10. State v. Casanova, 164 N.H. 563, 63 A.3d 169, 2013 N.H. LEXIS 11 (2013).

Adjudication of delinquency based upon misdemeanor sexual assault under RSA 632-A:2, I(a), and RSA 632-A:4, I, was not supported by the evidence. The complainant's statements that defendant "squeezed and rubbed" her breasts and "touched and rubbed" her private parts as they rode a school bus did not support a finding that she was overcome by the actual application of physical force, nor did her statement that defendant's conduct was "rough" and "hurt" her. In re D.B., 164 N.H. 46, 53 A.3d 646, 2012 N.H. LEXIS 116 (2012).

Rough, hurtful conduct is not, standing alone, among the circumstances the legislature has enumerated as a basis for a sexual assault conviction. Therefore, such evidence is insufficient to support a finding that the complainant was overcome by the application of physical force. In re D.B., 164 N.H. 46, 53 A.3d 646, 2012 N.H. LEXIS 116 (2012).

Because the child complainant's hearsay statements that defendant "licked his finger and put it into [the child's] private and moved it up and down." were properly admitted through the testimony of a pediatrician, there was sufficient evidence that defendant committed aggravated felonious sexual assault by digital penetration. State v. Munroe, 161 N.H. 618, 20 A.3d 871, 2011 N.H. LEXIS 34 (2011).

Given the victim's testimony that she was lying on her stomach and that she knew defendant was trying to touch her private because she could feel it, the trial court properly denied defendant's motion to dismiss an aggravated felonious sexual assault charge under RSA 632-A:2, II. State v. Carvell, — N.H. —, — A.3d —, 2011 N.H. LEXIS 38 (Mar. 29, 2011).

Victim's testimony was not sufficient to establish that defendant penetrated her vagina with his fingers during the incident in question; thus, defendant's conviction of aggravated felonious sexual assault under RSA 632-A:2, I(l) was plain error. The victim testified that defendant touched her vagina, but did not say that her pants were removed or that defendant's hands were underneath her clothing. State v. Guay, 162 N.H. 375, 33 A.3d 1166, 2011 N.H. LEXIS 121 (2011).

There was sufficient evidence to support convictions of aggravated felonious sexual assault and of felonious sexual assault under RSA 632-A:2 and RSA 632-A:3. The jury was free to accept or reject the victim's testimony, and the testimony of the victim and of the police officers provided more than sufficient evidence for a rational trier of fact to find guilt. State v. Oakes, 161 N.H. 270, 13 A.3d 293, 2010 N.H. LEXIS 149 (Dec. 7, 2010).

The evidence was not insufficient to support a conviction for aggravated felonious sexual assault under RSA 632-A:2. Defendant's arguments that the victim was unable to recall any of the time frames of the alleged assaults or what details she gave to police investigators and that her allegations changed over time went to the victim's credibility and the proper weight to be given to the evidence, questions which were for the jury to resolve; furthermore, the evidence was not all circumstantial, as the victim presented direct evidence of the sexual assaults. State v. Ericson, 159 N.H. 379, 986 A.2d 488, 2009 N.H. LEXIS 125 (2009).

Trial court erred in precluding defendant from cross examining the complainant in a sexual assault case about a prior false accusation of sexual assault because such examination was permitted under N.H. R. Evid. 608(b), and, given the nature of the case—a sexual assault case with no eyewitnesses other than the complainant and defendant—the complainant's testimony and credibility were crucial; further, defendant asserted several similarities between the two accusations, and while the prior accusation occurred seven years before the current charged offense, that time period was not so remote as to eliminate probity. The likelihood that the prior false accusation occurred, whatever the motivation behind it, weighed heavily in favor of admissibility and the evidence of a prior false accusation was not cumulative as to the complainant's credibility. State v. Kornbrekke, 156 N.H. 821, 943 A.2d 797, 2008 N.H. LEXIS 25 (2008).

Admission of hearsay statement of sexual assault victim's biological father regarding the timing of his report of his daughter's allegations of sexual assault by defendant, through testimony of a police officer, was error, as the statement was inadmissible hearsay that did not fall within any hearsay exception. The doctrine of "curative admissibility" did not apply since the State did not contend that the arguments and testimony presented by the defendant were themselves inadmissible; nor did the doctrine of "specific contradiction" apply as the defendant did not create a misleading advantage as the mere existence of contrary evidence did not mean that the defendant's initial theory and supporting evidence were misleading. Furthermore, the State had submitted other admissible testimony regarding the reasons for the father's delay in reporting the assault and because both sides had presented admissible evidence regarding the father's motivation to delay, the defendant did not create a misleading advantage and did not open the door. State v. Morrill, 154 N.H. 547, 914 A.2d 1206, 2006 N.H. LEXIS 196 (2006).

Victim's testimony, showing that the initial threat of injury made by defendant was implicit and ongoing throughout the assault, was sufficient to support defendant's convictions for aggravated felonious sexual assault. State v. Goupil, 154 N.H. 208, 908 A.2d 1256, 2006 N.H. LEXIS 146 (2006).

Circumstantial evidence of semen and saliva found on the victim's body and other circumstances were ample to support defendant's conviction of aggravated felonious sexual assault by surprise, and there was plenty of direct evidence indicating assault by digital penetration, particularly the victim's own account. State v. Flynn, 151 N.H. 378, 855 A.2d 1254, 2004 N.H. LEXIS 158 (2004).

Where a child victim used the words "privates," "crotch," and "pee pee" to describe the victim's genitalia and the State used a demonstrative aid to augment the victim's testimony, the victim's testimony was sufficient to establish a prima facie case of sexual assault under RSA 632-A:2, II; as a result, pursuant to RSA 632-A:6, I, no corroborating evidence was needed. State v. King, 151 N.H. 59, 855 A.2d 510, 2004 N.H. LEXIS 89 (2004), rehearing denied, 2004 N.H. LEXIS 167 (N.H. July 16, 2004).

Trial court did not violate U.S. Const. amends. VI, XIV and N.H. Const. pt. I, art. 15 Confrontation Clauses and did not violate N.H. R. Evid. 403, 608(b) by not allowing a defendant who was accused of sex crimes under RSA 629:1, 632-A:2, 632-A:3 to cross-examine the victim with evidence that she stole money from her employer since that evidence was prejudicial and was not probative of her credibility regarding the sex crimes. State v. Hokenstrom, 2003 N.H. LEXIS 214 (N.H. Feb. 14, 2003). (Unpublished opinion.)

Trial court properly denied defendant's motion for a mistrial in a prosecution for aggravated felonious sexual assault, RSA 632-A:2, I(i), because disputed testimony by the victim was not based on repressed memory, and therefore no pre-trial hearing on the reliability of the testimony was required. State v. Madore, 150 N.H. 221, 834 A.2d 389, 2003 N.H. LEXIS 166 (2003).

Although the victim could not remember whether she was wearing any clothing at the time of the assault, there was sufficient evidence for the jury to conclude beyond a reasonable doubt that the defendant touched the victim directly with his lips or tongue where victim testified that defendant touched her with his tongue and prosecution pointed out that cunnilingus could occur even if the victim were clothed since one can reach under, or pull aside, clothing with a hand in order to stimulate the vulva or clitoris with the lips or tongue. State v. Mason, 150 N.H. 53, 834 A.2d 339, 2003 N.H. LEXIS 138 (2003).

Supreme court affirmed convictions of defendant for one count of RSA 632-A:2 aggravated felonious sexual assault, and four counts of RSA 632-A:3 felonious sexual assault of the teenage daughter of his former wife, based, in part, on testimony of former wife, high school classmate, and physician. State v. Pelletier, 149 N.H. 243, 818 A.2d 292, 2003 N.H. LEXIS 34 (2003).

Supreme court affirmed adult male babysitter's conviction of four counts of RSA 632-A:2, II, aggravated felonious sexual assault (touching) of seven-year-old female; an officer's non-prejudicial

testimony of babysitter's unsolicited statements were admissible to show babysitter's state of mind. State v. Stott, 149 N.H. 170, 816 A.2d 1018, 2003 N.H. LEXIS 20 (2003).

Child's testimony that defendant touched her between her legs and touched her in her "private parts" and "private area" was sufficient to establish that defendant touched the child's genitalia for purposes of proving his guilt on a charge of aggravated felonious sexual assault in violation of RSA 632-A:2, II. State v. Blackstock, 147 N.H. 791, 802 A.2d 1169, 2002 N.H. LEXIS 83 (2002).

In defendant's trial for sexual assault, the trial court properly allowed the prosecution to introduce evidence that defendant physically assaulted his adopted daughter to explain the daughter's rationale for waiting seven years after the sexual assaults ended to report them. State v. Berry, 148 N.H. 88, 803 A.2d 593, 2002 N.H. LEXIS 98 (2002).

In prosecution for sexual assault, before defendant may cross-examine the victim about a prior false allegation of sexual assault, he must establish by clear and convincing evidence that the victim made such prior accusation. State v. Gordon, 146 N.H. 258, 770 A.2d 702, 2001 N.H. LEXIS 70 (2001), overruled in part, State v. Miller, 155 N.H. 246, 921 A.2d 942, 2007 N.H. LEXIS 51 (2007).

In a prosecution for aggravated felonious sexual assault, prosecutor's argument in closing that the victim's bruises were consistent with being dragged by the shoulders from a hot tub to defendant's couch constituted a reasonable inference based upon facts in evidence, and thus was not improper. State v. Walton, 146 N.H. 316, 771 A.2d 562, 2001 N.H. LEXIS 77 (2001).

Evidence was sufficient to permit a reasonable jury to find that the defendant digitally penetrated the victim on at least three occasions. State v. DeCosta, 146 N.H. 405, 772 A.2d 340, 2001 N.H. LEXIS 89 (2001).

In a prosecution for aggravated felonious sexual assault and felonious sexual assault committed by the defendant against his minor niece, the victim's use of the term "privates" to describe where the defendant allegedly touched her was sufficiently specific to establish that the defendant touched her vagina as charged. State v. Graham, 142 N.H. 357, 702 A.2d 322, 1997 N.H. LEXIS 103 (1997).

There was sufficient evidence from which a reasonable jury could have found penetration, where victim testified to "sexual intercourse" having occurred and to vaginal bleeding after one of the incidents. State v. Paglierani, 139 N.H. 37, 648 A.2d 209, 1994 N.H. LEXIS 105 (1994).

Trial court did not err in finding that five-year-old child met threshold requirements of competency. Evidence was sufficient to support defendant's convictions, despite apparent divergence among accounts of child victims and notwithstanding defendant's arguments that allegations arose in context of a bitter marital separation and that children may have gained their sexual knowledge elsewhere. State v. Briere, 138 N.H. 617, 644 A.2d 551, 1994 N.H. LEXIS 75 (1994).

Evidence was insufficient to establish digital penetration where the victim testified that the defendant put lotion on a rash on her vagina, but that he put his fingers on the outside of her vagina and not on the inside. State v. Chamberlain, 137 N.H. 414, 628 A.2d 704, 1993 N.H. LEXIS 93 (1993).

Court error at aggravated felonious sexual assault trial, allowing witness to testify indirectly that she believed the victim had been sexually assaulted by the defendant, was harmless, where opinion was not directed to specific inconsistency in victim's testimony, was cumulative, and was inconsequential compared to victim's damaging, vivid description of acts defendant forced her to perform. State v. Lemieux, 136 N.H. 329, 615 A.2d 635, 1992 N.H. LEXIS 171 (1992).

The inconsistent and uncorroborated testimony of a victim is not insufficient, as a matter of law, to support a conviction for aggravated felonious sexual assault. State v. Simpson, 133 N.H. 704, 582 A.2d 619, 1990 N.H. LEXIS 124 (1990).

Argument was rejected that court at trial for aggravated felonious sexual assault abused its discretion by admitting evidence of "prior bad acts" committed by defendant; evidence at issue constituted very threat which coerced the victim during the assaults in question. State v. Kulikowski, 132 N.H. 281, 564 A.2d 439, 1989 N.H. LEXIS 99 (1989).

A defendant charged with violating paragraph XI (now paragraph I(l)) of this section must be afforded the opportunity to show, by specific incidents of sexual conduct, that the victim had the experience and ability to contrive a statutory rape charge. State v. Howard, 121 N.H. 53, 426 A.2d 457, 1981 N.H. LEXIS 248 (1981).

19. Expert testimony

Testimony of a social worker and a police officer as to victims' tendencies to fail to contemporaneously report abuse and to recant or deny abuse was erroneously admitted expert testimony and was inadmissible lay testimony under N.H. R. Evid. 701 and 702 as, although the testimony was within the knowledge of the witnesses due to their training, it required knowledge beyond the ken of the average person; however the error was harmless as the victim testified in detail and defendant admitted the actions during a family meeting, and defendant's convictions for aggravated felonious sexual assault under RSA 632-A:2, felonious sexual assault under RSA 632-A:3, and misdemeanor sexual assault under RSA 632-A:4 were affirmed. State v. Gonzalez, 150 N.H. 74, 834 A.2d 354, 2003 N.H. LEXIS 142 (2003).

Admission of expert's testimony that victim presented a "symptom picture" consistent with sexual abuse was not harmless error, where testimony was lengthy, comprehensive, and directly linked to determination of defendant's guilt or innocence. State v. Silk, 138 N.H. 290, 639 A.2d 243, 1994 N.H. LEXIS 14 (1994).

Trial court erred in allowing social worker to give his opinion as to credibility of child victim's account of sexual assault by defendants because he could not provide an expert opinion as to the victim's testimony, nor a lay opinion based upon "common sense"; a common sense evaluation of the credibility of the witness was the province of the jury. State v. Huard, 138 N.H. 256, 638 A.2d 787, 1994 N.H. LEXIS 11 (1994).

20. Instructions

Trial court did not err when it denied defendant's request to instruct the jury to use the definition of "household members" contained in RSA 173-B:1 in his sexual assault trial with regard to his alleged assaults upon the minor daughter of an ex-girlfriend, who had commenced living with defendant, as RSA 632-A:2, I(j)(1), which he was charged as having violated, was specifically aimed at protecting victims between the ages of 13 and 16 who are members of the same household as accused and the defendant's proposed instruction based upon RSA 173-B:1, X(a) and (b) excluded minor children from the definition of household members. State v. Hearns, 151 N.H. 226, 855 A.2d 549, 2004 N.H. LEXIS 129 (2004).

Trial court's failure to give an instruction on consent was not reversible error because it caused no prejudice to the defendant; if the jury found the State proved all elements of the charged variant of aggravated felonious sexual assault, it would have to find the victim did not consent and if the jury found the State did not prove the element of concealment or surprise, the jury would be required to acquit the defendant. State v. Ramos, 149 N.H. 272, 821 A.2d 979, 2003 N.H. LEXIS 37 (2003).

Trial court properly instructed the jury in defendant's trial for aggravated felonious sexual assault, RSA 632-A:2, and felonious sexual assault, RSA 632-A:3; the trial court instructed the jury in accordance with the law applicable to the charged offenses, RSA 632-A:6(I), as that statute stated only that the victim's testimony needed no corroboration, and the trial court's jury instruction did not imply that defendant's testimony needed corroboration to be believed. State v. Cook, 148 N.H. 735, 813 A.2d 480, 2002 N.H. LEXIS 183 (2002).

The state alleged a time frame for the occurrence of the crime, rather than a specific time and date, and the defendant asserted a defense based on lack of opportunity within that time frame. Therefore, it was reversible error for the trial court to refuse to provide an instruction that the state was required to prove that the offense occurred within the time frame alleged in the indictment. State v. Williams, 137 N.H. 343, 629 A.2d 83, 1993 N.H. LEXIS 79 (1993), overruled, State v. Quintero, 162 N.H. 526, 34 A.3d 612, 2011 N.H. LEXIS 142 (2011).

At trial for aggravated felonious sexual assault, court did not err in refusing to give an instruction on contributing to the delinquency of a minor as a lesser-included offense, since contributing to the delinquency of a minor does not contain the elements of and need not be committed in the process of committing aggravated felonious sexual assault. State v. Lacourse, 127 N.H. 737, 506 A.2d 339, 1986

N.H. LEXIS 213 (1986).

If the evidence supports it, a defendant charged with aggravated felonious sexual assault is entitled to an instruction that if the jury should find the alleged penetration was necessary for the health, hygiene, or safety of the child, it must find the defendant not guilty. State v. Smith, 127 N.H. 433, 503 A.2d 774, 1985 N.H. LEXIS 463 (1985).

At trial for aggravated felonious sexual assault, no prejudice resulted from the lack of a jury instruction that penetration necessary for health, hygiene or safety reasons was a valid defense to the charge, since the defense in the case was that the penetration was accidental and the actual jury charge emphasized the requirement that the penetration was purposeful. State v. Smith, 127 N.H. 433, 503 A.2d 774, 1985 N.H. LEXIS 463 (1985).

Trial court's erroneous jury instruction that sexual assault was a lesser-included offense of aggravated felonious sexual assault did not require reversal of conviction, since trial court correctly defined the elements of the two offenses, and since the jury did not consider the lesser offense, because the defendant was convicted of the greater offense. State v. Smith, 127 N.H. 433, 503 A.2d 774, 1985 N.H. LEXIS 463 (1985).

Where indictment for aggravated felonious sexual assault charged defendant as both a resident of the victim's household and a blood relative and the trial court instructed the jury that proof of only one of the elements was necessary for a conviction, the instruction, phrased in the disjunctive, was in accord with paragraph X (now paragraph I(k)) of this section, and there was no prejudice occasioned by the discrepancy between the wording of the indictment and the instruction to the jury. State v. Langdon, 121 N.H. 1065, 438 A.2d 299, 1981 N.H. LEXIS 466 (1981).

21. Consecutive sentencing

Imposition of consecutive sentences for convictions on multiple counts of aggravated felonious sexual assault did not violate due process under N.H. Const. pt. I, art. 15 because of vagueness in that the language of RSA 632-A:10-a, RSA chapter 651 and judicial construction of that language puts a person of ordinary intelligence on notice that a person guilty of aggravated felonious sexual assault under RSA 632-A:2 may receive the maximum statutory sentence for each aggravated felonious sexual assault conviction. Duquette v. Warden, N.H. State Prison, 154 N.H. 737, 919 A.2d 767, 2007 N.H. LEXIS 10 (2007).

22. Proof of victim's age

In a case under RSA 632-A:2, when the victim testified that she learned her birth date from her mother, that she saw her birth certificate with the same date as recently as two months earlier, and that she celebrated her birthday on the same day each year, her testimony that she was 12 was sufficiently trustworthy and reliable under N.H. R. Evid. 803(19) so as not to require corroboration, and the State was not required to produce her birth certificate to satisfy its burden. Furthermore, there was no evidence that the victim could have a different date of birth. State v. Tayag, 159 N.H. 21, 977 A.2d 510, 2009 N.H. LEXIS 80 (2009).

23. Therapeutic relationship

Defendant's aggravated felonious sexual assault and sexual assault convictions under RSA 632-A:2, I(g)(1) and RSA 632-A:4, I were reversed because he had not provided "therapy" under RSA 632-A:1, VI to the victim, an inmate whom defendant met while serving as a "spiritual services coordinator" at a correctional institution. Having regular meetings centered on different topics which ultimately generated encouraging and helpful discussions did not give rise to a rational conclusion that defendant engaged in a planned action or a systematic cause or measure, procedure, technique or any particular approach in order to relieve the alleged victim's bodily, mental, or behavioral disorders; defendant's own characterization of his work as therapeutic in nature did not satisfy the statutorily defined dimensions of therapy. State v. Flodin, 159 N.H. 358, 986 A.2d 470, 2009 N.H. LEXIS 126 (2009).

24. Registration as sex offender

Gross sexual assault under Me. Rev. Stat. Ann. tit. 17-A, § 253(2)(D) was reasonably equivalent to aggravated felonious sexual assault under RSA 632-A:2, as New Hampshire's definition of "sexual penetration" in RSA 632-A:1, V is substantially similar to

Maine's definition of "sexual act" in Me. Rev. Stat. Ann. tit. 17-A, § 251(C). Accordingly, petitioner, who had pleaded guilty to violating the Maine statute, was required under RSA 651-B:1 to register for life as a sex offender. Doe v. N.H. Dep't of Safety, 160 N.H. 474, 999 A.2d 362, 2010 N.H. LEXIS 63 (2010).

25. Member of household

There was sufficient evidence that defendant, who was convicted of aggravated felonious sexual assault under RSA 632-A:2, I(j)(1), was a member of the same household as the victim, the daughter of his girlfriend. Although defendant and the victim's mother concealed their relationship from their children, he contributed to the maintenance of her household, spent every night at her home, and looked after her children. State v. Moncada, 161 N.H. 791, 20 A.3d 904, 2011 N.H. LEXIS 58 (2011).

Cited:

Cited in State v. Meloon, 116 N.H. 669, 366 A.2d 1176, 1976 N.H. LEXIS 443 (1976); Kanteles v. Wheelock, 439 F. Supp. 505, 1977 U.S. Dist. LEXIS 13414 (D.N.H. 1977); State v. Scott, 117 N.H. 996, 380 A.2d 1092, 1977 N.H. LEXIS 479 (1977); State v. Gregoire, 118 N.H. 140, 384 A.2d 132, 1978 N.H. LEXIS 360 (1978); State v. LaBranche, 118 N.H. 176, 385 A.2d 108, 1978 N.H. LEXIS 371 (1978); State v. Goodwin, 118 N.H. 862, 395 A.2d 1234, 1978 N.H. LEXIS 307 (1978); State v. Scarlett, 118 N.H. 904, 395 A.2d 1244, 1978 N.H. LEXIS 317 (1978); State v. Boisvert, 119 N.H. 174, 400 A.2d 48, 1979 N.H. LEXIS 268 (1979); State v. Boone, 119 N.H. 594, 406 A.2d 113, 1979 N.H. LEXIS 360 (1979); State v. Nash, 119 N.H. 728, 407 A.2d 365, 1979 N.H. LEXIS 377 (1979); State v. Isaac, 119 N.H. 971, 409 A.2d 1354, 1979 N.H. LEXIS 433 (1979); State v. St. John, 120 N.H. 61, 410 A.2d 1126, 1980 N.H. LEXIS 224 (1980); State v. Gullick, 120 N.H. 99, 411 A.2d 1113, 1980 N.H. LEXIS 237 (1980); State v. Staples, 120 N.H. 278, 415 A.2d 320, 1980 N.H. LEXIS 275 (1980); State v. Gonzales, 120 N.H. 805, 423 A.2d 608, 1980 N.H. LEXIS 393 (1980); Isaac v. Perrin, 659 F.2d 279, 1981 U.S. App. LEXIS 17363 (1st Cir. N.H. 1981); State v. Preston, 121 N.H. 147, 427 A.2d 32, 1981 N.H. LEXIS 269 (1981); State v. Perkins, 121 N.H. 713, 435 A.2d 504, 1981 N.H. LEXIS 415 (1981); State v. La Clair, 121 N.H. 743, 433 A.2d 1326, 1981 N.H. LEXIS 391 (1981); State v. Wonyetye, 122 N.H. 39, 441 A.2d 363, 1982 N.H. LEXIS 286 (1982); State v. Dukette, 122 N.H. 336, 444 A.2d 547, 1982 N.H. LEXIS 325 (1982); State v. Miskell, 122 N.H. 842, 451 A.2d 383, 1982 N.H. LEXIS 452 (1982); State v. Niquette, 122 N.H. 870, 451 A.2d 1292, 1982 N.H. LEXIS 482 (1982); State v. Stone, 122 N.H. 987, 453 A.2d 1272, 1982 N.H. LEXIS 505 (1982); State v. Chaisson, 123 N.H. 17, 458 A.2d 95, 1983 N.H. LEXIS 236 (1983); State v. Allard, 123 N.H. 209, 459 A.2d 259, 1983 N.H. LEXIS 253 (1983); State v. Guaraldi, 124 N.H. 93, 467 A.2d 233, 1983 N.H. LEXIS 365 (1983); State v. Mitchell, 124 N.H. 210, 470 A.2d 885, 1983 N.H. LEXIS 414 (1983); State v. Mitchell, 124 N.H. 247, 469 A.2d 1310, 1983 N.H. LEXIS 411 (1983); State v. Brown, 125 N.H. 346, 480 A.2d 901, 1984 N.H. LEXIS 265 (1984); State v. Morse, 125 N.H. 403, 480 A.2d 183, 1984 N.H. LEXIS 259 (1984); State v. Howland, 125 N.H. 497, 484 A.2d 1076, 1984 N.H. LEXIS 407 (1984); State v. Nadeau, 126 N.H. 120, 489 A.2d 623, 1985 N.H. LEXIS 257 (1985); State v. Munson, 126 N.H. 191, 489 A.2d 646, 1985 N.H. LEXIS 245 (1985); State v. Vanguilder, 126 N.H. 326, 493 A.2d 1116, 1985 N.H. LEXIS 326 (1985); State v. Ober, 126 N.H. 471, 493 A.2d 493, 1985 N.H. LEXIS 305 (1985); State v. Walsh, 126 N.H. 610, 495 A.2d 1256, 1985 N.H. LEXIS 367 (1985); State ex rel. McLellan v. Cavanaugh, 127 N.H. 33, 498 A.2d 735, 1985 N.H. LEXIS 397 (1985); State v. Campbell, 127 N.H. 112, 498 A.2d 330, 1985 N.H. LEXIS 376 (1985); State v. Guaraldi, 127 N.H. 303, 500 A.2d 360, 1985 N.H. LEXIS 444 (1985); State v. Decker, 127 N.H. 468, 503 A.2d 796, 1985 N.H. LEXIS 466 (1985); State v. Jones, 127 N.H. 515, 503 A.2d 802, 1985 N.H. LEXIS 454 (1985); State v. Parker, 127 N.H. 525, 503 A.2d 809, 1985 N.H. LEXIS 455 (1985); State v. Dukette, 127 N.H. 540, 506 A.2d 699, 1986 N.H. LEXIS 227 (1986); State v. Meekins, 127 N.H. 777, 508 A.2d 1048, 1986 N.H. LEXIS 230 (1986); State v. Lurvey, 127 N.H. 822, 508 A.2d 1074, 1986 N.H. LEXIS 239 (1986); State v. Smith, 127 N.H. 836, 508 A.2d 1082, 1986 N.H. LEXIS 229 (1986); State v. Judkins, 128 N.H. 223, 512 A.2d 427, 1986 N.H. LEXIS 264 (1986); State v. Oropallo, 128 N.H. 305, 512 A.2d 1130, 1986 N.H. LEXIS 281 (1986); In re Gene B., 128 N.H. 321, 512 A.2d 432, 1986 N.H. LEXIS 263 (1986); State v. Chapin, 128 N.H. 355, 513 A.2d 358, 1986 N.H. LEXIS 296 (1986); State v. Fennell, 128 N.H. 383, 513 A.2d 363, 1986 N.H. LEXIS 297 (1986); Vermont Mut. Ins. Co. v. Malcolm, 128 N.H. 521, 517 A.2d 800, 1986 N.H. LEXIS 339 (1986); State v. O'Leary, 128 N.H. 661, 517 A.2d 1174, 1986 N.H. LEXIS 326 (1986); State v. Wood, 128 N.H. 739, 519 A.2d 277, 1986 N.H. LEXIS 360 (1986); State v. Heath, 129 N.H. 102, 523 A.2d 82, 1986 N.H. LEXIS 395 (1986); State v. Howe, 129 N.H. 120, 523 A.2d 94, 1987 N.H. LEXIS 155 (1987); State v. Duff, 129 N.H. 731, 532 A.2d 1381, 1987 N.H. LEXIS 248 (1987); State v. Dean, 129 N.H. 744, 533 A.2d 333, 1987 N.H. LEXIS 263 (1987); State v. Bujnowski, 130 N.H. 1, 532 A.2d 1385, 1987 N.H. LEXIS 264 (1987); State v. Coppola, 130 N.H. 148, 536 A.2d 1236, 1987 N.H. LEXIS 298 (1987); State v. Colbath, 130 N.H. 316, 540 A.2d 1212, 1988 N.H. LEXIS 13 (1988); State v. Munnis, 130 N.H. 641, 546 A.2d 1060, 1988 N.H. LEXIS 46 (1988); State v. Dube, 130 N.H. 770, 547 A.2d 283, 1988 N.H. LEXIS 49 (1988); State v. King, 131 N.H. 173, 551 A.2d 973, 1988 N.H. LEXIS 102 (1988); State v. Knowles, 131 N.H. 274, 553 A.2d 274, 1988 N.H. LEXIS 127 (1988); State v. Wood, 132 N.H. 162, 562 A.2d 1312, 1989 N.H. LEXIS 85 (1989); State v. Johnson, 132 N.H. 279, 564 A.2d 444, 1989 N.H. LEXIS 94 (1989); State v. Blum, 132 N.H. 396, 566 A.2d 1131, 1989 N.H. LEXIS 113 (1989); State v. Bruce, 132 N.H. 465, 566 A.2d 1144, 1989 N.H. LEXIS 122 (1989); State v. Pond, 132 N.H. 472, 567 A.2d 992, 1989 N.H. LEXIS 129 (1989); State v. Hunter, 132 N.H. 556, 567 A.2d 564, 1989 N.H. LEXIS 143 (1989); State v. Cochran, 132 N.H. 670, 569 A.2d 756, 1990 N.H. LEXIS 10 (1990); State v. Colbath, 132 N.H. 708, 571 A.2d 260, 1990 N.H. LEXIS 15 (1990); State v. Allen, 133 N.H. 306, 577 A.2d 801, 1990 N.H. LEXIS 68 (1990); State v. Jernigan, 133 N.H. 396, 577 A.2d 1214, 1990 N.H. LEXIS 78 (1990); State v. Fennell, 133 N.H. 402, 578 A.2d 329, 1990 N.H. LEXIS 79 (1990); State v. Killam, 133 N.H. 458, 578 A.2d 850, 1990 N.H. LEXIS 87 (1990); State v. Letendre, 133 N.H. 555, 579 A.2d 1223, 1990 N.H. LEXIS 103 (1990); State v. Jones, 133 N.H. 562, 578 A.2d 864, 1990 N.H. LEXIS 101 (1990); State v. Wisowaty, 133 N.H. 604, 580 A.2d 1079, 1990 N.H. LEXIS 109 (1990); State v. Pond, 133 N.H. 738, 584 A.2d 770, 1990 N.H. LEXIS 133 (1990); State v. LaPorte, 134 N.H. 73, 587 A.2d 1237, 1991 N.H. LEXIS 25 (1991); State v. Bureau, 134 N.H. 220, 589 A.2d 1013, 1991 N.H. LEXIS 48 (1991); State v. Anctil, 134 N.H. 623, 598 A.2d 213, 1991 N.H. LEXIS 110 (1991); State v. Ellison, 135 N.H. 1, 599 A.2d 477, 1991 N.H. LEXIS 132 (1991); State v. Bergmann, 135 N.H. 97, 599 A.2d 502, 1991 N.H. LEXIS 158 (1991); State v. Chase, 135 N.H. 209, 600 A.2d 931, 1991 N.H. LEXIS 169 (1991); State v. Cooper, 135 N.H. 258, 603 A.2d 499, 1992 N.H. LEXIS 16 (1992); State v. Parra, 135 N.H. 306, 604 A.2d 567, 1992 N.H. LEXIS 31 (1992); State v. Chapman, 135 N.H. 390, 605 A.2d 1055, 1992 N.H. LEXIS 48 (1992); State v. Smith, 135 N.H. 524, 607 A.2d 611, 1992 N.H. LEXIS 71 (1992); State v. Eldredge, 135 N.H. 562, 607 A.2d 617, 1992 N.H. LEXIS 80 (1992); State v. Philbrick, 135 N.H. 729, 610 A.2d 353, 1992 N.H. LEXIS 109 (1992); State v. Gagne, 136 N.H. 101, 612 A.2d 899, 1992 N.H. LEXIS 135 (1992); State v. Ellsworth, 136 N.H. 115, 613 A.2d 473, 1992 N.H. LEXIS 144 (1992); State v. Huffman, 136 N.H. 149, 613 A.2d 476, 1992 N.H. LEXIS 149 (1992); State v. Demond, 136 N.H. 233, 614 A.2d 1342, 1992 N.H. LEXIS 160 (1992); State v. Wellington, 134 N.H. 79, 588 A.2d 372, 1991 N.H. LEXIS 20 (1991); State v. Stow, 136 N.H. 598, 620 A.2d 1023, 1993 N.H. LEXIS 8 (1993); State v. Brinkman, 136 N.H. 716, 621 A.2d 932, 1993 N.H. LEXIS 20 (1993); State v. Wade, 136 N.H. 750, 622 A.2d 832, 1993 N.H. LEXIS 25 (1993); State v. Killam, 137 N.H. 155, 626 A.2d 401, 1993 N.H. LEXIS 55 (1993); State v. McSheehan, 137 N.H. 180, 624 A.2d 560, 1993 N.H. LEXIS 59 (1993); State v. Weber, 137 N.H. 193, 624 A.2d 967, 1993 N.H. LEXIS 60 (1993); State v. Collins, 138 N.H. 217, 637 A.2d 153, 1994 N.H. LEXIS 3 (1994); State v. Cegelis, 138 N.H. 249, 638 A.2d 783, 1994 N.H. LEXIS 10 (1994); State v. Silk, 138 N.H. 290, 639 A.2d 243, 1994 N.H. LEXIS 14 (1994); State v. Besk, 138 N.H. 412, 640 A.2d 775, 1994 N.H. LEXIS 41 (1994); State v. Martin, 138 N.H. 508, 643 A.2d 946, 1994 N.H. LEXIS 57 (1994); State v. Brown, 138 N.H. 649, 644 A.2d 1082, 1994 N.H. LEXIS 83 (1994); State v. Little, 138 N.H. 657, 645 A.2d 665, 1994 N.H. LEXIS 80 (1994); State v. McLellan, 139 N.H. 132, 649 A.2d 843, 1994 N.H. LEXIS 121 (1994); State v. Crooker, 139 N.H. 226, 651 A.2d 470, 1994 N.H. LEXIS 128 (1994); State v. Panzera, 139 N.H. 235, 652 A.2d 136, 1994 N.H. LEXIS 138 (1994); State v. Telles, 139 N.H. 344, 653 A.2d 554, 1995 N.H. LEXIS 11 (1995); State v. Bernaby, 139 N.H. 420, 653 A.2d 1124, 1995 N.H. LEXIS 18 (1995); Reid v. Warden, New Hampshire State Prison, 139 N.H. 530, 659

A.2d 429, 1995 N.H. LEXIS 45 (1995); State v. Kirsch, 139 N.H. 647, 662 A.2d 937, 1995 N.H. LEXIS 67 (1995); State v. Locke, 139 N.H. 741, 663 A.2d 602, 1995 N.H. LEXIS 82 (1995); State v. Carter, 140 N.H. 1, 662 A.2d 289, 1995 N.H. LEXIS 86 (1995); Tsiatsios v. Tsiatsios, 140 N.H. 173, 663 A.2d 1335, 1995 N.H. LEXIS 120 (1995); State v. Horne, 140 N.H. 90, 663 A.2d 92, 1995 N.H. LEXIS 110 (1995); State v. Desmarais, 140 N.H. 196, 665 A.2d 348, 1995 N.H. LEXIS 125 (1995); State v. Laforest, 140 N.H. 286, 665 A.2d 1083, 1995 N.H. LEXIS 142 (1995); State v. Fecteau, 140 N.H. 498, 667 A.2d 1384, 1995 N.H. LEXIS 178 (1995); Mutter v. Town of Salem, 945 F. Supp. 402, 1996 U.S. Dist. LEXIS 16818 (D.N.H. 1996); State v. Martin, 142 N.H. 63, 694 A.2d 999, 1997 N.H. LEXIS 55 (1997); State v. Croft, 142 N.H. 76, 696 A.2d 1117, 1997 N.H. LEXIS 58 (1997); State v. Crosby, 142 N.H. 134, 697 A.2d 1377, 1997 N.H. LEXIS 63 (1997); State v. Ranger, 142 N.H. 140, 697 A.2d 505, 1997 N.H. LEXIS 65 (1997); State v. Boetti, 142 N.H. 255, 699 A.2d 585, 1997 N.H. LEXIS 86 (1997); State v. Walters, 142 N.H. 239, 698 A.2d 1244, 1997 N.H. LEXIS 81 (1997); State v. Thibedau, 142 N.H. 325, 702 A.2d 299, 1997 N.H. LEXIS 97 (1997); State v. Ellsworth, 142 N.H. 710, 709 A.2d 768, 1998 N.H. LEXIS 25 (1998); State v. Graf, 143 N.H. 294, 726 A.2d 1270, 1999 N.H. LEXIS 1 (1999); State v. Cannon, 146 N.H. 562, 776 A.2d 736, 2001 N.H. LEXIS 128 (2001); State v. Cole, 147 N.H. 374, 788 A.2d 248, 2001 N.H. LEXIS 227 (2001); State v. Mitchell, 148 N.H. 293, 808 A.2d 62, 2002 N.H. LEXIS 128 (2002); State v. McLellan, 149 N.H. 237, 817 A.2d 309, 2003 N.H. LEXIS 32 (2003); State v. Whittey, 149 N.H. 463, 821 A.2d 1086, 2003 N.H. LEXIS 64 (2003).

RESEARCH REFERENCES

New Hampshire Practice.
2-33 N.H.P. Criminal Practice & Procedure § 33.10.
2-33 N.H.P. Criminal Practice & Procedure § 33.54.

New Hampshire Bar Journal.
For article, "Understanding and Representing Adult Clients Who Are Victims of Domestic Abuse," see 35 N.H.B.J. 8. (1994).

632-A:3. Felonious Sexual Assault.

A person is guilty of a class B felony if such person:

I. Subjects a person to sexual contact and causes serious personal injury to the victim under any of the circumstances named in RSA 632-A:2; or

II. Engages in sexual penetration with a person, other than his legal spouse, who is 13 years of age or older and under 16 years of age where the age difference between the actor and the other person is 4 years or more; or

III. Engages in sexual contact with a person other than his legal spouse who is under 13 years of age.

IV. (a) Engages in sexual contact with the person, or causes the person to engage in sexual contact on himself or herself in the presence of the actor, when the actor is in a position of authority over the person and uses that authority to coerce the victim to submit under any of the following circumstances:

(1) When the actor has direct supervisory or disciplinary authority over the victim by virtue of the victim being incarcerated in a correctional institution, the secure psychiatric unit, or juvenile detention facility where the actor is employed; or

(2) When the actor is a probation or parole officer or a juvenile probation and parole officer who has direct supervisory or disciplinary authority over the victim while the victim is on parole or probation or under juvenile probation.

(b) Consent of the victim under any of the circumstances set forth in this paragraph shall not be considered a defense.

(c) For the purpose of this paragraph, "sexual contact" means the intentional touching of the person's sexual or intimate parts, including genitalia, anus, breasts, and buttocks, where such contact, or the causing of such contact, can reasonably be construed as being for the purpose of sexual arousal or gratification of the person in the position of authority, or the humiliation of the person being touched.

Source.
1975, 302:1. 1981, 415:4. 1985, 228:4, eff. Jan. 1, 1986. 1997, 220:3, eff. Jan. 1, 1998. 2003, 226:3, 4, eff. Jan. 1, 2004. 2006, 162:1, eff. January 1, 2007. 2008, 334:9, eff. January 1, 2009. 2010, 223:1, eff. January 1, 2011.

Amendments
—2010. The 2010 amendment added the IV(a) and IV(b) designations; added "or causes the person to engage in sexual contact on himself or herself in the presence of the actor" in the introductory language of IV(a); redesignated former IV(a) and IV(b) as IV(a)(1) and IV(a)(2); substituted "this paragraph" for "paragraph IV" in IV(b); and added IV(c).

—2008. The 2008 amendment substituted "4 years" for "3 years" in II.

—2006. Paragraph II: Inserted "where the age difference between the actor and the other person is 3 years or more" following "years of age".

—2003. Substituted "such person" for "he" in the introductory paragraph and rewrote par. IV.

—1997. Paragraph IV: Added.

—1985. Rewritten to the extent that a detailed comparison would be impracticable.

—1981. Inserted "other than his legal spouse" following "person".

Cross References.
Bail prohibited, see RSA 597:1-a.
Classification of crimes, see RSA 625:9.
Extended term of imprisonment, see RSA 651:6.
Limitations on civil actions brought by defendant against victim, see RSA 632-A:10-c.
Registration of criminal offenders, see RSA 651-B.
Sentences, see RSA 651.

NOTES TO DECISIONS

1. Privacy rights
2. Application
3. Mens rea
4. Indictment
5. Severance of charges
6. Separate acts
7. Consent
8. Defenses
9. Burden of proof
10. Evidence
11. Victim testimony
12. Expert testimony
13. Attempt
14. Instructions
15. Lesser included offenses

1. Privacy rights

Although this section lacked requirement of scienter it did not infringe on party's assumed federally protected privacy right to engage in consensual heterosexual intercourse with adults. Goodrow v. Perrin, 119 N.H. 483, 403 A.2d 864, 1979 N.H. LEXIS 325 (1979).

There is no privacy right to engage in sexual intercourse with a person the legislature has determined is unable to give consent, even if there is a protected privacy right to engage in heterosexual intercourse with other adults. Goodrow v. Perrin, 119 N.H. 483, 403 A.2d 864, 1979 N.H. LEXIS 325 (1979).

2. Application

Statutory rape applies to those under the age of sixteen years regardless of their emotional and sexual maturity. State v. Berry, 117 N.H. 352, 373 A.2d 355, 1977 N.H. LEXIS 337 (1977).

3. Mens rea

State did not have to prove defendant knew that a victim was under age of legal consent for statutory rape conviction under RSA 632-A:3(II) because legislature had amended statute many times and did not insert a mens rea pursuant to RSA 626:2(I) and did not provide a reasonable mistake of age defense. Thus, the offense remained a strict liability crime. State v. Holmes, 154 N.H. 723, 920 A.2d 632, 2007 N.H. LEXIS 9 (2007).

"Knowingly" is the appropriate mens rea for felonious sexual assault involving sexual penetration. State v. Goodwin, 140 N.H. 672, 671 A.2d 554, 1996 N.H. LEXIS 13 (1996).

The mens rea required for felonious sexual assault is "purposely." State v. Pond, 132 N.H. 472, 567 A.2d 992, 1989 N.H. LEXIS 129 (1989).

At trial for felonious sexual assault, court properly made no reference to the term "knowingly," which was mere surplusage in the indictments, and appropriately instructed the jury that they must find the defendant acted purposely to find him guilty. State v. Pond, 132 N.H. 472, 567 A.2d 992, 1989 N.H. LEXIS 129 (1989).

4. Indictment

Defendant charged with felonious sexual assault was not entitled to a bill of particulars specifying whether the victim was age twelve or thirteen at the time of the alleged offenses because the intent of the legislature in creating two classes of felony offenses for any act of sexual penetration committed against a child under sixteen years of age was to protect all young victims against sexual assault but to establish an enhanced penalty for assaults against younger victims. State v. Woodard, 146 N.H. 221, 769 A.2d 379, 2001 N.H. LEXIS 64 (2001).

Indictments on nine counts of felonious sexual assault did not violate defendant's constitutional guarantees against double jeopardy where each indictment accused the defendant of engaging in the act of sexual penetration with the victim when the victim was "either twelve or thirteen years old" and charged the defendant with a class B felony, and, because the victim's age was in question, the court limited the state to prosecuting the defendant only on class B felonies. State v. Woodard, 146 N.H. 221, 769 A.2d 379, 2001 N.H. LEXIS 64 (2001).

5. Severance of charges

Defendant's convictions of aggravated felonious sexual assault, RSA 632-A:2, and felonious sexual assault, RSA 632-A:3, III, were reversed, because under newly-adopted rules concerning severance which applied retroactively, the trial court erred in denying defendant's motion to sever the charges concerning the two child victims. State v. Tierney, 150 N.H. 339, 839 A.2d 38, 2003 N.H. LEXIS 196 (2003).

6. Separate acts

Each act of sexual contact under this section constitutes a separate offense of felonious sexual assault when such contact is with a person less than thirteen years of age. State v. Patch, 135 N.H. 127, 599 A.2d 1243, 1991 N.H. LEXIS 155 (1991).

7. Consent

Delay in making a complaint in a forceable rape case may be considered on question of credibility of complaining witness and of her state of mind regarding consent, but in case of alleged rape of child under age of sixteen, consent is not material; whatever relevance delay may have with respect to credibility was purely question of fact under circumstances of particular case. State v. Berry, 117 N.H. 352, 373 A.2d 355, 1977 N.H. LEXIS 337 (1977).

8. Defenses

Reasonable and honest belief that person is over age of consent is not a constitutional defense to statutory rape. Goodrow v. Perrin, 119 N.H. 483, 403 A.2d 864, 1979 N.H. LEXIS 325 (1979).

9. Burden of proof

In prosecution for statutory rape, state has burden of establishing identity of prosecutrix. State v. Ebelt, 121 N.H. 143, 427 A.2d 29, 1981 N.H. LEXIS 268 (1981).

10. Evidence

Six-year-old victim's inner thigh adjacent to her genitals was an "intimate part" of her body as defined by RSA 632-A:1, IV. Accordingly, there was sufficient evidence to support defendant's conviction of felonious sexual assault under RSA 632-A:3, III. State v. Bakunczyk, 164 N.H. 77, 53 A.3d 569, 2012 N.H. LEXIS 110 (2012).

There was sufficient evidence to support convictions of aggravated felonious sexual assault and of felonious sexual assault under RSA 632-A:2 and RSA 632-A:3. The jury was free to accept or reject the victim's testimony, and the testimony of the victim and of the police officers provided more than sufficient evidence for a rational trier of fact to find guilt. State v. Oakes, 161 N.H. 270, 13 A.3d 293, 2010 N.H. LEXIS 149 (Dec. 7, 2010).

Superior court properly refused to dismiss a felonious sexual assault charge under RSA 632-A:3 because defendant had not shown that the victim's statement that there was "merging" in her mind between admissible continuous memories and inadmissible repressed memories demonstrated that her memory of the admissible assault was no longer continuous. Nothing demonstrated that the victim had lost her ability to distinguish between these memories. State v. Gibson, 153 N.H. 454, 897 A.2d 957, 2006 N.H. LEXIS 47 (2006).

Trial court did not violate U.S. Const. amends. VI, XIV and N.H. Const. pt. I, art. 15 Confrontation Clauses and did not violate N.H. R. Evid. 403, 608(b) by not allowing a defendant who was accused of sex crimes under RSA 629:1, 632-A:2, 632-A:3 to cross-examine the victim with evidence that she stole money from her employer since that evidence was prejudicial and was not probative of her credibility regarding the sex crimes. State v. Hokenstrom, 2003 N.H. LEXIS 214 (N.H. Feb. 14, 2003). (Unpublished opinion.)

In prosecution for felonious sexual assault, the probative value of evidence of a homosexual relationship between defendant and the victim's mother was substantially outweighed by the danger of unfair prejudice. State v. Woodard, 146 N.H. 221, 769 A.2d 379, 2001 N.H. LEXIS 64 (2001).

In prosecution for felonious sexual assault, allowing reference to disclosures the victim had previously made to others about alleged assaults by defendant was not an abuse of discretion because the victim's testimony was relevant to establish that prior reports had been made and the prior reports were relevant to explain her delay in making the ultimate disclosure which led to defendant's arrest. State v. Woodard, 146 N.H. 221, 769 A.2d 379, 2001 N.H. LEXIS 64 (2001).

Victim's testimony and illustrations, together with testimony of victim's brother and investigating officer, were sufficient to support jury's verdict on counts alleging sexual contact, fellatio and cunnilingus. State v. Hodgdon, 143 N.H. 399, 725 A.2d 660, 1999 N.H. LEXIS 17 (1999).

In a prosecution for aggravated felonious sexual assault and felonious sexual assault committed by the defendant against his minor niece, the victim's use of the term "privates" to describe where the defendant allegedly touched her was sufficiently specific to establish that the defendant touched her vagina as charged. State v. Graham, 142 N.H. 357, 702 A.2d 322, 1997 N.H. LEXIS 103 (1997).

Trial court did not err in finding that five-year-old child met threshold requirements of competency. Evidence was sufficient to support defendant's convictions, despite apparent divergence among accounts of child victims and notwithstanding defendant's arguments that allegations arose in context of a bitter marital separation and that children may have gained their sexual knowledge elsewhere. State v. Briere, 138 N.H. 617, 644 A.2d 551, 1994 N.H. LEXIS 75 (1994).

In a prosecution for statutory rape, a birth certificate is not admissible as evidence of the age of the prosecutrix if the prosecutor fails to show that the prosecutrix is the person named in the certificate, nor is prosecutrix's testimony of her age admissible if based solely on the certificate. State v. Ebelt, 121 N.H. 143, 427 A.2d 29, 1981 N.H. LEXIS 268 (1981).

Absent proof that prosecutrix in statutory rape case and person named in birth certificate which the state claimed to be prosecutrix's were one and the same, the certificate was inadmissible as a matter of law as being irrelevant. State v. Ebelt, 121 N.H. 143, 427 A.2d 29, 1981 N.H. LEXIS 268 (1981).

Conviction for statutory rape of child under 16 must be reversed where the evidence of child's age was improperly admitted and there was thus insufficient evidence to sustain the verdict. State v. Ebelt, 121 N.H. 143, 427 A.2d 29, 1981 N.H. LEXIS 268 (1981).

11. Victim testimony

In a felonious sexual assault prosecution, a mistrial was not required on the ground that the victim stated during her testimony that she felt "very limited" in the testimony that she could give against defendant because, even in light of potentially prejudicial testimony by other witnesses, a jury could have construed the victim's statement of feeling very limited as an expression of frustration and confusion with limitations upon what she could testify to, and the statement did not clearly refer to defendant's past acts of violence toward the victims' mother. State v. Gibson, 153 N.H. 454, 897 A.2d 957, 2006 N.H. LEXIS 47 (2006).

12. Expert testimony

Testimony of a social worker and a police officer as to victims' tendencies to fail to contemporaneously report abuse and to recant or deny abuse was erroneously admitted expert testimony and was inadmissible lay testimony under N.H. R. Evid. 602 and 701 as, although the testimony was within the knowledge of the witnesses due to their training, it required knowledge beyond the ken of the average person; however, the error was harmless as the victim testified in detail and defendant admitted the actions during a family meeting, and defendant's convictions for aggravated felonious sexual assault under RSA 632-A:2, felonious sexual assault under RSA 632-A:3, and misdemeanor sexual assault under RSA 632-A:4 were affirmed. State v. Gonzalez, 150 N.H. 74, 834 A.2d 354, 2003 N.H. LEXIS 142 (2003).

Admission of expert's testimony that victim presented a "symptom picture" consistent with sexual abuse was not harmless error, where testimony was lengthy, comprehensive, and directly linked to determination of defendant's guilt or innocence. State v. Silk, 138 N.H. 290, 639 A.2d 243, 1994 N.H. LEXIS 14 (1994).

13. Attempt

In prosecution for attempted felonious sexual assault, State was required to prove beyond a reasonable doubt that defendant intended on engaging in sexual contact with a person, other than his legal spouse, who was under the age of thirteen. State v. Cobb, 143 N.H. 638, 732 A.2d 425, 1999 N.H. LEXIS 53 (1999).

14. Instructions

In its felonious sexual assault (FSA) charge, the trial court erroneously substituted the word "genitalia" for "buttocks," thereby effectively eliminating the distinction between the FSA charge and one of the aggravated felonious sexual assault charges. This required that the conviction and sentence on the FSA charge be vacated. State v. Munroe, 161 N.H. 618, 20 A.3d 871, 2011 N.H. LEXIS 34 (2011).

Under the plain error rule, instructing the jury that the mens rea for a felonious sexual assault charge was "knowingly" instead of "purposely" did not seriously affect the fairness, integrity or public reputation of judicial proceedings. The evidence that defendant acted purposely was overwhelming and essentially uncontroverted. State v. Ortiz, 162 N.H. 585, 34 A.3d 599, 2011 N.H. LEXIS 146 (2011).

In a prosecution for felonious sexual assault, where the trial court included an instruction that "the testimony of a victim of a sexual assault does not require corroboration," the court did not err

in refusing defendant's request to give the same instruction about the testimony of a defense witness because the statute regarding testimony in sexual assault cases states only that the victim's testimony needs no corroboration, not other witnesses who testify at trial. State v. Cook, 148 N.H. 735, 813 A.2d 480, 2002 N.H. LEXIS 183 (2002).

A jury instruction on transferred intent did not improperly amend the indictment where the court informed the jury that the state was required to prove purposeful penetration of the vagina and purposeful penetration of the anus, but that if the jury were to find that the defendant intended to purposely penetrate one area and with that purpose accidentally penetrated another area, the jury could find that element of the offense had been established. State v. Demmons, 137 N.H. 716, 634 A.2d 998, 1993 N.H. LEXIS 149 (1993).

15. Lesser included offenses

Simple assault under RSA 631:2-a, I(a), although perhaps a lesser-included offense of aggravated felonious sexual assault by means of application of physical force, is not a lesser-included offense of felonious sexual assault under RSA 632-A:3, III. "Unprivileged physical contact" is not an element of felonious sexual assault by means of sexual contact with a victim under the age of thirteen. State v. Michaud, 161 N.H. 785, 20 A.3d 1012, 2011 N.H. LEXIS 60 (2011).

Defendant, who was charged with violating RSA 632-A:3, III, by engaging in sexual contact with a person other than his legal spouse who was under 13, was not entitled to a lesser-included-offense instruction on simple assault under RSA 631:2-a, I(a). "Unprivileged physical contact" was not an element of felonious sexual assault under RSA 632-A:3, III. State v. Michaud, 161 N.H. 785, 20 A.3d 1012, 2011 N.H. LEXIS 60 (2011).

Cited:

Cited in State v. Scott, 117 N.H. 996, 380 A.2d 1092, 1977 N.H. LEXIS 479 (1977); State v. Goupil, 122 N.H. 857, 451 A.2d 1284, 1982 N.H. LEXIS 475 (1982); State v. Baker, 127 N.H. 801, 508 A.2d 1059, 1986 N.H. LEXIS 236 (1986); State v. Steer, 128 N.H. 490, 517 A.2d 797, 1986 N.H. LEXIS 334 (1986); State v. Walters, 128 N.H. 783, 519 A.2d 305, 1986 N.H. LEXIS 361 (1986); State v. Lacasse, 129 N.H. 651, 531 A.2d 327, 1987 N.H. LEXIS 236 (1987); State v. Lemire, 130 N.H. 552, 543 A.2d 425, 1988 N.H. LEXIS 23 (1988); State v. Woods, 130 N.H. 721, 546 A.2d 1073, 1988 N.H. LEXIS 74 (1988); State v. Hood, 131 N.H. 606, 557 A.2d 995, 1989 N.H. LEXIS 36 (1989); State v. Derby, 131 N.H. 760, 561 A.2d 504, 1989 N.H. LEXIS 57 (1989); State v. Blum, 132 N.H. 396, 566 A.2d 1131, 1989 N.H. LEXIS 113 (1989); State v. Cochran, 132 N.H. 670, 569 A.2d 756, 1990 N.H. LEXIS 10 (1990); State v. Cox, 133 N.H. 261, 575 A.2d 1320, 1990 N.H. LEXIS 46 (1990); State v. Jones, 133 N.H. 562, 578 A.2d 864, 1990 N.H. LEXIS 101 (1990); State v. Letourneau, 133 N.H. 565, 578 A.2d 865, 1990 N.H. LEXIS 99 (1990); State v. Zurita, 133 N.H. 719, 584 A.2d 758, 1990 N.H. LEXIS 134 (1990); State v. Anctil, 134 N.H. 623, 598 A.2d 213, 1991 N.H. LEXIS 110 (1991); State v. Bergmann, 135 N.H. 97, 599 A.2d 502, 1991 N.H. LEXIS 158 (1991); State v. Patch, 135 N.H. 127, 599 A.2d 1243, 1991 N.H. LEXIS 155 (1991); State v. Simonds, 135 N.H. 203, 600 A.2d 928, 1991 N.H. LEXIS 170 (1991); State v. Chase, 135 N.H. 209, 600 A.2d 931, 1991 N.H. LEXIS 169 (1991); State v. Guajardo, 135 N.H. 401, 605 A.2d 217, 1992 N.H. LEXIS 52 (1992); State v. Vaillancourt, 136 N.H. 206, 612 A.2d 1329, 1992 N.H. LEXIS 152 (1992); State v. Lemieux, 136 N.H. 329, 615 A.2d 635, 1992 N.H. LEXIS 171 (1992); State v. Weber, 137 N.H. 193, 624 A.2d 967, 1993 N.H. LEXIS 60 (1993); State v. Woodsum, 137 N.H. 198, 624 A.2d 1342, 1993 N.H. LEXIS 64 (1993); In re Hamel, 137 N.H. 488, 629 A.2d 802, 1993 N.H. LEXIS 111 (1993); State v. Degre, 137 N.H. 512, 629 A.2d 818, 1993 N.H. LEXIS 108 (1993); State v. Woveris, 138 N.H. 33, 635 A.2d 454, 1993 N.H. LEXIS 162 (1993); State v. LaFountain, 138 N.H. 225, 636 A.2d 1028, 1994 N.H. LEXIS 5 (1994); State v. Silk, 138 N.H. 290, 639 A.2d 243, 1994 N.H. LEXIS 14 (1994); State v. Hamel, 138 N.H. 392, 643 A.2d 953, 1994 N.H. LEXIS 35 (1994); State v. Brown, 138 N.H. 649, 644 A.2d 1082, 1994 N.H. LEXIS 83 (1994); State v. Little, 138 N.H. 657, 645 A.2d 665, 1994 N.H. LEXIS 80 (1994); State v. Weir, 138 N.H. 671, 645 A.2d 56, 1994 N.H. LEXIS 87 (1994); State v. Bonacorsi, 139 N.H. 28, 648 A.2d 469, 1994 N.H. LEXIS 103 (1994); State v. Taylor, 139 N.H. 96, 649 A.2d 375, 1994 N.H. LEXIS 116

(1994); State v. Kirsch, 139 N.H. 647, 662 A.2d 937, 1995 N.H. LEXIS 67 (1995); State v. Locke, 139 N.H. 741, 663 A.2d 602, 1995 N.H. LEXIS 82 (1995); In re Turgeon, 140 N.H. 52, 663 A.2d 82, 1995 N.H. LEXIS 98 (1995); State v. Lucius, 140 N.H. 60, 663 A.2d 605, 1995 N.H. LEXIS 97 (1995); State v. Cavaliere, 140 N.H. 108, 663 A.2d 96, 1995 N.H. LEXIS 103 (1995); State v. Desmarais, 140 N.H. 196, 665 A.2d 348, 1995 N.H. LEXIS 125 (1995); Millette v. Warden, N.H. State Prison, 141 N.H. 653, 692 A.2d 963, 1997 N.H. LEXIS 16 (1997); State v. Ranger, 142 N.H. 140, 697 A.2d 505, 1997 N.H. LEXIS 65 (1997); State v. Graham, 142 N.H. 357, 702 A.2d 322, 1997 N.H. LEXIS 103 (1997); State v. Sullivan, 142 N.H. 399, 702 A.2d 339, 1997 N.H. LEXIS 110 (1997); State v. Cole, 142 N.H. 519, 703 A.2d 658, 1997 N.H. LEXIS 125 (1997); State v. Ellsworth, 142 N.H. 710, 709 A.2d 768, 1998 N.H. LEXIS 25 (1998); State v. Paulsen, 143 N.H. 447, 726 A.2d 902, 1999 N.H. LEXIS 23 (1999); State v. Carlson, 146 N.H. 52, 767 A.2d 421, 2001 N.H. LEXIS 26 (2001); State v. Richard, 147 N.H. 340, 786 A.2d 876, 2001 N.H. LEXIS 221 (2001); State v. Cole, 147 N.H. 374, 788 A.2d 248, 2001 N.H. LEXIS 227 (2001); State v. Hall, 148 N.H. 671, 813 A.2d 501, 2002 N.H. LEXIS 208 (2002); State v. Mason, 150 N.H. 53, 834 A.2d 339, 2003 N.H. LEXIS 138 (2003); Duquette v. Warden, N.H. State Prison, 154 N.H. 737, 919 A.2d 767, 2007 N.H. LEXIS 10 (2007).

RESEARCH REFERENCES

New Hampshire Bar Journal.
For article, "Lex Loci: A Survey of New Hampshire Supreme Court Decisions," see 48 N.H.B.J. 78 (Spring 2007).

632-A:4. Sexual Assault.

I. A person is guilty of a class A misdemeanor under any of the following circumstances:

(a) When the actor subjects another person who is 13 years of age or older to sexual contact under any of the circumstances named in RSA 632-A:2.

(b) When the actor subjects another person, other than the actor's legal spouse, who is 13 years of age or older and under 16 years of age to sexual contact where the age difference between the actor and the other person is 5 years or more.

(c) In the absence of any of the circumstances set forth in RSA 632-A:2, when the actor engages in sexual penetration with a person, other than the actor's legal spouse, who is 13 years of age or older and under 16 years of age where the age difference between the actor and the other person is 4 years or less.

II. A person found guilty under subparagraph I(c) of this section shall not be required to register as a sexual offender under RSA 651-B.

III. (a) A person is guilty of a misdemeanor if such person engages in sexual contact or sexual penetration with another person, or causes the person to engage in sexual contact on himself or herself in the presence of the actor, when the actor is in a position of authority over the person under any of the following circumstances:

(1) When the actor has direct supervisory or disciplinary authority over the victim by virtue of the victim being incarcerated in a correctional institution, the secure psychiatric unit, or juvenile detention facility where the actor is employed; or

(2) When the actor is a probation or parole officer or a juvenile probation and parole officer who has direct supervisory or disciplinary authority over the victim while the victim is on parole or probation or under juvenile probation.

(b) Consent of the victim under any of the circumstances set forth in this paragraph shall not be considered a defense.

(c) For the purpose of this paragraph, "sexual contact" means the intentional touching of the person's sexual or intimate parts, including genitalia, anus, breasts, and buttocks, where such contact, or the causing of such contact, can reasonably be construed as being for the purpose of sexual arousal or gratification of the person in the position of authority, or the humiliation of the person being touched.

Source.
1975, 302:1. 1985, 228:5, eff. Jan. 1, 1986. 2003, 226:5, eff. Jan. 1, 2004; 316:7, eff. at 12:02 a.m., Jan. 1, 2004. 2005, 290:1, eff. January 1, 2006. 2008, 334:14, eff. January 1, 2009. 2010, 223:2, eff. January 1, 2011.

Amendments
—**2010.** The 2010 amendment added the III(a) and III(b) designations; added "or causes the person to engage in sexual contact on himself or herself in the presence of the actor" in the introductory language of III(a); redesignated former III(a) and III(b) as III(a)(1) and III(a)(2); substituted "this paragraph" for "paragraph III" in III(b); and added III(c).

—**2008.** The 2008 amendment substituted "4 years" for "3 years" in I(c).

—**2005.** Paragraph I: Added new subparagraph (b) and redesignated subparagraph (b) as (c).
Paragraph II: Substituted reference to "subparagraph I(c)" for "subparagraph I(b)".

—**2003.** Rewritten by chs. 226:5 and 316 to the extent that a detailed comparison would be impracticable.

—**1985.** Inserted "who is 13 years of age or older" following "another person".

Contingent 2003, ch. 226:9 amendment.
2003, 226:9, provided for amendment of this section. However, under the terms of 2003, 226:7, eff. July 1, 2003, the amendment did not take effect.

Cross References.
Classification of crimes, see RSA 625:9.
Limitations on civil actions brought by defendant against victim, see RSA 632-A:10-c.
Registration of criminal offenders, see RSA 651-B.
Sentences, see RSA 651.

NOTES TO DECISIONS

1. Construction with other laws
2. Consent
3. Lesser included offense
4. Evidence
5. Instructions
6. Therapeutic relationship

1. Construction with other laws
In order to establish sexual assault on the basis of RSA 632-A:2, IX (now RSA 632-A:2, I(i)), i.e. that the defendant, through concealment or by the element of surprise, was able to cause sexual penetration with the victim before the victim had an adequate chance to flee or resist, it is not necessary to prove sexual penetration. State v. Arris, 139 N.H. 469, 656 A.2d 828, 1995 N.H. LEXIS 31 (1995).

The distinguishing feature between the crimes of sexual assault and aggravated sexual assault is that a person must commit "sexual penetration" to be guilty of aggravated felonious sexual assault under RSA 632-A:2, but to be guilty of sexual assault under this section, he need only commit sexual contact under circumstances set forth in RSA 632-A:2. State v. Vonklock, 121 N.H. 697, 433 A.2d 1299, 1981 N.H. LEXIS 399 (1981), overruled in part, State v. Smith, 127 N.H. 433, 503 A.2d 774, 1985 N.H. LEXIS 463 (1985).

2. Consent

Once defendant charged with sexual assault raises the defense of consent, the burden of proving lack of consent shifts to the state. State v. Cooper, 135 N.H. 258, 603 A.2d 499, 1992 N.H. LEXIS 16 (1992).

Because consent is not a justification, lack of consent is not an element of the offense of sexual assault. State v. Cooper, 135 N.H. 258, 603 A.2d 499, 1992 N.H. LEXIS 16 (1992).

3. Lesser included offense

Sexual assault cannot be a lesser-included offense of aggravated felonious sexual assault because sexual assault requires element of "sexual contact" for purpose of sexual arousal or gratification, an element not required for a conviction of aggravated felonious sexual assault. State v. Smith, 127 N.H. 433, 503 A.2d 774, 1985 N.H. LEXIS 463 (1985).

State v. vonKlock, 121 NH 697, 433 A.2d 1299, 1981 N.H. LEXIS 399 (1981), is overruled to the extent it held that sexual assault is a lesser-included offense of aggravated felonious sexual assault. State v. Smith, 127 N.H. 433, 503 A.2d 774, 1985 N.H. LEXIS 463 (1985).

A person must necessarily commit the crime of sexual assault before he can commit aggravated felonious sexual assault inasmuch as there is no means by which a person could commit sexual penetration without engaging in sexual contact; therefore, sexual assault is a lesser included offense of aggravated felonious sexual assault. State v. Vonklock, 121 N.H. 697, 433 A.2d 1299, 1981 N.H. LEXIS 399 (1981), overruled in part, State v. Smith, 127 N.H. 433, 503 A.2d 774, 1985 N.H. LEXIS 463 (1985).

4. Evidence

Adjudication of delinquency based upon misdemeanor sexual assault under RSA 632-A:2, I(a), and RSA 632-A:4, I, was not supported by the evidence. The complainant's statements that defendant "squeezed and rubbed" her breasts and "touched and rubbed" her private parts as they rode a school bus did not support a finding that she was overcome by the actual application of physical force, nor did her statement that defendant's conduct was "rough" and "hurt" her. In re D.B., 164 N.H. 46, 53 A.3d 646, 2012 N.H. LEXIS 116 (2012).

Testimony of a social worker and a police officer as to victims' tendencies to fail to contemporaneously report abuse and to recant or deny abuse was erroneously admitted expert testimony and was inadmissible lay testimony under N.H. R. Evid. 701 and 702 as, although the testimony was within the knowledge of the witnesses due to their training, it required knowledge beyond the ken of the average person; however, the error was harmless as the victim testified in detail and defendant admitted the actions during a family meeting, and defendant's convictions for aggravated felonious sexual assault under RSA 632-A:2, felonious sexual assault under RSA 632-A:3, and misdemeanor sexual assault under RSA 632-A:4 were affirmed. State v. Gonzalez, 150 N.H. 74, 834 A.2d 354, 2003 N.H. LEXIS 142 (2003).

In defendant's trial for sexual assault, the trial court properly allowed the prosecution to introduce evidence that defendant physically assaulted his adopted daughter to explain the daughter's rationale for waiting seven years after the sexual assaults ended to report them. State v. Berry, 148 N.H. 88, 803 A.2d 593, 2002 N.H. LEXIS 98 (2002).

In prosecution for sexual assault, before defendant may cross-examine the victim about a prior false allegation of sexual assault, he must establish by clear and convincing evidence that the victim made such prior accusation. State v. Gordon, 146 N.H. 258, 770 A.2d 702, 2001 N.H. LEXIS 70 (2001), overruled in part, State v. Miller, 155 N.H. 246, 921 A.2d 942, 2007 N.H. LEXIS 51 (2007).

5. Instructions

Defendant charged with sexual assault was not entitled to mistrial on ground that jury had deliberated after receiving supplemental instruction which failed to include lack of consent, where, upon defendant's objection, court gave a new instruction which

properly required state to prove lack of consent beyond a reasonable doubt and directed jury to disregard initial supplemental instruction. State v. Cooper, 135 N.H. 258, 603 A.2d 499, 1992 N.H. LEXIS 16 (1992).

Trial court's erroneous jury instruction that sexual assault was a lesser-included offense of aggravated felonious sexual assault did not require reversal of conviction, since trial court correctly defined the elements of the two offenses, and since the jury did not consider the lesser offense, because the defendant was convicted of the greater offense. State v. Smith, 127 N.H. 433, 503 A.2d 774, 1985 N.H. LEXIS 463 (1985).

6. Therapeutic relationship

Defendant's aggravated felonious sexual assault and sexual assault convictions under RSA 632-A:2, I(g)(1) and RSA 632-A:4, I were reversed because he had not provided "therapy" under RSA 632-A:1, VI to the victim, an inmate whom defendant met while serving as a "spiritual services coordinator" at a correctional institution. Having regular meetings centered on different topics which ultimately generated encouraging and helpful discussions did not give rise to a rational conclusion that defendant engaged in a planned action or a systematic cause or measure, procedure, technique or any particular approach in order to relieve the alleged victim's bodily, mental, or behavioral disorders; defendant's own characterization of his work as therapeutic in nature did not satisfy the statutorily defined dimensions of therapy. State v. Flodin, 159 N.H. 358, 986 A.2d 470, 2009 N.H. LEXIS 126 (2009).

Cited:

Cited in State v. Scott, 117 N.H. 996, 380 A.2d 1092, 1977 N.H. LEXIS 479 (1977); Hudson v. Miller, 119 N.H. 141, 399 A.2d 612, 1979 N.H. LEXIS 257 (1979); State v. Perkins, 121 N.H. 713, 435 A.2d 504, 1981 N.H. LEXIS 415 (1981); State v. Lovely, 124 N.H. 690, 480 A.2d 847, 1984 N.H. LEXIS 295 (1984); State v. Decker, 127 N.H. 468, 503 A.2d 796, 1985 N.H. LEXIS 466 (1985); State v. Collins, 129 N.H. 488, 529 A.2d 945, 1987 N.H. LEXIS 219 (1987); State v. Vachon, 130 N.H. 37, 533 A.2d 384, 1987 N.H. LEXIS 266 (1987); State v. Chapman, 135 N.H. 390, 605 A.2d 1055, 1992 N.H. LEXIS 48 (1992); State v. Huffman, 136 N.H. 149, 613 A.2d 476, 1992 N.H. LEXIS 149 (1992); Tsiatsios v. Tsiatsios, 140 N.H. 173, 663 A.2d 1335, 1995 N.H. LEXIS 120 (1995); State v. Johnson, 144 N.H. 175, 738 A.2d 1284, 1999 N.H. LEXIS 95 (1999); State v. Cole, 147 N.H. 374, 788 A.2d 248, 2001 N.H. LEXIS 227 (2001).

RESEARCH REFERENCES

New Hampshire Bar Journal.
For article, "Minor Victims of Sexual Assault," see 26 N.H.B.J. 199 (1985).

632-A:5. Spouse as Victim; Evidence of Husband and Wife.

An actor commits a crime under this chapter even though the victim is the actor's legal spouse. Laws attaching a privilege against the disclosure of communications between husband and wife are inapplicable to proceedings under this chapter.

Source.
1975, 302:1. 1981, 415:1, eff. Aug. 22, 1981.

Amendments
—1981. Rewritten to the extent that a detailed comparison would be impractical.

NOTES TO DECISIONS

Cited:
Cited in State v. Boone, 119 N.H. 594, 406 A.2d 113, 1979 N.H. LEXIS 360 (1979).

632-A:6. Testimony and Evidence.

I. The testimony of the victim shall not be required to be corroborated in prosecutions under this chapter.

II. Prior consensual sexual activity between the victim and any person other than the actor shall not be admitted into evidence in any prosecution under this chapter.

III. Consent is no defense if, at the time of the sexual assault, the victim indicates by speech or conduct that there is not freely given consent to performance of the sexual act. A jury is not required to infer consent from a victim's failure to physically resist a sexual assault.

III-a. The victim's manner of dress at the time of the sexual assault shall not be admitted as evidence in any prosecution under this chapter to infer consent.

IV. At the request of a party the court shall, in cases under RSA 632-A, order witnesses excluded so that they cannot hear the testimony of other witnesses, and it may make the order of its own motion. This does not authorize exclusion of a party who is a natural person or a victim of the crime, or a person whose presence is shown by a party to be essential to the presentation of the party's cause.

V. In any sexual assault case under RSA 632-A where the victim is 16 years of age or younger, and the defense has listed as a witness or subpoenaed a parent or parents to testify in the case and requested that the parent or parents be sequestered, the court shall appoint a guardian ad litem to determine the best interests of the minor victim. The guardian ad litem shall make a recommendation to the court, based on the preferences and best interests of the victim, as to whether the parent or parents should be permitted to sit with the victim in the court room during the duration of the trial.

Source.

1975, 302:1. 1992, 254:7, eff. Jan. 1, 1993. 1996, 5:1, eff. May 17, 1996. 2005, 148:1, eff. January 1, 2006.

Amendments

—**2005.** Paragraph V: Added.

—**1996.** Paragraph III-a: Added.

—**1992.** Rewritten to the extent that a detailed comparison would be impracticable.

NOTES TO DECISIONS

1. Constitutionality
2. Applicability
3. Construction
4. Purpose
5. Depositions
6. Admissibility—Balancing factors
7. —Burden of proof
8. —Hearing
9. —Limitations
10. —Relevant evidence
11. —Inconsistent statements
12. —Procedure
13. Corroboration
14. Cross-examination of victim
15. Guardian ad litem
16. Jury instructions
17. Particular cases
18. Sequestration of witness

1. Constitutionality

The enactment of an amendment to RSA 632-A:6 would violate Part I, Article 37 of the New Hampshire Constitution where the amendment would, in criminal prosecutions for offenses set forth in RSA 632-A, for incest and endangering the welfare of a child or incompetent in violation of RSA 639, and for attempts and conspiracies to commit those crimes, and in civil suits for sexual assault, create a rebuttable presumption that evidence of any other sexual assault committed by the defendant is admissible for specified purposes. Opinion of the Justices (Prior Sexual Assault Evidence), 141 N.H. 562, 688 A.2d 1006, 1997 N.H. LEXIS 4 (1997).

The enactment of a bill to prohibit the introduction of evidence of the victim's manner of dress at the time of a sexual assault in order to infer consent would not be improper on the basis that it might result in preempting an accused's right to produce all proofs that may be favorable to the accused and cross-examine witnesses in violation of Part I, Article 15 of the New Hampshire Constitution. Opinion of the Justices (Certain Evidence in Sexual Assault Cases), 140 N.H. 22, 662 A.2d 294, 1995 N.H. LEXIS 87 (1995).

Although this section mandates the exclusion of evidence regarding a victim's prior consensual sexual activity with any person other than the defendant, the defendant's right to due process and confrontation of witnesses limits the prohibitive sweep of this section when the probative value of that evidence outweighs the prejudicial effect of its introduction. State v. Fennell, 133 N.H. 402, 578 A.2d 329, 1990 N.H. LEXIS 79 (1990).

This section, construed to allow defendant upon motion and out of presence of jury the opportunity to demonstrate that due process requires admission of prior consensual sexual activity between victim of sexual assault and any other person where its probative value in the particular case outweighs its prejudicial effect on the victim, is constitutional. State v. Howard, 121 N.H. 53, 426 A.2d 457, 1981 N.H. LEXIS 248 (1981).

Trial court's ruling that this section barred any evidence of prior sexual activity of prosecutrix with any person other than defendant, which precluded defendant from questioning prosecutrix with regard to her sexual activities on day preceding the alleged rape, violated defendant's constitutional right to rebut case against him by attempting to establish that prosecutrix had sexual relations with a person other than defendant and that such relations accounted for the presence of sperm in her vagina on the day of the alleged rape. State v. La Clair, 121 N.H. 743, 433 A.2d 1326, 1981 N.H. LEXIS 391 (1981).

2. Applicability

Rape shield doctrine does not apply when prior non-consensual conduct is at issue, although evidence of prior non-consensual sexual conduct would be subject to evidentiary standards for admissibility, including New Hampshire Rule of Evidence 403. State v. Frost, 141 N.H. 493, 686 A.2d 1172, 1996 N.H. LEXIS 132 (1996).

This section applies to sexual activity of rape victims under the age of thirteen. Therefore, rape shield law applied to prohibit defendant from cross-examining child victim about an allegation that victim had sexually molested defendant's son. State v. Besk, 138 N.H. 412, 640 A.2d 775, 1994 N.H. LEXIS 41 (1994).

3. Construction

This section authorizes a victim to claim a privilege of personal privacy which cannot be defeated without a defendant's offer to prove facts that could justify its invasion, followed by a hearing to establish those facts and to evaluate the strengths of the competing interests in privacy and effective confrontation. State v. Goulet, 129 N.H. 348, 529 A.2d 879, 1987 N.H. LEXIS 215 (1987).

This section creates a qualified privilege against disclosure of prior consensual sexual activity between the victim and anyone other than the defendant. State v. Dukette, 127 N.H. 540, 506 A.2d 699, 1986 N.H. LEXIS 227 (1986).

By excluding evidence of prior consensual sexual activity between the victim and any person other than the defendant, and thus sheltering the rape victim from inquiry into certain topics at trial, this section affords the victim a limited testimonial privilege. State v. Walsh, 126 N.H. 610, 495 A.2d 1256, 1985 N.H. LEXIS 367 (1985).

Under this section, the victim is the real party in interest, and her interests may differ from those of the state. State v. Walsh, 126 N.H. 610, 495 A.2d 1256, 1985 N.H. LEXIS 367 (1985).

4. Purpose

The legislature intended to create a testimonial privilege by enacting this section, the purpose of which was to protect the victim of rape from being subject to unnecessary embarrassment, prejudice and courtroom procedures that only serve to exacerbate the trauma of the rape itself; the underpinnings of that privilege are grounded in the constitutional right to privacy. State v. Miskell, 122 N.H. 842, 451 A.2d 383, 1982 N.H. LEXIS 452 (1982).

Intent of this section is to protect victims from being subject to unnecessary embarrassment, prejudices and courtroom procedures that only serve to exacerbate the trauma of rape. State v. Howard, 121 N.H. 53, 426 A.2d 457, 1981 N.H. LEXIS 248 (1981).

Legislative intent behind this section is to spare victim testifying at trial from unnecessary embarrassment, prejudice and harassment, and courts have obligation to protect rape victims from improper questions. State v. La Clair, 121 N.H. 743, 433 A.2d 1326, 1981 N.H. LEXIS 391 (1981).

5. Depositions

Trial court did not err when it precluded the defendant, who was accused of sexually and physically assaulting a prostitute that the defendant picked up, from questioning the victim at a deposition about the victim's past consensual sexual activity as a prostitute, because the defendant failed to demonstrate that the evidence of the victim's prior consensual sexual activity was relevant and that its probative value outweighed its prejudicial effect on the victim. State v. Higgins, 149 N.H. 290, 821 A.2d 964, 2003 N.H. LEXIS 41 (2003).

The testimonial privilege created by this section applies to depositions as well as at trial. State v. Miskell, 122 N.H. 842, 451 A.2d 383, 1982 N.H. LEXIS 452 (1982).

In prosecutions for sexual assault and related offenses, the same policies of this section are served by prohibiting questions concerning unrelated prior sexual activity in a deposition as are served by their prohibition at trial, since the major harassment and embarrassment occurs because the victim must answer the questions, not because she must answer them in public. State v. Miskell, 122 N.H. 842, 451 A.2d 383, 1982 N.H. LEXIS 452 (1982).

Although the control of discovery is within the sound discretion of the trial court, the court must be careful to protect the legitimate interests of the prosecutrix embodied in this section. State v. Miskell, 122 N.H. 842, 451 A.2d 383, 1982 N.H. LEXIS 452 (1982).

6. Admissibility—Balancing factors

In a sexual assault trial, defendant was properly prohibited from questioning, for impeachment purposes, the two victims regarding sexual activity between the two victims under RSA 632-A:6, II; the probative value of the testimony was outweighed by the prejudicial effect, as the victims had already impeached each other by offering conflicting testimony, and the questions would have been highly prejudicial. State v. Spaulding, 147 N.H. 583, 794 A.2d 800, 2002 N.H. LEXIS 34 (2002).

Requirement of due process and the right of confrontation limit application of rape shield law when evidence of the victim's prior sexual activity with people other than defendant has a probative value in the context of a particular case that outweighs its prejudicial effect on the victim. State v. Cannon, 146 N.H. 562, 776 A.2d 736, 2001 N.H. LEXIS 128 (2001).

The privilege against the admission of evidence under this section must yield if the defendant demonstrates that due process requires the admission of the evidence because its probative value outweighs its prejudicial effect. State v. Ellsworth, 136 N.H. 115, 613 A.2d 473, 1992 N.H. LEXIS 144 (1992).

The requirement of due process and the right of confrontation limit the application of the rape shield law when evidence of the victim's prior sexual activity with people other than the defendant has a probative value in the context of a particular case that outweighs its prejudicial effect on the victim; therefore, upon

motion by the defense, a hearing must be held to enable the trial court to evaluate the strengths of the competing interests in privacy and effective confrontation, permitting the defendant an opportunity to prove facts that could justify the invasion of the victim's privacy. State v. Cox, 133 N.H. 261, 575 A.2d 1320, 1990 N.H. LEXIS 46 (1990).

Inquiry into the prior consensual sexual activities of victims of aggravated felonious sexual assault is generally prohibited; nonetheless, due process and the right of confrontation require the admission of such evidence when its probative value in the context of the case outweighs its judicial effect. State v. Dean, 129 N.H. 744, 533 A.2d 333, 1987 N.H. LEXIS 263 (1987).

Despite literal language of this section, defendant in rape case must, upon motion, be given the opportunity to demonstrate that due process requires admission of evidence concerning past sexual activities of prosecutrix, because probative value of evidence outweighs its prejudicial effect on such prosecutrix. State v. La Clair, 121 N.H. 743, 433 A.2d 1326, 1981 N.H. LEXIS 391 (1981).

Defendant charged with sexual assault or related offenses must, upon motion, be given opportunity to demonstrate, out of presence of the jury, that due process requires admission of evidence of prior consensual sexual activity between victim and any other person other than the accused where the probative value in the context of the particular case outweighs its prejudicial effect on the victim. State v. Howard, 121 N.H. 53, 426 A.2d 457, 1981 N.H. LEXIS 248 (1981).

Since automatic and total exclusion of evidence of rape victim's prior consensual sexual activity is improper because it might preempt the accused's right to confront witnesses against him, admission of such evidence may be proper upon showing of particular relevance by the defendant in cases in which reputation of the rape victim and in which specific prior sexual activity of the victim may become relevant and its probative value may outweigh the detrimental impact of its introduction. State v. Howard, 121 N.H. 53, 426 A.2d 457, 1981 N.H. LEXIS 248 (1981).

7. —Burden of proof

At sexual assault trial, defendant carries the burden of establishing that due process requires the admission of evidence of prior consensual activity between the victim and any person other than the defendant. State v. Dean, 129 N.H. 744, 533 A.2d 333, 1987 N.H. LEXIS 263 (1987).

When a sexual assault victim has invoked the privilege of this section, a personal privilege that may be invoked not only at trial but at pre-trial proceedings, a defendant may defeat the privilege only by demonstrating a reasonable possibility that the information sought will produce the type of evidence that due process will require to be admitted at trial; an offer of proof may therefore be demanded before the privacy privilege must yield to questioning. State v. Baker, 127 N.H. 801, 508 A.2d 1059, 1986 N.H. LEXIS 236 (1986).

At a sexual assault trial, where the defendant requested a hearing to demonstrate that due process required the testimony of the victim under an exception to the privilege of this section, the request was not ineffective merely because defense counsel failed to make an offer of proof that admissible evidence would be produced, where the court did not request such an offer, and the request should not, therefore, have been denied. State v. Baker, 127 N.H. 801, 508 A.2d 1059, 1986 N.H. LEXIS 236 (1986).

Defendants charged with sexual assault and related offenses who wish the prosecutrix to answer questions in a deposition relating to the prosecutrix's prior sexual activity must show, in a hearing before the trial judge, that there is a reasonable possibility that the information sought will produce the type of evidence that due process will require to be admitted at trial under a limited exception to this section's exclusion of such evidence. State v. Miskell, 122 N.H. 842, 451 A.2d 383, 1982 N.H. LEXIS 452 (1982).

In cases of sexual assault and related offenses, the requirement that a defendant, seeking to have the prosecutrix answer questions in a deposition about certain instances of the prosecutrix's prior sexual activity, must show that there is a reasonable possibility that the information sought will produce the type of evidence that due process will require to be admitted at trial as a limited exception to this section's exclusion of such evidence is not satisfied by mere speculation that favorable information might be forthcoming, and a defendant must show that there is a reasonable likelihood that admissible information will be obtained. State v. Miskell, 122 N.H. 842, 451 A.2d 383, 1982 N.H. LEXIS 452 (1982).

In rape case where defendant seeks to introduce evidence of prior sexual activities of the prosecutrix, defendant must establish through medical evidence that the particular prior sexual activities of prosecutrix that he desires to raise are relevant to her physical condition. State v. La Clair, 121 N.H. 743, 433 A.2d 1326, 1981 N.H. LEXIS 391 (1981).

8. —Hearing

When defendant sought to cross-examine a sexual assault victim about her exposure to sexually explicit videos and paraphernalia, it was unnecessary to hold a Howard hearing, because neither the rape shield law nor the victim's prior sexual activity were implicated. State v. Currier, 148 N.H. 203, 808 A.2d 527, 2002 N.H. LEXIS 110 (2002).

In cases of sexual assault and related offenses, the fact that a prosecutrix is compelled to answer a question at a deposition under a limited exception to this section's exclusion of evidence of the prosecutrix's prior sexual activity does not necessarily mean that the question may be asked again at trial, since the defendant still must show at a hearing, out of the presence of the jury, that, in light of the answer given at the deposition, due process requires that she again must testify about certain instances of prior sexual activity. State v. Miskell, 122 N.H. 842, 451 A.2d 383, 1982 N.H. LEXIS 452 (1982).

Rape victim's right to sexual privacy is recognized to the extent that the hearings held on the admissibility of victim's prior sexual activity may, upon request of the victim and in the exercise of sound discretion of the trial court, be closed to those not a party to the proceeding. State v. Howard, 121 N.H. 53, 426 A.2d 457, 1981 N.H. LEXIS 248 (1981).

9. —Limitations

At a *Howard* hearing, intended to determine whether evidence of victim's sexual activity should be admitted notwithstanding rape shield law, evidence ruled admissible must be of consensual sexual behavior. State v. Cox, 133 N.H. 261, 575 A.2d 1320, 1990 N.H. LEXIS 46 (1990).

Despite this section's exclusion of evidence of a prosecutrix's prior sexual activity, such evidence could be relevant and admissible in certain limited circumstances where due process requires that the evidence be admitted because its probative value outweighs its possible prejudicial effect, but a defendant cannot parade the prosecutrix's entire sexual history, including her alleged predilection for promiscuity and indiscriminate sexual activity, before the jury. State v. Miskell, 122 N.H. 842, 451 A.2d 383, 1982 N.H. LEXIS 452 (1982).

In the exercise of its sound discretion in trying sexual assault and related cases, the trial court should be mindful of policy considerations underlying this section; court should limit admission of evidence of specific instances of victim's sexual conduct to the extent that it is possible without unduly infringing upon the defendant's constitutional right to confrontation. State v. Howard, 121 N.H. 53, 426 A.2d 457, 1981 N.H. LEXIS 248 (1981).

10. —Relevant evidence

In a prosecution for aggravated felonious sexual assault, trial court erred in denying defendant's motion to call witness to testify concerning complainant's prior consensual sexual activity where complainant opened the door to admission of the testimony when she testified that the reason she did not want to have sex with the defendant was because she "had a boyfriend." State v. Cannon, 146 N.H. 562, 776 A.2d 736, 2001 N.H. LEXIS 128 (2001).

In a prosecution for aggravated felonious sexual assault, where the central issue was whether complainant consented to having sexual intercourse with defendant, complainant's testimony served only to bolster her credibility regarding the issue of consent and, in such a circumstance, defendant was entitled to rebut this assertion because the probative value of proffered evidence concerning complainant's prior consensual sexual activity would outweigh its prejudicial effect on the victim. State v. Cannon, 146 N.H. 562, 776 A.2d 736, 2001 N.H. LEXIS 128 (2001).

In rape cases, protection from undue harassment afforded prosecutrix must yield to defendant's right to confront evidence against

him; therefore, sexual activities of a prosecutrix immediately prior to an alleged rape may be a relevant area for cross-examination, especially where the evidence may explain the physical injuries of the prosecutrix or the origin of semen. State v. La Clair, 121 N.H. 743, 433 A.2d 1326, 1981 N.H. LEXIS 391 (1981).

In statutory rape case involving a twelve-year-old victim, testimony concerning the claimed decadent sexual environment in which the victim lived could, in the discretion of the trial judge, be found relevant and admissible, provided that its admission was not otherwise barred by other rules of evidence. State v. Howard, 121 N.H. 53, 426 A.2d 457, 1981 N.H. LEXIS 248 (1981).

11. —Inconsistent statements

Where prosecutrix in rape case made inconsistent statements regarding her virginity, and they could have cast some doubts on her credibility, because prejudice to such prosecutrix resulting from the disclosure that she might not have been a virgin at the time of the alleged rape would have been minimal, defendant was entitled to opportunity to cross-examine her concerning her inconsistent statements. State v. La Clair, 121 N.H. 743, 433 A.2d 1326, 1981 N.H. LEXIS 391 (1981).

12. —Procedure

Defendant seeking to introduce evidence of complainant's prior sexual history must file a motion with the court not less than 45 days prior to trial. State v. Cannon, 146 N.H. 562, 776 A.2d 736, 2001 N.H. LEXIS 128 (2001).

In a prosecution for aggravated felonious sexual assault, defendant was not required to file Howard motion within the time limit because, even though he had notice of complainant's statements to police, knowledge of this information was not a sufficient basis upon which to file a motion; defendant could not have been expected to foresee that the State would present him with the opportunity to admit otherwise inadmissible testimony when it opened the door to its admission by asking complainant her reasons for not consenting to sexual intercourse with defendant. State v. Cannon, 146 N.H. 562, 776 A.2d 736, 2001 N.H. LEXIS 128 (2001).

13. Corroboration

Conviction for the crime of rape did not depend upon the corroboration of the prosecutrix's testimony. State v. Lemire, 115 N.H. 526, 345 A.2d 906, 1975 N.H. LEXIS 353 (1975). (Decided under prior law.)

14. Cross-examination of victim

Trial court was well within its discretion in limiting defendant's proposed cross-examination of victim to only that evidence relevant to her alleged motive to fabricate charges. The court properly prohibited the defendant from inquiring into any particular sexual acts of victim. State v. Rogers, 138 N.H. 503, 642 A.2d 932, 1994 N.H. LEXIS 56 (1994).

Concern that women who are victims of rape may be subject to unfair cross-examination and, in general, an unfair procedure, is proper, and courts have responsibility to protect rape victims from questions not within the proper bounds of cross-examination and which are designed only to harass, annoy or humiliate. State v. Howard, 121 N.H. 53, 426 A.2d 457, 1981 N.H. LEXIS 248 (1981).

15. Guardian ad litem

There was no error in the participation, at a sexual assault trial, of a guardian ad litem appointed by the court to protect the interests of the 15-year-old victim, given the young age of the victim, the importance to the victim of obtaining the full protection available to her under this section, and the limited involvement that the guardian ad litem had in the trial itself. State v. Walsh, 126 N.H. 610, 495 A.2d 1256, 1985 N.H. LEXIS 367 (1985).

16. Jury instructions

Instruction to jury at child sexual assault trial adequately apprised jury of weight to be given uncorroborated complaining witness' testimony, in accordance with statute, and trial court was not required to specifically instruct that although corroboration was not required, lack of corroboration could be considered. State v. Laurent, 144 N.H. 517, 744 A.2d 598, 1999 N.H. LEXIS 149 (1999).

Taken in context, court's instruction to jury did not impermissibly imply that jury was required to find defendant guilty if they found uncorroborated testimony of victim credible. State v. Marti, 143 N.H. 608, 732 A.2d 414, 1999 N.H. LEXIS 50 (1999).

17. Particular cases

Even if the trial court violated N.H. R. Evid. 615 and RSA 632-A:6, IV, by failing to sequester the victim's mother during the victim's testimony, any error was harmless. The conviction was supported by other substantial evidence, and the evidence did not support a conclusion that the mother tailored her testimony to the victim's testimony. State v. Guild, 163 N.H. 475, 44 A.3d 545, 2012 N.H. LEXIS 44 (2012).

In a case under RSA 632-A:2, when the victim testified that she learned her birth date from her mother, that she saw her birth certificate with the same date as recently as two months earlier, and that she celebrated her birthday on the same day each year, her testimony that she was 12 was sufficiently trustworthy and reliable under N.H. R. Evid. 803(19) so as not to require corroboration, and the State was not required to produce her birth certificate to satisfy its burden. Furthermore, there was no evidence that the victim could have a different date of birth. State v. Tayag, 159 N.H. 21, 977 A.2d 510, 2009 N.H. LEXIS 80 (2009).

Where a child victim used the words "privates," "crotch," and "pee pee" to describe the victim's genitalia and the State used a demonstrative aid to augment the victim's testimony, the victim's testimony was sufficient to establish a prima facie case of sexual assault under RSA 632-A:2, II; as a result, pursuant to RSA 632-A:6, I, no corroborating evidence was needed. State v. King, 151 N.H. 59, 855 A.2d 510, 2004 N.H. LEXIS 89 (2004), rehearing denied, 2004 N.H. LEXIS 167 (N.H. July 16, 2004).

In a prosecution for aggravated felonious sexual assault and felonious sexual assault by the defendant of his niece, the trial judge should have made a further inquiry to evaluate evidence proffered by the defendant regarding the niece's alleged sexual intercourse with other parties. In addition, the judge should have considered whether due process considerations required the admission of such evidence to explain evidence that the condition of the victim's hymen and vagina was consistent with that of a child who had sexual intercourse. State v. Cressey, 137 N.H. 402, 628 A.2d 696, 1993 N.H. LEXIS 83 (1993).

At sexual assault trial, court committed reversible error in its rulings that barred the jury from considering evidence of the complainant's openly sexually provocative behavior toward a group of men in the hours preceding the incident, as bearing on the defense of consent. State v. Colbath, 130 N.H. 316, 540 A.2d 1212, 1988 N.H. LEXIS 13 (1988).

In statutory rape case in which accused was charged with having had sexual relations with a girl under the age of thirteen, defendant had to be given opportunity to show, by specific incidents of sexual conduct, that the victim had the experience and ability to contrive a statutory rape charge. State v. Howard, 121 N.H. 53, 426 A.2d 457, 1981 N.H. LEXIS 248 (1981).

In rape case, where defendant's explanation of presence of sperm in the prosecutrix's vagina was plausible, supported by medical evidence and consistent with his defense that he never had had sexual relations with her, opportunity to present evidence in support of that explanation to the jury should have been granted. State v. La Clair, 121 N.H. 743, 433 A.2d 1326, 1981 N.H. LEXIS 391 (1981).

18. Sequestration of witness

When, in a criminal trial, a trial court has violated N.H. R. Evid. 615 and RSA 632-A:6, IV (2007) by failing to sequester a witness, a new trial is in order unless the State proves that any error was harmless beyond a reasonable doubt. An error in failing to sequester a witness may be harmless beyond a reasonable doubt if, even without the non-sequestered witness's testimony, the other evidence of the defendant's guilt is of an overwhelming nature, quantity, or weight and the non-sequestered witness's testimony is merely cumulative or inconsequential in relation to the strength of the State's evidence of guilt. State v. Guild, 163 N.H. 475, 44 A.3d 545, 2012 N.H. LEXIS 44 (2012).

Cited:

Cited in State v. Hardy, 120 N.H. 552, 419 A.2d 398, 1980 N.H. LEXIS 344 (1980); State v. Preston, 121 N.H. 147, 427 A.2d 32, 1981 N.H. LEXIS 269 (1981); State v. Wonyetye, 122 N.H. 39, 441 A.2d

363, 1982 N.H. LEXIS 286 (1982); State v. Shute, 122 N.H. 498, 446 A.2d 1162, 1982 N.H. LEXIS 392 (1982); State v. Simpson, 133 N.H. 704, 582 A.2d 619, 1990 N.H. LEXIS 124 (1990); Opinion of the Justices (Certain Evidence in Sexual Assault Cases), 140 N.H. 22, 662 A.2d 294, 1995 N.H. LEXIS 87 (1995); State v. Berrocales, 140 N.H. 647, 670 A.2d 1045, 1996 N.H. LEXIS 5 (1996); State v. Ellsworth, 142 N.H. 710, 709 A.2d 768, 1998 N.H. LEXIS 25 (1998); State v. Dewitt, 143 N.H. 24, 719 A.2d 570, 1998 N.H. LEXIS 65 (1998); State v. Walton, 146 N.H. 316, 771 A.2d 562, 2001 N.H. LEXIS 77 (2001).

RESEARCH REFERENCES

New Hampshire Court Rules Annotated.

Admissibility of evidence of prior sexual activity of victim, see Rule 412, Rules of Evidence, New Hampshire Court Rules Annotated.

New Hampshire Evidence Manual.

Douglas, New Hampshire Rules of Evidence Manual.

New Hampshire Bar Journal.

For article, "Historical Perspective: Rape Shield Law," see 24 N.H.B.J. 95 (July 1983).

For article, "Minor Victims of Sexual Assault," see 26 N.H.B.J. 199 (1985).

For article, "Open Door Doctrine Prevails Over the Rape Shield Law: State v. Cannon," see 43 N.H.B.J. 24 (Sept. 2002).

632-A:7. Limitations of Prosecutions.

[Repealed 1990, 213:3, eff. April 27, 1990.]

Former section(s).

Former RSA 632-A:7, which was derived from 1975, 302:1; 1986, 168:1; 1987, 158:1, related to limitations of prosecutions.

632-A:8. In Camera Testimony.

In the cases where the victim is under 16 years of age, the victim's testimony shall be heard in camera unless good cause is shown by the defendant. The record of the victim's testimony shall not be sealed and all other testimony and evidence introduced during the proceeding shall be public.

Source.

1979, 195:1, eff. Aug. 7, 1979.

NOTES TO DECISIONS

1. Constitutionality
2. Standards
3. Burden of proof

1. Constitutionality

This section does not comport with part I, article 15 of the New Hampshire Constitution or the Sixth Amendment to the Federal Constitution to the extent that it requires the defendant to bear the burden of proof when the state is the party seeking to close a courtroom. State v. Weber, 137 N.H. 193, 624 A.2d 967, 1993 N.H. LEXIS 60 (1993).

2. Standards

Party seeking to close courtroom to public must advance an overriding interest that is likely to be prejudiced, closure must be no broader than necessary to protect that interest, trial court must consider reasonable alternatives to closing the proceeding, and it must make findings adequate to support the closure. State v. Guajardo, 135 N.H. 401, 605 A.2d 217, 1992 N.H. LEXIS 52 (1992).

Trial court must determine on a case-by-case basis whether closure of courtroom is necessary to protect welfare of a minor victim; in making this determination, trial court may consider the minor victim's age, psychological maturity and understanding, the nature of the crime, the desires of the victim, and the interests of parents and relatives. State v. Guajardo, 135 N.H. 401, 605 A.2d 217, 1992 N.H. LEXIS 52 (1992).

Trial court is not required to withhold action on a request to close courtroom to the public during testimony of a minor victim until the victim is on the stand and becomes unable to testify. State v. Guajardo, 135 N.H. 401, 605 A.2d 217, 1992 N.H. LEXIS 52 (1992).

3. Burden of proof

In a prosecution for aggravated felonious sexual assault and felonious sexual assault, the trial court violated the defendant's constitutional right to a public trial by requiring him to show good cause why the courtroom should not be closed during the victim's testimony. State v. Weber, 137 N.H. 193, 624 A.2d 967, 1993 N.H. LEXIS 60 (1993).

RESEARCH REFERENCES

New Hampshire Bar Journal.

For article, "Minor Victims of Sexual Assault," see 26 N.H.B.J. 199 (1985).

632-A:9. Speedy Trial.

In any action under this chapter involving a victim 16 years of age or under or a victim 65 years of age or older, the court and the department of justice shall take appropriate action to ensure a speedy trial to minimize the length of time the victim must endure the stress of involvement in the proceeding. In ruling on any motion or request for a delay or continuance of proceedings, the court shall consider any adverse impact the delay or continuance may have on the well-being of the victim or any witness who is 16 years of age or under or 65 years of age or older. This provision establishes a right to a speedy trial for the victim and shall not be construed as creating any additional rights for the defendant.

Source.

1986, 225:2, eff. Jan. 1, 1987. 2003, 283:1, eff. Jan. 1, 2004.

Amendments

—2003. Substituted "16 years" for "13 years" in two places in the first and second sentences.

632-A:10. Prohibition from Child Care Service of Persons Convicted of Certain Offenses.

I. A person is guilty of a class A felony if, having been convicted in this or any other jurisdiction of any felonious offense involving child pornography, or of a felonious physical assault on a minor, or of any sexual assault, he knowingly undertakes employment or volunteer service involving the care, instruction or guidance of minor children, including, but not limited to, service as a teacher, a coach, or worker of any type in child athletics, a day care worker, a boy or girl scout master or leader or worker, a summer camp counselor or worker of any type, a guidance counselor, or a school administrator of any type.

II. A person is guilty of a class B felony if, having been convicted in this or any other jurisdiction of any of the offenses specified in paragraph I of this section, he knowingly fails to provide information of such conviction when applying or volunteering for service or employment of any type involving the care, instruction, or guidance of minor children, including, but not limited to, the types of services set forth in paragraph I.

III. A person is guilty of a class B felony if, having been convicted in this or any other jurisdiction of any of the offenses specified in paragraph I of this section, he knowingly fails to provide information of such conviction when making application for initial teacher certification in this state.

Source.

1988, 257:2, eff. Jan. 1, 1989.

Cross References.

Classification of crimes, see RSA 625:9.

Sentences, see RSA 651.

NOTES TO DECISIONS

Cited:

Cited in In re T.J.S., 141 N.H. 697, 692 A.2d 498, 1997 N.H. LEXIS 24 (1997).

632-A:10-a. Penalties.

Notwithstanding RSA 651:2, and except where an extended term is sought as provided in RSA 651:6:

I. A person convicted of aggravated felonious sexual assault under:

(a) RSA 632-A:2, I(*l*) shall be sentenced in accordance with subparagraph (b) and paragraphs II–V and may be sentenced to lifetime supervision under paragraph V.

(b) Any provision of RSA 632-A:2 shall be sentenced to a maximum sentence which is not to exceed 20 years and a minimum which is not to exceed ½ of the maximum.

II. If a court finds that a defendant has been previously convicted under RSA 632-A:2 or any other statute prohibiting the same conduct in another state, territory or possession of the United States, the defendant shall be sentenced to a maximum sentence which is not to exceed 40 years and a minimum which is not to exceed ½ of the maximum.

III. If the court finds that a defendant has been previously convicted of 2 or more offenses under RSA 632-A:2 or any other statute prohibiting the same conduct in another state, territory or possession of the United States, the defendant shall be sentenced to life imprisonment and shall not be eligible for parole at any time.

IV. In this section, the phrase "previously convicted" shall mean any conviction obtained by trial on the merits, or negotiated plea with the assistance of counsel and evidencing a knowing, intelligent and voluntary waiver of the defendant's rights, provided, however, that previous imprisonment is not required.

V. (a) When a defendant pleads or is found guilty of aggravated felonious sexual assault under RSA 632-A:2, I(*l*), the judge may include in sentencing, in addition to any other penalties provided by law, a special sentence of lifetime supervision by the department of corrections. The defendant shall comply with the conditions of lifetime supervision which are imposed by the court or the department of corrections. Violation of any terms of lifetime supervisions shall be deemed contempt of court. The special sentence of lifetime supervision shall begin upon the release of the offender from incarceration, parole or probation.

(b) A person sentenced to lifetime supervision under subparagraph (a) may petition the court for release from lifetime supervision. The court shall grant a petition for release from a special sentence of lifetime supervision if:

    (1) The person has not committed a crime for 15 years after his last conviction or release from incarceration, whichever occurs later; and

    (2) The person is not likely to pose a threat to the safety of others if released from supervision.

(c) Prior to granting any petition pursuant to subparagraph V(b), the court shall provide notice to the county attorney who prosecuted the case, the victim advocate, and the victim or victim's family and permit those parties to be heard on the petition. If the court denies the offender's petition, the offender may not file another application pursuant to this paragraph for 5 years from the date of the denial and shall include a risk assessment prepared at the offender's expense.

Source.
1992, 254:8, eff. Jan. 1, 1993. 1998, 7:1, 2, eff. Jan. 1, 1999; 1998, 240:5, eff. at 12:01 a.m., Jan. 1, 1999. 2006, 327:15, 16, eff. January 1, 2007.

Revision note.
This section was originally enacted as RSA 632-A:11 but was renumbered to avoid conflict with RSA 632-A:11, as previously enacted by 1992, 213:1.

Amendments
—2006. In the introductory paragraph, added the end of the sentence following "RSA 651:2".
Paragraph V(c): Added.

—1998. Paragraph I: Rewritten by ch. 7 to the extent that a detailed comparison would be impracticable.
Paragraph V: Added by ch. 7.
Chapter 240 rewrote subpar. (a).

NOTES TO DECISIONS

  1.   Construction
  1.5.   Consecutive sentences
  2.   Illustrative cases

1. Construction
Due process required proof beyond a reasonable doubt of prior sexual assault convictions used to enhance defendant's sentence to life in prison without parole under provisions of statute. State v. McLellan, 146 N.H. 108, 767 A.2d 953, 2001 N.H. LEXIS 36 (2001).

1.5 Consecutive sentences
Although N.H. Rev. Stat. Ann. §§ 651:2, 632-A:10-a, and 651:3 did not authorize consecutive sentences for defendant's convictions for several counts of aggravated felonious sexual assault, by repealing former N.H. Rev. Stat. Ann. § 651:3(III), the legislature intended to revive the common law authority for judges to impose

consecutive sentences. Duquette v. Warden, N.H. State Prison, 154 N.H. 737, 919 A.2d 767, 2007 N.H. LEXIS 10 (2007).

2. Illustrative cases
"Three strikes" provision for sex offenders did not require three separate proceedings, but, rather, three separate adjudications of guilt, so that multiple separate incidents adjudicated in a single trial counted as multiple prior felonies; the possibility of enhanced sentencing was not an element of the offense for purposes of due process, so the State's desire to seek an enhanced sentence did not have to be included in the indictment. State v. Melvin, 150 N.H. 134, 834 A.2d 247, 2003 N.H. LEXIS 152 (2003).

RESEARCH REFERENCES

New Hampshire Bar Journal.
For article, "Lex Loci: A Survey of New Hampshire Supreme Court Decisions," see 46 N.H.B.J. 68 (Fall 2005).

632-A:10-b. HIV Testing.

I. The state shall administer to any person convicted of any offense under this chapter, except violations of RSA 632-A:10 or RSA 632-A:19, a test to detect in such person the presence of the etiologic agent for acquired immune deficiency syndrome.

I-a. The results of such test shall be disclosed to the person convicted and to the office of victim/witness assistance. The office of victim/witness assistance is authorized to disclose the test results to the county attorney victim/witness advocates and to the victim. The victim may be notified whether or not the victim has requested notification.

II. Notwithstanding RSA 141-F:7 and RSA 141-F:8, the state shall disclose results of a test administered pursuant to paragraph I and RSA 141-F:5, IV, to any person convicted, to the office of victim/witness assistance and may disclose the results to the victim.

III. The state shall provide counseling to the victim and the person convicted for such an offense regarding HIV disease, HIV testing for the victim in accordance with applicable law and referral for appropriate health care and support services.

IV. For purposes of this section:

(a) "HIV" means "human immune deficiency virus" as defined in RSA 141-F:2, V.

(b) "Person convicted" includes persons adjudicated under juvenile proceedings.

(c) "Victim" means "victim" as defined in RSA 21-M:8-b, I(a).

Source.
1993, 138:1. 1994, 18:1, eff. June 21, 1994.

References in text.
RSA 632-A:19, referred to in par. I, was repealed by 1996, 293:2, eff. Aug. 9, 1996. See now RSA 651-B:9.

Amendments
—1994. Paragraph I: Deleted "at the request of a victim of any offense under this chapter, except violations of RSA 632-A:10 or RSA 632-A:19" preceding "administer" and substituted "of any offense under this chapter, except violations of RSA 632-A:10 or RSA 632-A:19" for "for such offense" following "convicted".
Paragraph I-a: Added.

Paragraph II: Substituted "to the office of victim/witness assistance and may disclose the results to" for "and" following "convicted".

NOTES TO DECISIONS

Cited:
Cited in Opinion of Justices, 137 N.H. 260, 628 A.2d 1069, 1993 N.H. LEXIS 99 (1993).

632-A:10-c. Limitations on Civil Actions.

I. In this section "victim" means a person alleging to have been subjected to aggravated felonious sexual assault as defined in RSA 632-A:2, felonious sexual assault, as defined in RSA 632-A:3 or sexual assault as defined in RSA 632-A:4. The term "victim" shall include the parent, guardian, or custodian of such person if the person is less than 18 years of age or if the person is mentally incapable of meaningfully understanding or participating in the legal process.

II. Neither the defendant in an aggravated felonious sexual assault, felonious sexual assault or a sexual assault case nor the parent or legal guardian of such defendant shall commence or maintain a civil action against a victim of the crime for which the defendant is charged if both of the following circumstances exist:

(a) The criminal action is pending in a trial court of this state, of another state, or of the United States.

(b) The civil action is based upon statements or reports made by the victim that pertain to an incident from which the criminal action is derived.

III. The court shall dismiss without prejudice a civil action commenced or maintained in violation of paragraph II.

IV. The period of limitations for the bringing of a civil action described in paragraph II is tolled for the period of time during which the criminal action is pending in a trial court of this state, or another state, or of the United States.

V. This section shall not apply:

(a) If the victim files a civil action based upon an incident from which the criminal action is derived against the defendant in the criminal action; or

(b) The court determines that there are reasonable grounds to believe that the delay would be prejudicial to the interest of justice.

Source.
1993, 356:1, eff. Aug. 5, 1993.

Applicability of enactment.
1993, 356:3, eff. Aug. 5, 1993, provided: "Section 1 of this act [which added this section] shall apply only if the criminal action against the defendant is based upon a crime allegedly committed after the effective date of this act [Aug. 5, 1993]."

Registration of Sexual Offenders

632-A:11–632-A:19.

[Repealed 1996, 293:2, eff. Aug. 9, 1996.]

Former section(s).
Former RSA 632-A:11, which was derived from 1992, 213:1 and 1993, 297:2, related to terms of registration of sexual offenders.
Former RSA 632-A:12, which was derived from 1992, 213:1, related to registration of sexual offenders.
Former RSA 632-A:13, which was derived from 1992, 213:1, related to the release of sexual offenders into the community.
Former RSA 632-A:14, which was derived from 1992, 213:1, related to duty of released sexual offenders to report current address to local law enforcement agency.
Former RSA 632-A:15, which was derived from 1992, 213:1, related to duty of released sexual offenders to report change of address to local law enforcement agency.
Former RSA 632-A:16, which was derived from 1992, 213:1 and 1993, 297:3, related to duration of registration of convicted sexual offenders.
Former RSA 632-A:17, which was derived from 1992, 213:1 and 1996, 174:1, related to confidentiality of records and information of convicted sexual offenders.
Former RSA 632-A:18, which was derived from 1992, 213:1, related to departmental rules relative to administrative procedures concerning convicted sexual offenders.
Former RSA 632-A:19, which was derived from 1992, 213:1, related to penalties for violations of provisions for convicted sexual offenders.

Applicability of RSA 651-B enactment.
1996, 293:3, eff. Aug. 9, 1996, provided:
"I. This act [which repealed RSA 632-A:11–632-A:19 and enacted RSA 651-B] shall apply to any sexual offender, irrespective of the date of conviction of the offense, who:
"(a) Is released into the community as provided in RSA 651-B:3 on or after July 16, 1993; or
"(b) Has been released but has not completed his sentence before July 16, 1993; or
"(c) Has completed his sentence not more than 6 years before January 1, 1994.
"II. This act shall apply to any offender against children, irrespective of the date of conviction of the offense, who:
"(a) Is released into the community as provided in RSA 651-B:3 on or after the effective date of this act; or
"(b) Has been released but has not completed his sentence before the effective date of this act."

DNA Testing of Sexual Offenders

632-A:20–632-A:24.

[Repealed 2002, 183:2, eff. May 15, 2002.]

Former section(s).
Former RSA 632-A:20–632-A:24, which were derived from 1996, 177:1, related to DNA testing of sexual offenders. See now RSA 651-C.

CHAPTER 633

INTERFERENCE WITH FREEDOM

SECTION
633:1.   Kidnapping.
633:2.   Criminal Restraint.

SECTION
633:3.   False Imprisonment.
633:3-a.   Stalking.
633:4.   Interference with Custody.
633:5.   Peonage.

Trafficking in Persons

633:6.   Definitions.
633:7.   Trafficking in Persons.
633:8.   Forfeiture of Items Used in Connection with Traffick-
             ing in Persons.
633:9.   Administrative Forfeiture of Items Used in Connection
             with Trafficking in Persons.
633:10.   Restitution and Compensation.

RESEARCH REFERENCES

New Hampshire Bar Journal.
For article, "Understanding and Representing Adult Clients Who Are Victims of Domestic Abuse," see 35 N.H.B.J. 8 (1994).

633:1. Kidnapping.

I. A person is guilty of kidnapping if he knowingly confines another under his control with a purpose to:

(a) Hold him for ransom or as a hostage; or

(b) Avoid apprehension by a law enforcement official; or

(c) Terrorize him or some other person; or

(d) Commit an offense against him.

I-a. A person is guilty of kidnapping if the person knowingly takes, entices away, detains, or conceals any child under the age of 18 and unrelated to the person by consanguinity, or causes such child to be taken, enticed away, detained, or concealed, with the intent to detain or conceal such child from a parent, guardian, or other person having lawful physical custody of such child. This paragraph shall not apply to law enforcement personnel or department of health and human services personnel engaged in the conduct of their lawful duties.

II. Kidnapping is a class A felony unless the actor voluntarily releases the victim without serious bodily injury and in a safe place prior to trial, in which case it is a class B felony.

Source.
1971, 518:1, eff. Nov. 1, 1973. 2001, 230:1, eff. Jan. 1, 2002.

Amendments
—**2001.** Paragraph I-a: Added.

Cross References.
Capital murder, see RSA 630:1.
Classification of crimes, see RSA 625:9.
Liability for reimbursement of public agency response service expenses, see RSA 153-A:23 et seq.
Physical force in defense of person, see RSA 627:4.
Registration of criminal offenders, see RSA 651-B.
Sentences, see RSA 651.

NOTES TO DECISIONS

1. Degree of offense
2. Serious bodily injury
3. Indictments
4. Questions for jury
5. Double jeopardy
6. Particular cases
7. Incidental confinements or movements

8. Appeal

1. Degree of offense
A defendant is guilty of the class A felony of kidnapping only if the jury finds that the evidence establishes both the elements of a class B felony of kidnapping and the elements of a class A felony, as set forth in this section. State v. LaRose, 127 N.H. 146, 497 A.2d 1224, 1985 N.H. LEXIS 389 (1985).

2. Serious bodily injury
"Serious bodily injury," within the terms of this section, includes within its definition the serious psychological injuries of a rape victim. State v. Goodwin, 118 N.H. 862, 395 A.2d 1234, 1978 N.H. LEXIS 307 (1978).

To support a finding of felony A kidnapping, the injury to the victim's physical or mental health must be severe, permanent or protracted in nature. State v. Goodwin, 118 N.H. 862, 395 A.2d 1234, 1978 N.H. LEXIS 307 (1978).

Not every aggravated felonious sexual assault will constitute sufficient serious bodily injury to make an accompanying kidnapping a class A felony as a matter of law. State v. Goodwin, 118 N.H. 862, 395 A.2d 1234, 1978 N.H. LEXIS 307 (1978).

3. Indictments
Kidnapping indictment provided sufficient notice to defendant that he was charged with a crime premised on purpose to engage in a sexual assault or act of lewdness against victim, and a bill of particulars was thus unnecessary to allow proper preparation for trial. State v. Hilton, 144 N.H. 470, 744 A.2d 96, 1999 N.H. LEXIS 139 (1999).

Trial court did not err in granting state's motion to strike language in kidnapping indictment, where there was no showing that ruling prejudiced defendant either in his ability to understand charges or prepare his defense, and defendant's conviction was for class B kidnapping, which defendant admitted was sufficiently charged in indictment. State v. Norgren, 136 N.H. 399, 616 A.2d 505, 1992 N.H. LEXIS 183 (1992).

4. Questions for jury
Sentence of the trial court imposed for the class A felony of kidnapping was vacated, and the case remanded to the trial court for sentencing consistent with class B felony standards, where jury was instructed by the trial judge only on the elements of the class B felony of kidnapping, and therefore the trial judge usurped the function of the jury as fact-finder, to determine if the elements necessary for a class A felony of kidnapping were present. State v. LaRose, 127 N.H. 146, 497 A.2d 1224, 1985 N.H. LEXIS 389 (1985).

Whether a rape victim has suffered serious physical or psychological injury to make an accompanying kidnapping a class A felony is a matter of fact and must be presented to the jury as would evidence of any other element of the crime. State v. Goodwin, 118 N.H. 862, 395 A.2d 1234, 1978 N.H. LEXIS 307 (1978).

Judge's decision at the time of sentencing that the evidence supported a conviction for felony A kidnapping was improper in that it invaded the domain of the jury. State v. Goodwin, 118 N.H. 862, 395 A.2d 1234, 1978 N.H. LEXIS 307 (1978).

5. Double jeopardy
Defendant was properly convicted and sentenced for separate kidnapping and criminal threatening charges, as each element of two offenses differed and each charge required different evidence, and therefore there was no double jeopardy violation; the kidnapping elements were set forth in RSA 633:1, I(c), and the criminal threatening elements were set forth in RSA 631:4, I(a), II(a)(2). State v. McKean, 147 N.H. 198, 785 A.2d 404, 2001 N.H. LEXIS 195 (2001).

6. Particular cases
Sufficient evidence supported defendant's attempted kidnapping conviction where the record revealed ample evidence from which a jury could conclude that defendant had the purpose to commit the crime of kidnapping, and the jury also heard testimony about statements made by defendant that pointed to his own consciousness of guilt. State v. Bean, 153 N.H. 380, 897 A.2d 946, 2006 N.H. LEXIS 45 (2006).

7. Incidental confinements or movements

Merger doctrine applied to the crime of attempted kidnapping, in violation of RSA 629:1 and 633:1, as the purpose of the doctrine was arguably even more germane in such a case, where actual confinement did not need to be proven. State v. Casanova, 164 N.H. 563, 63 A.3d 169, 2013 N.H. LEXIS 11 (2013).

Merger doctrine rendered it unlikely that the Legislature intended to criminalize restraint that was integral to other crimes, such that it was irrelevant whether the charges against defendant of attempted kidnapping and attempted aggravated felonious sexual assault, in violation of RSA 629:1, 633:1, and 632-A:2, were intended to prohibit different types of criminal activity; accordingly, the merger doctrine should have been employed. State v. Casanova, 164 N.H. 563, 63 A.3d 169, 2013 N.H. LEXIS 11 (2013).

New Hampshire Supreme Court agrees with the view taken by the majority of jurisdictions, and holds that a kidnapping conviction cannot rest on unlawful confinements or movements incidental to the commission of other felonies. Simply because the restraint takes place to facilitate another crime does not by itself render that restraint "merely incidental." State v. Brooks, 164 N.H. 272, 56 A.3d 1245, 2012 N.H. LEXIS 141 (2012).

8. Appeal

As defendant had sought dismissal in the trial court of a charge of attempted kidnapping, in violation of RSA 629:1 and 633:1, arguing that it was not independent of an attempted aggravated felonious sexual assault charge, even though his motion was denied the issue was properly preserved for review. State v. Casanova, 164 N.H. 563, 63 A.3d 169, 2013 N.H. LEXIS 11 (2013).

Cited:

Cited in State v. Osborne, 119 N.H. 427, 402 A.2d 493, 1979 N.H. LEXIS 346 (1979); State v. Gonzales, 120 N.H. 805, 423 A.2d 608, 1980 N.H. LEXIS 393 (1980); State v. Preston, 121 N.H. 147, 427 A.2d 32, 1981 N.H. LEXIS 269 (1981); State v. Taylor, 121 N.H. 489, 431 A.2d 775, 1981 N.H. LEXIS 356 (1981); State v. Preston, 122 N.H. 153, 442 A.2d 992, 1982 N.H. LEXIS 310 (1982); State v. Shute, 122 N.H. 498, 446 A.2d 1162, 1982 N.H. LEXIS 392 (1982); State v. Fernald, 123 N.H. 442, 462 A.2d 122, 1983 N.H. LEXIS 302 (1983); State v. Morse, 125 N.H. 403, 480 A.2d 183, 1984 N.H. LEXIS 259 (1984); State v. Dellorfano, 128 N.H. 628, 517 A.2d 1163, 1986 N.H. LEXIS 343 (1986); State v. O'Leary, 128 N.H. 661, 517 A.2d 1174, 1986 N.H. LEXIS 326 (1986); State v. Duff, 129 N.H. 731, 532 A.2d 1381, 1987 N.H. LEXIS 248 (1987); King v. Prudential Property & Casualty Ins. Co., 684 F. Supp. 347, 1988 U.S. Dist. LEXIS 4173 (D.N.H. 1988); State v. Guay, 130 N.H. 413, 543 A.2d 910, 1988 N.H. LEXIS 42 (1988); State v. Rathbun, 132 N.H. 28, 561 A.2d 505, 1989 N.H. LEXIS 54 (1989); State v. Wisowaty, 133 N.H. 604, 580 A.2d 1079, 1990 N.H. LEXIS 109 (1990); State v. Stow, 136 N.H. 598, 620 A.2d 1023, 1993 N.H. LEXIS 8 (1993).

633:2. Criminal Restraint.

I. A person is guilty of a class B felony if he knowingly confines another unlawfully in circumstances exposing him to risk of serious bodily injury.

II. The meaning of "confines another unlawfully", as used in this section and RSA 633:3, includes but is not limited to confinement accomplished by force, threat or deception or, in the case of a person who is under the age of 16 or incompetent, if it is accomplished without the consent of his parent or guardian.

Source.

1971, 518:1, eff. Nov. 1, 1973.

Revision note.

In par. II, substituted "RSA 633:3" for "the following section" for purposes of clarity.

Cross References.

Classification of crimes, see RSA 625:9.
Registration of criminal offenders, see RSA 651-B.

Sentences, see RSA 651.

NOTES TO DECISIONS

1. Elements
2. Children
3. Evidence
4. Double jeopardy

1. Elements

Unlawful confinement element of RSA 633:2 begins when the confinement is initiated and ends only when the victim both feels and is, in fact, free from the confinement. State v. Gibbs, 164 N.H. 439, 58 A.3d 656, 2012 N.H. LEXIS 169 (2012).

RSA 633:2, I, requires only a risk of serious bodily injury and does not establish separate crimes based upon the level or type of risk. State v. Gibbs, 164 N.H. 439, 58 A.3d 656, 2012 N.H. LEXIS 169 (2012).

In order to establish a "risk of serious bodily injury" under RSA 633:2, the State does not have to present evidence of an actual, identifiable risk of serious physical or mental injury. Had the legislature intended to require proof of an actual, identifiable risk in order for there to be criminal restraint, it certainly could have done so. State v. Burke, 162 N.H. 459, 33 A.3d 1194, 2011 N.H. LEXIS 125 (2011).

Criminal restraint has three elements: (1) the actor must act knowingly; (2) the victim must be exposed to the risk of serious bodily injury; and (3) the act must confine the victim unlawfully. State v. Bruce, 132 N.H. 465, 566 A.2d 1144, 1989 N.H. LEXIS 122 (1989).

2. Children

This section does not provide an unqualified exemption from prosecution for parents who unlawfully confine their own children. State v. Bruce, 132 N.H. 465, 566 A.2d 1144, 1989 N.H. LEXIS 122 (1989).

Under this section, non-parents are subject to prosecution for criminally restraining a child under sixteen, if the confinement, regardless of means, was accomplished without parental consent. State v. Bruce, 132 N.H. 465, 566 A.2d 1144, 1989 N.H. LEXIS 122 (1989).

3. Evidence

With regard to a charge of criminal restraint under RSA 633:2, the evidence was sufficient to establish a risk of serious bodily injury when defendant bound the hands of an elderly, disabled woman who needed her hands in order to get up from a seated position. It was foreseeable that she could rise from the sofa on which she was seated, lose her balance, and suffer a serious injury. State v. Burke, 162 N.H. 459, 33 A.3d 1194, 2011 N.H. LEXIS 125 (2011).

Evidence was sufficient to support defendant's conviction of criminal restraint of his victim, his wife; the jury heard evidence that defendant repeatedly stopped the victim from going upstairs or downstairs by holding onto her arms, standing in front of her, and physically restricting her movement. The jury also heard evidence that, before the first choking incident, defendant dragged the victim upstairs when she was trying to go downstairs, and that before the second choking incident, he pushed her upstairs when she was trying to go downstairs. State v. Pepin, 156 N.H. 269, 940 A.2d 221, 2007 N.H. LEXIS 182 (2007).

In the case of defendant charged with criminal restraint, where disputed evidence and statements of the complainant regarding her fear of rape and bodily injury suggested that she might suffer psychological injuries as a result of the incident, the evidence was relevant because it tended to prove an element of the offense, namely, that circumstances existed exposing the complainant to a risk of serious bodily injury. State v. Dustin, 122 N.H. 544, 446 A.2d 1186, 1982 N.H. LEXIS 381 (1982).

4. Double jeopardy

One of two counts of criminal restraint had to be vacated based on double jeopardy grounds under N.H. Const. pt. I, art. 16, as both the confinement and the risk of serious bodily injury were continuous during the period in question. The victim's confinement began from the time he was tied to a column in a basement, continued when he was brought upstairs and tied to a chair, and ended only when he was able to free himself; the victim was exposed to the risk of bodily injury throughout this period. State v. Gibbs, 164 N.H. 439, 58 A.3d 656, 2012 N.H. LEXIS 169 (2012).

Cited:

Cited in State v. Fecteau, 121 N.H. 1003, 437 A.2d 294, 1981 N.H. LEXIS 451 (1981); State v. Vachon, 130 N.H. 37, 533 A.2d 384, 1987 N.H. LEXIS 266 (1987); State v. Guajardo, 135 N.H. 401, 605 A.2d 217, 1992 N.H. LEXIS 52 (1992); State v. Horne, 140 N.H. 90, 663 A.2d 92, 1995 N.H. LEXIS 110 (1995).

633:3. False Imprisonment.

A person is guilty of a misdemeanor if he knowingly confines another unlawfully, as defined in RSA 633:2, so as to interfere substantially with his physical movement.

Source.
1971, 518:1, eff. Nov. 1, 1973.

Cross References.
Classification of crimes, see RSA 625:9.
Registration of criminal offenders, see RSA 651-B.
Sentences, see RSA 651.

NOTES TO DECISIONS

1. Elements
2. Evidence

1. Elements
The offense of false imprisonment consists of three elements: first, there must be a confinement or detention which restricts another person's free movement; second, the confinement must be unlawful, a requirement which is satisfied when the perpetrator acts without legal authority and the victim does not consent; and, third, the perpetrator must have knowledge of both the confinement and its unlawfulness. State v. Fecteau, 121 N.H. 1003, 437 A.2d 294, 1981 N.H. LEXIS 451 (1981).

2. Evidence
Where state, in prosecution for false imprisonment, adduced evidence that the defendant confined other persons and that the confinement was unlawful, but offered no evidence that the defendant knew that the confinement was unlawful or that it caused a prohibited result, trial court erred in denying defendant's motions to dismiss for insufficient evidence. State v. Fecteau, 121 N.H. 1003, 437 A.2d 294, 1981 N.H. LEXIS 451 (1981).

Cited:
Cited in State v. Taylor, 121 N.H. 489, 431 A.2d 775, 1981 N.H. LEXIS 356 (1981); State v. Vachon, 130 N.H. 37, 533 A.2d 384, 1987 N.H. LEXIS 266 (1987); MacDowell v. Manchester Fire Dep't, 769 F. Supp. 40, 1990 U.S. Dist. LEXIS 19059 (D.N.H. 1990); State v. Cegelis, 138 N.H. 249, 638 A.2d 783, 1994 N.H. LEXIS 10 (1994); State v. Horne, 140 N.H. 90, 663 A.2d 92, 1995 N.H. LEXIS 110 (1995); State v. Kidder, 150 N.H. 600, 843 A.2d 312, 2004 N.H. LEXIS 37 (2004).

RESEARCH REFERENCES

New Hampshire Practice.
8-3 N.H.P. Personal Injury-Tort & Insurance Practice §§ 3.03, 3.06.

633:3-a. Stalking.

I. A person commits the offense of stalking if such person:

(a) Purposely, knowingly, or recklessly engages in a course of conduct targeted at a specific person which would cause a reasonable person to fear for his or her personal safety or the safety of a member of that person's immediate family, and the person is actually placed in such fear;

(b) Purposely or knowingly engages in a course of conduct targeted at a specific individual, which the actor knows will place that individual in fear for his or her personal safety or the safety of a member of that individual's immediate family; or

(c) After being served with, or otherwise provided notice of, a protective order pursuant to RSA 173-B, RSA 458:16, or paragraph III-a of this section, or an order pursuant to RSA 597:2 that prohibits contact with a specific individual, purposely, knowingly, or recklessly engages in a single act of conduct that both violates the provisions of the order and is listed in paragraph II(a).

II. As used in this section:

(a) "Course of conduct" means 2 or more acts over a period of time, however short, which evidences a continuity of purpose. A course of conduct shall not include constitutionally protected activity, nor shall it include conduct that was necessary to accomplish a legitimate purpose independent of making contact with the targeted person. A course of conduct may include, but not be limited to, any of the following acts or a combination thereof:

(1) Threatening the safety of the targeted person or an immediate family member.

(2) Following, approaching, or confronting that person, or a member of that person's immediate family.

(3) Appearing in close proximity to, or entering the person's residence, place of employment, school, or other place where the person can be found, or the residence, place of employment or school of a member of that person's immediate family.

(4) Causing damage to the person's residence or property or that of a member of the person's immediate family.

(5) Placing an object on the person's property, either directly or through a third person, or that of an immediate family member.

(6) Causing injury to that person's pet, or to a pet belonging to a member of that person's immediate family.

(7) Any act of communication, as defined in RSA 644:4, II.

(b) "Immediate family" means father, mother, stepparent, child, stepchild, sibling, spouse, or grandparent of the targeted person, any person residing in the household of the targeted person, or any person involved in an intimate relationship with the targeted person.

III. [Repealed.]

III-a. A person who has been the victim of stalking as defined in this section may seek relief by filing a civil petition in the district court or the superior court in the county or district where the plaintiff or defendant resides. Upon a showing of stalking by a preponderance of the evidence, the court shall grant such relief as is necessary to bring about a cessation of stalking. The types of relief that may be granted, the procedures and burdens of proof to be applied in such proceedings, the methods of notice, service, and enforcement of such orders, and the penalties for violation thereof shall be the same as those set forth in RSA 173-B.

III-b. The minority of a plaintiff or defendant shall not preclude the court from issuing protective orders under this section.

III-c. Any order under this section shall be for a fixed period of time not to exceed one year, but may be extended by order of the court upon a motion by the plaintiff, showing good cause, with notice to the defendant, for one year after the expiration of the first order and thereafter each extension may be for up to 5 years, upon the request of the plaintiff and at the discretion of the court. The court shall review the order, and each renewal thereof and shall grant such relief as may be necessary to provide for the safety and well-being of the plaintiff. A defendant shall have the right to a hearing on the extension of any order under this paragraph to be held within 30 days of the extension. The court shall state in writing, at the respondent's request, its reason or reasons for granting the extension. The court shall retain jurisdiction to enforce and collect the financial support obligation which accrued prior to the expiration of the protective order.

III-d. (a) A protective order issued pursuant to this section, RSA 173-B:4, or RSA 173-B:5 shall not be construed to prohibit an attorney, or any person acting on the attorney's behalf, who is representing the defendant in an action brought under this chapter, or in any criminal proceeding concerning the abuse alleged under this chapter, from contacting the plaintiff for a legitimate purpose within the scope of the civil or criminal proceeding; provided, that the attorney or person acting on behalf of the attorney: identifies himself or herself as a representative of the defendant; acknowledges the existence of the protective order and informs the plaintiff that he or she has no obligation to speak; terminates contact with the plaintiff if the plaintiff expresses an unwillingness to talk; and ensures that any personal contact with the plaintiff occurs outside of the defendant's presence, unless the court has modified the protective order to permit such contact.

(b) A no-contact provision in a protective order issued pursuant to this section shall not be construed to:

(1) Prevent contact between counsel for represented parties; or

(2) Prevent a party from appearing at a scheduled court or administrative hearing; or

(3) Prevent a defendant or defendant's counsel from sending the plaintiff copies of any legal pleadings filed in court relating to the domestic violence petition or related civil or criminal matters.

(c) A violation of this paragraph may result in a finding of contempt of court.

IV. In any complaint, information, or indictment brought for the enforcement of any provision of this statute, it shall not be necessary to negate any exception, excuse, proviso, or exemption contained herein and the burden of proof of any exception, excuse, proviso, or exemption shall be upon the defendant.

V. Any law enforcement officer may arrest, without a warrant, any person that the officer has probable cause to believe has violated the provisions of this section when the offense occurred within 12 hours, regardless of whether the crime occurred in the presence of the officer. A law enforcement officer shall arrest a person when he has probable cause to believe a violation of the provisions of this section has occurred within the last 12 hours when the offense involves a violation of a protective order issued pursuant to RSA 173-B, RSA 458:16, or paragraph III-a of this section.

VI. (a) Any person convicted of a violation of this section and who has one or more prior stalking convictions in this state or another state when the second or subsequent offense occurs within 7 years following the date of the first or prior offense shall be guilty of a class B felony.

(b) In all other cases, any person who is convicted of a violation of this section shall be guilty of a class A misdemeanor.

VII. If any provision or application of this section or the application thereof to a person or circumstance is held invalid, the invalidity does not affect other provisions or applications of this section which can be given effect without the invalid provisions or applications, and to this end the provisions of this section are severable.

Source.
1993, 173:2, eff. July 26, 1993. 1994, 101:1, eff. May 11, 1994. 1997, 242:1–4, eff. Jan. 1, 1998. 2000, 151:1, 2, eff. Jan. 1, 2001. 2002, 62:1, eff. Jan. 1, 2003; 79:5, eff. Jan. 1, 2003. 2005, 284:2, eff. August 21, 2005. 2006, 214:2, eff. July 31, 2006.

Amendments
—**2006.** Paragraph III-d: Added.

—**2005.** Paragraph III-c: Added.

—**2002.** Paragraph III-b: Added by ch. 62.
Paragraph V: Chapter 79 substituted "12 hours" for "6 hours" in the first and second sentences.

—**2000.** Paragraphs I and II: Rewritten to the extent that a detailed comparison would be impracticable.
Paragraph III: Repealed.
Paragraph III-a: Inserted "civil" preceding "petition in the district court" in the first sentence.

—1997. Paragraph I(d)(5): Inserted "or paragraph III-a of this section" following "RSA 458:16" and made a stylistic change in the introductory paragraph.

Paragraph III: Substituted "the person's" for "his" following "RSA 630:1, II that" and inserted "or a person who has been served with a protective order issued pursuant to paragraph III-a of this section" following "this chapter".

Paragraph III-a: Added.

Paragraph V: Deleted "or" following "RSA 173-B" and added "or paragraph III-a of this section" following "RSA 458:16" in the second sentence.

—1994. Paragraph I(d)(5): Substituted "RSA 597:2" for "RSA 597:1-a, III" preceding "on a single" in the introductory paragraph.

Applicability of 2005 amendment. 2005, 284:3, eff. Aug. 21, 2005, provided: "This act shall apply to any order in effect under RSA 173-B:5, VI and RSA 633:3-a, III-c on the effective date of this act [August 21, 2005] as well as any order entered thereafter."

Cross References.
Classification of crimes, see RSA 625:9.
Sentences, see RSA 651.
Violating temporary restraining order by stalking, see RSA 458:16.

NOTES TO DECISIONS

1. Constitutionality
2. Construction
3. Construction with other laws
4. Applicability
5. Restraining order
6. Legitimate purpose
7. Sufficiency of evidence
8. Protective orders

1. Constitutionality

RSA 633:3-a, the stalking statute, is not vague in violation of the Due Process Clause or N.H. Const. pt. I, art. 15. The phrase "legitimate purpose" read in the context of the entire statute, coupled with an objective standard, does not give too much discretion to a trial court and does not require a person of common intelligence to guess at its meaning. Miller v. Blackden, 154 N.H. 448, 913 A.2d 742, 2006 N.H. LEXIS 184 (2006), rehearing denied, 2007 N.H. LEXIS 16 (N.H. Jan. 12, 2007).

Provisions of the New Hampshire stalking statute, subsections (I)(d)(5)(A) and (II)(b) of RSA 633:3-a, were not unconstitutionally vague either on their face or as applied to the defendant who was convicted of stalking his wife during their divorce proceedings by following her car in his car after the wife obtained a domestic violence restraining order against him. State v. Porelle, 149 N.H. 420, 822 A.2d 562, 2003 N.H. LEXIS 58 (2003).

2. Construction

Where a professor unleashed a tirade against a colleague, the false arrest claim based on a stalking charge failed because the issuing court had before it an officer's statement about the professor's conduct which provided sufficient information for a prudent person to believe that the professor had threatened the colleague's safety at least two times and that the colleague did fear for the colleague's safety. Collins v. Univ. of N.H., 664 F.3d 8, 2011 U.S. App. LEXIS 25146 (2011).

Neither the stalking statute nor case law requires the plaintiff to provide the specific dates upon which the prohibited acts occurred; rather, the statute requires "2 or more acts over a period of time, however short." Despres v. Hampsey, 162 N.H. 398, 33 A.3d 1133, 2011 N.H. LEXIS 123 (2011).

3. Construction with other laws

To the extent RSA 173-B:9, IV, and RSA 633:3-a, VI, conflict, RSA 173-B:9, IV, as the more specific statute, controls. Accordingly, when defendant was convicted of stalking, the trial court did not err in imposing felony sentences. State v. Moussa, 164 N.H. 108, 53 A.3d 630, 2012 N.H. LEXIS 117 (2012).

RSA 633:3-a, II(a)(7) provides that a course of conduct may include any act of communication as defined in RSA 644:4, II.

Under RSA 644:4, II, "communicates" means to impart a message by any method of transmission, including but not limited to telephoning. The statute does not require that the act of communication take place between the defendant and the intended victim. State v. Gubitosi, 152 N.H. 673, 886 A.2d 1029, 2005 N.H. LEXIS 159 (2005).

Since RSA 644:4, II did not require that the act of communication take place between the defendant and the intended victim, it was sufficient for the State to prove that defendant telephoned the restaurant with the intent to impart a message to the victim and that the telephone call was part of a course of conduct that reasonably made the victim fear for her safety. State v. Gubitosi, 152 N.H. 673, 886 A.2d 1029, 2005 N.H. LEXIS 159 (2005).

4. Applicability

Since the trial court issued a restraining order that explicitly noted that defendant had "no adequate remedy at law," implicit in that finding was the notion that the alleged victim had no remedy under the stalking statute, RSA 633:3-a, I(c). The final restraining order was one issued under the superior court's equitable powers. State v. Simone, 151 N.H. 328, 856 A.2d 17, 2004 N.H. LEXIS 148 (2004).

5. Restraining order

Defendant was not allowed to collaterally attack the validity of a temporary restraining order that was issued pursuant to RSA 173-B:3 in defending charges that he violated RSA 633:3-a and RSA 173-B:9, by stalking his wife, and the trial court did not err by denying his motion to dismiss the charges on grounds that the order had expired. State v. Small, 150 N.H. 457, 843 A.2d 932, 2004 N.H. LEXIS 3 (2004), rehearing denied, 2004 N.H. LEXIS 56 (N.H. Mar. 25, 2004).

6. Legitimate purpose

Although a stalking defendant, the business partner of plaintiff's former boyfriend, claimed that he was following plaintiff because the boyfriend had hired him as a licensed private detective to conduct surveillance of plaintiff, defendant had refused to testify why he was hired. Thus, he had failed to show that the purpose for which he was hired was lawful, and the trial court did not err when it ruled that defendant's conduct was not for a legitimate purpose. Miller v. Blackden, 154 N.H. 448, 913 A.2d 742, 2006 N.H. LEXIS 184 (2006), rehearing denied, 2007 N.H. LEXIS 16 (N.H. Jan. 12, 2007).

7. Sufficiency of evidence

Because the trial court failed to make specific factual findings to support its final stalking order, entered pursuant to RSA 633:3-a, and evidence pertaining to unnoticed allegations should not have been admitted, insufficient evidence supported the order, warranting vacation of the same and remand. Moreover, petitioner's assertion that her specific allegations were part of respondent's "ongoing pattern of behavior" did not satisfy the notice provision under RSA 173-B:3, I. South v. McCabe, 156 N.H. 797, 943 A.2d 779, 2008 N.H. LEXIS 23 (2008).

Because a daughter threatened the administrator of an assisted living center and other staff members, the acts constituted a course of conduct, as defined in RSA 633:3-a, II; therefore, the district court properly issued a stalking protective order under RSA ch. 173-B against the daughter and in favor of the administrator. Fisher v. Minichiello, 155 N.H. 188, 921 A.2d 385, 2007 N.H. LEXIS 45 (2007), rehearing denied, 2007 N.H. LEXIS 105 (N.H. May 23, 2007).

Stalking order entered against respondent pursuant to RSA 633:3-a was reversed, as the order was not supported by sufficient evidence where petitioner alleged that respondent met her in a parking lot, left her two voice messages, and claimed that she discovered pile of cigarette butts under the seat of her car, which were the brand that respondent smoked, but petitioner's claim that respondent left a pile of cigarette butts in petitioner's car was not included in the stalking petition, and thus the trial court erred in considering the claim. Furthermore, the record contained no eyewitness accounts or other direct evidence that respondent entered petitioner's residence after he removed the last of his belongings, the parking-lot encounter and the two subsequent telephone calls were not sufficient to support the issuance of a stalking order and the trial court had made no factual findings concerning the content of those calls. Comer v. Tracey, 156 N.H. 241, 931 A.2d 1245, 2007 N.H. LEXIS 169 (2007).

Final stalking protective order against an opponent was vacated because a trial court failed to make findings on the record that the opponent engaged in two or more specific acts over a period of time which evidenced a continuity of purpose; the final stalking order gave no indication of the facts relied on in issuing the order, nor the reasoning. Kiesman v. Middleton, 156 N.H. 479, 937 A.2d 917, 2007 N.H. LEXIS 210 (2007).

Evidence was sufficient to support the trial court's entry of a final protective order against defendant in a stalking petition. Defendant, a business partner of plaintiff's former boyfriend, had begun following plaintiff after she had the boyfriend arrested; plaintiff testified that police had told her to take precautions because defendant was watching her; defendant had followed plaintiff to her son's school and "stared her down"; defendant had parked near plaintiff's home with the lights off; and defendant had followed plaintiff to and from the courthouse when she filed her petition. Miller v. Blackden, 154 N.H. 448, 913 A.2d 742, 2006 N.H. LEXIS 184 (2006), rehearing denied, 2007 N.H. LEXIS 16 (N.H. Jan. 12, 2007).

Even without an explicit verbal threat of physical violence, defendant's unrelenting telephone calls and gifts to his victim, especially in light of his articulated history of emotional instability, could have been viewed as evidence that defendant was obsessed with his victim and posed a threat of physical violence to her under RSA 633:3-a, I(a); defendant's unwanted conduct continued even though the victim, the police, and the courts repeatedly and explicitly told him not to do so. State v. Simone, 152 N.H. 755, 887 A.2d 135, 2005 N.H. LEXIS 171 (2005).

Where a rational trier of fact could have found beyond a reasonable doubt that defendant knowingly engaged in a course of conduct targeted at the victim by driving through the parking lot of the restaurant where she was and then calling the restaurant and asking to speak to her, after being told by the police not to contact her, there was sufficient evidence to convict defendant of stalking. State v. Gubitosi, 152 N.H. 673, 886 A.2d 1029, 2005 N.H. LEXIS 159 (2005).

8. Protective orders

In a case where plaintiff sought a protective order based on stalking, the evidence supported the finding that defendant's behavior constituted a "course of conduct" under RSA 633:3-a. A "course of conduct" could include entering the targeted person's residence, and plaintiff testified to two occasions when defendant entered her apartment unannounced and without prior consent; even assuming that the evidence would not establish that each time defendant entered plaintiff's apartment unannounced and confronted her, she also was undressed and defendant made sexual remarks, the other elements of the trial court's finding were sufficient, as a matter of law, to establish a course of conduct. Despres v. Hampsey, 162 N.H. 398, 33 A.3d 1133, 2011 N.H. LEXIS 123 (2011).

In a case where plaintiff sought a protective order based on stalking, the trial court did not fail to make findings of two or more specific acts that constituted stalking. The trial court attached to its order two single-spaced pages summarizing the parties' testimony and concluding that on two or more occasions defendant engaged in the prohibited conduct by entering plaintiff's apartment unannounced and without prior consent and confronting her there. Despres v. Hampsey, 162 N.H. 398, 33 A.3d 1133, 2011 N.H. LEXIS 123 (2011).

In a case where plaintiff sought a protective order based on stalking, the record supported a finding that defendant encountered plaintiff when she was less than fully dressed and made sexual comments to her. These circumstances provided context and support for plaintiff's fear of defendant. Despres v. Hampsey, 162 N.H. 398, 33 A.3d 1133, 2011 N.H. LEXIS 123 (2011).

In a case where plaintiff sought a protective order based on stalking, the trial court did not fail to make findings as to the credibility of the witnesses. The trial court's order showed that of necessity, it weighed the evidence and found plaintiff more credible than defendant. Despres v. Hampsey, 162 N.H. 398, 33 A.3d 1133, 2011 N.H. LEXIS 123 (2011).

In seeking a protective order based on stalking, plaintiff testified

to at least two specific incidents of unwanted entry by defendant, and defendant himself testified regarding both specific incidents, claiming that each time he knocked on the door. Thus, the record did not support defendant's claim that plaintiff's allegations were too vague and nonspecific for him to defend against. Despres v. Hampsey, 162 N.H. 398, 33 A.3d 1133, 2011 N.H. LEXIS 123 (2011).

For a showing of "good cause" under RSA 633:3-a, III-c, the trial court must assess whether the current conditions are such that there is still a concern for the safety and wellbeing of the plaintiff; to do so, the trial court must review the circumstances of the original stalking and any violation of a protective order, and should also take into account any present and reasonable fear by the plaintiff. Where the trial court determines that the circumstances are such that, without a protective order, the plaintiff's safety and wellbeing would be in jeopardy, "good cause" warrants an extension of the order. MacPherson v. Weiner, 158 N.H. 6, 959 A.2d 206, 2008 N.H. LEXIS 127 (2008).

Trial court properly extended a protective order under RSA 633:3-a, III-c. Although defendant had complied with the order during the past 15 months, his actions in driving by plaintiff's home multiple times in violation of the protective order only 15 months earlier, together with plaintiff's reasonable fear, constituted good cause. MacPherson v. Weiner, 158 N.H. 6, 959 A.2d 206, 2008 N.H. LEXIS 127 (2008).

"Good cause" under RSA 633:3-a, III-c was not vague either on its face or as applied to defendant, the subject of a protective order that was extended at plaintiff's request; the statute provided notice to a person of ordinary intelligence that in addressing whether there was "good cause" for an extension, the court would take into account the original act and any subsequent acts, and it further provided notice that if the court found good cause, the extension might be for five years. Defendant knew or should have known that if he participated in activity that constituted stalking or violated conditions of the original stalking order, the court could issue an extended protective order; a statute was not unconstitutionally vague simply because it did not precisely apprise an individual of the standards by which the decision would be made. MacPherson v. Weiner, 158 N.H. 6, 959 A.2d 206, 2008 N.H. LEXIS 127 (2008).

Defendant's compliance with a protective order over the previous 15 months did not bar an extension. If the legislature intended to allow for an extension only when there was a violation of the prior order, the legislature would have included that restriction in the statute, which it did not; thus, a defendant's compliance with or violation of a protective order is a factor for the trial court to consider. MacPherson v. Weiner, 158 N.H. 6, 959 A.2d 206, 2008 N.H. LEXIS 127 (2008).

Trial court is in the best position to view the current circumstances, as well as the defendant's prior acts, and determine whether an extension of a protective order under the stalking statute is necessary for the safety and well-being of the plaintiff. Thus, the trial court has discretion to extend a protective order, although this discretion is not without limitation. MacPherson v. Weiner, 158 N.H. 6, 959 A.2d 206, 2008 N.H. LEXIS 127 (2008).

Cited:

Cited in State v. Weeks, 141 N.H. 248, 681 A.2d 86, 1996 N.H. LEXIS 85 (1996); State v. Gubitosi, 153 N.H. 79, 888 A.2d 1262, 2005 N.H. LEXIS 192 (2005).

RESEARCH REFERENCES

New Hampshire Bar Journal.

For article, "Lex Loci: A Survey of New Hampshire Supreme Court Decisions," see 47 N.H.B.J. 78 (Autumn 2006).

For article, "Beyond State v. Kidder: Defining a Defendant's Right to Contact Witnesses in Domestic Violence Cases," see 46 N.H.B.J. 22 (2005).

633:4. Interference with Custody.

I. A person is guilty of a class B felony if such person knowingly takes from this state or entices away from this state any child under the age of 18, or causes any such child to be taken from this state or enticed away from this state, with the intent to detain or conceal such child from a parent, guardian or other person having lawful parental rights and responsibilities as described in RSA 461-A.

II. A person is guilty of a misdemeanor if such person knowingly takes, entices away, detains or conceals any child under the age of 18, or causes any such child to be taken, enticed away, detained or concealed, with the intent to detain or conceal such child from a parent, guardian or other person having lawful parental rights and responsibilities as described in RSA 461-A.

III. It shall be an affirmative defense to a charge under paragraph I or II that the person so charged was acting in good faith to protect the child from real and imminent physical danger. Evidence of good faith shall include but shall not be limited to the filing of a nonfrivolous petition documenting such danger and seeking to modify the custody decree in a court of competent jurisdiction within this state. Such petition must be filed within 72 hours of termination of visitation rights.

IV. The affirmative defense set forth in paragraph III shall not be available if the person charged with the offense has left this state with the child.

Source.
1983, 390:1, eff. Aug. 21, 1983. 1998, 292:2, eff. Jan. 1, 1999. 2005, 273:16, eff. October 1, 2005.

Amendments
—2005. Paragraph I: Substituted "parental rights and responsibilities as described in RSA 461-A" for "physical custody or physical custodial rights as described in RSA 458:17, IV".
Paragraph II: Substituted "parental rights and responsibilities as described in RSA 461-A" for "physical custody or physical custodial rights as described in RSA 458:17".

—1998. Paragraphs I and II: Rewritten to the extent that a detailed comparison would be impracticable.

Use of federal locator services.
1983, 390:2, eff. Aug. 21, 1983, provided: "The commissioner of health and welfare [commissioner of health and human services] shall enter into an agreement with the United States Secretary of Health and Human Services, pursuant to 42 U.S.C.S. 663 under which the services of the Parent Locator Service established under 42 U.S.C.S. 653 shall be made available to this state for the purpose of determining the whereabouts of any absent parent or child in order to enforce the provisions of RSA 633:4 or to make or enforce a child custody determination."

Cross References.
Classification of crimes, see RSA 625:9.
Parental rights and responsibilities, see RSA 461-A.
Sentences, see RSA 651.
Uniform Child Custody Jurisdiction Act, see RSA 458-A.

633:5. Peonage.

I. An actor is guilty of a class A misdemeanor if such person knowingly holds a victim in a condition of involuntary servitude in satisfaction of a debt owed to the actor. In this section, "involuntary servitude" means a condition of servitude in which the victim is forced to work for the actor by the use or threat of physical restraint or physical injury, or by the use or threat of coercion through law or the legal process.

II. The use of the labor of any person incarcerated in a state or county correctional facility or municipal jail shall be exempt from this section.

Source.
2006, 237:1, eff. January 1, 2007.

Trafficking in Persons

633:6. Definitions.

In this subdivision:

I. "Commercial sex act" means any sex act because of which anything of value is given, promised to, or received, directly or indirectly, by any person.

II. "Sex act" means any act of sexual contact as defined in RSA 632-A:1, IV, any act of sexual penetration as defined in RSA 632-A:1, V, or any other sexually explicit conduct as defined in RSA 649-A:2.

III. "Sexually-explicit performance" means an act or show involving one or more sex acts, intended to arouse, satisfy the sexual desires of, or appeal to the prurient interests of patrons or viewers, whether public or private, live, photographed, recorded, or videotaped.

IV. "Serious harm" includes physical and non-physical harm. It can be any improper threat of a consequence sufficient under the circumstances to compel or coerce a reasonable person in the same situation to provide or continue to provide labor or services, or to engage in commercial sex acts or sexually explicit performances.

V. "Involuntary servitude" means a condition of compulsory service or labor, including commercial sex acts or sexually explicit performances, performed by one person, against his or her will, for the benefit of another. If a person willingly begins to perform the labor or service but later attempts to withdraw and is forced to remain and perform against his or her will, the service becomes involuntary. The payment of a wage or salary is not determinative of the question as to whether that person has been held in involuntary servitude.

Source.
2009, 211:1, eff. January 1, 2010.

633:7. Trafficking in Persons.

I. (a) It is a class A felony to knowingly subject a person to involuntary servitude, where the compulsion is accomplished by any of the following means:

(1) Causing or threatening to cause serious harm to any person.

(2) Confining the person unlawfully as defined in RSA 633:2, II, or threatening to so confine the person.

(3) Abusing legal process or threatening to bring legal action against the person relating to the person's legal status or potential criminal liability.

(4) Destroying, concealing, removing, confiscating, or otherwise making unavailable to that person any actual or purported passport or other immigration document, or any other actual or purported government identification document.

(5) Threatening to commit a crime against the person.

(6) False promise relating to the terms and conditions of employment, education, marriage, or financial support.

(7) Threatening to reveal any information sought to be kept concealed by the person which relates to the person's legal status or which would expose the person to criminal liability.

(8) Facilitating or controlling the person's access to an addictive controlled substance.

(9) Engaging in any scheme, plan, or pattern, whether overt or subtle, intended to cause the person to believe that, if he or she did not perform such labor, services, commercial sex acts, or sexually explicit performances, that such person or any person would suffer serious harm or physical restraint.

(10) Withholding or threatening to withhold food or medication that the actor has an obligation or has promised to provide to the person.

(11) Coercing a person to engage in any of the foregoing acts by requiring such in satisfaction of a debt owed to the actor.

(b) The means listed in subparagraphs (a)(4), (a)(10), and (a)(11) are not intended to criminalize the actions of a parent or guardian who requires his or her child to perform common household chores under threat of typical parental discipline.

(c) Notwithstanding RSA 651:2, a person convicted of an offense under subparagraph I(a) involving a commercial sex act or sexually explicit performance by a victim under the age of 18 shall be subject to a minimum term of not more than 10 years and a maximum term of not more than 30 years.

II. It is a class A felony to recruit, harbor, transport, provide, obtain, or otherwise make available a person, knowing or believing it likely that the person will be subjected to trafficking as defined in paragraph I. Notwithstanding RSA 651:2, a person convicted of an offense under this paragraph involving a victim under the age of 18 shall be subject to a minimum term of not more than 10 years and a maximum to be fixed by the court, if the offender knew or believed it likely that the victim would be coerced into engaging in a commercial sex act or sexually explicit performance.

III. Evidence of a trafficking victim's personal sexual history or history of commercial sexual activity shall not be admissible at trial.

Source.
2009, 211:1, eff. January 1, 2010.

633:8. Forfeiture of Items Used in Connection with Trafficking in Persons.

I. All offenses under this section shall qualify as offenses for forfeiture and thereby upon petition of the attorney general, shall be subject to forfeiture to the state and said property interest shall be vested in the state:

(a) All materials, products, and equipment of any kind used in violation of this section.

(b) Any property interest in any conveyance used in furtherance of an act which violates this section.

(c) Any moneys, coin, currency, negotiable instruments, securities, or other investments knowingly used or intended for use in violation of this section.

(d) Any books, records, ledgers, and research material, including formulae, microfilm, tapes, and any other data which are used or intended for use in felonious violation of this section.

(e) Any real property, including any right, title, leasehold interest, and other interest in the whole of any lot or tract of land and any appurtenances or improvements, which real property is knowingly used or intended for use, in any manner or part, in felonious violation of this section.

II. The state shall have a lien on any property subject to forfeiture under this section upon seizure thereof. Upon forfeiture, the state's title to the property relates back to the date of seizure.

III. (a) Property may be seized for forfeiture by any law enforcement agency designated by the department of justice, as follows:

(1) Upon process issued by any justice, associate justice, or special justice of the district or superior court. The court may issue a seizure warrant on an affidavit under oath demonstrating that probable cause exists for its forfeiture or that the property has been the subject of a previous final judgment of forfeiture in the courts of any state or of the United States. The application for process and the issuance, execution, and return of process shall be subject to applicable state law. The court may order that the property be seized and secured on such terms and conditions as are reasonable in the discretion of the court. Such order may include an order to a financial institution or to any fiduciary or bailee to require the entity to impound any property in its possession or control and not to release it except upon further order of the court. The order may be made on or in connection with a search warrant;

(2) Physically, without process on probable cause to believe that the property is subject to forfeiture under this section; or

(3) Constructively, without process on probable cause to believe that the property is subject to forfeiture under this section, by recording a

notice of pending forfeiture in the registry of deeds in the county where the real property is located or at the town clerk's office where the personal property is located stating that the state intends to seek forfeiture of the identified property pursuant to this section.

(b) A seizure for forfeiture without process under subparagraph (a)(2) or (a)(3) shall be reasonable if made under circumstances in which a warrantless seizure or arrest would be valid in accordance with state law.

IV. Upon seizure of any items or property interests the property shall not be subject to alienation, sequestration, or attachment but is deemed to be in the custody of the department of justice subject only to the order of the court.

V. Upon the seizure of any personal property, the person making or directing such seizure shall inventory the items or property interests and issue a copy of the resulting report to any person or persons having a recorded interest, or claiming an equitable interest in the item within 7 days of the seizure.

VI. Upon seizure of any real property, the person making or directing such seizure shall notify any person having a recorded interest or claiming an equitable interest in the property within 7 days of the seizure.

VII. The seizing agency shall cause an appraisal to be made of the property as soon as possible and shall promptly send to the department of justice a written request for forfeiture. This request shall include a statement of all facts and circumstances supporting forfeiture of the property, including the names of all witnesses then known, and the appraised value of the property.

VIII. The department of justice shall examine the facts and applicable law of the cases referred pursuant to paragraph VII, and if it is probable that the property is subject to forfeiture, shall cause the initiation of administrative or judicial proceedings against the property. If upon inquiry and examination, the department of justice determines that such proceedings probably cannot be sustained or that the ends of justice do not require the institution of such proceedings, the department shall make a written report of such findings and send a copy to the seizing agency, and, if appropriate, shall also authorize and direct the release of the property.

IX. The department of justice shall, within 60 days of the seizure, file a petition in the superior court having jurisdiction under this section. If no such petition is filed within 60 days, the items or property interest seized shall be released or returned to the owners.

X. Pending forfeiture and final disposition, the law enforcement agency making the seizure shall:

(a) Place the property under seal;

(b) Remove the property to a storage area for safekeeping;

(c) Remove the property to a place designated by the court;

(d) Request another agency to take custody of the property and remove it to an appropriate location within the state, or in the case of moneys, file a motion for transfer of evidence under RSA 595-A:6. Upon the court's granting of the motion, the moneys shall be immediately forwarded to an interest-bearing seized asset escrow account to be administered by the attorney general.

XI. The court may order forfeiture of all items or property interests under this section, except no item or property interest shall be subject to forfeiture unless the owner or owners thereof were consenting parties to a felonious violation of this section and had knowledge thereof.

XII. The department of justice may petition the superior court in the name of the state in the nature of a proceeding in rem to order forfeiture of items or property interests subject to forfeiture under the provisions of this section. Such petition shall be filed in the court having jurisdiction over any related criminal proceedings which could be brought under this section. Such proceeding shall be deemed a civil suit in equity in which the state shall have the burden of proving all material facts by a preponderance of the evidence and in which the owners or other persons claiming an exception pursuant to paragraph XI shall have the burden of proving such exception.

XIII. The court shall issue orders of notice to all persons who have a recorded interest or claim an equitable interest in said items or property interests seized under this section and shall schedule a hearing on the petition to be held within 90 days of the return date on said petition.

XIV. At the request of any party to the forfeiture proceeding, the court shall grant a continuance until the final resolution of any criminal proceedings which were brought against a party under this section and which arose from the transaction which gave rise to the forfeiture proceeding. No party's interest in property shall be forfeited unless a party has been found guilty of the underlying felonious charge.

XV. At the hearing, the court shall hear evidence and make findings of fact and rulings of law as to whether the property is subject to forfeiture under this section. Except in the case of proceeds, upon a finding that the property is subject to forfeiture the court shall determine whether the forfeiture of the property is not excessive in relation to the underlying criminal offense. In making this determination the court shall consider whether in addition to any other pertinent considerations:

(a) There is a substantial connection between the property to be forfeited and the underlying offense;

(b) Criminal activities conducted by or through the use of the property were extensive; and

(c) The value of the property to be forfeited greatly outweighs the cost of prosecution and the harm caused by the criminal conduct.

XVI. The court shall, thereupon, make a final order, from which all parties shall have a right of appeal. Final orders for forfeiture of property under this section shall be implemented by the department of justice and shall provide for disposition of the items or property interests by the state in any manner not prohibited by law, including payment of restitution to a victim of trafficking or sale at public auction. The department of justice shall pay the reasonable expenses of the forfeiture proceeding, seizure, storage, maintenance of custody, advertising, court costs, and notice of sale from any money forfeited and from the proceeds of any sale or public auction of forfeited items. All outstanding recorded liens on said items or property interests seized shall be paid in full upon conclusion of the court proceedings from the proceeds of any sale or public auction of forfeited items.

XVII. Overseas assets of persons convicted of trafficking in persons shall also be subject to forfeiture to the extent they can be retrieved by the government.

XVIII. After payment of costs outlined in paragraph XVI, any forfeited money and the proceeds of any sale or public auction of forfeited items shall first be used to satisfy any order of restitution or compensation imposed by the court. Any remaining funds shall go to the victims' assistance fund as defined in RSA 21-M:8-i.

Source.
2009, 211:1, eff. January 1, 2010.

633:9. Administrative Forfeiture of Items Used in Connection with Trafficking in Persons.

I. Interests in property subject to forfeiture under the provisions of RSA 633:8, I(a), I(b), I(c) excepting proceeds, and I(d), but not real property, shall be subject to administrative forfeiture by the department of justice provided that the total amount or value of such property does not exceed $75,000. The provisions of RSA 633:8 shall apply in any case of administrative forfeiture except as otherwise provided in this section.

II. The department of justice may administratively forfeit property seized under paragraph I of this section as follows:

(a) The department of justice shall provide a notice of intent to forfeit property administratively by publication for 3 consecutive weeks in a local newspaper of general circulation where the property was seized.

(b) In addition, to the extent practicable, the department of justice shall provide notice by certified mail return receipt addressee only requested, of intent to forfeit the property administratively to all persons having a recorded interest or claiming an equitable interest in the property seized.

(c) Notice by publication and by mail shall include:

(1) A description of the property;

(2) Its appraised value;

(3) The date and place of seizure;

(4) The violation of law alleged against the subject property;

(5) Instructions for filing a claim and posting bond or filing a petition for remission or mitigation; and

(6) Notice that the property will be forfeited to the state if a petition for remission or mitigation has not been filed in a timely manner or a claim has not been filed and bond has not been posted in a timely manner.

(d) Persons claiming an interest in the property may file petitions for remission or mitigation of forfeiture or file a claim and post bond with the department of justice within 30 days of the first notice by publication or 30 days from the receipt of written notice, whichever is later.

(e) It shall be the duty of the department of justice to inquire into the facts and circumstances surrounding petitions for remission or mitigation of forfeiture.

(f) The department of justice shall provide the seizing agency and the petitioner a written decision on each petition for remission or mitigation within 60 days of receipt of such petition unless the circumstances of the case require additional time in which case the department of justice shall notify the petitioner in writing and with specificity within the 60-day period that the circumstances of the case require additional time, and further notify the petitioner of the expected decision date.

(g) Any person claiming an interest in seized property may institute judicial review of the seizure and proposed forfeiture by timely filing with the department of justice a claim and bond to the state in the amount of 10 percent of the appraised value or in the penal sum of $2,500, whichever is less, with sureties to be approved by the department of justice, upon condition that in the case of forfeiture the claimant shall pay all costs and expenses of the proceedings at the discretion of the court. A sworn affidavit of indigency may be filed in lieu of a cost bond. Upon receipt of the claim and bond, or, if department of justice otherwise so elects, the department shall file with the court a petition in rem to order forfeiture of items or property interests subject to forfeiture under the provisions of this section. All judicial proceedings thereafter shall be conducted in accordance with the provisions of RSA 633:8. Any bonds received by the department of justice shall be held by it pending final disposition of the case.

(h) If no petitions or claims with bonds are timely filed, the department of justice shall prepare a written declaration of forfeiture of the subject property to the state and dispose of the property in accordance with this section and the department of justice rules, if any, relative to this section.

(i) If the petition is denied, the department of justice shall prepare a written declaration of forfeiture to the state and dispose of the property in accordance with this section and the department of justice rules, if any, relative to this section.

(j) A written declaration of forfeiture signed by the attorney general or designee pursuant to this chapter shall be deemed good and sufficient title to the forfeited property.

Source.

2009, 211:1, eff. January 1, 2010.

633:10. Restitution and Compensation.

I. A person convicted under this section shall be ordered by the court to pay restitution to the victim. Such restitution may include but not be limited to:

(a) Any economic loss compensable under RSA 651:62, in accordance with the provisions of RSA 651:61-a through RSA 651:67; and

(b) The value of the victim's labor as guaranteed under the minimum wage law and overtime provisions of the Fair Labor Standards Act or the state minimum wage law, whichever is greater.

II. To the extent not included in economic loss that is compensable under paragraph I, the court may also order a person convicted under this section to pay compensation as follows:

(a) Costs of medical and psychological treatment, including physical and occupational therapy and rehabilitation, at the court's discretion;

(b) Costs of necessary transportation, temporary housing, and child care, at the court's discretion;

(c) Return of property, cost of damage to property, or full value of property if destroyed or damaged beyond repair;

(d) Expenses incurred by a victim and any household members or other family members in relocating away from the defendant or his or her associates, including, but not limited to, deposits for utilities and telephone service, deposits for rental housing, temporary lodging and food expenses, clothing, and personal items; and

(e) Any and all other losses suffered by the victim as a result of an offense under this section.

III. The return of the victim to her or his home country or other absence of the victim from the jurisdiction shall not relieve the defendant of his or her restitution obligation.

IV. Except as otherwise provided in this section, the provisions of RSA 651:61-a through RSA 651:67 shall govern all restitution and compensation orders.

Source.

2009, 211:1, eff. January 1, 2010.

CHAPTER 634

DESTRUCTION OF PROPERTY

SECTION
634:1.   Arson.
634:2.   Criminal Mischief.
634:3.   Unauthorized Use of Propelled Vehicle or Animal.

634:1. Arson.

I. A person is guilty of arson if he knowingly starts a fire or causes an explosion which unlawfully damages the property of another.

II. Arson is a class A felony if the property damaged is:

(a) An occupied structure and the actor knew it was an occupied structure; or

(b) An historic structure.

III. Arson is a class B felony if:

(a) The property is either that of another or the actor's property, and the fire was started or the explosion caused for the purpose of collecting insurance on such property; or

(b) The actor purposely starts a fire or causes an explosion on anyone's property and thereby recklessly places another in danger of death or serious bodily injury, or places an occupied structure of another in danger of damage; or

(c) The property damaged is real estate; or

(d) The pecuniary loss caused is in excess of $1,000.

IV. All other arson is a misdemeanor.

V. As used in this section:

(a) "Occupied structure" has the same meaning as in RSA 635:1, III, and includes structures appurtenant to occupied structures and seasonal dwellings whether vacant or occupied;

(b) "Property" has the same meaning as in RSA 637:2, I;

(c) "Property of another" has the same meaning as in RSA 637:2, IV.

(d) "Historic structure" means any structure listed, or determined by the department of cultural resources to be eligible for listing, in the National Register of Historic Places, or designated as historic under state or local law.

Source.

1971, 518:1. 1975, 284:1, 2. 1994, 346:1, 2, eff. Jan. 1, 1995. 1998, 363:3, eff. Aug. 25, 1998.

Amendments

—1998. Paragraph V(d): Substituted "cultural resources" for "cultural affairs".

—1994. Paragraph II: Rewritten to the extent that a detailed comparison would be impractical.
Paragraph V(d): Added.

—1975. Paragraph III: Former subpar. (c) redesignated as subpar. (d) and a new subpar. (c) added.

Paragraph V: Rewritten to the extent that a detailed comparison would be impracticable.

Cross References.
Arson occurring as a result of riot, see RSA 644:1.
Classification of crimes, see RSA 625:9.
First degree murder, see RSA 630:1-a.
Insurance fraud, see RSA 638:20.
Involuntary admission for persons charged with arson found not competent to stand trial, see RSA 171-B.
Sentences, see RSA 651.
Use of force to prevent arson, see RSA 627:7.

NOTES TO DECISIONS

1. Purpose
2. Elements
3. Property of another
4. Indictment
5. Defenses
6. Evidence
7. Sentence

1. Purpose

The purpose of subparagraph V(c) of this section is to include within the sweep of the Criminal Code that property in which more than one person has an interest—e.g., partnership property, leased property, and property held by joint tenancy or by tenancy in common. State v. Marion, 122 N.H. 20, 440 A.2d 448, 1982 N.H. LEXIS 277 (1982).

2. Elements

For the purpose of interpreting this section, the word "unlawfully" means that the burning was not lawful, and does not require showing of the lack of the owner's consent. State v. Janvrin, 122 N.H. 75, 441 A.2d 1144, 1982 N.H. LEXIS 289 (1982).

In a prosecution under this section, the state is under no obligation to prove as an element of its affirmative case that the fire was set without the consent of the owner; consent is not an element that is presumed, nor does it have to be shown not to have been given. State v. Janvrin, 122 N.H. 75, 441 A.2d 1144, 1982 N.H. LEXIS 289 (1982).

Where defendant, who was charged with class A felony arson, never raised the issue of consent and asserted a defense that he had not set the fire, the trial judge was not required to instruct the jury that lack of permission or consent was an element of proof upon which the state had the burden, nor was it an element necessary to support a conviction upon indictment. State v. Janvrin, 122 N.H. 75, 441 A.2d 1144, 1982 N.H. LEXIS 289 (1982).

Aggravating factors set forth in this section are essential elements of state's case for felonious arson, and therefore are elements of the offense that must be proved by the state; as substantive elements of the offense, these facts are to be decided by the jury. State v. Champagne, 119 N.H. 118, 399 A.2d 287, 1979 N.H. LEXIS 253 (1979).

3. Property of another

A mortgagee's interest in a structure is sufficient so that the structure may also be considered to be the "property of another" within the meaning of this section. State v. Marion, 122 N.H. 20, 440 A.2d 448, 1982 N.H. LEXIS 277 (1982).

The second sentence of RSA 637:2, IV, defining "property of another," which is incorporated by reference into this section, does not exclude a mortgage interest; the sentence, by its terms, does not apply to real property and excludes only interests created by a conditional sales contract or other security agreement, interests which can arise only in personal property or fixtures. State v. Marion, 122 N.H. 20, 440 A.2d 448, 1982 N.H. LEXIS 277 (1982).

When a mortgagor knowingly starts a fire in a mortgaged structure that he knows is an "occupied structure," he is guilty of a class A felony. State v. Marion, 122 N.H. 20, 440 A.2d 448, 1982 N.H. LEXIS 277 (1982).

Where mortgage deed contained language in granting clause whereby the mortgagors had "given, granted, bargained, sold or by these presents do give, grant, bargain, sell, alien and enfeoff, convey and confirm" the premises unto the mortgagee, its succes-

sors and assigns "forever," the interest conveyed was more than a mere security interest and the interest of the mortgagee in the premises in question was a sufficient "property of another" to satisfy the requirement of this section. State v. Marion, 122 N.H. 20, 440 A.2d 448, 1982 N.H. LEXIS 277 (1982).

4. Indictment

For a conviction of arson under subparagraph II(a), the term "property" means "an occupied structure," thus, each occupied structure that is damaged is the "property of another" needed to sustain an indictment under the statute. State v. Ayotte, 146 N.H. 544, 776 A.2d 715, 2001 N.H. LEXIS 107 (2001).

In a prosecution on two counts of arson, fact that structure contained the businesses of two separate leaseholders was irrelevant under the definition of a single occupied structure; there was only one "occupied structure" damaged by the fire, and thus, only one conviction under subparagraph II(a) could be sustained. State v. Ayotte, 146 N.H. 544, 776 A.2d 715, 2001 N.H. LEXIS 107 (2001).

Where indictments identified the elements of arson specified in subparagraph III(a) of this section, the fact that they described the property as being owned by defendant, the mortgagor, did not impair their sufficiency. State v. Champagne, 125 N.H. 648, 484 A.2d 1161, 1984 N.H. LEXIS 381 (1984).

Indictment for arson which tracked the wording of paragraph I of this section alleged the nature of the offense with sufficient definiteness to withstand a motion to dismiss. State v. Champagne, 119 N.H. 118, 399 A.2d 287, 1979 N.H. LEXIS 253 (1979).

5. Defenses

Although it is difficult to imagine many instances where the burning of the occupied property of another would be lawful, the consensual burning of such property is usually not a prosecutable action. State v. Janvrin, 122 N.H. 75, 441 A.2d 1144, 1982 N.H. LEXIS 289 (1982).

Under this section, consent, as a defense, must be asserted and claimed by the defendant after appropriate notice pursuant to the Superior Court Rule 101, requiring notice of a criminal defense. State v. Janvrin, 122 N.H. 75, 441 A.2d 1144, 1982 N.H. LEXIS 289 (1982).

If indictment had charged defendant with intent to defraud insurer, consent by owner or ownership itself of burned property would not have been a defense to arson. State v. Champagne, 119 N.H. 118, 399 A.2d 287, 1979 N.H. LEXIS 253 (1979).

6. Evidence

For purposes of proving a conspiracy to commit arson, trial evidence amply supported the existence of an agreement between petitioner and his accomplice whereby petitioner paid his accomplice to set fire to his restaurant for purposes of collecting insurance proceeds; the accomplice's technical denial of an agreement to set the fire did not establish that no agreement existed as the factual circumstances that the accomplice described in his testimony, along with the evidence provided by other witnesses, showed that after some thought, the accomplice accepted petitioner's offer to burn the building in exchange for money and, based upon petitioner's offer, the accomplice set the fire, and petitioner paid him for his work. Nowaczyk v. Warden, N.H. State Prison, 2003 U.S. Dist. LEXIS 6912 (D.N.H. 2003).

Where defendant was charged with arson, evidence regarding prior fire that she reported from a location and at a time proximate to the charged fire was not admissible and was prejudicial to her case because, once she conceded at trial that she started the charged fire, her presence at the prior fire scene was no longer relevant to establish opportunity, and evidence of that fire was no longer relevant. State v. Ayotte, 146 N.H. 544, 776 A.2d 715, 2001 N.H. LEXIS 107 (2001).

Circumstantial evidence was sufficient to convict defendant of arson, despite lack of physical evidence tying him to the fire and despite his assertion that others had a superior motive to set the fire. State v. Alexander, 143 N.H. 216, 723 A.2d 22, 1998 N.H. LEXIS 97 (1998).

Evidence was sufficient to establish that the defendant, as an accomplice, committed two counts of attempted murder, one count of attempted arson, and one count of attempted falsification of evidence, where a witness testified that, mere hours after the incident, the defendant admitted that he had accompanied his coperpetrator to the scene of the crime, that they planned to rob whomever they discovered there, by violent means if necessary, that the defendant and the coperpetrator hid behind a bush while the latter twice shot at a car, that after the victims abandoned the car they searched it for valuables and money, and that there was an attempt to destroy the car following the search for valuables. State v. Laudarowicz, 142 N.H. 1, 694 A.2d 980, 1997 N.H. LEXIS 47 (1997).

7. Sentence

Where defendant was charged and convicted only of misdemeanor arson under paragraph IV of this section, court erred in upgrading the offense to a felony as part of the sentencing procedure. State v. Champagne, 119 N.H. 118, 399 A.2d 287, 1979 N.H. LEXIS 253 (1979).

Cited:

Cited in Welch v. Bergeron, 115 N.H. 179, 337 A.2d 341, 1975 N.H. LEXIS 253 (1975); State v. Doran, 117 N.H. 491, 374 A.2d 950, 1977 N.H. LEXIS 362 (1977); State v. Theodore, 118 N.H. 548, 392 A.2d 122, 1978 N.H. LEXIS 238 (1978); Heald v. Perrin, 123 N.H. 468, 464 A.2d 275, 1983 N.H. LEXIS 310 (1983); State v. Bertrand, 123 N.H. 719, 465 A.2d 912, 1983 N.H. LEXIS 340 (1983); State v. Holt, 124 N.H. 645, 474 A.2d 1031, 1984 N.H. LEXIS 228 (1984); State v. Fleming, 125 N.H. 238, 480 A.2d 107, 1984 N.H. LEXIS 365 (1984); State v. Abbis, 125 N.H. 646, 484 A.2d 1156, 1984 N.H. LEXIS 387 (1984); State v. Brooks, 126 N.H. 618, 495 A.2d 1258, 1985 N.H. LEXIS 366 (1985); State v. Corey, 127 N.H. 56, 497 A.2d 1196, 1985 N.H. LEXIS 400 (1985); Hopps v. Utica Mut. Ins. Co., 127 N.H. 508, 506 A.2d 294, 1985 N.H. LEXIS 476 (1985); State v. Gagne, 129 N.H. 93, 523 A.2d 76, 1986 N.H. LEXIS 380 (1986); State v. Maguire, 129 N.H. 165, 523 A.2d 120, 1987 N.H. LEXIS 161 (1987); State v. Murray, 129 N.H. 645, 531 A.2d 323, 1987 N.H. LEXIS 233 (1987); State v. Decoteau, 137 N.H. 106, 623 A.2d 1338, 1993 N.H. LEXIS 49 (1993); State v. Turgeon, 137 N.H. 544, 630 A.2d 276, 1993 N.H. LEXIS 117 (1993); State v. Dowdle, 148 N.H. 345, 807 A.2d 1237, 2002 N.H. LEXIS 133 (2002).

RESEARCH REFERENCES

New Hampshire Bar Journal.

For article, "Understanding and Representing Adult Clients Who Are Victims of Domestic Abuse," see 35 N.H.B.J. 8 (1994).

634:2. Criminal Mischief.

I. A person is guilty of criminal mischief who, having no right to do so nor any reasonable basis for belief of having such a right, purposely or recklessly damages property of another.

II. Criminal mischief is a class B felony if the actor purposely causes or attempts to cause:

(a) Pecuniary loss in excess of $1,500; or

(b) A substantial interruption or impairment of public communication, transportation, supply of water, gas, or power, or other public service; or

(c) Discharge of a firearm at an occupied structure, as defined in RSA 635:1, III; or

(d) Damage to private or public property, real or personal, when the actor knows that the property has historical, cultural, or sentimental value that cannot be restored by repair or replacement.

II-a. Criminal mischief is a class A misdemeanor if the actor purposely causes or attempts to cause pecuniary loss in excess of $100 and not more than $1,500.

III. All other criminal mischief is a misdemeanor.

IV. As used in this section, "property" has the same meaning as in RSA 637:2, I; "property of another" has the same meaning as in RSA 637:2, IV.

V. For purposes of determining pecuniary loss under subparagraph II(a), amounts involved in acts committed pursuant to one scheme or course of conduct participated in by the actor may be aggregated in determining the grade of the offense.

VI. Any person who is found guilty of criminal mischief under paragraph III of this section because he or she has vandalized, defaced, or destroyed any part of state or municipal property, or any natural geological formation, site, or rock surface located on public property that has been designated by the state or any of its political subdivisions or the federal government as a natural area or landmark shall be guilty of a class A misdemeanor and shall also make restitution for any damage he or she has caused.

VII. If the court determines that a motor vehicle was used to abet the commission of the act constituting criminal mischief, the court may suspend, for a period not to exceed 90 days, the driver's license of a person who is convicted of criminal mischief, or the driver's licenses of persons who are convicted of criminal mischief.

VIII. Any person who is found guilty of criminal mischief under this section because the person has purposely or recklessly damaged an emergency vehicle, emergency apparatus, or private vehicle containing emergency equipment, shall be liable for full restitution to the injured party.

IX. Any person who is found guilty of criminal mischief under this section because such person is a tenant, or a guest of such tenant, in a rental dwelling who has destroyed, disconnected, or otherwise rendered inoperable any smoke detector in the rental dwelling, or who has attempted the same in a rental dwelling, shall be guilty of a misdemeanor.

Source.

1971, 518:1. 1985, 201:1. 1986, 98:1. 1987, 182:1. 1991, 35:1. 1992, 269:12, eff. July 1, 1992. 1996, 225:2, eff. Jan. 1, 1997. 1997, 327:2, eff. Jan. 1, 1998. 2001, 283:1, eff. Sept. 14, 2001. 2003, 290:1, eff. Jan. 1, 2004. 2009, 193:1, eff. July 13, 2009. 2010, 239:1, eff. July 1, 2010. 2012, 133:1, eff. January 1, 2013.

Amendments

—2012. The 2012 amendment, in VI, substituted "state or municipal property" for "the 'Old Man of the Mountain'" and deleted "to the state" following "also make restitution."

—2010. The 2010 amendment substituted "$1,500" for "$1,000" in II(a) and II-a and made stylistic changes.

—2009. The 2009 amendment substituted "or any natural geological formation, site, or rock surface located on public property that has been designated by the state or any of its political subdivisions or the federal government as a natural area or landmark shall be guilty of a class A misdemeanor" for "shall" in VI and made stylistic changes.

—2003. Paragraph IX: Added.

—2001. Paragraph VIII: Added.

—1997. Paragraph VII: Added.

—1996. Paragraph I: Substituted "who" for "when" following "mischief", "for belief of having" for "to believe that he has" following "basis" and deleted "he" preceding "purposely".

Paragraph II: Added subpar. (d).

—**1992.** Paragraph II-a: Added.

—**1991.** Paragraph II: Added "or" following "service" in subpar. (b) and added subpar. (c).

—**1987.** Paragraph V: Rewritten to the extent that a detailed comparison would be impracticable.

—**1986.** Paragraph VI: Added.

—**1985.** Paragraph V: Added.

Applicability of 1992 amendment.

1992, 269:21, eff. July 1, 1992, provided that the amendment to this section by 1992, 269:12, shall apply to all offenses committed on or after July 1, 1992.

Cross References.

Classification of crimes, see RSA 625:9.

Criminal threatening, see RSA 631:4.

Performance of uncompensated public service by person convicted of criminal mischief, see RSA 651:2, VI-a.

Sentences, see RSA 651.

Use of force to prevent criminal mischief, see RSA 627:8.

Violating temporary restraining order by committing criminal mischief, see RSA 458:16.

NOTES TO DECISIONS

1. Construction generally
2. Evidence
3. Lesser-included offense

1. Construction generally

Where defendant was charged with the least serious variant of criminal mischief, the State was not required to prove pecuniary loss. State v. Hudson, 151 N.H. 688, 867 A.2d 412, 2005 N.H. LEXIS 11 (2005).

Because paragraph III of this section does not specify a classification, pursuant to RSA 625:9, IV(a)(2), defining class A misdemeanor, it must be categorized as a class A misdemeanor. State v. Bruce, 147 N.H. 37, 780 A.2d 1270, 2001 N.H. LEXIS 165 (2001).

The legislature did not intend that subsection II(b) apply to the interruption or impairment of cable television service and, therefore, the defendant did not violate the statute when he moved a satellite dish owned by a cable television company. State v. Wilson, 140 N.H. 44, 662 A.2d 954, 1995 N.H. LEXIS 91 (1995).

Property damage constitutes a pecuniary loss under this section, even where the victim receives insurance to cover the cost of repairing the damage. State v. Paris, 137 N.H. 322, 627 A.2d 582, 1993 N.H. LEXIS 78 (1993).

The intent requirement of this section relates to the causation, not the amount, of pecuniary loss. Thus, the state need not prove that the defendant intended to cause more than $1,000 in pecuniary losses. State v. Paris, 137 N.H. 322, 627 A.2d 582, 1993 N.H. LEXIS 78 (1993).

2. Evidence

Even if the trial court erred under N.H. R. Evid. 403 and 404(b) in admitting evidence of a physical altercation at a nightclub that occurred before defendant threw an iron through the screen of his girlfriend's television set, its admission was harmless because the evidence of guilt of class A misdemeanor criminal mischief was overwhelming. The evidence included the girlfriend's testimony that defendant threw the iron through the screen after learning that their relationship was over, photographs of the damaged television, the girlfriend's testimony about what she had paid for the television, defendant's confession that he damaged the television, and his admission that he meant to "screw up" the television. State v. Prudent, 161 N.H. 320, 13 A.3d 181, 2010 N.H. LEXIS 183

(2010).

There was sufficient evidence supporting defendant's conviction for criminal mischief where the testimony established that he ran over a small bush and left tire marks on the victim's driveway and lawn, and there was a fair inference that the lawn and the bush had value. State v. Hudson, 151 N.H. 688, 867 A.2d 412, 2005 N.H. LEXIS 11 (2005).

Evidence was sufficient to establish that the defendant caused pecuniary loss greater than $1,000 when he shot at the victim's car. An insurance adjuster estimated that repairing the car would cost $1,771.36, the victim's insurer paid $1,705.45 for the damage to his car, and the jury saw photographs and heard testimony detailing the damage caused by the defendant. State v. Paris, 137 N.H. 322, 627 A.2d 582, 1993 N.H. LEXIS 78 (1993).

3. Lesser-included offense

In prosecution for criminal mischief, defendant was expected to know that RSA 626:2, III, defines elements requiring proof that he acted recklessly as constituting a subset of the elements requiring proof that he acted purposely, and, thus, this section on its face gave him notice that recklessly causing damage to property is a lesser-included offense of purposely causing damage to property. State v. Bruce, 147 N.H. 37, 780 A.2d 1270, 2001 N.H. LEXIS 165 (2001).

In prosecution for criminal mischief, defendant could not complain that he had insufficient notice that the prosecution might request jury instructions on lesser-included offenses, including misdemeanor criminal mischief, where his own testimony provided the basis for the charges. State v. Bruce, 147 N.H. 37, 780 A.2d 1270, 2001 N.H. LEXIS 165 (2001).

Cited:

Cited in State v. Robidoux, 125 N.H. 169, 480 A.2d 67, 1984 N.H. LEXIS 360 (1984); State v. DeLong, 136 N.H. 707, 621 A.2d 442, 1993 N.H. LEXIS 18 (1993); State v. McMinn, 141 N.H. 636, 690 A.2d 1017, 1997 N.H. LEXIS 11 (1997); In re Ryan D., 146 N.H. 644, 777 A.2d 881, 2001 N.H. LEXIS 127 (2001).

RESEARCH REFERENCES

New Hampshire Practice.

8-5 N.H.P. Personal Injury-Tort & Insurance Practice § 5.02.

New Hampshire Bar Journal.

For article, "Understanding and Representing Adult Clients Who Are Victims of Domestic Abuse," see 35 N.H.B.J. 8 (1994).

634:3. Unauthorized Use of Propelled Vehicle or Animal.

I. A person is guilty of a misdemeanor if, knowing that he does not have the consent of the owner, he takes, operates, exercises control over, or otherwise uses a propelled vehicle or animal. A person who engages in any such conduct without the consent of the owner is presumed to know that he does not have such consent.

II. As used in this section, "propelled vehicle" has the same meaning as in RSA 637:9, III.

Source.

1971, 518:1, eff. Nov. 1, 1973.

Cross References.

Classification of crimes, see RSA 625:9.

Sentences, see RSA 651.

Cited:

Cited in State v. Stevens, 121 N.H. 287, 428 A.2d 1241, 1981 N.H. LEXIS 303 (1981); State v. Guay, 130 N.H. 413, 543 A.2d 910, 1988 N.H. LEXIS 42 (1988).

RESEARCH REFERENCES

New Hampshire Trial Bar News.

For article, "Presumptions in New Hampshire Law—A Guide Through the Impenetrable Jungle (Part II)," see 11 N.H. Trial Bar News 31, 34 n.112 (Fall 1991).

CHAPTER 635

UNAUTHORIZED ENTRIES

SECTION
635:1.   Burglary.
635:2.   Criminal Trespass.
635:3.   Trespassing Stock.
635:4.   Prescribed Manner of Posting.
635:5.   Penalty.

Cemeteries, Burial Grounds, Gravestones

635:6.   Interference With Cemetery or Burial Ground.
635:7.   Unlawful Possession or Sale of Gravestones and Gravesite Items.
635:8.   Penalties.

635:1. Burglary.

I. A person is guilty of burglary if he enters a building or occupied structure, or separately secured or occupied section thereof, with purpose to commit a crime therein, unless the premises are at the time open to the public or the actor is licensed or privileged to enter. It is an affirmative defense to prosecution for burglary that the building or structure was abandoned.

II. Burglary is a class B felony unless it is perpetrated in the dwelling of another at night, or if, in the commission of the offense, attempt at commission or in flight immediately after attempt or commission, the actor is armed with a deadly weapon or explosives or he purposely, knowingly or recklessly inflicts bodily injury on anyone; in which case it is a class A felony; except that if the person is armed with a deadly weapon and the deadly weapon is a firearm, he shall be sentenced in accordance with RSA 651:2, II-g.

III. "Occupied structure" shall mean any structure, vehicle, boat or place adapted for overnight accommodation of persons, or for carrying on business therein, whether or not a person is actually present. "Night" shall mean the period between 30 minutes past sunset and 30 minutes before sunrise.

IV. A person may not be convicted both for burglary and for the offense which it was his purpose to commit after the burglarious entry or for an attempt to commit that offense, unless the additional offense constitutes a class A felony.

V. A person is guilty of a misdemeanor if he makes or mends, or begins to make or mend, or knowingly has in his possession, an engine, machine, tool, or implement adapted and designed for cutting through, forcing or breaking open a building, room, vault, safe, or other depository, in order to steal therefrom money or other property, or to commit any other crime, knowing the same to be adapted and designed for the purpose aforesaid, with intent to use or employ or allow the same to be used or employed for such purpose.

Source.

1971, 518:1. 1990, 95:4, eff. June 12, 1990.

Amendments

—1990. Paragraph II: Added "except that if the person is armed with a deadly weapon and the deadly weapon is a firearm, he shall be sentenced in accordance with RSA 651:2, II-g" following "class A felony".

Cross References.

Classification of crimes, see RSA 625:9.
First degree murder, see RSA 630:1-a.
Physical force in defense of a person, see RSA 627:4.
Sentences, see RSA 651.
Unauthorized entry with intent to commit sabotage, see RSA 649:4.

NOTES TO DECISIONS

1. Intent
2. Intended offenses
3. Knowledge
4. Definitions
5. Indictment
6. Evidence
7. Jury instructions
8. License or privilege

1. Intent

To prove a charge of possession of burglary tools, the intent that must be established is a general intent to use the tools for a burglarious purpose, whenever and wherever the opportunity might present itself. State v. MacDonald, 129 N.H. 13, 523 A.2d 35, 1986 N.H. LEXIS 375 (1986).

In order to establish the intent element on a charge of possession of burglary tools, it is not necessary that the accused possess the tools with the intent to commit a particular burglary. State v. MacDonald, 129 N.H. 13, 523 A.2d 35, 1986 N.H. LEXIS 375 (1986).

In order to establish the intent element on a charge of possession of burglary tools, the state need not link the defendant to any past or future burglary. State v. MacDonald, 129 N.H. 13, 523 A.2d 35, 1986 N.H. LEXIS 375 (1986).

In a prosecution for possession of burglary tools, burglarious intent can be inferred from the number and combination of tools found in the defendant's possession. State v. MacDonald, 129 N.H. 13, 523 A.2d 35, 1986 N.H. LEXIS 375 (1986).

In a prosecution for possession of burglary tools, intent to commit a burglary can be inferred from the circumstances under which the tools were found. State v. MacDonald, 129 N.H. 13, 523 A.2d 35, 1986 N.H. LEXIS 375 (1986).

In a prosecution for possession of burglary tools, general burglarious intent may be inferred from the circumstances accompanying the possession and from the character of the objects; such intent may not be presumed from possession alone, and circumstances must exist from which a jury could draw a legitimate inference that the defendant had the requisite intent to use the tools for a burglarious purpose. State v. MacDonald, 129 N.H. 13, 523 A.2d 35, 1986 N.H. LEXIS 375 (1986).

Proof of a completed larceny within an allegedly burglarized building is not essential to establish the criminal intent required by paragraph I of this section. State v. Meloon, 124 N.H. 257, 469 A.2d 1316, 1983 N.H. LEXIS 400 (1983).

In prosecution for burglary, the fact that the defendant was found without any stolen items in his possession at the time of apprehension was not controlling on the issue of his intent at the time of his entry into the allegedly burglarized building, because this section requires that a purpose to commit a crime be proven but does not require proof of successful completion of a crime. State v. Meloon, 124 N.H. 257, 469 A.2d 1316, 1983 N.H. LEXIS 400 (1983).

Where there was substantial evidence that defendant was intoxicated when he allegedly broke into and entered dwelling in the nighttime with intent to commit rape, and the crime charged was one of specific intent and intent was a separate element of the crime, the jury could consider whether intoxication could prevent the formation of the requisite intent and the trial court erred in not so charging the jury. State v. Caldrain, 115 N.H. 390, 342 A.2d 628, 1975 N.H. LEXIS 318 (1975).

Evidence of a completed larceny within premises allegedly burglarized is not essential to establish intent to commit a crime therein, and unexplained entry by breaking coupled with suspicious attempt to conceal while in yard was sufficient evidence of intent to commit a crime within house. State v. Reed, 114 N.H. 377, 321 A.2d 581, 1974 N.H. LEXIS 282 (1974). (Decided under prior law.)

2. Intended offenses

Where defendant was acquitted on two charges of receiving stolen property, paragraph IV of this section did not bar a subsequent prosecution of defendant for the burglary in which the allegedly stolen property was taken, since the prohibition in paragraph IV relates to multiple convictions, not prosecutions. State v. Wonyetye, 129 N.H. 452, 529 A.2d 927, 1987 N.H. LEXIS 212 (1987).

Paragraph IV of this section bars a conviction for an intended offense when that offense is the sole objective of the burglary, but when there is more than one objective, paragraph IV will operate to preclude a conviction for the intended offense specified in the burglary indictment but will not bar a conviction for additional offenses intended at the time of the burglarious entry. State v. Robidoux, 125 N.H. 169, 480 A.2d 67, 1984 N.H. LEXIS 360 (1984).

3. Knowledge

A motion to quash a complaint charging possession of burglar's tools under paragraph V of this section, on the ground that the complaint did not expressly charge the defendant with knowledge of the burglarious suitability of the tools, was properly denied where the complaint did charge intent to use the tools to commit a burglary; since the defendant could not reasonably be found to have intended to use his tools to commit a burglary without knowledge that the tools were appropriate for that purpose, charging the intent was sufficient to charge the knowledge. State v. Allard, 128 N.H. 437, 514 A.2d 824, 1986 N.H. LEXIS 310 (1986).

4. Definitions

A person is "privileged" within the meaning of paragraph I of this section if he may naturally be expected to be on the premises often and in the normal course of his duties or habits. State v. Thaxton, 120 N.H. 526, 419 A.2d 392, 1980 N.H. LEXIS 341 (1980).

Testimony by owner of burglarized house that he had stayed there weekend prior to burglary and that it was furnished and livable was sufficient to make house a building or occupied structure within the terms of this section. State v. Lovett, 116 N.H. 571, 364 A.2d 880, 1976 N.H. LEXIS 414 (1976).

5. Indictment

Trial court did not constructively amend the indictment for attempted burglary under RSA 635:1, RSA 626:8, and RSA 629:1 by refusing to instruct the jury that the State had to prove that defendant himself removed a window screen. Because the indictment clearly alleged both principal and accomplice liability, it provided sufficient notice that defendant was charged with either removing the window screen himself or soliciting, aiding or attempting to aid another in removing it; the indictment was more than sufficient for defendant to prepare his defense because it put him on notice that the State would have to prove that he in some way solicited, aided, agreed or attempted to aid in the attempted burglary State v. Winward, 161 N.H. 533, 20 A.3d 338, 2011 N.H. LEXIS 21 (2011).

Indictment for attempted burglary was not inadequate under N.H. Const. pt. I, art. 15 because it did not allege what crime

defendant would have committed in furtherance of the burglary. Charging a defendant with attempted burglary did not require the State to specify the offense the defendant would have committed in furtherance of the burglary; furthermore, juror unanimity was required only for the elements of attempted burglary, not as to the crime or offense defendant would have committed in furtherance of the burglary. State v. Munoz, 157 N.H. 143, 949 A.2d 155, 2008 N.H. LEXIS 47 (2008).

Burglary indictment that identified burglarized building and utilized the words of this section was sufficient even though it did not allege ownership of burglarized building. State v. Meloon, 119 N.H. 76, 397 A.2d 1041, 1979 N.H. LEXIS 234 (1979).

6. Evidence

Error in admitting post-arrest statements of co-conspirators under N.H. R. Evid. 801(d)(2)(E) was harmless as to defendant's conviction for conspiracy to commit burglary under RSA 629:3 and RSA 635:1. Given defendant's admission that he intended to go to the victim's residence to assault the victim as well as evidence that he enlisted the help of others to do so, the alternative evidence of his guilt was overwhelming. State v. Rodriguez, 164 N.H. 800, 64 A.3d 962, 2013 N.H. LEXIS 45 (2013).

Evidence was sufficient to convict defendant of attempted burglary under RSA 629:1 and RSA 635:1. A rational trier of fact could have found that defendant took a substantial step towards committing the crime of burglary when, without the victim's permission, he pulled on the door of her screened-in porch; a rational trier of fact could also have found that he acted with the specific intent of committing a crime inside the victim's home. State v. Gordon, 161 N.H. 410, 13 A.3d 201, 2011 N.H. LEXIS 6 (2011).

In a trial for attempted burglary under RSA 635:1, RSA 626:8, and RSA 629:1, the evidence revealed more than defendant's mere presence at the scene. A witness saw three men fleeing from his home and later identified them; he found a bent window screen in the grass and testified that he was sure that one of the men removed the screen; another witness heard three men having a "panicked" conversation and then saw them fleeing together; the three men, including defendant, were found hiding near the scene; and when police questioned defendant regarding the whereabouts of any accomplices, he was uncooperative, physically aggressive and used vulgar language. State v. Winward, 161 N.H. 533, 20 A.3d 338, 2011 N.H. LEXIS 21 (2011).

Evidence was sufficient to support a burglary conviction and thus did not preclude a new trial on double jeopardy grounds. Defendant lived in the same apartment building as the victim, who testified that he would stare in to her apartment; defendant could easily access the apartment; defendant appeared nervous during police questioning and contradicted himself as to whether he had left his apartment; defendant purchased a car with $100 bills the day after the robbery, and the money stolen was in $100 bills; and defendant's print matched a latent print on the victim's dresser. State v. Langill, 161 N.H. 218, 13 A.3d 171, 2010 N.H. LEXIS 143 (2010).

There was no merit to defendant's argument that the evidence was insufficient to support his burglary conviction because a witness never identified defendant as the man to whom she sold a car the day after the burglary. The victim sufficiently identified the man as defendant because she described him as a certain woman's boyfriend, and the evidence at trial established that defendant lived with that woman at the time of the burglary. State v. Langill, 161 N.H. 218, 13 A.3d 171, 2010 N.H. LEXIS 143 (2010).

When defendant was accused of burglarizing an apartment on which he had co-signed a lease, the jury could have found beyond a reasonable doubt that he did not possess license or privilege to enter the apartment based on his violent entry into it and the facts that he had moved out, removed his personal property, and no longer had a key. State v. McMillan, 158 N.H. 753, 973 A.2d 287, 2009 N.H. LEXIS 74 (2009).

In a burglary case, defendant's heroin addiction at the time of the crime was relevant under N.H. R. Evid. 404(b) to show that he entered the victim's home with the motive to steal, as there was strong circumstantial evidence identifying him as the perpetrator and a nexus between his addiction and his motive to steal. Moreover, the evidence was not unduly prejudicial. State v. Costello, 159 N.H. 113, 977 A.2d 454, 2009 N.H. LEXIS 92 (2009).

Lack of privilege or license to enter burglarized premises can be proven circumstantially without testimony from all owners or occupiers of premises. State v. Flynn, 144 N.H. 567, 744 A.2d 1131, 1999 N.H. LEXIS 157 (1999).

Although co-renter of hotel room did not testify at burglary trial, circumstantial evidence was sufficient to support exclusion of all rational conclusions except that defendant was neither licensed nor privileged to enter couple's hotel room. State v. Flynn, 144 N.H. 567, 744 A.2d 1131, 1999 N.H. LEXIS 157 (1999).

Circumstantial evidence at burglary trial, that defendant was seen gaining access to a store by breaking a window, that defendant sought egress through the back door when he was aware of a police presence at or in the store, and defendant's statement to the police that the store had "looked like a good place to break into" was sufficient to warrant jury in finding that defendant was neither licensed nor privileged to enter the building. State v. Blow, 135 N.H. 640, 608 A.2d 1309, 1992 N.H. LEXIS 98 (1992).

7. Jury instructions

In a trial for attempted burglary, the trial court did not err in not giving a "mere presence" instruction. Its instruction made clear that to find defendant guilty, the jury had to conclude that he in some way actively aided or participated in the attempted burglary. State v. Winward, 161 N.H. 533, 20 A.3d 338, 2011 N.H. LEXIS 21 (2011).

Where instructions to jury followed language of this section rather than indictment, which in exact wording referred to crime of theft, instructions did not prejudice defendant, because jury could not have been misled. State v. Reardon, 121 N.H. 604, 431 A.2d 796, 1981 N.H. LEXIS 363 (1981).

In burglary trial where trial judge, during his instructions to jury, fully explained all of the elements of burglary and twice stated that the state was required to prove that the defendant entered building with "the purpose to commit a crime therein," trial court's refusal to give instruction requested by defendant concerning the issue of his intent to commit a crime at the time he entered the building was not an abuse of discretion. State v. Meloon, 119 N.H. 76, 397 A.2d 1041, 1979 N.H. LEXIS 234 (1979).

8. License or privilege

Holding a legal interest in property, such as a leasehold, is not dispositive on the issue of license or privilege; the fact finder must look beyond legal title and evaluate the totality of the circumstances in determining whether a defendant had license or privilege to enter. Thus, when defendant entered an apartment on which he had co-signed the lease before moving out, the trial court properly instructed the jury that it could consider all of the evidence, including defendant's legal title to the property, in determining whether he had license or privilege to enter; the instruction also provided a list of relevant, although not exclusive, factors, such as defendant's method of entry, his past entries, and the length of his separation from the victim, which adequately conveyed to the jury the meaning of the license or privilege element. State v. McMillan, 158 N.H. 753, 973 A.2d 287, 2009 N.H. LEXIS 74 (2009).

Purpose of the burglary statute to protect the occupant of property is achieved only if entry is prohibited whenever the defendant has no license or privilege to enter, regardless of whether he thinks he has or not. Thus, the trial court properly declined to give an instruction on the State's burden to prove that defendant knew he was not licensed or privileged to enter an apartment. State v. McMillan, 158 N.H. 753, 973 A.2d 287, 2009 N.H. LEXIS 74 (2009).

While defendant had some proprietary interest in an apartment as a co-lessee, this fact did not automatically give him license to enter under RSA 635:1. Unlike an entry into a public area, the entry here interfered with the security and safety of the occupant, thus implicating the very interests the burglary statute was designed to protect. State v. McMillan, — N.H. —, 973 A.2d 287, 2009 N.H. LEXIS 74 (May 29, 2009).

Cited:

Cited in State v. Farris, 114 N.H. 355, 320 A.2d 642, 1974 N.H. LEXIS 277 (1974); State v. Hanley, 116 N.H. 235, 356 A.2d 687, 1976 N.H. LEXIS 317 (1976); State v. Floyd, 116 N.H. 632, 365 A.2d 738, 1976 N.H. LEXIS 432 (1976); State v. Lainey, 117 N.H. 592, 375 A.2d 1162, 1977 N.H. LEXIS 388 (1977); State v. Noel, 119 N.H. 522, 404 A.2d 290, 1979 N.H. LEXIS 347 (1979); State v. White, 119 N.H. 567, 406 A.2d 291, 1979 N.H. LEXIS 356 (1979); State v. Gullick, 120 N.H. 99, 411 A.2d 1113, 1980 N.H. LEXIS 237 (1980); State v. Stevens, 121 N.H. 287, 428 A.2d 1241, 1981 N.H. LEXIS 303 (1981); State v. Cyr, 122 N.H. 1155, 453 A.2d 1315, 1982 N.H. LEXIS 531 (1982); State v. Reynolds, 122 N.H. 1161, 453 A.2d 1319, 1982 N.H. LEXIS 532 (1982); State v. Settle, 123 N.H. 34, 455 A.2d 1031, 1983 N.H. LEXIS 218 (1983); State v. McDuffee, 123 N.H. 184, 459 A.2d 251, 1983 N.H. LEXIS 249 (1983); Heald v. Perrin, 123 N.H. 468, 464 A.2d 275, 1983 N.H. LEXIS 310 (1983); State v. Zysk, 123 N.H. 481, 465 A.2d 480, 1983 N.H. LEXIS 322 (1983); State v. Stoehrer, 123 N.H. 661, 465 A.2d 905, 1983 N.H. LEXIS 330 (1983); State v. Berube, 123 N.H. 771, 465 A.2d 509, 1983 N.H. LEXIS 348 (1983); State v. Copeland, 124 N.H. 90, 467 A.2d 238, 1983 N.H. LEXIS 367 (1983); State v. Palamia, 124 N.H. 333, 470 A.2d 906, 1983 N.H. LEXIS 392 (1983); State v. Leuthner, 124 N.H. 638, 474 A.2d 1029, 1984 N.H. LEXIS 226 (1984); State v. Chaisson, 125 N.H. 810, 486 A.2d 297, 1984 N.H. LEXIS 320 (1984); State v. Vanguilder, 126 N.H. 326, 493 A.2d 1116, 1985 N.H. LEXIS 326 (1985); State v. Maya, 126 N.H. 590, 493 A.2d 1139, 1985 N.H. LEXIS 347 (1985); State v. Sprague, 127 N.H. 97, 497 A.2d 1212, 1985 N.H. LEXIS 380 (1985); In re Allen R., 127 N.H. 718, 506 A.2d 329, 1986 N.H. LEXIS 210 (1986); State v. Wellman, 128 N.H. 340, 513 A.2d 944, 1986 N.H. LEXIS 294 (1986); State v. Jaroma, 128 N.H. 423, 514 A.2d 1274, 1986 N.H. LEXIS 304 (1986); State v. Rau, 129 N.H. 126, 523 A.2d 98, 1987 N.H. LEXIS 154 (1987); State v. Meaney, 129 N.H. 448, 529 A.2d 384, 1987 N.H. LEXIS 193 (1987); State v. Pierce, 130 N.H. 7, 533 A.2d 34, 1987 N.H. LEXIS 252 (1987); State v. Coppola, 130 N.H. 148, 536 A.2d 1236, 1987 N.H. LEXIS 298 (1987); State v. Surette, 130 N.H. 531, 544 A.2d 823, 1988 N.H. LEXIS 38 (1988); State v. Reynolds, 131 N.H. 291, 556 A.2d 298, 1988 N.H. LEXIS 128 (1988); State v. Sampson, 132 N.H. 343, 565 A.2d 1040, 1989 N.H. LEXIS 104 (1989); State v. Fecteau, 132 N.H. 646, 568 A.2d 1187, 1990 N.H. LEXIS 1 (1990); State v. Jernigan, 133 N.H. 396, 577 A.2d 1214, 1990 N.H. LEXIS 78 (1990); State v. Letendre, 133 N.H. 555, 579 A.2d 1223, 1990 N.H. LEXIS 103 (1990); State v. Collins, 133 N.H. 609, 581 A.2d 69, 1990 N.H. LEXIS 115 (1990); State v. Whittey, 134 N.H. 310, 591 A.2d 1326, 1991 N.H. LEXIS 58 (1991); State v. Patten, 134 N.H. 319, 591 A.2d 1329, 1991 N.H. LEXIS 61 (1991); State v. Giordano, 134 N.H. 718, 599 A.2d 109, 1991 N.H. LEXIS 136 (1991); State v. Kiewert, 135 N.H. 338, 605 A.2d 1031, 1992 N.H. LEXIS 45 (1992); State v. Jaroma, 137 N.H. 143, 625 A.2d 1049, 1993 N.H. LEXIS 54 (1993); State v. Noel, 137 N.H. 384, 628 A.2d 692, 1993 N.H. LEXIS 88 (1993); State v. Yates, 137 N.H. 495, 629 A.2d 807, 1993 N.H. LEXIS 109 (1993); State v. Patten, 137 N.H. 627, 631 A.2d 921, 1993 N.H. LEXIS 134 (1993); State v. Giordano, 138 N.H. 90, 635 A.2d 482, 1993 N.H. LEXIS 172 (1993); State v. Panzera, 139 N.H. 235, 652 A.2d 136, 1994 N.H. LEXIS 138 (1994); State v. Fecteau, 140 N.H. 498, 667 A.2d 1384, 1995 N.H. LEXIS 178 (1995); United States v. Field, 39 F.3d 15, 1994 U.S. App. LEXIS 30689 (1st Cir. N.H. 1994); Millette v. Warden, N.H. State Prison, 141 N.H. 653, 692 A.2d 963, 1997 N.H. LEXIS 16 (1997); State v. Langill, 157 N.H. 77, 945 A.2d 1, 2008 N.H. LEXIS 39 (2008).

635:2. Criminal Trespass.

I. A person is guilty of criminal trespass if, knowing that he is not licensed or privileged to do so, he enters or remains in any place.

II. Criminal trespass is a misdemeanor for the first offense and a class B felony for any subsequent offense if the person knowingly or recklessly causes damage in excess of $1,500 to the value of the property of another.

III. Criminal trespass is a misdemeanor if:

   (a) The trespass takes place in an occupied structure as defined in RSA 635:1, III; or

   (b) The person knowingly enters or remains:

      (1) In any secured premises;

      (2) In any place in defiance of an order to leave or not to enter which was personally communicated to him by the owner or other autho-

rized person; or

    (3) In any place in defiance of any court order restraining him from entering such place so long as he has been properly notified of such order.

IV. All other criminal trespass is a violation.

V. In this section, "secured premises" means any place which is posted in a manner prescribed by law or in a manner reasonably likely to come to the attention of intruders, or which is fenced or otherwise enclosed in a manner designed to exclude intruders.

VI. In this section, "property," "property of another," and "value" shall be as defined in RSA 637:2, I, IV, and V, respectively.

Source.
1971, 518:1. 1979, 377:7, eff. Aug. 22, 1979. 2005, 125:1, eff. January 1, 2006. 2010, 239:2, eff. July 1, 2010.

Amendments
—2010. The 2010 amendment substituted "$1,500" for "$1,000" in II.

—2005. Added new par. II, redesignated former pars. II through IV as pars. III through V, and added par. VI, and in present par. V, deleted "as used" preceding "in this section".

—1979. Paragraph II(b)(3): Added.

Cross References.
Classification of crimes, see RSA 625:9.
Prescribed manner of posting, see RSA 635:4.
Sentences, see RSA 651.
Use of force to prevent or terminate criminal trespass, see RSA 627:7.
Violating temporary restraining order by committing criminal trespass, see RSA 458:16.

NOTES TO DECISIONS

1. Elements of offense
2. Eviction
3. Hunters
4. Jury instructions
5. Probable cause for arrest

1. Elements of offense
Because defendant's brother-in-law and his family had lived with the mother-in-law at her home for eight or nine years, he was an "authorized person" under RSA 635:2 who could exclude defendant, a non-resident, from the premises; therefore, the evidence was sufficient to sustain defendant's conviction for criminal trespass. State v. Ruff, 155 N.H. 536, 927 A.2d 489, 2007 N.H. LEXIS 91 (2007).

When defendant refused to leave the police station after being asked to do so, there was sufficient evidence to convict defendant of criminal trespass under former RSA 635:2, II(b) (now RSA 635:2, III(b)), because defendant received strong warnings to leave the station or risk being arrested. State v. Gaffney, 147 N.H. 550, 795 A.2d 243, 2002 N.H. LEXIS 24 (2002).

An essential element of the crime of criminal trespass is that the defendant know that he was not licensed or privileged to remain on the property. State v. Wentworth, 118 N.H. 832, 395 A.2d 858, 1978 N.H. LEXIS 302 (1978).

Even assuming defendant was invited onto nuclear power plant construction site, that fact had no bearing upon charge that she knew she was not licensed or privileged to remain on the property and that she improperly remained on the site after an order to leave was communicated to her. State v. Dupuy, 118 N.H. 848, 395 A.2d 851, 1978 N.H. LEXIS 304 (1978).

2. Eviction
That mortgagee had commenced a possessory action under RSA 540 did not bar mortgagee from availing itself of this section to evict mortgagor from the premises, since RSA 540:26 expressly reserved other remedies at common law and criminal trespass statutes merely codify such common law. Dieffenbach v. Buckley, 464 F. Supp. 670, 1979 U.S. Dist. LEXIS 14797 (D.N.H. 1979).

3. Hunters
A hunter may enter upon improved land of another and discharge firearms during a certain period of the year unless such land is posted. State v. Jenkins, 102 N.H. 545, 162 A.2d 613, 1960 N.H. LEXIS 76 (1960). (Decided under prior law.)

4. Jury instructions
Where trial judge, charging jury on elements of criminal trespass, first read aloud complaint which tracked this section word for word, then read this section to the jury, extensively explained this section and the words "knowing" and "knowingly" as those words appeared in this section, and explained the other elements of the offense, it was improbable that jury misunderstood. State v. Dupuy, 118 N.H. 848, 395 A.2d 851, 1978 N.H. LEXIS 304 (1978).

5. Probable cause for arrest
There was probable cause for defendant's arrest for criminal trespass. An officer received information that two men with a rental truck were parked at her home, the owners of which were out of town; when an officer approached the property, defendant immediately yelled something and got into a car; defendant appeared extremely nervous and admitted that he came to the property with the second man; the property owner called the officer and told him that the second man knew he was not supposed to be on the property and that she wanted both men arrested; and the officer knew that defendant had rented the truck and driven it to the property. State v. Newcomb, 161 N.H. 666, 20 A.3d 881, 2011 N.H. LEXIS 46 (2011).

Cited:
Cited in Daneker v. State, 117 N.H. 380, 373 A.2d 1322, 1977 N.H. LEXIS 341 (1977); State v. Linsky, 117 N.H. 866, 379 A.2d 813, 1977 N.H. LEXIS 450 (1977); State v. Cole, 118 N.H. 829, 395 A.2d 189, 1978 N.H. LEXIS 301 (1978); State v. Dorsey, 118 N.H. 844, 395 A.2d 855, 1978 N.H. LEXIS 303 (1978); State v. Koski, 120 N.H. 112, 411 A.2d 1122, 1980 N.H. LEXIS 240 (1980); State v. Gorman, 120 N.H. 685, 421 A.2d 141, 1980 N.H. LEXIS 378 (1980); State v. Brady, 120 N.H. 899, 424 A.2d 407, 1980 N.H. LEXIS 417 (1980); Koski v. Samaha, 648 F.2d 790, 1981 U.S. App. LEXIS 13062 (1st Cir. 1981); State v. Weitzman, 121 N.H. 83, 427 A.2d 3, 1981 N.H. LEXIS 265 (1981); Brady v. Samaha, 667 F.2d 224, 1981 U.S. App. LEXIS 15036 (1st Cir. N.H. 1981); State v. Chaisson, 125 N.H. 810, 486 A.2d 297, 1984 N.H. LEXIS 320 (1984); State v. Gagne, 129 N.H. 93, 523 A.2d 76, 1986 N.H. LEXIS 380 (1986); State v. Maguire, 129 N.H. 165, 523 A.2d 120, 1987 N.H. LEXIS 161 (1987); Kay v. New Hampshire Democratic Party, 821 F.2d 31, 1987 U.S. App. LEXIS 7635 (1st Cir. N.H. 1987); State v. Meaney, 129 N.H. 448, 529 A.2d 384, 1987 N.H. LEXIS 193 (1987); State v. Collins, 133 N.H. 609, 581 A.2d 69, 1990 N.H. LEXIS 115 (1990); State v. Mansfield, 134 N.H. 287, 592 A.2d 512, 1991 N.H. LEXIS 54 (1991); State v. Ellison, 135 N.H. 1, 599 A.2d 477, 1991 N.H. LEXIS 132 (1991); State v. Steed, 140 N.H. 153, 665 A.2d 1072, 1995 N.H. LEXIS 115 (1995).

RESEARCH REFERENCES

New Hampshire Bar Journal.
For article, "Understanding and Representing Adult Clients Who Are Victims of Domestic Abuse," see 35 N.H.B.J. 8 (1994).

635:3. Trespassing Stock.

If any person having the charge or custody of any sheep, goats, cattle, horses, or swine shall knowingly, recklessly, or negligently suffer or permit the same to enter upon, pass over, or remain upon any improved or enclosed land of another without written permission of the owner, occupant, or his agent, and thereby injures his crops, or property, he shall be guilty of a violation.

Source.
1971, 518:1, eff. Nov. 1, 1973.

Cross References.
Animals running at large, see RSA 467.
Classification of crimes, see RSA 625:9.
Sentences, see RSA 651.

635:4. Prescribed Manner of Posting.

A person may post his land to prohibit criminal trespass and physical activities by posting signs of durable material with any words describing the physical activity prohibited, such as "No Hunting or Trespassing", printed with block letters no less than 2 inches in height, and with the name and address of the owner or lessee of such land. Such signs shall be posted not more than 100 yards apart on all sides and shall also be posted at gates, bars and commonly used entrances. This section shall not prevent any owner from adding to the language required by this section.

Source.
1977, 284:1, eff. Aug. 21, 1977.

635:5. Penalty.

Any person who is found removing, defacing or destroying any sign, poster or property of another shall be guilty of a class B misdemeanor.

Source.
1977, 284:1. 1992, 269:13, eff. July 1, 1992.

Amendments
—**1992.** Inserted "class B" preceding "misdemeanor".

Applicability of 1992 amendment.
1992, 269:21, eff. July 1, 1992, provided that the amendment to this section by 1992, 269:13, shall apply to all offenses committed on or after July 1, 1992.

Cross References.
Classification of crimes, see RSA 625:9.
Sentences, see RSA 651.

Cemeteries, Burial Grounds, Gravestones

Cross References.
Cemeteries generally, see RSA 289.
Burials and disinterments generally, see RSA 290.

635:6. Interference With Cemetery or Burial Ground.

I. No person, without the written authorization of the owner of a burial plot, or the lineal descendant of the deceased, if such owner or lineal descendant is known, or the written authorization of the governing board of the municipality in which the burial plot lies, if the owner or lineal descendant is unknown, shall:

(a) Purposely or knowingly destroy, mutilate, injure or remove any tomb, monument, gravestone, marker, or other structure, or any portion or fragment thereof, placed or designed for a memorial of the dead, or any fence, railing, gate, curb, or plot delineator or other enclosure for the burial of the dead.

(b) Purposely or knowingly disturb the contents of any tomb or grave in any cemetery or burial ground.

II. The governing board of the municipality in which the burial plot lies shall not grant approval for the removal or disturbance of a tomb, monument, gravestone, marker, or plot delineator without first giving 30 days' notice, along with a report of the full circumstances, to the division of historical resources, that such approval has been requested. The governing board of the municipality shall maintain a record of the date, circumstances, and disposition of the request for removal or disturbance.

Source.
1987, 107:1, eff. May 6, 1987.

Cross References.
Abuse of corpse, see RSA 644:7.

635:7. Unlawful Possession or Sale of Gravestones and Gravesite Items.

No person shall possess or sell, offer for sale or attempt to sell, or transfer or dispose of any monument, gravestone, marker, or other structure, or any portion or fragment thereof, placed or designed for a memorial of the dead, or any fence, railing, gate, plot delineator, or curb, knowing or having reasonable cause to know that it has been unlawfully removed from a cemetery or burial ground.

Source.
1987, 107:1, eff. May 6, 1987.

635:8. Penalties.

Any person who is convicted of an offense under RSA 635:6 or 635:7 shall be guilty of a class B felony, and shall be ordered by the court to make restitution for damages resulting from the offense and for replacement of removed items.

Source.
1987, 107:1, eff. May 6, 1987.

Cross References.
Classification of crimes, see RSA 625:9.
Sentences, see RSA 651.

CHAPTER 636

ROBBERY

SECTION
636:1. Robbery.

636:1. Robbery.

I. A person commits the offense of robbery if, in the course of committing a theft, he:

(a) Uses physical force on the person of another and such person is aware of such force; or

(b) Threatens another with or purposely puts him in fear of immediate use of physical force.

II. An act shall be deemed "in the course of committing a theft" if it occurs in an attempt to commit theft, in an effort to retain the stolen property immediately after its taking, or in immediate flight after the attempt or commission.

III. Robbery is a class B felony, except that if the defendant:

(a) Was actually armed with a deadly weapon; or

(b) Reasonably appeared to the victim to be armed with a deadly weapon; or

(c) Inflicted or attempted to inflict death or serious injury on the person of another,
the offense is a class A felony, except that if the defendant was actually armed with a deadly weapon, and the deadly weapon was a firearm, he shall be sentenced in accordance with RSA 651:2, II-g.

Source.
1971, 518:1. 1990, 95:5, eff. June 12, 1990.

Amendments
—1990. Paragraph III: Added "except that if the defendant was actually armed with a deadly weapon, and the deadly weapon was a firearm, he shall be sentenced in accordance with RSA 651:2, II-g" following "class A felony".

Cross References.
Classification of crimes, see RSA 625:9.
First degree murder, see RSA 630:1-a.
Sentences, see RSA 651.
Theft, see RSA 637.
Use of force in property offenses, see RSA 627:8.

NOTES TO DECISIONS

1. Construction with other laws
2. Elements
3. Force
4. Classification of offense
5. Indictment
6. Double jeopardy
7. Evidence
8. Jury instructions

1. Construction with other laws

A pickpocket who merely snatches a wallet without using force of which the victim is aware has committed a theft but not a robbery. State v. Goodrum, 123 N.H. 77, 455 A.2d 1067, 1983 N.H. LEXIS 227 (1983).

2. Elements

Presence of one of three aggravating factors set forth in paragraph III of this section is an essential element of the class A felony of armed robbery. State v. Corey, 127 N.H. 56, 497 A.2d 1196, 1985 N.H. LEXIS 400 (1985).

Serious bodily injury as an element of robbery as a class A felony need not be inflicted in the course of the theft, provided that some force is used in the course of the theft and the infliction of serious bodily injury occurs at some point during the robbery. State v. Thresher, 122 N.H. 63, 442 A.2d 578, 1982 N.H. LEXIS 288 (1982).

To be guilty of armed robbery, a defendant must be actually armed with a deadly weapon, reasonably appear to the victim to be armed with a deadly weapon, or inflict or attempt to inflict death or serious bodily injury on another. State v. Burke, 122 N.H. 565, 448 A.2d 962, 1982 N.H. LEXIS 401 (1982).

The crime of robbery is the felonious taking from the person of another, by assault, or by violence and putting in fear. State v. Skillings, 98 N.H. 203, 97 A.2d 202, 1953 N.H. LEXIS 49 (1953). (Decided under prior law.)

3. Force

Any forcible taking of property from the possession of another by means which overcome resistance, however slight, is a taking by the infliction of actual injury, and so is by assault, and evidence of such taking will support a conviction for robbery. State v. Gorham, 55 N.H. 152, 1875 N.H. LEXIS 55 (1875). (Decided under prior law.)

4. Classification of offense

To upgrade the offense of robbery to a class A felony, at least one of the additional elements set out in paragraph III of this section must be specified in the indictment. State v. Shannon, 125 N.H. 653, 484 A.2d 1164, 1984 N.H. LEXIS 380 (1984).

5. Indictment

Indictment which failed to make any reference to intended victim was legally insufficient to charge defendant with attempted armed robbery, and trial court's instruction supplying that reference was an improper amendment of the indictment in violation of New Hampshire constitution. State v. Glanville, 145 N.H. 631, 765 A.2d 173, 2000 N.H. LEXIS 114 (2000).

The trial court impermissibly amended the indictment against the defendant where the indictment charged that the defendant, "in the course of committing a theft, ... purposely put [the victim] in fear of the immediate use of physical force by pointing a black colored revolver (a firearm) at him," and the court instructed the jury that they could convict the defendant if, inter alia, the defendant reasonably appeared to the victim to be armed with a deadly weapon. State v. Prevost, 141 N.H. 559, 689 A.2d 121, 1997 N.H. LEXIS 1 (1997).

An indictment charging a defendant with conduct amounting to a class A felony under paragraph III of this section must adequately inform defendant that he is being charged with that specific offense. State v. Shannon, 125 N.H. 653, 484 A.2d 1164, 1984 N.H. LEXIS 380 (1984).

Indictment which alleged that defendant purposely used physical force on another person by striking him about the head with a blunt instrument while demanding United States currency and that the person was aware of such force specified facts sufficient to inform defendant that he was charged with a class B felony under paragraph I of this section. State v. Shannon, 125 N.H. 653, 484 A.2d 1164, 1984 N.H. LEXIS 380 (1984).

An indictment charging robbery wherein the value of the goods alleged to have been taken is described as "Eighteen ($18.00) Dollars of the lawful currency and money of the United States of America of the value of Eighteen ($18.00) Dollars" is a sufficient description of the goods taken, it being unnecessary to describe each bill or coin in minute detail. State v. Canatella, 96 N.H. 202, 72 A.2d 507, 1950 N.H. LEXIS 144 (1950). (Decided under prior law.)

Since the gist of the offense of robbery is force and intimidation, particular allegations of the value of the property taken are less material than they would be if the charge were larceny. State v. Canatella, 96 N.H. 202, 72 A.2d 507, 1950 N.H. LEXIS 144 (1950).

(Decided under prior law.)

Where an indictment for robbery alleges force and intimidation but fails to make any reference to the use of guns by the accused, evidence by the complaining witness that guns were used by the accused in the commission of the robbery is admissible as a matter of identification of the particular accused, where other evidence introduced prior to this time showed that on that day the accused had a gun in his possession. State v. Canatella, 96 N.H. 202, 72 A.2d 507, 1950 N.H. LEXIS 144 (1950). (Decided under prior law.)

An indictment which charges the commission of the offense of robbery, which in its nature includes other inferior offenses, is not, for that reason, multifarious; a single count in an indictment may allege all the circumstances necessary to constitute two different crimes, where the offense described is a complicated one comprehending in itself many circumstances each of which is an offense when taken alone. State v. Gorham, 55 N.H. 152, 1875 N.H. LEXIS 55 (1875). (Decided under prior law.)

Where goods are stolen from the possession of a bailee, they may be described in the indictment charging robbery as the property of the bailor or of the bailee, although the goods were never in the real owner's possession but in that of the bailee only. State v. Gorham, 55 N.H. 152, 1875 N.H. LEXIS 55 (1875). (Decided under prior law.)

6. Double jeopardy

Defendant's armed robbery of jewelry store clerk and theft from store constituted two distinct acts involving different property and separated in time and space, and therefore evidence was sufficient to support two separate convictions without violating double jeopardy. State v. Ford, 144 N.H. 57, 738 A.2d 937, 1999 N.H. LEXIS 71 (1999).

Defendant committed theft when he removed diamond and sapphire from jewelry store display cases, and he then committed robbery when he threatened clerk with gun and demanded her bracelet and pendant; theft and robbery were separate acts of taking distinct from each other and each supported by its own set of facts, and separate sentences for theft and robbery were therefore not prohibited by "single larceny rule." State v. Ford, 144 N.H. 57, 738 A.2d 937, 1999 N.H. LEXIS 71 (1999).

Defendant's convictions for armed robbery under this section and assault under RSA 631:2 did not violate the double jeopardy clause of the federal constitution, since proof that defendant used physical force while in the course of committing theft is essential to a conviction for armed robbery, but it is not necessary that defendant be in the course of committing theft for a conviction under RSA 631:2, and the state must establish that defendant caused bodily injury to obtain a conviction under RSA 631:2, while bodily injury is not essential to a conviction for armed robbery. State v. Shannon, 125 N.H. 653, 484 A.2d 1164, 1984 N.H. LEXIS 380 (1984).

Where plaintiff was convicted of robbery while armed with a deadly weapon and of the felonious use of a firearm under RSA 650-A:1, where not a single difference in evidence was required, as the offenses were charged and proven in this case, the conviction for the felonious use of a firearm could not be supported under the double jeopardy clause of the state constitution. Heald v. Perrin, 123 N.H. 468, 464 A.2d 275, 1983 N.H. LEXIS 310 (1983), superseded by statute as stated in, State v. Nickles, 144 N.H. 673, 749 A.2d 290, 2000 N.H. LEXIS 9 (2000). (Superseded by statute, see RSA 651:2, II-g.)

7. Evidence

There was sufficient evidence to support defendant's conviction for being an accomplice to armed robbery when a witness testified that defendant told her and a decedent that he wanted to commit robbery, traveled with them to the house in question, directed her to park behind the house, and wore a ski mask and armed himself. Furthermore, defendant admitted that he was inside the house during the robbery and used force against the victim; a ski mask and a rubber glove recovered from the scene contained defendant's DNA; and the decedent was found wearing rubber gloves with a baseball bat nearby. State v. Noucas, — N.H. —, 70 A.3d 476, 2013 N.H. LEXIS 83 (July 16, 2013).

In defendant's trial for robbery, a trial court gave insufficient weight to the fact that the victim twice identified defendant as the man who attempted to rob him at knife point and gave too much weight to the discrepancies between the victim's description and defendant's actual attributes. As a rational juror could have found beyond a reasonable doubt that defendant robbed the victim, the identification evidence was sufficient to support the guilty verdict, and the due process and double jeopardy clauses were not violated; no objective basis sustained the trial court's conclusion that the victim's description varied too greatly from defendant's actual physical attributes such that the actual perpetrator was defendant's associate and not defendant. State v. Spinale, 156 N.H. 456, 937 A.2d 938, 2007 N.H. LEXIS 209 (2007).

For the state to prove that defendant committed the offense of armed robbery, it was necessary for the state to introduce evidence that the defendant was armed with a deadly weapon or reasonably appeared to be armed with a deadly weapon. State v. Wheeler, 132 N.H. 552, 567 A.2d 996, 1989 N.H. LEXIS 148 (1989).

The offense of robbery is sustained by proof of a felonious taking of property from the person of another by assault, although without putting the victim in fear. State v. Gorham, 55 N.H. 152, 1875 N.H. LEXIS 55 (1875). (Decided under prior law.)

8. Jury instructions

Trial court instructions to the jury on charge of robbery which separated the act of serious bodily injury and the act of force in conjunction with the theft were consistent with this section. State v. Thresher, 122 N.H. 63, 442 A.2d 578, 1982 N.H. LEXIS 288 (1982).

Cited:

Cited in State v. Lordan, 116 N.H. 479, 363 A.2d 201, 1976 N.H. LEXIS 387 (1976); State v. Dunbar, 117 N.H. 904, 379 A.2d 831, 1977 N.H. LEXIS 455 (1977); State v. Fraser, 120 N.H. 117, 411 A.2d 1125, 1980 N.H. LEXIS 241 (1980); State v. Heald, 120 N.H. 319, 414 A.2d 1288, 1980 N.H. LEXIS 273 (1980); State v. Perron, 122 N.H. 941, 454 A.2d 422, 1982 N.H. LEXIS 496 (1982); State v. Fernald, 123 N.H. 442, 462 A.2d 122, 1983 N.H. LEXIS 302 (1983); State v. Woodbury, 124 N.H. 218, 469 A.2d 1302, 1983 N.H. LEXIS 385 (1983); State v. Scarborough, 124 N.H. 363, 470 A.2d 909, 1983 N.H. LEXIS 417 (1983); State v. Beaudette, 124 N.H. 579, 474 A.2d 1012, 1984 N.H. LEXIS 355 (1984); State v. Crosman, 125 N.H. 527, 484 A.2d 1095, 1984 N.H. LEXIS 401 (1984); State v. Benoit, 126 N.H. 6, 490 A.2d 295, 1985 N.H. LEXIS 240 (1985); State v. Pierce, 126 N.H. 84, 489 A.2d 109, 1985 N.H. LEXIS 278 (1985); State v. Mayo, 127 N.H. 67, 497 A.2d 853, 1985 N.H. LEXIS 391 (1985); Colpitt v. Cunningham, 638 F. Supp. 1277, 1986 U.S. Dist. LEXIS 22572 (D.N.H. 1986); Lovely v. Cunningham, 796 F.2d 1, 1986 U.S. App. LEXIS 26377 (1st Cir. N.H. 1986); State v. Elbert, 128 N.H. 210, 512 A.2d 1114, 1986 N.H. LEXIS 280 (1986); State v. Dellorfano, 128 N.H. 628, 517 A.2d 1163, 1986 N.H. LEXIS 343 (1986); State v. Cross, 128 N.H. 732, 519 A.2d 272, 1986 N.H. LEXIS 351 (1986); State v. MacDonald, 129 N.H. 13, 523 A.2d 35, 1986 N.H. LEXIS 375 (1986); State v. Sullivan, 130 N.H. 64, 534 A.2d 384, 1987 N.H. LEXIS 279 (1987); State v. Riccio, 130 N.H. 376, 540 A.2d 1239, 1988 N.H. LEXIS 8 (1988); State v. Houtenbrink, 130 N.H. 385, 539 A.2d 714, 1988 N.H. LEXIS 17 (1988); State v. Guay, 130 N.H. 413, 543 A.2d 910, 1988 N.H. LEXIS 42 (1988); State v. Hamel, 130 N.H. 615, 547 A.2d 223, 1988 N.H. LEXIS 76 (1988); State v. Rathbun, 132 N.H. 28, 561 A.2d 505, 1989 N.H. LEXIS 54 (1989); State v. Dandurant, 132 N.H. 617, 567 A.2d 592, 1989 N.H. LEXIS 147 (1989); State v. Wheeler, 132 N.H. 552, 567 A.2d 996, 1989 N.H. LEXIS 148 (1989); State v. Letendre, 133 N.H. 555, 579 A.2d 1223, 1990 N.H. LEXIS 103 (1990); State v. Smagula, 133 N.H. 600, 578 A.2d 1215, 1990 N.H. LEXIS 107 (1990); State v. Torrence, 134 N.H. 24, 587 A.2d 1227, 1991 N.H. LEXIS 14 (1991); State v. Rezk, 135 N.H. 599, 609 A.2d 391, 1992 N.H. LEXIS 89 (1992); State v. Morales, 136 N.H. 616, 620 A.2d 1034, 1993 N.H. LEXIS 2 (1993); State v. Barton, 142 N.H. 391, 702 A.2d 336, 1997 N.H. LEXIS 109 (1997); State v. Williams, 143 N.H. 559, 729 A.2d 416, 1999 N.H. LEXIS 44 (1999); State v. Hatt, 144 N.H. 246, 740 A.2d 1037, 1999 N.H. LEXIS 107 (1999); State v. Velez, 150 N.H. 589, 842 A.2d 97, 2004 N.H. LEXIS 35 (2004); State v. Belton, 150 N.H. 741, 846 A.2d 526, 2004 N.H. LEXIS 67 (2004).

CHAPTER 637

THEFT

SECTION
637:1.   Consolidation.
637:2.   Definitions.
637:3.   Theft by Unauthorized Taking or Transfer.
637:3-a.   Willful Concealment.
637:4.   Theft by Deception.
637:5.   Theft by Extortion.
637:6.   Theft of Lost or Mislaid Property.
637:7.   Receiving Stolen Property.
637:7-a.   Possession of Property Without Serial Number.
637:8.   Theft of Services.
637:9.   Unauthorized Use of Propelled Vehicle or Rented Property.
637:10.   Theft by Misapplication of Property.
637:10-a. Use or Possession of Theft Detection Shielding Devices and Theft Detection Device Removers.
637:10-b. Fraudulent Retail Transactions.
637:10-c. Organized Retail Crime Enterprise.
637:11.   Penalties.

Cross References.
Insurance fraud, see RSA 638:20.
Robbery, see RSA 636:1.
Use of force in property offenses, see RSA 627:8.
Willful concealment and shoplifting, see RSA 644:17.

637:1. Consolidation.

Conduct denominated theft in this chapter constitutes a single offense embracing the separate offenses such as those heretofore known as larceny, larceny by trick, larceny by bailees, embezzlement, false pretense, extortion, blackmail, receiving stolen property. An accusation of theft may be supported by evidence that it was committed in any manner that would be theft under this chapter, notwithstanding the specification of a different manner in the indictment or information.

Source.
1971, 518:1, eff. Nov. 1, 1973.

NOTES TO DECISIONS

1. Construction
2. Pleadings
3. Forgery

1. Construction

Since the term "theft" was broadly-defined to include crimes "such as" larceny, embezzlement, false pretense, extortion, blackmail, and receiving stolen property, the list of crimes was merely illustrative rather than exhaustive; as a result, the term "theft" could include burglary with the purpose to commit a theft for the purpose of determining whether that crime qualified as a predicate theft offense for sentence enhancement purposes. Derosia v. Warden, N.H. State Prison, 149 N.H. 579, 826 A.2d 575, 2003 N.H. LEXIS 78 (2003), rehearing denied, 2003 N.H. LEXIS 111 (N.H. July 18, 2003).

Where defendant convicted of larceny of property in Massachusetts was also charged in New Hampshire with retaining the same property which he stole in Massachusetts, the plain language and legislative history of this section rebutted the defendant's assertion that the charge of retaining stolen property could not be prosecuted independently from the larceny charge. State v. McNally, 122 N.H. 892, 451 A.2d 1305, 1982 N.H. LEXIS 487 (1982).

Words "such as," in this section, render the list of crimes enumerated illustrative rather than exhaustive, so that prior conviction for forgery of check could be regarded as theft under this chapter. State v. Partlow, 117 N.H. 78, 369 A.2d 221, 1977 N.H. LEXIS 274 (1977).

2. Pleadings

Argument was rejected that the addition of certain facts in a bill of particulars for the indicted offense of theft by unauthorized taking introduced a different theory of the offense, changing it to theft by deception, since defendant was later tried and convicted for theft by unauthorized taking, and since this section provides that accusation of theft may be supported by evidence that it was committed in any manner that would be theft, notwithstanding the specification of a different manner in the indictment or information. State v. Stearns, 130 N.H. 475, 547 A.2d 672, 1988 N.H. LEXIS 72 (1988).

While this section allows great latitude in the proof that may suffice under a charge of theft and eliminates the need for formal pleading by multiple counts, indictments or complaints to ensure against the contingencies of proof, the utility of the statute is limited by the defendant's right, under State v. Harlan, 116 N.H. 598, 364 A.2d 1254, 1976 N.H. LEXIS 423 (1976), to fair notice sufficient to allow him to prepare a defense, and it does not follow from the fact that multiple pleadings may not be required that they should be forbidden. State v. Allison, 126 N.H. 111, 489 A.2d 620, 1985 N.H. LEXIS 255 (1985).

When the state wishes to leave open the possibility of proving more than one statutory method of committing theft, the preferred method of guarding against unfair or prejudicial surprise to the defendant is a formal statement of alternative charges at the start of the case. (Overruling State v. Harlan, 116 N.H. 598, 364 A.2d 1254, 1976 N.H. LEXIS 423 (1976), to the extent that it eliminated the possibility of alternative charges of theft arising from a single act or transaction.) State v. Allison, 126 N.H. 111, 489 A.2d 620, 1985 N.H. LEXIS 255 (1985).

3. Forgery

Because under prior law, defendant's prior conviction for check forgery in amount of $48.45 was equivalent to conviction of crime of false pretense, it could be regarded as theft for purposes of this section. State v. Partlow, 117 N.H. 78, 369 A.2d 221, 1977 N.H. LEXIS 274 (1977).

Cited:

Cited in State v. Hill, 115 N.H. 37, 332 A.2d 182, 1975 N.H. LEXIS 217 (1975); State v. Harlan, 116 N.H. 598, 364 A.2d 1254, 1976 N.H. LEXIS 423 (1976); Partlow v. Perrin, 117 N.H. 957, 379 A.2d 1273, 1977 N.H. LEXIS 470 (1977); State v. Harper, 126 N.H. 815, 498 A.2d 310, 1985 N.H. LEXIS 409 (1985); State v. Wonyetye, 129 N.H. 452, 529 A.2d 927, 1987 N.H. LEXIS 212 (1987).

637:2. Definitions.

The following definitions are applicable to this chapter:

I. "Property" means anything of value, including real estate, tangible and intangible personal property, captured or domestic animals and birds, written instruments or other writings representing or embodying rights concerning real or personal property, labor, services, or otherwise containing any thing of value to the owner, commodities of a public utility nature such as telecommunications, gas, electricity, steam, or water, and trade secrets, meaning the whole or any portion of any scientific or technical information, design, process, procedure, formula or invention which the owner thereof intends to be available only to persons selected by him.

II. "Obtain" means, in relation to property, to bring about a transfer of possession or of some other legally recognized interest in property, whether to the obtainer or another; in relation to labor or services, to secure performance thereof; and in relation to a trade secret, to make any facsimile, replica, photograph or other reproduction.

III. "Purpose to deprive" means to have the conscious object:

(a) To withhold property permanently or for so extended a period or to use under such circumstances that a substantial portion of its economic value, or of the use and benefit thereof, would be lost; or

(b) To restore the property only upon payment of a reward or other compensation; or

(c) To dispose of the property under circumstances that make it unlikely that the owner will recover it; or

(d) To appropriate the goods or merchandise of a merchant without paying the merchant's stated or advertised price.

IV. "Property of another" includes property in which any person other than the actor has an interest which the actor is not privileged to infringe, regardless of the fact that the actor also has an interest in the property and regardless of the fact that the other person might be precluded from civil recovery because the property was used in an unlawful transaction or was subject to forfeiture as contraband. Property in possession of the actor shall not be deemed property of another who has only a security interest therein, even if legal title is in the creditor pursuant to a conditional sales contract or other security agreement.

V. "Value" means the highest amount determined by any reasonable standard of property or services.

(a) Amounts involved in thefts committed pursuant to one scheme or course of conduct, whether from the same person or several persons, may be aggregated in determining the grade of the offense.

(b) The value of property or services obtained by the actor shall determine the grade of the offense, and such value shall not be offset against or reduced by the value of any property or services given by the actor in exchange.

(c) Each personal check or credit card shall have a value of $250.

VI. "Merchant" means the owner or operator of any place of business where merchandise is displayed, held, or stored, for sale to the public, or any agent or employee of such owner or operator.

Source.
1971, 518:1. 1986, 222:1, eff. Aug. 5, 1986. 2005, 36:1, eff. July 16, 2005. 2009, 209:2, 3, eff. January 1, 2010.

Amendments
—**2009.** The 2009 amendment added III(d) and VI and made a related change.

—**2005.** Paragraph V(c): Added.

—**1986.** Paragraph V: Rewritten to the extent that a detailed comparison would be impractical.

NOTES TO DECISIONS

1. Construction
2. Purpose
3. Indictment
4. Value obtained
5. Security interests
6. Course of conduct
7. —Aggregation of value

1. Construction
A mortgagee's interest in a structure is sufficient so that the structure may also be considered to be the "property of another" within the meaning of paragraph IV of this section. State v. Marion, 122 N.H. 20, 440 A.2d 448, 1982 N.H. LEXIS 277 (1982).

The second sentence of paragraph IV of this section, defining "property of another" does not exclude a mortgage interest; the sentence, by its terms, does not apply to real property and excludes only interests created by a conditional sales contract or other security agreement, interests which can arise only in personal property or fixtures. State v. Marion, 122 N.H. 20, 440 A.2d 448, 1982 N.H. LEXIS 277 (1982).

2. Purpose
The legislative history of the second sentence of paragraph IV of this section, defining "property of another" reveals that it was added only so that a purchaser in a conditional sales arrangement would not be guilty of theft when he treated the property as his own. State v. Marion, 122 N.H. 20, 440 A.2d 448, 1982 N.H. LEXIS 277 (1982).

3. Indictment
An indictment for a theft crime, of which an essential element is "a purpose to deprive," need not allege any one of the variants of "purpose to deprive" specifically, and the variants of the "purpose to deprive" mental state are not elements of the offense that must be specifically pleaded. State v. Erickson, 129 N.H. 515, 533 A.2d 23, 1987 N.H. LEXIS 253 (1987).

The three variants of paragraph III of this section are not elements that must necessarily be alleged in theft indictments requiring proof of intent to deprive. State v. Cote, 126 N.H. 514, 493 A.2d 1170, 1985 N.H. LEXIS 336 (1985).

4. Value obtained
Evidence that defendant took temporary possession of intimate photographs he found in his tenants' apartment, without the tenants' permission, and scanned those photographs into his computer, also without permission, was sufficient to sustain defendant's conviction for receiving stolen property; although defendant returned the original photographs, he kept a computer reproduction of the captured images, without permission, and it was these images he was convicted of unlawfully retaining. State v. Nelson, 150 N.H. 569, 842 A.2d 83, 2004 N.H. LEXIS 28 (2004).

Argument was rejected that state, at trial for theft by deception, failed to prove the value of the property which the defendant had obtained, based on defendant's contention that some portion of the stolen property was actually received by defendant's wife, where the defendant brought about the transfer and it was irrelevant under paragraph II of this section who received it. State v. Gruber, 132 N.H. 83, 562 A.2d 156, 1989 N.H. LEXIS 71 (1989).

5. Security interests
Lien held by service station for charges of towing and storing automobile was an interest in the automobile which the owner was not privileged to infringe, even though the service station had only a security interest, where the automobile was not in possession of the owner but rather in possession of the creditor. State v. Hill, 115 N.H. 37, 332 A.2d 182, 1975 N.H. LEXIS 217 (1975).

6. Course of conduct
Bill of particulars in prosecution for theft by deception adequately informed defendant that he was being charged with a course of conduct, and therefore there was no error in trial court's instructing jury that it could aggregate dollar amounts of individual thefts to determine grade of offense if thefts were committed as part of one scheme or course of conduct. State v. French, 146

N.H. 97, 776 A.2d 1253, 2001 N.H. LEXIS 35 (2001).

Two indictments could sustain a finding of a different scheme or course of conduct as to each indictment, notwithstanding that both indictments involved thefts from a single bank account during the same time frame. State v. Weeks, 137 N.H. 687, 635 A.2d 439, 1993 N.H. LEXIS 145 (1993).

In a prosecution for theft by unauthorized taking, the state bore the burden of proving that the defendant's conduct in each indictment was part of a general scheme or plan motivated by a continuing criminal impulse or intent. However, the state was not required to prove that the defendant's criminal intent continued on a daily, weekly, or monthly basis. State v. Weeks, 137 N.H. 687, 635 A.2d 439, 1993 N.H. LEXIS 145 (1993).

7. —Aggregation of value

Evidence supported the conclusion that each of three instances of extortion was committed pursuant to one scheme or course of conduct, where in each of the three instances, the professional relationships between the defendant and the victims were the same, threat to deny the victim a fulltime appointment as deputy sheriff was urged, and the funds that were extorted were in each case to be spent on defendant sheriff's reelection campaign, and therefore court properly aggregated the amounts involved in determining the grade of the offense. State v. O'Flynn, 126 N.H. 706, 496 A.2d 348, 1985 N.H. LEXIS 349 (1985).

Indictments were sufficient to allow aggregation of value under paragraph V of this section for purposes of establishing a basis for a class B felony where each indictment alleged a separate series of takings during one course of conduct encompassing separate long trips, each larceny within a series involving property of less than $ 100 in value but amounting in the aggregate for each trip to more than $100. State v. Sampson, 120 N.H. 251, 413 A.2d 590, 1980 N.H. LEXIS 268 (1980).

Cited:

Cited in State v. Theodore, 118 N.H. 548, 392 A.2d 122, 1978 N.H. LEXIS 238 (1978); State v. Noel, 119 N.H. 522, 404 A.2d 290, 1979 N.H. LEXIS 347 (1979); State v. Sampson, 120 N.H. 251, 413 A.2d 590, 1980 N.H. LEXIS 268 (1980); State v. Merski, 121 N.H. 901, 437 A.2d 710, 1981 N.H. LEXIS 435 (1981); State v. Kelly, 125 N.H. 484, 484 A.2d 1066, 1984 N.H. LEXIS 410 (1984); In re Dubuque, 46 B.R. 156, 1985 Bankr. LEXIS 6762 (Bankr. D.N.H. 1985); State v. Harper, 126 N.H. 815, 498 A.2d 310, 1985 N.H. LEXIS 409 (1985); State v. Guay, 130 N.H. 413, 543 A.2d 910, 1988 N.H. LEXIS 42 (1988); State v. Williams, 133 N.H. 631, 581 A.2d 78, 1990 N.H. LEXIS 111 (1990); State v. Hermsdorf, 135 N.H. 360, 605 A.2d 1045, 1992 N.H. LEXIS 42, (1992); State v. Paris, 137 N.H. 322, 627 A.2d 582, 1993 N.H. LEXIS 78 (1993).

637:3. Theft by Unauthorized Taking or Transfer.

I. A person commits theft if he obtains or exercises unauthorized control over the property of another with a purpose to deprive him thereof.

II. As used in this section and RSA 637:4 and 5, "obtain or exercise unauthorized control" includes but is not necessarily limited to conduct heretofore defined or known as common law larceny by trespassory taking, larceny by conversion, larceny by bailee, and embezzlement.

Source.
1971, 518:1, eff. Nov. 1, 1973.

NOTES TO DECISIONS

1. Double jeopardy
2. Lesser included offenses
3. Intent
4. Indictment
5. Bankruptcy of defendant
6. Evidence

7. Jury instructions

1. Double jeopardy

Defendant's armed robbery of jewelry store clerk and theft from store constituted two distinct acts involving different property and separated in time and space, and therefore evidence was sufficient to support two separate convictions without violating double jeopardy. State v. Ford, 144 N.H. 57, 738 A.2d 937, 1999 N.H. LEXIS 71 (1999).

Defendant committed theft when he removed diamond and sapphire from jewelry store display cases, and he then committed robbery when he threatened clerk with gun and demanded her bracelet and pendant; theft and robbery were separate acts of taking distinct from each other and each supported by its own set of facts, and separate sentences for theft and robbery were therefore not prohibited by "single larceny rule." State v. Ford, 144 N.H. 57, 738 A.2d 937, 1999 N.H. LEXIS 71 (1999).

2. Lesser included offenses

Since three essential elements contained in RSA 638:11, defining the crime of misapplication of property, are not contained within the definition of the crime of theft by unauthorized taking, a person need not have committed the former in the process of committing the latter. State v. Merski, 123 N.H. 564, 465 A.2d 491, 1983 N.H. LEXIS 323 (1983).

In prosecution for theft by unauthorized taking, the defendant was not entitled to an instruction on the elements of the misdemeanor of misapplication of property since the indictment accusing the defendant of violating this section did not invoke RSA 638:11, the misdemeanor misapplication statute, as a lesser-included offense. State v. Merski, 123 N.H. 564, 465 A.2d 491, 1983 N.H. LEXIS 323 (1983).

3. Intent

Court at trial of attorney for theft of client funds did not err in ruling that evidence of acute alcohol dependence was limited to insanity defense and could not be used to prove lack of specific intent to commit theft; case law distinguishes between intoxication and alcoholism, and expert testimony offered by defendant as to his acute alcoholism had no bearing on whether he was so intoxicated as to be unable to form specific intent to commit theft. State v. Sylvia, 136 N.H. 428, 616 A.2d 507, 1992 N.H. LEXIS 185 (1992).

There was no impropriety in prosecutor's closing argument at trial of attorney for theft of client funds, and therefore no curative instruction to jury was required; in arguing that defendant's inventory filings with probate court did not reflect that defendant had already spent portion of funds received, prosecutor did not misstate expert's testimony, but rather drew a reasonable inference from evidence as a whole that defendant knew that what he was doing with his client's funds was illegal. State v. Sylvia, 136 N.H. 428, 616 A.2d 507, 1992 N.H. LEXIS 185 (1992).

4. Indictment

In the case of defendant charged with two counts of theft by unauthorized taking and one count of attempted theft, where one of the indictments for theft by unauthorized taking specified all of the elements of the offense but did not describe the location or the means used by the defendant to gain unauthorized control over the victim's property, the defendant's motion to dismiss that indictment should have been granted, since the factual information contained in the indictment, including the date and place of the offense, the name of the victim, and the amount and type of property involved, was constitutionally insufficient to inform the defendant of the factual basis of the charge. State v. Stiles, 123 N.H. 680, 465 A.2d 908, 1983 N.H. LEXIS 333 (1983).

5. Bankruptcy of defendant

A debt arising from a conviction under this section is nondischargeable in bankruptcy under 11 U.S.C.S. § 523(a)(4). In re Dubuque, 46 B.R. 156, 1985 Bankr. LEXIS 6762 (Bankr. D.N.H. 1985).

6. Evidence

Defendant, a medical examiner, requested and received payment from the Commonwealth of Massachusetts for viewing bodies before they were cremated in New Hampshire and in fact viewed these bodies. Thus, a theft by taking charge was not supported by sufficient evidence, as a rational juror could not have found that defendant collected money from the Commonwealth of Massachusetts for services he failed to perform State v. Breed, 159 N.H. 61, 977 A.2d 463, 2009 N.H. LEXIS 88 (2009).

Where defendant used a power of attorney the victim gave to her to borrow money against his home and insurance policy, without his knowledge, deposited the funds into the victim's business account, and withdrew funds from that account to pay her personal expenses and where the evidence supported a jury's finding beyond a reasonable doubt that the victim did not know about, accept, or ratify defendant's spending practices, evidence was sufficient to support her conviction of theft by unauthorized taking or transfer in violation of RSA 637:3. State v. Emery, 152 N.H. 783, 887 A.2d 123, 2005 N.H. LEXIS 169 (2005).

Testimony of husband as to disappearance of his wife's wedding ring from hotel room, coupled with other circumstantial evidence, was sufficient to prove lack of wife's permission for defendant to possess her ring, and defendant's conviction for theft was therefore upheld. State v. Flynn, 144 N.H. 567, 744 A.2d 1131, 1999 N.H. LEXIS 157 (1999).

Evidence was sufficient to establish that various transactions engaged in by the defendant were unauthorized by the board of trustees for a home for the aged. The state introduced the minutes of the meetings of the board of trustees to show that there was no express authorization of various expenditures and the defendant could not seriously contend that he had implied authority to: (1) spend $1,250 to go to the Bahamas with his wife, (2) spend $1,783 for work done to his home, (3) give his friend $5,000, or (4) take a $25,000 "finder's fee" on a loan transaction where the terms of the loan provided that the finder's fee would be paid to the home. State v. Weeks, 137 N.H. 687, 635 A.2d 439, 1993 N.H. LEXIS 145 (1993).

7. Jury instructions

As the New Hampshire Supreme Court has never addressed the issue of whether a party to a joint checking account may be convicted of stealing from the other party by making unauthorized withdrawals, the trial court did not commit plain error by failing to give an instruction, sua sponte, that defendant could not be convicted under such circumstances. State v. Emery, 152 N.H. 783, 887 A.2d 123, 2005 N.H. LEXIS 169 (2005).

Cited:

Cited in State v. Hill, 115 N.H. 37, 332 A.2d 182, 1975 N.H. LEXIS 217 (1975); Bernier v. Wheelock, 116 N.H. 626, 365 A.2d 737, 1976 N.H. LEXIS 430 (1976); State v. Floyd, 116 N.H. 632, 365 A.2d 738, 1976 N.H. LEXIS 432 (1976); Bell v. Superior Court Sentence Review Div., 117 N.H. 474, 374 A.2d 659, 1977 N.H. LEXIS 358 (1977); State v. Mitchell, 118 N.H. 1, 381 A.2d 1198, 1978 N.H. LEXIS 328 (1978); State v. MacLeod, 119 N.H. 480, 402 A.2d 1338, 1979 N.H. LEXIS 343 (1979); State v. Noel, 119 N.H. 522, 404 A.2d 290, 1979 N.H. LEXIS 347 (1979); State v. Kelley, 120 N.H. 12, 413 A.2d 308, 1980 N.H. LEXIS 219 (1980); State v. Houle, 120 N.H. 160, 412 A.2d 736, 1980 N.H. LEXIS 252 (1980); State v. Sampson, 120 N.H. 251, 413 A.2d 590, 1980 N.H. LEXIS 268 (1980); State v. Merski, 121 N.H. 901, 437 A.2d 710, 1981 N.H. LEXIS 435 (1981); Chandler v. Perini Power Constructors, Inc., 520 F. Supp. 1152, 1981 U.S. Dist. LEXIS 14254 (D.N.H. 1981); State v. Cyr, 122 N.H. 1155, 453 A.2d 1315, 1982 N.H. LEXIS 531 (1982); State v. Chaisson, 123 N.H. 17, 458 A.2d 95, 1983 N.H. LEXIS 236 (1983); State v. Zysk, 123 N.H. 481, 465 A.2d 480, 1983 N.H. LEXIS 322 (1983); State v. Robinson, 123 N.H. 532, 465 A.2d 1201, 1983 N.H. LEXIS 317 (1983); State v. Fournier, 123 N.H. 777, 465 A.2d 898, 1983 N.H. LEXIS 349 (1983); State v. Copeland, 124 N.H. 90, 467 A.2d 238, 1983 N.H. LEXIS 367 (1983); State v. Beaudette, 124 N.H. 579, 474 A.2d 1012, 1984 N.H. LEXIS 355 (1984); State v. Steele, 125 N.H. 190, 480 A.2d 80, 1984 N.H. LEXIS 358 (1984); State v. Kelly, 125 N.H. 484, 484 A.2d 1066, 1984 N.H. LEXIS 410 (1984); State v. Chaisson, 125 N.H. 810, 486 A.2d 297, 1984 N.H. LEXIS 320 (1984); State v. Benoit, 126 N.H. 6, 490 A.2d 295, 1985 N.H. LEXIS 240 (1985); State v. Le Clair, 126 N.H. 479, 493 A.2d 498, 1985 N.H. LEXIS 308 (1985); State v. Harper, 126 N.H. 815, 498 A.2d 310, 1985 N.H. LEXIS 409 (1985); In re Carroll, 127 N.H. 390, 503 A.2d 750, 1985 N.H. LEXIS 458 (1985); State v. Rau, 129 N.H. 126, 523 A.2d 98, 1987 N.H. LEXIS 154 (1987); State v. Maguire, 129 N.H. 165, 523 A.2d 120, 1987 N.H. LEXIS 161 (1987);

State v. Bundy, 130 N.H. 382, 539 A.2d 713, 1988 N.H. LEXIS 14 (1988); State v. Guay, 130 N.H. 413, 543 A.2d 910, 1988 N.H. LEXIS 42 (1988); State v. Stearns, 130 N.H. 475, 547 A.2d 672, 1988 N.H. LEXIS 72 (1988); State v. Wisowaty, 133 N.H. 604, 580 A.2d 1079, 1990 N.H. LEXIS 109 (1990); State v. Williams, 133 N.H. 631, 581 A.2d 78, 1990 N.H. LEXIS 111 (1990); New England Ins. Co. v. Sylvia, 783 F. Supp. 6, 1991 U.S. Dist. LEXIS 19549 (D.N.H. 1991); State v. Patten, 134 N.H. 319, 591 A.2d 1329, 1991 N.H. LEXIS 61 (1991); State v. Decoteau, 137 N.H. 106, 623 A.2d 1338, 1993 N.H. LEXIS 49 (1993); State v. Wisowaty, 137 N.H. 298, 627 A.2d 572, 1993 N.H. LEXIS 74 (1993); State v. Richardson, 138 N.H. 162, 635 A.2d 1361, 1993 N.H. LEXIS 187 (1993); State v. Philbrook, 138 N.H. 601, 644 A.2d 66, 1994 N.H. LEXIS 71 (1994); State v. Emanuel, 139 N.H. 57, 649 A.2d 53, 1994 N.H. LEXIS 114 (1994); State v. Dolbeare, 140 N.H. 84, 663 A.2d 85, 1995 N.H. LEXIS 96 (1995); State v. Davis, 143 N.H. 8, 718 A.2d 1202, 1998 N.H. LEXIS 60 (1998); Gilsum v. Monadnock Regional Sch. Dist., 136 N.H. 32, 611 A.2d 625, 1992 N.H. LEXIS 121 (1992).

OPINIONS OF THE ATTORNEY GENERAL

Conversion of lottery tickets

Conversion of lottery tickets to cash by person entrusted by the government with those tickets would constitute the crime of misapplication of property, and under some circumstances could constitute the crime of theft by unauthorized taking, or theft by misapplication of property. Op. Atty. Gen. 86-51.

637:3-a. Willful Concealment.

I. A person is guilty of willful concealment if, without authority, he or she willfully conceals the goods or merchandise of any store while still upon the premises of such store. Goods or merchandise found concealed upon the person shall be prima facie evidence of willful concealment. Notwithstanding RSA 637:11, willful concealment shall be a misdemeanor.

II. A person commits theft if, with the purpose to deprive a merchant of goods or merchandise, he or she knowingly:

(a) Removes goods or merchandise from the premises of a merchant; or

(b) Alters, transfers, or removes any price marking affixed to goods or merchandise; or

(c) Causes the cash register or other sales recording device to reflect less than the merchant's stated or advertised price for the goods or merchandise; or

(d) Transfers goods or merchandise from the container in which such goods or merchandise were intended to be sold to another container.

Source.

2009, 209:1, eff. January 1, 2010.

Cross References.

Civil actions for theft, see RSA 507:8-f.
Classification of crimes, see RSA 625:9.
Penalties for theft, see RSA 637:11.
Sentences, see RSA 651.
Use of force by merchants, see RSA 627:8-a.

NOTES TO DECISIONS

1. Construction with other laws
2. Premises

1. Construction with other laws

Offense of shoplifting is sufficiently similar to theft to enable a prior conviction for shoplifting to be regarded as a conviction for theft which may be used to enhance penalty for theft under RSA 637:11, II(b). State v. Harper, 126 N.H. 815, 498 A.2d 310, 1985 N.H. LEXIS 409 (1985). (Decided under former RSA 644:17.)

2. Premises

Distinction between willful concealment and shoplifting under former RSA 644:17 occurs at the boundary of the merchant's "premises": within the boundary, the wrongful conduct constitutes "willful concealment"; outside the boundary, the wrongful conduct constitutes shoplifting. Given this distinction, the New Hampshire Supreme Court cannot conclude that the legislature intended the boundary of a merchant's premises to be delineated by its sales area. State v. Thiel, 160 N.H. 462, 999 A.2d 367, 2010 N.H. LEXIS 65 (2010).

It was error to hold that defendant, who was convicted of shoplifting under former RSA 644:17, II, left the merchant's premises when she was stopped outside of the sales area but within the vestibule of the store. State v. Thiel, 160 N.H. 462, 999 A.2d 367, 2010 N.H. LEXIS 65 (2010).

637:4. Theft by Deception.

I. A person commits theft if he obtains or exercises control over property of another by deception and with a purpose to deprive him thereof.

II. For the purposes of this section, deception occurs when a person purposely:

(a) Creates or reinforces an impression which is false and which that person does not believe to be true, including false impressions as to law, value, knowledge, opinion, intention or other state of mind. Provided, however, that an intention not to perform a promise, or knowledge that it will not be performed, shall not be inferred from the fact alone that the promise was not performed; or

(b) Fails to correct a false impression which he previously had created or reinforced and which he did not believe to be true, or which he knows to be influencing another to whom he stands in a fiduciary or confidential relationship; or

(c) Prevents another from acquiring information which is pertinent to the disposition of the property involved; or

(d) Fails to disclose a known lien, adverse claim or other legal impediment to the enjoyment of property which he transfers or encumbers in consideration for the property obtained, whether such impediment is or is not valid, or is or is not a matter of official record; or

(e) Misrepresents to or misleads any person, in any manner, so as to make that person believe that the person on whose behalf a solicitation or sales promotion is being conducted is a charitable trust or that the proceeds of such solicitation or sales promotion shall be used for charitable purposes, if such is not the fact.

III. Theft by deception does not occur, however, when there is only falsity as to matters having no pecuniary significance, or puffing by statements unlikely to deceive ordinary persons in the group addressed. "Puffing" means an exaggerated commendation of wares in communications addressed to the public or to a class or group.

IV. A person commits theft under this section notwithstanding that the victim has suffered no actual or net pecuniary loss.

Source.
1971, 518:1. 1986, 222:2. 1992, 239:4, eff. July 1, 1992.

Amendments
—**1992.** Paragraph II(d): Added "or" following "record". Paragraph II(e): Added.

—**1986.** Paragraph IV: Added.

NOTES TO DECISIONS

1. Constitutionality
2. Construction
3. Intent
4. Elements
5. Indictments
6. Evidence
7. Jury instructions
8. Jurisdiction
9. Joinder

1. Constitutionality

This section is not unconstitutionally ambiguous or vague. State v. Gruber, 132 N.H. 83, 562 A.2d 156, 1989 N.H. LEXIS 71 (1989).

2. Construction

This section is not applicable where the alleged victim, in a bargaining exchange, receives value in excess of the consideration paid. State v. Kelly, 125 N.H. 484, 484 A.2d 1066, 1984 N.H. LEXIS 410 (1984), superseded by statute as stated in, State v. Gruber, 132 N.H. 83, 562 A.2d 156, 1989 N.H. LEXIS 71 (1989).

3. Intent

In a prosecution for theft by deception, in which it was alleged that the defendant obtained from the victim a sum of money in excess of $1,000 by creating a false impression that the defendant would build a garage at the victim's residence, the state failed to prove the required intent. The defendant's conduct was as much indicative of an irresponsible member of the business community on the threshold of bankruptcy as it was of a thief whom the statute was intended to punish. State v. Sharon, 136 N.H. 764, 622 A.2d 840, 1993 N.H. LEXIS 27 (1993).

Where property is exchanged between two willing parties, even if fraud is committed, the deceiving party can only intend to deprive the victim of the value of the victim's property that exceeds the value of the property which the victim receives in exchange. State v. Kelly, 125 N.H. 484, 484 A.2d 1066, 1984 N.H. LEXIS 410 (1984), superseded by statute as stated in, State v. Gruber, 132 N.H. 83, 562 A.2d 156, 1989 N.H. LEXIS 71 (1989).

One of the elements of theft by deception is that defendant intend to deprive the owner of the property. State v. Murchaison, 118 N.H. 916, 395 A.2d 1250, 1978 N.H. LEXIS 320 (1978).

Where defendant was convicted of theft by deception, intent to deprive the owner of the property could be found from fact that defendant obtained it by deception and had not paid it back. State v. Murchaison, 118 N.H. 916, 395 A.2d 1250, 1978 N.H. LEXIS 320 (1978).

4. Elements

Defendant was not entitled to directed verdict since State was not required to prove that he obtained entire $25,000 lump sum workers' compensation settlement through theft by deception; value of property taken was not an element of the crime and, to obtain a conviction for class A felony theft by deception, State was only required to prove that property taken was valued at more than $1,000. State v. French, 146 N.H. 97, 776 A.2d 1253, 2001 N.H. LEXIS 35 (2001).

5. Indictments

Since defendant's actions of obtaining numerous loans from the elderly victim, purportedly for the purchase of a property, demonstrated a prior design that included the charged acts as part of its consummation, joinder was proper as to the 17 counts of theft by deception. State v. Schonarth, 152 N.H. 560, 883 A.2d 305, 2005 N.H. LEXIS 138 (2005), rehearing denied, 2005 N.H. LEXIS 156 (N.H. Oct. 25, 2005).

6. Evidence

Rational juror could find that defendant, a medical examiner, committed theft by deception by signing cremation certificates indicating he had viewed the remains of certain decedents when he had not done so and that he engaged in this conduct to receive fees. State v. Breed, 159 N.H. 61, 977 A.2d 463, 2009 N.H. LEXIS 88 (2009).

Where defendant used a power of attorney the victim gave to her to borrow money against his home and insurance policy, without his knowledge, deposited the funds into the victim's business account, and withdrew funds from that account to pay her personal expenses and where the evidence supported a jury's finding beyond a reasonable doubt that the victim did not know about, accept, or ratify defendant's spending practices, evidence was sufficient to support her conviction of theft by unauthorized taking or transfer in violation of RSA 637:3 and theft by deception in violation of RSA 637:4. State v. Emery, 152 N.H. 783, 887 A.2d 123, 2005 N.H. LEXIS 169 (2005).

7. Jury instructions

As the New Hampshire Supreme Court has never addressed the issue of whether a party to a joint checking account may be convicted of stealing from the other party by making unauthorized withdrawals, the trial court did not commit plain error by failing to give an instruction, sua sponte, that defendant could not be convicted under such circumstances. State v. Emery, 152 N.H. 783, 887 A.2d 123, 2005 N.H. LEXIS 169 (2005).

8. Jurisdiction

Under RSA 625:4, I(a), New Hampshire had jurisdiction over charges of theft by deception because defendant, a medical examiner, took money from the Commonwealth of Massachusetts by submitting medical examiner fee forms to a New Hampshire entity in New Hampshire that gave the false impression that he had examined bodies in New Hampshire. State v. Breed, 159 N.H. 61, 977 A.2d 463, 2009 N.H. LEXIS 88 (2009).

9. Joinder

Trial court did not err in joining theft by deception and fraudulent handling of recordable writings offenses when the trial court reasonably found that each fraudulent transaction or theft in which defendant, a medical examiner, engaged was part of an overarching plan of furthering his increasingly profitable relationship with a crematorium, and, in this way, the charges were mutually dependent. The trial court reasonably could have found that the defendant was not merely taking advantage of opportunities as they arose, but instead was exhibiting forethought and premeditation in his scheming. State v. Breed, 159 N.H. 61, 977 A.2d 463, 2009 N.H. LEXIS 88 (2009).

Cited:

Cited in State v. Harlan, 116 N.H. 598, 364 A.2d 1254, 1976 N.H. LEXIS 423 (1976); State v. Keyser, 117 N.H. 45, 369 A.2d 224, 1977 N.H. LEXIS 263 (1977); Hogan v. Robert H. Irwin Motors, 121 N.H. 737, 433 A.2d 1322, 1981 N.H. LEXIS 392 (1981); State v. Monahan, 125 N.H. 17, 480 A.2d 863, 1984 N.H. LEXIS 372 (1984); State v. Abbis, 125 N.H. 646, 484 A.2d 1156, 1984 N.H. LEXIS 387 (1984); State v. Allison, 126 N.H. 111, 489 A.2d 620, 1985 N.H. LEXIS 255 (1985); Dartmouth Motor Sales v. Wilcox, 128 N.H. 526, 517 A.2d 804, 1986 N.H. LEXIS 324 (1986); State v. Erickson, 129 N.H. 515, 533 A.2d 23, 1987 N.H. LEXIS 253 (1987); State v. Trainor, 130 N.H. 371, 540 A.2d 1236, 1988 N.H. LEXIS 9 (1988); State v. Tucker, 132 N.H. 31, 561 A.2d 1075, 1989 N.H. LEXIS 53 (1989); State v. Schachter, 133 N.H. 439, 577 A.2d 1222, 1990 N.H. LEXIS 81 (1990); State v. Matiyosus, 134 N.H. 686, 597 A.2d 1068, 1991 N.H. LEXIS 122 (1991); State v. Davis, 139 N.H. 185, 650 A.2d 1386, 1994 N.H. LEXIS 132 (1994); State v. Davis, 139 N.H. 185, 650 A.2d 1386, 1994 N.H. LEXIS 132 (1994).

RESEARCH REFERENCES

New Hampshire Trial Bar News.

For article, "Presumptions in New Hampshire Law—A Guide Through the Impenetrable Jungle (Part II)," see 11 N.H. Trial Bar News 31, 34 n.112 (Fall 1991).

637:5. Theft by Extortion.

I. A person is guilty of theft as he obtains or exercises control over the property of another by extortion and with a purpose to deprive him thereof.

II. As used in this section, extortion occurs when a person threatens to:

(a) Cause physical harm in the future to the person threatened or to any other person or to property at any time; or

(b) Subject the person threatened or any other person to physical confinement or restraint; or

(c) Engage in other conduct constituting a crime; or

(d) Accuse any person of a crime or expose him to hatred, contempt or ridicule; or

(e) Reveal any information sought to be concealed by the person threatened; or

(f) Testify or provide information or withhold testimony or information with respect to another's legal claim or defense; or

(g) Take action as an official against anyone or anything, or withhold official action, or cause such action or withholding; or

(h) Bring about or continue a strike, boycott or other similar collective action to obtain property which is not demanded or received for the benefit of the group which the actor purports to represent; or

(i) Do any other act which would not in itself substantially benefit him but which would harm substantially any other person with respect to that person's health, safety, business, calling, career, financial condition, reputation, or personal relationships.

Source.

1971, 518:1, eff. Nov. 1, 1973.

NOTES TO DECISIONS

1. Constitutionality
2. Applicability
3. Threats
4. "Substantially benefit"

1. Constitutionality

RSA 637:5, II(i) is not unconstitutionally vague under U.S. Const. amend. I or N.H. Const. pt. I, arts. 14 and 22, as the phrase "substantially benefit" gives clear notice to a person of ordinary intelligence that the statute prohibits a threat that will not provide him with some actual advantage that is real and definite. Furthermore, the statute was not unconstitutionally vague as applied to defendant, who had threatened to sue a beauty salon for discrimination and obtained a settlement despite neither being a client of the salon nor representing one, as defendant had a reasonable opportunity to know that the term "benefit" would require, at the very least, standing to bring the threatened suit. State v. Hynes, 159 N.H. 187, 978 A.2d 264, 2009 N.H. LEXIS 101 (2009), cert. denied, Hynes v. New Hampshire, 558 U.S. 1125, 130 S. Ct. 1083,

175 L. Ed. 2d 907, 2010 U.S. LEXIS 334 (2010).

RSA 637:5, II(i) was not overbroad under N.H. Const. pt. I, arts. 14, 22, and 32 or the First Amendment as applied to defendant, where he sought out the salon; sent a demand letter identifying himself as an attorney and threatening baseless litigation; and ultimately used the threat as leverage to obtain a settlement for his personal gain. Furthermore, the statute was not overbroad on its face, as the term "extortion" impliedly excludes legitimate claims to property through threats State v. Hynes, 159 N.H. 187, 978 A.2d 264, 2009 N.H. LEXIS 101 (2009), cert. denied, Hynes v. New Hampshire, 558 U.S. 1125, 130 S. Ct. 1083, 175 L. Ed. 2d 907, 2010 U.S. LEXIS 334 (2010).

2. Applicability

RSA 637:5, II(i) applied to the conduct of defendant, an attorney who obtained a settlement for his own personal gain from a beauty salon after threatening to sue it for discriminatory pricing despite the fact that he had no client and had not been a customer of the salon himself. There was no merit to defendant's argument that he had standing to sue under RSA 354-A:21-a, I; he had no preexisting relationship with the salon before threatening litigation and had suffered no direct, compensable harm. State v. Hynes, 159 N.H. 187, 978 A.2d 264, 2009 N.H. LEXIS 101 (2009), cert. denied, Hynes v. New Hampshire, 558 U.S. 1125, 130 S. Ct. 1083, 175 L. Ed. 2d 907, 2010 U.S. LEXIS 334 (2010).

3. Threats

Unlike the other provisions within RSA 637:5, II, the plain language of RSA 637:5, II(i) does not simply evaluate the type of threat that was made, but requires a court to consider both the threat's potential harm to the person threatened as well as its potential benefit to the person making the threat; thus, the court cannot simply evaluate the threat on its face and disregard the circumstances under which it was made, but must consider all of the circumstances surrounding that threat on a case-by-case basis. The New Hampshire Supreme Court, therefore, cannot conclude, as a matter of law, that there are no circumstances under which a threat to sue would constitute extortion. State v. Hynes, 159 N.H. 187, 978 A.2d 264, 2009 N.H. LEXIS 101 (2009), cert. denied, Hynes v. New Hampshire, 558 U.S. 1125, 130 S. Ct. 1083, 175 L. Ed. 2d 907, 2010 U.S. LEXIS 334 (2010).

Plain language of RSA 637:5, II(i) makes clear that it applies to a threat to do any act which would not in itself substantially benefit him but which would harm substantially another person. Thus, the statute neither explicitly, nor by implication, excludes a baseless threat to sue. State v. Hynes, 159 N.H. 187, 978 A.2d 264, 2009 N.H. LEXIS 101 (2009), cert. denied, Hynes v. New Hampshire, 558 U.S. 1125, 130 S. Ct. 1083, 175 L. Ed. 2d 907, 2010 U.S. LEXIS 334 (2010).

RSA 637:5, II(i) broadly considers the consequences of the threat, both to the person making it and to its intended recipient; furthermore, RSA 637:5, II(i) does not require there to be fear as a result of the threat, but, rather, only that there be substantial harm. The Supreme Court of New Hampshire does not believe that these terms are interchangeable. State v. Hynes, 159 N.H. 187, 978 A.2d 264, 2009 N.H. LEXIS 101 (2009), cert. denied, Hynes v. New Hampshire, 558 U.S. 1125, 130 S. Ct. 1083, 175 L. Ed. 2d 907, 2010 U.S. LEXIS 334 (2010).

To be extortionate, a threat need not be express; it may be implied in words and conduct. State v. O'Flynn, 126 N.H. 706, 496 A.2d 348, 1985 N.H. LEXIS 349 (1985).

The extraction of money from a subordinate under a threat of a promotion denial may be held to be extortionate. State v. O'Flynn, 126 N.H. 706, 496 A.2d 348, 1985 N.H. LEXIS 349 (1985).

Since sheriffs are charged with the responsibility of appointing their deputies, threats of sheriff to deny deputy appointments unless political contributions were made to his campaign was a threat to "withhold official action" under subparagraph II(g) of this section. State v. O'Flynn, 126 N.H. 706, 496 A.2d 348, 1985 N.H. LEXIS 349 (1985).

4. "Substantially benefit"

Phrase "substantially benefit" in RSA 637:5, II(i) is not so broad as to encompass an altruistic sense of accomplishment for ridding the world of a perceived injustice; indeed, this type of conceptual interpretation is far too abstract to constitute a substantial benefit

under this statute; it bespeaks of a societal goal, not personal gain. Thus, defendant's asserted general interest in ending discrimination was insufficient to satisfy the "substantially benefit" element. State v. Hynes, 159 N.H. 187, 978 A.2d 264, 2009 N.H. LEXIS 101 (2009), cert. denied, Hynes v. New Hampshire, 558 U.S. 1125, 130 S. Ct. 1083, 175 L. Ed. 2d 907, 2010 U.S. LEXIS 334 (2010).

Cited:

Cited in State v. Lovely, 124 N.H. 690, 480 A.2d 847, 1984 N.H. LEXIS 295 (1984); Lovely v. Cunningham, 796 F.2d 1, 1986 U.S. App. LEXIS 26377 (1st Cir. N.H. 1986).

637:6. Theft of Lost or Mislaid Property.

A person commits theft when:

I. He obtains property of another which he knows to have been lost or mislaid, or to have been delivered under a mistake as to the identity of the recipient or as to the nature or amount of the property, without taking reasonable measures to return the same to the owner, and

II. He has the purpose to deprive the owner of such property when he obtains the property or at any time prior to taking the measures designated in paragraph I.

Source.
1971, 518:1, eff. Nov. 1, 1973.

637:7. Receiving Stolen Property.

I. A person commits theft if he receives, retains, or disposes of the property of another knowing that it has been stolen, or believing that it has probably been stolen, with a purpose to deprive the owner thereof.

II. The knowledge or belief required for paragraph I is presumed in the case of a dealer who:

(a) Is found in possession or control of property stolen from 2 or more persons on separate occasions; or

(b) Has received other stolen property within the year preceding the receiving charged; or

(c) Being a dealer in property of the sort received, retained or disposed, acquires it for a consideration which he knows is far below its reasonable value, or

(d) Purchases property from a law enforcement officer working in an undercover capacity, or an agent of such law enforcement officer, where such property has been explicitly represented as stolen.

III. As used in this section, "receives" means acquiring possession, control or title or lending on the security of the property; and "dealer" means a person in the business of buying or selling goods.

Source.
1971, 518:1, eff. Nov. 1, 1973. 2001, 174:1, eff. Jan. 1, 2002.

Amendments
—2001. Paragraph II: Added "or" following "value" in subpar. (c) and added subpar. (d).

NOTES TO DECISIONS

1. Constitutionality

2. Construction with other laws
3. Knowledge
4. Belief
5. Possession
6. Ownership
7. Burden of proof
8. Evidence
9. Sentencing

1. Constitutionality

This section is not unconstitutionally over broad since it does not invade any area of protected freedom. State v. Chaisson, 123 N.H. 17, 458 A.2d 95, 1983 N.H. LEXIS 236 (1983); State v. Settle, 123 N.H. 34, 455 A.2d 1031, 1983 N.H. LEXIS 218 (1983).

This section is not unconstitutionally vague since the meaning of the phrase "believing that the property has probably been stolen" is clear, and it requires the state to prove beyond a reasonable doubt that the defendant believed that it was more likely than not that the property had been stolen. State v. Chaisson, 123 N.H. 17, 458 A.2d 95, 1983 N.H. LEXIS 236 (1983).

This section's definition of the crime of receiving stolen property is constitutional since the use of the word "probably" in the first sentence of paragraph I does not permit the state to convict a defendant without proving the defendant's required mental state beyond a reasonable doubt, but, on the contrary, requires the state to prove beyond a reasonable doubt that the defendant knew that the property was stolen or believed that it had probably been stolen. State v. Chaisson, 123 N.H. 17, 458 A.2d 95, 1983 N.H. LEXIS 236 (1983); State v. Settle, 123 N.H. 34, 455 A.2d 1031, 1983 N.H. LEXIS 218 (1983).

2. Construction with other laws

Defendant was properly barred from impeaching a witness under N.H. R. Evid. 609(a)(2) with a prior conviction of receiving stolen property under RSA 637:7, I. Receiving stolen property was not a crime that necessarily involved deceit, untruthfulness, or falsification and thus was not a crime of dishonesty or false statement under the pre-2007 version of the rule; under the current version of the rule, it was plainly not "readily determinable" that establishing the elements of the crime required proof of an act of dishonesty or false statement. State v. Holmes, 159 N.H. 173, 978 A.2d 909, 2009 N.H. LEXIS 104 (2009).

Unlike crimes such as perjury or false statement, receiving stolen property is not obviously dishonest; on its face, the New Hampshire statute does not impute dishonesty or mendacity to the crime for purposes of N.H. R. Evid. 609(a)(2). State v. Holmes, 159 N.H. 173, 978 A.2d 909, 2009 N.H. LEXIS 104 (2009).

N.H. R. Evid. 609(a)(2) was intended to include a narrow subset of criminal activity; at its broadest, the rule contemplates only crimes involving deceit, untruthfulness, or falsification. Only a limited number of crimes necessarily involve these elements, and receiving stolen property is not among them. State v. Holmes, 159 N.H. 173, 978 A.2d 909, 2009 N.H. LEXIS 104 (2009).

Conspiracy to receive stolen property, governed by RSA 629:3, is a separate and distinct crime from the crime of receiving stolen property. State v. Chaisson, 123 N.H. 17, 458 A.2d 95, 1983 N.H. LEXIS 236 (1983).

3. Knowledge

The essential element of guilty knowledge on the part of a receiver of stolen property can rarely be proven by direct evidence but it may be demonstrated by the surrounding facts or circumstances from which such knowledge may be inferred. State v. Stauff, 126 N.H. 186, 489 A.2d 140, 1985 N.H. LEXIS 244 (1985).

Knowledge that items one is receiving were stolen is a matter of fact which cannot ordinarily be proven by direct evidence, and in many instances knowledge must be inferred from circumstances known to the receiver at the time. State v. Casey, 113 N.H. 19, 300 A.2d 325, 1973 N.H. LEXIS 188 (1973). (Decided under prior law.)

Guilty knowledge, which can rarely be proven by direct evidence, may be proven by surrounding facts or circumstances from which guilty knowledge may be inferred. State v. Cote, 113 N.H. 647, 312 A.2d 687, 1973 N.H. LEXIS 342 (1973). (Decided under prior law.)

4. Belief

The "belief" standard in this section does not subject a defendant, charged under this section, to an undefined and/or lesser standard of culpability than that entailed by purposeful, knowing, reckless or negligent behavior, since for a defendant to believe that goods have probably been stolen is but another and, if anything, stronger way of stating that he is aware that such goods have probably been stolen. State v. Fennelly, 123 N.H. 378, 461 A.2d 1090, 1983 N.H. LEXIS 288 (1983).

5. Possession

Mere presence in the vicinity of stolen property unilluminated by other facts is insufficient proof of the element of possession to support a conviction of the crime of receiving stolen property. State v. Ward, 134 N.H. 626, 595 A.2d 508, 1991 N.H. LEXIS 112 (1991).

Constructive possession, whereby a defendant participates with another in possession of stolen goods, is sufficient to support a conviction of receiving stolen property. State v. Stauff, 126 N.H. 186, 489 A.2d 140, 1985 N.H. LEXIS 244 (1985).

Mere presence in the vicinity of stolen property unilluminated by other facts is insufficient proof of possession of the stolen property. State v. Stauff, 126 N.H. 186, 489 A.2d 140, 1985 N.H. LEXIS 244 (1985).

Possession need not be exclusive for one to possess stolen property; participation with another in the possession is sufficient. State v. Cote, 113 N.H. 647, 312 A.2d 687, 1973 N.H. LEXIS 342 (1973). (Decided under prior law.)

Defendant who drove codefendant to a place where codefendant picked up adding machine stolen two days earlier and then drove him to place where it was sold, accompanying codefendant while codefendant carried it inside and sold it, possessed the property. State v. Cote, 113 N.H. 647, 312 A.2d 687, 1973 N.H. LEXIS 342 (1973). (Decided under prior law.)

6. Ownership

At trial for receipt of stolen property, court properly denied defendant's motion to dismiss for insufficiency of evidence to prove ownership of the property, an automobile, where entity named as owner in indictment was "Ed Byrnes Chevrolet," and evidence at trial indicated ownership by the "dealers" and "Brynes Chevrolet, Inc.," since this section required proof only that the automobile was the property of another, and any distinction as to name of particular entity which owned automobile was irrelevant. State v. Stanley, 132 N.H. 571, 567 A.2d 575, 1989 N.H. LEXIS 146 (1989).

7. Burden of proof

In order for the state to convict on the charge of receiving stolen property, it must prove beyond a reasonable doubt that the property was stolen, that the defendant possessed the property, that he believed the property was stolen and that he intended to deprive the owners of the property. State v. Stauff, 126 N.H. 186, 489 A.2d 140, 1985 N.H. LEXIS 244 (1985).

8. Evidence

Evidence that defendant took temporary possession of intimate photographs he found in his tenants' apartment, without the tenants' permission, and scanned those photographs into his computer, also without permission, was sufficient to sustain defendant's conviction for receiving stolen property. State v. Nelson, 150 N.H. 569, 842 A.2d 83, 2004 N.H. LEXIS 28 (2004).

Evidence was sufficient to support a conviction based on the receipt of a stolen gun where the gun was stolen from a coin shop in Connecticut, the defendant and the perpetrator of the robbery were friends, and the defendant spent time with that perpetrator in Connecticut around the time the coin shop was robbed. State v. Prevost, 141 N.H. 647, 690 A.2d 1029, 1997 N.H. LEXIS 15 (1997).

Evidence was sufficient to establish that the defendant knew that an outboard motor was stolen where: (1) the defendant admitted that he paid only $1,200 for the motor, which had a retail value of approximately $6,500, (2) the defendant's explanation for why he took the motor to New Hampshire to be worked on, rather that having it worked on in Massachusetts, where he lived, was unlikely, and (3) the owner of the store where the defendant claimed to have purchased the motor testified that a document submitted by the defendant was not a receipt from his store and was not on a form used by his store, and that his store had never sold boats or boat motors. State v. Wong, 138 N.H. 56, 635 A.2d 470, 1993 N.H. LEXIS 157 (1993).

At trial for receipt of stolen property, handwritten document purporting to be a bill of sale transferring ownership of automobile to defendant was properly admitted over hearsay objection, since state did not offer the information for its truth, but to prove that the defendant had held himself out as the car's owner with authority that was inconsistent with the true owner's rights, thus indicating the requisite intent to deprive. State v. Stanley, 132 N.H. 571, 567 A.2d 575, 1989 N.H. LEXIS 146 (1989).

Circumstantial evidence which sheds light on the surrounding facts and circumstances is admissible in a case involving the receipt of stolen property. State v. Stauff, 126 N.H. 186, 489 A.2d 140, 1985 N.H. LEXIS 244 (1985).

In a prosecution for receiving three stolen firearms, evidence indicating that a joint burglary was being undertaken by defendant and two accomplices was relevant in demonstrating possession and knowledge of the stolen guns, since it could be inferred that the guns were intended to be used in the planned burglary. State v. Stauff, 126 N.H. 186, 489 A.2d 140, 1985 N.H. LEXIS 244 (1985).

Where defendant was a passenger in a stolen car, stolen firearms were within the passenger compartment of the car, so that it could reasonably be inferred that defendant knew of their presence, and the firearms were thrown from the car during a high-speed chase by police giving rise to an inference that defendant knew or believed them to be stolen, there was sufficient evidence upon which a rational trier of fact could have found that defendant possessed the stolen firearms and believed them to be stolen. State v. Stauff, 126 N.H. 186, 489 A.2d 140, 1985 N.H. LEXIS 244 (1985).

Where defendant was a passenger in a car which pulled away from the parking lot of a building where a burglar alarm had gone off, the car was stopped by police after a high-speed chase, inside the car were burglary tools, ammunition and a glove, stolen firearms, found along the chase route, on the right hand side of the road, matched ammunition found in the car, defendant was the only passenger on the right hand side of the car, fingerprints on one of the weapons matched those of another passenger in the car, and the presence of the glove was consistent with the lack of defendant's fingerprints on the weapons, there was sufficient evidence for the jury to infer that defendant possessed the stolen firearms. State v. Stauff, 126 N.H. 186, 489 A.2d 140, 1985 N.H. LEXIS 244 (1985).

9. Sentencing

Trial court erred in imposing an enhanced sentence under RSA 651:2, II-g. One of the elements of the offense for which defendant was convicted, felony receipt of stolen property under RSA 637:7 and RSA 637:11, I(b), was not the possession, use, or attempted use of a deadly weapon. State v. Mohamed, 159 N.H. 559, 986 A.2d 649, 2009 N.H. LEXIS 149 (2009).

Cited:

Cited in State v. Partlow, 117 N.H. 78, 369 A.2d 221, 1977 N.H. LEXIS 274 (1977); State v. Collins, 117 N.H. 198, 371 A.2d 1154, 1977 N.H. LEXIS 300 (1977); State v. Spade, 118 N.H. 186, 385 A.2d 115, 1978 N.H. LEXIS 373 (1978); State v. Scione, 118 N.H. 922, 395 A.2d 1252, 1978 N.H. LEXIS 323 (1978); State v. Hastings, 121 N.H. 465, 430 A.2d 1131, 1981 N.H. LEXIS 353 (1981); State v. Lurvey, 122 N.H. 190, 442 A.2d 592, 1982 N.H. LEXIS 316 (1982); State v. Dumont, 122 N.H. 866, 451 A.2d 1286, 1982 N.H. LEXIS 478 (1982); State v. McNally, 122 N.H. 892, 451 A.2d 1305, 1982 N.H. LEXIS 487 (1982); State v. Hebert, 122 N.H. 1089, 453 A.2d 1310, 1982 N.H. LEXIS 526 (1982); State v. Donovan, 123 N.H. 446, 462 A.2d 125, 1983 N.H. LEXIS 303 (1983); State v. Copeland, 124 N.H. 90, 467 A.2d 238, 1983 N.H. LEXIS 367 (1983); State v. McGann, 124 N.H. 101, 467 A.2d 571, 1983 N.H. LEXIS 368 (1983); State v. Sidebotham, 124 N.H. 682, 474 A.2d 1377, 1984 N.H. LEXIS 344 (1984); State v. Bell, 125 N.H. 425, 480 A.2d 906, 1984 N.H. LEXIS 253 (1984); State v. Lamb, 125 N.H. 495, 484 A.2d 1074, 1984 N.H. LEXIS 408 (1984); State v. Chaisson, 125 N.H. 810, 486 A.2d 297, 1984 N.H. LEXIS 320 (1984); State v. Donohue, 126 N.H. 182, 489 A.2d 139, 1985 N.H. LEXIS 242 (1985); State v. Cote, 126 N.H. 366, 493 A.2d 459, 1985 N.H. LEXIS 300 (1985); State v. Cote, 126 N.H. 514, 493 A.2d 1170, 1985 N.H. LEXIS 336 (1985); State v. Dumais, 126 N.H. 532, 493 A.2d 501, 1985 N.H. LEXIS 337 (1985); State v. Camargo, 126 N.H. 766, 498 A.2d 292, 1985 N.H.

LEXIS 418 (1985); State v. Harper, 126 N.H. 815, 498 A.2d 310, 1985 N.H. LEXIS 409 (1985); State v. Gray, 127 N.H. 348, 499 A.2d 1013, 1985 N.H. LEXIS 427 (1985); State v. McGann, 128 N.H. 186, 514 A.2d 1247, 1986 N.H. LEXIS 306 (1986); State v. Wellman, 128 N.H. 340, 513 A.2d 944, 1986 N.H. LEXIS 294 (1986); State v. Jaroma, 128 N.H. 423, 514 A.2d 1274, 1986 N.H. LEXIS 304 (1986); State v. Hammell, 128 N.H. 787, 519 A.2d 307, 1986 N.H. LEXIS 358 (1986); State v. Johnson, 129 N.H. 33, 523 A.2d 47, 1986 N.H. LEXIS 390 (1986); State v. Pugliese, 129 N.H. 442, 529 A.2d 925, 1987 N.H. LEXIS 226 (1987); State v. Wentzell, 131 N.H. 151, 551 A.2d 960, 1988 N.H. LEXIS 100 (1988); State v. Reynolds, 131 N.H. 291, 556 A.2d 298, 1988 N.H. LEXIS 128 (1988); State v. Brown, 132 N.H. 321, 565 A.2d 1035, 1989 N.H. LEXIS 112 (1989); State v. Bertrand, 133 N.H. 843, 587 A.2d 1219, 1991 N.H. LEXIS 8 (1991); State v. Murray, 134 N.H. 613, 598 A.2d 206, 1991 N.H. LEXIS 107 (1991); State v. Skidmore, 138 N.H. 201, 636 A.2d 64, 1993 N.H. LEXIS 181 (1993); State v. Jaroma, 139 N.H. 611, 660 A.2d 1131, 1995 N.H. LEXIS 63 (1995); Derosia v. Warden, N.H. State Prison, 149 N.H. 579, 826 A.2d 575, 2003 N.H. LEXIS 78 (2003).

RESEARCH REFERENCES

New Hampshire Trial Bar News.
For article, "Presumptions in New Hampshire Law—A Guide Through the Impenetrable Jungle (Part II)," see 11 N.H. Trial Bar News 31, 34, 43 nn.112–113, 36 (Fall 1991)

New Hampshire Bar Journal.
For article, "Criminal Theft of an Image: State v. Nelson and Federal Copyright Law," see 46 N.H.B.J. 48 (Fall 2005).

637:7-a. Possession of Property Without Serial Number.

I. No person shall knowingly remove, deface, alter, change, destroy, obliterate or mutilate, or cause to be removed, defaced, altered, changed, destroyed, obliterated or mutilated the identifying number or numbers or any other identifying mark on any machine, mechanical or electrical device or any other property. Anyone doing so with the intent thereby to conceal the identity of the item or to defraud a manufacturer, seller or purchaser, or to hinder competition in the areas of sales and servicing, or to prevent the detection of a crime shall be guilty of a misdemeanor.

II. Any person who buys, receives, possesses, sells or disposes of any machine, mechanical or electrical device or any other property knowing that the identification number or numbers or any other identifying mark on the item have been removed, defaced, altered, changed, destroyed, obliterated or mutilated shall be guilty of a misdemeanor. However, if a person discovering that the identification number or numbers or any other identifying mark have been removed, defaced, altered, changed, destroyed, obliterated or mutilated shall report the same to the nearest police station, he shall not be charged with violating this section. Further, said provisions do not apply to those persons who, on August 13, 1977, are lawfully in possession of that type of property described in paragraph I which does not have identifying numbers or marks or from which the identifying marks or numbers have been lost inadvertently.

III. The provisions of this section do not apply to those cases or instances where any of the changes or alterations enumerated in paragraph I have been customarily made or done in an established practice in the ordinary and regular conduct of business by the original manufacturer, or by his duly appointed direct representative, or under specific authorization from the original manufacturer.

IV. When property described in paragraph I comes into the custody of a law enforcement officer, it shall be considered stolen or embezzled property, and prior to being disposed of, shall have an identifying number engraved on it or embedded in it.

Source.
1977, 187:1, eff. Aug. 13, 1977.

Revision note.
In the third sentence of par. II, substituted "August 13, 1977" for "the effective date of this section" for purposes of clarity.

Cross References.
Classification of crimes, see RSA 625:9.
Sentences, see RSA 651.

NOTES TO DECISIONS

Probable cause for arrest
Although knowledge of the removal of the serial number from property is an element of the crime of possession of property without a serial number which must be proven at trial, proof that the defendant knew that the serial number had been removed was not required to establish probable cause for an arrest. State v. Crotty, 134 N.H. 706, 597 A.2d 1078, 1991 N.H. LEXIS 126 (1991).

637:8. Theft of Services.

I. A person commits theft if he obtains services which he knows are available only for compensation by deception, threat, force, or any other means designed to avoid the due payment therefor. "Deception" has the same meaning as in RSA 637:4, II, and "threat" the same meaning as in RSA 637:5, II.

II. A person commits theft if, having control over the disposition of services of another, to which he knows he is not entitled, he diverts such services to his own benefit or to the benefit of another who he knows is not entitled thereto.

III. As used in this section, "services" includes, but is not necessarily limited to, labor, professional service, public utility and transportation services, restaurant, hotel, motel, tourist cabin, rooming house and like accommodations, the supplying of equipment, tools, vehicles, or trailers for temporary use, telephone or telegraph service, gas, electricity, water or steam, admission to entertainment, exhibitions, sporting events or other events for which a charge is made.

IV. This section shall not apply to the attachment of private equipment to residential telephone lines unless the telephone company can prove that the attached equipment will cause direct harm to the telephone system. Attached equipment which is registered with the public utilities commission shall not require a protective interconnecting device. If the telephone company cites this section in its directories or other customer informational material, said company shall duplicate the entire section verbatim therein.

Source.
1971, 518:1. 1977, 175:1, eff. Aug. 7, 1977.

Amendments
—**1977.** Paragraph IV: Added.

Cross References.
Theft of computer services, see RSA 638:17, II.

NOTES TO DECISIONS

Cited:
Cited in State v. Hill, 115 N.H. 37, 332 A.2d 182, 1975 N.H. LEXIS 217 (1975); Hogan v. Robert H. Irwin Motors, 121 N.H. 737, 433 A.2d 1322, 1981 N.H. LEXIS 392 (1981); Greenberg v. Mynczywor, 667 F. Supp. 901, 1987 U.S. Dist. LEXIS 7712 (D.N.H. 1987).

637:9. Unauthorized Use of Propelled Vehicle or Rented Property.

I. A person is guilty of theft if:

(a) Having custody of a propelled vehicle pursuant to an agreement between himself or another and the owner thereof whereby the actor or another is to perform for compensation a specific service for the owner involving the maintenance, repair or use of such vehicle, he intentionally uses or operates the same, without the consent of the owner, for his own purposes in a manner constituting a gross deviation from the agreed purpose; or

(b) Having custody of a propelled vehicle pursuant to a rental or lease agreement with the owner thereof whereby such vehicle is to be returned to the owner at a specified time and place, he abandons the vehicle or willfully refuses or neglects to redeliver it to the owner in such manner as he may have agreed; or

(c) Having custody of any property pursuant to a rental or lease agreement whereby such property is to be returned in a specified manner, intentionally fails to comply with the terms of the agreement concerning return so as to render such failure a gross deviation from the agreement.

II. [Repealed.]

III. As used in this section, "propelled vehicle" means any automobile, airplane, motorcycle, motorboat or any other motor-propelled vehicle or vessel, or any boat or vessel propelled by sail, oar or paddle.

Source.
1971, 518:1. 1985, 176:1. 1992, 269:22, I, eff. July 1, 1992.

Amendments
—**1992.** Paragraph II: Repealed.

—**1985.** Paragraph I: Substituted "abandons the vehicle or willfully refuses or neglects to redeliver it to the owner in such manner as he may have agreed" for "intentionally fails to comply with the agreed terms concerning return of such vehicle, without the consent of the owner, for so lengthy a period beyond the specified time for return as to render his retention or possession or other failure to return a gross deviation from the agreement" following "place, he" in subpar. (b) and made other minor stylistic changes in the introductory clause.

Cross References.
Classification of crimes, see RSA 625:9.
Sentences, see RSA 651.

Cited:

Cited in State v. Murgatroy, 115 N.H. 717, 349 A.2d 600, 1975 N.H. LEXIS 408 (1975); State v. Wong, 125 N.H. 610, 486 A.2d 262, 1984 N.H. LEXIS 413 (1984); State v. Bailey, 127 N.H. 811, 508 A.2d 1066, 1986 N.H. LEXIS 243 (1986).

637:10. Theft by Misapplication of Property.

I. A person commits theft if he obtains property from anyone or personal services from an employee upon agreement, or subject to a known legal obligation, to make a specified payment or other disposition to a third person, whether from that property or its proceeds or from his own property to be reserved in an equivalent or agreed amount, if he purposely or recklessly fails to make the required payment or disposition and deals with the property obtained or withheld as his own.

II. Liability under paragraph I is not affected by the fact that it may be impossible to identify particular property as belonging to the victim at the time of the failure to make the required payment or disposition.

III. An officer or employee of the government or of a financial institution is presumed:

(a) To know of any legal obligation relevant to his liability under this section, and

(b) To have dealt with the property as his own if he fails to pay or account upon lawful demand, or if an audit reveals a shortage or falsification of his accounts.

IV. As used in this section:

(a) "Financial institution" means a bank, insurance company, credit union, safety deposit company, savings and loan association, investment trust, or other organization held out to the public as a place of deposit of funds or medium of savings or collective investment.

(b) "Government" means the United States, any state or any county, municipality or other political unit within territory belonging to the United States, or any department, agency, or subdivision of any of the foregoing, or any corporation or other association carrying out the functions of government or formed pursuant to interstate compact or international treaty.

Source.

1971, 518:1, eff. Nov. 1, 1973.

Sufficient evidence.

In a prosecution for theft by misapplication of property, under RSA 637:10, alleging that defendant treated his father's funds as his own instead of using them to pay his father's nursing home, defendant was not entitled to dismissal because it was undisputed that all but $ 50 of the father's income was to go to the nursing home, and the evidence showed defendant withdrew more money in cash from the father's accounts than he deposited, showing that he withdrew thousands of dollars of his father's money and that the money did not go to the nursing home, nor did defendant establish another account to receive the money, so a rational jury could have found beyond a reasonable doubt that the evidence excluded all rational conclusions except that defendant withheld payments from the nursing home and dealt with his father's money as his own. State v. Huffman, 154 N.H. 678, 918 A.2d 1279, 2007 N.H. LEXIS 3 (2007).

Cited:

Cited in State v. Heinz, 119 N.H. 717, 407 A.2d 814, 1979 N.H. LEXIS 382 (1979); State v. Dennehy, 127 N.H. 425, 503 A.2d 769, 1985 N.H. LEXIS 462 (1985); State v. Davis, 143 N.H. 8, 718 A.2d 1202, 1998 N.H. LEXIS 60 (1998).

OPINIONS OF THE ATTORNEY GENERAL

Conversion of lottery tickets

Conversion of lottery tickets to cash by person entrusted by the government with those tickets would constitute the crime of misapplication of property, and under some circumstances could constitute the crime of theft by unauthorized taking, or theft by misapplication of property. Op. Atty. Gen. 86-51.

RESEARCH REFERENCES

New Hampshire Trial Bar News.

For article, "Presumptions in New Hampshire Law—A Guide Through the Impenetrable Jungle (Part II)," see 11 N.H. Trial Bar News 31, 34 n.112 (Fall 1991).

637:10-a. Use or Possession of Theft Detection Shielding Devices and Theft Detection Device Removers.

I. A person commits unlawful use of a theft detection shielding device when he or she engages in the following acts:

(a) Knowingly manufactures, sells, offers for sale, or distributes a laminated or coated bag or device specially designed, marketed, and intended to be used to shield merchandise from detection by an electronic or magnetic theft alarm sensor.

(b) Knowingly possesses any laminated or coated bag or device specially designed, marketed, and intended to be used to shield merchandise from detection by an electronic or magnetic theft alarm sensor, with the intent to commit a theft.

II. A person commits unlawful possession of a theft detection device remover when he or she knowingly possesses any tool or device designed to allow the removal of any theft detection device from any merchandise, with the intent to use such tool to remove the detection device from the merchandise without the permission of the merchant or person owning or holding said merchandise.

III. Persons convicted of either the use or possession of theft detection shielding devices or theft detection device removers shall be guilty of a misdemeanor.

Source.

2000, 89:1, eff. April 27, 2000.

637:10-b. Fraudulent Retail Transactions.

I. A person shall be guilty of a misdemeanor if such person possesses, uses, transfers, manufactures, alters, counterfeits, or reproduces a retail sales receipt or universal product code label with the purpose to deprive a merchant of goods or merchandise.

II. A person shall be guilty of a class B felony if such person possesses, uses, transfers, manufactures, alters, counterfeits, or reproduces 5 or more retail sales receipts or universal product code labels, or any combination of 5 or more sales receipts or universal product code labels, or possesses a device designed or adapted to manufacture counterfeit retail sales receipts or universal product code labels with the purpose to deprive a merchant of goods or merchandise.

Source.
2009, 209:4, eff. January 1, 2010.

637:10-c. Organized Retail Crime Enterprise.

A person is guilty of a class B felony, and a class A felony for a second or subsequent offense, if he or she conspires with one or more persons to engage for profit in a scheme or course of conduct of theft as defined in RSA 637:3-a, II or RSA 637:10-b. A conviction under this section shall not merge with the conviction for any offense that is the object of the conspiracy.

Source.
2010, 239:13, eff. July 1, 2010.

637:11. Penalties.

I. Theft constitutes a class A felony if:
(a) The value of the property or services exceeds $1,500, or
(b) The property stolen is a firearm, or
(c) The actor is armed with a deadly weapon at the time of the theft, except that if the deadly weapon is a firearm, he shall be sentenced in accordance with RSA 651:2, II-g.

II. Theft constitutes a class B felony if:
(a) The value of the property or services is more than $1,000 but not more than $1,500, or
(b) The actor has been twice before convicted of theft of property or services, as a felony or class A misdemeanor, or
(c) The theft constitutes a violation of RSA 637:5, II(a) or (b), or
(d) The property or services stolen are from 3 separate business establishments within a 72-hour period, or
(e) The property is stolen with intent to resell or distribute. It would be prima facie evidence that the offense constitutes theft with intent to resell or distribute when the theft consists of goods or merchandise in quantities that would not normally be purchased for personal use or consumption, or
(f) The property received in violation of RSA 637:7 consists of goods or merchandise in quantities that would not normally be purchased for personal use or consumption, or

(g) The actor has twice before been convicted of offenses under RSA 637:3-a, II and the present and prior convictions were based on offenses committed within a 36-month period.

III. Theft constitutes a misdemeanor if the value of the property or services does not exceed $1,000.

Source.
1971, 518:1. 1977, 187:2. 1979, 266:1. 1990, 95:6. 1992, 269:14, 22, II, eff. July 1, 1992. 2001, 174:2, eff. Jan. 1, 2002. 2010, 239:3, eff. July 1, 2010.

Amendments
—2010. The 2010 amendment substituted "$1,500" for "$1,000" in I(a) and II(a); substituted "$1,000" for "$500" in II(a) and III; added II(e) through II(g); and made related changes.

—2001. Paragraph II: Added "or" following "RSA 637:5, II(a) or (b)" in subpar. (c) and added subpar. (d).

—1992. Deleted the introductory paragraph and inserted "as a felony or class A misdemeanor" following "services" in par. II(b).

—1990. Paragraph I(c): Added "except that if the deadly weapon is a firearm, he shall be sentenced in accordance with RSA 651:2, II-g" following "theft".

—1979. Paragraph II(b): Deleted "valued at one hundred dollars or less" following "services".

—1977. Paragraph II(a): Substituted "$500" for "one hundred dollars" preceding "but not more than" and "$1000" for "one thousand dollars" thereafter.
Paragraph III: Substituted "$500" for "one hundred dollars" following "exceed".

Applicability of 1992 amendment.
1992, 269:21, eff. July 1, 1992, provided that the amendments to this section by 1992, 269:14, 22, II, shall apply to all offenses committed on or after July 1, 1992.

Cross References.
Classification of crimes, see RSA 625:9.
Sentences, see RSA 651.

NOTES TO DECISIONS

1. Theft of firearm
2. Aggregation of theft counts
3. Prior convictions
4. Value of property or services
5. Sentencing
6. Construction

1. Theft of firearm
To determine whether a weapon is a firearm under this section, issue is whether the weapon is designed to, or is capable of, discharging a shot by gunpowder, not whether it was capable of discharge at the time of the offense; thus, where a defendant has been charged with theft of a firearm, state need not prove operability of the firearm at the time of the offense as an essential element. State v. Taylor, 136 N.H. 131, 612 A.2d 917, 1992 N.H. LEXIS 147 (1992).

2. Aggregation of theft counts
A defendant may not attempt to prove a common intent or scheme, in order to aggregate several class A felony theft counts into one class A felony, and thereby effect a conviction of no more than one class A felony. State v. Williams, 133 N.H. 631, 581 A.2d 78, 1990 N.H. LEXIS 111 (1990).

3. Prior convictions
Plain language of RSA 637:11, II(b), together with RSA 625:9, III and IV(a), expressed the legislature's intent to include out-of-state theft convictions as predicate sentence enhancement offenses. Thus, defendant, who had two theft convictions in another state,

could be charged with class B felony theft as a third offense under RSA 637:11, II(b). State v. Lukas, 164 N.H. 693, 62 A.3d 883, 2013 N.H. LEXIS 25 (2013).

Petitioner's prior burglary with the purpose to commit theft was a "theft" crime for the purpose of sentence enhancement and, thus, petitioner's prior conviction on that offense meant his sentence could be enhanced in regard to current conviction on one count of stolen property. Derosia v. Warden, N.H. State Prison, 149 N.H. 579, 826 A.2d 575, 2003 N.H. LEXIS 78 (2003), rehearing denied, 2003 N.H. LEXIS 111 (N.H. July 18, 2003).

Two prior convictions based on nolo contendere pleas could properly be put into evidence by the state for the purpose of invoking subparagraph II(b) of this section, where the collateral attack by the defendant on the validity of these prior convictions, based on the allegation that she was not properly apprised of the fact that after entry of her nolo pleas those convictions could be used for penalty enhancement, did not meet the requirement that allegations of involuntary or unknowing waiver of constitutional rights state the specific manner in which the guilty or nolo plea was in fact involuntary or without understanding. State v. Harper, 126 N.H. 815, 498 A.2d 310, 1985 N.H. LEXIS 409 (1985).

4. Value of property or services

Defendant was not entitled to directed verdict since State was not required to prove that he obtained entire $25,000 lump sum workers' compensation settlement through theft by deception; value of property taken was not an element of the crime and, to obtain a conviction for class A felony theft by deception, State was only required to prove that property taken was valued at more than $1,000. State v. French, 146 N.H. 97, 776 A.2d 1253, 2001 N.H. LEXIS 35 (2001).

At trial for theft, the state had the burden of proving the value of the property involved beyond a reasonable doubt. State v. Gray, 127 N.H. 348, 499 A.2d 1013, 1985 N.H. LEXIS 427 (1985).

Defendant's theft conviction was reversed, where evidence was insufficient to prove beyond a reasonable doubt the value of the property involved. State v. Gray, 127 N.H. 348, 499 A.2d 1013, 1985 N.H. LEXIS 427 (1985).

5. Sentencing

Trial court erred in imposing an enhanced sentence under RSA 651:2, II-g. One of the elements of the offense for which defendant was convicted, felony receipt of stolen property under RSA 637:7 and RSA 637:11, I(b), was not the possession, use, or attempted use of a deadly weapon. State v. Mohamed, 159 N.H. 559, 986 A.2d 649, 2009 N.H. LEXIS 149 (2009).

6. Construction

Because there is no ambiguity in RSA 637:11, II(b), the rule of lenity does not apply. State v. Lukas, 164 N.H. 693, 62 A.3d 883, 2013 N.H. LEXIS 25 (2013).

Cited:

Cited in State v. Harlan, 116 N.H. 598, 364 A.2d 1254, 1976 N.H. LEXIS 423 (1976); State v. Partlow, 117 N.H. 78, 369 A.2d 221, 1977 N.H. LEXIS 274 (1977); State v. Lantaigne, 117 N.H. 266, 371 A.2d 1170, 1977 N.H. LEXIS 313 (1977); Bell v. Superior Court Sentence Review Div., 117 N.H. 474, 374 A.2d 659, 1977 N.H. LEXIS 358 (1977); Partlow v. Perrin, 117 N.H. 957, 379 A.2d 1273, 1977 N.H. LEXIS 470 (1977); State v. Kelley, 120 N.H. 12, 413 A.2d 308, 1980 N.H. LEXIS 219 (1980); State v. Sampson, 120 N.H. 251, 413 A.2d 590, 1980 N.H. LEXIS 268 (1980); State v. Lemire, 121 N.H. 1, 424 A.2d 1135, 1981 N.H. LEXIS 238 (1981); State v. Hastings, 121 N.H. 465, 430 A.2d 1131, 1981 N.H. LEXIS 353 (1981); State v. Dumont, 122 N.H. 866, 451 A.2d 1286, 1982 N.H. LEXIS 478 (1982); State v. Cyr, 122 N.H. 1155, 453 A.2d 1315, 1982 N.H. LEXIS 531 (1982); Heald v. Perrin, 123 N.H. 468, 464 A.2d 275, 1983 N.H. LEXIS 310 (1983); State v. Robinson, 123 N.H. 532, 465 A.2d 1201, 1983 N.H. LEXIS 317 (1983); State v. Reynolds, 124 N.H. 428, 471 A.2d 1172, 1984 N.H. LEXIS 218 (1984); State v. Steele, 125 N.H. 190, 480 A.2d 80, 1984 N.H. LEXIS 358 (1984); State v. Fleming, 125 N.H. 238, 480 A.2d 107, 1984 N.H. LEXIS 365 (1984); State v. Kelly, 125 N.H. 484, 484 A.2d 1066, 1984 N.H. LEXIS 410 (1984); State v. Abbis, 125 N.H. 646, 484 A.2d 1156, 1984 N.H. LEXIS 387 (1984); State v. O'Flynn, 126 N.H. 706, 496 A.2d 348, 1985 N.H. LEXIS 349 (1985); State v. Camargo, 126 N.H. 766,

498 A.2d 292, 1985 N.H. LEXIS 418 (1985); State v. McGann, 128 N.H. 186, 514 A.2d 1247, 1986 N.H. LEXIS 306 (1986); State v. Wellman, 128 N.H. 340, 513 A.2d 944, 1986 N.H. LEXIS 294 (1986); State v. Hammell, 128 N.H. 787, 519 A.2d 307, 1986 N.H. LEXIS 358 (1986); Greenberg v. Mynczywor, 667 F. Supp. 901, 1987 U.S. Dist. LEXIS 7712 (D.N.H. 1987); State v. Gruber, 132 N.H. 83, 562 A.2d 156, 1989 N.H. LEXIS 71 (1989); State v. Paris, 137 N.H. 322, 627 A.2d 582, 1993 N.H. LEXIS 78 (1993).

CHAPTER 638

FRAUD

Forgery and Fraudulent Practices Generally

SECTION
638:1.	Forgery.
638:2.	Fraudulent Handling of Recordable Writings.
638:3.	Tampering with Public or Private Records.
638:4.	Issuing Bad Checks.
638:5.	Fraudulent Use of Credit Card.
638:5-a.	Fraudulent Communications Paraphernalia.
638:6.	Deceptive Business Practices.
638:6-a.	Dealing in Counterfeit Recordings.
638:6-b.	Dealing in Counterfeit Goods.
638:7.	Commercial Bribery.
638:8.	Sports Bribery.
638:9.	Fraud on Creditors.
638:10.	Frauds on Depositors.
638:11.	Misapplication of Property.
638:12.	Fraudulent Execution of Documents.
638:13.	Use and Possession of Slugs.
638:14.	Unlawful Simulation of Legal Process.
638:15.	Fraud on the Women, Infants, and Children (WIC) Program.
638:15-a.	False Academic Documentation.

Computer Crime

638:16.	Computer Crime; Definitions.
638:17.	Computer related offenses.
638:18.	Computer Crime Penalties.
638:19.	Venue.

Insurance Fraud

638:20.	Insurance Fraud.
638:20-a.	Venue.

Wireless Telephone Cloning

638:21.	Definitions.
638:22.	Criminal Acts Involving Cloned Phones and Telephone Cloning Paraphernalia; Possession or Use.
638:23.	Criminal Acts Involving Cloned Phones and Telephone Cloning Paraphernalia; Traffic and Manufacture; Exclusions.
638:24.	Restitution; Civil Action; Forfeiture.

Identity Fraud

638:25.	Definitions.
638:26.	Identity Fraud.
638:27.	Venue.

Illegal Use of Payment Card Scanning Device or Reencoder

638:28.	Definitions.
638:29.	Use of Scanning Device or Reencoder to Defraud Prohibited.

Cross References.

Charging intent to defraud, see RSA 601:5.

Fraudulent conveyances, see RSA 545-A.

Forgery and Fraudulent Practices Generally

638:1. Forgery.

I. A person is guilty of forgery if, with purpose to defraud anyone, or with knowledge that he is facilitating a fraud to be perpetrated by anyone, he:

(a) Alters any writing of another without his authority or utters any such altered writing; or

(b) Makes, completes, executes, authenticates, issues, transfers, publishes or otherwise utters any writing so that it purports to be the act of another, or purports to have been executed at a time or place or in a numbered sequence other than was in fact the case, or to be a copy of an original when no such original existed.

II. As used in this section, "writing" includes printing or any other method of recording information, checks, tokens, stamps, seals, credit cards, badges, trademarks, and other symbols of value, right, privilege, or identification.

III. Forgery is a class B felony if the writing is or purports to be:

(a) A security, revenue stamp, or any other instrument issued by a government, or any agency thereof; or

(b) A check, an issue of stocks, bonds, or any other instrument representing an interest in or a claim against property, or a pecuniary interest in or claim against any person or enterprise.

IV. All other forgery is a class B misdemeanor.

V. A person is guilty of a class B misdemeanor if he knowingly possesses any writing that is a forgery under this section or any device for making any such writing. It is an affirmative defense to prosecution under this paragraph that the possession was without an intent to defraud.

Source.
1971, 518:1. 1992, 269:15, eff. July 1, 1992.

Amendments
—1992. Inserted "class B" preceding "misdemeanor" in par. IV and the first sentence of par. V.

Applicability of 1992 amendment.
1992, 269:21, eff. July 1, 1992, provided that the amendment to this section by 1992, 269:15, shall apply to all offenses committed on or after July 1, 1992.

Cross References.
Classification of crimes, see RSA 625:9.
Forging election documents, see RSA 666:6.
Forging food or drug identification device, see RSA 146:1.
Forging motor vehicle certificate of title, see RSA 262:1.
Forged motor vehicle inspection sticker or registration validation decal, see RSA 262:16.
Forgery to obtain a controlled drug, see RSA 318-B:2.
Sentences, see RSA 651.

NOTES TO DECISIONS

1. Subject of forgery
2. Intent
3. Alteration of signed document
4. Indictment

1. Subject of forgery
Ordinarily the writing or instrument which may be the subject of forgery must be, or purport to be the act of another, or it must at the time be the property of another, or must be some writing or instrument under which others have acquired some rights, or have in some way become liable, and where these rights or liabilities are sought to be affected or changed by the alteration without their consent. State v. Young, 46 N.H. 266, 1865 N.H. LEXIS 64 (1865). (Decided under prior law.)

A forged writing or instrument must, in itself, be false, that is, fictitious, not genuine, a counterfeit, and not the true instrument which it purports to be, without regard to the truth or falsehood of the statement which the writing contains. State v. Young, 46 N.H. 266, 1865 N.H. LEXIS 64 (1865). (Decided under prior law.)

2. Intent
To constitute forgery it is not enough that the accused signed the name of another person to a promissory note without authority, but it must also have been done with an intent to defraud. Grafton Bank v. Flanders, 4 N.H. 239, 1827 N.H. LEXIS 55 (1827). (Decided under prior law.)

3. Alteration of signed document
Where A and B made a note for $20, payable to H, which note B took for the purpose of passing it to the payee H, but before he delivered it, B, without the knowledge or consent of A, altered it to $120 and then passed to H for that sum, B was guilty of forgery, since his act amounted to a fraudulent application of a real signature to a false instrument. Goodman v. Eastman, 4 N.H. 455, 1828 N.H. LEXIS 35 (1828). (Decided under prior law.)

4. Indictment
Requirement of this section that defendant act "with purpose to defraud anyone" did not require allegation in indictment as to specific person defendant intended to defraud by uttering a forged check, and therefore trial court erred in quashing indictment for insufficiency. State v. DeMatteo, 134 N.H. 296, 591 A.2d 1323, 1991 N.H. LEXIS 56 (1991).

Cited:
Cited in State v. Sheedy, 124 N.H. 738, 474 A.2d 1042, 1984 N.H. LEXIS 336 (1984); State v. Allegra, 129 N.H. 720, 533 A.2d 338, 1987 N.H. LEXIS 247 (1987); State v. Skidmore, 138 N.H. 201, 636 A.2d 64, 1993 N.H. LEXIS 181 (1993); State v. Koehler, 140 N.H. 469, 669 A.2d 788, 1995 N.H. LEXIS 173 (1995).

638:2. Fraudulent Handling of Recordable Writings.

A person is guilty of a class B felony if, with a purpose to deceive or injure anyone, he falsifies, destroys, removes or conceals any will, deed, mortgage, security instrument or other writing for which the law provides public recording.

Source.
1971, 518:1, eff. Nov. 1, 1973.

Cross References.
Classification of crimes, see RSA 625:9.
Sentences, see RSA 651.

NOTES TO DECISIONS

1. Applicability
2. Joinder

1. Applicability
Cremation certificates are not similar in nature to the documents enumerated in RSA 638:2, which affect property interests, and thus are not recordable writings within the meaning of the statute. Accordingly, defendant, a medical examiner, had not violated the statute by falsely signing such certificates. State v. Breed, 159 N.H. 61, 977 A.2d 463, 2009 N.H. LEXIS 88 (2009).

2. Joinder

Trial court did not err in joining theft by deception and fraudulent handling of recordable writings offenses when the trial court reasonably found that each fraudulent transaction or theft in which defendant, a medical examiner, engaged was part of an overarching plan of furthering his increasingly profitable relationship with a crematorium, and, in this way, the charges were mutually dependent. The trial court reasonably could have found that the defendant was not merely taking advantage of opportunities as they arose, but instead was exhibiting forethought and premeditation in his scheming. State v. Breed, 159 N.H. 61, 977 A.2d 463, 2009 N.H. LEXIS 88 (2009).

Cited:

Cited in State v. Dowdle, 148 N.H. 345, 807 A.2d 1237, 2002 N.H. LEXIS 133 (2002).

638:3. Tampering with Public or Private Records.

A person is guilty of a misdemeanor if, knowing he has no privilege to do so, he falsifies, destroys, removes or conceals any writing or record, public or private, with a purpose to deceive or injure anyone or to conceal any wrongdoing.

Source.
1971, 518:1, eff. Nov. 1, 1973.

Cross References.
Classification of crimes, see RSA 625:9.
Sentences, see RSA 651.

638:4. Issuing Bad Checks.

I. A person is guilty of issuing a bad check if he issues or passes a check for the payment of money and payment is refused by the drawee, except in cases where a legal stop payment order has been issued or where the drawee refuses payment for any other reason through no fault of the person who issued or passed the check.

I-a. A person who issues or passes a bad check is subject to prosecution in the jurisdiction in which he issued or passed the check.

II. For the purposes of this section, as well as in any prosecution for theft committed by means of a bad check, a person who issues a check for which payment is refused by the drawee is presumed to know that such check would not be paid if he had no account with the drawee at the time of issue.

III. It is an affirmative defense that the actor paid the amount of the check, together with all costs and protest fees, to the person to whom it was due, within 14 days after having received notice that payment was refused. The actor's failure to make such payment within 14 days after receiving notice that payment was refused shall be prima facie evidence of a violation of paragraph I of this section.

IV. (a) Issuing a bad check is:

(1) A class A felony if:

(A) The face amount of the check exceeds $1,500; or

(B) The defendant has 2 or more prior convictions under this section, the present and prior convictions were based on offenses com-

mitted within a 12-month period, and the aggregate face amount of the checks underlying the present and prior convictions exceeds $1,500;

(2) A class B felony if:

(A) The face amount of the check exceeds $1,000 but is not more than $1,500; or

(B) The defendant has 2 or more prior convictions under this section, the present and prior convictions were based on offenses committed within a 12-month period, and the aggregate face amount of the checks underlying the present and prior convictions exceeds $1,000 but does not exceed $1,500;

(3) A class A misdemeanor if the face amount of the check does not exceed $1,000 and the actor has been convicted of an offense under this section within the previous 12 months; and

(4) A class B misdemeanor in all other cases.

(b) In any prosecution under subparagraph IV(a), the prosecutor shall prove that the person issued or passed the check knowing or believing that the check would not be paid by the drawee.

(c) Face amounts involved in the issuance of bad checks committed pursuant to one scheme or course of conduct may be aggregated in determining the grade of the offense.

V. In addition to any other sentence which it imposes, the court shall, if restitution is authorized under RSA 651:63, order any person convicted of a violation of this section to make restitution to the person to whom the check was due. Such restitution shall include the amount of the check and may include all reasonable costs and protest fees.

VI. (a) Notwithstanding any other provision of law to the contrary, in any judicial proceeding under this section, a notarized or sworn statement by the bank official who is the keeper of records of the bank upon which the check was drawn shall be admissible as evidence at trial to prove the status or account balance of the person's account on the date the check was issued or passed. The admission of this statement shall eliminate the need for the keeper of records to personally appear and testify before the court.

(b) Nothing in this paragraph shall prevent the person who issued the check for which payment was refused from securing the appearance of the keeper of the records before the court by subpoena or other legal process.

Source.
1971, 518:1. 1979, 265:1. 1983, 378:1, 2. 1985, 163:1. 1989, 269:1–4. 1990, 153:1. 1993, 215:1, 2, eff. Jan. 1, 1994. 2010, 239:4, eff. July 1, 2010.

Amendments
—2010. The 2010 amendment added the IV(a)(1)(A) and IV(a)(2)(A) designations; substituted "$1,500" for "$1,000" in IV(a)(1)(A) and IV(a)(2)(A); added IV(a)(1)(B) and IV(a)(2)(B); substituted "$1,000" for "$500" in IV(a)(2)(A) and IV(a)(3); and made related and stylistic changes.

—1993. Paragraph IV(a): Rewrote subpar. (3) and added subpar. (4).

Paragraph IV(b): Substituted "subparagragph IV(a)" for "subparagraph IV(a)(1) or (2)" preceding "the prosecutor" in the first sentence and deleted the second sentence.

—1990. Paragraph IV: Rewritten to the extent that a detailed comparison would be impracticable.

—1989. Paragraph I: Rewritten to the extent that a detailed comparison would be impracticable.

Paragraph IV(c): Substituted "violation" for "misdemeanor".
Paragraph IV(e): Added.
Paragraph VI: Added.

—1985. Paragraph III: Substituted "14" for "ten" preceding "days" in the first sentence and added the second sentence.

—1983. Paragraph I-a. Added.
Paragraph V: Added.

—1979. Paragraph IV: Rewritten to the extent that a detailed comparison would be impracticable.

Cross References.
Civil liability for bad checks, see RSA 544-B.
Classification of crimes, see RSA 625:9.
Sentences, see RSA 651.

NOTES TO DECISIONS

1. Construction
2. Construction with other laws
3. Intent
4. Probable cause
5. Restitution

1. Construction
Postdated checks are not exempt from the prohibition contained in this section. State v. Fitanides, 141 N.H. 352, 683 A.2d 534, 1996 N.H. LEXIS 102 (1996).

2. Construction with other laws
Under 11 U.S.C.S. § 105, a bankruptcy court can enjoin state criminal proceedings where there in an affirmative showing that those proceedings are in fact employed merely as a collection device for recipients of bad checks and do not involve a true vindication of public rights. In re Milone, 73 B.R. 452, 1987 Bankr. LEXIS 691 (Bankr. D.N.H. 1987).

Under 11 U.S.C.S. § 105, a bankruptcy court may enjoin a criminal proceeding involving a bad check offense even though a restitution obligation may be imposed upon the bankrupt debtor in the criminal proceeding. In re Milone, 73 B.R. 452, 1987 Bankr. LEXIS 691 (Bankr. D.N.H. 1987).

3. Intent
Defendant's conviction of a felony count of issuing a bad check, RSA 638:4, I, IV(a)(1), had to be reversed, because the trial court erred in instructing the jury to consider defendant's belief as to his account balance on the date of the check where the defendant had told the payee that there were insufficient funds to cover the checks but that there would be sufficient funds shortly. By erroneously informing the jury that defendant's knowledge of an insufficient account balance on the date the check was issued was a necessary element of the crime, the court's answer could have misled the jury into thinking such knowledge was sufficient to meet the mens rea requirement for the crime. State v. Stewart, 155 N.H. 212, 921 A.2d 933, 2007 N.H. LEXIS 48 (2007).

Culpable mental state that State is required to prove is that defendant passed check knowing or believing that it would not be paid by drawee bank, and State need not prove that defendant never intended to pay the amount owed. State v. Fitanides, 141 N.H. 352, 683 A.2d 534, 1996 N.H. LEXIS 102 (1996).

4. Probable cause
Where police learned from payee that plaintiff's check had been refused by bank and that plaintiff had failed to respond to a demand letter, police could reasonably infer that plaintiff knew or believed his check would be refused by bank at the time he issued it, and thus police had probable cause to arrest plaintiff for a violation of this section. Hartgers v. Town of Plaistow, 141 N.H. 253, 681 A.2d 82, 1996 N.H. LEXIS 87 (1996).

5. Restitution
Restitution orders are not mandated in all bad check criminal cases; restitution is a discretionary matter and should only be ordered when (1) restitution will serve to rehabilitate the offender, (2) restitution will compensate the victim, and (3) no other compensation is available. In re Milone, 73 B.R. 452, 1987 Bankr. LEXIS 691 (Bankr. D.N.H. 1987).

Cited:
Cited in State v. Sheedy, 124 N.H. 738, 474 A.2d 1042, 1984 N.H. LEXIS 336 (1984); Leavitt v. Hamelin, 126 N.H. 670, 495 A.2d 1286, 1985 N.H. LEXIS 359 (1985); State v. Tucker, 132 N.H. 31, 561 A.2d 1075, 1989 N.H. LEXIS 53 (1989); State v. Schachter, 133 N.H. 439, 577 A.2d 1222, 1990 N.H. LEXIS 81 (1990); State v. Hermsdorf, 135 N.H. 360, 605 A.2d 1045, 1992 N.H. LEXIS 42, (1992); State v. Maynard, 137 N.H. 537, 629 A.2d 1345, 1993 N.H. LEXIS 116 (1993); State v. Smith, 141 N.H. 271, 681 A.2d 1215, 1996 N.H. LEXIS 90 (1996); State v. Smith, 141 N.H. 271, 681 A.2d 1215, 1996 N.H. LEXIS 90 (1996).

638:5. Fraudulent Use of Credit Card.

I. A person is guilty of fraudulent use of a credit card if he uses a credit card for the purpose of obtaining property or services with knowledge that:

(a) The card is stolen; or

(b) The card has been revoked or cancelled; or

(c) For any other reason his use of the card is unauthorized by either the issuer or the person to whom the credit card is issued.

II. "Credit card" means a writing or other evidence of an undertaking to pay for property or services delivered or rendered to or upon the order of a designated person or bearer.

III. (a) Fraudulent use of a credit card is:

(1) A class A felony if:

(A) Property or services are obtained which exceed the value of $1,500; or

(B) The defendant has 2 or more prior convictions under this section, the present and prior convictions were based on offenses committed within a 12-month period, and the aggregate amount of the property or services obtained by the defendant as part of those offenses exceeds $1,500;

(2) A class B felony if:

(A) Property or services are obtained which exceed the value of $1,000 but are not more than the value of $1,500; or

(B) The defendant has 2 or more prior convictions under this section, the present and prior convictions were based on offenses committed within a 12-month period, and the aggregate amount of the property or services obtained by the defendant as part of those offenses exceeds $1,000 but does not exceed $1,500; and

(3) A misdemeanor in all other cases.

(b) The value shall be determined according to the provisions of RSA 637:2, V.

Source.
1971, 518:1. 1979, 265:2, eff. Aug. 20, 1979. 2010, 239:5, eff. July 1, 2010.

Amendments
—2010. The 2010 amendment added the III(a)(1)(A) and III(a)(2)(A) designations; substituted "$1,500" for "$1,000" in III(a)(1)(A) and III(a)(2)(A); added III(a)(1)(B) and III(a)(2)(B); substituted "$1,000" for "$500" in III(a)(2)(A); substituted "shall" for "may" in III(b); and made related changes.

—1979. Paragraph III: Rewritten to the extent that a detailed comparison would be impracticable.

Cross References.
Classification of crimes, see RSA 625:9.
Defrauding an innkeeper by use of a credit card, see RSA 353:7 et seq.
Sentences, see RSA 651.

NOTES TO DECISIONS

Crime of dishonesty or false statement
In establishing the elements of RSA 638:5, I(a), the State must prove that a defendant knowingly used a stolen credit card to obtain goods or services; thus, because this act necessarily involves falsely claiming to be someone else, conviction under this statute clearly falls within N.H. R. Evid. 609(a)(2). Furthermore, even if the act constituting the attempt, e.g., entering a store, is not itself an act of dishonesty or false statement, the act is done with the purpose of ultimately posing as someone else and using that person's stolen credit card to obtain goods and services; thus, because the ultimate purpose is to commit an act of dishonesty, an attempt to commit credit card fraud comes within Rule 609(a)(2). State v. Long, 161 N.H. 364, 12 A.3d 1289, 2011 N.H. LEXIS 3 (2011).

Defendant was properly impeached under N.H. R. Evid. 609(a)(2) with attempted credit card fraud under RSA 638:5, I(a) and RSA 629:1, I. The act constituting the attempt was done with the purpose of ultimately posing as someone else and using that person's stolen credit card to obtain goods and services, an act of dishonesty. State v. Long, 161 N.H. 364, 12 A.3d 1289, 2011 N.H. LEXIS 3 (2011).

Cited:
Cited in State v. Hermsdorf, 135 N.H. 360, 605 A.2d 1045, 1992 N.H. LEXIS 42, (1992); State v. Merritt, 143 N.H. 714, 738 A.2d 343, 1999 N.H. LEXIS 63 (1999).

638:5-a. Fraudulent Communications Paraphernalia.

I. As used in this section, "fraudulent communications paraphernalia" means any device used or intended for use in obtaining any toll telecommunication or cable television service from a company providing either service by rearranging, tampering with, or making any unauthorized connection to any telephone or cable television instrument, equipment or facility of such company in order to avoid the payment, in whole or in part, of the lawful charge for such communication service or to conceal from any such company or any lawful authority, the existence or place of origin or termination of any such service.

II. Any person who wilfully creates, offers, or transfers to another any fraudulent communications paraphernalia or information for creating or using such paraphernalia shall be guilty of a class B felony.

III. Any person who wilfully possesses any fraudulent communications paraphernalia or information for creating or using such paraphernalia shall be guilty of a misdemeanor.

IV. Any person who communicates or causes to be communicated the number or code of an existing, canceled, revoked, expired, or nonexistent credit card issued by a company providing telecommunication services or the numbering or coding system which is employed in the issuance of such credit cards, or any method, scheme, instruction or information on how to fraudulently avoid payment for telecommunication services, with the intent that such number or coding system or information be used to fraudulently avoid the payment of any lawful charges imposed by such company, shall be guilty of a misdemeanor.

V. Any fraudulent communications paraphernalia prohibited under this section may be seized under warrant or incident to a lawful arrest, and, upon conviction of a person for violation of this section, such paraphernalia may be destroyed as contraband by such officers, agents or other persons as shall be designated for that purpose by the attorney general.

Source.
1981, 458:1, eff. Aug. 22, 1981.

Cross References.
Classification of crimes, see RSA 625:9.
Sentences, see RSA 651.

638:6. Deceptive Business Practices.

I. A person is guilty of a class B misdemeanor if, in the course of business, he:

(a) Uses or possesses for use, a false weight or measure, or any other device for falsely determining or recording any quality or quantity; or

(b) Sells, offers or exposes for sale, or delivers less than the represented quantity of any commodity or service; or

(c) Takes or attempts to take more than the represented quantity of any commodity or service when as buyer he furnishes the weight or measure; or

(d) Sells, offers or exposes for sale adulterated or mislabeled commodities. "Adulterated" means varying from the standard of composition or quality prescribed by or pursuant to any statute providing criminal penalties for such variance, or set by established commercial usage. "Mislabeled" means varying from the standard of truth or disclosure in labeling prescribed by or pursuant to any statute providing criminal penalties for such variance, or set by established commercial usage; or

(e) Makes a false or misleading statement in any advertisement addressed to the public or to a substantial segment thereof for the purpose of promoting the purchase or sale of property or services.

II. It is an affirmative defense to prosecution under this section that the defendant's conduct was not knowing or reckless.

Source.
1971, 518:1. 1992, 269:16, eff. July 1, 1992.

Amendments
—**1992.** Paragraph I: Inserted "class B" preceding "misdemeanor" in the introductory paragraph.

Applicability of 1992 amendment.
1992, 269:21, eff. July 1, 1992, provided that the amendment to this section by 1992, 269:16, shall apply to all offenses committed on or after July 1, 1992.

Cross References.
Classification of crimes, see RSA 625:9.
Regulation of business practices for consumer protection, see RSA 358-A.
Sentences, see RSA 651.

638:6-a. Dealing in Counterfeit Recordings.

I. As used in this section, "original recording" means any article on which sounds or images, or both, have been recorded with the authorization of the holder of the copyright for the material recorded. "Counterfeit recording" means any article on which sounds or images, or both, have been copied from an original recording, without the authorization of the holder of the copyright for the material recorded.

II. Any person who sells or rents counterfeit recordings, or possesses counterfeit recordings for the purpose of sale or rental, shall be guilty of a class A misdemeanor if a natural person, or guilty of a class B felony if any other person. Each individual counterfeit recording shall constitute a separate offense.

III. Possession of 5 or more duplicate copies or 20 or more individual copies of counterfeit recordings shall create a rebuttable presumption that such recordings are intended for sale or distribution in violation of this section.

Source.
1995, 175:3, eff. Jan. 1, 1996.

638:6-b. Dealing in Counterfeit Goods.

I. In this section, "counterfeit mark" means a spurious mark that:

(a) Is applied to, or attached to, or used in connection with in any way, any goods, or packaging of such goods, or any other component of any type or nature that is designed, marketed, or otherwise intended to be used on or in connection with any goods;

(b) Is identical to, or substantially indistinguishable from, a mark registered under RSA 350-A, or the laws of any other state, or that is recorded on the principal register in the United States Patent and Trademark Office and is in use, whether or not the defendant knew the mark was registered; and

(c) By the application or use of such mark, is likely to cause confusion, to cause mistake, or to deceive.

II. Any person who purposely or knowingly manufactures, displays, advertises, distributes, offers for sale, sells or possesses with intent to sell, or distributes any goods bearing or identified by a counterfeit mark shall be guilty of a class A misdemeanor for a first offense and a class B felony for any subsequent offense. Each individual good bearing or identified by a counterfeit mark shall constitute a separate offense.

III. Evidence that a person had possession, custody, or control of more than 25 items bearing a counterfeit mark shall be prima facie evidence that the person had possession with the intent to sell or distribute the items.

IV. Any goods that bear or consist of a counterfeit mark used in committing a violation of this section shall be subject to forfeiture to the state of New Hampshire and no property right shall exist in such property. At the conclusion of all criminal proceedings, the court shall order such items destroyed or disposed of in another manner with the written consent of the trademark owner.

V. (a) The following property is subject to forfeiture for an offense under this section:

(1) Any property used by the defendant in any manner to facilitate, aid, or abet, a violation of this section; and

(2) Any property constituting or derived from any proceeds obtained by the defendant, either directly or indirectly, as a result of a violation of this section.

(b) Such property may be seized by a law enforcement agency for forfeiture as follows:

(1) Pursuant to a search warrant or seizure warrant on an affidavit under oath demonstrating that probable cause exists for its forfeiture;

(2) Physically, on probable cause to believe that the property is subject to forfeiture; or

(3) Constructively, on probable cause to believe that the property is subject to forfeiture under this section, by recording a notice of pending forfeiture in the registry of deeds in the county where the real property is located or at the town clerk's office where the person's property is located stating that the state intends to seek forfeiture of the identified property pursuant to this section.

(c) A seizure for forfeiture without process under subparagraph (b)(2) or (b)(3) shall be reasonable if made under circumstances in which a warrantless seizure or arrest would be valid in accordance with state law.

(d) The seizing agency shall notify the defendant within 7 days of any seizure of property of its intent to forfeit the property pursuant to this section.

(e) The forfeiture of any property or item under this paragraph shall be governed by RSA 595-A:6. The state shall have the burden of proving by a preponderance of the evidence that the property is subject to forfeiture. Except in the case of proceeds, upon a finding that the property is subject to forfeiture, the court shall determine whether the forfeiture of the property is not excessive in relation to the underlying criminal offense. In making this determination, the court shall consider whether in addition to any pertinent considerations:

(1) There is a substantial connection between the property to be forfeited and the underlying offense;

(2) Criminal activities conducted by or through the use of the property were extensive; and

(3) The value of the property to be forfeited greatly outweighs the cost of prosecution and the harm caused by the criminal conduct.

(f) Final orders for forfeiture shall be implemented by the seizing agency and all proceeds of the forfeiture shall go to that agency.

(g) At the request of any party to the forfeiture proceeding, the court shall grant a continuance until the final resolution of any criminal proceedings which were brought against a party under this section and which arose from the transaction which gave rise to the forfeiture proceeding. No party's interest in property shall be forfeited unless a party has been found guilty of the underlying charge.

VI. The court may order a person convicted under this section to pay restitution pursuant to RSA 651:63 to the trademark owner and to any other person the court may determine. Any restitution ordered by the court shall include, but is not limited to, attorney's fees, court costs, and any other expenses incurred by the trademark owner in the investigation and prosecution of the case.

Source.
2009, 209:9, eff. July 15, 2009 (see contingent effective date note below). 2010, 312:1, eff. July 13, 2010.

Amendments
—**2010.** The 2010 amendment rewrote I; deleted "uses" following "manufactures" in the first sentence of II; rewrote III, which formerly read: "Any person having possession, custody, or control of more than 25 items bearing a counterfeit mark shall be presumed to possess said items with the intent to sell or distribute. Any state or federal certificate of registration of any intellectual property shall be prima facie evidence of the facts stated therein"; and added IV through VI.

Contingent effective date of 2009 enactment.
2009, 306:16, eff. July 31, 2009, provided: "If HB 471-FN [ch. 209] of the 2009 legislative session becomes law, then RSA 638:6-b as inserted by section 9 of that act shall not take effect on January 1, 2010, but shall take effect upon the passage [July 15, 2009] of HB 471-FN."

638:7. Commercial Bribery.

I. A person is guilty of commercial bribery when, without the consent of employer or principal, contrary to the best interests of the employer or principal:

(a) He confers, offers, or agrees to confer upon the employee, agent or fiduciary of such employer or principal, any benefit with the purpose of influencing the conduct of the employee, agent or fiduciary in relation to his employer's or principal's affairs; or

(b) He, as an employee, agent or fiduciary of such employer or principal, solicits, accepts or agrees to accept any benefit from another upon an agreement or understanding that such benefit will influence his conduct in relation to his employer's or principal's affairs: provided that this section does not apply to inducements made or accepted solely for the purpose of causing a change in employment by an employee, agent or fiduciary.

II. A person is also guilty of commercial bribery if he holds himself out to the public as being engaged in the business of making disinterested selection, appraisal or criticism of goods or services and he solicits, accepts, or agrees to accept any benefit to influence his selection, appraisal or criticism.

III. (a) Commercial bribery is:

(1) A class A felony if the value of the benefit referred to in paragraphs I and II is more than $1,500;

(2) A class B felony if the value of the benefit referred to in paragraphs I and II is more than $1,000, but is not more than $1,500; and

(3) A misdemeanor in all other cases.

(b) The value shall be determined according to the provisions of RSA 637:2, V.

Source.
1971, 518:1. 1979, 265:3–5, eff. Aug. 20, 1979. 2010, 239:6, eff. July 1, 2010.

Amendments
—**2010.** The 2010 amendment substituted "$1,500" for "$1,000" in III(a)(1) and III(a)(2); substituted "$1,000" for "$500" in III(a)(2); and made a stylistic change.

—**1979.** Paragraph I: Substituted "commercial bribery" for "a misdemeanor" following "guilty of" in the introductory clause.
Paragraph II: Inserted "also" preceding "guilty of" and substituted "commercial bribery" for "violation of this section" thereafter.
Paragraph III: Added.

Cross References.
Classification of crimes, see RSA 625:9.
Sentences, see RSA 651.

NOTES TO DECISIONS

Cited:
Cited in State v. Hermsdorf, 135 N.H. 360, 605 A.2d 1045, 1992 N.H. LEXIS 42, (1992).

638:8. Sports Bribery.

I. A person is guilty of sports bribery if:

(a) With a purpose to influence any participant or prospective participant not to give his best efforts in a publicly exhibited contest, he confers or offers or agrees to confer any benefit upon or threatens any injury to such participant or prospective participant; or

(b) With a purpose to influence an official in a publicly exhibited contest to perform his duties improperly, he confers or offers or agrees to confer any benefit upon or threatens any injury to such official; or

(c) With a purpose to influence the outcome of a publicly exhibited contest, he tampers with any person, animal or thing contrary to the rules and usages purporting to govern such a contest; or

(d) He knowingly solicits, accepts or agrees to accept any benefit, the giving of which would be criminal under subparagraph I(a) or (b).

II. (a) Sports bribery is:

(1) A class A felony if the benefit referred to in subparagraphs I(a), (b) or (d), or the value of the benefit gained or to be gained from influencing the outcome of a contest as referred to in subparagraph I(c), exceeds $1,500 or if the injury threatened in subparagraphs I(a) or (b) is a serious bodily injury;

(2) A class B felony in all other cases.

(b) The value shall be determined according to the provisions of RSA 637:2, V.

Source.
1971, 518:1. 1979, 265:6, eff. Aug. 20, 1979. 2010, 239:7, eff. July 1, 2010.

Amendments
—**2010.** The 2010 amendment substituted "$1,500" for "$1,000" in II(a)(1).

—**1979.** Rewritten to the extent that a detailed comparison would be impracticable.

Cross References.
Classification of crimes, see RSA 625:9.
Sentences, see RSA 651.

NOTES TO DECISIONS

Cited:
Cited in State v. Hermsdorf, 135 N.H. 360, 605 A.2d 1045, 1992 N.H. LEXIS 42, (1992).

638:9. Fraud on Creditors.

A person is guilty of a misdemeanor if:

I. He destroys, removes, conceals, encumbers, transfers or otherwise deals with property subject to a security interest with a purpose to hinder enforcement of that interest; or

II. Knowing that proceedings have been or are about to be instituted for the appointment of a person entitled to administer property for the benefit of creditors, he

(a) Destroys, removes, conceals, encumbers, transfers or otherwise deals with any property with a purpose to defeat or obstruct the claim of any creditor, or otherwise to obstruct the operation of any law relating to administration of property for the benefit of creditors; or

(b) Presents to any creditor or to an assignee for the benefit of creditors, orally or in writing, any statement relating to the debtor's estate, knowing that a material part of such statement is false.

Source.
1971, 518:1, eff. Nov. 1, 1973.

Cross References.
Classification of crimes, see RSA 625:9.
Sentences, see RSA 651.

NOTES TO DECISIONS

Fraudulent mortgage
In an indictment for falsely and fraudulently mortgaging personal property to prevent it from being taken on legal process for the mortgagor's debts, if the debt or obligation intended to be secured was falsely described in the condition of the mortgage, and the mortgage was made in whole or in part for the purpose of preventing the property mortgaged from being seized on legal process, this was a fraud on the creditors of the mortgagor, and the making of the mortgage was a violation of this section. State v. Marsh, 36 N.H. 196, 1858 N.H. LEXIS 55 (1858). (Decided under prior law.)

Where the accused falsely and fraudulently mortgaged his personal property to prevent it from being taken on legal process for his debts he was guilty under this section even though he was advised by counsel that the mortgage would be legal and valid. State v. Marsh, 36 N.H. 196, 1858 N.H. LEXIS 55 (1858). (Decided under prior law.)

In an indictment under this section for concealing the goods of a debtor to prevent their being taken for his debts, it was no defense to show that the accused, at the time of the concealment, held the goods under a fraudulent mortgage from the debtor, duly executed and recorded. State v. Johnson, 33 N.H. 441, 1856 N.H. LEXIS 97 (1856). (Decided under prior law.)

638:10. Frauds on Depositors.

A person is guilty of a misdemeanor if:

I. As an officer, manager, or other person participating in the direction of a financial institution, as defined in RSA 637:10, IV(a), he receives or permits receipt of a deposit or other investment knowing that the institution is or is about to become unable, from any cause, to pay its obligations in the ordinary course of business; and

II. He knows that the person making the payment to the institution is unaware of such present or prospective inability.

Source.
1971, 518:1, eff. Nov. 1, 1973.

Cross References.
Classification of crimes, see RSA 625:9.
Sentences, see RSA 651.

638:11. Misapplication of Property.

I. A person is guilty of a misdemeanor if he deals with property that has been entrusted to him as a fiduciary, or property of the government or of a financial institution, in a manner which he knows is a violation of his duty and which involves substantial risk of loss to the owner or to a person for whose benefit the property was entrusted.

II. As used in this section, "fiduciary" includes any person carrying on fiduciary functions on behalf of a corporation or other organization which is a fiduciary. "Government" and "financial institution" have the meanings given in RSA 637:10, IV. "Property" has the meaning given in RSA 637:2, I.

Source.
1971, 518:1, eff. Nov. 1, 1973.

Cross References.
Classification of crimes, see RSA 625:9.
Sentences, see RSA 651.

NOTES TO DECISIONS

1. Elements
2. Lesser included offense
3. Statute of limitations
4. Fiduciary

1. Elements
To convict a person under this section, the prosecution must prove three elements which are not elements of the crime of theft by unauthorized taking: (1) the property was entrusted to the defendant as a fiduciary; (2) the defendant dealt with the entrusted property in a manner which he knew constituted a breach of his fiduciary duty; and (3) the defendant dealt with the entrusted property in a manner which he knew involved a substantial risk of loss to the owner of the property or to a person for whose benefit the property was entrusted. State v. Merski, 123 N.H. 564, 465 A.2d 491, 1983 N.H. LEXIS 323 (1983).

2. Lesser included offense
Since three essential elements contained in the definition of the crime of misapplication of property are not contained within RSA 637:3, defining the crime of theft by unauthorized taking, a person need not have committed the former in the process of committing the latter. State v. Merski, 123 N.H. 564, 465 A.2d 491, 1983 N.H. LEXIS 323 (1983).

In prosecution for theft by unauthorized taking, the defendant was not entitled to an instruction on the elements of the misdemeanor of misapplication of property since the indictment accusing the defendant of violating RSA 637:3, the theft statute, did not invoke this section as a lesser-included offense. State v. Merski, 123 N.H. 564, 465 A.2d 491, 1983 N.H. LEXIS 323 (1983).

3. Statute of limitations
When an attorney revealed information about his former representation of a client because he believed it was reasonably necessary to prevent the client from committing criminal activity to the substantial detriment of the client's mother, under RSA 638:11, I, the applicable one year statute of limitations did not bar the client's prosecution because, even if the time period had run, a prosecution was allowed since a material element of the crime was fraud or a breach of a fiduciary duty. Because RSA 638:11, I, applies only in cases where a person "deals with property that has been entrusted to him as a fiduciary . . . in a manner which he knows is a violation of his duty and which involves substantial risk of loss to the owner or to a person for whose benefit the property was entrusted," the exception in RSA 625:8, III(a) applied.Lane's Case, 153 N.H. 10, 889 A.2d 3, 2005 N.H. LEXIS 178 (2005).

4. Fiduciary
An averment that funds were entrusted to the accused for the purpose of investing them in property did not sufficiently show that he was acting in a fiduciary capacity. State v. Goodwin, 101 N.H. 252, 139 A.2d 630, 1958 N.H. LEXIS 10 (1958). (Decided under prior law.)

OPINIONS OF THE ATTORNEY GENERAL

Conversion of lottery tickets
Conversion of lottery tickets to cash by person entrusted by the government with those tickets would constitute the crime of misapplication of property, and under some circumstances could constitute the crime of theft by unauthorized taking, or theft by misapplication of property. Op. Atty. Gen. 86-51.

638:12. Fraudulent Execution of Documents.

A person is guilty of a misdemeanor if, by deception or threat, he causes another to sign or execute any instrument which affects or is likely to affect the pecuniary interest of any person.

Source.
1971, 518:1, eff. Nov. 1, 1973.

Cross References.
Classification of crimes, see RSA 625:9.
Sentences, see RSA 651.

638:13. Use and Possession of Slugs.

I. A person is guilty of a violation if:
(a) With a purpose to defraud the supplier of property or a service offered or sold by means of a coin machine, he inserts, deposits or uses a slug in that machine; or
(b) He makes, possesses, or disposes of a slug with the purpose of enabling a person to use it fraudulently in a coin machine.

II. As used in this section, "coin machine" means any mechanical or electronic device or receptacle designed to receive a coin or bill of a certain denomination, or a token made for the purpose; and in return for the insertion or deposit thereof, automatically to offer, provide, assist in providing or permit the acquisition of property or a public or private service. "Slug" means any object which, by virtue of its size, shape or other quality, is capable of being inserted, deposited, or otherwise used in a coin machine as an improper substitute for a genuine coin, bill or token.

Source.
1971, 518:1. 1990, 60:4, eff. Jan. 1, 1991.

Amendments
—**1990.** Paragraph I: Substituted "violation" for "misdemeanor" in the introductory paragraph.

Cross References.
Classification of crimes, see RSA 625:9.
Sentences, see RSA 651.

638:14. Unlawful Simulation of Legal Process.

A person is guilty of a misdemeanor who, with a purpose to procure the compliance of another with a request made by such person, knowingly sends, mails or delivers to such person a notice or other writing which has no judicial or other sanction, but which in its format or appearance simulates a summons, complaint, court order or process, including, but not limited to, lien, indictment, warrant, injunction, writ, notice, pleading, subpoena, or order, or an insignia, seal or printed form of a federal, state or local government or an instrumentality thereof, or is otherwise calculated to induce a belief that it does have a judicial or other official sanction.

Source.
1971, 518:1, eff. Nov. 1, 1973. 2003, 168:2, eff. Jan. 1, 2004.

Amendments
—**2003.** Substituted "legal process" for "official notice" in the section catchline and inserted "including, but not limited to, lien, indictment, warrant, injunction, writ, notice, pleading, subpoena, or order" following "court order or process".

Cross References.
Classification of crimes, see RSA 625:9.
Sentences, see RSA 651.

638:15. Fraud on the Women, Infants, and Children (WIC) Program.

I. A person is guilty of fraud on the women, infants, and children program if he is a vendor who embezzles, purposely misapplies, steals, or obtains by fraud or theft any funds, assets, or property provided under RSA 132:12-a or if he receives, conceals, or retains such funds, assets, or property for his own use, knowing them to have been embezzled, purposely misapplied, stolen, or obtained by fraud or theft.

II. Fraud on the women, infants, and children program is:

(a) A class A felony where the value of the funds, assets, or property exceeds $1,500;

(b) A class B felony where the value of the funds, assets, or property exceeds $500, but is not more than $1,500;

(c) A misdemeanor in all other cases.

III. A person is guilty of a misdemeanor if he is a participant who:

(a) By a purposely false statement or misrepresentation or by impersonation or other purposely fraudulent act or device attempts to obtain or obtains funds under RSA 132:12-a to which he is not entitled.

(b) Purposely and knowingly aids or abets any person, by a purposely false statement or misrepresentation or by impersonation or other purposely fraudulent act or device, to attempt to obtain or obtain funds under RSA 132:12-a to which the person is not entitled.

(c) Purposely fails to disclose the receipt of property, wages, income, or resources or any change in circumstances that would affect his eligibility for assistance under RSA 132:12-a, to obtain funds or assistance to which he is not entitled.

Source.
1981, 307:4, eff. Aug. 15, 1981. 2010, 239:8, eff. July 1, 2010.

Amendments
—**2010.** The 2010 amendment substituted "$1,500" for "$1,000" in II(a) and II(b) and substituted "$500" for "$100" in II(b).

Cross References.
Classification of crimes, see RSA 625:9.
Fraudulent acts relating to public assistance, see RSA 167:17-b.
Sentences, see RSA 651.

NOTES TO DECISIONS

Cited:
Cited in State v. Hermsdorf, 135 N.H. 360, 605 A.2d 1045, 1992 N.H. LEXIS 42, (1992).

638:15-a. False Academic Documentation.

I. A person is guilty of a class A misdemeanor if such person knowingly does any of the following:

(a) Falsely creates, alters, or assists in the false creation or alteration of an academic degree.

(b) Solicits from another the false creation or alteration of an academic degree.

(c) Uses, offers, or presents as authentic a falsely created or altered academic degree.

(d) Sells, gives, purchases, or obtains, or assists in the selling, giving, purchasing, or obtaining of a false academic degree.

(e) Makes a false written representation relating to the person's academic degree, or makes a false written representation that the person has received an academic degree from a specific secondary, postsecondary, or professional institution, or governmental program, in the application for:

(1) Employment.

(2) Admission to any educational program.

(3) An award, honor, or other recognition.

(4) The issuance of an academic degree to the person himself or herself.

II. In this section, "academic degree" means a diploma, certificate, license, academic transcript, or other document which signifies or purports to signify the completion of the academic requirements of a secondary, postsecondary, professional, or governmental program of study.

Source.
2001, 46:1, eff. June 8, 2001.

Cross References.
Classification of crimes, see RSA 625:9.
Sentences, see RSA 651.

Computer Crime

638:16. Computer Crime; Definitions.

For the purpose of this subdivision:

I. "Access" means to instruct, communicate with, store data in, retrieve data from, intercept data from, or otherwise make use of any computer, computer network, computer program, computer software, computer data, or other computer resources.

II. "Authorization" means the express or implied consent given by a person to another to access or use said person's computer, computer network, computer program, computer software, password, identifying code, or personal identification number.

III. "Computer" means an electronic, magnetic, optical, electrochemical, or other high speed data processing device performing logical, arithmetic, or storage functions, and includes any data storage facility or communication facility directly related to or operating in conjunction with such device. The term "computer" includes any connected or directly-related device, equipment, or facility which enables the computer to store, retrieve, or communicate computer programs, computer data, or the results of computer operations to or from a person, another computer, or another device, but such term does not include an automated typewriter or typesetter, a portable hand-held calculator, or other similar device.

IV. "Computer contaminant" means any set of computer instructions that are designed to modify, damage, destroy, record, or transmit information within a computer, computer system, or computer network without the authorization of the owner of the information. They include, but are not limited to, a group of computer instructions commonly called viruses or worms, that are self-replicating or self-propagating and are designed to contaminate other computer programs or computer data, consume computer resources, modify, destroy, record, or transmit data, or in some other fashion usurp the normal operation of the computer, computer program, computer operations, computer services, or computer network.

V. "Computer data" means any representation of knowledge, facts, concepts, instruction, or other information computed, classified, processed, transmitted, received, retrieved, originated, stored, manifested, measured, detected, recorded, reproduced, handled, or utilized by a computer, computer network, computer program, or computer software, and may be in any medium, including, but not limited to, computer print-outs, microfilm, microfiche, magnetic storage media, optical storage media, punch paper tape, or punch cards, or it may be stored internally in read-only memory or random access memory of a computer or any other peripheral device.

VI. "Computer network" means a set of connected devices and communication facilities, including more than one computer, with the capability to transmit computer data among them through such communication facilities.

VII. "Computer operations" means arithmetic, logical, storage, display, monitoring, or retrieval functions or any combination thereof, and includes, but is not limited to, communication with, storage of data in or to, or retrieval of data from any device and the human manual manipulation of electronic magnetic impulses. A "computer operation" for a particular computer shall also mean any function for which that computer was designed.

VIII. "Computer program" means an ordered set of computer data representing instructions or statements, in a form readable by a computer, which controls, directs, or otherwise influences the functioning of a computer or computer network.

IX. "Computer software" means one or more computer programs, existing in any form, or any associated operational procedures, manuals, or other documentation.

X. "Computer services" means computer access time, computer data processing, or computer data storage, and the computer data processed or stored in connection therewith.

XI. "Computer supplies" means punch cards, paper tape, magnetic tape, magnetic disks or diskettes, optical disks or diskettes, disk or diskette packs, paper, microfilm, and any other tangible input, output, or storage medium used in connection with a computer, computer network, computer data, computer software, or computer program.

XII. "Computer resources" includes, but is not limited to, information retrieval, computer data processing, transmission and storage, and any other functions performed, in whole or in part, by the use of a computer, computer network, computer software, or computer program.

XIII. "Financial instrument" includes, but is not limited to, any check, draft, warrant, money order, note, certificate of deposit, letter of credit, bill of exchange, credit or debit card, transaction authorization mechanism, marketable security, or any computerized representation thereof.

XIV. "Owner" means any person who owns or leases or is a licensee of a computer, computer network, computer data, computer program, computer software, computer resources, or computer supplies.

XV. "Person" means any natural person, general partnership, limited partnership, trust, association, corporation, joint venture, or any state, county, or municipal government and any subdivision, branch, department, or agency thereof.

XVI. "Property" includes:

  (a) Real property;

  (b) Computers and computer networks;

  (c) Financial instruments, computer data, computer programs, computer software and all other personal property regardless of whether they are:

    (1) Tangible or intangible;

    (2) In a format readable by humans or by a computer;

    (3) In transit between computers or within a computer network or between any devices which comprise a computer; or

    (4) Located on any paper or in any device on which it is stored by a computer or by a human; and

  (d) Computer services.

Source.
  1985, 139:1, eff. Jan. 1, 1986. 2002, 261:1, eff. Jan. 1, 2003.

Amendments
  —2002. Rewritten to the extent that a detailed comparison would be impracticable.

638:17. Computer related offenses.

I. A person is guilty of the computer crime of unauthorized access to a computer or computer network when, knowing that the person is not authorized to do so, he or she knowingly accesses or causes to be accessed any computer or computer network without authorization. It shall be an affirmative defense to a prosecution for unauthorized access to a computer or computer network that:

(a) The person reasonably believed that the owner of the computer or computer network, or a person empowered to license access thereto, had authorized him or her to access; or

(b) The person reasonably believed that the owner of the computer or computer network, or a person empowered to license access thereto, would have authorized the person to access without payment of any consideration; or

(c) The person reasonably could not have known that his or her access was unauthorized.

II. A person is guilty of the computer crime of theft of computer services when he or she knowingly accesses or causes to be accessed or otherwise uses or causes to be used a computer or computer network with the purpose of obtaining unauthorized computer services.

III. A person is guilty of the computer crime of interruption of computer services when the person, without authorization, knowingly or recklessly disrupts or degrades or causes the disruption or degradation of computer services or denies or causes the denial of computer services to an authorized user of a computer or computer network.

IV. A person is guilty of the computer crime of misuse of computer or computer network information when:

(a) As a result of his or her accessing or causing to be accessed a computer or computer network, the person knowingly makes or causes to be made an unauthorized display, use, disclosure, or copy, in any form, of data residing in, communicated by, or produced by a computer or computer network; or

(b) The person knowingly or recklessly and without authorization:

(1) Alters, deletes, tampers with, damages, destroys, or takes data intended for use by a computer or computer network, whether residing within or external to a computer or computer network; or

(2) Intercepts or adds to data residing within a computer or computer network; or

(c) The person knowingly receives or retains data obtained in violation of subparagraph (a) or (b) of this paragraph; or

(d) The person knowingly uses or discloses any data he or she knows or believes was obtained in violation of subparagraph (a) or (b) of this paragraph.

V. A person is guilty of the computer crime of destruction of computer equipment when he or she, without authorization, knowingly or recklessly tampers with, takes, transfers, conceals, alters, damages, or destroys any equipment used in a computer or computer network, or knowingly or recklessly causes any of the foregoing to occur.

VI. A person is guilty of the computer crime of computer contamination if such person knowingly introduces, or causes to be introduced, a computer contaminant into any computer, computer program, or computer network which results in a loss of property or computer services.

Source.
1985, 139:1, eff. Jan. 1, 1986. 2002, 261:2, eff. Jan. 1, 2003.

Amendments
—**2002.** Substituted "computer or computer network" for "computer system" and "the person" for "he" wherever it appeared throughout the section, added par. VI, and made gender neutral changes throughout the section.

638:18. Computer Crime Penalties.

I. Computer crime constitutes a class A felony if the damage to or the value of the property or computer services exceeds $1,500, or if the person has previously been convicted of violating RSA 638:17, II, IV, or VI, or any other statute prohibiting the same conduct in another state, territory, or possession of the United States.

II. Computer crime constitutes a class B felony if:

(a) The damage to or the value of the property or computer services exceeds $1,000 but is not more than $1,500;

(b) The person recklessly engages in conduct which creates a risk of serious physical injury to another person; or

(c) The person is guilty of violating RSA 638:17, II, IV, or VI.

III. Computer crime is a misdemeanor if the damage to or the value of the property or computer services, if any, is $1,000 or less.

IV. If a person has gained money, property, or services or other consideration through the commission of any offense under RSA 638:17, upon conviction thereof, the court, in addition to any sentence of imprisonment or other form of sentence authorized by RSA 651, may, in lieu of imposing a fine, sentence the defendant to pay an amount, fixed by the court, not to exceed double the amount of the defendant's gain from the commission of such offense. In such case, the court shall make a finding as to the amount of the defendant's gain from the offense and, if the record does not contain sufficient evidence to support such finding, the court may conduct a hearing upon the issue. For the purpose of this section, "gain" means the amount of money or the value of property or computer services or other consideration derived.

V. For the purposes of this section:

(a) The value of property or computer services shall be:

(1) The market value of the property or computer services at the time of the violation; or

(2) If the property or computer services are unrecoverable, damaged, or destroyed as a result of a violation of RSA 638:17 the cost of reproducing or replacing the property or computer services at the time of the violation.

(b) Amounts included in violations of RSA 638:17 committed pursuant to one scheme or course of conduct, whether from the same person or several persons, may be aggregated in determining the grade of the offense.

(c) When the value of the property or computer services or damage thereto cannot be satisfactorily ascertained, the value shall be deemed to be $500.

Source.
1985, 139:1, eff. Jan. 1, 1986. 2007, 137:1, 2, eff. January 1, 2008. 2010, 239:9, 10, eff. July 1, 2010.

Amendments
—2010. The 2010 amendment substituted "$1,500" for "$1,000" in I; substituted "$1,000 but is not more than $1,500" for "$500" in II(a); substituted "$1,000" for "$500" in III; and substituted "$500" for "$250" in V(c).

—2007. Paragraph I: Added "or if the person has previously been convicted of violating RSA 638:17, II, IV, or VI, or any other statute prohibiting the same conduct in another state, territory, or possession of the United States".

Paragraph II: Made minor stylistic changes to subpars. (a) and (b) and added subpar. (c).

Cross References.
Classification of crimes, see RSA 625:9.
Sentences, see RSA 651.

638:19. Venue.

I. In any prosecution for a violation of RSA 638:17 the offense shall be deemed to have been committed in the town in which the act occurred or in which the computer system or part thereof involved in the violation was located.

II. In any prosecution for a violation of RSA 638:17 based upon more than one act in violation thereof, the offense shall be deemed to have been committed in any of the towns in which any of the acts occurred or in which a computer system or part thereof involved in a violation was located.

III. If any act performed in furtherance of the offenses prohibited by RSA 638:17 occurs in this state or if any computer system or part thereof accessed in violation of RSA 638:17 is located in this state, the offense shall be deemed to have occurred in this state.

Source.
1985, 139:1, eff. Jan. 1, 1986.

Insurance Fraud

Cross References.
Insurance fraud investigation unit, see RSA 417:23 et seq.

638:20. Insurance Fraud.

I. In this section:

(a) "Bidding" includes a bid made as any contractor, general contractor, or subcontractor.

(b) "Financial interest" means any direct or indirect interest in the entity, whether as an owner, partner, officer, manager, employee, agent, consultant, advisor, or representative, but does not include an employee who does not participate in management of the entity and ownership in a mutual or common investment fund that holds securities unless the person participates in the management of the fund.

(c) "Insurance policy" includes an actual or purported insurance policy.

(d) "Insurer" includes any insurance company, health maintenance organization, or reinsurance company, or broker or agent thereof, or insurance claims adjuster.

(e) "Participating in public works projects" means bidding or working on any public works project or holding any financial interest in any entity bidding or working on any public works project.

(f) "Public works project" means any construction project financed by public funds.

(g) "Statement" includes, but is not limited to, any notice, statement, proof of loss, bill of lading, receipt of payment, invoice, account, estimate of property damages, bill for service, diagnosis, prescription, hospital or doctor records, x-rays, test results, or other evidence of loss, injury, or expense.

II. A person is guilty of insurance fraud, if, such person knowingly and with intent to injure, defraud or deceive any insurer, conceals or causes to be concealed from any insurer a material statement, or presents or causes to be presented to any insurer, or prepares with knowledge or belief that it will be so presented, any written or oral statement including computer-generated documents, knowing that such statement contains any false, incomplete or misleading information which is material to:

(a) An application for the issuance of any insurance policy.

(b) The rating of any insurance policy.

(c) A claim for payment or benefit pursuant to any insurance policy.

(d) Premiums on any insurance policy.

(e) Payments made in accordance with the terms of any insurance policy.

III. A person is guilty as an accomplice to insurance fraud, if, with a purpose to injure, defraud or deceive any insurer, the person assists, abets, solicits or conspires with another to commit insurance fraud, as defined in paragraph II of this section.

IV. (a) Insurance fraud is:

(1) A class A felony if the value of the fraudulent portion of the claim for payment or other benefit pursuant to an insurance policy is more than $1,500.

(2) A class B felony if the value of the fraudulent portion of the claim for payment or other benefit pursuant to an insurance policy is more

than \$1,000, but not more than \$1,500.

    (3) A misdemeanor in all other cases.

V. [Repealed.]

VI. In addition to any other penalty authorized by law, any person convicted of violating subparagraphs II(a), (b), or (d) relative to a workers' compensation insurance policy shall, as a condition of his or her sentence, be prohibited from participating in any public works projects for a period of no less than one year and no more than 3 years and shall be ordered to pay restitution to its workers' compensation carrier, as determined by the sentencing court. Any person convicted of a third or subsequent violation may, as a condition of his or her sentence, be permanently banned from participating in any public works projects. For the purposes of this paragraph, "restitution" means the difference between the premium actually charged and the premium amount that would have been charged if accurate information had been provided to the carrier, provided that the carrier is not compensated by the offender more than once.

VII. The commissioner of the department of administrative services shall maintain a list of persons who have been banned from participating in public works projects under this section. Such list shall be a public record under 91-A.

Source.
  1991, 248:1. 1993, 239:4, 5, eff. Jan. 1, 1994. 1996, 285:25, eff. Jan. 1, 1997. 2001, 224:12, II, eff. Sept. 9, 2001. 2008, 378:5, 6, eff. January 1, 2009. 2010, 239:11, eff. July 1, 2010.

Amendments
  —2010. The 2010 amendment substituted "\$1,500" for "\$1,000" in IV(a)(1) and IV(a)(2) and substituted "\$1,000" for "\$500" in IV(a)(2).

  —2008. The 2008 amendment rewrote I to the extent that a detailed comparison would be impracticable; deleted I-a; and added VI and VII.

  —2001. Paragraph V: Repealed.

  —1996. Paragraph II: Substituted "such person knowingly and with intent" for "with a purpose" preceding "to injure", "conceals or causes to be concealed from any insurer a material statement" for "the person" preceding "or presents", and "which is material to" for "concerning" following "misleading information" in the introductory paragraph.

  —1993. Paragraph I-a: Added.
  Paragraph II: Rewritten to the extent that a detailed comparison would be impracticable.
  Paragraph III: Substituted "insurer" for "insurance company" following "deceive any" and "commit insurance fraud, as defined in paragraph II of this section" for "prepare or make any written or oral statement that is intended to be presented to any insurance company in connection with, or in support of, any claim for payment or other benefit pursuant to an insurance policy, knowing that such statement contains any false, incomplete or misleading information concerning any fact or thing material to such claim" following "another to".

Cross References.
  Classification of crimes, see RSA 625:9.
  Sentences, see RSA 651.

Cited:
  Cited in Grew's Case, 156 N.H. 361, 934 A.2d 537, 2007 N.H. LEXIS 193 (2007).

638:20-a. Venue.

I. In any prosecution for a violation of RSA 638:20, the offense shall be deemed to have been committed in any of the following locations:

    (a) The county or judicial district in which any element of the offense was committed;

    (b) The county or judicial district of the purported loss;

    (c) The county or judicial district in which the insurance policy provides coverage;

    (d) The county or judicial district in which the insurer or the insurer's agent received the false statement or application; or

    (e) The county or judicial district in which money was received for the fraudulent act.

II. If any violation of RSA 638:20 has been deemed to have occurred in any of the locations listed in paragraph I, the prosecution for all the related violations may be brought together in any of the counties or judicial districts.

Source.
  2013, 234:1, eff. January 1, 2014.

Wireless Telephone Cloning

Severability of enactment.
  1997, 298 was subject to a severability clause. See 1997, 298:31.

Statement of purpose.
  1997, 298:29, eff. Jan. 1, 1998, provided: "The purpose of sections 30–31 of this act [which enacted RSA 638:21–24], is to prohibit a person from unlawfully possessing, using, distributing, manufacturing, buying, or selling a cloned wireless telephone or other access device which is capable of unlawfully obtaining telecommunication services; to establish penalties for certain violations under certain conditions; to define certain terms; and, generally, to criminalize wireless telephone cloning and access device counterfeiting."

638:21. Definitions.

In this subdivision:

I. "Access device" means property consisting of any telephone calling card number, credit card number, account number, mobile identification number electronic serial number, personal identification number, or any other data intended to control or limit access to telecommunications or other computer networks in either human readable or computer readable form, either copy or original, that can be used to obtain telephone service.

II. "Clone" means to program or reprogram a wireless telephone or access device with an electronic serial number, mobile identification number, or personal identification number which has been obtained from a registered wireless telephone without the consent of the telecommunication service provider.

III. "Defaced access device" means any cloned wireless telephone or access device in either human readable or computer readable form, either copy or original, which has been removed, erased defaced, altered, destroyed, covered, or otherwise changed in any manner from its original configuration. In any prosecution regarding a defaced access device, any removal, erasure, defacement, alteration, destruction, covering, or other change in such access device from its original configuration performed by any person other than an authorized manufacturer of, or service provider to, access devices shall be presumed to be for an unlawful purpose.

IV. "Manufacture" means to produce or assemble, modify, alter, program, or re-program any wireless telephone or reader without the consent of the telecommunication service provider.

V. "Reader" means a device which is capable of, or has been manufactured, assembled, altered, modified, programmed, or re-programmed so as to be capable of acquiring or facilitating the acquisition of an electronic serial number, mobile identification number, personal identification number, or any code, or encoded or encrypted transmission, used in originating, facilitating, or transmitting telecommunication service without the consent of the telecommunication service provider.

VI. "Registered wireless telephone" means a wireless telephone registered with a telecommunication service provider for a fee as set by the telecommunication service provider.

VII. "Telecommunication service" means a service provided for a charge or compensation to facilitate the origination, transmission, emission, or reception of signs, signals, writings, images and sounds, or intelligence of any nature by telephone, including wireless telephone.

VIII. "Telecommunication service provider" means a person or entity providing telecommunication service including, but not limited to, a wireless telephone company which, for a fee, supplies the facility, cell site, wireless telephone switching office, registered wireless telephone, or other equipment.

IX. "Telephone cloning paraphernalia" means materials, including at least one of the items in subparagraph (a), (f), (g), or (h), that, when possessed in combination, are capable of creating a cloned cellular telephone. Telephone cloning paraphernalia includes, but is not limited to:

(a) Readers;

(b) Cellular telephones;

(c) Cables;

(d) EPROM chips;

(e) EPROM burners;

(f) Software for programming the cellular telephone with a false electronic serial number, mobile identification number, other identifiable data, or a combination of those items;

(g) Computers containing software described in subparagraph (f); and

(h) Lists of electronic serial number and mobile identification number combinations.

X. "Traffic" means to sell, buy, receive, possess, distribute, exchange, give, transfer, or dispose of an access device, defaced access device, reader, or cloned wireless telephone, or plans or instructions for making or assembling the same, to another, or to offer or agree to do the same.

XI. "Wireless telephone" means any equipment or instrument that transmits:

(a) Cellular telephone service;

(b) Personal communication service; or

(c) Any other commercial mobile radio service as defined in 47 C.F.R. 20.3.

Source.
1997, 298:30, eff. Jan. 1, 1998. 1998, 16:1, eff. April 15, 1998.

Amendments
—1998. Inserted "including at least one of the items in subparagraph (a), (f), (g), or (h)" in the introductory paragraph of par. IX.

Severability of enactment.
1997, 298 was subject to a severability clause. See 1997, 298:31.

638:22. Criminal Acts Involving Cloned Phones and Telephone Cloning Paraphernalia; Possession or Use.

I. A person is guilty of a misdemeanor if such person knowingly possesses or uses a cloned wireless telephone.

II. A person is guilty of a class B felony if such person knowingly possesses or uses telephone cloning paraphernalia, or possesses 2 or more unauthorized access devices or defaced access devices. The requisite knowledge or belief is presumed in the case of a person who is found in possession of 2 or more unauthorized access devices or defaced access devices.

Source.
1997, 298:30, eff. Jan. 1, 1998.

Severability of enactment.
1997, 298 was subject to a severability clause. See 1997, 298:31.

Cross References.
Classification of crimes, see RSA 625:9.
Sentences, see RSA 651.

638:23. Criminal Acts Involving Cloned Phones and Telephone Cloning Paraphernalia; Traffic and Manufacture; Exclusions.

A person is guilty of a class B felony if:

I. The person knowingly and with intent to defraud, traffics in or manufactures a cloned wireless telephone; or

II. The person knowingly and with the intent to defraud, traffics in one or more unauthorized access devices or defaced access devices; or

III. The person knowingly and with intent to defraud, traffics in or manufactures telephone cloning paraphernalia.

IV. The provisions of 638:22 and 638:23 do not apply to:

(a) Officers, employees, or agents of cellular telephone service providers who engage in conduct prohibited by this section for the purpose of constructing, maintaining, or conducting the radio telecommunication service or for law enforcement purposes pursuant to RSA 570-A;

(b) Law enforcement officers and public officials in charge of jails, police premises, sheriff's offices, department of corrections institutions, and other penal or correctional institutions, or any other person under the color of law, who engages in conduct prohibited by this section for the purpose of law enforcement or in the normal course of the officer's or official's employment activities or duties; and

(c) Officers, employees, or agents of federal or state agencies that are authorized under RSA 570-A to monitor or intercept cellular telephone service in the normal course of the officer's, employee's, or agent's employment.

Source.
1997, 298:30, eff. Jan. 1, 1998.

Severability of enactment.
1997, 298 was subject to a severability clause. See 1997, 298:31.

Cross References.
Classification of crimes, see RSA 625:9.
Sentences, see RSA 651.

638:24. Restitution; Civil Action; Forfeiture.

I. The court may, in addition to any other sentence authorized by law, sentence a person convicted of violating this subdivision to make restitution to the appropriate telecommunication service provider.

II. A telecommunication service provider aggrieved by a violation of this subdivision may, in a civil action in any court of competent jurisdiction, obtain appropriate relief, including preliminary and other equitable or declaratory relief, compensatory and punitive damages, reasonable investigation expenses, costs of suit, and attorney fees.

III. Any property used in committing, or to facilitate the commission of, offenses under this subdivision is subject to forfeiture, including but not limited to access devices, defaced access devices, readers, wireless telephones, cloned wireless telephones, computers, computer systems, computer networks, hardware, software, any data residing or stored in any of the foregoing, and radio frequency scanners.

Source.
1997, 298:30, eff. Jan. 1, 1998.

Severability of enactment.
1997, 298 was subject to a severability clause. See 1997, 298:31.

Identity Fraud

RESEARCH REFERENCES

New Hampshire Bar Journal.
For Attorney General article, "The Consumer Protection and Antitrust Bureau: An overview," see 45 N.H.B.J. 38 (2004).

638:25. Definitions.

In this subdivision:

I. "Personal identifying information" means any name, number, or information that may be used, alone or in conjunction with any other information, to assume the identity of an individual, including any name, address, telephone number, driver's license number, social security number, employer or place of employment, employee identification number, mother's maiden name, demand deposit account number, savings account number, credit card number, debit card number, personal identification number, account number, or computer password identification.

II. "Pose" means to falsely represent oneself, directly or indirectly, as another person or persons.

III. "Victim" means any person whose personal identifying information has been unlawfully obtained or recorded or any person or entity that provided money, credit, goods, services, or anything of value and has suffered financial loss as a direct result of the commission or attempted commission of a violation of this subdivision.

Source.
1999, 239:1, eff. Jan. 1, 2000.

638:26. Identity Fraud.

I. A person is guilty of identity fraud when the person:

(a) Poses as another person with the purpose to defraud in order to obtain money, credit, goods, services, or anything else of value;

(b) Obtains or records personal identifying information about another person without the express authorization of such person, with the intent to pose as such person;

(c) Obtains or records personal identifying information about a person without the express authorization of such person in order to assist another to pose as such person; or

(d) Poses as another person, without the express authorization of such person, with the purpose of obtaining confidential information about such person that is not available to the general public.

II. Identity fraud is a class A felony.

III. A person found guilty of violating any provisions of this section shall, in addition to the penalty under paragraph II, be ordered to make restitution for economic loss sustained by a victim as a result of such violation.

Source.
1999, 239:1, eff. Jan. 1, 2000. 2004, 233:1, eff. June 11, 2004.

Amendments
—2004. Paragraph II: Rewritten to the extent that a detailed comparison would be impracticable.

Cross References.
Classification of crimes, see RSA 625:9.
Sentences, see RSA 651.

638:27. Venue.

If any act performed in furtherance of the offenses prohibited by RSA 638:26 occurs in this state or if any victim of the offenses prohibited by RSA 638:26 resides in this state, the offense shall be deemed to have occurred in this state.

Source.
1999, 239:1, eff. Jan. 1, 2000.

Illegal Use of Payment Card Scanning Device or Reencoder

638:28. Definitions.

In this subdivision:

I. "Scanning device" means a scanner, reader, or any other electronic device that is used to access, read, scan, obtain, memorize, or store, temporarily or permanently, information encoded on the magnetic strip or stripe of a payment card.

II. "Reencoder" means an electronic device that places encoded information from the magnetic strip or stripe of a payment card onto the magnetic strip or stripe of a different payment card.

III. "Payment card" means a credit card, charge card, debit card, or any other card that is issued to an authorized card user and that allows the user to obtain, purchase, or receive goods, services, money, or anything else of value from a merchant.

IV. "Merchant" means an owner or operator of any retail mercantile establishment or any agent, employee, lessee, consignee, officer, director, franchisee, or independent contractor of such owner or operator. A merchant includes a person who receives from an authorized user of a payment card, or someone the person believes to be an authorized user, a payment card or information from a payment card, or what the person believes to be a payment card or information from a payment card, as the instrument for obtaining, purchasing or receiving goods, services, money, or anything else of value from the person.

Source.
2003, 210:1, eff. Aug. 29, 2003.

638:29. Use of Scanning Device or Reencoder to Defraud Prohibited.

I. A person is guilty of the crime of using a scanning device or reencoder to defraud when the person knowingly:

(a) Uses a scanning device to access, read, obtain, memorize, or store, temporarily or permanently, information encoded on the magnetic strip or stripe of a payment card without the permission of the authorized user of the payment card and with the intent to defraud the authorized user, the issuer of the authorized user's payment card, or a merchant; or

(b) Uses a reencoder to place information encoded on the magnetic strip or stripe of a payment card onto the magnetic strip or stripe of a different card without the permission of the authorized user of the card from which the information is being reencoded and with the intent to defraud the authorized user, the issuer of the authorized user's payment card, or a merchant.

II. Using a scanning device or reencoder to defraud is:

(a) A class B felony if such person has one or more prior convictions in this state or another state for the conduct described in this section.

(b) A class B felony if such person used a scanning device or reencoder to defraud 2 or more times in violation of this section.

(c) A misdemeanor in all other cases.

Source.
2003, 210:1, eff. Aug. 29, 2003.

Cross References.
Classification of crimes, see RSA 625:9.
Sentences, see RSA 651.

CHAPTER 639

OFFENSES AGAINST THE FAMILY

SECTION
639:1. Bigamy.
639:2. Incest.
639:3. Endangering Welfare of Child or Incompetent.
639:4. Non-Support.
639:5. Concealing Death of a Newborn.

639:1. Bigamy.

A person is guilty of a class B felony if, having a spouse and knowing that he is not legally eligible to marry, he marries another.

Source.
1971, 518:1, eff. Nov. 1, 1973.

Cross References.
Classification of crimes, see RSA 625:9.
Proof of marriage in indictment for bigamy, see RSA 457:41.
Sentences, see RSA 651.
Void marriages, see RSA 458:1 et seq.

NOTES TO DECISIONS

Evidence
On the trial of an indictment for bigamy the testimony of persons who were present and witnessed the former marriage ceremony was admissible to show the fact of such marriage. State v. Clark, 54 N.H. 456, 1874 N.H. LEXIS 64 (1874). (Decided under prior law.)
Testimony of a witness, that he was present at the marriage of the respondent in another state and that the services were per-

formed by the settled minister of the place, who was accustomed to officiating in such services in such instances, was sufficient evidence of a prior marriage. State v. Kean, 10 N.H. 347, 1839 N.H. LEXIS 20 (1839). (Decided under prior law.)

639:2. Incest.

I. A person is guilty of a class B felony if he or she marries or engages in sexual penetration as defined in RSA 632-A:1, V, or lives together with, under the representation of being married, a person 18 years or older whom he or she knows to be his or her ancestor, descendant, brother, or sister, of the whole or half blood, or an uncle, aunt, nephew, or niece; provided, however, that no person under the age of 18 shall be liable under this section if the other party is at least 3 years older at the time of the act. The relationships referred to herein include blood relationships without regard to legitimacy, stepchildren, and relationships of parent and child by adoption.

II. In cases of alleged incest where the victim is under the age of 18 when the alleged offense occurred, the statute of limitations shall run pursuant to RSA 625:8, III(d).

III. Notwithstanding the provisions of paragraph I, a person convicted of incest where the victim is under the age of 18 shall be sentenced to a maximum sentence which is not to exceed 20 years and a minimum which is not to exceed ½ the maximum. Notwithstanding the provisions of this paragraph, no person under 18 years of age shall be subject to any minimum sentence of imprisonment for a conviction of incest under this section.

Source.
1971, 518:1. 1986, 168:2, eff. Jan. 1, 1987. 2000, 173:2, 3, eff. May 24, 2000. 2008, 334:10, eff. January 1, 2009.

Amendments
—2008. The 2008 amendment in I, in the first sentence, substituted "engages in sexual penetration as defined in RSA 632-A:1, V" for "has sexual intercourse", added "18 years or older" and made stylistic changes.

—2000. Paragraph II: Inserted "when the alleged offense occurred" following "under the age of 18" and substituted "run pursuant to RSA 625:8, III(d)" for "not begin to run until the victim reaches the age of 18" following "limitations shall".
Paragraph III: Added.

—1986. Designated the existing provisions of the section as par. I and added par. II.

Cross References.
Annulment of record of conviction for offense under section, see RSA 651:5.
Classification of crimes, see RSA 625:9.
Marriages prohibited by law, see RSA 457:1 et seq.
Sentences, see RSA 651.
Sexual assault and related offenses, see RSA 632-A.
Void marriages, see RSA 458:1 et seq.

NOTES TO DECISIONS

Evidence
Where defendant was indicted for incest by intercourse, not marriage, with his daughter the state did not have to prove defendant's marriage to daughter's mother. State v. Dymond, 110 N.H. 228, 265 A.2d 9, 1970 N.H. LEXIS 138 (1970). (Decided under prior law.)

Testimony of mother that five-year-old daughter had told her father had "fooled around with me" was some evidence tending to establish material elements of attempt to commit incest and together with father's confession was sufficient for verdict of guilty by jury. State v. Pickard, 104 N.H. 11, 177 A.2d 401, 1962 N.H. LEXIS 3 (1962). (Decided under prior law.)

A charge of incest with the "daughter" of the accused is sustained by evidence of sexual relations with a stepdaughter. State v. Geddes, 101 N.H. 164, 136 A.2d 818, 1957 N.H. LEXIS 45 (1957). (Decided under prior law.)

Cited:
Cited in State v. Carroll, 120 N.H. 458, 417 A.2d 8, 1980 N.H. LEXIS 322 (1980); State v. Oropallo, 128 N.H. 305, 512 A.2d 1130, 1986 N.H. LEXIS 281 (1986); State v. Kulikowski, 132 N.H. 281, 564 A.2d 439, 1989 N.H. LEXIS 99 (1989).

639:3. Endangering Welfare of Child or Incompetent.

I. A person is guilty of endangering the welfare of a child or incompetent if he knowingly endangers the welfare of a child under 18 years of age or of an incompetent person by purposely violating a duty of care, protection or support he owes to such child or incompetent, or by inducing such child or incompetent to engage in conduct that endangers his health or safety.

II. In the prosecution of any person under this section, the tattooing or branding by any person of a child under the age of 18 constitutes endangering the welfare of such child.

III. In the prosecution of any person under this section, the solicitation by any person of a child under the age of 16 to engage in sexual activity as defined by RSA 649-A:2, III for the purpose of creating a visual representation as defined in RSA 649-A:2, IV, or to engage in sexual penetration as defined by RSA 632-A:1, V, constitutes endangering the welfare of such child.

IV. A person who pursuant to the tenets of a recognized religion fails to conform to an otherwise existing duty of care or protection is not guilty of an offense under this section.

V. A person who endangers the welfare of a child or incompetent by violating paragraph III of this section is guilty of a class B felony. All other violations of this section are misdemeanors.

VI. No person acting in accordance with the provisions of RSA 132-A shall be guilty of an offense under this section.

Source.
1971, 518:1. 1983, 448:1, eff. Aug. 23, 1983. 2002, 195:2, eff. Jan. 1, 2003. 2003, 40:2, eff. June 4, 2003.

Amendments
—2003. Paragraph VI: Added.

—2002. Paragraph II: Inserted "or branding" following "the tattooing".

—1983. Paragraph I: Substituted "endangering the welfare of a child or incompetent" for "a misdemeanor" following "guilty of" and "18 years of age" for "eighteen" following "child under".
Paragraph II: Substituted "18" for "eighteen" following "age of".
Paragraph III: Former par. III redesignated as par. IV and new

par. III added.

Paragraph IV: Redesignated from former par. III.

Paragraph V: Added.

Cross References.

Annulment of record of conviction for offense under section, see RSA 651:5.

Child pornography, see RSA 649-A.

Child Protection Act, see RSA 169-C.

Classification of crimes, see RSA 625:9.

Exposing minor to harmful materials, see RSA 571-B.

Registration of criminal offenders, see RSA 651-B.

Sentences, see RSA 651.

NOTES TO DECISIONS

1. Constitutionality
2. Solicitation
3. Indictment and information
4. Duty of care
5. Knowingly
6. Mens rea
7. Sufficiency of the evidence

1. Constitutionality

References in the child endangerment definition to knowing endangerment by purposely ignoring a duty to a child did not make the prohibition unconstitutionally vague, because many conceivable purposeful failures to perform less critical duties to a child could occur without knowingly exposing the child to danger. State v. Bortner, 150 N.H. 504, 841 A.2d 80, 2004 N.H. LEXIS 11 (2004).

2. Solicitation

Defendant is guilty of solicitation pursuant to RSA 639:3, III if defendant entices or strongly urges a child under the age of 16 to engage in sexual penetration, as the plain language of RSA 639:3, III does not incorporate the definition of criminal solicitation in RSA 629:2, I; the use of the term "solicits" in RSA 639:3, III is not synonymous with the use of the term "criminal solicitation" in RSA 629:2, I. State v. Laporte (in re State), 157 N.H. 229, 950 A.2d 147, 2008 N.H. LEXIS 55 (2008).

3. Indictment and information

Subdivision III of this section defines each act of soliciting a minor to engage in a single act of sexual penetration as a separate offense, and thus prosecution under this subdivision does not permit charging a course of conduct. State v. Paulsen, 143 N.H. 447, 726 A.2d 902, 1999 N.H. LEXIS 23 (1999).

Plain meaning of this section suggests that it is not necessary for the state to charge specific incidents of parental disregard or specific beatings, nor must the state allege a specific time frame in which the knowing endangerment took place in order to satisfy the material elements of the offense; an information which alleges a continuous course of conduct involving continuous acts or omissions constituting endangerment is sufficient to give specific notice to a defendant so that he or she can prepare a proper defense. State v. Portigue, 125 N.H. 352, 481 A.2d 534, 1984 N.H. LEXIS 266 (1984).

4. Duty of care

Defendant's representation was not constitutionally deficient under N.H. Const. art. I, § 15 or the Sixth Amendment because trial counsel failed to argue that the evidence did not support a finding that defendant owed the victim a duty of care as: (1) defendant's precise affinal relationship to the victim was not an element of an offense under RSA 639:3, I; and (2) defendant owed the victim a duty of care as defendant's contact with the victim came about through familial channels, and the arrangements for the victim's contact with defendant on the day of the assault were made between two adult family members. State v. Kepple, 155 N.H. 267, 922 A.2d 661, 2007 N.H. LEXIS 52 (2007).

5. Knowingly

An indictment that alleges that a defendant "knowingly" solicited a child under the age of 16 to engage in sexual penetration as defined by RSA 632-A:1, V satisfies the requirements of RSA 639:3, III, as the "knowingly" mental state in RSA 639:3, I applies to the

conduct defined in RSA 639:3, III. State v. Laporte (in re State), 157 N.H. 229, 950 A.2d 147, 2008 N.H. LEXIS 55 (2008).

6. Mens rea

For purposes of a charge of endangerment of a child, in violation of RSA 639:3, I, the mens rea of "knowingly" applies to all of the material elements except those to which the higher culpability of "purposely" has been specifically assigned. State v. Laporte (in re State), 157 N.H. 229, 950 A.2d 147, 2008 N.H. LEXIS 55 (2008).

7. Sufficiency of the evidence

There was sufficient evidence supporting a conviction of felony endangering the welfare of a child under RSA 639:3, III. From sexually suggestive photographs in evidence, a rational trier of fact could have concluded that in asking the victim to pose nude, defendant solicited her for a photograph that would be a lewd exhibition of the genitals; as for whether defendant engaged in "solicitation," a rational jury could find that defendant enticed the victim by playing to her ambition to be a model and that his request that she pose nude was the culmination of a sequence intended to gain her trust so that she would pose for pornography. State v. Lopez, 162 N.H. 153, 27 A.3d 713, 2011 N.H. LEXIS 79 (2011).

Cited:

Cited in State v. Vachon, 130 N.H. 37, 533 A.2d 384, 1987 N.H. LEXIS 266 (1987); State v. Huard, 138 N.H. 256, 638 A.2d 787, 1994 N.H. LEXIS 11 (1994).

639:4. Non-Support.

I. A person is guilty of non-support if such person knowingly fails to provide support which such person is legally obliged to provide and which such person can provide to a spouse, child or other dependent. The fine, if any, shall be paid or applied in whole or in part to the support of such spouse, child or other dependent as the court may direct.

II. In this section, non-support shall be:

(a) A class B felony if the arrearage of support has remained unpaid for a cumulative period of more than one year;

(b) A class B felony if the amount of the arrearage is more than $10,000;

(c) A class B felony if the obligor has been previously convicted of non-support under this section or if the obligor has been convicted of a similar criminal nonsupport offense in another state and the arrearage of support in this state has remained unpaid for a cumulative period of more than one year; or

(d) A class A misdemeanor in all other cases.

Source.

1971, 518:1. 1977, 588:14, eff. Sept. 16, 1977. 1999, 327:1, eff. Jan. 1, 2000.

Amendments

—1999. Designated the existing provisions of the section as par. I and substituted "of non-support if such person" for "of a misdemeanor if he" preceding "knowingly fails", "such person" for "he know he" preceding "is legally obliged" and "such person" for "he" preceding "can provide" in the first sentence of that paragraph and added par. II.

—1977. Added the second sentence.

Cross References.

Alternative method for support enforcement for dependent children, see RSA 161-C.

Assignment of wages for support of spouses and children, see RSA 458-B.

Classification of crimes, see RSA 625:9.
Sentences, see RSA 651.
Support of dependent children, see RSA 161-B.
Uniform Civil Liability for Support Act, see RSA 546-A.
Uniform Interstate Family Support Act, see RSA 546-B.

NOTES TO DECISIONS

Jurisdiction

Where jurisdiction of the father's person was obtained by his arrest within the state, a complaint charging the crime of nonsupport of his minor children residing in the state could be maintained against him under this section, notwithstanding the fact that he resided elsewhere. State v. Carr, 107 N.H. 477, 225 A.2d 178, 1966 N.H. LEXIS 217 (1966). (Decided under prior law.)

Cited:

Cited in Opinion of Justices, 121 N.H. 531, 431 A.2d 144, 1981 N.H. LEXIS 342 (1981).

639:5. Concealing Death of a Newborn.

A person is guilty of a class B felony if he knowingly conceals the corpse of a newborn child.

Source.
1971, 518:1, eff. Nov. 1, 1973.

Cross References.
Abuse of corpse, see RSA 644:7.
Burials and disinterments generally, see RSA 290.
Classification of crimes, see RSA 625:9.
Joining charges of murder and concealing death of a newborn child, see RSA 601:6-a.
Sentences, see RSA 651.

NOTES TO DECISIONS

Cited:

Cited in Wallace v. Wallace, 120 N.H. 675, 421 A.2d 134, 1980 N.H. LEXIS 377 (1980).

CHAPTER 639-A

METHAMPHETAMINE-RELATED CRIMES

SECTION
639-A:1.   Definitions.
639-A:2.   Prohibited Conduct.
639-A:3.   Penalties.
639-A:4.   Protective Custody for Health Screening; Reports Required.

639-A:1. Definitions.

In this chapter:

I. "Chemical substance" means a substance intended to be used as a precursor in the manufacture of methamphetamine or any other chemical intended to be used in the manufacture of methamphetamine.

II. "Child" means any person under the age of 18 years.

III. "Incapacitated adult" means a person 18 years of age or older who is incapacitated, as defined in RSA 161-F:43, VII.

IV. "Methamphetamine paraphernalia" means all equipment, products, and materials of any kind that are used, intended for use, or designed for use in manufacturing, injecting, ingesting, inhaling, or otherwise introducing methamphetamine into the human body.

V. "Methamphetamine waste products" means substances, chemicals, or items of any kind used in the manufacture of methamphetamine or any part of the manufacturing process, or the by-products or degradates of manufacturing methamphetamine.

Source.
2006, 135:1, eff. May 19, 2006.

639-A:2. Prohibited Conduct.

I. No person shall knowingly engage in any of the following activities in the presence of a child or incapacitated adult; in the residence of a child or an incapacitated adult; in a building, structure, conveyance, or outdoor location where a child or incapacitated adult might reasonably be expected to be present; within any drug-free school zone, as defined under RSA 193-B:1, II; in a room offered to the public for overnight accommodations; or in any multiple unit residential building:

(a) Manufacturing or attempting to manufacture methamphetamine.

(b) Storing any chemical substance.

(c) Storing or disposing of any methamphetamine waste products.

(d) Storing or disposing of any methamphetamine paraphernalia.

II. No person shall knowingly cause or permit a child or incapacitated adult to inhale, be exposed to, have contact with, or ingest methamphetamine, a chemical substance, or methamphetamine paraphernalia.

III. No person shall, with the intent to engage in any prohibited conduct under paragraph I, knowingly cause or permit any child or incapacitated adult to buy or otherwise obtain methamphetamine paraphernalia.

Source.
2006, 135:1, eff. May 19, 2006.

639-A:3. Penalties.

I. A person convicted of an offense under RSA 639-A:2 shall be guilty of a felony and, notwithstanding RSA 651:2, may be sentenced to imprisonment for not more than 5 years or a fine of up to $10,000, or both.

II. A prosecution or conviction under this chapter is not a bar to conviction of or punishment for any other crime committed by the defendant as part of the same conduct.

Source.
2006, 135:1, eff. May 19, 2006.

639-A:4. Protective Custody for Health Screening; Reports Required.

I. A peace officer shall, pursuant to RSA 169-C:6, take any child present in an area where any of the activities described in RSA 639-A:2 are taking place into protective custody. Upon taking a child into protective custody, the peace officer shall follow the procedures outlined in RSA 169-C:6 and shall report the matter to the department of health and human services as a suspected incident of abuse or neglect under RSA 169-C:29. The department shall investigate the report in accordance with RSA 169-C:34 and shall, as part of its investigation, screen the child for possible health concerns related to exposure to methamphetamine.

II. If a peace officer does not take a child into protective custody under this section, but has reason to believe that the child may have been exposed to methamphetamine, the peace office shall report the matter to the department of health and human services as a suspected incident of abuse or neglect under RSA 169-C:29. The department shall investigate the report in accordance with RSA 169-C:34 and may, as part of its investigation, screen the child for possible health concerns related to exposure to methamphetamine.

Source.
2006, 135:1, eff. May 19, 2006.

CHAPTER 640

CORRUPT PRACTICES

SECTION
640:1. Scope of Chapter.
640:2. Bribery in Official and Political Matters.
640:3. Improper Influence.
640:4. Compensation for Past Action.
640:5. Gifts to Public Servants.
640:6. Compensation for Services.
640:7. Purchase of Public Office.

Cross References.
Abuse of office, see RSA 643.
Accountability of magistrates and government officers, see New Hampshire Constitution, Part 1, Article 8.
Bribery or corruption in obtaining election or appointment disqualify person convicted from holding office, see New Hampshire Constitution, Part 2, Article 96.
Legislative ethics committee, see RSA 14-B.

640:1. Scope of Chapter.

Nothing in this chapter shall be construed to prohibit the giving or receiving of campaign contributions made for the purpose of defraying the costs of a political campaign, or the giving or receiving of any other thing exempt from the prohibition on gifts pursuant to RSA 15-B. No person shall be convicted of an offense solely on the evidence that a campaign contribution, or any other thing exempt from the prohibition on gifts pursuant to RSA 15-B was made to a public official, and that a vote, an appointment, or a nomination was subsequently made by the person to whose campaign or political party the contribution was made or who received the thing exempt from the prohibition on gifts pursuant to RSA 15-B.

Source.
1971, 518:1, eff. Nov. 1, 1973. 2007, 354:1, eff. September 15, 2007.

Amendments
—**2007.** Rewritten to the extent that a detailed comparison would be impracticable.

Cross References.
Political expenditures and contributions, see RSA 664.

640:2. Bribery in Official and Political Matters.

I. A person is guilty of a class B felony if:

(a) He promises, offers, or gives any pecuniary benefit to another with the purpose of influencing the other's action, decision, opinion, recommendation, vote, nomination, or other exercise of discretion as a public servant, party official, or voter; or

(b) Being a public servant, party official, candidate for electoral office, or voter, he solicits, accepts or agrees to accept any pecuniary benefit from another knowing or believing the other's purpose to be as described in subparagraph I(a), or fails to report to a law enforcement officer that he has been offered or promised a pecuniary benefit in violation of subparagraph I(a).

II. As used in this section and other sections of this chapter, the following definitions apply:

(a) "Public servant" means any officer or employee of the state or any political subdivision thereof, including judges, legislators, consultants, jurors, and persons otherwise performing a governmental function. A person is considered a public servant upon his election, appointment or other designation as such, although he may not yet officially occupy that position. A person is a candidate for electoral office upon his public announcement of his candidacy.

(b) "Party official" means any person holding any post in a political party whether by election, appointment or otherwise.

(c) "Pecuniary benefit" means any advantage in the form of money, property, commercial interest or anything else, the primary significance of which is economic gain; it does not include economic advantage applicable to the public generally, such as tax reduction or increased prosperity generally.

Source.
1971, 518:1, eff. Nov. 1, 1973.

Cross References.
Classification of crimes, see RSA 625:9.

Sentences, see RSA 651.

Cited:
Cited in Evans v. Hall, 118 N.H. 920, 396 A.2d 334, 1978 N.H. LEXIS 322 (1978).

640:3. Improper Influence.

I. A person is guilty of a class B felony if he:

(a) Threatens any harm to a public servant, party official or voter with the purpose of influencing his action, decision, opinion, recommendation, nomination, vote or other exercise of discretion; or

(b) Privately addresses to any public servant who has or will have an official discretion in a judicial or administrative proceeding any representation, argument or other communication with the purpose of influencing that discretion on the basis of considerations other than those authorized by law; or

(c) Being a public servant or party official, fails to report to a law enforcement officer conduct designed to influence him in violation of subparagraph (a) or (b) hereof.

II. "Harm" means any disadvantage or injury, to person or property or pecuniary interest, including disadvantage or injury to any other person or entity in whose welfare the public servant, party official, or voter is interested, provided that harm shall not be construed to include the exercise of any conduct protected under the First Amendment to the United States Constitution or any provision of the federal or state constitutions.

Source.
1971, 518:1, eff. Nov. 1, 1973. 2006, 43:1, eff. January 1, 2007.

Amendments
—2006. Paragraph II: Substituted "to person or property or pecuniary interest" for "pecuniary or otherwise", and added the proviso.

Cross References.
Classification of crimes, see RSA 625:9.
Sentences, see RSA 651.

640:4. Compensation for Past Action.

A person is guilty of a misdemeanor if:

I. Being a public servant, he solicits, accepts or agrees to accept any pecuniary benefit in return for having given a decision, opinion, recommendation, nomination, vote, otherwise exercised his discretion, or for having violated his duty; or

II. He promises, offers or gives any pecuniary benefit, acceptance of which would be a violation of paragraph I.

Source.
1971, 518:1, eff. Nov. 1, 1973.

Cross References.
Classification of crimes, see RSA 625:9.
Sentences, see RSA 651.

640:5. Gifts to Public Servants.

A person is guilty of a misdemeanor if:

I. Being a public servant he solicits, accepts or agrees to accept any pecuniary benefit from a person who is or is likely to become subject to or interested in any matter or action pending before or contemplated by himself or the governmental body with which he is affiliated; or

II. He knowingly gives, offers, or promises any pecuniary benefit prohibited by paragraph I.

Source.
1971, 518:1, eff. Nov. 1, 1973.

Cross References.
Classification of crimes, see RSA 625:9.
Sentences, see RSA 651.

640:6. Compensation for Services.

A person is guilty of a misdemeanor if:

I. Being a public servant, he solicits, accepts, or agrees to accept any pecuniary benefit in return for advice or other assistance in preparing or promoting a bill, contract, claim, or other transaction or proposal as to which he knows that he has or is likely to have an official discretion to exercise; or

II. He gives, offers or promises any pecuniary benefit, knowing that it is prohibited by paragraph I.

Source.
1971, 518:1, eff. Nov. 1, 1973.

Cross References.
Classification of crimes, see RSA 625:9.
Sentences, see RSA 651.

640:7. Purchase of Public Office.

A person is guilty of a misdemeanor if:

I. He solicits, accepts or agrees to accept, for himself, another person, or a political party, money or any other pecuniary benefit as compensation for his endorsement, nomination, appointment, approval or disapproval of any person for a position as a public servant or for the advancement of any public servant; or

II. He knowingly gives, offers or promises any pecuniary benefit prohibited by paragraph I.

Source.
1971, 518:1, eff. Nov. 1, 1973.

Cross References.
Classification of crimes, see RSA 625:9.
Sentences, see RSA 651.

CHAPTER 641

FALSIFICATION IN OFFICIAL MATTERS

SECTION
641:1.   Perjury.
641:2.   False Swearing.
641:3.   Unsworn Falsification.
641:4.   False Reports to Law Enforcement.

SECTION
641:5. Tampering With Witnesses and Informants.
641:6. Falsifying Physical Evidence.
641:7. Tampering With Public Records or Information.
641:8. False Filing With the Director of Charitable Trusts.

NOTES TO DECISIONS

Cited:

Cited in State v. Sands, 123 N.H. 570, 467 A.2d 202, 1983 N.H. LEXIS 362, 37 A.L.R.4th 904 (1983).

641:1. Perjury.

I. A person is guilty of a class B felony if in any official proceeding:

(a) He makes a false material statement under oath or affirmation, or swears or affirms the truth of a material statement previously made, and he does not believe the statement to be true; or

(b) He makes inconsistent material statements under oath or affirmation, both within the period of limitations, one of which is false and not believed by him to be true. In a prosecution under this section, it need not be alleged or proved which of the statements is false but only that one or the other was false and not believed by the defendant to be true.

II. "Official proceeding" means any proceeding before a legislative, judicial, administrative or other governmental body or official authorized by law to take evidence under oath or affirmation including a notary or other person taking evidence in connection with any such proceeding. "Material" means capable of affecting the course or outcome of the proceeding. A statement is not material if it is retracted in the course of the official proceeding in which it was made before it became manifest that the falsification was or would be exposed and before it substantially affected the proceeding. Whether a statement is material is a question of law to be determined by the court.

Source.

1971, 518:1, eff. Nov. 1, 1973.

Cross References.

Classification of crimes, see RSA 625:9.
Sentences, see RSA 651.

NOTES TO DECISIONS

0.5. Construction
 1. Construction with other laws
 2. Lesser included offense
 3. Official proceeding
 4. Materiality of statement
 5. Falsity
 6. Knowledge
 7. Oath or affirmation
 8. Burden of proof
 9. Evidence—Proof required
10. —Nature and sufficiency
11. —Admissibility
12. Jury instructions
13. Indictments and informations

0.5. Construction

RSA 641:1, I(a) provides that a person commits perjury if in any official proceeding, he makes a false material statement under oath or affirmation, or swears or affirms the truth of a material statement previously made, and he does not believe the statement to be true. Thus, the statute criminalizes the making of false statements, not the creation of false impressions. State v. Bisbee, — N.H. —, 69 A.3d 95, 2013 N.H. LEXIS 51 (May 14, 2013).

1. Construction with other laws

Since the only difference between the elements of the felony of perjury and the elements of the misdemeanor of false swearing set forth in RSA 641:2 is that of materiality, it necessarily follows that if a statement is material as a matter of law, then a defendant could not be guilty of false swearing. State v. Sands, 123 N.H. 570, 467 A.2d 202, 1983 N.H. LEXIS 362, 37 A.L.R.4th 904 (1983).

2. Lesser included offense

In prosecution for perjury, after the trial court properly determined that the defendant's false statements were material, the court did not violate the defendant's rights under the fifth, eighth and fourteenth amendments to the United States Constitution by declining to instruct the jury on the lesser included offense of false swearing, since the finding of materiality precluded a finding of guilty on the lesser included offense. Sands v. Cunningham, 617 F. Supp. 1551, 1985 U.S. Dist. LEXIS 15393 (D.N.H. 1985).

In prosecutions for perjury, where the trial court determined that the allegedly false statements were material as a matter of law, the defendants' argument that that determination deprived them of their right to have the jury determine whether they were guilty of the lesser-included offense of false swearing under RSA 641:2, which contains no requirement of materiality, was without merit; where a statement is material, a defendant could not be guilty of false swearing, but must be guilty either of perjury or of no offense at all, and therefore, a "lesser-included offense" charge would not be warranted. State v. Sands, 123 N.H. 570, 467 A.2d 202, 1983 N.H. LEXIS 362, 37 A.L.R.4th 904 (1983).

3. Official proceeding

In a prosecution for perjury, the determination whether the allegedly false statements were made at an official proceeding is ultimately a question of fact for the jury. State v. Sands, 123 N.H. 570, 467 A.2d 202, 1983 N.H. LEXIS 362, 37 A.L.R.4th 904 (1983).

Commissioner who was appointed to take defendant's deposition in civil litigation that gave rise to perjury prosecution was a "person taking evidence in connection with an official proceeding," namely the civil litigation, and the deposition could form the basis of a perjury conviction under paragraph II of this section. State v. Sands, 123 N.H. 570, 467 A.2d 202, 1983 N.H. LEXIS 362, 37 A.L.R.4th 904 (1983).

4. Materiality of statement

In prosecution for perjury, withdrawal from jury consideration of the issue of the materiality of the false statement did not violate the defendant's rights under the sixth and seventh amendments to the United States Constitution since determination of the materiality of the statement is a legal question properly reserved for the trial court. Sands v. Cunningham, 617 F. Supp. 1551, 1985 U.S. Dist. LEXIS 15393 (D.N.H. 1985).

The question of materiality in a prosecution for perjury, the examination of the often complex relationship between the allegedly false statements and the official proceeding, is a legal issue for the court. State v. Sands, 123 N.H. 570, 467 A.2d 202, 1983 N.H. LEXIS 362, 37 A.L.R.4th 904 (1983).

Since materiality as an element of the crime of perjury involves the legal relationship between certain facts which are to be found by the jury, this section correctly categorizes materiality as a question of law. State v. Sands, 123 N.H. 570, 467 A.2d 202, 1983 N.H. LEXIS 362, 37 A.L.R.4th 904 (1983).

By properly categorizing the element of materiality in this section as a question of law for the trial court, the legislature has clearly recognized that this element is not subject to the mandates of RSA 625:10, which requires that each element of an offense be proved beyond a reasonable doubt. State v. Sands, 123 N.H. 570,

467 A.2d 202, 1983 N.H. LEXIS 362, 37 A.L.R.4th 904 (1983).

In prosecutions for perjury, as a legal issue, the determination of materiality did not fall within the constitutional requirement for jury determination of all factual elements, and the constitutional rights of defendants were fully safeguarded when the trial court submitted all factual elements to the jury. State v. Sands, 123 N.H. 570, 467 A.2d 202, 1983 N.H. LEXIS 362, 37 A.L.R.4th 904 (1983).

Where a charge of perjury is based on allegedly false testimony given by the accused on the trial of another case, in order to sustain the charge of perjury the matter sworn to must have been material to the issues on trial, for if it was of no importance, though false, it is not perjury, and testimony which has no tendency to change the opinion of the jury or the judgment of the court is considered immaterial. State v. Norris, 9 N.H. 96, 1837 N.H. LEXIS 21 (1837). (Decided under prior law.)

5. Falsity

If defendant honestly believes her statements to be true, even if in fact they are false, the state has failed to prove defendant guilty of perjury. State v. Maya, 127 N.H. 684, 506 A.2d 308, 1986 N.H. LEXIS 221 (1986).

At trial for perjury, objective falsity of the defendant's statements are an element to be considered by the jury in determining the subjective state of mind of the defendant. State v. Maya, 127 N.H. 684, 506 A.2d 308, 1986 N.H. LEXIS 221 (1986).

6. Knowledge

It is perjury for one to swear that a certain fact did not occur at a certain time and place if he has no knowledge whether or not it did or did not occur. State v. Gates, 17 N.H. 373, 1845 N.H. LEXIS 109 (1845). (Decided under prior law.)

7. Oath or affirmation

This section establishes a general requirement that an oath be administered but makes no reference to the timing of the oath or to any need for subsequent confirmation by subscription, which are formalities which are irrelevant to the oath's objective to impress upon the individual his obligation to tell the truth. State v. Sands, 123 N.H. 570, 467 A.2d 202, 1983 N.H. LEXIS 362, 37 A.L.R.4th 904 (1983).

8. Burden of proof

At trial for perjury, state bears the burden of proving the three elements of the offense beyond a reasonable doubt to gain a conviction. State v. Maya, 127 N.H. 684, 506 A.2d 308, 1986 N.H. LEXIS 221 (1986).

9. Evidence—Proof required

There is no indication that the repeal of the former perjury statute (Laws 1967, 358:1), which had specifically abolished the common-law rule requiring proof by a particular number of witnesses and type of evidence, was intended to resurrect the common-law rule; there is no reason to treat the proof required in a perjury case any differently from that required for other serious offenses, such as murder and rape. State v. Sands, 123 N.H. 570, 467 A.2d 202, 1983 N.H. LEXIS 362, 37 A.L.R.4th 904 (1983).

10. —Nature and sufficiency

Evidence was sufficient to support defendant's conviction of perjury since, from evidence presented, jury could have found beyond a reasonable doubt that defendant transferred money to his father within six months prior to completing his financial affidavit, and that defendant therefore perjured himself by responding "N/A" to question in affidavit regarding whether any such transfers were made. State v. Atkins, 145 N.H. 256, 761 A.2d 484, 2000 N.H. LEXIS 54 (2000).

As long as the evidence establishes guilt beyond a reasonable doubt, perjury may be established entirely by circumstantial evidence. State v. Sands, 123 N.H. 570, 467 A.2d 202, 1983 N.H. LEXIS 362, 37 A.L.R.4th 904 (1983); State v. Maya, 127 N.H. 684, 506 A.2d 308, 1986 N.H. LEXIS 221 (1986).

Proof of the objective falsity of defendant's statements cannot alone suffice to prove the necessary subjective element of perjury. State v. Maya, 127 N.H. 684, 506 A.2d 308, 1986 N.H. LEXIS 221 (1986).

A deposition or affidavit which is inadmissible at trial may form the basis of a perjury conviction. State v. Sands, 123 N.H. 570, 467 A.2d 202, 1983 N.H. LEXIS 362, 37 A.L.R.4th 904 (1983).

11. —Admissibility

In prosecution for perjury, where the elements of materiality, falsity and mental state were intertwined and evidence pertaining to materiality was also relevant as to whether the defendant believed that his statements were false, admission of the evidence relating to materiality did not deny defendant his right to a fair trial under the fifth and fourteenth amendments to the United States Constitution. Sands v. Cunningham, 617 F. Supp. 1551, 1985 U.S. Dist. LEXIS 15393 (D.N.H. 1985).

12. Jury instructions

Where trial court in prosecution for perjury instructed the jury that the state was required to prove beyond a reasonable doubt that the defendant did not believe the questioned statements to be true, and also instructed the jury that the state did not have to prove that the defendant believed the statements to be false, the overall charge was fundamentally sound and did not violate the defendant's due process rights by removing the question of mens rea from the jury. Sands v. Cunningham, 617 F. Supp. 1551, 1985 U.S. Dist. LEXIS 15393 (D.N.H. 1985).

In prosecutions for perjury, the trial judge correctly instructed the jury that the state was not required to prove beyond a reasonable doubt that the defendants believed or knew their statements to be false, but only that they did not believe the statements to be true. State v. Sands, 123 N.H. 570, 467 A.2d 202, 1983 N.H. LEXIS 362, 37 A.L.R.4th 904 (1983).

13. Indictments and informations

Indictments for perjury under RSA 641:1, I(a) were not insufficient under N.H. Const. pt. I, art. 15 and the Fourteenth Amendment because they did not allege specific statements. An indictment that attributes a false statement to a defendant does not fail for insufficiency even though the statement represents a summary of the defendant's testimony. State v. Bisbee, — N.H. —, 69 A.3d 95, 2013 N.H. LEXIS 51 (May 14, 2013).

In evaluating the sufficiency of a perjury indictment, the trial court need not compare the allegedly perjurious statement with the defendant's prior testimony. Whether the defendant made the statements alleged in the indictments raises an issue of proof that is distinct from the indictment's sufficiency. State v. Bisbee, — N.H. —, 69 A.3d 95, 2013 N.H. LEXIS 51 (May 14, 2013).

Cited:

Cited in State v. Gage, 116 N.H. 656, 366 A.2d 501, 1976 N.H. LEXIS 440 (1976); Kozerski v. Smith, 555 F. Supp. 212, 1983 U.S. Dist. LEXIS 20099 (D.N.H. 1983); State v. Cook, 135 N.H. 702, 609 A.2d 742, 1992 N.H. LEXIS 107 (1992); State v. Hutchins, 144 N.H. 669, 746 A.2d 447, 2000 N.H. LEXIS 8 (2000).

RESEARCH REFERENCES

New Hampshire Code of Administrative Rules.
Rules of the Public Utilities Commission, Puc 202.01, New Hampshire Code of Administrative Rules Annotated.

641:2. False Swearing.

A person is guilty of a misdemeanor if:

I. He makes a false statement under oath or affirmation or swears or affirms the truth of such a statement previously made and he does not believe the statement to be true if:

(a) The falsification occurs in an official proceeding, as defined in RSA 641:1, II, or is made with a purpose to mislead a public servant in performing his official function; or

(b) The statement is one which is required by law to be sworn or affirmed before a notary or other person authorized to administer oaths; or

II. He makes inconsistent statements under oath or affirmation, both within the period of limitations, one of which is false and not believed by him to be true. In a prosecution under this section, it need not be alleged or proved which of the statements is false but only that one or the other was false and not believed by the defendant to be true.

III. No person shall be guilty under this section if he retracts the falsification before it becomes manifest that the falsification was or would be exposed.

Source.
1971, 518:1, eff. Nov. 1, 1973.

Cross References.
Classification of crimes, see RSA 625:9.
Sentences, see RSA 651.

NOTES TO DECISIONS

1. Construction with other laws
2. Lesser included offense

1. Construction with other laws
Since the only difference between the elements of the felony of perjury set forth in RSA 641:1 and the elements of the misdemeanor of false swearing is that of materiality, it necessarily follows that if a statement is material as a matter of law, then a defendant could not be guilty of false swearing. State v. Sands, 123 N.H. 570, 467 A.2d 202, 1983 N.H. LEXIS 362, 37 A.L.R.4th 904 (1983).

2. Lesser included offense
In prosecutions for perjury under RSA 641:1, where the trial court determined that the allegedly false statements were material as a matter of law, the defendants' argument that that determination deprived them of their right to have the jury determine whether they were guilty of the lesser-included offense of false swearing under this section, which contains no requirement of materiality, was without merit; where a statement is material, a defendant could not be guilty of false swearing, but must be guilty either of perjury or of no offense at all, and therefore, a "lesser-included offense" charge would not be warranted. State v. Sands, 123 N.H. 570, 467 A.2d 202, 1983 N.H. LEXIS 362, 37 A.L.R.4th 904 (1983).

Cited:
Cited in Kozerski v. Smith, 555 F. Supp. 212, 1983 U.S. Dist. LEXIS 20099 (D.N.H. 1983).

RESEARCH REFERENCES

New Hampshire Code of Administrative Rules.
Rules of the Public Utilities Commission, Puc 202.08, New Hampshire Code of Administrative Rules Annotated.

641:3. Unsworn Falsification.

A person is guilty of a misdemeanor if:

I. He or she makes a written or electronic false statement which he or she does not believe to be true, on or pursuant to a form bearing a notification authorized by law to the effect that false statements made therein are punishable; or

II. With a purpose to deceive a public servant in the performance of his or her official function, he or she:

(a) Makes any written or electronic false statement which he or she does not believe to be

true; or

(b) Knowingly creates a false impression in a written application for any pecuniary or other benefit by omitting information necessary to prevent statements therein from being misleading; or

(c) Submits or invites reliance on any writing which he or she knows to be lacking in authenticity; or

(d) Submits or invites reliance on any sample, specimen, map, boundary mark, or other object which he or she knows to be false.

III. No person shall be guilty under this section if he or she retracts the falsification before it becomes manifest that the falsification was or would be exposed.

Source.
1971, 518:1, eff. Nov. 1, 1973. 2003, 158:2, eff. June 17, 2003.

Amendments
—2003. Inserted "or electronic" following "makes a written" in par. I and following "any written" in subpar. II(a), inserted "or her" following "his" in par. II; and inserted "or she" following "he" throughout the section.

Cross References.
Classification of crimes, see RSA 625:9.
Sentences, see RSA 651.

NOTES TO DECISIONS

Particular cases
State conceded that it was unaware of any provision of law authorizing municipal police to create forms which stated that making false written statements on the form was punishable as unsworn falsification. Therefore, defendant's unsworn falsification conviction under RSA 641:3, I, had to be reversed. State v. Stowe, 162 N.H. 464, 34 A.3d 678, 2011 N.H. LEXIS 128 (2011).

Cited:
Cited in State v. La Clair, 121 N.H. 743, 433 A.2d 1326, 1981 N.H. LEXIS 391 (1981); Kozerski v. Smith, 555 F. Supp. 212, 1983 U.S. Dist. LEXIS 20099 (D.N.H. 1983).

641:4. False Reports to Law Enforcement.

A person is guilty of a misdemeanor if he:

I. Knowingly gives or causes to be given false information to any law enforcement officer with the purpose of inducing such officer to believe that another has committed an offense; or

II. Knowingly gives or causes to be given information to any law enforcement officer concerning the commission of an offense, or the danger from an explosive or other dangerous substance, knowing that the offense or danger did not occur or exist or knowing that he has no information relating to the offense or danger.

Source.
1971, 518:1, eff. Nov. 1, 1973.

Cross References.
Classification of crimes, see RSA 625:9.
Sentences, see RSA 651.

NOTES TO DECISIONS

1. Application

2. Construction with other law
3. Sufficiency of evidence

1. Application

Where, upon being arrested for traffic violations, defendant provided the name and address of someone later described as his friend, it was clearly his intent to convince the police that someone other than he had been driving the vehicle, and the State properly concluded that his actions violated this section; that the false information did not actually impede the investigation was irrelevant. State v. Hill, 146 N.H. 568, 781 A.2d 979, 2001 N.H. LEXIS 114 (2001).

2. Construction with other law

Where defendant provided a false identification upon being arrested for traffic violations and was charged under statute prohibiting false reports to law enforcement, it was irrelevant that he could also have been charged under RSA 265:4, I(b) which prohibits an individual "while driving or in charge of a motor vehicle" from "giv[ing] false information to a law enforcement officer that would hinder law enforcement officer from properly identifying the person in charge of such a motor vehicle." State v. Hill, 146 N.H. 568, 781 A.2d 979, 2001 N.H. LEXIS 114 (2001).

3. Sufficiency of evidence

When defendant was accused of falsely claiming that her husband sent her text messages in violation of a protective order, the evidence was sufficient to support her convictions of falsifying physical evidence under RSA 641:6, II and of false report under RSA 641:4, I. An officer presented evidence that defendant had made false statements about meeting with him, which showed consciousness of guilt; there was evidence, including video recordings, that defendant used a phone to leave messages to herself; and there was evidence contradicting her claim that she was not in California when she placed a telephone call. State v. Ruggiero, 163 N.H. 129, 35 A.3d 616, 2011 N.H. LEXIS 190 (Dec. 28, 2011).

Cited.

Cited in McGranahan v. Dahar, 119 N.H. 758, 408 A.2d 121, 1979 N.H. LEXIS 381 (1979); State v. La Clair, 121 N.H. 743, 433 A.2d 1326, 1981 N.H. LEXIS 391 (1981); State v. MacManus, 130 N.H. 256, 536 A.2d 203, 1987 N.H. LEXIS 283 (1987); State v. Davis, 133 N.H. 211, 575 A.2d 4, 1990 N.H. LEXIS 49 (1990).

641:5. Tampering With Witnesses and Informants.

A person is guilty of a class B felony if:

I. Believing that an official proceeding, as defined in RSA 641:1, II, or investigation is pending or about to be instituted, he attempts to induce or otherwise cause a person to:

(a) Testify or inform falsely; or

(b) Withhold any testimony, information, document or thing; or

(c) Elude legal process summoning him to provide evidence; or

(d) Absent himself from any proceeding or investigation to which he has been summoned; or

II. He commits any unlawful act in retaliation for anything done by another in his capacity as witness or informant; or

III. He solicits, accepts or agrees to accept any benefit in consideration of his doing any of the things specified in paragraph I.

Source.
1971, 518:1, eff. Nov. 1, 1973.

Cross References.
Classification of crimes, see RSA 625:9.

Sentences, see RSA 651.

NOTES TO DECISIONS

1. Constitutionality
2. Construction
3. Person tampered with
4. Mens rea
5. Evidence
6. Severance of charges
7. Jury instructions

1. Constitutionality

On its face, the use of the word "person" in this section is sufficient to give an individual actual notice of the prohibited conduct and does not permit a standardless sweep; therefore, the section is not void for vagueness. Kilgus v. Cunningham, 602 F. Supp. 735, 1985 U.S. Dist. LEXIS 22685 (D.N.H. 1985), aff'd without op., 782 F.2d 1025, 1985 U.S. App. LEXIS 25950 (1st Cir. 1985).

Subparagraph I(a) of this section is not unconstitutionally over broad; an individual's right to speak to a potential witness with the intent of tampering with that witness is minuscule in comparison to the state's interest in discovering the truth in official proceedings and investigations. Kilgus v. Cunningham, 602 F. Supp. 735, 1985 U.S. Dist. LEXIS 22685 (D.N.H. 1985), aff'd without op., 782 F.2d 1025, 1985 U.S. App. LEXIS 25950 (1st Cir. 1985).

Subparagraph I(a) of this section is not unconstitutionally vague, since the description of the proscribed conduct is sufficiently specific to give fair notice of the prohibited behavior, regardless of the fact that it is forbidden as to all people, and not only as to witnesses and informants. State v. Kilgus, 125 N.H. 739, 484 A.2d 1208, 1984 N.H. LEXIS 375 (1984).

When the public interest in discovering the truth in official proceedings, protected by subparagraph I(a) of this section, is balanced against an individual's right to speak with the intent to tamper with a potential witness, the individual's right is miniscule and not protected by the First Amendment to the United States Constitution. State v. Kilgus, 125 N.H. 739, 484 A.2d 1208, 1984 N.H. LEXIS 375 (1984).

2. Construction

Witness tampering is a crime based on the attempt to induce false testimony and, therefore, this section focuses upon the defendant's intent, rather than upon the actions of the person tampered with, or the outcome of the pending investigation. Kilgus v. Cunningham, 602 F. Supp. 735, 1985 U.S. Dist. LEXIS 22685 (D.N.H. 1985), aff'd without op., 782 F.2d 1025, 1985 U.S. App. LEXIS 25950 (1st Cir. 1985).

This section focuses on the defendant's intent, rather than the actions of the person tampered with, or the outcome of the pending investigation. State v. Kilgus, 125 N.H. 739, 484 A.2d 1208, 1984 N.H. LEXIS 375 (1984).

Subparagraph I(a) of this section contains no language which indicates a limitation upon the nature of the testimony intended to be falsified. State v. Kilgus, 125 N.H. 739, 484 A.2d 1208, 1984 N.H. LEXIS 375 (1984).

There is no language in subparagraph I(a) of this section requiring that a person intend to obstruct justice. State v. Kilgus, 125 N.H. 739, 484 A.2d 1208, 1984 N.H. LEXIS 375 (1984).

3. Person tampered with

In order to support a conviction under subparagraph I(a) of this section, it is not necessary that a person tampered with actually inform or testify so as to become an informant or witness; it is only necessary that the defendant believe that the person is a potential witness when attempting to induce the person to testify or inform falsely. Kilgus v. Cunningham, 602 F. Supp. 735, 1985 U.S. Dist. LEXIS 22685 (D.N.H. 1985), aff'd without op., 782 F.2d 1025, 1985 U.S. App. LEXIS 25950 (1st Cir. 1985).

The meaning of the word "person" in subparagraph I(a) of this section is clear and unambiguous; it refers generally to all people without limitation as to their status as witnesses or informants. State v. Kilgus, 125 N.H. 739, 484 A.2d 1208, 1984 N.H. LEXIS 375 (1984).

Since the word "person" in this section is clear and unambiguous, the title of this section does not affect the meaning of this section and, therefore, does not require that the "person" actually become a witness or informant. State v. Kilgus, 125 N.H. 739, 484 A.2d 1208, 1984 N.H. LEXIS 375 (1984).

Under the language of this section it is not necessary that the person tampered with actually inform or testify so as to become an "informant" or a "witness"; it is only necessary that defendant believe that the person was a potential witness. State v. Kilgus, 125 N.H. 739, 484 A.2d 1208, 1984 N.H. LEXIS 375 (1984).

4. Mens rea

An indictment for witness tampering which stated that the defendant "intentionally" attempted to induce one to testify falsely, rather than using the statutory term "purposely," sufficiently alleged the requisite culpable mental state, since the two terms are synonymous. State v. Brewer, 127 N.H. 799, 508 A.2d 1058, 1986 N.H. LEXIS 232 (1986).

Trial court used the proper mens rea when it instructed the jury that defendant indicted for violating subparagraph I(a) of this section had to act purposely when he attempted to get a person to give the police false information. State v. Kilgus, 125 N.H. 739, 484 A.2d 1208, 1984 N.H. LEXIS 375 (1984).

5. Evidence

Where defendant offered money, baseball tickets, and a job to a witness to testify falsely, the evidence was sufficient to convict defendant for witness tampering and the trial court did not err in denying defendant's motion for a directed verdict. State v. DiNapoli, 149 N.H. 514, 823 A.2d 744, 2003 N.H. LEXIS 69 (2003).

At trial for witness tampering arising out of defendant's retaliatory actions against his daughter for her participation in an initial child abuse or neglect hearing, court properly denied motion in limine to exclude all evidence pertaining to the abuse or neglect hearing under confidentiality provision of Child Protection Act. State v. Baird, 133 N.H. 637, 581 A.2d 1313, 1990 N.H. LEXIS 110 (1990).

Jury at witness tampering trial could reasonably infer from totality of evidence presented that defendant knew that his statements regarding his thirteen-year-old daughter's willingness to engage in sexual intercourse were untrue, even though prosecution was unable to present to the jury any direct evidence of the defendant's state of mind. State v. Baird, 133 N.H. 637, 581 A.2d 1313, 1990 N.H. LEXIS 110 (1990).

Under subparagraph I(a) of this section no proof of a connection between the matter under investigation and the information to be falsified is required, except that the defendant have knowledge of a pending investigation. State v. Kilgus, 125 N.H. 739, 484 A.2d 1208, 1984 N.H. LEXIS 375 (1984).

6. Severance of charges

Trial court properly denied defendant's motion to sever two witness tampering charges against him for trial because the charges were related parts of a common plan designed to cause a jury to have a reasonable doubt about his guilt of an underlying arson charge, and the two offenses were mutually dependent, as the success of one witness tampering scheme depended on the success of the other, and defendant was not denied a fair determination of his guilt or innocence because a jury could distinguish the evidence and apply the law intelligently to each offense. State v. Michaud, 150 N.H. 359, 839 A.2d 35, 2003 N.H. LEXIS 198 (2003).

7. Jury instructions

In instructing the jury on the elements of witness tampering, the trial court erred when it id not simply instruct the jury that the State was not required to prove that the witness failed to attend defendant's district court trial—it stated that whether or not she appeared "does not matter." Whether the witness's appearance at the district court proceedings should have been a factor in the jury's evaluation of evidence in the witness tampering trial was an issue of fact, and the trial court's instruction invaded the exclusive province of the jury. State v. Jones, — N.H. —, — A.3d —, 2012 N.H. LEXIS 104 (July 3, 2012).

Cited:

Cited in State v. Black, 116 N.H. 836, 368 A.2d 1177, 1976 N.H. LEXIS 481 (1976); State v. Donovan, 120 N.H. 603, 419 A.2d 1102,

1980 N.H. LEXIS 350 (1980); State v. Miner, 122 N.H. 86, 441 A.2d 1150, 1982 N.H. LEXIS 291 (1982); State v. Whitney, 125 N.H. 636, 484 A.2d 1158, 1984 N.H. LEXIS 393 (1984); State v. Bemis, 127 N.H. 490, 503 A.2d 789, 1985 N.H. LEXIS 471 (1985); State v. Roberts, 131 N.H. 512, 556 A.2d 302, 1989 N.H. LEXIS 20 (1989); State v. Sammataro, 135 N.H. 579, 607 A.2d 135, 1992 N.H. LEXIS 85 (1992); State v. Mason, 150 N.H. 53, 834 A.2d 339, 2003 N.H. LEXIS 138 (2003).

641:6. Falsifying Physical Evidence.

A person commits a class B felony if, believing that an official proceeding, as defined in RSA 641:1, II, or investigation is pending or about to be instituted, he:

I. Alters, destroys, conceals or removes any thing with a purpose to impair its verity or availability in such proceeding or investigation; or

II. Makes, presents or uses any thing which he knows to be false with a purpose to deceive a public servant who is or may be engaged in such proceeding or investigation.

Source.
1971, 518:1, eff. Nov. 1, 1973.

Cross References.
Classification of crimes, see RSA 625:9.
Sentences, see RSA 651.

NOTES TO DECISIONS

1. Construction
2. Sufficiency of evidence
3. Elements
4. Relevance of altered evidence

1. Construction

While under standard rules of statutory construction, none of the terms "alters," "destroys," "conceals," or "removes" used in RSA 641:6 may be redundant or superfluous, the terms need not be mutually exclusive; it is possible to conceal something without removing it and to remove something, with the intent to impair its availability, without concealing it. Thus the terms "conceals" and "removes" in RSA 641:6 have independent significance. State v. Daoud, 158 N.H. 334, 965 A.2d 1136, 2009 N.H. LEXIS 19 (2009).

Single act may theoretically constitute one or more of the variants of RSA 641:6 and, thus, the State may simultaneously prosecute multiple charges which constitute the same offense based on a single act or transaction provided it seeks a single conviction and each charge alleges a distinct, alternative method of committing the offense. State v. Daoud, 158 N.H. 334, 965 A.2d 1136, 2009 N.H. LEXIS 19 (2009).

2. Sufficiency of evidence

When defendant was accused of falsely claiming that her husband sent her text messages in violation of a protective order, the evidence was sufficient to support her convictions of falsifying physical evidence under RSA 641:6, II and of false report under RSA 641:4, I. An officer presented evidence that defendant had made false statements about meeting with him, which showed consciousness of guilt; there was evidence, including video recordings, that defendant used a phone to leave messages to herself; and there was evidence contradicting her claim that she was not in California when she placed a telephone call. State v. Ruggiero, 163 N.H. 129, 35 A.3d 616, 2011 N.H. LEXIS 190 (Dec. 28, 2011).

Defendant, who denied being the driver in an automobile accident, concealed his car key in his shoe and was indicted only on the "removes" variant of the falsifying evidence statute. Nevertheless, that defendant might have concealed the key in his shoe did not prevent his conduct from satisfying the elements of the "removes" variant of the offense, for which there was ample evidence at trial. State v. Daoud, 158 N.H. 334, 965 A.2d 1136, 2009 N.H. LEXIS 19

(2009).

Sufficient evidence supported a conviction of falsifying physical evidence under RSA 641:6. A rational juror could have found that defendant, who disappeared after an accident, altered the appearance of his feet to make them appear consistent with his statement of events, including his claim that he crossed a river and was exposed to the elements; there was expert testimony that he could have injured his feet intentionally by soaking them in cold water and that the injury was not frostbite. State v. Dodds, 159 N.H. 239, 982 A.2d 377, 2009 N.H. LEXIS 112 (2009).

Trial court erred in finding defendant juvenile delinquent for falsifying physical evidence because there was insufficient evidence to prove that defendant altered, destroyed, concealed, or removed the package of cigarettes when defendant threw the pack containing contraband onto the floor of the crowded high school corridor and fled from the police; defendant's actions constituted a simple abandonment of the cigarette pack because the pack was not hidden, buried or secreted from the officer's vision or attention. In re Juvenile 2003-187, 151 N.H. 14, 846 A.2d 1207, 2004 N.H. LEXIS 81 (2004).

Evidence was sufficient to establish that the defendant, as an accomplice, committed two counts of attempted murder, one count of attempted arson, and one count of attempted falsification of evidence, where a witness testified that, mere hours after the incident, the defendant admitted that he had accompanied his coperpetrator to the scene of the crime, that they planned to rob whomever they discovered there, by violent means if necessary, that the defendant and the coperpetrator hid behind a bush while the latter twice shot at a car, that after the victims abandoned the car they searched it for valuables and money, and that there was an attempt to destroy the car following the search for valuables. State v. Laudarowicz, 142 N.H. 1, 694 A.2d 980, 1997 N.H. LEXIS 47 (1997).

3. Elements

Language of RSA 641:6 does not make admissibility of the evidence at trial an element of the offense of falsifying physical evidence. State v. McGurk, 157 N.H. 765, 958 A.2d 1005, 2008 N.H. LEXIS 119 (2008).

Possession of a controlled substance required proof that defendant knowingly possessed a controlled drug, and falsifying physical evidence required the State to prove that defendant, believing that there was a proceeding pending, knowingly altered, destroyed, concealed or removed anything, and did so with a purpose to impair its availability; thus, although each offense arose out of the same act of ingesting marijuana, they were separate offenses and there was no violation of the Double Jeopardy Clauses of the United States and New Hampshire Constitutions. State v. McGurk, 157 N.H. 765, 958 A.2d 1005, 2008 N.H. LEXIS 119 (2008).

4. Relevance of altered evidence

When defendant was accused of violating RSA 641:6, I by altering the appearance of his feet to make them appear consistent with his statement of events, his uninjured feet would not have been irrelevant to an investigation. Because defendant, who disappeared for 27 hours after an accident, claimed that he did not recall much of what happened after the accident, any injury or absence thereof would have been relevant to officials trying to reconstruct what had occurred. State v. Dodds, 159 N.H. 239, 982 A.2d 377, 2009 N.H. LEXIS 112 (2009).

Cited:

Cited in State v. St. Laurent, 122 N.H. 540, 446 A.2d 1185, 1982 N.H. LEXIS 387 (1982); State v. Beland, 138 N.H. 735, 645 A.2d 79, 1994 N.H. LEXIS 96 (1994); State v. Duguay, 142 N.H. 221, 698 A.2d 5, 1997 N.H. LEXIS 79 (1997).

641:7. Tampering With Public Records or Information.

A person is guilty of a misdemeanor if he:

I. Knowingly makes a false entry in or false alteration of any thing belonging to, received, or kept by the government for information or record, or required by law to be kept for information of the government; or

II. Presents or uses any thing knowing it to be false, and with a purpose that it be taken as a genuine part of information or records referred to in paragraph I; or

III. Purposely and unlawfully destroys, conceals, removes or otherwise impairs the verity or availability of any such thing.

Source.
  1971, 518:1, eff. Nov. 1, 1973.

Cross References.
  Classification of crimes, see RSA 625:9.
  Sentences, see RSA 651.

641:8. False Filing With the Director of Charitable Trusts.

A person shall be guilty of a class B felony if he knowingly makes a false entry in or false alteration of any registration statement, annual report or other information required to be filed with the director of charitable trusts.

Source.
  1992, 239:3, eff. July 1, 1992.

Cross References.
  Classification of crimes, see RSA 625:9.
  Sentences, see RSA 651.

CHAPTER 642

OBSTRUCTING GOVERNMENTAL OPERATIONS

SECTION
642:1.   Obstructing Government Administration.
642:2.   Resisting Arrest or Detention.
642:3.   Hindering Apprehension or Prosecution.
642:3-a. Taking a Firearm From a Law Enforcement Officer.
642:4.   Aiding Criminal Activity.
642:5.   Compounding.
642:6.   Escape.
642:7.   Implements for Escape and Other Contraband.
642:8.   Bail Jumping.
642:9.   Assaults by Prisoners.
642:10.   Obstructing Report of Crime or Injury.

642:1. Obstructing Government Administration.

I. A person is guilty of a misdemeanor if that person uses intimidation, actual or threatened force or violence, simulated legal process, or engages in any other unlawful conduct with a purpose to hinder or interfere with a public servant, as defined in RSA 640:2, II, performing or purporting to perform an official function or to retaliate for the performance or purported performance of such a function.

II. Flight by a person charged with an offense, refusal by anyone to submit to arrest, or any such interference in connection with a labor dispute with the government shall be prosecuted under the statutes governing such matters and not under this section.

III. In this section, "simulated legal process" means a document or order which purports to have been issued by a court or filed or recorded for the purpose of exercising jurisdiction or representing a claim against a person or property, or for the purpose of directing a person to appear before a court or tribunal, or to perform or refrain from performing a specified act, but which the actor knows was not lawfully issued or rendered in accordance with the applicable statutes, rules, regulations, or ordinances of the federal, state, or local government, or a political subdivision thereof. "Simulated legal process" includes any document that purports to be a summons, lien, indictment, complaint, warrant, injunction, writ, notice, pleading, subpoena, or order.

IV. For any offense committed under paragraph I that involved the use of simulated legal process, the court may impose the following remedies, in addition to any criminal penalties authorized under RSA 651:

(a) Such appropriate injunctive relief as the court may deem necessary to prevent continued violations of this section.

(b) Restitution to the public official for any out-of-pocket expenses incurred as a result of the simulated legal process, including legal fees.

Source.
1971, 518:1, eff. Nov. 1, 1973. 2003, 168:1, eff. Jan. 1, 2004.

Amendments
—**2003.** Rewritten to the extent that a detailed comparison would be impractical.

Cross References.
Classification of crimes, see RSA 625:9.
Sentences, see RSA 651.

NOTES TO DECISIONS

1. Acts constituting offense
2. No political protest exception
3. Evidence sufficient for conviction

1. Acts constituting offense
State properly charged defendant with acts constituting a violation of this section where the offense the defendant was about to commit was resisting arrest. State v. Diamond, 146 N.H. 691, 785 A.2d 887, 2001 N.H. LEXIS 144 (2001).

Where evidence showed that defendant did not just refuse to move after being ordered to do so, but actually stepped in front of the arresting officer, notwithstanding its alleged political motivation, his conduct fell within the scope of the offense covered by this section. State v. Diamond, 146 N.H. 691, 785 A.2d 887, 2001 N.H. LEXIS 144 (2001).

2. No political protest exception
Because this section is not ambiguous, while defendant invoked legislative history, he offered no justification for looking beyond the plain language of the statute, which contains no express exception for political protest. State v. Diamond, 146 N.H. 691, 785 A.2d 887, 2001 N.H. LEXIS 144 (2001).

3. Evidence sufficient for conviction
Sufficient evidence existed to convict defendants of obstructing government administration where defendants prevented a wildlife officer from leaving a field while the officer was performing his official function of checking fields for deer and illegal hunters. State v. Briggs, 147 N.H. 431, 790 A.2d 792, 2002 N.H. LEXIS 8 (2002).

Cited:
Cited in State v. Blodgett, 129 N.H. 163, 523 A.2d 119, 1987 N.H. LEXIS 158 (1987).

642:2. Resisting Arrest or Detention.

A person is guilty of a misdemeanor when the person knowingly or purposely physically interferes with a person recognized to be a law enforcement official, including a probation or parole officer, seeking to effect an arrest or detention of the person or another regardless of whether there is a legal basis for the arrest. A person is guilty of a class B felony if the act of resisting arrest or detention causes serious bodily injury, as defined in RSA 625:11, VI, to another person. Verbal protestations alone shall not constitute resisting arrest or detention.

Source.
1971, 518:1. 1983, 347:2. 1992, 85:1. 1995, 237:3, eff. Jan. 1, 1996. 2007, 191:1, eff. January 1, 2008.

Amendments
—**2007.** Added the second sentence.

—**1995.** Substituted "the person" for "he" following "misdemeanor when", inserted "including a probation or parole officer" following "law enforcement official" and substituted "the person" for "himself" following "detention of" in the first sentence.

—**1992.** Inserted "physically" preceding "interferes" in the first sentence and added the second sentence.

—**1983.** Inserted "knowingly or" preceding "purposely".

Cross References.
Classification of crimes, see RSA 625:9.
Duty to submit to arrest, see RSA 594:5.
Resisting arrest by forest fire control personnel, see RSA 227-L:14.
Sentences, see RSA 651.

NOTES TO DECISIONS

1. Construction
2. Evidence
3. Classification.
4. Sentence

1. Construction
Supreme Court of New Hampshire construes the phrase "seeking to effect an arrest or detention" in RSA 642:2 as including the entire course of events during which law enforcement officers seek to secure and maintain physical control of an individual, attendant to accomplishing the intended law enforcement duty. Whether a defendant's resistive conduct occurred while law enforcement was seeking to effect an arrest or detention must be assessed on a case-by-case basis, objectively viewing the continuum of events as a whole. N.H. v. Lindsey, 158 N.H. 703, 973 A.2d 314, 2009 N.H. LEXIS 67 (2009).

Construing the resisting arrest statute so that all resistance that occurs after the moment in which an individual comes under the control of law enforcement officers is no longer culpable neither accords with the fair import of the statute nor promotes justice. The New Hampshire Supreme Court agrees with those jurisdictions that hold that effecting an arrest or detention is not necessarily an instantaneous event and should not be assessed by parsing out discrete, snapshot moments in time. N.H. v. Lindsey, 158 N.H. 703, 973 A.2d 314, 2009 N.H. LEXIS 67 (2009).

New Hampshire Supreme Court rejects a reliance upon the meaning of "seizure" within the constitutional context to aid in the interpretation of key terms in the resisting arrest statute. While concepts involving the restraint upon a person's liberty, such as arrest, detention and seizure, may overlap in various legal contexts, the legislature's intended meaning of the phrase "seeking to effect an arrest or detention" within the context of the resisting arrest statute controls. N.H. v. Lindsey, 158 N.H. 703, 973 A.2d 314, 2009 N.H. LEXIS 67 (2009).

Because the word "detain" did not have to be applied in a criminal context to the exclusion of other applications, defendant could be convicted for resisting arrest or detention under RSA 642:2 where defendant knowingly or purposely physically interfered with being taken into protective custody under RSA 172-B:3. State v. Kelley, 153 N.H. 481, 899 A.2d 236, 2006 N.H. LEXIS 62 (2006).

At trial for simple assault and resisting arrest, regardless of whether chief of police properly or improperly ordered arresting officer to tow defendant's vehicle, defendant enjoyed no privilege to use self-help to prevent removal of his property or to effect its return nor was he entitled to resist arrest; any such privileges that may have existed at common law had been statutorily superseded. State v. Haas, 134 N.H. 480, 596 A.2d 127, 1991 N.H. LEXIS 88 (1991).

Because this section is clear on its face and unambiguous, resort to legislative history is not necessary for its construction. State v. Reid, 134 N.H. 418, 594 A.2d 160, 1991 N.H. LEXIS 81 (1991).

Under this section the requisite mental state, "knowingly," applies to each material element of the offense, and therefore in order to convict, a finding that defendant subjectively knew that the individual effecting the arrest was a law enforcement official is required. State v. Reid, 134 N.H. 418, 594 A.2d 160, 1991 N.H. LEXIS 81 (1991).

This section does not create two different crimes, one for resisting arrest and the other for resisting detention, but rather defines the offense so as to avoid defenses based on a technical distinction between arrest and other forms of seizures of the person falling short of a full-blown arrest. State v. Fleury, 116 N.H. 577, 364 A.2d 625, 1976 N.H. LEXIS 416 (1976).

2. Evidence

Once officers handcuffed and forced defendant to lie on the floor, his subsequent conduct of yelling, attempting to get off the floor where he had been instructed to stay, and kicking, pushing, and "bull-rushing" at an officer was culpable under the resisting arrest statute. Thus, a reasonable juror could have concluded that the brief time period in which defendant was face down on the floor while handcuffed did not serve to conclude the process of seeking to effect his detention, and the evidence was sufficient to support his conviction. N.H. v. Lindsey, 158 N.H. 703, 973 A.2d 314, 2009 N.H. LEXIS 67 (2009).

Jury could rationally conclude from evidence at trial that defendant resisted arrest in a manner consistent with identifying facts set forth in information, and variance between information and proof at trial was minimal and was insufficient to upset jury's verdict. State v. Smith, 144 N.H. 1, 736 A.2d 1236, 1999 N.H. LEXIS 66 (1999).

3. Classification.

Complaints for simple assault under RSA 631:2-a and for resisting arrest under RSA 642:2 did not allege a crime that involved as an element an act of violence or a threat of violence for purposes of class A misdemeanor classification under RSA 625:9, IV(c)(1). The variant of simple assault alleged here involved causing unprivileged physical contact, not bodily injury, and the resisting arrest statute could be violated by conduct that fell short of causing or attempting to cause bodily injury. State v. Blunt, 164 N.H. 679, 62 A.3d 1285, 2013 N.H. LEXIS 27 (2013).

4. Sentence

Because RSA 651:6, I(g) applies only to "crimes defined in RSA 631," it is not applicable to a conviction on a resisting arrest charge, since that offense is found in RSA ch. 642. State v. Blunt, 164 N.H. 679, 62 A.3d 1285, 2013 N.H. LEXIS 27 (2013).

Cited:

Cited in State v. Hamilton, 123 N.H. 686, 465 A.2d 495, 1983 N.H. LEXIS 334 (1983); State v. Baldwin, 124 N.H. 770, 475 A.2d 522, 1984 N.H. LEXIS 341 (1984); State v. Gagne, 129 N.H. 93, 523 A.2d 76, 1986 N.H. LEXIS 380 (1986); State v. Blodgett, 129 N.H. 163, 523 A.2d 119, 1987 N.H. LEXIS 158 (1987); State v. Letendre, 133 N.H. 555, 579 A.2d 1223, 1990 N.H. LEXIS 103 (1990); State v. Murray, 135 N.H. 369, 605 A.2d 676, 1992 N.H. LEXIS 41 (1992); State v. Cavanaugh, 138 N.H. 193, 635 A.2d 1382, 1993 N.H. LEXIS 183 (1993); In re Justin D., 144 N.H. 450, 743 A.2d 829, 1999 N.H. LEXIS 132 (1999); State v. Diamond, 146 N.H. 691, 785 A.2d 887, 2001 N.H. LEXIS 144 (2001); Collins v. City of Manchester, 208 F. Supp. 2d 123, 2002 U.S. Dist. LEXIS 12585 (D.N.H. 2002).

642:3. Hindering Apprehension or Prosecution.

I. A person is guilty of an offense if, with a purpose to hinder, prevent or delay the discovery, apprehension, prosecution, conviction or punishment of another for the commission of a crime, he:

(a) Harbors or conceals the other; or

(b) Provides such person a weapon, transportation, disguise or other means for avoiding discovery or apprehension; or

(c) Warns such person of impending discovery or apprehension; or

(d) Conceals, destroys or alters any physical evidence that might aid in the discovery, apprehension or conviction of such person; or

(e) Obstructs by force, intimidation or deception anyone from performing an act which might aid in the discovery, apprehension, prosecution or conviction of such person; or

(f) Having knowledge that an investigative or law enforcement officer has been authorized or has applied for authorization under RSA 570-A to intercept a telecommunication or oral communication, or under RSA 570-B to install and use a pen register or trap and trace device, gives notice of the possible interception or installation and use to any person.

II. The offense is a misdemeanor unless the actor knows that the charge made or liable to be made against the other is murder or a class A felony, in which case it is a class B felony.

Source.

1971, 518:1. 1988, 25:6. 1995, 280:10, I, eff. Aug. 20, 1995.

Amendments

—1995. Paragraph I: Substituted "telecommunication" for "wire" following "intercept a" in subpar. (f).

—1988. Paragraph I: Added "or" following "such person" at the end of subpar. (e) and added subpar. (f).

Cross References.

Classification of crimes, see RSA 625:9.
Sentences, see RSA 651.

NOTES TO DECISIONS

1. Construction
2. Construction with other laws
3. Scope
4. Intent
5. Harboring
6. Indictments

1. Construction

Convicting a defendant of harboring or concealing another under RSA 642:3, I(a) requires proof of a physical act of assistance beyond merely lying in response to police inquiries about the other's whereabouts. Accordingly, when defendant lied to police who were attempting to serve an arrest warrant on her daughter about her daughter's whereabouts, then went to the police station with her daughter less than an hour later for the daughter to turn herself in, the evidence was insufficient to support her conviction. State v. Durgin, 158 N.H. 51, 959 A.2d 196, 2008 N.H. LEXIS 134 (2008).

There is no legislative intent to exclude wives or other relatives from the scope of this section. State v. Maloney, 126 N.H. 235, 490 A.2d 772, 1985 N.H. LEXIS 287 (1985).

2. Construction with other laws

A driver's exercise of the right to refuse a chemical test under former RSA 265:84 (see now RSA 265-A:4), governing implied consent, cannot result in charges being brought for destroying evidence within the meaning of this section. State v. Schneider, 124 N.H. 242, 470 A.2d 887, 1983 N.H. LEXIS 418 (1983).

3. Scope

This section covers not only aid to felons, but also to misdemeanants. State v. Laponsee, 115 N.H. 56, 333 A.2d 447, 1975 N.H. LEXIS 222 (1975).

4. Intent

Mental state required to convict defendant of hindering apprehension under RSA 642:3, I(a), was an intent to hinder apprehension or prosecution; defendant needed only act with an intent to harbor or conceal a person from apprehension or discovery, which was found from the fact that the police informed defendant that they were investigating a crime that occurred in the area and asked defendant whether he knew the suspect, whether defendant knew who owned a car parked out front, and whether anyone else was in defendant's apartment. State v. Brown, 155 N.H. 164, 930 A.2d 410, 2007 N.H. LEXIS 43 (2007), rehearing denied, 2007 N.H. LEXIS 158 (N.H. Aug. 20, 2007).

Prosecution need not show hindering apprehension of another for a crime to have been defendant's sole intent in order to convict him of that offense if jury could reasonably find from the evidence presented that an obstructive purpose was present. State v. Kelley, 120 N.H. 14, 413 A.2d 300, 1980 N.H. LEXIS 220 (1980).

5. Harboring

Where defendant who was convicted of hindering apprehension of a criminal had been informed that the police possessed a warrant for her husband's arrest and then took steps to inform her husband of this and to secrete him from the police, defendant's acts constituted harboring of a criminal. State v. Maloney, 126 N.H. 235, 490 A.2d 772, 1985 N.H. LEXIS 287 (1985).

6. Indictments

Indictment sufficiently informed defendant that she was being charged with a felony offense because it alleged that underlying crime, in relation to which defendant hindered authorities, was armed robbery. Subdivision II of this section does not require that defendant know the legal classification of the underlying armed robbery. State v. Williams, 143 N.H. 559, 729 A.2d 416, 1999 N.H. LEXIS 44 (1999).

Cited:

Cited in State v. Wilkinson, 136 N.H. 170, 612 A.2d 926, 1992 N.H. LEXIS 141 (1992).

642:3-a. Taking a Firearm From a Law Enforcement Officer.

I. Whoever knowingly takes a firearm:

(a) From the person of a law enforcement officer, while such officer is engaged in the performance of official duties; and

(b) Against that officer's will; or attempts to do so, shall be punished as provided in paragraph II.

II. The punishment for an offense under this section is:

(a) In the case of an offense other than an attempt, or an offense that is an attempt during which the firearm is discharged (other than intentionally by the officer), a class A felony; and

(b) In the case of any other offense that is an attempt, a class B felony.

III. It shall be an affirmative defense to prosecution under this section if an individual acts to disarm an officer engaging in felonious conduct or conduct so reckless as to endanger the lives of others. However, a conviction resulting from that conduct need not be obtained to present this defense.

IV. A term of imprisonment imposed under this section shall not run concurrently with any other term of imprisonment imposed with respect to the same criminal episode.

V. In this section:

(a) "Firearm" has the meaning given that term in section 921 of Title 18 of the United States Code.

(b) "Law enforcement officer" means law enforcement officer as defined in RSA 630:1, II.

Source.

1999, 166:1, eff. Jan. 1, 2000.

Cross References.

Classification of crimes, see RSA 625:9.

Sentences, see RSA 651.

642:4. Aiding Criminal Activity.

A person is guilty of a misdemeanor if he purposely aids another who has committed a crime in profiting or benefiting from the criminal activity, as by safeguarding the proceeds thereof or converting the proceeds into negotiable funds.

Source.

1971, 518:1, eff. Nov. 1, 1973.

Cross References.

Classification of crimes, see RSA 625:9.

Sentences, see RSA 651.

642:5. Compounding.

A person is guilty of a misdemeanor if he:

I. Solicits, accepts, or agrees to accept any benefit as consideration for his refraining from initiating or aiding in a criminal prosecution; or

II. Confers, offers, or agrees to confer any benefit upon another as consideration for such person refraining from initiating or aiding in a criminal prosecution.

III. It is an affirmative defense that the value of the benefit did not exceed an amount which the actor believed to be due as restitution or indemnification for the loss caused, or to be caused by the offense.

Source.

1971, 518:1, eff. Nov. 1, 1973.

Cross References.

Classification of crimes, see RSA 625:9.

Sentences, see RSA 651.

642:6. Escape.

I. A person is guilty of an offense if he escapes from official custody.

II. "Official custody" means arrest, custody in a penal institution, an institution for confinement of juvenile offenders or other confinement pursuant to an order of a court.

III. The offense is a class A felony if the actor employs force against any person or threatens any person with a deadly weapon to effect the escape, except that if the deadly weapon is a firearm, he shall be sentenced in accordance with RSA 651:2, II-g. Otherwise it is a class B felony.

IV. If a person is convicted of the offense of escape under this section, the term of imprisonment authorized by RSA 651:2, II or RSA 651:6 shall be added to the portion of the term which remained unserved at the time of the commission of the offense.

Source.

1971, 518:1. 1975, 458:3, 4. 1990, 95:7, eff. June 12, 1990.

Amendments

—1990. Paragraph III: Added "except that if the deadly weapon is a firearm, he shall be sentenced in accordance with RSA 651:2, II-g" following "escape" in the first sentence.

—1975. Paragraph III: Rewritten to the extent that a detailed comparison would be impracticable.

Paragraph IV: Added.

Cross References.

Classification of crimes, see RSA 625:9.

Failure to report by person released for employment or under suspended sentence deemed escape, see RSA 651:24.

Loss of good conduct credits for escape, see RSA 651-A:22.

Sentences, see RSA 651.

Use of physical force to prevent escape, see RSA 627:5.

NOTES TO DECISIONS

1. Elements
2. Types of confinement
3. Double jeopardy
4. Mens rea
5. Evidence
6. Admissions

1. Elements

Defendant committed a crime of violence within the meaning of U.S. Sentencing Guidelines Manual § 4B1.2(a)(2) for career offender enhancement purposes under U.S. Sentencing Guidelines Manual § 4B1.1 when his predicate offense consisted of escaping from official custody by failing to return to a halfway house after a break, a Class B felony escape under RSA 642:6, even though defendant escaped by stealth and injured no one in the process. United States v. Winn, 364 F.3d 7, 2004 U.S. App. LEXIS 6950 (1st Cir. N.H. 2004).

Under this section the state need only prove that the defendant was in custody pursuant to a valid court order; the name of the county from which the order emanated is not an element of the offense, but is surplusage. State v. Woodman, 125 N.H. 381, 480 A.2d 169, 1984 N.H. LEXIS 250 (1984).

2. Types of confinement

RSA 642:6 distinguishes between Class A and Class B felony escapes based on the use of force or of a deadly weapon, but does not distinguish among types of confinement or institutions. United States v. Winn, 364 F.3d 7, 2004 U.S. App. LEXIS 6950 (1st Cir. N.H. 2004).

3. Double jeopardy

In indictment for crime of escape from state prison where respondent alleged previous administrative discipline as former jeopardy, it was proper for trial court to refuse to receive evidence of nature and extent of such discipline in presence of jury and to consider it only on question of sentence for crime of escape. State v. Gonyer, 102 N.H. 527, 162 A.2d 172, 1960 N.H. LEXIS 72 (1960). (Decided under prior law.)

Conviction for crime of escape from state prison under this section did not constitute double jeopardy in violation of NH Const., Part 1, Art. 16, by mere fact that respondent had previously been subjected to limited administrative discipline as authorized by RSA 622:14. State v. Gonyer, 102 N.H. 527, 162 A.2d 172, 1960 N.H. LEXIS 72 (1960). (Decided under prior law.)

4. Mens rea

Mental element of the crime of escape is satisfied by proof that the defendant acted knowingly when he departed from official custody without authority. State v. Stone, 127 N.H. 747, 506 A.2d 345, 1986 N.H. LEXIS 214 (1986).

In prosecution for escape the state need not prove a specific intent by the defendant to remain free beyond some limited period. State v. Stone, 127 N.H. 747, 506 A.2d 345, 1986 N.H. LEXIS 214 (1986).

"Knowledge" is the minimum level of mental culpability that the state must prove to sustain a prosecution under this section; consequently, proof that a defendant "negligently" or "recklessly" escaped from official custody is legally insufficient to sustain a conviction of violating this section. State v. Aldrich, 124 N.H. 43, 466 A.2d 938, 1983 N.H. LEXIS 356 (1983).

A defendant may be properly convicted of escape based upon evidence that he "knowingly" departed from official custody without authority; under this section, the state does not have to prove that the defendant "purposely" escaped from official custody. State v. Aldrich, 124 N.H. 43, 466 A.2d 938, 1983 N.H. LEXIS 356 (1983).

Requiring the state to prove only "knowledge" rather than "purpose" as the mens rea requirement under this section not only is consistent with the prevailing authority regarding the culpable mental state for the offense of escape, but also comports with the fair import of this section and promotes justice. State v. Aldrich, 124 N.H. 43, 466 A.2d 938, 1983 N.H. LEXIS 356 (1983).

5. Evidence

In prosecution for escape from official custody, where the defendant's indictment alleged that he did not report for work when granted temporary release for that purpose and did not return to the half-way house to which his commitment had been transferred at the appointed time, and where the only evidence of his failure to report to work was certain inadmissible hearsay, the allegation that the defendant did not report for work was not an essential element of the escape charge, in light of the allegation that the defendant did not return to the half-way house at the appointed time, and proof that the defendant knowingly failed to report to the half-way house was sufficient to sustain a conviction under this section. State v. Aldrich, 124 N.H. 43, 466 A.2d 938, 1983 N.H. LEXIS 356 (1983).

In prosecution for escape from official custody, the admission into evidence of a logbook kept at a half-way house indicating the whereabouts of inmates who left the facility on work release, although improper under the hearsay rule, was harmless error, since the allegation that the defendant did not report for work was not an essential element of the escape charge and since there was sufficient evidence to support a finding that the defendant failed to return to the half-way house. State v. Aldrich, 124 N.H. 43, 466 A.2d 938, 1983 N.H. LEXIS 356 (1983).

In prosecution for escape from official custody, where the trial judge instructed the jury that it would have to find that the state proved both that the defendant did not report for work and that he did not return to the half-way house at the appointed time, and the only evidence of defendant's failure to report to work was certain inadmissible hearsay, the proof that the defendant did not return to the half-way house was a sufficient independent basis to support the guilty verdict since the allegation in the indictment that he failed to report for work was not an essential element of the escape offense. State v. Aldrich, 124 N.H. 43, 466 A.2d 938, 1983 N.H. LEXIS 356 (1983).

6. Admissions

An escaped convict is not entitled to a trial after recapture, except upon the issue of his identity, and his refusal to litigate this question when opportunity is afforded him is an admission that he is the person the state alleges him to be. In re Moebus, 73 N.H. 350, 62 A. 170, 1905 N.H. LEXIS 53 (1905) (Decided under prior law.); Petition of Moebus, 74 N.H. 213, 66 A. 641, 1907 N.H. LEXIS 25 (1907). (Decided under prior law.)

Cited:
Cited in Bell v. Superior Court Sentence Review Div., 117 N.H. 474, 374 A.2d 659, 1977 N.H. LEXIS 358 (1977); Hudson v. Miller, 119 N.H. 141, 399 A.2d 612, 1979 N.H. LEXIS 257 (1979); State v. Sampson, 125 N.H. 544, 484 A.2d 1104, 1984 N.H. LEXIS 397 (1984); State v. Batchelder, 126 N.H. 700, 496 A.2d 346, 1985 N.H. LEXIS 351 (1985); State v. Perra, 127 N.H. 533, 503 A.2d 814, 1985 N.H. LEXIS 456 (1985); Gangi v. Cunningham, 127 N.H. 780, 508 A.2d 1050, 1986 N.H. LEXIS 235 (1986); State v. Joncas, 131 N.H. 476, 554 A.2d 841, 1989 N.H. LEXIS 11 (1989); State v. Polito, 132 N.H. 410, 566 A.2d 183, 1989 N.H. LEXIS 107 (1989); N.H. v. Burgess, 156 N.H. 746, 943 A.2d 727, 2008 N.H. LEXIS 18 (2008).

642:7. Implements for Escape and Other Contraband.

A person is guilty of a class B felony if:

I. He knowingly provides a person in official custody, as defined in RSA 642:6, II, with anything which may facilitate such person's escape or the possession of which by such person is contrary to law or regulation, or in any other manner facilitates such person's escape; or

II. Being a person in official custody, as defined in RSA 642:6, II, he knowingly procures, makes or possesses anything which may facilitate escape.

Source.
1971, 518:1, eff. Nov. 1, 1973.

Cross References.
Classification of crimes, see RSA 625:9.
Sentences, see RSA 651.

NOTES TO DECISIONS

Constitutionality

As applied to defendant, a person in official custody who possessed a mop handle which had been fashioned into a double-ended spear or fighting stick by the addition of metal prongs at both ends, this section was not unconstitutionally vague, since it would inform any reasonable person that possession of a mop handle, as so modified, would be prohibited. State v. Foster, 120 N.H. 654, 421 A.2d 127, 1980 N.H. LEXIS 371 (1980).

This section was not unconstitutional for vagueness and overbreadth as applied to prison inmates, one of whom allegedly possessed 2 jackknife blades, one of whom allegedly possessed a knife-like instrument, one of whom was allegedly found with materials constituting elements of an explosive device and one of whom was alleged to have made a dummy to facilitate his escape, as any reasonable person seeking compliance with provisions of this section would understand such items to be proscribed. State v. Hewitt, 116 N.H. 711, 366 A.2d 487, 1976 N.H. LEXIS 455 (1976), aff'd, Bisson v. New Hampshire, 429 U.S. 1081, 97 S. Ct. 1088, 51 L. Ed. 2d 528, 1977 U.S. LEXIS 596 (1977).

Cited:
Cited in N.H. v. Burgess, 156 N.H. 746, 943 A.2d 727, 2008 N.H. LEXIS 18 (2008).

642:8. Bail Jumping.

I. A person is guilty of an offense if, after having been released with or without bail, he:

(a) knowingly fails to appear before a court as required by the conditions of his release; or

(b) knowingly fails to surrender for service of sentence pursuant to a court order.

II. It is an affirmative defense to a prosecution under this section that uncontrollable circumstances prevented the person from appearing or surrendering and that the person did not contribute to the creation of such circumstances in reckless disregard of the requirement that he appear or surrender, and that he appeared or surrendered as soon as such circumstances ceased to exist.

III. If the person was released:

(a) In connection with a charge of, or while awaiting sentence, surrender for service of sentence, or appeal after conviction for:

(1) An offense punishable by death, life imprisonment, or imprisonment of a maximum term of 15 years or more, he shall be fined not more than $10,000 or imprisoned for not more than 15 years, or both;

(2) An offense punishable by imprisonment for a term of more than one year, but less than 15 years, he shall be fined not more than $5,000 or imprisoned for not more than 7 years, or both;

(3) A Class A or Class B misdemeanor, he shall be fined not more than $2,000 or imprisoned for not more than one year, or both;

(4) A violation, he shall be fined not more than $1,500; or

(b) For appearance as a material witness, he shall be fined not more than $1,000 or imprisoned for not more than one year, or both.

IV. A term of imprisonment imposed pursuant to this section shall be consecutive to the sentence of imprisonment for any other offense.

Source.
1971, 518:1. 1986, 37:1. 1988, 110:10. 1990, 50:1. 1992, 269:7, eff. July 1, 1992.

Amendments
—1992. Paragraph III(a)(3): Inserted "class A or class B" preceding "misdemeanor".

—1990. Paragraph III(a): Substituted "term of more than one year" for "maximum term of 7 years or more" following "imprisonment for a" in subpar. (2), deleted "or" at the end of subpar. (3) and added subpar. (4).

—1988. Paragraph III: Rewritten to the extent that a detailed comparison would be impracticable.
Paragraph IV: Added.

—1986. Rewritten to the extent that a detailed comparison would be impracticable.

Applicability of 1992 amendment.

1992, 269:21, eff. July 1, 1992, provided that the amendment to this section by 1992, 269:7, shall apply to all offenses committed on or after July 1, 1992.

Cross References.

Bail and recognizances generally, see RSA 597.

Classification of crimes, see RSA 625:9.

Sentences, see RSA 651.

NOTES TO DECISIONS

Cited:

Cited in State v. Moccia, 120 N.H. 298, 414 A.2d 1275, 1980 N.H. LEXIS 283 (1980); Duquette v. Warden, N.H. State Prison, 154 N.H. 737, 919 A.2d 767, 2007 N.H. LEXIS 10 (2007).

642:9. Assaults by Prisoners.

I. Any person held in official custody who commits an assault under RSA 631 is guilty of an offense under this section.

II. An inmate is guilty of aggravated assault on a corrections staff member when, with intent to harass, threaten, or alarm a person whom the inmate knows or reasonably should know to be an employee of such facility, or an employee of the department of corrections, or an employee of any law enforcement agency, the inmate causes or attempts to cause such employee to come in contact with blood, seminal fluid, urine, or feces by throwing or expelling such fluid or material.

II-a. An inmate is guilty of aggravated harassment of an employee when, with intent to harass, annoy, threaten, or alarm a person who the inmate knows or reasonably should know is an employee of such facility, or the department of corrections, or any law enforcement agency, the inmate causes or attempts to cause such employee to come into contact with blood, seminal fluid, urine, feces, emesis, or saliva by throwing or expelling such substance either directly or indirectly at the employee, thus contaminating the employee's work environment.

III. For the purposes of this section:

(a) "Official custody" means custody in a penal institution or other confinement by an order of a court.

(b) "Inmate" means a person committed by law to the custody of the commissioner of the department of corrections, a person in pretrial confinement, any person incarcerated in a local detention facility operated by a county department of corrections, or a person in detention at a police department.

(c) "Facility" means a correctional facility or local correctional facility hospital, operated by the state or a county department of corrections, or a police department.

IV. The offense is a class B felony if it is an aggravated assault or harassment as defined in paragraph II or II-a, or if the offense committed is simple assault as defined under RSA 631:2-a unless committed in a fight entered into by mutual consent, in which case it is a misdemeanor. The offense is a

class A felony if the offense committed is first degree or second degree assault as defined under RSA 631:1 or RSA 631:2.

V. If a person is convicted of the offense of assault under this section, the term of imprisonment authorized by RSA 651:2, II or RSA 651:6 shall be consecutive to and not concurrent with any other sentence to be served.

Source.

1985, 80:1, eff. Jan. 1, 1986. 2000, 113:1, eff. Jan. 1, 2001. 2010, 174:1, 2, eff. January 1, 2011.

Amendments

—2010. The 2010 amendment added II-a; rewrote III(b), which formerly read: "'Inmate' means an offender, as defined in RSA 21-H:2, VII, a person in pretrial confinement, or any person incarcerated in a local detention facility"; in III(c), added "state or a county" and "or a police department"; and in the first sentence of IV, added "or harassment" and substituted "paragraph II or II-a" for "paragraph II."

—2000. Added new par. II, redesignated former pars. II–IV as present pars. III–V, and rewrote present par. III, and inserted "it is an aggravated assault as defined in paragraph II, or if" in the first sentence of present par. IV.

Cross References.

Classification of crimes, see RSA 625:9.

Sentences, see RSA 651.

NOTES TO DECISIONS

1. Indictment
2. Elements
3. Legislative history and/or intent
4. Jury instructions

1. Indictment

It was error to dismiss indictments under RSA 642:9, II. Defendant's alleged conduct of throwing or expelling feces or urine onto the floor, or underneath his cell door and onto the floor, causing a corrections employee to clean it up, fell within the scope of the statute, which did not require that the substances be thrown or expelled at an officer. State v. Spade, 161 N.H. 248, 13 A.3d 855, 2010 N.H. LEXIS 147 (2010).

Indictment was not duplicitous as charging the felony offense of assault by a prisoner and also charging misdemeanor offense of simple assault, since the indictment could only be read to charge the felony. State v. Wright, 126 N.H. 643, 496 A.2d 702, 1985 N.H. LEXIS 362 (1985).

Indictment charging felony offense of assault by a prisoner and using language that was consistent with misdemeanor offense of simple assault did not charge two different offenses and was not, therefore, duplicitous, since the common law assault necessary to prove felony offense of assault by a prisoner included purposely causing bodily injury, which is the definition of misdemeanor offense of simple assault under RSA 631:2-a. State v. Wright, 126 N.H. 643, 496 A.2d 702, 1985 N.H. LEXIS 362 (1985). (Decided under prior law.)

Where indictment charging assault by a prisoner alleged that bodily injury to victim had consisted of soreness and bruises to the groin, knee and neck, it was not necessary at trial to prove every detail of these injuries; so long as there was some proof of bodily injury as alleged, cumulative or superfluous details were properly disregarded as surplusage. State v. Wright, 126 N.H. 643, 496 A.2d 702, 1985 N.H. LEXIS 362 (1985). (Decided under prior law.)

2. Elements

According to the plain language of RSA 642:9, II, to be guilty of aggravated assault, the inmate must have thrown or expelled an enumerated bodily substance, causing or attempting to cause the employee to come in contact with such substance, with the intent to harass, threaten or alarm. Nothing in the statute's plain language requires the inmate to throw or expel such substance at an employee who is physically present. State v. Spade, 161 N.H. 248, 13 A.3d 855, 2010 N.H. LEXIS 147 (2010).

3. Legislative history and/or intent

Legislative history demonstrates that the primary purposes for the enactment of RSA 642:9 were threefold: (1) protecting corrections employees from exposure to disease through coming in contact with certain bodily fluids or materials; (2) promoting respect and dignity for corrections staff by protecting them from humiliation and degradation caused by inmates using bodily waste to harass them; and (3) ensuring that inmates who repeatedly misbehave toward corrections employees by throwing or expelling bodily substances, but who already have had their existing prison terms extended to the maximum, could be subject to criminal punishment as a deterrent. State v. Spade, 161 N.H. 248, 13 A.3d 855, 2010 N.H. LEXIS 147 (2010).

Language of RSA 642:9, II, as compared to that of the assault provisions under RSA ch. 631, evinces a legislative intent to proscribe a broader range of conduct than just throwing or expelling an enumerated bodily substance at an employee in order to harass, threaten, or alarm that person. State v. Spade, 161 N.H. 248, 13 A.3d 855, 2010 N.H. LEXIS 147 (2010).

4. Jury instructions

Even if defendant presented sufficient evidence to support a mutual combat instruction on the class B felony charge of assault by a prisoner, he had failed to establish that he was prejudiced by the trial court's failure to give the instruction. The instruction was relevant only to the class B felony charge, and defendant did not receive a sentence for that offense. State v. Matton, — N.H. —, 69 A.3d 90, 2013 N.H. LEXIS 54 (May 14, 2013).

Cited:

Cited in State v. Goodnow, 140 N.H. 38, 662 A.2d 950, 1995 N.H. LEXIS 93 (1995); State v. Tallard, 143 N.H. 228, 723 A.2d 574, 1998 N.H. LEXIS 95 (1998).

642:10. Obstructing Report of Crime or Injury.

I. A person shall be guilty of an offense under this section who disconnects, damages, disables, removes, or uses physical force or intimidation to block access to any telephone, radio, or other electronic communication device with a purpose to obstruct, prevent, or interfere with:

(a) The report of any criminal offense to any law enforcement agency; or

(b) The report of any bodily injury or property damage to any law enforcement agency; or

(c) A request for ambulance or emergency medical assistance to any governmental agency, or any hospital, doctor, or other medical service provider.

II. It shall be an affirmative defense to prosecution under this section that the actor reasonably believed his conduct to be necessary to prevent a criminal false alarm.

III. Obstructing report of a crime or injury is a misdemeanor.

Source.

1994, 304:1, eff. Jan. 1, 1995.

Cross References.

Classification of crimes, see RSA 625:9.

Sentences, see RSA 651.

CHAPTER 643

ABUSE OF OFFICE

SECTION

643:1.   Official Oppression.

643:2.   Misuse of Information.

Cross References.

Corrupt practices, see RSA 640.

False statements by public officials relative to public works or contracts, see RSA 96.

Personal interest of public official in business transactions with public, see RSA 95.

643:1. Official Oppression.

A public servant, as defined in RSA 640:2, II, is guilty of a misdemeanor if, with a purpose to benefit himself or another or to harm another, he knowingly commits an unauthorized act which purports to be an act of his office; or knowingly refrains from performing a duty imposed on him by law or clearly inherent in the nature of his office.

Source.

1971, 518:1, eff. Nov. 1, 1973.

Cross References.

Classification of crimes, see RSA 625:9.

Sentences, see RSA 651.

NOTES TO DECISIONS

1.   Neglect of official duty
2.   Indictment

1. Neglect of official duty

If the moderator of a school district meeting wilfully refused to make a vote certain by a poll of the voters when duly required, he was liable for neglect of his official duty under this section. State v. Waterhouse, 71 N.H. 488, 53 A. 304, 1902 N.H. LEXIS 66 (1902). (Decided under prior law.)

2. Indictment

An indictment against overseers of the poor for neglect of duty had to allege that the accused wilfully neglected their duty as such overseers, or contain other terms equivalent thereto, and where an indictment charged that the overseers of the poor, though requested to grant relief did not and would not grant it, but disregarded their duty as such overseers and neglected and refused to grant the relief, such indictment was insufficient, since it did not charge any wilful and intentional neglect of duty. State v. Hoit, 23 N.H. 355, 1851 N.H. LEXIS 135 (1851). (Decided under prior law.)

Where an indictment charged that the defendants were, on a certain day, overseers of the poor of a town, and disregarded their duty as such overseers by neglecting and refusing to relieve and maintain a pauper, judgment would not be arrested after verdict because the indictment did not allege that the accused acted as overseers of the poor of the town, or accepted the office, nor because it failed to allege more fully that it was the duty of the accused to relieve and maintain the pauper. State v. Hoit, 23 N.H. 355, 1851 N.H. LEXIS 135 (1851). (Decided under prior law.)

Cited:

Cited in McGranahan v. Dahar, 119 N.H. 758, 408 A.2d 121, 1979

N.H. LEXIS 381 (1979); Lourie v. Keene State College, 121 N.H. 233, 428 A.2d 902, 1981 N.H. LEXIS 299 (1981).

643:2. Misuse of Information.

A public servant, as defined in RSA 640:2, II, is guilty of a misdemeanor if, knowing that official action is contemplated or in reliance on information which he has acquired by virtue of his office or from another public servant, he:

I. Acquires or divests himself of a pecuniary interest in any property, transaction or enterprise which may be affected by such action or information; or

II. Speculates or wagers on the basis of such action or information; or

III. Knowingly aids another to do any of the foregoing.

Source.
1971, 518:1, eff. Nov. 1, 1973.

Cross References.
Classification of crimes, see RSA 625:9.
Sentences, see RSA 651.

NOTES TO DECISIONS

Purpose
By enactment of this section, legislature created a duty not to misuse information, the purpose of which is to prevent government officials from using inside information for their own personal gain, and as such created a statutory conflict of interest provision enforceable either civilly or criminally. Evans v. Hall, 118 N.H. 920, 396 A.2d 334, 1978 N.H. LEXIS 322 (1978).

CHAPTER 644

BREACHES OF THE PEACE AND RELATED OFFENSES

SECTION
644:1.   Riot.
644:2.   Disorderly Conduct.
644:2-a.   Exposing the Public to Toxic Biological or Chemical Substances.
644:2-b.   Prohibition on Funeral Protests.
644:3.   False Public Alarms.
644:3-a.   False Fire Alarms.
644:3-b.   False Fire Alarms Resulting in Injury or Death.
644:3-c.   Unlawful Interference With Fire Alarm Apparatus.
644:4.   Harassment.
644:5.   Intoxication. [Repealed.]
644:5-a.   Inhaling Toxic Vapors for Effect.
644:6.   Loitering or Prowling.
644:7.   Abuse of Corpse.
644:8.   Cruelty to Animals.
644:8-a.   Exhibitions of Fighting Animals.
644:8-aa.   Animals in Motor Vehicle.
644:8-b.   Docking Tail of Horse.
644:8-c.   Animal Use in Science Classes and Science Fairs.
644:8-d.   Maiming or Causing the Death of or Willful Interference with Police Dogs or Horses.
644:8-e.   Willful Interference With Organizations or Projects Involving Animals or With Animal Facilities.
644:8-f.   Transporting Dogs in Pickup Trucks.
644:9.   Violation of Privacy.
644:10.   Violation of Privacy of Messages. [Repealed.]
644:11.   Criminal Defamation.
644:12.   Emergency Calls.
644:13.   Unauthorized Use of Firearms and Firecrackers.
SECTION
644:14.   Selling Air Rifles or Paint Ball Guns to Young Persons.
644:15.   Furnishing Arms to Persons Under 16.
644:16.   Exposing Poisons.
644:16-a.   Sale or Use of Stink Bombs.
644:16-b.   Sale or Use of Smoke Bombs.
644:17.   Willful Concealment and Shoplifting. [Repealed.]
644:17-a.   Civil Damages; Willful Concealment and Shoplifting. [Repealed.]
644:18.   Facilitating a Drug or Underage Alcohol House Party.
644:19.   Unauthorized Recording in a Motion Picture Theater.
644:20.   Criminal Street Gang; Solicitation.

644:1. Riot.

I. A person is guilty of riot if:

(a) Simultaneously with 2 or more other persons, he engages in tumultuous or violent conduct and thereby purposely or recklessly creates a substantial risk of causing public alarm; or

(b) He assembles with 2 or more other persons with the purpose of engaging soon thereafter in tumultuous or violent conduct, believing that 2 or more other persons in the assembly have the same purpose; or

(c) He assembles with 2 or more other persons with the purpose of committing an offense against the person or property of another whom he supposes to be guilty of a violation of the law, believing that 2 or more other persons in the assembly have the same purpose.

II. Any person who refuses to comply with a lawful order to withdraw given to him immediately prior to, during, or immediately following a violation of paragraph I is guilty of riot. It is no defense to liability under this paragraph that withdrawal must take place over private property; provided, however, that no person so withdrawing shall incur criminal or civil liability by virtue of acts reasonably necessary to accomplish the withdrawal.

III. Upon the request of a police officer, any person present during a violation of paragraph I or II shall render assistance, other than the use of force, in the suppression of such violations. Any person refusing to render such assistance is guilty of a misdemeanor.

IV. Riot is a class B felony if, in the course of and as a result of the conduct, any person suffers physical injury, or substantial property damage or arson occurs, or the defendant was armed with a deadly weapon, or knowingly throws or causes to propel any object or substance of any kind at any uniformed law enforcement officer or uniformed emergency responder, regardless of whether such object actually strikes the uniformed law enforcement officer or uniformed emergency responder, except that if the deadly weapon was a firearm, he or she shall be sentenced in accordance with RSA 651:2, II-g. Otherwise, it is a misdemeanor.

V. (a) If the conduct comprising the offense of riot occurred within any municipality in which a student housing facility owned by a public institution of higher education is located, or in any adjacent municipality, the following penalties may be imposed, in addition to those set forth in RSA 651:

(1) The court may order the individual not to enter the campus of any public institution of higher education in this state as follows:

(A) If the offense is a felony, for a period of time not to exceed 2 years following the imposition of sentence or the completion of any term of imprisonment.

(B) If the offense is a misdemeanor, for a period of time not to exceed one year following the imposition of sentence or the completion of any term of imprisonment.

(2) The court may order the individual to pay restitution to the public institution of higher education and, if appropriate, any municipality for expenses incurred as a result of the riot. The amount shall be reasonable and shall not exceed the individual's fair and reasonable share of the costs.

(b) An order issued under this section shall not apply to any of the following:

(1) Entering onto the campus of a public institution of higher education to obtain medical treatment.

(2) Traveling on a public roadway situated on the campus of a public institution of higher education for the purpose of traveling to a location other than on such campus.

(c) For the purposes of this section, "public institution of higher education" shall include any public community college, public college, or public university.

Source.
1971, 518:1. 1990, 95:8, eff. June 12, 1990. 2004, 87:1, eff. May 7, 2004; 168:1, eff. Jan. 1, 2005.

Amendments
—2004. Paragraph IV: Ch. 168 inserted "or knowingly throws or causes to propel any object or substance of any kind at any uniformed law enforcement officer or uniformed emergency responder" following "armed with a deadly weapon" and "or she" following "he" in the first sentence.
Paragraph V: Added by ch. 87.

—1990. Paragraph IV: Added "except that if the deadly weapon was a firearm, he shall be sentenced in accordance with RSA 651:2, II-g" at the end of the first sentence.

Cross References.
Classification of crimes, see RSA 625:9.
Sentences, see RSA 651.

NOTES TO DECISIONS

1. Purpose
2. Construction
3. Self-defense
4. Withdrawal
5. Evidence

1. Purpose
The state has an indisputable and substantial interest in protecting its citizens against riots and other forms of unlawful mob activity, which is precisely the evil against which this section is directed. State v. Albers, 113 N.H. 132, 303 A.2d 197, 1973 N.H. LEXIS 217 (1973). (Decided under prior law.)

2. Construction
The offense specified in paragraph IV of this section is not an offense separate from the one specified in paragraph I, but rather is an aggravated status of that same offense. State v. Belkner, 117 N.H. 462, 374 A.2d 938, 1977 N.H. LEXIS 357 (1977).

3. Self-defense
Self-defense is an available defense to riot. State v. McMinn, 141 N.H. 636, 690 A.2d 1017, 1997 N.H. LEXIS 11 (1997).

It was error for the court to refuse to instruct the jury with regard to self-defense in a prosecution for riot where there was evidence that a three-on-one beating of the victim never occurred and that the defendant acted, throughout the altercation, under a reasonable belief that his conduct was necessary to defend himself from two others. State v. McMinn, 141 N.H. 636, 690 A.2d 1017, 1997 N.H. LEXIS 11 (1997).

4. Withdrawal
The fact that mob action at the particular location ceased after the command to withdraw was given did not excuse the respondent, who remained at the scene, from compliance with either the command or this section. State v. Galvin, 107 N.H. 441, 224 A.2d 574, 1966 N.H. LEXIS 209 (1966). (Decided under prior law.)

5. Evidence
Any error in excluding certain testimony was harmless and thus did not violate due process under N.H. Const. pt. I, art. 15 and the Fifth and Fourteenth Amendments. The alternative evidence of defendant's guilt of second-degree murder under RSA 630:1-b, I(b), and of riot under RSA 644:1, I, including eyewitness testimony, was of an overwhelming nature, and the testimony was cumulative. State v. Garcia, 162 N.H. 426, 33 A.3d 1087, 2011 N.H. LEXIS 126 (2011).

644:2. Disorderly Conduct.

A person is guilty of disorderly conduct if:

I. He knowingly or purposely creates a condition which is hazardous to himself or another in a public place by any action which serves no legitimate purpose; or

II. He or she:

(a) Engages in fighting or in violent, tumultuous or threatening behavior in a public place; or

(b) Directs at another person in a public place obscene, derisive, or offensive words which are likely to provoke a violent reaction on the part of an ordinary person; or

(c) Obstructs vehicular or pedestrian traffic on any public street or sidewalk or the entrance to any public building; or

(d) Engages in conduct in a public place which substantially interferes with a criminal investigation, a firefighting operation to which RSA 154:17 is applicable, the provision of emergency medical treatment, or the provision of other emergency services when traffic or pedestrian management is required; or

(e) Knowingly refuses to comply with a lawful order of a peace officer to move from or remain away from any public place; or

III. He purposely causes a breach of the peace, public inconvenience, annoyance or alarm, or recklessly creates a risk thereof, by:

(a) Making loud or unreasonable noises in a public place, or making loud or unreasonable noises in a private place which can be heard in a public place or other private places, which noises would disturb a person of average sensibilities; or

(b) Disrupting the orderly conduct of business in any public or governmental facility; or

(c) Disrupting any lawful assembly or meeting of persons without lawful authority.

III-a. When noise under subparagraph III(a) is emanating from a vehicle's sound system or any portable sound system located within a vehicle, a law enforcement officer shall be considered a person of average sensibilities for purposes of determining whether the volume of such noise constitutes a breach of the peace, public inconvenience, annoyance, or alarm, and the officer may take enforcement action to abate such noise upon detecting the noise, or upon receiving a complaint from another person.

IV. (a) Whenever a peace officer has probable cause to believe that a serious threat to the public health or safety is created by a flood, storm, fire, earthquake, explosion, riot, ongoing criminal activity that poses a risk of bodily injury, or other disaster, the officer may close the area where the threat exists and the adjacent area necessary to control the threat or to prevent its spread, for the duration of the threat, until related law enforcement, fire, and emergency medical service operations are complete, by means of ropes, markers, uniformed emergency service personnel, or any other reasonable means, to any persons not authorized by a peace officer or emergency services personnel to enter or remain within the closed area.

(b) Peace officers may close the immediate area surrounding any emergency field command post activated for the purpose of abating any threat enumerated in this paragraph to any unauthorized persons, whether or not the field command post is located near the source of the threat.

(c) Any unauthorized person who knowingly enters an area closed pursuant to this paragraph or who knowingly remains within the area after receiving a lawful order from a peace officer to leave shall be guilty of disorderly conduct.

V. In this section:

(a) "Lawful order" means:

(1) A command issued to any person for the purpose of preventing said person from committing any offense set forth in this section, or in any section of Title LXII or Title XXI, when the officer has reasonable grounds to believe that said person is about to commit any such offense, or when said person is engaged in a course of conduct which makes his commission of such an offense imminent;

(2) A command issued to any person to stop him from continuing to commit any offense set forth in this section, or in any section of Title LXII or Title XXI, when the officer has reasonable grounds to believe that said person is presently engaged in conduct which constitutes any such offense; or

(3) A command not to enter or a command to leave an area closed pursuant to paragraph IV, provided that a person may not lawfully be ordered to leave his or her own home or business.

(b) "Public place" means any place to which the public or a substantial group has access. The term includes, but is not limited to, public ways, sidewalks, schools, hospitals, government offices or facilities, and the lobbies or hallways of apartment buildings, dormitories, hotels or motels.

VI. Disorderly conduct is a misdemeanor if the offense continues after a request by any person to desist; otherwise, it is a violation.

Source.
1971, 518:1. 1983, 200:1. 1985, 309:1, eff. Jan. 1, 1986. 2005, 192:1, 2, eff. June 30, 2005; 260:2, eff. July, 22, 2005; 260:3, eff. June 30, 2005.

Amendments
—2005. Paragraph II: Inserted "or she" in the introductory paragraph and inserted "or remain away from" in subpar. (e).
Paragraph III-a: Added.
Paragraphs IV through VI: Added new par. IV, redesignated former par. IV as present par. V, and in that paragraph, added subpar. (a)(3), and redesignated former par. V as par. VI.

—1985. Paragraph I: Inserted "or purposely" following "knowingly".
Paragraph II: Deleted "knowingly" following "he" in the introductory clause, added "knowingly" preceding "refuses" in subpar. (e), and made other minor stylistic changes.
Paragraph III: Rewrote the introductory clause and substituted "making" for "makes" in two places in subpar. (a) and "disrupting" for "disrupts" in subpars. (b) and (c).

—1983. Rewritten to the extent that a detailed comparison would be impracticable.

Contingent 2005, 260:1 amendment. 2005, 260:1, provided for amendment of paragraph IV(c). However, under the terms of 2005, 260:4, eff. July 22, 2005, the amendment did not take effect.

Cross References.
Classification of crimes, see RSA 625:9.
Sentences, see RSA 651.

NOTES TO DECISIONS

1. Constitutionality
2. Elements
3. Language
4. Complaint
5. Particular conduct
6. Plain error

1. Constitutionality
RSA 644:2, II(e), the disorderly conduct statute, did not facially violate defendant's right to free speech under the First Amendment or N.H. Const. pt. I, art. 22. It was tailored to advance only the legitimate, content-neutral goal of allowing police officials to disperse those on the brink of engaging in unlawful conduct. State v. Biondolillo, 164 N.H. 370, 55 A.3d 1034, 2012 N.H. LEXIS 152 (2012).

RSA 644:2, II(e), the disorderly conduct statute, did not violate the First Amendment or N.H. Const. pt. I, art. 22 as applied to defendant. It was not the content of his speech that caused his arrest, but the fact that he was interfering with an officer's performance of his duties. State v. Biondolillo, 164 N.H. 370, 55 A.3d 1034, 2012 N.H. LEXIS 152 (2012).

This section, if it regulates speech, is no more than a reasonable regulation of the time, place and manner of that speech, and does not violate state constitutional right of free speech, since it neither restricts nondisruptive speech, nor forecloses opportunities for speech altogether. State v. Comley, 130 N.H. 688, 546 A.2d 1066, 1988 N.H. LEXIS 50 (1988).

Where paragraph I of this section provided that a person who refused to comply with a lawful order of the police to move from a public place was guilty of disorderly conduct, it was unconstitutionally over broad. State v. Nickerson, 120 N.H. 821, 424 A.2d 190, 1980 N.H. LEXIS 397 (1980), superseded by statute as stated in, State v. Biondolillo, 164 N.H. 370, 55 A.3d 1034, 2012 N.H. LEXIS 152 (2012).

2. Elements

Where defendant's offensive remarks to employees and customers of a tanning salon were not likely to provoke a violent reaction, the trial court misinterpreted the disorderly conduct statute, under RSA 644:2, II(b), and the evidence was insufficient to support defendant's convictions. State v. Boulais, 150 N.H. 216, 834 A.2d 380, 2003 N.H. LEXIS 165 (2003).

Where a citizen testified that she was stunned by defendant's disrespectful behavior towards police officers at the police station, and three police officers supported this testimony, there was sufficient evidence to convict defendant of disorderly conduct under RSA 644:2, III(a). State v. Gaffney, 147 N.H. 550, 795 A.2d 243, 2002 N.H. LEXIS 24 (2002).

Someone other than arresting officer must be disturbed for there to be a public disturbance within the meaning of this section. State v. Murray, 135 N.H. 369, 605 A.2d 676, 1992 N.H. LEXIS 41 (1992).

Where complaint charged defendant with purposely making unreasonable noises on a public way in violation of this section without charging that she made the noises with a conscious object to cause public inconvenience, annoyance, or alarm, or that she recklessly created such a risk, it should have been dismissed, since it did not charge all the essential elements of the offense for which she was purportedly being prosecuted. State v. Laponsee, 115 N.H. 56, 333 A.2d 447, 1975 N.H. LEXIS 222 (1975).

3. Language

Defendant's conviction for disorderly conduct could not stand where it was not supported by evidence that anyone other than arresting officers heard defendant shout vulgarities. State v. Murray, 135 N.H. 369, 605 A.2d 676, 1992 N.H. LEXIS 41 (1992).

Where words used by defendant charged with rude and disorderly conduct in a public place, on the basis of language he used to describe certain persons, did not refer to persons present at the time, situation did not involve fighting words, which are subject to greater regulation because of their inherent capacity to cause breach of peace. State v. Oliveira, 115 N.H. 559, 347 A.2d 165, 1975 N.H. LEXIS 363 (1975).

However distasteful the language used by the defendant, conviction for rude and disorderly conduct in a public place could not be based solely on the use of a crude phrase like "F—k the political pigs" while exhorting people to attend an upcoming meeting of the city council to emphasize community club's need for increased funding. State v. Oliveira, 115 N.H. 559, 347 A.2d 165, 1975 N.H. LEXIS 363 (1975).

Where there was evidence that any unwilling listeners could have retreated without forfeiting their right to return when the dance resumed, their mere presumed presence was not a sufficient basis to convict for rude and disorderly behavior in a public place based on language used in speech given at a dance. State v. Oliveira, 115 N.H. 559, 347 A.2d 165, 1975 N.H. LEXIS 363 (1975).

Where defendant convicted of rude and disorderly conduct on the basis of language used to describe certain persons during a speech did not exhort the crowd to violence and there was no violent reaction to the speech, situation did not present a clear and present danger of riot, disorder or other immediate threat to public safety, peace or order. State v. Oliveira, 115 N.H. 559, 347 A.2d 165, 1975 N.H. LEXIS 363 (1975).

The test of what was offensive language within the meaning of this section was not subjective, depending upon whether the words actually caused offense to the person addressed; but the test was the tendency of the words to cause such resentment as would provoke the average person to fight. State v. Chaplinsky, 91 N.H. 310, 18 A.2d 754, 1941 N.H. LEXIS 15 (1941), aff'd, Chaplinsky v. New Hampshire, 315 U.S. 568, 62 S. Ct. 766, 86 L. Ed. 1031, 1942

U.S. LEXIS 851 (1942), superseded by statute as stated in, Fallin v. City of Huntsville, 865 So. 2d 473, 2003 Ala. Crim. App. LEXIS 19 (Ala. Crim. App. 2003). (Decided under prior law.)

It was no defense to a complaint that the offensive words used express the truth, since this section made no distinction between truthful and untruthful expressions, but prohibited both alike. (Decided under prior law); State v. Chaplinsky, 91 N.H. 310, 18 A.2d 754, 1941 N.H. LEXIS 15 (1941), aff'd, Chaplinsky v. New Hampshire, 315 U.S. 568, 62 S. Ct. 766, 86 L. Ed. 1031, 1942 U.S. LEXIS 851 (1942), superseded by statute as stated in, Fallin v. City of Huntsville, 865 So. 2d 473, 2003 Ala. Crim. App. LEXIS 19 (Ala. Crim. App. 2003). (Decided under prior law.)

Where a union official yelled the term "scab" at a fellow workman and his wife as the latter were driving peaceably along the public highway, not close to the plant where either worked and not going to or coming from work, such facts supported a finding of a violation of this section, since the epithets spoken by the defendant were not instruments of information or peaceful persuasion but were offensive, derisive, and annoying words, likely in the setting here, to provoke retaliation. State v. Dyer, 98 N.H. 59, 94 A.2d 718, 1953 N.H. LEXIS 13 (1953). (Decided under prior law.)

4. Complaint

A complaint charging the respondents with disorderly conduct by using profane words and engaging in loud talk sufficiently informed them that they were being prosecuted under the provisions of this section and was sufficiently definite to enable them to defend and in the event of conviction to protect them from later prosecution for the same offense. State v. O'Neill, 105 N.H. 15, 191 A.2d 528, 1963 N.H. LEXIS 4 (1963). (Decided under prior law.)

5. Particular conduct

There was sufficient evidence to support defendant's conviction under RSA 644:2, II(e), as defendant demonstrated a design to interfere with an officer's efforts to complete his inquiry into the safety of a child by interfering with the officer's attempts to talk to the child's parents about a complaint he had received. Furthermore, there was not insufficient evidence of a criminal investigation, as the nature of the sort of investigation here often called upon the police to ascertain whether a caretaker was endangering the child's welfare or otherwise harming the child; moreover, during the investigation the officer learned that the mother had an outstanding arrest warrant. State v. Biondolillo, 164 N.H. 370, 55 A.3d 1034, 2012 N.H. LEXIS 152 (2012).

Where a professor unleashed a tirade against a colleague, the false arrest claim based on a disorderly conduct charge failed because there was probable cause for the professor's arrest on the disorderly conduct charge, and the professor's argument regarding an alleged distinction between crimes and violations under New Hampshire law was rejected. Collins v. Univ. of N.H., 664 F.3d 8, 2011 U.S. App. LEXIS 25146 (2011).

Defendant's conviction of disorderly conduct under RSA 644:2, III(b) was not supported by sufficient evidence where the charge was based on an incident in which defendant said he would or might shoot up the school if a teacher did not hug him, and the teacher testified that the students in her class did not react to defendant's comment, which tended to show there was no disruption, and the State did not present evidence that students became unruly or were unable to pay attention to their lessons because police detectives were present at the school to investigate, and therefore no rational trier of fact could have found beyond a reasonable doubt that defendant disrupted the orderly conduct of business at the school. State v. McCooey, 148 N.H. 86, 802 A.2d 1216, 2002 N.H. LEXIS 95 (2002).

Defendant who yelled, kicked and swore as police officers took her into custody in a public place recklessly created a risk of causing public inconvenience, annoyance or alarm within the meaning of this section. State v. Murphy, 117 N.H. 75, 369 A.2d 189, 1977 N.H. LEXIS 272 (1977).

Where a town selectman continually interrupted another selectman who had the floor according to the chairman's ruling, argued with the chairman and refused to come to order, chairman had authority to order him from the room, and since chairman could properly ask for assistance of a police officer in removing him, officer's order to defendant to step outside was lawful order, and on basis of these facts, defendant could properly be found guilty of disorderly conduct. State v. Dominic, 117 N.H. 573, 376 A.2d 124, 1977 N.H. LEXIS 384 (1977).

6. Plain error

There was no basis under the plain error rule to reverse defendant's conviction under RSA 644:2, II(e). Even assuming that certain hypothetical applications of the current statute might pose vagueness concerns, in no sense was the controlling law "settled" against the trial court's decision as applied to the defendant. State v. Biondolillo, 164 N.H. 370, 55 A.3d 1034, 2012 N.H. LEXIS 152 (2012).

Cited:

Cited in State v. Hamilton, 123 N.H. 686, 465 A.2d 495, 1983 N.H. LEXIS 334 (1983); Roe v. Sugar River Mills Assocs., 820 F. Supp. 636, 1993 U.S. Dist. LEXIS 6525 (D.N.H. 1993); Parker v. City of Nashua, 76 F.3d 9, 1996 U.S. App. LEXIS 1682 (1st Cir. N.H. 1996); State v. Bernard, 158 N.H. 43, 959 A.2d 193, 2008 N.H. LEXIS 133 (2008).

644:2-a. Exposing the Public to Toxic Biological or Chemical Substances.

Any person who knowingly delivers or causes the delivery of a biological or chemical substance to a governmental facility, school, business, hospital, office building, or similar facility open to the public, with the purpose of causing bodily injury or evacuation of such facility, shall be guilty of a class A felony.

Source.

2002, 222:9, eff. Jan. 1, 2003.

Cross References.

Classification of crimes, see RSA 625:9.
Sentences, see RSA 651.

644:2-b. Prohibition on Funeral Protests.

I. In this section, "funeral" means the ceremonies, processions, and memorial services held in connection with the burial or cremation of the dead.

II. It shall be unlawful for any person to engage in picketing or other protest activities at any location at which a funeral is held, within one hour prior to the commencement of any funeral, and until one hour following the cessation of any funeral, if such picketing or other protest activities:

(a) Take place within 150 feet of a road, pathway, or other route of ingress to or egress from cemetery property and include, as part of such activities, any individual willfully making or assisting in the making of any noise or diversion that disturbs or tends to disturb the peace or good order of the funeral, memorial service, or ceremony; or

(b) Are within 300 feet of such cemetery and impede the access to or egress from such cemetery.

III. Each day on which a violation of this section occurs shall constitute a separate offense. Violation of this section is a class B misdemeanor, unless committed by a person who has previously pled guilty to or been found guilty of a violation of this section, in which case the violation is a class A misdemeanor.

Source.

2007, 370:2, eff. September 15, 2007.

Cross References.

Classification of crimes, see RSA 625:9.
Sentences, see RSA 651.

644:3. False Public Alarms.

I. Any person who directly or indirectly communicates to any governmental agency that commonly deals with emergencies involving danger to life or property a report known by him to be false regarding a fire, explosion, or other catastrophe or emergency, shall be guilty of a misdemeanor; except if the report concerns the presence of a biological or chemical substance, the offense shall constitute a class B felony.

II. Any person who directly or indirectly communicates to any school, business, office building, hospital, or similar facility open to the public, a report concerning the presence of a biological or chemical substance, knowing such report is false, shall be guilty of a class B felony.

III. Any person who knowingly delivers, or causes the delivery of any substance the actor knows could reasonably be perceived as a biological or chemical substance, with the purpose of causing fear or terrorism and with reckless disregard for the risk that emergency services will be dispatched as a result of such delivery, shall be guilty of a class B felony.

IV. This section shall not apply to false alarms subject to RSA 644:3-a or RSA 644:3-b, or false reports under RSA 158:38.

Source.

1971, 518:1. 1975, 25:1. 1981, 553:3, eff. Aug. 29, 1981. 2002, 222:8, eff. Jan. 1, 2003.

Amendments

—2002. Designated the existing provisions of the section as par. I and in that paragraph, added "except if the report concerns the presence of a biological or chemical substance, the offense shall constitute a class B felony" following "misdemeanor" in the first sentence and deleted the second sentence, and added pars. II–IV.

—1981. Rewritten to the extent that a detailed comparison would be impracticable.

—1975. Substituted "any governmental" for "a fire department or other government" preceding "agency" and "an" for "a fire" preceding "explosion" in the first sentence and added the second sentence.

Cross References.

Calling 911 to make false alarm, see RSA 106-H:13.
Classification of crimes, see RSA 625:9.
Sentences, see RSA 651.

NOTES TO DECISIONS

1. Conduct constituting violation
2. Sufficiency of evidence

1. Conduct constituting violation

Plain meaning of these terms "communicate," "indirectly," and "report" does not require that an indirect communication occur solely by spoken word from the mouth of a defendant; to the contrary, a defendant could make known or "communicate" an emergency through his conduct—such as by evading search and rescue. Thus, the acts of failing to return from an undisclosed location, evading search and rescue personnel, and of doing so knowingly constituted conduct that "indirectly communicated" a report of an emergency. State v. Dodds, 159 N.H. 239, 982 A.2d 377, 2009 N.H. LEXIS 112 (2009).

2. Sufficiency of evidence

There was sufficient evidence to support a false public alarms conviction. A reasonable juror could have found that defendant, who disappeared for 27 hours after a car accident, failed to return from an undisclosed location and failed to communicate his location, evading search and rescue personnel; there was medical testimony that cast doubt upon his claims that he suffered memory loss and hypothermia. State v. Dodds, 159 N.H. 239, 982 A.2d 377, 2009 N.H. LEXIS 112 (2009).

644:3-a. False Fire Alarms.

Any person who knowingly gives or aids or abets in giving any false alarm of fire, by any means, is guilty of a misdemeanor.

Source.
1975, 25:2, eff. May 3, 1975.

Cross References.
Classification of crimes, see RSA 625:9.
Sentences, see RSA 651.

644:3-b. False Fire Alarms Resulting in Injury or Death.

Any person who knowingly gives or aids or abets in giving any false alarm of fire, by any means, is guilty of a class B felony if bodily injury or death is sustained by any person as a result thereof.

Source.
1975, 25:2, eff. May 3, 1975.

Cross References.
Classification of crimes, see RSA 625:9.
Sentences, see RSA 651.

644:3-c. Unlawful Interference With Fire Alarm Apparatus.

A person who knowingly tampers with, interferes with or impairs any public fire alarm apparatus, wire or associated equipment is guilty of a class B felony.

Source.
1975, 25:2, eff. May 3, 1975.

Cross References.
Classification of crimes, see RSA 625:9.
Sentences, see RSA 651.

644:4. Harassment.

I. A person is guilty of a misdemeanor, and subject to prosecution in the jurisdiction where the communication originated or was received, if such person:

(a) Makes a telephone call, whether or not a conversation ensues, with no legitimate communicative purpose or without disclosing his or her identity and with a purpose to annoy, abuse, threaten, or alarm another; or

(b) Makes repeated communications at extremely inconvenient hours or in offensively coarse language with a purpose to annoy or alarm another; or

(c) Insults, taunts, or challenges another in a manner likely to provoke a violent or disorderly response; or

(d) Knowingly communicates any matter of a character tending to incite murder, assault, or arson; or

(e) With the purpose to annoy or alarm another, communicates any matter containing any threat to kidnap any person or to commit a violation of RSA 633:4; or a threat to the life or safety of another; or

(f) With the purpose to annoy or alarm another, having been previously notified that the recipient does not desire further communication, communicates with such person, when the communication is not for a lawful purpose or constitutionally protected.

II. As used in paragraph I, "communicates" means to impart a message by any method of transmission, including but not limited to telephoning or personally delivering or sending or having delivered any information or material by written or printed note or letter, package, mail, courier service or electronic transmission, including electronic transmissions generated or communicated via a computer. For purposes of this section, "computer" means a programmable, electronic device capable of accepting and processing data.

III. In any complaint or information brought for the enforcement of RSA 644:4, I(f), it shall not be necessary for the state to negate any exception, excuse, proviso, or exemption contained therein and the burden of proof of any exception, excuse, proviso, or exemption shall be upon the defendant.

IV. A person shall be guilty of a class B felony if the person violates RSA 644:4, I(a) under circumstances involving making telephone calls to a telephone number that he or she knows is being used, at the time of the calls, to facilitate the transportation of voters to polling places or otherwise to support voting or registering to vote.

Source.
1971, 518:1. 1994, 354:1, eff. Jan. 1, 1995. 1999, 141:1, eff. June 25, 1999. 2005, 138:1, eff. January 1, 2006. 2009, 320:1, eff. August 7, 2009.

Amendments
—**2009.** The 2009 amendment added IV.

—**2005.** Paragraph I(a): Inserted "with no legitimate communicative purpose or without disclosing his or her identity and" preceding "with a purpose to annoy" and "abuse, threaten" thereafter.

—**1999.** Paragraph II: Added "including electronic transmissions generated or communicated via a computer" following "electronic transmission" at the end of the first sentence and added the second sentence.

—**1994.** Rewritten to the extent that a detailed comparison would be impracticable.

Cross References.
Classification of crimes, see RSA 625:9.
Sentences, see RSA 651.

NOTES TO DECISIONS

1. Constitutionality
2. Construction with other laws
3. Evidence
4. Repeated communications
5. Legislative history

1. Constitutionality

Because the court had previously found RSA 644:4, I(b) not to be overbroad under the First Amendment, the trial court could properly consider defendant's repeated messages containing extraordinarily offensive and coarse language in determining that defendant had harassed plaintiff as defined in RSA 644:4, I(b). Thompson v. D'errico, 163 N.H. 20, 35 A.3d 584, 2011 N.H. LEXIS 185 (2011).

RSA 644:4, I(b) is not overbroad on its face under the First Amendment. With its requirement of repeated communications that either occur at extremely inconvenient hours or contain offensively coarse language and its requirement that these repeated communications be made with the purpose to annoy or alarm another, its scope is narrowly tailored to the illegal communications sought to be prevented. State v. Gubitosi, 157 N.H. 720, 958 A.2d 962, 2008 N.H. LEXIS 116 (2008).

Supreme Court of New Hampshire's decision in Brobst does not require that RSA 644:4, I(b) include both inconvenient hour and offensive language elements in order to pass muster as not being overbroad under the First Amendment. Brobst simply highlights, in hypothetical fashion, some potential characteristics of communications where the State may have a legitimate interest, and does not compel their inclusion in RSA 644:4, I(b). State v. Gubitosi, 157 N.H. 720, 958 A.2d 962, 2008 N.H. LEXIS 116 (2008).

Even if it were assumed that a savings clause in RSA 644:4, I(f), was an affirmative defense to harassment and the burdens of proof were not shifted, the statute is unconstitutionally overbroad and violates N.H. Const. art. 15, pt. I, and U.S. Const. amends. I, V, XIV. State v. Pierce, 152 N.H. 790, 887 A.2d 132, 2005 N.H. LEXIS 172 (2005).

RSA 644:4, I(a) prohibited all phone calls placed with intent to alarm, and encompassed too large an area of protected speech; the statute was facially overbroad, and a trial court's dismissal of harassment charges brought against defendant was affirmed. State v. Brobst, 151 N.H. 420, 857 A.2d 1253, 2004 N.H. LEXIS 163 (2004). (Decided prior to the 2005 amendment to 644:4, I(a).)

2. Construction with other laws

RSA 633:3-a, II(a)(7) provides that a course of conduct may include any act of communication as defined in RSA 644:4, II. Under RSA 644:4, II, "communicates" means to impart a message by any method of transmission, including but not limited to telephoning. The statute does not require that the act of communication take place between the defendant and the intended victim. State v. Gubitosi, 152 N.H. 673, 886 A.2d 1029, 2005 N.H. LEXIS 159 (2005).

3. Evidence

Since RSA 644:4, II did not require that the act of communication take place between the defendant and the intended victim, it was sufficient for the State to prove that defendant telephoned the restaurant with the intent to impart a message to the victim and that the telephone call was part of a course of conduct that reasonably made the victim fear for her safety. State v. Gubitosi, 152 N.H. 673, 886 A.2d 1029, 2005 N.H. LEXIS 159 (2005).

Trial court's finding of abuse in issuing protective order was not supported by sufficient evidence that husband committed abuse in the form of harassment because the incidents the wife described were either too distant in time or were too non-specific to constitute harassment where she testified that (1) 11 years before she filed her request, the husband struck her in anger; (2) 8 years prior to the request, the husband pushed her into a slide during an argument; and (3) the husband threatened during an argument some months prior to the request to make her life a living hell if she did not

comply with his wishes. Fillmore v. Fillmore, 147 N.H. 283, 786 A.2d 849, 2001 N.H. LEXIS 206 (2001).

4. Repeated communications

Plain and ordinary meaning of "repeated communications," within the overall context of RSA 644:4 is the renewed, frequent, or constant imparting of a message by any method of transmission. In re Alex C., 161 N.H. 231, 13 A.3d 347, 2010 N.H. LEXIS 146 (2010).

Juvenile defendant's conduct of sending 20 instant messages to the victim within 56 minutes constituted "repeated communications" under RSA 644:4, I(b). In re Alex C., 161 N.H. 231, 13 A.3d 347, 2010 N.H. LEXIS 146 (2010).

5. Legislative history

Legislative history of RSA 644:4, I(b) indicates an intent to provide for a broad proscription against harassment via the internet, the electronic transmissions of computers, and the technological advances therein. In re Alex C., 161 N.H. 231, 13 A.3d 347, 2010 N.H. LEXIS 146 (2010).

Cited:

Cited in State v. Sorrell, 120 N.H. 472, 416 A.2d 1375, 1980 N.H. LEXIS 326 (1980); State v. Cantara, 123 N.H. 737, 465 A.2d 887, 1983 N.H. LEXIS 341 (1983); Duchesnaye v. Munro Enters., 125 N.H. 244, 480 A.2d 123, 1984 N.H. LEXIS 284 (1984).

RESEARCH REFERENCES

New Hampshire Practice.
3-5 N.H.P. Family Law § 5.04.

644:5. Intoxication.

[Repealed 1979, 378:3, eff. Aug. 22, 1979.]

Former section(s).
Former RSA 644:5, which was derived from 1971, 518:1, related to intoxication.

644:5-a. Inhaling Toxic Vapors for Effect.

A person is guilty of a violation if he or she purposely smells or inhales the fumes of any substance having the property of releasing toxic vapors, for the purpose of causing a condition of intoxication, euphoria, excitement, exhilaration, stupefaction, or dulled senses of the nervous system, or possesses, buys or sells any such substance for the purpose of violating or aiding another to violate this section. This section does not apply to the inhalation of anesthesia for medical or dental purposes.

Source.
1971, 518:1, eff. Nov. 1, 1973. 2005, 112:1, eff. January 1, 2006.

Amendments
—**2005.** Inserted "or she" following "he" in the first sentence and deleted the third through sixth sentences.

Cross References.
Classification of crimes, see RSA 625:9.
Sentences, see RSA 651.

644:6. Loitering or Prowling.

I. A person commits a violation if he knowingly appears at a place, or at a time, under circumstances that warrant alarm for the safety of persons or property in the vicinity. Circumstances which may be considered in determining whether such alarm is warranted include, but are not limited to, when the actor:

(a) Takes flight upon appearance of a law enforcement official or upon questioning by such an official.

(b) Manifestly endeavors to conceal himself or any object.

(c) Has in his possession tools or other property which would lead a reasonable person to believe a crime was about to be perpetrated.

(d) Examines entrances to a structure which the actor has no authority or legitimate purpose to enter.

II. Prior to any arrest under this section, unless flight or other circumstances make it impossible, a law enforcement official shall afford the actor the opportunity to dispel any alarm which would otherwise be warranted, by requesting him to identify himself and give an account for his presence and conduct. Failure to identify or account for oneself, absent other circumstances, however, shall not be grounds for arrest.

III. No person shall be convicted under this section if the law enforcement official did not comply with paragraph II or if it appears at trial that the explanation he gave of his conduct and purposes was true and, if believed by the law enforcement official at the time, would have dispelled the alarm. In such cases, any record of the arrest made under authority of paragraph I shall be expunged.

IV. In this section, "entrances" means any part of a structure through which entry or egress could be made.

Source.
1971, 518:1. 1985, 255:1, eff. Jan. 1, 1986.

Amendments
—**1985.** Rewritten to the extent that a detailed comparison would be impracticable.

Cross References.
Classification of crimes, see RSA 625:9.
Sentences, see RSA 651.

NOTES TO DECISIONS

Particular conduct

This section did not provide justification for police officer to search passenger compartment of pick-up truck occupied by two men and parked in a parking lot at 1:00 a.m., even though passenger made a furtive gesture in placing an object beside the seat; there was no indication that the men intended to commit a crime which threatened public safety, nor was there any indication they intended to leave the truck, and furthermore, officer failed to afford the men opportunity to dispel any alarm. State v. Dodier, 135 N.H. 134, 600 A.2d 913, 1991 N.H. LEXIS 152 (1991).

Cited:

Cited in State v. Graca, 142 N.H. 670, 708 A.2d 393, 1998 N.H. LEXIS 18 (1998); State v. Graca, 142 N.H. 670, 708 A.2d 393, 1998 N.H. LEXIS 18 (1998).

RESEARCH REFERENCES

New Hampshire Practice.
1-3 N.H.P. Criminal Practice & Procedure § 3.04.
1-3 N.H.P. Criminal Practice & Procedure § 3.07.

644:7. Abuse of Corpse.

A person is guilty of a misdemeanor if he unlawfully removes, conceals or destroys a corpse or any part thereof.

Source.
1971, 518:1, eff. Nov. 1, 1973.

Cross References.
Anatomical gifts, see RSA 291-A.
Burials and disinterments generally, see RSA 290.
Classification of crimes, see RSA 625:9.
Concealing death of a newborn, see RSA 639:5.
Dead bodies for scientific study, see RSA 291.
Disturbance of burial grounds and unlawful removal, possession or sale of tombstones or gravesite items, see RSA 635:6 et seq.
Sentences, see RSA 651.

644:8. Cruelty to Animals.

I. In this section, "cruelty" shall include, but not be limited to, acts or omissions injurious or detrimental to the health, safety or welfare of any animal, including the abandoning of any animal without proper provision for its care, sustenance, protection or shelter.

II. In this section, "animal" means a domestic animal, a household pet or a wild animal in captivity.

II-a. In this section, "shelter" or "necessary shelter" for dogs shall mean any natural or artificial area which provides protection from the direct sunlight and adequate air circulation when that sunlight is likely to cause heat exhaustion of a dog tied or caged outside. Shelter from the weather shall allow the dog to remain clean and dry. Shelter shall be structurally sound and have an area within to afford the dog the ability to stand up, turn around and lie down, and be of proportionate size as to allow the natural body heat of the dog to be retained.

III. A person is guilty of a misdemeanor for a first offense, and of a class B felony for a second or subsequent offense, who:

(a) Without lawful authority negligently deprives or causes to be deprived any animal in his possession or custody necessary care, sustenance or shelter;

(b) Negligently beats, cruelly whips, tortures, mutilates or in any other manner mistreats or causes to be mistreated any animal;

(c) Negligently overdrives, overworks, drives when overloaded, or otherwise abuses or misuses any animal intended for or used for labor;

(d) Negligently transports any animal in his possession or custody in a manner injurious to the health, safety or physical well-being of such animal;

(e) Negligently abandons any animal previously in his possession or custody by causing such animal to be left without supervision or adequate provision for its care, sustenance or shelter; or

(f) Otherwise negligently permits or causes any animal in his possession or custody to be subjected to cruelty, inhumane treatment or unnecessary suffering of any kind.

III-a. A person is guilty of a class B felony who purposely beats, cruelly whips, tortures, or mutilates any animal or causes any animal to be beaten, cruelly whipped, tortured, or mutilated.

IV. (a) In addition to being guilty of crimes as provided in paragraphs III and III-a, any person charged with cruelty to animals may have his or her animal confiscated by the arresting officer and, upon said person's conviction of cruelty to animals, the court may dispose of said animal in any manner it decides. Courts shall give cases in which animals have been confiscated by an arresting officer priority on the court calendar. The costs, if any, incurred in boarding and treating the animal, pending disposition of the case, and in disposing of the animal, upon a conviction of said person for cruelty to animals, shall be borne by the person so convicted. In addition, the court may prohibit any person convicted of animal cruelty from having future ownership or custody of other animals for any period of time the court deems reasonable or impose any other reasonable restrictions on the person's future ownership or custody of animals as necessary for the protection of the animals.

(b) If a person convicted of cruelty to animals appeals the conviction and any confiscated animal remains in the custody of the arresting officer or the officer's designee pending disposition of the appeal, in order for the appellant to maintain a future interest in the animal, the trial court may require the appellant to post a bond or other security in an amount not exceeding $2,000 for each animal in custody for costs expected to be incurred for the board and care of the animal during the appeal. If the conviction is affirmed on appeal, the costs incurred for the board and care of the animal shall be paid to the custodian from the posted security and the balance, if any, returned to the person who posted it.

IV-a. (a) Except as provided in subparagraphs (b) and (c) any appropriate law enforcement officer, animal control officer, or officer of a duly licensed humane society may take into temporary protective custody any animal when there is probable cause to believe that it has been or is being abused or neglected in violation of paragraphs III or III-a when there is a clear and imminent danger to the animal's health or life and there is not sufficient time to obtain a court order. Such officer shall leave a written notice indicating the type and number of animals taken into protective custody, the name of the officer, the time and date taken, the reason it was taken, the procedure to have the animal returned and any other relevant information. Such notice shall be left at the location where the animal was taken into custody. The officer shall provide for proper care and housing of any animal taken into protective custody under this paragraph. If, after 7 days, the animal has not been returned or claimed, the officer shall petition the municipal or district court seeking either permanent custody or a one-

week extension of custody or shall file charges under this section. If a week's extension is granted by the court and after a period of 14 days the animal remains unclaimed, the title and custody of the animal shall rest with the officer on behalf of the officer's department or society. The department or society may dispose of the animal in any lawful and humane manner as if it were the rightful owner. If after 14 days the officer or the officer's department determines that charges should be filed under this section, the officer shall petition the court.

(b) For purposes of subparagraph (a) the investigating officer for livestock, as defined in RSA 427:38, III, shall be accompanied by a veterinarian licensed under RSA 332-B or the state veterinarian who shall set the probable cause criteria for taking the animal or animals.

(c) (1) For purposes of subparagraph (a), for facilities licensed to conduct live running or harness horseracing or live dog racing pursuant to RSA 284, the appropriate law enforcement officer, animal control officer, or officer of a duly licensed humane society shall:

(A) Notify the director of the racing and charitable gaming commission of the circumstances arising under subparagraph (a);

(B) Enter the grounds of the facility with the director of the racing and charitable gaming commission or such person designated by the director of the racing and charitable gaming commission;

(C) Take such horses or dogs into temporary protective custody as determined by the director of the racing and charitable gaming commission or such person designated by the director of the racing and charitable gaming commission; and

(D) Comply with subparagraph (a) after taking a horse or dog from a facility licensed pursuant to RSA 284 into temporary protective custody.

(2) This paragraph shall not preempt existing or enforcement authority of the racing and charitable gaming commission, pursuant to RSA 284 or rules and regulations adopted pursuant to such authority.

V. A veterinarian licensed to practice in the state shall be held harmless from either criminal or civil liability for any decisions made for services rendered under the provisions of this section or RSA 435:11–16. Such a veterinarian is, therefore, under this paragraph, protected from a lawsuit for his part in an investigation of cruelty to animals.

Source.
1971, 518:1. 1975, 460:1. 1979, 23:1. 1981, 575:2. 1982, 8:4. 1983, 231:2. 1985, 72:3. 1989, 57:1. 1994, 234:1–3, eff. Jan. 1, 1995. 1998, 283:1, eff. Jan. 1, 1999. 1999, 152:1, eff. Jan. 1, 2000; 308:1, eff. Sept. 14, 1999. 2000, 4:1, eff. Feb. 4, 2000. 2008, 240:1, eff. January 1, 2009; 288:1, 2, eff. July 1, 2008.

Revision note.
References to "pari-mutuel commission" have been changed to

"racing and charitable gaming commission" throughout the section in light of the amendments by 2008, 25:1, eff. July 11, 2008.

Amendments

—2008. The 2008 amendment by Chapter 240, in II-a, in the first sentence added "and adequate air circulation", substituted "the" for "inclement" preceding "weather" and added "allow the dog to remain clean and dry" at the end; and in the second sentence, added "Shelter shall be structurally sound and" at the beginning.

The 2008 amendment by Chapter 288, in IV-a(a), in the first sentence, substituted "subparagraphs (b) and (c)" for "subparagraph (b)" and added "or is being" preceding "abused or neglected"; rewrote IV-a(c) to the extent that a detailed comparison would be impracticable.

—2000. Paragraph II-a: Added.

—1999. Paragraph IV: Designated the existing provisions of the paragraph as subpar. (a) and added subpar. (b).

Paragraph IV-a(a): Substituted "the officer's" for "his" in the sixth and eighth sentences and "the officer" for "he" in the eighth sentence.

Paragraph IV-a(b): Substituted "investigating" for "appropriate law enforcement" preceding "officer for" and deleted "domestic animals, as defined in RSA 436:1, II, or" thereafter, inserted "accompanied by" preceding "a veterinarian" and added "who shall set the probable cause criteria for taking the animal or animals".

Paragraph IV-a(c): Added.

—1998. Paragraph IV: Inserted "or her" preceding "animal confiscated" in the first sentence and added the second and fourth sentences.

—1994. Paragraph III: Rewrote the introductory paragraph to the extent that a detailed comparison would be impracticable.

Paragraph III-a. Added.

Paragraph IV: Substituted "crimes" for "a misdemeanor" preceding "as provided in" and "paragraphs III and III-a" for "paragraph III" thereafter in the first sentence.

Paragraph IV-a: Substituted "paragraphs III or III-a" for "paragraph III" following "violation of" in the first sentence.

—1989. Paragraph IV-a: Added.

—1985. Paragraph V: Substituted "RSA 435:11–16" for "RSA 575-C" at the end of the first sentence.

—1983. Paragraph V: Substituted "RSA 575-C" for "RSA 575-B" at the end of the first sentence.

—1982. Paragraph V: Added.

—1981. Paragraph I: Substituted "or" for "and" preceding "shelter".

Paragraph III: Substituted "negligently" for "knowingly" wherever it appeared and deleted "or purposely" preceding "beats" in subpar. (b).

—1979. Paragraph IV: Added.

—1975. Rewritten to the extent that a detailed comparison would be impracticable.

Contingent 2008 amendment.

2008, 240:2 provided for amendment of this section. However, under the terms of 2008, 288:3, eff. July 1, 2008, the amendment did not take effect.

Cross References.

Animals in motor vehicle, see RSA 644:8-aa.

Animal use in science classes and science fairs, see RSA 644:8-c.

Application of section to wolf hybrids, see RSA 466-A:2.

Classification of crimes, see RSA 625:9.

Cropping ear of dog, see RSA 466:40.

Docking tail of horse, see RSA 644:8-b.

Exhibitions of fighting animals, see RSA 644:8-a.

Exposing poisonous substance with intent that it be eaten by a dog, see RSA 466:42-a.

Exposing poisons for the destruction of animals, see RSA 644:16.

Sale of pets and disposition of unclaimed animals, see RSA 437.

Sentences, see RSA 651.

Treatment of horses, see RSA 435:11 et seq.

NOTES TO DECISIONS

1. Accomplice liability
2. Disposition of animal

1. Accomplice liability

The crime of accomplice to negligent cruelty to animals exists under New Hampshire law. State v. Anthony, 151 N.H. 492, 861 A.2d 773 (2004).

Where defendant assisted her husband in binding binding a colt's four legs together with the purpose of leaving the colt on the ground, which caused the colt to suffer pain and injury, defendant was guilty as an accomplice to negligent cruelty to animals under RSA 644:8 and RSA 626:8, as the jury could properly have concluded defendant intentionally aided her husband in confining the horse but was unaware of the result, i.e., a substantial and unjustifiable risk that the animal's attempts to free itself would injure it and cause it pain. State v. Anthony, 151 N.H. 492, 861 A.2d 773 (2004).

2. Disposition of animal

Before an animal could be destroyed in pursuance of this section the owner had to be given notice of such proposed action and an opportunity to be heard thereon. Carter v. Colby, 71 N.H. 230, 51 A. 904, 1902 N.H. LEXIS 9 (1902). (Decided under prior law.)

644:8-a. Exhibitions of Fighting Animals.

I. No person shall keep, breed, or train any bird, dog, or other animal, with the intent that it or its offspring shall be engaged or used in an exhibition of fighting, or shall establish or promote an exhibition of the fighting thereof. Whoever violates the provisions of this paragraph shall be guilty of a class B felony.

II. Any person present at any place or building when preparations are being made for an exhibition of such fighting with intent to be present at such exhibition, or present at, aiding in or contributing to, such an exhibition, shall be guilty of a class B felony.

III. All animals so kept, bred, or trained by a person charged with violating the provisions of paragraph I may be seized by the arresting officer, pursuant to RSA 595-A:6 and RSA 644:8. Upon said person's conviction, said animals may, at the discretion of the court, be destroyed in a humane manner by a licensed veterinarian. The costs, if any, incurred in boarding the animals, pending disposition of the case, and in disposing of the animals, upon a conviction of said person for violating paragraph I, shall be borne by the person so convicted.

IV. Upon conviction of a violation of this section, all animals used or to be used in training, fighting, or baiting, and all equipment, paraphernalia, and money involved in a violation of this section may be forfeited to the state at the discretion of the court, pursuant to RSA 595-A:6. Proceeds of any such forfeiture shall be used to reimburse local government and state agencies for the costs of prosecution of animal fighting cases. Proceeds which are not needed for such reimbursement shall be deposited in the companion animal neutering fund, established in RSA 437-A:4-a.

V. In addition to other penalties prescribed by law, the court may issue an order prohibiting a person who is convicted of a violation of this section from owning or possessing any animals within the species that is the subject of the conviction, or any animals kept for the purpose of training, fighting, or baiting, for a period of time determined by the court.

Source.
1979, 30:1, eff. June 5, 1979. 2003, 98:1, eff. Jan. 1, 2004. 2008, 326:1, eff. January 1, 2009.

Amendments
—2008. The 2008 amendment added IV and V.

—2003. Paragraph I: Inserted "breed" preceding "or train" and "or its offspring" preceding "shall be engaged" in the first sentence and deleted "in the case of dogs, and a misdemeanor in the case of birds or other animals" following "class B felony" in the second sentence.
   Paragraph II: Deleted "in the case of dogs, and a misdemeanor in the case of birds or other animals" following "class B felony".
   Paragraph III: Inserted "bred" preceding "or trained" and added "pursuant to RSA 595-A:6 and RSA 644:8" in the first sentence.

Cross References.
Classification of crimes, see RSA 625:9.
Sentences, see RSA 651.

644:8-aa. Animals in Motor Vehicle.

I. It shall be cruelty to confine an animal in a motor vehicle or other enclosed space in which the temperature is either so high or so low as to cause serious harm to the animal. "Animal" means a domestic animal, household pet, or wild animal held in captivity.

II. Any person in violation of this section shall be guilty of a misdemeanor as set forth in RSA 644:8.

III. Any law enforcement officer or agent of a licensed humane organization may take action necessary to rescue a confined animal endangered by extreme temperatures, and to remove the threat of further serious harm.

IV. No officer or agent taking action under paragraph III shall be liable for damage reasonably necessary to rescue the confined animal.

Source.
1981, 575:1, eff. July 7, 1981.

Cross References.
Classification of crimes, see RSA 625:9.
Sentences, see RSA 651.

644:8-b. Docking Tail of Horse.

If any person shall cut the bone of the tail of a horse for the purpose of docking the tail, or shall cause or knowingly permit the same to be done upon the premises of which he is in control, or shall assist in or be present at such cutting, he shall be guilty of a misdemeanor. Written permission from the state veterinarian shall be obtained by a licensed veterinarian to perform surgical operations pursuant to this section. The state veterinarian shall promulgate rules relative to granting authorization for such operation.

Source.
1979, 263:1, eff. Aug. 20, 1979.

Cross References.
Administrative Procedure Act, see RSA 541-A.
Classification of crimes, see RSA 625:9.
Sentences, see RSA 651.

644:8-c. Animal Use in Science Classes and Science Fairs.

I. In this section:
   (a) "Animal" means any member of the kingdom of Animalia.
   (b) "Vertebrate animal" means any animal belonging to the subphylum Vertebrata of the phylum Chordata, and specifically includes all mammals, fishes, birds, reptiles and amphibians.

II. Live vertebrate animals shall not be used in experiments or observational studies, with the following exceptions:
   (a) Observational studies may be made of the normal living patterns of wild animals, in the free living state or in zoological parks, gardens, or aquaria.
   (b) Observational studies may be made of the living patterns of vertebrate animals in the classroom.
   (c) Observational studies on bird egg embryos are permitted. However, if normal bird embryos are to be allowed to hatch, satisfactory humane consideration shall be made for disposal of the baby birds.
   (d) Vertebrate animal cells such as red blood cells or other tissue cells, plasma or serum, or anatomical specimens, such as organs, tissues, or skeletons, may be used in experiments or observational studies.

III. No school principal, administrator or teacher shall allow any live vertebrate animal to be used in any elementary or secondary school, or in any activity associated with such school, such as science fairs, as part of a scientific experiment or procedure in which the health of the animal is interfered with, or in which pain, suffering, or distress is caused. Such experiments and procedures include, but are not limited to, surgery, anesthetization, and the inducement by any means of painful, lethal, or pathological conditions through techniques that include, but are not limited to:
   (a) Administration of drugs;
   (b) Exposure to pathogens, ionizing radiation, carcinogens, or to toxic or hazardous substances;
   (c) Deprivation; or
   (d) Electric shock or other distressing stimuli.

IV. All experiments on live vertebrate animals which are not prohibited by this section shall be carried out under the supervision of a competent science teacher who shall be responsible for ensuring that the student has the necessary comprehension for the study to be undertaken.

V. No person shall, in the presence of a pupil in any elementary or secondary school, perform any of the procedures or experiments described in paragraph III or exhibit any vertebrate animal that has been used in such manner. Dissection of any dead animal, or portions thereof, shall be confined to the presence of students engaged in the study to be promoted by the dissections.

VI. Science fair projects originating in other states that do not conform with the provisions of this section shall not be exhibited within the state.

VII. Any live animal kept in any elementary or secondary school shall be housed and cared for in a humane and safe manner and shall be the personal responsibility of the teacher or other adult supervisor of the project or study.

VIII. Ordinary agricultural procedures taught in animal husbandry courses shall not be prohibited by this section.

IX. Any person who violates this section is guilty of a misdemeanor.

Source.
1985, 54:1, eff. June 22, 1985.

Cross References.
Classification of crimes, see RSA 625:9.
Sentences, see RSA 651.

644:8-d. Maiming or Causing the Death of or Willful Interference with Police Dogs or Horses.

I. Whoever willfully tortures, beats, kicks, strikes, mutilates, injures, disables, or otherwise mistreats, or whoever willfully causes the death of a dog or horse owned or employed by or on behalf of a law enforcement agency and whoever knows that such dog or horse is owned or employed by or on behalf of a law enforcement agency shall be guilty of a class B felony.

II. Whoever willfully interferes or attempts to interfere with the lawful performance of a dog or horse owned or employed by or on behalf of a law enforcement agency and whoever knows that such dog or horse is owned or employed by or on behalf of a law enforcement agency shall be guilty of a misdemeanor.

Source.
1988, 203:1. 1994, 111:1, eff. Jan. 1, 1995. 1998, 365:1, eff. Jan. 1, 1999.

Amendments
—1998. Rewritten to the extent that a detailed comparison would be impracticable.

—1994. Added "maiming or causing the death of or" preceding "willfull" in the section catchline, designated the existing provisions of the section as par. I, and added par. II.

Cross References.
Classification of crimes, see RSA 625:9.
Sentences, see RSA 651.

644:8-e. Willful Interference With Organizations or Projects Involving Animals or With Animal Facilities.

I. Whoever willfully causes bodily injury or willfully interferes with any property, including animals or records, used by any organization or project involving animals, or with any animal facility shall be guilty of a class A misdemeanor.

II. Whoever in the course of a violation of paragraph I causes serious bodily injury to another individual or economic loss in excess of $10,000 shall be guilty of a class B felony, and may be subject to an order of restitution pursuant to RSA 651:63.

III. For the purposes of this section:

(a) "An organization or project involving animals" means:

(1) A commercial or academic enterprise that uses animals for food or fiber production, agriculture, research, education, or testing.

(2) Any lawful competitive animal event, including but not limited to conformation shows or obedience trials, field trials, agility events, hunts, sled races, or training activities.

(3) Any fair or similar event intended to advance the agricultural arts and sciences.

(b) "Animal facilities" means any vehicle, building, structure, research facility, or premises where an animal is kept, handled, housed, exhibited, bred or offered for sale.

(c) "Economic loss" means "economic loss" as defined in RSA 651:62, III.

IV. Nothing in this section shall be construed to restrict any constitutional, statutory, regulatory or common law right.

Source.
1993, 170:1, eff. May 24, 1993.

Cross References.
Classification of crimes, see RSA 625:9.

644:8-f. Transporting Dogs in Pickup Trucks.

I. No person driving a pickup truck shall transport any dog in the back of the vehicle on a public way, unless the space is enclosed or has side and tail racks to a height of at least 46 inches extending vertically from the floor, the dog is cross tethered to the vehicle, the dog is protected by a secured container or cage, or the dog is otherwise protected, in a manner which will prevent the dog from being thrown or from falling or jumping from the vehicle.

II. Notwithstanding paragraph I, this section shall not apply to the following:

(a) A dog being used by a farmer or farm employee while actually engaged in farming activities requiring the services of a dog; or

(b) A hunting dog being used at a hunting site or between hunting sites by a licensed hunter who is in possession of all applicable licenses and permits for the species being pursued during the legal season for such activity.

III. Any person who violates this section shall be guilty of a violation.

Source.
1996, 191:1, eff. Jan. 1, 1997.

644:9. Violation of Privacy.

I. A person is guilty of a class A misdemeanor if such person unlawfully and without the consent of the persons entitled to privacy therein, installs or uses:

(a) Any device for the purpose of observing, photographing, recording, amplifying, broadcasting, or in any way transmitting images or sounds of the private body parts of a person including the genitalia, buttocks, or female breasts, or a person's body underneath that person's clothing; or

(b) In any private place, any device for the purpose of observing, photographing, recording, amplifying or broadcasting, or in any way transmitting images or sounds in such place; or

(c) Outside a private place, any device for the purpose of hearing, recording, amplifying, broadcasting, observing, or in any way transmitting images, location, movement, or sounds originating in such place which would not ordinarily be audible, visible, or comprehensible outside such place.

II. As used in this section, "private place" means a place where one may reasonably expect to be safe from surveillance including public restrooms, locker rooms, the interior of one's dwelling place, or any place where a person's private body parts including genitalia, buttocks, or female breasts may be exposed.

III. A person is guilty of a class A misdemeanor if that person knowingly disseminates or causes the dissemination of any photograph or video recording of himself or herself engaging in sexual activity with another person without the express consent of the other person or persons who appear in the photograph or videotape. In this paragraph, "disseminate" and "sexual activity" shall have the same meaning as in RSA 649-A:2.

III-a. A person is guilty of a misdemeanor if, for the purpose of arousing or gratifying the person's sexual desire, he or she knowingly views another person, without that person's knowledge or consent, in a place where one would have a reasonable expectation of privacy. For purposes of this paragraph, "views" means looking at another person with the unaided eye or any device intended to improve visual acuity.

IV. A person is guilty of a misdemeanor if such person knowingly enters any residential curtilage, as defined in RSA 627:9, I, or any other private place as defined in paragraph II of this section, without

lawful authority and looks into the residential structure thereon or other private place with no legitimate purpose.

V. Paragraphs I and II shall not be construed to impair or limit any otherwise lawful activities of law enforcement personnel, nor are paragraphs I and II intended to limit employees of governmental agencies or other entities, public or private, who, in the course and scope of their employment and supported by articulable suspicion, attempt to capture any type of visual image, sound recording, or other physical impression of a person during an investigation, surveillance, or monitoring of conduct to obtain evidence of suspected illegal activity, the suspected violation of any administrative rule or regulation, a suspected fraudulent insurance claim, or any other suspected fraudulent conduct or activity involving a violation of law, or pattern of business practices adversely affecting the public health or safety.

Source.
1971, 518:1. 1995, 280:9, eff. Aug. 20, 1995. 2003, 256:1, eff. Jan. 1, 2004. 2004, 212:1, 2, eff. June 11, 2004. 2005, 264:1, eff. January 1, 2006. 2008, 334:7, eff. January 1, 2009. 2012, 76:1, eff. January 1, 2013.

Amendments
—2012. The 2012 amendment, in I(c), added "observing," "location, movement," and "visible."

—2008. The 2008 amendment added III-a.

—2005. Paragraph II: Inserted "the interior of one's dwelling place" following "locker rooms".
Paragraphs IV and V: Redesignated former paragraph IV as paragraph V and added new paragraph IV.

—2004. Paragraphs I–IV: Rewritten to the extent that a detailed comparison would be impracticable.

—2003. Paragraph III: Added.

—1995. Paragraph I: Substituted "such person" for "he" following "misdemeanor if" in the introductory paragraph.

Cross References.
Classification of crimes, see RSA 625:9.
Sentences, see RSA 651.
Wiretapping and eavesdropping generally, see RSA 570-A.

NOTES TO DECISIONS

Construction
Classroom from which money was taken was not school custodian's personal space, and thus it was not a place in which he could reasonably expect to be safe from surveillance; classroom was therefore not a "private place" within meaning of statute prohibiting violations of privacy. State v. McLellan, 144 N.H. 602, 744 A.2d 611, 1999 N.H. LEXIS 162 (1999).

644:10. Violation of Privacy of Messages.

[Repealed 1975, 385:4, eff. Aug. 6, 1975.]

Former section(s).
Former RSA 644:10, which was derived from 1971, 518:1, related to interception and disclosure of privately communicated messages.

644:11. Criminal Defamation.

I. A person is guilty of a class B misdemeanor if he purposely communicates to any person, orally or in writing, any information which he knows to be false and knows will tend to expose any other living person to public hatred, contempt or ridicule.

II. As used in this section "public" includes any professional or social group of which the victim of the defamation is a member.

Source.
1971, 518:1. 1992, 269:17, eff. July 1, 1992.

Amendments
—1992. Paragraph I: Inserted "class B" preceding "misdemeanor".

Applicability of 1992 amendment.
1992, 269:21, eff. July 1, 1992, provided that the amendment to this section by 1992, 269:17, shall apply to all offenses committed on or after July 1, 1992.

Cross References.
Classification of crimes, see RSA 625:9.
Defamation by radio or television, see RSA 507-A.
Limitation period for civil action for libel or slander, see RSA 508:4.
Sentences, see RSA 651.

NOTES TO DECISIONS

Construction
New Hampshire has clearly expressed its interest in protecting nonresidents from in-state libels as well as in safeguarding its populace from falsehoods: paragraph I of this section bears no restriction to libels of which residents are the victim, and former RSA 300:14 was amended in 1971 to specifically delete the requirement that a tort be committed against a resident of New Hampshire. Keeton v. Hustler Magazine, Inc., 465 U.S. 770, 104 S. Ct. 1473, 79 L. Ed. 2d 790, 1984 U.S. LEXIS 40 (1984).

644:12. Emergency Calls.

A person is guilty of a class B misdemeanor if he purposely refuses to yield the use of a telephone party line upon being informed that it is needed for any call to summon fire, police or medical assistance; to invoke or operate the civil defense system; or otherwise to deal with an immediate threat to life or health.

Source.
1971, 518:1. 1992, 269:18, eff. July 1, 1992.

Amendments
—1992. Inserted "class B" preceding "misdemeanor".

Applicability of 1992 amendment.
1992, 269:21, eff. July 1, 1992, provided that the amendment to this section by 1992, 269:18, shall apply to all offenses committed on or after July 1, 1992.

Cross References.
Classification of crimes, see RSA 625:9.
Sentences, see RSA 651.

644:13. Unauthorized Use of Firearms and Firecrackers.

I. A person is guilty of a violation if, within the compact part of a town or city, such person fires or discharges any cannon, gun, pistol, or other firearm, except by written permission of the chief of police or governing body.

II. For the purposes of this section, "compact part" means the territory within a town or city comprised of the following:

(a) Any nonresidential, commercial building, including, but not limited to, industrial, educational, or medical buildings, plus a perimeter 300 feet wide around all such buildings without permission of the owner.

(b) Any park, playground, or other outdoor public gathering place designated by the legislative body of the city or town.

(c) Any contiguous area containing 6 or more buildings which are used as either part-time or permanent dwellings and the spaces between them where each such building is within 300 feet of at least one of the others, plus a perimeter 300 feet wide around all the buildings in such area.

Source.
1971, 518:1. 1991, 164:1, eff. Jan. 1, 1992. 1996, 161:1, 2, eff. Aug. 2, 1996.

Amendments
—1996. Paragraph I: Substituted "such person" for "he" following "town or city" and deleted "or fires or discharges any rockets, squibs, or firecrackers" following "firearm".
Paragraph II: Rewrote subpar. (a) and added subpar. (c).

—1991. Designated the existing provisions of the section as par. I, inserted "or city" following "town" and substituted "governing body" for "selectman" following "police or" in that paragraph and added par. II.

Cross References.
Careless discharge of firearms while hunting or target practicing, see RSA 207:37-a.
Classification of crimes, see RSA 625:9.
Felonious use of firearms, see RSA 650-A.
Fireworks generally, see RSA 160-B.
Sentences, see RSA 651.

NOTES TO DECISIONS

1. Purpose
2. Definitions

1. Purpose
This section was designed to prohibit certain things done to cause disturbance and excitement and did not apply to the use of explosives in the course of business. Honnon v. Kerr, 85 N.H. 386, 159 A. 121, 1932 N.H. LEXIS 89 (1932). (Decided under prior law.)

2. Definitions
The term "compact part", as used in this section, meant such part of a city so inhabited in relation to the surrounding vicinity as to render it dangerous to the public to have firearms discharged. Cote v. Sears, Roebuck & Co., 86 N.H. 238, 166 A. 279, 1933 N.H. LEXIS 34 (1933). (Decided under prior law.)

644:14. Selling Air Rifles or Paint Ball Guns to Young Persons.

If any person shall sell, barter, rent, lend, or give an air rifle or paint ball gun to a person under the age of 18, without the written consent of the parent or guardian, as the case may be, such person shall be guilty of a violation. Air rifles and paint ball guns may be used in New Hampshire only in the home of the person under 18 under parental supervision or on an approved range under responsible adult supervision. Air rifles or paint ball guns may be possessed by a person under 18 only in his or her own home under parental supervision or on the way to or from an approved range that is under the supervision of a responsible adult such as an instructor in gun safety or marksmanship.

Source.
1971, 518:1, eff. Nov. 1, 1973. 1999, 44:1, eff. Jan. 1, 2000.

Amendments
—1999. Inserted "or paint ball guns" following "air rifles" in the section catchline and in the third sentence, "or paint ball gun" following "air rifle" in the first sentence, and "and paint ball guns" following "air rifles" in the second sentence; substituted "such person" for "he" following "case may be" in the second sentence; and inserted "or her" following "in his" in the third sentence.

Cross References.
Classification of crimes, see RSA 625:9.
Sentences, see RSA 651.

644:15. Furnishing Arms to Persons Under 16.

I. Any person who shall sell, barter, hire, lend, or give to any person under the age of 16 years any cartridges or shotshells suitable for discharging in any rifle, pistol, revolver, or shotgun shall be guilty of a violation.

II. This section shall not apply to:

(a) Fathers, mothers, grandparents, or guardians of such children.

(b) Individuals instructing such children in the safe use of firearms during a supervised firearms training program, provided the child's parent or legal guardian has granted the child permission to participate in such program.

(c) Licensed hunters accompanying such children while lawfully taking wildlife.

(d) Individuals supervising such children using firearms during a lawful shooting event or activity.

Source.
1971, 518:1, eff. Nov. 1, 1973. 2006, 73:3, eff. April 28, 2006.

Amendments
—2006. Rewritten to the extent that a detailed comparison would be impracticable.

Cross References.
Classification of crimes, see RSA 625:9.
Criminal liability of persons furnishing firearms to minors for hunting purposes, see RSA 207:2-a.
Furnishing pistol or revolver to minor, see RSA 159:12.
Sentences, see RSA 651.

644:16. Exposing Poisons.

If any person shall in any way or place purposely expose an active poison or deadly substance for the destruction of any animal, or for any other purpose except the destruction of rats or other vermin in his own building or upon his crops, he shall be guilty of a violation.

Source.
1971, 518:1, eff. Nov. 1, 1973.

Cross References.
Classification of crimes, see RSA 625:9.
Exposing poisonous substance with intent that it be eaten by a dog, see RSA 466:42-a.
Pesticides controls, see RSA 430:28 et seq.
Sentences, see RSA 651.
Taking fish by use of poisonous substance prohibited, see RSA 211:7.

644:16-a. Sale or Use of Stink Bombs.

I. In this section, "stink bomb" means any device designed for the primary purpose of giving off a noxious or offensive odor when used.

II. Any person who sells, barters, lends or gives to any person a stink bomb, and any person who uses a stink bomb in a public place shall be guilty of a violation.

Source.
1975, 294:1, eff. Aug. 6, 1975.

Cross References.
Classification of crimes, see RSA 625:9.
Sentences, see RSA 651.

644:16-b. Sale or Use of Smoke Bombs.

I. In this section, "smoke bomb" means any kind of device containing chemicals which when ignited gives off dense clouds of smoke.

II. With the exception of persons or groups, including law enforcement organizations, who use smoke bombs for training purposes or to protect property or lives, any person who sells, barters, lends or gives to any person a smoke bomb and any person who uses a smoke bomb in a public place shall be guilty of a violation.

Source.
1977, 402:1, eff. Sept. 3, 1977.

Cross References.
Classification of crimes, see RSA 625:9.
Sentences, see RSA 651.

644:17. Willful Concealment and Shoplifting.

[Repealed 2009, 209:10, eff. January 1, 2010.]

Former section(s).
Former RSA 644:17, which was derived from 1971, 518:1 and 1981, 344:1, related to willful concealment and shoplifting. For present provisions, see RSA 637:3-a.

644:17-a. Civil Damages; Willful Concealment and Shoplifting.

[Repealed 1992, 106:4, eff. Oct. 31, 1992.]

Former section(s).

Former RSA 644:17-a, which was derived from 1986, 222:5, and 1992, 269:20, related to civil damages for willful concealment or shoplifting. See now RSA 544-C.

644:18. Facilitating a Drug or Underage Alcohol House Party.

I. A person shall be guilty of a misdemeanor if such person owns or has control of the occupied structure, dwelling, or curtilage, where a drug or underage alcohol house party is held and such person knowingly commits an overt act in furtherance of the occurrence of the drug or underage alcohol house party knowing persons under the age of 21 possess or intend to consume alcoholic beverages or use controlled drugs at such drug or underage alcohol house party.

II. It is an affirmative defense to prosecution under this section if a person gives timely notice to a law enforcement official of the occurrence of the drug or underage alcohol house party or engages in other conduct designed to prevent the occurrence of such party, or takes action to terminate such party once underway.

III. In this section, "drug or underage alcohol house party" means a gathering of 5 or more people under the age of 21 at any occupied structure, dwelling, or curtilage, who are unrelated to the person who owns such occupied structure, dwelling, or curtilage or has control thereof, where at least one person under the age of 21 unlawfully possesses or consumes an alcoholic beverage or controlled drug. "Occupied structure" has the same meaning as in RSA 635:1, and "dwelling" and "curtilage" have the same meaning as in RSA 627:9.

IV. The provisions of this section shall not apply to the use of alcoholic beverages at legally protected religious observances or activities, or to those persons using a controlled drug under a physician's care where the use of the drug is consistent with the directions of a physician.

Source.

2004, 25:1, eff. April 12, 2004.

Effective Date.

2004, 162:2, amended the effective date of HB 464 (2004, 25:2) to be effective upon its passage (April 12, 2004).

644:19. Unauthorized Recording in a Motion Picture Theater.

I. In this section:

(a) "Audiovisual recording function" means the capability of a device to record or transmit a motion picture or any part thereof by means of any technology now known or later developed.

(b) "Motion picture theater" means a movie theater, screening room, or other venue that is being utilized primarily for the exhibition of a motion picture at the time of the offense.

II. Any person who knowingly operates the audiovisual recording function of any device in a motion picture theater, while a motion picture is being exhibited and without the written consent of the motion picture theater owner, commits a crime punishable as provided in paragraph III.

III. Unauthorized operation of a recording device shall be a class A misdemeanor for a first offense and a class B felony for a second or subsequent offense.

IV. This section does not prevent any lawfully authorized investigative, law enforcement, protective, or intelligence gathering employee or agent, of the local, state, or federal government or a duly authorized private investigator, from operating any audiovisual recording device in a motion picture theater, as part of lawfully authorized investigative, protective, law enforcement, or intelligence gathering activities.

V. This section does not apply to a person who operates the audiovisual recording function of a device in a retail establishment solely to demonstrate the use of that device for sales purposes.

VI. Nothing in this section prevents prosecution, instead of prosecution pursuant to this section, under any provision of law providing for a greater penalty.

Source.

2005, 70:2, eff. January 1, 2006.

644:20. Criminal Street Gang; Solicitation.

Any person who solicits, invites, recruits, encourages, or otherwise causes or attempts to cause another individual to become a member of, remain in, or actively participate in what the person knows to be a criminal street gang, as defined in RSA 651:6, I-a(c), shall be guilty of a class A felony.

Source.

2008, 379:3, eff. March 31, 2009.

CHAPTER 645

PUBLIC INDECENCY

SECTION
645:1.   Indecent Exposure and Lewdness.
645:1-a.   Public Urination or Defecation.
645:2.   Prostitution and Related Offenses.
645:3.   Adultery.

645:1. Indecent Exposure and Lewdness.

I. A person is guilty of a misdemeanor if such person fornicates, exposes his or her genitals, or performs any other act of gross lewdness under circumstances which he or she should know will likely cause affront or alarm.

II. A person is guilty of a class B felony if:

(a) Such person purposely performs any act of sexual penetration or sexual contact on himself or herself or another in the presence of a child who is less than 16 years of age.

(b) Such person purposely transmits to a child who is less than 16 years of age, or an individual whom the actor reasonably believes is a child who is less than 16 years of age, an image of himself or herself fornicating, exposing his or her genitals, or performing any other act of gross lewdness.

(c) Having previously been convicted of an offense under paragraph I, or of an offense that includes the same conduct under any other jurisdiction, the person subsequently commits an offense under paragraph I.

III. A person shall be guilty of a class A felony if having previously been convicted of 2 or more offenses under paragraph II, or a reasonably equivalent statute in another state, the person subsequently commits an offense under this section.

Source.
1971, 518:1. 1992, 254:10. 1993, 297:1, eff. Jan. 1, 1994. 1999, 321:1, eff. Jan. 1, 2000. 2008, 323:5, eff. January 1, 2009.

Amendments
—2008. The 2008 amendment rewrote the section to the extent that a detailed comparison would be impracticable.

—1999. Rewritten to the extent that a detailed comparison would be impracticable.

—1993. Rewritten to the extent that a detailed comparison would be impracticable.

—1992. Rewritten to the extent that a detailed comparison would be impracticable.

Cross References.
Classification of crimes, see RSA 625:9.
Registration of criminal offenders, see RSA 651-B.
Sentences, see RSA 651.

NOTES TO DECISIONS

1. Sufficient evidence
2. Mens rea

1. Sufficient evidence
Evidence was sufficient to support a conviction where a witness testified on more than one occasion that she saw the defendant's hands "on his penis," as, based on this testimony, a fair inference could be drawn that she saw his genitals. State v. Devaney, 139 N.H. 473, 657 A.2d 832, 1995 N.H. LEXIS 37 (1995).

2. Mens rea
Trial court erred in instructing jury that "recklessly" was the required mens rea for guilt under this section; proper standard was "knowingly," and defendant's conviction was therefore reversed and the matter remanded. State v. Bergen, 141 N.H. 61, 677 A.2d 145, 1996 N.H. LEXIS 47 (1996).

Cited:
Cited in In re Turgeon, 140 N.H. 52, 663 A.2d 82, 1995 N.H. LEXIS 98 (1995).

645:1-a. Public Urination or Defecation.

A person is guilty of a violation if such person urinates or defecates in a public place, other than a public restroom, under circumstances where the person knew or should have known would likely cause affront or alarm to another.

Source.
2008, 70:1, eff. January 1, 2009.

645:2. Prostitution and Related Offenses.

I. A person is guilty of a misdemeanor if the person:

(a) Solicits, agrees to perform, or engages in sexual contact as defined in RSA 632-A:1, IV or sexual penetration as defined in RSA 632-A:1, V, in return for consideration; or

(b) Induces or otherwise purposely causes another to violate subparagraph (a); or

(c) Transports another into or within this state with the purpose of promoting or facilitating such other in engaging in conduct in violation of subparagraph (a); or

(d) Not being a legal dependent incapable of self support, knowingly is supported in whole or in part by the proceeds of violation of subparagraph (a); or

(e) Knowingly permits a place under such person's control to be used for violation of subparagraph (a); or

(f) Pays, agrees to pay, or offers to pay another person to engage in sexual contact as defined in RSA 632-A:1, IV or sexual penetration as defined in RSA 632-A:1, V, with the payor or with another person.

II. A person is guilty of a class B felony if such person violates the provisions of subparagraphs (b), (c), (d), or (e) of paragraph I and the violation:

(a) Involves another person who is under the age of 18; or

(b) Involved compelling another person by force or intimidation.

III. A person is guilty under this section regardless of the sex of the persons involved.

IV. It shall be an affirmative defense to a charge under subparagraph I(a) that the defendant engaged in the conduct because he or she was the victim of trafficking in persons, as defined in RSA 633:7.

Source.
1971, 518:1. 1977, 311:1. 1985, 228:6. 1991, 82:1. 1993, 168:1, 2, eff. June 23, 1993. 1995, 229:1–3, eff. Jan. 1, 1996. 2009, 211:2, eff. January 1, 2010.

Amendments
—2009. The 2009 amendment added IV.

—1995. Paragraph I: Substituted "the person" for "he" following "misdemeanor if" in the introductory clause, inserted "agrees to perform" following "solicits" in subpar. (a), substituted "such person's" for "his" following "place under" in subpar. (e).
Paragraph II: Substituted "such person" for "he" following "felony if" in the introductory paragraph.

—1993. Paragraph I(a): Inserted "sexual contact as defined in RSA 632-A:1, IV or" following "engages in".
Paragraph I(f): Substituted "contact as defined in RSA 632-A:1, IV or sexual penetration as defined in RSA 632-A:1, V" for "conduct" following "with the payor".

—1991. Paragraph I: Made a minor stylistic change at the end of subpar. (e) and added subpar. (f).

—1985. Rewritten to the extent that a detailed comparison would be impracticable.

—1977. Paragraph I(a): Rewritten to the extent that a detailed comparison would be impracticable.

Cross References.

Classification of crimes, see RSA 625:9.

Registration of criminal offenders, see RSA 651-B.

Sentences, see RSA 651.

NOTES TO DECISIONS

1. Constitutionality
2. Construction
3. Corporate liability

1. Constitutionality

RSA 645:2, the prostitution statute, is not substantially overbroad under N.H. Const. pt. I, art. 22 and the First and Fourteenth Amendments, as the possibility that it can be applied in an unconstitutional manner is exceedingly slight and as it does not target speech; thus, any applications of the statute that infringe upon protected conduct can be remedied on a case-by-case basis. Thus, defendant, who had offered to pay two people to have sexual intercourse while he watched, could be prosecuted under it. State v. Theriault, 157 N.H. 215, 949 A.2d 678, 2008 N.H. LEXIS 56 (2008).

RSA 645:2, I(f) was overbroad under N.H. Const. pt. I, art. 22 when applied to the specific facts of the case, where defendant offered to pay a couple for engaging in sexual intercourse while he videotaped them. The only evidence in the record as to defendant's intent was that he intended to make pornography, which as a general rule could be banned only if obscene; the State had not charged defendant with offering to pay the couple to engage in sexual contact, which under RSA 632-A:1, IV would have required the State to prove that he acted for the purpose of sexual arousal or gratification and thus engaged in conduct that was not constitutionally protected. State v. Theriault, 158 N.H. 123, 960 A.2d 687, 2008 N.H. LEXIS 138 (2008).

2. Construction

Subparagraph I(b) of this section does not require proof that the defendant received consideration. State v. Steer, 128 N.H. 490, 517 A.2d 797, 1986 N.H. LEXIS 334 (1986).

The factual allegations in indictments on charges of causing juveniles to engage in prostitution in violation of subparagraph I(b) of this section did not require that the state prove at trial that the defendant received consideration for the acts of the persons involved in the prostitution since immaterial or superfluous allegations need not be proven at trial. State v. Steer, 128 N.H. 490, 517 A.2d 797, 1986 N.H. LEXIS 334 (1986).

This section proscribes neither patronizing a prostitute nor the conduct of a would-be patron who desires to give money in return for receiving sexual services. State v. Chandonnet, 124 N.H. 778, 474 A.2d 578, 1984 N.H. LEXIS 331 (1984).

3. Corporate liability

Evidence was sufficient to show that a fraternity knowingly permitted a place under its control to be used for prostitution where the fraternity hired strippers for a party, guests were told that if they paid more money the dancers would do more, on more than one occasion guests were led to a mattress that was brought into the room by the fraternity brothers to perform oral sex in exchange for money, at least one guest performed oral sex on the dancer for "quite a while," and the fraternity president testified that he "was very well in control" of the party. State v. Zeta Chi Fraternity, 142 N.H. 16, 696 A.2d 530, 1997 N.H. LEXIS 50 (1997), cert. denied, Zeta Chi Fraternity v. New Hampshire, 522 U.S. 995, 118 S. Ct. 558, 139 L. Ed. 2d 400, 1997, 1997 U.S. LEXIS 7080 (1997).

645:3. Adultery.

A person is guilty of a class B misdemeanor if, being a married person, he engages in sexual intercourse with another not his spouse or, being unmarried, engages in sexual intercourse with another known by him to be married.

Source.

1971, 518:1. 1992, 269:19, eff. July 1, 1992.

Amendments

—1992. Inserted "class B" preceding "misdemeanor".

Applicability of 1992 amendment.

1992, 269:21, eff. July 1, 1992, provided that the amendment to this section by 1992, 269:19, shall apply to all offenses committed on or after July 1, 1992.

Cross References.

Classification of crimes, see RSA 625:9.

Sentences, see RSA 651.

NOTES TO DECISIONS

Homosexual relationships

Upon review pursuant to N.H. Sup. Ct. 8, it was determined that the trial court erred in denying a wife's female lover's motion to dismiss a husband's divorce action claiming adultery pursuant to RSA 458:7, II as a ground for divorce; under both RSA 458:7, II and the New Hampshire criminal adultery statute, RSA 654:3, sexual intercourse was required for a finding of adultery, and intercourse could only occur between a man and a woman, and therefore homosexual relationships were not defined as adultery. In re Blanchflower, 150 N.H. 226, 834 A.2d 1010, 2003 N.H. LEXIS 167 (2003).

CHAPTER 646

OFFENSES AGAINST THE FLAG

[Repealed 1990, 135:3, eff. April 19, 1990.]

Former section(s).

Former RSA 646, comprising RSA 646:1 and 646:2, which was derived from 1971, 518:1, related to offenses against the flag. See now RSA 646-A.

CHAPTER 646-A

DESECRATION OF THE FLAG

SECTION

646-A:1. Definitions.

646-A:2. Desecration Prohibited.

646-A:3. Destruction of a Worn Flag of the United States Allowed.

646-A:4. Penalties.

646-A:1. Definitions.

In this chapter:

I. "Desecration" means the act of diverting from a sacred purpose or use to which a flag has been devoted by another individual or group of individuals. The act of desecration shall include burning, defacing, mutilating, destroying or trampling upon the flag.

II. "Flag of the United States" means any flag that is the commonly accepted "stars and stripes" or that flag described in Executive Order #10834 of President Eisenhower, August 25, 1959, and succeeding attachments to such Executive Order.

III. "Properly displayed" means any flag of the United States attached to a public or private building by means of a pole or any other attachment which renders the flag of the United States to be displayed according to commonly accepted flag etiquette; any flag of the United States displayed in a cemetery to mark a memorial or veteran's gravesite; any flag of the United States displayed for a certain period of time to mark a national holiday; any flag of the United States which is historic and is maintained in a display case for public viewing; or any flag of the United States displayed in accordance with Public Law 623, approved June 22, 1942 and amendments thereto.

Source.
1990, 135:2, eff. April 19, 1990.

References in text.
Executive Order #10834, referred to in par. II, is set out in a note under 4 U.S.C.S. § 1.
Public Law 623, approved June 22, 1942, referred to in par. III, is classified to 4 U.S.C.S. §§ 4–10 and 36 U.S.C.S. § 301.

646-A:2. Desecration Prohibited.

I. It shall be unlawful to knowingly desecrate a flag of the United States while it is properly displayed.
II. It shall be unlawful to knowingly desecrate a flag of the United States while it is the property of another.

Source.
1990, 135:2, eff. April 19, 1990.

646-A:3. Destruction of a Worn Flag of the United States Allowed.

When the flag of the United States is worn or frayed or torn or in such a condition that it is no longer a fitting emblem of the United States, it should be destroyed in a dignified manner, preferably by burning privately.

Source.
1990, 135:2, eff. April 19, 1990.

646-A:4. Penalties.

Whoever knowingly casts contempt upon the flag of the United States by desecrating the flag when it is properly displayed or is the property of another shall be guilty of a misdemeanor.

Source.
1990, 135:2, eff. April 19, 1990.

Cross References.
Classification of crimes, see RSA 625:9.
Sentences, see RSA 651.

CHAPTER 647

GAMBLING OFFENSES

SECTION
647:1.   Lotteries.
647:2.   Gambling.

NOTES TO DECISIONS

Cited:
Cited in State v. Cutting, 114 N.H. 200, 317 A.2d 553, 1974 N.H. LEXIS 237 (1974).

647:1. Lotteries.

A person is guilty of a misdemeanor if he knowingly and unlawfully:
I. Conducts a lottery or disposes or offers to dispose of property in any way whereby the payment for such property is, in whole or in part, induced by the hope of gain by luck or chance; or
II. Sells, offers for sale, or possesses for the purpose of sale, any lottery ticket or other thing which is evidence that the purchaser will be entitled to a share or chance in a lottery or deposits for mailing any such ticket or thing, or notice of the drawing of a lottery; or
III. Publishes or deposits for mailing information as to the location or identity of the person where or from whom a ticket or other thing described in paragraph II may be obtained.
IV. "Unlawfully" means not specifically authorized by law.

Source.
1971, 518:1, eff. Nov. 1, 1973.

Cross References.
Classification of crimes, see RSA 625:9.
Complaint or indictment, see RSA 601:9.
Sentences, see RSA 651.

NOTES TO DECISIONS

1. Consideration
2. Separate wagers
3. Gifts
4. Buying lottery ticket for another

1. Consideration
To constitute a lottery a consideration of value must be given for the opportunity to participate therein. State v. Eames, 87 N.H. 477, 183 A. 590, 1936 N.H. LEXIS 83 (1936). (Decided under prior law.)

2. Separate wagers
In making a lottery by the acceptance of separate wagers from the same person on the same day on the results of different horse races, each wager accepted constituted a separate lottery and was a separate and distinct offense. State v. Donovan, 97 N.H. 190, 84 A.2d 405, 1951 N.H. LEXIS 49 (1951). (Decided under prior law.)

3. Gifts

This section did not prohibit the making of a gift the recipient of which was selected by chance. State v. Eames, 87 N.H. 477, 183 A. 590, 1936 N.H. LEXIS 83 (1936). (Decided under prior law.)

4. Buying lottery ticket for another

Conviction for violating this section by selling a Massachusetts megabucks ticket to another person was vacated and complaint dismissed; simply buying a lottery ticket for another is not a crime under this section, whose overall purpose is to prohibit private, for-profit lotteries. State v. Powell, 132 N.H. 562, 567 A.2d 568, 1989 N.H. LEXIS 134 (1989).

Cited:

Cited in Boys' Club v. Attorney Gen., 122 N.H. 325, 444 A.2d 541, 1982 N.H. LEXIS 351 (1982).

647:2. Gambling.

I. A person is guilty of a misdemeanor if such person knowingly and unlawfully:

(a) Permits gambling in any place under the person's control.

(b) Gambles, or loans money or any thing of value for the purpose of aiding another to gamble.

(c) Possesses a gambling machine.

I-a. (a) A person is guilty of a misdemeanor if such person conducts, finances, manages, supervises, directs, or owns all or part of a business and such person knowingly and unlawfully permits gambling on the premises of the business.

(b) A person is guilty of a class B felony if such person conducts, finances, manages, supervises, directs, or owns all or part of a business and such person knowingly and unlawfully conducts, finances, manages, supervises, or directs any gambling activity on the business premises which does any of the following:

(1) Has had gross revenue of $2,000 in any single day.

(2) Has been or remains in substantially continuous operation for a period in excess of 10 days.

(3) Accepts wagers exceeding $5,000 during any 30 day period on future contingent events.

I-b. A person is guilty of a class B felony if a person knowingly and unlawfully promotes gambling on a gambling machine. If the offense continues over consecutive days, the person shall be charged with a single continuing offense. Notwithstanding RSA 651:2, IV, any person convicted under this paragraph shall be fined not less than $5,000 per day for each gambling machine used or intended for use.

II. For purposes of this section:

(a) "Antique gambling machine" means any device or equipment at least 25 years old which is in the possession of a collector and which is not maintained or operated for gambling purposes.

(b) "Collector" means a person who for nostalgic reasons, monetary investment, or personal interest acquires antique gambling machines as defined in subparagraph (a) for personal display or retention.

(c) "Family entertainment center" means a place of business having at least 50 games or devices designed and manufactured only for bona fide amusement purposes on premises which are operated for the entertainment of the general public and tourists as a bona fide entertainment facility and not having more than 15 percent of the total games or machines being redemption slot machines or redemption poker machines.

(d) "Gambling" means to risk something of value upon a future contingent event not under one's control or influence, upon an agreement or understanding that something of value will be received in the event of a certain outcome. For the purposes of this subparagraph, the phrase "something of value" shall include a sweepstakes ticket or other item obtained in conjunction with the purchase of goods or services that entitles the holder to a share or chance in a sweepstakes where, but for the opportunity to enter the sweepstakes, the value of purchased goods or services is insufficient to justify the purchase or the inducement to purchase the goods or services is the opportunity to play on a gambling machine.

(e) "Gambling machine" means any device or equipment which is capable of being used to play sweepstakes or games of chance and which discharges money, or anything that may be exchanged for money, cash equivalent, debit card, merchandise credit card, or opportunities to enter sweepstakes or play games of chance, or displays any symbol entitling a person to receive such a prize.

(f) "Redemption slot machine" or "redemption poker machine" means any device or equipment which operates by means of the insertion of a coin or token and which may entitle the person playing or operating the game or machine the opportunity of additional chances or free plays or to receive points or coupons which may be exchanged for merchandise only, excluding cash and alcoholic beverages, provided the value for such points or coupons does not exceed 2½ cents for each credit on the game or machine.

(g) "Unlawfully" means not specifically authorized by law or not solely for amusement, without stake or possibility of gain or loss.

(h) "Sweepstakes" means any game, advertising scheme or plan, or other promotion which, with or without payment of any consideration, a person may enter to win or become eligible to receive any prize, the determination of which is based upon chance. For purposes of this chapter, the term includes only those sweepstakes that an entrant can enter, play or otherwise interact with using a gambling machine furnished by the sweepstakes operator or an affiliate or person under contract with the operator, in an establishment controlled by, affiliated with, or contracting with the operator.

III. All implements, equipment, and apparatus used in violation of this section shall be forfeited.

IV. An antique gambling machine in the possession of a collector and which is not maintained or operated for gambling purposes shall not be subject to the provisions of this section.

V. This section shall not apply to:

(a) Dispenser devices approved by the racing and charitable gaming commission which are located at the regular meeting place of, or at a facility owned, leased, or utilized by, a charitable organization licensed under RSA 287-E:20.

(b) A family entertainment center having redemption slot machines or redemption poker machines.

(c) Cruise ships which are equipped with gambling machines whose primary purpose is touring. Any such cruise ship shall be allowed to temporarily enter New Hampshire coastal waters and ports for up to 48 hours, provided that all gambling machines on board are not in use or capable of being used while in New Hampshire coastal waters and ports. For the purposes of this paragraph "cruise ship" means any vessel which is capable of providing overnight accommodations for 500 or more people.

VI. Any violation of this chapter may be enjoined by the superior court, upon petition of the attorney general, county attorney, or the police chief within the jurisdiction in which the violation is alleged to have occurred.

Source.
1971, 518:1. 1978, 23:1, 2. 1985, 124:1. 1987, 114:2. 1995, 75:3, eff. May 9, 1995; 300:1, eff. Aug. 20, 1995. 1999, 277:1, eff. Jan. 1, 2000. 2004, 97:8, eff. July 10, 2004; 257:14, eff. Jan. 1, 2005. 2008, 25:1, eff. July 11, 2008. 2012, 256:7-10, eff. June 18, 2012.

Amendments
—2012. The 2012 amendment added I-b, II(h), and VI; added the second sentence of II(d); in II(e), substituted "play sweepstakes or games of chance and which discharges" for "which discharge," "cash equivalent, debit card, merchandise credit card, or opportunities to enter sweepstakes or play games of chance, or displays" for "or to display," and "such a prize" for "money"; and made a stylistic change.

—2008. The 2008 amendment substituted "racing and charitable gaming commission" for "pari-mutuel commission" in V(a).

—2004. Paragraph V(a): Ch. 97 substituted "lottery commission" for "sweepstakes commission".
Ch. 257 substituted "pari-mutuel commission" for "lottery commission".

—1999. Paragraph I-a: Added.

—1995. Chapter 43 rewrote section to the extent that a detailed comparison would be impracticable.
Chapter 300 amended par. V generally and deleted par. VI.

—1987. Paragraph VII: Added.

—1985. Paragraph IV: Substituted "at least 25 years old" for "manufactured prior to 1941" following "equipment" in the third sentence.

—1978. Paragraph IV: Added the third sentence.
Paragraph VI: Added.

Cross References.
Classification of crimes, see RSA 625:9.
Sentences, see RSA 651.

NOTES TO DECISIONS

1. Control
2. Intent
3. Complaint
4. Evidence
5. Horse races
6. Wagering
7. Sentencing
8. Forfeiture

1. Control
Defendant could be found in control of premises resorted to for gambling where he was an incorporator and the secretary-treasurer of club renting the premises from him, kept an extension of his private telephone in the club, and a witness testified he had placed bets with defendant, who once refused payment on a win in the numbers game, and that defendant was present when another man accepted bets and a police officer testified that during a raid on the club a telephone caller asked for defendant and placed a bet with the officer upon being told defendant was not present. State v. George, 113 N.H. 703, 313 A.2d 401, 1973 N.H. LEXIS 356 (1973). (Decided under prior law.)

2. Intent
It was not necessary to establish an offense under this section that both the person who placed the bet and the one who received it had a mutual criminal intent; it was sufficient that the person receiving the bet accepted it either expressly or constructively with intention of violating the section. State v. Del Bianco, 96 N.H. 436, 78 A.2d 519, 1951 N.H. LEXIS 181 (1951). (Decided under prior law.)

3. Complaint
Where party was charged with accepting five dollar bill from designated person and entering into an agreement with him to bet four dollars for him on outcome of horse race at state park, the complaint was sufficient to charge a violation of this section. State v. Kachadoorian, 104 N.H. 29, 177 A.2d 398, 1962 N.H. LEXIS 8 (1962). (Decided under prior law.)

4. Evidence
At trial for permitting gambling on corporation's premises, evidence was sufficient to find guilt beyond a reasonable doubt where video poker machines located on premises were activated by the insertion of money, and where employees kept log of points earned by players and paid players according to number of points logged if players returned to the premises on a subsequent day. State v. Pinardville Athletic Club, 134 N.H. 462, 594 A.2d 1284, 1991 N.H. LEXIS 96 (1991).

In a complaint charging the respondent with accepting an illegal bet on a horse race to be run at an out-of-state track it was not essential that the state prove that the race was actually run. State v. Groulx, 106 N.H. 44, 203 A.2d 641, 1964 N.H. LEXIS 34 (1964). (Decided under prior law.)

Evidence showing that party bet money for another at a pari-mutuel window of park where betting was permitted by RSA 284 did not establish violation of this section. State v. Kachadoorian, 104 N.H. 29, 177 A.2d 398, 1962 N.H. LEXIS 8 (1962). (Decided under prior law.)

5. Horse races
A bet or wager on a horse race was a gambling contract which was prohibited by this section, except as pari-mutuel horse racing and gambling was permitted and regulated by other statutes. State v. Del Bianco, 96 N.H. 436, 78 A.2d 519, 1951 N.H. LEXIS 181 (1951). (Decided under prior law.)

6. Wagering
A wager is not of itself an offense against the criminal law, and is not gambling, but a wager on a game or sport is gambling. In re Opinion of Justices, 73 N.H. 625, 63 A. 505, 1906 N.H. LEXIS 46 (1906). (Decided under prior law.)

7. Sentencing

Trial court's judgment imposing a fine of $160,000 on defendant who was convicted of 80 counts of gambling was not excessive or disproportionate to the offenses. State v. Enderson, 148 N.H. 252, 804 A.2d 448, 2002 N.H. LEXIS 116 (2002).

8. Forfeiture

Dismissal by the district court of a criminal charge at the conclusion of the state's case did not operate to collaterally estop the state from prosecuting the subsequent forfeiture proceeding arising out of the same conduct, and the state was not, therefore, precluded from pursuing its libel for decree of forfeiture. In re Three Video Poker Machs., 129 N.H. 416, 529 A.2d 905, 1987 N.H. LEXIS 211 (1987).

Cited:

Cited in State v. Rowman, 116 N.H. 41, 352 A.2d 737, 1976 N.H. LEXIS 259 (1976); State v. Beland, 138 N.H. 735, 645 A.2d 79, 1994 N.H. LEXIS 96 (1994).

CHAPTER 648

SUBVERSIVE ACTIVITIES

[Repealed 1994, 29:1, eff. June 21, 1994.]

Former section(s).

Former RSA 648, comprising RSA 648:1–648:21, which was derived from 1971, 518:1 and 1986, 12:4, I, related to subversive activities.

NOTES TO DECISIONS

1. Constitutionality
2. Constitutional rights
3. Federal legislation
4. Investigation
5. Report

1. Constitutionality

The provisions of this section which contained definitions of "subversive organization," "foreign subversive organization," and "subversive person," and the provisions of section 10 of this chapter which required the signing of an oath and provided penalties were unduly vague and violated the due process requirement of the United States Constitution. Opinion of Justices, 108 N.H. 62, 228 A.2d 165, 1967 N.H. LEXIS 121 (1967). (Decided under prior law.)

2. Constitutional rights

Where 1955 report on subversive activities in New Hampshire dealt primarily with "world-wide communism" and federal government, and there was no showing of present danger of sedition against the state itself, the only area to which the authority of the state extended, defendant was justified in refusing to answer questions regarding his Communist affiliations prior to the effective date of this chapter, since the state's interest was too remote and conjectural to override the guarantee of the First Amendment. Maynard v. De Gregory, 106 N.H. 262, 209 A.2d 712, 1965 N.H. LEXIS 143 (1965). (Decided under prior law.)

3. Federal legislation

The enactment by Congress of legislation which defined and penalized sedition and subversive activities against the government of the United States, the states or any of their subdivisions did not preclude state legislation on the same subject matter. Nelson v. Wyman, 99 N.H. 33, 105 A.2d 756, 1954 N.H. LEXIS 10 (1954). (Decided under prior law.)

4. Investigation

This section did not require that there be a violation of law before legislative investigation could be set in motion, but only required that there be reasonable and reliable information "relating" to violations of provisions of subversive activities act. Wyman v. De Gregory, 103 N.H. 214, 169 A.2d 1, 1961 N.H. LEXIS 18 (1961),

aff'd, De Gregory v. Attorney Gen., 368 U.S. 19, 82 S. Ct. 137, 7 L. Ed. 2d 86, 1961 U.S. LEXIS 295 (1961), aff'd, Tinsley v. Richmond, 368 U.S. 18, 82 S. Ct. 137, 7 L. Ed. 2d 86, 1961 U.S. LEXIS 293 (1961). (Decided under prior law.)

5. Report

Provision that results of investigation shall be reported to legislature together with attorney general's "recommendations," if any, for legislation, clearly indicated that legislature demanded a report as to whether further legislation in field of subversive activities was required. Wyman v. De Gregory, 103 N.H. 214, 169 A.2d 1, 1961 N.H. LEXIS 18 (1961), aff'd, De Gregory v. Attorney Gen., 368 U.S. 19, 82 S. Ct. 137, 7 L. Ed. 2d 86, 1961 U.S. LEXIS 295 (1961), aff'd, Tinsley v. Richmond, 368 U.S. 18, 82 S. Ct. 137, 7 L. Ed. 2d 86, 1961 U.S. LEXIS 293 (1961). (Decided under prior law.)

CHAPTER 649

SABOTAGE PREVENTION

SECTION
649:1.   Definitions.
649:2.   Intentional Injury to or Interference with Property.
649:3.   Intentionally Defective Workmanship.
649:4.   Attempts.
649:5.   Conspirators.
649:6.   Witnesses' Privileges.
649:7.   Unlawful Entry on Property.
649:8.   Questioning and Detaining Suspected Persons.
649:9.   Closing and Restricting Use of Highway.
649:10.   Rights of Labor.
649:11.   Relation to Other Statutes.
649:12.   When in Force.

649:1. Definitions.

As used in this chapter:

I. "Highway" includes any private or public street, way or other place used for travel to or from property.

II. "Highway commissioner" means the commissioner of the department of transportation, the city council of a city or board of selectmen of a town having authority under then existing law to discontinue the use of the highway which it is desired to restrict or close to public use and travel.

III. "Public utility" includes any pipeline, gas, electric, heat, water, oil, sewer, telephone, telegraph, radio, railway, railroad, airplane, transportation, communication or other system, by whomsoever owned or operated for public use.

Source.

1971, 518:1, eff. Nov. 1, 1973.

Revision note.

In par. II, substituted "commissioner of the department of transportation" for "state highway commissioner" pursuant to 1985, 402:6.

649:2. Intentional Injury to or Interference with Property.

Whoever intentionally destroys, impairs, injures, interferes or tampers with real or personal property with reasonable grounds to believe that such act will hinder, delay or interfere with the preparation of the United States or of any of the states for defense or for war, or with the prosecution of war by the United

States, or by any country with which the United States shall then maintain friendly relations, shall be guilty of a class A felony. Provided, if such person so acts with the intent to hinder, delay or interfere with the preparation of the United States or of any of the states for defense or for war, or with the prosecution of war by the United States or by any country with which the United States shall then maintain friendly relations, the minimum punishment shall be imprisonment for not less than one year.

Source.
1971, 518:1, eff. Nov. 1, 1973.

Cross References.
Classification of crimes, see RSA 625:9.
Sentences, see RSA 651.

649:3. Intentionally Defective Workmanship.

Whoever intentionally makes or causes to be made or omits to note on inspection any defect in any article or thing with reasonable grounds to believe that such article or thing is intended to be used in connection with the preparation of the United States or any of the states for defense or for war, or for the prosecution of war by the United States, or by any country with which the United States shall then maintain friendly relations, or that such article or thing is one of a number of similar articles or things, some of which are intended so to be used, shall be guilty of a class A felony. Provided, if such person so acts or so fails to act with the intent to hinder, delay or interfere with the preparation of the United States or of any of the states for defense or for war, or with the prosecution of war by the United States or by any country with which the United States shall then maintain friendly relations, the minimum punishment shall be imprisonment for not less than one year.

Source.
1971, 518:1, eff. Nov. 1, 1973.

Cross References.
Classification of crimes, see RSA 625:9.
Sentences, see RSA 651.

649:4. Attempts.

Whoever attempts to commit any of the crimes defined by this chapter shall be liable to ½ the punishment prescribed for the completed crime. In addition to the acts which constitute an attempt to commit a crime under the law of this state, the solicitation or incitement of another to commit any of the crimes defined by this chapter not followed by the commission of the crime, the collection or assemblage of any materials with the intent that the same are to be used then or at a later time in the commission of such crime, or the entry, with or without permission, of a building, enclosure or other premises of another with the intent to commit any

such crime therein or thereon shall constitute an attempt to commit such crime.

Source.
1971, 518:1, eff. Nov. 1, 1973.

Cross References.
Attempt generally, see RSA 629:1.

649:5. Conspirators.

If 2 or more persons conspire to commit any crime defined by this chapter, each of such persons is guilty of conspiracy and subject to the same punishment as if he had committed the crime which he conspired to commit, whether or not any act be done in furtherance of the conspiracy. It shall not constitute any defense or ground of suspension of judgment, sentence or punishment on behalf of any person prosecuted under this section, that any of his fellow conspirators has been acquitted, has not been arrested or convicted, is not amenable to justice or has been pardoned or otherwise discharged before or after conviction.

Source.
1971, 518:1, eff. Nov. 1, 1973.

Cross References.
Conspiracy generally, see RSA 629:3.

RESEARCH REFERENCES

New Hampshire Court Rules Annotated.
Statements of coconspirators not hearsay, see Rule 801(d)(2)(E), Rules of Evidence, New Hampshire Court Rules Annotated.

649:6. Witnesses' Privileges.

No person shall be excused from attending and testifying, or producing any books, papers, or other documents before any court, magistrate, referee or grand jury upon any investigation, proceeding or trial, for or relating to or concerned with a violation of any section of this chapter or attempt to commit such violation, upon the ground or for the reason that the testimony or evidence, documentary or otherwise, required of him by the state may tend to convict him of a crime or to subject him to a penalty or forfeiture; but no person shall be prosecuted or subjected to any penalty or forfeiture for or on account of any transaction, matter or thing concerning which he may so testify or produce evidence, documentary or otherwise, and no testimony so given or produced shall be received against him, upon any criminal investigation, proceeding or trial, except upon a prosecution for perjury or contempt of court based upon the giving or producing of such testimony.

Source.
1971, 518:1, eff. Nov. 1, 1973.

Cross References.
Perjury, see RSA 641:1.

Privilege against self-incrimination, see United States Constitution, Amendment V and New Hampshire Constitution, Part 1, Article 15.

649:7. Unlawful Entry on Property.

Any individual, partnership, association, corporation, municipal corporation or state or any political subdivision thereof engaged in, or preparing to engage in, the manufacture, transportation or storage of any product to be used in the preparation of the United States or of any of the states for defense or for war or in the prosecution of war by the United States, or by any country with which the United States shall then maintain friendly relations, or the manufacture, transportation, distribution or storage of gas, oil, coal, electricity or water, or any of said natural or artificial persons operating any public utility, whose property, except where it fronts on water or where there are entrances for railway cars, vehicles, persons or things, is surrounded by a fence or wall, or a fence or wall and buildings, may post around his or its property at each gate, entrance, dock or railway entrance and every 100 feet of water front a sign reading "No Entry Without Permission." Whoever without permission of such owner shall wilfully enter upon premises so posted shall be guilty of a misdemeanor.

Source.
1971, 518:1, eff. Nov. 1, 1973.

Cross References.
Classification of crimes, see RSA 625:9.
Sentences, see RSA 651.

649:8. Questioning and Detaining Suspected Persons.

Any peace officer or any person employed as watchman, guard, or in a supervisory capacity on premises posted as provided in RSA 649:7 may stop any person found on any premises to which entry without permission is forbidden by said section and may detain him for the purpose of demanding, and may demand, of him his name, address and business in such place. If said peace officer or employee has reason to believe from the answers of the person so interrogated that such person has no right to be in such place, said peace officer shall forthwith release such person or he may arrest such person without a warrant on the charge of violating the provisions of RSA 649:7; and said employee shall forthwith release such person or turn him over to a peace officer, who may arrest him without a warrant on the charge of violating the provisions of said section.

Source.
1971, 518:1, eff. Nov. 1, 1973.

649:9. Closing and Restricting Use of Highway.

Any individual, partnership, association, corporation, municipal corporation or state or any political subdivision thereof engaged in or preparing to engage in the manufacture, transportation or storage of any product to be used in the preparation of the United States or any of the states for defense or for war or in the prosecution of war by the United States, or by any country with which the United States shall then maintain friendly relations, or in the manufacture, transportation, distribution or storage of gas, oil, coal, electricity or water, or any of said natural or artificial persons operating any public utility, who has property so used which he or it believes will be endangered if public use and travel is not restricted or prohibited on one or more highways or parts thereof upon which such property abuts, may petition the appropriate highway commissioner to close one or more of said highways or parts thereof to public use and travel or to restrict by order the use and travel upon one or more of said highways or parts thereof. Upon receipt of such petition, the highway commissioner shall set a day for hearing and give notice thereof by publication in a newspaper having general circulation in the city, town or county in which such property is located, such notice to be at least 7 days prior to the date set for hearing. If after hearing the highway commissioner determines that the public safety and the safety of the property of the petitioner so require, they shall by suitable order close to public use and travel or reasonably restrict the use of and travel upon one or more of said highways or parts thereof, provided, the highway commissioner may issue written permits to travel over the highways so closed or restricted to responsible and reputable persons for such term, under such conditions and in such form as said commissioner may prescribe. Appropriate notices in letters at least 3 inches high shall be posted conspicuously at each end of any highway so closed or restricted by such order. The highway commissioner may at any time revoke or modify any order so made. Whoever violates any order made under this section shall be guilty of a misdemeanor.

Source.
1971, 518:1, eff. Nov. 1, 1973.

649:10. Rights of Labor.

Nothing in this chapter shall be construed to impair, curtail or destroy the rights of employees and their representatives to self-organization, to form, join, or assist labor organizations, to bargain collectively through representatives of their own choosing, and to engage in concerted activities, for the purpose of collective bargaining or other mutual aid or protection nor to make strikes illegal.

Source.
1971, 518:1, eff. Nov. 1, 1973.

649:11. Relation to Other Statutes.

All acts and parts of acts inconsistent with this chapter are hereby suspended in their application to any proceedings hereunder. If conduct prohibited by this chapter is also made unlawful by another or other laws, the offender may be convicted for the violation of this chapter or of such other law or laws.

Source.
    1971, 518:1, eff. Nov. 1, 1973.

649:12. When in Force.

This chapter, and all orders made under it shall be in force until May 15, 1945, and thereafter whenever the governor and council shall by proclamation declare a state of emergency to exist; provided, any violation hereof, committed while this chapter is in force, may be prosecuted and punished thereafter, whether or not this chapter is in force at the time of such prosecution and punishment.

Source.
    1971, 518:1, eff. Nov. 1, 1973.

CHAPTER 649-A

CHILD PORNOGRAPHY

SECTION
649-A:1.   Declaration of Findings and Purposes.
649-A:2.   Definitions.
649-A:3.   Possession of Child Sexual Abuse Images.
649-A:3-a. Distribution of Child Sexual Abuse Images.
649-A:3-b. Manufacture of Child Sexual Abuse Images.
649-A:4.   Exemption.
649-A:5.   Justifiable Dissemination.
649-A:6.   Proving Age of Child.
649-A:7.   Discovery.

Cross References.
    Annulment of record of conviction for offense under chapter, see RSA 651:5, XI.
    Endangering welfare of child, see RSA 639:3.
    Exposing minor to harmful materials, see RSA 571-B.
    Intentional contribution to the delinquency of a minor, see RSA 169-B:41.
    Obscene matter, see RSA 650.

649-A:1. Declaration of Findings and Purposes.

I. The legislature finds that there has been a proliferation of exploitation of children through their use as subjects in sexual performances. The care of children is a sacred trust and should not be abused by those who seek to profit through a commercial network based upon the exploitation of children. The public policy of the state demands the protection of children from exploitation through sexual performances.

II. It is the purpose of this chapter to facilitate the prosecution of those who exploit children in the manner specified in paragraph I. In accordance with the United States Supreme Court's decision in New York v. Ferber, this chapter makes the dissemination of visual representations of children under the age of 16 engaged in sexual activity illegal irrespective of whether the visual representations are legally obscene; and the legislature urges law enforcement

officers to aggressively seek out and prosecute those who violate the provisions of this chapter.

Source.
    1983, 448:2, eff. Aug. 23, 1983.

References in text.
    The United States Supreme Court's decision in New York v. Ferber, referred to in par. II, is published at New York v. Ferber, 458 U.S. 747, 102 S. Ct. 3348, 73 L. Ed. 2d 1113, 1982 U.S. LEXIS 12 (1982).

Cross References.
    Computer pornography and child exploitation prevention, see RSA 649-B.

NOTES TO DECISIONS

Morphed images
    Defendant's conviction on nine counts of possession of child pornography, pursuant to RSA 649-A:3, had to be reversed, as application of that statute to defendant's possession of morphed images of children's heads and necks superimposed on the bodies of naked adult females violated defendant's First Amendment right to free speech. The state did not have a compelling interest in protecting children under such circumstances because none of the underage children were depicted performing sex acts, and, thus, the children were not being sexually exploited. State v. Zidel, 156 N.H. 684, 940 A.2d 255, 2008 N.H. LEXIS 5 (2008).

Cited:
    Cited in State v. Steer, 128 N.H. 490, 517 A.2d 797, 1986 N.H. LEXIS 334 (1986); State v. Cobb, 143 N.H. 638, 732 A.2d 425, 1999 N.H. LEXIS 53 (1999); State v. Ravell, 155 N.H. 280, 922 A.2d 685, 2007 N.H. LEXIS 58 (2007).

649-A:2. Definitions.

In this chapter:

I. "Child" means any person under the age of 18 years.

II. "Disseminate" means to import, publish, produce, print, manufacture, distribute, sell, lease, exhibit, or display.

III. "Sexually explicit conduct" means human masturbation, the touching of the actor's or other person's sexual organs in the context of a sexual relationship, sexual intercourse actual or simulated, normal or perverted, whether alone or between members of the same or opposite sex or between humans and animals, or any lewd exhibitions of the buttocks, genitals, flagellation, bondage, or torture. Sexual intercourse is simulated when it depicts explicit sexual intercourse that gives the appearance of the consummation of sexual intercourse, normal or perverted.

IV. "Visual representation" means any visual depiction, including any photograph, film, video, digital image, picture, or computer or computer-generated image or picture, whether made or produced by electronic, mechanical, or other means, of sexually explicit conduct, where:

(a) The production of such visual depiction involves the use of a child engaging in or being engaged in sexually explicit conduct; or

(b) Such visual depiction is a digital image, computer image, or computer-generated image of a child engaging in or being engaged in sexually explicit conduct; or

(c) Such visual depiction has been created, adapted, or modified to appear that an identifiable child is engaging in or being engaged in sexually explicit conduct.

V. (a) "Identifiable child" means a person:

(1) Who was a child at the time the visual depiction was created, adapted, or modified; or

(2) Whose image as a child was used in creating, adapting, or modifying the visual depiction; and

(3) Who is recognizable as an actual person by the person's face, likeness, or other distinguishing characteristic, such as a unique birthmark or other recognizable feature.

(b) The term "identifiable child" shall not be construed to require proof of the actual identity of the identifiable child.

VI. "Previous conviction" or "previously convicted" means having been convicted by a jury or a judge, or having plead guilty prior to the commission of the current offense. For purposes of this paragraph, a previous conviction need not have been affirmed on appeal.

VII. "Computer" means an electronic, magnetic, optical, electrochemical, or other high speed data processing device performing logical, arithmetic, or storage functions, and includes any data storage facility or communications facility directly related to or operating in conjunction with such device, but such term does not include an automated typewriter or typesetter, a portable hand held calculator, or other similar device.

Source.
1983, 448:2, eff. Aug. 23, 1983. 2008, 323:1, eff. January 1, 2009.

Amendments
—2008. The 2008 amendment rewrote the section to the extent that a detailed comparison would be impracticable.

NOTES TO DECISIONS

1. Construction
2. Age of subjects

1. Construction
Statutory language in child pornography case showed a legislative intent to treat displaying or possessing of each photograph as a separate offense. State v. Cobb, 143 N.H. 638, 732 A.2d 425, 1999 N.H. LEXIS 53 (1999).

This section does not require that visual representation involve the use of an actual child, and review of photographic collages supported trial court's conclusion that each depicted a child engaged in sexual activity, as prohibited by statute. State v. Cobb, 143 N.H. 638, 732 A.2d 425, 1999 N.H. LEXIS 53 (1999).

2. Age of subjects
State was required to prove that photographs depicted persons under age of sixteen, and determination of age of subjects in each photograph was for the trier of fact, relying on everyday observations and common experiences. State v. Cobb, 143 N.H. 638, 732 A.2d 425, 1999 N.H. LEXIS 53 (1999).

Cited:
Cited in State v. Ravell, 155 N.H. 280, 922 A.2d 685, 2007 N.H. LEXIS 58 (2007).

649-A:3. Possession of Child Sexual Abuse Images.

I. No person shall knowingly:

(a) Buy, procure, possess, or control any visual representation of a child engaging in sexually explicit conduct; or

(b) Bring or cause to be brought into this state any visual representation of a child engaging in sexually explicit conduct.

II. An offense under this section shall be a class A felony if such person has had no previous convictions in this state or another jurisdiction for the conduct prohibited by paragraph I. Upon conviction of an offense under this section based on an indictment alleging that the person has been previously convicted of an offense under this section or a reasonably equivalent offense in another jurisdiction, the defendant may be sentenced to a maximum sentence not to exceed 20 years and a minimum sentence not to exceed ½ of the maximum sentence.

III. It shall be an affirmative defense to a charge of violating paragraph I of this section that the defendant:

(a) Possessed less than 3 images of any visual depiction proscribed by that paragraph; and

(b) Promptly and in good faith, and without retaining or allowing any person, other than a law enforcement agency, to access any visual depiction or copy thereof:

(1) Took reasonable steps to destroy each such visual depiction; or

(2) Reported the matter to a law enforcement agency and afforded that agency access to each such visual depiction.

Source.
1983, 448:2. 1991, 27:1, eff. Jan. 1, 1992. 1998, 361:1, eff. Jan. 1, 1999. 2008, 323:1, eff. January 1, 2009.

Amendments
—2008. The 2008 amendment rewrote the section to the extent that a detailed comparison would be impracticable.

—1998. Rewritten to the extent that a detailed comparison would be impracticable.

—1991. Paragraph I: Substituted "a felony" for "an offense" following "guilty or" in the introductory clause.
Paragraph II: Substituted "an" for "the" preceding "offense" and inserted "under paragraph I" in the introductory clause and substituted "paragraph I" for "this section" following "prohibited by" in subpars. (a) and (b).
Paragraph III: Added.

Cross References.
Classification of crimes, see RSA 625:9.
Computer pornography and child exploitation prevention, see RSA 649-B.
Registration of criminal offenders, see RSA 651-B.
Sentences, see RSA 651.

NOTES TO DECISIONS

1. Construction
2. Probable cause for search warrant
3. Double jeopardy
4. Evidence
5. Indictment

1. Construction

Defendant's conviction on nine counts of possession of child pornography, pursuant to RSA 649-A:3, had to be reversed, as application of that statute to defendant's possession of morphed images of children's heads and necks superimposed on the bodies of real naked adult females violated defendant's First Amendment right to free speech. The state did not have a compelling interest in protecting children under such circumstances because none of the underage children were depicted performing sex acts, and, thus, the children were not being sexually exploited. State v. Zidel, 156 N.H. 684, 940 A.2d 255, 2008 N.H. LEXIS 5 (2008).

This section does not require that visual representation involve the use of an actual child, and review of photographic collages supported trial court's conclusion that each depicted a child engaged in sexual activity, as prohibited by statute. State v. Cobb, 143 N.H. 638, 732 A.2d 425, 1999 N.H. LEXIS 53 (1999).

Statutory language in child pornography case showed a legislative intent to treat displaying or possessing of each photograph as a separate offense. State v. Cobb, 143 N.H. 638, 732 A.2d 425, 1999 N.H. LEXIS 53 (1999).

In order to prevail on charges of child pornography under this section, it is not necessary that the state prove that the defendant intended to profit. State v. Steer, 128 N.H. 490, 517 A.2d 797, 1986 N.H. LEXIS 334 (1986).

The language in RSA 649-A:1 referring to persons who seek to profit through a commercial network based upon the exploitation of children cannot be read as grafting an element of intent to profit into the offenses enumerated in this section. State v. Steer, 128 N.H. 490, 517 A.2d 797, 1986 N.H. LEXIS 334 (1986).

2. Probable cause for search warrant

Affidavit seeking a search warrant for child pornography adequately established probable cause for such a warrant, without providing copies of the images defendant was alleged to possess, or detailed factual descriptions of them, because it alleged that defendant admitted that about 25 percent of the image files on his computer and disks contained child pornography, and this admission provided a sufficient "other indicia of probable cause" to issue a search warrant. State v. Dowman, 151 N.H. 162, 855 A.2d 524, 2004 N.H. LEXIS 109 (2004).

3. Double jeopardy

Convictions for both delivering and possessing the same video clip under RSA 649-A:3 subjected defendant to multiple punishments and violated double jeopardy under N.H. Const. pt. I, art. 16. Proof that defendant delivered the clip was proof that he possessed it, and his possession of the clip was a continuing offense. State v. Farr, 160 N.H. 803, 7 A.3d 1276, 2010 N.H. LEXIS 111 (2010).

Possessing a single visual representation of child pornography may be considered separate possessions for double jeopardy purposes only if the evidence indicates that the possessions are separated in space or time or that they were intended for different purposes or transactions. Close proximity in space and time is indicative of unitary conduct; likewise, lack of evidence indicating that the defendant had a separate intent or purpose with regard to his possessions of the single visual representation is not necessarily fatal to the determination that the possessions were separate, but, in the absence of other factors, is strongly corroborative of unitary conduct. State v. Farr, 160 N.H. 803, 7 A.3d 1276, 2010 N.H. LEXIS 111 (2010).

Defendant could be punished in one county for five images containing pornographic images of children that defendant possessed on a CD-ROM and punished in another county for the identical five images he possessed on his computer hard drive without violating double jeopardy. The possession of any visual representation of a child engaging in sexual activity constituted a separate offense, regardless of whether that visual representation was a duplicate copy of another visual representation. State v. Ravell, 155 N.H. 280, 922 A.2d 685, 2007 N.H. LEXIS 58 (2007), rehearing denied, 2007 N.H. LEXIS 109 (N.H. June 8, 2007).

4. Evidence

Having viewed the video clip in question, the court concluded that a rational trier of fact, viewing all of the evidence and all reasonable inferences from it in the light most favorable to the State, could have found beyond a reasonable doubt that the clip depicted a child younger than sixteen. State v. Farr, 160 N.H. 803, 7 A.3d 1276, 2010 N.H. LEXIS 111 (2010).

In a child pornography case, the State is not required to present evidence beyond the images themselves to establish that a real child is depicted. That is not to say that there are no circumstances under which the trial court may find expert testimony helpful; however, the admission or exclusion of expert testimony is within the trial court's sound discretion. State v. Clark, 158 N.H. 13, 959 A.2d 229, 2008 N.H. LEXIS 128 (2008).

In a child pornography case, the trial court could reasonably have concluded that each image depicted a real child without the aid of expert testimony. Indeed, contrary to defendant's assertion, the exhibits admitted at trial were not of such inferior quality or insufficient size as to make this determination impossible; furthermore, although not required to do so, the State did present expert testimony in this regard. State v. Clark, 158 N.H. 13, 959 A.2d 229, 2008 N.H. LEXIS 128 (2008).

In a child pornography case, reliance upon the automatic record created of images merely viewed on a computer, irrespective of any prompting by the user, is problematic because the images contained in temporary Internet files or unallocated space may not always be the result of the computer user seeking out or downloading the image. The relevant inquiry thus becomes whether the defendant knowingly possessed the images, in that he exerted some control over them, or whether the presence of the images on his computer was merely inadvertent; this inquiry is a question of fact. State v. Clark, 158 N.H. 13, 959 A.2d 229, 2008 N.H. LEXIS 128 (2008).

In a child pornography case, there was no merit to defendant's argument that the State failed to prove that he knowingly possessed certain images because they were located in either deleted files or in unallocated hard drive space on his computer. Defendant, communicating with a detective posing as a fictitious child, stated that he possessed child pornography and that he would bring some with him on a disc when he met the child; furthermore, another image that was a trial exhibit was saved to defendant's hard drive, and there was evidence of additional images found on defendant's computer. State v. Clark, 158 N.H. 13, 959 A.2d 229, 2008 N.H. LEXIS 128 (2008).

5. Indictment

Under RSA 649-A:3, time is not an element of the crime; therefore, any discrepancy as to the date of possession is not fatal to the State's case, as long as possession can be found on or about the date alleged in the indictment. Thus, when defendant did not dispute that an image was last viewed on May 5, 2003, prior to the indictment date and within the statute of limitations, he could be found guilty of possessing child pornography even though the indictment alleged that he possessed it on August 3, 2003. State v. Clark, 158 N.H. 13, 959 A.2d 229, 2008 N.H. LEXIS 128 (2008).

649-A:3-a. Distribution of Child Sexual Abuse Images.

I. No person shall:

(a) Knowingly sell, exchange, or otherwise transfer, or possess with intent to sell, exchange, or otherwise transfer any visual representation of a child engaging in or being engaged in sexually explicit conduct;

(b) Knowingly publish, exhibit, or otherwise make available any visual representation of a child engaging in or being engaged in sexually explicit conduct.

II. (a) If such person has had no previous convictions in this state or another state for the conduct prohibited by paragraph I, the defendant may be sentenced to a maximum sentence not to exceed 20 years and a minimum sentence not to exceed ½ of the maximum. Upon conviction of an offense under this section based on an indictment alleging that the person has been previously convicted of an offense under this section or a reasonably equivalent offense in an out-of-state jurisdiction, the defendant may be sentenced to a maximum sentence not to exceed 30 years and a minimum sentence not to exceed ½ of the minimum.

(b) If such person has no previous convictions in this state or another state for the conduct prohibited in paragraph I, and is convicted under subparagraph I(b) with having less than 3 images or visual representations, the defendant will be guilty of a class B felony.

III. Nothing in this chapter shall be construed to limit any law enforcement agency from possessing or displaying or otherwise make available any images as may be necessary to the performance of a valid law enforcement function.

Source.
2008, 323:2, eff. January 1, 2009.

649-A:3-b. Manufacture of Child Sexual Abuse Images.

I. No person shall knowingly create, produce, manufacture, or direct a visual representation of a child engaging in or being engaged in sexually explicit conduct, or participate in that portion of such visual representation that consists of a child engaging in or being engaged in sexually explicit conduct.

II. If such person has had no previous convictions in this state or another state for the conduct prohibited in this section, the defendant may be sentenced to a maximum sentence not to exceed 30 years and a minimum sentence not to exceed ½ of the maximum. Upon conviction of an offense under this section based on an indictment alleging that the person has been previously convicted of an offense under this section or a reasonably equivalent offense in an out-of-state jurisdiction, a person may be sentenced to life imprisonment or for such term as the court may order.

Source.
2008, 323:2, eff. January 1, 2009.

649-A:4. Exemption.

A person shall not be guilty of a violation under this chapter if he is a librarian, or a paid or volunteer member of a library staff working under the supervision of a librarian, engaged in the normal course of his employment, or if he is regularly employed by anybody as a motion picture projectionist, stage employee or spotlight operator, cashier, doorman, usher, candy stand attendant, porter or in any other nonmanagerial or nonsupervisory capacity in a motion picture theatre; provided that he has no financial interest, other than his employment, which employment does not encompass compensation based upon any proportion of the gross receipts, in the promotion of a sexual performance for sale,

rental or exhibition or in the promotion, presentation or direction of any sexual performance, and provided further that he is not in any way responsible for acquiring such material for sale, rental or exhibition.

Source.
1983, 448:2, eff. Aug. 23, 1983.

NOTES TO DECISIONS

Cited:
Cited in State v. Steer, 128 N.H. 490, 517 A.2d 797, 1986 N.H. LEXIS 334 (1986).

649-A:5. Justifiable Dissemination.

It is an affirmative defense to prosecution under this chapter that dissemination was:

I. Restricted to institutions or persons having scientific, medical, educational, governmental or other similar justification for possessing a visual representation of a child engaging in sexual activity; or

II. Of the same material available in the same or another form in any public library in the state.

Source.
1983, 448:2, eff. Aug. 23, 1983. 1998, 361:2, eff. Jan. 1, 1999.

Amendments
—1998. Designated the existing provisions of the section as par. I, added "or" following "activity" at the end of that paragraph, and added par. II.

649-A:6. Proving Age of Child.

Whether a child depicted in a visual representation is a minor for the purposes of this chapter is a question of fact for the jury and may be found by expert or lay testimony, or by viewing the images.

Source.
2008, 323:3, eff. January 1, 2009.

649-A:7. Discovery.

I. In any criminal proceeding, any material that constitutes a visual representation of a child engaging in or being engaged in sexually explicit conduct shall remain in the care, custody, and control of the state or the court.

II. The state shall provide ample opportunity for the defendant, his or her attorney, or any individual the defendant may seek to qualify to furnish expert testimony at trial, or any expert retained in anticipation of criminal litigation or for preparation for trial, to inspect, view, and examine the property or material at a state facility.

III. Upon a defense motion or by agreement of the parties establishing that it is necessary to copy, photograph, duplicate, or otherwise reproduce such material or property in order to prepare a defense, the court may authorize such action, provided that the court's order include a protective order prohibiting disclosure of the material or property to any one other than the defendant, his or her attorney, or any individual the defendant may seek to qualify to furnish expert testimony at trial, or any expert retained in anticipation of criminal litigation or for preparation for trial. The court protective order shall require that all such material or property provided to the defense be kept secure against theft and inadvertent disclosure to any other person and be maintained in a manner which deters copying or dissemination. Any person either handling or viewing such material or property shall sign a non-disclosure agreement agreeing to refrain from copying or publishing any visual representation of a child engaging in or being engaged in sexually explicit conduct. Any person who views any of the images shall certify in writing that he or she has not knowingly kept any material or property which would qualify as an image of child sexual abuse under state or federal law, and that all materials, property, and signed non-disclosure agreements shall be returned to the state at the end of the case.

Source.
2008, 323:3, eff. January 1, 2009.

CHAPTER 649-B

COMPUTER PORNOGRAPHY AND CHILD EXPLOITATION PREVENTION

SECTION
649-B:1. Short Title.
649-B:2. Definition.
649-B:3. Computer Pornography Prohibited.
649-B:4. Certain Uses of Computer Services Prohibited.
649-B:5. Owners or Operators of Computer Services Liable.
649-B:6. State Criminal Jurisdiction.

649-B:1. Short Title.

This chapter shall be known and may be cited as the "Computer Pornography and Child Exploitation Prevention Act of 1998."

Source.
1998, 361:1, eff. Jan. 1, 1999.

649-B:2. Definition.

In this chapter, "child" means any person under the age of 16 years.

Source.
1998, 361:3, eff. Jan. 1, 1999.

649-B:3. Computer Pornography Prohibited.

I. No person shall knowingly:
(a) Compile, enter into, or transmit by means of computer;
(b) Make, print, publish, or reproduce by other computerized means;
(c) Cause or allow to be entered into or transmitted by means of computer; or

(d) Buy, sell, receive, exchange, or disseminate by means of computer, any notice, statement, or advertisement, or any minor's name, telephone number, place of residence, physical characteristics, or other descriptive or identifying information, for purposes of facilitating, encouraging, offering, or soliciting sexual conduct of or with any child, or the visual depiction of such conduct.

II. Any person who violates the provisions of this section is guilty of a class B felony.

Source.
1998, 361:3, eff. Jan. 1, 1999.

649-B:4. Certain Uses of Computer Services Prohibited.

I. No person shall knowingly utilize a computer on-line service, internet service, or local bulletin board service to seduce, solicit, lure, or entice a child or another person believed by the person to be a child, to commit any of the following:
(a) Any offense under RSA 632-A, relative to sexual assault and related offenses.
(b) Indecent exposure and lewdness under RSA 645:1.
(c) Endangering a child as defined in RSA 639:3, III.

II. (a) A person who violates the provisions of paragraph I shall be guilty of a class A felony if such person believed the child was under the age of 13, otherwise such person shall be guilty of a class B felony.
(b) A person convicted under paragraph I based on an indictment alleging that the person has been previously convicted of an offense under this section or a reasonably equivalent offense in an out-of-state jurisdiction shall be charged as a class A felony. If the indictment also alleges that the person believed that the child was under the age of 13, the person may be sentenced to a maximum sentence not to exceed 20 years and a minimum sentence not to exceed 10 years.
(c) If the person has been previously convicted 2 or more times for an offense under this section or a reasonably equivalent statute in another state, the person may be sentenced to a maximum term not to exceed 30 years.

III. It shall not be a defense to a prosecution under this section that the victim was not actually a child so long as the person reasonably believed that the victim was a child.

Source.
1998, 361:3, eff. Jan. 1, 1999. 2008, 323:4, eff. January 1, 2009.

Amendments
—**2008.** The 2008 amendment rewrote the section to the extent that a detailed comparison would be impracticable.

NOTES TO DECISIONS

1. Construction
2. Evidence sufficient

3. Elements

1. Construction

Nowhere in the plain and ordinary meaning of "solicit, seduce, lure, or entice" in RSA 649-B:4 does the New Hampshire Supreme Court discern any requirement that the defendant must explicitly or affirmatively ask the victim to engage in sexual penetration. State v. Farrington, 161 N.H. 440, 20 A.3d 291, 2011 N.H. LEXIS 11 (2011).

2. Evidence sufficient

Defendant's conviction for violating RSA 649-B:4, I, was affirmed, where a rational jury could have concluded beyond a reasonable doubt that the evidence excluded all rational conclusions except that defendant believed the person with whom he was conversing in an on-line chat room was 14 as purported by the person's screen name profile. State v. Lacasse, 153 N.H. 670, 917 A.2d 184, 2006 N.H. LEXIS 86 (2006).

3. Elements

Crime proscribed by the legislature in RSA 649-B:4, I(a) is an attempt to seduce, solicit, lure, or entice a person believed to be a child under the age of sixteen; thus, the crime is complete when the defendant uses the Internet in an effort to solicit a child, or a person believed to be a child, to engage in sexual activity. It is the conduct of attempting or trying to seduce or solicit that the legislature is prohibiting. State v. Moscone, 161 N.H. 355, 13 A.3d 137, 2011 N.H. LEXIS 1 (2011).

Word "attempt" in RSA 649-B:4, I(a) does not incorporate the attempt statute, RSA 629:1, I, or the mental state of "purposely." Accordingly, under RSA 626:2, I, the mental state of "knowingly" applies to all of the material elements of RSA 649-B:4, I(a), and the trial court did not err in its jury instruction as to the mental state required for conviction. State v. Moscone, 161 N.H. 355, 13 A.3d 137, 2011 N.H. LEXIS 1 (2011).

There was sufficient evidence to support a conviction of prohibited uses of computer services under RSA 649-B:4 when defendant told the victim that he found her attractive, repeatedly asked to meet her in person, and made other flirtatious and sexually graphic remarks to her. He did not have to explicitly ask her to engage in sexual intercourse. State v. Farrington, 161 N.H. 440, 20 A.3d 291, 2011 N.H. LEXIS 11 (2011).

RESEARCH REFERENCES

New Hampshire Bar Journal.

For article, "Lex Loci: A Survey of New Hampshire Supreme Court Decisions," see 46 N.H.B.J. 76 (Summer 2005).

649-B:5. Owners or Operators of Computer Services Liable.

I. It shall be a class A misdemeanor for any owner or operator of a computer on-line service, Internet service, or local bulletin board service knowingly to permit a subscriber to utilize the service to commit a violation of this chapter.

II. Any out-of-state computer service company doing business in New Hampshire which receives a subpoena from the state of New Hampshire resulting from an investigation of a violation of this chapter shall respond to such subpoena within 14 days. Failure to respond may result in the suspension or revocation of such company's right to do business in New Hampshire.

Source.

1998, 361:3, eff. Jan. 1, 1999.

649-B:6. State Criminal Jurisdiction.

A person is subject to prosecution for engaging in any conduct proscribed by this chapter within this state, or for engaging in such conduct outside this state if by such conduct the person commits a violation of this chapter involving a child or an individual the person believes to be a child, residing within this state.

Source.

1998, 361:3, eff. Jan. 1, 1999.

CHAPTER 650

OBSCENE MATTER

General Provisions

SECTION
650:1.   Definitions.
650:2.   Offenses.
650:3.   Exemption.
650:4.   Justifiable and Non-Commercial Private Dissemination.
650:5.   Evidence; Adjudication of Obscenity.

Preliminary Hearing

650:6.   Preliminary Hearing.

Legislative intent

1976, 46:6, eff. June 1. 1976, provided: "It is the express intent of the general court that RSA 571-B relating to exposing minors to harmful materials and RSA 650 [this chapter] relating to obscene matter shall be enforced to apply only to those persons actually responsible for the production and dissemination of pornographic or obscene materials."

NOTES TO DECISIONS

Cited:

Cited in Dover News v. City of Dover, 117 N.H. 1066, 381 A.2d 752, 1977 N.H. LEXIS 500 (1977).

General Provisions

650:1. Definitions.

In this chapter:

I. "Disseminate" means to import, publish, produce, print, manufacture, distribute, sell, lease, exhibit or display.

II. "Knowledge" means general awareness of the nature of the content of the material.

III. "Material" means any printed matter, visual representation, live performance or sound recording including, but not limited to, books, magazines, motion picture films, pamphlets, phonographic records, pictures, photographs, figures, statues, plays, dances or other representation or embodiment of the obscene. Undeveloped photographs, molds, printing plates, and the like, shall be deemed obscene material notwithstanding that processing or other acts may be required to make the obscenity patent or to disseminate it.

IV. Material is "obscene" if, considered as a whole, to the average person

(a) When applying the contemporary standards of the county within which the obscenity offense was committed, its predominant appeal is to the prurient interest in sex, that is, an interest in lewdness or lascivious thoughts;

(b) It depicts or describes sexual conduct in a manner so explicit as to be patently offensive; and

(c) It lacks serious literary, artistic, political or scientific value.

V. "Predominant appeal" shall be judged with reference to ordinary adults unless it appears from the character of the material or the circumstances of its dissemination to be designed for children or other specially susceptible audience.

VI. "Sexual conduct" means human masturbation, sexual intercourse, actual or simulated, normal or perverted, whether alone or between members of the same or opposite sex or between humans and animals, any depiction or representation of excretory functions, any lewd exhibitions of the genitals, flagellation or torture in the context of a sexual relationship. Sexual intercourse is simulated when it depicts explicit sexual intercourse which gives the appearance of the consummation of sexual intercourse, normal or perverted.

VII. "Child" means a person under the age of 18.

Source.

1971, 518:1. 1976, 46:3. 1977, 199:3. 1994, 60:1, eff. Jan. 1, 1995.

Amendments

—1994. Paragraph VI: Deleted "or any touching of the genitals, pubic areas or buttocks of the human male or female, or the breasts of the female" following "perverted" in the first sentence.

—1977. Paragraph VII: Added.

—1976. Rewritten to the extent that a detailed comparison would be impracticable.

NOTES TO DECISIONS

1. Constitutionality
2. Determination of obscenity
3. Distributors

1. Constitutionality

In determining requisite scienter for conviction on offense of delivering obscene material, paragraph II of this section is constitutional. State v. Manchester News Co., 118 N.H. 255, 387 A.2d 324, 1978 N.H. LEXIS 392 (1978), appeal dismissed, Manchester News Co. v. New Hampshire, 439 U.S. 949, 99 S. Ct. 343, 58 L. Ed. 2d 340, 1978 U.S. LEXIS 3691 (1978).

Provisions of this section purporting to apply different standards to material designed for children from that designed for adults are constitutional. Opinion of Justices, 115 N.H. 226, 337 A.2d 777, 1975 N.H. LEXIS 267 (1975).

This section was constitutional, since it was designed to limit regulation of obscenity to those materials which primarily sought to exploit unhealthy, antisocial attitudes toward sexual conduct by graphically depicting or representing such conduct in a patently offensive manner, leaving nothing to the imagination, and having

as a theme sex for the sake of sex alone. State v. Harding, 114 N.H. 335, 320 A.2d 646, 1974 N.H. LEXIS 272 (1974). (Decided under prior law.)

2. Determination of obscenity

Whether allegedly obscene material could be found by the average person applying contemporary community standards to appeal to the prurient interest in sex and whether it lacked literary, artistic, political or scientific value were for the trier of fact. State v. Harding, 114 N.H. 335, 320 A.2d 646, 1974 N.H. LEXIS 272 (1974). (Decided under prior law.)

3. Distributors

Inclusion of the terms "distribute" and "sell" in paragraph I of this section indicates legislature's intent to include distributors of obscene material within the scope of this chapter. State v. Manchester News Co., 118 N.H. 255, 387 A.2d 324, 1978 N.H. LEXIS 392 (1978), appeal dismissed, Manchester News Co. v. New Hampshire, 439 U.S. 949, 99 S. Ct. 343, 58 L. Ed. 2d 340, 1978 U.S. LEXIS 3691 (1978).

Cited:

Cited in State v. DeCosta, 146 N.H. 405, 772 A.2d 340, 2001 N.H. LEXIS 89 (2001).

650:2. Offenses.

I. A person is guilty of a misdemeanor if he commits obscenity when, with knowledge of the nature of content thereof, he:

(a) Sells, delivers or provides, or offers or agrees to sell, deliver or provide, any obscene material; or

(b) Presents or directs an obscene play, dance or performance, or participates in that portion thereof which makes it obscene; or

(c) Publishes, exhibits or otherwise makes available any obscene material; or

(d) Possesses any obscene material for purposes of sale or other commercial dissemination; or

(e) Sells, advertises or otherwise commercially disseminates material, whether or not obscene, by representing or suggesting that it is obscene.

II. A person who commits any of the acts specified in subparagraphs (a) through (e) of paragraph I with knowledge that such act involves a child in material deemed obscene pursuant to this chapter is guilty of:

(a) A class B felony if such person has had no prior convictions in this state or another state for the conduct described in this paragraph;

(b) A class A felony if such person has had one or more prior convictions in this state or another state for the conduct described in this paragraph.

III. For the second and for each subsequent violation of paragraph I, such person shall be guilty of a class B felony.

Source.

1971, 518:1. 1976, 46:4. 1977, 199:2. 1983, 448:3. 1994, 60:2, eff. Jan. 1, 1995.

Amendments

—1994. Paragraph III: Added.

—1983. Paragraph II: Rewritten to the extent that a detailed comparison would be impracticable.

—1977. Paragraph I: Designated existing introductory paragraph as par. I and redesignated former pars. I-V as subpars. (a) to (e) respectively.

Paragraph II: Added.

—1976. Paragraph I: Substituted "material" for "writing, picture, record or other representation or embodiment of the obscene" following "any obscene".

Cross References.

Classification of crimes, see RSA 625:9.

Registration of criminal offenders, see RSA 651-B.

Sentences, see RSA 651.

NOTES TO DECISIONS

1. Constitutionality
2. Construction
3. Knowledge
4. Distributors
5. Evidence

1. Constitutionality

This section was not constitutionally defective for imposing a broad ban on the sale or distribution of obscene material in New Hampshire. State v. Harding, 114 N.H. 335, 320 A.2d 646, 1974 N.H. LEXIS 272 (1974). (Decided under prior law.)

2. Construction

The provisions of this section punishing the possession and distribution of obscene literature involved solely the punishment of individuals rather than the forfeiture of the obscene literature; the fact that the same magazine was involved in a prosecution of different individuals did not convert the criminal action from a proceeding against the person into one in rem. State v. Hentschel, 98 N.H. 382, 101 A.2d 456, 1953 N.H. LEXIS 86 (1953). (Decided under prior law.)

The prior acquittal of a distributor of a magazine, where the sole issue was whether a particular issue of the magazine was obscene, was not res judicata of a prosecution against another defendant charged with having in his control with intent to sell the same issue of the same magazine, alleged to be obscene. State v. Hentschel, 98 N.H. 382, 101 A.2d 456, 1953 N.H. LEXIS 86 (1953). (Decided under prior law.)

3. Knowledge

In order to be guilty of distributing obscene material, defendant need not have had knowledge that material was obscene, but must be shown to have had knowledge of nature of contents thereof. State v. Manchester News Co., 118 N.H. 255, 387 A.2d 324, 1978 N.H. LEXIS 392 (1978), appeal dismissed, Manchester News Co. v. New Hampshire, 439 U.S. 949, 99 S. Ct. 343, 58 L. Ed. 2d 340, 1978 U.S. LEXIS 3691 (1978).

An information charging distributor with delivering issue of magazine with knowledge of nature of contents of magazine, alleged to be obscene, sufficiently apprised distributor that he was being charged with having knowledge of contents of magazine and it was not necessary for state to allege how or when distributor acquired knowledge, or which of its agents possessed knowledge of magazine's contents. State v. Manchester News Co., 118 N.H. 255, 387 A.2d 324, 1978 N.H. LEXIS 392 (1978), appeal dismissed, Manchester News Co. v. New Hampshire, 439 U.S. 949, 99 S. Ct. 343, 58 L. Ed. 2d 340, 1978 U.S. LEXIS 3691 (1978).

4. Distributors

Language of this section manifests legislature's intent to attach criminal liability to more than just person or corporation responsible for decision to produce obscene material and legislature clearly intended to include those individuals and corporations distributing obscene material. State v. Manchester News Co., 118 N.H. 255, 387 A.2d 324, 1978 N.H. LEXIS 392 (1978), appeal dismissed, Manchester News Co. v. New Hampshire, 439 U.S. 949, 99 S. Ct. 343, 58 L. Ed. 2d 340, 1978 U.S. LEXIS 3691 (1978).

5. Evidence

In prosecution for exhibiting obscenity, the State must, through reasonable diligence, attempt to produce the alleged obscene material; if it is unable to do so and can reasonably explain the failure to the trial court, then testimonial evidence that explicitly describes the material may be sufficient to prove that the material is obscene, however, in such a situation, the State must lay a proper foundation demonstrating that the witness is qualified to describe with sufficient detail the alleged obscene material. State v. DeCosta, 146 N.H. 405, 772 A.2d 340, 2001 N.H. LEXIS 89 (2001).

Cited:

Cited in Eames v. Rudman, 115 N.H. 91, 333 A.2d 157, 1975 N.H. LEXIS 232 (1975); State v. Luv Pharmacy, 118 N.H. 398, 388 A.2d 190, 1978 N.H. LEXIS 426, 16 A.L.R.4th 1304 (1978).

650:3. Exemption.

A motion picture projectionist or motion picture machine operator who is regularly employed by anybody to operate a projecting machine in a public motion picture theatre shall not be guilty of a violation under this chapter because of the picture which is being projected if he is required to project it as part of his employment.

Source.

1971, 518:1, eff. Nov. 1, 1973.

650:4. Justifiable and Non-Commercial Private Dissemination.

It is an affirmative defense to prosecution under this chapter that dissemination was restricted to:

I. Institutions or persons having scientific, educational, governmental or other similar justification for possessing obscene material; or

II. Non-commercial dissemination to personal associates of the accused who are not under 18 years of age.

Source.

1971, 518:1, eff. Nov. 1, 1973.

650:5. Evidence; Adjudication of Obscenity.

In any prosecution under this chapter, evidence shall be admissible to show:

I. The character of the audience for which the material was designed or to which it was directed;

II. What the predominant appeal of the material would be for ordinary adults or any special audience to which it was directed;

III. The degree of public acceptance of the material in this state;

IV. Appeal to prurient interest, or absence thereof, in advertising or other promotion of the material; and

V. The good repute of the author, creator, publisher or other person from whom the material originated;

VI. Expert testimony and testimony of the author, creator, publisher or other person from whom the material originated, relating to factors entering into determination of the issue of obscenity.

Source.
1971, 518:1. 1976, 46:5, eff. June 1, 1976.

Amendments
—1976. Paragraph II: Deleted "and what effect, if any, it would probably have on conduct of such people" following "directed".

Paragraph III: Former par. IV redesignated as par. III, substituted "this state" for "the United States" following "material in" at the end of that paragraph, and former par. III deleted.

Paragraph IV: Former par. IV redesignated as par. III and former par. V redesignated as par. IV.

Paragraph V: Former par. V redesignated as par. IV and former par. VI redesignated as par. V.

Paragraph VI: Former par. VI redesignated as par. V and former par. VII redesignated as par. VI.

Paragraph VII: Former par. VII redesignated as par. VI.

Preliminary Hearing

650:6. Preliminary Hearing.

I. No recognized or established school, museum, public library or governmental agency, nor any person acting as an employee or agent of such institution, shall be arrested, charged or indicted for any violation of a provision of this chapter until such time as the material involved has first been the subject of an adversary hearing wherein such institution or person is made a defendant, and, after such material is declared by the court to be obscene matter, such institution or person continues to engage in the conduct prohibited by this chapter. The sole issue at the hearing shall be whether the material is obscene matter.

II. The adversary hearing prescribed in paragraph I of this section may be initiated only by complaint of the county attorney or the attorney general. Hearing on the complaint shall be held in the superior court of the county in which the alleged violation occurs. Notice of the complaint and of the hearing shall be given by registered mail or personal service. The notice shall state the nature of the violation, the date, place and time of the hearing, and the right to present and cross-examine witnesses. In addition to the defendant, any other interested party may appear at the hearing in opposition to the complaint and may present and cross-examine witnesses. For the purposes of this paragraph, the term "interested party" includes, but is not limited to the manufacturer of the material alleged to be harmful to minors.

III. The state or any defendant may appeal from a judgment. Such appeal shall not stay the judgment. Any defendant engaging in conduct prohibited by this chapter subsequent to notice of the judgment finding the material to be obscene matter shall be subject to criminal prosecution notwithstanding the appeal from the judgment.

Source.
1979, 397:2, eff. Aug. 22, 1979.

CHAPTER 650-A

FELONIOUS USE OF FIREARMS

SECTION
650-A:1.   Felonious Use of Firearms.

Cross References.
Involuntary admission for persons charged with felonious use of a deadly weapon found not competent to stand trial, see RSA 171-B.

650-A:1. Felonious Use of Firearms.

A person is guilty of a class B felony if he commits or attempts to commit any felony when armed with a pistol, revolver, rifle, shotgun or any other firearm. For any subsequent offense, a person shall be guilty of a class A felony.

Source.
1977, 403:1, eff. Sept. 3, 1977.

Cross References.
Classification of crimes, see RSA 625:9.
Felonious use of body armor, see RSA 650-B.
Felonious use of teflon-coated, armor-piercing and exploding bullets and cartridges, see RSA 159:18.
Mandatory minimum sentence, see RSA 651:2, II-b.
Possession of dangerous weapons by convicted felons, see RSA 159:3.
Possession of dangerous weapon by person arrested, see RSA 159:15.
Sentences, see RSA 651.
Unauthorized use of firearms, see RSA 644:13.

NOTES TO DECISIONS

1.   Construction
2.   Double jeopardy
3.   Sentence

1. Construction
A pellet gun is not a "firearm" within the meaning of this section, since a firearm acts by force of gunpowder and a pellet is propelled by pneumatic force. State v. Beaudette, 124 N.H. 579, 474 A.2d 1012, 1984 N.H. LEXIS 355 (1984).

2. Double jeopardy
Imposition of consecutive sentences for first degree assault and the felonious use of a firearm violated constitutional guarantee against double jeopardy, because the underlying crime of knowing assault was itself enhanced by the use of a deadly weapon, and the perpetrator could therefore not be properly sentenced a second time for the felonious use of the firearm. State v. Houtenbrink, 130 N.H. 385, 539 A.2d 714, 1988 N.H. LEXIS 17 (1988).

Where a criminal defendant's use of a gun is used to trigger "enhancement" provisions in felonies contained in this title, so as to raise certain criminal acts from class B to class A felonies, it will generally follow that the felonious use of a firearm cannot also be charged for commission of the same felony with the same gun because the elements of neither crime will require a single difference in evidence at trial. Heald v. Perrin, 123 N.H. 468, 464 A.2d 275, 1983 N.H. LEXIS 310 (1983), superseded by statute as stated in, State v. Nickles, 144 N.H. 673, 749 A.2d 290, 2000 N.H. LEXIS 9 (2000). (But see RSA 651:2, II-g).

Whether this section could be the basis for a conviction in addition to a conviction for the underlying felony depends on the elements of the felony charged and the evidence which will be required to sustain each offense. Heald v. Perrin, 123 N.H. 468, 464 A.2d 275, 1983 N.H. LEXIS 310 (1983), superseded by statute as stated in, State v. Nickles, 144 N.H. 673, 749 A.2d 290, 2000 N.H. LEXIS 9 (2000). (But see RSA 651:2, II-g).

Where plaintiff was convicted under RSA 636:1 of robbery while armed with a deadly weapon, and of the felonious use of a firearm, where not a single difference in evidence was required, as the offenses were charged and proven in this case, the conviction for the felonious use of a firearm could not be supported under the double jeopardy clause of the state constitution. Heald v. Perrin, 123 N.H. 468, 464 A.2d 275, 1983 N.H. LEXIS 310 (1983), superseded by statute as stated in, State v. Nickles, 144 N.H. 673, 749 A.2d 290, 2000 N.H. LEXIS 9 (2000). (But see RSA 651:2, II-g).

3. Sentence

The plain language as well as the legislative history of this section and RSA 651:2, governing sentencing of persons convicted of felonious use of a firearm, evince a clear legislative intent to provide for a mandatory consecutive sentence for the use of a firearm in the commission of all felonies, including armed robbery. Heald v. Perrin, 123 N.H. 468, 464 A.2d 275, 1983 N.H. LEXIS 310 (1983), superseded by statute as stated in, State v. Nickles, 144 N.H. 673, 749 A.2d 290, 2000 N.H. LEXIS 9 (2000). (But see RSA 651:2, II-g).

Cited:

Cited in State v. Fraser, 120 N.H. 117, 411 A.2d 1125, 1980 N.H. LEXIS 241 (1980); State v. Heald, 120 N.H. 319, 414 A.2d 1288, 1980 N.H. LEXIS 273 (1980); State v. Purrington, 122 N.H. 458, 446 A.2d 451, 1982 N.H. LEXIS 377 (1982); State v. Fernald, 123 N.H. 442, 462 A.2d 122, 1983 N.H. LEXIS 302 (1983); State v. Lessard, 123 N.H. 788, 465 A.2d 516, 1983 N.H. LEXIS 329 (1983); State v. Elbert, 125 N.H. 1, 480 A.2d 854, 1984 N.H. LEXIS 371 (1984); State v. Elbert, 128 N.H. 210, 512 A.2d 1114, 1986 N.H. LEXIS 280 (1986); State v. Taylor, 136 N.H. 131, 612 A.2d 917, 1992 N.H. LEXIS 147 (1992); State v. Drake, 139 N.H. 662, 662 A.2d 265, 1995 N.H. LEXIS 69 (1995); State v. Hennessey, 142 N.H. 149, 697 A.2d 930, 1997 N.H. LEXIS 68 (1997).

CHAPTER 650-B

FELONIOUS USE OF BODY ARMOR

SECTION
650-B:1. Definition.
650-B:2. Felonious Use of Body Armor.

650-B:1. Definition.

In this chapter, "body armor" means any device designed to be worn on the body which is bullet resistant and is designed and intended to provide ballistic and trauma protection.

Source.
1983, 193:1, eff. Aug. 14, 1983.

650-B:2. Felonious Use of Body Armor.

I. A person is guilty of a class B felony if he commits or attempts to commit any felony while using or wearing body armor.

II. Neither the whole nor any part of a sentence of imprisonment imposed for a violation of this section shall be served concurrently with any other term of imprisonment.

Source.
1983, 193:1, eff. Aug. 14, 1983. 1996, 260:1, eff. Jan. 1, 1997.

Amendments
—1996. Paragraph I: Deleted "misdemeanor or" preceding "felony while using".

Cross References.
Classification of crimes, see RSA 625:9.
Felonious use of armor-piercing bullets or cartridges, see RSA 159:18.
Felonious use of firearms, see RSA 650-A.
Sentences, see RSA 651.

NOTES TO DECISIONS

1. Constitutionality
2. Mens rea

1. Constitutionality
This section is not unconstitutionally overbroad or vague; even if it is susceptible to an expansive reading, and no constitutional violation exists absent an impingement on some protected right. State v. Haines, 142 N.H. 692, 709 A.2d 762, 1998 N.H. LEXIS 23 (1998).

2. Mens rea
This section requires that defendant act "knowingly," not "purposely." State v. Haines, 142 N.H. 692, 709 A.2d 762, 1998 N.H. LEXIS 23 (1998).

CHAPTER 650-C

NEGLIGENT STORAGE OF FIREARMS

SECTION
650-C:1. Negligent Storage of Firearms.

650-C:1. Negligent Storage of Firearms.

I. Nothing in this section shall be construed to reduce or limit any existing right to purchase and own firearms or ammunition, or both, or to provide authority to any state or local agency to infringe upon the privacy of any family, home or business except by lawful warrant.

II. As used in this section, "child," "juvenile" or "youth" shall mean any person under 16 years of age.

III. Any person who stores or leaves on premises under that person's control a loaded firearm, and who knows or reasonably should know that a child is likely to gain access to the firearm without the permission of the child's parent or guardian, is guilty of a violation if a child gains access to a firearm and:

(a) The firearm is used in a reckless or threatening manner;

(b) The firearm is used during the commission of any misdemeanor or felony; or

(c) The firearm is negligently or recklessly discharged.

IV. Any person who violates paragraph III shall be fined not more than $1,000.

V. This section shall not apply whenever any of the following occurs:

(a) The child has completed firearm safety instructions by a certified firearms safety instructor or has successfully completed a certified hunter safety course.

(b) The firearm is kept secured in a locked box, gun safe, or other secure locked space, or in a location which a reasonable person would believe to be secure, or is secured with a trigger lock or similar device that prevents the firearm from discharging.

(c) The firearm is carried on the person or within such a close proximity thereto so that the individual can readily retrieve and use the firearm as if carried on the person.

(d) The child obtains or obtains and discharges the firearm in a lawful act of self-defense or defense of another person.

(e) The person who keeps a loaded firearm on any premises which are under such person's custody or control has no reasonable expectation, based on objective facts and circumstances, that a child is likely to be present on the premises.

(f) The child obtains the firearm as a result of an illegal entry of any premises by any person or an illegal taking of the firearm from the premises of the owner without permission of the owner.

VI. A parent or guardian of a child who is injured or who dies of an accidental shooting shall be prosecuted under this section only in those instances in which the parent or guardian behaved in a grossly negligent manner.

VII. Licensees shall conspicuously post at each purchase counter the following warning in bold type not less than one inch in height: "IT IS IMPORTANT THAT THE OWNER OF A FIREARM SEEK FIREARM SAFETY INSTRUCTIONS FROM A CERTIFIED FIREARMS INSTRUCTOR AND KEEP FIREARMS SECURED FROM UNAUTHORIZED USE." A licensee failing to display this warning to the purchaser of a firearm shall be guilty of a violation.

Source.
2000, 267:1, eff. Jan. 1, 2001.

Cross References.
Classification of crimes, see RSA 625:9.
Sentences, see RSA 651.

CHAPTER 651

SENTENCES

General Provisions

SECTION
651:1.   Applicability.
651:2.   Sentences and Limitations.
651:3.   Calculation of Periods.
651:4.   Presentence Investigation.
651:4-a.   Victims of Certain Violent Crimes Against a Person Permitted to Speak Before Sentencing and at Sentence Reduction or Suspension Hearings.
651:4-b.   Presentence Investigation of Members and Veterans of the Armed Forces.
651:5.   Annulment of Criminal Records.
651:6.   Extended Term of Imprisonment.
651:7.   Release from State Prison. [Repealed.]

Insane Persons

651:8.   Certificate of Jury.
651:8-a.   Plea of Insanity.
651:8-b.   Hospitalization; Persons Acquitted by Reason of Insanity.
651:9.   Committal. [Repealed.]
651:9-a.   Committal.
651:10.   Discharge or Transfer from Prison.
651:11.   Transfer from County Correctional Facility.
651:11-a.   Duration of Committal Orders.
651:11-b.   Rights of Persons Transferred to State Hospital.

Death Sentences

Sentence to State Prison

651:15.   Sentence to State Prison.
651:16.   Solitary Confinement. [Repealed.]

Sentence to County Correctional Facility

651:17.   Year or Less.
651:18.   Place; Reduction in Sentence.

Discretionary Sentences

651:19.   Release for Purpose of Gainful Employment, Rehabilitation or Home Confinement.
651:19-a.   Day Reporting Program.
651:20.   Incarceration Under Suspended Sentence.
651:21.   Terms on Revocation of Suspended Sentence.
651:22.   Jurisdiction Over and Disposition of Wages and Income.
651:23.   Change of Place of Confinement. [Repealed.]
651:24.   Failure to Report Deemed Escape.
651:25.   Release from State Prison.

Conditional Sentence of Fine or Imprisonment

Sentences Against Corporations

651:28.   Default.

Employment of Prisoners on State Roads, etc.

Employment of County Correctional Facility Prisoners

651:36-a.   Uncompensated Public Service by Prisoners.

Parole of Prisoners

Out-Of-State Parolee Supervision

651:56.   Execution of Compact Authorized. [Repealed.]

Review of State Prison Sentences

651:57.   Review Division.
651:58.   Application for Review.
651:59.   Review Procedure.
651:60.   Amendment of Sentence.
651:61.   Records.
651:61-a.   Statement of Purpose.

Restitution

651:62.   Definitions.
651:63.   Restitution Authorized.
651:64.   Time and Method of Restitution.
651:65.   Civil Actions.
651:66.   Revocation of Restitution.
651:67.   Failure to Make Restitution.

Uncompensated Public Service

651:68.   Uncompensated Public Service.
651:69.   Compensation.
651:70.   Liability.

Cross References.
Assaults by prisoners, see RSA 642:9.
Department of corrections, see RSA 21-H.
Escape, see RSA 642:6.
Excessive fines and cruel and unusual punishments prohibited, see New Hampshire Constitution, Part 1, Article 33.

Fines, costs and discharges, see RSA 618.

Implements for escape and other contraband, see RSA 642:7.

Interstate Corrections Compact, see RSA 622-B.

New England Interstate Corrections Compact, see RSA 622-A.

Parole of delinquents, see RSA 170-H.

Parole of prisoner, see RSA 651-A.

Penalties to be proportioned to offenses, see New Hampshire Constitution, Part 1, Article 18.

Rendition of prisoners as witnesses, see RSA 613-A.

True design of punishment, see New Hampshire Constitution, Part 1, Article 18.

Youth development center, see RSA 621.

NOTES TO DECISIONS

Discretion of court

Sentencing is within the discretion of the trial court unless the sentence is grossly disproportionate to the crime. State v. Wheeler, 120 N.H. 496, 416 A.2d 1384, 1980 N.H. LEXIS 331 (1980), overruled in part, State v. Landry, 131 N.H. 65, 550 A.2d 94, 1988 N.H. LEXIS 83 (1988).

RESEARCH REFERENCES

Workers' Compensation Manual.

Employees Covered, see § 5.02.

General Provisions

651:1. Applicability.

I. The provisions of this chapter govern the sentencing for every offense, whether defined within or outside the code, except as provided by RSA 630.

II. This chapter does not deprive the court of any authority conferred by law to decree a forfeiture of property, suspend or cancel a license, remove a person from office, or impose any other civil penalty. Any appropriate order exercising that authority may be included as part of the judgment of conviction.

Source.

1971, 518:1. 1973, 370:1, eff. Nov. 1, 1973.

Amendments

—**1973.** Paragraph I: Deleted "other than murder" following "offense" and added "except as provided by RSA 630" following "code".

NOTES TO DECISIONS

1. Sentence for homicide
2. Suspension of license

1. Sentence for homicide

When RSA 630:1-a, III, this section, and RSA 651:20, I(a), are read together, RSA 651:20, I(a), cannot be construed to allow persons convicted of first degree murder to petition for sentence suspension; such a construction, if adopted, would defeat the underlying legislative intent of these statutes by providing new opportunities for first degree murderers to return to society. State v. Farrow, 140 N.H. 473, 667 A.2d 1029, 1995 N.H. LEXIS 174 (1995).

Although RSA 651:20, I(a), confers general discretion upon a sentencing court to suspend a sentence, RSA 630:1-a, III, and this section clearly and specifically limit the court's authority in sentencing first degree murderers and, because RSA 630:1-a, III, and this section, provide specific exceptions to the more general rule found in RSA 651:20, I(a), they control. State v. Farrow, 140 N.H. 473, 667 A.2d 1029, 1995 N.H. LEXIS 174 (1995).

Although court has authority under RSA 651:20 to suspend a

sentence that has already been imposed or is being executed, such authority is specifically made inapplicable to all sentences imposed for first degree murder under RSA 630:1-a, III by virtue of this section. State v. Smith, 119 N.H. 674, 406 A.2d 135, 1979 N.H. LEXIS 353 (1979).

2. Suspension of license

This section granted no authority to suspend or revoke a license, and court could not revoke license of person found guilty of negligent homicide. State v. Buckingham, 121 N.H. 339, 430 A.2d 135, 1981 N.H. LEXIS 315 (1981). (RSA 630:3, III now provides for revocation of driving license following conviction of negligent homicide.)

Cited:

Cited in State v. Thayer, 118 N.H. 819, 395 A.2d 500, 1978 N.H. LEXIS 299 (1978); State v. Perkins, 121 N.H. 713, 435 A.2d 504, 1981 N.H. LEXIS 415 (1981); State v. Philbrick, 127 N.H. 353, 499 A.2d 1341, 1985 N.H. LEXIS 426 (1985); State v. Gatchell, 150 N.H. 642, 843 A.2d 332, 2004 N.H. LEXIS 42 (2004); State v. Horner, 153 N.H. 306, 893 A.2d 683, 2006 N.H. LEXIS 28 (2006).

651:2. Sentences and Limitations.

I. A person convicted of a felony or a Class A misdemeanor may be sentenced to imprisonment, probation, conditional or unconditional discharge, or a fine.

II. If a sentence of imprisonment is imposed, the court shall fix the maximum thereof which is not to exceed:

(a) Fifteen years for a class A felony,

(b) Seven years for a class B felony,

(c) One year for a class A misdemeanor,

(d) Life imprisonment for murder in the second degree, and, in the case of a felony only, a minimum which is not to exceed ½ of the maximum, or if the maximum is life imprisonment, such minimum term as the court may order.

II-a. A person convicted of murder in the first degree shall be sentenced as provided in RSA 630:1-a.

II-b. A person convicted of a second or subsequent offense for the felonious use of a firearm, as provided in RSA 650-A:1, shall, in addition to any punishment provided for the underlying felony, be given a minimum mandatory sentence of 3 years imprisonment. Neither the whole nor any part of the additional sentence of imprisonment hereby provided shall be served concurrently with any other term nor shall the whole or any part of such additional term of imprisonment be suspended. No action brought to enforce sentencing under this section shall be continued for sentencing, nor shall the provisions of RSA 651-A relative to parole apply to any sentence of imprisonment imposed.

II-c. [Repealed.]

II-d. A person convicted of manslaughter shall be sentenced as provided in RSA 630:2, II.

II-e. To the minimum sentence of every person who is sentenced to imprisonment for a maximum of more than one year shall be added a disciplinary period equal to 150 days for each year of the minimum term of the sentence, to be prorated for any part of the year. The presiding justice shall certify, at the time of sentencing, the minimum term of the sentence and the additional disciplinary period required under this paragraph. This additional disciplinary period may be reduced for good conduct as provided in RSA 651-A:22. There shall be no addition to the sentence under this section for the period of pre-trial confinement for which credit against the sentence is awarded pursuant to RSA 651-A:23.

II-f. A person convicted of violating RSA 159:3-a, I shall be sentenced as provided in RSA 159:3-a, II and III.

II-g. If a person is convicted of a felony, an element of which is the possession, use or attempted use of a deadly weapon, and the deadly weapon is a firearm, such person may be sentenced to a maximum term of 20 years' imprisonment in lieu of any other sentence prescribed for the crime.

III. A person convicted of a class B misdemeanor may be sentenced to conditional or unconditional discharge, a fine, or other sanctions, which shall not include incarceration or probation but may include monitoring by the department of corrections if deemed necessary and appropriate.

III-a. A person convicted of a violation may be sentenced to conditional or unconditional discharge, or a fine.

IV. A fine may be imposed in addition to any sentence of imprisonment, probation, or conditional discharge. The limitations on amounts of fines authorized in subparagraphs (a) and (b) shall not include the amount of any civil penalty, the imposition of which is authorized by statute or by a properly adopted local ordinance, code, or regulation. The amount of any fine imposed on:

(a) Any individual may not exceed $4,000 for a felony, $2,000 for a class A misdemeanor, $1,200 for a class B misdemeanor, and $1,000 for a violation.

(b) A corporation or unincorporated association may not exceed $100,000 for a felony, $20,000 for a misdemeanor and $1,000 for a violation. A writ of execution may be issued by the court against the corporation or unincorporated association to compel payment of the fine, together with costs and interest.

(c) If a defendant has gained property through the commission of any felony, then in lieu of the amounts authorized in paragraphs (a) and (b), the fine may be an amount not to exceed double the amount of that gain.

V. (a) A person may be placed on probation if the court finds that such person is in need of the supervision and guidance that the probation service can provide under such conditions as the court may impose. The period of probation shall be for a period to be fixed by the court not to exceed 5 years for a felony and 2 years for a class A misdemeanor. Upon petition of the probation officer or the probationer, the period may be terminated sooner by the court if the conduct of the probationer warrants it.

(b) In cases of persons convicted of felonies or class A misdemeanors, or in cases of persons found to be habitual offenders within the meaning of RSA

259:39 and convicted of an offense under RSA 262:23, the sentence may include, as a condition of probation, confinement to a person's place of residence for not more than one year in case of a class A misdemeanor or more than 5 years in case of a felony. Such home confinement may be monitored by a probation officer and may be supplemented, as determined by the department of corrections or by the county department of corrections, by electronic monitoring to verify compliance.

(c) Upon recommendation by the department of corrections or by the county department of corrections, the court may, as a condition of probation, order an incarceration-bound offender placed in an intensive supervision program as an alternative to incarceration, under requirements and restrictions established by the department of corrections or by the county department of corrections.

(d) Upon recommendation by the department of corrections or by the county department of corrections, the court may sentence an incarceration-bound offender to a special alternative incarceration program involving short term confinement followed by intensive community supervision.

(e) The department of corrections and the various county departments of corrections shall adopt rules governing eligibility for home confinement, intensive supervision and special alternative incarceration programs.

(f) Any offender placed in a home confinement, intensive supervision or special alternative incarceration program who violates the conditions or restrictions of probation shall be subject to immediate arrest by a probation officer or any authorized law enforcement officer and brought before the court for an expeditious hearing pending further disposition.

(g) The court may include, as a condition of probation, restitution to the victim as provided in RSA 651:62–67 or performance of uncompensated public service as provided in RSA 651:68–70.

(h) In cases of a person convicted of a felony or class A misdemeanor, a court may require such person to be screened and/or evaluated for risk of substance use disorders at an impaired driver care management program (IDCMP) approved by the department of health and human services, and to comply with the treatment plan developed by the IDCMP as established under RSA 265-A:40, if the evidence demonstrates that substances were a contributing factor in the commission of the offense and if such person has the ability to pay the fees for the program in full.

(i) The court may include, as a condition of probation for a felony offense, a jail sentence of up to 30 days that a probation/parole officer may impose in segments of one to 7 days over the course of the probation period, in response to any violation of a condition of probation, in lieu of a violation of probation hearing. Such jail sanction shall be served at the county jail facility closest to or in reasonable proximity to where the probationer is under supervision.

VI. (a) A person may be sentenced to a period of conditional discharge if such person is not imprisoned and the court is of the opinion that probationary supervision is unnecessary, but that the defendant's conduct should be according to conditions determined by the court. Such conditions may include:

(1) Restrictions on the defendant's travel, association, place of abode, such as will protect the victim of the crime or insure the public peace;

(2) An order requiring the defendant to attend counselling or any other mode of treatment the court deems appropriate;

(3) Restitution to the victim; and

(4) Performance of uncompensated public service as provided in RSA 651:68–70.

(b) The period of a conditional discharge shall be 3 years for a felony and one year for a misdemeanor or violation. However, if the court has required as a condition that the defendant make restitution or reparation to the victim of the defendant's offense or that the defendant perform uncompensated public service and that condition has not been satisfied, the court may, at any time prior to the termination of the above periods, extend the period for a felony by no more than 2 years and for a misdemeanor or violation by no more than one year in order to allow the defendant to satisfy the condition. During any period of conditional discharge the court may, upon its own motion or on petition of the defendant, discharge the defendant unconditionally if the conduct of the defendant warrants it. The court is not required to revoke a conditional discharge if the defendant commits an additional offense or violates a condition.

VI-a. [Repealed.]

VI-b. A person sentenced to conditional discharge under paragraph VI may apply for annulment of the criminal record under RSA 651:5.

VII. When a probation or a conditional discharge is revoked, the defendant may be fined, as authorized by paragraph IV, if a fine was not imposed in addition to the probation or conditional discharge. Otherwise the defendant shall be sentenced to imprisonment as authorized by paragraph II.

VIII. A person may be granted an unconditional discharge if the court is of the opinion that no proper purpose would be served by imposing any condition or supervision upon the defendant's release. A sentence of unconditional discharge is for all purposes a final judgment of conviction.

Source.

1971, 518:1. 1973, 370:2. 1974, 34:13, 14. 1977, 397:1; 403:2. 1979, 126:6; 377:8. 1981, 397:1. 1982, 36:2. 1983, 382:8. 1986, 156:4. 1988, 19:4. 1989, 295:2. 1990, 95:1. 1991, 355:102. 1992, 19:1; 269:8–10; 284:85, 86, XIII. 1994, 192:1, 2, eff. July 1, 1994. 1995, 237:4, eff. Jan. 1, 1996. 1996, 93:2–9, eff. Jan. 1, 1997. 1998, 366:3, eff. June 26, 1998. 1999, 158:4, eff. June 28, 1999. 2006, 163:1, eff. January 1, 2007. 2006, 260:33, eff. January 1, 2007. 2010, 247:12, eff. July 1, 2010. 2010S, 1:24, eff. June 10, 2010. 2011 268:2, eff. November 13, 2011. 2012, 228:10, eff. January 1, 2013. 2013, 156:8, eff. July 1, 2013.

Revision note.

In par. II-b, substituted "RSA 651-A" for "RSA 651" and in par. II-e, substituted "RSA 651-A:22" for "RSA 651:55-b" and "RSA 651-A:23" for "RSA 651:55-c". RSA 651:37–651:56, relative to parole, were repealed by 1983, 461, which enacted RSA 651-A, which deals with the subject matter formerly covered by the repealed sections.

Amendments

—2013. The 2013 amendment, in the first sentence of V(i), substituted "up to 30 days" for "one to 5 days" and added "segments of one to 7 days over the course of the probation period, in" and made a stylistic change.

—2012. The 2012 amendment, in V(h), substituted "require such person to be screened and/or evaluated for risk of substance use disorders at an impaired driver care management program (IDCMP) approved by the department of health and human services, and to comply with the treatment plan developed by the IDCMP as" for "sentence such person to 7 consecutive 24-hour periods to be served at the 7-day multiple DWI offender intervention program," substituted "substances were" for "alcohol was," substituted "if such person has the ability to pay" for "provided that space is available in the program and such person pays," and deleted "prior to admission" at the end.

—2011. The 2011 amendment deleted the former second and third sentences of II-g.

—2010. The 2010 amendment by Chapter 247 added V(i).

The 2010 amendment by Chapter 1 (Spec. Sess.), in V(h), deleted "state-operated" preceding "7-day multiple" and substituted "offender intervention program" for "offender intervention detention center program."

—2006. Paragraph II-b: In the first sentence, inserted "a second or subsequent offense for" following "convicted of", deleted "minimum mandatory sentence of one year imprisonment for a first offense and a" following "be given a", and substituted "3 years" for "3 years'" preceding "imprisonment" and deleted "for any subsequent offense" thereafter.

Paragraph V(h): Substituted "RSA 265-A:40" for "RSA 172-B:2-b".

—1999. Paragraph II-c: Repealed.

—1998. Paragraph V(h): Added.

—1996. Paragraph II-e: Substituted "the" for "his" preceding "sentence" in the first sentence.

Paragraph II-g: Substituted "such person" for "he" preceding "may be sentenced" in the first sentence and "the person" for "he" preceding "shall be given", and "such person" for "he" preceding "has been previously" in the second sentence.

Paragraph III: Rewritten to the extent that a detailed comparison would be impracticable.

Paragraph III-a: Added.

Paragraph V(a): Substituted "that such person" for "he" following "court finds" in the first sentence and "and 2 years for a class A misdemeanor" for "2 years for a misdemeanor and one year for a violation" following "felony" in the second sentence.

Paragraph V(b): Inserted "class A" in two places in the first sentence.

Paragraph V(f): Deleted "his" preceding "probation shall".

Paragraph VI(a): Substituted "such person" for "he" following "discharge if" and "defendant's conduct should be" for "defendant should conduct himself" preceding "according" in the introductory paragraph.

Paragraph VI(b): Substituted "the defendant's" for "his" preceding "offense" in the second sentence.

—1995. Paragraph VI-b: Added.

—1994. Paragraph V(g): Added.

Paragraph VI: Rewritten to the extent that a detailed comparison would be impracticable.

—1992. Paragraph I: Chapter 269 inserted "a class A" preceding "misdemeanor".

Paragraph II(c): Chapter 269 inserted "class A" preceding "misdemeanor".

Paragraph III: Chapter 269 inserted "class B misdemeanor or a" preceding "violation".

Paragraph IV(a): Chapter 269 inserted "$1,200 for a class B misdemeanor" preceding "and $1,000".

Paragraph V: Rewritten by ch. 19 to the extent that a detailed comparison would be impracticable.

Paragraph VI: Chapter 284 deleted "and" at the end of clause (b), added "and" at the end of clause (c) and added clause (d) of the second sentence, added the third sentence, and inserted "or that the defendant perform community service" following "offense" in the fifth sentence.

Paragraph VI-a: Repealed by ch. 284.

—1991. Paragraph IV(a): Substituted "$4,000" for "$2,000", "$2,000" for "$1,000" and "$1,000" for "$500".

Paragraph IV(b): Substituted "$100,000" for "$50,000", "$20,000" for "$10,000" and "$1,000" for "$500" in the first sentence.

—1990. Paragraph II-g: Added.

—1989. Paragraph II-f: Added.

—1988. Paragraph IV: Added the second sentence in the introductory paragraph.

—1986. Paragraph V: Added the fourth through ninth sentences.

—1983. Paragraph IV(a): Substituted "$2,000" for "two thousand dollars", "$1,000" for "one thousand dollars", and "$500" for "one hundred dollars".

—1982. Paragraph II-e: Added.

—1981. Paragraph II-b: Rewritten to the extent that a detailed comparison would be impracticable.

—1979. Paragraphs II-c and II-d: Added by ch. 126.
Paragraph VI: Chapter 377 added the second sentence.

—1977. Paragraph II-b: Added by ch. 403.
Paragraph VI-a: Added by ch. 397.

—1974. Paragraph II(d): Added "in the second degree" following "murder".
Paragraph II-a: Added.

—1973. Paragraph II: Added subpar. (d) and "or if the maximum is life imprisonment, such minimum term as the court may order" following "maximum" at the end of the paragraph.

Severability of enactment.
Paragraph II-e of this section is subject to a severability clause.

Applicability of 2013 amendment.
2013, 156:11, eff. July 1, 2013, provided: "The provisions of sections 1–8 of this act shall apply to:
"I. Any person who is on parole or eligible for parole, on or after the effective date of this act; and
"II. Any person who, on or after the effective date of this act, has violated the conditions of parole after a hearing pursuant to RSA 651-A:17."

Applicability of 1992 amendment.
1992, 269:21, eff. July 1, 1992, provided that the amendments to this section by 1992, 269:8–10, shall apply to all offenses committed on or after July 1, 1992.

Effect of 1982 amendment on prior law.
1982, 36:9, eff. May 22, 1982, provided: "Any person convicted of a crime any element of which occurred prior to the effective date of this act [May 22, 1982] shall be subject to the sentencing, parole and credit for good conduct provisions of the law as such provisions existed immediately prior to the effective date of this act [May 22, 1982]. Such provisions of law shall be continued in effect, only for such purpose, as if this act [Laws 1982, 36] were not in force."

Transition Provision; Phasing-out Multiple DWI Offender Intervention Program (M.O.P.) for the Impaired Driver Care Management Program (IDCMP).
2012, 228:11, eff. January 1, 2013, provided: "If a person was sentenced to the multiple DWI offender intervention program (M.O.P.) under RSA 651:2, V(h) or RSA 265-A:18 prior to January 1, 2013, and the person has not successfully completed the multiple DWI offender intervention program as of January 30, 2013, then such person shall be required to participate in the impaired driver care management program (IDCMP) as established under RSA 265-A:40."

Cross References.
Administrative Procedure Act, see RSA 541-A.
Discretionary sentences, see RSA 651:19 et seq.
Extended term of imprisonment, see RSA 651:6.
Limitation on time for bringing petition to suspend sentence, see RSA 651:20.
Mandatory sentences for habitual motor vehicle offenders, see RSA 262:23.
Probation, see RSA 504-A.
Probationers and parolees generally, see RSA 504-A.
Sentence for bail jumping, see RSA 642:8.
Sentence to house of correction or jail, see RSA 651:17 et seq.
Sentence to make restitution, see RSA 651:61-a et seq.
Sentence to state prison, see RSA 651:15.

NOTES TO DECISIONS

1. Constitutionality
2. Construction
3. Validity of statute
4. Discretion of court
5. Mandatory language
6. Consecutive sentences
7. Disciplinary period
8. Suspended sentence
9. Conditional discharge
10. Probation violation
11. Double jeopardy
12. Unanimity requirement
13. Deadly weapon
14. Amendment of sentence
15. Probation
16. Miscellaneous

1. Constitutionality
Imposition of a mandatory sentence of three to six years in state prison under RSA 651:2, II-g for conviction of criminal threatening under RSA 631:4 did not violate N.H. Const. pt. I, art. 18 or U.S. Const. amends. VIII and XIV. Defendant failed to persuade the court that the sentencing scheme was unconstitutional because it necessarily resulted in sentences that were disproportionate. State v. Bird, 161 N.H. 31, 8 A.3d 146, 2010 N.H. LEXIS 125 (2010).

2. Construction
RSA 651:21 provides no vehicle for importing into RSA 651:20 the temporal limits upon probation within RSA 651:2, V, as that would be limiting the greater by the constraints placed upon the lesser. State v. Moran, 158 N.H. 318, 965 A.2d 1024, 2009 N.H. LEXIS 12 (2009).
Since the commitment to prison of a mentally deranged person accused of crime was not a sentence within the meaning of this section, it had no application in such cases. State v. Johnson, 96 N.H. 4, 69 A.2d 515, 1949 N.H. LEXIS 3 (1949). (Decided under prior law.)

3. Validity of statute
RSA 651:2, II-e, enacted during a special session called by the Governor of New Hampshire pursuant to N.H. Const. pt. II, art. 50, was not invalid for having been outside of the matters enumerated in the Governor's resolution. N.H. Const. pt. II, art. 5 conferred on

the legislature the "full power and authority" to make laws, whether in regular or special session. Starr v. Governor, 154 N.H. 174, 910 A.2d 1247, 2006 N.H. LEXIS 140 (2006), rehearing denied, 2006 N.H. LEXIS 193 (N.H. Nov. 27, 2006).

Inmate's challenge to RSA 651:2, II-e on grounds that the legislature did not follow its own procedures when it enacted that statute presented a nonjusticiable political question. Starr v. Governor, 154 N.H. 174, 910 A.2d 1247, 2006 N.H. LEXIS 140 (2006), rehearing denied, 2006 N.H. LEXIS 193 (N.H. Nov. 27, 2006).

Assuming arguendo that the due process protections provided by N.H. Const. pt. I, art. 15 applied to the passage of legislation, an inmate's due process rights were not violated by the enactment of RSA 651:2, II-e, as the session during which this occurred was open to the public, as required by RSA 91-A:1-a, I(a) and 91-A:2, II. Starr v. Governor, 154 N.H. 174, 910 A.2d 1247, 2006 N.H. LEXIS 140 (2006), rehearing denied, 2006 N.H. LEXIS 193 (N.H. Nov. 27, 2006).

4. Discretion of court

Trial court did not abuse its discretion in imposing a twenty-to-forty year sentence for defendant's convictions of manslaughter and first degree assault in connection with death of seven-month-old child; there was no requirement that all sentences for a particular crime be identical, and court considered all relevant factors, including misrepresentations defendant made regarding cause of victim's injuries, fact that shaking incident was not the only instance of abuse, and defendant's lack of remorse. State v. Hammond, 144 N.H. 401, 742 A.2d 532, 1999 N.H. LEXIS 129 (1999).

Within this section's parameters, judge has broad discretion to assign different sentences, suspend sentence, or grant probation. State v. W.J.T. Enters., 136 N.H. 490, 618 A.2d 806, 1992 N.H. LEXIS 211 (1992).

This section demonstrates a continuing intent by the legislature to provide the sentencing judge with options to adapt his or her sentence to a particular individual in the manner best suited to accomplish the constitutional objectives of punishment, rehabilitation and deterrence. State v. W.J.T. Enters., 136 N.H. 490, 618 A.2d 806, 1992 N.H. LEXIS 211 (1992).

Within the parameters set by this section, the sentencing judge has broad discretion to assign different sentences, suspend sentence, or grant probation in order to achieve the goals of punishment, deterrence, protection of society and rehabilitation. State v. Evans, 127 N.H. 501, 506 A.2d 695, 1985 N.H. LEXIS 478 (1985).

Trial judges are vested with broad discretionary powers with regard to sentencing; they may provide for terms of imprisonment, probation, conditional or unconditional discharge, or a fine. State v. Rau, 129 N.H. 126, 523 A.2d 98, 1987 N.H. LEXIS 154 (1987).

Trial judges have broad authority under this section to provide for extended terms of imprisonment, a range of fines, probation, and conditional or unconditional discharge. Stapleford v. Perrin, 122 N.H. 1083, 453 A.2d 1304, 1982 N.H. LEXIS 525 (1982).

This section and RSA 651:20, authorizing suspended sentences, demonstrate an intent by the legislature to provide the sentencing judge with options to adapt his sentence to a particular individual in the manner best suited to accomplish the constitutional objectives of punishment, rehabilitation and deterrence. State v. Burroughs, 113 N.H. 21, 300 A.2d 315, 1973 N.H. LEXIS 189 (1973).

5. Mandatory language

Because RSA 651:2, II-g made it clear that it applied when a defendant had been convicted of a felony, an element of which was the possession, use or attempted use of a firearm, absent a specific finding by the jury, RSA 651:2, II-g was not applicable. Thus, the trial court erred in sentencing defendant to the minimum mandatory sentence where the appellate court could not determine in light of the jury instructions, whether the offense for which defendant was actually convicted included the element of possession of a firearm. State v. Henderson, 154 N.H. 95, 907 A.2d 968, 2006 N.H. LEXIS 128 (2006).

In a prosecution of defendant for possession of a firearm by a felon, in violation of RSA 159:3, the trial court erred in applying the mandatory minimum sentencing provision of RSA 651:2, II-g, where the indictments to which defendant pled guilty did not allege that defendant possessed, used, or attempted to use a firearm. State v. Taylor, 152 N.H. 719, 886 A.2d 1012, 2005 N.H. LEXIS 164 (2005).

Minimum mandatory sentence provision of subdivision II-g applied to defendant's felony conviction of reckless conduct with a deadly weapon under RSA 631:3, II. State v. Haines, 142 N.H. 692, 709 A.2d 762, 1998 N.H. LEXIS 23 (1998).

Where the defendant was convicted for driving after being certified as an habitual offender in violation of RSA 262:23, the court did not have the authority to sentence him to 12 months of probation and concurrent home confinement and, instead, was required to impose a minimum mandatory sentence of one year imprisonment since his convictions underlying his habitual offender certification included a conviction for DWI; a contrary result was not required by this section which empowers a trial court to impose a sentence that "may include, as a condition of probation," home confinement since this statute does not purport to abrogate the imposition of a mandatory sentence and simply gives the trial court the power to impose home confinement when probation is otherwise appropriate. State v. Langille (In re State), 139 N.H. 705, 661 A.2d 766, 1995 N.H. LEXIS 76 (1995).

The plain language as well as the legislative history of RSA 650-A:1, governing felonious use of firearms, and paragraph II-b of this section, governing sentencing of persons convicted of felonious use of a firearm, evince a clear legislative intent to provide for a mandatory consecutive sentence for the use of a firearm in the commission of all felonies, including armed robbery. Heald v. Perrin, 123 N.H. 468, 464 A.2d 275, 1983 N.H. LEXIS 310 (1983), superseded by statute as stated in, State v. Nickles, 144 N.H. 673, 749 A.2d 290, 2000 N.H. LEXIS 9 (2000)(superseded by enactment of RSA 651:2, II-g).

6. Consecutive sentences

Although RSA 651:2, 632-A:10-a, and 651:3 did not authorize consecutive sentences for defendant's convictions for several counts of aggravated felonious sexual assault, by repealing former RSA 651:3, III, the legislature intended to revive the common law authority for judges to impose consecutive sentences. Duquette v. Warden, N.H. State Prison, 154 N.H. 737, 919 A.2d 767, 2007 N.H. LEXIS 10 (2007).

7. Disciplinary period

Disciplinary period may be added to the minimum term of a sentence even if the sum of time to be served will then exceed one-half the maximum term of the sentence. State v. Wheeler, 127 N.H. 337, 499 A.2d 1005, 1985 N.H. LEXIS 449 (1985).

8. Suspended sentence

Suspension of sentences is not obligatory; rather, suspension can occur on satisfaction of a condition imposed, or not at all. State v. W.J.T. Enters., 136 N.H. 490, 618 A.2d 806, 1992 N.H. LEXIS 211 (1992).

9. Conditional discharge

Where defendant pleaded guilty to a charge of felony arson and was given a one-year suspended sentence with the additional statement "conditional discharge if merited," the defendant's sentence did not incorporate a one-year conditional discharge, contrary to the defendant's argument on appeal, and the trial court had no authority to impose a one-year conditional discharge under paragraph VI of this section, since the defendant pleaded guilty to a felony, the sentencing judge could not impose a sentence that included a conditional discharge for a period more or less than three years. State v. Michael B., 124 N.H. 590, 474 A.2d 564, 1984 N.H. LEXIS 349 (1984).

Where defendant pleaded guilty to a charge of felony arson and was given a one-year suspended sentence, with the additional statement "conditional discharge if merited," the supreme court remanded the case to the superior court for a rehearing by the original sentencing judge on the matter of conditional discharge alone, since it was unclear whether a sentence of conditional discharge was imposed, and while the language used by the sentencing judge might support the conclusion that a sentence of conditional discharge was imposed, the sentencing judge did not clearly specify the conditions that would control the defendant's right to a discharge after three years, as appeared to be contemplated by paragraph VI of this section. State v. Michael B., 124 N.H. 590, 474 A.2d 564, 1984 N.H. LEXIS 349 (1984).

10. Probation violation

After defendant was placed on probation for possession of a controlled drug, under RSA 318-B:2, a class B felony, and his violation of probation was found, to the extent the term of his probation was extended beyond five years, the trial court's judgment was plain error, under N.H. Sup. Ct. R. 16-A, because a term of probation exceeding the five-year maximum allowable under RSA 651:2, V(a) was illegal. State v. Matey, 153 N.H. 263, 891 A.2d 592, 2006 N.H. LEXIS 11 (2006).

After defendant was placed on probation for possession of a controlled drug, under RSA 318-B:2, a class B felony, and his violation of probation was found, it was not plainly erroneous, under N.H. Sup. Ct. R. 16-A, for a trial court to resentence him to a longer period of probation, as long as that period did not exceed the five-year maximum in RSA 651:2, V(a), because the law on the propriety of such a sentence was not clear at the time it was imposed. State v. Matey, 153 N.H. 263, 891 A.2d 592, 2006 N.H. LEXIS 11 (2006).

Paragraph VII of this section authorizes courts to impose fines or imprisonment upon probation violation up to the balance of the maximum which could have been imposed originally. State v. White, 131 N.H. 555, 556 A.2d 308, 1989 N.H. LEXIS 26 (1989).

11. Double jeopardy

Double jeopardy provision of State Constitution was not violated by sentence enhancement under statute requiring minimum mandatory sentence for firearms, in combination with enhancement of reckless conduct from misdemeanor to Class B felony for use of deadly weapon. State v. Haines, 142 N.H. 692, 709 A.2d 762, 1998 N.H. LEXIS 23 (1998).

12. Unanimity requirement

Constitutional mandate of unanimity in the jury verdict to enhance the defendant's sentences was met because, in light of the jury instructions as a whole and the evidence presented at trial, a reasonable jury would understand that the deadly weapon element of both the criminal threatening charges against the defendant exclusively referred to the use of a firearm. Therefore, the guilty verdicts reflected a unanimous conclusion that the defendant used a firearm, and no other object, as a deadly weapon to commit the crimes. State v. Higgins, 149 N.H. 290, 821 A.2d 964, 2003 N.H. LEXIS 41 (2003).

13. Deadly weapon

When defendant was convicted of being a felon in possession of a firearm under RSA 159:3, I, it was plain error to sentence him to the minimum mandatory sentence pursuant to RSA 651:2, II-g. The elements of the crime did not include a showing that the firearm was a deadly weapon, and a firearm was not a deadly weapon per se. State v. Charest, 164 N.H. 252, 55 A.3d 960, 2012 N.H. LEXIS 135 (2012).

Trial court did not violate the federal Constitution in imposing an enhanced sentence pursuant to RSA 651:2, II-g. Any Apprendi violation in not charging the enhancement factor in the indictment was harmless, as a grand jury would have found a shotgun to be a deadly weapon and a firearm; furthermore, there was no prejudice to defendant, as the issue of an enhanced sentence under RSA 651:2, II-g did not arise until defendant requested that the trial court instruct the jury on reckless second degree assault as a lesser included offense of attempted murder. State v. Fichera, 160 N.H. 660, 7 A.3d 1151, 2010 N.H. LEXIS 98 (2010).

Any error arising out of the failure of the trial court to instruct the jury regarding use of a firearm under RSA 651:2, II-g was harmless. The jury could only have found defendant guilty of a second-degree assault charge if it also found he used a firearm. State v. Fichera, 160 N.H. 660, 7 A.3d 1151, 2010 N.H. LEXIS 98 (2010).

Trial court did not err in imposing a mandatory minimum sentence under RSA 651:2, II-g. In light of the language of the indictment and the evidence presented at trial, a reasonable jury would have understood that to find defendant guilty it had to find that defendant used a firearm as a deadly weapon. State v. Bird, 161 N.H. 31, 8 A.3d 146, 2010 N.H. LEXIS 125 (2010).

RSA 651:2, VII, provided that violations of probation could be punished only through the imposition of a fine or a term of imprisonment. Thus, it was error to revoke defendant's license for violation of his probation. State v. Pandelena, 161 N.H. 326, 13 A.3d 239, 2010 N.H. LEXIS 184 (Dec. 22, 2010).

Standard language included in a defendant's mittimus that "violations of probation or any of the terms of this sentence may result in revocation of probation and imposition of any sentence within the legal limits for the underlying offense" does not permit a trial court to sentence a defendant to anything other than a fine or imprisonment for a probation violation. A mittimus cannot confer on the trial court a sentencing power not granted to it by the legislature. State v. Pandelena, 161 N.H. 326, 13 A.3d 239, 2010 N.H. LEXIS 184 (Dec. 22, 2010).

Although the trial court erred in imposing a sentence enhancement under RSA 651:2, II-g without having instructed the jury that it had to find that defendant used a firearm during the armed robbery, the court declined to reverse under the plain error rule of N.H. Sup. Ct. R. 16-A. The evidence that defendant used a firearm during the robbery was overwhelming and essentially uncontroverted. State v. Russell, 159 N.H. 475, 986 A.2d 515, 2009 N.H. LEXIS 141 (2009).

Trial court erred in imposing an enhanced sentence under RSA 651:2, II-g. One of the elements of the offense for which defendant was convicted, felony receipt of stolen property under RSA 637:7 and RSA 637:11, I(b), was not the possession, use, or attempted use of a deadly weapon. State v. Mohamed, 159 N.H. 559, 986 A.2d 649, 2009 N.H. LEXIS 149 (2009).

Requirement of possession, use, or attempted use of a deadly weapon as an element of RSA 651:2, II-g applies only to a defendant's current conviction; under the three-year provision, the nature of the defendant's prior felony conviction is immaterial because it is relevant only with respect to the six-year provision. Thus, when defendant was convicted of being a felon in possession of a dangerous weapon, it was immaterial that his underlying felony of negligent homicide had not involved use or possession of a weapon. State v. Crie, 154 N.H. 403, 913 A.2d 767, 2006 N.H. LEXIS 179 (2006).

RSA 651:2, II-g is plain and unambiguous. It provides a three-year minimum sentence if three conditions are met: (1) the defendant is convicted of a felony; (2) one of the elements of the crime is possession, use or attempted use of a deadly weapon; and (3) the deadly weapon is a firearm. State v. Crie, 154 N.H. 403, 913 A.2d 767, 2006 N.H. LEXIS 179 (2006).

Where an indictment specifically alleges that a defendant had firearms in his possession, the offense as alleged under RSA 159:3 is within the scope of RSA 651:2, II-g. State v. Crie, 154 N.H. 403, 913 A.2d 767, 2006 N.H. LEXIS 179 (2006).

14. Amendment of sentence

A sentence in excess of the prescribed maximum may be amended. State v. Richard, 99 N.H. 126, 106 A.2d 194, 1954 N.H. LEXIS 26 (1954). (Decided under prior law.)

15. Probation

There was no error under RSA 651:2 in sentencing defendant to a stand-committed prison term of one to three years and probation for two years on the same charge, as portions of the maximum term of imprisonment remained unimposed. State v. Martin, 164 N.H. 687, 62 A.3d 864, 2013 N.H. LEXIS 26 (2013).

Under RSA 651:2, it was error to sentence defendant, who was convicted of unfair and deceptive trade practices, to 12 months in jail, two years of probation, and a $2,000 fine, with the fine suspended on the condition that he pay $4,000 in restitution. Although a trial court had discretion to sentence a defendant to incarceration, impose a fine, or impose a combination of the two, it could not sentence a defendant to both statutory maximums if it also imposed probation. State v. Sideris, 157 N.H. 258, 951 A.2d 164, 2008 N.H. LEXIS 60 (2008).

Trial court committed plain error by sentencing defendant to 12 months in jail, a $2,000 fine and two years probation for misdemeanor simple assault constituting a violation of his probation because under RSA 651:2, the trial court, in order to impose probation, was required to retain a portion of its sentencing power as an enforcement mechanism; the trial court's failure to do so was plain error. RSA 651:2, VII mandates that probation violations be enforced exclusively through imposing a fine, under RSA 651:2, IV, or imprisonment under RSA 651:2, II; although the trial court has discretion to sentence a defendant to incarceration, impose a fine, or a combination of the two, it may not sentence a defendant to both statutory maximums if it also imposes probation. State v. Hancock, 156 N.H. 301, 934 A.2d 551, 2007 N.H. LEXIS 183 (2007).

16. Miscellaneous

Read as a whole, a sentencing order committed defendant to state prison, and a drug court program, as set forth in the sentencing order, was neither a "day reporting" program nor "home confinement"; thus, RSA 651:19 and RSA 651:19-a, which defendant argued entitled him to pretrial confinement credit for the drug court program, did not apply. Furthermore, to the extent that defendant argued that conditioning the suspension of his sentence upon successful completion of the drug court program was unlawful because the sentence was not issued pursuant to RSA 651:19 and RSA 651:19-a, he was mistaken, as his sentence was authorized by RSA 651:2, I, II, and RSA 651:20. State v. Dimaggio, 163 N.H. 497, 44 A.3d 468, 2012 N.H. LEXIS 45 (2012).

Where a professor unleashed a tirade against a colleague, the false arrest claim based on a disorderly conduct charge failed because there was probable cause for the professor's arrest on the disorderly conduct charge, and the professor's argument regarding an alleged distinction between crimes and violations under New Hampshire law was rejected. Collins v. Univ. of N.H., 664 F.3d 8, 2011 U.S. App. LEXIS 25146 (2011).

Cited:

Cited in State v. Belanger, 114 N.H. 616, 325 A.2d 789, 1974 N.H. LEXIS 333 (1974); Doe v. State, 114 N.H. 714, 328 A.2d 784, 1974 N.H. LEXIS 359 (1974); State v. Dunphy, 114 N.H. 740, 328 A.2d 787, 1974 N.H. LEXIS 363 (1974); State v. Payne, 115 N.H. 595, 347 A.2d 157, 1975 N.H. LEXIS 370 (1975); State v. McMillan, 116 N.H. 126, 352 A.2d 702, 1976 N.H. LEXIS 283 (1976); State v. Taschler, 116 N.H. 218, 356 A.2d 697, 1976 N.H. LEXIS 312 (1976); State v. Pratt, 116 N.H. 385, 359 A.2d 642, 1976 N.H. LEXIS 360 (1976); Nichols v. Helgemoe, 117 N.H. 57, 369 A.2d 614, 1977 N.H. LEXIS 266 (1977); State v. Komisarek, 118 N.H. 524, 388 A.2d 1263, 1978 N.H. LEXIS 230 (1978); State v. Roe, 118 N.H. 690, 393 A.2d 553, 1978 N.H. LEXIS 271 (1978); State v. Thayer, 118 N.H. 819, 395 A.2d 500, 1978 N.H. LEXIS 299 (1978); State v. Wentworth, 118 N.H. 832, 395 A.2d 858, 1978 N.H. LEXIS 302 (1978); State v. Holland, 119 N.H. 200, 399 A.2d 976, 1979 N.H. LEXIS 275 (1979); Grindle v. Miller, 119 N.H. 214, 400 A.2d 787, 1979 N.H. LEXIS 280 (1979); State v. Mullen, 119 N.H. 703, 406 A.2d 698, 1979 N.H. LEXIS 352 (1979); State v. Fraser, 120 N.H. 117, 411 A.2d 1125, 1980 N.H. LEXIS 241 (1980); State v. Sampson, 120 N.H. 251, 413 A.2d 590, 1980 N.H. LEXIS 268 (1980); State v. Morehouse, 120 N.H. 738, 424 A.2d 798, 1980 N.H. LEXIS 406 (1980); Koski v. Samaha, 648 F.2d 790, 1981 U.S. App. LEXIS 13062 (1st Cir. 1981); McCollester v. Keene, 514 F. Supp. 1046, 1981 U.S. Dist. LEXIS 12208 (D.N.H. 1981); State v. Darcy, 121 N.H. 220, 427 A.2d 516, 1981 N.H. LEXIS 283 (1981); State v. Buckingham, 121 N.H. 339, 430 A.2d 135, 1981 N.H. LEXIS 315 (1981); Opinion of Justices, 121 N.H. 531, 431 A.2d 144, 1981 N.H. LEXIS 342 (1981); State v. Perkins, 121 N.H. 713, 435 A.2d 504, 1981 N.H. LEXIS 415 (1981); State v. Peabody, 121 N.H. 1075, 438 A.2d 305, 1981 N.H. LEXIS 469 (1981); State v. Dumont, 122 N.H. 866, 451 A.2d 1286, 1982 N.H. LEXIS 478 (1982); Kozerski v. Smith, 555 F. Supp. 212, 1983 U.S. Dist. LEXIS 20099 (D.N.H. 1983); State v. Toto, 123 N.H. 619, 465 A.2d 894, 1983 N.H. LEXIS 344 (1983); State v. Morrill, 123 N.H. 707, 465 A.2d 882, 1983 N.H. LEXIS 338 (1983); State v. Hamilton, 123 N.H. 686, 465 A.2d 495, 1983 N.H. LEXIS 334 (1983); La Vallee v. Perrin, 124 N.H. 33, 466 A.2d 932, 1983 N.H. LEXIS 354 (1983); State v. Shannon, 125 N.H. 653, 484 A.2d 1164, 1984 N.H. LEXIS 380 (1984); State v. Goding, 126 N.H. 50, 489 A.2d 579, 1985 N.H. LEXIS 241 (1985); Sands v. Cunningham, 617 F. Supp. 1551, 1985 U.S. Dist. LEXIS 15393 (D.N.H. 1985); State v. Langone, 127 N.H. 49, 498 A.2d 731, 1985 N.H. LEXIS 399 (1985); State v. LaRose, 127 N.H. 146, 497 A.2d 1224, 1985 N.H. LEXIS 389 (1985); State v. Philbrick, 127 N.H. 353, 499 A.2d 1341, 1985 N.H. LEXIS 426 (1985); State v. Elbert, 128 N.H. 210, 512 A.2d 1114, 1986 N.H. LEXIS 280 (1986); State v. Deflorio, 128 N.H. 309, 512 A.2d 1133, 1986 N.H. LEXIS 286 (1986); State v. Allen, 128 N.H. 390, 514 A.2d 1263, 1986 N.H. LEXIS 309 (1986); Private Truck Council v. State, 128 N.H. 466, 517 A.2d 1150, 1986 N.H. LEXIS 342 (1986); State v. Pliskaner, 128 N.H. 486, 517 A.2d 795, 1986 N.H.

LEXIS 329 (1986); Greenberg v. Mynczywor, 667 F. Supp. 901, 1987 U.S. Dist. LEXIS 7712 (D.N.H. 1987); State v. Ingerson, 130 N.H. 112, 536 A.2d 161, 1987 N.H. LEXIS 292 (1987); State v. Houtenbrink, 130 N.H. 385, 539 A.2d 714, 1988 N.H. LEXIS 17 (1988); Op. Atty. Gen. 86-51; Lillios v. Justices of New Hampshire Dist. Court, 735 F. Supp. 43, 1990 U.S. Dist. LEXIS 4130 (D.N.H. 1990); State v. Field, 132 N.H. 760, 571 A.2d 1276, 1990 N.H. LEXIS 17 (1990); State v. Corson, 134 N.H. 430, 593 A.2d 248, 1991 N.H. LEXIS 77 (1991); Opinion of Justices, 135 N.H. 549, 608 A.2d 874, 1992 N.H. LEXIS 214 (1992); State v. Huot, 136 N.H. 96, 612 A.2d 362, 1992 N.H. LEXIS 131 (1992); State v. Fitzgerald, 137 N.H. 23, 622 A.2d 1245, 1993 N.H. LEXIS 29 (1993); State v. Little, 138 N.H. 657, 645 A.2d 665, 1994 N.H. LEXIS 80 (1994); State v. Woods, 139 N.H. 399, 654 A.2d 960, 1995 N.H. LEXIS 12 (1995); State v. Little, 138 N.H. 657, 645 A.2d 665, 1994 N.H. LEXIS 80 (1994); State v. Hatt, 144 N.H. 246, 740 A.2d 1037, 1999 N.H. LEXIS 107 (1999); State v. Duquette, 145 N.H. 374, 761 A.2d 520, 2000 N.H. LEXIS 72 (2000).

RESEARCH REFERENCES

New Hampshire Court Rules Annotated.

Terms of conditional discharge, see Rule 106, Rules of the Superior Court, New Hampshire Court Rules Annotated.

New Hampshire Practice.

8-4 N.H.P. Personal Injury-Tort & Insurance §§ 4.03, 4.05.
16-50 N.H.P. Municipal Law & Taxation § 50.02.

New Hampshire Bar Journal.

For article, "Lex Loci: A Survey of New Hampshire Supreme Court Decisions," see 48 N.H.B.J. 78 (Spring 2007).

For article, "Lex Loci: A Survey of New Hampshire Supreme Court Decisions," see 47 N.H.B.J. 44 (Winter 2007).

651:3. Calculation of Periods.

I. A sentence of imprisonment commences when it is imposed if the defendant is in custody or surrenders into custody at that time. Otherwise, it commences when he becomes actually in custody. All the time actually spent in custody prior to the time he is sentenced shall be credited in the manner set forth in RSA 651-A:23 against the maximum term of imprisonment that is imposed and against any minimum term authorized by RSA 651:2 or 6.

II. If a court determines that the defendant violated the conditions of his probation or conditional discharge but reinstates the probation or discharge, the period between the date of the violation and the date of restoration is not computed as part of the period of probation or discharge.

III. [Repealed.]

Source.

1971, 518:1. 1975, 158:2. 1976, 32:1, eff. July 26, 1976.

Revision note.

In the third sentence of par. I, substituted "RSA 651-A:23" for "RSA 651:55-c". RSA 651:55-c was repealed by 1983, 461, which enacted RSA 651-A:23, which deals with the subject matter of the repealed section.

Amendments
—**1976.** Paragraph I: Inserted "in the manner set forth in RSA 651:55-c" following "credited" in the third sentence.

—**1975.** Paragraph III: Repealed.

NOTES TO DECISIONS

1. Construction
2. Credit

3. Extradition

1. Construction

Although RSA 651:2, 632-A:10-a, and 651:3 did not authorize consecutive sentences for defendant's convictions for several counts of aggravated felonious sexual assault, by repealing former RSA 651:3, III, the legislature intended to revive the common law authority for judges to impose consecutive sentences. Duquette v. Warden, N.H. State Prison, 154 N.H. 737, 919 A.2d 767, 2007 N.H. LEXIS 10 (2007).

As used in the statute, the term "custody" necessarily presupposes a form of custody over which New Hampshire can exercise its control. State v. Harnum, 142 N.H. 195, 697 A.2d 1380, 1997 N.H. LEXIS 75 (1997), overruled, State v. Duran, 158 N.H. 146, 960 A.2d 697, 2008 N.H. LEXIS 139 (2008).

2. Credit

"Awaiting and during trial" encompasses all time from the moment of arrest through the completion of the trial and sentencing; in so holding, the Supreme Court of New Hampshire joins the overwhelming majority of jurisdictions that have decided this issue. State v. Harnum, 142 N.H. 195, 697 A.2d 1380, 1997 N.H. LEXIS 75 (1997), is overruled. State v. Duran, 158 N.H. 146, 960 A.2d 697, 2008 N.H. LEXIS 139 (2008).

Where the trial court allocated 71 days of pretrial credit toward the State Prison sentences and the remaining 365 days toward the misdemeanor sentence, defendant lost any opportunity to earn time off of his house of correction sentence for good behavior and thus could serve more time than a similarly situated offender who furnished bail; accordingly, the allocation of pretrial credit was vacated. State v. Edson, 153 N.H. 45, 889 A.2d 420, 2005 N.H. LEXIS 179 (2005).

Defendant was not entitled to pretrial confinement credit for time spent released on bail under conditions requiring home confinement and electronic monitoring, since restrictions on defendant's liberty did not rise to level of control associated with incarceration in jail. State v. Duquette, 145 N.H. 374, 761 A.2d 520, 2000 N.H. LEXIS 72 (2000).

The presentence credit provision of paragraph I of this section and RSA 651-A:23 stem principally from the recognition that presentence detention is often the result of indigency. State v. Decker, 127 N.H. 468, 503 A.2d 796, 1985 N.H. LEXIS 466 (1985).

One principle underlying the presentence credit provision of paragraph I of this section and RSA 651-A:23 is that an indigent offender unable to furnish bail should serve no more and no less time in confinement than an otherwise identically situated offender who succeeds in furnishing bail. State v. Decker, 127 N.H. 468, 503 A.2d 796, 1985 N.H. LEXIS 466 (1985).

The presentence credit provision of paragraph I of this section and RSA 651-A:23 mandate that a prisoner is to receive credit for all jail time—neither more nor less—served before sentencing which relates to the criminal episode for which the prisoner is sentenced, but does not receive credit greater than the number of days of his presentencing confinement. State v. Decker, 127 N.H. 468, 503 A.2d 796, 1985 N.H. LEXIS 466 (1985).

Trial court properly applied presentence credit provision of paragraph I of this section and RSA 651-A:23 in denying defendant multiple credit for his period of pretrial confinement, where defendant contended he was entitled to credit toward each of his three consecutive sentences, since a prisoner should not receive credit greater than the number of days of his presentencing confinement. State v. Decker, 127 N.H. 468, 503 A.2d 796, 1985 N.H. LEXIS 466 (1985).

Imposition of sentence for conspiracy to commit murder as of date of sentencing was proper, and defendant was not entitled to credit against sentence for time spent in custody from date of murder or from date of arrest on charge of raping person who was later killed to keep her from talking in rape trial. State v. Colby, 116 N.H. 790, 368 A.2d 587, 1976 N.H. LEXIS 471 (1976).

3. Extradition

Because term "awaiting and during trial" under RSA 651-A:23 encompasses all time from the moment of arrest through the completion of the trial and sentencing, defendant was entitled to credit for pretrial confinement in Colombia while awaiting extradition. State v. Duran, 158 N.H. 146, 960 A.2d 697, 2008 N.H.

LEXIS 139 (2008).

The statute does not allow pretrial confinement credit to fugitives from New Hampshire justice who are awaiting extradition in another state. State v. Harnum, 142 N.H. 195, 697 A.2d 1380, 1997 N.H. LEXIS 75 (1997), overruled, State v. Duran, 158 N.H. 146, 960 A.2d 697, 2008 N.H. LEXIS 139 (2008).

Cited:

Cited in State v. McMillan, 115 N.H. 268, 339 A.2d 21, 1975 N.H. LEXIS 283 (1975); State v. McMillan, 116 N.H. 126, 352 A.2d 702, 1976 N.H. LEXIS 283 (1976); State v. Lordan, 116 N.H. 479, 363 A.2d 201, 1976 N.H. LEXIS 387 (1976); In re Dubuque, 46 B.R. 156, 1985 Bankr. LEXIS 6762 (Bankr. D.N.H. 1985); State v. Philbrick, 127 N.H. 353, 499 A.2d 1341, 1985 N.H. LEXIS 426 (1985); State v. Rau, 129 N.H. 126, 523 A.2d 98, 1987 N.H. LEXIS 154 (1987); State v. Huot, 136 N.H. 96, 612 A.2d 362, 1992 N.H. LEXIS 131 (1992); State v. Wisowaty, 137 N.H. 298, 627 A.2d 572, 1993 N.H. LEXIS 74 (1993).

651:4. Presentence Investigation.

I. The court may, in its discretion, order a presentence investigation for a defendant convicted of a felony or a misdemeanor; provided that, upon the recommendation of the prosecution, the court shall order a presentence investigation report where the felony or misdemeanor was violent and the court has reason to believe that the defendant committed a similar act within the past year. The report shall include a recommendation as to disposition, together with reference to such material disclosed by the investigation as supports such recommendation.

II. Before imposing sentence, the court shall take such steps as may be necessary so that the defendant is advised, by counsel or otherwise, as the situation warrants, of the factual contents of any presentence investigation, and afforded a fair opportunity to contest them. The sources of confidential information need not, however, be disclosed.

Source.

1971, 518:1. 1975, 158:1. 1979, 377:9. 1995, 237:5, eff. Jan. 1, 1996. 2009, 183:1, eff. January 1, 2010. 2010, 239:12, eff. July 1, 2010.

Amendments

—2010. The 2010 amendment, in I, deleted the former first sentence, which read: "No person convicted of a felony and no person convicted of a felony or misdemeanor who is a member or veteran of the armed forces, shall be sentenced before a written report of a presentence investigation has been presented to and considered by the court, unless waived by defendant and the state, or by the court" and added "felony or" twice in the first sentence; substituted "contest" for "controvert" in the first sentence of II; and made stylistic changes.

—2009. The 2009 amendment added "and no person convicted of a felony or misdemeanor who is a member or veteran of the armed forces" in the first sentence of I.

—1995. Paragraph I: Added "or by the court" following "and the state" in the first sentence.

—1979. Paragraph I: Added proviso at the end of the second sentence.

—1975. Paragraph II: Rewritten to the extent that a detailed comparison would be impracticable.

NOTES TO DECISIONS

1. Construction

2.   Report—Unavailable
3.   —Disclosure of information
4.   —Waiver
5.   —Time of preparation
6.   —Time of filing
7.   —Oral
8.   —Sentencing recommendation

1. Construction

Neither this section nor court rule relating to probation reports entitled defendant to interview woman whose allegation of a prior sexual assault by defendant was contained in presentence report; verified information provided to defendant prior to sentencing afforded him a fair and reasonable opportunity to rebut allegation, and there was thus compliance with section and rule. State v. Tufts, 136 N.H. 517, 618 A.2d 818, 1992 N.H. LEXIS 202 (1992).

2. Report—Unavailable

No error resulted from failure to prepare written presentence investigation report prior to sentencing for felony conviction, where availability of lengthy documentation regarding the defendant's social and psychological history substantially complied with requirements of this section. State v. Giordano, 134 N.H. 718, 599 A.2d 109, 1991 N.H. LEXIS 136 (1991).

When a presentence report is unavailable at the time of sentencing, the defendant would ordinarily be entitled to postponement until one is presented and considered. State v. Schulte, 119 N.H. 36, 398 A.2d 63, 1979 N.H. LEXIS 232 (1979).

3. —Disclosure of information

Fact that probation officer may have relied upon information from documents withheld from the defendant as privileged did not render the presentence probation report improper. State v. Cote, 129 N.H. 358, 530 A.2d 775, 1987 N.H. LEXIS 217 (1987).

4. —Waiver

Defendants have a right not to talk to a probation officer prior to conviction, and such a refusal does not constitute a waiver of a presentence report under paragraph I of this section. State v. Schulte, 119 N.H. 36, 398 A.2d 63, 1979 N.H. LEXIS 232 (1979).

5. —Time of preparation

Where presentence investigation report was prepared before conclusion of trial for robbery and second-degree murder, there was no reversible error in the trial court's reliance on the report, even though the report did not take into account the defendant's allegation that testimony of an accomplice was inconsistent, since this section was substantially complied with and the credibility of the accomplice's testimony was evaluated by the jury and judge, who had presided at the trial and was able to draw his own conclusions about the significance and value of the testimony. State v. Thresher, 122 N.H. 63, 442 A.2d 578, 1982 N.H. LEXIS 288 (1982).

6. —Time of filing

Filing of presentence probation report with the court two days before the sentencing hearing was not untimely, and paragraph II of this section was substantially complied with, where defendant was notified at the time the report was filed; further, defendant made no motion for more time to rebut the information contained in the report, and therefore waived his timeliness claim on appeal. State v. Cote, 129 N.H. 358, 530 A.2d 775, 1987 N.H. LEXIS 217 (1987).

7. —Oral

Where defendant had been on probation on a previous charge and his probation officer was present in the courthouse at the time of sentencing and probation officer testified under oath regarding defendant and made his recommendations regarding sentencing, there was substantial compliance with the purpose of this section despite request by defendant that sentencing be postponed until

written probation department presentence report could be obtained. State v. Schulte, 119 N.H. 36, 398 A.2d 63, 1979 N.H. LEXIS 232 (1979).

8. —Sentencing recommendation

The trial court erred, in case of defendant charged with receiving stolen property, when it ordered the probation department not to make a sentencing recommendation in its presentence investigation report, since the defendant and the state were entitled by this section to have the trial judge receive and consider the sentencing recommendation of the probation department. State v. Fennelly, 123 N.H. 378, 461 A.2d 1090, 1983 N.H. LEXIS 288 (1983).

Cited:

Cited in State v. Lordan, 116 N.H. 479, 363 A.2d 201, 1976 N.H. LEXIS 387 (1976); State v. Dufield, 119 N.H. 28, 398 A.2d 818, 1979 N.H. LEXIS 229 (1979); State v. Heinz, 119 N.H. 717, 407 A.2d 814, 1979 N.H. LEXIS 382 (1979); Roy v. Perrin, 122 N.H. 88, 441 A.2d 1151, 1982 N.H. LEXIS 292 (1982); State v. Stone, 122 N.H. 987, 453 A.2d 1272, 1982 N.H. LEXIS 505 (1982); State v. Taylor, 139 N.H. 96, 649 A.2d 375, 1994 N.H. LEXIS 116 (1994).

651:4-a. Victims of Certain Violent Crimes Against a Person Permitted to Speak Before Sentencing and at Sentence Reduction or Suspension Hearings.

Before a judge sentences or suspends or reduces the sentence of any person for capital, first degree or second degree murder, attempted murder, manslaughter, aggravated felonious sexual assault, felonious sexual assault, first degree assault, or negligent homicide committed in consequence of being under the influence of intoxicating liquor or controlled drugs, the victim of the offense, or the victim's next of kin if the victim has died, shall have the opportunity to address the judge. The victim or victim's next of kin may appear personally or by counsel and may reasonably express his views concerning the offense, the person responsible, and the need for restitution. The prosecutor, the person to be sentenced, and the attorney for the person to be sentenced shall have the right to be present when the victim or victim's next of kin so addresses the judge. The judge may consider the statements of the victim or next of kin made pursuant to this section when imposing sentence or making a decision regarding sentence reduction or sentence suspension.

Source.
1983, 319:4. 1992, 254:11. 1994, 394:2, eff. June 10, 1994.

Amendments
—1994. Added "and at sentence reduction or suspension hearings" following "sentencing" in the section catchline, inserted "or suspends or reduces the sentence of" preceding "any person" in the first sentence, and added "or making a decision regarding sentence reduction or sentence suspension" following "imposing sentence" in the fourth sentence.

—1992. Inserted "of Certain Violent Crimes Against a Person" following "Victims" in the section catchline and "manslaughter" preceding "aggravated" and "felonious sexual assault" preceding "first degree" in the first sentence.

Cross References.

Victim or victim's next of kin permitted to speak at parole hearing, see RSA 651-A:11-a.

651:4-b. Presentence Investigation of Members and Veterans of the Armed Forces.

I. When a defendant appears in court and is convicted of a crime, the court shall inquire whether the defendant is currently serving in or is a veteran of the armed forces.

II. If the defendant is currently serving in the armed forces or is a veteran and has been diagnosed as having a mental illness by a qualified psychiatrist or clinical psychologist or physician, the court may:

(a) Order that the person preparing the presentence investigation report under RSA 651:4, I consult with the United States Department of Veterans Affairs, the adjutant general, the state office of veterans services, or another agency or person with suitable knowledge or experience, for the purpose of providing the court with information regarding treatment options available to the defendant, including federal, state, and local programming; and

(b) Consider the treatment recommendations of any diagnosing or treating mental health professionals together with the treatment options available to the defendant in imposing sentence.

Source.

2009, 183:2, eff. January 1, 2010. 2010, 119:7, eff. July 31, 2010.

Amendments

—2010. The 2010 amendment substituted "office of veterans services" for "veterans council" in II(a).

651:5. Annulment of Criminal Records.

I. Except as provided in paragraphs V–VIII, the record of arrest, conviction and sentence of any person may be annulled by the sentencing court at any time in response to a petition for annulment which is timely brought in accordance with the provisions of this section if in the opinion of the court, the annulment will assist in the petitioner's rehabilitation and will be consistent with the public welfare. The court may grant or deny an annulment without a hearing, unless a hearing is requested by the petitioner.

II. Any person whose arrest has resulted in a finding of not guilty, or whose case was dismissed or not prosecuted, may petition for annulment of the arrest record or court record, or both, at any time in accordance with the provisions of this section.

III. Except as provided in RSA 265-A:21 or in paragraphs V and VI, any person convicted of an offense may petition for annulment of the record of arrest, conviction, and sentence when the petitioner has completed all the terms and conditions of the sentence and has thereafter been convicted of no other crime, except a motor vehicle offense classified as a violation other than driving while intoxicated under RSA 265-A:2, I, RSA 265:82, or RSA 265:82-a

for a period of time as follows:

(a) For a violation, one year, unless the underlying conviction was for an offense specified under RSA 259:39.

(b) For a class B misdemeanor except as provided in subparagraph (f), 3 years.

(c) For a class A misdemeanor except as provided in subparagraph (f), 3 years.

(d) For a class B felony except as provided in subparagraph (g), 5 years.

(e) For a class A felony, 10 years.

(f) For sexual assault under RSA 632-A:4, 10 years.

(g) For felony indecent exposure or lewdness under RSA 645:1, II, 10 years.

IV. If a petition for annulment is denied, no further petition shall be brought more frequently than every 3 years thereafter.

V. No petition shall be brought and no annulment granted in the case of any violent crime, of any crime of obstruction of justice, or of any offense for which the petitioner was sentenced to an extended term of imprisonment under RSA 651:6.

VI. If a person has been convicted of more than one offense, no petition for annulment shall be brought and no annulment granted:

(a) If annulment of any part of the record is barred under paragraph V; or

(b) Until the time requirements under paragraphs III and IV for all offenses of record have been met.

VI-a. A conviction for an offense committed under the laws of another state which would not be considered an offense under New Hampshire law, shall not count as a conviction for the purpose of obtaining an annulment under this section.

VII. If, prior to disposition by the court of a petition for annulment, the petitioner is charged with an offense conviction for which would bar such annulment under paragraph V or VI(a) or would extend the time requirements under paragraphs III, IV and VI(b), the petition shall not be acted upon until the charge is disposed.

VIII. Any petition for annulment which does not meet the requirements of paragraphs III–VI shall be dismissed without a hearing.

IX. When a petition for annulment is timely brought, the court shall require the department of corrections to report to the court concerning any state or federal convictions, arrests or prosecutions of the petitioner and any other information which the court believes may aid in making a determination on the petition. The department shall charge the petitioner a fee of $100 to cover the cost of such investigation unless the petitioner demonstrates that he or she is indigent, or has been found not guilty, or the case has been dismissed or not prosecuted in accordance with paragraph II. The department of safety shall charge the successful petitioner a fee of $100 for researching and correcting the criminal history record accordingly, unless the petitioner demonstrates that he or she is indigent, or has been found not guilty, or the case has been dismissed or not prosecuted in accordance with paragraph II. The court shall provide a copy of the petition to the prosecutor of the underlying offense and permit them to be heard regarding the interest of justice in regard to the petition.

X. Upon entry of an order of annulment:

(a) The person whose record is annulled shall be treated in all respects as if he or she had never been arrested, convicted or sentenced, except that, upon conviction of any crime committed after the order of annulment has been entered, the prior conviction may be considered by the court in determining the sentence to be imposed, and may be counted toward habitual offender status under RSA 259:39.

(b) The court shall issue the person a certificate stating that such person's behavior after the conviction has warranted the issuance of the order, and that its effect is to annul the arrest, conviction, and sentence, and shall notify the state police criminal records unit, the prosecuting agency, and the arresting agency.

(c) The court records relating to an annulled arrest, conviction, or sentence shall be sealed and available only to the person whose record was annulled, his or her attorney, a court for sentencing pursuant to subparagraph (a), law enforcement personnel for legitimate law enforcement purposes, or as otherwise provided in this section.

(d) Upon payment of a fee not to exceed $100 to the state police, the state police criminal records unit shall remove the annulled criminal record and inform all appropriate state and federal agencies of the annulment.

(e) The arresting agency and the prosecuting agency shall clearly identify in their respective files and in their respective electronic records that the arrest or conviction and sentence have been annulled.

(f) In any application for employment, license or other civil right or privilege, or in any appearance as a witness in any proceeding or hearing, a person may be questioned about a previous criminal record only in terms such as "Have you ever been arrested for or convicted of a crime that has not been annulled by a court?"

XI. Nothing in this section shall affect any right:

(a) Of the person whose record has been annulled to appeal from the conviction or sentence or to rely on it in bar of any subsequent proceedings for the same offense; or

(b) Of law enforcement officers to maintain arrest and conviction records and to communicate information regarding the annulled record of arrest or conviction to other law enforcement officers for legitimate investigative purposes or in defense of any civil suit arising out of the facts of the arrest, or to the police standards and training council solely for the purpose of assisting the council in determining the fitness of an individual to serve as a law enforcement officer, in any of which cases such information shall not be disclosed to any other person.

XII. [Repealed.]

XIII. As used in this section, "violent crime" means:

(a) Capital murder, first or second degree murder, manslaughter, or class A felony negligent homicide under RSA 630;

(b) First degree assault under RSA 631:1;

(c) Aggravated felonious sexual assault or felonious sexual assault under RSA 632-A;

(d) Kidnapping or criminal restraint under RSA 633;

(e) Class A felony arson under RSA 634:1;

(f) Robbery under RSA 636;

(g) Incest under RSA 639:2, III or endangering the welfare of a child by solicitation under RSA 639:3, III; or

(h) Any felonious child pornography offense under RSA 649-A.

XIV. As used in this section, "crime of obstruction of justice" means:

(a) Tampering with witnesses or informants under RSA 641:5 or falsifying evidence under RSA 641:6; or

(b) Any felonious offense of obstructing governmental operations under RSA 642.

XV. A petition for annulment of any record of arrest, conviction, and sentence authorized by this section may be brought in the supreme court with respect to any such record in the supreme court, provided that no record in the supreme court relating to an opinion published in the New Hampshire Reports may be annulled.

XVI. A journalist or reporter shall not be subject to civil or criminal penalties for publishing or broadcasting:

(a) That a person had a criminal record that has been annulled, including the content of that record.

(b) That a person has a criminal record, including the content of such record, without reporting that the record has been annulled, if the journalist or reporter does not have knowledge of the annulment.

XVII. No person or entity, whether public or private, shall be subject to civil or criminal penalties for not removing from public access or making corrections to a report or statement that a person has a criminal record, including the content of such record, if thereafter the criminal record was annulled. This provision shall apply to any report or statement, regardless of its format.

Source.

1971, 518:1. 1985, 205:2. 1986, 49:1; 189:1. 1988, 238:6. 1991, 159:1. 1992, 269:11. 1994, 224:1, eff. May 27, 1994. 1998, 325:2, eff. Jan. 1, 1999. 2002, 269:1, eff. Jan. 1, 2003. 2006, 163:3, eff. January 1, 2007; 260:34, eff. January 1, 2007. 2008, 62:4, eff. July 20, 2008; 104:1, eff. January 1, 2009. 2009, 144:131, eff. July 1, 2009. 2011,

219:1–3, eff. June 28, 2011. 2012, 249:1, 2, eff. January 1, 2013. 2013, 123:1, eff. August 24, 2013.

Amendments

—2013. The 2013 amendment substituted "be sealed and available only to the person whose record was annulled, his or her attorney, a court for sentencing pursuant to subparagraph (a), law enforcement personnel for legitimate law enforcement purposes, or as otherwise provided in this section" for "remain public documents. However, the court shall clearly identify on the file and in the electronic record that the arrest or conviction and sentence have been annulled" in X(c) and rewrote X(d), which formerly read: "The state police criminal records unit shall add an entry to the subject's record of arrest, conviction, or sentence in the criminal history database stating that the record has been annulled."

—2012. The 2012 amendment, in X(b), deleted "record of" following "to annul the" and added "the prosecuting agency"; added X(c) through X(e); redesignated former X(c) as X(f); deleted XII; and made stylistic changes.

—2011. The 2011 amendment, in I, deleted "after hearing" following "of the court" and added the second sentence; added "or court record, or both" in II; in XII, added "or she, having knowledge of the annulment, knowingly" and "and paragraphs XVI–XVII"; and added XVI and XVII.

—2009. The 2009 amendment added the third sentence of IX and made stylistic changes.

—2008. The 2008 amendment by Chapter 62 added "RSA 265:82, or RSA 265:82-a" in the introductory language of III.
The 2008 amendment by Chapter 104 added XV.

—2006. Paragraph III: Chapter 260 substituted "265-A:21" for "265:82-c" and "265-A:2, I" for "265:82".
Paragraph XIII(g): Chapter 163 inserted "III" following "639:2".

—2002. Paragraph VI-a: Added.

—1998. Paragraph III(a): Added "unless the underlying conviction was for an offense specified under RSA 259:39".

—1994. Rewritten to the extent that a detailed comparison would be impractical.

—1992. Paragraph XVI: Added.

—1991. Paragraph V: Deleted "or district court probation officer" following "corrections" in the first sentence and added the second sentence.

—1988. Paragraph XV: Rewrote the first sentence and added the second sentence.

—1986. Chapter 49 rewrote section to the extent that a detailed comparison would be impractical.
Chapter 189 reenacted the section without change.

—1985. Paragraph XI: Added.

Applicability of 2013 amendment.
2013, 123:2, eff. August 24, 2013, provided: "The provisions of this act shall apply to any criminal record annulled between January 1, 2013 and the effective date of this act."

Applicability of 2012 amendment.
2012, 249:3, eff. January 1, 2013, provided: "The provisions of section 1 of this act shall apply to criminal charges annulled on or after the effective date of this act."

Applicability of 1994 amendment.
1994, 224:2, eff. Jan. 1, 1995, provided: "The provisions of section 1 of this act [which amended this section] shall apply in the case of any petition for annulment brought after the effective date of this act [Jan. 1, 1995], except that any person convicted of a misdemeanor before the effective date of this act shall have the option of applying for annulment under the laws in effect at the time of sentencing."

Applicability of 1992 amendment.
1992, 269:21, eff. July 1, 1992, provided that the amendment to this section by 1992, 269:11, shall apply to all offenses committed on or after July 1, 1992.

Cross References.
Annulment of record of conviction for possession of controlled drug, see RSA 318-B:28-a.
Classification of crimes, see RSA 625:9.
Sentences, see RSA 651.

NOTES TO DECISIONS

1. Constitutionality
2. Construction
3. Construction with other law
4. Retroactive application
5. Estoppel effect
6. Evidence
7. Hearing on petition
8. Discretion of court
9. Adults sentenced to imprisonment
10. Fines
11. Unconditional discharge
12. Continued for sentence
13. Crimes carrying enhanced penalties for subsequent convictions
14. Particular cases
15. Tests and standards

1. Constitutionality
The application of the 1994 amendments to this section, which lengthened the time until an application for annulment could be brought, to all petitions for annulment brought after the effective date of the amendments, regardless of the date of the conviction at issue, did not violate the ex post facto provisions of either the New Hampshire or United States Constitutions. State v. Comeau, 142 N.H. 84, 697 A.2d 497, 1997 N.H. LEXIS 59 (1997).
The defendant had no vested right to seek annulment of his criminal record under the version of the statute which was in effect at the time of his conviction, which allowed an application for annulment one year after the completion of his sentence, and, therefore, the application of the version of the statute which was in effect at the time of his application for annulment, which allowed an application 10 years after the completion of his sentence, did not violate part I, article 23 of the New Hampshire Constitution. State v. Burr, 142 N.H. 89, 696 A.2d 1114, 1997 N.H. LEXIS 60 (1997).
This section is within the legislative power and is not an unconstitutional infringement upon the prerogative of the governor to pardon. Doe v. State, 114 N.H. 714, 328 A.2d 784, 1974 N.H. LEXIS 359 (1974).

2. Construction
While RSA 651:5, XII, imposes criminal liability on one who discloses an annulled record, the statute does not provide a civil remedy to the person whose record is disclosed. Moreover, the statute provides that the person whose record is annulled shall be treated in all respects as if he had never been arrested, convicted or sentenced; it did not enshroud the record itself with a cloak of secrecy for purposes of the tort of invasion of privacy by public disclosure of private facts. Lovejoy v. Linehan, 161 N.H. 483, 20 A.3d 274, 2011 N.H. LEXIS 13 (2011).
This section effectively erases the conviction but does not prevent introduction of evidence of the incident that underlies the conviction. Panas v. Harakis, 129 N.H. 591, 529 A.2d 976, 1987 N.H. LEXIS 224 (1987).

3. Construction with other law
Where RSA 651:5, III(d) would permit a petition for annulment of a conviction to be filed sooner than seven years following a Controlled Drug Act (CDA) conviction, then CDA's seven-year minimum period, set forth in RSA 318-B:28-a, controls; however, for any CDA conviction involving a sentence longer than two years, the five and ten-year provisions of RSA 651:5, III(d) and (e) control, and the CDA's seven-year minimum is not violated. State v. Patterson,

145 N.H. 462, 764 A.2d 901, 2000 N.H. LEXIS 91 (2000).

Trial court did not err in ruling that ten-year period set forth in RSA 651:5 governed defendant's petition to annul his Controlled Drug Act conviction, and thus that his petition was premature. State v. Patterson, 145 N.H. 462, 764 A.2d 901, 2000 N.H. LEXIS 91 (2000).

4. Retroactive application

The application of the 1994 amendments to this section, which lengthened the time until an application for annulment could be brought, to all petitions for annulment brought after the effective date of the amendments, regardless of the date of the conviction at issue, did not violate the ex post facto provisions of either the New Hampshire or United States Constitutions. State v. Comeau, 142 N.H. 84, 697 A.2d 497, 1997 N.H. LEXIS 59 (1997).

The 1994 amendments to the statute, which lengthened the time until an application for annulment could be brought, was intended to apply to all petitions for annulment brought after the effective date of the amendments, regardless of the date of the conviction at issue. State v. Comeau, 142 N.H. 84, 697 A.2d 497, 1997 N.H. LEXIS 59 (1997).

The defendant was not entitled to seek annulment of his criminal record under the version of the statute which was in effect at the time of his conviction, which allowed an application for annulment one year after the completion of his sentence, on the basis that his plea agreement incorporated the prior annulment statute as a term or condition as the plea agreement, signed by both the defendant and his attorney, was devoid of any references to the prior statute or to the annulment of criminal records generally. State v. Burr, 142 N.H. 89, 696 A.2d 1114, 1997 N.H. LEXIS 60 (1997).

A record of conviction and sentence prior to the effective date of this section may be annulled under this section. Doe v. State, 114 N.H. 714, 328 A.2d 784, 1974 N.H. LEXIS 359 (1974).

5. Estoppel effect

This section clearly requires, except for narrowly drawn exceptions dealing with later convictions, that the applicant shall be treated "in all respects" as if he had never been convicted; therefore, an annulled conviction cannot be given collateral estoppel effect. Brown v. Brown, 133 N.H. 442, 577 A.2d 1227, 1990 N.H. LEXIS 86 (1990).

6. Evidence

A civil litigant was properly prohibited by this section from using defendant's annulled conviction to establish the occurrence of an assault. Brown v. Brown, 133 N.H. 442, 577 A.2d 1227, 1990 N.H. LEXIS 86 (1990).

7. Hearing on petition

Trial court did not err in summarily dismissing defendant's second petition for annulment of his conviction, since RSA 651:5, VIII mandated dismissal, without hearing, of any petition not meeting requirements of RSA 651:5, III. State v. Patterson, 145 N.H. 462, 764 A.2d 901, 2000 N.H. LEXIS 91 (2000).

In enacting this section the legislature intended the defendant to be afforded a hearing on his petition. State v. Meister, 125 N.H. 435, 480 A.2d 200, 1984 N.H. LEXIS 245 (1984).

8. Discretion of court

Paragraph V of this section mandates the exercise of the trial court's discretion in deciding whether to grant a petition for an annulment. State v. Meister, 125 N.H. 435, 480 A.2d 200, 1984 N.H. LEXIS 245 (1984).

9. Adults sentenced to imprisonment

The fact that paragraph III of this section provides for annulment when imprisonment is part of the sentence only when the defendant is a minor would prevent an annulment under paragraph I when probation is combined with imprisonment for an adult. State v. Roger A., 121 N.H. 19, 424 A.2d 1139, 1981 N.H. LEXIS 243 (1981). (Decided under prior law.)

Paragraph I of this section does not apply to a person who has received a sentence of both imprisonment and probation. State v. Doe, 117 N.H. 259, 372 A.2d 279, 1977 N.H. LEXIS 311 (1977). (Decided under prior law.)

10. Fines

Imposition of a fine in addition to a conditional discharge does not prevent annulment under paragraph I of this section. State v. Roger A., 121 N.H. 19, 424 A.2d 1139, 1981 N.H. LEXIS 243 (1981). (Decided under prior law.)

A sentence of a fine may be annulled under paragraph III of this section, since the punishment of a fine is included in the greater punishment of imprisonment. Doe v. State, 114 N.H. 714, 328 A.2d 784, 1974 N.H. LEXIS 359 (1974). (Decided under prior law.)

11. Unconditional discharge

Criminal case marked "continued for sentence" is not an unconditional discharge required before sentencing court can annul record of conviction and sentence under paragraph II of this section. State v. Doe, 117 N.H. 259, 372 A.2d 279, 1977 N.H. LEXIS 311 (1977). (Decided under prior law.)

12. Continued for sentence

Where no request for imposition of a period of imprisonment or sentence has been made by the state for many years following the conviction of a person under twenty-one years of age, marking of the case as "continued for sentence" may be treated as a lesser included punishment for purposes of paragraph III of this section. State v. Roe, 118 N.H. 690, 393 A.2d 553, 1978 N.H. LEXIS 271 (1978). (Decided under prior law.)

Where a defendant requests that his cases be brought forward for imposition of sentence in order that he may have standing to file a petition for annulment, neither expiration of time limitations for prosecutions nor passage of maximum period of imprisonment provided for particular offenses deprives the court of jurisdiction to bring forward convictions which have been marked "continued for sentence" for imposition of sentence. State v. Roe, 118 N.H. 690, 393 A.2d 553, 1978 N.H. LEXIS 271 (1978). (Decided under prior law.)

13. Crimes carrying enhanced penalties for subsequent convictions

The fact that a defendant has been convicted of a crime for which the legislature has provided an enhanced penalty for a second offense is a factor which may be considered by a trial court in determining whether to annul the defendant's record of conviction under this section; it cannot, however, absent a specific mandate of the legislature, be the sole determinative factor. State v. Meister, 125 N.H. 435, 480 A.2d 200, 1984 N.H. LEXIS 245 (1984).

In deciding whether to grant an annulment of the record of conviction for an offense for which the legislature has provided an enhanced penalty for a second offense, a trial court must weigh the possibility that an individual might commit a second offense and, because of the annulment, avoid the enhanced penalty, against the possible rehabilitative value of annulling the defendant's record of conviction and thereby relieving him or her of the disadvantages resulting from a permanent criminal record. State v. Meister, 125 N.H. 435, 480 A.2d 200, 1984 N.H. LEXIS 245 (1984).

A trial court, prior to sentencing for an offense for which the legislature has provided an enhanced penalty for a second offense, should require every defendant to attest, under oath, to any prior convictions he may have had for the same offense, including those for which the records of conviction have been annulled under this section. State v. Meister, 125 N.H. 435, 480 A.2d 200, 1984 N.H. LEXIS 245 (1984).

14. Particular cases

Trial court erred in denying defendant's petitions under RSA 651:5 to annul the records of two 2004 "arrests." There was no evidence that any charges were filed or any other action taken with regard to these arrests; moreover, the record did not show that these incidents even involved actual arrests. State v. Baker, 164 N.H. 296, 55 A.3d 1001, 2012 N.H. LEXIS 138 (2012).

Trial court had stated that based in part upon two reported arrests, it was not persuaded that annulling defendant's convictions was consistent with the public welfare. Because the court was unable to determine on the record how the trial court would have ruled had it not considered those arrests, which it should have annulled, the court remanded the case for further proceedings. State v. Baker, 164 N.H. 296, 55 A.3d 1001, 2012 N.H. LEXIS 138 (2012).

Someone's prior violation of the law is relevant to assessing his fitness to enforce it. Thus, there was no error in the trial court's citation of RSA 651:5, XI(b), to support its conclusion that because plaintiff sought to obtain, via public election, the position of chief law enforcement officer, his annulled conviction was, as a matter of law, of legitimate public concern for purposes of the tort of invasion of privacy by public disclosure of private facts. Lovejoy v. Linehan, 161 N.H. 483, 20 A.3d 274, 2011 N.H. LEXIS 13 (2011).

15. Tests and standards

Legislature has already determined that certain crimes are eligible for annulment, and others are not. Accordingly, it would be inconsistent with legislative intent for a trial court to deny a petition to annul the record of an offense, which the legislature has determined is eligible for annulment, solely because the defendant was convicted of that offense. State v. Baker, 164 N.H. 296, 55 A.3d 1001, 2012 N.H. LEXIS 138 (2012).

In deciding whether annulment is consistent with the public welfare, the trial court should weigh the factors in favor of annulment, such as evidence of the defendant's exemplary conduct and character since his last conviction, against the public interest in keeping his convictions a matter of public record; thus, in exercising its discretion, the court may consider such factors as the number and circumstances of the convictions at issue, the defendant's age at the time of each conviction, the time span of the convictions, and the particular manner in which annulment would aid the defendant's rehabilitation—for example, by allowing him to obtain a professional license or to pursue a calling otherwise prohibited to those convicted of a crime. By identifying potential factors, the Supreme Court of New Hampshire does not intend to limit the court's discretion to consider any relevant factor. State v. Baker, 164 N.H. 296, 55 A.3d 1001, 2012 N.H. LEXIS 138 (2012).

Cited:

Cited in State v. Michael B., 124 N.H. 590, 474 A.2d 564, 1984 N.H. LEXIS 349 (1984).

RESEARCH REFERENCES

New Hampshire Court Rules Annotated.

Application to annul record of conviction and sentence, see Rule 108, Rules of the Superior Court, and Rule 2.18 of the District and Municipal Courts, New Hampshire Court Rules Annotated.

Impeachment of witness by evidence of conviction of crime, see Rule 609, Rules of Evidence, New Hampshire Court Rules Annotated.

New Hampshire Practice.

2A-38 N.H.P. Criminal Practice & Procedure § 38.04.

New Hampshire Trial Bar News.

For article, "Trial Practice—The Law of Depositions: A Quiz", see 14 N.H. Trial Bar News 19, 20 (Summer 1993).

651:6. Extended Term of Imprisonment.

I. A convicted person may be sentenced according to paragraph III if the jury also finds beyond a reasonable doubt that such person:

(a) Based on the circumstances for which he or she is to be sentenced, has knowingly devoted himself or herself to criminal activity as a major source of livelihood;

(b) Has been subjected to a court-ordered psychiatric examination on the basis of which the jury finds that such person is a serious danger to others due to a gravely abnormal mental condition;

(c) Has manifested exceptional cruelty or depravity in inflicting death or serious bodily injury on the victim of the crime;

(d) Has committed an offense involving the use of force against a person with the intention of taking advantage of the victim's age or physical disability;

(e) Has committed or attempted to commit any of the crimes defined in RSA 631 or 632-A against a person under 13 years of age;

(f) Was substantially motivated to commit the crime because of hostility towards the victim's religion, race, creed, sexual orientation as defined in RSA 21:49, national origin or sex;

(g) Has knowingly committed or attempted to commit any of the crimes defined in RSA 631 where he or she knows the victim was, at the time of the commission of the crime, a law enforcement officer, a paid firefighter, volunteer firefighter, on-call firefighter, or licensed emergency medical care provider as defined in RSA 153-A:2, V acting in the line of duty;

(h) Was an on-duty law enforcement officer at the time that he or she committed or attempted to commit any of the crimes defined in RSA 631;

(i) Has committed a crime listed in RSA 193-D:1 in a safe school zone under RSA 193-D;

(j) Possesses a radio device with the intent to use that device in the commission of robbery, burglary, theft, gambling, stalking, or a violation of any provision of RSA 318-B. In this section, the term "radio device" means any device capable of receiving a wireless transmission on any frequency allocated for law enforcement use, or any device capable of transmitting and receiving a wireless transmission;

(k) Has committed or attempted to commit negligent homicide as defined in RSA 630:3, I against a person under 13 years of age who was in the care of, or under the supervision of, the defendant at the time of the offense;

(*l*) Has committed or attempted to commit any of the crimes defined in RSA 637 or RSA 638 against a victim who is 65 years of age or older or who has a physical or mental disability and that in perpetrating the crime, the defendant intended to take advantage of the victim's age or a physical or mental condition that impaired the victim's ability to manage his or her property or financial resources or to protect his or her rights or interests;

(m) Has committed or attempted to commit aggravated felonious sexual assault in violation of RSA 632-A:2, I(*l*) or RSA 632-A:2, II where the defendant was 18 years of age or older at the time of the offense;

(n) Has committed or attempted to commit aggravated felonious sexual assault in violation of RSA 632-A:2, III, and one or more of the acts comprising the pattern of sexual assault was an offense under RSA 632-A:2, I(*l*) or RSA 632-A:2, II, or both, and the defendant was 18 years of age or older when the pattern of sexual assault began;

(*o*) Has purposely, knowingly, or recklessly with extreme indifference to the value of human life committed an act or acts constituting first degree assault as defined in RSA 631:1 against a person under 13 years of age where the serious bodily injury has resulted in brain damage or physical disability to the child that is likely to be permanent;

(p) Has committed murder as defined in RSA 630:1-b against a person under 13 years of age;

(q) Has knowingly committed any of the following offenses as a criminal street gang member, or for the benefit of, at the direction of, or in association with any criminal street gang, with the purpose to promote, further, or assist in any such criminal conduct by criminal street gang members:

(1) Violent crime as defined in RSA 651:5, XIII.

(2) A crime involving the distribution, sale, or manufacture of a controlled drug under RSA 318-B:2.

(3) Class A felony theft where the property stolen was a firearm.

(4) Unlawful sale of a pistol or a revolver.

(5) Witness tampering.

(6) Criminal street gang solicitation as defined in RSA 644:20; or

(r) Has committed an offense under RSA 637 where such person knowingly activated an audible alarm system to avoid detection or apprehension, or cause a distraction during the commission of the offense.

I-a. As used in this section:

(a) "Law enforcement officer" means a sheriff or deputy sheriff of any county, a state police officer, a constable or police officer of any city or town, an official or employee of any prison, jail, or corrections institution, a probation-parole officer, a juvenile probation and parole officer, or a conservation officer.

(b) "Criminal street gang member" means an individual to whom 2 or more of the following apply:

(1) Admits to criminal street gang membership;

(2) Is identified as a criminal street gang member by a law enforcement officer, parent, guardian, or documented reliable informant;

(3) Resides in or frequents a particular criminal street gang's area and adopts its style of dress, its use of hand or other signs, tattoos, or other physical markings, and associates with known criminal street gang members; or

(4) Has been arrested more than once in the company of individuals who are identified as criminal street gang members by law enforcement, for offenses that are consistent with usual criminal street gang activity.

(c) "Criminal street gang" means a formal or informal ongoing organization, association, or group of 3 or more persons, which has as one of its primary objectives or activities the commission of criminal activity, whose members share a common name, identifying sign, symbol, physical marking, style of dress, or use of hand sign, and whose members individually or collectively have engaged in the commission, attempted commission, solicitation to commit, or conspiracy to commit 2 or more the following offenses, or a reasonably equivalent offense in another jurisdiction, on separate occasions within the preceding 3 years:

(1) Violent crimes, as defined in RSA 651:5, XIII;

(2) Distribution, sale, or manufacture of a controlled drug in violation of RSA 318-B:2;

(3) Class A felony theft;

(4) Unlawful sale of a pistol or revolver; or

(5) Witness tampering.

II. A convicted person may be sentenced according to the terms of paragraph III if the court finds, and includes such findings in the record, that such person:

(a) Has twice previously been convicted in this state, or in another jurisdiction, on sentences in excess of one year;

(b) Has previously been convicted of a violation of RSA 630:3, II, RSA 265-A:3, I(b) or II(b), or any crime in any other jurisdiction involving driving or attempting to drive a motor vehicle under the influence of controlled drugs, prescription drugs, over-the-counter drugs, or any other chemical substances, natural or synthetic, which impair a person's ability to drive or intoxicating liquors, or both, and such person has committed a crime as defined under RSA 630:3, II or RSA 265-A:3, I(b) or II(b); or

(c) Has twice previously been convicted in this state or any other jurisdiction, for driving or attempting to drive a motor vehicle under the influence of intoxicating liquors or controlled drugs, prescription drugs, over-the-counter drugs, or any other chemical substances, natural or synthetic, which impair a person's ability to drive, or both, and such person has committed a crime as defined under RSA 630:3, II or RSA 265-A:3, I(b) or II(b).

III. If authorized by paragraph I or II, and if written notice of the possible application of this section is given the defendant at least 21 days prior to the commencement of jury selection for his or her trial, a defendant may be sentenced to an extended term of imprisonment. An extended term is, for a person convicted of:

(a) Any felony, other than murder or manslaughter, a minimum to be fixed by the court of not more than 10 years and a maximum to be fixed by the court of not more than 30 years;

(b) A misdemeanor, a minimum to be fixed by the court of not more than 2 years and a maximum to be fixed by the court of not more than 5 years;

(c) Manslaughter, a minimum to be fixed by the court of not more than 20 years and a maximum to be fixed by the court of not more than 40 years;

(d) Murder, life imprisonment;

(e) Two or more offenses under RSA 632-A:2, life imprisonment without parole;

(f) A third offense under RSA 632-A:3, life imprisonment; or

(g) Any of the crimes listed under RSA 651:6, I(j), a minimum to be fixed by the court of not less than 90 days and a maximum of not more than one year.

IV. If authorized by subparagraphs I(m), (n), or (o) and if notice of the possible application of this section is given to the defendant prior to the commencement of trial:

(a) There is a presumption that a person shall be sentenced to a minimum to be fixed by the court of not less than 25 years and a maximum of life imprisonment unless the court makes a determination that the goals of deterrence, rehabilitation, and punishment would not be served, based on the specific circumstances of the case, by such a sentence and the court makes specific written findings in support of the lesser sentence. Before the court can determine whether the presumption has been overcome, the court shall consider, but is not limited to, the following factors:

(1) Age of victim at time of offense.

(2) Age of the defendant at the time of the offense.

(3) Relationship between defendant and victim.

(4) Injuries to victim.

(5) Use of force, fear, threats, or coercion to the victim or another.

(6) Length of time defendant offended against victim.

(7) Number of times defendant offended against victim.

(8) Number of other victims.

(9) Acceptance of responsibility by defendant.

(10) Defendant's criminal history.

(11) Use of a weapon.

(12) Medical or psychological condition of the victim at the time of the assault.

(b) The sentence shall also include, in addition to any other penalties provided by law, a special sentence of lifetime supervision by the department of corrections. The defendant shall comply with the conditions of lifetime supervision which are imposed by the court or the department of corrections. Violation of any of the conditions of lifetime supervision shall be deemed contempt of court. The special sentence of lifetime supervision shall begin upon the offender's release from incarceration, parole, or probation. A defendant who is sentenced to lifetime supervision pursuant to this paragraph shall not be eligible for release from the lifetime supervision pursuant to RSA 632-A:10-a, V(b).

(c) Any decision by the superior court under subparagraph (a) may be reviewed by the sentence review division of the superior court at the request of the defendant or at the request of the state pursuant to RSA 651:58.

V. If authorized by subparagraph I(p) and if notice of the possible application of this section is given to the defendant prior to the commencement of trial, a person shall be sentenced to an extended term of imprisonment as follows: a minimum to be fixed by the court of not less than 35 years and a maximum

of life imprisonment.

VI. A person shall be sentenced according to the terms of paragraph VII if the court finds, and includes such findings in the record, that such person:

(a) (1) Committed a violation of RSA 632-A:2, I(*l*), RSA 632-A:2, II, or RSA 632-A:2, III, in which one or more of the acts comprising the pattern of sexual assault was an offense under RSA 632-A:2, I(*l*) or RSA 632-A:2, II, or both, after having previously been convicted of an offense in violation of one of the aforementioned offenses or any other statute prohibiting the same conduct in another state, territory or possession of the United States, and

(2) The person committed the subsequent offense while released on bail on the earlier offense or the sentence for the earlier conviction involved a term of incarceration, probation, parole, or other supervised release; or

(b) (1) Committed a violation of RSA 631:1 after having previously been convicted of an offense in violation of RSA 631:1, or any other statute prohibiting the same conduct in another state, territory or possession of the United States, if the earlier offense also involved a victim under 13 years of age where the serious bodily injury resulted in brain damage or physical disability to the child that is likely to be permanent; and

(2) The person committed the subsequent offense while released on bail on the earlier offense or the sentence for the earlier conviction involved a term of incarceration, probation, parole, or other supervised release; or

(c) (1) Committed a violation of RSA 630:1-b after having previously been convicted of an offense in violation of RSA 630:1-b, or any other statute prohibiting the same conduct in another state, territory, or possession of the United States; and

(2) The person committed the subsequent offense while released on bail on the earlier offense or the sentence for the earlier conviction involved a term of incarceration, probation, parole, or other supervised release.

VII. If the court has made the findings authorized by RSA 651:6, VI, and if notice of the possible application of this section is given to the defendant prior to the commencement of trial, a person shall be sentenced to an extended term of imprisonment of life without parole.

Source.

1971, 518:1. 1973, 370:3. 1981, 511:1. 1985, 228:7, 8. 1990, 68:1; 140:2, XI. 1992, 3:1. 1994, 355:4, eff. Sept. 1, 1994. 1995, 131:1, 2, eff. May 24, 1995. 1996, 198:1, eff. Jan. 1, 1997. 1997, 108:16, eff. Jan. 1, 1998. 1998, 301:1, 2, eff. Aug. 25, 1998. 1999, 296:2, eff. Sept. 14, 1999. 2003, 33:1, eff. Jan. 1, 2004. 2006, 89:1, 2, eff. January 1, 2007; 197:1, eff. January 1, 2007; 260:35, eff. January 1, 2007; 327:17–20, eff. January 1, 2007; 327:20 (to the extent it enacts 651:6, IV–V), eff. at 12:01 a.m., January 1, 2007. 2007, 110:1, eff.

June 11, 2007. 2008, 379:1, 2, eff. March 31, 2009. 2009, 209:5, eff. January 1, 2010. 2012, 267:18, eff. January 1, 2013.

Revision note.

In par. I, made a minor change in punctuation and added "or" at the end of subpar. (f) in view of the amendment to this section by 1990, 68:1.

Editor's Note.

2006, 327:18 purportedly "repealed and reenacted RSA 651:6, I(k)–(l)"; this section makes a punctuation change to subpara. (k) and to subpara. (l), which was originally added by 2006, 89:1, and adds new subparagraphs (m) through (p).

Amendments

—2012. The 2012 amendment added "prescription drugs, over-the-counter drugs, or any other chemical substances, natural or synthetic, which impair a person's ability to drive" in II(b) and II(c).

—2009. The 2009 amendment added I(r) and made related changes.

—2008. The 2008 amendment in I, added I(q) and made related changes; and in I-a, added designation I-a(a), in I-a(a), substituted "means" for "is" following "a sheriff" and added I-a(b) and I-a(c).

—2007. Paragraph III: Inserted "written" preceding "notice of the" and "at least 21 days" following "the defendant" and "jury selection for his or her" following "commencement of" in the first sentence.

—2006. Paragraph I(j): Chapter 327 deleted "or" at the end of the sentence following "transmission".

Paragraph I(l)–(p): Added (See editor's note above).

Paragraph II(b): Chapter 260 substituted "265-A:3" for "265:82-a" twice, and inserted "or attempting to drive".

Paragraph II(c): Chapter 260 inserted "or attempting to drive" following "for driving" and substituted "265-A:3" for "265:82-a".

Paragraph III: Chapter 327 deleted subpar. (g), made stylistic changes and redesignated former subpar. (h) to be subpar. (g).

Paragraphs IV–VII: Added by Chapter 327.

Paragraph I: Chapter 89 made minor stylistic changes in subpars. (j) and (k) and added subpar. (l).

Paragraph I: Chapter 89 substituted "an offense" for "a felony" following "committed" in subpar. (d).

Paragraph I(g): Chapter 197 inserted "a paid firefighter, volunteer firefighter, on-call firefighter, or licensed emergency medical care provider as defined in RSA 153-A:2, V" preceding "acting in the line of duty".

—2003. Rewritten to the extent that a detailed comparison would be impracticable.

—1999. Paragraph I-a: Added.

—1998. Paragraph I: Substituted "a convicted person" for "If a court finds that a convicted person is 18 years of age or older, he" at the beginning of the introductory paragraph and added subpar. (n).

—1997. Paragraph I(g): Inserted "as defined in RSA 21:49" following "sexual orientation".

—1996. Paragraph I: Inserted "stalking" following "gambling" in the first sentence in subpar. (k) and added subpars. (l) and (m).

—1995. Paragraph I(j): Substituted "such person" for "he" preceding "has committed" and added "or" following "RSA 193-D".

Paragraph I(k): Added.

Paragraph II(e): Substituted "I(l)" for "XI" following "RSA 632-A:2".

Paragraph II(f): Added.

—1994. Paragraph I(i): Added "or" following "RSA 631".

Paragraph I(j): Added.

—1992. Paragraph I: Made a minor change in punctuation and added "or" at the end of subpar. (g) and added subpars. (h) and (i).

—1990. Paragraph I(e): Chapter 140 substituted "disability" for "handicap" following "physical".

Paragraph I(g): Added by ch. 68.

—1985. Paragraph I(e): Added "or" following "physical handicap".

Paragraph I(f): Added.

Paragraph II(c): Made minor changes in punctuation.

Paragraphs II(d), II(e): Added.

—1981. Rewritten to the extent that a detailed comparison would be impracticable.

—1973. Paragraph II(c): Added.

Applicability of 2007 amendment.

2007, 110:2, eff. June 11, 2007, provided that the amendments to this section, by section 1 of the act, shall apply only to trials commencing at least 60 days after the effective date of this act.

Construction of 1997 amendment.

1997, 108:17, eff. Jan. 1, 1998, provided: "Nothing in this act [which amended this section and RSA 21-I:42, 21-I:52, 21-I:58, 151:21, 151:21-b, 354-A:1, 354-A:2, 354-A:5-354-A:8, 354-A:10, 354-A:17] shall be interpreted to permit adoptions by homosexuals or to allow marriage of persons of the same sex."

Cross References.

Registration of criminal offenders, see RSA 651-B.

NOTES TO DECISIONS

1. Construction
2. Application
3. Double jeopardy
4. Prior imprisonment
5. Prior convictions
6. Cruelty or depravity—Due process
7. —Defined
8. —Inchoate crimes
9. —After infliction of injury
10. —Findings
11. —Particular cases
12. Pretrial notice
13. Plea bargaining
14. Evidence

1. Construction

Despite the change from "imprisoned" to "convicted," RSA 651:6, II(a), still requires a trial court to find, before it imposes an extended term of incarceration, that the defendant: (1) was previously imprisoned twice, resulting from; and (2) sentences in excess of one year. State v. Matton, 163 N.H. 411, 42 A.3d 830, 2012 N.H. LEXIS 36 (Mar. 23, 2012).

Because the phrase "convicted on sentences in excess of one year" in RSA 651:6, II(a) was ambiguous, and the statute's legislative history neither expressly addressed suspended sentences nor clearly indicated what types of convictions the legislature intended to include within the phrase, the court applied the rule of lenity and resolved the ambiguity in defendant's favor. Thus, a sentence imposing an extended term of imprisonment based on suspended sentences was unlawful. State v. Dansereau, 157 N.H. 596, 956 A.2d 310, 2008 N.H. LEXIS 97 (2008).

On its face, RSA 651:6, II(a), which refers to "convicted on sentences in excess of one year," is ambiguous. State v. Dansereau, 157 N.H. 596, 956 A.2d 310, 2008 N.H. LEXIS 97 (2008).

Former RSA 651:6, II(c) (see now RSA 651:6, II(a)), requires that a court make two findings at the time of sentencing: two prior convictions, resulting in imprisonments on sentences in excess of one year each; there is nothing in the plain language of the statute or the statutory scheme to indicate that the phrase "previously been imprisoned" means prior to the date of the commission of the third offense. State v. Hammell, 147 N.H. 313, 787 A.2d 850, 2001 N.H. LEXIS 218 (2001).

Word "also" in former RSA 651:6, I(f) (now I(e)), which applied where defendant had committed or attempted to commit any of the crimes defined in RSA 631 or RSA 632-A against a person under 13 years of age, referred to the defendant's age and not to the underlying offense; therefore, the crime was a more serious offense and defendant's sentence was extended because of his victim's age. State v. Cole, 147 N.H. 374, 788 A.2d 248, 2001 N.H. LEXIS 227 (2001).

A county correctional officer is a law enforcement officer within meaning of subdivision I(h), and assaults by inmates on county correctional officers acting in the line of duty may be punished by enhanced sentences. State v. Tallard, 143 N.H. 228, 723 A.2d 574, 1998 N.H. LEXIS 95 (1998).

The phrase "in excess of one year" contained in this section modifies the word "sentences" and the "sentence" which governs for purposes of applying the statute is the maximum term. State v. Kiewert, 135 N.H. 338, 605 A.2d 1031, 1992 N.H. LEXIS 45 (1992).

This section is not vague and provides adequate guidance to a sentencing judge. La Vallee v. Perrin, 124 N.H. 33, 466 A.2d 932, 1983 N.H. LEXIS 354 (1983).

2. Application

Because RSA 651:6, I(g) applies only to "crimes defined in RSA 631," it is not applicable to a conviction on a resisting arrest charge, since that offense is found in RSA ch. 642. State v. Blunt, 164 N.H. 679, 62 A.3d 1285, 2013 N.H. LEXIS 27 (2013).

Trial court erred in sentencing misdemeanor defendant to prison for more than one year for offenses that were charged by information and not by indictment, since his extended terms were based on punishment related to offenses themselves and not upon his recidivism. State v. Ouellette, 145 N.H. 489, 764 A.2d 914, 2000 N.H. LEXIS 96 (2000).

Misdemeanor assault defendant did not waive his right to indictment by stipulating that he knew victim was a law enforcement officer acting in the line of duty at time of assault. State v. Ouellette, 145 N.H. 489, 764 A.2d 914, 2000 N.H. LEXIS 96 (2000).

In imposing sentence enhancement based on prior convictions, trial court could properly sentence defendant to prison terms exceeding one year for crimes charged by information; portion of extended terms that exceeded maximum generally applicable sentence did not transform charged misdemeanor offenses into crimes required to be charged by indictment. State v. Smith, 144 N.H. 1, 736 A.2d 1236, 1999 N.H. LEXIS 66 (1999).

District court judge may not sentence a convicted criminal defendant to the enhanced penalties provided in this section; maximum sentence which a district court may impose for a given crime is one year in the county correctional facility. Kiluk v. Potter, 133 N.H. 67, 572 A.2d 1157, 1990 N.H. LEXIS 26 (1990).

Prosecutor does not offend due process considerations in recommending an enhanced sentence when the defendant does not plead guilty. State v. Gallant, 133 N.H. 138, 574 A.2d 385, 1990 N.H. LEXIS 44 (1990).

This section, on its face, does not apply only to defendants who assert their right to plead not guilty and seek a jury trial. La Vallee v. Perrin, 124 N.H. 33, 466 A.2d 932, 1983 N.H. LEXIS 354 (1983).

Selective use of this section, even if applied only to those who opt for trial and not to those who plead, is constitutionally permissible. La Vallee v. Perrin, 124 N.H. 33, 466 A.2d 932, 1983 N.H. LEXIS 354 (1983).

Nothing in this section prevents a judge, either upon recommendation of the prosecutor or upon his own motion, from utilizing this section in a plea situation. La Vallee v. Perrin, 124 N.H. 33, 466 A.2d 932, 1983 N.H. LEXIS 354 (1983).

3. Double jeopardy

The was no violation of the protection against double jeopardy found in part I, article 16 of the New Hampshire Constitution when an extended sentence of 10 to 30 years was imposed on the defendant for aggravated felonious sexual assault based on the age of the victim, notwithstanding the contention that the sentence was improper because the victim's age had already been used to elevate the offense from a class B felony to a class A felony; the defendant was only convicted once and sentenced once, and there was no violation. State v. Hennessey, 142 N.H. 149, 697 A.2d 930, 1997 N.H. LEXIS 68 (1997).

4. Prior imprisonment

Trial court did not err in imposing an extended term of imprisonment. At the time the State filed its notices, defendant had

been imprisoned only once; however, prior to his sentencing, defendant's prior suspended sentence had been imposed, resulting in a second term of imprisonment in excess of one year. State v. Russo, 164 N.H. 585, 62 A.3d 798, 2013 N.H. LEXIS 16 (2013).

Trial court properly denied defendant's motion to preclude the State from seeking an extended term of incarceration under RSA 651:6, II(a). The requirements of the statute were satisfied because defendant had served two terms of imprisonment resulting from sentences in excess of one year. State v. Matton, 163 N.H. 411, 42 A.3d 830, 2012 N.H. LEXIS 36 (Mar. 23, 2012).

Evidence of one of defendant's alleged two prior sentences for more than a year's imprisonment was insufficient when it consisted solely of a copy of a police criminal record, with no copy of the judgment of conviction or the mittimus; therefore, resentencing to a non-enhanced sentence was required. State v. Scognamiglio, 150 N.H. 534, 842 A.2d 109, 2004 N.H. LEXIS 17 (2004).

Although sentencing court misconstrued this section as requiring two prior incarcerations for periods in excess of one year, court's error was harmless, as defendant was twice previously imprisoned on sentences in excess of one year. State v. Kiewert, 135 N.H. 338, 605 A.2d 1031, 1992 N.H. LEXIS 45 (1992).

Imposition of an extended imprisonment under former subparagraph I(c) of this section was dependent on proof of previous periods of imprisonment, and proof of prior convictions was not sufficient although it could be presumed that prior prison terms were preceded by convictions. State v. Gosselin, 117 N.H. 115, 370 A.2d 264, 1977 N.H. LEXIS 281 (1977)(decided under prior law).

Imposition of an extended term of imprisonment upon a finding defendant has twice previously been imprisoned on sentence in excess of a year is not dependent upon a request from the prosecution, either orally or by written motion or otherwise. State v. Bailey, 115 N.H. 149, 335 A.2d 659, 1975 N.H. LEXIS 247 (1975).

5. Prior convictions

Prior convictions obtained when defendant was not represented by counsel and had not knowingly and intelligently waived his right to counsel could not be used as basis for an enhanced sentence under this section. State v. Gosselin, 117 N.H. 115, 370 A.2d 264, 1977 N.H. LEXIS 281 (1977).

6. Cruelty or depravity—Due process

"Exceptional cruelty or depravity," as used in subparagraph I(d) (now I(c)) of this section, is a valid sentencing consideration, subject to the relaxed due process considerations which apply in sentencing hearings. La Vallee v. Perrin, 124 N.H. 33, 466 A.2d 932, 1983 N.H. LEXIS 354 (1983).

7. —Defined

Where terms "cruelty" and "depravity" are not defined in this section, the terms will be ascribed their usual and common meaning; "cruel" is defined as "disposed to inflict pain in a wanton, insensate manner" or "given to killing or mangling or to tormenting" and, "depraved" is defined as "marked by debasement." State v. Morehouse, 120 N.H. 738, 424 A.2d 798, 1980 N.H. LEXIS 406 (1980).

8. —Inchoate crimes

The legislature intended to apply subparagraph I(d) (now I(c)) of this section to an inchoate crime such as conspiracy; it did not intend to limit its application to a killer and exclude persons who planned the murder and dispatched the killer. State v. Colby, 116 N.H. 790, 368 A.2d 587, 1976 N.H. LEXIS 471 (1976).

9. —After infliction of injury

Defendant could not avoid imposition of extended sentence pursuant to subparagraph I(d) (now I(c)) of this section by showing cruelty and depravity after inflicting serious bodily injury rather than before or during the infliction of serious bodily injury. State v. Woodard, 121 N.H. 970, 437 A.2d 273, 1981 N.H. LEXIS 443 (1981).

10. —Findings

Trial court should enunciate specific findings of fact based upon the evidence that supports finding of exceptional cruelty or depravity under subparagraph I(d) (now I(c)) of this section so as to allow enhancement of a sentence. State v. Morehouse, 120 N.H. 738, 424

A.2d 798, 1980 N.H. LEXIS 406 (1980).

In sentencing proceedings following conviction of attempted first-degree murder, trial court's finding of cruelty or depravity due to accused's actions of repeatedly striking the victim on the head with a metal hammer, which finding resulted in an enhanced sentence, was a valid sentencing criterion and did not violate accused's right to due process of law. State v. Morehouse, 120 N.H. 738, 424 A.2d 798, 1980 N.H. LEXIS 406 (1980).

11. —Particular cases

Nineteen stab wounds together with the demands for unnatural sexual acts were sufficient manifestation of cruelty or depravity to justify extended sentence imposed by the trial court. State v. Woodard, 121 N.H. 970, 437 A.2d 273, 1981 N.H. LEXIS 443 (1981).

12. Pretrial notice

Trial court did not err in imposing an extended term of imprisonment because the State's notices failed to specify the prior convictions upon which it intended to rely. There was no evidence that defendant suffered any prejudice from the State's failure to specify which prior convictions it intended to rely upon. State v. Russo, 164 N.H. 585, 62 A.3d 798, 2013 N.H. LEXIS 16 (2013).

Because the notice of intent to seek enhanced sentence purported to authorize a sentence beyond that which the district division had the power to impose under RSA 502-A:11, the State's filing of that notice in the circuit court was wholly ineffective. Furthermore, there was no merit to the State's position that the RSA 651:6 notice could nonetheless be treated as a "proxy" for the notice required by RSA 625:9, IV(c)(2), as not only was the RSA 651:6 notice devoid of any indication that its purpose was to authorize the imposition of class A misdemeanor penalties, but the notice was not filed at or before the defendant's arraignment. State v. Blunt, 164 N.H. 679, 62 A.3d 1285, 2013 N.H. LEXIS 27 (2013).

State was not required to notify defendant of application of this section before defendant's retrial where state had provided written notice of intent to seek extended sentence prior to first trial, nothing had occurred between the two trials which would warrant belief that extended sentence would not again be sought, and it was clear during plea negotiations prior to second trial that state intended to press for extended sentence at the second trial. State v. Hurlburt, 135 N.H. 143, 603 A.2d 493, 1991 N.H. LEXIS 157 (1991), cert. denied, Hurlburt v. New Hampshire, 503 U.S. 1008, 112 S. Ct. 1770, 118 L. Ed. 2d 430, 1992 U.S. LEXIS 2629 (1992).

The trial court did not abuse its discretion in denying defendant's motion to continue a trial based on the prosecution's amended notice, on the first day of trial, of its intent to seek extended term sentencing; notice complied with statutory requirements and did not deny defendant the opportunity to refute the basis for seeking the extended sentencing, since no new grounds were set forth in the amended notice, but only the addition of charges to which it applied. State v. Reid, 134 N.H. 418, 594 A.2d 160, 1991 N.H. LEXIS 81 (1991).

Purpose of pretrial notice requirement of this section is to give the defendant an opportunity to offer evidence to refute the findings required by this section. State v. Coppola, 130 N.H. 148, 536 A.2d 1236, 1987 N.H. LEXIS 298 (1987).

Although a prosecutor will be prudent to specify the applicable criteria for extended sentences under this section, as part of the pretrial notice requirement, the failure so to specify will not render this section inapplicable in the absence of actual prejudice. State v. Coppola, 130 N.H. 148, 536 A.2d 1236, 1987 N.H. LEXIS 298 (1987).

Pretrial notice requirement of this section will give the defendant an opportunity to offer evidence to refute the findings required by this section. State v. Toto, 123 N.H. 619, 465 A.2d 894, 1983 N.H. LEXIS 344 (1983).

The requirement that notice be given to the defendant prior to trial of the possible application of this section is not limited to those instances in which the prosecutor seeks application of this section. State v. Toto, 123 N.H. 619, 465 A.2d 894, 1983 N.H. LEXIS 344 (1983).

Because the legislature has not established any distinction based on the individual invoking this section, and because application of the section, either at the request of the prosecutor or by the judge sua sponte, may result in a substantial increase in one's penalty, it appears that the requirement of this section that notice be given to the defendant prior to trial of the possible application of this section was intended to apply even when the judge seeks to apply it sua sponte. State v. Toto, 123 N.H. 619, 465 A.2d 894, 1983 N.H. LEXIS 344 (1983).

In the case of a defendant convicted of unauthorized possession of a narcotic drug, where the court sua sponte imposed an extended term of imprisonment pursuant to this section, even though no notice of the possible application of the section had been given to the defendant prior to trial, the trial court erred in sentencing the defendant in accordance with this section because notice was not given prior to commencement of trial. State v. Toto, 123 N.H. 619, 465 A.2d 894, 1983 N.H. LEXIS 344 (1983).

13. Plea bargaining

Prosecutor's request that defendant waive his right to appeal in exchange for an unenhanced sentence recommendation did not violate defendant's due process rights, where offer was made in course of negotiations in which both parties were on equal footing. State v. Gallant, 133 N.H. 138, 574 A.2d 385, 1990 N.H. LEXIS 44 (1990).

14. Evidence

Defendant's parole officer, who testified that he had custody of both state prison and parole board records concerning defendant, which included copies of previous conviction orders and other prison and parole board records, whose status as custodian of these records was not challenged as being improper by defendant, properly testified from the commitment orders for purpose of imposing extended prison term under former subparagraph I(c) (see now II) of this section. State v. Gosselin, 117 N.H. 115, 370 A.2d 264, 1977 N.H. LEXIS 281 (1977).

Cited:

Cited in State v. McPhail, 116 N.H. 440, 362 A.2d 199, 1976 N.H. LEXIS 377 (1976); State v. Martineau, 116 N.H. 797, 368 A.2d 592, 1976 N.H. LEXIS 472 (1976); State v. La Roche, 117 N.H. 127, 370 A.2d 631, 1977 N.H. LEXIS 283 (1977); State v. Leclair, 118 N.H. 214, 385 A.2d 831, 1978 N.H. LEXIS 383 (1978); State v. Champagne, 119 N.H. 118, 399 A.2d 287, 1979 N.H. LEXIS 253 (1979); State v. Lavallee, 119 N.H. 207, 400 A.2d 480, 1979 N.H. LEXIS 278 (1979); State v. Hudson, 119 N.H. 963, 409 A.2d 1349, 1979 N.H. LEXIS 431 (1979); State v. Heald, 120 N.H. 319, 414 A.2d 1288, 1980 N.H. LEXIS 273 (1980); State v. Beaupre, 123 N.H. 155, 459 A.2d 233, 1983 N.H. LEXIS 243 (1983); State v. Dean, 129 N.H. 744, 533 A.2d 333, 1987 N.H. LEXIS 263 (1987); State v. Vachon, 130 N.H. 37, 533 A.2d 384, 1987 N.H. LEXIS 266 (1987); Stewart v. Cunningham, 131 N.H. 68, 550 A.2d 96, 1988 N.H. LEXIS 84 (1988); State v. Wisowaty, 133 N.H. 604, 580 A.2d 1079, 1990 N.H. LEXIS 109 (1990); Hurlburt v. Cunningham, 802 F. Supp. 585, 1992 U.S. Dist. LEXIS 14744 (D.N.H. 1992); State v. Wisowaty, 137 N.H. 298, 627 A.2d 572, 1993 N.H. LEXIS 74 (1993); State v. Cole, 142 N.H. 519, 703 A.2d 658, 1997 N.H. LEXIS 125 (1997); State v. Porter, 144 N.H. 96, 738 A.2d 1271, 1999 N.H. LEXIS 78 (1999); State v. White, 145 N.H. 544, 765 A.2d 156, 2000 N.H. LEXIS 107 (2000).

RESEARCH REFERENCES

New Hampshire Practice.

2-33 N.H.P. Criminal Practice & Procedure § 33.10.

651:7. Release from State Prison.

[Repealed 1973, 370:39, eff. Nov. 1, 1973.]

Former section(s).

Former RSA 651:7, which was derived from 1971, 518:1, related to early release for good conduct.

Insane Persons

Cross References.

Insanity defense, see RSA 628:2.

Interstate Compact on the Mentally Disordered Offender, see RSA 126-C.

651:8. Certificate of Jury.

Whenever the grand jury shall omit to find an indictment against a person, for the reason of insanity or mental derangement, or a person prosecuted for an offense shall be acquitted by the petit jury for the same reason, such jury shall certify the same to the court.

Source.
1971, 518:1, eff. Nov. 1, 1973.

NOTES TO DECISIONS

Constitutionality
This section is mandated unconstitutional by state due process clause in that grand jury proceedings are secret and without adversaries, cross-examination of witnesses does not take place, written record from which appeal may be taken is not required, accused may be compelled to appear without benefit of counsel present, hearsay evidence is considered, and probable cause rather than proof beyond reasonable doubt is standard by which determinations are made. Novosel v. Helgemoe, 118 N.H. 115, 384 A.2d 124, 1978 N.H. LEXIS 356 (1978), superseded by statute as stated in, State v. Blair, 143 N.H. 669, 732 A.2d 448, 1999 N.H. LEXIS 57 (1999).

This section offends the due process clause of the fourteenth amendment since it empowers the grand jury to make a conclusive finding of fact that an accused is insane or mentally deranged in a secret, non-adversarial setting, with no cross-examination of witnesses; there is no requirement of a written transcript from which an appeal may be taken; the accused may be compelled to appear before the grand jury and has no right to have an attorney present; the grand jury can consider hearsay and illegally obtained evidence; no psychiatric examination of the accused precedes the grand jury's finding; and the standard guiding the grand jury is that of probable cause. Kanteles v. Wheelock, 439 F. Supp. 505, 1977 U.S. Dist. LEXIS 13414 (D.N.H. 1977).

Since certification of insanity pursuant to this section has the same effect upon the accused as a finding of not guilty by reason of insanity in that it presupposes that he committed the crime charged, and once the grand jury finds him insane, the accused stands to suffer loss of liberty and the stigma of criminal commitment without being convicted of a crime, it is at this stage where due process safeguards should attach. Kanteles v. Wheelock, 439 F. Supp. 505, 1977 U.S. Dist. LEXIS 13414 (D.N.H. 1977).

This section and [former] RSA 651:9, authorizing committal of a person certified insane or mentally deranged, deny equal protection of the laws since the method and process of determining insanity are different in civil and criminal commitment proceedings, based merely on the fact of pending criminal charges, thereby constituting an impermissible classification. Kanteles v. Wheelock, 439 F. Supp. 505, 1977 U.S. Dist. LEXIS 13414 (D.N.H. 1977).

Cited:
Cited in In re Sargent, 116 N.H. 77, 354 A.2d 404, 1976 N.H. LEXIS 270 (1976); State v. Gregoire, 118 N.H. 140, 384 A.2d 132, 1978 N.H. LEXIS 360 (1978); State v. Novosel, 120 N.H. 176, 412 A.2d 739, 1980 N.H. LEXIS 245 (1980).

RESEARCH REFERENCES

New Hampshire Bar Journal.
For article, "Shuffling the Insanity Defense: Novosel v. Helgemoe," see 20 N.H.B.J. 226 (July 1979).

651:8-a. Plea of Insanity.

Any person prosecuted for an offense may plead that he is not guilty by reason of insanity or mental derangement. If such a plea is accepted by the state's counsel, such counsel shall certify the same to the court.

Source.
1975, 243:1, eff. Aug. 3, 1975.

NOTES TO DECISIONS

1. Presumption of sanity
2. Trial procedure
3. Advice to accused
4. Burden of proof

1. Presumption of sanity
Sanity is properly in the nature of a policy presumption because it is inherent in human nature, is a natural and normal condition of mankind and is not properly an element of the crime. Novosel v. Helgemoe, 118 N.H. 115, 384 A.2d 124, 1978 N.H. LEXIS 356 (1978), superseded by statute as stated in, State v. Blair, 143 N.H. 669, 732 A.2d 448, 1999 N.H. LEXIS 57 (1999).

2. Trial procedure
If the state disputes the insanity of the accused at the time of the commission of the crime, the matter will be tried solely on the question of insanity because the plea of not guilty by reason of insanity is one of confession and avoidance and admits that the accused committed the acts alleged. Novosel v. Helgemoe, 118 N.H. 115, 384 A.2d 124, 1978 N.H. LEXIS 356 (1978), superseded by statute as stated in, State v. Blair, 143 N.H. 669, 732 A.2d 448, 1999 N.H. LEXIS 57 (1999).

3. Advice to accused
Court must inform accused and must find that accused understands, that by pleading not guilty by reason of insanity and having state agree to it, he will be subject to proceeding which could result in his involuntary hospitalization for life until or unless earlier discharged, released, or transferred by due course of law if found to be dangerous to go at large. Novosel v. Helgemoe, 118 N.H. 115, 384 A.2d 124, 1978 N.H. LEXIS 356 (1978), superseded by statute as stated in, State v. Blair, 143 N.H. 669, 732 A.2d 448, 1999 N.H. LEXIS 57 (1999).

4. Burden of proof
The affirmative defense of insanity must be proven by clear and convincing evidence. State v. Rullo, 120 N.H. 149, 412 A.2d 1009, 1980 N.H. LEXIS 248 (1980), superseded by statute as stated in, State v. Blair, 143 N.H. 669, 732 A.2d 448, 1999 N.H. LEXIS 57 (1999).

651:8-b. Hospitalization; Persons Acquitted by Reason of Insanity.

I. If a person is found not guilty by reason of insanity at the time of the offense charged, he shall be committed to the secure psychiatric unit until such time as he is eligible for release pursuant to paragraph IV.

II. A hearing shall be conducted not later than 40 days following a verdict of not guilty by reason of insanity, at which the defendant shall be represented by counsel. The state and the defendant shall be offered the opportunity to present evidence and to cross-examine witnesses who appear at the hearing.

III. Prior to the date of the hearing pursuant to paragraph II, the court shall order that a psychiatric or psychological examination of the defendant be conducted, and that a psychiatric or psychological report be filed with the court, with copies provided to the defendant and to the attorney for the state.

IV. If, after the hearing, the court finds by clear and convincing evidence that the acquitted person is presently suffering from a mental disease or defect as a result of which his or her release would create a substantial risk of bodily injury to himself or herself or another, or serious damage to the property of another, the court shall commit the person pursuant to the provisions of RSA 651:9-a and RSA 651:11-a. The court shall supply a copy of the report ordered pursuant to paragraph III to the secure psychiatric unit or other treatment facility in which the person is confined. The existence of clear and convincing evidence that a person's release would create a substantial risk of bodily injury to himself or herself or another person or serious damage to the property of another shall be presumed, subject to rebuttal by the acquitted person, where the person has been found not guilty by reason of insanity of an offense involving bodily injury or serious damage to property of another, or substantial risk of such injury or damage.

Source.
1987, 405:1, eff. July 25, 1987. 2010, 46:2, eff. May 18, 2010.

Amendments
—2010. The 2010 amendment added the second sentence of IV and made stylistic changes.

NOTES TO DECISIONS

Cited:
Cited in In re Sanborn, 130 N.H. 430, 545 A.2d 726, 1988 N.H. LEXIS 40 (1988); State v. Blair, 143 N.H. 669, 732 A.2d 448, 1999 N.H. LEXIS 57 (1999).

651:9. Committal.

[Repealed 1985, 337:8, eff. July 1, 1985.]

Former section(s).
Former RSA 651:9, which was derived from 1971, 518:1 and 1975, 388:6, related to committal of persons certified insane or mentally deranged. See now RSA 651:9-a.

Committal or transfer of persons previously committed or transferred.
1985, 337:10, eff. July 1, 1985, provided: "All persons previously committed or transferred to New Hampshire hospital under RSA 623:1, 651:9, and 651:11 shall be committed or transferred to the secure psychiatric unit."

651:9-a. Committal.

In either of the cases aforesaid the court, if it is of the opinion that it will be dangerous that such person should go at large, shall commit him to the secure psychiatric unit for 5 years unless earlier discharged, released or transferred by due course of law.

Source.
1975, 388:1. 1985, 337:4, eff. July 1, 1985.

Amendments
—1985. Substituted "secure psychiatric unit for 5 years" for "state hospital for life until or" preceding "unless".

Cross References.
Committal of accused for pre-trial psychiatric examination, see RSA 135:17.
Committal of persons confined in jails or houses of correction, see RSA 651:11.
Discharge by governor and council, see RSA 651:10.
Duration of committal orders, see RSA 651:11-a.
Evidence required to commit accused acquitted by reason of insanity, see New Hampshire Constitution, Part 1, Article 15.
Procedure for examination and commitment of persons acquitted by reason of insanity, see RSA 651:8-b.
Secure psychiatric unit, see RSA 622:40 et seq.

NOTES TO DECISIONS

1. Constitutionality
2. Examination of defendant
3. Release
4. Proof required

1. Constitutionality
This section and RSA 651:8, authorizing the grand jury to certify that a person is insane or mentally deranged, deny equal protection of the laws, since the method and process of determining insanity are different in civil and criminal commitment proceedings, based merely on the fact of pending criminal charges, thereby constituting an impermissible classification. Kanteles v. Wheelock, 439 F. Supp. 505, 1977 U.S. Dist. LEXIS 13414 (D.N.H. 1977). (Decided under former RSA 651:9.)

2. Examination of defendant
A superior court had authority under this section to order a post-trial psychiatric evaluation of a defendant found not guilty by reason of insanity for purposes of determining whether the defendant would be dangerous if allowed to go at large. State v. Mercier, 128 N.H. 57, 509 A.2d 1246, 1986 N.H. LEXIS 255 (1986). (Decided under former RSA 651:9.)

3. Release
Once the threshold determination has been made that a person is dangerous within meaning of this section and is to be committed pursuant thereto, trial court has authority to order the person released provided certain terms and conditions are met. State v. Radford, 118 N.H. 722, 393 A.2d 561, 1978 N.H. LEXIS 278 (1978). (Decided under former RSA 651:9.)

4. Proof required
In a criminal case, when there is an initial commitment proceeding under this section following a verdict or plea of insanity, the requirements for predicting dangerousness are in practice the same as those in a civil commitment proceeding under former RSA 135-B:26. State v. Mercier, 128 N.H. 57, 509 A.2d 1246, 1986 N.H. LEXIS 255 (1986). (Decided under former RSA 651:9.)
In an initial criminal commitment proceeding under this section following a verdict of insanity, a rational trier of fact could have found dangerousness beyond a reasonable doubt on the basis of the evidentiary facts where it was shown that the defendant had a history of violent acts of robbery; suffered from antisocial personality disorder, post-traumatic stress disorder, and the effects of substance abuse; and his clinical diagnosis was poor. State v. Mercier, 128 N.H. 57, 509 A.2d 1246, 1986 N.H. LEXIS 255 (1986). (Decided under former RSA 651:9.)
To commit accused under this section required proof beyond reasonable doubt. Novosel v. Helgemoe, 118 N.H. 115, 384 A.2d 124, 1978 N.H. LEXIS 356 (1978), superseded by statute as stated in, State v. Blair, 143 N.H. 669, 732 A.2d 448, 1999 N.H. LEXIS 57 (1999). (Decided under former RSA 651:9.)

Cited:
Cited in Gibbs v. Helgemoe, 116 N.H. 825, 367 A.2d 1041, 1976 N.H. LEXIS 478 (1977); State v. Kupchun, 117 N.H. 412, 373 A.2d 1325, 1977 N.H. LEXIS 348 (1977); In re Sanborn, 130 N.H. 430, 545 A.2d 726, 1988 N.H. LEXIS 40 (1988); State v. Blair, 143 N.H. 669, 732 A.2d 448, 1999 N.H. LEXIS 57 (1999).

651:10. Discharge or Transfer from Prison.

The governor and council or the superior court may discharge any such person from prison, or shall transfer any prisoner who is insane to the secure psychiatric unit, to be kept at the expense of the state, whenever they are satisfied that such discharge or transfer will be conducive to the health and comfort of the person and the welfare of the public.

Source.

1971, 518:1. 1975, 388:2. 1985, 337:5, eff. July 1, 1985.

Amendments

—1985. Substituted "secure psychiatric unit" for "state hospital" and deleted "there" preceding "kept at the expense of the state" in the first sentence and deleted the second and third sentences.

—1975. Substituted "shall" for "may" preceding "transfer" in the first sentence and added the second and third sentences.

Cross References.

Duration of committal orders, see RSA 651:11-a.
Secure psychiatric unit, see RSA 622:40 et seq.

NOTES TO DECISIONS

1. Construction
2. Liability for support

1. Construction

The term "prisoner" in this section refers to one in prison under a criminal sentence. In re Sargent, 116 N.H. 77, 354 A.2d 404, 1976 N.H. LEXIS 270 (1976).

The words "to be there kept at the expense of the state" in this section refer to prisoners who have been transferred pursuant to this section, not to those who have not been indicted or have been acquitted or have pleaded not guilty by reason of insanity and subsequently committed on the ground that it would be dangerous for them to go at large. In re Sargent, 116 N.H. 77, 354 A.2d 404, 1976 N.H. LEXIS 270 (1976).

2. Liability for support

The state was chargeable with the support of an insane person transferred to the state prison from the asylum by order of the governor and council until he was discharged therefrom according to law, and the state's liability for his support did not terminate at the expiration of the term for which he was sentenced to prison. New Hampshire Asylum for Insane v. Belknap County, 69 N.H. 174, 44 A. 928, 1897 N.H. LEXIS 12 (1897). (Decided under prior law.)

Cited:

Cited in Novosel v. Helgemoe, 118 N.H. 115, 384 A.2d 124, 1978 N.H. LEXIS 356 (1978).

651:11. Transfer from County Correctional Facility.

If any insane person is confined in a county correctional facility, the superior court shall order him to be committed to the secure psychiatric unit.

Source.

1971, 518:1. 1975, 388:3. 1985, 337:6. 1988, 89:30, eff. June 17, 1988.

Amendments

—1988. Substituted "County Correctional Facility" for "Jail" following "Transfer from" in the section catchline and "a county correctional facility" for "jail, or a house of correction" following "confined in" in the text.

—1985. Substituted "secure psychiatric unit" for "state hospital" at the end of the first sentence and deleted the second and third sentences.

—1975. Substituted "shall" for "may" preceding "order" in the first sentence, deleted "if it thinks it expedient" at the end of that sentence and added the second and third sentences.

Committal or transfer of persons previously committed or transferred.

1985, 337:10, eff. July 1, 1985, provided: "All persons previously committed or transferred to New Hampshire hospital under RSA 623:1, 651:9, and 651:11 shall be committed or transferred to the secure psychiatric unit."

Cross References.

Duration of committal orders, see RSA 651:11-a.
Secure psychiatric unit, see RSA 622:40 et seq.

651:11-a. Duration of Committal Orders.

I. Orders of committal to the secure psychiatric unit made pursuant to this chapter shall be valid for 5 years. For the order to be renewed, another judicial hearing must be held. At the renewal hearing, when the court is satisfied by clear and convincing evidence that the person suffers from a mental disorder and that it would be dangerous for him to go at large, the court shall renew the order of committal.

II. Without otherwise limiting the discretion of the court, a court shall find it would be dangerous for a person to go at large if:

(a) He has been found not guilty by reason of insanity of a crime; and

(b) The physical act or acts constituting the crime of which the person was found not guilty by reason of insanity caused death or serious bodily injury as defined in RSA 625:11, VI, to him or another, or created a grave risk of death or serious bodily injury to him or another; and

(c) The person suffers from the mental disorder or a substantially similar mental condition as existed at the time he committed the act or acts which constituted the crime of which he was found not guilty by reason of insanity.

III. Without otherwise limiting the discretion of the court, a court may find that it would be dangerous for a person to go at large if:

(a) He has been found not guilty by reason of insanity of a crime; and

(b) The physical act or acts constituting the crime of which the person was found not guilty by reason of insanity resulted in damage to the property of another, or created a grave risk of damage to the property of another, or caused harm or a risk of harm to himself or another; and

(c) The person suffers from the mental disorder or a substantially similar mental condition as existed at the time he committed the act or acts which constituted the crime of which he was found not guilty by reason of insanity.

IV. The following provisions shall apply after the court renews the order of committal pursuant to paragraph I of this section:

(a) If the court renews the order of committal but finds by clear and convincing evidence that the person's release under certain conditions, including, but not limited to, a prescribed regimen of medical, psychiatric, or psychological care or treatment, would no longer create a substantial risk of bodily injury to himself or another person or serious damage to property of another, the court may:

(1) Order that he be conditionally discharged under conditions the court finds appropriate, including any prescribed regimen of medical, psychiatric, or psychological care or treatment that has been prepared for him, which has been certified to the court as appropriate by the commissioner of the department of corrections or his designee or by the director of another facility not within the department of corrections in which he is committed, and which has been found by the court to be appropriate; and

(2) Order, as an explicit condition of release, that he comply with the conditions imposed by the court, including any prescribed regimen of medical, psychiatric, or psychological care or treatment.

(b) The court at any time may, after a hearing employing the same criteria as a hearing pursuant to subparagraph (a), modify or eliminate the conditions imposed, including any prescribed regimen of medical, psychiatric, or psychological care or treatment.

(c) The commissioner of the department of corrections or the director of another program or facility not within the department of corrections responsible for administering a condition or regimen imposed on a person conditionally discharged under subparagraph (a) shall notify the attorney general and the court having jurisdiction over the person of any failure of the person to comply with the condition or regimen, or of any other circumstances which create a reasonable likelihood that it is dangerous for the person to remain conditionally discharged. Upon such notice, or upon other probable cause to believe that the person has failed to comply with the condition or prescribed regimen of medical, psychiatric, or psychological treatment, or that other circumstances exist which create a reasonable likelihood that it is dangerous for the person to remain conditionally discharged, the person may be arrested, and, upon arrest, shall be taken without unnecessary delay before the court having jurisdiction over him. The court shall, after a hearing, determine whether the person should be remanded to the secure psychiatric unit or to another suitable facility on the basis that in light of his failure to comply with the conditions imposed by the court, including any prescribed regimen of medical, psychiatric, or psychological care or treatment, or because of other circumstances, his continued release would create a substantial risk of bodily injury to himself or another person or serious damage to property of another.

Source.
1975, 388:4. 1977, 180:1. 1982, 34:2. 1985, 337:7. 1987, 13:2, eff. June 2, 1987.

Amendments
—1987. Paragraph IV: Rewritten to the extent that a detailed comparison would be impracticable.

—1985. Paragraph I: Substituted "secure psychiatric unit" for "New Hampshire hospital" preceding "made pursuant" in the first sentence and "clear and convincing evidence that the person" for "proof beyond a reasonable doubt that the hospital patient" preceding "suffers" in the third sentence.

—1982. Rewritten to the extent that a detailed comparison would be impracticable.

—1977. Added the last sentence and made minor changes in phraseology.

Cross References.
Procedure for examination and commitment of persons acquitted by reason of insanity, see RSA 651:8-b.
Secure psychiatric unit, see RSA 622:40 et seq.

NOTES TO DECISIONS

1. Constitutionality
2. Construction with other laws
3. Application—Generally
4. —Retrospective
5. Legal representation
6. Burden of proof
7. Dangerous persons
8. Medical records

1. Constitutionality
Paragraph II of this section, creating an irrebuttable presumption of dangerousness based on the patient's past dangerous act and on the fact that the mental condition which led to his acquittal by reason of insanity has not substantially changed, is invalid, in that it denies insanity acquittees their due process right to be given a chance to defeat the presumption with additional evidence. State v. Robb, 125 N.H. 581, 484 A.2d 1130, 1984 N.H. LEXIS 310 (1984).

2. Construction with other laws
The language of this section, "that it would be dangerous for him to go at large," does not set a more difficult standard than RSA 135-B:26 (now RSA 135-C:34), governing civil involuntary commitment, with its language "as to create a potentially serious likelihood of danger to himself or others"; the two sections are merely different ways of saying the same thing. State v. Paradis, 123 N.H. 68, 455 A.2d 1070, 1983 N.H. LEXIS 225 (1983).

3. Application—Generally
This section applies to persons committed under former RSA 651:9 (now RSA 651:9-a) when the grand jury omits to find an indictment for reason of insanity or the petit jury acquits for the same reason. Gibbs v. Helgemoe, 116 N.H. 825, 367 A.2d 1041, 1976 N.H. LEXIS 478 (1977), superseded by statute as stated in, In re Sanborn, 130 N.H. 430, 545 A.2d 726, 1988 N.H. LEXIS 40 (1988).

4. —Retrospective
For purposes of determining the retrospectivity of a statute governing recommitment to psychiatric facilities of defendants found not guilty by reason of insanity, the date of the defendant's insanity plea, not the date of the underlying alleged criminal conduct, determines whether application of a particular recommitment statute is retrospective. Iandolo v. Powell, 134 N.H. 630, 595 A.2d 510, 1991 N.H. LEXIS 111 (1991).
1982 amendment of paragraph I of this section, extending validity of commitment order from two to five years, violated prohibition against retrospective or ex post facto laws of the New Hampshire Constitution, part 1, article 23, when applied to a patient committed prior to the date of the amendment, since it operated to shift the burden of initiating judicial review of the commitment status for patients who were committed prior to the

amendment and who desired to review their commitment status more frequently than the five-year review provided by the amendment. State v. Ballou, 125 N.H. 304, 481 A.2d 260, 1984 N.H. LEXIS 270 (1984).

5. Legal representation

When the state petitions to recommit a defendant under paragraph I of this section, the state must initiate the proceedings, and the defendant is guaranteed legal representation in accordance with Superior Court Administrative Rule 11-7. State v. Ballou, 125 N.H. 304, 481 A.2d 260, 1984 N.H. LEXIS 270 (1984).

6. Burden of proof

Paragraph I of this section implicitly places the burden of petitioning the court for a hearing and the burden of proof, should a hearing be requested sooner than the five years provided in paragraph I, on the patient. State v. Ballou, 125 N.H. 304, 481 A.2d 260, 1984 N.H. LEXIS 270 (1984).

At a hearing held pursuant to this section, the state is the moving party and is therefore assigned the burden of proof, but at an interim hearing held pursuant to a defendant's petition for release prior to expiration of a committal order, the defendant is the party asserting the affirmative issue and must bear the burden of proof. State v. Hesse, 117 N.H. 329, 373 A.2d 345, 1977 N.H. LEXIS 331 (1977).

7. Dangerous persons

Since this section contains no words of possible limitation, and since it is unlikely that the legislature would have limited its application so as not to include a mentally ill arsonist or anyone else whose mental illness creates a significant risk of substantial damage to valuable property, it is not confined only to danger to persons but extends also to property. State v. Paradis, 123 N.H. 68, 455 A.2d 1070, 1983 N.H. LEXIS 225 (1983).

8. Medical records

Information obtained by office of attorney general regarding medical records of treatment of defendant committed to state hospital following plea or verdict of not guilty by reason of insanity to criminal charge shall be used only in hearings before superior court pertaining to recommitment and for no other purpose, and trial court may take whatever further steps it may deem necessary, such as holding closed hearing, to prevent public disclosure of information; except for these proceedings, such information remains privileged. State v. Kupchun, 117 N.H. 412, 373 A.2d 1325, 1977 N.H. LEXIS 348 (1977).

Order of superior court, in hearing on whether court's committal order of defendant to state hospital following plea of not guilty by reason of insanity to criminal charge should be renewed, granting state access to medical records of treatment of defendant at state hospital and stating that hospital's physicians and psychologists might disclose all information which had a bearing on defendant's dangerousness or mental condition, did not violate statutory physician-patient or psychologist-client privileges or other rights of defendant. State v. Kupchun, 117 N.H. 412, 373 A.2d 1325, 1977 N.H. LEXIS 348 (1977).

Cited:

Cited in Kanteles v. Wheelock, 439 F. Supp. 505, 1977 U.S. Dist. LEXIS 13414 (D.N.H. 1977); Novosel v. Helgemoe, 118 N.H. 115, 384 A.2d 124, 1978 N.H. LEXIS 356 (1978); State v. Gregoire, 118 N.H. 140, 384 A.2d 132, 1978 N.H. LEXIS 360 (1978); Hudson v. Miller, 119 N.H. 141, 399 A.2d 612, 1979 N.H. LEXIS 257 (1979); Grindle v. Miller, 119 N.H. 214, 400 A.2d 787, 1979 N.H. LEXIS 280 (1979); In re Brenda H., 119 N.H. 382, 402 A.2d 169, 1979 N.H. LEXIS 320 (1979); State v. Merski, 121 N.H. 901, 437 A.2d 710, 1981 N.H. LEXIS 435 (1981); State v. Lister, 122 N.H. 603, 448 A.2d 395, 1982 N.H. LEXIS 410 (1982); State v. Bertrand, 123 N.H. 719, 465 A.2d 912, 1983 N.H. LEXIS 340 (1983); In re Kathleen M., 126 N.H. 379, 493 A.2d 472, 1985 N.H. LEXIS 312 (1985); State v. Mercier, 128 N.H. 57, 509 A.2d 1246, 1986 N.H. LEXIS 255 (1986); In re Sanborn, 130 N.H. 430, 545 A.2d 726, 1988 N.H. LEXIS 40 (1988); State v. Westcott, 134 N.H. 692, 597 A.2d 1072, 1991 N.H. LEXIS 124 (1991).

RESEARCH REFERENCES

New Hampshire Court Rules Annotated.

Procedure for Parole, Discharge and Off-Ground Privileges from the New Hampshire Hospital Under RSA 135:28, 29 and 30-a, and for all Recommittal Petitions Under RSA 651:11-a, see N.H. Superior Ct. Admin R. 11-1 through 11-15.

New Hampshire Trial Bar News.

For article, "Presumptions in New Hampshire Law—A Guide Through the Impenetrable Jungle (Part II)," see 11 N.H. Trial Bar News 31, 43 nn.112, 119 (Fall 1991).

651:11-b. Rights of Persons Transferred to State Hospital.

Persons committed or transferred to the state hospital pursuant to this chapter shall be granted the rights set forth in RSA 135-C:55-59.

Source.

1975, 388:4. 1994, 248:10, eff. June 2, 1994.

Amendments

—1994. Substituted "RSA 135-C:55-59" for "RSA 135-B:42-46" following "set forth in".

NOTES TO DECISIONS

Cited:

Cited in Gibbs v. Helgemoe, 116 N.H. 825, 367 A.2d 1041, 1976 N.H. LEXIS 478 (1977); State v. Kupchun, 117 N.H. 412, 373 A.2d 1325, 1977 N.H. LEXIS 348 (1977).

Death Sentences

651:12–651:14.

[Repealed 1973, 370:36, eff. Nov. 1, 1973.]

Former section(s).

Former RSA 651:12–14, which were derived from 1971, 518:1, related to death sentences. See now RSA 630:5 and 630:6.

Sentence to State Prison

651:15. Sentence to State Prison.

Whenever the sentence for an offense is to be imprisonment for a maximum of more than one year, the sentence shall be served in the state prison.

Source.

1971, 518:1. 1981, 228:1, eff. Aug. 10, 1981.

Amendments

—1981. Rewrote the catchline, substituted "served" for "that the offender be imprisoned" following "shall be" in the first sentence and deleted the second sentence.

Cross References.

Adoption of standards regarding behavior and responsibilities of inmates, see RSA 21-H:14.

Approved absences from state prison, see RSA 623-A.

Release from state prison for purpose of gainful employment or rehabilitation, see RSA 651:25.

Review of state prison sentences, see RSA 651:57 et seq.

State prison, see RSA 622.

Temporary removal of prisoners, see RSA 623.

NOTES TO DECISIONS

Cited:

Cited in Laaman v. Helgemoe, 437 F. Supp. 269, 1977 U.S. Dist. LEXIS 15128 (D.N.H. 1977); State v. Peabody, 121 N.H. 1075, 438 A.2d 305, 1981 N.H. LEXIS 469 (1981); Kiluk v. Potter, 133 N.H. 67, 572 A.2d 1157, 1990 N.H. LEXIS 26 (1990); State v. Horner, 153 N.H. 306, 893 A.2d 683, 2006 N.H. LEXIS 28 (2006).

651:16. Solitary Confinement.

[Repealed 1981, 228:2, eff. Aug. 10, 1981.]

Former section(s).

Former RSA 651:16, which was derived from 1971, 518:1, related to when a sentence to solitary confinement would be served.

Sentence to County Correctional Facility

Revision note.

Substituted "County Correctional Facility" for "House of Correction or Jail" in the subdivision heading for purposes of conformity with RSA 651:18, as amended by 1988, 89:31, eff. June 17, 1988.

Cross References.

County departments of correction, see RSA 30-B. Temporary removal of prisoners, see RSA 623.

651:17. Year or Less.

I. Whenever a person is sentenced either

(a) For a misdemeanor under the provisions of RSA 651:2; or

(b) For a felony under the provisions of RSA 651:2; or

(c) For an extended term of imprisonment under RSA 651:6, and the maximum term thereof does not exceed one year.

II. The sentence shall be that the offender be confined to hard labor, for the term ordered by the court, in the county correctional facility of the county in which the crime was committed if such county has a correctional facility, or in the county correctional facility designated by agreement in RSA 30-B:1.

Source.

1971, 518:1, eff. Nov. 1, 1973. 2003, 237:11, eff. Jan. 1, 2004. 2007, 93:8, eff. August 10, 2007.

Revision note.

Substituted "correctional facility" for "house of correction, or in jail" following "county" in par. II for purposes of conformity with RSA 651:18, as amended by 1988, 89:31, eff. June 17, 1988.

Amendments

—2007. Paragraph II: Added "if such county has a correctional facility, or in the county correctional facility designated by agreement in RSA 30-B:1" at the end.

—2003. Paragraph II: Substituted "of the county in which the crime was committed" for "except where otherwise expressly provided".

NOTES TO DECISIONS

Cited:

Cited in Kiluk v. Potter, 133 N.H. 67, 572 A.2d 1157, 1990 N.H. LEXIS 26 (1990).

651:18. Place; Reduction in Sentence.

I. Persons liable to commitment to a correctional facility for any offense shall be committed to the county correctional facility in the county in which the crime was committed.

II. Any prisoner whose conduct while in the custody of the superintendent of a county correctional facility has been meritorious may be issued a permit and discharged by the superintendent of the county department of corrections when he has served ⅔ of his minimum sentence, provided it shall appear to the superintendent to be a reasonable probability that he will remain at liberty without violating the law and will conduct himself as a good citizen.

Source.

1971, 518:1. 1973, 370:32. 1988, 89:31. 1991, 316:1, eff. July 1, 1991. 2003, 237:14, eff. July 7, 2003.

Amendments

—2003. Rewritten to the extent that a detailed comparison would be impracticable.

—1991. Added the second sentence.

—1988. Rewritten to the extent that a detailed comparison would be impracticable.

—1973. Rewritten to the extent that a detailed comparison would be impracticable.

NOTES TO DECISIONS

Pretrial credit

Where the trial court allocated 71 days of pretrial credit toward the State Prison sentences and the remaining 365 days toward the misdemeanor sentence, defendant lost any opportunity to earn time off of his house of correction sentence for good behavior and thus could serve more time than a similarly situated offender who furnished bail; accordingly, the allocation of pretrial credit was vacated. State v. Edson, 153 N.H. 45, 889 A.2d 420, 2005 N.H. LEXIS 179 (2005).

Cited:

Cited in State v. Wentworth, 118 N.H. 832, 395 A.2d 858, 1978 N.H. LEXIS 302 (1978); State v. Dumont, 122 N.H. 866, 451 A.2d 1286, 1982 N.H. LEXIS 478 (1982); State v. Philbrick, 127 N.H. 353, 499 A.2d 1341, 1985 N.H. LEXIS 426 (1985); State v. Evans, 127 N.H. 501, 506 A.2d 695, 1985 N.H. LEXIS 478 (1985).

Discretionary Sentences

651:19. Release for Purpose of Gainful Employment, Rehabilitation or Home Confinement.

I. A sentencing court may recommend at the time of sentencing, or the superintendent of the county correctional facility may, at any time during the sentence, allow any person who has been committed to a correctional institution other than state prison under a criminal sentence to be released therefrom for the purpose of obtaining and working at gainful employment, for the performance of uncompensated public service as provided in RSA 651:68–70, under the terms of a day reporting program, provided the correctional facility has a day reporting program, or to serve the sentence under home confinement, provided the correctional facility has a home confinement program.

II. If the sentencing court recommends a person for release and the superintendent determines the person is inappropriate for such release, the court shall be notified and, at the request of the defendant, a hearing may be scheduled.

III. If the sentencing court does not include a recommendation for release pursuant to paragraph I in its order, but at any time during the sentence the superintendent deems such a release to be conducive to the person's rehabilitation, the court and the prosecutor shall be notified and, at the request of the prosecutor, a hearing may be scheduled. The decision of the superintendent for release under this paragraph shall stand unless, following the hearing, the court orders otherwise.

IV. In any case, the defendant shall first serve 14 consecutive days prior to eligibility for home confinement, or for such other purpose as the court or the superintendent may deem conducive to his or her rehabilitation, for such times or intervals of time and under such terms and conditions as the rules and regulations of the correctional facility may allow or as the court may order. Any part of a day spent in the free community, or in home confinement, under such a release order shall be counted as a full day toward the serving of the sentence unless otherwise provided by the court. If a person violates the terms and conditions laid down for his or her conduct, custody, and employment, he or she shall be returned to the correctional facility. The superintendent may then require that the balance of the person's sentence be spent in actual confinement.

Source.
1971, 518:1. 1994, 192:3, eff. July 1, 1994. 2000, 307:3, eff. Jan. 1, 2001. 2003, 237:12, eff. Jan. 1, 2004. 2007, 149:1, eff. August 17, 2007. 2013, 277:1, eff. September 22, 2013.

Amendments
—2013. The 2013 amendment added the I, II, and IV designations; substituted "recommend at the time of sentencing, or the superintendent of the county correctional facility may, at any time during the sentence, allow" for "order" in I; added "sentencing court recommends a person for release and the" in II; added III; added "or the superintendent" in the first sentence of IV; and made a stylistic change.

—2007. Inserted "under the terms of a day reporting program, provided the correctional facility has a day reporting program" following "RSA 651:68–70" in the first sentence.

—2003. Rewritten to the extent that a detailed comparison would be impracticable.

—2000. Deleted "or" preceding "rehabilitation" and inserted "or home confinement" thereafter in the section catchline; inserted "or to serve the sentence under home confinement, provided the offender first serves 8 consecutive weekends or 14 consecutive days prior to eligibility for home confinement" following "RSA 651:68–70" in the first sentence, "or in home confinement" following "free community" in the second sentence and made minor stylistic changes throughout the section.

—1994. Inserted "for the performance of uncompensated public service as provided in RSA 651:68–70" following "employment" in the first sentence.

Cross References.
Failure to report as ordered deemed escape, see RSA 651:24.

NOTES TO DECISIONS

Applicability
Read as a whole, a sentencing order committed defendant to state prison, and a drug court program, as set forth in the sentencing order, was neither a "day reporting" program nor "home confinement"; thus, RSA 651:19 and RSA 651:19-a, which defendant argued entitled him to pretrial confinement credit for the drug court program, did not apply. Furthermore, to the extent that defendant argued that conditioning the suspension of his sentence upon successful completion of the drug court program was unlawful because the sentence was not issued pursuant to RSA 651:19 and RSA 651:19-a, he was mistaken, as his sentence was authorized by RSA 651:2, I, II, and RSA 651:20. State v. Dimaggio, 163 N.H. 497, 44 A.3d 468, 2012 N.H. LEXIS 45 (2012).

Cited:
Cited in State v. Linsky, 117 N.H. 866, 379 A.2d 813, 1977 N.H. LEXIS 450 (1977); State v. Philbrick, 127 N.H. 353, 499 A.2d 1341, 1985 N.H. LEXIS 426 (1985); State v. Evans, 127 N.H. 501, 506 A.2d 695, 1985 N.H. LEXIS 478 (1985).

RESEARCH REFERENCES

New Hampshire Practice.
2-33 N.H.P. Criminal Practice & Procedure § 33.12.

651:19-a. Day Reporting Program.

I. The superintendent of a county correctional facility may establish a day reporting program in lieu of incarceration for certain offenders as deemed appropriate by the superintendent. Such release shall be for such terms or intervals of time and under such terms and conditions as may be permitted by the facility's rules and regulations or as the court may order. Any part of a day spent in the free community under such a release order shall be counted as a full day toward the serving of the sentence unless otherwise provided by the sentencing court.

II. The sentencing court may order any person who has been committed to a correctional institution other than state prison to be released therefrom for the purpose of participating in a day reporting program, provided the county correctional facility has established such a program.

Source.
2007, 149:2, eff. August 17, 2007.

NOTES TO DECISIONS

Applicability
Read as a whole, a sentencing order committed defendant to state prison, and a drug court program, as set forth in the sentencing order, was neither a "day reporting" program nor "home confinement"; thus, RSA 651:19 and RSA 651:19-a, which defendant argued entitled him to pretrial confinement credit for the drug court program, did not apply. Furthermore, to the extent that defendant argued that conditioning the suspension of his sentence upon successful completion of the drug court program was unlawful because the sentence was not issued pursuant to RSA 651:19 and RSA 651:19-a, he was mistaken, as his sentence was authorized by RSA 651:2, I, II, and RSA 651:20. State v. Dimaggio, 163 N.H. 497, 44 A.3d 468, 2012 N.H. LEXIS 45 (2012).

651:20. Incarceration Under Suspended Sentence.

I. Notwithstanding any other provision of law, except as provided in subparagraphs (a), (b), and (c), the sentence to imprisonment of any person may be suspended by the sentencing court at the time of imposition of the sentence or at any time thereafter in response to a petition to suspend sentence which is timely brought in accordance with the limitations set forth below in subparagraphs (a), (b), and (c).

(a) Any person sentenced to state prison for a minimum term of 6 years or more shall not bring a petition to suspend sentence until such person has served at least 4 years or ⅔ of his minimum sentence, whichever is greater, and not more frequently than every 3 years thereafter. Any person sentenced to state prison for a minimum term of less than 6 years shall not bring a petition to suspend sentence until such person has served at least ⅔ of the minimum sentence, or the petition has been authorized by the sentencing court. For the purposes of this subparagraph:

(1) For concurrent terms of imprisonment, the minimum term shall be satisfied by serving the longest minimum term imposed, and the maximum term shall be satisfied by serving the longest maximum term.

(2) For consecutive terms of imprisonment, the minimum terms of each sentence shall be added to arrive at an aggregate minimum term, and the maximum terms of each sentence shall be added to arrive at an aggregate maximum term.

(b) A petition to suspend the sentence of any state prisoner may be brought at any time if, prior to the petition being filed, the commissioner of the department of corrections has found that the prisoner is a suitable candidate for suspension of sentence.

(c) A petition to suspend the sentence of any state prisoner may be brought at any time by the attorney general in recognition of substantial assistance by the inmate in the investigation or prosecution of a serious felony offense.

(d) Petitions filed which do not meet the criteria in (a), (b), or (c) above shall be dismissed without a hearing.

II. A person whose sentence has been suspended may be required to report to the institution to which he has been sentenced to be incarcerated during weekends or at such times or intervals of time as the court may direct, except that weekend sentence provisions do not apply to the New Hampshire state prison. Time so spent in said institution shall be deducted from the maximum term, and where there are both a minimum and maximum term, from both. Any part of a day spent in the institution shall count as a full day toward the sentence.

III. As a condition of any suspension of sentence, the court may include restitution to the victim, as provided in RSA 651:62–67, performance of uncompensated public service as provided in RSA 651:68–70, and such other conditions as the court may determine.

Source.
1971, 518:1. 1979, 407:3. 1981, 516:1. 1982, 36:3. 1990, 266:3. 1992, 254:13. 1994, 129:1, eff. July 22, 1994; 192:5, eff. July 1, 1994. 1996, 286:5, eff. July 1, 1997. 2008, 114:1, eff. January 1, 2009.

Amendments
—2008. The 2008 amendment in the introductory language of I(a), added "for a minimum term of 6 years or more" in the first sentence and added the second and third sentences; added I(a)(1) and I(a)(2).

—1996. Paragraph III: Substituted "and" for "or" preceding "such other conditions" and made a minor change in punctuation.

—1994. Paragraph I: Rewritten by ch. 129 to the extent that a detailed comparison would be impracticable.
Paragraph III: Added by ch. 192.

—1992. Rewritten to the extent that a detailed comparison would be impracticable.

—1990. Added the second sentence and substituted "a person whose sentence has been suspended" for "he" preceding "may be required" in the third sentence.

—1982. Added "except that weekend sentence provisions do not apply to the New Hampshire state prison" following "direct" at the end of the second sentence and deleted the fifth sentence.

—1981. Rewritten to the extent that a detailed comparison would be impracticable.

—1979. Substituted "no later than 180 days after imposition of the sentence, unless otherwise ordered by the court at the time of sentencing" for "at any time while any part thereof remains unserved" following "at the time of sentence or" in the first sentence.

Severability of enactment.
This section is subject to a severability clause.

Applicability of 1994 amendment.
1994, 129:2, eff. July 22, 1994, provided that the amendments to paragraph I of this section by section 1 of the act shall apply to all petitions brought after July 22, 1994.

Effect of 1982 amendment on prior law.
See note under RSA 651:2.

Cross References.
Failure to report as ordered deemed escape, see RSA 651:24.
Suspension of mandatory sentence of habitual motor vehicle offender, see RSA 262:23.
Suspension of mandatory sentence of person convicted of felonious use of a firearm, see RSA 651:2.

NOTES TO DECISIONS

1. Constitutionality
2. Construction with other laws
3. Applicability
4. Discretion of court
5. Sentence for homicide
6. Evidentiary hearing
7. Premature petitions
8. Time limitations

1. Constitutionality

Prior to 1992 amendment, this section clearly proscribed all suspension petitions for two years after sentencing, regardless of the length of sentence, and this proscription did not violate constitutional guarantees of equal protection to defendants who were sentenced to less than two years in prison; since all defendants with similar sentences were treated similarly under this section, the fact that defendants who were sentenced to more than two years in prison might petition for suspension after those who were sentenced to shorter terms had been released did not mean that those in the first group were better off than those in the second group, and the proscription reasonably achieved its goal of preserving or expanding the court's power to suspend sentences while lightening its workload by means of a rule that reduced the number of frivolous petitions for suspension without impinging on any fundamental individual rights. State v. Callaghan, 125 N.H. 449, 480 A.2d 209, 1984 N.H. LEXIS 249 (1984).

2. Construction with other laws

RSA 651:21 provides no vehicle for importing into RSA 651:20 the temporal limits upon probation within RSA 651:2, V, as that would be limiting the greater by the constraints placed upon the lesser. State v. Moran, 158 N.H. 318, 965 A.2d 1024, 2009 N.H. LEXIS 12 (2009).

Provisions of this section were in no way suspended or repealed by enactment of RSA 651:57–61, creating a sentence review division. State v. Lemire, 116 N.H. 395, 359 A.2d 644, 1976 N.H. LEXIS 363 (1976).

RSA 651:57–61, creating a sentence review division, does not preclude the superior court from considering a petition to reduce sentence as a petition for suspension of sentence under this section and RSA 651:21. State v. Lemire, 116 N.H. 395, 359 A.2d 644, 1976 N.H. LEXIS 363 (1976).

Motor vehicle laws habitual offenders provision that a person convicted thereunder shall, notwithstanding the provisions of the Criminal Code, be sentenced to imprisonment for not less than a year nor more than five years, and that no portion of the minimum mandatory sentence shall be suspended, being more specific and recent than this section's provision that notwithstanding any other provision of law, the sentence to imprisonment of any person may be suspended, controlled and took priority. State v. Dean, 115 N.H. 520, 345 A.2d 408, 1975 N.H. LEXIS 352 (1975).

3. Applicability

Read as a whole, a sentencing order committed defendant to state prison, and a drug court program, as set forth in the sentencing order, was neither a "day reporting" program nor "home confinement"; thus, RSA 651:19 and RSA 651:19-a, which defendant argued entitled him to pretrial confinement credit for the drug court program, did not apply. Furthermore, to the extent that defendant argued that conditioning the suspension of his sentence upon successful completion of the drug court program was unlawful because the sentence was not issued pursuant to RSA 651:19 and RSA 651:19-a, he was mistaken, as his sentence was authorized by RSA 651:2, I, II, and RSA 651:20. State v. Dimaggio, 163 N.H. 497, 44 A.3d 468, 2012 N.H. LEXIS 45 (2012).

Trial court's imposition of deferred sentences, which were implicitly authorized by the legislature, was not imposition of terms that were consecutive to a suspended sentence pursuant to RSA 651:20, as they were presumed to be concurrent to one another where the sentencing order did not indicate otherwise; however, the trial court decided to impose the suspended and deferred sentences at different times based on the circumstances of the case. State v. Almodovar, 158 N.H. 548, 969 A.2d 479, 2009 N.H. LEXIS 46 (2009).

Reviewing RSA ch. 651 as a whole, the word "sentence" plainly and unambiguously denotes the punishment prescribed by a court in relation to a conviction on a single offense. Therefore, RSA 651:20, I(a) permits an inmate serving multiple, consecutive sentences to bring a petition to suspend an individual sentence after serving at least four years or two-thirds of the minimum term of that sentence, whichever is greater. State v. Horner, 153 N.H. 306, 893 A.2d 683, 2006 N.H. LEXIS 28 (2006), rehearing denied, 2006 N.H. LEXIS 74 (N.H. Apr. 26, 2006).

Although a trial court might have suspended defendant's sentence conditioned upon the completion of a sexual offender treatment program, thereby circumventing the time limitations in RSA 651:20, the trial court's ruling, which at most created the opportunity for defendant to return to court, prove that he had successfully completed the program, and argue that the trial court should suspend two-and-one-half years from his minimum sentence, was subject to the mandatory time limitations in RSA 651:20, I(a). State v. Horner, 153 N.H. 306, 893 A.2d 683, 2006 N.H. LEXIS 28 (2006),

rehearing denied, 2006 N.H. LEXIS 74 (N.H. Apr. 26, 2006).

Trial court's reinterpretation of its authority to suspend defendant's sentence in light of the time limitations in RSA 651:20, I(a), which resulted in the trial court denying defendant's motion seeking the suspension that the trial court indicated he could seek after his successful completion of a sexual offender treatment program, was not unconstitutional and did not violate the doctrine against judicial ex post facto decisions under either the U.S. Constitution or the New Hampshire State Constitution. State v. Horner, 153 N.H. 306, 893 A.2d 683, 2006 N.H. LEXIS 28 (2006), rehearing denied, 2006 N.H. LEXIS 74 (N.H. Apr. 26, 2006).

A suspended sentence may be imposed or probation revoked for acts committed by a defendant after imposition of the sentence but before commencement of the suspended sentence or probationary term. State v. Kierstead, 141 N.H. 803, 693 A.2d 410, 1997 N.H. LEXIS 41 (1997).

To apply statutory amendment governing suspension of sentences to preexisting petition for sentence suspension would violate constitutional proscription against ex post facto laws, because new law could operate to keep petitioner in prison longer than old law. State v. Reynolds, 138 N.H. 519, 642 A.2d 1368, 1994 N.H. LEXIS 59 (1994).

Suspension of sentences is not obligatory; rather, suspension can occur on satisfaction of a condition imposed, or not at all. State v. W.J.T. Enters., 136 N.H. 490, 618 A.2d 806, 1992 N.H. LEXIS 211 (1992).

Trial judge sentence requiring defendants in solid waste transfer facility case to either clean up transfer site or serve second six-months of one-year imprisonment was proper, as it did not involve restitution, defendants were familiar with environmental enforcement procedures, defendants desired to clean up site anyway, and sufficiency of clean up could be determined. State v. W.J.T. Enters., 136 N.H. 490, 618 A.2d 806, 1992 N.H. LEXIS 211 (1992).

The legislature intended that the 1979 and 1981 amendments to this section apply to all defendants under sentence at the time the provisions went into effect, since it did not limit their applicability only to those committing crimes after those dates. State v. Theodosopoulos, 123 N.H. 287, 461 A.2d 100, 1983 N.H. LEXIS 279 (1983), overruled in part, State v. Reynolds, 138 N.H. 519, 642 A.2d 1368, 1994 N.H. LEXIS 59 (1994).

Trial court correctly ruled that defendant sentenced on April 18, 1981, was not eligible in April 1982 to seek a suspension of his sentence, and neither the 1979 nor the 1981 version of this section subjected the defendant to an ex post facto law because, although the revisions modified the previously unlimited right to seek a suspension of sentence, they did not deprive the defendant of a meaningful opportunity to seek a suspension of his sentence. State v. Theodosopoulos, 123 N.H. 287, 461 A.2d 100, 1983 N.H. LEXIS 279 (1983), overruled in part, State v. Reynolds, 138 N.H. 519, 642 A.2d 1368, 1994 N.H. LEXIS 59 (1994).

Where defendant filed a motion for suspension of sentence in April 1982 for sentences imposed in April 1981, the trial court should also have applied the 1981 version of this section, rather than denying the motion based solely upon the 1979 version, since the 1981 version was in effect when the defendant filed his motion for suspension. State v. Theodosopoulos, 123 N.H. 287, 461 A.2d 100, 1983 N.H. LEXIS 279 (1983), overruled in part, State v. Reynolds, 138 N.H. 519, 642 A.2d 1368, 1994 N.H. LEXIS 59 (1994).

4. Discretion of court

Text of RSA 651:20 makes clear that its subparagraphs are the only legislative limitations upon the judicial exercise of authority to suspend incarceration. State v. Moran, 158 N.H. 318, 965 A.2d 1024, 2009 N.H. LEXIS 12 (2009).

This section demonstrates a continuing intent by the legislature to provide the sentencing judge with options to adapt his or her sentence to a particular individual in the manner best suited to accomplish the constitutional objectives of punishment, rehabilitation and deterrence. State v. W.J.T. Enters., 136 N.H. 490, 618 A.2d 806, 1992 N.H. LEXIS 211 (1992).

Within this section's parameters, judge has broad discretion to assign different sentences, suspend sentence, or grant probation. State v. W.J.T. Enters., 136 N.H. 490, 618 A.2d 806, 1992 N.H. LEXIS 211 (1992).

This section provided for essentially discretionary judgment by sentencing judge, and therefore indigent defendant seeking sentence suspension pursuant to section had no procedural due process right to assistance of counsel under Fourteenth Amendment to Federal Constitution. State v. Gibbons, 135 N.H. 320, 605 A.2d 214, 1992 N.H. LEXIS 38 (1992).

This section and RSA 651:2, governing sentences and limitations, demonstrate an intent by the legislature to provide the sentencing judge with options to adapt his sentence to a particular individual in the manner best suited to accomplish the constitutional objectives of punishment, rehabilitation and deterrence. State v. Burroughs, 113 N.H. 21, 300 A.2d 315, 1973 N.H. LEXIS 189 (1973).

5. Sentence for homicide

Although this section confers general discretion upon a sentencing court to suspend a sentence, RSA 630:1-a, III and RSA 651:1, I, clearly and specifically limit the court's authority in sentencing first degree murderers and, because RSA 630:1-a, III, and RSA 651:1, I, provide specific exceptions to the more general rule found in this section they control. State v. Farrow, 140 N.H. 473, 667 A.2d 1029, 1995 N.H. LEXIS 174 (1995).

When RSA 630:1-a, III, RSA 651:1, I, and this section are read together, this section cannot be construed to allow persons convicted of first degree murder to petition for sentence suspension; such a construction, if adopted, would defeat the underlying legislative intent of these statutes by providing new opportunities for first degree murderers to return to society. State v. Farrow, 140 N.H. 473, 667 A.2d 1029, 1995 N.H. LEXIS 174 (1995).

Although court has authority under this section to suspend a sentence that has already been imposed or is being executed, such authority is, by RSA 651:1, specifically made inapplicable to all sentences imposed for first degree murder under RSA 630:1-a, III. State v. Smith, 119 N.H. 674, 406 A.2d 135, 1979 N.H. LEXIS 353 (1979).

6. Evidentiary hearing

Trial court properly denied defendant's petition pursuant to RSA 651:20 to suspend unserved consecutive sentences, but erred in refusing to hold a hearing and give reasons for the denial as to the sentence defendant was currently serving, as the petition was filed in a timely fashion. State v. Duquette, 153 N.H. 315, 893 A.2d 709, 2006 N.H. LEXIS 27 (2006).

The superior court did not err in denying the defendant's request for a hearing on his motion for a sentence suspension. The court not only had before it the defendant's motion for sentence modification and the defendant's four-page personal letter in support thereof, it also held a chambers conference on the record with counsel for the defendant and the state in attendance, at which the defendant's counsel was permitted to set forth the facts that he believed entitled his client to an evidentiary hearing. State v. Roy, 138 N.H. 97, 635 A.2d 486, 1993 N.H. LEXIS 166 (1993).

7. Premature petitions

Trial court lacked authority under RSA 651:20, I(a) to hear defendant's petition to suspend his sentence because three years had not elapsed since the filing of his last petition. Under RSA 651:20, I(d), the trial court had been obliged to dismiss the premature petition. State v. Fischer, 152 N.H. 205, 876 A.2d 232, 2005 N.H. LEXIS 77 (2005).

8. Time limitations

With the enactment of the Criminal Code in 1971, the three-year cap was omitted from RSA 651:20, the new statute governing the exercise of suspension authority. The Supreme Court of New Hampshire presumes that this omission was deliberate. State v. Moran, 158 N.H. 318, 965 A.2d 1024, 2009 N.H. LEXIS 12 (2009).

Trial court's sentencing discretion with respect to suspending misdemeanor incarceration is bounded on a case-by-case basis only by constitutional limitations. Accordingly, there was no merit to defendant's argument that under RSA 651:20, the length of elapsed time exceeded the trial court's authority to suspend incarceration for a misdemeanor State v. Moran, 158 N.H. 318, 965 A.2d 1024, 2009 N.H. LEXIS 12 (2009).

Trial court properly denied defendant's motion for a sentence suspension after his successful completion of sex offender program where, although the trial court had indicated at sentencing that defendant could apply for a sentence suspension upon completion of the program, the time limitations in RSA 651:20, I(a) had not been

satisfied and, as the time requirements were mandatory, a suspension was not available to defendant. State v. Horner, 153 N.H. 306, 893 A.2d 683, 2006 N.H. LEXIS 28 (2006), rehearing denied, 2006 N.H. LEXIS 74 (N.H. Apr. 26, 2006).

Cited:

Cited in State v. Linsky, 117 N.H. 866, 379 A.2d 813, 1977 N.H. LEXIS 450 (1977); State v. Shea, 117 N.H. 1007, 380 A.2d 1099, 1977 N.H. LEXIS 483 (1977); State v. Mullen, 119 N.H. 703, 406 A.2d 698, 1979 N.H. LEXIS 352 (1979); State v. Peabody, 121 N.H. 1075, 438 A.2d 305, 1981 N.H. LEXIS 469 (1981); State v. Philbrick, 127 N.H. 353, 499 A.2d 1341, 1985 N.H. LEXIS 426 (1985); State v. Rau, 129 N.H. 126, 523 A.2d 98, 1987 N.H. LEXIS 154 (1987); State v. Ingerson, 130 N.H. 112, 536 A.2d 161, 1987 N.H. LEXIS 292 (1987); State v. Rothe, 142 N.H. 483, 703 A.2d 884, 1997 N.H. LEXIS 122 (1997).

RESEARCH REFERENCES

New Hampshire Court Rules Annotated.
Subdivision of suspended sentence, see Rule 103, Rules of the Superior Court, New Hampshire Court Rules Annotated.

New Hampshire Practice.
2-33 N.H.P. Criminal Practice & Procedure § 33.22.

651:21. Terms on Revocation of Suspended Sentence.

Upon revocation of any suspended sentence the court may order that the defendant serve such sentence in full or in such parts and at such times as is deemed best, may further suspend any part not ordered to be served upon such terms and conditions as the court may order and may place the defendant on probation during the time any portion of the sentence remains suspended.

Source.
1971, 518:1, eff. Nov. 1, 1973.

Cross References.
Failure to report as ordered deemed escape, see RSA 651:24.
Probation, see RSA 504-A.

NOTES TO DECISIONS

1. Construction with other laws
2. Application
3. Deferred sentence

1. Construction with other laws

RSA 651:21 provides no vehicle for importing into RSA 651:20 the temporal limits upon probation within RSA 651:2, V, as that would be limiting the greater by the constraints placed upon the lesser. State v. Moran, 158 N.H. 318, 965 A.2d 1024, 2009 N.H. LEXIS 12 (2009).

Provisions of this section were in no way suspended or repealed by enactment of RSA 651:57–61, creating a sentence review division. State v. Lemire, 116 N.H. 395, 359 A.2d 644, 1976 N.H. LEXIS 363 (1976).

RSA 651:57–61, creating a sentence review division, does not preclude the superior court from considering a petition to reduce sentence as a petition for suspension of sentence under this section and RSA 651:20. State v. Lemire, 116 N.H. 395, 359 A.2d 644, 1976 N.H. LEXIS 363 (1976).

2. Application

This section did not apply, where court declined either to impose or suspend or further defer remainder of previously deferred one-to-three-year term, and thus no "portion of the sentence remained suspended." State v. Burgess, 141 N.H. 51, 677 A.2d 142, 1996 N.H. LEXIS 46 (1996).

3. Deferred sentence

The statute does not permit a court to impose probation near the end of the period of the deferral of a sentence upon the defendant's motion to suspend the sentence. State v. Rothe, 142 N.H. 483, 703 A.2d 884, 1997 N.H. LEXIS 122 (1997).

Cited:

Cited in State v. Dean, 115 N.H. 520, 345 A.2d 408, 1975 N.H. LEXIS 352 (1975); State v. Ingerson, 130 N.H. 112, 536 A.2d 161, 1987 N.H. LEXIS 292 (1987).

651:22. Jurisdiction Over and Disposition of Wages and Income.

In any criminal case, in addition to such other terms and conditions as may be imposed by the court, a defendant who has received a suspended sentence or who has been released under RSA 651:19 may be required by the court to surrender to the department of corrections or other agency designated by the court all or part of his wages or other income, less standard payroll deduction required by law, earned during the time he is not confined under the sentence. The court may direct that, after deducting therefrom the cost of his maintenance while not confined, the balance be applied as needed for restitution payments made to authorized claimants pursuant to RSA 651:62 through 66 and for the support and maintenance of his dependents. Any balance after such applications shall be deposited in a savings account to be released to him or applied as needed for restitution payments or the support of his dependents as the court may order, or applied to the designated cost of room and board at the institution for the period of time during which the inmate is working before the expiration of his sentence. Upon expiration of his sentence the balance remaining shall be paid to him or his order.

Source.

1971, 518:1. 1981, 329:3, eff. Aug. 16, 1981.

Revision note.

In the first sentence, substituted "department of corrections" for "probation department" pursuant to 1983, 461:4. 1983, 461:6 transferred all powers, duties and functions of the probation department to the department of corrections.

Amendments

—**1981.** Rewritten to the extent that a detailed comparison would be impracticable.

651:23. Change of Place of Confinement.

[Repealed 2003, 237:15, III, eff. Jan. 1, 2004.]

Former section(s).

Former RSA 651:23, which was derived from 1971, 518:1, related to change of place of confinement.

651:24. Failure to Report Deemed Escape.

Any person released under RSA 651:19 or RSA 651:19-a, or ordered confined under RSA 651:20 or 21 who willfully fails to report as ordered shall be deemed to have escaped from the institution to which he has been sentenced and upon conviction shall be subject to the punishment provided for escape therefrom.

Source.

1971, 518:1, eff. Nov. 1, 1973. 2007, 149:3, eff. August 17, 2007.

Amendments

—**2007.** Inserted "or RSA 651:19-a" following "under RSA 651:19" and deleted "for confinement" following "fails to report".

Cross References.

Escape, see RSA 642:6.

NOTES TO DECISIONS

Cited:

Cited in State v. Perra, 127 N.H. 533, 503 A.2d 814, 1985 N.H. LEXIS 456 (1985).

651:25. Release from State Prison.

I. The commissioner of corrections may release any person who has been committed to the state prison at any time during the term of sentence for the purpose of obtaining and working at gainful employment, for the performance of uncompensated public service as provided in RSA 651:68–70, or for such other purpose as may be deemed conducive to his rehabilitation, for such times or intervals of time and under such terms and conditions as may be prescribed by the commissioner pursuant to RSA 541-A, provided, however, that a prisoner who has not served sufficient time to be eligible for parole may be released under this section only if the sentencing court and the prosecutor of the underlying offense have been notified of the proposed release, and there has been no objection within 10 days of the notice by either the sentencing court or the prosecutor of the underlying offense. If the prosecutor of the underlying offense objects to the proposed release, the prosecutor shall submit in writing to the sentencing court the reasons for objecting. The sentencing court shall, within 10 days of receipt of the prosecutor's objection, schedule a hearing on the proposed release. The sentencing court shall then approve or deny the proposed release. The commissioner of corrections may permit inmates of the state prison, who volunteer to do so, to be gainfully employed outside the institution when such employment is considered in their best interest and the best interest of the state. Inmates may be so employed by the state or by public or private employers.

II. The rates of pay and other conditions of employment of a person released for work shall be the same as those paid or required in the locality in which the work is performed. An inmate so employed shall surrender to the commissioner of corrections his total earnings less payroll deductions authorized by law, including income taxes. After deducting from the earnings of each person an amount determined to be the cost of the person's keep, the commissioner shall:

(a) Allow the person to draw from the balance a sufficient sum to cover his incidental expenses;

(b) Credit to his account such amount as seems necessary to accumulate a reasonable sum to be paid to him on his release;

(c) Cause to be paid such part of any additional balance as is needed for restitution payments to authorized claimants pursuant to RSA 651:62 through 66;

(d) Cause to be paid such part of any additional balance as is needed for the support of the person's dependents and notify the overseer of public welfare of the town, in which the person's dependents reside, of such support payments;

(e) Pay the balance to the person when he is released.

III. Any part of a day a prisoner is employed outside the walls of the institution shall count as a full day toward the serving of his sentence as though served inside the walls. An inmate so employed outside shall be subject to the rules and regulations of the institution and be under the direction and control of the officers thereof.

IV. If an inmate released for work escapes or fails to return inside the walls of the institution as required by the rules or the orders of the officers thereof or if on administrative home confinement, knowingly leaves a place without authority to do so, such inmate shall be punished as provided by RSA 642:6. The commissioner of corrections may at any time recall a prisoner from such release status if the commissioner believes or has reason to believe the peace, safety, welfare, or security of the community may be endangered by the prisoner being under such release status.

V. A prisoner authorized to work at paid employment in the community under this section may be required to pay, and the commissioner of corrections is authorized to collect, such cost incident to the prisoner's confinement as the commissioner deems appropriate and reasonable. Such collections shall be deposited with the state treasurer as a part of the general revenue of the state.

VI. A low-risk, nonviolent prisoner who has not served sufficient time to be eligible for parole as provided in RSA 651-A:6, I, may be released on parole notwithstanding such provision, subject to the other provisions of RSA 651-A, provided that the following requirements are met before the parole board schedules a hearing on the proposed parole:

(a) The prisoner has been sentenced to the state prison for an offense other than capital, first degree or second degree murder, attempted murder, manslaughter, aggravated felonious sexual assault, felonious sexual assault or first degree assault;

(b) The prisoner has been assigned a course of programs or treatment, has successfully completed such course, and has been found by the commissioner of corrections to be a suitable candidate for early parole;

(c) The commissioner of corrections has submitted findings and a recommendation for early parole to the parole board; and

(d) The commissioner of corrections has notified the sentencing court and the prosecutor of the underlying offense of the proposed parole, and the court has not objected in writing within 20 days of such notice.

VII. (a) The commissioner of corrections may release a prisoner who is serving a New Hampshire state sentence to the custody and control of the United States Immigration and Customs Enforcement if all of the following requirements are satisfied:

(1) The department of corrections receives an order of deportation for the prisoner from the United States Immigration and Customs Enforcement;

(2) The prisoner has served at least 1/3 of the minimum sentences imposed by the court;

(3) The prisoner was not convicted of a violent crime, or any crime of obstruction of justice, or sentenced to an extended term of imprisonment under RSA 651:6; and

(4) The prisoner was not convicted of a sexual offense as defined in RSA 651-B:1, V.

(b) If a prisoner who is released from his or her state sentence pursuant to this section returns illegally to the United States, on notification from any federal or state law enforcement agency that the prisoner is in custody, the commissioner of corrections shall revoke the prisoner's release and immediately file a detainer seeking the prisoner's return to the custody of the department of corrections to serve the remainder of his or her sentence.

Source.
1971, 518:1. 1975, 179:1. 1981, 205:1, 2; 329:4. 1993, 45:1, eff. April 8, 1993. 1994, 192:4, eff. July 1, 1994. 1995, 237:6, eff. Jan. 1, 1996. 2002, 181:1, 2, eff. Jan. 1, 2003. 2009, 144:63, eff. July 1, 2009.

Revision note.
Substituted "commissioner of corrections" and "commissioner" for "warden", "warden of the state prison" and "board of trustees of the state prison" pursuant to 1983, 461:4. 1983, 461:3 terminated the position of warden of the state prison and transferred all powers, duties and functions of that position to the commissioner of corrections. 1983, 461:2 abolished the board of trustees of the state prison and transferred all powers, duties and functions of the board to the commissioner of corrections.

In the first sentence of par. I, deleted "in accordance with policies adopted by the board of trustees of the state prison" preceding "pursuant to RSA 541-A" as no longer necessary in light of 1983, 461, which transferred all powers, duties and functions of the warden and the board of trustees of the state prison to the commissioner of corrections.

At the beginning of par. IV, substituted "an inmate released for work" for "he" for purposes of clarity.

Amendments
—2009. The 2009 amendment added VII.

—2002. Paragraph I: Substituted "and the prosecutor of the underlying offense have been" for "has been" following "sentencing court" and "there has been no objection within 10 days of the notice by either the sentencing court or the prosecutor of the underlying offense" for "has not objected within 10 days of receipt of such notice" at the end of the first sentence and added the second through fourth sentences.

Paragraph VI(d): Inserted "and the prosecutor of the underlying offense" following "sentencing court".

—1995. Paragraph IV: Substituted "or if on administrative home confinement, knowingly leaves a place without authority to do so, such inmate" for "he" following "officers thereof" in the first sentence and substituted "the commissioner" for "he" preceding "believes or has" in the second sentence.

—1994. Paragraph I: Inserted "for the performance of uncompensated public service as provided in RSA 651:68–70" following "employment" in the first sentence and made minor changes in phraseology in the third sentence.

—1993. Paragraph VI: Added.

—1981. Paragraph I: Chapter 205 deleted "the state board of parole and" following "prescribed by", added "in accordance with policies adopted by the board of trustees of the state prison pursuant to RSA 541-A" preceding "provided" and substituted "10" for "ten" preceding "days" in the first sentence.

Paragraph II: Chapter 329 redesignated former subpars. (c) and (d) as subpars. (d) and (e) respectively and added a new subpar. (c).

Paragraph IV: Chapter 205 substituted "RSA 642:6" for "RSA 622:13" at the end of the first sentence and deleted the third sentence.

—1975. Designated existing provisions of section as pars. I–V, made minor changes in style and substituted "board of trustees of the state prison" for "New Hampshire state board of parole" preceding "deems appropriate" in the first sentence of par. V.

Cross References.
Adoption of rules by commissioner generally, see RSA 21-H:13.

NOTES TO DECISIONS

1. Purpose
2. Due process
3. Discretion

1. Purpose
Rehabilitation is clearly the legislative purpose underlying the work release program. Rich v. Powell, 130 N.H. 455, 544 A.2d 29, 1988 N.H. LEXIS 31 (1988).

2. Due process
The regulations implementing the program established by this section provide a prisoner participating in a halfway house work release program with a liberty interest, implicating due process protections, in remaining in the halfway house. Brennan v. Cunningham, 813 F.2d 1, 1987 U.S. App. LEXIS 2754 (1st Cir. N.H. 1987).

3. Discretion
On the basis of this section and the regulations promulgated pursuant thereto, the warden has the authority to monitor a prisoner's behavior and has wide discretion to revoke work release. Brennan v. Cunningham, 126 N.H. 600, 493 A.2d 1213, 1985 N.H. LEXIS 348 (1985).

Cited:
Cited in State v. Peabody, 121 N.H. 1075, 438 A.2d 305, 1981 N.H. LEXIS 469 (1981); State v. Aldrich, 124 N.H. 43, 466 A.2d 938, 1983 N.H. LEXIS 356 (1983).

Conditional Sentence of Fine or Imprisonment

651:26, 651:27.

[Repealed 1973, 370:33, eff. Nov. 1, 1973.]

Former section(s).
Former RSA 651:26 and 651:27, which were derived from 1971, 518:1, related to term of and committal to a conditional sentence of fine or imprisonment.

Sentences Against Corporations

651:28. Default.

Whenever a corporation indicted under a statute fails to appear, after being duly served with process or an order of notice, its default shall be recorded, the charges in the indictment taken to be true, and judgment shall be rendered accordingly.

Source.
1971, 518:1, eff. Nov. 1, 1973.

Employment of Prisoners on State Roads, etc.

651:29–651:36.

[Repealed 1973, 370:34, eff. Nov. 1, 1973.]

Former section(s).
Former RSA 651:29–651:36, which were derived from 1971, 518:1, related to employment of prisoners for construction, improvement and maintenance of highways.

Employment of County Correctional Facility Prisoners

Revision note.
Substituted "Correctional Facility" for "Jail or House of Correction" preceding "Prisoners" in the subdivision heading for purposes of conformity with RSA 651:36-a, as amended by 1988, 89:32, eff. June 17, 1988.

651:36-a. Uncompensated Public Service by Prisoners.

The county commissioners of any county may authorize the superintendent of the county correctional facility to make arrangements with officials of a city or town to have prisoners from the county correctional facilities perform uncompensated public service at municipality-owned grounds or property. Prisoners sent from the county correctional facility shall be in the custody of the superintendent of county correctional facilities or designee.

Source.
1973, 322:1. 1988, 89:32, eff. June 17, 1988. 1997, 237:1, eff. Aug. 17, 1997.

Amendments
—1997. Rewritten to the extent that a detailed comparison would be impracticable.

—1988. Substituted "county correctional facilities" for "county jail or house of correction" following "prisoners from the" in the first sentence and rewrote the second sentence.

Cross References.
Employment of offenders generally, see RSA 30-B:17–21.

Parole of Prisoners

651:37–651:55-c.

[Repealed 1983, 461:33, eff. July 1, 1983.]

Former section(s).

Former RSA 651:37, which was derived from 1971, 518:1 and 1973, 370:85, related to the composition and duties of the state parole board. See now RSA 651-A:3 and 651-A:4.

Former RSA 651-A:38, which was derived from 1971, 518:1, related to the appointment of a state parole officer.

Former RSA 651:39, which was derived from 1971, 518:1, related to the salary of the state parole officer.

Former RSA 651:40, which was derived from 1971, 518:1, related to employment of clerical assistance by the state parole officer.

Former RSA 651:41, which was derived from 1971, 518:1, related to duties of the state parole officer.

Former RSA 651:42, which was derived from 1971, 518:1, related to the appointment of assistant parole officers.

Former RSA 651:43, which was derived from 1971, 518:1, related to the payment of expenses incurred by the state parole officer and assistant parole officers.

Former RSA 651:44, which was derived from 1971, 518:1, related to law enforcement agencies providing assistance to the state parole officer.

Former RSA 651:45, which was derived from 1971, 518:1; 1973, 370:37; 1975, 244:1, 506:1; 1981, 216:1; and 1982, 36:4, related to terms of release. See now RSA 651-A:6.

Former RSA 651:45-a, which was derived from 1973, 370:38; 1974, 34:7; and 1982, 36:5, related to eligibility for release of prisoners serving a sentence of life imprisonment. See now RSA 651-A:7.

Former RSA 651:45-b, which was derived from 1973, 370:38 and 1974, 34:8, related to eligibility for parole of persons convicted of psycho-sexual murder. See now RSA 651-A:8.

Former RSA 651:45-c, which was derived from 1973, 370:38 and 1974 34:9, related to certification of psycho-sexual murder. See now RSA 651-A:9.

Former RSA 651:45-d, which was derived from 1973, 370:38, defined psycho-sexual murder. See now RSA 651-A:10.

Former RSA 651:45-e, which was derived from 1981, 216:2 and 1983, 319:1, 2, related to notice of parole hearings. See now RSA 651-A:11.

Former RSA 651:46, which was derived from 1971, 518:1, and previously repealed by 1973, 370:42, related to release to the custody of the parole board and reporting to the state parole officer.

Former RSA 651:47, which was derived from 1971, 518:1, related to reduction of maximum sentence while on parole. See now RSA 651-A:12.

Former RSA 651:48, which was derived from 1971, 518:1, related to suspension of supervision of parolees who entered the armed service of the United States. See now RSA 651-A:13.

Former RSA 651:49, which was derived from 1971, 518:1, related to early discharge for good conduct. See now RSA 651-A:14.

Former RSA 651:50, which was derived from 1971, 518:1, related to complaints and hearings for violations of parole. See now RSA 651-A:15 and 651-A:17.

Former RSA 651:51, which was derived from 1971, 518:1, related to recommittal of parole violators. See now RSA 651-A:17 and 651-A:18.

Former RSA 651:52, which was derived from 1971, 518:1 and 1973, 370:40, related to the effect of recommittal for violation of parole. See now RSA 651-A:19.

Former RSA 651:53, which was derived from 1971, 518:1, and previously repealed by 1973, 370:42, related to deductions from the maximum term of recommitted parolees.

Former RSA 651:54, which was derived from 1971, 518:1, related to final discharge of paroled prisoners. See now RSA 651-A:21.

Former RSA 651:55, which was derived from 1971, 518:1, and previously repealed by 1973, 370:42, related to reduction of a prisoner's minimum term for donation of blood.

Former RSA 651:55-a, which was derived from 1973, 370:41 and 1975 61:1, and previously repealed by 1982, 36:6, related to credits for donation of blood.

Former RSA 651:55-b, which was derived from 1973, 370:41; 1979, 319:1, 407:1, 4; and 1982, 36:7, related to credits for good conduct. See now RSA 651-A:22.

Former RSA 651:55-c, which was derived from 1973, 370:41 and 1976, 32:2, related to credit for confinement prior to sentencing. See now RSA 651-A:23.

Out-Of-State Parolee Supervision

651:56. Execution of Compact Authorized.

[Repealed 1983, 461:33, eff. July 1, 1983.]

Former section(s).

Former RSA 651:56, which was derived from 1971, 518:1, related to an interstate compact permitting prisoners on probation or parole to reside in another state. See now RSA 651-A:25.

Review of State Prison Sentences

Cross References.

Habeas corpus, see RSA 534.

Review of transfer to secure psychiatric unit, see RSA 622:45.

NOTES TO DECISIONS

Construction with other laws

Enactment of this subdivision in no way suspended or repealed RSA 651:20, 21, providing for suspension of sentence. State v. Lemire, 116 N.H. 395, 359 A.2d 644, 1976 N.H. LEXIS 363 (1976).

Cited:

Cited in State v. McMillan, 116 N.H. 126, 352 A.2d 702, 1976 N.H. LEXIS 283 (1976); State v. Fraser, 120 N.H. 117, 411 A.2d 1125, 1980 N.H. LEXIS 241 (1980).

RESEARCH REFERENCES

New Hampshire Court Rules Annotated.

Rules, see Sentence Review Division Rules, Rules of the Superior Court, New Hampshire Court Rules Annotated.

651:57. Review Division.

The chief justice of the superior court shall appoint 3 superior court justices, senior justices, or retired superior court justices to constitute a board of 3 members to act as a review division of the court and shall designate one of these judges as division chairman. The term shall be for 3 years. The division shall meet at the times and places as its business requires, as determined by the chairman. The decision of 2 members is sufficient to determine any matter before the review division. No member may sit or act on a review of a sentence imposed by him. If the review to be acted on by the division is a review of a sentence imposed by a member serving on the review division or if it is inexpedient for a member to attend at the time for which a meeting is called, the division chairman shall designate a superior court justice, a retired superior court justice, or a senior superior court justice to act as an alternate in place of the absent or disqualified member. The review division may appoint a secretary-clerk, whose compensation shall be fixed by the review division and paid by the state.

Source.

1975, 267:1. 1976, 25:1. 1979, 407:2. 1981, 186:1. 1988, 81:2, eff. April 15, 1988.

Amendments

—1988. Substituted "senior justices, or retired superior court justices" for "or judicial referees" preceding "to constitute" in the first sentence and "a superior court justice, a retired superior court justice, or a senior superior court justice" for "from among the superior court, a justice" following "shall designate" in the sixth sentence.

—1981. Deleted "and a member of the superior court as an alternate" following "referees" in the first sentence and rewrote the sixth sentence.

—1979. Substituted "a member of the superior court as an alternate" for "3 superior court justices or judicial referees, as alternates" following "referees and" in the first sentence, rewrote the second sentence, deleted the former third sentence and substituted "division chairman" for "chief justice" preceding "shall designate" in the sixth sentence and "the" for "an" thereafter.

—1976. Substituted "3" for "two" following "referees and" in the first sentence and preceding "alternates" in the third sentence and made minor changes in phraseology.

NOTES TO DECISIONS

Cited:

Cited in Bell v. Superior Court Sentence Review Div., 117 N.H. 474, 374 A.2d 659, 1977 N.H. LEXIS 358 (1977); State v. Goodwin, 118 N.H. 862, 395 A.2d 1234, 1978 N.H. LEXIS 307 (1978); In re Turgeon, 140 N.H. 52, 663 A.2d 82, 1995 N.H. LEXIS 98 (1995).

651:58. Application for Review.

I. Any person sentenced to a term of one year or more in the state prison, except in any case in which a different sentence could not have been imposed, or the state of New Hampshire, may file with the clerk of the superior court for the county in which the judgment was rendered an application for review of the sentence by the review division. The application may be filed within 30 days after the date the sentence was imposed, but not thereafter except for good cause shown. The filing of an application for review shall not stay the execution of the sentence.

II. Upon imposition of the sentence the person sentenced shall be given oral and written notice of his or her right to make such a request. This notice shall include a statement that review of the sentence may result in a decrease or increase of the minimum or maximum term within the limits fixed by law. A form for making the application shall accompany the notice. If an application is filed, the clerk shall forthwith transmit it to the review division and shall notify the chief justice and the judge who imposed the sentence of the filing.

III. The sentencing judge may transmit to the review division a statement of his reasons for imposing the sentence, and shall transmit such a statement within 7 days if requested to do so by the review division.

Source.

1975, 267:1, eff. Aug. 5, 1975. 2001, 45:1, eff. Jan. 1, 2002. 2009, 24:1, eff. July 7, 2009.

Amendments

—2009. The 2009 amendment, in the first sentence of II, substituted "person sentenced shall be given" for "clerk shall give" and deleted "to the person sentenced" following "written notice"; and made a stylistic change.

—2001. Paragraph I: Inserted "or the state of New Hampshire" in the first sentence.

NOTES TO DECISIONS

1. Constitutionality
2. Certiorari review
3. Retrospective effect

1. Constitutionality

RSA 651:58, I and II provide a defendant with statutory notice of the State of New Hampshire's right to seek a review of his sentence, and the extent to which jurisdiction was retained to either increase or decrease the imposed sentence after a hearing conducted by the division. Therefore, RSA 651:58, I does not violate the Due Process Clause of the U.S. Constitution. In re Evans, 154 N.H. 142, 908 A.2d 796, 2006 N.H. LEXIS 130 (2006), cert. denied, Evans v. New Hampshire, 549 U.S. 1310, 127 S. Ct. 1888, 167 L. Ed. 2d 374, 2007 U.S. LEXIS 3671 (2007).

RSA 651:58, I, which allows a state to seek an increase in an inmate's sentence within one year, does not violate the Double Jeopardy Clause of the U.S. Constitution because a defendant has no "expectation of finality" until the sentence review process has concluded. In re Evans, 154 N.H. 142, 908 A.2d 796, 2006 N.H. LEXIS 130 (2006), cert. denied, Evans v. New Hampshire, 549 U.S. 1310, 127 S. Ct. 1888, 167 L. Ed. 2d 374, 2007 U.S. LEXIS 3671 (2007).

As the purpose of amended RSA 651:58, I, which allowed New Hampshire to seek an increase in an inmate's sentence within one year, was remedial rather than punitive, application of RSA 651:58, I to a petitioner who had committed the crimes before its enactment did not violate the Ex Post Facto Clause of the U.S. Constitution, U.S. Const. art. I, § 10. In re Evans, 154 N.H. 142, 908 A.2d 796, 2006 N.H. LEXIS 130 (2006), cert. denied, Evans v. New Hampshire, 549 U.S. 1310, 127 S. Ct. 1888, 167 L. Ed. 2d 374, 2007 U.S. LEXIS 3671 (2007).

As RSA 651:58, I provides for notice to the defendant that the imposed sentence may be increased after a review hearing before the sentencing review board, he or she has no expectation of finality until the 30-day period to request a sentence review has passed. Because this limited appeal does not involve a retrial or approximate the ordeal of a trial on the basic issue of guilt or innocence, RSA 651:58, I does not violate the Double Jeopardy Clause of the New Hampshire Constitution. In re Guardarramos-Cepeda, 154 N.H. 7, 904 A.2d 609, 2006 N.H. LEXIS 112 (2006).

As RSA 651:58, I and II provide that a defendant must be given both statutory and actual notice of the State's right to seek a review of his sentence within 30 days of the imposition of that sentence, and the extent to which jurisdiction is retained to either increase or decrease the sentence after a hearing conducted by a sentencing review board, RSA 651:58, I does not violate the Due Process Clause of the New Hampshire Constitution. In re Guardarramos-Cepeda, 154 N.H. 7, 904 A.2d 609, 2006 N.H. LEXIS 112 (2006).

2. Certiorari review

State's petition for certiorari review of defendant's sentence was granted as defendant was not sentenced to an enhanced sentence for driving while intoxicated and certiorari was the only avenue by which the State could appeal the sentencing order. State v. Marcoux (In re State), 154 N.H. 118, 908 A.2d 155, 2006 N.H. LEXIS 126 (2006).

3. Retrospective effect

District court did not err in dismissing an inmate's habeas claim that application of a post-conviction procedural change to the state's sentencing laws in RSA 651:58 violated the Ex Post Facto Clause because the court could not say that the state court "unreasonably applied" the U.S. Supreme Court's significant risk test. Evans v. Gerry, 647 F.3d 30, 2011 U.S. App. LEXIS 15031

(2011).

As the amendment to RSA 651:58, I created a procedural change in the statute by altering who made the final sentencing decision, but not the legal standards for that decision, the legislature presumably intended RSA 651:58, I, as amended, to apply retrospectively. In re Evans, 154 N.H. 142, 908 A.2d 796, 2006 N.H. LEXIS 130 (2006), cert. denied, Evans v. New Hampshire, 549 U.S. 1310, 127 S. Ct. 1888, 167 L. Ed. 2d 374, 2007 U.S. LEXIS 3671 (2007).

Cited:

Cited in State v. Church, 115 N.H. 537, 345 A.2d 392, 1975 N.H. LEXIS 355 (1975); Bell v. Superior Court Sentence Review Div., 117 N.H. 474, 374 A.2d 659, 1977 N.H. LEXIS 358 (1977); State v. Goodwin, 118 N.H. 862, 395 A.2d 1234, 1978 N.H. LEXIS 307 (1978); State v. Cote, 129 N.H. 358, 530 A.2d 775, 1987 N.H. LEXIS 217 (1987); In re Turgeon, 140 N.H. 52, 663 A.2d 82, 1995 N.H. LEXIS 98 (1995).

RESEARCH REFERENCES

New Hampshire Court Rules Annotated.

Application following incarceration, see Rule 3, Sentence Review Division Rules, Rules of the Superior Court, New Hampshire Court Rules annotated.

Late applications, see Rule 8, Sentence Review Division Rules, Rules of the Superior Court, New Hampshire Court Rules Annotated.

Sentences subject to review, see Rules 12 and 13, Sentence Review Division Rules, Rules of the Superior Court, New Hampshire Court Rules Annotated.

New Hampshire Bar Journal.

For article, "Lex Loci: A Survey of New Hampshire Supreme Court Decisions," see 47 N.H.B.J. 78 (Autumn 2006).

651:59. Review Procedure.

I. The review division has jurisdiction: to consider an appeal with or without a hearing; to review the judgment insofar as it relates to the sentence imposed; to review any other sentence imposed when the sentence appealed from was imposed, notwithstanding the partial execution of any such sentence; to amend the judgment by ordering substituted therefor a different appropriate sentence or sentences; or to make any other disposition of the case which could have been made at the time of the imposition of the sentence or sentences under review.

II. The review division may require the production of any records, documents, exhibits or other things connected with the proceedings. The superior court shall by rule establish forms for appeals hereunder and may by rule make such other regulations of procedure relative thereto, consistent with law, as justice requires.

Source.

1975, 267:1, eff. Aug. 5, 1975.

NOTES TO DECISIONS

1. Constitutional issues
2. Increase of sentence

1. Constitutional issues

District court did not err in dismissing an inmate's habeas claim that application of a post-conviction procedural change to the state's sentencing laws in RSA 651:58 violated the Ex Post Facto

Clause because the court could not say that the state court "unreasonably applied" the U.S. Supreme Court's significant risk test. Evans v. Gerry, 647 F.3d 30, 2011 U.S. App. LEXIS 15031 (2011).

Sentence division lacked jurisdiction to determine the constitutionality of a sentence; because the sentence review division's finding that defendants' due process rights were violated at sentencing was a constitutional issue, it was well beyond division's statutory jurisdiction, and the finding was vacated. In re State (Sentence Review Div.), 150 N.H. 296, 837 A.2d 291, 2003 N.H. LEXIS 184 (2003).

2. Increase of sentence

Superior court sentence review division had authority to increase sentences where the appropriateness of the sentences was the very subject of appeal to it by prisoner given adequate notice that division might find sentence too short as well as too long and nothing in procedure created any realistic likelihood of vindictiveness. Bell v. Superior Court Sentence Review Div., 117 N.H. 474, 374 A.2d 659, 1977 N.H. LEXIS 358 (1977).

Constitutional requirements of due process do not require statement of reasons which justify increase of sentence in sentence review proceedings where it is the appropriateness of original sentence which is the very issue on appeal to board. Bell v. Superior Court Sentence Review Div., 117 N.H. 474, 374 A.2d 659, 1977 N.H. LEXIS 358 (1977).

Increased sentences in sentence review proceedings do not have to be based on events occurring after original sentence. Bell v. Superior Court Sentence Review Div., 117 N.H. 474, 374 A.2d 659, 1977 N.H. LEXIS 358 (1977).

Cited:

Cited in State v. Goodwin, 118 N.H. 862, 395 A.2d 1234, 1978 N.H. LEXIS 307 (1978); Allard v. Power, 122 N.H. 27, 440 A.2d 450, 1982 N.H. LEXIS 279 (1982); State v. Stone, 122 N.H. 987, 453 A.2d 1272, 1982 N.H. LEXIS 505 (1982).

RESEARCH REFERENCES

New Hampshire Court Rules Annotated.

Decisions regarding sentence, see Rule 14, Sentence Review Division Rules, Rules of the Superior Court, New Hampshire Court Rules Annotated.

Factors considered in decision, see Rule 20, Sentence Review Division Rules, Rules of the Superior Court, New Hampshire Court Rules Annotated.

Material requiring production, see Rule 15, Sentence Review Division Rules, Rules of the Superior Court, New Hampshire Court Rules Annotated.

Matters which will be considered, see Rule 15, Sentence Review Division Rules, Rules of the Superior Court, New Hampshire Court Rules Annotated.

Matters which will not be considered, see Rule 16, Sentence Review Division Rules, Rules of the Superior Court, New Hampshire Court Rules Annotated.

Personal appearance by defendant and counsel required to increase sentence, see Rule 17, Sentence Review Division Rules, Rules of the Superior Court, New Hampshire Court Rules Annotated.

Right of applicant to appear and be represented by counsel, see Rule 17, Sentence Review Division Rules, Rules of the Superior Court, New Hampshire Court Rules Annotated.

Scope of review, see Rule 22, Sentence Review Division Rules, Rules of the Superior Court, New Hampshire Court Rules Annotated.

651:60. Amendment of Sentence.

If the judgment is amended by an order substituting a different sentence or sentences or disposition of the case, the review division or any member thereof shall resentence the defendant or make any other disposition of the case in accordance with the order of the review division. Time served on a sentence appealed from shall be deemed to have been served on a substituted sentence.

Source.
1975, 267:1, eff. Aug. 5, 1975.

NOTES TO DECISIONS

Cited:
Cited in Bell v. Superior Court Sentence Review Div., 117 N.H. 474, 374 A.2d 659, 1977 N.H. LEXIS 358 (1977); State v. Goodwin, 118 N.H. 862, 395 A.2d 1234, 1978 N.H. LEXIS 307 (1978).

651:61. Records.

The secretary-clerk shall attend all sittings of the review division, shall record all appointments to the division, notifying the clerk of the superior court in each county thereof, and shall record the proceedings of the division.

Source.
1975, 267:1, eff. Aug. 5, 1975.

NOTES TO DECISIONS

Cited:
Cited in Bell v. Superior Court Sentence Review Div., 117 N.H. 474, 374 A.2d 659, 1977 N.H. LEXIS 358 (1977).

RESEARCH REFERENCES

New Hampshire Court Rules Annotated.
Inspection of record book, see Rule 6, Sentence Review Division Rules, Rules of the Superior Court, New Hampshire Court Rules Annotated.

651:61-a. Statement of Purpose.

I. The legislature finds and declares that the victims of crimes often suffer losses through no fault of their own and for which there is no compensation. It also finds that repayment, in whole or in part, by the offender to the victim can operate to rehabilitate the offender. It is the purpose of this act to establish a presumption that the victim will be compensated by the offender who is responsible for the loss. Restitution by the offender can serve to reinforce the offender's sense of responsibility for the offense, to provide the offender the opportunity to pay the offender's debt to society and to the victim in a constructive manner, and to ease the burden of the victim as a result of the criminal act.

II. The legislature does not intend that restitution be contingent upon an offender's current ability to pay or upon the availability of other compensation. The legislature intends that the court increase, to the maximum extent feasible, the number of instances in which victims receive restitution. The legislature does not intend the use of restitution to result in preferential treatment for offenders with substantial financial resources.

Source.
1996, 286:6, eff. July 1, 1997.

NOTES TO DECISIONS

Burden of proof
If the State bears the burden of proving that a defendant is, in fact, responsible for a victim's loss, then, pursuant to the language of RSA 651:61-a, I, the court must presume that the defendant will compensate the victim and the party wishing to rebut this presumption would, logically, bear the burden of proof. State v. Shannon, 155 N.H. 135, 920 A.2d 1163, 2007 N.H. LEXIS 40 (2007).

Restitution

Purpose.
1981, 329:1, eff. Aug. 16, 1981 provided:

"I. The legislature finds and declares that the victims of crimes often suffer losses through no fault of their own and for which there is no compensation. It also finds that repayment, in whole or in part, by the offender to the victim of his crime can operate to rehabilitate the offender in certain instances. It is the purpose of this act to encourage the compensation of victims by the person most responsible for the loss incurred by the victim, the offender. Restitution by the offender can serve to reinforce the offender's sense of responsibility for the offense, to provide him the opportunity to pay his debt to society and to his victim in a constructive manner, and to ease the burden of the victim as a result of the criminal conduct.

"II. The legislature recognizes that a crime is an offense against society as a whole, not only against the victim of the crime, and that restitution for victims is therefore ancillary to the central objectives of the criminal law. It intends restitution to be applied only when other purposes of sentencing can be appropriately served. It does not intend the use of restitution to result in preferential treatment for offender with substantial financial resources."

Cross References.
Restitution for vandalism committed by minors, see RSA 169-B:45.

Restitution to government for losses incurred as a result of food stamp fraud, see RSA 167:17-c.

Restitution to state for illegal taking or possession of game animals, game birds or fur bearing animals, see RSA 207:55.

NOTES TO DECISIONS

1. Construction
2. Criteria for awarding restitution
3. Amounts recoverable
4. Insurers

1. Construction

Since RSA 651:65 provides that a victim's right to civil relief against a criminal defendant is not impaired by restitution award, and under RSA 651:66, governing revocation of restitution, the beneficiary for a restitution award may lose the right to receive payment upon the successful petition of the defendant, an order of restitution under this subdivision is not equivalent to an award of civil damages. State v. Fleming, 125 N.H. 238, 480 A.2d 107, 1984 N.H. LEXIS 365 (1984).

2. Criteria for awarding restitution

Restitution to a victim of crime may be ordered when three criteria are met: (1) restitution will serve to rehabilitate the offender, (2) restitution will compensate the victim, and (3) no other compensation is available. State v. Fleming, 125 N.H. 238, 480 A.2d 107, 1984 N.H. LEXIS 365 (1984).

3. Amounts recoverable

The legislature intended restitution under this subdivision to cover only those losses included in RSA 651:62, III, defining economic loss. State v. Fleming, 125 N.H. 238, 480 A.2d 107, 1984 N.H. LEXIS 365 (1984).

Since the definition of economic loss in RSA 651:62, III, is limited by the phrase "pecuniary detriment," only those losses which are easily ascertained and measured, that is, only liquidated amounts, should be recovered under this subdivision. State v. Fleming, 125 N.H. 238, 480 A.2d 107, 1984 N.H. LEXIS 365 (1984).

4. Insurers

Insurer that has compensated its insured for consequences of a crime is not a "victim" suffering loss as a "direct result" of criminal conduct within the meaning of this subdivision, and insurer is therefore not eligible for statutory restitution. State v. Springer, 133 N.H. 223, 574 A.2d 1381, 1990 N.H. LEXIS 56 (1990).

651:62. Definitions.

As used in this subdivision, unless the context otherwise indicates:

I. "Claimant" means a victim, dependent, or any person legally authorized to act on behalf of the victim.

II. "Dependent" means any person who was wholly or partially dependent upon the victim for care and support when the crime was committed.

III. "Economic loss" means out-of-pocket losses or other expenses incurred as a direct result of a criminal offense, including:

(a) Reasonable charges incurred for reasonably needed products, services and accommodations, including but not limited to charges for medical and dental care, rehabilitation, and other remedial treatment and care including mental health services for the victim or, in the case of the death of the victim, for the victim's spouse and immediate family;

(b) Loss of income by the victim or the victim's dependents;

(c) The value of damaged, destroyed, or lost property;

(d) Expenses reasonably incurred in obtaining ordinary and necessary services in lieu of those the injured or deceased victim would have performed, if the crime had not occurred, for the benefit of the victim or the victim's dependents;

(e) Reasonable expenses related to funeral and burial or crematory services for the decedent victim.

IV. "Offender" means any person convicted of a criminal or delinquent act.

V. "Restitution" means money or service provided by the offender to compensate a victim for economic loss, or to compensate any collateral source subrogated to the rights of the victim, which indemnifies a victim for economic loss under this subdivision.

VI. "Victim" means a person or claimant who suffers economic loss as a result of an offender's criminal conduct or the good faith effort of any person attempting to prevent or preventing the criminal conduct.

Source.

1981, 329:2. 1994, 190:1, eff. Sept. 21, 1994. 1996, 286:7, eff. July 1, 1997.

Amendments
—1996. Rewritten to the extent that a detailed comparison would be impracticable.

—1994. Paragraph V: Inserted "or to any collateral source subrogated to the rights of the victim, which indemnifies a victim for personal injury, death or economic loss" preceding "under this".

NOTES TO DECISIONS

1. Violations
2. Economic losses
3. Victim
4. Nature of restitution
5. Apportionment
6. Future expenses

1. Violations

A violation is a "crime" within the meaning of the statute, and a person who commits a violation is an "offender" within the meaning of the statute and can be sentenced to pay restitution. State v. Woods, 139 N.H. 399, 654 A.2d 960, 1995 N.H. LEXIS 12 (1995).

2. Economic losses

While use of the term "including" may limit the applicability of the general term "pecuniary detriment" to the types of economic losses particularized therein, mental health services, such as counseling services, are sufficiently similar to "medical costs" to fall within the scope of the definition of "economic loss" under RSA 651:62; thus, it was not error to award restitution for mental health services with respect to crimes committed in 1986 to 1987. To the extent that the prior statute was ambiguous with respect to whether mental health services were included, the 1996 amendment that first specified "mental health services" is more properly viewed as an attempt to resolve any ambiguity rather than as a change in legal rights. State v. Gibson, 160 N.H. 445, 999 A.2d 240, 2010 N.H. LEXIS 67 (2010).

RSA 651:62, III(b) does not provide an avenue of recovery for a minor victim's mother who has suffered loss of income. State v. McCarthy, 150 N.H. 389, 839 A.2d 22, 2003 N.H. LEXIS 204 (2003).

Defendant may be held liable for economic losses directly resulting from factual allegations that support conduct covered by conviction. Where several factors contribute to loss suffered by victim, court should apportion costs so that restitution reasonably represents amount of loss victim sustained as a result of offense. State v. Eno, 143 N.H. 465, 727 A.2d 981, 1999 N.H. LEXIS 26 (1999).

3. Victim

Trial court erred in ordering the payment of restitution directly to a counselor. The version of the restitution statute in effect in 1986 to 1987, when the crimes were committed, defined "victim" as a person who suffered economic loss as a direct result of the offender's criminal conduct, and the counselor did not fall within this category; furthermore, the State conceded that the counselor was not a "collateral source subrogated to the rights of the victim." State v. Gibson, 160 N.H. 445, 999 A.2d 240, 2010 N.H. LEXIS 67 (2010).

Although a minor victim's mother suffered lost wages caring for the minor after defendant assaulted him, the mother was not entitled to restitution because she was not a "victim or the victim's dependent," under RSA 651:62, III(b). State v. McCarthy, 150 N.H. 389, 839 A.2d 22, 2003 N.H. LEXIS 204 (2003).

4. Nature of restitution

Restitution is not an element of the offense. Rather, it is money provided by the offender to compensate a victim for economic loss. State v. Schwartz, 160 N.H. 68, 993 A.2d 220, 2010 N.H. LEXIS 29 (2010).

5. Apportionment

It was error when the trial court, finding that it was not possible to apportion the counseling required for the victim between what was necessitated by the abuse for which defendant was convicted and what was necessitated by the other alleged abuse perpetrated by defendant, ordered restitution covering all counseling costs. The State had to prove that the conduct for which the defendant was convicted was a substantial factor in producing the injury that required the treatment, and the trial court had not made such a finding. State v. Gibson, 160 N.H. 445, 999 A.2d 240, 2010 N.H. LEXIS 67 (2010).

6. Future expenses

Remand was required when it appeared that the amount that the trial court ordered to remain in trust for future counseling for the victim might have been influenced by its erroneous ruling regarding the apportionment of counseling costs. State v. Gibson, 160 N.H. 445, 999 A.2d 240, 2010 N.H. LEXIS 67 (2010).

Cited:

Cited in State v. Fleming, 125 N.H. 238, 480 A.2d 107, 1984 N.H. LEXIS 365 (1984); State v. Springer, 133 N.H. 223, 574 A.2d 1381, 1990 N.H. LEXIS 56 (1990); State v. W.J.T. Enters., 136 N.H. 490, 618 A.2d 806, 1992 N.H. LEXIS 211 (1992).

651:63. Restitution Authorized.

I. Any offender may be sentenced to make restitution in an amount determined by the court. In any case in which restitution is not ordered, the court shall state its reasons therefor on the record or in its sentencing order. Restitution may be ordered regardless of the offender's ability to pay and regardless of the availability of other compensation; however, restitution is not intended to compensate the victim more than once for the same injury. A restitution order is not a civil judgment.

II. Restitution ordered shall be in addition to any other penalty or fine and may be a condition of probation or parole. Restitution, if ordered, may also be a condition of any work release program administered under RSA 651:19 or RSA 651:25.

III. The making of a restitution order shall not affect the right of a victim to compensation under RSA 21-M:8-h, except to the extent that restitution is actually collected pursuant to the order. The offender shall reimburse the victims' assistance fund for any payments made by the fund to the victim pursuant to RSA 21-M:8-h after the restitution order is satisfied. Refused or unclaimed restitution payments shall be made to the victims' assistance fund.

IV. The court's determination of the amount of restitution shall not be admissible as evidence in a civil action. The court shall reduce any civil damage awards by restitution ordered and paid to the victim. Restitution orders shall survive bankruptcy.

V. The court shall add 17 percent to the total restitution payment as an administrative fee to be paid by the offender. Such administrative fee shall be divided into the following components, to be designated as follows: 15 percent shall be continually appropriated to a special fund for the division of field services, department of corrections, $22,500 of which shall lapse to the general fund at the end of each quarter should that amount be received, to maximize restitution collections, directly or through agents of contractors selected by the department; and 2 percent for the victims' assistance fund. Unexpended account balances in the special fund for the division of field services in excess of $50,000 at the end of the fiscal year shall lapse to the general

fund. Administrative fees shall be paid by the offender in addition to and when each restitution payment is made.

VI. Restitution, administrative fines and fees, and other fees collected, except for supervision fees pursuant to RSA 504-A:13, shall be allocated on a pro-rata basis by the commissioner of corrections or his or her designee when payments are insufficient to cover the full amount due for each of these balances, except that restitution to victims shall have priority over all other allocations.

VII. On or before July 1, 1997, and each year thereafter until July 1, 2000, the division of field services, department of corrections, shall submit an annual budget plan to the joint legislative fiscal committee. The division of field services, department of corrections, shall have the authority to hire temporary personnel and to procure equipment and expend relevant operating expenses as may be necessary to implement this chapter.

Source.

1981, 329:2, eff. Aug. 16, 1981. 1996, 286:7, eff. July 1, 1997; 286:19, eff. July 1, 2001. 1999, 261:6, eff. July 1, 1999. 2008, 120:33, eff. August 2, 2008.

Amendments

—2008. The 2008 amendment added the third sentence of V.

—1999. Paragraph VI: Inserted "by the commissioner of corrections or his or her designee" following "basis" and added "except that restitution to victims shall have priority over all other allocations" at the end of the paragraph.

—1996. Chapter 286:7 rewrote section to the extent that a detailed comparison would be impracticable.

Chapter 286:19 rewrote par. V.

Repeal of 1996, 286:19 amendment.

2001, 176:1, eff. July 5, 2001, provided for the repeal of the amendment to par. V of this section by 1996, 286:19, which was to have taken effect July 1, 2001.

Cross References.

Restitution to victim's assistance fund, see RSA 21-M:8-*l*.

NOTES TO DECISIONS

1. Criteria for ordering restitution
2. Due process
3. Particular cases
4. Burden of proof
5. Amount

1. Criteria for ordering restitution

Three criteria must be met in order to warrant restitution: (1) restitution will serve to rehabilitate the offender; (2) restitution will compensate the victim; and (3) no other compensation is available. State v. Stearns, 130 N.H. 475, 547 A.2d 672, 1988 N.H. LEXIS 72 (1988).

In considering whether criterion for restitution is met, that no other compensation is available, defendant who contests a restitution order has not shown that other compensation is available merely by showing that a plaintiff could bring a civil suit for damages and that the defendant is not indigent. State v. Stearns, 130 N.H. 475, 547 A.2d 672, 1988 N.H. LEXIS 72 (1988).

Restitution orders are not mandated in all bad check criminal cases; restitution is a discretionary matter and should only be ordered when (1) restitution will serve to rehabilitate the offender, (2) restitution will compensate the victim, and (3) no other compensation is available. In re Milone, 73 B.R. 452, 1987 Bankr. LEXIS 691 (Bankr. D.N.H. 1987).

2. Due process

An order for restitution is part of the sentencing process, and federal constitutional right to due process applied to defendant's restitution hearing. State v. Eno, 143 N.H. 465, 727 A.2d 981, 1999 N.H. LEXIS 26 (1999).

3. Particular cases

Because the trial court never independently considered the amount of restitution, but incorrectly ruled that it was bound by the amount set by the Department of Corrections, the award had to be vacated and the case remanded so that the trial court could determine the amount of restitution and whether the award of any portion of the restitution amount would result in the victim receiving an impermissible double recovery. State v. Bent, 163 N.H. 237, 37 A.3d 390, 2012 N.H. LEXIS 12 (2012).

Trial court properly ordered defendant to pay restitution to the victim. The victim suffered economic loss as a result of defendant's criminal conduct whereby he incurred medical bills for treatment of his broken jaw, and the record supported a finding that the victim's injuries were causally connected to defendant's hitting him. State v. Schwartz, 160 N.H. 68, 993 A.2d 220, 2010 N.H. LEXIS 29 (2010).

Trial court properly ordered defendant under RSA 651:63, I, to pay for the victim's future counseling costs. Nothing in these statutes precluded a trial court from ordering a defendant to pay restitution for future economic losses caused by his or her crime. State v. Oakes, 161 N.H. 270, 13 A.3d 293, 2010 N.H. LEXIS 149 (Dec. 7, 2010).

Trial court properly ordered a defendant to pay a victim restitution for jewelry stolen in the state where the victim's representative stated that she had not reported the losses at issue in this case to the authorities in another state and the defendant failed to provide the record from the other proceeding to show that he had fully compensated the victim for the claimed losses. State v. Shannon, 155 N.H. 135, 920 A.2d 1163, 2007 N.H. LEXIS 40 (2007).

Where restitution was statutorily authorized by RSA 651:63, I and defendant knew that the victim's civil case had settled, defendant's failure to argue that the sentence allegedly provided dual recovery barred a challenge to the sentence three years later. State v. Chesbrough, 151 N.H. 105, 849 A.2d 141, 2004 N.H. LEXIS 97 (2004).

Where defendant was ordered to pay restitution to a humane society for costs incurred as a result of defendant's cruelty to 20 dogs, and the humane society had received donations directly related to defendant's case that exceeded the amount of the humane society's claimed losses, defendant, nonetheless, was properly required to pay restitution under RSA 651:63, I, because nothing in the statute precluded victims from receiving both restitution and voluntary public donations. State v. Burr, 147 N.H. 102, 782 A.2d 914, 2001 N.H. LEXIS 176 (2001).

4. Burden of proof

If the State bears the burden of proving that a defendant is, in fact, responsible for a victim's loss, then, pursuant to the language of RSA 651:61-a, I, the court must presume that the defendant will compensate the victim and the party wishing to rebut this presumption would, logically, bear the burden of proof. State v. Shannon, 155 N.H. 135, 920 A.2d 1163, 2007 N.H. LEXIS 40 (2007).

5. Amount

While under RSA 651:64, the Department of Corrections has authority to set the time and method of restitution payments and to enforce a restitution order, under RSA 651:63, only the trial court has the authority to set the amount of restitution. State v. Bent, 163 N.H. 237, 37 A.3d 390, 2012 N.H. LEXIS 12 (2012).

Cited:

Cited in State v. Fleming, 125 N.H. 238, 480 A.2d 107, 1984 N.H. LEXIS 365 (1984); State v. Springer, 133 N.H. 223, 574 A.2d 1381, 1990 N.H. LEXIS 56 (1990); State v. Schachter, 133 N.H. 439, 577 A.2d 1222, 1990 N.H. LEXIS 81 (1990); State v. W.J.T. Enters., 136 N.H. 490, 618 A.2d 806, 1992 N.H. LEXIS 211 (1992).

651:64. Time and Method of Restitution.

I. The time and method of restitution payments or performance of restitution services shall be specified by the department of corrections. Monetary restitution may be by lump sum, or by periodic installments in any amounts. The court shall not be required to reduce the total obligation as a result of the offender's inability to pay. The offender shall bear the burden of demonstrating lack of ability to pay. Restitution shall be paid by the offender to the department of corrections unless otherwise ordered by the court. Monetary restitution shall not bear interest. Restitution shall be made to any collateral source or subrogee, if authorized by that source and after restitution to the victim, and to the victims' assistance fund, if applicable, has been satisfied. Restitution shall be a continuing obligation of the offender's estate and shall inure to the benefit of the victim's estate, provided that no indebtedness shall pass to any heir of the offender's estate.

II. The department of corrections shall have continuing authority over the offender for purposes of enforcing restitution until the restitution order is satisfied.

III. The department may garnish the offender's wages for the purpose of ensuring payment of victim restitution.

Source.

1981, 329:2. 1994, 190:2, eff. Sept. 21, 1994. 1996, 286:7, eff. July 1, 1997.

Amendments

—1996. Rewritten to the extent that a detailed comparison would be impracticable.

—1994. Added the third sentence and deleted "in those cases" preceding "the corrections" in the fourth sentence.

NOTES TO DECISIONS

Amount

While under RSA 651:64, the Department of Corrections has authority to set the time and method of restitution payments and to enforce a restitution order, under RSA 651:63, only the trial court has the authority to set the amount of restitution. State v. Bent, 163 N.H. 237, 37 A.3d 390, 2012 N.H. LEXIS 12 (2012).

Cited:

Cited in State v. Springer, 133 N.H. 223, 574 A.2d 1381, 1990 N.H. LEXIS 56 (1990).

651:65. Civil Actions.

This subdivision does not bar, suspend, or otherwise affect any right or liability for damages, penalty, forfeiture or other remedy authorized by law to be recovered or enforced in a civil action, regardless of whether the conduct involved in such civil action constitutes an economic loss. Any restitution ordered and paid shall be deducted from the amount of any judgment awarded in a civil action brought by the victim or other authorized claimant against the offender based on the same facts. If the restitution ordered and made was work restitution, the reasonable value of the services may be deducted from any such judgment.

Source.
  1981, 329:2, eff. Aug. 16, 1981.

NOTES TO DECISIONS

Cited:
  Cited in State v. Fleming, 125 N.H. 238, 480 A.2d 107, 1984 N.H. LEXIS 365 (1984); State v. Stearns, 130 N.H. 475, 547 A.2d 672, 1988 N.H. LEXIS 72 (1988); State v. Springer, 133 N.H. 223, 574 A.2d 1381, 1990 N.H. LEXIS 56 (1990).

651:66. Revocation of Restitution.

The supervising agency, or the offender who has been sentenced to pay restitution and has not inexcusably defaulted in payment thereof, may at any time petition the court which sentenced him for a revocation of any unpaid portion of the restitution. If the court finds that the circumstances which warranted the imposition of the restitution have changed, or that it would otherwise be unjust to require payment, the court may revoke the unpaid portion of the restitution in whole or in part, or modify the time and method of payment.

Source.
  1981, 329:2, eff. Aug. 16, 1981.

NOTES TO DECISIONS

Cited:
  Cited in State v. Fleming, 125 N.H. 238, 480 A.2d 107, 1984 N.H. LEXIS 365 (1984); State v. Springer, 133 N.H. 223, 574 A.2d 1381, 1990 N.H. LEXIS 56 (1990).

651:67. Failure to Make Restitution.

I. Any offender who is sentenced to make restitution under RSA 651:63, and who purposely violates the court's order by either failing to make restitution or by defaulting in the payment or performance of the restitution authorized, may be prosecuted for contempt.

II. In the case of a juvenile offender, restitution must be paid before the juvenile's eighteenth birthday, or for any person sentenced pursuant to RSA 169-B:4, before his nineteenth birthday. Any offender who fails to make restitution as ordered before the termination of juvenile court jurisdiction may be prosecuted, as an adult, for contempt.

Source.
  1981, 329:2. 1985, 130:1, eff. Jan. 1, 1986.

Amendments
  —1985. Designated existing provisions of section as par. I, inserted "purposely" preceding "violates" and substituted "may be prosecuted for" for "shall be guilty of" preceding "contempt" in that paragraph, and added par. II.

NOTES TO DECISIONS

Cited:
  Cited in State v. Fleming, 125 N.H. 238, 480 A.2d 107, 1984 N.H. LEXIS 365 (1984); State v. Springer, 133 N.H. 223, 574 A.2d 1381, 1990 N.H. LEXIS 56 (1990).

Uncompensated Public Service

651:68. Uncompensated Public Service.

The performance of uncompensated public service of a sort that in the opinion of the court, the commissioner of the department of corrections, the superintendent of a county correctional facility, or the parole board will foster respect for those interests violated by the defendant's conduct may be ordered:

I. By the sentencing court as a condition of probation, conditional discharge, release under RSA 651:19, or suspension of sentence;

II. By the commissioner of the department of corrections as a condition of release under RSA 651:25;

III. By the superintendent of a county correctional facility; or

IV. By the parole board as a condition of parole.

Source.
  1994, 192:6, eff. July 1, 1994. 2007, 149:4, eff. August 17, 2007.

Amendments
  —2007. Inserted "the superintendent of a county correctional facility" following "corrections" in the introductory paragraph and added new par. III and redesignated former par. III as par. IV.

NOTES TO DECISIONS

  1. Relation to other statutes
  2. Particular cases

1. Relation to other statutes
  Plain language of the immunity statute, read within the sentencing scheme, demonstrates that RSA 651:70 is limited to "uncompensated public service" ordered by a government entity authorized under RSA 651:68. Chatman v. Brady, 162 N.H. 362, 33 A.3d 1103, 2011 N.H. LEXIS 115 (2011).

2. Particular cases
  Plain language of RSA 651:70 showed that it was limited to "uncompensated public service" ordered by a government entity authorized under RSA 651:68. Because at the time plaintiff entered a work program in 2007, RSA 651:68 did not give county correctional authorities the authority to order such service, defendants were not immune under RSA 651:70. Chatman v. Brady, 162 N.H. 362, 33 A.3d 1103, 2011 N.H. LEXIS 115 (2011).

651:69. Compensation.

No individual who performs uncompensated public service under this subdivision for a person or organization shall receive any benefits that are provided to other employees.

Source.
  1994, 192:6, eff. July 1, 1994.

651:70. Liability.

No person or organization who utilizes the services of any person performing uncompensated public service under this subdivision shall be liable for any damages sustained by an individual while performing such services for the benefit of the person or organization or any damages caused by that person unless the person or organization is guilty of gross negligence.

Source.

1994, 192:6, eff. July 1, 1994.

NOTES TO DECISIONS

1. Construction.
2. Particular cases

1. Construction.

Plain language of the immunity statute, read within the sentencing scheme, demonstrates that RSA 651:70 is limited to "uncompensated public service" ordered by a government entity authorized under RSA 651:68. Chatman v. Brady, 162 N.H. 362, 33 A.3d 1103, 2011 N.H. LEXIS 115 (2011).

2. Particular cases

Plain language of RSA 651:70 showed that it was limited to "uncompensated public service" ordered by a government entity authorized under RSA 651:68. Because at the time plaintiff entered a work program in 2007, RSA 651:68 did not give county correctional authorities the authority to order such service, defendants were not immune under RSA 651:70. Chatman v. Brady, 162 N.H. 362, 33 A.3d 1103, 2011 N.H. LEXIS 115 (2011).

CHAPTER 651-A

PAROLE OF PRISONERS

SECTION
651-A:1.   Purpose of Parole.
651-A:2.   Definitions.
651-A:3.   Adult Parole Board; Establishment; Procedures.
651-A:4.   Duties; Adult Parole Board.
651-A:5.   Executive Assistant.
651-A:6.   Terms of Release.
651-A:7.   Eligibility for Release; Life Sentences.
651-A:8.   Eligibility for Parole; Persons Convicted of Psycho-Sexual Murder.
651-A:9.   Psycho-Sexual Murder Certified.
651-A:10.   Psycho-Sexual Murder Defined.
651-A:10-a. Medical Parole.
651-A:11.   Notice of Hearings.
651-A:11-a. Victims Permitted to Speak at Parole Hearings.
651-A:12.   Reduction of Maximum Sentence While on Parole.
651-A:13.   Suspension of Supervision.
651-A:14.   Early Discharge for Good Conduct.
651-A:15.   Complaint for Violation of Parole. [Repealed.]
651-A:15-a. Arrest of Parolees.
651-A:16.   Report Required.
651-A:16-a. Intermediate Sanction.
651-A:17.   Parole Revocation.
651-A:18.   Revocation Required.
651-A:19.   Effect of Recommittal.
651-A:20.   Parole Records.
651-A:21.   Final Discharge.
651-A:22.   Credits for Good Conduct.
651-A:23.   Credit for Confinement Prior to Sentencing.
651-A:24.   Administrative Attachment.
651-A:25.   Execution of Compact Authorized.

Interstate Compact for Adult Offender Supervision

651-A:26.   Definitions.
651-A:27.   Interstate Commission Established.
651-A:28.   Powers and Duties of the Interstate Commission.
651-A:29.   Organization and Operation of the Interstate Commission.
651-A:30.   Officers and Staff of the Interstate Commission.
651-A:31.   Activities of the Interstate Commission.
651-A:32.   Rulemaking.
651-A:33.   Oversight, Enforcement, and Dispute Resolution.
651-A:34.   Finance.
651-A:35.   Compacting States, Amendment.
651-A:36.   Withdrawal, Default, Termination, and Judicial Enforcement.
651-A:37.   Severability and Construction.
651-A:38.   Binding Effect.

Cross References.

Appointment and authority of probation-parole officers, see RSA 21-H:8.

Department of corrections generally, see RSA 21-H.

International prisoner transfers, see RSA 622-C.

Parole of delinquents, see RSA 170-H.

Probationers and parolees generally, see RSA 504-A.

NOTES TO DECISIONS

Cited:

Cited in State v. Elbert, 125 N.H. 1, 480 A.2d 854, 1984 N.H. LEXIS 371 (1984).

651-A:1. Purpose of Parole.

It is the intent of the legislature that the state parole system provide a means of supervising and rehabilitating offenders without continued incarceration and a means by which prisoners can be aided in the transition from prison to society. It is also the intent of the legislature that the policies, procedures and actions of the adult parole board and the department of corrections relative to the administration of this system emphasize the need to protect the public from criminal acts by parolees.

Source.

1983, 461:16. 1991, 342:1, eff. Jan. 1, 1992.

Revision note.

Substituted "adult parole board" for "state parole board". RSA 651:37, which provided for the establishment of the state board of parole, was repealed by 1983, 461, which enacted RSA 651-A:3, which provides for the establishment of the adult parole board.

Substituted "department of corrections" for "department of probation" pursuant to 1983, 461:4. 1983, 461:6 transferred all powers, duties and functions of the probation department to the department of corrections.

Amendments

—1991. Inserted "supervising and" preceding "rehabilitating" in the first sentence and substituted "emphasize" for "demonstrate recognition of" following "system" in the second sentence.

Cited:

Cited in Cable v. Warden, State Prison, 140 N.H. 395, 666 A.2d 967, 1995 N.H. LEXIS 154 (1995); Knowles v. Warden, 140 N.H. 387, 666 A.2d 972, 1995 N.H. LEXIS 158 (1995).

651-A:2. Definitions.

As used in this chapter:

I. "Prisoner" means any adult person who has been committed to the custody of the commissioner of corrections.

II. "Parole" means a conditional release from the state prison which allows a prisoner to serve the remainder of his term outside the prison, contingent upon compliance with the terms and conditions of parole as established by the parole board.

III. "Board" means the adult parole board.

IV. "Commissioner" means the commissioner of corrections.

V. "Department" means the department of corrections.

VI. "Nonviolent offense" shall include all criminal offenses, except those defined as violent crimes in RSA 651:5, XIII and the following:

(a) RSA 173-B:9, violation of protective order.

(b) RSA 631:2, second degree assault.

(c) RSA 631:3, felony reckless conduct.

(d) RSA 631:4, criminal threatening involving the use of a deadly weapon.

(e) RSA 633:3-a, stalking.

(f) RSA 635:1, burglary.

(g) RSA 641:5, tampering with witnesses and informants.

(h) RSA 650-A:1, felonious use of firearms.

VII. "Intermediate sanction program" means a community-based day or residential program that is designed for use as a swift and certain sanction for a parole violation, in lieu of parole revocation.

Source.
1983, 461:16, eff. July 1, 1983. 2010, 247:5, eff. July 1, 2010.

Amendments
—2010. The 2010 amendment added VI and VII.

651-A:3. Adult Parole Board; Establishment; Procedures.

I. There shall be an adult parole board with 7 members. The members of the board shall be appointed by the governor with the consent of the council for staggered terms of 5 years or until their successors are appointed. No member shall serve more than 2 consecutive terms. A vacancy on the board shall be filled for the unexpired term. The governor shall designate one member as chairman, and the chairman shall designate one other member to serve as chairman in his absence. In the case of a revocation hearing an attorney of the board shall be present at the hearing. Board members shall be paid $100 a day plus mileage at the state employee rate while engaged in parole hearings or administrative meetings.

II. The board shall hold at least 24 parole hearings each year and may hold more hearings as necessary. Each parole hearing shall be held by a hearing panel consisting of exactly 3 members of the board. The board shall establish operating procedures which provide for rotation of board members among hearing panels.

Source.
1983, 461:16. 1994, 305:2, eff. July 1, 1994. 1995, 257:3, eff. July 1, 1995.

Amendments
—1995. Paragraph I: Substituted "$100" for "$50" following "shall be paid" in the seventh sentence.

—1994. Paragraph I: Substituted "7" for "5" preceding "members" in the first sentence and added the sixth sentence.

Membership to board.
1983, 461:17, eff. July 1, 1983, provided: "The incumbent members of the state parole board [established by RSA 651:37, which was repealed by 1983, 461:33] as of the effective date of this act shall become members of the adult parole board and shall complete their terms. The governor shall appoint additional members as needed. To provide for staggered terms, one new member shall be appointed for a 3 year term and the remaining new members shall be appointed to full 5 year terms. The governor shall determine which initial appointments shall be for less than full terms and shall designate the chairman of the new board. Alternate members shall be appointed to full 5 year terms."

Cross References.
Notice of hearings, see RSA 651-A:11.

Organization of executive branch of government generally, see RSA 21-G.

Victim or victim's next of kin permitted to speak at parole hearing, see RSA 651-A:11-a.

651-A:4. Duties; Adult Parole Board.

The board shall:

I. Be responsible for paroling prisoners from the state prison, subject to the applicable provisions of this chapter;

II. Have legal custody of all persons released on parole until they receive their discharge or are recommitted to the prison;

III. Adopt rules, pursuant to RSA 541-A, relative to:

(a) The parole process, including the conduct of parole hearings;

(b) Criteria used to evaluate prospective parolees;

(c) Conditions for the conduct of parolees; and

(d) Procedures for revocation of parole.

(e) Procedures for medical parole.

Source.
1983, 461:16, eff. July 1, 1983. 2004, 218:4, eff. June 11, 2004.

Amendments
—2004. Paragraph III(e): Added.

NOTES TO DECISIONS

1. Parolee's rights
2. Review
3. Authority of parole board

1. Parolee's rights

The parole board has broad authority and discretion, but they are limited by the constitutional rights of the parolee. Martel v. Hancock, 115 N.H. 237, 339 A.2d 9, 1975 N.H. LEXIS 271 (1975). (Decided under prior law.)

2. Review

On petition for habeas corpus, review of the actions of the parole board is necessarily restricted, and they will be upheld unless it is shown as a matter of law that they were arbitrary or capricious, or void for lack of the requisite statutory process. Martel v. Hancock, 115 N.H. 237, 339 A.2d 9, 1975 N.H. LEXIS 271 (1975). (Decided under prior law.)

3. Authority of parole board

A parole board has the independent authority to require an inmate to complete a sexual offender program before he is released on parole, and such a condition does not constitute an improper augmentation of the inmate's sentence. Cable v. Warden, State Prison, 140 N.H. 395, 666 A.2d 967, 1995 N.H. LEXIS 154 (1995). (Decided under prior law.)

Cited:

Cited in Bussiere v. Cunningham, 132 N.H. 747, 571 A.2d 908, 1990 N.H. LEXIS 19 (1990); Knowles v. Warden, 140 N.H. 387, 666 A.2d 972, 1995 N.H. LEXIS 158 (1995).

651-A:5. Executive Assistant.

The board may appoint an executive assistant who shall be an unclassified employee and shall serve at its pleasure. The salary of the executive assistant shall be that established in RSA 94:1-a.

Source.
1983, 461:16, eff. July 1, 1983.

651-A:6. Terms of Release.

I. Any prisoner released on parole shall be given a permit by the board to be at liberty from prison during the unexpired portion of the maximum term of his or her sentence. The decision to release a prisoner shall be governed by the following rules:

(a) A prisoner may be released on parole upon the expiration of the minimum term of his or her sentence, minus any credits received pursuant to RSA 651-A:23, plus the disciplinary period added to such minimum under RSA 651:2, II-e, any part of which is not reduced for good conduct as provided in RSA 651-A:22, provided that there shall appear to the adult parole board, after having given the notice required in RSA 651-A:11, to be a reasonable probability that the prisoner will remain at liberty without violating the law and will conduct himself or herself as a good citizen.

(b) [Repealed.]

(c) A prisoner who has not been previously paroled, or who was recommitted to prison more than one year prior to the expiration of the maximum term of his or her sentence, shall be released on parole at least 9 months prior to the expiration of the maximum term of his or her sentence, unless the parole board votes to deny such release. This provision shall not apply to any prisoner who is the subject of a pending petition for civil commitment pursuant to RSA 135-E. In the event that the prisoner is not civilly committed, he or she shall be released on parole for the remainder of his or her sentence.

II. [Repealed.]

III. The release of prisoners sentenced to the state prison in accordance with sentencing provisions of law in effect prior to November 1, 1973, shall be governed by the law in effect immediately prior to November 1, 1973. However, except for prisoners serving sentences pursuant to conviction of murder in violation of RSA 585:1, murder which is psychosexual in nature as defined in RSA 607:41-d, and manslaughter in the first degree in violation of RSA 585:8, and for the purpose of determining eligibility for release on parole only, the minimum term of a prisoner who has been sentenced in accordance with sentencing provisions in effect prior to November 1, 1973, shall be deemed to be either the longest minimum sentence which could have been imposed for a class A felony under RSA 651:2, II, or his actual minimum sentence, whichever is shorter.

IV. Prior to the release of any inmate on parole from the state prison, or upon termination of the inmate's sentence to the state prison, the commissioner and the department of safety shall provide a nondriver's picture identification card pursuant to RSA 260:21 to the inmate upon release if the inmate does not already possess a valid driver license or nondriver's picture identification card. The failure of the commissioner and the department of safety to provide the inmate with the required nondriver's picture identification card prior to appearance before the parole board shall not constitute a cause for delaying the inmate's release on parole, if approved.

Source.
1983, 461:16. 1991, 342:3, eff. Jan. 1, 1992. 2008, 101:1, eff. July 26, 2008; 277:4, eff. August 26, 2008. 2010, 247:6, eff. July 1, 2010; 247:6 (see effective date note below). 2011, 244:1, 2, eff. July 13, 2011. 2013, 156:10, eff. July 1, 2013.

References in text.
RSA 651:3, III, referred to in par. II, was repealed prior to the enactment of this section. For the present counterparts of the repealed provision, see RSA 642:6, III, IV.

RSA 585:1, 607:41-d, and 585:8, referred to in par. III, were repealed prior to the enactment of this section. For the present counterparts of the repealed provisions, see RSA 630:1 to 630:1-b, 651-A:10, and 630:2, respectively.

Revision note.
In par. I, substituted "RSA 651-A:23" for "RSA 651:55-c" and "adult parole board" for "state board of parole". RSA 651:37, which provided for the establishment of the state board of parole, and RSA 651:55-c were repealed by 1983, 461, which enacted RSA 651-A:3, which provides for establishment of the adult parole board, and RSA 651-A:23, which deals with the subject matter formerly covered by RSA 651:55-c.

In par. III, substituted "November 1, 1973" for "the effective date of this title" and "said effective date" for purposes of clarity.

Amendments
—2013. The 2013 amendment deleted I(b).

—2011. The 2011 amendment added "who has not been previously convicted of a sexually violent offense as defined in RSA 135-E:2, XI, aggravated felonious sexual assault pursuant to RSA 632-A:2, felonious sexual assault pursuant to RSA 632-A:3, sexual assault pursuant to RSA 632-A:4, I(a)-(b), kidnapping pursuant to RSA 633:1, I, first degree assault pursuant to RSA 631:1, I, possession of child sexual abuse images pursuant to RSA 649-A:3, I, or distribution of child sexual abuse images pursuant to RSA 649-A:3-a, I" in I(b); added "unless the parole board votes to deny such release" in I(b) and the first sentence of I(c); and made stylistic changes.

—2010. The 2010 amendment by Chapter 247:6, effective July 1, 2010, added the introductory language of I; redesignated former I as I(a); deleted the former second sentence of I(a), which read: "Any prisoner so released shall be given a permit by the board to be at liberty from prison during the unexpired portion of the maximum term of his sentence"; added I(b); and made stylistic changes.
The 2010 amendment by Chapter 247:6 (see effective date note below) added I(c).

—2008. The 2008 amendment by Chapter 101 deleted II.
The 2008 amendment by Chapter 277 added IV.

—1991. Paragraph II: Substituted "total of the 2 longest sentences, subject to the provisions of RSA 651-A:14" for "longest of said sentences" following "computed from the".

Effective Date.
2010, 247:13, II, eff. July 1, 2010, provided that RSA 651-A:6, I(b) as inserted by section 6 of this act shall apply to any person sentenced to the state prison on or after the effective date of this act.
2010, 247:13, III, eff. July 1, 2010, provided that RSA 651-A:6, I(c) as inserted by section 6 of this act shall apply to any person incarcerated in the state prison with 9 months or more remaining until the expiration of his or her maximum sentence as of October 1, 2010 or thereafter.

Applicability of 2013 amendment.
2013, 156:11, eff. July 1, 2013, provided: "The provisions of sections 1–8 of this act shall apply to:
"I.   Any person who is on parole or eligible for parole, on or after the effective date of this act; and
"II.   Any person who, on or after the effective date of this act, has violated the conditions of parole after a hearing pursuant to RSA 651-A:17."

Cross References.
Conditions for parole of low-risk, nonviolent prisoners prior to serving minimum term of sentence, see RSA 651:25.
Exception for low-risk, nonviolent prisoners, see RSA 651:25.
Performance of uncompensated public service as condition of parole, see RSA 651:68.
Restitution as a condition of parole, see RSA 651:63.

NOTES TO DECISIONS

Construction
This section does not provide prisoners with a "level two" liberty interest in obtaining parole. Bussiere v. Cunningham, 132 N.H. 747, 571 A.2d 908, 1990 N.H. LEXIS 19 (1990).

Cited:
Cited in State ex rel. McLellan v. Cavanaugh, 127 N.H. 33, 498 A.2d 735, 1985 N.H. LEXIS 397 (1985); Baker v. Cunningham, 128 N.H. 374, 513 A.2d 956, 1986 N.H. LEXIS 300 (1986); State v. Gibbons, 135 N.H. 320, 605 A.2d 214, 1992 N.H. LEXIS 38 (1992); Cable v. Warden, State Prison, 140 N.H. 395, 666 A.2d 967, 1995 N.H. LEXIS 154 (1995); Knowles v. Warden, 140 N.H. 387, 666 A.2d 972, 1995 N.H. LEXIS 158 (1995).

651-A:7. Eligibility for Release; Life Sentences.

A prisoner serving a sentence of life imprisonment, except one convicted of murder in the first degree, one convicted of murder which was psycho-sexual in nature and committed prior to April 15, 1974, or one sentenced under RSA 632-A:10-a, III, may be given a life permit at any time after having served 18 years. Eighteen years shall be deemed the minimum term of his sentence for the purposes of this section, minus any credits received pursuant to RSA 651-A:23, plus the disciplinary period added to such minimum under RSA 651:2, II-e, any part of which is not reduced for good conduct as provided in RSA 651-A:22, provided that there shall appear to said board to be a reasonable probability that he will remain at liberty without violating the law and will conduct himself as a good citizen. The provisions of this section shall not apply to a prisoner serving a life sentence when the court, pursuant to RSA 630:1-b, II, has specified a minimum term other than that prescribed in this section.

Source.
1983, 461:16. 1992, 254:9, eff. Jan. 1, 1993.

Revision note.
Substituted "RSA 632-A:10-a, III" for "RSA 632-A:11, III" in the first sentence to conform to the renumbering of that section.

Amendments
—1992. Deleted "or" following "degree" and inserted "or one sentenced under RSA 632-A:11, III" following "1974" in the first sentence.

Cross References.
Psycho-sexual murder defined, see RSA 651-A:10.

NOTES TO DECISIONS

Cited:
Cited in Baker v. Cunningham, 128 N.H. 374, 513 A.2d 956, 1986 N.H. LEXIS 300 (1986); Bussiere v. Cunningham, 132 N.H. 747, 571 A.2d 908, 1990 N.H. LEXIS 19 (1990).

651-A:8. Eligibility for Parole; Persons Convicted of Psycho-Sexual Murder.

A prisoner serving a sentence of life imprisonment who has been convicted of murder which was psycho-sexual in nature and committed prior to April 15, 1974, shall not be eligible for parole until he shall have served 40 years minus any credits earned under the provisions of RSA 651-A:22 and RSA 651-A:23 and until the board shall recommend to the superior court that said prisoner should be released on parole. The superior court shall have a hearing on the recommendation of the board at which all interested parties, including the attorney general, may appear and present evidence. If it shall appear to the superior court after said hearing that there is a reasonable probability that the prisoner will remain at liberty without violating the law and will conduct himself as a good citizen, the court may order him released on parole with such conditions as it may deem just.

Source.
1983, 461:16, eff. July 1, 1983.

Cross References.
Psycho-sexual murder defined, see RSA 651-A:10.

NOTES TO DECISIONS

Constitutional law
Defendant convicted of first degree murder which at time of commission of crime would have subjected him to life imprisonment without parole was not subjected to an ex post facto law when sentenced under later legislation which provided sentence of life imprisonment with eligibility for parole after 40 years if murder was certified as being psycho-sexual in nature, since later legislation operated to mitigate penalty, not to increase or modify punishment to his detriment. State v. Breest, 116 N.H. 734, 367 A.2d 1320, 1976 N.H. LEXIS 463 (1976). (Decided under prior law.)

651-A:9. Psycho-Sexual Murder Certified.

Whenever any person is convicted of murder, committed prior to April 15, 1974, the presiding justice shall certify, at the time of sentencing, whether or not such murder was psycho-sexual in nature.

Source.
1983, 461:16, eff. July 1, 1983.

Cross References.
Psycho-sexual murder defined, see RSA 651-A:10.

NOTES TO DECISIONS

Time of certification
Where defendant convicted of first degree murder had started sentence of life imprisonment at time trial judge certified, at next term of court, that the murder was psycho-sexual in nature, which resulted in extending time in which defendant would be eligible for parole from 18 to 40 years, trial judge did not act contrary to appellate court's rulings holding that superior court could review a valid sentence after expiration of term of court if defendant had not started to serve it but could not reduce a sentence which was being served, since in this case there was no complete or valid sentence until trial court complied with requirements of this section. State v. Breest, 116 N.H. 734, 367 A.2d 1320, 1976 N.H. LEXIS 463 (1976). (Decided under prior law.)

651-A:10. Psycho-Sexual Murder Defined.

For the purposes of RSA 651-A:7, 8 and 9, the phrase "murder which is psycho-sexual in nature" means murder in which there is evidence that the offender has committed sexual assault or abuse or attempted sexual assault or abuse of the victim before or after death.

Source.
1983, 461:16, eff. July 1, 1983.

Cross References.
Sexual assault, see RSA 632-A:4.

NOTES TO DECISIONS

1. Constitutionality

2. Construction

1. Constitutionality
This section, which defined murder which is psycho-sexual in nature, was not unconstitutionally vague, since it provided ample notice of its purpose and prohibitions in such a manner that men of common intelligence did not need to guess at its intent. State v. Breest, 116 N.H. 734, 367 A.2d 1320, 1976 N.H. LEXIS 463 (1976). (Decided under prior law.)

2. Construction
This section, which defined murder which is psycho-sexual in nature, did not create a new and distinct criminal charge requiring a new finding of fact which was not a part of the charge of murder in the first degree for which defendant was tried. State v. Breest, 116 N.H. 734, 367 A.2d 1320, 1976 N.H. LEXIS 463 (1976). (Decided under prior law.)

651-A:10-a. Medical Parole.

I. Upon the recommendation of the commissioner of the department of corrections and the administrative director of forensic and medical services, after review of the information provided by a physician licensed pursuant to RSA 329, the parole board may grant medical parole to an inmate residing in a state correctional facility, regardless of the time remaining on his or her sentence, provided all of the following conditions apply:

(a) The inmate has a terminal, debilitating, incapacitating, or incurable medical condition or syndrome, as certified by a physician licensed pursuant to RSA 329, and, if requested by the parole board, at least one additional physician licensed pursuant to RSA 329.

(b) The cost of medical care, treatment, and resources for the inmate is determined to be excessive.

(c) The parole board has determined that the inmate will not be a danger to the public, and that there is a reasonable probability that the inmate will not violate the law while on medical parole and will conduct himself or herself as a good citizen.

II. The administrative director of forensic and medical services, on behalf of an inmate, may petition the parole board for hearing to determine if the inmate is eligible for medical parole and if the inmate is eligible, shall submit the parole plan to the parole board.

III. Medical parole shall only be granted by a majority vote which includes at least 3 votes of the members who are present and voting.

IV. The parole board may request, as a condition of medical parole, that such inmate submit to periodic medical examinations while on medical parole and comply with any other parole conditions imposed by the parole board. The administrative director of forensic and medical services, after review of any such medical examination shall report the findings to the parole board. If the parole board, after review of such findings, determines that the parolee no longer has a terminal, debilitating, incapacitating, or incurable medical condition or syndrome, the medical parole shall be revoked and the parolee shall be returned to the custody of the state.

V. Notwithstanding RSA 504-A:5, a medical parolee who is arrested under the authority of RSA 504-A:4 or RSA 651-A:25 shall be detained at the medical unit or infirmary of the appropriate state correctional facility closest to the location where he or she was arrested.

VI. An inmate who has been sentenced to life in prison without parole or sentenced to death shall not be eligible for medical parole under this section. Nothing in this provision or law shall be construed to create a right to medical parole for any inmate.

VII. Notwithstanding RSA 167:18-a, the state shall be responsible for all medicaid costs incurred, net of federal reimbursement, for any inmate granted medical parole under this section, until the earliest date on which parole could have been granted had the inmate not been granted medical parole.

VIII. [Repealed.]

Source.
2004, 218:3, eff. June 11, 2004; 218:5, eff. July 1, 2005. 2007, 263:19, eff. July 1, 2008. 2012, 134:1, eff. August 4, 2012.

Amendments
—**2012.** The 2012 amendment substituted "which includes at least 3 votes of the members who are present and voting" for "of the full 7-member parole board" in III.

—**2007.** Paragraph VII: Substituted "RSA 167:18-a" for "RSA 167:18-b".

—**2004.** Paragraph VIII: Repealed.

651-A:11. Notice of Hearings.

I. At least 15 and not more than 30 days prior to any parole hearing, the adult parole board shall twice publish, in a newspaper of general circulation within the county where the offense occurred, a notice stating the intention of the person to seek parole and shall post notice stating the intent of the person to seek parole in the adult parole board section of the department of corrections' Internet site. Said notices shall include the name and birth date of the applicant and the date, time, and location of the parole hearing.

II. At least 15 and not more than 30 days prior to any parole hearing, the adult parole board shall send by first class mail to each chief of police and county attorney of the place where the offense occurred, where the person resided prior to conviction, or where the person intends to reside after release, a copy of the information described in paragraph I.

II-a. At least 15 and not more than 30 days prior to any parole hearing, the adult parole board shall provide a copy of the information described in paragraph I to the department of corrections which shall send a copy of such information by first class mail to the victim of the person seeking parole, or to the next of kin of such victim if the victim has died, if request for such notice has been filed with the department of corrections. The victim or next of kin so requesting shall keep the department of corrections apprised of his or her current mailing address.

III. The adult parole board shall conduct no parole hearing without first having met the notice requirements of this section.

Source.
1983, 416:6, eff. July 1, 1983; 319:1, 2, eff. Aug. 17, 1983. 2013, 156:1, 2, eff. July 1, 2013.

Revision note.
Substituted "adult parole board" for "state board of parole". RSA 651:37, which provided for the establishment of the state board of parole, was repealed by 1983, 461, which enacted RSA 651-A:3, which provides for the establishment of the adult parole board.

Amendments
—**2013.** The 2013 amendment, in I, added "and shall post notice stating the intent of the person to seek parole in the adult parole board section of the department of corrections' Internet site" in the first sentence and in the second sentence, added "and birth date" and "time"; in the first sentence of II-a, substituted "provide" for "send" and "to the department of corrections which shall send a copy of such information by first class mail to the" for "by first class mail to the"; substituted "department of corrections" for "board" in the first and second sentence of II-a; and made stylistic changes.

—**1983.** Paragraph I: Amended generally.
Paragraph II: Deleted "to the commissioner of safety and" preceding "to each" and "county sheriff" thereafter.
Paragraph II-a: Added.

Applicability of 2013 amendment.
2013, 156:11, eff. July 1, 2013, provided: "The provisions of sections 1–8 of this act shall apply to:
"I. Any person who is on parole or eligible for parole, on or after the effective date of this act; and
"II. Any person who, on or after the effective date of this act, has violated the conditions of parole after a hearing pursuant to RSA 651-A:17."

Cross References.
Requirements relating to hearings generally, see RSA 651-A:3.
Victim or victim's next of kin permitted to speak at parole hearing, see RSA 651-A:11-a.

651-A:11-a. Victims Permitted to Speak at Parole Hearings.

The victim of any person seeking parole, or the victim's next of kin if the victim has died, shall have the right to appear at the parole hearing of such person, personally or by counsel, and to reasonably express his views concerning the offense and the person responsible.

Source.
1983, 319:3, eff. Aug. 17, 1983.

Cross References.
Victim or victim's next of kin permitted to speak before sentencing, see RSA 651:4-a.

NOTES TO DECISIONS

Cited:
Cited in Baker v. Cunningham, 128 N.H. 374, 513 A.2d 956, 1986 N.H. LEXIS 300 (1986).

651-A:12. Reduction of Maximum Sentence While on Parole.

Any person who is on parole from the state prison on a permit under the provisions of this chapter may be granted a reduction of maximum term of his sentence equal to ⅓ of the period of time during which the parolee is at liberty on said permit, provided that said parolee is not recommitted to the state prison or has not been cited as a parole violator, pursuant to the provisions of this chapter. The parolee may be granted a discharge at the expiration of his maximum sentence less deductions provided for in this chapter.

Source.
1983, 461:16, eff. July 1, 1983.

Cross References.
Credit for confinement prior to sentencing, see RSA 651-A:23.
Credits for good conduct, see RSA 651-A:22.
Early discharge of parolee for good conduct, see RSA 651-A:14.
Effect of recommittal, see RSA 651-A:19.

651-A:13. Suspension of Supervision.

In the case of a paroled prisoner who has entered the armed service of the United States, the board may suspend all parole supervision of said person during the period he so serves and is subject to military law. Upon the termination of such service by honorable discharge the board may, in its discretion, give the prisoner a final discharge.

Source.
1983, 461:16, eff. July 1, 1983.

651-A:14. Early Discharge for Good Conduct.

Whenever the board finds that the parolee is no longer in need of supervision because of his good conduct it may issue him a certificate of discharge.

Source.
1983, 461:16, eff. July 1, 1983.

Cross References.
Credits for good conduct, see RSA 651-A:22.

651-A:15. Complaint for Violation of Parole.

[Repealed 1986, 156:14, II, eff. May 28, 1986.]

Former section(s).
Former RSA 651-A:15, which was derived from 1983, 461:16, related to complaint for violation of parole. See now RSA 504-A:4.

651-A:15-a. Arrest of Parolees.

Any parolee may be arrested and detained by a probation or parole officer in accordance with RSA 504-A:4-6.

Source.
1986, 156:5, eff. May 28, 1986.

Cross References.
Revocation of parole, see RSA 651-A:17.

651-A:16. Report Required.

I. The department may report any parolee who violates the conditions of his parole to the parole board. However, the department shall, within 30 days of official knowledge of such an occurrence,

submit a report on any parolee who:

(a) Is arrested for any felony or misdemeanor offense;

(b) Is convicted of any felony, misdemeanor or other offense; provided, however, that the department need only report traffic offenses deemed to be serious traffic offenses under RSA 265;

(c) Absconds from supervision for a period of 30 days or more;

(d) Commits 3 or more parole violations of any type within a 12 month period; or

(e) Is placed in an intermediate sanction by a probation/parole officer in lieu of revocation.

II. This report shall include information on the circumstances of the alleged violation as well as a recommendation as to whether parole should be revoked.

Source.
1983, 461:16, eff. July 1, 1983. 2010, 247:7, eff. July 1, 2010. 2013, 156:3, eff. July 1, 2013.

Amendments
—2013. The 2013 amendment deleted "program" following "intermediate sanction" in I(e).

—2010. The 2010 amendment added I(e) and made related changes.

Applicability of 2013 amendment.
2013, 156:11, eff. July 1, 2013, provided: "The provisions of sections 1–8 of this act shall apply to:
"I. Any person who is on parole or eligible for parole, on or after the effective date of this act; and
"II. Any person who, on or after the effective date of this act, has violated the conditions of parole after a hearing pursuant to RSA 651-A:17."

Cross References.
Classification of crimes, see RSA 625:9.

651-A:16-a. Intermediate Sanction.

I. The commissioner shall establish a 7-day residential sanction located in a halfway house facility.

II. Probation/parole officers may place a parolee in an intermediate sanction in lieu of a parole revocation hearing only if the offender agrees to participate.

Source.
2010, 247:8, eff. July 1, 2010. 2013, 156:4, eff. July 1, 2013.

Amendments
—2013. The 2013 amendment deleted "program" following "sanction" in the section heading and in II and substituted "a 7-day residential sanction" for "one or more intermediate sanction programs to include a 7-day residential program" in I.

Applicability of enactment.
2010, 247:13, IV, eff. July 1, 2010, provided that RSA 651-A:16-a as inserted by section 8 of this act shall apply to any person who is on parole as of October 1, 2010 or thereafter.

651-A:17. Parole Revocation.

Any parolee arrested under RSA 651-A:15-a shall be entitled to a hearing before the board within 45 days, in addition to any preliminary hearing which is required under RSA 504-A:5. The parolee shall have the right to appear and be heard at the revocation hearing. The board shall have power to subpoena witnesses, pay said witnesses such fees and expenses as allowed under RSA 516:16, and administer oaths in any proceeding or examination instituted before or conducted by it, and to compel, by subpoena duces tecum, the production of any accounts, books, contracts, records, documents, memoranda, papers or tangible objects of any kind. If the board, after a hearing, finds that the parolee has violated the conditions of parole, violated the law, or associated with criminal companions and in its judgment should be returned to the custody of the commissioner of corrections, the board shall revoke the parole. A prisoner whose parole is revoked shall be recommitted to the custody of the commissioner of corrections. This provision shall not apply to a parolee who has accepted an option, offered by a probation/parole officer, to participate in an intermediate sanction program and has waived his or her right to counsel and to a preliminary hearing under RSA 504-A:5.

Source.
1983, 461:16. 1986, 156:6. 1987, 180:1, eff. Jan. 1, 1988. 1996, 93:10, eff. Jan. 1, 1997. 2010, 247:9, eff. July 1, 2010.

Amendments
—2010. The 2010 amendment substituted "RSA 504-A:5" for "RSA 504-A:6" in the first sentence and added the last sentence.

—1996. Substituted "45 days" for "30 days" in the first sentence and deleted "his" following "conditions of" and substituted "the" for "his" preceding "parole" in the fourth sentence.

—1987. Added the third sentence.

—1986. Substituted "RSA 651-A:15-a" for "RSA 651-A:15" in the first sentence and "the revocation" for "this" preceding "hearing" in the second sentence and added "in addition to any preliminary hearing which is required under RSA 504-A:6" following "30 days" at the end of the first sentence.

Applicability of 2013 amendment.
2013, 156:11, eff. July 1, 2013, provided: "The provisions of sections 1–8 of this act shall apply to:
"I. Any person who is on parole or eligible for parole, on or after the effective date of this act; and
"II. Any person who, on or after the effective date of this act, has violated the conditions of parole after a hearing pursuant to RSA 651-A:17."

Cross References.
Effect of recommittal, see RSA 651-A:19.

NOTES TO DECISIONS

1. Due process
2. Jurisdiction
3. Waiver
4. Review
5. Habeas relief

1. Due process
Liberty of parolee could be terminated only in accordance with requisite procedural due process, including right, after due notice, to inquiry by uninvolved judicial or administrative officer who would conduct a preliminary hearing to determine whether there was probable cause to believe that arrested parolee had committed acts which constituted a violation of parole conditions. Belton v. Vitek, 113 N.H. 183, 304 A.2d 362, 1973 N.H. LEXIS 230 (1973). (Decided under prior law.)

2. Jurisdiction
A parolee, by leaving this state in violation of his unexpired parole, could not convert his subsequent convictions and confinements in prisons of other jurisdictions into a waiver of this state's jurisdiction to enforce a warrant for a violation of parole. Peare v. State, 107 N.H. 197, 219 A.2d 289, 1966 N.H. LEXIS 154 (1966). (Decided under prior law.)

Sentence imposed upon prisoner for second crime while still in legal custody of state parole board and prior to its revocation of parole permit, to commence only upon expiration of prior sentence, was in effect return of prisoner to parole board for recommittal to prison under original sentence and hence board's jurisdiction to commit him to prison was not superseded by superior court. Tsoukalas v. Hancock, 102 N.H. 417, 158 A.2d 296, 1960 N.H. LEXIS 46 (1960). (Decided under prior law.)

3. Waiver
No violation of RSA 651-A:15-a, RSA 651-A:17 or of N.H. Code Admin. R. Ann. Parole 208.01(b) took place when, after the State requested a continuance, a parolee's revocation hearing was held 49 days after the last of three hearing dates which had been rescheduled at the parolee's request; the 45-day period in both provisions creates a right to a hearing within 45 days of arrest which does not recur each time a hearing is rescheduled, and the parolee had expressly waived his right to a hearing each time he requested a continuance. Debonis v. Warden, N.H. State Prison, 153 N.H. 603, 903 A.2d 993, 2006 N.H. LEXIS 78 (2006).

4. Review
Although the legislature has not provided a procedure to appeal revocation of parole, habeas corpus is an available remedy and the superior court has jurisdiction to review actions of the parole board. Martel v. Hancock, 115 N.H. 237, 339 A.2d 9, 1975 N.H. LEXIS 271 (1975). (Decided under prior law.)

5. Habeas relief
Petitioner was not entitled to habeas relief based on respondents' alleged failure to hold a parole revocation hearing within 45 days of her arrest under RSA 651-A:17. Because she conceded that there was no prejudice, her Fourteenth Amendment due process claim failed, and habeas relief was not available for the alleged statutory violation alone. Barnet v. Warden, 159 N.H. 465, 986 A.2d 579, 2009 N.H. LEXIS 131 (2009).

Cited:
Cited in Reynolds v. Cunningham, 131 N.H. 312, 556 A.2d 300, 1988 N.H. LEXIS 141 (1988).

651-A:18. Revocation Required.

I. The board may revoke the parole of any parolee who:
   (a) Violates the conditions of his parole;
   (b) Violates the law; or
   (c) Associates with criminal companions.
II. The board shall revoke the parole of any parolee who:
   (a) Is convicted of a felony; or
   (b) Absconds from parole supervision for a period of 60 days or more.
III–V. [Repealed.]

Source.
1983, 461:16. 1986, 156:14, III. 1991, 342:2. 1993, 26:1, eff. April 8, 1993.

Amendments
—1993. Paragraphs IV, V: Repealed.

—1991. Paragraph IV: Added.
Paragraph V: Added.

—1986. Paragraph III: Repealed.

Cross References.
Classification of crimes, see RSA 625:9.
Revocation of parole generally, see RSA 651-A:17.

NOTES TO DECISIONS

Application

Trial court did not err in relying upon RSA 651-A:19 in denying defendant pretrial confinement credit when defendant was arrested for burglary after being arrested for a parole violation. When the judge accepted and entered defendant's guity plea to the burglary charges, parole revocation became mandatory under RSA 651-A:18, II(a); consequently, under RSA 651-A:19, the time between defendant's return to prison after his arrest on the parole violation warrant and his conviction on the burglary charges, which effectively constituted revocation of his parole, was to be considered as time served as a portion of the maximum sentence. State v. Forest, 163 N.H. 616, 44 A.3d 563, 2012 N.H. LEXIS 72 (2012).

651-A:19. Effect of Recommittal.

I. A prisoner who is recommitted shall serve 90 days in prison before being placed back on parole or the remainder of his or her maximum sentence, whichever is shorter, or may be subject to an extended term of recommittal pursuant to paragraphs III and IV. The time between the return of the parolee to prison after arrest and revocation of parole shall be considered as time served as a portion of the maximum sentence. The 90-day recommittal period may be calculated from the date of the arrest or from the date of the hearing, as ordered by the parole board.

II. Prisoners who are recommitted shall be provided access to focused, evidence-based programming aimed at reengaging parolees in their parole plan.

III. The parole board may impose an extended term of recommittal for greater than 90 days if:

(a) The prisoner has previously been found true for a parole violation on his or her current sentence or another sentence for which he or she was concurrently serving a term of parole; or

(b) The prisoner was on parole for a sexual offense as defined in RSA 651-B:1, V or an offense against a child as defined in RSA 651-B:1, VII; and

(1) The conduct underlying the parole violation is related to his or her offense or offending pattern; or

(2) The prisoner has displayed a combination of dynamic risk factors, including but not limited to, homelessness, loss of supports, substance abuse, or non-compliance with treatment, as determined by the department of corrections sexual offender treatment program staff; or

(3) Both subparagraphs (1) and (2); or

(c) The prisoner was on parole for a violent crime as defined in RSA 651:5, XIII; or

(d) The nature of the conduct underlying the parole violation constitutes a criminal act or is otherwise so serious as to warrant an extended period of recommittal.

IV. (a) A prisoner may be brought before the parole board at any time during the 90-day term of recommittal to determine whether a longer term is warranted if:

(1) The prisoner did not meaningfully participate in the evidence-based programming during the 90-day recommittal period; or

(2) The prisoner received one or more major disciplinary violations during the 90-day recommittal period.

(b) The prisoner shall be provided notice of the hearing and the basis of the parole board's consideration of an extended term.

V. The imposition of an extended term of recommittal pursuant to paragraph III or IV shall be supported by written findings and a written order.

VI. Any prisoner who is subject to an extended term of recommittal shall, upon request, be entitled to a hearing before the parole board after serving 6 months of his or her term of recommittal and every 6 months thereafter.

VII. At the revocation hearing, the parole board may impose a term of recommittal for less than 90 days if:

(a) The prisoner has not been previously found true for a parole violation on his or her current sentence or another sentence for which he or she was concurrently serving a term of parole;

(b) The prisoner was not on parole for a sexual offense as defined in RSA 651-B:1, V or an offense against a child as defined in RSA 651-B:1, VII;

(c) The prisoner was not on parole for a violent crime as defined in RSA 651:5, XIII;

(d) The parole violation is not substantially related to his or her offense or offending pattern; and

(e) The parole board determines that a lesser period of recommittal will aid in the rehabilitation of the parolee.

Source.
1983, 461:16, eff. July 1, 1983. 2010, 247:10, eff. July 1, 2010. 2011, 244:3, eff. July 13, 2011. 2013, 156:5–7, eff. July 1, 2013.

Amendments
—2013. The 2013 amendment added the last sentence of I and in III(a) and VII(a), substituted "found true" for "recommitted" and added "on his or her current sentence or another sentence for which he or she was concurrently serving a term of parole."

—2011. The 2011 amendment added "or may be subject to an extended term of recommittal pursuant to paragraphs III and IV" in the first sentence of I; substituted "provided access to" for "housed separately in a prison housing unit that provides" in II; and added III through VII.

—2010. The 2010 amendment added the I designation; in I, in the first sentence, substituted "shall serve 90 days in prison before being placed back on parole or the remainder" for "may, at any time before the expiration" and "whichever is shorter" for "except as provided in RSA 651-A:18, be paroled again" and deleted the former second sentence, which read: "If not paroled, a prisoner who is recommitted shall serve the remainder of his maximum sentence minus any credits to which he may thereafter become entitled under RSA 651-A:22 and 23 and less the period of time the prisoner was at liberty in satisfactory compliance with the terms and conditions of his parole"; added II; and made stylistic changes.

Applicability of 2013 amendment.
2013, 156:11, eff. July 1, 2013, provided: "The provisions of sections 1–8 of this act shall apply to:
"I.   Any person who is on parole or eligible for parole, on or after the effective date of this act; and
"II.   Any person who, on or after the effective date of this act, has violated the conditions of parole after a hearing pursuant to RSA 651-A:17."

Applicability of enactment.
2010, 247:13, IV, eff. July 1, 2010, provided that RSA 651-A:19 as inserted by section 10 of this act shall apply to any person who is on parole as of October 1, 2010 or thereafter.

NOTES TO DECISIONS

1. Construction
2. Credits

1. Construction
Under the doctrine of expressio unius est exclusio alterius, in light of the reference in the first sentence of former RSA 651-A:19, I, to both the maximum sentence and the 90-day recommitment period, the inclusion of only "maximum sentence" in the second sentence, addressing how to apply credit for time served post-arrest/pre-revocation, indicates that the legislature intended this credit to be applied solely to reduce the maximum sentence and not to reduce the recommitment period (unless necessary to avoid exceeding the maximum sentence). Gentry v. Warden, 163 N.H. 280, 37 A.3d 433, 2012 N.H. LEXIS 18 (2012).
Former RSA 651-A:19 did not permit the parole board to credit the time habeas petitioner spent in confinement between his arrest and revocation of his parole against his ninety-day recommitment period. Gentry v. Warden, 163 N.H. 280, 37 A.3d 433, 2012 N.H. LEXIS 18 (2012).
Period of confinement for inability to furnish bail prior to conviction and sentence was not to be considered as "time between the return of the parolee to prison after his arrest and revocation of the [parole] permit" within the meaning of this section, which provided for credit toward time parolee was to serve for violation of parole. Tsoukalas v. Hancock, 102 N.H. 417, 158 A.2d 296, 1960 N.H. LEXIS 46 (1960). (Decided under prior law.)

2. Credits
Trial court did not err in relying upon RSA 651-A:19 in denying defendant pretrial confinement credit when defendant was arrested for burglary after being arrested for a parole violation. When the judge accepted and entered defendant's guilty plea to the burglary charges, parole revocation became mandatory under RSA 651-A:18, II(a); consequently, under RSA 651-A:19, the time between defendant's return to prison after his arrest on the parole violation warrant and his conviction on the burglary charges, which effectively constituted revocation of his parole, was to be considered as time served as a portion of the maximum sentence. State v. Forest, 163 N.H. 616, 44 A.3d 563, 2012 N.H. LEXIS 72 (2012).

651-A:20. Parole Records.

The adult parole board or its designee shall have access to all parole records of the department. The board shall review the records of the department for each parolee in its custody at least once every 36 months.

Source.
1983, 461:16, eff. July 1, 1983.

Revision note.
Substituted "adult parole board" for "board of parole" for purpose of conformity with RSA 651-A:3.

Cross References.
Parole board records exempt from right to know law, see RSA 91-A:5.

651-A:21. Final Discharge.

I. Upon the expiration of the term of his maximum sentence as provided in RSA 651-A:18 and 19, a paroled prisoner shall be entitled to receive a final discharge, provided that at the time of such expiration no proceedings are pending for his recommitment. Such proceedings shall be deemed to be pending when a warrant has been issued or an arrest has been made under RSA 651-A:15-a.

II. For each parolee affected by this section, the board shall determine the amount of time the parolee was at liberty while in noncompliance with the terms and conditions of parole, as specified in RSA 651-A:19. The board may recommit the parolee to the state prison for a period not to exceed the amount of time so determined.

Source.
1983, 461:16. 1986, 156:7, eff. May 28, 1986.

Amendments
—1986.   Paragraph I: Substituted "provided in RSA 651-A:18 and 19" for "herein provided" in the first sentence and "RSA 651-A:15-a" for "RSA 651-A:15" in the second sentence, inserted "or an arrest has been made" following "warrant has been issued" in the second sentence, and made other minor stylistic changes.

Cross References.
Probationers and parolees generally, see RSA 504-A.
Revocation of parole, see RSA 651-A:17.

651-A:22. Credits for Good Conduct.

I. The commissioner of corrections shall, on a monthly basis, review the conduct of each prisoner subject to parole to determine whether the prisoner shall receive credit for good conduct as provided in this section.

II. The commissioner shall by rule determine the standards for the earning of credit for good conduct. Such rules shall not be subject to the provisions of RSA 541-A. Such rules shall establish standards for prisoners to receive credit for participating in programs designed to reduce recidivism of participants, as determined by the commissioner.

III. If, as a result of the review provided in paragraph I, the commissioner determines that a prisoner has exhibited good conduct, he may reduce the additional disciplinary period provided in RSA 651:2, II-e of such prisoner by up to 12-½ days for each month during which the prisoner has exhibited such good conduct.

IV. Credits may be granted subject to the provisions of this section provided that:
(a) Any prisoner who escapes from the state prison or from custody of any person charged with his custodial safekeeping, or from the limits of his minimum custody or community corrections boundaries or agreements will automatically suffer the loss of all accrued good conduct credits. This loss is

in addition to and not in lieu of any other administrative or judicial punishment later imposed for the escape.

(b) Any serious act of misconduct or insubordination, or persistent refusal to conform to prison regulations during his confinement shall subject the prisoner to the loss of all or any portion of such credits, at the discretion of the commissioner.

(c) The commissioner at his discretion may restore all or part of the good conduct credits lost under subparagraphs (a) or (b) should the prisoner later demonstrate exemplary behavior.

(d) Provided further, that upon a prisoner's release on parole any such credits earned prior to his release shall not thereafter be lost.

V. Any good conduct credit earned against a maximum sentence by a prisoner before August 22, 1979, except for loss in the manner provided by this section, shall be unaffected by enactment of this section.

Source.

1983, 461:16. 1987, 180:2, eff. Jan. 1, 1988. 2010, 247:11, eff. July 1, 2010.

Revision note.

In pars. I–IV, substituted "commissioner of corrections" and "commissioner" for "warden of the state prison" and "warden" pursuant to 1983, 461:4. 1983, 461:3 terminated the position of warden of the state prison and transferred all powers, duties and functions of that position to the commissioner of corrections.

Amendments

—2010. The 2010 amendment added the last sentence of II.

—1987. Paragraph III: Deleted "and the maximum sentence" following "RSA 651:2, II-e".

Cross References.

Early discharge for good conduct, see RSA 651-A:14.

NOTES TO DECISIONS

Cited:

Cited in State ex rel. McLellan v. Cavanaugh, 127 N.H. 33, 498 A.2d 735, 1985 N.H. LEXIS 397 (1985); Gangi v. Cunningham, 127 N.H. 780, 508 A.2d 1050, 1986 N.H. LEXIS 235 (1986).

651-A:23. Credit for Confinement Prior to Sentencing.

Any prisoner who is confined to the state prison, any house of correction, any jail or any other place shall be granted credit against both the maximum and minimum terms of his sentence equal to the number of days during which the prisoner was confined in jail awaiting and during trial prior to the imposition of sentence and not under any sentence of confinement. The clerk of the court sentencing a prisoner shall record in the mittimus the number of days of such confinement, and the credit provided for herein shall be calculated on the basis of such information.

Source.

1983, 461:16, eff. July 1, 1983.

NOTES TO DECISIONS

1. Generally
2. Extradition
3. Time credited
4. Consecutive sentences

1. Generally

One principle underlying RSA 651:3, I and this section is that an indigent offender unable to furnish bail should serve no more and no less time in confinement than an otherwise identically situated offender who succeeds in furnishing bail. State v. Decker, 127 N.H. 468, 503 A.2d 796, 1985 N.H. LEXIS 466 (1985).

RSA 651:3, I and this section stem principally from the recognition that presentence detention is often the result of indigency. State v. Decker, 127 N.H. 468, 503 A.2d 796, 1985 N.H. LEXIS 466 (1985).

2. Extradition

Because term "awaiting and during trial" under RSA 651-A:23 encompasses all time from the moment of arrest through the completion of the trial and sentencing, defendant was entitled to credit for pretrial confinement in Colombia while awaiting extradition. State v. Duran, 158 N.H. 146, 960 A.2d 697, 2008 N.H. LEXIS 139 (2008).

The statute does not extend pretrial confinement credit to fugitives from New Hampshire justice who are awaiting extradition in another state. State v. Harnum, 142 N.H. 195, 697 A.2d 1380, 1997 N.H. LEXIS 75 (1997), overruled, State v. Duran, 158 N.H. 146, 960 A.2d 697, 2008 N.H. LEXIS 139 (2008).

3. Time credited

When defendant was arrested for a parole violation before being arrested for burglary and remained incarcerated at least in part as a result of the parole violation, his incarceration was not exclusively related to the burglary for which he was sentenced. Thus, trial court was not mandated to grant pretrial confinement credit under RSA 651-A:23. State v. Forest, 163 N.H. 616, 44 A.3d 563, 2012 N.H. LEXIS 72 (2012).

Trial court did not err in relying upon RSA 651-A:19 in denying defendant pretrial confinement credit when defendant was arrested for burglary after being arrested for a parole violation. When the judge accepted and entered defendant's guilty plea to the burglary charges, parole revocation became mandatory under RSA 651-A:18, II(a); consequently, under RSA 651-A:19, the time between defendant's return to prison after his arrest on the parole violation warrant and his conviction on the burglary charges, which effectively constituted revocation of his parole, was to be considered as time served as a portion of the maximum sentence. State v. Forest, 163 N.H. 616, 44 A.3d 563, 2012 N.H. LEXIS 72 (2012).

Although RSA 651-A:23 does not require a sentencing court to award pretrial confinement credit in circumstances where the defendant also is being held in custody for a parole violation, nothing in the statute prohibits the court from doing so. State v. Forest, 163 N.H. 616, 44 A.3d 563, 2012 N.H. LEXIS 72 (2012).

Where the trial court allocated 71 days of pretrial credit toward the State Prison sentences and the remaining 365 days toward the misdemeanor sentence, defendant lost any opportunity to earn time off of his house of correction sentence for good behavior and thus could serve more time than a similarly situated offender who furnished bail; accordingly, the allocation of pretrial credit was vacated. State v. Edson, 153 N.H. 45, 889 A.2d 420, 2005 N.H. LEXIS 179 (2005).

Defendant was not entitled to pretrial confinement credit for time spent released on bail under conditions requiring home confinement and electronic monitoring, since restrictions on defendant's liberty did not rise to level of control associated with incarceration in jail. State v. Duquette, 145 N.H. 374, 761 A.2d 520, 2000 N.H. LEXIS 72 (2000).

"Awaiting and during trial" encompasses all time from the moment of arrest through the completion of the trial and sentencing; in so holding, the Supreme Court of New Hampshire joins the overwhelming majority of jurisdictions that have decided this issue. State v. Harnum, 142 N.H. 195, 697 A.2d 1380, 1997 N.H. LEXIS 75 (1997), is overruled. State v. Duran, 158 N.H. 146, 960 A.2d 697,

2008 N.H. LEXIS 139 (2008).

RSA 651:3, I and this section mandate that a prisoner is to receive credit for all jail time—neither more nor less—served before sentencing which relates to the criminal episode for which the prisoner is sentenced, but does not receive credit greater than the number of days of his presentencing confinement. State v. Decker, 127 N.H. 468, 503 A.2d 796, 1985 N.H. LEXIS 466 (1985).

4. Consecutive sentences

Trial court properly applied RSA 651:3, I and this section in denying defendant multiple credit for his period of pretrial confinement, where defendant contended he was entitled to credit toward each of his three consecutive sentences, since a prisoner should not receive credit greater than the number of days of his presentencing confinement. State v. Decker, 127 N.H. 468, 503 A.2d 796, 1985 N.H. LEXIS 466 (1985).

Cited:

Cited in State v. Philbrick, 127 N.H. 353, 499 A.2d 1341, 1985 N.H. LEXIS 426 (1985).

651-A:24. Administrative Attachment.

The parole board shall be administratively attached to the department of corrections. The department shall provide budgeting, recordkeeping, and related clerical assistance to the board. The commissioner shall have no administrative authority over the board, its executive assistant or its duties.

Source.

1983, 461:16, eff. July 1, 1983.

651-A:25. Execution of Compact Authorized.

The governor of this state is hereby authorized and directed to execute a compact on behalf of the state of New Hampshire with any of the United States legally joining therein in the form substantially as follows:

A Compact entered into by and among the contracting states, signatories hereto, with the consent of the Congress of the United States of America, granted by an act entitled "An Act Granting the Consent of Congress to any two or more States to enter into Agreements or Compacts for Cooperative Effort and Mutual Assistance in the Prevention of Crime and for other purposes."

The contracting states solemnly agree:

I. That it shall be competent for the duly constituted judicial and administrative authorities of a state party to this compact, herein called "sending state," to permit any person convicted of an offense within such state and placed on probation or released on parole to reside in any other state party to this compact, herein called "receiving state," while on probation or parole, if (a) Such person is in fact a resident of or has his family residing within the receiving state and can obtain employment there; (b) Though not a resident of the receiving state and not having his family residing there, the receiving state consents to such person being sent there. Before granting such permission, opportunity shall be granted to the receiving state to investigate the home and prospective employment of such person. A resident of the receiving state, within the meaning of this section, is one who has been an actual inhabitant of such state continuously for more than one year prior to his coming to the sending state and has not resided within the sending state more than 6 continuous months immediately preceding the commission of the offense for which he has been convicted.

II. That each receiving state will assume the duties of visitation of and supervision over probationers or parolees of any sending state and in the exercise of those duties will be governed by the same standards that prevail for its own probationers and parolees.

III. That duly accredited officers of a sending state may at all times enter a receiving state and there apprehend and retake any person on probation or parole. For that purpose no formalities will be required other than establishing the authority of the officer and the identity of the person to be retaken. All legal requirements to obtain extradition of fugitives from justice are hereby expressly waived on the part of states party hereto, as to such persons. The decision of the sending state to retake a person on probation or parole shall be conclusive upon and not reviewable within the receiving state; provided, however, that if at the time when a state seeks to retake a probationer or parolee there should be pending against him within the receiving state any criminal charge, or he should be suspected of having committed within such state a criminal offense, he shall not be retaken without the consent of the receiving state until discharge from prosecution or from imprisonment for such offense.

III-a. Notwithstanding any other law to the contrary, any hearings, including final revocation hearings, to which a probationer or parolee is entitled prior to incarceration or reincarceration for a violation of probation or parole may, at the discretion of the court or parole board involved, be held before the appropriate court or parole board of the receiving state. In such event, the appropriate court or parole board of the sending state shall transfer jurisdiction of the case to the appropriate court of the receiving state.

IV. That the duly accredited officers of the sending state will be permitted to transport prisoners being retaken through any and all states parties to this compact, without interference.

V. That the governor of each state may designate an officer who, acting jointly with like officers of other contracting states, if and when appointed, shall promulgate such rules and regulations as may be deemed necessary to more effectively carry out the terms of this compact.

VI. That this compact shall become operative immediately upon its execution by any state as between it and any other state or states so executing. When executed it shall have the full force and effect of law within such state, the form of execution to be in accordance with the laws of the executing state.

VII. That this compact shall continue in force and remain binding upon each executing state until renounced by it. The duties and obligations hereunder of a renouncing state shall continue as to parolees or probationers residing therein at the time of withdrawal until retaken or finally discharged by the sending state. Renunciation of this compact shall be by the same authority which executed it, by sending 6 months' notice in writing of its intention to withdraw from the compact to the other states party hereto.

VIII. It is hereby declared that the word "state" as used in this subdivision means any one of the several states and Alaska, Hawaii, the Commonwealth of Puerto Rico, the Virgin Islands, and the District of Columbia. It is hereby recognized and further declared that pursuant to the consent and authorization contained in Section 112(b) of title 4 of the United States Code as added by Public Law 970-84th Congress, Chapter 941-2d Session, this state shall be a party to said Interstate Compact for the Supervision of Parolees and Probationers with any additional jurisdiction legally joining therein when such jurisdiction shall have enacted said compact, in accordance with the terms thereof.

IX. An individual who is on parole or probation in another state, who is present in this state without the permission of the officer of this state designated under paragraph V of this section, and who does not leave this state within 7 days after being notified in writing by a law enforcement officer that the individual may not remain in this state without the permission of the designated officer, is guilty of a class B felony.

X. Within 24 hours after a law enforcement officer has notified an individual that he or she may not remain within the state without the permission of the designated officer, the law enforcement officer shall report the notification to the designated officer. An individual who is on parole or probation in another state may not remain in this state without the permission of the officer of this state designated under paragraph V of this section. In a prosecution for an offense under this section, an individual's good faith belief that he or she had received permission to be present in this state is an affirmative defense if the individual acted in reasonable reliance upon the written statements of an authorized officer of this state or the state in which the individual is on parole or probation. This defense is not available to a person who remains present in this state after being notified in writing by the designated officer of this state that the individual does not have permission to be present.

Source.
1983, 461:16. 1993, 112:2, eff. July 3, 1993. 2000, 300:1, eff. Jan. 1, 2001.

References in text.
The Act of Congress referred to in the introductory paragraph of the Compact is classified to 4 U.S.C.S. § 112.

Revision note.
In par. VIII, substituted "Section 112(b)" of title 4 of the United States Code for "Section 111(b)" to conform the reference to the renumbering of that section.

Amendments
—2000. Added pars. IX and X.

—1993. Paragraph III-a: Added.

Operative date of paragraph III-a.
1993, 112:2, eff. July 3, 1993, provided: "Section 2 of this act [which added par. III-a of this section] shall become operative immediately upon its execution by any state as between it and any other state or states so executing. When executed it shall have the full force and effect of law within such state, the form of execution to be in accordance with the laws of the executing state."

NOTES TO DECISIONS

1.. Constitutionality
2.. Sufficiency of indictment

1. Constitutionality
RSA 651-A:25, IX is not void for vagueness under the federal Constitution on the ground that it fails to provide people of ordinary intelligence a reasonable opportunity to understand what conduct it prohibits. No one of ordinary intelligence, told to leave New Hampshire because he or she does not have permission to stay, would believe that he or she may return to New Hampshire without permission. State v. Lamarche, 157 N.H. 337, 950 A.2d 172, 2008 N.H. LEXIS 67 (2008).

2. Sufficiency of indictment
Indictment for being in New Hampshire without permission while on probation in another state was not insufficient under the federal Constitution. It was not necessary that the indictment allege that defendant failed to leave the state within seven days; it only needed to allege that he was in the state without permission more than seven days after he was told to leave. State v. Lamarche, 157 N.H. 337, 950 A.2d 172, 2008 N.H. LEXIS 67 (2008).

Cited:
Cited in Goss v. State, 142 N.H. 915, 714 A.2d 225, 1998 N.H. LEXIS 59 (1998).

Interstate Compact for Adult Offender Supervision

Purpose.
2003, 230:1, eff. Jan. 1, 2004, provided:

"I. The compacting states to this Interstate compact recognize that each state is responsible for the supervision of adult offenders in the community who are authorized pursuant to the bylaws and rules of this compact to travel across state lines both to and from each compacting state in such a manner as to, track the location of offenders, transfer supervision authority in an orderly and efficient manner, and when necessary, return offenders to the originating jurisdictions.

"II. The compacting states also recognize that Congress, by enacting the Crime Control Act, 4 U.S.C. Section 112 (1965), has authorized and encouraged compacts for cooperative efforts and mutual assistance in the prevention of crime.

"III. It is the purpose of this compact and the interstate commission created hereunder, through means of joint and cooperative action among the compacting states, to provide the framework for the promotion of public safety and protect the rights of victims through the control and regulation of the interstate movement of offenders in the community, to provide for the effective tracking, supervision, and rehabilitation of these offenders by the sending and receiving states, and to equitably distribute the costs, benefits and obligations of the compact among the compacting states.

"IV. In addition, this compact will, create an interstate commission which will establish uniform procedures to manage the movement between states of adults placed under community supervision and released to the community under the jurisdiction of courts, paroling authorities, corrections or other criminal justice agencies which will adopt rules to achieve the purpose of this compact, ensure an opportunity for input and timely notice to victims and to jurisdictions where defined offenders are authorized to travel or to relocate across state lines, establish a system of uniform data collection, access to information on active cases by authorized criminal justice officials, and regular reporting of compact activities to heads of state councils, state executive, judicial, and legislative branches and criminal justice administrators, monitor compliance with rules governing interstate movement of offenders and initiate interventions to address and correct non-compliance, and coordinate training and education regarding regulations of interstate movement of offenders for officials involved in such activity.

"V. The compacting states recognize that there is no right of any offender to live in another state and that duly accredited officers of a sending state may at all times enter a receiving state and there apprehend and retake any offender under supervision subject to the provisions of this compact and bylaws and rules adopted hereunder. It is the policy of the compacting states that the activities conducted by the interstate commission created herein are the formation of public policies and are therefore public business."

651-A:26. Definitions.

As used in this compact:

I. "Adult" means both individuals legally classified as adults and juveniles treated as adults by court order, statute, or operation of law.

II. "Bylaws" mean those bylaws established by the interstate commission for its governance, or for directing or controlling the interstate commission's actions or conduct.

III. "Compact administrator" means the individual in each compacting state appointed pursuant to the terms of this compact responsible for the administration and management of the state's supervision and transfer of offenders subject to the terms of this compact, the rules adopted by the interstate commission and policies adopted by the state council under this compact.

IV. "Compacting state" means any state which has enacted the enabling legislation for this compact.

V. "Commissioner" means the voting representative of each compacting state appointed pursuant to this compact.

VI. "Interstate commission" means the interstate commission for adult offender supervision established by this compact.

VII. "Member" means the commissioner of a compacting state or designee, who shall be a person officially connected with the commissioner.

VIII. "Non-compacting state" means any state which has not enacted the enabling legislation for this compact.

IX. "Offender" means an adult placed under, or subject, to supervision as the result of the commission of a criminal offense and released to the community under the jurisdiction of courts, paroling authorities, corrections, or other criminal justice agencies.

X. "Person" means any individual, corporation, business enterprise, or other legal entity, either public or private.

XI. "Rules" means acts of the interstate commission, duly adopted pursuant to this compact, substantially affecting interested parties in addition to the interstate commission, which shall have the force and effect of law in the compacting states.

XII. "State" means a state of the United States, the District of Columbia and any other territorial possessions of the United States.

XIII. "State council" means the resident members of the state council for interstate adult offender supervision created by each state under this compact.

Source.
2003, 230:2, eff. Jan. 1, 2004.

651-A:27. Interstate Commission Established.

I. The compacting states hereby create the interstate commission for adult offender supervision. The interstate commission shall be a body corporate and joint agency of the compacting states. The interstate commission shall have all the responsibilities, powers and duties set forth herein, including the power to sue and be sued, and such additional powers as may be conferred upon it by subsequent action of the respective legislatures of the compacting states in accordance with the terms of this compact.

II. The interstate commission shall consist of commissioners selected and appointed by resident members of a state council for interstate adult offender supervision for each state. While each member state may determine the membership of its own state council, its membership must include at least one representative from the legislative, judicial, and executive branches of government, victims groups and compact administrators. Each state council shall appoint as its commissioner the compact administrator from that state to serve on the interstate commission in such capacity under or pursuant to applicable law of the member state. Each compacting state retains the right to determine the qualifications of the compact administrator who shall be appointed by the state council or by the governor in consultation with the legislature and the judiciary. In addition to appointment of its' commissioner to the National Interstate Commission, each state council shall exercise oversight and advocacy concerning its participation in interstate commission activities and other duties as may be determined by each member state, including but not limited to, development of policy concerning operations and procedures of the compact within that state.

III. In addition to the commissioners who are the voting representatives of each state, the interstate commission shall include individuals who are not commissioners but who are members of interested organizations; such non-commissioner members must include a member of the national organizations of governors, legislators, state chief justices, attorneys general and crime victims. All non-commissioner members of the interstate commission shall be ex-officio, non-voting members. The interstate commission may provide in its bylaws for such additional, ex-officio, non-voting members as it deems necessary.

IV. Each compacting state represented at any meeting of the interstate commission is entitled to one vote. A majority of the compacting states shall constitute a quorum for the transaction of business, unless a larger quorum is required by the bylaws of the interstate commission.

V. The interstate commission shall meet at least once each calendar year. The chairperson may call additional meetings and, upon the request of 27 or more compacting states, shall call additional meetings. Public notice shall be given of all meetings and meetings shall be open to the public.

VI. The interstate commission shall establish an executive committee which shall include commission officers, members and others as shall be determined by the bylaws. The executive committee shall have the power to act on behalf of the interstate commission during periods when the interstate commission is not in session, with the exception of rulemaking and/or amendment to the compact. The executive committee oversees the day-to-day activities managed by the executive director and interstate commission staff; administers enforcement and compliance with the provisions of the compact, its bylaws and as directed by the interstate commission and performs other duties as directed by the commission or set forth in the bylaws.

Source.
2003, 230:2, eff. Jan. 1, 2004.

651-A:28. Powers and Duties of the Interstate Commission.

The interstate commission shall have the following powers:

I. To adopt a seal and suitable bylaws governing the management and operation of the interstate commission.

II. To adopt rules which shall have the force and effect of statutory law and shall be binding in the compacting states to the extent and in the manner provided in this compact.

III. To oversee, supervise and coordinate the interstate movement of offenders subject to the terms of this compact and any bylaws adopted and rules adopted by the compact commission.

IV. To enforce compliance with compact provisions, interstate commission rules, and bylaws, using all necessary and proper means, including but not limited to, the use of judicial process.

V. To establish and maintain offices.

VI. To purchase and maintain insurance and bonds.

VII. To borrow, accept, or contract for services of personnel, including, but not limited to, members and their staffs.

VIII. To establish and appoint committees and hire staff which it deems necessary for the carrying out of its functions including, but not limited to, an executive committee as required by this compact which shall have the power to act on behalf of the interstate commission in carrying out its powers and duties hereunder.

IX. To elect or appoint such officers, attorneys, employees, agents, or consultants, and to fix their compensation, define their duties and determine their qualifications; and to establish the interstate commission's personnel policies and programs relating to, among other things, conflicts of interest, rates of compensation, and qualifications of personnel.

X. To accept any and all donations and grants of money, equipment, supplies, materials, and services, and to receive, utilize, and dispose of same.

XI. To lease, purchase, accept contributions or donations of, or otherwise to own, hold, improve, or use any property, real, personal, or mixed.

XII. To sell, convey, mortgage, pledge, lease, exchange, abandon, or otherwise dispose of any property, real, personal or mixed.

XIII. To establish a budget and make expenditures and levy dues as provided in this compact.

XIV. To sue and be sued.

XV. To provide for dispute resolution among compacting states.

XVI. To perform such functions as may be necessary or appropriate to achieve the purposes of this compact.

XVII. To report annually to the legislatures, governors, judiciary, and state councils of the compacting states concerning the activities of the interstate commission during the preceding year. Such reports shall also include any recommendations that may have been adopted by the interstate commission.

XVIII. To coordinate education, training and public awareness regarding the interstate movement of offenders for officials involved in such activity.

XIX. To establish uniform standards for the reporting, collecting, and exchanging of data.

Source.
2003, 230:2, eff. Jan. 1, 2004.

651-A:29. Organization and Operation of the Interstate Commission.

The interstate commission shall, by a majority of the members, within 12 months of the first interstate commission meeting, adopt bylaws to govern its conduct as may be necessary or appropriate to carry out the purposes of the compact, including, but not limited to:

I. Establishing the fiscal year of the interstate commission;

II. Establishing an executive committee and such other committees as may be necessary;

III. Providing reasonable standards and procedures for the establishment of committees, and governing any general or specific delegation of any authority or function of the interstate commission;

IV. Providing reasonable procedures for calling and conducting meetings of the interstate commission, and ensuring reasonable notice of each such meeting;

V. Establishing the titles and responsibilities of the officers of the interstate commission;

VI. Providing reasonable standards and procedures for the establishment of the personnel policies and programs of the interstate commission. Notwithstanding any civil service or other similar laws of any compacting state, the bylaws shall exclusively govern the personnel policies and programs of the interstate commission;

VII. Providing a mechanism for winding up the operations of the interstate commission and the equitable return of any surplus funds that may exist upon the termination of the compact after the payment or reserving of all of its debts and obligations;

VIII. Providing transition rules for start up administration of the compact; and

IX. Establishing standards and procedures for compliance and technical assistance in carrying out the compact.

Source.
2003, 230:2, eff. Jan. 1, 2004.

651-A:30. Officers and Staff of the Interstate Commission.

I. The interstate commission shall, by a majority of the members, elect from among its members a chairperson and a vice chairperson, each of whom shall have such authorities and duties as may be specified in the bylaws. The chairperson or, in his or her absence or disability, the vice chairperson, shall preside at all meetings of the interstate commission. The officers so elected shall serve without compensation or remuneration from the interstate commission; provided that subject to the availability of budgeted funds, the officers shall be reimbursed for any actual and necessary costs and expenses incurred by them in the performance of their duties and responsibilities as officers of the interstate commission.

II. The interstate commission shall, through its executive committee, appoint or retain an executive director for such period, upon such terms and conditions and for such compensation as the interstate commission may deem appropriate. The executive director shall serve as secretary to the interstate commission, and hire and supervise such other staff as may be authorized by the interstate commission, but shall not be a member.

III. The interstate commission shall maintain its corporate books and records in accordance with the bylaws.

IV. The members, officers, executive director and employees of the interstate commission shall be immune from suit and liability, either personally or in their official capacity, for any claim for damage to or loss of property or personal injury or other civil liability caused or arising out of any actual or alleged act, error or omission that occurred within the scope of interstate commission employment, duties or responsibilities; provided, that nothing in this paragraph shall be construed to protect any such person from suit and/or liability for any damage, loss, injury or liability caused by the intentional or willful and wanton misconduct of any such person.

V. The interstate commission shall defend the commissioner of a compacting state, or his or her representatives or employees, or the interstate commission's representatives or employees, in any civil action seeking to impose liability, arising out of any actual or alleged act, error or omission that occurred within the scope of interstate commission employment, duties or responsibilities, or that the defendant had a reasonable basis for believing occurred within the scope of interstate commission employment, duties or responsibilities; provided, that the actual or alleged act, error or omission did not result from intentional wrongdoing on the part of such person.

VI. The interstate commission shall indemnify and hold the commissioner of a compacting state, the appointed designee or employees, or the interstate commission's representatives or employees, harmless in the amount of any settlement or judgment obtained against such persons arising out of any actual or alleged act, error or omission that occurred within the scope of interstate commission employment, duties or responsibilities, or that such persons had a reasonable basis for believing occurred within the scope of interstate commission employment, duties or responsibilities, provided, that the actual or alleged act, error or omission did not result from gross negligence or intentional wrongdoing on the part of such person.

Source.
2003, 230:2, eff. Jan. 1, 2004.

651-A:31. Activities of the Interstate Commission.

I. The interstate commission shall meet and take such actions as are consistent with the provisions of this compact.

II. Except as otherwise provided in this compact and unless a greater percentage is required by the bylaws, in order to constitute an act of the interstate commission, such act shall have been taken at a meeting of the interstate commission and shall have received an affirmative vote of a majority of the members present.

III. Each member of the interstate commission shall have the right and power to cast a vote to which that compacting state is entitled and to participate in the business and affairs of the interstate commission. A member shall vote in person on behalf of the state and shall not delegate a vote to another member state. However, a state council shall appoint another authorized representative, in the absence of the commissioner from that state, to cast a vote on behalf of the member state at a specified meeting. The bylaws may provide for members' participation in meetings by telephone or other means of telecommunication or electronic communication. Any voting conducted by telephone, or other means of telecommunication or electronic communication shall be subject to the same quorum requirements of meetings where members are present in person.

IV. The interstate commission shall meet at least once during each calendar year. The chairperson of the interstate commission may call additional meetings at any time and, upon the request of a majority of the members, shall call additional meetings.

V. The interstate commission's bylaws shall establish conditions and procedures under which the interstate commission shall make its information and official records available to the public for inspection or copying. The interstate commission may exempt from disclosure any information or official records to the extent they would adversely affect personal privacy rights or proprietary interests. In promulgating such rules, the interstate commission may make available to law enforcement agencies records and information otherwise exempt from disclosure, and may enter into agreements with law enforcement agencies to receive or exchange information or records subject to non-disclosure and confidentiality provisions.

VI. Public notice shall be given of all meetings and all meetings shall be open to the public, except as set forth in the rules or as otherwise provided in the compact. The interstate commission shall adopt rules consistent with the principles contained in the "Government in Sunshine Act," 5 U.S.C. Section 552(b), as may be amended. The interstate commission and any of its committees may close a meeting to the public where it determines by two-thirds vote that an open meeting would be likely to:

(a) Relate solely to the interstate commission's internal personnel practices and procedures.

(b) Disclose matters specifically exempted from disclosure by statute.

(c) Disclosure of trade secrets or commercial or financial information which is privileged or confidential.

(d) Involve accusing any person of a crime, or formally censuring any person.

(e) Disclose information of a personal nature where disclosure would constitute a clearly unwarranted invasion of personal privacy.

(f) Disclose investigatory records compiled for law enforcement purposes.

(g) Disclose information contained in or related to examination, operating or condition reports prepared by, or on behalf of or for the use of, the interstate commission with respect to a regulated entity for the purpose of regulation or supervision of such entity.

(h) Disclose information, the premature disclosure of which would significantly endanger the life of a person or the stability of a regulated entity.

(i) Specifically relate to the interstate commission's issuance of a subpoena, or its participation in a civil action or proceeding.

VII. For every meeting closed pursuant to this provision, the interstate commission's chief legal officer shall publicly certify that, in his or her opinion, the meeting may be closed to the public, and shall reference each relevant exemptive provision. The interstate commission shall keep minutes which shall fully and clearly describe all matters discussed in any meeting and shall provide a full and accurate summary of any actions taken, and the reasons therefor, including a description of each of the views expressed on any item and the record of any roll call vote reflected in the vote of each member on the question. All documents considered in connection with any action shall be identified in such minutes.

VIII. The interstate commission shall collect standardized data concerning the interstate movement of offenders as directed through its bylaws and rules which shall specify the data to be collected, the means of collection and data exchange and reporting requirements.

Source.
2003, 230:2, eff. Jan. 1, 2004.

651-A:32. Rulemaking.

I. The interstate commission shall adopt rules, pursuant to RSA 541-A, to effectively and efficiently achieve the purposes of the compact including transition rules governing administration of the compact during the period in which it is being considered and enacted by the states;

II. Rulemaking shall occur pursuant to the criteria set forth in this section and the bylaws and rules adopted pursuant hereunder. Such rulemaking shall substantially conform to the principles of the federal Administrative Procedure Act, 5 U.S.C.S. section 551 et seq., and the Federal Advisory Committee Act, 5 U.S.C.S. app. 2, section 1 et seq., as may be amended (hereinafter "APA").

III. All rules and amendments shall become binding as of the date specified in each rule or amendment.

IV. If a majority of the legislatures of the compacting states rejects a rule, by enactment of a statute or resolution in the same manner used to adopt the compact, then such rule shall have no further force and effect in any compacting state.

V. When promulgating a rule, the interstate commission shall:

(a) Publish the proposed rule stating with particularity the text of the rule which is proposed and the reason for the proposed rule.

(b) Allow persons to submit written data, facts, opinions and arguments, which information shall be publicly available.

(c) Provide an opportunity for an informal hearing.

(d) Adopt a final rule and its effective date, if appropriate, based on the rulemaking record.

VI. Not later than sixty days after a rule is adopted, any interested person may file a petition in the United States district court for the District of Columbia or in the federal district court where the interstate commission's principal office is located for judicial review of such rule. If the court finds that the interstate commission's action is not supported by substantial evidence, in the rulemaking record, the court shall hold the rule unlawful and set it aside.

VII. Subjects to be addressed within 12 months after the first meeting must at a minimum include:

(a) Notice to victims and opportunity to be heard.

(b) Offender registration and compliance.

(c) Violations/returns.

(d) Transfer procedures and forms.

(e) Eligibility for transfer.

(f) Collection of restitution and fees from offenders.

(g) Data collection and reporting.

(h) The level of supervision to be provided by the receiving state.

(i) Transition rules governing the operation of the compact and the interstate commission during all or part of the period between the effective date of the compact and the date on which the last eligible state adopts the compact.

(j) Mediation, arbitration and dispute resolution.

IX. Upon determination by the interstate commission that an emergency exists, it may adopt an emergency rule which shall become effective immediately upon adoption, provided that the usual rulemaking procedures provided hereunder shall be retroactively applied to said rule as soon as reasonably possible, in no event later than 90 days after the effective date of the rule.

Source.
2003, 230:2, eff. Jan. 1, 2004.

651-A:33. Oversight, Enforcement, and Dispute Resolution.

I. The interstate commission shall oversee the interstate movement of adult offenders in the compacting states and shall monitor such activities being administered in non-compacting states which may significantly affect compacting states.

II. The courts and executive agencies in each compacting state shall enforce this compact and shall take all actions necessary and appropriate to effectuate the compact's purposes and intent. In any judicial or administrative proceeding in a compacting state pertaining to the subject matter of this compact which may affect the powers, responsibilities or actions of the interstate commission, the interstate commission shall be entitled to receive all service of process in any such proceeding, and shall have standing to intervene in the proceeding for all purposes.

III. The compacting states shall report to the interstate commission on issues or activities of concern to them, and cooperate with and support the interstate commission in the discharge of its duties and responsibilities.

IV. The interstate commission shall attempt to resolve any disputes or other issues which are subject to the compact and which may arise among compacting states and non-compacting states.

V. The interstate commission shall enact a law or adopt a rule providing for both mediation and binding dispute resolution for disputes among the compacting states.

Source.
2003, 230:2, eff. Jan. 1, 2004.

651-A:34. Finance.

I. The interstate commission shall pay or provide for the payment of the reasonable expenses of its establishment, organization and ongoing activities.

II. The interstate commission shall levy on and collect an annual assessment from each compacting state to cover the cost of the internal operations and activities of the interstate commission and its staff which must be in a total amount sufficient to cover the interstate commission's annual budget as approved each year. The aggregate annual assessment amount shall be allocated based upon a formula to be determined by the interstate commission, taking into consideration the population of the state and the volume of interstate movement of offenders in each compacting state and shall adopt rules binding upon all compacting states which govern said assessment.

III. The interstate commission shall not incur any obligations of any kind prior to securing the funds adequate to meet the same, nor shall the interstate commission pledge the credit of any of the compacting states, except by and with the authority of the compacting state.

IV. The interstate commission shall keep accurate accounts of all receipts and disbursements. The receipts and disbursements of the interstate commission shall be subject to the audit and accounting procedures established under its bylaws. However, all receipts and disbursements of funds handled by the interstate commission shall be audited yearly by a certified or licensed public accountant and the report of the audit shall be included in and become part of the annual report of the interstate commission.

Source.
   2003, 230:2, eff. Jan. 1, 2004.

651-A:35. Compacting States, Amendment.

I. Any state, as defined in this compact, is eligible to become a compacting state.

II. The compact shall become effective and binding upon legislative enactment of the compact into law by no less than 35 of the states. The initial effective date shall be the later of July 1, 2001, or upon enactment into law by the 35th jurisdiction. Thereafter it shall become effective and binding, as to any other compacting state, upon enactment of the compact into law by that state. The governors of non-member states or their designees will be invited to participate in interstate commission activities on a non-voting basis prior to adoption of the compact by all states and territories of the United States.

III. Amendments to the compact may be proposed by the interstate commission for enactment by the compacting states. No amendment shall become effective and binding upon the interstate commission and the compacting states unless and until it is enacted into law by unanimous consent of the compacting states.

Source.
   2003, 230:2, eff. Jan. 1, 2004.

651-A:36. Withdrawal, Default, Termination, and Judicial Enforcement.

I. Once effective, the compact shall continue in force and remain binding upon each and every compacting state; provided, that a compacting state may withdraw from the compact by enacting a statute specifically repealing the statute which enacted the compact into law.

II. The effective date of withdrawal is the effective date of the repeal.

III. The withdrawing state shall immediately notify the chairperson of the interstate commission in writing upon the introduction of legislation repealing this compact in the withdrawing state.

IV. The interstate commission shall notify the other compacting states of the withdrawing state's intent to withdraw within sixty days of its receipt thereof.

V. The withdrawing state is responsible for all assessments, obligations and liabilities incurred through the effective date of withdrawal, including any obligations, the performance of which extend beyond the effective date of withdrawal.

VI. Reinstatement following withdrawal of any compacting state shall occur upon the withdrawing state reenacting the compact or upon such later date as determined by the interstate commission.

VII. If the interstate commission determines that any compacting state has at any time defaulted in the performance of any of its obligations or responsibilities under this compact, the bylaws or any duly adopted rules, the interstate commission may impose any or all of the following penalties:

(a) Fines, fees and costs in such amounts as are deemed to be reasonable as fixed by the interstate commission.

(b) Remedial training and technical assistance as directed by the interstate commission.

(c) Suspension and termination of membership in the compact. Suspension shall be imposed only after all other reasonable means of securing compliance under the bylaws and rules have been exhausted. Immediate notice of suspension shall be given by the interstate commission to the governor, the chief justice or chief judicial officer of the state; the majority and minority leaders of the defaulting state's legislature, and the state council. The grounds for default include, but are not limited to, failure of a compacting state to perform such obligations or responsibilities imposed upon it by this compact, interstate commission bylaws, or duly adopted rules. The interstate commission shall immediately notify the defaulting state in writing of the penalty imposed by the interstate commission on the defaulting state pending a cure of the default. The interstate commission shall stipulate the conditions and the time period within which the defaulting state must cure its default. If the defaulting state fails to cure the default within the time period specified by the interstate commission, in addition to any other penalties imposed herein, the defaulting state may be terminated from the compact upon an affirmative vote of a majority of the compacting states and all rights, privileges and benefits conferred by this compact shall be terminated from the effective date of suspension.

VIII. Within 60 days of the effective date of termination of a defaulting state, the interstate commission shall notify the governor, the chief justice or chief judicial officer and the majority and minority leaders of the defaulting state's legislature and the state council of such termination.

IX. The defaulting state is responsible for all assessments, obligations and liabilities incurred through the effective date of termination including any obligations, the performance of which extends beyond the effective date of termination.

X. The interstate commission shall not bear any costs relating to the defaulting state unless otherwise mutually agreed upon between the interstate commission and the defaulting state.

XI. Reinstatement following termination of any compacting state requires both a reenactment of the compact by the defaulting state and the approval of the interstate commission pursuant to the rules.

XII. The interstate commission may, by majority vote of the members, initiate legal action in the United States district court for the District of Columbia or, at the discretion of the interstate commission, in the federal district where the interstate commission has its offices to enforce compliance with the provisions of the compact, its duly adopted rules and bylaws, against any compacting state in default. In the event judicial enforcement is necessary the prevailing party shall be awarded all costs of such litigation including reasonable attorneys fees.

XIII. The compact dissolves effective upon the date of the withdrawal or default of the compacting state which reduces membership in the compact to one compacting state.

XIV. Upon the dissolution of this compact, the compact becomes null and void and shall be of no further force or effect, and the business and affairs of the interstate commission shall be wound up and any surplus funds shall be distributed in accordance with the bylaws.

Source.
2003, 230:2, eff. Jan. 1, 2004.

651-A:37. Severability and Construction.

I. The provisions of this compact shall be severable, and if any phrase, clause, sentence or provision is deemed unenforceable, the remaining provisions of the compact shall be enforceable.

II. The provisions of this compact shall be liberally constructed to effectuate its purposes.

Source.
2003, 230:2, eff. Jan. 1, 2004.

651-A:38. Binding Effect.

I. Nothing herein prevents the enforcement of any other law of a compacting state that is not inconsistent with this compact.

II. All compacting states' laws conflicting with this compact are superseded to the extent of the conflict.

III. All lawful actions of the interstate commission, including all rules and bylaws adopted by the interstate commission, are binding upon the compacting states.

IV. All agreements between the interstate commission and the compacting states are binding in accordance with their terms.

V. Upon the request of a party to a conflict over meaning or interpretation of interstate commission actions, and upon a majority vote of the compacting states, the interstate commission may issue advisory opinions regarding such meaning or interpretation.

VI. In the event any provision of this compact exceeds the constitutional limits imposed on the legislature of any compacting state, the obligations, duties, powers or jurisdiction sought to be conferred by such provision upon the interstate commission shall be ineffective and such obligations, duties, powers or jurisdiction shall remain in the compacting state and shall be exercised by the agency

thereof to which such obligations, duties, powers or jurisdiction are delegated by law in effect at the time this compact becomes effective.

Source.
2003, 230:2, eff. Jan. 1, 2004.

CHAPTER 651-B

REGISTRATION OF CRIMINAL OFFENDERS

SECTION
651-B:1.   Definitions.
651-B:2.   Registration.
651-B:3.   Release of Certain Sexual Offenders Into the Community; Duties.
651-B:4.   Duty to Report.
651-B:4-a. Registration of Online Identifiers.
651-B:5.   Change of Registration Information; Duty to Inform.
651-B:6.   Duration of Registration.
651-B:7.   Availability of Information to the Public and Law Enforcement.
651-B:8.   Rules.
651-B:9.   Penalty.
651-B:10.   Hearing.
651-B:11.   Registration Fee.
651-B:12.   Application.

Applicability of RSA 651-B enactment.
1996, 293:3, eff. Aug. 9, 1996, provided:

"I. This act [which repealed RSA 632-A:11–632-A:19 and enacted RSA 651-B] shall apply to any sexual offender, irrespective of the date of conviction of the offense, who:

"(a) Is released into the community as provided in RSA 651-B:3 on or after July 16, 1993; or

"(b) Has been released but has not completed his sentence before July 16, 1993; or

"(c) Has completed his sentence not more than 6 years before January 1, 1994.

"II. This act shall apply to any offender against children, irrespective of the date of conviction of the offense, who:

"(a) Is released into the community as provided in RSA 651-B:3 on or after the effective date of this act; or

"(b) Has been released but has not completed his sentence before the effective date of this act."

651-B:1. Definitions.

In this chapter:

I. "Department" means the department of safety.

II. "Division" means the division of state police, department of safety.

III. "Local law enforcement agency" means the chief of police in the city or town where the person resides or is temporarily domiciled, or, if the municipality has no police chief or if the person resides in an unincorporated place, the division.

IV. "Sexual offender" means a person who is required to register for any sexual offense.

V. "Sexual offense" means the following offenses, including an accomplice to, or an attempt, conspiracy, or solicitation to commit, any of the following offenses, where the victim was 18 years of age or older at the time of the offense:

(a) Capital murder, RSA 630:1, I(e); first degree murder, RSA 630:1-a, I(b)(1); aggravated felonious sexual assault, RSA 632-A:2; felonious sexual assault, 632-A:3; sexual assault, 632-A:4, I(a) or RSA 632-A:4, III; violation of privacy, RSA 644:9, I(a) or RSA 644:9, III-a; second or subsequent offense within a 5-year period for indecent exposure and lewdness, RSA 645:1, I(a).

(b) A law of another state, country, territory, tribal territory, or the federal government reasonably equivalent to a violation listed in subparagraph (a). For purposes of this section, the term "country" refers to Canada, Great Britain, Australia, and New Zealand, as well as any other country that the United States State Department has determined has an independent judiciary that generally enforces the right to a fair trial.

(c) Any offense for which the offender is required to register pursuant to the law in the jurisdiction where the conviction occurred.

(d) Any other criminal offense which is not specifically listed in subparagraph (a) if the court finds by clear and convincing evidence at the time of conviction or sentencing that the person committed the offense as a result of sexual compulsion or for purposes of sexual gratification and protection of the public would be furthered by requiring the person to register. In determining whether the offender should be required to register, the court may consider the offender's prior criminal history and any other relevant information. If the court determines that the offender should be required to register, the court shall determine whether the offender should be required to register pursuant to the requirements of a tier I, tier II, or tier III offender. In determining in which tier the offender should register, the court shall consider the nature of other offenses that are currently listed in each tier; the extent to which public safety would be furthered; whether the victim was a minor when the offense occurred; and any other relevant factors. The hearing at which such a determination is made shall comply with due process requirements, including a right to appeal the finding. The court shall provide the defendant an opportunity to be heard on the issue prior to the imposition of the registration requirement and shall state on the record the reasons for its findings and the reasons for requiring registration.

VI. "Offender against children" means a person who is required to register for an offense against a child.

VII. "Offense against a child" means the following offenses, including an accomplice to, or an attempt, conspiracy, or solicitation to commit, any of the following offenses:

(a) Any of the following offenses, where the victim was under the age of 18 at the time of the offense: capital murder, RSA 630:1, I(e); first degree murder, RSA 630:1-a, 1(b)(1); aggravated felonious sexual assault, RSA 632-A:2; felonious sexual assault, RSA 632-A:3; sexual assault, RSA 632-A:4, I(a) or RSA 632-A:4, III; kidnapping, RSA 633:1; criminal restraint, RSA 633:2; false imprisonment, RSA 633:3; incest, RSA 639:2; violation of privacy, RSA 644:9, I(a) or RSA 644:9, III-a; a second or subsequent offense within a 5-year period for indecent exposure and lewdness, RSA 645:1, 1(a); indecent exposure and lewdness, RSA 645:1, I(b), RSA 645:1, II, and RSA 645:1, III; or prostitution, RSA 645:2.

(b) Intentional contribution to the delinquency of a minor, RSA 169-B:41, II; sexual assault, RSA 632-A:4, I(b) if the actor was 18 years of age or older at the time of the offense; endangering the welfare of a child, RSA 639:3, III; child pornography, RSA 649-A:3, RSA 649-A:3-a and RSA 649-A:3-b; computer pornography, RSA 649-B:3; certain uses of computer services prohibited, RSA 649-B:4; or obscene matters, RSA 650:2, II.

(c) A law of another state, country, territory, tribal territory, or the federal government reasonably equivalent to a violation listed in subparagraph (a) or (b). For purposes of this section, the term "country" refers to Canada, Great Britain, Australia, and New Zealand, as well as any other country that the United States State Department has determined has an independent judiciary that generally enforces the right to a fair trial.

(d) Any offense involving a victim under the age of 18 for which the offender is required to register pursuant to the law in the jurisdiction where the conviction occurred.

(e) Any other criminal offense which is not specifically listed in subparagraph (a) if the court finds by clear and convincing evidence at the time of conviction or sentencing that the person committed the offense as a result of sexual compulsion or for purposes of sexual gratification and protection of the public would be furthered by requiring the person to register. In determining whether the offender is required to register, the court may consider the offender's prior criminal history and any other relevant information. If the court determines that the offender is required to register, the court shall determine if the offender shall register as a tier I, tier II, or tier III offender. In determining the tier in which the offender is to be registered, the court shall consider the nature of other offenses that are currently listed in each tier, the extent to which public safety would be furthered, whether the victim was a minor when the offense occurred, and any other relevant factors. The hearing at which such a determination is made shall comply with due process requirements, including a right to appeal the findings. The defendant shall have the opportunity to be heard prior to the imposition of the registration requirement, and the court shall state on the record the reasons for its findings and the reasons for requiring registration.

VIII. "Tier I offender" means a sexual offender or offender against children who is required to register pursuant to RSA 651-B:1, V(d) or RSA 651-B:1, VII(e), or is required to register as a result of any of the following offenses:

(a) RSA 632-A:4, I(a); RSA 632-A:4, I(b); RSA 632-A:4, III; RSA 644:9, I(a); RSA 644:9, III-a; or a second or subsequent offense within a 5-year period for indecent exposure and lewdness, RSA 645:1, I.

(b) A law of another state, territory, tribal territory, or the federal government reasonably equivalent to a violation listed in subparagraph (a).

(c) Any out-of-state offense for which the offender is required to register in the state where the conviction occurred and the division determines the offender is a tier I offender.

(d) Any offense not listed in subparagraph (a) where the court determined the offender is a tier I offender and required the offender to register.

IX. "Tier II offender" means a sexual offender or offender against children who is required to register pursuant to RSA 651-B:1, V(d) or RSA 651-B:1, VII(e), or is required to register as a result of any of the following offenses:

(a) RSA 169-B:41, II; RSA 632-A:3, I; RSA 632-A:3, II; RSA 632-A:3, IV if the victim was 13 years of age or older but less than 18 years of age; RSA 633:2; RSA 633:3; RSA 639:3, III; RSA 645:1, II; RSA 645:1, III; RSA 645:2; RSA 649-A:3; RSA 649-A:3-a; RSA 649-A:3-b; RSA 649-B:3; RSA 649-B:4; or RSA 650:2, II.

(b) A law of another state, territory, tribal territory, or the federal government reasonably equivalent to a violation listed in subparagraph (a).

(c) Any out-of-state offense for which the offender is required to register in the state where the conviction occurred and the division determines the offender is a tier II offender.

(d) The offender is required to register as a result of more than one sexual offense or offense against a child.

(e) Any offense not listed in subparagraph (a) where the court determined the offender is a tier II offender and required the offender to register.

X. "Tier III offender" means a sexual offender or offender against children who is required to register pursuant to RSA 651-B:1, V(d) or RSA 651-B:I, VII(e), or is required to register as a result of any of the following:

(a) RSA 630:1, I(e), RSA 630:1-a, I(b)(1), RSA 632-A:2, RSA 632-A:3, III, RSA 632-A:3, IV if the victim was under the age of 13, RSA 633:1; or RSA 639:2.

(b) Any sexual offense or offense against a child if the offender was sentenced to an extended term of imprisonment pursuant to RSA 651:6.

(c) Any person civilly committed as a sexually violent predator pursuant to RSA 135-E.

(d) A law of another state, territory, tribal territory, or the federal government reasonably equivalent to a violation listed in subparagraph (a).

(e) Any out-of-state offense for which the offender is required to register in the state where the conviction occurred, and the division determines the offender is a tier III offender.

(f) The offender is required to register as a result of more than 2 sexual offenses or offenses against a child.

(g) Any offense not listed in subparagraph (a) where the court determined the offender is a tier III offender and required the offender to register.

XI. (a) "Required to register" means that a sexual offender or offender against children was charged with an offense or an attempt, conspiracy, solicitation, or as an accomplice to commit a sexual offense or offense against a child that resulted in one of the following outcomes:

(1) Conviction.

(2) A finding of not guilty by reason of insanity.

(3) An adjudication as a juvenile delinquent and the court at the time of the dispositional hearing finds, pursuant to RSA 169-B:19, that the juvenile is required to register.

(4) An adjudication of juvenile delinquency or its equivalent in another state or territory of the United States if the juvenile is required to register under the laws of that jurisdiction.

(5) An order committing the person as a sexually violent predator pursuant to RSA 135-E.

(b) A juvenile certified to stand trial as an adult, who is convicted, found not guilty by reason of insanity, or committed as a sexually violent predator, shall be treated as an adult for all purposes under this chapter.

XII. "SOR system" means the division of state police sex offender registry system.

XIII. Notwithstanding RSA 21:6-a, "residence" means a place where a person is living or temporarily staying for more than a total of 5 days during a one-month period, such as a shelter or structure that can be located by a street address, including, but not limited to, houses, apartment buildings, motels, hotels, homeless shelters, and recreational and other vehicles.

Source.

1996, 293:1, eff. Aug. 9, 1996. 1999, 177:3, eff. Aug. 30, 1999; 321:2, eff. Jan. 1, 2000. 2003, 316:8, eff. Jan. 1, 2004. 2004, 69:1, eff. Jan. 1, 2005. 2005, 214:1–3, eff. January 1, 2006; 290:2, eff. January 1, 2006. 2006, 162:4, eff. January 1, 2007; 327:1–4, eff. January 1, 2007. 2008, 323:9, eff. January 1, 2009 (see editor's note below); 334:1, eff. January 1, 2009. 2009, 306:3, eff. July 31, 2009. 2010, 78:1–6, eff. January 1, 2011.

Editor's note.

2008, 323:9, eff. January 1, 2009, purports to amend par. V(b) of this section by adding references to 649-A:3-a and 649-A:3-b. However, this amendment was adopted apparently without consideration of the amendment of this section by 2008, 334:1, eff. January 1, 2009, which substantially rewrote the section. In order to reconcile the conflicting amendments and give effect to the intent of 2008, 323:9, the references to 649-A:3-a and 649-A:3-b have been inserted in par. VII(b) following the reference to 649-A:3.

2008, 323:10, eff. January 1, 2009, purports to amend par. I of RSA 651-B:6 by adding references to RSA 649-A:3-a (distribution of child sexual abuse images) and RSA 649-A:3-b (manufacture of child sexual abuse images). However, this amendment was adopted apparently without consideration of the amendment of RSA 651-B:6 by 2008, 334:4, which rewrote the section to eliminate the specific statutory references in favor of Tier I, Tier II and Tier III offender classifications as defined by this section (as amended by 2008, 334:1, eff. January 1, 2009). Therefore, in order to reconcile these conflicting amendments, the references to RSA 649-A:3-a and 649-A:3-b have been added to the Tier II offender definition found in par. IX(a) of this section.

Amendments

—2010. The 2010 amendment added "including an accomplice to, or an attempt, conspiracy, or solicitation to commit, any of the following offenses" in the introductory language of V and VII; substituted "pursuant to the law in the jurisdiction" for "in the state" in V(c) and VII(d); added "if the victim was 13 years of age or older but less than 18 years of age" in IX(a); in X(a), added "RSA 632-A:3, IV if the victim was under the age of 13" and "or RSA 639:2"; and made a related change.

—2009. The 2009 amendment added "or a" preceding "second or" and substituted "RSA 645:1, I" for "RSA 645:1, I(a)" in V(a); substituted "RSA 645:1, I" for "RSA 645:1, 1(a)" and deleted "RSA 645:1, I(b)" in VII(a); rewrote VII(b); substituted "RSA 645:1, I" for "RSA 645:1, I(a); or RSA 645:, I(b)" in VII(a); added "RSA 649-A:3-a; RSA 649-A:3-b" and "II" following "RSA 650:2" in IX(a); and made related changes.

—2008. The 2008 amendment rewrote the section to the extent that a detailed comparison would be impracticable.

—2006. Paragraph III: Rewritten to the extent that a detailed comparison would be impracticable.

Paragraph V(a): Chapter 162 inserted "RSA 632-A:2, RSA 632-A:3" preceding "RSA 633:1" and inserted "RSA" preceding "633:2", "633:3", "639:2" and "645:2".

Paragraph V(c): Chapter 327 made a punctuation change.

Paragraph V(d): Added by Chapter 327.

Paragraph VII: Chapter 327 rewrote to the extent that a detailed comparison would be impracticable.

Paragraph VIII: Added by Chapter 327.

—2005. Paragraph III: Rewritten to the extent that a detailed comparison would be impracticable.

Paragraph V: Substituted "is required to register as a result" for "has been convicted" in the introductory paragraph.

Paragraph VII: Added.

Paragraph III: In subparagraph (a), inserted "632-A:4, I(b) if the actor was 21 years of age or older at the time of the offense".

—2004. Paragraph III: Inserted "or acquitted by reason of insanity" following "convicted" in the introductory paragraph.

—2003. Paragraph III(a): Inserted "I(a)" following "RSA 632-A:4".

—1999. Paragraph III(a): Deleted "or" preceding "645:1, II" and inserted "or 645:1, III" thereafter.

Paragraph V(a): Inserted "639:2" following "633:3".

Paragraph V(b): Inserted "649-B:3, 649-B:4" following "649-A:3".

Applicability of enactment.

See note preceding this section.

Applicability of 2010 amendment.

2010, 78:9, eff. January 1, 2011, provided: "RSA 651-B shall apply to any sexual offender or offender against children, regardless of the date of conviction, juvenile delinquency adjudication, finding of not guilty by reason of insanity, or commitment under RSA 135-E."

Applicability of 2003 amendment.

2003, 316:6, eff. September 20, 2003, provided that the amendment to this section, by section 8 of the act, shall apply to any person required to be registered pursuant to RSA 651-B:2 as of September 20, 2003.

NOTES TO DECISIONS

1. Equivalency of offenses
2. Evidence
3. Construction
4. Attempts

1. Equivalency of offenses

Department of Safety (DOS) erred in relying upon a police interview transcript in determining whether sex offenses were equivalent under RSA 651-B:1. Under N.H. Code Admin. R. Ann. Saf.-C 5502.01(c), the DOS was limited to making a comparison of the elements of the New Hampshire statute to the elements of the other jurisdiction's statute. Doe v. N.H. Dep't of Safety, 160 N.H. 474, 999 A.2d 362, 2010 N.H. LEXIS 63 (2010).

Gross sexual assault under Me. Rev. Stat. Ann. tit. 17-A, § 253(2)(D) was reasonably equivalent to aggravated felonious sexual assault under RSA 632-A:2, as New Hampshire's definition of "sexual penetration" in RSA 632-A:1, V is substantially similar to Maine's definition of "sexual act" in Me. Rev. Stat. Ann. tit. 17-A, § 251(C). Accordingly, petitioner, who had pleaded guilty to violating the Maine statute, was required under RSA 651-B:1 to register for life as a sex offender. Doe v. N.H. Dep't of Safety, 160 N.H. 474, 999 A.2d 362, 2010 N.H. LEXIS 63 (2010).

2. Evidence

Unlike sentencing, sex offender registration has the administrative purpose of providing a means for law enforcement agencies in the State to share information regarding the whereabouts and levels of dangerousness of convicted sex offenders. While considering whether the evidence required to sustain the out-of-state jurisdiction's conviction would necessarily sustain a conviction under a New Hampshire statute might be relevant in the context of sentencing for subsequent offenses, it is not relevant to the purpose of sex offender registration. Doe v. N.H. Dep't of Safety, 160 N.H. 474, 999 A.2d 362, 2010 N.H. LEXIS 63 (2010).

3. Construction

Because the prefatory language to RSA 651-B:1, VII(a), includes attempt crimes, a court must construe the phrase "where the victim was under the age of 18" in light of that language. In context, therefore, the phrase cannot refer only to crimes in which there is an actual victim under the age of eighteen, but must also refer to attempt crimes in which the offender subjectively believed that such a victim existed. Czyzewski v. N.H. Dep't of Safety, — N.H. —, 70 A.3d 444, 2013 N.H. LEXIS 65 (June 5, 2013).

4. Attempts

When petitioner was convicted of attempted sexual assault based on an online chat with a detective he believed to be a minor girl, he was required to register as a sexual offender. The phrase "where the victim was under the age of 18" in RSA 651-B:1, VII, included attempt crimes in which the offender subjectively believed a victim existed; thus, all that was required here was that the petitioner entertained a subjective -- albeit incorrect -- belief that he was going to meet a minor and commit the elements that constituted his crime of conviction. Czyzewski v. N.H. Dep't of Safety, — N.H. —, 70 A.3d 444, 2013 N.H. LEXIS 65 (June 5, 2013).

651-B:2. Registration.

I. Every sexual offender or offender against children shall be registered with the department of safety, division of state police, as provided in this chapter.

II. Upon receipt of information pursuant to RSA 106-B:14 concerning the disposition of any charges against any sex offender or offender against children, the division shall register such person and shall include the relevant information in the SOR system.

III. Upon receipt from any out-of-state law enforcement agency of information that a sex offender or offender against children has moved to New Hampshire, the division shall register such person and shall include the relevant information in the SOR system.

IV. The information that a person is required to register on the public list as a sexual offender or offender against children, including his or her qualifying offense or offenses, shall be available to law enforcement through the offender's criminal record and motor vehicle record. If an offender's obligation to register terminates for any reason, the department shall notify the division of motor vehicles of the change and the offender's motor vehicle record shall no longer reflect that the person is required to register as a sexual offender or offender against children.

Source.
1996, 293:1, eff. Aug. 9, 1996. 2006, 327:5, eff. January 1, 2007. 2008, 334:2, eff. January 1, 2009.

Amendments
—2008. The 2008 amendment substituted "SOR" for "law enforcement name search (LENS)" in II and substituted "SOR" for "LENS" in III.

—2006. Paragraph I: Substituted "chapter" for "subdivision".
Paragraph II: Substituted "the disposition of any charges against" for "the conviction of".
Paragraph IV: Added.

Applicability of enactment.
See note preceding RSA 651-B:1.

651-B:3. Release of Certain Sexual Offenders Into the Community; Duties.

I. (a) When a person is convicted of a sexual offense or offense against a child that results in the person being required to register, the court shall notify the offender in writing and advise the offender of his or her duty to report under this chapter. The offender shall acknowledge in writing that he or she has received such notice. The court shall forward a copy of the notice to the division along with a copy of each offense for which he or she was convicted, including a copy of any indictment, complaint, juvenile petition, mittimus, or other court orders. The division shall enter such information into the SOR system.

(b) Upon release of any sexual offender or offender against children required to register, whether on probation, parole, conditional or unconditional release, completion of sentence, release from secure psychiatric care, release into the community after involuntary commitment, release from a juvenile detention facility, or for any other reason, the official in charge of such release shall notify the offender of the offender's duty to report under this chapter. The offender shall acknowledge in writing that he has received such notice. The official shall obtain the address at which the offender expects to reside upon release and shall report such address to the department. The department shall inform the local law enforcement agency in the city or town where the offender expects to reside. The local law enforcement agency in the city or town where the offender expects to reside may notify the superintendent of the school administrative unit and the principal of any school within its jurisdiction of the address at which the offender expects to reside. If such notification occurs, the local law enforcement agency shall also notify the superintendent of the school administrative unit and the principal of any school within its jurisdiction of any changes to the offender's information made pursuant to RSA 651-B:5. The division shall enter the information concerning the offender's release and notification in the SOR system.

II. Upon receipt from any out-of-state law enforcement agency of information that a sex offender or offender against children has moved to New Hampshire, the department shall obtain the address at which the offender expects to reside and shall inform the local law enforcement agency. The local law enforcement agency in the city or town where the offender expects to reside may notify the superintendent of the school administrative unit and the principal of any school within its jurisdiction of the address at which the offender expects to reside. The department shall locate and shall serve notice upon such offender of the offender's duty to report under this chapter. Service by the department is not required if the offender has already registered with the local law enforcement agency in which the offender resides or is located as required by this chapter. At the time of the initial registration, the offender shall acknowledge in writing that the offender has received notice of the duty to report. The division shall enter the information concerning the offender's location in New Hampshire and notification in the SOR system. This paragraph shall not apply to a sexual offender or offender against children who has moved to New Hampshire and has registered with a local law enforcement agency.

III. Semi-annually, the department shall verify, in person, the address at which the offender resides or by sending a letter by certified non-forwarding mail to the offender. The address verification shall occur prior to the offender's birthday and again prior to the offender's 6-month semi-annual registration. The address verification shall remind the offender of the obligation to register in person. The offender shall sign the address verification and return it to the officer, if the address verification was made in person, or to the department within 10 business days of receipt.

IV. In the discretion of the local law enforcement agency or the department, such agency or the department may affirmatively verify the address of any offender within that agency's jurisdiction through in-person contact at the home or residence of the offender.

Source.

1996, 293:1, eff. Aug. 9, 1996. 2005, 214:4, eff. January 1, 2006. 2006, 162:2, eff. January 1, 2007; 327:6 (amendments to RSA 651-B:3, II), eff. at 12:01 a.m., January 1, 2007; 327:6 (all other amendments), eff. January 1, 2007. 2007, 319:2, eff. September 14, 2007. 2008, 323:11, eff. at 12:01 a.m., January 1, 2009; 334:3, eff. January 1, 2009.

Amendments

—2008. The 2008 amendment by Chapter 323 added IV.

The 2008 amendment by Chapter 334, added I(a); redesignated former I(a) as I(b); in the seventh sentence of I(b) and in the sixth sentence of II, substituted "SOR" for "LENS"; and rewrote III to the extent that a detailed comparison would be impracticable.

—2007. Paragraph I: Inserted "in the city or town" following "enforcement agency" in the fourth sentence and added the fifth and sixth sentences.

Paragraph II: Added the second sentence.

—2006. Paragraph I: Chapter 327 inserted "release into the community after involuntary commitment, release from a juvenile detention facility" following "psychiatric care" in the first sentence.

Paragraph II: Chapter 327 added the last part of the first sentence following "New Hampshire", added the third sentence, and in the fourth sentence, substituted "at the time of the initial registration, the" for "the" at the beginning, deleted "such" preceding "notice" and added "of the duty to report" at the end, and deleted the former fifth sentence.

Paragraph III: Added by Chapter 327.

Paragraph II: Chapter 162 added the last sentence.

—2005. Paragraph I: Substituted "required to register" for "after conviction" and inserted "release from secure psychiatric care" in the first sentence.

Effective date of amendments

—2006. 2006, 327:29, II, eff. June 26, 2006, provided that the amendment to par. II shall take effect January 1, 2007, at 12:01 a.m.

Applicability of enactment.

See note preceding RSA 651-B:1.

651-B:4. Duty to Report.

I. Any sexual offender or offender against children residing in this state shall report in person to the local law enforcement agency. The offender shall report in person as set forth in this section within 5 business days after the person's release, or within 5 business days after the person's date of establishment of residence, employment, or schooling in New Hampshire. If an offender has more than one residence, the offender shall report in person to the local law enforcement agency having jurisdiction over his or her primary residence and report the addresses of all his or her residences, including those outside of New Hampshire. The division shall notify the local law enforcement agencies having jurisdiction over the offender's other residences of the offender's address in their jurisdiction. Thereafter, the offender shall report as follows:

(a) Every tier III offender shall report in person quarterly, within 5 business days after each anniversary of the offender's date of birth and every 3 months thereafter.

(b) Every tier I and tier II offender shall report in person semi-annually, within 5 business days after each anniversary of the offender's date of birth and every 6 months thereafter.

II. Any nonresident offender shall report in person to the local law enforcement agency having jurisdiction over the place of employment or school. In the event a nonresident offender required to register under this paragraph does not have a principal place of employment in this state, the offender shall register in person with the department in Concord.

III. Each time a sexual offender or offender against children is required to report, the offender shall provide the following information:

(a) Name and any aliases.

(b) Address of any permanent residence and address of any current temporary residence, within the state or out-of-state, and mailing address. A post office box shall not be provided in lieu of a physical residential address. If the offender cannot provide a definite address, he or she shall provide information about all places where he or she habitually lives.

(c) Name, address, and date of any employment or schooling. For purposes of this section, the term "employment" includes volunteer work or work without remuneration. If the offender does not have a fixed place of work, he or she shall provide information about all places he or she generally works, and any regular routes of travel.

(d) Any professional licenses or certifications that authorize the offender to engage in an occupation or carry out a trade or business.

(e) Make, model, color, and license plate or registration number and state of registration of any vehicle, watercraft, or aircraft owned or regularly operated by the offender, and the place or places where such vehicles, watercraft, or aircraft are regularly kept.

(f) Date of birth, including any alias date of birth used by the offender.

(g) Social security number.

(h) Physical description to include identifying marks such as scars and tattoos.

(i) Telephone numbers for both fixed location and cell phones.

(j) Passport, travel, and immigration documents.

(k) The name, address, and phone number of any landlord, if the offender resides in rental property.

IV. In addition to the information required pursuant to paragraph III, the department, at the time of the offender's registration, may require the offender to submit the following:

(a) A photograph taken by the law enforcement agency each time the person is required to report to the law enforcement agency under this section.

(b) A DNA sample, if such sample has not already been provided.

(c) A set of major case prints, including fingerprints and palm prints of the offender.

(d) A photocopy of a valid driver's license or identification card issued to the offender. The consent of the registrant shall not be necessary to obtain this information. Such information may be used in the performance of any valid law enforcement function.

V. At periodic intervals, not less frequently than once each month, the commissioner of the department of corrections, the superintendent of each county department of corrections, and the commissioner of the department of health and human services shall forward to the division a statement identifying every sexual offender and offender against children who is confined in a facility under its control and who is eligible for any unsupervised work detail, release into the community following secure psychiatric care, or other assignment which may bring the offender into contact with members of the public. These statements shall include the information required in paragraph III and may include the information set forth in paragraph IV. In no event shall the statements include the identity of any victim.

VI. In addition to the requirements imposed under this section, the following provisions shall apply to any sexual offender or offender against children who is sentenced to an extended term of imprisonment pursuant to RSA 651:6, I(b):

(a) Every 90 days after the date of the offender's initial release or commencement of parole, the department shall mail a nonforwardable verification form to the offender's last reported address.

(b) The offender shall mail the verification form to the department within 10 days after receipt of the form.

(c) The verification form shall be signed by the offender, and state that the offender still resides at the address last reported to the local law enforcement agency.

Source.
1996, 293:1, eff. Aug. 9, 1996. 2000, 177:1, eff. Jan. 1, 2001. 2001, 233:1, eff. Jan. 1, 2002. 2002, 241:3, eff. May 17, 2002. 2003, 316:1, eff. Sept. 20, 2003. 2005, 214:5, eff. January 1, 2006. 2006, 327:7, eff. January 1, 2007. 2008, 334:4, eff. January 1, 2009. 2009, 306:5, eff. July 31, 2009. 2010, 78:7, eff. January 1, 2011.

Amendments
—2010. The 2010 amendment, in III(e), deleted "Vehicle" at the beginning, added "or registration," added "watercraft, or aircraft" twice, and substituted "operated" for "driven."

—2009. The 2009 amendment rewrote III(a), which formerly read: "Name, aliases, electronic mail addresses, and any instant messaging, chat, or other Internet communication name identities."

—2008. The 2008 amendment rewrote the section to the extent that a detailed comparison would be impracticable.

—2006. Paragraph I: Rewritten to the extent that a detailed comparison would be impracticable.

—2005. Paragraph I(a)(1): Rewrote the first sentence.

—2003. Paragraph I(a): Redesignated the existing provisions as subpar. (1) and in that subparagraph, deleted "be required to" following "chapter shall" in the first sentence and made minor changes in the punctuation in the second sentence and added subpar. (2).
Paragraph I(b): Substituted "shall" for "is required to" following "calendar year" in the first sentence.

—2002. Paragraph I(a): Deleted "and" following "mailing address" and inserted "and place of employment or schooling" following "temporary domicile" in the first sentence.

—2001. Paragraph I: Designated the first and second sentences as subpar. (a); added subpar. (b); and designated the third and fourth sentences as subpar. (c).

—2000. Paragraph I: Rewritten to the extent that a detailed comparison would be impracticable.

Applicability of enactment.
See note preceding RSA 651-B:1.

Applicability of 2010 amendment.
2010, 78:9, eff. January 1, 2011, provided: "RSA 651-B shall apply to any sexual offender or offender against children, regardless of the date of conviction, juvenile delinquency adjudication, finding of not guilty by reason of insanity, or commitment under RSA 135-E."

Applicability of 2003 amendment.
2003, 316:6, eff. September 20, 2003, provided that the amendment to this section, by section 1 of the act, shall apply to any person required to be registered pursuant to RSA 651-B:2 as of September 20, 2003.

NOTES TO DECISIONS

1. Time limitation
2. Lifetime registration

1. Time limitation
Defendant was entitled to have vacated his conviction for failure to register with police under RSA 651-B:4, I, because his guilty plea to the charge was not knowing and voluntary as he was not informed by either the trial court or the complaint that the statute afforded him 30 days in which to register after he moved to New Hampshire, and, thus, his due process rights under N.H. Const. pt. 1, art. 15, were violated; further, the 30-day time period was an element of the offense pursuant to RSA 625:11, III(a) as it was included in the definition of the offense. State v. Offen, 156 N.H. 435, 938 A.2d 879, 2007 N.H. LEXIS 203 (2007).

2. Lifetime registration
Phrase "more than one offense" in RSA 651-B:6, III, was not intended to apply to two misdemeanor sexual assault convictions arising from a single criminal episode; therefore, the lifetime registration requirement does not apply when the defendant had two misdemeanor sexual assault convictions arising from the same criminal episode. Accordingly, the trial court properly dismissed two indictments for felony failure to report as a sexual offender under RSA 651-B:4 and RSA 651-B:5. State v. McKeown, 159 N.H. 434, 986 A.2d 583, 2009 N.H. LEXIS 132 (2009).

651-B:4-a. Registration of Online Identifiers.

In addition to any other information a person who is required to register is required to provide pursuant to RSA 651-B:4, such person shall report any online identifier such person uses or intends to use. For purposes of this section, "online identifier" includes all of the following: electronic mail address, instant message screen name, user identification, user profile information, and chat or other Internet communication name or identity information. Such person shall report any changes to an existing online identifier, or the creation of any new online identifier to law enforcement before using the online identifier.

Source.
2008, 323:6, eff. at 12:01 a.m., January 1, 2009.

NOTES TO DECISIONS

1. Constitutionality
2. Online identifier

1. Constitutionality
RSA 651-B:4-a was not unconstitutionally vague when applied to defendant, who was accused of failing to notify authorities of his Myspace account. The phrase "user profile information" provided a person of ordinary intelligence a reasonable opportunity to understand the conduct it prohibited—namely, the failure by a sex offender to report the creation of, or changes to, an online profile. State v. White, 164 N.H. 418, 58 A.3d 643, 2012 N.H. LEXIS 163 (2012).

Sex offender registration form that defendant was required to sign did not render impermissibly vague the application to him of RSA 651-B:4-a. From the form, defendant could fairly be charged with knowledge that he had to report "user profile information" and the other statutory examples of online identifiers; neither the statute nor the form promoted arbitrary enforcement or unfettered police discretion, as the statute provided five specific examples of the online information and activities subject to the reporting requirement. State v. White, 164 N.H. 418, 58 A.3d 643, 2012 N.H. LEXIS 163 (2012).

2. Online identifier
Myspace account includes "user profile information," which, therefore, is an "online identifier" subject to the reporting requirement of RSA 651-B:4-a. Accordingly, it was error to dismiss an indictment against defendant for failing to report his Myspace account. State v. White, 164 N.H. 418, 58 A.3d 643, 2012 N.H. LEXIS 163 (2012).

651-B:5. Change of Registration Information; Duty to Inform.

I. When there is a change to any of the information that a sexual offender or offender against children is required to report pursuant to this chapter, the offender shall give written notification of the new information to the local law enforcement agency to which he or she last reported under RSA 651-B:4 within 5 business days of such change of information. In addition, any time a sex offender or offender against children changes residence, employment, or schooling, the offender shall report in person to the local law enforcement agency having jurisdiction over the offender's previous place of residence, place of employment, or school within 5 business days. The local law enforcement agency receiving notice of the change of registration information shall forward a copy to the division within 5 days after receipt. The division shall notify the local law enforcement agency at the new place of residence, place of employment, or school, or the appropriate out-of-state law enforcement agency if the new place of residence, place of employment, or school is outside New Hampshire. The division shall include any new information in the SOR system.

II. Upon receipt of notice that an offender has changed residence, employment, or schooling to a place outside New Hampshire, the division shall notify the appropriate out-of-state law enforcement agency of that information. Within 10 business days after reporting the change of residence, employment, or schooling to the New Hampshire law enforcement agency, the offender shall report to the appropriate out-of-state law enforcement agency having jurisdiction over the new place of residence, place of employment, or school. If the offender fails to report to the appropriate out-of-state law enforcement agency the division shall maintain the offender's information in the SOR system.

III. The local law enforcement agency in the city or town where the offender resides may notify the superintendent of the school administrative unit and the principal of any school within its jurisdiction of a new place of residence, a change of name, or a change of an alias, of a person required to be registered under this chapter.

Source.
1996, 293:1, eff. Aug. 9, 1996. 1999, 160:2, eff. Jan. 1, 2000. 2001, 233:2, eff. Jan. 1, 2002. 2002, 241:4, eff. May 17, 2002. 2006, 327:8, eff. January 1, 2007. 2007, 319:3, eff. September 14, 2007. 2008, 334:4, eff. January 1, 2009.

Amendments
—2008. The 2008 amendment rewrote the section to the extent that a detailed comparison would be impracticable.

—2007. Inserted "Residence" preceding "Name, or Alias" and deleted "or Address" thereafter in section heading and designated the existing provisions of the section as par. I and added par. II.

—2006. Rewritten to the extent that a detailed comparison would be impracticable.

—2002. Paragraph III: Added.

—2001. Designated the existing provisions of the section as par. I, and in that paragraph, substituted "RSA 651-B:4, I(a)" for "this chapter" and inserted "or she" following "which he" in the first sentence and added par. II.

—1999. Inserted "Name or Alias, or" in the section catchline, "or their name or alias" following "residence" and "name, or alias" in two places in the first sentence, and inserted "or change-of-name" following "change-of-address" in the last sentence.

Applicability of enactment.
See note preceding RSA 651-B:1.

NOTES TO DECISIONS

Lifetime registration
Phrase "more than one offense" in RSA 651-B:6, III, was not intended to apply to two misdemeanor sexual assault convictions arising from a single criminal episode; therefore, the lifetime registration requirement does not apply when the defendant had two misdemeanor sexual assault convictions arising from the same criminal episode. Accordingly, the trial court properly dismissed two indictments for felony failure to report as a sexual offender under RSA 651-B:4 and RSA 651-B:5. State v. McKeown, 159 N.H. 434, 986 A.2d 583, 2009 N.H. LEXIS 132 (2009).

651-B:6. Duration of Registration.

I. All tier II or tier III offenders shall be registered for life.

II. All tier I offenders shall be registered for a 10-year period from the date of release, provided that any such registration period shall not run concurrently with any registration period resulting from a subsequent violation or attempted violation of an offense for which the person is required to register.

III. (a) (1) All tier III offenders shall remain on the public list contained in RSA 651-B:7 for life.

(2) A tier II offender may petition the superior court to have his or her name and information removed from the public list. The petition shall not be filed prior to the completion of all the terms and conditions of the sentence and in no case earlier than 15 years after the date of release. The petition shall be accompanied by a risk assessment prepared by a qualified psychiatrist or psychologist at the offender's expense. The court may grant the petition if the offender has not been convicted of any felony, class A misdemeanor, sex offense, or offense against a child, has successfully completed any periods of supervised release, probation, or parole, and has successfully completed an appropriate sex offender treatment program as determined by the court. If the court denies the petition, the offender shall not file another petition for 5 years from the date of denial.

(3) A tier I offender may petition the superior court to have his or her name and other information removed from the public list. The petition shall not be filed prior to the completion of all the terms and conditions of the sentence and in no case earlier than 5 years after the date of release. The petition shall be accompanied by a risk assessment prepared by a qualified psychiatrist or psychologist at the offender's expense. The court may grant the petition if the offender has not been convicted of any felony, class A misdemeanor, sexual offense, or offense against a child, has successfully completed any periods of supervised release, probation, or parole, and has successfully completed an appropriate sex offender treatment program as determined by the court.

(b) Prior to granting any petition to remove an offender from the public list, the court shall provide notice to the county attorney who prosecuted the case, the victim advocate, and the victim or victim's family, and permit those parties to be heard on the petition. Prior to any decision granting the application, the court shall provide the victim with the opportunity to address the court. The victim may appear personally, or by counsel, or may provide a written statement to reasonably express his or her views concerning the offense, the person responsible, and the need for maintaining the registration requirement. The judge shall consider the statements of the victim pursuant to this section when making a decision regarding the application. The judge shall grant the application, after a hearing, only where, in the opinion of the court, removal from

the registration requirements will assist the individual in the individual's rehabilitation and will be consistent with the public welfare.

IV. Registration of any juvenile required to register pursuant to RSA 651-B:1, XI(a)(3) or (4) shall end when the juvenile turns 17 years of age unless the court which adjudicated the juvenile as a delinquent retains jurisdiction over the juvenile pursuant to RSA 169-B:4, V, in which case registration of the juvenile shall end when the court terminates jurisdiction over the juvenile's case. When the registration of a juvenile terminates, the department shall remove information relating to the juvenile from the SOR system and records of the juvenile's registration shall be handled in accordance with RSA 169-B:35 and RSA 169-B:36.

Source.
1996, 293:1, eff. Aug. 9, 1996. 1999, 177:4, 5, eff. Aug. 30, 1999; 321:3, eff. Jan. 1, 2000. 2002, 241:2, eff. May 17, 2002. 2003, 316:9, eff. Jan. 1, 2004. 2005, 214:6, eff. January 1, 2006. 2006, 162:3, eff. January 1, 2007; 327:9, 10, eff. January 1, 2007. 2008, 334:4, eff. January 1, 2009.

Amendments
—2008. The 2008 amendment rewrote the section to the extent that a detailed comparison would be impracticable.

—2006. Paragraph I: Chapter 162 inserted "632-A:2" following "169-B:41, II".
Paragraph II: Chapter 162 inserted "or (b)" following "RSA 632-A:4, I(a)".
Paragraph III: Chapter 327 inserted "of a violation" following "as a result".
Paragraph IV: Added by Ch. 327.

—2005. Rewritten to the extent that a detailed comparison would be impracticable.

—2003. Paragraph II: Inserted "I(a)" following "RSA 632-A:4".

—2002. Paragraph II: Inserted "or" preceding "645:2, I" and deleted "or 649-A:3, III" thereafter.

—1999. Paragraph I: Chapter 177 inserted "639:2" following "633:2" and "649-B:3, 649-B:4" preceding "or 650:2".
Chapter 321 deleted "or" preceding "632-A:3" and inserted "or 645:1, III" thereafter.
Paragraph III: Inserted "has been convicted of more that one offense listed in RSA 651-B:1, III or RSA 651-B:1, V, or who" following "children who".

Repeal of prospective amendment by 2008, 323:10.
2009, 306:15, II, eff. July 31, 2009, provided for the repeal of 2008, 323:10, which amended par. I to be effective January 1, 2009.

Applicability of enactment.
See note preceding RSA 651-B:1.

Applicability of 2003 amendment.
2003, 316:6, eff. September 20, 2003, provided that the amendment to this section, by section 9 of the act, shall apply to any person required to be registered pursuant to RSA 651-B:2 as of September 20, 2003.

NOTES TO DECISIONS

Construction
Phrase "more than one offense" in RSA 651-B:6, III, was not intended to apply to two misdemeanor sexual assault convictions arising from a single criminal episode; therefore, the lifetime registration requirement does not apply when the defendant had two misdemeanor sexual assault convictions arising from the same criminal episode. Accordingly, the trial court properly dismissed

two indictments for felony failure to report as a sexual offender under RSA 651-B:4 and RSA 651-B:5. State v. McKeown, 159 N.H. 434, 986 A.2d 583, 2009 N.H. LEXIS 132 (2009).

651-B:7. Availability of Information to the Public and Law Enforcement.

I. Except as provided in this section, the records established and information collected pursuant to the provisions of this chapter shall not be considered "public records" subject to inspection under RSA 91-A:4. However, nothing in this chapter shall be construed to limit any law enforcement agency from making any use or disclosure of any such information as may be necessary for the performance of a valid law enforcement function. Nothing in this chapter shall be construed to limit an individual's ability to obtain access to the individual's own records, or to limit access to a person's criminal record under the provisions of RSA 106-B:14, including address information obtained under the provisions of this chapter.

II. The division shall maintain a list of all tier I, tier II, and tier III offenders required to register pursuant to this chapter. The list shall also include all offenders about whom the division receives notice pursuant to RSA 651-B:4, V. In addition to the information contained on the public list pursuant to paragraph III, the law enforcement list shall include all information reported to the local law enforcement agency or the department pursuant to RSA 651-B:4. In addition, the information shall include the text of the statute under which the offender was convicted and the criminal history of the offender. The list maintained pursuant to this paragraph shall not be available to the public but shall be available to law enforcement officials for valid law enforcement purposes.

III. (a) The division shall maintain a separate public list of all tier I, tier II, and tier III offenders who are required to register as a result of an offense against a child, any offenders about whom the division receives notice pursuant to RSA 651-B:4, V that will be required to register as a result of an offense against children, and any offender who is required to register for more than one sexual offense or offense against a child. The public list shall include all of the following information:

(1) Offender's name, alias, age, race, sex, date of birth, height, weight, hair and eye color, and any other relevant physical description.

(2) Address of any permanent residence and address of any temporary residence, within the state or out-of-state.

(3) The offense for which the individual is required to register and the text of the provision of law defining the offense, and any other sex offense for which the individual has been convicted.

(4) The date and court of the adjudication on the offense for which the individual is registered.

(5) Outstanding arrest warrants, and the information listed in subparagraphs (a)(1)–(3), for any sexual offender or offender against children who has not complied with the obligation to register under this chapter.

(6) Criminal history of the offender, including the date of all convictions and the status of parole, probation, or supervised release, and registration status.

(7) A photograph of the individual.

(8) The address of any place where the individual is or will be a student.

(9) [Repealed.]

(b) Where such information is available, the public list may also include:

(1) Information on the profile of the victim of the individual's offense.

(2) The method of approach utilized by the individual.

(c) The public list shall not include:

(1) The identity of any victim either directly or indirectly. Sexual offenders convicted under RSA 632-A:2 shall be listed on the public list in a manner which does not disclose, directly or indirectly, that the victim and the defendant were related or members of the same household. For sexual offenders convicted under RSA 632-A:2, I, no specific reference to any statutory subparagraph shall appear on the public list.

(2) The social security number of the offender.

(3) Arrests of the offender which did not result in a conviction.

(4) The name of the employer or school which the offender attends.

(5) Information about a juvenile delinquent required to register pursuant to RSA 651-B:1, XI (a)(3) or (4).

IV. (a) The public list shall be made available to interested members of the public upon request to a local law enforcement agency. The department of safety shall also make the list available to the public through the use of the department's official public Internet website. The Internet website shall be available to the public in a manner that will permit the public to obtain relevant information for each sex offender by a single query for any given zip code or geographic radius set by the user. The website may include additional search parameters as determined by the department.

(b) Local law enforcement agencies may photograph, at the time of the registration, any individual who is required to be registered pursuant to this chapter. The consent of the registrant shall not be necessary. Such photographs may be used in the performance of any valid law enforcement function.

(c) In the discretion of the local law enforcement agency, such agency may affirmatively notify the public that an offender who is included on the public list received by the agency pursuant to subparagraph IV(a) is residing in the community.

V. Local law enforcement agencies, employees of local law enforcement agencies, county and state officials, municipal and school officials, and munici-palities and school districts shall be immune from civil and criminal liability for good faith conduct under this chapter, including any decision to provide or not provide affirmative notification to the public pursuant to subparagraph IV(c). Nothing in this paragraph shall be deemed to grant any such immu-nity to any person for that person's reckless or wanton conduct.

VI. [Repealed.]

Source.

1996, 293:1, eff. Aug. 9, 1996. 1998, 239:2, eff. Jan. 1, 1999. 1999, 321:4, eff. Jan. 1, 2000. 2000, 177:2, 3, eff. Jan. 1, 2001. 2002, 241:1, eff. May 17, 2002. 2003, 316:2–4, eff. Sept. 20, 2003. 2005, 214:7, 8, eff. January 1, 2006. 2006, 162:5, eff. January 1, 2007; 327:11, eff. January 1, 2007; 327:11 (amendment to II(a)), eff. at 12:01 a.m., January 1, 2007. 2008, 334:4, eff. January 1, 2009. 2009, 306:6, 15, III, eff. July 31, 2009. 2010, 78:8, eff. January 1, 2011.

Amendments
—2010.   The 2010 amendment deleted III(a)(9).

—2009.   The 2009 amendment added III(a)(9) and deleted VI.

—2008.   The 2008 amendment rewrote the section to the extent that a detailed comparison would be impracticable.

—2006.   Paragraphs II(a)(1) and (2): Repealed by Chapter 162.
Paragraph II: In subpar. (a), Chapter 327 added subpars. (1) and (2) and redesignated former subpars. (1) through (6) to be subpars. (3) through (8) (former subparagraphs (1) and (2) were repealed by Chapter 162 as noted above), in subpar. (5), deleted "convicted" preceding "individual" and inserted "required to register" thereaf-ter, added the second and third sentences in subpar. (b)(3), and added subpar. (c).
Paragraph IV(c): Added by Chapter 327.
Paragraph V: In the first sentence, inserted "municipal and school officials, and municipalities and school districts" preceding "shall be immune" and added the end of the sentence following "under this chapter", and made a stylistic change.
Paragraph VI(a): In the first sentence, Chapter 327 substituted "is required to register as a result" for "has been convicted", deleted "convicted" preceding "individual" and inserted "required to regis-ter" thereafter, and substituted "adjudications" for "convictions", deleted "following conviction" following "date of release" in the second sentence, and added the last two sentences.

—2005.   Paragraph II(a): Substituted "are required to register as a result" for "have been convicted" in the introductory paragraph.
Paragraph II(b)(1)(B): Substituted "is required to register" for "was convicted".
Paragraph II(b)(1)(C): Substituted "adjudication on the offense" for "conviction".
Paragraph III: Rewritten to the extent that a detailed compari-son would be impracticable.
Paragraph VI(a): Deleted "more than" preceding "3 years" and inserted "or less" thereafter in the first sentence.

—2003.   Paragraph II: Rewritten to the extent that a detailed comparison would be impracticable.
Paragraph IV(a): Rewrote the sixth sentence to the extent that a detailed comparison would be impracticable.
Paragraph VI: Added.

—2002.   Paragraph IV: Designated the existing provisions of the paragraph as subpar. (a) and in that paragraph inserted "through written, electronic, computerized, or other accessible means" fol-lowing "periodic intervals" in the first sentence, substituted "a local law" for "the local law" in the second sentence, and added the third sentence, and added subpar. (b).

—2000.   Paragraph II(b)(1)(D): Added.
Paragraph IV: Substituted "provide" for "forward" preceding "a

copy of" in the first sentence, and "the state" for "a specified city or town" at the end of the fourth sentence.

—1999.   Paragraph II(a): Added new subpar. (5) and redesig-nated former subpar. (5) as present subpar. (6).

—1998.   Rewritten to the extent that a detailed comparison would be impracticable.

Effective date.

2006, 327:29(II) provided that RSA 651-B:7, II(a), inserted by 2006, 327:11, is effective at 12:01 a.m., January 1, 2007.

Applicability of enactment.
See note preceding RSA 651-B:1.

Applicability of 2010 amendment.
2010, 78:9, eff. January 1, 2011, provided: "RSA 651-B shall apply to any sexual offender or offender against children, regard-less of the date of conviction, juvenile delinquency adjudication, finding of not guilty by reason of insanity, or commitment under RSA 135-E."

Applicability of 2003 amendment.
2003, 316:6, eff. September 20, 2003, provided that the amend-ments to this section, by sections 2–4 of the act, shall apply to any person required to be registered pursuant to RSA 651-B:2 as of September 20, 2003.

Repeal of 2008, 323:7 amendment.
2009, 306:15, I, eff. July 31, 2009, provided for the repeal of the amendment to par. II(b)(1)(F) by 2008, 323:7.

651-B:8. Rules.

The department shall adopt rules, pursuant to RSA 541-A, relative to forms and procedures for the administration of this chapter.

Source.
1996, 293:1, eff. Aug. 9, 1996.

Applicability of enactment.
See note preceding RSA 651-B:1.

651-B:9. Penalty.

I. A sexual offender or offender against children who is required to register under this chapter and who negligently fails to comply with the require-ments of this chapter shall be guilty of a misdemeanor.

II. A sexual offender or offender against children who is required to register under this chapter and who knowingly fails to comply with the require-ments of this chapter shall be guilty of a class B felony. An offender who is required to register for a period of 10 years following his or her release, pursuant to RSA 651-B:6, II, shall be required to register for an additional 10 years from the date of conviction for violating this paragraph. The obliga-tion to register for an additional 10 years from the date of conviction for violating this paragraph shall be consecutive to the registration period imposed pursuant to RSA 651-B:6 and shall be imposed even if the original registration period has elapsed.

III. A sexual offender or offender against children previously convicted pursuant to paragraph II who is required to register under this chapter and who knowingly fails to comply with the requirements of this chapter shall be guilty of a class A felony. An offender who is required to register for a period of 10 years following his or her release, pursuant to RSA 651-B:6, II, who is convicted for violating this paragraph shall be required to register for life.

IV. The penalties imposed under paragraphs I–III shall not apply to juveniles required to register pursuant to RSA 651-B:1, XI(a)(3) or (4). The court with jurisdiction over such juveniles may impose an appropriate disposition for a violation of this section.

V. Any person who violates the provisions of RSA 651-B:7 shall be guilty of a violation.

VI. A sexual offender or offender against children who knowingly provides false information in response to any of the requirements of this chapter shall be guilty of a class B felony.

VII. A person is guilty of a class B felony if the person has reason to believe that a sexual offender or offender against children is not complying, or has not complied, with the requirements of this chapter and who purposely assists the offender in eluding any law enforcement agency that is seeking to find the offender to question the offender about, or to arrest the offender for, his or her noncompliance with the requirements of this chapter, and engages in any of the following acts or omissions:

(a) Withholds information from, or does not notify, the law enforcement agency about the offender's noncompliance with the requirements of this chapter, and, if known, the whereabouts of the offender;

(b) Harbors, or attempts to harbor, or assists another person in harboring or attempting to harbor, the offender;

(c) Conceals or attempts to conceal, or assists another person in concealing or attempting to conceal, the offender;

(d) Provides information to the law enforcement agency regarding the offender which the person knows to be false information; or

(e) Warns the offender that the law enforcement agency is attempting to locate the offender.

VIII. (a) Except as provided in subparagraph (b), any sexual offender or offender against children who is required to register under this chapter who is convicted of aggravated felonious sexual assault pursuant to RSA 632-A:2, or felonious sexual assault pursuant to RSA 632-A:3, or sexual assault pursuant to RSA 632-A:4, and who initiates contact with the victim of the offense at any time shall be guilty of a class A misdemeanor. In this paragraph, "contact" means any action to communicate with the victim either directly or indirectly, including, but not limited to, using any form of electronic communication, leaving items, or causing another to communicate in such fashion.

(b) Subparagraph (a) shall not apply to contact between a sexual offender or an offender against children and a victim where there is an ongoing relationship between the victim and the offender that existed prior to the commission of the offense and that necessitates contact between them, such as the shared custody of a child or an emergency involving a shared sibling or parent, provided that any contact by the offender shall be strictly limited to the immediate issue that needs to be communicated.

Source.
1996, 293:1, eff. Aug. 9, 1996. 2000, 177:4, eff. Jan. 1, 2001. 2005, 214:9, eff. January 1, 2006. 2006, 327:12, eff. January 1, 2007. 2008, 334:5, eff. January 1, 2009. 2010, 75:1, eff. January 1, 2011.

Amendments
—**2010.** The 2010 amendment added VIII.

—**2008.** The 2008 amendment substituted "XI(a)(3) or (4)" for "VII(a)(3) or (4)" at the end of the first sentence in IV.

—**2006.** Paragraph I: Substituted "misdemeanor" for "violation".
Paragraph II: Substituted "class B felony" for "misdemeanor" in the first sentence and added the second and third sentences.
Paragraph III: In the first sentence, deleted "of a misdemeanor" following "convicted" and substituted "class A" for "class B", and added the second sentence.
Paragraph IV: Added.
Paragraph V: Redesignated from former paragraph IV.
Paragraphs VI, VII: Added.

—**2005.** Inserted "who is required to register under this chapter and" in pars. I through III.

—**2000.** Added new par. III and redesignated former par. III as par. IV.

Applicability of enactment.
See note preceding RSA 651-B:1.

Cross References.
Classification of crimes, see RSA 625:9.

NOTES TO DECISIONS

Cited:
Cited in State v. Offen, 156 N.H. 435, 938 A.2d 879, 2007 N.H. LEXIS 203 (2007).

651-B:10. Hearing.

I. Any offender required to register for an offense committed in another state, country, territory, or tribal territory, or under federal law that is determined to be a reasonably equivalent offense to an offense listed RSA 651-B:1, V(a) or RSA 651-B:1, VII(a) or (b) may appeal that determination to the commissioner. The offender shall, within 10 days of notification, request a hearing on the matter before the commissioner. If such a request is made, the commissioner shall promptly schedule and conduct a hearing pursuant to rules adopted under RSA 541-A. The offender shall have the right to appeal the commissioner's decision in superior court.

II. Any offender required to register for an offense in the state of conviction pursuant to RSA 651-B:1, V(c), RSA 651-B:1, VII(d), or RSA 651-B:1, XI(a)(4) may petition the superior court for a hearing to review the registration requirement. In determining whether the offender should be required to register, the court may consider the facts of underlying the out-of-state conviction, the offender's prior criminal history, the extent to which public safety would be furthered by requiring the offender to register, and any other relevant information. If the court determines that the offender is required to register, the court shall determine whether the offender is required to register as a tier I, tier II, or tier III offender. In determining the appropriate tier, the court shall consider the nature of other offenses that are currently listed in each tier, the seriousness of the offender's offense, the extent to which public safety would be furthered, whether the victim was a minor when the offense occurred, and any other relevant factors. The hearing at which such a determination is made shall comply with due process requirements, including a right to appeal the findings. The court shall provide the defendant an opportunity to be heard on the issue and shall state on the record the reasons for its findings and the reasons for requiring registration.

III. Any individual required to be registered as a result of any violation or attempted violation of RSA 632-A:3, II in effect prior to January 1, 2009, or RSA 632-A:2, III if the acts constituting the pattern were in violation of RSA 632-A:3, II in effect prior to January 1, 2009, provided that the age difference between the individual required to register and the victim was less than 4 years at the time of the offense and the person has no other adjudications requiring registration under RSA 651-B:2, may file with the clerk of the superior court for the county in which the judgment was rendered an application for review of the registration requirement. No application shall be granted without a hearing, during which the prosecuting attorney and the victim or victim's family shall have an opportunity to be heard. Notice of the hearing shall be provided no less than 30 days prior to the hearing. The victim may appear personally or through a representative, and may reasonably express his or her views concerning the offense, the offender, and the need for continuing the registration requirement. If the court denies the application, the offender shall not file another application for 5 years from the date of the denial.

Source.
2003, 316:5, eff. Sept. 20, 2003. 2008, 334:6, eff. January 1, 2009. 2009, 306:7, eff. July 31, 2009.

Amendments
—2009. The 2009 amendment added III.

—2008. The 2008 amendment rewrote the section to the extent that a detailed comparison would be impracticable.

Applicability of enactment.
See note preceding RSA 651-B:1.
2003, 316:6, eff. September 20, 2003, provided that section 5 of the act, which enacted this section, shall apply to any person required to be registered pursuant to RSA 651-B:2 as of September 20, 2003.

651-B:11. Registration Fee.

I. An offender shall pay a fee of $50 to the department within 10 days of the registration that occurs within the month of the anniversary of his or her birth. Such payment shall be made in person or shall be mailed to the department. The department shall retain $40 of this amount to be used to defray the costs of maintaining the sex offender registry. Such funds shall be nonlapsing and shall be continually appropriated to the department for such use. The department shall forward the remaining $10 to the law enforcement agency which registered the offender within the month of the anniversary of the offender's birth to defray any costs associated with implementing the provisions of this chapter. The department shall forward these fees to the registering law enforcement agencies in a manner determined by the department but no less frequently than once a year.

II. An offender who cannot afford to pay the fee shall, within 10 days of registration, request a waiver of the fee and a hearing on the matter before the commissioner. In order to be considered for a waiver, the offender shall submit a financial affidavit on a form provided by the department. The division may at its discretion request such a waiver on behalf of an offender. If such a request is made, the commissioner shall promptly schedule and conduct a hearing pursuant to rules adopted under RSA 541-A, unless the commissioner or commissioner's designee determines a hearing is not necessary and waives the fee based on the offender's financial affidavit, or at the written request of the division. At the hearing, the burden shall be on the offender to prove that he or she is indigent. The offender may appeal the commissioner's decision to the superior court. Under no circumstances shall the offender's request for a hearing or indigency relieve the offender of the obligation to register as required pursuant to this chapter.

III. Notwithstanding RSA 651-B:9, an offender who violates the provisions of this section shall be guilty of a violation for a first offense and a misdemeanor for a second or subsequent offense.

Source.
2006, 327:13, eff. January 1, 2007. 2007, 337:13, eff. January 1, 2008. 2008, 334:6, eff. January 1, 2009.

Amendments
—2008. The 2008 amendment rewrote the section to the extent that a detailed comparison would be impracticable.

—2007. Paragraph I: Deleted "at the time of the offender's initial registration and" preceding "semi-annually" and "at the time of the offender's re-registration" thereafter in the first sentence.

NOTES TO DECISIONS

1. Constitutionality
2. Nature of fee

1. Constitutionality
RSA 651-B:11, I, requiring sex offenders to pay a $17 semi-annual fee, was not an ex post facto law under N.H. Const. pt. I, art. 23. It was not imposed as punishment, but to defray the costs of maintaining the sex offender registry; moreover, because the fee was imposed at the time of registration, which occurred upon a sex offender's release from prison, the requirements of registration and

payment of the fee occurred prospectively, not retrospectively. Horner v. Governor, 157 N.H. 400, 951 A.2d 180, 2008 N.H. LEXIS 76 (2008).

2. Nature of fee

RSA 651-B:11, I, requiring sex offenders to pay a $17 semiannual fee, was not a tax, but a fee, and thus did not violate N.H. Const. pt. I, art. 12 and N.H. Const. pt. II, art. 5. The charge was not intended to raise additional revenue but was used solely to support a governmental regulatory activity made necessary by the actions of those required to pay the charge. Horner v. Governor, 157 N.H. 400, 951 A.2d 180, 2008 N.H. LEXIS 76 (2008).

651-B:12. Application.

Whenever possible, the provisions of this chapter shall be interpreted and applied consistent with the provisions of the federal Jacob Wetterling Act, as amended.

Source.

2006, 327:13, eff. January 1, 2007.

References in Text.

The federal Jacob Wetterling Act, referred to in this section, is codified at 42 U.S.C.S. § 14071.

CHAPTER 651-C

DNA TESTING OF CRIMINAL OFFENDERS

SECTION.
651-C:1.   Definitions.
651-C:2.   DNA Analysis Required.
651-C:3.   Dissemination of Information in DNA Database.
651-C:4.   Unauthorized Dissemination or Use of DNA Database Information; Obtaining DNA Samples Without Authority; Penalties.
651-C:5.   Expungement of DNA Database Records Upon Reversal or Dismissal of Conviction.
651-C:6.   Cost.
651-C:7.   Applicability. [Repealed.]

RESEARCH REFERENCES

New Hampshire Bar Journal.

For Attorney General article, "The New Hampshire Office of Chief Medical Examiner: Medicolegal Death Investigation in the Granite State," see 45 N.H.B.J. 14 (2004).

For article, "A Vision of Justice: The Future of the New Hampshire Courts," see 45 N.H.B.J. 12 (2005).

651-C:1. Definitions.

In this chapter:

I. "CODIS" means the Combined DNA Index System, the FBI's national DNA identification index system.

II. "Department" means the department of safety.

III. "Division" means the division of state police, department of safety.

IV. "DNA" means deoxyribonucleic acid.

V. "DNA record" means the DNA identification information stored in the state DNA database or CODIS for the purpose of generating investigative leads or supporting statistical interpretation of DNA test results. The DNA record is the objective form of the DNA analysis test and may include numerical representation of DNA fragment lengths, digital images of autoradiographs, discrete allele assignment numbers, and similar characteristics obtained from a DNA sample which are of value in establishing the identity of individuals. A DNA record may not specify the presence, absence, or alteration of any gene or chromosome.

VI. "DNA sample" means a blood, tissue, hair follicle, or other biological sample provided by any person or submitted to the division pursuant to this subdivision for analysis or storage or both.

VII. "FBI" means the Federal Bureau of Investigation.

VIII, IX. [Repealed.]

Source.

2002, 183:1, eff. May 15, 2002. 2010, 208:2, eff. August 24, 2010.

Amendments

—**2010.** The 2010 amendment deleted VIII and IX.

651-C:2. DNA Analysis Required.

I. Upon intake or prior to the release of any offender after conviction for the commission of any sexual offense, as defined in RSA 651-B:1, V, or any offense against a child as defined in RSA 651-B:1, VII, or any other felony offense prohibited by the laws of this or another state or federal law, whether on probation, conditional or unconditional release, completion of sentence, or release for any other reason, such person shall have a DNA sample taken for DNA analysis to determine identification characteristics specific to the person.

II. The analysis shall be performed under the direction of the division, following procedures in conformance with the federal "DNA Identification Act of 1994". Identifying characteristics of the resulting DNA profile shall be stored by the division in a DNA database compatible with and maintained by the CODIS system. Information in the database shall be made available only as provided in RSA 651-C:3.

III. The division shall prescribe procedures compatible with the Federal Bureau of Investigation's requirements for the CODIS program, to be used in the collection, submission, identification, analysis, storage, and disposition of DNA samples and DNA records obtained pursuant to this subdivision.

IV. The division may contract with third parties for the purposes of this subdivision. Any DNA sample sent to third parties for analysis shall be coded to maintain confidentiality concerning the donor of the sample.

V. A certificate and the results of the analysis shall be admissible in any court as evidence of the facts stated in the analysis.

VI. A law enforcement officer may use such means as are reasonably necessary to detain, restrain, and collect a DNA sample from an individual who refuses to cooperate in the collection of a sample.

VII. If the initial DNA sample collected from an individual is found to be deficient, a new sample shall be collected.

VIII. Any person required under this chapter to submit a DNA sample, including a juvenile offender who is required to submit a DNA sample prior to the juvenile's eighteenth birthday, who knowingly refuses to submit such sample for a period of 30 days after receiving notice from the division, the department of corrections, probation, parole, or other authorized representative of law enforcement shall be guilty of a class A misdemeanor.

IX. Any entry into the database which is found to be erroneous shall not prohibit law enforcement officials from the legitimate use of the information in the furtherance of a criminal investigation.

X. Any authorized individual collecting a DNA sample shall be immune from civil liability, provided such person acts with reasonable care under the circumstances.

Source.
2002, 183:1, eff. May 15, 2002. 2010, 208:1, eff. August 24, 2010.

References in text.
The federal "DNA Identification Act of 1994," referred to in par. II, is principally classified to 42 U.S.C.S. § 14131 et seq.

Amendments
—2010. The 2010 amendment, in I, substituted "sexual offense, as defined in RSA 651-B:1, V, or any offense against a child as defined in RSA 651-B:1, VII, or any other felony offense prohibited by the laws of this or another state or federal law" for "offense defined in RSA 651-C:1, VIII or IX, or commission of a similar offense prohibited by federal law or the laws of another state" and deleted "or prior to the release of any juvenile offender after a finding of delinquency" following "other reason."

Applicability of 2010 amendment.
2010, 208:3, eff. August 24, 2010, provided:
"I. Section 1 of this act shall apply to those persons who are incarcerated in a state or county correctional facility, or on probation or parole, for a felony offense, or who are required to register under RSA 651-B, on or after the effective date of this act.
"II. The provisions of RSA 651-C in effect prior to the effective date of this act shall apply to those persons convicted of a violent crime as defined in that chapter, on or after July 1, 2003, and to persons incarcerated in a state or county correctional facility, or on probation or parole, for a violent crime as defined in RSA 651-C:1, IX, on or after July 1, 2003.
"III. The provisions of RSA 651-C in effect prior to the effective date of this act shall apply to those persons convicted of a sexual offense listed under RSA 651-C:1, VIII, on or after August 2, 1996, and to persons incarcerated in a state or county correctional facility for a sexual offense listed under RSA 651-C:1, VIII, on or after August 2, 1996."

Cross References.
Classification of crimes, see RSA 625:9.
Sentences, see RSA 651.

651-C:3. Dissemination of Information in DNA Database.

I. It shall be the duty of the division to receive DNA samples and to analyze, classify, and store the DNA records of DNA samples submitted pursuant to this subdivision, and to make such information available to federal, state, and local law enforcement officers upon request made in furtherance of an official investigation of any criminal offense. Such law enforcement officers shall use such information only for the purposes of criminal investigations and prosecutions, or as necessary to the functions of an office of chief medical examiner. A request may be made by personal contact, mail, or electronic means. The name of the person making the request and the purpose for which the information is requested shall be maintained on file with the division. The information contained in the database shall not be a public record for the purposes of RSA 91-A, and shall not be available for inspection by any unauthorized individual.

II. The commissioner of the department of safety shall adopt rules under RSA 541-A to govern the methods of obtaining information from the state DNA database and CODIS and procedures for verification of the identity and authority of the requester.

III. Upon request, a copy of the request for a search shall be furnished to any person identified and charged with an offense as the result of a search of information in the database. Only when a sample or DNA record supplied by the person making the request satisfactorily matches a profile in the database shall the existence of data in the database be confirmed or identifying information from the database be disseminated.

IV. The division may create a separate statistical database comprised of DNA records of persons whose identities are unknown. Nothing in this subdivision shall prohibit the department from sharing or otherwise disseminating the information in the statistical database with law enforcement or criminal justice agencies within or without the state.

Source.
2002, 183:1, eff. May 15, 2002.

651-C:4. Unauthorized Dissemination or Use of DNA Database Information; Obtaining DNA Samples Without Authority; Penalties.

I. Any person who, without authority, disseminates information contained in the DNA database shall be guilty of a class B misdemeanor. Any person who disseminates, receives, or otherwise uses or attempts to use information in the database, knowing that such dissemination, receipt, or use is for a purpose other than as authorized by the provisions of this subdivision, shall be guilty of a class A misdemeanor. Except as authorized by law, any person who, for purposes of having a DNA analysis performed, obtains or attempts to obtain any sample submitted to the forensic science laboratory for analysis shall be guilty of a class B felony.

II. The division may use DNA samples for forensic validation and forensic protocol development, provided that all personally identifying information shall be removed and shall not be used.

III. The department and its employees shall not be liable for the erroneous collection and entry of a DNA sample into the database where the collection and entry were made in good faith reliance that the individual was convicted of a qualifying offense under RSA 651-C:2, I.

Source.

2002, 183:1, eff. May 15, 2002.

Cross References.

Classification of crimes, see RSA 625:9.

Sentences, see RSA 651.

651-C:5. Expungement of DNA Database Records Upon Reversal or Dismissal of Conviction.

I. A person whose DNA record has been included in the database pursuant to this chapter may request expungement on the grounds that the criminal conviction on which the authority for including such person's DNA record was based has been reversed or the case dismissed, provided that such person requesting expungement has no other criminal convictions which would require inclusion of his or her record in the database. The department shall purge all records and identifiable information in the database pertaining to the person and destroy all samples from the person upon receipt of a written request for expungement pursuant to this section and a certified copy of the court order reversing and dismissing the conviction.

II. The DNA record of any juvenile sex offender shall be maintained in the database and shall not be automatically expunged from the database upon that individual's reaching the age of adulthood.

Source.

2002, 183:1, eff. May 15, 2002. 2003, 101:1, eff. Jan. 1, 2004.

Amendments

—2003. Paragraph I: Substituted "or" for "and" following "been reversed" and added the proviso in the first sentence.

651-C:6. Cost.

The court, upon conviction, may order the offender to pay the cost of testing. The court shall include a statement describing the responsibility for the cost of testing in the sentencing order.

Source.

2002, 183:1, eff. May 15, 2002.

651-C:7. Applicability.

[Repealed 2010, 208:2, II, eff. August 24, 2010.]

Former section(s).

Former RSA 651-C:7, which was derived from 2002, 183:1, related to the applicability of RSA 651-C for DNA testing of criminal offenders.

CHAPTER 651-D

POST-CONVICTION DNA TESTING

SECTION

651-D:1.   Definitions.

651-D:2.   Post-Conviction DNA Testing of Biological Material.

651-D:3.   Preservation of Biological Material for DNA Testing.

651-D:4.   DNA Testing and Analysis.

651-D:5.   Victim Services.

RESEARCH REFERENCES

New Hampshire Bar Journal.

For Attorney General article, "The New Hampshire Office of Chief Medical Examiner: Medicolegal Death Investigation in the Granite State," see 45 N.H.B.J. 14 (2004).

For article, "A Vision of Justice: The Future of the New Hampshire Courts," see 45 N.H.B.J. 12 (2005).

651-D:1. Definitions.

In this chapter:

I. "Department" means the department of safety.

II. "Division" means the division of state police, department of safety.

III. "DNA" means deoxyribonucleic acid.

IV. "DNA sample" means a blood, tissue, or hair follicle sample provided by any person or submitted to the division for analysis or storage or both.

V. "Investigating agency" means the law enforcement agency that investigated a case resulting in a conviction in which biological material was collected as evidence during the course of the investigation.

Source.

2004, 239:1, eff. June 15, 2004.

RESEARCH REFERENCES

New Hampshire Bar Journal.

For article, "House Bill 640: Proposed Statute on Post-Conviction DNA Testing," see 44 N.H.B.J. 28 (Sept. 2003).

651-D:2. Post-Conviction DNA Testing of Biological Material.

I. A person in custody pursuant to the judgment of the court may, at any time after conviction or adjudication as a delinquent, petition the court for forensic DNA testing of any biological material. The petition shall, under penalty of perjury:

(a) Explain why the identity of the petitioner was or should have been a significant issue during court proceedings notwithstanding the fact that the petitioner may have pled guilty or nolo contendere, or made or is alleged to have made an incriminating statement or admission as to identity.

(b) Explain why, in light of all the circumstances, the requested DNA testing will exonerate the petitioner and demonstrate his or her innocence by proving that the petitioner has been misidentified as the perpetrator of, or accomplice to, the crime for which the petitioner was convicted.

(c) Make every reasonable attempt to identify both the evidence that should be tested and the specific type of DNA testing which is sought.

(d) Explain why the evidence sought to be tested by the petitioner was not previously subjected to DNA testing, or explain how the evidence can be subjected to retesting with different DNA techniques that provide a reasonable probability of reliable and probative results.

II. The court shall notify the office of the attorney general, or the county attorney who prosecuted the case, of a petition made under this section and shall afford an opportunity to respond. Upon receiving notice of a petition made under this section, the attorney general, or county attorney who prosecuted the case, shall take such steps as are necessary to ensure that any remaining biological material obtained in connection with the case or investigation is preserved pending the completion of proceedings under this section.

III. The court may order DNA testing pursuant to an application made under this section upon finding that the petitioner has established each of the following factors by clear and convincing evidence:

(a) The evidence to be tested was secured in relation to the investigation or prosecution that resulted in the petitioner's conviction or sentence, and is available and in a condition that would permit the DNA testing that is requested in the motion.

(b) The evidence to be tested has been subject to a chain of custody sufficient to establish it has not been substituted, tampered with, replaced, or altered in any material aspect.

(c) The evidence sought to be tested is material to the issue of the petitioner's identity as the perpetrator of, or accomplice to, the crime.

(d) DNA results of the evidence sought to be tested would be material to the issue of the petitioner's identity as the perpetrator of, or accomplice to, the crime that resulted in his or her conviction or sentence.

(e) If the requested DNA testing produces exculpatory results, the testing will constitute new, noncumulative material evidence that will exonerate the petitioner by establishing that he or she was misidentified as the perpetrator or accomplice to the crime.

(f) The evidence sought to be tested was not previously tested using DNA technology or the technology requested was not available at the time of trial.

(g) If DNA or other forensic testing previously was done in connection with the case, the requested DNA test would provide results that are significantly more discriminating and probative on a material issue of identity, and would have a reasonable probability of contradicting prior test results.

(h) The testing requested employs a method generally accepted within the relevant scientific community.

(i) The motion is timely and not unreasonably delayed.

IV. If the court grants the motion for DNA testing, the court's order shall:

(a) Identify the specific evidence to be tested and the DNA technology to be used.

(b) If the court ordered different testing than requested by the petitioner, the court shall explain why the different test was ordered.

(c) Designate the New Hampshire state police forensic laboratory to conduct the test. However, the court, upon a showing of good cause, may order testing by another laboratory or agency accredited by the American Society of Crime Laboratory Directors/Laboratory Accreditation Board (ASCLD/LAB) or the National Forensic Science Training Center, if requested by the petitioner.

(d) [Repealed.]

V. The cost of DNA testing ordered under this section shall be paid by the petitioner, or by the state, if the petitioner is indigent as determined by the court. The court may appoint counsel for an indigent petitioner under this section.

VI. (a) If the results of DNA testing conducted under this section are unfavorable to the petitioner, the court shall dismiss the application and in cases where the petitioner was convicted of a sexual offense, the court shall forward the test results to the New Hampshire state prison, sex offender program.

(b) In addition to any other substantive or procedural remedies provided by applicable law, if the results of DNA testing conducted under this section are favorable to the petitioner, the court shall order a hearing and shall enter any order that serves the interests of justice, including an order vacating and setting aside the judgment, discharging the petitioner if the petitioner is in custody, resentencing the petitioner, or granting a new trial.

VII. Nothing in this chapter shall be construed to limit the circumstances under which a person may obtain DNA testing or other post-conviction relief under any other provision of state or federal law.

Source.

2004, 239:1, eff. June 15, 2004. 2010, 299:2, 3, 6, eff. September 11, 2010.

Amendments

—**2010.** The 2010 amendment added "notwithstanding the fact that the petitioner may have pled guilty or nolo contendere, or made or is alleged to have made an incriminating statement or admission as to identity" in I(a); added the second sentence of IV(c); and deleted IV(d).

651-D:3. Preservation of Biological Material for DNA Testing.

I. The investigating agency shall preserve any biological material obtained in connection with a criminal or delinquency investigation or prosecution for 5 years from the date of conviction or adjudication, or as long as any person connected with that case or investigation remains in custody, whichever is longer.

II. The investigating agency may, however, petition the court to destroy or otherwise dispose of biological material after 5 years even if a person connected with the case is still in custody. If the investigating agency petitions the court to destroy evidence before the person is released from custody, the investigating agency must serve a copy of the petition to destroy biological evidence on the person who remains in custody, any counsel of record, and the prosecuting agency. The investigating agency may destroy biological material 90 days after filing a petition, unless the investigating agency receives:

(a) A court order preventing the destruction of biological evidence; or

(b) A motion to preserve biological evidence on the grounds that the person in custody intends to file a petition for post-conviction DNA testing pursuant to RSA 651-D:2 within 180 days of the motion to preserve.

Source.
2004, 239:1, eff. June 15, 2004.

651-D:4. DNA Testing and Analysis.

I. The DNA testing and analysis under this chapter shall be performed under the direction of the division, following procedures in conformance with the federal "DNA Identification Act of 1994". Identifying characteristics of the resulting DNA profile shall be stored and maintained by the division consistent with division policy.

II. The division shall prescribe procedures to be used in the collection, submission, identification, analysis, storage, and disposition of DNA samples and all DNA information obtained pursuant to this chapter.

III. The division may contract with third parties for the purposes of this chapter. Any DNA sample sent to third parties for analysis shall be coded to maintain confidentiality concerning the donor of the sample.

IV. A certificate and the results of the analysis shall be admissible in any court as evidence of the facts stated in the analysis.

Source.
2004, 239:1, eff. June 15, 2004.

651-D:5. Victim Services.

When post-conviction DNA testing is being considered by the court, the state shall, upon request, reactivate victim services for the victim of the crime being reinvestigated during the reinvestigation of the case, during the pendency of the proceedings, and, as determined by the court after consultation with the victim and/or victim advocate, following final adjudication of the case.

Source.
2010, 299:1, eff. September 11, 2010.

CHAPTER 651-E

INTERBRANCH CRIMINAL AND JUVENILE JUSTICE COUNCIL

SECTION
651-E:1.   Council Established.
651-E:2.   Membership and Compensation.
651-E:3.   Duties.
651-E:4.   Chairperson; Quorum.
651-E:5.   Report.

Interbranch Criminal and Juvenile Justice Council; Development of Mental Health Screening Procedures.

2010, 250:2, eff. July 6, 2010, provided:

"I. The interbranch criminal and juvenile justice council (ICJJC) established in RSA 651-E shall develop procedures for the identification of a criminal defendant who may have a mental illness, estimate the cost of implementing the procedures, and make recommendations for the best method of implementing the procedures. The procedures shall:

"(a) Establish a mechanism for determining which criminal defendants will be subjected to an assessment.

"(b) Establish a mechanism to ensure that a defendant's participation in an assessment is voluntary.

"(c) Provide for the assessment of psychological or behavioral conditions that may indicate a need for emergency intervention, treatment during incarceration, referral for community services, or an evaluation for competency to stand trial.

"(d) Provide that such assessment may be conducted using simplified instruments.

"(e) Ensure that the results of the screening shall be provided to defense counsel immediately upon availability.

"(f) Provide that the results of the screening shall not be accessible by law enforcement agencies, the prosecuting attorney, or the public, and may not be used during the trial or sentencing of any criminal defendant.

"II. The ICJJC shall prepare a written report detailing the procedures and other findings required under paragraph I, and shall submit such report to the speaker of the house of representatives, the president of the senate, the chief justice of the New Hampshire supreme court, the governor, the house clerk, and the senate clerk, no later than one year from the effective date of this section."

651-E:1. Council Established.

There is established an interbranch criminal and juvenile justice council to provide leadership, communication, and coordination among those involved in or affected by the criminal and juvenile justice systems.

Source.
2008, 201:1, eff. June 16, 2008.

651-E:2. Membership and Compensation.

I. The members of the council shall be as follows:

(a) The governor, or designee.

(b) Two members of the senate, appointed by the president of the senate.

(c) Three members of the house of representatives, one of whom shall be from the criminal justice and public safety committee, and one of whom shall be from the children and family law committee, appointed by the speaker of the house of representatives.

(d) The chief justice of the supreme court, or designee.

(e) The attorney general, or designee.

(f) The commissioner of the department of corrections, or designee.

(g) The commissioner of the department of safety, or designee.

(h) The commissioner of the department of health and human services, or designee.

(i) The director of the division of juvenile justice services, department of health and human services, or designee.

(j) The director of the division of field services, department of corrections, or designee.

(k) The director of police standards and training, or designee.

(l) The director of victim/witness services, department of justice, or designee.

(m) The chief justice of the superior court, or designee.

(n) The administrative judge of the district court, or designee.

(o) The administrative judge of the judicial branch family division, or designee.

(p) The executive director of the judicial council.

(q) The president of the county attorneys affiliate of the New Hampshire Association of Counties, or designee.

(r) The president of the county corrections superintendents affiliate of the New Hampshire Association of Counties, or designee.

(s) The president of the New Hampshire Association of Chiefs of Police, or designee.

(t) The executive director of the New Hampshire Public Defender, or designee.

(u) The president of the New Hampshire Association of Criminal Defense Lawyers, or designee.

(v) The executive director of the New Hampshire Civil Liberties Union, or designee.

(w) The chairperson of the governor's commission on alcohol and drug abuse prevention, intervention, and treatment services, or designee.

II. Legislative members of the council shall receive mileage at the legislative rate when attending to the duties of the council.

Source.
2008, 201:1, eff. June 16, 2008. 2009, 199:1, eff. September 13, 2009.

Amendments
—**2009.** The 2009 amendment, in I(c), substituted "Three members" for "Two members" and added "one of whom shall be from the criminal justice and public safety committee, and one of whom shall be from the children and family law committee"; added I(h); and redesignated former I(h) through I(v) as I(i) through I(w).

651-E:3. Duties.

The council shall:

I. Identify, study, develop, and implement effective criminal and juvenile justice policy.

II. Promote the effective allocation and use of public and private resources within the criminal and juvenile justice system.

III. Foster effective communication, understanding, cooperation, and coordination among those involved in, or affected by, the criminal and juvenile justice system.

IV. Inform and engage the public regarding criminal and juvenile justice matters.

Source.
2008, 201:1, eff. June 16, 2008.

651-E:4. Chairperson; Quorum.

I. The members of the council shall elect a chairperson from among the members. The first meeting of the council shall be called by the speaker of the house of representatives or the speaker's designee. The first meeting of the council shall be held within 45 days of the effective date of this section. Twelve members of the council shall constitute a quorum.

II. The chairperson may invite any person to provide information in council meetings, provided there is no objection from the council.

Source.
2008, 201:1, eff. June 16, 2008. 2009, 199:2, eff. September 13, 2009.

Amendments
—**2009.** The 2009 amendment added the I designation and added II.

651-E:5. Report.

The council shall submit an annual report beginning on November 1, 2008, together with its findings and any recommendations for proposed legislation to the speaker of the house of representatives, the senate president, the house clerk, the senate clerk, the governor, and the state library.

Source.
2008, 201:1, eff. June 16, 2008.

CHAPTER 651-F

INFORMATION AND ANALYSIS CENTER

SECTION
651-F:1.   Definitions.
651-F:2.   Purpose and Duties.
651-F:3.   Advisory Committee.
651-F:4.   Management.
651-F:5.   Intelligence Functions of the Center.
651-F:6.   Security of Data.
651-F:7.   Penalties.
651-F:8.   Audit Requirement and Disclosure.

Contingent 2010 amendment.
2010, 208:9, eff. June 25, 2010, provided in part: "If HB 587-FN

[ch. 82] of the 2010 legislative session becomes law, then sections 5–8 of this act shall take effect as provided in section 10 of this act."

Prospective repeal of chapter.

Repeal of prospective repeal of chapter. 2010, 208:8, provided for the repeal of this chapter on December 31, 2014; however, this provision was repealed by 2013, 150:1, eff. August 27, 2013.

Statement of Purpose.

2010, 82:1, eff. May 19, 2010, provided: "The purpose of this chapter is to describe the operation of an information and analysis center within the department of safety and to ensure that the operation of such a center does not violate the rights accorded to citizens under the federal and state constitutions, to ensure the accuracy of information collected, analyzed, and retained, to ensure information is safeguarded, according to standards set by the federal and state government, and to ensure that proper practices are in place for the prompt expunging of any personally identifiable data related to innocent persons or innocent activities."

651-F:1. Definitions.

In this chapter:

I. "Criminal intelligence information" means information and data that have been determined through evaluation to be relevant to the identification of actual and impending criminal activity by an individual or group that is reasonably suspected of involvement in criminal or terrorist activity, and meets valid criminal intelligence suspicion criteria. Criminal activity shall not include motor vehicle-related offenses.

II. "Criminal intelligence system" means the arrangements, equipment, facilities, and procedures used for the receipt, analysis, storage, interagency sharing, or dissemination of criminal intelligence information.

III. "Information and analysis center" means an organizational entity within the department of safety that compiles, analyzes, and disseminates information in support of efforts to anticipate, identify, prevent, mitigate, respond to, and recover from natural and human-caused threats to the state and its people or to the United States, on behalf of the single government agency and also operates an inter-jurisdictional intelligence sharing system on behalf of 2 or more participating agencies, whether called a criminal intelligence system, information and analysis center, fusion center, or by any other name.

IV. "Intelligence data" means information and data gathered from a number of sources that, when analyzed and evaluated, provides the basis for decision making to help ensure the safety and well-being of the people of New Hampshire from actual or impending criminal or terrorist activity.

V. "Inter-jurisdictional intelligence system" means an intelligence system that involves 2 or more participating agencies representing different governmental units or jurisdictions.

VI. "Participating agency" means an agency of a local, county, state, federal, or other governmental unit that exercises homeland security, emergency management, law enforcement, or criminal investigation authority and is authorized to submit and receive criminal intelligence data through an inter-jurisdictional intelligence system. A participating agency may be a member or non-member of an inter-jurisdictional intelligence system.

VII. "Personally identifiable data" means data or information that contains a person's name, date or place of birth, social security number, address, employment history, credit history, financial information, account numbers, cellular telephone, voice over Internet protocol or landline telephone numbers, biometric identifiers including fingerprints, facial photographs or images, retinal scans, DNA/RNA, or other identifying data unique to that individual.

VIII. "Reasonably suspected" means information received and evaluated by a law enforcement officer or intelligence analyst in consideration of his or her training and experience and the facts and circumstances under which it was received that would cause a prudent person to conclude that there are sufficient facts to believe that the information is relevant to and will aid in the detection, discovery, or interruption of actual, planned, or impending criminal or terrorist activity by an individual or group.

IX. "Validation of information" means the procedures governing the periodic review of criminal intelligence and personally identifiable data to assure its continuing compliance with system submission criteria.

Source.

2010, 82:2, eff. May 19, 2010.

Contingent 2010 amendment.

See note set out preceding this section.

Prospective repeal of chapter.

See note set out preceding this section.

651-F:2. Purpose and Duties.

I. The information and analysis center shall gather information on natural and human-caused threats to the state, its people, and environment. The center shall:

(a) Gather, monitor, and analyze information from a variety of sources, examine the information, and document its significance, veracity, and possible impact on the state and its people.

(b) Evaluate critical infrastructure and key resource assets of the state and assist the director of the division of homeland security and emergency management and the director of state police in better protecting these assets.

(c) Gather available information from federal, state, and local sources and provide situational awareness, disaster intelligence, and early warning of possible terrorist activities or events, including but not limited to chemical, biological, explosive, radioactive, and nuclear threats, natural hazards, severe weather conditions, traffic hazards, fuel shortages, threats to the transportation, energy, and agricultural infrastructures, public health threats, and hazardous materials incidents.

(d) Track criminal activity in the state and provide information to the attorney general, and state, county, and local law enforcement officials to assist with the deployment of resources, to aid in the investigation of crimes, and to assist in minimizing possible conflicts in situations where 2 or more agencies are investigating the same suspect or case.

(e) Participate in planning for and monitoring various special events that might involve threats to public safety and assist the commissioner of the department of safety, the director of homeland security and emergency management, and political subdivisions in anticipating threats and adequately protecting against them.

II. The center shall monitor information from a variety of open and classified sources, analyze that information, and provide information that serves the homeland security, public safety, and emergency management needs of the state. The center shall assist in the development and use of real-time metrics in the effective and efficient deployment of public safety resources.

III. Information provided by the center shall include but not be limited to a daily report to the governor, the commissioner of the department of safety, the director of the division of state police, and the director of homeland security and emergency management that summarizes significant events or information from the previous 24-hour period that could have a significant effect on the health and safety of New Hampshire citizens and visitors, special reports regarding significant situations as they arise, responses to ad hoc requests for public safety data and information from public safety agencies, and ad hoc requests for data and analysis that will assist the department of safety in deployment of its resources.

IV. The center may allow the attendance, on detached duty with appropriate security clearances, of representatives of local police departments, county sheriffs' departments, the 911 mapping unit, the department of health and human services, the Federal Bureau of Investigation, and the Department of Homeland Security who shall be subject to the provisions of this chapter regarding access to information.

Source.
2010, 82:2, eff. May 19, 2010; 208:5, eff. August 24, 2010.

Amendments
—2010. The 2010 amendment deleted "Until June 30, 2013, the center may allow attendance of employees of" following "human services" in IV and made related and stylistic changes.

Contingent 2010 amendment.
See note set out preceding RSA 651-F:1.

Prospective repeal of chapter.
See note set out preceding RSA 651-F:1.

651-F:3. Advisory Committee.

I. The intelligence subcommittee of the advisory council on emergency preparedness and security (ACEPS) established under RSA 21-P:48 shall serve as an advisory committee to the information and analysis center, meeting periodically at the call of the chair or the commissioner of the department of safety to review the operations of the center and provide advice to the commissioner regarding security, privacy, data technology, the protection of civil rights, and other matters.

II. The attorney general or designee, and a representative of a civil liberties organization, appointed by the governor and council, shall meet with the intelligence subcommittee of ACEPS at least annually to receive reports regarding the operation of the center and provide added input to best insure the protection of civil rights and personal privacy.

III. The assistant commissioner of the department of safety shall provide ongoing oversight over the operations of the center, and shall ensure that the center compiles a report on its activities to be incorporated with the department of safety's annual report to the governor and council.

IV. On or before November 30, 2013, the advisory council on emergency preparedness and security shall report to the governor, the speaker of the house of representatives, the president of the senate, and the chairpersons of the house and senate finance committees on the progress and accomplishments of the information and analysis center and shall include recommendations for any legislative changes and whether or not the operations of the center should continue.

Source.
2010, 82:2, eff. May 19, 2010; 208:6, eff. August 24, 2010.

Amendments
—2010. The 2010 amendment added IV.

Contingent 2010 amendment.
See note set out preceding RSA 651-F:1.

Prospective repeal of chapter.
See note set out preceding RSA 651-F:1.

651-F:4. Management.

I. Persons working at the center shall be subject to background investigations and appropriate levels of security clearances. Security policies shall govern admittance to the center and the access to and release of data. The co-managers of the center shall develop and maintain an internal manual of procedures for persons working in the center. The manual shall be approved by the commissioner of the department of safety. Supplemental job descriptions for state personnel working within high security areas of the center shall include the requirement to obtain security clearances.

II. All personnel assigned to the center shall receive appropriate training for the functions they will perform.

III. The activities of the information and analysis center shall be budgeted as a specific activity code within the biennial budget of the department of safety and subject to the same level of program review and financial audit by the office of the legislative budget assistant as all other budgeted functions of state agencies.

Source.
2010, 82:2, eff. May 19, 2010.

Contingent 2010 amendment.
See note set out preceding RSA 651-F:1.

Prospective repeal of chapter.
See note set out preceding RSA 651-F:1.

651-F:5. Intelligence Functions of the Center.

I. Each participating agency, as a condition of access to the center, shall comply with the requirements of this chapter governing the collection, analysis, evaluation, maintenance, sharing, and expunging of information and data included as part of the inter-jurisdictional system.

II. Nothing in this chapter shall prevent the center from gathering and disseminating non-criminal data such as traffic crash information, weather information, and other data and information relevant and useful to the non-criminal deployment of public safety resources; provided however, that the center shall not receive, obtain, use, or retain any personally identifiable data in connection with such activities other than that publicly available for individuals licensed by the state to engage in certain occupations and professions that may be needed to respond to emergencies, and contact data regarding persons in charge of or responsible for responding to incidents at critical infrastructure sites.

III. Except as provided in paragraph II, the center may collect, use, or retain personally identifiable data as part of criminal intelligence information only.

IV. The operations and policies of criminal intelligence systems in this state shall be no less stringent than those established by the United States Department of Justice in 28 C.F.R. part 23. To the extent that, in this chapter or elsewhere, the state provides greater protection of civil rights and personal privacy than applicable federal law, state law shall take precedence.

V. Criminal intelligence data may be shared on a case-by-case basis only with law enforcement, homeland security, or counter-terrorism agencies for detective, investigative, preventive, anti-terrorism, or intelligence activity only when the information is within the law enforcement or investigative jurisdiction of the receiving agency, or may assist in preventing a crime.

VI. Criminal intelligence data may be shared with officials charged with monitoring or auditing the system's compliance with this chapter and any rules or policies adopted to implement this chapter.

VII. Except as provided elsewhere in this chapter, the information and analysis center shall share criminal intelligence data only with agencies qualified to receive this information and data under this chapter and that have procedures in place regarding information and data receipt, maintenance, security, dissemination, and expunging that are consistent with constitutional and civil liberties safeguards set forth in this chapter, unless determined to be reasonably necessary to prevent impending danger to life or property.

(a) The center shall collect and maintain criminal intelligence information concerning an individual only if there is a reasonable suspicion that the individual is involved in criminal conduct or activity, or terrorist activity, and the information is directly relevant to that conduct or activity.

(b) The center shall not collect or maintain criminal intelligence information about the political, religious, or social views, associations, or activities of any individual or group, association, corporation, business, partnership, or other organization unless such information relates directly to criminal or terrorist conduct or activity and there is reasonable suspicion that the subject of the information is or may be involved in criminal or terrorist conduct or activity.

(c) If the information is received from an inter-jurisdictional source, the center is responsible for establishing that no information is entered in violation of federal or state laws, either through examination of supporting information submitted by a participating agency or by inspection and audit procedures established by the center.

(d) The center or authorized recipient of information shall disseminate criminal or terrorist intelligence only when there is a need to know and a right to know the information in the performance of a law enforcement or anti-terrorism activity. The center shall disseminate criminal intelligence information only to law enforcement authorities who shall agree to follow procedures of the center regarding information receipt, maintenance, security, and dissemination which are consistent with 28 C.F.R. part 23 or state law where state law provides greater protection of civil rights and personal privacy. This paragraph shall not limit the dissemination of an assessment of criminal intelligence information to a government official or other individual under circumstances where such dissemination is necessary to avoid imminent danger to life or property.

VIII. The information and analysis center shall implement administrative, technical, and physical safeguards to protect against unauthorized access, improper use or retention of personally identifiable data, and intentional or unintentional damage. A record indicating to whom information has been disseminated, the reason for the release of the information, and the date of each dissemination outside the center shall be kept and clearly labeled to indicate the levels of sensitivity, levels of confidence, and the identity of the submitting agency or agencies and controlling officials.

IX. The information and analysis center shall establish written definitions for the need to know and the right to know standards for dissemination to other agencies as provided in subparagraph VII(d) and shall be responsible for establishing the existence of the requester's need to know and right to know the information requested, either through inquiry or by delegation of this responsibility to a properly trained participating agency that is subject to routine audit and inspection procedures established by the center.

X. Criminal intelligence information including personally identifiable data retained in the criminal intelligence system shall be reviewed and validated for continuing compliance with system submission criteria before the expiration of the information's retention period, which in no event shall be longer than 5 years. After the initial 5 years, the retention period may be extended in one-year increments subject to annual review, if the state police commander of the center believes that there is a reasonable possibility of ongoing criminal activity sufficient to retain the information for the additional time. The commander shall annually submit to the assistant commissioner of the department of safety a listing of files that are being retained beyond the 5-year period.

XI. The information and analysis center shall implement security policies and procedures to ensure that remote access to intelligence information and personally identifiable data is available only to authorized system users and only on a case-by-case basis.

XII. The commissioner of the department of safety or a designee with general policy making authority who has been designated with such control by the commissioner, and who has certified in writing that he or she takes full responsibility for the system's compliance with the provisions of this chapter shall have control and supervision of information and collection by the information and analysis center.

Source.
2010, 82:2, eff. May 19, 2010.

Contingent 2010 amendment.
See note set out preceding RSA 651-F:1.

Prospective repeal of chapter.
See note set out preceding RSA 651-F:1.

651-F:6. Security of Data.

I. The center shall utilize effective and technologically advanced computer software and hardware designs to prevent unauthorized access to the information contained in the system. The center shall restrict access to its facilities, operating environment, and documentation to authorized organizations and personnel.

II. The center shall store information in the system in such a manner that it cannot be modified, destroyed, accessed, or purged without authorization.

III. The center shall institute procedures to protect criminal intelligence and terrorism intelligence information from unauthorized access, theft, sabotage, fire, flood, or other natural or human-made disaster.

IV. The center shall adopt procedures for implementing its authority to screen, reject for employment, transfer, or remove personnel authorized to have direct access to the system and may only authorize and utilize a remote, off-premises system database to the extent that it complies with these security requirements and is under the exclusive control of the center.

V. The center shall adopt procedures to assure that only information relevant to the center's purpose, as defined in this chapter, is retained. Such procedures shall provide for the periodic review of information and the destruction of any information which is misleading, obsolete, or otherwise unreliable, and shall require that any recipient agencies be advised of such changes which involve errors or corrections. All information retained as a result of periodic review shall reflect the name of the reviewer, date of review, and an explanation of the decision to retain. Information retained in the system shall be reviewed and validated for continuing compliance with system submission criteria before the expiration of its retention period, which in no event shall be longer than 5 years.

VI. The center shall make remote terminal access to intelligence information available to a participating agency, provided the agency has adequate policies and procedures in place to insure that the information is accessible only to authorized users. Such access shall be on a case-by-case basis only.

VII. There shall be no purchase or use of any electronic, mechanical, or other device for surveillance purposes that is in violation of the provisions of the Electronic Communications Privacy Act of 1986, RSA 570-A:1 through RSA 570-A:11, or any other applicable federal or state statute related to civil rights, personal privacy, personally identifiable data, or wiretapping and surveillance.

VIII. The intelligence operations of the center shall not interfere with the lawful activities of any other federal or state department or agency.

IX. In addition to the penalties set forth in RSA 651-F:7, the center shall adopt internal sanctions for unauthorized access, utilization, or disclosure of information contained in the system.

X. The center and any participating inter-jurisdictional agencies shall maintain information documenting each submission to the system. Each submission shall demonstrate compliance with center entry criteria. Such submissions shall be made available for reasonable audit and inspection by center representatives who shall conduct participating agency inspections and audits in such a manner as to protect the confidentiality and sensitivity of participating agency intelligence records.

Source.
2010, 82:2, eff. May 19, 2010.

Contingent 2010 amendment.
See note set out preceding RSA 651-F:1.

Prospective repeal of chapter.
See note set out preceding RSA 651-F:1.

651-F:7. Penalties.

I. Any person who purposely obtains, receives, uses, disseminates to an unauthorized individual, or retains any personally identifiable information on individuals in contravention of the provisions of this chapter shall be guilty of a felony and subject to a fine of $1,000 for each such violation. Prosecutions under this section shall be the responsibility of the attorney general.

II. An aggrieved individual may bring suit for civil penalties for up to $10,000 or actual damages, whichever is greater, for a violation of this section, but no action against the state shall exceed the limits to which the state has waived its sovereign immunity. The court may also award court costs and reasonable attorney's fees.

Source.
2010, 82:2, eff. May 19, 2010; 208:7, eff. August 24, 2010.

Amendments
—2010. The 2010 amendment rewrote the section to the extent that a detailed comparison would be impracticable.

Contingent 2010 amendment.
See note set out preceding RSA 651-F:1.

Prospective repeal of chapter.
See note set out preceding RSA 651-F:1.

651-F:8. Audit Requirement and Disclosure.

The department of safety shall maintain and conduct periodic audits of data access performed by personnel assigned to the center at least annually. The audit shall consist of a review of authorized credentials of persons accessing the data, a random sampling of data input quality and the type and reason for data access, and a review of the policy and procedures that govern data entry, access, and purging. The department shall report its findings in an annual report to the speaker of the house of representatives, the president of the senate, the governor, the intelligence subcommittee of the advisory council on emergency preparedness and security established under RSA 21-P:48, the attorney general, and the representative of the civil liberties organization designated under RSA 651-F:3, II.

Source.
2010, 82:2, eff. May 19, 2010.

Contingent 2010 amendment.
See note set out preceding RSA 651-F:1.

Prospective repeal of chapter.
See note set out preceding RSA 651-F:1.

User's Guide to the Index

Two guidelines for using this index are:

(1) *Consult the most pertinent subject.* For example, if you were looking in an evidence book for information about depositions, you would start with DEPOSITIONS rather than broader headings like EVIDENCE, TESTIMONY or WITNESSES. The broader headings may also exist, but to find the material more quickly, look for the specific subject first.

(2) *Cross references.* Pay close attention to and make full use of the index cross references. An index cross reference directs the index user to go to another part of the index to find treatment.

The index benefits from customer suggestions. Especially helpful are popular names or legal terms specific to your area of practice. We are grateful for your assistance in the ongoing improvement of the index.

To make comments or suggestions to improve this index or for assistance in locating material within this index, please use one of the following methods:

- Toll Free Number: 1-800-897-7922.
- Email: LNG-CHO-Indexing@lexisnexis.com

For issues not directly related to the Index, such as missing pages, ordering or other customer service information, you may contact Customer Service via a toll-free number, 1-800-833-9844, or by toll-free fax at 1-800-828-8341.

Index

A

ABANDONED PROPERTY.
Burglary, affirmative defense, 635:1.

ABANDONMENT.
Children, incompetents, 639:3.

ABORTION.
Homicide, 630:1.
Medico-legal cases.
    Medical examiner to investigate, 611-B:11.

ABSENCE AND ABSENTEES.
Limitation of action, 625:8.

ABUSE OF OFFICE.
Conflict of interest, 643:2.
Oppression by official, 643:1.
Speculation, privileged information, 643:2.

ACADEMIC DEGREES.
False academic documentation, 638:15-a.

ACCIDENTS.
Death due to accidental or unintentional injury.
    Medico-legal cases.
        Medical examiner to investigate, 611-B:11.

ACCOMPLICES AND ACCESSORIES.
Conduct of another, liability for, 626:8.
Immunity, 626:8.
Insurance fraud, 638:20.
Obstructing justice, 642:3.
    After the fact, 642:4.
Public assistance, 167:17-b.
Suicide, causing or aiding, 630:4.
Victim of offense, 626:8.

ACTIONS AND PROCEEDINGS.
Civil actions.
    Brought by defendant, sexual assault, 632-A:10-c.
    Code affecting, 625:5.
    Justification of act affecting remedy, 627:1.
Commencement, 625:8.
Drug dealer liability, 318-C:1 to 318-C:18.
    See DRUG DEALER LIABILITY.
Indictment commencing, 625:8.
Information commencing, 625:8.
Statute of Limitations.
    See STATUTE OF LIMITATIONS.
Warrant commencing, 625:8.
Wireless telephone cloning, 638:24.

ACTOR.
Defined, 625:11.

ADMINISTRATIVE ORDER.
Mistaken belief, defense of, 626:3.

ADMINISTRATIVE PROCEEDINGS.
Falsifications, 641:1.

ADMINISTRATIVE SERVICES DEPARTMENT.
Commissioner.
    Indigent defendant representation, records, 604-A:10.

ADOPTION.
Incest, 639:2.

ADULTERATED OR MISLABELED GOODS.
Fraud by, 638:6.

ADULTERY.
Misdemeanor, 645:3.

ADULT OFFENDER SUPERVISION.
Interstate compact, 651-A:26 to 651-A:38.

ADVERSE CLAIM.
Theft by failure to disclose, 637:4.

ADVERTISING.
Alcoholic beverages.
    Consumer specialties, 179:30.
    Product advertising, 179:28.
    Restrictions, 179:31.
    Retailer specialties, 179:29.
    Sign restrictions, 179:25.
False or misleading statements, 638:6.
Obscene matter, 650:2, 650:5.
Wire or oral communication intercepting devices, 570-A:3.

AERONAUTICS.
Controlled drugs.
    Sale to captain, 318-B:5.
    Use, limitations on, 318-B:8.

AEROSOL SELF-DEFENSE SPRAY WEAPONS.
Criminal use, 159:23.

AFFIRMATIVE DEFENSE.
Bad checks, 638:4.
Bail jumping, 642:8.
Burden of proof, 626:7.
Burglary, 635:1.
Child pornography, 649-A:5.
Counterfeit drugs, 318-B:2-b.
Custody, interference with, 633:4.
Deceptive business practices, 638:6.
Entrapment, 626:5.
Establishing, burden of, 626:7.
Forgery, 638:1.
Insanity, 628:2.
Obscene matter, 650:4.
Renunciation of.
    Attempt to commit crime, 629:1.
    Conspiracy, 629:3.
    Criminal solicitation, 629:2.
Restitution, 642:5.
Unauthorized access to computer system, 638:17.

AGE.
Air rifles, sale to minor, 644:14.
Criminal responsibility, 628:1.
Death penalty, 630:1.
Firearms, furnishing to minor, 644:15.
Incapacity, 628:1.
Incest, 639:2.
Prostitution, 645:2.
Sexual assault, 632-A:2, 632-A:3.
Tattooing of minor, 639:3.
Welfare of child, endangering, 639:3.

AGED PERSONS.
Criminal neglect of elderly, disabled or impaired adults, 631:8.

AGGRESSION.
Force to prevent, justification, 627:4.

AGREEMENT ON DETAINERS.
Application, 606-A:4.
Appropriate court, defined, 606-A:2.
Compact administrator, 606-A:6.
Definition, 606-A:2.
Enactment of agreement, 606-A:1.
Enforcement, 606-A:3.
Warden, duty of, 606-A:5.

I-1

AGRICULTURAL VANDALISM, 539:9.

AIDERS AND ABETTORS.
Accomplices and accessories.
See ACCOMPLICES AND ACCESSORIES.

AIDS.
Testing sexual offenders, 632-A:10-b.

AIRLINES.
Passengers, justification for use of force, 627:6.
Services, theft of, 637:8.
Threatening safety on, 631:4.

AIRPLANE.
Joyriding, 637:9.

AIR RIFLES.
Minors, sale to, 644:14.

AIR SPACE.
Jurisdiction, 625:4.

ALARM.
False reports, 641:4.
Breach of peace, 644:3.
Public service, sentence to perform, 651:2.

ALCOHOLIC BEVERAGES.
Admission price or fee by licensee.
Exchange of coupon, ticket or check for beverages, 179:41.
Adulteration, 179:16.
Advertising.
Illuminated signs, 179:25.
Product display, 179:28.
Specialties.
Consumer, 179:30.
Retailer, 179:29.
Age.
Misrepresenting, 179:9.
Posting age requirements, 179:18.
Alteration of premises, 179:53.
**Amusement machines provided by on-sale or off-sale
licensees,** 179:19.
Attempt by person under 21 to purchase, 179:10-a.
Bar, serving patrons at, 179:27.
Beer.
Container sizes, 179:33.
Samples, distribution, 179:31.
Specialty beers having alcohol content greater than 12 percent.
Label requirements, 179:40-a.
Beverage.
Delinquent accounts, licensees reporting, 179:13.
Sales, reports of, 179:14.
Transportation of, 179:15.
Billboard.
Advertising, 179:31.
Bottles, containers and packages.
Specialty beers having alcohol content greater than 12 percent.
Label requirements, 179:40-a.
Brew pub licenses.
Prohibited interest of holder of license, 179:11.
Champagne brunch.
Advertising by on-sale licensees, 179:31.
Cider, sale of.
Drinking age, sale to person under, 179:6.
Commercial accounts.
On-sale and off-sale licensees extending credit through medium
of, 179:43.
Concessions, leasing or renting, 179:48.
Consumption.
Enforcement activity verifying noncompliance, 179:5-b.
Containers.
Beer, 179:33.
Requirements, 179:33.
Wine, 179:34.
Corporate officers, notification of change in, 179:55.
Coupon offers, 179:31.
Coupons exchanged for beverages, admission price or fee,
179:41.

ALCOHOLIC BEVERAGES —Cont'd
Credit cards.
On-sale and off-sale licensees extending credit through medium
of, 179:43.
Credit sales of, 179:43.
Dancing provided by on-sale licensees, 179:19.
Darts allowed in defined areas, 179:19.
Delinquency of licensee in making payment of accounts,
179:13.
Delivery slips, retention of, 179:33.
Distributor.
Credits, limitations on, 179:13.
Delinquent accounts, reporting, 179:13.
Invoices, 179:33.
Prices, 179:33.
Retention, 179:35.
Prohibited interests, 179:11.
Sales, reports of, 179:14.
Drinking age, 179:5.
Documentation required, 179:8.
Identification card.
False, 179:9.
Lending to another, 179:9.
Possession by person under, 179:10.
Required, 179:8.
Withdrawal of, 179:9.
Sales to persons under.
Cider, 179:6.
Defenses, 179:7.
Drive-in windows prohibited, 179:53.
Employees and employment.
Liquor commissioner or employees, prohibitions, 179:21.
State officials, prohibitions, 179:21.
Employment, licensed places.
Age.
Employment of minors, 179:23.
Aliens, 179:20.
Bartenders, 179:23.
Citizens, 179:20.
Drinking while working, 179:20.
Felons, 179:23.
Fines and penalties.
Employment intervention by state officials, 179:22.
Intervention by state officials, 179:22.
Manager, change of, 179:24.
Minors, 179:23.
Sign restrictions, 179:25.
Waiters and waitresses, 179:23.
Enforcement proceedings and penalties.
False statements at hearings, 179:56.
Fines.
Administrative, 179:57.
Deposited into general fund, 179:61.
Hearings, 179:56.
Penalties, 179:58.
Suspension or revocation as sanction, 179:57.
Entertainment provided by on-sale licensees, 179:19.
Fake ID used for purposes of purchasing, 179:9.
False identification.
Manufacture, sale and possession, 179:62.
Fees.
Delinquent accounts, failure to report, 179:13.
Fines and penalties.
Age, misrepresenting, 179:9.
General penalty, 179:58.
Identification cards, misuse of, 179:9.
Payments, 179:61.
Forfeiture, 179:3.
Driving while intoxicated, 179:4.
Protective custody, persons in, 179:4.
Foyers in on-sale establishments.
Consumption in prohibited, 179:27.
Free drinks, serving of, 179:44.
Gambling or wagering prohibited on licensees' premises,
179:19.

ALCOHOLIC BEVERAGES —Cont'd
Hallways of on-sale establishments.
  Consumption in prohibited, 179:27.
Happy hour.
  Advertising references, 179:31.
Identification card.
  False, 179:9.
  Lending to another, 179:9.
  Withdrawal of, 179:9.
Illuminated signs, prohibition on advertising, 179:25.
Importers.
  Prohibited interests, 179:11.
Intoxication.
  Protective custody, forfeiture of liquor and beverages, 179:4.
Invoices, 179:33.
  Commission, submission to, 179:38.
  Retention, 179:35.
Kegs, 179:5-a.
Kitchens of on-sale establishments.
  Consumption in prohibited, 179:27.
Licenses.
  Brew pubs.
    Prohibited interest of licensee, 179:11.
  Delinquency of on-sale or off-sale licensee in making payments
    of accounts, 179:13.
  Entertainment and dancing provided by on-sale licensees,
    179:19.
  Fines, administrative, 179:57.
  Off-sale licensees.
    Number held, unrestricted, 179:11.
  Penalties for violations, 179:58.
  Posting of, required, 179:51.
  Prohibited interests, licensees, 179:11.
  Revocation, 179:57.
  Suspension, 179:57.
Lighting requirements for on-sale licensees, 179:51.
Liquor investigators, 179:59.
  Interference with, 179:60.
Listing of retail prices in newspapers, magazines, etc.,
  179:31.
Loiter on premises, licensees not to allow intoxicated
  persons to, 179:50.
Manufacturers.
  Delinquent accounts, reporting, 179:13.
  Prohibited interests.
    Beverage manufacturers, 179:11.
  Sales, reports of, 179:14.
Minors.
  Enforcement activity verifying noncompliance, 179:5-b.
  House parties.
    Facilitating a drug or underage alcohol house party, 644:18.
Misrepresenting age for purposes of purchasing, 179:9.
Off-sale licensees.
  Hours of sale, 179:17.
  Special license restriction, 179:47.
On-sale licensees.
  Congregating of patrons, 179:27.
  Fire certificates, 179:26.
  Health certificates, 179:26.
  Hours of sale, 179:17.
  Package deals, 179:42.
  Serving restrictions, 179:27.
  Substitution of brands, 179:40.
Outdoor internally illuminated screen displays.
  Advertising prohibited, 179:31.
Package deals, 179:42.
Packaging requirements, 179:33.
Penalties for violations, 179:58.
Permitting persons under 21 years of age to possess or
  consume, 179:5.
Possession.
  Enforcement activity verifying noncompliance, 179:5-b.
Premises restrictions.
  Alteration of premises, 179:53.
  Beverage taps in view of public, 179:54.
  Concessions, leasing or renting, 179:48.

ALCOHOLIC BEVERAGES —Cont'd
Premises restrictions —Cont'd
  Conduct requirements, 179:50.
  Corporate officers, notification of change in, 179:55.
  Lighting requirements, 179:50.
  Loitering on premises, 179:50.
  Posting of licenses, 179:52.
  Surplus liquor and beverage, storage of, 179:49.
Prices.
  Listing of retail prices in newspapers, magazines, etc., 179:31.
  Wholesale distributors to make current prices available to
    commission, 179:33.
Product displays.
  Furnished by industry members, 179:28.
Prohibited interests, licensees, 179:11.
Promotion requirements, 179:33.
Purchase of supplies by licensees, 179:32.
Removal of open table wine from premises, 179:27-a.
Restrooms.
  Consumption in restrooms prohibited in on-sale
    establishments, 179:27.
Retailer advertising specialties, 179:29.
Retail prices listed in newspapers, magazines, etc., 179:31.
Sales.
  Credit sales, 179:43.
  Enforcement activity verifying noncompliance, 179:5-b.
  Hours of, 179:17.
  Prohibited, 179:5.
  Slips, retention of, 179:35.
Samples, distribution, 179:31.
Samples for tastings.
  Consumption on premises, 179:44.
Seated at tables or booths.
  Serving at on-sale establishments, 179:29.
Serving restrictions on-sale establishments, 179:27.
Sign restrictions, 179:25.
Sound trucks advertising prohibited, 179:31.
Specially advertising by retailers, 179:29.
Standing at bar or drink rails.
  Serving of patrons in on-sale establishments, 179:27.
Substitution of brands, 179:40.
Surplus liquor and beverage, storing of, 179:49.
Tastings of beverage, liquor or wine on premises, 179:44.
Ticket exchanged for beverages or as admission price or
  fee, 179:41.
Transportation of.
  Beverages, 179:15.
  Unlawful.
    Forfeiture, 179:3.
    Generally, 179:1.
    Seizure, 179:2.
  Wine, 179:15.
    Removal of open table wine from premises, 179:27-a.
Unlawful possession.
  Drinking age, person under, 179:10.
  Forfeiture, 179:3.
  Generally, 179:1.
  Seizure, 179:2.
Vendors.
  Prohibited interests.
    Beverage vendors, 179:11.
Violations.
  Enforcement activity verifying noncompliance, 179:5-b.
Wine.
  Bottles, 179:34.
  Containers, 179:34.
  Removal of open table wine from premises, 179:27-a.
  Samples, distribution, 179:31.
  Size of listed wine available for purchase, registration required.
    Transportation of, 179:15.
Wine coolers.
  Samples, distribution, 179:31.

ALCOHOLISM.
Alcoholics, protective custody of, 172-B:3.
Defined terms, 172-B:1.

ALCOHOLISM —Cont'd
Prevention and treatment services, 172-B:2.
Sliding fee scale, 172-B:2.

ALIAS.
Criminal offender registration.
Change of name or alias.
Duty to notify, 651-B:5.

ALIENS.
Pistols and revolvers, sale to, 159:8.

ALTERATIONS.
Computer equipment, 638:17.
Physical evidence, 641:6.
Serial numbers, removing or defacing, 637:7-a.

AMMUNITION.
Armor-piercing, felonious use of, 159:18.
Exploding, felonious use of, 159:18.
Teflon-coated, felonious use of, 159:18.

AMUSEMENTS.
Alcoholic beverages, licensed premises, 179:19.

ANIMALS.
Cruelty to, 644:8.
Animals in motor vehicles, 644:8-aa.
Horses, docking of tail, 644:8-b.
Transporting dogs in pickup trucks, 644:8-f.
Fighting, promotion and exhibition of, 644:8-a.
Motor vehicles.
Confinement in, 644:8-aa.
Transporting dogs in pickup trucks, 644:8-f.
Stray beasts, theft of, 637:6.
Tampering with, fraud, 638:8.
Theft generally.
See THEFT.
Trespassing, 635:3.
Unauthorized use of, 634:3.
Use in science classes and fairs, 644:8-c.
Veterinarian, protection from lawsuit, 644:8.
Willful interference with organizations or projects involving, 644:8-e.

ANNULMENT.
Conviction and sentence, records, 651:5.
Criminal records.
Possession of controlled drug, 318-B:28-a.
Violent crime, defined, 651:5.

ANTICIPATORY OFFENSES.
Attempt, 629:1.
Conspiracy, 629:3.
Criminal solicitation, 629:2.

ANTIQUES.
Gun cane, defined, 159:1.
Pistols or revolvers, defined, 159:1.

APPEAL AND REVIEW.
Bail.
Order for release or detention, 597:6-e.
Pending appeal, 597:1-a.

APPEALS.
Convictions in municipal or district court, 502-A:12, 599:1
to 599:4.
Enforcement of original sentence, 599:4.
Failure to prosecute appeal, 599:3.
Petition, 599:1-a, 599:1-b.
Records, 599:1-c.
Right of appeal, 599:1.
Criminal offender DNA testing.
Expungement of DNA database records on reversal of
conviction, 651-C:5.
Forfeitures, personal property, 617:9.
State, appeals by, 606:10.
Surety of the peace, 608:3.
Failure to prosecute appeal, 608:5.
Order, 608:4.

APPLICABILITY.
Prior offenses, prosecution and sentence, 625:2.
Territorial jurisdiction, 625:4.

APPREHENSION.
Obstructing justice, 642:3.

ARMED ROBBERY.
Felony, 650-A:1.
Murder during, 630:1-a.

ARMED SERVICES IDENTIFICATION CARD.
Tobacco products purchases.
Proof of age of purchaser, 126-K:3.

ARMOR-PIERCING BULLETS.
Crimes, 159:18.

ARRAIGNMENT.
Arrest without warrant, 594:19-a, 612:14.
Extradited person, 612:14.
Fresh pursuit, person arrested, 614:2, 614:8.
Release pending, 597:2.
Time for, 594:20-a.
Venue, 602:2.

ARREST.
Aid to officer, 594:6.
Arrest, defined, 594:1.
Arrest records, 594:14-a.
Breach of the peace, order of judge, 594:11.
Duty to obey, 594:12.
Citizen's arrest, justifiable use of force, 627:5.
Conference, friends or counsel, 594:16.
Failure to permit, penalty, 594:17.
Conveying prisoner, 594:8.
County fair security guards.
Detention powers, 627:8-b.
Courtrooms.
Judge ordering, 594:11.
Duties to obey, 594:12.
Power, 594:1-a.
Deadly force, use of, 594:4, 627:5.
Definitions, 594:1.
Demand for assistance, 594:6.
Detention of suspect, 594:2.
Arrest with or without warrant, 594:19-a.
Order of judge for arrest, 594:11.
Superintendent, authority of, 594:21-a.
Time and place, 594:20-a.
Domestic violence.
Abuse, 173-B:10.
Violation of protective order, 173-B:9.
Escape from, 642:6.
Implements for and contraband, 642:7.
Extradition.
Arresting officer, authority of, 612:9.
Failure to appear, arrest without warrant, 612:18.
Prior to requisition, 612:13.
Without warrant, 612:14.
Failure to appear, 612:18.
Felony, defined, 594:1.
Force, permissible, 594:4, 627:5.
Resisting arrest, 594:5.
Fresh pursuit.
Arrest, authority to make.
Interstate, 614:1.
Intra-state, 614:7.
Limitations, 614:3, 614:10.
Defined, 614:5, 614:9.
Judge ordering, 594:11.
Duty to obey, 594:12.
National guard.
Members.
Authority of, 594:1.
Notice of.
To county attorney, 594:10-a.
To relatives, counsel or friends.
Failure to give, penalty, 594:17.

ARREST —Cont'd
Notice of —Cont'd
To relatives, counsel or friends —Cont'd
Required, 594:15.
Officer, defined, 594:1.
Order of judge for arrest, 594:11.
Duty to obey, 594:12.
Parolees, 651-A:15-a.
Peace officer, defined, 594:1.
Phone call, right to, 594:15.
Failure to permit, penalty, 594:17.
Physical force, justification.
Assisting officer, 627:5.
Deadly force, 627:4.
Non-deadly force, 627:5.
Retreat from use of force, 627:4.
Questioning suspect, 594:2.
Weapons, search for, 594:3.
Reasonable grounds, arrest without warrant, 594:10.
Records, 594:14-a.
Resistance to, 642:2.
Resisting arrest, 594:5, 642:2.
Restraint, permissible force, 594:4.
Resisting arrest, 594:5.
Rights of person detained, 594:15.
Failure to give, penalty, 594:17.
Searches during, justification, 627:5.
Search incident to.
Weapons, search for, 594:3.
Stalking, 633:3-a.
Summons instead of arrest, 594:14.
Unreasonable force, 594:4.
Resisting arrest, 594:5.
Warrants for, 594:7.
Conveying prisoners, 594:8.
Detention of person, 594:19-a.
Place and time of, 594:20-a.
Not in possession of officer, 594:9.
Powers of officer, 594:7.
Weapons, search for, 594:3.
Without warrant, 594:10.
Detention of person, 594:19-a.
Place and time of, 594:20-a.
Domestic violence, 173-B:10.
Release of person, 594:18-a.
Stalking, 633:3-a.
Violation order, protective, 173-B:9.
Witnesses summoned from without state, exemption from arrest, 613:4.
Wrong offense, effect of charge of, 594:13.

ARSON.
Commitment evaluation, 135:17-a.
Death associated with fire or explosion.
Medico-legal cases.
Investigation by medical examiner, 611-B:11.
Felony, 634:1.
Force to prevent, justification, 627:7.
Historic structures, defined, 634:1.
Misdemeanor, 634:1.
Murder resulting, 630:1-a.
Rioting, 644:1.

ASSASSINATION.
First degree murder, 630:1-a.

ASSAULT.
Assaults by prisoners, 642:9.
Bodily harm.
Danger of, 631:3.
First degree assault, 631:1.
Second degree assault, 631:2.
Simple assault, 631:2-a.
Charging assaults, 601:7.
Children and fetuses, 631:2.
Criminal threatening, 631:4.
Deadly weapon.
Negligent injury, 631:2-a.

ASSAULT —Cont'd
Deadly weapon —Cont'd
Purposely or knowingly causing bodily injury, 631:1.
Reckless injury, 631:2.
First degree, 631:1.
Government administration, interference with, 642:1.
Indifference to human life.
Simple assault, 631:2-a.
Law enforcement officer, extended sentence, 651:6.
Minors, employment in child care service after conviction for assault on, 632-A:10.
Reckless conduct.
Second degree assault, 631:2.
Simple assault, 631:2-a.
Second degree, 631:2.
Sexual assault.
See SEXUAL RELATIONS.
Simple assault, 631:2-a.

ASSEMBLY.
Evacuation of place of assembly.
Threatening crime of violence causing, 631:4.

ATHLETICS.
Anabolic steroids.
Defined, 318-B:1.
Prohibitions, 318-B:26.
Bribery, 638:8.

ATTEMPTS.
Aggravated assault, 631:2.
Burglary, 635:1.
Commission of offense, 625:4.
In another jurisdiction, 625:4.
Inchoate crimes, 629:1.
Conduct out of state, jurisdiction, 625:4.
Methamphetamine, crimes relating to.
Manufacturing, 318-D:2.
Murder, penalty, 651:2.
Penalties, inchoate crimes, 629:1.
Renunciation, affirmative defense, 629:1.
Sabotage, penalty, 649:4.
Suicide, causing or aiding, 630:4.

ATTORNEY GENERAL.
Extradition, 612:4.
Forfeiture reports, drug assets, 318-B:17-d.
Incompetent person released to community, 135:17-b.
Office of the chief medical examiner.
Generally, 611-B:1 to 611-B:31.
See MEDICAL EXAMINERS.

ATTORNEYS AT LAW.
County attorneys.
Death investigations by medical examiners.
Report upon completion, 611-B:20.
Court-appointed attorneys.
Pleas, entering, 605:1, 605:2.
Indigent defendant representation.
General provisions, 604-A:1 to 604-A:10.
Public defenders, 604-B:1 to 604-B:8.
Right to counsel.
Extradition, 612:10.

AUTOPSIES.
Medical examiners.
Office of the chief medical examiner.
Generally, 611-B:1 to 611-B:31.
See MEDICAL EXAMINERS.

B

BAD CHECKS.
Fraud by, 638:4.

BADGES.
Forging of, 638:1.
Unlawful simulation, 638:14.

BAIL AND RECOGNIZANCES.
Appeal.
  Convictions in municipal or district court.
    Recognizance of appellant, 599:2.
  District and municipal court records, filing copies, 597:10.
  Order for release or detention, 597:6-e.
  Pending, 597:1-a.
Appellate proceedings, 597:1-a.
  Records, copies of, 597:10.
Bail commissioners.
  Appointment, 597:15.
  District courts, 597:15-a.
  Educational requirements, 597:18-a.
  Fees, 597:20.
  Powers, 597:18.
  Returns, 597:19.
  Salaried public officers, fees, 597:20.
  Sunday bail, 597:21.
  Term, 597:17.
Binding over, copies of records, 597:6, 597:11.
Capital offenses, 597:1, 597:1-c.
Cash bail, 597:10.
Default.
  Arraignment, venue, 602:2.
  Bench warrant, 597:37.
  Commitment, 597:7.
  Complainant, payment to, 597:38.
  Declaration of, 597:36.
  Defective records, 597:35.
  Detention, 597:7-a.
  Fees, 597:38-a.
  Forfeiture, declaration of, 597:31.
  Judgment for forfeiture, 597:33.
  Recovery of forfeiture, 597:31.
  Sanctions, 597:7-a.
  Striking off default, 597:32.
  Subsequent bail, 597:8.
  Venue, 597:34.
  Witnesses, 597:23.
Deposit in lieu of security, 597:2.
Detention.
  Appeal.
    Detention order, 597:6-e.
    Pending, 597:1-a.
  Authority generally, 597:1.
  Breach of conditions of release, 597:7-a.
  Default of recognizance, 597:7-a.
  Material witness, 597:6-d.
  Probationers and parolees, 597:1-d.
  Review of order, 597:6-e.
  Sentence, pending, 597:1-a.
  Witnesses, 597:6-d.
Discharge of bail.
  Court, surrender in, 597:27.
  Inability to procure bail, 597:39.
  Jailer, surrender to, 597:28.
  New bail, 597:29.
  Surrender prevented, excusing surrender, 597:30.
District courts.
  Binding over, copies of records, 597:11.
  Superior court appearance, bailing for, 597:6.
Extradition, 612:15.
  Conditions of bond, 612:16.
  Failure to appear, forfeiture, 612:18.
Fines and penalties, 597:12, 597:13.
  Offense committed while on release, 597:14-b.
First degree murder, 597:1, 597:1-c.
Forfeitures and actions.
  Bench warrant, 597:37.
  Complainant, payment to, 597:38.
  Declaration, 597:36.
  Declaration of, 597:31, 597:36.
  Default, 597:31.
  Defective records, 597:35.
  Forfeiture, 597:31.
  Judgment for forfeiture, 597:33.

BAIL AND RECOGNIZANCES —Cont'd
Forfeitures and actions —Cont'd
  Motor vehicle violations, 597:38-b.
  Striking off default, 597:32.
  Venue, 597:34.
Form of.
  Condition, 597:25.
  Continuances, 597:25.
  Irregularities, effect of, 597:35.
  Sureties to state, 597:24.
  Variations, 597:26.
Fresh pursuit, person arrested, 614:2, 614:8.
Inability to procure, 597:39.
Insufficient bail, liability for, 597:13.
Jumping bail, 642:8.
  Extradition.
    Arrest prior to requisition, 612:13.
    From this state, 612:22.
    Other state, 612:3.
Life imprisonment, offenses punishable by, 597:1-c.
Minors, 597:14.
Money deposited, 597:2, 597:3.
Murder, 597:4.
  First degree, 597:1, 597:1-c.
No-contact provision in bail order, 597:2.
Other county, offense committed in, 597:40.
  Court or justice named in warrant, 597:41.
  Return of recognizance, 597:42.
Pending sentence or appeal, 597:1-a.
Probationers and parolees, 597:1-d.
Probation violations.
  Release of defendant pending trial, 597:2.
  When hearing may be required, 597:5-a.
Professional bondsmen.
  Notice to local law enforcement.
    Searching for violators of conditions of release, 597:7-b.
Records of bail and orders.
  Appeals, 597:10.
  Subsequent bail, discharge from commitment, 597:9.
Recovery agents.
  Searching for violators of conditions of release.
    Notice to local law enforcement, 597:7-b.
Release.
  Appeal.
    Pending, 597:1-a.
    Release order, 597:6-e.
  Arraignment, pending, 597:2.
  Authority generally, 597:1.
  Conditions, 597:2.
    Amendment of, motion for, 597:6-e.
    Breach of, 597:7-a.
    Review, 597:6-e.
  Material witness, 597:6-d.
  Penalty, offense committed while on release, 597:14-b.
  Review of order, 597:6-e.
  Revocation of order.
    Grounds, 597:7-a.
    Hearing, 597:7-a.
    Motion for, 597:6-e.
  Sentence, pending, 597:1-a.
  Trial, pending, 597:2.
  Violation of conditions, 597:7-a.
  Witness, 597:6-d.
Required, 597:5.
  Persons detained for probation violation, 597:5-a.
Sentence, pending, 597:1-a.
Subsequent bail, commitment on default, 597:7.
  Application for discharge, orders, etc., 597:9.
  Bail commissioners, 597:21.
Summons instead of, 594:14.
Sundays, 597:21.
Sureties to state, 597:24.
Surrender prevented, excusing surrender, 597:30.
Trial, pending, 597:2.
Variations, 597:26.

BAIL AND RECOGNIZANCES —Cont'd
Witnesses, 597:22.
  Default, commitment, 597:23.
  Material witnesses, 597:6-d.

BAIL COMMISSIONERS.
Appointment, 597:15.
District courts, 597:15-a.
Educational requirements, 597:18-a.
Fees, 597:20.
Powers, 597:18.
Returns, 597:19.
Salaried public officers, fees, 597:20.
Sunday bail, 597:21.
Term, 597:17.

BAILMENT.
Larceny by, 637:3.
Misapplication of property, 637:10.
Theft, 637:3.

BANKS AND BANKING.
Checks.
  Bad checks, 638:4.
  Forgery, 638:1.
Fraud on depositors, 638:10.
Property, misapplication of.
  Fraud, 638:11.
  Theft by, 637:10.
Recordable writings, fraudulent handling, 638:2.
Records, tampering with, 638:3.

BARBITURATES.
Barbiturate-type drugs, defined, 318-B:1.

BAWDYHOUSE.
Permitting, 645:2.

BELIEF OR KNOWLEDGE.
Bad checks, 638:4.

BENEVOLENT SOCIETIES.
Property, misapplication of, 638:11.

BETTING.
Alcoholic beverage licensees.
  Permitting gambling or wagering on premises prohibited, 179:19.

BIGAMY.
Felony, 639:1.

BILLBOARDS.
Alcoholic beverage advertising or promotion prohibited, 179:31.

BILLIES.
Possession of, penalty, 159:15.

BIRDS.
Theft, 637:2.

BLACKJACKS.
Carrying or selling, 159:16.

BLACKMAIL.
Extortion by, 637:5.

BLOOD TESTS.
DNA.
  Post-conviction DNA testing, 651-D:1 to 651-D:5.
  See POST-CONVICTION DNA TESTING.

BOATS.
Burglary, 635:1.
Joyriding, 634:3.
Negligent homicide, 630:3.
Theft, 637:9.
Unauthorized use, 634:3.

BODILY HARM.
Arson, 634:1.
Burglary, inflicting during, 635:1.
Consent of victim as defense, 626:6.
Criminal restraint, 633:2.

BODILY HARM —Cont'd
Deadly weapon, defined, 625:11.
Extortion, theft by, 637:5.
First degree assault, 631:1.
Kidnapping, 633:1.
Party official, corrupt practice, 640:3.
Public servant, corrupt practice, 640:3.
Reckless conduct, placing in danger of, 631:3.
Rioting, 644:1.
Robbery, injury due to, 636:1.
Second degree assault, 631:2.
Serious bodily injury, defined, 625:11.
Simple assault, 631:2-a.
Threatening, 631:4.
  Corrupt practice, 640:3.
Voter, corrupt practice, 640:3.

BODY ARMOR.
Defined, 650-B:1.
Felonious use of, 650-B:2.

BOMBS.
False report, 641:4, 644:3.
  Public service, sentence to perform, 651:2.
Stink bombs, sale or use, 644:16-a.

BONDS.
Forging of, 638:1.
Tampering with, 638:3.

BONDS, SURETY.
Surety of the peace, 608:1 to 608:10.
  See SURETY OF THE PEACE.

BOOKS AND PAPERS.
Forging of, 638:1.
Tobacco tax, 78:18.

BORDELLO.
Permitting, 645:2.

BOYCOTT.
Extortion by, 637:5.

BRASS KNUCKLES.
Carrying or selling, 159:16.
Possession of, 159:15.

BRAWLING.
Disturbing the peace, 644:2.

BREACH OF PEACE.
Abuse of corpse, 644:7.
Abusive language or gestures, 644:2.
  Telephone calls, 644:4.
Air rifles, sale to minors, 644:14.
Animals, cruelty, 644:8.
Arrest.
  Order of justice, 594:11.
Bomb scare, 644:3.
Brawling, 644:2.
Broadcasting and amplification, invasion of privacy, 644:9.
Criminal defamation, 644:11.
Cruelty to animals, 644:8.
Dead body, abuse of, 644:7.
Defamation, 644:11.
Disaster, falsely reporting, 644:3.
Disorderly conduct, 644:2.
False public alarms, 644:3.
Fighting, 644:2.
Fire alarms, falsely reporting, 644:3-a.
Firearms, 644:13.
  Furnishing to minors, 644:15.
Firecrackers, 644:13.
Harassment, 644:4.
Loitering, 644:6.
Minors.
  Air rifle, sale to, 644:14.
  Firearms, furnishing to, 644:15.
  Toxic vapors, inhaling for effect, 644:5-a.
Mobs, rioting, 644:1.

BREACH OF PEACE —Cont'd
Noisy conduct, 644:2.
Obscene language or gestures, 644:2.
  Telephone calls, 644:4.
Party line, denial for emergency, 644:12.
Pedestrian traffic, obstructing, 644:2.
Photographs, invasion of privacy, 644:9.
Poisons, exposing, 644:16.
Privacy, violation of, 644:9.
Private place, defined, 644:9.
Public, defined.
  Criminal defamation, 644:11.
  Disorderly conduct, 644:2.
Recordings, invasion of privacy, 644:9.
Riot, 644:1.
Smoke bombs, sale or use of, 644:16-b.
Telephone.
  Emergency, denial to use, 644:12.
  Harassment by, 644:4.
Threatening behavior, 644:2.
  Creating panic, 631:4.
Toxic vapors.
  Inhaling for effect, 644:5-a.
Traffic, obstructing, 644:2.
Vehicular traffic, obstructing, 644:2.
Vigilantes, 644:1.

BREAKING OR ENTERING.
Burglary, 635:1.
  Murder during, 630:1-a.
Criminal trespass, 635:2.
Livestock, trespassing, 635:3.
Night, defined, 635:1.
Occupied structure, defined, 635:1.

BREW PUBS.
Prohibited interest of holder of license, 179:11.

BRIBERY.
Candidate for office, 640:2.
Commercial bribery, 638:7.
Corrupt practice, 640:2.
Party official, 640:2.
Public officer or employee, 640:2.
Sports bribery, 638:8.
Voter, 640:2.

BROTHEL.
Permitting, 645:2.

BUILDINGS.
Abandoned buildings, burglary, 635:1.
Arson, 634:1.
Burglary, 635:1.
Criminal trespass, 635:2.
Evacuation.
  Criminal threatening, 631:4.
Occupied structure, defined.
  Arson, 634:1.
  Burglary, 635:1.
Secured premise, defined, 635:2.
Threat of crime of violence causing evacuation, 631:4.

BULLETPROOF VESTS.
Felonious use of body armor, 650-B:1, 650-B:2.

BULLETS.
**Felonious use of teflon-coated, armor-piercing and
    exploding bullets,** 159:18.

BULLET WOUNDS.
Failure to report, 631:6.

BURDEN OF PROOF.
Affirmative defense, 626:7.
Controlled drug act, 318-B:22.
Drug dealer liability.
  Participation in illegal drug market.
    Standard of proof, 318-C:13.
Drug offense, forfeiture of items used in connection with,
    318-B:17-b.

BURDEN OF PROOF —Cont'd
False swearing, 641:2.
Insanity, 628:2.
Perjury, 641:1.
Principle of, 625:10.
Swearing falsely, 641:2.

BURGLAR TOOLS.
Possession of, 635:1.

BURGLARY.
Armed burglary, murder during, 630:1-a.
Felony, 635:1.
Force to prevent, justification, 627:4.
Misdemeanor, 635:1.
Murder during, 630:1.

BURIAL GROUNDS.
Cemeteries.
  See CEMETERIES.

BUSES.
Threatening safety on, 631:4.

BUSINESS.
Deceptive practices, 638:6.
Extortion, 637:5.

C

CABLE TELEVISION.
Service, fraudulent communications paraphernalia,
    638:5-a.

CALENDARS.
Alcoholic beverages.
  Retailer advertising specialties, 179:29.

CANNABIS.
Penalties, 318-B:26.

CAPITAL PUNISHMENT.
Capital murder, 630:1.
  Hanging, 630:5.
    Place, witnesses, 630:6.
Jury in capital cases, NH Const Pt 1 Art 16.
Murder.
  Rights of accused, 604:1.

CARNAL ABUSE.
Sexual Relations.
  See SEXUAL RELATIONS.

CAR PHONES.
Wireless telephone cloning, 638:21 to 638:24.

CARRIERS.
Threatening safety on, 631:4.

CELLULAR TELEPHONES.
Wireless telephone cloning, 638:21 to 638:24.
  Civil action by telecommunication service providers, 638:24.
  Criminal acts, 638:22, 638:23.
  Definitions, 638:21.
  Forfeiture of property used in committing offense, 638:24.
  Restitution, 638:24.

CEMETERIES.
Burial plots, interference with.
  Penalty, 635:8.
  Prohibited, 635:6.
Fences.
  Destruction, mutilation or removal of.
    Penalty, 635:8.
    Prohibited, 635:6.
  Possession, sale or disposition of.
    Penalty, 635:8.
    Prohibited, 635:7.
Graves, disturbance of contents of.
  Penalty, 635:6.
  Prohibited, 635:8.

CEMETERIES —Cont'd
Gravestones.
Destruction, mutilation or removal of.
Penalty, 635:8.
Prohibited, 635:6.
Possession, sale or disposition of.
Penalty, 635:8.
Prohibited, 635:7.
Markers.
Destruction, mutilation or removal of.
Penalty, 635:8.
Prohibited, 635:6.
Possession, sale or disposition of.
Penalty, 635:8.
Prohibited, 635:7.
Monuments.
Destruction, mutilation or removal of.
Penalty, 635:8.
Prohibited, 635:6.
Possession, sale or disposition of.
Penalty, 635:8.
Prohibited, 635:7.
Tombs.
Destruction, mutilation or removal of.
Penalty, 635:8.
Prohibited, 635:6.
Disturbance of contents of.
Penalty, 635:8.
Prohibited, 635:6.

CERTIFIED MAIL.
Chemical analysis, physical evidence, drug act violations, 318-B:26-a.

CHAMPAGNE BRUNCHES.
Advertising by on-sale alcoholic beverage licensees, 179:31.

CHANGE OF NAME.
Criminal offender registration.
Duty to notify, 651-B:5.

CHARITABLE ORGANIZATIONS.
Gambling machines, possession of, 647:2.

CHECKS.
Bad checks, 638:4.
Forgery, 638:1.

CHILD CARE.
Employment after conviction for offense against minor, 632-A:10.

CHILD CUSTODY.
Kidnapping.
Acts constituting, 633:1.

CHILD DAY CARE AGENCIES.
Criminal justification.
Physical force by persons with special responsibilities.
Necessary force to be limited to minimum physical contact necessary, 627:6.

CHILD PLACEMENT.
Court-ordered placements.
Indigent defendant representation, 604-A:1-a.
Indigent defendant representation.
Funding.
Additional funding, 604-A:1-b.

CHILD PORNOGRAPHY, 649-A:1 to 649-A:7.
Affirmative defense, 649-A:5.
Age of child.
Proving, 649-A:6.
Child, defined, 649-A:2.
Child care service, employment after conviction, 632-A:10.
Defenses, 649-A:5.
Definitions, 649-A:2.
Discovery, 649-A:7.
Disseminate, defined, 649-A:2.
Distribution, 649-A:3-a.

CHILD PORNOGRAPHY —Cont'd
Felonies, 649-A:3.
Child care service, employment after conviction, 632-A:10.
Findings, declaration of, 649-A:1.
Justifiable dissemination, 649-A:5.
Librarians, exemption, 649-A:4.
Manufacture, 649-A:3-b.
Offenses, 649-A:3.
Prior convictions, 649-A:3.
Purpose of law governing, 649-A:1.
Sexual activity, defined, 649-A:2.
Theater employees, exemption, 649-A:4.
Visual representation, defined, 649-A:2.
Welfare of child, endangering, 639:3.

CHILD PROTECTION.
Obscene Matter.
See OBSCENE MATTER.
Welfare of child, endangering, 639:3.

CHILDREN.
Minors generally.
See MINORS.

CHOICE OF EVILS.
Justification, 627:3.

CIDER.
Sale of.
Drinking age, sale to person under, 179:6.

CIGARETTES AND CIGARS.
Sales.
Licensees, unauthorized sales to, 78:12-a.
Youth access to and use of tobacco products, 126-K:1 to 126-K:14.
See MINORS.

CIVIL ACTIONS.
Code affecting, 625:5.
Justification of act affecting remedy, 627:1.
Victims, losses, recovery, 651:65.
Wireless telephone cloning, 638:24.

CIVIL PROCEDURE.
Witnesses.
General provisions, 516:1 to 516:38.
See WITNESSES.

CLINICS.
Gunshot wounds, reporting, 631:6.

CLOCKS.
Alcoholic beverages.
Retailer advertising specialties, 179:29.

CLONING.
Wireless telephone cloning, 638:21 to 638:24.

CLUBS.
Property, misapplication of, 638:11.

COASTERS.
Alcoholic beverages.
Retail advertising specialties, 179:29.

COCAINE.
Cocaine-type drugs, defined, 318-B:1.

COERCION.
Criminal liability, 626:1.
Duress or Coercion.
See DURESS OR COERCION.
Suicide, causing or aiding, 630:4.
Threatening safety of person or public, 631:4.

COIN-OPERATED MACHINES.
Slugs, use of, 638:13.

COMMERCIAL BRIBERY.
Fraud, 638:7.

COMMITMENT.
Corrections department.
Psychiatric unit, 622:45, 622:52.

COMMITMENT —Cont'd

Defendants, competency.
Confidentiality of information related to evaluation, 135:17-c.
Hearing on competency, 135:17-a.
Notification if discharged to community, 135:17-b.
Sentence and punishment generally.
See SENTENCE AND PUNISHMENT.

COMMON CARRIERS.
Controlled drug act, exemption, 318-B:15.

COMMON LAW.
Insanity, defense of, 628:2.
Offenses defined by statute, 625:6.

COMMUNICATIONS.
Harassment, 644:4.
Interruption of, 634:2.
Obstructing justice, 642:3.
Party line, refusing to yield, 644:12.
Services.
Defined as property, 637:2.
Theft of, 637:8.
Telephone, harassment, 644:4.

COMPACTS.
Adult offender supervision, 651-A:26 to 651-A:38.
Corrections.
Interstate corrections compact, 622-B:1 to 622-B:3.
New England interstate corrections compact, 622-A:1 to 622-A:3.
Detainers.
Agreement on detainers, 606-A:1 to 606-A:6.
New England interstate corrections compact, 622-A:1 to 622-A:3.
Parole.
Execution of compact authorized, 651-A:25.

COMPETENCY OF DEFENDANT.
Commitment to hospital for observation, 135:17.
Evaluation for permanent commitment, 135:17-a.

COMPETING HARMS.
Justification, 627:3.

COMPLICITY.
Terminating prior to commission of offense, 626:8.

COMPOUNDING CRIME.
Misdemeanor, 642:5.

COMPROMISE AND SETTLEMENT.
Witnesses.
Disclosure of information about confidential settlement agreements, 516:33-a.

COMPUTER CRIMES.
Computer contamination, 638:17.
Definitions, 638:16.
Misuse of computer or computer network information, 638:17.
Offenses, 638:17.
Penalties, 638:18.
Unauthorized access to a computer or computer network, 638:17.
Venue, 638:19.

COMPUTER PORNOGRAPHY AND CHILD EXPLOITATION PREVENTION, 649-B:1 to 649-B:6.
Citation of act, 649-B:1.
Definition of "child," 649-B:2.
Felonies, 649-B:3, 649-B:4.
Jurisdiction.
State criminal jurisdiction, 649-B:6.
Misdemeanors.
Owners or operators of computer services, 649-B:5.
Owners or operators of computer services, liability, 649-B:5.
Title of act, 649-B:1.

CONCEALING MERCHANDISE.
Computer equipment, 638:17.

CONCEALING MERCHANDISE —Cont'd
Corpse, 644:7.
Creditors, defrauding by, 638:9.
Criminal, harboring, 642:3.
Evidence, 642:3.
Newborn, death of, 639:5.
Physical evidence, 641:6.
Public records or information, 641:7.
Recordable writings, 638:2.
Records, public or private, 638:3.
Statute of limitations, tolling of, 625:8.
Willful concealment.
Prohibited acts, 637:3-a.
Use of force by merchants, 627:8-a.

CONDITIONAL SALES.
Theft by, 637:2.

CONDUCT.
Another, liability for conduct of, 626:8.
Attempt, conduct constituting, 629:1.
Defined, 625:11.
Justifiable conduct.
See JUSTIFICATION.
Liability for conduct of another, 626:8.
Reckless conduct.
Manslaughter, 630:2.
Murder, 630:1-b.
Theft, conduct constituting, 637:1.
Voluntary act, criminal liability, 626:1.

CONFIDENTIALITY OF INFORMATION.
Autopsy reports.
Death investigations by medical examiners.
Confidential medical records, 611-B:21.
Clergy.
Privileged communications, 516:35.
Criminal justice information system, 106-K:6.
Defendants, competency.
Confidentiality of information related to evaluation, 135:17-c.
Drug abuse, records for treatment of, 318-B:12-a.
Drug control, physician-patient relationship, 318-B:21.
Physician-patient, drug control, 318-B:21.
Prescriptions.
Patient-identifiable and prescriber-identifiable data.
Restrictions on business use, 318-B:12.
Substance abuse treatment and rehabilitation, 172:13.
Weapons.
Criminal background check by department of safety, 159-D:2.

CONFINEMENT.
Criminal restraint, 633:2.
Escape from, 642:6.
Implements for and contraband, 642:7.
Extortion by, 637:5.
False imprisonment, 633:3.
Probation, home confinement, 651:2.
Stalking, 594:10, 633:3-a.

CONFISCATION.
Animals, cruelty to, 644:8.

CONFLICT OF INTEREST.
Abuse of office, 643:2.

CONGRESS, REPRESENTATIVE IN.
Murder of, 630:1-a.

CONSENT.
Boats, joyriding, 634:3.
Bodily harm, consent of victim, 626:6.
Defense.
Victim consenting, 626:6.
Drug user giving, 626:6.
Immaturity of victim, 626:6.
Incompetent giving, 626:6.
Insanity of victim, 626:6.
Intoxicated person giving, 626:6.
Joyriding, 634:3.

CONSENT —Cont'd
Sexual assault.
  Aggravated felonious, 632-A:2.
Sporting event, risk of bodily harm, 626:6.
Vehicles, authorized use, 634:3.
Victim consenting, defense of, 626:6.

CONSERVATION OFFICER.
Murder of, death penalty, 630:1.

CONSPIRACY.
Commission of offense, 625:4.
  In another jurisdiction, 625:4.
Conduct out of state, 625:4.
Controlled drugs, 318-B:26.
  Drug enterprise leader, 318-B:2.
Inchoate crimes, 629:3.
Organized retail crime enterprise, 637:10-c.
Out of state conduct, 625:4.
Penalties.
  Inchoate crimes, 629:3.
Sabotage, 649:5.

CONSTABLE.
Murder of, death penalty, 630:1.

CONSTITUTION OF NEW HAMPSHIRE.
Bill of Rights, NH Const Pt 1 Arts 15 to 19, 33.
  Capital cases.
    Jury trial, NH Const Pt 1 Art 16.
  Jury trial.
    Jurors, NH Const Pt 1 Art 21.
  Penalties proportioned to offenses, NH Const Pt 1 Art 18.
  Rights of accused, NH Const Pt 1 Art 15.
  Venue of prosecutions, NH Const Pt 1 Art 17.
Excessive bail, fines and punishments prohibited, NH Const Pt 1 Art 33.
Habeas corpus, NH Const Pt 2 Art 91.
Searches and seizures, NH Const Pt 1 Art 19.

CONSTRUCTION.
Civil actions, affecting on, 625:5.
Fair import, 625:3.
Strictly construed, 625:3.

CONTEMPT.
Accusation, theft by extortion, 637:5.
Bail, violation of conditions of release, 597:7-a.
Criminal defamation, 644:11.
Restitution, failure to make, 651:67.

CONTESTANTS.
Tampering with, 638:8.

CONTRABAND.
Fraudulent communications paraphernalia, 638:5-a.
Implements for escape, 642:7.
Search warrants.
  Affidavit by applicant, 595-A:4.
  Assistance in execution of warrant, 595-A:8.
  Custody of seized goods, 595-A:6.
  Daytime search, 595-A:2.
  Disposition of goods seized, 595-A:6.
  Execution, 595-A:8.
  Form.
    Application for warrant, 595-A:4.
    Warrant, 595-A:3.
  Inventory of goods seized, 595-A:5.
  Issuance, 595-A:1.
  Nighttime search, 595-A:2.
  Oath, applicant under, 595-A:4.
  Property, defined, 595-A:9.
  Purposes for issuance, 595-A:1.
  Receipt for goods seized, 595-A:5.
  Requisites for, 595-A:2.
  Return of warrant, 595-A:5.
    Time for, 595-A:7.
  Safekeeping of seized goods, 595-A:6.
  Scope of statute, 595-A:9.
  Seizure of goods, 595-A:6.

CONTROLLED SUBSTANCES.
Abuse of drugs.
  Defined, 318-B:1.
  Treatment for, 318-B:12-a.
Administer, defined, 318-B:1.
Administering, 318-B:2.
Advanced emergency medical care providers.
  Affirmative defense to prosecution, 318-B:2-b.
  Possession and administration of prescription drugs, 318-B:10.
Affirmative defenses, 318-B:2-b.
Aircraft.
  Captain.
    Sales to, 318-B:5.
  Use, limitations on, 318-B:8.
Anabolic steroid.
  Defined, 318-B:1.
  Prohibitions, 318-B:26.
Cannabis-type drugs.
  Defined, 318-B:1.
  Prescription for cancer patients, 318-B:10.
Chemical analysis, certificate, 318-B:26-a.
Common carriers, exempted, 318-B:15.
Common nuisance, maintaining, 318-B:16.
Communications not privileged, 318-B:21.
Compounding, 318-B:2.
Confiscated drugs, disposal of, 318-B:17.
Conspiracy.
  Drug enterprise leader, 318-B:2.
  Penalties, 318-B:26.
Controlled drug analog.
  Defined, 318-B:1.
  Penalties, 318-B:26.
  Prohibited acts, 318-B:2.
Convictions.
  Annulment of record, 318-B:28-a.
  Burden of proof, 318-B:22.
  Drug enterprise leader, 318-B:2.
  Federal law, effect of acquittal or conviction under, 318-B:29.
  Licensing board, notice to, 318-B:18.
  Prior offenses, 318-B:27.
Counterfeit drugs.
  Acts prohibited, 318-B:2.
  Affirmative defense, 318-B:2-b.
Definitions, 318-B:1.
Dentist.
  Defined, 318-B:1.
  Labeling containers, 318-B:13.
Director.
  Defined, 318-B:1.
  Rulemaking authority, 318-B:24.
  Scheduling of substances, 318-B:1-a.
Dispensing, 318-B:2.
Disposal.
  Law enforcement officers, 318-B:17.
Drug abuse, treatment for, 318-B:12-a.
Drug dealer liability, 318-C:1 to 318-C:18.
  See DRUG DEALER LIABILITY.
Drug enterprise leader, 318-B:2.
Drug paraphernalia.
  Acts prohibited, 318-B:2.
  Defined, 318-B:1.
  Penalties, 318-B:26.
Enforcement, 318-B:23.
Exempted preparations, 318-B:11.
False statements to obtain, 318-B:2.
Federal narcotic laws.
  Defined, 318-B:1.
  Effect of acquittal or conviction under, 318-B:29.
Fines and penalties, 318-B:26.
Flunitrazepam.
  Penalties, 318-B:26.
Foreign countries, sales in, 318-B:5.
Forfeitures.
  Items used in connection with drug offense, 318-B:17-b.
    Administrative forfeiture, 318-B:17-d.
    Drug forfeiture fund, 318-B:17-c.

CONTROLLED SUBSTANCES —Cont'd
Forfeitures —Cont'd
 Law enforcement officers, 318-B:17.
 Unlawful possession, 318-B:17.
Habit forming, warning of, 318-B:13.
Hospitals.
 Records required, 318-B:12.
 Sales to, 318-B:5.
 Use, limitations on, 318-B:8.
House parties.
 Facilitating a drug or underage alcohol house party, 644:18.
Individuals.
 Exemptions, 318-B:15.
Inspections, right of entry, 318-B:25.
Inventories, 318-B:1.
Labels.
 False or forged, 318-B:2.
 Prescriptions, 318-B:13.
Laboratory.
 Defined, 318-B:1.
 Records required, 318-B:12.
 Sales to, 318-B:5.
 Use, limitations on, 318-B:8.
Licenses.
 Convictions, notice of, 318-B:18.
 Required, 318-B:3.
 Suspension or revocation, 318-B:18.
Manufacture, 318-B:2.
 Labels, 318-B:13.
 Manufacturer, defined, 318-B:1.
 Records required, 318-B:12.
 Sales by, 318-B:5.
Marijuana, possession, penalty, 318-B:26.
Methadone administration for alcohol and drug abuse treatment, 318-B:10.
Methadone maintenance program, prohibited, 318-B:10.
Minors, treatment for drug abuse, 318-B:12-a.
 Prohibited acts, 318-B:2.
Nurse.
 Administering.
  Affirmative defense to prosecution, 318-B:2-b.
 Defined, 318-B:1.
 Dispensing of, labeling, 318-B:13.
Official written order.
 Defined, 318-B:1.
 Pharmacists, sales by, 318-B:9.
 Sales, required for, 318-B:5.
 Signatures on, 318-B:7.
Outdated drugs, disposal of, 318-B:17-a.
Paramedics.
 Administration by, 318-B:10.
 Affirmative defense to prosecution, 318-B:2-b.
 Possession for emergency use, 318-B:10.
Penalties, 318-B:26.
Pharmacist.
 Affirmative defense to prosecution, 318-B:2-b.
 Defined, 318-B:1.
 Inspections, right of entry, 318-B:25.
 Labels, 318-B:13.
 Official written orders, 318-B:9.
 Records required, 318-B:12.
 Right of entry, inspections, 318-B:25.
 Sales by, 318-B:9.
 Sales to, 318-B:5.
Physicians.
 Affirmative defense to prosecution, 318-B:2-b.
 Cannabis-type drugs, prescribing for patient, 318-B:9, 318-B:10.
 Defined, 318-B:1.
 Labeling containers, 318-B:13.
 Sales to, 318-B:5.
Possession, 318-B:2.
 Lawful possession, 318-B:6.
 Licensees, 318-B:5.
Potential for abuse, defined, 318-B:1.

CONTROLLED SUBSTANCES —Cont'd
Practitioner.
 Communications not privileged, 318-B:21.
 Defined, 318-B:1.
 Professional use, 318-B:10.
 Records required, 318-B:12.
 Sales to, 318-B:5.
Preparations exempted, 318-B:11.
Prescribing, 318-B:2.
Prescriptions.
 Defined, 318-B:1.
 Labeling, 318-B:13.
 Pharmacists, sales by, 318-B:9.
Prior offenses, 318-B:27.
Professional use, 318-B:10.
Prohibited acts, 318-B:2.
Prosecutions.
 Burden of proof, 318-B:22.
 Convictions, notice to license board, 318-B:22.
 Federal law, effect of acquittal or conviction under, 318-B:29.
 Prior offenses, 318-B:27.
 Theft, 318-B:2.
Public health services division.
 Rules and regulations, 318-B:24.
Records.
 Confidentiality, 318-B:12.
 Convictions, annulment, 318-B:28-a.
 Drug abuse, treatment for, 318-B:12-a.
 Required, 318-B:12.
 Treatment for drug abuse, 318-B:12-a.
 Unlawful possession, disposal of confiscated drugs, 318-B:17.
Registered nurse, professional use of, 318-B:10.
Report of forfeitures, 318-B:17-f.
Right of entry, inspections, 318-B:25.
Rulemaking authority, 318-B:24.
 Scheduling of substances, 318-B:1-a.
Sale.
 Defined, 318-B:1.
 Manufacturer, 318-B:5.
 Official written order required, 318-B:5.
 Pharmacists, conditions for, 318-B:9.
 Prohibition, 318-B:2.
 Wholesaler, 318-B:5.
Scheduling, 318-B:1-a.
 Certain drugs, 318-B:1-c.
 Tests, 318-B:1-b.
Severability, 318-B:30.
Ship master.
 Sales to, 318-B:5.
 Use, limitations on, 318-B:8.
State food, drug and cosmetic laws, defined, 318-B:1.
Treatment for drug abuse, 318-B:12-a.
Unlawful possession, forfeiture, disposal, 318-B:17.
Use of, common nuisance, maintaining, 318-B:16.
Veterinarian.
 Defined, 318-B:1.
 Labeling containers, 318-B:13.
 Professional use, 318-B:10.
Warehousemen, exempted, 318-B:15.
Wholesaler.
 Defined, 318-B:1.
 Labels, 318-B:13.
 Records required, 318-B:12.
 Sales by, 318-B:5.

CONVERSION.
Larceny by, 637:3.

CONVICTED PERSONS, 607-A:1 to 607-A:8.
Certificate of discharge, 607-A:5.
DNA testing of criminal offenders.
 Generally, 651-C:1 to 651-C:6.
Rights lost, 607-A:2.
Rights retained, 607-A:3.
Savings provisions, 607-A:4.
Severability, 607-A:8.
Surety of the peace order on conviction, 608:8.

CONVICTED PERSONS —Cont'd
Uniform act on status of convicted persons.
   Severability, 607-A:8.
   Short title, 607-A:7.
Uniformity of interpretation, 607-A:6.
Validity, 607-A:8.

CONVICTION.
Annulment of record, 651:5.
Burden of proof, 625:10.
Disability or legal disadvantage.
   Violations, 625:9.
Obstructing justice, 642:3.
Reasonable doubt, 625:10.
Record, annulment of, 651:5.
Sentence and Punishment.
   See SENTENCE AND PUNISHMENT.
Violations, disability or legal disadvantage, 625:9.

COP-KILLER BULLETS.
Crimes.
   Felonious use, 159:18.

CORPORAL PUNISHMENT.
Justification, 627:6.

CORPORATIONS.
Actor, defined, 625:11.
Corporate records, tampering with, 638:3.
Felonies, classification of crime, 625:9.
Fines, limitations, 651:2.
   Default, 651:28.
He, defined, 625:11.
Misdemeanors, classification of offense, 625:9.
Person, defined, 625:11.
Violations, classification of offense, 625:9.

CORPSE.
Abuse of, 644:7.
Newborn, concealing death of, 639:5.

CORRECTIONS DEPARTMENT.
Adult parole board.
   Administrative attachment to department, 651-A:24.
Commitment.
   Psychiatric unit, 622:45, 622:52.
Interstate corrections compact, 622-B:1 to 622-B:3.
New England interstate corrections compact, 622-A:1 to 622-A:3.
New Hampshire youth development center, 621:1 to 621:34.
Parole, 651-A:1 to 651-A:25.
State prisons, 622:2 to 622:58.
Youth development center, 621:1 to 621:34.

CORRECTIONS OFFICERS.
Murder of, death penalty, 630:1.

CORRUPT PRACTICES.
Bodily harm, threats of, 640:3.
Bribery, 640:2.
Campaign contributions.
   Chapter not construed to prohibit, 640:1.
Candidate, bribery of, 640:2.
Compensation.
   Past action, 640:4.
   Services, 640:6.
Consultants, bribery of, 640:2.
Definitions, 640:2, 640:3.
Gifts to public servants, 640:5.
Harm, defined, 640:3.
Improper influence, 640:3.
Intimidation, 640:3.
Judges, bribery of, 640:2.
Jurors, bribery of, 640:2.
Legislators, bribery of, 640:2.
Party official.
   Bodily harm, threat of, 640:3.
   Bribery, 640:2.
   Defined, 640:2.
   Improper influence, 640:3.

CORRUPT PRACTICES —Cont'd
Past action, compensation for, 640:4.
Pecuniary benefit, defined, 640:2.
Political parties.
   Applicability, 640:1.
Public office, purchase of, 640:7.
Public servant.
   Bodily harm, threat of, 640:3.
   Bribery, 640:2.
   Compensation for services, 640:6.
   Defined, 640:2.
   Gifts to, 640:5.
   Improper influence, 640:3.
   Past action, compensation for, 640:4.
   Services, compensation for, 640:6.
Reporting.
   Bribe offers, 640:2.
   Improper influence, 640:3.
Scope, 640:1.
Soliciting bribe, 640:2.
Threats, improper influence, 640:3.
Trade associations, pecuniary benefits, 640:2.
Voter.
   Bodily harm, threat of, 640:3.
   Bribery, 640:2.
   Improper influence, 640:3.

COSTS.
Criminal offender DNA testing, 651-C:6.

COUNTERFEIT RECORDINGS, DEALING IN, 638:6-a.

COUNTY CORRECTIONAL FACILITIES.
Commitment to, 651:18.
Discharge from, 651:18.
Insane persons, transfer of, 651:11.
Municipally-owned grounds or property.
   Prisoners performing uncompensated public service, 651:36-a.
Sentence, 651:17.

COUNTY DEPARTMENTS OF CORRECTIONS.
Prisoners.
   Expense of maintenance, 651:18.

COUNTY FAIR SECURITY GUARDS.
Detention powers, 627:8-b.

COUPONS.
Alcoholic beverages.
   Coupon offers, restrictions, 179:31.
   Exchange for beverages, admission price or fee, 179:41.

COURTHOUSES.
Weapons.
   Carrying weapons into courtrooms, 159:19.

COURT ORDERS.
Simulating unlawfully, 638:11.

COURTS.
Bailiffs.
   Arrest, power of, 594:1-a.
Firearms, possession in, 159:5, 159:19.
Law enforcement officers, possession of firearms, 159:19.
Security.
   Arrest.
      Judge ordering, 594:11.
      Powers of, 594:1-a.
   Firearms, possession of, 159:5, 159:19.
Sheriffs.
   Responsibility for court security, 594:1-a.

CREDIT CARDS.
Alcoholic beverages.
   On-sale and off-sale licensees extending credit through medium of, 179:43.
Defined, 638:5.
Forging, 638:1.
Fraudulent use, 638:5.

CREDIT CARDS —Cont'd
Payment card scanning device or reencoder.
　Use to defraud, 638:29.
　　Definitions, 638:28.
Telecommunications, defrauding, 638:5-a.

CREDITORS.
Defrauding, 638:9.

CREDIT UNION.
Depositors, frauds on, 638:10.
Property, misapplication of.
　Fraud, 638:11.
　Theft by, 638:10.

CRIMINAL JUSTICE INFORMATION SYSTEM, 106-K:1 to
　106-K:7.
Board, 106-K:5.
Confidentiality of information, 106-K:6.
Criminal penalties for violations, 106-K:7.
Definitions, 106-K:1.
Design and implementation, 106-K:4.
Elements, 106-K:3.
Established, 106-K:2.
Master name index, 106-K:3.
Penalties for violations, 106-K:7.
Purpose and function, 106-K:4.
Requirements, 106-K:3.
When records to be expunged, 106-K:3.

CRIMINAL MISCHIEF.
Felony, 634:2.
Misdemeanor, 634:2.
Old Man of the Mountain, vandalizing, 634:2.
Public service, sentence to perform, 651:2.

CRIMINAL NEGLECT OF ELDERLY, DISABLED OR
　IMPAIRED ADULTS, 631:8.

CRIMINAL OFFENDER DNA TESTING, 651-C:1 to 651-C:6.
Costs, 651-C:6.
Definitions, 651-C:1.
Dissemination of information in DNA database, 651-C:3.
　Unauthorized dissemination, 651-C:4.
Evidence.
　Certificate and results of DNA analysis.
　　Admissibility, 651-C:2.
Expungement of DNA database records.
　Reversal or dismissal of conviction, 651-C:5.
Immunities.
　Erroneous collection and entry of DNA sample into database in
　　good faith, 651-C:4.
Procedures, 651-C:2.
Prohibited acts, 651-C:4.
Requirement of DNA analysis, 651-C:2.
Unauthorized dissemination or use of DNA database
　information, 651-C:4.

CRIMINAL OFFENDER REGISTRATION, 651-B:1 to
　651-B:12.
Change of address of registrant, 651-B:5.
Confidentiality of records, 651-B:7.
Definitions, 651-B:1.
Duration of registration, 651-B:6.
Penalties for noncompliance, 651-B:9.
Registration requirement generally, 651-B:2.
Release of sexual offenders into community, 651-B:3.
Reporting requirements of registrant, 651-B:4.
Rules promulgation, 651-B:8.

CRIMINAL RECORD CHECKS.
Firearms sales.
　Department of safety as point of contact for federal
　　government, 159-D:1 to 159-D:3.

CRIMINAL RECORDS.
Record of conviction, annulment.
　Possession of controlled drug, 318-B:28-a.

CRIMINAL RESTRAINT.
Felony, 633:2.

CRIMINAL SOLICITATION, 630:1.

CRIMINAL THREATENING, 631:4.
Court or judicial officers, 631:4-a.

CRIMINAL TRESPASS.
Conditions of, 635:2.
Posting property, 635:4.
　Defacing or removing signs, 635:5.

CROPS.
Livestock damaging, 635:3.
Vandalism, 539:9.

CRUELTY.
Animals, 644:8.
Animal use in science classes and fairs, 644:8-c.
Children, 639:3.

CULPABILITY.
Accomplice, 626:8.
Conduct of another, liability for, 626:8.
Conspiracy, inchoate crimes, 629:3.
Element of an offense, 625:11.
Felony, 626:2.
Ignorance, effect of, 626:3.
Inchoate crimes.
　Conspiracy, 629:3.
　Solicitation to commit crime, 629:2.
Misdemeanor, 626:2.
Mistake, effect of, 626:3.
Murder, 626:2, 630:1.
Reckless conduct, 631:3.
Solicitation to commit crime.
　Inchoate crimes, 629:2.
Violation, 626:2.

CURTILAGE.
Defined, 627:9.

CUSTODY.
Escape from, 642:6.
　Implements for and contraband, 642:7.
Interference with, 633:4.

D

DAGGERS.
Carrying or selling, penalty, 159:16.

DAMAGES.
Civil liability, affect on, 625:5.
Drug dealer liability.
　Generally, 318-C:1 to 318-C:18.
　　See DRUG DEALER LIABILITY.
Information and analysis center violations, 651-F:7.
Trespass by livestock, 635:2.

DANCING PROVIDED BY ON-SALE ALCOHOLIC
　BEVERAGE LICENSEES, 179:19.

DARTS.
Alcoholic beverage licensees.
　Use of darts in defined areas, 179:19.

DATE RAPE DRUGS.
Controlled drugs, 318-B:1-c.
Penalties, 318-B:26.

DEAD BODY.
Abuse of, 644:7.

DEADLY FORCE.
Justification.
　Arresting law enforcement officer, 627:5.
　Arson, prevention of, 627:5.
　Assisting officer, 627:5.
　Burglary, preventing, 627:4.
　Citizen's arrest, 627:5.
　Defined, 627:9.
　Felonies, preventing, 627:5.
　Kidnapping, preventing, 627:4.

DEADLY FORCE —Cont'd
Justification —Cont'd
  Penal guards, use of, 627:5.
  Premises, defense of, 627:4.
  Self-defense, 627:4.
  Sex offenses, preventing, 627:4.
  Weapons, use of, 627:9.

DEADLY WEAPON.
Burglary, with, 635:1.
Defined, 625:11.
Escapee using, 642:6.
Firearms, felonious use of, 650-A:1.
First degree assault, 631:1.
Homicide, 630:1.
Rioting with, 644:1.
Robbery, 636:1.
Second degree assault, 631:2.
Simple assault, 631:2-a.
Theft with, penalty, 637:11.

DEALER.
Stolen property, 637:7.

DEATH.
Explosives.
  Death or bodily injury, 158:18.
False fire alarms, death resulting, 644:3-b.
Investigation by medical examiner.
  Medico-legal cases.
    Autopsies, 611-B:17.
      Expenses, 611-B:27-a.
      Reports by medical examiner, 611-B:21.
    Body tissue and body fluids.
      Retention, disposition, 611-B:18.
    Charge of body.
      Medical examiner to take, 611-B:13.
    Child death.
      Report to bureau of maternal and child health, 611-B:22.
    Claims for fees.
      Assistant deputy medical examiners, 611-B:27.
    Compensation.
      Assistant deputy medical examiners, 611-B:27.
    Confidential medical records, 611-B:21.
    Forensic science laboratory.
      Investigations by.
        Supervising medical examiner requiring, 611-B:19.
    Medical records, 611-B:14-a.
    Medico-legal investigation fund, 611-B:28.
    Money and other personal property of deceased.
      Medical examiner to take charge of, 611-B:16.
    Postmortem examinations, 611-B:15.
    Release of body.
      Completion of examination, 611-B:24.
        Unclaimed bodies, 611-B:25.
      Death report to person taking custody of body, 611-B:26.
    Reporting medico-legal deaths.
      Mandatory reporting, 611-B:12.
    Report to county attorney.
      Completion of investigation, 611-B:20.
    Survey of body and surroundings, 611-B:14.
    Unidentified human remains.
      Dental examination, 611-B:23.
      Release of body, 611-B:25.
      Retention, disposition, 611-B:18.
  Office of the chief medical examiner.
    Generally, 611-B:1 to 611-B:31.
Newborn child.
  Concealing death, 601:6-a, 639:5.
Reporting medico-legal deaths.
  Mandatory reporting, 611-B:12.
Robbery, death due to, 636:1.

DEATH PENALTY.
Capital murder, 630:1.
Injection, lethal, 630:5.
Place of execution, 630:6.
Witnesses, 630:6.

DECEPTION.
Business practices, 638:6.
Counterfeit recordings, 638:6-a.
Criminal restraint, 633:2.
Documents, fraudulent execution, 638:12.
Physical evidence, falsifying, 641:6.
Public officials, 641:3.
Serial numbers, removing or altering, 637:7-a.
Services, theft of, 637:8.
Suicide, causing or aiding, 630:4.
Theft by, 637:4.

DECISION OF COURT.
Mistaken belief founded upon, 626:3.

DEEDS.
Fraud, 638:2.

DEFAMATION.
Criminal defamation, 644:11.
Forfeitures, personal property, 617:2 to 617:4.

DEFAULT.
Omission.
  Defined by statute, 625:6.
Omission of duty, 625:4.

DEFECATION.
Public defecation, 645:1-a.

DEFENDANT.
Burden of proof, 625:10.
Innocence, presumption of, 625:10.
Trial of, 606:3.

DEFENSES.
Affirmative defense.
  Bail jumping, 642:8.
  Burden of proof, 626:7.
  Burglary, 635:1.
  Child pornography, 649-A:5.
  Custody, interference with, 633:4.
  Entrapment, 626:5.
  Establishing, burden of, 626:7.
  Laser pointing device used in organized meeting or training class, 631:3-a.
  Obscene matter, 650:4.
  Renunciation of.
    Attempt to commit crime, 629:1.
    Conspiracy, 629:3.
    Criminal solicitation, 629:2.
  Restitution, 642:5.
Attempt to commit crime, renunciation of, 629:1.
Bail jumping, 642:8.
Bigamy, 639:1.
Bodily harm, consent of victim, 626:6.
Burden of proof, 625:10.
Burglary, 635:1.
Child pornography, 649-A:5.
Consent of victim, 626:6.
Conspiracy, renunciation of, 629:3.
Criminal solicitation, renunciation of, 629:2.
Custody, interference with, 633:4.
Deceptive business practices, 638:6.
Disproving, 626:7.
Element of an offense negating statute of limitations, 625:11.
Entrapment, 626:5.
Ignorance, 626:3.
Immunity from liability.
  Conspiracy, 629:3.
  Criminal solicitation, 629:2.
Incapacity.
  Conspiracy, 629:3.
  Criminal solicitation, 629:2.
Insanity defense, 628:2.
  Commitment to hospital for observation, 135:17.
  Confidentiality of information related to evaluation, 135:17-c.
  Evaluation for permanent commitment, 135:17-a.
  Notification if discharged to community, 135:17-b.

DEFENSES —Cont'd

Intoxication, 626:4.

Irresponsibility.
  Conspiracy, 629:3.
  Criminal solicitation, 629:2.

Justification, mistake supporting, 626:3.

Justification generally, 627:1 to 627:9.
  See JUSTIFICATION.

Mistake, 626:3.

Obscene matter, 650:4.

Presumptions, 626:7.

Prior offenses, procedural provisions, 625:2.

Prostitution.
  Trafficking in persons, 645:2.

Renunciation of.
  Attempt to commit crime, 629:1.
  Conspiracy, 629:3.
  Criminal solicitation, 629:2.

Solicitation to commit crime, renunciation of, 629:2.

Tobacco products purchases.
  Proof of age of purchaser, 126-K:3.

DEFINED TERMS.

Abuse.
  Domestic violence, 173-B:1.

Abuse of drugs, 172:1.
  Controlled drug act, 318-B:1.

Academic degree.
  False academic documentation, 638:15-a.

Access, 638:16.
  Criminal justice information system, 106-K:7.

Access device.
  Wireless telephone cloning, 638:21.

Acting chief medical examiner.
  Office of the chief medical examiner, 611-B:1.

Act of violence.
  Classification of misdemeanors, 625:9.

Actor, 625:11.
  Sexual assault, 632-A:1.

Administer.
  Controlled drugs, 318-B:1.

Administration of criminal justice.
  Criminal justice information system, 106-K:1.

Administrative release to parole.
  Youth development center, 621:3.

Adult.
  Criminal neglect of elderly, disabled or impaired adults, 631:8.
  Interstate compact for adult offender supervision, 651-A:26.

Adulterated, 638:6.

Advanced emergency medical care provider.
  Controlled drug act, 318-B:1.

Advanced registered nurse practitioner.
  Controlled drug act, 318-B:1.

Aerosol self-defense spray weapon, 159:20.

Affinity, 632-A:1.

Aggrieved person.
  Electronic surveillance, 570-A:1.

Alcohol abuser, 172-B:1.

Alcoholic, 172-B:1.

Alcoholism, 172-B:1.

Amphetamine-type drugs, 318-B:1.
  Study, treatment and care of inebriates, 172:1.

Anabolic steroid, 318-B:1.

Anhydrous ammonia.
  Methamphetamine, crimes relating to, 318-D:1.

Animal, 644:8, 644:8-aa.
  Confining animals in motor vehicle, 644:8-aa.
  Cruelty generally, 644:8.
  Use in science classes and fairs, 644:8-c.

Another, 630:1.

Antique gambling machine, 647:2.

Antique pistol.
  Pistols and revolvers, 159:1.

Applicant.
  Domestic violence, 173-B:1.

Approved alcohol treatment program, 172-B:1.

Arrest, 594:1.

DEFINED TERMS —Cont'd

Assistant deputy medical examiner.
  Office of the chief medical examiner, 611-B:1.

Audiovisual recording function.
  Unauthorized recording in a theater, 644:19.

Authorization.
  Computer crime, 638:16.

Bail agent.
  Notice to law enforcement agencies, 597:7-b.

Barbiturate-type drugs, 318-B:1.
  Study, treatment and care of inebriates, 172:1.

Blasting caps, 158:29.

Body armor, 650-B:1.

Boosters, 158:29.

Bylaws.
  Interstate compact for adult offender supervision, 651-A:26.

Cannabis-type drugs, 318-B:1.
  Study, treatment and care of inebriates, 172:1.

Caregiver.
  Criminal neglect of elderly, disabled or impaired adults, 631:8.

Certified alcohol and drug abuse counselor, 172:1.

Certified substance abuse treatment facility, 172:1.

Chemical substance.
  Methamphetamine-related crimes, 639-A:1.

Chief medical examiner, 611-B:1.

Child.
  Child pornography and child exploitation prevention, 649-B:2.
  Computer pornography and child exploitation prevention, 649-B:2.
  Methamphetamine-related crimes, 639-A:1.
  Negligent storage of firearms, 650-C:1.
  Obscene matter, 650:1.
  Pornography, 649-A:2.

Cigarette.
  Tobacco tax, 78:1.
  Youth access to and use of tobacco products, 126-K:2.

Claimant, 651:62.

Clandestine lab sites.
  Methamphetamine, crimes relating to, 318-D:1.

Client.
  Alcoholism and alcohol abuse, 172-B:1.
  Study, treatment and care of inebriates, 172:1.

Clone.
  Wireless telephone cloning, 638:21.

Cocaine-type drugs, 318-B:1.
  Study, treatment and care of inebriates, 172:1.

CODIS.
  Criminal offender DNA testing, 651-C:1.

Coin machine, 638:13.

Collector, 647:2.

Commercial sex act.
  Trafficking in persons, 633:6.

Communications common carrier.
  Electronic surveillance, 570-A:1.

Compact administrator.
  Interstate compact for adult offender supervision, 651-A:26.

Compacting state.
  Interstate compact for adult offender supervision, 651-A:26.

Compact part of town or city (firearms statute), 644:13.

Comprehensive drug abuse prevention and control act of 1970.
  Controlled drugs, 318-B:1.

Computer, 638:16.
  Child pornography, 649-A:2.

Computer contaminant.
  Computer crime, 638:16.

Computer data.
  Computer crime, 638:16.

Computer network, 638:16.

Computer operations.
  Computer crime, 638:16.

Computer pornography and child exploitation prevention, 649-B:2.

Computer program, 638:16.

Computer resources.
  Computer crime, 638:16.

DEFINED TERMS —Cont'd
Computer services, 638:16.
Computer software, 638:16.
Computer supplies.
　Computer crime, 638:16.
Computer system, 638:16.
Conduct, 625:11.
Confines another unlawfully, 633:2.
Contact.
　Domestic violence, 173-B:1.
Contents.
　Electronic surveillance, 570-A:1.
Controlled drug analog, 318-B:1.
Controlled drugs, 318-B:1.
Coordinator.
　Domestic violence, 173-B:1.
Counterfeit mark.
　Dealing in counterfeit goods, 638:6-b.
Counterfeit recording, 638:6-a.
Course of conduct, 633:3-a.
Crack cocaine, 318-B:1.
Credit card, 638:5.
Criminal intelligence information.
　Information and analysis center, 651-F:1.
Criminal intelligence system.
　Information and analysis center, 651-F:1.
Criminal justice agency.
　Criminal justice information system, 106-K:1.
Criminal justice information, 106-K:1.
Cross orders for relief.
　Domestic violence, 173-B:1.
Cruelty, 644:8.
Curtilage, 627:9.
Data, 638:16.
Deadly force, 627:9.
Deadly weapon, 625:11.
　Domestic violence, 173-B:1.
Dealer, 637:7.
Death investigation.
　Office of the chief medical examiner, 611-B:1.
Deception.
　Services, theft of, 637:8.
Defaced access device.
　Wireless telephone cloning, 638:21.
Delay electric igniters, 158:29.
Delinquent.
　Youth development center, 621:3.
Delinquent child.
　Youth development center, 621:3.
Dentist.
　Controlled Drug Act, 318-B:1.
Dependent, 651:62.
Deputy chief medical examiner, 611-B:1.
Desecration, 646-A:1.
Designated alcohol counselor, 172-B:1.
Designated drug counselor.
　Study, treatment and care of inebriates, 172:1.
Designee.
　Office of the chief medical examiner, 611-B:1.
Detention.
　Youth development center, 621:3.
Detonators, 158:29.
Detoxification, 172-B:1.
Director.
　Controlled drugs, 318-B:1.
Disabled adult.
　Criminal neglect of elderly, disabled or impaired adults, 631:8.
Dispense.
　Controlled drugs, 318-B:1.
Disposition.
　Criminal justice information system, 106-K:1.
Disseminate, 649-A:2, 650:1.
DNA.
　Criminal offender DNA testing, 651-C:1.
　Post-conviction DNA testing, 651-D:1.

DEFINED TERMS —Cont'd
DNA record.
　Criminal offender DNA testing, 651-C:1.
DNA sample.
　Criminal offender DNA testing, 651-C:1.
　Post-conviction DNA testing, 651-D:1.
Domestic violence, 173-B:1.
Driver's license information.
　Criminal justice information system, 106-K:1.
Drug abuser, 172:1.
Drug dependence, 318-B:1.
　Study, treatment and care of inebriates, 172:1.
Drug dependent person, 172:1, 318-B:1.
Drug paraphernalia, 318-B:1.
Dwelling, 627:9.
E-cigarette.
　Sales and use by minors, 126-K:2.
Economic loss, 651:62.
Educational institution, hazing, 631:7.
Elderly adult.
　Criminal neglect of elderly, disabled or impaired adults, 631:8.
Electric squibs, 158:29.
Electronic defense weapon, 159:20.
Element of an offense, 625:11.
Emergency response.
　Methamphetamine, crimes relating to, 318-D:1.
Executive authority.
　Extradition, 612:1.
Explicit or implicit threat, 633:3-a.
Explosive bombs, 158:29.
Explosives, 158:29.
Family entertainment center, 647:2.
Family or household member, 173-B:1.
FBI.
　Criminal offender DNA testing, 651-C:1.
Federal food and drug laws, 318-B:1.
Felony.
　Arrests in criminal cases, 594:1.
Fiduciary, 638:11.
Financial institution.
　Fraud, 638:11.
　Theft, 637:10.
Financial instrument.
　Computer crime, 638:16.
Firearm.
　Domestic violence, 173-B:1.
First degree assault, 631:1.
Flag of the United States, 646-A:1.
Foreign protective order.
　Domestic violence, 173-B:1.
Fraudulent communications paraphernalia, 638:5-a.
Fresh pursuit.
　Interstate, 614:5.
　Intrastate, 614:9.
Fund.
　Domestic violence, 173-B:1.
Funeral.
　Prohibition on funeral protests, 644:2-b.
Fuse lighters, 158:29.
Gambling, 647:2.
Gambling machine, 647:2.
Genital openings, 632-A:1.
Government.
　Fraud, 638:11.
　Theft, 637:10.
Governor.
　Extradition, 612:1.
Grantee.
　Domestic violence, 173-B:1.
Gun cane.
　Pistols and revolvers, 159:1.
Hallucinogenic drugs, 318-B:1.
　Study, treatment and care of inebriates, 172:1.
Harm, 640:3.
HE, 625:11.
High explosive, 158:9-a.

DEFINED TERMS —Cont'd

Highway, 649:1.

Highway commissioner, 649:1.

HIV, 632-A:10-b.

Identifiable child.
  Child pornography, 649-A:2.

Illegal drug.
  Drug dealer liability act, 318-C:4.

Illegal drug market.
  Drug dealer liability act, 318-C:4.

Illegal drug market target community.
  Drug dealer liability act, 318-C:4.

Impaired adult.
  Criminal neglect of elderly, disabled or impaired adults, 631:8.

Incapacitated.
  Alcoholism and alcohol abuse, 172-B:1.
  Study, treatment and care of inebriates, 172:1.

Incapacitated adult.
  Methamphetamine-related crimes, 639-A:1.

Individual drug user.
  Drug dealer liability act, 318-C:4.

Infernal machine, 158:29.

Information and analysis center.
  Safety department, 651-F:1.

Intellectual property.
  Dealing in counterfeit goods, 638:6-b.

Intelligence data.
  Information and analysis center, 651-F:1.

Inter-jurisdictional intelligence system.
  Information and analysis center, 651-F:1.

Intermediate sanction program.
  Parole, 651-A:2.

Interstate commission.
  Interstate compact for adult offender supervision, 651-A:26.

In the course of committing a theft, 636:1.

Intimate partners, 173-B:1.

Intimidates, 633:3-a.

Intoxicated, 172-B:1.
  Study, treatment and care of inebriates, 172:1.

Investigating agency.
  Post-conviction DNA testing, 651-D:1.

Investigative or law enforcement officer.
  Electronic surveillance, 570-A:1.

Involuntary servitude.
  Peonage, 633:5.
  Trafficking in persons, 633:6.

Judge of competent jurisdiction.
  Electronic surveillance, 570-A:1.

Juvenile.
  Negligent storage of firearms, 650-C:1.

Keg.
  Alcoholic beverages, 179:5-a.

Knowingly, culpable mental state, 626:2.

Knowledge, 650:1.

Laboratory, 318-B:1.

Law enforcement officer, 630:1.
  Controlled drugs, 318-B:1.

Lawful order, 644:2.

Level 1 offense.
  Drug dealer liability act, 318-C:4.

Level 2 offense.
  Drug dealer liability act, 318-C:4.

Level 3 offense.
  Drug dealer liability act, 318-C:4.

Level 4 offense.
  Drug dealer liability act, 318-C:4.

Licensed manufacturer.
  Tobacco tax, 78:1.

Licensed retailer.
  Tobacco tax, 78:1.

Licensed sub-jobber.
  Tobacco tax, 78:1.

Licensed vending machine operator.
  Tobacco tax, 78:1.

Licensed wholesaler.
  Tobacco tax, 78:1.

DEFINED TERMS —Cont'd

Licensee.
  Tobacco tax, 78:1.
  Youth access to and use of tobacco products, 126-K:2.

Liquid nicotine.
  Sales and use by minors, 126-K:2.

Local law enforcement agency.
  Registration of criminal offenders, 651-B:1.

Manufacture.
  Wireless telephone cloning, 638:21.

Manufacturer.
  Controlled Drug Act, 318-B:1.
  Tobacco tax, 78:1.
  Youth access to and use of tobacco products, 126-K:2.

Martial arts weapons, 159:24.

Material.
  Falsifying official matters, 641:1.
  Obscene matter, 650:1.

Material element of an offense, 625:11.

Medical examiner.
  Office of the chief medical examiner, 611-B:1.

Medico-legal cases.
  Medical examiners, 611-B:11.

Member.
  Criminal justice information system, 106-K:1.
  Interstate compact for adult offender supervision, 651-A:26.

Member user.
  Criminal justice information system, 106-K:1.

Merchant.
  Theft, 637:2.

Methamphetamine paraphernalia.
  Methamphetamine-related crimes, 639-A:1.

Methamphetamine waste products.
  Methamphetamine-related crimes, 639-A:1.

Minor.
  Youth access to and use of tobacco products, 126-K:2.

Minority.
  Youth development center, 621:3.

Miscarriage, 631:1.
  Stillbirth, 631:1.

Mislabeled, 638:6.

Missing adult, 106-J:1.

Missing person with developmental disabilities, 106-J:3.

Missing senior citizen, 106-J:3.

Morphine-type drugs, 318-B:1.
  Study, treatment and care of inebriates, 172:1.

Motion picture theater.
  Unauthorized recording in a theater, 644:19.

Motor vehicle records.
  Criminal justice information system, 106-K:1.

Murder, 630:1.

Murder which is psycho-sexual in nature.
  Parole, 651-A:10.

Mutual order for relief.
  Domestic violence, 173-B:1.

Narcotic drugs, 318-B:1.

Neglect.
  Criminal neglect of elderly, disabled or impaired adults, 631:8.

Negligent homicide, 630:2.

Negligently, culpable mental state, 626:2.

Night, 635:1.

Non-compacting state.
  Interstate compact for adult offender supervision, 651-A:26.

Non-deadly force, 627:9.

Nonviolent offense.
  Parole, 651-A:2.

Nurse, 318-B:1.

Obtaining, 637:2.

Obtain or exercise unauthorized control, 637:3.

Occupied structure.
  Arson, 634:1.
  Burglary, 635:1.

Offender, 651:62.
  Interstate compact for adult offender supervision, 651-A:26.

Offender against children.
  Registration of criminal offenders, 651-B:1.

DEFINED TERMS —Cont'd
Officers.
　Arrests in criminal cases, 594:1.
Official custody.
　Assaults by prisoners, 642:9.
　Escape, 642:6.
Official proceeding, 641:1.
Official written order, 318-B:1.
One or more persons, 629:3.
Online identifier.
　Registration of criminal offenders, 651-B:4-a.
Optometrist.
　Controlled drugs, 318-B:1.
Oral communication.
　Electronic surveillance, 570-A:1.
Organization.
　Hazing, 631:7.
Organized crime.
　Electronic surveillance, 570-A:1.
Original recording, 638:6-a.
Other stimulant and depressant drugs, 172:1, 318-B:1.
Owner.
　Computer crime, 638:16.
Parole, 651-A:2.
　Youth development center, 621:3.
Participate in the illegal drug market.
　Drug dealer liability act, 318-C:4.
Participating agency.
　Information and analysis center, 651-F:1.
Party official, 640:2.
Pattern of sexual assault, 632-A:1.
Peace officer.
　Arrests in criminal cases, 594:1.
Pecuniary benefit, 640:2.
Period of illegal drug use.
　Drug dealer liability act, 318-C:4.
Person.
　Computer crimes, 638:16.
　Controlled Drug Act, 318-B:1.
　Convicted, 632-A:10-b.
　Criminal neglect of elderly, disabled or impaired adults, 631:8.
　Drug dealer liability act, 318-C:4.
　Electronic surveillance, 570-A:1.
　Generally, 625:11.
　Interstate compact for adult offender supervision, 651-A:26.
　Tobacco tax, 78:1.
　Youth access to and use of tobacco products, 126-K:2.
Personal identifying information.
　Identity fraud, 638:25.
Personal information.
　Criminal justice information system, 106-K:1.
Personally identifiable data.
　Information and analysis center, 651-F:1.
Pharmacist.
　Controlled drugs, 318-B:1.
Pharmacy.
　Controlled Drug Act, 318-B:1.
Physician.
　Controlled Drug Act, 318-B:1.
Pistols, 159:1.
Place of illegal drug activity.
　Drug dealer liability act, 318-C:4.
Place of participation.
　Drug dealer liability act, 318-C:4.
Podiatrist.
　Controlled drugs, 318-B:1.
Pose.
　Identity fraud, 638:25.
Post-mortem examination.
　Office of the chief medical examiner, 611-B:1.
Potential for abuse, 318-B:1.
Practitioner.
　Controlled drugs, 318-B:1.
Practitioner-patient relationship.
　Controlled drugs, 318-B:1.
Predominant appeal, 650:1.

DEFINED TERMS —Cont'd
Premium cigars.
　Tobacco tax, 78:1.
Prescribe, 318-B:1.
Prescription.
　Controlled Drug Act, 318-B:1.
Previous conviction.
　Child pornography, 649-A:2.
Primers, percussion fuses, combination fuses and time fuses, 158:29.
Prisoner, 651-A:2.
　Parole, 651-A:2.
Private place, 644:9.
Program.
　Domestic violence, 173-B:1.
Propelled vehicle, 634:3, 637:9.
Properly displayed, 646-A:1.
Property.
　Arson, 634:1.
　Computer crimes, 638:16.
　Criminal mischief, 634:2.
　Criminal threatening, 631:4.
　Fraudulent misapplication, 638:11.
　Theft, 637:2.
Property of another.
　Arson, 634:1.
　Criminal mischief, 634:2.
　Criminal threatening, 631:4.
　Theft, 637:2.
Protective custody.
　Alcoholism and alcohol abuse, 172-B:1.
　Study, treatment and care of inebriates, 172:1.
Psycho-sexual murder, 651-A:10.
Public.
　Criminal defamation, 644:11.
　Disorderly conduct, 644:2.
Public educational facility.
　Youth access to and use of tobacco products, 126-K:2.
Public place, 644:2.
Public servant, 640:2.
Public utility, 649:1.
Puffing, 637:4.
Purposely.
　Culpable mental state, 626:2.
　Murder, 630:1-a.
Purpose to deprive.
　Theft, 637:2.
Qualified.
　Psychiatric evaluation, insanity defense, 135:17.
Reader.
　Wireless telephone cloning, 638:21.
Reasonably suspected.
　Information and analysis center, 651-F:1.
Receives, 637:7.
Recklessly, culpable mental state, 626:2.
Recovery agent.
　Notices to law enforcement, 597:7-b.
Redemption poker machine, 647:2.
Redemption slot machine, 647:2.
Registered wireless telephone, 638:21.
Registry number, 318-B:1.
Remediation.
　Methamphetamine, crimes relating to, 318-D:1.
Removal.
　Methamphetamine, crimes relating to, 318-D:1.
Required to register.
　Registration of criminal offenders, 651-B:1.
Residence.
　Registration of criminal offenders, 651-B:1.
Restitution, 651:62.
Retailer.
　Tobacco tax, 78:1.
　Youth access to and use of tobacco products, 126-K:2.
Retaliation, 632-A:1.
Revolvers, 159:1.

DEFINED TERMS —Cont'd
Rolling paper.
  Access to tobacco products by minors, 126-K:2.
Rule.
  Interstate compact for adult offender supervision, 651-A:26.
Sale.
  Controlled Drug Act, 318-B:1.
  Tobacco tax, 78:1.
Sampler.
  Tobacco tax, 78:1.
  Youth access to and use of tobacco products, 126-K:2.
Scanning device.
  Use of payment card scanning device to defraud, 638:28.
Second degree assault, 631:2.
Secured premise, 635:2.
Sell.
  Tobacco tax, 78:1.
Serious bodily injury, 625:11.
Serious harm.
  Trafficking in persons, 633:6.
Serious personal injury, 632-A:1.
Services, 637:8.
Sex act.
  Trafficking in persons, 633:6.
Sexual conduct, 650:1.
Sexual contact, 632-A:1.
  Felonious sexual assault, 632-A:3.
Sexually explicit conduct.
  Child pornography, 649-A:2.
Sexually-explicit performance.
  Trafficking in persons, 633:6.
Sexual offender.
  Registration, 651-B:1.
Sexual offense.
  Registration of criminal offenders, 651-B:1.
Sexual penetration, 632-A:1.
Simple assault, 631:2-a.
Slug, 638:13.
Smoke bomb, 644:16-b.
SOR system.
  Registration of criminal offenders, 651-B:1.
Stalk, 633:3-a.
State.
  Extradition, 612:1.
  Interstate compact for adult offender supervision, 651-A:26.
State council.
  Interstate compact for adult offender supervision, 651-A:26.
State food, drug and cosmetic laws, 318-B:1.
Stink bomb, 644:16-a.
Strangulation.
  Assault, 631:2.
Student hazing, 631:7.
Sub-jobber.
  Tobacco tax, 78:1.
  Youth access to and use of tobacco products, 126-K:2.
Substantial step, 629:1.
Supervising medical examiner.
  Office of the chief medical examiner, 611-B:1.
Sweepstakes.
  Gambling, 647:2.
Telecommunications.
  Electronic surveillance, 570-A:1.
Telecommunication service.
  Wireless telephone cloning, 638:21.
Telecommunication service provider.
  Wireless telephone cloning, 638:21.
Telephone cloning paraphernalia, 638:21.
Telephone consultation.
  Office of the chief medical examiner, 611-B:1.
Therapy, 632-A:1.
Threat, 637:8.
Threat of violence.
  Classification of misdemeanors, 625:9.
Tier I offender.
  Registration of criminal offenders, 651-B:1.

DEFINED TERMS —Cont'd
Tier II offender.
  Registration of criminal offenders, 651-B:1.
Tier III offender.
  Registration of criminal offenders, 651-B:1.
Tobacco products.
  Tobacco tax, 78:1.
  Youth access to and use of tobacco products, 126-K:2.
Tracer fuses, 158:29.
Traffic.
  Wireless telephone cloning, 638:21.
Treatment.
  Alcoholism and alcohol abuse, 172-B:1.
Unlawfully.
  Gambling, 647:2.
  Lottery, 647:1.
Unvented space heater, 158:28.
Validation of information.
  Information and analysis center, 651-F:1.
Value, 637:2.
  Gambling, 647:2.
Vending machine.
  Tobacco tax, 78:1.
  Youth access to and use of tobacco products, 126-K:2.
Vending machine operator.
  Tobacco tax, 78:1.
  Youth access to and use of tobacco products, 126-K:2.
Vertebrate animals, 644:8-c.
Veterinarian.
  Controlled Drug Act, 318-B:1.
Victim, 651:62.
  Identity fraud, 638:25.
Victim/witness assistance, office of, 632-A:10-b.
Violations, 625:9.
Visual representation, 649-A:2.
Wholesaler.
  Controlled Drug Act, 318-B:1.
  Tobacco tax, 78:1.
  Youth access to and use of tobacco products, 126-K:2.
Wholesale sales price.
  Tobacco tax, 78:1.
WIC program, 638:15.
Wireless telephone.
  Wireless telephone cloning, 638:21.
Writing, 638:1.
Youth.
  Negligent storage of firearms, 650-C:1.

DELINQUENT CHILDREN.
Youth development center, 621:1 to 621:34.
  See YOUTH DEVELOPMENT CENTER.

DENTISTS AND DENTAL HYGIENISTS.
Controlled drugs, labeling containers, 318-B:13.
Defined.
  Controlled drug act, 318-B:1.

DEPORTATION.
State prison.
  Release from, 651:25.

DEPOSITIONS.
Discovery depositions, 517:13.
Expert witnesses, 516:29-b.

DEPOSITORS.
Frauds on, 638:10.

DEPRAVED HEART MURDER.
Homicide, 630:1-b.

DEPUTY SHERIFF.
Murder of, death penalty, 630:1.

DESTRUCTION.
Computer equipment, 638:17.
Corpse, 644:7.
Creditors, defrauding by, 638:9.
Evidence, 642:3.
Physical evidence, 641:6.

DESTRUCTION —Cont'd
Public records or information, 638:3, 641:7.
Recordable writings, 638:2.
Records, public or private, 638:3, 641:7.

DETAINERS.
Agreement on detainers, 606-A:1 to 606-A:6.

DETENTION.
Force to effect, justification, 627:5.
Resistance to, 642:2.

DEVELOPMENTALLY DISABLED.
Alert program for missing persons.
　Definitions, 106-J:3.
　Establishment of program, 106-J:4.
　Issuance and cancellation of alert, 106-J:4.
　Rulemaking, 106-J:5.
Neglect.
　Criminal neglect of elderly, disabled or impaired adults, 631:8.

DIRK-KNIVES.
Carrying or selling, 159:16.

DISABLED PERSONS.
Neglect.
　Criminal neglect of elderly, disabled or impaired adults, 631:8.

DISCHARGE OF FIREARM AT OCCUPIED STRUCTURE.
Criminal mischief, 634:2.

DISCOVERY, 604:1-a.
Child pornography, 649-A:7.
Obstructing justice, 642:3.

DISEASES.
Cancer.
　Cannabis-type drugs, prescription for, 318-B:9, 318-B:10.
HIV.
　Request by victim, 632-A:10-b.

DISGUISE.
Criminal, furnishing to, 642:3.

DISORDERLY CONDUCT.
Breach of the peace, 644:2.

DISORDERLY HOUSE.
Permitting, 645:2.

DISTRICT COURTS.
Appeals.
　Convictions in municipal or district court, 599:1 to 599:4.
　Superior court appeals, 502-A:12.
Bail, 597:6.
Bail commissioners, 597:15-a.
Records.
　Copies on.
　　Appeal, 597:10.
　　Binding over, 597:11.

DIVORCE.
Restraining orders, 597:7-a.

DNA.
Post-conviction DNA testing, 651-D:1 to 651-D:5.
　See POST-CONVICTION DNA TESTING.

DNA TESTING OF CRIMINAL OFFENDERS, 651-C:1 to
　651-C:6.
See CRIMINAL OFFENDER DNA TESTING.

DOCUMENTS.
Fraudulent execution, 638:12.

DOGS.
Police dogs, interference with, 644:8-d.
Transporting in pickup trucks, 644:8-f.

DOMESTIC VIOLENCE, PROTECTION OF PERSONS.
Abuse, defined, 173-B:1.
Arrest, 173-B:10.
　Violation of protective order, 173-B:9.
Best interest of child, 173-B:4.

DOMESTIC VIOLENCE, PROTECTION OF PERSONS
　—Cont'd
Custody of children, 173-B:5.
　Temporary order, 173-B:4.
Emergency care, immunity from liability, 173-B:12.
Evidence, rules of inapplicable, 173-B:3.
Family or household member, defined, 173-B:1.
Financial support, 173-B:5.
Good Samaritan, immunity from liability, 173-B:12.
Grant program.
　Commissioner.
　　Duties, 173-B:17.
　Compensation for coordinating program, 173-B:19.
　Confidentiality, 173-B:22.
　Coordinator.
　　Compensation, 173-B:19.
　　Duties, 173-B:20.
　　Selection, 173-B:18.
　Direct service grantees, criteria for selection, 173-B:21.
　Established, 173-B:16.
　Fund.
　　Established, 173-B:15.
　Referral, 173-B:23.
　Rights reserved, 173-B:24.
Guardian ad litem, 173-B:6.
Hearing, 173-B:3.
Household goods, rights to, 173-B:5.
Intimate partners, defined, 173-B:1.
Jurisdiction and venue, 173-B:2.
Law enforcement agencies, notice of orders, 173-B:8.
Minority not a preclusion for services, 173-B:7.
Notice of orders, transmission to local law enforcement
　agency, 173-B:8.
Notification to department of safety, 173-B:5.
Orders.
　Permissible contact, 173-B:5-a.
Police officers, protection by, 173-B:10.
Protective orders, 173-B:5.
　Permissible contact, 173-B:5-a.
　Temporary, 173-B:4.
　Violation, arrest and detention, 597:7-a.
Relief.
　Court granting, 173-B:5.
　Judicial notice of support obligation, 173-B:14.
　Minors protected, 173-B:3.
　Petition for, 173-B:3.
　Protective orders, 173-B:5.
　　Enforceable, 173-B:13.
　　Foreign, enforceable, 173-B:13.
　　Support orders, enforcement, 173-B:14.
　　Temporary, 173-B:4.
　　Violation, 173-B:9, 597:7-a.
　Supreme court, questions of law, 173-B:3.
　Temporary relief, 173-B:4.
Rights and remedies of victims, 173-B:10.
Service of process.
　Order, 173-B:8.
　Petition, 173-B:3.
Severability, 173-B:25.
Stalking.
　Relief granted to persons victim of stalking, 633:3-a.
Temporary relief, 173-B:4.
Treatment, batterer's counseling may be ordered, 173-B:5.
Victims.
　Notification of rights, 173-B:11.
　Rights and remedies available, 173-B:11.
Violation of order.
　Notice in order, 173-B:5.
　Protective order, 173-B:9.

DOUBLE JEOPARDY.
Constitution of New Hampshire, NH Const Pt 1 Art 16.

DRINKING AGE, 179:5.

DRIVE-IN WINDOWS.
Alcoholic beverage on-sale of off-sale licensees, 179:53.

DRIVERS' LICENSES.
Criminal mischief.
　Suspension, 634:2.
Tobacco products purchases.
　Proof of age of purchaser, 126-K:3.

DRIVE YOURSELF.
Theft of vehicle, 637:9.

DRIVING WHILE INTOXICATED.
Forfeiture of liquor or beverages, 179:4.
Fresh pursuit, interstate.
　Arrest, authority to make, 614:1.
　Reciprocity requirement, 614:1-a.

DRUG ADDICTS.
Consent, user giving, 626:6.
Negligent homicide, 630:3.
Treatment of, 318-B:12-a.

DRUG DEALER LIABILITY, 318-C:1 to 318-C:18.
Absence of criminal conviction.
　Action not barred, 318-C:13.
Attachment.
　Prejudgment attachment, 318-C:14.
Attorney fees, recovery, 318-C:6, 318-C:7.
Comparative responsibility, 318-C:11.
Contribution among and recovery from multiple
　defendants, 318-C:12.
Criminal conviction.
　Estoppel from denying participation, 318-C:13.
Definitions, 318-C:4.
Economic damages, recovery, 318-C:6, 318-C:7.
Execution on judgments, 318-C:14.
Illegal drug market community, 318-C:9.
Injury resulting from individual's use.
　Persons who may bring action for, 318-C:6.
　Recovering for, 318-C:5.
　Requirements for individual user's right to bring action,
　　318-C:7.
Insurance or indemnification.
　Third party restrictions, 318-C:8.
Intra-family tort immunity.
　Law not altered, 318-C:17.
Joinder of parties, 318-C:10.
Legislative findings and declaration, 318-C:3.
Liability for participation in the illegal drug market,
　318-C:5.
Limited recovery of damages, 318-C:7.
Non-economic damages, recovery, 318-C:6.
Notice.
　Filing of action, 318-C:16.
Persons who may bring action, 318-C:6.
Prosecution attorneys.
　Representation of governmental entity, 318-C:16.
Purpose of chapter, 318-C:2.
Recovery of damages, 318-C:6.
Severability, 318-C:18.
Standard of proof of participation, 318-C:13.
Statute of limitations, 318-C:15.
Stay until completion of criminal investigation, 318-C:16.
Third party restrictions, 318-C:8.
Title of chapter, 318-C:1.

DRUGS.
Animals, administering to, 638:8.
Controlled substances, 318-B:1 to 318-B:30.
　See CONTROLLED SUBSTANCES.
Drug dealer liability, 318-C:1 to 318-C:18.
　See DRUG DEALER LIABILITY.
Methamphetamine.
　See METHAMPHETAMINE.

DRUGS AND CONTROLLED SUBSTANCES.
Cannabis.
　Penalties, 318-B:26.

DRUNKARDS AND DRUNKENNESS.
Intoxication.
　See INTOXICATION.

DUELING.
Justification, 627:4.

DURESS OR COERCION.
Criminal liability, 626:1.
Extortion, theft by, 637:5.
Prostitution, 645:2.
Public administration, 640:2.
Robbery, 636:1.
Suicide, causing or aiding, 630:4.
Theft of services, 637:8.
Threatening safety of person or public, 631:4.

DWELLINGS.
Arson, 634:1.
Defined, 627:9.

E

EAVESDROPPING.
General provisions, 570-A:1 to 570-A:11.
　See WIRETAPPING AND EAVESDROPPING.

ECONOMIC WEALTH.
Theft, 637:2.

EDUCATION.
False academic documentation, 638:15-a.
Youth development center, 621:1 to 621:34.
　See YOUTH DEVELOPMENT CENTER.

EFFECTIVE DATE.
Criminal Code, 625:2.

ELDERLY.
Criminal neglect of elderly, disabled or impaired adults,
　631:8.
Sexual assault, speedy trial, 632-A:9.
Use of force against, 651:6.

ELECTIONS.
Convicted persons, rights lost, 607-A:2.
Corrupt Practices.
　See CORRUPT PRACTICES.
Voters.
　Bodily harm, threat of, 640:3.
　Bribery, 640:2.
　Improper influence, 640:3.

ELECTRICAL DEVICES.
Appliances and equipment.
　Nonconformance with standards.
　　Rulemaking, enforcement of law, 158:24.
　　Unlawful sales, 158:23.
Serial numbers, removing or altering, 637:7-a.
Space heaters, unvented.
　Sales or installation violations, 158:28.

ELECTRIC FENCES, 158:26, 158:27.

ELECTRICITY.
Services.
　Defined as property, 637:2.
　Theft of, 637:8.

ELECTRONIC DEFENSE WEAPONS.
Criminal use, 159:23.
Possession by felons, 159:21.
Sales to minors, 159:22.

ELECTRONIC DEVICES.
Privacy, invasion of, 644:9.

ELECTRONIC TRANSACTIONS.
Search warrants.
　Electronic appearance, authorization and signature, 595-A:4-a.

ELEMENT OF AN OFFENSE.
Defined, 625:11.
Offenses.
　See OFFENSES.

EMBEZZLEMENT.
Larceny by, 637:3.
Property, misapplication of, 638:11.
Search warrants, 595-A:1.
Theft generally.
　See THEFT.

EMERGENCIES.
False reports, 644:3.
Gunshot wounds, reporting, 631:6.
Law enforcement officers.
　Natural disasters.
　　Closure of area posing threat to public health and safety,
　　　644:2.
Medical treatment, justifiable use of force, 627:6.
Party line, refusal to yield, 644:12.

EMERGENCY MEDICAL AND TRAUMA SERVICES.
Methamphetamine-related crimes.
　Manufacturing.
　　Injury resulting from manufacturing activities, 318-D:3.
Restitution.
　Criminal mischief.
　　Damaging emergency vehicle or apparatus, 634:2.

EMERGENCY MEDICAL CARE PROVIDERS.
Drugs.
　Counterfeit, affirmative defense to prosecution, 318-B:2-b.
　Prescription, possession and administration of, 318-B:10.

ENCUMBRANCES.
Creditors, defrauding by, 638:9.

ENTERING.
Breaking or entering.
　See BREAKING OR ENTERING.

ENTERTAINMENT.
Admission to, theft of, 637:8.
Obscene matter, 650:2.

ENTERTAINMENT PROVIDED BY ON-SALE ALCOHOLIC
　　BEVERAGE LICENSEES, 179:19.

ENTRAPMENT.
Affirmative defense, 626:5.

EQUIPMENT.
Rental services, theft of, 637:8.
Serial numbers, removing or altering, 637:7-a.

ESCAPE.
Deadly weapon employed in, 642:6.
Force to prevent, justification, 627:5.
Good conduct credits, loss of, 651-A:22.
Implements for and contraband, 642:7.
Imprisonment, additional time, 642:6.
Obstructing justice, 642:6.

ESTATES.
Prisoners, cost of care of, 622:53.

EVACUATION OF BUILDING.
Criminal threatening, 631:4.

EVASION.
Kidnapping to avoid apprehension, 633:1.

EVIDENCE.
Accusation of theft, 637:1.
Burden of proof, 625:10.
Concealing, 642:3.
Controlled drug chemical analysis certificate, 318-B:26-a.
Criminal offender DNA testing.
　Certificate and results of DNA analysis.
　　Admissibility, 651-C:2.
Defenses, establishment of, 626:7.
Destruction of, 642:3.
Falsification, physical evidence, 641:6.
Grand juries, multicounty, 600-A:5.
Ignorance, defense of, 626:3.
Insanity, defense of, 628:2.
Mistake, defense of, 626:3.

EVIDENCE —Cont'd
Obscene matter, 650:5.
　Defense, 650:4.
Perjury, 641:1.
Physical evidence, falsifying, 641:6.
Post-conviction DNA testing, 651-D:2.
Rebutting, during trial, 606:6.
Restitution.
　Admissibility of court's determination of amount, 651:63.
Sexual assault, 632-A:6.
　Testimony, in camera, 632-A:8.
Staleness, limitation of action, 625:8.
Tampering with.
　Physical evidence, 641:6.
　Public records, 641:7.
　Witnesses, 641:5.
Tobacco products purchases.
　Proof of age of purchaser.
　　Prima facie evidence of innocence, 126-K:3.
Wiretapping and eavesdropping, prohibition of use of
　　intercepted wire or oral communications devices,
　　570-A:6.
Witnesses.
　General provisions, 516:1 to 516:38.
　　See WITNESSES.

EXCUSE.
Element of an offense, 625:11.

EXHIBITIONS.
Admission to, theft of, 637:8.

EXPERIMENTS.
Use of live animals, 644:8-c.

EXPERT WITNESSES.
Video teleconference to take testimony.
　Criminal cases, 516:37.
　Motor vehicle violations, 516:38.

EXPLODING BULLETS, 159:18.

EXPLOSIONS AND EXPLOSIVES.
Access to information, 158:9-g.
Adjutant general.
　Control of storage, sale and use, 158:19.
Arson, 634:1.
Bomb scare, 641:4.
　Public service, sentence to perform, 651:2.
Burglary, 635:1.
Certificates of competency, 158:9-h.
Class A explosives, 158:30.
　Possession violations, penalties, 158:32.
　Seizure, notice requirements, 158:33.
Class B explosives, 158:30.
Class B special fireworks, rulemaking, 158:9-f.
Class C explosives, 158:30.
Criminal penalties.
　Transportation, 158:17, 158:18.
Death or bodily injuries, transportation, 158:18.
False reports, criminal penalties, 158:38.
Fire department investigations, 158:31.
High explosives, larceny, 158:9-e.
Infernal machines.
　Possession violations, penalties, 158:35.
Licenses, 158:9-a to 158:9-h.
　Application for, 158:9-b.
　Forms, 158:9-d.
　Information regarding, availability, 158:9-g.
Malicious explosion, penalties, 158:34.
Molotov cocktails, violations, 158:37.
Packages, labeling for transport, 158:16.
Penalties, 158:25.
Police investigations, 158:31.
Possession, 158:9, 158:32.
Reporting falsely, 641:4.
Simulated explosives, placement violations, 158:38-a.
Smoke bombs, sale or use of, 644:16-b.

EXPLOSIONS AND EXPLOSIVES —Cont'd
Storage.
    Control, by adjutant general, 158:19.
    Fees, 158:9-c.
    Rulemaking, 158:9-f.
Throwing or placing explosives, violations, penalties,
    158:36.
Transportation, 158:17, 158:18.
    Unlawful acts, 158:11.
Unlawful use, 158:29 to 158:40.
    Exceptions, 158:39.

EXPORTS AND IMPORTS.
Tobacco tax, importations.
    Inspection, right of entry, 78:26.

EX POST FACTO.
Prosecution and sentencing, applicable law, 625:2.

EXPOSURE.
Indecent exposure, 645:1.
Poisons, 644:16.

EXPUNGEMENT OF RECORDS.
Criminal justice information system, 106-K:3.
Criminal offender DNA testing.
    Reversal or dismissal of conviction, 651-C:5.

EXTENDED TERM OF IMPRISONMENT, 651:6.

EXTORTION.
Sexual assault, 632-A:2.
Theft, 637:1, 637:5.

EXTRADITION, 612:1 to 612:30.
Arrest.
    Arresting officer, authority of, 612:9.
    Failure to appear, arrest without warrant, 612:18.
    Prior to requisition, 612:13.
    Without warrant, 612:14.
        Failure to appear, 612:18.
Asylum not granted, 612:28.
    Awaiting trial in other state, 612:5.
Bail, 612:5.
    Conditions of bond, 612:16.
    Failure to appear, forfeiture, 612:18.
Bail jumping.
    Arrest prior to requisition, 612:13.
    From this state, 612:22.
    Other state, 612:3.
Civil actions, immunity from process, 612:25.
Confinement in jail, 612:12.
    Awaiting requisition, 612:15.
    Extension of time, 612:17.
Criminal prosecution.
    Immunity not granted, 612:28.
    In this state, persons awaiting, 612:19.
Custody, pending habeas corpus hearing outcome, 612:10.
Executive authority, defined, 612:1.
Expenses of extradition, 612:24.
Fugitives from justice, duty of governor.
    From this state, 612:22.
    Other states demanding, 612:2.
Governor.
    Defined, 612:1.
    Investigation by, 612:4.
    Without governor's warrant, 612:5-a.
Guilt or innocence, inquiry into, 612:20.
Habeas corpus.
    Application for, 612:10.
    Custody, 612:10.
    Procedure, 612:10.
    Waiver of extradition, 612:26.
Imprisoned person in other state, 612:5.
Interpretation of statute, 612:29.
Investigation by governor, 612:4.
Persons not present at time crime committed, 612:6.
Probation and parole violations.
    Arrest prior to requisition, 612:13.
    From this state, 612:22.

EXTRADITION —Cont'd
Probation and parole violations —Cont'd
    Other state, 612:3.
Right to counsel, 612:10.
Severability, 612:30.
State, defined, 612:1.
Waiver of extradition, 612:26.
    Custody, 612:26.
    Presigned, 612:5-a.
    State prisons, approved absences, 623-A:6.
    This state, 612:27.
Warrant.
    Application for requisition, 612:23.
    Commitment to await requisition, 612:15.
    Execution, 612:8.
    Issuance, recital of facts, 612:7.
    Noncompliance, penalty, 612:11.
    Other state, form of demand, 612:3.
    Recall, issuance of alias, 612:21.

F

FACSIMILE.
Theft by, 637:2.

FALSE ALARMS.
Fire alarms, 644:3-a.
Misdemeanor, 641:4.
Public alarms, 644:3.
    Public service, sentence to perform, 651:2.

FALSE FILING.
Charitable trusts, director of, 641:8.

FALSE IDENTIFICATION.
Alcoholic beverage purchases, 179:9.

FALSE IMPRISONMENT.
Misdemeanor, 633:3.
Sexual assault, 632-A:2.

FALSE PRETENSES.
Obtaining property by, 637:1.
Theft, 637:4.

FALSE REPORTS.
Misdemeanor, 641:4.
Public alarms, 644:3.
    Public service, sentence to perform, 651:2.

FALSE SWEARING.
Misdemeanor, 641:2.

FALSE WEIGHT OR MEASURE.
Fraud by, 638:6.

FALSIFICATION.
Administrative proceedings, 641:1.
Alarm, falsely reporting, 641:4.
Alteration, physical evidence, 641:6.
Application, false writing, 641:3.
Bomb scare, 641:4.
Burden of proof.
    False swearing, 641:2.
    Perjury, 641:1.
    Swearing falsely, 641:2.
Charitable trusts, director of, false filing, 641:8.
Concealment.
    Physical evidence, 641:6.
    Public records or information, 641:7.
Deceiving public official, 641:3.
    Physical evidence, falsifying, 641:6.
Destruction.
    Physical evidence, 641:6.
    Public records or information, 641:7.
Evidence, falsifying physical evidence, 641:6.
Explosives, reporting falsely, 641:4.
False alarms, 641:4.
False swearing, 641:2.
Fire alarms, 641:4, 644:3-a.

FALSIFICATION —Cont'd
Informants, tampering with, 641:5.
Information, tampering with public information, 641:7.
Judicial proceedings, 641:1.
Law enforcement, false reports, 641:4.
Legislative proceedings, 641:1.
Misapplication of property, theft by, 637:10.
Notary.
  Perjury before, 641:1.
  Swearing falsely before, 641:2.
Official matters.
  Administrative proceedings, 641:1.
  Informants, tampering with, 641:5.
  Judicial proceedings, 641:1.
  Law enforcement, false reports to, 641:4.
  Legislative proceedings, 641:1.
  Material, defined, 641:1.
  Notary.
    Perjury before, 641:1.
    Swearing falsely before, 641:2.
  Official proceeding, defined, 641:1.
  Perjury, 641:1.
  Physical evidence, tampering with, 641:6.
  Public records and information, tampering with, 641:7.
  Swearing falsely, 641:2.
  Unsworn falsification, 641:3.
  Witnesses, tampering with, 641:5.
Official proceeding, defined, 641:1.
Omission of information, 641:3.
Perjury, 641:1.
  Subornation, 641:5.
Physical evidence, 641:6.
Process, eluding, 641:5.
Recordable writings, 638:2.
Records, public or private, 638:3.
  Tampering with, 641:7.
Removal, physical evidence, 641:6.
  Public records or information, 641:7.
Swearing falsely, 641:2.
Unsworn falsification, 641:3.
Witnesses, tampering with, 641:5.

FAMILY, OFFENSES AGAINST.
Bigamy, 639:1.
Child, endangering welfare of, 639:3.
Incest, 639:2.
Incompetent, endangering welfare of, 639:3.
Newborn, concealing death of, 639:5.
Non-support, 639:4.
  Child or incompetent, 639:3.

FEAR.
Threats producing, 631:4.

FEDERAL FOOD AND DRUG LAWS.
Defined, 318-B:1.

FEDERAL NARCOTICS LAWS.
Defined, 318-B:1.
Effect of acquittal or conviction under, 318-B:29.

FEES AND COSTS.
Bail commissioners, 597:20.
Criminal record annulment, investigation, 651:5.
Explosives.
  Blasting operations, certificates of competency, 158:9-h.
  Licenses, 158:9-c.
Pistols and revolvers, license to carry, 159:6.
Sex offender registration, 651-B:11.
Tobacco tax.
  Licenses, 78:2.
Witnesses, 516:16 to 516:18.
  Limitations, 516:18.

FELONIES.
Accomplices and accessories, 642:3.
  After the fact, 642:4.
Adulteration.
  Alcoholic beverages, 179:16.

FELONIES —Cont'd
Aerosol self-defense spray weapons.
  Criminal use, 159:23.
Aggravated felonious sexual assault, 632-A:2.
Alcoholic beverages.
  Adulteration, 179:16.
  False identification.
    Manufacture, sale and possession, 179:62.
  Increasing alcoholic content, 179:16.
  Interference with business practices at licensed establishments, 179:22.
  Liquor license violations, 179:58.
  Penalties in general, 179:58.
Apprehension, hindering, 642:3.
Armor-piercing bullets, 159:18.
Arrest, aiding escape from, 642:6.
Arson, 643:1.
Assaults.
  By prisoners, 642:9.
  On minors, employment in child care service after conviction, 632-A:10.
Bad checks, 638:4.
Bigamy, 639:1.
Billies.
  Possession by convicted felons, 159:3.
Blackjacks.
  Possession by convicted felons, 159:3.
Body armor, felonious use of, 650-B:2.
Bribery.
  Commercial bribery, 638:7.
  Official and political matters, 640:2.
  Sports bribery, 638:8.
Bullets.
  Felonious use of teflon-coated, armor-piercing and exploding bullets, 159:18.
Burglary, 635:1.
Career criminal possession of firearm, 159:3-a.
Cemeteries or burial grounds, interference with, 635:8.
Child.
  Assault on, employment in child care service after conviction for, 632-A:10.
  Endangering welfare of, 639:3.
  Pornography, 649-A:3.
    Child care service, employment after conviction, 632-A:10.
    Distribution, 649-A:3-a.
    Manufacture, 649-A:3-b.
Child care service, employment after conviction, 632-A:10.
Classification, 625:9.
Commercial bribery, 638:7.
Communications paraphernalia, fraudulent, creation or usage, 638:5-a.
Computer pornography and child exploitation prevention, 649-B:3, 649-B:4.
Computer related offenses, 638:18.
Contraband, providing, 642:7.
Conviction, hindering, 642:3.
Cop-killer bullets, 159:18.
Counterfeit recordings, 638:6-a.
Courtrooms.
  Carrying weapons into courtrooms, 159:19.
Credit card, fraudulent use, 638:5.
Criminal.
  Mischief, 634:2.
  Restraint, 633:2.
Cruelty to animals, 644:8.
Culpability, 626:2.
Custody, interference with, 633:4.
Daggers.
  Possession by convicted felons, 159:3.
Dangerous weapons.
  Possession by convicted felons, 159:3.
Defined, 625:9.
Dirk-knives.
  Possession by convicted felons, 159:3.
Discovery, hindering, 642:3.

FELONIES —Cont'd
Electronic defense weapons.
    Criminal use, 159:23.
    Possession by felons, 159:21.
Escape.
    Aiding, 642:6.
    Implements of, providing, 642:7.
Evidence, falsifying physical evidence, 641:6.
Exploding bullets or cartridges, 159:18.
False filing with director of charitable trusts, 641:8.
False fire alarms, death resulting, 644:3-b.
Felon possession of dangerous weapon, 159:3.
Felons, transfer of firearms to, 159:7.
Fines, limitations, 651:2.
Fire alarms, tampering with, 644:3-c.
Firearms.
    Felonious use of, 650-A:1.
    Possession by career criminals, 159:3-a.
    Possession by convicted felons, 159:3.
    Transfers to felons, 159:7.
First degree assault, 631:1.
Force to prevent, justification, 627:5.
Forgery, 638:1.
Gravestones and gravesite items, possession or sale, 635:8.
Incest, 639:2.
Incompetent, endangering welfare of, 639:3.
Influencing public official improperly, 640:3.
Informants, tampering with, 641:5.
Kidnapping, 633:1.
Limitation of action, 625:8.
Mace.
    Criminal use, 159:23.
Malicious mischief, 634:2.
Manslaughter, 630:2.
Metallic knuckles.
    Possession by convicted felons, 159:3.
Negligent homicide, 630:3.
Newborn, concealing death of, 639:5.
Obscene matter, 650:2.
Pepper spray.
    Criminal use, 159:23.
Perjury, 641:1.
Physical evidence, falsification, 641:6.
Pistol canes, 159:19-a.
    Possession by convicted felons, 159:3.
Pistols.
    Carrying without license, 159:4.
    False information in purchasing, 159:11.
    Possession by career criminals, 159:3-a.
    Possession by convicted felons, 159:3.
    Sale without license, 159:10.
    Transfers to felons, 159:7.
Prosecution, hindering, 642:3.
Prostitution, 645:2.
Protection orders, violation of.
    Conjunction with another crime, 173-B:9.
Public officials.
    Bribery, 640:2.
    Influencing improperly, 640:3.
Punishment, hindering, 642:3.
Reckless conduct, use of deadly weapon, 631:3.
Recordable writings, fraudulent handling, 638:2.
Revolvers.
    Carrying without license, 159:4.
    Possession by career criminals, 159:3-a.
    Possession by convicted felons, 159:3.
    Transfers to felons, 159:7.
Rifles.
    Possession by career criminals, 159:3-a.
Rioting, 644:1.
Robbery, 636:1.
Running of time, 625:8.
Sabotage.
    Injuring or interfering with property, 649:2.
    Workmanship intentionally defective, 649:3.
Second degree assault, 631:2.

FELONIES —Cont'd
Sentence and limitations, 651:2.
    Annulment of criminal record, 651:2.
    Extended term, 651:6.
    Firearms, felonious use of, 651:2.
Sentencing.
    Presentence investigation.
        Military forces and veterans, 651:4-b.
Sexual assault, 632-A:2, 632-A:3.
    Child care service, employment after conviction, 632-A:10.
Shotguns.
    Possession by career criminals, 159:3-a.
Slingshots.
    Possession by convicted felons, 159:3.
Sporting event, fixing of, 638:8.
Stalking, 633:3-a.
Stilettos.
    Possession by convicted felons, 159:3.
Stun guns.
    Criminal use, 159:23.
    Possession by felons, 159:21.
Suicide, causing or aiding, 630:4.
Switch blade knives.
    Possession by convicted felons, 159:3.
Sword canes, 159:19-a.
    Possession by convicted felons, 159:3.
Taxes.
    Tobacco.
        Stamps, 78:12.
            Required, 78:14.
Teflon-coated bullets, 159:18.
Theft, 637:11.
Threatening safety of person or public, 631:4.
Tobacco.
    Stamps, 78:12.
        Required, 78:14.
Utilities, impairing, 634:2.
WIC program, 638:15.
Wireless telephone cloning, 638:22, 638:23.
Witnesses, tampering with, 641:5.

FELONS.
Alcoholic beverages.
    Employment in licensed places, 179:23.
Pistols and revolvers, possession and sale to, prohibited,
    159:3, 159:7.

FEMALE CONVICTS, STATE PRISONS, 622:33-a to 622:37.

FENCES.
Cemetery fences.
    Destruction, mutilation or removal of.
        Penalty, 635:8.
        Prohibited, 635:6.
    Possession, sale or disposition of.
        Penalty, 635:8.
        Prohibited, 635:7.

FETUS.
Assault, 631:2.
Murder, 630:1.

FIDUCIARIES.
Breach of duty, 625:8.
Commercial bribery, 638:7.
Property, misapplication of.
    Fraud, 638:11.
    Theft by, 637:10.

FIGHTING.
Animals, prohibition against promotion and exhibition of,
    644:8-a.
Disorderly conduct, 644:2.

FINANCIAL CONDITION.
Harm to, extortion, 637:5.

FINANCIAL INSTITUTION.
Defined, 638:11.
Fraud on depositors, 638:10.

FINANCIAL INSTITUTION —Cont'd
Property, misapplication of.
> Fraud, 638:11.
> Theft by, 637:10.

FINES.
Alcoholic beverages, 179:61.
> Administrative fines, 179:57.
> Liquor license violations, 179:57.
> Misrepresenting age, 179:9.
> Unlawful possession, 179:10.
Arrests.
> Aid to officers.
>> Refusal to give required aid, 594:6.
Attempt to commit crime, 629:1.
Bail jumping, 642:8.
Career criminal possession of firearm, 159:3-a.
Cemeteries or burial grounds, interference with, 635:8.
Civil actions, affect on, 625:5.
Computer related offenses, 638:18.
Conspiracy, 629:3.
Controlled drug act, 318-B:26.
Criminal solicitation, 629:2.
Discharge of one committed in default of payment.
> Committal for nonpayment, term, 618:9.
> Costs, 618:14.
>> Liability for, 618:15.
> Effect, 618:13.
> Payment of balance, 618:8.
> Petition for discharge, 618:10.
> Procedure for discharge, 618:11.
> Selectmen, discharge by, 618:12.
Drug paraphernalia, 318-B:26.
Enforcement.
> Place of committal, 618:6.
> Writ of execution, 618:7.
Explosives.
> Infernal machines, possession, 158:35.
> Malicious explosion, 158:34.
> Possession, violations, 158:32.
> Throwing or placing explosives, violations, 158:36.
Firearms.
> Possession by career criminals, 159:3-a.
General issue, 616:8.
Gravestones and gravesite items, possession or sale, 635:8.
Imposition and payment, 618:1 to 618:5.
> County.
>> Payment by, 618:5.
>> Payment to, 618:4.
> Payment, to whom, 618:3.
>> Clerk, to, 618:3-a.
> Use, for whose, 618:2.
Information and analysis center violations, 651-F:7.
Justice, disqualification of, 616:7.
Limitation of action, 616:9.
Limitations, 651:2.
Methamphetamine-related crimes, 639-A:3.
> Anhydrous ammonia.
>> Prohibited conduct, 318-D:5.
> Manufacturing, 318-D:2.
>> Injury resulting from manufacturing activities, 318-D:3.
Negligent storage of firearms, 650-C:1.
Old Man of the Mountain, vandalizing, 634:2.
Penal sanctions, defined by statute, 625:6.
Pistols.
> Possession by career criminals, 159:3-a.
> Sales to nonresidents, 159:8-b.
Revolvers.
> Possession by career criminals, 159:3-a.
> Sales to nonresidents, 159:8-b.
Rifles.
> Possession by career criminals, 159:3-a.
Sabotage, attempting, 649:4.
Shotguns.
> Possession by career criminals, 159:3-a.
Theft, 637:11.
Time, computation of, 616:6.

FINES —Cont'd
Tobacco.
> Person misrepresenting age, 126-K:6.
> Possession and use by minors, 126-K:6.
> Sale and distribution to persons under eighteen years of age, 126-K:4.
>> Note from adult possessed by minor, 126-K:8.
> Samples distributed in public place, 126-K:5.
> Selling in packages without Surgeon General's warning, 126-K:8.
> Single cigarette sales, 126-K:8.
> Use of products on public educational facility grounds, 126-K:7.
Tobacco tax.
> Importation of certain tobacco products, 78:34.

FIREARMS.
Career criminals, armed, 159:3-a.
Deadly weapon, defined, 625:11.
Discharge at occupied structure.
> Criminal mischief, 634:2.
Felonious use of, 650-A:1.
Minor, furnishing to, 644:15.
Unauthorized use, 644:13.

FIRECRACKERS.
Unauthorized use, 644:13.

FIRES.
Arson, 634:1.
Death associated with fire or explosion.
> Medico-legal cases.
>> Investigation by medical examiner, 611-B:11.
False alarms, 644:3-a.
> Injury or death resulting, 644:3-b.
False reports, 644:3.
Fire alarm apparatus, interference with, 644:3-c.
Party line, refusal to yield, 644:12.

FIXERS.
Sporting events, 638:8.

FLAGS.
United States, flag of.
> Defined, 646-A:1.
> Desecration.
>> Defined, 646-A:1.
>> Penalties, 646-A:4.
>> Prohibited, 646-A:2.
> Destruction of worn flag, 646-A:3.
> Properly displayed, defined, 646-A:1.
> Worn, destruction of, 646-A:3.

FLAK JACKETS.
Felonious use of body armor, 650-B:1, 650-B:2.

FLUNITRAZEPAM.
Controlled drugs, 318-B:1-c, 318-B:26.

FOOD STAMP PROGRAM.
Criminal penalties.
> Violations, 167:17-c.
Prohibited acts, 167:17-b.
Violations.
> Prohibited acts, 167:17-b.

FORCE AND VIOLENCE.
Criminal restraint, 633:2.
> Murder during, 630:1-a.
Justification generally.
> See JUSTIFICATION.
Obstructing justice, 642:1.
Prostitution, 645:2.
Robbery, 636:1.
Services, theft of, 637:8.
Sexual assault, 632-A:3.

FOREIGN LAW.
Effect of, jurisdiction, 625:4.

FORFEITURES.
Civil actions, affect on, 625:5.
Counterfeit goods, 638:6-b.

FORFEITURES —Cont'd
Drug offenses.
Law enforcement officers, 318-B:17.
Drugs.
Controlled drugs, 318-B:17.
Findings required, 318-B:17-b.
Guidelines required, 318-B:17-e.
Items used in connection with offenses, 318-B:1.
Administrative forfeiture, 318-B:17-d.
Not guilty finding, no forfeiture allowed, 318-B:17-b.
Report of, 318-B:17-d, 318-B:17-f.
Execution, 616:3.
Gambling equipment, 647:2.
Jurisdiction, 616:1.
Personal property, 617:1 to 617:10.
Appeal, 617:9.
Claimant, delivery to, 617:6.
Costs, 617:8.
Destruction order for, 617:10.
Libel, 617:2.
Notice, 617:4.
Warrant, 617:3.
Sales, 617:5.
Seizure, 617:1.
Trial by jury, 617:7.
Right of town, 616:4.
Selectmen, powers of, 616:5.
Tobacco tax.
Unstamped tobacco products.
Appeal of forfeiture, 78:31-a.
Tobacco tax, unstamped products, 78:16.
Trafficking in persons.
Forfeiture of items used in connection with, 633:8.
Administrative forfeiture, 633:9.
Use, for whose, 616:2.
Weapons, 159:16.
Wireless telephone cloning, 638:24.

FORGERY AND COUNTERFEITING.
Controlled drugs, obtaining by, 318-B:2.
Dealing in counterfeit goods, 638:6-b.
Fraud by, 638:1.

FORMULAE.
Theft of, 637:2.

FORNICATION.
Misdemeanor, 645:1.

FRATERNAL SOCIETIES.
Property, misapplication of, 638:11.

FRAUD AND DECEIT.
Adulterated or mislabeled goods, 638:6.
Advertisements, false or misleading statements, 638:6.
Affirmative defense.
Bad checks, 638:4.
Deceptive business practices, 638:6.
Forgery, 638:1.
Agent, commercial bribery, 638:7.
Animals, tampering with, 638:8.
Arson, to defraud, 634:1.
Bad checks, 638:4.
Badges.
Forging of, 638:1.
Unlawful simulation, 638:14.
Banks.
Checks.
Bad checks, 638:4.
Forgery, 638:1.
Fraud on depositors, 638:10.
Property, misapplication of, 638:11.
Recordable writings, fraudulent handling, 638:2.
Records, tampering with, 638:3.
Belief or knowledge, bad checks, 638:4.
Benevolent societies, misapplication of property, 638:11.
Bodily harm, sporting events, fixing of, 638:8.
Bonds.
Forging of, 638:1.

FRAUD AND DECEIT —Cont'd
Bonds —Cont'd
Tampering with, 638:3.
Books and papers, forging of, 638:1.
Bribery.
Commercial bribery, 638:7.
Sporting events, 638:8.
Cable television service, defrauding, 638:5-a.
Checks.
Bad checks, 638:4.
Forgery, 638:1.
Clubs, misapplication of property, 638:11.
Coin-operated machines, slugs, 638:13.
Commercial bribery, 638:7.
Communications paraphernalia, use, 638:5-a.
Complaint, unlawful simulation, 638:14.
Concealment.
Creditors, defrauding by, 638:9.
Recordable writings, 638:2.
Records, public or private, 638:3.
Contestants, tampering with, 638:8.
Controlled drugs, obtaining by, 318-B:2.
Corporate records, tampering with, 638:3.
Counterfeit recordings, dealing in, 638:6-a.
Court order, unlawful simulation, 638:11.
Credit card.
Defined, 638:5.
Forging of, 638:1.
Fraudulent use, 638:5.
Creditors, defrauding, 638:9.
Credit union.
Depositors, frauds on, 638:10.
Property, misapplication of, 638:11.
Dealing in counterfeit goods, 638:6-b.
Deception.
Business practices, 638:6.
Documents, fraudulent execution, 638:12.
Deeds, fraudulent handling, 638:2.
Depositors, frauds on, 638:10.
Destruction.
Computer equipment, 638:17.
Creditors, defrauding by, 638:9.
Recordable writings, 638:2.
Records, public or private, 638:3.
Documents, fraudulent execution, 638:12.
Doping animals, 638:8.
Embezzlement, misapplication of property, 638:11.
Encumbrances to defraud creditors, 638:9.
Evidence, physical evidence, falsification, 641:6.
False academic documentation, 638:15-a.
False weight or measure, 638:6.
Falsification.
Public or private records, 638:3.
Recordable writings, 638:2.
Records, public or private, 638:3.
Fiduciary.
Commercial bribery, 638:7.
Property, misapplication of, 638:11.
Financial institution.
Defined, 638:11.
Fraud on depositors, 638:10.
Property, misapplication of, 638:11.
Fixing sporting events, 638:8.
Forgery, 638:1.
Fraternal societies, misapplication of property, 638:11.
Fraudulent communications paraphernalia, defined,
638:5-a.
Fraudulent retail transactions, 637:10-b.
Government, defined, 638:11.
Identity fraud, 638:25 to 638:29.
Inducement, commercial bribery, 638:7.
Innkeeper, 637:8.
Insignia.
Forging of, 638:1.
Unlawful simulation, 638:14.

FRAUD AND DECEIT —Cont'd
Instruments.
　Executing fraudulently, 638:12.
　Forging of, 638:1.
　Fraudulent handling, 638:2.
Insurance company.
　Instability, 638:10.
　Property, misapplication of, 638:11.
Insurance fraud, 638:20.
　Venue, 638:20-a.
Interruption of computer services, 638:17.
Investment trust.
　Fraud on depositors, 638:10.
　Property, misapplication of, 638:11.
Knowledge or belief, bad checks, 638:4.
Limitation of action, 625:8.
Measure, deceptive practices, 638:6.
Misapplication of property, 638:11.
Mislabeled, defined, 638:6.
Mislabeled goods, 638:6.
Misuse of computer information system, 638:17.
Mortgages, fraudulent handling, 638:2.
Notice, simulation of official notice, 638:14.
Payment card scanning device or reencoder.
　Use to defraud, 638:29.
　　Definitions, 638:28.
Physical evidence, falsification, 641:6.
Possession.
　Forged instruments, 638:1.
　Slugs, 638:13.
Process, unlawful simulation, 638:11.
Property.
　Credit cards, fraudulent use, 638:5.
　Fraud on creditors, 638:9.
　Misapplication, 638:11.
　Slugs used to obtain, 638:13.
Recordable writings, fraudulent handling, 638:2.
Records, tampering with, 638:3.
Removal.
　Defrauding creditors, 638:9.
　Recordable writings, 638:2.
　Records, public or private, 638:3.
Revenue stamp, forging of, 638:1.
Running of time, 625:8.
Safety deposit company.
　Fraud on depositors, 638:10.
　Property, misapplication of, 637:10, 638:11.
Savings and loan associations.
　Fraud on depositors, 638:10.
　Property, misapplication of, 638:11.
Seals.
　Forging of, 638:1.
　Unlawful simulation, 638:14.
Securities.
　Forging of, 638:1.
　Fraudulent handling, 638:2.
Services.
　Credit cards, fraudulent use, 638:5.
　Slugs used to obtain, 638:13.
　Theft of, 637:8.
Short weight, 638:6.
Simulation, official notice, 638:14.
Slugs, possession and use of, 638:13.
Societies, misapplication of property, 638:11.
Sports bribery, 638:8.
Stamps, forging of, 638:1.
Statements, false or misleading, 638:6.
Stocks.
　Forging of, 638:1.
　Tampering with, 638:3.
Suicide, causing or aiding, 630:4.
Summons, unlawful simulation, 638:14.
Symbols, forging of, 638:1.
Tampering with records, 638:3.
Telecommunication, defrauding, 638:5-a.
Theft, 637:4.

FRAUD AND DECEIT —Cont'd
Theft of computer services, 638:17.
Threats.
　Documents, fraudulent execution of, 638:12.
　Sporting events, fixing of, 638:8.
Time, bad checks, 638:4.
Tokens, forgery, 638:1.
Trademarks, forging of, 638:1.
Trades union, misapplication of property, 638:11.
Transfers to defraud creditors, 638:9.
Unauthorized access to computer system, 638:17.
Vending machines, slugs, 638:13.
Weights and measures, 638:6.
WIC program, 638:15.
Wills, fraudulent handling, 638:2.
Writings, forgery of, 638:1.

FRAUDULENT RETAIL TRANSACTIONS, 637:10-b.

FREEDOM, ABRIDGEMENT OF.
Criminal restraint, 633:2.
False imprisonment, 633:3.
Kidnapping, 633:1.
Stalking, 594:10, 633:3-a.

FREE DRINKS.
Alcoholic beverage licensee serving, 179:44.

FRESH PURSUIT.
Arrest, authority to make.
　Interstate, 614:1.
　Intra-state, 614:7.
　Limitations, 614:3, 614:10.
Court hearing.
　Interstate, 614:2.
　Intra-state, 614:8.
Defined.
　Interstate, 614:5.
　Intra-state, 614:9.
Intoxicated drivers.
　Arrest, authority to make, 614:1.
　Reciprocity requirement, 614:1-a.
Severability, 614:6.
State, defined, 614:4.

FUMES.
Glue sniffing, 644:5-a.

FUNERALS.
Picketing or protest activities.
　Prohibition, 644:2-b.

G

GAMBLING.
Alcoholic beverage licensees.
　Permitting on premises prohibited, 179:19.
Equipment for, 647:2.
Lottery, 647:1.

GANGS.
Criminal street gang solicitation, 644:20.

GARAGE.
Joyriding, 637:9.

GARNISHMENT OF WAGES.
Restitution, 651:64.

GAS SERVICE.
Defined as property, 637:2.
Interruption of, 634:2.
Theft of, 637:8.

GENERAL COURT.
Bribery of members, 640:2.
Intimidation of members, 640:3.
Perjury before, 641:1.

GENETIC TESTING.
Criminal offender DNA testing, 651-C:1 to 651-C:6.
  See CRIMINAL OFFENDER DNA TESTING.
Post-conviction DNA testing, 651-D:1 to 651-D:5.
  See POST-CONVICTION DNA TESTING.

GENITALS.
Genital openings, defined, 632-A:1.
Indecent exposure, 645:1.

GIFTS.
Public servants, corrupt practice, 640:5.

GLASSWARE.
Alcoholic beverages.
  Retailer advertising specialties, 179:29.

GLUE SNIFFING.
Intoxication.
  Habitual offenders, 644:5-a.

GOOD FAITH.
Bigamy, 639:1.

GOODS.
Lost or mislaid, theft of, 637:6.

GOOD SAMARITAN.
Immunity from liability, domestic violence, 173-B:12.

GOVERNMENT.
Property, misapplication of.
  Fraud, 638:11.
  Theft by, 637:10.

GOVERNMENTAL AGENCIES.
Obscene matter, 650:6.

GOVERNOR.
Murder of, 630:1-a.

GRAFFITI.
Criminal threatening, 631:4.

GRAND JURY.
Clerk, 600:5.
Drawing jurors, 600:1.
Indictments.
  Generally, 601:1 to 601:9.
  Multicounty grand juries, 600-A:6, 600-A:7.
Minutes, 600:5.
Multicounty grand juries, 600-A:1 to 600-A:8.
  Applicable law, 600-A:4.
  Application for, 600-A:1.
  Consolidation, 600-A:6.
  Evidence, presentation, 600-A:5.
  Indictment, 600-A:6.
    Costs and expenses, 600-A:8.
    Prosecution of, 600-A:7.
  Order convening, contents of, 600-A:2.
  Term, 600-A:3.
  Venue, designation, 600-A:6.
Oaths, 600:3.
  Witnesses, to, 600:4.
Venires, issuance in emergencies, 600:2.

GRAVES.
Disturbance of contents of, 635:6.
Possession, sale or disposition of gravesite items, 635:7.
Removal, concealment or destruction of corpse, 644:7.

GUARDIANS AD LITEM.
Sexual assault, minor victims, 632-A:6.

GUEST HOUSE.
Services, theft of, 637:8.

GUNSHOT WOUNDS.
Reporting, 631:6.

H

HABEAS CORPUS.
Extradition.
  Application for, 612:10.
  Custody, 612:10.
  Procedure, 612:10.
  Waiver of extradition, 612:26.

HABITUAL OR REPEAT OFFENDERS.
Glue sniffing, 644:5-a.
Theft, 637:11.

HANDICAPPED.
Use of force against, 651:6.

HAPPY HOUR.
Alcoholic beverage advertising references, 179:31.

HARASSMENT.
Misdemeanor, 644:4.

HARBORING.
Criminal, 642:3.

HARM.
Bodily Harm.
  See BODILY HARM.
Defined, corrupt practice, 640:3.

HATE CRIMES.
Extended term of imprisonment, 651:6.

HATRED.
Accusation, theft by extortion, 637:5.
Criminal defamation, 644:11.

HAZARDOUS SUBSTANCES.
Methamphetamine-related crimes.
  Prohibited acts enumerated, 639-A:2.

HAZING.
Student hazing, 631:7.

HEALTH.
Harm to, theft by extortion, 637:5.

HEALTH AND HUMAN SERVICES DEPARTMENT.
Incompetent person released to community, 135:17-b.
Youth services center, 621-A:1 to 621-A:11.
  See YOUTH SERVICES CENTER.

HEALTH MAINTENANCE ORGANIZATIONS.
Insurance fraud, 638:20.

HINDERING.
Apprehension or prosecution, 642:3.

HOMICIDE.
Abortion, 630:1.
Aiding and abetting, suicide, 630:4.
Another, defined, 630:1.
Arson, murder resulting, 630:1.
Attempted suicide, aiding or abetting, 630:4.
Boats, negligent homicide, 630:3.
Burglary, murder during, 630:1.
Capital cases.
  Indictments, 601:6.
Capital murder, 630:1.
  Rights of accused, 604:1.
  Sentencing procedure, 630:5.
Criminal solicitation, suicide, 630:4.
Deadly weapon, use of, 630:1-b.
Death penalty, 630:1.
Deception, inducing suicide, 630:4.
Deliberation, murder, 630:1-b.
Depraved heart murder, 630:1-b.
Drug addiction, negligent homicide, 630:3.
Drunkenness, negligent homicide, 630:3.

HOMICIDE —Cont'd
Duress, inducing suicide, 630:4.
Emotional disturbance, 630:2.
Fetus, 630:1.
First degree murder, 630:1-a.
Indictments.
    Charging manner of death, 601:6.
Indifference to human life, 630:1-b.
Intentional killing, 630:1.
Intoxication, negligent homicide, 630:3.
Jurisdiction, 625:4.
Limitation of action, 625:8.
Malice, murder, 630:1-b.
Manslaughter, 630:2.
Mental disturbance, 630:2.
Negligent homicide, 630:3.
Newborn, concealment of death of, 639:5.
Parole.
    Murder which is psycho-sexual in nature, 651-A:8 to 651-A:10.
Premeditated murder, 630:1-a.
Prosecution, time for, 625:8.
Provocation, manslaughter, 630:2.
Recklessness.
    Manslaughter, 630:2.
    Murder, 630:1-b.
Second degree murder, 630:1-b.
Soliciting person to.
    Commit suicide, 630:4.
    Murder, 630:1.
Suicide, 630:4.
Time for prosecution, 625:8.
Vehicles, negligent homicide, 630:3.
Weapon, use of deadly weapon, 630:1-a.

HORSES.
Docking of tail prohibited, 644:8-b.
Police horses, interference with, 644:8-d.

HOSPITALS AND OTHER HEALTH FACILITIES.
Controlled drugs.
    Inventories, 318-B:12.
    Records required, 318-B:12.
    Sales to, 318-B:5.
    Use, limitations on, 318-B:8.
Gunshot wounds, reporting, 631:6.
Mentally ill.
    Confidentiality of information related to evaluation, 135:17-c.
    Notification if discharged to community, 135:17-b.

HOSTAGES.
Kidnapping generally.
    See KIDNAPPING.

HOTEL.
Services, theft of, 637:8.

HOUSE OF CORRECTION.
Escape from, 642:6.
    Contraband, implements for escape, 642:7.
Prisons and Prisoners generally.
    See PRISONS AND PRISONERS.
Sentence to, 651:17.

HOUSE OF ILL FAME.
Permitting, 645:2.

HOUSE PARTIES.
Facilitating a drug or underage alcohol house party, 644:18.

HUMAN IMMUNODEFICIENCY VIRUS.
Testing sexual offenders, 632-A:10-b.

HYPNOSIS.
Culpable mental state, 626:2.

I

IDENTIFICATION CARDS.
Alcoholic beverage purchases.
    False card used for purposes of purchasing, 179:9.
Tobacco products purchasers.
    Proof of age of purchaser, 126-K:3.

IDENTITY FRAUD, 638:25 to 638:29.
Definitions, 638:25.
Elements of offense, 638:26.
Penalties, 638:26.
Venue, 638:27.

IGNORANCE.
Effect of, 626:3.

ILLEGITIMATE CHILDREN.
Newborn, concealment of death of, 639:5.

IMMUNITIES.
Criminal offender DNA testing.
    Erroneous collection and entry of DNA sample into database in good faith, 651-C:4.
Domestic violence, providing emergency care, 173-B:12.
Expungement of records.
    Journalists reporting, 651:5.
Privileges and Immunities.
    See PRIVILEGES AND IMMUNITIES.
Witnesses in criminal cases, 516:34.

INCAPACITY.
Age of, 628:1.
Defense of.
    Conspiracy, 629:3.
    Criminal solicitation, 629:2.

INCEST.
Felony, 639:2.
Statute of limitations, 639:2.

INCHOATE CRIMES.
Affirmative defense.
    Renunciation.
        Attempt to commit crime, 629:1.
        Conspiracy, 629:3.
        Criminal solicitation, 629:2.
Attempt to commit crime, 629:1.
Conspiracy, 629:3.
Corroborative conduct, 629:1.
Culpability.
    Conspiracy, 629:3.
    Solicitation to commit crime, 629:2.
Defense.
    Affirmative defense, renunciation of.
        Attempt to commit crime, 629:1.
        Conspiracy, 629:3.
        Criminal solicitation, 629:2.
    Immunity from liability.
        Conspiracy, 629:3.
        Criminal solicitation, 629:2.
    Incapacity.
        Conspiracy, 629:3.
        Criminal solicitation, 629:2.
    Irresponsibility.
        Conspiracy, 629:3.
        Criminal solicitation, 629:2.
Incapacity, defense of.
    Conspiracy, 629:3.
    Criminal solicitation, 629:2.
Inducement to commit crime, 629:2.
Irresponsibility, defense of.
    Conspiracy, 629:3.
    Criminal solicitation, 629:2.

INCHOATE CRIMES —Cont'd
Jurisdiction, 625:4.
Notice, renunciation of conspiracy, 629:3.
Omission constituting attempt, 629:1.
One or more persons, defined, 629:3.
Participation in conspiracy, 629:3.
Penalties.
   Attempt to commit crime, 629:1.
   Conspiracy, 629:3.
   Criminal solicitation, 629:2.
Renunciation.
   Attempt to commit crime, 629:1.
   Conspiracy, 629:3.
   Solicitation to commit crime, 629:2.
Sabotage, 649:4.
Solicitation to commit crime, 629:2.
Substantial step, 629:1.

INCOMPETENTS.
Consent, giving of, 626:6.
Non-support, 639:3, 639:4.
Physical force to safeguard, justification, 627:6.
Welfare of, endangering, 639:3.

INCORRIGIBLES.
Youth development center, 621:27.

INDECENCY.
Deviate sexual relations.
   Murder during, 630:1-a.
Fornication, 645:1.
Indecent exposure, 645:1.
Lewdness, 645:1.
Prostitution, 645:2.

INDEMNIFICATION.
Medical examiner, 611-B:6.

INDICTMENTS, INFORMATIONS, AND COMPLAINTS.
Additional charges, 601:3.
Extradition, complaint against fugitive, 612:3, 612:13, 612:14.
Formal errors, 601:8.
Grand jury.
   Indictments generally, 601:1 to 601:9.
   Multicounty grand juries, 600-A:6.
      Prosecution of indictments, 600-A:7.
Intent to defraud, 601:5.
Prosecution, commencement of, 625:8.
Sufficiency, 601:4.
Waiver, 601:2, 601:3-a.

INDIGENT DEFENDANT REPRESENTATION, 604-A:1 to 604-A:10.
Appointment of counsel, 604-A:2.
   Additional inquiry, 604-A:2-a.
   Contract attorneys, 604-A:2-b.
   Duration of appointments, 604-A:3.
   Financial ability of defendant to obtain counsel, 604-A:2-c, 604-A:2-d.
   Substitution of appointments, 604-A:3.
Commissioner of administrative services, recordkeeping, 604-A:10.
Compensation of counsel, 604-A:4.
   Limitation, 604-A:5.
Contract attorneys, 604-A:2-b.
Contract services, 604-A:6-a.
Expenses, payment of, 604-A:8.
   Repayment to state, 604-A:9.
Financial ability of defendant to obtain counsel, 604-A:2-c.
   Partial liability, 604-A:2-d.
Funding.
   Additional funding, 604-A:1-b.
Neglected or abused children, 604-A:1-a.
Public defenders, 604-B:1 to 604-B:8.
Records, 604-A:10.
Representation, generally, 604-A:1.
Rules and regulations, 604-A:7.
   Rulemaking, 604-A:10.

INDIGENT DEFENDANT REPRESENTATION —Cont'd
Services other than counsel, 604-A:6.

INDUCEMENT.
Solicitation generally.
   See SOLICITATION.

INFANT.
Minors generally.
   See MINORS.

INFANTICIDE.
Newborn, concealing death of, 639:5.

INFORMATION.
Child care service employment, convictions for offenses against minor, failure to provide, 632-A:10.
Computer system information, misuse of, 638:17.
Prosecution, commencement of, 625:8.
Recording information, forgery, 638:1.

INJUNCTION.
Domestic violence, protective orders, 173-B:5.
Pistols and revolvers.
   Licensing violations, 159:6-e.

INNOCENCE.
Presumption of, 625:10.

INNS.
Services, theft of, 637:8.

INSANE PERSONS.
Acquittal.
   Certificate of jury, 651:8.
   Committal, 651:9-a.
   Court orders, duration, 651:11-a.
   Hospitalization, 651:8-b, 651:10, 651:11.
   Rights of persons, 651:11-b.
Consent, giving of, 626:6.
County correctional facility, transfer from, 651:11.
Defense of insanity, 628:2.
Plea of insanity, 651:8-a.

INSIGNIA.
Forging, 638:1.
Simulating unlawfully, 638:14.

INSPECTIONS.
Controlled drugs, right of entry, 318-B:25.
Drug stores.
   Controlled drugs, right of entry, 318-B:23.
Pharmacies.
   Controlled drugs, right of entry, 318-B:23.

INSTRUMENTS.
Executing fraudulently, 638:12.
Forging, 638:1.
Fraudulent handling, 638:2.
Theft, 637:2.

INSURANCE AND INSURANCE COMPANIES.
Arson, to defraud, 634:1.
Fraud, 638:20.
   Venue, 638:20-a.
Property, misapplication of.
   Fraud, 638:11.
   Theft by, 637:10.
Receipt of deposits, instability, 638:10.

INSURANCE FRAUD, 638:20.
Venue of prosecution, 638:20-a.

INTENTIONALLY.
Culpability generally.
   See CULPABILITY.

INTERBRANCH CRIMINAL AND JUVENILE JUSTICE COUNCIL, 651-E:1 to 651-E:5.
Chairperson, 651-E:4.
Duties, 651-E:3.
Established, 651-E:1.
Meetings, 651-E:4.
Members, 651-E:2.

INTERBRANCH CRIMINAL AND JUVENILE JUSTICE
        COUNCIL —Cont'd
Quorum, 651-E:4.
Report.
    Annual report, 651-E:5.

INTERPRETERS.
Wiretapping and eavesdropping.
    Use of interpreters, 570-A:9-b.

INTERRUPTION.
Computer services, 638:17.
Public services, 634:2.

INTERSTATE COMPACT FOR ADULT OFFENDER
        SUPERVISION.
Interstate commission, 651-A:26 to 651-A:38.

INTIMIDATION.
Government administration, 642:1.
Prostitution, 645:2.
Student hazing, 631:7.
Threats generally.
    See THREATS.

INTOXICATION.
Consent, giving of, 626:6.
Culpable mental state, 626:2.
Defense of, 626:4.
Negligent homicide, 630:3.
Protective custody, forfeiture of alcoholic beverages, 179:4.
Sexual assault.
    Incapacitating victim by administering intoxicating substance,
        632-A:2.

INTRUSION.
Burglary, 635:1.
Criminal trespass, 635:2.
No trespassing signs, posting, 635:4.
    Defacing or removing signs, penalty, 635:5.
Trespass by livestock, 635:3.

INVENTION.
Theft of, 637:2.

INVESTIGATIONS.
Presentence investigation.
    Military forces and veterans, 651:4-b.

INVESTMENT TRUST.
Fraud on depositors, 638:10.
Property, misapplication of.
    Fraud, 638:11.
    Theft by, 637:10.

INVOLUNTARY SERVITUDE.
Peonage.
    Involuntary servitude to pay a debt, 633:5.

IRRESPONSIBILITY.
Responsibility.
    See RESPONSIBILITY.

J

JAILS.
Extradition, detention of person, 612:12.

J-ONE.
Criminal justice information system, 106-K:1 to 106-K:7.
    See CRIMINAL JUSTICE INFORMATION SYSTEM.

JOSTLING.
Robbery, 636:1.

JOYRIDING.
Misdemeanor, 634:3.
Theft of vehicle, 637:9.

JUDGES.
Bribery, 640:2.
Intimidation, 640:3.
Threats against court or judicial officers, 631:4-a.

JUDGMENTS AND DECREES.
Force to execute, justification, 627:2.
Mistaken belief, founded upon, 626:3.

JUDICIAL BRANCH FAMILY DIVISION.
Domestic violence.
    Jurisdiction, 173-B:2.
    Petitions alleging abuse, 173-B:3.
    Relief, 173-B:5.
    Temporary orders, 173-B:4.
Jurisdiction.
    Domestic violence, 173-B:2.

JUDICIAL OFFICER.
Capital murder, causing death of, 630:1.

JURISDICTION.
Bad checks, 638:4.
Computer pornography and child exploitation prevention.
    State criminal jurisdictions, 649-B:6.
Domestic violence.
    Judicial branch family division, 173-B:2.
Element of an offense establishing, 625:11.
Judicial branch family division.
    Domestic violence, 173-B:2.
Telephone harassment, 644:4.
Territorial jurisdiction, 625:4.

JURORS.
Bribery, 640:2.
Intimidation, 640:3.

JURY.
Custody of, 606:5.
Grand jury.
    Multicounty grand juries, 600-A:1 to 600-A:8.
Impaneling, 606:1.
Oaths, 606:2.
Waiver of jury trial, 606:7.

JUSTICE DEPARTMENT.
Drug asset forfeiture guidelines, adoption of, 318-B:17-e.
Forfeiture report, 318-B:17-d.
Office of the chief medical examiner, 611-B:1 to 611-B:31.
    See MEDICAL EXAMINERS.

JUSTICE OF THE PEACE.
Arrest.
    Breach of peace, 594:11, 594:12.
Bail commissioner, 597:15.

JUSTIFICATION, 627:1 to 627:9.
Aggression, force to prevent, 627:4.
Arrest.
    Physical force.
        Assisting officer, 627:5.
        Deadly force, 627:4.
        Non-deadly force, 627:5.
        Retreat from use of force, 627:4.
    Searches during, 627:5.
Arson, deadly force to prevent, 627:7.
Burglary, deadly force to prevent, 627:4.
Choice of evils, 627:3.
Citizen's arrest, use of force, 627:5.
Competing harms, 627:3.
Conduct justifiable, 627:1.
Corporal punishment, 627:6.
Criminal.
    Liability.
        Reckless conduct, 627:3.
        Use of force, 627:2.
    Mischief, force to prevent, 627:8.
    Trespass, non-deadly force, 627:7.
Deadly force.
    Arresting law enforcement officer, use by, 627:5.
    Arson, prevention of, 627:7.
    Assisting officer, 627:5.
    Burglary, preventing, 627:4.
    Citizen's arrest, 627:5.
    Defined, 627:9.

JUSTIFICATION —Cont'd
Deadly force —Cont'd
Felonies, preventing, 627:5.
Kidnapping, preventing, 627:4.
Penal guards, use of, 627:5.
Premises, defense of, 627:4.
Self-defense, 627:4.
Sex offenses, preventing, 627:4.
Weapons, use of, 627:9.
Defense of.
Justifiable conduct, 627:1.
Mistake supporting, 626:3.
Person, 627:4.
Property, 627:7, 627:8.
Definitions, 627:9.
Detention, deadly force to effect, 627:5.
Dueling, 627:4.
Element of an offense, defined, 625:11.
Escape, deadly force to prevent, 627:5.
Felonies, deadly force to prevent, 627:5.
Force to protect.
Person, 627:4.
Property, 627:7, 627:8.
Incompetents, physical force to safeguard, 627:6.
Judgments, force to execute, 627:2.
Kidnapping, force to prevent, 627:4.
Military duty, use of force, 627:2.
Minors, physical force to discipline, 627:6.
Mistake supporting defense, 626:3.
Motion picture theater owners.
Use of force, 627:8-a.
Negligent conduct, criminal liability, 627:3.
Non-deadly force.
Assisting officer, 627:5.
Citizen's arrest, 627:5.
Criminal trespass, 627:7.
Defined, 627:9.
Property, protection of, 627:7.
Self-defense, 627:4.
Orders, force to execute, 627:2.
Penal guards, use of force, 627:5.
Personal safety, self-defense, 627:4.
Physical force, 627:2.
Airline captain maintaining order, 627:6.
Arrest.
Assisting officer, 627:5.
Deadly force, 627:4, 627:5.
Non-deadly force, 627:5.
Retreat from use of force, 627:4.
Assemblies, maintaining order in, 627:6.
Assisting public servant, 627:2.
Citizen's arrest, 627:5.
Criminal.
Liability, 627:2.
Mischief, prevention of, 627:8.
Trespass, 627:7.
Detention, effecting by use of, 627:5.
Emergency medical treatment, 627:6.
Felonies, preventing, 627:5.
Incompetents, use to safeguard, 627:6.
Judgments, execution of, 627:2.
Kidnapping, force to prevent, 627:4.
Malicious use of, 627:6.
Merchants, use of, 627:8-a.
Military duty, 627:2.
Minors, disciplining, 627:6.
Orders, execution of, 627:2.
Parent or guardian using, 627:6.
Physician treating patient, 627:6.
Process, execution of, 627:2.
Property.
Destruction, choice of evils, 627:3.
Protection of, 627:7.
Recovery of, 627:8.
Public duty, execution of, 627:2.
Railroad employees maintaining order, 627:6.

JUSTIFICATION —Cont'd
Physical force —Cont'd
Reckless use of, 627:6.
Recovery of property, 627:8.
Robbery, prevention of, 627:8.
Sea captain maintaining order, 627:6.
Self-defense, 627:4.
Sex offenses, preventing forcible violation, 627:4.
Suicide, prevention of, 627:6.
Teachers using, 627:6.
Vehicles, maintaining order in, 627:6.
Premises, deadly force in defense of, 627:4.
Private citizen, physical force, use of, 627:5.
Process, force to execute, 627:2.
Property.
Destruction, choice of evils, 627:3.
Protection of, 627:7.
Recovery of, physical force, 627:8.
Provoking non-deadly force, 627:4.
Public duty, use of force, 627:2.
Reckless conduct, criminal liability, 627:3.
Retreat from use of deadly force, 627:4.
Robbery, physical force to prevent, 627:8.
Searches during arrest, 627:5.
Self-defense, use of force, 627:4.
Sex offenses, force to prevent, 627:4.
Teachers, physical force to discipline, 627:6.
Unlawful combat, 627:4.
Weapons, use of, 627:9.
Deadly force to prevent use of, 627:5.
Withdrawal, non-deadly force use of, 627:4.

JUVENILE DELINQUENTS.
Detention.
Sexual assault by person in position of authority, 632-A:3.
Incapacity, age of, 628:1.

JUVENILE JUSTICE ADVISORY BOARD, 621-A:9 to 621-A:11.

JUVENILE OFFENDER.
Escape, 642:6.
Implements for and contraband, 642:7.

JUVENILE PROCEEDINGS.
Interbranch criminal and juvenile justice council, 651-E:1 to 651-E:5.

K

KIDNAPPING.
Deviate sexual relations.
Murder during, 630:1-a.
Felony, 633:1.
Force to prevent, justification, 627:4.
Minor, responsibility of, 628:1.
Murder during, death penalty, 630:1.
Trafficking in persons, 633:6 to 633:10.

KNIFE.
Deadly weapon, defined, 625:11.
Martial arts weapons.
Sales to minors, 159:24.

KNOWLEDGE.
Adultery, 645:3.
Arrest, resistance to, 642:2.
Bad checks, 638:4.
Culpable mental state, 626:2.
Defined, obscene matter, 650:1.
Detention, resistance to, 642:2.
First degree assault, 631:1.
Second degree assault, 631:2.
Simple assault, 631:2-a.

KNUCKLES, BRASS.
Carrying or selling, 159:16.
Possession, 159:15.

L

LABELS AND LABELING.
Alcoholic beverages.
　Specialty beers having alcohol content greater than 12 percent.
　　Label requirements, 179:40-a.
Drugs.
　Controlled drugs, 318-B:13.
　Prescriptions.
　　Controlled drugs, 318-B:13.
Explosives.
　Explosives packaged for transportation, 158:16.
Mislabeled goods, 638:6.
Pharmacists.
　Controlled drugs, 318-B:13.

LABOR.
Services.
　Defined as property, 637:2.
　Theft of, 637:8.
Unions, property, misapplication of, 638:11.

LABORATORIES.
Controlled drugs.
　Laboratory, defined, 318-B:1.
　Records required, 318-B:12.
　Sales to, 318-B:5.
　Use, limitations on, 318-B:8.

LAND.
Jurisdiction, 625:4.
Posting, no trespassing signs, 635:4.
　Defacing or removing signs, penalty, 635:5.

LANDMARKS.
Criminal mischief.
　Penalties, 634:2.

LARCENY.
Lost or mislaid property, theft of, 637:6.
Theft generally.
　See THEFT.

LASCIVIOUSNESS.
Misdemeanor, 645:1.

LASER POINTING DEVICES.
Criminal conduct involving, 631:3-a.

LAW ENFORCEMENT OFFICERS.
Assault of, extended term of imprisonment for, 651:6.
Chief medical examiner and other medical examiners.
　Assistance in police training, 611-B:8.
Crimes against.
　Extended term of imprisonment, 651:6.
Criminal justice information system, 106-K:1 to 106-K:7.
　See CRIMINAL JUSTICE INFORMATION SYSTEM.
Emergencies.
　Closure of area posing threat to public health and safety,
　　644:2.
Explosions.
　Investigations, 158:31.
Laser pointing devices.
　Knowingly shining beam at law enforcement officer, 631:3-a.
Methamphetamine-related crimes.
　Manufacturing.
　　Injury resulting from manufacturing activities, 318-D:3.
　Protective custody of child for health screening, 639-A:4.
Missing adults, duties of law enforcement officers, 106-J:1,
　106-J:2.
Murder of, death penalty, 630:1.
Riots.
　Closure of area posing threat to public health and safety,
　　644:2.
Training.
　Chief medical examiner and other medical examiners.
　　Assistance in police training, 611-B:8.
Transportation, duties regarding.
　Alcoholism prevention and treatment services, 172-B:3.

LEGISLATORS.
Bribery, 640:2.
Intimidation, 640:3.

LEWDNESS.
Misdemeanor, 645:1.

LIABILITY.
Accomplice, conduct of another, liability for, 626:8.
Bigamy, 639:1.
Civil liability, affect on, 625:5.
Coercion, 626:1.
Conduct of another, 626:8.
Criminal liability, 625:7.
　Arson, 634:1.
　Culpable mental state, 626:2.
　Ignorance or mistake, effect of, 626:3.
Drug dealer liability.
　See DRUG DEALER LIABILITY.
Duress and coercion, 626:1.
Ignorance, effect of, 626:3.
Immunity from as defense.
　Conspiracy, 629:3.
　Criminal solicitation, 629:2.
Justification.
　Reckless conduct, 627:3.
　Use of force, 627:2.
Knowingly acting, 626:2.
Mistaken, effect of, 626:3.
Negligently acting, 626:2.
Possession or control of thing, termination, 626:1.
Purposely or recklessly acting, 626:2.
Rioting, 644:1.
Voluntary act, criminal liability, 626:1.

LIBEL.
Forfeitures.
　Personal property, 617:2.
　　Notice, 617:4.
　　Warrant, 617:3.

LICENSES AND PERMITS.
Controlled drugs.
　Convictions, notice of, 318-B:18.
　Required, 318-B:3.
　Suspension or revocation, 318-B:18.
Explosives, 158:9-a to 158:9-h.
Pistols and revolvers.
　Injunctive relief, violations of licensing sections, 159:6-e.
　Nonresidents, 159:6, 159:6-d, 159:8-a.
　Remedies, refusal of licensing entity to comply with provisions,
　　159:6-f.
　Sale of, 159:8.
　　Sale without license, 159:10.
　To carry, 159:6.
Tobacco tax, 78:2 to 78:6-a, 78:12-a.

LIENS.
Theft by failure to disclose, 637:4.
Tobacco tax stamps.
　Licensed wholesalers.
　　Lien in lieu of bond, 78:9.

LIMITATIONS.
**Animals, confined in motor vehicles, officer or agent
　rescuing,** 644:8-aa.
Prior offenses, prosecution and sentence, 625:2.
Statute of Limitations.
　See STATUTE OF LIMITATIONS.

LIQUOR COMMISSION.
Books and papers, requiring production of, 179:56.
Employment prohibited, 179:21.
Enforcement policy, 179:56.
Hearings, 179:56.
Inspections of license plates.
　Generally, 179:57.
Rulemaking authority.
　Enforcement policy, 179:50.
Witnesses, summoning, 179:56.

LIQUOR TASTINGS, 179:44.

LIVESTOCK.
Trespassing, 635:3.
Vandalism to, 539:9.

LOANS.
Gambling loans, 647:2.

LOCAL OPTION.
Alcoholic beverages.
  Malt beverages, 179:1.
  Petition for, 179:1.

LOITERING.
Violation, 644:6.

LOST PROPERTY.
Theft of, 637:5.

LOTTERIES.
Indictments, 601:9.
Unlawful conduct, 647:1.

M

MAGAZINES.
Alcoholic beverages.
  Listing of retail prices, 179:31.

MAIL.
Lottery tickets, 647:1.

MALICE.
Murder, 630:1-b.
Physical force, malicious use of, 627:6.

MALICIOUS MISCHIEF.
Property damage, 634:2.
Public service, sentence to perform, 651:2.

MANSLAUGHTER.
Defined, 630:2.
Minor, responsibility of, 628:1.

MANUFACTURERS AND MANUFACTURING.
Controlled drugs, 318-B:2.
  Labels, 318-B:13.
  License for, 318-B:3.
    Required, 318-B:3.
  Manufacturer, defined, 318-B:1.
  Records, required, 318-B:12.
  Sales by, 318-B:5.
Manufacturer, defined, 318-B:1.

MARIHUANA.
Defined, 318-B:1.

MARRIAGE.
Adultery, 645:3.
Bigamy, 639:1.
Incest, 639:2.
Prostitution, 645:2.

MARTIAL ARTS WEAPONS.
Sale of, 159:24.

MATERIAL ELEMENT OF AN OFFENSE.
Defined, 625:11.

MEASURES.
Deceptive practice, 638:6.

MEDICAL EXAMINERS.
Office of the chief medical examiner, 611-B:1 to 611-B:31.
  Acting chief medical examiner.
    Designation by chief medical examiner, 611-B:4.
    Qualifications, 611-B:4.
  Administrative, clerical and technical assistants.
    Employment, 611-B:10.
  Assistant deputy medical examiners.
    Appointment, 611-B:5.
    Claims for fees, 611-B:27.
    Compensation, 611-B:27.

MEDICAL EXAMINERS —Cont'd
Office of the chief medical examiner —Cont'd
  Assistant deputy medical examiners —Cont'd
    Powers, 611-B:5.
    Qualifications, 611-B:5.
  Autopsies, 611-B:17.
    Expenses, 611-B:27-a.
    Reports made by medical examiners, 611-B:21.
  Chief medical examiner.
    Authority, 611-B:2.
    Nominated by attorney general, 611-B:2.
    Qualifications, 611-B:2.
    Rulemaking authority, 611-B:2.
    Supervision of office, 611-B:2, 611-B:7.
    Term of office, 611-B:2.
  Confidential medical records, 611-B:21.
  Definitions, 611-B:1.
  Deputy chief medical examiner.
    Acting chief medical examiner.
      Absence of chief medical examiner, 611-B:3.
    Appointment, 611-B:3.
    Qualifications, 611-B:3.
  Established within department of justice, 611-B:2.
  Expert assistance.
    Employment of persons skilled in science or pathology.
      Authority of supervising medical examiner, 611-B:9.
  Indemnification of medical examiner, 611-B:6.
  Laboratories, morgues and other technical facilities.
    Agreements with colleges and universities, medical schools
      or hospitals for use, 611-B:8.
  Medico-legal cases, death investigations.
    Autopsies, 611-B:17.
      Expenses, 611-B:27-a.
      Reports made by medical examiners, 611-B:21.
    Body tissue or body fluids.
      Retention, disposal, 611-B:18.
    Charge of body.
      Medical examiner to take, 611-B:13.
    Child death.
      Report to bureau of maternal and child health, 611-B:22.
    Claims for fees.
      Assistant deputy medical examiners, 611-B:27.
    Compensation.
      Assistant deputy medical examiners, 611-B:27.
    Confidential medical records, 611-B:21.
    Death report to person taking custody of body, 611-B:26.
    Defined, 611-B:11.
    Dental examination.
      Unidentified body, 611-B:23.
    Forensic science laboratory.
      Investigations by.
        Supervising medical examiner requiring, 611-B:19.
    Investigations, 611-B:11.
    Medical records, 611-B:14-a.
    Medico-legal investigation fund, 611-B:28.
    Money and other personal property of deceased.
      Medical examiner to take charge of, 611-B:16.
    Postmortem examinations, 611-B:15.
    Release of body.
      Completion of examination, 611-B:24.
        Unclaimed bodies, 611-B:25.
      Death report to person taking custody of body, 611-B:26.
    Reporting medico-legal deaths.
      Mandatory reporting, 611-B:12.
    Report to county attorney.
      Completion of investigation, 611-B:20.
    Survey of body and surroundings, 611-B:14.
    Unclaimed bodies.
      Release of body, 611-B:25.
    Unidentified human remains.
      Dental examination, 611-B:23.
      Release of body, 611-B:25.
      Skeletal remains recovered.
        Retention, disposal, 611-B:18.
  Medico-legal investigation fund, 611-B:28.

MEDICAL EXAMINERS —Cont'd
Office of the chief medical examiner —Cont'd
Missing persons investigations.
  Dental records.
    Destruction, person found, 611-B:31.
    Identification by scoring probabilities, 611-B:30.
    Requesting, 611-B:29.
Money and other personal property of deceased.
  Medical examiner to take charge of, 611-B:16.
Oath of office, 611-B:11.
Supervision of office, 611-B:7.
Training of police officers.
  Assistance, 611-B:8.

MEDICAL MARIJUANA.
Criminal prosecution.
Sale to non-qualifying patient or non-designated caregiver, 318-B:2, 318-B:26.

MEDICAL RECORDS.
Confidentiality of information.
Death investigations by medical examiners, 611-B:21.
Death investigations by medical examiners, 611-B:14-a.
Missing person investigations.
Dental records.
  Requesting, 611-B:29 to 611-B:31.
State prisons.
Secure psychiatric unit, 622:47.

MENTALLY ILL.
Consent of, not defense, 626:6.
Criminal liability, 628:2.
Criminal neglect of elderly, disabled or impaired adults, 631:8.
Endangering welfare of, 639:3.
Homicide, 630:2.
Hospitals.
Commitment for observation, 135:17.
Confidentiality of information related to evaluation, 135:17-c.
Indigent defendant representation.
Appointment of counsel, 604-A:2.
Insanity defense, 628:2.
Commitment to hospital for observation, 135:17.
Confidentiality of information related to evaluation, 135:17-c.
Evaluation for permanent commitment, 135:17-b.
Hearing on competency, 135:17-a.
Notification if discharged to community, 135:17-b.
Manslaughter, 630:2.
Neglect.
Criminal neglect of elderly, disabled or impaired adults, 631:8.
Physical force, use of, 627:6.
Sexual assault, 632-A:2.

MENU CARDS.
Alcoholic beverages.
Retailers' advertising specialties, 179:29.

MERCHANT.
Shoplifting, person detained, 627:8-a.

METALLIC KNUCKLES.
Carrying or selling, 159:16.
Possession of, 159:15.

METHAMPHETAMINE.
Conveyances of property on which methamphetamine produced.
Disclosures, 318-D:4.
Crimes relating to, 318-D:1 to 318-D:5, 639-A:1 to 639-A:4.
Anhydrous ammonia.
  Prohibited conduct, 318-D:5.
Convictions under controlled drugs provisions considered prior offense, 318-B:27.
Definitions, 318-D:1, 639-A:1.
Manufacturing, 318-D:2.
  Conveyances of real property on which methamphetamine produced, 318-D:2.
  Injury resulting from manufacturing activities, 318-D:3.
Penalties, 318-B:26, 639-A:3.
Prohibited acts enumerated, 639-A:2.

METHAMPHETAMINE —Cont'd
Crimes relating to —Cont'd
Protective custody of child for health screening, 639-A:4.

MILITARY AFFAIRS.
Paroled prisoner entering armed forces.
Suspension of supervision, 651-A:13.
Presentence investigation, 651:4-b.

MILITARY DUTY.
Force, justifiable use of, 627:2.

MINORS.
Adopted children, incest, 639:2.
Air rifles, sale to, 644:14.
Alcoholic beverages.
Advertising containing references to, 179:31.
Attempt to purchase, 179:10-a.
Cider, sales to, 179:6.
Employment of, 179:23.
Entertaining in licensed places, 179:19.
False identification to purchase, 179:9.
Furnishing to, 179:5.
Misrepresenting age, 179:9.
Possessing or consuming, allowing or permitting, 179:5.
Statement as to age, 179:8.
Unlawful possession, 179:10.
Assault of.
Child care service, employment after conviction, 632-A:10.
Sexual assault. See within this heading, "Sexual assault."
Bail and recognizances, 597:14.
Child pornography, 649-A:1 to 649-A:7.
Child pornography generally.
See CHILD PORNOGRAPHY.
Criminal restraint, 633:2.
Custody, interference with, 633:4.
Death investigation by medical examiner.
Report to bureau of maternal and child health, 611-B:22.
Death penalty, 630:1.
Drug abuse, treatment for, 318-B:12-a.
Electronic defense weapons, sale to, 159:22.
Firearms, furnishing to, 644:15.
Force to discipline, justification, 627:6.
Glue sniffing, 644:5-a.
Incapacity, age of, 628:1.
Incest, 639:2.
Juvenile justice advisory board, 621-A:9 to 621-A:11.
Kidnapping, 633:1.
Methamphetamine-related crimes.
Definitions, 639-A:1.
Penalties, 639-A:3.
Prohibited acts relating to children, 639-A:2.
Protective custody of child for health screening, 639-A:4.
Newborn, concealing death of, 639:5.
New Hampshire youth development center, 621:1 to 621:34.
Non-support, 639:3, 639:4.
Obscene matter involving, 650:2.
Obscenity.
Child pornography, 649-A:1 to 649-A:7.
Offenders against children.
Registration, 651-B:1, 651-B:2.
Pistols or revolvers, purchase of, 159:12.
Registration of criminal offenders generally, 651-B:1 to 651-B:12.
Responsibility of, 628:1.
Sexual assault, 632-A:2, 632-A:3.
Child care service, employment after conviction, 632-A:10.
Speedy trial, 632-A:9.
Testimony, in camera, 632-A:8.
Stepchildren, incest, 639:2.
Tattooing, 639:3.
Tobacco products.
Access to and use, 126-K:1 to 126-K:14.
  Administrative warnings, 126-K:12.
  Civil infractions.
    Distributing samples in public place, 126-K:5.
    Selling, giving or furnishing products to minors, 126-K:4.
    Minor possessing note from adult requesting, 126-K:8.

MINORS —Cont'd
Tobacco products —Cont'd
Access to and use —Cont'd
Civil infractions —Cont'd
Selling of product in packages without Surgeon General's warning, 126-K:8.
Single cigarette sales, 126-K:8.
Community service.
Minors purchasing, possessing or using products, 126-K:6.
Definitions, 126-K:2.
Documentation proving age, furnishing on purchase, 126-K:3.
Enforcement of provisions, 126-K:9.
Fines.
Assessment by commission, 126-K:12.
Deposit into general fund, 126-K:11.
Distributing samples in public place, 126-K:5.
List of names and addresses of persons against whom fines assessed, 126-K:12.
Minors purchasing, possessing or using products, 126-K:6.
Payment, 126-K:11.
Selling, giving or furnishing products to minors, 126-K:4.
Minor possessing note from adult requesting, 126-K:8.
Selling products in packages without Surgeon General's warning, 126-K:8.
Single cigarette sales, 126-K:8.
Use of products on public educational facility grounds, 126-K:7.
Law enforcement officers.
Jurisdiction to enforce provisions, 126-K:9.
License to sell tobacco products.
Suspension or revocation.
Powers of commission, 126-K:12.
List of names and addresses of persons against whom fines and penalties assessed, 126-K:12.
Local laws, ordinances and regulations, 126-K:14.
Misrepresenting age for purpose of purchasing products, 126-K:6.
Note from adult requesting sale, gift or delivery.
Selling, giving or furnishing products to minor with note, 126-K:8.
Prohibited, 126-K:4.
Proof of age of purchaser, 126-K:3.
Prosecution of violations by local, county or state law enforcement officials, 126-K:12.
Public educational facility or grounds of facility.
Use of tobacco products, 126-K:7.
Purchase, possession or use of product by minor, 126-K:6.
Purposes, 126-K:1.
Rulemaking, 126-K:10.
Samples.
Distributing or offering to distribute in public place, 126-K:5.
Selling, giving or furnishing products to minors.
Note from adult requesting sale, gift or delivery, 126-K:8.
Severability of provisions, 126-K:13.
Single cigarette sales prohibited, 126-K:8.
Surgeon General's warning.
Products to be sold in original packaging bearing, 126-K:8.
Suspension of license to sell tobacco products.
Selling, giving or furnishing products to minors, 126-K:4.
Weapons.
Negligent storage of firearms.
Child likely to gain access, 650-C:1.
Welfare of, endangering, 639:3.
Witnesses.
Civil cases, 516:25-a.
Youth development center, 621:1 to 621:34.
Youth services center, 621-A:1 to 621-A:11.

MISAPPLICATION OF PROPERTY.
Fraud, 638:11.
Theft by, 637:10.

MISAPPROPRIATION.
Lost or mislaid property, 637:6.
Property, 625:8.
Prosecution, running of time, 625:8.

MISBRANDING.
Fraud, 638:6.

MISCARRIAGES.
Assault, 631:1, 631:2.

MISCHIEF.
Criminal mischief, 634:2.
Force to prevent, justification, 627:8.

MISDELIVERY.
Lost or mislaid goods, theft of, 637:6.

MISDEMEANORS.
Accomplices and accessories, 642:3.
After the fact, 642:4.
Adulteration.
Alcoholic beverages, 179:16.
Adultery, 645:3.
Aerosol self-defense spray weapons.
Criminal use, 159:23.
Alcoholic beverages.
Adulteration, 179:16.
False identification.
Manufacture, sale and possession, 179:62.
Hours of sale violations, 179:17.
Increasing alcoholic content, 179:16.
Liquor investigators.
Interference with, 179:60.
Liquor license violations, 179:58.
Misrepresenting age, 179:9.
Penalties in general, 179:58.
Animals.
Confined in motor vehicles, 644:8-aa.
Cruelty to, 644:8.
Willful interference with organizations and projects involving, 644:8-e.
Apprehension, hindering, 642:3.
Arrest.
Aiding escape from, 642:6.
Resistance to, 642:2.
Violation of requirements, 594:17.
Arson, 634:1.
Bad checks, 638:4.
Bail and recognizance.
Bail agents and recovery agents.
Failure to notify local law enforcement, 597:7-b.
Bail jumping, penalty, 642:8.
Billies.
Possession or use in committing a crime, 159:15.
Blackjacks.
Carrying or selling, 159:16.
Bomb scare, 641:4.
Brass knuckles.
Carrying or selling, 159:16.
Possession or use in committing a crime, 159:15.
Bribery, 638:7.
Burglar tools, possession of, 635:1.
Burglary, 635:1.
Carrying or selling weapons, 159:16.
Child, endangering welfare of, 639:3.
Classification, 625:9.
Commercial bribery, 638:7.
Communications paraphernalia, fraudulent, possession, 638:5-a.
Compensating public official.
Past action, 640:4.
Services, 640:6.
Compounding crime, 642:5.
Computer pornography and child exploitation prevention.
Owners or operators of computer services, 649-B:5.
Computer related offenses, 638:18.
Conflict of interest, 643:2.
Conviction, hindering, 642:3.
Corpse, abuse of, 644:7.
Counterfeit recordings, 638:6-a.
Credit card, fraudulent use, 638:5.
Creditors, defrauding, 638:9.

MISDEMEANORS —Cont'd
Criminal.
  Defamation, 644:11.
  Mischief, 634:2.
  Threats, 631:4.
  Trespass, 635:2.
Cruelty to animals, 644:8.
Culpability, requirement of, 626:2.
Custody, interference with, 633:4.
Daggers.
  Carrying or selling, 159:16.
Dangerous weapons.
  Possession or use in committing a crime, 159:15.
Dead bodies, abusing, 644:7.
Deceptive business practices, 638:6.
Detention, resistance to, 642:2.
Dirk-knives.
  Carrying or selling, 159:16.
Discovery, hindering, 642:3.
Disorderly conduct, 644:2.
Documents, fraudulent execution, 638:12.
Dogs, police, interference with, 644:8-d.
Eavesdropping, 644:9.
Electronic defense weapons.
  Criminal use, 159:23.
Escape, aiding, 642:6.
Extradition.
  Noncompliance with rights of accused person, 612:11.
False.
  Alarms, 641:4, 644:3, 644:3-a.
  Imprisonment, 633:3.
  Swearing, 641:2.
Falsification not under oath, 641:3.
Fines, limitations, 651:2.
Forgery, 638:1.
Fraud on.
  Creditors, 638:9.
  Depositors, 638:10.
Gambling, 647:2.
Government administration, obstruction of, 642:1.
Gunshot wounds, failure to report, 631:6.
Harassment, 644:4.
Horses, police, interference with, 644:8-d.
Incompetent, endangering welfare of, 639:3.
Indecent exposure, 645:1.
Joyriding, 634:3, 635:5, 637:9.
Knives.
  Sales of martial arts weapons to minors, 159:24.
Limitation of action, 625:8.
Lottery, conduct of, 647:1.
Mace.
  Criminal use, 159:23.
Malicious mischief, 634:2.
Martial arts weapons.
  Sales to minors, 159:24.
Metallic knuckles.
  Carrying or selling, 159:16.
  Possession or use in committing a crime, 159:15.
Non-support, 639:4.
  Child or incompetent, 639:3.
No trespassing signs, removal or defacement of, 635:5.
Nunchaku.
  Sales of martial arts weapons to minors, 159:24.
Obscene matter, 650:2.
Obstructing government administration, 642:1.
Official notice, simulation of, 638:14.
Oppression by official, 643:1.
Party line, refusal to yield, 644:12.
Pepper spray.
  Criminal use, 159:23.
Pistol canes, 159:19-a.
Pistols and revolvers.
  Changing identification marks, 159:13.
  False information in purchasing, 159:11.
  Possession or use in committing a crime, 159:15.
  Sales to minors, 159:12.

MISDEMEANORS —Cont'd
Possession of weapons, 159:15.
Posted land, removing or defacing signs, 635:5.
Privacy, violation of, 644:9.
Property, misapplication of, 638:11.
Prosecution, hindering, 642:3.
Prostitution, 645:2.
Protective orders, violation of, 173-B:9.
Public officers and employees.
  Conflict of interest, 643:2.
  Official oppression, 643:1.
Public official, compensation for.
  Past action, 640:4.
  Services, 640:6.
Public records, tampering with, 641:7.
Punishment, hindering, 642:3.
Reckless conduct, 631:3.
Records, tampering with, 638:3.
  Public records, 641:7.
Registration of criminal offenders.
  Noncompliance, 651-B:9.
Resisting arrest, 642:2.
Rioting, 644:1.
Running of time, 625:8.
Sabotage, unlawful entry, 649:7.
Saps.
  Carrying or selling, 159:16.
  Possession or use in committing a crime, 159:15.
Sentence and limitations, 651:2.
  Annulment of criminal record, 651:2.
  Extended term, 651:6.
Sexual assault, 632-A:4.
Short weight, 638:6.
Simple assault, 631:2-a.
Slugs, possession and use of, 638:13.
Slung shots.
  Carrying or selling, 159:16.
  Possession or use in committing a crime, 159:15.
Spears.
  Sales of martial arts weapons to minors, 159:24.
Stalking, 633:3-a.
Stilettos.
  Carrying or selling, 159:16.
Stun guns.
  Criminal use, 159:23.
Suicide, causing or aiding, 630:4.
Swearing falsely, 641:2.
Switchblade knives.
  Carrying or selling, 159:16.
Sword canes, 159:19-a.
Swords.
  Sales of martial arts weapons to minors, 159:24.
Telephone, denying emergency use of, 644:12.
Theft, 637:11.
Threatening property, 631:4.
Threatening safety of person or public, 631:4.
Throwing darts.
  Sales of martial arts weapons to minors, 159:24.
Throwing stars.
  Sales of martial arts weapons to minors, 159:24.
Unsworn falsification, 641:3.
Use of animals in science classes and fairs, 644:8-c.
Violations, charged as, 625:9.
Weapons.
  Carrying or selling, 159:16.
  Possession, 159:15.
Weights and measures, fraud, 638:6.
WIC program, misrepresentation, 638:15.
Wireless telephone cloning.
  Possessing or using cloned wireless telephone, 638:22.

MISLAID PROPERTY.
Theft of, 637:6.

MISSING PERSONS.
Developmentally disabled persons, alert program.
  Definitions, 106-J:3.

MISSING PERSONS —Cont'd
Developmentally disabled persons, alert program —Cont'd
 Establishment of program, 106-J:4.
 Issuance and cancellation of alert, 106-J:4.
 Rulemaking, 106-J:5.
Investigation by law enforcement or medical examiner.
 Dental records.
  Destruction, missing person found, 611-B:31.
  Identification by scoring probabilities, 611-B:30.
  Requesting, 611-B:29.
Missing adults, duties of law enforcement officers, 106-J:1, 106-J:2.
Senior citizen alert program.
 Definitions, 106-J:3.
 Establishment of program, 106-J:4.
 Issuance and cancellation of alert, 106-J:4.
 Rulemaking, 106-J:5.

MISTAKE.
Boats, unauthorized use, 634:3.
Defense of, 626:3.
Effect of, 626:3.
Joyriding, 634:3.
Justification as defense, 626:3.
Lost or mislaid property, theft of, 637:6.
Vehicles, unauthorized use, 634:3.

MISUSE.
Computer system information, 638:17.

MITIGATION.
Prior offenses, procedural provisions, 625:2.

MOBILE RADIO SERVICE.
Wireless telephone cloning.
 Civil action by providers, 638:24.
 Criminal acts, 638:22, 638:23.
 Definitions, 638:21.
 Forfeiture of property, 638:24.
 Restitution, 638:24.

MOBS.
Rioting, 644:1.

MODEL DRUG DEALER LIABILITY ACT, 318-C:1 to 318-C:18.
 See DRUG DEALER LIABILITY.

MOLOTOV COCKTAILS, 158:37.

MONEY.
Lost or mislaid, theft of, 637:6.

MONUMENTS.
Cemeteries.
 See CEMETERIES.

MORTGAGES.
Fraudulent handling, 638:2.

MOTEL.
Services, theft of, 637:8.

MOTION PICTURES.
Child pornography, 649-A:2.
 Exemption, 649-A:4.
Obscene matter, 650:2.
 Projectionists, 650:3.
Theater owners.
 When use of force justified, 627:8-a.
Unauthorized recording in a theater, 644:19.

MOTORBOATS.
Joyriding, 637:9.
Negligent homicide, 630:3.
Theft of, 637:9.

MOTORCYCLE.
Joyriding, 637:9.
Theft of, 637:9.

MOTOR VEHICLES.
Animals, confined in, 644:8-aa.
 Transporting dogs in pickup trucks, 644:8-f.

MOTOR VEHICLES —Cont'd
Disorderly conduct for excessive volume, 644:2.
Dogs.
 Transporting in pickup trucks, 644:8-f.
Driver's license.
 Criminal mischief.
  Suspension, 634:2.
 Tobacco products purchases.
  Proof of age of purchaser, 126-K:3.
Joyriding, 637:9.
Negligent homicide, 630:2.
Noise.
 Disorderly conduct for excessive volume, 644:2.
Rental services, theft of, 637:8.
Serial numbers, removing or altering, 637:7-a.
Violations.
 Forfeitures of recognizances, 597:38-b.

MULTICOUNTY GRAND JURIES, 600-A:1 to 600-A:8.
Applicable law, 600-A:4.
Application for, 600-A:1.
Consolidation, 600-A:6.
Evidence, presentation, 600-A:5.
Indictment, 600-A:6.
 Costs and expenses, 600-A:8.
 Prosecution of, 600-A:7.
Order convening, contents of, 600-A:2.
Term, 600-A:3.
Venue, designation, 600-A:6.

MUNICIPAL COURTS.
Appeals.
 Criminal convictions in municipal or district court, 599:1 to 599:4.

MURDER.
Another, defined, 630:1.
Arson, murder resulting, 630:1-a.
Attempt to commit, 629:1.
 Sentence, 651:2.
Capital murder, 630:1.
 Sentencing procedures, 630:5.
Classification of crime, 625:9.
Conspiracy, 629:3.
Culpability, requirement of, 626:2.
Deadly weapon, 630:1-b.
Death penalty, 630:1.
 Injection, lethal, 630:5.
 Place of execution, 630:6.
 Witnesses, 630:6.
First degree murder, 630:1-a.
 Minor, responsibility of, 628:1.
Jurisdiction, 625:4.
Law enforcement officer, death penalty, 630:1.
Limitation of action, 625:8.
Minor, responsibility of, 628:1.
Parole, 651-A:7.
 Psycho-sexual murder, 651-A:8.
Presumptions, 630:1-b.
Prosecution, time for, 625:8.
Psycho-sexual murder, 651-A:8.
 Certification by court, 651-A:9.
 Defined, 651-A:10.
Reckless conduct, 630:1-b.
Robbery, murder during, 630:1-a.
Second degree murder, 630:1-b.
 Minor, responsibility of, 628:1.
Sentence, 651:2.
 Capital murder, procedure for, 630:5.
 Extended term, 651:6.
Sexual assault, murder during, 630:1-a.
Time for prosecution, 625:8.

MUSEUMS.
Obscene matter, 650:6.

MUTILATION.
Corpse, 644:7.
Flags, 646-A:1.

MUTILATION —Cont'd
No trespassing signs, 635:5.

N

NAMES.
Change of name.
Criminal offender registration.
Duty to notify, 651-B:5.

NATIONAL GUARD.
Activation.
State service.
Arrest, power of, 594:1.
Adjutant general.
Explosives.
Control of storage, sale and use, 158:19.
Arrest.
Powers of, 594:1.

NEGLIGENCE.
Culpable mental state, 626:2.
Firearms.
Negligent storage of firearms, 650-C:1.
Livestock trespassing, 635:3.
Negligent conduct, criminal liability, 627:3.
Negligent homicide, 630:3.
Simple assault, 631:2-a.
Trespass by livestock, 635:3.

NEGLIGENT HOMICIDE.
Defined, 630:3.

NEWBORN.
Death of, concealment, 639:5.

NEW ENGLAND INTERSTATE CORRECTIONS COMPACT,
622-A:1 to 622-A:3.

NEW HAMPSHIRE YOUTH DEVELOPMENT CENTER,
621:1 to 621:34.

NEWSPAPERS.
Alcoholic beverages.
Listing of retail prices, 179:31.

NIGHT.
Defined, burglary, 635:1.

NOISE.
Breach of peace, 644:2.
Motor vehicles.
Disorderly conduct for excessive volume, 644:2.

NON-DEADLY FORCE.
Justification.
Assisting officer, 627:5.
Citizen's arrest, 627:5.
Criminal trespass, preventing, 627:7.
Defined, 627:9.
Property, protection of, 627:7.
Self-defense, 627:4.

NONRESIDENTS.
Pistols or revolvers.
License for, 159:6, 159:6-d.
Sale to, 159:8-a.
Penalty, 159:8-b.
Tobacco tax, stamps and metering machines, 78:13.

NON-SUPPORT.
Minor or incompetent, 639:3.
Misdemeanor, 639:4.

NOTARY PUBLIC.
Perjury before, 641:1.
Swearing falsely before, 641:2.

NOTICE.
Conspiracy, renunciation of, 629:3.
Drug dealer liability.
Filing of action, 318-C:16.

NOTICE —Cont'd
Forfeitures of personal property, libel, 617:4.
Incompetent persons, release to community, 135:17-b.
Insanity, defense of, 628:2.
Official notice, simulation of, 638:14.
Parole hearings, 651-A:11.
Renunciation of conspiracy, 629:3.
State prisons, psychiatric unit, notification of granting of
off-grounds privileges, 622:49.

NUDITY.
Obscene Matter.
See OBSCENE MATTER.

NUISANCES.
Drugs, maintaining common nuisance, 318-B:16.

NUNCHAKU.
Sales of martial arts weapons to minors, 159:24.

NURSES AND NURSING.
Controlled drugs.
Administering, 318-B:10.
Nurse, defined, 318-B:1.
Definitions.
Controlled drug act, 318-B:1.

O

OATHS.
Jurors, 606:2.
Medical examiners, 611-B:11.

OBSCENE MATTER.
Adjudication of, 650:5.
Adversary hearing, 650:6.
Advertising, 650:2, 650:5.
Affirmative defense, 650:4.
Artistic merits, 650:5.
Child, defined, 650:1.
Dances, 650:2.
Defenses, 650:4.
Definitions, 650:1.
Disseminate, defined, 650:1.
Educational.
Justification, 650:4.
Merits, 650:5.
Evidence, 650:5.
Defense, 650:4.
Felony, child involved, 650:2.
Governmental agencies, 650:6.
Hearing, 650:6.
Knowledge, defined, 650:1.
Literary merits, 650:5.
Material, defined, 650:1.
Misdemeanor, 650:2.
Motion pictures, 650:2.
Projectionist, 650:3.
Museums, 650:6.
Obscene, defined, 650:1.
Plays, 650:2.
Predominant appeal, defined, 650:1.
Preliminary hearing, 650:6.
Publication, 650:2.
Public libraries, 650:6.
Reputation of producer, 650:5.
Schools, 650:6.
Scientific.
Justification, 650:4.
Merit, 650:5.
Sexual conduct, defined, 650:1.
Theaters, 650:2.

OBSCENITY.
Child pornography, 649-A:1 to 649-A:7.
Disorderly conduct, 644:2.
Telephone calls, 644:4.

OBSTRUCTING JUSTICE.
Accomplice or accessory, 642:3.
  After the fact, 642:4.
Affirmative defense, restitution, 642:5.
Apprehension, hindering, 642:3.
Arrest.
  Escape from, 642:6.
    Implements for and contraband, 642:7.
  Resistance to, 642:2.
Assault, interference with government administration,
  642:1.
Bail jumping, 642:8.
Compounding crime, 642:5.
Concealing criminal, 642:3.
Confinement, escape from, 642:6.
  Implements for and contraband, 642:7.
Contraband, implements for escape, 642:7.
Conviction, hindering, 642:3.
Custody, escape from, 642:6.
  Implements for and contraband, 642:7.
Deadly weapon, escapee using, 642:6.
Detention, resistance to, 642:2.
Discovery, hindering, 642:3.
Disguise, furnishing criminal, 642:3.
Escape, 642:6.
  Deadly weapon, employed in, 642:6.
  Implements for and contraband, 642:7.
Evidence, concealing or destroying, 642:3.
Force, interference with government administration, 642:1.
Government administration, generally, 642:1.
Harboring criminal, 642:3.
House of correction, escape from, 642:6.
  Contraband, implements for escape, 642:7.
Intimidation, interference with government
  administration, 642:1.
Juvenile offender, escape, 642:6.
  Implements for and contraband, 642:7.
Obstructing report of crime or injury, offense of, 642:10.
Official custody, escape from, 642:6.
Penal institution, escape from, 642:6.
  Implements for and contraband, 642:7.
Prison, escape from, 642:6.
  Contraband, implements for escape, 642:7.
Prosecuting, hindering, 642:3.
Punishment, hindering, 642:3.
Reimbursement, compounding crime, 642:5.
Restitution, affirmative defense, 642:5.
Transportation, furnishing criminal, 642:3.
Victim, compounding crime, 642:5.
Violence, interference with government administration,
  642:1.
Warning to avoid discovery, 642:3.
Weapon, providing criminal, 642:3.
Witness, compounding crime, 642:5.

OFFENSES.
Classification of, 625:9.
  Limitation of action, 625:8.
Computer related offenses, 638:17.
Conduct out of state, 625:4.
Culpability, element of an offense, 625:11.
Defined by statute, 625:6.
Element of an offense.
  Burden of proof, 625:10.
  Conduct of another, liability for, 626:8.
  Consent of victim, as defense, 626:6.
  Defined, 625:11.
  Intoxication as defense, 626:4.
  Jurisdiction, 625:4.
    Establishing, 625:11.
Excuse, element of an offense, 625:11.
Family, Offenses Against.
  See FAMILY, OFFENSES AGAINST.
Hypnosis, culpable mental state, 626:2.
Inchoate offenses.
  Jurisdiction, 625:4.
Intoxication, culpable mental state, 626:2.

OFFENSES —Cont'd
Jurisdiction.
  Conduct out of state, 625:4.
  Element of an offense establishing, 625:11.
  Out of state conduct, 625:4.
Justification.
  Element of an offense, defined, 625:11.
Limitation of action, 625:8.
Material element of an offense.
  Culpability, requirements of, 626:2.
  Defined, 625:11.
Oral communications, notice of, 642:3.
Out of state conduct, jurisdiction, 625:4.
Outside code, applicability, 625:7.
Pen registers, notice of use of, 642:3.
Possession, criminal liability, 626:1.
Prior offenses, prosecution of, 625:2.
Risk, culpable mental state, 626:2.
Tracing devices, notice of use of, 642:3.
Venue.
  Computer related offenses, 638:19.
  Element of an offense establishing, 625:11.
Voluntary act, criminal liability, 626:1.
Wire interception, notice of, 642:3.

OFFICE OF THE CHIEF MEDICAL EXAMINER, 611-B:1 to
  611-B:31.
See MEDICAL EXAMINERS.

OLD MAN OF THE MOUNTAIN.
Vandalizing, 634:2.

OMISSION.
Attempt to commit crime, 629:1.
Conduct, defined, 625:11.
Constituting attempt to commit crime, 629:1.
Default of duty, 625:4.
Defined by statute, 625:6.
Information in official matters, 641:3.
Voluntary omission, criminal liability, 626:1.

ORDERS.
Force to execute, justification, 627:2.

ORGANIZED CRIME.
Retail crime enterprise, 637:10-c.

OUT OF STATE.
Foreign law, jurisdiction, 625:4.
Parole, 651-A:25.

OVERT ACT.
Conspiracy, 629:3.
Jurisdiction, 625:4.

P

PAGER SERVICE.
Wireless telephone cloning, 638:21 to 638:24.
  Civil action by providers, 638:24.
  Criminal acts, 638:22, 638:23.
  Definitions, 638:21.
  Forfeiture of property, 638:24.
  Restitution, 638:24.

PANDERING.
Misdemeanor, 645:2.

PANIC.
Criminal threats causing fear of, 631:4.
Fear-producing threats, 631:4.

PAPER NAPKINS.
Alcoholic beverages.
  Retailers' advertising specialties, 179:29.

PARAMEDICS.
Controlled drugs, emergency use of, 318-B:10.

PARAPHERNALIA.
Methamphetamine paraphernalia, 639-A:2.

PARENT AND CHILD.
Notice requirements.
　Intoxicated or incapacitated minors in protective custody,
　　172-B:3.
Physical force, justifiable use, 627:6.
Youth development center.
　Costs, parents or estate of child to contribute, 621:31.

PAROLE, 651-A:1 to 651-A:25.
Adult parole board, 651-A:3, 651-A:4.
　Department of corrections.
　　Administrative attachment to, 651-A:24.
　Executive assistant, 651-A:5.
　Hearings.
　　Notice, 651-A:11.
　　Revocation of parole, 651-A:17.
　　Victims permitted to speak, 651-A:11-a.
Arrest of parolee, 651-A:15-a.
Board.
　Administrative attachment, 651-A:24.
　Defined, 651-A:2.
　Duties, 651-A:4.
　Established, 651-A:3.
　Executive assistant, 651-A:5.
　Hearings.
　　Notice of, 651-A:11.
　　Number required, 651-A:3.
　　Procedures, 651-A:3.
　　Revocation of parole, 651-A:17.
　　Testimony by victims or next of kin, 651-A:11-a.
　Records, access and review, 651-A:20.
Commissioner, defined, 651-A:2.
Compact.
　Execution authorized, 651-A:25.
Confinement prior to sentencing, credits, 651-A:23.
Credits.
　Confinement prior to sentencing, 651-A:23.
　Good conduct, 651-A:22.
　Life sentence, 651-A:7.
　Psycho-sexual murder, 651-A:8.
Defined, 651-A:2.
Department, defined, 651-A:2.
Discharge.
　Final discharge, 651-A:21.
　Good conduct, early discharge, 651-A:14.
First degree murder, 630:1-a.
Good conduct, 651-A:22.
　Credits, 651-A:22.
　Early discharge, 651-A:14.
　Life sentence, 651-A:7.
　Psycho-sexual murder, 651-A:8.
Hearings.
　Notice, 651-A:11.
　Revocation of parole, 651-A:17.
　Victims permitted to speak, 651-A:11-a.
Intermediate sanction, 651-A:16-a.
Interstate compact, 651-A:25.
Interstate compact for adult offender supervision, 651-A:26
　　to 651-A:38.
　Activities of interstate commission, 651-A:31.
　Amendment of compact, 651-A:35.
　Binding effect, 651-A:38.
　Construction of compact, 651-A:37.
　Default, 651-A:36.
　Dispute resolution, 651-A:33.
　Eligibility to be compacting state, 651-A:35.
　Enforcement, 651-A:33.
　Establishment of interstate commission, 651-A:27.
　Financing of expenses of interstate commission, 651-A:34.
　Judicial enforcement, 651-A:36.
　Officers and staff of interstate commission, 651-A:30.
　Organization and operation of interstate commission, 651-A:29.
　Oversight, 651-A:33.
　Powers and duties of interstate commission, 651-A:28.
　Rulemaking, 651-A:32.
　Severability, 651-A:37.
　Termination of compact, 651-A:36.

PAROLE —Cont'd
Interstate compact for adult offender supervision —Cont'd
　Withdrawal from compact, 651-A:36.
Legislative intent, 651-A:1.
Life sentence, 651-A:7.
　Eligibility for release, 651-A:7.
　Psycho-sexual murder, 651-A:8.
Maximum sentence.
　Discharge upon expiration of, 651-A:21.
　Reduction of, 651-A:12.
Medical parole, 651-A:10-a.
Military service.
　Suspension of supervision, 651-A:13.
Minimum term.
　Expiration of, 651-A:6.
　Life sentence, 651-A:7.
Murder, 651-A:7.
　First degree murder, 630:1-a.
　Psycho-sexual murder.
　　Certification by sentencing judge, 651-A:9.
　　Defined, 651-A:10.
　　Eligibility for parole, 651-A:8.
Officer, murder of, death penalty for, 630:1.
Out of state parolee, supervision, 651-A:25.
Prisoner, defined, 651-A:2.
Psycho-sexual murder, 651-A:8.
　Certification by court, 651-A:9.
　Defined, 651-A:10.
Purpose of, 651-A:1.
Records, 651-A:20.
Release.
　Early, recommended, 651:25.
　Life sentence, 651-A:7.
　Terms of, 651-A:6.
Re-parole, eligibility, 651-A:18.
Reports.
　Violations of conditions, 651-A:16.
Revocation, 651-A:17, 651-A:18.
　Effect of recommittal, 651-A:19.
　Grounds, 651-A:18.
　Hearing, 651-A:17.
　Recommittal, 651-A:17.
　　Effect of, 651-A:19.
Supervision.
　Out of state parolee, 651-A:25.
　Suspension of, 651-A:13.
Terms of release, 651-A:6.
Victims of crime.
　Right to speak at hearings, 651-A:11-a.
Violation of.
　Extradition, 612:3, 612:23.
　Report, 651-A:16.
　Revocation of parole, 651-A:17, 651-A:18.

PAROLE OFFICERS.
Sexual assault.
　Sexual contact by person in possession of authority over victim,
　　632-A:3.

PARTY LINE.
Refusal to yield, 644:12.

PASSPORTS.
Tobacco products purchasers.
　Proof of age of purchaser, 126-K:3.

PAYMENT CARD SCANNING DEVICE OR REENCODER.
Use to defraud, 638:29.
　Definitions, 638:28.

PEEPING TOMS.
Violation of privacy, 644:9.

PENAL INSTITUTION.
Escape from, 642:6.
　Contraband and implements for escape, 642:7.

PENAL SANCTIONS.
Offenses defined by statute, 625:6.

PENETRATION.
Defined, 632-A:1.
Sexual assault, 632-A:2, 632-A:3.

PEN REGISTERS.
Obstructing justice, 642:3.

PEPPER SPRAY.
Criminal use of aerosol self-defense spray weapons, 159:23.

PERJURY.
Felony, 641:1.
Subornation, 641:5.

PERSON.
Defined, 625:11.

PERSONAL COMMUNICATION SERVICE.
Wireless telephone cloning, 638:21 to 638:24.
  Civil action by providers, 638:24.
  Criminal acts, 638:22, 638:23.
  Definitions, 638:21.
  Forfeiture of property, 638:24.
  Restitution, 638:24.

PERSONAL PROPERTY.
Forfeitures, 617:1 to 617:10.
Theft, 637:2.

PHARMACISTS AND PHARMACIES.
Board.
  Rulemaking authority.
    Controlled drugs, 318-B:24.
Compounding.
  Labels, 318-B:13.
Controlled Drug Act, 318-B:1.
Controlled drugs and prescriptions.
  Electronic prescriptions, 318-B:9.
  Requirements for prescriptions issued by practitioners,
    318-B:9.
Prescription drugs.
  Prescriptions.
    Labeling.
      Controlled drugs, 318-B:13.
Prescriptions.
  Controlled drugs.
    Confidentiality, 318-B:12.
    Forging or altering, 318-B:2.
    Pharmacists, sale by, 318-B:9.
    Prescription, defined, 318-B:1.

PHOTOGRAPH.
Child pornography, 649-A:2.
Obscene Matter generally.
  See OBSCENE MATTER.
Privacy, invasion of, 644:9.
Theft by, 637:2.

PHYSICAL FORCE.
Justification, 627:2.
  Airplanes, maintaining order on, 627:6.
  Arrest.
    Assisting officer, 627:5.
    Deadly force, 627:4.
    Non-deadly force, 627:5.
    Retreat from use of force, 627:4.
  Assemblies, maintaining order in, 627:6.
  Assisting public servant, 627:2.
  Citizen's arrest, 627:5.
  Criminal.
    Liability, 627:2.
    Mischief, preventing, 627:8.
    Trespass, 627:7.
  Detention, effecting by use of, 627:5.
  Emergency medical treatment, 627:6.
  Felonies, preventing, 627:5.
  Incompetents, use to safeguard, 627:6.
  Judgments, execution of, 627:2.
  Kidnapping, force to prevent, 627:4.
  Malicious use of, 627:6.
  Military duty, 627:2.

PHYSICAL FORCE —Cont'd
Justification —Cont'd
  Minors, disciplining, 627:6.
  Orders, execution of, 627:2.
  Parent or guardian using, 627:6.
  Physician treating patient, 627:6.
  Process, execution of, 627:2.
  Property.
    Protection of, 627:7.
    Recovery of, 627:8.
  Public duty, execution of, 627:2.
  Railroads, maintaining order on, 627:6.
  Reckless use of, 627:6.
  Recovery of property, 627:8.
  Robbery, prevention of, 627:8.
  Self-defense, 627:4.
  Sex offenses, preventing forcible violation, 627:4.
  Suicide, prevention of, 627:6.
  Teachers using, 627:6.
  Vehicles, maintaining order in, 627:6.
  Vessels, maintaining order on, 627:6.
Robbery, 636:1.

PHYSICAL INJURY.
Bodily Harm generally.
  See BODILY HARM.

PHYSICIANS AND SURGEONS.
Controlled drugs.
  Communications not privileged, 318-B:21.
  Labeling containers, 318-B:13.
  Physician, defined, 318-B:1.
  Prescriptions written by practitioners, requirements, 318-B:9.
  Sales to, 318-B:5.
Definitions.
  Felony, 625:9.
Gunshot wounds, reporting, 631:6.
**Medical associations and corporations, licenses for
    controlled drugs,** 318-B:3.
Physical force, justifiable use, 627:6.
Physician, defined.
  Controlled Drug Act, 318-B:1.
Prescriptions.
  Controlled drugs.
    Requirements, 318-B:9.
Sexual assault.
  Reporting, victim consent, 631:6.

PICK POCKETING.
Robbery, 636:1.

PICKUP TRUCKS.
Transporting dogs, 644:8-f.

PIMPING.
Misdemeanor, 645:2.

PIRACY OF MOTION PICTURES.
Unauthorized recording in a theater, 644:19.

PIRATING RECORDS AND TAPES, 638:6-a.

PISTOL CANE.
Criminal use of, 159:19-a.
Gun cane, defined, 159:1.

PISTOLS AND REVOLVERS.
Antique pistol or revolver, defined, 159:1.
Bullets and cartridges, armor piercing or exploding.
  Felonious use, 159:18.
Career criminals, armed, 159:3-a.
Carrying without license, 159:4, 159:5.
Crimes.
  Changing identification marks, 159:13.
  False information in purchasing, 159:11.
  Possession or use in committing a crime, 159:15.
  Sales to minors, 159:12.
  Sale without license, 159:10.
Dangerous weapons.
  Carrying or selling, 159:16.
  Exceptions, 159:17.

PISTOLS AND REVOLVERS —Cont'd
Dangerous weapons —Cont'd
  Possession on arrest, 159:15.
Defined, 159:1.
Exceptions.
  Proof of, 159:5-a.
Fees.
  License to carry, 159:6.
Felons.
  Career criminals, armed, 159:3-a.
  Possession of, 159:3, 159:8.
  Sales prohibited, 159:7.
Identifying marks, altering, 159:13.
Licenses and permits.
  Carrying without, 159:4.
  Injunctive relief, violations of licensing sections, 159:6-e.
  Nonresident, 159:6, 159:6-d.
  Remedies, refusal of licensing entity to comply with provisions, 159:6-f.
  Sale of, 159:8.
    Without license, 159:10.
  To carry, 159:6, 159:6-d.
  Violations.
    Proceedings on, 159:6-e.
    Remedies, 159:6-f.
Minors purchasing, 159:12.
Nonresident.
  Sale to, 159:8-a.
    Penalty, 159:8-b.
Pistol, defined, 159:1.
Purchase.
  False information, 159:11.
  Minors, 159:12.
  Nonresidents, 159:8-a.
    Penalty, 159:8-b.
Revolver, defined, 159:1.
Sales.
  Individuals selling, 159:14.
  License for, 159:8.
  Minors purchasing, 159:12.
  Nonresident, 159:8-a.
    Penalty, 159:8-b.
  Without license, 159:10.

PLACE OF TRIAL.
Territorial jurisdiction, 625:4.

PLEAS.
Lesser offense, 605:3.
Nolo contendere, 605:6.
Nonacceptance of, 605:4.
Refusal to plead, 605:5.

POISONS.
Exposure to, 644:16.

POLICE.
Arrest.
  Notice of, to county attorney, 594:10-a.
  Use of deadly force, 594:4.
  Without warrant, when permitted, 594:10.
Assault crimes, officer as victim or perpetrator, 651:6.
Chief medical examiner and other medical examiners.
  Assistance in police training, 611-B:8.
Courtroom, possession of firearms in, 159:19.
Dogs, willful interference with, 644:8-d.
Firearms, possession, 159:5.
  Courtrooms, 159:19.
Horses, willful interference with, 644:8-d.
Officer, murder of, death penalty for, 630:1.
Powers.
  National guard members when in active state service, 594:1.

POLITICAL PARTIES.
Party official.
  Bodily harm, threat of, 640:3.
  Bribery, 640:2.
  Improper influence, 640:3.

POPULAR NAME.
Citation, 625:1.
Controlled Drug Act, 318-B:1 to 318-B:30.
  See CONTROLLED SUBSTANCES.
Kimberly Goss Act, 597:1-d.

PORNOGRAPHY.
Child pornography, 649-A:1 to 649-A:7.
Computer pornography and child exploitation prevention, 649-B:1 to 649-B:6.
  See COMPUTER PORNOGRAPHY AND CHILD EXPLOITATION PREVENTION.

POSSESSION.
Burglar tools, 635:1.
Criminal liability, 626:1.
Forged instruments, 638:1.
Gambling equipment, 647:2.
Slugs, 638:13.
Stolen property, 637:7.

POST-CONVICTION DNA TESTING, 651-D:1 to 651-D:5.
Definitions, 651-D:1.
Generally, 651-D:2, 651-D:4.
Preservation of biological material for, 651-D:3.
Victim services, 651-D:5.

POSTMORTEM EXAMINATIONS.
Medico-legal cases, 611-B:15.
Office of the chief medical examiner.
  Generally, 611-B:1 to 611-B:31.
    See MEDICAL EXAMINERS.

POWER SERVICE.
Interruption of, 634:2.

PRESCRIPTIONS.
Confidentiality of information.
  Patient-identifiable and prescriber-identifiable data.
    Restrictions on business use, 318-B:12.
Controlled drugs, 318-B:9.

PRESENTENCE INVESTIGATION, 651:4.

PRESIDENT OF THE UNITED STATES.
Murder of, 630:1-a.

PRESUMPTION.
Defenses, jury, consideration of, 626:7.
Innocence, burden of proof, 625:10.
Misapplication of property, theft by, 637:10.
Murder, 630:1-b.
Stalking.
  Acting knowingly, 633:3-a.
Stolen property, receipt of, 637:7.

PRIOR LAW.
Applicability, 625:2.

PRISON LABOR.
State prisons, 622:26 to 622:32.

PRISONS AND PRISONERS.
Admission of intoxicated or incapacitated persons to protective custody, 172-B:3.
Assault by prisoners, 642:9.
Court appearances by prisoner, 623:1-a.
Day reporting program.
  In lieu of incarceration, 651:19-a.
Estates, cost of care of, 622:53.
Female inmates.
  State prisons, 622:33-a to 622:38, 622:33-a to 622:39.
International prisoner transfers, 622-C:1.
Interstate corrections compact, 622-B:1 to 622-B:3.
  Articles, 622-B:2.
  Commissioner or corrections, authority, 622-B:3.
  Name, 622-B:1.
Methamphetamine-related crimes, 639-A:3.
  Anhydrous ammonia.
    Prohibited conduct, 318-D:5.
  Manufacturing.
    Injury resulting from manufacturing activities, 318-D:3.

PRISONS AND PRISONERS —Cont'd

New England interstate corrections compact, 622-A:1 to 622-A:3.

Commissioner or corrections, authority, 622-A:3.

Compact, articles, 622-A:2.

Name, 622-A:1.

Parole generally, 651-A:1 to 651-A:25.

See PAROLE.

Penal guards.

Murder of, death penalty, 630:1.

Use of force, 627:5.

Regular visiting hours, establishment, 594:16.

Sentence.

Review division, 651:57.

Suspended.

Conditions for granting, 651:20.

Public service, uncompensated.

Compensation prohibited, 651:69.

Condition of, 651:68.

Liability, waiver of, 651:70.

Weekend service of term, 651:20.

Sentencing to imprisonment.

Day reporting program.

In lieu of incarceration, 651:19-a.

Sexual assault by person in position of authority over victim.

Victim incarcerated in correctional institution, 632-A:3.

State prisons, 622:2 to 622:58.

Approved absences, 623-A:1 to 623-A:9.

Duration of, 623-A:4.

Eligibility for, 623-A:2.

Expenses, 623-A:5.

Interpretation of chapter, 623-A:9.

Purposes of, 623-A:3.

Regulations, authority to establish, 623-A:1.

Status during absence, 623-A:7.

Violation of terms of, 623-A:8.

Waiver of extradition, 623-A:6.

Civil process, one held on.

Committal of, 622:17.

Detention of, 622:18.

Commissioner of corrections.

Communication by inmates with, 622:15.

Duties of, 622:7.

Failure of, 622:20.

Judgment against, execution, 622:19.

Powers of, 622:5.

Committals, 622:8.

Communication by inmates with commissioner of corrections, 622:15.

Cost of care, reimbursement by inmates, 622:53 to 622:58.

Definitions, 622:53.

Financial resources form, 622:54.

Legal costs, 622:57.

Post-imprisonment action for, 622:56.

Recovered moneys, deposit of, 622:58.

Delivery of articles to prisoners.

Penalty, 622:25.

Regulations, 622:24.

Discharged prisoners.

Supplies, 622:16.

Discipline, 622:14.

Female convicts, 622:33-a to 622:38, 622:33-a to 622:39.

Care and custody, 622:33-a.

Cost of maintenance, 622:37.

Expenses of confinement, 622:34-a.

Good behavior, 622:35.

Return of, 622:36.

Transfer of, 622:36.

Illegal privileges, 622:11.

Medical care, copayments, 622:31-a.

Mittimus, 622:9.

Prisoner's fund, 622:7-a.

Prison labor and products, 622:26 to 622:32.

Application of earnings, 622:31.

Earnings of prisoner, 622:29 to 622:32.

PRISONS AND PRISONERS —Cont'd

State prisons —Cont'd

Prison labor and products —Cont'd

Goods, sales of, 622:27.

Industries inventory account, 622:28-a.

Misconduct, effect of, 622:32.

Products, sales of, 622:26.

Source of payment, 622:30.

State agencies, provision of products for, 622:28.

Privileges.

Illegal, 622:11.

Psychiatric unit, 622:40 to 622:52.

Commitment, 622:45, 622:52.

Definitions, 622:40.

Detention, 622:51, 622:52.

Discharge, 622:48.

Establishment of, 622:41.

Hearings for commitment, detention or parole, 622:52.

Investigation of detention, 622:51.

Medical records, 622:47.

Off-grounds privileges, notification of granting of, 622:49.

Parole, 622:50, 622:52.

Staffing, 622:43.

Treatment standards, 622:46.

Religious ministrations, 622:22.

Religious preferences, 622:23.

Restitution.

Use of payments to defray the operating expenses of prisons, 622:32.

Return, 622:9.

Secure psychiatric unit, 622:40 to 622:52.

Security force, 622:38.

Authority, 622:39.

Superintendence, 622:2.

Supplies, discharged prisoners, 622:16.

Transfers to, 623:2.

United States prisoners, 622:10.

Victim's fund, 622:7-b.

Visitation, 622:6.

Wardens, 622:2-a.

Temporary removal of prisoners, 623:1 to 623:4.

Court appearances, 623:1-a.

Emergency, 623:1.

Illness, 623:1.

Procedure for transfer, 623:4.

State prisons, transfers from, 623:2.

Uncompensated public service by prisoners at county correctional facilities.

Performing services at municipally-owned grounds or property, 651:36-a.

Witnesses.

Rendition of prisoners as witnesses, 613-A:1 to 613-A:11.

PRIVACY.

Invasion of, 644:9.

PRIVILEGES AND IMMUNITIES.

Accomplice, conviction of, 626:8.

Liability, immunity from as defense.

Conspiracy, 629:3.

Criminal solicitation, 629:2.

Sabotage, witnesses, 649:6.

PROBABLE CAUSE.

Wiretapping, 570-A:9.

PROBATION.

Alternative incarceration program, 651:2.

Extradition for violations.

Arrest prior to requisition, 612:13.

From this state, 612:22, 612:23.

Other state, 612:3.

Home confinement, 651:2.

Intensive supervision program, 651:2.

Interstate compact for adult offender supervision, 651-A:26 to 651-A:38.

Officer, murder of, death penalty for, 630:1.

PROBATION —Cont'd
Officers.
  Sexual assault.
    Sexual contact with person.
      Actor in position of authority over, 632-A:3.
Restitution to victim as condition, 651:2.
Sentence and limitations, 651:2.
Termination, 651:2.
Violation of terms.
  Bail and recognizance.
    Release of defendant pending trial, 597:2.
    When hearing may be required, 597:5-a.

PROCESS.
Eluding, falsifications, 641:5.
Execution, justifiable use of force, 627:2.
Service.
  See SERVICE OF PROCESS.
Simulation of, 638:11.

PROFESSION.
Harm to, extortion, 637:5.

PROFESSIONAL SERVICES.
Theft of, 637:8.

PROPELLED VEHICLES.
Defined.
  Unauthorized use, 634:3.
Negligent homicide, 630:3.
Theft of, 637:9.
Unauthorized use, 634:3.

PROPERTY.
Abandoned property, burglary, 635:1.
Arson, 634:1.
Burglary, 635:1.
Communications, interruption of, 634:2.
Credit cards, fraudulent use, 638:5.
Creditors, defrauding, 638:9.
Criminal mischief, 634:2.
Criminal trespass, 635:2.
Defined.
  Arson, 634:1.
  Computer related offenses, 638:16.
  Criminal mischief, 634:2.
  Criminal threatening, 631:4.
  Theft, 637:2.
Force, justifiable use of.
  Destruction of, 627:3.
  Protection of, 627:7.
  Recovery of, 627:8.
Fraud.
  Credit cards, 638:5.
  Creditors, defrauding, 638:9.
  Misapplication of property, 638:11.
  Slugs used to obtain, 638:13.
Gas service, interruption of, 634:2.
Livestock trespassing, 635:3.
Lost property, theft of, 637:6.
Malicious mischief, 634:3.
Misapplication of.
  Fraud, 638:11.
  Theft by, 637:10.
Mislaid property, theft of, 637:6.
Occupied structure, defined.
  Arson, 634:1.
  Burglary, 635:1.
Power service, interruption of, 634:2.
Property of another, defined.
  Arson, 634:1.
  Criminal mischief, 634:2.
Robbery, 636:1.
Sabotage.
  Injuring or interfering with, 649:2.
  Posting, 649:7.
  Trespass.
    Arrest, 649:8.
    Attempting sabotage, 649:4.

PROPERTY —Cont'd
Sabotage —Cont'd
  Trespass —Cont'd
    Detention, 649:8.
    Unlawful entry, 649:7.
Secured premises, trespass on, 635:2.
Slugs used to obtain, 638:13.
Stolen property, receipt of, 637:7.
Theft generally.
  See THEFT.
Transportation, interruption of, 634:2.
Unauthorized use, 637:9.
Valuation, computer related offenses, 638:18.
Vehicles, unauthorized use, 637:9.
Water supply, interruption of, 634:2.

PROPERTY DAMAGE.
Rioting, 644:1.

PROSECUTIONS.
Bad checks, 638:4.
Commencement of, 625:8.
Limitation of action, 625:8.
Obstructing justice, 642:3.
Prior offenses, 625:2.
Running of time, 625:8.

PROSECUTORS.
Compensation for service, 610:2.

PROSTITUTION.
Defenses.
  Trafficking in persons, 645:2.
Degree of offense, 645:2.

PROTECTION ORDERS.
Stalking, 633:3-a.

PROVOCATION.
Manslaughter, 630:2.

PUBLIC ASSISTANCE.
Violations.
  Criminal penalties, 167:17-c.
  Prohibited acts, 167:17-b.

PUBLICATION.
Child pornography, 649-A:3.
  Distribution, 649-A:3-a.
  Manufacture, 649-A:3-b.
Highway closing, sabotage, 649:9.
Lottery tickets, 647:1.
Obscene Matter generally.
  See OBSCENE MATTER.

PUBLIC DEFENDERS, 604-B:1 to 604-B:8.
Allocation of cases, 604-B:6.
Alternate public defender program, 604-B:8.
Contract, 604-B:4.
Indigent defendants, representation, 604-B:2.
Limitation, 604-B:3.
Minors, representation, 604-B:2.
Responsibilities, 604-B:7.
Supervision, 604-B:5.

PUBLIC HEALTH SERVICES, DIVISION OF.
Controlled drugs.
  Rulemaking authority, 318-B:24.
Director.
  Rulemaking authority.
    Controlled drugs, 318-B:24.

PUBLIC INDECENCY.
Adultery, 645:3.
Deviate sexual relations, 645:2.
Fornication, 645:1.
Indecent exposure, 645:1.
Lewd and lascivious conduct, 645:1.
Prostitution, 645:2.

PUBLIC LIBRARIES.
Obscene matter, 650:6.

PUBLIC OFFICE.
Purchase of, 640:7.

PUBLIC OFFICERS AND EMPLOYEES.
Alcoholic beverage licenses.
  Time limit on elected state officials from holding after leaving
    office, 179:21.
Bribery, 640:2.
Compensation for.
  Past action, 640:4.
  Services, 640:6.
Conflict of interest, 643:2.
Convicted persons, rights lost, 607-A:2.
Extortion, theft by, 637:5.
Gifts to, corrupt practice, 640:5.
Information, misuse of, 643:2.
Intimidating, 640:3.
Misconduct.
  Limitation of action, 625:8.
  Running of time, 625:8.
Neglect of duty, 643:1.
Oppression, 643:1.
Past action, compensation for, 640:4.
Public office, purchase of, 640:7.
Services, compensation for, 640:6.
Speculation, privileged information, 643:2.
Threatening, corrupt practice, 640:3.

PUBLIC SAFETY.
Threats against, 631:4.

PUBLIC SERVANT.
Public Officers and Employees generally.
  See PUBLIC OFFICERS AND EMPLOYEES.

PUBLIC SERVICE.
Sentencing to perform, 651:2.

PUBLIC UTILITIES.
Defined, sabotage prevention, 649:1.
Interruption of, 634:2.
Sabotage Prevention generally.
  See SABOTAGE PREVENTION.
Services.
  Defined as property, 637:2.
  Theft of, 637:8.
Theft of utility services as trespass, 539:7.

PUFFING.
Theft by deception, 637:4.

PUNISHMENT.
Sentence and Punishment.
  See SENTENCE AND PUNISHMENT.

PURPOSELY.
Culpable mental state, 626:2.
Defined, murder, 630:1-a.

R

RACE OF VICTIM.
Extended term of imprisonment.
  Hate crimes, 651:6.

RADIO.
Expungement of records.
  Immunity of journalists reporting, 651:5.

RADIO AND TELEVISION.
Alcoholic beverages.
  Listing of retail prices, 179:31.

RAILROADS.
Threatening safety on, 631:4.

RANSOM.
Kidnapping for, 633:1.

RAPE.
Sexual Relations.
  See SEXUAL RELATIONS.

REASONABLE DOUBT.
Burden of proof, 625:10.

RECKLESS CONDUCT.
Arson, 634:1.
Bodily harm, placing in danger of, 631:3.
Criminal liability, 627:3.
Criminal mischief, 634:2.
Criminal threatening, 631:4.
Culpability, 631:3.
Culpable mental state, 626:2.
Disorderly conduct, 644:2.
Livestock trespassing, 635:3.
Malicious mischief, 634:2.
Manslaughter, 630:2.
Murder, 630:1-b.
Rioting, 644:1.
Second degree assault, 631:2.
Simple assault, 631:2-a.
Trespass by livestock, 635:3.

RECORDABLE WRITINGS.
Fraudulent handling, 638:2.

RECORDS.
Annulment of criminal record, 651:2, 651:5.
Appeals.
  Convictions in municipal or district court, 599:1-c.
Arrest records, 594:14-a.
Criminal convictions, annulment.
  Possession of controlled drug, 318-B:28-a.
Criminal offender registration.
  Availability of information to public, 651-B:7.
Indigent defendant representation, 604-A:10.
Missing persons investigations.
  Dental records, 611-B:29 to 611-B:31.
Parole, 651-A:20.
Tampering with, 638:3.
  Public records, 641:7.
Youth services center, 621-A:7.
  Accounting, 621:6.
  Children committed or detained, 621:15.

RECOVERY.
Civil actions, affect on, 625:5.
Property, justifiable use of force, 627:8.

REGISTRATION OF CRIMINAL OFFENDERS, 651-B:1 to
    651-B:12.
Address, residence or mailing address.
  Duty to report, 651-B:4.
Applicability of provisions, 651-B:12.
Change of address or place of residence.
  Duty to report, 651-B:4, 651-B:5.
Change of registration information.
  Duty to notify, 651-B:5.
Confidentiality of records, 651-B:7.
Definitions, 651-B:1.
Duration of registration, 651-B:6.
Failure to comply with requirements.
  Penalties, 651-B:9.
Fee, 651-B:11.
Hearing on decision offense requires registration.
  Nonresident or federal offenders, 651-B:10.
Information available to public, 651-B:7.
List of individuals registered.
  Duty to maintain, 651-B:7.
Nonresident offenders entering state.
  Duty to report, 651-B:4.
  Hearing on decision offense requires registration, 651-B:10.
Offenders against children.
  Defined, 651-B:1.
  Registration required, 651-B:2.
Online identifier.
  Registration required, 651-B:4-a.
Penalties for noncompliance, 651-B:9.
Photographing individual required to register, 651-B:7.
  Offender filing required report, 651-B:4.

REGISTRATION OF CRIMINAL OFFENDERS —Cont'd
Records.
  Availability of information to public, 651-B:7.
Release of sexual offenders into community, 651-B:3.
Reporting requirements of registrant, 651-B:4.
Requirement of registration, 651-B:2.
  Duration, 651-B:6.
  Penalties for failure to comply, 651-B:9.
Rules promulgation by department, 651-B:8.
Sexual offenders.
  Defined, 651-B:1.
  Duration of registration, 651-B:6.
  Registration required, 651-B:2.
  Release into community, 651-B:3.

REIMBURSEMENT.
Obstructing justice, 642:5.

RELIGIOUS BELIEFS.
Extended term of imprisonment.
  Hate crimes, 651:6.
Welfare of child, endangering, 639:3.

REMEDIES.
Civil actions.
  Affect on, 625:5.
  Justifiable acts affecting, 627:1.

REMOVAL.
Corpse, 644:7.
Creditors, defrauding by, 638:9.
Physical evidence, 641:6.
Public records or information, 641:7.
Recordable writings, 638:2.
Records, public or private, 638:3.

RENTALS.
Equipment, theft of, 637:8.
Services, unauthorized use of, 637:9.

RENUNCIATION.
Affirmative defense of.
  Attempt to commit crime, 629:1.
  Conspiracy, 629:3.
  Criminal solicitation, 629:2.

REPAIRMEN.
Unauthorized use of vehicle, 637:9.

REPLICA.
Theft by, 637:2.

REPORTS.
Criminal offender registration.
  Persons required to be registered, 651-B:4.
Death investigations by medical examiners.
  Autopsy reports, 611-B:21.
  Child death.
    Report to bureau of maternal and child health, 611-B:22.
  Completion of death investigations, 611-B:20.
  Death report to person taking custody of body, 611-B:26.
Information and analysis center, 651-F:3.
Interbranch criminal and juvenile justice council.
  Annual report, 651-E:5.
Medico-legal deaths.
  Mandatory reporting, 611-B:12.
Parole.
  Violations of conditions, 651-A:16.
Witnesses.
  Expert witnesses, 516:29-b.

REPRESENTATIVE IN CONGRESS.
Murder of, 630:1-a.

REPRODUCTION.
Theft by, 637:2.

REPUTATION.
Harm to.
  Defamation, 644:11.
  Extortion, 637:5.

RESPONSIBILITY.
Immaturity, 628:1.
Insanity, 628:2.
Irresponsibility, defense of.
  Conspiracy, 629:3.
  Criminal solicitation, 629:2.
Minors, 628:1.

RESTAURANTS.
Services, theft of, 637:8.

RESTITUTION.
Administrative fee, 651:63.
Affirmative defense, 642:5.
Amount of restitution, court's determination.
  Admissibility as evidence in civil action, 651:63.
Authority to sentence offender to make restitution, 651:63.
Authorized, 651:63.
Bad checks, 638:4.
Cemeteries or burial grounds, damages to, 635:8.
Civil actions, 651:65.
Collateral source or subrogee, 651:64.
Defaulting, payment or order, 651:67.
Definitions, 651:62.
Emergency medical and trauma services.
  Criminal mischief.
    Damaging emergency vehicle or apparatus, 634:2.
Failure to make, 651:67.
Garnishment of wages, 651:64.
Gravestones and gravesite items, replacement of, 635:8.
In addition to other penalty or fine, 651:63.
Lack of ability to pay, 651:64.
Lump sum or periodic installments of monetary restitution, 651:64.
Methamphetamine, crimes relating to.
  Manufacturing.
    Emergency response and cleanup costs, 318-D:2.
    Removal or remediation costs, 318-D:2.
Old Man of the Mountain, vandalism, 634:2.
Payment, time and method, 651:64.
Prisons and prisoners.
  State prisons.
    Use of payments to defray the operating expenses of prisons, 622:32.
Release for employment.
  Sentence and Punishment.
    See SENTENCE AND PUNISHMENT.
Revocation of, 651:66.
Statement of purpose, 651:61-a.
Suspended sentence.
  Condition of, 651:20.
Time and method of payments or performance, 651:64.
Wireless telephone cloning, 638:24.

RESTROOMS.
Alcoholic beverages.
  Consumption in restrooms prohibited in on-sale establishments, 179:27.

RETAIL THEFT.
Willful concealment.
  Prohibited acts, 637:3-a.

RETREAT.
Physical force, 627:4.

REVELATION.
Extortion, theft by, 637:5.

REVENUE STAMPS.
Forging, 638:1.

REWARDS, OFFER OF, 610:1.

RIDICULE.
Accusation, theft by extortion, 637:5.
Criminal defamation, 644:11.

RIGHT OF ENTRY.
Drugs, controlled drugs, inspections, 318-B:25.
Pharmacies, controlled drug inspections, 318-B:25.

RIGHT OF ENTRY —Cont'd
Tobacco tax, inspections, 78:26.

RIGHTS OF ACCUSED PERSONS.
Discovery, criminal matters, 604:1-a.

RIGHT TO COUNSEL.
Extradition, 612:10.

RIOTS.
Inciting, 644:1.
Law enforcement officers.
Closure of area posing threat to public health and safety, 644:2.

ROBBERY.
Generally, 636:1.
Murder during, 630:1-a.
Physical force to prevent, 627:8.
Theft generally.
See THEFT.

ROOMING HOUSE.
Services, theft of, 637:8.

S

SABOTAGE PREVENTION.
Attempts, penalty, 649:4.
Collective bargaining, effect on, 649:10.
Conspiracy, 649:5.
Force of statute, 649:12.
Highway, defined, 649:1.
Highway commissioner, defined, 649:1.
Highways, closing or restricting use, 649:9.
Impairment of property, 649:2.
Inconsistent laws, 649:11.
Labor, rights of, 649:10.
Posting property, 649:7.
Property.
Injuring or interfering with, 649:2.
Posting, 649:7.
Trespass.
Arrest, 649:8.
Attempting sabotage, 649:4.
Detention, 649:8.
Unlawful entry, 649:7.
Publication, highway closing or restricting use, 649:9.
Public utility, defined, 649:1.
Tampering with property, 649:2.
Trespass.
Arrest, 649:8.
Attempt at sabotage, 649:4.
Detention, 649:8.
Unlawful entry, 649:7.
Witnesses, privileges and immunity, 649:6.
Workmanship intentionally defective, 649:3.

SAFE SCHOOL ZONES.
Extended term of imprisonment for crime committed in, 651:6.

SAFETY DEPARTMENT.
Information and analysis center, 651-F:1 to 651-F:8.
Advisory committee, 651-F:3.
Audits, 651-F:8.
Definitions, 651-F:1.
Disclosures, 651-F:8.
Duties, 651-F:2.
Intelligence functions, 651-F:5.
Management, 651-F:4.
Penalties for violations, 651-F:7.
Purpose, 651-F:2.
Security of data, 651-F:6.

SAFETY DEPOSIT COMPANY.
Fraud on depositors, 638:10.
Property, misapplication of.
Fraud, 638:11.

SAFETY DEPOSIT COMPANY —Cont'd
Property, misapplication of —Cont'd
Theft by, 637:10.

SAPS.
Carrying or selling, 159:16.
Possession or use in committing a crime, 159:15.

SAVINGS AND LOAN ASSOCIATIONS.
Fraud on depositors, 638:10.
Property, misapplication of.
Fraud, 638:11.
Theft by, 637:10.

SCHOOL BUSES.
Audio recording inside of a school bus, 570-A:2.

SCHOOLS.
Experiments or observation involving live animals, 644:8-c.
Obscene matter, 650:6.
Student hazing, 631:7.
Tobacco products.
Use in public educational facility or on grounds of facility, 126-K:7.
Public educational facility defined, 126-K:2.

SCIENCE CLASSES.
Experiments involving live animals, 644:8-c.

SCIENCE FAIRS.
Experiments involving live animals, 644:8-c.

SCIENTIFIC INFORMATION.
Theft of, 637:2.

SEAL.
Forging of, 638:1.
Simulating unlawfully, 638:14.
State seal.
Extradition warrant, 612:7.

SEARCHES AND SEIZURES.
Arrest, 627:5.
Search for weapons, 594:3.
Constitution of New Hampshire, NH Const Pt 1 Art 19.
Drug offenses, seizure of items used in connection with, 318-B:17-b.
Forfeitures.
Personal property, 617:1.
Gambling equipment, 647:2.
Tobacco tax.
Seizure of unstamped tobacco products, 78:16.
Appeal, 78:31-a.
Warrants.
Affidavit by applicant, 595-A:4.
Assistance in execution of warrant, 595-A:8.
Custody of seized goods, 595-A:6.
Daytime search, 595-A:2.
Disposition of goods seized, 595-A:6.
Execution, 595-A:8.
Form.
Application for warrant, 595-A:4.
Warrant, 595-A:3.
Inventory of goods seized, 595-A:5.
Issuance, 595-A:1.
Nighttime search, 595-A:2.
Oath, applicant under, 595-A:4.
Property, defined, 595-A:9.
Purposes for issuance, 595-A:1.
Receipt for goods seized, 595-A:5.
Return of warrant, 595-A:5.
Time for, 595-A:7.
Safekeeping of seized goods, 595-A:6.
Scope of statute, 595-A:9.
Seizure of goods, 595-A:6.

SEARCH WARRANTS.
Affidavit by applicant, 595-A:4.
Assistance in execution of warrant, 595-A:8.
Custody of seized goods, 595-A:6.
Daytime search, 595-A:2.

SEARCH WARRANTS —Cont'd
Disposition of goods seized, 595-A:6.
Electronic appearance, authorization and signature,
  595-A:4-a.
Execution, 595-A:8.
Form.
  Application for warrant, 595-A:4.
  Warrant, 595-A:3.
Inventory of goods seized, 595-A:5.
Issuance, 595-A:1.
Nighttime search, 595-A:2.
Oath, applicant under, 595-A:4.
Property, defined, 595-A:9.
Purposes for issuance, 595-A:1.
Receipt for goods seized, 595-A:5.
Requisites for, 595-A:2.
Return of warrant, 595-A:5.
  Time for, 595-A:7.
Safekeeping of seized goods, 595-A:6.
Scope of statute, 595-A:9.
Seizure of goods, 595-A:6.
Telecommunication of appearance, authorization and
  signature, 595-A:4-a.

SECRETARY OF STATE.
Licenses.
  Weapons, 159:8.
Service of process.
  Tobacco dealer out of state, 78:13.

SECURE PSYCHIATRIC UNIT.
Insane persons, transfer from county correctional facility,
  651:11.

SECURITIES.
Forging of, 638:1.
Fraudulent handling of, 638:2.
Tampering with, 638:3.

SELF-DEFENSE.
Generally, 627:4.
Law enforcement officers, 627:5.

SENIOR CITIZENS.
Alert program for missing persons.
  Definitions, 106-J:3.
  Establishment of program, 106-J:4.
  Issuance and cancellation of alert, 106-J:4.
  Rulemaking, 106-J:5.

SENTENCE AND PUNISHMENT.
Aerosol self-defense spray weapons, criminal use of,
  159:23.
Aggravating factors.
  Extended term of imprisonment, 651:6.
Amendment of sentence, 651:60.
Annulment of record, 651:5.
Assault.
  By or against law enforcement officer, 651:6.
  By prisoners, 642:9.
  Sexual assault, 632-A:10-a.
Assault by prisoners, 642:9.
Attempt to commit murder, 651:2.
Authority of court, 651:1.
Bail.
  Offense committed while on release, 597:14-b.
  Pending sentence or appeal, 597:1-a.
Bail jumping, 642:8.
Capital murder, 630:1.
Career criminal, armed, 159:3-a, 651:2.
Commitment.
  Defendants, competency.
    Commitment to hospital, 135:17.
    Evaluation for permanent commitment, 135:17.
Computation of time, 651:3.
  Parole, 651-A:6.
Conditional discharge, 651:2.
  Public service, uncompensated.
    Compensation prohibited, 651:69.

SENTENCE AND PUNISHMENT —Cont'd
Conditional discharge —Cont'd
  Public service, uncompensated —Cont'd
    Condition of, 651:68.
    Liability, waiver of, 651:70.
Corporations, fines against, 651:2.
  Default, 651:28.
County correctional facility, sentence to, 651:17.
Criminal mischief, performance of public service, 651:2.
Day reporting program.
  In lieu of incarceration, 651:19-a.
Death penalty, 630:1.
  Injection, lethal, 630:5.
  Place of execution, 630:6.
  Witnesses, 630:6.
Disciplinary period, 651:2.
Discretionary sentences, public service, release for, 651:19.
Elderly or handicapped, use of force against, 651:6.
Electronic defense weapons.
  Criminal use of, 159:23.
  Felons, possession by, 159:21.
Expunging record, 651:5.
Extended term, 651:6.
False public alarm, performance of public service, 651:2.
Felonies.
  Presentence investigation.
    Military forces and veterans, 651:4-b.
Firearms, felonious use of, 651:2.
First degree murder, 630:1.
Habitual offenders, 651:6.
Hard labor.
  County correctional facility, 651:17.
  State prison, 651:15.
Imprisonment, 651:2.
  Bail jumping, 642:8.
Insane persons.
  Certificate of jury, 651:8.
  Committal, 651:9-a.
  Court orders, duration, 651:11-a.
  Discharge from prison, 651:10.
  Hospitalization, 651:8-b, 651:10, 651:11.
  Plea of insanity, 651:8-a.
  Rights of, 651:11-b.
  Transfer from prison, 651:10.
Interstate compact for adult offender supervision, 651-A:26
  to 651-A:38.
Jail sentence to, 651:17.
Life imprisonment.
  Bail and recognizance for offenses punishable by, 597:1-c.
Manslaughter, 630:2.
Murder, 651:2.
  Capital murder, 630:1.
  Extended term, 651:6.
  First degree murder, 630:1-a.
  Second degree murder, 630:1-b, 651:2.
Parole generally, 651-A:1 to 651-A:25.
  See PAROLE.
Petition to suspend sentence.
  Time for bringing, 651:20.
Pistol cane, criminal use of, 159:19-a.
Place of confinement.
  Reduction in sentence, 651:18.
Presentence investigation, 651:4.
  Military forces and veterans, 651:4-b.
Prior offenses, 625:2.
Prison terms.
  Day reporting program.
    In lieu of incarceration, 651:19-a.
  Parole, 651-A:1 to 651-A:25.
Probation, 651:2.
  Public service, uncompensated.
    Compensation prohibited, 651:69.
    Condition of, 651:68.
    Liability, waiver of, 651:70.
Psycho-sexual murder.
  Certification by court, 651-A:9.

SENTENCE AND PUNISHMENT —Cont'd
Psycho-sexual murder —Cont'd
  Defined, 651-A:10.
Public service.
  Hours of performance, 651:2.
  Release for, 651:19.
Records.
  Annulment of criminal record, 651:2.
  Expunging, 651:5.
Reduction in sentence, 651:18.
Release, early, recommended, 651:25.
Release for employment, 651:19.
  Failure to return, 651:24, 651:25.
  Recall of status, 651:25.
  Wages and income, 651:22, 651:25.
    Dependents, support, 651:22, 651:25.
    Maintenance, deduction for, 651:22.
    Restitution payments, 651:22, 651:25.
Restitution generally.
  See RESTITUTION.
Review.
  Amendment of sentence, 651:60.
  Application, 651:58.
  Division, 651:57.
  Procedure, 651:59.
  Records, 651:61.
  Review division, 651:57.
Second degree murder, 630:1.
Sexual assault, 632-A:10-a.
State prison, sentence to, 651:15.
State prison sentences, review of, 651:25.
Suspended sentence, 651:2.
  Conditions for granting, 651:20.
  Public service, uncompensated.
    Compensation prohibited, 651:69.
    Condition of, 651:68.
    Liability, waiver of, 651:70.
  Revocation, 651:21.
  Weekend service of term, 651:20.
Sword cane, criminal use of, 159:19-a.
Time, calculation of, 651:3.
  Parole, 651-A:6.
Unconditional discharge, 651:2.
Victims permitted to speak, 651:4-a.
Weekend service of term, 651:20.

SERIAL NUMBERS.
Removing or altering, 637:7-a.

SERVICE OF PROCESS.
Definition of summons, 613:1.
Domestic violence.
  Order, 173-B:8.
  Petition, 173-B:3.
Pistol and revolver licensing violations.
  Petition for injunctive relief, 159:6-e.
Tobacco dealer, 78:13.
Witnesses.
  Exemption from service of process, 613:4.
    Rendition of prisoners as witnesses, 613-A:8.

SERVICES.
Computer services.
  Defined, 638:16.
  Offenses, 638:17.
  Penalties, 638:18.
Credit card, fraudulent use of, 638:5.
Defined, 637:8.
Property, defined as, 637:2.
Slugs used to obtain, 638:13.
Theft of.
  Generally, 637:8.
  Misapplication, 637:10.

SEX OFFENSES.
Trafficking in persons, 633:6 to 633:10.

SEXUAL ASSAULT.
Age, pattern of sexual assault, 632-A:2.

SEXUAL ASSAULT —Cont'd
Aggravated felonious sexual assault, 632-A:2.
Bail pending sentence or appeal, 597:1-a.
Civil actions, by defendant, 632-A:10-c.
Consent, 632-A:2.
DNA testing of criminal offenders generally, 651-C:1 to
    651-C:6.
Felonious sexual assault, 632-A:3.
Pattern of sexual assault, defined, 632-A:1.
Registration of criminal offenders generally, 651-B:1 to
    651-B:12.
Sexual offenders, HIV testing, 632-A:10-b.
Sexual relations.
  See SEXUAL RELATIONS.
Victims.
  Guardian ad litem for minor victims, 632-A:6.

SEXUAL OFFENDER REGISTRATION, 651-B:1 to 651-B:12.
See REGISTRATION OF CRIMINAL OFFENDERS.

SEXUAL OFFENDERS.
DNA testing of criminal offenders generally, 651-C:1 to
    651-C:6.
HIV, testing of, 632-A:10-b.

SEXUAL ORIENTATION.
Extended term of imprisonment.
  Hate crimes, 651:6.

SEXUAL RELATIONS.
Adultery, 645:3.
Age.
  Pattern of sexual assault, 632-A:2.
  Sexual assault, 632-A:2, 632-A:3.
Assault.
  Sexual assault, 632-A:4.
    Aggravated felonious, 632-A:2.
    Consent, 632-A:6.
    Definitions, 632-A:1, 632-A:2.
    Felonious, 632-A:3.
    Generally, 632-A:4.
    Murder during, 630:1-a.
    Penalties, 632-A:10-a.
    Sentences, 632-A:10-a.
    Speedy trial, 632-A:9.
    Testimony.
      Exclusion of witnesses, 632-A:6.
      In camera, 632-A:8.
    Victims.
      Civil actions, brought by defendants, 632-A:10-c.
      Request for HIV testing of offender, 632-A:10-b.
      Right to speedy trial, 632-A:9.
  Testimony.
    Exclusion of witnesses, 632-A:6.
    In camera, 632-A:8.
Bodily harm, 632-A:3.
Child, endangering welfare of, 639:3.
Definitions, 632-A:1.
Dress of victim at time of assault.
  Evidence, 632-A:6.
Evidence, sexual assault, 632-A:6.
Felonies, 632-A:2, 632-A:3.
Force and violence, 632-A:3.
  Threatening, 632-A:2.
Force to prevent, justification, 627:4.
Fornication, 645:1.
Incest, 639:2.
Indecent exposure, 645:1.
Kidnapping, 632-A:2.
Mental incapacity, sexual assault, 632-A:2.
Misdemeanor, sexual assault, 632-A:4.
Offenses.
  Pattern of sexual assault, defined, 632-A:1.
Prostitution, 645:2.
Sexual assault, 632-A:4.
  Aggravated felonious, 632-A:2.
    Minor, responsibility of, 628:1.
  Child care service, employment after conviction, 632-A:10.

SEXUAL RELATIONS —Cont'd
Sexual assault —Cont'd
　Consent, 632-A:6.
　Definitions, 632-A:1, 632-A:2.
　Evidence, 632-A:6.
　Felonious, 632-A:3.
　Generally, 632-A:4.
　Misdemeanor, 632-A:4.
　Murder during, 630:1-a.
　Penalties, 632-A:10-a.
　Sentences, 632-A:10-a.
　Speedy trial, 632-A:9.
　Spouse as victim, 632-A:5.
　Testimony, 632-A:5.
　　In camera, 632-A:8.
　Victims, right to speedy trial, 632-A:9.
Supervisory authority.
　Sexual assault by person in position of authority over victim,
　　632-A:3.
Testimony, sexual assault.
　Exclusion of witnesses, 632-A:6.
　In camera, 632-A:8.

SHERIFF.
Courts.
　Responsibility for court security, 594:1-a.
Firearms, possession of, 159:5.
　Courtrooms, 159:19.
Murder of, death penalty, 630:1.

SHIPS AND SHIPPING.
Burglary on, 635:1.
Masters.
　Controlled drugs.
　　Sales to, 318-B:5.
　　Use, limitations on, 318-B:8.
Threatening safety on, 631:4.
Unauthorized use of, 634:3, 637:9.

SHOPLIFTING.
Suspect, detention of, 627:8-a.

SHORT WEIGHT.
Fraud, 638:6.

SHOWS.
Obscene matter, 650:1.

SIGNS.
Alcoholic beverage licensees, 179:25.

SLANDER.
Forfeitures, personal property, 617:2 to 617:4.

SLAVERY.
Involuntary servitude to pay a debt.
　Peonage, 633:5.

SLOT MACHINES.
Gambling device, possession of, 647:2.

SLUGS.
Possession and use of, 638:13.

SLUNG SHOTS.
Carrying or selling, 159:16.
Possession or use in committing a crime, 159:15.

SMOKE BOMBS.
Sale or use of, 644:16-b.

SNOWMOBILES.
Local regulation, 215-C:31.

SOLICITATION.
Bribe.
　Commercial bribe, 638:7.
　Official and political matters, 640:2.
　Sporting event, 638:8.
Commission of offense.
　In another jurisdiction, 625:4.
　Inchoate crimes, 629:2.
Conduct of another, liability for, 626:8.

SOLICITATION —Cont'd
Criminal solicitation to cause death, death penalty, 630:1.
Deception, theft by, 637:4.
Prostitution, 645:2.
Suicide, commission of, 630:4.

SPEARS.
Sale of martial arts weapons to minors, 159:24.

SPORTING EVENTS.
Admission to, theft of, 637:8.
Bribery, 638:8.

STALKING.
Crime established and defined, 633:3-a.
Warrantless arrest, 594:10.

STAMPS.
Forging of, 638:1.
Tobacco products, tax stamps.
　Discount for, 78:9.
　Evidence of payments, 78:7.
　Nonresidents, 78:13.
　Resale, redemption, 78:10.
　Sale, discount for, 78:9.
　Time for affixing, 78:12.
　Unstamped products.
　　Penalties, 78:14, 78:16.
　Unused or uncancelled, 78:10.

STATE POLICE.
Director.
　Pistols and revolvers, sale, 159:8.
Police generally.
　See POLICE.

STATE PRISONS, 622:2 to 622:58.

STATE SEAL.
Extradition warrant, 612:7.

STATE TREASURER.
Tobacco stamp revenues, 78:9.

STATUTE OF LIMITATIONS.
Absentees, 625:8.
Drug dealer liability, 318-C:15.
Incest, 639:2.
Limitation of actions, 625:8.
Offenses classified, 625:8.
Running of time, 625:8.
Sexual assault.
　Civil actions by defendant, 632-A:10-c.

STEAM.
Services.
　Defined as property, 637:2.
　Theft of, 637:8.

STILETTOS.
Carrying or selling, penalty, 159:16.

STILLBIRTHS.
Assault, 631:1, 631:2.

STINK BOMBS.
Sale or use, 644:16-a.

STOCKS.
Forging of, 638:1.
Fraudulent handling of, 638:2.
Tampering with, 638:3.

STOLEN PROPERTY.
Receiving, 637:7.
Search warrants.
　Affidavit by applicant, 595-A:4.
　Assistance in execution of warrant, 595-A:8.
　Custody of seized goods, 595-A:6.
　Daytime search, 595-A:2.
　Disposition of goods seized, 595-A:6.
　Execution, 595-A:8.
　Form.
　　Application for warrant, 595-A:4.

STOLEN PROPERTY —Cont'd
Search warrants —Cont'd
Form —Cont'd
Warrant, 595-A:3.
Inventory of goods seized, 595-A:5.
Issuance, 595-A:1.
Nighttime search, 595-A:2.
Oath, applicant under, 595-A:4.
Property, defined, 595-A:9.
Purposes for issuance, 595-A:1.
Receipt for goods seized, 595-A:5.
Requisites for, 595-A:2.
Return of warrant, 595-A:5.
Time for, 595-A:7.
Safekeeping of seized goods, 595-A:6.
Scope of statute, 595-A:9.
Seizure of goods, 595-A:6.
Theft generally.
See THEFT.

STORAGE.
Firearms.
Negligent storage of, 650-C:1.

STORES.
Alcoholic beverages.
State stores.
Local option, 179:1.

STRANGULATION, 631:2.

STREET GANGS.
Criminal street gang solicitation, 644:20.

STRIKES.
Extortion by, 637:5.

STUDENT HAZING.
Prohibited, 631:7.

STUN GUNS.
Criminal use of, 159:23.
Felons.
Possession prohibited, 159:21.
Sale to minors, 159:22.

SUBPOENAS.
Parole.
Adult parole board.
Revocation hearings, 651-A:17.

SUBSTANCE ABUSE.
Defined terms, 172:1.
Dependency examinations, court orders, 172:13.
Intoxicated persons.
Treatment and services, 172:15.
Treatment and rehabilitation program.
Client records, confidentiality, 172:13.
Intoxicated persons, 172:15.
Voluntary admissions, 172:13.

SUBSTANTIAL STEP.
Defined, 629:1.

SUICIDE.
Causing or aiding, 630:4.
Medico-legal cases.
Medical examiner to investigate, 611-B:11.
Use of physical force to prevent, 627:6.

SUMMONS.
Arrest, summons instead of, 594:14.
Simulating unlawfully, 638:14.

SUNDAYS.
Arrested persons, detention of, 594:20-a.
Bail on, 597:21.

SUPERIOR COURT.
Bail, 597:4, 597:6, 597:40.
Bail commissioners.
Appointment, 597:15.
District courts, 597:15-a.

SUPERIOR COURT —Cont'd
Bail commissioners —Cont'd
Educational requirements, 597:18-a.
Fees, 597:20.
Powers, 597:18.
Returns, 597:19.
Salaried public officers, fees, 597:20.
Sunday bail, 597:21.
Term, 597:17.
Pistol and revolver licensing violations.
Petition for injunctive relief, 159:6-e.
Recognizance, 597:6, 597:40.
Copies, delivery of, 597:11.
Youth development center, discharge, 621:26.

SUPREME COURT.
Weapons, law enforcement officers wearing in court, 159:19.

SURETY OF THE PEACE, 608:1 to 608:10.
Appeals, 608:3.
Failure to prosecute, 608:5.
Order, 608:4.
Certifying to court, 608:7.
Committal by surety, 608:10.
Recognizing after, 608:6.
Complaint, 608:1.
Order, 608:2.
Conviction order on, 608:8.
Order.
Appeals, 608:4.
Complaint, 608:2.
Conviction, on, 608:8.
View, on, 608:9.

SUSPENDED SENTENCE, 651:20.

SWITCHBLADE KNIVES.
Carrying or selling, penalty, 159:16.

SWORD CANES.
Criminal use of, 159:19-a.

SWORDS.
Sale of martial arts weapons to minors, 159:24.

SYMBOLS.
Forging of, 638:1.

T

TARGET SHOOTING.
Pistols and revolvers, license to carry, 159:6, 159:6-d.

TASTINGS OF BEVERAGES, LIQUOR OR WINE, 179:44.

TATTOO.
Minor, 639:3.

TAXATION.
Tobacco tax, 78:1 to 78:34.
Additions to tax, 78:18-a.
Additives.
Information to be obtained and made available to the public, 78:12-e.
Deficiency.
Additions to tax, 78:18-a.
Definitions, 78:1.
Direct tax upon consumer at retail, 78:7-a.
Distribution of revenues, 78:32.
Education trust fund.
Distribution of revenues, 78:26.
Foreign state's tax stamp or indicia.
Possession of tobacco products bearing, 78:14-a.
Importation of certain tobacco products prohibited, 78:33.
Imposition of tax, 78:7.
Products other than cigarettes, 78:7-c.
Inspections, 78:26.

TAXATION —Cont'd
Tobacco tax —Cont'd
Labels.
  Placement of labels.
    Requirements for importation of certain tobacco products, 78:34.
Licenses, 78:2 to 78:6-a.
  Sales to licensee who does not possess valid or current license, 78:12-a.
  Suspension or revocation.
    Sale and distribution violations, 126-K:12.
Metering machines in lieu of stamps, 78:11.
  Authorization to use, 78:13.
Presumption of pre-collection, 78:7-a.
Rate, 78:7.
  Products other than cigarettes, 78:7-c.
Records.
  Taxpayer records, 78:18.
Stamps, 78:9.
  Affixing, 78:12.
    Authorization to affix stamps, 78:13.
  Foreign state's tax stamps.
    Possession of tobacco products bearing, 78:14-a.
  Redemption or refund, 78:10.
  Resale, 78:10.
  Unstamped tobacco products, 78:14.
    Forfeiture, 78:16.
      Appeal of forfeiture, 78:31-a.
Vending machines.
  Defined, 78:1.
  Records of operators, 78:18.
  Seals, 78:2.

TAX EXEMPTIONS.
New Hampshire veterans' home, tobacco tax, 78:7-b.
Tobacco tax, 78:7-b.

TEACHERS.
Physical force to discipline, use of, 627:6.

TECHNICAL INFORMATION.
Theft of, 637:2.

TEFLON-COATED BULLETS, 159:18.

TELECOMMUNICATIONS.
Abusive language, 644:4.
Emergency calls, obstruction of, 644:12.
Fraudulent paraphernalia, use to defraud, 638:5-a.
Harassment by, 644:4.
Services.
  Defined as property, 637:2.
  Theft of, 637:8.
Wireless telephone cloning, 638:21 to 638:24.
  Civil action by providers, 638:24.
  Criminal acts, 638:22, 638:23.
  Definitions, 638:21.
  Forfeiture of property, 638:24.
  Restitution, 638:24.

TELEVISION.
Expungement of records.
  Immunity of journalists reporting, 651:5.

TERRITORIAL JURISDICTION.
Jurisdiction.
  See JURISDICTION.

TERRORISM.
Toxic biological or chemical substances.
  Exposing the public to, 644:2-a.
  False public alarms, 644:3.

TERRORIZING.
Criminal threatening, 631:4.

TESTIMONY.
Sexual assault, 632-A:6, 632-A:8.

THEATERS.
Motion pictures.
  Theater owners.
    When use of force justified, 627:8-a.
  Unauthorized recording in a theater, 644:19.
Obscene matter, 650:2.

THEFT.
Accusation of a crime, theft by extortion, 637:7.
Adverse claim, theft by failure to disclose, 637:4.
Airplane.
  Services, theft of, 637:8.
  Unauthorized use, 637:9.
Animals, 637:2.
  Stray beasts, 637:6.
Bad checks, 638:4.
Bailment, larceny by, 637:3.
Bank, misapplication of property, 637:10.
Birds, 637:2.
Boats, unauthorized use, 637:9.
Bodily harm, extortion, 637:5.
Boycott, extortion, 637:5.
Burglar tools, possession of, 635:1.
Burglary, 635:1.
Communications, services of, 637:8.
  Defined as property, 637:2.
Computer equipment, 638:17.
Computer services, 638:17.
Conditional sales, 637:2.
Conduct constituting, 637:1.
Conversion, larceny by, 637:3.
Credit union, misapplication of property, 637:10.
Deadly weapon, theft with, penalty, 637:11.
Dealer, defined, stolen property, 637:7.
Deception, 637:4.
  Services, theft of, 637:4.
Definitions, 637:2.
Economic wealth, defined as property, 637:2.
Electricity, services of, 637:8.
  Defined as property, 637:2.
Embezzlement, larceny by, 637:3.
Entertainment, admission to, 637:8.
Exercise of control, theft by, 637:4.
Extortion, theft by, 637:1, 637:5.
Facsimile, theft by, 637:2.
False pretenses, theft by, 637:4.
Fiduciary, misapplication of property, 637:10.
Financial institution, defined, 637:10.
Formulae, 637:2.
Fraud and deceit, 637:4.
  Services, theft of, 637:4.
Fraudulent retail transactions, 637:10-b.
Gas, services of, 637:8.
  Defined as property, 637:2.
Government, misapplication of property, 637:10.
Guest house, services of, 637:8.
Habitual offender, penalty, 637:11.
Hotel, services of, 637:8.
Information, withholding to obtain control, 637:4.
Instruments, 637:2.
Insurance company, misapplication of property, 637:10.
Invention, 637:2.
Investment trust, misapplication of property, 637:10.
Labor, services of, 637:8.
  Defined as property, 637:2.
Larceny, generally, 637:3.
Lien, failure to disclose, theft by, 637:4.
Limitation of action, 625:8.
Lost property, 637:6.
Misapplication of property, 637:10.
Mislaid property, 637:6.
Motel, service of, 637:8.
Motor vehicles.
  Rental services, theft of, 637:8.
  Unauthorized use, 637:9.
Obtain, defined, 637:2.
Organized retail crime enterprise, 637:10-c.

THEFT —Cont'd
Penalties, 637:11.
Personal property, 637:2.
Photograph, obtaining by, 637:2.
Presumption.
　Misapplication of property, theft by, 637:10.
　Stolen property, 637:7.
Professional services, 637:8.
Propelled vehicles, unauthorized use, 637:9.
Property, defined, 637:2.
Property of another, defined, 637:2.
Prosecution, running of time, 625:8.
Public utilities, services of, 637:8.
　Defined as property, 637:2.
Puffing and deception, 637:4.
Purpose to deprive, defined, 637:2.
Receives, defined, 637:7.
Receiving stolen property, 637:7.
Rental equipment, 637:8.
　Joyriding, 637:9.
Reproduction, theft by, 637:2.
Restaurants, theft of services, 637:8.
Robbery, 636:1.
Safety deposit company, misapplication of property,
　637:10.
Savings and loan association, misapplication of property,
　637:10.
Scientific information, 637:2.
Serial numbers, removing or altering, 637:7-a.
Services, theft of, 637:8.
　Defined as property, 637:2.
Sporting events, admissions to, 637:8.
Steam, services of, 637:8.
　Defined as property, 637:2.
Stolen property, receipt of, 637:7.
Stray beasts, 637:6.
Technical information, 637:2.
Telecommunications, services of, 637:8.
　Defined as property, 637:2.
Tools, rental services, 637:8.
Trade secrets, 637:2.
Trespassory taking, 637:3.
Trickery and deception, 637:4.
Unauthorized use of vehicles, 637:9.
Utilities, services of, 637:8.
　Defined as property, 637:2.
　Trespass, 539:7.
Value, defined, 637:2.
Vehicles.
　Services, theft of, 637:8.
　Unauthorized use, 637:9.
Vessels, unauthorized use, 637:9.
Water, services of, 637:8.
　Defined as property, 637:2.
Willful concealment.
　Prohibited acts, 637:3-a.
　Use of force by merchants, 627:8-a.
Written instruments, 637:2.

THEFT DETECTION DEVICE REMOVERS.
Use or possession, 637:10-a.

THEFT DETECTION SHIELDING DEVICES.
Use or possession, 637:10-a.

THREATS.
Court or judicial officers, 631:4-a.
Criminal.
　Restraint, 633:2.
Criminal threatening, 631:4.
Defined, services, theft of, 637:8.
Disorderly conduct, 644:2.
Documents, fraudulent execution, 638:12.
Extortion, theft by, 637:5.
Legislators, corrupt practice, 640:3.
Party official, corrupt practice, 640:3.
Prostitution, 645:2.
Public officers and employees, corrupt practice, 640:3.

THREATS —Cont'd
Services, theft of, 637:8.
Sexual assault, 632-A:2.
Sporting events, fixing of, 638:8.
Voter, corrupt practice, 640:3.

THROWING DARTS.
Sale of martial arts weapons to minors, 159:24.

TICKETS.
Alcoholic beverages.
　Admission price or fee of licensee, 179:41.

TIME.
Bad checks, 638:4.
Effective date, 625:2.
Limitation of action, 625:8.
Night, burglary, 635:1.
Prosecutions, limitation of action, 625:8.
Running of, limitation period, 625:8.
Sentences, calculation of time, 651:3.
　Parole, 651-A:6.

TOBACCO PRODUCTS.
Additives.
　Access and dissemination of information required, 78:12-e.
Age of purchaser, proof, 126-K:3.
Control program.
　Definitions, 126-K:16.
　Establishment of program, 126-K:15.
　Funding, 126-K:15.
List of additives.
　Access and dissemination of information, 78:12-e.
Minors, 126-K:1 to 126-K:14.
　Administrative warnings, 126-K:12.
　Definitions, 126-K:2.
　Distribution to, 126-K:4.
　　Minor possessing note from adult requesting, 126-K:8.
　Documentation furnished upon purchase, 126-K:3.
　Enforcement authority, 126-K:9.
　Fines.
　　Payment, deposit, 126-K:11.
　　Power of commission to assess, 126-K:12.
　List of persons against whom fines and penalties assessed,
　　126-K:12.
　Local laws, ordinances and regulations, 126-K:14.
　Misrepresenting age to procure, 126-K:4.
　Possession and use, 126-K:6.
　Proof of age of purchaser, 126-K:3.
　Prosecution of violations, 126-K:12.
　Public educational facility or facility grounds.
　　Use of products on, 126-K:7.
　Purposes of provisions, 126-K:1.
　Rolling paper.
　　Defined, 126-K:2.
　　Prohibited acts, 126-K:4-a.
　Rulemaking, 126-K:10.
　Sale and distribution to minors prohibited.
　　Rolling paper, 126-K:4-a.
　Samples.
　　Distribution in public place, 126-K:5.
　Severability, 126-K:13.
　Single cigarette sales prohibited, 126-K:8.
　Surgeon General's warnings.
　　Products sold in original packaging bearing, 126-K:8.
Proof of age of purchaser, 126-K:3.
Public educational facility.
　Use of products in facility or on grounds of facility, 126-K:7.
Sale and distribution.
　Minors.
　　Rolling paper, 126-K:4-a.
Sales.
　Licenses, unauthorized sales to, 78:12-a.
　Minors, 126-K:4.
　　Note from adult requesting sale, 126-K:8.
　Single cigarettes, 126-K:8.
　Surgeon General's warning.
　　Original packages bearing, 126-K:8.

TOBACCO PRODUCTS —Cont'd
Samples.
  Distribution in public place, 126-K:5.
Single cigarette sales, 126-K:8.
Surgeon General's warnings.
  Products sold in original packaging bearing, 126-K:8.
Tobacco use prevention fund and control program,
      126-K:15 to 126-K:18.
  Fund, 126-K:15.
  Grants, 126-K:17.
  Rulemaking, 126-K:18.
Vending machines.
  Youth access to and use of tobacco products, 126-K:1 to
      126-K:14.

TOBACCO TAX.
Additions to tax, 78:18-a.
Affixing stamps, penalty, 78:12.
Books and papers, production of, 78:18.
Cigarette, defined, 78:1.
Commissioner, defined, 78:1.
Consumer tax, 78:7, 78:7-a.
Definitions, 78:1.
Display of license, 78:2.
Distribution of revenues, 78:32.
Evidence of payment, 78:7.
Exemption, 78:7-b.
Fees.
  Licenses, 78:2.
Fines and penalties.
  License, failure to obtain, 78:2.
  Unstamped products, 78:14.
Forfeitures, unstamped products, 78:16.
Importation of certain tobacco products prohibited, 78:33,
      78:34.
Importations.
  Inspections, right of entry, 78:26.
Imposition of tax, 78:7.
Labels.
  Placement of labels.
      Requirements for importation of certain tobacco products,
        78:34.
Licenses, 78:2 to 78:6-a.
  Denial of application, 78:6-a.
  Display of, 78:2.
  Expiration, 78:4.
  Fees, 78:2.
  Lack of, penalty, 78:2.
  Renewal, 78:4.
  Required, 78:2.
  Revocation, 78:6.
  Sales to licensee who does not possess valid or current license,
      78:12-a.
  Suspension, 78:6.
  Suspension or revocation.
      Appeal of order, 78:31-a.
  Term of, 78:4.
  Vending machines, 78:2.
Manufacturer.
  Defined, 78:1.
  Metering machines, 78:11.
  Stamps, discount for, 78:9.
      Time for affixing, 78:12.
      Transfer of stamps, 78:10.
Metering machines, tax stamps.
  Nonresidents, 78:13.
Nature of tax, 78:7-a.
New Hampshire veterans' home, exemption, 78:7-b.
Nonresidents, stamps and meters, 78:13.
Out-of-state, stamps and meters, 78:13.
Possession of tobacco products of foreign states, 78:14-a.
Premium cigars.
  Defined, 78:1.
  Exemption from tax, 78:7-c.
Rate of tax, 78:7.
Records, preservation of, 78:18.

TOBACCO TAX —Cont'd
Retailer.
  Defined, 78:1.
  Metering machines, 78:11.
  Tax stamps.
      Sale to, 78:9.
      Time for affixing, 78:12.
      Transfer of, 78:10.
Sampler.
  Defined, 78:1.
Smokeless tobacco.
  Exemption, 78:12.
  Tax imposed, 78:7-c.
Stamps.
  Unstamped tobacco products.
      Forfeiture.
        Appeal, 78:31-a.
Sub-jobber.
  Defined, 78:1.
  Metering machines, 78:11.
  Tax stamps.
      Discount for, 78:9.
      Time for affixing, 78:12.
      Transfer of, 78:10.
Tax stamps.
  Destroyed, refund of purchase price, 78:10.
  Discount for, 78:9.
  Evidence of payments, 78:7.
  Metering machines.
      Nonresidents, 78:13.
  Nonresidents, 78:13.
  Purchase, failure to pay amount owing, 78:9.
  Resale, redemption, 78:10.
  Sale, discount for, 78:9.
  Time for affixing, 78:12.
  Unstamped products.
      Penalties, 78:14, 78:16.
  Unused or uncancelled, 78:10.
Time.
  Payment of tax, 78:7.
  Records, preservation of, 78:18.
  Stamps, affixing, 78:12.
Tobacco products, defined, 78:1.
Unlicensed tobacco product vending machines, sealing by
      commissioner, 78:2.
Vending machines.
  Defined, 78:1.
  Operator.
      Defined, 78:1.
      Metering machines, 78:11.
      Stamps, sale to, 78:9.
        Time for affixing, 78:12.
        Transfer of, 78:10.
  Seals, 78:2.
Wholesaler.
  Defined, 78:1.
  Metering machines, 78:11.
  Stamps.
      Discount for, 78:9.
      Time for affixing, 78:12.
      Transfer of, 78:10.

TOKENS.
Forgery of, 638:1.

TOLLING.
Statute of limitations, 625:8.

TOMBS.
Cemeteries.
  See CEMETERIES.

TOOLS.
Burglar's tools, possession of, 635:1.
Rental services, theft of, 637:8.

TOURIST CABINS.
Services, theft of, 637:8.

TOWNS.
Licenses.
Pistols or revolvers, sale of, 159:8.
Selectmen.
Powers, 616:5.

TOXIC BIOLOGICAL OR CHEMICAL SUBSTANCES.
Exposing the public to, 644:2-a.
False public alarms, 644:3.

TOXIC VAPORS.
Inhaling for effect, 644:5-a.

TRACING DEVICES.
Obstructing justice, 642:3.

TRADEMARKS.
Forging of, 638:1.

TRADE SECRETS.
Theft of, 637:2.

TRAFFIC.
Obstructing, 644:2.

TRAFFICKING IN PERSONS, 633:6 to 633:10.
Compensation, 633:10.
Definitions, 633:6.
Felonies, 633:7.
Forfeiture of items used in connection with, 633:8.
Administrative forfeiture, 633:9.
Prohibitions, 633:7.
Prostitution.
Affirmative defenses, 645:2.
Restitution, 633:10.

TRAILERS.
Rental services, theft of, 637:8.

TRANSFERS.
Computer equipment, unauthorized, 638:17.
Creditors, defrauding by, 638:9.

TRANSPORTATION.
Criminal, furnishing to, 642:3.
Interruption of, 634:2.
Persons, promotion of sexual offenses, 645:2.
Services, theft of, 637:8.
Threatening safety on, 631:4.

TREES AND TIMBER.
Agricultural vandalism, 539:9.

TRESPASS.
Agricultural vandalism, 539:9.
Burglary, 635:1.
Criminal trespass, 635:2.
Force to prevent, justification, 627:7.
Livestock trespassing, 635:3.
Posting land, 635:4.
Defacing or removing signs, penalty, 635:5.
Sabotage.
Arrest, 649:8.
Attempt at sabotage, 649:4.
Detention, 649:8.
Unlawful entry, 649:7.
Theft by trespassory taking, 637:3.
Willful trespass.
Utility services, theft of, 539:7.

TRIAL, 606:1 to 606:10.
Appeals by state, 606:10.
Bail pending, 597:2.
Challenges, 606:9.
Defendant, 606:3.
State, 606:4.
Custody of jury, 606:5.
Evidence.
Rebutting, 606:6.
Forfeitures.
Personal property, 617:7.
Imprisonment not exceeding one year, offenses punishable by, 606:8.

TRIAL —Cont'd
Sexual assault, speedy trial, 632-A:9.
Waiver of jury trial, 606:7.

TRUCKS.
Transporting dogs in pickup trucks, 644:8-f.

U

UNAUTHORIZED RECORDING IN A MOTION PICTURE THEATER, 644:19.

UNEMPLOYMENT COMPENSATION.
Offenses, limitation of action, 625:8.

UNIFORM ACT ON STATUS OF CONVICTED PERSONS, 607-A:1 to 607-A:8.

UNIFORM CRIMINAL EXTRADITION LAW, 612:1 to 612:30.

UNIFORM RENDITION OF PRISONERS AS WITNESSES IN CRIMINAL PROCEEDINGS ACT, 613-A:1 to 613-A:11.

UNINCORPORATED ASSOCIATIONS.
Actor, defined, 625:11.
Felonies, classification of crime, 625:9.
Fines, limitations, 651:2.
He, defined, 625:11.
Misdemeanors, classification of offense, 625:9.
Person, defined, 625:11.
Violations, classification of offense, 625:9.

UNIVERSITIES AND COLLEGES.
False academic documentation, 638:15-a.

UNLAWFUL ENTRY.
Burglary, 635:1.
Criminal trespass, 635:2.
No trespassing signs, posting, 635:4.
Defacing or removing signs, penalty, 635:5.

URINATION.
Public urination, 645:1-a.

UTILITIES.
Interruption of, 634:2.
Sabotage prevention generally.
See SABOTAGE PREVENTION.
Services.
Defined as property, 637:2.
Theft of, 637:8.

V

VANDALISM.
Agricultural vandalism, 539:9.
Criminal mischief, 634:2.
Criminal threatening, 631:4.
Old Man of the Mountain, 634:2.

VEHICLES.
Burglary, 635:1.
Negligent homicide, 630:3.
Rental services, theft of, 637:8.
Unauthorized use, 634:3, 637:9.

VENDING MACHINES.
Slugs, use in, 638:13.
Tobacco products.
Youth access to and use of tobacco products, 126-K:1 to 126-K:14.
See TOBACCO PRODUCTS.

VENUE.
Arraignment, 602:2.
Bail and recognizance.
Default, 597:34.
Computer crimes, 638:19.
Defaulters, bail, 602:2.
Element of an offense establishing, 625:11.

VENUE —Cont'd
Grand jury.
   Multicounty grand juries, 600-A:6.
Identity fraud, 638:27.
Insurance.
   Fraud, 638:20-a.
More than one county, parts of offense in, 602:1.
Pistols and revolvers.
   Petition for injunctive relief, 159:6-e.
Recognizance, action on, 597:34.

VESSELS.
Burglary on, 635:1.
Theft of, 637:9.
Threatening safety on, 631:4.
Unauthorized use of, 634:3.

VETERANS.
Presentence investigation, 651:4-b.

VETERANS' HOME.
Tobacco tax exemption, 78:7-b.

VETERINARIANS.
Controlled drugs.
   Labeling containers, 318-B:13.
   Professional use, 318-B:10.
   Veterinarian, defined, 318-B:1.
Veterinarian, defined.
   Controlled drug act, 318-B:1.

VICE PRESIDENT OF THE UNITED STATES.
Murder of, 630:1-a.

VICTIMS.
Confidential communications.
   Defined, 173-C:1.
   Disclosure of.
      Appeal of, 173-C:9.
      Consent of victim required, 173-C:2.
      Criminal proceedings, 173-C:2.
   Domestic violence.
      Center.
         Defined, 173-C:1.
         Location of, privileged, 173-C:6.
      Counselor.
         Child abuse, duty to report, 173-C:10.
         Defined, 173-C:1.
   Failure to testify, 173-C:8.
   Privilege.
      Assertion of, 173-C:3.
      Confidentiality, third person present, 173-C:2.
      Limitation on, 173-C:5.
      Scope of, 173-C:2.
      Termination of, 173-C:2.
      Waiver of, 173-C:3.
         Involuntary, 173-C:7.
         Partial, 173-C:4.
   Sexual assault.
      Counselor.
         Child abuse, duty to report, 173-C:10.
         Defined, 173-C:1.
      Rape crisis center.
         Defined, 173-C:1.
         Location of, privileged, 173-C:6.
   Victim, defined, 173-C:1.
HIV testing, disclosure of results, 632-A:10-b.
Incest, minor victim, 639:2.
Incompetent person released to community.
   Notice, 135:17-b.
Parole.
   Right to speak at hearings, 651-A:11-a.
Permitted to speak at parole hearing, 651-A:11-a.
Permitted to speak before sentencing, 651:4-a.
Post-conviction DNA testing service reactivation, 651-D:5.
Restitution generally.
   See RESTITUTION.
Right to speak.
   Sentence reduction hearings, 651:4-a.

VICTIMS —Cont'd
Right to speak —Cont'd
   Suspension hearings, 651:4-a.
Sexual assault, right to speedy trial, 632-A:9.
Sexual assault or abuse.
   HIV testing, disclosure of results, 632-A:10-b.
   Release of medical data, 631:6.
   Right to speedy trial, 632-A:9.

VIDEO TELECONFERENCED TESTIMONY.
Expert witnesses.
   Criminal cases, 516:37.
   Motor vehicle violations, 516:38.

VIOLATIONS.
Air rifles, sale to minors, 644:14.
Arrest, summons instead of, 594:14.
Bail, summons instead of, 594:14.
Classification, 625:9.
Criminal trespass, 635:2.
Culpability, 626:2.
Defined, 625:9.
Disability or legal disadvantage on conviction, 625:9.
Disorderly conduct, 644:2.
Electronic defense weapon, sale to minor, 159:22.
Firearms.
   Minors, furnishing to, 644:15.
   Unauthorized use of, 644:13.
Firecrackers, 644:13.
Legal disadvantage or disability on conviction, 625:9.
Limitation of action, 625:8.
Livestock trespassing, 635:3.
Loitering, 644:6.
Misdemeanors charged as, 625:9.
Poisons, exposure of, 644:16.
Sentence and limitations, 651:2.
Simple assault, mutual consent to fight, 631:2-a.
Stink bombs, sale or use, 644:16-a.
Theft, penalty, 637:11.
Toxic vapors, inhaling for effect, 644:5-a.
Trespass by livestock, 635:3.

VOLUNTARY ACT.
Requirement, 626:1.

VOTERS.
Bodily harm, threat of, 640:3.
Bribery, 640:2.
Improper influence, 640:3.

W

WAGE GARNISHMENT.
Restitution, 651:64.

WARDENS.
Agreement on detainers, 606-A:5.
State prisons, 622:2-a.

WAREHOUSES.
Controlled drug act, exemption, 318-B:15.

WARRANTS.
Default of bail, bench warrant for recovery of forfeiture, 597:37.
Extradition.
   Application for requisition, 612:23.
   Commitment to await requisition, 612:15.
   Execution, 612:8.
   Issuance, recital of facts, 612:7.
   Noncompliance, penalty, 612:11.
   Other state, form of demand, 612:3.
   Recall, issuance of alias, 612:21.
Forfeitures of personal property, libel, 617:3.
Prosecution, commencement of, 625:8.

WATER.
Jurisdiction, 625:4.

WATER SUPPLY.
Interruption of, 634:2.
Services.
    Defined as property, 637:2.
    Theft of, 637:8.

WEAPONS.
Aerosol self-defense spray weapons, criminal use of,
    159:23.
Arrest, search for weapons, 594:3.
Attempts to purchase firearms illegally, 159-D:3.
Billies, possession of, 159:15.
Blackjack, carrying or selling, 159:16.
Brass knuckles.
    Carrying or selling, 159:16.
    Possession of, 159:15.
Career criminal, armed, 159:3-a.
Courthouses.
    Carrying weapons into courtrooms, 159:19.
Criminal record checks, 159-D:3.
    Firearms sales.
        Department of safety as point of contact for federal
            government, 159-D:1 to 159-D:3.
Dagger, carrying or selling, 159:16.
Deadly force to prevent use, 627:5.
Deadly weapon.
    Burglary, armed with, 635:1.
    Defined, 625:11.
    Escapee using, 642:6.
    First degree assault, 631:1.
    Murder, 630:1-b.
    Rioting with, 644:1.
    Robbery, 636:1.
    Second degree assault, 631:2.
    Simple assault, 631:2-a.
    Theft with, 637:11.
Death associated with firearms or weapons.
    Medico-legal cases.
        Medical examiner to investigate, 611-B:11.
Dirk-knife, carrying or selling, 159:16.
Electronic defense weapons.
    Criminal use of, 159:23.
    Felons, possession prohibited, 159:21.
    Sale to minors, 159:22.
Felonious use of teflon-coated, armor-piercing and
    exploding bullets, 159:18.
Firearms.
    Discharge at occupied structure.
        Criminal mischief, 634:2.
    Felonious use of, 650-A:1.
    Theft of, 637:11.
Furnishing to criminal, 642:3.
Gun cane, defined, 159:1.
Handguns.
    State jurisdiction over, 159:26.
Law enforcement officers.
    Taking firearm from law enforcement officer, 642:3-a.
Mace.
    Criminal use of aerosol self-defense spray weapons, 159:23.
Martial arts weapons.
    Sales to minors, 159:24.
Martial arts weapons, sale of, 159:24.
Medico-legal cases.
    Medical examiner to investigate, 611-B:11.
Metallic knuckles.
    Carrying or selling, 159:16.
    Possession of, 159:15.
Minors.
    Negligent storage of firearms.
        Child likely to gain access, 650-C:1.
Negligent storage of firearms, 650-C:1.
Pepper spray.
    Criminal use of aerosol self-defense spray weapons, 159:23.
Pistol canes, 159:19-a.
Pistols and revolvers.
    Aliens, sale to, 159:8.
    Antique pistol or revolver, defined, 159:1.

WEAPONS —Cont'd
Pistols and revolvers —Cont'd
    Carrying without license, 159:4.
    Convicted felons.
        Career criminals, 159:3-a.
        Possession prohibited, 159:3.
        Sales to, prohibited, 159:7.
    Dangerous weapons.
        Carrying or selling, 159:16.
        Exceptions, 159:17.
        Possession on arrest, 159:15.
    Defined, 159:1.
    Exceptions, 159:5, 159:17.
    Fees, license to carry, 159:6, 159:6-d.
    Felons.
        Permit to purchase, 159:7.
        Possession of, 159:3.
    Identifying marks, altering, 159:13.
    Licenses and permits.
        Carrying without, 159:4.
        Confidentiality of, 159:6-a.
        Injunctive relief, violation of licensing sections, 159:6-e.
        Licensing entity refusing to comply with provisions, remedy,
            159:6-f.
        Nonresident, 159:6, 159:6-d.
        Sale of, 159:8, 159:10.
        Suspension or revocation, appeal, 159:6-b, 159:6-c.
        To carry, 159:6, 159:6-d.
    Minors purchasing, 159:12.
    Nonresident.
        Sale to, 159:8-a, 159:8-b.
    Pistol, defined, 159:1.
    Purchase.
        False information, 159:11.
        Felons, permit for, 159:7.
        Minors, 159:12.
        Nonresidents, penalty, 159:8-a, 159:8-b.
    Records, purchases and sales, 159:8.
    Revolver, defined, 159:1.
    Sales.
        Individual selling, 159:14.
        License for, 159:8.
        Minors, purchasing, 159:12.
        Nonresidents, penalty, 159:8-a, 159:8-b.
        Without license, 159:10.
Preemption of municipal ordinances.
    State authority, 159:26.
Self-defense weapons.
    Defined, 159:20.
Slung shot.
    Carrying or selling, 159:16.
    Possession of, 159:15.
State jurisdiction over, 159:26.
Stiletto, carrying or selling, 159:16.
Storage.
    Negligent storage of firearms, 650-C:1.
Stun guns.
    Criminal use of, 159:23.
    Felons.
        Possession prohibited, 159:21.
    Sale to minors, 159:22.
Switchblade knife, carrying or selling, 159:16.
Sword canes, 159:19-a.
Use of, justification, 627:9.
Voluntarily surrendered firearms, 159:25.

WEIGHTS AND MEASURES.
Fraud, 638:6.

WHOLESALERS.
Controlled drugs.
    Labels, 318-B:13.
    License, 318-B:3.
        Required, 318-B:3.
    Records required, 318-B:12.
    Sales by, 318-B:5.
    Wholesaler, defined, 318-B:1.

WHOLESALERS —Cont'd
Defined, controlled drug act, 318-B:1.

WIC.
Program, fraud, 638:15.

WILLFUL CONCEALMENT.
Prohibited acts, 637:3-a.
Use of force by merchants, 627:8-a.

WILLS.
Fraudulent handling, 638:2.

WINE COOLERS.
Samples, distribution, 179:31.

WINE TASTINGS, 179:44.

WIRE INTERCEPTION.
Obstructing justice, 642:3.

WIRELESS TELEPHONE CLONING, 638:21 to 638:24.
Civil action by providers, 638:24.
Criminal acts, 638:22, 638:23.
Definitions, 638:21.
Forfeiture of property, 638:24.
Restitution, 638:24.

WIRETAPPING AND EAVESDROPPING, 570-A:1 to 570-A:11.
Advertising of wire or oral communication intercepting devices prohibited, 570-A:3.
Civil damages, recovery authorized, 570-A:11.
Confiscation of wire or oral communication intercepting devices, 570-A:4.
Crimes and offenses, 570-A:1 to 570-A:11.
Disclosure and use of intercepted or oral communications, authorization, 570-A:8.
Distribution of wire or oral communication intercepting devices prohibited, 570-A:3.
Evidence, prohibition of use of intercepted devices as, 570-A:6.
Interception of wire or oral communications.
Authorization, 570-A:7.
Interpreters, use of, 570-A:9-b.
Manufacture of wire or oral communication intercepting devices prohibited, 570-A:3.
Possession of wire or oral communication intercepting devices prohibited, 570-A:3.
Procedure for interception of wire or oral communications, 570-A:9.
Reports concerning intercepted communications, 570-A:10.
Witnesses, immunity, 570-A:5.

WITNESSES, 516:1 to 516:38.
Affirmation, 516:20.
Attendance of, 516:1 to 516:7-a.
Competency, 516:19 to 516:28.
Affirmation, 516:20.
Interest as party, 516:22.
Negotiated paper, 516:26.
Party deponent, 516:23.
Religious opinions, 516:21.
Confidential settlement agreements.
Disclosure of information about agreements, 516:33-a.
Defined, 613:1.
Disappearance, limitation of action, 625:8.
Exclusion and segregation, sexual assault cases, 632-A:6.
Expert witnesses.
Disclosure of expert testimony, 516:29-b.
Testimony, 516:29-a.
Disclosure, 516:29-b.
Video teleconference to take testimony.
Criminal cases, 516:37.
Motor vehicle violations, 516:38.
Fees, 516:16 to 516:18.
Limitations, 516:18.
Immunities, 570-A:5.
Interest as party, 516:22.
Law enforcement officers.
Fees, 516:16, 516:16-a.

WITNESSES —Cont'd
Law enforcement officers —Cont'd
Written policy directives, 516:36.
Material, bail jumping, penalty, 642:8.
Material witnesses, release or detention, 597:6-d.
Minors.
Civil cases, 516:25-a.
Nonresident officers of corporations, 516:8 to 516:15.
Duty to testify, 516:9.
Fees, 516:13.
Double fees, 516:14.
Obstructing justice, 642:5.
Party deponent, 516:23.
Prisoners.
Rendition of prisoners as witnesses, 613-A:1 to 613-A:11.
Recognizances.
Commitment in default of, 597:23.
For appearance, 597:22.
Religious leaders, 516:35.
Religious opinions of, 516:21.
Rendition of prisoners as witnesses, 613-A:1 to 613-A:11.
Arrest, exemption from, 613-A:8.
Compliance, 613-A:7.
Conditions, 613-A:4.
Court order, 613-A:3.
Definitions, 613-A:1.
Exceptions, 613-A:5.
Service of process, exemption from, 613-A:8.
Severability clause, 613-A:11.
Short title, 613-A:10.
Summons from another state to testify in this state, 613-A:6.
Terms, 613-A:4.
Uniformity of interpretation, 613-A:9.
Witnesses summoned from this state to testify in another, 613-A:2.
Sabotage, privileges and immunities, 649:6.
Service of process.
Exemption from service, 613:4.
Rendition of prisoners as witnesses, 613-A:8.
Summons, 516:5.
Sexual assault cases, exclusion, 632-A:6.
Summoning from without state, 613:1 to 613:6.
Arrest, exemption, 613:4.
Constitutionality, 613:6.
Definitions, 613:1.
Service of process, exemption, 613:4.
Uniformity of interpretation, 613:5.
Summons.
Clerks, issue by, 516:2.
Defined, 613:1.
Deposition, issue for, 516:4.
Justices, issued by, 516:3.
Neglecting to attend, 516:6.
Nonresident officers of corporations, 516:15.
Penalty, 516:7.
Nonresident officers of corporations, 516:10.
Commissioner, issuance of summons by, 516:12.
Service of summons, 516:11.
Tampering with, 641:5.
Victim as witness, 516:7-a.
Video teleconference to take testimony of experts.
Criminal cases, 516:37.
Motor vehicle violations, 516:38.
Wills, 516:28.
Wiretapping and eavesdropping, 570-A:5.

WOMEN.
Prisons and prisoners.
Female inmates, 622:33-a to 622:37.

WOUNDS.
Gunshot wounds, reporting, 631:6.

WRIT OF EXECUTION.
Fines and costs, compelling payment, 651:2.

WRITTEN INSTRUMENTS.
Forgery, 638:1.

WRITTEN INSTRUMENTS —Cont'd
Theft, 637:2.

Y

YOUTH ACCESS TO AND USE OF TOBACCO PRODUCTS,
    126-K:1 to 126-K:14.
See TOBACCO PRODUCTS.

YOUTH DEVELOPMENT CENTER, 621:1 to 621:34.
Accounting, 621:6.
Administration, 621:1.
Apprehending.
    Authority to, 621:33.
    Transportation cost, reimbursement, 621:34.
Board.
    Contract for, 621:20.
    Payment of, 621:21.
Books and records, 621:6.
Bylaws, 621:7.
Care of children, 621:9.
Children's funds, 621:30.
Commitment.
    Error of court, child committed elsewhere, 621:16.
    Extended commitment, 621:9-a.
    Records, 621:15.
    United States, 621:17.
Contraband, 621:32.
Costs, parents or estate of child to contribute, 621:31.
Definitions, 621:3.
Detention, 621:18.
Discharge, 621:19.
    Superior court, by, 621:26.

YOUTH DEVELOPMENT CENTER —Cont'd
Duties of department, 621:12.
Duties relative to property, 621:4.
Error of court, child committed elsewhere, 621:16.
Extended commitment to center, 621:9-a.
Fire code compliance, 621:8.
Incorrigibles, 621:27.
Juvenile justice advisory board, 621-A:9 to 621-A:11.
Orders, 621:29.
Philosophy, 621:2.
Population, limits, 621:10.
Records.
    Accounting, 621:6.
    Children committed or detained, 621:15.
Release, 621:19.
    Changes in conditions of, 621:25.
    Effect of, 621:24.
    Remands in conditions of, 621:25.
Religious preference, 621:23.
Residential care, children in, 621:22.
Superior court, discharge by, 621:26.
Transfer, modification, 621:28.
United States, commitment by, 621:17.

YOUTH SERVICES CENTER, 621-A:1 to 621-A:11.
Admission, 621-A:6.
Definitions, 621-A:1.
Health and human services department.
    Commissioner.
        Powers and duties, 621-A:4.
Juvenile justice advisory board, 621-A:9 to 621-A:11.
Purposes, 621-A:5.
Records, 621-A:7.

Notes